MAP PAGES

106

O EUROPE AND
OUNTRY INDEX
R ENDPAPER

108
110
166

SWEDEN
FINLAND
ESTONIA
LATVIA

UKRAINE

KAZAKHSTAN

MONGOLIA

RUSSIA

HUNGARY
MOLDOVA
CROATIA ROMANIA
SERBIA
ALBANIA BULG
GREECE

104
TURKEY
GEORGIA
ARM. AZER.
TURKMENISTAN UZBEKISTAN
KYRGYZSTAN
TAJIK.

114
112
NORTH
KOREA
JAPAN
SOUTH
KOREA

128
130
SYRIA
IRAQ
IRAN

122
AFGHAN
124

116

CHINA

137
JORDAN
KUWAIT

EGYPT
LIBYA
SAUDI
ARABIA
QATAR
U.A.E.
OMAN

PAKISTAN
NEPAL

126
INDIA
BANGLA-
DESH

120
MYANMAR
LAOS

TAIWAN

Tropic of Cancer

CHAD
SUDAN
ERITREA
YEMEN

SOUTH
SUDAN
ETHIOPIA
DJIBOUTI
SOMALIA

118
THAILAND
CAMB. VIETNAM

PHILIPPINES

PACIFIC
OCEAN

156

121
121

CENTRAL
AFRICAN
REP.

142
CONGO
(DEM. REP OF THE)
UGANDA KENYA
RWANDA
BURUNDI
TANZANIA

SRI
LANKA

131

121 MALAYSIA

INDONESIA

Equator

141

PAPUA
NEW GUINEA

119
E. TIMOR

INDIAN
OCEAN

146

148
150

154

ANGOLA
ZAMBIA MALAWI
141
141
ZIMBABWE MOZAMBIQUE
MADAGASCAR

150

NAMIBIA
141

Tropic of Capricorn

BOTSWANA
SWAZILAND

152

154

SOUTH
AFRICA LESOTHO

AUSTRALIA

NEW
ZEALAND

AP SYMBOLS

ADMINISTRATION

— International boundaries
--- International boundaries (undefined or disputed)

···· Internal boundaries
National parks

PERU Country names
KENT Administrative area names

International boundaries show the *de facto* situation where there are rival claims to territory

PHYSICAL FEATURES

Perennial streams
Intermittent streams
Sand deserts

Intermittent lakes
Swamps and marshes
Permanent ice and glaciers

▲ 8848 Elevations in metres
▼ 8500 Sea depths in metres
1134 Height of lake surface above sea level in metres

The Royal Geographical Society

ESSENTIAL
WORLD
ATLAS

The Royal Geographical Society

ESSENTIAL
WORLD
ATLAS

PHILIP'S

PHILIP'S would like to thank **Richard Chiles** and the staff at
NPA Satellite Mapping, CGG Services (UK) Ltd, Edenbridge,
Kent, UK (www.npa.cgg.com)
for sourcing and processing the satellite imagery that appears in the atlas.

First published in Great Britain in 2013 by Philip's,
a division of Octopus Publishing Group Limited
(www.octopusbooks.co.uk)
Carmelite House, 50 Victoria Embankment, London EC4Y 0DZ
An Hachette UK Company (www.hachette.co.uk)

Third edition 2018
Reprinted 2019

Copyright © 2018 Philip's

Cartography by Philip's

ISBN 978–1–84907–482–7

A CIP catalogue record for this book is available from the British Library.

All rights reserved. Apart from any fair dealing for the purpose of private
study, research, criticism or review, as permitted under the Copyright, Designs
and Patents Act, 1988, no part of this publication may be reproduced, stored
in a retrieval system, or transmitted in any form or by any means, electronic,
electrical, chemical, mechanical, optical, photocopying, recording, or otherwise,
without prior written permission. All enquiries should be addressed to
the Publisher.

Printed in Malaysia

Details of other Philip's titles and services can be found on our website at:
www.philips-maps.co.uk

Front cover image: Anton Balazh/Shutterstock

Royal Geographical Society
with IBG

Advancing geography
and geographical learning

PHILIP'S World Atlases are published in association with THE ROYAL GEOGRAPHICAL SOCIETY (WITH THE INSTITUTE OF BRITISH GEOGRAPHERS).

The Society was founded in 1830 and given a Royal Charter in 1859 for 'the advancement of geographical science'. It holds historical collections of national and international importance, many of which relate to the Society's association with and support for scientific exploration and research from the 19th century onwards. It was pivotal in establishing geography as a teaching and research discipline in British universities close to the turn of the century, and has played a key role in geographical and environmental education ever since.

Today the Society is a leading world centre for geographical learning – supporting education, teaching, research and expeditions, and promoting public understanding of the subject. The Society welcomes those interested in geography as members. For further information, please visit the website at: **www.rgs.org**

Join us!

Royal Geographical Society
with IBG

Advancing geography
and geographical learning

Find out more about your world.

Visit our website www.rgs.org/joinus
to join the Society to discover:

● Why is the world changing and
what are the consequences?

● Enhance your understanding
of the world through Geography

● Be challenged and entertained
by great achievers

Royal Geographical Society (with IBG) 1 Kensington Gore London SW7 2AR
☎ +44 (0) 20 7591 3000 📠 +44 (0) 20 7591 3001

Image © NASA

USER GUIDE

The reference maps which form the main body of this atlas have been prepared in accordance with the highest standards of international cartography to provide an accurate and detailed representation of the Earth. The scales and projections used have been carefully chosen to give balanced coverage of the world, while emphasizing the most densely populated and economically significant regions. A hallmark of Philip's mapping is the use of hill shading and relief colouring to create a graphic impression of landforms: this makes the maps exceptionally easy to read. However, knowledge of the key features employed in the construction and presentation of the maps will enable the reader to derive the fullest benefit from the atlas.

MAP SEQUENCE

The atlas covers the Earth continent by continent: first Europe; then its land neighbour Asia (mapped north before south, in a clockwise sequence), then Africa, Australia and Oceania, North America and South America. This is the classic arrangement adopted by most cartographers since the 16th century. For each continent,

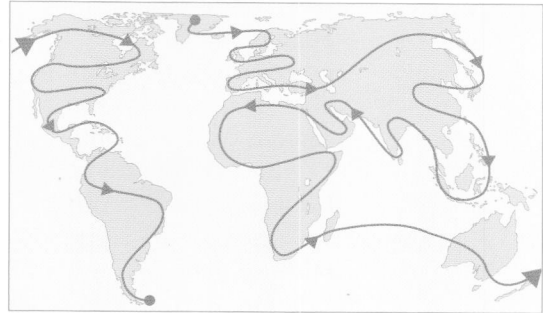

there are maps at a variety of scales. First, physical relief and political maps of the whole continent; then a series of larger-scale maps of the regions within the continent, each followed, where required, by still larger-scale maps of the most important or densely populated areas. The governing principle is that by turning the pages of the atlas, the reader moves steadily from north to south through each continent, with each map overlapping its neighbours.

MAP PRESENTATION

With very few exceptions (for example, for the Arctic and Antarctica), the maps are drawn with north at the top, regardless of whether they are presented upright or sideways on the page. In the borders will be found the map title; a locator diagram showing the area covered; continuation arrows showing the page numbers for maps of adjacent areas; the scale; the projection used; the degrees of latitude and longitude; and the letters and figures used in the index for locating place names and geographical features. Physical relief maps also have a height reference panel identifying the colours used for each layer of contouring.

MAP SYMBOLS

Each map contains a vast amount of detail which can only be conveyed clearly and accurately by the use of symbols. Points and circles of varying sizes locate and identify the relative importance of towns and cities; different styles of type are employed for administrative, geographical and regional place names to aid identification. A variety of pictorial symbols denote landforms such as glaciers, marshes and coral reefs, and man-made structures including roads, railways, airports and canals. International borders are shown by red lines. Where neighbouring countries are in dispute, for example in parts of the Middle East, the maps show the *de facto* boundary between nations, regardless of the legal or historical situation. The symbols are explained on the front endpaper of the atlas.

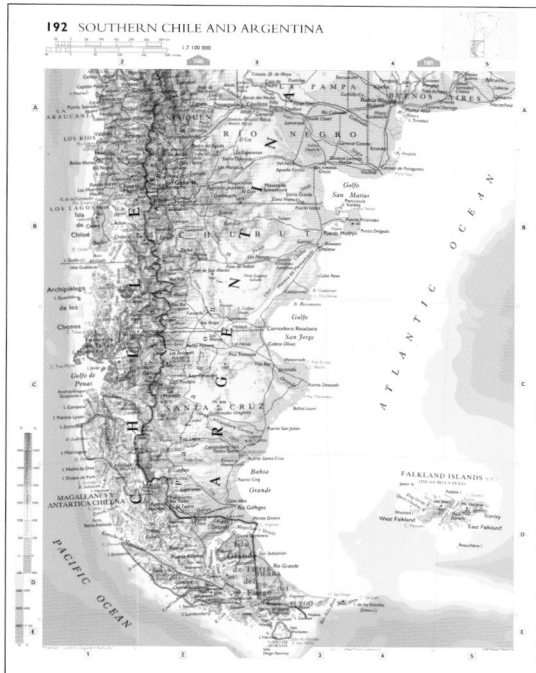

MAP SCALES

1:16 000 000
1 inch = 252 statute miles

The scale of each map is given in the numerical form known as the 'representative fraction'. The first figure is always one, signifying one unit of distance on the map; the second figure, usually in millions, is the number by which the map must be multiplied to give the equivalent distance on the Earth's surface. Calculations can easily be made in centimetres and kilometres, by dividing the Earth units figure by 100 000 (i.e. deleting the last five 0s). Thus 1:1 000 000 means 1 cm = 10 km. The calculation for inches and miles is more laborious, but 1 000 000 divided by 63 360 (the number of inches in a mile) shows that 1:1 000 000 means approximately 1 inch = 16 miles. The table below provides distance equivalents for scales down to 1:50 000 000.

LARGE SCALE		
1:1 000 000	1 cm = 10 km	1 inch = 16 miles
1:2 500 000	1 cm = 25 km	1 inch = 39.5 miles
1:5 000 000	1 cm = 50 km	1 inch = 79 miles
1:6 000 000	1 cm = 60 km	1 inch = 95 miles
1:8 000 000	1 cm = 80 km	1 inch = 126 miles
1:10 000 000	1 cm = 100 km	1 inch = 158 miles
1:15 000 000	1 cm = 150 km	1 inch = 237 miles
1:20 000 000	1 cm = 200 km	1 inch = 316 miles
1:50 000 000	1 cm = 500 km	1 inch = 790 miles
SMALL SCALE		

MEASURING DISTANCES

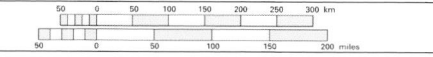

Although each map is accompanied by a scale bar, distances cannot always be measured with confidence because of the distortions involved in portraying the curved surface of the Earth on a flat page. As a general rule, the larger the map scale (that is, the lower the number of Earth units in the representative fraction), the more accurate and reliable will be the distance measured. On small-scale maps such as those of the world and of entire continents, measurement may only be accurate

along the 'standard parallels', or central axes, and should not be attempted without considering the map projection.

MAP PROJECTIONS

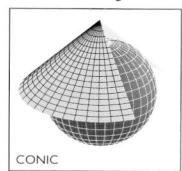
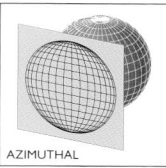
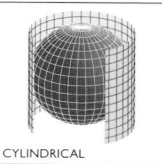

Unlike a globe, no flat map can give a true scale representation of the world in terms of area, shape and position of every region. Each of the numerous systems that have been devised for projecting the curved surface of the Earth on to a flat page involves the sacrifice of accuracy in one or more of these elements. The variations in shape and position of landmasses such as Alaska, Greenland and Australia, for example, can be quite dramatic when different projections are compared. For this atlas, the guiding principle has been to select projections that involve the least distortion of size and distance. The projection used for each map is noted in the border. Most fall into one of three categories – conic, azimuthal or cylindrical – whose basic concepts are shown above. Each involves plotting the forms of the Earth's surface on a grid of latitude and longitude lines, which may be shown as parallels, curves or radiating spokes.

LATITUDE AND LONGITUDE

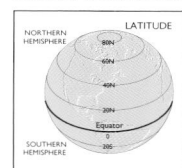
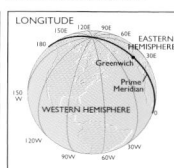
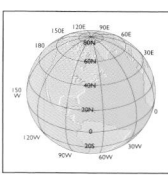

Accurate positioning of individual points on the Earth's surface is made possible by reference to the geometrical system of latitude and longitude. Latitude *parallels* are drawn west–east around the Earth and numbered by degrees north and south of the equator, which is designated 0° of latitude. Longitude *meridians* are drawn north–south and numbered by degrees east and west of the *prime meridian*, 0° of longitude, which passes through Greenwich in England. By referring to these co-ordinates and their subdivisions of minutes (1/60th of a degree) and seconds (1/60th of a minute), any place on Earth can be located to within a few hundred metres. Latitude and longitude are indicated by blue lines on the maps; they are straight or curved according to the projection employed. Reference to these lines is the easiest way of determining the relative positions of places on different maps, and for plotting compass directions.

NAME FORMS

For ease of reference, both English and local name forms appear in the atlas. Oceans, seas and countries are shown in English throughout the atlas; country names may be abbreviated to their commonly accepted form (for example, Germany, not The Federal Republic of Germany). Conventional English forms are also used for place names on the smaller-scale maps of the continents. However, local name forms are used on all large-scale and regional maps, with the English form given in brackets only for important cities – the large-scale map of Russia and Northern Asia thus shows Moskva (Moscow). For countries which do not use a Roman script, place names have been transcribed according to the systems adopted by the British and US Geographic Names Authorities. For China, the Pin Yin system has been used, with some more widely known forms appearing in brackets, as with Beijing (Peking). Both English and local names appear in the index, the English form being cross-referenced to the local form.

CONTENTS

WORLD STATISTICS

COUNTRIES	8
CITIES	9
CLIMATE	10–11
PHYSICAL DIMENSIONS	12–13

IMAGES OF EARTH

PARIS, FRANCE	16
COPENHAGEN, DENMARK	17
ST PETERSBURG, RUSSIA	18
BUDAPEST, HUNGARY	19
BARCELONA, SPAIN	20
DUBAI, UNITED ARAB EMIRATES	21
KATHMANDU, NEPAL	22
KOLKATA, INDIA	23
BANGKOK, THAILAND	24
BEIJING, CHINA	25
KHARTOUM, SUDAN	26
LAGOS, NIGERIA	27
BRAZZAVILLE, CONGO/KINSHASA, D.R. CONGO	28
DAR ES SALAAM, TANZANIA	29
MELBOURNE, AUSTRALIA	30
CHRISTCHURCH, NEW ZEALAND	31
OTTAWA, CANADA	32
NEW YORK, UNITED STATES OF AMERICA	33
MEMPHIS, UNITED STATES OF AMERICA	34
LAS VEGAS, UNITED STATES OF AMERICA	35
LOS ANGELES, UNITED STATES OF AMERICA	36
MEXICO CITY, MEXICO	37
BRASILIA, BRAZIL	38
SAO PAULO, BRAZIL	39

OCEAN SEAFLOORS

ARCTIC OCEAN SEAFLOOR	41
ATLANTIC OCEAN SEAFLOOR	42–43
PACIFIC OCEAN SEAFLOOR	44–45
INDIAN OCEAN SEAFLOOR	46
SOUTHERN OCEAN SEAFLOOR	47

WORLD MAPS

THE WORLD: PHYSICAL 1:84 000 000	50–51
THE WORLD: POLITICAL 1:84 000 000	52–53
ARCTIC OCEAN 1:31 100 000	54
ANTARCTICA 1:31 100 000	55
ATLANTIC OCEAN 1:45 000 000	56
GREENLAND 1:11 100 000	57

EUROPE

EUROPE: PHYSICAL 1:17 800 000	58
EUROPE: POLITICAL 1:17 800 000	59
SCANDINAVIA 1:5 300 000 Iceland 1:5 300 000 Færoe Islands 1:5 300 000	60–61
DENMARK AND SOUTHERN SWEDEN 1:2 200 000	62–63
IRELAND 1:1 800 000	64
SCOTLAND 1:1 800 000 Orkney Islands 1:1 800 000 Shetland Islands 1:1 800 000	65
ENGLAND AND WALES 1:1 800 000 Isles of Scilly 1:1 800 000	66–67
BRITISH ISLES 1:4 400 000	68
NETHERLANDS, BELGIUM AND LUXEMBOURG 1:2 200 000	69
NORTHERN FRANCE 1:2 200 000	70–71
SOUTHERN FRANCE 1:2 200 000	72–73
CENTRAL EUROPE 1:4 400 000	74–75
GERMANY AND SWITZERLAND 1:2 200 000	76–77
AUSTRIA, CZECHIA AND SLOVAKIA 1:2 200 000	78–79
HUNGARY, ROMANIA AND THE LOWER DANUBE 1:2 200 000	80–81
POLAND AND THE SOUTHERN BALTIC 1:2 200 000	82–83
BALTIC STATES, BELARUS AND UKRAINE 1:4 400 000	84–85
THE VOLGA BASIN AND THE CAUCASUS 1:4 400 000	86–87
WESTERN SPAIN AND PORTUGAL 1:2 200 000	88–89
EASTERN SPAIN 1:2 200 000 Menorca 1:2 200 000	90–91
NORTHERN ITALY, SLOVENIA AND CROATIA 1:2 200 000	92–93
SOUTHERN ITALY 1:2 200 000	94–95
THE BALKANS 1:2 200 000	96–97
SOUTHERN GREECE AND WESTERN TURKEY 1:2 200 000	98–99
THE BALEARICS, THE CANARIES AND MADEIRA 1:900 000 / 1:1 800 000	100
MALTA, CRETE, CORFU, RHODES AND CYPRUS 1:900 000 / 1:1 200 000	101

ASIA

ASIA: PHYSICAL 1:44 400 000	102
ASIA: POLITICAL 1:44 400 000	103
TURKEY AND TRANSCAUCASIA 1:4 400 000	104–105
RUSSIA AND NORTHERN ASIA 1:17 800 000	106–107
KAZAKHSTAN AND CENTRAL ASIA 1:8 900 000	108–109
CHINA AND THE FAR EAST 1:13 300 000 Hong Kong, Macau and Shenzhen 1:890 000	110–111

JAPAN 112–113
1:4 400 000
Ryukyu Islands 1:4 400 000

NORTHERN CHINA AND KOREA 114–115
1:5 300 000

SOUTHERN CHINA AND TAIWAN 116–117
1:5 300 000
Hainan 1:5 300 000

INDONESIA AND THE PHILIPPINES 118–119
1:11 100 000
Java and Madura 1:6 700 000
Bali 1:1 800 000

MAINLAND SOUTH-EAST ASIA 120–121
1:5 300 000
Ko Phuket 1:900 000
Ko Samui 1:900 000
Pinang 1:900 000
Singapore 1:900 000

SOUTH ASIA 122–123
1:8 900 000

NORTHERN INDIA, PAKISTAN
    AND NEPAL 124–125
1:5 300 000
Jammu and Kashmir 1:5 300 000

SOUTHERN INDIA AND SRI LANKA 126–127
1:5 300 000
Lakshadweep Islands 1:5 300 000
Andaman and Nicobar Islands 1:5 300 000

THE MIDDLE EAST 128–129
1:6 200 000

THE NEAR EAST 130
1:2 200 000

ARABIA AND THE HORN OF AFRICA 131
1:13 300 000

AFRICA

AFRICA: PHYSICAL 132
1:37 300 000

AFRICA: POLITICAL 133
1:37 300 000

NORTHERN AFRICA 134–135
1:13 300 000
Azores 1:13 300 000
Cape Verde Islands 1:8 900 000

MOROCCO, ALGERIA AND TUNISIA 136
1:7 100 000

EGYPT 137
1:7 100 000

WEST AFRICA 138–139
1:7 100 000

CENTRAL AND SOUTHERN AFRICA 140–141
1:13 300 000
Seychelles 1:2 200 000
Réunion 1:2 200 000
Mauritius 1:2 200 000
Comoros 1:7 100 000
Madagascar 1:13 300 000

EAST AFRICA 142–143
1:7 100 000

SOUTHERN AFRICA 144–145
1:7 100 000

INDIAN OCEAN 146
1:45 000 000

AUSTRALIA AND OCEANIA

AUSTRALIA AND OCEANIA:
    PHYSICAL AND POLITICAL 147
1:44 400 000

WESTERN AUSTRALIA 148–149
1:7 100 000

EASTERN AUSTRALIA 150–151
1:7 100 000
Whitsunday Islands 1:2 200 000
Tasmania 1:7 100 000
Torres Strait 1:7 100 000

SOUTH-EASTERN AUSTRALIA 152–153
1:3 500 000

NEW ZEALAND – NORTH ISLAND 154
1:3 100 000
Fiji 1:5 300 000

NEW ZEALAND – SOUTH ISLAND 155
1:3 100 000
Tahiti and Moorea 1:900 000
Chatham Islands 1:3 100 000

PACIFIC OCEAN 156–157
1:48 000 000

NORTH AMERICA

NORTH AMERICA: PHYSICAL 158
1:31 100 000

NORTH AMERICA: POLITICAL 159
1:31 100 000

CANADA 160–161
1:13 300 000
Northern Canada 1:13 300 000

WESTERN CANADA 162–163
1:6 200 000

EASTERN CANADA 164–165
1:6 200 000

UNITED STATES 166–167
1:13 300 000
Hawai'i 1:13 300 000
Alaska 1:13 300 000

UNITED STATES – WEST 168–169
1:6 250 000

CENTRAL AND SOUTHERN
    CALIFORNIA AND
    WESTERN WASHINGTON 170–171
1:2 200 000

UNITED STATES – MIDWEST
    AND NORTH-EAST 172–173
1:6 250 000

NORTH-EASTERN UNITED STATES 174–175
1:2 200 000

UNITED STATES – SOUTH 176–177
1:6 250 000

SOUTH-EASTERN UNITED STATES 178–179
1:2 200 000

MEXICO 180–181
1:7 100 000

CENTRAL AMERICA AND
    the WEST INDIES 182–183
1:7 100 000
Jamaica 1:2 700 000
Guadeloupe 1:1 800 000
Martinique 1:1 800 000
Puerto Rico 1:2 700 000
Virgin Islands 1:1 800 000
St Lucia 1:890 000
Barbados 1:890 000

SOUTH AMERICA

SOUTH AMERICA: PHYSICAL 184
1:31 100 000

SOUTH AMERICA: POLITICAL 185
1:31 100 000

SOUTH AMERICA – NORTH 186–187
1:14 200 000
Trinidad and Tobago 1:2 200 000

PERU AND THE CENTRAL ANDES 188
1:7 100 000

NORTH-EASTERN BRAZIL 189
1:7 100 000

CENTRAL SOUTH AMERICA 190–191
1:7 100 000

SOUTHERN CHILE AND ARGENTINA 192
1:7 100 000

INDEX TO WORLD
    MAPS 193–288

WORLD STATISTICS: COUNTRIES

This alphabetical list includes the principal countries and territories of the world. If a territory is not completely independent, the country it is associated with is named. The area figures give the total area of land, inland water and ice. The population figures are 2017 estimates where available. The annual income is the Gross Domestic Product per capita (PPP) in US dollars. The figures are the latest available, usually 2017 estimates.

Country/Territory	Area km² Thousands	Area miles² Thousands	Population Thousands	Capital	Annual Income US $
Afghanistan	652	252	34,125	Kabul	1,900
Albania	28.7	11.1	3,048	Tirana	12,500
Algeria	2,382	920	40,969	Algiers	15,100
American Samoa (US)	0.20	0.08	52	Pago Pago	13,000
Andorra	0.47	0.18	86	Andorra La Vella	49,900
Angola	1,247	481	29,310	Luanda	6,800
Anguilla (UK)	0.10	0.04	17	The Valley	12,200
Antigua & Barbuda	0.44	0.17	95	St John's	26,300
Argentina	2,780	1,074	44,293	Buenos Aires	20,700
Armenia	29.8	11.5	3,045	Yerevan	9,100
Aruba (Netherlands)	0.19	0.07	115	Oranjestad	25,300
Australia	7,741	2,989	23,232	Canberra	49,900
Austria	83.9	32.4	8,754	Vienna	49,200
Azerbaijan	86.6	33.4	9,961	Baku	17,400
Azores (Portugal)	2.2	0.86	246	Ponta Delgada	15,197
Bahamas	13.9	5.4	330	Nassau	25,100
Bahrain	0.69	0.27	1,411	Manama	51,800
Bangladesh	144	55.6	157,827	Dhaka	4,200
Barbados	0.43	0.17	292	Bridgetown	17,500
Belarus	208	80.2	9,550	Minsk	18,600
Belgium	30.5	11.8	11,491	Brussels	46,300
Belize	23.0	8.9	360	Belmopan	8,300
Benin	113	43.5	11,039	Porto-Novo	2,200
Bermuda (UK)	0.05	0.02	71	Hamilton	85,700
Bhutan	47.0	18.1	758	Thimphu	8,700
Bolivia	1,099	424	11,138	La Paz/Sucre	7,500
Bosnia-Herzegovina	51.2	19.8	3,856	Sarajevo	11,400
Botswana	582	225	2,215	Gaborone	18,100
Brazil	8,514	3,287	207,353	Brasília	15,500
Brunei	5.8	2.2	444	Bandar Seri Begawan	76,700
Bulgaria	111	42.8	7,102	Sofia	21,600
Burkina Faso	274	106	20,108	Ouagadougou	1,900
Burundi	27.8	10.7	11,467	Bujumbura	800
Cabo Verde	4.0	1.6	561	Praia	6,900
Cambodia	181	69.9	16,204	Phnom Penh	4,000
Cameroon	475	184	24,995	Yaoundé	3,400
Canada	9,971	3,850	35,624	Ottawa	48,100
Canary Is. (Spain)	7.2	2.8	2,105	Las Palmas/Santa Cruz	19,900
Cayman Is. (UK)	0.26	0.10	58	George Town	43,800
Central African Republic	623	241	5,625	Bangui	700
Chad	1,284	496	12,076	Ndjaména	2,400
Chile	757	292	17,789	Santiago	24,600
China	9,597	3,705	1,379,303	Beijing	16,600
Colombia	1,139	440	47,699	Bogotá	14,500
Comoros	2.2	0.86	808	Moroni	1,600
Congo	342	132	4,955	Brazzaville	6,700
Congo (Dem. Rep. of the)	2,345	905	83,301	Kinshasa	800
Cook Is. (NZ)	0.24	0.09	9	Avarua	12,300
Costa Rica	51.1	19.7	4,930	San José	17,200
Côte d'Ivoire (Ivory Coast)	322	125	24,185	Yamoussoukro	3,900
Croatia	56.5	21.8	4,292	Zagreb	24,100
Cuba	111	42.8	11,147	Havana	11,900
Curaçao (Netherlands)	0.44	0.17	150	Willemstad	15,000
Cyprus	9.3	3.6	1,222	Nicosia	36,600
Czechia	78.9	30.5	10,675	Prague	35,200
Denmark	43.1	16.6	5,606	Copenhagen	49,600
Djibouti	23.2	9.0	865	Djibouti	3,600
Dominica	0.75	0.29	74	Roseau	12,000
Dominican Republic	48.5	18.7	10,734	Santo Domingo	17,000
East Timor	14.9	5.7	1,291	Dili	5,000
Ecuador	284	109	16,291	Quito	11,000
Egypt	1,001	387	97,041	Cairo	13,000
El Salvador	21.0	8.1	6,172	San Salvador	8,900
Equatorial Guinea	28.1	10.8	778	Malabo	34,900
Eritrea	118	45.4	5,919	Asmara	1,400
Estonia	45.1	17.4	1,252	Tallinn	31,500
Ethiopia	1,104	426	105,350	Addis Ababa	2,100
Falkland Is. (UK)	12.2	4.7	3	Stanley	96,200
Faroe Is. (Denmark)	1.4	0.54	51	Tórshavn	40,000
Fiji	18.3	7.1	921	Suva	9,900
Finland	338	131	5,518	Helsinki	44,000
France	552	213	67,106	Paris	43,600
French Guiana (France)	90.0	34.7	250	Cayenne	8,300
French Polynesia (France)	4.0	1.5	281	Papeete	17,000
Gabon	268	103	1,772	Libreville	19,300
Gambia, The	11.3	4.4	2,051	Banjul	1,700
Georgia	69.7	26.9	4,926	Tbilisi	10,600
Germany	357	138	80,594	Berlin	50,200
Ghana	239	92.1	27,500	Accra	4,600
Gibraltar (UK)	0.006	0.002	29	Gibraltar Town	61,700
Greece	132	50.9	10,768	Athens	27,800
Greenland (Denmark)	2,176	840	58	Nuuk	37,600
Grenada	0.34	0.13	112	St George's	14,700
Guadeloupe (France)	1.7	0.66	402	Basse-Terre	7,900
Guam (US)	0.55	0.21	167	Agana	30,500
Guatemala	109	42.0	15,461	Guatemala City	8,200
Guinea	246	94.9	12,414	Conakry	2,000
Guinea-Bissau	36.1	13.9	1,792	Bissau	1,800
Guyana	215	83.0	738	Georgetown	8,300
Haiti	27.8	10.7	10,647	Port-au-Prince	1,800
Honduras	112	43.3	9,039	Tegucigalpa	5,500
Hungary	93.0	35.9	9,851	Budapest	28,900
Iceland	103	39.8	340	Reykjavik	52,100
India	3,287	1,269	1,281,936	New Delhi	7,200
Indonesia	1,905	735	260,581	Jakarta	12,400
Iran	1,648	636	82,022	Tehran	20,000
Iraq	438	169	39,192	Baghdad	17,000
Ireland	70.3	27.1	5,011	Dublin	72,600
Israel	20.6	8.0	8,300	Jerusalem	36,200
Italy	301	116	62,138	Rome	38,000
Jamaica	11.0	4.2	2,991	Kingston	9,200
Japan	378	146	126,451	Tokyo	42,700
Jordan	89.3	34.5	10,248	Amman	12,500
Kazakhstan	2,725	1,052	18,557	Astana	26,100
Kenya	580	224	47,616	Nairobi	3,500
Kiribati	0.73	0.28	108	Tarawa	1,900
Korea, North	121	46.5	25,248	Pyo˘ngyang	1,700
Korea, South	99.3	38.3	51,181	Seoul	39,400
Kosovo	10.9	4.2	1,895	Pristina	10,400
Kuwait	17.8	6.9	2,875	Kuwait City	69,700
Kyrgyzstan	200	77.2	5,789	Bishkek	3,700
Laos	237	91.4	7,127	Vientiane	7,400
Latvia	64.6	24.9	1,945	Riga	27,300
Lebanon	10.4	4.0	6,230	Beirut	19,500
Lesotho	30.4	11.7	1,958	Maseru	3,900
Liberia	111	43.0	4,689	Monrovia	900
Libya	1,760	679	6,653	Tripoli	9,800
Liechtenstein	0.16	0.06	38	Vaduz	139,100
Lithuania	65.2	25.2	2,824	Vilnius	31,900
Luxembourg	2.6	1.0	594	Luxembourg	109,100
Macedonia (FYROM)	25.7	9.9	2,104	Skopje	15,200
Madagascar	587	227	25,054	Antananarivo	1,600
Madeira (Portugal)	0.78	0.30	289	Funchal	25,800
Malawi	118	45.7	19,196	Lilongwe	1,200
Malaysia	330	127	31,382	Kuala Lumpur/Putrajaya	28,900
Maldives	0.30	0.12	393	Malé	19,200
Mali	1,240	479	17,885	Bamako	2,200
Malta	0.32	0.12	416	Valletta	42,500
Marshall Is.	0.18	0.07	75	Majuro	3,400
Martinique (France)	1.1	0.43	371	Fort-de-France	14,400
Mauritania	1,026	396	3,759	Nouakchott	4,500
Mauritius	2.0	0.79	1,356	Port Louis	21,600
Mayotte (France)	0.37	0.14	213	Mamoudzou	4,900
Mexico	1,958	756	124,575	Mexico City	19,500
Micronesia, Fed. States of	0.70	0.27	104	Palikir	3,400
Moldova	33.9	13.1	3,474	Kishinev	5,700
Monaco	0.002	0.0008	31	Monaco	115,700
Mongolia	1,567	605	3,068	Ulan Bator	12,600
Montenegro	14.0	5.4	643	Podgorica	17,400
Montserrat (UK)	0.10	0.39	5	Brades	8,500
Morocco	447	172	33,987	Rabat	8,600
Mozambique	802	309	26,574	Maputo	1,300
Myanmar (Burma)	677	261	55,124	Rangoon/Naypyidaw	6,300
Namibia	824	318	2,485	Windhoek	11,500
Nauru	0.02	0.008	10	Yaren	12,200
Nepal	147	56.8	29,384	Katmandu	2,700
Netherlands	41.5	16.0	17,085	Amsterdam/The Hague	53,600
New Caledonia (France)	18.6	7.2	279	Nouméa	31,100
New Zealand	271	104	4,510	Wellington	38,500
Nicaragua	130	50.2	6,026	Managua	5,800
Niger	1,267	489	19,245	Niamey	1,200
Nigeria	924	357	190,632	Abuja	5,900
Northern Mariana Is. (US)	0.46	0.18	52	Saipan	13,300
Norway	324	125	5,320	Oslo	70,600
Oman	310	119	3,424	Muscat	45,500
Pakistan	796	307	204,925	Islamabad	5,400
Palau	0.46	0.18	21	Melekeok	16,700
Panama	75.5	29.2	3,753	Panamá	24,300
Papua New Guinea	463	179	6,910	Port Moresby	3,800
Paraguay	407	157	6,944	Asunción	9,800
Peru	1,285	496	31,037	Lima	13,300
Philippines	300	116	104,256	Manila	8,200
Poland	323	125	38,476	Warsaw	29,300
Portugal	88.8	34.3	10,840	Lisbon	30,300
Puerto Rico (US)	8.9	3.4	3,352	San Juan	37,900
Qatar	11.0	4.2	2,314	Doha	124,900
Réunion (France)	2.5	0.97	845	St-Denis	6,200
Romania	238	92.0	21,530	Bucharest	24,000
Russia	17,075	6,593	142,258	Moscow	27,900
Rwanda	26.3	10.2	11,901	Kigali	2,100
St Kitts & Nevis	0.26	0.10	52	Basseterre	26,800
St Lucia	0.54	0.21	164	Castries	13,500
St Vincent & Grenadines	0.39	0.15	102	Kingstown	11,600
Samoa	2.8	1.1	200	Apia	5,700
San Marino	0.06	0.02	34	San Marino	59,500
São Tomé & Príncipe	0.96	0.37	201	São Tomé	3,200
Saudi Arabia	2,150	830	28,572	Riyadh	55,300
Senegal	197	76.0	14,669	Dakar	2,700
Serbia	77.5	29.9	7,111	Belgrade	15,200
Seychelles	0.46	0.18	94	Victoria	28,900
Sierra Leone	71.7	27.7	6,163	Freetown	1,800
Singapore	0.68	0.26	5,889	Singapore City	90,500
Slovakia	49.0	18.9	5,446	Bratislava	32,900
Slovenia	20.3	7.8	1,972	Ljubljana	34,100
Solomon Is.	28.9	11.2	648	Honiara	2,100
Somalia	638	246	11,031	Mogadishu	400
South Africa	1,221	471	54,842	Cape Town/Pretoria	13,400
Spain	498	192	48,958	Madrid	38,200
Sri Lanka	65.6	25.3	22,409	Colombo	13,000
Sudan	1,886	728	37,346	Khartoum	4,600
Sudan, South	620	239	13,026	Juba	1,500
Suriname	163	63.0	592	Paramaribo	13,900
Swaziland (eSwatini)	17.4	6.7	1,467	Mbabane	9,900
Sweden	450	174	9,960	Stockholm	51,300
Switzerland	41.3	15.9	8,236	Bern	61,400
Syria	185	71.5	18,029	Damascus	2,900
Taiwan	36.0	13.9	23,508	Taipei	49,800
Tajikistan	143	55.3	8,469	Dushanbe	3,100
Tanzania	945	365	53,951	Dodoma	3,300
Thailand	513	198	68,414	Bangkok	17,800
Togo	56.8	21.9	7,965	Lomé	1,600
Tonga	0.65	0.25	106	Nuku'alofa	5,600
Trinidad & Tobago	5.1	2.0	1,218	Port of Spain	31,200
Tunisia	164	63.2	11,404	Tunis	12,000
Turkey	775	299	80,845	Ankara	26,500
Turkmenistan	488	188	5,351	Ashkhabad	18,700
Turks & Caicos Is. (UK)	0.43	0.17	53	Cockburn Town	29,100
Tuvalu	0.03	0.01	11	Fongafale	3,800
Uganda	241	93.1	39,570	Kampala	2,400
Ukraine	604	233	44,034	Kiev	8,700
United Arab Emirates	83.6	32.3	5,927	Abu Dhabi	68,200
United Kingdom	242	93.4	64,769	London	43,600
United States of America	9,629	3,718	326,626	Washington, DC	59,500
Uruguay	175	67.6	3,361	Montevideo	22,400
Uzbekistan	447	173	29,749	Tashkent	7,000
Vanuatu	12.2	4.7	283	Port-Vila	2,800
Vatican City	0.0004	0.0002	1	Vatican City	
Venezuela	912	352	31,304	Caracas	12,400
Vietnam	332	128	96,160	Hanoi	6,900
Virgin Is. (UK)	0.15	0.06	35	Road Town	42,300
Virgin Is. (US)	0.35	0.13	107	Charlotte Amalie	36,100
Yemen	528	204	28,037	Sana'	2,300
Zambia	753	291	15,972	Lusaka	4,000
Zimbabwe	391	151	13,805	Harare	2,300

WORLD STATISTICS: CITIES

This list shows the principal cities with more than 900,000 inhabitants. The figures are taken from the most recent census or estimate available and as far as possible are the population of the metropolitan area or urban agglomeration. The list includes Metropolitan Statistical Areas from the United States Census Bureau. All the figures are in thousands. Local name forms have been used for the smaller cities (for example, Antwerpen).

AFGHANISTAN
Kabul 5,056
ALGERIA
Algiers 2,676
ANGOLA
Luanda 5,985
Huambo 1,409
ARGENTINA
Buenos Aires 15,482
Córdoba 1,528
Rosario 1,409
Mendoza 1,030
San Miguel de Tucumán 933
ARMENIA
Yerevan 1,036
AUSTRALIA
Sydney 4,580
Melbourne 4,316
Brisbane 2,275
Perth 1,931
Adelaide 1,276
AUSTRIA
Vienna 1,773
AZERBAIJAN
Baku 2,483
BANGLADESH
Dhaka 18,898
Chittagong 4,751
Khulna 1,010
BELARUS
Minsk 1,934
BELGIUM
Brussels 2,076
Antwerpen 1,002
BOLIVIA
Santa Cruz 2,254
La Paz 1,854
Cochabamba 1,305
BRAZIL
São Paulo 21,519
Rio de Janeiro 13,063
Belo Horizonte 5,816
Brasília 4,311
Fortaleza 4,005
Recife 3,797
Salvador 3,663
Pôrto Alegre 3,642
Curitiba 3,598
Campinas 3,134
Goiânia 2,368
Belém 2,236
Manaus 2,110
Vitória 1,674
Santos 1,674
São Luís 1,483
Maceió 1,305
Joinville 1,255
Florianópolis 1,243
Natal 1,205
João Pessoa 1,124
Teresina 979
BULGARIA
Sofia 1,234
BURKINA FASO
Ouagadougou 1,234
CAMBODIA
Phnom Penh 1,827
CAMEROON
Yaoundé 3,343
Douala 3,161
CANADA
Toronto 6,170
Montréal 4,049
Vancouver 2,561
Calgary 1,392
Ottawa 1,366
Edmonton 1,322
CHAD
Ndjamena 1,362
CHILE
Santiago 6,582
Valparaiso 919
CHINA
Shanghai 25,202
Beijing 22,063
Chongqing 14,144
Guangzhou, Guangdong 13,659
Tianjin 11,896
Shenzhen 10,919
Chengdu 8,077
Wuhan 8,060
Nanjing, Jiangsu 7,842
Dongguan, Guangdong 7,513
Hong Kong 7,414
Foshan 7,151
Hangzhou 6,917
Shenyang 6,561
Xi'an, Shaanxi 6,392
Suzhou, Jiangsu 6,093
Harbin 5,673
Xiamen 5,037
Qingdao 4,804
Dalian 4,733
Zhengzhou 4,686
Jinan, Shandong 4,241
Zhongshan 4,118
Shantou 4,075
Changsha 3,999
Kunming 3,939
Changchun 3,907
Ürümqi 3,774
Taiyuan, Shanxi 3,617
Nanning 3,478
Fuzhou, Fujian 3,474
Shijiazhuang 3,472
Hefei 3,451
Wenzhou 3,428
Ningbo 3,365

Wuxi, Jiangsu 3,169
Guiyang 3,017
Tangshan 2,959
Lanzhou 2,841
Changzhou, Jiangsu 2,720
Nanchang 2,653
Huizhou 2,533
Zibo 2,501
Weifang 2,342
Yantai 2,247
Shaoxing 2,224
Huai'an 2,212
Luoyang 2,135
Nantong 2,135
Haikou 2,070
Baotou 2,034
Xuzhou 1,994
Hohhot 1,906
Yangzhou 1,841
Yinchuan 1,796
Linyi 1,782
Handan 1,771
Taizhou, Zhejiang 1,741
Liuzhou 1,706
Daqing 1,700
Zhuhai 1,614
Jiangmen 1,612
Datong 1,602
Anshan 1,584
Putian 1,583
Xiangyang 1,576
Yancheng 1,566
Wuhu 1,563
Jilin 1,549
Quanzhou 1,498
Qiqihar 1,488
Jining, Shandong 1,422
Cixi 1,407
Xining 1,394
Hengyang 1,379
Chaozhou 1,366
Huainan 1,365
Yichang 1,355
Fushun 1,295
Tai'an 1,260
Anyang 1,241
Taizhou, Jiangsu 1,238
Zhanjiang 1,195
Lianyungang 1,186
Suqian 1,170
Qinhuangdao 1,168
Yiwu 1,167
Baoding 1,135
Rizhao 1,130
Zhuzhou 1,118
Nanchong 1,117
Mianyang 1,106
Benxi 1,100
Zhenjiang 1,091
Jinhua 1,088
Yingkou 1,087
Guilin 1,072
Jinzhou 1,072
Chifeng 1,067
Jiaxing 1,061
Puning 1,059
Nanyang 1,058
Xiangtan 1,054
Baoji 1,054
Zaozhuang 1,049
Pingdingshan 1,049
Ruian 1,036
Huaibei 1,033
Tengzhou 1,031
Xinxiang 1,021
Dongying 1,017
Zhangjiakou 1,008
Suzhou 1,001
Jingzhou 989
Jieyang 984
Yueyang 978
Liuan 977
Fuyang 940
Yueqing 931
Wenling 927
Liuyang 925
COLOMBIA
Bogotá 10,165
Medellín 4,032
Cali 2,718
Barranquilla 2,027
Bucaramanga 1,255
Cartagena 1,134
CONGO
Brazzaville 2,012
Pointe-Noire 1,029
CONGO (DEM. REP. OF THE)
Kinshasa 12,566
Mbuji-Mayi 2,189
Lubumbashi 2,181
Kananga 1,271
Kisangani 1,120
Bukavu 917
COSTA RICA
San José 1,198
CÔTE D'IVOIRE (IVORY COAST)
Abidjan 5,188
CUBA
Havana 2,122
CZECHIA
Prague 1,335
DENMARK
Copenhagen 1,294
DOMINICAN REPUBLIC
Santo Domingo 3,097

ECUADOR
Guayaquil 2,804
Quito 1,783
EGYPT
Cairo 19,486
Alexandria 4,950
EL SALVADOR
San Salvador 1,106
ETHIOPIA
Addis Ababa 3,408
FINLAND
Helsinki 1,199
FRANCE
Paris 11,011
Lyon 1,636
Marseilles 1,628
Lille 1,035
Nice 979
Toulouse 963
Bordeaux 911
GEORGIA
Tbilisi 1,143
GERMANY
Berlin 3,593
Hamburg 1,847
Munich 1,468
Cologne 1,047
GHANA
Kumasi 2,836
Accra 2,358
GREECE
Athens 3,044
GUATEMALA
Guatemala City 3,076
GUINEA
Conakry 2,045
HAITI
Port-au-Prince 2,579
HONDURAS
Tegucigalpa 1,170
San Pedro Sula 911
HUNGARY
Budapest 1,712
INDIA
Delhi 27,197
Mumbai 21,690
Kolkata 15,119
Bengaluru 10,819
Chennai 10,435
Hyderabad 9,489
Ahmedabad 7,796
Surat 6,149
Pune 6,037
Jaipur 3,638
Lucknow 3,369
Kanpur 3,074
Nagpur 2,759
Coimbatore 2,733
Calicut 2,685
Indore 2,566
Thrissur 2,554
Kochi 2,553
Malappuram 2,466
Kannur 2,400
Patna 2,286
Bhopal 2,202
Thiruvananthapuram 2,093
Agra 2,067
Vadodara 2,049
Vishakhapatnam 2,030
Vijayawada 1,884
Nashik 1,879
Ludhiana 1,765
Rajkot 1,695
Madurai 1,654
Meerut 1,609
Varanasi 1,592
Kollam 1,553
Jamshedpur 1,505
Srinagar 1,500
Raipur 1,492
Aurangabad 1,416
Jabalpur 1,370
Tiruppur 1,359
Jodhpur 1,352
Asansol 1,348
Allahabad 1,332
Ranchi 1,324
Amritsar 1,304
Dhanbad 1,284
Gwalior 1,276
Kota 1,238
Chandigarh 1,185
Bareilly 1,171
Bhilainagar-Durg 1,161
Tiruchchirapalli 1,146
Mysore 1,128
Aligarh 1,096
Moradabad 1,085
Guwahati 1,077
Hubli-Dharwad 1,056
Bhubaneswar 1,054
Salem 1,042
Solapur 1,042
Jalandhar 992
Saharanpur 917
INDONESIA
Jakarta 10,660
Surabaya 2,909
Bandung 2,618
Medan 2,261
Semarang 1,670
Batam 1,606
Makassar 1,558
Palembang 1,469
Denpasar 1,247
Pekanbaru 1,216
Bogor 1,130

Bandar Lampung 1,130
Padang 936
Samarinda 924
IRAN
Tehran 8,604
Mashhad 3,160
Esfahan 1,950
Karaj 1,913
Shiraz 1,770
Tabriz 1,617
Ahvaz 1,273
Qom 1,264
Kermanshah 923
IRAQ
Baghdad 6,988
Mosul 1,806
Arbil 1,237
Basra 1,065
As Sulaymaniyah 1,079
Najaf 950
IRELAND
Dublin 1,201
ISRAEL
Tel Aviv-Yafo 3,717
Haifa 1,115
ITALY
Rome 3,756
Milan 3,109
Naples 2,195
Turin 1,773
JAPAN
Tokyo–Yokohama 38,241
Osaka–Kobe 20,415
Nagoya 9,456
Fukuoka–Kitakyushu 5,478
Shizuoka–Hamamatsu 3,605
Sapporo 2,558
Hiroshima 2,186
Sendai 2,053
JORDAN
Amman 1,160
KAZAKHSTAN
Almaty 1,547
KENYA
Nairobi 4,235
Mombasa 1,182
KOREA, NORTH
Pyŏngyang 2,884
KOREA, SOUTH
Seoul 9,791
Busan 3,190
Incheon 2,738
Daegu 2,240
Gwangju 1,654
Daejeon 1,592
Yongin 1,131
Suwon 1,113
Changwon 1,036
Seongnam 979
Goyang 960
Ulsan 911
KUWAIT
Kuwait City 2,963
LAOS
Vientiane 1,104
LEBANON
Beirut 2,277
LIBERIA
Monrovia 1,349
LIBYA
Tripoli 1,133
MADAGASCAR
Antananarivo 2,873
MALAWI
Lilongwe 987
MALAYSIA
Kuala Lumpur 7,254
Johor Bahru 955
MALI
Bamako 2,795
MAURITANIA
Nouakchott 1,014
MEXICO
Mexico City 21,321
Guadalajara 4,995
Monterrey 4,663
Puebla 3,079
Toluca 2,249
Tijuana 2,075
León 1,881
Ciudad Juárez 1,413
Torreón 1,376
Querétaro 1,332
San Luis Potosí 1,188
Mérida 1,104
Mexicali 1,071
Aguascalientes 1,069
Cuernavaca 1,019
Chihuahua 974
Saltillo 974
Morelia 947
Tampico 944
Acapulco 915
Cancún 911
Veracruz 906
Reynosa 901
MONGOLIA
Ulan Bator 1,463
MOROCCO
Casablanca 3,581
Rabat 2,043
Fès 1,222
Marrakesh 1,203
Tangier 1,050
MOZAMBIQUE
Maputo 1,223
Matola 1,018

MYANMAR (BURMA)
Rangoon 5,011
Mandalay 1,227
Naypyidaw 1,063
NEPAL
Katmandu 1,266
NETHERLANDS
Amsterdam 1,108
Rotterdam 997
NEW ZEALAND
Auckland 1,377
NICARAGUA
Managua 1,165
NIGER
Niamey 1,125
NIGERIA
Lagos 14,234
Kano 3,777
Ibadan 3,337
Abuja 2,737
Port Harcourt 2,592
Benin City 1,594
Onitsha 1,223
Kaduna 1,085
Aba 1,003
Uyo 950
Ilorin 901
NORWAY
Oslo 1,019
PAKISTAN
Karachi 17,636
Lahore 9,245
Faisalabad 3,789
Rawalpindi 2,659
Gujranwala 2,265
Multan 2,020
Hyderabad 1,855
Peshawar 1,840
Islamabad 1,502
Quetta 1,189
Bahawalpur 992
PANAMA
Panamá 1,744
PARAGUAY
Asunción 2,456
PERU
Lima 10,247
PHILIPPINES
Manila 13,322
Davao 1,694
Cebu 981
Zamboanga 983
POLAND
Warsaw 1,732
PORTUGAL
Lisbon 2,921
Porto 1,310
PUERTO RICO
San Juan 2,457
ROMANIA
Bucharest 1,864
RUSSIA
Moscow 12,340
St Petersburg 5,008
Novosibirsk 1,499
Yekaterinburg 1,384
Nizhniy Novgorod 1,189
Kazan 1,164
Chelyabinsk 1,162
Omsk 1,160
Samara 1,159
Rostov 1,095
Ufa 1,069
Volgograd 1,019
Krasnoyarsk 1,018
Perm 973
Voronezh 915
RWANDA
Kigali 1,333
SAUDI ARABIA
Riyadh 6,704
Jedda 4,245
Mecca 1,827
Medina 1,325
Dammam 1,106
SENEGAL
Dakar 3,792
SERBIA
Belgrade 1,183
SIERRA LEONE
Freetown 1,052
SINGAPORE
Singapore City 5,811
SOMALIA
Mogadishu 2,394
SOUTH AFRICA
Johannesburg 9,823
Cape Town 3,736
Durban 2,929
Pretoria 2,189
Port Elizabeth 1,194
Vereeniging 1,173
SPAIN
Madrid 6,325
Barcelona 5,356
SUDAN
Khartoum 5,409
SWEDEN
Stockholm 1,529
SWITZERLAND
Zürich 1,274
SYRIA
Aleppo 3,752
Damascus 2,632
Homs 1,762
Hamah 1,368
TAIWAN
Taipei 2,677

Kaohsiung 1,530
T'aichung 1,259
TANZANIA
Dar es Salaam 5,717
Mwanza 943
THAILAND
Bangkok 9,617
Samut Prakan 2,143
TOGO
Lomé 1,016
TUNISIA
Tunis 2,028
TURKEY
Istanbul 14,557
Ankara 4,949
Izmir 3,138
Bursa 2,022
Adana 1,926
Gaziantep 1,604
Konya 1,257
Antalya 1,126
Diyarbakir 950
Kayseri 933
UGANDA
Kampala 2,093
UKRAINE
Kiev 2,987
Kharkov 1,435
Odessa 1,011
Dnepropetrovsk 938
Donetsk 921
UNITED ARAB EMIRATES
Dubai 2,596
Sharjah 1,387
Abu Dhabi 1,214
UNITED KINGDOM
London 10,549
Manchester 2,690
Birmingham 1,552
Glasgow 1,232
UNITED STATES OF AMERICA
New York 18,627
Los Angeles 12,334
Chicago 8,772
Miami 5,911
Dallas–Fort Worth 5,891
Houston 5,869
Philadelphia 5,622
Atlanta 5,350
Washington, DC 5,070
Boston 4,264
Phoenix–Mesa 4,205
Detroit 3,604
Seattle 3,307
San Francisco 3,301
San Diego 3,152
Minneapolis–St Paul 2,834
Tampa–St Petersburg 2,729
Denver 2,672
Las Vegas 2,405
Baltimore 2,285
Riverside–San Bernardino 2,282
St Louis 2,192
San Antonio 2,122
Portland 2,049
Sacramento 1,985
Orlando 1,805
Austin 1,800
Cleveland 1,768
Charlotte 1,751
San Jose 1,749
Pittsburgh 1,713
Cincinnati 1,706
Indianapolis 1,698
Kansas City 1,631
Columbus 1,550
Virginia Beach–Norfolk 1,465
Milwaukee 1,418
Raleigh 1,234
Jacksonville 1,207
Providence 1,197
Nashville 1,152
Memphis 1,120
Salt Lake City 1,120
Richmond 1,054
Louisville 1,051
Hartford 975
Oklahoma 946
Tucson 935
New Orleans 927
Buffalo 905
URUGUAY
Montevideo 1,726
UZBEKISTAN
Tashkent 2,281
VENEZUELA
Caracas 2,934
Maracaibo 2,262
Valencia 1,781
Maracay 1,206
Barquisimeto 1,051
VIETNAM
Ho Chi Minh City 7,700
Hanoi 3,948
Can Tho 1,307
Haiphong 1,145
Da Nang 1,006
YEMEN
Sana' 3,229
Aden 939
ZAMBIA
Lusaka 2,396
ZIMBABWE
Harare 1,525

WORLD STATISTICS: CLIMATE

Rainfall and temperature figures are provided for more than 70 cities. As climate is affected by altitude, the height of the weather station for each city is shown in metres beneath its name. For each location, the top row of figures shows the total rainfall or snow in millimetres, and the bottom row the average temperature in degrees Celsius; the total annual rainfall and average annual temperature are at the end of the rows. The map opposite shows the city locations.

EUROPE

CITY	JAN.	FEB.	MAR.	APR.	MAY	JUNE	JULY	AUG.	SEPT.	OCT.	NOV.	DEC.	YEAR
Athens, Greece 107 m	62	37	37	23	23	14	6	7	15	51	56	71	402
	10	10	12	16	20	25	28	28	24	20	15	11	18
Berlin, Germany 55 m	42	33	41	37	54	69	56	58	45	37	44	55	571
	−1	0	4	9	14	17	19	18	15	9	5	1	9
Istanbul, Turkey 14 m	87	71	63	43	33	25	24	24	44	71	85	107	655
	5	6	7	11	16	20	23	23	20	16	12	8	14
Lisbon, Portugal 77 m	111	110	69	54	44	16	3	4	33	62	93	103	702
	11	12	14	16	17	20	22	23	21	18	14	12	17
London, UK 5 m	54	40	37	37	46	45	57	59	49	57	64	48	593
	4	5	7	9	12	16	18	17	15	11	8	5	11
Málaga, Spain 33 m	61	51	62	46	26	5	1	3	29	64	64	62	474
	12	13	16	17	19	29	25	26	23	20	16	13	18
Moscow, Russia 156 m	39	38	36	37	53	58	88	71	58	45	47	54	624
	−13	−10	−4	6	13	16	18	17	12	6	−1	−7	4
Odessa, Ukraine 64 m	57	62	30	21	34	34	42	37	37	13	35	71	473
	−3	−1	2	9	15	20	22	22	18	12	9	1	10
Paris, France 75 m	56	46	35	42	57	54	59	64	55	50	51	50	619
	3	4	8	11	15	18	20	19	17	12	7	4	12
Rome, Italy 17 m	71	62	57	51	46	37	15	21	63	99	129	93	744
	8	9	11	14	18	22	25	25	22	17	13	10	16
Shannon, Ireland 2 m	94	67	56	53	61	57	77	79	86	86	96	117	929
	5	5	7	9	12	14	16	16	14	11	8	6	10
Stockholm, Sweden 44 m	43	30	25	31	34	45	61	76	60	48	53	48	554
	−3	−3	−1	5	10	15	18	17	12	7	3	0	7

ASIA

CITY	JAN.	FEB.	MAR.	APR.	MAY	JUNE	JULY	AUG.	SEPT.	OCT.	NOV.	DEC.	YEAR
Bangkok, Thailand 2 m	8	20	36	58	198	160	160	175	305	206	66	5	1,397
	26	28	29	30	29	29	28	28	28	28	26	25	28
Beirut, Lebanon 34 m	191	158	94	53	18	3	3	3	5	51	132	185	892
	14	14	16	18	22	24	27	28	26	24	19	16	21
Colombo, Sri Lanka 7 m	89	69	147	231	371	224	135	109	160	348	315	147	2,365
	26	26	27	28	28	27	27	27	27	27	26	26	27
Harbin, China 160 m	6	5	10	23	43	94	112	104	46	33	8	5	488
	−18	−15	−5	6	13	19	22	21	14	4	−6	−16	3
Ho Chi Minh, Vietnam 9 m	15	3	13	43	221	330	315	269	335	269	114	56	1,984
	26	27	29	30	29	28	28	28	27	27	27	26	28
Hong Kong, China 33 m	33	46	74	137	292	394	381	361	257	114	43	31	2,162
	16	15	18	22	26	28	28	28	27	25	21	18	23
Jakarta, Indonesia 8 m	300	300	211	147	114	97	64	43	66	112	142	203	1,798
	26	26	27	27	27	27	27	27	27	27	27	26	27

ASIA (continued)

CITY	JAN.	FEB.	MAR.	APR.	MAY	JUNE	JULY	AUG.	SEPT.	OCT.	NOV.	DEC.	YEAR
Kabul, Afghanistan 1,815 m	34	60	68	72	23	1	6	2	2	4	19	22	313
	−3	−1	6	13	18	22	25	24	20	14	7	3	12
Karachi, Pakistan 4 m	13	10	8	3	3	18	81	41	13	<3	3	5	196
	19	20	24	28	30	31	30	29	28	28	24	20	26
Kolkata, India 6 m	10	31	36	43	140	297	325	328	252	114	20	5	1,600
	20	22	27	30	30	30	29	29	29	28	23	19	26
Manama, Bahrain 5 m	8	18	13	8	3	0	0	0	0	0	18	18	81
	17	18	21	25	29	32	33	34	31	28	24	19	26
Mumbai, India 11 m	3	3	3	3	18	485	617	340	264	64	13	3	1,809
	24	24	26	28	30	29	27	27	27	28	27	26	27
New Delhi, India 218 m	23	18	13	8	13	74	180	172	117	10	3	10	640
	14	17	23	28	33	34	31	30	29	26	20	15	25
Omsk, Russia 85 m	15	8	8	13	31	51	51	51	28	25	18	20	318
	−22	−19	−12	−1	10	16	18	16	10	1	−11	−18	−1
Qazaly, Kazakhstan 63 m	10	10	13	13	15	5	5	8	8	10	13	15	125
	−12	−11	−3	6	18	23	25	23	16	8	−1	−7	7
Shanghai, China 7 m	48	58	84	94	94	180	147	142	130	71	51	36	1,135
	4	5	9	14	20	24	28	28	23	19	12	7	16
Singapore 10 m	252	173	193	188	173	173	170	196	178	208	254	257	2,413
	26	27	28	28	28	28	28	27	27	27	27	27	27
Tehran, Iran 1,220 m	46	38	46	36	13	3	3	3	3	8	20	31	246
	2	5	9	16	21	26	30	29	25	18	12	6	17
Tokyo, Japan 6 m	48	74	107	135	147	165	142	152	234	208	97	56	1,565
	3	4	7	13	17	21	25	26	23	17	11	6	14
Ulan Bator, Mongolia 1,325 m	3	3	3	5	10	28	76	51	23	5	5	3	208
	−26	−21	−13	−1	6	14	16	14	8	−1	−13	−22	−3
Verkhoyansk, Russia 100 m	5	5	3	5	8	23	28	25	13	8	8	5	134
	−50	−45	−32	−15	0	12	14	9	2	−15	−38	−48	−17

AFRICA

CITY	JAN.	FEB.	MAR.	APR.	MAY	JUNE	JULY	AUG.	SEPT.	OCT.	NOV.	DEC.	YEAR
Addis Ababa, Ethiopia 2,450 m	3	3	25	135	213	201	206	239	102	28	3	0	1,151
	19	20	20	20	19	18	18	19	21	22	21	20	20
Antananarivo, Madag. 1,372 m	300	279	178	53	18	8	8	10	18	61	135	287	1,356
	21	21	21	19	18	15	14	15	17	19	21	21	19
Cairo, Egypt 116 m	5	4	4	1	1	0	0	0	0	1	4	6	26
	13	15	18	21	25	28	28	28	26	24	20	15	22
Cape Town, S.Africa 17 m	15	8	18	48	79	84	89	66	43	31	18	10	508
	21	21	20	17	14	13	12	13	14	16	18	19	17
Jo'burg, S.Africa 1,665 m	114	109	89	38	25	8	8	8	23	56	107	125	709
	20	20	18	16	13	10	11	13	16	18	19	20	16

CITY	JAN.	FEB.	MAR.	APR.	MAY	JUNE	JULY	AUG.	SEPT.	OCT.	NOV.	DEC.	YEAR
AFRICA (continued)													
Khartoum, Sudan	3	3	3	3	3	8	53	71	18	5	3	0	158
390 m	24	25	28	31	33	34	32	31	32	32	28	25	29
Kinshasa, Congo (D.R.)	135	145	196	196	158	8	3	3	31	119	221	142	1,354
325 m	26	26	27	27	26	24	23	24	25	26	26	26	25
Lagos, Nigeria	28	46	102	150	269	460	279	64	140	206	69	25	1,836
3 m	27	28	29	28	28	26	26	25	26	26	28	28	27
Lusaka, Zambia	231	191	142	18	3	3	3	0	3	10	91	150	836
1,277 m	21	22	21	21	19	16	16	18	22	24	23	22	21
Monrovia, Liberia	31	56	97	216	516	973	996	373	744	772	236	130	5,138
23 m	26	26	27	27	26	25	24	25	25	25	26	26	26
Nairobi, Kenya	38	64	125	211	158	46	15	23	31	53	109	86	958
820 m	19	19	19	19	18	16	16	16	18	19	18	18	18
Timbuktu, Mali	1	0	0	1	4	16	54	74	29	4	0	0	183
301 m	22	24	28	32	34	35	32	30	32	31	28	23	29
Tunis, Tunisia	64	51	41	36	18	8	3	8	33	51	48	61	419
66 m	10	11	13	16	19	23	26	27	25	20	16	11	18
Walvis Bay, Namibia	3	5	8	3	3	3	3	3	3	3	3	3	23
7 m	19	19	19	18	17	16	15	14	14	15	17	18	18
AUSTRALIA, NEW ZEALAND AND ANTARCTICA													
Alice Springs, Aust.	43	33	28	10	15	13	8	8	8	18	31	38	252
579 m	29	28	25	20	15	12	12	14	18	23	26	28	21
Christchurch, NZ	56	43	48	48	66	66	69	48	46	43	48	56	638
10 m	16	16	14	12	9	6	6	7	9	12	14	16	11
Darwin, Australia	386	312	254	97	15	3	3	3	13	51	119	239	1,491
30 m	29	29	29	29	28	26	25	26	28	29	30	29	28
Mawson, Antarctica	11	30	20	10	44	180	4	40	3	20	0	0	362
14 m	0	−5	−10	−14	−15	−16	−18	−18	−19	−13	−5	−1	−11
Perth, Australia	8	10	20	43	130	180	170	149	86	56	20	13	881
60 m	23	23	22	19	16	14	13	13	15	16	19	22	18
Sydney, Australia	89	102	127	135	127	117	117	76	73	71	73	73	1,181
42 m	22	22	21	18	15	13	12	13	15	18	19	21	17
NORTH AMERICA													
Anchorage, USA	20	18	15	10	13	18	41	66	66	56	25	23	371
40 m	−11	−8	−5	2	7	12	14	13	9	2	−5	−11	2
Chicago, USA	51	51	66	71	86	89	84	81	79	66	61	51	836
251 m	−4	−3	2	9	14	20	23	22	19	12	5	−1	10
Churchill, Canada	15	13	18	23	32	44	46	58	51	43	39	21	402
13 m	−28	−26	−20	−10	−2	6	12	11	5	−2	−12	−22	−7
Edmonton, Canada	25	19	19	22	43	77	89	78	39	17	16	25	466
676 m	−15	−10	−5	4	11	15	17	16	11	6	−4	−10	3
Honolulu, USA	104	66	79	48	25	18	23	28	36	48	64	104	643
12 m	23	18	19	20	22	24	25	26	26	24	22	19	22
Houston, USA	89	76	84	91	119	117	99	99	104	94	89	109	1,171
12 m	12	13	17	21	24	27	28	29	26	22	16	12	21

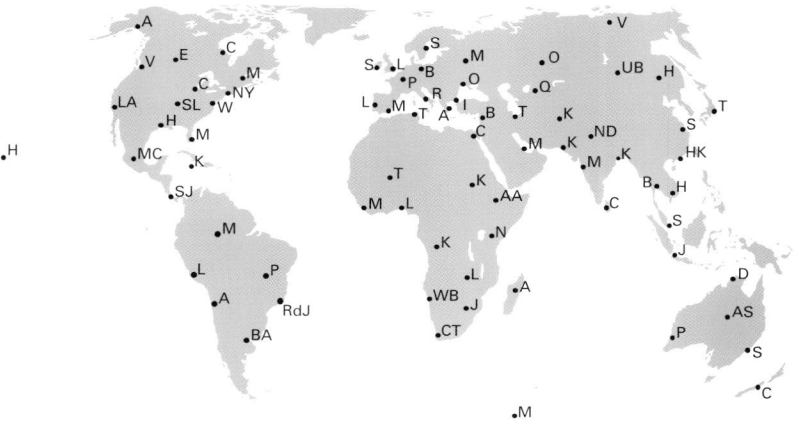

CITY	JAN.	FEB.	MAR.	APR.	MAY	JUNE	JULY	AUG.	SEPT.	OCT.	NOV.	DEC.	YEAR
NORTH AMERICA (continued)													
Kingston, Jamaica	23	15	23	31	102	89	38	91	99	180	74	36	800
34 m	25	25	25	26	26	28	28	28	27	27	26	26	26
Los Angeles, USA	79	76	71	25	10	3	3	3	5	15	31	66	381
95 m	13	14	14	16	17	19	21	22	21	18	16	14	17
Mexico City, Mexico	13	5	10	20	53	119	170	152	130	51	18	8	747
2,309 m	12	13	16	18	19	19	17	18	18	16	14	13	16
Miami, USA	71	53	64	81	173	178	155	160	203	234	71	51	1,516
8 m	20	20	22	23	25	27	28	28	27	25	22	21	24
Montréal, Canada	72	65	74	74	66	82	90	92	88	76	81	87	946
57 m	−10	−9	−3	−6	13	18	21	20	15	9	2	−7	6
New York City, USA	94	97	91	81	81	84	107	109	86	89	76	91	1,092
96 m	−1	−1	3	10	16	20	23	23	21	15	7	2	11
St Louis, USA	58	64	89	97	114	114	89	86	81	74	71	64	1,001
173 m	0	1	7	13	19	24	26	26	22	15	8	2	14
San José, Costa Rica	15	5	20	46	229	241	211	241	305	300	145	41	1,798
1,146 m	19	19	21	21	22	21	21	21	21	20	20	19	20
Vancouver, Canada	154	115	101	60	52	45	32	41	67	114	150	182	1,113
14 m	3	5	6	9	12	15	17	17	14	10	6	4	10
Washington, DC, USA	86	76	91	84	94	99	112	109	94	74	66	79	1,064
22 m	1	2	7	12	18	23	25	24	20	14	8	3	13
SOUTH AMERICA													
Antofagasta, Chile	0	0	0	3	3	3	5	3	3	3	3	0	13
94 m	21	21	20	18	16	15	14	14	15	16	18	19	17
Buenos Aires, Arg.	122	123	154	107	92	50	53	63	78	139	131	103	1,215
27 m	23	23	21	17	13	9	10	11	13	15	19	22	16
Lima, Peru	3	3	3	3	5	5	8	8	8	3	3	3	41
120 m	23	24	24	22	19	17	17	16	17	18	19	21	20
Manaus, Brazil	249	231	262	221	170	84	58	38	46	107	142	203	1,811
44 m	28	28	28	27	28	28	28	29	29	29	29	28	28
Paraná, Brazil	287	236	239	102	13	3	3	5	28	127	231	310	1,582
260 m	23	23	23	23	23	21	21	22	24	24	24	23	23
Rio de Janeiro, Brazil	125	122	130	107	79	53	41	43	66	79	104	137	1,082
61 m	26	26	25	24	22	21	21	21	21	22	23	25	23

WORLD STATISTICS: PHYSICAL DIMENSIONS

Each topic list is divided into continents and within a continent the items are listed in order of size. The bottom part of many of the lists is selective in order to give examples from as many different countries as possible. The order of the continents is as in the atlas, Europe through to South America. The world top ten are shown in square brackets; in the case of mountains this has not been done because the world top 30 are all in Asia. The figures are rounded as appropriate.

WORLD, CONTINENTS, OCEANS

THE WORLD

	km²	miles²	%
The World	509,450,000	196,672,000	–
Land	149,450,000	57,688,000	29.3
Water	360,000,000	138,984,000	70.7
Asia	44,500,000	17,177,000	29.8
Africa	30,302,000	11,697,000	20.3
North America	24,241,000	9,357,000	16.2
South America	17,793,000	6,868,000	11.9
Antarctica	14,100,000	5,443,000	9.4
Europe	9,957,000	3,843,000	6.7
Australia and Oceania	8,557,000	3,303,000	5.7
Pacific Ocean	155,557,000	60,061,000	46.4
Atlantic Ocean	76,762,000	29,638,000	22.9
Indian Ocean	68,556,000	26,470,000	20.4
Southern Ocean	20,327,000	7,848,000	6.1
Arctic Ocean	14,056,000	5,427,000	4.2

SEAS

PACIFIC

	km²	miles²
South China Sea	2,974,600	1,148,500
Bering Sea	2,268,000	875,000
Sea of Okhotsk	1,528,000	590,000
East China and Yellow Sea	1,249,000	482,000
Sea of Japan	1,008,000	389,000
Gulf of California	162,000	62,500
Bass Strait	75,000	29,000

ATLANTIC

	km²	miles²
Caribbean Sea	2,766,000	1,068,000
Mediterranean Sea	2,516,000	971,000
Gulf of Mexico	1,543,000	596,000
Hudson Bay	1,232,000	476,000
North Sea	575,000	223,000
Black Sea	462,000	178,000
Baltic Sea	422,170	163,000
Gulf of St Lawrence	238,000	92,000

INDIAN

	km²	miles²
Red Sea	438,000	169,000
Persian Gulf	239,000	92,000

MOUNTAINS

EUROPE

		m	ft
Elbrus	Russia	5,642	18,510
Dykh Tau	Russia	5,203	17,070
Shkhara	Russia/Georgia	5,201	17,064
Koshtan Tau	Russia	5,152	16,903
Kazbek	Russia/Georgia	5,047	16,558
Pushkin	Russia/Georgia	5,033	16,512
Katyn Tau	Russia/Georgia	4,979	16,335
Shota Rustaveli	Russia/Georgia	4,860	15,945
Mont Blanc	France/Italy	4,808	15,774
Monte Rosa	Italy/Switzerland	4,634	15,203
Dom	Switzerland	4,545	14,911
Liskamm	Switzerland	4,527	14,852
Weisshorn	Switzerland	4,505	14,780
Tebulos	Russia/Georgia	4,492	14,737
Taschorn	Switzerland	4,490	14,730
Matterhorn/Cervino	Italy/Switzerland	4,478	14,691
Mont Maudit	France/Italy	4,465	14,649
Bazar Dyuzi	Russia/Azerbaijan	4,462	14,639
Grandes Jorasses	France/Italy	4,208	13,806
Jungfrau	Switzerland	4,158	13,642
Barre des Ecrins	France	4,102	13,458
Gran Paradiso	Italy	4,061	13,323
Piz Bernina	Italy/Switzerland	4,049	13,284
Eiger	Switzerland	3,970	13,025
Grossglockner	Austria	3,797	12,457
Mulhacén	Spain	3,478	11,411
Etna	Italy	3,323	10,902
Zugspitze	Germany	2,962	9,718
Olympus	Greece	2,917	9,570
Galdhøpiggen	Norway	2,469	8,100
Ben Nevis	UK	1,345	4,411

ASIA

		m	ft
Everest	China/Nepal	8,850	29,035
K2 (Godwin Austen)	China/Kashmir	8,611	28,251
Kanchenjunga	India/Nepal	8,598	28,208
Lhotse	China/Nepal	8,516	27,939
Makalu	China/Nepal	8,481	27,824
Cho Oyu	China/Nepal	8,201	26,906
Dhaulagiri	Nepal	8,167	26,795
Manaslu	Nepal	8,156	26,758
Nanga Parbat	Kashmir	8,126	26,660
Annapurna	Nepal	8,078	26,502
Gasherbrum	China/Kashmir	8,068	26,469
Broad Peak	China/Kashmir	8,051	26,414
Xixabangma Feng	China	8,012	26,286
Gayachung Kang	Nepal	7,897	25,909
Himalchuli	Nepal	7,893	25,896
Disteghil Sar	Kashmir	7,885	25,869
Nuptse	Nepal	7,879	25,849
Kangbachen	Nepal	7,858	25,781
Khunyang Chhish	Kashmir	7,852	25,761
Masherbrum	Kashmir	7,821	25,659
Nanda Devi	India	7,817	25,646
Rakaposhi	Kashmir	7,788	25,551
Batura	Kashmir	7,785	25,541
Namche Barwa	China	7,782	25,531
Kamet	India	7,756	25,447
Soltoro Kangri	Pakistan	7,742	25,400
Gurla Mandhata	China	7,728	25,354
Trivor	Pakistan	7,720	25,328
Kongur Shan	China	7,719	25,324
Jannu	Nepal	7,710	25,295
Tirich Mir	Pakistan	7,690	25,229
K'ula Shan	Bhutan/China	7,543	24,747
Pik Imeni Ismail Samani	Tajikistan	7,495	24,590
Demavend	Iran	5,604	18,386
Ararat	Turkey	5,165	16,945
Gunong Kinabalu	Malaysia (Borneo)	4,101	13,455
Yu Shan	Taiwan	3,952	12,966
Fuji-San	Japan	3,776	12,388

AFRICA

		m	ft
Kilimanjaro	Tanzania	5,895	19,340
Mt Kenya	Kenya	5,199	17,057
Ruwenzori (Margherita)	Uganda/Congo (D.R.)	5,109	16,762
Meru	Tanzania	4,565	14,977
Ras Dashen	Ethiopia	4,533	14,872
Karisimbi	Rwanda/Congo (D.R.)	4,507	14,787
Mt Elgon	Kenya/Uganda	4,321	14,176
Batu	Ethiopia	4,307	14,130
Guna	Ethiopia	4,231	13,882
Toubkal	Morocco	4,165	13,665
Irhil Mgoun	Morocco	4,071	13,356
Mt Cameroun	Cameroon	4,070	13,353
Amba Ferit	Ethiopia	3,875	13,042
Pico del Teide	Spain (Tenerife)	3,718	12,198
Thabana Ntlenyana	Lesotho	3,482	11,424
Emi Koussi	Chad	3,415	11,204
Mt aux Sources	Lesotho/South Africa	3,282	10,768
Piton des Neiges	Réunion	3,069	10,069

OCEANIA

		m	ft
Puncak Jaya	Indonesia	4,884	16,024
Puncak Trikora	Indonesia	4,730	15,518
Puncak Mandala	Indonesia	4,702	15,427
Mt Wilhelm	Papua New Guinea	4,508	14,790
Mauna Kea	USA (Hawai'i)	4,205	13,796
Mauna Loa	USA (Hawai'i)	4,169	13,678
Aoraki Mt Cook	New Zealand	3,724	12,218
Mt Popomanaseu	Solomon Islands	2,439	8,002
Mt Orohena	French Polynesia (Tahiti)	2,241	7,352
Mt Kosciuszko	Australia	2,228	7,310

NORTH AMERICA

		m	ft
Denali (Mt McKinley)	USA (Alaska)	6,190	20,310
Mt Logan	Canada	5,959	19,551
Pico de Orizaba	Mexico	5,610	18,405
Mt St Elias	USA/Canada	5,489	18,008
Popocatépetl	Mexico	5,452	17,887

NORTH AMERICA (continued)

		m	ft
Mt Foraker	USA (Alaska)	5,304	17,401
Iztaccihuatl	Mexico	5,230	17,159
Mt Lucania	Canada	5,226	17,146
Mt Steele	Canada	5,073	16,644
Mt Bona	USA (Alaska)	5,005	16,420
Mt Blackburn	USA (Alaska)	4,996	16,391
Mt Sanford	USA (Alaska)	4,949	16,237
Mt Wood	Canada	4,840	15,880
Nevado de Toluca	Mexico	4,690	15,387
Mt Fairweather	USA (Alaska)	4,663	15,298
Mt Hunter	USA (Alaska)	4,442	14,573
Mt Whitney	USA	4,418	14,495
Mt Elbert	USA	4,399	14,432
Mt Harvard	USA	4,395	14,419
Mt Rainier	USA	4,392	14,409
Blanca Peak	USA	4,372	14,344
Longs Peak	USA	4,345	14,255
Tajumulco	Guatemala	4,220	13,845
Grand Teton	USA	4,197	13,770
Mt Waddington	Canada	4,019	13,186
Mt Robson	Canada	3,954	12,972
Chirripó Grande	Costa Rica	3,819	12,529
Pico Duarte	Dominican Rep.	3,175	10,417

SOUTH AMERICA

		m	ft
Aconcagua	Argentina	6,962	22,841
Ojos del Salado	Argentina/Chile	6,863	22,615
Monte Pissis	Argentina	6,793	22,287
Nevado Huascarán	Peru	6,768	22,205
Cerro Bonete	Argentina	6,759	22,175
Cerro Llullaillaco	Argentina/Chile	6,739	22,110
Cerro Mercedario	Argentina/Chile	6,720	22,047
Yerupaja	Peru	6,632	21,758
Nevado de Tres Cruces	Argentina/Chile	6,620	21,719
Tupungato	Argentina/Chile	6,570	21,555
Sajama	Bolivia	6,520	21,391
Coropuna	Peru	6,425	21,079
Illimani	Bolivia	6,402	21,004
Ausangate	Peru	6,384	20,945
Nevado de Cachi	Argentina	6,380	20,932
Cerro del Toro	Argentina	6,380	20,932
Siula Grande	Peru	6,356	20,853
Chimborazo	Ecuador	6,267	20,561
Incahuasi	Argentina/Chile	6,218	20,400
Alpamayo	Peru	5,947	19,511
Cerro Galan	Argentina	5,912	19,396
Cotapaxi	Ecuador	5,896	19,344
Pico Cristóbal Colón	Colombia	5,775	18,947
Pico Bolivar	Venezuela	4,981	16,342

ANTARCTICA

	m	ft
Vinson Massif	4,897	16,066
Mt Kirkpatrick	4,528	14,855
Mt Markham	4,349	14,268

OCEAN DEPTHS

ATLANTIC OCEAN

	m	ft	
Puerto Rico (Milwaukee) Deep	8,604	28,232	[7]
Cayman Trench	7,680	25,197	[10]
Gulf of Mexico	5,203	17,070	
Mediterranean Sea	5,121	16,801	
Black Sea	2,211	7,254	
North Sea	660	2,165	
Baltic Sea	463	1,519	
Hudson Bay	258	846	

INDIAN OCEAN

	m	ft
Java Trench	7,450	24,442
Red Sea	2,635	8,454
Persian Gulf	73	239

PACIFIC OCEAN

	m	ft	
Mariana Trench	11,022	36,161	[1]
Tonga Trench	10,882	35,702	[2]
Japan Trench	10,554	34,626	[3]
Kuril Trench	10,542	34,587	[4]
Mindanao Trench	10,497	34,439	[5]
Kermadec Trench	10,047	32,962	[6]

PACIFIC OCEAN (continued)

		m	ft	
Peru–Chile Trench		8,050	26,410	[8]
Aleutian Trench		7,822	25,662	[9]

ARCTIC OCEAN

		m	ft
Molloy Deep		5,608	18,399

SOUTHERN OCEAN

		m	ft
South Sandwich Trench		7,235	23,737

LAND LOWS

		m	ft
Caspian Sea	Europe	−28	−92
Dead Sea	Asia	−422	−1,384
Lake Assal	Africa	−156	−512
Lake Eyre North	Oceania	−16	−52
Death Valley	North America	−86	−282
Laguna del Carbón	South America	−105	−344

RIVERS

EUROPE

		km	miles
Volga	Caspian Sea	3,700	2,300
Danube	Black Sea	2,850	1,770
Ural	Caspian Sea	2,535	1,575
Dnieper	Black Sea	2,285	1,420
Kama	Volga	2,030	1,260
Don	Black Sea	1,990	1,240
Pechora	Arctic Ocean	1,790	1,110
Oka	Volga	1,480	920
Belaya	Kama	1,420	880
Dniester	Black Sea	1,400	870
Vyatka	Kama	1,370	850
Rhine	North Sea	1,320	820
Northern Dvina	Arctic Ocean	1,290	800
Desna	Dnieper	1,190	740
Elbe	North Sea	1,145	710
Vistula	Baltic Sea	1,090	675
Loire	Atlantic Ocean	1,020	635

ASIA

		km	miles	
Yangtse	Pacific Ocean	6,380	3,960	[3]
Yenisey–Angara	Arctic Ocean	5,550	3,445	[5]
Huang Ho	Pacific Ocean	5,464	3,395	[6]
Ob–Irtysh	Arctic Ocean	5,410	3,360	[7]
Mekong	Pacific Ocean	4,500	2,800	[9]
Amur	Pacific Ocean	4,442	2,760	
Lena	Arctic Ocean	4,402	2,735	
Irtysh	Ob	4,250	2,640	
Yenisey	Arctic Ocean	4,090	2,540	
Ob	Arctic Ocean	3,680	2,285	
Indus	Indian Ocean	3,100	1,925	
Brahmaputra	Indian Ocean	2,900	1,800	
Syrdarya	Aral Sea	2,860	1,775	
Salween	Indian Ocean	2,800	1,740	
Euphrates	Indian Ocean	2,700	1,675	
Vilyuy	Lena	2,650	1,645	
Kolyma	Arctic Ocean	2,600	1,615	
Amudarya	Aral Sea	2,540	1,578	
Ural	Caspian Sea	2,535	1,575	
Ganges	Indian Ocean	2,510	1,560	
Si Kiang	Pacific Ocean	2,100	1,305	
Irrawaddy	Indian Ocean	2,010	1,250	
Tarim–Yarkand	Lop Nur	2,000	1,240	
Tigris	Indian Ocean	1,900	1,180	

AFRICA

		km	miles	
Nile	Mediterranean	6,695	4,160	[1]
Congo	Atlantic Ocean	4,670	2,900	[8]
Niger	Atlantic Ocean	4,180	2,595	
Zambezi	Indian Ocean	3,540	2,200	
Oubangi/Uele	Congo (D.R.)	2,250	1,400	
Kasai	Congo (D.R.)	1,950	1,210	
Shaballe	Indian Ocean	1,930	1,200	
Orange	Atlantic Ocean	1,860	1,155	
Cubango	Okavango Delta	1,800	1,120	
Limpopo	Indian Ocean	1,770	1,100	
Senegal	Atlantic Ocean	1,640	1,020	
Volta	Atlantic Ocean	1,500	930	

AUSTRALIA

		km	miles
Murray–Darling	Southern Ocean	3,750	2,330
Darling	Murray	3,070	1,905
Murray	Southern Ocean	2,575	1,600
Murrumbidgee	Murray	1,690	1,050

NORTH AMERICA

		km	miles	
Mississippi–Missouri	Gulf of Mexico	5,971	3,710	[4]
Mackenzie	Arctic Ocean	4,240	2,630	
Missouri	Mississippi	4,088	2,540	

NORTH AMERICA (continued)

		km	miles
Mississippi	Gulf of Mexico	3,782	2,350
Yukon	Pacific Ocean	3,185	1,980
Rio Grande	Gulf of Mexico	3,030	1,880
Arkansas	Mississippi	2,340	1,450
Colorado	Pacific Ocean	2,330	1,445
Red	Mississippi	2,040	1,270
Columbia	Pacific Ocean	1,950	1,210
Saskatchewan	Lake Winnipeg	1,940	1,205
Snake	Columbia	1,670	1,040
Churchill	Hudson Bay	1,600	990
Ohio	Mississippi	1,580	980
Brazos	Gulf of Mexico	1,400	870
St Lawrence	Atlantic Ocean	1,170	730

SOUTH AMERICA

		km	miles	
Amazon	Atlantic Ocean	6,450	4,010	[2]
Paraná–Plate	Atlantic Ocean	4,500	2,800	[10]
Purus	Amazon	3,350	2,080	
Madeira	Amazon	3,200	1,990	
São Francisco	Atlantic Ocean	2,900	1,800	
Paraná	Plate	2,800	1,740	
Tocantins	Atlantic Ocean	2,750	1,710	
Orinoco	Atlantic Ocean	2,740	1,700	
Paraguay	Paraná	2,550	1,580	
Pilcomayo	Paraná	2,500	1,550	
Araguaia	Tocantins	2,250	1,400	
Juruá	Amazon	2,000	1,240	
Xingu	Amazon	1,980	1,230	
Ucayali	Amazon	1,900	1,180	
Uruguay	Plate	1,610	1,000	

LAKES

EUROPE

		km²	miles²
Lake Ladoga	Russia	17,700	6,800
Lake Onega	Russia	9,700	3,700
Saimaa system	Finland	8,000	3,100
Vänern	Sweden	5,500	2,100

ASIA

		km²	miles²	
Caspian Sea	Asia	371,000	143,000	[1]
Lake Baikal	Russia	30,500	11,780	[8]
Tonlé Sap	Cambodia	20,000	7,700	
Lake Balkhash	Kazakhstan	18,500	7,100	
Dongting Hu	China	12,000	4,600	
Aral Sea	Kazakhstan/ Uzbekistan	6,800	2,620	
Issyk Kul	Kyrgyzstan	6,200	2,400	
Koko Nur	China	5,700	2,200	
Poyang Hu	China	5,000	1,900	
Lake Khanka	China/Russia	4,400	1,700	
Lake Van	Turkey	3,500	1,400	

AFRICA

		km²	miles²	
Lake Victoria	East Africa	68,000	26,300	[3]
Lake Tanganyika	Central Africa	33,000	13,000	[6]
Lake Malawi/Nyasa	East Africa	29,600	11,430	[9]
Lake Chad	Central Africa	25,000	9,700	
Lake Bangweulu	Zambia	9,840	3,800	
Lake Turkana	Ethiopia/Kenya	8,500	3,290	
Lake Volta	Ghana	8,480	3,270	
Lake Kariba	Zambia/Zimbabwe	5,380	2,150	
Lake Albert	Uganda/Congo (D.R.)	5,300	2,050	
Lake Nasser	Egypt/Sudan	5,250	2,030	
Lake Mweru	Zambia/Congo (D.R.)	4,920	1,900	
Lake Kyoga	Uganda	4,430	1,710	
Lake Tana	Ethiopia	3,620	1,400	
Lake Cabora Bassa	Mozambique	2,750	1,070	
Lake Rukwa	Tanzania	2,600	1,000	
Lake Mai-Ndombe	Congo (D.R.)	2,300	890	

AUSTRALIA

		km²	miles²
Lake Eyre	Australia	8,900	3,400
Lake Torrens	Australia	5,800	2,200
Lake Gairdner	Australia	4,800	1,900

NORTH AMERICA

		km²	miles²	
Lake Superior	Canada/USA	82,350	31,800	[2]
Lake Huron	Canada/USA	59,600	23,010	[4]
Lake Michigan	USA	58,000	22,400	[5]
Great Bear Lake	Canada	31,800	12,280	[7]
Great Slave Lake	Canada	28,500	11,000	[10]
Lake Erie	Canada/USA	25,700	9,900	
Lake Winnipeg	Canada	24,400	9,400	
Lake Ontario	Canada/USA	19,500	7,500	
Lake Nicaragua	Nicaragua	8,200	3,200	
Lake Athabasca	Canada	8,100	3,100	
Smallwood Reservoir	Canada	6,530	2,520	
Reindeer Lake	Canada	6,400	2,500	
Nettilling Lake	Canada	5,500	2,100	

SOUTH AMERICA

		km²	miles²
Lake Titicaca	Bolivia/Peru	8,300	3,200
Lake Poopo	Bolivia	2,800	1,100

ISLANDS

EUROPE

		km²	miles²	
Great Britain	UK	229,880	88,700	[8]
Iceland	Atlantic Ocean	103,000	39,800	
Ireland	Ireland/UK	84,400	32,600	
Novaya Zemlya (N.)	Russia	48,200	18,600	
Spitsbergen	Norway	39,000	15,100	
Novaya Zemlya (S.)	Russia	33,200	12,800	
Sicily	Italy	25,500	9,800	
Sardinia	Italy	24,000	9,300	
Nordaustlandet	Norway	15,000	5,600	
Corsica	France	8,700	3,400	
Crete	Greece	8,350	3,200	
Sjælland	Denmark	6,850	2,600	

ASIA

		km²	miles²	
Borneo	South-east Asia	744,360	287,400	[3]
Sumatra	Indonesia	473,600	182,860	[6]
Honshu	Japan	230,500	88,980	[7]
Sulawesi (Celebes)	Indonesia	189,000	73,000	
Java	Indonesia	126,700	48,900	
Luzon	Philippines	104,700	40,400	
Mindanao	Philippines	101,500	39,200	
Hokkaido	Japan	78,400	30,300	
Sakhalin	Russia	74,060	28,600	
Sri Lanka	Indian Ocean	65,600	25,300	
Taiwan	Pacific Ocean	36,000	13,900	
Kyushu	Japan	35,700	13,800	
Hainan	China	34,000	13,100	
Timor	South-east Asia	33,600	13,000	
Shikoku	Japan	18,800	7,300	
Halmahera	Indonesia	18,000	6,900	
Ceram	Indonesia	17,150	6,600	
Sumbawa	Indonesia	15,450	6,000	
Flores	Indonesia	15,200	5,900	
Samar	Philippines	13,100	5,100	
Negros	Philippines	12,700	4,900	
Bangka	Indonesia	12,000	4,600	
Palawan	Philippines	12,000	4,600	
Panay	Philippines	11,500	4,400	
Sumba	Indonesia	11,100	4,300	
Mindoro	Philippines	9,750	3,800	

AFRICA

		km²	miles²	
Madagascar	Indian Ocean	587,040	226,660	[4]
Socotra	Indian Ocean	3,600	1,400	
Réunion	Indian Ocean	2,500	965	
Tenerife	Atlantic Ocean	2,350	900	
Mauritius	Indian Ocean	1,865	720	

OCEANIA

		km²	miles²	
New Guinea	Indonesia/Papua NG	821,030	317,000	[2]
New Zealand (S.)	Pacific Ocean	150,500	58,100	
New Zealand (N.)	Pacific Ocean	114,700	44,300	
Tasmania	Australia	67,800	26,200	
New Britain	Papua New Guinea	37,800	14,600	
New Caledonia	Pacific Ocean	19,100	7,400	
Viti Levu	Fiji	10,500	4,100	
Hawai'i	Pacific Ocean	10,450	4,000	
Bougainville	Papua New Guinea	9,600	3,700	
Guadalcanal	Solomon Islands	6,500	2,500	
Vanua Levu	Fiji	5,550	2,100	
New Ireland	Papua New Guinea	3,200	1,200	

NORTH AMERICA

		km²	miles²	
Greenland	Atlantic Ocean	2,175,600	839,800	[1]
Baffin Island	Canada	508,000	196,100	[5]
Victoria Island	Canada	212,200	81,900	[9]
Ellesmere Island	Canada	212,000	81,800	[10]
Cuba	Caribbean Sea	110,860	42,800	
Newfoundland	Canada	110,680	42,700	
Hispaniola	Dominican Rep./Haiti	76,200	29,400	
Banks Island	Canada	67,000	25,900	
Devon Island	Canada	54,500	21,000	
Melville Island	Canada	42,400	16,400	
Vancouver Island	Canada	32,150	12,400	
Somerset Island	Canada	24,300	9,400	
Jamaica	Caribbean Sea	11,400	4,400	
Puerto Rico	Atlantic Ocean	8,900	3,400	
Cape Breton Island	Canada	4,000	1,500	

SOUTH AMERICA

		km²	miles²
Tierra del Fuego	Argentina/Chile	47,000	18,100
Falkland Islands (East)	Atlantic Ocean	6,800	2,600
South Georgia	Atlantic Ocean	4,200	1,600
Galapagos (Isabela)	Pacific Ocean	2,250	870

IMAGES OF EARTH

Stretching from Windsor in the west to Southend-on-Sea in the east, this image covers all of Greater London and the lower valley of the river Thames. Alongside the dark shapes of the reservoirs in the west, the runway pattern of London's major international airport, Heathrow, can be seen. Further downstream, towards the sea, the light area on the north bank of the river is the brand new seaport, Thames Gateway, built to handle the largest container vessels. The original settlement of London was founded by the Romans as the lowest bridging point of the river in AD 47 and called 'Londinium'. The city is now a global financial centre and its diverse cultural highlights attract tourists from all over the world. The current population is over 10 million people.

[Map page 67] *USGS / NPA Satellite Mapping, CGG Services (UK) Ltd*

The capital and largest city in France, Paris is considered one of the world's most elegant cities. Spanning both banks of the river Seine as it flows north-west toward the English Channel, the pattern of wide 19th century boulevards is easily visible. Railways, built in the same century, radiate from the city, further strengthening its position as the hub of France. By the end of the 20th century, the metropolitan area had spread across much of the land within a 30 km (20 mile) radius of the Ile de la Cité. However, many old neighbourhoods remain and Parisians say their city is really a collection of 100 villages. The alleyways of the Latin Quarter, on the left (or south) bank, with their many bookshops and cafés comprise a district with a typically Bohemian air.

[Map page 71] *Copernicus Sentinel data 2016 / NPA Satellite Mapping, CGG Services (UK) Ltd*

The strait shown here is called the Øresund ('The Sound') and it is one of the main entrances into the Baltic Sea for commercial shipping sailing as far east as St Petersburg and including the ports in Sweden, Finland, the Baltic states and Poland. To the west of it lies Denmark and its capital city København (Copenhagen). On the eastern shore is Sweden with the third largest city, Malmö. Connecting the two is the Øresund Bridge. Opened in 2000, it is a bridge for two-thirds of its length, but runs in a tunnel for the final 4 km (2.5 miles) into Denmark, to avoid disruption of flights at Copenhagen International Airport because of its height. The construction of the bridge has changed this trans-national region's economy – Swedes can now visit Copenhagen very easily and many Danes have bought property in southern Sweden and commute to work.

[Map page 63] *USGS Landsat / NPA Satellite Mapping, CGG Services (UK) Ltd*

St Petersburg's position at the mouth of the river Neva, where it meets the Gulf of Finland in the Baltic Sea, has allowed it to flourish as a major sea port. The dock area can be seen in the centre left of the image. But this city has a greater significance to the Russian people than just being a centre of trade and industry. It is one of Europe's most sparkling cities, steeped in history and culture. St Petersburg (known as Leningrad between 1924 and 1991) provided the backdrop for three major revolutions, with the most significant being the October Revolution that led to the overthrow of the Tsars and the rise of the communist party. Now visitors crowd to see the legacy of the imperial age that is preserved in the many palaces, museums and art galleries, the greatest of which is The Hermitage. [Map page 84]

Satellite image by Planet Labs, distributed by NPA Satellite Mapping, CGG Services (UK) Ltd

The origins of this city on the Danube lie in the amalgamation, in 1873, of the old city of Buda on the right bank of the river and the newer town of Pest on the left. Budapest can be seen as the concentration of buildings either side of the river just below the centre of the image. The country's industries are concentrated in, and around, this capital city to a degree seldom seen in other European countries. In the top of the image can be seen the abrupt curve of the 'Danube Bend'. Between Esztergom (in the top-left of the image) and Szentendre (north of Budapest) the river executes a sharp right turn to the south. The Danube connects four capital cities as it flows towards the Black Sea: Vienna, Bratislava, Budapest and Belgrade.

[Map page 80] *USGS / NPA Satellite Mapping, CGG Services (UK) Ltd*

Barcelona is the chief city of Catalonia and lies on the north-east coast of Spain facing the Mediterranean Sea. As well as being the second largest city in Spain, it is also the country's largest sea-port and main industrial and commercial centre. The large harbour is clearly visible in this image, as is the airport, close to the coast, in the south. Inland from the northern dock area lies the heart of the old city – the Barri Gòtic. Bounding the western edge of the old town is the wide tree-lined boulevard of La Rambla. This was once a riverbed, but is now a river of perambulating local residents and tourists. The old dock area at the seaward end of La Rambla, and the nearby hill of Montjuïc, were transformed when Barcelona hosted the 1992 Summer Olympics. Modern architects, such as Antonio Gaudí, have also left their mark on the city. [Map page 90]

Copernicus Sentinel data 2016 / NPA Satellite Mapping, CGG Services (UK) Ltd

Dubai is the capital city of the second largest of the seven states that make up the United Arab Emirates. Although the state does have some oil reserves, Dubai's current wealth has grown out of trade and financial services. In the 1960s the town consisted of low houses of only one or two storeys. In contrast, the city is now known for its iconic high-rise towers including the Burj Khalifa, currently the world's tallest building soaring to 828.8 m (2,722 ft). The most striking features seen along the coast in this image are the artificial islands in the shape of palm trees (Palm Jumeirah and Palm Jebel Ali) and a world map. The aim behind these massive construction projects is to make Dubai a major tourist destination. [Map page 129]

Satellite image by Planet Labs, distributed by NPA Satellite Mapping, CGG Services (UK) Ltd

Nestling in a fertile valley in the foothills of the Himalayas at a height of 1,400 m (4,600 ft), Kathmandu occupies a position between the heights of the snow-capped mountains to the north and the plains of India to the south. The labyrinthine old city centre, and the outer areas of more European-style buildings, are home to around 8% of the population of Nepal. The surrounding geographical conditions have encouraged agriculture, and Kathmandu's position between India and China established the city as an early trading centre. Kathmandu has been a magnet for tourists from the hippies of the 1960s to those now visiting the historic and religious sites, and venturing further out to Nepal's national parks and its trekking and mountaineering opportunities. [Map page 125]
USGS Landsat / NPA Satellite Mapping, CGG Services (UK) Ltd

This stunning image shows the location of Kolkata (Calcutta), the purple/grey area in the north-west quadrant, running along the east bank of the Hugli River. The city is the third largest in India with a population of over 15 million people. It grew rapidly after the East India Company founded it as a commercial centre and port in the late 17th century. Until 1911, it was the capital of India. To the south and east can be seen the myriad waterways and channels of the Ganges Delta, flowing into the Bay of Bengal. The large islands are called 'The Sundarbans'. It is the world's largest delta and, due to the huge amount of silt deposited there, is constantly changing. It is also one of the most fertile areas of the world and is consequently densely populated, despite the danger of flooding.

[Map page 125] *USGS / NPA Satellite Mapping, CGG Services (UK) Ltd*

The old city of Bangkok at the head of the Gulf of Thailand, once known as the 'Venice of the East', is a place of 'klongs' (canals) and 'wats' (temples or monasteries). This core has now been overwhelmed by an ever-expanding and chaotic megalopolis of over nine million people. Until recently, transport infrastructure has failed to keep pace with the needs of the population, but there has been a major investment in public transport and four rapid transit lines are now in operation. The loops of the Chao Phraya river can be seen meandering through the centre of the image. Much of the land surrounding the city was once swamp, but has now been drained for agriculture. [Map page 120]
USGS / NPA Satellite Mapping, CGG Services (UK) Ltd

The imperial heart of Beijing, the 'Forbidden City' can be seen within the dark square just to the right of the series of lakes in the centre of this image. Beijing became the imperial capital of the Ming dynasty in 1421, and the grid-like street pattern of wide, broad streets has been preserved. The city sits at the northern end of the North China Plain and, with a population of over 22 million in the metropolitan area, is the second largest city in China after Shanghai. The growth of the city follows the sequence of concentric ring roads which are clearly seen in this image. Beijing Capital International Airport, seen top right, handles over 95 million passengers per year and is the second busiest in the world. [Map page 114]
USGS / NPA Satellite Mapping,
CGG Services (UK) Ltd

The city was founded in the early 19th century as a strategic settlement by the Egyptians, who ruled the area at that time. However its location, where the Nîl el Azraq (Blue Nile), flowing west from Lake Tana in Ethiopia, joins the Nîl el Abyad (White Nile), flowing north from Lake Victoria in Uganda, soon meant that it became a major trading and commercial centre. It then became the capital city of Sudan. From here the Nahr en Nîl (River Nile) flows north to its delta on the Mediterranean Sea, passing through Cairo in Egypt. The city itself is in the fork created by the confluence of the two rivers. To the north of this, on the east bank of the Nile, is El Khartûm Bahrî (North Khartoum) and opposite that, Omdurmàn. Together, this 'Greater Khartoum' area comprises a population of over 5 million people. [Map page 135]

USGS Landsat / NPA Satellite Mapping, CGG Services (UK) Ltd

With a population of over 14 million, the city is one of the fastest growing urban areas in Africa. It was the capital of Nigeria from 1914 until 1991, when a newly built capital was established at Abuja. The original settlement, and port, was on the smallest island visible and from there it has expanded, as communications links have developed and improved. Its port, Apapa, has become the gateway for Nigerian agricultural and mineral exports, as well as oil, and has modern container facilities. The bright white area at the entry to Lagos Lagoon is a large reclamation project called Eko Atlantic. As well as being a major urban development, it will also act as a flood defence system for Victoria Island. [Map page 139]
USGS / NPA Satellite Mapping, CGG Services (UK) Ltd

Two capital cities face each other across the Congo river to the west of the Malebo (formerly) Stanley Pool. On the northern bank lies Brazzaville, capital of the Republic of the Congo and across the water sprawls Kinshasa, the capital of the Democratic Republic of the Congo. Brazzaville became the capital of French Equatorial Africa and expanded rapidly after World War II when it was the headquarters of the Free French Forces in Africa. The adventurer, Sir Henry Morton Stanley, acquired the rights to the area and named it Léopoldville after his patron Léopold II of the Belgians. It was renamed Kinshasa in 1966. The growth of both cities is the result of their location on the Congo river. Brazzaville is at the lowest navigable point on the Congo-Oubangi river system and became a major trans-shipment point. Kinshasa became the focus of both river and rail communications that extend far inland.

[Map page140] *USGS / NPA Satellite Mapping, CGG Services (UK) Ltd*

Dar es Salaam, no longer the capital of
Tanzania, is the largest town and main
seaport in the country. It handles most
of Tanzania's exports and also those
of neighbouring, landlocked, Zambia.
Founded in 1862 by the Sultan of Zanzibar
its name, which is of Arabic-Swahili
origin, means 'haven of peace'. Maybe not
so peaceful in 1916 when it was captured
from Germany by the British during World
War I and, as Tanganyika, remained a
British territory until independence in
1961. In 1964, Tanganyika and Zanzibar
united to establish the United Republic of
Tanzania. Although the city lost its place
as the capital city to Dodoma in 1974, it
has remained the focus of government
and trade in the country. [Map page 142]

*Satellite image by Planet Labs,
distributed by NPA Satellite Mapping,
CGG Services (UK) Ltd*

State capital of Victoria, and Australia's second largest city, Melbourne stands astride the Yarra river. Its establishment by settlers from Tasmania in 1835 was given a boost as a result of the Victoria gold rush in the 1850s. Many fine buildings date from this era and gave the city centre a stately, colonial appeal. However, post World War II immigration, mainly from southern Europe, engendered a more modern and multi-cultural atmosphere. Height restrictions on buildings were lifted in the 1950s and skyscrapers were built. In recent years, there has been much urban regeneration of the dock areas. Its location, climate and vibrant cultural life have led to Melbourne being regarded as one of the most desirable places to live.

[Map page 153] *Satellite image by Planet Labs, distributed by NPA Satellite Mapping, CGG Services (UK) Ltd*

Christchurch nestles at the base of Banks Peninsula on South Island, New Zealand. It is the largest city on South Island and is the centre of one of the country's most productive wheat, grain, and sheep-rearing areas. It was founded in 1851 as a Church of England settlement and until recently some fine buildings from that era could still be seen. However, one building that has not survived intact is the Gothic-style cathedral that was severely damaged in the earthquake of 2011. New Zealand's location on the Pacific rim means that it is vulnerable to earth-quakes. This earthquake, which followed one in September of the previous year, resulted in 185 deaths. Following these earthquakes, a programme of wholesale demolition and reconstruction has begun with plans for extensive expansion of residential areas. Christchurch remains as a tourist hub acting as a stopover point for trips to the Southern Alps. [Map page 155]

Copernicus Sentinel data 2016 / NPA Satellite Mapping, CGG Services (UK) Ltd

Ottawa was founded in 1826 by Colonel By and was subsequently named Bytown. Its name was changed to Ottawa in 1854, a few years before the British queen, Victoria, chose it as the capital of Canada. The city stands on the south bank of the Ottawa river that can be seen flowing across the middle of this image. Most of the major public buildings, including the inspiring gothic-style Parliament complex, cluster round the Rideau Canal. This historic canal was declared to be an UNESCO World Heritage Site in 2007. The city has a wealth of world-class museums, as well as attractive parks and gardens, all of which contribute to Ottawa offering a high quality of living for its residents and visitors.

[Map page 164] *Copernicus Sentinel data 2016 / NPA Satellite Mapping, CGG Services (UK) Ltd*

New York is at the centre of a conurbation which now spreads from Yonkers in the north of this image to Coney Island in the the south. Founded at the start of the 17th century as a trading post on Manhattan island at the mouth of Hudson river (centre), its fine natural harbour allowed it to flourish. Its greatest period of growth was during the 19th and 20th centuries when it became the gateway to the New World for millions of European immigrants. New York is now the most important financial and trading centre in the country, still focused on Manhattan island. The John F. Kennedy International Airport, visible in the lower right of the image, overlooks the islands and tidal estuary of the Jamaica Bay Wildlife Refuge. [Map page 175]

Satellite image by Planet Labs, distributed by NPA Satellite Mapping, CGG Services (UK) Ltd

Memphis, on the mighty Mississippi river,
conjures up images from the past
of steamboats from the plantation era.
Also evoked are sounds of blues
and rock'n'roll from its musical past.
Graceland, the former mansion home
of Elvis Presley, to the south of the city
centre, is still a major tourist attraction. It
is the second most visited house in the US
– the White House in Washington being
the first. The Mississippi, running down
the image, separates the main part of the
city in the extreme south-west corner of
Tennessee from Arkansas on the western
bank. Its geographic location has been
central to the city's growth: firstly using
the river for transport then becoming an
intersection point for five major railways.
In more recent times the airport, lying
south-east of the city centre, became the
world's second busiest cargo airport.

[Map page 177] *Copernicus Sentinel
data 2017 / NPA Satellite Mapping,
CGG Services (UK) Ltd*

Nestling in the extreme south-east of the state of Nevada is the startling city of Las Vegas. A city of over-the-top glitz and glamour set in the midst of an unforgiving and arid landscape. It began as a Mormon settlement in 1855 and grew into a modestly sized agricultural town at the beginning of the 20th century. Its rise to greatness came as a result of Nevada's liberal gaming laws which allowed gambling and casinos to flourish. Las Vegas is now one of the world's top tourist destinations. To the east of the city can be seen Lake Mead, created by the building of the Hoover Dam on the Colorado river. Constructed during the years of the Great Depression in the 1930s, the dam was built to control flooding, provide irrigation and supply hydroelectric power. [Map page 171]
USGS / NPA Satellite Mapping, CGG Services (UK) Ltd

Los Angeles, the 'City of Angels', is the second largest metropolitan area in the USA after New York. Its location on the Pacific coast, warm and sunny climate, have long made it a magnet for those seeking a better life and maybe even fame and fortune in 'Tinseltown', a nickname that nods towards the movie industry based in the hills of Hollywood. Santa Catalina Island, in the south of the image, is separated from the mainland by the San Pedro Channel. The flora, fauna, reefs and shipwrecks are a major attraction for thousands of 'Angelenos' on holiday. [Map page 171]

USGS / NPA Satellite Mapping, CGG Services (UK) Ltd

Mexico City lies in exceptionally thin air high on Mexico's central plateau at 2,200 m (7,350ft) above sea level. The city of over 21 million people sprawls over a vast area of 1,485 sq km (573 sq miles). Over half of all Mexicans employed in industry work here, but this does not disguise the fact that thousands of people still live in abject poverty. By the 1990s the city was one of the most polluted in the world, but since then strenuous efforts have resulted in a dramatic improvement in air quality. Older polluting factories are being closed and there has been significant investment in public transport systems, and attempts have been made to control private car use. [Map page 181]

USGS / NPA Satellite Mapping, CGG Services (UK) Ltd

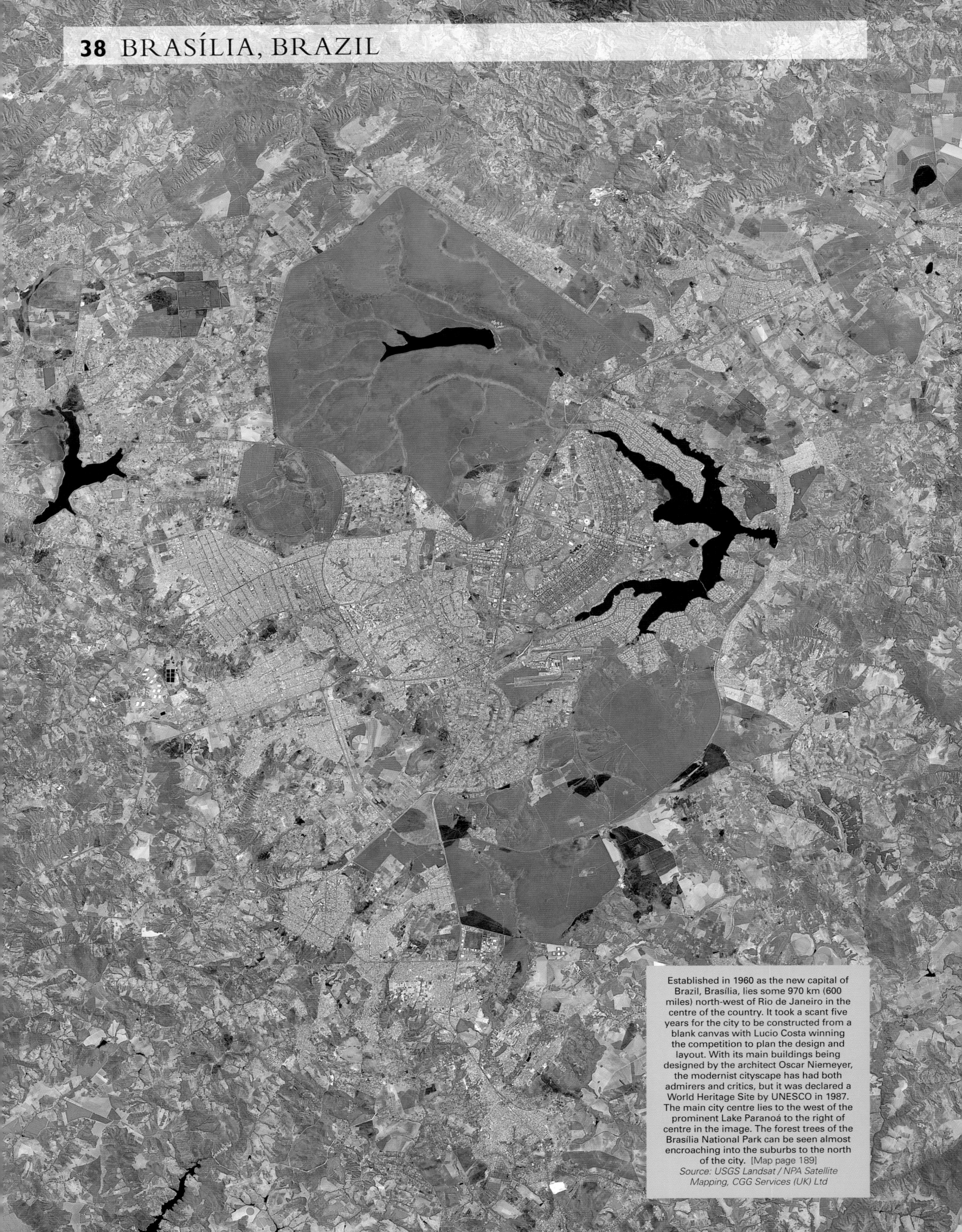

Established in 1960 as the new capital of Brazil, Brasília, lies some 970 km (600 miles) north-west of Rio de Janeiro in the centre of the country. It took a scant five years for the city to be constructed from a blank canvas with Lucio Costa winning the competition to plan the design and layout. With its main buildings being designed by the architect Oscar Niemeyer, the modernist cityscape has had both admirers and critics, but it was declared a World Heritage Site by UNESCO in 1987. The main city centre lies to the west of the prominent Lake Paranoá to the right of centre in the image. The forest trees of the Brasília National Park can be seen almost encroaching into the suburbs to the north of the city. [Map page 189]
Source: USGS Landsat / NPA Satellite Mapping, CGG Services (UK) Ltd

Lying almost exactly on the Tropic of Capricorn, and about 350 km (220 miles) south-west of Rio de Janeiro, is the industrial city of São Paulo. It also acts as Brazil's main financial centre. It does not, however, neglect the arts, and it is home to many great museums and hosts the renowned São Paulo Art Biennial. The city is separated from the coast by the escarpment of Serra de Mar which can be seen at the bottom of this image. It rivals Mexico City as one of the fastest growing cities in the world. [Map page 191]
USGS / NPA Satellite Mapping, CGG Services (UK) Ltd

OCEAN SEAFLOORS

– GREAT BARRIER REEF, AUSTRALIA –
First explored by Captain James Cook in 1770 and lying just off the east coast of Queensland, the Great Barrier Reef is composed of some 2,900 individual reefs and over 900 islands, a few of which are shown on this image. Designated a UNESCO World Heritage Site and protected as a Marine Park, this fragile environment is home to over 1,500 species of fish and 400 species of coral, as well as turtles, whales, and many species of birds.

[Map page 150]

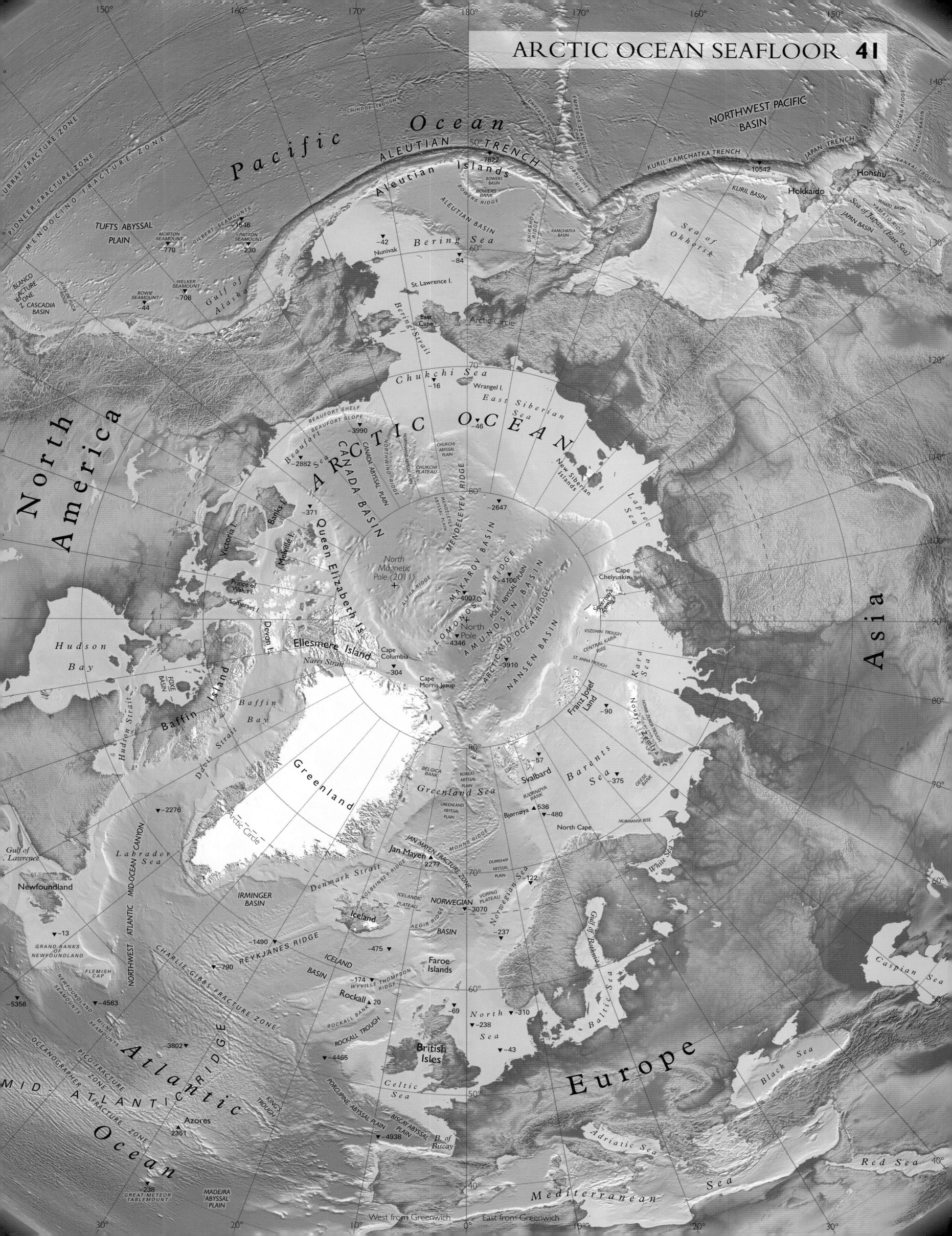

Pacific Ocean

ALEUTIAN TRENCH

NORTHWEST PACIFIC BASIN

Aleutian Islands

CHINOOK TROUGH

EMPEROR SEAMOUNT

OBRUCHEV RISE

KURIL-KAMCHATKA TRENCH

JAPAN TRENCH

Honshu

10542

KURIL BASIN

Hokkaido

Sea of Okhotsk

Sea of Japan (East Sea)

JAPAN BASIN

7822

BOWERS RIDGE

SHIRSHOV RIDGE

ALEUTIAN BASIN

KAMCHATKA BASIN

Bering Sea

−42

−84

Nunivak

60°

St. Lawrence I.

Arctic Circle

East Cape

Bering Strait

70°

Chukchi Sea

−16

Wrangel I.

East Siberian Sea

Laptev Sea

NEW Siberian Islands

Cape Chelyuskin

Severnaya Zemlya

−46

ARCTIC OCEAN

80°

BEAUFORT SHELF

Beaufort Slope

−3990

NORTHWIND ABYSSAL PLAIN

CHUKCHI ABYSSAL PLAIN

CHUKCHI PLATEAU

MENDELEYEV RIDGE

MENDELEEV ABYSSAL PLAIN

−2647

Beaufort Sea

−2882

CANADA ABYSSAL PLAIN

CANADA BASIN

−371

Banks I.

Victoria I.

Melville I.

Queen Elizabeth Is.

MAKAROV BASIN

ALPHA RIDGE

North Magnetic Pole (2011)

−40070

POLE ABYSSAL PLAIN

−4100

LOMONOSOV RIDGE

North Pole

−4346

AMUNDSEN BASIN

ARCTIC MID-OCEAN RIDGE

NANSEN BASIN

−3910

VOZONIN TROUGH

CENTRAL KARA RISE

ST. ANNA TROUGH

Kara Sea

Asia

90°

Prince of Wales I.

Somerset I.

Devon I.

NORTH AMERICA

Hudson Bay

FOXE BASIN

Baffin Island

Ellesmere Island

Cape Columbia

−304

Nares Strait

Cape Morris Jesup

Franz Josef Land

−90

Novaya Zemlya

80°

Baffin Bay

Hudson Strait

Davis Strait

Greenland

Barents Sea

−375

GEESE BANK

−57

Svalbard

Bjørnøya

536

−480

North Cape

MURMANSK RISE

White Sea

70°

Labrador Sea

−2276

Arctic Circle

BELGICA BANK

BOREAS ABYSSAL PLAIN

Greenland Sea

GREENLAND ABYSSAL PLAIN

MOHNS RIDGE

JAN MAYEN FRACTURE ZONE

Jan Mayen

2277

BJØRNØYA BANK

−122

Norwegian Sea

Gulf of Bothnia

Newfoundland

MID-ATLANTIC RIDGE

NORTHWEST ATLANTIC

LABRADOR CANYON

IRMINGER BASIN

Denmark Strait

KOLBEINSEY RIDGE

Iceland

ICELAND BASIN

AEGIR RIDGE

VORING PLATEAU

−3070

NORWEGIAN BASIN

−237

Caspian Sea

−13

GRAND BANKS OF NEWFOUNDLAND

FLEMISH CAP

NEWFOUNDLAND SEAMOUNTS

−5356

−4563

CHARLIE-GIBBS FRACTURE ZONE

REYKJANES RIDGE

−1490

−790

−475

ICELAND BASIN

Faroe Islands

−174

THOMPSON RIDGE

WYVILLE THOMPSON RIDGE

Rockall

20

ROCKALL BANK

ROCKALL TROUGH

−69

North Sea

−310

−238

Baltic Sea

Black Sea

−43

PICO FRACTURE ZONE

−3802

OCEANOGRAPHER FRACTURE ZONE

MILNE SEAMOUNTS

MID-ATLANTIC RIDGE

Atlantic

Azores

2351

−4465

British Isles

Celtic Sea

PORCUPINE ABYSSAL PLAIN

KING'S TROUGH

Europe

Adriatic Sea

−238

GREAT METEOR TABLEMOUNT

MADEIRA ABYSSAL PLAIN

−4938

BISCAY ABYSSAL PLAIN

B. of Biscay

Mediterranean Sea

Red Sea

Ocean

West from Greenwich

East from Greenwich

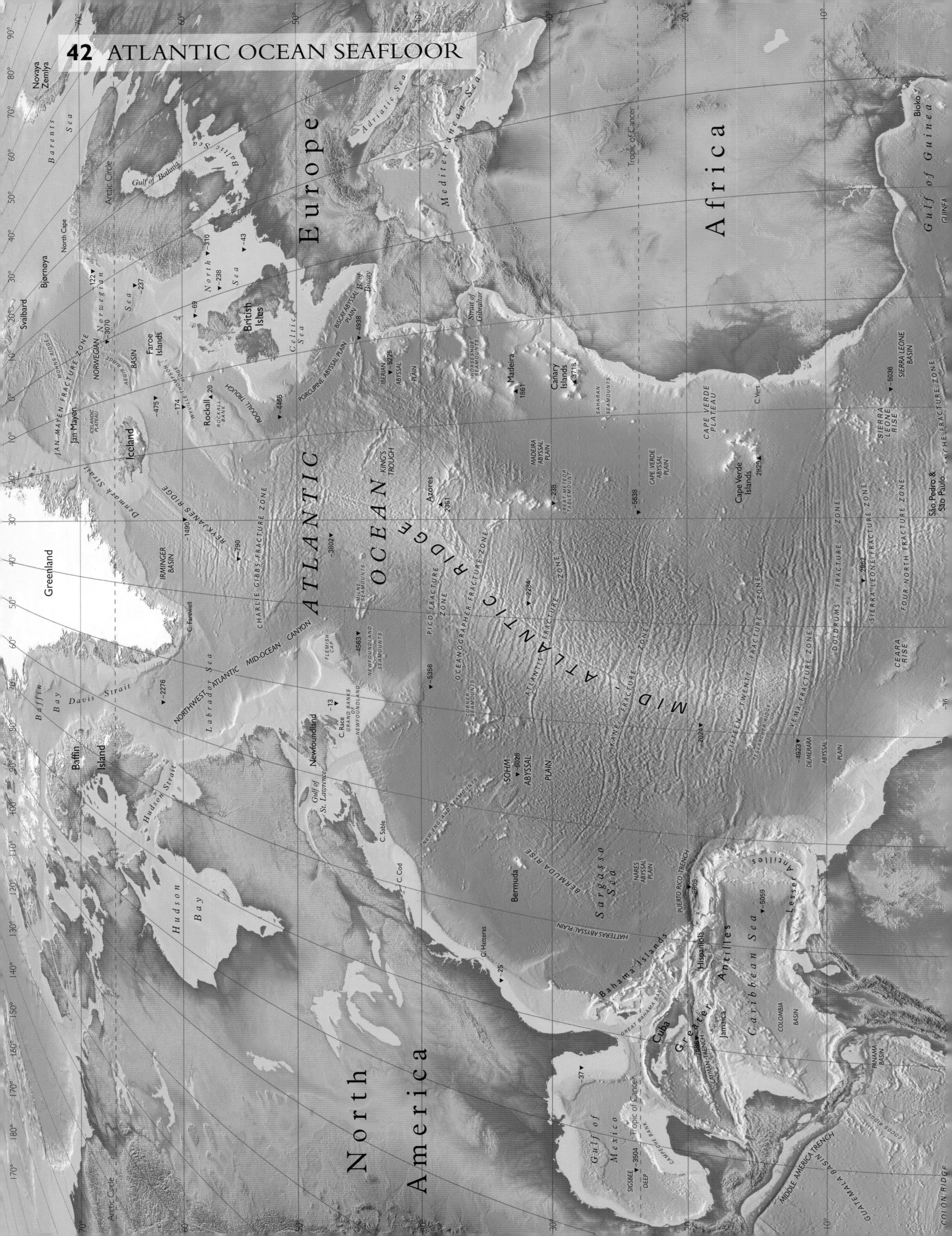

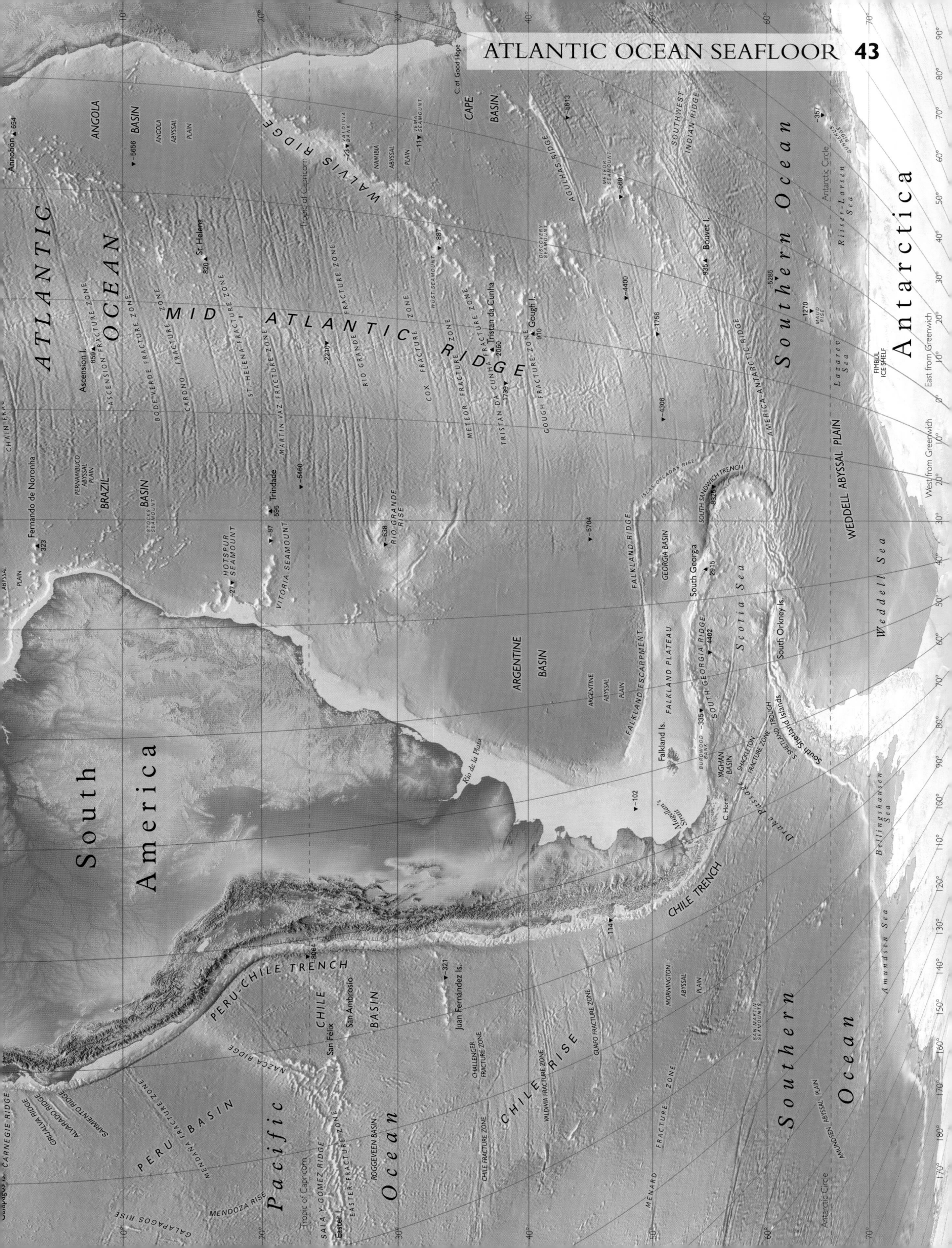

ATLANTIC

OCEAN

Annobón ▲ 654

ANGOLA

▼ 5656 BASIN

ANGOLA
ABYSSAL
PLAIN

CAPE

BASIN

▲ 5613

SOUTHWEST

INDIAN RIDGE

▲ 357

VALDIVIA
BANK

NAMIBIA
ABYSSAL
PLAIN

−23 ▼

C. of Good Hope

Southern Ocean

Antarctic Circle

Riiser-Larsen Sea

Antarctica

WALVIS RIDGE

−11 ▼ VEMA
SEAMOUNT

▼ −560

AGULHAS RIDGE

METEOR
SEAMOUNT

Bouvet I.

▼ −935

MAUD
RISE

MID- ATLANTIC

Ascension I.
859 ▼

ASCENSION FRACTURE ZONE

820 ▼ St. Helena

BODE-VERDE FRACTURE ZONE

CARDNO FRACTURE ZONE

ST. HELENA FRACTURE ZONE

2210 ▼

RIO GRANDE FRACTURE ZONE

COX FRACTURE ZONE

−887 ▼

DISCOVERY
SEAMOUNT

▼ −4400

▼ 1270

FIMBUL
ICE SHELF

East from Greenwich

CHAIN FRAZ.

Fernando de Noronha

PERNAMBUCO
ABYSSAL
PLAIN

323 ▼

BRAZIL

BASIN

STOCKS SEAMOUNT

▼ 5460

Trindade

595

87 ▼
HOTSPUR
SEAMOUNT

−27 ▼

VITORIA SEAMOUNT

MARTIN-VAZ FRACTURE ZONE

ATLANTIC RIDGE

2060 ▼

1739 ▼

Tristan da Cunha
Gough I.

TRISTAN DA CUNHA FRACTURE ZONE

METEOR FRACTURE ZONE

910

GOUGH FRACTURE ZONE

▼ −4306

AMERICA-ANTARCTIC RIDGE

Lazarev Sea

West from Greenwich

WEDDELL ABYSSAL PLAIN

Weddell Sea

ABYSSAL
PLAIN

−638 ▼

RIO GRANDE
RISE

▼ −5704

▲ −5285

FALKLAND RIDGE

ISLAS ORCADAS RISE

SOUTH SANDWICH TRENCH

−8227 ▼

South
America

Río de la Plata

ARGENTINE

BASIN

ARGENTINE
ABYSSAL
PLAIN

FALKLAND ESCARPMENT

FALKLAND PLATEAU

GEORGIA BASIN

South Georgia

SOUTH GEORGIA RIDGE

4402 ▼

2915

Scotia Sea

South Orkney Is.

Pacific

Ocean

Tropic of Capricorn

Easter I.

San Félix
San Ambrosio

SALA-Y-GOMEZ RIDGE

NAZCA RIDGE

CHILE

BASIN

Juan Fernández Is.

CHALLENGER
FRACTURE ZONE

CHILE FRACTURE ZONE

EASTER FRACTURE ZONE

MENDANA FRACTURE ZONE

−321 ▼

VALDIVIA FRACTURE ZONE

GUAFO FRACTURE ZONE

CHILE RISE

−102 ▼

−114 ▼

Falkland Is.

−335 ▼

BURDWOOD
BANK

YAGHAN
BASIN

C. Horn

SHACKLETON
FRACTURE ZONE

Magellan Strait

S. Shetland Islands

S. Shetland Is.

SOUTH SHETLAND TRENCH

Pirie Is.

DRAKE PASSAGE

CHILE TRENCH

PERU-CHILE TRENCH

3084 ▼

PERU BASIN

ROGGEVEEN BASIN

MENDOZA RISE

MORNINGTON
ABYSSAL
PLAIN

MENARD FRACTURE ZONE

SAN MARTIN
SEAMOUNTS

Southern

Ocean

Amundsen Sea

Bellingshausen
Sea

AMUNDSEN ABYSSAL PLAIN

SAN MARTIN ABYSSAL PLAIN

Antarctic Circle

GALAPAGOS RISE

CARNEGIE RIDGE

GRIJALVA RIDGE

SARMIENTO RIDGE

Arctic Circle

Asia

Bering Sea

Sea of Okhotsk
−1000

Kamchatka

ALEUTIAN ISLANDS
ALEUTIAN TRENCH

KURIL BASIN

NORTHWEST PACIFIC BASIN

EMPEROR SEAMOUNT CHAIN

CHINOOK TROUGH

HESS RISE

Hokkaidō
−10542

Sea of Japan (East Sea)
YAMATO RIDGE

Honshū
−8412
JAPAN TRENCH

SHATSKY RISE
−2450

Yellow Sea

East China Sea

MID-PACIFIC SEAMOUNTS

Midway Is. −13

HAWAIIAN

Taiwan

NANSEI SHOTO TRENCH

Tropic of Cancer

Bay of Bengal

Gulf of Tonkin

Hainan

South China Sea

Luzon

PHILIPPINE

WEST MARIANA BASIN

MARIANA RIDGE

MARIANA TROUGH

EAST MARIANA BASIN

MAPMAKERS SEAMOUNTS

Maudin Sun

Andaman Is. −732

Andaman Sea
ANDAMAN BASIN −4267

Philippine Islands
−10057

PHILIPPINE BASIN

Philippine Sea

CHALLENGER DEEP −11022

MARIANA TRENCH

Micronesia

MARSHALL SEAMOUNTS

Marshall Is.

CENTRAL PACIFIC BASIN

Ceylon
Dondra Head

Nicobar Is. −642

Gulf of Thailand

PALAWAN TROUGH

Sulu Sea
SULU BASIN

Mindanao

Palau Is.

PALAU TRENCH
YAP TRENCH

EAURIPIK RISE

WEST CAROLINE BASIN

CAROLINE SEAMOUNTS

EAST CAROLINE BASIN

−791
Pohnpei

PACIFIC

Equator

CEYLON PLAIN −1550

COCOS BASIN

SUNDA SHELF

Celebes Sea
CELEBES BASIN

MELANESIAN BASIN

Phoenix Is.

AFANASY NIKITIN SEAMOUNT

NINETYEAST RIDGE

Sumatra

Borneo

Celebes

Seram Sea

ONTONG JAVA PLATEAU

SOLOMON RISE

MID-INDIAN OCEAN BASIN

MENTAWAI BASIN

Java Sea

SOUTH MAKASSAR BASIN

NORTH BANDA BASIN

Banda Sea

Bismarck Sea

New Britain
−8940
NEW BRITAIN TRENCH

Java

Flores Sea Is.

SOUTH BANDA BASIN

New Guinea

Melanesia

SUNDA TRENCH (JAVA TRENCH)

Christmas I. −7125 −361

−6204

Timor

Arafura Sea

PAPUA PLATEAU

Solomon Sea
−8322

−9165

WEST FIJI BASIN

Samoa Is.

Indian Ocean

Cocos Is.

OSBORN PLATEAU

INVESTIGATOR RIDGE

ROO RISE

NORTH AUSTRALIAN BASIN

Timor Sea

ARAFURA SHELF

Torres Str.

Gulf of Carpentaria

CORAL SEA BASIN

QUEENSLAND PLATEAU

Coral Sea

Great Barrier Reef

New Caledonia

Espiritu Santo

WEST FIJI BASIN

Fiji Is.

Niue

HORIZON RIDGE

GASCOYNE PLAIN

EXMOUTH PLATEAU

SAHUL SHELF

−570

SOUTH FIJI BASIN

WHARTON BASIN

WALLABY PLATEAU

NORTH WEST C.
CUVIER BASIN

Tropic of Capricorn

Tropic of Capricorn

BATAVIA KNOLL

CUVIER PLATEAU
C. Inscription

Australia

LORD HOWE RISE

NEW CALEDONIA TROUGH

NORFOLK RIDGE

LAU RIDGE

JAU BASIN

−10822

EAST INDIAMAN RIDGE

GULDEN DRAAK KNOLL

PERTH BASIN

NATURALISTE FRACTURE ZONE

BROUWER SEAMOUNT −5748

NATURALISTE PLATEAU
C. Leeuwin

Norfolk I. −319

SOUTH FIJI BASIN

DIRCK HARTOG RIDGE

BROKEN RIDGE

DIAMANTINA FRACTURE ZONE

−6602

North I.

−10047

TONGA TRENCH

KERMADEC TRENCH

LOUISV

SOUTHEAST INDIAN RIDGE

Amsterdam I. −881
St. Paul Is. −284

SOUTH AUSTRALIAN BASIN

Bass Str.

TASMAN ABYSSAL PLAIN

Tasman Sea

New Zealand

CHATHAM RISE
Chatham Is.

DEL CAÑO RISE

Crozet Is.
−1090 −4590

Kerguelen Is. −1850

AUSTRALIAN ANTARCTIC DISCORDANCE

Tasmania

EAST TASMAN PLATEAU

TASMAN BASIN

South I.

Bounty Is.
BOUNTY TROUGH
−60
BOUNTY PLATEAU
Antipodes I.

CHALLENGER PLATEAU

CROOK

Auckland Is.
CAMPBELL PLATEAU

BOLLONS SEAMOUNT

EFNA SEAMOUNT
CONRAD RISE

Heard I. −274
−2745

KERGUELEN PLATEAU

Macquarie I.

Campbell I. −272

−6240

ELAN BANK

VALDIVIA ABYSSAL PLAIN

AMERY BASIN

AUSTRALIAN-ANTARCTIC BASIN

SOUTH INDIAN ABYSSAL PLAIN
−4650

Dumont d'Urville Sea

HJORT TROUGH

−6800

Southern

ENDERBY ABYSSAL PLAIN
−6739

C. Borley
−5325

PRINCESS ELIZABETH TROUGH

Davis Sea

Vincennes Bay

Porpose Sea

Ocean

Antarctic Circle

Prydz Bay

Paulding Bay

Balleny Is.

Scott I. −50

East from Greenwich

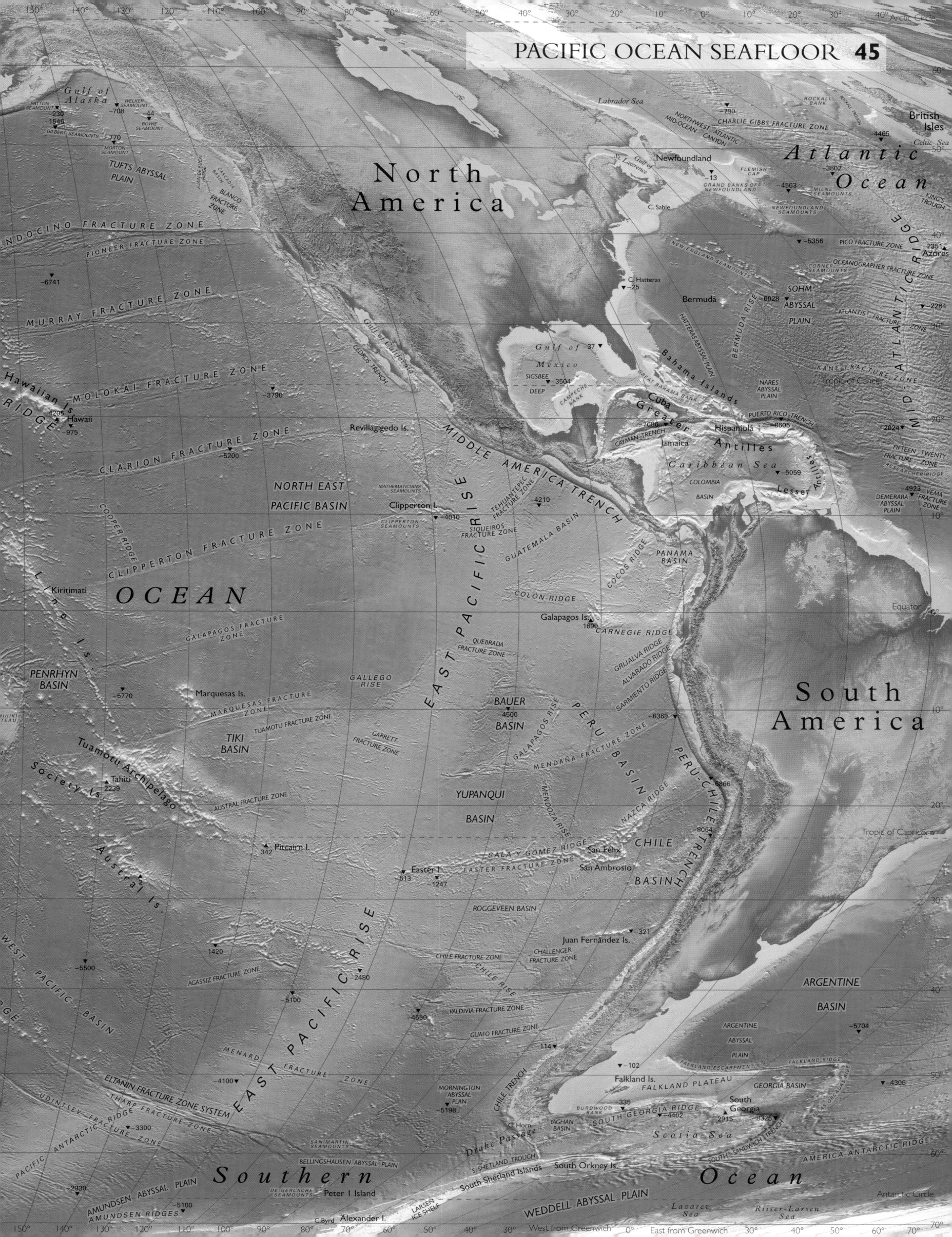

Arctic Circle

150° 140° 130° 120° 110° 100° 90° 80° 70° 60° 50° 40° 30° 20° 10° 0° 10° 20° 30° 40°

North America

Atlantic Ocean

Gulf of Alaska
PATTON SEAMOUNT
-230
-1546
GILBERT SEAMOUNTS
WELKER SEAMOUNT
-708
BOWIE SEAMOUNT
-44
770
MORTON SEAMOUNT

TUFTS ABYSSAL PLAIN

Labrador Sea

NORTHWEST ATLANTIC MID-OCEAN CANYON

CHARLIE GIBBS FRACTURE ZONE
-790

ROCKALL BANK
ROCKALL TROUGH

British Isles
-4485
Celtic Sea

Newfoundland
-13
Gulf of St. Lawrence
St. Lawrence

FLEMISH CAP
GRAND BANKS OF NEWFOUNDLAND

-3802

MILNE SEAMOUNTS
KING'S TROUGH

-4563

C. Sable

INDOCINO FRACTURE ZONE

PIONEER FRACTURE ZONE

JUAN DE FUCA RIDGE
GORDA RIDGE
BLANCO FRACTURE ZONE

-6741

MURRAY FRACTURE ZONE

NEW ENGLAND SEAMOUNTS
-5356
PICO FRACTURE ZONE
OCEANOGRAPHER FRACTURE ZONE
-2351
Azores

ATLANTIS FRACTURE ZONE
-2284

Gulf of California

C. Hatteras
-25

Bermuda

BERMUDA RISE
-6028

SOHM ABYSSAL PLAIN

Hawaiian Is.
RIDGE

Hawaii
-4205
-975

MOLOKAI FRACTURE ZONE

CEDROS TRENCH

-3790

Gulf of Mexico
-37

SIGSBEE DEEP
-3504

CAMPECHE BANK

GREAT BAHAMA BANK

Bahama Islands

HATTERAS ABYSSAL PLAIN

KANE FRACTURE ZONE
Tropic of Cancer

NARES ABYSSAL PLAIN

MID-ATLANTIC RIDGE

Revillagigedo Is.

CLARION FRACTURE ZONE
-5200

MATHEMATICIANS SEAMOUNTS

MIDDLE AMERICA TRENCH

Cuba
Greater Antilles
-7686
CAYMAN TRENCH
Jamaica
Hispaniola
PUERTO RICO TRENCH
-8605

-2024

FIFTEEN - TWENTY FRACTURE ZONE
RESEARCHER RIDGE

NORTH EAST PACIFIC BASIN

Clipperton I.
CLIPPERTON SEAMOUNTS
-4010

TEHUANTEPEC FRACTURE ZONE
SIQUEIROS FRACTURE ZONE
-4210

GUATEMALA BASIN

COCOS RIDGE

PANAMA BASIN

Caribbean Sea
COLOMBIA BASIN

Lesser Antilles
-5059

-4923
DEMERARA ABYSSAL PLAIN

VEMA FRACTURE ZONE
10°

CLIPPERTON FRACTURE ZONE

COOPER RIDGE

OCEAN

Kiritimati
Line Is.

GALAPAGOS FRACTURE ZONE

COLON RIDGE

Galapagos Is.
1690
CARNEGIE RIDGE

Equator

PENRHYN BASIN

-5770

Marquesas Is.

MARQUESAS FRACTURE ZONE

GALLEGO RISE

QUEBRADA FRACTURE ZONE

BAUER BASIN
-4500

GALAPAGOS RISE

PERU BASIN

GRIJALVA RIDGE
ALVARADO RIDGE
SARMIENTO RIDGE

-6369

South America

TUAMOTU FRACTURE ZONE

TIKI BASIN

GARRETT FRACTURE ZONE

MENDAÑA FRACTURE ZONE

NAZCA RIDGE

PERU-CHILE TRENCH
-6866

10°

Society Is.
Tahiti
2239

Tuamotu Archipelago

AUSTRAL FRACTURE ZONE

YUPANQUI BASIN

MENDOZA RISE

-8064

20°
Tropic of Capricorn

EAST PACIFIC RISE

Austral Is.

342
Pitcairn I.

Easter I.
-613
-1247

SALA Y GÓMEZ RIDGE
EASTER FRACTURE ZONE

San Felix
San Ambrosio

CHILE BASIN

-1420

ROGGEVEEN BASIN

Juan Fernández Is.
-321

30°

WEST PACIFIC BASIN

-5500

AGASSIZ FRACTURE ZONE
-2480

CHILE FRACTURE ZONE

CHALLENGER FRACTURE ZONE

CHILE RISE

ARGENTINE BASIN

-5704

-5100

VALDIVIA FRACTURE ZONE

GUAFO FRACTURE ZONE

-4550

114

40°

MENARD FRACTURE ZONE

-4100

EAST PACIFIC RISE

ELTANIN FRACTURE ZONE SYSTEM
THARP FRACTURE ZONE

RIDGE

UDINTSEV FRACTURE ZONE

PACIFIC ANTARCTIC RIDGE

-3300

-102

Falkland Is.

MORNINGTON ABYSSAL PLAIN
-5198

BURDWOOD BANK
335

CHILE TRENCH

FALKLAND ESCARPMENT
FALKLAND PLATEAU

South Georgia
2915
-8325

GEORGIA BASIN
-4306

FALKLAND RIDGE

50°

Southern

2930

-5100
AMUNDSEN ABYSSAL PLAIN
AMUNDSEN RIDGES

SAN MARTIN SEAMOUNTS

BELLINGSHAUSEN ABYSSAL PLAIN

DE GERLACHE SEAMOUNTS
Peter I Island

C.Byrd Alexander I.

C. Horn
YAGHAN BASIN
Drake Passage

S.SHETLAND TROUGH
South Shetland Islands

LARSEN ICE SHELF

SOUTH GEORGIA RIDGE
-4402

South Orkney Is.

WEDDELL ABYSSAL PLAIN

Lazarev Sea

SOUTH SANDWICH TRENCH

Scotia Sea

AMERICA-ANTARCTIC RIDGE

Riiser-Larsen Sea

Ocean

Antarctic Circle

West from Greenwich 0° East from Greenwich

150° 140° 130° 120° 110° 100° 90° 80° 70° 60° 50° 40° 30° 20° 10° 0° 10° 20° 30° 40° 50° 60° 70°

Asia

Africa

Australia

Antarctica

Mediterranean Sea

Red Sea
−2211

Persian Gulf
60

Gulf of Oman
OMAN BASIN

Tropic of Cancer

Equator

Tropic of Capricorn

Antarctic Circle

Arabian Sea
ARABIAN BASIN

W. SHEBA RIDGE
Gulf of Aden
SHEBA RIDGE
Socotra
Ras Asir

OWEN FRACTURE ZONE

SADKO SEAMOUNT
−2758

CARLSBERG RIDGE
−5827

Laccadive Is.

Bay of Bengal
Maudin Sun

Andaman Is. ▲732
Andaman Sea
ANDAMAN BASIN
−4267

Gulf of Tonkin
Hainan

Taiwan

Yellow Sea

South China Sea
SOUTH CHINA BASIN

SOMALI BASIN

Pemba
Zanzibar

Seychelles
SEYCHELLES BANK
▲905
−13
AMIRANTE TRENCH
−5273
FORTUNE BANK

MASCARENE PLATEAU

C. Delgado
Comoro Is.
Agalega Is.
MASCARENE BASIN
Tromelin

SAYA DE MALHA BANK
−7
NAZARETH BANK
CARGADOS CARAJOS BANK
396 ▲ Rodrigues I.
RODRIGUES RIDGE

−2194

COCO-DE-MER SEAMOUNTS

MABAHISS FRACTURE ZONE
SEALARK FRACTURE ZONE
VITYAZ FRACTURE ZONE
−6402
VEMA FRACTURE ZONE
ARGO FRACTURE ZONE
MARIE CELESTE FRACTURE ZONE

MID-INDIAN RIDGE

Maldives
CHAGOS TROUGH CHAGOS-LACCADIVE RIDGE

C. Comorin
Ceylon
Dondra Head

Nicobar Is. ▲642

Gulf of Thailand

SUNDA SHELF

Borneo

Equator

−22

Java Sea
Sunda Is.
Java

Chagos Arch.
CHAGOS BANK
−5408

CEYLON PLAIN
−1550
AFANASY NIKITIN SEAMOUNT

MID-INDIAN OCEAN BASIN

COCOS BASIN

OSBORN PLATEAU

NINETYEAST RIDGE

INVESTIGATOR RIDGE

MENTAWAI BASIN
Mentawai Is.
Sumatra
Str. of Malacca

SUNDA TRENCH (JAVA)
SUNDA TROUGH

Christmas I.
▲361
Cocos Is. ▲5
−7125
JAVA TRENCH
ROO RISE
−6204
NORTH AUSTRALIAN BASIN

INDIAN OCEAN

ARGO FRACTURE ZONE
WILSHAW RIDGE
−5194
MASCARENE PLAIN
828 ▲ Mauritius
Réunion 3069

SOUTHWEST INDIAN RIDGE

MADAGASCAR RIDGE

Madagascar

Bassas da India
Europa

MOZAMBIQUE CHANNEL

MOZAMBIQUE BASIN

MADAGASCAR BASIN

HORIZON RIDGE
GASCOGNE PLAIN
EXMOUTH PLATEAU

WHARTON BASIN

WALLABY PLATEAU
North West C.
CUVIER BASIN
CUVIER PLATEAU
C. Inscription

SOUTHEAST INDIAN RIDGE

−2067

BROKEN RIDGE

EAST INDIAMAN RIDGE
BATAVIA KNOLL
GULDEN DRAAK KNOLL

PERTH BASIN
NATURALISTE FRACTURE ZONE
BROUWER SEAMOUNT
−5746
NATURALISTE PLATEAU
C. Leeuwin

Australia

NATAL VALLEY

MOZAMBIQUE ESCARPMENT

C. of Good Hope
C. Agulhas
AGULHAS BANK
TRANSKEI BASIN
−5371
AGULHAS PLATEAU
AGULHAS BASIN

DISCOVERY II FRACTURE ZONE
INDOMED FRACTURE ZONE
GALLIENI FRACTURE ZONE
ATLANTIS FRACTURE ZONE
MELVILLE FRACTURE ZONE

CROZET BASIN

Amsterdam I. ▲881
St. Paul Is. ▲284

−8000

DIAMANTINA FRACTURE ZONE

AUSTRALIAN ANTARCTIC DISCORDANCE

−3902

PRINCE EDWARD FRACTURE ZONE

DEL CAÑO RISE
Prince Edward Is.
1230
1090
Crozet Is. ▲
−4590
Kerguelen Is. ▲
1850

Heard I.
2745
KERGUELEN-GAUSSBERG PLATEAU

LENA SEAMOUNT
CONRAD RISE

ELAN BANK

SOUTHEAST INDIAN RIDGE

AUSTRALIAN-ANTARCTIC BASIN

−6739

ENDERBY ABYSSAL PLAIN

VALDIVIA ABYSSAL PLAIN

AMERY BASIN
PRINCESS ELIZABETH TROUGH

Southern

SOUTH INDIAN ABYSSAL PLAIN

Ocean

−1270
MAUD RISE

Antarctic Circle

Lazarev Sea
Riiser-Larsen Sea

Cosmonaut Sea
C. Borley

Prydz Bay

Vincennes Bay
Paulding Bay
Porpoise Bay

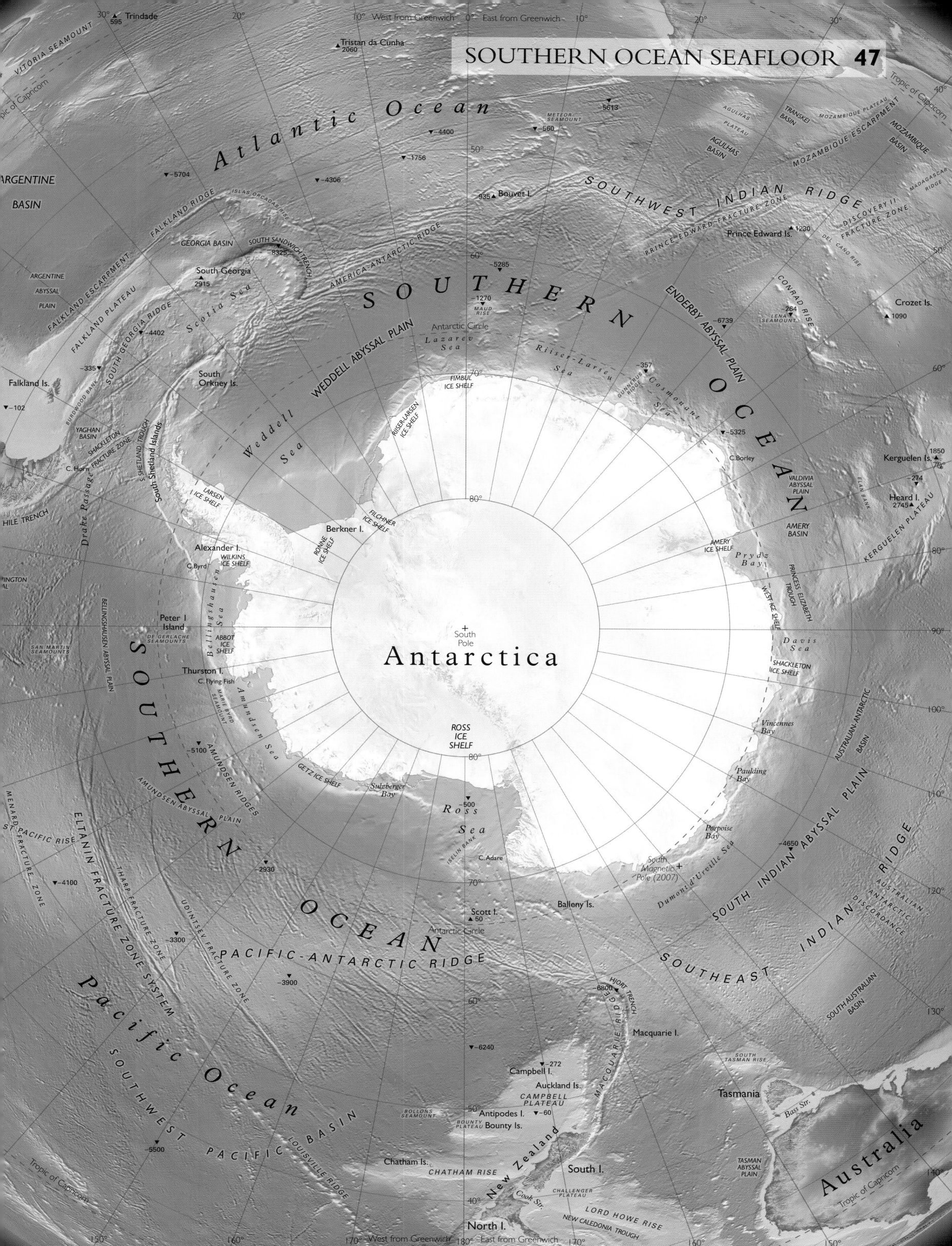

Trindade
595

VITORIA SEAMOUNT

Tristan da Cunha
2060

Atlantic Ocean

-5613

-4400   METEOR
SEAMOUNT -560

30°   20°   10° West from Greenwich   0°   East from Greenwich   10°   20°   30°   40° Tropic of Capricorn

AGULHAS
PLATEAU   TRANSKEI   MOZAMBIQUE PLATEAU
BASIN

50°   -1756   AGULHAS   MOZAMBIQUE ESCARPMENT   MOZAMBIQUE
BASIN   BASIN

-5704   -4306   S O U T H W E S T   I N D I A N   R I D G E

ARGENTINE
BASIN   935 Bouvet I.   PRINCE EDWARD FRACTURE ZONE   DISCOVERY II
FRACTURE ZONE

GEORGIA BASIN   SOUTH SANDWICH TRENCH   Prince Edward Is. 1230   DEL CANO RISE   MADAGASCAR PLATEAU

FALKLAND RIDGE   ISLAS ORCADAS RISE   -8325   AMERICA-ANTARCTIC RIDGE   60°   CONRAD RISE   Crozet Is.
1090

ARGENTINE   South Georgia   S O U T H E R N   264   LENA
ABYSSAL   2915   -6739   SEAMOUNT
PLAIN   FALKLAND PLATEAU   Scotia Sea   -5285

SOUTH GEORGIA RIDGE   -4402   -1270   ENDERBY ABYSSAL PLAIN   50°
-335   MAUD
RISE   -274
Falkland Is.   Antarctic Circle   Kerguelen Is. 1850   70°
BURDWOOD BANK   Lazarev   Sea   Riiser-Larsen   -357   Heard I.
-102   South   Sea   GUNNERUS RIDGE   2745
Orkney Is.   WEDDELL ABYSSAL PLAIN   70°   -5325   ELAN BANK

YAGHAN   FIMBUL   O C E A N   C. Borley   KERGUELEN PLATEAU
BASIN   ICE SHELF   COSMONAUT   VALDIVIA
SHACKLETON   Weddell   RIISER-LARSEN   Sea   ABYSSAL
FRACTURE ZONE   ICE SHELF   PLAIN

C. Horn   Sea   AMERY   80°
South Shetland Islands   80°   BASIN   Prydz
CHILE TRENCH   LARSEN   FILCHNER   AMERY   Bay   PRINCESS ELIZABETH TROUGH
ICE SHELF   ICE SHELF   Berkner I.   ICE SHELF

Drake Passage   RONNE   WEST ICE SHELF
Alexander I.   ICE SHELF   90°
WASHINGTON   WILKINS   G.Byrd   Davis
ICE SHELF   Sea
BELLINGSHAUSEN ABYSSAL PLAIN   + South   SHACKLETON
Pole   ICE SHELF

Peter I   Antarctica
Island
DE GERLACHE
SEAMOUNTS   Bellingshausen   ABBOT
Sea   ICE SHELF   100°
SAN MARTIN
SEAMOUNTS   Thurston I.   Vincennes
C. Flying Fish   Bay

MARIE BYRD   ROSS
SEAMOUNT   ICE   Paulding   AUSTRALIAN-ANTARCTIC
SHELF   Bay   BASIN

-5100   Amundsen   80°
AMUNDSEN RIDGES   Sea   GETZ ICE SHELF   Porpoise
Bay
EAST PACIFIC RISE   AMUNDSEN ABYSSAL   -500   Ross   Dumont d'Urville Sea   -4650
PLAIN   Sulzberger   Sea   SOUTH INDIAN ABYSSAL PLAIN   140°
Bay   South   AUSTRALIAN
MENARD   ISELIN BANK   Magnetic +   ANTARCTIC
FRACTURE ZONE   -2930   C. Adare   Pole (2007)   DISCORDANCE

S O U T H E R N   70°   120°
-4100   THARP FRACTURE ZONE   Balleny Is.   SOUTHEAST   SOUTH AUSTRALIAN
BASIN

Scott I.   50   INDIAN RIDGE
-3300   UDINTSEV FRACTURE ZONE   Antarctic Circle   130°
O C E A N
PACIFIC-ANTARCTIC RIDGE   60°
-3900   HJORT TRENCH   SOUTH
-6800   TASMAN RISE

Pacific   *Ocean*   -6240   MACQUARIE RIDGE   Macquarie I.

Campbell I. 272   TASMAN
-5500   Auckland Is.   ABYSSAL
SOUTH WEST PACIFIC BASIN   CAMPBELL   Tasmania   PLAIN
PLATEAU   Bass Str.
BOLLONS   50°   Antipodes I. -60
SEAMOUNT   BOUNTY   Bass Str.
PLATEAU   Bounty Is.
Chatham Is.   CHATHAM RISE   South I.   *Australia*
LOUISVILLE RIDGE   CHALLENGER   Tropic of Capricorn
PLATEAU
Cook Str.   LORD HOWE RISE
Tropic of Capricorn   North I.   NEW CALEDONIA TROUGH

150°   160°   170° West from Greenwich   180°   East from Greenwich   170°   160°   150°   140°

WORLD
MAPS

Equatorial Scale 1:84 000 000

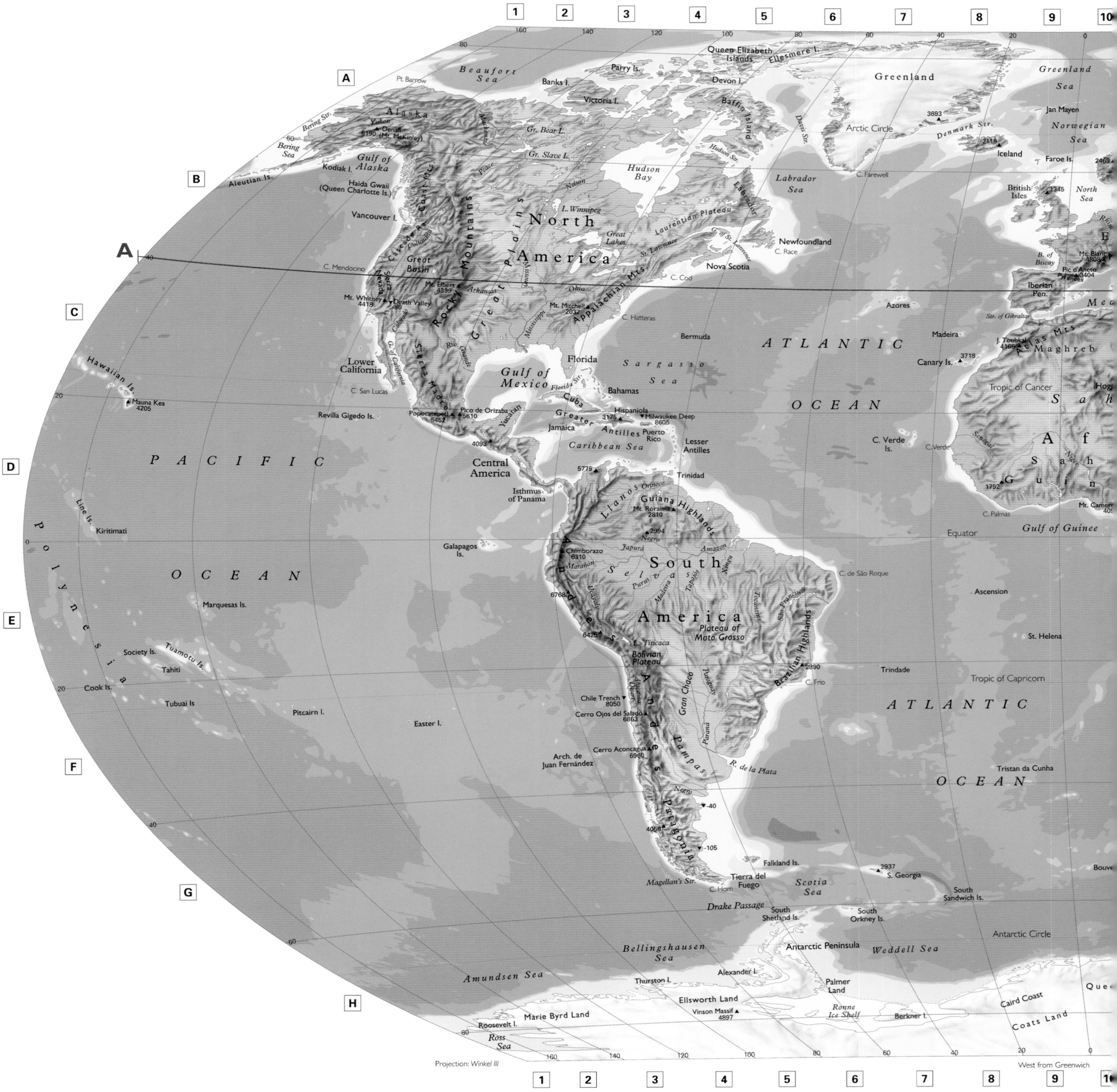

A B C D E F G H

1 2 3 4 5 6 7 8 9 10

Beaufort Sea
Pt. Barrow
Banks I.
Victoria I.
Parry Is.
Queen Elizabeth Islands
Devon I.
Ellesmere I.
Greenland
Greenland Sea
Jan Mayen
3693
Denmark Str.
2116
Iceland
Norwegian Sea
Faroe Is.
2468

Bering Str.
Alaska
Denali 6190 (Mt McKinley)
Gulf of Alaska
Kodiak I.
Aleutian Is.
Haida Gwaii (Queen Charlotte Is.)
Vancouver I.
Gr. Bear L.
Gr. Slave L.
Baffin Island
Hudson Str.
Hudson Bay
Labrador Sea
Arctic Circle
C. Farewell
British Isles
1345
North Sea

North America
L. Winnipeg
Nelson
Great Lakes
Laurentian Plateau
G. of St. Lawrence
St. Lawrence
Newfoundland
C. Race
Nova Scotia
Labrador

Rocky Mountains
Great Plains
Great Basin
Sierra Nevada
Mt. Elbert 4399
Ohio
Arkansas
Mississippi
Appalachian Mts.
C. Cod
C. Hatteras
Bermuda
B. of Biscay
Mt. Blanc 4808
Pic d'Aneto 3404
Iberian Pen.

Mt. Whitney 4418
Death Valley
Mt. Mitchell 2037
Azores
Madeira
Canary Is. 3718
Str. of Gibraltar
Atlas Mts.
Maghreb

Hawaiian Is.
Mauna Kea 4205
Lower California
C. San Lucas
Sierra Madre
Revilla Gigedo Is.
Popocatepetl 5452
Pico de Orizaba 5610
Yucatan
Gulf of Mexico
Florida Str.
Florida
Cuba
Bahamas
Greater Antilles
Hispaniola 3126
Jamaica
Milwaukee Deep 8605
Puerto Rico
Lesser Antilles
Caribbean Sea
Sargasso Sea
ATLANTIC OCEAN
C. Verde
C. Verde Is.
Tropic of Cancer
Sahara
Africa

PACIFIC OCEAN
Central America
Isthmus of Panama
4093
5775
Trinidad
Llanos
Orinoco
Mt. Roraima 2810
Guiana Highlands
2964
C. Palmas
Equator
Gulf of Guinea
1752

Line Is.
Kiritimati
Galapagos Is.
Chimborazo 6310
Marañón
Japurá
Amazon
South America
Selvas
Purus
Madeira
Tapajos
C. de São Roque
Ascension

Polynesia
Marquesas Is.
6768
Negro
Ucayali
Juruá
St. Helena

Society Is.
Tahiti
Tuamotu Is.
Cook Is.
Tubuai Is.
Pitcairn I.
Easter I.
6425
L. Titicaca
Bolivian Plateau
Plateau of Mato Grosso
Brazilian Highlands
2890
C. Fno
Paraná
São Francisco
Trindade
Tropic of Capricorn
ATLANTIC OCEAN

Chile Trench 8050
Cerro Ojos del Salado 6863
Gran Chaco
Pilcomayo
Arch. de Juan Fernández
Cerro Aconcagua 6960
Pampas
R. de la Plata
Negro
-40
Tristan da Cunha
OCEAN

Patagonia
4058
-105
Falkland Is.
2937
S. Georgia
South Sandwich Is.

Magellan's Str.
Tierra del Fuego
C. Horn
Drake Passage
Scotia Sea
South Shetland Is.
South Orkney Is.
Antarctic Circle
Bouvet

Amundsen Sea
Bellingshausen Sea
Antarctic Peninsula
Weddell Sea
Queen
Thurston I.
Alexander I.
Palmer Land
Ross Sea
Roosevelt I.
Marie Byrd Land
Ellsworth Land
Vinson Massif 4897
Ronne Ice Shelf
Berkner I.
Caird Coast
Coats Land

Projection: Winkel III
West from Greenwich

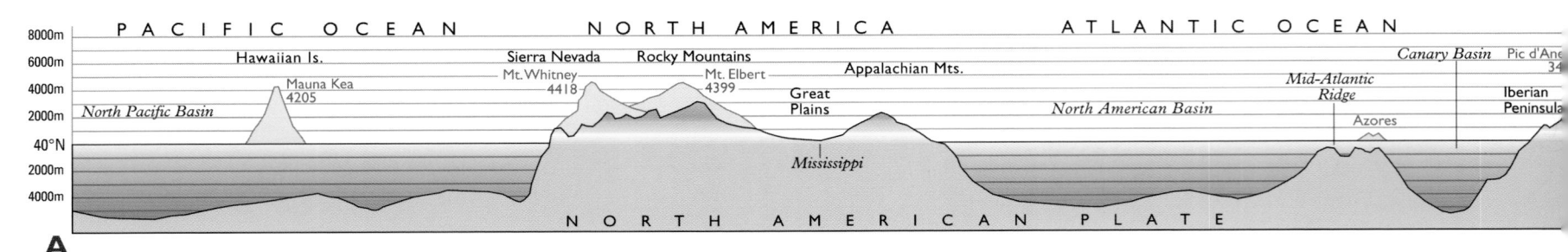

8000m
6000m
4000m
2000m
40°N
2000m
4000m

PACIFIC OCEAN   NORTH AMERICA   ATLANTIC OCEAN
Hawaiian Is.
Mauna Kea 4205
North Pacific Basin
Sierra Nevada
Mt. Whitney 4418
Rocky Mountains
Mt. Elbert 4399
Great Plains
Appalachian Mts.
Mississippi
North American Basin
Mid-Atlantic Ridge
Azores
Canary Basin
Pic d'Aneto 34
Iberian Peninsula

NORTH AMERICAN PLATE

A

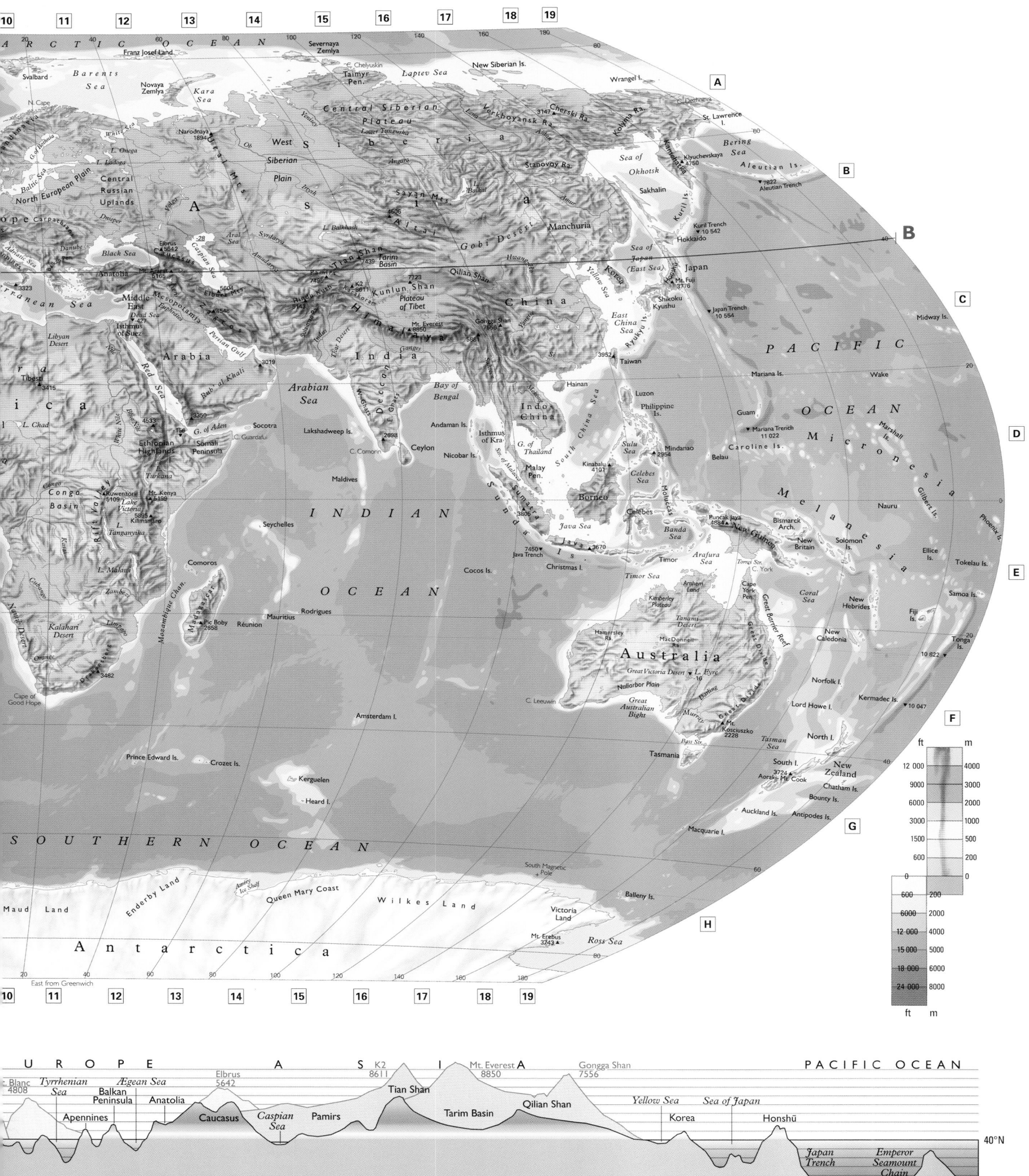

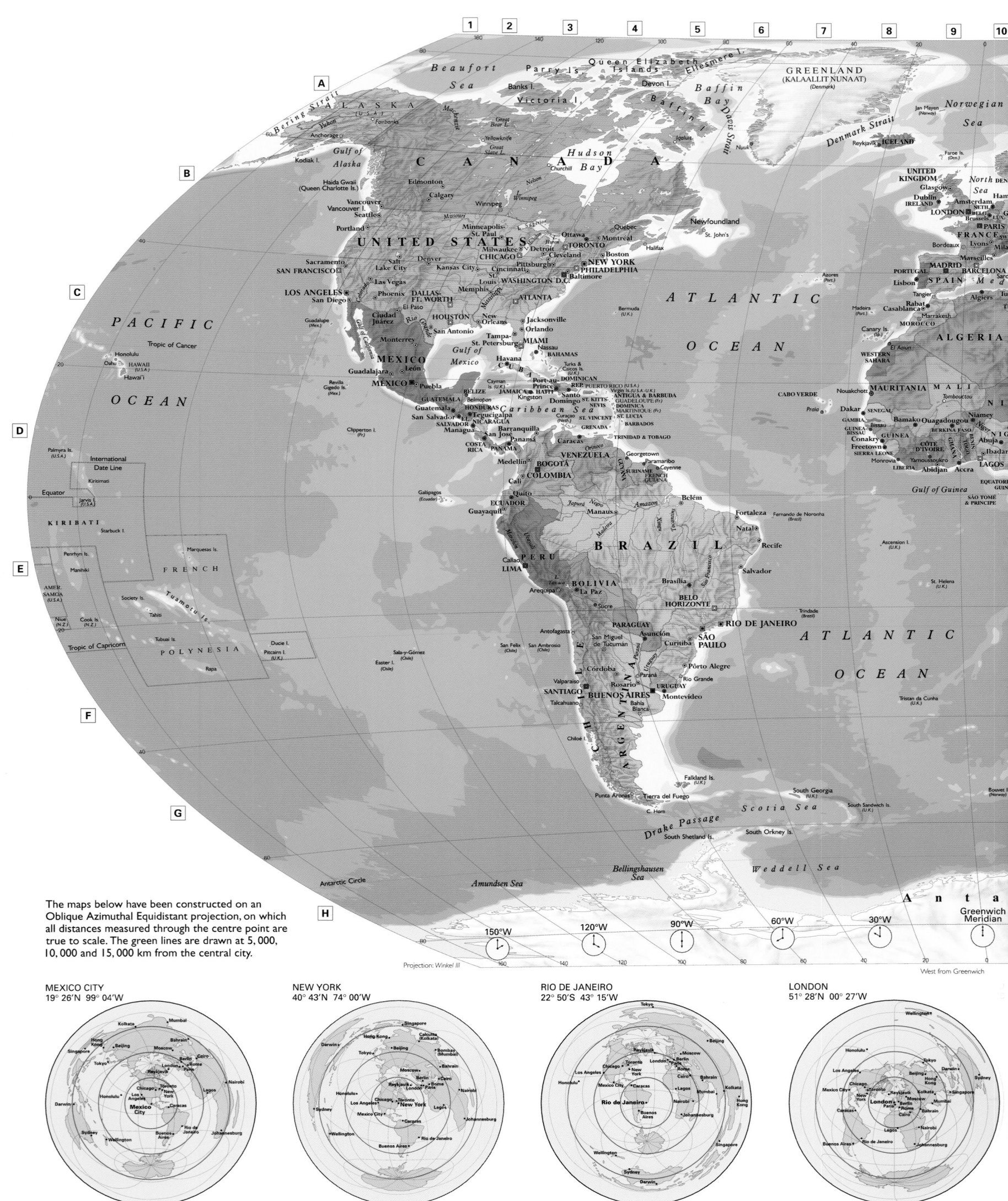

The maps below have been constructed on an Oblique Azimuthal Equidistant projection, on which all distances measured through the centre point are true to scale. The green lines are drawn at 5, 000, 10, 000 and 15, 000 km from the central city.

Projection: Winkel III

West from Greenwich

MEXICO CITY
19° 26'N 99° 04'W

NEW YORK
40° 43'N 74° 00'W

RIO DE JANEIRO
22° 50'S 43° 15'W

LONDON
51° 28'N 00° 27'W

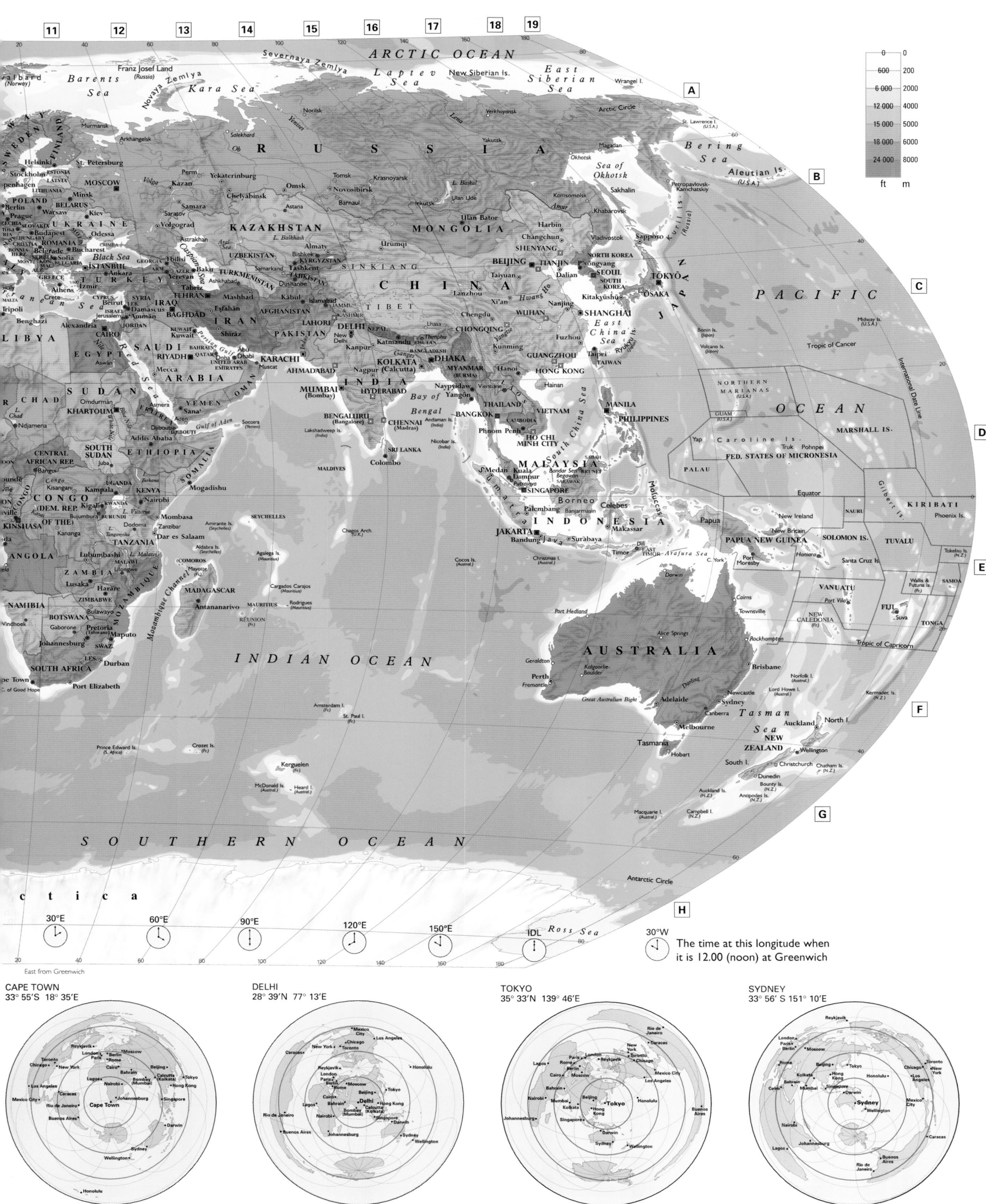

COPYRIGHT PHILIP'S

1:31 100 000

Projection : Zenithal Equidistant

West from Greenwich | East from Greenwich

COPYRIGHT PHILIP'S

Legend:
- Maximum extent of sea ice
- Minimum extent of sea ice
- Ice caps and permanent ice shelf

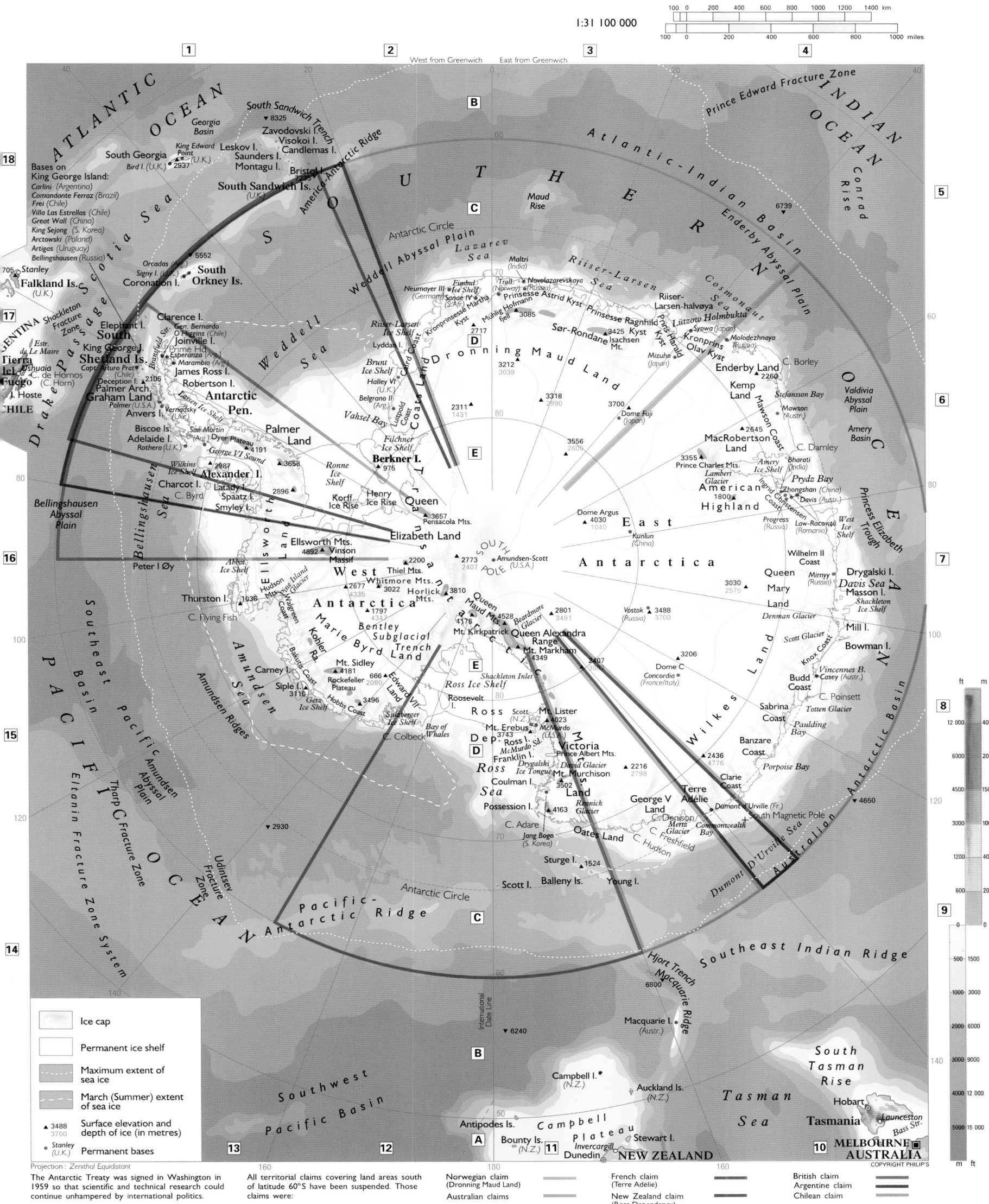

1:31 100 000

Projection: Zenithal Equidistant

The Antarctic Treaty was signed in Washington in 1959 so that scientific and technical research could continue unhampered by international politics.

All territorial claims covering land areas south of latitude 60°S have been suspended. Those claims were:

Norwegian claim (Dronning Maud Land)	French claim (Terre Adélie)	British claim
Australian claims	New Zealand claim (Ross Dependency)	Argentine claim
		Chilean claim

COPYRIGHT PHILIP'S

Legend:
- Ice cap
- Permanent ice shelf
- Maximum extent of sea ice
- March (Summer) extent of sea ice
- ▲ 3488 / 3700 Surface elevation and depth of ice (in metres)
- • Stanley (U.K.) Permanent bases

Bases on King George Island:
Carlini (Argentina)
Comandante Ferraz (Brazil)
Frei (Chile)
Villa Las Estrellas (Chile)
Great Wall (China)
King Sejong (S. Korea)
Arctowski (Poland)
Artigas (Uruguay)
Bellingshausen (Russia)

Equatorial Scale 1:45 000 000

ATLANTIC OCEAN

CANADA
Hudson Bay
Churchill
Belcher Is.
C. Henrietta Maria
L. Winnipeg
Regina
Winnipeg
Nelson
James Bay
Albany
Moosonee
L. Superior
Minneapolis
St. Paul
L. Michigan
L. Huron
Chicago
Detroit
Omaha
Pittsburgh
St. Louis
Ohio
L. Erie
L. Ontario
Toronto
Ottawa
Montréal
Québec
St. Lawrence
UNITED STATES
Missouri
Mississippi
Appalachian Mts.
Arkansas
Red
Tennessee
Alabama
Atlanta
Charleston
New York
Philadelphia
Baltimore
Washington D.C.
Boston
C. Cod
Chesapeake Bay
C. Hatteras
Jacksonville
Orlando
Houston
Galveston
New Orleans
Miami
Nassau
Gulf of Mexico
Sigsbee Deep 3504
Tampico
G. de Campeche
Veracruz
MEXICO
BELIZE
GUATEMALA
Guatemala
EL SALVADOR
HONDURAS
NICARAGUA
COSTA RICA
PANAMA
Panamá
G. de Panamá
Canal de Yucatan
La Habana
CUBA
Santiago de Cuba
JAMAICA
Kingston
HAITI
DOM. REP.
Santo Domingo
San Juan
PUERTO RICO (U.S.A.)
West Indies
BAHAMAS
Tropic of Cancer
Florida Strait
Sargasso Sea
Bermuda (U.K.)
Hamilton
Hatteras Abyssal Plain
New England Seamounts
Corner Seamounts
Sohm Abyssal Plain
Bermuda Rise
6028
Nares Abyssal Plain
5638

ATLANTIC OCEAN
Mid Atlantic Ridge

GREENLAND (Denmark)
Nuuk
Ittoqqortoormiit
Nunap Isua (K. Farvel)
Hudson Str.
C. Chidley
Labrador Sea
Hamilton Inlet
Str. of Belle Isle
Newfoundland
Gulf of St. Lawrence
St. John's
C. Race
Cape Breton I.
Halifax
Grand Banks of Newfoundland
Flemish Cap
Tasiilaq
Denmark Strait
Davis Strait
Northwest Atlantic Mid-Ocean Canyon
Charlie Gibbs Fracture Zone
ICELAND
Reykjavík
Oraefajökull 2119
Reykjanes Ridge
Rockall (U.K.)
Rockall Trough
Porcupine Abyssal Plain
King's Trough
5225
Azores-Biscay Rise
Açores (Port.)
Ponta Delgada
2351

Norwegian Sea
Norwegian Basin
Trondheim
Tórshavn
Føroyar (Den.)
NORWAY
Bergen
Oslo
Stockholm
Göteborg
Malmö
København
DENMARK
North Sea
UNITED KINGDOM
Glasgow
Liverpool
Dublin
IRELAND
London
Celtic Sea
English Channel
Le Havre
Paris
FRANCE
Bay of Biscay
Biscay Abyssal Plain
A Coruña
C. Fisterra
Vigo
Porto
PORTUGAL
Lisboa
Madrid
SPAIN
Bordeaux
Marseille
Barcelona
Is. Baleares
Mt. Blanc 4808
GERMANY
Berlin
Hamburg
Amsterdam
NETH.
BELG.
Brussel
Wien
AUSTRIA
SWITZ.
Milano
Roma
NÁPOLI
ITALY
Corse
Sardegna
Sicilia
Mediterranean Sea
POLAND
Warszawa
Gdansk
CZECHIA
SLOVAKIA
HUNGARY
Zagreb
CROATIA
BOS. H.
Adriatic Sea
MALTA
Alger
Tunis
TUNISIA
Tarābulus
Str. of Gibraltar
Tanger
Rabat
Casablanca
MOROCCO
Marrakech
Funchal
Madeira (Port.)
Is. Canarias (Sp.) 3718
Las Palmas
El Aaiún
WESTERN SAHARA
Saharan Seamounts
ALGERIA
Sahara
Chott Djerid
Chott Melghir 3008

MAURITANIA
Nouakchott
Nouâdhibou
Ras Nouâdhibou
Cape Verde Abyssal Plain
Cape Verde Plateau
CABO VERDE
Praia
2829
Dakar
SENEGAL
C. Vert
GAMBIA
Banjul
GUINEA-BISSAU
GUINEA
Conakry
Freetown
SIERRA LEONE
St-Louis
Tombouctou
MALI
Bamako
Kayes
Senegal
Ouagadougou
BURKINA FASO
NIGER
NIGERIA
Kano
Kano
Niger
Benue
Lagos
Accra
GHANA
CÔTE D'IVOIRE
Abidjan
LIBERIA
Monrovia
Sekondi-Takoradi
Sierra Leone Rise
Sierra Leone Basin
Port Harcourt
CAMEROON
Douala
4070
EQUATORIAL GUINEA
Bioko
SÃO TOMÉ & PRÍNCIPE
Libreville
GABON
Gulf of Guinea
Guinea Basin
7758
6537
Annobón (Eq. Guinea)
Equator
São Pedro & São Paulo (Brazil)
7292

COLOMBIA
Bogotá
Cali
Quito
ECUADOR
Cotopaxi 5897
Chimborazo 6310
Guayaquil
G. de Guayaquil
Iquitos
Pta. Pariñas
VENEZUELA
Caracas
Barranquilla
Sierra Nevada de Santa Marta
Maracaibo
G. de Venezuela
Curaçao
ARUBA
Port of Spain
TRINIDAD & TOBAGO
GRENADA
ST. VINCENT
BARBADOS
ST. LUCIA
MARTINIQUE (Fr.)
DOMINICA
GUADELOUPE (Fr.)
Leeward Is.
ANTIGUA
ST. KITTS
Windward Is.
Caribbean Sea
Colombian Basin
Panama Canal
G. del Darién
Sierra Parima
Mt. Roraima 2810
Orinoco
Meta
GUYANA
Georgetown
SURINAME
Paramaribo
FRENCH GUIANA
Cayenne
C. Orange
Demerara Abyssal Plain
Ceara Rise
Ceara Abyssal Plain

BRAZIL
Amazonas
Manaus
Negro
Japurá
Putumayo
Branco
Santarém
Belém
São Luís
Fortaleza
Natal
Recife
Maceió
Salvador
Atol das Rocas
Fernando de Noronha (Brazil)
C. de São Roque
Pernambuco Abyssal Plain
Brazil Basin
Ascension I. (U.K.) 859
5656
St. Helena (U.K.) 820
PERU
Lima
Trujillo
Purus
Madeira
Ucayali
Marañón
Tapajós
Xingu
Tocantins
Araguaia
São Francisco
Brasília
Goiânia
La Paz
BOLIVIA
Nevado Ancohuma 6550
L. Titicaca
Arica
Iquique
Belo Horizonte
2890
Vitória Seamount
Martin Vaz
Trindade (Brazil)
Hotspur Seamount
Banco Abrolhos
Serra do Mar
São Tomé
C. Frio
Rio de Janeiro
Santos
São Paulo
Curitiba
Tropic of Capricorn
Angola
Luanda
ANGOLA
Lobito
Benguela
Namibe
Angola Basin
Angola Abyssal Plain
NAMIBIA
Walvis Bay
C. Fria
Pointe Noire
Walvis Ridge

PARAGUAY
Asunción
Gran Chaco
Pilcomayo
Paraná
Salado
San Miguel de Tucumán
Ojos del Salado 6893
ARGENTINA
Córdoba
Rosario
Santa Fe
URUGUAY
Montevideo
Buenos Aires
Rio de la Plata
Pôrto Alegre
L. dos Patos
Bahía Blanca
Colorado
Pampas
CHILE
Aconcagua 6962
Valparaíso
Santiago
Concepción
Arch. de Juan Fernández (Chile)
San Ambrosio (Chile)
Antofagasta 8062
Peru-Chile Trench
Nasca Ridge
Chile Basin
PACIFIC OCEAN
Puerto Montt
I. de Chiloé
Arch. de los Chonos
Pen. de Taitao
Chile Rise
Patagonia
G. San Matías
Pen. Valdés
G. San Jorge
Chubut
Est. de Magallanes (Magellan Str.) 705
Tierra del Fuego
C. de Hornos
Punta Arenas
I. Santa Inés
Rio Grande Rise
638
SOUTH AFRICA
Cape Town
C. of Good Hope
Cape Basin
Port Nolloth
Lüderitz (Namibus)
Nambia Abyssal Plain
411
Discovery Seamount
887
5457
Agulhas Ridge
Tristan da Cunha (U.K.) 2062
Inaccessible I. (U.K.)
Gough I. (U.K.) 910
Argentine Basin
Argentine Abyssal Plain
5704
Falkland Is. (U.K.)
Stanley
Falkland Plateau
Falkland Ridge
Burdwood Bank
Shag Rocks
Georgia Basin
South Georgia (U.K.)
Grytviken
Mt. Paget 2937
South Sandwich Trench 8325
Bouvetøya (Nor.)

ATLANTIC OCEAN

ft / m scale
12000 / 4000
9000 / 3000
6000 / 2000
3000 / 1000
1500 / 500
600 / 200
0 / 0
600 / 200
3000 / 1000
6000 / 2000
12000 / 4000
18000 / 6000
24000 / 8000

West from Greenwich

Projection: Mollweide

COPYRIGHT PHILIP'S

1:11 100 000

100   0   100   200   300   400   500 km
100   0   50   100   150   200   250   300   350 miles

54

ARCTIC OCEAN

3548

Nansen Basin

McKinley Sea

Kvitøya
4270

Nordaust-landet
Kong Karls Land

Cape Columbia

Lincoln Sea

Kap Morris Jesup
Oodaaq
1920   Frederik E. Hyde Fjord
Nansen Land   Peary Land
Jørgen Brønlund Fjord
Independence Fjord
Station Nord
Nordostrundingen

Nordkapp
Ny-Ålesund   Prins Nortontoppen
1717
Karls   Longleardbyen   Storfjorden
Forland
Barentsburg   Sjuøyane
Svalbard   Edgeøya
(Spitsbergen)   3431
(Norway)
Serkapp

CANADA

Axel Heiberg I.
Nansen Sound
Eureka
Meighen I.
1626
Lake Hazen
QUTTINIRPAAQ NAT. PARK
2616
Alert
Robeson Chan.
Victoria Fjord

Ellesmere Island
2437
Hans I. Chan.
Nyeboe Land
Wulff Land
Warming Land
Hall Land
Petermann Gletscher
Washington Land

Kronprins Frederik Land
Hellprin Land
Academy Gletscher
Danmark Fjord
Mylius Erichsen Land
Kronprins Christian Land
Ingolf Fjord
Mallemukfjeld

GREENLAND SEA

Kennedy Chan.
Kane Basin
Smith Sound
Nares Strait
Humboldt Gletscher
Sermersuaq

Coburg I.
Ellef Fiord
Grise Fiord
Jones Sd.
Kap Atholl
Inglefield Land
Qeqertarsuaq (Thule)
Siorapaluk
Knud Rasmussen Land

Hovgaard Ø
Nioghalvfjerdsfjorden
Norske Øer
Jøkel-bugten
Franske Øer
Île de France
Germania Land
Danmarkshavn
Store Koldewey

Baffin Bay

Devon Island
Uummannaq (Dundas) (Thule Air Base)
Kap York
Lauge Koch Kyst
Melville Bugt

Steenstrup Gletscher

2170

Dronning Margrethe II Land
Shannon Ø
Hochstetter Forland

GRØNLANDS NATIONALPARK

Ole Romer Land
Danborg
Zackenberg
Wollaston Forland
Clavering Ø

QAASUITSUP

Nuussuaq (Kraulshavn)
Upernavik
Kangersuatsiaq
Upernavik Kujalleq

2935

Baffin I.

Clyde River (Kangiqtugaapik)
2469

Nunavik
Illorsuit

Andrée Land
Walterhausen Gletscher
2940
Petermann Bjerg
Ymer Ø
Kejserr Franz Joseph Fd.
Geographical Society Ø
Mestersvig
Traill Ø

Maarmorilik

3238

Kong Oscar Fjord
Stauning Alper
Uunartoq Qeqertoq (Warming I.)
Renland
Jameson Land
Ittoqqortoormiit (Scoresbysund)
Milne Land
Ittaqjimmiut
Scoresby Sund
Uunartoq
(Kangertittivaq)   Kangikajik
Kap Brewster

Beerenberg   Jan Mayen
2277   (Norway)
Olonkinbyen

GREENLAND (KALAALLIT NUNAAT)

Qeqertarsuaq (Disko)
Sullorsuaq
Ikerasak
Uummannaq
2082
Saqqaq
Kangerluk
Qeqertarsuaq (Godhavn)
Disko Bugt
Aasiaat (Egedesminde)
Ilulissat (Jakobshavn)
Qasigiannguit (Christianshåb)
Ikamiut
Kangaatsiaq

(Denmark)

SERMERSOOQ

C. Dyer
Nordre Strømfjord

Kong Frederik IX's Land

Sisimiut (Holsteinsborg)
Kangerlussuaq (Søndre Strømfjord)
Itilleq
Søndre Strømfjord
Kangaamiut

Gunnbjørn Fjeld
3693
Blosseville Kyst
Kap Dalton

Kangerdlugssuaq

Kap Gustav Holm

Icelandic Plateau

Mohns Ridge

Arctic Circle

QEQQATA

Maniitsoq (Sukkertoppen)

Mt. Forel
3380
Helheim Gletscher
Kuummiut
Ikkatteq
Kulusuk
Isortoq
Tasiilaq (Ammassalik)

Horn
Ísafjörður
Breidafjörður

Eyjafjörður
Húsavík   Neskaupstaður
Akureyri
Hínaflói   Blöndúós
Höfn
Vatnajökull
2119   Öræfajökull

Dronning

Nuuk (Godthåb)
Kapisillit
Kangerluarsoruseq (Færingehavn)
Qeqertarsuatsiaat (Fiskenæsset)

Ingrid Land

2850

Gyldenløve Fjord
Kap Møsting
Kap Moltke
Kap Skjold

Kong Frederik VI's Kyst

ICELAND

Faxaflói
Reykjavík
Vestmannaeyjar
Heimaey
Surtsey

Paamiut (Frederikshåb)
Narsalik
Kangilinnguit (Grønnedal)
Arsuk
Ivittuut   Narsaq
Qaqortoq (Julianehåb)
Narsarsuaq
Alluitsup Paa (Sydprøven)

KUJALLEQ

Timmiarmiut
Mogens Heinesen Fjord

ATLANTIC OCEAN

Labrador Sea

Davis Strait

Denmark Strait

Reykjanes Ridge

Nanortalik
Lindenow Fjord
2045
Nunap Isua (Kap Farvel)
Nalumasortoq
Prins Christian Sund

ft   m
3000   1000
1200   400
600   200
0
200   600
500   1500
1000   3000
2000   6000
3000   9000
4000   12000
m   ft

1:17 800 000

100 0 100 200 300 400 500 600 700 800 km
100 0 100 200 300 400 500 miles

COPYRIGHT PHILIP'S

West Siberian Lowlands

Ob
Pelym
Belaya
Sosva
Kama Res.
Kama

Obshchi Syrt
Kirgiziya Steppe
Ural
Caspian Depression
Caspian Sea
Agrakhan Pen.

Ural Mountains

Timan Ridge
Vychegda Lowlands
Northern Urals
Kama
Sura
Vyatka
Vetluga
Kuybyshev Res.
Volga
Volgograd Res.
Volga Hts.

Pechora
N. Dvina
Mezen
Sukhona
Oka
Volga
Don
Khoper
Medveditsa

Barents Sea
Kanin Pen.
Cheshka Bay
Kola Pen.
White Sea
Dvina B.
Onega Bay

Caucasus
Transcaucasia
Elbruz 5642
Kazbek
Terek
Kuma
Kuban
Pontine Mts.
Kurdistan
Anatolia (Asia Minor)
Taurus Mts.
Mesopotamia
Tigris
Euphrates
L. Van
L. Urmia
Ararat 5165

Central Russian Uplands
Donets Basin
Donets
Don
Sea of Azov
Crimea
Str. of Kerch
Ukraine
Dnieper
Desna
Kremenchuk Res.
Kakhovka Res.
Tsimlyansk Res.
Manych

Black Sea
C. Ince

Lapland
L. Inari
Tana
L. Oulu
North Cape
Nordkinn

Onega
L. Onega
L. Ladoga
L. Ilmen
Valdai Hills
Rybinsk Res.
L. Chudskoye
Prut
Siret
Dniester
Dnieper
Kiev Res.
Pripet
E. Bug
W. Bug
W. Dvina
Niemen
Desna

Finland
G. of Finland
L. Saimaa
G. of Bothnia
Åland
Gulf of Riga
Baltic Sea
Gotland
Öland
Bornholm
Gulf of Gdansk

European Plain
North European Plain
Vistula
Warta
Oder
Elbe
Odra

Carpathians
Tatra 2655
Plain of Hungary
Balaton
Tisza
Maros
Danube
Transylvanian Alps 2543
Moldavia
Wallachia
Dinaric Alps
Balkans
Rhodope 2925
Pindus
Olympus 2917
Northern Sporades
Euboea
Aegean Sea
Cyclades
Dodecanese
Rhodes
Crete
Sea of Crete
C. Matapan
Peloponnese
Ionian Is.
Ionian Sea
Str. of Otranto

Scandinavia
Norwegian Sea
Vesterålen
Lofoten
Kebnekaise 2117
Glittertind 2472
Galdhøpiggen 2469
Sognefjorden
Hardangervidda
Jotunheim
Trondheimsfjorden
Dovrefjell
Dalälven
Klar
Vänern
Vättern
Glåma
Gothenburg

Skagerrak
Kattegat
Jutland
Zealand
Fyn
Lolland

Atlantic Ocean
Iceland
Hvannadalshnúkur
Vatnajökull
Reykjavik
Faxaflói
Breiðafjörður
Arctic Circle
Faroe Is.
Shetland Is.
Orkney
Fair Isle
Hebrides
Outer Hebrides
Great Britain
British Isles
Grampian Mts.
Ben Nevis 1343
Pennines
Snowdon 1085
Ireland
Lough Neagh
Irish Sea
Rockall
Lands End
English Channel
Channel Is.
Brittany
Celtic Sea
Bay of Biscay
North Sea
German Bight
Heligoland
Rhine
Weser
Ijsselmeer
Dogger

Shannon
Cabbage

North Sea weather forecast areas:
VIKING, FORTIES, CROMARTY, FORTH, TYNE, DOGGER, FISHER, GERMAN BIGHT, HUMBER, THAMES, DOVER, WIGHT, PORTLAND, PLYMOUTH, BISCAY, FINISTERRE, SOLE, LUNDY, FASTNET, IRISH SEA, SHANNON, ROCKALL, MALIN, HEBRIDES, BAILEY, FAIR ISLE, FAEROES, SOUTH EAST ICELAND, FITZROY

Rhine
Seine
Loire
Garonne
Massif Central
Puy de Sancy 1886
Cévennes
Dordogne
Rhône
Saône
Gironde
Pyrenees
Cantabrian Mts.
Picos de Europa
Iberian Peninsula
Ebro
Duero
Old Castile
New Castile
Sierra Morena
Andalusia
Sierra Nevada 3478
Guadalquivir
Guadiana
Tagus
Serra da Estrela
C. Finisterre
C. da Roca
C. St. Vincent
C. Trafalgar
Str. of Gibraltar

Alps
Mont Blanc 4807
Monte Rosa 4634
Matterhorn 4478
Gran Paradiso 4061
Jungfrau 4158
Grossglockner 3797
L. Constance
L. Geneva
L. Como
L. Garda
L. Maggiore
Po
Gulf of Venice
Adriatic Sea
Apennines
Gran Sasso d'Italia 2914
Tiber
Ligurian Sea
Corsica 2710
Sardinia
Elba
Tyrrhenian Sea
Str. of Bonifacio
Sicily
Etna 3323
Str. of Messina
Vesuvius 1277
Calabria
Malta
Pantelleria
C. Bon
Balearic Is.
Minorca
Majorca
Ibiza

Harz 1142
Erzgebirge
Bohemian Forest
Sudeten
Moravian Hts.
Bohemia
Black Forest
Vosges
Jura
Inn
Danube
Drave
Sava
Morava

Mediterranean Sea
Africa
Plateau of the Shotts
Er Rif

Ore Mts.
Thuringia

m / ft elevation scale:
5000, 4000, 3000, 2000, 1000, 400, 200, 0
15 000, 12 000, 9000, 6000, 3000, 1200, 600, 0
200–600, 2000, 4000, 6000
600–200, 6000, 12 000

West from Greenwich   East from Greenwich

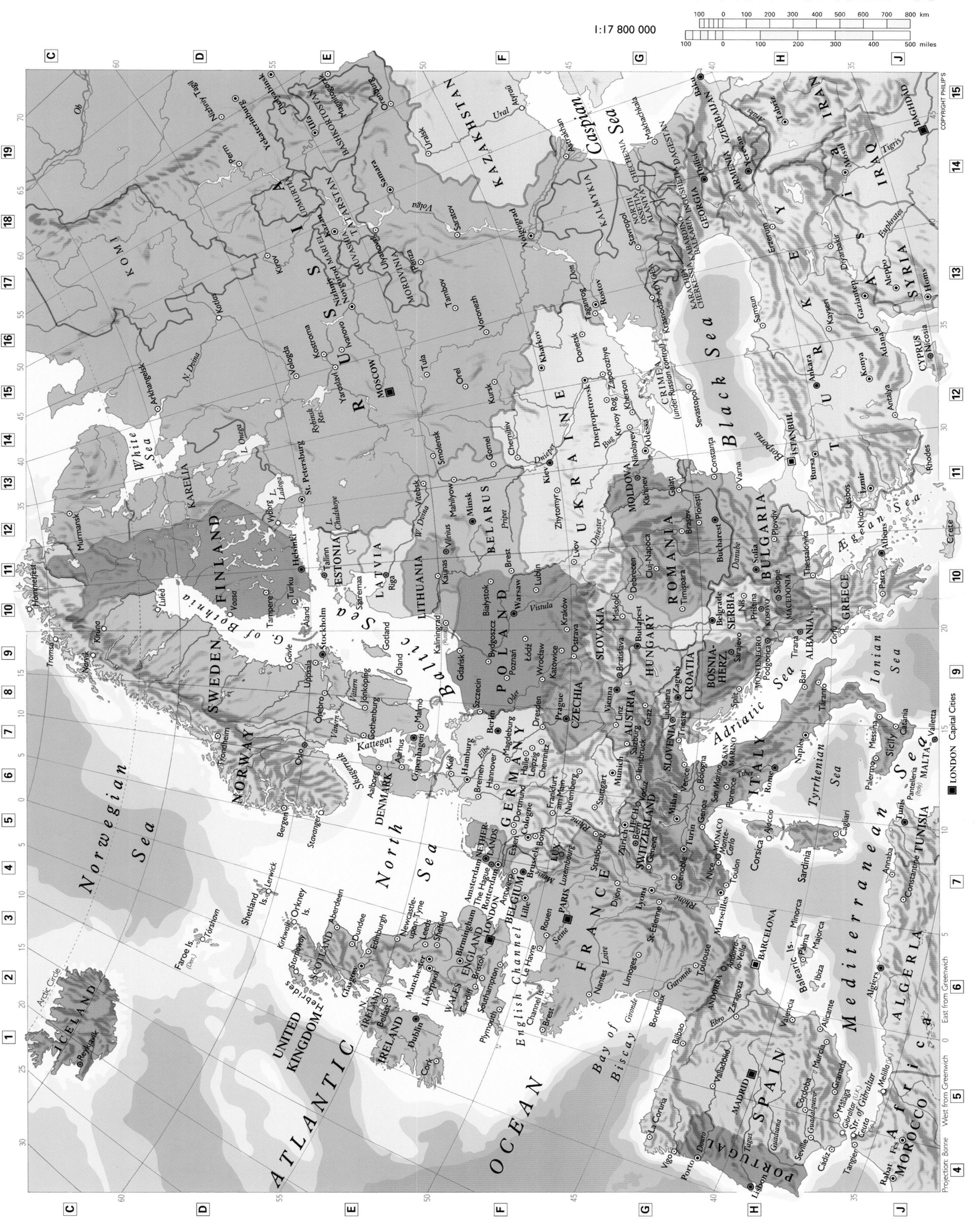

1:17 800 000

COPYRIGHT PHILIP'S

■ LONDON Capital Cities

Projection: Bonne   West from Greenwich   East from Greenwich

1:5 300 000

50 0 25 50 75 100 125 150 175 km
50 0 25 50 75 100 125 miles

106

Grid references: A B C D E F across top and bottom; 2–26 along sides

BARENTS SEA

R U S S I A

KARELIA

F I N L A N D

Lapland

S W E D E N

N O R W A Y

ATLANTIC OCEAN

Gulf of Bothnia

Major places (selection):

Murmansk · Kola · Pechenga · Nikel · Kirkenes · Vadsø · Vardø · Varanger halvøya · Nordkapp · Honningsvåg · Hammerfest · Alta · Tromsø · Narvik · Harstad · Bodø · Mo i Rana · Mosjøen · Namsos · Trondheim · Steinkjer · Levanger · Ålesund · Molde · Kristiansund · Bergen · Florø · Måløy

Kolari · Kittilä · Sodankylä · Ivalo · Inari · Kautokeino · Karasjok · Enontekiö · Muonio · Rovaniemi · Kemijärvi · Salla · Kuusamo · Tornio · Kemi · Oulu · Raahe · Kajaani · Kuhmo · Nurmes · Kuopio · Iisalmi · Joensuu · Lieksa · Jyväskylä · Tampere · Vaasa (Vasa) · Kokkola · Pietarsaari (Jakobstad) · Pori · Rauma · Lahti · Mikkeli · Savonlinna · Kouvola · Lappeenranta · Imatra · Vyborg

Kiruna · Gällivare · Jokkmokk · Boden · Luleå · Piteå · Skellefteå · Umeå · Örnsköldsvik · Härnösand · Sundsvall · Hudiksvall · Söderhamn · Bollnäs · Östersund · Storuman · Sorsele · Arvidsjaur · Lycksele · Vilhelmina · Strömsund · Sveg · Mora · Ljusdal

ICELAND on same scale

Reykjavík · Akureyri · Keflavík · Höfn · Vík · Vatnajökull · Hofsjökull · Langjökull · Mýrdalsjökull · Ísafjörður · Selfoss · Borgarnes · Egilsstaðir · Húsavík · Faxaflói · Breiðafjörður · Arctic Circle · West from Greenwich

FAEROE ISLANDS on same scale

Tórshavn · Streymoy · Eysturoy · Vágar · Sandoy · Suðuroy · Nordoyar · Føroyar (Faeroe Is.) (Den.)

ATLANTIC OCEAN

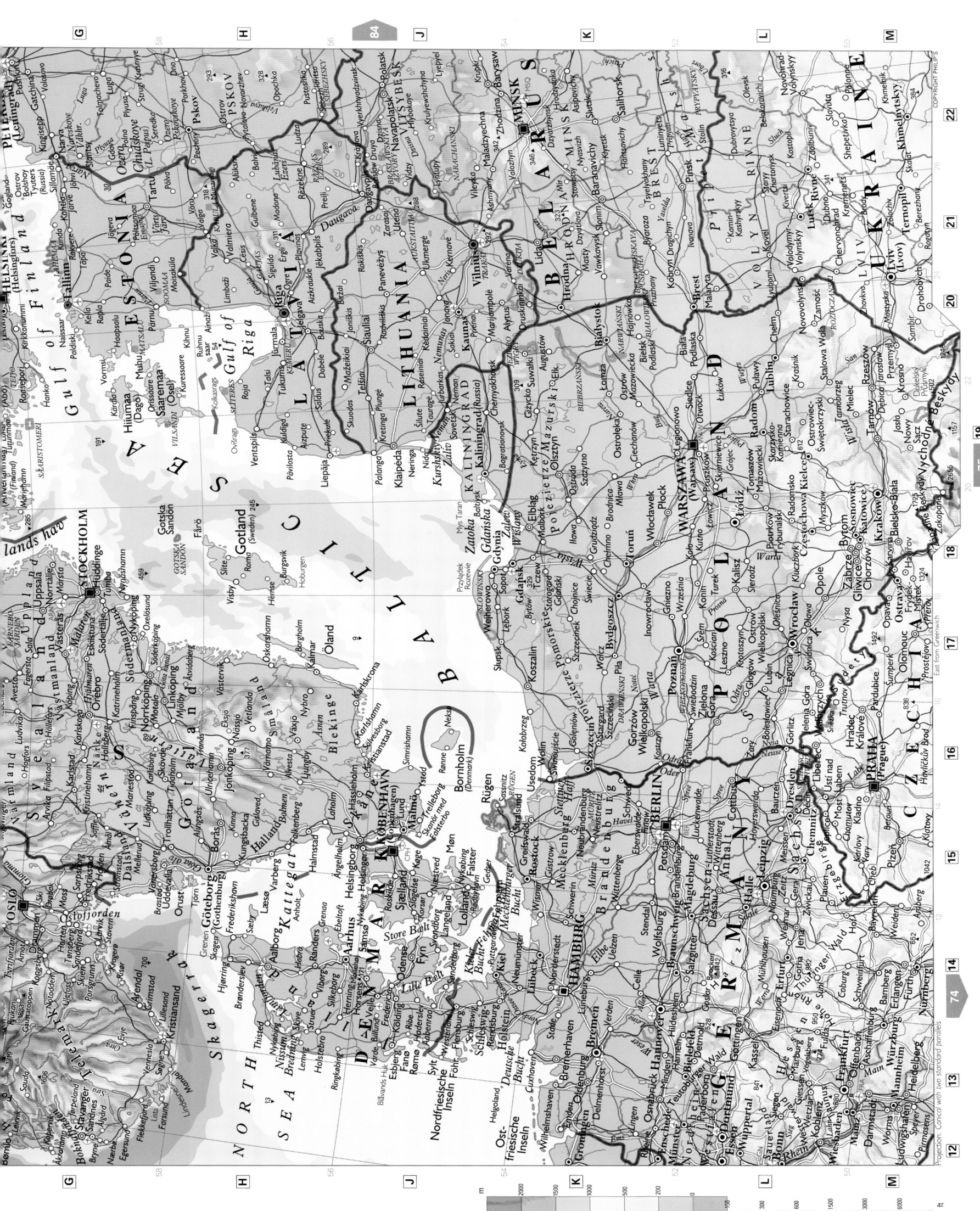

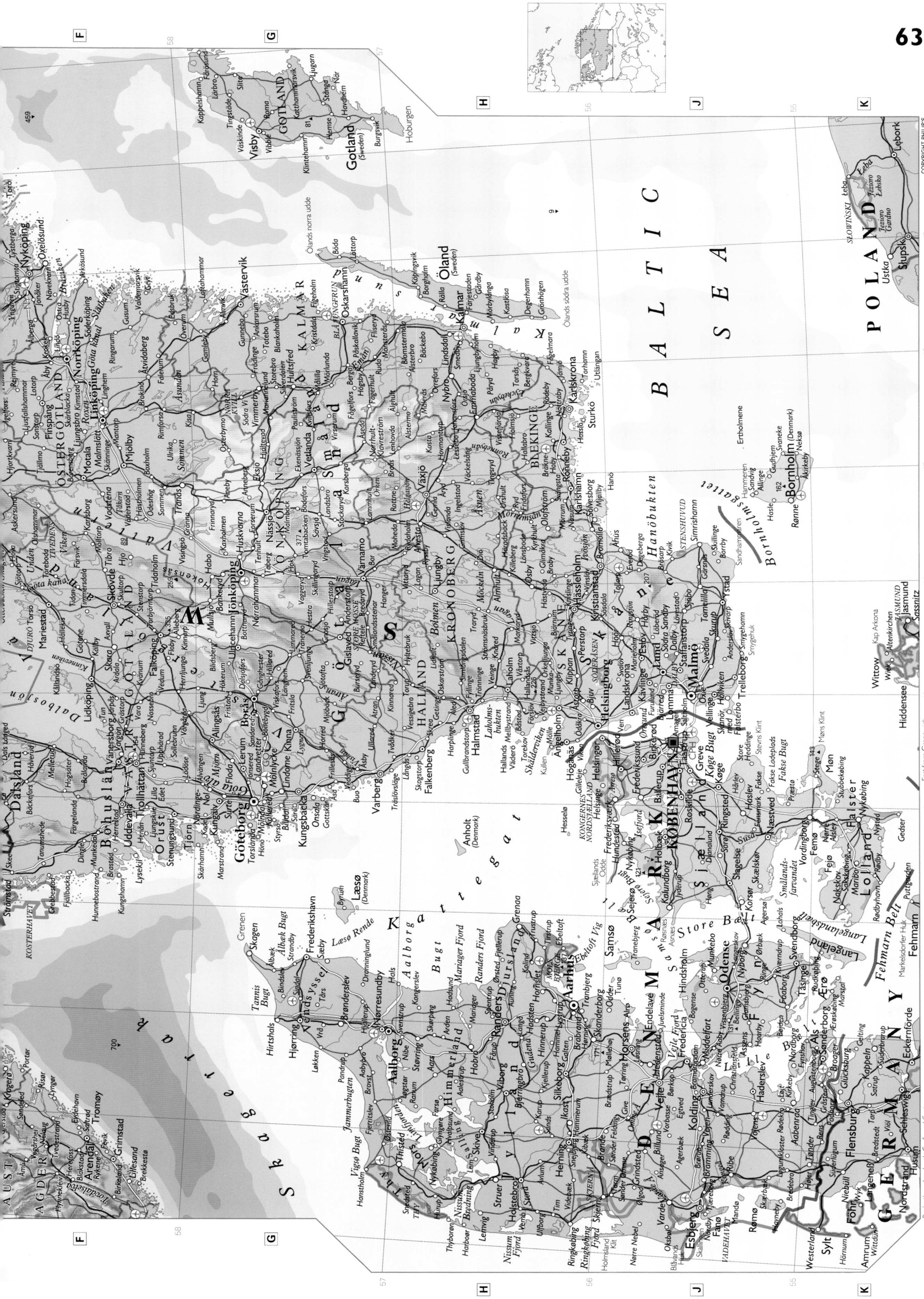

POLAND

BALTIC SEA

GOTLAND (Sweden)

Gotland (Sweden)

ÖLAND

Öland (Sweden)

KALMAR

SMÅLAND

ÖSTERGÖTLAND

JÖNKÖPING

KRONOBERG

BLEKINGE

HALLAND

VÄSTRA GÖTALAND

BOHUSLÄN

Dalsland

SKÅNE

Bornholm (Denmark)

Hanöbukten

Bornholmsgattet

AUST-AGDER

Skagerrak

Kattegat

Aalborg Bugt

Jylland

Vendsyssel

Himmerland

Djursland

Thy

SJÆLLAND

KØBENHAVN

NORDSJÆLLAND

FYN

Langeland

Lolland

Falster

Møn

DENMARK

GERMANY

Store Bælt

Fehmarn Belt

Fehmarn

Læsø (Denmark)

Anholt (Denmark)

Nyköping
Norrköping
Linköping
Motala
Mjölby
Visby
Kalmar
Karlskrona
Växjö
Halmstad
Varberg
Falkenberg
Borås
Göteborg
Trollhättan
Vänersborg
Uddevalla
Helsingborg
Landskrona
Malmö
Trelleborg
Ystad
Kristianstad
Hässleholm
Ronneby
Rønne
 Stupsk
Ustka
Lębork
Łeba

Aalborg
Hjørring
Frederikshavn
Skagen
Randers
Århus
Viborg
Holstebro
Herning
Silkeborg
Horsens
Vejle
Fredericia
Kolding
Esbjerg
Varde
Ribe
Odense
Svendborg
Nyborg
Slagelse
Næstved
Roskilde
Helsingør
Hillerød
Holbæk
Kalundborg
Korsør
Nykøbing
Sønderborg
Åbenrå
Haderslev
Flensburg
Husum
Nordstrand
Eckernförde
Schleswig

Copyright Philip's

Projection: Lambert's Conformal Conic

East from Greenwich

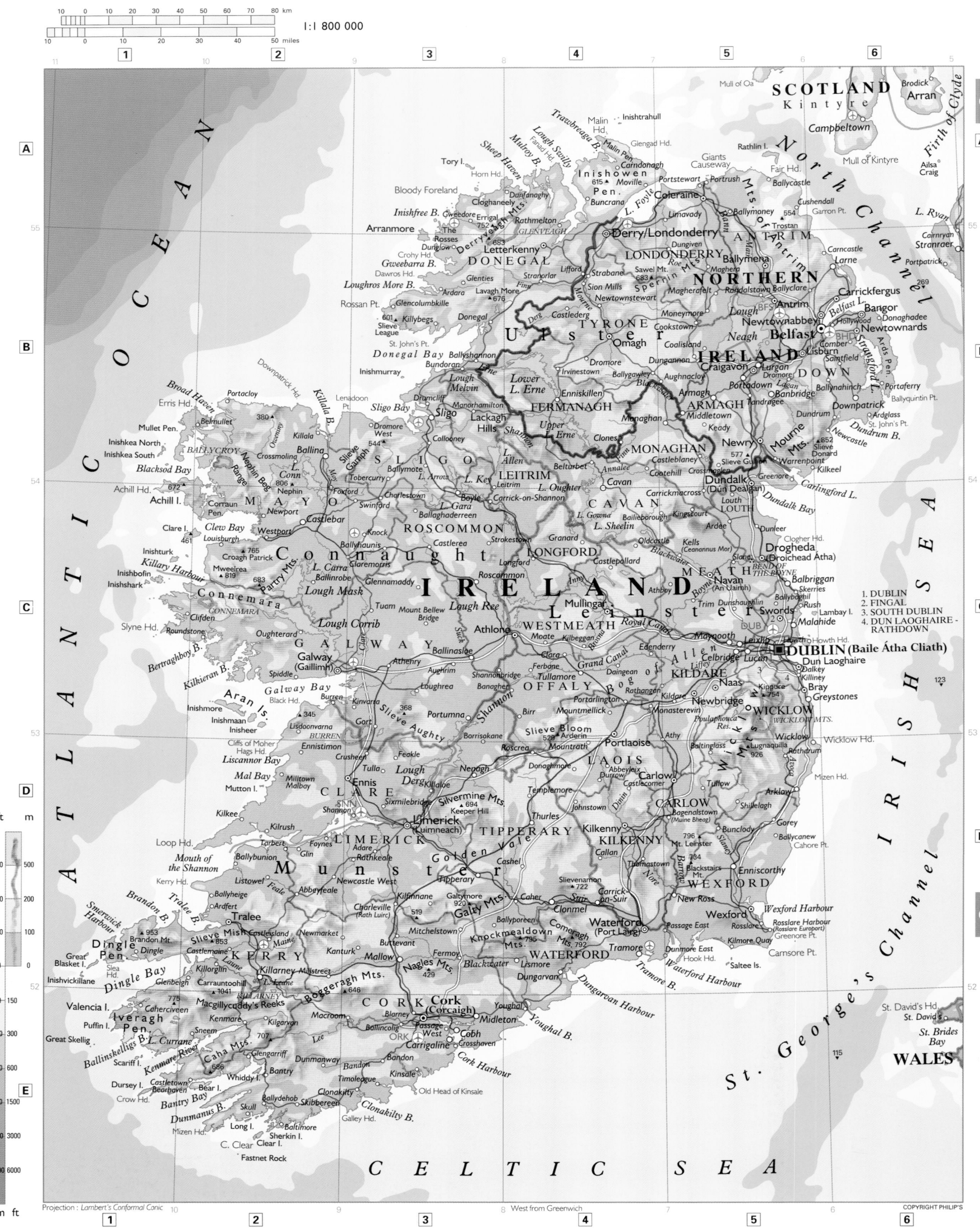

1 : 1 800 000

1. DUBLIN
2. FINGAL
3. SOUTH DUBLIN
4. DUN LAOGHAIRE - RATHDOWN

Projection : Lambert's Conformal Conic

West from Greenwich

COPYRIGHT PHILIP'S

1:1 800 000

10   0   10   20   30   40   50   60   70   80 km
10   0   10   20   30   40   50 miles

Key to Scottish unitary authorities on map

1 ABERDEEN CITY
2 DUNDEE CITY
3 WEST DUNBARTONSHIRE
4 EAST DUNBARTONSHIRE
5 GLASGOW CITY
6 INVERCLYDE
7 RENFREWSHIRE
8 EAST RENFREWSHIRE
9 NORTH LANARKSHIRE
10 FALKIRK
11 CLACKMANNANSHIRE
12 WEST LOTHIAN
13 CITY OF EDINBURGH
14 MIDLOTHIAN

ORKNEY IS. on same scale

ORKNEY
North Ronaldsay
Papa Westray
Westray
Rousay
Eday
Sanday
Shapinsay
Stronsay
Brough Hd.
Mainland
Stromness
Kirkwall
St. Mary's
Burray
Hoy
Scapa Flow
South Ronaldsay
Burwick
Dunnet Hd. Stroma
Duncansby Head
John o' Groats
Pentland Firth
Thurso
Sinclair's Bay

SHETLAND IS. on same scale

Muckle Flugga
Unst
Haroldswick
Yell
Fetlar
Esha Ness
Yell Sound
Ulsta
Out Skerries
Sullom Voe
Whalsay
St. Magnus Bay
Papa Stour
Voe
Bressay
Walls
Scalloway
Lerwick
Foula
West Burra
Boddam
Sumburgh Hd.

Projection: Lambert's Conformal Conic

COPYRIGHT PHILIP'S

ATLANTIC OCEAN

NORTH SEA

SCOTLAND

NORTHERN IRELAND

ENGLAND

Belfast
Newcastle-upon-Tyne

Stornoway
Lewis
EILEAN SIAR (WESTERN ISLES)
Harris
OUTER HEBRIDES
North Uist
Benbecula
South Uist
Barra
Skye
Cuillin Hills
INNER HEBRIDES
Mull
Tiree
Coll
Islay
Jura
Colonsay
Oronsay
Arran
Kintyre
Campbeltown

C. Wrath
Durness
Tongue
Thurso
Wick
Caithness
Sutherland
NORTH WEST HIGHLANDS
Ben Hope
Ben More Assynt
Ullapool
Lairg
Helmsdale
Brora
Golspie
Dornoch
Tain
Dingwall
Inverness
Moray Firth
Lossiemouth
Elgin
Forres
Nairn
Buckie
Banff
Macduff
Fraserburgh
Peterhead
Buchan
Huntly
ABERDEENSHIRE
Inverurie
Aberdeen
Fort William
Ben Nevis
Glen Coe
Rannoch Moor
Grampian Mountains
CAIRNGORMS
Ballater
Braemar
Stonehaven
ANGUS
Brechin
Montrose
Forfar
Arbroath
PERTH AND KINROSS
Pitlochry
Aberfeldy
Perth
Dundee
FIFE
St. Andrews
Crieff
Callander
STIRLING
Stirling
Alloa
Dunfermline
Firth of Forth
ARGYLL AND BUTE
Oban
LOCH LOMOND TROSSACHS
Loch Lomond
Helensburgh
Dumbarton
Greenock
Paisley
GLASGOW
East Kilbride
Hamilton
Motherwell
Coatbridge
Airdrie
Cumbernauld
Falkirk
EDINBURGH
Livingston
Musselburgh
Dunbar
EAST LOTHIAN
Ayr
Prestwick
Troon
Kilmarnock
NORTH AYRSHIRE
EAST AYRSHIRE
SOUTH AYRSHIRE
Girvan
Stranraer
SOUTH LANARKSHIRE
Lanark
Biggar
Peebles
SCOTTISH BORDERS
Galashiels
Selkirk
Hawick
Jedburgh
Cheviot Hills
Berwick-upon-Tweed
DUMFRIES & GALLOWAY
Dumfries
Lockerbie
Annan
Solway Firth
Gretna
Carlisle
CUMBRIA
Penrith
NORTHUMBERLAND
Morpeth
DURHAM

West from Greenwich

ft   m
3000 1000
1500   600
600   200
300   100
0   0
50   150
100   300
200   600
500 1500
1000 3000
m   ft

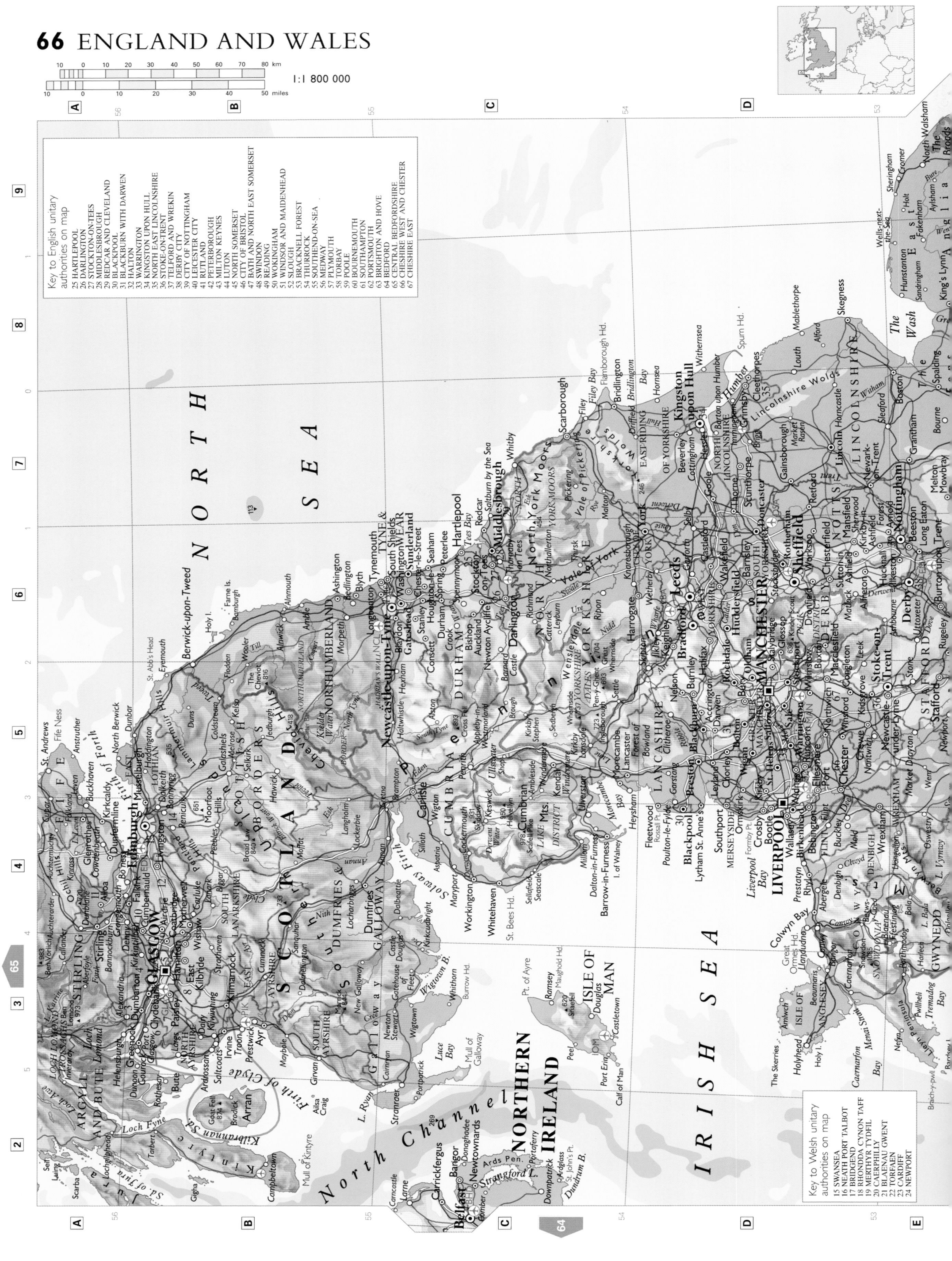

10 0   10 20 30 40 50 60 70 80 km
10 0   10   20   30   40   50 miles

1:1 800 000

65
64

Key to English unitary
authorities on map

25 HARTLEPOOL
26 DARLINGTON
27 STOCKTON-ON-TEES
28 MIDDLESBROUGH
29 REDCAR AND CLEVELAND
30 BLACKPOOL
31 BLACKBURN WITH DARWEN
32 HALTON
33 WARRINGTON
34 KINGSTON UPON HULL
35 NORTH EAST LINCOLNSHIRE
36 STOKE-ON-TRENT
37 TELFORD AND WREKIN
38 DERBY CITY
39 CITY OF NOTTINGHAM
40 LEICESTER CITY
41 RUTLAND
42 PETERBOROUGH
43 MILTON KEYNES
44 LUTON
45 NORTH SOMERSET
46 CITY OF BRISTOL
47 BATH AND NORTH EAST SOMERSET
48 SWINDON
49 READING
50 WOKINGHAM
51 WINDSOR AND MAIDENHEAD
52 SLOUGH
53 BRACKNELL FOREST
54 THURROCK
55 SOUTHEND-ON-SEA
56 MEDWAY
57 PLYMOUTH
58 TORBAY
59 POOLE
60 BOURNEMOUTH
61 SOUTHAMPTON
62 PORTSMOUTH
63 BRIGHTON AND HOVE
64 BEDFORD
65 CENTRAL BEDFORDSHIRE
66 CHESHIRE WEST AND CHESTER
67 CHESHIRE EAST

Key to Welsh unitary
authorities on map

15 SWANSEA
16 NEATH PORT TALBOT
17 BRIDGEND
18 RHONDDA CYNON TAFF
19 MERTHYR TYDFIL
20 CAERPHILLY
21 BLAENAU GWENT
22 TORFAEN
23 CARDIFF
24 NEWPORT

NORTH

SEA

IRISH

SEA

North Channel

NORTHERN
IRELAND

ISLE OF
MAN

SCOTLAND

NORTHUMBERLAND

CUMBRIA

DURHAM

NORTH YORKSHIRE

LANCASHIRE

Newcastle-upon-Tyne
Sunderland
Middlesbrough
Hartlepool
Darlington
Scarborough
Whitby
York
Leeds
Bradford
Harrogate
MANCHESTER
Liverpool
Chester
Sheffield
Derby
Nottingham
Stoke-on-Trent
Lincoln
Kingston upon Hull

Edinburgh
GLASGOW
Carlisle
Berwick-upon-Tweed
St. Andrews

The Wash

LINCOLNSHIRE

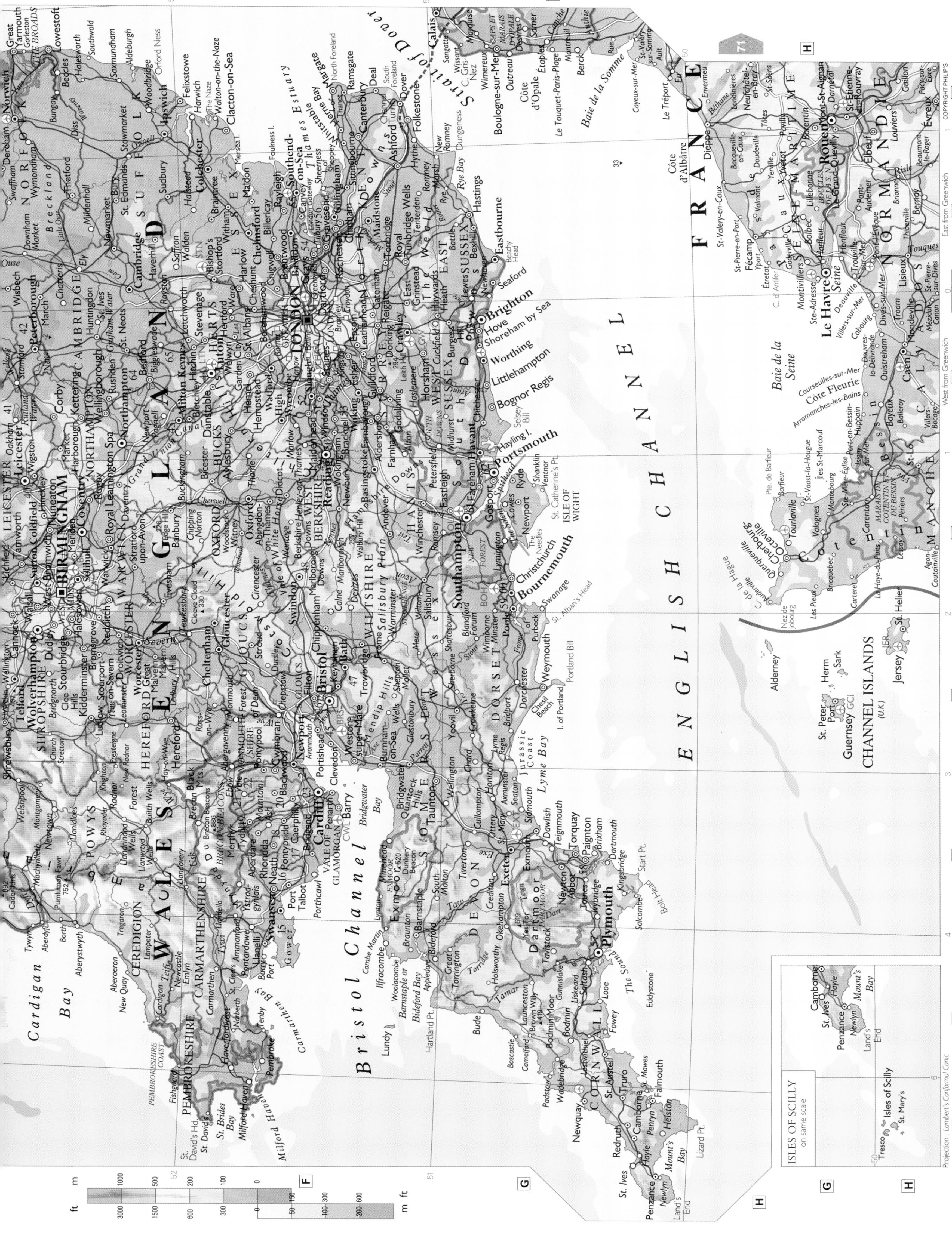

FRANCE

NORMANDIE

ENGLISH CHANNEL

Bristol Channel

Cardigan Bay

WALES

ENGLAND

LONDON

BIRMINGHAM

Isle of Wight

CHANNEL ISLANDS (U.K.)

ISLES OF SCILLY
on same scale

Isles of Scilly
St. Mary's
Tresco

Projection: Lambert's Conformal Conic

COPYRIGHT PHILIP'S

East from Greenwich

West from Greenwich

50 0 25 50 75 100 125 150 175 km
50 0 25 50 75 100 125 miles

1:4 400 000

ATLANTIC OCEAN

NORWAY
Bergen
Osøyro
Stord
Bømlo
Leirvik
Haugesund
Kopervik
Åkrahamn
Boknafjorden
Stavanger
Sandnes
Bryne
Nærbø
Askøyna

NORTH SEA

Shetland Is. (U.K.)
Yell
Unst
Fetlar
Mainland
Lerwick
Foula
Fair Isle

Orkney Is.
Westray
Sanday
Stronsay
North Rona
Mainland
Kirkwall
Hoy
South Ronaldsay
Pentland Firth

C. Wrath
Thurso
Wick
Helmsdale

Flannan Is.
Stornoway
Lewis
Harris
North Minch
Ullapool
Lairg
Golspie
Tain
Invergordon
Dingwall
Moray Firth
Buckie
Banff
Fraserburgh
Peterhead

St. Kilda (U.K.)
North Uist
Benbecula
South Uist
Barra

Outer Hebrides
Sea of the Hebrides
Inner Hebrides

Skye
Portree
Nairn
Inverness
Elgin
Huntly
Inverurie
Glen Mor
Aviemore
CAIRNGORMS
Don
Aberdeen

North West Highlands
Rum
Eigg
Malaig
Fort William
Ben Nevis
Glen Mor
L. Ness
SCOTLAND
Grampian Mts.
Dee
Ballater
Stonehaven

Coll
Tiree
Tobermory
Mull
Iona
Oban
L. Awe
L. Lomond
L. LOMOND & TROSSACHS
Perth
Dundee
St. Andrews
Forfar
Arbroath
Montrose

Colonsay
Jura
Islay
Dumbarton
Greenock
Stirling
Dunfermline
Glenrothes
Kirkcaldy
Dunbar

GLASGOW
Paisley
East Kilbride
Cumbernauld
Hamilton
EDINBURGH
Berwick-upon-Tweed

Campbeltown
Arran
Irvine
Kilmarnock
Ayr
Southern Uplands
Galashiels
Hawick
Jedburgh
Cheviot Hills
Alnwick

Tory I.
Arranmore
Buncrana
Letterkenny
Coleraine
Ballymena
Larne
Malin Hd.
GLENVEAGH
Lifford
Donegal
Omagh
NORTHERN IRELAND
Lough Neagh
Antrim
Bangor
Belfast
Lisburn
Craigavon
Armagh
Newry

North Channel
Girvan
Dumfries
Kirkcudbright
Stranraer
Workington
Carlisle
Hexham
NORTHUMBERLAND
Newcastle-upon-Tyne
South Shields
Sunderland
Gateshead
Durham
Hartlepool
Redcar

Firth of Clyde

Ballina
Castlebar
Westport
Sligo
Enniskillen
Clones
Cavan
Dundalk
Drogheda
UNITED KINGDOM

Douglas
I. of Man
Whitehaven
Cumbrian Mts.
LAKE DISTRICT
Barrow-in-Furness
Lancaster
Darlington
Stockton-on-Tees
Middlesbrough
N. YORK MOORS
Scarborough

IRELAND
Achill I.
L. Corrib
Lough Mask
Connemara
Galway B.
Galway
Aran Is.
Roscommon
Longford
Lough Ree
Mullingar
Athlone
Kells
Boyne
Liffey
DUBLIN
Dun Laoghaire
Bray

IRISH SEA

Blackpool
Preston
Blackburn
Burnley
Keighley
Bolton
Halifax
Huddersfield
Harrogate
Leeds
Bradford
York
Kingston upon Hull
Beverley
Bridlington

Holyhead
Anglesey
Bangor
Colwyn Bay
Chester
Crewe
Stockport
MANCHESTER
LIVERPOOL
Warrington
Oldham
Sheffield
Rotherham
Doncaster
Scunthorpe
Grimsby
Humber
Lincoln
Louth
Skegness
Boston

Lough Derg
Ennis
Nenagh
Thurles
Limerick
Tipperary
Kilkenny
Carlow
Wicklow Mts.
Snowdon
SNOWDONIA
Wrexham
Chesterfield
Mansfield
Nottingham
Derby
Stoke-on-Trent
Cardigan Bay
Cambrian Mts.
Shrewsbury
Telford
Stafford
Leicester
Grantham
The Wash
King's Lynn
Cromer
THE BROADS

Kilrush
Listowel
Tralee
Dingle
Killarney
Mallow
Clonmel
Carrick-on-Suir
Waterford
Wexford
Rosslare
St. George's Channel
Fishguard
Haverfordwest
Milford Haven
Pembroke
PEMBROKESHIRE COAST

Macgillycuddy's Reeks
Valencia
C. Clear
Bantry
Kinsale
Cork
Bandon
Cóbh
Youghal
Dungarvan

Aberystwyth
WALES
Llanelli
Swansea
Neath
Port Talbot
Rhondda
Cardiff
Barry
Bristol Channel
Weston-super-Mare

ENGLAND
Wolverhampton
BIRMINGHAM
Redditch
Worcester
Coventry
Rugby
Nuneaton
Northampton
Corby
Peterborough
Ely
Bury St. Edmunds
Thetford
Norwich
Great Yarmouth
Lowestoft

Hereford
Gloucester
Cheltenham
Leamington Spa
Royal
Bedford
Cambridge
Ipswich
Harwich
Felixstowe
Colchester

Merthyr Tydfil
BRECON BEACONS
Brecon
Newport
Cwmbran
Cotswold Hills
Oxford
Milton Keynes
Stevenage
Hemel Hempstead
Luton
Harlow
Chelmsford
Basildon
Southend-on-Sea

EXMOOR
Barnstaple
Exmoor
Taunton
Bridgwater
High Wycombe
Slough
Reading
Newbury
Swindon
Bath
LONDON
Reigate
Chatham
Maidstone
Margate
Canterbury
Dover

Yeovil
Salisbury
Basingstoke
Guildford
Crawley
Ashford
Folkestone
Winchester
SOUTH DOWNS
Hastings

Bude
Bideford
Bournemouth
Poole
Southampton
Portsmouth
Fareham
Havant
Worthing
Brighton
Eastbourne

Newquay
Truro
Exeter
Exmouth
Torbay
Weymouth
Isle of Wight
Newport

DARTMOOR
Dartmoor
Plymouth
St. Austell
Falmouth
Penzance
Land's End
Isles of Scilly

CELTIC SEA

English Channel

NETHERLANDS
Texel
Den Helder
Alkmaar
Haarlem
's-Gravenhage (Den Haag)
Hoek van Holland
ROTTERDAM
Dordrecht
Zeeland
Vlissingen

Zeebrugge
Oostende
Brugge
Gent
Mechelen
Antwerpen
BELGIUM
BRUSSELS (Bruxelles)
Tournai

Dunkerque
Calais
Gris Nez
Boulogne-sur-Mer
Le Touquet-Paris-Plage
St-Omer
Béthune
Bruay-la-Buissiere
Bruay-la-Lens
LILLE
Tourcoing
Roubaix
Villeneuve-d'Ascq
Valenciennes
Cambrai

Abbeville
Le Tréport
Dieppe
Fécamp
Le Havre
Pays de Caux
Amiens
St. Quentin
Laon
Picardie
FRANCE
Rouen
Seine
Elbeuf
Bolbec

Str. of Dover
Alderney
C. de la Hague
Pte. de Barfleur
Cherbourg-Octeville
Valognes
Guernsey
St. Peter Port
Sark
Cotentin
Bayeux
Caen
Lisieux
Trouville-sur-Mer
Channel Is. (U.K.)
Jersey
St. Helier

Projection: Conical with two standard parallels

East from Greenwich
West from Greenwich
COPYRIGHT PHILIP'S

61
74

1:2 200 000

NORTH SEA

UNITED KINGDOM

NETHERLANDS

BELGIUM

FRANCE

GERMANY

LUXEMBOURG

Major places (selected):

AMSTERDAM, 's-Gravenhage (Den Haag), ROTTERDAM, Utrecht, Haarlem, Leiden, Delft, Dordrecht, Breda, Tilburg, Eindhoven, 's-Hertogenbosch (Den Bosch), Nijmegen, Arnhem, Apeldoorn, Deventer, Zwolle, Enschede, Hengelo, Almelo, Groningen, Leeuwarden, Assen, Emmen, Hoogeveen, Meppel, Den Helder, Alkmaar, Hilversum, Amersfoort, Gouda, Zoetermeer, Almere, Lelystad, Hoorn, Enkhuizen, Zaanstad

Texel, Vlieland, Terschelling, Ameland, Schiermonnikoog, Waddeneilanden, Waddenzee

Brugge, Gent (Gand), Antwerpen, BRUSSEL (Bruxelles), Leuven, Mechelen, Oostende, Roeselare, Kortrijk, Hasselt, Maastricht, Liège, Namur, Charleroi, Mons, La Louvière, Tournai, Verviers, Aachen, Genk, Roermond, Venlo

LILLE, Dunkerque, Calais, Boulogne-sur-Mer, Arras, Lens, Douai, Valenciennes, Cambrai, Amiens, St-Quentin, Beauvais, Compiègne, Reims, Charleville-Mézières, Sedan, PARIS, Versailles, Meaux, Châlons-en-Champagne, Nancy, Metz, Thionville, Verdun

LUXEMBOURG, Esch-sur-Alzette, Differdange, Ettelbruck, Diekirch, Arlon

Düsseldorf, Köln, Bonn, Essen, Dortmund, Bochum, Duisburg, Oberhausen, Mülheim, Krefeld, Mönchengladbach, Wuppertal, Gelsenkirchen, Recklinghausen, Münster, Osnabrück, Bremerhaven, Oldenburg, Emden, Wilhelmshaven, Koblenz, Wiesbaden, Mainz, Saarbrücken, Trier, Kaiserslautern, Strasbourg

Ostfriesische Inseln, Helgoland, Norderney, Borkum

NORD-PAS-DE-CALAIS, PICARDIE, HAUTS-DE-FRANCE, ARDENNES, GRAND EST, SEINE-ET-MARNE, NORDRHEIN-WESTFALEN, RHEINLAND-PFALZ, SAARLAND, NIEDERSÄCHSISCHES WATTENMEER

FRIESLAND, GRONINGEN, DRENTHE, OVERIJSSEL, FLEVOLAND, NOORD-HOLLAND, ZUID-HOLLAND, ZEELAND, NOORD-BRABANT, LIMBURG, GELDERLAND, UTRECHT

VLAANDEREN, OOST-VLAANDEREN, WEST-VLAANDEREN, BRABANT, HAINAUT, NAMUR

THE BROADS

High-speed rail routes

Underlined towns give their name to the administrative area in which they stand.

COPYRIGHT PHILIP'S

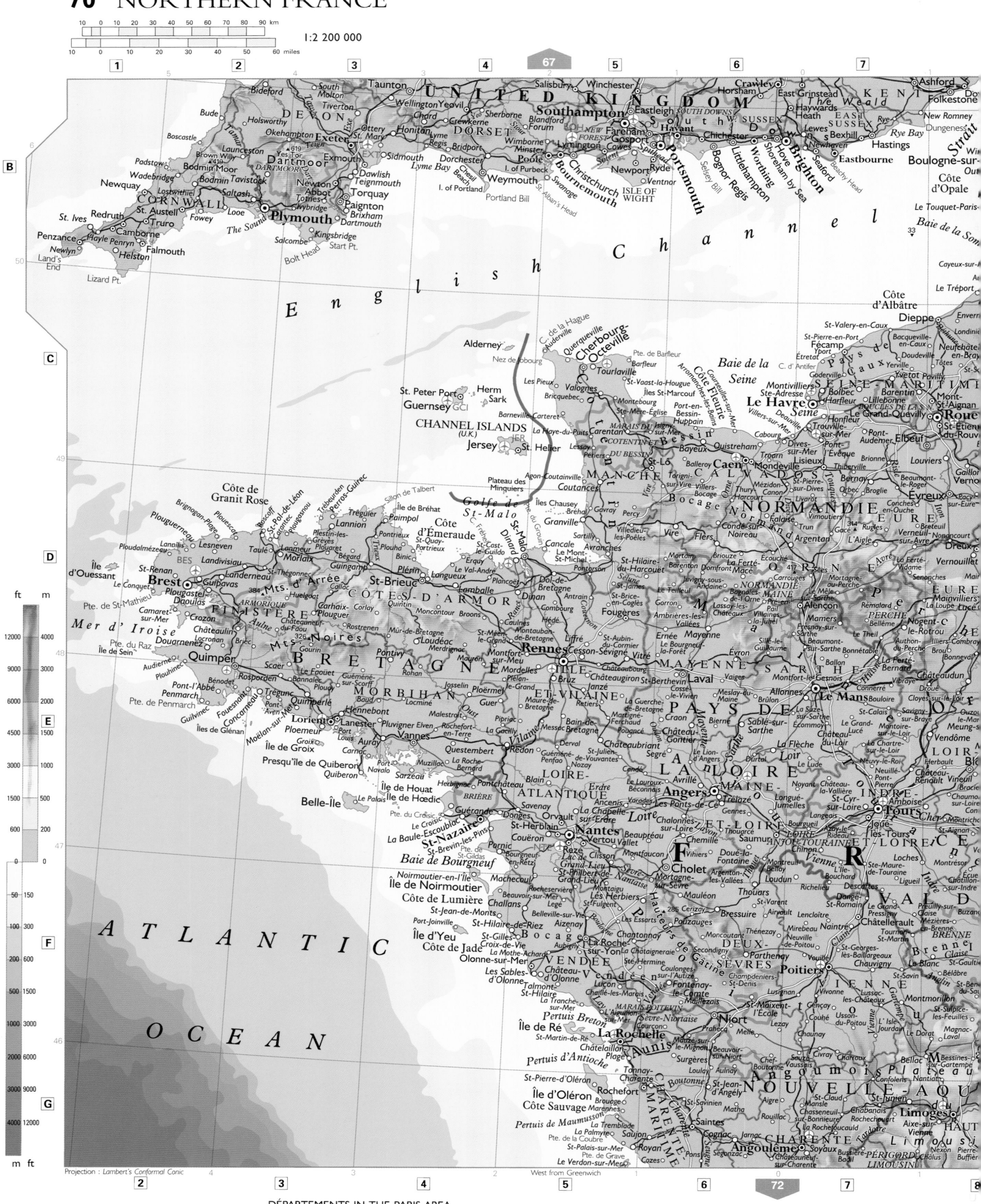

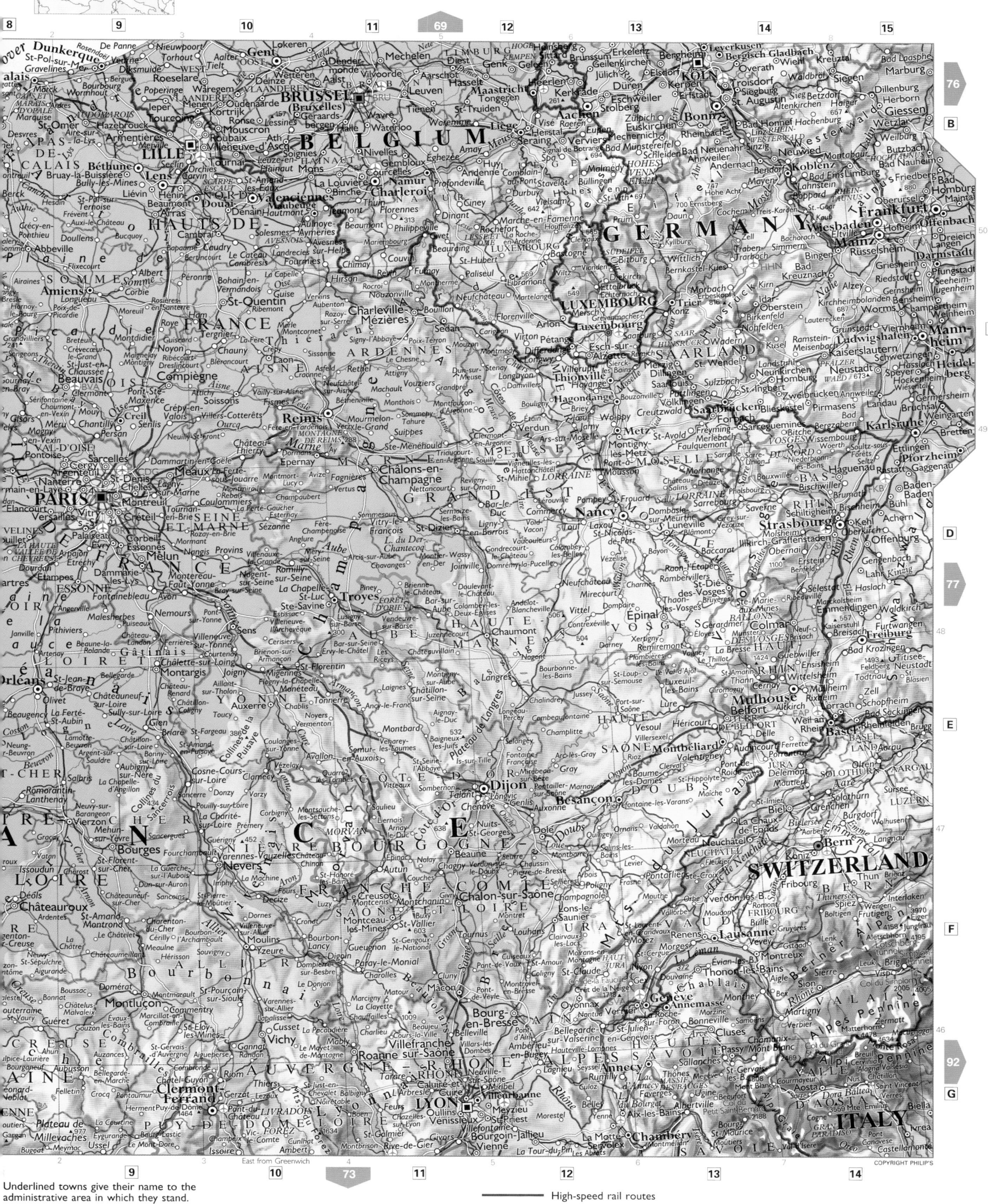

Underlined towns give their name to the
administrative area in which they stand.

——— High-speed rail routes

COPYRIGHT PHILIP'S

1:2 200 000

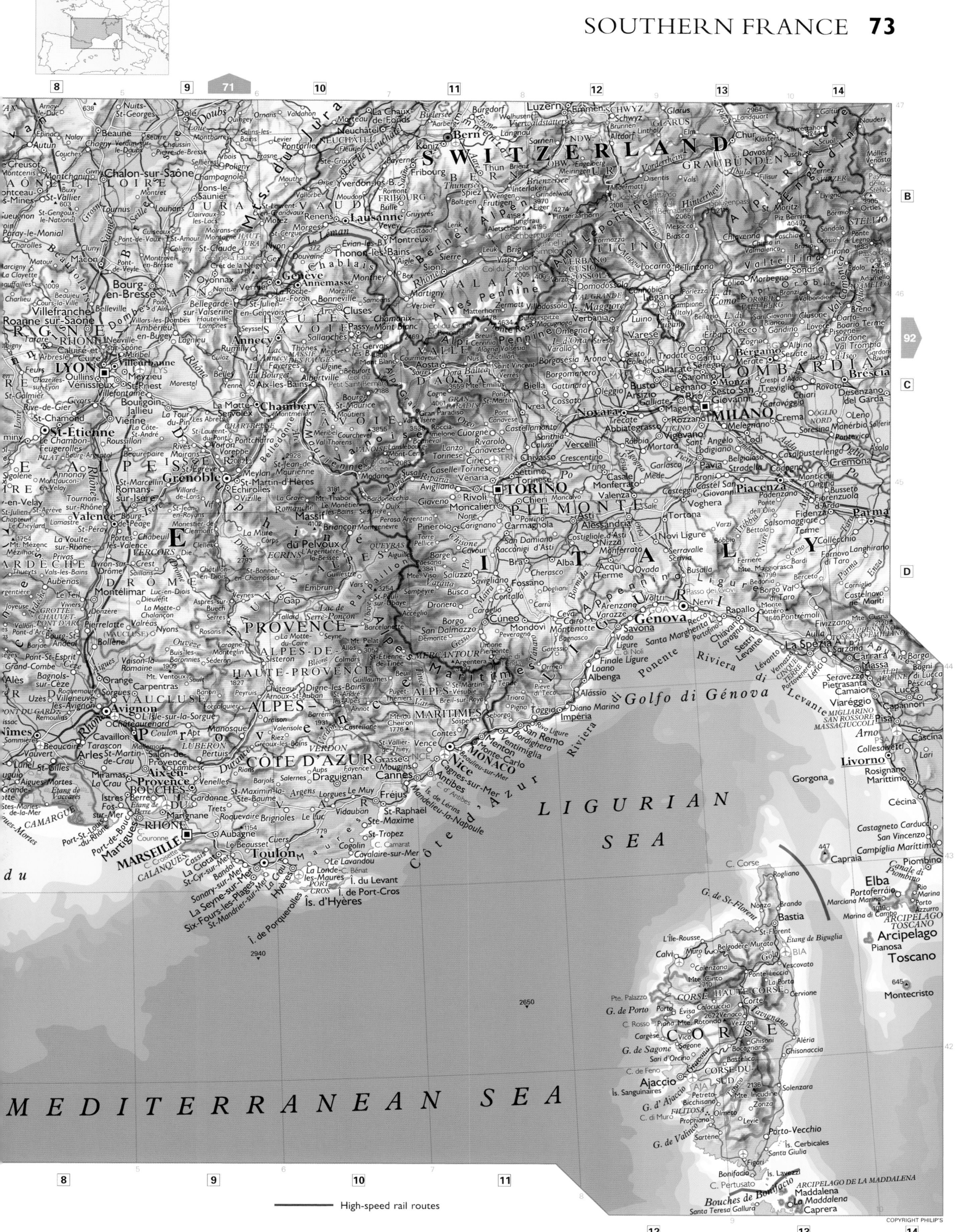

High-speed rail routes

COPYRIGHT PHILIP'S

1:4 400 000

50 0 25 50 75 100 125 150 175 km
50 0 25 50 75 100 125 miles

NORTH SEA

BALTIC SEA

DENMARK

UNITED KINGDOM

NETHERLANDS

AMSTERDAM
's-Gravenhage (Den Haag)
ROTTERDAM

BELGIUM
BRUSSEL (Bruxelles)

LUXEMBOURG

GERMANY

HAMBURG
Bremen
Hannover
BERLIN
Magdeburg
Leipzig
Dresden
KÖLN (Cologne)
Düsseldorf
Dortmund
Essen
Bonn
Frankfurt
Wiesbaden
Mannheim
Stuttgart
Nürnberg
München (Munich)
Kiel
Rostock
Lübeck
Schwerin
Szczecin

FRANCE

PARIS
LILLE
Reims
Metz
Strasbourg
Nancy
Dijon
LYON
Grenoble
MARSEILLE
Nice
MONACO

SWITZERLAND

ZÜRICH
Bern
Genève
Basel
LIECHTENSTEIN
Vaduz

AUSTRIA

Innsbruck
Salzburg
Graz
Wien

CZECH

PRAHA (Prague)
Plzeň
Karlovy Vary

ITALY

MILANO
TORINO (Turin)
Venezia (Venice)
Bologna
Genova
Verona
Trento
Bolzano

SLOVENIA

Ljubljana
ZAGREB

CROATIA

ADRIATIC SEA

Projection: Conical with two standard parallels

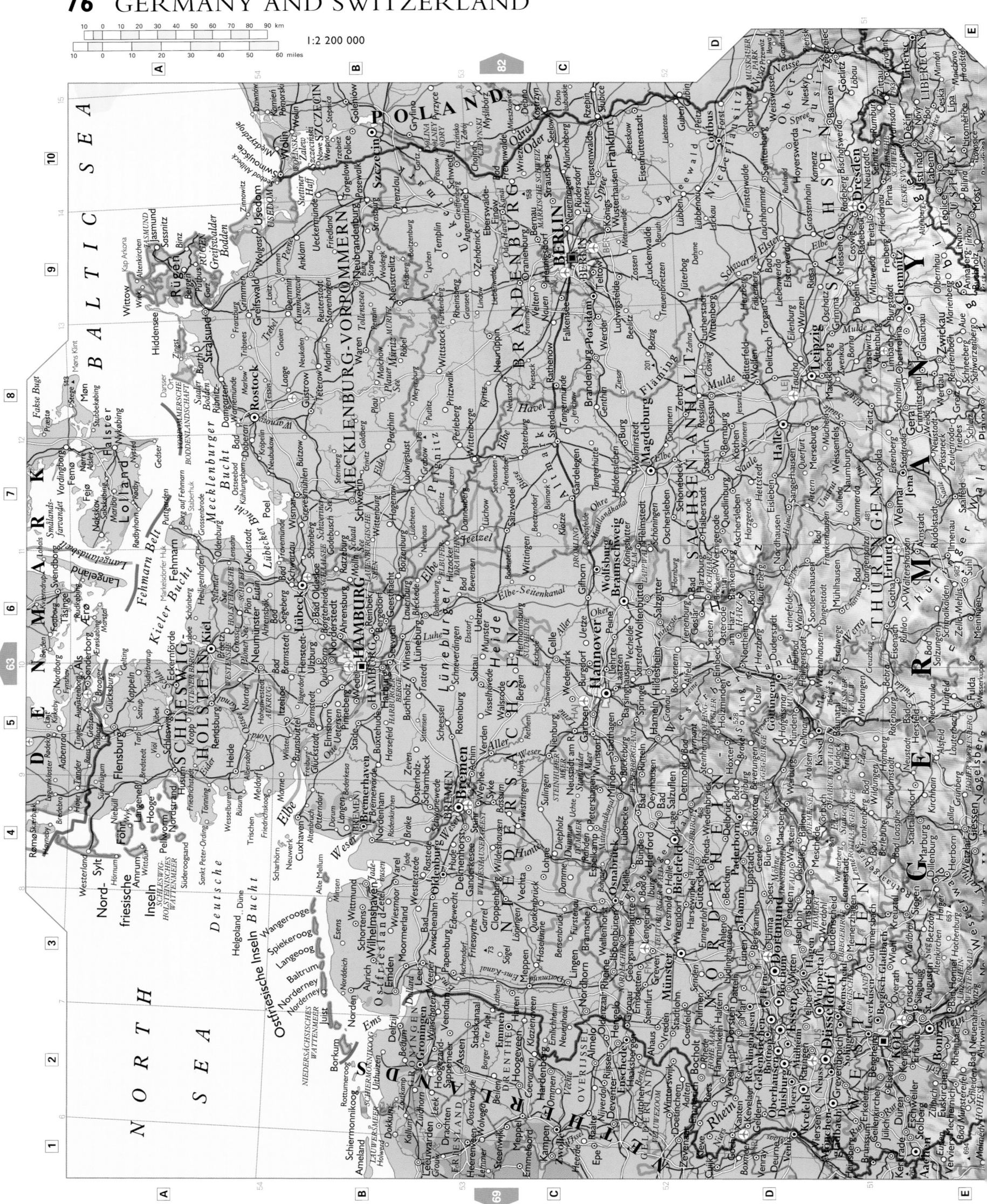

COPYRIGHT PHILIP'S

Projection : Lambert's Conformal Conic

East from Greenwich

————— High-speed rail routes

Underlined towns give their name to the administrative area in which they stand.

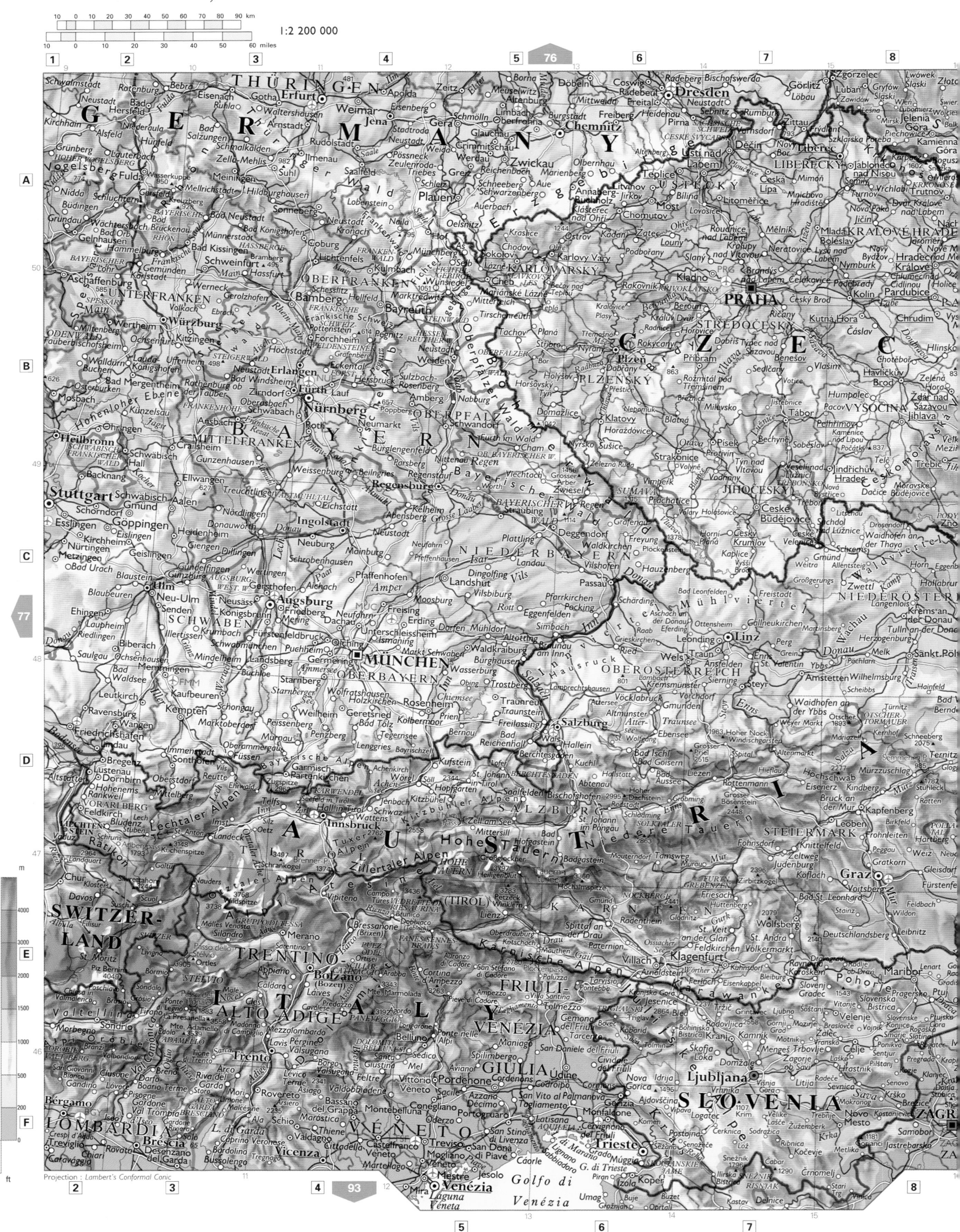

Underlined towns give their name to the
administrative area in which they stand.

1:2 200 000

Administrative divisions in Croatia:
1 Brodsko-Posavska
2 Koprivničko-Križevačka
4 Medimurska
5 Osječko-Baranjska
6 Požeško-Slavonska
8 Virovitičko-Podravska
9 Vukovarsko-Srijemska

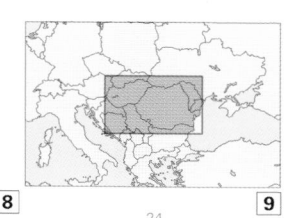

Underlined towns give their name to the
administrative area in which they stand.

COPYRIGHT PHILIP'S

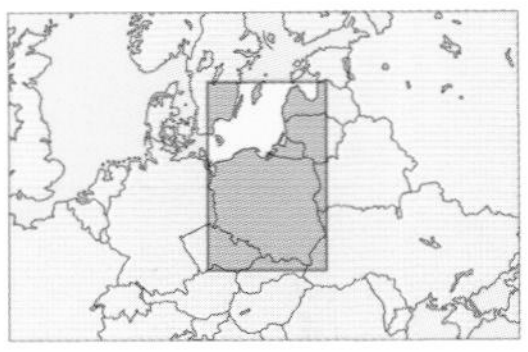

1:2 200 000

10 0 10 20 30 40 50 60 70 80 90 km
10 0 10 20 30 40 50 60 miles

Gulf of Riga

LATVIA

LITHUANIA

ŠIAULIAI

TELŠIAI

TAURAGĖ

KLAIPĖDA

KALININGRAD (Russia)

MARIJAMPOLĖ

WARMIŃSKO-MAZURSKIE

POMORSKIE

ZACHODNIO- POMORSKIE

S W E D E N

KALMAR

Gotland (Sweden)

Öland (Sweden)

Bornholm (Denmark)

BORNHOLMS AMT.

B A L T I C   S E A

Riga
Jūrmala
Kaunas
Hrodna
Gdańsk
Gdynia
Sopot
Elbląg
Malbork
Klaipėda
Liepāja
Ventspils
Šiauliai
Koszalin
Słupsk
Olsztyn
Szczecin
Świnoujście

Curonian Spit
Vistula Spit
Zatoka Gdańska
Neman
Nemunas

Visby
Kalmar
Karlskrona
Jönköping
Växjö

Underlined towns give their name to the administrative area in which they stand.

COPYRIGHT PHILIP'S

Projection : Lambert's Conformal Conic

East from Greenwich

A large reference map showing Poland and the southern Baltic region, with countries including Germany, Czechia, Slovakia, Ukraine, Belarus and Austria, and Polish administrative regions such as Pomorskie, Mazowieckie, Wielkopolskie, Lubelskie, Podkarpackie, Małopolskie, Śląskie, Opolskie, Dolnośląskie, Lubuskie, Łódzkie and Świętokrzyskie. Major cities labelled include Warszawa, Kraków, Łódź, Wrocław, Poznań, Gdańsk, Szczecin, Bydgoszcz, Toruń, Lublin, Białystok, Kielce, Radom, Częstochowa, Katowice, Brno, Ostrava, Wien area.

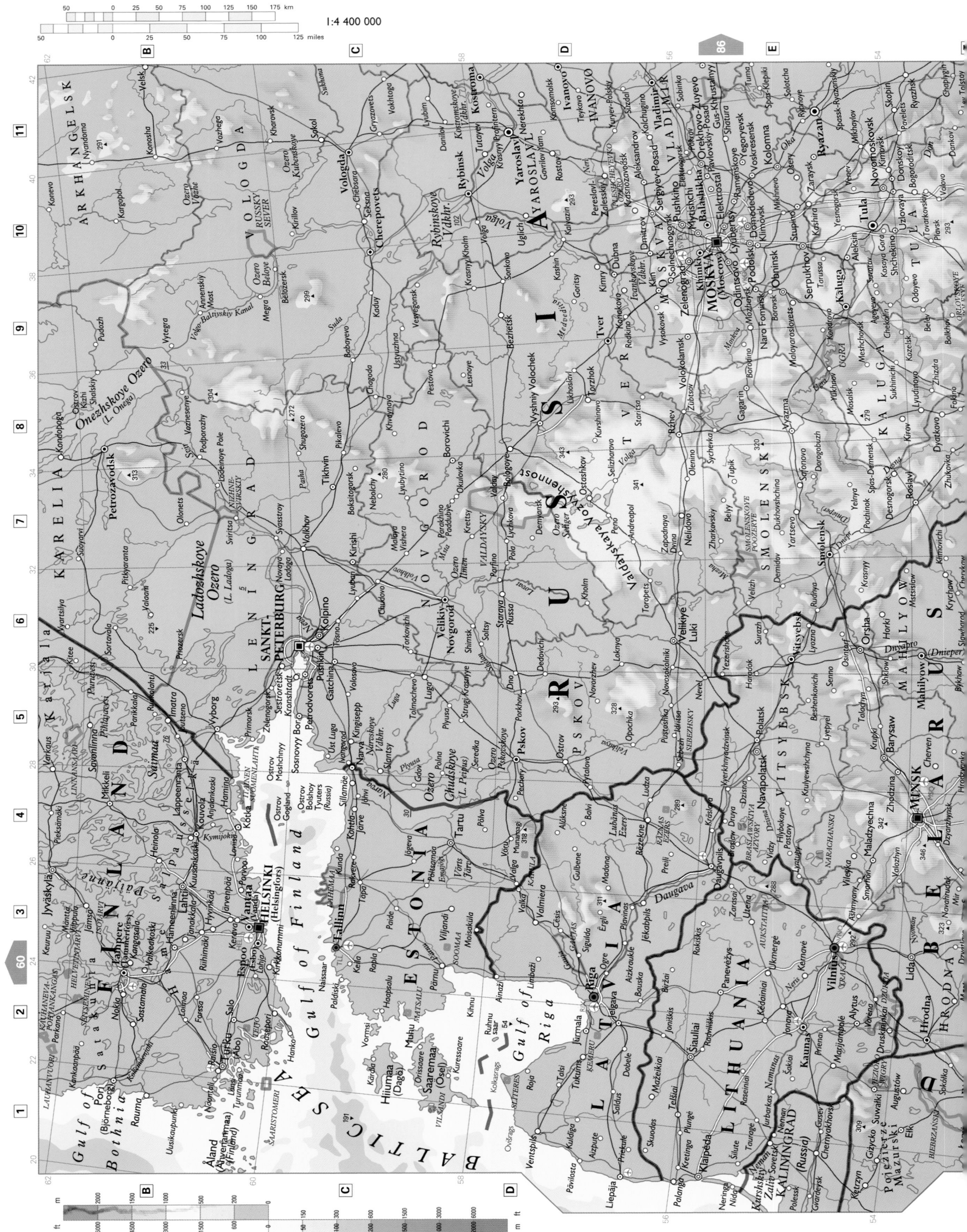

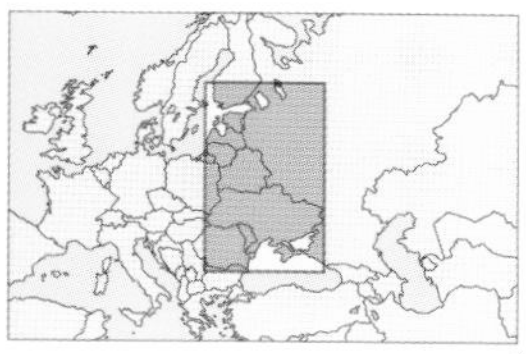

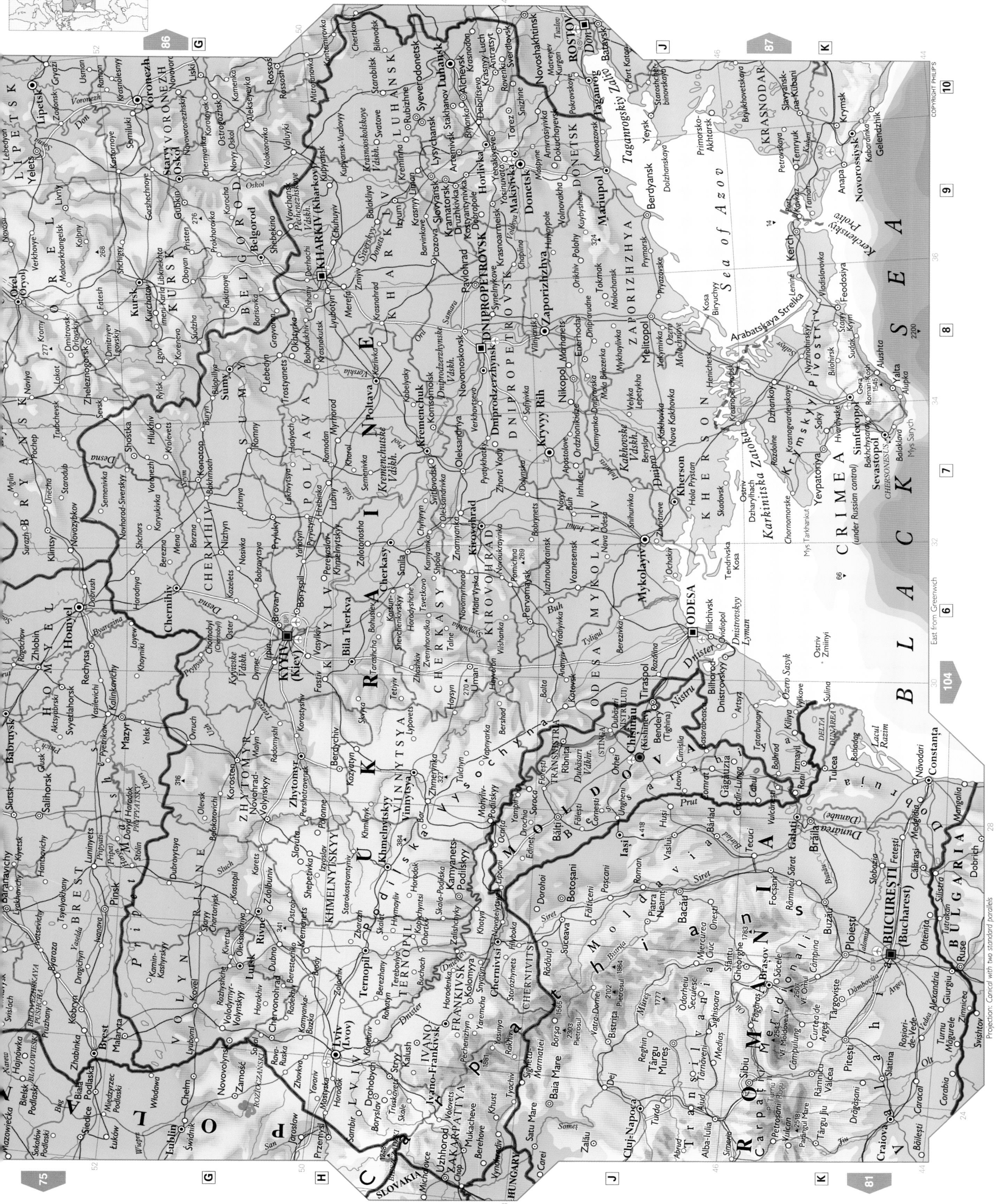

BLACK SEA
Sea of Azov
U K R A I N E
R O M A N I A
MOLDOVA
CRIMEA
(under Russian control)
KYIV (Kiev)
ODESA
KHARKIV (Kharkov)
DNIPROPETROVSK
DONETSK
LUHANSK
ZAPORIZHZHYA
MYKOLAYIV
KHERSON
POLTAVA
CHERKASY
KIROVOHRAD
VINNYTSYA
ZHYTOMYR
CHERNIHIV
SUMY
RIVNE
VOLYN
LVIV
TERNOPIL
KHMELNYTSKYY
CHERNIVTSI
IVANO-FRANKIVSK
ZAKARPATTYA
Chişinău (Kishinev)
BUCUREŞTI (Bucharest)
Constanţa
VORONEZH
ROSTOV
KRASNODAR
BELGOROD
KURSK
Homyel
Brest
Pinsk
Mazyr
Simferopol
Sevastopol
Kerch
Yalta
Mariupol
Melitopol
Berdyansk
Kryvyy Rih
Kremenchuk
Bila Tserkva
Uman
Chernihiv
Lutsk
Rivne
Lviv (Lvov)
Chernivtsi
Iaşi
Galaţi
Brăila
Ploieşti
Braşov
Cluj-Napoca
Craiova
BULGARIA
HUNGARY
SLOVAKIA
Dnister
Dnipro
Prut
Danube
Desna
Prypyat
Siret
Carpaţii Meridionali
Projection: Conical with two standard parallels
East from Greenwich
COPYRIGHT PHILIP'S
86
87
75
81
104

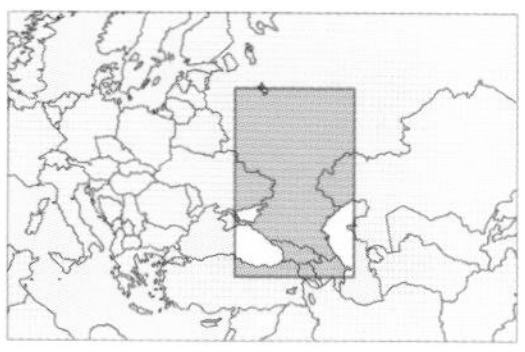

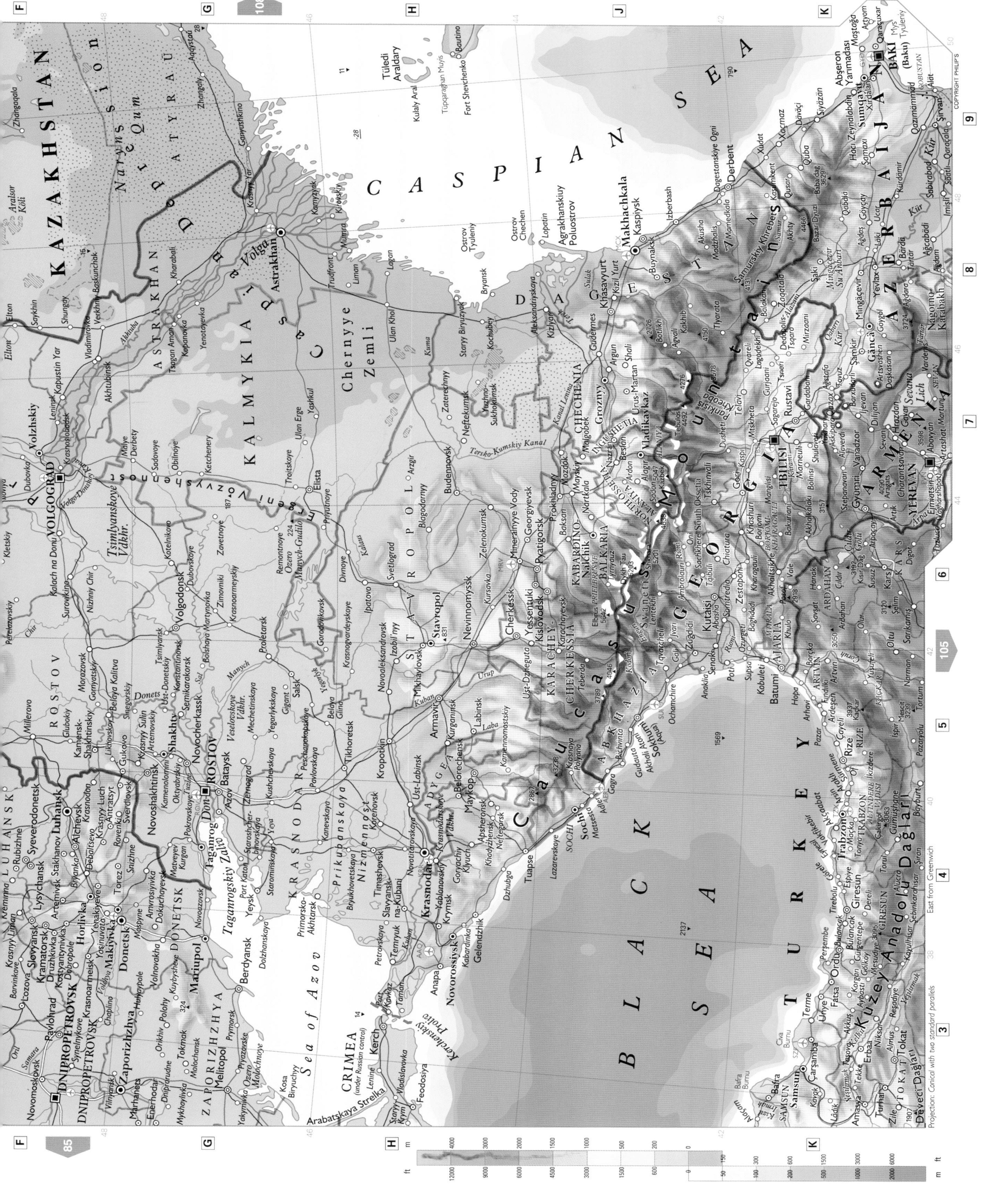

CASPIAN SEA

BLACK SEA

Sea of Azov

KAZAKHSTAN

RUSSIA / (region labels) KALMYKIA, Chernyye Zemli, ASTRAKHAN, STAVROPOL, KRASNODAR, ROSTOV, DONETSK, LUHANSK, ZAPORIZHZHYA, CRIMEA (under Russian control)

DAGESTAN, CHECHENIA, INGUSHETIA, NORTH OSSETIA, KABARDINO-BALKARIA, KARACHAY-CHERKESSIA, ADYGEA, ABKHAZIA, AJARIA, SOUTH OSSETIA

GEORGIA, ARMENIA, AZERBAIJAN, TURKEY

Caucasus Mountains

Volga, Don, Donets, Kuban, Manych, Kuma, Terek, Sulak, Kür

Tsimlyanskoye Vdkhr., Veselovskoye Vdkhr.

Major towns: VOLGOGRAD, Astrakhan, Makhachkala, Derbent, BAKI (Baku), Sumqayıt, Şamaxı, Gäncä, YEREVAN, TBILISI, Kutaisi, Batumi, Sochi, Krasnodar, ROSTOV, Taganrog, Novorossiysk, DNIPROPETROVSK, ZAPORIZHZHYA, Mariupol, Donetsk, Stavropol, Pyatigorsk, Kislovodsk, Nalchik, Vladikavkaz, Grozny, Elista, Volzhskiy, Volgodonsk, Salsk, Armavir, Maykop, Tuapse, Trabzon, SAMSUN, RIZE, Kutaisi, Poti, Sukhumi, Nevinnomyssk, Cherkessk, Yessentuki, Kizlyar, Buynaksk, Izberbash, Qusar, Şäki, Mingäçevir

COPYRIGHT PHILIP'S

East from Greenwich

Projection: Conical with two standard parallels

Scale bar (elevation): ft / m — 4000 3000 2000 1500 1000 500 200 0 50 100 200 600 1500 3000 6000 ft; m 6000 4500 3000 1500 600 300 150 0 -150 -300 -600 m

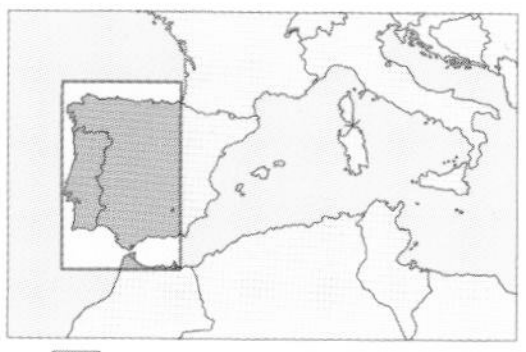

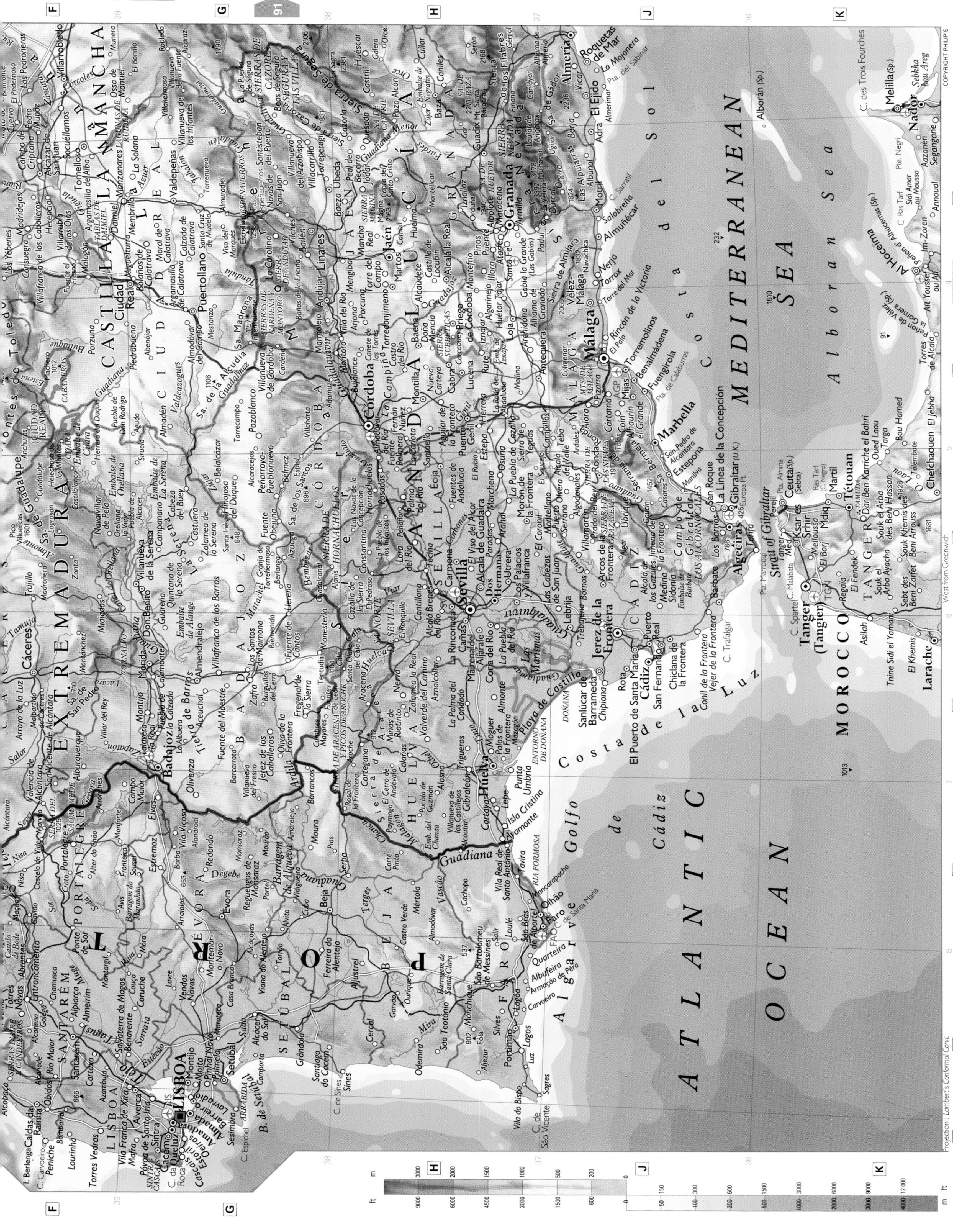
ATLANTIC OCEAN
MEDITERRANEAN SEA
Golfo de Cádiz
Alboran Sea
Costa de la Luz
Costa del Sol
Strait of Gibraltar
EXTREMADURA
CASTILLA-LA MANCHA
ANDALUCÍA
PORTUGAL
MOROCCO
LISBOA
Sevilla
Córdoba
Granada
Málaga
Cádiz
Huelva
Badajoz
Cáceres
Jaén
Almería
Gibraltar (U.K.)
Ceuta (Sp.)
Tanger (Tangier)
Tétouan
Faro
Évora
Setúbal
High-speed rail routes
West from Greenwich
Projection: Lambert's Conformal Conic
COPYRIGHT PHILIP'S

1:2 200 000

High-speed rail routes

COPYRIGHT PHILIP'S

Projection: Lambert's Conformal Conic

1:2 200 000

Underlined towns give their name to the
administrative area in which they stand

Brodsko-Posavska	4 Medimurska	8 Virovitičko-Podravska	
Koprivničko-Križevačka	6 Požeško-Slavonska	10 Zagreba čka	
Krapinsko-Zagorska	7 Varaždinska		High-speed rail routes

COPYRIGHT PHILIP'S

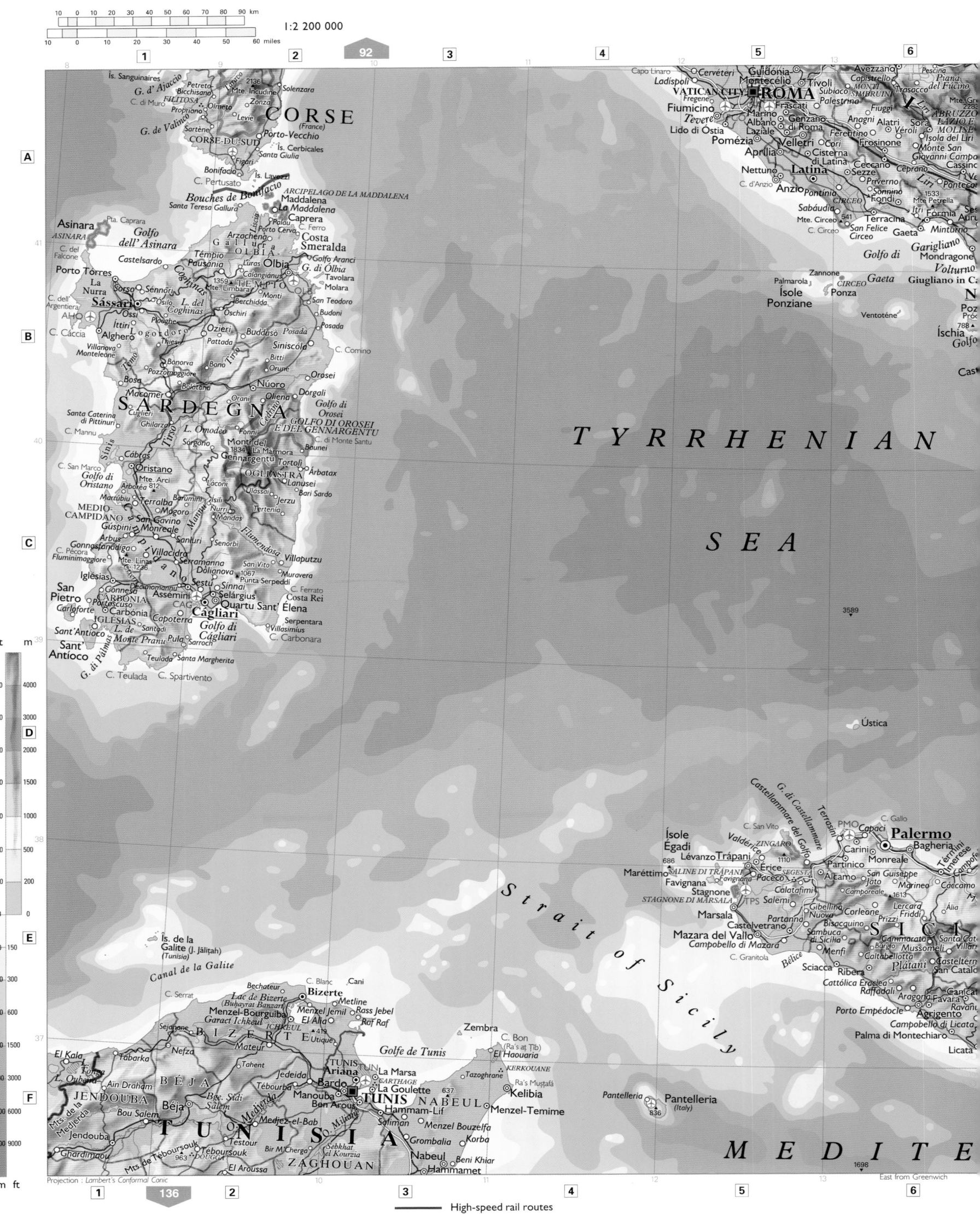

1:2 200 000

Projection : Lambert's Conformal Conic

High-speed rail routes

ADRIATIC

SEA

Strait of Otranto

GREECE

Golfo di
Táranto

IONIAN

SEA

RRANEAN SEA

COPYRIGHT PHILIP'S

Underlined towns give their name to the
administrative area in which they stand.

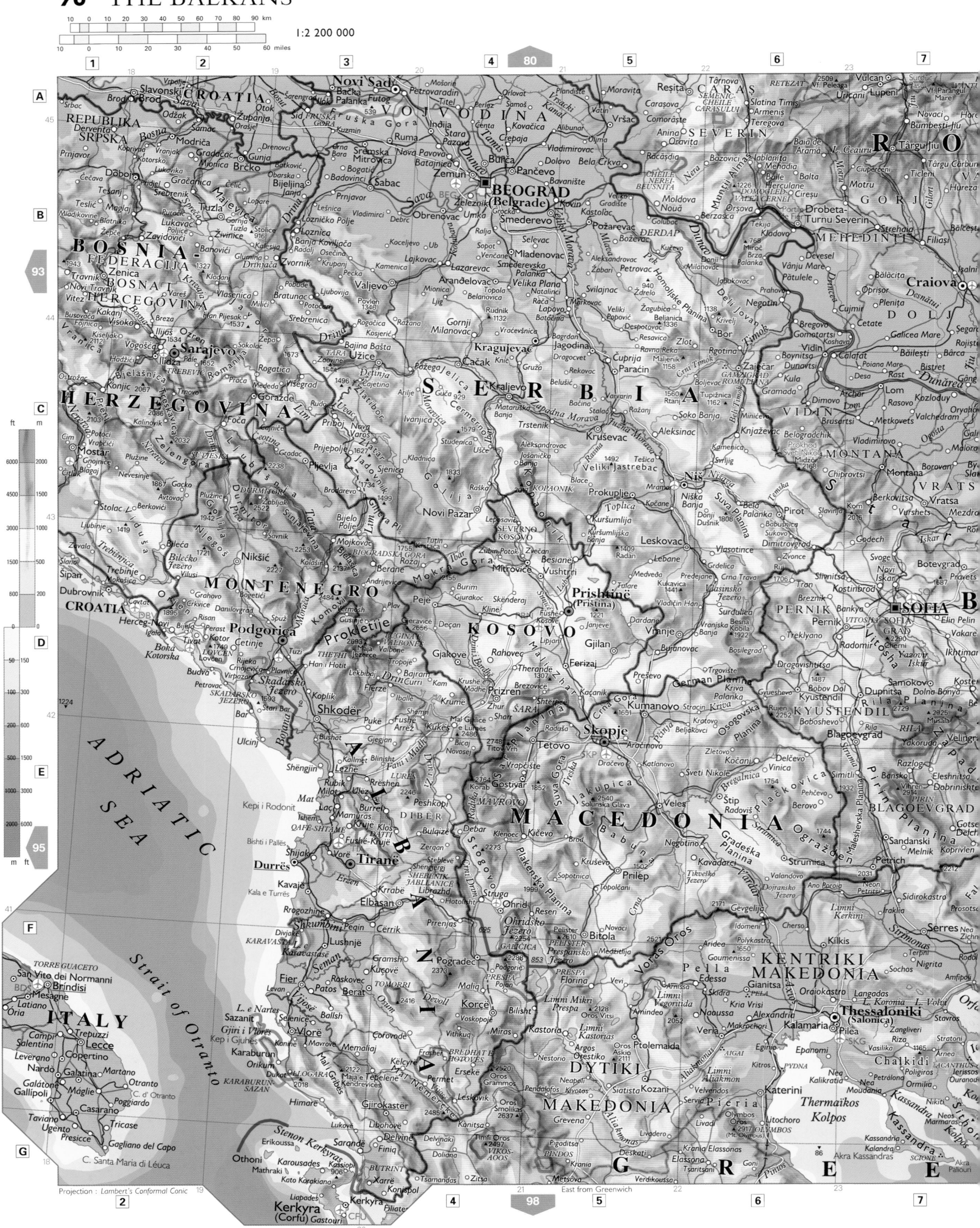

1:2 200 000

Projection : Lambert's Conformal Conic

East from Greenwich

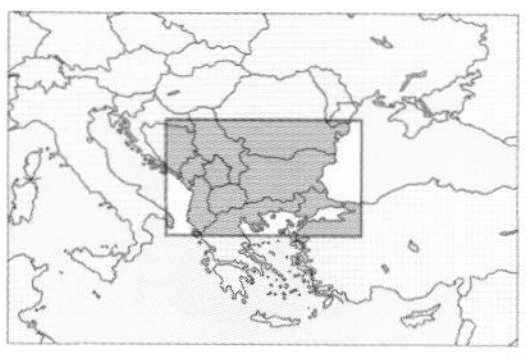

ROMANIA

BULGARIA

TURKEY

B L A C K   S E A

Marmara Denizi (Sea of Marmara)

Sea of Thrace

Bucureşti (Bucharest)

Constanţa

Varna

Burgas

Plovdiv

İSTANBUL

BURSA

Edirne

Galaţi

Brăila

Buzău

Ploieşti

Piteşti

Ruse

Pleven

Veliko Tarnovo

Stara Zagora

Pazardzhik

Haskovo

Kırklareli

Tekirdağ

Çanakkale

Çorlu

Üsküdar

Kartal

Gebze

Kocaeli (İzmit)

İstanbul Boğazı (Bosporus)

Gelibolu Yarımadası

Çanakkale Boğazı (Dardanelles)

ANATOLIKI MAKEDONIA

Kavala

Komotini

Xanthi

Alexandroupoli

Underlined towns give their name to the administrative area in which they stand.

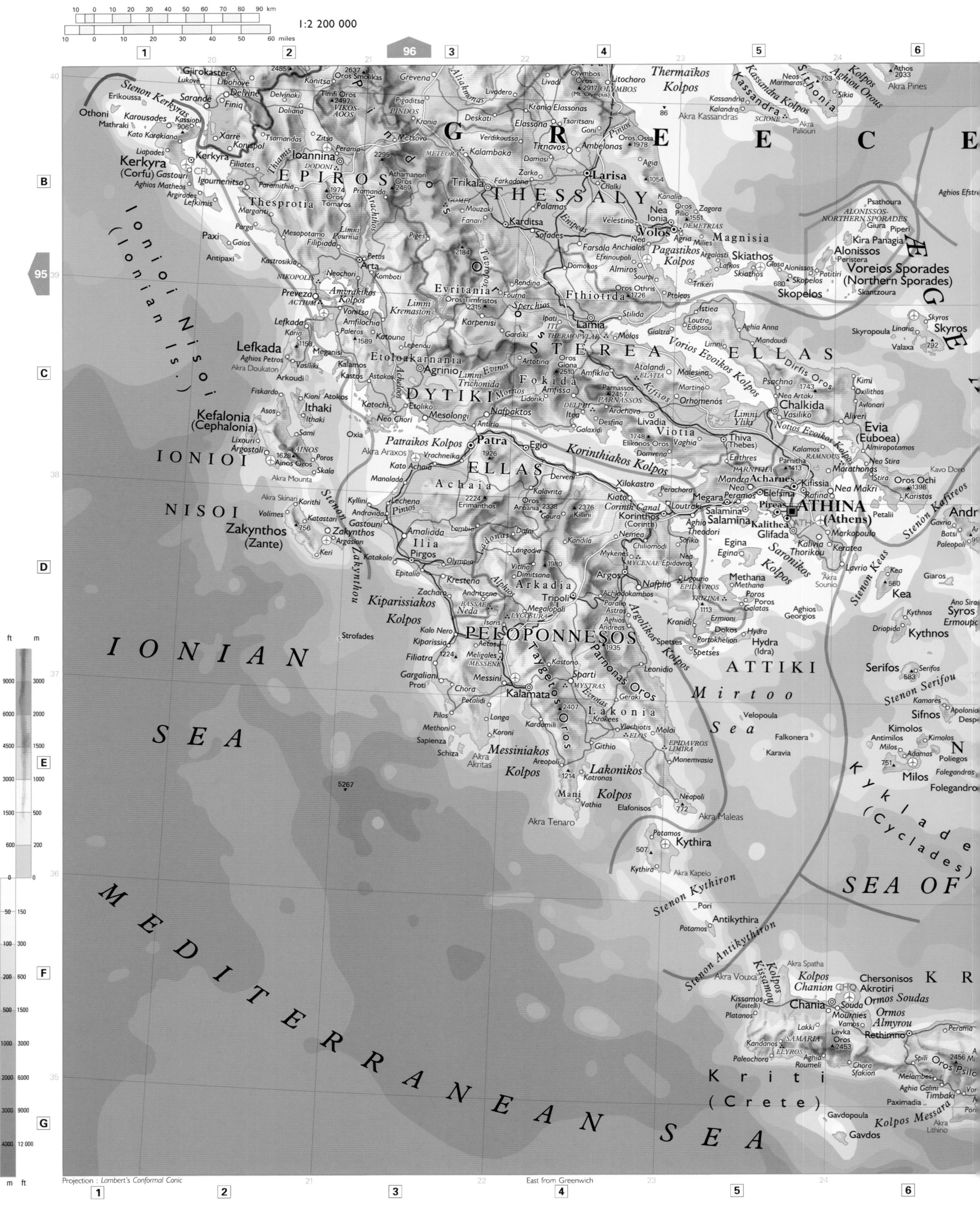

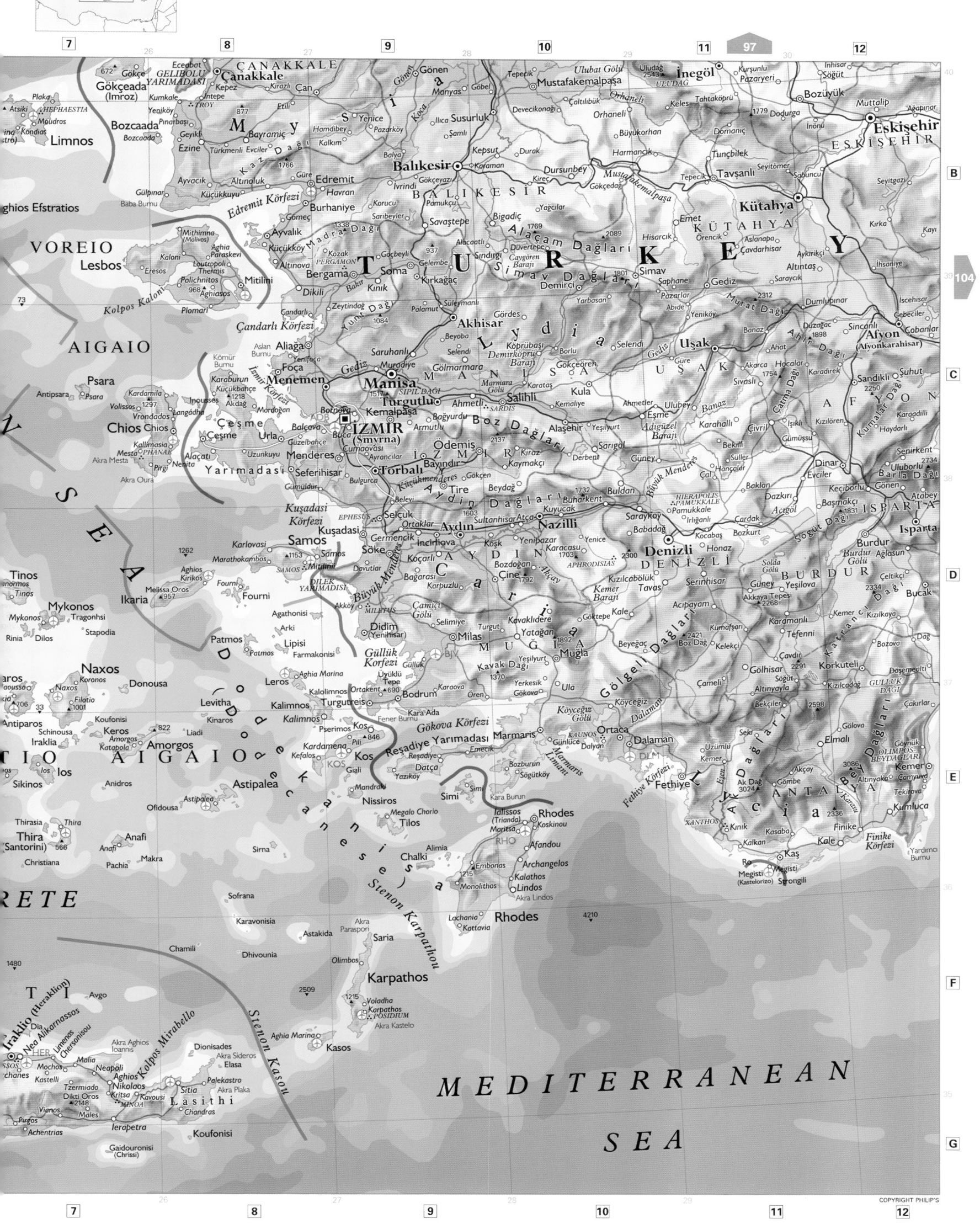

COPYRIGHT PHILIP'S

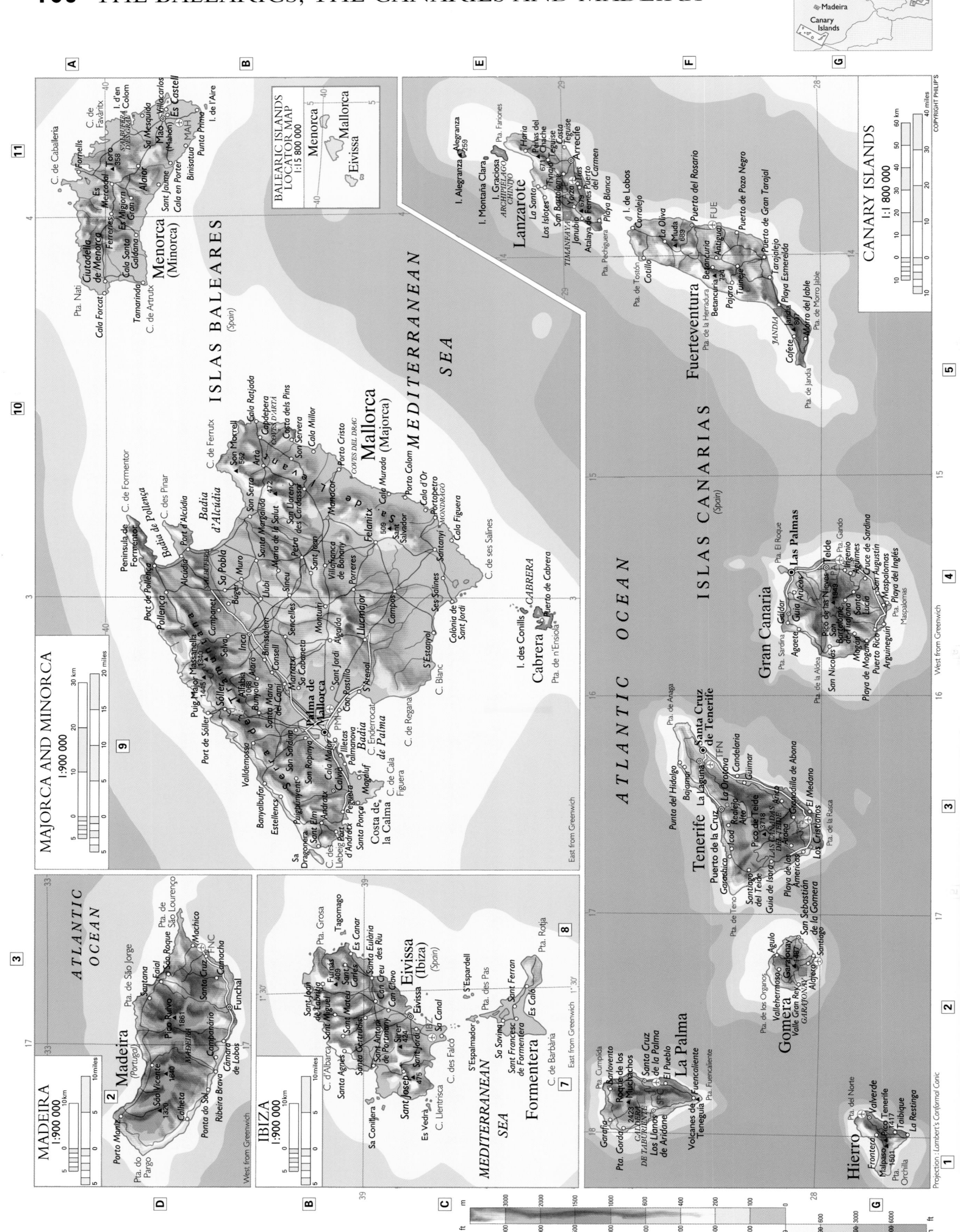

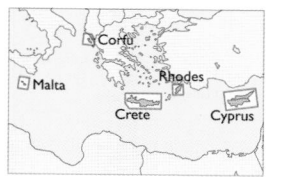

CRETE
1:1 200 000

MALTA
1:900 000

CORFU
1:900 000

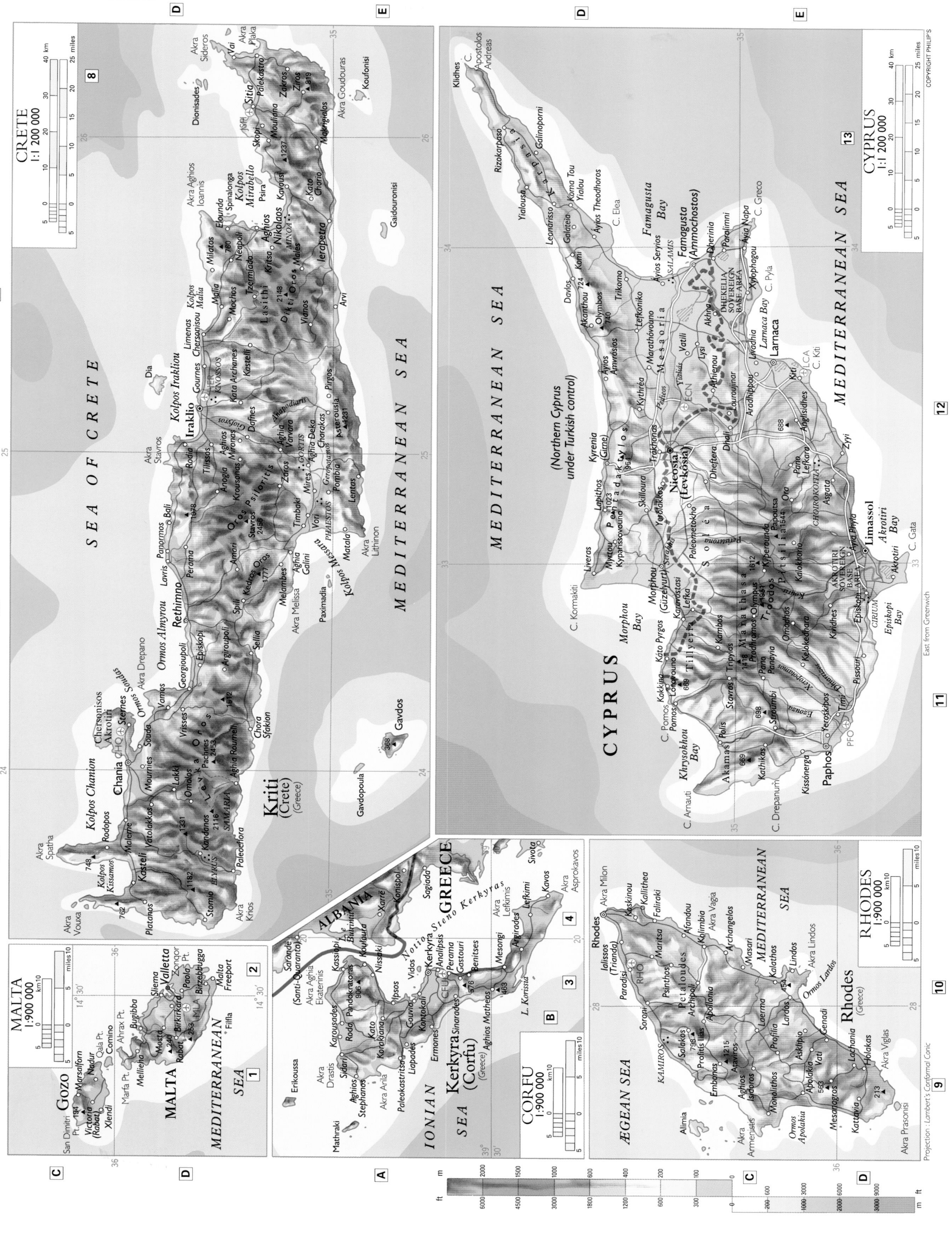

RHODES
1:900 000

CYPRUS
1:1 200 000

SEA OF CRETE

Kriti (Crete) (Greece)

Chania · Iraklio · Rethimno · Ierapetra · Sitia · Knossos

MEDITERRANEAN SEA

CYPRUS

(Northern Cyprus under Turkish control)

Nicosia (Levkosia) · Famagusta (Ammochostos) · Larnaca · Limassol · Paphos · Kyrenia (Girne) · Morphou

AKROTIRI SOVEREIGN BASE AREA · DHEKELIA SOVEREIGN BASE AREA

MALTA

Valletta · Sliema · Victoria (Rabat) · Gozo · Comino

MEDITERRANEAN SEA

Kerkyra (Corfu) (Greece)

ALBANIA · **GREECE**

IONIAN SEA

Rhodes (Greece)

AEGEAN SEA

East from Greenwich

Projection: Lambert's Conformal Conic

COPYRIGHT PHILIP'S

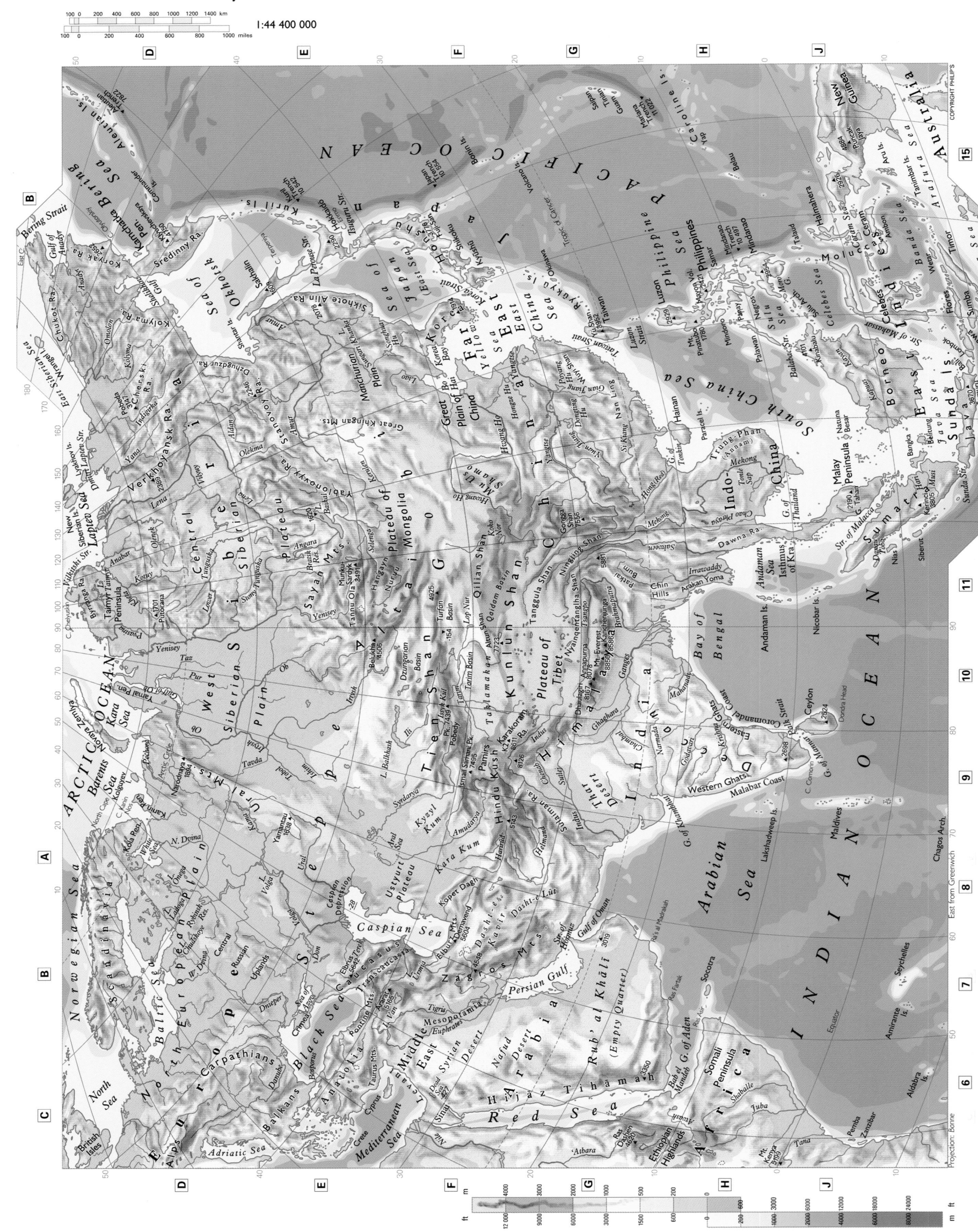

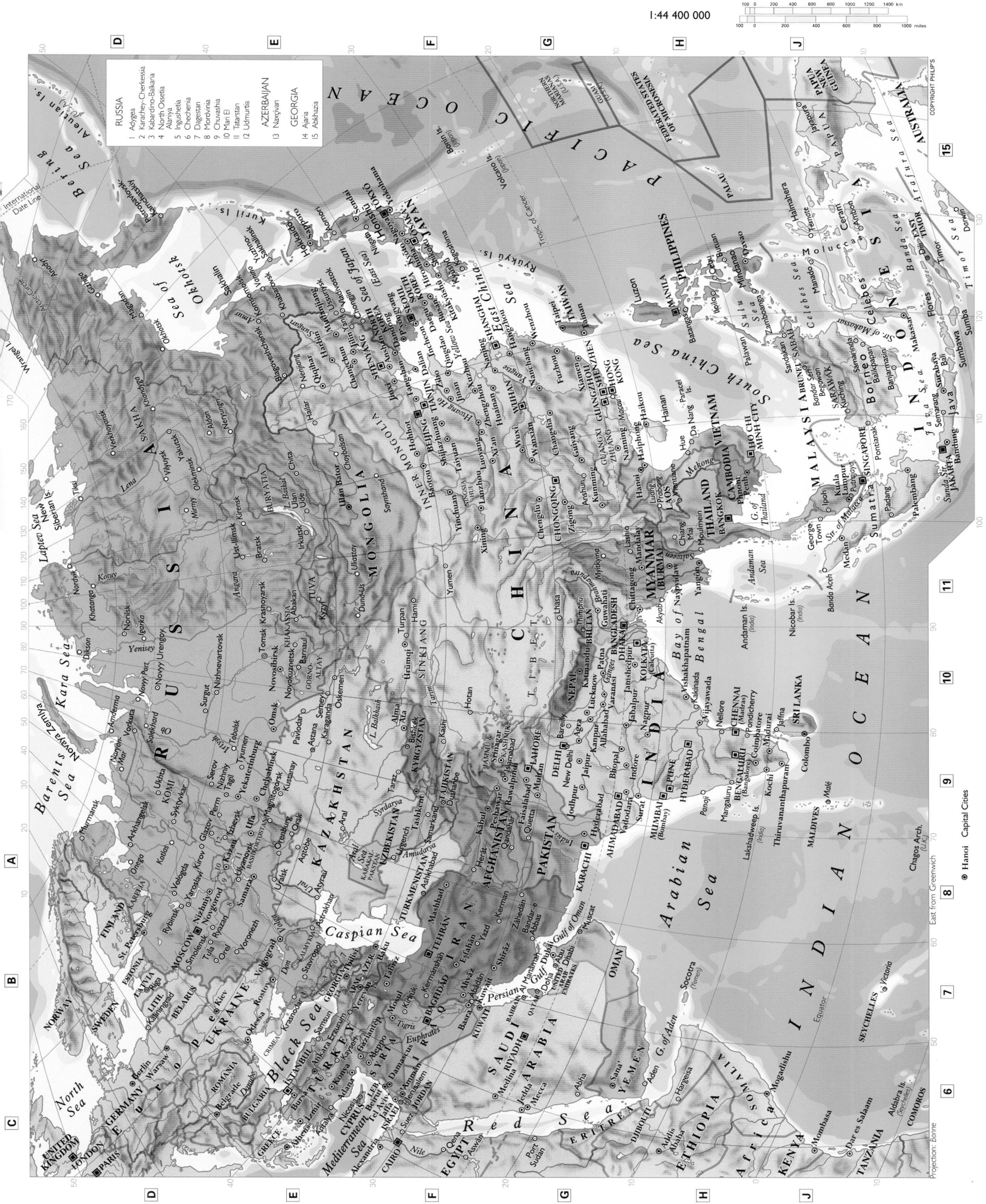

1:44 400 000

COPYRIGHT PHILIP'S

RUSSIA
1 Adygea
2 Karachey-Cherkessia
3 Kabardino-Balkaria
4 North Ossetia
5 Ingushetia
6 Chechenia
7 Dagestan
8 Mordvinia
9 Chuvashia
10 Mari El
11 Tatarstan
12 Udmurtia

AZERBAIJAN
13 Naxçivan

GEORGIA
14 Ajaria
15 Abkhazia

Projection: Bonne

◉ Hanoi   Capital Cities

1 : 4 400 000

50 0 25 50 75 100 125 150 175 km
50 0 25 50 75 100 125 miles

BULGARIA

BLACK SEA

Stara Zagora · Yambol · Aytos · Burgas · Nos Emine

Kırklareli · Edirne · Pınarhisar · İğneada · İğneada Burnu

Babaeski · Vize · Saray · Çerkezköy

Lüleburgaz · Çatalca

Uzunköprü · Muratlı · Çorlu

İpsala · Keşan · Malkara · Tekirdağ · Silivri · **İSTANBUL** · Kartal · Kocaeli (İzmit) · Sakarya (Adapazarı)

Enez · Şarköy · İstanbul Boğazı (Bosporus) · Gebze · Darıca

Marmara Denizi (Sea of Marmara)

Gökçeada · Gelibolu · Kapı Dağ · Yalova · Orhangazi · Gemlik · İznik Gölü

Çanakkale · Biga · Bandırma · Mudanya · Yenişehir · İznik

TROY · Çan · Gönen · Karacabey · **BURSA**

Bayramiç · Edremit · Balya · Mustafakemalpaşa · ULUDAĞ 2543

Edremit Körfezi · Ayvacık · Burhaniye · BALIKESİR · Dursunbey · Domaniç

Lesbos · Bergama · Soma · Demirci · Simav · Gediz · **Eskişehir** · Polatlı

Chios · Foça · Menemen · Akhisar · Kırkağaç · Kula · Uşak · Afyon (Afyonkarahisar) · Çay

İZMİR (Smyrna) · Turgutlu · Manisa · Salihli · Alaşehir · Eşme · Uşak

Çeşme · Urla · Torbalı · Ödemiş · Sarıgöl · SANDIKLI · Şuhut

Seferihisar · Selçuk · Tire · Nazilli · Buldan · Denizli · Dinar

Samos · Kuşadası · Aydın · İncirliova · Karacasu · Çardak · Burdur

Söke · Bozdoğan · Tavas · Acıgöl · Isparta

Didim · Milas · Muğla · Kale · Burdur

Bodrum · Ören · Ula · Köyceğiz · Tefenni · Bucak

GREECE

Rhodes · Marmaris · Dalaman · Ortaca · Fethiye · Kalkan · Kaş · Kale · Finike · Kumluca · Kemer · **ANTALYA** · Serik · Aksu · Manavgat · Alanya · Gazipaşa

ANKARA · Kırıkkale · Kırşehir · Nevşehir · **KAYSERİ** · Talas

Kütahya · Eskişehir · Sivrihisar · Kulu · Aksaray · Niğde

Tuz Gölü · Şereflikoçhisar · Derinkuyu · Ereğli · Ulukışla

Akşehir · Beyşehir · **KONYA** · Karapınar · Karaman · Ereğli

Toros Dağları

ADANA · Kahramanmaraş · Osmaniye · **GAZİANTEP** (Antep) · Nizip

Tarsus · Mersin (İçel) · Silifke · İskenderun · Kilis

MEDITERRANEAN SEA

CYPRUS · Nicosia · Famagusta · Kyrenia · Morphou · Larnaca · Limassol · Paphos · Troodos · (Northern Cyprus under Turkish control)

Al Lādhiqīyah (Latakia) · Ḥamāh · **HIMṢ** (Homs) · Tarābulus (Tripoli) · **BAYRŪT** (Beirut) · Sür · Saydā

LEBANON · **DIMASHQ** (Damascus) · Jaramānah

SYRIA · **ḤALAB** (Aleppo)

HEFA (Haifa) · Netanya · Teverya · Nazareth

ISRAEL · **TEL AVIV-YAFO** · **WEST BANK** · Jerusalem · **AMMÂN**

JORDAN

Projection: Conical with two standard parallels

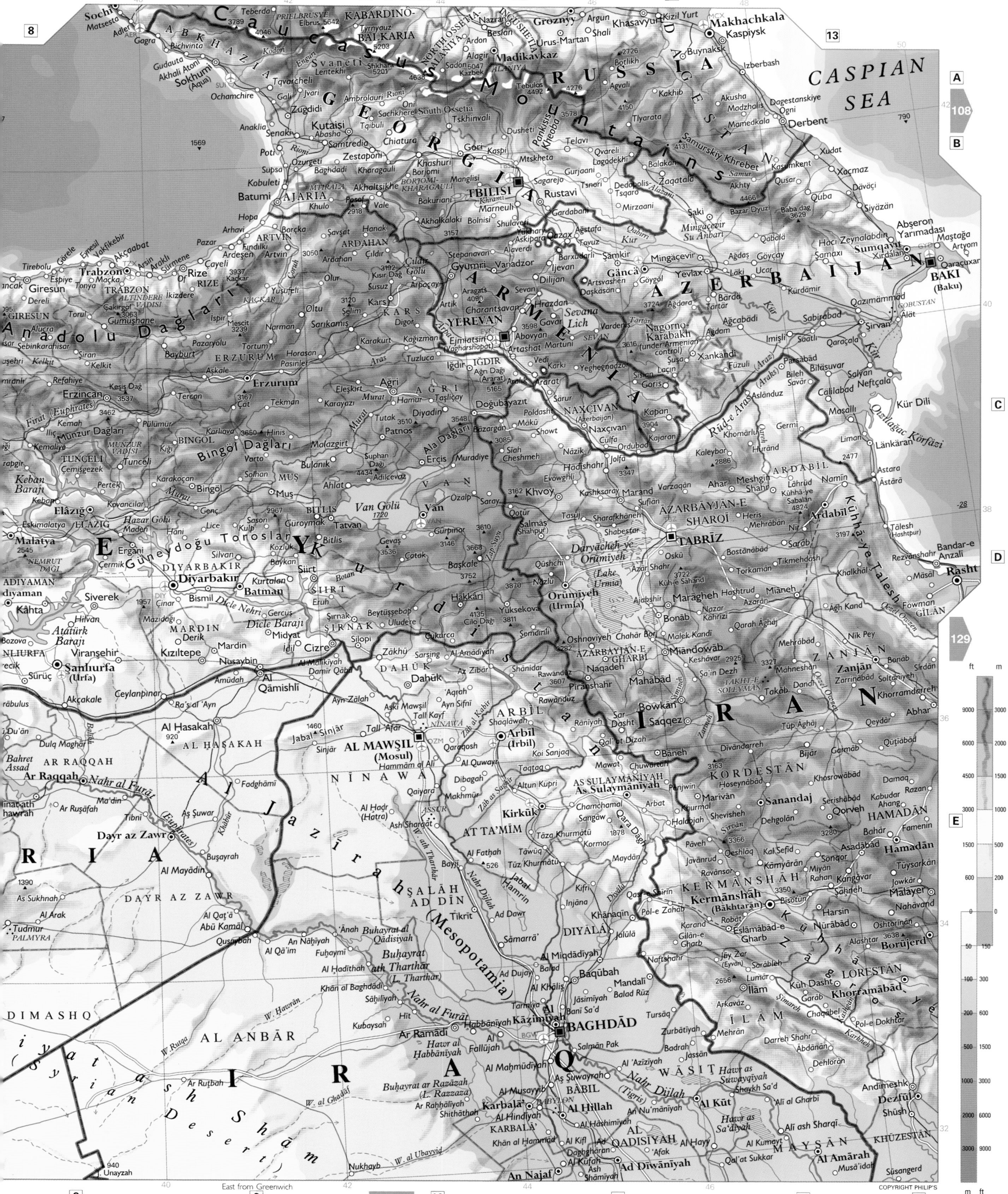

Underlined towns give their name
to the administrative area in which they stand

East from Greenwich

COPYRIGHT PHILIP'S

100 0 100 200 300 400 500 600 700 800 km

1:17 800 000

100   0   100   200   300   400   500 miles

RUSSIA
1 Adygea
2 Karachey-Cherkessia
3 Kabardino-Balkaria
4 North Ossetia-Alaniya
5 Ingushetia
6 Chechenia
7 Dagestan
8 Mordvinia
9 Chuvashia
10 Mari El
11 Tatarstan
12 Udmurtia
13 Khakassia

AZERBAIJAN
14 Naxçıvan

GEORGIA
15 Ajaria
16 Abkhazia

Projection: Conical Orthomorphic with two standard parallels

East from Greenwich

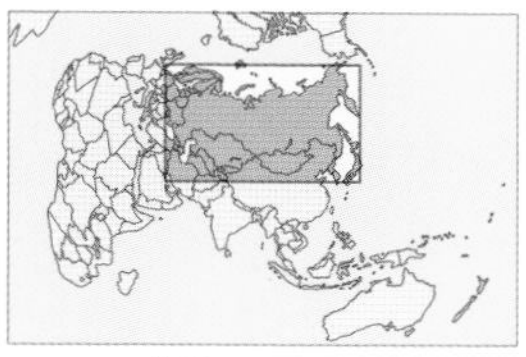

ARCTIC OCEAN

Severnaya Zemlya

East Siberian Sea

Laptev Sea

Chukchi Sea

Bering Sea

Sea of Okhotsk

Sea of Japan (East Sea)

R U S S I A

Poluostrov Taymyr

Gory Byrranga

SAKHA

Verkhoyanskiy Khrebet

Khrebet Cherskogo

Stanovoy Khrebet

Khrebet Dzhugdzur

Kamchatka

Poluostrov Kamchatka

Kurilskiye Ostrova

Sakhalin

Khrebet Sikhote Alin

Norilsk
Yakutsk
Tiksi
Khatanga
Olenek
Vilyuysk
Mirnyy
Lensk
Bratsk
Irkutsk
Ulan-Ude
Chita
Blagoveshchensk
Khabarovsk
Komsomolsk-na-Amur
Vladivostok
Petropavlovsk-Kamchatskiy
Magadan
Yuzhno-Sakhalinsk
Krasnoyarsk

MONGOLIA

ULAANBAATAR

Hangayn Nuruu

Gobi

Altay

(Aerhtai Shan)

C H I N A

(Manchuria)

Dong bei

BEIJING
HOHHOT
BAOTOU
ZHANGJIAKOU
TANGSHAN
SHENYANG
ANSHAN
FUSHUN
CHANGCHUN
HARBIN
QIQIHAR
DAQING
JIAMUSI
JIXI
MUDANJIANG
JILIN
FUYU
CHIFENG

NORTH KOREA
PYONGYANG
NAMP'O
Hamhŭng
Wŏnsan
Chŏngjin
Dandong

SOUTH KOREA
SEOUL
INCHEON
DAEJEON
DAEGU
BUSAN
GWANGJU

JAPAN
Hokkaidō
SAPPORO
Hakodate
Aomori
Akita
Honshū
Niigata
KYOTO
OSAKA
KOBE
Kanazawa

Bering Str.

St. Lawrence I. (U.S.A.)

International Date Line

Arctic Circle

Underlined towns give their name to the administrative area in which they stand.

COPYRIGHT PHILIP'S

Oz. Baykal
Ulan Ude
Bukachacha
Chita
Sretensk
Shilka
Mangui
Gulian
Shimanovsk
Zeya
Svobodnyy
Chegdomyn
Aleksandrovsk-Sakhalinskiy
Poronaysk
Mys Terpeniya

B

Yablonovyy Khrebet
Nerchinsk
Olovyannaya
Priargunsk
Krasnokamensk
Borzya
Manzhouli
Yakeshi
Hailar
(Hulunbuir)
Arxan
Solon
Baruun-Urt
Tamsagbulag

Genhe
Ergun Youqi
Jagdaqi
Blagoveshchensk
Heihe
(Aihui)
Nenjiang
Nehe
Bei'an
Hailun
Tieli
QIQIHAR
Anda
Suihua
HARBIN
Acheng
FUYU
Shuangcheng
Da'an
Hegang
Fujin
Qianjin
Tongjiang
JIAMUSI
Shuangyashan
Qitaihe
Hulin
Mishan
JIXI
Bikin

Obluchye
Birobidzhan
Khabarovsk
Vanino
Tongliao

RUSSIA

Khrebet Sikhote Alin
Tatarskiy Proliv
Sakhalin
Dolinsk
Yuzhno-Sakhalinsk
Kholmsk
La Perouse Str.
Rebun-To
Wakkanai
Ostrov Kunashir
Kitami
Asahikawa
HOKKAIDŌ
SAPPORO
Otaru
Muroran
Kushiro

C

COPYRIGHT PHILIP'S

HONG KONG, MACAU AND SHENZHEN
1:890 000

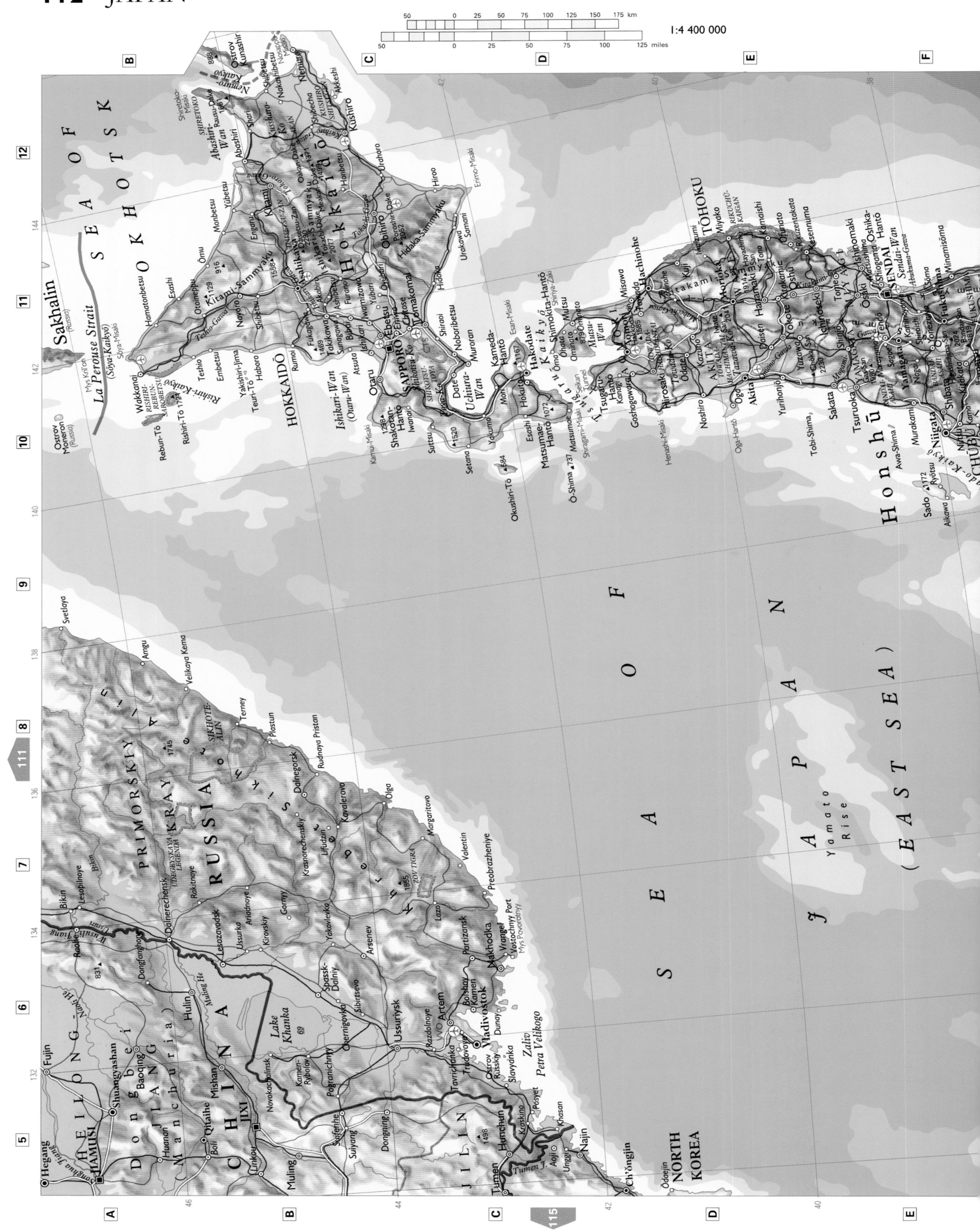

50   0   25   50   75   100   125   150   175 km
50   0   25   50   75   100   125 miles

1:4 400 000

SEA OF OKHOTSK

Sakhalin
(Russia)

La Perouse Strait
(Sōya-Kaikyō)

HOKKAIDŌ

SAPPORO

SEA OF JAPAN (EAST SEA)

Yamato Rise

TŌHOKU

SENDAI

Honshū

CHŪBU

RUSSIA

PRIMORSKIY KRAY

SIKHOTE-ALIN

Vladivostok

Lake Khanka

CHINA

HEILONGJIANG

Manchuria

JILIN

NORTH KOREA

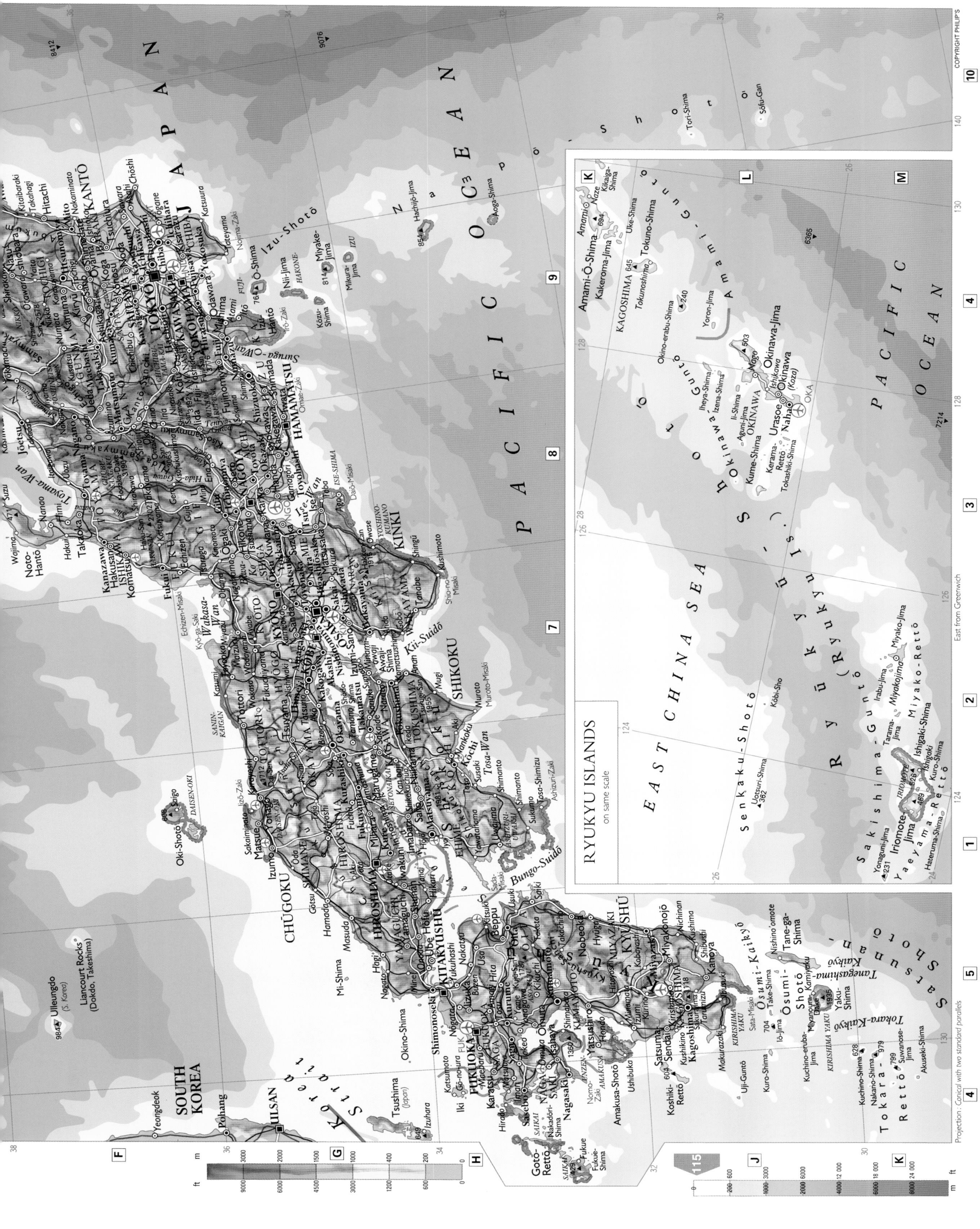

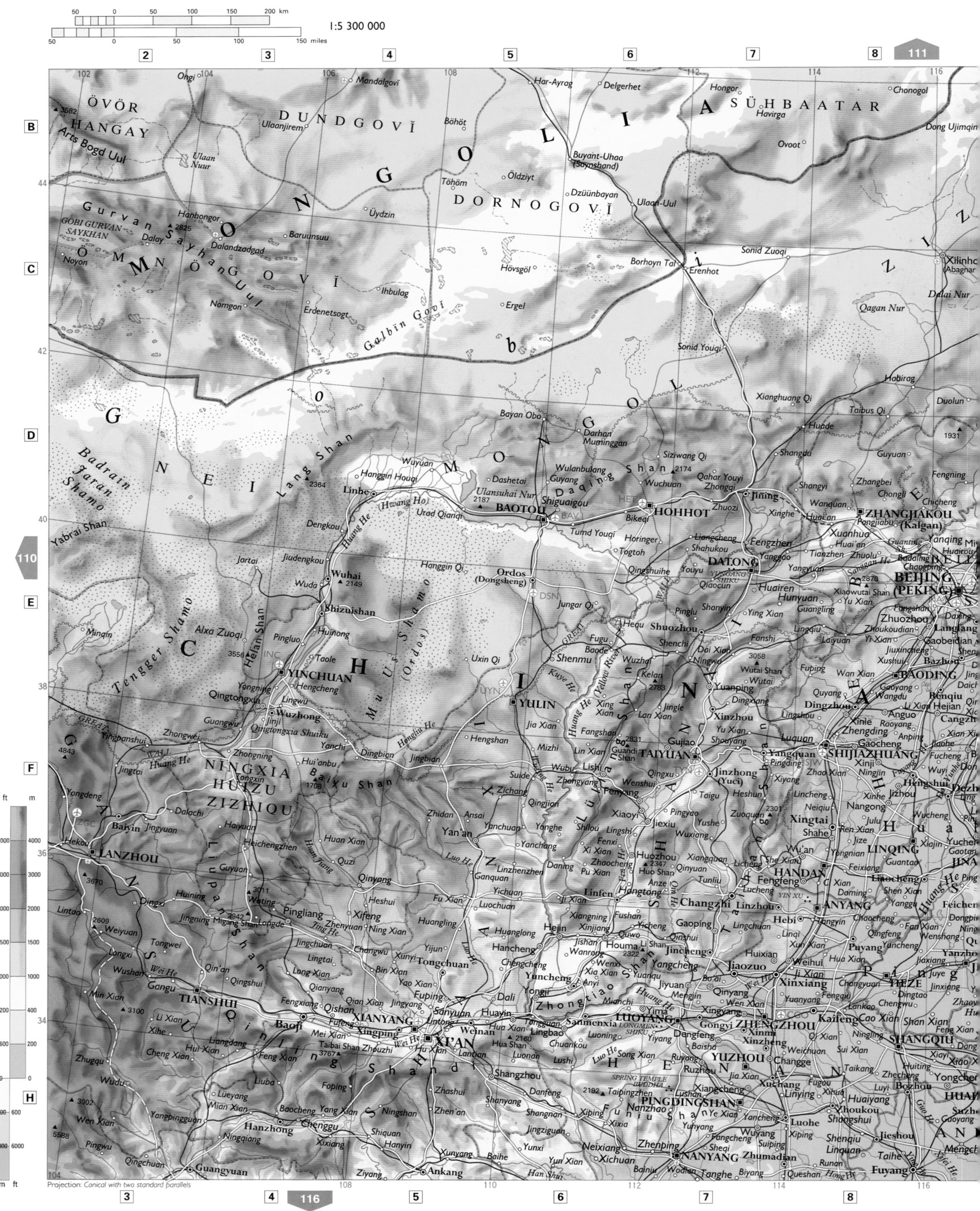

Projection: Conical with two standard parallels

B

RUSSIA

Horqin Youyi Qianqi
(Ulanhot)

HARBIN Bin Xian
Zhenlai
Maoxing Zhaoyuan Shuangcheng Acheng Yanshou
Baicheng Da'an Songhua Changchunling Shangzhi Linkou HXI Novokachalinsk
Taonan HEILONGJIANG
Anguang Qagan Yimianpo Hengdaohezi Muling
Nur Qian Sanchahe Wuchang Maqiaohe Lake
Huolin Gol Tuquan Gorlos Beitaolaizhao Yushu Shanhetun Hailin Xiaochengzi Khanka
Hulin He Tongyu Qian'an Kaishan MUDANJIANG Pogranichnyy
Shenjinzi Nong'an Dehui Shulan Muling Suiyang Suifenhe
Zhanyu Beizhengzhen JILIN Ning'an Dongning
Xinkai He Taipingchuan Fulongquan Changling Huaidezhen Jiutai Jiaohe Dongjingcheng Ussuriysk
Xi Ujimqin Qi Jarud Qi Horqin Zuoqi Zhongqi Maolin CHANGCHUN JILIN Xinzhan Emu Dunhua Daxinggou Razdolnoye
1949 Xebert CGO Fanjiatun Yongji Huangsongdian Ha Wangqing Tavrichanka
Bairin Ar Horqin Qi Shuangyang Yitong Chunyang Mingyuegue Shixian Golenki
Zuoqi Kailu Tongliao Shuangliao Lishu Gongzhuling Panshi Huadian Antu Tumen Vladivostok
Linxi Xar Moron He Jargalang Siping Liaoyuan Huija Longjing Yanji Hunchun Kraskino C
Bairin Youqi Xilao He Bamiancheng Xifeng Dongfeng Huinan Quanyang Baihe Helong Hoeryong Posyet Khasan
Ongniud Qi Laoha He Changtu Kangping Meihekou Jingyu Songjianghe 1677 Changbai Shan Musan Aoji 42
2020 Hure Qi Xiawa Wutonghaolai Faku Tiefa Kaiyuan Luhe Baishan Paekdu-san Puryong Unggi
CHIFENG Aohan Qi Fuxin Zhangwu Xinlitun Tieling Qingyuan Hunjiang Linjiang 2744 Nanam Puyong Najin
(Ulanhad) Heishui Xinmin Liao He Shanchengzhen Jiangyuan Chunggang-up Changbai 2541 Ch'ŏngjin
Beipiao Qinghemen Piao'ertun Shiren Fusong Tonghua Huch'ang Kyŏngsŏng
Weichang 1885 Ningcheng Heishan SHENYANG FUSHUN Tianshifu Huanren 1846 Manp'o Hapsu Ōdaejin D
Chaoyang Beizhen Sujiatun SHE Benxi Qinghecheng Ji'an Kasan-dong Hyesan Kapsan Kilchu
Chengle Jianping Liaozhong Anping Kuandian Yalu Wiwŏn Puksubaek-san Musudan
Longhua Lingyuan Gongchangling Kanggye 2522 Kimch'aek
Pingquan LIAONING ANSHAN Pyŏktong Ch'osan Changjin- P'ungsan (Sŏngjin)
Chengde Liaoyang Haicheng Koin ho Iwŏn Tanch'ŏn
Jinzhou Panjin Niuzhuang Supung Changjin Pujŏn-ho Kwangdong Pukch'ŏng
Luanhe Lingyuan Jinzhou 1846 Dashiqiao Shuiku Sinhung Changhŭngni Sinch'ang
Jianchang HUXI Tianzhuangtai Yingkou Fengcheng Taegwan Pukch'ŏng 40
Xingcheng Huludao Xinglongtai Boyuquan Gaizhou Xiuyan Pakch'ŏn Pukch'in Oro Hongwon
Shangbancheng Kuancheng 1846 Shuangshanzi Wanfu 1131 Bayun Shan Dandong Uiju Huichon Hamhŭng Hŭngnam
Zunhua Qian'an Liaodong Langtou Dongang Sinŭiju Pukchin Sinpung Hongwon
Fengrun Lulong Gushan Sinamp'o Kusŏng Kujang Oro
Liugou Wan Wafangdian Xiongyuecheng Pyongyang Ch'ŏngju Pakch'ŏn NORTH Tongjosŏn-man
YANGSHAN TIANJIN SHI Fuji Qinhuangdao Changli Baoding Bandao Zhuanghe Yalu Jiang Sŏnch'ŏn Anju KOREA Ch'ŏngyang E
Qinhuangdao Linxi Leting Pulandian Changshan Sinmi-do Sukch'ŏn Sunch'on Yŏnghŭng Wŏnsan
TIANJIN Hangu Jingtang (Xinjin) Pikou Sukch'ŏn P'yŏngsong Kowŏn Munch'ŏn
Tanggu Caofeidian Jinzhou Qundao Cho-do Sunan Kangdong Anbyŏn
Dagu Changli (Jin Xian) (China) KOREA P'YŎNGYANG Chunghwa Tongyang Kojŏ
Oikou Lüshun DALIAN Bay NAMP'O Suan Kosan Kosŏng SEA OF
Huanghua 465 DLC (Lüda) Sariwŏn Sepo-ri Hoeyang 1638 JAPAN
Huanghuagang Bo Hai Haixia Chaeryŏng Sinmak Pyŏnggang Changdo-a Gangseong
Yonshan Miaodao Nam-ch'ŏn Cheorwon Hwacheon 38 (EAST SEA)
BO HAI Qundao Changyŏn Sinch'ŏn Kŭmch'ŏn Pyŏnggang Hwacheon Yang-yang
Qingyun (China) Haeju Kaesŏng Panmunjom 1708 Sokcho
Wudi Dongyinggang Korea Ongjin Yŏnan Munsan Uijeongbu Chuncheon Ulleungdo
Huimin Penglai Baengnyeongdo GOYANG SEOUL Hongcheon 984 (S. Korea)
Hang He Longkou Daxindian Bay (S. Korea) Bucheon SEONGNAM Hoengseong Donghae F
Laizhou YANTAI INCHEON Ansan Anyang Wonju Gangneung
Zhanhua Wan Huang Xian Fushan Weihai Gyeonggi-man SUWON Yong-in Yeongwol Samcheok
Binzhou Dongying Zhaoyuan Muping Chengshan Jiao Pyeongtaek Chungju Jecheon Uljin
Dajiao Qixia 923 Wendeng Cheonan Yecheon Yeongju
ZIBO Huantai Shouguang Changyi Rongcheng SOUTH Andong Yeongdeok
Linzi Hanting Laiyang Seosan Cheongju Heunghae
Mashangcun Yidu Fangzi Laixi Haiyang Boryeong KOREA Sangju Uiseong 36
Shan WEIFANG Jimo Seosan Gongju DAEJEON Gimcheon Yeongcheon Pohang
Zhoucun XINTAI Anqiu Gaomi Chengyang Boryeong Nonsan Yeongdong Waegwan Gyeongju
Boshan Lingqu Zhucheng Lancun TAO Gangyeong Yeongdong Gumi
AN'AN Laiwu 1108 Jiaozhou QINGDAO Anmyeondo Iksan DAEGU Cheongdo
XINTAI Mengyin Yishui Huangdao Gunsan Jeonju Gyeongsan ULSAN
 DONG Yi'nan Wulian Jiaonan Jiaozhou Wan Buan Geochang Hamyang Miryang G
Pingyi Ju Xian YELLOW SEA Jeong-eup Namwon Jirisan 1915 Jinju Masan Gimhae
Rizhao (HUANG HAI) GWANGJU Damyang Chang-won PUS BUSAN
Fei Xian Tangtou Naju Hadong Sacheon Geoje
Fengzhou Lanshantou Suncheon Gwangyang Tong-yeong
ZAOZHUANG Linshu Ganyu Mokpo Boseong Beolgyo Yeosu
Linyi Haizhou Wan Lianyungang Boseong 649 Tsushima
Jiawang LINYI Hanzhuang Pizhou Tancheng Jangheung Haenam Izuhara (Japan) 34
Cangshan Heuksando Jindo Korea Strait
XINYI LIANYUNGANG (S. Korea) Jindo
XUZHOU Yaowan Chenjiagang Soheuksando Iki Karatsu 113
Shuangzhai Xiangshui (S. Korea) JAPAN Kashima Imari
Suining Da Yunhe Guannan Jeju Haehyŏp Hallim Saeba H
SUQIAN Binhai Jeju-do (S. Korea) Hallasan Nakadōri-Shima Ōmura Isahaya
Siyang Funing Jeju Daejeong Hamyeong Nagasaki
Sihong Huaiyin HUAI'AN Sheyang Seogwipo Namjeju Fukue-Shima Kuchinotsu
Lingbi Hongze Chuzhou Baoying Liuzhuang 429
Sixian Hu XINGHUA YANCHENG
Guzhen Wuhe Gaoyou Dafeng
Bengbu Fengyang Baiju Dongtai

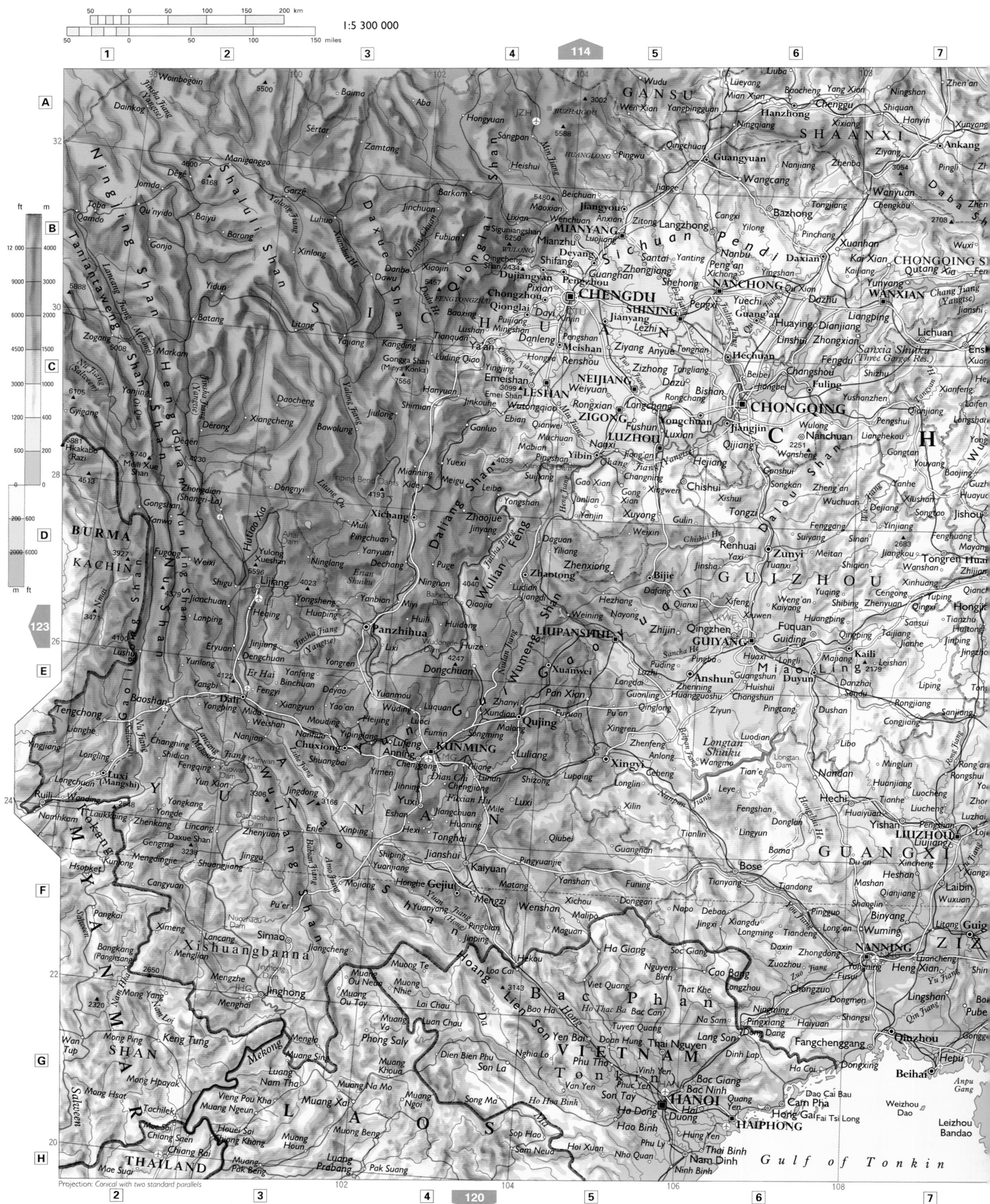

Projection: Conical with two standard parallels

8 9 10 115 11 12 13 14

SOUTH
CHINA
SEA

HAINAN
on same scale

HAINAN
Dao
(China)

CHINA

Gulf of
Tonkin

VIETNAM

Luzon
Strait

East from Greenwich

COPYRIGHT PHILIP'S

1:11 100 000

Projection: Mercator

East from Greenwich

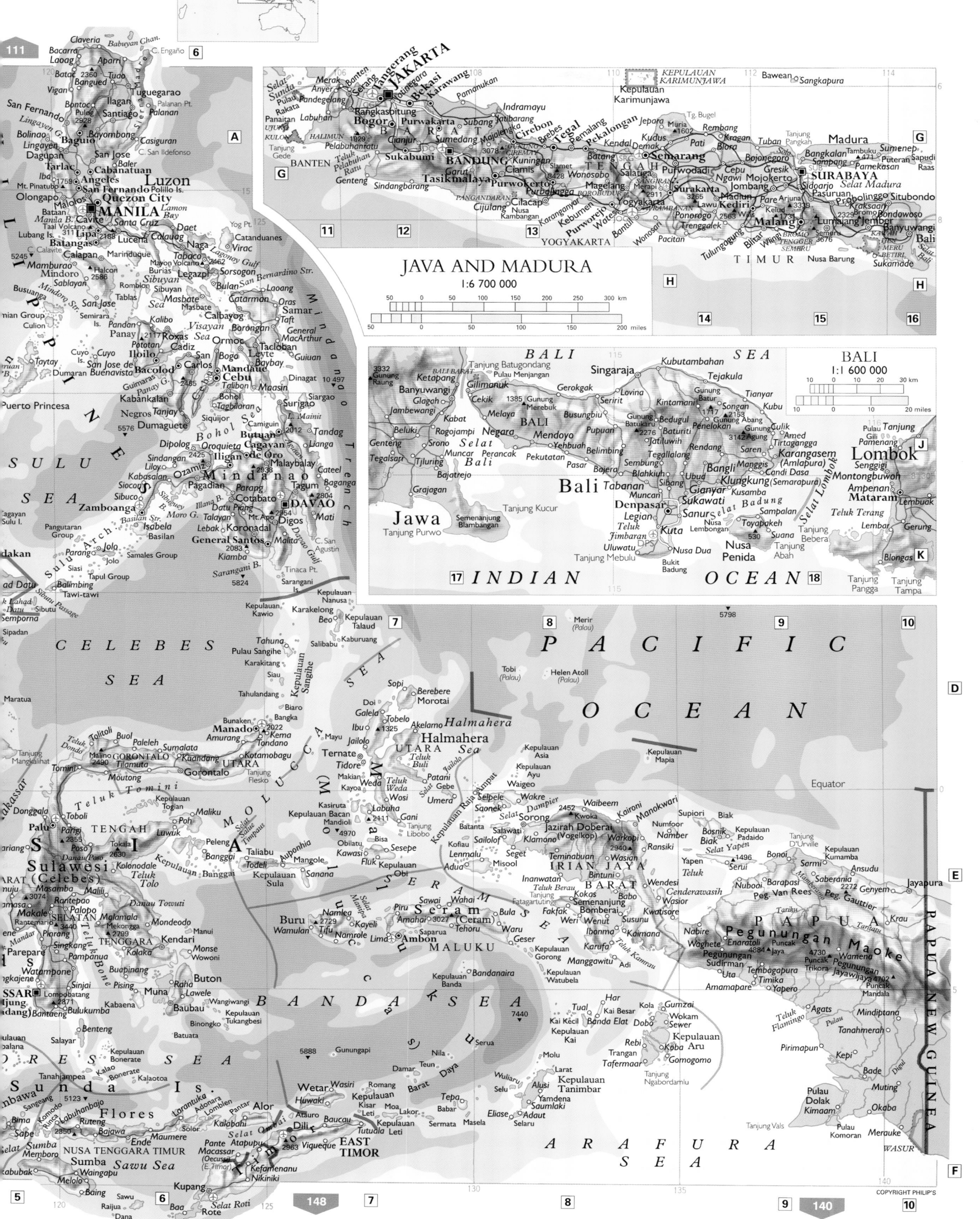

1:5 300 000

COPYRIGHT PHILIP'S

b

Gulf of Thailand

KO SAMUI
1:900 000

Ko Samui

Chong Phangan
Ban Sam Rong
Laem Sam Rong
Ban Mae Nam
Na Thon
Ko Thong Yang
Chaweng
Khao Phiu 635
Ben Lamai
Ben Hua Thanon
Ban Thong
Kut
Ko Matsum
Laem
Hin Khom
Ko Taen
Chong Samui
Ko Rap
Ban Na Bo

KO SAMUI
1:900 000
Ko Ang Thong
MU KO
ANG THONG
Ko Phaluai
Ko Thalu
Ko Chuak
Ko Nok
Ta Phao
Don Sak

a

KO PHUKET
1:900 000

Ko Yao
Ko Yao Noi
Ko Yao Yai
AO
PHANGNGA
Ko Raya Ring
Ban Khlong
Khian
Laem Rang
Nakha Yai
Ko Yamu
Ban Bong Rong
Ban Bong Khu
Amphoe
Phra
Ko Maphrao
Laem Nga
Phuket
Ao Makham
Ko Lon
Takua Thung
Ban Khuan
Nai Yong
Ao
Kung
Kao 442
Ban Phok Chit
Ao Supam
Ko Mai Thon
Khok Kloi
Ban Tha Nun
Ban Tha Rua
Ban Wa
Amphoe
Kathu 520
Amphoe
Thalang
Ban Ao Tu Kun
SIRINAT
HKT
Ban Sakhu
Muang Mai
Ko Phara
Laem Phan Wa
Ao Karon
Ban Kata
Ao Rawai
Ban Katoi
Ko Hae
Ao Patong
Ban Patong
Laem
Son
Ao Karon
Ban Katoi
Ao Kata
Laem Phrom Thep
Ko Phuket

ANDAMAN SEA

c

Selat Utara
Tanjung Tokong
George Town
Butterworth
Kepala
Bates
Bukit
Tengah
Bukit
Mertajam
Teluk Bahang
Tanjung Muka
Pulau
Tikus
Tanjung
Bungah
Ayer
Itam
Batu
Feringghi
Bukit
Bendera 833
342
PEN
Teluk
Kumbar
Balik Pulau
Bayan
Lepas
Gelugur
Gedung
Simpang
Ampat
Pulau
Jerejak
Pulau
Aman
Kuala
Kerian
Gertak
Sanggul
Tanjung
Gertak Sanggul
Pulau Kendi

**Pulau
Pinang**

PINANG
1:900 000

d

Straits of Singapore

Pulau Bintan
Pulau
Batam
BTH
Nongsa
Ngoyan
BATAM
INDONESIA
Sekupang
Bulang
Pulau Senang
Kampong Punggol
Kampong Tanjung
Langsat
Kampong
Peneperang
Telok
Ramunia
Tanjung
Penawar
Desaru
191
Kangkar
Chemaran
Sungai
Tiram
Kampong
Gelang Patah
Bukit
Nil
Kota
SINGAPORE
Johor
Bahru
Jurong
Sentosa
Serangoon
Queenstown
MALAYSIA

SINGAPORE
1:900 000

1:900 000

40 km
25 miles

8

M U N G

Cao Nguyen
2287
Da Lat
1818
Dran
Di Linh
Phan Rang–Thap Cham
Ba Ngoi
Cam Ranh
Ca Na
Ca Na
Phan Ri
Cua
Phan Thiet
Vinh Phan Thiet
Cu Lao Cham
Hon Hai

7

108

1580
Bao Loc
Bien Hoa
Long Khanh
Ba Ria
Vung Tau

J

THANH PHO HO CHI MINH
(Saigon)
My Tho
Ben Tre
Tra Vinh
Mekong
Vinh Long
CAN THO
Soc Trang
Bac Lieu
Ca Mau
Nam Can
Hon Khoai

PHNOM PENH
Tonlé Sap
Takeo
Kampot
Kep
Kampong Saom
(Sihanoukville)
Koh Kong

SOUTH CHINA SEA

Gulf of Thailand

Ko Chang
Ko Kut
Koh Kong
Koh Rong

Thailand

Prachuap Khirikhan
Chumphon
Ko Tao
Ko Phangan
Na Thon
Ko Samui
Surat Thani

**Kho Khot Kra
(Isthmus of Kra)**

Nakhon Si Thammarat
Phatthalung
Songkhla
Hat Yai
Yala
Narathiwat
Kota Bharu
KELANTAN
TERENGGANU
Kuala Terengganu
Kuantan
PAHANG
G. Tahan
2190
Cameron Highlands
Ipoh
PERAK
Taiping
Butterworth
George Town
PINANG
Alor Setar
KEDAH
PERLIS
Pulau Langkawi

MALAYSIA
**PENINSULAR
MALAYSIA**

Pulau Tioman
P. Aur
Mersing
JOHOR
Kluang
Batu Pahat
Muar
Melaka
MELAKA
**NEGERI
SEMBILAN**
Seremban
Port Dickson
SELANGOR
KUALA LUMPUR
Klang
Port Klang
Kajang

Straits of Malacca

**SUMATERA
UTARA**
Medan
Tebingtinggi
Pematangsiantar
GUNUNG
LEUSER
ACEH
Langsa

INDONESIA

Johor Bahru
SINGAPORE
BATAM
BTH
Bintan
Tanjungpinang
RIAU
Dumai
Pakanbaru

104 East from Greenwich

Kyun zu
(Mergui Archipelago)
Myeik
(Mergui Archipelago)

Projection: Conical with two standard parallels

9000 3000
6000 2000
4500 1500
3000 1000
2400 800
1800 600
1200 400
600 200
0
200 600
3000 1000
6000 2000
ft m

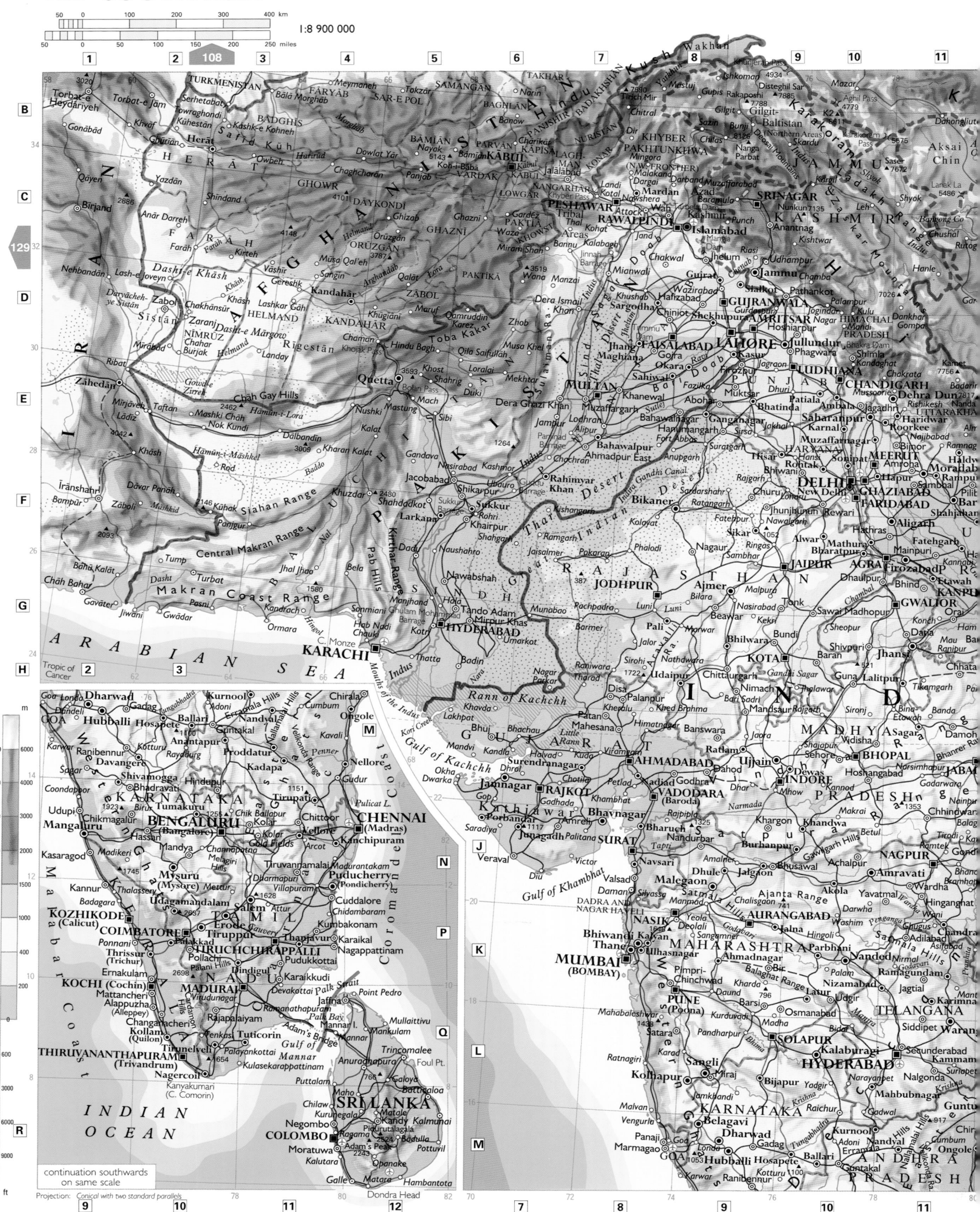

JIANG UYGUR ZIZHIQU Muz Tag
(SINKIANG)
·Pulu
Lun Shan
7723
Hoh Xil Shan
4767
Kunlun
Shankou
Maqên
Gangri 6282
Huang He
Maqu
B
·Maqên
6094
QINGHAI
34
Yushu
Dainkog
Dogai Coring
Bayan Har Shan
Huang He
C
Gyaring Hu
4237
Ngoring Hu
XIZANG
C H I N A
Dêngqên
Garzê
32
Tanggula (Dangla) Shan
Yushu
Dainkog
Ningjing Shan
Xinlong
ZIZHIQU
5180 Tanggula
Shankou
Baiyü
Dêgê
D
6714
Kangrinboqê Feng (Kailash)
Dongco
Amdo
Nagqu
Nangqên
Qamdo
SICHUAN
Markam
Yidun
Xinlong
30
116
Mapam
Yumco
Siling Co
4495
Nu Jiang
Lhorong
Bomi
Zhaxizê
Litang
Yajiang
E
Ombu
Coqên
Xainza
Nam Co
4627
Lhünzub
Namcha
Barwa
Gongbo'gyamda
Nyingchi
Gogên
Zayü
Hkakabo Razi
(Thala La)
6740
Zhongdian
28
Tangra
Yumco
Lhasa
Nyainqentanglha Shan
7088
5891
Nizamghat
Weixi
5596
Lijiang
F

BAY OF BENGAL

INDIAN OCEAN

1:5 300 000

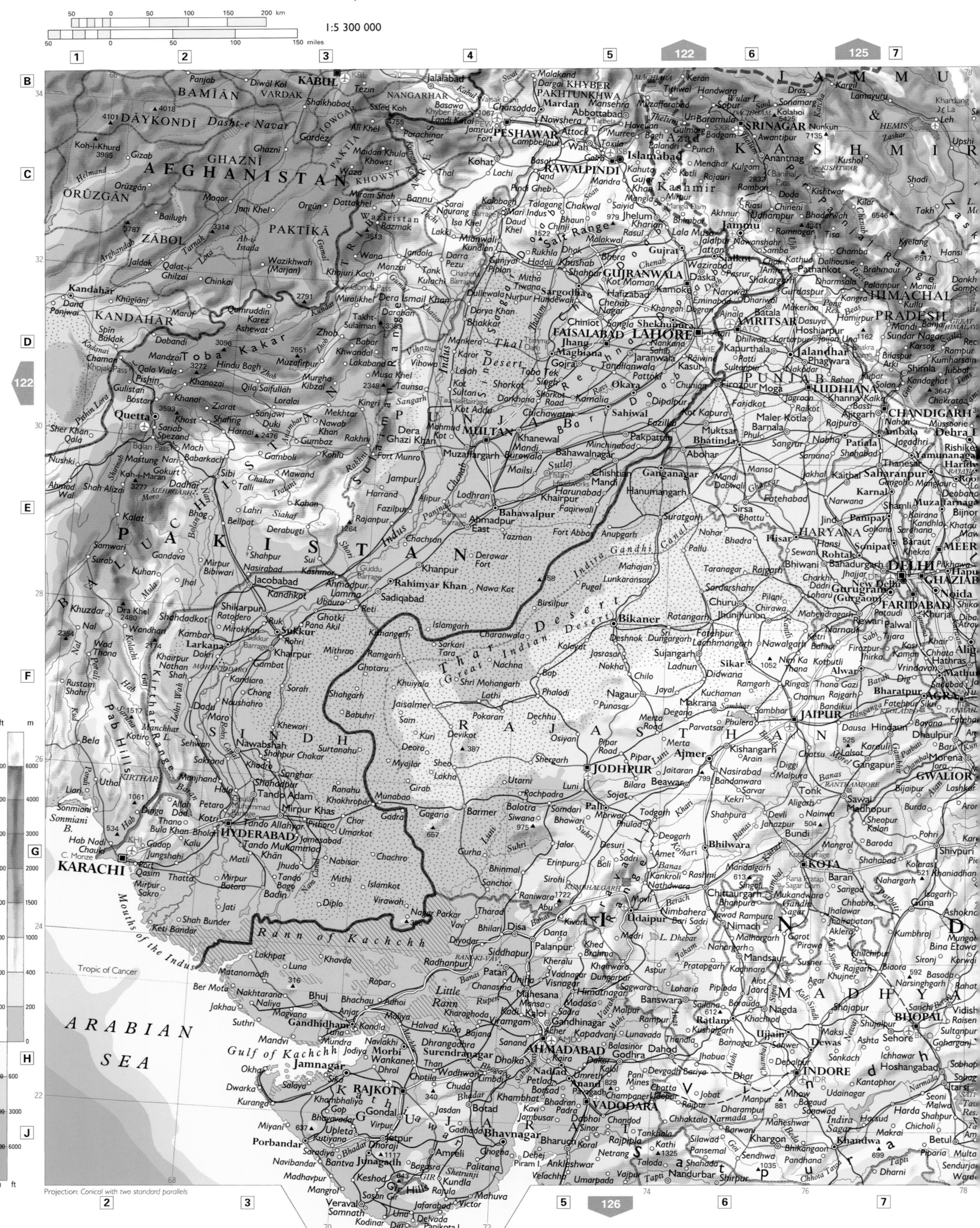

1:5 300 000

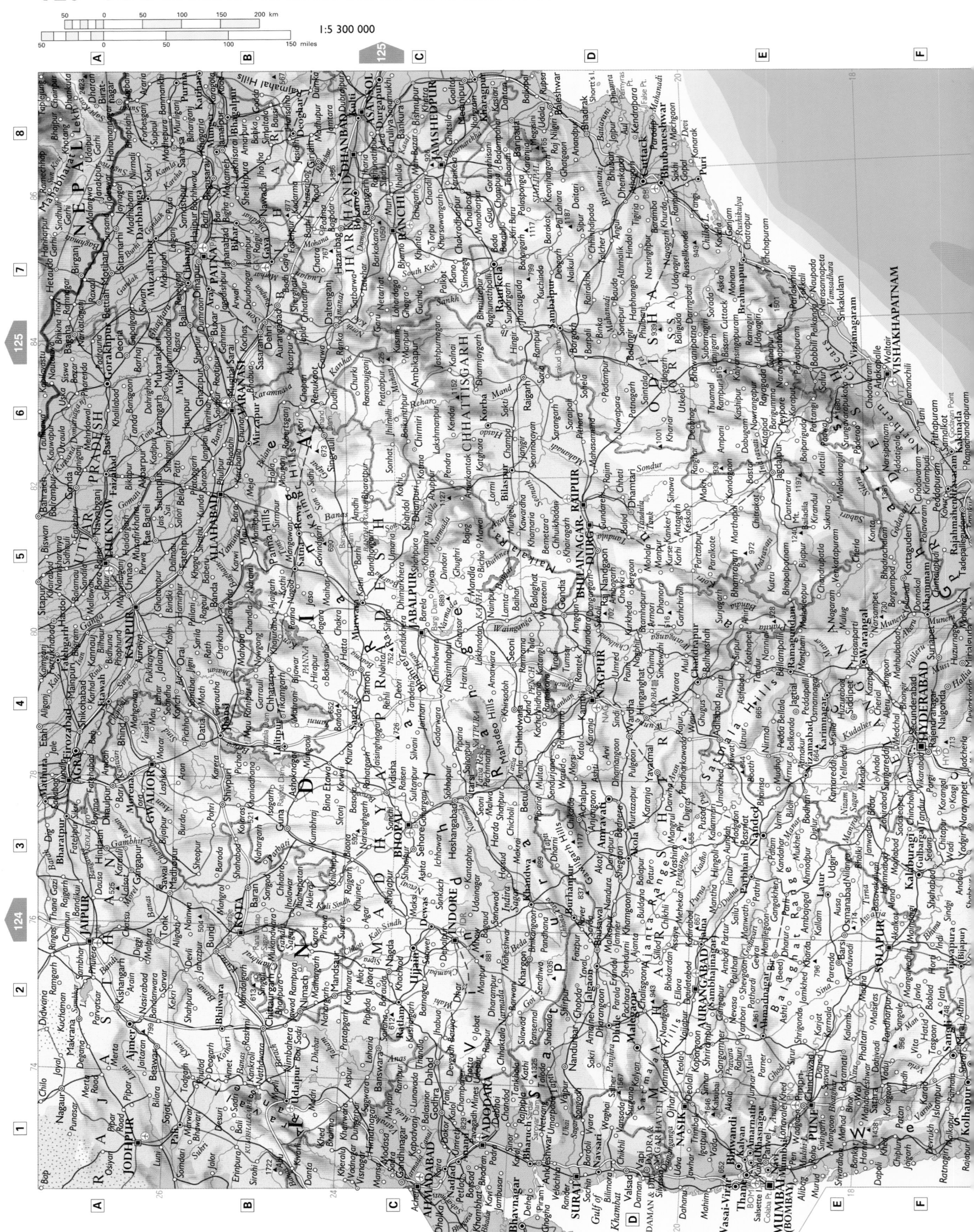

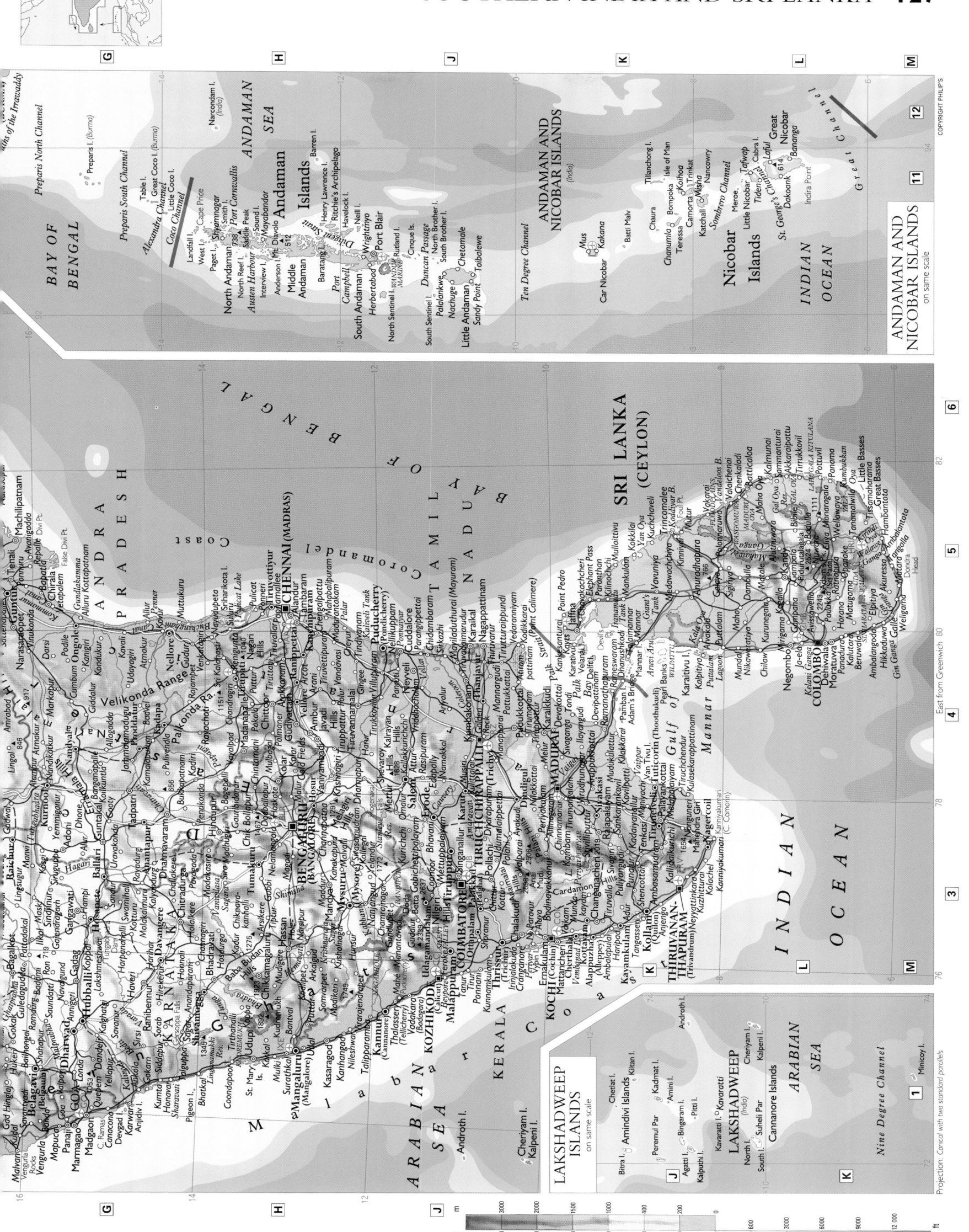

COPYRIGHT PHILIP'S

ANDAMAN AND
NICOBAR ISLANDS
on same scale

LAKSHADWEEP
ISLANDS
on same scale

Projection: Conical with two standard parallels

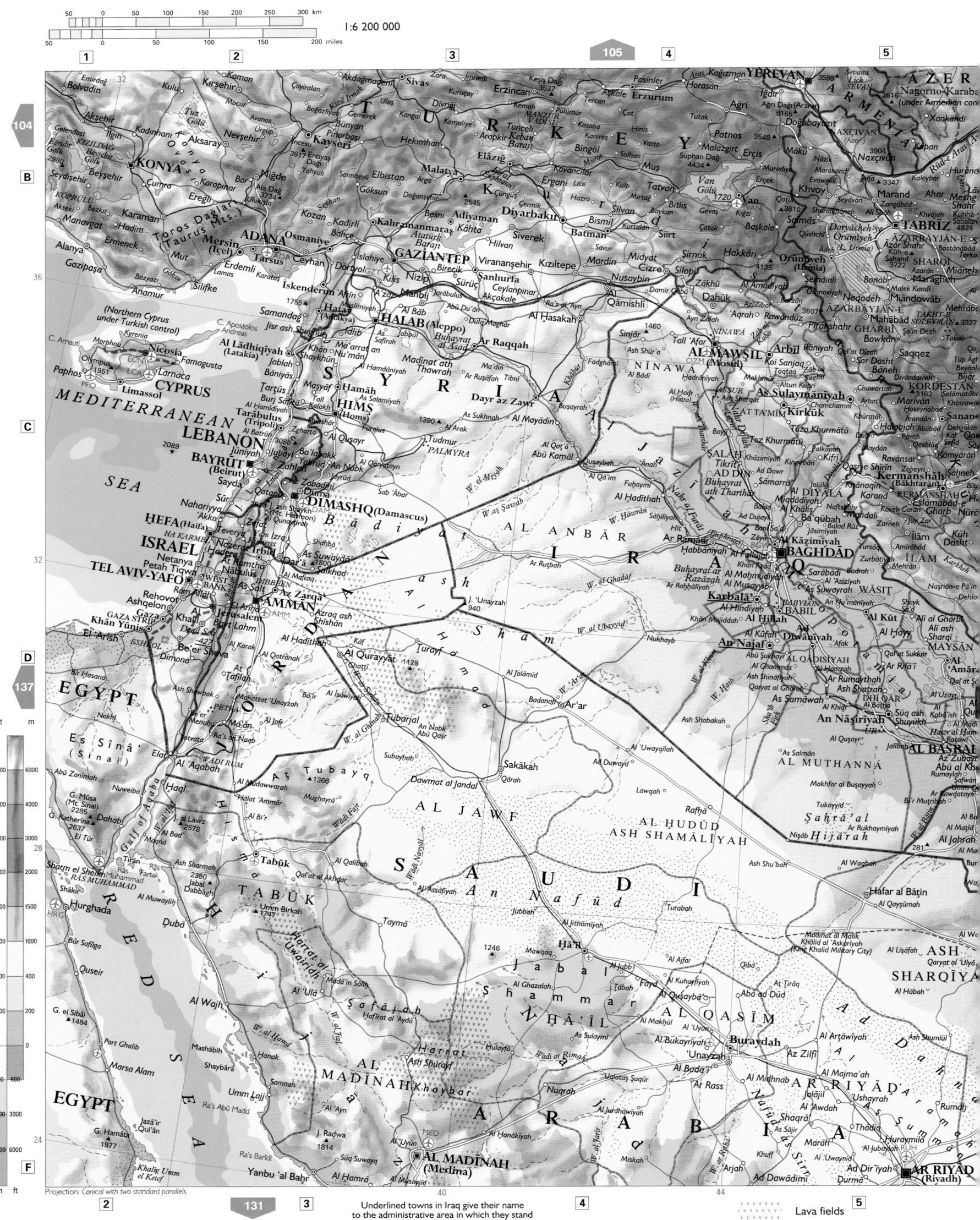

Projection: Conical with two standard parallels

Underlined towns in Iraq give their name
to the administrative area in which they stand

v v v v v   Lava fields

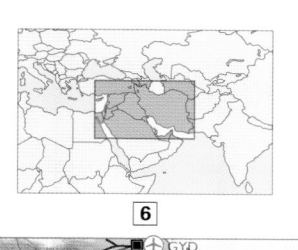

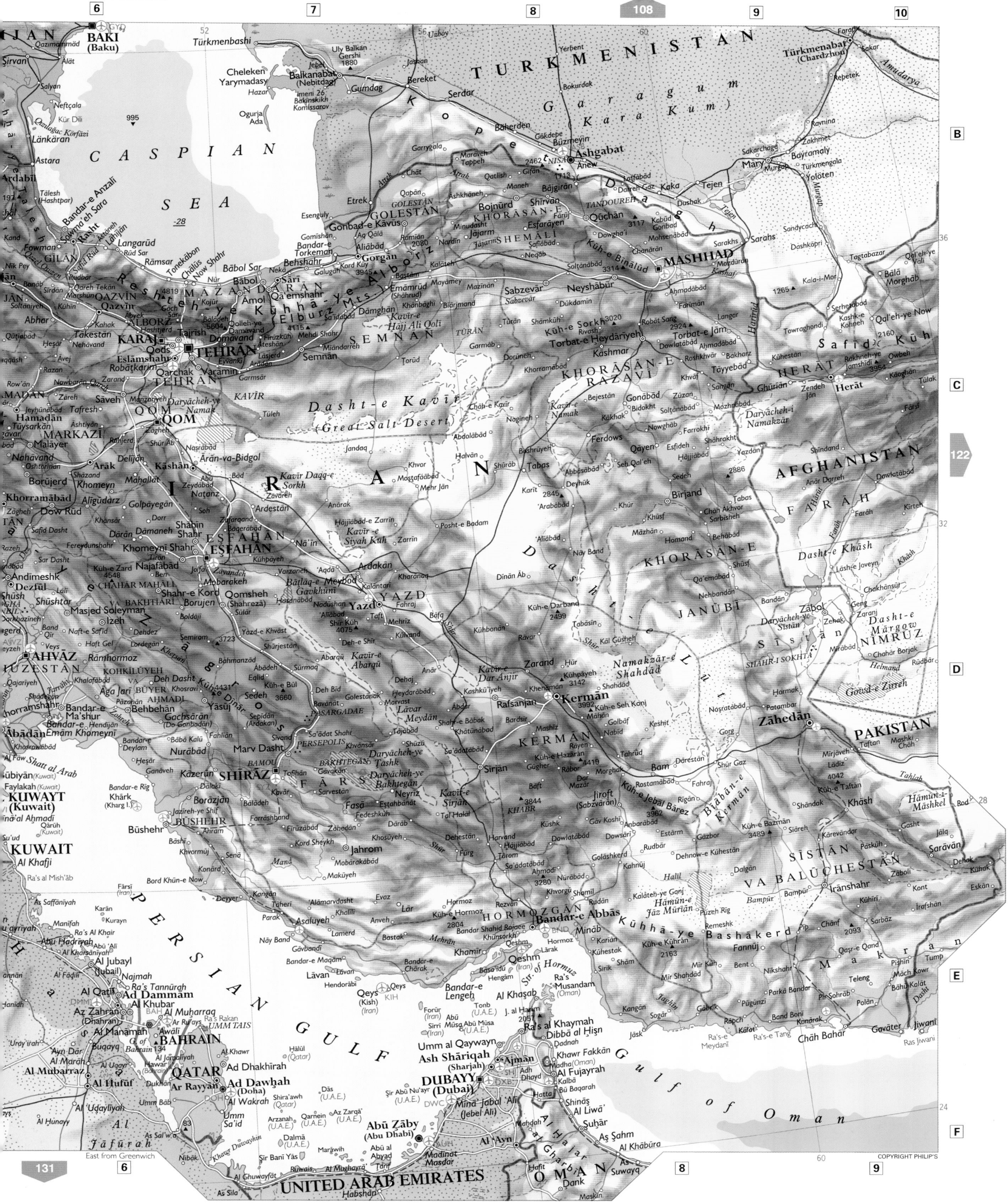

1:2 200 000

10 0 10 20 30 40 50 60 70 80 90 km
10 0 10 20 30 40 50 60 miles

CYPRUS

Paphos
PFO
Episkopi · Kividhes · Zyyi
Limassol
Akrotiri
Bay
Episkopi Bay
C. Gata

2775

2089

M E D I T E R R A N E A N

S E A

HIMS (Homs)
Al Hamidiyah
Tall Kalakh · Shinshar · Furqlus
Al Mina'
ASH SHAMAL
Al Hirmil · Al Qusayr
Tarabulus (Tripoli)
Zgharta · Qurnat as Sawda' 3088
Bsharri · Al Labwah · 2464 · Al Qaryatayn
Al Batrun
Jubayl · Qartaba · An Nabk · Bi'r Ghadir
Ibrahim
Ba'labakk · Yabrud
Juniyah
2628 · J. Sannin
BAYRUT (Beirut)
BEY
Bikfayya · Alayh · Zahlah · Singhaya
Ash Shuwayfat · Jayrud
Ad Damur
LEBANON
JABAL LUBNAN
1942 · J. al Barak
Sayda (Sidon) · Az Zabadani · Dumayr · Khan Abu Shamat
Jazzin · ash Shaykh · Barada
An Nabatiyah at Tahta
AL JANUB
Mt. Hermon 2814 · Darayya · DIMASHQ (Damascus)
Sur (Tyre) · Marj 'Uyun · Al Khiyam · Qatana · Jaramanah
Qiryat Shemona · Q. Mas'ada · Al Kiswah · Al Hajanah
Ma'alot-Tarshiha · 1197 · Al Qunaytirah · Buraq
Nahariyya · Hagalil · Ar Rafid · As Sanamayn
'Akko (Acre) · Zefat · Golan · W. al Harir · Shabba · AS SUWAYDA
Mifraz Hefa · (Galilee) · Yam Kinneret (Sea of Galilee) · Fiq · Shaykh Miskin
Qiryat Yam · HAZAFON · Karmi'el · Saham al Jawlan · Dar'a · As Suwayda · Salah 1800
HEFA (Haifa) · Qiryat Ata · Teverya (Tiberias) · -210
Har Ha Karmel 546 · HA KARMEL · Nazerat (Nazareth) · Yarmuk · Irbid
TEL MEGIDDO · Afula · Taiyiba · Malah
Umm el Fahm · Bet She'an · Irbid
CAESAREA · Shomron · Tirat Zevi · AJLUN · Al Mafraq · Umm al Qittayn
Hadera · SAMARIA · 'Ajlun · Umm al Daraj · DIBBEEN · 1247 · Jarash
Netanya · Jenin · Tubas · JARASH
ISRAEL
HAMERKAZ · Nabulus · N. az Zarqa · AL MAFRAQ
Herzliyya · Tulkarm · Ra'anana
Bene Beraq · Kefar Sava
TEL AVIV-YAFO · Petah Tiqwa · SHILOH · AL BALQA'
Bat Yam · Ramat Gan · Tila' al 'Ali · Az Zarqa
Holon · Lod · WEST BANK · As Salt · Ar Rusayfah
Rishon le Ziyyon · Ramla · Ram Allah · 289 · AMMAN
Yavne · Rehovot · El Ariha (Jericho) · Wadi as Sir · Az Zarqa
Ashdod · Na'ur · Al Quwaysimah · Azraq ash Shishan · AMM
Qiryat Mal'akhi · Bet Shemesh · Jerusalem (Yerushalayim / Al Quds) · Ma'daba · AZ ZARQA
Ashqelon · Qiryat Gat · Bayt Lahm (Bethlehem) · MA'DABA
Beit Lahiya · N. Shiqma · TEL LAKHISH · MA'DABA
GAZA STRIP · Jabalya · Gaza · El Khalil (Hebron) · Dhiban · UMM AR RASAS · Al Hadithah
Sederot · Wadi al Haydan
Deir al Balah · Nuseirat · Rahat · Zahiriyya · En Gedi · AL 'ASIMA
Khan Yunis · ESHKOL · -422
Rafah · Be'er Sheva (Beersheba) · Arad · MASADA · Al Qatranah
Bur Sa'id (Port Said) · 'En Boqeq · W. al Mujib
Bur Fu'ad · Al Karak · Al Ghadaf
BUR SA'ID · Ras Burun · El Daheir · Bor Mashash · AL KARAK · Al Mazar
Sabkhet el Bardawil · El 'Arish · Dimona · 1305
Khalig el Tina · Bir el 'Abd · Bir el Gararat · Bir Lahfan · Sedom · 333 · W. al Hasa · JORDAN
Ramani · Bir Kaseiba · HADAROM · W. Bar
Bir el 'Abd · W. 'Arish · At Tafilah · Ba'ir
El Qantara · Bir Qatia · Bir el Duweidar · SHAMAL SINI · Qezi'ot · AT TAFILAH
Bir el Jafir · Abu 'Aweigila · Dana
Wahid · Bir Madkur · Birein · Sede Boqer · -121
Ismâ'ilîya · 892 · El Quseima · Muweilih · Mizpe Ramon · Nijil · Al Jafr
ISMA-ILIYA · Bir el Malhi · Rujm Tal'at al Jamaliya · 1736
Khamsa · Bir Hasana · Bir Beida · Hanegev (Negev Desert) · PETRA · Ma'an
El Buheirat el Murrat el Kubra (Great Bitter L.) · G. Yi 'Allaq 1094 · Wadi Musa · MA'AN
Gineifa · Bir el Thamada · W. el Bruk · W. Qnaiya · El 'Agrud · N. Paran · N. Hiyyon · Ras 'an Naqb
EGYPT · El Wabeira · Mamarr Mitla · Bir Gebel Hisn · W. Madhasin · El Kuntilla · Al 'Aqabah
ES SINA (Sinai) · Ain Sudr · Nakhl · El Thamad · Bi'r Abu Muhammad · Yotvata · Mahattat ash Shidiya
El Suweis (Suez) · Bur Taufiq · 948 · W. el Agaba · N. Girafi · Ras 'an Naqb · 1435
Adabiya · 'Uyun Musa · g. el Kabrit · Bir el Biarat · 1592 · WADI RUM · SAUDI
Ras Sudr · JANUB SINI · Bir el Mari · 1754 · Batn al Ghul · ARABIA
Ghubbet el Bus · W. Abu Ga'da · W. Abel Gein · Bir Taba · Rum · At Tubayq
Abu Sandug 1272 · Ras Matarma · 1165 · Elat · Al Aqabah · Al Mudawwarah
Bir Wuseit · Haql
EL SUWEIS
Gulf of 'Aqaba

SYRIA
DIMASHQ
DARA
Al Quṭayfah

Projection: Polyconic

East from Greenwich

=== 1974 Cease Fire Lines

COPYRIGHT PHILIP'S

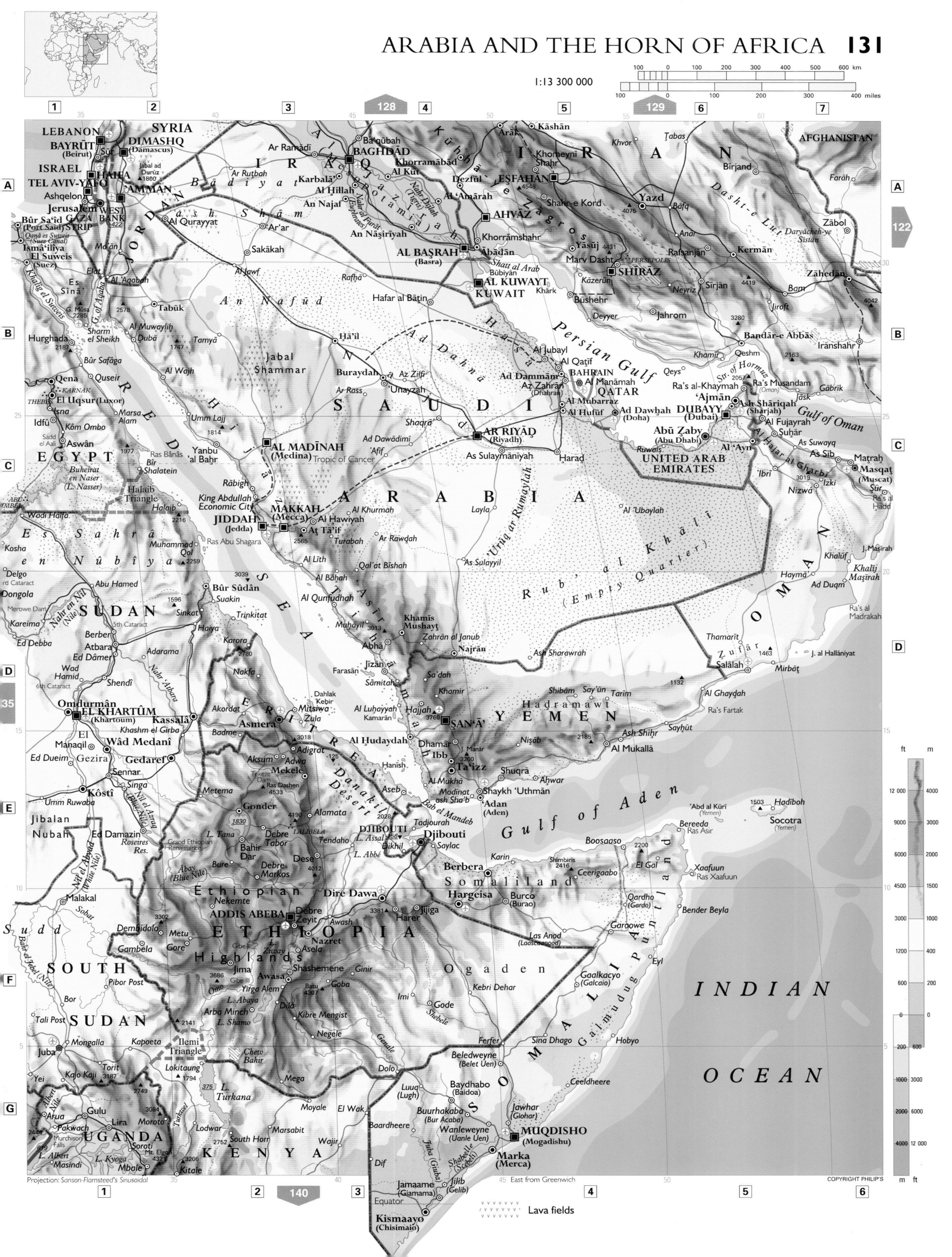

1:13 300 000

100   0   100   200   300   400   500   600 km
100   0   100   200   300   400 miles

LEBANON
BAYRŪT
(Beirut)
SYRIA
DIMASHQ
(Damascus)
Sūr
Jabal ad
Durūz
1800
Ar Ramādī
BAGHDĀD
Ba'qūbah
Arāk
Kāshān
AFGHANISTAN
Khvor
Ṭabas
Birjand
Farāh

ISRAEL
TEL AVIV-YAFO
HAIFA
AMMAN
Ar Ruṭbah
Karbalā'
Al Ḥillah
An Najaf
Khorramābād
Al Kūt
Dezfūl
EṢFAHĀN
4548
Khomeyni
Shahr
Yazd
4075
Birjand
Farāh
Zābol

A
Jerusalem
WEST
BANK
GAZA
STRIP
Būr Sa'īd
(Port Said)
Iṣmā'īliya
El Suweis
(Suez)
422
Al Qurayyāt
Ar'ar
An Nāṣirīyah
AHVĀZ
Khorramshahr
Ābādān
Marv Dasht
Yāsūj 4431
PERSEPOLIS
SHĪRĀZ
Rafsanjān
Kermān
Anār
Daryācheh-ye
Sīstān
Zāhedān
4042

Qanā es Suweis (Suez Canal)
Sharm
el Sheikh
G. Mūsa
2285
Elat
Al 'Aqabah
Sakākah
AL BAṢRAH
(Basra)
Shaṭṭ al 'Arab
Būbiyān
Khārk
AL KUWAYT
KUWAIT
Bandar-e Abbās
Īrānshahr

B
Hurghada
Būr Safāga
2187
Tabūk
Al Muwayliḥ
Dubā
Tamyā
2578
1747
An Nafūd
Ḥā'il
Ad Dahnā
Al Jubayl
Al Qaṭīf
BAHRAIN
Al Manāmah
QATAR
Ad Dawḥah
(Doha)
Hafar al Bāṭin
Būshehr
Deyyer
Khamīr
Qeshm
2057
Str. of Hormuz
Ra's al-Khaymah
Ra's Musandam
(Oman)
Jāsk
Gābrik
3280

Qena
Quseir
Al Wajh
Tamyā
Jabal
Shammar
Burãydah
Az Zilfī
Ar Rass
'Unayzah
Ad Dammām
Az Zahrān
(Dhahran)
Al Mubarraz
'Ajmān
Ash Shāriqah
(Sharjah)
DUBAYY
(Dubai)
Al Fujayrah
Ṣuḥār
As Suwayq
2163
Qeys

KARNAK
THEBES
El Uqsur (Luxor)
Isna
Idfū
Kôm Ombo
Umm Lajj
1814
Rābigh
SAUDI
Shaqrā'
AR RIYĀḌ
(Riyadh)
Al Ḥufūf
Abū Ẓaby
(Abu Dhabi)
Ruwais
UNITED ARAB
EMIRATES
Al 'Ayn
Ibrī
Nizwā
3019
Izki
Maṭraḥ
Masqaṭ
(Muscat)
Shūr
As Sīb

C
EGYPT
Aswān
1977
Sadd
el 'Ali
Buheirat
en Naser
(L. Nasser)
Bîr
Shalatein
2216
Halaib
Halaib
Triangle
ABU
MBEA
Ras Bânas
King Abdullah
Economic City
MAKKAH
(Mecca)
JIDDAH
(Jedda)
ARABIA
Ad Dawādimī
'Afīf
As Sulaymāniyah
Layla
Ḥarad
Al 'Ubaylah
Al Khurmah
2565
Aṭ Ṭā'if
Ar Rawḍah
Tropic of Cancer
OMAN
3019
Ra's al
Madrakah
Khalūf
J. Maṣīrah
Khalīj
Maṣīrah

Wâdi Halfa
Es
Sahrâ
en
Nûbîya
Delgo
3rd Cataract
Dongola
Kareima
Merowe Dam
Kosha
Muhammad
Qol
2259
Rābigh
Al Līth
Qal'at Bīshah
As Sulayyil
Rub' al Khālī
(Empty Quarter)
Ūrūq ar Rumaylah
Ash Sharawrah
Thamarīt
1463
Hayma'
Ad Duqm
Ṣalālah
Mirbāṭ
Zufār
J. al Hallāniyat

D
SUDAN
Abu Hamed
Berber
Atbara
Ed Dâmer
Wad
Hamid
6th Cataract
Shendî
Nahr 'Atbara
Adarama
Karora
Haiya
1596
Sinkat
Bûr Sûdân
Suakin
Trinkitat
3039
Al Bāḥah
Al Qunfudhah
Muḥāyil
3013
Abhā
Khamis
Mushayṭ
Zahrān al Janub
Najrān
2780
Sāmitah
Farasān
Jīzān
Sa'dah
Khamir
Shibām
Say'ūn
Tarīm
2185
Al Ghaydah
1132
Ra's Fartak

E
35
Omdurmân
EL KHARTÛM
(Khartoum)
KASSALÂ
Asmera
ERITREA
Akordat
Mitsiwa
Dahlak
Kebir
Zula
Al Luḥayyah
Kamarān
Hajjah
3760
ṢAN'Ā'
Dhamār
J. Manār
Ibb
3200
Ta'izz
Al Mukallā
Ash Shiḥr
Sayḥūt
Ra's Fartak

El Manãqil
Wâd Medanî
Gedaref
Khashm el Girba
Badme
Adigrat
3018
Aksum
Adwa
Mekele
Ras Dashen
4533
Metema
Hanish
Al Ḥudaydah
Zabīd
Shuqrā
Aḥwar
Madīnat
ash Sha'b
Adan
(Aden)

F
El Dueim
Gezira
Sennar
Kôstî
Umm Ruwaba
Singa
Gonder
L. Tana
1830
4190
Alamata
Debre
Tabor
Bahir
Dar
Dese
4012
Abay
(Blue Nile)
Bure
Debre
Markos
Nekemte
ADDIS ABEBA
Debre
Zeyit
Grand Ethiopian
Renaissance Dam
L. Abbé
L. Assal
156
Dikhil
DJIBOUTI
Tadjourah
Tendaho
Danakil
Desert
Bab el Mandeb
Djibouti
Saylac
Boosaaso
Karin
'Abd al Kūrī
(Yemen)
1503
Hadībo
Bereeda
Ras Asir
Socotra
(Yemen)
Gulf of Aden

SOUTH
SUDAN
Malakal
Sobat
Jibalan
Nubah
Ed Damazin
Roseires Res.
Dembidolo
Metu
Gambela
Gore
3302
Nil el Azraq
(Blue Nile)
Nil el Abyad
(White Nile)
Ethiopian
Highlands
Jima
3686
Awasa
Nazret
Awash
3381
Harer
Jijiga
Diré Dawa
Hargeisa
Berbera
Burco
(Burao)
Qardho
(Gardo)
Shimbiris
2416
Ceerigaabo
El Gal
Xaafuun
Ras Xaafuun
Bender Beyla
2200
INDIAN
Somaliland

Asela
Shashemene
Ginir
Goba
Batu
4307
Ogaden
Las Anod
(Laascaanood)
Garoowe
Galkayo
(Galcaio)
Eyl

Pibor Post
Bor
Tali Post
Jibalan
Yirga Alem
Gibe I
Arba Minch
L. Abaya
Dila
Kibre Mengist
Negele
Gode
Imi
Kebri Dehar
Shebele
Ferfer
Sina Dhago
Hobyo
Ceeldheere

G
Juba
Mongalla
Torit
Yei
Kajo Kaji
3187
Ilemi
Triangle
Lokitaung
1794
Chew
Bahir
Mega
Moyale
Dolo
Luuq
(Lugh)
Baydhabo
(Baidoa)
Beledweyne
(Belet Uen)
Wanleweyne
(Uanle Uen)
Jawhar
(Giohar)
MUQDISHO
(Mogadishu)
Buurhakaba
(Bur Acaba)
INDIAN
OCEAN

UGANDA
Gulu
Lira
Moroto
3084
Mt Elgon
4321
L. Kyoga
Mbale
KENYA
Lodwar
2752
South Horn
L. Turkana
Marsabit
375
Wajir
El Wak
Baardheere
Dif
Buulobarde
Marka
(Merca)

Projection: Sanson-Flamsteed's Sinusoidal

Kismaayo
(Chisimaio)
Jamaame
(Giamama)
Jilib
(Gelib)
Equator

Lava fields

East from Greenwich

COPYRIGHT PHILIP'S

ft   m
12 000   4000
9000   3000
6000   2000
       1500
3000   1000
       600
1200   400
600   200
       0
200   600
1000   3000
2000   6000
4000 12 000
m   ft

1:37 300 000

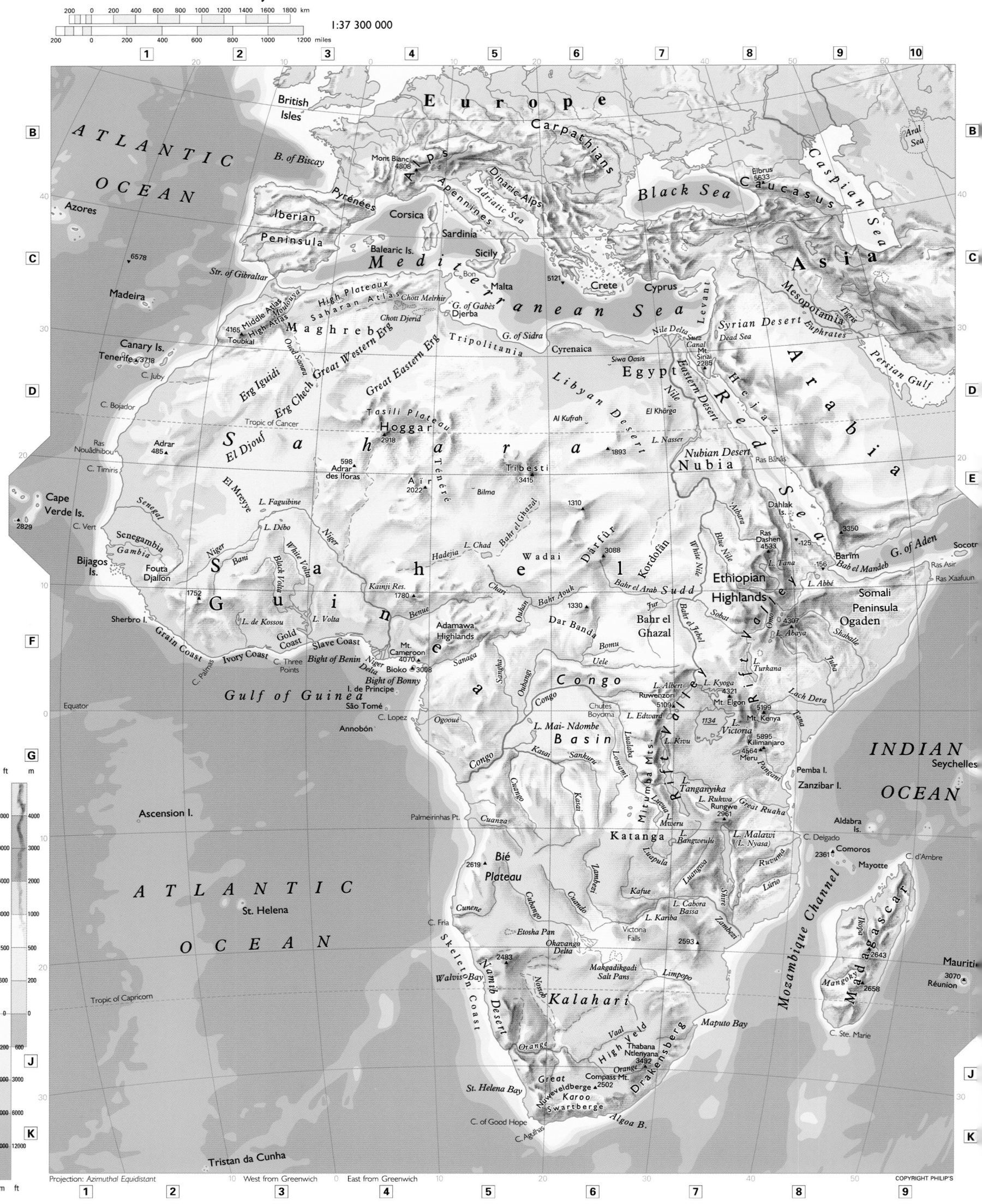

COPYRIGHT PHILIP'S

Projection: *Azimuthal Equidistant*   West from Greenwich   East from Greenwich

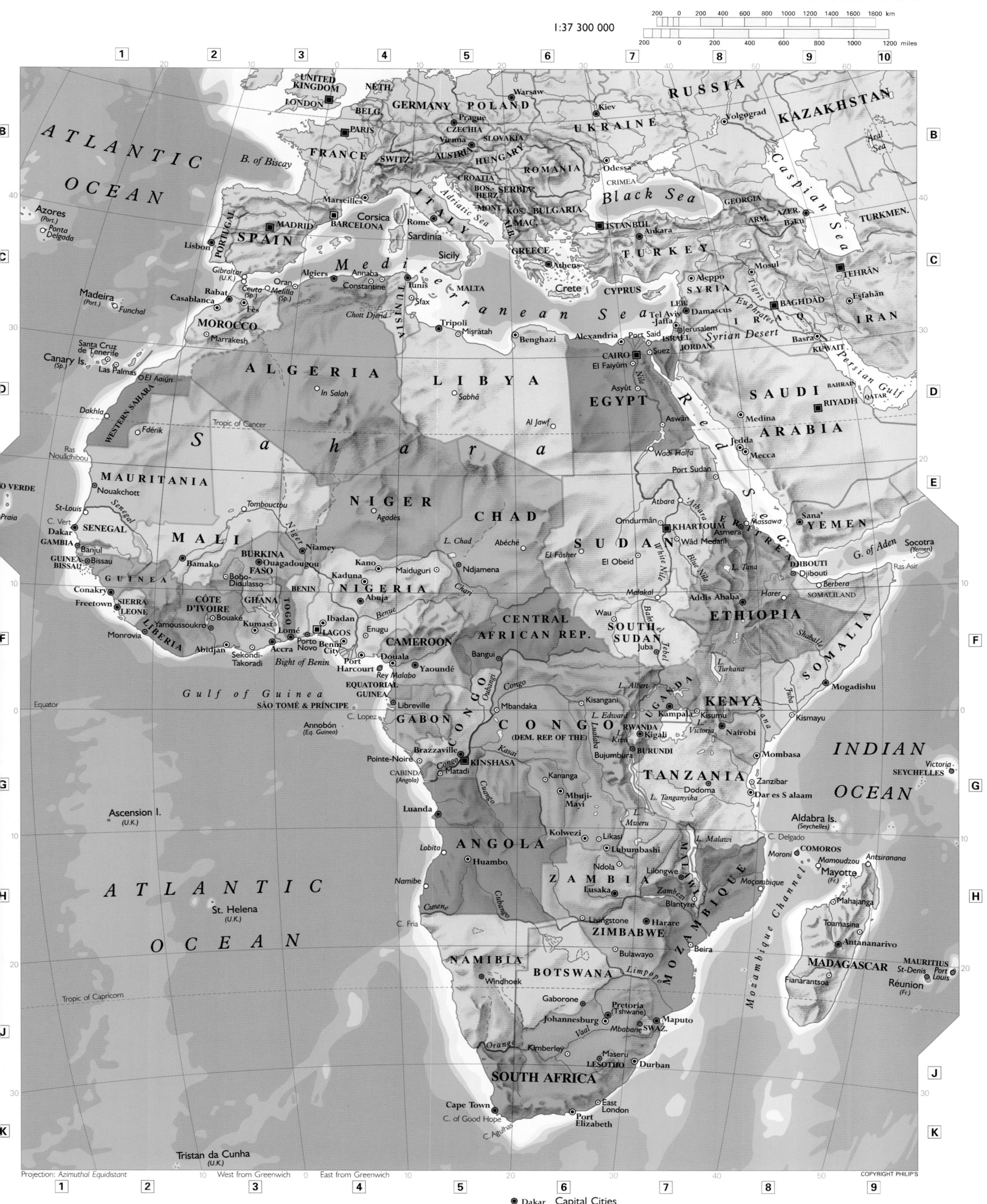

1:37 300 000

Projection: Azimuthal Equidistant   West from Greenwich   East from Greenwich   COPYRIGHT PHILIP'S

● Dakar   Capital Cities

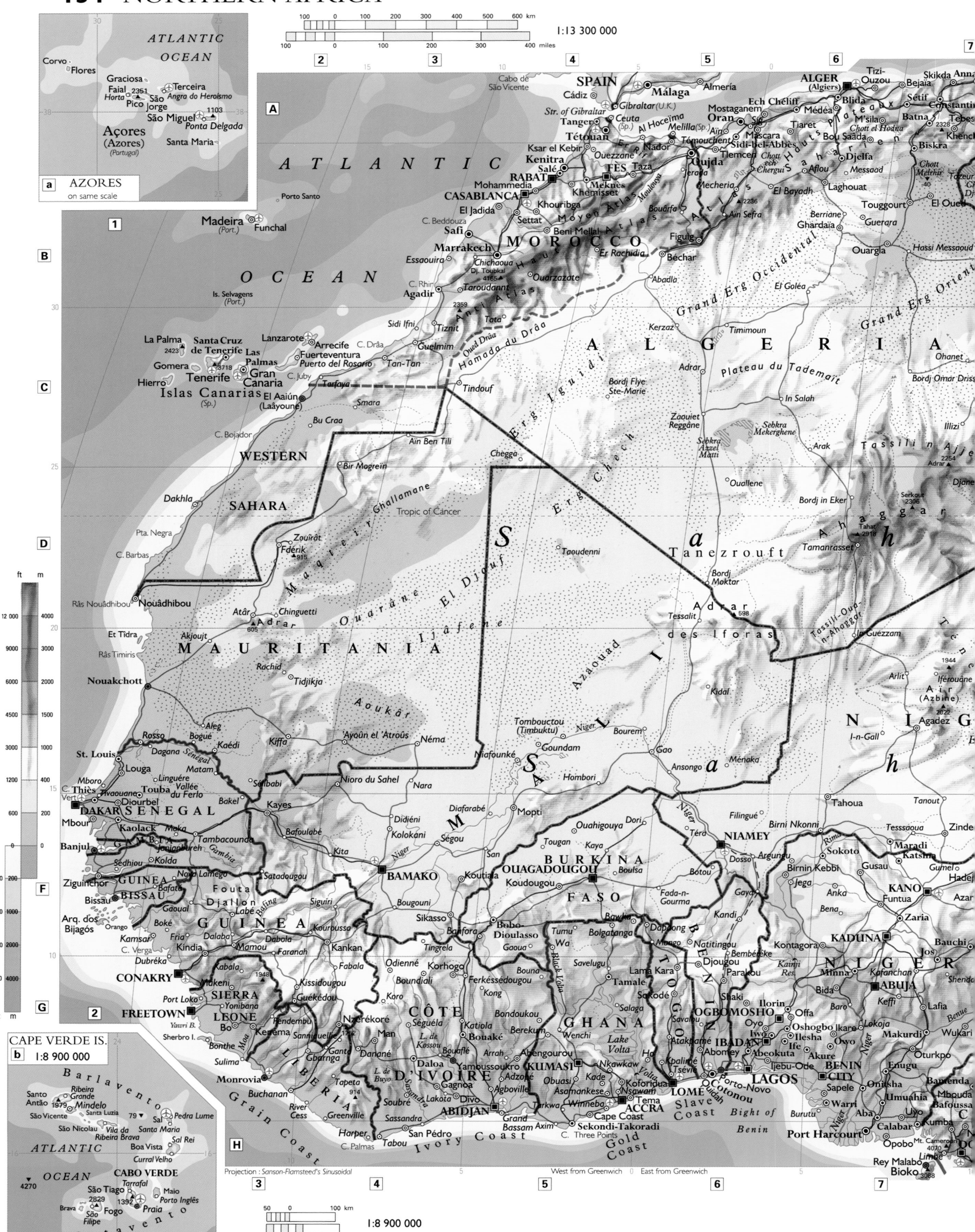

Lava fields

COPYRIGHT PHILIPS

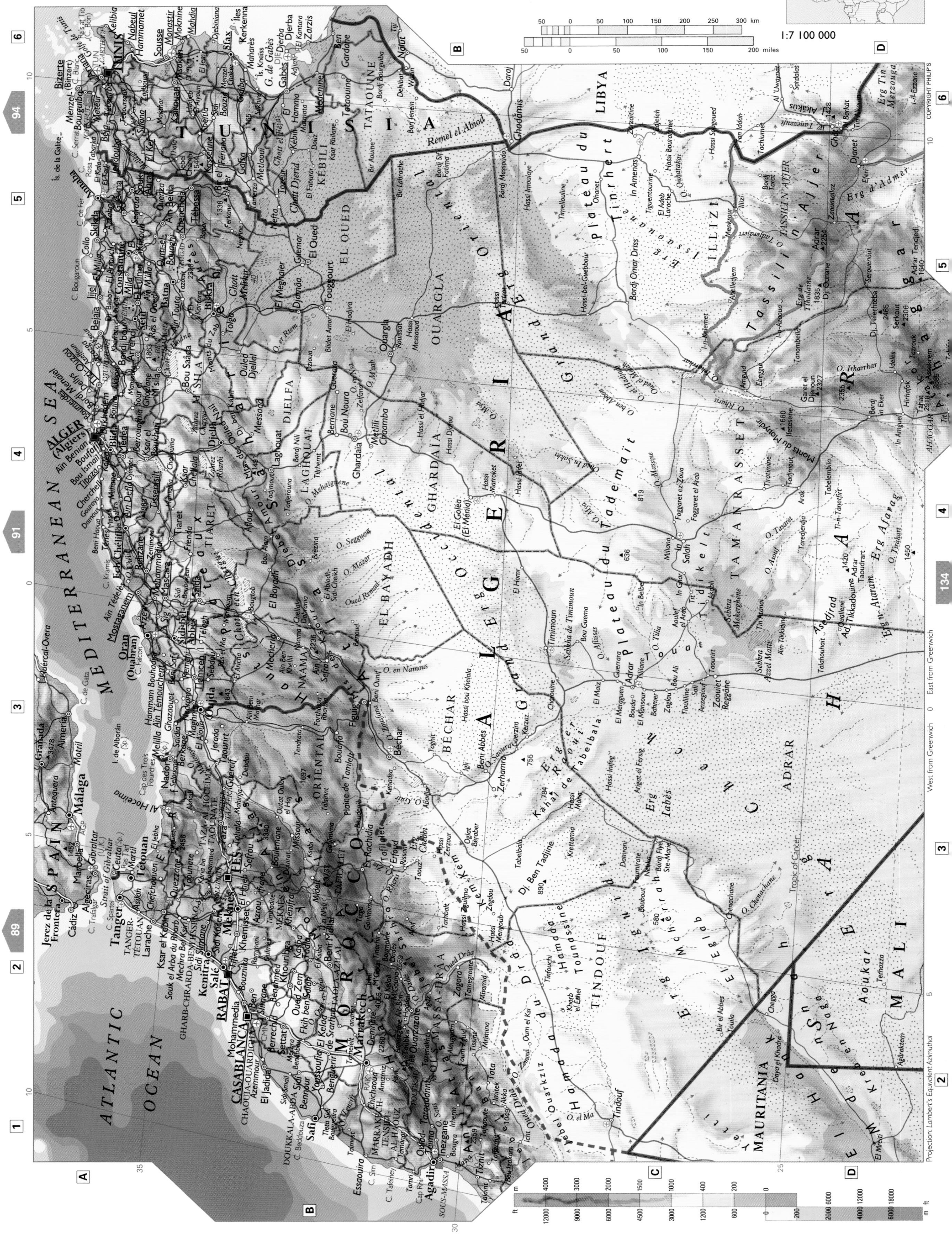

1:7 100 000

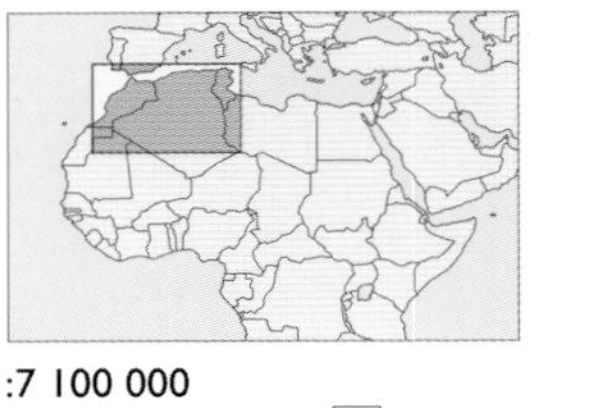

LIBYA

TUNISIA

ALGERIA

MOROCCO

MAURITANIA

MALI

SPAIN

MEDITERRANEAN SEA

ATLANTIC OCEAN

ALGER (Algiers)

TUNIS

RABAT

CASABLANCA

Marrakech

Oran (Ouahran)

Tanger

FÈS

MEKNÈS

Tropic of Cancer

Plateau du Tinrhert

Plateau du Tademaït

Grand Erg Oriental

Grand Erg Occidental

Tassili n'Ajjer

OUARGLA

EL OUED

KÉBILI

TATAOUINE

LAGHOUAT

DJELFA

GHARDAÏA

BÉCHAR

ADRAR

TAMANRASSET

TINDOUF

ILLIZI

Erg Tin Merzouga

Erg d'Admer

Ghadāmis

East from Greenwich

West from Greenwich

Projection: Lambert's Equidistant Azimuthal

COPYRIGHT PHILIP'S

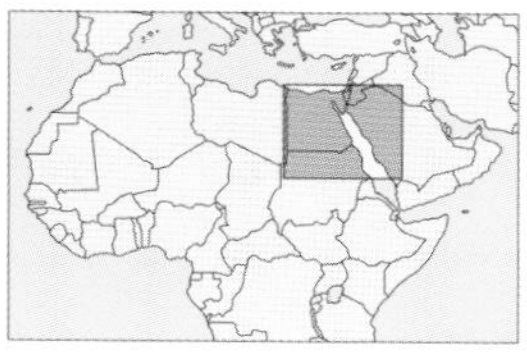

50 0 50 100 150 200 250 300 km

1:7 100 000

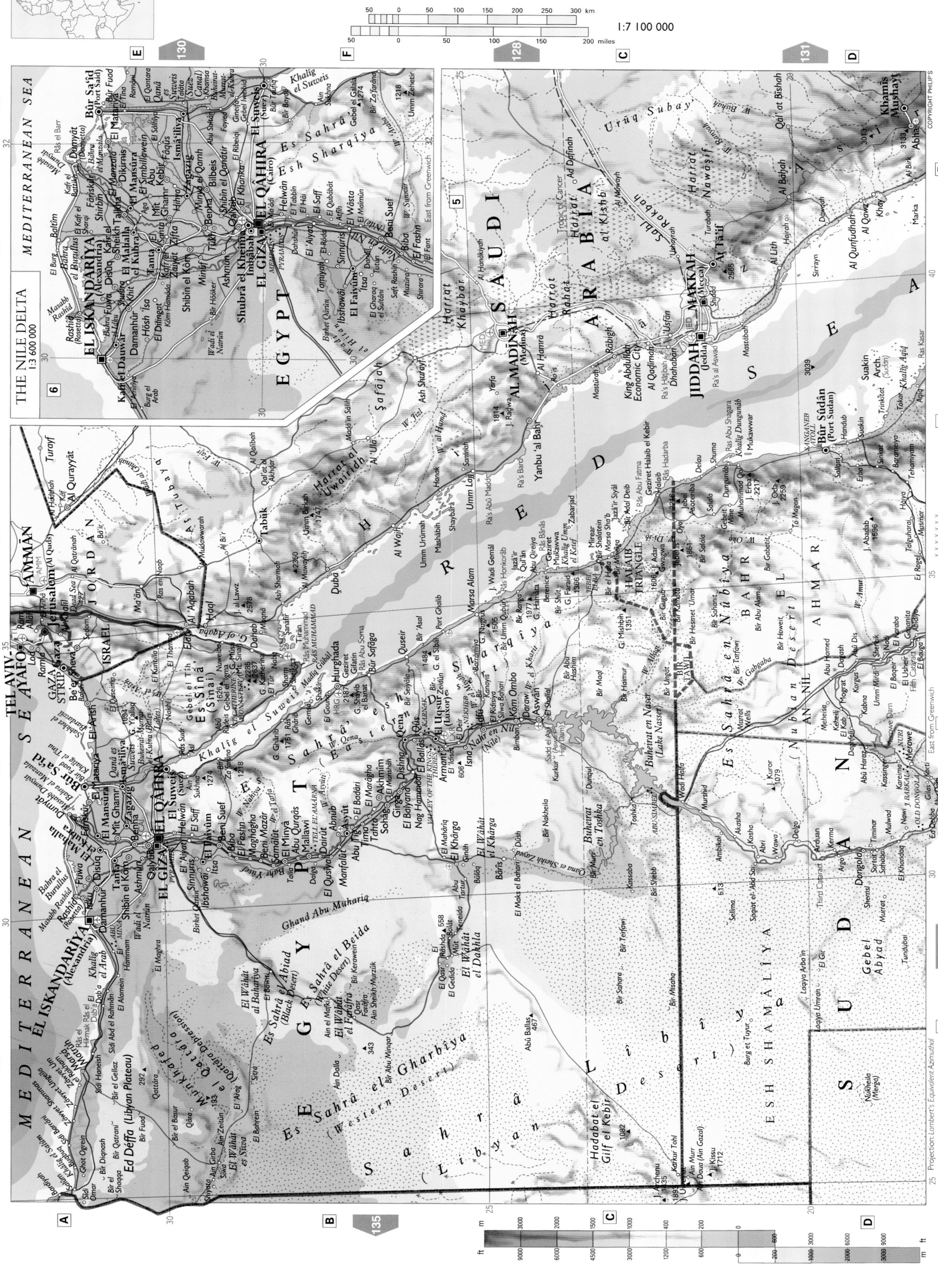

50 0 50 100 150 200 miles

COPYRIGHT PHILIP'S

THE NILE DELTA
1:3 600 000

MEDITERRANEAN SEA

E G Y P T

S A U D I   **A R A B I A**

J O R D A N

I S R A E L

S U D A N

R E D   S E A

Es Sahrâ el Gharbîya (Western Desert)

Sahrâ Lîbîya (Libyan Desert)

EL QÂHIRA (Cairo)

EL GIZA

EL ISKANDARÎYA (Alexandria)

AMMÂN (Al Quds)

Jerusalem

GAZA STRIP

TEL AVIV-YAFO

AL MADÎNAH (Medina)

MAKKAH (Mecca)

JIDDAH (Jedda)

Bûr Sûdân (Port Sudan)

Khamîs Mushayt

Es Sahra en Nûbîya (Nubian Desert)

Tropic of Cancer

East from Greenwich

Lava fields

Projection: Lambert's Equivalent Azimuthal

ft m 9000 3000 6000 2000 4500 1500 3000 1000 1200 600 400 200 0 200-600

1:7 100 000

134

Projection: Lambert's Equivalent Azimuthal

West from Green...

Underlined towns give their name to the
administrative area in which they stand.

Administrative division in Côte d'Ivoire:
1 Sassandra-Marahoué

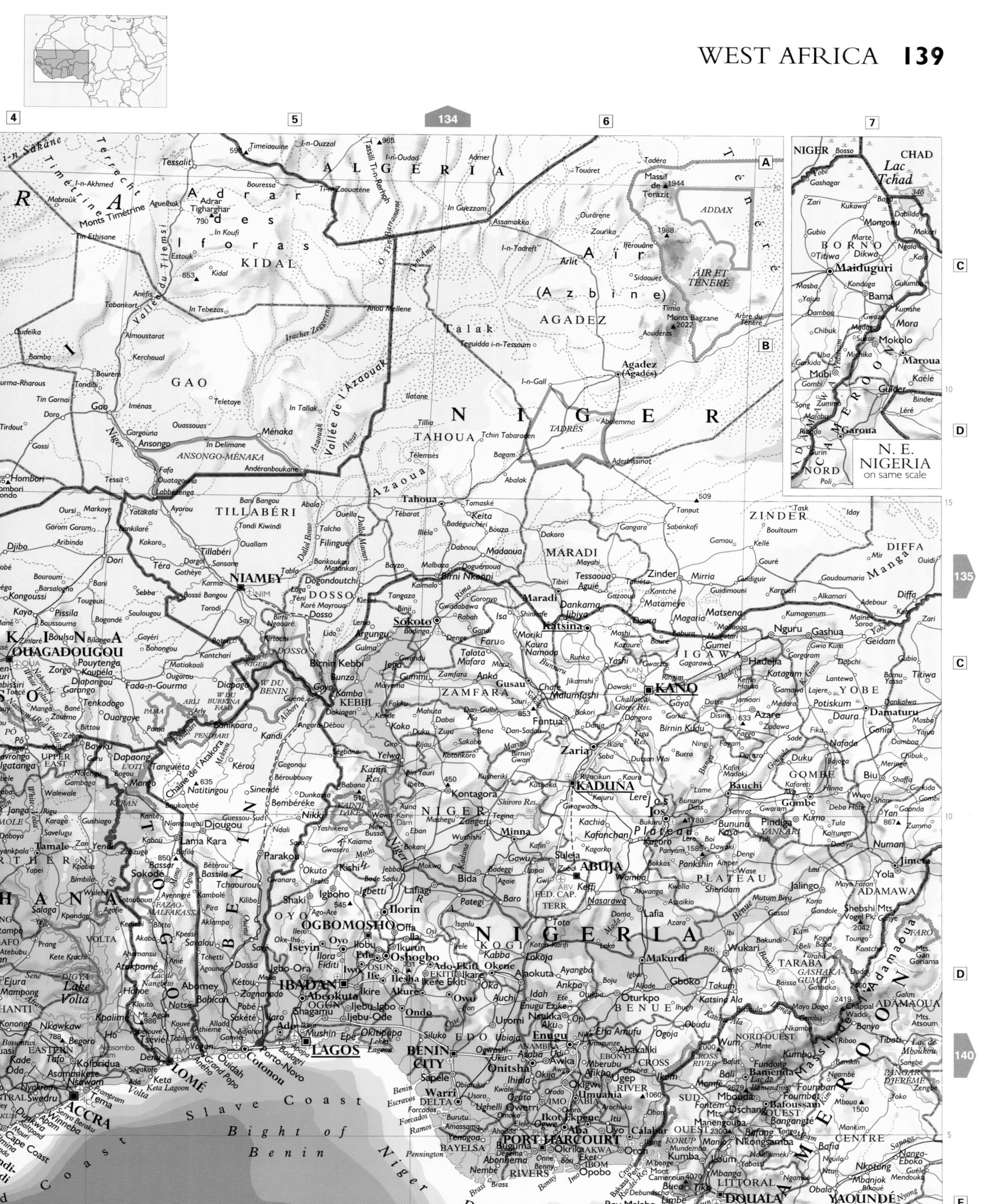

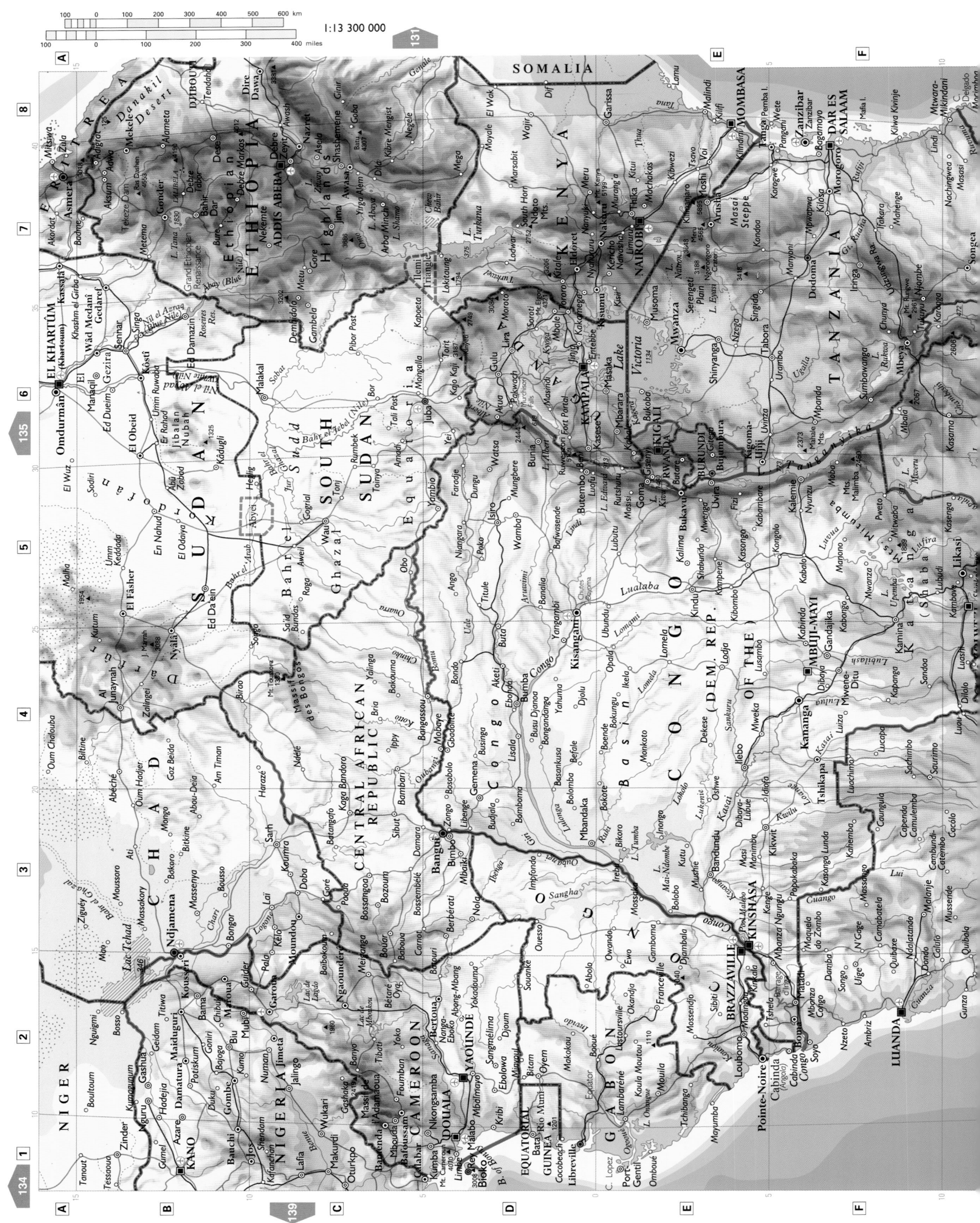

1:13 300 000

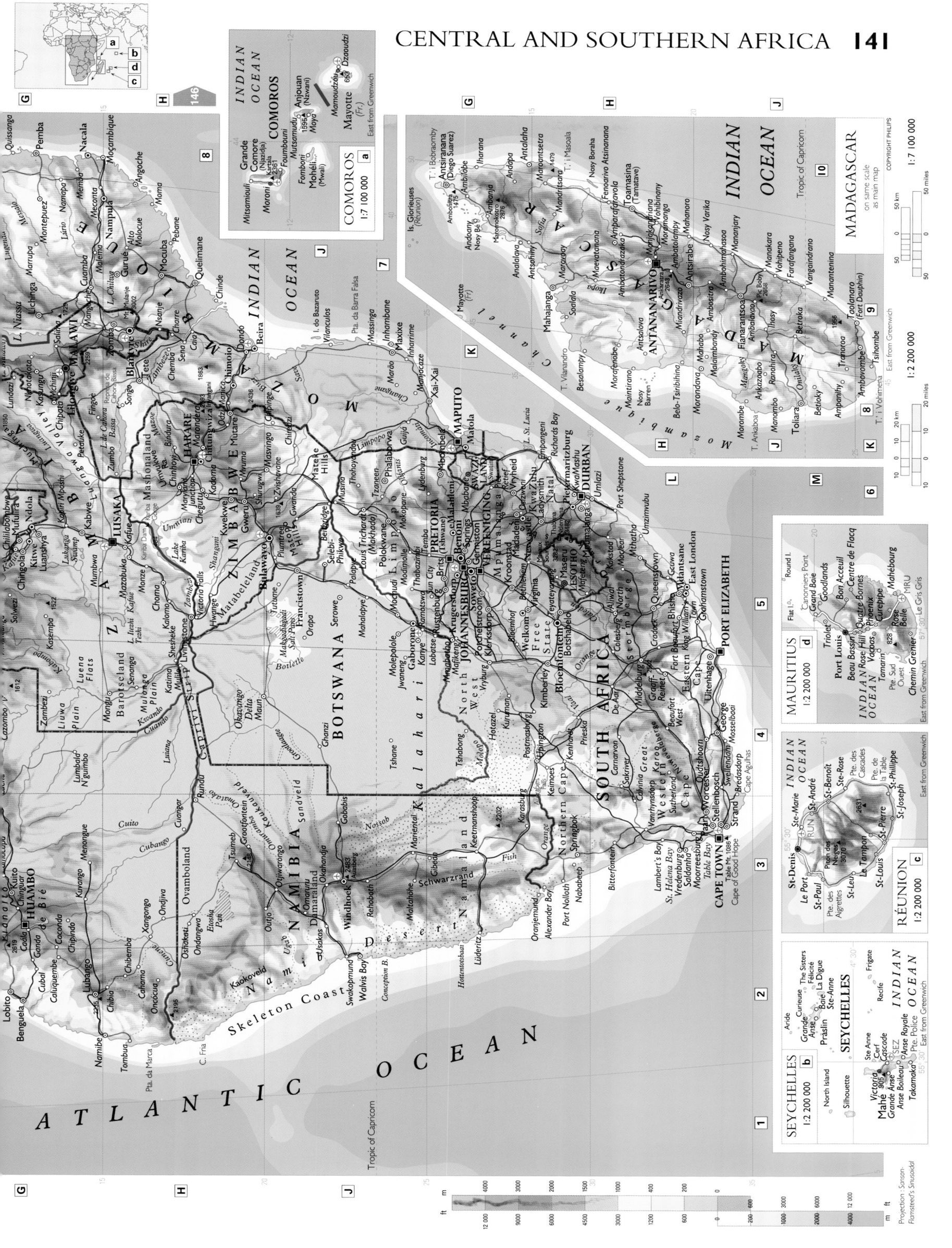

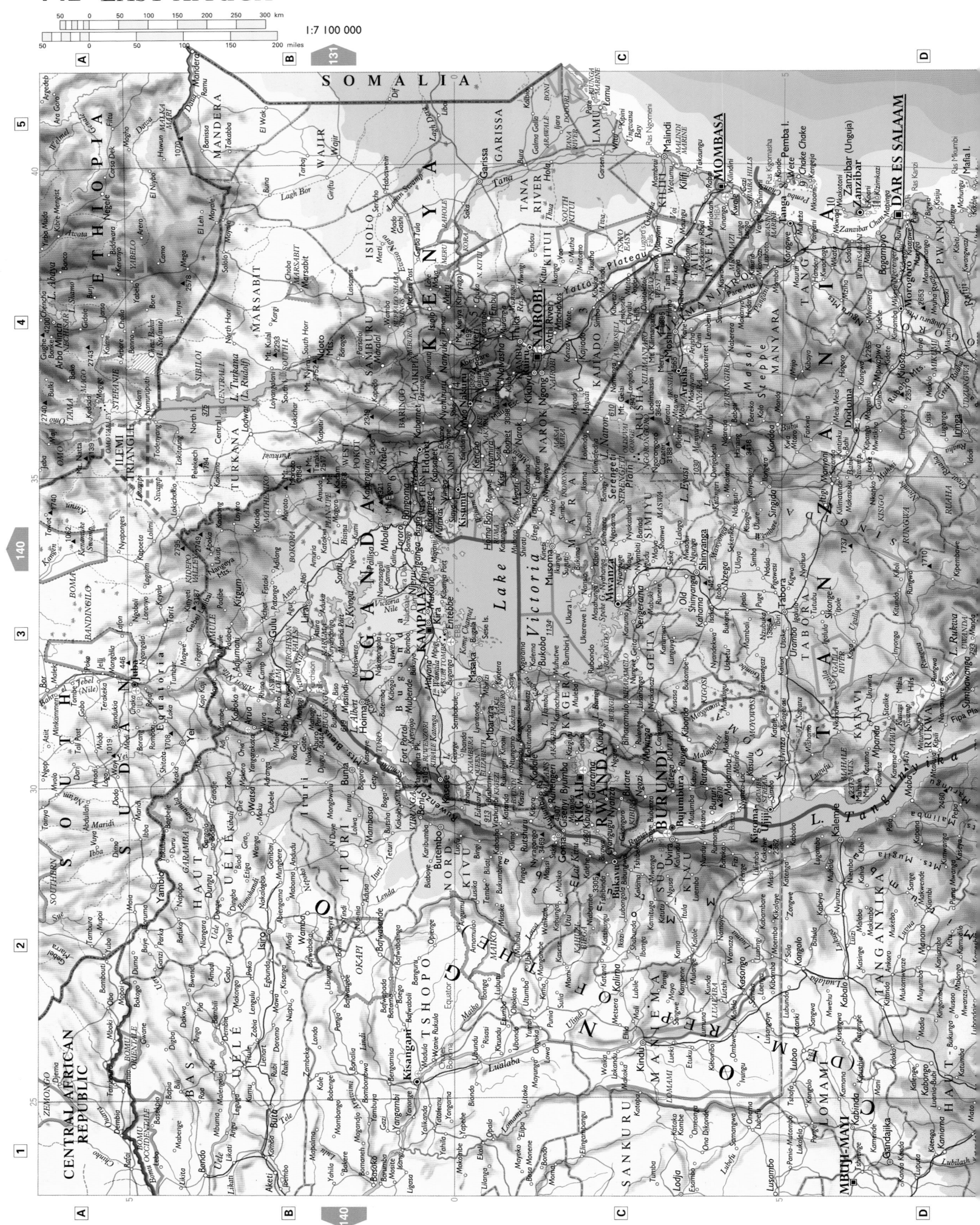

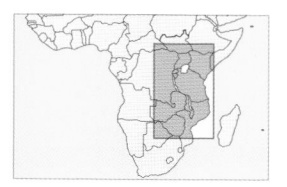

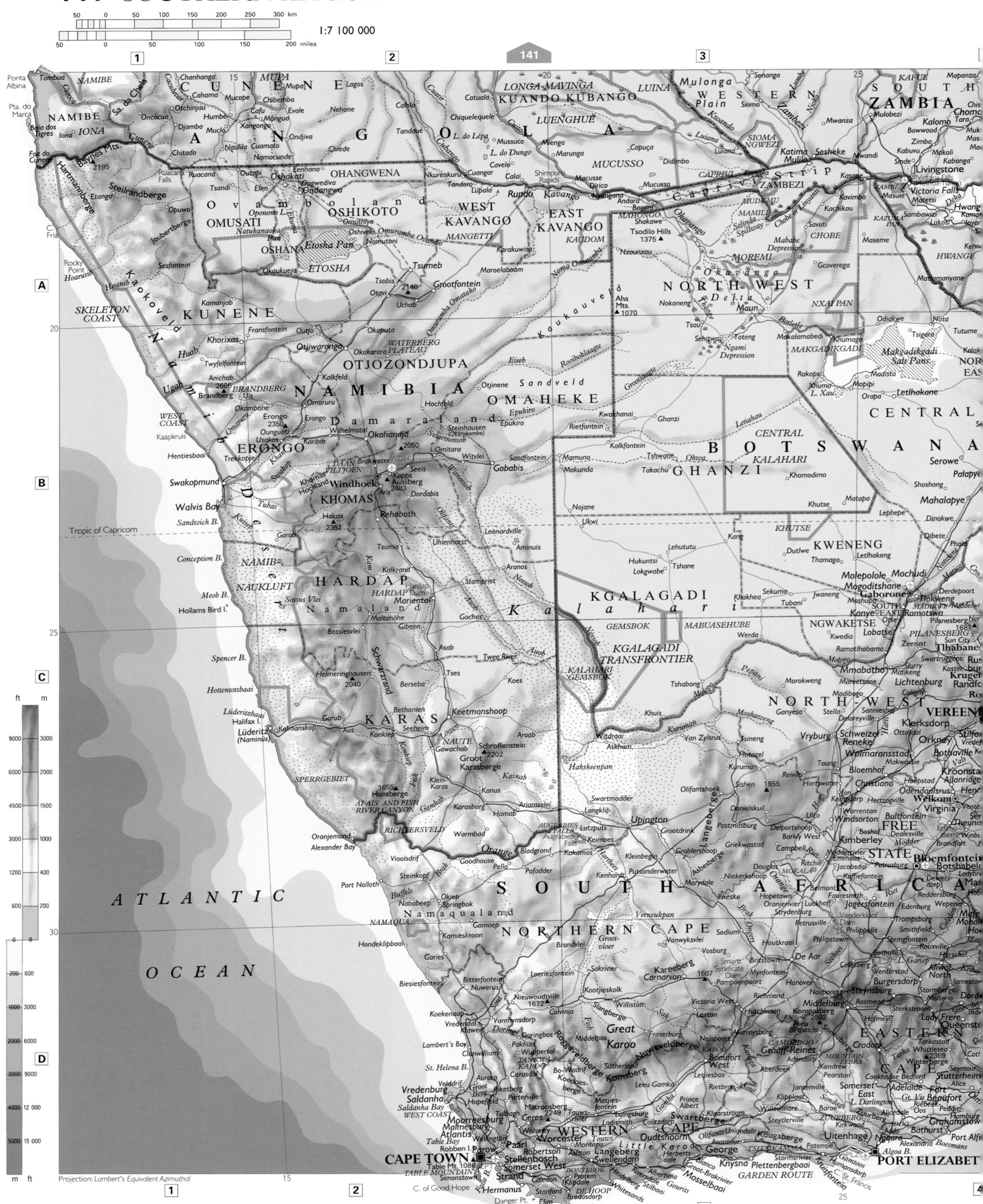

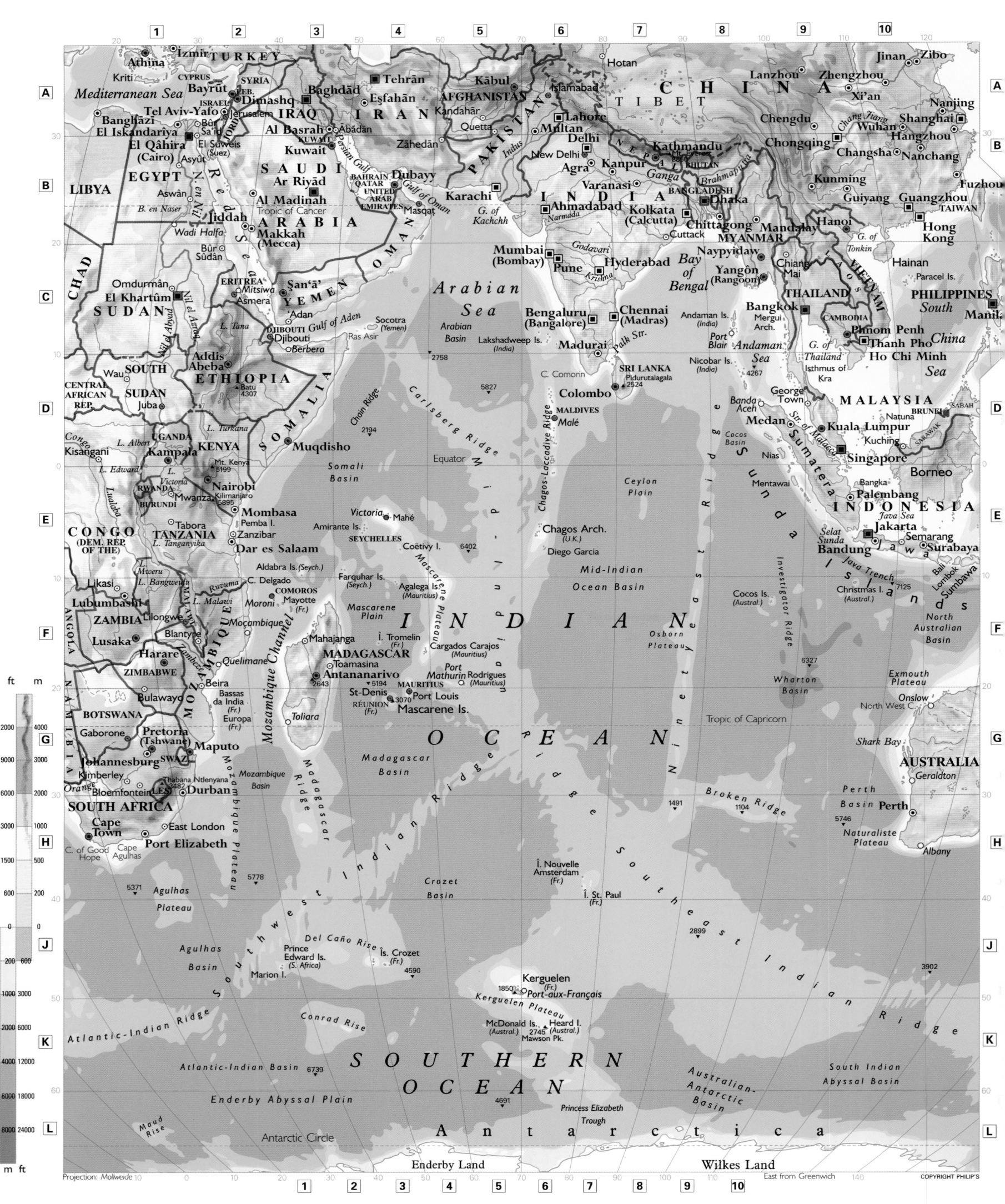

Projection: Mollweide

East from Greenwich

COPYRIGHT PHILIP'S

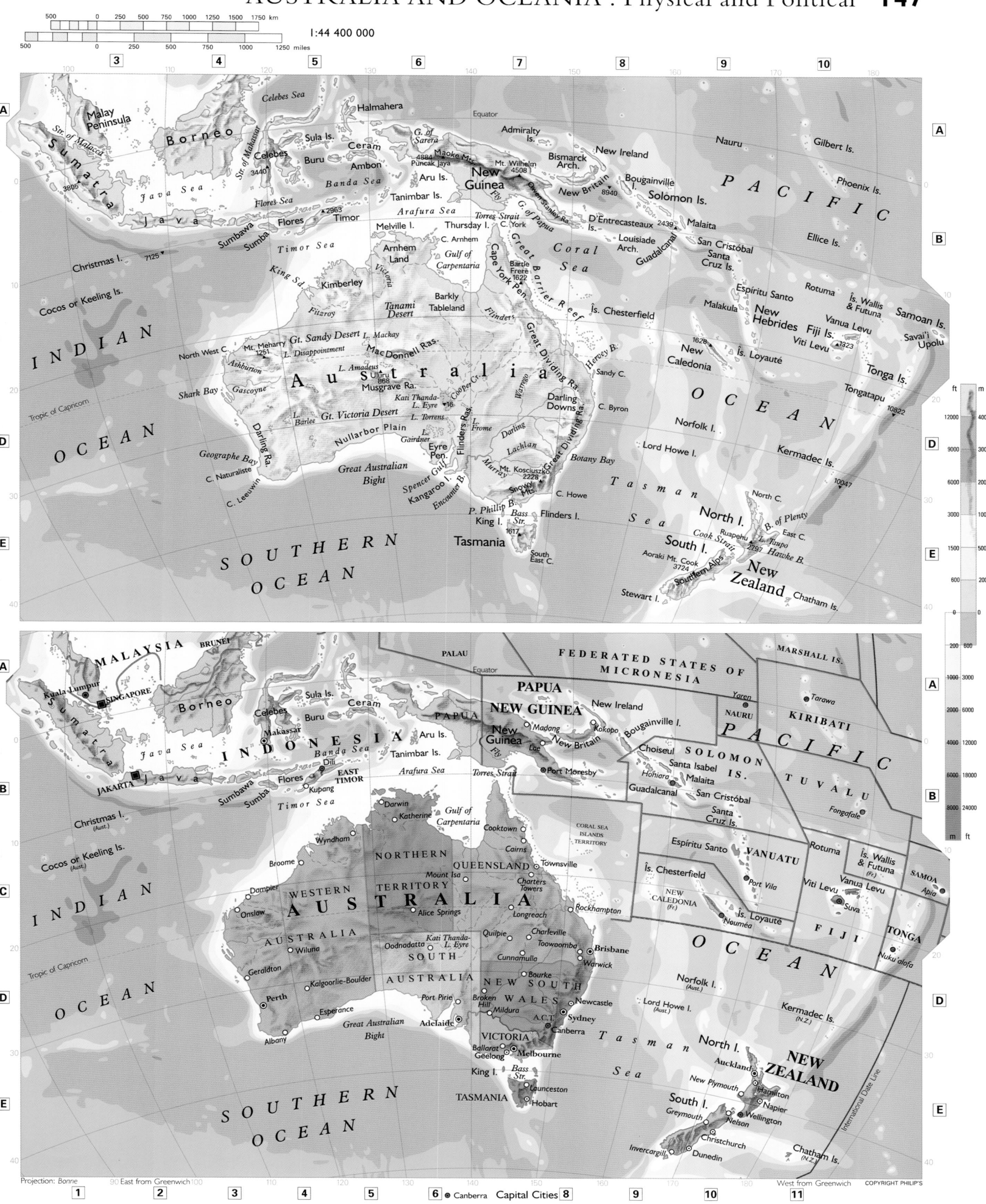

1:44 400 000

500   0   250   500   750   1000   1250   1500   1750 km
500   0   250   500   750   1000   1250 miles

Physical Map

A
Malay Peninsula
Str. of Malacca
Borneo
Celebes Sea
Halmahera
Sula Is.
Celebes
Ceram
Buru
Ambon
G. of Sarera
Admiralty Is.
New Ireland
Nauru
Gilbert Is.
Equator
Sumatra
3805
Str. of Makassar
3440
Maoke Mts.
4884
Puncak Jaya
Mt. Wilhelm
4508
New
Guinea
Fly
Owen Stanley Ra.
Bismarck Arch.
New Britain
8940
Bougainville
Solomon Is.
PACIFIC
Phoenix Is.

B
Java Sea
Banda Sea
Aru Is.
Tanimbar Is.
Flores Sea
2963
Arafura Sea
Torres Strait
C. York
G. of Papua
D'Entrecasteaux
2439
Malaita
Ellice Is.
Java
Sumbawa
Sumba
Flores
Timor
Melville I.
Thursday I.
C. Arnhem
Coral
Sea
Louisiade Arch.
Guadalcanal
San Cristóbal
Santa Cruz Is.
Espíritu Santo
Rotuma
Îs. Wallis & Futuna
Samoan Is.
Savai'i
Upolu

C
Timor Sea
Arnhem Land
Gulf of Carpentaria
Cape York Pen.
Great Barrier Reef
Îs. Chesterfield
Malakula
New Hebrides
Vanua Levu
Fiji Is.
Christmas I.
7125
Kimberley
Barkly Tableland
1628
New Caledonia
Viti Levu
1323
Cocos or Keeling Is.
King Sd.
Victoria
Tanami Desert
Flinders
Great Dividing Ra.
Hervey B.
Îs. Loyauté
Tonga Is.
Fitzroy

D
INDIAN
North West C.
Mt. Meharry 1251
Gt. Sandy Desert
L. Mackay
L. Disappointment
MacDonnell Ras.
L. Amadeus
Uluru 868
Musgrave Ra.
Kati Thanda–L. Eyre 16
Cooper Cr.
Warrego
Sandy C.
Darling Downs
C. Byron
Norfolk I.
Tongatapu
10822
Ashburton
Australia
OCEAN
Shark Bay
Gascoyne
L. Barlee
Gt. Victoria Desert
L. Torrens
L. Frome
Darling
Lachlan
Murray
Lord Howe I.
Kermadec Is.
10047

E
OCEAN
Geographe Bay
C. Naturaliste
C. Leeuwin
Darling Ra.
Nullarbor Plain
L. Gairdner
Great Australian Bight
Spencer Gulf
Kangaroo I.
Encounter B.
Eyre Pen.
Flinders Ras.
Mt. Kosciuszko 2228
Snowy Mts.
C. Howe
Botany Bay
Tasman Sea
North C.
North I.
B. of Plenty
East C.
Ruapehu 2797
Tuapo
Hawke B.
P. Phillip B.
King I.
1617
Bass Str.
Flinders I.
South East C.
Tasmania
South I.
Cook Strait
Aoraki Mt. Cook 3724
Southern Alps
New Zealand
Chatham Is.
Stewart I.
SOUTHERN OCEAN

ft   m
12000   4000
9000   3000
2000
1500   500
600   200
0   0
200   600
1000   3000
2000   6000
4000   12000
6000   18000
8000   24000
m   ft

Political Map

A
MALAYSIA
BRUNEI
Kuala Lumpur
SINGAPORE
Borneo
Sula Is.
Ceram
Buru
PALAU
PAPUA
FEDERATED STATES OF MICRONESIA
MARSHALL IS.
Equator
PAPUA NEW GUINEA
New Ireland
Yaren
Tarawa
NAURU
KIRIBATI
PACIFIC

B
Sumatra
INDONESIA
Makassar
Celebes
Java Sea
Banda Sea
Aru Is.
Tanimbar Is.
New Guinea
Madang
Kokopo
New Britain
Bougainville I.
Lae
Choiseul
Santa Isabel
SOLOMON IS.
JAKARTA
Java
Dili
EAST TIMOR
Sumbawa
Sumba
Flores
Kupang
Arafura Sea
Torres Strait
Fly
Port Moresby
Honiara
Malaita
Guadalcanal
San Cristóbal
Fongafale
Christmas I. (Aust.)
Timor Sea
Santa Cruz Is.
TUVALU

C
Cocos or Keeling Is. (Aust.)
Darwin
Katherine
Gulf of Carpentaria
Cooktown
CORAL SEA ISLANDS TERRITORY
Espíritu Santo
VANUATU
Rotuma
Îs. Wallis & Futuna (Fr.)
SAMOA
Wyndham
NORTHERN
Cairns
Port Vila
Vanua Levu
Apia
INDIAN
Broome
TERRITORY
QUEENSLAND
Townsville
Îs. Chesterfield
NEW CALEDONIA (Fr.)
Viti Levu
Suva
Dampier
WESTERN
Mount Isa
Charters Towers
Nouméa
Îs. Loyauté
FIJI
TONGA
Onslow
AUSTRALIA
Alice Springs
Longreach
Rockhampton
OCEAN
Nuku'alofa

D
OCEAN
AUSTRALIA
SOUTH
Charleville
Toowoomba
Brisbane
Norfolk I. (Aust.)
Wiluna
Quilpie
Cunnamulla
Warwick
Geraldton
Oodnadatta
Kati Thanda–L. Eyre
AUSTRALIA
Bourke
NEW SOUTH WALES
Newcastle
Lord Howe I. (Aust.)
Kermadec Is. (N.Z.)
Kalgoorlie-Boulder
Broken Hill
Mildura
A.C.T.
Sydney
Perth
Port Pirie
Canberra
North I.
NEW ZEALAND
Esperance
Adelaide
VICTORIA
Tasman Sea
Auckland

E
Albany
Great Australian Bight
Ballarat
Geelong
Melbourne
New Plymouth
Hamilton
Napier
King I.
Bass Str.
Launceston
South I.
Wellington
Greymouth
Nelson
TASMANIA
Hobart
Invercargill
Christchurch
Dunedin
Chatham Is. (N.Z.)
SOUTHERN OCEAN

m   ft
2000   6000
4000   12000
6000   18000
8000   24000
m   ft

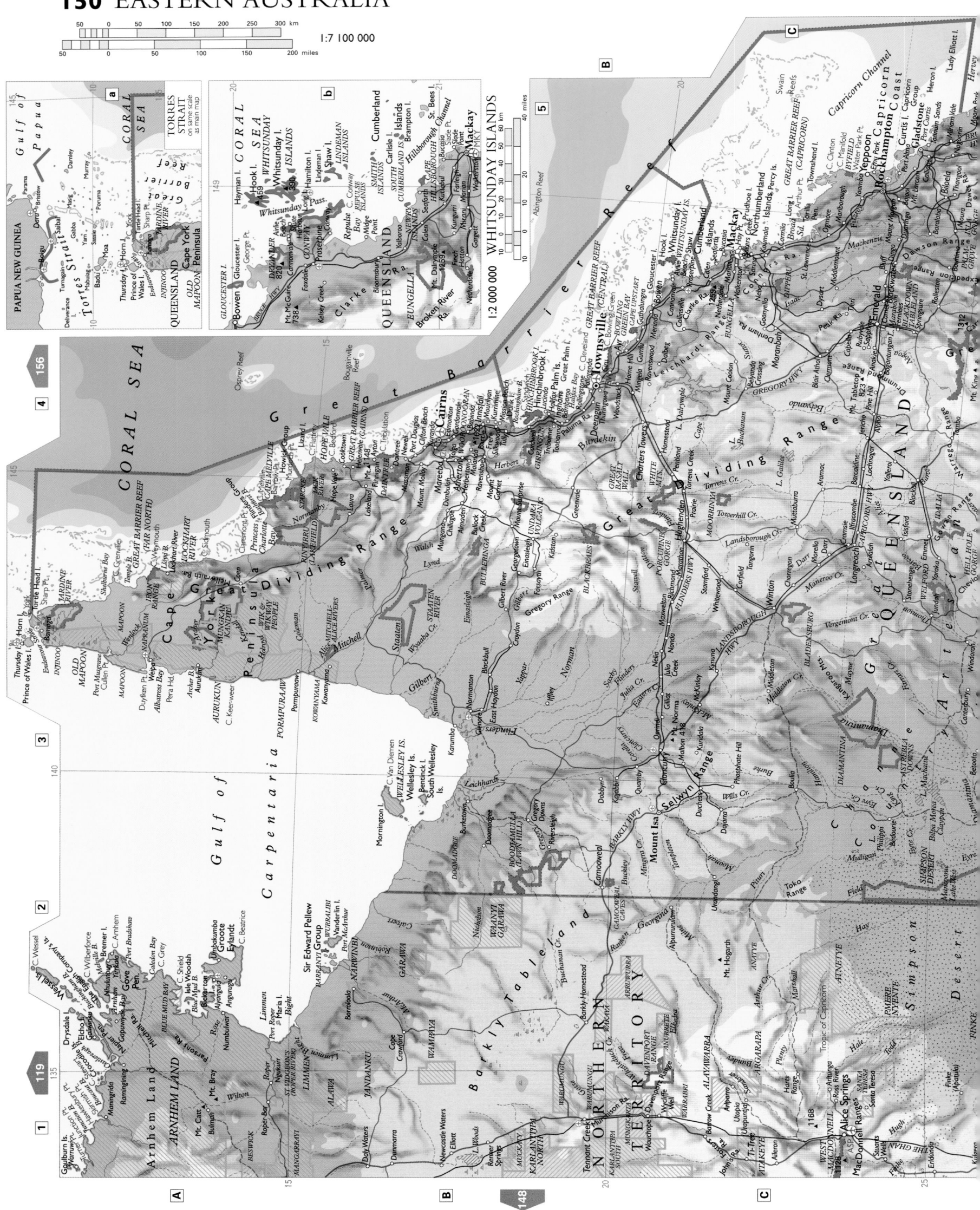

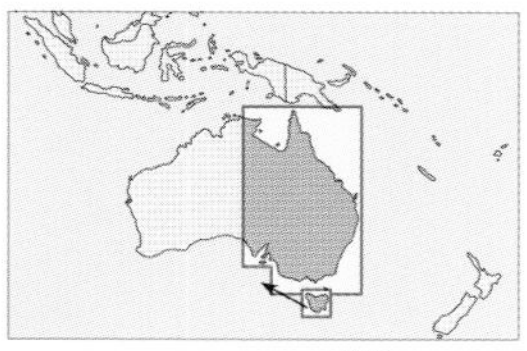

COPYRIGHT PHILIP'S

EASTERN AUSTRALIA

SOUTH AUSTRALIA

NEW SOUTH WALES

TASMAN SEA

Bass Strait

TASMANIA

BRISBANE · SYDNEY · Canberra · MELBOURNE · ADELAIDE · Hobart · Newcastle · Wollongong

Aboriginal lands

Projection: Bonne

East from Greenwich

1:3 500 000

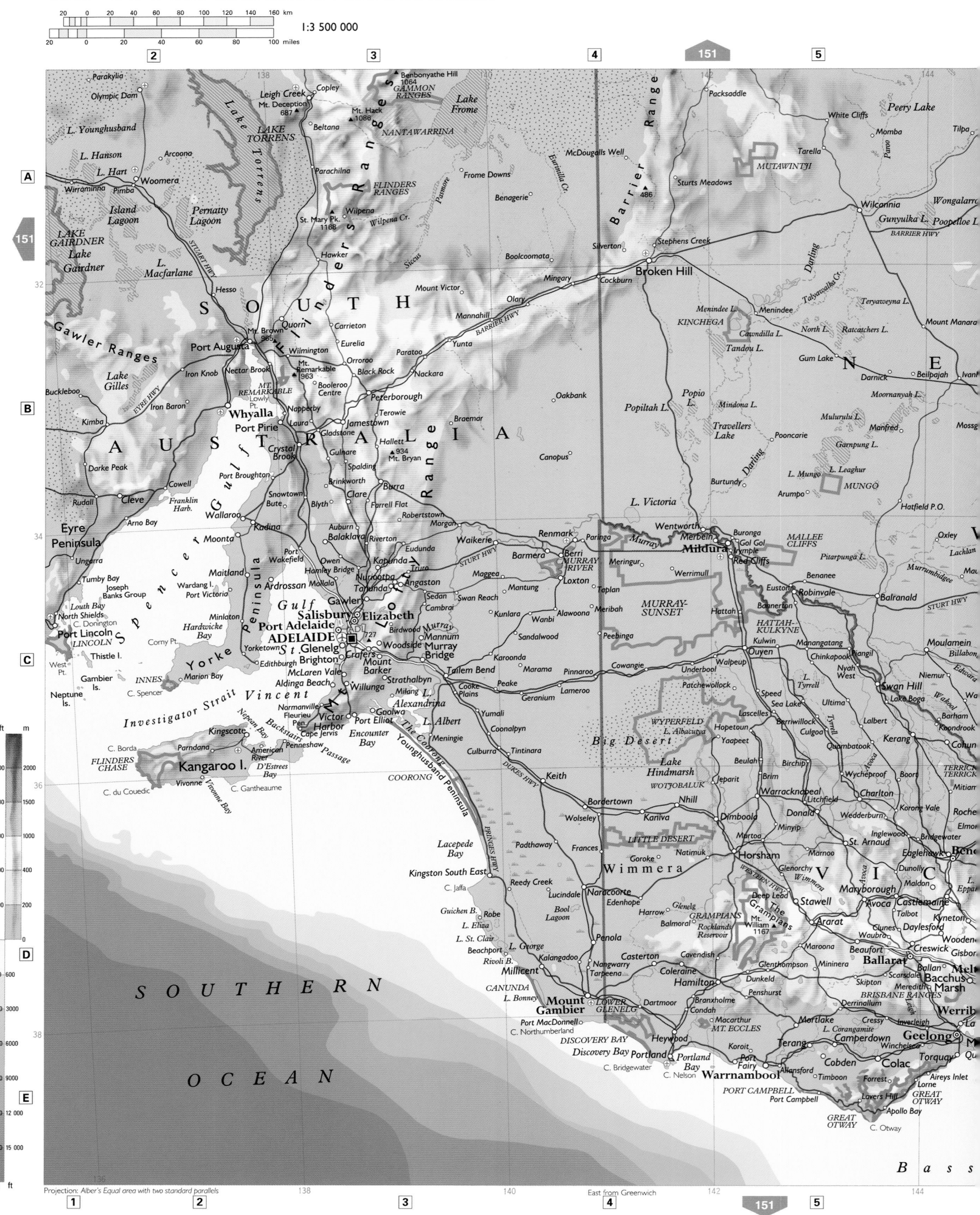

Projection: Alber's Equal area with two standard parallels

East from Greenwich

T A S M A N

S E A

East from Greenwich

COPYRIGHT PHILIP'S

6 7 8 9 10

Aboriginal lands

10 0 20 40 60 80 100 120 140 km
10 0 20 40 60 80 100 miles

1:3 100 000

1 **2** **3** **4**

173 174 175 176

A

C. Reinga
Waitiki Landing
North C.
C. Maria van Diemen
Parengarenga Harbour
Houhora Heads
Rangaunu B.
Ninety Mile Beach
Awanui
Mongonui
Doubtless Bay
Whangaroa Harb.
C. Karikari
Cavalli Is.
35

Ahipara B.
Kaitaia
Waitangi
Kerikeri
Kaeo
NORTHLAND
Russell
Herekino
Okaihau
Raihia
Opua
C. Brett
Kohukohu
Rawene
Kaikohe
Kawakawa
Whangaruru Harb.
▲744
Moerewa

B

Hokianga Harbour
Omapere
Waipoua Forest
Donnelly's Crossing
Hikurangi
Kamo
▲781
Poor Knights Is.
Aranga
Whangarei
Waiotira
Onerahi
Kirikopuni
Whangarei Harb.
Morsden Point
Bream Hd.
Dargaville
Maungaturoto
Waipu
Bream B.
Bream Tail
Hen & Chickens Is.
36

Te Kopuru
Paparoa
Ruawai
Wellsford
Needles Pt.
Port Fitzroy
Great Barrier I.
Matakana
I. 722 627
Tryphena
Kaipara Harbour
Helensville
Snells Beach
C. Rodney
Colville Chan.
Cuvier I.
Warkworth
Kawau I.
C. Colville
Port Charles
Hauraki G.
892▲
Mercury Is.

C

AUCKLAND
Whangaparaoa Pen.
Coromandel
Ostend
Mercury B.
Takapuna
Waiheke I.
Whitianga
AUCKLAND
Mount Wellington
AK
Howick
Otahuhu
846
Tairua
Coromandel Pen.
Piha
Onehunga
Papakura
Pauanui
37
Muriwai Beach
Papatoetoe
Firth of Thames
Manukau
Pukekohe
Thames
Manukau Harbour
Waiuku
Tuakau
Mercer
Whangamata
Waikato
Te Kauwhata
L. Waikare
Mayor I.
Waihi

D

WAIKATO
Huntly
Waihi Beach
Paeroa
Te Aroha
Katikati
BAY OF PLENTY
Whakaari (White I.)
Glen Afton
Ngaruawahia
Waitoa
Tauranga Harb.
C. Runaway
Hicks Bay
Glen Massey
Morrinsville
Matakana I.
Motiti I.
Te Araroa
Raglan Harbour
Hamilton
Tauranga
Mount Maunganui
Te Kaha
Raglan
Cambridge
Matamata
Te Puke
Edgecumbe
1067▲1753
Ruatoria
38
Aotea Harbour
Leamington
Tirau
Paengaroa
Whakatane
Hikurangi▲
Kawhia Harbour
Te Awamutu
Arapuni
L. Rotorua
Matata
Ohiwa Harbour
Opotiki
Waipiro Bay
Albatross Pt.
Kihikihi
Momaku
Kawerau
Tokomaru Bay
Tirua Pt.
Otorohanga
Ngongotaha
L. Rotoiti
Te Teko
Taneatua
Waitomo Caves
Rotorua
Mt. Tarawera▲
GISBORNE

E

Te Kuiti
Tokoroa
Kinleith
Mangakino
Waiotapu
Tolaga Bay
1111
Mokau
Aria
Mangaokino
Atiamuri
Galatea
Matawai
Puha
Te Karaka
North Taranaki Bight
Ongarue
Mokai
Wairakei
TE UREWERA
Murupara
Ngatapa
Ormond
Gisborne
Waitara
Pukearuhe
Okahukura
Taupo
369 L. Taupo
Rangitaiki
Tuahine Pt.
Poverty B.
Manunui
Taumarunui
1392 L. Waikaremoana
39
New Plymouth
Tahora
Owhango
Tokaanu
Turangi
Tuai
Waikaremoana
TARANAKI
Okato
Inglewood
Whangamomona
Mt. Ngauruhoe 2287▲
Ahimanawa Ra.
Frasertown
Mt. Taranaki or Mt. Egmont 2518▲
Midhirst
Mt. Tongariro 1968▲
Tarawera
Mohaka
Wairoa
C. Egmont
Huiroa
TONGARIRO
Ruapehu
1728
403▲
Waikokopu
Rahotu
Stratford
Ruapehu▲ 2797
Kaweka Ra.
Putorino
Mahia Pen.
Egmont
Kaponga
Eltham
746
Ohakune
Rangataua
Waiouru
Portland I.
Table C.
Opunake
Kapuni
Normanby
Raetihi
Kaimanawa Mts.
Bay View
Manaia
Hawera
Pipiriki
Taihape
Ngaruroro
Taradale
Napier
South Taranaki Bight
Patea
Waverley
Maxwell
Mangaweka
Clive
C. Kidnappers
Waitotara
Wanganui
Waiouru
Apiti
1733
Hastings
Hawke Bay
40
Wanganui
Castlecliff
Hunterville
Mangaweka
Opapa
Havelock North

F

MANAWATU-WANGANUI
Turakina
Marton
Halcombe
Norsewood
Otane
HAWKE'S BAY
Bulls
Feilding
Ormondville
Waipawa
Rongotea
Rangitikei
Dannevirke
Waipukurau
Takapau
112
Bunnythorpe
Ashhurst
Woodville
Porangahau
Palmerston North
Manawatu
Pahiatua
Weber
Foxton
Longburn
C. Turnagain
Herbertville

G

Shannon
803
Levin
Eketahuna
Alfredton
C. Farewell
Farewell Spit
Otaki
Tinui
PACIFIC
Golden Bay
C. Stephens
Stephens I.
Kapiti I.
157 Mt. Mikimiki
Collingwood
Rangitoto ke te tonga (D'Urville I.)
French Pass
Mauriceville
Castlepoint
Kahurangi Pt.
Takaka
Separation Pt.
OCEAN
ABEL TASMAN
Paraparaumu
Masterton
Riwaka
Tasman
Porirua
Carterton
Motueka
Bay
Pelorus Sd.
Johnsonville
Greytown
NELSON
1203
Lower Hutt
Featherston
Martinborough
Wairau
Havelock
Stoke
Queen Charlotte Sd.
Arapawa I.
Picton
Paekakariki
Upper Hutt
WELLINGTON
41
Tadmor
Richmond
Petone
Wainuiomata
Flat Pt.
Nelson
Belgrove 1756
Tuamarina
Wellington
Wairarapa
Brightwater
Mt. Richmond
L. Onoke
665
Wakefield
Richmond Ra.
Port Nicholson
Eastbourne
665
Mt. Owen
Renwick
Blenheim
Palliser B.
1875▲
Glenhope
Cloudy B.
Ruamahanga
Aorangi Mts.
981
C. Palliser

H

Lyell
2120 1780
Seddon
Awatere
3122
Murchison
TASMAN
NELSON LAKES
L. Rotoiti
Ward
C. Campbell

TASMAN SEA

NORTH ISLAND (Te Ika-a-Māui)

PACIFIC OCEAN

ft / m
9000 / 3000
6000 / 2000
3000 / 1000
1200 / 400
600 / 200
0 / 0
200 / 600
1000 / 3000
1500 / 4500
3000 / 9000
m / ft

Projection: Conical with two standard parallels

East from Greenwich

COPYRIGHT PHILIP'S

1 **2** **3** **4** **5** **6** **7** **8**

FIJI a
1:5 300 000

50 0 50 100 150 200 km
50 0 50 100 150 miles

178 E 180

Great Sea Reef
Kia
Ringgold Is.
Udu Pt.
PACIFIC
Yaqaga
Labasa
Nukubua Bay
Rabi
Yasawa
Yadua
Bua
Vanua Levu 1031▲
Natewa Bay
Buca
Qamea
OCEAN
Nacula
Nabouwalu
Savusavu
Somosomo
Taveuni
Naitaba
Viwa
Naviti
Bligh Water
Savusavu Bay
Kanacea
Vanua Balavu
Waya
Vomo
Rakiraki
Nasau
Koro
Vatu Vara
Mago
Lomaloma
Manuca Group
Lautoka
Mba
Tavua
Tomaniivi 1323
Lawaki
Levuka
Wakaya
Cicia
Tuvuca
Malolo
Nadi
Naval
Ovalau
Batiki
Nairai
Nayau
Sigatoka
Keiyasi
Navua
Viti Levu
Vunidawa
Korovou
Sawaleke
KORO
Lakeba Passage
Tubou
Korolevu
Nausori
Gau
SEA
Lakeba
Oneata
Yanuca
Beqa
Suva
Vanua Vatu
Moce
FIJI
Vatulele
Moala
Southern Lau Group
Namuka-i-lau
Kadavu Passage
Ono
Matuku
Yagasa Cluster
Kadavu
Tavuki
Levu
Yunisea
Totoya
Kabara
Fulaga
Ogea Driki
178 E East from Greenwich 180 West from Greenwich Ogea Levu

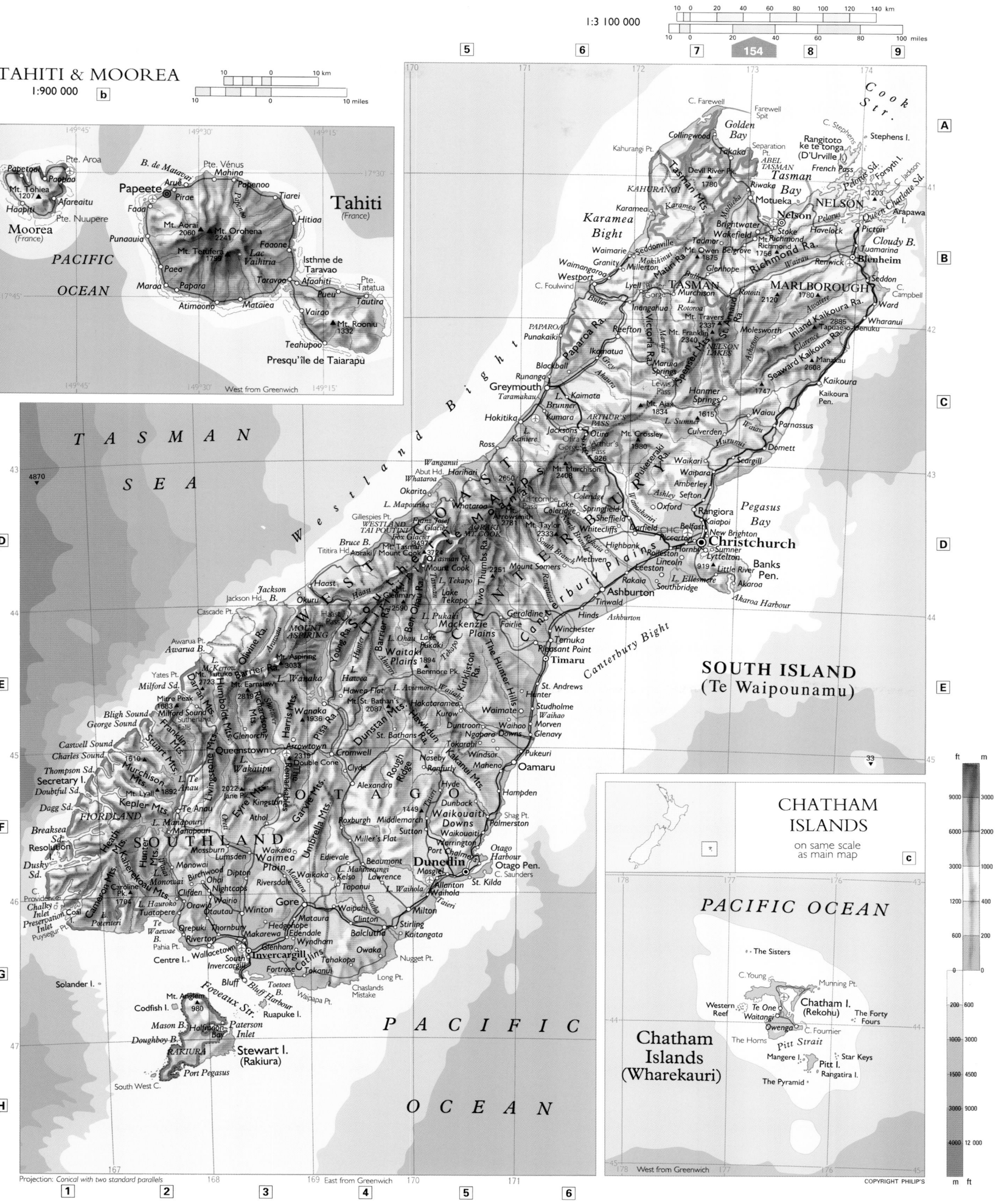

TAHITI & MOOREA
1:900 000 **b**

Moorea
(France)

Mt. Tohiea
1207 ▲

Papeete ⊙

PACIFIC
OCEAN

Tahiti
(France)

Mt. Aorai
2060 ▲   ▲ Mt. Orohena
2241

Mt. Terufera
1799

Lac
Vaihiria

Isthme de
Taravao

Pte. Tatutua

▲ Mt. Rooniu
1332

Presqu'île de Taiarapu

West from Greenwich

TASMAN

SEA

C. Farewell

Farewell
Spit

Cook
Str.

Collingwood   *Golden*
Bay   Takaka

Kahurangi Pt.

C. Stephens

Stephens I.

Rangitoto
ke te tonga
(D'Urville I.)

Separation
Pt.

French Pass

Pelorus Sd.   Forsyth I.
Jackson

Devil River Pk
1780

Tasman
Bay

Riwaka
Motueka

Nelson ⊙

Queen Charlotte Sd.

Arapawa
I.

1203

Picton

KAHURANGI

Tasman Mts.

Karamea

Brightwater
Stoke
Wakefield
Tadmor

Mt Owen
1875

Mt. Richmond
1756

Richmond Ra.

Havelock

Cloudy B.

Tuamarina

Blenheim

Karamea
Bight

Waimarie

Seddonville
Granity
Millerton

Mokihinui

Belgrove
Glenhope

TASMAN

Murchison

L.
Rotoiti

NELSON
LAKES

Renwick

Seddon

C.
Campbell

Westport

Waimangaroo

C. Foulwind

PAPAROA

Lyell
Gorge

Inangahua

Buller

Victoria Ra.

Mt. Franklin
2340

Mt. Travers
2337

St. Arnaud Ra.

Spencer Mts.

Awatere

2120

Ward

Wharanui

MARLBOROUGH

1780

Inland Kaikoura Ra.

2885

Molesworth

Tapuae-o-uku
2885

Seaward Kaikoura Ra.

Clarence

Manakau
2608

Wairau

Benmore

Punakaiki

Blackball

Grey

Ahaura

L. Kaimata

Reefton

Maruia
Springs

Lewis
Pass

Hanmer
Springs

Kaikoura

Runanga

Greymouth

Taramakau

L. Brunner

Kumara

Ikamatua

Mt. Ajax
1834

Mt. Crossley
1980

Waiau

1615

L. Sumner

Parnassus

Kaikoura
Pen.

WESTLAND
BIGHT

Hokitika

Jacksons

ARTHUR'S
PASS

Otira
Gorge

Arthur's
Pass
926

Puketeraki Ra.

Culverden

Hurunui

Domett

Ross

Kaniere

Mt. Murchison
2408

Waikari
Waipara

Amberley

Hawdon

Seargill

43

Wanganui

SOUTH ISLAND

Abut Hd.

Whataroa

Harihari

Okarito

Westland
Tai Poutini

Gillespies Pt.

L. Mapourika

2650

Main Divide

Whitcombe
Pass

L.
Coleridge

Mt. Murchison

Arrowsmith
2781

Springfield
Sheffield

Whitecliffs
Darfield

Oxford
Rangiora
Kaiapoi

Pegasus
Bay

Belfast

New Brighton

Christchurch

CHCH

Franz Josef
Glacier

Fox Glacier

Aoraki/
MT COOK

Mt. Taylor
2333

Rakaia

Highbank

Rolleston

Sumner
Lyttelton

Ricearton

Banks
Pen.

Bruce B.

Mt. Tasman
3497

Aoraki/
Mount Cook
3724

Tasman Gl.

Mount Cook

2251

Mount Somers

South Branch

Methven

Lincoln
Leeston

919

Little River

Akaroa

Tititira Hd.

L. Tekapo

Two Thumbs Ra.

Hinds

Ashburton

Southbridge

L. Ellesmere

Akaroa Harbour

Okuru

Haast

Glenmary
2590

Benn Ra.

L. Tekapo

Geraldine
Fairlie

Tinwald

Akaroa

Jackson Hd.
B.

Cascade Pt.

Haast
Pass

Ben Ohau Ra.

Mt.
3027

L. Ohau

L. Pukaki

Mackenzie
Plains

Winchester
Pleasant Point

Timaru

Canterbury Bight

SOUTH ISLAND
(Te Waipounamu)

Awarua Pt.
Awarua B.

Yates Pt.

MOUNT
ASPIRING

Mt. Aspiring
3033

Young Ra.

L. Hawea

Hunter

Waitaki Plains
1894

Benmore Pk.

Kirkliston Ra.

St. Andrews

Hunter

Milford Sd.

Mt. McKerrow
2723

Barrier Ra.

Olivine Ra.

L. Wanaka

Hawea Flat

The Hunter Hills

Milford Sound

Mitre Peak
1683

Sutherland
Falls

Mt. Earnslaw
2819

Richardson Mts.

Wanaka
1936

Mt St. Bathan's
2087

Hakataramea

Waimate

33

Bligh Sound

George Sound

Harris Mts.

Pisa Ra.

Hawkdun Mts.

Kurow

Waihao
Morven
Glenavy

Caswell Sound

Humboldt Mts.

Stuart Mts.

Glenorchy

Arrowtown

Cromwell

Dunstan Mts.

St. Bathans

Duntroon

Ngapara
Downs

Oamaru

Charles Sound

1610

Franklin Mts.

Queenstown

2319

Double Cone

Clyde

Naseby

Tokarahi

Pukeuri

Thompson Sd.

L. Te
Anau

Eyre Mts.

L. Wakatipu

Alexandra

Rough
Ridge

Ranfurly

Windsor

Maheno

Secretary I.

The Remarkables

Kingston

Roxburgh

Middlemarch

Kakanui Mts.

Hampden

Doubtful Sd.

2022

Jane Pk.

Athol

Dagg Sd.

Mt. Lyall
1892

Hyde

Dunback

Shag Pt.

FIORDLAND

Garvie Mts.

1449

Palmerston

Breaksea
Sd.

Murchison
Mts.

Lumsden

Mossburn

Waikaia

Umbrella Mts.

Beaumont

Sutton

Waikouaiti
Downs

Waikouaiti

Resolution
I.

SOUTHLAND

Dipton

Miller's Flat

Waimea
Plain

Otago
Harbour

Dusky
Sd.

Hunter
Mts.

Kaherekoau Mts.

Monowai

Ohai
Birchwood

Edievale

Dunedin

Otago Pen.

Mosgiel

C. Saunders

Providence

Cameron Mts.

Caroline
Pk.
1704

Riversdale

Mataura

Waipahi

Lawrence

Tapanui

Clutha

Allanton
Waihola

St. Kilda

Chalky
Inlet
Coal I.

Preservation
Inlet

L. Hauroko

Orawia
Otautau

Gore

Winton

Taieri

Hedgehope
Edendale

Clinton

Milton

Puysegur Pt.

Te
Waewae
B.

Tuatapere

Wairio
Nightcaps

Balclutha

Stirling
Kaitangata

Solander I.

Pahia Pt.

Riverton

Orepuki
Thornbury

Wyndham

Owaka

Nugget Pt.

Centre I.

Makarewa

Glenham

Invercargill

Fortrose

Catlins

Tahakopa

Wallacetown
South
Invercargill

Toetoes

Long Pt.

Bluff

Bluff Harbour

Waipapa Pt.

Chaslands
Mistake

Mt. Anglem
980

Codfish I.

Foveaux Str.

Ruapuke I.

PACIFIC

Mason B.

Doughboy B.

Halfmoon
Bay

Paterson
Inlet

RAKIURA

Stewart I.
(Rakiura)

Port Pegasus

South West C.

OCEAN

Projection: Conical with two standard parallels

East from Greenwich

CHATHAM
ISLANDS

on same scale
as main map **c**

PACIFIC OCEAN

The Sisters

C. Young

Munning Pt.

Western
Reef

Te One

Waitangi

Chatham I.
(Rekohu)

The Forty
Fours

Owenga

C. Fournier

Chatham
Islands
(Wharekauri)

The Horns

Pitt Strait

Mangere I.

Pitt I.

Star Keys

Rangatira I.

The Pyramid

West from Greenwich

COPYRIGHT PHILIP'S

ft   m

9000   3000

6000   2000

3000   1000

1200   400

600   200

0   0

200   600

1000   3000

1500   4500

3000   9000

4000   12 000

m   ft

RUSSIA
Yekaterinburg
Tomsk
Moskva
Volga
Novosibirsk
Irkutsk
Chita
Oб
Lena
Okhotsk
Sea of Okhotsk
Poluostrov Kamchatka
Komandorskiye Ostrova (Russia)
Near Is. (U.S.A.)
Aleutian Basin
Beri Sea
Andreano (U.S.A.)

KAZAKHSTAN
Astana (Aqmola)
Semey
Oz. Baykal
Balqash Köl
Aral Sea
Almaty
 MONGOLIA
Ulaanbaatar
Blagoveshchensk
Amur
Khabarovsk
Sakhalin
Petropavlovsk-Kamchatskiy
Shirshov Ridge
-7822
Chinook Trough
Aleutian Trench
Aleutia

KYRGYZSTAN
Toshkent
Ürümqi
Altai
Changchun
Harbin
Vladivostok
Hakodate
La Perouse Str.
Kurilskiye Ostrova (Russia)
Kuril-Kamchatka Trench
-10,542
Northwest

TAJIKISTAN
AFGHANISTAN
Kabul
Srinagar
Kunlun Shan
CHINA
Lanzhou
Beijing
Tianjin
Taiyuan
NORTH KOREA
Shenyang
Dalian
SOUTH KOREA
Seoul
Sapporo
Sea of Japan
Pacific
Emperor Seamount Chain
Shatsky Rise

PAKISTAN
Lahore
Delhi
Himalaya
XIZANG
Lhasa
8850
Everest
Xi'an
Qingdao
Kyoto
Osaka
Fuji-San 3776
Tokyo
Yokohama
JAPAN
Nagoya
Sendai
Kyushu
Shikoku
Yellow Sea
Tamu Massif
1980
Tamu
-10,554
Japan Trench
Ho

Kanpur
Nanjing
Wuhan
Chongqing
Changsha
Shanghai
Hangzhou
East China Sea
Okinawa
Ryukyu-retto (Japan)
Kazan-Retto (Japan)
Minami-Tori-Shima (Japan)
Midway Is. (U.S.A.)
Basin

INDIA
Ganga
BANGLADESH
Kolkata (Calcutta)
Dhaka
Kunming
Fuzhou
Guangzhou
Macau
Hong Kong
Taipei
TAIWAN
Philippine Sea
Iwo-Jima (Japan)
Ogasawara Gunto (Japan)
Kyushu-Palau Ridge
Izu-Ozima-Ridge
Wake I. (U.S.A.)
Mid-Pacific Mou
Lisianski I. (U.S.A.)

Hyderabad
MYANMAR
Mandalay
LAOS
Hanoi
Hainan
C. Engano
Luzon
Paracel Is.
Manila
West Mariana Basin
NORTHERN MARIANAS (U.S.A.)
Tinian
Saipan
East Mariana Basin
MARSHALL IS.
Bikini Atoll
Enewetak Atoll
Ratak Chain
P A

Bay of Bengal
Andaman Is. (India)
THAILAND
Bangkok
CAMBODIA
VIETNAM
Phnom Penh
Thanh Pho Ho Chi Minh
South China Sea
Mindoro
PHILIPPINES
Samar
Palawan
Philippine Basin
Mariana Trench
Challenger 11,022 Deep
-10,497
GUAM (U.S.A.)
Yap
Micro
Kwajalein
Jaluit I.
Majuro
Ralik Chain

Chennai (Madras)
Nicobar Is. (India)
G. of Thailand
Samar
Sulu Sea
Mindanao
Davao
4101
Melekeok
Caroline Is.
Chuuk
nesia
Butaritari

SRI LANKA
Colombo
Kuala Lumpur
MALAYSIA
Sea
Celebes Sea
FED. STATES OF MICRONESIA
PALAU
West Caroline Basin
Eauripik Rise
Pohnpei
Palikir
East Caroline Basin
Me
Melanesian Basin
Tarawa
Yaren
Gilbert Is.
Banaba
Howland I. (U.
Baker I. (U.
Pacif
Centr

PEN. MALAYSIA
Singapore
SARAWAK
BRUNEI
SABAH
Borneo
Halmahera
Sulawesi
Seram
Buru
Puncak Jaya 4884
PAPUA
Solomon Rise
NAURU
la
K I

Sumatera
Palembang
INDONESIA
Makassar
Banda Sea
7440
PAPUA NEW GUINEA
Admiralty Is.
New Ireland
Bismarck Arch.
New
Abaringani
Enderbury
Phoenix Is.
O

Java Sea
Jakarta
Jawa
Surabaya
Flores Sea
Flores
Bali
Dili
EAST TIMOR
Timor
Sumbawa
Sumba
Guinea
Lae
Kokopo
New Britain
Bougainville
SOLOMON IS.
s
a
Fongafale
TUVALU
Tokelau (N.Z.)

Selat Sunda
Sunda Islands
Java Trench
Christmas I. (Austral.)
Arafura Sea
Torres Strait
C. York
Louisiade Arch.
Port Moresby
Honiara
Guadalcanal
Santa Cruz I.
9165
Rotuma
Îs. Wallis & Futuna (Fr.)
SAMO
Apia

Cocos Is. (Austral.)
North Australian Basin
C. Arnhem
Darwin
Gulf of Carpentaria
Great Barrier Reef
Coral Sea Basin
Espíritu Santo
VANUATU
Port Vila
Vanua Levu
Viti Levu
Suva
FIJI
West Fiji Basin
7570
Nuku'alofa
TON

Exmouth Plateau
Broome
Cairns
Coral Sea
Î. Chesterfield
New Caledonia Trough
Tonga Trench

Wharton Basin
North West C.
Townsville
Great Dividing Ra.
NEW CALEDONIA (Fr.)
Nouméa
Îs. Loyauté
Norfolk Ridge
South Fiji Basin
10,822
Tonga Tr

INDIAN
Mount Isa
AUSTRALIA
Alice Springs
Rockhampton
Middleton Basin
Lord Howe
Norfolk I. (Austral.)
Kermadec Is. (N.Z.)
Kermadec Trench
10,047

OCEAN
Geraldton
Kati Thanda-L. Eyre
Brisbane
Lord Howe I. (Austral.)
South Fiji Basin

Broken Ridge
Perth Basin
Perth
Naturaliste Plateau
Albany
Great Australian Bight
Adelaide
Sydney
Canberra
Mt. Kosciuszko 2228
Murray
Darling
Tasman Sea
NEW ZEALAND
Auckland
Chatham Rise
Chatham Is. (N.Z.)

Nouvelle Amsterdam (Fr.)
Î. St. Paul (Fr.)
Mid-Indian Ridge
South Australian Basin
Melbourne
Bass Str.
Tasmania
Hobart
East Tasman Plateau
Tasman Basin
Wellington
Aoraki Mt. Cook 3724
Christchurch
Dunedin
Bounty Trough
Bounty Is. (N.Z.)

Îs. Crozet (Fr.)
SOUTHERN
South Tasman Rise
Invercargill
Campbell I. (N.Z.)
Campbell Plateau
Antipodes Is. (N.Z.)

Kerguelen (Fr.)
OCEAN
Auckland Is. (N.Z.)

Heard I. (Austral.)
Macquarie I. (Austral.)

ft m
12 000 4000
9000 3000
6000 2000
3000 1000
1500 500
600 200
0 0
200 600
1000 3000
2000 6000
4000 12 000
6000 18 000
8000 24 000
m ft

Arctic Circle

ALASKA (U.S.A.)
Anchorage
5959
Bristol Bay
Juneau
Gulf of Alaska
Is. (U.S.A.)

Tufts
Abyssal
Plain

C A N A D A

Prince of Wales I. (U.S.A.)
Prince Rupert
Haida Gwaii (Queen Charlotte Is.) (Canada)

Edmonton
Calgary
Regina
Winnipeg
L. Winnipeg
Newfoundland

Vancouver
Vancouver I.
Victoria
Seattle
Portland
Boise
Snake

St. Lawrence
Québec
Montréal
Ottawa
St. John's

Minneapolis
L. Superior
L. Michigan
L. Huron
Toronto
Detroit
L. Ontario
L. Erie
Buffalo
Boston

Northeast

Mendocino Fracture Zone
C. Mendocino

Salt Lake City
Denver
Chicago
Pittsburgh
New York
Philadelphia
Baltimore
Washington D.C.

Sacramento
6741
Missouri
Colorado
Kansas City
St. Louis
Cincinnati

San Francisco
4418

Murray Fracture Zone

UNITED STATES
Oklahoma City
Memphis
Atlanta
C. Hatteras

A T L A N T I C

Pacific

Los Angeles
San Diego
Phoenix
Dallas

Guadalupe (Mex.)
Ciudad Juárez
Houston
San Antonio
New Orleans
Tampa
Jacksonville

Bermuda (U.K.)

Sargasso Sea

Molokai Fracture Zone
Gulf of Mexico
Monterrey
Miami
BAHAMAS

O C E A N

Tropic of Cancer

Basin
C. San Lucas

an Ridge

Honolulu
Kauai
Oahu
Maui
HAWAIIAN IS. (U.S.A.)
4205
Hilo
Hawaii

La Habana
Canal de Yucatán
CUBA
West Indies

Guadalajara
Mexico
5610
Puebla
Mérida
7680
HAITI
DOMINICAN REP.
JAMAICA
Kingston
8605
PUERTO RICO (U.S.A.)
Leeward Is.

Johnston I. (U.S.A.)

Clarion Fracture Zone
Is. Revilla Gigedo (Mex.)

Acapulco
Middle America Trench
6662
BELIZE
GUATEMALA
HONDURAS
Guatemala
Caribbean Sea
BARBADOS

C I F I C

San Salvador
EL SALVADOR
NICARAGUA
Managua
Barranquilla
Maracaibo
Windward Is.

North West Christmas I. Ridge

Palmyra Is. (U.S.A.)

Î. Clipperton (Fr.)

Clipperton Fracture Zone

Guatemala Basin

COSTA RICA
San José
Colón
PANAMA
Panamá

I. del Coco (Costa Rica)
Cocos Ridge
Panama Basin

Caracas
Orinoco
VENEZUELA

asin

Teraina
Tabuaeran
Kiritimati

Medellín
I. de Malpelo (Colombia)
Bogotá
Cali
COLOMBIA

E A N
Jarvis I. (U.S.A.)

Galápagos Fracture Zone

Galápagos (Ecuador)
Carnegie Ridge
Quito
ECUADOR

Malden I.
Starbuck I.

Equator

B A T I

Guayaquil
Iquitos
C. Pariñas

Amazonas

BRAZIL

ains I.
Pukapuka
Manihiki
Penrhyn (Tongareva)

Manihiki
Plateau
Vostok I.

Nuku Hiva
Caroline I. (Millennium I.)
Flint I.
Hiva Oa
Îs. Marquises

Marquesas Fracture Zone

Trujillo

ER.
OA
S.A.)
Suwarrow Is.

Yupanqui
Basin

6369
PERU
Lima

Cook Is. (N.Z.)
Îs. de la Société
Bora Bora
Huahine
Raiatea
Papeete
Tahiti
Rangiroa
Îs. Tuamotu

Mendaña
Fracture Zone

Cusco
L. Titicaca
Arequipa
Nevado Ancohuma 6550

ue I.
.Z.)
Aitutaki
Atiu
Rarotonga
Mangaia
Mururoa
Îs. Gambier

FRENCH POLYNESIA

6866
La Paz
BOLIVIA
Peru–
Arica

Îs. Tubuai

Oeno I.
Henderson I.
Pitcairn I. (U.K.)
Ducie I.
Rapa

Tropic of Capricorn

Easter Fracture Zone
Sala-y-Gómez (Chile)
I. de Pascua (Chile)

Sala-y-Gómez Ridge

San Felix (Chile)
San Ambrosio (Chile)

Iquique
Chile
Antofagasta
8050
PARAGUAY

San Miguel de Tucumán
Asunción

Pôrto Alegre

S o u t h w e s t

Roggeveen
Basin

Arch. de Juan Fernández (Chile)
Aconcagua 6982

Córdoba
Valparaíso
Rosario

URUGUAY
Montevideo

P a c i f i c

Challenger Fracture Zone

Santiago
Concepción

Buenos Aires
Río de la Plata

ATLANTIC

B a s i n

Menard Fracture Zone

ARGENTINA

OCEAN
6212

Pacific-Antarctic Ridge

S o u t h e a s t
P a c i f i c   B a s i n

Punta Arenas
C. de Hornos
Est. de Magallanes
Tierra del Fuego
Drake Passage

Falkland Is. (U.K.)

South Georgia (U.K.)

COPYRIGHT PHILIP'S

100 0 200 400 600 800 1000 1200 1400 km

1:31 100 000

100 0 200 400 600 800 1000 miles

Projection: Bonne

West from Greenwich

COPYRIGHT PHILIP'S

1:31 100 000

100 0 200 400 600 800 1000 1200 1400 km

100 0 200 400 600 800 1000 miles

B A B

RUSSIA
Asia
St. Lawrence I.
Bering Strait
Bering Sea

ARCTIC OCEAN
International Date Line

GREENLAND (Denmark)
ICELAND
Reykjavik
Denmark Strait

Queen Elizabeth Is.
Ellesmere I.
Beaufort Sea
Baffin Bay
Davis Strait
Nuuk

ALASKA (USA)
Yukon
Fairbanks
Anchorage
Kodiak I.
Gulf of Alaska
Porcupine
Arctic Circle
Victoria I.
NORTHWEST TERRITORIES
YUKON
Whitehorse
Juneau
Mackenzie
Great Bear L.
Back
Great Slave L.
Yellowknife
Dubawnt
NUNAVUT
Iqaluit
Hudson Strait

Baffin Island

CANADA

Hudson Bay

BRITISH COLUMBIA
Skeena
Fraser
Peace
Athabasca
ALBERTA
Edmonton
Calgary
SASKATCHEWAN
Saskatchewan
Regina
Churchill
Nelson
MANITOBA
L. Winnipeg
Winnipeg
ONTARIO
Eastmain
QUÉBEC
St. Lawrence
NEWFOUNDLAND & LABRADOR
St-John's
St-Pierre et Miquelon (Fr.)

Victoria
Vancouver
WASHINGTON
Olympia
Seattle
Portland
Salem
OREGON
Columbia
MONTANA
Helena
IDAHO
Boise
Snake
Missouri
WYOMING
NORTH DAKOTA
Bismarck
SOUTH DAKOTA
MINNESOTA
Minneapolis-St. Paul
WISCONSIN
Madison
Milwaukee
L. Superior
L. Michigan
MICHIGAN
Lansing
Detroit
L. Huron
L. Ontario
TORONTO
Buffalo
Ottawa
Montréal
Québec
MAINE
Augusta
NEW BRUNSWICK
Fredericton
PRINCE EDWARD I.
Charlottetown
NOVA SCOTIA
Halifax
VT.
N.H.
Concord
MASS.
Boston
Providence
Hartford
NEW YORK
NEW YORK
Cleveland
Pittsburgh
PA.
N.J.
PHILADELPHIA
Baltimore
WASHINGTON D.C.
MD.
DEL.
Richmond

IOWA
ILLINOIS
INDIANA
OHIO
Columbus
W.VA.
VIRGINIA
KENTUCKY
TENNESSEE
NORTH CAROLINA
Raleigh
Charlotte
SOUTH CAROLINA
Columbia
Charleston

NEBRASKA
Lincoln
NEVADA
UTAH
Salt Lake City
Carson City
Sacramento
SAN FRANCISCO
San Jose
CALIFORNIA
Las Vegas
LOS ANGELES
San Diego
Tijuana
Mexicali
UNITED STATES
COLORADO
Denver
KANSAS
Topeka
Kansas City
St. Louis
MISSOURI
Springfield
Indianapolis
Cincinnati
CHICAGO
Nashville
Memphis
Little Rock
ARKANSAS
OKLAHOMA
Oklahoma City
Santa Fe
Albuquerque
ARIZONA
Phoenix
Tucson
NEW MEXICO
El Paso
Ciudad Juárez
TEXAS
DALLAS-FT. WORTH
Austin
HOUSTON
San Antonio
Birmingham
ALABAMA
MISSISSIPPI
Jackson
Montgomery
GEORGIA
ATLANTA
Baton Rouge
LOUISIANA
New Orleans
Tallahassee
Jacksonville
FLORIDA
Orlando
Tampa-St. Petersburg
MIAMI

PACIFIC OCEAN

Guadalupe (Mex.)
Tropic of Cancer
Revilla Gigedo Is. (Mex.)

Hermosillo
Culiacán
Río Grande
MÉXICO
Monterrey
Torreón
San Luis Potosí
Guadalajara
León
Querétaro
MÉXICO
Toluca
Puebla
Acapulco

Gulf of Mexico

Havana
CUBA
Cayman Is. (U.K.)
JAMAICA
Kingston
BAHAMAS
Nassau
Turks & Caicos Is. (U.K.)
Bermuda (U.K.)

ATLANTIC OCEAN

Florida Str.

Mérida
Belmopan
BELIZE
GUATEMALA
Guatemala
San Salvador
EL SALVADOR
HONDURAS
Tegucigalpa
NICARAGUA
Managua
L. Nicaragua
COSTA RICA
San José
PANAMA
Panamá

Caribbean Sea

HAITI
Port-au-Prince
DOMINICAN REP.
Santo Domingo
PUERTO RICO (U.S.A.)
San Juan

Barranquilla
Maracaibo
VENEZUELA
COLOMBIA
Medellín
South America

Projection: Bonne

West from Greenwich

7 ■ MÉXICO Capital Cities 8 9 10 11 12

COPYRIGHT PHILIP'S

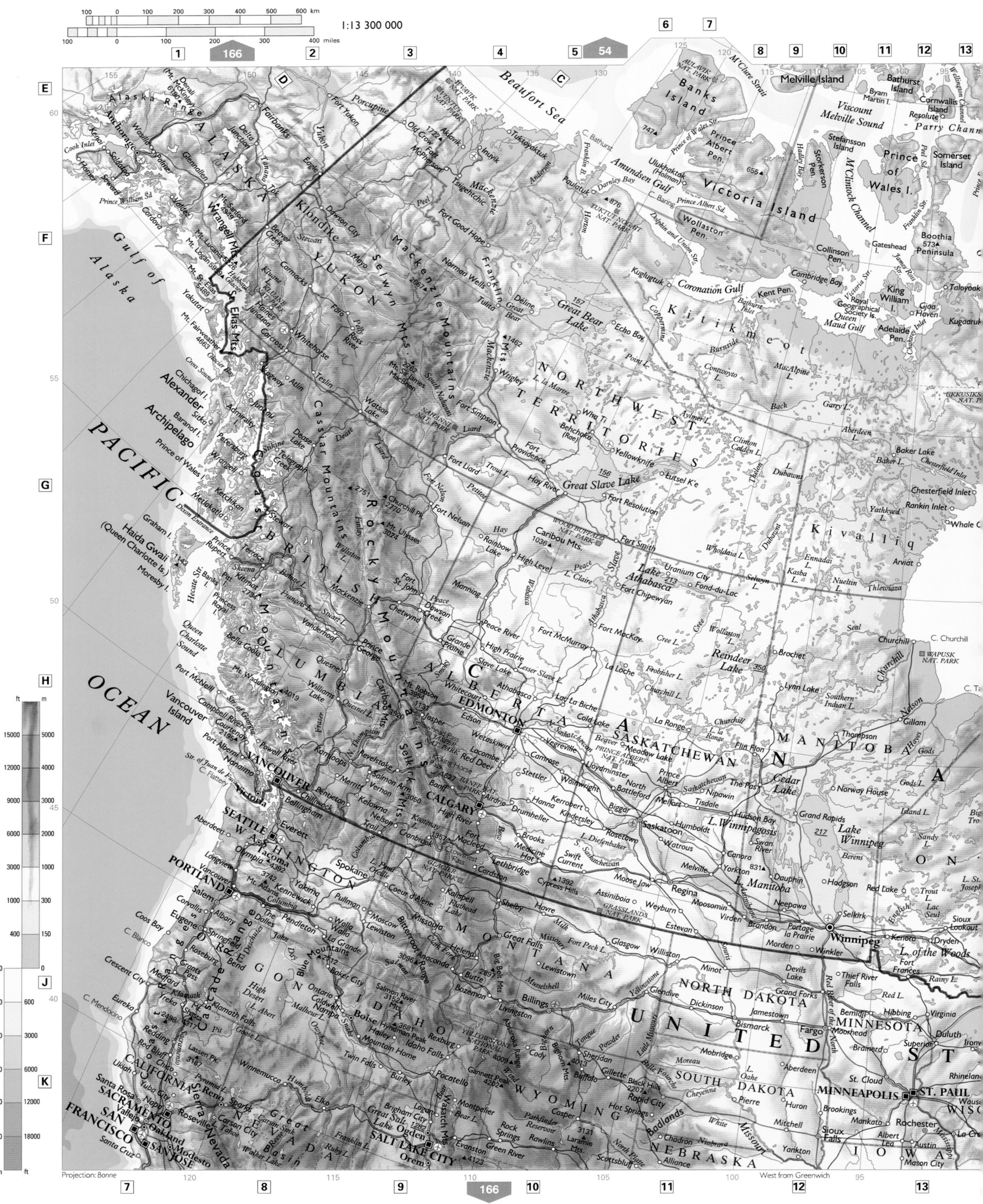

1:13 300 000

Projection: Bonne

West from Greenwich

54

57

NORTHERN CANADA
continuation northwards on same scale as main map

ARCTIC OCEAN

GREENLAND (KALAALLIT NUNAAT) (Denmark)

Kronprins Frederik Land
Kap Columbia
Alert
Lincoln Sea
Nyeboe Land
Peary Channel
QUTTINIRPAAQ NAT. PARK
Barbeau Pk.
Lake Hazen
Petermann Gletscher
Sermersuaq (Humboldt Gletscher)
C. Thomas Hubbard
Meighen I.
Nansen Sd.
Greely Fiord
Eureka
Agassiz Icecap
Knud Rasmussen Land
Axel Heiberg Island
Sverdrup Islands
Ellef Ringnes Island
Amund Ringnes I.
King Christian I.
Mackenzie King I.
Borden Island
Brock I.
Prince Patrick Island
Emerald I.
Lougheed I.
Norwegian Bay
Graham I.
Cornwall I.
Prince of Wales I.
Qegertarsuaq (Thule)
Qaanaaq (Thule)
Uummannaq (Dundas)
Lauge Koch Kyst
Kap York
Melville Bugt
Eglinton I.
N.W.T.
Parry Islands
Melville Island
Bathurst Island
Byam Martin I.
Cornwallis Island
Grinnell Pen.
NUNAVUT
Devon Island
Grise Fiord
Jones Sound
Coburg I.
M'Clure Strait
Viscount Melville Sound
Stefansson Island
Lowther I.
Resolute
Prince of Wales I.
Somerset Island
Parry Channel
Prince Regent Inlet
Brodeur Pen.
Nanisivik
Arctic Bay
Borden Pen.
Bylot I.
Eclipse Sd.
Pond Inlet
Lancaster Sound
SIRMILIK NAT. PARK
Baffin Bay

ARCTIC OCEAN

Island
Sound
Lancaster Sound
SIRMILIK NAT. PARK
Nanisivik
Arctic Bay
Borden Pen.
Bylot I.
Eclipse Sd.
Pond Inlet
GREENLAND (Denmark)
Baffin Bay
Nunavik
C. Adair
Clyde River
C. Raper
Iglulik
Rowley
Hall Beach
Spicer Is.
Air Force I.
Prince Charles I.
Home B.
Qikiqtarjuaq
Melville Peninsula
Foxe Basin
AUYUITTUQ NAT. PARK
Cumberland Peninsula
Pangnirtung
Koukdjuak
C. Dyer
Baffin Island (Qikiqtaaluk)
Davis Strait
Netilling L.
Cumberland Sd.
Hoare B.
C. Mercy
Repulse Bay
NUNAVUT
Amadjuak L.
Iqaluit
Meta Incognita Peninsula
Frobisher Bay
Kimmirut
Vansittart I.
C. Dorchester
Foxe Pen.
Hall Peninsula
Resolution I.
Southampton
Salisbury
Mill I.
Coral Harbour
Bell Pen.
Nottingham
Charles I.
Salluit
Digges Is.
Ivujivik
Quaqtaq
Akpatok I.
Coats I.
Kangiqsujuaq
Cratère du Nouveau-Québec
C. Chidley
TORNGAT MTS. NAT. PARK
Mansel I.
Péninsule d'Ungava
Kangirsuk
Ungava Bay
Killiniq I.
Mt. d'Iberville / Mt. Caubvick
Hebron
Smith I.
Arnaud
L. Payne
Feuilles
Kangiqsualujjuaq
George
Nain
Ottawa Is.
Puvirnituq
Inukjuak
Labrador Sea
Hopedale
Hudson Bay
Sleeper Is.
King George Is.
L. Minto
Mélèzes
Nunavik
Caniapiscau
Baleine
C. Harrison
Rigolet
Cartwright
NEWFOUNDLAND & LABRADOR
Port Hope Simpson
Sanikiluaq
Bakers Dozen Is.
L. à l'Eau Claire
Smallwood Rés.
Labrador
Kawawachikamach
North West River
Happy Valley–Goose Bay
St. Lewis
Belcher Is.
C. Henrietta Maria
Kuujjuarapik
Grande Baleine
L. Bienville
Schefferville
Churchill Falls
Churchill
St. Augustin
Str. of Belle Isle
Belle Isle
C. Bauld
St. Anthony
Grey Is.
Peawanuck
Winisk
James Bay
Chisasibi
La Grande
Kanaaupscow
Petitsikapau L.
Esker
Labrador City
Fermont
Ashuanipi
Romaine
Baie Verte
Notre Dame B.
Long Range Mts.
Lewisporte
Gander
Bonavista
Twin Is.
Akimiski I.
Wemindji
Eastmain
Ontario
Attawapiskat
Fort Albany
Charlton
Rupert
L. Mistassini
L. Albanel
L. Caniapiscau
Rés. Gouin
Gagnon
Manicouagan Rés.
Manicouagan
Havre-St-Pierre
Natashquan
Deer Lake
Corner Brook
Grand Falls-Windsor
Newfoundland
Trinity B.
Corbonear
St. John's
Placentia
Avalon
C. Race
Moosonee
Albany
Waskaganish
Mistassini
Groulx
Sept-Îles
Port-Cartier
Dét. de Jacques-Cartier
Î. d'Anticosti
Stephenville
Channel-Port aux Basques
ST-PIERRE et MIQUELON (Fr.)
Placentia B.
Marystown
Nakina
Kapiskau
Hearst
L. Matagami
Matagami
Chibougamau
Dolbeau-Mistassini
Baie-Comeau
Matane
Gaspé
Gaspésie
Dét. d'Honguedo
Gulf of St. Lawrence
Cabot Strait
C. Ray
C. North
Sydney
Glace Bay
Geraldton
Cochrane
Amos
Val-d'Or
Rés. Cabonga
Alma
Chicoutimi
Rimouski
Campbellton
Bathurst
Chaleur B.
Îs. de la Madeleine
Cape Breton I.
Port Hawkesbury
New Glasgow
Antigonish
Timmins
Kirkland Lake
Rouyn-Noranda
L. Abitibi
L. St-Jean
Roberval
Jonquière
Rivière-du-Loup
Edmundston
Miramichi
PRINCE EDWARD I.
Summerside
Charlottetown
Northumberland Str.
Amherst
Truro
Dartmouth
Halifax
Sydney
Thunder Bay
Marathon
Chapleau
New Liskeard
Saguenay
La Tuque
Shawinigan
Trois-Rivières
Grand Falls
Woodstock
Fredericton
NEW BRUNSWICK
Moncton
NOVA SCOTIA
Windsor
Bridgewater
Liverpool
Sable I. (Nova Scotia)
Wawa
Sault Ste. Marie
Elliot Lake
Sudbury
North Bay
Pembroke
Québec
Lévis
Thetford Mines
Drummondville
St-Hyacinthe
Sherbrooke
MAINE
Bangor
Augusta
St-Georges
Saint John
B. of Fundy
Digby
Yarmouth
C. Sable
Superior
Houghton
Marquette
Manistique
Menominee
Green Bay
Manitoulin
Georgian Bay
Parry Sound
Huntsville
Orillia
Barrie
OTTAWA
Hull
Outaouais
Mont-Laurier
Cornwall
Montpelier
VERMONT
NEW HAMPSHIRE
Concord
Manchester
Portland
MILWAUKEE
Grand Rapids
Flint
Sarnia
London
DETROIT
Windsor
L. Erie
Cleveland
Toledo
Lake Michigan
Traverse City
Cadillac
Sheboygan
TORONTO
Kitchener
Hamilton
Niagara Falls
BUFFALO
ROCHESTER
Syracuse
Albany
Elmira
Binghamton
NEW YORK
PENNSYLVANIA
Erie
Jamestown
Oshawa
L. Ontario
Peterborough
Owen Sound
Brockville
Kingston
Belleville
Burlington
Lake Champlain
Adirondack Mts.
Lowell
BOSTON
MASS.
Springfield
CONN.
HARTFORD
New Haven
PROVIDENCE
Lewiston
C. Cod
Portland

ATLANTIC OCEAN

COPYRIGHT PHILIP'S

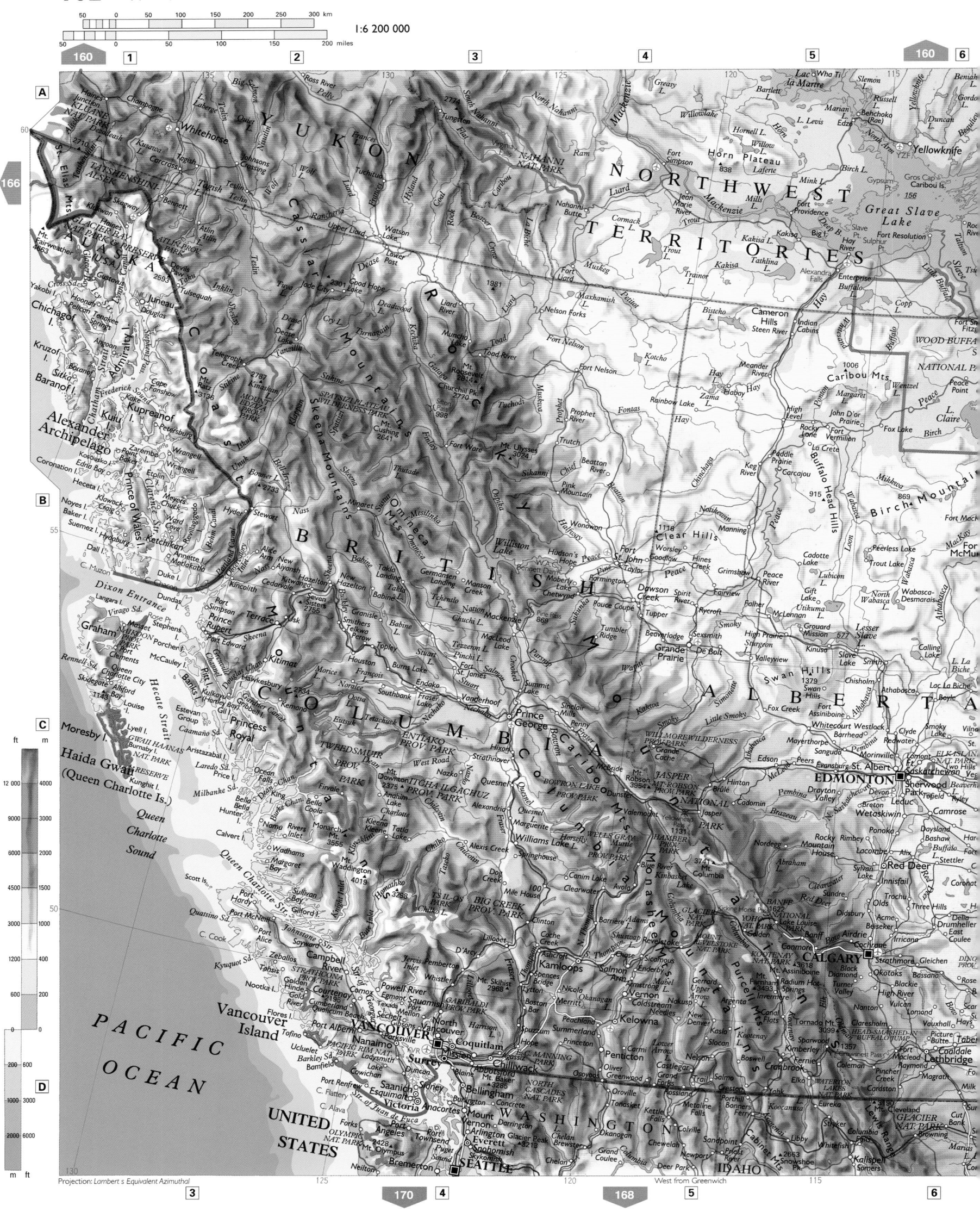

Projection: Lambert's Equivalent Azimuthal

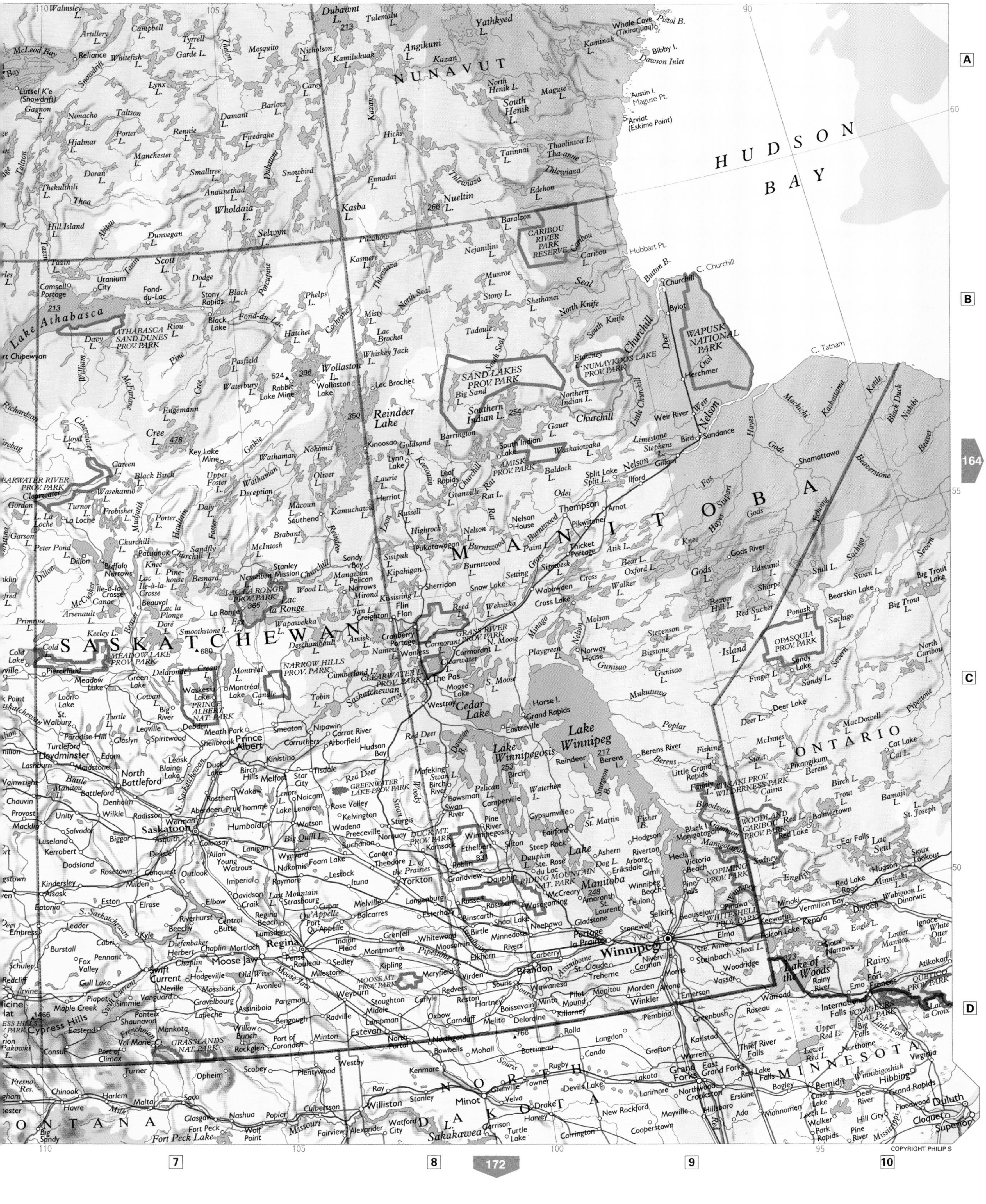

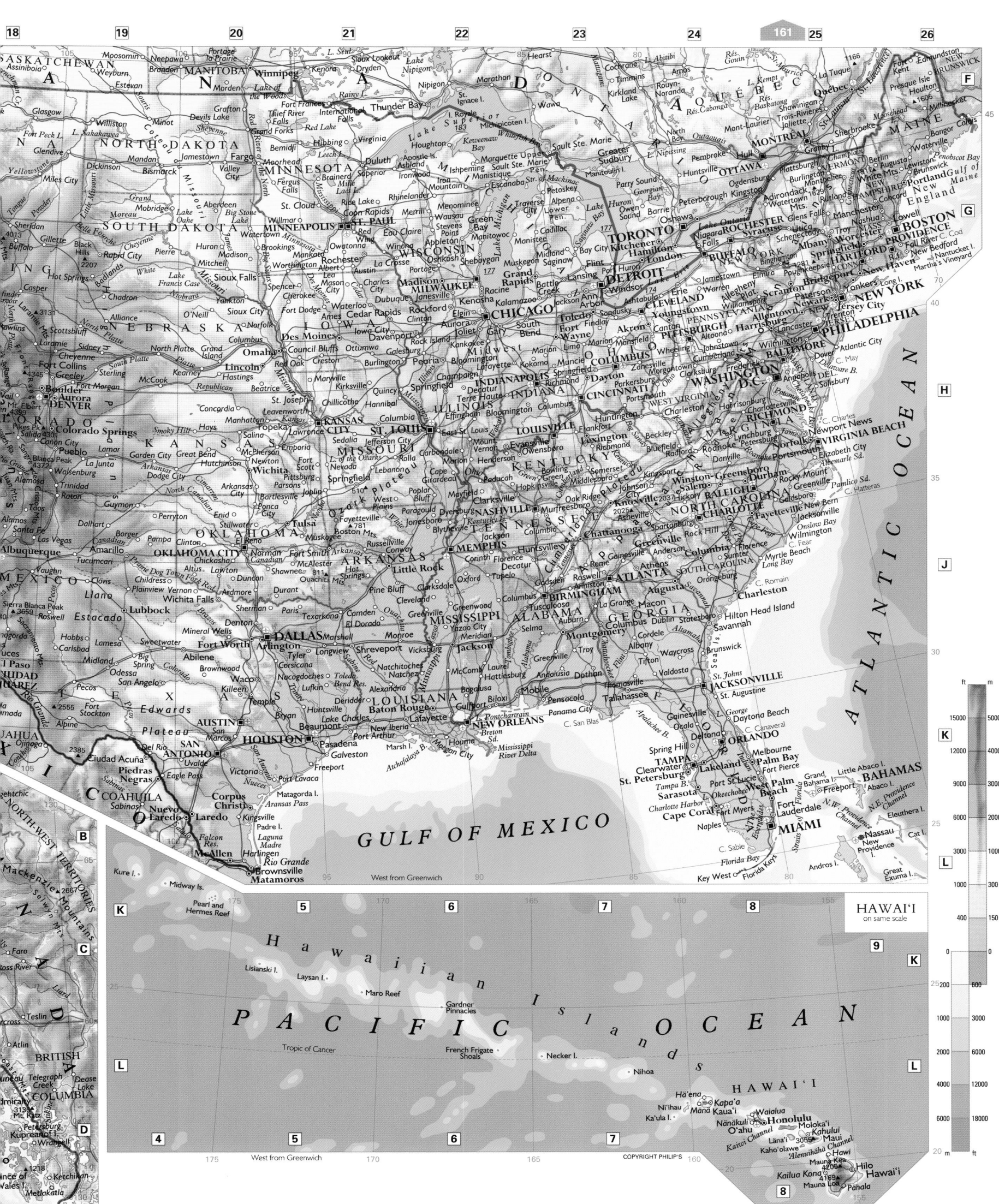

SASKATCHEWAN
Moosomin Neepawa
Assiniboia Weyburn Brandon Portage Winnipeg Kenora Sioux Lookout Lake Hearst
Estevan Morden Lake of Dryden Nipigon Timmins Amos La Tuque Fort
the Woods Marathon Cochrane Rouyn- Noranda Kempt Québec Edmundston Kent
Glasgow Williston Grafton Fort Frances Rés. Les. Presque Isle Houlton
Fort Peck L. Minot Devils Lake Thief River International Falls Thunder Bay Cabonga St-Maurice Shawinigan Québec MAINE
Glendive Falls Kirkland Lake Trois-Rivières Sherbrooke
Dickinson Bismarck Jamestown Fargo Bemidji Duluth Lake Greater Sudbury MONTRÉAL Granby Waterville
Miles City Mandan Valley City Moorhead Ironwood Sudbury L. Nipissing Hull OTTAWA Montpelier Bangor
NORTH DAKOTA Fergus Falls St. Cloud Iron Mountain Parry Sound Georgian Pembroke Huntsville Ogdensburg Plattsburgh Burlington Augusta
SOUTH DAKOTA MINNESOTA Brainerd Manistique Bay Peterborough Kingston Adirondack Watertown VERMONT NEW Portland Gulf of
Aberdeen MINNEAPOLIS ST. PAUL WISCONSIN Green Bay TORONTO Oshawa ROCHESTER Syracuse Glens Falls HAMPSHIRE Concord BOSTON
Pierre Watertown Eau Claire Appleton Kitchener London Hamilton NiagaraFalls BUFFALO Utica Albany Troy Manchester Worcester PROVIDENCE
Rapid City Brookings Madison MILWAUKEE Racine DETROIT Cleveland Erie Scranton NEW YORK
Huron Sioux Falls Rochester La Crosse Kenosha Windsor Akron Youngstown PENNSYLVANIA Allentown NEW YORK
IOWA CHICAGO South Bend Toledo PITTSBURGH Harrisburg PHILADELPHIA
NEBRASKA Des Moines Rockford Fort Wayne OHIO COLUMBUS WASHINGTON BALTIMORE
Omaha Lincoln Peoria INDIANAPOLIS Dayton CINCINNATI WEST VIRGINIA D.C. Atlantic City
KANSAS ST. LOUIS Springfield Louisville Frankfort RICHMOND VIRGINIA BEACH
KANSAS CITY MISSOURI KENTUCKY VIRGINIA Norfolk
COLORADO Wichita Springfield NASHVILLE Knoxville RALEIGH
DENVER Tulsa TENNESSEE NORTH CAROLINA
OKLAHOMA CITY MEMPHIS CHARLOTTE
Albuquerque OKLAHOMA ARKANSAS Little Rock ATLANTA Columbia SOUTH CAROLINA Charleston
DALLAS BIRMINGHAM GEORGIA Savannah
Fort Worth MISSISSIPPI ALABAMA Montgomery
El Paso TEXAS Shreveport Jackson JACKSONVILLE
Odessa Austin LOUISIANA Mobile FLORIDA
SAN ANTONIO HOUSTON Baton Rouge NEW ORLEANS Orlando
CIUDAD JUÁREZ Pasadena Gulfport TAMPA
COAHUILA Galveston St. Petersburg Fort Myers MIAMI
Corpus Christi GULF OF MEXICO BAHAMAS
Nuevo Laredo West from Greenwich Nassau
McAllen Brownsville Matamoros Key West Florida Bay Andros I.

ATLANTIC OCEAN

HAWAI'I
on same scale

PACIFIC OCEAN

Hawaiian Islands

HAWAI'I

Honolulu
O'ahu
Maui
Hawai'i
Hilo

COPYRIGHT PHILIP'S
West from Greenwich

1:2 200 000

WESTERN WASHINGTON REGION
on same scale

COPYRIGHT PHILIP'S

West from Greenwich

Projection: Bonne

Lava fields

1:2 200 000

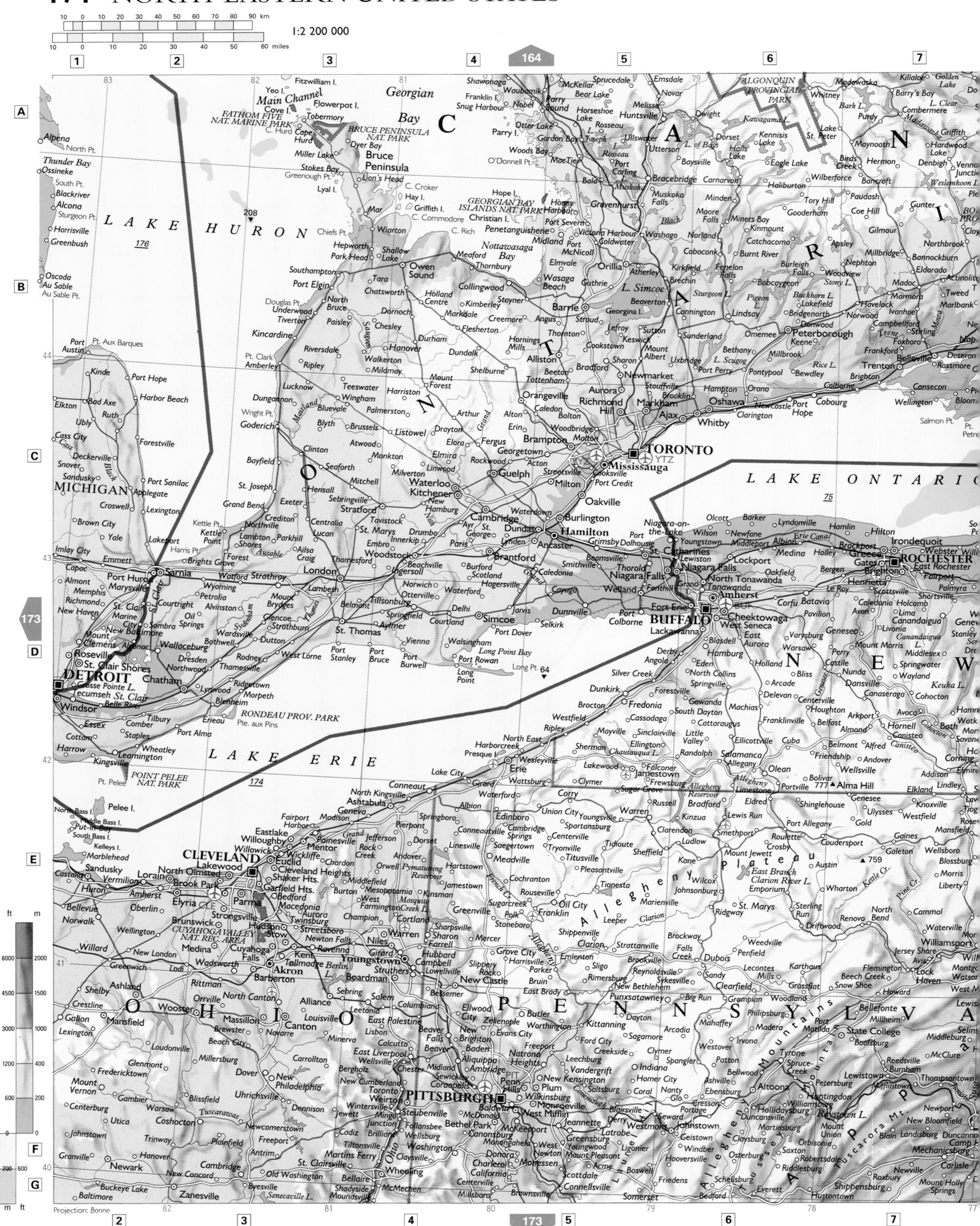

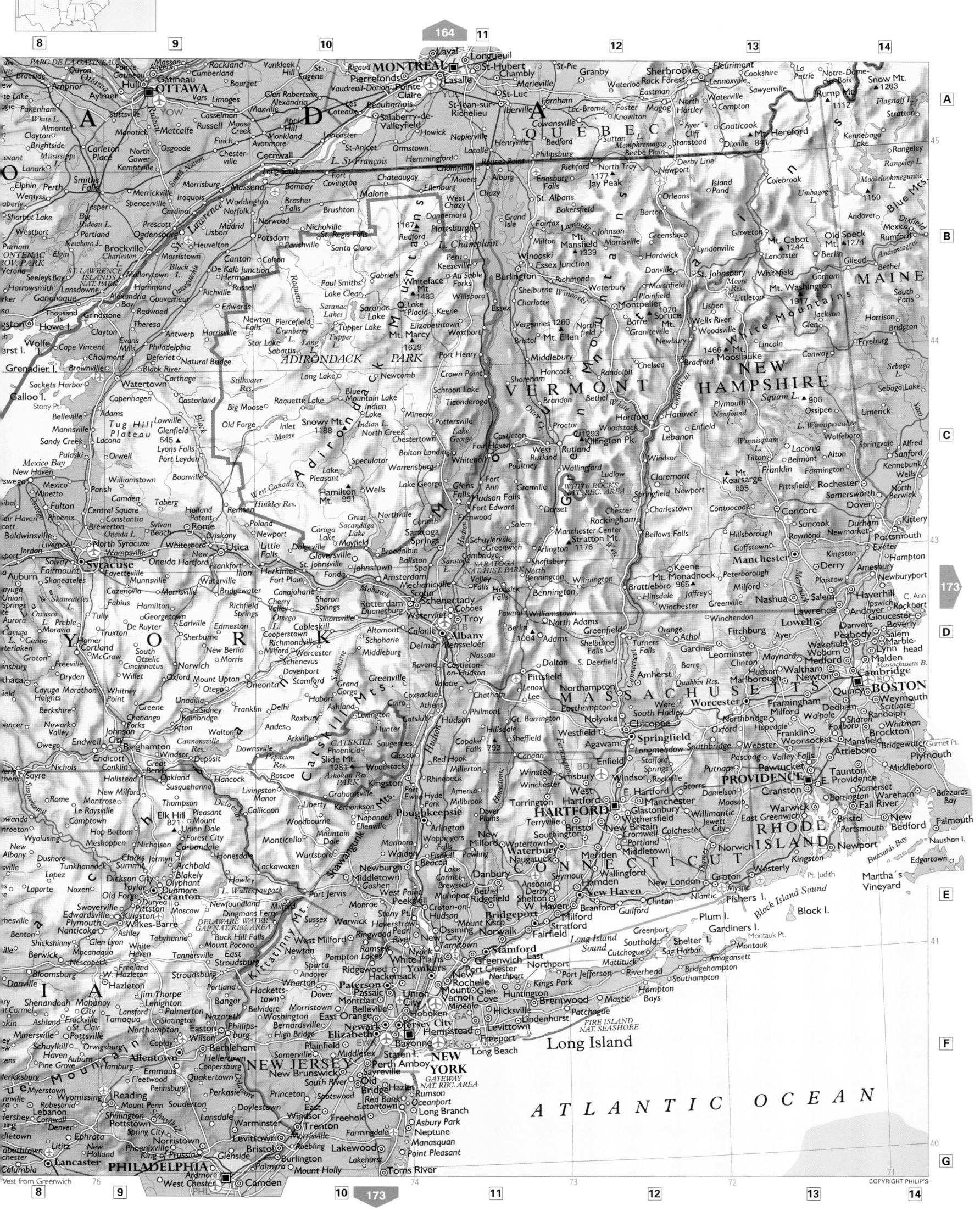

A

B

C

173

D

E

F

G

ATLANTIC OCEAN

Long Island

COPYRIGHT PHILIP'S

1:2 200 000

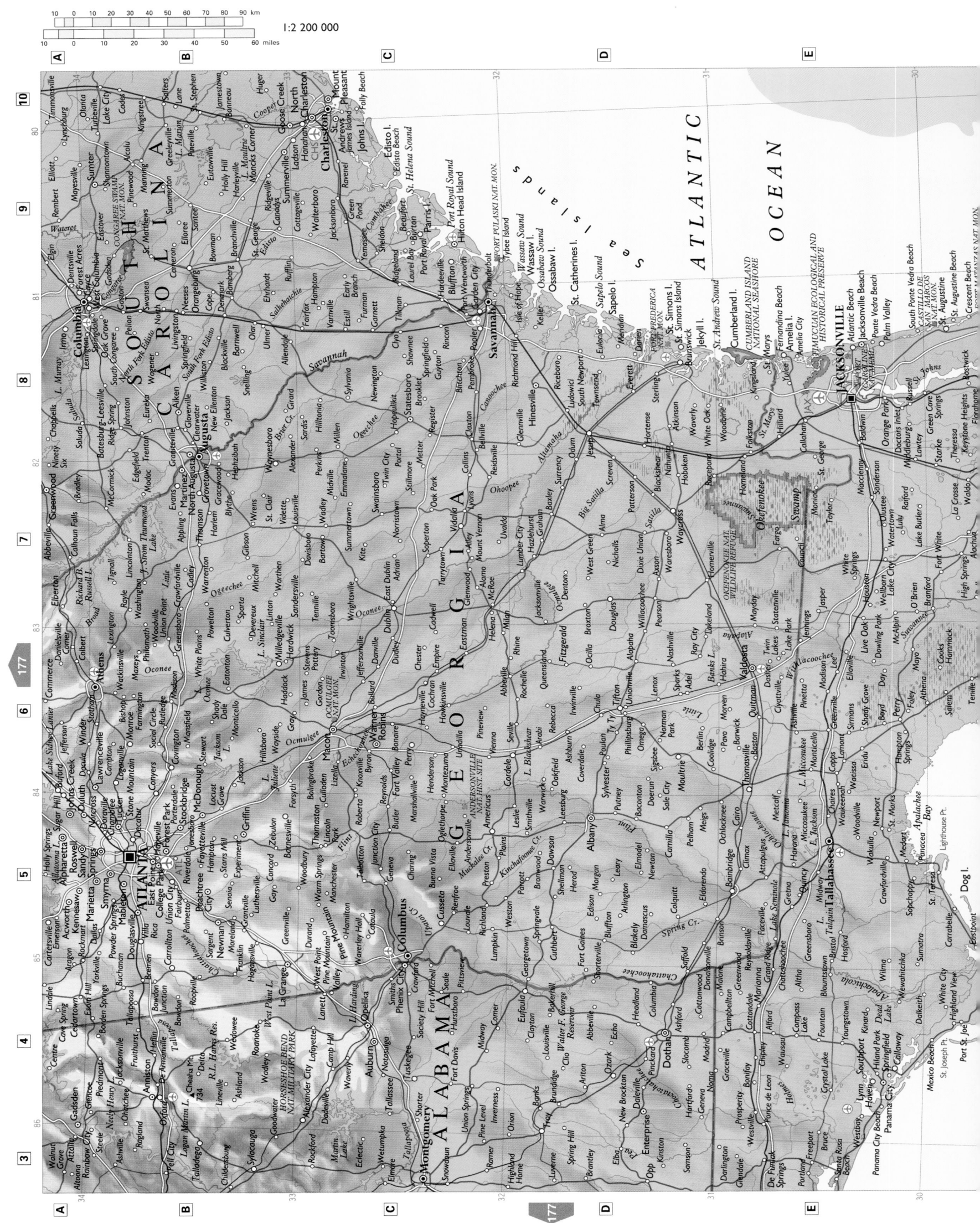

COPYRIGHT PHILIPS

F L O R I D A

GULF OF MEXICO

Major cities and places

ORLANDO
TAMPA
St. Petersburg
Clearwater
Miami
West Palm Beach
Fort Lauderdale
Hollywood
Miami Beach
Coral Gables
Hialeah
Kendall
Homestead

Flagler Beach, Ormond by the Sea, Ormond Beach, Daytona Beach, Port Orange, New Smyrna Beach, Edgewater, Titusville, Merritt Island, KENNEDY SPACE CENTER, Cape Canaveral, Cocoa Beach, Cocoa, Rockledge, Melbourne, Palm Bay, Malabar, Grant, Micco, Sebastian, Wabasso, Vero Beach, Gifford, Indrio, Fort Pierce, Port St. Lucie, St. Lucie, Jensen Beach, Stuart, Port Salerno, Hobe Sound, Jupiter, Juno Beach, Riviera Beach, West Palm Beach, Palm Beach, Lake Worth, Lantana, Boynton Beach, Delray Beach, Boca Raton, Deerfield Beach, Pompano Beach, Sunrise, Plantation, Davie, Pembroke Pines, Coral Springs, Margate, Tamarac, Oakland Park, Hallandale Beach, North Miami Beach, Surfside, North Miami, Miami Shores, North Miami, Westwood Lakes, South Miami, Cutler Ridge, Goulds, Florida City, Leisure City, Naranja

CANAVERAL NATIONAL SEASHORE

Merritt Island, Indian Harbour Beach, Satellite Beach, Indialantic

Lake Okeechobee, Lake Kissimmee, Lake Istokpoga

Crescent Lake, Lake George, Lake Harris, Lake Apopka, Lake Tohopekaliga

WALT DISNEY WORLD RESORT

Kissimmee, St. Cloud, Davenport, Haines City, Winter Haven, Lake Wales, Lake Alfred, Auburndale, Bartow, Frostproof, Avon Park, Sebring, Lake Placid, Venus, Palmdale, Moore Haven, Clewiston, Pahokee, South Bay, Belle Glade, Canal Point

BIG CYPRESS NAT. PRESERVE

EVERGLADES NATIONAL PARK

BISCAYNE NAT. PARK

Key Largo, Elliott Key, Key Biscayne

Naples, Bonita Springs, Fort Myers, Cape Coral, North Fort Myers, Punta Gorda, Port Charlotte, North Port, Venice, Sarasota, Bradenton, Palmetto, Bee Ridge, Osprey, Nokomis, Englewood, Grove City, Boca Grande, Gasparilla I., Sanibel, Captiva I., Pine I., San Carlo Park, Fort Myers Beach, Estero, Immokalee, La Belle, Marco Island, C. Romano, Goodland, Everglades City, Ochopee, Copeland

DE SOTO NAT. MEMORIAL

Dunedin, Palm Harbor, Tarpon Springs, New Port Richey, Holiday, Port Richey, Spring Hill, Weeki Wachee, Bayport, Hudson, Lutz, Zephyrhills, Dade City, Trilby, Lacoochee, Brooksville, Inverness, Homosassa Springs, Crystal River, Dunnellon, Citrus Springs, Beverly Hills, Ocala, Silver Springs, Belleview, Summerfield, Lady Lake, Leesburg, Eustis, Mount Dora, Tavares, Apopka, Altamonte Springs, Longwood, Winter Park, Oviedo, Sanford, Deltona, De Land, De Leon Springs, Pierson, Lake Helen, Orange City

Ocklawaha, Umatilla, Groveland, Clermont, Winter Garden, Ocoee, Winter Park, Casselberry, Belle Isle

Chiefland, Bronson, Williston, Archer, Micanopy, Reddick, Anthony, Citra, Orange Lake, Kendrick, Raleigh, Morriston, Lebanon Station, Coleman, Wildwood, Bushnell, Floral City

Cedar Key, Waccasassa Bay, Suwannee Sound, Crystal Bay, Gulf Hammock, Otter Creek, Inglis, Yankeetown

L. Griffin, L. Weir, L. Harris, L. Apopka, L. Tohopekaliga, E. L. Tohopekaliga, L. Kissimmee

SUWANNEE R., St. Johns, Kissimmee, Peace, Myakka, Withlacoochee, Caloosahatchee, Fisheating Cr., Hicpochee, Hillsboro Canal, Miami Canal, North New River Canal, W. Palm Beach Canal, Tamiami Canal

Lake Woodruff, Blue Cypress Lake, Lakewood Park, Fellsmere, Kenansville, Fort Drum, Basinger, Okeechobee, Brighton, Cornwell, Indiantown, Port Mayaca, Port Mayaca

---

Inset: FLORIDA KEYS

Continuation southwards on same scale

GULF OF MEXICO

EVERGLADES NAT. PARK, Flamingo, Florida Bay, C. Sable, Key Largo, Tavernier, Islamorada, Layton, Long Key, Marathon, Key Colony Beach, Big Pine Key, Summerland Key, Stock Island, Key West, Marquesas Keys

Florida Keys, Straits of Florida

Inset: WESTERN FLORIDA / ALABAMA

Continuation westwards on same scale

ALABAMA — FLORIDA

GULF OF MEXICO

Apalachicola, Apalachicola Bay, St. Vincent I., C. St. George, Eastpoint, Sumatra, Wewahitchka, Port St. Joe, St. Joseph Bay, C. San Blas, St. Joe, Highland View, Wewahitchka, Blountstown, Bristol, Hosford, Wilma, Greenwood, Grand Ridge, Marianna, Cottondale, Chipley, Alford, Campbellton, Graceville, Malone, Greenwood, Campbellton, Bonifay, Westville, De Funiak Springs, Ponce de Leon, Freeport, Portland, Bruce, Santa Rosa Beach, Destin, Fort Walton Beach, Mary Esther, Valparaiso, Niceville, Crestview, Baker, Milligan, Holt, Munson, Blackwater, Milton, Bagdad, Pace, Pensacola, Gulf Breeze, Warrington, Myrtle Grove, West Pensacola, Perdido Bay, Pensacola Bay, Escambia Bay, Century, Walnut Hill, McDavid, Cottonwood, Barrineau Park, Molino, Cantonment, Florala, Paxton, Florala, Panama City, Panama City Beach, Lynn Haven, Callaway, Parker, Springfield, Youngstown, Fountain, Compass Lake, Crystal Lake, Mexico Beach, Gulf Islands Nat. Seashore, Santa Rosa I., Gulf Breeze, Perdido Key

PROJECTION: Albers Equal Area

50 0 50 100 150 200 250 300 km

1:7 100 000

50 0 50 100 150 200 miles

State names in Central Mexico

1 DISTRITO FEDERAL   3 GUANAJUATO   5 MÉXICO   7 QUERÉTARO
2 AGUASCALIENTES   4 HIDALGO   6 MORELOS 8 TLAXCALA

Projection: Bi-polar oblique Conical Orthomorphic

West from Greenwich

COPYRIGHT PHILIP'S

1:7 100 0

50 0 50 100 150 200 250 300 km
50 0 50 100 150 200 miles

JAMAICA
1:2 700 000
10 0 10 20 30 40 50 km
10 0 10 20 30 miles

CARIBBEAN SEA

Montego Bay
MBJ
Lucea
Falmouth
Runaway Bay
St. Ann's Bay
Galina Point
Negril
Cambridge
Wakefield
Ocho Rios
Port Maria
South Negril Pt.
The Cockpit Country
Mount Denham 985
Dry Harbour Mountains
Moneague
Annotto Bay
Savanna-la-Mar
Maggotty
Don Figuereroa Mts.
Linstead
Blue Mountains
John Crow
Port Antonio
Black River
Mandeville
Santa Cruz Mts.
Spanish Town
2256
Blue Mountain Peak
Morant Point
Great Pedro Bluff
May Pen
Portmore
Old Harbour
Kingston
KIN
Morant Bay
Port Morant
Alligator Pond
Portland Bight
Portland Point

Gulf of Mexico

MERIDA
YUCATAN
Campeche
CAMPECHE
MEXICO
QUINTANA ROO
BELIZE
GUATEMALA
HONDURAS
TEGUCIGALPA
EL SALVADOR
SAN SALVADOR
NICARAGUA
MANAGUA
COSTA RICA
SAN JOSE
PANAMÁ

FLORIDA
U.S.A.
MIAMI
LA HABANA (Havana)
CUBA
Cayman Islands (U.K.)
JAMAICA
Kingston

CARIBBEAN SEA

GUADELOUPE AND MARTINIQUE
1:1 800 000
10 0 10 20 30 40 50 60 km
10 0 10 20 30 40 miles

GUADELOUPE (Fr.)
MARTINIQUE (Fr.)

PACIFIC OCEAN

Isthmus of Panama

ATLANTIC OCEAN

PUERTO RICO 1:2 700 000 [d]
10 0 10 20 30 40 50 km
10 0 10 20 30 miles

PUERTO RICO (U.S.A.)

Pta. Agujereada · Isabela · Barceloneta
Aguadilla · Arecibo · Manati · Vega Baja · **San Juan** · Rio Grande
San Sebastian · Utuado · Bayamón · Carolina · Fajardo · Dewey
Mayagüez · Adjuntas · Cordillera Central · Caguas · Naguabo · Culebra
Cerro de Punta 1338 · Cayey · Humacao · Vieques · Esperanza
San German · Uroyan Yauco · Coamo · Yabucoa
Pta. Aguila · Guanica · Ponce · Guayama
I. Caja de Muertos

VIRGIN ISLANDS 1:1 800 000 [e]
10 0 10 20 30 km
10 0 10 20 miles

Rufling Pt. · The Settlement
Anegada · East Pt.
Virgin Islands (U.K.)
Jost Van Dyke I. · Guana I. · Virgin Gorda
Hans Lollik I. · Tortola · 521 · Beef I. · Spanish Town
Virgin Is. (U.S.A.) · Cruz Bay · Road Town · Peter I.
Charlotte Amalie · St. Thomas I. · St. John I.

ST. LUCIA 1:890 000 [f]
5 0 10 km
5 0 10 miles

Cap Point · Pte. Hardy · Esperance Bay
Gros Islet · Marquis
Castries · Girard
Anse la Raye · Dennery
Canaries · Millet · Trou Gras Pt.
Soufrière · Mt. Gimie 950 · Micoud
Soufrière Bay · 750 Petit Piton · Vierge Pt.
Gros Piton Pt. · 796 Gros Piton · UVF · **ST. LUCIA**
Choiseul · Laborie · Vieux Fort · C. Moule à Chique

BARBADOS 1:890 000 [g]
5 0 10 km
5 0 10 miles

ATLANTIC OCEAN
Crab Hill · North Point · Spring Hall
Fustic · Boscobelle
Portland · 245 Belleplaine
Speightstown · **BARBADOS**
Westmoreland · 340 · Bathsheba · Hillcrest
Alleynes Bay · Mt. Hillaby · Martin's Bay
Holetown · Massiah Street · Ragged Pt.
Black Rock · Jackson · Bridgefield · Six Cross Roads
Ivy · Ellerton · Edey · The Crane
Bridgetown · Oistins · St. Martins
Carlisle Bay · Worthing · Chancery Lane
Oistins Bay · South Point

ATLANTIC OCEAN

MAS

Arthur's Town · New Bight · Cat I.
San Salvador I. · Conception I. · Rum Cay
Long I. · Tropic of Cancer
Clarence Town · Crooked I. Passage · Samana Cay
Albert Town · Crooked I. · Plana Cays
Snug Corner · Acklins I.
Cay Verde · Mira por vos Cay · Mayaguana Passage · Mayaguana I.
Santo Domingo · Caicos Passage
Hogsty Reef · Turks & Caicos Is. (U.K.) · PLS · Caicos Is.
Little Inagua I. · Cockburn Town
Lake Rose · Turks Is. · Turks Island Passage
INAGUA · Silver Bank Passage · Mouchoir Bank · Navidad Bank
Great Inagua I. · Matthew Town · Silver Bank
Moa · Alejandro de Humboldt
Baracoa · Pta. de Maisi
Guantanamo · Paso de los Vientos (Windward Passage)
GUANTANAMO BAY (U.S.A.)

ATLANTIC OCEAN
Puerto Rico Trench
Milwaukee Deep 8605
Cap-Haïtien · Monte Cristi · LA ISABELA · POP · Santiago de los Caballeros · San Francisco de Macorís · Nagua · Samana
Jean Rabel · Port-de-Paix · Puerto Plata · Cordillera · La Vega · Sánchez · Sabana de la Mar
Cap-à-Foux · Fort Liberté · Central · Pico Duarte 3175 · Hato Mayor · C. Engaño
G. de la Gonâve · Gonaives · Hinche · HAITISES · PUJ · Higüey
St-Marc · **DOMINICAN REP.** · San Pedro de Macorís
Jérémie · Î. de la Gonâve · **HAITI** · **SANTO** · L. Enriquillo · La Romana
Dame Marie · **PORT-AU-PRINCE** · PAP · SDQ · B. de Yuma
Massif de la Hotte · Petit Goâve · 2680 · SIERRA DE BAHORUCO · ESTE · Isla Saona
Les Cayes · Aquin · Jacmel · Azua de Compostela · Baní · San Cristóbal · I. Saona
Pointe-à-Gravois · Pedernales · Barahona · Mona Passage · Isla Mona (U.S.A.)
Î. à Vache · I. Beata · C. Beata · 5500 · Muertas Trough

Hispaniola
Antilles
Greater Antilles

Beata Ridge
4530

CARIBBEAN SEA

Colombian Basin

Venezuelan Basin
I. de Aves (Venezuela)
5420

Virgin Gorda · Anegada · Sombrero (U.K.)
Aguadilla · Arecibo · **SAN JUAN** · Virgin Is. (U.K.) · Anguilla (U.K.)
Bayamón · Carolina · St. Thomas · Tortola · Road Town · Anegada Passage
1338 · Fajardo · Charlotte Amalie · Virgin Is. (U.S.A.) · St-Martin (Fr.)
Ponce · Caguas · Culebra · Christiansted · St. Maarten (Neth.) · St-Barthélemy (Fr.)
Mayagüez · Guayama · Vieques · Virgin Is. · Saba (Neth.) · Barbuda
PUERTO RICO (U.S.A.) · St. Croix · St. Eustatius (Neth.) · Mt. Liamuiga 1156 · **ANTIGUA & BARBUDA**
Frederiksted · Basseterre · SKB · St. John's
Redonda · Nevis · **ST. KITTS & NEVIS** · ANU · Antigua
Montserrat (U.K.) · 914 · Soufrière Hills · Guadeloupe Passage
Ste-Rose · PTP · Le Moule · La Désirade
GUADELOUPE (Fr.) · 1467 · **Pointe-à-Pitre**
Basse-Terre · Marie-Galante (Fr.) · Grand-Bourg
I. des Saintes (Fr.) · Dominica Passage
Portsmouth · 1447 · **DOMINICA**
Morne Diablotin · DOM · Roseau · MORNE
TROIS PITONS · Martinique Passage
Mt. Pelée 1397 · Ste-Marie
Fort-de-France · Le Robert · Rivière-Pilote
FDF · **MARTINIQUE** (Fr.)
St. Lucia Channel
Castries · 950 · UVF · **ST. LUCIA**
Soufrière · St. Vincent Passage
St. Vincent · SVD · Speightstown · BGI
Kingstown · 340 · **Bridgetown**
Bequia · **BARBADOS**
Tobago · Canouan · **ST. VINCENT & THE GRENADINES**
Carriacou · The Grenadines · Grenadines Basin
840 · St. George's · **GRENADA** · GND

Leeward Islands
Windward Islands
Lesser Antilles
Aves Ridge
Grenada Basin

ABC Islands · **Lesser Antilles**
Oranjestad · Aruba (Neth.) · Curaçao (Neth.) · AUA · Bonaire (Neth.)
C. San Roman · Pen. de Paraguaná · Willemstad · CUR
Pta. Gallinas · MACURIA · Punto Fijo
GUAJIRA · Puerto Bolívar · Pta. Espada · MEDANOS DE CORO · Ic. Las Aves (Ven.)
Pen. de la Guajira · Puerto Cumarebo · Is. Los Roques (Ven.)
Uribia · Golfo de Venezuela · Coro · La Vela · ARC. LOS ROQUES
Ríohacha · Maicao · Punta Cardón · I. Orchila (Ven.)
Santa Marta · TAYRONA · San Rafael · I. Blanquilla (Ven.) · Is. Los Hermanos (Ven.)
SA. NEVADA DE STA. MARTA · MENE DE MAUROA · Tucacas · HENRI PITTIER · NUEVA ESPARTA · Is. Los Testigos (Ven.) · Tobago
COLOMBIA · Ciénaga · Santa Marta 2775 · Mene de Mauroa · Puerto Cabello · MIRANDA · CERRO EL COPEY 957 · La Asunción · Port of Spain
Soledad · Fundación · La Concepción · Altagracia · CUEVA DE LA QUEBRADA DEL TORO · MAIQUETIA · LAGUNA DE LA RESTINGA · Porlamar · Scarborough
Sabanalarga · Valledupar · Villa del Rosario · Cabimas · CARABOBO · **CARACAS** · CCS · I. de Margarita · PMV
Baranoa · Agustín Codazzi · Ciudad Ojeda · CARARA · San Felipe · **VALENCIA** · Los Teques · I. La Tortuga (Ven.) · Cumaná · **TRINIDAD & TOBAGO**
Calamar · CÉSAR · Machiques · Lago de Maracaibo · **LARA** · YARACUY · Villa de Cura · Ocumare del Tuy · MOCHIMA 2640 · Carúpano · Güiria · Arima
Zambrano · **MARACAIBO** · MAR · Santa Rita · **BARQUISIMETO** · Yaritagua · San Juan de los Morros · Río Caribe · SUCRE · Caicara · POS · Río Claro
Carmen · PERIJA · Trujillo · Betijoque · FALCÓN · San Carlos · Aragua de Barcelona · Anaco · MONAGAS · San Fernando · Serpent's Mouth
Mompós · ZULIA · CIENAGAS DEL CATATUMBO · **PORTUGUESA** · **Barcelona** · Cantaura · Maturín · MARIUSA · DELTA AMACURO
Magangué · El Banco · Valera · El Guache · El Baúl · Valle de la Pascua · El Tigre · Tucupita
San Carlos del Zulia · MÉRIDA · CARORA · GUARICO · Santa María de Ipire
Ocaña · NORTE DE SANTANDER · SIERRA NEVADA · **Mérida** · Barinas · Calabozo · **ANZOÁTEGUI** · Los Barrancos
BOLÍVAR · CATATUMBO-BARI · Pico Bolívar · Ciudad Bolivia · Libertad · GUARICO · **Ciudad Guayana**
Simiti · Cúcuta · **TÁCHIRA** · **BARINAS** · San Fernando de Apure · **Ciudad Bolívar** · El Pao · Sierra Imataca
Caucasia · San Cristóbal · Guasdualito · Bruzual · APURE · AGUARO GUARIQUITO · Upata
VENEZUELA · Achaguas · **ORINOCO** · Mapire · Guasipati · El Callao
Calcara · Caicara · Embalse de Guri · Tumeremo

West from Greenwich
186
4000 3000 2000 1500 1000 400 200 0
12 000 9000 6000 4500 3000 1200 600 0 ft
600 1000 2000 3000 4000 6000 8000 m

COPYRIGHT PHILIP'S

1:31 100 000

Projection: Lambert's Azimuthal Equal Area

COPYRIGHT PHILIP'S

1:31 100 000

100 0   200   400   600   800   1000 1200 1400 km

100 0   200   400   600   800   1000 miles

1 **2** **3** **4** **5** **6** **7**

Tropic of Cancer

Havana   BAHAMAS   Turks & Caicos Is.
C U B A   (U.K.)

Cayman Is.   HAITI   DOMINICAN
  (U.K.)   REP.   San Juan   Virgin Is.(U.S.A. - U.K.)
                 Port-au-   Santo   PUERTO   Anguilla (U.K.)
JAMAICA Kingston Prince   Domingo   RICO   St. Martin (Fr. - Neth.)
                      (U.S.A.)   ANTIGUA &
MEXICO   BELIZE   BARBUDA
                           Basse-Terre GUADELOUPE
GUATEMALA HONDURAS   DOMINICA   (Fr.)
                               Fort-de-France MARTINIQUE
Guatemala Tegucigalpa   (Fr.)
                          Castries   ST. LUCIA
San Salvador NICARAGUA   ST. VINCENT   BARBADOS
EL SALVADOR   Kingstown   Bridgetown
   Managua   Oranjestad CURAÇAO GRENADA   St. George's
         San José   ARUBA   (Neth.)   Port of
COSTA   (Neth.) Willemstad   Spain TRINIDAD &
RICA   Panamá   TOBAGO
          Barranquilla   Maracaibo   Caracas
     G. of   Cartagena   Barquisimeto Valencia
     Darién   Orinoco   Ciudad Guayana
          Cúcuta
I. del Coco   Medellín Bucaramanga VENEZUELA   Georgetown
 (Costa Rica)   San Cristóbal   Paramaribo
                          BOGOTÁ   GUYANA
I. de Malpelo   Cali   Boa Vista SURINAME Cayenne
  (Colombia)   COLOMBIA   RORAIMA   C. Orange
                                          FRENCH
                                           GUIANA
                              AMAPÁ
Galapagos Is.   Quito   Macapá   Equator
  (Ecuador)   ECUADOR   Napo   Marajó
         Guayaquil   Putumayo Japurá   I.   Belém
    G. of Guayaquil   Iquitos Marañón   Amazon   Santarém   São Luís
                                                              Fortaleza
                  AMAZONAS   Amazon   P A R Á   Teresina
                     Juruá   Madeira   MARANHÃO   CEARÁ
       Chiclayo   Purus   Tapajós   Imperatriz   RIO G.
       Trujillo   Xingu   DO NORTE Natal
PERÚ Chimbote   Pôrto Velho   Tocantins   PIAUÍ   Campina Grande João
                  Rio Branco   Parnaíba   Pessoa
            ACRE   RONDÔNIA   Palmas   PERNAMBUCO Recife
         Callao   Madre de Dios   TOCANTINS   ALAGOAS
              LIMA   B R A Z I L   Maceió
            Cusco   Mamoré   SERGIPE Aracaju
                              MATO GROSSO   GOIÁS Brasília   B A H Í A
           Arequipa   L. Titicaca   BOLIVIA   DIS. FED.
                          La Paz   Cochabamba   Cuiabá   Goiânia   São Francisco Salvador
                          Sucre   Santa Cruz   MINAS GERAIS
              Iquique   Paraguay   MATO GROSSO   BELO   ESPÍRITO
                                                DO SUL   Ribeirão HORIZONTE SANTO
                                              Campo   Prêto   Juiz   Vitória
         Antofagasta   PARAGUAY   Grande   Paraná   SÃO PAULO de Fora   Campos
                          Salta   SÃO PAULO Campinas R. DE J.
                                  Pilcomayo   PARANÁ   SÃO   Niterói RIO DE
            San Miguel   Asunción   PAULO   Santos JANEIRO
            de Tucumán   Paraná   Curitiba
                  Resistencia Corrientes   SANTA CATARINA
                                     Uruguay   Florianópolis
                                     RIO GRANDE
                                     DO SUL
         San Félix   Córdoba   Santa Fé   Pôrto Alegre
          (Chile)   San Juan Rosario   Paraná   Pelotas
       San Ambrosio   A   URUGUAY
         (Chile)   Viña del Mar   Mendoza R
Arch. de Juan Fernández Valparaíso   G   Montevideo
        (Chile) Robinson SANTIAGO   E
               Crusoe   Talca   N   BUENOS AIRES
                                  T   La Plata Río de la Plata
                   Concepción   I   Mar del Plata
                             N   Bahía
                   Neuquén   A   Colorado Blanca
             Valdivia   Negro   Viedma
            Puerto Montt C
                        H   Chubut
                        I
                        L   Comodoro Rivadavia
                        E   Gulf of San Jorge
         Gulf of Penas
                                      West Falkland FALKLAND IS.
                                                (U.K.)
                              Magellan's Str.   Stanley
                   Punta Arenas   East Falkland
                          Tierra del Fuego
                                C. Horn   South Georgia
                                                      (U.K.)

P A C I F I C
O C E A N

A T L A N T I C
O C E A N

C a r i b b e a n   S e a

A T L A N T I C
O C E A N

Tropic of Capricorn

A   **B**   **C**   **D**   **E**   **F**   **G**   **H**

Projection: *Lambert's Azimuthal Equal Area*

1   **2**
■ **LIMA** Capital Cities

60 West from Greenwich 50

COPYRIGHT PHILIP'S

3   **4**   **5**   **6**   **7**

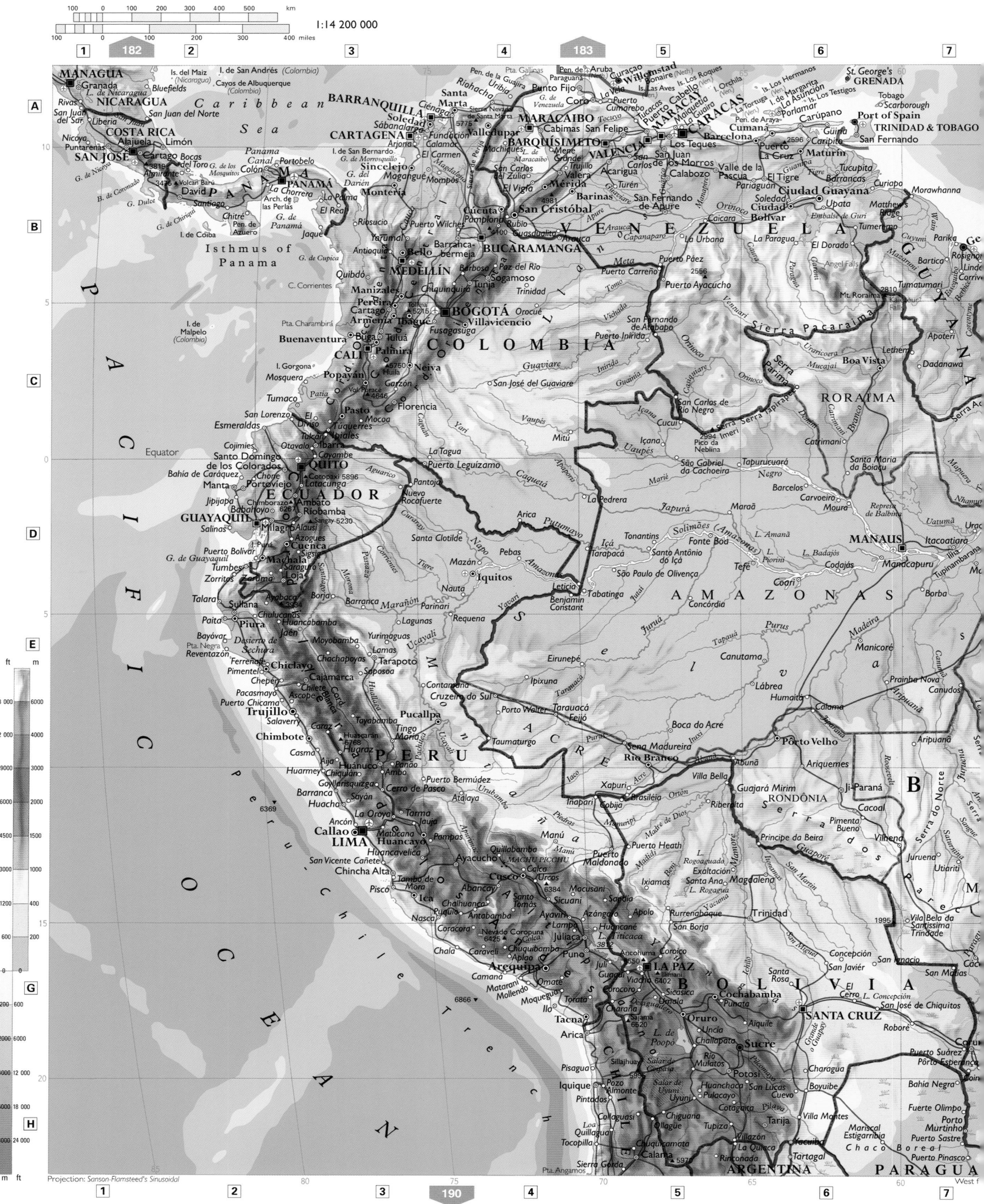

Projection: Sanson-Flamsteed's Sinusoidal

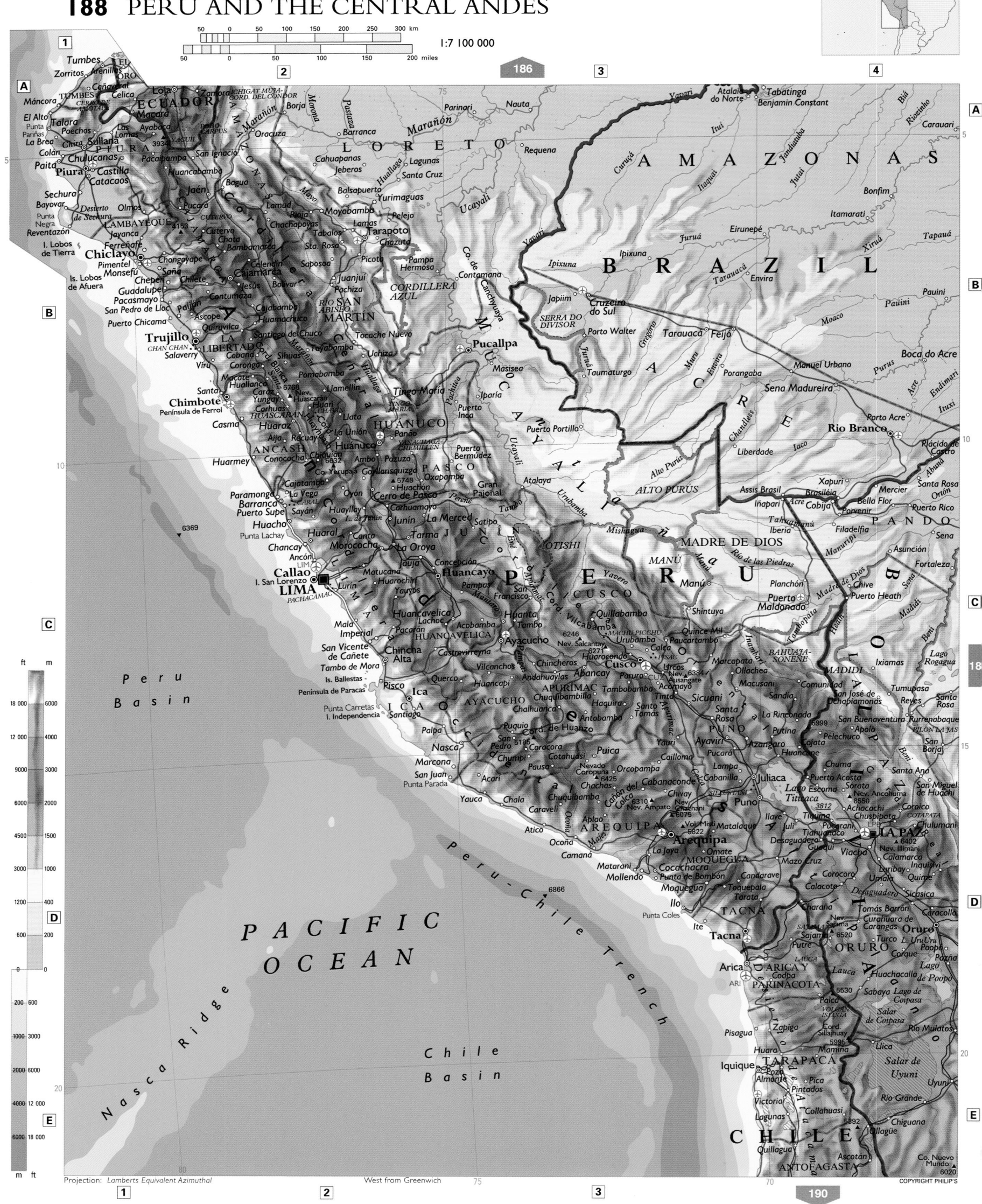

1:7 100 000

Projection: Lamberts Equivalent Azimuthal   West from Greenwich   COPYRIGHT PHILIP'S

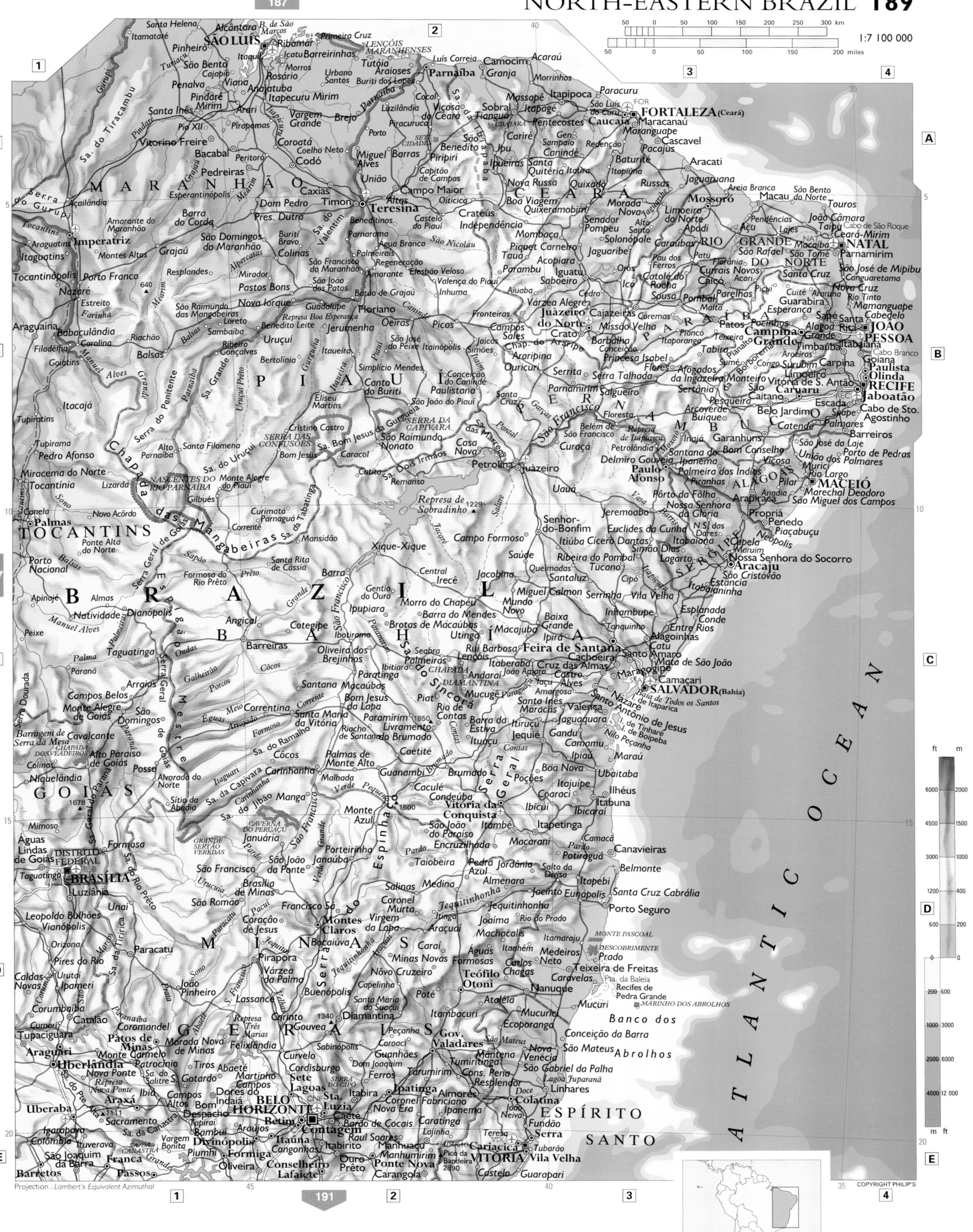

50 0 50 100 150 200 250 300 km

1:7 100 000

50 0 50 100 150 200 miles

Projection : Lambert's Equivalent Azimuthal

COPYRIGHT PHILIP'S

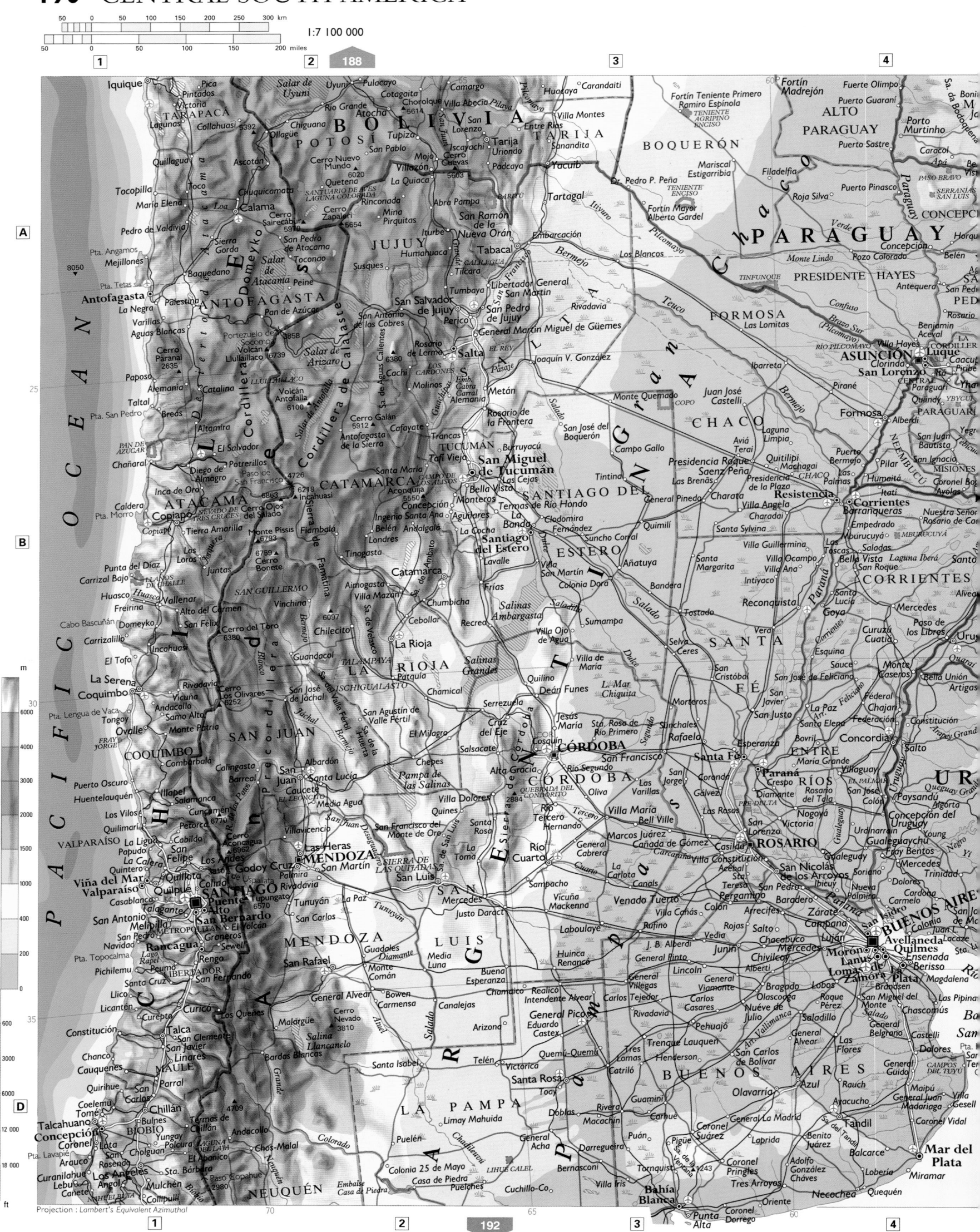

VITÓRIA
Vila
Velha

BELO
HORIZONTE
Contagem
CNF

A T L A N T I C

O C E A N

Tropic of Capricorn

RIO DE JANEIRO

SÃO PAULO

CAMPINAS

CURITIBA

JOINVILLE

FLORIANÓPOLIS

SANTA
CATARINA

B R A Z I L

P A R A N Á

R I O   G R A N D E

D O   S U L

PORTO ALEGRE

Pelotas

Rio Grande

Lagoa dos Patos

M A T O   G R O S S O
D O   S U L

MISIONES

U A Y

ONTEVIDEO

25

30

35

5304

50 0 50 100 150 200 250 300 km
50 0 50 100 150 200 miles

1:7 100 000

Map labels

ARAUCO · Mulchén · Colonia 25 de Mayo · Puelches · Bernascom · Coronel Pringles · Tres Arroyos · Benito Juárez · Balcarce
Cañete · Angol · Collipulli · Loncopué · Casa de Piedra · Villa Iris · Tornquist 1243 · Coronel · Aldofo González Cháves · Loberia
Capitán Pastene · Victoria · Curacautín · Copahue 2985 · Anelo · Casa de Piedra · LA PAMPA · BUENOS AIRES · Quequén
I. Mocha · Galvarino · Lautaro · 3124 · Las Lajas · Barda del Medio · Cipolletti · Villa Regina · Mayor Buratovich · Necochea
Temuco · Cherquenco · Zapala · Neuquén · Allen · General Roca · Fortín Uno · Río Colorado · Choele Choel · I. Trinidad
Carahue · Cunco · NEUQUÉN · Picún · Embalse Ezequiel Ramos Mexía · Chelforó · Colorado · Bahía Blanca · Punta Alta
Puerto Saavedra · Nueva Imperial · Villarrica · Paso de los Indios · Leufú · Negro · Lamarque · Coronel Dorrego · Médanos
Pitrufquén · Toltén · LA ARAUCANÍA · Freire · PANGUIPULLI · LANÍN · San Martín de los Andes · Piedra del Águila · La Esperanza · RÍO NEGRO · General Conesa · Stroeder · B. Anegada
Valdivia · LOS RÍOS · Lago Ranco · Junín de los Andes · Sierra Colorada · Valcheta · San Antonio Oeste · Carmen de Patagones · Viedma · Punta Rasa
Corral · La Unión · Futrono · Embalse Piedra del Águila · El Cuy · Los Menucos · Aguada Cecilio · General Lorenzo Vintter
Osorno · Río Bueno · Puyehue · NAHUEL HUAPÍ · San Carlos de Bariloche · Maquinchao · El Caín · Salina Gualicho
Bahía Mansa · Ensenada · Nahuel Huapí · Ingeniero Jacobacci · Sierra Grande · Golfo San Matías · Península Valdés
Río Negro · Mte. Tronador 3554 · El Bolsón · Quetrequile 1879 · Cona Niyeu · Puerto Pirámides · Punta Delgado
Puerto Varas · Puerto Montt · HORNOPIREN 1572 · El Maitén · Gastre · Telsen · Puerto Lobos · Puerto Madryn
Los Muermos · Maullín · Ancud · LOS ALERCES · El Bolsón · Gan Gan · Puerto Pirámides · Rawson · Trelew
G. de los Coronados · Isla de Chiloé · Castro · Achao · LOS ALERCES · Esquel · Gualjaina · CHUBUT · Gaimán · Trelew
LOS LAGOS · Quellón · Chaitén 2404 · Corcovado 2440 · Tecka · Pampa de Agnia · Las Plumas · Embalse Florentino Ameghino
C. Quilán · Boca del Guafo · Yelcho · Corcovado 2070 · Paso de Indios · Chubut · Cabo Raso
I. Guafo · Palena · José de San Martín · Gran Laguna Salada · Camarones · B. Camarones · C. Dos Bahías
Islas Guaitecas · QUEULAT · Río Pico 1651 · Chico · B. Bustamante
Archipiélago de los Chonos · ISLA MAGDALENA · Puerto Cisnes · L. General Vintter · L. Fontana · L. Musters · L. Colhué Huapi · Golfo San Jorge
I. Guamblin · RÍO SIMPSON · Alto Río Senguerr · Facundo · Sarmiento · Comodoro Rivadavia
Puerto Aisén · Coyhaique · Mayo · Río Mayo · Holdich · Caleta Olivia
C. Taitao · LOS HUEMULES · Vol. Hudson 2500 · Balmaceda · Los Monos · Las Heras · Pico Truncado
Peninsula de Taitao 1372 · L. General Carrera (L. Buenos Aires) · Perito Moreno · Fitz Roy · Mazarredo · C. Tres Puntas · C. Blanco
Mte. San Valentín 4058 · Chile Chico · Los Antiguos · CUEVA DE LAS MANOS · Jaramillo · Deseado
Golfo de Penas · Cochrane · Puerto Deseado
Archipiélago Guayaneco · LAGUNA SAN RAFAEL · Cerro Arenales 3437 · Mte. San Lorenzo 3706 · Pueyrredón · Bajo Caracoles · Pta. Medanosa
I. Campana · I. Javier · Las Horquetas 2215 · Lago Posadas
I. Patricio Lynch · Cerro Melizo Sur 3050 · Mt. Inés 1120 · Gobernador Gregores · Bahía Laura
I. Esmeralda · SANTA CRUZ · Altiplanicie Central · Puerto San Julián
I. Mornington · I. Wellington · Cerro Fitz Roy 3405 · L. Viedma · Tres Lagos · Chico · Laguna del Carbón –108
G. Ladrillero · G. Trinidad · Cerro Murallón 2831 · Shehuen · Comandante Luis Piedra Buena · MONTE LEÓN
I. Madre de Dios · I. Duque de York · LOS GLACIARES · Lago Argentino · Santa Cruz · Puerto Santa Cruz
C. Santiago · B. Salvación · Chatham · El Calafate · Estancia Monte León
I. Hanover · TORRES DEL PAINE · Cerro Paine Grande 2884 · Esperanza · Bahía Grande · Puerto Coig
MAGALLANES Y ANTÁRTICA CHILENA · Yacimiento Río Turbio · Güer Aike
C. Jorge · Puerto Natales · El Turbio · Gallegos · Río Gallegos
Arch. Reina Adelaida · Almirante Montt · Morro Chico · PALI-AIKE · Monte Dinero
Estrecho de Magallanes · Pen. Muñoz · Punta Delgada · C. Vírgenes
C. Deseado · I. Desolación · Seno Skyring · Cerro Sombrero · (Magellan's Strait)
Santa Inés · Seno de Otway · I. Riesco · Porvenir · San Sebastián · Isla Grande de Tierra del Fuego
HERNANDO DE MAGALLANES · Punta Arenas · Pen. de Brunswick · Cameron · Río Grande
Clarence I. · Dawson · B. Inútil · TIERRA DEL FUEGO
Capitán Aracena · Mte. Sarmiento 2246 · 822 · DEL
ALBERTO DE AGOSTINI · YENDEGAIA · Mte. Darwin 2488 · FUEGO · Ushuaia · L. Fagnano · C. San Diego · 1120 · I. de los Estados (Staten I.)
I. Stewart · Gordon · Canal Beagle · Puerto Williams · I. Picton · Nueva
I. Londonderry · I. Hoste · I. Navarino · I. Lennox
B. Cook · Pen. Hardy · B. Nassau
Is. L'Hermite · Islas Wollaston · Cabo de Hornos (Cape Horn)
Islas Diego Ramírez

LOS LAGOS · CHILE · PATAGONIA · ARGENTINA

PACIFIC OCEAN

ATLANTIC OCEAN

Falkland Islands

FALKLAND ISLANDS (U.K.) (ISLAS MALVINAS)
Jason Is. · Pebble I. · C. Dolphin
King George B. · Queen Charlotte B. · Mt. Adam 700 · Mt. Usborne 705
Weddell I. · West Falkland · Falkland Sound · Port Darwin · Stanley · East Falkland
C. Meredith · Beauchêne I.

Elevation scale

ft	m
9000	3000
6000	2000
4500	1500
3000	1000
1200	400
600	200
0	0
600	200
3000	1000
6000	2000
12 000	4000
ft	m

INDEX TO WORLD MAPS

HOW TO USE THE INDEX

The index contains the names of all the principal places and features shown on the World Maps. Each name is followed by an additional entry in italics giving the country or region within which it is located. The alphabetical order of names composed of two or more words is governed primarily by the first word, then by the second, and then by the country or region name that follows. This is an example of the rule:

Mir *Niger*	14°5N 11°59E	**139** C7
Mīr Kūh *Iran*	26°22N 58°55E	**129** E8
Mīr Shahdād *Iran*	26°15N 58°29E	**129** E8
Mira *Italy*	45°26N 12°8E	**93** C9

Physical features composed of a proper name (Erie) and a description (Lake) are positioned alphabetically by the proper name. The description is positioned after the proper name and is usually abbreviated:

Erie, L. *N. Amer.*	42°15N 81°0W	**174** D4

Where a description forms part of a settlement or administrative name, however, it is always written in full and put in its true alphabetical position:

Mount Isa *Australia*	20°42S 139°26E	**150** C2

Names beginning with M' and Mc are indexed as if they were spelled Mac. Names beginning St. are alphabetized under Saint, but Sankt, Sint, Sant', Santa and San are all spelt in full and are alphabetized accordingly. If the same place name occurs two or more times in the index and all are in the same country, each is followed by the name of the administrative subdivision in which it is located.

The geographical co-ordinates which follow each name in the index give the latitude and longitude of each place. The first co-ordinate indicates latitude – the distance north or south of the Equator. The second co-ordinate indicates longitude – the distance east or west of the Greenwich Meridian. Both latitude and longitude are measured in degrees and minutes (there are 60 minutes in a degree).

The latitude is followed by N(orth) or S(outh) and the longitude by E(ast) or W(est).

The number in bold type which follows the geographical co-ordinates refers to the number of the map page where that feature or place will be found. This is usually the largest scale at which the place or feature appears.

The letter and figure that are immediately after the page number give the grid square on the map page, within which the feature is situated. The letter represents the latitude and the figure the longitude. A lower-case letter immediately after the page number refers to an inset map on that page.

In some cases the feature itself may fall within the specified square, while the name is outside. This is usually the case only with features that are larger than a grid square.

Rivers are indexed to their mouths or confluences, and carry the symbol → after their names. The following symbols are also used in the index: ■ country, ☑ overseas territory or dependency, □ first-order administrative area, △ national park, ⌂ other park (provincial park, nature reserve or game reserve), ❂ Australian Aboriginal land, ✈ (LHR) principal airport (and location identifier).

HOW TO PRONOUNCE PLACE NAMES

English-speaking people usually have no difficulty in reading and pronouncing correctly English place names. However, foreign place name pronunciations may present many problems. Such problems can be minimized by following some simple rules. However, these rules cannot be applied to all situations, and there will be many exceptions.

1. In general, stress each syllable equally, unless your experience suggests otherwise.
2. Pronounce the letter 'a' as a broad 'a' as in 'arm'.
3. Pronounce the letter 'e' as a short 'e' as in 'elm'.
4. Pronounce the letter 'i' as a cross between a short 'i' and long 'e', as the two 'i's in 'California'.
5. Pronounce the letter 'o' as an intermediate 'o' as in 'soft'.
6. Pronounce the letter 'u' as an intermediate 'u' as in 'sure'.
7. Pronounce consonants hard, except in the Romance-language areas where 'g's are likely to be pronounced softly like 'j' in 'jam'; 'j' itself may be pronounced as 'y'; and 'x's may be pronounced as 'h'.
8. For names in mainland China, pronounce 'q' like the 'ch' in 'chin', 'x' like the 'sh' in 'she', 'zh' like the 'j' in 'jam', and 'z' as if it were spelled 'dz'. In general, pronounce 'a' as in 'father', 'e' as in 'but', 'i' as in 'keep', 'o' as in 'or', and 'u' as in 'rule'.

Moreover, English has no diacritical marks (accent and pronunciation signs), although some languages do. The following is a brief and general guide to the pronunciation of those most frequently used in the principal Western European languages.

		Pronunciation as in
French	é	day and shows that the 'e' is to be pronounced; e.g. Orléans.
	è	mare
	î	used over any vowel and does not affect pronunciation; shows contraction of the name, usually omission of 's' following a vowel.
	ç	's' before 'a', 'o' and 'u'.
	ë, ï, ü	over 'e', 'i' and 'u' when they are used with another vowel and shows that each is to be pronounced.
German	ä	fate
	ö	fur
	ü	no English equivalent; like French 'tu'.
Italian	à, é	over vowels and indicates stress.
Portuguese	ã, õ	vowels pronounced nasally.
	ç	boss
	á	shows stress.
	ô	shows that a vowel has an 'i' or 'u' sound combined with it.
Spanish	ñ	canyon
	ü	pronounced as 'w' and separately from adjoining vowels.
	á	usually indicates that this is a stressed vowel.

ABBREVIATIONS

A.C.T. – Australian Capital Territory
A.R. – Autonomous Region
Afghan. – Afghanistan
Afr. – Africa
Ala. – Alabama
Alta. – Alberta
Amer. – America(n)
Ant. – Antilles
Arch. – Archipelago
Ariz. – Arizona
Ark. – Arkansas
Atl. Oc. – Atlantic Ocean
B. – Baie, Bahía, Bay, Bucht, Bugt
B.C. – British Columbia
Bangla. – Bangladesh
Barr. – Barrage
Bos.-H. – Bosnia-Herzegovina
C. – Cabo, Cap, Cape, Coast
C.A.R. – Central African Republic
C. Prov. – Cape Province
Calif. – California
Cat. – Catarata
Cent. – Central
Chan. – Channel
Colo. – Colorado
Conn. – Connecticut
Cord. – Cordillera
Cr. – Creek
D.C. – District of Columbia
Del. – Delaware
Dem. – Democratic
Dep. – Dependency
Des. – Desert
Dét. – Détroit
Dist. – District
Dj. – Djebel
Dom. Rep. – Dominican Republic
E. – East
El Salv. – El Salvador
Eq. Guin. – Equatorial Guinea
Est. – Estrecho
Falk. Is. – Falkland Is.
Fd. – Fjord
Fla. – Florida
Fr. – French
G. – Golfe, Golfo, Gulf, Guba, Gebel
Ga. – Georgia
Gt. – Great, Greater
Guinea-Biss. – Guinea-Bissau
H.K. – Hong Kong
H.P. – Himachal Pradesh
Hants. – Hampshire
Harb. – Harbor, Harbour
Hd. – Head
Hts. – Heights
I.(s). – Île, Ilha, Insel, Isla, Island, Isle
Ill. – Illinois
Ind. – Indiana
Ind. Oc. – Indian Ocean
J. – Jabal, Jebel
Jaz. – Jazīrah
Junc. – Junction
K. – Kap, Kapp
Kans. – Kansas
Kep. – Kepulauan
Ky. – Kentucky
L. – Lac, Lacul, Lago, Lagoa, Lake, Limni, Loch, Lough
La. – Louisiana
Ld. – Land
Liech. – Liechtenstein
Lux. – Luxembourg
Mad. P. – Madhya Pradesh
Madag. – Madagascar
Man. – Manitoba
Mass. – Massachusetts
Md. – Maryland
Me. – Maine
Medit. S. – Mediterranean Sea
Mich. – Michigan
Minn. – Minnesota
Miss. – Mississippi
Mo. – Missouri
Mont. – Montana
Mozam. – Mozambique
Mt.(s) – Mont, Montaña, Mountain
Mte. – Monte
Mti. – Monti
N. – Nord, Norte, North, Northern, Nouveau, Nahal, Nahr
N.B. – New Brunswick
N.C. – North Carolina
N. Cal. – New Caledonia
N. Dak. – North Dakota
N.H. – New Hampshire
N.I. – North Island
N.J. – New Jersey
N. Mex. – New Mexico
N.S. – Nova Scotia
N.S.W. – New South Wales
N.W.T. – North West Territory
N.Y. – New York
N.Z. – New Zealand
Nac. – Nacional
Nat. – National
Nebr. – Nebraska
Neths. – Netherlands
Nev. – Nevada
Nfld & L.. – Newfoundland and Labrador
Nic. – Nicaragua
O. – Oued, Ouadi
Occ. – Occidentale
Okla. – Oklahoma
Ont. – Ontario
Or. – Orientale
Oreg. – Oregon
Os. – Ostrov
Oz. – Ozero
P. – Pass, Passo, Pasul, Pulau
P.E.I. – Prince Edward Island
Pa. – Pennsylvania
Pac. Oc. – Pacific Ocean
Papua N.G. – Papua New Guinea
Pass. – Passage
Peg. – Pegunungan
Pen. – Peninsula, Péninsule
Phil. – Philippines
Pk. – Peak
Plat. – Plateau
Prov. – Province, Provincial
Pt. – Point
Pta. – Ponta, Punta
Pte. – Pointe
Qué. – Québec
Queens. – Queensland
R. – Rio, River
R.I. – Rhode Island
Ra. – Range
Raj. – Rajasthan
Recr. – Recreational, Récréatif
Reg. – Region
Rep. – Republic
Res. – Reserve, Reservoir
Rhld-Pfz. – Rheinland-Pfalz
S. – South, Southern, Sur
Si. Arabia – Saudi Arabia
S.C. – South Carolina
S. Dak. – South Dakota
S.I. – South Island
S. Leone – Sierra Leone
Sa. – Serra, Sierra
Sask. – Saskatchewan
Scot. – Scotland
Sd. – Sound
Sev. – Severnaya
Sib. – Siberia
Sprs. – Springs
St. – Saint
Sta. – Santa
Ste. – Sainte
Sto. – Santo
Str. – Strait, Stretto
Switz. – Switzerland
Tas. – Tasmania
Tenn. – Tennessee
Terr. – Territory, Territoire
Tex. – Texas
Tg. – Tanjung
Trin. & Tob. – Trinidad & Tobago
U.A.E. – United Arab Emirates
U.K. – United Kingdom
U.S.A. – United States of America
Univ. – University, Université, Universidad
Ut. P. – Uttar Pradesh
Va. – Virginia
Vdkhr. – Vodokhranilishche
Vdskh. – Vodoskhovyshche
Vf. – Vírful
Vic. – Victoria
Vol. – Volcano
Vt. – Vermont
W. – Wadi, West
W. Va. – West Virginia
Wall. & F. Is. – Wallis and Futuna Is.
Wash. – Washington
Wis. – Wisconsin
Wlkp. – Wielkopolski
Wyo. – Wyoming
Yorks. – Yorkshire

A

A Baiuca Spain 43°19N 8°29W 88 B2
A Baña = San Vicenzo Spain 42°58N 8°46W 88 C2
A Cañiza Spain 42°13N 8°16W 88 C2
A Carballa Spain 43°13N 8°54W 88 B2
A Carreira Spain 43°21N 8°12W 88 B2
A Coruña Spain 43°20N 8°25W 88 B2
A Coruña □ Spain 43°10N 8°30W 88 B2
A Cruz do Incio Spain 42°39N 7°21W 88 C3
A Estrada Spain 42°43N 8°27W 88 C2
A Feira do Monte Spain 43°12N 7°34W 88 B3
A Fonsagrada Spain 43°8N 7°4W 88 B3
A Guarda Spain 41°56N 8°52W 88 D2
A Gudiña Spain 42°4N 7°8W 88 C3
A Pobre Spain 42°58N 7°3W 88 C3
A Ramallosa Spain 42°45N 8°30W 88 C2
A Rúa Spain 42°24N 7°6W 88 C3
A Serra de Outes Spain 42°52N 8°55W 88 C2
A Shau Vietnam 16°6N 107°22E 120 D6
Aabenraa Denmark 55°3N 9°25E 63 J3
Aabybro Denmark 57°10N 9°44E 63 G3
Aachen Germany 50°45N 6°6E 76 E2
Aalborg Denmark 57°2N 9°54E 63 G3
Aalborg Bugt Denmark 56°50N 10°35E 63 H4
Aalen Germany 48°51N 10°6E 77 G6
Aalestrup Denmark 56°42N 9°29E 63 H3
Aalst Belgium 50°56N 4°2E 69 D4
Aalten Neths. 51°56N 6°35E 69 C6
Aalter Belgium 51°5N 3°28E 69 C3
Äänekoski Finland 62°36N 25°44E 60 E21
Aarau Switz. 47°23N 8°4E 77 H4
Aarberg Switz. 47°2N 7°16E 77 H3
Aare → Switz. 47°33N 8°14E 77 H4
Aargau □ Switz. 47°26N 8°10E 77 H4
Aarhus Denmark 56°8N 10°11E 63 H4
Aars Denmark 56°48N 9°30E 63 H3
Aarschot Belgium 50°59N 4°49E 69 D4
Aasiaat Greenland 68°43N 52°56W 57 D5
Aba China 32°59N 101°42E 116 A3
Aba Dem. Rep. of the Congo 3°58N 30°17E 142 B3
Aba Nigeria 5°10N 7°19E 139 D6
Abaco I. Bahamas 26°25N 77°10W 182 A4
Abadab, J. Sudan 18°54N 35°56E 137 D4
Ābādān Iran 30°22N 48°20E 129 D6
Ābādeh Iran 31°8N 52°40E 129 D7
Abadin Spain 43°21N 7°29W 88 B3
Abadla Algeria 31°2N 2°45W 136 B3
Abaeté Brazil 19°9S 45°27W 189 D1
Abaeté → Brazil 18°2S 45°12W 189 D1
Abaetetuba Brazil 1°40S 48°50W 187 D9
Abagnar Qi = Xilinhot China 43°52N 116°2E 114 C9
Abah, Tanjung Indonesia 8°46S 115°38E 119 K18
Abai Paraguay 25°58S 55°54W 191 B4
Abakaliki Nigeria 6°22N 8°2E 139 D6
Abakan Russia 53°40N 91°10E 109 B12
Abala Niger 14°56N 3°22E 139 C5
Abalak Niger 15°22N 6°21E 139 B6
Abalemma Niger 16°12N 7°50E 139 B6
Abana Turkey 41°59N 34°1E 104 B6
Abancay Peru 13°35S 72°55W 188 C3
Abang, Gunung Indonesia 8°16S 115°25E 119 J18
Abano Terme Italy 45°22N 11°46E 93 C8
Abarán Spain 38°12N 1°23W 91 G3
Abariringa Kiribati 2°50S 171°40W 156 H10
Abarqū Iran 31°10N 53°20E 129 D7
Abasha Georgia 42°11N 42°13E 87 J6
Abashiri Japan 44°0N 144°15E 112 B12
Abashiri-Wan Japan 44°0N 144°30E 112 C12
Abaújszántó Hungary 48°16N 21°12E 80 B6
Abava → Latvia 57°6N 21°54E 82 A8
Ābay = Nîl el Azraq → Sudan 15°38N 32°31E 135 E12
Abay Kazakhstan 49°38N 72°53E 109 C8
Abaya, L. Ethiopia 6°30N 37°50E 131 F2
Abaza Russia 52°39N 90°6E 109 B12
Abbadia di Fiastra ⌂ Italy 43°12N 13°24E 93 E10
Abbadia San Salvatore Italy 42°53N 11°41E 93 F8
'Abbāsābād Iran 33°34N 58°23E 129 C8
Abbay = Nîl el Azraq → Sudan 15°38N 32°31E 135 E12
Abbaye, Pt. U.S.A. 46°58N 88°8W 172 B9
Abbé, L. Ethiopia 11°8N 41°47E 131 E3
Abbeville France 50°6N 1°49E 71 B8
Abbeville Ala., U.S.A. 31°34N 85°15W 178 D4
Abbeville Ga., U.S.A. 31°59N 83°18W 178 D6
Abbeville La., U.S.A. 29°58N 92°8W 176 G8
Abbeville S.C., U.S.A. 34°11N 82°23W 178 A7
Abbeyfeale Ireland 52°23N 9°18W 64 D2
Abbeyleix Ireland 52°54N 7°22W 64 D4
Abbiategrasso Italy 45°24N 8°54E 92 C5
Abbot Ice Shelf Antarctica 73°0S 92°0W 55 D16
Abbotsford Canada 49°5N 122°20W 162 D4
Abbottabad Pakistan 34°10N 73°15E 124 B5
Abbou, O. ben → Algeria 28°32N 5°14E 136 C5
ABC Islands W. Indies 12°15N 69°0W 183 D6
Abd al Kūrī Yemen 12°5N 52°20E 131 E5
Ābdānān Iran 32°56N 47°28E 105 F12
Ābdar Iran 30°16N 55°19E 129 D7
'Abdolābād Iran 34°12N 56°30E 129 C8
Abdulino Russia 53°42N 53°40E 108 B4
Abdulpur Bangla. 24°15N 88°59E 125 G13
Abéché Chad 13°50N 20°35E 135 F10
Abejar Spain 41°48N 2°47W 90 D2
Abel Tasman △ N.Z. 40°59S 173°3E 155 A8
Abengourou Côte d'Ivoire 6°42N 3°27W 138 D4
Abenójar Spain 38°53N 4°21W 89 G6
Åbenrå = Aabenraa Denmark 55°3N 9°25E 63 J3
Abensberg Germany 48°48N 11°51E 77 G7
Abeokuta Nigeria 7°3N 3°19E 139 D5
Aberaeron U.K. 52°15N 4°15W 67 E3
Aberayron = Aberaeron U.K. 52°15N 4°15W 67 E3
Aberchirder U.K. 57°34N 2°37W 65 D6
Abercorn Australia 25°12S 151°5E 151 D5
Abercrombie River △ Australia 34°5S 149°40E 153 C8
Aberdare U.K. 51°43N 3°27W 67 F4
Aberdare △ Kenya 0°22S 36°44E 142 C4
Aberdare Ra. Kenya 0°15S 36°50E 142 C4
Aberdaugleddau = Milford Haven U.K. 51°42N 5°7W 67 F2
Aberdeen Australia 32°9S 150°56E 153 B9
Aberdeen Canada 52°20N 106°8W 163 C7
Aberdeen China 22°14N 114°8E 111 a
Aberdeen S. Africa 32°28S 24°2E 144 D3
Aberdeen U.K. 57°9N 2°5W 65 D6
Aberdeen Idaho, U.S.A. 42°57N 112°50W 168 E7
Aberdeen Md., U.S.A. 39°31N 76°10W 173 F15
Aberdeen Miss., U.S.A. 33°49N 88°33W 177 E10
Aberdeen S. Dak., U.S.A. 45°28N 98°29W 172 C4
Aberdeen Wash., U.S.A. 46°59N 123°50W 170 D3
Aberdeen City □ U.K. 57°10N 2°10W 65 D6
Aberdeen L. Canada 64°30N 99°0W 160 E12
Aberdeenshire □ U.K. 57°17N 2°36W 65 D6
Aberdovey = Aberdyfi U.K. 52°33N 4°3W 67 E3
Aberdyfi U.K. 52°33N 4°3W 67 E3
Aberfeldy U.K. 56°37N 3°51W 65 E5
Aberfoyle U.K. 56°11N 4°23W 65 E4
Abergavenny U.K. 51°49N 3°1W 67 F4
Abergele U.K. 53°17N 3°35W 66 D4
Abergwaun = Fishguard U.K. 52°0N 4°58W 67 E3
Aberhonddu = Brecon U.K. 51°57N 3°23W 67 F4
Abermaw = Barmouth U.K. 52°44N 4°4W 66 E3
Abernathy U.S.A. 33°50N 101°51W 176 E4
Aberpennar = Mountain Ash U.K. 51°40N 3°23W 67 F4
Abert, L. U.S.A. 42°38N 120°14W 168 E3
Abertawe = Swansea U.K. 51°37N 3°57W 67 F4
Aberteifi = Cardigan U.K. 52°5N 4°40W 67 E3
Aberystwyth U.K. 52°25N 4°5W 67 E3
Abhā Si. Arabia 18°0N 42°34E 137 D5
Abhar Iran 36°9N 49°13E 105 D13
Abhayapuri India 26°24N 90°38E 125 F14
Abia □ Nigeria 5°30N 7°35E 139 D6
Abide Turkey 38°55N 29°20E 99 C11
Abidiya Sudan 18°18N 34°3E 137 D3
Abidjan Côte d'Ivoire 5°26N 3°58W 138 D4
Abidjan □ Côte d'Ivoire 5°20N 4°0W 138 D4
Abilene Kans., U.S.A. 38°55N 97°13W 172 F5
Abilene Tex., U.S.A. 32°28N 99°43W 176 E5
Abingdon U.S.A. 36°43N 81°59W 173 G13
Abingdon-on-Thames U.K. 51°40N 1°17W 67 F6
Abington Reef Australia 18°0S 149°35E 150 B4
Abiod, Remel el Tunisia 31°45N 9°35E 136 B5
Abisko △ Sweden 68°18N 18°44E 60 B18
Abitau → Canada 59°53N 109°3W 163 B7
Abitibi → Canada 51°3N 80°55W 164 B3
Abitibi, L. Canada 48°40N 79°40W 164 C4
Abkhaz Republic = Abkhazia □ Georgia 43°12N 41°5E 87 J5
Abkhazia □ Georgia 43°12N 41°5E 87 J5
Abminga Australia 26°8S 134°51E 151 D1
Abnûb Egypt 27°18N 31°4E 137 B3
Åbo = Turku Finland 60°30N 22°19E 84 B2
Abohar India 30°10N 74°10E 124 D6
Aboisso Côte d'Ivoire 5°30N 3°5W 138 D4
Abomey Benin 7°10N 2°5E 139 D5
Abong-Mbang Cameroon 4°0N 13°8E 140 D2
Abonnema Nigeria 4°41N 6°49E 139 E6
Abony Hungary 47°12N 20°3E 80 C5
Aboso Ghana 5°23N 1°57W 138 D4
Abou-Deïa Chad 11°20N 19°20E 135 F9
Abovyan Armenia 40°16N 44°37E 87 K7
Aboyne U.K. 57°4N 2°47W 65 D6
Abra Pampa Argentina 22°43S 65°42W 190 A2
Abraham L. Canada 52°15N 116°35W 162 C5
Abrantes Portugal 39°24N 8°7W 89 F2
Abreojos, Pta. Mexico 26°50N 113°40W 180 B2
Abri Sudan 20°50N 30°27E 137 C3
Abrolhos, Banco dos Brazil 18°0S 38°0W 189 D3
Abrud Romania 46°19N 23°5E 80 D8
Abruzzo □ Italy 42°15N 14°0E 93 F10
Absaroka Range U.S.A. 44°45N 109°50W 168 D9
Abşeron Yarımadası Azerbaijan 40°28N 49°57E 87 K9
Abtenau Austria 47°33N 13°21E 78 D6
Abu India 24°41N 72°50E 124 G5
Abū al Abyad U.A.E. 24°11N 53°50E 129 E7
Abū al Khaşīb Iraq 30°25N 48°0E 128 D5
Abū 'Alī Si. Arabia 27°20N 49°27E 129 E6
Abū 'Alī → Lebanon 34°25N 35°50E 130 A4
Abu Ballas Egypt 24°26N 27°36E 137 C2
Abu Dhabi = Abū Ẓāby U.A.E. 24°28N 54°22E 129 E7
Abu Dis Sudan 19°12N 33°38E 137 D3
Abū Du'ān Syria 36°25N 38°15E 105 D8
Abu el Gaĭn, W. → Egypt 29°35N 33°30E 130 F2
Abu Fatma, Ras Sudan 22°25N 36°25E 137 C4
Abu Ga'da, W. → Egypt 29°15N 32°53E 130 F1
Abū Ḩadrīyah Si. Arabia 27°20N 48°58E 129 E6
Abu Hamed Sudan 19°32N 33°13E 137 D3
Abu Haraz Sudan 19°8N 32°18E 137 D3
Abū Kamāl Syria 34°30N 41°0E 105 E9
Abu Kebir Egypt 30°43N 31°40E 137 E7
Abū Madd, Ra's Si. Arabia 24°50N 37°7E 128 E3
Abu Mena = Abu Mina Egypt 30°51N 29°40E 137 E6
Abu Mina Egypt 30°51N 29°40E 137 E6
Abū Mūsā U.A.E. 25°52N 55°3E 129 E7
Abū Qaşr Si. Arabia 30°21N 38°34E 128 D3
Abu Qireiya Egypt 24°5N 35°28E 137 C4
Abu Qurqâs Egypt 28°1N 30°44E 137 F7
Abu Shagara, Ras Sudan 21°4N 37°19E 137 C4
Abu Simbel Egypt 22°18N 31°40E 137 C3
Abu Soma, Râs Egypt 26°51N 33°58E 137 B3
Abū Şukhayr Iraq 31°54N 44°30E 105 G11
Abu Sultân Egypt 30°24N 32°21E 137 E8
Abu Tig Egypt 27°4N 31°15E 137 B3
Abu Zabad Sudan 12°25N 29°10E 135 F11
Abū Ẓāby U.A.E. 24°28N 54°22E 129 E7
Abū Zeydābād Iran 33°54N 51°45E 129 C6
Abuja Nigeria 9°5N 7°32E 139 D6
Abukuma-Gawa → Japan 38°6N 140°52E 112 E10
Abukuma-Sammyaku Japan 37°30N 140°45E 112 F10
Abunã Brazil 9°40S 65°20W 186 E5
Abunã → Brazil 9°41S 65°20W 186 E5
Aburo Dem. Rep. of the Congo 2°4N 30°53E 142 B3
Abut Hd. N.Z. 43°7S 170°15E 155 D5
Åby Sweden 58°40N 16°10E 63 F10
Aby, Lagune Côte d'Ivoire 5°15N 3°14W 138 D4
Abyei □ Sudan 9°30N 28°30E 135 G11
Ābyek Iran 36°4N 50°33E 129 B6
Academy Gletscher Greenland 82°2N 34°0W 57 A7
Acadia △ U.S.A. 44°20N 68°13W 173 C19
Açailândia Brazil 4°57S 47°30W 189 A1
Acajutla El Salv. 13°36N 89°50W 182 D2
Acámbaro Mexico 20°2N 100°44W 180 D4
Acanthus Greece 40°27N 23°47E 96 F7
Acaponeta Mexico 22°30N 105°22W 180 C3
Acapulco Mexico 16°51N 99°55W 181 D5
Acapulco Trench Pac. Oc. 12°0N 88°0W 180 D4
Acaraí, Serra Brazil 1°50N 57°50W 186 C7
Acarai Mts. = Acaraí, Serra Brazil 1°50N 57°50W 186 C7
Acaraú Brazil 2°53S 40°7W 189 A2
Acari Brazil 6°31S 36°38W 189 B3
Acari Peru 15°25S 74°36W 188 D3
Acarigua Venezuela 9°33N 69°12W 186 B5
Acatlán Mexico 18°12N 98°3W 181 D5
Acayucán Mexico 17°57N 94°55W 181 D6
Accéglio Italy 44°28N 7°0E 92 D4
Accomac U.S.A. 37°43N 75°40W 173 G16
Accous France 43°0N 0°36W 72 E3
Accra Ghana 5°35N 0°6W 139 D4
Accrington U.K. 53°45N 2°22W 66 D5
Acebal Argentina 33°20S 60°50W 190 C3
Aceh □ Indonesia 4°15N 97°30E 118 D1
Acerra Italy 40°57N 14°22E 95 B7
Aceuchal Spain 38°39N 6°30W 89 G4
Achacachi Bolivia 16°3S 68°43W 188 D4
Achaia Greece 38°5N 21°45E 98 C3
Achalpur India 21°22N 77°32E 126 D3
Achao Chile 42°28S 73°30W 192 B2
Acharnes Greece 38°5N 23°44E 98 C5
Acheloos → Greece 38°19N 21°7E 98 C3
Acheng China 45°30N 126°58E 115 B14
Achenkirch Austria 47°32N 11°45E 78 D4
Achensee Austria 47°26N 11°45E 78 D4
Achentrias Greece 34°59N 25°13E 99 G7
Acher India 23°10N 72°32E 124 H5
Achern Germany 48°37N 8°4E 77 G4
Acheron → N.Z. 42°16S 173°4E 155 C8
Achill Hd. Ireland 53°58N 10°15W 64 C1
Achill I. Ireland 53°58N 10°1W 64 C1
Achim Germany 53°1N 9°2E 76 B5
Achinsk Russia 56°20N 90°20E 107 D10
Achladokambos Greece 37°31N 22°35E 98 D4
Acıgöl Turkey 37°50N 29°50E 99 D11
Acıpayam Turkey 37°26N 29°22E 99 D11
Acireale Italy 37°37N 15°10E 95 E8
Ackerman U.S.A. 33°19N 89°11W 177 E10
Acklins I. Bahamas 22°30N 74°0W 183 B5
Acme Canada 51°33N 113°30W 162 C6
Acme U.S.A. 40°8N 79°26W 174 F5
Acobamba Peru 12°52S 74°35W 188 C3
Acomayo Peru 13°55S 71°38W 188 C3
Aconcagua, Cerro Argentina 32°39S 70°0W 190 C2
Aconquija, Mt. Argentina 27°0S 66°0W 190 B2
Acopiara Brazil 6°6S 39°27W 189 B3
Açores, Is. dos Atl. Oc. 38°0N 27°0W 134 a
Acornhoek S. Africa 24°37S 31°2E 145 B5
Acquapendente Italy 42°44N 11°52E 93 F8
Acquasanta Terme Italy 42°46N 13°24E 93 F10
Acquasparta Italy 42°41N 12°33E 93 F9
Acquaviva delle Fonti Italy 40°54N 16°50E 95 B9
Ácqui Terme Italy 44°41N 8°28E 92 D5
Acraman, L. Australia 32°2S 135°23E 151 E2
Acre = 'Akko Israel 32°55N 35°4E 130 C4
Acre □ Brazil 9°1S 71°0W 188 B3
Acre → Brazil 8°45S 67°22W 188 B4
Acri Italy 39°29N 16°23E 95 C9
Acs Hungary 47°42N 18°2E 80 C3
Actinolite Canada 44°32N 77°19W 174 B7
Actium Greece 38°57N 20°45E 98 C2
Acton Canada 43°38N 80°3W 174 C4
Açu Brazil 5°34S 36°54W 189 B3
Acworth U.S.A. 34°4N 84°41W 178 A5
Ad Dafinah Si. Arabia 23°18N 41°58E 137 C5
Ad Daghghāran Iraq 32°8N 44°55E 105 G11
Ad Dahnā Si. Arabia 24°30N 48°10E 131 C4
Ad Dammām Si. Arabia 26°20N 50°5E 129 E6
Ad Dāmūr Lebanon 33°43N 35°27E 130 B4
Ad Dawādimī Si. Arabia 24°35N 44°15E 128 E5
Ad Dawḩah Qatar 25°15N 51°35E 129 E6
Ad Dawr Iraq 34°27N 43°47E 105 E10
Ad Dhakhīrah Qatar 25°44N 51°33E 129 E6
Ad Dir'īyah Si. Arabia 24°44N 46°35E 128 E5
Ad Dīwānīyah Iraq 32°0N 45°0E 105 F11
Ad Dujayl Iraq 33°51N 44°14E 105 F11
Ad Duwayd Si. Arabia 30°15N 42°17E 128 D4
Ada Ghana 5°44N 0°40E 139 D5
Ada Serbia 45°49N 20°9E 80 E5
Ada Minn., U.S.A. 47°18N 96°31W 172 B5
Ada Okla., U.S.A. 34°46N 96°41W 176 D6
Adabiya Egypt 29°53N 32°28E 130 F1
Adair, C. Canada 71°30N 71°34W 161 C17
Adaja → Spain 41°32N 4°52W 88 D6
Adak U.S.A. 51°45N 176°45W 166 E4
Adak I. U.S.A. 51°45N 176°45W 166 E4
Adam, Mt. Falk. Is. 51°34S 60°4W 192 D4
Adama = Nazret Ethiopia 8°32N 39°22E 131 F2
Adamaoua □ Cameroon 6°30N 13°30E 139 D7
Adamaoua, Massif de l' Cameroon 7°20N 12°20E 139 D7
Adamawa □ Nigeria 9°20N 12°30E 139 D7
Adamawa Highlands = Adamaoua, Massif de l' Cameroon 7°20N 12°20E 139 D7
Adamello, Mt. Italy 46°9N 10°30E 92 B7
Adamello ⌂ Italy 46°4N 10°28E 92 B7
Adaminaby Australia 36°0S 148°45E 153 D8
Adams Mass., U.S.A. 42°38N 73°7W 175 D11
Adams N.Y., U.S.A. 43°49N 76°1W 175 C8
Adams Wis., U.S.A. 43°57N 89°49W 172 D9
Adams, Mt. U.S.A. 46°12N 121°30W 170 D5
Adam's Bridge Sri Lanka 9°15N 79°40E 127 K4
Adams L. Canada 51°10N 119°40W 162 C5
Adam's Peak Sri Lanka 6°48N 80°30E 127 L5
Adamuz Spain 38°2N 4°32W 89 G6
'Adan Yemen 12°45N 45°0E 131 E4
Adana Turkey 37°0N 35°16E 104 D6
Adana □ Turkey 37°0N 35°30E 104 D6
Adanero Spain 40°56N 4°36W 88 E6
Adang, Ko Thailand 6°33N 99°18E 121 J2
Adapazarı = Sakarya Turkey 40°48N 30°25E 104 B4
Adar Gwagwa, J. Sudan 22°15N 35°20E 137 C4
Adarama Sudan 17°10N 34°52E 135 E12
Adare Ireland 52°34N 8°47W 64 D3
Adare, C. Antarctica 71°0S 171°0E 55 D11
Adaut Indonesia 8°8S 131°7E 119 F8
Adavale Australia 25°52S 144°32E 151 D3
Adda → Italy 45°8N 9°53E 92 C6
Addatigala India 17°31N 82°3E 126 F6
Addis Ababa = Addis Abeba Ethiopia 9°2N 38°42E 131 F2
Addis Abeba Ethiopia 9°2N 38°42E 131 F2
Addison U.S.A. 42°1N 77°14W 174 D7
Addo S. Africa 33°32S 25°45E 144 D4
Addo △ S. Africa 33°30S 25°50E 144 D4
Adebour Niger 13°17N 11°50E 139 C7
Ādeh Iran 37°42N 45°11E 128 B5
Adel U.S.A. 31°8N 83°25W 178 D6
Adel Bagrou Mauritania 15°29N 6°57W 138 B3
Adelaide Australia 34°52S 138°30E 152 C3
Adelaide S. Africa 32°42S 26°20E 144 D4
Adelaide I. Antarctica 67°15S 68°30W 55 C17
Adelaide Pen. Canada 68°15N 97°30W 160 D12
Adelaide River Australia 13°15S 131°7E 148 B5
Adelaide Village Bahamas 25°0N 77°31W 182 A4
Adelanto U.S.A. 34°35N 117°22W 171 L9
Adele I. Australia 15°32S 123°9E 148 C3
Adélie, Terre Antarctica 68°0S 140°0E 55 C10
Adelie Land = Adélie, Terre Antarctica 68°0S 140°0E 55 C10
Adelong Australia 35°16S 148°4E 153 C8
Adelsk Belarus 53°24N 23°47E 82 E10
Adelunga Toghi Uzbekistan 42°7N 70°58E 109 D8
Ademuz Spain 40°5N 1°13W 90 E3
Aden = 'Adan Yemen 12°45N 45°0E 131 E4
Aden, G. of Ind. Oc. 12°30N 47°30E 131 E4
Adendorp S. Africa 32°15S 24°30E 144 D3
Aderbissinat Niger 15°34N 7°54E 139 B6
Adh Dhayd U.A.E. 25°17N 55°53E 129 E7
Adhoi India 23°26N 70°32E 124 H4
Adi Indonesia 4°15S 133°30E 119 E8
Adieu, C. Australia 32°0S 132°10E 149 F5
Adieu Pt. Australia 15°14S 124°35E 148 C3
Adige → Italy 45°9N 12°20E 93 C9
Adigrat Ethiopia 14°20N 39°26E 131 E2
Adıgüzel Barajı Turkey 38°13N 29°14E 99 C11
Adilabad India 19°33N 78°20E 126 E4
Adilcevaz Turkey 38°47N 42°43E 105 C10
Adirondack ⌂ U.S.A. 44°0N 74°20W 175 C10
Adirondack Mts. U.S.A. 44°0N 74°0W 175 C10
Adis Abeba = Addis Abeba Ethiopia 9°2N 38°42E 131 F2
Adıyaman Turkey 37°45N 38°16E 105 D8
Adıyaman □ Turkey 37°30N 38°10E 105 D8
Adjim Tunisia 33°47N 10°50E 136 B6
Adjohon Benin 6°41N 2°32E 139 D5
Adjud Romania 46°7N 27°10E 81 D12
Adjumani Uganda 3°20N 31°50E 142 B3
Adjuntas Puerto Rico 18°10N 66°43W 183 d
Adlavik Is. Canada 55°0N 58°40W 165 B8
Adler Russia 43°28N 39°52E 87 J4
Admer Algeria 20°21N 5°27E 139 A6
Admer, Erg d' Algeria 24°0N 9°5E 136 D5
Admiralty G. Australia 14°20S 125°55E 148 B4
Admiralty Gulf ◎ Australia 14°16S 125°52E 148 B4
Admiralty I. U.S.A. 57°30N 134°30W 162 B2
Admiralty Inlet Canada 72°30N 86°0W 161 C14
Admiralty Is. Papua N. G. 2°0S 147°0E 147 B7
Adnan Menderes, İzmir ✈ (ADB) Turkey 38°23N 27°6E 99 C9
Ado Nigeria 6°36N 2°56E 139 D5
Ado-Ekiti Nigeria 7°38N 5°12E 139 D6
Adolfo González Chaves Argentina 38°2S 60°5W 190 D3
Adolfo Ruiz Cortines, Presa Mexico 27°15N 109°6W 180 B3
Adonara Indonesia 8°15S 123°5E 119 F6
Adoni India 15°33N 77°18E 127 G3
Adony Hungary 47°6N 18°52E 80 C3
Adour → France 43°32N 1°32W 72 E2
Adra India 23°30N 86°42E 125 H12
Adra Spain 36°43N 3°3W 89 J7
Adrano Italy 37°40N 14°50E 95 E7
Adrar Algeria 27°51N 0°19W 136 C3
Adrar Mauritania 20°30N 7°30W 134 D3
Adrar □ Algeria 25°45N 1°0E 136 C4
Adrar □ Mauritania 20°10N 10°0W 138 A3
Adrar des Iforas Africa 19°40N 1°40E 139 B5
Ádria Italy 45°3N 12°3E 93 C9
Adrian Ga., U.S.A. 32°33N 82°35W 178 C7
Adrian Mich., U.S.A. 41°54N 84°2W 173 E11
Adrian Tex., U.S.A. 35°16N 102°40W 176 D3
Adriatic Sea Medit. S. 43°0N 16°0E 58 G9
Adua Indonesia 1°45S 129°50E 119 E7
Adur India 9°8N 76°40E 127 K3
Adwa Ethiopia 14°15N 38°52E 131 E2
Adygea □ Russia 45°0N 40°0E 87 H5
Adzhar Republic = Ajaria □ Georgia 41°30N 42°0E 87 K6
Adzopé Côte d'Ivoire 6°7N 3°49W 138 D4
Aegae = Aigai Greece 40°28N 22°19E 96 F6
Ægean Sea Medit. S. 38°30N 25°0E 99 C7
Aerhtai Shan Mongolia 46°40N 92°45E 109 C12
Ærø Denmark 54°52N 10°25E 63 K4
Ærøskøbing Denmark 54°53N 10°24E 63 K4
Aetdia-Akarnania = Etoloakarnania Greece 38°45N 21°18E 98 C3
Aetos Greece 37°15N 21°50E 98 D3
Afaahiti Tahiti 17°45S 149°17W 155 b
'Afak Iraq 32°4N 45°15E 105 F11
Afandou Greece 36°18N 28°12E 101 C10
Afarag, Erg Algeria 23°50N 2°47E 136 D4
Afghanistan ■ Asia 33°0N 65°0E 122 C4
Afikpo Nigeria 5°53N 7°54E 139 D6
Aflisses, O. → Algeria 28°40N 0°50E 136 C4
Aflou Algeria 34°7N 2°3E 136 B4
Afogados da Ingàzeira Brazil 7°45S 37°39W 189 B3
Afognak I. U.S.A. 58°15N 152°30W 166 D9
Afragóla Italy 40°55N 14°18E 95 B7
Afram → Ghana 7°0N 0°50W 139 D4
Africa 10°0N 20°0E 132 E6
'Afrīn Syria 36°32N 36°50E 104 D7
Afşin Turkey 38°14N 36°55E 104 C7
Afton N.Y., U.S.A. 42°14N 75°32W 175 D9
Afton Wyo., U.S.A. 42°44N 110°56W 168 E8
Afuá Brazil 0°15S 50°20W 187 D8
'Afula Israel 32°37N 35°17E 130 C4
Afyon Turkey 38°45N 30°33E 99 C12
Afyon □ Turkey 38°25N 30°30E 99 C12
Afyonkarahisar = Afyon Turkey 38°45N 30°33E 99 C12
Aga Egypt 30°55N 31°10E 137 E7
Āgā Jarī Iran 30°42N 49°50E 129 D6
Agadès = Agadez Niger 16°58N 7°59E 139 B6
Agadez Niger 16°58N 7°59E 139 B6
Agadir Morocco 30°28N 9°55W 136 B2
Agaete Canary Is. 28°6N 15°43W 100 F4
Agaie Nigeria 9°1N 6°18E 139 D6
Agalega Is. Mauritius 11°0S 57°0E 146 F4
Ağapınar Turkey 39°48N 30°47E 99 B12
Agar India 23°40N 76°2E 124 H7
Agar → India 21°0N 82°57E 126 D6
Agartala India 23°50N 91°23E 123 H17
Agăş Romania 46°28N 26°15E 81 D11
Agassiz Canada 49°14N 121°46W 162 D4
Agassiz Icecap Canada 80°15N 76°0W 161 A16
Agats Indonesia 5°33S 138°0E 119 F9
Agatti I. India 10°50N 72°12E 127 J1
Agattu I. U.S.A. 52°25N 173°35E 166 E2
Agawam U.S.A. 42°5N 72°37W 175 D12
Agbélouvé Togo 6°35N 1°14E 139 D5
Agboville Côte d'Ivoire 5°55N 4°15W 138 D4
Ağcabädi Azerbaijan 40°5N 47°27E 87 K8
Ağdam Azerbaijan 40°0N 46°58E 87 K8
Ağdara Azerbaijan 40°13N 46°49E 87 K8
Ağdaş Azerbaijan 40°44N 47°22E 87 K8
Agde France 43°19N 3°28E 72 E7
Agde, C. d' France 43°16N 3°28E 72 E7
Agdz Morocco 30°47N 6°30W 136 B2
Agdzhabedi = Ağcabädi Azerbaijan 40°5N 47°27E 87 K8
Agen France 44°12N 0°38E 72 D4
Agerbæk Denmark 55°36N 8°48E 63 J2
Agersø Denmark 55°13N 11°12E 63 J5
Ageyevo Russia 54°10N 36°27E 84 E9
Aggteleki △ Hungary 48°27N 20°36E 80 B5
Āgh Kand Iran 37°15N 48°4E 105 D13
Aghathonisi Greece 37°28N 27°0E 99 D8
Aghia Anna Greece 38°52N 23°24E 98 C5
Aghia Deka Greece 35°3N 24°58E 101 D6
Aghia Ekaterinis, Akra Greece 39°50N 19°50E 101 A3
Aghia Galini Greece 35°6N 24°41E 101 D6
Aghia Marina Kasos, Greece 35°27N 26°53E 99 F8
Aghia Marina Leros, Greece 37°11N 26°48E 99 D8
Aghia Paraskevi Greece 39°14N 26°21E 99 B8
Aghia Roumeli Greece 35°14N 23°58E 98 F5
Aghia Varvara Greece 35°8N 25°1E 101 D7
Aghiasos Greece 39°5N 26°23E 99 B8
Aghio Theodori Greece 37°55N 23°9E 98 D5
Aghion Oros □ Greece 40°25N 24°6E 97 F8
Aghios Andreas Greece 37°21N 22°45E 98 D4
Aghios Efstratios Greece 39°34N 24°58E 98 B6
Aghios Georgios Greece 37°28N 23°57E 98 D5
Aghios Ioannis, Akra Greece 35°20N 25°40E 101 D7
Aghios Isidoros Greece 36°9N 27°51E 101 C9
Aghios Kirikos Greece 37°34N 26°17E 99 D8
Aghios Matheos Greece 39°30N 19°47E 101 B3
Aghios Mironas Greece 35°15N 25°1E 99 F7
Aghios Nikolaos Greece 35°11N 25°41E 101 D7
Aghios Petros Greece 38°40N 20°36E 98 C2
Aghios Stephanos Greece 39°46N 19°39E 101 A3
Aghiou Orous, Kolpos Greece 40°6N 24°0E 96 F7
Aghireşu Romania 46°53N 23°15E 81 D8
Agia Greece 39°43N 22°45E 98 B4
Aginskoye Russia 51°6N 114°32E 107 D12
Agjert Mauritania 16°23N 9°17W 138 B3
Ağlasun Turkey 37°39N 30°31E 99 D12
Agly → France 42°46N 3°3E 72 F7
Agnew Australia 28°1S 120°31E 149 E3
Agnibilékrou Côte d'Ivoire 7°10N 3°11W 138 D4
Agnita Romania 45°59N 24°40E 81 E9
Agnone Italy 41°48N 14°22E 93 G11
Ago-Are Nigeria 8°30N 3°25E 139 D5
Agofie Ghana 8°27N 0°15E 139 D5
Agogna → Italy 45°4N 8°54E 92 C5
Agoitz = Aoiz Spain 42°46N 1°22W 90 C3
Agön Sweden 61°34N 17°23E 62 C11
Agon-Coutainville France 49°2N 1°34W 70 C5
Agordo Italy 46°18N 12°2E 93 B9
Agori India 24°33N 82°57E 125 G10
Agouna Benin 7°39N 1°47E 139 D5
Agout → France 43°47N 1°41E 72 E5
Agra India 27°17N 77°58E 124 F7
Agrakhanskiy Poluostrov Russia 43°42N 47°36E 87 J8
Agramunt Spain 41°48N 1°6E 90 D6
Ágreda Spain 41°51N 1°55W 90 D3
Ağri Turkey 39°44N 43°3E 105 C10
Ağri □ Turkey 39°45N 43°5E 105 C10
Agri → Italy 40°13N 16°44E 95 B9
Ağri Dağı Turkey 39°50N 44°15E 105 C11
Ağri Karakose = Ağri Turkey 39°44N 43°3E 105 C10
Agria Greece 39°20N 23°1E 98 B5
Agrigento Italy 37°19N 13°34E 94 E6
Agrinio Greece 38°37N 21°27E 98 C3
Agrópoli Italy 40°21N 14°59E 95 B7
Ağstafa Azerbaijan 41°7N 45°27E 87 K7
Água Branca Brazil 5°50S 42°40W 189 B2
Agua Caliente Mexico 32°29N 116°59W 171 N10
Agua Caliente Springs U.S.A. 32°56N 116°19W 171 N10
Água Clara Brazil 20°25S 52°45W 187 H8
Agua Fria ⌂ U.S.A. 34°14N 112°0W 169 J8
Agua Hechicera Mexico 32°28N 116°15W 171 N10
Agua Prieta Mexico 31°18N 109°34W 180 A3
Aguada Cecilio Argentina 40°51S 65°51W 192 B3
Aguadilla Puerto Rico 18°26N 67°10W 183 d
Aguadulce Panama 8°15N 80°32W 182 E3
Aguanga U.S.A. 33°27N 116°51W 171 M10
Aguanish Canada 50°14N 62°2W 165 B7
Aguanish → Canada 50°13N 62°5W 165 B7
Aguapey → Argentina 29°7S 56°36W 190 B4
Aguaray Guazú → Paraguay 24°47S 57°19W 190 A4
Aguarico → Ecuador 0°59S 75°11W 186 D3
Aguaro-Guariquito △ Venezuela 8°20N 66°35W 183 E6
Aguas → Spain 41°20N 0°30W 90 D4
Aguas Blancas Chile 24°15S 69°55W 190 A2
Aguas Calientes, Sierra de Argentina 25°26S 66°40W 190 B2
Águas Formosas Brazil 17°5S 40°57W 189 D2
Águas Lindas de Goiás Brazil 15°46S 48°15W 189 D1
Aguascalientes Mexico 21°53N 102°18W 180 C4
Aguascalientes □ Mexico 22°0N 102°20W 180 C4
Agudo Spain 38°59N 4°52W 89 G6
Águeda Portugal 40°34N 8°27W 88 E2
Agueda → Spain 41°2N 6°56W 88 D4
Aguelhok Mali 19°29N 0°52E 139 B5
Aguié Niger 13°31N 7°46E 139 C6
Aguila, Punta Puerto Rico 17°57N 67°13W 183 d
Aguilafuente Spain 41°13N 4°7W 88 D6
Aguilar de Campóo Spain 42°47N 4°15W 88 C6
Aguilar de la Frontera Spain 37°31N 4°40W 89 H6
Aguilares Argentina 27°26S 65°35W 190 B2
Águilas Spain 37°23N 1°35W 91 H3
Agüimes Canary Is. 27°58N 15°27W 100 G4
Aguja, C. de la Colombia 11°18N 74°12W 184 B3
Agujereada, Pta. Puerto Rico 18°30N 67°8W 183 d
Agulhas, C. S. Africa 34°52S 20°0E 144 D3
Agulhas Ridge Atl. Oc. 42°0S 15°0E 56 L13
Agulo Canary Is. 28°11N 17°12W 100 F2
Agung, Gunung Indonesia 8°20S 115°28E 118 F5
Aguni-Jima Japan 26°30N 127°10E 113 L3
Agur Uganda 2°28N 32°55E 142 B3
Agusan → Phil. 9°0N 125°30E 119 C7
Ağva Turkey 41°8N 29°51E 97 E13
Agvali Russia 42°36N 46°8E 87 J8
Aha Mts. Botswana 19°45S 21°0E 144 A3
Ahaggar Algeria 23°0N 6°30E 136 D5
Ahaggar △ Algeria 23°0N 4°5E 136 D4
Ahai Dam China 27°21N 100°30E 116 D3
Ahal □ Turkmenistan 37°0N 57°0E 108 E5
Ahamansu Ghana 7°38N 0°35E 139 D5
Ahar Iran 38°35N 47°0E 105 C12
Ahat Turkey 38°39N 29°47E 99 C11
Ahaura → N.Z. 42°21S 171°34E 155 C6
Ahaus Germany 52°4N 7°0E 76 C2
Ahelledjem Algeria 26°37N 6°58E 136 C5
Ahimanawa Ra. N.Z. 39°3S 176°30E 154 F5
Ahipara B. N.Z. 35°5S 173°5E 154 B2
Ahir Dağı Turkey 38°45N 30°10E 99 C12
Ahiri India 19°30N 80°0E 126 E5
Ahlat Turkey 38°45N 42°29E 105 C10
Ahlen Germany 51°45N 7°53E 76 D3
Ahmad Wal Pakistan 29°18N 65°58E 124 E1
Ahmadabad India 23°0N 72°40E 124 H5
Aḩmadābād Khorāsān, Iran 35°3N 60°50E 129 C9
Aḩmadābād Khorāsān, Iran 35°49N 59°42E 129 C8
Aḩmadī Iran 27°56N 56°42E 129 E8
Ahmadnagar India 19°7N 74°46E 126 E2
Ahmadpur India 18°40N 76°57E 126 E3
Ahmadpur East Pakistan 29°12N 71°10E 124 E4
Ahmadpur Lamma Pakistan 28°19N 70°3E 124 E4
Ahmedabad = Ahmadabad India 23°0N 72°40E 124 H5
Ahmednagar = Ahmadnagar India 19°7N 74°46E 126 E2
Ahmetbey Turkey 41°26N 27°34E 97 E11
Ahmetler Turkey 38°28N 29°5E 99 C11
Ahmetli Turkey 38°32N 27°57E 99 C9
Ahoada Nigeria 5°8N 6°36E 139 D6
Ahome Mexico 25°55N 109°11W 180 B3
Ahoskie U.S.A. 36°17N 76°59W 177 C16
Ahr → Germany 50°32N 7°16E 76 E3
Ahram Iran 28°52N 51°16E 129 D6
Ahrax Pt. Malta 36°0N 14°22E 101 D1
Ahrensbök Germany 54°2N 10°35E 76 A6
Ahrensburg Germany 53°40N 10°13E 76 B6
Ahtopol Bulgaria 42°6N 27°56E 97 D11
Ahuachapán El Salv. 13°54N 89°52W 182 D2
Ahun France 46°4N 2°5E 71 F9
Ahuriri → N.Z. 44°31S 170°12E 155 E5
Åhus Sweden 55°56N 14°18E 63 J8
Ahvāz Iran 31°20N 48°40E 129 D6
Ahvenanmaa = Åland Finland 60°15N 20°0E 61 F19
Aḩwar Yemen 13°30N 46°40E 131 E4
Ahzar → Mali 15°30N 3°20E 139 B5
Ai → India 26°26N 90°44E 125 F14
Ai-Ais Namibia 27°54S 17°59E 144 C2
Ai-Ais and Fish River Canyon △ Namibia 24°45S 17°15E 144 B2
Aichach Germany 48°27N 11°8E 77 G7
Aichi □ Japan 35°0N 137°15E 113 G8
Aigai Greece 40°28N 22°19E 96 F6
Aigle Switz. 46°18N 6°58E 77 J2
Aignay-le-Duc France 47°40N 4°43E 71 E11
Aigoual, Mt. France 44°8N 3°35E 72 D7
Aigre France 45°54N 0°1E 72 C4
Aigrettes, Pte. des Réunion 21°3S 55°13E 141 c
Aiguá Uruguay 34°13S 54°46W 191 C5
Aigueperse France 46°3N 3°13E 71 F10
Aigues → France 44°7N 4°43E 73 D8
Aigues-Mortes France 43°35N 4°12E 73 E8
Aigues-Mortes, G. d' France 43°31N 4°3E 73 E8
Aigües-Tortes i Estany de St. Maurici △ Spain 42°38N 0°31E 90 C4
Aiguilles France 44°47N 6°51E 73 D10

Aiguillon *France* 44°18N 0°21E **72 D4**
Aigurande *France* 46°27N 1°49E **71 F8**
Aihui = Heihe *China* 50°10N 127°30E **111 A14**
Aija *Peru* 9°50S 77°45W **188 B2**
Aikawa *Japan* 38°2N 138°15E **112 E9**
Aiken *U.S.A.* 33°34N 81°43W **178 B8**
Ailao Shan *China* 24°0N 101°20E **116 F3**
Aileron *Australia* 22°39S 133°20E **150 C1**
Ailey *U.S.A.* 32°11N 82°34W **178 C7**
Aillant-sur-Tholon
   France 47°52N 3°20E **71 E10**
Aillik *Canada* 55°11N 59°18W **165 A8**
Ailsa Craig *Canada* 43°8N 81°33W **174 C3**
Ailsa Craig *U.K.* 55°15N 5°6W **65 F3**
Aim *Russia* 59°0N 133°55E **107 D14**
Aimogasta *Argentina* 28°33S 66°50W **190 B2**
Aimorés *Brazil* 19°30S 41°4W **189 D2**
Ain □ *France* 46°5N 5°20E **71 F12**
Ain → *France* 45°45N 5°11E **73 C9**
Aïn Beïda *Algeria* 35°50N 7°29E **136 A5**
Aïn Ben Khellil *Algeria* 33°15N 0°49W **136 B3**
Aïn Ben Tili *Mauritania* 25°59N 9°27W **134 C4**
Aïn Beni Mathar *Morocco* 34°1N 2°0W **136 B3**
Aïn Dalla *Egypt* 27°20N 27°23E **137 B2**
Aïn Defla *Algeria* 36°16N 1°58E **136 A4**
Aïn Defla □ *Algeria* 36°10N 2°10E **136 A4**
Aïn el Mafki *Egypt* 27°30N 28°15E **137 B2**
Aïn Girba *Egypt* 29°20N 25°14E **137 B2**
Aïn M'lila *Algeria* 36°2N 6°35E **136 A5**
Aïn Murr *Sudan* 21°50N 25°59E **137 C2**
Aïn Qeiqab *Egypt* 29°42N 24°55E **137 B1**
Aïn Sefra *Algeria* 32°47N 0°37W **136 B3**
Aïn Sheikh Murzûk
   Egypt 26°47N 27°45E **137 B2**
Aïn Sudr *Egypt* 29°50N 33°6E **130 F2**
Aïn Sukhna *Egypt* 29°32N 32°20E **138 J8**
Aïn Tédélès *Algeria* 36°0N 0°21E **136 A4**
Aïn Témouchent *Algeria* 35°16N 1°8W **136 A3**
Aïn Témouchent □
   Algeria 35°20N 1°5W **136 A3**
Aïn Tikkidine *Algeria* 25°33N 1°24E **136 C4**
Aïn Touta *Algeria* 35°26N 5°54E **136 A5**
Aïn Zeitûn *Egypt* 29°10N 25°48E **137 B2**
Aïn Zorah *Morocco* 34°37N 3°32W **136 B3**
Aïnaži *Latvia* 57°50N 24°24E **84 D3**
Ainos Oros *Greece* 38°9N 20°40E **98 C2**
Ainsworth *U.S.A.* 42°33N 99°52W **172 C4**
Aiquile *Bolivia* 18°10S 65°10W **186 G5**
Aïr *Niger* 18°30N 8°0E **139 B6**
Aïr et Ténéré △ *Niger* 18°12N 9°56E **139 B6**
Air Force I. *Canada* 67°58N 74°5W **161 D17**
Air Hitam *Malaysia* 1°55N 103°11E **121 M4**
Airaines *France* 49°58N 1°55E **71 C8**
Airdrie *Canada* 51°18N 114°2W **162 C6**
Airdrie *U.K.* 55°52N 3°57W **65 F5**
Aire → *France* 49°18N 4°49E **71 C11**
Aire *U.K.* 53°43N 0°55W **66 E7**
Aire, I. de l' *Spain* 39°48N 4°16E **100 B11**
Aire-sur-la-Lys *France* 50°37N 2°22E **71 B9**
Aire-sur-l'Adour *France* 43°42N 0°15W **72 E3**
Aireys Inlet *Australia* 38°29S 144°5E **152 F6**
Airlie Beach *Australia* 20°16S 148°43E **150 b**
Airvault *France* 46°50N 0°8W **70 F6**
Aisch → *Germany* 49°46N 10°58E **75 F6**
Aisne □ *France* 49°42N 3°40E **71 C10**
Aisne → *France* 49°26N 2°50E **71 C9**
Ait *India* 25°54N 79°14E **125 G8**
Aït Ben Haddou *Morocco* 31°3N 7°7W **136 B3**
Aitana, Sierra de *Spain* 38°35N 0°24W **91 G4**
Aitkin *U.S.A.* 46°32N 93°42W **172 B7**
Aitutaki *Cook Is.* 18°52S 159°45W **157 J12**
Aiuaba *Brazil* 6°38S 40°7W **189 D3**
Aiud *Romania* 46°19N 23°44E **81 D8**
Aix-en-Provence *France* 43°32N 5°27E **73 E9**
Aix-la-Chapelle = Aachen
   Germany 50°45N 6°6E **76 E2**
Aix-les-Bains *France* 45°41N 5°53E **73 C9**
Aixe-sur-Vienne *France* 45°47N 1°9E **72 C5**
Aíyina = Egina *Greece* 37°45N 23°26E **98 D5**
Aizawl *India* 23°40N 92°44E **123 H18**
Aizenay *France* 46°44N 1°38W **70 F5**
Aizkraukle *Latvia* 56°36N 25°11E **84 D3**
Aizpute *Latvia* 56°43N 21°40E **82 B8**
Aizuwakamatsu *Japan* 37°30N 139°56E **112 F9**
Ajabshīr *Iran* 37°30N 45°54E **105 D11**
Ajaccio *France* 41°55N 8°40E **73 G12**
Ajaccio, G. d' *France* 41°52N 8°40E **73 G12**
Ajai △ *Uganda* 2°52N 31°16E **142 B3**
Ajaigarh *India* 24°52N 80°16E **125 G9**
Ajalpan *Mexico* 18°22N 97°15W **181 D5**
Ajanta *India* 20°30N 75°48E **126 D2**
Ajanta Ra. *India* 20°28N 75°50E **126 D2**
Ajaokuta *Nigeria* 7°28N 6°42E **139 D6**
Ajari Rep. = Ajaria □
   Georgia 41°30N 42°0E **87 K6**
Ajaria □ *Georgia* 41°30N 42°0E **87 K6**
Ajax *Canada* 43°50N 79°1W **174 C5**
Ajax, Mt. *N.Z.* 42°35S 172°5E **155 D5**
Ajdâbiyā *Libya* 30°54N 20°4E **135 B10**
Ajdovščina *Slovenia* 45°54N 13°54E **91 C10**
Ajitgarh *India* 30°47N 76°41E **124 D7**
Ajka *Hungary* 47°4N 17°31E **80 C2**
'Ajlûn *Jordan* 32°18N 35°47E **130 C4**
'Ajlûn □ *Jordan* 32°18N 35°47E **130 C4**
'Ajmân *U.A.E.* 25°25N 55°30E **129 E7**
Ajmer *India* 26°28N 74°37E **124 F6**
Ajnala *India* 31°50N 74°48E **126 D6**
Ajo *U.S.A.* 32°22N 112°52W **169 K7**
Ajo, C. de *Spain* 43°31N 3°35W **88 B7**
Ak Dağ *Turkey* 36°30N 30°0E **99 E11**
Ak Dağlar *Turkey* 39°32N 36°12E **104 C7**
Ak Dağları *Turkey* 39°0N 37°50E **104 C7**
Ak-Dovurak *Russia* 51°11N 90°36E **109 D10**
Akaba *Turkey* 8°10N 1°2E **139 D5**
Akabira *Japan* 43°33N 142°5E **112 C11**
Akabli *Algeria* 26°49N 1°31E **136 C4**
Akademika Obrucheva, Khrebet
   Russia 51°50N 96°0E **109 B13**
Akagera △ *Rwanda* 1°31S 30°33E **142 C3**
Akalkot *India* 17°32N 76°13E **126 B3**
Akamas *Cyprus* 35°3N 32°18E **101 D11**
Akan △ *Japan* 43°20N 144°20E **112 C12**
Akanthou *Cyprus* 35°22N 33°45E **101 D12**
Akaroa *N.Z.* 43°49S 172°59E **155 D7**
Akaroa Harbour *N.Z.* 43°54S 172°55E **155 D7**
Akasha *Sudan* 21°10N 30°32E **137 C3**
Akashi *Japan* 34°45N 134°58E **113 G7**
Akbarpur *Bihar, India* 24°39N 83°58E **125 G10**
Akbarpur *Ut. P., India* 26°25N 82°32E **125 F10**

Akbou *Algeria* 36°31N 4°31E **136 A4**
Akbulak *Russia* 51°1N 55°37E **108 B5**
Akçaabat *Turkey* 41°1N 39°34E **105 B8**
Akçadağ *Turkey* 38°27N 37°42E **104 C7**
Akçakale *Turkey* 36°41N 38°56E **105 D8**
Akçakoca *Turkey* 41°5N 31°8E **104 B4**
Akçaova *Turkey* 41°3N 29°57E **97 E13**
Akçay *Turkey* 36°36N 29°34E **99 E11**
Akçay → *Turkey* 37°50N 28°15E **99 D10**
Akdağ *Turkey* 38°33N 26°30E **99 C8**
Akdağmadeni *Turkey* 39°39N 35°53E **104 C6**
Akdoğan = Lysi *Cyprus* 35°8N 33°41E **101 D12**
Akelamo *Indonesia* 1°35N 129°40E **119 D7**
Åkers styckebruk
   Sweden 59°15N 17°5E **62 E11**
Åkersberga *Sweden* 59°29N 18°18E **62 E12**
Akeru → *India* 17°25N 80°5E **126 F5**
Aketi
   Dem. Rep. of the Congo 2°38N 23°47E **140 D4**
Akhali Atoni *Georgia* 43°7N 40°50E **87 J5**
Akhalkalaki *Georgia* 41°27N 43°25E **87 K6**
Akhaltsikhe *Georgia* 41°40N 43°0E **87 K6**
Akhisar *Turkey* 38°56N 27°48E **99 C9**
Akhmîm *Egypt* 26°31N 31°47E **137 B3**
Akhna *Cyprus* 35°3N 33°47E **101 D12**
Akhnur *India* 32°52N 74°45E **125 C6**
Akhtuba → *Russia* 47°41N 46°55E **87 G8**
Akhtubinsk *Russia* 48°13N 46°7E **87 F8**
Akhty *Russia* 41°30N 47°45E **87 K8**
Akhtyrka = Okhtyrka
   Ukraine 50°25N 35°0E **85 G8**
Aki *Japan* 33°30N 133°54E **113 H6**
Akimiski I. *Canada* 52°50N 81°30W **164 B3**
Akıncı Burnu *Turkey* 36°19N 35°46E **104 D6**
Akıncılar = Louroujina
   Cyprus 35°0N 33°28E **101 E12**
Akiōta *Japan* 34°36N 132°19E **113 G6**
Akita *Japan* 39°45N 140°7E **112 E10**
Akita □ *Japan* 39°40N 140°30E **112 E10**
Akjoujt *Mauritania* 19°45N 14°15W **138 B2**
Akka *Mali* 15°24N 4°11W **138 B4**
Akka *Morocco* 29°22N 8°9W **136 C2**
Akkaraipattu *Sri Lanka* 7°13N 81°51E **127 L5**
Akkeshi *Japan* 43°2N 144°51E **112 C12**
'Akko *Israel* 32°55N 35°4E **130 C4**
Akköy *Turkey* 37°29N 27°15E **99 D9**
Akkuş *Turkey* 40°47N 37°0E **104 B7**
Aklampa *Benin* 8°15N 2°10E **139 D5**
Aklavik *Canada* 68°12N 135°0W **160 D4**
Aklera *India* 24°26N 76°32E **124 G7**
Akmenrags *Latvia* 56°50N 21°4E **82 B8**
Akmonte = Almonte
   Spain 37°13N 6°38W **89 H4**
Aknoul *Morocco* 34°40N 3°55W **136 B3**
Akō *Japan* 34°45N 134°24E **113 G7**
Ako *Nigeria* 10°19N 10°48E **139 C7**
Akola *Maharashtra, India* 20°42N 77°2E **126 D3**
Akola *Maharashtra, India* 19°32N 74°3E **126 E2**
Akonolinga *Cameroon* 3°50N 12°18E **139 E7**
Akor *Mali* 14°59N 6°58W **138 C3**
Akordat *Eritrea* 15°30N 37°40E **137 D4**
Akosombo Dam *Ghana* 6°20N 0°5E **139 D5**
Akot *India* 21°10N 77°10E **126 D3**
Akoupé *Côte d'Ivoire* 6°23N 3°54W **138 D4**
Akpatok I. *Canada* 60°25N 68°8W **161 E18**
Åkrahamn *Norway* 59°15N 5°10E **61 G11**
Akranes *Iceland* 64°19N 22°5W **60 D2**
Akreijit *Mauritania* 18°19N 9°11W **138 B3**
Akritas, Akra *Greece* 36°43N 21°54E **98 E3**
Akron *Colo., U.S.A.* 40°10N 103°13W **168 F12**
Akron *Ohio, U.S.A.* 41°5N 81°31W **174 E3**
Akrotiri *Cyprus* 34°36N 32°57E **101 E11**
Akrotíri, Ákra *Greece* 40°26N 25°27E **97 F9**
Akrotiri Bay *Cyprus* 34°35N 33°10E **101 E12**
Aksai Chin *China* 35°15N 79°55E **125 B8**
Aksaray *Turkey* 38°25N 34°2E **104 C5**
Aksaray □ *Turkey* 38°20N 33°45E **104 C5**
Aksay = Aqsay
   Kazakhstan 51°11N 53°0E **108 B4**
Akşehir *Turkey* 38°18N 31°30E **104 C4**
Akşehir Gölü *Turkey* 38°30N 31°25E **104 C4**
Akstafa = Ağstafa
   Azerbaijan 41°7N 45°27E **87 K7**
Aksu *China* 41°5N 80°10E **109 D10**
Aksu *Turkey* 36°57N 30°50E **104 D4**
Aksu → *Turkey* 36°52N 30°57E **104 D4**
Aksu He → *China* 40°26N 80°59E **109 D10**
Aksum *Ethiopia* 14°5N 38°40E **131 E2**
Aktash *Russia* 55°2N 52°3E **86 C11**
Akto *China* 39°5N 75°59E **109 E9**
Aktsyabrski *Belarus* 52°38N 28°53E **75 B15**
Aktyubinsk = Aqtöbe
   Kazakhstan 50°17N 57°10E **108 B5**
Aku *Nigeria* 6°40N 7°18E **139 D6**
Akure *Nigeria* 7°15N 5°5E **139 D6**
Akuressa *Sri Lanka* 6°5N 80°29E **127 L5**
Akureyri *Iceland* 65°40N 18°6W **60 D4**
Akuseki-Shima *Japan* 29°27N 129°37E **113 K4**
Akusha *Russia* 42°18N 47°30E **87 J8**
Akwa-Ibom □ *Nigeria* 4°30N 7°30E **139 E6**
Akwanga *Nigeria* 8°55N 8°23E **139 D6**
Akyab = Sittwe
   Myanmar 20°18N 92°45E **123 J18**
Akyazı *Turkey* 40°40N 30°38E **104 B4**
Al 'Adan = 'Adan
   Yemen 12°45N 45°0E **131 E4**
Al Ahsâ = Hasa
   Si. Arabia 25°50N 49°0E **129 E6**
Al Ajfar *Si. Arabia* 27°26N 43°0E **128 E4**
Al Amādīyah *Iraq* 37°5N 43°30E **128 B4**
Al 'Amārah *Iraq* 31°55N 47°15E **105 G12**
Al Anbār □ *Iraq* 32°0N 42°0E **128 C4**
Al 'Aqabah *Jordan* 29°31N 35°0E **130 H4**
Al 'Aqabah □ *Jordan* 29°40N 35°5E **130 H4**
Al Arak *Syria* 34°38N 38°35E **105 E8**
Al 'Āsimah □ *Jordan* 31°40N 36°30E **130 D5**
Al 'Assāfīyah *Si. Arabia* 28°17N 38°59E **128 D3**
Al 'Awdah *Si. Arabia* 25°4N 38°44E **128 E3**
Al 'Ayn *Si. Arabia* 25°4N 38°6E **128 E3**
Al 'Ayn *U.A.E.* 24°15N 55°45E **129 E7**
Al 'Azīzīyah *Iraq* 32°54N 45°4E **105 F11**
Al Bāb *Syria* 36°23N 37°29E **104 D7**
Al Bad' *Si. Arabia* 28°28N 35°1E **128 D2**
Al Bad'i *Si. Arabia* 22°0N 46°35E **128 C4**
Al Bādī *Iraq* 35°56N 41°32E **128 C4**

Al Bāḩah *Si. Arabia* 20°1N 41°28E **137 C5**
Al Baḩrah *Kuwait* 29°40N 47°52E **128 D5**
Al Baḩral Mayyit = Dead Sea
   Asia 31°30N 35°30E **130 D4**
Al Balqā' □ *Jordan* 32°5N 35°45E **130 C4**
Al Bārūk, J. *Lebanon* 33°59N 35°40E **130 B4**
Al Başrah *Iraq* 30°30N 47°50E **128 D5**
Al Baṭḩā *Iraq* 31°6N 45°53E **128 D5**
Al Batrûn *Lebanon* 34°15N 35°40E **130 A4**
Al Baydā *Libya* 32°50N 21°44E **135 B10**
Al Biqā □ *Lebanon* 34°10N 36°10E **130 A5**
Al Bi'r *Si. Arabia* 28°51N 36°16E **128 D3**
Al Bukayrīyah *Si. Arabia* 26°9N 43°40E **128 E4**
Al Burayj *Syria* 34°15N 36°46E **130 A5**
Al Fadilī *Si. Arabia* 26°58N 49°10E **129 E6**
Al Fallūjah *Iraq* 33°20N 43°55E **105 F10**
Al Fatḩah *Iraq* 35°3N 43°33E **105 E10**
Al Fāw *Iraq* 30°0N 48°30E **129 D6**
Al Fujayrah *U.A.E.* 25°7N 56°18E **129 E8**
Al Ghadaf, W. →
   Jordan 31°26N 36°43E **130 D5**
Al Ghammās *Iraq* 31°45N 44°37E **128 D5**
Al Ghazālah *Si. Arabia* 26°48N 41°19E **128 E4**
Al Ghuwayfāt *U.A.E.* 24°10N 51°38E **129 E6**
Al Ḩadīthah *Iraq* 34°0N 41°13E **105 E10**
Al Ḩadīthah *Si. Arabia* 31°28N 37°8E **130 D6**
Al Ḩadr *Iraq* 35°35N 42°44E **105 E10**
Al Ḩājānah *Syria* 33°20N 36°33E **130 B5**
Al Ḩajal al Gharbī
   Oman 24°10N 56°15E **129 E8**
Al Ḩāmad *Si. Arabia* 31°30N 39°30E **128 D3**
Al Ḩamdānīyah *Syria* 35°25N 36°50E **128 C3**
Al Ḩamīdīyah *Syria* 34°42N 35°57E **130 A4**
Al Ḩammār *Iraq* 30°57N 46°51E **128 D5**
Al Ḩamrā' *Si. Arabia* 24°2N 38°55E **128 E3**
Al Ḩamzah *Iraq* 31°43N 44°58E **128 D5**
Al Ḩarīqah
   Si. Arabia 24°51N 40°31E **128 E4**
Al Ḩarūj al Aswad *Libya* 27°0N 17°10E **135 C9**
Al Ḩasakah *Iraq* 36°35N 40°45E **105 D9**
Al Ḩasakah □ *Syria* 36°40N 40°50E **105 D9**
Al Ḩāshimīyah *Iraq* 32°22N 44°39E **105 G11**
Al Ḩayy *Iraq* 32°5N 46°5E **105 F12**
Al Ḩillah *Iraq* 32°30N 44°25E **105 F11**
Al Ḩindīyah *Iraq* 32°30N 44°10E **105 F11**
Al Ḩirmil *Lebanon* 34°26N 36°24E **130 A5**
Al Hoceïma *Morocco* 35°8N 3°58W **136 A3**
Al Ḩudaydah *Yemen* 14°50N 43°0E **131 E3**
Al Ḩudud ash Shamālīyah □
   Si. Arabia 29°10N 42°30E **128 D4**
Al Ḩufūf *Si. Arabia* 25°25N 49°45E **129 E6**
Al Ḩumaydah
   Si. Arabia 29°14N 34°56E **128 D2**
Al Ḩunayy *Si. Arabia* 25°58N 48°45E **129 E6**
Al Īsāwīyah *Si. Arabia* 30°43N 37°59E **128 D3**
Al Jafr *Jordan* 30°18N 36°14E **130 E5**
Al Jāfūrah *Si. Arabia* 25°0N 50°15E **129 E6**
Al Jaghbūb *Libya* 29°42N 24°38E **135 C10**
Al Jahrah *Kuwait* 29°25N 47°40E **128 D5**
Al Jalāmīd *Si. Arabia* 31°20N 40°6E **128 D4**
Al Jamaliyah *Qatar* 25°37N 51°5E **129 E6**
Al Janūb □ *Lebanon* 33°20N 35°20E **130 B4**
Al Jawf *Libya* 24°10N 23°24E **135 D10**
Al Jawf □ *Si. Arabia* 29°30N 39°30E **128 D3**
Al Jazair = Algeria ■
   Africa 28°30N 2°0E **136 C4**
Al Jazirah *Iraq* 33°30N 44°0E **105 E10**
Al Jithāmīyah *Si. Arabia* 27°41N 41°43E **128 E4**
Al Jubayl *Si. Arabia* 27°0N 49°50E **129 E6**
Al Jubaylah *Si. Arabia* 24°55N 46°25E **128 E5**
Al Jubb *Si. Arabia* 27°11N 42°17E **128 E4**
Al Junaynah *Sudan* 13°27N 22°45E **135 F10**
Al Kabā'ish *Iraq* 30°58N 47°0E **128 D5**
Al Karak *Jordan* 31°11N 35°42E **130 D4**
Al Karak □ *Jordan* 31°0N 36°0E **130 E5**
Al Kāzimīyah *Iraq* 33°22N 44°18E **105 F11**
Al Khābūrah *Oman* 23°57N 57°5E **129 F8**
Al Khafjī *Si. Arabia* 28°24N 48°29E **129 E6**
Al Khalīl = Hebron
   West Bank 31°32N 35°6E **130 D4**
Al Khāliş *Iraq* 33°49N 44°32E **105 F11**
Al Kharsānīyah
   Si. Arabia 27°13N 49°18E **129 E6**
Al Khaşab *Oman* 26°14N 56°15E **129 E8**
Al Khawr *Qatar* 25°41N 51°30E **129 E6**
Al Khiḍr *Iraq* 31°12N 45°33E **128 D5**
Al Khiyām *Lebanon* 33°20N 35°36E **130 B4**
Al Khubar *Si. Arabia* 26°17N 50°12E **129 E6**
Al Khums *Libya* 32°40N 14°17E **135 B8**
Al Khurmah *Si. Arabia* 21°54N 42°3E **131 C3**
Al Kiflī *Iraq* 32°13N 44°22E **105 G11**
Al Kiswah *Syria* 33°23N 36°14E **130 B5**
Al Kūfah *Iraq* 32°2N 44°24E **105 F11**
Al Kufrah *Libya* 24°17N 23°15E **135 D10**
Al Kuhayfiyah *Si. Arabia* 27°12N 43°3E **128 E4**
Al Kumayt *Iraq* 32°30N 46°52E **105 G12**
Al Kūt *Iraq* 32°30N 46°0E **105 F11**
Al Kuwayt *Kuwait* 29°30N 48°0E **128 D5**
Al Labwah *Lebanon* 34°11N 36°20E **130 A5**
Al Lādhiqīyah *Syria* 35°30N 35°45E **104 E6**
Al Lādhiqīyah □ *Syria* 35°45N 36°0E **104 E6**
Al Lith *Si. Arabia* 20°9N 40°15E **137 C5**
Al Liwā' *Oman* 24°31N 56°36E **129 E8**
Al Luḩayyah *Yemen* 15°45N 42°40E **131 E3**
Al Madīnah *Iraq* 30°57N 47°16E **128 D5**
Al Madīnah *Si. Arabia* 24°35N 39°52E **128 E3**
Al Mafraq *Jordan* 32°17N 36°14E **130 C5**
Al Mafraq □ *Jordan* 32°17N 37°15E **130 C5**
Al Maghreb = Morocco ■
   N. Afr. 32°0N 5°50W **134 B4**
Al Maḩmūdīyah *Iraq* 33°3N 44°21E **105 F11**
Al Majma'ah *Si. Arabia* 25°57N 45°22E **128 E5**
Al Makhruq, W. →
   Jordan 31°28N 37°0E **130 D6**
Al Makhūl *Si. Arabia* 34°59N 39°57E **128 C3**
Al Manāmah *Bahrain* 26°10N 50°30E **129 E6**
Al Maqwa' *Kuwait* 29°10N 47°59E **128 D5**
Al Marāḩ *Si. Arabia* 25°35N 49°35E **129 E6**
Al Marj *Libya* 32°25N 20°30E **135 B10**
Al Maţlā *Kuwait* 29°24N 47°40E **128 D5**
Al Mawşil *Iraq* 36°15N 43°5E **105 B10**
Al Mayadin *Syria* 35°1N 40°27E **105 C9**
Al Mazār *Jordan* 31°4N 35°41E **130 D4**
Al Midhnab *Si. Arabia* 25°50N 44°18E **128 E5**
Al Minā' *Lebanon* 34°24N 35°49E **130 A4**
Al Miqdādīyah *Iraq* 34°0N 45°0E **105 F11**
Al Mubarraz *Si. Arabia* 25°30N 49°40E **129 E6**
Al Mudawwarah *Jordan* 29°19N 36°0E **130 F5**
Al Mughayrā' *U.A.E.* 24°5N 53°32E **129 E7**
Al Muḩarraq *Bahrain* 26°15N 50°40E **129 E6**
Al Mukallā *Yemen* 14°33N 49°2E **131 E4**

Al Mukhā *Yemen* 13°18N 43°15E **131 E3**
Al Musayjid *Si. Arabia* 24°5N 39°5E **128 E3**
Al Musayyib *Iraq* 32°49N 44°20E **105 F11**
Al Muthanná □ *Iraq* 30°30N 45°15E **128 D5**
Al Muwayh *Si. Arabia* 22°1N 41°37E **137 C5**
Al Muwaylih *Si. Arabia* 27°40N 35°30E **128 E2**
Al Owuho = Otukpa
   Nigeria 7°9N 7°41E **139 D6**
Al Qādisīyah □ *Iraq* 32°0N 45°0E **128 D5**
Al Qā'im *Iraq* 34°21N 41°7E **105 E9**
Al Qalībah *Si. Arabia* 28°24N 37°42E **128 D3**
Al Qāmishlī *Syria* 37°2N 41°14E **105 D9**
Al Qaryatayn *Syria* 34°12N 37°13E **130 A6**
Al Qaşīm □ *Si. Arabia* 26°0N 43°0E **128 E4**
Al Qaţ'a *Syria* 34°40N 40°48E **105 C9**
Al Qaţīf *Si. Arabia* 26°35N 50°0E **129 E6**
Al Qaţrānah *Jordan* 31°12N 36°6E **130 D5**
Al Qaţrūn *Libya* 24°56N 15°3E **135 D8**
Al Qawz *Si. Arabia* 18°58N 41°26E **137 D5**
Al Qayşūmah *Si. Arabia* 28°20N 46°7E **128 D5**
Al Quds = Jerusalem
   Israel/West Bank 31°47N 35°10E **130 D4**
Al Qunayţirah *Syria* 33°5N 35°45E **130 B4**
Al Qunfudhah *Si. Arabia* 19°3N 41°4E **137 D5**
Al Qurayyāt *Si. Arabia* 31°20N 37°20E **128 D3**
Al Qurnah *Iraq* 31°1N 47°25E **128 D5**
Al Quşayr *Iraq* 30°39N 45°50E **128 D5**
Al Quşayr *Syria* 34°31N 36°34E **130 A5**
Al Quţayfah *Syria* 33°44N 36°36E **130 B5**
Al Quwaysimah *Jordan* 31°55N 35°57E **130 D5**
Al 'Ubaylah *Si. Arabia* 21°59N 50°57E **131 C5**
Al 'Uḍayliyah *Si. Arabia* 25°8N 49°18E **129 E6**
Al 'Ulā *Si. Arabia* 26°35N 38°0E **128 E3**
Al 'Uqayr *Si. Arabia* 25°40N 50°15E **129 E6**
Al 'Uwaynid *Si. Arabia* 24°50N 46°0E **128 E5**
Al 'Uwayqīlah
   Si. Arabia 30°30N 42°10E **128 D4**
Al 'Uyūn *Ḩijāz,
   Si. Arabia* 24°33N 39°35E **128 E3**
Al 'Uyūn *Najd,
   Si. Arabia* 26°30N 43°50E **128 E4**
Al Wajh *Si. Arabia* 26°10N 36°30E **128 E3**
Al Wakrah *Qatar* 25°10N 51°40E **129 E6**
Al Waqbah *Si. Arabia* 28°48N 45°33E **128 D5**
Al Wari'ah *Si. Arabia* 27°51N 47°25E **128 D5**
Al Yaman = Yemen ■
   Asia 15°0N 44°0E **131 E3**
Ala *Italy* 45°45N 11°0E **92 C4**
Ala Archa △
   Kyrgyzstan 42°32N 74°28E **109 D8**
Ala Dağ *Turkey* 37°44N 35°9E **128 B2**
Ala Dağları *Turkey* 39°15N 43°33E **105 C10**
Ala Tau *Asia* 45°30N 80°40E **109 C10**
Ala Tau Shankou = Dzungarian
   Gate Asia 45°0N 82°0E **109 C10**
Alabama □ *U.S.A.* 33°0N 87°0W **177 E11**
Alabama → *U.S.A.* 31°8N 87°57W **177 F11**
Alabaster *U.S.A.* 33°15N 86°49W **177 E11**
Alaca *Turkey* 40°10N 34°51E **104 B6**
Alacahöyük *Turkey* 40°15N 34°35E **104 B6**
Alaçam *Turkey* 41°36N 35°36E **104 B6**
Alaçam Dağları *Turkey* 39°18N 28°49E **99 B10**
Alacant = Alicante
   Spain 38°23N 0°30W **91 G4**
Alaçatı *Turkey* 38°15N 26°22E **99 C8**
Alachua *U.S.A.* 29°47N 82°30W **178 F17**
Alaejos *Spain* 41°18N 5°13W **88 D5**
Alaer *China* 40°30N 81°16E **109 D10**
Alagna Valsésia *Italy* 45°51N 7°56E **92 C4**
Alagoa Grande *Brazil* 7°3S 35°35W **189 B3**
Alagoas □ *Brazil* 9°0S 36°0W **189 C3**
Alagoinhas *Brazil* 12°7S 38°20W **189 C3**
Alagón *Spain* 41°46N 1°12W **90 D3**
Alagón → *Spain* 39°44N 6°53W **88 F4**
Alaheaieatnu = Altaelva →
   Norway 69°54N 23°17E **60 B20**
Alai Range *Asia* 39°45N 72°0E **109 D8**
Alaior *Spain* 39°57N 4°8E **100 B11**
Alajero *Canary Is.* 28°3N 17°13W **100 F2**
Alajuela *Costa Rica* 10°2N 84°8W **182 D3**
Alaknanda → *India* 30°8N 78°36E **125 D8**
Alakol *Kazakhstan* 46°0N 81°5E **109 C10**
Alakurtti *Russia* 66°58N 30°25E **60 C24**
Alamarvdasht *Iran* 27°37N 52°59E **129 E7**
Alameda *Calif., U.S.A.* 37°46N 122°15W **170 H4**
Alameda *N. Mex.,
   U.S.A.* 35°11N 106°37W **169 J10**
Alamo *Ga., U.S.A.* 32°9N 82°47W **178 C7**
Alamo *U.S.A.* 32°12N 115°10W **171 H11**
Alamogordo *U.S.A.* 32°54N 105°57W **169 K11**
Alamos *Mexico* 27°1N 108°56W **180 B3**
Alamosa *U.S.A.* 37°28N 105°52W **169 H11**
Alampur *India* 15°55N 78°6E **127 G4**
Åland *Finland* 60°15N 20°0E **61 F19**
Aland *India* 17°36N 76°35E **126 F3**
Alandroal *Portugal* 38°41N 7°24W **89 G3**
Ålands hav *Europe* 60°0N 19°30E **61 G18**
Ålandsbro *Sweden* 62°40N 17°51E **62 B11**
Alandur *India* 13°0N 80°15E **127 H5**
Alange, Embalse d' *Spain* 38°45N 6°18W **89 G4**
Alanís *Spain* 38°3N 5°43W **89 G5**
Alaniya = North Ossetia-
   Alaniya □ *Russia* 43°30N 44°30E **87 J7**
Alaniya □ *Russia* 42°55N 44°0E **87 J7**
Alanya *Turkey* 36°38N 32°0E **104 D5**
Alapaha *U.S.A.* 31°23N 83°13W **178 D6**
Alapayevsk *Russia* 57°52N 61°42E **106 D7**
Alar del Rey *Spain* 42°38N 4°20W **88 C6**
Alarcón, Embalse de
   Spain 39°36N 2°10W **91 G3**
Alaró *Spain* 39°42N 2°47E **100 B9**
Alaşehir *Turkey* 38°23N 28°30E **99 C10**
Alashtar *Iran* 33°51N 48°15E **105 E13**
Alaska □ *U.S.A.* 64°0N 154°0W **166 C5**
Alaska, G. of *Pac. Oc.* 58°0N 145°0W **160 F7**
Alaska Peninsula
   U.S.A. 56°0N 159°0W **166 D8**
Alaska Range *U.S.A.* 62°50N 151°0W **160 E11**
Alássio *Italy* 44°1N 8°10E **92 D6**
Ãlãt *Azerbaijan* 39°58N 49°25E **87 L9**
Alatau Shan = Ala Tau
   Asia 45°30N 80°40E **109 C10**
Alatri *Italy* 41°44N 13°21E **93 G10**
Alatyr *Russia* 54°45N 46°35E **86 C8**
Alatyr → *Russia* 54°52N 46°36E **86 C8**
Alausí *Ecuador* 2°0S 78°50W **186 D3**

Álava = Araba/Álava □
   Spain 42°48N 2°28W **90 C2**
Alava, C. *U.S.A.* 48°10N 124°44W **170 B2**
Alaverdi *Armenia* 41°15N 44°37E **87 K7**
Alavo = Alavus *Finland* 62°35N 23°36E **60 E20**
Alavus *Finland* 62°35N 23°36E **60 E20**
Alawa ◌ *Australia* 15°42S 134°39E **150 B1**
Alawoona *Australia* 34°45S 140°30E **152 C4**
Alayawarra ◌
   Australia 22°0S 134°30E **150 C1**
'Alayh *Lebanon* 33°46N 35°33E **130 B4**
Alayköy = Yerolakkos
   Cyprus 35°11N 33°15E **101 D12**
Alazani → *Azerbaijan* 41°5N 46°40E **87 K8**
Alba *Italy* 44°42N 8°2E **92 D5**
Alba □ *Romania* 46°10N 23°30E **81 D8**
Alba de Tormes *Spain* 40°50N 5°30W **88 E5**
Alba-Iulia *Romania* 46°8N 23°39E **81 D8**
Albac *Romania* 46°28N 22°58E **80 D7**
Albacete *Spain* 39°0N 1°50W **91 F3**
Albacete □ *Spain* 38°50N 2°0W **91 G3**
Albacutya, L. *Australia* 35°45S 141°58E **152 C4**
Ålbæk *Denmark* 57°36N 10°25E **63 G4**
Ålbæk Bugt *Denmark* 57°35N 10°40E **63 G4**
Albaida *Spain* 38°51N 0°31W **91 G4**
Albalate de las Nogueras
   Spain 40°22N 2°18W **90 E2**
Albalate del Arzobispo
   Spain 41°6N 0°31W **90 D4**
Alban *France* 43°53N 2°28E **72 E6**
Albanel, L. *Canada* 50°55N 73°12W **164 B5**
Albania ■ *Europe* 41°0N 20°0E **96 E4**
Albano Laziale *Italy* 41°44N 12°39E **93 G9**
Albany *Australia* 35°1S 117°58E **149 G2**
Albany *Ga., U.S.A.* 31°35N 84°10W **178 D5**
Albany *N.Y., U.S.A.* 42°39N 73°45W **175 D11**
Albany *Oreg., U.S.A.* 44°38N 123°6W **168 D2**
Albany *Tex., U.S.A.* 32°44N 99°18W **176 E5**
Albany → *Canada* 52°17N 81°31W **164 B3**
Albarca, C. d' *Spain* 39°4N 1°22E **100 B7**
Albardón *Argentina* 31°20S 68°30W **190 C2**
Albarracín *Spain* 40°25N 1°26W **90 E3**
Albarracín, Sierra de
   Spain 40°30N 1°30W **90 E3**
Albatera *Spain* 38°11N 0°52W **91 G4**
Albâtre, Côte d' *France* 49°55N 0°50E **70 C7**
Albatross B. *Australia* 12°45S 141°30E **150 A3**
Albatross Pt. *N.Z.* 38°7S 174°44E **154 E3**
Albegna → *Italy* 42°30N 11°11E **93 F8**
Albemarle *U.S.A.* 35°21N 80°12W **177 D14**
Albemarle Sd. *U.S.A.* 36°5N 76°0W **177 C16**
Albenga *Italy* 44°3N 8°13E **92 D5**
Alberche → *Spain* 39°58N 4°46W **88 F6**
Alberdi *Paraguay* 26°14S 58°20W **190 B4**
Albères, Mts. *France* 42°28N 2°56E **72 F6**
Ålberga *Sweden* 58°44N 16°35E **63 F10**
Alberga → *Australia* 27°6S 135°33E **151 D2**
Alberga *Germany* 54°8N 9°17E **76 A5**
Albersdorf *Germany* 54°8N 9°17E **76 A5**
Albert *France* 50°0N 2°38E **71 C9**
Albert, L. *Africa* 1°30N 31°0E **142 B3**
Albert, L. *Australia* 35°30S 139°10E **152 C3**
Albert Edward Ra.
   Australia 18°17S 127°57E **148 C4**
Albert Lea *U.S.A.* 43°39N 93°22W **172 D7**
Albert Nile → *Uganda* 3°36N 32°2E **142 B3**
Albert Town *Bahamas* 22°37N 74°33W **183 B5**
Alberta □ *Canada* 54°40N 115°0W **162 C6**
Alberti *Argentina* 35°1S 60°16W **190 D3**
Albertinia *S. Africa* 34°11S 21°34E **144 D3**
Albertirsa *Hungary* 47°14N 19°37E **80 C4**
Alberto de Agostini △
   Chile 54°38S 71°37W **192 G2**
Alberton *Canada* 46°50N 64°0W **165 C7**
Albertville *France* 45°40N 6°22E **73 C10**
Albertville *U.S.A.* 34°16N 86°13W **177 D11**
Albi *France* 43°56N 2°9E **72 E6**
Albia *U.S.A.* 41°2N 92°48W **172 E7**
Albina *Suriname* 5°37N 54°15W **187 B7**
Albina, Ponta *Angola* 15°52S 11°44E **144 A1**
Albino *Italy* 45°46N 9°47E **92 C6**
Albion *Mich., U.S.A.* 42°15N 84°45W **173 D11**
Albion *Nebr., U.S.A.* 41°42N 98°0W **172 E4**
Albion *Pa., U.S.A.* 41°53N 80°22W **174 E4**
Albocàsser *Spain* 40°21N 0°1E **90 E5**
Albolote *Spain* 37°14N 3°39W **89 H7**
Alborán *Medit. S.* 35°57N 3°0W **89 K7**
Alboran Sea *Medit. S.* 36°0N 3°0W **89 K7**
Alborea *Spain* 39°17N 1°24W **91 F3**
Ålborg = Aalborg *Denmark* 57°2N 9°54E **63 G3**
Ålborg Bugt = Aalborg Bugt
   Denmark 56°50N 10°35E **63 H4**
Alborz, Reshteh-ye Kūhhā-ye
   Iran 36°0N 52°0E **129 C7**
Albox *Spain* 37°23N 2°8W **91 H2**
Albstadt *Germany* 48°13N 9°1E **75 G5**
Albufeira *Portugal* 37°5N 8°15W **89 H2**
Albula → *Switz.* 46°38N 9°28E **75 J5**
Albuñol *Spain* 36°48N 3°11W **89 J7**
Albuquerque *U.S.A.* 35°5N 106°39W **169 J10**
Albuquerque, Cayos de
   Caribbean 12°10N 81°50W **182 D3**
Alburg *U.S.A.* 44°59N 73°18W **175 B11**
Alburno, Mte. *Italy* 40°33N 15°17E **95 B8**
Alburquerque *Spain* 39°15N 6°59W **89 F4**
Albury *Australia* 36°3S 146°56E **153 D7**
Alby *Sweden* 62°30N 15°28E **62 B9**
Alcácer do Sal *Portugal* 38°22N 8°33W **89 G2**
Alcáçovas *Portugal* 38°23N 8°9W **89 G2**
Alcalá de Guadaira
   Spain 37°20N 5°50W **89 H5**
Alcalá de Henares *Spain* 40°28N 3°22W **88 E7**
Alcalá de los Gazules
   Spain 36°29N 5°43W **89 J5**
Alcalá del Júcar *Spain* 39°12N 1°26W **91 F3**
Alcalá del Río *Spain* 37°31N 5°59W **89 H5**
Alcalá la Real *Spain* 37°27N 3°57W **89 H7**
Álcamo *Italy* 37°59N 12°55E **94 E5**
Alcanadre → *Spain* 41°43N 0°12W **90 D4**
Alcanar *Spain* 40°33N 0°28E **90 E5**
Alcañices *Spain* 41°41N 6°21W **88 D4**
Alcañiz *Spain* 41°2N 0°8W **90 D4**
Alcântara *Brazil* 2°20S 44°30W **189 A2**
Alcântara *Spain* 39°41N 6°57W **88 F4**

Alcántara, Embalse de
   Spain 39°44N 6°50W **88 F4**
Alcantarilla *Spain* 37°59N 1°12W **91 H3**
Alcaracejos *Spain* 38°24N 4°58W **89 G6**
Alcaraz *Spain* 38°40N 2°29W **91 G2**
Alcaraz, Sierra de *Spain* 38°40N 2°20W **91 G2**
Alcaudete *Spain* 37°35N 4°5W **89 H6**
Alcázar de San Juan
   Spain 39°24N 3°12W **89 F7**
Alchevsk *Ukraine* 48°30N 38°45E **85 H10**
Alcira = Alzira *Spain* 39°9N 0°30W **91 F4**
Alcobaça *Portugal* 39°32N 8°58W **89 F2**
Alcobendas *Spain* 40°32N 3°38W **88 E7**
Alcolea del Pinar *Spain* 41°2N 2°28W **90 D2**
Alcoma *U.S.A.* 27°54N 81°29W **179 H8**
Alcorcón *Spain* 40°20N 3°48W **88 E7**
Alcoutim *Portugal* 37°25N 7°28W **89 H3**
Alcova *U.S.A.* 42°34N 106°43W **168 E10**
Alcoy *Spain* 38°43N 0°30W **91 G4**
Alcubierre, Sierra de
   Spain 41°45N 0°22W **90 D4**
Alcublas *Spain* 39°48N 0°43W **90 F4**
Alcúdia *Spain* 39°51N 3°7E **100 B10**
Alcúdia, B. d' *Spain* 39°47N 3°15E **100 B10**
Alcúdia, Sierra de la
   Spain 38°34N 4°30W **89 G6**
Aldabra Is. *Seychelles* 9°22S 46°28E **133 G8**
Aldama *Mexico* 22°55N 98°4W **181 C5**
Aldan *Russia* 58°40N 125°30E **107 D13**
Aldan → *Russia* 63°28N 129°35E **107 C13**
Aldea, Pta. de la
   Canary Is. 28°0N 15°50W **100 G4**
Aldeburgh *U.K.* 52°10N 1°37E **67 E9**
Alder Pk. *U.S.A.* 35°53N 121°22W **170 K5**
Alderney *U.K.* 49°42N 2°11W **67 H5**
Aldershot *U.K.* 51°15N 0°44W **67 F7**
Aldinga Beach
   Australia 35°17S 138°27E **152 C3**
Åled *Sweden* 56°44N 12°57E **63 H6**
Aledo *U.S.A.* 41°12N 90°45W **172 E8**
Aleg *Mauritania* 17°3N 13°55W **138 B2**
Alegranza *Canary Is.* 29°23N 13°32W **100 E6**
Alegranza, I. *Canary Is.* 29°23N 13°32W **100 E6**
Alegre *Brazil* 20°50S 41°30W **191 A7**
Alegrete *Brazil* 29°40S 56°0W **191 B4**
Aleksandriya = Oleksandriya
   Kirovohrad, Ukraine 48°42N 33°3E **85 H7**
Aleksandriya = Oleksandriya
   Rivne, Ukraine 50°37N 26°19E **75 C14**
Aleksandriyskaya
   Russia 43°58N 47°14E **87 J8**
Aleksandrov *Russia* 56°23N 38°44E **84 D10**
Aleksandrov Gay *Russia* 50°9N 48°34E **86 E9**
Aleksandrovac *Serbia* 43°28N 21°3E **96 C5**
Aleksandrovac *Serbia* 44°28N 21°13E **96 B5**
Aleksandrovka = Oleksandrivka
   Ukraine 48°55N 32°20E **85 H7**
Aleksandrovo *Bulgaria* 43°14N 24°51E **97 C8**
Aleksandrovsk-Sakhalinskiy
   Russia 50°50N 142°20E **111 A17**
Aleksandrów Kujawski
   Poland 52°53N 18°43E **83 F5**
Aleksandrów Łódzki
   Poland 51°49N 19°17E **83 G6**
Aleksandry, Zemlya
   Russia 80°25N 48°0E **106 A5**
Alekseyevka *Samara,
   Russia* 52°35N 51°17E **86 D10**
Alekseyevka *Voronezh,
   Russia* 50°43N 38°40E **85 G10**
Aleksin *Russia* 54°31N 37°9E **84 E9**
Aleksinac *Serbia* 43°31N 21°42E **96 C5**
Além Paraíba *Brazil* 21°52S 42°41W **191 A7**
Alemania *Argentina* 25°40S 65°30W **190 B2**
Alemania *Chile* 25°10S 69°55W **190 B2**
Alençon *France* 48°27N 0°4E **70 D7**
Alenquer *Brazil* 1°56S 54°46W **187 D8**
'Alenuihāhā Channel
   U.S.A. 20°30N 156°0W **167 C4**
Alépé *Côte d'Ivoire* 5°29N 3°40W **138 D4**
Aleppo = Ḩalab *Syria* 36°10N 37°15E **104 D7**
Alerce Andino △ *Chile* 41°33S 72°29W **192 B2**
Alerce Costero △ *Chile* 40°10S 73°30W **192 B2**
Aléria *France* 42°5N 9°26E **73 F13**
Alert *Canada* 83°2N 60°0W **161 A20**
Aleru *India* 17°39N 79°3E **126 F4**
Alès *France* 44°9N 4°5E **73 D8**
Aleşd *Romania* 47°3N 22°22E **80 C7**
Alessándria *Italy* 44°54N 8°37E **92 D5**
Ålesund *Norway* 62°28N 6°12E **61 E5**
Alet-les-Bains *France* 42°59N 2°14E **72 F6**
Aletschhorn *Switz.* 46°28N 8°0E **77 J4**
Aleutian Basin *Pac. Oc.* 57°0N 177°0E **156 B9**
Aleutian Is. *Pac. Oc.* 52°0N 175°0W **156 B10**
Aleutian Range *U.S.A.* 60°0N 154°0W **166 D9**
Aleutian Trench
   Pac. Oc. 48°0N 180°0E **54 D17**
Alexander *Ga., U.S.A.* 33°1N 81°53W **178 B8**
Alexander *N. Dak.,
   U.S.A.* 47°51N 103°39W **172 B2**
Alexander, Mt.
   Australia 28°58S 120°16E **149 E3**
Alexander Arch. *U.S.A.* 56°0N 136°0W **160 E6**
Alexander Bay *S. Africa* 28°40S 16°30E **144 C2**
Alexander City *U.S.A.* 32°56N 85°58W **178 C4**
Alexander I. *Antarctica* 69°0S 70°0W **55 C17**
Alexandra *Australia* 37°8S 145°40E **153 D6**
Alexandra *N.Z.* 45°14S 169°25E **155 F4**
Alexandra Channel
   Myanmar 14°7N 93°13E **127 G11**
Alexandra Falls
   Canada 60°29N 116°18W **162 A5**
Alexandria = El Iskandarîya
   Egypt 31°13N 29°58E **137 B3**
Alexandria *B.C.,
   Canada* 52°35N 122°27W **162 C4**
Alexandria *Ont.,
   Canada* 45°19N 74°38W **175 A10**
Alexandria *Romania* 43°57N 25°24E **81 G10**
Alexandria *S. Africa* 33°38S 26°28E **144 D4**
Alexandria *U.K.* 55°59N 4°35W **65 F4**
Alexandria *La., U.S.A.* 31°18N 92°27W **176 F8**
Alexandria *Minn.,
   U.S.A.* 45°53N 95°22W **172 C6**
Alexandria *Va., U.S.A.* 38°49N 77°5W **175 F13**
Alexandria Bay *U.S.A.* 44°20N 75°55W **175 B9**
Alexandrina, L.
   Australia 35°25S 139°10E **152 C3**
Alexandroupoli *Greece* 40°50N 25°54E **97 F9**

Alexis → Canada 52°33N 56°8W 165 B8
Alexis Creek Canada 52°10N 123°20W 162 C4
Aley → Russia 52°51N 83°36E 109 B10
Aleysk Russia 52°40N 83°0E 109 B10
Alfabia Spain 39°44N 2°44E 100 B9
Alfambra Spain 40°33N 1°5W 90 E3
Alfândega da Fé Portugal 41°20N 6°59W 88 D4
Alfaro Spain 42°10N 1°50W 90 C3
Alfatar Bulgaria 43°59N 27°13E 97 C11
Alfeld Germany 51°59N 9°50E 76 D5
Alfenas Brazil 21°20S 46°10W 191 A6
Alföld Hungary 46°30N 20°0E 80 D5
Alfonsine Italy 44°30N 12°3E 93 D9
Alford Aberds., U.K. 57°14N 2°41W 65 D6
Alford Lincs., U.K. 53°15N 0°10E 66 D8
Alford U.S.A. 30°42N 85°24W 178 E4
Alfred Maine, U.S.A. 43°29N 70°43W 175 C14
Alfred N.Y., U.S.A. 42°16N 77°48W 174 D7
Alfredton N.Z. 40°41S 175°54E 154 G4
Alfreton U.K. 53°6N 1°24W 66 D6
Alfta Sweden 61°21N 16°4E 62 C10
Algaida Spain 39°33N 2°53E 100 B9
Algar Spain 36°40N 5°39W 89 J5
Ålgård Norway 58°46N 5°53E 61 G11
Algarinejo Spain 37°19N 4°9W 89 H6
Algarve Portugal 36°58N 8°20W 89 J2
Algeciras Spain 36°9N 5°28W 89 J5
Algemesí Spain 39°11N 0°27W 91 F4
Alger Algeria 36°42N 3°8E 136 A4
Alger □ Algeria 36°45N 3°10E 91 J8
Alger ✕ (ALG) Algeria 36°39N 3°13E 91 J8
Algeria ■ Africa 28°30N 2°0E 136 C4
Algha Kazakhstan 49°53N 57°20E 108 C5
Alghero Italy 40°33N 8°19E 94 B1
Älghult Sweden 57°0N 15°35E 63 G9
Algiers = Alger Algeria 36°42N 3°8E 136 A4
Algoa B. S. Africa 33°50S 25°45E 144 D4
Algodonales Spain 36°54N 5°24W 89 J5
Algodones Dunes
U.S.A. 32°50N 115°5W 171 N11
Algodor → Spain 39°55N 3°53W 88 F7
Algoma U.S.A. 44°36N 87°26W 172 C10
Algona U.S.A. 43°4N 94°14W 172 D6
Algonac U.S.A. 42°37N 82°32W 174 D2
Algonquin ⌂ Canada 45°50N 78°30W 164 C4
Algorta Spain 43°21N 2°59W 90 B2
Algorta Uruguay 32°25S 57°24W 190 C4
Alhama de Almería
Spain 36°57N 2°34W 89 J8
Alhama de Aragón
Spain 41°18N 1°54W 90 D3
Alhama de Granada
Spain 37°0N 3°59W 89 H7
Alhama de Murcia Spain 37°51N 1°25W 91 H3
Alhambra U.S.A. 34°5N 118°7W 171 L8
Alhaurín el Grande
Spain 36°39N 4°41W 89 J6
Alhucemas = Al Hoceïma
Morocco 35°8N 3°58W 136 A3
'Alī al Gharbī Iraq 32°30N 46°45E 105 F12
'Alī ash Sharqī Iraq 32°7N 46°44E 105 F12
Āli Bayramlı = Şirvan
Azerbaijan 39°59N 48°52E 87 L9
'Alī Khēl Afghan. 33°57N 69°43E 124 C3
Alī Shāh Iran 38°9N 45°50E 128 B5
Ália Italy 37°47N 13°43E 94 E6
'Alīābād Golestān, Iran 36°40N 54°33E 129 B7
'Alīābād Khorāsān, Iran 32°30N 57°30E 129 C8
'Alīābād Kordestān, Iran 35°4N 46°58E 128 C5
'Alīābād Yazd, Iran 31°41N 53°49E 129 D7
Aliade Nigeria 7°18N 8°29E 139 D6
Aliaga Spain 40°40N 0°42W 90 E4
Aliağa Turkey 38°47N 26°59E 99 C8
Aliakmonas → Greece 40°30N 22°36E 96 F6
Alibag India 18°38N 72°56E 126 E1
Alibori → Benin 11°56N 3°17E 139 C5
Alibunar Serbia 45°5N 20°57E 80 E5
Alicante Spain 38°23N 0°30W 91 G4
Alicante □ Spain 38°30N 0°37W 91 G4
Alicante ✕ (ALC) Spain 38°14N 0°36W 91 G4
Alice S. Africa 32°48S 26°55E 144 D4
Alice U.S.A. 27°45N 98°5W 176 H5
Alice → Queens.,
Australia 24°2S 144°50E 150 C3
Alice → Queens.,
Australia 15°35S 142°20E 150 B3
Alice, Punta Italy 39°24N 17°9E 95 C10
Alice Arm Canada 55°29N 129°31W 162 B3
Alice Springs Australia 23°40S 133°50E 150 C1
Alicedale S. Africa 33°15S 26°4E 144 D4
Aliceville U.S.A. 33°8N 88°9W 177 E10
Alicudi Italy 38°33N 14°20E 95 D7
Aliganj India 27°30N 79°10E 125 F8
Aligarh Raj., India 25°55N 76°15E 124 G7
Aligarh Ut. P., India 27°55N 78°10E 124 F8
Alīgūdarz Iran 33°25N 49°45E 129 C6
Alijó Portugal 41°16N 7°27W 88 D3
Alimia Greece 36°16N 27°43E 101 C9
Alingsås Sweden 57°56N 12°31E 63 G6
Alipur Pakistan 29°25N 70°55E 124 E4
Alipur Duar India 26°30N 89°35E 123 F16
Aliquippa U.S.A. 40°37N 80°15W 174 F4
Alishan Taiwan 23°31N 120°48E 117 F13
Aliste → Spain 41°34N 5°58W 88 D5
Alitus = Alytus Lithuania 54°24N 24°3E 84 E3
Aliveri Greece 38°24N 24°2E 98 C6
Aliwal North S. Africa 30°45S 26°45E 144 D4
Alix Canada 52°24N 113°11W 162 C6
Aljezur Portugal 37°18N 8°49W 89 H2
Aljustrel Portugal 37°55N 8°10W 89 H2
Alkamari Niger 13°27N 11°10E 139 C7
Alkhanay △ Russia 51°0N 113°30E 107 D12
Alkmaar Neths. 52°37N 4°45E 69 B4
All American Canal
U.S.A. 32°45N 115°15W 171 N11
Allada Benin 6°41N 2°9E 139 D5
Allagadda India 15°8N 78°30E 127 G4
Allagash → U.S.A. 47°5N 69°3W 173 B19
Allah Dad Pakistan 25°38N 67°34E 124 G2
Allahabad India 25°25N 81°58E 125 G9
Allan Canada 51°53N 106°4W 163 C7
Allanche France 45°14N 2°57E 72 C6
Allanridge S. Africa 27°45S 26°40E 144 C4
Allansford Australia 38°26S 142°39E 152 E5
Allanton N.Z. 45°55S 170°15E 155 F5
Allaqi, Wadi → Egypt 23°7N 32°47E 137 C3
Allariz Spain 42°11N 7°50W 88 C3
Allassac France 45°15N 1°29E 72 C5
Allatoona L. U.S.A. 34°10N 84°44W 178 A5
Älleberg Sweden 58°8N 13°36E 63 F7
Allegany U.S.A. 42°6N 78°30W 174 D6
Allegheny → U.S.A. 40°27N 80°1W 174 F5
Allegheny Mts.
U.S.A. 38°15N 80°10W 173 F13
Allegheny Plateau
U.S.A. 41°30N 78°30W 173 E14
Allegheny Res. U.S.A. 41°50N 79°0W 174 E6
Allègre France 45°12N 3°41E 72 C7
Allègre, Pte. Guadeloupe 16°22N 61°46W 182 b
Allen Argentina 38°58S 67°50W 192 A3
Allen, Bog of Ireland 53°15N 7°0W 64 C5
Allen, L. Ireland 54°8N 8°4W 64 B3
Allendale U.S.A. 33°1N 81°18W 178 B8
Allende Mexico 28°20N 100°51W 180 B4
Allentown U.S.A. 40°37N 75°29W 175 F9
Allentsteig Austria 48°41N 15°20E 78 C8
Alleppey = Alappuzha
India 9°30N 76°28E 127 K3
Allepuz Spain 40°29N 0°44W 90 E4
Aller → Germany 52°56N 9°12E 76 C5
Alleynes B. Barbados 13°13N 59°39W 183 g
Alliance Nebr., U.S.A. 42°6N 102°52W 172 D2
Alliance Ohio, U.S.A. 40°55N 81°6W 174 F3
Allier □ France 46°25N 2°40E 71 F9
Allier → France 46°57N 3°4E 71 F10
Alliford Bay Canada 53°12N 131°58W 162 C2
Alligator Pond Jamaica 17°52N 77°34W 182 a
Allinagaram India 10°2N 77°30E 127 J3
Allinge Denmark 55°17N 14°50E 63 J8
Alliston Canada 44°9N 79°52W 174 B5
Alloa U.K. 56°7N 3°47W 65 E5
Allones France 48°20N 1°40E 70 D8
Allora Australia 28°2S 152°0E 151 D5
Allos France 44°15N 6°38E 73 D10
Alluitsup Paa Greenland 60°30N 45°35W 57 E6
Allur India 14°40N 80°4E 127 G5
Allur Kottapatnam
India 15°24N 80°7E 127 G5
Alma Canada 48°35N 71°40W 165 C5
Alma Ga., U.S.A. 31°33N 82°28W 178 D7
Alma Kans., U.S.A. 39°1N 96°17W 172 F5
Alma Mich., U.S.A. 43°23N 84°39W 173 D11
Alma Nebr., U.S.A. 40°6N 99°22W 172 E4
Alma Wis., U.S.A. 44°20N 91°55W 172 C8
Alma Ata = Almaty
Kazakhstan 43°15N 76°57E 109 D9
Alma Hill U.S.A. 42°2N 78°0W 174 D7
Almacelles Spain 41°43N 0°27E 90 D5
Almada Portugal 38°41N 9°8W 89 G1
Almaden Australia 17°22S 144°40E 150 B3
Almadén Spain 38°49N 4°52W 89 G6
Almalyk = Olmaliq
Uzbekistan 40°50N 69°35E 109 D7
Almanor, L. U.S.A. 40°14N 121°9W 168 F3
Almansa Spain 38°51N 1°5W 91 G3
Almanza Spain 42°39N 5°3W 88 C5
Almanzor, Pico Spain 40°15N 5°18W 88 E5
Almanzora → Spain 37°14N 1°46W 91 H3
Almas Brazil 11°33S 47°9W 189 C1
Almaş, Munţii Romania 44°49N 22°12E 80 F7
Almaty Kazakhstan 43°15N 76°57E 109 D9
Almaty □ Kazakhstan 44°30N 78°0E 109 D9
Almazán Spain 41°30N 2°30W 90 D2
Almazora Spain 39°57N 0°3W 90 F4
Almeirim Brazil 1°30S 52°34W 187 D8
Almeirim Portugal 39°12N 8°37W 89 F2
Almelo Neths. 52°22N 6°42E 69 B6
Almenar de Soria Spain 41°43N 2°12W 90 D2
Almenara Brazil 16°11S 40°42W 189 D2
Almenara Spain 39°46N 0°14W 90 F4
Almenara, Sierra de
Spain 37°34N 1°32W 91 H3
Almendra, Embalse de
Spain 41°10N 6°5W 88 D4
Almendralejo Spain 38°41N 6°26W 89 G4
Almere Neths. 52°20N 5°15E 69 B5
Almería Spain 36°52N 2°27W 89 J8
Almería □ Spain 37°20N 2°20W 91 H2
Almería, G. de Spain 36°41N 2°28W 91 J2
Almetyevsk Russia 54°53N 52°20E 86 C11
Älmhult Sweden 56°33N 14°8E 63 H8
Almirante Panama 9°10N 82°30W 182 E3
Almirante Montt, G.
Chile 51°52S 72°50W 192 D2
Almiropotamos Greece 38°16N 24°11E 98 C6
Almiros Greece 39°11N 22°45E 98 B4
Almodôvar Portugal 37°31N 8°2W 89 H2
Almodóvar del Campo
Spain 38°43N 4°10W 89 G6
Almodóvar del Río Spain 37°48N 5°1W 89 H5
Almond U.S.A. 42°19N 77°44W 174 D7
Almont U.S.A. 42°55N 83°3W 174 D1
Almonte Canada 45°14N 76°12W 175 A8
Almonte Spain 37°13N 6°38W 89 H4
Almora India 29°38N 79°40E 125 E8
Almoradí Spain 38°7N 0°46W 91 G4
Almoroux Spain 40°14N 4°24W 88 E6
Almoustarat Mali 17°35N 0°8E 139 B5
Ålmsta Sweden 59°58N 18°50E 62 E12
Almudévar Spain 42°3N 0°35W 90 C4
Almuñécar Spain 36°43N 3°41W 89 J7
Almunge Sweden 59°53N 18°3E 62 E12
Almuradiel Spain 38°32N 3°28W 89 G7
Almus Turkey 40°22N 36°54E 104 B7
Almvik Sweden 57°49N 16°30E 63 G10
Almyrou, Ormos
Greece 35°23N 24°20E 101 D6
Alness U.K. 57°41N 4°16W 65 D4
Alnif Morocco 31°10N 5°8W 136 B2
Alnmouth U.K. 55°24N 1°37W 66 B6
Alnwick U.K. 55°24N 1°42W 66 B6
Aloi Uganda 2°16N 33°10E 142 B3
Alon Myanmar 22°12N 95°5E 123 H19
Alonissos Greece 39°9N 23°50E 98 B5
Alonissos-Northern Sporades △
Greece 39°15N 24°5E 98 B6
Alor Indonesia 8°15S 124°30E 119 F6
Alor Setar Malaysia 6°7N 100°22E 121 J3
Álora Spain 36°49N 4°46W 89 J6
Alosno Spain 37°33N 7°7W 89 H3
Alot India 23°56N 75°40E 124 H6
Alougoum Morocco 30°17N 6°56W 136 B2
Aloysius, Mt. Australia 26°0S 128°38E 149 E4
Alpaugh U.S.A. 35°53N 119°29W 170 K7
Alpe Apuane △ Italy 44°4N 10°15E 92 D7
Alpedrinha Portugal 40°6N 7°27W 88 E3
Alpena U.S.A. 45°4N 83°27W 174 A1
Alpercatas → Brazil 6°2S 44°19W 189 B2
Alpes-de-Haute-Provence □
France 44°8N 6°10E 73 D10
Alpes-Maritimes □
France 43°55N 7°10E 73 E11
Alpha Australia 23°39S 146°37E 150 C4
Alpha Ridge Arctic 84°0N 118°0W 54 A2
Alpharetta U.S.A. 34°5N 84°18W 178 A5
Alphen aan den Rijn
Neths. 52°7N 4°40E 69 B4
Alphios → Greece 37°40N 21°33E 98 D3
Alpiarça Portugal 39°15N 8°35W 89 F2
Alpine Ariz., U.S.A. 33°51N 109°9W 169 K9
Alpine Calif., U.S.A. 32°50N 116°46W 171 N10
Alpine Tex., U.S.A. 30°22N 103°40W 176 F3
Alpine △ Australia 36°56S 148°10E 153 D7
Alps Europe 46°30N 9°30E 74 E5
Alpu Turkey 39°46N 30°58E 104 C4
Alpurrurulam
Australia 20°59S 137°50E 150 C2
Alqueta, Barragem do
Portugal 38°20N 7°25W 89 G3
Alrø Denmark 55°52N 10°5E 63 J4
Als Denmark 54°59N 9°55E 63 K3
Alsask Canada 51°21N 109°59W 163 C7
Alsasua Spain 42°54N 2°10W 90 C2
Alsek → U.S.A. 59°10N 138°12W 162 B1
Alsfeld Germany 50°44N 9°16E 76 E5
Alsta Norway 65°58N 12°40E 60 D15
Alsterbro Sweden 56°57N 15°55E 63 H9
Alstermo Sweden 56°58N 15°38E 63 H9
Alston U.K. 54°49N 2°25W 66 C5
Alta Norway 69°57N 23°10E 60 B20
Alta, Sierra Spain 40°31N 1°30W 90 E3
Alta Gracia Argentina 31°40S 64°30W 190 C3
Alta Murgia △ Italy 40°55N 16°30E 95 B9
Alta Sierra U.S.A. 35°42N 118°33W 171 K8
Altaelva → Norway 69°54N 23°17E 60 B20
Altafjorden Norway 70°5N 23°5E 60 A20
Altai = Aerhtai Shan
Mongolia 46°40N 92°45E 109 C12
Altai = Gorno-Altay □
Russia 51°0N 86°0E 109 B11
Altai △ Russia 50°30N 85°30E 109 B11
Altamaha → U.S.A. 31°20N 81°20W 178 D8
Altamira Brazil 3°12S 52°10W 187 D8
Altamira Chile 25°47S 69°51W 190 B2
Altamira Mexico 22°24N 97°55W 181 C5
Altamira, Cuevas de
Spain 43°20N 4°5W 88 B6
Altamont U.S.A. 42°42N 74°2W 175 D10
Altamura Italy 40°49N 16°33E 95 B9
Altanbulag Mongolia 50°16N 106°30E 110 A10
Altar Mexico 30°43N 111°44W 180 A2
Altar, Gran Desierto de
Mexico 31°50N 114°10W 180 B2
Altata Mexico 24°40N 107°55W 180 C3
Altavista U.S.A. 37°6N 79°17W 173 G14
Altay China 47°48N 88°10E 109 C11
Altay Mongolia 46°22N 96°15E 110 B8
Altdorf Switz. 46°52N 8°36E 77 J4
Alte Mellum Germany 53°43N 8°10E 76 B4
Altea Spain 38°38N 0°2W 91 G4
Altenberg Germany 50°45N 13°45E 76 E9
Altenbruch Germany 53°49N 8°46E 76 B4
Altenburg Germany 50°59N 12°25E 76 E8
Altenkirchen
Mecklenburg-Vorpommern,
Germany 54°38N 13°22E 76 A9
Altenkirchen Rhld-Pfz.,
Germany 50°41N 7°39E 76 E3
Altenmarkt Austria 47°43N 14°39E 78 D7
Alter do Chão Portugal 39°12N 7°40W 89 F3
Altha U.S.A. 30°34N 85°8W 178 E4
Altınkaya Barajı
Turkey 41°18N 35°30E 104 B6
Altınoluk Turkey 39°34N 26°45E 99 B8
Altınova Turkey 39°12N 26°47E 99 B8
Altıntaş Turkey 39°4N 30°7E 99 B12
Altınyaka Turkey 36°33N 30°20E 99 E12
Altınyayla Turkey 37°0N 29°33E 99 D11
Altiplano Bolivia 17°0S 68°0W 188 D4
Altkirch France 47°37N 7°15E 71 E14
Altmark Germany 52°45N 11°30E 76 C7
Altmühl → Germany 48°54N 11°52E 77 G7
Altmühltal △ Germany 48°55N 11°15E 77 G7
Altmunster Austria 47°54N 13°45E 78 D6
Alto Adige = Trentino-Alto
Adige □ Italy 46°30N 11°20E 93 B8
Alto Araguaia Brazil 17°15S 53°20W 187 G8
Alto Cuchumatanes =
Cuchumatanes, Sierra de los
Guatemala 15°35N 91°25W 182 C1
Alto del Carmen Chile 28°46S 70°30W 190 B1
Alto Douro Portugal 41°6N 7°47W 88 D3
Alto Garda Bresciano ⌂
Italy 45°42N 10°38E 92 C7
Alto Ligonha Mozam. 15°30S 38°11E 143 F4
Alto Molocue Mozam. 15°50S 37°35E 143 F4
Alto Paraguay □
Paraguay 21°0S 58°30W 190 A4
Alto Paraíso de Goiás
Brazil 14°7S 47°31W 189 C1
Alto Paraná □
Paraguay 25°30S 54°50W 191 B5
Alto Parnaíba Brazil 9°6S 45°57W 189 B1
Alto Purús → Peru 9°12S 70°28W 188 B3
Alto Río Senguerr
Argentina 45°2S 70°50W 192 C2
Alto Santo Brazil 5°31S 38°15W 189 B3
Alto Tajo ⌂ Spain 40°44N 2°30W 90 E2
Alton Canada 43°54N 80°5W 174 C4
Alton U.K. 51°9N 0°59W 67 F7
Alton Ill., U.S.A. 38°53N 90°11W 172 F8
Alton N.H., U.S.A. 43°27N 71°13W 175 C13
Altona Canada 49°6N 97°33W 163 D9
Altoona Ala., U.S.A. 34°2N 86°20W 178 A3
Altoona Pa., U.S.A. 40°31N 78°24W 174 F6
Altos Brazil 5°3S 42°28W 189 B2
Altötting Germany 48°12N 12°39E 77 G8
Altsasu = Alsasua Spain 42°54N 2°10W 90 C2
Altstätten Switz. 47°22N 9°33E 77 H5
Altun Kupri Iraq 35°45N 44°9E 105 E11
Altun Shan China 38°30N 88°0E 109 E11
Alturas U.S.A. 41°29N 120°32W 168 F3
Altus U.S.A. 34°38N 99°20W 176 D5
Altyn-Emel △
Kazakhstan 44°40N 78°26E 109 D9
Alucra Turkey 40°22N 38°47E 105 B8
Alūksne Latvia 57°24N 27°3E 84 D4
Alunda Sweden 60°4N 18°5E 62 D12
Alunite U.S.A. 35°59N 114°55W 171 K12
Alupka Ukraine 44°23N 34°2E 85 K8
Alur India 15°24N 77°15E 127 E3
Alushta Ukraine 44°40N 34°25E 85 K8
Alusi Indonesia 7°35S 131°40E 119 F8
Alustante Spain 40°36N 1°40W 90 E3
Alutgama Sri Lanka 6°26N 79°59E 127 L4
Alutnuwara Sri Lanka 7°19N 80°59E 127 L5
Aluva India 10°8N 76°24E 127 J3
Alva U.S.A. 36°48N 98°40W 176 C5
Alvaiázere Portugal 39°49N 8°23W 88 F2
Älvängen Sweden 57°58N 12°8E 63 G6
Alvão ⌂ Portugal 41°22N 7°48W 88 D3
Alvarado Mexico 18°46N 95°46W 181 D5
Alvarado U.S.A. 32°24N 97°13W 176 E6
Álvaro Obregón, Presa
Mexico 27°52N 109°52W 180 B3
Älvdalen Sweden 61°13N 14°4E 62 C8
Alvear Argentina 29°5S 56°30W 190 B4
Alverca Portugal 38°56N 9°1W 89 G1
Alvesta Sweden 56°54N 14°35E 63 H8
Alvinston Canada 42°49N 81°52W 174 D3
Alvito Portugal 38°15N 7°58W 89 G3
Älvkarleby Sweden 60°34N 17°26E 62 D11
Alvord Desert U.S.A. 42°30N 118°25W 168 E4
Älvros Sweden 62°3N 14°38E 62 B8
Älvsbyn Sweden 65°40N 21°0E 60 D19
Alwar India 27°38N 76°34E 124 F7
Alwaye = Aluva India 10°8N 76°24E 127 J3
Alxa Zuoqi China 38°50N 105°40E 114 E3
Alyangula Australia 13°55S 136°30E 150 A2
Alyata = Ālāt Azerbaijan 39°58N 49°25E 87 L9
Alyth U.K. 56°38N 3°13W 65 E5
Alytus Lithuania 54°24N 24°3E 84 E3
Alzada U.S.A. 45°2N 104°25W 168 D11
Alzamay Russia 55°33N 98°39E 107 D10
Alzey Germany 49°45N 8°7E 77 F4
Alzira Spain 39°9N 0°30W 91 F4
Am Timan Chad 11°0N 20°10E 135 F10
Amådalen Sweden 61°20N 14°44E 62 C8
Amadeus, L. Australia 24°54S 131°0E 149 D5
Amadi
Dem. Rep. of the Congo 3°40N 26°40E 142 B2
Amadi South Sudan 5°29N 30°25E 135 G12
Amadjuak L. Canada 65°0N 71°8W 161 E17
Amadora Portugal 38°45N 9°13W 89 G1
Amagansett U.S.A. 40°59N 72°9W 175 F12
Amagasaki Japan 34°42N 135°23E 113 G7
Amager Denmark 55°36N 12°35E 63 J6
Amagi Japan 33°25N 130°39E 113 H5
Amagunze Nigeria 6°20N 7°40E 139 D6
Amahai Indonesia 3°20S 128°55E 119 E7
Amaiun-Maia Spain 43°12N 1°29W 90 B3
Amakusa = Hondo
Japan 32°27N 130°12E 113 H5
Amakusa-Shotō Japan 32°15N 130°10E 113 H5
Åmål Sweden 59°3N 12°42E 62 E6
Amalapuram India 16°35N 81°55E 127 F5
Amalfi Italy 40°38N 14°36E 95 B7
Amaliada Greece 37°47N 21°22E 98 D3
Amalner India 21°5N 75°5E 126 D2
Amamapare Indonesia 4°53S 136°38E 119 E9
Amambaí Brazil 23°5S 55°13W 191 A4
Amambaí → Brazil 23°22S 53°56W 191 A5
Amambay □ Paraguay 23°0S 56°0W 191 A4
Amambay, Cordillera de
S. Amer. 23°0S 55°45W 191 A4
Amami Japan 28°22N 129°27E 113 K4
Amami-Guntō Japan 27°16N 129°21E 113 L4
Amami-Ō-Shima
Japan 28°16N 129°21E 113 K4
Aman, Pulau Malaysia 5°16N 100°24E 121 c
Amaná, L. Brazil 2°35S 64°40W 186 D6
Amanat → India 24°7N 84°4E 125 G11
Amanda Park U.S.A. 47°28N 123°55W 170 C3
Amankeldi Kazakhstan 50°10N 65°10E 108 B7
Amantea Italy 39°8N 16°4E 95 C9
Amapá Brazil 2°5N 50°50W 187 C8
Amapá □ Brazil 1°40N 52°0W 187 C8
Amarante Brazil 6°14S 42°50W 189 B2
Amarante Portugal 41°16N 8°5W 88 D2
Amarante do Maranhão
Brazil 5°36S 46°45W 189 B1
Amaranth Canada 50°36N 98°43W 163 C9
Amaravati → India 11°0N 78°15E 127 J4
Amareleja Portugal 38°12N 7°13W 89 G3
Amargosa Brazil 13°2S 39°36W 189 C3
Amargosa → U.S.A. 36°14N 116°51W 171 J10
Amargosa Desert
U.S.A. 36°40N 116°30W 171 J10
Amargosa Range
U.S.A. 36°20N 116°45W 171 J10
Amari Greece 35°13N 24°40E 101 D6
Amarillo U.S.A. 35°13N 101°50W 176 D4
Amarkantak India 22°40N 81°45E 125 H9
'Amârna, Tell el Egypt 27°38N 30°52E 137 B3
Amarnath India 19°12N 73°22E 126 E1
Amaro, Mte. Italy 42°5N 14°5E 93 F11
Amarpur India 25°5N 87°0E 125 G12
Amarwara India 22°18N 79°10E 125 H8
Amasra Turkey 41°45N 32°23E 104 B5
Amassama Nigeria 5°1N 6°2E 139 D6
Amasya Turkey 40°40N 35°50E 104 B6
Amasya □ Turkey 40°40N 35°50E 104 B6
Amata Australia 26°9S 131°9E 149 E5
Amatikulu S. Africa 29°3S 31°33E 145 C5
Amatitlán Guatemala 14°29N 90°38W 182 D1
Amatrice Italy 42°38N 13°17E 93 F10
Amay Belgium 50°33N 5°19E 69 D5
Amazon = Amazonas →
S. Amer. 0°5S 50°0W 187 D8
Amazonas □ Brazil 5°0S 65°0W 186 E6
Amazonas □ Peru 5°0S 78°0W 188 B2
Amazonas → S. Amer. 0°5S 50°0W 187 D8
Ambad India 19°38N 75°50E 126 E2
Ambagarh Chowki
India 20°47N 80°43E 126 D5
Ambah India 26°43N 78°13E 124 F8
Ambajogal India 18°44N 76°23E 126 E3
Ambala India 30°23N 76°56E 124 D7
Ambalangoda Sri Lanka 6°15N 80°5E 127 L5
Ambalantota Sri Lanka 6°7N 81°1E 127 L5
Ambalapulai India 9°25N 76°25E 127 K3
Ambalavao Madag. 21°50S 46°56E 141 J9
Ambanja Madag. 13°40S 48°27E 141 G9
Ambarchik Russia 69°40N 162°20E 107 C17
Ambarlı Turkey 40°58N 28°40E 97 E12
Ambasamudram India 8°43N 77°25E 127 K3
Ambato Ecuador 1°5S 78°42W 186 D3
Ambato, Sierra de
Argentina 28°25S 66°10W 190 B2
Ambatolampy Madag. 19°20S 47°35E 141 H9
Ambatondrazaka
Madag. 17°55S 48°28E 141 H9
Ambelonas Greece 39°45N 22°22E 98 B4
Amberg Germany 49°26N 11°52E 77 F7
Ambergris Cay Belize 18°0N 87°55W 181 D7
Ambérieu-en-Bugey
France 45°57N 5°20E 73 C9
Amberley Canada 44°2N 81°43W 174 B3
Amberley N.Z. 43°9S 172°44E 155 D7
Ambert France 45°33N 3°44E 72 C7
Ambidédi Mali 14°35N 11°47W 138 C2
Ambikapur India 23°15N 83°15E 125 H10
Ambikol Sudan 21°20N 30°50E 137 C3
Ambilobé Madag. 13°10S 49°3E 141 G9
Amble U.K. 55°20N 1°36W 66 B6
Ambleside U.K. 54°26N 2°58W 66 C5
Ambo Peru 10°5S 76°10W 188 C2
Ambohitra Madag. 12°30S 49°10E 141 G9
Amboise France 47°24N 1°2E 70 E8
Ambon Indonesia 3°43S 128°12E 119 E7
Amboseli, L. Kenya 2°40S 37°10E 142 C4
Amboseli △ Kenya 2°37S 37°13E 142 C4
Ambositra Madag. 20°31S 47°25E 141 J9
Ambovombe Madag. 25°11S 46°5E 141 K9
Amboy U.S.A. 34°33N 115°45W 171 L11
Amboyna Cay
S. China Sea 7°50N 112°50E 118 C4
Ambridge U.S.A. 40°36N 80°14W 174 F4
Ambriz Angola 7°48S 13°8E 140 F2
Ambrolauri Georgia 42°31N 43°9E 105 A10
Ambur India 12°48N 78°43E 127 H4
Amchitka I. U.S.A. 51°32N 179°0E 166 E3
Amderma Russia 69°45N 61°30E 106 C7
Amdhi India 23°51N 81°27E 125 H9
Amdo China 32°20N 91°40E 110 E7
Ameca Mexico 20°33N 104°2W 180 C4
Ameca → Mexico 20°41N 105°18W 180 C3
Amecameca de Juárez
Mexico 19°8N 98°46W 181 D5
Amed Indonesia 8°19S 115°39E 119 J18
Ameland Neths. 53°27N 5°45E 69 A5
Amélia Italy 42°33N 12°25E 93 F9
Amelia City U.S.A. 30°35N 81°28W 178 E8
Amelia I. U.S.A. 30°40N 81°25W 178 E8
Amendolara Italy 39°57N 16°35E 95 C9
Amenia U.S.A. 41°51N 73°33W 175 E11
America-Antarctica Ridge
S. Ocean 59°0S 16°0W 55 B2
American Falls U.S.A. 42°47N 112°51W 168 E7
American Falls Res.
U.S.A. 42°47N 112°52W 168 E7
American Fork
U.S.A. 40°23N 111°48W 168 F8
American Highland
Antarctica 73°0S 75°0E 55 D6
American River
Australia 35°47S 137°46E 152 C2
American Samoa ☒
Pac. Oc. 14°20S 170°0W 157 J11
Americana Brazil 22°45S 47°20W 191 A6
Americus U.S.A. 32°4N 84°14W 178 C5
Amerigo Vespucci, Firenze ✕
(FLR) Italy 43°49N 11°13E 93 E8
Amersfoort Neths. 52°9N 5°23E 69 B5
Amersfoort S. Africa 26°59S 29°53E 145 C4
Amery Basin S. Ocean 68°15S 74°30E 55 C6
Amery Ice Shelf
Antarctica 69°30S 72°0E 55 C6
Amerzgane Morocco 31°4N 7°14W 136 B2
Ames = Bertamirans
Spain 42°54N 8°38W 88 C2
Ames U.S.A. 42°2N 93°37W 172 D7
Amesbury U.S.A. 42°51N 70°56W 175 D14
Amet India 25°18N 73°56E 124 G5
Amfiklia Greece 38°38N 22°35E 98 C4
Amfilochia Greece 38°52N 21°9E 98 C3
Amfipoli Greece 40°48N 23°52E 96 F7
Amfissa Greece 38°32N 22°22E 98 C4
Amga Russia 60°50N 132°0E 107 C14
Amga → Russia 62°38N 134°32E 107 C14
Amgaon India 21°22N 80°22E 126 D5
Amgu Russia 45°45N 137°15E 112 B8
Amguid Algeria 26°26N 5°22E 136 C5
Amgun → Russia 52°56N 139°38E 107 D14
Amherst Canada 45°48N 64°8W 165 C7
Amherst Mass.,
U.S.A. 42°23N 72°31W 175 D12
Amherst N.Y., U.S.A. 42°59N 78°48W 174 D6
Amherst Ohio, U.S.A. 41°24N 82°14W 174 E2
Amherst I. Canada 44°8N 76°43W 175 B8
Amherstburg Canada 42°6N 83°6W 164 D3
Amiata, Mte. Italy 42°53N 11°37E 93 F8
Amidon U.S.A. 46°29N 103°19W 172 B2
Amiens France 49°54N 2°16E 71 C9
Amindeo Greece 40°42N 21°42E 96 F5
Amindivi Is. India 11°23N 72°23E 127 J1
Amini I. India 11°6N 72°45E 127 J1
Aminuis Namibia 23°43S 19°21E 144 B2
Amīrābād Iran 33°20N 46°16E 128 C5
Amirante Is. Seychelles 6°0S 53°0E 102 J7
Amisk ⌂ Canada 56°43N 98°0W 163 B9
Amisk L. Canada 54°35N 102°15W 163 C8
Amistad, Presa de la
Mexico 29°26N 101°3W 180 B4
Amistad ⌂ U.S.A. 29°32N 101°12W 176 G4
Amite U.S.A. 30°44N 90°30W 177 F9
Amizmiz Morocco 31°12N 8°15W 136 B2
Amla India 21°56N 78°7E 124 J8
Amlapura Indonesia 8°27S 115°37E 119 J18
Amlia I. U.S.A. 52°4N 173°30W 166 E5
Amlwch U.K. 53°24N 4°20W 66 D3
'Ammān Jordan 31°57N 35°52E 130 D4
'Ammān ✕ (AMM)
Jordan 31°45N 36°2E 130 D5
Ammanford U.K. 51°48N 3°59W 67 F4
Ammassalik = Tasiilaq
Greenland 65°40N 37°20W 57 D7
Ammerån → Sweden 63°9N 16°13E 62 A10
Ammersee Germany 48°0N 11°7E 77 G7
Ammochostos = Famagusta
Cyprus 35°8N 33°55E 101 D12
Ammon U.S.A. 43°28N 111°58W 168 E8
Amnat Charoen
Thailand 15°51N 104°38E 120 E5
Amnura Bangla. 24°37N 88°25E 125 G13
Amo Jiang → China 23°0N 101°50E 116 F3
Āmol Iran 36°23N 52°20E 129 B7
Amorgos Greece 36°50N 25°57E 99 E7
Amory U.S.A. 33°59N 88°29W 177 E10
Amos Canada 48°35N 78°5W 164 C4
Åmot Norway 59°57N 9°54E 61 G13
Åmot Sweden 60°58N 16°27E 62 D10
Åmotfors Sweden 59°47N 12°22E 62 E6
Amour, Djebel Algeria 33°42N 1°37E 136 B4
Amoy = Xiamen
China 24°25N 118°4E 117 E12
Ampang Malaysia 3°8N 101°45E 121 L3
Ampani India 19°35N 82°38E 126 E6
Ampanihy Madag. 24°40S 44°45E 141 J8
Ampato, Nevado Peru 15°40S 71°56W 188 D3
Ampenan Indonesia 8°34S 116°4E 119 K18
Amper Nigeria 9°25N 9°40E 139 D6
Amper → Germany 48°29N 11°55E 77 G7
Ampezzo Italy 46°25N 12°48E 93 B9
Amphitrite Group
S. China Sea 16°50N 112°20E 118 A4
Amphoe Kathu Thailand 7°55N 98°21E 121 a
Amphoe Thalang Thailand 8°1N 98°20E 121 a
Amposta Spain 40°43N 0°34E 90 E5
Amqui Canada 48°28N 67°27W 165 C6
Amrabad India 16°23N 78°50E 127 F4
Amravati India 20°55N 77°45E 126 D3
Amreli India 21°35N 71°17E 124 J4
Amritsar India 31°35N 74°57E 124 D6
Amroha India 28°53N 78°30E 125 E8
Amrum Germany 54°38N 8°22E 76 A4
Amsterdam Neths. 52°23N 4°54E 69 B4
Amsterdam U.S.A. 42°56N 74°11W 175 D10
Amsterdam ✕ (AMS)
Neths. 52°18N 4°45E 69 B4
Amsterdam I. = Nouvelle
Amsterdam, Î.
Ind. Oc. 38°30S 77°30E 146 H6
Amstetten Austria 48°7N 14°51E 78 C7
'Amūdah Syria 37°6N 40°55E 105 D9
Amudarya
Turkmenistan 37°53N 65°15E 108 E7
Amudarya →
Uzbekistan 43°58N 59°34E 108 D5
Amukta Pass U.S.A. 52°0N 171°0W 166 E5
Amund Ringnes I.
Canada 78°20N 96°25W 161 B12
Amundsen Abyssal Plain
S. Ocean 65°0S 125°0W 55 C14
Amundsen Basin Arctic 87°30N 80°0E 54 A
Amundsen Gulf Canada 71°0N 124°0W 160 C7
Amundsen Ridges
S. Ocean 69°15S 123°0W 55 C14
Amundsen-Scott
Antarctica 90°0S 166°0E 55 E
Amundsen Sea
Antarctica 72°0S 115°0W 55 D15
Amungen Sweden 61°10N 15°40E 62 C9
Amuntai Indonesia 2°28S 115°25E 118 E5
Amur → Russia 52°56N 141°10E 107 D15
Amur, W. → Sudan 18°56N 33°34E 137 D3
Amurang Indonesia 1°5N 124°40E 119 D6
Amurrio Spain 43°3N 3°0W 90 B1
Amursk Russia 50°14N 136°54E 107 D14
Amusco Spain 42°10N 4°28W 88 C6
Amvrakikos Kolpos
Greece 39°0N 20°55E 98 C2
Amvrosiyivka Ukraine 47°43N 38°30E 85 J10
Amyderya = Amudarya →
Uzbekistan 43°58N 59°34E 108 D5
An Bang, Dao = Amboyna Cay
S. China Sea 7°50N 112°50E 118 C4
An Bien Vietnam 9°45N 105°0E 121 H5
An Hoa Vietnam 15°40N 108°5E 120 E7
An Khe Vietnam 13°57N 108°51E 120 F7
An Nabatīyah at Tahta
Lebanon 33°23N 35°27E 130 B4
An Nabk Syria 34°2N 36°44E 130 A5
An Nafūd Si. Arabia 28°15N 41°0E 128 D4
An Nāḥīyah Iraq 34°26N 41°33E 105 E9
An Najaf Iraq 32°3N 44°15E 105 G11
An Nāşirīyah Iraq 31°0N 46°15E 128 D5
An Nhon = Binh Dinh
Vietnam 13°55N 109°7E 120 F7
An Nîl □ Sudan 19°30N 33°0E 137 D3
An Nu'ayrīyah
Si. Arabia 27°30N 48°30E 129 E6
An Nu'mānīyah Iraq 32°32N 45°25E 105 F11
An Ros = Rush Ireland 53°31N 6°6W 64 C5
An Thoi, Quan Dao
Vietnam 9°58N 104°0E 121 H5
Anabar → Russia 73°8N 113°36E 107 B12
Anaconda U.S.A. 46°8N 112°57W 168 C7
Anacortes U.S.A. 48°30N 122°37W 170 B4
Anadarko U.S.A. 35°4N 98°15W 176 D5
Anadia Brazil 9°42S 36°18W 189 B3
Anadia Portugal 40°26N 8°27W 88 E2
Anadolu Turkey 39°0N 30°0E 104 C5
Anadyr Russia 64°35N 177°20E 107 C18
Anadyr → Russia 64°55N 176°5E 107 C18
Anadyrskiy Zaliv
Russia 64°0N 180°0E 107 C19
Anafi Greece 36°22N 25°48E 99 E7
Anaga, Pta. de
Canary Is. 28°34N 16°9W 100 F3
Anagni Italy 41°44N 13°9E 93 G10
'Ānah Iraq 34°25N 42°0E 105 E10
Anaheim U.S.A. 33°50N 117°55W 171 M9
Anahim Lake Canada 52°28N 125°18W 162 C3
Anai Mudi India 10°12N 77°4E 127 J3
Anaimalai Hills India 10°20N 76°40E 127 J3
Anajatuba Brazil 3°16S 44°37W 189 A2
Anakapalle India 17°42N 83°6E 126 F6
Anakie Australia 23°32S 147°45E 150 C4
Anaklia Georgia 42°22N 41°35E 87 J5
Analalava Madag. 14°35S 48°0E 141 G9
Analipsis Greece 39°36N 19°55E 101 A3
Anambar → Pakistan 30°15N 68°50E 124 D3
Anambas, Kepulauan
Indonesia 3°20N 106°30E 118 D3
Anambas Is. = Anambas,
Kepulauan Indonesia 3°20N 106°30E 118 D3
Anambra □ Nigeria 6°20N 7°0E 139 D6
Anamosa U.S.A. 42°7N 91°17W 172 D8
Anamur Turkey 36°8N 32°58E 104 D5
Anamur Burnu Turkey 36°2N 32°47E 104 D5
Anan Japan 33°54N 134°40E 113 H7
Anand India 22°32N 72°59E 124 H5
Anandapuram India 14°5N 75°12E 127 G2
Anandpur India 21°16N 86°13E 126 D8
Ananes Greece 36°33N 24°9E 98 E6
Anangu Pitjantjatjara ☼
Australia 27°0S 132°0E 149 E5
Anantapur India 14°39N 77°42E 127 G3
Anantnag India 33°45N 75°10E 125 C6
Ananyiv Ukraine 47°44N 29°58E 81 C14
Anapa Russia 44°55N 37°25E 85 K9
Anapodiaris → Greece 34°59N 25°20E 101 E7
Anápolis Brazil 16°15S 48°50W 187 G9
Anapu → Brazil 1°53S 50°53W 187 D8

Anār Iran 30°55N 55°13E 129 D7
Anārak Iran 33°25N 53°40E 129 C7
Anarisfjällen Sweden 63°6N 13°10E 62 A7
Anas → India 23°26N 74°0E 124 H5
Anatolia = Anadolu Turkey 39°0N 30°0E 104 C5
Anatoliki Makedonia kai Thraki □ Greece 41°10N 24°30E 97 E8
Añatuya Argentina 28°20S 62°50W 190 B3
Anatye ✪ Australia 22°29S 137°3E 150 C2
Anaunethad L. Canada 60°55N 104°25W 163 A8
Anbyŏn N. Korea 39°1N 127°35E 115 E14
Ancares, Sierra dos Spain 42°51N 6°52W 88 C4
Ancares ⌂ Spain 42°50N 6°40W 88 C4
Ancash □ Peru 9°30S 77°45W 188 B2
Ancaster Canada 43°13N 79°59W 174 C5
Ancenis France 47°21N 1°10W 70 E5
Ancho, Canal Chile 50°0S 74°20W 192 D2
Anchor Bay U.S.A. 38°48N 123°34W 170 G3
Anchorage U.S.A. 61°13N 149°54W 160 E2
Anchuras Spain 39°29N 4°50W 89 F6
Anchuthengu India 8°40N 76°46E 127 K3
Anci China 39°20N 116°40E 114 E9
Ancohuma, Nevado Bolivia 16°0S 68°50W 188 D4
Ancón Peru 11°50S 77°10W 188 C2
Ancona Italy 43°38N 13°30E 93 E10
Ancud Chile 42°0S 73°50W 192 B2
Ancud, G. de Chile 42°0S 73°0W 192 B2
Ancy-le-Franc France 47°46N 4°10E 71 E11
Anda China 46°24N 125°19E 111 B14
Andacollo Argentina 37°10S 70°42W 190 D1
Andacollo Chile 30°14S 71°6W 190 C1
Andahuaylas Peru 13°40S 73°25W 188 C3
Andalgalá Argentina 27°40S 66°30W 190 B2
Åndalsnes Norway 62°35N 7°43E 60 E12
Andalucía □ Spain 37°35N 5°0W 89 H6
Andalusia = Andalucía □ Spain 37°35N 5°0W 89 H6
Andalusia U.S.A. 31°18N 86°29W 177 F11
Andaman & Nicobar Is. □ India 10°0N 93°0E 127 K11
Andaman Is. Ind. Oc. 12°30N 92°45E 127 H11
Andaman Sea Ind. Oc. 13°0N 96°0E 118 B1
Andamooka Australia 30°27S 137°9E 151 E2
Andapa Madag. 14°39S 49°39E 141 G9
Andara Namibia 18°2S 21°9E 144 A3
Andaraí Brazil 12°48S 41°20W 189 C2
Andelot-Blancheville France 48°15N 5°18E 71 D12
Andenes Norway 69°19N 16°18E 60 B17
Andenne Belgium 50°28N 5°5E 69 D5
Andéranboukane Mali 15°26N 3°2E 139 B5
Andermatt Switz. 46°38N 8°35E 77 J4
Andernach Germany 50°26N 7°24E 76 E3
Andernos-les-Bains France 44°44N 1°6W 72 D2
Anderslöv Sweden 55°26N 13°19E 63 J7
Anderson Australia 38°31S 145°26E 153 E6
Anderson Alaska, U.S.A. 64°25N 149°15W 166 C10
Anderson Calif., U.S.A. 40°27N 122°18W 168 F2
Anderson Ind., U.S.A. 40°10N 85°41W 173 E11
Anderson Mo., U.S.A. 36°39N 94°27W 172 G6
Anderson S.C., U.S.A. 34°31N 82°39W 177 D13
Anderson → Canada 69°42N 129°0W 160 D6
Anderson I. India 12°46N 92°43E 127 H11
Andersonville U.S.A. 32°12N 84°9W 178 C5
Andersonville ⌂ U.S.A. 32°12N 84°1W 178 C5
Anderstorp Sweden 57°19N 13°39E 63 G7
Andes U.S.A. 42°12N 74°47W 175 D10
Andes, Cord. de los S. Amer. 20°0S 68°0W 188 E4
Andfjorden Norway 69°10N 16°20E 60 B17
Andhra, L. India 18°54N 73°32E 126 E1
Andhra Pradesh □ India 18°0N 79°0E 126 F4
Andijon Uzbekistan 41°10N 72°15E 109 D8
Andijon □ Uzbekistan 40°45N 72°20E 109 D8
Andikíthira = Antikythira Greece 35°52N 23°15E 98 F5
Andīmeshk Iran 32°27N 48°21E 105 F13
Andímilos = Antimilos Greece 36°47N 24°12E 98 E6
Andíparos = Antiparos Greece 37°0N 25°3E 99 D7
Andípaxoi = Antipaxi Greece 39°9N 20°13E 98 B2
Andípsara = Antipsara Greece 38°30N 25°29E 99 C7
Andizhan = Andijon Uzbekistan 41°10N 72°15E 109 D8
Andkhvoy Afghan. 36°52N 65°8E 109 E7
Andoain Spain 43°13N 2°1W 90 B2
Andoany Madag. 13°25S 48°16E 141 G9
Andol India 17°51N 78°4E 126 F4
Andola India 16°57N 76°50E 126 F3
Andong S. Korea 36°40N 128°43E 115 F15
Andorra Spain 40°59N 0°28W 90 E4
Andorra ■ Europe 42°30N 1°30E 72 F5
Andorra La Vella Andorra 42°31N 1°32E 72 F5
Andover U.K. 51°12N 1°29W 67 F6
Andover Kans., U.S.A. 37°43N 97°7W 172 G5
Andover Maine, U.S.A. 44°38N 70°45W 175 B14
Andover Mass., U.S.A. 42°40N 71°8W 175 D13
Andover N.J., U.S.A. 40°59N 74°45W 175 F10
Andover N.Y., U.S.A. 42°10N 77°48W 174 D7
Andover Ohio, U.S.A. 41°36N 80°34W 174 E4
Andøya Norway 69°10N 15°50E 60 B16
Andradina Brazil 20°54S 51°23W 187 H8
Andratx Spain 39°39N 2°25E 100 B9
Andravida Greece 37°54N 21°16E 98 D3
Andreanof Is. U.S.A. 51°30N 176°0W 166 E4
Andreapol Russia 56°40N 32°17E 84 D7
Andrée Land Greenland 73°40N 26°0W 57 C8
Andrews S.C., U.S.A. 33°27N 79°34W 177 E15
Andrews Tex., U.S.A. 32°19N 102°33W 176 E3
Andreyevka Russia 52°19N 51°55E 86 D10
Ándria Italy 41°13N 16°17E 95 A9
Andrijevica Montenegro 42°45N 19°48E 96 D3
Andritsena Greece 37°29N 21°52E 98 D3
Andros Greece 37°50N 24°57E 98 D6
Andros I. Bahamas 24°30N 78°0W 182 B4
Andros Town Bahamas 24°43N 77°47W 182 B4
Androth I. India 10°50N 73°41E 127 J1
Andrychów Poland 49°51N 19°18E 83 J6
Andselv Norway 69°4N 18°34E 60 B18
Andújar Spain 38°3N 4°5W 89 G6
Andulo Angola 11°25S 16°45E 140 G3
Aneby Sweden 57°48N 14°49E 63 G8
Anéfis Mali 18°2N 0°36E 139 B5
Anegada Br. Virgin Is. 18°45N 64°20W 183 e
Anegada, B. Argentina 40°20S 62°20W 192 B4
Anegada Passage W. Indies 18°15N 63°45W 183 C7
Anécho Togo 6°12N 1°34E 139 D5
Añelo Argentina 38°20S 68°45W 192 A3
Anenni-Noi Moldova 46°53N 29°15E 81 D14
Aneto, Pico de Spain 42°37N 0°40E 90 C5
Ānew Turkmenistan 37°52N 58°31E 108 E5
Anfu China 27°21N 114°40E 117 D10
Ang Mo Kio Singapore 1°23N 103°50E 121 d
Ang Thong Thailand 14°35N 100°31E 120 E3
Ang Thong, Ko Thailand 9°37N 99°41E 121 b
Ang Thong, Mu Ko △ Thailand 9°40N 99°43E 121 b
Angamos, Punta Chile 23°1S 70°32W 190 A1
Angara → Russia 58°5N 94°20E 107 D10
Angara-Débou Benin 11°19N 3°3E 139 C5
Angarsk Russia 52°30N 104°0E 110 A9
Angas Hills Australia 23°0S 127°50E 148 D4
Angaston Australia 34°30S 139°8E 152 C3
Ånge Sweden 62°31N 15°35E 62 B9
Ángel, Salto = Angel Falls Venezuela 5°57N 62°30W 186 B6
Ángel de la Guarda, I. Mexico 29°20N 113°25W 180 B2
Angel Falls Venezuela 5°57N 62°30W 186 B6
Angeles Phil. 15°9N 120°33E 119 A6
Ängelholm Sweden 56°15N 12°50E 63 H6
Angels Camp U.S.A. 38°4N 120°32W 170 G6
Ängelsberg Sweden 59°58N 16°0E 62 E10
Ångermanälven → Sweden 63°0N 17°20E 62 A11
Ångermanland Sweden 63°36N 17°45E 60 E17
Angermünde Germany 53°0N 14°0E 76 B9
Angers Canada 45°31N 75°29W 175 A9
Angers France 47°30N 0°35W 70 E6
Angerville France 48°19N 2°0E 71 D9
Ångesån → Sweden 66°16N 22°47E 60 C20
Angical Brazil 12°0S 44°42W 189 C2
Angikuni L. Canada 62°12N 99°59W 163 A9
Angkor Cambodia 13°22N 103°50E 120 F4
Angledool Australia 29°5S 147°55E 151 D4
Anglem, Mt. N.Z. 46°45S 167°53E 155 G2
Anglès Spain 41°57N 2°38E 90 D7
Anglesey U.K. 53°17N 4°20W 66 D3
Anglesey, Isle of □ U.K. 53°16N 4°18W 66 D3
Anglet France 43°29N 1°31W 72 E2
Angleton U.S.A. 29°10N 95°26W 176 G7
Anglin → France 46°42N 0°52E 72 B4
Anglisidhes Cyprus 34°51N 33°27E 101 E12
Anglure France 48°35N 3°50E 71 D10
Angmagssalik = Tasiilaq Greenland 65°40N 37°20W 57 D7
Ango Dem. Rep. of the Congo 4°10N 26°5E 142 B2
Angoche Mozam. 16°8S 39°55E 143 F4
Angoche, I. Mozam. 16°20S 39°50E 143 F4
Angol Chile 37°56S 72°45W 190 D1
Angola Ind., U.S.A. 41°38N 85°0W 173 E11
Angola N.Y., U.S.A. 42°38N 79°2W 174 D5
Angola ■ Africa 12°0S 18°0E 141 G3
Angola Abyssal Plain Atl. Oc. 15°0S 2°0E 56 H12
Angola Basin Atl. Oc. 15°0S 3°0E 56 H12
Angoulême France 45°39N 0°10E 72 C4
Angoumois France 45°50N 0°25E 72 C4
Angra do Heroismo Azores 38°39N 27°13W 134 a
Angra dos Reis Brazil 23°0S 44°10W 191 A7
Angrapa → Russia 54°37N 21°54E 82 D8
Angren Uzbekistan 41°1N 70°12E 109 D8
Angtassom Cambodia 11°1N 104°41E 121 G5
Angu Dem. Rep. of the Congo 3°23N 24°30E 142 B1
Anguang China 45°15N 123°45E 115 B12
Anguilla ☑ W. Indies 18°14N 63°5W 183 C7
Angul India 20°51N 85°6E 126 D7
Anguo China 38°28N 115°15E 114 E8
Angurugu Australia 14°0S 136°25E 150 A2
Angus Canada 44°19N 79°53W 174 B5
Angus □ U.K. 56°46N 2°56W 65 E6
Angwa → Zimbabwe 16°0S 30°23E 145 A5
Anhanduí → Brazil 21°46S 52°9W 191 A5
Anholt Denmark 56°42N 11°33E 63 H5
Anhua China 28°23N 111°12E 117 C8
Anhui □ China 32°0N 117°0E 117 B11
Anhwei = Anhui □ China 32°0N 117°0E 117 B11
Anichab Namibia 21°0S 14°46E 144 B1
Anidros Greece 36°38N 25°43E 99 E7
Anié Togo 7°42N 1°8E 139 D5
Animas → U.S.A. 36°43N 108°13W 169 H9
Anin Myanmar 15°36N 97°50E 120 E1
Anina Romania 45°6N 21°51E 80 E6
Aninoasa Romania 44°47N 24°10E 81 F9
Anjalankoski Finland 60°45N 26°51E 84 B4
Anjangaon India 21°10N 77°20E 126 D3
Anjar = Hawsh Mūssā Lebanon 33°45N 35°55E 130 B4
Anjar India 23°6N 70°10E 124 H4
Anjengo = Anchuthengu India 8°40N 76°46E 127 K3
Anji China 30°46N 119°40E 117 B12
Anjidiv I. India 14°40N 74°10E 127 G2
Anjou France 47°20N 0°15W 70 E6
Anjouan Comoros Is. 12°15S 44°20E 141 a
Anjozorobe Madag. 18°22S 47°52E 141 H9
Anju N. Korea 39°36N 125°40E 115 E13
Anka Nigeria 12°13N 5°58E 139 C6
Ankaboa, Tanjona Madag. 21°58S 43°20E 141 J8
Ankang China 32°40N 109°1E 114 H5
Ankara Turkey 39°57N 32°54E 104 C5
Ankara □ Turkey 39°55N 32°50E 104 C5
Ankaratra Madag. 19°25S 47°12E 141 H9
Ankarsrum Sweden 57°41N 16°20E 63 G10
Ankazoabo Madag. 22°18S 44°31E 141 J8
Ankeny U.S.A. 41°44N 93°36W 172 E7
Anklam Germany 53°51N 13°41E 76 B9
Ankleshwar India 21°38N 73°3E 126 D1
Ankola India 14°40N 74°18E 127 G2
Ankoro Dem. Rep. of the Congo 6°45S 26°55E 142 D2
Ankpa Nigeria 7°22N 7°38E 139 D6
Anlong China 25°2N 105°27E 116 E5
Anlong Veng Cambodia 14°14N 104°5E 120 E5
Anlu China 31°15N 113°45E 117 B9
Anmyeondo S. Korea 36°25N 126°25E 115 F14
Ånn Sweden 63°19N 12°33E 62 A6
Ann, C. U.S.A. 42°38N 70°35W 175 D14
Ann Arbor U.S.A. 42°17N 83°45W 173 D12
Anna Russia 51°28N 40°23E 86 E5
Anna U.S.A. 37°28N 89°15W 172 G9
Annaba Algeria 36°50N 7°46E 136 A5
Annaba □ Algeria 36°12N 7°45E 136 A5
Annaberg-Buchholz Germany 50°34N 13°0E 76 E9
Annalee → Ireland 54°2N 7°24W 64 B4
Annam = Trung Phan Vietnam 17°0N 109°0E 120 D6
Annamitique, Chaîne Asia 17°0N 106°0E 120 D6
Annan U.K. 54°59N 3°16W 65 G5
Annan → U.K. 54°58N 3°16W 65 G5
Annapolis U.S.A. 38°59N 76°30W 173 F15
Annapolis Royal Canada 44°44N 65°32W 165 D6
Annapurna Nepal 28°34N 83°50E 125 E10
Annean, L. Australia 26°54S 118°14E 149 E2
Anneberg Sweden 57°44N 14°49E 63 G8
Annecy France 45°55N 6°8E 73 C10
Annecy, Lac d' France 45°52N 6°10E 73 C10
Annemasse France 46°12N 6°16E 71 F13
Annenskiy Most Russia 60°45N 37°10E 84 B9
Annette I. U.S.A. 55°9N 131°28W 162 B2
Annigeri India 15°26N 75°26E 127 G2
Anning China 24°55N 102°26E 116 E4
Anniston U.S.A. 33°39N 85°50W 178 B4
Annobón Atl. Oc. 1°25S 5°36E 133 G4
Annonay France 45°15N 4°40E 73 C8
Annot France 43°58N 6°38E 73 E10
Annotto B. Jamaica 18°17N 76°45W 182 a
Annsjön Sweden 63°19N 12°34E 62 A6
Annville U.S.A. 40°20N 76°31W 175 F8
Annweiler Germany 49°12N 7°57E 77 F3
Ano Poroia Greece 41°17N 23°2E 96 E7
Ano Siros Greece 37°29N 24°56E 98 D6
Anogia Greece 35°16N 24°52E 101 D6
Anou Mellene Mali 17°29N 0°33E 139 B5
Anoumaba Côte d'Ivoire 6°23N 4°38W 138 D4
Anping Hebei, China 38°15N 115°30E 114 E8
Anping Liaoning, China 41°5N 123°30E 115 D12
Anpu Gang China 21°25N 109°50E 116 G7
Anqing China 30°30N 117°3E 117 B11
Anqiu China 36°25N 119°10E 115 F10
Anren China 26°43N 113°18E 117 D9
Ansager Denmark 55°43N 8°45E 63 J2
Ansai China 36°50N 109°20E 114 F5
Ansan S. Korea 37°21N 126°52E 115 F14
Ansbach Germany 49°28N 10°34E 77 F6
Anse Boileau Seychelles 4°43S 55°29E 141 b
Anse la Raye St. Lucia 13°55N 61°3W 183 f
Anse Royale Seychelles 4°44S 55°31E 141 b
Ansfelden Austria 48°12N 14°17E 78 C7
Anshan China 41°5N 122°58E 115 D12
Anshun China 26°18N 105°57E 116 D5
Ansião Portugal 39°56N 8°27W 88 F2
Ansley U.S.A. 41°18N 99°23W 172 E4
Ansó Spain 42°51N 0°48W 90 C4
Ansoáin Spain 42°50N 1°38W 90 C3
Anson U.S.A. 32°45N 99°54W 176 E5
Anson B. Australia 13°20S 130°6E 148 B5
Ansongo Mali 15°25N 0°35E 139 B5
Ansongo-Ménaka ⌂ Mali 15°3N 1°37E 139 B5
Ansonia U.S.A. 41°21N 73°5W 175 E11
Anstruther U.K. 56°14N 2°41W 65 E6
Ansudu Indonesia 2°11S 139°22E 119 E9
Antabamba Peru 14°40S 73°0W 188 C3
Antagarh India 20°6N 81°9E 126 D5
Antakya = Hatay Turkey 36°14N 36°10E 104 D7
Antalaha Madag. 14°57S 50°20E 141 G10
Antalya Turkey 36°52N 30°45E 104 D4
Antalya □ Turkey 36°50N 30°45E 104 D4
Antalya ✕ (AYT) Turkey 36°54N 30°47E 104 D4
Antalya Körfezi Turkey 36°15N 31°30E 104 D4
Antananarivo Madag. 18°55S 47°31E 141 H9
Antarctic Pen. Antarctica 67°0S 60°0W 55 C18
Antarctica 90°0S 0°0 55 E3
Antelope Zimbabwe 21°2S 28°31E 143 G2
Antep = Gaziantep Turkey 37°6N 37°23E 104 D7
Antequera Paraguay 24°8S 57°7W 190 A4
Antequera Spain 37°5N 4°33W 89 H6
Antero, Mt. U.S.A. 38°41N 106°15W 168 G10
Anthony Fla., U.S.A. 29°18N 82°7W 179 F7
Anthony Kans., U.S.A. 37°9N 98°2W 172 G4
Anthony N. Mex., U.S.A. 32°0N 106°36W 169 K10
Anti Atlas Morocco 30°0N 8°30W 136 C2
Anti-Lebanon = Sharqi, Al Jabal ash Lebanon 33°40N 36°10E 130 B5
Antibes France 43°34N 7°6E 73 E11
Antibes, C. d' France 43°31N 7°7E 73 E11
Anticosti, Î. d' Canada 49°30N 63°0W 165 C7
Antifer, C. d' France 49°41N 0°10E 70 C7
Antigo U.S.A. 45°9N 89°9W 172 C9
Antigonish Canada 45°38N 61°58W 165 C7
Antigua Canary Is. 28°24N 14°1W 100 F5
Antigua Guatemala 14°34N 90°41W 182 D1
Antigua W. Indies 17°0N 61°50W 183 C7
Antigua & Barbuda ■ W. Indies 17°20N 61°48W 183 C7
Antikythira Greece 35°52N 23°15E 98 F5
Antilla Cuba 20°40N 75°50W 182 B4
Antilles = West Indies Cent. Amer. 15°0N 65°0W 183 D7
Antimilos Greece 36°47N 24°12E 98 E6
Antioch U.S.A. 38°1N 121°48W 170 G5
Antioche, Pertuis d' France 46°6N 1°20W 72 B2
Antioquia Colombia 6°40N 75°55W 186 B3
Antiparos Greece 37°0N 25°3E 99 D7
Antipaxi Greece 39°9N 20°13E 98 B2
Antipodes Is. Pac. Oc. 49°45S 178°40E 156 M9
Antipsara Greece 38°30N 25°29E 99 C7
Antirio Greece 38°20N 21°46E 98 C3
Antlers U.S.A. 34°14N 95°37W 176 D7
Antofagasta Chile 23°50S 70°30W 190 A1
Antofagasta □ Chile 24°0S 69°0W 190 A2
Antofagasta de la Sierra Argentina 26°5S 67°20W 190 B2
Antofalla Argentina 25°30S 68°5W 190 B2
Antofalla, Salar de Argentina 25°40S 67°45W 190 B2
Anton U.S.A. 33°49N 102°10W 176 E3
Antonina Brazil 25°26S 48°42W 191 B6
Antrain France 48°28N 1°30W 70 D5
Antratsyt Ukraine 48°7N 39°5E 85 H10
Antrim U.K. 54°43N 6°14W 64 B5
Antrim U.S.A. 40°7N 81°21W 174 F3
Antrim □ U.K. 54°56N 6°25W 64 B5
Antrim, Mts. of U.K. 55°3N 6°14W 64 A5
Antrim Plateau Australia 18°8S 128°20E 148 C4
Antrodoco Italy 42°25N 13°5E 93 F10
Antropovo Russia 58°24N 43°6E 86 A6
Antsalova Madag. 18°40S 44°37E 141 H8
Antsirabe Madag. 19°55S 47°2E 141 H9
Antsiranana Madag. 12°25S 49°20E 141 G9
Antsohihy Madag. 14°50S 47°59E 141 G9
Antu China 42°30N 128°20E 115 C15
Antwerp = Antwerpen Belgium 51°13N 4°25E 69 C4
Antwerp U.S.A. 44°12N 75°37W 175 B9
Antwerpen Belgium 51°13N 4°25E 69 C4
Antwerpen □ Belgium 51°15N 4°40E 69 C4
Anupgarh India 29°10N 73°10E 124 E5
Anuppur India 23°6N 81°41E 125 H9
Anuradhapura Sri Lanka 8°22N 80°28E 127 K5
Anurrete ✪ Australia 20°50S 135°38E 150 C2
Anveh Iran 27°23N 54°11E 129 E7
Anvers = Antwerpen Belgium 51°13N 4°25E 69 C4
Anvers I. Antarctica 64°30S 63°40W 55 C17
Anwen China 29°4N 120°26E 117 C13
Anxi Fujian, China 25°2N 118°12E 117 E12
Anxi Gansu, China 40°30N 95°43E 110 C8
Anxian China 31°40N 104°25E 116 B5
Anxiang China 29°27N 112°11E 117 C9
Anxious B. Australia 33°24S 134°45E 151 E1
Anyama Côte d'Ivoire 5°30N 4°3W 138 D4
Anyang China 36°5N 114°21E 114 F8
Anyang S. Korea 37°23N 126°55E 115 F14
Anyer Indonesia 6°4S 105°53E 119 G11
Anyi Jiangxi, China 28°49N 115°25E 117 C10
Anyi Shanxi, China 35°2N 111°2E 114 G6
Anyuan China 25°9N 115°21E 117 E10
Anyue China 30°9N 105°50E 116 B5
Anza U.S.A. 33°35N 116°39W 171 M10
Anze China 36°10N 112°12E 114 F7
Anzeglouf Algeria 26°50N 0°1E 136 C4
Anzhero-Sudzhensk Russia 56°10N 86°0E 106 D9
Ánzio Italy 41°27N 12°37E 94 A5
Ao Makham Thailand 7°50N 98°24E 121 a
Ao Phangnga △ Thailand 8°10N 98°32E 121 a
Aoga-Shima Japan 32°28N 139°46E 113 H9
Aohan Qi China 43°18N 119°43E 115 C10
Aoiz Spain 42°46N 1°22W 90 C3
Aoji N. Korea 42°31N 130°23E 115 C16
Aomen = Macau China 22°12N 113°33E 117 F9
Aomori Japan 40°45N 140°45E 112 D10
Aomori □ Japan 40°45N 140°40E 112 D10
tAonach, An = Nenagh Ireland 52°52N 8°11W 64 D3
Aonla India 28°16N 79°11E 125 E8
Aorai, Mt. Tahiti 17°34S 149°30W 155 b
Aoraki Mount Cook N.Z. 43°36S 170°9E 155 D5
Aoral, Phnum Cambodia 12°0N 104°15E 121 G5
Aorangi Ra. N.Z. 41°28S 175°22E 154 H4
Aosta Italy 45°45N 7°20E 92 C4
Aotea Harbour N.Z. 38°0S 174°50E 154 E3
Aotearoa = New Zealand ■ Oceania 40°0S 176°0E 154 G5
Aoudéras Niger 17°45N 8°20E 139 B6
Aoukâr Mauritania 17°40N 10°0W 138 B3
Aoulef el Arab Algeria 26°55N 1°2E 136 C4
Aozou, Couloir d' Chad 22°0N 19°0E 135 D9
Apá → S. Amer. 22°6S 58°2W 190 A4
Apache U.S.A. 34°54N 98°22W 176 D5
Apache Junction U.S.A. 33°25N 111°33W 169 K8
Apalachee B. U.S.A. 30°0N 84°0W 178 E5
Apalachicola U.S.A. 29°43N 84°59W 178 F5
Apalachicola → U.S.A. 29°43N 84°58W 178 F5
Apalachicola B. U.S.A. 29°40N 85°0W 178 F3
Apam Ghana 5°19N 0°42W 139 D4
Apapa Nigeria 6°26N 3°21E 139 D5
Apaporis → Colombia 1°23S 69°25W 186 D5
Aparados da Serra △ Brazil 29°10S 50°8W 191 B5
Aparri Phil. 18°22N 121°38E 119 A6
Apateu Romania 46°36N 21°47E 80 D6
Apatin Serbia 45°40N 19°0E 80 E4
Apatity Russia 67°34N 33°22E 60 C25
Apatula = Finke Australia 25°34S 134°35E 150 D1
Apatzingán Mexico 19°5N 102°21W 180 D4
Apeldoorn Neths. 52°13N 5°57E 69 B5
Apen Germany 53°13N 7°48E 76 B3
Apennines = Appennini Italy 44°30N 10°0E 92 D7
Aphrodisias Turkey 37°42N 28°46E 99 D10
Api Nepal 30°0N 80°57E 110 F5
Apia Samoa 13°50S 171°50W 147 C11
Apiacás, Serra dos Brazil 9°50S 57°0W 186 E7
Apies → S. Africa 25°15S 28°8E 145 C4
Apinajé Brazil 11°31S 48°18W 189 C1
Apiti N.Z. 39°58S 175°54E 154 F4
Apizaco Mexico 19°25N 98°8W 181 D5
Aplao Peru 16°0S 72°40W 188 D3
Apo, Mt. Phil. 6°53N 125°14E 119 C7
Apodi Brazil 5°39S 37°48W 189 B3
Apolakia Greece 36°5N 27°48E 101 C9
Apolakia, Ormos Greece 36°5N 27°45E 101 C9
Apolda Germany 51°2N 11°32E 76 D7
Apollo Bay Australia 38°45S 143°40E 152 E5
Apollonia = Sūsah Libya 32°52N 21°59E 135 B10
Apollonia Greece 36°15N 27°58E 101 C9
Apolo Bolivia 14°30S 68°30W 188 C4
Apolonia Greece 36°58N 24°43E 98 E6
Apopa El Salv. 13°48N 89°10W 182 D2
Apopka U.S.A. 28°40N 81°31W 179 G8
Apopka, L. U.S.A. 28°37N 81°37W 179 G8
Aporé → Brazil 19°27S 50°57W 187 G8
Apostle Is. U.S.A. 47°0N 90°40W 172 B8
Apostle Islands ⌂ U.S.A. 46°55N 91°0W 172 B8
Apóstoles Argentina 28°0S 56°0W 191 B4
Apostolos Andreas, C. Cyprus 35°42N 34°35E 101 D13
Apostolovo Ukraine 47°39N 33°39E 85 J7
Apoteri Guyana 4°2N 58°32W 186 C7
Appalachian Mts. U.S.A. 38°0N 80°0W 173 G14
Äppelbo Sweden 60°29N 14°1E 62 D8
Appennino Lucano-Val d'Agri-Lagonegrese ⌂ Italy 40°5N 16°10E 95 B9
Appennino Tosco-Emiliano ⌂ Italy 44°10N 10°25E 92 D7
Appennini Italy 44°30N 10°0E 92 D7
Appennino Ligure Italy 44°30N 9°0E 92 D6
Appenzell-Ausser Rhoden □ Switz. 47°23N 9°23E 77 H5
Appenzell-Inner Rhoden □ Switz. 47°20N 9°25E 77 H5
Appiano Italy 46°28N 11°15E 93 B8
Apple Hill Canada 45°13N 74°46W 175 A10
Apple Valley U.S.A. 34°32N 117°14W 171 L9
Appleby-in-Westmorland U.K. 54°35N 2°29W 66 C5
Appledore U.K. 51°3N 4°13W 67 F3
Appleton U.S.A. 44°16N 88°25W 172 C9
Appling U.S.A. 33°33N 82°19W 178 B7
Approuague → Fr. Guiana 4°30N 51°57W 187 C8
Apricena Italy 41°47N 15°27E 93 G12
Aprília Italy 41°36N 12°39E 94 A5
Apsheronsk Russia 44°28N 39°42E 87 H4
Apsley Canada 44°45N 78°6W 174 B6
Apt France 43°53N 5°24E 73 E9
Apuane, Alpi Italy 44°7N 10°14E 92 D7
Apucarana Brazil 23°55S 51°33W 191 A5
Apulia = Púglia □ Italy 41°15N 16°15E 95 A9
Apure → Venezuela 7°37N 66°25W 186 B5
Apurímac □ Peru 14°0S 73°0W 188 C3
Apurímac → Peru 12°17S 73°56W 188 C3
Apuseni, Munții Romania 46°30N 22°45E 80 D7
Āq Qālā Iran 37°10N 54°30E 129 B7
Aqaba = Al 'Aqabah Jordan 29°31N 35°0E 130 F4
Aqaba, G. of Red Sea 29°0N 34°40E 128 D2
'Aqabah, Khalīj al = Aqaba, G. of Red Sea 29°0N 34°40E 128 D2
Aqadyr Kazakhstan 48°17N 74°50E 109 C8
Āqchah Afghan. 36°56N 66°11E 109 E7
'Aqdā Iran 32°26N 53°37E 129 C7
Aqīq Sudan 18°14N 38°12E 137 D4
Aqīq, Khalīg Sudan 18°20N 38°10E 137 D4
Aqköl Kazakhstan 51°59N 70°56E 109 B8
Aqmola □ Kazakhstan 51°30N 70°0E 109 B8
'Aqrah Iraq 36°46N 43°45E 105 D10
Aqsay Kazakhstan 51°11N 53°0E 108 B4
Aqshataū Kazakhstan 47°59N 74°3E 109 C8
Aqsū Ongtüstik Qazaqstan, Kazakhstan 42°25N 69°50E 109 D7
Aqsū Pavlodar, Kazakhstan 52°2N 76°55E 109 B9
Aqsūgek Kazakhstan 44°37N 74°30E 109 D8
Aqtaū Mangghystaū, Kazakhstan 43°39N 51°12E 108 D4
Aqtaū Qaraghandy, Kazakhstan 50°14N 73°3E 109 B8
Aqtöbe Kazakhstan 50°17N 57°10E 108 B5
Aqtoghay Kazakhstan 46°57N 79°40E 109 C9
Aqua = Sokhumi Georgia 43°0N 41°0E 87 J5
Aquidauana Brazil 20°30S 55°50W 187 H7
Aquila Mexico 18°36N 103°30W 180 D4
Aquileia Italy 45°46N 13°22E 93 C10
Aquiles Serdán Mexico 28°36N 105°53W 180 B3
Aquin Haiti 18°16N 73°24W 183 C5
Ar Horqin Qi China 43°45N 120°0E 115 C11
Ar Rafīd Syria 32°57N 35°52E 130 C4
Ar Raḩḩālīyah Iraq 32°44N 43°23E 105 F10
Ar Ramādī Iraq 33°25N 43°20E 105 F10
Ar Ramthā Jordan 32°34N 36°0E 130 C5
Ar Raqqah Syria 35°59N 39°8E 105 E8
Ar Raqqah □ Syria 36°20N 39°10E 105 D8
Ar Rashidiya = Er Rachidia Morocco 31°58N 4°20W 136 B3
Ar Rass Si. Arabia 25°50N 43°40E 128 E4
Ar Rawḑah Si. Arabia 21°16N 42°50E 131 C3
Ar Rayyan Qatar 25°17N 51°25E 129 E6
Ar Rifā'ī Iraq 31°50N 46°10E 128 D5
Ar Riyāḑ Si. Arabia 24°41N 46°42E 128 E5
Ar Ru'ays Qatar 26°8N 51°12E 129 E6
Ar Rukhaymīyah Iraq 29°22N 45°38E 128 D5
Ar Rumaythah Iraq 31°31N 45°12E 128 D5
Ar Ruşāfah Syria 35°45N 38°49E 105 E8
Ar Ruţbah Iraq 33°0N 40°15E 105 F9
Ara India 25°35N 84°32E 125 G11
Arab U.S.A. 34°19N 86°30W 177 D11
'Arab, Bahr el → South Sudan 9°0N 29°30E 135 G11
Arab, Khalîg el Egypt 30°55N 29°0E 137 E6
Arab, Shatt al → Asia 29°57N 48°34E 129 D6
'Araba, W. → Egypt 28°19N 33°11E 137 F8
'Arabābād Iran 33°2N 57°41E 129 C8
Araban Turkey 37°28N 37°44E 104 D7
Arabatskaya Strelka Ukraine 45°40N 35°0E 85 K8
Araba/Álava □ Spain 42°48N 2°28W 90 C2
Arabba Italy 46°30N 11°52E 93 B8
Arabi U.S.A. 31°50N 83°44W 178 D6
Arabia Asia 25°0N 45°0E 102 F6
Arabian Basin Ind. Oc. 11°30N 65°0E 146 C5
Arabian Desert = Sharqîya, Es Sahrâ esh Egypt 27°30N 32°30E 137 B3
Arabian Gulf = Persian Gulf Asia 27°0N 50°0E 129 E6
Arabian Sea Ind. Oc. 16°0N 65°0E 102 G8
Araç Turkey 41°15N 33°21E 104 B5
Aracaju Brazil 10°55S 37°4W 189 C3
Aracati Brazil 4°30S 37°44W 189 A3
Araçatuba Brazil 21°10S 50°30W 191 A5
Aracena Spain 37°53N 6°38W 89 H4
Aracena, Sierra de Spain 37°50N 6°50W 89 H4
Arachova Greece 38°28N 22°35E 98 C4
Arachthos → Greece 39°20N 21°4E 98 B3
Aračinovo Macedonia 42°1N 21°34E 96 D5
Araçuai Brazil 16°52S 42°4W 189 D2
Araçuaí → Brazil 16°46S 42°2W 189 D2
'Arad Israel 31°15N 35°12E 130 D4
Arad Romania 46°10N 21°20E 80 D6
Arad □ Romania 46°20N 22°0E 80 D6
Arādān Iran 35°21N 52°30E 129 C7
Aradhippou Cyprus 34°57N 33°36E 101 E12
Arafura Sea E. Indies 9°0S 135°0E 147 B6
Aragats Armenia 40°30N 44°15E 87 K7
Aragon U.S.A. 34°2N 85°3W 178 A4
Aragón □ Spain 41°25N 0°40W 90 D4
Aragón → Spain 42°13N 1°44W 90 C3
Aragona Italy 37°24N 13°27E 94 E6
Araguacema Brazil 8°50S 49°20W 187 E9
Araguaia → Brazil 5°21S 48°41W 187 E9
Araguaína Brazil 7°12S 48°12W 189 B1
Araguari Brazil 18°38S 48°11W 189 D1
Araguari → Brazil 1°15N 49°55W 187 C9
Araguatins Brazil 5°38S 48°7W 189 B1
Arahal Spain 37°15N 5°33W 89 H5
Arain India 26°27N 75°2E 124 F6
Araioses Brazil 2°53S 41°55W 189 A2
Arak Algeria 25°20N 3°45E 136 C4
Arāk Iran 34°0N 49°40E 129 C6
Arakan = Rakhine □ Myanmar 19°0N 94°15E 123 K18
Arakan Coast Myanmar 19°0N 94°0E 123 K19
Arakan Yoma Myanmar 20°0N 94°40E 123 K19
Arakkonam India 13°7N 79°43E 127 H4
Araklı Turkey 41°6N 40°2E 105 B9
Araks = Aras, Rūd-e → Asia 40°5N 48°29E 105 B13
Araks → Iran 39°10N 47°10E 108 E3
Aral Kazakhstan 46°41N 61°45E 108 C6
Aral Mangy Qaraqumy Kazakhstan 46°50N 63°10E 108 C6
Aral Sea Asia 45°0N 58°20E 108 C5
Aral Tengizi = Aral Sea Asia 45°0N 58°20E 108 C5
Aralık Turkey 39°52N 44°31E 105 C11
Aralkum Asia 44°30N 60°35E 108 D6
Aralsk = Aral Kazakhstan 46°41N 61°45E 108 C6
Aralskoye More = Aral Sea Asia 45°0N 58°20E 108 C5
Aralsor, Ozero = Aralsor Köli Kazakhstan 49°5N 48°12E 87 F9
Aralsor Köli Kazakhstan 49°5N 48°12E 87 F9
Aramac Australia 22°58S 145°14E 150 C4
Aran → India 19°55N 78°12E 126 E4
Aran, Val de Spain 42°50N 0°55E 90 C5
Aran I. = Arranmore Ireland 55°0N 8°30W 64 A3
Aran Is. Ireland 53°6N 9°38W 64 C2
Aranda de Duero Spain 41°39N 3°42W 88 D7
Arandān Iran 35°23N 46°55E 128 C5
Aranđelovac Serbia 44°18N 20°34E 96 B4
Aranga N.Z. 35°44S 173°40E 154 B2
Arani India 12°43N 79°19E 127 H4
Aranjuez Spain 40°1N 3°40W 88 E7
Aranos Namibia 24°9S 19°7E 144 B2
Aransas Pass U.S.A. 27°55N 97°9W 176 H6
Aranyaprathet Thailand 13°41N 102°30E 120 F4
Araouane Mali 18°55N 3°30W 138 B4
Arapahoe U.S.A. 40°18N 99°54W 172 E4
Arapawa I. N.Z. 41°11S 174°17E 155 B9
Arapey Grande → Uruguay 30°55S 57°49W 190 C4
Arapgir Turkey 39°5N 38°30E 105 C8
Arapiraca Brazil 9°45S 36°39W 189 B3
Arapis, Akra Greece 40°27N 24°0E 97 F8
Arapongas Brazil 23°29S 51°28W 191 A5
Arapuni N.Z. 38°4S 175°39E 154 E4
Ar'ar Si. Arabia 30°59N 41°2E 128 D4
Araranguá Brazil 29°0S 49°30W 191 B6
Araraquara Brazil 21°50S 48°0W 187 H9
Ararás, Serra das Brazil 25°0S 53°10W 191 B5
Ararat Armenia 39°48N 44°50E 105 C11
Ararat Australia 37°16S 142°58E 152 D5
Ararat, Mt. = Ağrı Dağı Turkey 39°50N 44°15E 105 C11
Arari Brazil 3°28S 44°47W 189 A2
Araria India 26°9N 87°33E 125 F12
Araripe, Chapada do Brazil 7°20S 40°0W 189 B3
Araripina Brazil 7°33S 40°34W 189 B2
Araruama, L. de Brazil 22°53S 42°12W 191 A7
Araruna Brazil 6°52S 35°44W 189 B3
Aras, Rūd-e → Asia 40°5N 48°29E 105 B13
Aratâne Mauritania 18°24N 8°32W 138 B3
Arauca Colombia 7°0N 70°40W 186 B4
Arauca → Venezuela 7°24N 66°35W 186 B5
Arauco Chile 37°16S 73°25W 190 D1
Araújos Brazil 19°56S 45°14W 189 D1
Aravalli Range India 25°0N 73°30E 124 G5
Arawale ⌂ Kenya 1°24S 40°9E 142 C5
Arawhata → N.Z. 44°0S 168°40E 155 E3
Araxá Brazil 19°35S 46°55W 189 D1
Araxos, Akra Greece 38°13N 21°20E 98 C3
Araya, Pen. de Venezuela 10°40N 64°0W 186 A6
Arba Minch Ethiopia 6°0N 37°30E 131 F2
Arbat Iraq 35°25N 45°35E 105 E11
Árbatax Italy 39°56N 9°42E 94 C2
Arbīl Iraq 36°15N 44°5E 105 D11
Arbīl □ Iraq 36°20N 44°20E 105 D11
Arboga Sweden 59°24N 15°52E 62 E9
Arbois France 46°55N 5°46E 71 F12
Arboréa Italy 39°46N 8°35E 94 C1
Arborfield Canada 53°6N 103°39W 163 C8
Arborg Canada 50°54N 97°13W 163 C9
Arbre du Ténéré Niger 17°50N 10°4E 139 B7
Arbroath U.K. 56°34N 2°35W 65 E6
Arbuckle U.S.A. 39°1N 122°3W 170 F4
Arbus Italy 39°30N 8°33E 94 C1
Arc → France 45°34N 6°12E 73 C10
Arc-lès-Gray France 47°28N 5°34E 71 E12
Arcachon France 44°40N 1°10W 72 D2
Arcachon, Bassin d' France 44°42N 1°10W 72 D2
Arcade U.S.A. 42°32N 78°25W 174 D6
Arcadia Greece 37°30N 22°20E 98 D4
Arcadia Fla., U.S.A. 27°13N 81°52W 179 H8
Arcadia La., U.S.A. 32°33N 92°55W 176 E8
Arcadia Pa., U.S.A. 40°47N 78°51W 174 F6
Arcata U.S.A. 40°52N 124°5W 168 F1
Arcévia Italy 43°30N 12°56E 93 E9
Archanes Greece 35°16N 25°11E 99 F7
Archangelsk = Arkhangelsk Russia 64°38N 40°36E 106 C5
Archangelos Greece 36°13N 28°7E 101 C10
Archar Bulgaria 43°50N 22°54E 96 C6
Archbald U.S.A. 41°30N 75°32W 175 E9
Archena Spain 38°9N 1°16W 91 G3
Archer U.S.A. 29°32N 82°32W 179 F7
Archer → Australia 13°28S 141°41E 150 A3
Archer B. Australia 13°20S 141°30E 150 A3
Archer Bend = Mungkan Kandju △ Australia 13°35S 142°52E 150 A3

Archers Post Kenya 0°35N 37°35E 142 B4
Arches △ U.S.A. 38°45N 109°25W 168 G9
Archidona Spain 37°6N 4°22W 89 H6
Archipel-de-Mingan △ Canada 50°13N 63°10W 165 B7
Archipiélago Chinijo △ Canary Is. 29°20N 13°30W 100 E6
Archipiélago Los Roques △ Venezuela 11°50N 66°44W 183 D6
Arci, Mte. Italy 39°47N 8°45E 94 C1
Arcidosso Italy 42°52N 11°33E 93 F8
Arcila = Asilah Morocco 35°29N 6°0W 136 A2
Arcipelago de la Maddalena △ Italy 41°14N 9°24E 94 A2
Arcipelago Toscano △ Italy 42°45N 10°15E 92 F7
Arcis-sur-Aube France 48°32N 4°10E 71 D11
Arckaringa Cr. → Australia 28°10S 135°22E 151 D2
Arco Italy 45°55N 10°53E 92 C7
Arco U.S.A. 43°38N 113°18W 168 E7
Arcoona Australia 31°2S 137°1E 152 A2
Arcos de Jalón Spain 41°12N 2°16W 90 D2
Arcos de la Frontera Spain 36°45N 5°49W 89 J5
Arcos de Valdevez Portugal 41°55N 8°22W 88 D2
Arcot India 12°53N 79°20E 127 H4
Arcoverde Brazil 8°25S 37°4W 189 B3
Arcozelo Portugal 40°32N 7°47W 88 E3
Arctic Bay Canada 73°1N 85°7W 161 C14
Arctic Mid-Ocean Ridge Arctic 87°0N 90°0E 54 A
Arctic Ocean Arctic 78°0N 160°0W 54 B18
Arctic Red River = Tsiigehtchic Canada 67°15N 134°0W 160 D5
Arctowski Antarctica 62°30S 58°0W 55 C18
Arda → Bulgaria 41°40N 26°30E 97 E10
Arda → Italy 45°2N 10°2E 92 C7
Ardabīl Iran 38°15N 48°18E 105 C13
Ardabīl □ Iran 38°15N 48°20E 129 B6
Ardahan Turkey 41°7N 42°41E 105 B10
Ardahan □ Turkey 41°10N 42°50E 105 B10
Ardakān = Sepīdān Iran 30°20N 52°5E 129 D7
Ardakān Iran 32°19N 53°59E 129 C7
Ardala Sweden 58°22N 13°19E 63 F7
Ardales Spain 36°53N 4°51W 89 J6
Ardara Ireland 54°46N 8°25W 64 B3
Ardas → Greece 41°40N 26°30E 97 E10
Ardèche □ France 44°42N 4°16E 73 D8
Ardèche → France 44°16N 4°39E 73 D8
Ardee Ireland 53°52N 6°33W 64 C5
Arden Canada 44°43N 76°56W 174 B8
Arden Denmark 56°46N 9°52E 63 H3
Arden Calif., U.S.A. 38°36N 121°33W 170 G5
Arden Nev., U.S.A. 36°1N 115°14W 171 J11
Ardenne Belgium 49°50N 5°5E 69 E5
Ardennes = Ardenne Belgium 49°50N 5°5E 69 E5
Ardennes □ France 49°35N 4°40E 71 C11
Ardentes France 46°45N 1°50E 71 F8
Arderin Ireland 53°2N 7°39W 64 C4
Ardeşen Turkey 41°12N 41°2E 105 B9
Ardestān Iran 33°20N 52°25E 129 C7
Ardfert Ireland 52°20N 9°47W 64 D2
Ardglass U.K. 54°16N 5°36W 64 B6
Ardhéa = Aridea Greece 40°58N 22°3E 96 F6
Ardila → Portugal 38°12N 7°28W 89 G3
Ardino Bulgaria 41°34N 25°9E 97 E9
Ardivachar Pt. U.K. 57°23N 7°26W 65 D1
Ardlethan Australia 34°22S 146°53E 153 C7
Ardmore Okla., U.S.A. 34°10N 97°8W 176 D6
Ardmore Pa., U.S.A. 40°2N 75°17W 175 F9
Ardnamurchan, Pt. of U.K. 56°43N 6°14W 65 E2
Ardnave Pt. U.K. 55°53N 6°20W 65 F2
Ardon Russia 43°10N 44°18E 87 J7
Ardore Italy 38°11N 16°10E 95 D9
Ardres France 50°50N 1°59E 71 B8
Ardrossan Australia 34°26S 137°53E 152 C2
Ardrossan U.K. 55°39N 4°49W 65 F4
Ards Pen. U.K. 54°33N 5°34W 64 B6
Arduan Sudan 19°54N 30°20E 137 D3
Ardud Romania 47°37N 22°52E 80 C7
Åre Sweden 63°22N 13°15E 62 A7
Arecibo Puerto Rico 18°29N 66°43W 183 d
Areia Branca Brazil 5°0S 37°0W 189 A3
Arena, Pt. U.S.A. 38°57N 123°44W 170 G3
Arenal Honduras 15°21N 86°50W 182 C2
Arenales, Cerro Chile 47°5S 73°40W 192 C2
Arenas = Las Arenas Spain 43°17N 4°50W 88 B6
Arenas de San Pedro Spain 40°12N 5°5W 88 E5
Arendal Norway 58°28N 8°46E 61 G13
Arendsee Germany 52°52N 11°27E 76 C7
Arenys de Mar Spain 41°35N 2°33E 90 D7
Arenzano Italy 44°24N 8°41E 92 D5
Areopoli Greece 36°40N 22°22E 98 E4
Arequipa Peru 16°20S 71°30W 188 D3
Arequipa □ Peru 16°0S 72°50W 188 D3
Arès France 44°47N 1°8W 72 D2
Arévalo Spain 41°3N 4°43W 88 D6
Arezzo Italy 43°25N 11°53E 93 E8
Arga Turkey 38°21N 37°59E 128 B3
Arga → Spain 42°18N 1°47W 90 C3
Argalasti Greece 39°13N 23°13E 98 B5
Argamasilla de Alba Spain 39°8N 3°5W 89 F7
Argamasilla de Calatrava Spain 38°44N 4°4W 89 G6
Arganda del Rey Spain 40°19N 3°26W 88 E7
Arganil Portugal 40°13N 8°3W 88 E2
Argarapa ☼ Australia 22°20S 134°58E 150 C1
Argelès-Gazost France 43°0N 0°6W 72 E3
Argelès-sur-Mer France 42°34N 3°1E 72 F7
Argens → France 43°24N 6°44E 73 E10
Argent, Côte d' France 44°15N 1°30W 72 D2
Argent-sur-Sauldre France 47°33N 2°25E 71 E9
Argenta Canada 50°11N 116°56W 162 C5
Argenta Italy 44°37N 11°50E 93 D8
Argentan France 48°45N 0°1W 70 D6
Argentário, Mte. Italy 42°24N 11°9E 93 F8
Argentat France 45°6N 1°56E 72 C5
Argentera Italy 44°12N 7°5E 92 D4
Argenteuil France 48°56N 2°15E 71 D9
Argentia Canada 47°18N 53°58W 165 C9
Argentiera, C. dell' Italy 40°44N 8°8E 94 B1
Argentina ■ S. Amer. 35°0S 66°0W 185 G4
Argentine Abyssal Plain Atl. Oc. 46°0S 52°0W 56 L6
Argentine Basin Atl. Oc. 45°0S 45°0W 56 L7
Argentino, L. Argentina 50°10S 73°0W 192 D2
Argenton-les-Vallées France 46°59N 0°27W 70 F6
Argenton-sur-Creuse France 46°36N 1°30E 71 F8
Argeş □ Romania 45°0N 24°45E 81 F9
Argeş → Romania 44°5N 26°38E 81 F11
Arghandab → Afghan. 31°30N 64°15E 124 D1
Argirades Greece 39°27N 19°58E 101 B3
Argiroupoli Greece 35°17N 24°20E 101 D6
Argo Sudan 19°28N 30°30E 137 D3
Argolikos Kolpos Greece 37°20N 22°52E 98 D4
Argonne France 49°10N 5°0E 71 C12
Argos Greece 37°40N 22°43E 98 D4
Argos Orestiko Greece 40°27N 21°18E 96 F5
Argostoli Greece 38°11N 20°29E 98 C2
Arguedas Spain 42°11N 1°36W 90 C3
Arguello, Pt. U.S.A. 34°35N 120°39W 171 L6
Arguineguín Canary Is. 27°46N 15°41W 100 G4
Argun Russia 43°18N 45°52E 87 J7
Argun → Russia 53°20N 121°28E 111 A13
Argungu Nigeria 12°40N 4°31E 139 C5
Argus Pk. U.S.A. 35°52N 117°26W 171 K9
Argyle, L. Australia 16°20S 128°40E 148 C4
Argyll & Bute □ U.K. 56°13N 5°28W 65 E3
Arhavi Turkey 41°21N 41°18E 105 B9
Århus = Aarhus Denmark 56°8N 10°11E 63 H4
Aria N.Z. 38°33S 175°0E 154 E4
Ariadnoye Russia 45°8N 134°25E 112 B7
Ariamsvlei Namibia 28°9S 19°51E 144 C2
Ariana, L' Tunisia 36°52N 10°12E 136 A6
Ariana, L' □ Tunisia 36°50N 9°52E 136 A5
Ariano Irpino Italy 41°9N 15°5E 95 A8
Aribinda Burkina Faso 14°17N 0°52W 139 C4
Arica Chile 18°32S 70°20W 188 D3
Arica Colombia 2°0S 71°50W 186 D4
Arica y Parinacota □ Chile 17°40S 69°50W 188 D4
Arico Canary Is. 28°9N 16°29W 100 F3
Arid, C. Australia 34°1S 123°10E 149 F3
Arida Japan 34°5N 135°8E 113 G7
Aride Seychelles 4°13S 55°40E 141 b
Aridea Greece 40°58N 22°3E 96 F6
Ariège □ France 42°56N 1°30E 72 F5
Ariège → France 43°30N 1°25E 72 E5
Aries → Romania 46°24N 23°20E 81 D8
Arīhā Syria 35°49N 36°35E 104 E7
Arigat el Fersig Algeria 27°35N 2°7W 136 C3
Arihā Israel 31°51N 35°27E 137 A4
Arila, Akra Greece 39°43N 19°39E 101 A3
Arilje Serbia 43°44N 20°7E 96 C4
Arima Trin. & Tob. 10°38N 61°17W 183 D7
Arinos → Brazil 10°25S 58°20W 186 F7
Ario de Rosales Mexico 19°12N 101°43W 180 D4
Ariogala Lithuania 55°16N 23°28E 82 C10
Aripo, Mt. Trin. & Tob. 10°45N 61°15W 187 K15
Aripuanã Brazil 9°25S 60°30W 186 E6
Aripuanã → Brazil 5°7S 60°25W 186 E6
Ariquemes Brazil 9°55S 63°6W 186 E6
Arisaig U.K. 56°55N 5°51W 65 E3
Arish, W. el → Egypt 31°9N 33°49E 137 E8
Aristazabal I. Canada 52°40N 129°10W 162 C3
Ariton U.S.A. 31°36N 85°43W 178 D4
Ariyalur India 11°8N 79°8E 127 J4
Ariza Spain 41°19N 2°3W 90 D2
Arizaro, Salar de Argentina 24°40S 67°50W 190 A2
Arizona Argentina 35°45S 65°25W 190 D2
Arizona □ U.S.A. 34°0N 112°0W 169 J8
Arizpe Mexico 30°20N 110°10W 180 A2
'Arjah Si. Arabia 24°43N 44°17E 128 E5
Årjäng Sweden 59°24N 12°8E 62 E6
Arjeplog Sweden 66°3N 17°54E 60 C17
Arjepluovve = Arjeplog Sweden 66°3N 17°54E 60 C17
Arjona Colombia 10°14N 75°22W 186 A3
Arjona Spain 37°56N 4°4W 89 H6
Arjuna Indonesia 7°49S 112°34E 119 G15
Arka Russia 60°15N 142°0E 107 C15
Arkadak Russia 51°58N 43°30E 86 E6
Arkadelphia U.S.A. 34°7N 93°4W 176 D8
Arkadia Greece 37°30N 22°20E 98 D4
Arkaig, L. U.K. 56°59N 5°10W 65 E3
Arkalgud India 12°46N 76°3E 127 H3
Arkalyk = Arqalyk Kazakhstan 50°13N 66°50E 109 B7
Arkansas □ U.S.A. 35°0N 92°30W 176 D8
Arkansas → U.S.A. 33°47N 91°4W 176 E9
Arkansas City U.S.A. 37°4N 97°2W 172 G5
Arkaroola Australia 30°20S 139°22E 151 E2
Arkavāz Iran 33°22N 46°35E 105 F12
Arkhangelsk Russia 64°38N 40°36E 106 C5
Arkhangelskoye Russia 51°32N 40°58E 86 E5
Arki Greece 37°24N 26°44E 99 D8
Arki India 31°9N 76°58E 124 D7
Arklow Ireland 52°48N 6°10W 64 D5
Arkona, Kap Germany 54°42N 13°26E 76 A9
Arkösund Sweden 58°29N 16°56E 63 F10
Arkoudi Greece 38°33N 20°43E 98 C2
Arkport U.S.A. 42°24N 77°42W 174 D7
Arkticheskiy, Mys Russia 81°10N 95°0E 107 A10
Arkul Russia 57°17N 50°3E 86 B10
Arkville U.S.A. 42°9N 74°37W 175 D10
Årla Sweden 59°17N 16°40E 62 E10
Arlanda, Stockholm ✕ (ARN) Sweden 59°41N 17°56E 62 E11
Arlanza → Spain 42°6N 4°9W 88 C6
Arlanzón → Spain 42°3N 4°17W 88 C6
Arlbergpass Austria 47°9N 10°12E 78 D3
Arlbergtunnel Austria 47°9N 10°12E 78 D3
Arles France 43°41N 4°40E 73 E8
Arli Burkina Faso 11°35N 1°28E 139 C5
Arli △ Burkina Faso 11°35N 1°28E 139 C5
Arlington S. Africa 28°1S 27°53E 145 C4
Arlington Ga., U.S.A. 31°26N 84°44W 178 D5
Arlington N.Y., U.S.A. 41°42N 73°54W 175 E11
Arlington Oreg., U.S.A. 45°43N 120°12W 168 D3
Arlington S. Dak., U.S.A. 44°22N 97°8W 172 C5
Arlington Tex., U.S.A. 32°44N 97°6W 176 E6
Arlington Va., U.S.A. 38°53N 77°7W 173 F15
Arlington Vt., U.S.A. 43°5N 73°9W 175 C11
Arlington Wash., U.S.A. 48°12N 122°8W 170 B4
Arlington Heights U.S.A. 42°5N 87°59W 172 D10
Arlit Niger 19°0N 7°38E 134 E7
Arlon Belgium 49°42N 5°49E 69 E5
Arlparra Australia 22°11S 134°30E 150 C1
Arltunga Australia 23°26S 134°41E 150 C1
Armação de Pêra Portugal 37°6N 8°22W 89 H2
Armadale Australia 32°9S 116°0E 149 F2
Armagh U.K. 54°21N 6°39W 64 B5
Armagh □ U.K. 54°18N 6°37W 64 B5
Armagnac France 43°50N 0°10E 72 E4
Armançon → France 47°59N 3°30E 71 E10
Armando Bermudez △ Dom. Rep. 19°3N 71°0W 183 C5
Armant Egypt 25°37N 32°32E 137 B3
Armatree Australia 31°26S 148°28E 153 A8
Armavir Russia 45°2N 41°7E 87 H5
Armenia Colombia 4°35N 75°45W 186 C3
Armenia ■ Asia 40°20N 45°0E 87 K7
Armeniş Romania 45°13N 22°17E 80 E7
Armenistis, Akra Greece 36°8N 27°42E 101 C9
Armentières France 50°40N 2°50E 71 B9
Armidale Australia 30°30S 151°40E 153 A9
Armilla Spain 37°9N 3°37W 89 H7
Armori India 20°28N 79°59E 126 D4
Armorique ⌂ France 48°22N 3°50W 70 D3
Armour U.S.A. 43°19N 98°21W 172 D4
Armstrong B.C., Canada 50°25N 119°10W 162 C5
Armstrong Ont., Canada 50°18N 89°4W 164 B2
Armur India 18°48N 78°16E 126 E4
Armutlu Bursa, Turkey 40°31N 28°50E 97 F12
Armutlu İzmir, Turkey 38°24N 27°34E 99 C9
Arnarfjörður Iceland 65°48N 23°40W 60 D2
Arnaud → Canada 59°59N 69°46W 161 F18
Arnauti, C. Cyprus 35°6N 32°17E 101 D11
Arnay-le-Duc France 47°10N 4°27E 71 E11
Arnea Greece 40°30N 23°38E 96 F7
Arnedillo Spain 42°13N 2°14W 90 C2
Arnedo Spain 42°12N 2°5W 90 C2
Arnett U.S.A. 36°8N 99°46W 176 C5
Arnhem Neths. 51°58N 5°55E 69 C5
Arnhem, C. Australia 12°20S 137°30E 150 A2
Arnhem B. Australia 12°20S 136°10E 150 A2
Arnhem Land Australia 13°10S 134°30E 150 A1
Arnhem Land ☼ Australia 12°50S 134°50E 150 A1
Arnissa Greece 40°47N 21°49E 96 F5
Arno → Italy 43°41N 10°17E 92 E7
Arno Bay Australia 33°54S 136°34E 152 B2
Arnold U.K. 53°1N 1°7W 66 D6
Arnold Calif., U.S.A. 38°15N 120°21W 170 G6
Arnold Mo., U.S.A. 38°26N 90°23W 172 F8
Arnoldstein Austria 46°33N 13°43E 78 E6
Arnon → France 47°13N 2°1E 71 E9
Arnot Canada 55°56N 96°41W 163 B9
Arnøya Norway 70°9N 20°40E 60 A19
Arnprior Canada 45°26N 76°21W 175 A8
Arnsberg Germany 51°24N 8°5E 76 D4
Arnsberger Wald ⌂ Germany 51°25N 8°20E 76 D4
Arnstadt Germany 50°50N 10°56E 76 E6
Aroab Namibia 26°41S 19°39E 144 C2
Aroania Oros Greece 37°56N 22°12E 98 D4
Aroche Spain 37°56N 6°57W 89 H4
Arochuku Nigeria 5°21N 7°54E 139 D6
Aroeiras Brazil 7°31S 35°41W 189 B3
Arolsen Germany 51°23N 9°2E 76 D5
Aron India 25°57N 77°56E 124 G6
Aron → France 46°50N 3°28E 71 F10
Arona Canary Is. 28°6N 16°40W 100 F3
Arona Italy 45°46N 8°34E 92 C5
Aros → Mexico 29°9N 107°57W 180 B3
Arousa, Ría de → Spain 42°28N 8°57W 88 C2
Arpa → Asia 39°28N 44°56E 105 C11
Arpaçay Turkey 40°50N 43°19E 105 B10
Arpajon France 48°36N 2°15E 71 D9
Arpajon-sur-Cère France 44°53N 2°28E 72 D6
Arpaşu de Jos Romania 45°47N 24°37E 81 E9
Arqalyk Kazakhstan 50°13N 66°50E 109 B7
Arrah = Ara India 25°35N 84°32E 125 G11
Arrah Côte d'Ivoire 6°40N 3°58W 138 D4
Arraias Brazil 12°56S 46°57W 189 C1
Arraiolos Portugal 38°44N 7°59W 89 G3
Arran U.K. 55°34N 5°12W 65 F3
Arranmore Ireland 55°0N 8°30W 64 A3
Arras France 50°17N 2°46E 71 B9
Arrasate Spain 43°4N 2°30W 90 B2
Arrats → France 44°6N 0°52E 72 D4
Arreau France 42°54N 0°22E 72 F4
Arrecife Canary Is. 28°57N 13°37W 100 F6
Arrecifes Argentina 34°6S 60°9W 190 C3
Arrée, Mts. d' France 48°26N 3°55W 70 D3
Arresø Denmark 55°58N 12°6E 63 J6
Arriaga Mexico 16°14N 93°54W 181 D6
Arribes del Duero ⌂ Spain 41°11N 6°39W 88 D4
Arrilalah Australia 23°43S 143°54E 150 C3
Arrino Australia 29°30S 115°40E 149 E2
Arriondas Spain 43°23N 5°11W 88 B5
Arrojado → Brazil 13°24S 44°20W 189 C2
Arromanches-les-Bains France 49°20N 0°38W 70 C6
Arronches Portugal 39°8N 7°16W 89 F3
Arros → France 43°40N 0°2W 72 E3
Arrow, L. Ireland 54°3N 8°19W 64 B3
Arrowsmith, Mt. N.Z. 43°20S 170°55E 155 D5
Arrowtown N.Z. 44°57S 168°50E 155 E3
Arroyo de la Luz Spain 39°30N 6°38W 89 F4
Arroyo Grande U.S.A. 35°7N 120°35W 171 K6
Ars Iran 37°9N 47°46E 128 B5
Ars-sur-Moselle France 49°5N 6°4E 71 C13
Arsenault L. Canada 55°6N 108°32W 163 B7
Arsenev Russia 44°10N 133°15E 112 B6
Arsiero Italy 45°48N 11°21E 93 C8
Arsikere India 13°15N 76°15E 127 H3
Arsin Turkey 41°8N 39°55E 105 B8
Arsk Russia 56°10N 49°50E 86 B9
Årsunda Sweden 60°31N 16°45E 62 D10
Arta Greece 39°8N 21°2E 98 B3
Artà Spain 39°41N 3°21E 100 B10
Artà, Coves d' Spain 39°40N 3°24E 100 B10
Artashat Armenia 40°0N 44°35E 105 B11
Arteaga Mexico 18°28N 102°25W 180 D4
Arteixo = A Baiuca Spain 43°19N 8°29W 88 B2
Artem = Artyom Azerbaijan 40°28N 50°20E 87 K10
Artem Russia 43°22N 132°13E 112 C6
Artemivsk Ukraine 48°35N 38°0E 85 H9
Artemovsk Russia 54°45N 93°35E 107 D10
Artemovskiy Russia 47°45N 40°16E 87 G5
Artenay France 48°5N 1°50E 71 D8
Artern Germany 51°22N 11°18E 76 D7
Artesa de Segre Spain 41°54N 1°3E 90 D6
Artesia = Mosomane Botswana 24°2S 26°19E 144 B4
Artesia U.S.A. 32°51N 104°24W 169 K11
Arthington Liberia 6°35N 10°45W 138 D2
Arthur Canada 43°50N 80°32W 174 C4
Arthur → Australia 41°2S 144°40E 151 G3
Arthur Cr. → Australia 22°30S 136°25E 150 C2
Arthur Pt. Australia 22°7S 150°3E 150 C5
Arthur River Australia 33°20S 117°2E 149 F2
Arthur's Pass N.Z. 42°54S 171°35E 155 C6
Arthur's Pass △ N.Z. 42°53S 171°42E 155 C6
Arthur's Town Bahamas 24°38N 75°42W 183 B4
Artigas Antarctica 62°30S 58°0W 55 C18
Artigas Uruguay 30°20S 56°30W 190 C4
Artik Armenia 40°38N 43°58E 87 K6
Artillery L. Canada 63°9N 107°52W 163 A7
Artois France 50°20N 2°30E 71 B9
Artotina Greece 38°42N 22°2E 98 C4
Artova Turkey 40°5N 36°28E 104 B7
Artrutx, C. de Spain 39°55N 3°49E 100 B10
Arts Bogd Uul Mongolia 44°40N 102°20E 114 B2
Artsvashen Armenia 40°38N 45°30E 105 B11
Artsyz Ukraine 46°4N 29°26E 81 D14
Artux China 39°40N 76°10E 109 E9
Artvin Turkey 41°14N 41°44E 105 B9
Artvin □ Turkey 41°10N 41°50E 105 B9
Artyk Russia 64°12N 145°6E 107 C15
Artyom Azerbaijan 40°28N 50°20E 87 K10
Aru, Kepulauan Indonesia 6°0S 134°30E 119 F8
Aru Is. = Aru, Kepulauan Indonesia 6°0S 134°30E 119 F8
Arua Uganda 3°1N 30°58E 142 B3
Aruanã Brazil 14°54S 51°10W 187 F8
Aruba ☒ W. Indies 12°30N 70°0W 183 D6
Arucas Canary Is. 28°7N 15°32W 100 F4
Arudy France 43°7N 0°28W 72 E3
Arué Tahiti 17°31S 149°30W 155 b
Arumpo Australia 33°48S 142°55E 152 B5
Arun → Nepal 26°55N 87°10E 125 F12
Arun → U.K. 50°49N 0°33W 67 G7
Arunachal Pradesh □ India 28°0N 95°0E 123 F19
Aruppukkottai India 9°31N 78°8E 127 K4
Arusha Tanzania 3°20S 36°40E 142 C4
Arusha □ Tanzania 3°20S 36°30E 142 C4
Arusha △ Tanzania 3°16S 36°47E 142 C4
Arusha Chini Tanzania 3°32S 37°20E 142 C4
Aruvi → Sri Lanka 8°48N 79°53E 127 K4
Aruwimi → Dem. Rep. of the Congo 1°13N 23°36E 142 B1
Arvada Colo., U.S.A. 39°48N 105°5W 168 G11
Arvada Wyo., U.S.A. 44°39N 106°8W 168 D10
Arvakalu Sri Lanka 8°20N 79°58E 127 K4
Arvayheer Mongolia 46°15N 102°48E 110 B9
Arve → France 46°11N 6°8E 71 F13
Arvi Greece 34°59N 25°28E 101 E7
Arvi India 20°59N 78°16E 126 D4
Arviat Canada 61°6N 93°59W 163 A10
Arvidsjaur Sweden 65°35N 19°10E 60 D18
Arvika Sweden 59°40N 12°36E 62 E6
Arvin U.S.A. 35°12N 118°50W 171 K8
Arwal India 25°15N 84°41E 125 G11
Arxan China 47°11N 119°57E 111 B12
Åryd Sweden 56°49N 14°59E 63 H8
Arys Kazakhstan 42°26N 68°48E 109 D7
Arzachena Italy 41°5N 9°23E 94 A2
Arzamas Russia 55°27N 43°55E 86 C6
Arzanah U.A.E. 24°47N 52°34E 129 E7
Arzew Algeria 35°50N 0°23W 136 A3
Arzgir Russia 45°18N 44°23E 87 H7
Arzignano Italy 45°31N 11°20E 93 C8
Arzúa Spain 42°56N 8°9W 88 C2
Aš Czechia 50°13N 12°12E 78 A5
Ås Sweden 63°15N 14°34E 62 A8
As Pontes de García Rodríguez Spain 43°27N 7°50W 88 B3
As Safā Syria 33°10N 37°0E 130 B6
As Saffānīyah Si. Arabia 27°55N 48°50E 129 E6
As Safīrah Syria 36°5N 37°21E 104 D7
Aş Şahm Oman 24°10N 56°53E 129 E8
As Sājir Si. Arabia 25°11N 44°36E 128 E5
As Salamīyah Syria 35°1N 37°2E 104 E7
As Salmān Iraq 30°30N 44°32E 128 D5
As Salţ Jordan 32°2N 35°43E 130 C4
As Sal'w'a Qatar 24°23N 50°50E 129 E6
As Samāwah Iraq 31°15N 45°15E 128 D5
As Sanamayn Syria 33°3N 36°10E 130 B5
As Sila' U.A.E. 24°4N 51°45E 129 E6
As Sukhnah Syria 34°52N 38°52E 105 E8
As Sulaymānīyah Iraq 35°35N 45°29E 105 E11
As Sulaymānīyah □ Iraq 35°50N 45°30E 105 E11
As Sulaymī Si. Arabia 26°17N 41°21E 128 E4
As Sulayyil Si. Arabia 20°27N 45°34E 131 C4
As Summān Si. Arabia 25°0N 47°0E 128 E5
Aş Şuwar Syria 35°30N 40°38E 105 E9
As Suwaydā' Syria 32°40N 36°30E 130 C5
As Suwaydā' □ Syria 32°45N 36°45E 130 C5
As Suwayq Oman 23°51N 57°26E 129 F8
Aş Şuwayrah Iraq 32°55N 45°0E 105 F11
Åsa Sweden 57°21N 12°8E 63 G6
Asab Namibia 25°30S 18°0E 144 C2
Asaba Nigeria 6°12N 6°38E 139 D6
Asad, Buḩayrat al Syria 36°0N 38°15E 105 D8
Asadābād Iran 34°47N 48°7E 105 E13
Asafo Ghana 6°20N 2°40W 138 D4
Asahi Japan 35°43N 140°39E 113 G10
Asahi-Gawa → Japan 34°36N 133°58E 113 G6
Asahigawa = Asahikawa Japan 43°46N 142°22E 112 C11
Asahikawa Japan 43°46N 142°22E 112 C11
Asaluyeh Iran 27°29N 52°37E 129 E7
Asamankese Ghana 5°50N 0°40W 139 D4
Asan → India 26°37N 78°24E 125 F8
Asansol India 23°40N 87°1E 125 H12
Åsarna Sweden 62°39N 14°22E 62 B8
Asbesberge S. Africa 29°0S 23°0E 144 C3
Asbestos Canada 45°47N 71°58W 165 C5
Asbury Park U.S.A. 40°13N 74°1W 175 F10
Åsby Sweden 57°14N 12°18E 63 G6
Ascea Italy 40°8N 15°17E 95 B8
Ascensión Mexico 31°6N 107°59W 180 A3
Ascensión, B. de la Mexico 19°40N 87°30W 181 D7
Ascension I. Atl. Oc. 7°57S 14°23W 133 G2
Aschach an der Donau Austria 48°22N 14°2E 78 C7
Aschaffenburg Germany 49°58N 9°6E 77 F5
Aschendorf Germany 53°3N 7°19E 76 B3
Aschersleben Germany 51°45N 11°29E 76 D7
Asciano Italy 43°14N 11°33E 93 E8
Áscoli Piceno Italy 42°51N 13°34E 93 F10
Áscoli Satriano Italy 41°11N 15°32E 95 A8
Ascope Peru 7°46S 79°8W 188 B2
Ascotán Chile 21°45S 68°17W 190 A2
Aseb Eritrea 13°0N 42°40E 131 E3
Åseda Sweden 57°10N 15°20E 63 G9
Asedjrad Algeria 24°51N 1°29E 136 D4
Asela Ethiopia 8°0N 39°0E 131 F2
Åsen Sweden 61°17N 13°50E 62 C7
Asenovgrad Bulgaria 42°1N 24°51E 97 D8
Asfeld France 49°27N 4°5E 71 C11
Asfûn el Matâ'na Egypt 25°26N 32°30E 137 B3
Asgabat = Ashgabat Turkmenistan 37°58N 58°24E 129 B8
Asgata Cyprus 34°46N 33°15E 101 E12
Ash Fork U.S.A. 35°13N 112°29W 169 J7
Ash Grove U.S.A. 37°19N 93°35W 172 G7
Ash Shabakah Iraq 30°49N 43°39E 128 D4
Ash Shamāl □ Lebanon 34°25N 36°0E 130 A5
Ash Shāmīyah Iraq 31°55N 44°35E 105 G11
Ash Shāriqah U.A.E. 25°23N 55°26E 129 E7
Ash Sharmah Si. Arabia 28°1N 35°16E 128 D2
Ash Sharqāt Iraq 35°27N 43°16E 105 E10
Ash Shaţrah Iraq 31°30N 46°10E 128 D5
Ash Shawbak Jordan 30°32N 35°34E 128 D2
Ash Shiḩr Yemen 14°45N 49°36E 131 E4
Ash Shināfīyah Iraq 31°35N 44°39E 128 D5
Ash Shu'bah Si. Arabia 28°54N 44°44E 128 D5
Ash Shumlūl Si. Arabia 26°31N 47°20E 128 E5
Ash Shūr'a Iraq 35°58N 43°13E 128 C4
Ash Shurayf Si. Arabia 25°43N 39°14E 128 E3
Ash Shuwayfāt Lebanon 33°45N 35°30E 130 B4
Asha Russia 55°0N 57°16E 108 B5
Ashanti □ Ghana 7°30N 1°30W 139 D4
Ashbourne U.K. 53°2N 1°43W 66 D6
Ashburn U.S.A. 31°43N 83°39W 178 D6
Ashburton N.Z. 43°53S 171°48E 155 D6
Ashburton → Australia 21°40S 114°56E 148 D1
Ashburton, North Branch → N.Z. 43°54S 171°44E 155 D6
Ashburton, South Branch → N.Z. 43°54S 171°44E 155 D6
Ashcroft Canada 50°40N 121°20W 162 C4
Ashdod Israel 31°49N 34°35E 130 D3
Ashdown U.S.A. 33°40N 94°8W 176 E7
Asheboro U.S.A. 35°43N 79°49W 177 D15
Ashern Canada 51°11N 98°21W 163 C9
Asherton U.S.A. 28°27N 99°46W 176 G5
Asheville U.S.A. 35°36N 82°33W 177 D13
Ashewat Pakistan 31°22N 68°32E 124 D3
Asheweig → Canada 54°17N 87°12W 164 B2
Ashford Australia 29°15S 151°3E 151 D5
Ashford U.K. 51°8N 0°53E 67 F8
Ashford U.S.A. 31°11N 85°14W 178 D4
Ashgabat Turkmenistan 37°58N 58°24E 129 B8
Ashhurst N.Z. 40°16S 175°45E 154 G4
Ashibetsu Japan 43°31N 142°11E 112 C11
Ashikaga Japan 36°28N 139°29E 113 F9
Ashington U.K. 55°11N 1°33W 66 B6
Ashizuri-Uwakai △ Japan 32°56N 132°32E 113 H6
Ashizuri-Zaki Japan 32°44N 133°0E 113 H6
Ashkarkot Afghan. 33°3N 67°58E 124 C2
Ashkhabad = Ashgabat Turkmenistan 37°58N 58°24E 129 B8
Āshkhāneh Iran 37°26N 56°55E 129 B8
Ashland Ala., U.S.A. 33°16N 85°50W 178 B4
Ashland Kans., U.S.A. 37°11N 99°46W 172 G4
Ashland Ky., U.S.A. 38°28N 82°38W 173 F12
Ashland Maine, U.S.A. 46°38N 68°24W 173 B19
Ashland Mont., U.S.A. 45°36N 106°16W 168 D10
Ashland Ohio, U.S.A. 40°52N 82°19W 174 F2
Ashland Oreg., U.S.A. 42°12N 122°43W 168 E2
Ashland Pa., U.S.A. 40°45N 76°22W 175 F8
Ashland Va., U.S.A. 37°46N 77°29W 173 G15
Ashland Wis., U.S.A. 46°35N 90°53W 172 B8
Ashley N. Dak., U.S.A. 46°2N 99°22W 172 B4
Ashley Pa., U.S.A. 41°12N 75°55W 175 E9
Ashley → N.Z. 43°17S 172°44E 155 D7
Ashmore and Cartier Is. Ind. Oc. 12°15S 123°0E 148 B3
Ashmore Reef Australia 12°14S 123°5E 148 B3
Ashmûn Egypt 30°18N 30°58E 137 E7
Ashmyany Belarus 54°26N 25°52E 75 A13
Ashokan Res. U.S.A. 41°56N 74°13W 175 E10
Ashoknagar India 24°34N 77°43E 126 B3
Ashqelon Israel 31°42N 34°35E 130 D3
Ashta India 23°1N 76°43E 124 H7
Ashtabula U.S.A. 41°52N 80°47W 174 E4
Ashti Maharashtra, India 21°12N 78°11E 126 D4
Ashti Maharashtra, India 18°50N 75°15E 126 E2
Āshtiyān Iran 34°31N 50°0E 129 C6
Ashton S. Africa 33°50S 20°5E 144 D3
Ashton U.S.A. 44°4N 111°27W 168 D8
Ashuanipi, L. Canada 52°45N 66°15W 165 B6
Ashuapmushuan → Canada 48°37N 72°20W 164 C5
Ashur = Assur Iraq 35°27N 43°15E 105 E10
Ashville Ala., U.S.A. 33°50N 86°15W 178 B3
Ashville Fla., U.S.A. 30°37N 83°39W 178 E6
Ashville Pa., U.S.A. 40°34N 78°33W 174 F6
'Āşī → Asia 36°1N 35°59E 104 D6
Asia 45°0N 75°0E 102 E9
Asia, Kepulauan Indonesia 1°0N 131°13E 119 D8
Asiago Italy 45°52N 11°30E 93 C8
Asifabad India 19°20N 79°24E 126 E4
Asilah Morocco 35°29N 6°0W 136 A2
Asinara Italy 41°4N 8°16E 94 A1
Asinara, G. dell' Italy 41°0N 8°30E 94 A1
Asino Russia 57°0N 86°0E 106 D9
Asipovichy Belarus 53°19N 28°33E 75 B15
'Asīr Si. Arabia 18°40N 42°30E 137 D5
Asir, Ras Somalia 11°55N 51°10E 131 E5
Aska India 19°2N 84°42E 126 E7
Askale Turkey 39°55N 40°41E 105 C9
Askersund Sweden 58°53N 14°55E 63 F8
Askham S. Africa 26°59S 20°47E 144 C3
Askī Mawşil Iraq 36°30N 42°44E 105 D10
Askim Norway 59°35N 11°10E 61 G14
Askio, Oros Greece 40°25N 21°35E 96 F5
Askja Iceland 65°3N 16°48W 60 D5
Asklipio Greece 36°4N 27°56E 101 C9
Askøyna Norway 60°29N 5°10E 60 F11
Asl Egypt 29°33N 32°44E 137 F8
Aslan Burnu Turkey 38°44N 26°45E 99 C8
Aslanapa Turkey 39°13N 29°52E 99 B11
Aslānduz Iran 39°26N 47°24E 105 C12
Asmara = Asmera Eritrea 15°19N 38°55E 131 D2
Asmera Eritrea 15°19N 38°55E 131 D2
Asnæs Denmark 55°40N 11°0E 63 J4
Åsnen Sweden 56°37N 14°45E 63 H8
Asni Morocco 31°17N 7°58W 136 B2
Aso Kujū △ Japan 32°53N 131°6E 113 H5
Asola Italy 45°13N 10°25E 92 C7
Asos Greece 38°22N 20°33E 98 C2
Asoteriba, Jebel Sudan 21°51N 36°30E 137 C4
Asouf, O. → Algeria 25°40N 2°8E 136 C4
Aspatria U.K. 54°47N 3°19W 66 C4
Aspe Spain 38°20N 0°40W 91 G4
Aspen U.S.A. 39°11N 106°49W 168 G10
Aspendos Turkey 36°54N 31°7E 104 D4
Aspermont U.S.A. 33°8N 100°14W 176 E4
Aspet France 43°1N 0°48E 72 E4
Aspiring, Mt. N.Z. 44°23S 168°46E 155 E3
Aspres-sur-Buëch France 44°32N 5°44E 73 D9
Asprokavos, Akra Greece 39°21N 20°6E 101 B4
Aspromonte △ Italy 38°9N 15°58E 95 D8
Aspur India 23°58N 74°7E 124 H6
Asquith Canada 52°8N 107°13W 163 C7
Assab = Aseb Eritrea 13°0N 42°40E 131 E3
Assâba □ Mauritania 16°40N 11°40W 138 B2
Assâba, Massif de l' Mauritania 16°10N 11°45W 138 B2
Assagny △ Côte d'Ivoire 5°10N 4°58W 138 D4
Assaikio Nigeria 8°34N 8°55E 139 D6
Assal, L. Djibouti 11°40N 42°26E 131 E3
Assam □ India 26°0N 93°0E 123 G18
Assamakka Niger 19°21N 5°38E 139 B6
Assateague Island ⌂ U.S.A. 38°15N 75°10W 173 F16
Assaye India 20°15N 75°53E 126 D2
Asse Belgium 50°24N 4°10E 69 D4
Assekrem Algeria 23°16N 5°49E 136 D5
Assémini Italy 39°17N 9°0E 94 C1
Assen Neths. 53°0N 6°35E 69 A6
Assens Denmark 55°16N 9°55E 63 J3
Assini Côte d'Ivoire 5°9N 3°17W 138 D4
Assiniboia Canada 49°40N 105°59W 163 D7
Assiniboine → Canada 49°53N 97°8W 163 D9
Assiniboine, Mt. Canada 50°52N 115°39W 162 C5
Assis Brazil 22°40S 50°20W 191 A5
Assis Brasil Brazil 10°55S 69°32W 188 C4
Assisi Italy 43°4N 12°37E 93 E9
Assur Iraq 35°27N 43°15E 105 E10
Assynt, L. U.K. 58°10N 5°3W 65 C3
Astaffort France 44°4N 0°40E 72 D4
Astakida Greece 35°53N 26°50E 99 F8
Astakos Greece 38°32N 21°5E 98 C3
Astana Kazakhstan 51°10N 71°30E 109 B8
Āstāneh Iran 37°17N 49°59E 129 B6
Astara Azerbaijan 38°30N 48°50E 105 C13
Āstārā Iran 38°20N 48°52E 105 C13
Astarabad = Gorgān Iran 36°55N 54°30E 129 B7
Asterousia Greece 34°59N 25°3E 101 E7
Asti Italy 44°54N 8°12E 92 D5
Astipalea Greece 36°32N 26°22E 99 E8
Astorga Spain 42°29N 6°8W 88 C4
Astoria U.S.A. 46°11N 123°50W 170 D3
Åstorp Sweden 56°6N 12°55E 63 H6
Astrakhan Russia 46°25N 48°5E 87 G9
Astrakhan □ Russia 47°45N 46°20E 87 G8
Astrebla Downs Australia 24°12S 140°34E 150 C3
Astudillo Spain 42°12N 4°22W 88 C6
Asturias □ Spain 43°15N 6°0W 88 B5
Asturias ✕ (OVD) Spain 43°33N 6°3W 88 B4
Asunción Bolivia 11°46S 67°50W 188 C4
Asunción Paraguay 25°10S 57°30W 190 B4
Asunción Nochixtlán Mexico 17°28N 97°14W 181 D5
Åsunden Sweden 58°0N 15°51E 63 F9
Aswa → Uganda 3°43N 31°55E 142 B3
Aswa-Lolim ⌂ Uganda 2°43N 31°35E 142 B3
Aswad, Ra's al Si. Arabia 21°20N 39°0E 137 C4
Aswân Egypt 24°4N 32°57E 137 C3
Aswan High Dam = Sadd el Aali Egypt 23°54N 32°54E 137 C3
Asyût Egypt 27°11N 31°4E 137 B3
Asyûti, Wadi → Egypt 27°11N 31°16E 137 B3
Aszód Hungary 47°39N 19°28E 80 C4
At-Bashy Kyrgyzstan 41°10N 75°48E 109 D9
At Ţafīlah Jordan 30°45N 35°30E 130 E4
At Ţafīlah □ Jordan 30°45N 35°30E 130 E4
Aţ Ţā'if Si. Arabia 21°5N 40°27E 137 C5
At Ta'mīm □ Iraq 35°30N 44°20E 128 C5
Aţ Ţirāq Si. Arabia 27°19N 44°33E 128 E5
Aţ Ţubayq Si. Arabia 29°30N 37°0E 128 D3
Aţ Ţunayb Jordan 31°48N 35°57E 130 D4
Atabey Turkey 37°57N 30°39E 99 D12
Atacama □ Chile 27°30S 70°0W 190 B2
Atacama, Desierto de Chile 24°0S 69°20W 190 A2
Atacama, Salar de Chile 23°30S 68°20W 190 A2
Atakeye ☼ Australia 22°30S 133°45E 148 D5
Atakor Algeria 23°27N 5°31E 136 D5
Atakpamé Togo 7°31N 1°13E 139 D5
Atalandi Greece 38°39N 22°58E 98 C4
Atalaya Peru 10°45S 73°50W 188 C3
Atalaya de Femes Canary Is. 28°56N 13°47W 100 F6
Ataléia Brazil 18°3S 41°6W 189 D2
Atami Japan 35°5N 139°4E 113 G9
Atamyrat Turkmenistan 37°50N 65°12E 109 E7
Atapuerca, Cueva de Spain 42°22N 3°32W 88 C7
Atapupu Indonesia 9°0S 124°51E 119 F6
Atâr Mauritania 20°30N 13°5W 134 D3
Ataram, Erg n- Algeria 23°57N 2°0E 136 D4
Atarfe Spain 37°13N 3°40W 89 H7
Atari Pakistan 30°56N 74°2E 124 D6
Atascadero U.S.A. 35°29N 120°40W 170 K6
Atasū Kazakhstan 48°30N 71°0E 109 C8
Atatürk, İstanbul ✕ (IST) Turkey 40°59N 28°49E 97 F12
Atatürk Barajı Turkey 37°28N 38°30E 105 D8
Atauro E. Timor 8°10S 125°30E 119 F7
Ataviros Greece 36°12N 27°50E 101 C9

Atbara Sudan 17°42N 33°59E 135 E12
'Atbara, Nahr → Sudan 17°40N 33°56E 137 D3
Atbasar Kazakhstan 51°48N 68°20E 109 E7
Atbashi = At-Bashy Kyrgyzstan 41°10N 75°48E 109 E9
Atça Turkey 37°53N 28°13E 99 D10
Atchafalaya B. U.S.A. 29°25N 91°25W 176 G9
Atchison U.S.A. 39°34N 95°7W 172 F6
Atebubu Ghana 7°47N 1°0W 139 D4
Ateca Spain 41°20N 1°49W 90 D3
Aterno → Italy 42°11N 13°51E 93 F10
Āteshān Iran 35°35N 52°37E 129 C7
Atesine, Alpi Italy 46°55N 11°30E 93 B8
Atessa Italy 42°4N 14°27E 93 F11
Atfih Egypt 29°25N 31°15E 137 F7
Ath Belgium 50°38N 3°47E 69 D3
Athabasca Canada 54°45N 113°20W 162 C6
Athabasca → Canada 58°40N 110°50W 163 B6
Athabasca, L. Canada 59°15N 109°15W 163 B7
Athabasca Sand Dunes → Canada 59°4N 108°43W 163 B7
Athagarh India 20°32N 85°37E 126 D7
Athboy Ireland 53°36N 6°56W 64 C5
Athena U.S.A. 29°59N 83°30W 178 F6
Athenry Ireland 53°18N 8°44W 64 C3
Athens = Athina Greece 37°58N 23°43E 98 D5
Athens Ala., U.S.A. 34°48N 86°58W 177 D11
Athens Ga., U.S.A. 33°57N 83°23W 178 B6
Athens N.Y., U.S.A. 42°16N 73°49W 175 D11
Athens Ohio, U.S.A. 39°20N 82°6W 173 F12
Athens Pa., U.S.A. 41°57N 76°31W 175 E8
Athens Tenn., U.S.A. 35°27N 84°36W 177 D12
Athens Tex., U.S.A. 32°12N 95°51W 176 E7
Atherley Canada 44°37N 79°20W 174 B5
Atherton Australia 17°17S 145°30E 150 B4
Athi River Kenya 1°28S 36°58E 142 C4
Athiéme Benin 6°37N 1°40E 139 D5
Athienou Cyprus 35°3N 33°32E 101 D12
Athina Greece 37°58N 23°43E 98 D5
Athina ✈ (ATH) Greece 37°56N 23°56E 98 D5
Athinai = Athina Greece 37°58N 23°43E 98 D5
Athlone Ireland 53°25N 7°56W 64 C4
Athmallik India 20°43N 84°32E 126 D7
Athni India 16°44N 75°6E 124 C2
Athol N.Z. 45°30S 168°35E 155 F3
Athol U.S.A. 42°36N 72°14W 175 D12
Atholl, Forest of U.K. 56°51N 3°50W 65 E5
Atholl, Kap Greenland 75°26N 69°30W 57 B4
Atholville Canada 47°59N 66°43W 165 C6
Athos Greece 40°9N 24°22E 97 F8
Athy Ireland 53°0N 7°0W 64 C5
Ati Chad 13°13N 18°20E 135 F9
Atiak Uganda 3°12N 32°2E 142 B3
Atiamuri N.Z. 38°24S 176°5E 154 C5
Atico Peru 16°14S 73°40W 188 D3
Atienza Spain 41°12N 2°52W 90 D2
Atik L. Canada 55°15N 96°0W 163 B9
Atikaki Canada 51°30N 95°31W 163 C9
Atikameg → Canada 52°30N 82°46W 164 B3
Atikokan Canada 48°45N 91°37W 164 C1
Atikonak L. Canada 52°40N 64°32W 165 B7
Atimaono Tahiti 17°46S 149°28W 155 b
Atirampattinam India 10°28N 79°20E 127 J4
Atiu Cook Is. 20°0S 158°10W 157 J12
Atka Russia 60°50N 151°48E 107 C16
Atka I. U.S.A. 52°7N 174°30W 166 E5
Atkarsk Russia 51°55N 45°2E 89 F7
Atkinson Ga., U.S.A. 31°13N 81°47W 178 D8
Atkinson Nebr., U.S.A. 42°32N 98°59W 172 D4
Atlanta Ga., U.S.A. 33°45N 84°23W 178 B5
Atlanta Tex., U.S.A. 33°7N 94°10W 176 E7
Atlanta Hartsfield-Jackson Int. ✈ (ATL) U.S.A. 33°38N 84°26W 178 B5
Atlantic U.S.A. 41°24N 95°1W 172 E6
Atlantic Beach U.S.A. 30°20N 81°24W 178 E8
Atlantic City U.S.A. 39°21N 74°27W 173 F16
Atlantic-Indian Basin Antarctica 60°0S 30°0E 55 B4
Atlantic Ocean 0°0S 20°0W 56 F8
Atlantis S. Africa 33°34S 18°29E 144 D2
Atlas Mts. = Haut Atlas Morocco 32°30N 5°0W 136 B3
Atlin Canada 59°31N 133°41W 162 B2
Atlin, L. Canada 59°26N 133°45W 162 B2
Atlin → Canada 59°10N 134°30W 162 B2
Atmakur Andhra Pradesh, India 14°37N 79°40E 127 G4
Atmakur Andhra Pradesh, India 15°53N 78°35E 127 G4
Atmakur Telangana, India 18°45N 78°33E 126 E4
Atmore U.S.A. 31°2N 87°29W 178 D2
Atoka U.S.A. 34°23N 96°8W 176 D6
Atokos Greece 38°28N 20°49E 98 C2
Atolia U.S.A. 35°19N 117°37W 171 K9
Atqasuk U.S.A. 70°28N 157°24W 166 A8
Atrai → Bangla. 24°7N 89°22E 125 G13
Atrak = Atrek → Turkmenistan 37°35N 53°58E 129 B8
Ātran Sweden 57°7N 12°57E 63 B6
Ātran → Sweden 56°53N 12°30E 63 H6
Atrauli India 28°2N 78°20E 124 E8
Atrek → Turkmenistan 37°35N 53°58E 129 B8
Atri Italy 42°35N 13°58E 93 F10
Atsiki Greece 39°56N 25°13E 99 B7
Atsoum, Mts. Cameroon 6°41N 12°57E 139 D7
Atsuta Japan 43°24N 141°26E 112 C10
Attalla U.S.A. 34°1N 86°6W 178 A3
Attapeu Laos 14°48N 106°50E 120 E6
Attapulgus U.S.A. 30°45N 84°29W 178 E5
Attawapiskat Canada 52°57N 82°18W 164 B3
Attawapiskat → Canada 52°57N 82°24W 164 B3
Attawapiskat L. Canada 52°18N 87°54W 164 B2
Attersee Austria 47°55N 13°32E 78 D6
Attica = Attiki Greece 37°10N 23°40E 98 D5
Attica Ind., U.S.A. 40°18N 87°15W 172 E10
Attica Ohio, U.S.A. 41°4N 82°53W 174 E2
Attichy France 49°25N 3°3E 71 C11
Attigny France 49°28N 4°35E 71 C11
Attikamagen L. Canada 55°0N 66°30W 165 B6
Attiki Greece 37°10N 23°40E 98 D5
Attock Pakistan 33°52N 72°20E 124 C5
Attopu = Attapeu Laos 14°48N 106°50E 120 E6
Attunga Australia 30°55S 150°50E 153 A9

Attur India 11°35N 78°30E 127 J4
Atuel → Argentina 36°17S 66°50W 190 D2
Atura Uganda 2°7N 32°20E 142 B3
Åtvidaberg Sweden 58°12N 16°0E 63 F10
Atwater U.S.A. 37°21N 120°37W 170 H6
Atwood Canada 43°40N 81°1W 174 C3
Atwood U.S.A. 39°48N 101°3W 172 F3
Atyraū Kazakhstan 47°5N 52°0E 108 C4
Au Sable U.S.A. 44°25N 83°20W 174 B1
Au Sable → U.S.A. 44°25N 83°20W 173 C12
Au Sable Forks U.S.A. 44°27N 73°41W 175 B11
Au Sable Pt. U.S.A. 44°20N 83°20W 174 B1
Auas Honduras 15°29N 84°20W 182 C3
Auasberg Namibia 22°37S 17°13E 144 B2
Aubagne France 43°17N 5°37E 73 E9
Aubenas France 48°15N 4°10E 71 D11
Aubenton France 49°50N 4°12E 71 C11
Auberry U.S.A. 37°7N 119°29W 170 H7
Aubigny-sur-Nère France 47°30N 2°24E 71 E9
Aubin France 44°33N 2°15E 72 D6
Aubrac, Mts. d' France 44°40N 3°2E 72 D7
Auburn Ala., U.S.A. 32°36N 85°29W 178 C4
Auburn Calif., U.S.A. 38°54N 121°4W 170 G5
Auburn Ind., U.S.A. 41°22N 85°4W 172 E11
Auburn Maine, U.S.A. 44°6N 70°14W 173 C18
Auburn N.Y., U.S.A. 42°56N 76°34W 175 D8
Auburn Nebr., U.S.A. 40°23N 95°51W 172 E6
Auburn Pa., U.S.A. 40°36N 76°6W 175 F8
Auburn Wash., U.S.A. 47°18N 122°14W 170 C4
Auburn Ra. Australia 25°15S 150°30E 151 D5
Auburndale U.S.A. 28°4N 81°48W 178 G5
Aubusson France 45°57N 2°11E 72 C6
Auce Latvia 56°28N 22°53E 82 B9
Auch France 43°39N 0°36E 72 E4
Auchi Nigeria 7°6N 6°13E 139 D6
Auchterarder U.K. 56°18N 3°41W 65 E5
Auchtermuchty U.K. 56°18N 3°13W 65 E5
Auckland N.Z. 36°52S 174°46E 154 C3
Auckland □ N.Z. 36°50S 175°0E 154 C3
Auckland Is. Pac. Oc. 50°40S 166°5E 156 N8
Aude □ France 43°8N 2°28E 72 E6
Aude → France 43°13N 3°14E 72 E7
Auden Canada 50°14N 87°53W 164 B2
Auderville France 49°43N 1°57W 70 C5
Audierne France 48°1N 4°34W 70 D2
Audincourt France 47°30N 6°50E 71 E13
Audubon U.S.A. 41°43N 94°56W 172 E6
Auerbach Germany 50°30N 12°24E 76 E8
Augathella Australia 25°48S 146°35E 151 D4
Aughnacloy U.K. 54°25N 6°59W 64 B5
Aughrim Ireland 53°18N 8°19W 64 C3
Augrabies Falls S. Africa 28°35S 20°20E 144 C3
Augrabies Falls △ S. Africa 28°40S 20°22E 144 C3
Augsburg Germany 48°25N 10°52E 77 G6
Augsburg-Westliche Wälder △ Germany 48°20N 10°40E 77 G6
Augusta Australia 34°19S 115°9E 149 F2
Augusta Italy 37°13N 15°13E 95 E8
Augusta Ark., U.S.A. 35°17N 91°22W 176 D9
Augusta Ga., U.S.A. 33°28N 81°58W 178 C6
Augusta Kans., U.S.A. 37°41N 96°59W 172 G5
Augusta Maine, U.S.A. 44°19N 69°47W 173 C19
Augusta Mont., U.S.A. 47°30N 112°24W 168 C7
Augustenborg Denmark 54°57N 9°53E 63 K3
Augustów Poland 53°51N 23°0E 82 E9
Augustus, Mt. Australia 24°20S 116°50E 149 D2
Augustus I. Australia 15°20S 124°30E 148 C3
Aujuittuq = Grise Fiord Canada 76°25N 82°57W 161 B15
Aukrug Germany 54°5N 9°46E 76 A5
Aukštaitija △ Lithuania 55°15N 26°0E 61 J22
Aukum U.S.A. 38°34N 120°43W 170 G6
Aul India 20°41N 86°39E 126 D8
Aulavik △ Canada 73°42N 119°55W 160 C8
Auld, L. Australia 22°25S 123°50E 148 D3
Āūliekōl Kazakhstan 52°32N 62°45E 108 D8
Aulifeltet Norway 60°30N 11°21E 62 D5
Aulla Italy 44°12N 9°58E 92 D6
Aulnay France 46°2N 0°22W 72 B3
Aulnoye-Aymeries France 50°12N 3°50E 71 B10
Ault France 50°8N 1°26E 70 B8
Ault U.S.A. 40°35N 104°44W 168 F11
Aulus-les-Bains France 42°49N 1°19E 72 F5
Aumale France 49°46N 1°46E 71 C8
Aumont-Aubrac France 44°43N 3°17E 72 D7
Auna Nigeria 10°9N 4°42E 139 C5
Aundah India 19°32N 77°3E 126 E3
Auning Denmark 56°26N 10°22E 63 H4
Aunis France 46°5N 0°50W 72 B3
Auponhia Indonesia 1°58S 125°27E 119 E7
Aur, Pulau Malaysia 2°35N 104°10E 121 L5
Auraiya India 26°28N 79°33E 125 F8
Aurangabad Bihar, India 24°45N 84°18E 125 G11
Aurangabad Maharashtra, India 19°50N 75°23E 126 E2
Auray France 47°40N 2°59W 70 E4
Aurès Algeria 35°8N 6°30E 136 A5
Aurich Germany 53°28N 7°28E 76 B3
Auronzo di Cadore Italy 46°33N 12°26E 93 B9
Aurora Canada 44°0N 79°28W 174 C5
Aurora S. Africa 32°40S 18°29E 144 D2
Aurora Colo., U.S.A. 39°43N 104°49W 168 G11
Aurora Ill., U.S.A. 41°45N 88°19W 172 E9
Aurora Mo., U.S.A. 36°58N 93°43W 172 G7
Aurora N.Y., U.S.A. 42°45N 76°42W 175 D8
Aurora Nebr., U.S.A. 40°52N 98°0W 172 E5
Aurora Ohio, U.S.A. 41°21N 81°20W 174 E3
Aurukun Australia 13°20S 141°45E 150 A3
Aus Namibia 26°35S 16°12E 144 C2
Ausa India 18°15N 76°30E 126 E3
Ausable → Canada 43°19N 81°46W 174 C3
Auschwitz = Oświęcim Poland 50°2N 19°11E 83 H6

Auski Roadhouse Australia 22°22S 118°43E 148 D2
Austen Harbour Canada 12°55N 92°45E 127 H11
Austerlitz = Slavkov u Brna Czechia 49°10N 16°52E 79 B9
Austin Minn., U.S.A. 43°40N 92°58W 172 D7
Austin Nev., U.S.A. 39°30N 117°4W 168 G5
Austin Pa., U.S.A. 41°38N 78°6W 174 E6
Austin Tex., U.S.A. 30°17N 97°45W 176 F6
Austin, L. Australia 27°40S 118°0E 149 E2
Austin I. Canada 61°10N 94°0W 163 A10
Austra Norway 65°8N 11°55E 60 D14
Austral Is. = Tubuaï, Îs. French Polynesia 25°0S 150°0W 157 K13
Austral Seamount Chain Pac. Oc. 24°0S 150°0W 157 K13
Australia ■ Oceania 23°0S 135°0E 147 D6
Australian-Antarctic Basin S. Ocean 60°0S 120°0E 55 C9
Australian Capital Territory □ Australia 35°30S 149°0E 153 C8
Australind Australia 33°17S 115°42E 149 F2
Austria ■ Europe 47°0N 14°0E 78 E7
Austvågøya Norway 68°20N 14°40E 60 B16
Auterive France 43°21N 1°29E 72 E5
Authie → France 50°22N 1°38E 71 B8
Authon-du-Perche France 48°12N 0°54E 70 D7
Autlán de Navarro Mexico 19°46N 104°22W 180 D4
Autun France 46°58N 4°17E 71 F11
Auvergne France 45°20N 2°55E 72 C6
Auvergne, Mts. d' France 45°20N 2°55E 72 C6
Auvergne-Rhône-Alpes □ France 45°30N 5°0E 73 C8
Auvézère → France 45°12N 0°50E 72 C4
Auxerre France 47°48N 3°32E 71 E10
Auxi-le-Château France 50°15N 2°8E 71 B9
Auxonne France 47°10N 5°20E 71 E12
Auyuittuq △ Canada 67°30N 66°0W 161 D18
Auzances France 46°2N 2°30E 71 F9
Auzangate, Nevado Peru 13°47S 71°13W 188 C3
Av-Dovurak Russia 51°17N 91°35E 107 D10
Ava U.S.A. 36°57N 92°40W 172 G7
Avachinskaya Sopka Russia 53°15N 158°50E 107 D16
Avallon France 47°30N 3°53E 71 E10
Avalon U.S.A. 33°21N 118°20W 171 M8
Avalon Pen. Canada 47°30N 53°20W 165 C9
Avanigadda India 16°0N 80°56E 127 G5
Avanos Turkey 38°43N 34°51E 104 C6
Avantas Greece 40°57N 25°56E 99 F9
Avaré Brazil 23°4S 48°58W 191 A6
Avawatz Mts. U.S.A. 35°40N 116°30W 171 K10
Avdan Dağı Turkey 40°23N 29°46E 97 F13
Aveiro Brazil 3°10S 55°5W 187 D7
Aveiro Portugal 40°37N 8°38W 88 E2
Aveiro □ Portugal 40°40N 8°35W 88 E2
Āvej Iran 35°40N 49°15E 129 C6
Avellaneda Argentina 34°40S 58°22W 190 C4
Avellino Italy 40°54N 14°47E 95 B7
Avenal U.S.A. 36°0N 120°8W 170 K6
Aversa Italy 40°58N 14°12E 95 B7
Avery U.S.A. 47°15N 115°49W 168 C6
Aves, I. de W. Indies 15°45N 63°55W 183 C7
Aves, Is. las Venezuela 12°0N 67°30W 183 D6
Avesnes-sur-Helpe France 50°8N 3°55E 71 B10
Avesnois → France 50°10N 3°45E 71 B10
Avesta Sweden 60°9N 16°10E 62 D10
Aveyron □ France 44°22N 2°45E 72 D6
Aveyron → France 44°5N 1°16E 72 D5
Avezzano Italy 42°2N 13°25E 93 F10
Avgo Greece 35°33N 25°37E 99 F7
Aviá Terai Argentina 26°45S 60°50W 190 B3
Aviano Italy 46°4N 12°36E 93 B9
Aviemore U.K. 57°12N 3°50W 65 D5
Aviemore, L. N.Z. 44°37S 170°18E 155 E5
Avignon France 43°57N 4°50E 73 E8
Avigliana Italy 45°7N 4°43E 73 E8
Ávila Spain 40°39N 4°43W 88 E6
Ávila □ Spain 40°30N 5°0W 88 E6
Ávila, Sierra de Spain 40°40N 5°15W 88 E5
Avila Beach U.S.A. 35°11N 120°44W 171 K6
Avilés Spain 43°35N 5°57W 88 B5
Aviño Spain 43°36N 8°8W 88 B2
Avintes Portugal 41°7N 8°33W 88 D2
Avis Portugal 39°4N 7°53W 89 F3
Avis U.S.A. 41°11N 77°19W 174 E7
Avissawella Sri Lanka 6°56N 80°11E 127 L5
Aviz = Avis Portugal 39°4N 7°53W 89 F3
Avize France 48°59N 4°1E 71 D11
Avlonari Greece 38°31N 24°8E 98 C6
Avlum Denmark 56°16N 8°47E 63 H2
Avoca Australia 37°5S 143°26E 152 D5
Avoca U.S.A. 42°25N 77°25W 174 D7
Avoca → Australia 35°40S 143°43E 152 C5
Avoca → Ireland 52°48N 6°10W 64 D5
Avola Canada 51°45N 119°19W 162 C5
Avola Italy 36°56N 15°7E 95 F8
Avon U.S.A. 43°55N 77°45W 174 D7
Avon → Australia 31°40S 116°7E 149 F2
Avon → Bristol, U.K. 51°29N 2°41W 67 F5
Avon → Dorset, U.K. 50°44N 1°46W 67 G6
Avon → Warks., U.K. 52°0N 2°8W 67 E5
Avon Park U.S.A. 27°36N 81°31W 178 H5
Avondale Zimbabwe 17°43S 30°58E 143 F3
Avonlea Canada 50°0N 105°0W 163 D8
Avonmore Canada 45°10N 74°58W 175 A10
Avonmouth U.K. 51°30N 2°42W 67 F5
Avramov Bulgaria 42°45N 26°38E 97 C10
Avranches France 48°40N 1°20W 70 D5
Avre → France 48°47N 1°20E 70 D8
Avrig Romania 45°43N 24°21E 81 E9
Avrillé France 47°30N 0°35W 70 E6
Avtovac Bos.-H. 43°9N 18°35E 97 C8
Awa-Shima Japan 38°27N 139°14E 112 E9
Awaji Nigeria 24°5N 83°13E 125 G10
Awaji-Shima Japan 34°30N 134°50E 113 G7
'Awālī Bahrain 26°0N 50°30E 131 E6
Awantipur India 33°55N 75°3E 125 C6
Awanui N.Z. 35°4S 173°17E 154 B4
Awarja → India 17°5N 76°15E 126 F3
Awarua B. N.Z. 44°28S 168°4E 155 F1
Awarua Pt. N.Z. 44°15S 168°5E 155 F1
Awasa Ethiopia 7°2N 38°28E 137 F5
Awash Ethiopia 9°1N 40°10E 137 F5
Awaso Ghana 6°15N 2°22W 138 D4
Awat China 40°35N 80°24E 109 D10

Awatere → N.Z. 41°37S 174°10E 155 B9
Awbārī Libya 26°46N 12°57E 135 C8
Awbārī, Idehan Libya 27°10N 11°30E 135 C8
Awe, L. U.K. 56°17N 5°16W 65 E3
Awgu Nigeria 6°4N 7°24E 139 D6
Awjilah Libya 29°8N 21°7E 135 C10
Awka Nigeria 6°12N 7°5E 139 D6
Ax-les-Thermes France 42°44N 1°50E 72 F5
Axat France 42°48N 2°13E 72 F6
Axel Heiberg I. Canada 80°0N 90°0W 161 B14
Axim Ghana 4°51N 2°15W 138 E4
Axintele Romania 44°37N 26°47E 81 F11
Axios → Greece 40°57N 22°35E 96 F6
Axminster U.K. 50°46N 3°0W 67 G4
Axson U.S.A. 31°17N 82°44W 178 E7
Axvall Sweden 58°23N 13°34E 63 F7
Ay France 49°3N 4°1E 71 C11
Ayabaca Peru 4°40S 79°53W 188 A2
Ayabe Japan 35°20N 135°20E 113 G7
Ayacucho Argentina 37°5S 58°20W 190 D4
Ayacucho Peru 13°0S 74°0W 188 C3
Ayacucho □ Peru 14°0S 74°0W 188 C3
Ayaguz = Ayaköz Kazakhstan 48°10N 80°10E 109 E9
Ayakkum Hu China 37°30N 89°20E 109 E11
Ayaköz Kazakhstan 48°10N 80°10E 109 E9
Ayaköz → Kazakhstan 46°40N 79°14E 109 E9
Ayakudi India 10°28N 77°56E 127 J3
Ayamé Côte d'Ivoire 5°35N 3°9W 138 D4
Ayamonte Spain 37°12N 7°24W 89 H3
Ayan Russia 56°30N 138°16E 107 D14
Ayancık Turkey 41°57N 34°35E 104 B6
Ayangba Nigeria 7°31N 7°8E 139 D6
Ayas Turkey 40°2N 32°21E 104 B5
Ayaviri Peru 14°50S 70°35W 188 C3
Āybak Afghan. 36°15N 68°5E 109 E7
Aybastı Turkey 40°41N 37°23E 104 B7
Aydarko'l Ko'li Uzbekistan 40°50N 67°10E 109 D7
Aydın Turkey 37°51N 27°51E 104 D2
Aydın Dağları Turkey 38°0N 28°0E 99 D9
Aydıngkol Hu China 49°51N 89°15E 108 E3
Ayenngré Togo 8°40N 1°1E 139 D5
Ayer U.S.A. 42°34N 71°35W 175 D13
Ayer Hitam Malaysia 5°24N 100°16E 121 c
Ayerbe Spain 42°17N 0°41W 90 C4
Ayers Cliff Canada 45°10N 72°3W 175 A12
Ayers Rock = Uluru Australia 25°23S 131°5E 149 E5
Ayeyarwady = Ayeyawadi → Myanmar 15°50N 95°6E 123 M19
Ayeyawadi → Myanmar 15°50N 95°6E 123 M19
Ayia Napa Cyprus 34°59N 34°0E 101 E13
Ayia Phyla Cyprus 34°43N 33°1E 101 E12
Áyios Amvrósios Cyprus 35°20N 33°35E 101 D12
Áyios Seryios Cyprus 35°12N 33°53E 101 D12
Áyios Theodhoros Cyprus 35°22N 34°1E 101 D13
Áyios Yeóryios = Aghios Georgios Greece 37°28N 23°57E 98 D5
Aykhal Russia 66°0N 111°30E 107 C12
Aykirikçi Turkey 39°8N 30°9E 99 B12
Aylesbury U.K. 51°49N 0°49W 67 F7
Aylmer Canada 42°46N 80°59W 174 D4
Aylmer, L. Canada 64°5N 108°30W 160 E11
Ayn Dār Si. Arabia 25°55N 49°10E 129 E7
Ayn Sifni Iraq 36°41N 43°20E 105 D10
Ayn Zālah Iraq 36°45N 42°35E 105 D10
Ayna Spain 38°34N 2°3W 91 G2
Ayolas Paraguay 27°10S 56°59W 190 B4
Ayon, Ostrov Russia 69°50N 169°0E 107 C17
Ayora Spain 39°3N 1°3W 91 F3
Ayorou Niger 14°53N 1°0E 139 C5
'Ayoûn el 'Atroûs Mauritania 16°38N 9°37W 138 B3
Ayr Australia 19°35S 147°25E 150 B4
Ayr Canada 43°17N 80°27W 174 C4
Ayr U.K. 55°28N 4°38W 65 F4
Ayr → U.K. 55°28N 4°38W 65 F4
Ayrancı Turkey 37°21N 33°41E 104 D5
Ayrancılar Turkey 38°7N 27°18E 99 C9
Ayre, Pt. of I. of Man 54°25N 4°21W 66 C3
Ayrıbaba Turkmenistan 37°50N 66°34E 109 E7
Aysén □ Chile 46°30S 73°0W 192 F2
Ayteke Bi Kazakhstan 45°48N 62°6E 108 C6
Ayton Australia 15°56S 145°22E 150 B4
Aytos Bulgaria 42°42N 27°16E 97 D11
Aytoska Planina Bulgaria 42°45N 27°30E 97 D11
Ayu, Kepulauan Indonesia 0°35N 131°5E 119 D8
Ayutla Guatemala 14°40N 92°10W 182 D1
Ayutla de los Libres Mexico 16°54N 99°13W 181 D5
Ayutthaya = Phra Nakhon Si Ayutthaya Thailand 14°25N 100°30E 120 E3
Ayvacık Turkey 39°36N 26°24E 104 C2
Ayvalık Turkey 39°20N 26°46E 99 B8
Az Zabadānī Syria 33°43N 36°5E 130 B5
Az Ẓāhirīyah West Bank 31°25N 34°58E 130 D3
Az Zahrān Si. Arabia 26°10N 50°7E 129 E6
Az Zarqā Jordan 32°5N 36°4E 130 C5
Az Zarqā' U.A.E. 24°53N 53°4E 129 E7
Az Zarqā □ Jordan 32°5N 36°4E 130 C5
Az Zāwiyah Libya 32°52N 12°56E 135 B8
Az Zībār Iraq 36°52N 44°4E 105 D11
Az Zilfī Si. Arabia 26°12N 44°52E 128 E5
Az Zubayr Iraq 30°26N 47°40E 128 D5
Azahar, Costa del Spain 40°0N 0°5E 90 F5
Azambuja Portugal 39°4N 8°51W 89 F2
Azamgarh India 26°5N 83°13E 125 F10
Azangaro Peru 14°55S 70°13W 188 C3
Azaouad Mali 19°0N 3°0W 138 B4
Azaouak, Vallée de l' Mali 15°50N 3°20E 138 B6
Āzar Shahr Iran 37°45N 45°59E 105 D11
Azara Nigeria 8°22N 9°12E 139 D7
Azarán Iran 37°25N 47°16E 105 D12
Āzārbāyjān = Azerbaijan ■ Asia 40°20N 48°0E 87 K9
Āzārbāyjān-e Gharbī □ Iran 37°0N 44°30E 128 B5

Āzārbāyjān-e Sharqī □ Iran 37°20N 47°0E 128 B5
Azare Nigeria 11°55N 10°10E 139 C7
Azay-le-Rideau France 47°16N 0°30E 70 E7
A'zāz Syria 36°36N 37°4E 104 D7
Azbine = Aïr Niger 18°30N 8°0E 139 B6
Azeffoun Algeria 36°51N 4°22E 136 A4
Azemmour Morocco 33°20N 9°20W 136 B2
Azerbaijan ■ Asia 40°20N 48°0E 87 K9
Azezo Ethiopia 12°28N 37°15E 137 E4
Azimganj India 24°14N 88°16E 125 G13
Aznā Iran 33°30N 49°16E 128 C5
Azogues Ecuador 2°35S 78°0W 186 D3
Azores = Açores, Is. dos Atl. Oc. 38°0N 27°0W 134 a
Azores-Biscay Rise Atl. Oc. 42°0N 20°0W 56 D9
Azov Russia 47°3N 39°25E 87 G4
Azov, Sea of Europe 46°0N 36°30E 85 J9
Azovskoye More = Azov, Sea of Europe 46°0N 36°30E 85 J9
Azpeitia Spain 43°12N 2°19W 90 B2
Azraq ash Shīshān Jordan 31°50N 36°49E 130 D5
Azrou Morocco 33°28N 5°19W 136 B3
Aztec U.S.A. 36°49N 107°59W 169 H10
Azua de Compostela Dom. Rep. 18°25N 70°44W 183 C5
Azuaga Spain 38°16N 5°39W 89 G5
Azuara Spain 41°15N 0°53W 90 D4
Azuer → Spain 39°8N 3°36W 89 F7
Azuero, Pen. de Panama 7°30N 80°30W 182 E3
Azuga Romania 45°27N 25°31E 81 E10
Azul Argentina 36°42S 59°43W 190 D4
Azumino Japan 36°20N 137°50E 113 F8
Azur, Côte d' France 43°25N 7°10E 73 E11
Azusa U.S.A. 34°8N 117°52W 179 L9
Azzaba Algeria 36°48N 7°6E 136 A6
Azzano Décimo Italy 45°52N 12°56E 93 C9
Azzel Matti, Sebkra Algeria 26°10N 0°43E 136 C4

B

Ba Be △ Vietnam 22°25N 105°37E 120 A5
Ba Don Vietnam 17°45N 106°26E 120 D6
Ba Dong Vietnam 9°40N 106°33E 121 H6
Ba Ngoi Vietnam 11°54N 109°10E 121 G7
Ba Ria Vietnam 10°30N 107°10E 121 G6
Ba Tri Vietnam 10°2N 106°36E 121 G6
Ba Vì △ Vietnam 21°1N 105°22E 120 B5
Ba Xian = Bazhou China 39°8N 116°22E 114 E9
Baa Indonesia 10°50S 123°0E 148 B3
Baalbek = Ba'labakk Lebanon 34°0N 36°10E 130 B5
Baamonde Spain 43°7N 7°44W 88 B3
Baardheere Somalia 2°20N 42°27E 131 G3
Baarle-Nassau Belgium 51°27N 4°56E 69 C4
Bab el Mandeb Red Sea 12°35N 43°25E 131 E3
Baba Bulgaria 42°44N 23°59E 96 D7
Bābā, Koh-i- Afghan. 34°30N 67°0E 109 F7
Baba Budan Hills India 13°30N 75°44E 127 H2
Baba Burnu Turkey 39°29N 26°2E 99 B8
Baba dağ Azerbaijan 41°0N 48°19E 87 K9
Bābā Kalū Iran 30°7N 50°49E 129 D6
Babaçulândia Brazil 7°13S 47°46W 189 D9
Babadag Romania 44°53N 28°44E 81 F13
Babaeski Turkey 41°26N 27°6E 99 E11
Babahoyo Ecuador 1°40S 79°30W 186 D3
Babai = Sarju → India 27°21N 81°23E 125 F9
Babai → Nepal 28°10N 82°21E 125 E10
Babana Nigeria 10°31N 3°46E 139 C5
Babar Algeria 35°10N 7°6E 136 A5
Babar Indonesia 8°0S 129°30E 119 F7
Babar Pakistan 31°7N 69°32E 124 D3
Babarkach Pakistan 29°45N 68°0E 124 E3
Babayevo Russia 59°24N 35°55E 84 C8
Babb U.S.A. 48°51N 113°27W 168 B7
Babenhausen Germany 49°57N 8°57E 77 F4
Bābeni Romania 44°59N 24°11E 81 F9
Baberu India 25°33N 80°43E 125 G9
Babi Besar, Pulau Malaysia 2°25N 103°59E 121 L4
Babia Gora Europe 49°38N 19°38E 83 J6
Babian Jiang → China 22°55N 101°47E 116 F3
Bābil □ Iraq 32°30N 44°30E 128 C5
Babimost Poland 52°10N 15°49E 83 F2
Babinda Australia 17°20S 145°56E 150 B4
Babine → Canada 55°22N 126°37W 162 B3
Babine L. Canada 54°48N 126°0W 162 C3
Babo Indonesia 2°30S 133°30E 119 E8
Babócsa Hungary 46°2N 17°21E 80 D2
Bābol Iran 36°40N 52°50E 129 B7
Bābol Sar Iran 36°45N 52°45E 129 B7
Babor, Dj. Algeria 36°31N 5°25E 136 A5
Baborów Poland 50°7N 18°1E 83 H5
Baboua C.A.R. 5°49N 14°58E 140 C2
Babruysk Belarus 53°10N 29°15E 75 B15
Babson Park U.S.A. 27°49N 81°32W 178 H5
Babuhri India 26°49N 69°43E 124 F1
Babuna Macedonia 41°30N 21°40E 96 E5
Babura Nigeria 12°51N 9°59E 139 C6
Babusar Pass Pakistan 35°12N 73°59E 125 B5
Babušnica Serbia 43°7N 22°27E 96 C6
Babuyan Chan. Phil. 18°40N 121°30E 119 A6
Babylon Iraq 32°34N 44°22E 105 F11
Bac Serbia 45°29N 19°15E 81 E8
Bac = Moldova 46°55N 29°26E 81 D14
Bac Can Vietnam 22°8N 105°49E 120 A5
Bac Giang Vietnam 21°16N 106°11E 116 G6
Bac Lieu Vietnam 9°17N 105°43E 121 H5
Bac Ninh Vietnam 21°13N 106°4E 116 G6
Bac Phan Vietnam 22°0N 105°0E 116 G5
Bacabal Brazil 4°15S 44°45W 189 D10
Bacalar Mexico 18°43N 88°27W 181 D7
Bacan, Kepulauan Indonesia 0°35S 127°30E 119 E7
Bacarra Phil. 18°15N 120°37E 119 A6
Bacău Romania 46°35N 26°55E 81 D12
Bacău □ Romania 46°30N 26°45E 81 D11
Baccarat France 48°28N 6°42E 71 D13
Bacchus Marsh Australia 37°43S 144°27E 152 D6
Bacerac Mexico 30°18N 108°50W 180 A3
Băcești Romania 46°50N 27°11E 81 D12

Bach Long Vi, Dao Vietnam 20°10N 107°40E 120 B6
Bach Ma △ Vietnam 16°11N 107°49E 120 D6
Bacharach Germany 50°3N 7°44E 77 E3
Bachhwara India 25°35N 85°54E 125 G11
Bachu China 39°46N 78°34E 108 E9
Bačina Serbia 43°42N 21°23E 96 C5
Back → Canada 65°10N 104°0W 160 D11
Bačka Palanka Serbia 45°17N 19°27E 80 E4
Bačka Topola Serbia 45°49N 19°39E 80 E4
Bäckebo Sweden 56°53N 16°4E 63 H10
Bäckefors Sweden 58°48N 12°9E 63 F6
Bäckhammar Sweden 59°10N 14°11E 62 E8
Bački Petrovac Serbia 45°29N 19°32E 80 E4
Backnang Germany 48°56N 9°26E 77 G5
Backstairs Passage Australia 35°40S 138°5E 152 C3
Bacolod Phil. 10°40N 122°57E 119 B6
Baconton U.S.A. 31°23N 84°10W 178 D5
Bacqueville-en-Caux France 49°47N 1°0E 70 C8
Bács-Kiskun □ Hungary 46°43N 19°30E 80 D4
Bácsalmás Hungary 46°8N 19°17E 80 D4
Bacuk Malaysia 6°4N 102°25E 121 J4
Bácum Mexico 27°33N 110°5W 180 B2
Bād Iran 33°41N 52°1E 129 C7
Bad → U.S.A. 44°21N 100°22W 172 C3
Bad Aussee Austria 47°43N 13°45E 78 D6
Bad Axe U.S.A. 43°48N 83°0W 174 C2
Bad Bergzabern Germany 49°6N 7°59E 77 F3
Bad Berleburg Germany 51°2N 8°26E 76 D4
Bad Bevensen Germany 53°5N 10°35E 76 B6
Bad Bramstedt Germany 53°55N 9°53E 76 B5
Bad Brückenau Germany 50°18N 9°47E 77 E5
Bad Doberan Germany 54°6N 11°53E 76 A7
Bad Driburg Germany 51°43N 9°1E 76 D5
Bad Ems Germany 50°20N 7°43E 77 E3
Bad Frankenhausen Germany 51°21N 11°5E 76 D7
Bad Freienwalde Germany 52°46N 14°1E 76 C10
Bad Goisern Austria 47°38N 13°38E 78 D6
Bad Harzburg Germany 51°52N 10°34E 76 D6
Bad Hersfeld Germany 50°52N 9°42E 76 E5
Bad Hofgastein Austria 47°17N 13°6E 78 D6
Bad Homburg Germany 50°13N 8°38E 77 E4
Bad Honnef Germany 50°38N 7°13E 76 E3
Bad Iburg Germany 52°10N 8°3E 76 C4
Bad Ischl Austria 47°44N 13°38E 78 D6
Bad Kissingen Germany 50°11N 10°4E 76 E6
Bad Königshofen Germany 50°17N 10°28E 77 E6
Bad Kreuznach Germany 49°50N 7°51E 77 F3
Bad Krozingen Germany 47°54N 7°42E 77 H3
Bad Laasphe Germany 50°56N 8°25E 76 E4
Bad Langensalza Germany 51°5N 10°38E 76 D6
Bad Lauterberg Germany 51°38N 10°28E 76 D6
Bad Leonfelden Austria 48°31N 14°18E 78 C7
Bad Liebenwerda Germany 51°31N 13°24E 76 D9
Bad Mergentheim Germany 49°28N 9°42E 77 F5
Bad Münstereifel Germany 50°33N 6°46E 76 E2
Bad Nauheim Germany 50°21N 8°43E 77 E4
Bad Neuenahr-Ahrweiler Germany 50°32N 7°5E 76 E3
Bad Neustadt Germany 50°18N 10°13E 77 E6
Bad Oeynhausen Germany 52°12N 8°46E 76 C4
Bad Oldesloe Germany 53°48N 10°22E 76 B6
Bad Orb Germany 50°13N 9°22E 77 E5
Bad Pyrmont Germany 51°59N 9°16E 76 D5
Bad Reichenhall Germany 47°43N 12°54E 77 H8
Bad Säckingen Germany 47°33N 7°56E 77 H3
Bad Salzuflen Germany 52°5N 8°45E 76 C4
Bad Sankt Leonhard Austria 46°58N 14°47E 78 E7
Bad Schwartau Germany 53°55N 10°41E 76 B6
Bad Segeberg Germany 53°56N 10°17E 76 B6
Bad Tölz Germany 47°46N 11°34E 77 H7
Bad Urach Germany 48°29N 9°25E 77 G5
Bad Vöslau Austria 47°58N 16°13E 79 D9
Bad Waldsee Germany 47°55N 9°45E 77 H5
Bad Wildungen Germany 51°7N 9°7E 76 D5
Bad Wimpfen Germany 49°13N 9°11E 77 F5
Bad Windsheim Germany 49°30N 10°25E 77 F6
Bad Zwischenahn Germany 53°12N 8°1E 76 B4
Bada Barabil India 22°7N 85°24E 125 H11
Badagara = Vadakara India 11°35N 75°40E 127 J2
Badagri Nigeria 6°25N 2°55E 139 D5
Badain Jaran Shamo China 40°23N 102°0E 110 C9
Badajós, L. Brazil 3°15S 62°50W 186 D6
Badajoz Spain 38°50N 6°59W 89 G4
Badajoz □ Spain 38°40N 6°30W 89 G4
Badakhshān □ Afghan. 36°30N 71°0E 109 E8
Badaling China 40°20N 116°0E 114 D9
Badalona Spain 41°26N 2°15E 90 D7
Badalzai Afghan. 29°50N 65°35E 124 E1
Badami India 15°55N 75°41E 127 G2
Badampahar India 22°10N 86°10E 126 D8
Badanah Si. Arabia 30°58N 41°30E 128 D4
Badarinath India 30°45N 79°30E 125 D8
Badas, Kepulauan Indonesia 0°45N 107°5E 118 D5
Baddo → Pakistan 28°0N 64°20E 127 A1
Bade Indonesia 7°10S 139°35E 119 F9
Badeggi Nigeria 9°1N 6°8E 139 D6
Baden Austria 48°1N 16°13E 79 C9
Baden Switz. 47°28N 8°18E 78 E3
Baden-Baden Germany 48°44N 8°13E 77 G4
Baden-Württemberg □ Germany 48°20N 8°40E 77 G4
Badgam India 34°1N 74°45E 125 B6
Badgastein Austria 47°7N 13°9E 78 D6
Badger Canada 49°0N 56°4W 165 C8
Badger U.S.A. 36°38N 119°1W 170 J7
Badgingarra △ Australia 30°23S 115°22E 149 F2
Badia Polésine Italy 45°6N 11°29E 93 C8
Badiar △ Guinea 13°37N 13°11W 138 C2

Badin Pakistan 24°38N 68°54E 124 G3
Badinka ⌓ Mali 13°31N 9°28W 138 C3
Badlands U.S.A. 43°55N 102°30W 172 D2
Badlands △ U.S.A. 43°38N 102°56W 172 D2
Badme Africa 14°43N 37°48E 131 E2
Badnera India 20°48N 77°44E 126 D3
Badogo Mali 11°2N 8°13W 138 C3
Badoumbé Mali 13°42N 10°15W 138 C2
Badrah Iraq 33°6N 45°58E 105 F11
Badrain Jaran Shamo China 40°40N 103°20E 114 D2
Badrinath India 30°44N 79°29E 125 D8
Badu Australia 10°7S 142°11E 150 a
Badulla Sri Lanka 7°1N 81°7E 127 L5
Badung, Bukit Indonesia 8°49S 115°10E 119 K18
Badung, Selat Indonesia 8°40S 115°22E 119 K18
Badvel India 14°45N 79°3E 127 G4
Baena Spain 37°37N 4°20W 89 H6
Baengnyeongdo S. Korea 37°57N 124°40E 115 F13
Baerami Australia 32°27S 150°27E 153 B9
Baetov Kyrgyzstan 41°13N 74°54E 109 D8
Baeza Spain 37°57N 3°25W 89 H7
Bafang Cameroon 5°9N 10°11E 139 D7
Bafatá Guinea-Biss. 12°8N 14°40W 138 C2
Baffin B. N. Amer. 72°0N 64°0W 158 B13
Baffin I. Canada 68°0N 75°0W 161 D17
Bafia Cameroon 4°40N 11°10E 139 E7
Bafilo Togo 9°22N 1°22E 139 D5
Bafing → Mali 13°49N 10°50W 138 C2
Bafing △ Mali 12°38N 10°28W 138 C2
Bafliyūn Syria 36°37N 36°59E 128 B3
Bafoulabé Mali 13°50N 10°55W 138 C2
Bafoussam Cameroon 5°28N 10°25E 139 D7
Bāfq Iran 31°40N 55°25E 129 D7
Bafra Turkey 41°34N 35°54E 104 B6
Bafra Burnu Turkey 41°45N 36°2E 104 B7
Bāft Iran 29°15N 56°38E 129 D8
Bafut Cameroon 6°6N 10°2E 139 D7
Bafwasende Dem. Rep. of the Congo 1°3N 27°5E 142 B2
Bagaha India 27°6N 84°5E 126 A7
Bagalkot India 16°10N 75°40E 127 F2
Bagam Niger 15°43N 6°35E 139 B6
Bagamoyo Tanzania 6°28S 38°55E 142 D4
Bagan Datoh Malaysia 3°59N 100°47E 121 L3
Bagan Serai Malaysia 5°1N 100°32E 121 K3
Baganga Phil. 7°34N 126°33E 119 C7
Bagani Namibia 18°7S 21°41E 144 A3
Bagansiapiapi Indonesia 2°12N 100°50E 118 D2
Bagasra India 21°30N 71°0E 124 J4
Bagaud India 22°19N 75°53E 124 H6
Bagdad Calif., U.S.A. 34°35N 115°53W 171 L11
Bagdad Fla., U.S.A. 30°36N 87°2W 179 E2
Bagdarin Russia 54°26N 113°36E 107 D12
Bagé Brazil 31°20S 54°15W 191 C5
Bagenalstown Ireland 52°42N 6°58W 64 D5
Bagepalli India 13°47N 77°47E 127 H3
Bageshwar India 29°51N 79°46E 125 E8
Bagevadi India 16°35N 75°58E 126 F2
Baggs U.S.A. 41°2N 107°39W 168 F10
Bagh Pakistan 33°59N 73°45E 125 C5
Baghain → India 25°32N 81°1E 125 G9
Baghdād Iraq 33°20N 44°23E 105 F11
Baghdadi Georgia 42°5N 42°49E 105 A10
Bagheria Italy 38°5N 13°30E 94 D6
Baghlān Afghan. 32°12N 68°46E 109 F7
Baghlān □ Afghan. 36°0N 68°30E 109 E7
Bagley U.S.A. 47°32N 95°24W 172 B6
Baglung Nepal 28°16N 83°36E 125 E10
Bagnara Cálabra Italy 38°17N 15°48E 95 D8
Bagnasco Italy 44°18N 8°2E 92 D5
Bagnères-de-Bigorre France 43°5N 0°9E 72 E4
Bagnères-de-Luchon France 42°47N 0°38E 72 F4
Bagni di Lucca Italy 44°1N 10°35E 92 D7
Bagno di Romagna Italy 43°50N 11°57E 93 E8
Bagnoles-de-l'Orne France 48°32N 0°25W 70 D6
Bagnols-sur-Cèze France 44°10N 4°36E 73 D8
Bagnorégio Italy 42°37N 12°5E 93 F9
Bago Myanmar 17°20N 96°29E 123 L20
Bagodar India 24°5N 85°52E 125 G11
Bagrationovsk Russia 54°23N 20°39E 82 D7
Bagrdan Serbia 44°5N 21°11E 96 B5
Bagua Peru 5°35S 78°22W 188 B2
Baguio Phil. 16°26N 120°34E 119 A6
Bağyurdu Turkey 38°25N 27°41E 99 C9
Bagzane, Monts Niger 17°43N 8°45E 139 B6
Bahabón de Esgueva Spain 41°52N 3°43W 88 D7
Bahadurganj India 26°16N 87°49E 125 F12
Bahadurgarh India 28°40N 76°57E 124 E7
Bahama, Canal Viejo de W. Indies 22°10N 77°30W 182 B4
Bahamas ■ N. Amer. 24°0N 75°0W 183 B5
Bahār Iran 34°54N 48°26E 105 E13
Baharampur India 24°2N 88°27E 125 G13
Baharîya, El Wâhât al Egypt 28°0N 28°50E 137 F6
Baharu Pandan = Pandan Malaysia 1°32N 103°46E 121 d
Bahawalnagar Pakistan 30°0N 73°15E 124 E5
Bahawalpur Pakistan 29°24N 71°40E 124 E4
Bahçe Turkey 37°13N 36°34E 104 D7
Bahçecik Turkey 40°41N 29°44E 97 F13
Bäherden Turkmenistan 38°25N 57°26E 129 B8
Baheri India 28°45N 79°34E 125 E8
Bahgul → India 27°45N 79°36E 125 F8
Bahi Tanzania 5°58S 35°21E 142 D4
Bahi Swamp Tanzania 6°10S 35°0E 142 D4
Bahía = Salvador Brazil 13°0S 38°30W 189 C3
Bahía □ Brazil 12°0S 42°0W 189 C2
Bahía, Is. de la Honduras 16°45N 86°15W 182 C2
Bahía Blanca Argentina 38°35S 62°13W 190 D3
Bahía de Caráquez Ecuador 0°40S 80°27W 186 D2
Bahía de Los Angeles Mexico 28°56N 113°34W 180 B2
Bahía Honda Cuba 22°54N 83°10W 182 B3
Bahía Kino Mexico 28°47N 111°58W 180 B2
Bahía Laura Argentina 48°10S 66°30W 192 C3
Bahía Mansa Chile 40°33S 73°46W 192 B2
Bahía Negra Paraguay 20°5S 58°5W 186 H7
Bahir Dar Ethiopia 11°37N 37°10E 131 E2
Bahmanzād Iran 31°15N 51°47E 129 D6
Bahmer Algeria 27°32N 0°10W 136 C3
Bahr el Ahmar □ Sudan 20°0N 35°0E 137 D4
Bahraich India 27°38N 81°37E 125 F9
Bahrain ■ Asia 26°0N 50°35E 129 E6
Bahror India 27°51N 76°20E 124 F7
Bāhū Kalāt Iran 25°43N 61°25E 129 E9
Bai Mali 13°35N 3°28W 138 C4
Bai Bung, Mui = Ca Mau, Mui Vietnam 8°38N 104°44E 121 H5
Bai Thuong Vietnam 19°54N 105°23E 120 C5
Baia de Aramă Romania 45°0N 22°50E 80 E7
Baia Mare Romania 47°40N 23°35E 81 C8
Baia-Sprie Romania 47°41N 23°43E 81 C8
Baião Brazil 2°40S 49°40W 187 D9
Baïbokoum Chad 7°46N 15°43E 135 G9
Baicheng Jilin, China 45°38N 122°42E 115 B12
Baicheng Xinjiang Uygur, China 41°46N 81°52E 109 D10
Băicoi Romania 45°3N 25°52E 81 E10
Baidoa = Baydhabo Somalia 3°8N 43°30E 131 G3
Baie-Comeau Canada 49°12N 68°10W 165 C6
Baie-St-Paul Canada 47°28N 70°32W 165 C5
Baie Ste-Anne Seychelles 4°18S 55°45E 141 b
Baie-Trinité Canada 49°25N 67°20W 165 C6
Baie Verte Canada 49°55N 56°12W 165 C8
Baignes-Ste-Radegonde France 45°23N 0°25W 72 C3
Baigneux-les-Juifs France 47°31N 4°39E 71 E11
Baihar India 22°6N 80°33E 125 H9
Baihe Hubei, China 32°50N 110°5E 117 A8
Baihe Jilin, China 42°27N 128°9E 115 C15
Baihetan Dam China 27°11N 102°54E 116 D4
Ba'ījī Iraq 35°0N 43°30E 105 E10
Baijnath India 29°55N 79°37E 125 E8
Baikal, L. = Baykal, Oz. Russia 53°0N 108°0E 107 D11
Baikonur = Bayqonyr Kazakhstan 45°40N 63°20E 108 C6
Baikunthpur India 23°15N 82°33E 125 H10
Bailadila, Mt. India 18°43N 81°15E 126 E5
Baile Átha Cliath = Dublin Ireland 53°21N 6°15W 64 C5
Baile Átha Fhirdhia = Ardee Ireland 53°52N 6°33W 64 C5
Baile Átha Í = Athy Ireland 53°0N 7°0W 64 C5
Baile Átha Luain = Athlone Ireland 53°25N 7°56W 64 C4
Baile Átha Troim = Trim Ireland 53°33N 6°48W 64 C5
Baile Brigín = Balbriggan Ireland 53°37N 6°11W 64 C5
Băile Govora Romania 45°5N 24°11E 81 E9
Băile Herculane Romania 44°53N 22°26E 80 F7
Băile Olănești Romania 45°12N 24°14E 81 E9
Baile Sear = Baleshare U.K. 57°31N 7°22W 65 D1
Băile Tușnad Romania 46°9N 25°51E 81 D10
Bailén Spain 38°8N 3°48W 89 G7
Băilești Romania 44°1N 23°20E 81 F8
Bailhongal India 15°55N 74°53E 127 G2
Bailieborough Ireland 53°56N 6°59W 64 C5
Baima China 33°0N 100°26E 116 A3
Bain-de-Bretagne France 47°50N 1°40W 70 E5
Bainbridge Ga., U.S.A. 30°55N 84°35W 178 E5
Bainbridge N.Y., U.S.A. 42°18N 75°29W 175 D9
Bainbridge Island U.S.A. 47°38N 122°32W 170 C4
Baine China 42°0N 128°0E 111 C14
Baing Indonesia 10°14S 120°34E 119 F6
Bainiu China 32°50N 112°15E 117 A9
Baiona Spain 42°6N 8°52W 88 C2
Bā'ir Jordan 30°45N 36°55E 130 E5
Baird Mts. U.S.A. 67°0N 160°0W 166 B8
Bairiki = Tarawa Kiribati 1°30N 173°0E 156 G9
Bairin Youqi China 43°30N 118°35E 115 C10
Bairin Zuoqi China 43°58N 119°15E 115 C10
Bairnsdale Australia 37°48S 147°36E 153 D7
Baisha China 34°20N 112°32E 114 G7
Baisha Li China 19°12N 109°20E 117 a
Baishan = Hunjiang China 41°54N 126°26E 115 D14
Baishan China 42°43N 127°14E 115 C14
Baissa Nigeria 7°14N 10°38E 139 D7
Baitadi Nepal 29°35N 80°25E 125 E9
Baitarani → India 20°45N 86°48E 126 D8
Baixa Grande Brazil 11°57S 40°11W 189 C2
Baixa Limia-Sierra do Xurés ⌓ Spain 41°59N 8°2W 88 D2
Baiyin China 36°45N 104°14E 114 F3
Baiyü China 31°16N 98°50E 116 B2
Baiyu Shan China 37°15N 107°30E 114 F4
Baj Baj India 22°30N 88°5E 125 H13
Baja Hungary 46°12N 18°59E 80 D3
Baja, Pta. Mexico 29°58N 115°49W 180 B1
Baja California Mexico 31°10N 115°12W 180 A1
Baja California □ Mexico 30°0N 115°0W 180 B2
Baja California Sur □ Mexico 25°50N 111°50W 180 B2
Bajag India 22°40N 81°21E 125 H9
Bajamar Canary Is. 28°33N 16°20W 100 F3
Bajana India 23°7N 71°49E 124 H4
Bajatrejo Indonesia 8°29S 114°19E 119 J17
Bajawa Indonesia 8°47S 120°59E 119 F6
Bajera Indonesia 8°31S 115°2E 119 J18
Bājgīrān Iran 37°36N 58°24E 129 B8
Bajimba, Mt. Australia 29°17S 152°6E 151 D5
Bajina Bašta Serbia 43°58N 19°35E 96 C3
Bajmok Serbia 45°57N 19°24E 80 E4
Bajo Boquete Panama 8°46N 82°27W 182 E3
Bajo Caracoles Argentina 47°27S 70°56W 192 C2
Bajo Nuevo Caribbean 15°40N 78°50W 182 C4
Bajoga Nigeria 10°57N 11°20E 139 C7
Bajool Australia 23°40S 150°35E 150 C5
Bak Hungary 46°43N 16°51E 80 D1
Bakar Croatia 45°18N 14°32E 93 C11
Bakassi Pen. Cameroon 4°42N 8°20E 139 E6
Bakel Senegal 14°56N 12°20W 138 C2
Baker Calif., U.S.A. 35°16N 116°4W 171 K10
Baker Fla., U.S.A. 30°48N 86°41W 179 E3
Baker Mont., U.S.A. 46°22N 104°17W 168 C11
Baker, Canal Chile 47°45S 74°45W 192 C2
Baker, L. Canada 64°0N 96°0W 160 E12
Baker, Mt. U.S.A. 48°50N 121°49W 168 B3
Baker City U.S.A. 44°47N 117°50W 168 D5
Baker I. Pac. Oc. 0°10N 176°35W 156 G10
Baker I. U.S.A. 55°20N 133°40W 162 B2
Baker L. Australia 26°54S 126°5E 149 E4
Baker Lake Canada 64°20N 96°3W 160 E12
Bakerhill U.S.A. 31°47N 85°18W 178 D4
Bakers Creek Australia 21°13S 149°7E 150 C4
Bakers Dozen Is. Canada 56°45N 78°45W 164 A4
Bakersfield Calif., U.S.A. 35°23N 119°1W 171 K8
Bakersfield Vt., U.S.A. 44°45N 72°48W 175 B12
Bakharden = Bäherden Turkmenistan 38°25N 57°26E 129 B8
Bakhchysaray Ukraine 44°40N 33°45E 85 K7
Bakhmach Ukraine 51°10N 32°45E 85 G7
Bākhtarān = Kermānshāh Iran 34°23N 47°0E 105 E12
Bākhtarān = Kermānshāh □ Iran 34°0N 46°30E 128 C5
Bakhtegān, Daryācheh-ye Iran 29°40N 53°50E 129 D7
Bakhtegān △ Iran 29°51N 53°40E 129 D7
Bakı Azerbaijan 40°29N 49°56E 87 K9
Bakır → Turkey 38°55N 27°0E 99 C9
Bakırdaği Turkey 38°13N 35°46E 104 C6
Bakkafjörður Iceland 66°2N 14°48W 60 C6
Bakkagerði Iceland 65°31N 13°49W 60 D7
Baklan Turkey 38°0N 29°36E 99 C11
Bako Côte d'Ivoire 9°8N 7°40W 138 D3
Bakony Hungary 47°10N 17°30E 80 C2
Bakony Forest = Bakony Hungary 47°10N 17°30E 80 C2
Bakori Nigeria 11°34N 7°25E 139 C6
Bakouma C.A.R. 5°40N 22°56E 140 C4
Baksan Russia 43°42N 43°32E 87 J6
Bakswaho India 24°15N 79°18E 125 G8
Baku = Bakı Azerbaijan 40°29N 49°56E 87 K9
Bakundi Nigeria 8°2N 10°45E 139 D7
Bakuriani Georgia 41°44N 43°31E 105 B10
Bakutis Coast Antarctica 74°0S 120°0W 55 D15
Baky = Bakı Azerbaijan 40°29N 49°56E 87 K9
Bala Canada 45°1N 79°37W 174 A5
Bala Senegal 14°1N 13°8W 138 C2
Balâ Turkey 39°32N 33°6E 104 C5
Bala U.K. 52°54N 3°36W 66 E4
Bala, L. U.K. 52°53N 3°37W 66 E4
Bālā Morghāb Afghan. 35°35N 63°20E 108 E6
Balabac I. Phil. 8°0N 117°0E 118 C5
Balabac Str. E. Indies 7°53N 117°5E 118 C5
Balabagh Afghan. 34°25N 70°12E 124 B4
Ba'labakk Lebanon 34°0N 36°10E 130 B5
Balabalangan, Kepulauan Indonesia 2°20S 117°30E 118 E5
Bălăciţa Romania 44°23N 23°8E 81 F8
Balad Iraq 34°0N 44°9E 105 F11
Balad Rūz Iraq 33°42N 45°5E 105 F11
Bālādeh Fārs, Iran 29°17N 51°56E 129 D6
Bālādeh Māzandaran, Iran 36°12N 51°48E 129 B6
Balaghat India 21°49N 80°12E 126 D5
Balaghat Ra. India 18°50N 76°30E 126 E3
Balaguer Spain 41°50N 0°50E 90 D5
Balakän Azerbaijan 41°43N 46°24E 87 K8
Balakhna Russia 56°25N 43°32E 86 B6
Balaklava Australia 34°7S 138°22E 152 C3
Balaklava Ukraine 44°30N 33°30E 85 K7
Balakliya Ukraine 49°28N 36°55E 85 H9
Balakovo Russia 52°4N 47°55E 86 D8
Balamau India 27°10N 80°21E 125 F9
Bălan Romania 46°39N 25°49E 81 D10
Balancán Mexico 17°48N 91°32W 181 D6
Balangir India 20°43N 83°35E 126 D6
Balapur India 20°40N 76°45E 126 D3
Balashikha Russia 55°48N 37°58E 84 E9
Balashov Russia 51°30N 43°10E 86 E6
Balasinor India 22°57N 73°23E 124 H5
Balasore = Baleshwar India 21°35N 87°3E 126 D8
Balassagyarmat Hungary 48°4N 19°15E 80 B4
Balât Egypt 25°36N 29°19E 137 B2
Balaton Hungary 46°50N 17°40E 80 D2
Balaton-Felvidéki △ Hungary 46°52N 17°30E 80 D2
Balatonboglár Hungary 46°46N 17°40E 80 D2
Balatonfüred Hungary 46°58N 17°54E 80 D2
Balatonszentgyörgy Hungary 46°41N 17°19E 80 D2
Balazote Spain 38°54N 2°9W 91 G2
Balbieriškis Lithuania 54°32N 23°53E 82 D10
Balbigny France 45°49N 4°11E 73 C8
Balbina, Represa de Brazil 2°0S 59°30W 186 D7
Balboa Panama 8°57N 79°34W 182 E4
Balbriggan Ireland 53°37N 6°11W 64 C5
Balcarce Argentina 38°0S 58°10W 190 D4
Balcarres Canada 50°50N 103°35W 163 C8
Bălcești Romania 44°37N 23°57E 81 F8
Balchik Bulgaria 43°28N 28°11E 97 C12
Balclutha N.Z. 46°15S 169°45E 155 G4
Balcones Escarpment U.S.A. 29°30N 99°15W 176 G5
Balçova Turkey 38°22N 27°4E 99 C9
Bald I. Australia 34°57S 118°27E 149 F2
Bald Knob U.S.A. 35°19N 91°34W 176 D9
Baldock L. Canada 56°33N 97°57W 163 B9
Baldwin Fla., U.S.A. 30°18N 81°59W 178 E8
Baldwin Mich., U.S.A. 43°54N 85°51W 173 D11
Baldwin Pa., U.S.A. 40°21N 79°58W 174 F5
Baldwinsville U.S.A. 43°10N 76°20W 175 C8
Baldy Peak U.S.A. 33°54N 109°34W 169 K9
Bale Croatia 45°4N 13°46E 93 C10
Baleares, Is. Spain 39°30N 3°0E 100 B10
Balearic Is. = Baleares, Is. Spain 39°30N 3°0E 100 B10
Baleia, Pta. da Brazil 17°40S 39°7W 189 D3
Baleine → Canada 58°15N 67°40W 165 A6
Baleine, Petite R. de la → Canada 56°0N 76°45W 164 A4
Băleni Romania 45°48N 27°51E 81 E12
Baler Phil. 15°46N 121°34E 119 A6
Baleshare U.K. 57°31N 7°22W 65 D1
Baleshwar India 21°35N 87°3E 126 D8
Baley Russia 51°36N 116°37E 107 D12
Balezino Russia 58°2N 53°6E 86 B11
Balfate Honduras 15°48N 86°25W 182 C2
Balgo Australia 20°9S 127°58E 148 D4
Balharshah India 19°50N 79°23E 126 E4
Bali Cameroon 5°54N 10°0E 139 D7
Bali Greece 35°25N 24°47E 101 D6
Bali India 25°11N 73°17E 124 G5
Bali Indonesia 8°20S 115°0E 118 F4
Bali □ Indonesia 8°20S 115°0E 118 F5
Bali, Selat Indonesia 8°18S 114°25E 119 J17
Bali Barat △ Indonesia 8°12S 114°35E 119 J17
Bali Sea Indonesia 8°0S 115°0E 119 J17
Balia S. Leone 9°22N 11°1W 138 D2
Baliapal India 21°40N 87°17E 125 J12
Baligród Poland 49°20N 22°17E 83 J9
Baliguda India 20°12N 83°55E 126 D6
Balik Pulau Malaysia 5°21N 100°14E 121 c
Balıkeşir Turkey 39°39N 27°53E 99 B9
Balıkeşir □ Turkey 39°45N 28°0E 99 B9
Balīkh → Syria 35°52N 39°12E 105 E8
Balıklıçeşme Turkey 40°18N 27°5E 97 F11
Balikpapan Indonesia 1°10S 116°55E 118 E5
Balimbing Phil. 5°5N 119°58E 119 C5
Baling Malaysia 5°41N 100°55E 121 K3
Bälinge Sweden 59°57N 17°33E 62 E11
Balingen Germany 48°16N 8°51E 77 G4
Balinţ Romania 45°48N 21°54E 80 E6
Balkan □ Turkmenistan 40°0N 54°30E 108 D5
Balkan Mts. = Stara Planina Bulgaria 43°15N 23°0E 96 C7
Balkanabat Turkmenistan 39°30N 54°22E 129 B7
Balkh Afghan. 36°44N 66°47E 109 E7
Balkh □ Afghan. 36°50N 67°0E 109 E7
Balkhash = Balqash Kazakhstan 46°50N 74°50E 106 E8
Balkhash, Ozero = Balqash Köli Kazakhstan 46°0N 74°50E 109 C8
Balkonda India 18°52N 78°21E 126 E4
Ballachulish U.K. 56°41N 5°8W 65 E3
Balladonia Australia 32°27S 123°51E 149 F3
Ballaghadereen Ireland 53°55N 8°34W 64 C3
Ballan Australia 37°35S 144°13E 152 D6
Ballarat Australia 37°33S 143°50E 152 D5
Ballard, L. Australia 29°20S 120°40E 149 E3
Ballari India 15°10N 76°56E 127 G3
Ballater U.K. 57°3N 3°3W 65 D5
Ballé Mali 15°18N 8°33W 138 B3
Ballenas, Canal de Mexico 29°10N 113°29W 180 B2
Balleny Is. Antarctica 66°30S 163°0E 55 C11
Balleroy France 49°11N 0°50W 70 C6
Ballerup Denmark 55°43N 12°21E 63 J6
Ballestas, Is. Peru 13°44S 76°25W 188 C2
Ballı Turkey 40°50N 27°3E 97 F11
Ballia India 25°46N 84°12E 125 G11
Ballina Australia 28°50S 153°31E 151 D5
Ballina Ireland 54°7N 9°9W 64 B2
Ballinasloe Ireland 53°20N 8°13W 64 C3
Ballincollig Ireland 51°53N 8°33W 64 E3
Ballinger U.S.A. 31°45N 99°57W 176 F5
Ballinrobe Ireland 53°38N 9°13W 64 C2
Ballinskelligs B. Ireland 51°48N 10°13W 64 E1
Ballon France 48°10N 0°14E 70 D7
Ballons des Vosges ⌓ France 48°0N 7°0E 71 E14
Ballsh Albania 40°36N 19°44E 96 F3
Ballston Spa U.S.A. 43°0N 73°51W 175 D11
Ballyboghil Ireland 53°32N 6°16W 64 C5
Ballybunion Ireland 52°31N 9°40W 64 D2
Ballycanew Ireland 52°37N 6°19W 64 D5
Ballycastle U.K. 55°12N 6°15W 64 A5
Ballyclare U.K. 54°46N 6°0W 64 B5
Ballycroy △ Ireland 54°5N 9°50W 64 B2
Ballydehob Ireland 51°34N 9°28W 64 E2
Ballygawley U.K. 54°27N 7°2W 64 B4
Ballyhaunis Ireland 53°46N 8°46W 64 C3
Ballyheigue Ireland 52°23N 9°49W 64 D2
Ballymena U.K. 54°52N 6°17W 64 B5
Ballymoney U.K. 55°5N 6°31W 64 A5
Ballymote Ireland 54°5N 8°31W 64 B3
Ballynahinch U.K. 54°24N 5°54W 64 B6
Ballyporeen Ireland 52°16N 8°6W 64 D3
Ballyquintin Pt. U.K. 54°20N 5°30W 64 B6
Ballyshannon Ireland 54°30N 8°11W 64 B3
Balmaceda Chile 46°0S 71°50W 192 C2
Balmaseda Spain 43°11N 3°12W 90 B1
Balmazújváros Hungary 47°37N 21°21E 80 C6
Balmertown Canada 51°4N 93°41W 163 C10
Balmoral Australia 37°15S 141°48E 152 D4
Balmorhea U.S.A. 30°59N 103°45W 176 F3
Balneário Camboriú Brazil 26°59S 48°38W 191 B6
Balochistan = Baluchistan □ Pakistan 27°30N 65°0E 122 F4
Balod India 20°44N 81°13E 126 D5
Balonne → Australia 28°47S 147°56E 151 D4
Balotra India 25°50N 72°14E 124 G5
Balpyq Bī Kazakhstan 44°52N 78°12E 109 D9
Balqash Kazakhstan 46°50N 74°50E 106 E8
Balqash Köli Kazakhstan 46°0N 74°50E 109 C8
Balrampur India 27°30N 82°20E 125 F10
Balranald Australia 34°38S 143°33E 152 C5
Balş Romania 44°22N 24°5E 81 F9
Balsapuerto Peru 5°48S 76°33W 188 B2
Balsas → Maranhão, Brazil 7°15S 44°35W 189 B2
Balsas → Tocantins, Brazil 9°58S 47°52W 189 B1
Balsas → Mexico 17°55N 102°10W 180 D4
Balsas del Norte Mexico 18°0N 99°46W 181 D5
Bålsta Sweden 59°35N 17°30E 62 E11
Balta Romania 44°54N 22°38E 80 F7
Balta Ukraine 47°56N 29°45E 81 C14
Balta Ialomiţei Romania 44°20N 27°55E 81 F12
Baltaköl Kazakhstan 43°7N 67°46E 109 D7
Baltanás Spain 41°56N 4°15W 88 D6
Bălţi Moldova 47°48N 27°58E 81 C12
Baltic Sea Europe 57°0N 19°0E 61 H18
Baltîm Egypt 31°35N 31°10E 137 E7
Baltimore Ireland 51°29N 9°22W 64 E2
Baltimore Md., U.S.A. 39°17N 76°36W 173 F15
Baltimore Ohio, U.S.A. 39°51N 82°36W 174 G2
Baltimore-Washington Int. ✈ (BWI) U.S.A. 39°10N 76°40W 173 F15
Baltinglass Ireland 52°56N 6°43W 64 D5
Baltit Pakistan 36°15N 74°40E 125 A6
Baltiysk Russia 54°41N 19°58E 82 D6
Baltrum Germany 53°43N 7°24E 76 B3
Baluchistan □ Pakistan 27°30N 65°0E 122 F4
Baluqtybulaq Kazakhstan 50°51N 51°8E 86 E10
Balurghat India 25°15N 88°44E 125 G13
Balvi Latvia 57°8N 27°15E 84 D4
Balya Turkey 39°44N 27°35E 99 B9
Balykchy Kyrgyzstan 42°26N 76°12E 109 D9
Balyqshy Kazakhstan 47°4N 51°52E 108 C4
Bam Iran 29°7N 58°14E 129 D8
Bama China 24°8N 107°12E 116 E6
Bama Nigeria 11°33N 13°41E 139 C7
Bamaga Australia 10°50S 142°25E 150 A3
Bamaji L. Canada 51°9N 91°25W 164 B1
Bamako Mali 12°34N 7°55W 138 C3
Bamba Mali 17°5N 1°24W 139 B4
Bambamarca Peru 6°36S 78°32W 188 B2
Bambara Maoundé Mali 13°26N 4°3W 138 B4
Bambari C.A.R. 5°40N 20°35E 140 C4
Bambaroo Australia 18°50S 146°10E 150 B4
Bambaya Guinea 10°55N 13°38W 138 D2
Bamberg Germany 49°54N 10°54E 77 F6
Bamberg U.S.A. 33°18N 81°2W 178 B8
Bambey Senegal 14°42N 16°28W 138 C1
Bambili Dem. Rep. of the Congo 3°40N 26°0E 142 B2
Bamboi Ghana 8°13N 2°1W 138 D4
Bambuí Brazil 20°1S 45°58W 189 E1
Bamburgh U.K. 55°37N 1°43W 66 B6
Bamenda Cameroon 5°57N 10°11E 139 D7
Bamendjing, L. de Cameroon 5°50N 10°30E 139 D7
Bamfield Canada 48°45N 125°10W 162 D3
Bāmīān Afghan. 34°49N 67°49E 109 F7
Bāmīān □ Afghan. 35°0N 67°0E 122 B5
Bamiancheng China 43°15N 124°2E 115 C13
Bamkin Cameroon 6°3N 11°27E 139 D7
Bamou △ Iran 29°45N 52°35E 129 D7
Bampūr Iran 27°15N 60°21E 129 E9
Bampūr → Iran 27°24N 59°0E 129 E8
Ban Burkina Faso 14°5N 2°27W 138 C4
Ban Ao Tu Khun Thailand 8°9N 98°20E 121 a
Ban Ban Laos 19°31N 103°30E 120 C4
Ban Bang Hin Thailand 9°32N 98°35E 121 H2
Ban Bang Khu Thailand 7°57N 98°23E 121 a
Ban Bang Rong Thailand 8°3N 98°25E 121 a
Ban Bo Phut Thailand 9°33N 100°2E 121 b
Ban Chaweng Thailand 9°32N 100°3E 121 b
Ban Chiang Thailand 17°30N 103°10E 120 D4
Ban Chiang Klang Thailand 19°25N 100°55E 120 C3
Ban Choho Thailand 15°2N 102°9E 120 E4
Ban Dan Lan Hoi Thailand 17°0N 99°35E 120 D2
Ban Don = Surat Thani Thailand 9°6N 99°20E 121 H2
Ban Don Vietnam 12°53N 107°48E 120 F6
Ban Don, Ao → Thailand 9°20N 99°25E 121 H2
Ban Dong Thailand 19°30N 100°59E 120 C3
Ban Hong Thailand 18°18N 98°50E 120 C2
Ban Hua Thanon Thailand 9°26N 100°1E 121 b
Ban Kantang Thailand 7°25N 99°31E 121 J2
Ban Karon Thailand 7°51N 98°18E 121 a
Ban Kata Thailand 7°50N 98°18E 121 a
Ban Keun Laos 18°22N 102°35E 120 C4
Ban Khai Thailand 12°46N 101°18E 120 F3
Ban Kheun Laos 20°13N 101°7E 120 B3
Ban Khlong Khian Thailand 8°10N 98°26E 121 a
Ban Khlong Kua Thailand 6°57N 100°8E 121 J3
Ban Khuan Thailand 8°20N 98°25E 121 a
Ban Ko Yai Chim Thailand 11°17N 99°26E 121 G2
Ban Laem Thailand 13°13N 99°59E 120 F2
Ban Lamai Thailand 9°28N 100°3E 121 b
Ban Lao Ngam Laos 15°28N 106°10E 120 E6
Ban Le Kathe Thailand 15°49N 98°53E 120 E2
Ban Lo Po Noi Thailand 8°1N 98°34E 121 a
Ban Mae Chedi Thailand 19°11N 99°31E 120 C2
Ban Mae Nam Thailand 9°34N 100°0E 121 b
Ban Mae Sariang Thailand 18°10N 97°56E 120 C1
Ban Mê Thuôt = Buon Ma Thuot Vietnam 12°40N 108°3E 120 F7
Ban Mi Thailand 15°3N 100°32E 120 E3
Ban Muang Mo Laos 19°4N 103°58E 120 C4
Ban Na Bo Thailand 9°19N 99°41E 121 b
Ban Na San Thailand 8°53N 99°52E 121 H2
Ban Na Tong Laos 20°56N 101°47E 120 B3
Ban Nam Bac Laos 20°38N 102°20E 120 B4
Ban Nammi Laos 17°7N 105°40E 120 D5
Ban Nong Bok Laos 17°5N 104°48E 120 D5
Ban Nong Pling Thailand 15°40N 100°10E 120 E3
Ban Pak Chan Thailand 10°32N 98°51E 121 G2
Ban Patong Thailand 7°54N 98°18E 121 a
Ban Phai Thailand 16°4N 102°44E 120 D4
Ban Phak Chit Thailand 8°0N 98°24E 121 a
Ban Pong Thailand 13°50N 99°55E 120 F2
Ban Rawai Thailand 7°47N 98°20E 121 a
Ban Ron Phibun Thailand 8°9N 99°51E 121 H2
Ban Sakhu Thailand 8°4N 98°18E 121 a
Ban Sanam Chai Thailand 7°33N 100°25E 121 J3
Ban Tak Thailand 17°2N 99°4E 120 D2
Ban Tako Thailand 14°5N 102°40E 120 E4
Ban Tha Nun Thailand 8°12N 98°18E 121 a
Ban Tha Rua Thailand 7°59N 98°22E 121 a
Ban Tha Yu Thailand 8°17N 98°22E 121 a
Ban Thong Krut Thailand 9°25N 99°57E 121 b
Ban Xien Kok Laos 20°54N 100°39E 120 B3
Ban Yen Nhan Vietnam 20°57N 106°2E 120 B6
Banaba Kiribati 0°45S 169°50E 156 H8
Banagher Ireland 53°11N 7°59W 64 C3
Banalia Dem. Rep. of the Congo 1°32N 25°5E 142 B2
Banam Cambodia 11°20N 105°17E 121 G5
Banamba Mali 13°29N 7°22W 138 C3
Banana Is. S. Leone 8°7N 13°15W 138 D2
Bananal, I. do Brazil 11°30S 50°30W 187 F8
Bananga India 6°57N 93°54E 127 L11
Banaras = Varanasi India 25°22N 83°0E 125 G10
Banas → Gujarat, India 23°45N 71°25E 124 H4
Banas → Mad. P., India 24°15N 81°30E 125 G9
Bânâs, Ras Egypt 23°57N 35°59E 137 C4
Banaz Turkey 38°46N 29°46E 99 C11
Banaz → Turkey 38°12N 29°14E 99 C11
Banbridge U.K. 54°22N 6°16W 64 B5
Banbury U.K. 52°4N 1°20W 67 E6
Banchory U.K. 57°3N 2°29W 65 D6
Bancroft Canada 45°3N 77°51W 174 A7
Band Romania 46°30N 24°25E 81 D9
Band Bonī Iran 25°30N 59°33E 129 E8
Band Qīr Iran 31°39N 48°53E 129 D6
Banda Mad. P., India 24°3N 78°57E 125 G8
Banda Maharashtra, India 15°49N 73°52E 127 G1
Banda Ut. P., India 25°30N 80°26E 125 G9
Banda, Kepulauan Indonesia 4°37S 129°50E 119 E7
Banda Aceh Indonesia 5°35N 95°20E 118 C1
Banda Banda, Mt. Australia 31°10S 152°28E 153 A10
Banda Elat Indonesia 5°40S 133°5E 119 F8
Banda Is. = Banda, Kepulauan Indonesia 4°37S 129°50E 119 E7
Banda Sea Indonesia 6°0S 130°0E 119 F8
Bandai-Asahi △ Japan 37°38N 140°5E 112 F10
Bandai-San Japan 37°36N 140°4E 112 F10
Bandama → Côte d'Ivoire 6°32N 4°30W 138 D3
Bandama Blanc → Côte d'Ivoire 6°55N 5°30W 138 D4
Bandama Rouge → Côte d'Ivoire 6°55N 5°30W 138 D4
Bandān Iran 31°23N 60°44E 129 D9
Bandanaira Indonesia 4°32S 129°54E 119 E7
Bandanwara India 26°9N 74°38E 124 F6
Bandar = Machilipatnam India 16°12N 81°8E 127 F5
Bandar-e Abbās Iran 27°15N 56°15E 129 E8
Bandar-e Anzalī Iran 37°30N 49°30E 105 D13
Bandar-e Bushehr = Būshehr Iran 28°55N 50°55E 129 D6
Bandar-e Chārak Iran 26°45N 54°20E 129 E7
Bandar-e Deylam Iran 30°5N 50°10E 129 D6
Bandar-e Emām Khomeynī Iran 30°30N 49°5E 129 D6
Bandar-e Lengeh Iran 26°35N 54°58E 129 E7
Bandar-e Maqām Iran 26°56N 53°29E 129 E7
Bandar-e Ma'shur Iran 30°35N 49°10E 129 D6
Bandar-e Rīg Iran 29°29N 50°38E 129 D6
Bandar-e Torkeman Iran 37°0N 54°10E 129 B7
Bandar Labuan Malaysia 5°20N 115°14E 118 C5
Bandar Lampung Indonesia 5°20S 105°10E 118 F3
Bandar Maharani = Muar Malaysia 2°3N 102°34E 121 L4
Bandar Penggaram = Batu Pahat Malaysia 1°50N 102°56E 121 M4
Bandar Seri Begawan Brunei 4°52N 115°0E 118 D5
Bandar Shahid Rajaee Iran 27°7N 56°4E 129 E8
Bandar Sri Aman Malaysia 1°15N 111°32E 118 D4
Bandawe Malawi 11°58S 34°5E 143 E3
Bande Spain 42°3N 7°58W 88 C3
Bandeira, Pico da Brazil 20°26S 41°47W 189 E2
Bandera Argentina 28°55S 62°20W 190 B3
Banderas, B. de Mexico 20°40N 105°25W 180 C3
Bandhavgarh India 23°40N 81°2E 125 H9
Bandhavgarh △ India 23°45N 81°10E 126 C5
Bandi → India 26°12N 75°47E 124 F6
Bandia → India 19°2N 80°28E 126 E5
Bandiagara Mali 14°12N 3°29W 138 C4
Bandiagara, Falaise de Mali 14°14N 3°29W 138 D4
Bandikui India 27°3N 76°34E 124 F7
Bandipur △ India 11°45N 76°30E 127 J3
Bandırma Turkey 40°20N 28°0E 97 F11
Bandjarmasin = Banjarmasin Indonesia 3°20S 114°35E 118 E4
Bandol France 43°8N 5°46E 73 E9
Bandon Ireland 51°44N 8°44W 64 E3
Bandon → Ireland 51°43N 8°37W 64 E3
Bandula Mozam. 19°0S 33°7E 143 F3
Bandundu Dem. Rep. of the Congo 3°15S 17°22E 140 E3
Bandung Indonesia 6°54S 107°36E 118 F3
Bané Burkina Faso 11°42N 0°15W 139 C4
Băneasa Romania 45°56N 27°55E 81 E12
Bāneh Iran 35°59N 45°53E 105 E11
Banes Cuba 21°0N 75°42W 183 B4
Banff Canada 51°10N 115°34W 162 C5
Banff U.K. 57°40N 2°33W 65 D6
Banff △ Canada 51°30N 116°15W 162 C5
Banfora Burkina Faso 10°40N 4°40W 138 C4
Bang Fai → Laos 16°57N 104°45E 120 D5
Bang Hieng → Laos 16°10N 105°10E 120 D5
Bang Krathum Thailand 16°34N 100°18E 120 D3
Bang Lang △ Thailand 5°58N 101°19E 121 K3
Bang Lang Res. Thailand 6°6N 101°17E 121 J3
Bang Mun Nak Thailand 16°2N 100°23E 120 D3
Bang Pa In Thailand 14°14N 100°35E 120 E3
Bang Rakam Thailand 16°45N 100°7E 120 D3
Bang Saphan Thailand 11°14N 99°28E 121 G2
Bang Thao Thailand 7°59N 98°18E 121 a
Bangaduni I. India 21°34N 88°52E 125 J13
Bangala Dam Zimbabwe 21°7S 31°25E 143 G3
Bangalore = Bengaluru India 12°59N 77°40E 127 H3
Banganapalle India 15°19N 78°14E 127 G4
Banganga → India 27°6N 77°25E 124 F6
Bangangté Cameroon 5°8N 10°32E 139 D7
Bangaon India 23°0N 88°47E 125 H13
Bangassou C.A.R. 4°55N 23°7E 140 D4
Banggai Indonesia 1°34S 123°30E 119 E6
Banggai, Kepulauan Indonesia 1°40S 123°30E 119 E6
Banggai Arch. = Banggai, Kepulauan Indonesia 1°40S 123°30E 119 E6
Banggi, Pulau Malaysia 7°17N 117°12E 118 C5
Banghāzī Libya 32°11N 20°3E 135 B10
Bangka Sulawesi, Indonesia 1°50N 125°5E 119 D7
Bangka Sumatera, Indonesia 2°0S 105°50E 118 E3
Bangka, Selat Indonesia 2°30S 105°30E 118 E3
Bangka-Belitung □ Indonesia 2°30S 107°0E 118 E3
Bangkalan Indonesia 7°2S 112°46E 119 G15
Bangkang Myanmar 22°4N 99°1E 116 F2
Bangkinang Indonesia 0°18N 101°5E 118 D2
Bangko Indonesia 2°5S 102°9E 118 E2
Bangkok Thailand 13°45N 100°35E 120 F3
Bangkok, Bight of Thailand 12°55N 100°30E 120 F3
Bangla = Paschimbanga □ India 23°0N 88°0E 125 H13
Bangladesh ■ Asia 24°0N 90°0E 123 H17
Bangli Indonesia 8°27S 115°21E 119 J18
Bangolo Côte d'Ivoire 7°1N 7°29W 138 D3
Bangong Co China 33°45N 78°43E 125 C8
Bangor Down, U.K. 54°40N 5°40W 64 B6
Bangor Gwynedd, U.K. 53°14N 4°8W 66 D3

Bangor Maine, U.S.A. 44°48N 68°46W 173 C19
Bangor Pa., U.S.A. 40°52N 75°13W 175 F9
Bangued Phil. 17°40N 120°37E 119 A6
Bangui C.A.R. 4°23N 18°35E 140 D3
Banguru
  Dem. Rep. of the Congo 0°30N 27°10E 142 B2
Bangweulu, L. Zambia 11°0S 30°0E 143 E3
Bangweulu Swamp
  Zambia 11°20S 30°15E 143 E3
Banhine △ Mozam. 22°49S 32°55E 145 B5
Bani Burkina Faso 13°43N 0°10W 139 C4
Bani Dom. Rep. 18°16N 70°22W 183 C5
Bani → Mali 14°30N 4°12W 138 C4
Bani, Jebel Morocco 29°16N 8°0W 136 C2
Bani Bangou Niger 15°3N 2°42E 139 B5
Banī Sa'd Iraq 33°34N 44°32E 105 F11
Bania Côte d'Ivoire 9°4N 3°6W 138 D4
Banihal Pass India 33°30N 75°12E 125 C6
Banikoara Benin 11°18N 2°26E 139 C5
Banissa Kenya 3°55N 40°19E 142 B5
Bāniyās Syria 35°10N 36°0E 104 E6
Banja India 24°53N 86°55E 125 G12
Bankas Mali 14°4N 3°31W 138 C4
Bankeryd Sweden 57°53N 14°6E 63 G8
Banket Zimbabwe 17°27S 30°19E 143 F3
Bankilaré Niger 14°35N 0°44E 139 C5
Bankipore India 25°35N 85°10E 123 G14
Bankot India 17°58N 73°2E 126 F1
Banks U.S.A. 31°49N 85°51W 178 D4
Banks I. = Moa
  Australia 10°11S 142°16E 150 A4
Banks I. B.C., Canada 53°20N 130°0W 162 C3
Banks I. N.W.T.,
  Canada 73°15N 121°30W 160 C7
Banks L. U.S.A. 31°2N 83°6W 178 D6
Banks Pen. N.Z. 43°45S 173°15E 155 D8
Banks Str. Australia 40°40S 148°10E 151 G4
Bankura India 23°11N 87°18E 125 H12
Bankya Bulgaria 42°43N 23°8E 96 D7
Banmankhi India 25°53N 87°11E 125 F10
Bann → Armagh, U.K. 54°30N 6°31W 64 B5
Bann → L'derry., U.K. 55°8N 6°41W 64 A5
Bannalec France 47°57N 3°42W 70 E3
Bannang Sata Thailand 6°16N 101°16E 121 J3
Bannerton Australia 34°42S 142°47E 152 C5
Banning U.S.A. 33°56N 116°53W 171 M10
Bannockburn Canada 44°39N 77°33W 174 B7
Bannockburn U.K. 56°5N 3°55W 65 E5
Bannockburn
  Zimbabwe 20°17S 29°48E 143 G2
Bannu Pakistan 33°0N 70°18E 122 C7
Bano India 22°40N 84°55E 125 H11
Bañolas = Banyoles Spain 42°16N 2°44E 90 C7
Banon France 44°2N 5°38E 73 D9
Baños de la Encina Spain 38°10N 3°46W 89 G1
Baños de Molgas Spain 42°15N 7°40W 88 C3
Bánovce nad Bebravou
  Slovakia 48°44N 18°16E 79 C11
Banovići Bos.-H. 44°25N 18°32E 80 F3
Bansagar Dam India 24°11N 81°17E 126 B5
Bansgaon India 25°53N 87°11E 125 F10
Banská Bystrica
  Slovakia 48°46N 19°14E 79 C12
Banská Štiavnica
  Slovakia 48°25N 18°55E 79 C11
Bansko Bulgaria 41°52N 23°28E 96 E7
Banskobystrický □
  Slovakia 48°30N 19°0E 79 C12
Banswara India 23°32N 74°24E 124 H6
Bantaeng Indonesia 5°32S 119°56E 119 F5
Bantaji → Nigeria 8°6N 10°5E 139 D7
Banteay Prei Nokor
  Cambodia 11°56N 105°40E 121 G5
Banten □ Indonesia 6°30S 106°0E 119 G11
Bantry Ireland 51°41N 9°27W 64 E2
Bantry B. Ireland 51°37N 9°44W 64 E2
Bantva India 21°29N 70°12E 124 J4
Bantval India 12°55N 75°0E 127 H2
Banya Bulgaria 42°33N 24°50E 97 D8
Banya, Pta. de la Spain 40°33N 0°36E 90 E5
Banyak, Kepulauan
  Indonesia 2°10N 97°10E 118 D1
Banyalbufar Spain 39°42N 2°31E 100 B9
Banyeres de Mariola
  Spain 38°44N 0°38W 91 G4
Banyo Cameroon 6°52N 11°45E 139 D7
Banyoles Spain 42°16N 2°44E 90 C7
Banyuls-sur-Mer France 42°28N 3°8E 72 F7
Banyuwangi Indonesia 8°13S 114°21E 119 J17
Banzare Coast Antarctica 68°0S 125°0E 55 C9
Bao Ha Vietnam 22°11N 104°21E 116 F5
Bao Lac Vietnam 22°57N 105°40E 120 A5
Bao Loc Vietnam 11°32N 107°48E 121 G6
Bao'an China 22°34N 113°52E 111 a
Baocheng China 33°12N 106°56E 116 A4
Baode China 39°1N 111°5E 114 E6
Baodi China 39°38N 117°20E 115 E9
Baoding China 38°50N 115°28E 114 E8
Baoji China 34°20N 107°5E 114 H4
Baojing China 28°45N 109°41E 116 C7
Baokang China 31°54N 111°12E 117 B8
Baoshan Shanghai, China
  31°24N 121°28E 117 B13
Baoshan Yunnan, China 25°10N 99°5E 116 E2
Baotou China 40°32N 110°2E 114 D6
Baoulé → Mali 12°36N 9°45W 138 C3
Baoxing China 30°24N 102°50E 116 B4
Baoying China 33°17N 119°20E 117 A12
Bayou = Ledong China 18°41N 109°5E 117 a
Bap India 27°23N 72°18E 124 F5
Bapatla India 15°55N 80°30E 127 G5
Bapaume France 50°7N 2°50E 71 B9
Bāqerābād Iran 33°45N 51°38E 129 C6
Ba'qūbah Iraq 33°45N 44°50E 105 F11
Baquedano Chile 23°20S 69°52W 190 A2
Bar Ukraine 49°4N 27°40E 75 D14
Bar Montenegro 42°8N 19°6E 96 D3
Bar Bigha India 25°21N 85°47E 125 G11
Bar Harbor U.S.A. 44°23N 68°13W 173 C19
Bar-le-Duc France 48°47N 5°10E 71 D12
Bar-sur-Aube France 48°14N 4°40E 71 D11
Bar-sur-Seine France 48°7N 4°22E 71 D11
Bara India 25°16N 81°43E 125 G9
Bara Romania 45°57N 22°3E 81 C12
Bara Banki India 26°55N 81°12E 125 F8
Barabai Indonesia 2°32S 115°34E 118 E5

Baraboo U.S.A. 43°28N 89°45W 172 D9
Baracoa Cuba 20°20N 74°30W 183 B5
Baradā → Syria 33°33N 36°34E 130 B5
Baradero Argentina 33°52S 59°29W 190 C4
Baradine Australia 30°56S 149°4E 153 A4
Baraga U.S.A. 46°47N 88°30W 172 B9
Bārāganul Romania 44°49N 27°31E 81 F12
Baragoi Kenya 1°47N 36°47E 142 B4
Barah → India 27°42N 77°5E 124 F6
Barahona Dom. Rep. 18°13N 71°7W 183 C5
Barail Range India 25°15N 93°20E 123 G18
Barajas, Madrid ✈ (MAD)
  Spain 40°26N 3°34W 88 E7
Barakaldo Spain 43°18N 2°59W 90 B2
Barakar → India 24°7N 86°14E 125 G12
Barakee △ Australia 31°37S 151°53E 153 A9
Barakot India 21°33N 84°59E 125 J11
Barakpur India 22°47N 88°21E 125 H13
Baralaba Australia 24°13S 149°50E 150 C4
Baralzon L. Canada 60°0N 98°3W 163 B9
Baramati India 18°11N 74°33E 126 E2
Baramba India 20°25N 85°23E 126 D7
Barameiya Sudan 18°32N 36°38E 137 D4
Baramula India 34°15N 74°20E 125 B6
Baran India 25°9N 76°40E 124 G7
Baran → Pakistan 25°13N 68°17E 124 G3
Barañain Spain 42°48N 1°40W 90 C3
Baranavichy Belarus 53°10N 26°0E 75 B14
Barani Burkina Faso 13°9N 3°51W 138 C4
Baranof U.S.A. 57°5N 134°50W 162 B2
Baranof I. U.S.A. 57°0N 135°0W 160 F4
Baranów Sandomierski
  Poland 50°29N 21°30E 83 H11
Baranya □ Hungary 46°0N 18°15E 80 E3
Barão de Cocais Brazil 19°56S 43°28W 189 D2
Barão de Grajaú Brazil 6°45S 43°1W 189 B2
Baraolt Romania 46°5N 25°34E 81 D10
Baraona Spain 41°17N 2°39W 90 D2
Barapasi Indonesia 2°15S 137°5E 119 E9
Barasat India 22°46N 88°31E 125 H13
Barat Daya, Kepulauan
  Indonesia 7°30S 128°0E 119 F7
Baratang I. India 12°13N 92°45E 127 H11
Barataria B. U.S.A. 29°20N 89°55W 177 G10
Barauda India 23°33N 75°15E 124 H6
Baraut India 29°13N 77°7E 124 E7
Barbacena Brazil 21°15S 43°56W 191 A7
Barbados ■ W. Indies 13°10N 59°30W 183 d
Barbalha Brazil 7°19S 39°17W 189 B3
Barban Croatia 45°5N 14°2E 93 C11
Barbària, C. de Spain 38°39N 1°24E 100 C7
Barbaros Turkey 40°54N 27°27E 97 B11
Barbas, C. W. Sahara 22°20N 16°42W 134 D2
Barbastro Spain 42°2N 0°5E 90 C5
Barbate Spain 36°13N 5°56W 89 J5
Barberino di Mugello
  Italy 44°0N 11°15E 93 E8
Barberton S. Africa 25°42S 31°2E 145 D5
Barberton U.S.A. 41°1N 81°39W 174 E3
Barberville U.S.A. 29°11N 81°26W 179 F8
Barbezieux-St-Hilaire
  France 45°28N 0°9W 72 C3
Barbosa Colombia 5°57N 73°37W 186 B4
Barbourville U.S.A. 36°52N 83°53W 173 G12
Barbuda W. Indies 17°30N 61°40W 183 C7
Bârca Romania 43°59N 23°36E 81 G8
Barcaldine Australia 23°43S 145°6E 150 C4
Barcarrota Spain 38°31N 6°51W 89 G4
Barcellona Pozzo di Gotto
  Italy 38°9N 15°13E 95 D8
Barcelona Spain 41°22N 2°10E 90 D7
Barcelona Venezuela 10°10N 64°40W 186 A6
Barcelona □ Spain 41°30N 2°0E 90 D7
Barcelona, El Prat ✈ (BCN)
  Spain 41°18N 2°5E 90 D7
Barcelonnette Puerto Rico 18°27N 66°32W 183 d
Barcelonnette France 44°23N 6°40E 73 D10
Barcelos Brazil 1°0S 63°0W 188 D6
Barcin Poland 52°52N 17°55E 83 F4
Barclayville Liberia 4°48N 8°10W 138 E3
Barcoo → Australia 25°30S 142°50E 150 D3
Barcs Hungary 45°58N 17°28E 80 E2
Barczewo Poland 53°50N 20°42E 82 E7
Bárða Azerbaijan 40°25N 47°10E 87 K8
Barda del Medio
  Argentina 38°45S 68°11W 192 A3
Bardas Blancas
  Argentina 35°49S 69°45W 190 D2
Bardawīl, Sabkhet el
  Egypt 31°10N 33°15E 130 D2
Barddhaman India 23°14N 87°39E 125 H12
Bardejov Slovakia 49°18N 21°15E 79 B14
Bardera = Baardheere
  Somalia 2°20N 42°27E 131 G3
Bardi Italy 44°38N 9°44E 92 D6
Bardīyah Libya 31°45N 25°5E 128 E3
Bardoli India 21°12N 73°5E 126 D1
Bardolino Italy 45°33N 10°43E 92 C7
Bardonécchia Italy 45°5N 6°42E 92 C3
Bardsey I. U.K. 52°45N 4°47W 66 E3
Bardstown U.S.A. 37°49N 85°28W 173 G11
Bareilly India 28°22N 79°27E 125 E8
Barela India 23°6N 80°3E 125 H9
Barellan Australia 34°16S 146°24E 153 C7
Barentin France 49°33N 0°58E 70 C7
Barenton France 48°38N 0°50W 70 D6
Barents Sea Arctic 73°0N 39°0E 54 B8
Barentsøya Svalbard 78°25N 21°20E 57 B13
Barfleur France 49°40N 1°17W 70 C5
Barfleur, Pte. de France 49°42N 1°16W 70 C5
Barga India 44°4N 10°29E 92 D7
Bargara Australia 24°50S 152°25E 150 C5
Bargarh India 21°20N 83°37E 126 D6
Bargas Spain 39°56N 4°3W 88 F6
Barge Italy 44°43N 7°20E 92 D4
Bargi Dam India 22°59N 80°0E 128 C5
Barguzin Russia 53°37N 109°37E 107 D11
Barh India 25°29N 85°46E 125 G11
Barhaj India 26°18N 83°44E 125 F10
Barham Australia 35°36S 144°8E 152 C6
Barharwa India 24°52N 87°47E 125 G12
Barhi India 24°15N 85°25E 125 G11
Bari India 26°39N 77°39E 124 F7
Bari Italy 41°8N 16°51E 95 A9
Bari Doab Pakistan 30°20N 73°0E 124 D5
Bari Sadri India 24°28N 74°30E 124 G6

Bari Sardo Italy 39°50N 9°38E 94 C2
Bariadi Tanzania 2°48S 34°0E 142 C3
Barīdī, Ra's Si. Arabia 24°17N 37°31E 128 E3
Barīm Yemen 12°39N 43°25E 132 E8
Barinas Venezuela 8°36N 70°15W 186 B4
Baring, C. Canada 70°0N 117°30W 160 D8
Baring □ India 0°40N 36°0E 142 B4
Baringo, L. Kenya 0°47N 36°16E 142 B4
Baripada India 21°57N 86°45E 126 D8
Bâris Egypt 24°42N 30°31E 137 C3
Barisal Bangla. 22°45N 90°20E 123 H17
Barisal □ Bangla. 22°45N 90°20E 123 H17
Barisan, Pegunungan
  Indonesia 3°30S 102°15E 118 E2
Barito → Indonesia 4°0S 114°50E 118 E4
Baritú △ Argentina 23°43S 64°40W 190 A3
Barjac France 44°20N 4°22E 73 D8
Barjols France 43°34N 6°2E 73 E10
Barjūj, Wadi → Libya 25°26N 12°12E 135 C8
Bark L. Canada 45°27N 77°51W 174 A7
Barkakana India 23°37N 85°29E 125 H11
Barkal, J. Sudan 18°32N 31°50E 137 D3
Barkam China 31°51N 102°28E 116 B4
Barker China 43°20N 78°33W 174 C6
Barkley, L. U.S.A. 37°1N 88°14W 177 C10
Barkley Sound
  Canada 48°50N 125°10W 162 D3
Barkly East S. Africa 30°58S 27°33E 144 D4
Barkly Homestead
  Australia 19°52S 135°50E 150 B2
Barkly Tableland
  Australia 17°50S 136°40E 150 B2
Barkly West S. Africa 28°5S 24°31E 144 C3
Barkol Kazak Zizhixian
  China 43°37N 93°2E 110 C7
Barla Dağı Turkey 38°5N 30°40E 99 C12
Bârlad Romania 46°15N 27°38E 81 D12
Bârlad → Romania 45°38N 27°32E 81 E12
Barlee, L. Australia 29°15S 119°30E 149 E2
Barlee, Mt. Australia 24°38S 128°13E 149 D4
Barletta Italy 41°19N 16°17E 95 A9
Barlinek Poland 53°0N 15°15E 83 F2
Barlovento Cabo Verde 17°0N 25°0W 134 b
Barlovento Canary Is. 28°48N 17°48W 102 F2
Barlow L. Canada 62°0N 103°0W 163 A8
Barmedman Australia 34°9S 147°21E 153 C7
Barmer India 25°45N 71°20E 124 G4
Barmera Australia 34°15S 140°28E 152 C4
Barmouth U.K. 52°44N 4°4W 66 E3
Barmstedt Germany 53°47N 9°46E 76 B5
Barna → India 25°21N 83°3E 125 G10
Barnagar India 23°7N 75°19E 124 H6
Barnala India 30°23N 75°33E 124 D6
Barnard → Australia 31°34S 151°25E 153 A9
Barnard Castle U.K. 54°33N 1°55W 66 C6
Barnaul Russia 53°20N 83°40E 109 B10
Barnes U.S.A. 36°2S 144°49E 152 D6
Barnesville Ga., U.S.A. 33°3N 84°9W 178 D5
Barnesville Minn.,
  U.S.A. 46°43N 96°28W 172 B5
Barnet □ U.K. 51°38N 0°9W 67 F7
Barneveld Neths. 52°7N 5°36E 69 B5
Barneville-Carteret
  France 49°23N 1°46W 70 C5
Barnhart U.S.A. 31°8N 101°10W 176 F4
Barnsley U.K. 53°34N 1°27W 66 D6
Barnstable U.S.A. 41°42N 70°18W 173 E18
Barnstaple U.K. 51°5N 4°4W 67 F3
Barnstaple Bay = Bideford Bay
  U.K. 51°5N 4°20W 67 F3
Barnwell U.S.A. 33°15N 81°23W 178 D6
Baro Nigeria 8°35N 6°18E 139 D6
Baroda = Vadodara
  India 22°20N 73°10E 124 H5
Baroda India 25°29N 76°35E 124 G7
Baroe S. Africa 33°13S 24°33E 144 D3
Baron Ra. Australia 23°30S 127°45E 148 D4
Barong China 31°3N 99°20E 116 B2
Barotseland Zambia 15°0S 24°0E 141 H4
Barouéli Mali 13°4N 6°50W 138 C3
Barpali India 21°11N 83°35E 126 D6
Barpeta India 26°20N 91°10E 123 F17
Barqa Libya 27°0N 23°0E 135 C10
Barques, Pt. Aux U.S.A. 44°4N 82°58W 174 C4
Barquisimeto Venezuela 10°4N 69°19W 186 A5
Barr, Ras el Egypt 31°32N 31°50E 137 E7
Barr Smith Range
  Australia 27°4S 120°20E 149 E3
Barra Brazil 11°5S 43°10W 189 C2
Barra Gambia 13°28N 16°32W 138 C1
Barra U.K. 57°0N 7°29W 65 E1
Barra, Pta. Mozam. 23°48S 35°32E 145 B6
Barra, Sd. of U.K. 57°4N 7°25W 65 D1
Barra da Estiva Brazil 13°38S 41°19W 189 C2
Barra de Navidad
  Mexico 19°12N 104°41W 180 D4
Barra do Corda Brazil 5°30S 45°10W 189 B1
Barra do Garças Brazil 15°54S 52°16W 187 G8
Barra do Mendes Brazil 11°43S 42°4W 189 C2
Barra do Piraí Brazil 22°30S 43°50W 191 A7
Barra Falsa, Pta. da
  Mozam. 22°58S 35°37E 145 B6
Barra Hd. U.K. 56°47N 7°40W 65 E1
Barra Mansa Brazil 22°35S 44°12W 191 A7
Barraba Australia 30°21S 150°35E 153 A9
Barrackpur = Barakpur
  India 22°47N 88°21E 125 H13
Barrafranca Italy 37°22N 14°12E 95 E7
Barrāmīya Egypt 25°4N 33°47E 137 B3
Barranca Lima, Peru 10°45S 77°50W 188 C2
Barranca Loreto, Peru 4°50S 76°50W 188 B2
Barranca del Cobre
  Mexico 27°18N 107°40W 180 B3
Barrancabermeja
  Colombia 7°0N 73°50W 186 B4
Barrancas Venezuela 8°55N 62°5W 186 B6
Barrancos Portugal 38°10N 6°58W 89 G4
Barranqueras Argentina 27°30S 59°0W 190 B4
Barranquilla Colombia 11°0N 74°50W 186 A4
Barras Brazil 4°15S 42°18W 189 B2
Barraute Canada 48°26N 77°38W 172 A9
Barre Mass., U.S.A. 42°25N 72°6W 173 D17
Barre Vt., U.S.A. 44°12N 72°30W 175 B12
Barreal Argentina 31°33S 69°28W 190 C2
Barreiras Brazil 12°8S 45°0W 189 C2
Barreirinhas Brazil 2°30S 42°50W 189 A2
Barreiro Portugal 38°39N 9°5W 89 G1
Barreiros Brazil 8°49S 35°12W 189 C3
Barrême France 43°57N 6°23E 73 E10
Barren, Nosy Madag. 18°25S 43°40E 141 H8

Barren I. India 12°16N 93°51E 127 H11
Barretos Brazil 20°30S 48°35W 189 E1
Barrhead Canada 54°10N 114°24W 162 C6
Barrie Canada 44°24N 79°40W 174 B5
Barrier, C. N.Z. 36°25S 175°32E 154 C4
Barrier Ra. Australia 31°0S 141°30E 152 A4
Barrier Ra. Otago, N.Z. 44°15S 169°32E 155 E3
Barrier Ra. W. Coast,
  N.Z. 44°30S 168°30E 155 E3
Barrière Canada 51°12N 120°7W 162 C4
Barrineau Park U.S.A. 30°42N 87°26W 179 E2
Barrington L. Canada 41°44N 71°18W 175 E13
Barrington L. Canada 56°55N 100°15W 163 B8
Barrington Tops
  Australia 32°6S 151°28E 153 B9
Barrington Tops △
  Australia 32°4S 151°25E 153 B9
Barringun Australia 29°1S 145°41E 151 D4
Barron U.S.A. 45°24N 91°51W 172 C6
Barrow → Ireland 52°25N 6°58W 64 D5
Barrow, Pt. U.S.A. 71°23N 156°29W 166 A8
Barrow Creek
  Australia 21°30S 133°55E 150 C1
Barrow I. Australia 20°45S 115°20E 148 D2
Barrow-in-Furness U.K. 54°7N 3°14W 66 C4
Barrow Pt. Australia 14°20S 144°40E 150 A3
Barrow Ra. Australia 26°0S 127°40E 149 E4
Barrow Str. Canada 74°20N 95°0W 161 C13
Barruecopardo Spain 41°4N 6°40W 88 D4
Barruelo de Santullán
  Spain 42°54N 4°17W 88 C6
Barry U.K. 51°24N 3°16W 67 F4
Barry's Bay Canada 45°29N 77°41W 174 A7
Barsalogho Burkina Faso 13°25N 1°3W 139 C4
Barsat Pakistan 36°10N 72°45E 125 A5
Barsham Syria 35°21N 40°33E 105 E9
Barshatas Kazakhstan 48°10N 78°39E 109 C9
Barsi India 18°10N 75°50E 126 E2
Barsinghausen Germany 52°18N 9°28E 76 C5
Barstow Calif., U.S.A. 34°54N 117°1W 171 L9
Barth Germany 54°22N 12°42E 76 A8
Bartica Guyana 6°25N 58°40W 186 B7
Bartin Turkey 41°38N 32°21E 104 B5
Bartle Frere Australia 17°27S 145°50E 150 B4
Bartlesville U.S.A. 36°45N 95°59W 176 C7
Bartlett Calif., U.S.A. 36°29N 118°2W 170 J8
Bartlett Tenn., U.S.A. 35°12N 89°52W 177 D10
Bartlett, L. Canada 63°5N 118°20W 162 A5
Bartolomeu Dias
  Mozam. 21°10S 35°8E 143 G4
Barton U.S.A. 44°45N 72°11W 175 B12
Barton-upon-Humber
  U.K. 53°41N 0°25W 66 D7
Bartoszyce Poland 54°15N 20°55E 82 D7
Bartow Fla., U.S.A. 27°54N 81°50W 179 H8
Bartow Ga., U.S.A. 32°53N 82°29W 178 D7
Barú, Volcan Panama 8°55N 82°35W 182 E3
Barumba
  Dem. Rep. of the Congo 1°3N 23°37E 142 B1
Barúmini Italy 39°42N 8°59E 94 C1
Baruba, Nusa
  Indonesia 8°30S 113°30E 119 H15
Baruth Germany 52°4N 13°30E 76 C9
Baruun Urt Mongolia 46°46N 113°15E 111 B11
Baruunsuu Mongolia 43°43N 105°35E 114 C3
Barvinkove Ukraine 48°57N 37°0E 85 H9
Barwani India 22°2N 74°57E 124 H6
Barwice Poland 53°44N 16°21E 82 E3
Barwon → Australia 30°54N 83°44W 178 E6
Barxudarlı Azerbaijan 41°0N 45°14E 105 B11
Barycz → Poland 51°42N 16°15E 83 G3
Barysaw Belarus 54°17N 28°28E 75 A15
Barysh Russia 53°39N 47°8E 86 D8
Barzān Iraq 36°55N 44°3E 128 B5
Bârzava Romania 46°7N 21°59E 80 D6
Bas-Rhin □ France 48°40N 7°30E 71 D14
Bas-Sandaoua □
  Côte d'Ivoire 5°30N 7°0W 138 D3
Bašaïd Serbia 45°38N 20°25E 80 D5
Bāsa'idū Iran 26°35N 55°20E 129 E7
Basal Pakistan 33°33N 72°13E 124 C5
Basankusu
  Dem. Rep. of the Congo 1°5N 19°50E 140 D3
Basarabeasca Moldova 46°21N 28°58E 81 D13
Basarabi Romania 44°10N 28°26E 81 F13
Basarabia = Bessarabiya
  Moldova 47°0N 28°10E 75 E15
Basauri Spain 43°13N 2°53W 90 B2
Basavakalyan India 17°52N 76°57E 126 F3
Basawa Afghan. 34°15N 70°50E 124 B4
Bascuñán, C. Chile 28°52S 71°35W 190 B1
Basel Switz. 47°35N 7°35E 77 H3
Basel-Landschaft □
  Switz. 47°26N 7°45E 77 H3
Basento → Italy 40°20N 16°55E 95 B9
Bashākerd, Kūhhā-ye
  Iran 26°42N 58°35E 129 E8
Bashaw Canada 52°35N 112°58W 162 C6
Bāshī Iran 28°41N 51°4E 129 D6
Bashkand = Artsvashen
  Armenia 40°38N 45°30E 105 B11
Bashkir Republic =
  Bashkortostan □
  Russia 54°0N 57°0E 108 D7
Bashkiria = Bashkortostan □
  Russia 52°58N 56°30E 108 D5
Bashkortostan □
  Russia 54°0N 57°0E 108 D7
Bashtanivka Ukraine 45°46N 29°29E 81 E14
Basilan Phil. 6°35N 122°0E 119 C6
Basilan Str. Phil. 6°50N 122°0E 119 C6
Basildon U.K. 51°34N 0°28E 67 F8
Basilé Eq. Guin. 3°42N 8°48E 139 E6
Basilé, Pico de Eq. Guin. 3°36N 8°49E 139 E6
Basilicata □ Italy 40°30N 16°30E 95 B9
Basim = Washim India 20°3N 77°0E 126 D3
Basin U.S.A. 44°23N 108°2W 168 D9
Basingstoke U.K. 51°15N 1°5W 67 F6
Basirhat India 22°40N 88°54E 125 H13
Baška Croatia 44°58N 14°45E 93 D11
Başkale Turkey 38°20N 44°5E 105 C10
Baskatong, Rés.
  Canada 46°46N 75°50W 164 C4
Basle = Basel Switz. 47°35N 7°35E 77 H3
Basmat India 19°15N 77°12E 126 E3
Basoda India 23°52N 77°54E 124 H7
Basoko
  Dem. Rep. of the Congo 1°16N 23°40E 142 B1

Basque, Côte France 43°30N 2°0W 72 E2
Basque, Pays France 43°15N 1°20W 72 E2
Basque Provinces = País Vasco □
  Spain 42°50N 2°45W 90 C2
Basra = Al Baṣrah Iraq 30°30N 47°50E 128 D5
Bass Str. Australia 39°15S 146°30E 151 F4
Bassae Greece 37°26N 21°53E 98 D3
Bassano Canada 50°48N 112°20W 162 C6
Bassano del Grappa
  Italy 45°46N 11°44E 93 C8
Bassar Togo 9°19N 0°57E 139 D5
Bassas da India Ind. Oc. 22°0S 39°0E 143 G4
Basse-Pointe Martinique 14°52N 61°8W 182 c
Basse Santa-Su
  Gambia 13°13N 14°15W 138 C2
Basse-Terre Guadeloupe 16°0N 61°44W 182 b
Basse Terre Trin. & Tob. 10°7N 61°19W 187 K15
Bassein = Pathein
  Myanmar 16°45N 94°30E 123 L19
Basses, Pte. des
  Guadeloupe 15°52N 61°17W 182 b
Basseterre
  St. Kitts & Nevis 17°17N 62°43W 183 C7
Bassett U.S.A. 42°35N 99°32W 172 D4
Bassi India 30°44N 76°21E 124 D7
Bassigny France 48°0N 5°30E 71 E12
Bassikounou Mauritania 15°55N 6°1W 138 B3
Bassila Benin 9°1N 1°46E 139 D5
Bassum Germany 52°50N 8°40E 76 C4
Bastak Iran 27°15N 54°25E 129 E7
Bastām Iran 36°29N 55°4E 129 B7
Bastar India 19°15N 81°40E 126 F6
Basti India 26°52N 82°55E 125 F10
Bastia France 42°40N 9°30E 73 F13
Bastogne Belgium 50°1N 5°43E 69 D5
Bastrop La., U.S.A. 32°47N 91°55W 176 E9
Bastrop Tex., U.S.A. 30°7N 97°19W 176 F6
Basuo = Dongfang
  China 18°50N 108°33E 117 a
Bat Yam Israel 32°2N 34°44E 130 C3
Bata Eq. Guin. 1°57N 9°50E 140 D1
Bataan □ Phil. 14°40N 120°25E 119 B6
Bataan Romania 46°1N 22°4E 80 D7
Batabanó Cuba 22°41N 82°18W 182 B3
Batabanó, G. de Cuba 22°30N 82°30W 182 B3
Batac Phil. 18°3N 120°34E 119 A6
Batagai Russia 67°38N 134°38E 107 C14
Batajnica Serbia 44°54N 20°17E 96 B4
Batak Bulgaria 41°57N 24°12E 97 E8
Batak Bulgaria 31°48N 75°12E 124 D6
Batama
  Dem. Rep. of the Congo 0°58N 26°33E 142 B2
Batamay Russia 63°30N 129°15E 107 C13
Batang China 30°1N 99°0E 116 B2
Batang Indonesia 6°55S 109°45E 119 G13
Batangafo C.A.R. 7°25N 18°20E 140 C3
Batangas Phil. 13°35N 121°10E 119 B6
Batanta Indonesia 0°55S 130°40E 119 E8
Bataís Brazil 20°54S 47°37W 191 A6
Batavia Spain 43°0N 78°11W 174 D6
Bataysk Russia 47°3N 39°45E 85 J10
Batchelor Australia 13°4S 131°1E 148 B5
Batdambang Cambodia 13°7N 103°12E 120 F4
Batemans B. Australia 35°40S 150°12E 153 C9
Batemans Bay
  Australia 35°44S 150°11E 153 C9
Batesburg-Leesville
  U.S.A. 33°54N 81°33W 178 D8
Batesville Ark., U.S.A. 35°46N 91°39W 176 D8
Batesville Miss.,
  U.S.A. 34°19N 89°57W 177 D10
Batesville Tex., U.S.A. 28°58N 99°37W 176 G5
Bath Canada 44°11N 76°47W 175 B8
Bath U.K. 51°23N 2°22W 67 F5
Bath Maine, U.S.A. 43°55N 69°49W 173 D19
Bath N.Y., U.S.A. 42°20N 77°19W 174 D7
Bath & North East Somerset □
  U.K. 51°21N 2°27W 67 F5
Batheay Cambodia 11°59N 104°57E 121 G5
Bathsheba Barbados 13°13N 59°32W 183 g
Bathurst Australia 33°25S 149°31E 153 B8
Bathurst Canada 47°37N 65°43W 165 D10
Bathurst S. Africa 33°30S 26°50E 144 D4
Bathurst, C. Canada 70°34N 128°0W 160 B7
Bathurst B. Australia 14°16S 144°25E 150 A3
Bathurst Harb.
  Australia 43°15S 146°10E 151 G4
Bathurst I. Australia 11°30S 130°10E 148 B5
Bathurst I. Canada 76°0N 100°30W 161 B11
Bathurst Inlet Canada 66°50N 108°1W 160 D10
Batie Burkina Faso 9°53N 2°53W 138 D4
Batikala Fiji 17°48S 179°10E 154 a
Batken Kyrgyzstan 40°3N 70°50E 109 D8
Batken □ Kyrgyzstan 39°50N 71°10E 109 D8
Batlow Australia 35°31S 148°9E 153 C8
Batman Turkey 37°55N 41°5E 105 C9
Baṭn al Ghūl Jordan 29°36N 35°56E 130 F4
Batna Algeria 35°34N 6°15E 136 A6
Batna □ Algeria 35°30N 5°55E 136 A6
Batočina Serbia 44°7N 21°5E 96 B5
Batoka Zambia 16°45S 27°15E 143 F2
Baton Rouge U.S.A. 30°27N 91°11W 176 F9
Batong, Ko Thailand 6°32N 99°12E 121 J2
Batopilas Mexico 27°1N 107°44W 180 B3
Batouri Cameroon 4°30N 14°25E 140 D2
Båtsfjord Norway 70°38N 29°39E 60 A23
Batsi Greece 37°54N 24°47E 98 D6
Battambang = Batdambang
  Cambodia 13°7N 103°12E 120 F4
Batti Malv India 8°50N 92°51E 127 K11
Batticaloa Sri Lanka 7°43N 81°45E 127 L5
Battipáglia Italy 40°37N 14°58E 95 B7
Battle U.K. 50°55N 0°30E 67 G8
Battle → Canada 52°43N 108°15W 162 C7
Battle Creek U.S.A. 42°19N 85°11W 173 D11
Battle Ground U.S.A. 45°47N 122°32W 168 D3
Battle Harbour Canada 52°16N 55°35W 165 B8
Battle Lake U.S.A. 46°17N 95°43W 172 B5
Battle Mountain
  U.S.A. 40°38N 116°56W 168 F5
Battlefields Zimbabwe 18°37S 29°47E 143 F2
Battleford Canada 52°45N 108°15W 162 C7
Battonya Hungary 46°16N 21°3E 80 E6
Batu Ethiopia 6°55N 39°45E 131 F2
Batu Malaysia 3°15N 101°40E 121 L3

Batu, Kepulauan
  Indonesia 0°30S 98°25E 118 E1
Batu Ferringhi Malaysia 5°28N 100°15E 121 c
Batu Gajah Malaysia 4°28N 101°3E 121 K3
Batu Is. = Batu, Kepulauan
  Indonesia 0°30S 98°25E 118 E1
Batu Pahat Malaysia 1°50N 102°56E 121 M4
Batu Puteh, Gunung
  Malaysia 4°15N 101°31E 121 K3
Batuata Indonesia 6°12S 122°42E 119 F6
Batugondang, Tanjung
  Indonesia 8°6S 114°29E 119 J17
Batukaru, Gunung
  Indonesia 8°20S 115°5E 119 J18
Batumi Georgia 41°39N 41°44E 87 K5
Batu Sar Pakistan 36°30N 74°31E 125 A6
Baturaja Indonesia 4°11S 104°15E 118 E2
Baturité Brazil 4°28S 38°45W 189 A3
Baturiti Indonesia 8°19S 115°11E 119 J18
Batys Qazaqstan □
  Kazakhstan 50°0N 50°0E 108 C3
Bau Malaysia 1°25N 110°9E 118 D4
Baubau Indonesia 5°25S 122°38E 119 F6
Baucau E. Timor 8°27S 126°27E 119 F7
Bauchi Nigeria 10°22N 9°48E 139 C6
Bauchi □ Nigeria 10°30N 10°0E 139 C7
Baud France 47°52N 3°1W 70 E3
Bauda India 20°50N 84°25E 126 D7
Baudette U.S.A. 48°43N 94°36W 172 A6
Bauer, C. Australia 32°44S 134°4E 151 E1
Bauhinia Australia 24°35S 149°18E 150 C4
Baukau = Baucau
  E. Timor 8°27S 126°27E 119 F7
Bauld, C. Canada 51°38N 55°26W 161 G20
Baume-les-Dames
  France 47°22N 6°22E 71 E13
Baunatal Germany 51°14N 9°24E 76 D5
Baunei Italy 40°2N 9°40E 94 B2
Baure Nigeria 12°52N 9°50E 139 C6
Bauru Brazil 22°10S 49°0W 191 A6
Bausi India 24°48N 87°1E 125 G12
Bauska Latvia 56°24N 24°15E 82 B11
Bautino Kazakhstan 44°35N 50°14E 87 H10
Bautzen Germany 51°10N 14°26E 76 D10
Bauya S. Leone 8°12N 12°38W 138 D2
Bavănāt Iran 30°28N 53°27E 129 D7
Bavanište Serbia 44°49N 20°55E 80 F5
Bavaria = Bayern □
  Germany 48°50N 12°0E 77 G7
Båven Sweden 59°0N 16°56E 62 E10
Bavispe → Mexico 29°15N 109°11W 180 B3
Baw Baw △ Australia 37°50S 146°17E 153 D7
Bawdwin Myanmar 23°5N 97°20E 123 H20
Bawean Indonesia 5°46S 112°35E 118 F4
Bawku Ghana 11°3N 0°19W 139 C4
Bawlake Myanmar 19°11N 97°21E 123 K20
Bawolung China 28°50N 101°16E 116 C3
Baxley U.S.A. 31°47N 82°21W 178 D7
Baxter U.S.A. 46°21N 94°17W 172 B6
Baxter Springs U.S.A. 37°2N 94°44W 172 G6
Baxter State △ U.S.A. 46°5N 68°57W 173 B19
Bay City Mich., U.S.A. 43°36N 83°54W 173 D12
Bay City Tex., U.S.A. 28°59N 95°58W 176 G7
Bay Is. = Bahía, Is. de la
  Honduras 16°45N 86°15W 182 C2
Bay Minette U.S.A. 30°53N 87°46W 177 F11
Bay of Plenty □ N.Z. 38°0S 177°0E 154 C5
Bay Roberts Canada 47°36N 53°16W 165 C9
Bay St. Louis U.S.A. 30°19N 89°20W 177 F10
Bay Springs U.S.A. 31°59N 89°17W 177 F10
Bay View N.Z. 39°25S 176°50E 154 F5
Baya
  Dem. Rep. of the Congo 11°53S 27°25E 143 E2
Bayamo Cuba 20°20N 76°40W 182 B4
Bayamón Puerto Rico 18°24N 66°9W 183 d
Bayan Har Shan China 34°0N 98°0E 110 E8
Bayan Hot = Alxa Zuoqi
  China 38°50N 105°40E 114 E3
Bayan Lepas Malaysia 5°17N 100°16E 121 c
Bayan Obo China 41°52N 109°59E 114 D5
Bayan-Ovoo = Erdenetsogt
  Mongolia 42°55N 106°5E 114 C4
Bayana India 26°55N 77°18E 124 F7
Bayanaūyl Kazakhstan 50°45N 75°45E 109 B9
Bayanbulak China 43°20N 84°0E 110 B5
Bayanhongor Mongolia 46°8N 102°43E 110 B9
Bayard N. Mex., U.S.A. 32°46N 108°8W 169 K9
Bayard Nebr., U.S.A. 41°45N 103°20W 172 E2
Bayay Phil. 10°40N 124°55E 119 B6
Bayburt Turkey 40°15N 40°20E 105 B9
Bayburt □ Turkey 40°25N 40°15E 105 B9
Baydaratskaya Guba
  Russia 69°0N 67°30E 108 C7
Baydhabo Somalia 3°8N 43°30E 131 G3
Bayelsa □ Nigeria 4°30N 6°0E 139 E6
Bayerische Alpen
  Germany 47°30N 11°30E 77 H7
Bayerische Rhön
  Germany 50°10N 10°5E 77 E6
Bayerischer Spessart △
  Germany 49°58N 10°15E 77 F6
Bayerischer Wald
  Germany 48°58N 12°50E 77 G8
Bayern □ Germany 48°50N 12°0E 77 G7
Bayeux France 49°17N 0°42W 70 C6
Bayfield Canada 43°34N 81°42W 174 C3
Bayfield U.S.A. 46°49N 90°49W 172 B7
Bayındır Turkey 38°13N 27°39E 99 C9
Baykal, Oz. Russia 53°0N 108°0E 107 D11
Baykan Turkey 38°7N 41°44E 105 C9
Baymak Russia 52°36N 58°19E 108 D5
Baynes Mts. Namibia 17°15S 13°0E 144 A1
Bayombong Phil. 16°30N 121°10E 119 A6
Bayon France 48°30N 6°20E 71 D13
Bayona = Baiona Spain 42°7N 8°51W 88 C2
Bayonet Point U.S.A. 28°20N 82°41W 179 G7
Bayonne France 43°30N 1°28W 72 E2
Bayonne U.S.A. 40°40N 74°6W 175 F11 c
Bayovar Peru 5°50S 81°0W 188 B1
Bayport U.S.A. 28°32N 82°39W 179 G7
Bayqongyr Kazakhstan 45°40N 63°20E 108 E7
Bayram-Ali = Bayramaly
  Turkmenistan 37°37N 62°10E 108 F7
Bayramaly
  Turkmenistan 37°37N 62°10E 108 F7
Bayramiç Turkey 39°48N 26°36E 99 B8
Bayreuth Germany 49°56N 11°35E 77 F7
Bayrischzell Germany 47°41N 12°0E 77 H8
Bayrūt Lebanon 33°53N 35°31E 130 B4

Bays, L. of Canada 45°15N 79°4W 174 A5
Bayshore U.S.A. 26°43N 81°50W 179 J8
Baysville Canada 45°9N 79°7W 174 A5
Bayt Lahm West Bank 31°43N 35°12E 130 D4
Baytik Shan China 45°15N 90°50E 109 C12
Baytown U.S.A. 29°43N 94°59W 176 D7
Bayuquan China 40°16N 122°8E 115 D12
Bayzo Niger 13°52N 4°35E 139 C5
Baza Spain 37°30N 2°47W 89 H8
Bazar Dyuzi Russia 41°12N 47°50E 87 K8
Bazardüzü = Bazar Dyuzi
  Russia 41°12N 47°50E 87 K8
Bāzārgān Iran 39°22N 44°26E 105 C11
Bazarny Karabulak
  Russia 52°20N 46°29E 86 D8
Bazarnyy Syzgan Russia 53°45N 46°40E 86 D8
Bazaruto, I. do Mozam. 21°40S 35°28E 145 B6
Bazaruto △ Mozam. 21°42S 35°26E 145 B6
Bazas France 44°27N 0°13W 72 D3
Bazhong China 31°52N 106°46E 116 B6
Bazhou China 39°8N 116°22E 114 E9
Bazmān, Kūh-e Iran 28°4N 60°1E 129 D9
Baztan = Elizondo Spain 43°12N 1°30W 90 B2
Bé, Nosy Madag. 13°25S 48°15E 141 G9
Beach U.S.A. 46°58N 104°0W 172 B2
Beach City U.S.A. 40°39N 81°35W 174 F3
Beachville Canada 43°5N 80°49W 174 C4
Beachy Hd. U.K. 50°44N 0°15E 67 G8
Beacon Australia 30°26S 117°52E 149 F2
Beacon U.S.A. 41°30N 73°58W 175 E11
Beaconsfield Australia 41°11S 146°48E 151 G4
Beagle, Canal S. Amer. 55°0S 68°30W 192 G3
Beagle Bay Australia 16°58S 122°40E 148 C3
Beagle Bay △ Australia 16°15S 123°0E 148 C3
Beagle G. Australia 12°15S 130°25E 148 B5
Béal an Átha = Ballina
  Ireland 54°7N 9°9W 64 B2
Béal Átha na Sluaighe =
  Ballinasloe Ireland 53°20N 8°13W 64 C2
Beals Cr. → U.S.A. 32°10N 100°51W 176 E4
Beamsville Canada 43°12N 79°28W 174 C5
Bear → Calif., U.S.A. 38°56N 121°36W 170 G5
Bear → Utah, U.S.A. 41°30N 112°8W 166 E7
Béar, C. France 42°31N 3°8E 72 F7
Bear I. = Bjørnøya Arctic 74°30N 19°0E 54 B8
Bear I. Ireland 51°38N 9°50W 64 E2
Bear L. Canada 56°8N 96°0W 163 B9
Bear L. U.S.A. 41°59N 111°21W 168 F8
Beardmore Canada 49°36N 87°57W 164 C2
Beardmore Glacier
  Antarctica 84°30S 170°0E 55 E11
Beardstown U.S.A. 40°1N 90°26W 172 E8
Bearma → India 24°20N 79°51E 125 G8
Béarn France 43°20N 0°30W 72 E3
Bearpaw Mts. U.S.A. 48°12N 109°30W 168 B9
Bearskin Lake Canada 53°58N 91°2W 164 B1
Beas → India 31°10N 74°59E 124 D6
Beas de Segura Spain 38°15N 2°53W 89 G8
Beasain Spain 43°3N 2°11W 90 B2
Beata, C. Dom. Rep. 17°40N 71°30W 183 C5
Beata, I. Dom. Rep. 17°34N 71°31W 183 C5
Beatrice Zimbabwe 18°15S 30°55E 143 F3
Beatrice U.S.A. 40°16N 96°45W 172 E5
Beatton → Canada 56°15N 120°45W 162 B4
Beatton River Canada 57°26N 121°20W 162 B4
Beatty U.S.A. 36°54N 116°46W 170 J10
Beau Bassin Mauritius 20°13S 57°27E 141 d
Beaucaire France 43°48N 4°39E 73 E6
Beauce, Plaine de la
  France 48°10N 1°45E 71 D8
Beauceville Canada 46°13N 70°46W 165 C5
Beauchêne, I. Falk. Is. 52°55S 59°15W 192 G5
Beaudesert Australia 27°59S 153°0E 151 D5
Beaufort Australia 37°25S 143°25E 152 D5
Beaufort France 45°44N 6°34E 73 C10
Beaufort Malaysia 5°30N 115°40E 118 C5
Beaufort N.C., U.S.A. 34°43N 76°40W 177 D16
Beaufort S.C., U.S.A. 32°26N 80°40W 178 E5
Beaufort Sea Arctic 72°0N 140°0W 158 B5
Beaufort West S. Africa 32°18S 22°36E 144 D3
Beaugency France 47°47N 1°38E 71 E8
Beauharnois Canada 45°20N 73°52W 175 A11
Beaujeu France 46°10N 4°35E 71 F11
Beaujolais France 46°0N 4°22E 71 F11
Beaulieu → Canada 62°3N 113°11W 162 A6
Beaulieu-sur-Dordogne
  France 44°58N 1°50E 72 D5
Beaulieu-sur-Mer
  France 43°42N 7°20E 73 E11
Beauly U.K. 57°30N 4°28W 65 D4
Beauly → U.K. 57°29N 4°27W 65 D4
Beaumaris U.K. 53°16N 4°6W 66 D3
Beaumont Belgium 50°15N 4°14E 69 D4
Beaumont N.Z. 45°50S 169°33E 155 F4
Beaumont Calif.,
  U.S.A. 33°57N 116°59W 171 M9
Beaumont Tex., U.S.A. 30°5N 94°6W 176 F7
Beaumont-de-Lomagne
  France 43°53N 1°0E 72 E5
Beaumont-du-Périgord
  France 44°45N 0°46E 72 D4
Beaumont-le-Roger
  France 49°4N 0°47E 70 C7
Beaumont-sur-Sarthe
  France 48°13N 0°8E 70 D7
Beaune France 47°2N 4°50E 71 E11
Beaune-la-Rolande France 48°4N 2°25E 71 D9
Beaupré Canada 47°3N 70°54W 165 C5
Beaupréau France 47°12N 1°0W 70 E6
Beauraing Belgium 50°7N 4°57E 69 D4
Beaurepaire France 45°25N 5°3E 73 C9
Beausejour Canada 50°5N 96°35W 163 C9
Beauvais France 49°25N 2°8E 71 C9
Beauval France 50°9N 107°37W 163 B7
Beauvoir-sur-Mer France 46°55N 2°2W 70 F4
Beauvoir-sur-Niort
  France 46°12N 0°30W 72 B3
Beaver Okla., U.S.A. 36°49N 100°31W 176 C4
Beaver Utah, U.S.A. 38°17N 112°38W 168 G7
Beaver → B.C.,
  Canada 59°52N 124°20W 162 B4
Beaver → Ont., Canada 55°55N 87°48W 164 A2
Beaver → Sask.,
  Canada 55°26N 107°45W 163 B7
Beaver → U.S.A. 36°35N 99°30W 176 C5
Beaver City U.S.A. 40°8N 99°50W 172 E4
Beaver Creek Canada 63°0N 141°0W 160 E3

Beaver Dam U.S.A. 43°28N 88°50W 172 D9
Beaver Falls U.S.A. 40°46N 80°20W 174 F4
Beaver Hill L. Canada 54°5N 94°50W 163 C10
Beaver I. U.S.A. 45°40N 85°33W 173 C11
Beavercreek U.S.A. 39°43N 84°11W 173 F11
Beaverhill L. Canada 53°27N 112°32W 162 C6
Beaverlodge Canada 55°11N 119°29W 162 B5
Beaverstone →
  Canada 54°59N 89°25W 164 B2
Beaverton Canada 44°26N 79°9W 174 B5
Beaverton U.S.A. 45°29N 122°48W 170 E4
Beawar India 26°3N 74°18E 124 F6
Bebedouro Brazil 21°0S 48°25W 191 A6
Bebera, Tanjung
  Indonesia 8°44S 115°51E 119 K18
Bebington U.K. 53°22N 3°0W 66 D4
Bebra Germany 50°58N 9°48E 76 E5
Becán Mexico 18°34N 89°31W 181 D7
Bécancour Canada 46°20N 72°26W 173 B17
Beccles U.K. 52°27N 1°35E 67 E9
Bečej Serbia 45°36N 20°3E 80 E5
Beceni Romania 45°23N 26°48E 81 E11
Becerreá Spain 42°51N 7°10W 88 C3
Béchar Algeria 31°38N 2°18W 136 B4
Béchar □ Algeria 30°15N 3°5E 136 B4
Becharof L. U.S.A. 57°56N 156°23W 166 D8
Becharre = Bsharri
  Lebanon 34°15N 36°0E 130 A5
Bechyně Czechia 49°17N 14°29E 78 B7
Beckley U.S.A. 37°47N 81°11W 173 G13
Beckum Germany 51°45N 8°2E 76 D4
Beclean Romania 47°11N 24°11E 81 C9
Bečov nad Teplou Czechia 50°5N 12°49E 78 A6
Bečva → Czechia 49°31N 17°20E 79 B10
Bédar Spain 37°11N 1°59W 91 H3
Bédarieux France 43°37N 3°10E 72 E7
Bédarrides France 44°2N 4°54E 73 D9
Beddouza, C. Morocco 32°33N 9°9W 136 B2
Bederkesa Germany 53°37N 8°50E 76 B4
Bedford Canada 45°7N 72°59W 175 A12
Bedford S. Africa 32°40S 26°10E 144 D4
Bedford U.K. 52°8N 0°28W 67 E7
Bedford Ind., U.S.A. 38°52N 86°29W 172 F10
Bedford Iowa, U.S.A. 40°40N 94°44W 172 E6
Bedford Ohio, U.S.A. 41°23N 81°32W 174 E3
Bedford Pa., U.S.A. 40°1N 78°30W 174 F6
Bedford Va., U.S.A. 37°20N 79°31W 173 G14
Bedford, C. Australia 15°14S 145°21E 150 B4
Bedków Poland 51°36N 19°44E 83 G6
Bednja → Croatia 46°20N 16°52E 93 B13
Bednodemyanovsk
  Russia 53°55N 43°15E 86 D6
Bedok Singapore 1°19N 103°56E 121 d
Bedónia Italy 44°30N 9°38E 92 D6
Bedourie Australia 24°30S 139°30E 150 C2
Bedti → India 14°50N 74°44E 127 G2
Bedugul Indonesia 8°17S 115°10E 119 J18
Bedum Neths. 53°18N 6°36E 64 A6
Będzin Poland 50°19N 19°7E 83 H6
Bee Ridge U.S.A. 27°17N 82°29W 179 H7
Beebe Plain Canada 45°1N 72°9W 175 A12
Beech Creek U.S.A. 41°5N 77°36W 174 E7
Beechworth Australia 36°22S 146°43E 153 D7
Beechy Canada 50°53N 107°24W 163 C7
Beef I. Br. Virgin Is. 18°26N 64°30W 183 e
Beelitz Germany 52°14N 12°58E 76 C8
Beenleigh Australia 27°43S 153°10E 151 D5
Be'er Sheva Israel 31°15N 34°48E 130 D3
Beerenberg Norway 71°0N 8°20W 57 C10
Beersheba = Be'er Sheva
  Israel 31°15N 34°48E 130 D3
Beeskow Germany 52°10N 14°15E 76 C10
Beestekraal S. Africa 25°23S 27°38E 145 C4
Beeston U.K. 52°56N 1°14W 66 E6
Beeton Canada 44°5N 79°47W 174 B5
Beetzendorf Germany 52°42N 11°6E 76 C7
Beeville U.S.A. 28°24N 97°45W 176 G6
Befale
  Dem. Rep. of the Congo 0°25N 20°45E 140 D4
Bega Australia 36°41S 149°51E 153 D8
Bega, Canalul Romania 45°37N 20°46E 80 E5
Bégard France 48°38N 3°18W 70 D3
Beğendik Turkey 40°55N 26°34E 97 F10
Begoro Ghana 6°23N 0°23W 139 D4
Begusarai India 25°24N 86°9E 125 G12
Behābād Iran 32°24N 59°47E 129 C8
Behala India 22°30N 88°18E 125 H13
Behbehān Iran 30°30N 50°15E 129 D6
Behchoko Canada 62°50N 116°3W 162 A5
Behm Canal U.S.A. 55°10N 131°0W 162 B2
Behshahr Iran 36°45N 53°35E 129 B7
Bei Jiang → China 23°2N 112°58E 117 F9
Bei Shan China 41°30N 96°0E 110 B8
Bei'an China 48°10N 126°20E 111 B14
Beibei China 29°47N 106°22E 116 C6
Beichuan China 31°55N 104°39E 116 B5
Beida, Es Sahrâ al
  Egypt 27°50N 28°45E 137 B2
Beihai China 21°28N 109°6E 116 G7
Beijing China 39°53N 116°21E 114 E9
Beijing Capital Int. ✈ (PEK)
  China 40°5N 116°35E 114 D9
Beijing Shi □ China 39°55N 116°20E 114 E9
Beilen Neths. 52°52N 6°27E 69 B6
Beiliu China 22°41N 110°21E 117 F8
Beilngries Germany 49°2N 11°28E 77 F7
Beilpajah Australia 32°54S 143°52E 152 B5
Beinn na Faoghla = Benbecula
  U.K. 57°26N 7°21W 65 D1
Beipan Jiang → China 24°55N 106°5E 116 E6
Beipiao China 41°52N 120°32E 115 D11
Beira Mozam. 19°50S 34°52E 143 F3
Beirut = Bayrūt Lebanon 33°53N 35°31E 130 B4
Beiseker Canada 51°23N 113°32W 162 C6
Beit Lāhīyā Gaza Strip 31°33N 34°30E 130 D3
Beit Lahm = Bayt Lahm
  West Bank 31°43N 35°12E 130 D4
Beitaolaizhao China 44°58N 125°58E 115 B13
Beitbridge Zimbabwe 22°5S 30°0E 143 G3
Beitun China 47°22N 87°4E 109 F11
Beiuș Romania 46°40N 22°21E 80 D7
Beizhen China 41°38N 121°54E 115 D11
Beizhengzhen China 44°31N 123°30E 115 B12
Beja Portugal 38°2N 7°53W 89 G3
Beja □ Portugal 37°55N 7°55W 89 H3
Béja Tunisia 36°43N 9°12E 136 A5
Béja □ Tunisia 36°40N 9°29E 136 A5

Bejaïa Algeria 36°42N 5°2E 136 A5
Bejaïa □ Algeria 36°40N 4°55E 136 A4
Béjar Spain 40°23N 5°46W 88 E5
Bejestān Iran 34°30N 58°5E 129 C8
Bekaa Valley = Al Biqā
  Lebanon 34°10N 36°10E 130 A5
Bekasi Indonesia 6°14S 106°59E 119 G12
Bekçiler Turkey 36°56N 29°44E 99 E11
Bekdash Turkmenistan 41°34N 52°32E 108 D4
Békés Hungary 46°47N 21°9E 80 D6
Békés □ Hungary 46°45N 21°0E 80 D6
Békéscsaba Hungary 46°47N 21°9E 80 D6
Bekili Turkey 38°17N 29°27E 99 C11
Bekily Madag. 24°13S 45°19E 145 C8
Bekok Malaysia 2°20N 103°7E 121 L4
Bekwai Ghana 6°30N 1°34W 139 D4
Bela India 25°50N 82°0E 125 G10
Bela Pakistan 26°12N 66°20E 124 F2
Bela Bela S. Africa 24°51S 28°19E 145 B4
Bela Crkva Serbia 44°55N 21°27E 80 E6
Bela Palanka Serbia 43°13N 22°17E 96 C6
Bela Vista Brazil 22°12S 56°20W 190 A4
Bela Vista Mozam. 26°10S 32°44E 145 C5
Bélâbre France 46°34N 1°8E 72 B5
Belagavi India 15°55N 74°35E 127 G2
Belalcázar Spain 38°35N 5°10W 89 G5
Belan → India 24°2N 81°45E 125 G9
Belanovica Serbia 44°15N 20°23E 96 B4
Belau ■ = Palau ■ Palau 7°30N 134°30E 58 G5
Belau = Palau ■ Palau 7°30N 134°30E 58 G5
Belawan Indonesia 3°33N 98°32E 118 D1
Belaya → Russia 54°40N 56°0E 108 D6
Belaya Glina Russia 46°5N 40°48E 87 G5
Belaya Kalitva Russia 48°13N 40°50E 87 F5
Belaya Tserkov = Bila Tserkva
  Ukraine 49°45N 30°10E 75 D16
Belaya Zemlya, Ostrova
  Russia 81°36N 62°18E 106 A7
Belcești Romania 47°19N 27°7E 81 C12
Belcher Is. Canada 56°15N 78°45W 164 A3
Belchite Spain 41°18N 0°43W 90 D4
Belden U.S.A. 40°2N 121°17W 170 E5
Belebey Russia 54°7N 54°7E 108 D6
Beledweyne Somalia 4°30N 45°5E 131 G4
Belém Brazil 1°20S 48°30W 187 D9
Belém de São Francisco
  Brazil 8°46S 38°58W 189 B3
Belén Argentina 27°40S 67°5W 190 B2
Belén Paraguay 23°30S 57°6W 190 A4
Belen Turkey 36°31N 36°10E 104 D7
Belen U.S.A. 34°40N 106°46W 169 J10
Belene Bulgaria 43°39N 25°10E 97 C9
Bélesta France 42°55N 1°56E 72 F5
Belet Uen = Beledweyne
  Somalia 4°30N 45°5E 131 G4
Belev Russia 53°50N 36°5E 84 F9
Belevi Turkey 38°0N 27°28E 99 C9
Belfair U.S.A. 47°27N 122°50W 170 C4
Belfast S. Africa 25°42S 30°2E 145 C5
Belfast U.K. 54°37N 5°56W 64 B6
Belfast Maine, U.S.A. 44°26N 69°1W 173 C19
Belfast N.Y., U.S.A. 42°21N 78°7W 174 D6
Belfast L. U.K. 54°40N 5°50W 64 B6
Belfield U.S.A. 46°53N 103°12W 172 B2
Belfort France 47°38N 6°50E 71 E13
Belfort, Territoire de □
  France 47°40N 6°55E 71 E13
Belfry U.S.A. 45°9N 109°1W 168 D9
Belgaum = Belagavi
  India 15°55N 74°35E 127 G2
Belgioioso Italy 45°10N 9°19E 92 C6
Belgium ■ Europe 50°30N 5°0E 69 D4
Belgodère France 42°35N 9°1E 73 F13
Belgorod Russia 50°35N 36°35E 85 G9
Belgorod □ Russia 50°45N 36°45E 85 G9
Belgorod-Dnestrovskiy =
  Bilhorod-Dnistrovskyy
  Ukraine 46°11N 30°23E 85 J6
Belgrade = Beograd
  Serbia 44°50N 20°37E 96 B4
Belgrade U.S.A. 45°47N 111°11W 168 D8
Belgrano II Antarctica 77°52S 34°37W 55 D1
Belgrove N.Z. 41°27S 172°59E 155 D4
Belhaven U.S.A. 35°33N 76°37W 177 D16
Béli Guinea-Biss. 11°51N 13°56W 138 C2
Beli Drim → Europe 42°6N 20°25E 96 C4
Beli Manastir Croatia 45°45N 18°36E 80 E3
Beli Timok → Serbia 43°53N 22°14E 96 C6
Bélice → Italy 37°35N 12°55E 94 F5
Belimbing Indonesia 8°24S 115°12E 119 J18
Belinskiy Russia 52°58N 43°25E 86 D6
Belinyu Indonesia 1°35S 105°50E 118 E3
Beliton Is. = Belitung
  Indonesia 3°10S 107°50E 118 E3
Belitung Indonesia 3°10S 107°50E 118 E3
Beliu Romania 46°30N 22°0E 80 D7
Belize ■ Cent. Amer. 17°0N 88°30W 181 D7
Belize Barrier Reef Belize 17°9N 88°3W 181 D7
Belize City Belize 17°25N 88°10W 181 D7
Beljakovci Macedonia 42°6N 21°59E 96 D5
Beljanica Serbia 44°8N 21°43E 96 B5
Belkovskiy, Ostrov
  Russia 75°32N 135°44E 107 B14
Bell U.S.A. 29°45N 82°52W 178 F7
Bell → Canada 49°48N 77°38W 164 C4
Bell I. Canada 50°46N 55°35W 165 B8
Bell-Irving → Canada 56°12N 129°5W 162 B3
Bell Peninsula Canada 63°50N 82°0W 161 E15
Bell Ville Argentina 32°40S 62°40W 190 C3
Bella Italy 40°45N 15°32E 95 B8
Bella Bella Canada 52°10N 128°10W 162 C3
Bella Coola Canada 52°25N 126°40W 162 C3
Bella Flor Bolivia 11°9S 67°49W 188 C4
Bella Unión Uruguay 30°15S 57°40W 190 C4
Bella Vista Corrientes,
  Argentina 28°33S 59°0W 190 B4
Bella Vista Tucuman,
  Argentina 27°10S 65°25W 190 B2
Bellac France 46°7N 1°3E 72 B5
Bellágio Italy 45°59N 9°15E 92 C6
Bellaire U.S.A. 40°1N 80°45W 174 F4
Bellária Italy 44°9N 12°28E 93 B9
Bellata Australia 29°53S 149°46E 151 D4
Belle Fourche U.S.A. 44°40N 103°51W 172 C2
Belle Fourche →
  U.S.A. 44°26N 102°18W 172 C2
Belle Glade U.S.A. 26°41N 80°40W 179 J9

Belle-Île France 47°20N 3°10W 70 E3
Belle Isle Canada 51°57N 55°25W 165 B8
Belle Isle, Str. of
  Canada 51°30N 56°30W 165 B8
Belle Plaine U.S.A. 41°54N 92°17W 172 E7
Belle River Canada 42°18N 82°43W 174 D2
Belle Yella Liberia 7°24N 10°0W 138 D3
Belledonne France 45°20N 6°10E 73 C10
Bellefontaine U.S.A. 40°22N 83°46W 173 E12
Bellefonte U.S.A. 40°55N 77°47W 174 F7
Bellegarde France 47°59N 2°26E 71 E9
Bellegarde-en-Marche
  France 45°59N 2°18E 72 C6
Bellegarde-sur-Valserine
  France 46°4N 5°50E 71 F12
Bellême France 48°22N 0°34E 70 D7
Belleoram Canada 47°31N 55°25W 165 C8
Belleplaine Barbados 13°15N 59°34E 183 g
Belleview U.S.A. 29°4N 82°3W 179 F7
Belleville Canada 44°10N 77°23W 174 B7
Belleville France 46°7N 4°45E 71 F11
Belleville Ill., U.S.A. 38°31N 89°59W 172 F9
Belleville Kans., U.S.A. 39°50N 97°38W 172 F5
Belleville N.J., U.S.A. 40°47N 74°9W 175 F10
Belleville N.Y., U.S.A. 43°46N 76°10W 175 C8
Belleville-sur-Vie France 46°46N 1°25W 70 F5
Bellevue Idaho, U.S.A. 43°28N 114°16W 168 E6
Bellevue Nebr., U.S.A. 41°9N 95°54W 172 E6
Bellevue Ohio, U.S.A. 41°17N 82°51W 174 E2
Bellevue Wash.,
  U.S.A. 47°37N 122°12W 170 C4
Belley France 45°46N 5°41E 73 C9
Bellin = Kangirsuk
  Canada 60°0N 70°0W 161 F18
Bellinge Denmark 55°20N 10°20E 63 J4
Bellingen Australia 30°25S 152°50E 153 A10
Bellingham U.S.A. 48°46N 122°29W 170 B4
Bellingshausen Abyssal Plain
  S. Ocean 64°0S 90°0W 55 C17
Bellingshausen Sea
  Antarctica 66°0S 80°0W 55 C17
Bellinzona Switz. 46°11N 9°1E 77 J5
Bello Colombia 6°20N 75°33W 186 B3
Bellows Falls U.S.A. 43°8N 72°27W 175 C12
Bellpat Pakistan 29°0N 68°5E 124 E3
Bellpuig Spain 41°37N 1°1E 90 D6
Belluno Italy 46°9N 12°13E 93 B9
Bellville U.S.A. 32°9N 81°59W 178 E6
Bellwood U.S.A. 40°36N 78°20W 174 F6
Bélmez Spain 38°17N 5°17W 89 G5
Belmont Australia 33°4S 151°42E 153 B9
Belmont Canada 42°53N 81°5W 174 D3
Belmont S. Africa 29°28S 24°22E 144 C3
Belmont U.S.A. 42°14N 78°2W 174 D6
Belmonte Brazil 16°0S 39°0W 189 E3
Belmonte Portugal 40°21N 7°20W 88 E3
Belmonte Spain 39°34N 2°43W 91 F2
Belmopan Belize 17°18N 88°30W 181 D7
Belmullet Ireland 54°14N 9°58W 64 B2
Belo Horizonte Brazil 19°55S 43°56W 189 D2
Belo Jardim Brazil 8°20S 36°26W 189 B3
Belo-Tsiribihina Madag. 19°40S 44°30E 141 H8
Belogorsk = Bilohirsk
  Ukraine 45°0N 34°35E 85 K8
Belogorsk Russia 51°0N 128°20E 107 D13
Belogradchik Bulgaria 43°53N 22°42E 96 C6
Belogradets Bulgaria 43°22N 27°18E 97 C11
Beloha Madag. 25°10S 45°3E 145 D8
Beloit Kans., U.S.A. 39°28N 98°6W 172 F4
Beloit Wis., U.S.A. 42°31N 89°2W 172 D9
Belokorovichi Ukraine 51°7N 28°2E 75 C15
Belomorsk Russia 64°35N 34°54E 106 C4
Belonia India 23°15N 91°30E 123 H17
Belopolye = Bilopillya
  Ukraine 51°14N 34°20E 85 G8
Belorechensk Russia 44°46N 39°52E 87 H4
Beloretsk Russia 53°58N 58°24E 108 D5
Belorussia = Belarus ■
  Europe 53°30N 27°0E 75 B14
Beloslav Bulgaria 43°11N 27°42E 97 C11
Belousovka Kazakhstan 50°8N 82°31E 109 B10
Belovezhskaya Pushcha =
  Białowieska △ Poland 52°43N 23°50E 83 F10
Belovo Bulgaria 42°13N 24°1E 97 D8
Belovo Russia 54°30N 86°0E 109 B11
Beloyarskiy Russia 63°42N 66°40E 106 C7
Beloye, Ozero Russia 60°10N 37°35E 84 B9
Beloye More Russia 66°30N 38°0E 58 B13
Belozem Bulgaria 42°12N 25°2E 97 D9
Belozersk Russia 60°1N 37°45E 84 B9
Belpasso Italy 37°35N 14°58E 95 E7
Belpre U.S.A. 39°17N 81°34W 173 F13
Belrain India 28°23N 80°5E 125 E9
Belt U.S.A. 47°23N 110°55W 168 C8
Beltana Australia 30°48S 138°25E 152 A2
Belterra Brazil 2°45S 55°0W 187 D8
Beltinci Slovenia 46°37N 16°20E 93 B13
Belton U.S.A. 31°3N 97°28W 176 F6
Beltsy = Bălți Moldova 47°48N 27°58E 81 C12
Belturbet Ireland 54°6N 7°26W 64 B4
Belukha Russia 49°50N 86°50E 109 C11
Belušič Serbia 43°50N 21°10E 96 C5
Belvedere Maríttimo
  Italy 39°37N 15°52E 95 C8
Belvès France 44°46N 1°0E 72 D5
Belvidere Ill., U.S.A. 42°15N 88°50W 172 D8
Belvidere N.J., U.S.A. 40°50N 75°5W 175 F9
Belvis de la Jara Spain 39°45N 4°57W 88 F6
Belyando → Australia 21°38S 146°50E 150 C4
Belyando Crossing
  Australia 21°32S 146°51E 150 C4
Belyuen Australia 12°34S 130°42E 148 B5
Belyy Russia 55°49N 32°58E 84 D7
Belyy, Ostrov Russia 73°30N 71°0E 106 B8
Belyy Yar Russia 58°26N 84°39E 106 D9
Belyye Vody = Aqsū
  Kazakhstan 42°25N 69°50E 109 D7
Belz Ukraine 50°23N 24°1E 83 H10
Belzec Poland 50°23N 23°26E 83 H10
Belzig Germany 52°8N 12°35E 76 C8
Belzoni U.S.A. 33°11N 90°29W 178 E7
Bełżyce Poland 51°11N 22°17E 83 G9
Bembéréke Benin 10°11N 2°43E 139 C5
Bembesi Zimbabwe 20°0S 28°58E 143 G2
Bembesi → Zimbabwe 18°57S 27°47E 143 F2
Bembézar → Spain 37°45N 5°13W 89 H5
Bembibre Spain 42°37N 6°25W 88 C4

Bemboka Australia 36°35S 149°41E 153 D8
Bemetara India 21°42N 81°32E 125 J9
Bemidji U.S.A. 47°28N 94°53W 172 B6
Ben Iran 32°32N 50°45E 129 C6
Ben Boyd △ Australia 37°0S 149°55E 153 D8
Ben Cruachan U.K. 56°26N 5°8W 65 E3
Ben Dearg U.K. 57°47N 4°56W 65 D4
Ben En → Vietnam 19°37N 105°30E 120 C5
Ben Gardane Tunisia 33°11N 11°11E 136 B6
Ben Halls Gap △
  Australia 31°37S 151°1E 153 A9
Ben Hope U.K. 58°25N 4°36W 65 C4
Ben Lawers U.K. 56°32N 4°14W 65 E4
Ben Lomond N.S.W.,
  Australia 30°1S 151°43E 151 E5
Ben Lomond Tas.,
  Australia 41°38S 147°42E 151 G4
Ben Lomond U.K. 56°11N 4°38W 65 E4
Ben Lomond △
  Australia 41°33S 147°39E 151 G4
Ben Luc Vietnam 10°39N 106°29E 121 G6
Ben Macdhui U.K. 57°4N 3°40W 65 D5
Ben Mhor U.K. 57°15N 7°18W 65 D1
Ben More Argyll & Bute,
  U.K. 56°26N 6°1W 65 E2
Ben More Stirling, U.K. 56°23N 4°32W 65 E4
Ben More Assynt U.K. 58°8N 4°52W 65 C4
Ben Nevis U.K. 56°48N 5°1W 65 E3
Ben Ohau Ra. N.Z. 44°1S 170°4E 155 E5
Ben Quang Vietnam 17°3N 106°55E 120 D6
Ben Slimane Morocco 33°38N 7°7W 136 B2
Ben Tadjine, Djebel
  Algeria 29°0N 3°30E 136 C5
Ben Tre Vietnam 10°14N 106°23E 121 G6
Ben Vorlich U.K. 56°21N 4°14W 65 E4
Ben Wyvis U.K. 57°40N 4°35W 65 D4
Bena Nigeria 11°20N 5°50E 139 C6
Benaco, L. di = Garda, L. di
  Italy 45°40N 10°41E 92 C7
Benagerie Australia 31°25S 140°22E 152 A4
Benahmed Morocco 33°4N 7°9W 136 B2
Benalla Australia 36°30S 146°0E 153 D7
Benalmádena Spain 36°36N 4°34W 89 J6
Benambra, Mt.
  Australia 36°31S 147°34E 153 D7
Benanee Australia 34°31S 142°52E 152 C5
Benares = Varanasi
  India 25°22N 83°0E 125 G10
Bénat, C. France 43°5N 6°22E 73 E10
Benavente Portugal 38°59N 8°49W 89 G2
Benavente Spain 42°2N 5°43W 88 C5
Benavides U.S.A. 27°36N 98°25W 176 H5
Benavides de Órbigo
  Spain 42°30N 5°54W 88 C5
Benbecula U.K. 57°26N 7°21W 65 D1
Benbonyathe Hill
  Australia 30°25S 139°11E 152 A3
Bend U.S.A. 44°4N 121°19W 168 D3
Bendemeer Australia 30°53S 151°8E 153 A9
Bender Beyla Somalia 9°30N 50°48E 133 C6
Bendery = Tighina Moldova 46°50N 29°30E 81 D14
Bendigo Australia 36°40S 144°15E 152 D6
Bendorf Germany 50°25N 7°35E 76 E3
Bené Beraq Israel 32°6N 34°51E 130 C3
Beneditinos Brazil 5°27S 42°22W 189 B2
Benedito Leite Brazil 7°13S 44°34W 189 B2
Bénéna Mali 13°9N 4°17W 138 C4
Benešov Czechia 49°46N 14°41E 78 B7
Benevento Italy 41°8N 14°45E 95 A7
Benfeld France 48°22N 7°34E 71 D14
Beng Mealea Cambodia 13°28N 104°14E 120 F5
Benga Mozam. 16°11S 33°40E 143 F3
Bengal, Bay of Ind. Oc. 15°0N 90°0E 123 M17
Bengaluru India 12°59N 77°40E 127 H3
Bengbis Cameroon 3°27N 12°36E 139 E7
Bengbu China 32°58N 117°20E 117 A11
Benghazi = Banghāzī
  Libya 32°11N 20°3E 135 B10
Bengkalis Indonesia 1°30N 102°10E 118 D2
Bengkulu Indonesia 3°50S 102°12E 118 E2
Bengkulu □ Indonesia 3°48S 102°16E 118 E2
Bengough Canada 49°25N 105°10W 163 D7
Bengtsfors Sweden 59°2N 12°14E 63 E6
Benguela Angola 12°37S 13°25E 141 G2
Benguérua, I. Mozam. 21°58S 35°28E 145 B6
Benha Egypt 30°26N 31°8E 137 C7
Beni
  Dem. Rep. of the Congo 0°30N 29°27E 142 B2
Beni → Bolivia 10°23S 65°24W 186 C4
Beni Abbès Algeria 30°5N 2°5W 136 B3
Beni Hammad Algeria 35°49N 4°47E 136 A4
Beni Haoua Algeria 36°30N 1°30E 136 A4
Beni Mazâr Egypt 28°32N 30°44E 137 C7
Beni Mellal Morocco 32°21N 6°21W 136 B3
Beni Ounif Algeria 32°0N 1°10W 136 B3
Beni Saf Algeria 35°17N 1°15W 136 A4
Beni Suef Egypt 29°5N 31°6E 137 C7
Beniah L. Canada 63°23N 112°17W 162 A6
Benicarló Spain 40°23N 0°23E 90 E5
Benicássim Spain 40°3N 0°9E 90 E5
Benidorm Spain 38°33N 0°9W 91 G4
Benin ■ Africa 10°0N 2°0E 139 D5
Benin → Nigeria 5°45N 5°4E 139 D6
Benin, Bight of W. Afr. 5°0N 3°0E 139 E5
Benin City Nigeria 6°20N 5°31E 139 D6
Benissa Spain 38°43N 0°3E 91 G5
Benito Juárez Argentina 37°40S 59°43W 190 D4
Benitses Greece 39°32N 19°55E 101 A3
Benjamin Aceval
  Paraguay 24°58S 57°34W 190 A4
Benjamin Constant
  Brazil 4°40S 70°15W 186 D4
Benjamin Hill Mexico 30°10N 111°10W 180 B2
Benkelman U.S.A. 40°3N 101°32W 172 E3
Benkovac Croatia 44°2N 15°37E 93 D12
Benmore Pk. N.Z. 44°25S 170°8E 155 E3
Bennett Canada 59°51N 135°0W 162 B2
Bennett, L. Australia 22°50S 131°2E 148 D5
Bennetta, Ostrov
  Russia 76°21N 148°56E 107 B15
Bennettsville U.S.A. 34°37N 79°41W 177 D15
Bennichchâb
  Mauritania 19°32N 15°12W 138 B1
Bennington N.H. 43°0N 71°55W 175 D11
Bennington Vt., U.S.A. 42°53N 73°12W 175 D11

Benoni S. Africa 26°11S 28°18E 145 C4
Benoud Algeria 32°20N 0°16E 136 B4
Benque Viejo del Carmen
  Belize 17°5N 89°8W 181 D7
Bensheim Germany 49°40N 8°38E 77 F4
Benson Ariz., U.S.A. 31°58N 110°18W 169 L8
Benson Minn., U.S.A. 45°19N 95°36W 172 B6
Bent Iran 26°20N 59°31E 129 E8
Benteng Indonesia 6°10S 120°30E 119 F6
Bentinck I. Australia 17°3S 139°35E 150 B2
Bentinck I. Myanmar 11°45N 98°3E 121 G2
Bentley Subglacial Trench
  Antarctica 80°0S 115°0W 55 E15
Bento Gonçalves Brazil 29°10S 51°31W 191 B5
Benton Ark., U.S.A. 34°34N 92°35W 176 D8
Benton Calif., U.S.A. 37°48N 118°32W 170 H8
Benton Ill., U.S.A. 38°0N 88°55W 172 F9
Benton Pa., U.S.A. 41°12N 76°23W 175 E8
Benton Harbor U.S.A. 42°6N 86°27W 172 D10
Bentong Malaysia 3°31N 101°55E 121 L3
Bentonville U.S.A. 36°22N 94°13W 176 C7
Benue → Nigeria 7°20N 8°45E 139 D6
Benue □ Nigeria 7°48N 6°46E 139 D6
Benxi China 41°20N 123°48E 115 D12
Beo Indonesia 4°25N 126°50E 119 D7
Beograd Serbia 44°50N 20°37E 96 B4
Beograd ✈ (BEG) Serbia 44°49N 20°17E 96 B4
Beolgyo S. Korea 34°51N 127°21E 115 G14
Beoumi Côte d'Ivoire 7°45N 5°23W 138 D3
Beppu Japan 33°15N 131°30E 113 H5
Beqa Fiji 18°23S 178°8E 154 a
Beqaa Valley = Al Biqā
  Lebanon 34°10N 36°10E 130 A5
Ber Mota India 23°27N 68°34E 124 H3
Bera, Tasik Malaysia 3°15N 102°38E 121 L4
Berach → India 25°15N 75°2E 124 G6
Berane Montenegro 42°51N 19°52E 96 C3
Berastagi Indonesia 3°11N 98°31E 121 L2
Berat Albania 40°43N 19°59E 96 F3
Berau = Tanjungredeb
  Indonesia 2°9N 117°29E 118 D5
Berau, Teluk Indonesia 2°30S 132°30E 119 E8
Berber Sudan 18°0N 34°0E 135 E12
Berbera Somalia 10°30N 45°2E 133 C5
Berbérati C.A.R. 4°15N 15°40E 140 D3
Berbice → Guyana 6°20N 57°32W 186 B7
Berceto Italy 44°31N 9°59E 92 D6
Berchidda Italy 40°47N 9°10E 94 D3
Berchtesgaden Germany 47°38N 13°0E 77 H8
Berchtesgaden △
  Germany 47°34N 12°55E 77 H8
Berck France 50°25N 1°36E 71 B8
Berdichev = Berdychiv
  Ukraine 49°57N 28°30E 75 D15
Berdsk Russia 54°47N 83°2E 109 B9
Berdyansk Ukraine 46°45N 36°50E 85 J9
Berdychiv Ukraine 49°57N 28°30E 75 D15
Berea U.S.A. 37°34N 84°17W 173 G11
Berebere Indonesia 2°25N 128°45E 119 D7
Bereeda Somalia 11°45N 51°0E 133 B6
Berehomet Ukraine 48°15N 25°19E 81 D10
Berehove Ukraine 48°15N 22°35E 80 B7
Bereket Turkmenistan 39°16N 55°32E 108 F6
Berekum Ghana 7°29N 2°34W 138 D4
Berenice Egypt 24°2N 35°25E 137 C4
Berens → Canada 52°25N 97°2W 163 C9
Berens I. Canada 52°18N 97°18W 163 C9
Berens River Canada 52°25N 97°0W 163 C9
Beresfield Australia 32°50S 151°40E 153 B9
Beresford U.S.A. 43°5N 96°46W 172 D5
Berestechko Ukraine 50°22N 25°5E 75 C13
Bereşti Romania 46°6N 27°50E 81 D12
Beretău → Romania 46°59N 21°7E 80 D6
Berettyó → Hungary 46°59N 21°7E 80 D6
Berettyóújfalu Hungary 47°13N 21°33E 80 C6
Bereza = Byaroza
  Belarus 52°31N 24°51E 75 B13
Berezhany Ukraine 49°26N 24°58E 75 D13
Berezina = Byarezina →
  Belarus 52°33N 30°14E 75 B16
Berezivka Ukraine 47°14N 30°55E 85 J6
Berezna Ukraine 51°35N 31°46E 85 G6
Bereznik Russia 62°51N 42°40E 106 C5
Berezniki Russia 59°24N 56°46E 106 D6
Berezovo Russia 64°0N 65°0E 106 C7
Berezyne Ukraine 47°12N 29°16E 81 D14
Berga Spain 42°6N 1°48E 90 C6
Berga Sweden 57°14N 16°3E 63 G10
Bergama Turkey 39°8N 27°11E 99 B9
Bérgamo Italy 45°41N 9°43E 92 C6
Bergara Spain 43°6N 2°25W 90 B2
Bergby Sweden 60°57N 17°2E 62 D11
Berge Norway 59°34N 8°10E 62 E2
Bergeforsen Sweden 62°32N 17°23E 62 B11
Bergen Mecklenburg-Vorpommern,
  Germany 54°25N 13°25E 76 A9
Bergen Niedersachsen,
  Germany 52°49N 9°57E 76 C5
Bergen Neths. 52°40N 4°43E 69 B4
Bergen Norway 60°20N 5°20E 63 E8
Bergen op Zoom Neths. 51°28N 4°18E 69 C4
Bergerac France 44°51N 0°30E 72 D4
Bergheim Germany 50°58N 6°38E 76 E2
Bergholz U.S.A. 40°31N 80°53W 174 F4
Bergisch Gladbach
  Germany 50°59N 7°8E 76 E3
Bergisches Land △
  Germany 51°0N 7°20E 76 E3
Bergkamen Germany 51°37N 7°38E 76 D3
Bergkvara Sweden 56°23N 16°5E 63 H10
Bergshamra Sweden 59°38N 18°37E 62 E12
Bergsjö Sweden 61°59N 17°3E 62 C11
Bergstrasse-Odenwald
  Germany 49°45N 8°55E 77 F4
Bergues France 50°58N 2°24E 71 B9
Bergviken Sweden 61°15N 16°40E 62 C10
Bergville S. Africa 28°52S 29°18E 145 C4
Berhala, Selat Indonesia 1°0S 104°15E 118 E2
Berhampore = Baharampur
  India 24°2N 88°27E 125 G13
Berhampur = Brahmapur
  India 19°15N 84°54E 126 E7
Berheci → Romania 45°58N 27°28E 81 E12
Bering Glacier
  U.S.A. 60°20N 143°30W 166 C11
Bering Sea Pac. Oc. 58°0N 171°0E 166 D2
Bering Strait Pac. Oc. 65°30N 169°0W 166 D6
Beringovskiy Russia 63°3N 179°19E 107 C18

erisso *Argentina* 34°56S 57°50W **190** C4
erja *Spain* 36°50N 2°56W **89** B8
erkane *Morocco* 34°52N 2°20W **136** B3
erkeley *U.S.A.* 37°51N 122°16W **170** H4
erkner I. *Antarctica* 79°30S 50°00W **55** D18
erkovitsa *Bulgaria* 43°16N 23°8E **96** C7
erkshire *U.S.A.* 42°19N 76°11W **175** D8
erkshire Downs *U.K.* 51°33N 1°29W **67** F6
erlanga *Spain* 38°17N 5°50W **89** G5
erlenga I., *Portugal* 39°25N 9°30W **89** F1
erlin *Germany* 52°31N 13°23E **76** C9
erlin, Ga., U.S.A. 31°4N 83°37W **177** F4
erlin Md., U.S.A. 38°20N 75°13W **173** F16
erlin N.H., U.S.A. 44°28N 71°11W **175** B13
erlin N.Y., U.S.A. 42°42N 73°23W **175** D11
erlin Wis., U.S.A. 43°58N 88°57W **172** D9
erlin L. U.S.A. 41°3N 81°0W **174** E4
erlin Tegel ✈ (TXL)
 Germany 52°35N 13°14E **76** C9
ermagui *Australia* 36°23S 150°4E **153** D9
ermeja, Sierra *Spain* 36°30N 5°11W **89** J5
ermejo → *Formosa,*
 Argentina 26°51S 58°23W **190** B4
ermejo → *San Juan,*
 Argentina 32°30S 67°30W **190** C2
ermejo, Paso = Uspallata, P. de
 Argentina 32°37S 69°22W **190** C2
ermen, L. *Canada* 53°35N 68°55W **165** B6
ermeo *Spain* 43°25N 2°47W **90** B2
ermuda ☑ *Atl. Oc.* 32°18N 64°45W **159** F13
ermuda Rise *Atl. Oc.* 30°30N 65°0W **56** C5
ern *Switz.* 46°57N 7°28E **77** J3
ern □ *Switz.* 46°45N 7°40E **77** J3
ernalda *Italy* 40°24N 16°41E **95** B9
ernalillo *U.S.A.* 35°18N 106°33W **169** J10
ernardo de Irigoyen
 Argentina 26°15S 53°40W **191** B5
ernardo O'Higgins △
 Chile 48°50S 75°36W **192** C1
ernasconi *Argentina* 40°43N 74°34W **175** F10
ernau *Bayern, Germany* 47°47N 12°22E **77** H8
ernau *Brandenburg,*
 Germany 52°40N 13°35E **76** C9
ernay *France* 49°5N 0°35E **70** C7
ernburg *Germany* 51°47N 11°44E **76** D7
erndorf *Austria* 47°59N 16°1E **78** D9
erne = Bern *Switz.* 46°57N 7°28E **77** J3
erne □ = Bern *Switz.* 46°45N 7°40E **77** J3
erner Alpen *Switz.* 46°27N 7°35E **77** J3
erneray *U.K.* 57°43N 7°11W **65** D1
ernina I. *Australia* 24°50S 113°12E **149** D1
ernina, Piz *Switz.* 46°20N 9°54E **77** J5
ernkastel-Kues *Germany* 49°54N 7°4E **77** D2
eroun *Czechia* 49°57N 14°5E **78** B7
erounka → *Czechia* 50°0N 14°22E **78** B7
erovo *Macedonia* 41°38N 22°51E **96** E6
erre, Étang de *France* 43°27N 5°5E **73** E9
erre-l'Étang *France* 43°27N 5°2E **73** E9
errechid *Morocco* 33°18N 7°36W **136** B2
erri *Australia* 34°14S 140°35E **152** C4
erriane *Algeria* 32°50N 3°46E **136** B4
erridale *Australia* 36°22S 148°48E **153** D8
errigan *Australia* 35°38S 145°49E **152** C5
erriwillock *Australia* 35°36S 142°59E **152** C5
errouaghia *Algeria* 36°10N 2°53E **136** A4
erry *Australia* 34°46S 150°43E **153** D9
erry *France* 46°50N 2°0E **71** F8
erry Is. *Bahamas* 25°40N 77°50W **182** A4
errydale *U.S.A.* 30°53N 87°3W **179** E2
erryessa, L. U.S.A. 38°31N 122°6W **170** G4
erryville *U.S.A.* 36°22N 93°34W **176** C8
erseba *Namibia* 26°0S 17°46E **144** C2
ersenbrück *Germany* 52°34N 7°56E **76** C3
ershad *Ukraine* 48°22N 29°31E **81** B14
ertamans *Spain* 52°54N 8°38W **88** C2
erthold *U.S.A.* 48°19N 101°44W **172** A3
erthoud *U.S.A.* 40°19N 105°5W **168** F11
ertincourt *France* 50°5N 2°58E **71** B9
ertolínia *Brazil* 7°38S 43°57W **189** B2
ertoua *Cameroon* 4°30N 13°45E **140** D2
ertraghboy B. *Ireland* 53°22N 9°54W **64** C2
eruniy *Uzbekistan* 41°41N 60°45E **108** D6
eruwala *Sri Lanka* 6°30N 80°0E **127** L4
erwick *U.S.A.* 41°3N 76°14W **175** E8
erwick-upon-Tweed
 U.K. 55°46N 2°0W **66** B6
erwyn Mts. *U.K.* 52°54N 3°26W **66** E4
eryslav *Ukraine* 46°50N 33°30E **85** J7
erzasca *Romania* 44°39N 21°58E **80** F6
erzence *Hungary* 46°12N 17°11E **80** D2
esal *Pakistan* 35°4N 73°56E **125** B5
esalampy *Madag.* 16°43S 44°29E **141** H8
esançon *France* 47°15N 6°2E **71** E13
esar *Indonesia* 2°40S 116°0E **118** E5
eshenkovichi *Belarus* 55°2N 29°29E **84** E5
esianē *Kosovo* 42°54N 21°10E **96** D5
eška *Serbia* 45°8N 20°6E **80** E5
eslan *Russia* 43°15N 44°28E **87** D7
esna Kobila *Serbia* 42°31N 22°10E **96** D6
esnard L. *Canada* 55°25N 106°0W **163** B7
esni *Turkey* 37°41N 37°52E **104** D7
esor, N. → *Egypt* 31°28N 34°22E **130** D3
essarabka = Basarabeasca
 Moldova 46°21N 28°58E **81** D13
essarabiya = Basarabia
 Moldova 47°0N 28°10E **75** E15
essèges *France* 44°18N 4°8E **73** D8
essemer, Ala., U.S.A. 33°24N 86°58W **177** E11
essemer, Mich., U.S.A. 46°29N 90°3W **172** B8
essemer Pa., U.S.A. 40°59N 80°30W **174** E4
essin *France* 49°18N 1°0W **70** C6
Bessines-sur-Gartempe
 France 46°6N 1°22E **72** B5
eswick *Australia* 14°34S 132°53E **148** B5
eswick *U.S.A.* 14°31S 132°51E **148** B5
Bet She'an *Israel* 32°30N 35°30E **130** C4
Bet Shemesh *Israel* 31°44N 35°0E **130** D4
Betancuria *Canary Is.* 28°25N 14°3W **100** F5
Betanzos *Spain* 43°15N 8°12W **88** B2
Bétaré Oya *Cameroon* 5°40N 14°5E **140** D2
Bétera *Spain* 39°35N 0°28W **91** F4
Bétérou *Benin* 9°12N 2°16E **139** D5
Bethal *S. Africa* 26°27S 29°28E **145** C4
Bethanien *Namibia* 26°31S 17°8E **144** C2
Bethany *Canada* 44°11N 78°34W **174** B6
Bethany Mo., U.S.A. 40°16N 94°2W **172** E6
Bethany S.C., U.S.A. 35°31N 97°38W **176** D6
Bethel *Alaska, U.S.A.* 60°48N 161°45W **166** C7

Bethel *Conn., U.S.A.* 41°22N 73°25W **175** E11
Bethel *Maine, U.S.A.* 44°25N 70°47W **175** B14
Bethel *Vt., U.S.A.* 43°50N 72°38W **175** C12
Bethel Park *U.S.A.* 40°19N 80°2W **174** F4
Béthenville *France* 49°18N 4°23E **71** C11
Bethlehem = Bayt Lahm
 West Bank 31°43N 35°12E **130** D4
Bethlehem *S. Africa* 28°14S 28°18E **145** C4
Bethlehem *U.S.A.* 40°37N 75°23W **175** F9
Bethulie *S. Africa* 30°30S 25°59E **144** D4
Béthune *France* 50°30N 2°38E **71** B9
Béthune → *France* 49°53N 1°4E **70** C8
Bethungra *Australia* 34°45S 147°51E **153** C7
Betim *Brazil* 19°58S 44°13W **189** D2
Betioky *Madag.* 23°48S 44°20E **141** J8
Betong *Malaysia* 1°24N 111°31E **118** D4
Betong *Thailand* 5°45N 101°5E **121** K3
Betoota *Australia* 25°45S 140°42E **150** D3
Betpaqdala *Kazakhstan* 45°45N 70°30E **109** C8
Betroka *Madag.* 23°16S 46°0E **141** J9
Betsiamites *Canada* 48°56N 68°40W **165** C6
Betsiamites → *Canada* 48°56N 68°38W **165** C6
Bettendorf *U.S.A.* 41°32N 90°30W **172** E8
Bettiah *India* 26°48N 84°33E **125** F11
Bettna *Sweden* 58°55N 16°38E **63** F10
Béttola *Italy* 44°47N 9°36E **92** D6
Betul *India* 21°58N 77°59E **126** D3
Betws-y-Coed *U.K.* 53°5N 3°48W **66** D4
Betxi *Spain* 39°56N 0°12W **90** F4
Betzdorf *Germany* 50°46N 7°52E **76** E3
Beuil *France* 44°6N 6°59E **73** D10
Beulah *Australia* 35°58S 142°29E **152** C5
Beulah *Mich., U.S.A.* 44°38N 86°6W **172** C9
Beulah *N. Dak., U.S.A.* 47°16N 101°47W **172** B3
Beuvron → *France* 47°29N 1°15E **70** E8
Beveren *Belgium* 51°12N 4°16E **69** C4
Beverley *Australia* 32°9S 116°56E **149** F2
Beverley *U.K.* 53°51N 0°26W **66** D7
Beverly *U.S.A.* 42°33N 70°53W **175** D14
Beverly Hills *Calif.,*
 U.S.A. 34°5N 118°24W **171** L8
Beverly Hills *Fla.,*
 U.S.A. 28°55N 82°28W **179** G7
Beverungen *Germany* 51°39N 9°22E **76** D5
Bewas → *India* 23°59N 79°21E **125** H8
Bewdley *Canada* 44°5N 78°19W **174** B6
Bex *Switz.* 46°15N 7°1E **77** J3
Bexhill *U.K.* 50°51N 0°29E **67** G8
Bey Dağları *Turkey* 36°38N 30°29E **99** E12
Beyănli *Iran* 36°0N 47°51E **128** C5
Beyazköy *Turkey* 41°21N 27°42E **97** C11
Beyçayırı *Turkey* 40°15N 26°55E **97** F10
Beydağ *Turkey* 38°5N 28°13E **99** D10
Beyeğaç *Turkey* 37°14N 28°53E **99** D10
Beyin *Ghana* 5°1N 2°41W **138** D4
Beykoz *Turkey* 41°7N 29°7E **97** E13
Beyla *Guinea* 8°30N 8°38W **138** D3
Beynat *France* 45°8N 1°44E **72** C5
Beyneu *Kazakhstan* 45°18N 55°9E **108** C5
Beyoba *Turkey* 38°48N 27°47E **99** C9
Beyoğlu *Turkey* 41°1N 28°58E **97** E12
Beypore → *India* 11°10N 75°47E **127** J2
Beyşehir *Turkey* 37°41N 31°45E **104** D4
Beyşehir Gölü *Turkey* 37°41N 31°33E **104** D4
Beytüşşebap *Turkey* 37°35N 43°10E **105** D10
Bezdan *Serbia* 45°50N 18°57E **80** E3
Bezhetsk *Russia* 57°47N 36°39E **84** D9
Béziers *France* 43°20N 3°12E **72** E7
Bezwada = Vijayawada
 India 16°31N 80°39E **126** F5
Bhabua *India* 25°3N 83°37E **125** G10
Bhachau *India* 23°20N 70°16E **124** H4
Bhadar → *Gujarat,*
 India 22°17N 72°20E **124** H5
Bhadar → *Gujarat,*
 India 21°27N 69°47E **124** J3
Bhadarwah *India* 32°58N 75°46E **125** C6
Bhadgaon = Bhaktapur
 Nepal 27°38N 85°24E **125** F11
Bhadohi *India* 25°25N 82°34E **125** G10
Bhadra *India* 29°8N 75°14E **124** E6
Bhadra → *India* 14°0N 75°20E **127** H2
Bhadrachalam *India* 17°40N 80°53E **126** F5
Bhadrak *India* 21°10N 86°30E **126** D8
Bhadravati *India* 13°49N 75°40E **127** H2
Bhag *Pakistan* 29°2N 67°49E **124** E2
Bhagalpur *India* 25°10N 87°0E **125** G12
Bhagirathi → *Paschimanga,*
 India 23°25N 88°23E **125** H13
Bhagirathi → *Uttarakhand,*
 India 30°8N 78°35E **125** D8
Bhainsa *India* 19°10N 77°58E **126** E3
Bhakkar *Pakistan* 31°40N 71°5E **124** D4
Bhakra Dam *India* 31°30N 76°45E **124** D7
Bhaktapur *Nepal* 27°38N 85°24E **125** F11
Bhalki *India* 18°2N 77°13E **126** E3
Bhamo *Myanmar* 24°15N 97°15E **123** G20
Bhamragarh *India* 19°30N 80°40E **126** E5
Bhandara *India* 21°5N 79°42E **126** D4
Bhanpura *India* 24°31N 75°44E **124** G6
Bhanrer Ra. *India* 23°40N 79°45E **125** H8
Bhaptiahi *India* 26°19N 86°44E **125** F12
Bharat = India ■ *Asia* 20°0N 78°0E **122** K11
Bharatpur *Chhatisgarh,*
 India 23°44N 81°46E **125** H9
Bharatpur *Raj., India* 27°15N 77°30E **124** F7
Bharatpur *Nepal* 27°34N 84°10E **125** F11
Bharno *India* 23°14N 84°53E **125** H11
Bharuch *India* 21°47N 73°0E **124** J5
Bharsaigh, Caolas = Barra, Sd. of
 U.K. 57°4N 7°25W **65** D1
Bhatarsaigh = Vatersay
 U.K. 56°55N 7°32W **65** E1
Bhatghar L. *India* 18°10N 73°48E **126** E1
Bhatinda *India* 30°15N 74°57E **124** D6
Bhatkal *India* 13°58N 74°35E **127** H1
Bhatpara *India* 22°50N 88°25E **125** H13
Bhattu *India* 29°36N 75°19E **124** E6
Bhaun *Pakistan* 32°55N 72°40E **124** C5
Bhaunagar = Bhavnagar
 India 21°45N 72°10E **124** D1
Bhavani *India* 11°27N 77°43E **127** J3
Bhavani → *India* 21°45N 72°10E **124** J5
Bhawanipatna *India* 19°55N 83°10E **126** E6
Bhawari *India* 25°42N 73°4E **124** E5
Bhayavadar *India* 21°51N 70°15E **124** J4

Bhearnaraigh = Berneray
 U.K. 57°43N 7°11W **65** D1
Bhera *Pakistan* 32°29N 72°57E **124** C5
Bheri → *Nepal* 28°47N 81°18E **125** E9
Bhikangaon *India* 21°52N 75°57E **124** J6
Bhilai = Bhilainagar-Durg
 India 21°13N 81°26E **126** D5
Bhilainagar-Durg *India* 21°13N 81°26E **126** D5
Bhilsa = Vidisha *India* 23°28N 77°53E **124** H7
Bhilwara *India* 25°25N 74°38E **124** G6
Bhima → *India* 16°25N 77°17E **126** F3
Bhimavaram *India* 16°30N 81°30E **127** F5
Bhimbar *Pakistan* 32°59N 74°3E **125** C6
Bhind *India* 26°30N 78°46E **125** F8
Bhinga *India* 27°43N 81°56E **125** F9
Bhinmal *India* 25°0N 72°15E **124** G5
Bhisho *S. Africa* 32°50S 27°23E **144** D4
Bhiwandi *India* 19°20N 73°0E **126** E1
Bhiwani *India* 28°50N 76°9E **124** E7
Bhogava → *India* 22°26N 72°20E **124** H5
Bhojpur *Nepal* 27°10N 87°3E **125** F12
Bhokardan *India* 20°16N 75°46E **126** D2
Bhola *Bangla.* 22°45N 90°35E **123** H17
Bholari *Pakistan* 25°19N 68°13E **124** G3
Bhongir *India* 17°30N 78°56E **126** F4
Bhopal *India* 23°20N 77°30E **124** H7
Bhopalpatnam *India* 18°52N 80°23E **126** E5
Bhor *India* 18°12N 73°53E **126** E1
Bhuban *India* 20°53N 85°50E **126** D7
Bhubaneshwar *India* 20°15N 85°50E **126** D7
Bhuj *India* 23°15N 69°49E **124** H3
Bhumiphol Res.
 Thailand 17°20N 98°40E **120** D2
Bhusawal *India* 21°3N 75°46E **126** D2
Bhutan ■ *Asia* 27°25N 90°30E **123** F17
Biafra, B. of = Bonny, Bight of
 Africa 3°30N 9°20E **139** E6
Biak *Indonesia* 1°10S 136°6E **119** E9
Biała *Poland* 50°24N 17°40E **83** H4
Biała → *Poland* 50°3N 20°55E **83** H7
Biała Piska *Poland* 53°37N 22°5E **82** E9
Biała Podlaska *Poland* 52°4N 23°6E **83** F10
Biała Rawska *Poland* 51°48N 20°29E **83** G7
Białobrzegi *Poland* 51°39N 20°57E **83** G7
Białogard *Poland* 54°2N 15°58E **82** D2
Białowieski □ *Poland* 52°43N 23°50E **83** F10
Białowieża *Poland* 52°41N 23°49E **83** F10
Biały Bór *Poland* 53°53N 16°51E **82** E3
Białystok *Poland* 53°10N 23°10E **83** E10
Biancavilla *Italy* 37°38N 14°52E **95** E7
Bianco *Italy* 38°5N 16°9E **95** D9
Biankouma *Côte d'Ivoire* 7°50N 7°40W **138** D3
Biaora *India* 23°56N 76°56E **124** H7
Biärjmand *Iran* 36°6N 55°53E **129** B7
Biaro *Indonesia* 2°5N 125°26E **119** D7
Biarritz *France* 43°29N 1°33W **72** E2
Biasca *Switz.* 46°22N 8°58E **77** J4
Biba *Egypt* 28°55N 31°0E **137** C7
Bibai *Japan* 43°19N 141°52E **112** C10
Bibbiena *Italy* 43°42N 11°49E **93** E8
Bibby I. *Canada* 61°55N 93°0W **163** A10
Bibei → *Spain* 42°24N 7°13W **88** C3
Biberach *Germany* 48°5N 9°47E **77** G5
Bibiani *Ghana* 6°30N 2°8W **138** D4
Bibile *Sri Lanka* 7°10N 81°25E **127** L5
Bibungwa
 Dem. Rep. of the Congo 2°40S 28°15E **142** C2
Bicaj *Albania* 42°0N 20°25E **96** C4
Bicaz *Romania* 46°53N 26°5E **81** D11
Bicazu Ardelean
 Romania 46°51N 25°56E **81** D10
Biccari *Italy* 41°23N 15°12E **95** A8
Bicester *U.K.* 51°54N 1°9W **67** F6
Bicheno *Australia* 41°52S 148°18E **151** G4
Bichia *India* 22°27N 80°42E **125** H9
Bichvinta *Georgia* 43°9N 40°21E **87** A5
Bickerton I. *Australia* 13°45S 136°10E **150** A2
Bicske *Hungary* 47°29N 18°38E **80** C3
Bida = Bir *India* 19°4N 75°46E **126** E2
Bida *Nigeria* 9°3N 5°58E **139** D6
Bidar *India* 17°55N 77°35E **126** F3
Biddeford *U.S.A.* 43°30N 70°28W **173** D18
Bideford *U.K.* 51°1N 4°13W **67** F3
Bideford Bay *U.K.* 51°5N 4°20W **67** F3
Bidhuna *India* 26°49N 79°31E **125** F8
Bidokht *Iran* 34°20N 58°46E **129** C8
Bidor *Malaysia* 4°6N 101°15E **121** K3
Bidyadanga *Australia* 18°45S 121°43E **148** C3
Bie *Sweden* 59°5N 16°12E **62** E10
Bié, Planalto de *Angola* 12°0S 16°0E **141** G3
Bieber *U.S.A.* 41°7N 121°8W **168** F3
Biebrza → *Poland* 53°13N 22°25E **83** E9
Biebrzański △ *Poland* 53°36N 22°45E **83** E9
Biecz *Poland* 49°44N 21°15E **83** J8
Biel *Switz.* 47°8N 7°14E **77** H3
Bielawa *Poland* 50°43N 16°37E **83** H3
Bielefeld *Germany* 52°1N 8°33E **76** C4
Bielersee *Switz.* 47°6N 7°5E **77** H3
Biella *Italy* 45°34N 8°3E **92** C5
Bielsk Podlaski *Poland* 52°47N 23°12E **83** F10
Bielsko-Biała *Poland* 49°50N 19°2E **83** J6
Bien Hoa *Vietnam* 10°57N 106°49E **121** G6
Bienne = Biel *Switz.* 47°8N 7°14E **77** H3
Bienvenida *Spain* 38°18N 6°12W **89** G4
Bienville, L. *Canada* 55°5N 72°40W **164** A5
Bierné *France* 47°49N 0°33W **70** E6
Bierun *Poland* 50°6N 19°6E **83** H6
Bierutów *Poland* 51°7N 17°32E **83** G4
Biescas *Spain* 42°37N 0°20W **90** C4
Biese → *Germany* 52°53N 11°46E **76** C7
Biesiesfontein *S. Africa* 30°57S 17°58E **144** D2
Bieszczadzki □ *Poland* 49°5N 22°43E **83** J9
Bietigheim-Bissingen
 Germany 48°58N 9°8E **77** G5
Bieżuń *Poland* 52°58N 19°55E **83** F6
Biferno → *Italy* 41°59N 15°2E **93** G12
Bifoun *Gabon* 0°5S 10°23E **140** E2
Big B. = Awarua B.
 N.Z. 46°28S 168°4E **155** D2
Big B. *Canada* 55°43N 60°35W **165** A7
Big Bear City *U.S.A.* 34°16N 116°51W **171** L10
Big Bear Lake *U.S.A.* 34°15N 116°56W **171** L10
Big Belt Mts. *U.S.A.* 46°30N 111°25W **168** C8
Big Bend *Swaziland* 26°50S 31°58E **145** D5
Big Bend △ *U.S.A.* 29°20N 103°5W **176** G3
Big Black → *U.S.A.* 32°3N 91°4W **176** E9
Big Blue → *U.S.A.* 39°35N 96°34W **172** F5
Big Buddha
 Hong Kong, China 22°15N 113°54E **111** a
Big Creek *U.S.A.* 37°11N 119°14W **170** H7

Big Creek △ *Canada* 51°18N 123°10W **162** C4
Big Cypress △ *U.S.A.* 26°0N 81°10W **179** J8
Big Cypress Swamp
 U.S.A. 26°15N 81°30W **179** J8
Big Desert *Australia* 35°45S 141°10E **151** F3
Big Falls *U.S.A.* 48°31N 93°48W **172** A7
Big Fork → *U.S.A.* 48°31N 93°43W **172** A7
Big Horn Mts. = Bighorn Mts.
 U.S.A. 44°25N 107°0W **168** D10
Big I. *Canada* 61°7N 116°45W **162** A5
Big Lake *U.S.A.* 31°12N 101°28W **176** F4
Big Moose *U.S.A.* 43°49N 74°58W **175** C10
Big Muddy Cr. →
 U.S.A. 48°8N 104°36W **168** B11
Big Pine *U.S.A.* 37°10N 118°17W **170** H8
Big Pine Key *U.S.A.* 24°40N 81°21W **179** L8
Big Piney *U.S.A.* 42°32N 110°7W **168** E8
Big Quill L. *Canada* 51°55N 104°30W **163** C8
Big Rapids *U.S.A.* 43°42N 85°29W **173** D11
Big Rideau L. *Canada* 44°40N 76°15W **175** B8
Big River *Canada* 53°50N 107°0W **163** C7
Big Run *U.S.A.* 40°57N 78°55W **174** F6
Big Sable Pt. *U.S.A.* 44°3N 86°1W **172** C10
Big Salmon →
 Canada 61°52N 134°55W **162** A2
Big Sand L. *Canada* 57°45N 99°45W **163** B9
Big Sandy *U.S.A.* 48°11N 110°7W **168** B8
Big Sandy → *U.S.A.* 38°25N 82°36W **173** F12
Big Sandy Cr. = Sandy Cr. →
 U.S.A. 41°51N 109°47W **168** F9
Big Sandy Cr. →
 U.S.A. 38°7N 102°29W **168** G12
Big Satilla Cr. → *U.S.A.* 31°27N 82°3W **178** D7
Big Sioux → *U.S.A.* 42°29N 96°27W **172** D5
Big South Fork △
 U.S.A. 36°27N 84°47W **177** C12
Big Spring *U.S.A.* 32°15N 101°28W **176** E4
Big Stone City *U.S.A.* 45°18N 96°28W **172** C5
Big Stone Gap *U.S.A.* 36°52N 82°47W **173** G12
Big Stone L. *U.S.A.* 45°30N 96°35W **172** C5
Big Sur *U.S.A.* 36°15N 121°48W **170** J5
Big Timber *U.S.A.* 45°50N 109°57W **168** D9
Big Trout L. *Canada* 53°40N 90°0W **164** B2
Big Trout Lake *Canada* 53°45N 90°0W **164** B2
Biga *Turkey* 40°13N 27°14E **97** F11
Biga → *Turkey* 40°20N 27°4E **97** F11
Bigadiç *Turkey* 39°22N 28°7E **99** B10
Biganos *France* 44°39N 0°59W **72** D3
Biggar *Canada* 52°4N 108°0W **163** C7
Biggar *U.K.* 55°38N 3°32W **65** F5
Bigge I. *Australia* 14°35S 125°10E **148** B4
Biggenden *Australia* 25°31S 152°4E **151** D5
Biggleswade *U.K.* 52°5N 0°14W **67** E7
Biggs *U.S.A.* 39°25N 121°43W **170** F5
Bighorn *U.S.A.* 46°10N 107°27W **168** C10
Bighorn → *U.S.A.* 46°10N 107°28W **168** C10
Bighorn Canyon △
 U.S.A. 45°10N 108°0W **168** D10
Bighorn L. *U.S.A.* 44°55N 108°15W **168** D9
Bighorn Mts. *U.S.A.* 44°25N 107°0W **168** D10
Bignona *Senegal* 12°52N 16°14W **138** C1
Bigorre *France* 43°10N 0°5E **72** E4
Bigstone L. *Canada* 53°42N 95°44W **163** C9
Biguglia, Étang de
 France 42°36N 9°29E **73** F13
Bigwa *Tanzania* 7°10S 39°10E **142** D4
Bihać *Bos.-H.* 44°49N 15°57E **93** D12
Bihar *India* 25°5N 85°40E **125** G11
Bihar □ *India* 25°0N 86°0E **125** G12
Biharamulo *Tanzania* 2°25S 31°25E **142** C3
Biharamulo △ *Tanzania* 2°24S 31°26E **142** C3
Biharkeresztes *Hungary* 47°8N 21°44E **80** C6
Bihor □ *Romania* 47°0N 22°10E **80** D7
Bihor, Munţii *Romania* 46°29N 22°47E **80** D7
Bijagós, Arquipélago dos
 Guinea-Biss. 11°15N 16°10W **138** C1
Bijaipur *India* 26°2N 77°20E **124** F7
Bijapur = Vijayapura
 India 16°50N 75°55E **126** F2
Bijapur *India* 18°50N 80°50E **126** E5
Bijār *Iran* 35°52N 47°35E **105** E12
Bijauri *Nepal* 28°6N 82°20E **125** E10
Bijawar *India* 24°38N 79°30E **125** G8
Bijela *Montenegro* 42°28N 18°39E **96** D2
Bijeljina *Bos.-H.* 44°46N 19°14E **80** F4
Bijie *China* 27°20N 105°16E **116** D5
Bijnor *India* 29°27N 78°11E **124** E8
Bikaner *India* 28°2N 73°18E **124** E5
Bikapur *India* 26°30N 82°7E **125** F10
Bikeqi *China* 40°43N 111°20E **114** D6
Bikfayya *Lebanon* 33°55N 35°41E **130** B4
Bikin *Russia* 46°50N 134°20E **112** A7
Bikin → *Russia* 46°51N 134°2E **112** A7
Bikini Atoll *Marshall Is.* 12°0N 167°30E **156** F8
Bikita *Zimbabwe* 20°6S 31°41E **145** B5
Bikku Bitti *Libya* 22°0N 19°12E **135** D9
Bikoué *Cameroon* 3°55N 11°50E **139** E7
Bila Tserkva *Ukraine* 49°45N 30°10E **75** D16
Bilanga *Burkina Faso* 12°33N 0°25W **139** C5
Bilara *India* 26°14N 73°53E **124** F5
Bilaspur *Chhattisgarh,*
 India 22°2N 82°15E **125** H10
Bilaspur *Punjab, India* 31°19N 76°50E **124** D7
Biläsuvar *Azerbaijan* 39°27N 48°32E **105** C13
Bilauk Taungdan
 Thailand 13°0N 99°0E **120** F2
Bilauri *Nepal* 28°41N 80°21E **125** E9
Bilbao *Spain* 43°16N 2°56W **90** B2
Bilbao ✈ (BIO) *Spain* 43°18N 2°57W **90** B2
Bilbeis *Egypt* 30°25N 31°34E **137** C7
Bilbo = Bilbao *Spain* 43°16N 2°56W **90** B2
Bilbor *Romania* 47°6N 25°30E **81** C10
Bilche-Zolote *Ukraine* 48°47N 25°53E **81** D10
Bilçureşti *Romania* 44°44N 25°48E **81** F10
Bildudalur *Iceland* 65°41N 23°36W **60** D2
Bílé Karpaty *Europe* 49°5N 18°0E **79** B11
Bílé Patra → *Italy* 45°50N 58°55W **165** B8
Bileća *Bos.-H.* 42°53N 18°27E **96** D2
Bilecik *Turkey* 40°5N 30°5E **104** B4
Bilecikó *Turkey* 40°0N 30°0E **104** B3
Bilecko Jezero *Bos.-H.* 42°48N 18°28E **96** D2
Bileh Savār *Iran* 39°21N 48°21E **105** C13
Bilgoraj *Poland* 50°33N 22°42E **83** H9
Bilgram *India* 27°11N 80°2E **125** F9
Bilhaur *India* 26°51N 80°5E **125** F9
Bilhorod-Dnistrovskyy
 Ukraine 46°11N 30°23E **85** J6
Bilibino *Russia* 68°3N 166°20E **107** C17
Bilibiza *Mozam.* 12°30S 40°20E **143** E5
Bilimora *India* 20°45N 72°57E **126** D1

Bilisht *Albania* 40°37N 21°2E **96** F5
Bi'r Muṭribah *Kuwait* 29°54N 47°17E **128** D5
Bi'r Nakheila *Egypt* 24°1N 30°50E **137** C3
Bi'r Qatia *Egypt* 30°58N 32°45E **130** E1
Bi'r Qatrani *Egypt* 30°55N 26°10E **137** A2
Bi'r Ranga *Egypt* 24°25N 35°15E **137** C4
Bi'r Sahara *Egypt* 22°54N 28°40E **137** C3
Bir Seiyâla *Egypt* 26°10N 33°50E **137** B3
Bi'r Shalatein *Egypt* 23°5N 35°25E **137** C4
Bi'r Shebb *Egypt* 22°25N 29°40E **137** C2
Bir Shût *Egypt* 23°50N 35°15E **137** C4
Bi'r Terfawi *Egypt* 22°57N 28°55E **137** C2
Bi'r Umm Qubûr *Egypt* 24°35N 34°2E **137** C4
Bi'r Za'farâna *Egypt* 29°10N 32°40E **137** B8
Bi'r Zeidûn *Egypt* 25°45N 33°40E **137** B3
Biräk *Libya* 27°31N 14°20E **135** C8
Biramféro *Guinea* 11°40N 9°10W **138** C3
Biratnagar *Nepal* 26°27N 87°17E **125** F12
Birawa
 Dem. Rep. of the Congo 2°20S 28°48E **142** C2
Birch → *Canada* 58°28N 112°17W **162** B6
Birch Hills *Canada* 52°59N 105°25W **163** C7
Birch I. *Canada* 52°26N 99°54W **163** C9
Birch L. N.W.T., Canada 62°4N 116°33W **162** A5
Birch L. Ont., Canada 51°23N 92°18W **164** B1
Birch Mts. *Canada* 57°30N 113°10W **162** B6
Birch River *Canada* 52°24N 101°6W **163** C8
Birchip *Australia* 35°56S 142°55E **152** C5
Birchiş *Romania* 45°58N 22°9E **80** E7
Birchwood *N.Z.* 45°55S 167°53E **155** F2
Bird *Canada* 56°30N 94°13W **163** B10
Bird I. = Aves, I. de
 W. Indies 15°45N 63°55W **183** C7
Bird I. *S. Georgia* 54°0S 38°3W **55** B1
Birds Creek *Canada* 45°6N 77°52W **174** A7
Birdsville *Australia* 25°51S 139°20E **150** D2
Birdum Cr. → *Australia* 15°14S 133°0E **148** C5
Birdwood *Australia* 34°51S 138°58E **152** C2
Birecik *Turkey* 37°2N 38°0E **105** D8
Birein *Israel* 30°50N 34°28E **130** E3
Bireuen *Indonesia* 5°14N 96°39E **118** C1
Birganj *Nepal* 27°1N 84°52E **125** F11
Birifo *Gambia* 13°30N 13°58E **139** C2
Birigüi *Brazil* 21°18S 50°16W **191** A5
Birjand *Iran* 32°53N 59°13E **129** C8
Birka *Sweden* 59°20N 17°32E **62** E11
Birkenfeld *Germany* 49°38N 7°9E **77** F3
Birkenhead *U.K.* 53°23N 3°2W **66** D4
Birkerød *Denmark* 55°50N 12°25E **63** J6
Birket Qârûn *Egypt* 29°30N 30°40E **137** C7
Birkfeld *Austria* 47°21N 15°45E **78** D8
Birkhadem *Algeria* 36°43N 3°3E **136** A4
Bîrlad = Bârlad
 Romania 46°15N 27°38E **81** D12
Birmingham *U.K.* 52°29N 1°52W **67** E6
Birmingham *U.S.A.* 33°31N 86°48W **177** E11
Birmingham Int. ✈ (BHX)
 U.K. 52°26N 1°45W **67** E6
Birmitrapur *India* 22°24N 84°46E **126** C7
Birni Ngaouré *Niger* 13°5N 2°51E **139** C5
Birni Nkonni *Niger* 13°55N 5°15E **139** C6
Birni Gwari *Nigeria* 11°0N 6°45E **139** C6
Birni Kebbi *Nigeria* 12°32N 4°12E **139** C5
Birni Kudu *Nigeria* 11°30N 9°29E **139** C6
Birobidzhan *Russia* 48°50N 132°50E **111** B15
Birr *Ireland* 53°6N 7°54W **64** C4
Birrie → *Australia* 29°43S 146°37E **151** D4
Birsilpur *India* 28°11N 72°15E **124** E5
Birsk *Russia* 55°25N 55°30E **106** D6
Birtle *Canada* 50°30N 101°5W **163** C8
Birur *India* 13°30N 75°55E **122** N9
Biryuchiy *Ukraine* 46°10N 35°0E **85** J8
Biržai *Lithuania* 56°11N 24°45E **84** D3
Birżebbuġa *Malta* 35°50N 14°32E **100** D2
Bisa *Indonesia* 1°15S 127°28E **119** E7
Bisáccia *Italy* 41°1N 15°22E **95** A8
Bisacquino *Italy* 37°42N 13°15E **94** E6
Bisalpur *India* 28°14N 79°48E **125** E8
Bisbee *U.S.A.* 31°27N 109°55W **169** L9
Biscarrosse *France* 44°22N 1°20W **72** D2
Biscarrosse et de Parentis, Étang
 de *France* 44°21N 1°10W **72** D2
Biscay, B. of *Atl. Oc.* 45°0N 2°0W **58** F5
Biscay Abyssal Plain
 Atl. Oc. 45°0N 8°0W **56** B11
Biscayne B. *U.S.A.* 25°25N 80°12W **179** K9
Biscayne B. *U.S.A.* 25°40N 80°12W **179** K9
Biscéglie *Italy* 41°14N 16°30E **95** A9
Bischheim *France* 48°37N 7°46E **71** D14
Bischofshofen *Austria* 47°26N 13°14E **78** D6
Bischofswerda *Germany* 51°7N 14°10E **76** D10
Bischwiller *France* 48°46N 7°50E **71** D14
Biscoe I. *Antarctica* 66°0S 67°0W **55** C17
Biscotasing *Canada* 47°18N 82°9W **164** C3
Biševo *Croatia* 42°57N 16°3E **93** F13
Bishah, W. →
 Si. Arabia 21°24N 43°26E **137** C5
Bishan *China* 29°33N 106°12E **116** C6
Bishkek *Kyrgyzstan* 42°54N 74°46E **108** D8
Bishnupur *India* 23°8N 87°20E **125** H12
Bisho = Bhisho *S. Africa* 32°50S 27°23E **144** D4
Bishoftu = Debre Zeyit
 Ethiopia 8°50N 39°0E **131** F2
Bishop *Calif., U.S.A.* 37°22N 118°24W **170** H8
Bishop *Ga., U.S.A.* 33°49N 83°26W **178** B6
Bishop *Tex., U.S.A.* 27°35N 97°48W **176** H6
Bishop Auckland *U.K.* 54°39N 1°40W **66** C6
Bishop's Falls *Canada* 49°2N 55°30W **165** C8
Bishop's Stortford *U.K.* 51°52N 0°10E **67** F8
Bisignano *Italy* 39°37N 16°17E **95** C9
Bisina, L. *Uganda* 1°38N 33°56E **142** B3
Biskra *Algeria* 34°50N 5°44E **136** B7
Biskupiec *Poland* 53°53N 20°58E **82** E8
Bismarck *U.S.A.* 46°48N 100°47W **172** B3
Bismarck Arch.
 Papua N.G. 2°30S 150°0E **147** D6
Bismark *Germany* 52°40N 11°33E **76** C7
Bismil *Turkey* 37°51N 40°40E **105** D9
Biso *Uganda* 1°44N 31°26E **142** B3
Bison *U.S.A.* 45°31N 102°28W **172** C2
Bīsotūn *Iran* 34°23N 47°26E **105** E12
Bispgården *Sweden* 63°2N 16°40E **62** A10
Bissagos = Bijagós, Arquipélago
 dos *Guinea-Biss.* 11°15N 16°10W **138** C1
Bissam Cuttack *India* 19°31N 83°31E **126** E6
Bissau *Guinea-Biss.* 11°45N 15°45W **138** C1
Bissikrima *Guinea* 10°50N 10°58W **138** C2
Bissorã *Guinea-Biss.* 12°16N 15°35W **138** C1

Bistcho L. Canada 59°45N 118°50W 162 B5
Bistreţ Romania 43°54N 23°23E 81 G8
Bistrica = Ilirska-Bistrica Slovenia 45°34N 14°14E 93 C11
Bistriţa Romania 47°9N 24°35E 81 C9
Bistriţa → Romania 46°30N 26°57E 81 D11
Bistriţa Năsăud □ Romania 47°15N 24°30E 81 C9
Bistriţei, Munţii Romania 47°15N 25°40E 81 C10
Biswan India 27°29N 81°2E 125 F9
Bisztynek Poland 54°8N 20°53E 82 D7
Bitam Gabon 2°5N 11°25E 140 D2
Bitburg Germany 49°58N 6°31E 77 F2
Bitche France 49°2N 7°25E 71 C14
Bithynia Turkey 40°40N 31°0E 104 B4
Bitkine Chad 11°59N 18°13E 135 F9
Bitlis Turkey 38°20N 42°3E 105 C10
Bitlis □ Turkey 38°20N 42°5E 105 C10
Bitola Macedonia 41°1N 21°20E 96 E5
Bitolj = Bitola Macedonia 41°1N 21°20E 96 E5
Bitonto Italy 41°6N 16°41E 95 A9
Bitra I. India 11°33N 72°9E 127 J1
Bitter Creek U.S.A. 41°33N 108°33W 168 F9
Bitter L. = Buheirat-Murrat-el-Kubra Egypt 30°18N 32°26E 137 E8
Bitterfeld-Wolfen Germany 51°37N 12°20E 76 D8
Bitterfontein S. Africa 31°1S 18°32E 144 D2
Bitterroot → U.S.A. 46°52N 114°7W 168 C6
Bitterroot Range U.S.A. 46°0N 114°20W 168 C6
Bitterwater U.S.A. 36°23N 121°0W 170 J6
Bitti Italy 40°29N 9°23E 94 B2
Bittou Burkina Faso 11°17N 0°18W 139 C4
Biu Nigeria 10°40N 12°3E 139 C7
Bivolari Romania 47°31N 27°27E 81 C12
Bivolu, Vf. Romania 47°16N 25°58E 81 C10
Biwa-Ko Japan 35°15N 136°10E 113 G8
Biwabik U.S.A. 47°32N 92°21W 172 B7
Bixad Romania 47°56N 23°28E 81 C8
Bixby U.S.A. 35°57N 95°53W 176 D7
Biya → Russia 52°25N 85°0E 109 B11
Biyang China 32°38N 113°21E 117 A9
Biysk Russia 52°40N 85°0E 109 B11
Bizana S. Africa 30°50S 29°52E 145 D4
Bizen Japan 34°43N 134°8E 113 G7
Bizerte Tunisia 37°15N 9°50E 136 A5
Bizerte □ Tunisia 37°5N 9°35E 136 A5
Bizkaia □ Spain 43°15N 2°45W 90 B2
Bjargtangar Iceland 65°30N 24°30W 60 D1
Bjärnum Sweden 56°17N 13°43E 63 H7
Bjästa Sweden 63°12N 18°29E 62 A12
Bjelasica Montenegro 42°50N 19°40E 96 D3
Bjelašnica Bos.-H. 43°43N 18°9E 80 G3
Bjelovar Croatia 45°56N 16°49E 93 C13
Bjerringbro Denmark 56°23N 9°39E 63 H3
Björbo Sweden 60°27N 14°44E 62 D8
Björklinge Sweden 60°2N 17°33E 62 D11
Björkö Sweden 59°52N 19°2E 62 E13
Björneborg = Pori Finland 61°29N 21°48E 84 B1
Björneborg Sweden 59°14N 14°16E 62 E8
Bjørnevatn Norway 69°40N 30°0E 60 B24
Bjørnøya Arctic 74°30N 19°0E 54 B8
Bjursås Sweden 60°44N 15°25E 62 D9
Bjuv Sweden 56°5N 12°55E 63 H6
Bla Mali 12°56N 5°47W 138 C3
Blå Jungfrun △ Sweden 57°16N 16°47E 63 G10
Blace Serbia 43°18N 21°17E 96 C5
Blachownia Poland 50°49N 18°56E 83 H5
Black = Da → Vietnam 21°15N 105°20E 116 G5
Black → Canada 44°42N 79°19W 174 B5
Black → Ariz., U.S.A. 33°44N 110°13W 169 K8
Black → Ark., U.S.A. 35°38N 91°20W 176 D9
Black → La., U.S.A. 31°16N 91°50W 176 F9
Black → Mich., U.S.A. 42°59N 82°27W 174 D2
Black → N.Y., U.S.A. 43°59N 76°4W 175 C8
Black → Wis., U.S.A. 43°57N 91°22W 172 D8
Black Bay Pen. Canada 48°38N 88°21W 164 C2
Black Birch L. Canada 56°53N 107°45W 163 B7
Black Canyon of the Gunnison ⌓ U.S.A. 38°40N 107°35W 168 G10
Black Diamond Canada 50°45N 114°14W 162 C6
Black Duck → Canada 56°51N 89°2W 164 A2
Black Forest = Schwarzwald Germany 48°30N 8°20E 77 G4
Black Forest U.S.A. 39°0N 104°43W 168 G11
Black Hd. Ireland 53°9N 9°16W 64 C2
Black Hills U.S.A. 44°0N 103°45W 172 D2
Black I. Canada 51°12N 96°30W 163 C9
Black L. Canada 59°12N 105°15W 163 B7
Black L. Mich., U.S.A. 45°28N 84°16W 173 C11
Black L. N.Y., U.S.A. 44°31N 75°36W 175 B9
Black Lake Canada 59°11N 105°20W 163 B7
Black Mesa U.S.A. 36°58N 102°58W 176 C3
Black Mountain Australia 30°18S 151°39E 153 A9
Black Mt. = Mynydd Du U.K. 51°52N 3°50W 67 F4
Black Mts. U.K. 51°55N 3°7W 67 F4
Black Range U.S.A. 33°15N 107°50W 169 K10
Black River Jamaica 18°0N 77°50W 182 a
Black River U.S.A. 44°0N 75°47W 175 C9
Black River Falls U.S.A. 44°18N 90°51W 172 C8
Black Rock Australia 32°50S 138°44E 152 B3
Black Rock Barbados 13°7N 59°37W 183 g
Black Rock Desert U.S.A. 41°10N 118°50W 168 F4
Black Sea Eurasia 43°30N 35°0E 58 G12
Black Tickle Canada 53°28N 55°45W 165 B8
Black Volta → Africa 8°41N 1°33W 138 D4
Black Warrior → U.S.A. 32°32N 87°51W 177 E11
Blackall Australia 24°25S 145°45E 150 C4
Blackball N.Z. 42°22S 171°26E 155 C6
Blackbraes △ Australia 19°10S 144°10E 150 B3
Blackbull Australia 17°55S 141°45E 150 B3
Blackburn U.K. 53°45N 2°29W 66 D5
Blackburn, Mt. U.S.A. 61°44N 143°26W 166 C11
Blackburn with Darwen □ U.K. 53°45N 2°29W 66 D5
Blackdown Tableland △ Australia 23°52S 149°8E 150 C4
Blackfoot U.S.A. 43°11N 112°21W 168 E7
Blackfoot → U.S.A. 46°52N 113°53W 168 C7
Blackfoot Res. U.S.A. 42°55N 111°39W 168 E8
Blackman U.S.A. 30°56N 86°38W 179 E3
Blackpool U.K. 53°49N 3°3W 66 D4
Blackpool □ U.K. 53°49N 3°3W 66 D4
Blackriver U.S.A. 44°46N 83°17W 174 B1
Blacks Harbour Canada 45°3N 66°49W 165 C6
Blacksburg U.S.A. 37°14N 80°25W 173 G13
Blackshear U.S.A. 31°18N 82°14W 178 D7
Blackshear, L. U.S.A. 31°51N 83°56W 178 D6
Blacksod B. Ireland 54°6N 10°0W 64 B1
Blackstairs Mt. Ireland 52°33N 6°48W 64 D5
Blackstone U.S.A. 37°5N 78°0W 173 G14
Blackstone Ra. Australia 26°0S 128°30E 149 E4
Blackville U.S.A. 33°22N 81°16W 178 B8
Blackwater = West Road → Canada 53°18N 122°53W 162 C4
Blackwater Australia 23°35S 148°53E 150 C4
Blackwater → Meath, Ireland 53°39N 6°41W 64 C4
Blackwater → Waterford, Ireland 52°4N 7°52W 64 D4
Blackwater → U.K. 54°31N 6°35W 64 B5
Blackwater → U.S.A. 30°36N 87°2W 179 E2
Blackwell U.S.A. 36°48N 97°17W 176 C6
Blackwells Corner U.S.A. 35°37N 119°47W 171 K7
Blackwood U.K. 51°39N 3°12W 67 F4
Bladensburg △ Australia 22°30S 142°59E 150 C3
Blaenau Ffestiniog U.K. 53°0N 3°56W 66 E4
Blaenau Gwent □ U.K. 51°48N 3°12W 67 F4
Blåfjella-Skjækerfjella △ Norway 64°15N 13°8E 60 D15
Blagaj Bos.-H. 43°16N 17°55E 96 C1
Blagnac France 43°37N 1°23E 72 E5
Blagnac, Toulouse ✕ (TLS) France 43°37N 1°22E 72 E5
Blagodarnyy Russia 45°7N 43°37E 87 H6
Blagoevgrad Bulgaria 42°2N 23°5E 96 D7
Blagoevgrad □ Bulgaria 42°2N 23°5E 96 D7
Blagoveshchensk Russia 50°20N 127°30E 111 A14
Blahkiuh Indonesia 8°31S 115°12E 119 J18
Blain France 47°29N 1°45W 70 E5
Blain U.S.A. 40°20N 77°31W 174 F7
Blaine Minn., U.S.A. 45°10N 93°13W 172 C7
Blaine Wash., U.S.A. 48°59N 122°45W 170 B4
Blaine Lake Canada 52°51N 106°52W 163 C7
Blair U.S.A. 41°33N 96°8W 172 E5
Blair Athol Australia 22°42S 147°31E 150 C4
Blair Atholl U.K. 56°46N 3°50W 65 E5
Blairgowrie U.K. 56°35N 3°21W 65 E5
Blairsden U.S.A. 39°47N 120°37W 170 F6
Blairsville U.S.A. 40°26N 79°16W 174 F5
Blaj Romania 46°10N 23°57E 81 D8
Blakang Mati, Pulau Singapore 1°15N 103°50E 121 d
Blake Pt. U.S.A. 48°11N 88°25W 172 A9
Blakely Ga., U.S.A. 31°23N 84°56W 178 D5
Blakely Pa., U.S.A. 41°28N 75°37W 175 E9
Blambangan, Semenanjung Indonesia 8°42S 114°29E 119 K17
Blâmont France 48°35N 6°50E 71 D13
Blanc, C. Spain 39°21N 2°51E 100 B9
Blanc, C. Tunisia 37°15N 9°56E 136 A5
Blanc, Mont Europe 45°48N 6°50E 73 C10
Blanca, B. Argentina 39°10S 61°30W 192 A4
Blanca, Cord. Peru 9°10S 77°35W 188 B2
Blanca, Costa Spain 38°25N 0°10W 91 G4
Blanca Peak U.S.A. 37°35N 105°29W 169 H11
Blanche, C. Australia 33°1S 134°9E 151 E1
Blanche, L. S. Austral., Australia 29°15S 139°40E 151 D2
Blanche, L. W. Austral., Australia 22°25S 123°17E 148 D3
Blanchisseuse Trin. & Tob. 10°48N 61°18W 187 K15
Blanco S. Africa 33°55S 22°23E 144 D3
Blanco U.S.A. 30°6N 98°25W 176 F5
Blanco → Argentina 30°20S 68°42W 190 C2
Blanco, C. Costa Rica 9°34N 85°8W 182 E2
Blanco, C. U.S.A. 42°51N 124°34W 168 E1
Blanda → Iceland 65°37N 20°9W 60 D3
Blandford Forum U.K. 50°51N 2°9W 67 G5
Blanding U.S.A. 37°37N 109°29W 169 H9
Blanes Spain 41°40N 2°48E 90 D7
Blangy-sur-Bresle France 49°55N 1°37E 71 C8
Blanice → Czechia 49°10N 14°5E 78 B7
Blankaholm Sweden 57°36N 16°31E 63 G10
Blankenberge Belgium 51°20N 3°9E 69 C3
Blankenburg Germany 51°47N 10°57E 76 D6
Blanquefort France 44°55N 0°38W 72 D3
Blanquilla, I. Venezuela 11°51N 64°37W 183 D7
Blanquillo Uruguay 32°53S 55°37W 191 C4
Blansko Czechia 49°22N 16°40E 79 B9
Blantyre Malawi 15°45S 35°0E 143 F4
Blarney Ireland 51°56N 8°33W 64 E3
Blasdell U.S.A. 42°48N 78°50W 174 D6
Błaszki Poland 51°38N 18°30E 83 G5
Blatná Czechia 49°25N 13°52E 78 B6
Blato Croatia 42°56N 16°48E 93 F13
Blaubeuren Germany 48°24N 9°46E 77 G5
Blaustein Germany 48°25N 9°53E 77 G5
Blåvands Huk Denmark 55°33N 8°4E 63 J2
Blaydon U.K. 54°58N 1°42W 66 C6
Blaye France 45°8N 0°40W 72 C3
Blaye-les-Mines France 44°1N 2°8E 72 D6
Blayney Australia 33°32S 149°14E 153 B8
Blaze, Pt. Australia 12°56S 130°11E 148 B5
Błażowa Poland 49°53N 22°7E 83 J9
Bleckede Germany 53°17N 10°43E 76 B6
Bled Slovenia 46°27N 14°7E 93 B11
Bleiburg Austria 46°35N 14°49E 78 E7
Blejeşti Romania 44°19N 25°27E 81 F10
Blekinge Sweden 56°25N 15°20E 61 H16
Blekinge □ Sweden 56°20N 15°20E 63 H9
Blenheim Canada 42°20N 82°0W 174 D3
Blenheim N.Z. 41°38S 173°57E 155 B8
Bléone → France 44°5N 6°0E 73 D10
Blérancourt France 49°31N 3°9E 71 C10
Bletchley U.K. 51°59N 0°44W 67 F7
Bleus, Monts Dem. Rep. of the Congo 1°30N 30°30E 142 B3
Blida Algeria 36°30N 2°49E 136 A4
Blida □ Algeria 36°35N 3°0E 136 A4
Blidet Amor Algeria 32°59N 5°58E 136 B5
Blidö Sweden 59°37N 18°53E 62 E12
Blidsberg Sweden 57°56N 13°30E 63 G7
Blieskastel Germany 49°14N 7°12E 77 F3
Bligh Sound N.Z. 44°47S 167°32E 155 E2
Bligh Water Fiji 17°0S 178°0E 154 a
Blind River Canada 46°10N 82°58W 164 C3
Blinisht Albania 41°52N 19°59E 96 E3
Bliss Idaho, U.S.A. 42°56N 114°57W 168 E6
Bliss N.Y., U.S.A. 42°34N 78°15W 174 D6
Blissfield U.S.A. 40°24N 81°58W 174 F3
Blitar Indonesia 8°5S 112°11E 119 H15
Blitchton U.S.A. 32°12N 81°26W 178 C8
Blitta Togo 8°23N 1°6E 139 D5
Block I. U.S.A. 41°11N 71°35W 175 E13
Block Island Sd. U.S.A. 41°15N 71°40W 175 E13
Bloemfontein S. Africa 29°6S 26°7E 144 C4
Bloemhof S. Africa 27°38S 25°32E 144 C4
Blois France 47°35N 1°20E 70 E8
Blomskog Sweden 59°16N 12°2E 62 E6
Blomstermåla Sweden 56°59N 16°21E 63 H10
Blönduós Iceland 65°40N 20°12W 60 D3
Blongas Indonesia 8°53S 116°2E 119 K19
Błonie Poland 52°12N 20°37E 83 F7
Bloodvein → Canada 51°47N 96°43W 163 C9
Bloody Foreland Ireland 55°10N 8°17W 64 A3
Bloomer U.S.A. 45°6N 91°29W 172 C8
Bloomfield Canada 43°59N 77°14W 174 C7
Bloomfield Iowa, U.S.A. 40°45N 92°25W 172 E7
Bloomfield N. Mex., U.S.A. 36°43N 107°59W 169 H10
Bloomfield Nebr., U.S.A. 42°36N 97°39W 172 D5
Bloomington Ill., U.S.A. 40°28N 89°0W 172 E9
Bloomington Ind., U.S.A. 39°10N 86°32W 172 F10
Bloomington Minn., U.S.A. 44°50N 93°17W 172 C7
Bloomsburg U.S.A. 41°0N 76°27W 175 F8
Bloomsbury Australia 20°48S 148°38E 150 b
Blora Indonesia 6°57S 111°25E 119 G14
Blossburg U.S.A. 41°41N 77°4W 174 E7
Blosseville Kyst Greenland 68°50N 26°30W 57 D8
Blouberg S. Africa 23°8S 28°59E 145 B4
Blountstown U.S.A. 30°27N 85°3W 178 E4
Bludenz Austria 47°10N 9°50E 78 D2
Blue Cypress L. U.S.A. 27°44N 80°45W 179 H9
Blue Earth U.S.A. 43°38N 94°6W 172 D6
Blue Hole △ Belize 17°9N 88°40W 182 C2
Blue Lagoon △ Zambia 15°28S 27°26E 143 F2
Blue Mesa Res. U.S.A. 38°28N 107°20W 168 G10
Blue Mountain Lake U.S.A. 43°51N 74°27W 175 C10
Blue Mountain Pk. Jamaica 18°3N 76°36W 182 a
Blue Mt. U.S.A. 40°30N 76°30W 175 F8
Blue Mts. Australia 33°40S 150°15E 153 B9
Blue Mts. Jamaica 18°3N 76°36W 182 a
Blue Mts. Maine, U.S.A. 44°50N 70°35W 175 B14
Blue Mts. Oreg., U.S.A. 45°0N 118°20W 168 D4
Blue Mts. △ Australia 34°2S 150°15E 153 C9
Blue Mud B. Australia 13°30S 136°0E 150 A2
Blue Mud Bay ✪ Australia 13°25S 136°2E 150 A2
Blue Nile = Nîl el Azraq → Sudan 15°38N 32°31E 135 E12
Blue Rapids U.S.A. 39°41N 96°39W 172 F5
Blue Ridge U.S.A. 36°40N 80°50W 173 G13
Blue River Canada 52°6N 119°18W 162 C5
Bluefield U.S.A. 37°15N 81°17W 173 G13
Bluefields Nic. 12°20N 83°50W 182 D3
Bluevale Canada 43°51N 81°15W 174 C3
Bluff Australia 23°35S 149°4E 150 C4
Bluff N.Z. 46°37S 168°20E 155 G3
Bluff U.S.A. 37°17N 109°33W 169 H9
Bluff Harbour N.Z. 46°36S 168°21E 155 G3
Bluff Knoll Australia 34°24S 118°15E 149 F2
Bluff Pt. Australia 27°50S 114°5E 149 E1
Bluffton Ga., U.S.A. 31°31N 84°52W 178 D5
Bluffton Ind., U.S.A. 40°44N 85°11W 173 E11
Bluffton S.C., U.S.A. 32°14N 80°52W 178 C9
Blumenau Brazil 27°0S 49°0W 191 B6
Blunt U.S.A. 44°31N 99°59W 172 C4
Bly U.S.A. 42°24N 121°3W 168 E3
Blyde River Canyon ⌓ S. Africa 24°37S 31°2E 145 B5
Blyth Australia 33°49S 138°28E 152 B3
Blyth Canada 43°44N 81°26W 174 C3
Blyth U.K. 55°8N 1°31W 66 B6
Blythe Calif., U.S.A. 33°37N 114°36W 171 M12
Blythe Ga., U.S.A. 33°17N 82°12W 178 B7
Blytheville U.S.A. 35°56N 89°55W 177 D10
Bo S. Leone 7°55N 11°50W 138 D2
Bo Duc Vietnam 11°58N 106°50E 121 G6
Bo Hai China 39°0N 119°0E 115 E10
Bo Hai Haixia Asia 38°25N 121°10E 115 E11
Bo Xian = Bozhou China 33°55N 115°41E 114 H8
Boa Esperança, Represa Brazil 6°50S 43°50W 189 B2
Boa Nova Brazil 14°22S 40°10W 189 C2
Boa Viagem Brazil 5°7S 39°44W 189 B3
Boa Vista Brazil 2°48N 60°30W 186 C6
Boa Vista Cabo Verde 16°0N 22°49W 134 b
Boaco Nic. 12°29N 85°35W 182 D2
Bo'ai China 35°10N 113°3E 114 G7
Boal Spain 43°25N 6°49W 88 B4
Boalsburg U.S.A. 40°47N 77°49W 174 F7
Boane Mozam. 26°6S 32°19E 145 C5
Boao China 19°8N 110°34E 117 a
Boardman U.S.A. 41°2N 80°40W 174 E4
Boath India 19°20N 78°20E 126 E4
Bobadah Australia 32°19S 146°41E 153 B7
Bobai China 22°17N 109°59E 116 F7
Bobbili India 18°35N 83°30E 126 E6
Bóbbio Italy 44°46N 9°23E 92 D6
Bobcaygeon Canada 44°33N 78°33W 174 B6
Boblad India 17°13N 75°26E 126 F2
Böblingen Germany 48°40N 9°1E 77 G5
Bobo-Dioulasso Burkina Faso 11°8N 4°13W 138 C4
Bobolice Poland 53°58N 16°37E 82 E3
Bobonong Botswana 21°58S 28°20E 145 B4
Boboshevo Bulgaria 42°9N 23°0E 96 D7
Bobov Dol Bulgaria 42°20N 23°0E 96 D6
Bóbr → Poland 52°4N 15°4E 83 F2
Bobraomby, Tanjon' i Madag. 12°40S 49°10E 141 G9
Bobrov Russia 51°5N 40°2E 86 E5
Bobrovytsya Ukraine 50°45N 31°23E 85 G6
Bobruysk = Babruysk Belarus 53°10N 29°15E 75 B15
Bobrynets Ukraine 48°4N 32°5E 85 H7
Boby, Pic Madag. 22°12S 46°55E 141 J9
Boca del Río Mexico 19°5N 96°4W 181 D5
Boca do Acre Brazil 8°50S 67°27W 188 B4
Boca Grande U.S.A. 26°45N 82°16W 179 J7
Boca Raton U.S.A. 26°21N 80°5W 179 J9
Bocaiúva Brazil 17°7S 43°49W 189 D2
Bocanda Côte d'Ivoire 7°5N 4°31W 138 D4
Bocas del Dragón = Dragon's Mouths Trin. & Tob. 11°0N 61°50W 187 K15
Bocas del Toro Panama 9°15N 82°20W 182 E3
Boceguillas Spain 41°20N 3°39W 88 D7
Bochmanivka Ukraine 47°40N 29°34E 81 C14
Bochnia Poland 49°58N 20°27E 83 J7
Bocholt Germany 51°50N 6°36E 76 D2
Bochum = Senwabarana S. Africa 23°17S 29°7E 145 B4
Bochum Germany 51°28N 7°13E 76 D3
Bockenem Germany 52°1N 10°8E 76 C6
Boćki Poland 52°39N 23°3E 83 F10
Bocognano France 42°5N 9°4E 73 F13
Bocoyna Mexico 27°52N 107°35W 180 B3
Bocşa Romania 45°21N 21°47E 80 E6
Boda Dalarna, Sweden 61°1N 15°13E 62 C9
Böda Kalmar, Sweden 57°15N 17°3E 63 G11
Boda Västernorrland, Sweden 62°52N 16°39E 62 B10
Bodafors Sweden 57°48N 14°23E 63 G8
Bodaybo Russia 57°50N 114°0E 107 D12
Boddam U.K. 59°56N 1°17W 65 B7
Boddington Australia 32°50S 116°30E 149 F2
Bode Sadu Nigeria 9°0N 4°47E 139 D5
Bodega Bay U.S.A. 38°20N 123°3W 170 G3
Boden Sweden 65°50N 21°42E 60 D19
Bodensee Europe 47°35N 9°25E 77 H5
Bodenteich Germany 52°50N 10°42E 76 C6
Bodh Gaya India 24°41N 84°59E 125 G11
Bodhan India 18°40N 77°44E 126 E3
Bodinayakkanur India 10°2N 77°10E 127 J3
Bodinga Nigeria 12°58N 5°10E 139 C6
Bodmin U.K. 50°28N 4°43W 67 G3
Bodmin Moor U.K. 50°33N 4°36W 67 G3
Bodø Norway 67°17N 14°24E 60 C16
Bodrog → Hungary 48°11N 21°22E 80 B6
Bodrum Turkey 37°3N 27°30E 99 D9
Bódva → Hungary 48°19N 20°45E 80 B5
Boën France 45°44N 4°1E 73 C8
Boende Dem. Rep. of the Congo 0°24S 21°12E 140 E4
Boeotia = Viotia Greece 38°20N 23°0E 98 C5
Boerne U.S.A. 29°47N 98°44W 176 G5
Boesmans → S. Africa 33°42S 26°39E 144 D4
Boffa Guinea 10°16N 14°3W 138 C2
Bogalusa U.S.A. 30°47N 89°52W 177 F10
Bogan → Australia 30°20S 146°55E 153 A7
Bogan Gate Australia 33°7S 147°49E 153 B7
Bogandé Burkina Faso 13°2N 0°8W 139 C4
Bogantungan Australia 23°41S 147°17E 150 C4
Bogata U.S.A. 33°28N 95°13W 176 E7
Bogatić Serbia 44°51N 19°30E 96 B3
Boğazkale Turkey 40°2N 34°37E 104 B6
Boğazlıyan Turkey 39°11N 35°14E 104 C6
Bogda Shan China 43°35N 89°40E 109 D11
Bogen Sweden 60°4N 12°33E 62 D6
Bogense Denmark 55°34N 10°5E 63 J4
Bogetići Montenegro 42°41N 18°58E 96 D2
Boggabilla Australia 28°36S 150°24E 151 D5
Boggabri Australia 30°45S 150°5E 153 A9
Boggeragh Mts. Ireland 52°2N 8°55W 64 D3
Boglan = Solhan Turkey 38°57N 41°3E 105 C9
Bognes Norway 68°13N 16°5E 60 B17
Bognor Regis U.K. 50°47N 0°40W 67 G7
Bogo Phil. 11°3N 124°0E 119 B6
Bogodukhov = Bohodukhiv Ukraine 50°9N 35°33E 85 G8
Bogong, Mt. Australia 36°47S 147°17E 153 D7
Bogor Indonesia 6°36S 106°48E 118 F3
Bogoroditsk Russia 53°47N 38°8E 84 F10
Bogorodsk Russia 56°4N 43°30E 86 B6
Bogoso Ghana 5°38N 2°3W 138 D4
Bogotá Colombia 4°34N 74°0W 186 C4
Bogotol Russia 56°15N 89°50E 106 D9
Bogou Togo 10°40N 0°12E 139 C5
Bogra Bangla. 24°51N 89°22E 123 G16
Boguchanskoye Vdkhr. Russia 58°42N 99°9E 107 D10
Boguchany Russia 58°40N 97°30E 107 D10
Boguchar Russia 49°55N 40°32E 86 F5
Bogué Mauritania 16°45N 14°10W 138 B2
Boguszów-Gorce Poland 50°45N 16°12E 83 H3
Bohain-en-Vermandois France 49°59N 3°28E 71 C10
Bohdan Ukraine 48°2N 24°22E 81 B9
Bohemian Forest = Böhmerwald Germany 49°8N 13°14E 77 F9
Bohena Cr. → Australia 30°17S 149°42E 153 A8
Bohinjska Bistrica Slovenia 46°17N 14°1E 93 B11
Böhmerwald Germany 49°8N 13°14E 77 F9
Bohmte Germany 52°22N 8°19E 76 C4
Bohodukhiv Ukraine 50°9N 35°33E 85 G8
Bohol □ Phil. 9°50N 124°10E 119 C6
Bohol Sea Phil. 9°0N 124°0E 119 C6
Bohongou Burkina Faso 12°30N 0°40E 139 C5
Böhönye Hungary 46°25N 17°28E 80 D2
Bohorodchany Ukraine 48°48N 24°32E 81 B9
Bohorok Indonesia 3°30N 98°12E 121 L2
Böhöt Mongolia 45°13N 108°16E 114 B5
Bohu China 41°58N 86°37E 109 D11
Bohuslän Sweden 58°25N 12°0E 63 F5
Bohuslev Ukraine 49°33N 30°56E 85 H6
Boi Nigeria 9°35N 9°27E 139 D6
Boi, Pta. do Brazil 23°55S 45°15W 191 A6
Boiaçu Brazil 0°27S 61°46W 186 D6
Boigu Australia 9°16S 142°13E 150 a
Boileau, C. Australia 17°40S 122°7E 148 C3
Boipariguda India 18°46N 82°26E 126 E6
Boipeba, I. de Brazil 13°39S 38°55W 189 C3
Boiro Spain 42°39N 8°54W 88 C2
Boise U.S.A. 43°37N 116°13W 168 E5
Boise City U.S.A. 36°44N 102°31W 176 C3
Boissevain Canada 49°15N 100°5W 163 D8
Böite → Italy 46°5N 12°5E 93 B9
Boitzenburg Germany 53°16N 13°35E 76 B9
Boizenburg Germany 53°23N 10°43E 76 B6
Bojador, C. W. Sahara 26°0N 14°30W 134 C3
Bojana → Albania 41°52N 19°22E 96 E3
Bojano Italy 41°29N 14°29E 95 A7
Bojanowo Poland 51°43N 16°42E 83 G3
Bøjden Denmark 55°6N 10°7E 63 J4
Bojnūrd Iran 37°30N 57°20E 129 B8
Bojonegoro Indonesia 7°11S 111°54E 119 G14
Boju Nigeria 7°22N 7°55E 139 D6
Boka Serbia 45°22N 20°52E 80 E5
Boka Kotorska Montenegro 42°23N 18°32E 96 D2
Bokala Côte d'Ivoire 8°31N 4°33W 138 D4
Bokani Nigeria 9°28N 5°10E 139 D6
Bokaro India 23°46N 85°55E 125 H11
Boké Guinea 10°56N 14°17W 138 C2
Bokhara → Australia 29°55S 146°42E 151 D4
Bokkos Nigeria 9°17N 9°1E 139 D6
Boknafjorden Norway 59°14N 5°40E 61 G11
Bokor △ Cambodia 10°50N 104°1E 121 G5
Bokora ⌓ Uganda 2°12N 31°32E 142 B3
Bokoro Chad 12°25N 17°14E 135 F9
Bokpyin Myanmar 11°18N 98°42E 121 G2
Boksitogorsk Russia 59°22N 33°50E 84 C7
Bokungu Dem. Rep. of the Congo 0°35S 22°50E 140 E4
Bol Croatia 43°18N 16°38E 93 E13
Bolama Guinea-Biss. 11°30N 15°30W 138 C1
Bolan → Pakistan 28°38N 67°42E 124 E2
Bolan Pass Pakistan 29°50N 67°20E 122 E5
Bolaños → Mexico 21°12N 104°5W 180 C4
Bolaños de Calatrava Spain 38°54N 3°40W 89 G7
Bolayır Turkey 40°31N 26°45E 97 F10
Bolbec France 49°30N 0°30E 70 C7
Boldājī Iran 31°56N 51°3E 129 D6
Boldeşti-Scăeni Romania 45°3N 26°2E 81 E11
Bole China 44°55N 81°37E 109 C10
Bole Ghana 9°3N 2°23W 138 D4
Bolekhiv Ukraine 49°0N 23°57E 81 B8
Bolesławiec Poland 51°17N 15°37E 83 G2
Bolgatanga Ghana 10°44N 0°53W 139 C4
Bolgrad = Bolhrad Ukraine 45°40N 28°32E 81 E13
Bolhrad Ukraine 45°40N 28°32E 81 E13
Bolinao Phil. 16°23N 119°54E 119 A5
Bolingbrooke U.S.A. 32°57N 83°48W 178 C6
Bolintin-Vale Romania 44°27N 25°46E 81 F10
Bolívar Peru 7°18S 77°48W 188 B2
Bolivar Mo., U.S.A. 37°37N 93°25W 172 G7
Bolivar N.Y., U.S.A. 42°4N 78°10W 174 D6
Bolivar Tenn., U.S.A. 35°12N 89°0W 177 D10
Bolívar, Pico Venezuela 8°32N 71°2W 183 E5
Bolivia ■ S. Amer. 17°6S 64°0W 186 G6
Bolivian Plateau = Altiplano Bolivia 17°0S 68°0W 188 D4
Boljevac Serbia 43°51N 21°58E 96 C5
Bolkhov Russia 53°25N 36°0E 84 F9
Bolków Poland 50°55N 16°6E 83 H3
Bollebygd Sweden 57°40N 12°35E 63 G6
Bollène France 44°18N 4°45E 73 D8
Bollnäs Sweden 61°21N 16°24E 62 C10
Bollon Australia 28°2S 147°29E 151 D4
Bollstabruk Sweden 62°59N 17°40E 62 B11
Bolmen Sweden 56°55N 13°40E 63 H7
Bolnisi Georgia 41°26N 44°32E 87 K7
Bolobo Dem. Rep. of the Congo 2°6S 16°20E 140 E3
Bologna Italy 44°29N 11°20E 93 D8
Bologna ✕ (BLQ) Italy 44°34N 11°16E 93 D8
Bologoye Russia 57°55N 34°5E 84 D8
Bolomba Dem. Rep. of the Congo 0°35N 19°0E 140 D3
Bolonchén Mexico 20°1N 89°45W 181 D7
Bolótana Italy 40°20N 8°52E 94 B1
Boloven, Cao Nguyen Laos 15°10N 106°30E 120 E6
Bolpur India 23°40N 87°45E 125 H12
Bolsena Italy 42°39N 11°59E 93 F8
Bolsena, L. di Italy 42°36N 11°56E 93 F8
Bolshakovo Russia 54°53N 21°40E 82 D8
Bolshaya Chernigovka Russia 52°6N 50°52E 86 D10
Bolshaya Glushitsa Russia 52°28N 50°30E 86 D10
Bolshaya Martynovka Russia 47°19N 41°37E 87 G5
Bolshaya Vradiyevka Ukraine 47°50N 30°40E 85 J6
Bolshevik, Ostrov Russia 78°30N 102°0E 107 B11
Bolshoy Anyuy → Russia 68°30N 160°49E 107 C17
Bolshoy Begichev, Ostrov Russia 74°20N 112°30E 107 B12
Bolshoy Kamen Russia 43°7N 132°19E 112 C6
Bolshoy Kavkas = Caucasus Mountains Eurasia 42°50N 44°0E 87 J7
Bolshoy Lyakhovskiy, Ostrov Russia 73°35N 142°0E 107 B15
Bolshoy Tyuters, Ostrov Russia 59°51N 27°13E 84 C4
Bolsward Neths. 53°3N 5°32E 69 A5
Bolt Head U.K. 50°12N 3°48W 67 G4
Boltaña Spain 42°28N 0°4E 90 C5
Boltigen Switz. 46°38N 7°24E 77 J3
Bolton Canada 43°54N 79°45W 174 C5
Bolton U.K. 53°35N 2°26W 66 D5
Bolton Landing U.S.A. 43°32N 73°35W 175 C11
Bolu Turkey 40°45N 31°35E 104 B4
Bolu □ Turkey 40°40N 31°30E 104 B4
Bolungavík Iceland 66°9N 23°15W 60 C2
Boluo China 23°3N 114°21E 117 F10
Bolvadin Turkey 38°45N 31°4E 104 C4
Bolzano Italy 46°31N 11°22E 93 B8
Bom Conselho Brazil 9°10S 36°41W 189 B3
Bom Despacho Brazil 19°43S 45°15W 189 D1
Bom Jesus Brazil 9°4S 44°22W 189 B2
Bom Jesus da Gurguéia, Serra Brazil 9°0S 43°0W 189 B2
Bom Jesus da Lapa Brazil 13°15S 43°25W 189 C2
Boma Dem. Rep. of the Congo 5°50S 13°4E 140 F2
Bomaderry Australia 34°52S 150°37E 153 C9
Bombala Australia 36°56S 149°15E 153 D8
Bombarral Portugal 39°15N 9°9W 89 F1
Bombay = Mumbai India 18°56N 72°50E 126 E1
Bombay U.S.A. 44°56N 74°34W 175 B10
Bombedor, Pta. Venezuela 9°53N 61°37W 187 L15
Bomberai, Semenanjung Indonesia 3°0S 133°0E 119 E8
Bomboma Dem. Rep. of the Congo 2°25N 18°55E 140 D3
Bombombwa Dem. Rep. of the Congo 1°40N 25°40E 142 B2
Bomi China 29°50N 95°45E 110 F8
Bomi Liberia 7°1N 10°38W 138 D2
Bomili Dem. Rep. of the Congo 1°45N 27°5E 142 B2
Bømlo Norway 59°37N 5°13E 61 G11
Bomokandi → Dem. Rep. of the Congo 3°39N 26°8E 142 B2
Bompoka India 8°15N 93°13E 127 K11
Bomu → C.A.R. 4°40N 22°30E 140 D4
Bon, C. = Ra's aţ Tib Tunisia 37°1N 11°2E 136 A6
Bon Acceuil Mauritius 20°10S 57°39E 141 d
Bon Echo ⌓ Canada 44°55N 77°16W 174 B7
Bon Sar Pa Vietnam 12°24N 107°35E 120 F6
Bonāb Āzarbājān-e Sharqī, Iran 37°20N 46°4E 105 D12
Bonāb Zanjān, Iran 36°35N 48°41E 105 D13
Bonaigarh India 21°50N 84°57E 125 J11
Bonaire U.S.A. 32°33N 83°36W 178 C6
Bonaire W. Indies 12°10N 68°15W 183 D6
Bonampak Mexico 16°44N 91°5W 181 D6
Bonang Australia 37°11S 148°41E 153 D8
Bonanza Nic. 13°54N 84°35W 182 D3
Bonaparte Arch. Australia 14°0S 124°30E 148 B3
Boñar Spain 42°52N 5°19W 88 C5
Bonar Bridge U.K. 57°54N 4°20W 65 D4
Bonasse Trin. & Tob. 10°5N 61°54W 187 K15
Bonaventure Canada 48°5N 65°32W 165 C6
Bonavista Canada 48°40N 53°5W 165 C9
Bonavista, C. Canada 48°42N 53°5W 165 C9
Bonavista B. Canada 48°45N 53°25W 165 C9
Bondeno Italy 44°53N 11°25E 93 D8
Bondo Dem. Rep. of the Congo 3°55N 23°53E 142 B1
Bondokodi Indonesia 9°33S 119°0E 148 A2
Bondoukou Côte d'Ivoire 8°2N 2°47W 138 D4
Bondowoso Indonesia 7°55S 113°49E 119 G15
Bone, Teluk Indonesia 4°10S 120°50E 119 E6
Bonerate Indonesia 7°25S 121°5E 119 F6
Bonerate, Kepulauan Indonesia 6°30S 121°10E 119 F6
Bo'ness U.K. 56°1N 3°37W 65 E5
Bonete, Cerro Argentina 27°55S 68°40W 190 B2
Bong Son = Hoai Nhon Vietnam 14°28N 109°1E 120 E7
Bongaigaon India 26°28N 90°34E 110 F7
Bongandanga Dem. Rep. of the Congo 1°24N 21°3E 140 D4
Bongor Chad 10°35N 15°20E 135 F9
Bongos, Massif des C.A.R. 8°40N 22°25E 140 C4
Bongouanou Côte d'Ivoire 6°42N 4°15W 138 D4
Bonham U.S.A. 33°35N 96°11W 176 E6
Boni Mali 15°3N 2°10W 138 B4
Boni ⌓ Kenya 1°35S 41°18E 142 C5
Bonifacio France 41°24N 9°10E 73 G13
Bonifacio, Bouches de Medit. S. 41°12N 9°15E 94 A2
Bonifay U.S.A. 30°47N 85°41W 178 E4
Bonin Is. = Ogasawara Gunto Pac. Oc. 27°0N 142°0E 156 E6
Bonita Springs U.S.A. 26°21N 81°47W 179 J8
Bonkoukou Niger 14°0N 3°15E 139 C5
Bonn Germany 50°46N 7°6E 76 E3
Bonnat France 46°20N 1°54E 71 F8
Bonne Terre U.S.A. 37°55N 90°33W 172 G8
Bonneau U.S.A. 33°16N 79°58W 178 B10
Bonners Ferry U.S.A. 48°42N 116°19W 168 B5
Bonnétable France 48°11N 0°25E 70 D7
Bonneval France 45°22N 7°3E 73 C11
Bonneval-sur-Arc France 48°11N 1°24E 70 D8
Bonneville France 46°4N 6°24E 71 F13
Bonney, L. Australia 37°50S 140°20E 152 D4
Bonnie Doon Australia 37°2S 145°53E 153 D6
Bonnie Rock Australia 30°29S 118°22E 149 F2
Bonny Nigeria 4°25N 7°13E 139 E6
Bonny → Nigeria 4°20N 7°10E 139 E6
Bonny, Bight of Africa 3°30N 9°20E 139 E6
Bonny Hills Australia 31°36S 152°51E 153 A10
Bonny-sur-Loire France 47°33N 2°50E 71 E9
Bonnyrigg U.K. 55°53N 3°6W 65 F5
Bonnyville Canada 54°20N 110°45W 163 C6
Bono Italy 40°25N 9°2E 94 B2
Bonoi Indonesia 1°45S 137°41E 119 E9
Bonorva Italy 40°25N 8°46E 94 B1
Bonsall U.S.A. 33°16N 117°14W 171 M9
Bontang Indonesia 0°10N 117°30E 118 D5
Bontebok △ S. Africa 34°5S 20°28E 144 D3
Bonthe S. Leone 7°30N 12°33W 138 D2
Bontoc Phil. 17°7N 120°58E 119 A6
Bonyeri Ghana 5°1N 2°46W 138 D4
Bonyhád Hungary 46°18N 18°32E 80 D3
Bonython Ra. Australia 23°40S 128°45E 148 D4
Booderee △ Australia 35°12S 150°42E 153 C9
Boodjamulla △ Australia 18°15S 138°6E 150 B2
Bookabie Australia 31°50S 132°41E 149 F5
Booker U.S.A. 36°27N 100°32W 176 C4
Bool Lagoon Australia 37°7S 140°40E 152 D4
Boola Guinea 8°22N 8°41W 138 D3
Boolcoomata Australia 31°57S 140°33E 152 A4
Booleroo Centre Australia 32°53S 138°21E 152 B3
Booligal Australia 33°58S 144°53E 153 B6
Böön Tsagaan Nuur Mongolia 45°35N 99°9E 110 B8
Boonah Australia 27°58S 152°41E 151 D5
Boone Iowa, U.S.A. 42°4N 93°53W 172 D7
Boone N.C., U.S.A. 36°13N 81°41W 177 C14
Booneville Ark., U.S.A. 35°8N 93°55W 176 D8
Booneville Miss., U.S.A. 34°39N 88°34W 177 D10
Boonville Calif., U.S.A. 39°1N 123°22W 170 F3
Boonville Ind., U.S.A. 38°3N 87°16W 172 F10
Boonville Mo., U.S.A. 38°58N 92°44W 172 F7
Boonville N.Y., U.S.A. 43°29N 75°20W 175 C9
Boorabbin △ Australia 31°30S 120°10E 149 F3
Boorindal Australia 30°22S 146°11E 151 E4
Boorowa Australia 34°28S 148°44E 153 C8
Boort Australia 36°7S 143°46E 152 D5
Boosaaso Somalia 11°12N 49°18E 131 E4
Boothia, Gulf of Canada 71°0N 90°0W 160 C14
Boothia Pen. Canada 71°0N 94°0W 160 C13
Bootle U.K. 53°28N 3°1W 66 D4

Booué *Gabon* 0°5S 11°55E **140** E2
Bopolu *Liberia* 7°4N 10°29W **138** D2
Boppard *Germany* 50°13N 7°35E **77** E3
Boquilla, Presa de la
  Mexico 27°31N 105°30W **180** B3
Boquillas del Carmen
  Mexico 29°11N 102°58W **180** B4
Bor *Czechia* 49°41N 12°45E **78** B5
Bor *Russia* 56°28N 43°59E **86** B7
Bor *Serbia* 44°5N 22°7E **96** B6
Bor *South Sudan* 6°10N 31°40E **135** G2
Bor *Sweden* 57°9N 14°10E **63** G8
Bor *Turkey* 37°54N 34°32E **104** D6
Bor Mashash *Israel* 31°7N 34°50E **130** D3
Bora Bora
  French Polynesia 16°30S 151°45W **157** J12
Borah Peak *U.S.A.* 44°8N 113°47W **168** D7
Boraha, Nosy *Madag.* 16°50S 49°55E **141** H9
Borankul *Kazakhstan* 46°11N 54°25E **108** C4
Borås *Sweden* 57°43N 12°56E **63** G6
Borāzjān *Iran* 29°22N 51°10E **129** D6
Borba *Brazil* 4°12S 59°34W **186** D7
Borba *Portugal* 38°26N 7°26W **89** G3
Borborema, Planalto da
  Brazil 7°0S 37°0W **189** B3
Borča *Serbia* 44°52N 20°28E **96** B4
Borcea *Romania* 44°20N 27°45E **81** F12
Borça *Turkey* 41°25N 41°41E **105** B9
Bord Khūn e Now *Iran* 28°3N 51°28E **129** D6
Borda, C. *Australia* 35°45S 136°34E **152** C2
Bordeaux *France* 44°50N 0°36W **72** D3
Bordeaux ✈ (BOD)
  France 44°50N 0°35W **72** D3
Borden *Australia* 34°3S 118°12E **149** F2
Borden-Carleton
  Canada 46°18N 63°47W **165** C7
Borden I. *Canada* 78°30N 111°30W **161** B9
Borden Pen. *Canada* 73°0N 83°0W **161** C15
Borden Springs *U.S.A.* 33°56N 85°28W **178** B4
Border Ranges △
  Australia 28°24S 152°56E **151** D5
Borders = Scottish Borders □
  U.K. 55°35N 2°50W **65** F6
Bordertown *Australia* 36°19S 140°45E **152** D4
Borðeyri *Iceland* 65°12N 21°6W **60** D3
Bordighera *Italy* 43°46N 7°39E **92** D4
Bordj bou Arreridj *Algeria* 36°4N 4°45E **136** A4
Bordj Bourguiba *Tunisia* 32°12N 10°2E **136** B6
Bordj Flye Ste-Marie
  Algeria 27°19N 2°32W **136** C3
Bordj in Eker *Algeria* 24°9N 5°3E **136** D5
Bordj Menaïel *Algeria* 36°46N 3°43E **136** A4
Bordj Messouda *Algeria* 30°12N 9°25E **136** B6
Bordj Mokhtar *Algeria* 21°20N 0°56E **134** D6
Bordj Nili *Algeria* 33°28N 3°2E **136** B4
Bordj Omar Driss
  Algeria 28°10N 6°40E **136** B5
Bordj Sif Fatima *Algeria* 31°6N 8°41E **136** B5
Bordj Tarat *Algeria* 25°55N 9°3E **136** C5
Borehamwood *U.K.* 51°40N 0°15W **67** F7
Borek Wielkopolski
  Poland 51°54N 17°11E **83** G4
Borensberg *Sweden* 58°34N 15°17E **63** F9
Borgå = Porvoo *Finland* 60°24N 25°40E **84** B3
Borgampad *India* 17°39N 80°52E **126** F5
Borgarnes *Iceland* 64°32N 21°50W **60** D3
Børgefjellet *Norway* 65°20N 13°45E **60** D15
Borger *Neths.* 52°54N 6°44E **69** B6
Borger *U.S.A.* 35°39N 101°24W **176** D4
Borgholm *Sweden* 56°52N 16°39E **63** H10
Bórgia *Italy* 38°49N 16°30E **95** D9
Borgo San Dalmazzo
  Italy 44°20N 7°30E **92** D4
Borgo San Lorenzo *Italy* 43°57N 11°23E **93** E8
Borgo Val di Taro *Italy* 44°29N 9°46E **92** D6
Borgo Valsugana *Italy* 46°3N 11°27E **93** B8
Borgomanero *Italy* 45°42N 8°28E **92** C5
Borgorose *Italy* 42°11N 13°13E **93** F10
Borgosésia *Italy* 45°43N 8°16E **92** C5
Borhoyn Tal *Mongolia* 43°50N 111°58E **114** C6
Bori *Nigeria* 4°42N 7°21E **139** E6
Borigumma *India* 19°3N 82°33E **126** H5
Borikhane *Laos* 18°33N 103°43E **120** C4
Borisoglebsk *Russia* 51°27N 42°5E **86** E6
Borisov = Barysaw
  Belarus 54°17N 28°28E **75** A15
Borisovka *Russia* 50°36N 36°1E **85** G9
Borja *Peru* 4°20S 77°40W **186** D3
Borja *Spain* 41°48N 1°34W **90** D3
Borjas Blancas = Les Borges
  Blanques *Spain* 41°31N 0°52E **90** D5
Borjomi *Georgia* 41°48N 43°28E **87** K6
Børkop *Denmark* 55°39N 9°39E **63** J3
Borkou *Chad* 18°15N 18°50E **135** E9
Borkum *Germany* 53°34N 6°40E **76** B2
Borlänge *Sweden* 60°29N 15°26E **62** D9
Borley, C. *Antarctica* 66°15S 52°30E **55** C5
Borlu *Turkey* 38°44N 28°27E **99** C10
Bórmida → *Italy* 44°23N 8°13E **92** D5
Bórmio *Italy* 46°28N 10°22E **92** B7
Borna *Germany* 51°7N 12°29E **76** D8
Borne Sulinowo *Poland* 53°35N 16°35E **83** B3
Borneo *E. Indies* 1°0N 115°0E **118** D5
Bornholm *Denmark* 55°10N 15°0E **63** J8
Bornholmsgattet *Europe* 55°15N 14°20E **63** J8
Borno □ *Nigeria* 11°30N 13°0E **139** C7
Bornos *Spain* 36°48N 5°42W **89** J4
Bornova *Turkey* 38°27N 27°14E **99** C9
Bornu Yassa *Nigeria* 12°14N 12°25E **139** C7
Borobudur △
  Indonesia 7°36S 110°12E **119** G14
Borodino *Russia* 55°31N 35°40E **84** E8
Borodyanka *Ukraine* 50°39N 29°15E **81** C14
Borogontsy *Russia* 62°42N 131°8E **107** C14
Boromo *Burkina Faso* 11°45N 2°58W **138** C4
Boron *U.S.A.* 35°0N 117°39W **171** L9
Borongan *Phil.* 11°37N 125°26E **119** B7
Borotou *Côte d'Ivoire* 8°46N 7°30W **138** D3
Borovan *Bulgaria* 43°27N 23°45E **96** C7
Borovichi *Russia* 58°25N 33°55E **84** C7
Borovsk *Russia* 55°12N 36°24E **84** E9
Borovskoy *Kazakhstan* 53°48N 64°12E **108** A7
Borrby *Sweden* 55°27N 14°10E **63** J8
Borrego Springs
  U.S.A. 33°15N 116°23W **171** M10
Borriol *Spain* 40°4N 0°4W **90** E4
Borrisokane *Ireland* 53°0N 8°7W **64** D3
Borroloola *Australia* 16°4S 136°17E **150** B2

Borșa *Maramureș,*
  Romania 47°41N 24°50E **81** C9
Borsad *India* 22°25N 72°54E **124** H5
Borsec *Romania* 46°57N 25°34E **81** D10
Borshchiv *Ukraine* 48°48N 26°3E **81** B11
Borsod-Abaúj-Zemplén □
  Hungary 48°20N 21°0E **80** B6
Bort-les-Orgues *France* 45°24N 2°29E **72** C6
Bortala = Bole *China* 44°55N 81°37E **109** C12
Borth *U.K.* 52°29N 4°2W **67** E3
Börtnan *Sweden* 62°45N 13°50E **62** B7
Borūjerd *Iran* 33°55N 48°50E **128** C6
Boryeong *S. Korea* 36°21N 126°36E **115** F14
Borynya *Ukraine* 49°4N 23°0E **83** J10
Boryslav *Ukraine* 49°18N 23°28E **83** J10
Boryspil *Ukraine* 50°21N 30°59E **85** G6
Borzhomi = Borjomi
  Georgia 41°48N 43°28E **87** K6
Borzna *Ukraine* 51°18N 32°26E **85** G7
Borzya *Russia* 50°24N 116°31E **111** A12
Bosa *Italy* 40°18N 8°30E **94** B1
Bosanska Dubica = Dubica
  Bos.-H. 45°10N 16°50E **93** C13
Bosanska Gradiška = Gradiška
  Bos.-H. 45°10N 17°15E **80** E2
Bosanska Kostajnica = Kostajnica
  Bos.-H. 45°11N 16°33E **93** C13
Bosanska Krupa
  Bos.-H. 44°53N 16°10E **93** D13
Bosanski Brod = Brod
  Bos.-H. 45°10N 18°0E **80** E2
Bosanski Novi = Novi Grad
  Bos.-H. 45°2N 16°22E **93** C13
Bosanski Petrovac
  Bos.-H. 44°35N 16°21E **93** D13
Bosanski Šamac = Šamac
  Bos.-H. 45°3N 18°29E **80** E3
Bosansko Grahovo
  Bos.-H. 44°12N 16°26E **93** D13
Boscastle *U.K.* 50°41N 4°42W **67** G3
Boscobelle *Barbados* 13°17N 59°35W **183** g
Bose *China* 23°53N 106°35E **118** E5
Boseong *S. Korea* 34°46N 127°5E **115** G14
Boshan *China* 36°28N 117°49E **115** F9
Boshof *S. Africa* 28°31S 25°13E **144** C4
Boshrūyeh *Iran* 33°50N 57°30E **129** C8
Bosilegrad *Serbia* 42°30N 22°27E **96** D6
Boskovice *Czechia* 49°29N 16°40E **79** B9
Bosna → *Bos.-H.* 45°4N 18°29E **80** E2
Bosna i Hercegovina = Bosnia-
  Herzegovina ■ *Europe* 44°0N 18°0E **80** G2
Bosnia-Herzegovina ■
  Europe 44°0N 18°0E **80** G2
Bosnik *Indonesia* 1°5S 136°10E **119** E9
Bosobolo
  Dem. Rep. of the Congo 4°15N 19°50E **140** D3
Bosporus = İstanbul Boğazı
  Turkey 41°5N 29°3E **97** E13
Bosque Farms *U.S.A.* 35°51N 106°42W **169** J10
Bosra = Buşra ash Shām
  Syria 32°30N 36°25E **130** C5
Bossangoa *C.A.R.* 6°35N 17°30E **140** C3
Bossé Bangou *Niger* 13°20N 1°18E **139** C5
Bossier City *U.S.A.* 32°31N 93°44W **176** E8
Bossiesvlei *Namibia* 25°1S 16°44E **144** C2
Bosso *Niger* 13°43N 13°19E **139** C7
Bosso, Dallol → *Niger* 12°25N 2°50E **139** C5
Bostan *Pakistan* 30°26N 67°2E **124** D2
Bostānābād *Iran* 37°50N 46°50E **105** D12
Bosten Hu *China* 41°55N 87°40E **109** D11
Boston *U.K.* 52°59N 0°2W **66** E7
Boston *Ga., U.S.A.* 30°47N 83°47W **178** F6
Boston *Mass., U.S.A.* 42°22N 71°3W **175** D13
Boston Bar *Canada* 49°52N 121°30W **162** D4
Boston Mts., U.S.A.* 35°42N 93°15W **176** D8
Bostwick *U.S.A.* 29°46N 81°38W **178** F8
Bosumtwi, L. *Ghana* 6°30N 1°25W **139** D4
Bosut → *Croatia* 45°20N 18°45E **80** E3
Boswell *Canada* 49°28N 116°45W **162** D5
Boswell *U.S.A.* 40°10N 79°2W **174** F5
Botad *India* 22°15N 71°40E **124** H4
Botan → *Turkey* 37°57N 42°2E **105** D10
Botany B. *Australia* 33°58S 151°11E **147** E8
Botene *Laos* 17°35N 101°12E **120** D3
Botev *Bulgaria* 42°44N 24°52E **97** D8
Botevgrad *Bulgaria* 42°55N 23°47E **96** D7
Bothaville *S. Africa* 27°23S 26°34E **144** C4
Bothnia, G. of *Europe* 62°0N 20°0E **60** F19
Bothwell *Australia* 42°20S 147°1E **151** G4
Bothwell *Canada* 42°38N 81°52W **174** D3
Boticas *Portugal* 41°41N 7°40W **88** D3
Botletle → *Botswana* 20°10S 23°15E **144** B3
Botlikh *Russia* 42°39N 46°11E **87** J8
Botna → *Moldova* 46°45N 29°34E **81** D14
Botoroaga *Romania* 44°8N 25°32E **81** F11
Botoșani *Romania* 47°42N 26°41E **81** C11
Botoșani □ *Romania* 47°50N 26°50E **81** C11
Botou *Burkina Faso* 12°42N 1°59E **139** C5
Botou *China* 38°4N 116°34E **114** E8
Botricello *Italy* 38°56N 16°51E **95** D9
Botro *Côte d'Ivoire* 7°51N 5°19W **138** D3
Botshabelo *S. Africa* 29°14S 26°44E **144** C4
Botswana ■ *Africa* 22°0S 24°0E **144** B3
Bottineau *U.S.A.* 48°50N 100°27W **172** A3
Bottnaryd *Sweden* 57°47N 13°50E **63** G7
Bottrop *Germany* 51°31N 6°58E **76** D2
Botucatu *Brazil* 22°55S 48°30W **191** A6
Botum Sakor △
  Indonesia 11°5N 103°15E **121** G4
Botwood *Canada* 49°6N 55°23W **165** C8
Bou Alam *Algeria* 33°50N 1°26E **136** B4
Bou Ali *Algeria* 27°11N 0°4W **136** C3
Bou Guema *Algeria* 28°49N 0°19E **136** C4
Bou Ismaïl *Algeria* 36°38N 2°42E **136** A4
Bou Izakarn *Morocco* 29°12N 9°46E **136** C3
Boû Naga *Mauritania* 18°49N 13°20W **138** B2
Bou Noura *Algeria* 32°39N 3°43E **136** B4
Boû Rjeïmât *Mauritania* 19°4N 15°13W **138** B1
Bou Saâda *Algeria* 35°11N 4°9E **136** A4
Bou Salem *Tunisia* 36°45N 9°2E **136** A3
Bouafle *Côte d'Ivoire* 7°1N 5°47W **138** D3
Bouaké *Côte d'Ivoire* 7°40N 5°2W **138** D3
Bouar *C.A.R.* 6°0N 15°40E **140** C3
Bouârfa *Morocco* 32°32N 1°58W **136** B3
Boubout *Algeria* 27°26N 4°30W **136** C3
Boucaut B. *Australia* 12°0S 134°25E **150** A1
Bouches-du-Rhône □
  France 43°37N 5°2E **73** E9
Bouclé de Baoulé △ *Mali* 13°53N 9°0W **138** C3

Boucles de la Seine Normande △
  France 49°32N 0°35E **70** C7
Bouctouche *Canada* 46°30N 64°45W **165** C7
Bouda *Algeria* 27°50N 0°27W **136** C3
Boudenib *Morocco* 31°59N 3°31W **136** B3
Boufarik *Algeria* 36°34N 2°58E **136** A4
Bougainville, C.
  Australia 13°57S 126°4E **148** B4
Bougainville I.
  Papua N. G. 6°0S 155°0E **147** B8
Bougainville Reef
  Australia 15°30S 147°5E **150** B4
Bougaroun, C. *Algeria* 37°6N 6°30E **136** A5
Bougie = Bejaïa *Algeria* 36°42N 5°2E **136** A5
Bougouni *Mali* 11°30N 7°20W **138** C3
Bougtob *Algeria* 34°2N 0°55E **136** B4
Bouillon *Belgium* 49°44N 5°3E **69** E5
Bouïra *Algeria* 36°20N 3°59E **136** A4
Bouïra □ *Algeria* 36°15N 3°55E **136** A4
Boukombé *Benin* 10°13N 1°9E **139** C5
Boulal *Mali* 15°8N 8°21W **138** C2
Boulazac *France* 45°10N 0°47E **72** C4
Boulder *Colo., U.S.A.* 40°1N 105°17W **168** F11
Boulder *Mont., U.S.A.* 46°14N 112°7W **168** C7
Boulder City *U.S.A.* 35°58N 114°49W **171** K12
Boulder Creek *U.S.A.* 37°7N 122°7W **170** H4
Boulder Dam = Hoover Dam
  U.S.A. 36°1N 114°44W **171** K12
Bouli *Mauritania* 15°17N 12°18W **138** B2
Boulia *Australia* 22°52S 139°51E **150** C2
Bouligny *France* 49°17N 5°45E **71** C12
Boulogne → *France* 47°12N 1°47W **70** E5
Boulogne-sur-Gesse
  France 43°18N 0°38E **72** E4
Boulogne-sur-Mer *France* 50°42N 1°36E **71** B8
Bouloire *France* 47°59N 0°45E **70** E7
Boulouli *Mali* 15°30N 9°25W **138** C3
Boulsa *Burkina Faso* 12°39N 0°34W **139** C4
Boultoum *Niger* 14°45N 10°22E **139** C7
Bouma △ *Fiji* 16°50S 179°52W **154** a
Boumalne Dadès
  Morocco 31°25N 6°0W **136** B3
Boûmdeïd *Mauritania* 17°25N 11°50W **138** B2
Boumerdès *Algeria* 36°46N 3°28E **136** A4
Boumerdès □ *Algeria* 36°45N 3°40E **136** A4
Boun Neua *Laos* 21°38N 101°54E **120** B3
Boun Tai *Laos* 21°23N 101°58E **120** B3
Bouna *Côte d'Ivoire* 9°10N 3°0W **138** D4
Boundary Peak
  U.S.A. 37°51N 118°21W **170** H8
Boundiali *Côte d'Ivoire* 9°30N 6°20W **138** D3
Bountiful *U.S.A.* 40°53N 111°52W **168** F8
Bounty Is. *Pac. Oc.* 48°0S 178°30E **156** M9
Bounty Trough *Pac. Oc.* 46°0S 178°0E **156** M9
Boura *Mali* 12°25N 4°33W **138** C4
Bourbon-Lancy *France* 46°37N 3°45E **71** F10
Bourbon-l'Archambault
  France 46°36N 3°4E **71** F10
Bourbonnais *France* 46°28N 3°0E **71** F10
Bourbonne-les-Bains
  France 47°54N 5°45E **71** E12
Bourbourg *France* 50°56N 2°12E **71** B9
Bourdel L. *Canada* 56°43N 74°10W **164** A5
Bourem *Mali* 17°0N 0°24W **139** B4
Bourg *France* 45°3N 0°34W **72** C3
Bourg-Argental *France* 45°18N 4°32E **73** C8
Bourg-de-Péage *France* 45°2N 5°3E **73** C9
Bourg-en-Bresse *France* 46°13N 5°12E **71** F12
Bourg-Lastic *France* 45°39N 2°35E **72** C6
Bourg-Madame *France* 42°26N 1°55E **72** F5
Bourg-St-Andéol *France* 44°23N 4°39E **73** D8
Bourg-St-Maurice
  France 45°35N 6°46E **73** C10
Bourganeuf *France* 45°57N 1°45E **72** C5
Bourgas = Burgas
  Bulgaria 42°33N 27°29E **97** D11
Bourges *France* 47°9N 2°25E **71** E9
Bourget *Canada* 45°26N 75°9W **175** A9
Bourget, Lac du *France* 45°44N 5°52E **73** C9
Bourgneuf, B. de *France* 47°3N 2°10W **70** E4
Bourgneuf-en-Retz *France* 47°2N 1°58W **70** E5
Bourgogne -Franche-Comté □
  France 47°0N 5°0E **71** E11
Bourgoin-Jallieu *France* 45°36N 5°17E **73** C9
Bourgueil *France* 47°17N 0°10E **70** E7
Bourke *Australia* 30°8S 145°55E **151** E4
Bourne *France* 52°47N 0°22E **66** E7
Bournemouth *U.K.* 50°43N 1°52W **67** G6
Bournemouth □ *U.K.* 50°43N 1°52W **67** G6
Bouroum *Burkina Faso* 13°37N 0°39W **139** C4
Bouse *U.S.A.* 33°56N 114°0W **171** M13
Boussac *France* 46°22N 2°13E **71** F9
Boussé *Burkina Faso* 12°39N 1°53W **139** C4
Bousso *Chad* 10°34N 16°52E **135** F9
Boussouma
  Burkina Faso 12°52N 1°13W **139** C4
Boutilimit *Mauritania* 17°45N 14°40W **138** B2
Boutonne → *France* 45°54N 0°50W **72** C3
Bouvet I. = Bouvetøya
  Antarctica 54°26S 3°24E **56** M12
Bouvetøya *Antarctica* 54°26S 3°24E **56** M12
Bouxwiller *France* 48°49N 7°27E **71** D14
Bouza *Niger* 14°29N 6°2E **139** C6
Bouznika *Morocco* 33°46N 7°6W **136** B2
Bouzonville *France* 49°17N 6°32E **71** C13
Bova Marina *Italy* 37°56N 15°55E **95** E8
Bovalino *Italy* 38°10N 16°10E **95** D9
Bovenkarspel *Neths.* 52°42N 5°13E **69** B5
Bovec *Slovenia* 46°20N 13°33E **93** B10
Bovill *U.S.A.* 46°51N 116°24W **168** C5
Bovino *Italy* 41°15N 15°20E **95** A8
Bovril *Argentina* 31°21S 59°26W **190** C4
Bow → *Canada* 49°57N 111°41W **162** C6
Bow Island *Canada* 49°50N 111°23W **168** B9
Bowbells *U.S.A.* 48°48N 102°15W **172** A2
Bowdle *U.S.A.* 45°27N 99°39W **172** C4
Bowdon *U.S.A.* 33°32N 85°15W **178** B4
Bowelling *Australia* 33°25S 116°30E **149** F2
Bowen *Argentina* 35°0S 67°31W **190** D2
Bowen *Australia* 20°0S 148°16E **150** J6
Bowen Mts. *Australia* 37°0S 147°50E **153** C4
Bowers Basin *Pac. Oc.* 54°0N 180°0E **54** D11
Bowers Ridge *Pac. Oc.* 54°0N 180°0E **54** D11
Bowie *Ariz., U.S.A.* 32°19N 109°29W **169** K9
Bowie *Tex., U.S.A.* 33°34N 97°51W **176** E6
Bowkān *Iran* 36°31N 46°12E **105** D12
Bowland, Forest of *U.K.* 54°0N 2°30W **66** D5
Bowling Green *Fla.,*

Bowling Green *Ky.,*
  U.S.A. 36°59N 86°27W **172** G10
Bowling Green *Ohio,*
  U.S.A. 41°23N 83°39W **173** E12
Bowling Green, C.
  Australia 19°19S 147°25E **150** B4
Bowling Green Bay △
  Australia 19°26S 146°57E **150** B4
Bowman *N. Dak.,*
  U.S.A. 46°11N 103°24W **172** B2
Bowman S.C., U.S.A.* 33°21N 80°41W **178** B9
Bowmanville = Clarington
  Canada 65°0S 104°0E **55** C8
Bowmore *U.K.* 55°45N 6°17W **65** F2
Bowral *Australia* 34°26S 150°27E **153** C9
Bowraville *Australia* 30°37S 152°52E **151** E5
Bowron → *Canada* 54°3N 121°50W **162** C4
Bowron Lake △
  Canada 53°10N 121°5W **162** C4
Bowser L. *Canada* 56°30N 129°30W **162** B3
Bowsman *Canada* 52°14N 101°12W **163** C8
Bowwood *Zambia* 17°5S 26°20E **143** F2
Box Cr. → *Australia* 34°10S 143°50E **151** E3
Boxholm *Sweden* 58°12N 15°3E **63** F9
Boxmeer *Neths.* 51°38N 5°56E **69** C5
Boxtel *Neths.* 51°36N 5°20E **69** C5
Boyabat *Turkey* 41°28N 34°47E **104** B6
Boyalıca *Turkey* 40°29N 29°33E **97** F13
Boyang *China* 29°0N 116°38E **117** C11
Boyce *U.S.A.* 31°23N 92°40W **176** F8
Boyd L. *Canada* 52°46N 76°42W **164** B4
Boyle *Canada* 54°35N 112°49W **162** B6
Boyle *Ireland* 53°59N 8°18W **64** C3
Boyne → *Ireland* 53°43N 6°15W **64** C5
Boyne, Bend of the
  Ireland 53°41N 6°27E **64** C5
Boyne City *U.S.A.* 45°13N 85°1W **173** C11
Boynitsa *Bulgaria* 43°58N 22°32E **96** C6
Boynton Beach *U.S.A.* 26°32N 80°4W **179** J9
Boyoma, Chutes
  Dem. Rep. of the Congo 0°35N 25°23E **142** B2
Boysen Res. *U.S.A.* 43°25N 108°11W **168** E9
Boyuibe *Bolivia* 20°25S 63°17W **186** G6
Boyup Brook *Australia* 33°50S 116°23E **149** F2
Boz Burun *Turkey* 40°32N 28°46E **97** F12
Boz Dağ *Turkey* 37°18N 29°11E **99** D11
Boz Dağları *Turkey* 38°20N 28°0E **99** C10
Bozburun *Turkey* 36°43N 28°4E **99** E10
Bozcaada *Turkey* 39°49N 26°3E **104** C2
Bozdoğan *Turkey* 37°40N 28°17E **99** D10
Bozeman *U.S.A.* 45°41N 111°2W **168** D8
Bozen = Bolzano *Italy* 46°31N 11°22E **93** B8
Bozhou *China* 33°55N 115°41E **114** H8
Bozkir *Turkey* 37°11N 32°14E **104** D5
Bozkurt *Turkey* 37°50N 29°37E **99** D11
Bozouls *France* 44°28N 2°43E **72** D6
Bozoum *C.A.R.* 6°25N 16°35E **140** C3
Bozova *Antalya, Turkey* 37°11N 30°18E **99** D12
Bozova *Sanlıurfa, Turkey* 37°21N 38°32E **105** D8
Bozovici *Romania* 44°56N 22°0E **80** F7
Bozüyük *Turkey* 39°54N 30°0E **99** B12
Bozyazı *Turkey* 36°6N 33°0E **128** B2
Bra *Italy* 44°42N 7°51E **92** D4
Braås *Sweden* 57°4N 15°3E **63** G9
Brabant □ *Belgium* 50°46N 4°30E **69** D4
Brabant L. *Canada* 55°58N 103°43W **163** B8
Brabrand *Denmark* 56°9N 10°7E **63** H4
Brač *Croatia* 43°20N 16°40E **93** E13
Bracadale, L. *U.K.* 57°20N 6°30W **65** D2
Bracciano *Italy* 42°6N 12°10E **93** F9
Bracciano, L. di *Italy* 42°7N 12°14E **93** F9
Bracebridge *Canada* 45°2N 79°19W **174** A5
Bracieux *France* 47°30N 1°30E **70** E8
Bräcke *Sweden* 62°45N 15°26E **62** B9
Brackettville *U.S.A.* 29°19N 100°25W **176** G4
Brački Kanal *Croatia* 43°24N 16°40E **93** E13
Bracknell *U.K.* 51°25N 0°43W **67** F7
Bracknell Forest □ *U.K.* 51°25N 0°44W **67** F7
Brad *Romania* 46°10N 22°50E **80** D7
Bradano → *Italy* 40°23N 16°51E **95** B9
Bradenton *U.S.A.* 27°30N 82°34W **179** H7
Bradford *Canada* 44°7N 79°34W **174** B5
Bradford *U.K.* 53°47N 1°45W **66** D6
Bradford *Pa., U.S.A.* 41°58N 78°38W **174** E6
Bradford *Vt., U.S.A.* 43°59N 72°9W **175** C12
Bradley *Ark., U.S.A.* 33°6N 93°39W **176** E8
Bradley *Calif., U.S.A.* 35°52N 120°48W **170** K6
Bradley Institute
  Zimbabwe 17°7S 31°25E **143** F3
Bradley Junction
  U.S.A. 27°48N 81°59W **179** H8
Brady *U.S.A.* 31°9N 99°20W **176** F5
Brædstrup *Denmark* 55°58N 9°37E **63** J3
Braemar *Australia* 33°12S 139°35E **152** B3
Braeside *Canada* 45°28N 76°24W **175** A8
Braga *Portugal* 41°35N 8°25W **88** D2
Braga □ *Portugal* 41°30N 8°25W **88** D2
Bragadiru *Romania* 43°46N 25°31E **81** G10
Bragado *Argentina* 35°2S 60°27W **190** D3
Bragança *Brazil* 1°0S 47°2W **187** D9
Bragança *Portugal* 41°48N 6°50W **88** D4
Bragança □ *Portugal* 41°30N 6°45W **88** D4
Bragança Paulista
  Brazil 22°55S 46°32W **191** A6
Brahestad = Raahe
  Finland 64°40N 24°28E **60** D21
Brahmanbaria *Bangla.* 23°58N 91°15E **123** H17
Brahmani → *India* 20°39N 86°46E **126** D8
Brahmapur *India* 19°15N 84°54E **126** E7
Brahmaputra → *Asia* 23°40N 90°35E **125** H13
Braich-y-pwll *U.K.* 52°47N 4°46W **66** E3
Braidwood *Australia* 35°27S 149°49E **153** C8
Braila *Romania* 45°19N 27°59E **81** E12
Brainerd *U.S.A.* 46°22N 94°12W **172** B8
Braintree *U.K.* 51°53N 0°34E **67** F8
Brak → *S. Africa* 29°35S 22°55E **144** C3
Brakel *Germany* 51°43N 9°11E **76** D5
Brakna □ *Mauritania* 17°0N 13°20W **138** B2
Brakwater *Namibia* 22°28S 17°3E **144** B2
Bralorne *Canada* 50°50N 122°50W **162** C4
Bramhall *U.K.* 53°22N 2°10W **66** E5
Brämön *Sweden* 62°14N 17°40E **62** B11
Brampton *Canada* 43°45N 79°45W **174** C5
Brampton *U.K.* 54°57N 2°44W **66** C5
Brampton I. *Australia* 20°49S 149°16E **150** b
Bramsche *Germany* 52°24N 7°59E **76** C3
Branchville *U.S.A.* 33°15N 80°49W **178** B8
Branco → *Brazil* 1°20S 61°50W **186** D6
Branco, C. *Brazil* 7°9S 34°47W **189** B4
Brandberg *Namibia* 21°10S 14°33E **144** B1
Brandberg △ *Namibia* 21°10S 14°30E **144** B1
Brande *Denmark* 55°57N 9°8E **63** J3
Brandenburg = Neubrandenburg
  Germany 53°33N 13°15E **76** B9
Brandenburg *Germany* 52°25N 12°33E **76** C8
Brandenburg □ *Germany* 52°50N 13°0E **76** C9
Brandfort *S. Africa* 28°40S 26°30E **144** C4
Brandon *France* 46°34N 4°30E **71** F11
Brandon *Canada* 49°50N 99°57W **163** D9
Brandon *Fla., U.S.A.* 27°56N 82°17W **179** H7
Brandon *Vt., U.S.A.* 43°48N 73°6W **175** C11
Brandon B. *Ireland* 52°17N 10°8W **64** D1
Brandon Mt. *Ireland* 52°15N 10°15W **64** D1
Brandsen *Argentina* 35°10S 58°15W **190** D4
Brandvlei *S. Africa* 30°25S 20°30E **144** D3
Brandýs nad Labem
  Czechia 50°10N 14°40E **78** A7
Branford *Conn., U.S.A.* 41°17N 72°49W **175** E12
Branford *Fla., U.S.A.* 29°58N 82°56W **178** F7
Braniewo *Poland* 54°25N 19°50E **82** A8
Bransfield Str. *Antarctica* 63°0S 59°0W **55** C18
Branson *U.S.A.* 36°39N 93°13W **172** G7
Brantford *Canada* 43°10N 80°15W **174** C4
Brantley *U.S.A.* 31°35N 86°16W **178** D3
Brantôme *France* 45°22N 0°39E **72** C4
Branxholme *Australia* 37°52S 141°49E **152** D4
Branxton *Australia* 32°38S 151°21E **153** B9
Branzi *Italy* 46°1N 9°46E **92** B6
Bras d'Or L. *Canada* 45°50N 60°50W **165** C7
Brasher Falls *U.S.A.* 44°49N 74°47W **175** B10
Brasil = Brazil ■ *S. Amer.* 12°0S 50°0W **187** F8
Brasil, Planalto *Brazil* 18°0S 46°30W **184** E6
Brasília *Brazil* 11°0S 68°45W **188** C4
Brasília *Distrito Federal,*
  Brazil 15°47S 47°55W **189** D1
Brasília *Minas Gerais,*
  Brazil 16°12S 44°26W **189** D2
Brasília Legal *Brazil* 3°49S 55°36W **187** D7
Braslaw *Belarus* 55°38N 27°0E **75** B13
Braslawskiya Azyory △
  Belarus 55°36N 27°3E **84** E4
Braslovče *Slovenia* 46°21N 15°3E **93** B12
Braşov *Romania* 45°38N 25°35E **81** E10
Braşov □ *Romania* 45°45N 25°15E **81** E10
Brass *Nigeria* 4°35N 6°14E **139** E6
Brass → *Nigeria* 4°15N 6°13E **139** E6
Brassac-les-Mines *France* 45°24N 3°20E **72** C7
Brasschaat *Belgium* 51°19N 4°27E **69** C4
Brassey, Banjaran
  Malaysia 5°0N 117°15E **118** D5
Brassey Ra. *Australia* 25°8S 122°15E **149** E3
Brasstown Bald
  U.S.A. 34°53N 83°49W **177** D13
Brastad *Sweden* 58°23N 11°30E **63** F5
Bratan = Morozov
  Bulgaria 42°30N 25°10E **97** D9
Brateș *Romania* 45°50N 27°42E **81** E12
Bratislava *Slovakia* 48°10N 17°7E **79** C10
Bratislava M.R. Štefánik ✈ (BTS)
  Slovakia 48°15N 17°20E **79** C10
Bratislavský □ *Slovakia* 48°15N 17°20E **79** C10
Bratsigovo *Bulgaria* 42°1N 24°22E **97** D8
Bratsk *Russia* 56°10N 101°30E **107** D11
Bratskoye Vdkhr.
  Russia 56°0N 101°40E **107** D11
Brattleboro *U.S.A.* 42°51N 72°34W **175** D12
Bratunac *Bos.-H.* 44°13N 19°21E **80** F3
Braunau am Inn *Austria* 48°15N 13°3E **78** C6
Braunschweig *Germany* 52°15N 10°31E **76** C6
Brava *Cabo Verde* 15°0N 24°40W **134** g
Brava, Costa *Spain* 41°30N 3°0E **90** D8
Bravicea *Moldova* 47°35N 28°27E **81** C13
Bråviken *Sweden* 58°38N 16°32E **63** F10
Bravo del Norte, Rio = Grande,
  Rio → *N. Amer.* 25°58N 97°9W **176** J6
Brawley *U.S.A.* 32°59N 115°31W **171** N11
Bray *Ireland* 53°13N 6°7W **64** C5
Bray, Mt. *Australia* 14°0S 134°30E **150** A1
Bray, Pays de *France* 49°46N 1°26E **70** C7
Bray-sur-Seine *France* 48°25N 3°14E **71** D10
Brazeau → *Canada* 52°55N 115°14W **162** C5
Brazil *U.S.A.* 39°32N 87°8W **172** F10
Brazil ■ *S. Amer.* 12°0S 50°0W **187** F8
Brazil Basin *Atl. Oc.* 15°0S 25°0W **56** H9
Brazilian Highlands = Brasil,
  Planalto *Brazil* 18°0S 46°30W **184** E6
Brazo Sur → *S. Amer.* 25°21S 57°42W **190** B4
Brazos → *U.S.A.* 28°53N 95°23W **176** G7
Brazzaville *Congo* 4°9S 15°12E **140** E3
Brčko *Bos.-H.* 44°54N 18°46E **80** E3
Brda → *Poland* 53°8N 18°8E **83** E5
Brdy *Czechia* 49°43N 13°58E **78** B6
Bré = Bray *Ireland* 53°13N 6°7W **64** C5
Breaden, L. *Australia* 25°51S 125°28E **149** E4
Breaksea Sd. *N.Z.* 45°35S 166°35E **154** F1
Bream B. *N.Z.* 35°56S 174°28E **154** B6
Bream Hd. *N.Z.* 35°51S 174°36E **154** B6
Bream Tail *N.Z.* 36°3S 174°36E **154** C6
Breas *Chile* 25°29S 70°24W **190** B1
Breaza *Romania* 45°11N 25°40E **81** E10
Brebes *Indonesia* 6°52S 109°3E **119** G13
Brechin *Canada* 44°32N 79°10W **174** B5
Brechin *U.K.* 56°44N 2°39W **65** E6
Brecht *Belgium* 51°21N 4°38E **69** C4
Breckenridge *Colo.,*
  U.S.A. 39°29N 106°3W **168** G10
Breckenridge *Minn.,*
  U.S.A. 46°16N 96°35W **172** B5
Breckenridge *Tex.,*
  U.S.A. 32°45N 98°54W **176** E5
Breckland *U.K.* 52°30N 0°40E **67** E8
Brecon *U.K.* 51°57N 3°23W **67** F4
Brecon Beacons △ *U.K.* 51°53N 3°26W **67** F4

Bramming *Denmark* 55°28N 8°42E **63** J2
Brämön *Sweden* 62°14N 17°40E **62** B11
Brampton *Canada* 43°45N 79°45W **174** C5
Brampton *U.K.* 54°57N 2°44W **66** C5
Brampton I. *Australia* 20°49S 149°16E **150** b
Bramsche *Germany* 52°24N 7°59E **76** C3
Branchville *U.S.A.* 33°15N 80°49W **178** B8
Branco → *Brazil* 1°20S 61°50W **186** D6
Branco, C. *Brazil* 7°9S 34°47W **189** B4
Brandberg *Namibia* 21°10S 14°33E **144** B1
Brandberg △ *Namibia* 21°10S 14°30E **144** B1
Brande *Denmark* 55°57N 9°8E **63** J3
Brandenburg = Neubrandenburg
  Germany 53°33N 13°15E **76** B9
Brandenburg *Germany* 52°25N 12°33E **76** C8
Brandenburg □ *Germany* 52°50N 13°0E **76** C9
Brandfort *S. Africa* 28°40S 26°30E **144** C4
Brandon *France* 46°34N 4°30E **71** F11
Brandon *Canada* 49°50N 99°57W **163** D9
Brandon *Fla., U.S.A.* 27°56N 82°17W **179** H7
Brandon *Vt., U.S.A.* 43°48N 73°6W **175** C11
Brandon B. *Ireland* 52°17N 10°8W **64** D1
Brandon Mt. *Ireland* 52°15N 10°15W **64** D1
Brandsen *Argentina* 35°10S 58°15W **190** D4
Brandvlei *S. Africa* 30°25S 20°30E **144** D3
Brandýs nad Labem
  Czechia 50°10N 14°40E **78** A7
Branford *Conn., U.S.A.* 41°17N 72°49W **175** E12
Branford *Fla., U.S.A.* 29°58N 82°56W **178** F7
Braniewo *Poland* 54°25N 19°50E **82** A8
Bransfield Str. *Antarctica* 63°0S 59°0W **55** C18
Branson *U.S.A.* 36°39N 93°13W **172** G7
Brantford *Canada* 43°10N 80°15W **174** C4
Brantley *U.S.A.* 31°35N 86°16W **178** D3
Brantôme *France* 45°22N 0°39E **72** C4
Branxholme *Australia* 37°52S 141°49E **152** D4
Branxton *Australia* 32°38S 151°21E **153** B9
Branzi *Italy* 46°1N 9°46E **92** B6
Bras d'Or L. *Canada* 45°50N 60°50W **165** C7
Brasher Falls *U.S.A.* 44°49N 74°47W **175** B10
Brasil = Brazil ■ *S. Amer.* 12°0S 50°0W **187** F8
Brasil, Planalto *Brazil* 18°0S 46°30W **184** E6
Brasília *Brazil* 11°0S 68°45W **188** C4
Brasília *Distrito Federal,*
  Brazil 15°47S 47°55W **189** D1
Brasília *Minas Gerais,*
  Brazil 16°12S 44°26W **189** D2
Brasília Legal *Brazil* 3°49S 55°36W **187** D7
Braslaw *Belarus* 55°38N 27°0E **75** B13
Braslawskiya Azyory △
  Belarus 55°36N 27°3E **84** E4
Braslovče *Slovenia* 46°21N 15°3E **93** B12
Braşov *Romania* 45°38N 25°35E **81** E10
Braşov □ *Romania* 45°45N 25°15E **81** E10
Brass *Nigeria* 4°35N 6°14E **139** E6
Brass → *Nigeria* 4°15N 6°13E **139** E6
Brassac-les-Mines *France* 45°24N 3°20E **72** C7
Brasschaat *Belgium* 51°19N 4°27E **69** C4
Brassey, Banjaran
  Malaysia 5°0N 117°15E **118** D5
Brassey Ra. *Australia* 25°8S 122°15E **149** E3
Brasstown Bald
  U.S.A. 34°53N 83°49W **177** D13
Brastad *Sweden* 58°23N 11°30E **63** F5
Bratan = Morozov
  Bulgaria 42°30N 25°10E **97** D9
Brateș *Romania* 45°50N 27°42E **81** E12
Bratislava *Slovakia* 48°10N 17°7E **79** C10
Bratislava M.R. Štefánik ✈ (BTS)
  Slovakia 48°15N 17°20E **79** C10
Bratislavský □ *Slovakia* 48°15N 17°20E **79** C10
Bratsigovo *Bulgaria* 42°1N 24°22E **97** D8
Bratsk *Russia* 56°10N 101°30E **107** D11
Bratskoye Vdkhr.
  Russia 56°0N 101°40E **107** D11
Brattleboro *U.S.A.* 42°51N 72°34W **175** D12
Bratunac *Bos.-H.* 44°13N 19°21E **80** F3
Braunau am Inn *Austria* 48°15N 13°3E **78** C6
Braunschweig *Germany* 52°15N 10°31E **76** C6
Brava *Cabo Verde* 15°0N 24°40W **134** g
Brava, Costa *Spain* 41°30N 3°0E **90** D8
Bravicea *Moldova* 47°35N 28°27E **81** C13
Bråviken *Sweden* 58°38N 16°32E **63** F10
Bravo del Norte, Rio = Grande,
  Rio → *N. Amer.* 25°58N 97°9W **176** J6
Brawley *U.S.A.* 32°59N 115°31W **171** N11
Bray *Ireland* 53°13N 6°7W **64** C5
Bray, Mt. *Australia* 14°0S 134°30E **150** A1
Bray, Pays de *France* 49°46N 1°26E **70** C7
Bray-sur-Seine *France* 48°25N 3°14E **71** D10
Brazeau → *Canada* 52°55N 115°14W **162** C5
Brazil *U.S.A.* 39°32N 87°8W **172** F10
Brazil ■ *S. Amer.* 12°0S 50°0W **187** F8
Brazil Basin *Atl. Oc.* 15°0S 25°0W **56** H9
Brazilian Highlands = Brasil,
  Planalto *Brazil* 18°0S 46°30W **184** E6
Brazo Sur → *S. Amer.* 25°21S 57°42W **190** B4
Brazos → *U.S.A.* 28°53N 95°23W **176** G7
Brazzaville *Congo* 4°9S 15°12E **140** E3
Brčko *Bos.-H.* 44°54N 18°46E **80** E3
Brda → *Poland* 53°8N 18°8E **83** E5
Brdy *Czechia* 49°43N 13°58E **78** B6
Bré = Bray *Ireland* 53°13N 6°7W **64** C5
Breaden, L. *Australia* 25°51S 125°28E **149** E4
Breaksea Sd. *N.Z.* 45°35S 166°35E **154** F1
Bream B. *N.Z.* 35°56S 174°28E **154** B6
Bream Hd. *N.Z.* 35°51S 174°36E **154** B6
Bream Tail *N.Z.* 36°3S 174°36E **154** C6
Breas *Chile* 25°29S 70°24W **190** B1
Breaza *Romania* 45°11N 25°40E **81** E10
Brebes *Indonesia* 6°52S 109°3E **119** G13
Brechin *Canada* 44°32N 79°10W **174** B5
Brechin *U.K.* 56°44N 2°39W **65** E6
Brecht *Belgium* 51°21N 4°38E **69** C4
Breckenridge *Colo.,*
  U.S.A. 39°29N 106°3W **168** G10
Breckenridge *Minn.,*
  U.S.A. 46°16N 96°35W **172** B5
Breckenridge *Tex.,*
  U.S.A. 32°45N 98°54W **176** E5
Breckland *U.K.* 52°30N 0°40E **67** E8
Brecon *U.K.* 51°57N 3°23W **67** F4
Brecon Beacons △ *U.K.* 51°53N 3°26W **67** F4

Bredasdorp *S. Africa* 34°33S 20°2E **144** D3
Bredbo *Australia* 35°58S 149°10E **153** C8
Bredebro *Denmark* 55°4N 8°50E **63** J2
Bredhat e Hotovës △
  Albania 40°18N 20°25E **96** F4
Bredstedt *Germany* 54°37N 8°55E **76** A4
Bredy *Russia* 52°26N 60°21E **108** B6
Bree *Belgium* 51°8N 5°35E **69** C5
Bregalnica → *Macedonia* 41°43N 22°9E **96** E5
Bregenz *Austria* 47°30N 9°45E **78** D2
Bregovo *Bulgaria* 44°9N 22°39E **96** B6
Bréhal *France* 48°53N 1°30W **70** D5
Bréhat, Î. de *France* 48°51N 3°0W **70** D4
Breiðafjörður *Iceland* 65°15N 23°15W **60** D2
Breil-sur-Roya *France* 43°56N 7°31E **73** E11
Breisach *Germany* 48°1N 7°36E **77** G3
Brejo *Brazil* 3°41S 42°47W **189** A2
Bremanger *Norway* 61°51N 5°0E **63** A1
Bremen *Germany* 53°4N 8°47E **76** B4
Bremen *U.S.A.* 33°43N 85°9W **178** B4
Bremen □ *Germany* 53°33N 8°30E **76** B4
Bremer Bay *Australia* 34°21S 119°20E **149** F2
Bremer I. *Australia* 12°5S 136°45E **150** A2
Bremerhaven *Germany* 53°33N 8°36E **76** B4
Bremerton *U.S.A.* 47°34N 122°37W **170** C4
Bremervörde *Germany* 53°29N 9°8E **76** B5
Brenes *Spain* 37°32N 5°54W **89** H5
Brenham *U.S.A.* 30°10N 96°24W **176** F6
Brenne △ *France* 46°44N 1°14E **72** B5
Brenner Pass *Austria* 47°2N 11°30E **78** E4
Brennerpass *Austria* 47°2N 11°30E **78** E4
Breno *Italy* 45°57N 10°18E **92** C7
Brent *U.S.A.* 32°56N 87°10W **177** E11
Brenta → *Italy* 45°11N 12°18E **93** C9
Brentwood *U.K.* 51°37N 0°19E **67** F8
Brentwood *Calif.,*
  U.S.A. 37°56N 121°42W **170** H5
Brentwood *N.Y.,*
  U.S.A. 40°47N 73°15W **175** F11
Bréscia *Italy* 45°33N 10°15E **92** C7
Breskens *Neths.* 51°23N 3°33E **69** C3
Breslau = Wrocław *Poland* 51°5N 17°5E **83** G4
Bresle → *France* 50°4N 1°22E **70** B8
Bressanone *Italy* 46°43N 11°39E **93** B8
Bressay *U.K.* 60°9N 1°6W **65** A7
Bresse *France* 46°50N 5°10E **71** F12
Bressuire *France* 46°51N 0°30W **70** F6
Brest *Belarus* 52°10N 23°40E **75** B12
Brest *France* 48°24N 4°31W **70** D2
Brest □ *Belarus* 52°30N 26°10E **75** B13
Brest-Litovsk = Brest
  Belarus 52°10N 23°40E **75** B12
Bretagne *France* 48°10N 3°0W **70** D3
Bretçu *Romania* 46°7N 26°18E **81** D11
Bretenoux *France* 44°54N 1°51E **72** D5
Breteuil *Eure, France* 48°50N 0°57E **70** D7
Breteuil *Oise, France* 49°38N 2°18E **71** C9
Breton *Canada* 53°7N 114°28W **162** C6
Breton, Pertuis *France* 46°17N 1°25W **72** B2
Breton Sd. *U.S.A.* 29°35N 89°15W **177** G10
Brett, C. *N.Z.* 35°10S 174°20E **154** B3
Bretten *Germany* 49°2N 8°42E **77** F4
Breuil-Cervínia *Italy* 45°56N 7°38E **92** C4
Brevard *U.S.A.* 35°14N 82°44W **177** D13
Brewarrina *Australia* 30°0S 146°51E **151** E4
Brewer *U.S.A.* 44°48N 68°46W **173** C19
Brewer, Mt. *U.S.A.* 36°44N 118°28W **170** J8
Brewerville *Liberia* 6°26N 10°47W **138** D2
Brewster *N.Y., U.S.A.* 41°24N 73°36W **175** E11
Brewster *Ohio, U.S.A.* 40°43N 81°36W **174** F3
Brewster *Wash., U.S.A.* 48°6N 119°47W **168** B4
Brewster, Kap = Kangikajik
  Greenland 70°7N 22°0W **57** C7
Brewton *U.S.A.* 31°7N 87°4W **177** E11
Breyten *S. Africa* 26°16S 30°0E **145** C5
Breza *Bos.-H.* 44°2N 18°16E **80** F3
Brežice *Slovenia* 45°54N 15°35E **93** C12
Brézina *Algeria* 33°4N 1°14E **136** B4
Březnice *Czechia* 49°32N 13°57E **78** B6
Breznik *Bulgaria* 42°44N 22°55E **96** D6
Brezno *Slovakia* 48°50N 19°40E **79** C12
Brezoi *Romania* 45°21N 24°15E **81** E9
Brezovica *Kosovo* 42°15N 21°3E **96** D5
Brezovo *Bulgaria* 42°21N 25°5E **97** D9
Briançon *France* 44°54N 6°39E **73** D10
Briare *France* 47°38N 2°45E **71** E9
Briático *Italy* 38°43N 16°3E **95** D9
Bribie I. *Australia* 27°0S 153°10E **151** D5
Bribri *Costa Rica* 9°38N 82°50W **182** E3
Bridgefield *Barbados* 13°9N 59°36W **183** g
Bridgehampton
  U.S.A. 40°56N 72°19W **175** F12
Bridgend *U.K.* 51°30N 3°34W **67** F4
Bridgend □ *U.K.* 51°36N 3°36W **67** F4
Bridgeport *Calif.,*
  U.S.A. 38°15N 119°14W **170** G7
Bridgeport *Conn.,*
  U.S.A. 41°11N 73°12W **175** E11
Bridgeport *N.Y., U.S.A.* 43°9N 75°58W **175** C9
Bridgeport *Nebr.,*
  U.S.A. 41°40N 103°6W **172** E2
Bridgeport *Tex., U.S.A.* 33°13N 97°45W **176** E6
Bridger *U.S.A.* 45°18N 108°55W **168** D9
Bridger Pk. *U.S.A.* 41°11N 107°0W **168** F10
Bridgeton *U.S.A.* 39°26N 75°14W **173** F16
Bridgetown *Australia* 33°58S 116°7E **149** F2
Bridgetown *Barbados* 13°6N 59°37W **183** g
Bridgetown *Canada* 44°55N 65°18W **165** D6
Bridgewater *Canada* 44°25N 64°31W **165** D7
Bridgewater *Tas.,*
  Australia 42°44S 147°14E **151** G4
Bridgewater *Vic.,*
  Australia 36°36S 143°59E **152** D5
Bridgewater *Mass.,*
  U.S.A. 41°59N 70°58W **175** E14
Bridgewater *N.Y.,*
  U.S.A. 42°53N 75°15W **175** D9
Bridgewater, C.
  Australia 38°23S 141°23E **152** E4
Bridgnorth *U.K.* 52°32N 2°25W **67** E5
Bridgton *U.S.A.* 44°3N 70°42W **175** B14
Bridgwater *U.K.* 51°8N 2°59W **67** F5
Bridgwater B. *U.K.* 51°15N 3°15W **67** F4
Bridlington *U.K.* 54°5N 0°12W **66** C7
Bridlington B. *U.K.* 54°4N 0°10W **66** C7
Bridport *Australia* 40°59S 147°23E **151** G4
Bridport *U.K.* 50°44N 2°45W **67** G5
Briec *France* 48°6N 4°0W **70** D2

Brienne-le-Château
 France 48°24N 4°30E **71** D11
Brienon-sur-Armançon
 France 47°59N 3°38E **71** E10
Brienz *Switz.* 46°46N 8°2E **77** J4
Brienzersee *Switz.* 46°44N 7°53E **77** J3
Brier Cr. → *U.S.A.* 32°44N 81°26W **178** C8
Brière → *France* 47°22N 2°13W **70** E4
Brig *Switz.* 46°18N 7°59E **77** J3
Brigg *U.K.* 53°34N 0°28W **66** D7
Brigham City *U.S.A.* 41°31N 112°1W **168** F7
Bright *Australia* 36°42S 146°56E **153** D7
Brighton *Australia* 35°5S 138°30E **152** C3
Brighton *Canada* 44°2N 77°44W **174** B7
Brighton *Trin. & Tob.* 10°15N 61°39W **187** K15
Brighton *U.K.* 50°49N 0°7W **67** G7
Brighton *Fla., U.S.A.* 27°14N 81°6W **179** H8
Brighton *N.Y., U.S.A.* 43°8N 77°34W **174** C7
Brightside *Canada* 45°7N 75°30W **175** A8
Brightwater *N.Z.* 41°22S 173°9E **155** B8
Brignogan-Plage *France* 48°40N 4°20W **70** D2
Brignoles *France* 43°25N 6°5E **73** E10
Brihuega *Spain* 40°45N 2°52W **90** E2
Brikama *Gambia* 13°15N 16°45W **138** C1
Brilliant *U.S.A.* 40°15N 80°39W **174** F4
Brilon *Germany* 51°23N 8°35E **76** D4
Brim *Australia* 36°3S 142°27E **152** D5
Brindabella △ *Australia* 35°14S 148°5E **153** C8
Brindisi *Italy* 40°39N 17°55E **95** B10
Brinje *Croatia* 44°59N 15°9E **93** D12
Brinkley *U.S.A.* 34°53N 91°12W **176** D9
Brinkworth *Australia* 33°42S 138°26E **152** B3
Brinnon *U.S.A.* 47°41N 122°54W **170** C4
Brinson *U.S.A.* 30°59N 84°44W **178** E5
Brion, Î. *Canada* 47°46N 61°26W **165** C7
Brionne *France* 49°11N 0°43E **70** C7
Brioski *Croatia* 44°55N 13°45E **93** D10
Brioude *France* 45°18N 3°24E **72** C7
Briouze *France* 48°42N 0°23W **70** D6
Brisay *Canada* 54°26N 70°31W **165** B5
Brisbane *Australia* 27°25S 153°2E **151** D5
Brisbane → *Australia* 27°24S 153°9E **151** D5
Brisbane ✈ (BNE)
 Australia 27°35S 153°7E **151** D5
Brisbane Ranges △
 Australia 37°47S 144°16E **152** D6
Brisbane Water △
 Australia 33°26S 151°13E **153** B9
Brisighella *Italy* 44°13N 11°46E **93** D8
Bristol *U.K.* 51°26N 2°35W **67** F5
Bristol *Conn., U.S.A.* 41°40N 72°57W **175** E12
Bristol *Fla., U.S.A.* 30°26N 84°59W **178** E5
Bristol *Pa., U.S.A.* 40°6N 74°51W **175** F10
Bristol *R.I., U.S.A.* 41°40N 71°16W **175** E13
Bristol *Tenn., U.S.A.* 36°36N 82°11W **177** C13
Bristol *Vt., U.S.A.* 44°8N 73°4W **175** B11
Bristol, City of □ *U.K.* 51°27N 2°36W **67** F5
Bristol B. *U.S.A.* 58°0N 160°0W **166** D8
Bristol Channel *U.K.* 51°18N 4°30W **67** F3
Bristol I. *Antarctica* 58°45S 28°0W **5** B1
Bristol L. *U.S.A.* 34°28N 115°41W **171** L11
Bristow *U.S.A.* 35°50N 96°23W **176** D6
Britain = Great Britain
 Europe 54°0N 2°15W **58** E5
British Columbia □
 Canada 55°0N 125°15W **162** C3
British Indian Ocean Terr. =
 Chagos Arch. ☑ *Ind. Oc.* 6°0S 72°0E **146** E6
British Isles *Europe* 54°0N 4°0W **68** D5
British Mts. *N. Amer.* 68°50N 140°0W **166** B12
British Virgin Is. ☑
 W. Indies 18°30N 64°30W **183** e
Brits *S. Africa* 25°37S 27°48E **145** C4
Britstown *S. Africa* 30°37S 23°30E **144** D3
Britt *Canada* 45°46N 80°34W **164** C3
Brittany = Bretagne □
 France 48°10N 3°0W **70** D3
Britton *U.S.A.* 45°48N 97°45W **172** C5
Brive-la-Gaillarde *France* 45°10N 1°32E **72** C5
Briviesca *Spain* 42°32N 3°19W **88** C7
Brixen = Bressanone
 Italy 46°43N 11°39E **93** B8
Brixham *U.K.* 50°23N 3°31W **67** G4
Brnaze *Croatia* 43°41N 16°40E **93** E13
Brněnský = Jihomoravský □
 Czechia 49°5N 16°30E **79** B9
Brno *Czechia* 49°10N 16°35E **79** B9
Broach = Bharuch *India* 21°47N 73°0E **126** D1
Broad → *Ga., U.S.A.* 33°59N 82°39W **178** D3
Broad → *S.C., U.S.A.* 34°1N 81°4W **177** D14
Broad Arrow *Australia* 30°23S 121°15E **149** F3
Broad Haven *Ireland* 54°20N 9°55W **64** B2
Broad Law *U.K.* 55°30N 3°21W **65** F5
Broad Pk. = Faichan Kangri
 India 35°48N 76°34E **128** B7
Broad Sd. *Australia* 22°0S 149°45E **150** C4
Broadalbin *U.S.A.* 43°4N 74°12W **175** C10
Broadback → *Canada* 51°21N 78°52W **164** B4
Broadford *Australia* 37°14S 145°4E **153** D6
Broadhurst Ra.
 Australia 22°30S 122°30E **148** D3
Broads, The *U.K.* 52°45N 1°30E **66** E9
Broadus *U.S.A.* 45°27N 105°25W **168** D11
Broager *Denmark* 54°53N 9°40E **63** K3
Broby *Sweden* 56°15N 14°7E **63** H6
Brocēni *Latvia* 56°42N 22°32E **62** B9
Brochet *Canada* 57°53N 101°40W **163** B8
Brochet, L. *Canada* 58°36N 101°35W **163** B8
Brock I. *Canada* 77°52N 114°19W **161** B9
Brocken *Germany* 51°47N 10°37E **76** D6
Brockhurst *Australia* 32°9S 148°38E **153** B8
Brocklesby *Australia* 35°48S 146°40E **153** C7
Brockport *U.S.A.* 43°13N 77°56W **174** C7
Brockton *U.S.A.* 42°5N 71°1W **175** D13
Brockville *Canada* 44°35N 75°41W **175** B9
Brockway *Mont.,*
 U.S.A. 47°18N 105°45W **168** C11
Brockway *Pa., U.S.A.* 41°15N 78°47W **174** E6
Brocton *U.S.A.* 42°23N 79°26W **174** D5
Brod *Bos.-H.* 45°10N 18°0E **80** E2
Brod *Macedonia* 41°32N 21°17E **96** C4
Brodarevo *Serbia* 43°14N 19°44E **96** C3
Brodeur Pen. *Canada* 72°30N 88°10W **161** C14
Brodick *U.K.* 55°35N 5°9W **65** F3
Brodnica *Poland* 53°15N 19°25E **83** E6
Brody *Ukraine* 50°5N 25°10E **75** C13
Brogan *U.S.A.* 44°15N 117°31W **168** D5
Broglie *France* 49°0N 0°30E **70** C7
Brok *Poland* 52°43N 21°52E **83** F8
Broken Arrow *U.S.A.* 36°3N 95°48W **176** C7

Broken Bow *Nebr.,*
 U.S.A. 41°24N 99°38W **172** E4
Broken Bow *Okla.,*
 U.S.A. 34°2N 94°44W **176** D7
Broken Bow Lake
 U.S.A. 34°9N 94°40W **176** D7
Broken Hill *Australia* 31°58S 141°29E **152** A4
Broken Ridge *Ind. Oc.* 30°0S 94°0E **5** E13
Broken River Ra.
 Australia 21°0S 148°22E **150** b
Brokind *Sweden* 58°13N 15°42E **63** F9
Bromley *U.K.* 51°24N 0°2E **67** F8
Bromo, Gunung
 Indonesia 7°56N 112°57E **119** H15
Bromo Tengger Semeru △
 Indonesia 7°56S 112°57E **119** H15
Bromölla *Sweden* 56°5N 14°28E **63** H6
Bromsgrove *U.K.* 52°21N 2°2W **67** E5
Brønderslev *Denmark* 57°16N 9°57E **63** G3
Brong-Ahafo □ *Ghana* 7°50N 2°0W **138** D4
Broni *Italy* 45°4N 9°16E **92** C6
Bronkhorstspruit
 S. Africa 25°46S 28°45E **145** C4
Brønnøysund *Norway* 65°28N 12°14E **60** D15
Bronson *U.S.A.* 29°27N 82°39W **179** F7
Bronte *Italy* 37°47N 14°50E **95** E7
Bronwood *U.S.A.* 31°50N 84°22W **178** D5
Brook Park *U.S.A.* 41°23N 81°48W **174** E4
Brookhaven *U.S.A.* 31°35N 90°26W **177** F9
Brookings *Oreg., U.S.A.* 42°3N 124°17W **168** E1
Brookings *S. Dak.,*
 U.S.A. 44°19N 96°48W **172** C5
Brooklet *U.S.A.* 32°23N 81°40W **178** C8
Brooklin *Canada* 43°55N 78°55W **174** C6
Brooklyn Park *U.S.A.* 45°6N 93°23W **172** C7
Brooks *Canada* 50°35N 111°55W **162** C6
Brooks Range *U.S.A.* 68°0N 152°0W **166** B9
Brooksville *U.S.A.* 28°33N 82°23W **179** G6
Brookton *Australia* 32°22S 117°0E **149** F2
Brookville *U.S.A.* 41°10N 79°5W **174** E5
Broom, L. *U.K.* 57°55N 5°15W **65** D3
Broome *Australia* 18°0S 122°15E **148** C3
Broons *France* 48°20N 2°16W **70** D4
Brora *U.K.* 58°0N 3°52W **65** C5
Brora → *U.K.* 58°0N 3°51W **65** C5
Brørup *Denmark* 55°29N 9°1E **63** J2
Brösarp *Sweden* 55°43N 14°6E **63** J8
Brosna → *Ireland* 53°14N 7°58W **64** C4
Broșteni *Mehedinți,*
 Romania 44°45N 22°59E **80** F7
Broșteni *Suceava,*
 Romania 47°14N 25°43E **81** C10
Brotas de Macaúbas
 Brazil 12°0S 42°38W **189** C2
Brothers *U.S.A.* 43°49N 120°36W **168** E3
Brou *France* 48°13N 1°11E **70** D8
Brouage *France* 45°52N 1°4W **72** C2
Brough *U.K.* 54°32N 2°18W **66** C5
Brough Hd. *U.K.* 59°8N 3°20W **65** B5
Broughton Island = Qikiqtarjuaq
 Canada 67°33N 63°0W **161** D19
Broumov *Czechia* 50°35N 16°20E **79** A9
Brovary *Ukraine* 50°34N 30°48E **85** G6
Brovst *Denmark* 57°6N 9°31E **63** G3
Brown, L. *Australia* 31°5S 118°15E **149** F2
Brown, Mt. *Australia* 32°30S 138°0E **152** B3
Brown, Pt. *Australia* 32°32S 133°50E **151** E1
Brown City *U.S.A.* 43°13N 82°59W **174** C2
Brown Willy *U.K.* 50°35N 4°37W **67** G3
Brownfield *U.S.A.* 33°11N 102°17W **176** E3
Browning *U.S.A.* 48°34N 113°1W **168** B7
Brownsville *Oreg.,*
 U.S.A. 44°24N 122°59W **168** D2
Brownsville *Pa., U.S.A.* 40°1N 79°53W **174** F5
Brownsville *Tenn.,*
 U.S.A. 35°36N 89°16W **177** D10
Brownsville *Tex.,*
 U.S.A. 25°54N 97°30W **176** H6
Brownville *U.S.A.* 44°0N 75°59W **175** C9
Brownwood *U.S.A.* 31°43N 98°59W **176** F5
Browse I. *Australia* 14°7S 123°33E **148** B3
Broxton *U.S.A.* 31°38N 82°53W **178** D7
Bruas *Malaysia* 4°30N 100°47E **121** K3
Bruay-la-Buissière *France* 50°29N 2°33E **71** B9
Bruce *Australia* 35°28N 85°49W **178** C4
Bruce, Mt. *Australia* 22°37S 118°8E **148** D2
Bruce B. *N.Z.* 43°35S 169°42E **155** D4
Bruce Pen. *Canada* 45°0N 81°30W **174** B3
Bruce Peninsula △
 Canada 45°14N 81°36W **174** A3
Bruce Rock *Australia* 31°52S 118°8E **149** F2
Bruche → *France* 48°34N 7°43E **71** D14
Bruchsal *Germany* 49°7N 8°35E **77** F4
Bruck an der Leitha
 Austria 48°1N 16°47E **79** C9
Bruck an der Mur
 Austria 47°24N 15°16E **78** D8
Brue → *U.K.* 51°13N 2°59W **67** F5
Bruges = Brugge *Belgium* 51°13N 3°13E **69** C3
Brugg *Switz.* 47°29N 8°11E **77** H4
Brugge *Belgium* 51°13N 3°13E **69** C3
Bruin *U.S.A.* 41°3N 79°43W **174** E5
Brûk, W. el → *Egypt* 30°15N 33°50E **130** E2
Bruksvallarna *Sweden* 62°38N 12°27E **62** B6
Brûlé *Canada* 53°15N 117°58W **162** C5
Brûlé, L. *Canada* 53°35N 64°44W **165** B7
Brûlon *France* 47°58N 0°15W **70** E6
Brumado *Brazil* 14°14S 41°40W **189** C2
Brumado → *Brazil* 14°13S 41°40W **189** C2
Brumath *France* 48°43N 7°40E **71** D14
Brumunddal *Norway* 60°53N 10°56E **60** F14
Brundidge *U.S.A.* 31°43N 85°49W **178** D4
Bruneau *U.S.A.* 42°53N 115°48W **168** E6
Bruneau → *U.S.A.* 42°56N 115°57W **168** E6
Bruneck = Brunico *Italy* 46°48N 11°56E **93** B8
Brunei = Bandar Seri Begawan
 Brunei 4°52N 115°0E **118** D5
Brunei ■ *Asia* 4°50N 115°0E **118** D5
Brunflo *Sweden* 63°5N 14°50E **62** A8
Brunico *Italy* 46°48N 11°56E **93** B8
Brunnen *Switz.* 46°59N 8°37E **77** J4
Brunner, L. *N.Z.* 42°37S 171°27E **155** C6
Brunnsberg *Sweden* 61°17N 13°6E **62** B8
Brunssum *Neths.* 50°57N 5°59E **69** D5
Brunswick = Braunschweig
 Germany 52°15N 10°31E **76** C6
Brunswick *Ga., U.S.A.* 31°10N 81°30W **178** D8
Brunswick *Maine,*
 U.S.A. 43°55N 69°58W **173** D19

Brunswick *Md.,*
 U.S.A. 39°19N 77°38W **173** F15
Brunswick *Mo., U.S.A.* 39°26N 93°8W **172** F7
Brunswick *Ohio, U.S.A.* 41°14N 81°51W **174** E3
Brunswick, Pen. de
 Chile 53°30S 71°30W **192** D2
Brunswick B. *Australia* 15°15S 124°50E **148** C3
Brunswick Junction
 Australia 33°15S 115°50E **149** F2
Brunt Ice Shelf *Antarctica* 75°30S 25°0W **5** D2
Bruntál *Czechia* 49°59N 17°27E **79** B10
Brus Laguna *Honduras* 15°47N 84°35W **182** C3
Brusartsi *Bulgaria* 43°40N 23°5E **96** C7
Brush *U.S.A.* 40°15N 103°37W **168** F12
Brushton *U.S.A.* 44°50N 74°31W **175** B10
Brusio *Switz.* 46°14N 10°8E **77** J6
Brusque *Brazil* 27°5S 49°0W **191** B6
Brussel *Belgium* 50°51N 4°21E **69** D4
Brussel ✈ (BRU) *Belgium* 50°54N 4°29E **69** D5
Brussels = Brussel
 Belgium 50°51N 4°21E **69** D4
Brussels *Canada* 43°44N 81°15W **174** C3
Brusy *Poland* 53°53N 17°43E **82** E4
Bruthen *Australia* 37°42S 147°50E **153** D7
Bruxelles = Brussel
 Belgium 50°51N 4°21E **69** D4
Bruyères *France* 48°10N 6°40E **71** D13
Bruz *France* 48°1N 1°46W **70** D5
Brwinów *Poland* 52°9N 20°40E **83** F7
Bryagovo *Bulgaria* 41°58N 25°8E **97** E9
Bryan *Ohio, U.S.A.* 41°28N 84°33W **173** E11
Bryan *Tex., U.S.A.* 30°40N 96°22W **176** F6
Bryan, Mt. *Australia* 33°30S 139°5E **152** B3
Bryanka *Ukraine* 48°32N 38°45E **85** H10
Bryansk *Bryansk, Russia* 53°13N 34°25E **85** F8
Bryansk *Dagestan, Russia* 44°20N 47°10E **87** H8
Bryansk □ *Russia* 53°10N 33°10E **85** E7
Bryce Canyon △
 U.S.A. 37°30N 112°10W **169** H7
Bryne *Norway* 58°44N 5°38E **61** G11
Bryson City *U.S.A.* 35°26N 83°27W **177** D13
Bryukhovetskaya
 Russia 45°48N 39°0E **85** K10
Brza Palanka *Serbia* 44°28N 22°27E **96** B6
Brzeg *Poland* 50°52N 17°30E **83** H4
Brzeg Dolny *Poland* 51°16N 16°41E **83** G3
Brześć Kujawski *Poland* 52°36N 18°55E **83** F5
Brzesko *Poland* 49°59N 20°34E **83** J7
Brzeziny *Poland* 51°49N 19°42E **83** G6
Brzozów *Poland* 49°41N 22°3E **83** J9
Bsharri *Lebanon* 34°15N 36°0E **130** A5
Bu Baqarah *U.A.E.* 25°35N 56°25E **129** E8
Bu Craa *W. Sahara* 26°45N 12°50W **134** C3
Bū Ḩasā *U.A.E.* 23°30N 53°20E **129** F7
Bua *Fiji* 16°48S 178°37E **154** a
Bua *Sweden* 57°14N 12°7E **63** G6
Bua Yai *Thailand* 15°33N 102°26E **120** E4
Buan *S. Korea* 35°44N 126°44E **115** G14
Buapinang *Indonesia* 4°40S 121°30E **119** E6
Buba *Guinea-Biss.* 11°40N 14°59W **138** C2
Bubanza *Burundi* 3°6S 29°23E **142** C2
Bubaque *Guinea-Biss.* 11°16N 15°51W **138** C1
Bubi → *Zimbabwe* 22°0S 31°7E **145** B5
Būbiyān *Kuwait* 29°45N 48°15E **129** D6
Buca *Fiji* 16°38S 179°52E **154** a
Buca *Turkey* 38°22N 27°11E **99** C9
Bucak *Turkey* 37°28N 30°36E **99** D12
Bucaramanga *Colombia* 7°0N 73°0W **186** B4
Bucasia *Australia* 21°2S 149°10E **150** b
Buccaneer Arch.
 Australia 16°7S 123°20E **148** C3
Buccino *Italy* 40°38N 15°22E **95** B8
Buccoo Reef
 Trin. & Tob. 11°10N 60°51W **187** J16
Bucecea *Romania* 47°47N 26°28E **81** C11
Bucegi △ *Romania* 45°25N 25°25E **81** E10
Buchach *Ukraine* 49°5N 25°25E **75** D13
Buchan *U.K.* 57°32N 2°21W **65** D6
Buchan Ness *U.K.* 57°29N 1°46W **65** D7
Buchanan *Canada* 51°40N 102°45W **163** C8
Buchanan *Liberia* 5°57N 10°2W **138** D2
Buchanan *U.S.A.* 33°48N 85°11W **178** B4
Buchanan, L. *Queens.,*
 Australia 21°35S 145°52E **150** C4
Buchanan, L. *W. Austral.,*
 Australia 25°33S 123°2E **149** E3
Buchanan, L. *U.S.A.* 30°45N 98°25W **176** F5
Buchanan Cr. →
 Australia 19°13S 136°33E **150** B2
Buchans *Canada* 48°50N 56°52W **165** C8
Bucharest = București
 Romania 44°27N 26°10E **81** F11
Buchen *Germany* 49°32N 9°20E **77** F5
Bucheon *S. Korea* 37°28N 126°45E **115** F14
Buchholz *Germany* 53°19N 9°52E **76** B5
Buchloe *Germany* 48°1N 10°44E **77** G6
Buchon, Pt. *U.S.A.* 35°15N 120°54W **170** K6
Buciumi *Romania* 47°7N 23°11E **80** C8
Buck Hill Falls *U.S.A.* 41°11N 75°16W **175** E9
Bückeburg *Germany* 52°16N 9°2E **76** C5
Buckeye Lake *U.S.A.* 39°55N 82°29W **174** G2
Buckhannon *U.S.A.* 39°0N 80°8W **173** F13
Buckhaven *U.K.* 56°11N 3°3W **65** E5
Buckhorn L. *Canada* 44°29N 78°23W **174** B6
Buckie *U.K.* 57°41N 2°58W **65** D6
Buckingham *Canada* 45°37N 75°24W **164** C4
Buckingham *U.K.* 51°59N 0°57W **67** F7
Buckingham B.
 Australia 12°10S 135°40E **150** A2
Buckingham Canal *India* 14°0N 80°5E **127** H5
Buckinghamshire □
 U.K. 51°53N 0°55W **67** F7
Buckle Hd. *Australia* 14°26S 127°52E **148** B4
Buckleboo *Australia* 32°54S 136°12E **152** B2
Buckley *U.K.* 53°10N 3°5W **66** D4
Buckley → *Australia* 20°10S 138°49E **150** C2
Bucklin *U.S.A.* 37°33N 99°38W **172** G4
Bucks L. *U.S.A.* 39°54N 121°12W **170** F5
Bucquoy *France* 50°9N 2°43E **71** B9
București *Romania* 44°27N 26°10E **81** F11
București Otopeni ✈ (OTP)
 Romania 44°30N 26°11E **81** F11
Bucyrus *U.S.A.* 40°48N 82°59W **173** E12
Budacu, Vf. *Romania* 47°7N 25°41E **81** C10
Budalin *Myanmar* 22°20N 95°10E **123** H19
Budaörs *Hungary* 47°27N 18°57E **80** C3
Budapest *Hungary* 47°29N 19°5E **80** C4
Budapest □ *Hungary* 47°29N 19°5E **80** C4

Budapest Ferihegy ✈ (BUD)
 Hungary 47°26N 19°14E **80** C4
Budaun *India* 28°5N 79°10E **125** E8
Budawang △ *Australia* 35°10S 150°12E **153** C9
Budd Coast *Antarctica* 68°0S 112°0E **5** C8
Budderoo △ *Australia* 34°35S 150°41E **153** C9
Buddusò *Italy* 40°35N 9°15E **94** D2
Bude *U.K.* 50°49N 4°34W **67** G3
Budennovsk *Russia* 44°50N 44°10E **87** H7
Budești *Romania* 44°13N 26°30E **81** F11
Budeyi *Ukraine* 48°3N 29°16E **81** B14
Budge Budge = Baj Baj
 India 22°30N 88°5E **125** H13
Budgewoi *Australia* 33°13S 151°34E **153** B9
Budia *Spain* 40°38N 2°46W **90** E2
Büdingen *Germany* 50°16N 9°7E **77** E5
Budjala
 Dem. Rep. of the Congo 2°50N 19°40E **140** D3
Budo-Sungai Padi △
 Thailand 6°19N 101°42E **121** J3
Budoni *Italy* 40°40N 9°45E **94** D2
Búdrio *Italy* 44°32N 11°32E **93** D8
Budva *Montenegro* 42°17N 18°50E **96** D2
Budzyń *Poland* 52°54N 16°59E **83** E3
Buea *Cameroon* 4°10N 9°9E **139** E6
Buellton *U.S.A.* 34°37N 120°12W **171** L6
Buena Esperanza
 Argentina 34°45S 65°15W **190** C2
Buena Park *U.S.A.* 33°52N 117°59W **171** M9
Buena Vista *Colo.,*
 U.S.A. 38°51N 106°8W **168** G10
Buena Vista *Ga.,*
 U.S.A. 32°19N 84°31W **178** C5
Buena Vista *Va.,*
 U.S.A. 37°44N 79°21W **173** G14
Buena Vista Lake Bed
 U.S.A. 35°12N 119°18W **171** K7
Buenaventura *Colombia* 3°53N 77°4W **186** C3
Buenaventura *Mexico* 29°51N 107°29W **180** B3
Buendía, Embalse de
 Spain 40°25N 2°43W **90** E2
Buenópolis *Brazil* 17°54S 44°11W **189** D2
Buenos Aires *Argentina* 34°36S 58°22W **190** C4
Buenos Aires *Costa Rica* 9°10N 83°20W **182** E3
Buenos Aires □
 Argentina 36°30S 60°0W **190** D4
Buenos Aires, L. = General
 Carrera, L. *S. Amer.* 46°35S 72°0W **192** C2
Buffalo *Mo., U.S.A.* 37°39N 93°6W **172** G7
Buffalo *N.Y., U.S.A.* 42°53N 78°53W **174** D6
Buffalo *Okla., U.S.A.* 36°50N 99°38W **176** C5
Buffalo *S. Dak., U.S.A.* 45°35N 103°33W **172** C2
Buffalo *Wyo., U.S.A.* 44°21N 106°42W **168** D10
Buffalo → *Canada* 60°5N 115°5W **162** A5
Buffalo → *S. Africa* 28°43S 30°37E **145** C5
Buffalo → *U.S.A.* 36°14N 92°9W **176** C8
Buffalo Head Hills
 Canada 57°25N 115°55W **162** B5
Buffalo L. *Alta.,*
 Canada 52°27N 112°54W **162** C6
Buffalo L. *N.W.T.,*
 Canada 60°12N 115°25W **162** A5
Buffalo Narrows
 Canada 55°51N 108°29W **163** B7
Buffalo Springs ☆ *Kenya* 0°32N 37°35E **142** B4
Buffels → *S. Africa* 29°36S 17°3E **144** C2
Buford *U.S.A.* 34°7N 83°59W **178** B6
Bug = Buh → *Ukraine* 46°59N 31°58E **85** J6
Bug → *Poland* 52°31N 21°5E **83** F8
Buga *Colombia* 4°0N 76°15W **186** C3
Bugala I. *Uganda* 0°40S 32°20E **142** C3
Buganda *Uganda* 0°0 31°30E **142** C3
Buganga *Uganda* 0°3S 32°0E **142** C3
Bugeat *France* 45°36N 1°55E **72** C5
Bugel, Tanjung
 Indonesia 6°26S 111°3E **119** G14
Búger *Spain* 39°45N 2°59E **100** B9
Bugibba *Malta* 35°57N 14°25E **101** D1
Bugojno *Bos.-H.* 44°2N 17°25E **80** F2
Bugsuk I. *Phil.* 8°12N 117°18E **118** C5
Bugulma *Russia* 54°33N 52°48E **108** D6
Buguma *Nigeria* 4°42N 6°55E **139** E6
Bugungu → *Uganda* 2°17N 31°50E **142** B3
Buguruslan *Russia* 53°39N 52°26E **108** D6
Buh → *Ukraine* 46°59N 31°58E **85** J6
Buharkent *Turkey* 37°58N 28°44E **99** D10
Buheirat-Murrat-el-Kubra
 Egypt 30°18N 32°26E **137** E8
Buhera *Zimbabwe* 19°18S 31°29E **145** A5
Bühl *Germany* 48°40N 8°8E **77** G4
Buhl *U.S.A.* 42°36N 114°46W **168** E6
Buhuşi *Romania* 46°41N 26°45E **81** D11
Bui △ *Ghana* 8°21N 2°21W **138** D4
Buila-Vanturariţa △
 Romania 45°15N 24°0E **81** E8
Builth Wells *U.K.* 52°9N 3°25W **67** E4
Buinsk *Russia* 55°0N 48°18E **86** C9
Buique *Brazil* 8°37S 37°9W **189** D3
Buir Nur *Mongolia* 47°50N 117°42E **111** B12
Buis-les-Baronnies
 France 44°17N 5°16E **73** D9
Buitrago del Lozoya
 Spain 40°58N 3°38W **88** E7
Bujalance *Spain* 37°54N 4°23W **89** H6
Bujanovac *Serbia* 42°28N 21°44E **96** C5
Bujaraloz *Spain* 41°29N 0°10W **90** D4
Buje *Croatia* 45°24N 13°39E **93** C10
Buji *China* 22°37N 114°5E **111** a
Bujumbura *Burundi* 3°16S 29°18E **142** C2
Būk *Hungary* 47°22N 16°45E **80** C1
Buk *Poland* 52°21N 16°30E **83** F3
Bukachacha *Russia* 52°55N 116°50E **107** D12
Bukama
 Dem. Rep. of the Congo 9°10S 25°50E **143** D2
Bukavu
 Dem. Rep. of the Congo 2°20S 28°52E **142** C2
Bukene *Tanzania* 4°15S 32°48E **142** C3
Bukhara = Buxoro
 Uzbekistan 39°48N 64°25E **108** E6
Bukhoro = Buxoro
 Uzbekistan 39°48N 64°25E **108** E6
Bukima *Tanzania* 1°50S 33°25E **142** C3
Bukit Bendera *Malaysia* 5°25N 100°15E **121** c
Bukit Mertajam
 Malaysia 5°22N 100°28E **121** c
Bukit Nil *Malaysia* 1°22N 104°12E **121** d
Bukit Tengah *Malaysia* 5°21N 100°28E **121** c
Bukittinggi *Indonesia* 0°20S 100°20E **118** E2
Bükk *Hungary* 48°0N 20°30E **80** B5

Bukkapatnam *India* 14°14N 77°46E **127** G3
Bükki △ *Hungary* 48°3N 20°30E **80** B5
Bukoba *Tanzania* 1°20S 31°49E **142** C3
Bukum, Pulau *Singapore* 1°14N 103°46E **121** d
Bukuru *Nigeria* 9°42N 8°48E **139** D6
Bukuya *Uganda* 0°40N 31°52E **142** B3
Bula *Guinea-Biss.* 12°7N 15°43W **138** C1
Bula *Indonesia* 3°6S 130°30E **119** E8
Bulan *Phil.* 12°40N 123°52E **119** B6
Bulancak *Turkey* 40°56N 38°14E **105** B6
Bulanık *Turkey* 39°4N 42°14E **105** C10
Būlāq *Egypt* 25°10N 30°38E **137** B3
Bulawayo *Zimbabwe* 20°7S 28°32E **143** G2
Buldan *Turkey* 38°2N 28°50E **99** C10
Buldana *India* 20°30N 76°18E **126** D3
Buldir I. *U.S.A.* 52°21N 175°56E **166** E3
Bulenga *Ghana* 9°56N 2°12W **138** D4
Bulgan *Mongolia* 48°45N 103°34E **110** B9
Bulgar *Russia* 54°57N 49°4E **86** C9
Bulgaria ■ *Europe* 42°35N 25°30E **97** C9
Bulgheria, Monte *Italy* 40°4N 15°26E **95** B8
Bulgurca *Turkey* 38°9N 27°9E **99** C9
Buli, Teluk *Indonesia* 0°48N 128°25E **119** D7
Buliluyan, C. *Phil.* 8°20N 117°15E **118** C5
Bulkley → *Canada* 55°15N 127°40W **162** B3
Bull Shoals L. *U.S.A.* 36°22N 92°35W **176** C8
Bullaque → *Spain* 38°59N 4°17W **89** G6
Bullara *Australia* 22°40S 114°3E **149** D1
Bullard *U.S.A.* 32°8N 95°19W **176** E6
Bulls *Australia* 38°2N 1°40W **91** G3
Bulle *Switz.* 46°37N 7°3E **77** J3
Buller → *N.Z.* 41°44S 171°36E **155** B6
Buller, Mt. *Australia* 37°10S 146°28E **153** D7
Buller Gorge *N.Z.* 41°40S 172°10E **155** B7
Bulleringa △ *Australia* 17°39S 143°56E **150** B3
Bullhead City *U.S.A.* 35°8N 114°32W **171** K12
Bulli *Australia* 34°15S 150°57E **153** C9
Büllingen *Belgium* 50°25N 6°16E **69** D6
Bullock Creek
 Australia 17°43S 144°31E **150** B3
Bulloo → *Australia* 28°43S 142°30E **151** D3
Bulloo L. *Australia* 28°43S 142°25E **151** D3
Bully-les-Mines *France* 50°27N 2°44E **71** B9
Bulman *Australia* 13°39S 134°20E **150** A1
Bulnes *Chile* 36°42S 72°19W **190** D1
Bulqizë *Albania* 41°30N 20°21E **96** E4
Bulsar = Valsad *India* 20°40N 72°58E **126** D1
Bultfontein *S. Africa* 28°18S 26°10E **144** C4
Bulukumba *Indonesia* 5°33S 120°11E **119** F6
Bulun *Russia* 70°37N 127°30E **107** B13
Bulungkol *China* 38°36N 74°58E **109** E8
Bumba
 Dem. Rep. of the Congo 2°13N 22°30E **140** D4
Bumbah, Khalīj *Libya* 32°20N 23°15E **135** B10
Bumbeşti-Jiu *Romania* 45°10N 23°24E **81** E8
Bumbiri I. *Tanzania* 1°40S 31°55E **142** C3
Bumbuna *S. Leone* 9°2N 11°49W **138** D2
Bumhpa Bum
 Myanmar 26°51N 97°14E **123** F20
Bumi → *Zimbabwe* 17°0S 28°20E **143** F2
Buna *Kenya* 2°58N 39°30E **142** B4
Bunaken *Indonesia* 1°37N 124°46E **119** D6
Bunazi *Tanzania* 1°3S 31°23E **142** C3
Bunbah, Khalīj = Bumbah, Khalīj
 Libya 32°20N 23°15E **135** B10
Bunbury *Australia* 33°20S 115°35E **149** F2
Bunclody *Ireland* 52°39N 6°40W **64** D5
Buncrana *Ireland* 55°8N 7°27W **64** A4
Bundaberg *Australia* 24°54S 152°22E **151** C5
Bundanoon *Australia* 34°40S 150°16E **153** C9
Bünde *Germany* 52°11N 8°35E **76** C4
Bundey → *Australia* 21°46S 135°37E **150** C2
Bundi *India* 25°30N 75°35E **124** G6
Bundjalung △
 Australia 29°16S 153°21E **153** D5
Bundoran *Ireland* 54°28N 8°18W **64** B3
Bundure *Australia* 35°10S 146°1E **153** C7
Bung Kan *Thailand* 18°23N 103°37E **120** C4
Bunga → *Nigeria* 11°23N 9°56E **139** C6
Bungay *U.K.* 52°27N 1°28E **67** E9
Bungendore *Australia* 35°14S 149°30E **153** C8
Bungil Cr. → *Australia* 27°5S 149°5E **151** C4
Bungle Bungle = Purnululu △
 Australia 17°20S 128°20E **148** C4
Bungo-Suidō *Japan* 33°0N 132°15E **113** H6
Bungoma *Kenya* 0°34N 34°34E **142** B3
Bungotakada *Japan* 33°35N 131°25E **113** H5
Bungu *Tanzania* 7°35S 39°0E **142** D4
Bunia
 Dem. Rep. of the Congo 1°35N 30°20E **142** B3
Bunji *Pakistan* 35°45N 74°40E **125** B6
Bunkie *U.S.A.* 30°57N 92°11W **176** F8
Bunnell *U.S.A.* 29°28N 81°16W **179** F8
Buñol *Spain* 39°25N 0°47W **91** F4
Bunsuru → *Nigeria* 13°21N 6°23E **139** C5
Buntok *Indonesia* 1°40S 114°58E **118** E4
Bununu Dass *Nigeria* 10°5N 9°31E **139** D6
Bununu Kasa *Nigeria* 9°51N 9°32E **139** D6
Bunza *Nigeria* 12°8N 4°0E **139** C5
Buol *Indonesia* 1°15N 121°32E **119** D6
Buon Brieng *Vietnam* 13°9N 108°12E **120** F7
Buon Ho *Vietnam* 12°57N 108°18E **120** F7
Buong Long *Cambodia* 13°44N 106°59E **120** F6
Buorkhaya, Mys
 Russia 71°50N 132°40E **107** B14
Buqayq *Si. Arabia* 26°0N 49°45E **129** E6
Buqbuq *Egypt* 31°29N 25°29E **137** A2
Bur Acaba = Buurhakaba
 Somalia 3°12N 44°20E **131** G3
Būr Fuad *Egypt* 31°15N 32°20E **137** A2
Būr Safâga *Egypt* 26°43N 33°57E **128** D2
Būr Sa'īd *Egypt* 31°16N 32°18E **137** D6
Būr Sūdân *Sudan* 19°32N 37°9E **137** D4
Būr Taufiq *Egypt* 29°54N 32°32E **137** D6
Bura *Kenya* 1°4S 39°58E **142** C4
Burakin *Australia* 30°31S 117°10E **149** F2
Burang *China* 30°28N 81°10E **123** E9
Burao = Burco *Somalia* 9°32N 45°32E **131** F4
Buras *U.S.A.* 29°21N 89°32W **176** G9
Buraydah *Si. Arabia* 26°20N 43°59E **128** E4

Burbank *U.S.A.* 34°12N 118°18W **171** L8
Burcher *Australia* 33°30S 147°16E **153** B8
Burco *Somalia* 9°32N 45°32E **131** F4
Burda *India* 25°50N 77°35E **124** G7
Burdekin → *Australia* 19°38S 147°25E **150** B4
Burdur *Turkey* 37°45N 30°17E **99** D12
Burdur □ *Turkey* 37°45N 30°10E **99** D12
Burdur Gölü *Turkey* 37°44N 30°10E **99** D12
Burdwan = Barddhaman
 India 23°14N 87°39E **125** H12
Burdwood Bank *Atl. Oc.* 54°0S 59°0W **192** D5
Bure *Ethiopia* 10°40N 37°4E **131** E2
Bure → *U.K.* 52°38N 1°43E **66** E9
Burela *Spain* 43°39N 7°24E **88** A3
Büren *Germany* 51°33N 8°35E **76** D4
Bureskoye Vdkhr.
 Russia 50°16N 130°20E **107** D14
Bureya → *Russia* 49°27N 129°30E **107** D13
Burford *Canada* 43°7N 80°27W **174** C4
Burg *Germany* 52°16N 11°51E **76** C7
Burg auf Fehmarn
 Germany 54°28N 11°9E **76** A7
Burg el Arab *Egypt* 30°54N 29°32E **137** E6
Burg et Tuyur *Sudan* 20°55N 27°56E **137** C2
Burg Stargard *Germany* 53°29N 13°18E **76** B9
Burgas *Bulgaria* 42°33N 27°29E **97** D11
Burgas □ *Bulgaria* 42°30N 27°0E **97** D11
Burgaski Zaliv *Bulgaria* 42°30N 27°39E **97** D11
Burgdorf *Switz.* 52°27N 10°1E **76** C6
Burgdorf *Switz.* 47°3N 7°37E **77** H3
Burgenland □ *Austria* 47°20N 16°20E **79** D9
Burgeo *Canada* 47°37N 57°38W **165** C8
Burgersdorp *S. Africa* 31°0S 26°20E **144** D4
Burgess, Mt. *Australia* 30°50S 121°5E **149** F3
Burghausen *Germany* 48°9N 12°49E **78** D7
Burghead *U.K.* 57°43N 3°30W **65** D5
Búrgio *Italy* 37°36N 13°17E **94** E6
Burglengenfeld *Germany* 49°12N 12°2E **77** F8
Burgohondo *Spain* 40°26N 4°47W **88** E6
Burgos *Spain* 42°21N 3°41W **88** C7
Burgos □ *Spain* 42°21N 3°42W **88** C7
Burgstädt *Germany* 50°54N 12°49E **76** E8
Burgsvik *Sweden* 57°3N 18°19E **63** G12
Burguillos del Cerro
 Spain 38°23N 6°35W **89** G4
Burhaniye *Turkey* 39°30N 26°58E **99** B9
Burhanpur *India* 21°18N 76°14E **126** D3
Burhi Gandak →
 India 25°20N 86°37E **125** G12
Burhner → *India* 22°43N 80°31E **125** H9
Burias I. *Phil.* 12°55N 123°5E **119** B6
Burica, Pta. *Costa Rica* 8°3N 82°51W **182** E3
Burien *U.S.A.* 47°28N 122°20W **170** C4
Burigi, L. *Tanzania* 2°2S 31°22E **142** C3
Burigi △ *Tanzania* 2°20S 31°6E **142** C3
Burim *Kosovo* 42°45N 20°24E **96** D4
Burin *Canada* 47°1N 55°14W **165** C8
Buriram *Thailand* 15°0N 103°0E **120** E4
Buriti Bravo *Brazil* 5°50S 43°50W **189** B2
Buriti dos Lopes *Brazil* 3°10S 41°52W **189** B2
Burkburnett *U.S.A.* 34°6N 98°34W **176** D5
Burke → *Australia* 23°12S 139°33E **150** C2
Burke Chan. *Canada* 52°10N 127°30W **162** C3
Burketown *Australia* 17°45S 139°33E **150** B2
Burkhan Khaldun
 Mongolia 48°45N 108°40E **111** B10
Burkina Faso ■ *Africa* 12°0N 1°0W **138** C4
Burk's Falls *Canada* 45°37N 79°24W **164** C4
Burlada *Spain* 42°49N 1°36W **90** C3
Burleigh Falls *Canada* 44°33N 78°12W **174** B6
Burley *U.S.A.* 42°32N 113°48W **168** E7
Burlingame *U.S.A.* 37°35N 122°21W **170** H4
Burlington *Canada* 43°18N 79°45W **174** C5
Burlington *Colo.,*
 U.S.A. 39°18N 102°16W **168** G12
Burlington *Iowa,*
 U.S.A. 40°49N 91°14W **172** E8
Burlington *Kans.,*
 U.S.A. 38°12N 95°45W **172** F6
Burlington *N.C., U.S.A.* 36°6N 79°26W **177** C15
Burlington *N.J., U.S.A.* 40°4N 74°51W **175** F10
Burlington *Vt., U.S.A.* 44°29N 73°13W **175** B11
Burlington *Wash.,*
 U.S.A. 48°28N 122°20W **170** B4
Burlington *Wis.,*
 U.S.A. 42°41N 88°17W **172** D9
Burma = Myanmar ■
 Asia 21°0N 96°30E **123** J20
Burnaby I. *Canada* 52°25N 131°19W **162** C2
Burnet *U.S.A.* 30°45N 98°14W **176** F5
Burney *U.S.A.* 40°53N 121°40W **168** F3
Burnham *U.S.A.* 40°38N 77°34W **174** F7
Burnham-on-Sea *U.K.* 51°14N 3°0W **67** F5
Burnie *Australia* 41°4S 145°56E **151** G4
Burnley *U.K.* 53°47N 2°14W **66** D5
Burns *U.S.A.* 43°35N 119°3W **168** E4
Burns Junction
 U.S.A. 42°47N 117°51W **168** E5
Burns Lake *Canada* 54°14N 125°45W **162** C3
Burnside → *Canada* 66°51N 108°4W **160** D10
Burnside, L. *Australia* 25°22S 123°0E **149** E3
Burnsville *U.S.A.* 44°47N 93°17W **172** C7
Burnt River *Canada* 44°41N 78°42W **174** B6
Burntwood → *Canada* 56°8N 96°34W **163** B9
Burntwood L. *Canada* 55°22N 100°26W **163** B8
Buronga *Australia* 34°18S 142°22E **152** C5
Burqān *Kuwait* 29°0N 47°57E **128** D5
Burqin *China* 47°43N 87°0E **109** C11
Burra *Australia* 33°40S 138°55E **152** B3
Burra *Nigeria* 11°0N 8°56E **139** C6
Burragorang, L.
 Australia 33°52S 150°37E **153** B9
Burray *U.K.* 58°51N 2°54W **65** C6
Burrel *Albania* 41°36N 20°1E **96** E4
Burren △ *Ireland* 53°9N 9°5W **64** C2
Burren Junction
 Australia 30°7S 148°58E **151** E4
Burrendong, L.
 Australia 32°45S 149°10E **153** B8
Burriana *Spain* 39°50N 0°4W **91** F4
Burrinjuck, L. *Australia* 35°0S 148°36E **153** C8
Burro, Serranías del
 Mexico 29°0N 102°0W **180** B4
Burrow Hd. *U.K.* 54°41N 4°24W **65** G4
Burrowa-Pine Mountain △
 Australia 36°6S 147°45E **153** D7
Burrum Coast △
 Australia 25°13S 152°36E **151** C5
Burruyacú *Argentina* 26°30S 64°40W **190** B3
Burry Port *U.K.* 51°41N 4°15W **67** F3
Bursa *Turkey* 40°15N 29°5E **97** F13

Bursa □ *Turkey* 40°1N 29°5E **104** B3
Burseryd *Sweden* 57°12N 13°17E **63** G7
Burstall *Canada* 50°39N 109°54W **163** C17
Burton *Ohio, U.S.A.* 41°28N 81°8W **174** E4
Burton, L. *Canada* 54°45N 78°20W **172** A4
Burton, S.C., U.S.A. 32°26N 80°43W **178** C9
Burton, L. *Canada* 54°45N 78°20W **172** A4
Burton upon Trent *U.K.* 52°48N 1°38W **66** E6
Burtundy *Australia* 33°45S 142°15E **152** B5
Buru *Indonesia* 3°30S 126°30E **119** E7
Burullus, Bahra el *Egypt* 31°25N 31°0E **137** E7
Burûn, Râs *Egypt* 31°14N 33°7E **130** D2
Burundi ■ *Africa* 3°15S 30°0E **142** C3
Bururi *Burundi* 3°57S 29°37E **142** C2
Burutu *Nigeria* 5°20N 5°29E **139** D6
Burwell *U.S.A.* 41°47N 99°8W **172** E4
Burwick *U.K.* 58°45N 2°58W **65** C5
Bury *U.K.* 53°35N 2°17W **66** D5
Bury St. Edmunds *U.K.* 52°15N 0°43E **67** E8
Buryatia □ *Russia* 53°0N 110°0E **107** D12
Bürylbaytal *Kazakhstan* 44°56N 74°0E **108** D8
Buryn *Ukraine* 51°13N 33°50E **85** G7
Burzenin *Poland* 51°28N 18°47E **83** G5
Busalla *Italy* 44°34N 8°57E **92** D5
Busango Swamp
  Zambia 14°15S 25°45E **143** E2
Busaso = Boosaaso
  Somalia 11°12N 49°18E **131** E4
Buşayrah *Syria* 35°9N 40°26E **105** E9
Busca *Italy* 44°31N 7°29E **92** D4
Bushat *Albania* 41°58N 19°34E **96** E3
Büsheir *Iran* 28°55N 50°55E **129** D6
Büshehr □ *Iran* 28°20N 51°45E **129** D6
Bushenyi *Uganda* 0°35S 30°10E **142** C2
Bushire = Büshehr
  Iran 28°55N 50°55E **129** D6
Bushnell *U.S.A.* 28°40N 82°7W **179** G7
Bushtyna *Ukraine* 48°3N 23°28E **81** B8
Busie *Ghana* 10°29N 2°22E **138** C4
Businga
  Dem. Rep. of the Congo 3°16N 20°59E **140** D4
Büsingen *Germany* 47°42N 8°41E **77** H4
Busko-Zdrój *Poland* 50°28N 20°42E **83** H7
Busovača *Bos.-H.* 44°6N 17°53E **80** F2
Buşra ash Shām *Syria* 32°30N 36°25E **130** C5
Busselton *Australia* 33°42S 115°15E **149** F2
Busseto *Italy* 44°59N 10°2E **92** D7
Bussière-Badil *France* 45°35N 0°36E **72** C4
Bussol, Proliv *Russia* 46°30N 151°0E **107** E16
Bussolengo *Italy* 45°28N 10°51E **92** C7
Bussum *Neths.* 52°16N 5°10E **69** B5
Bustamante, B.
  Argentina 45°5S 66°18W **192** C3
Busto, C. *Spain* 43°34N 6°28W **88** B4
Busto Arsizio *Italy* 45°37N 8°51E **92** C5
Busu Djanoa
  Dem. Rep. of the Congo 1°43N 21°23E **140** D4
Busuanga I. *Phil.* 12°10N 120°0E **119** B6
Büsum *Germany* 54°7N 8°51E **76** A4
Busungbiu *Indonesia* 8°16S 114°58E **119** J17
Buta
  Dem. Rep. of the Congo 2°50N 24°53E **142** B1
Butare *Rwanda* 2°31S 29°52E **142** C2
Butaritari *Kiribati* 3°30N 174°0E **156** G9
Bute *Australia* 33°51S 138°0E **152** B3
Bute *U.K.* 55°48N 5°2W **65** F3
Bute Inlet *Canada* 50°40N 124°53W **162** C4
Butembo *Uganda* 1°9N 31°37E **142** B3
Butembo
  Dem. Rep. of the Congo 0°9N 29°18E **142** B2
Buteni *Romania* 46°19N 22°7E **80** D7
Butera *Italy* 37°11N 14°11E **95** E7
Butere *Kenya* 0°13N 34°30E **142** B3
Butha-Buthe *Lesotho* 28°47S 28°14E **145** C4
Butiaba *Uganda* 1°50N 31°20E **142** B3
Butler *Ga., U.S.A.* 32°33N 84°14W **178** C3
Butler *Mo., U.S.A.* 38°16N 94°20W **172** F6
Butler *Pa., U.S.A.* 40°52N 79°54W **174** F5
Buton *Indonesia* 5°0S 122°45E **119** E6
Butrint □ *Albania* 39°45N 20°1E **96** G4
Butte *Mont., U.S.A.* 46°0N 112°32W **168** D7
Butte *Nebr., U.S.A.* 42°58N 98°51W **172** D4
Butte Creek → *U.S.A.* 39°12N 121°56W **170** F5
Butterworth = Gcuwa
  S. Africa 32°20S 28°11E **145** D4
Butterworth *Malaysia* 5°24N 100°23E **121** c
Buttfield, Mt. *Australia* 24°45S 128°9E **149** D4
Button B. *Canada* 58°45N 94°23W **163** B10
Buttonwillow *U.S.A.* 35°24N 119°28W **171** K7
Butty Hd. *Australia* 33°54S 121°39E **149** F3
Butuan *Phil.* 8°57N 125°33E **119** D7
Butuku-Luba *Eq. Guin.* 3°29N 8°33E **139** E6
Butung = Buton
  Indonesia 5°0S 122°45E **119** E6
Buturlinovka *Russia* 50°50N 40°35E **86** E5
Butwal *Nepal* 27°33N 83°31E **125** E10
Butzbach *Germany* 50°25N 8°40E **77** E4
Bützow *Germany* 53°50N 11°56E **76** B7
Buurhakaba *Somalia* 3°12N 44°20E **131** G3
Buxa Duar *India* 27°45N 89°35E **125** F13
Buxar *India* 25°34N 83°58E **125** G10
Buxoro *Uzbekistan* 39°48N 64°25E **108** E6
Buxtehude *Germany* 53°28N 9°39E **76** B5
Buxton *U.K.* 53°16N 1°54W **66** D6
Buxy *France* 46°44N 4°40E **71** F11
Buy *Russia* 58°28N 41°28E **86** A5
Buyant-Uhaa
  Mongolia 44°55N 110°11E **114** B6
Buynaksk *Russia* 42°48N 47°7E **87** J8
Buyo *Côte d'Ivoire* 6°21N 7°5W **138** D3
Buyo, L. de *Côte d'Ivoire* 6°16N 7°10W **138** D3
Büyük Menderes →
  Turkey 37°28N 27°11E **99** D9
Büyükçekmece *Turkey* 41°2N 28°35E **97** E12
Büyükkarıştıran
  Turkey 41°18N 27°33E **97** E11
Büyükkemikli Burnu
  Turkey 40°18N 26°14E **97** F10
Büyükkonuk = Komi
  Cyprus 35°24N 34°0E **101** D13
Büyükorhan *Turkey* 39°46N 28°56E **99** B10
Büyükyoncalı *Turkey* 41°22N 28°5E **97** E12
Buyun Shan *China* 40°4N 122°43E **115** D12
Buzançais *France* 46°54N 1°25E **70** F8
Buzău *Romania* 45°10N 26°50E **81** E11
Buzău □ *Romania* 45°20N 26°0E **81** E11
Buzău → *Romania* 45°26N 27°44E **81** E12
Buzău, Pasul *Romania* 45°35N 26°12E **81** E11
Buzen *Japan* 33°35N 131°5E **113** H5

Buzet *Croatia* 45°24N 13°58E **93** C10
Buzi → *Mozam.* 19°50S 34°43E **143** F3
Buziaş *Romania* 45°38N 21°36E **80** E6
Büzmeyin *Turkmenistan* 38°3N 58°12E **129** B8
Buzuluk *Russia* 52°48N 52°12E **108** B4
Buzuluk → *Russia* 50°15N 42°7E **86** E6
Buzzards Bay *U.S.A.* 41°45N 70°37W **175** E14
Bwana Mkubwa *Zambia* 13°8S 28°38E **143** E2
Bwindi △ *Uganda* 1°2S 29°42E **142** C2
Byala *Ruse, Bulgaria* 43°28N 25°44E **97** C9
Byala *Varna, Bulgaria* 42°53N 27°55E **97** C11
Byala Slatina *Bulgaria* 43°26N 23°58E **96** C7
Byam Martin I.
  Canada 75°15N 104°15W **161** B11
Byarezina → *Belarus* 52°33N 30°14E **75** B16
Byaroza *Belarus* 52°31N 24°51E **75** B13
Byblos = Jubayl *Lebanon* 34°5N 35°39E **130** A4
Bychawa *Poland* 51°1N 22°36E **83** G9
Byczyna *Poland* 51°7N 18°12E **83** G5
Bydgoszcz *Poland* 53°10N 18°0E **83** E5
Byelorussia = Belarus ■
  Europe 53°30N 27°0E **75** B14
Byers *U.S.A.* 39°43N 104°14W **168** G11
Byesville *U.S.A.* 39°58N 81°32W **174** G3
Byfield △ *Australia* 22°52S 150°45E **150** C5
Bykhaw *Belarus* 53°31N 30°14E **75** B16
Bykhov = Bykhaw
  Belarus 53°31N 30°14E **75** B16
Bykovo *Russia* 49°50N 45°25E **86** F7
Bylas *U.S.A.* 33°8N 110°7W **169** K8
Bylot *Canada* 58°25N 94°8W **163** B10
Bylot I. *Canada* 73°13N 78°34W **161** C16
Byram *U.S.A.* 32°11N 90°15W **177** E9
Byrd, C. *Antarctica* 69°38S 76°7W **55** C17
Byrock *U.S.A.* 30°40S 146°27E **153** A7
Byron *U.S.A.* 32°39N 83°46W **178** C5
Byron, C. *Australia* 28°43S 153°38E **151** D5
Byron Bay *Australia* 28°43S 153°37E **151** D5
Byrranga, Gory *Russia* 75°0N 100°0E **107** B11
Byrranga Mts. = Byrranga, Gory
  Russia 75°0N 100°0E **107** B11
Byrum *Denmark* 57°16N 11°0E **63** G5
Byske *Sweden* 64°57N 21°11E **60** D19
Byskeälven → *Sweden* 64°57N 21°13E **60** D19
Bystrytsya → *Dolnośląskie,*
  Poland 51°12N 16°55E **83** G3
Bystrzyca → *Lubelskie,*
  Poland 51°21N 22°46E **83** G9
Bystrzyca Kłodzka
  Poland 50°19N 16°39E **83** H3
Bytča *Slovakia* 49°13N 18°34E **79** B11
Bytkiv *Ukraine* 48°38N 24°28E **81** D8
Bytom *Poland* 50°25N 18°54E **83** H5
Bytom Odrzański *Poland* 51°44N 15°48E **83** G2
Bytów *Poland* 54°10N 17°30E **82** D4
Byumba *Rwanda* 1°35S 30°4E **142** C3
Bzenec *Czechia* 48°58N 17°18E **79** C10
Bzura → *Poland* 52°25N 20°15E **83** F7

C

C.W. McConaughy, L.
  U.S.A. 41°14N 101°40W **172** E3
Ca → *Vietnam* 18°45N 105°45E **120** C5
Ca Mau *Vietnam* 9°7N 105°8E **121** H5
Ca Mau, Mui *Vietnam* 8°38N 104°44E **121** H5
Ca Na *Vietnam* 11°20N 108°54E **121** G7
Caacupé *Paraguay* 25°23S 57°5W **190** B4
Caaguazú □ *Paraguay* 26°5S 55°31W **191** B4
Caála *Angola* 12°46S 15°30E **141** G3
Caamaño Sd. *Canada* 52°55N 129°25W **162** C3
Caazapá *Paraguay* 26°8S 56°19W **190** B4
Caazapá □ *Paraguay* 26°10S 56°0W **191** B4
Cabana *Peru* 7°30S 78°30W **188** E3
Cabana de Bergantiños = A
  Carballa *Spain* 43°13N 8°54W **88** B2
Cabanaconde *Peru* 15°38S 71°58W **188** D3
Cabañaquinta *Spain* 43°10N 5°38W **88** B5
Cabanatuan *Phil.* 15°30N 120°58E **119** A6
Cabañeros △ *Spain* 39°18N 4°35W **89** F6
Cabanes *Spain* 40°9N 0°2E **90** E5
Cabanilla *Peru* 15°36S 70°28W **188** D3
Cabano *Canada* 47°40N 68°56W **185** B6
Čabar *Croatia* 45°36N 14°39E **93** C11
Cabazon *U.S.A.* 33°55N 116°47W **171** M10
Cabedelo *Brazil* 7°0S 34°50W **189** D12
Cabeza del Buey *Spain* 38°44N 5°13W **89** G5
Cabezón de la Sal *Spain* 43°18N 4°14W **88** B6
Cabhán, An = Cavan
  Ireland 54°0N 7°22W **64** B4
Cabildo *Chile* 32°30S 71°5W **190** C1
Cabimas *Venezuela* 10°23N 71°25W **186** A4
Cabinda *Angola* 5°33S 12°11E **140** F2
Cabinda □ *Angola* 5°0S 12°30E **140** F2
Cabinet Mts. *U.S.A.* 48°10N 115°50W **168** B6
Cabo Blanco *Argentina* 47°15S 65°47W **192** C3
Cabo de Gata-Níjar △
  Spain 36°51N 2°6W **91** J2
Cabo de Hornos △
  Chile 55°42S 67°20W **192** J3
Cabo de Santo Agostinho
  Brazil 8°20S 34°55W **189** B4
Cabo Frio *Brazil* 22°51S 42°3W **191** A7
Cabo Pantoja *Peru* 1°0S 75°10W **186** D3
Cabo Pulmo △
  Mexico 23°20N 109°28W **180** C3
Cabo Raso *Argentina* 44°20S 65°15W **192** B3
Cabo San Lucas
  Mexico 22°53N 109°54W **180** C3
Cabo Verde ■ *Atl. Oc.* 16°0N 24°0W **134** b
Cabonga, Réservoir
  Canada 47°20N 76°40W **164** C4
Caboolture *Australia* 27°5S 152°58E **151** D5
Cabora Bassa Dam = Cahora
  Bassa, Lago de
  Mozam. 15°20S 32°50E **143** F3
Caborca *Mexico* 30°37N 112°6W **180** A2
Cabot, Mt. *U.S.A.* 44°30N 71°25W **185** B13
Cabot Hd. *Canada* 45°14N 81°17W **174** A3
Cabot Str. *Canada* 47°15N 59°40W **165** C8
Cabourg *France* 49°17N 0°7W **70** C6
Cabra *Spain* 37°30N 4°28W **89** H6
Cabra del Santo Cristo
  Spain 37°42N 3°16W **89** H7
Cabra I. *India* 41°18N 93°50E **127** L11
Cábras *Italy* 39°56N 8°32E **94** C1
Cabrera *Spain* 39°8N 2°57E **100** B9

Cabrera, Sierra de la
  Spain 42°12N 6°40W **88** C4
Cabrera △ *Spain* 39°13N 2°53E **91** F7
Cabri *Canada* 50°35N 108°25W **163** C7
Cabriel → *Spain* 39°14N 1°3W **91** F3
Caçador *Brazil* 26°47S 51°0W **191** B5
Čačak *Serbia* 43°54N 20°20E **96** C4
Caçapava do Sul *Brazil* 30°30S 53°30W **191** C5
Cáccamo *Italy* 37°56N 13°40E **94** E6
Cacém *Portugal* 38°46N 9°18W **89** G1
Cáceres *Brazil* 16°5S 57°40W **186** G7
Cáceres *Spain* 39°26N 6°23W **89** F4
Cáceres □ *Spain* 39°45N 6°0W **89** F5
Cache Bay *Canada* 46°22N 80°0W **164** C4
Cache Cr. → *U.S.A.* 38°42N 121°42W **170** G5
Cache Creek *Canada* 50°48N 121°19W **162** C4
Cacheu *Guinea-Biss.* 12°25S 16°0W **190** A1
Cachi *Argentina* 25°5S 66°10W **190** B2
Cachimbo, Serra do
  Brazil 9°30S 55°30W **187** E7
Cachinal de la Sierra
  Chile 24°58S 69°32W **190** A2
Cachoeira *Brazil* 12°30S 39°0W **189** D3
Cachoeira do Sul *Brazil* 30°3S 52°53W **191** C5
Cachoeiro de Itapemirim
  Brazil 20°51S 41°7W **191** A7
Cachopo *Portugal* 37°20N 7°49W **89** H3
Cacine *Guinea-Biss.* 11°8N 14°57W **138** C1
Cacoal *Brazil* 11°32S 61°18W **186** F6
Cacólo *Angola* 10°9S 19°21E **140** G3
Caconda *Angola* 13°48S 15°8E **141** G3
Caculé *Brazil* 14°30S 42°13W **189** D2
Cadaqués *Spain* 42°17N 3°17E **90** C8
Cadca *Slovakia* 49°26N 18°45E **79** B11
Caddo *U.S.A.* 34°7N 96°16W **176** D6
Cader Idris *U.K.* 52°42N 3°53W **67** E4
Cadereyta de Jiménez
  Mexico 25°36N 100°0W **180** B5
Cades *U.S.A.* 33°47N 79°47W **178** B10
Cadí, Serra del *Spain* 42°17N 1°42E **90** C6
Cadí-Moixeró △ *Spain* 42°17N 1°44W **90** C3
Cadibarrawirracanna, L.
  Australia 28°52S 135°27E **151** D2
Cadillac *France* 44°38N 0°20W **72** D3
Cadillac *U.S.A.* 44°15N 85°24W **173** C11
Cádiz *Phil.* 10°57N 123°15E **119** B6
Cádiz *Spain* 36°30N 6°20W **89** J4
Cadiz *Calif., U.S.A.* 34°30N 115°28W **171** L11
Cadiz *Ohio, U.S.A.* 40°22N 81°0W **174** F4
Cádiz, G. de *Spain* 36°40N 7°0W **89** J3
Cádiz L. *U.S.A.* 34°18N 115°24W **171** L11
Cadley *U.S.A.* 33°32N 82°40W **178** B7
Cadney Park *Australia* 27°55S 134°3E **151** D1
Cadomin *Canada* 53°2N 117°20W **162** C5
Cadotte Lake *Canada* 56°26N 116°23W **162** B5
Cadours *France* 43°44N 1°2E **72** E5
Cadoux *Australia* 30°46S 117°7E **149** F2
Cadwell *U.S.A.* 32°20N 83°3W **178** D6
Caen *France* 49°10N 0°22W **70** C6
Caerdydd = Cardiff □ *U.K.* 51°29N 3°10W **67** F4
Caerfyrddin = Carmarthen
  U.K. 51°52N 4°19W **67** F3
Caergybi = Holyhead
  U.K. 53°18N 4°38W **66** D3
Caernarfon *U.K.* 53°8N 4°16W **66** D3
Caernarfon B. *U.K.* 53°4N 4°40W **66** D3
Caernarvon = Caernarfon
  U.K. 53°8N 4°16W **66** D3
Caerphilly *U.K.* 51°35N 3°13W **67** F4
Caerphilly □ *U.K.* 51°37N 3°12W **67** F4
Caesarea *Israel* 32°30N 34°53E **130** C3
Caeté *Brazil* 19°55S 43°40W **189** D2
Caetité *Brazil* 13°50S 42°32W **189** D2
Cafayate *Argentina* 26°2S 66°0W **190** B2
Cafu *Angola* 16°30S 15°8E **144** A2
Cagayan de Oro *Phil.* 8°30N 124°40E **119** C6
Cagli *Italy* 43°33N 12°39E **93** E9
Cágliari *Italy* 39°13N 9°7E **94** C2
Cágliari, G. di *Italy* 39°8N 9°11E **94** C2
Cagnano Varano *Italy* 41°49N 15°47E **93** G12
Cagnes-sur-Mer *France* 43°40N 7°9E **73** E11
Caguán → *Colombia* 0°8S 74°18W **186** D4
Caguas *Puerto Rico* 18°14N 66°2W **183** d
Caha Mts. *Ireland* 51°45N 9°40W **64** E2
Cahama *Angola* 16°17S 14°19E **144** A1
Caherciveen *Ireland* 51°56N 10°14W **64** E1
Cahir *Ireland* 52°22N 7°56W **64** D4
Cahora Bassa, Lago de
  Mozam. 15°20S 32°50E **143** F3
Cahore Pt. *Ireland* 52°33N 6°12W **64** D5
Cahors *France* 44°27N 1°27E **72** D5
Cahuapanas *Peru* 5°15S 77°0W **186** E3
Cahuita *Puerto Rico* 18°14N 66°2W **183** d
Cai Bau, Dao *Vietnam* 21°10N 107°27E **116** G6
Cai Be *Vietnam* 10°20N 106°2E **121** G6
Cai Nuoc *Vietnam* 8°56N 105°1E **121** H5
Caia *Mozam.* 17°51S 35°24E **143** F4
Caianda *Angola* 11°2S 23°31E **143** E5
Caibarién *Cuba* 22°30N 79°30W **182** B4
Caibiran *Venezuela* 7°38N 66°10W **186** B5
Caicara *Venezuela* 7°38N 66°10W **186** B5
Caicó *Brazil* 6°20S 37°0W **189** B3
Caicos Is.
  Turks & Caicos 21°40N 71°40W **183** B5
Caicos Passage
  W. Indies 22°45N 72°45W **183** B5
Caidian *China* 30°35N 114°2E **117** B10
Caiguna *Australia* 32°16S 125°29E **149** F4
Caillooma *Peru* 15°9S 71°45W **188** D3
Cainari *Moldova* 46°41N 29°3E **81** D14
Caird Coast *Antarctica* 75°0S 25°0W **55** D1
Cairn Gorm *U.K.* 57°7N 3°39W **65** D5
Cairngorm Mts. *U.K.* 57°6N 3°42W **65** D5
Cairnryan *U.K.* 54°59N 5°1W **65** G3
Cairns *Australia* 16°57S 145°45E **150** B4
Cairns L. *Canada* 51°42N 94°30W **163** C10
Cairo = El Qâhira *Egypt* 30°2N 31°13E **137** E7
Cairo *Ga., U.S.A.* 30°52N 84°13W **178** F5
Cairo *Ill., U.S.A.* 37°0N 89°11W **172** G9
Cairo *N.Y., U.S.A.* 42°18N 74°0W **175** D10
Cairo Montenotte *Italy* 44°23N 8°16E **92** D5
Caiseal = Cashel *Ireland* 52°30N 7°53W **64** D4
Caisleán an Bharraigh
  = Castlebar
  Ireland 53°52N 9°18W **64** C2
Caithness *U.K.* 58°25N 3°35W **65** C5
Caithness, Ord of *U.K.* 58°8N 3°36W **65** C5
Caja de Muertos, I.
  Puerto Rico 17°54N 66°32W **183** d
Cajamarca *Peru* 7°5S 78°28W **188** E3
Cajabamba *Peru* 7°38S 78°4W **188** B2

Cajamarca □ *Peru* 6°15S 78°50W **188** E3
Cajapió *Brazil* 2°58S 44°48W **189** A2
Cajarc *France* 44°29N 1°50E **72** D5
Cajatambo *Peru* 10°30S 77°2W **188** C2
Cajàzeiras *Brazil* 6°52S 38°30W **189** B3
Cajetina *Serbia* 43°47N 19°42E **96** C3
Çakirgol *Turkey* 40°33N 39°40E **105** B8
Çakırlar *Turkey* 36°52N 30°33E **99** E12
Čakovec *Croatia* 46°23N 16°26E **93** B13
Çal *Turkey* 38°4N 29°23E **99** C11
Cala → *Spain* 37°38N 6°5W **89** H4
Cala Cadolar, Punta de = Rotja,
  Pta. *Spain* 38°38N 1°35E **91** G6
Cala d'Or *Spain* 39°23N 3°14E **100** B10
Cala en Porter *Spain* 39°52N 4°8E **100** B11
Cala Figuera *Spain* 39°27N 2°31E **100** B9
Cala Figuera, C. de *Spain* 39°27N 2°31E **100** B9
Cala Forcat *Spain* 40°0N 3°47E **100** B10
Cala Major *Spain* 39°33N 2°37E **100** B9
Cala Mezquida = Sa Mesquida
  Spain 39°55N 4°16E **100** B11
Cala Millor *Spain* 39°35N 3°22E **100** B10
Cala Murada *Spain* 39°27N 3°17E **100** B10
Cala Ratjada *Spain* 39°43N 3°27E **100** B10
Cala Santa Galdana
  Spain 39°56N 3°58E **100** B10
Calabar *Nigeria* 4°57N 8°20E **139** E6
Calabogie *Canada* 45°18N 76°43W **175** A8
Calabozo *Venezuela* 9°0N 67°28W **186** B5
Calábria □ *Italy* 39°0N 16°30E **95** C9
Calábria △ *Italy* 39°6N 16°35E **95** C9
Calaburras, Pta. de *Spain* 36°30N 4°38W **89** J6
Calaceite *Spain* 41°1N 0°11E **90** D5
Calacoto *Bolivia* 17°16S 68°38W **188** D4
Calacuccia *France* 42°21N 9°1E **73** F13
Calafat *Romania* 43°58N 22°59E **80** G7
Calafell *Spain* 41°11N 1°34E **90** D6
Calahorra *Spain* 42°18N 1°59W **90** C3
Calais *France* 50°57N 1°56E **71** B8
Calais *U.S.A.* 45°11N 67°17W **173** C20
Calalaste, Cord. de
  Argentina 25°0S 67°0W **190** B2
Calama *Brazil* 8°0S 62°50W **186** E6
Calama *Chile* 22°30S 68°55W **190** A2
Calamar *Colombia* 10°15N 74°55W **186** A4
Calamarca *Bolivia* 16°55S 68°9W **188** D4
Calamian Group *Phil.* 11°50N 119°55E **119** B5
Calamocha *Spain* 40°50N 1°17W **90** E3
Calamonte *Spain* 38°53N 6°23W **89** G4
Calañas *Spain* 37°40N 6°53W **89** H4
Calanda *Spain* 40°56N 0°15W **90** E4
Calang *Indonesia* 4°37N 95°37E **118** D1
Calangiánus *Italy* 40°56N 9°11E **94** B2
Calanques △ *France* 43°14N 5°30E **73** E9
Calánscio, Sarīr *Libya* 27°30N 22°30E **135** C10
Calapan *Phil.* 13°25N 121°7E **119** B6
Călărași *Moldova* 47°16N 28°19E **81** C13
Călărași *Romania* 44°12N 27°20E **81** F12
Călărași □ *Romania* 44°10N 27°0E **81** F12
Calasparra *Spain* 38°14N 1°41W **91** G3
Calatafimi *Italy* 37°55N 12°52E **94** E5
Calatayud *Spain* 41°20N 1°40W **90** D3
Călăţele *Romania* 46°46N 23°1E **80** D8
Calato = Kalathos *Greece* 36°9N 28°8E **99** E10
Calauag *Phil.* 13°55N 122°15E **119** B6
Calavà, C. *Italy* 38°11N 14°55E **95** D7
Calavite, C. *Phil.* 13°26N 120°20E **119** B6
Calbayog *Phil.* 12°4N 124°38E **119** B6
Calca *Peru* 13°22S 72°0W **188** C3
Calcasieu L. *U.S.A.* 29°55N 93°18W **176** G8
Calcium *U.S.A.* 44°1N 75°50W **175** B9
Calcutta = Kolkata
  India 22°34N 88°21E **125** H13
Calcutta *U.S.A.* 40°40N 80°34W **174** F4
Caldaro *Italy* 46°25N 11°14E **92** B8
Caldas da Rainha *Portugal* 39°24N 9°8W **89** F1
Caldas de Reis *Spain* 42°36N 8°39W **88** C2
Caldas Novas *Brazil* 17°45S 48°38W **189** D1
Calder → *U.K.* 53°44N 1°22W **66** D6
Caldera *Chile* 27°5S 70°55W **190** B1
Caldera de Taburiente △
  Canary Is. 28°43N 17°52W **100** F2
Caldwell *Idaho, U.S.A.* 43°40N 116°41W **168** E5
Caldwell *Kans., U.S.A.* 37°2N 97°37W **172** G5
Caldwell *Tex., U.S.A.* 30°32N 96°42W **176** F6
Caledon *Canada* 43°51N 79°51W **174** C5
Caledon *S. Africa* 34°14S 19°26E **144** D2
Caledon → *S. Africa* 30°31S 26°5E **144** D4
Caledon B. *Australia* 12°45S 137°0E **150** A2
Caledonia *Canada* 43°7N 79°58W **174** C5
Caledonia *N.Z.* 42°58N 77°51W **174** D7
Calella *Spain* 41°37N 2°40E **90** D7
Calemba *Angola* 16°0S 15°44E **144** A2
Calen *Australia* 20°56S 148°48E **150** b
Calenzana *France* 50°11N 3°14E **71** B10
Calera, La *Chile* 32°40S 71°10W **190** C1
Caleta Olivia *Argentina* 46°25S 67°29W **192** C3
Caletones *Chile* 34°6S 70°27W **190** C1
Calexico *U.S.A.* 32°40N 115°30W **171** N11
Calf of Man *I. of Man* 54°3N 4°48W **66** C3
Calgary *Canada* 51°0N 114°10W **162** C6
Calheta *Madeira* 32°44N 17°11W **100** D2
Calhoun *U.S.A.* 34°30N 84°57W **178** B4
Calhoun Falls *U.S.A.* 34°6N 82°36W **178** C6
Cali *Colombia* 3°25N 76°35W **186** C3
Calicut = Kozhikode
  India 11°15N 75°43E **127** J2
Caliente *U.S.A.* 37°37N 105°51W **171** H11
California *Mo., U.S.A.* 38°38N 92°34W **172** F7
California *Pa., U.S.A.* 40°4N 79°54W **174** F5
California □ *U.S.A.* 37°30N 119°30W **170** H7
California, Baja, T.N. = Baja
  California □ *Mexico* 30°0N 115°0W **180** B2
California, Baja, T.S. = Baja
  California Sur □
  Mexico 25°50N 111°50W **180** B2
California, G. de *Mexico* 27°0N 111°0W **180** B2
California City *U.S.A.* 35°10N 117°55W **171** K9
California Hot Springs
  U.S.A. 35°51N 118°41W **171** K8
Călilabad *Azerbaijan* 39°12N 48°29E **105** C13
Calilegua △ *Argentina* 23°45S 64°50W **190** B3
Călimănești *Romania* 45°14N 24°20E **81** E8
Călimani, Munţii
  Romania 47°12N 25°0E **81** C9
Călimani △ *Romania* 47°7N 25°10E **81** C9

Calipatria *U.S.A.* 33°8N 115°31W **171** M11
Calistoga *U.S.A.* 38°35N 122°35W **170** G4
Calitri *Italy* 40°54N 15°26E **95** B8
Calitzdorp *S. Africa* 33°33S 21°42E **144** D3
Callabonna, L.
  Australia 29°40S 140°5E **151** D3
Callac *France* 48°25N 3°27W **70** D3
Callahan *U.S.A.* 30°34N 81°50W **178** E8
Callan *Ireland* 52°32N 7°24W **64** D4
Callander *U.K.* 56°15N 4°13W **65** E4
Callao *Peru* 12°3S 77°8W **188** C2
Callaway *U.S.A.* 30°8N 85°35W **178** F4
Callicoon *U.S.A.* 41°46N 75°3W **175** E9
Calling Lake *Canada* 55°15N 113°12W **162** B6
Calliope *Australia* 24°0S 151°16E **150** C5
Callosa de Segura *Spain* 38°7N 0°53W **91** G4
Callosa d'En Sarrià *Spain* 38°40N 0°8W **91** G4
Calma, Costa de la *Spain* 39°28N 2°26E **100** B9
Calne *U.K.* 51°26N 2°0W **67** F6
Calola *Angola* 16°25S 17°48E **144** A2
Calonge *Spain* 41°52N 3°5E **90** D8
Caloosahatchee →
  U.S.A. 26°31N 82°1W **179** J7
Calore → *Italy* 41°11N 14°28E **95** A7
Caloundra *Australia* 26°45S 153°10E **151** D5
Calpe *Spain* 38°39N 0°3E **91** G5
Calpella *U.S.A.* 39°14N 123°12W **170** F3
Calpine *U.S.A.* 39°40N 120°27W **170** F6
Calstock *Canada* 49°47N 84°9W **164** C3
Caltabellotta *Italy* 37°35N 13°13E **94** E6
Caltagirone *Italy* 37°14N 14°31E **95** E7
Caltanissetta *Italy* 37°29N 14°4E **95** E7
Çaltılıbük *Turkey* 39°57N 28°36E **97** G12
Calulo *Angola* 10°1S 14°56E **140** G2
Caluso *Italy* 45°18N 7°53E **92** C4
Calvados □ *France* 49°5N 0°15W **70** C6
Calvert → *Australia* 16°17S 137°44E **150** B2
Calvert I. *Canada* 51°30N 128°0W **162** C3
Calvert Ra. *Australia* 24°0S 122°30E **148** D3
Calvi *France* 42°34N 8°45E **73** F12
Calvià *Spain* 39°34N 2°31E **100** B9
Calvillo *Mexico* 21°51N 102°43W **180** C4
Calvinia *S. Africa* 31°28S 19°45E **144** D2
Calvo, Mte. *Italy* 41°44N 15°46E **93** G12
Calwa *U.S.A.* 36°42N 119°46W **170** J7
Calzada Almuradiel = Almuradiel
  Spain 38°32N 3°28W **89** G7
Calzada de Calatrava
  Spain 38°42N 3°46W **89** G7
Cam → *U.K.* 52°21N 0°16E **67** E8
Cam Lam = Ba Ngoi
  Vietnam 11°54N 109°10E **121** G7
Cam Pha *Vietnam* 21°7N 107°18E **116** G6
Cam Ranh *Vietnam* 11°54N 109°12E **121** G7
Cam Xuyen *Vietnam* 18°15N 106°0E **120** C6
Camabatela *Angola* 8°20S 15°26E **140** F3
Camacá *Brazil* 15°24S 39°30W **189** D3
Camaçari *Brazil* 12°41S 38°18W **189** D3
Camacha *Madeira* 32°41N 16°49W **100** D3
Camacupa *Angola* 11°58S 17°22E **141** G3
Camaguey *Cuba* 21°20N 77°55W **182** B4
Camaiore *Italy* 43°56N 10°18E **92** E7
Camamu *Brazil* 13°57S 39°7W **189** D3
Camaná *Peru* 16°30S 72°50W **188** D3
Camanche Res. *U.S.A.* 38°14N 121°1W **170** G5
Camaquã *Brazil* 30°51S 51°49W **191** C5
Camaquã → *Brazil* 31°17S 51°47W **191** C5
Câmara de Lobos
  Madeira 32°39N 16°59W **100** D3
Camarat, C. *France* 43°12N 6°41E **73** E10
Çamardı *Turkey* 37°49N 34°58E **104** D6
Camarès *France* 43°49N 2°53E **72** E6
Camaret-sur-Mer *France* 48°16N 4°37W **70** D2
Camargo *Mexico* 26°19N 98°50W **181** B5
Camargue *France* 43°34N 4°34E **73** E8
Camargue △ *France* 43°30N 4°40E **73** E8
Camarillo *U.S.A.* 34°13N 119°2W **171** L7
Camariñas *Spain* 43°8N 9°12W **88** B1
Camarón, C. *Honduras* 16°0N 85°5W **182** C2
Camarones *Argentina* 44°50S 65°40W **192** B3
Camarones, B.
  Argentina 44°45S 65°35W **192** B3
Camas *U.S.A.* 45°35N 122°24W **170** E4
Camas Valley *U.S.A.* 43°2N 123°40W **168** E2
Camballin *Australia* 17°59S 124°12E **148** D4
Cambará *Brazil* 23°2S 50°5W **191** A5
Cambay = Khambhat
  India 22°23N 72°33E **124** H8
Cambay, G. of = Khambhat, G. of
  India 20°45N 72°30E **124** J8
Cambil *Spain* 37°40N 3°33W **89** H7
Cambo-les-Bains *France* 43°22N 1°23W **72** E3
Cambodia ■ *Asia* 12°15N 105°0E **120** F5
Camborne *U.K.* 50°12N 5°19W **67** G2
Cambrai *France* 50°11N 3°14E **71** B10
Cambria *U.S.A.* 35°34N 121°5W **170** K5
Cambrian Mts. *U.K.* 52°3N 3°57W **67** E4
Cambridge *Canada* 43°23N 80°15W **174** C4
Cambridge *Jamaica* 18°18N 77°54W **182** a
Cambridge *N.Z.* 37°54S 175°29E **154** D4
Cambridge *U.K.* 52°12N 0°8E **67** E8
Cambridge *Mass.,*
  U.S.A. 42°23N 71°7W **175** D13
Cambridge *Minn.,*
  U.S.A. 45°34N 93°13W **172** C7
Cambridge *N.Y., U.S.A.* 43°2N 73°22W **175** C11
Cambridge *Nebr.,*
  U.S.A. 40°17N 100°10W **172** E3
Cambridge *Ohio, U.S.A.* 40°1N 81°35W **174** F3
Cambridge Bay
  Canada 69°10N 105°0W **160** D11
Cambridge G.
  Australia 14°55S 128°15E **148** B4
Cambridge Springs
  U.S.A. 41°48N 80°4W **174** E4
Cambridgeshire □ *U.K.* 52°25N 0°7W **67** E7
Cambrils *Spain* 41°8N 1°3E **90** D6
Cambuci *Brazil* 21°35S 41°55W **191** A7
Cambundi-Catembo
  Angola 10°10S 17°35E **140** G3
Camden *Australia* 34°1S 150°43E **153** B5
Camden *Ala., U.S.A.* 31°59N 87°17W **177** F11
Camden *Ark., U.S.A.* 33°35N 92°50W **176** E8
Camden *Maine, U.S.A.* 44°13N 69°4W **173** C19
Camden *N.J., U.S.A.* 39°55N 75°7W **175** G9
Camden *N.Y., U.S.A.* 43°20N 75°45W **175** C9

Camden *S.C., U.S.A.* 34°16N 80°36W **177** D14
Camden Sd. *Australia* 15°27S 124°25E **148** C3
Camdenton *U.S.A.* 38°1N 92°45W **172** F7
Camelford *U.K.* 50°37N 4°42W **67** G3
Çameli *Turkey* 37°5N 29°24E **99** D11
Camenca *Moldova* 48°3N 28°42E **81** B13
Camerino *Italy* 43°8N 13°4E **93** E10
Camerón *Chile* 53°38S 69°39W **192** D2
Cameron *Ariz., U.S.A.* 35°53N 111°25W **169** J8
Cameron *La., U.S.A.* 29°48N 93°20W **176** G8
Cameron *Mo., U.S.A.* 39°44N 94°14W **172** F6
Cameron *Tex., U.S.A.* 30°51N 96°59W **176** F6
Cameron Highlands
  Malaysia 4°27N 101°22E **121** K3
Cameron Hills *Canada* 59°48N 118°0W **162** B5
Cameron Mts. *N.Z.* 46°1S 167°0E **155** G2
Cameroon ■ *Africa* 6°0N 12°30E **135** G7
Cameroota *Italy* 40°2N 15°21E **95** B8
Cameroun → *Cameroon* 4°0N 9°35E **139** E6
Cameroun, Mt. *Cameroon* 4°13N 9°10E **139** E6
Cametá *Brazil* 2°12S 49°30W **187** D9
Çamiçi Gölü *Turkey* 37°29N 27°28E **99** D9
Camilla *U.S.A.* 31°14N 84°12W **178** D5
Caminha *Portugal* 41°50N 8°50W **88** D2
Camino *U.S.A.* 38°44N 120°41W **170** G6
Camlıbel = Myrtou
  Cyprus 35°18N 33°4E **101** D12
Cammal *U.S.A.* 41°24N 77°28W **174** E7
Cammarata *Italy* 37°38N 13°38E **94** E6
Camocim *Brazil* 2°55S 40°50W **189** A2
Camonica, Val *Italy* 46°10N 10°20E **92** B7
Camooweal *Australia* 19°56S 138°7E **150** B2
Camooweal Caves △
  Australia 20°1S 138°11E **150** B2
Camopi *Fr. Guiana* 3°12N 52°17W **187** C8
Camorta *India* 8°8N 93°30E **127** K11
Camp Hill *Ala., U.S.A.* 32°48N 85°39W **178** C4
Camp Hill *Pa., U.S.A.* 40°14N 76°55W **174** F8
Camp Nelson *U.S.A.* 36°8N 118°39W **171** J8
Camp Pendleton
  U.S.A. 33°13N 117°24W **171** M9
Camp Verde *U.S.A.* 34°34N 111°51W **169** J8
Camp Wood *U.S.A.* 29°40N 100°1W **176** G4
Campagna *Italy* 40°40N 15°6E **95** B8
Campana *Italy* 34°10S 58°55W **190** C4
Campana, I. *Chile* 48°20S 75°20W **192** C1
Campanário *Madeira* 32°39N 17°2W **100** D2
Campanario *Spain* 38°52N 5°36W **89** G5
Campanet *Spain* 39°46N 2°58E **100** B9
Campánia □ *Italy* 41°0N 14°30E **95** B7
Campas del Tuyú △
  Argentina 36°17S 56°50W **190** D4
Campbell *S. Africa* 28°48S 23°44E **144** C3
Campbell *Calif., U.S.A.* 37°17N 121°57W **170** H5
Campbell *Fla., U.S.A.* 28°16N 81°27W **179** H5
Campbell *Ohio, U.S.A.* 41°5N 80°37W **174** E4
Campbell *C. N.Z.* 41°47S 174°18E **155** B9
Campbell I. *Pac. Oc.* 52°30S 169°0E **156** N8
Campbell L. *Canada* 63°14N 106°55W **163** A7
Campbell Plateau
  S. Ocean 50°0S 170°0E **55** L1
Campbell River *Canada* 50°5N 125°20W **162** C3
Campbellford *Canada* 44°18N 77°48W **174** B7
Campbellpur *Pakistan* 33°46N 72°26E **124** C5
Campbellsville *U.S.A.* 37°21N 85°20W **173** G11
Campbellton *Canada* 47°57N 66°43W **165** C6
Campbelltown *U.S.A.* 50°57N 85°24W **178** E4
Campbellton
  Australia 34°4S 150°49E **153** C9
Campbeltown *U.K.* 55°26S 5°36W **65** F3
Campeche *Mexico* 19°51N 90°32W **181** D6
Campeche □ *Mexico* 19°0N 90°30W **181** D6
Campeche, Banco
  Mexico 22°30N 88°0W **181** C7
Campeche, Golfo de
  Mexico 19°30N 93°0W **181** D6
Câmpeni *Romania* 46°22N 23°3E **80** D8
Camperdown *Australia* 38°14S 143°9E **152** C5
Camperville *Canada* 51°59N 100°9W **163** C8
Campi Salentina *Italy* 40°24N 18°1E **95** B11
Câmpia Turzii *Romania* 46°34N 23°53E **81** D8
Campidano *Italy* 39°30N 8°40E **94** C1
Campíglia Maríttima
  Italy 43°4N 10°37E **92** E7
Campillo de Altobuey
  Spain 39°36N 1°49W **91** F3
Campillos *Spain* 37°4N 4°51W **89** H6
Câmpina *Romania* 45°10N 25°45E **81** E9
Campina Grande *Brazil* 7°20S 35°47W **189** D3
Campinas *Brazil* 22°50S 47°0W **191** A6
Campione *Italy* 45°58N 8°58E **73** C12
Campli *Italy* 42°43N 13°41E **93** F10
Campo de Criptana *Spain* 39°24N 3°7W **89** F7
Campo de Gibraltar
  Spain 36°15N 5°25W **89** J5
Campo de los Alisos △
  Argentina 27°15S 66°0W **190** B2
Campo Formoso *Brazil* 10°30S 40°20W **189** D2
Campo Grande *Brazil* 20°25S 54°40W **187** H8
Campo Maior *Brazil* 4°50S 42°12W **189** B2
Campo Maior *Portugal* 39°2N 7°7W **89** F3
Campo Mourão *Brazil* 24°3S 52°22W **191** A5
Campo Túres *Italy* 46°53N 11°55E **92** B8
Campobasso *Italy* 41°34N 14°39E **95** A7
Campobello di Licata
  Italy 37°15N 13°55E **94** E6
Campobello di Mazara
  Italy 37°38N 12°45E **94** E5
Campofelice di Roccella
  Italy 37°58N 13°53E **94** E6
Campomarino *Italy* 41°57N 15°2E **93** G12
Camporrobles *Spain* 39°39N 1°24W **90** F3
Campos *Brazil* 21°50S 41°20W **191** A7
Campos Belos *Brazil* 13°10S 47°3W **189** D2
Campos Altos *Brazil* 19°47S 46°10W **189** D1
Campos del Paraíso = Carrascosa
  del Campo *Spain* 40°2N 2°45W **90** E2
Campos Novos *Brazil* 27°21S 51°50W **191** B5
Campos Sales *Brazil* 7°0S 40°25W **189** C2
Camprodon *Spain* 42°19N 2°23E **90** C7
Campton *Fla., U.S.A.* 30°53N 86°31W **178** F4
Campton *U.S.A.* 37°44N 83°33W **173** G12
Camptonville *U.S.A.* 39°27N 121°3W **170** F5
Camptown *U.S.A.* 41°44N 76°14W **175** E8
Câmpulung *Romania* 45°17N 25°3E **81** E9
Câmpulung Moldovenesc
  Romania 47°32N 25°30E **81** C10

Câmpuri *Romania* 46°0N 26°50E **81 D11**
Campville *U.S.A.* 29°40N 82°7W **178 F7**
Camrose *Canada* 53°0N 112°50W **162 C6**
Camsell Portage
  Canada 59°37N 109°15W **163 B7**
Çamuva *Turkey* 36°30N 30°30E **99 E12**
Çan *Turkey* 40°2N 27°3E **97 F11**
Can Clavo *Spain* 38°57N 1°27E **100 C7**
Can Creu *Spain* 38°58N 1°28E **100 C7**
Can Gio *Vietnam* 10°25N 106°58E **121 G6**
Can Pastilla *Spain* 39°32N 2°42E **100 B9**
Can Tho *Vietnam* 10°2N 105°46E **121 G5**
Canaan *U.S.A.* 42°2N 73°20W **175 D11**
Canacona *India* 15°1N 74°4E **127 G2**
Canada ■ *N. Amer.* 60°0N 100°0W **160 G11**
Canada Abyssal Plain
  Arctic 80°0N 140°0W **54 B18**
Canada Basin *Arctic* 75°0N 145°0W **54 B18**
Cañada de Gómez
  Argentina 32°40S 61°30W **190 C3**
Canadian *U.S.A.* 35°55N 100°23W **176 D4**
Canadian ➔ *U.S.A.* 35°28N 95°3W **176 D7**
Canadian Shield *Canada* 53°0N 75°0W **158 D12**
Canadys *U.S.A.* 33°3N 80°37W **178 B9**
Canajoharie *U.S.A.* 42°54N 74°35W **175 D10**
Çanakkale *Turkey* 40°8N 26°24E **97 F10**
Çanakkale □ *Turkey* 40°0N 26°25E **97 F10**
Çanakkale Boğazı
  Turkey 40°17N 26°32E **97 F10**
Canal Flats *Canada* 50°10N 115°48W **162 C5**
Canal Point *U.S.A.* 26°52N 80°38W **179 J9**
Canalejas *Argentina* 35°15S 66°34W **190 D2**
Canals *Argentina* 33°35S 62°53W **190 C3**
Canals *Spain* 38°58N 0°35W **91 G4**
Canandaigua *U.S.A.* 42°54N 77°17W **174 D7**
Canandaigua L. *U.S.A.* 42°47N 77°19W **174 D7**
Cananea *Mexico* 31°0N 110°18W **180 A2**
Canarias, Is. *Atl. Oc.* 28°30N 16°0W **100 F4**
Canaries *St. Lucia* 13°55N 61°4W **183 f**
Canarreos, Arch. de los
  Cuba 21°35N 81°40W **182 B3**
Canary Is. = Canarias, Is.
  Atl. Oc. 28°30N 16°0W **100 F4**
Canaseraga *U.S.A.* 42°27N 77°45W **174 D7**
Canastra, Serra da
  Brazil 20°0S 46°20W **189 E1**
Canatlán *Mexico* 24°31N 104°47W **180 C4**
Canaveral, C. *U.S.A.* 28°27N 80°32W **179 G9**
Canaveral ➔ *U.S.A.* 28°28N 80°34W **179 G9**
Cañaverulas *Spain* 40°24N 2°38W **90 E2**
Canavieiras *Brazil* 15°39S 39°0W **189 D3**
Canbelego *Australia* 31°32S 146°18E **153 A7**
Canberra *Australia* 35°15S 149°8E **153 C8**
Canby *Calif., U.S.A.* 41°27N 120°52W **168 F3**
Canby *Minn., U.S.A.* 44°43N 96°16W **172 C5**
Canby *Oreg., U.S.A.* 45°16N 122°42W **170 E4**
Cancale *France* 48°40N 1°50W **70 D5**
Canche ➔ *France* 50°31N 1°39E **71 B8**
Canchungo *Guinea-Biss.* 12°26N 16°5W **138 C1**
Canchyuaya, Cordillera de
  Peru 7°30S 74°0W **188 B3**
Cancún *Mexico* 21°8N 86°44W **181 C7**
Candandchú *Peru* 42°47N 0°32W **90 C4**
Candarave *Peru* 17°15S 70°13W **188 D3**
Çandarlı *Turkey* 38°56N 26°56E **99 C8**
Çandarlı Körfezi *Turkey* 38°52N 26°55E **99 C8**
Candás *Spain* 43°35N 5°45W **88 B5**
Candé *France* 47°34N 1°2W **70 E5**
Candela *Italy* 41°8N 15°31E **95 A8**
Candelaria *Argentina* 27°29S 55°44W **191 B4**
Candelaria *Canary Is.* 28°22N 16°22W **100 F3**
Candelario ➔ *Spain* 40°20N 5°46W **88 E5**
Candeleda *Spain* 40°10N 5°14W **88 E5**
Candelo *Australia* 36°47S 149°43E **153 C8**
Candi Dasa *Indonesia* 8°30S 115°34E **119 J18**
Candia = Iraklio *Greece* 35°20N 25°12E **101 D7**
Candle L. *Canada* 53°50N 105°18W **163 C7**
Candlemas I. *Antarctica* 57°3S 26°40W **55 B1**
Cando *U.S.A.* 48°32N 99°12W **172 A4**
Canea = Chania *Greece* 35°30N 24°4E **101 D6**
Canela *Brazil* 10°15S 48°25W **189 C1**
Canelli *Italy* 44°43N 8°17E **92 D5**
Canelones *Uruguay* 34°32S 56°17W **191 C4**
Canet-Plage *France* 42°42N 3°2E **72 F7**
Canet de Mar *Spain* 41°35N 2°35E **90 D7**
Cañete *Chile* 37°50S 73°30W **190 D1**
Cañete *Spain* 40°3N 1°54W **90 E3**
Cañete de las Torres
  Spain 37°53N 4°19W **89 H6**
Cangas *Spain* 42°16N 8°47W **88 C2**
Cangas de Onís *Spain* 43°21N 5°8W **88 B5**
Cangas del Narcea *Spain* 43°10N 6°32W **88 B4**
Cangnan *China* 27°30N 120°23E **117 D13**
Cangshan *China* 34°50N 118°2E **115 G10**
Canguaretama *Brazil* 6°20S 35°5W **189 D3**
Canguçu *Brazil* 31°22S 52°43W **191 C5**
Canguçu, Serra do
  Brazil 31°20S 52°40W **191 C5**
Cangxi *China* 31°47N 105°59E **116 B5**
Cangzhou *China* 38°19N 116°52E **114 E9**
Caniapiscau ➔
  Canada 56°40N 69°30W **165 A6**
Caniapiscau, L. *Canada* 54°10N 69°55W **165 B6**
Canicattì *Italy* 37°21N 13°51E **94 E6**
Canicattini Bagni *Italy* 37°2N 15°4E **95 E8**
Canigou *France* 42°31N 2°27E **72 F6**
Caniles *Spain* 37°26N 2°43W **89 H8**
Canim Lake *Canada* 51°47N 120°54W **162 C4**
Canindé *Brazil* 4°22S 39°19W **189 A3**
Canindé ➔ *Brazil* 6°15S 42°52W **189 B2**
Canindeyu □ *Paraguay* 24°10S 55°0W **191 A4**
Canino *Italy* 42°32N 11°45E **93 F8**
Canisteo *U.S.A.* 42°16N 77°36W **174 D7**
Canisteo ➔ *U.S.A.* 42°7N 77°8W **174 D7**
Cañitas de Felipe Pescador
  Mexico 23°36N 102°43W **180 C4**
Cañizal *Spain* 41°12N 5°22W **88 D5**
Canjáyar *Spain* 37°1N 2°44W **89 H8**
Çankırı *Turkey* 40°40N 33°37E **104 B5**
Çankırı □ *Turkey* 40°40N 33°30E **104 B5**
Cankuzo *Burundi* 3°10S 30°31E **142 C3**
Canmore *Canada* 51°7N 115°18W **162 C5**
Cann River *Australia* 37°35S 149°7E **153 D8**
Canna *U.K.* 57°3N 6°33W **65 D2**
Cannanore = Kannur
  India 11°53N 75°27E **127 J2**
Cannanore Is. *India* 10°30N 72°30E **127 J1**
Cannes *France* 43°32N 7°1E **73 E11**

Canning Town = Port Canning
  India 22°23N 88°40E **125 H13**
Cannington *Canada* 44°20N 79°2W **174 B5**
Cannóbio *Italy* 46°4N 8°42E **92 B5**
Cannock *U.K.* 52°41N 2°1W **67 E5**
Cannonball ➔
  U.S.A. 46°26N 100°35W **172 B3**
Cannondale Mt.
  Australia 25°13S 148°57E **150 D4**
Cannonsville Res.
  U.S.A. 42°4N 75°22W **175 D9**
Cannonvale *Australia* 20°17S 148°43E **150 B4**
Canoas *Brazil* 29°56S 51°11W **191 B5**
Canoe L. *Canada* 55°10N 108°15W **163 B7**
Cañon City *U.S.A.* 38°27N 105°14W **168 G11**
Cañon de Río Blanco △
  Mexico 18°43N 97°15W **181 D5**
Cañon del Río Lobos △
  Spain 41°46N 3°28W **88 D7**
Canonniers Pt. *Mauritius* 20°2S 57°32E **141 d**
Canoochee ➔ *U.S.A.* 31°59N 81°19W **178 D8**
Canopus *Australia* 33°29S 140°42E **152 B4**
Canora *Canada* 51°40N 102°30W **163 C9**
Canosa di Púglia *Italy* 41°13N 16°4E **95 A9**
Canso *Canada* 45°20N 61°0W **165 C7**
Canso, Str. of *Canada* 45°37N 61°22W **165 C7**
Canta *Peru* 11°29S 76°37W **188 C2**
Cantabria □ *Spain* 43°10N 4°0W **88 B7**
Cantabria, Sierra de
  Spain 42°40N 2°30W **90 C2**
Cantabrian Mts. = Cantábrica,
  Cordillera *Spain* 43°0N 5°10W **88 C5**
Cantábrica, Cordillera
  Spain 43°0N 5°10W **88 C5**
Cantal □ *France* 45°4N 2°45E **72 C6**
Cantal, Plomb du *France* 45°3N 2°45E **72 C6**
Cantanhede *Portugal* 40°20N 8°36W **88 E2**
Cantavieja *Spain* 40°31N 0°25W **90 E4**
Čantavir *Serbia* 45°55N 19°46E **80 E4**
Cantemir *Moldova* 46°17N 28°14E **81 D13**
Canterbury *Australia* 25°23S 141°53E **150 D3**
Canterbury *U.K.* 51°16N 1°6E **67 F9**
Canterbury □ *N.Z.* 43°45S 171°19E **155 D6**
Canterbury Bight *N.Z.* 44°16S 171°55E **155 E6**
Canterbury Plains
  N.Z. 43°55S 171°22E **155 D6**
Cantil *U.S.A.* 35°18N 117°58W **171 K9**
Cantillana *Spain* 37°36N 5°50W **89 H5**
Canto do Buriti *Brazil* 8°7S 42°58W **189 B2**
Canton = Guangzhou
  China 23°6N 113°13E **117 F9**
Canton *Ga., U.S.A.* 34°14N 84°29W **177 D12**
Canton *Ill., U.S.A.* 40°33N 90°2W **172 E8**
Canton *Miss., U.S.A.* 32°37N 90°2W **177 E9**
Canton *Mo., U.S.A.* 40°8N 91°32W **172 E8**
Canton *N.Y., U.S.A.* 44°36N 75°10W **175 B9**
Canton *Ohio, U.S.A.* 40°48N 81°23W **174 F3**
Canton *Pa., U.S.A.* 41°39N 76°51W **174 E8**
Canton *S. Dak., U.S.A.* 43°18N 96°35W **172 D5**
Canton L. *U.S.A.* 36°6N 98°35W **176 C5**
Cantonment *U.S.A.* 30°37N 87°20W **179 D2**
Cantù *Italy* 45°44N 9°8E **92 C6**
Canudos *Brazil* 7°13S 58°5W **186 D7**
Canumã ➔ *Brazil* 3°55S 59°10W **186 D7**
Canutama *Brazil* 6°30S 64°20W **186 E6**
Canutillo *U.S.A.* 31°55N 106°36W **176 F1**
Canvey Island *U.K.* 51°31N 0°37E **67 F8**
Canyon *U.S.A.* 34°59N 101°55W **176 D4**
Canyon De Chelly △
  U.S.A. 36°10N 109°20W **169 H9**
Canyonlands △ *U.S.A.* 38°15N 110°0W **169 G9**
Canyons of the Ancients △
  U.S.A. 37°30N 108°55W **169 H9**
Canyonville *U.S.A.* 42°56N 123°17W **168 E2**
Cao Bang *Vietnam* 22°40N 106°15E **116 F6**
Cao He ➔ *China* 40°10N 124°32E **115 D13**
Cao Lanh *Vietnam* 10°27N 105°38E **121 G5**
Cao Xian *China* 34°50N 115°35E **114 G8**
Caofeidian *China* 38°56N 118°32E **115 E10**
Cáorle *Italy* 45°36N 12°53E **93 C9**
Cap-aux-Meules
  Canada 47°23N 61°52W **165 C7**
Cap-Chat *Canada* 49°6N 66°40W **165 C6**
Cap-de-la-Madeleine
  Canada 46°22N 72°31W **164 C5**
Cap-Haïtien *Haiti* 19°40N 72°20W **183 C5**
Cap Pt. *St. Lucia* 14°7N 60°57W **183 f**
Capac *U.S.A.* 43°1N 82°56W **174 C2**
Capáccio *Italy* 40°25N 15°5E **95 B8**
Capaci *Italy* 38°10N 13°14E **94 D6**
Capanaparo ➔ *Venezuela* 7°1N 67°7W **186 B5**
Capánnori *Italy* 43°50N 10°34E **92 E7**
Caparaó △ *Brazil* 20°25S 41°46W **189 E2**
Capbreton *France* 43°39N 1°26W **72 E2**
Capdenac *France* 44°34N 2°5E **72 D6**
Capdepera *Spain* 39°42N 3°26E **90 F8**
Cape ➔ *Australia* 20°59S 146°51E **150 C4**
Cape Arid △ *Australia* 33°58S 123°13E **149 F3**
Cape Barren I.
  Australia 40°25S 148°15E **151 G4**
Cape Basin *Atl. Oc.* 37°0S 7°0W **56 K12**
Cape Breton Highlands △
  Canada 46°50N 60°40W **165 C7**
Cape Breton I. *Canada* 46°0N 60°30W **165 C7**
Cape Charles *U.S.A.* 37°16N 76°1W **173 G15**
Cape Coast *Ghana* 5°5N 1°15W **139 D4**
Cape Cod △ *U.S.A.* 41°56N 70°6W **173 E18**
Cape Coral *U.S.A.* 26°33N 81°57W **179 J8**
Cape Crawford
  Australia 16°41S 135°43E **150 B2**
Cape Dorset = Kinngait
  Canada 64°14N 76°32W **161 E16**
Cape Fear ➔ *U.S.A.* 33°53N 78°1W **177 E15**
Cape Girardeau *U.S.A.* 37°19N 89°32W **172 G9**
Cape Hatteras △
  U.S.A. 35°30N 75°28W **177 D17**
Cape Hillsborough △
  Australia 20°54S 149°2E **150 b**
Cape Jervis *Australia* 35°40S 138°5E **152 C3**
Cape Lambert
  Australia 20°36S 117°11E **148 D2**
Cape Le Grand △
  Australia 33°54S 122°26E **149 F3**
Cape Lookout △
  U.S.A. 35°45N 76°25W **177 D16**
Cape May *U.S.A.* 38°56N 74°56W **173 F16**
Cape May Point
  U.S.A. 38°56N 74°58W **173 F16**

Cape Melville △
  Australia 14°26S 144°28E **150 A3**
Cape Mount △ *Liberia* 6°44N 11°24W **138 D2**
Cape Range △ *Australia* 22°3S 114°0E **148 D1**
Cape St. George
  Canada 48°28N 59°14W **165 C8**
Cape Tormentine
  Canada 46°8N 63°47W **165 C7**
Cape Town *S. Africa* 33°55S 18°22E **144 D2**
Cape Upstart △
  Australia 19°45S 147°48E **150 B4**
Cape Verde Abyssal Plain
  Atl. Oc. 23°0N 26°0W **56 D9**
Cape Verde Is. = Cabo Verde ■
  Atl. Oc. 16°0N 24°0W **134 b**
Cape Verde Plateau
  Atl. Oc. 18°0N 20°0W **56 E10**
Cape Vincent *U.S.A.* 44°8N 76°20W **175 B8**
Cape York Peninsula
  Australia 12°0S 142°30E **150 A3**
Capela *Brazil* 10°30S 37°0W **189 C3**
Capelinha *Brazil* 17°42S 42°31W **189 D2**
Capella *Australia* 23°2S 148°1E **150 C4**
Capendu *France* 43°11N 2°31E **72 E6**
Capertree *Australia* 33°6S 149°58E **153 B8**
Capestang *France* 43°20N 3°2E **72 E7**
Capesterre-Belle-Eau
  Guadeloupe 16°4N 61°36W **182 b**
Capesterre-de-Marie-Galante
  Guadeloupe 15°53N 61°14W **182 b**
Capim ➔ *Brazil* 1°40S 47°47W **187 D9**
Capistrello *Italy* 41°57N 13°23E **93 G10**
Capitan *U.S.A.* 33°35N 105°35W **169 K11**
Capitán Aracena, I.
  Chile 54°10S 71°20W **192 D2**
Capitán Arturo Prat
  Antarctica 63°0S 61°0W **55 C17**
Capitán Pastene *Chile* 38°13S 73°1W **192 A2**
Capitão de Campos
  Brazil 4°40S 41°55W **189 A2**
Capitol Reef △ *U.S.A.* 38°15N 111°10W **169 G8**
Capitola *U.S.A.* 36°59N 121°57W **170 J5**
Capivara, Serra da
  Brazil 14°35S 45°0W **189 C2**
Capizzi *Italy* 37°51N 14°29E **95 E7**
Capoche ➔ *Mozam.* 15°35S 33°0E **143 F3**
Capodichino, Nápoli ✈ (NAP)
  Italy 40°53N 14°16E **95 B7**
Capodistria = Koper
  Slovenia 45°31N 13°44E **93 C10**
Caporetto = Kobarid
  Slovenia 46°15N 13°30E **93 B10**
Capoterra *Italy* 39°11N 8°58E **94 C1**
Cappadocia *Turkey* 39°0N 35°0E **104 C6**
Capps *U.S.A.* 30°24N 83°54W **178 E6**
Capraia *Italy* 43°2N 9°50E **92 E6**
Capraia, Pta. *Italy* 41°7N 8°19E **94 A1**
Caprarola *Italy* 42°19N 12°14E **93 F9**
Caprera *Italy* 41°12N 9°28E **94 A2**
Capri *Italy* 40°33N 14°14E **95 B7**
Capricorn Coast
  Australia 23°16S 150°49E **150 C5**
Capricorn Group
  Australia 23°30S 151°55E **150 C5**
Capricorn Ra.
  Australia 23°20S 116°50E **148 D2**
Caprino Veronese *Italy* 45°36N 10°47E **92 C7**
Caprivi □ *Namibia* 17°55S 22°37E **144 A3**
Caprivi Strip *Namibia* 18°0S 23°0E **144 A3**
Caps et Marais d'Opale △
  France 50°40N 2°0E **71 B9**
Captains Flat *Australia* 35°35S 149°27E **153 C8**
Captieux *France* 44°18N 0°16W **72 D3**
Captiva *U.S.A.* 26°31N 82°11W **179 J7**
Capulin Volcano △
  U.S.A. 36°47N 103°58W **176 C3**
Caquetá ➔ *Colombia* 1°15S 69°15W **186 D5**
Car Nicobar *India* 9°10N 92°47E **127 K11**
Caracal *Romania* 44°8N 24°22E **81 F9**
Caracas *Venezuela* 10°30N 66°55W **186 A5**
Caracol *Belize* 16°45N 89°6W **182 C2**
Caracol *Mato Grosso do Sul,
  Brazil* 22°18S 57°1W **190 A4**
Caracol *Piauí, Brazil* 9°15S 43°22W **189 B2**
Caracollo *Bolivia* 17°39S 67°10W **188 D4**
Caragabal *Australia* 33°49S 147°45E **153 B7**
Caráglio *Italy* 44°25N 7°26E **92 D4**
Carahue *Chile* 38°43S 73°12W **192 A2**
Caraí *Brazil* 17°12S 41°42W **189 D2**
Carajas *Brazil* 6°5S 50°23W **187 E8**
Carajás, Serra dos *Brazil* 6°0S 51°30W **187 E8**
Caral *Peru* 10°53S 77°31W **188 C2**
Carangola *Brazil* 20°44S 42°5W **189 E2**
Caransebeş *Romania* 45°28N 22°18E **80 E7**
Carantec *France* 48°40N 3°55W **70 D3**
Caraquet *Canada* 47°48N 64°57W **165 C6**
Caraş Severin □
  Romania 45°20N 22°10E **80 E7**
Caraşova *Romania* 45°11N 21°51E **80 E6**
Caratasca, L. de
  Honduras 15°20N 83°40W **182 C3**
Caratinga *Brazil* 19°50S 42°10W **189 D2**
Caraúbas *Brazil* 5°43S 37°33W **189 B3**
Caravaca de la Cruz *Spain* 38°8N 1°52W **91 G3**
Caravággio *Italy* 45°30N 9°38E **92 C6**
Caravela *Guinea-Biss.* 11°30N 16°30W **138 C1**
Caravelas *Brazil* 17°45S 39°15W **189 D3**
Caraveli *Peru* 15°45S 73°25W **188 D3**
Caravelle, Presqu'île de la
  Martinique 14°46N 60°48W **182 c**
Caraz *Peru* 9°3S 77°47W **188 B2**
Carazinho *Brazil* 28°16S 52°46W **191 B5**
Carballo *Moldova* 45°52N 28°27E **81 E13**
Carballino = O Carballiño
  Spain 42°26N 8°5W **88 C2**
Carballo *Spain* 43°13N 8°41W **88 B2**
Carberry *Canada* 49°50N 99°25W **163 D9**
Carbó *Mexico* 29°42N 110°58W **180 B2**
Carbón, L. del
  Argentina 49°35S 68°21W **192 C3**
Carbonara, C. *Italy* 39°6N 9°31E **94 C2**
Carbondale *Colo.,
  U.S.A.* 39°24N 107°13W **168 G10**
Carbondale *Ill., U.S.A.* 37°44N 89°13W **172 G9**
Carbondale *Pa., U.S.A.* 41°35N 75°30W **175 E9**
Carbonear *Canada* 47°42N 53°13W **165 C10**
Carboneras *Spain* 36°59N 1°53W **91 J3**
Carboneras de Guadazón
  Spain 39°54N 1°50W **90 F3**
Carbónia *Italy* 39°10N 8°30E **94 C1**
Carbonne *France* 43°18N 1°11E **72 E5**

Carcabuey *Spain* 37°27N 4°17W **89 H6**
Carcagente = Carcaixent
  Spain 39°8N 0°28W **91 F4**
Carcaixent *Spain* 39°8N 0°28W **91 F4**
Carcajou *Canada* 57°47N 117°6W **162 B5**
Carcarana ➔
  Argentina 32°27S 60°48W **190 C3**
Carcasse, C. *Haiti* 18°30N 74°28W **183 C5**
Carcassonne *France* 43°13N 2°20E **72 E6**
Carcoar *Australia* 33°36S 149°8E **153 B8**
Carcross *Canada* 60°13N 134°45W **162 A2**
Çardak *Çanakkale,
  Turkey* 40°22N 26°43E **97 F10**
Çardak *Denizli, Turkey* 37°49N 29°39E **99 D11**
Cardamon Hills *India* 9°30N 77°15E **127 K3**
Cardamon Mts. = Kravanh,
  Chuor Phnum
  Cambodia 12°0N 103°32E **121 G4**
Cardeña *Spain* 38°16N 4°20W **89 G6**
Cárdenas *Cuba* 23°0N 81°30W **182 B3**
Cárdenas *San Luis Potosi,
  Mexico* 22°0N 99°38W **181 C5**
Cárdenas *Tabasco,
  Mexico* 17°59N 93°22W **181 D6**
Cardener ➔ *Spain* 41°41N 1°51E **90 D6**
Cardenete *Spain* 39°46N 1°41W **90 F3**
Cardiel, L. *Argentina* 48°55S 71°10W **192 C2**
Cardiff *U.K.* 51°29N 3°10W **67 F4**
Cardiff □ *U.K.* 51°31N 3°12W **67 F4**
Cardiff-by-the-Sea
  U.S.A. 33°1N 117°17W **171 M9**
Cardigan *U.K.* 52°5N 4°40W **67 E3**
Cardigan B. *U.K.* 52°30N 4°30W **67 E3**
Cardinal *Canada* 44°47N 75°23W **175 B9**
Cardona *Spain* 41°56N 1°40E **90 D6**
Cardona *Uruguay* 33°53S 57°18W **190 C4**
Cardston *Canada* 49°15N 113°20W **162 D6**
Cardwell *Australia* 18°14S 146°2E **150 B4**
Careen L. *Canada* 57°0N 108°11W **163 B7**
Carei *Romania* 47°40N 22°29E **80 C7**
Carentan *France* 49°19N 1°15W **70 C5**
Carey *U.S.A.* 43°19N 113°57W **168 E7**
Carey, L. *Australia* 29°0S 122°15E **149 E3**
Carey L. *Canada* 62°12N 102°55W **163 A8**
Careysburg *Liberia* 6°27N 10°29W **138 D2**
Cargados Carajos *Ind. Oc.* 17°0S 59°0E **146 F4**
Cargèse *France* 42°7N 8°35E **73 F12**
Carhaix-Plouguer
  France 48°18N 3°36W **70 D3**
Carhuamayo *Peru* 10°51S 76°4W **188 C2**
Carhuas *Peru* 9°15S 77°39W **188 B2**
Carhué *Argentina* 37°10S 62°50W **190 D3**
Caria *Turkey* 37°20N 28°10E **99 D10**
Cariacica *Brazil* 20°16S 40°25W **189 E2**
Cariati *Italy* 39°30N 16°57E **95 C9**
Caribbean Sea *W. Indies* 15°0N 75°0W **183 D5**
Cariboo Mts. *Canada* 53°0N 121°0W **162 C4**
Caribou *U.S.A.* 46°52N 68°1W **173 B19**
Caribou ➔ *Man.,
  Canada* 59°20N 94°44W **163 B10**
Caribou ➔ *N.W.T.,
  Canada* 61°27N 125°45W **162 A3**
Caribou I. *Canada* 47°22N 85°49W **164 C2**
Caribou Is. *Canada* 61°55N 113°15W **162 A6**
Caribou Mts. *Man.,
  Canada* 59°21N 96°10W **163 B9**
Caribou Mts. *Canada* 59°12N 115°40W **162 B5**
Caribou River △
  Canada 59°35N 96°35W **163 B9**
Caribrod = Dimitrovgrad
  Serbia 43°2N 22°48E **96 C1**
Carichic *Mexico* 27°56N 107°3W **180 B3**
Carignan *France* 49°38N 5°10E **71 C12**
Carignano *Italy* 44°55N 7°40E **92 D4**
Carinda *Australia* 30°28S 147°41E **153 A7**
Cariñena *Spain* 41°20N 1°13W **90 D3**
Carinhanha *Brazil* 14°15S 44°46W **189 D2**
Carinhanha ➔ *Brazil* 14°20S 43°47W **189 D2**
Carini *Italy* 38°8N 13°11E **94 D6**
Cariño *Spain* 43°45N 7°50W **88 B3**
Cariñola *Italy* 41°11N 13°58E **94 A6**
Carinthia = Kärnten □
  Austria 46°52N 13°30E **78 E6**
Caripito *Venezuela* 10°8N 63°6W **186 A6**
Cariré *Brazil* 3°57S 40°27W **189 A2**
Carlet *Spain* 39°14N 0°31W **91 F4**
Carleton, Mt. *Canada* 47°23N 66°53W **165 C6**
Carleton Place *Canada* 45°8N 76°9W **175 A8**
Carletonville *S. Africa* 26°23S 27°22E **144 C4**
Cârlibaba *Romania* 47°35N 25°8E **81 C10**
Carlin *U.S.A.* 40°43N 116°7W **168 F5**
Carlingford L. *U.K.* 54°3N 6°9W **64 B5**
Carlini Base *Antarctica* 62°30S 58°0W **55 C18**
Carlinville *U.S.A.* 39°17N 89°53W **172 F9**
Carlisle *U.K.* 54°54N 2°56W **66 C5**
Carlisle *U.S.A.* 40°12N 77°12W **174 F7**
Carlisle B. *Barbados* 13°5N 59°37W **183 g**
Carlisle I. *Australia* 20°49S 149°18E **150 b**
Carlit, Pic *France* 42°35N 1°55E **72 E5**
Carloforte *Italy* 39°8N 8°18E **94 C1**
Carlos Casares
  Argentina 35°32S 61°20W **190 D3**
Carlos Chagas *Brazil* 17°43S 40°45W **189 D2**
Carlos Tejedor
  Argentina 35°25S 62°25W **190 D3**
Carlow *Ireland* 52°50N 6°56W **64 D5**
Carlow □ *Ireland* 52°43N 6°50W **64 D5**
Carlsbad *Calif., U.S.A.* 33°10N 117°21W **171 M9**
Carlsbad *N. Mex.,
  U.S.A.* 32°25N 104°14W **169 K11**
Carlsbad Caverns △
  U.S.A. 32°10N 104°35W **169 K11**
Carlsberg Ridge *Ind. Oc.* 1°0N 66°0E **146 D5**
Carluke *U.K.* 55°45N 3°50W **65 F5**
Carlyle *Canada* 49°40N 102°20W **163 D8**
Carmacks *Canada* 62°5N 136°16W **160 E4**
Carman *Canada* 49°30N 98°0W **163 D9**
Carmarthen *U.K.* 51°52N 4°19W **67 F3**
Carmarthen B. *U.K.* 51°40N 4°30W **67 F3**
Carmarthenshire □ *U.K.* 51°55N 4°13W **67 F3**
Carmaux *France* 44°3N 2°10E **72 D6**
Carmel *U.S.A.* 41°26N 73°41W **175 E11**
Carmel, Mt. = Ha Karmel, Har
  Israel 32°45N 35°3E **130 C4**
Carmel Valley *U.S.A.* 36°29N 121°43W **170 J5**
Carmel-by-the-Sea
  U.S.A. 36°33N 121°55W **170 J5**
Carmelo *Uruguay* 34°0S 58°20W **190 C4**

Carmen *Bolivia* 11°40S 67°51W **188 C4**
Carmen *Paraguay* 27°13S 56°12W **191 B4**
Carmen, I. *Mexico* 25°57N 111°12W **180 B2**
Carmen de Patagones
  Argentina 40°50S 63°0W **192 B4**
Cármenes *Spain* 42°58N 5°34W **88 C5**
Carmensa *Argentina* 35°15S 67°40W **190 D2**
Carmi *Canada* 49°36N 119°8W **162 D5**
Carmi *U.S.A.* 38°5N 88°10W **172 F9**
Carmila *Australia* 21°55S 149°24E **150 C4**
Carmona *Costa Rica* 10°0N 85°15W **182 E2**
Carmona *Spain* 37°28N 5°42W **89 H5**
Carn Ban *U.K.* 57°7N 4°15W **65 D4**
Carn Eige *U.K.* 57°17N 5°8W **65 D3**
Carn France *France* 47°35N 3°6W **70 E2**
Carnamah *Australia* 29°41S 115°53E **149 E2**
Carnarvon *Australia* 24°51S 113°42E **149 D1**
Carnarvon *S. Africa* 30°56S 22°8E **144 D3**
Carnarvon △ *Australia* 24°54S 148°2E **150 C4**
Carnarvon Ra. *Queens.,
  Australia* 25°15S 148°30E **150 D4**
Carnarvon Ra. *W. Austral.,
  Australia* 25°20S 120°45E **149 E3**
Carnatic *India* 12°40N 77°50E **127 K3**
Carnation *U.S.A.* 47°39N 121°55W **170 C5**
Carncastle *U.K.* 54°54N 5°53W **64 B6**
Carndonagh *Ireland* 55°16N 7°15W **64 A4**
Carnduff *Canada* 49°10N 101°50W **163 D8**
Carnegie *U.S.A.* 40°24N 80°5W **174 F4**
Carnegie, L. *Australia* 26°5S 122°30E **149 E3**
Carnegie Ridge *Pac. Oc.* 1°0S 87°0W **157 H19**
Carney I. *Antarctica* 74°0S 121°0W **55 D14**
Carnic Alps = Karnische Alpen
  Europe 46°36N 13°0E **78 E6**
Carniche Alpi = Karnische Alpen
  Europe 46°36N 13°0E **78 E6**
Carnot *C.A.R.* 4°59N 15°56E **140 D3**
Carnot, C. *Australia* 34°57S 135°38E **151 E2**
Carnoustie *U.K.* 56°30N 2°42W **65 E6**
Carnsore Pt. *Ireland* 52°10N 6°22W **64 D5**
Caro *U.S.A.* 43°29N 83°24W **173 D12**
Caroga Lake *U.S.A.* 43°8N 74°28W **175 C10**
Carol City *U.S.A.* 25°56N 80°14W **177 J14**
Carolina *Brazil* 7°10S 47°30W **189 B1**
Carolina *Puerto Rico* 18°23N 65°58W **183 d**
Carolina, S. *Africa* 26°5S 30°6E **145 C5**
Caroline I. *Kiribati* 9°58S 150°13E **157 H12**
Caroline Is. *Micronesia* 8°0N 150°0E **156 G6**
Caroline Pk. *N.Z.* 45°57S 167°15E **155 F2**
Caroní ➔ *Venezuela* 8°21N 62°43W **186 B6**
Caroona *Australia* 31°24S 150°26E **153 B9**
Carpathians *Europe* 49°30N 21°0E **75 D11**
Carpații Meridionali
  Romania 45°30N 25°0E **81 E9**
Carpentaria, G. of
  Australia 14°0S 139°0E **150 A2**
Carpentras *France* 44°3N 5°2E **73 D9**
Carpi *Italy* 44°47N 10°53E **92 D7**
Carpina *Brazil* 7°51S 35°15W **189 B3**
Carpinteria *U.S.A.* 34°24N 119°31W **171 L7**
Carpio *Spain* 41°13N 5°7W **88 D5**
Carr Boyd Ra.
  Australia 16°15S 128°35E **148 C4**
Carra, L. *Ireland* 53°41N 9°14W **64 C2**
Carrabelle *U.S.A.* 29°51N 84°40W **178 F5**
Carraig Mhachaire Rois =
  Carrickmacross
  Ireland 53°59N 6°43W **64 C5**
Carraig na Siúire = Carrick-on-
  Suir *Ireland* 52°21N 7°24W **64 D4**
Carral *Spain* 43°14N 8°21W **88 B2**
Carranya ◎ *Australia* 19°13S 127°46E **148 C4**
Carrara *Italy* 44°5N 10°6E **92 D7**
Carrascosa del Campo
  Spain 40°2N 2°45W **90 E2**
Carrauntoohill *Ireland* 52°0N 9°45W **64 D2**
Carretas, Punta *Peru* 14°12S 76°17W **188 C2**
Carrick-on-Shannon
  Ireland 53°57N 8°7W **64 C3**
Carrick-on-Suir *Ireland* 52°21N 7°24W **64 D4**
Carrickfergus *U.K.* 54°43N 5°49W **64 B6**
Carrickmacross *Ireland* 53°59N 6°43W **64 C5**
Carrieton *Australia* 32°25S 138°31E **152 B3**
Carrigaline *Ireland* 51°48N 8°23E **64 E3**
Carrillo *Mexico* 26°54N 103°55W **180 B4**
Carrington *U.S.A.* 47°27N 99°8W **172 B4**
Carrión ➔ *Spain* 41°53N 4°32W **88 D6**
Carrión de los Condes
  Spain 42°20N 4°37W **88 C6**
Carrizal Bajo *Chile* 28°5S 71°20W **190 B1**
Carrizalillo *Chile* 29°5S 71°30W **190 B1**
Carrizo Cr. ➔
  U.S.A. 36°55N 103°55W **169 H12**
Carrizo Plain △
  U.S.A. 35°11N 119°47W **170 K7**
Carrizo Springs *U.S.A.* 28°31N 99°52W **176 G5**
Carrizozo *U.S.A.* 33°38N 105°53W **169 K11**
Carroll *U.S.A.* 42°4N 94°52W **172 D6**
Carrollton *Ga., U.S.A.* 33°35N 85°5W **178 B4**
Carrollton *Ill., U.S.A.* 39°18N 90°24W **172 F8**
Carrollton *Ky., U.S.A.* 38°41N 85°11W **173 F11**
Carrollton *Ohio, U.S.A.* 40°34N 81°5W **174 F3**
Carron ➔ *U.K.* 57°53N 4°22W **65 D4**
Carron, L. *U.K.* 57°22N 5°35W **65 D3**
Carrot ➔ *Canada* 53°50N 101°17W **163 C8**
Carrot River *Canada* 53°17N 103°35W **163 C8**
Carrouges *France* 48°34N 0°10W **70 D6**
Carrù *Italy* 44°29N 7°52E **92 D4**
Carruthers *Canada* 52°52N 109°16W **163 C7**
Çarşamba *Turkey* 41°11N 36°44E **104 B6**
Carsóli *Italy* 42°6N 13°5E **93 F10**
Carson *Calif., U.S.A.* 33°49N 118°16W **171 M8**
Carson *N. Dak., U.S.A.* 46°25N 101°34W **172 B3**
Carson ➔ *U.S.A.* 39°45N 118°40W **168 G4**
Carson City *U.S.A.* 39°10N 119°46W **170 F7**
Carson Sink *U.S.A.* 39°50N 118°25W **168 G4**
Cartagena *Colombia* 10°25N 75°33W **186 A3**
Cartagena *Spain* 37°38N 0°59W **91 H4**
Cartago *Colombia* 4°45N 75°55W **186 C3**
Cartago *Costa Rica* 9°50N 83°55W **182 E3**
Cártama *Spain* 36°43N 4°39W **89 J6**
Cartaxo *Portugal* 39°10N 8°47W **89 F2**
Cartaya *Spain* 37°16N 7°9W **89 H3**
Carter Bar *U.K.* 55°21N 2°29W **65 F6**

Cartersville *U.S.A.* 34°10N 84°48W **178 A5**
Carterton *N.Z.* 41°2S 175°31E **154 H4**
Carthage *Tunisia* 36°52N 10°20E **94 F3**
Carthage *Ill., U.S.A.* 40°25N 91°8W **172 E8**
Carthage *Mo., U.S.A.* 37°11N 94°19W **172 G6**
Carthage *N.Y., U.S.A.* 43°59N 75°37W **175 C9**
Carthage *Tex., U.S.A.* 32°9N 94°20W **176 E7**
Cartier I. *Australia* 12°31S 123°29E **148 B3**
Cartwright *Canada* 53°41N 56°58W **165 B8**
Caruaru *Brazil* 8°15S 35°55W **189 B3**
Carúpano *Venezuela* 10°39N 63°15W **186 A6**
Caruthersville *U.S.A.* 36°11N 89°39W **172 G9**
Carvin *France* 50°30N 2°57E **71 B9**
Carvoeiro *Brazil* 1°0S 61°59W **186 D6**
Carvoeiro, C. *Portugal* 39°21N 9°24W **89 F1**
Cary *U.S.A.* 35°47N 78°46W **177 D15**
Cas-gwent = Chepstow
  U.K. 51°38N 2°41W **67 F5**
Casa, Pas de la = Envalira, Port d'
  Europe 42°33N 1°43E **90 C6**
Casa Branca *Portugal* 38°29N 8°12W **89 G2**
Casa de Piedra
  Argentina 38°5S 67°28W **190 D2**
Casa de Piedra, Embalse
  Argentina 38°5S 67°32W **190 D2**
Casa Grande *U.S.A.* 32°53N 111°45W **169 K8**
Casa Nova *Brazil* 9°25S 41°5W **189 B2**
Casablanca *Chile* 33°20S 71°25W **190 C1**
Casablanca *Morocco* 33°36N 7°36W **136 B4**
Casablanca △ *Morocco* 40°24N 80°5W **174 F4**
Casacalenda *Italy* 41°44N 14°51E **93 G11**
Casalbordino *Italy* 42°9N 14°35E **93 F11**
Casale Monferrato *Italy* 45°8N 8°27E **92 C5**
Casalmaggiore *Italy* 44°59N 10°26E **92 D7**
Casalpusterlengo *Italy* 45°11N 9°39E **92 C6**
Casamance *Senegal* 13°0N 15°30W **138 C1**
Casamance ➔ *Senegal* 12°33N 16°46W **138 C1**
Casarano *Italy* 40°0N 18°10E **95 B11**
Casares *Spain* 36°27N 5°16W **89 J5**
Casas Ibáñez *Spain* 39°17N 1°30W **91 F3**
Casasimarro *Spain* 39°22N 2°3W **91 F2**
Casatejada *Spain* 39°54N 5°40W **88 F5**
Casavieja *Spain* 40°17N 4°46W **88 E6**
Cascada de Basaseachic △
  Mexico 28°9N 108°15W **180 B3**
Cascade *Seychelles* 4°39S 55°29E **141 b**
Cascade *Idaho, U.S.A.* 44°31N 116°2W **168 D5**
Cascade *Mont., U.S.A.* 47°16N 111°42W **168 C8**
Cascade Locks *U.S.A.* 45°40N 121°54W **170 E5**
Cascade Pt. *N.Z.* 44°1S 168°20E **155 E3**
Cascade Ra. *U.S.A.* 47°0N 121°30W **170 D5**
Cascade Res. *U.S.A.* 44°32N 116°3W **168 D5**
Cascades, Pte. des
  Réunion 21°9S 55°51E **141 c**
Cascais *Portugal* 38°41N 9°25W **89 G1**
Cascavel *Ceará, Brazil* 4°7S 38°14W **189 A3**
Cascavel *Paraná, Brazil* 24°57S 53°28W **191 A5**
Cáscina *Italy* 43°41N 10°33E **92 E7**
Casco B. *U.S.A.* 43°45N 70°0W **173 D18**
Caselle Torinese *Italy* 45°10N 7°39E **92 C4**
Caserta *Italy* 41°4N 14°20E **95 A7**
Casey *Antarctica* 66°0S 76°0E **55 C8**
Caseyr, Raas = Asir, Ras
  Somalia 11°55N 51°10E **131 E5**
Cashel *Ireland* 52°30N 7°53W **64 D4**
Casiguran *Phil.* 16°22N 122°7E **119 A6**
Casilda *Argentina* 33°10S 61°10W **190 C3**
Casimcea *Romania* 44°45N 28°23E **81 F13**
Casino *Australia* 28°52S 153°3E **151 D5**
Casiquiare ➔ *Venezuela* 2°1N 67°7W **186 C5**
Casitas *Peru* 3°54S 80°39W **188 A1**
Čáslav *Czechia* 49°54N 15°22E **78 B8**
Casma *Peru* 9°30S 78°20W **188 B2**
Casmalia *U.S.A.* 34°50N 120°32W **171 L6**
Casnewydd = Newport
  U.K. 51°35N 3°0W **67 F5**
Cásola Valsénio *Italy* 44°12N 11°40E **93 D8**
Cásoli *Italy* 42°7N 14°18E **93 F11**
Caspe *Spain* 41°14N 0°1W **90 D4**
Casper *U.S.A.* 42°51N 106°19W **168 E10**
Caspian Depression
  Eurasia 47°0N 48°0E **87 D13**
Caspian Sea *Eurasia* 43°0N 50°0E **88 B7**
Cass City *U.S.A.* 43°36N 83°10W **174 C1**
Cass Lake *U.S.A.* 47°23N 94°37W **172 B6**
Casseda de la Selva *Spain* 41°53N 2°52E **90 D7**
Cassadaga *U.S.A.* 42°20N 79°19W **174 D5**
Cassano allo Iónio *Italy* 39°47N 16°20E **95 C9**
Casselberry *U.S.A.* 28°41N 81°20W **179 G9**
Casselman *Canada* 45°19N 75°5W **175 A9**
Casselton *U.S.A.* 46°54N 97°13W **172 B5**
Cassiar Mts. *Canada* 59°30N 130°30W **162 B2**
Cassilis *Australia* 32°3S 149°58E **153 B8**
Cassino *Italy* 41°30N 13°49E **94 A6**
Cassis *France* 43°14N 5°32E **73 E9**
Cassville *U.S.A.* 36°41N 93°52W **172 G7**
Castagneto Carducci
  Italy 43°9N 10°36E **92 E7**
Castaic *U.S.A.* 34°30N 118°38W **171 L8**
Castalia *U.S.A.* 41°24N 82°49W **174 E2**
Castanhal *Brazil* 1°18S 47°55W **187 D9**
Castara *Trin. & Tob.* 11°17N 60°42W **187 J16**
Casteddu = Cágliari *Italy* 39°13N 9°7E **94 C2**
Castéggio *Italy* 45°1N 9°8E **92 C6**
Castejón de Monegros
  Spain 41°37N 0°15W **90 D4**
Castèl del Monte *Italy* 41°5N 16°16E **95 A9**
Castèl di Sangro *Italy* 41°47N 14°6E **93 G11**
Castèl San Giovanni *Italy* 45°4N 9°26E **92 C6**
Castèl San Pietro Terme
  Italy 44°24N 11°35E **93 D8**
Castelbuono *Italy* 37°56N 14°5E **95 E7**
Castelfidardo *Italy* 43°28N 13°33E **93 E10**
Castelfiorentino *Italy* 43°36N 10°58E **92 E7**
Casteljaloux *France* 44°19N 0°6E **72 D4**
Castell-Nedd = Neath
  U.K. 51°39N 3°48W **67 F4**
Castellabate *Italy* 40°17N 14°57E **95 B7**
Castellammare, G. di
  Italy 38°8N 12°54W **94 D5**
Castellammare del Golfo
  Italy 38°1N 12°53E **94 D5**
Castellammare di Stábia
  Italy 40°42N 14°29E **95 B7**
Castellamonte *Italy* 45°23N 7°42E **92 C4**
Castellane *France* 43°50N 6°31E **73 E10**
Castellaneta *Italy* 40°38N 16°56E **95 B9**
Castelli *Argentina* 36°7S 57°47W **190 D4**
Castelló de la Plana *Spain* 39°58N 0°3W **90 E4**

Castellón de la Plana □ 40°15N 0°5W 90 E4
Castellote Spain 40°48N 0°15W 90 E4
Castelmáuro Italy 41°50N 14°43E 93 G11
Castelnau-de-Médoc France 45°2N 0°48W 72 C3
Castelnau-Magnoac France 43°17N 0°31E 72 E4
Castelnaudary France 43°20N 1°58E 72 E5
Castelnaudary S. Africa 36°52S 149°24E 153 D4
Castelnovo ne' Monti Italy 44°26N 10°24E 92 D7
Castelnuovo di Val di Cécina Italy 43°12N 10°59E 92 E7
Castelo Brazil 20°33S 41°14W 189 E2
Castelo Branco Portugal 39°50N 7°31W 88 F3
Castelo Branco □ Portugal 39°52N 7°45W 88 F3
Castelo de Paiva Portugal 41°2N 8°16W 88 D2
Castelo de Vide Portugal 39°25N 7°27W 89 F3
Castelo do Piauí Brazil 5°20S 41°33W 189 D2
Castelsardo Italy 40°55N 8°43E 94 B1
Castelsarrasin France 44°2N 1°7E 72 D5
Casteltérmini Italy 37°32N 13°39E 94 E6
Castelvetrano Italy 37°41N 12°47E 94 E5
Casterton Australia 37°30S 141°30E 152 D4
Castets France 43°52N 1°6W 72 E2
Castiglion Fiorentino Italy 43°20N 11°55E 93 E8
Castiglione del Lago Italy 43°7N 12°3E 93 E9
Castiglione della Pescáia Italy 42°46N 10°53E 92 F7
Castiglione delle Stiviere Italy 45°23N 10°29E 92 C7
Castilblanco Spain 39°17N 5°5W 89 F5
Castile U.S.A. 42°38N 78°3W 174 D6
Castilla Peru 5°12S 80°38W 188 B1
Castilla, Playa de Spain 37°0N 6°33W 89 J4
Castilla-La Mancha □ Spain 39°30N 3°30W 89 F7
Castilla y Leon □ Spain 42°0N 5°0W 88 D6
Castillo de Locubín Spain 37°32N 3°56W 89 H7
Castillo de San Marcos △ U.S.A. 29°54N 81°19W 178 F8
Castillon-en-Couserans France 42°56N 1°1E 72 F5
Castillonès France 44°39N 0°37E 72 D4
Castillos Uruguay 34°12S 53°52W 191 C5
Castle Dale U.S.A. 39°13N 111°1W 168 G8
Castle Douglas U.K. 54°56N 3°56W 65 G5
Castle Rock Colo., U.S.A. 39°22N 104°51W 168 G2
Castle Rock Wash., U.S.A. 46°17N 122°54W 170 D4
Castlebar Ireland 53°52N 9°18W 64 C2
Castlebay U.K. 56°57N 7°31W 65 E1
Castleblayney Ireland 54°7N 6°44W 64 B5
Castlecliff N.Z. 39°57S 175°5E 154 F4
Castlecomer Ireland 52°48N 7°14W 64 D4
Castlederg U.K. 54°42N 7°36W 64 B4
Castleford U.K. 53°43N 1°21W 66 D6
Castlegar Canada 49°20N 117°40W 162 D5
Castleisland Ireland 52°14N 9°28W 64 D2
Castlemaine Australia 37°2S 144°12E 152 D6
Castlemaine Ireland 52°10N 9°42W 64 D2
Castlepoint N.Z. 40°54S 176°15E 154 G5
Castlepollard Ireland 53°41N 7°19W 64 C4
Castlerea Ireland 53°46N 8°29W 64 C3
Castlereagh → Australia 30°12S 147°32E 153 A7
Castlereagh B. Australia 12°10S 135°10E 150 A2
Castleton U.S.A. 43°37N 73°11W 175 C11
Castleton-on-Hudson U.S.A. 42°31N 73°45W 175 D11
Castletown I. of Man 54°5N 4°38W 66 C3
Castletown Bearhaven Ireland 51°39N 9°55W 64 E2
Castor Canada 52°15N 111°50W 162 C6
Castor → Canada 53°24N 78°58W 164 B4
Castorland U.S.A. 43°53N 75°31W 175 C9
Castres France 43°37N 2°13E 72 E6
Castricum Neths. 52°33N 4°40E 69 B4
Castries St. Lucia 14°2N 60°58W 183 f
Castril Spain 37°48N 2°46W 89 H8
Castro Brazil 24°45S 50°0W 191 A6
Castro Chile 42°30S 73°50W 192 B2
Castro Alves Brazil 12°46S 39°33W 189 C3
Castro del Río Spain 37°41N 4°29W 89 H6
Castro-Urdiales Spain 43°23N 3°11W 88 B7
Castro Valley U.S.A. 37°41N 122°5W 170 H4
Castro Verde Portugal 37°41N 8°4W 89 H2
Castrojeriz Spain 42°23N 4°9W 88 C6
Castropol Spain 43°32N 7°0W 88 B4
Castroreale Italy 38°6N 15°12E 95 D8
Castrovillari Italy 39°49N 16°12E 95 C9
Castroville U.S.A. 36°46N 121°45W 170 J5
Castrovirreyna Peru 13°20S 75°18W 188 C2
Castuera Spain 38°43N 5°37W 89 G5
Çat Turkey 39°40N 41°3E 105 C9
Cat Ba, Dao Vietnam 20°50N 107°0E 120 B6
Cat Ba □ Vietnam 20°47N 107°3E 120 B6
Cat I. Bahamas 24°30N 75°30W 183 B4
Cat L. Canada 51°40N 91°50W 164 B1
Cat Lake Canada 51°40N 91°50W 164 B1
Cat Tien △ Vietnam 11°25N 107°17E 121 G6
Čata Slovakia 47°58N 18°38E 79 D11
Catacamas Honduras 14°54N 85°56W 182 D2
Catacaos Peru 5°20S 80°45W 188 E1
Cataguases Brazil 21°23S 42°39W 191 A7
Çatak Turkey 38°1N 43°8E 105 C10
Catalão Brazil 18°10S 47°57W 189 D1
Çatalca Turkey 41°30N 31°59E 104 B4
Catalina Canada 48°31N 53°4W 165 C10
Catalina Chile 25°13S 69°43W 190 B2
Catalina U.S.A. 32°30N 110°50W 169 K8
Catalonia = Cataluña □ Spain 41°40N 1°15E 90 D6
Cataluña □ Spain 41°40N 1°15E 90 D6
Çatalzeytin Turkey 41°59N 34°12E 104 B6
Catamarca Argentina 28°30S 65°50W 190 B2
Catamarca □ Argentina 27°0S 65°50W 190 B2
Catanduanes □ Phil. 13°50N 124°20E 119 B6
Catanduva Brazil 21°5S 48°58W 191 A6
Catánia Italy 37°30N 15°6E 95 E8
Catánia, G. di Italy 37°10N 15°30E 95 E8
Catanzaro Italy 38°54N 16°35E 95 D9
Cataman Phil. 12°28N 124°35E 119 B6
Catatumbo-Bari △ Colombia 9°3N 73°12W 183 E5

Cataula U.S.A. 32°39N 84°52W 178 C5
Catchacoma Canada 44°44N 78°19W 174 B6
Cateel Phil. 7°47N 126°24E 119 C7
Catembe Mozam. 26°0S 32°33E 145 C5
Catende Brazil 8°40S 35°43W 189 D3
Caterham U.K. 51°15N 0°4W 67 F7
Cathair na Mart = Westport Ireland 53°48N 9°31W 64 C2
Cathcart Australia 36°52S 149°24E 153 D4
Cathcart S. Africa 32°18S 27°10E 144 D4
Cathedral City U.S.A. 33°47N 116°28W 171 M10
Cathedral Rock △ Australia 30°24S 152°15E 153 A10
Cathlamet U.S.A. 46°12N 123°23W 170 D3
Catió Guinea-Biss. 11°17N 15°15W 138 C1
Catita Brazil 9°31S 43°1W 189 B2
Catoche, C. Mexico 21°35N 87°5W 181 C7
Catolé do Rocha Brazil 6°21S 37°45W 189 B3
Cátria, Mte. Italy 43°28N 12°42E 93 E9
Catrilló Argentina 36°26S 63°24W 190 D3
Catrimani Brazil 0°27N 61°41W 186 C6
Catrimani → Brazil 0°28N 61°44W 186 C6
Catskill U.S.A. 42°14N 73°52W 175 D11
Catskill △ U.S.A. 42°8N 74°39W 175 D10
Catskill Mts. U.S.A. 42°10N 74°25W 175 D10
Catt, Mt. U.S.A. 13°49S 134°23E 150 A1
Cattaraugus U.S.A. 42°20N 78°52W 174 D6
Catterick U.K. 54°23N 1°37W 66 C6
Cattólica Italy 43°58N 12°44E 93 E9
Cattólica Eraclea Italy 37°26N 13°24E 94 E6
Catu Brazil 12°21S 38°23W 189 C3
Catuala Angola 16°25S 19°2E 144 A2
Catuane Mozam. 26°48S 32°18E 145 C5
Catur Mozam. 13°45S 35°30E 143 E4
Caubvick, Mt. = Iberville, Mt. d' Canada 58°50N 63°50W 161 F19
Cauca → Colombia 8°54N 74°28W 186 B4
Caucaia Brazil 3°40S 38°35W 189 A3
Caucasus Mountains Eurasia 42°50N 44°0E 87 J7
Caucete Argentina 31°38S 68°20W 190 C2
Caudete Spain 38°42N 1°2W 91 G3
Caudry France 50°7N 3°22E 71 B10
Cauese Mts. Mozam. 15°14S 30°33E 143 F3
Caulnes France 48°18N 2°10W 70 D4
Caulónia Italy 38°23N 16°24E 95 D9
Caungula Angola 8°26S 18°38E 140 F3
Cauquenes Chile 36°0S 72°22W 190 D1
Caura → Venezuela 7°38N 64°53W 186 B6
Cauresi → Mozam. 17°8S 33°0E 143 F3
Căuşani Moldova 46°35N 29°25E 81 D14
Causapscal Canada 48°19N 67°12W 165 C6
Caussade Canada 44°10N 1°33E 72 D5
Causse-Méjean France 44°18N 3°42E 72 D7
Causses du Quercy △ France 44°35N 1°35E 72 D5
Cauterets France 42°52N 0°8E 72 F3
Cauvery → India 11°9N 78°52E 127 J4
Caux, Pays de France 49°38N 0°35E 70 C7
Cava de' Tirreni Italy 40°42N 14°42E 95 B7
Cávado → Portugal 41°32N 8°48W 88 D2
Cavagrande del Cassibile △ Italy 36°58N 15°6E 95 F8
Cavaillon France 43°50N 5°2E 73 E9
Cavalaire-sur-Mer France 43°10N 6°33E 73 E10
Cavalcante Brazil 13°48S 47°30W 189 C1
Cavalese Italy 46°17N 11°27E 93 B8
Cavalier U.S.A. 48°48N 97°37W 172 A5
Cavalla = Cavally → Africa 4°22N 7°32W 138 E3
Cavalla △ Liberia 5°8N 7°20W 138 D3
Cavalli Is. N.Z. 35°0S 173°58E 154 B2
Cavally → Africa 4°22N 7°32W 138 E3
Cavan Ireland 54°0N 7°22W 64 B4
Cavan □ Ireland 54°1N 7°16W 64 C4
Cavárzere Italy 45°8N 12°5E 93 C9
Çavdarhisar Turkey 39°12N 29°37E 99 D11
Çavdır Turkey 37°10N 29°42E 99 D11
Cave Creek U.S.A. 33°50N 111°57W 169 K8
Cave Spring U.S.A. 34°6N 85°20W 178 A4
Cavelleria, C. de Spain 40°5N 4°5E 100 A11
Cavenagh Ra. Australia 26°12S 127°55E 149 E4
Cavendish Australia 37°31S 142°2E 152 D5
Caverna do Peruaçu △ Brazil 15°0S 44°35W 189 D2
Caviana, I. Brazil 0°10N 50°10W 187 C8
Cavite Phil. 14°29N 120°54E 119 B6
Cavnic Romania 47°40N 23°52E 81 C8
Cavour Italy 44°47N 7°22E 92 D4
Cavtat Croatia 42°35N 18°13E 96 D2
Cawndilla L. Australia 32°30S 142°15E 152 B5
Cawnpore = Kanpur India 26°28N 80°20E 125 F9
Caxias Brazil 4°55S 43°20W 189 A2
Caxias do Sul Brazil 29°10S 51°10W 191 B5
Çay Turkey 38°35N 31°1E 104 C4
Cay Sal Bank Bahamas 23°45N 80°0W 182 B4
Cayambe Ecuador 0°3N 78°8W 186 C3
Çaycuma Turkey 41°25N 32°4E 104 B5
Çayeli Turkey 41°5N 40°45W 105 B9
Cayenne Fr. Guiana 5°5N 52°18W 187 B8
Cayey Puerto Rico 18°7N 66°10W 183 d
Caygören Baraji Turkey 39°15N 28°12E 99 B10
Çayırhan Turkey 39°17N 35°38E 104 C6
Cayırova = Áyios Theodhoros Cyprus 35°22N 34°1E 101 D13
Caylus France 44°15N 1°47E 72 D5
Cayman Brac W. Indies 19°43N 79°49W 182 C4
Cayman Is. ■ Cayman Is. 19°40N 80°30W 182 C3
Cayman Trench Caribbean 17°0N 83°0W 158 H11
Cayres France 44°55N 3°42E 72 D7
Cayuga Canada 42°59N 79°50W 174 D5
Cayuga U.S.A. 42°54N 76°44W 175 D8
Cayuga Heights U.S.A. 42°27N 76°29W 175 D8
Cayuga L. U.S.A. 42°41N 76°41W 175 D8
Cazalla de la Sierra Spain 37°56N 5°45W 89 H5
Căzăneşti Romania 44°36N 27°3E 81 F11
Cazaubon France 43°56N 0°3W 72 E3
Cazaux et de Sanguinet, Étang de France 44°29N 1°10W 72 D2
Cazenovia U.S.A. 42°56N 75°51W 175 D9

Cazères France 43°13N 1°5E 72 E5
Cazin Bos.-H. 44°57N 15°57E 93 D12
Čazma Croatia 45°45N 16°39E 93 C13
Cazombo Angola 11°54S 22°56E 141 G4
Cazorla Spain 37°55N 3°2W 89 H7
Cazorla, Sierra de Spain 38°5N 2°55W 89 G8
Cea → Spain 42°0N 5°36W 88 C5
Ceadir-Lunga Moldova 46°3N 28°51E 81 D13
Ceahlău □ Romania 46°58N 25°55E 81 D10
Ceamurlia de Jos Romania 44°43N 28°47E 81 F13
Ceanannus Mor = Kells Ireland 53°44N 6°53W 64 C5
Ceará = Fortaleza Brazil 3°45S 38°35W 189 A3
Ceará □ Brazil 5°0S 40°0W 189 B3
Ceará Abyssal Plain Atl. Oc. 0°0 36°30W 56 F7
Ceará-Mirim Brazil 5°38S 35°25W 189 B3
Ceara Rise Atl. Oc. 4°30N 43°30W 56 F7
Ceatharlach = Carlow Ireland 52°50N 6°56W 64 D5
Ceauru, L. Romania 44°58N 23°11E 81 F8
Cébaco, I. de Panama 7°33N 81°9W 182 E3
Cebollar Argentina 29°10S 66°35W 190 B2
Cebollera, Sierra Spain 42°0N 2°30W 90 D2
Cebreros Spain 40°27N 4°28W 88 E6
Cebu Phil. 10°18N 123°54E 119 B6
Čečava Bos.-H. 44°42N 17°44E 80 F7
Ceccano Italy 41°34N 13°20E 94 A6
Cece Hungary 46°46N 18°39E 80 D3
Cechi Côte d'Ivoire 6°15N 4°25E 138 D4
Cecil Plains Australia 27°30S 151°11E 151 D5
Cécina Italy 43°19N 10°31E 92 E7
Cécina → Italy 43°18N 10°29E 92 E7
Ceclavín Spain 39°50N 6°45W 88 F4
Cedar → U.S.A. 41°17N 91°21W 172 E8
Cedar City U.S.A. 37°41N 113°4W 169 H7
Cedar Creek Res. U.S.A. 32°11N 96°4W 176 E6
Cedar Falls Iowa, U.S.A. 42°32N 92°27W 172 D7
Cedar Falls Wash., U.S.A. 47°25N 121°45W 170 C5
Cedar Key U.S.A. 29°8N 83°2W 179 F6
Cedar L. Canada 53°10N 100°0W 163 C9
Cedar Park U.S.A. 30°30N 97°49W 176 F6
Cedar Rapids U.S.A. 41°59N 91°40W 172 E8
Cedartown U.S.A. 34°1N 85°15W 178 A4
Cedarvale Canada 55°1N 128°22W 162 B3
Cedarville S. Africa 30°23S 29°3E 145 D4
Cedeira Spain 43°39N 8°2W 88 B2
Cedral Mexico 23°50N 100°45W 180 C4
Cedrino → Italy 40°11N 9°42E 94 B2
Cedro Brazil 6°34S 39°3W 189 E3
Cedros, I. Mexico 28°12N 115°15W 180 B1
Cedros, I. Trin. & Tob. 10°16N 61°54W 183 D7
Ceduna Australia 32°7S 133°46E 151 E1
Cedynia Poland 52°53N 14°12E 81 C5
Cée Spain 42°57N 9°10W 88 C1
Ceel Gaal Somalia 10°58N 50°20E 135 E5
Ceel Waaq Kenya 2°49N 40°56E 140 D8
Ceeldheere Somalia 3°50N 47°8E 131 G4
Ceerigaabo Somalia 10°35N 47°20E 135 E4
Cefalù Italy 38°2N 14°1E 95 D7
Cega → Spain 41°33N 4°46W 88 D6
Ceglid Hungary 47°11N 19°47E 80 C4
Céglie Messápica Italy 40°39N 17°31E 95 B10
Cehegín Spain 38°6N 1°48W 91 G3
Cehu-Silvaniei Romania 47°24N 23°9E 81 C8
Ceica Romania 46°53N 22°10E 80 D7
Ceira → Portugal 40°13N 8°16W 88 E2
Çekerek Turkey 40°4N 35°29E 104 B6
Cekik Indonesia 8°12S 114°27E 119 J17
Čeládkovice Czechia 50°10N 14°46E 78 A7
Celano Italy 42°5N 13°33E 93 F10
Celanova Spain 42°9N 7°58W 88 C3
Celaque △ Honduras 14°30N 88°43W 182 D2
Celaya Mexico 20°31N 100°37W 180 C4
Celbridge Ireland 53°20N 6°32W 64 C5
Celebes = Sulawesi Indonesia 2°0S 120°0E 119 E6
Celebes Sea Indonesia 3°0N 123°0E 119 D6
Celendin Peru 6°52S 78°10W 188 E3
Čelić Bos.-H. 44°43N 18°49E 80 F3
Celina U.S.A. 40°33N 84°35W 173 E11
Celinac Bos.-H. 44°44N 17°22E 80 F2
Celje Slovenia 46°16N 15°18E 93 B12
Celldömölk Hungary 47°16N 17°10E 80 C2
Celle Germany 52°37N 10°4E 76 C6
Celorico da Beira Portugal 40°38N 7°24W 88 E3
Celtic Sea Atl. Oc. 50°9N 9°34W 68 F2
Çeltikçi Turkey 37°32N 30°29E 99 D12
Çemişgezek Turkey 39°3N 38°56E 105 C8
Cenderawasih, Teluk Indonesia 3°0S 135°20E 119 E9
Cengong China 27°13N 108°44E 116 D7
Ceno → Italy 44°43N 10°5E 92 D7
Centallo Italy 44°30N 7°35E 92 D4
Centelles Spain 41°50N 2°14E 90 D7
Centennial U.S.A. 39°34N 104°52W 168 G11
Center N. Dak., U.S.A. 47°7N 101°18W 172 B3
Center Tex., U.S.A. 31°48N 94°11W 176 F7
Center Hill U.S.A. 28°38N 82°3W 179 G7
Centerburg U.S.A. 40°18N 82°42W 174 F2
Centerville Calif., U.S.A. 36°44N 119°30W 170 J7
Centerville Iowa, U.S.A. 40°44N 92°52W 172 E7
Centerville Pa., U.S.A. 40°3N 79°59W 174 F5
Centerville Tenn., U.S.A. 35°47N 87°28W 177 D11
Centerville Tex., U.S.A. 31°16N 95°59W 176 F7
Cento Italy 44°43N 11°17E 93 D8
Central = Tsentralnyy □ Russia 52°0N 40°0E 106 D4
Central □ Botswana 22°0S 26°30E 144 B4
Central □ Ghana 5°10N 1°10W 139 D4
Central □ Malawi 13°30S 33°30E 143 E3
Central □ Zambia 14°25S 28°50E 143 E2
Central, Cordillera Colombia 5°0N 75°0W 186 C4
Central, Cordillera Costa Rica 10°10N 84°5W 182 D3
Central, Cordillera Dom. Rep. 19°15N 71°0W 183 C5
Central, Cordillera Peru 7°0S 77°30W 188 B2
Central, Cordillera Puerto Rico 18°8N 66°35W 183 d
Central African Rep. ■ Africa 7°0N 20°0E 135 G4

Central America America 12°0N 85°0W 158 H11
Central Australia ◇ Australia 22°30S 128°30E 148 D4
Central Bedfordshire □ U.K. 52°5N 0°20W 67 E7
Central Butte Canada 50°48N 106°31W 163 C7
Central City Colo., U.S.A. 39°48N 105°31W 168 G11
Central City Ky., U.S.A. 37°18N 87°7W 172 G10
Central City Nebr., U.S.A. 41°7N 98°0W 172 E4
Central Desert ◇ Australia 19°56S 130°46E 148 C5
Central I. Kenya 3°30N 36°0E 142 B4
Central Island △ Kenya 3°23N 36°1E 142 B4
Central Japan Int. ✈ (NGO) Japan 34°53N 136°45E 113 G8
Central Kalahari △ Botswana 22°36S 23°58E 144 B3
Central Makran Range Pakistan 26°30N 64°15E 122 F4
Central Pacific Basin Pac. Oc. 8°0N 175°0W 156 G10
Central Patricia Canada 51°30N 90°9W 164 B1
Central Point U.S.A. 42°23N 122°55W 168 E2
Central Russian Uplands Europe 54°0N 36°0E 58 E13
Central Siberian Plateau Russia 65°0N 105°0E 102 B12
Central Square U.S.A. 43°17N 76°9W 175 C8
Centralia Canada 43°17N 81°28W 174 C3
Centralia Ill., U.S.A. 38°32N 89°8W 172 F9
Centralia Mo., U.S.A. 39°13N 92°8W 172 F7
Centralia Wash., U.S.A. 46°43N 122°58W 170 D4
Centre □ Cameroon 4°45N 12°0E 139 E7
Centre de Flacq Mauritius 20°12S 57°43E 141 d
Centre-Val de Loire □ France 47°30N 1°30E 70 E8
Centreville N.Y., U.S.A. 42°28N 78°14W 174 D6
Centreville Pa., U.S.A. 41°44N 79°45W 174 E5
Century U.S.A. 30°58N 87°16W 179 E2
Cenxi China 22°57N 110°57E 117 F8
Čeotina → Bos.-H. 43°36N 18°50E 96 C2
Cephalonia = Kefalonia Greece 38°15N 20°30E 98 C2
Čepin Croatia 45°32N 18°34E 80 E3
Ceprano Italy 41°33N 13°31E 94 A6
Ceptura Romania 45°1N 26°21E 81 E11
Cepu Indonesia 7°9S 111°35E 119 G14
Ceram = Seram Indonesia 3°10S 129°0E 119 E7
Ceram Sea = Seram Sea Indonesia 2°30S 128°30E 119 E7
Cée France 42°26N 3°10E 72 F7
Cerbicales, Îs. France 41°33N 9°22E 73 G13
Cercal Portugal 37°48N 8°40W 89 H2
Cerdanya Spain 42°22N 1°35E 90 C6
Cère → France 44°55N 1°49E 72 D5
Cerea Italy 45°12N 11°13E 93 C8
Ceredigion □ U.K. 52°16N 4°15W 67 E3
Ceres Argentina 29°55S 61°55W 190 B3
Ceres S. Africa 33°21S 19°18E 144 D2
Ceres U.S.A. 37°35N 120°57W 170 H6
Cerésio, L. di = Lugano, L. di Switz. 46°0N 9°0E 92 C6
Céret France 42°30N 2°42E 72 F6
Cerf Seychelles 4°38S 55°40E 141 b
Cergy France 49°2N 2°4E 71 C9
Cerignola Italy 41°17N 15°53E 95 A8
Cerigo = Kythira Greece 36°8N 23°0E 98 D5
Cérilly France 46°37N 2°50E 71 F9
Cerisiers France 48°8N 3°30E 71 D10
Cerizay France 46°50N 0°40W 70 F6
Çerkeş Turkey 40°49N 32°52E 104 B5
Çerkezköy Turkey 41°17N 28°0E 97 E12
Cerknica Slovenia 45°48N 14°21E 93 C11
Cerkovica Bulgaria 43°41N 24°56E 97 C8
Cermerno Serbia 43°35N 20°25E 96 C4
Çermik Turkey 38°9N 39°26E 105 C8
Cerna → Romania 44°38N 23°58E 81 F8
Cernavodă Romania 44°22N 28°3E 81 F13
Cernay France 47°44N 7°10E 71 E14
Cernik Croatia 45°17N 17°22E 80 E2
Çërrik Albania 41°2N 19°58E 96 E3
Cerritos Mexico 22°25N 100°16W 180 C4
Cerro Cofre de Perote △ Mexico 19°29N 97°8W 181 D5
Cerro Corá △ Paraguay 22°36S 56°0W 191 A4
Cerro de Pasco Peru 10°45S 76°10W 188 C2
Cerro del Copey △ Venezuela 10°59N 63°53W 183 D7
Cerro Saroche △ Venezuela 10°10N 69°35W 183 D6
Cerro Sombrero Chile 52°45S 69°15W 192 D3
Cerros Colorados, Embalse Argentina 38°30S 68°50W 190 A3
Certaldo Italy 43°33N 11°2E 92 E8
Cervaro → Italy 41°30N 15°52E 95 A8
Cervati, Monte Italy 40°17N 15°29E 95 B8
Cerventes Australia 30°31S 115°3E 149 F2
Cervera Spain 41°40N 1°16E 90 D6
Cervera de Pisuerga Spain 42°51N 4°30W 88 C6
Cervera del Río Alhama Spain 42°2N 1°58W 90 C3
Cervéteri Italy 42°0N 12°6E 93 F9
Cérvia Italy 44°15N 12°22E 93 D9
Cervignano del Friuli Italy 45°49N 13°20E 93 C10
Cervinara Italy 41°1N 14°37E 95 A7
Cervione France 42°20N 9°29E 73 F13
Cervo Spain 43°40N 7°24W 88 B3
Cesena Italy 44°8N 12°15E 93 D9
Cesenático Italy 44°12N 12°22E 93 D9
Cēsis Latvia 57°18N 25°15E 84 D3
Česká Lípa Czechia 50°45N 14°30E 78 A7
Česká Rep. = Czechia ■ Europe 50°0N 15°0E 78 B8
Česká Třebová Czechia 49°54N 16°27E 79 B9
České Budějovice Czechia 48°55N 14°25E 78 C7

České Švýcarsko △ Czechia 50°50N 14°15E 78 A7
České Velenice Czechia 48°45N 14°57E 78 C7
Českobudějovický = Jihočeský □ Czechia 49°8N 14°35E 78 B7
Českomoravská Vrchovina Czechia 49°30N 15°40E 78 B8
Český Brod Czechia 50°4N 14°52E 78 A7
Český Krumlov Czechia 48°43N 14°21E 78 C7
Český Těšín Czechia 49°45N 18°39E 79 B11
Česma → Croatia 45°35N 16°29E 93 C13
Çeşme Turkey 38°20N 26°23E 99 C8
Çeşme Yarımadası Turkey 38°20N 26°30E 99 C8
Cessnock Australia 32°50S 151°21E 153 B9
Cesson-Sévigné France 48°7N 1°36W 70 D5
Cestas France 44°44N 0°41W 72 D3
Cestos → Liberia 5°40N 9°10W 138 D3
Cestos Sehnkwehn □ Liberia 5°40N 9°10W 138 D3
Cetate Romania 44°7N 23°2E 80 F8
Cetin Grad Croatia 45°9N 15°45E 93 C12
Cetina → Croatia 43°26N 16°42E 93 E13
Cetinje Montenegro 42°23N 18°59E 96 D2
Cetraro Italy 39°31N 15°55E 95 C8
Ceuta N. Afr. 35°52N 5°18W 134 A4
Ceva Italy 44°23N 8°2E 92 D5
Cévennes France 44°10N 3°50E 72 D7
Cévennes △ France 44°15N 3°45E 72 D7
Ceyhan Turkey 37°4N 35°47E 104 D6
Ceyhan → Turkey 36°38N 35°40E 104 D6
Ceylanpınar Turkey 36°50N 40°2E 105 D9
Ceylon = Sri Lanka ■ Asia 7°30N 80°50E 127 L5
Ceylon Plain Ind. Oc. 4°0S 82°0E 146 E7
Cèze → France 44°6N 4°43E 73 D8
Cha-am Thailand 12°48N 99°58E 120 F2
Chabanais France 45°52N 0°48E 72 C4
Chabeuil France 44°54N 5°3E 73 D9
Chablais France 46°20N 6°36E 71 F13
Chablis France 47°47N 3°48E 71 E10
Chabounia Algeria 35°30N 2°38E 136 A4
Chacabuco Argentina 34°40S 60°27W 190 C3
Chacao, Canal Chile 41°47S 73°42W 192 B2
Chachani, Nevado Peru 16°11S 71°31W 188 D3
Chachapoyas Peru 6°15S 77°50W 188 B2
Chachasp Peru 15°30S 72°15W 188 D3
Chachoengsao Thailand 13°42N 101°5E 120 F3
Chachran Pakistan 28°55N 70°30E 124 E5
Chachro Pakistan 25°5N 70°15E 124 G4
Chaco □ Argentina 26°30S 61°0W 190 B3
Chaco □ Paraguay 26°0S 60°0W 190 B3
Chaco → U.S.A. 36°46N 108°39W 169 H9
Chaco Austral S. Amer. 27°0S 59°30W 190 B4
Chaco Boreal S. Amer. 22°0S 60°0W 186 H6
Chaco Central S. Amer. 24°0S 61°0W 190 A4
Chaco Culture △ U.S.A. 36°3N 107°58W 169 H10
Chacon, C. U.S.A. 54°42N 132°0W 162 C2
Chad ■ Africa 15°0N 17°15E 135 F8
Chad, L. = Tchad, L. Chad 13°30N 14°30E 135 F8
Chadileuvú → Argentina 37°46S 66°0W 190 D2
Chadiza Zambia 14°45S 32°27E 143 E3
Chadron U.S.A. 42°50N 103°0W 172 D2
Chadyr-Lunga = Ceadîr-Lunga Moldova 46°3N 28°51E 81 D13
Chae Hom Thailand 18°43N 99°35E 120 C2
Chae Son △ Thailand 18°42N 99°20E 120 C2
Chaem → Thailand 18°11N 98°38E 120 C2
Chaeryŏng N. Korea 38°24N 125°36E 115 E13
Chafe Nigeria 11°56N 6°55E 139 C6
Chagai Hills = Chāh Gay Hills Afghan. 29°30N 64°0E 122 E3
Chagda Russia 58°45N 130°38E 107 D14
Chagdo Kangri China 34°15N 84°10E 109 F10
Chaghcharān Afghan. 34°31N 65°15E 109 F17
Chagny France 46°57N 4°45E 71 F11
Chagoda Russia 59°10N 35°15E 106 C4
Chagos Arch. ☒ Ind. Oc. 6°0S 72°0E 146 E6
Chagres △ Panama 9°33N 79°37W 182 E4
Chaguanas Trin. & Tob. 10°30N 61°26W 187 K15
Chaguaramas Venezuela 9°33N 66°0W 183 D6
Chāh Ākhvor Iran 32°41N 59°40E 129 C8
Chāh Bahar Iran 25°20N 60°40E 129 E9
Chāh-e Kavīr Iran 34°29N 56°52E 129 C8
Chāh Gay Hills Afghan. 29°30N 64°0E 122 E3
Chahār Borj Iran 37°10N 55°20E 129 B7
Chahār Borjak Afghan. 30°17N 62°3E 122 D3
Chahār Mahāll va Bakhtīārī □ Iran 32°0N 49°0E 129 C6
Chai Badan Thailand 15°12N 101°8E 120 E3
Chaibasa India 22°42N 85°49E 125 H7
Chaillé-les-Marais France 46°25N 1°2W 72 B2
Chain Ridge Ind. Oc. 5°0N 90°0E 146 D4
Chainat Thailand 15°11N 100°8E 120 E3
Chainpur Nepal 27°17N 87°19E 125 F12
Chaires U.S.A. 30°26N 84°7W 178 E5
Chaitén Chile 42°55S 72°38W 192 B2
Chaiya Thailand 9°23N 99°14E 121 H2
Chaiyaphum Thailand 15°48N 102°2E 120 E4
Chaj Doab Pakistan 32°15N 73°0E 124 C5
Chajari Argentina 30°42S 58°0W 190 C4
Chak Amru Pakistan 32°22N 75°11E 124 C6
Chakar → Pakistan 29°29N 75°11E 124 E3
Chake Chake Tanzania 5°15S 39°45E 142 D4
Chakhānsūr Afghan. 31°10N 62°0E 122 D3
Chakonipau, L. Canada 56°18N 68°30W 165 A6
Chakradharpur India 22°45N 85°40E 125 H11
Chakwal Pakistan 32°56N 72°53E 124 C5
Chala Peru 15°48S 74°20W 188 D3
Chalais France 45°16N 0°3E 72 C4
Chalakudi India 10°18N 76°20E 127 J3
Chalchihuites Mexico 23°29N 103°53W 180 C4
Chalcis = Chalkida Greece 38°27N 23°42E 98 C5
Chálette-sur-Loing France 48°1N 2°44E 71 D9
Chaleur B. Canada 47°55N 65°30W 165 C6
Chalfant U.S.A. 37°32N 118°21W 170 H8
Chalhuanca Peru 14°15N 73°15W 188 C3
Chalindrey France 47°43N 5°26E 71 E12
Chaling China 26°58N 113°30E 117 D9
Chalisgaon India 20°30N 75°10E 124 J9
Chalk River Canada 46°1N 77°27W 164 C7
Chalkar, Ozero = Shalkar Köli Kazakhstan 50°35N 51°47E 86 D1

Chalki Dodekanisa, Greece 36°17N 27°35E 99 E9
Chalki Thessaly, Greece 39°36N 22°30E 98 B4
Chalkida Greece 38°27N 23°42E 98 C5
Chalkidiki Greece 40°25N 23°20E 96 F7
Chalky Inlet N.Z. 46°3S 166°31E 155 G1
Challakere India 14°19N 76°39E 127 K3
Challans France 46°50N 1°52W 70 F5
Challapata Bolivia 18°53S 66°50W 186 G5
Challawa Gorge Res. Nigeria 11°54N 8°25E 139 C6
Challenger Deep Pac. Oc. 11°30N 142°0E 156 F6
Challenger Fracture Zone Pac. Oc. 35°0S 105°0W 157 L17
Challis U.S.A. 44°30N 114°14W 168 D6
Chalmette U.S.A. 29°56N 89°57W 177 G10
Chaloem Rattanakosin △ Thailand 14°40N 99°17E 120 E2
Chalon-sur-Saône France 46°48N 4°50E 71 F11
Chalong Thailand 7°50N 98°22E 121 a
Chalonnes-sur-Loire France 47°20N 0°45W 70 E6
Châlons-en-Champagne France 48°58N 4°20E 71 D11
Chálten, Cerro = Fitz Roy, Cerro Argentina 49°17S 73°5W 192 C2
Chālus France 45°39N 0°58E 72 C4
Chālūs Iran 36°38N 51°26E 129 B6
Cham Germany 49°13N 12°39E 77 F8
Cham, Cu Lao Vietnam 15°57N 108°30E 120 E7
Chama U.S.A. 36°54N 106°35W 169 H10
Chamaicó Argentina 35°3S 64°58W 190 D3
Chaman Pakistan 30°58N 66°25E 122 D5
Chamba India 32°35N 76°10E 124 C7
Chamba Tanzania 11°37S 37°0E 143 E4
Chambal → India 26°29N 79°15E 125 F8
Chambal India 26°29N 79°15E 125 F8
Chamberlain U.S.A. 43°49N 99°20W 172 D4
Chamberlain → Australia 15°30S 127°54E 148 C4
Chamberlain L. U.S.A. 46°14N 69°19W 173 B19
Chambers U.S.A. 35°11N 109°26W 169 J9
Chambersburg U.S.A. 39°56N 77°40W 173 F15
Chambéry France 45°34N 5°55E 73 C9
Chambeshi → Zambia 11°53S 29°48E 140 G6
Chambi, Jebel Tunisia 35°11N 8°39E 136 A5
Chamblee U.S.A. 33°53N 84°18W 178 B5
Chambly Canada 45°27N 73°17W 175 A11
Chambord Canada 48°25N 72°6W 165 C5
Chamboulive France 45°26N 1°42E 72 C5
Chamchamal Iraq 35°32N 44°50E 105 E11
Chamela Mexico 19°32N 105°5W 180 D3
Chamical Argentina 30°22S 66°27W 190 C2
Chamkar Luong Cambodia 11°0N 103°45E 121 G4
Chamoli India 30°24N 79°21E 125 D8
Chamonix-Mont Blanc France 45°55N 6°51E 73 C10
Chamouchuane = Ashuapmushuan → Canada 48°37N 72°20W 164 C5
Champa India 22°2N 82°43E 125 H10
Champagne Canada 60°49N 136°30W 162 A1
Champagne France 48°40N 4°20E 71 D11
Champagnole France 46°45N 5°55E 71 F12
Champaign U.S.A. 40°7N 88°15W 172 E9
Champaner India 22°29N 73°32E 124 H5
Champassak Laos 14°53N 105°52E 120 E5
Champawat India 29°20N 80°6E 125 E9
Champdeniers-St-Denis France 46°29N 0°25W 72 B3
Champdoré, L. Canada 55°55N 65°49W 165 A6
Champeix France 45°37N 3°8E 72 C7
Champion U.S.A. 41°19N 80°51W 174 E4
Champlain U.S.A. 44°59N 73°27W 175 B11
Champlain, L. U.S.A. 44°40N 73°20W 175 B11
Champlitte France 47°36N 5°31E 71 E12
Champotón Mexico 19°21N 90°43W 181 D6
Champua India 22°5N 85°40E 125 H11
Chamrajnagar India 11°52N 76°52E 127 J3
Chamusca Portugal 39°21N 8°29W 89 F2
Chan Chan Peru 8°7S 79°0W 188 B2
Chañaral Chile 26°23S 70°40W 190 B1
Chanārān Iran 36°39N 59°6E 129 B8
Chanasma India 23°44N 72°5E 124 H5
Chancay Peru 11°32S 77°25W 188 C2
Chancery Lane Barbados 13°3N 59°30W 183 g
Chanco Chile 35°44S 72°32W 190 D1
Chand India 21°57N 79°7E 125 J8
Chandan Chauki India 28°33N 80°47E 125 E8
Chandannagar India 22°52N 88°24E 125 H13
Chandausi India 28°27N 78°49E 125 E8
Chandeleur Is. U.S.A. 29°55N 88°57W 177 G10
Chandeleur Sd. U.S.A. 29°55N 89°0W 177 G10
Chandigarh India 30°43N 76°47E 124 D7
Chandil India 22°58N 86°3E 125 H12
Chandler Australia 27°0S 133°19E 151 E1
Chandler Ariz., U.S.A. 33°18N 111°50W 169 K8
Chandler Okla., U.S.A. 35°42N 96°53W 176 D6
Chandless → Brazil 9°8S 69°51W 186 E5
Chandod India 21°59N 73°28E 124 J5
Chandpur Bangla. 23°8N 90°45E 125 H17
Chandra Greece 35°3N 26°8E 99 F8
Chandragiri India 13°35N 79°19E 127 H4
Chandrapur India 19°57N 79°25E 128 G3
Chandrupatla India 18°33N 80°24E 125 K8
Chanf Iran 26°38N 60°29E 129 E9
Chang Pakistan 26°59N 68°30E 124 F3
Chang, Ko Thailand 12°0N 102°23E 121 G4
Chang, Ko Thailand 9°50N 98°27E 121 H2
Ch'ang Chiang = Chang Jiang → China 31°48N 121°10E 117 B13
Chang Jiang → China 31°48N 121°10E 117 B13
Chang-won S. Korea 35°16N 128°37E 115 G15
Changan India 22°48N 113°48E 111 a
Changanacheri India 9°25N 76°31E 127 K3
Changanassery = Changanacheri India 9°25N 76°31E 127 K3
Changane → Mozam. 24°30S 33°30E 145 C5
Changbai China 41°25N 128°5E 115 D15
Changbai Shan China 42°20N 129°0E 115 C15
Changchiak'ou = Zhangjiakou China 40°48N 114°55E 114 D8
Ch'angchou = Changzhou China 31°47N 119°58E 117 B12

Changchun China 43°57N 125°17E 115 C13
Changchunling
 China 45°18N 125°27E 115 B13
Changde China 29°4N 111°35E 117 C8
Changdo-ri N. Korea 38°30N 127°40E 115 E14
Changfeng China 32°28N 117°10E 117 A11
Changge China 34°13N 113°46E 114 G7
Changhai = Shanghai
 China 31°15N 121°26E 117 B13
Changhua China 30°12N 119°12E 117 B12
Changhua Taiwan 24°2N 120°30E 117 E13
Changhŭngni
 N. Korea 40°24N 128°19E 115 D15
Changi Singapore 1°23N 103°59E 121 d
Changi, Singapore ✈ (SIN)
 Singapore 1°23N 103°59E 121 d
Changji China 44°1N 87°19E 109 D11
Changjiang China 19°20N 108°55E 117 a
Changjiang Shuiku
 China 22°29N 113°27E 111 a
Changjin N. Korea 40°27N 127°15E 115 D14
Changjin-ho N. Korea 40°30N 127°15E 115 D14
Changle China 25°59N 119°27E 117 E12
Changli China 39°40N 119°13E 115 E10
Changlun Malaysia 6°25N 100°26E 121 J3
Changning Hunan,
 China 26°28N 112°22E 117 D9
Changning Sichuan,
 China 28°40N 104°56E 116 C5
Changning Yunnan,
 China 24°45N 99°30E 116 E2
Changping China 40°14N 116°12E 114 C9
Changsha China 28°12N 113°0E 117 C9
Changshan China 28°55N 118°27E 117 C12
Changshan Qundao
 China 39°11N 122°32E 115 E12
Changshou China 29°50N 107°4E 116 C6
Changshu China 31°38N 120°43E 117 B13
Changshun China 26°3N 106°25E 116 D6
Changtai China 24°35N 117°42E 117 E11
Changting China 25°50N 116°22E 117 E11
Changtu China 42°46N 124°6E 115 C13
Changuinola Panama 9°26N 82°31W 182 E3
Changwu Guangxi Zhuangzu,
 China 23°25N 111°17E 117 F8
Changwu Shaanxi,
 China 35°10N 107°45E 114 G4
Changxing China 31°0N 119°55E 117 B12
Changyang China 30°30N 111°10E 117 B8
Changyi China 36°40N 119°30E 115 F10
Changyŏn N. Korea 38°15N 125°6E 115 E13
Changyuan China 35°15N 114°42E 114 G8
Changzhi China 36°10N 113°6E 114 F7
Changzhou China 31°47N 119°58E 117 B12
Chanhanga Angola 16°0S 14°8E 144 A1
Chania Greece 35°30N 24°4E 101 D6
Chanion, Kolpos Greece 35°33N 23°55E 101 D5
Chanlar = Goygöl
 Azerbaijan 40°37N 46°12E 87 K8
Channagiri India 14°2N 75°56E 127 G2
Channapatna India 12°40N 77°15E 127 H3
Channel Is. U.K. 49°19N 2°24W 67 H5
Channel Is. U.S.A. 33°40N 119°15W 171 M7
Channel Islands △
 U.S.A. 34°0N 119°24W 171 L7
Channel-Port aux Basques
 Canada 47°30N 59°9W 165 C8
Channel Tunnel Europe 51°0N 1°30E 67 F9
Channing U.S.A. 35°41N 102°20W 176 D3
Chantada Spain 42°36N 7°46W 88 C3
Chanthaburi Thailand 12°38N 102°12E 120 F4
Chantilly France 49°12N 2°29E 71 C9
Chantonnay France 46°40N 1°3W 70 F5
Chantrey Inlet
 Canada 67°48N 96°20W 160 D12
Chanumla India 8°19N 93°5E 127 K11
Chanute U.S.A. 37°41N 95°27W 172 G6
Chany, Ozero Russia 54°49N 77°29E 109 B9
Chanza → Spain 37°32N 7°30W 89 H3
Chao Hu China 31°30N 117°30E 117 B11
Chao Phraya →
 Thailand 13°40N 100°31E 120 F3
Chao Phraya Lowlands
 Thailand 15°30N 100°0E 120 E3
Chaocheng China 36°4N 115°37E 114 F8
Chaohu China 31°38N 117°50E 117 B11
Chaouia-Ouardigha □
 Morocco 33°0N 7°30W 136 B2
Chaoyang Guangdong,
 China - 23°17N 116°30E 117 F11
Chaoyang Liaoning,
 China 41°35N 120°22E 115 D11
Chaozhou China 23°42N 116°32E 117 F11
Chapada Diamantina △
 Brazil 12°52S 41°30W 189 C2
Chapada dos Veadeiros △
 Brazil 14°0S 47°30W 189 C1
Chapaev Kazakhstan 50°25N 51°10E 86 E10
Chapais Canada 49°47N 74°51W 164 C5
Chapala Mozam. 15°50S 37°35E 143 F4
Chapala, L. de Mexico 20°15N 103°0W 180 C4
Chapayevsk Russia 53°0N 49°40E 86 D9
Chapecó Brazil 27°14S 52°41W 191 B5
Chapel Hill U.S.A. 35°55N 79°4W 177 D15
Chapleau Canada 47°50N 83°24W 164 C3
Chaplin Canada 50°28N 106°40W 163 C7
Chaplin L. Canada 50°22N 106°36W 163 C7
Chaplino Ukraine 48°8N 36°15E 85 H9
Chaplygin Russia 53°15N 40°0E 84 F11
Chappell U.S.A. 41°6N 102°28W 172 E2
Chappells U.S.A. 34°11N 81°52W 178 A8
Chapra = Chhapra
 India 25°48N 84°44E 125 G11
Chaqâbel Iran 33°16N 47°50E 105 F12
Chara Russia 56°54N 118°20E 107 C12
Charadai Argentina 27°35S 59°55W 190 B4
Charagua Bolivia 19°45S 63°10W 186 G6
Charakas Greece 35°1N 25°7E 101 D7
Charambirá, Punta
 Colombia 4°16N 77°32W 186 C3
Charaña Bolivia 17°30S 69°25W 188 D4
Charantsavan Armenia 40°35N 44°41E 87 K7
Charanwala India 27°51N 72°10E 124 F5
Charata Argentina 27°13S 61°14W 190 B3
Charcas Mexico 23°8N 101°7W 180 C4
Charcot I. Antarctica 70°0S 75°0W 55 C17
Chard U.K. 50°52N 2°58W 67 G5
Chardon U.S.A. 41°35N 81°12W 174 E3
Chardzhou = Türkmenabat
 Turkmenistan 39°6N 63°34E 129 B9

Charente □ France 45°50N 0°16E 72 C4
Charente → France 45°57N 1°5W 72 C2
Charente-Maritime □
 France 45°45N 0°45W 72 C3
Charenton-du-Cher
 France 46°44N 2°39E 71 F9
Chari → Chad 12°58N 14°31E 135 F8
Chārīkār Afghan. 35°0N 69°10E 109 E7
Charing U.S.A. 32°28N 84°22W 178 C5
Chariton U.S.A. 41°1N 93°19W 172 E7
Chariton → U.S.A. 39°19N 92°58W 172 F7
Chärjew = Türkmenabat
 Turkmenistan 39°6N 63°34E 129 B9
Charkhari India 25°24N 79°45E 125 G8
Charkhi Dadri India 28°37N 76°17E 124 E7
Charleroi Belgium 50°24N 4°27E 69 D4
Charleroi U.S.A. 40°9N 79°57W 174 F5
Charles, C. U.S.A. 37°7N 75°58W 173 G16
Charles, Peak
 Australia 32°52S 121°11E 149 F3
Charles City U.S.A. 43°4N 92°41W 172 D7
Charles de Gaulle, Paris ✈ (CDG)
 France 49°0N 2°22E 71 D9
Charles I. Canada 62°39N 74°15W 161 E17
Charles L. Canada 59°50N 110°33W 163 B6
Charles Sound N.Z. 45°2S 167°4E 155 F2
Charles Town U.S.A. 39°17N 77°52W 173 F15
Charlesbourg Canada 46°51N 71°16W 173 B18
Charleston Ill., U.S.A. 39°30N 88°10W 172 F9
Charleston Miss., U.S.A. 34°1N 90°4W 177 D9
Charleston Mo., U.S.A. 36°55N 89°21W 172 G9
Charleston S.C.,
 U.S.A. 32°46N 79°56W 178 C10
Charleston W. Va.,
 U.S.A. 38°21N 81°38W 173 F13
Charleston L. Canada 44°32N 76°0W 175 B9
Charleston Peak
 U.S.A. 36°16N 115°42W 171 J11
Charlestown Ireland 53°58N 8°48W 64 C3
Charlestown S. Africa 27°26S 29°53E 145 C4
Charlestown Ind.,
 U.S.A. 38°27N 85°40W 173 F11
Charlestown N.H.,
 U.S.A. 43°14N 72°25W 175 C12
Charlestown of Aberlour
 U.K. 57°28N 3°14W 65 D5
Charleville Australia 26°24S 146°15E 151 D4
Charleville Ireland 52°21N 8°40W 64 D3
Charleville-Mézières
 France 49°44N 4°40E 71 C11
Charlevoix U.S.A. 45°19N 85°16W 173 C11
Charlie Gibbs Fracture Zone
 Atl. Oc. 52°45N 35°30W 56 A8
Charlieu France 46°10N 4°10E 71 F11
Charlotte Mich.,
 U.S.A. 42°34N 84°50W 173 D11
Charlotte N.C., U.S.A. 35°13N 80°50W 177 D14
Charlotte Vt., U.S.A. 44°19N 73°16W 175 B11
Charlotte Amalie
 U.S. Virgin Is. 18°21N 64°56W 183 a
Charlotte-Douglas Int. ✈ (CLT)
 U.S.A. 35°12N 80°56W 177 D14
Charlotte Harbor U.S.A. 26°57N 82°4W 179 J7
Charlotte L. Canada 52°12N 125°19W 162 C3
Charlottenberg Sweden 59°54N 12°17E 62 E6
Charlottesville U.S.A. 38°2N 78°30W 173 F14
Charlottetown Nfld. & L.,
 Canada 52°46N 56°7W 165 B8
Charlottetown P.E.I.,
 Canada 46°14N 63°8W 165 C7
Charlotteville
 Trin. & Tob. 11°20N 60°33W 187 J16
Charlton Australia 36°16S 143°24E 152 D5
Charlton I. Canada 52°0N 79°20W 164 B4
Charmes France 48°22N 6°17E 71 D13
Charny Canada 46°43N 71°15W 165 C5
Charnyany Belarus 51°59N 24°12E 83 G11
Charolles France 46°27N 4°16E 71 F11
Chârost France 47°0N 2°7E 71 F9
Charouine Algeria 29°0N 0°15W 136 C3
Charre Mozam. 17°13S 35°10E 143 F4
Charroux France 46°9N 0°25E 72 B4
Charsadda Pakistan 34°7N 71°45E 124 B4
Charters Towers
 Australia 20°5S 146°13E 150 C4
Chartres France 48°29N 1°30E 70 D8
Chartreuse △ France 45°22N 5°42E 73 C9
Charysh → Russia 52°22N 83°45E 109 B10
Chascomús Argentina 35°30S 58°0W 190 D4
Chase Canada 50°50N 119°41W 162 C5
Chasefu Zambia 11°55S 33°8E 143 E3
Chashma Barrage
 Pakistan 32°27N 71°20E 124 C4
Chaslands Mistake
 N.Z. 46°38S 169°22E 155 G4

Châteauroux France 46°50N 1°40E 71 F8
Châteauvillain France 48°2N 4°55E 71 D11
Châteaux, Pte. des
 Guadeloupe 16°15N 61°10W 182 b
Châtel-Guyon France 45°55N 3°4E 72 C7
Châtelaillon-Plage France 46°5N 1°5W 72 B2
Châtellerault France 46°50N 0°30E 70 F7
Châtelus-Malvaleix France 46°18N 2°1E 71 F9
Chatham = Miramichi
 Canada 47°2N 65°28W 165 C6
Chatham Canada 42°24N 82°11W 174 D2
Chatham U.K. 51°22N 0°32E 67 F8
Chatham U.S.A. 42°21N 73°36W 175 D11
Chatham Is. Pac. Oc. 44°0S 176°40W 155 c
Chatham Rise Pac. Oc. 43°30S 180°0E 156 M10
Châtillon Italy 45°45N 7°37E 92 C4
Châtillon-Coligny France 47°50N 2°51E 71 E9
Châtillon-en-Diois France 44°41N 5°29E 73 D9
Châtillon-sur-Indre
 France 46°59N 1°10E 70 F8
Châtillon-sur-Loire
 France 47°35N 2°44E 71 E9
Châtillon-sur-Seine
 France 47°50N 4°33E 71 E11
Chatmohar Bangla. 24°15N 89°15E 125 G13
Chatra India 24°12N 84°56E 125 G11
Chatrapur India 19°22N 85°2E 126 E7
Chats, L. des Canada 45°30N 76°20W 175 A8
Chatsu India 26°36N 75°57E 124 F6
Chatsworth Canada 44°27N 80°54W 174 B4
Chatsworth Zimbabwe 19°38S 31°13E 143 F3
Chāttagām = Chittagong
 Bangla. 22°19N 91°48E 123 H17
Chattahoochee U.S.A. 30°42N 84°51W 178 E5
Chattahoochee →
 U.S.A. 30°54N 84°57W 178 E5
Chattanooga U.S.A. 35°3N 85°19W 177 D12
Chatteris U.K. 52°28N 0°2E 67 E8
Chatturat Thailand 15°40N 101°51E 120 E3
Chau Doc Vietnam 10°42N 105°7E 121 G5
Chaudes-Aigues France 44°51N 3°1E 72 D7
Chauffailles France 46°13N 4°20E 71 F11
Chaukan Pass
 Myanmar 27°8N 97°10E 123 F20
Chaumont France 48°7N 5°8E 71 D12
Chaumont U.S.A. 44°4N 76°8W 175 B8
Chaumont-en-Vexin
 France 49°16N 1°53E 71 C8
Chaumont-sur-Loire
 France 47°29N 1°11E 70 E8
Chaunay France 46°13N 0°9E 72 B4
Chaunskaya G. Russia 69°0N 169°0E 107 C17
Chauny France 49°37N 3°12E 71 C10
Chausey, Îs. France 48°52N 1°49W 70 D5
Chaussin France 46°59N 5°22E 71 F12
Chautara Nepal 27°46N 85°42E 125 F11
Chautauqua L. U.S.A. 42°10N 79°24W 174 D5
Chauvigny France 46°34N 0°39E 70 F7
Chauvin Canada 52°45N 110°10W 163 C6
Chavakachcheri
 Sri Lanka 9°39N 80°9E 127 K5
Chavanges France 48°30N 4°35E 71 D11
Chavash Varmane △
 Russia 54°50N 47°10E 86 C8
Chaves Brazil 0°15S 49°55W 187 D9
Chaves Portugal 41°45N 7°32W 88 D3
Chavín de Huantar
 Peru 9°35S 77°10W 188 B2
Chawang Thailand 8°25N 99°30E 121 H2
Chazelles-sur-Lyon
 France 45°39N 4°22E 73 C8
Chazuta Peru 6°30S 76°0W 188 B2
Chazy U.S.A. 44°53N 73°26W 175 B11
Cheaha Mt. U.S.A. 33°29N 85°49W 178 B4
Cheb Czechia 50°9N 12°28E 78 A5
Chebbi, Erg Africa 31°12N 3°58W 136 B3
Cheboksarskoye Vdkhr.
 Russia 56°13N 46°58E 86 B8
Cheboksary Russia 56°8N 47°12E 86 B8
Cheboygan U.S.A. 45°39N 84°29W 173 C11
Chebsara Russia 59°10N 38°59E 84 C10
Chech, Erg Africa 25°0N 2°15W 136 D3
Chechelnyk Ukraine 48°13N 29°22E 81 B14
Chechen, Ostrov Russia 43°59N 47°40E 87 H8
Chechenia □ Russia 43°30N 45°29E 87 J7
Checheno-Ingush Republic =
 Chechenia □ Russia 43°30N 45°29E 87 J7
Chechnya = Chechenia □
 Russia 43°30N 45°29E 87 J7
Checiny Poland 50°46N 20°28E 83 H7
Checotah U.S.A. 35°28N 95°31W 176 D7
Chedabucto B. Canada 45°25N 61°8W 165 C7
Cheduba I. Myanmar 18°45N 93°40E 123 K18
Cheektowaga U.S.A. 42°54N 78°45W 174 D6
Cheepie Australia 26°33S 145°1E 151 D4
Chef-Boutonne France 46°7N 0°4W 72 B3
Chefchaouen Morocco 35°9N 5°15W 136 A3
Chegdomyn Russia 51°7N 133°1E 107 D14
Chegga Mauritania 25°27N 5°40W 134 C4
Chegutu Zimbabwe 18°10S 30°14E 143 F3
Chehalis U.S.A. 46°40N 122°58W 170 D3
Chehalis → U.S.A. 46°57N 123°50W 170 D3
Cheile Bicazului-Hăşmaş △
 Romania 46°55N 25°50E 81 D10
Cheile Nerei-Beusnita △
 Romania 44°56N 21°52E 80 F6
Cheiron, Mt. du France 43°49N 6°58E 73 E10
Cheju = Jeju S. Korea 33°31N 126°32E 115 H14
Cheju-do = Jeju-do
 S. Korea 33°29N 126°34E 115 H14
Cheju Str. = Jeju Haehyop
 S. Korea 34°0N 126°30E 115 H14
Chek Lap Kok China 22°18N 113°56E 111 a
Chek Lap Kok ✈ (HKG)
 China 22°19N 113°57E 111 a
Chekalin Russia 54°10N 36°10E 84 E9
Chekhovo Russia 54°33N 20°43E 82 D7
Chekiang = Zhejiang □
 China 29°0N 120°0E 117 C13
Chela, Sa. da Angola 16°20S 13°20E 144 A1
Chelan U.S.A. 47°51N 120°1W 168 C3
Chelan, L. U.S.A. 48°11N 120°30W 168 B3
Cheleken = Hazar
 Turkmenistan 39°34N 53°16E 108 E4
Cheleken Yarymadasy
 Turkmenistan 39°30N 53°15E 129 B2
Chelforó Argentina 39°0S 66°33W 192 A3
Chéliff, O. → Algeria 36°0N 0°8E 136 A4

Chelkar = Shalqar
 Kazakhstan 47°48N 59°39E 108 C5
Chellala Dahrania Algeria 33°2N 0°1E 136 B4
Chelles France 48°53N 2°35E 71 D9
Chelm Poland 51°8N 23°30E 83 G10
Chelmno Poland 53°20N 18°30E 83 E5
Chelmsford U.K. 51°44N 0°29E 67 F8
Chełmża Poland 53°10N 18°39E 83 E5
Chelsea Australia 38°5S 145°8E 153 E6
Chelsea U.S.A. 43°59N 72°27W 175 C12
Cheltenham U.K. 51°54N 2°4W 67 F5
Chelva Spain 39°45N 1°0W 90 F4
Chelyabinsk Russia 55°10N 61°24E 108 A6
Chelyuskin, C. = Chelyuskin, Mys
 Russia 77°30N 103°0E 107 B11
Chelyuskin, Mys
 Russia 77°30N 103°0E 107 B11
Chemainus Canada 48°55N 123°42W 170 B3
Chemba Mozam. 17°9S 34°53E 141 H6
Chembar = Belinskiy
 Russia 53°0N 43°25E 86 D6
Chemillé France 47°14N 0°45W 70 E6
Chemin Grenier
 Mauritius 20°29S 57°28E 141 d
Chemnitz Germany 50°51N 12°54E 76 C8
Chemult U.S.A. 43°14N 121°47W 168 E3
Chen, Gora Russia 65°16N 141°50E 107 C15
Chenab → Pakistan 30°23N 71°2E 124 D4
Chenab Nagar Pakistan 31°45N 72°55E 124 D5
Chenachane Algeria 26°0N 4°15W 136 C3
Chenachane, O. →
 Algeria 25°20N 3°20W 136 C3
Chenango Forks
 U.S.A. 42°15N 75°51W 175 D9
Chenchiang = Zhenjiang
 China 32°11N 119°26E 117 A12
Cheney U.S.A. 47°30N 117°35W 168 C5
Cheng Xian China 33°43N 105°42E 114 H3
Chengalpattu India 12°42N 79°58E 127 H4
Chengbu China 26°18N 110°16E 117 D8
Chengcheng China 35°8N 109°56E 114 G5
Chengchou = Zhengzhou
 China 34°45N 113°34E 114 G7
Chengde China 40°59N 117°58E 115 D10
Chengdong Hu China 32°15N 116°20E 117 A11
Chengdu China 30°38N 104°2E 116 B5
Chengdu Shuangliu Int. ✈ (CTU)
 China 30°35N 103°57E 116 B4
Chenggong China 24°52N 102°56E 116 D5
Chenggu China 33°10N 107°21E 116 A6
Chenghai China 23°30N 116°42E 117 F11
Chengjiang China 24°39N 103°0E 116 D5
Chengkou China 31°54N 108°31E 116 B7
Chengmai China 19°50N 109°58E 117 a
Chengshan Jiao
 China 37°25N 122°44E 115 F12
Ch'engtu = Chengdu
 China 30°38N 104°2E 116 B5
Chengwu China 34°58N 115°50E 114 G8
Chengxi Hu China 32°15N 116°10E 117 A11
Chengyang China 36°18N 120°21E 115 F11
Chenjiagang China 34°23N 119°47E 115 G10
Chenkaladi Sri Lanka 7°47N 81°35E 127 L5
Chennai India 13°8N 80°19E 127 H5
Chenôve France 47°16N 5°1E 71 E12
Chenxi China 28°2N 110°12E 117 C8
Chenzhou China 25°47N 113°1E 117 E9
Cheo, Eilean a' = Skye
 U.K. 57°15N 6°10W 65 D2
Cheo Reo Vietnam 13°20N 108°25E 120 F7
Cheom Ksan Cambodia 14°13N 104°56E 120 E5
Cheonan S. Korea 36°48N 127°9E 115 F14
Cheongdo S. Korea 35°38N 128°42E 115 G15
Cheongju S. Korea 36°39N 127°27E 115 F14
Cheorwon S. Korea 38°15N 127°10E 115 E14
Chepelare Bulgaria 41°44N 24°40E 97 E8
Chepelarska → Bulgaria 42°9N 24°54E 97 D8
Chepén Peru 7°15S 79°23W 188 B2
Chepes Argentina 31°20S 66°35W 190 C2
Chepo Panama 9°10N 79°6W 182 E4
Chepstow U.K. 51°38N 2°41W 67 F5
Chequamegon B.
 U.S.A. 46°39N 90°51W 172 B8
Cher □ France 47°10N 2°30E 71 E9
Cher → France 47°21N 0°29E 70 E7
Chéradi Italy 40°27N 17°10E 95 B10
Cherasco Italy 44°39N 7°51E 92 D4
Cheraw U.S.A. 34°42N 79°53W 177 D15
Cherbourg-Octeville
 France 49°39N 1°40W 70 C5
Cherchell Algeria 36°35N 2°12E 136 A4
Cherdakly Russia 54°25N 48°50E 86 C9
Cherdyn Russia 60°24N 56°29E 86 B6
Cheremkhovo Russia 53°8N 103°1E 110 A3
Cherepanovo Russia 54°15N 83°30E 109 B10
Cherepovets Russia 59°5N 37°55E 84 C9
Chergui, Chott ech
 Algeria 34°21N 0°25E 136 B4
Chergui, Zahrez Algeria 35°11N 3°31E 136 B4
Cherial India 17°55N 78°59E 126 F4
Cherikov = Cherykaw
 Belarus 53°32N 31°20E 75 B16
Cheriyam I. India 10°9N 73°40E 127 J1
Cherkasy Ukraine 49°27N 32°4E 85 H7
Cherkasy □ Ukraine 48°55N 30°50E 85 H6
Cherkessk Russia 44°15N 42°5E 87 H6
Cherla India 18°5N 80°49E 126 E5
Cherlak Russia 54°15N 74°55E 109 B8
Chernaya Russia 70°30N 89°10E 107 B9
Chernelytsya Ukraine 48°49N 25°26E 81 B10
Cherni Bulgaria 42°35N 23°18E 96 D7
Chernigov = Chernihiv
 Ukraine 51°28N 31°20E 85 G6
Chernihiv Ukraine 51°28N 31°20E 85 G6
Chernihiv □ Ukraine 51°28N 31°30E 85 G6
Chernivtsi Chernivtsi,
 Ukraine 48°15N 25°52E 81 B10
Chernivtsi Vinnytsi,a
 Ukraine 48°30N 28°9E 81 B15
Chernivtsi □ Ukraine 48°15N 25°55E 81 B10
Chernobyl = Chornobyl
 Ukraine 51°20N 30°15E 75 C16
Chernogorsk Russia 53°49N 91°18E 110 A6
Chernomorskoye =
 Chornomorske
 Ukraine 45°31N 32°40E 85 K7
Chernovtsy = Chernivtsi
 Ukraine 48°15N 25°52E 81 B10
Chernyakhovsk Russia 54°36N 21°48E 82 D8
Chernyanka Russia 50°56N 37°49E 85 G9

Chernysheyskiy
 Russia 63°0N 112°30E 107 C12
Chernyye Zemli Russia 46°10N 46°0E 87 H8
Cherokee Iowa, U.S.A. 42°45N 95°33W 172 D6
Cherokee Okla., U.S.A. 36°45N 98°21W 176 C5
Cherokee Village
 U.S.A. 36°18N 91°31W 176 C9
Cherokees, Grand Lake O' The
 U.S.A. 43°59N 72°27W 175 C12
Cherquenco Chile 38°35S 72°0W 192 A2
Cherrapunji India 25°17N 91°47E 123 G17
Cherry Valley U.S.A. 42°45N 95°57W 172 D6
Cherskiy Russia 68°45N 161°18E 107 C17
Cherskogo Khrebet
 Russia 65°0N 143°0E 107 C15
Cherso = Cres Croatia 41°5N 22°4E 96 E6
Chersonesus Ukraine 44°37N 33°30E 85 K7
Chersonisos Greece 35°18N 25°22E 101 D7
Chersonisos Akrotiri
 Greece 35°40N 24°10E 101 D6
Cherthala India 9°42N 76°20E 127 K3
Chertkovo Russia 49°25N 40°19E 85 H11
Cherven Belarus 53°45N 28°28E 75 B15
Cherven-Bryag Bulgaria 43°17N 24°7E 97 C8
Chervonoarmiyske
 Ukraine 45°47N 28°44E 81 E13
Chervonohrad Ukraine 50°25N 24°10E 75 C13
Cherwell → U.K. 51°44N 1°14W 67 F6
Cherykaw Belarus 53°32N 31°20E 75 B16
Chesapeake U.S.A. 36°49N 76°16W 173 G15
Chesapeake B. U.S.A. 38°0N 76°10W 173 F14
Cheshire East □ U.K. 53°15N 2°15W 66 D5
Cheshire West and Chester □
 U.K. 53°15N 2°40W 66 D5
Cheshskaya Guba
 Russia 67°20N 47°0E 106 C5
Cheshunt U.K. 51°43N 0°1W 67 F7
Chesil Beach U.K. 50°37N 2°33W 67 G5
Chesley Canada 44°17N 81°5W 174 B3
Cheste Spain 39°30N 0°41W 91 F4
Chester U.K. 53°12N 2°53W 66 D5
Chester Calif., U.S.A. 40°19N 121°14W 168 F3
Chester Ga., U.S.A. 32°24N 83°9W 178 C6
Chester Ill., U.S.A. 37°55N 89°49W 172 G9
Chester Mont., U.S.A. 48°31N 110°58W 168 B9
Chester Pa., U.S.A. 39°51N 75°22W 173 F16
Chester S.C., U.S.A. 34°43N 81°12W 177 D14
Chester Vt., U.S.A. 43°16N 72°36W 175 C12
Chester W. Va., U.S.A. 40°37N 80°34W 174 F4
Chester-le-Street U.K. 54°51N 1°34W 66 C6
Chesterfield U.K. 53°15N 1°25W 66 D6
Chesterfield, Îs. N. Cal. 19°52S 158°15E 147 C8
Chesterfield Inlet
 Canada 63°30N 90°45W 160 E13
Chesterton Ra.
 Australia 25°30S 147°27E 151 D4
Chesterton Range △
 Australia 26°16S 147°22E 151 D4
Chestertown U.S.A. 43°40N 73°48W 175 C11
Chesterville Canada 45°6N 75°14W 175 A9
Chesuncook L. U.S.A. 46°0N 69°21W 173 C19
Chetamale India 10°43N 92°33E 127 J11
Chéticamp Canada 46°37N 60°59W 165 C7
Chetlat I. India 11°42N 72°42E 127 J1
Chetrosu Moldova 48°5N 27°54E 81 B12
Chetumal Mexico 18°30N 88°20W 181 D7
Chetumal, B. de
 Cent. Amer. 18°40N 88°10W 181 D7
Chetwynd Canada 55°45N 121°36W 162 B4
Cheung Chau China 22°13N 114°1E 111 a
Chevanceaux France 45°18N 0°14W 72 C3
Cheviot, The U.K. 55°29N 2°9W 66 B5
Cheviot Hills U.K. 55°20N 2°30W 66 B5
Cheviot Ra. Australia 25°20S 143°45E 150 D3
Chew Bahir Ethiopia 4°40N 36°50E 131 G2
Chewelah U.S.A. 48°17N 117°43W 168 B5
Chewore △ Zimbabwe 16°0S 29°52E 143 F2
Cheyenne Okla., U.S.A. 35°37N 99°40W 176 D5
Cheyenne Wyo.,
 U.S.A. 41°8N 104°49W 168 F11
Cheyenne → U.S.A. 44°41N 101°18W 172 C3
Cheyenne Wells
 U.S.A. 38°49N 102°21W 168 G12
Cheyne B. Australia 34°35S 118°50E 149 F2
Cheyur India 12°21N 80°0E 127 H5
Chhabra India 24°40N 76°54E 124 G7
Chhaktala India 22°6N 74°11E 124 H6
Chhapra India 25°48N 84°44E 125 G11
Chhata India 27°42N 77°30E 124 F7
Chhatarpur Jharkhand,
 India 24°23N 84°11E 125 G11
Chhatarpur Mad. P.,
 India 24°55N 79°35E 125 G8
Chhatrapur India 20°47N 85°40E 126 E7
Chhattisgarh □ India 22°0N 82°0E 125 J10
Chhep Cambodia 13°45N 105°24E 120 F5
Chhindwara Mad. P.,
 India 23°3N 79°29E 125 H8
Chhindwara Mad. P.,
 India 22°2N 78°59E 125 H8
Chhlong Cambodia 12°15N 105°58E 121 F5
Chhota Tawa → India 22°14N 76°36E 124 H7
Chhoti Kali Sindh →
 India 24°2N 75°31E 124 G6
Chhuikhadan India 21°32N 80°59E 125 J9
Chhuk Cambodia 10°46N 104°28E 121 G5
Chi → Thailand 15°11N 104°43E 120 E5
Chi Thanh Vietnam 13°17N 109°16E 120 F7
Chiai Taiwan 23°29N 120°25E 117 F13
Chiali Taiwan 23°29N 120°9E 117 F13
Chianciano Terme Italy 43°2N 11°49E 93 E8
Chiang Dao, Doi
 Thailand 19°23N 98°54E 120 C2
Chiang Kham Thailand 19°32N 100°18E 120 C3
Chiang Khan Thailand 17°52N 101°36E 120 D3
Chiang Khong
 Thailand 20°17N 100°24E 116 G3
Chiang Mai Thailand 18°47N 98°59E 120 C2
Chiang Rai Thailand 19°52N 99°50E 120 C2
Chiang Saen Thailand 20°16N 100°5E 116 G3
Chianti Italy 43°32N 11°26E 93 E8
Chiapa de Corzo Mexico 16°42N 93°0W 181 D6
Chiapas □ Mexico 16°30N 92°30W 181 D6
Chiapas, Sa. Madre de
 Mexico 15°40N 93°0W 181 D6
Chiaramonte Gulfi Italy 37°1N 14°42E 95 F7
Chiaravalle Italy 43°36N 13°19E 93 E10

Chiaravalle Centrale
 Italy 38°41N 16°25E 95 D9
Chiari Italy 45°32N 9°56E 92 C6
Chiatura Georgia 42°15N 43°17E 87 J6
Chiautla de Tapia
 Mexico 18°18N 98°36W 181 D5
Chiávari Italy 44°19N 9°19E 92 D6
Chiavenna Italy 46°19N 9°24E 92 B6
Chiba Japan 35°30N 140°7E 113 G10
Chiba □ Japan 35°30N 140°20E 113 G10
Chibabava Mozam. 20°17S 33°35E 145 B5
Chibemba Cunene, Angola 15°48S 14°8E 141 H2
Chibemba Huila, Angola 16°20S 15°20E 144 A2
Chibi Zimbabwe 20°18S 30°25E 145 B5
Chibia Angola 15°10S 13°42E 141 H2
Chibougamau Canada 49°56N 74°24W 164 C5
Chibougamau, L.
 Canada 49°50N 74°20W 164 C5
Chibuk Nigeria 10°52N 12°50E 139 C7
Chibuto Mozam. 24°40S 33°33E 145 B5
Chic-Chocs, Mts.
 Canada 48°55N 66°0W 165 C6
Chicacole = Srikakulam
 India 18°14N 83°58E 126 E6
Chicago U.S.A. 41°52N 87°38W 172 E10
Chicago Heights
 U.S.A. 41°30N 87°38W 172 E10
Chichagof I. U.S.A. 57°30N 135°30W 160 F4
Chichaoua Morocco 31°32N 8°44W 136 B2
Chichawatni Pakistan 30°32N 72°42E 124 D5
Chichén-Itzá Mexico 20°37N 88°35W 181 C7
Chicheng China 40°55N 115°55E 114 D8
Chichester U.K. 50°50N 0°47W 67 G7
Chichester Ra.
 Australia 22°12S 119°15E 148 D2
Chichibu Japan 35°59N 139°10E 113 F9
Chichibu-Tama-Kai △
 Japan 35°52N 138°42E 113 G9
Ch'ich'ihaerh = Qiqihar
 China 47°26N 124°0E 111 B13
Chicholi India 22°1N 77°40E 124 H8
Chickasaw △ U.S.A. 34°26N 97°0W 176 D6
Chickasha U.S.A. 35°3N 97°58W 176 D6
Chiclana de la Frontera
 Spain 36°26N 6°9W 89 J4
Chiclayo Peru 6°42S 79°50W 188 B2
Chico U.S.A. 39°44N 121°50W 170 F5
Chico → Chubut,
 Argentina 44°0S 67°0W 192 B3
Chico → Santa Cruz,
 Argentina 50°0S 68°30W 192 D3
Chicoa Mozam. 15°36S 32°20E 143 F3
Chicomo Mozam. 24°31S 34°6E 145 B5
Chicomostoc Mexico 22°28N 102°46W 180 C4
Chicontepec Mexico 20°58N 98°10W 181 C5
Chicopee U.S.A. 42°9N 72°37W 175 D12
Chicoutimi Canada 48°28N 71°5W 165 C5
Chicualacuala Mozam. 22°6S 31°42E 145 B5
Chidambaram India 11°20N 79°45E 127 J4
Chidenguele Mozam. 24°55S 34°11E 145 B5
Chidley, C. Canada 60°23N 64°26W 161 E14
Chiducuane Mozam. 24°35S 34°25E 145 B5
Chiede Angola 17°15S 16°22E 144 A2
Chiefland U.S.A. 29°29N 82°52W 179 F7
Chiefs Pt. Canada 44°41N 81°18W 174 B3
Chiem Hoa Vietnam 22°12N 105°17E 120 A5
Chiemsee Germany 47°53N 12°28E 77 H8
Chiengi Zambia 8°45S 29°10E 143 D2
Chiengmai = Chiang Mai
 Thailand 18°47N 98°59E 120 C2
Chienti → Italy 43°18N 13°45E 93 E10
Chieri Italy 45°1N 7°49E 92 C4
Chiers → France 49°39N 4°59E 71 C11
Chiesa in Valmalenco
 Italy 46°16N 9°51E 92 B6
Chiese → Italy 45°8N 10°25E 92 C7
Chieti Italy 42°21N 14°10E 93 F11
Chifeng China 42°18N 118°58E 115 C10
Chigirin Ukraine 49°4N 32°38E 85 H7
Chignecto B. Canada 45°30N 64°40W 165 C7
Chiguana Bolivia 21°0S 67°58W 190 A2
Chigwell U.K. 51°37N 0°6E 67 F8
Chihli, G. of = Bo Hai
 China 39°0N 119°0E 115 E10
Chihuahua Mexico 28°38N 106°5W 180 B3
Chihuahua □ Mexico 28°30N 106°0W 180 B3
Chiili = Shieli
 Kazakhstan 44°20N 66°15E 109 E7
Chik Bollapur India 13°25N 77°45E 127 H3
Chikalda India 21°24N 77°19E 126 D3
Chikhli Andhra, India 20°45N 73°4E 126 C1
Chikhli Maharashtra,
 India 19°51N 76°35E 126 D3
Chikkamagaluru India 13°15N 75°45E 127 H2
Chikodi India 16°26N 74°38E 127 F2
Chikwawa Malawi 16°2S 34°50E 143 F3
Chilanga Zambia 15°33S 28°16E 143 F2
Chilapa Mexico 17°36N 99°10W 181 D5
Chilas Pakistan 35°25N 74°5E 125 B6
Chilaw Sri Lanka 7°30N 79°50E 127 L4
Chilcotin → Canada 51°44N 122°23W 162 C4
Childers Australia 25°15S 152°17E 151 D5
Childersburg U.S.A. 33°16N 86°21W 178 B3
Childress U.S.A. 34°25N 100°13W 176 D4
Chile ■ S. Amer. 35°0S 72°0W 190 D1
Chile Chico Chile 46°33S 71°44W 192 C2
Chile Rise Pac. Oc. 38°0S 92°0W 157 L18
Chilecito Argentina 29°10S 67°30W 190 B2
Chilete Peru 7°10S 78°50W 188 B2
Chilia, Brațul →
 Romania 45°14N 29°42E 81 E14
Chilik = Shelek
 Kazakhstan 43°33N 78°17E 109 E9
Chililabombwe Zambia 12°18S 27°43E 143 E2
Chilim Pakistan 35°5N 75°5E 125 B6
Chilin = Jilin China 43°44N 126°30E 115 C14
Chiliomodi Greece 37°48N 22°51E 98 D4
Chilka L. India 19°40N 85°25E 126 D7
Chilko → Canada 52°0N 123°40W 162 C4
Chilko L. Canada 51°20N 124°10W 162 C4
Chillagoe Australia 17°7S 144°33E 150 B3
Chillán Chile 36°40S 72°10W 190 D1
Chillicothe Ill., U.S.A. 40°55N 89°29W 172 E8
Chillicothe Mo., U.S.A. 39°48N 93°33W 172 F7
Chillicothe Ohio,
 U.S.A. 39°20N 82°59W 173 F12
Chilliwack Canada 49°10N 121°54W 162 D4
Chilo India 27°25N 73°32E 124 F5
Chiloane, I. Mozam. 20°40S 34°55E 145 B6

Chiloé, I. de *Chile* 42°30S 73°50W **192** B2
Chiloé △ *Chile* 42°11S 73°59W **192** B2
Chilpancingo *Mexico* 17°33N 99°30W **181** D5
Chiltern *Australia* 36°10S 146°36E **153** D7
Chiltern Hills *U.K.* 51°40N 0°53W **67** F7
Chilton *U.S.A.* 44°2N 88°10W **172** C9
Chilubi *Zambia* 11°5S 29°58E **143** E2
Chilubula *Zambia* 10°14S 30°51E **143** E3
Chilumba *Malawi* 10°28S 34°12E **143** E3
Chilung *Taiwan* 25°3N 121°45E **117** E13
Chilwa, L. *Malawi* 15°15S 35°40E **143** F4
Chimaltitán *Mexico* 22°22N 102°12E **180** D4
Chimán *Panama* 8°45N 78°40W **182** E4
Chimanimani *Zimbabwe* 19°48S 32°52E **145** A5
Chimanimani △
  Zimbabwe 19°48S 33°0E **145** A5
Chimay *Belgium* 50°3N 4°20E **69** D4
Chimayo *U.S.A.* 36°0N 105°56W **169** J11
Chimba *Zambia* 9°54S 31°28E **143** D3
Chimbarazo *Ecuador* 1°29S 78°55W **186** D3
Chimbote *Peru* 9°0S 78°35W **186** E2
Chimboy *Uzbekistan* 42°57N 59°47E **108** D5
Chimkent = Shymkent
  Kazakhstan 42°18N 69°36E **109** D7
Chimoio *Mozam.* 19°4S 33°30E **143** F3
Chimpembe *Zambia* 9°31S 29°33E **143** D2
Chimur *India* 20°30N 79°23E **126** D4
Chin □ *Myanmar* 22°0N 93°0E **123** H18
Chin Hills *Myanmar* 22°30N 93°30E **123** H18
Chin Ling Shan = Qinling Shandi
  China 33°50N 108°10E **114** H5
China *Mexico* 25°42N 99°14W **181** B5
China ■ *Asia* 30°0N 110°0E **111** E11
China, Great Plain of
  Asia 35°0N 115°0E **102** E13
China Lake *U.S.A.* 35°44N 117°37W **171** K9
Chinan = Jinan *China* 36°38N 117°1E **114** F9
Chinandega *Nic.* 12°35N 87°12W **182** D2
Chinati Peak *U.S.A.* 29°57N 104°29W **176** G2
Chincha Alta *Peru* 13°25S 76°7W **188** F3
Chinchaga → *Canada* 58°53N 118°20W **162** B5
Chincheros *Peru* 13°30S 73°44W **188** C3
Chinchilla *Australia* 26°45S 150°38E **151** D5
Chinchilla de Monte Aragón
  Spain 38°53N 1°40W **91** G3
Chincholi *India* 17°28N 77°26E **126** E3
Chinchorro, Banco
  Mexico 18°35N 87°22W **181** D7
Chinchou = Jinzhou
  China 41°5N 121°3E **115** D11
Chincoteague *U.S.A.* 37°56N 75°23W **173** G16
Chinde *Mozam.* 18°35S 36°30E **143** F4
Chindwin →
  Myanmar 21°26N 95°15E **123** J19
Chineni *India* 33°2N 75°15E **125** C6
Chinga *Mozam.* 15°13S 38°35E **143** F4
Chingola *Zambia* 12°31S 27°53E **143** E2
Chingole *Malawi* 13°4S 34°17E **143** E3
Ch'ingtao = Qingdao
  China 36°5N 120°20E **115** F11
Chinguetti *Mauritania* 20°25N 12°24W **134** D3
Chingune *Mozam.* 20°33S 34°58E **145** B5
Chinhanguanine
  Mozam. 25°21S 32°30E **145** C5
Chinhoyi *Zimbabwe* 17°20S 30°8E **143** F3
Chiniot *Pakistan* 31°45N 73°0E **124** D5
Chinipas *Mexico* 27°23N 108°32W **180** B3
Chinji *Pakistan* 32°42N 72°22E **124** C5
Chinju = Jinju
  S. Korea 35°12N 128°2E **115** G15
Chinkapook *Australia* 35°11S 142°57E **152** C5
Chinko → *C.A.R.* 4°50N 23°53E **140** D4
Chinle *U.S.A.* 36°9N 109°33W **169** H9
Chinmen *Taiwan* 24°26N 118°19E **117** E12
Chinmen Tao *Taiwan* 24°26N 118°23E **117** E12
Chinnamanur *India* 9°50N 77°24E **127** K3
Chinnampo = Namp'o
  N. Korea 38°52N 125°10E **115** E13
Chino *Japan* 35°59N 138°9E **113** G9
Chino *U.S.A.* 34°1N 117°41W **171** L9
Chino Valley *U.S.A.* 34°45N 112°27W **169** J7
Chinon *France* 47°10N 0°15E **70** E7
Chinook *U.S.A.* 48°35N 109°14W **168** B9
Chinook Trough
  Pac. Oc. 44°0N 175°0W **156** C10
Chinsali *Zambia* 10°30S 32°2E **143** E3
Chinsura = Chunchura
  India 22°53N 88°27E **125** H13
Chintalapudi *India* 17°4N 80°59E **126** F5
Chintamani *India* 13°26N 78°3E **127** H4
Chióggia *Italy* 45°13N 12°17E **93** C9
Chios *Greece* 38°27N 26°9E **99** C8
Chipata *Zambia* 13°38S 32°28E **143** E3
Chiperceni *Moldova* 47°31N 28°50E **81** C13
Chipindo *Angola* 13°49S 15°48E **141** G3
Chipinge *Zimbabwe* 20°13S 32°28E **143** G3
Chipinge △ *Zimbabwe* 20°14S 33°0E **143** G3
Chipiona *Spain* 36°44N 6°26W **89** J4
Chipley *U.S.A.* 30°47N 85°32W **178** F4
Chiplun *India* 17°31N 73°34E **126** F1
Chipman *Canada* 46°6N 65°53W **165** C6
Chipoka *Malawi* 13°57S 34°28E **143** E3
Chippenham *U.K.* 51°27N 2°6W **67** F5
Chippewa → *U.S.A.* 44°25N 92°5W **172** C7
Chippewa Falls *U.S.A.* 44°56N 91°24W **172** C8
Chipping Norton *U.K.* 51°56N 1°32W **67** F6
Chiprovtsi *Bulgaria* 43°24N 22°52E **96** C6
Chiputneticook Lakes
  N. Amer. 45°35N 67°35W **173** C20
Chiquián *Peru* 10°10S 77°0W **188** C2
Chiquibul △ *Belize* 16°49N 88°52W **182** C2
Chiquimula *Guatemala* 14°51N 89°37W **182** D2
Chiquinquira *Colombia* 5°37N 73°50W **186** B4
Chir → *Russia* 48°30N 43°0E **87** F6
Chirala *India* 15°50N 80°26E **127** E5
Chiramba *Mozam.* 16°55S 34°39E **143** F3
Chirawa *India* 28°14N 75°42E **124** E6
Chirchiq *Uzbekistan* 41°29N 69°35E **109** D7
Chiredzi *Zimbabwe* 21°0S 31°38E **145** C5
Chiricahua △ *U.S.A.* 32°0N 109°20W **169** K9
Chiricahua Peak
  U.S.A. 31°51N 109°18W **169** L9
Chirikof I. *U.S.A.* 55°50N 155°40W **166** D8
Chiriquí, G. de *Panama* 8°0N 82°10W **182** E3
Chiriquí, L. de *Panama* 9°10N 82°0W **182** E3
Chirivira Falls
  Zimbabwe 21°10S 32°12E **143** G3
Chirmiri *India* 23°15N 82°20E **125** H10
Chirnogi *Romania* 44°7N 26°32E **81** F11
Chirpan *Bulgaria* 42°10N 25°19E **97** D9

Chirripó Grande, Cerro
  Costa Rica 9°29N 83°29W **182** E3
Chirundu *Zimbabwe* 16°3S 28°50E **145** A4
Chisamba *Zambia* 14°55S 28°20E **143** E2
Chisapani *Nepal* 28°37N 81°16E **125** E9
Chisasibi *Canada* 53°50N 79°0W **164** B4
Ch'ishan *Taiwan* 22°44N 120°31E **117** F13
Chisholm *Canada* 54°55N 114°10W **162** C6
Chisholm *U.S.A.* 47°29N 92°53W **172** B7
Chishtian Mandi
  Pakistan 29°50N 72°55E **124** E5
Chishui *China* 28°30N 105°42E **116** D5
Chishui He → *China* 28°49N 105°50E **116** C5
Chisimaio = Kismaayo
  Somalia 0°22S 42°32E **131** H3
Chisimba Falls *Zambia* 10°12S 30°56E **143** E3
Chişinău *Moldova* 47°2N 28°50E **81** C13
Chişinău ✈ (KIV)
  Moldova 47°3N 28°46E **81** C13
Chişineu Criş *Romania* 46°32N 21°37E **80** D6
Chisone → *Italy* 44°49N 7°25E **92** D4
Chisos Mts. *U.S.A.* 29°5N 103°15W **176** G3
Chistopol *Russia* 55°25N 50°38E **86** C10
Chita *Russia* 52°0N 113°35E **111** A11
Chitapur *India* 17°10N 77°5E **126** F3
Chitipa *Malawi* 9°41S 33°19E **143** D3
Chitose *Japan* 42°49N 141°39E **112** C10
Chitradurga *India* 14°14N 76°24E **127** G3
Chitrakot *India* 19°10N 81°40E **126** E5
Chitral *Pakistan* 35°50N 71°56E **128** B7
Chitravati → *India* 14°45N 78°15E **127** G4
Chitré *Panama* 7°59N 80°27W **182** E3
Chittagong *Bangla.* 22°19N 91°48E **125** H17
Chittagong □ *Bangla.* 24°5N 91°0E **123** G17
Chittaurgarh *India* 24°52N 74°38E **124** G6
Chittoor *India* 13°15N 79°5E **127** H4
Chittur *India* 10°40N 76°45E **127** J3
Chitungwiza *Zimbabwe* 18°0S 31°6E **143** F3
Chiusi *Italy* 43°1N 11°57E **93** E8
Chiva *Spain* 39°27N 0°41W **91** F4
Chivasso *Italy* 45°11N 7°53E **92** C4
Chivay *Peru* 15°40S 71°33W **188** D3
Chive *Bolivia* 12°23S 68°35W **188** C4
Chivhu *Zimbabwe* 19°2S 30°52E **143** F3
Chivilcoy *Argentina* 34°55S 60°0W **190** C4
Chiwanda *Tanzania* 11°23S 34°55E **143** E3
Chixi *China* 22°0N 112°58E **117** G9
Chizarira △ *Zimbabwe* 17°44S 27°52E **143** F2
Chizarira Ra. *Zimbabwe* 17°36S 27°45E **143** F2
Chizela *Zambia* 13°8S 25°0E **143** E2
Chkalov = Orenburg
  Russia 51°45N 55°6E **108** B5
Chkolovsk *Russia* 56°50N 43°10E **86** B6
Chloride *U.S.A.* 35°25N 114°12W **171** K12
Chlumec nad Cidlinou
  Czechia 50°9N 15°29E **78** A8
Chmielnik *Poland* 50°37N 20°43E **83** H7
Cho-do *N. Korea* 38°30N 124°40E **115** E13
Cho Phuoc Hai
  Vietnam 10°26N 107°18E **121** G6
Choa Chu Kang
  Singapore 1°22N 103°41E **121** d
Choba △ *Botswana* 18°37S 24°23E **144** A4
Chocianów *Poland* 51°27N 15°55E **83** G2
Chociwel *Poland* 53°29N 15°21E **82** E2
Chocolate Mts.
  U.S.A. 33°15N 115°15W **171** M11
Choctawhatchee →
  U.S.A. 30°25N 86°8W **178** E3
Choctawhatchee B.
  U.S.A. 30°20N 86°20W **179** E3
Chodavaram *Andhra Pradesh,
  India* 17°50N 82°57E **126** F6
Chodavaram *Andhra Pradesh,
  India* 17°27N 81°46E **126** F5
Chodecz *Poland* 52°24N 19°2E **83** F6
Chodov *Czechia* 50°15N 12°45E **78** A5
Chodziez *Poland* 52°58N 16°58E **83** F3
Choele Choel *Argentina* 39°11S 65°40W **192** A3
Choghā Zanbil *Iran* 32°1N 48°32E **129** C6
Choghā Zanbil *St. Lucia* 13°47N 61°3W **183** f
Choiseul *Solomon Is.* 7°0S 156°40E **147** B8
Choix *Mexico* 26°43N 108°17W **180** B3
Chojna *Poland* 52°58N 14°25E **83** F1
Chojnice *Poland* 53°42N 17°32E **82** E4
Chojnów *Poland* 51°18N 15°58E **83** G2
Chokai-San *Japan* 39°6N 140°3E **112** E10
Choke Canyon Res.
  U.S.A. 28°30N 98°20W **176** G5
Chokurdakh *Russia* 70°38N 147°55E **107** B15
Chokwé *Mozam.* 24°32S 32°59E **145** B5
Cholame *U.S.A.* 35°44N 120°18W **170** K6
Cholet *France* 47°4N 0°52W **70** E6
Cholguan *Chile* 37°10S 72°3W **190** D1
Choloma *Honduras* 15°37N 87°57W **182** C2
Cholpon-Ata *Kyrgyzstan* 42°40N 77°0E **109** D9
Choluteca *Honduras* 13°20N 87°14W **182** D2
Choluteca → *Honduras* 13°0N 87°20W **182** D2
Chom Bung *Thailand* 13°37N 99°36E **120** F2
Chom Thong *Thailand* 18°25N 98°41E **120** C2
Choma *Zambia* 16°48S 26°59E **143** F2
Chomolungma = Everest, Mt.
  Nepal 28°5N 86°58E **125** E12
Chomun *India* 27°15N 75°40E **124** F6
Chomutov *Czechia* 50°28N 13°23E **78** A6
Chon Buri *Thailand* 13°21N 101°1E **120** F3
Chon Thanh *Vietnam* 11°24N 106°36E **121** G6
Chone *Ecuador* 0°40S 80°0W **186** D3
Chong Kai *Cambodia* 13°57N 103°35E **120** F4
Chong Mek *Thailand* 15°10N 105°27E **120** E5
Chong Phangan *Thailand* 9°39N 100°0E **121** b
Chong Samui *Thailand* 9°38N 99°55E **121** b
Chongde *China* 30°32N 120°26E **117** B13
Ch'ongjin *N. Korea* 41°47N 129°50E **115** D15
Chongli *China* 40°58N 115°15E **114** D8
Chongming *China* 31°38N 121°25E **117** B13
Chongming Dao
  China 31°40N 121°30E **117** B13
Chongoni Rock Art
  Malawi 14°17S 34°16E **143** E3
Chongoyape *Peru* 6°35S 79°25W **188** B2
Ch'ŏngp'yŏng
  N. Korea 39°47N 127°23E **115** E14
Chongqing *Chongqing,
  China* 29°35N 106°25E **116** C6
Chongqing *Sichuan,
  China* 30°38N 103°40E **116** B4
Chongqing □ *China* 30°0N 108°0E **116** C6
Chongqing Jiangbei Int. ✈ (CKG)
  China 29°35N 106°38E **116** C6

Chongqing Shi □ *China* 30°0N 108°0E **116** C6
Chongren *China* 27°46N 116°3E **117** D11
Chonguene *Mozam.* 25°3S 33°49E **145** C5
Chongwe *Zambia* 15°21S 28°42E **143** F2
Chonju *S. Korea* 35°50N 127°4E **115** G14
Chongzuo *China* 22°23N 107°20E **116** F6
Chonogol *Mongolia* 45°54N 115°22E **114** B8
Chonos, Arch. de los
  Chile 45°0S 75°0W **192** C2
Chop *Ukraine* 48°26N 22°12E **80** B7
Chopda *India* 21°20N 75°15E **126** D2
Chopim → *Brazil* 25°35S 53°5W **191** B5
Chor *Pakistan* 25°31N 69°46E **124** G3
Chora *Greece* 37°3N 21°42E **98** D3
Chora Sfakion *Greece* 35°15N 24°9E **101** D6
Chorbat La *India* 34°42N 76°37E **125** B7
Chorley *U.K.* 53°39N 2°38W **66** D5
Chorna *Ukraine* 47°36N 29°20E **81** C14
Chornobyl *Ukraine* 51°20N 30°15E **75** C16
Chornomorske *Ukraine* 45°31N 32°40E **85** K7
Chorolque, Cerro
  Bolivia 20°59S 66°5W **190** A2
Choroszcz *Poland* 53°10N 22°59E **83** E9
Chorregon *Australia* 22°40S 143°32E **150** C3
Chorro el Indio △
  Venezuela 7°43N 72°9W **183** E5
Chortkiv *Ukraine* 49°2N 25°46E **75** D13
Chorzele *Poland* 53°15N 20°55E **83** E7
Chorzów *Poland* 50°18N 18°57E **83** H5
Chos-Malal *Argentina* 37°20S 70°15W **190** D1
Ch'osan *N. Korea* 40°50N 125°47E **115** D13
Choszczno *Poland* 53°7N 15°25E **82** E2
Chota *Peru* 6°33S 78°39W **188** B2
Choteau *U.S.A.* 47°49N 112°11W **168** C7
Chotěboř *Czechia* 49°43N 15°40E **78** B8
Chotila *India* 22°23N 71°15E **124** H4
Chotta Udepur *India* 22°19N 74°1E **124** H6
Chowchilla *U.S.A.* 37°7N 120°16W **170** H6
Choybalsan *Mongolia* 48°4N 114°30E **111** B11
Choyr *Mongolia* 46°24N 108°30E **111** B10
Chrisoupoli *Greece* 40°58N 24°42E **97** F8
Chríssi = Gaidouronísi
  Greece 34°53N 25°41E **101** E7
Christchurch *N.Z.* 43°33S 172°47E **155** D7
Christchurch *U.K.* 50°44N 1°47W **67** G6
Christian I. *Canada* 44°50N 80°12W **174** B4
Christian Sd. *U.S.A.* 55°56N 134°40W **167** D13
Christiana *Greece* 36°14N 25°13E **99** E7
Christiana *S. Africa* 27°52S 25°8E **144** C4
Christiansfeld *Denmark* 55°21N 9°29E **63** J3
Christiansted
  U.S. Virgin Is. 17°45N 64°42W **183** C7
Christie B. *Canada* 62°32N 111°10W **163** A6
Christina → *Canada* 56°40N 111°3W **163** B6
Christmas Cr. →
  Australia 18°29S 125°23E **148** C4
Christmas I. = Kiritimati
  Kiribati 1°58N 157°27W **157** G12
Christmas I. *Ind. Oc.* 10°30S 105°40E **146** F9
Christopher, L.
  Australia 24°49S 127°42E **149** D4
Chrudim *Czechia* 49°58N 15°43E **78** B8
Chrzanów *Poland* 50°10N 19°21E **83** H6
Chtimba *Malawi* 10°35S 34°13E **143** E3
Chū = Shū *Kazakhstan* 43°36N 73°42E **109** D8
Chū → Shū →
  Kazakhstan 45°0N 67°44E **109** D7
Chu → *Vietnam* 19°53N 105°45E **120** C5
Chu Lai *Vietnam* 15°28N 108°45E **120** E7
Chu Mom Ray △
  Vietnam 14°29N 107°38E **120** E6
Chu Se *Vietnam* 13°40N 108°8E **120** E7
Chuadanga *Bangla.* 23°38N 88°51E **125** H13
Chuak, Ko *Thailand* 9°28N 99°41E **121** b
Ch'uanchou = Quanzhou
  China 24°55N 118°34E **117** E12
Chuankou *China* 34°20N 110°59E **114** G6
Chubbuck *U.S.A.* 42°55N 112°28W **168** E7
Chūbu □ *Japan* 36°45N 137°30E **113** F8
Chūbu-Sangaku △
  Japan 36°30N 137°40E **113** F8
Chubut □ *Argentina* 43°30S 69°0W **192** B3
Chubut → *Argentina* 43°20S 65°5W **192** B3
Chuçand = Khŭjand
  Tajikistan 40°17N 69°37E **109** D7
Chuchi L. *Canada* 55°12N 124°30W **162** B4
Chuda *India* 22°29N 71°41E **124** H4
Chudovo *Russia* 59°10N 31°41E **84** C6
Chudskoye, Ozero
  Russia 58°13N 27°30E **84** G5
Chugach Mts. *U.S.A.* 60°45N 147°0W **166** C10
Chūgoku □ *Japan* 35°0N 133°0E **113** G6
Chūgoku-Sanchi *Japan* 35°0N 133°0E **113** G6
Chuguev = Chuhuyiv
  Ukraine 49°55N 36°45E **85** H9
Chugwater *U.S.A.* 41°46N 104°50W **168** F11
Chuhuyiv *Ukraine* 49°55N 36°45E **85** H9
Chuka *Kenya* 0°20S 37°39E **142** C4
Chukchi Plateau *Arctic* 78°0N 165°0W **54** B17
Chukchi Sea *Russia* 68°0N 175°0W **107** C19
Chukotskiy, Mys
  Russia 64°14N 173°8W **166** C5
Chukotskiy Poluostrov
  Russia 66°0N 174°0W **166** B5
Chukotskoye Nagorye
  Russia 68°0N 175°0E **107** C18
Chula *U.S.A.* 31°33N 83°32W **178** D6
Chula Vista *U.S.A.* 32°38N 117°5W **171** N9
Chulband → *India* 20°40N 79°54E **126** D5
Chulucanas *Peru* 5°8S 80°10W **188** B1
Chulumani *Bolivia* 16°24S 67°31W **188** D4
Chulym → *Russia* 57°43N 83°51E **106** D9
Chum Phae *Thailand* 16°40N 102°6E **120** D4
Chum Saeng *Thailand* 15°55N 100°15E **120** E3
Chuma *Bolivia* 15°25S 68°56W **188** D4
Chumar *India* 32°40N 78°35E **125** C8
Chumbicha *Argentina* 29°0S 66°10W **190** B2
Chumerna *Bulgaria* 42°45N 25°55E **97** D9
Chumikan *Russia* 54°40N 135°10E **107** D14
Chumphon *Thailand* 10°35N 99°14E **121** G2
Chumpi *Peru* 15°4S 73°46W **188** D3
Chumuare *Mozam.* 14°31S 31°50E **143** E3
Chuna → *Russia* 57°47N 94°37E **107** D10
Chun'an *China* 29°35N 119°3E **117** C12
Chuncheon *S. Korea* 37°58N 127°44E **115** F14
Chunchura *India* 22°53N 88°27E **125** H13
Chunga *Zambia* 15°0S 26°2E **143** F2
Chunggang-ŭp
  N. Korea 41°48N 126°48E **115** D14

Chunghwa *N. Korea* 38°52N 125°47E **115** E13
Chungju *S. Korea* 36°58N 127°58E **115** F14
Chungking = Chongqing
  China 29°35N 106°25E **116** C6
Chungli *Taiwan* 24°57N 121°13E **117** E13
Chungt'iaoshan = Zhongtiao
  Shan *China* 35°0N 111°10E **114** G6
Chungyang Shanmo
  Taiwan 23°10N 121°0E **117** F13
Chunian *Pakistan* 30°57N 74°0E **124** D6
Chunya *Tanzania* 8°30S 33°27E **143** D3
Chunyang *China* 43°38N 129°23E **115** C15
Chupara Pt.
  Trin. & Tob. 10°49N 61°22W **187** K15
Chuquibamba *Peru* 15°47S 72°44W **188** D3
Chuquibambilla *Peru* 14°7S 72°41W **188** D3
Chuquicamata *Chile* 22°15S 69°0W **190** A2
Chur *Switz.* 46°52N 9°32E **77** J5
Churachandpur *India* 24°20N 93°40E **123** G18
Church Stretton *U.K.* 52°32N 2°48W **67** E5
Churchill *Canada* 58°47N 94°11W **163** B10
Churchill → *Man.,
  Canada* 58°47N 94°12W **163** B10
Churchill → *Nfld. & L.,
  Canada* 53°19N 60°10W **165** B7
Churchill, C. *Canada* 58°46N 93°12W **163** B10
Churchill Falls *Canada* 53°36N 64°19W **165** B7
Churchill L. *Canada* 55°55N 108°20W **163** B7
Churchill Pk. *Canada* 58°10N 125°10W **162** B3
Churki *India* 23°50N 83°12E **125** H10
Churu *India* 28°20N 74°50E **124** E6
Churún Merú = Angel Falls
  Venezuela 5°57N 62°30W **186** B6
Chushal *India* 33°40N 78°40E **125** C8
Chuska Mts. *U.S.A.* 36°15N 108°50W **169** H9
Chusovoy *Russia* 58°22N 57°50E **106** D6
Chuspipata *Bolivia* 16°18S 67°48W **188** D4
Chust *Uzbekistan* 41°0N 71°13E **109** D8
Chute-aux-Outardes
  Canada 49°7N 68°24W **165** C6
Chuuk = Truk
  Micronesia 7°25N 151°46E **156** G7
Chuvash Republic = Chuvashia □
  Russia 55°30N 47°0E **86** C8
Chuvashia □ *Russia* 55°30N 47°0E **86** C8
Chuwārtah *Iraq* 35°43N 45°34E **105** C11
Chuxiong *China* 25°2N 101°28E **116** E3
Chüy □ *Kyrgyzstan* 42°55N 75°15E **109** D9
Chüy → *Kyrgyzstan* 42°25N 75°16E **109** D9
Chuzhou *China* 32°19N 118°20E **117** A12
Chynadiyeve *Ukraine* 48°29N 22°50E **80** B7
Chyulu Hills *Kenya* 2°35S 37°50E **142** C4
Ci Xian *China* 36°20N 114°25E **114** F8
Ciacova *Romania* 45°35N 21°10E **80** E6
Ciamis *Indonesia* 7°20S 108°21E **119** G13
Cianjur *Indonesia* 6°49S 107°8E **119** G12
Cianorte *Brazil* 23°37S 52°37W **191** A5
Cibola *U.S.A.* 33°17N 114°42W **171** M12
Cicero *U.S.A.* 41°51N 87°44W **172** E10
Cicero Dantas *Brazil* 10°36S 38°23W **189** E11
Cicia *Fiji* 17°45S 179°18W **154** a
Cícia *Turkey* 36°30N 34°0E **104** D5
Cidacos → *Spain* 42°21N 1°38W **90** C3
Cide *Turkey* 41°53N 33°1E **104** B5
Ciechanów *Poland* 52°52N 20°38E **83** F7
Ciechanowiec *Poland* 52°40N 22°31E **83** F9
Ciechocinek *Poland* 52°53N 18°45E **83** F5
Ciego de Ávila *Cuba* 21°50N 78°50W **182** B4
Ciénaga *Colombia* 11°1N 74°15W **186** A4
Cienfuegos *Cuba* 22°10N 80°30W **182** B3
Cierp-Gaud *France* 42°55N 0°40E **72** F4
Cíes, Is. *Spain* 42°12N 8°55W **88** C2
Cieszanów *Poland* 50°14N 23°8E **83** H10
Cieszyn *Poland* 49°45N 18°35E **83** J5
Cieza *Spain* 38°17N 1°23W **91** G3
Cifteler *Turkey* 39°22N 31°2E **104** C4
Cifuentes *Spain* 40°47N 2°37W **90** E2
Cihanbeyli *Turkey* 38°40N 32°55E **104** C5
Cihuatlán *Mexico* 19°14N 104°35W **180** D4
Cijara, Embalse de *Spain* 39°18N 4°52W **89** F6
Cijara △ *Spain* 39°18N 4°52W **89** F6
Cijulang *Indonesia* 7°42S 108°27E **119** G13
Cilacap *Indonesia* 7°43S 109°0E **119** G13
Çıldır *Turkey* 41°7N 43°8E **105** B10
Çıldır Gölü *Turkey* 41°5N 43°15E **105** B10
Cilento e Vallo di Diano △
  Italy 40°15N 15°20E **95** B8
Cili *China* 29°30N 111°8E **117** C8
Cilibia *Romania* 45°4N 27°4E **81** E12
Cilicia *Turkey* 36°30N 35°0E **104** D5
Cixerri → *Italy* 39°17N 8°59E **94** C1
Cixi *China* 30°17N 121°19E **117** B13
Cizre *Turkey* 37°19N 42°10E **105** D10
Clackmannanshire □
  U.K. 56°10N 3°43W **65** E5
Clacton-on-Sea *U.K.* 51°47N 1°11E **67** F9
Clain → *France* 46°47N 0°33E **70** F7
Claire, L. *Canada* 58°35N 112°5W **162** B6
Clairton *U.S.A.* 40°18N 79°53W **174** F5
Clairvaux-les-Lacs
  France 46°35N 5°45E **71** F12
Claise → *France* 46°56N 0°42E **72** B5
Clallam Bay *U.S.A.* 48°15N 124°16W **170** B2
Clamecy *France* 47°12N 3°31E **71** E10
Clanton *U.S.A.* 32°51N 86°38W **177** E11
Clanwilliam *S. Africa* 32°11S 18°52E **144** D2
Clara *Ireland* 53°21N 7°37W **64** C4
Claraville *U.S.A.* 35°24N 118°20W **171** K8
Clare *Australia* 33°50S 138°37E **152** B2
Clare □ *Ireland* 52°45N 9°0W **64** D3
Clare → *Ireland* 53°20N 9°2W **64** C2
Clare I. *Ireland* 53°47N 10°0W **64** C1
Claremont *Calif., U.S.A.* 34°6N 117°43W **171** L9
Claremont *N.H., U.S.A.* 43°23N 72°20W **175** D12
Claremont Pt. *Australia* 14°1S 143°41E **150** A3
Claremore *U.S.A.* 36°19N 95°36W **176** C6
Claremorris *Ireland* 53°45N 9°0W **64** C3
Clarence → *Australia* 29°25S 153°22E **153** D5
Clarence → *N.Z.* 42°10S 173°56E **155** D5
Clarence, I. *Chile* 54°0S 72°0W **192** G2
Clarence I. *Antarctica* 61°10S 54°0W **55** C18
Clarence Str. *Australia* 12°0S 131°0E **148** B5
Clarence Town
  Bahamas 23°6N 74°59W **183** B5
Clarendon *Pa., U.S.A.* 41°47N 79°6W **174** E5

Clarendon *Tex.,
  U.S.A.* 34°56N 100°53W **176** D4
Clarenville *Canada* 48°10N 54°1W **165** C9
Claresholm *Canada* 50°2N 113°33W **162** D6
Clarinda *U.S.A.* 40°44N 95°2W **172** E6
Clarington *Canada* 43°55N 78°41W **174** C6
Clarion *Iowa, U.S.A.* 42°44N 93°44W **172** D7
Clarion *Pa., U.S.A.* 41°13N 79°23W **174** E5
Clarion → *U.S.A.* 41°7N 79°41W **174** E5
Clarion Fracture Zone
  Pac. Oc. 20°0N 120°0W **158** H7
Clark *U.S.A.* 44°53N 97°44W **172** C5
Clark, Pt. *Canada* 44°4N 81°45W **174** B3
Clark Fork *U.S.A.* 48°9N 116°11W **168** B5
Clark Fork → *U.S.A.* 48°9N 116°15W **168** B5
Clarkdale *U.S.A.* 34°46N 112°3W **169** J7
Clarke City *Canada* 50°12N 66°38W **165** B6
Clarke I. *Australia* 40°32S 148°10E **151** G4
Clarke Ra. *Australia* 20°40S 148°30E **150** b
Clark's Harbour
  Canada 43°25N 65°38W **165** D6
Clarks Hill L. = J. Strom
  Thurmond L. *U.S.A.* 33°40N 82°12W **178** E7
Clarks Summit *U.S.A.* 41°30N 75°42W **175** E9
Clarksburg *U.S.A.* 39°17N 80°30W **173** F13
Clarksdale *U.S.A.* 34°12N 90°35W **177** D9
Clarkston *U.S.A.* 46°25N 117°3W **168** C5
Clarksville *Ark., U.S.A.* 35°28N 93°28W **176** D8
Clarksville *Tenn.,
  U.S.A.* 36°32N 87°21W **177** C11
Clarksville *Tex., U.S.A.* 33°37N 95°3W **176** E7
Clatskanie *U.S.A.* 46°6N 123°12W **170** D3
Claude *U.S.A.* 35°7N 101°22W **176** D4
Claveria *Phil.* 18°37N 121°4E **119** A6
Clavering Ø *Greenland* 74°15N 21°0W **57** C8
Claxton *U.S.A.* 32°10N 81°55W **178** C8
Clay *U.S.A.* 38°17N 121°10W **170** G5
Clay Center *U.S.A.* 39°23N 97°8W **172** F5
Claypool *U.S.A.* 33°25N 110°51W **169** K8
Claysburg *U.S.A.* 40°17N 78°27W **174** F6
Claysville *U.S.A.* 40°7N 80°25W **174** F4
Clayton *Canada* 45°11N 76°19W **175** A8
Clayton *Ala., U.S.A.* 31°53N 85°27W **178** E4
Clayton *N. Mex.,
  U.S.A.* 36°27N 103°11W **169** H12
Clayton *N.Y., U.S.A.* 44°14N 76°5W **175** B8
Clear, C. *Ireland* 51°25N 9°32W **64** E2
Clear, L. *Canada* 45°26N 77°12W **174** A7
Clear Hills *Canada* 56°40N 119°30W **162** B5
Clear I. *Ireland* 51°26N 9°30W **64** E2
Clear L. *U.S.A.* 39°2N 122°47W **170** F4
Clear Lake *Iowa, U.S.A.* 43°8N 93°23W **172** D7
Clear Lake *S. Dak.,
  U.S.A.* 44°45N 96°41W **172** C5
Clear Lake Res. *U.S.A.* 41°56N 121°5W **168** F3
Clearfield *Pa., U.S.A.* 41°2N 78°27W **174** E6
Clearfield *Utah, U.S.A.* 41°7N 112°2W **168** F7
Clearlake *U.S.A.* 38°57N 122°38W **170** G4
Clearwater *Canada* 51°38N 120°2W **162** C4
Clearwater *U.S.A.* 27°59N 82°48W **179** H7
Clearwater → *Alta.,
  Canada* 52°22N 114°57W **162** C6
Clearwater → *Alta.,
  Canada* 56°44N 111°23W **163** B6
Clearwater L. *Canada* 56°44N 110°53W **163** B6
Clearwater Lake △
  Canada 54°0N 101°0W **163** C8
Clearwater Mts. *U.S.A.* 46°5N 115°20W **168** C6
Clearwater River △
  Canada 56°55N 109°10W **163** B7
Cleburne *U.S.A.* 32°21N 97°23W **176** E6
Clee Hills *U.K.* 52°26N 2°35W **67** E5
Cleethorpes *U.K.* 53°33N 0°3W **66** D7
Cleeve Cloud *U.K.* 51°56N 2°0W **67** F6
Clelles *France* 44°50N 5°38E **73** D9
Clemson *U.S.A.* 34°41N 82°50W **177** D13
Clerke Reef *Australia* 17°22S 119°20E **148** C2
Clermont *Australia* 22°49S 147°39E **150** C4
Clermont *France* 49°23N 2°24E **71** C9
Clermont-en-Argonne
  France 49°5N 5°4E **71** C12
Clermont-Ferrand *France* 45°46N 3°4E **72** D7
Clermont-l'Hérault
  France 43°38N 3°26E **72** E7
Clerval *France* 47°25N 6°30E **71** E13
Clervaux *Lux.* 50°4N 6°2E **69** D6
Cles *Italy* 46°22N 11°2E **92** B8
Cleve *Australia* 33°43S 136°30E **152** B2
Clevedon *U.K.* 51°26N 2°52W **67** F5
Cleveland *Miss., U.S.A.* 33°45N 90°43W **177** E9
Cleveland *Ohio, U.S.A.* 41°29N 81°41W **174** E3
Cleveland *Okla., U.S.A.* 36°19N 96°28W **176** C6
Cleveland *Tenn.,
  U.S.A.* 35°10N 84°53W **177** D12
Cleveland *Tex., U.S.A.* 30°21N 95°5W **176** F7
Cleveland, C. *Australia* 19°11S 147°1E **150** B4
Cleveland, Mt. *U.S.A.* 48°56N 113°51W **168** B7
Cleveland Heights
  U.S.A. 41°31N 81°33W **174** E3
Clew B. *Ireland* 53°50N 9°49W **64** C2
Clewiston *U.S.A.* 26°45N 80°56W **179** H7
Clifden *Ireland* 53°29N 10°1W **64** C1
Clifden *N.Z.* 46°1S 167°42E **155** G2
Cliffdell *U.S.A.* 46°56N 121°5W **170** D5
Cliffy Hd. *Australia* 35°1S 116°29E **149** G2
Clifton *Australia* 27°59S 151°53E **153** D5
Clifton *Ariz., U.S.A.* 33°3N 109°18W **169** K9
Clifton *Colo., U.S.A.* 39°7N 108°25W **168** G9
Clifton *Tex., U.S.A.* 31°47N 97°35W **176** F6
Clifton Beach *Australia* 16°46S 145°39E **150** B4
Climax *Canada* 49°10N 108°20W **163** D7
Clinch → *U.S.A.* 35°53N 84°29W **177** D12
Clingmans Dome
  U.S.A. 35°34N 83°30W **177** D13
Clint *U.S.A.* 31°35N 106°14W **169** L10
Clinton *B.C., Canada* 51°6N 121°35W **162** C4
Clinton *Ont., Canada* 43°37N 81°32W **174** C3
Clinton *N.Z.* 46°12S 169°23E **155** G2
Clinton *Ark., U.S.A.* 35°36N 92°28W **176** D8
Clinton *Conn., U.S.A.* 41°17N 72°32W **175** E12
Clinton *Ill., U.S.A.* 40°9N 88°57W **172** E9
Clinton *Ind., U.S.A.* 39°40N 87°24W **172** F9
Clinton *Iowa, U.S.A.* 41°51N 90°12W **172** E8
Clinton *Mass., U.S.A.* 42°25N 71°41W **175** D13
Clinton *Miss., U.S.A.* 32°20N 90°20W **177** E9
Clinton *Mo., U.S.A.* 38°22N 93°46W **172** F7

Clinton N.C., U.S.A. 35°0N 78°22W **177 D15**
Clinton Okla., U.S.A. 35°31N 98°58W **176 D5**
Clinton S.C., U.S.A. 34°29N 81°53W **177 D14**
Clinton Tenn., U.S.A. 36°6N 84°8W **177 C12**
Clinton Wash., U.S.A. 47°59N 122°21W **170 C4**
Clinton, C. U.S.A. 22°30S 150°45E **150 C5**
Clinton Colden L. Canada 63°58N 107°27W **160 E10**
Clio U.S.A. 31°43N 85°37W **178 D4**
Clipperton, Î. Pac. Oc. 10°18N 109°13W **157 F17**
Clipperton Fracture Zone Pac. Oc. 19°0N 122°0W **157 G16**
Clisham U.K. 57°58N 6°49W **65 D2**
Clisson France 47°5N 1°16W **70 E5**
Clitheroe U.K. 53°53N 2°22W **66 E5**
Clive N.Z. 39°36S 176°58E **154 F5**
Clo-oose Canada 48°39N 124°49W **170 B2**
Cloates, Pt. Australia 22°43S 113°40E **148 D1**
Clocolan S. Africa 28°55S 27°34E **145 C4**
Clodomira Argentina 27°35S 64°14W **190 B3**
Cloghaneely Ireland 55°8N 8°5W **64 A3**
Clogher Hd. Ireland 53°48N 6°14W **64 C5**
Clonakilty Ireland 51°37N 8°53W **64 E3**
Clonakilty B. Ireland 51°35N 8°51W **64 E3**
Cloncurry Australia 20°40S 140°28E **150 C3**
Cloncurry Ireland 53°25N 6°48W **64 C5**
Cloncurry → Australia 18°37S 140°40E **150 B3**
Clondalkin Ireland 53°19N 6°25W **64 C5**
Clones Ireland 54°11N 7°15W **64 B4**
Clonmel Ireland 52°21N 7°42W **64 D4**
Cloppenburg Germany 52°51N 8°1E **76 C4**
Cloquet U.S.A. 46°43N 92°28W **172 B7**
Clorinda Argentina 25°16S 57°45W **190 B4**
Cloud Peak U.S.A. 44°23N 107°11W **168 D10**
Cloudcroft U.S.A. 32°58N 105°45W **169 K11**
Cloudy B. N.Z. 41°25S 174°10E **155 B9**
Cloverdale U.S.A. 38°48N 123°1W **170 G4**
Clovis Calif., U.S.A. 36°49N 119°42W **170 J7**
Clovis N. Mex., U.S.A. 34°24N 103°12W **169 J12**
Cloyes-sur-le-Loir France 48°0N 1°14E **70 E8**
Cloyne Ireland 51°51N 8°13W **64 E3**
Cluain Meala = Clonmel Ireland 52°21N 7°42W **64 D4**
Club Terrace Australia 37°35S 148°58E **153 D8**
Cluj □ Romania 46°45N 23°30E **81 D8**
Cluj-Napoca Romania 46°47N 23°38E **81 D8**
Clunes Australia 37°20S 143°45E **152 D5**
Cluny France 46°26N 4°38E **71 F11**
Cluses France 46°5N 6°35E **71 F13**
Clusone Italy 45°53N 9°57E **92 C6**
Clutha → N.Z. 46°20S 169°49E **155 G4**
Clwyd → U.K. 53°19N 3°31W **66 D4**
Clyattville U.S.A. 30°42N 83°19W **178 E6**
Clyde Canada 54°9N 113°39W **162 C6**
Clyde N.Z. 45°12S 169°20E **155 F4**
Clyde U.S.A. 43°5N 76°52W **174 C8**
Clyde → U.K. 55°55N 4°30W **65 F4**
Clyde, Firth of U.K. 55°22N 5°1W **65 F3**
Clyde River Canada 70°30N 68°30W **161 C18**
Clydebank U.K. 55°54N 4°23W **65 F4**
Clymer N.Y., U.S.A. 42°1N 79°37W **174 D5**
Clymer Pa., U.S.A. 40°40N 79°1W **174 D5**
Clyo U.S.A. 32°29N 81°16W **178 C8**
Ćmielów Poland 50°53N 21°31E **83 H8**
Côa → Portugal 41°5N 7°6W **88 D3**
Coachella U.S.A. 33°41N 116°10W **171 M10**
Coachella Canal U.S.A. 32°43N 114°57W **171 N12**
Coahoma U.S.A. 32°18N 101°18W **176 E4**
Coahuayana → Mexico 18°41N 103°45W **180 D4**
Coahuila □ Mexico 27°20N 102°0W **180 B4**
Coal → Canada 59°39N 126°57W **162 B3**
Coal I. N.Z. 46°8S 166°40E **155 G1**
Coalane Mozam. 17°48S 37°2E **143 F4**
Coalcomán Mexico 18°47N 103°9W **180 D4**
Coaldale Canada 49°45N 112°35W **162 D6**
Coalgate U.S.A. 34°32N 96°13W **176 D6**
Coalinga U.S.A. 36°9N 120°21W **170 J6**
Coalisland U.K. 54°33N 6°42W **64 B5**
Coalville U.K. 52°44N 1°23W **66 E6**
Coalville U.S.A. 40°55N 111°24W **168 F8**
Coamo Puerto Rico 18°5N 66°22W **183 d**
Coaraci Brazil 14°38S 39°32W **189 C3**
Coari Brazil 4°8S 63°7W **186 D6**
Coast Mts. Canada 55°0N 129°20W **162 C3**
Coast Ranges U.S.A. 39°0N 123°0W **170 G4**
Coatbridge U.K. 55°52N 4°6W **65 F4**
Coatepec Mexico 19°27N 96°58W **181 D5**
Coatepeque Guatemala 14°46N 91°55W **182 D1**
Coatesville U.S.A. 39°59N 75°50W **173 F16**
Coaticook Canada 45°10N 71°46W **175 A13**
Coats I. Canada 62°30N 83°0W **161 E15**
Coats Land Antarctica 77°0S 25°0W **55 D1**
Coatzacoalcos Mexico 18°7N 94°25W **181 D6**
Cobá Mexico 20°31N 87°45W **181 C7**
Cobadin Romania 44°5N 28°13E **81 F13**
Cobalt Canada 47°25N 79°42W **164 C4**
Cobán Guatemala 15°30N 90°21W **182 C1**
Çobanlar Turkey 38°41N 30°47E **99 C12**
Cobar Australia 31°27S 145°48E **153 A6**
Cobargo Australia 36°20S 149°55E **153 D8**
Cobbannah Australia 37°37S 147°13E **153 D7**
Cobberas, Mt. Australia 36°53S 148°12E **153 D8**
Cobden Australia 38°20S 143°3E **152 E5**
Cobh Ireland 51°51N 8°17W **64 E3**
Côbh, An = Cobh Ireland 51°51N 8°17W **64 E3**
Cobija Bolivia 11°0S 68°50W **186 G5**
Cobleskill U.S.A. 42°41N 74°29W **175 D10**
Coboconk Canada 44°39N 78°48W **174 B6**
Cobourg Canada 43°58N 78°10W **174 C6**
Cobourg Pen. Australia 11°20S 132°15E **148 B5**
Cobram Australia 35°54S 145°40E **153 C6**
Cóbué Mozam. 12°0S 34°58E **143 G3**
Coburg Germany 50°15N 10°58E **77 E6**
Coburg I. Canada 75°57N 79°26W **161 B16**
Coca Spain 41°13N 4°32W **88 D6**
Cocachacra Peru 17°5S 71°45W **188 D3**
Cocal Brazil 3°28S 41°34W **189 A2**
Cocanada = Kakinada India 16°57N 82°11E **126 F6**
Cocentaina Spain 38°45N 0°27W **91 G4**
Cochabamba Bolivia 17°26S 66°10W **186 G5**
Cochem Germany 50°9N 7°9E **77 E6**
Cochemane Mozam. 17°0S 32°54E **143 F3**
Cochin = Kochi India 9°58N 76°20E **127 K3**

Cochin China = Nam Phan Vietnam 10°30N 106°0E **121 G6**
Cochran Alta., Canada 51°11N 114°30W **162 C6**
Cochrane Ont., Canada 49°0N 81°0W **164 C3**
Cochrane Chile 47°15S 72°33W **192 C2**
Cochrane → Canada 59°0N 103°40W **163 B8**
Cochrane, L. Chile 47°10S 72°0W **192 C2**
Cochranton U.S.A. 41°31N 80°3W **174 E4**
Cockburn Australia 32°5S 141°0E **152 B4**
Cockburn, Canal Chile 54°30S 72°0W **192 D2**
Cockburn I. Canada 45°55N 83°22W **164 C3**
Cockburn Ra. Australia 15°46S 128°0E **148 C4**
Cockermouth U.K. 54°40N 3°22W **66 C4**
Cockklebiddy Australia 32°0S 126°3E **149 F4**
Cockpit Country, The Jamaica 18°15N 77°45W **182 a**
Coco → Cent. Amer. 15°0N 83°8W **182 D3**
Coco, I. del Pac. Oc. 5°25N 87°55W **157 G19**
Coco Channel Asia 13°45N 93°10E **127 H11**
Cocoa U.S.A. 28°21N 80°44W **179 G6**
Cocoa Beach U.S.A. 28°19N 80°37W **179 G6**
Cocobeach Gabon 0°59N 9°34E **140 D1**
Cocoparra △ Australia 34°10S 146°12E **153 C7**
Cocora Romania 44°45N 27°3E **81 F12**
Côcos Brazil 14°10S 44°33W **189 C2**
Côcos → Brazil 14°54S 44°48W **189 C2**
Cocos B. Trin. & Tob. 10°24N 61°2W **187 K15**
Cocos Basin Ind. Oc. 1°0N 94°0E **146 D8**
Cocos I. = Coco, I. del Pac. Oc. 5°25N 87°55W **157 G19**
Cocos Is. Ind. Oc. 12°10S 96°55E **146 F8**
Cocos Ridge Pac. Oc. 4°0N 88°0W **157 G19**
Cod, C. U.S.A. 42°5N 70°10W **173 D18**
Codajás Brazil 3°55S 62°0W **186 D6**
Codfish I. N.Z. 46°47S 167°38E **155 G2**
Codigoro Italy 44°49N 12°8E **93 D9**
Codó Brazil 4°30S 43°55W **189 A2**
Codogno Italy 45°9N 9°42E **92 C6**
Codróipo Italy 45°58N 13°0E **93 C10**
Codru, Munţii Romania 46°30N 22°15E **80 D7**
Cody U.S.A. 44°32N 109°3W **168 D9**
Coe Hill Canada 44°52N 77°50W **174 B7**
Coelemu Chile 36°30S 72°48W **190 D1**
Coelho Neto Brazil 4°15S 43°0W **189 A2**
Coen Australia 13°52S 143°12E **150 A3**
Coesfeld Germany 51°56N 7°10E **76 D3**
Coetivy I. Seychelles 7°8S 56°16E **146 E4**
Coeur d'Alene U.S.A. 47°41N 116°46W **168 C5**
Coeur d'Alene L. U.S.A. 47°32N 116°49W **168 C5**
Coevorden Neths. 52°40N 6°44E **69 B6**
Cofete Canary Is. 28°6N 14°23W **100 F5**
Coffeyville U.S.A. 37°2N 95°37W **172 G6**
Coffin B. Australia 34°38S 135°28E **151 E2**
Coffin Bay Australia 34°37S 135°29E **151 E2**
Coffin Bay → Australia 34°34S 135°19E **151 E2**
Coffin Bay Peninsula Australia 34°32S 135°15E **151 E2**
Coffs Harbour Australia 30°16S 153°5E **153 A10**
Cofrentes Spain 39°13N 1°5W **91 F3**
Cogâlnic = Kohylnyk → Ukraine 45°49N 29°40E **81 E14**
Cogealac Romania 44°36N 28°36E **81 F13**
Coghinas → Italy 40°55N 8°48E **94 B1**
Coghinas, L. del Italy 40°46N 9°3E **94 B2**
Cognac France 45°41N 0°20W **72 C3**
Cogne Italy 45°37N 7°21E **92 C4**
Cogolin France 43°15N 6°32E **73 E10**
Cogolludo Spain 40°59N 3°10W **90 E1**
Cohocton U.S.A. 42°30N 77°30W **174 D7**
Cohocton → U.S.A. 42°9N 77°6W **174 D7**
Cohoes U.S.A. 42°46N 73°42W **175 D11**
Cohuna Australia 35°45S 144°15E **152 C6**
Coiba, I. de Panama 7°30N 81°40W **182 E3**
Coig → Argentina 51°0S 69°10W **192 D3**
Coigeach, Rubha U.K. 58°6N 5°26W **65 D3**
Coihaique Chile 45°35S 71°45W **192 C2**
Coimbatore India 11°2N 76°59E **127 J3**
Coimbra Brazil 19°55S 57°48W **188 G7**
Coimbra Portugal 40°15N 8°27W **88 E2**
Coimbra □ Portugal 40°12N 8°25W **88 E2**
Coín Spain 36°40N 4°48W **89 J6**
Coipasa, L. de Bolivia 19°12S 68°7W **188 G4**
Coipasa, Salar de Bolivia 19°26S 68°9W **188 G4**
Cojata Peru 15°2S 69°20W **188 G5**
Cojimies Ecuador 0°20N 80°0W **186 C3**
Cojocna Romania 46°45N 23°50E **81 D8**
Cojutepeque El Salv. 13°41N 88°54W **182 D2**
Čoka Serbia 45°57N 20°12E **80 E5**
Cokeville U.S.A. 42°5N 110°57W **168 E8**
Colaba Pt. India 18°53N 72°48E **126 E1**
Colac Australia 38°21S 143°35E **152 E5**
Colachel = Kolachel India 8°10N 77°15E **127 K3**
Colán Peru 5°0S 81°0W **188 E1**
Colatina Brazil 19°32S 40°37W **189 D2**
Colbeck, C. Antarctica 77°6S 157°48W **55 D13**
Colborne Canada 44°0N 77°53W **174 C7**
Colby U.S.A. 39°24N 101°3W **172 F3**
Colca → Peru 15°55S 72°43W **186 G4**
Colca, Cañón del Peru 15°0S 72°0W **188 D3**
Colchester U.K. 51°54N 0°55E **67 F8**
Colchester U.S.A. 41°35N 72°20W **175 E12**
Cold L. Canada 54°33N 110°5W **163 C7**
Cold Lake Canada 54°27N 110°10W **163 C7**
Coldstream Canada 50°13N 119°11W **162 C5**
Coldstream U.K. 55°39N 2°15W **65 F6**
Coldwater Kans., U.S.A. 37°16N 99°20W **172 G4**
Coldwater Mich., U.S.A. 41°57N 85°0W **173 E11**
Coleambally Australia 34°49S 145°52E **153 C6**
Colebrook Australia 42°31S 147°21E **150 G4**
Colebrook U.S.A. 44°54N 71°30W **175 B13**
Coleman Canada 49°40N 114°30W **162 D6**
Coleman Fla., U.S.A. 28°48N 82°4W **179 G7**
Coleman Tex., U.S.A. 31°50N 99°26W **176 F5**
Coleman → Australia 15°6S 141°38E **150 B3**
Colenso S. Africa 28°44S 29°50E **145 D4**
Coleraine Australia 37°36S 141°40E **152 D4**
Coleraine U.K. 55°8N 6°41W **64 A5**
Coleridge, L. N.Z. 43°17S 171°30E **155 D6**
Coleroon → India 11°25N 79°50E **127 J4**
Colesberg S. Africa 30°45S 25°5E **144 D4**

Coleville U.S.A. 38°34N 119°30W **170 G7**
Colfax Calif., U.S.A. 39°6N 120°57W **170 F6**
Colfax La., U.S.A. 31°31N 92°42W **176 F8**
Colfax Wash., U.S.A. 46°53N 117°22W **168 C5**
Colhué Huapi, L. Argentina 45°30S 69°0W **192 C3**
Colibași = Mioveni Romania 44°56N 24°54E **81 F9**
Colibași Moldova 45°43N 28°11E **81 E13**
Cólico Italy 46°8N 9°22E **92 B6**
Coligny France 46°23N 5°21E **71 F12**
Coligny S. Africa 26°17S 26°15E **145 C4**
Colima Mexico 19°14N 103°43W **180 D4**
Colima □ Mexico 19°10N 104°0W **180 D4**
Colima, Nevado de Mexico 19°33N 103°38W **180 D4**
Colina Chile 33°13S 70°45W **190 C1**
Colina do Norte Guinea-Biss. 12°28N 15°0W **138 C2**
Colinas Goiás, Brazil 14°15S 48°2W **189 C1**
Colinas Maranhão, Brazil 6°0S 44°10W **189 B2**
Colindres Spain 43°24N 3°27W **88 B7**
Coll U.K. 56°39N 6°34W **65 E2**
Collahuasi Chile 21°5S 68°45W **190 A2**
Collarada, Peña Spain 42°43N 0°29W **90 C4**
Collarenebri Australia 29°33S 148°34E **151 D4**
Colle di Val d'Elsa Italy 43°25N 11°7E **92 E8**
Collécchio Italy 44°45N 10°10E **92 D7**
Colleen Bawn Zimbabwe 21°0S 29°12E **143 G2**
College U.S.A. 64°52N 147°49W **166 C10**
College Park U.S.A. 33°39N 84°27W **178 B5**
College Station U.S.A. 30°37N 96°21W **176 F6**
Collesalvetti Italy 43°34N 10°27E **92 E7**
Colli Euganei △ Italy 45°18N 11°43E **93 C8**
Collie N.S.W., Australia 31°41S 148°18E **153 A8**
Collie W. Austral., Australia 33°22S 116°8E **149 F2**
Collier B. Australia 16°10S 124°15E **148 C3**
Collier Ra. Australia 24°45S 119°10E **149 D2**
Collier Range △ Australia 24°39S 119°7E **149 D2**
Collierville U.S.A. 35°3N 89°40W **177 D10**
Collina, Passo di Italy 44°2N 10°56E **92 D7**
Collingwood Canada 44°29N 80°13W **174 B4**
Collingwood N.Z. 40°41S 172°40E **155 A7**
Collins Canada 50°17N 89°27W **164 B2**
Collins U.S.A. 32°11N 82°7W **178 D7**
Collins Bay Canada 44°14N 76°36W **175 B8**
Collinson Pen. Canada 69°58N 101°24W **160 D11**
Collinsville Australia 20°30S 147°56E **150 C4**
Collipulli Chile 37°55S 72°30W **190 D1**
Collo Algeria 36°58N 6°37E **136 A5**
Collooney Ireland 54°11N 8°29W **64 B3**
Colmar France 48°5N 7°20E **71 D14**
Colmars France 44°11N 6°39E **73 D10**
Colmenar Spain 36°54N 4°20W **89 J6**
Colmenar de Oreja Spain 40°6N 3°25W **88 E7**
Colmenar Viejo Spain 40°39N 3°47W **88 E7**
Colo → Australia 33°25S 150°52E **153 B9**
Cologne = Köln Germany 50°56N 6°57E **76 E2**
Colom, I. d'en Spain 39°58N 4°16E **100 B11**
Colomb-Béchar = Béchar Algeria 31°38N 2°18W **136 B3**
Colombey-les-Belles France 48°32N 5°54E **71 D12**
Colombey-les-Deux-Églises France 48°13N 4°50E **71 D11**
Colômbia Brazil 20°10S 48°40W **189 E1**
Colombia ■ S. Amer. 3°45N 73°0W **186 C4**
Colombian Basin Caribbean 14°0N 76°0W **182 D4**
Colombo Sri Lanka 6°56N 79°58E **127 L4**
Colomiers France 43°36N 1°21E **72 E5**
Colón B. Aires, Argentina 33°53S 61°7W **190 C3**
Colón Entre Ríos, Argentina 32°12S 58°10W **190 C4**
Colón Cuba 22°42N 80°54W **182 B3**
Colón Panama 9°20N 79°54W **182 E4**
Colón, Arch. de Ecuador 0°0 91°0W **184 D1**
Colonia 25 de Mayo Argentina 37°48S 67°41W **192 A3**
Colònia de Sant Jordi Spain 39°19N 2°59E **100 B9**
Colonia del Sacramento Uruguay 34°25S 57°50W **190 C4**
Colonia Dora Argentina 28°34S 62°59W **190 B3**
Colonial Beach U.S.A. 38°15N 76°58W **173 F15**
Colonie U.S.A. 42°43N 73°50W **175 D11**
Colonna, C. Italy 39°2N 17°12E **95 C10**
Colonsay Canada 51°59N 105°52W **163 C7**
Colonsay U.K. 56°5N 6°12W **65 E2**
Colorado □ U.S.A. 39°30N 105°30W **168 G11**
Colorado → Argentina 39°50S 62°8W **192 A4**
Colorado → N. Amer. 31°45N 114°40W **169 K6**
Colorado → U.S.A. 28°36N 95°59W **176 G7**
Colorado City U.S.A. 32°24N 100°52W **176 E4**
Colorado Plateau U.S.A. 37°0N 111°0W **169 H8**
Colorado River Aqueduct U.S.A. 33°50N 117°23W **171 L12**
Colorado Springs U.S.A. 38°50N 104°49W **168 G11**
Colorno Italy 44°56N 10°23E **92 D7**
Colotlán Mexico 22°6N 103°16W **180 C4**
Colquitt U.S.A. 31°10N 84°44W **178 D5**
Colstrip U.S.A. 45°53N 106°38W **168 D10**
Colton U.S.A. 44°33N 74°56W **175 B10**
Columbia La., U.S.A. 31°15N 89°50W **177 F10**
Columbia Ky., U.S.A. 37°6N 85°18W **173 G11**
Columbia La., U.S.A. 32°6N 92°5W **176 E8**
Columbia Miss., U.S.A. 31°15N 89°50W **177 F10**
Columbia Mo., U.S.A. 38°57N 92°20W **172 F8**
Columbia Pa., U.S.A. 40°2N 76°30W **175 F8**
Columbia S.C., U.S.A. 34°0N 81°2W **178 B8**
Columbia Tenn., U.S.A. 35°37N 87°2W **177 D11**
Columbia → N. Amer. 46°15N 124°5W **170 D2**
Columbia, C. Canada 83°0N 70°0W **161 A18**
Columbia, District of □ U.S.A. 38°55N 77°0W **173 F15**
Columbia, Mt. Canada 52°8N 117°20W **162 C5**
Columbia Basin U.S.A. 46°45N 119°5W **168 C4**
Columbia Falls U.S.A. 48°23N 114°11W **168 B6**
Columbia Mts. Canada 52°0N 119°0W **162 C5**
Columbia Plateau U.S.A. 44°0N 117°30W **168 E5**
Columbiana U.S.A. 40°53N 80°42W **174 F4**
Columbretes, Is. Spain 39°50N 0°30E **90 F5**
Columbus Ga., U.S.A. 32°28N 84°59W **178 D5**

Columbus Ind., U.S.A. 39°13N 85°55W **173 F11**
Columbus Kans., U.S.A. 37°10N 94°50W **172 G6**
Columbus Miss., U.S.A. 33°30N 88°25W **177 E10**
Columbus Mont., U.S.A. 45°38N 109°15W **168 D9**
Columbus N. Mex., U.S.A. 31°50N 107°38W **169 L10**
Columbus Nebr., U.S.A. 41°26N 97°22W **172 E5**
Columbus Ohio, U.S.A. 39°58N 83°0W **173 F12**
Columbus Tex., U.S.A. 29°42N 96°33W **176 G6**
Colunga Spain 43°29N 5°16W **88 B5**
Colusa U.S.A. 39°13N 122°1W **170 F4**
Colville U.S.A. 48°33N 117°54W **168 B5**
Colville → U.S.A. 70°25N 150°30W **166 A9**
Colville, C. N.Z. 36°29S 175°21E **154 C4**
Colville Channel N.Z. 36°25S 175°27E **154 C4**
Colwood Canada 48°26N 123°29W **170 B3**
Colwyn Bay U.K. 53°18N 3°44W **66 D4**
Comácchio Italy 44°42N 12°11E **93 D9**
Comalcalco Mexico 18°16N 93°13W **181 D6**
Comallo Argentina 41°0S 70°5W **192 B2**
Comana Romania 44°10N 26°10E **81 F11**
Comanche U.S.A. 31°54N 98°36W **176 F5**
Comandante Ferraz Antarctica 62°30S 58°0W **55 C18**
Comandante Luis Piedrabuena Argentina 49°59S 68°54W **192 C3**
Comănești Romania 46°25N 26°26E **81 D11**
Comarnic Romania 45°15N 25°38E **81 E10**
Comayagua Honduras 14°25N 87°37W **182 D2**
Combahee → U.S.A. 32°31N 80°31W **178 D9**
Combara Australia 31°10S 148°22E **153 A8**
Combarbalá Chile 31°11S 71°2W **190 C1**
Combe Martin U.K. 51°12N 4°3W **67 F3**
Combeaufontaine France 47°38N 5°54E **71 E12**
Comber Canada 42°14N 82°33W **174 D2**
Comber U.K. 54°33N 5°45W **64 B6**
Combermere Canada 45°22N 77°37W **174 A7**
Comblain-au-Pont Belgium 50°29N 5°35E **69 D5**
Combourg France 48°25N 1°46W **70 D5**
Comboyne Australia 31°34S 152°27E **153 A10**
Combrailles France 46°8N 2°8E **71 F9**
Combronde France 45°58N 3°5E **72 C7**
Comer Ala., U.S.A. 32°2N 85°23W **178 C4**
Comer Ga., U.S.A. 34°4N 83°8W **178 B6**
Comeragh Mts. Ireland 52°18N 7°34W **64 D4**
Comet Australia 23°36S 148°38E **150 C4**
Comilla Bangla. 23°28N 91°10E **123 H17**
Comino Malta 36°1N 14°20E **101 C1**
Comino, C. Italy 40°32N 9°49E **94 B2**
Cómiso Italy 36°56N 14°36E **95 F7**
Comitán de Domínguez Mexico 16°15N 92°8W **181 D6**
Commentry France 46°20N 2°46E **71 F9**
Commerce Ga., U.S.A. 34°12N 83°28W **178 B6**
Commerce Tex., U.S.A. 33°15N 95°54W **176 E7**
Commercy France 48°43N 5°34E **71 D12**
Committee B. Canada 68°30N 86°30W **161 D14**
Commodore, C. Canada 44°47N 80°54W **174 B4**
Commonwealth B. Antarctica 67°0S 144°0E **55 C10**
Commoron Cr. → Australia 28°22S 150°8E **151 D5**
Communism Pk. = imeni Ismail Samani, Pik Tajikistan 39°0N 72°2E **109 E8**
Como Italy 45°47N 9°5E **92 C6**
Como, L. di Italy 46°0N 9°11E **92 B6**
Comodoro Rivadavia Argentina 45°50S 67°40W **192 C3**
Comoé → Côte d'Ivoire 5°12N 3°44W **138 D4**
Comoé △ Côte d'Ivoire 9°0N 3°35W **138 D4**
Comorâște Romania 45°10N 21°35E **80 E6**
Comorin, C. = Kannyakumari India 8°3N 77°40E **127 K3**
Comoros ■ Ind. Oc. 12°10S 44°15E **141 a**
Comox Canada 49°42N 124°55W **162 D4**
Compass Lake U.S.A. 30°36N 85°24W **178 E4**
Compiègne France 49°24N 2°50E **71 C9**
Comporta Portugal 38°22N 8°46W **89 G2**
Compostela Mexico 21°14N 104°55W **180 C4**
Comprida, I. Brazil 24°50S 47°42W **191 A6**
Compton Canada 45°14N 71°49W **175 A13**
Compton U.S.A. 33°53N 118°13W **171 M8**
Comrat Moldova 46°18N 28°40E **81 E13**
Comunidad Peru 13°59S 69°20W **188 C4**
Con Cuong Vietnam 19°2N 104°54E **120 C5**
Con Dao □ Vietnam 8°42N 106°31E **121 H6**
Con Son, Dao Vietnam 8°41N 106°37E **121 H6**
Cona Niyeu Argentina 41°58S 67°0W **192 B3**
Conakry Guinea 9°29N 13°49W **138 D2**
Conara Australia 41°50S 147°26E **151 G4**
Conargo Australia 35°16S 145°10E **153 C6**
Concarneau France 47°52N 3°56W **70 E2**
Conceição Brazil 7°33S 38°31W **189 E3**
Conceição Mozam. 18°47S 36°7E **143 F4**
Conceição da Barra Brazil 18°35S 39°45W **189 D2**
Conceição do Araguaia Brazil 8°0S 49°2W **187 E9**
Conceição do Canindé Brazil 7°54S 41°34W **189 E2**
Concepción Argentina 27°20S 65°35W **190 B2**
Concepción Bolivia 16°15S 62°8W **186 G6**
Concepción Chile 36°50S 73°0W **190 D1**
Concepción Paraguay 23°22S 57°26W **190 A4**
Concepción Peru 11°54S 75°19W **188 C2**
Concepción □ Chile 37°0S 72°30W **190 D1**
Concepción, Est. de Chile 50°30S 74°55W **192 D2**
Concepción, L. Bolivia 17°20S 61°20W **186 G6**
Concepción, Pta. Mexico 26°53N 111°50W **180 B2**
Concepción del Oro Mexico 24°38N 101°25W **180 C4**
Concepción del Uruguay Argentina 32°35S 58°20W **190 C4**
Conception, Pt. U.S.A. 34°27N 120°28W **171 L6**
Conception B. Canada 47°45N 53°0W **165 C10**
Conception B. Namibia 23°55S 14°22E **144 B1**
Conception I. Bahamas 23°52N 75°9W **183 B4**
Conception Zimbabwe 17°27S 30°56E **143 F3**
Conchas Dam U.S.A. 35°22N 104°11W **169 J11**
Conches-en-Ouche France 48°58N 0°56E **70 D7**
Concho U.S.A. 34°28N 109°36W **169 J9**

Concho → U.S.A. 31°34N 99°43W **176 F5**
Conchos → Chihuahua, Mexico 29°35N 104°25W **180 B4**
Conchos → Tamaulipas, Mexico 24°55N 97°38W **181 B5**
Concord Calif., U.S.A. 37°59N 122°2W **170 H4**
Concord Ga., U.S.A. 33°5N 84°27W **178 B5**
Concord N.C., U.S.A. 35°25N 80°35W **177 D14**
Concord N.H., U.S.A. 43°12N 71°32W **175 C13**
Concordia Antarctica 75°6S 123°23E **55 C9**
Concórdia Argentina 31°20S 58°2W **190 C4**
Concórdia Amazonas, Brazil 4°36S 66°36W **186 D5**
Concórdia Sta. Catarina, Brazil 27°14S 52°1W **191 B5**
Concordia Mexico 23°17N 106°4W **180 C3**
Concrete U.S.A. 48°32N 121°45W **168 B3**
Condah Australia 37°57S 141°44E **152 D4**
Condamine Australia 26°56S 150°9E **151 D5**
Condat France 45°21N 2°46E **72 C6**
Conde Brazil 11°49S 37°37W **189 C3**
Conde U.S.A. 45°9N 98°6W **172 C4**
Condé-sur-Noireau France 48°51N 0°33W **70 D6**
Condeúba Brazil 14°52S 42°0W **189 C2**
Condobolin Australia 33°4S 147°6E **153 B7**
Condom France 43°57N 0°22E **72 E4**
Condon U.S.A. 45°14N 120°11W **168 D3**
Conegliano Italy 45°53N 12°18E **93 C9**
Conejera, I. = Conills, I. des Spain 39°11N 2°58E **100 B9**
Conejos Mexico 26°14N 103°53W **180 B4**
Conero △ Italy 43°32N 13°35E **93 E10**
Confolens France 46°2N 0°40E **72 B4**
Confuso → Paraguay 25°9S 57°34W **190 B4**
Congaree → U.S.A. 33°44N 80°38W **178 B9**
Congaree △ U.S.A. 33°47N 80°47W **178 B9**
Congaz Moldova 46°7N 28°36E **81 E13**
Conghua China 23°36N 113°31E **117 F9**
Congjiang China 25°43N 108°52E **116 E7**
Congleton U.K. 53°10N 2°13W **66 D5**
Congo Brazil 7°48S 36°40W **189 E3**
Congo (Brazzaville) = Congo ■ Africa 1°0S 16°0E **140 E3**
Congo (Kinshasa) = Congo, Dem. Rep. of the ■ Africa 3°0S 23°0E **140 E4**
Congo ■ Africa 1°0S 16°0E **140 E3**
Congo → Africa 6°4S 12°24E **140 F2**
Congo, Dem. Rep. of the ■ Africa 3°0S 23°0E **140 E4**
Congo Basin Africa 0°10S 24°30E **140 E4**
Congonhas Brazil 20°30S 43°52W **189 E2**
Congress U.S.A. 34°9N 112°51W **169 J7**
Conguillío △ Chile 38°40S 71°42W **192 A2**
Conil de la Frontera Spain 36°17N 6°10W **89 J4**
Conills, I. des Spain 39°11N 2°58E **100 B9**
Coniston Canada 46°29N 80°51W **164 C3**
Conjeeveram = Kanchipuram India 12°52N 79°45E **127 H4**
Conklin Canada 55°38N 111°5W **163 B6**
Conklin U.S.A. 42°2N 75°49W **175 D9**
Conn, L. Ireland 54°3N 9°15W **64 B2**
Connacht □ Ireland 53°43N 9°12W **64 C2**
Conneaut U.S.A. 41°57N 80°34W **174 E4**
Connecticut □ U.S.A. 41°30N 72°45W **175 E12**
Connecticut → U.S.A. 41°16N 72°20W **175 E12**
Connell U.S.A. 46°40N 118°52W **168 C4**
Connellsville U.S.A. 40°1N 79°35W **174 F5**
Connemara Ireland 53°29N 9°45W **64 C2**
Connemara △ Ireland 53°32N 9°52W **64 C2**
Connerré France 48°3N 0°30E **70 D7**
Connersville U.S.A. 39°39N 85°8W **173 F11**
Connors Ra. Australia 21°40S 149°10E **150 C4**
Conoble Australia 32°55S 144°33E **153 B6**
ConocOcha Peru 10°7S 77°18W **186 E3**
Conques France 44°36N 2°23E **72 D6**
Conquest Canada 51°32N 107°14W **163 C7**
Conrad U.S.A. 48°10N 111°57W **168 B8**
Conran, C. Australia 37°49S 148°44E **153 D8**
Conroe U.S.A. 30°19N 95°27W **176 F7**
Conselheiro Lafaiete Brazil 20°40S 43°48W **189 E2**
Conselheiro Pena Brazil 19°10S 41°30W **189 D2**
Consell Spain 39°40N 2°49E **100 B9**
Conselve Italy 45°14N 11°52E **93 C8**
Consett U.K. 54°51N 1°50W **66 C6**
Consort Canada 52°1N 110°46W **163 C8**
Constance = Konstanz Germany 47°40N 9°10E **77 H5**
Constance, L. = Bodensee Europe 47°35N 9°25E **77 H5**
Constanţa Romania 44°14N 28°38E **81 F13**
Constanţa □ Romania 44°15N 28°15E **81 F13**
Constantina Spain 37°51N 5°40W **89 H5**
Constantine □ Algeria 36°25N 6°42E **136 A5**
Constantine Algeria 36°25N 6°42E **136 A5**
Constitución Chile 35°20S 72°30W **190 D1**
Constitución Uruguay 31°0S 57°50W **190 C4**
Constitución de 1857 △ Mexico 32°4N 115°55W **180 A1**
Consuegra Spain 39°28N 3°36W **89 F7**
Consul Canada 49°20N 109°30W **163 D7**
Contact U.S.A. 41°46N 114°45W **168 F6**
Contagem Brazil 19°55S 44°5W **189 E2**
Contai India 21°54N 87°46E **125 J12**
Contamana Peru 7°19S 74°55W **186 E4**
Contas → Brazil 14°17S 39°1W **189 C3**
Contes France 43°49N 7°19E **73 E11**
Contoocook U.S.A. 43°13N 71°45W **175 C13**
Contra Costa Mozam. 25°9S 33°30E **145 C5**
Contres France 47°24N 1°26E **70 E8**
Contrexéville France 48°10N 5°53E **71 D12**
Contumaza Peru 7°21S 78°57W **186 E3**
Contwoyto L. Canada 65°42N 110°50W **160 D9**
Conversano Italy 40°58N 17°7E **95 B10**
Conway = Conwy U.K. 53°17N 3°50W **66 D4**
Conway = Conwy → U.K. 53°17N 3°50W **66 D4**
Conway Ark., U.S.A. 35°5N 92°26W **176 D8**
Conway N.H., U.S.A. 43°59N 71°7W **175 C13**

Conway S.C., U.S.A. 33°51N 79°3W **177 D15**
Conway, C. Australia 20°34S 148°46E **150 b**
Conway, L. Australia 28°17S 135°35E **151 D2**
Conwy U.K. 53°17N 3°50W **66 D4**
Conwy □ U.K. 53°10N 3°44W **66 D4**
Conwy → U.K. 53°17N 3°50W **66 D4**
Conyers U.S.A. 33°40N 84°1W **178 B5**
Coober Pedy Australia 29°1S 134°43E **151 D1**
Cooch Behar = Koch Bihar India 26°22N 89°29E **123 F14**
Cooinda Australia 13°15S 130°5E **148 B5**
Cook Australia 30°37S 130°25E **149 F5**
Cook, B. Chile 55°10S 70°0W **192 D2**
Cook, C. Canada 50°8N 127°55W **162 C2**
Cook, Mt. = Aoraki Mount Cook N.Z. 43°36S 170°9E **155 D6**
Cook Inlet U.S.A. 60°0N 152°0W **160 D4**
Cook Is. ☑ Pac. Oc. 17°0S 160°0W **157 J12**
Cook Strait N.Z. 41°15S 174°29E **154 H3**
Cooke Plains Australia 35°23S 139°34E **152 C3**
Cookeville U.S.A. 36°10N 85°30W **177 C12**
Cookhouse S. Africa 32°44S 25°47E **144 D4**
Cooks Hammock U.S.A. 29°56N 83°17W **178 F6**
Cooks Harbour Canada 51°36N 55°52W **165 B8**
Cookshire Canada 45°25N 71°38W **175 A13**
Cookstown Canada 44°11N 79°42W **174 B5**
Cookstown U.K. 54°38N 6°45W **64 B5**
Cooksville Canada 43°35N 79°38W **174 C5**
Cooktown Australia 15°30S 145°16E **150 B4**
Coolabah Australia 31°1S 146°43E **153 A7**
Cooladdi Australia 26°37S 145°23E **151 D4**
Coolah Australia 31°48S 149°41E **153 A8**
Coolah Tops △ Australia 31°52S 150°0E **153 A9**
Coolamon Australia 34°46S 147°8E **153 C7**
Coolangatta Australia 28°11S 153°29E **151 D5**
Coolgardie Australia 30°55S 121°8E **149 F3**
Coolidge Ariz., U.S.A. 32°59N 111°31W **169 K8**
Coolidge Ga., U.S.A. 31°1N 83°52W **178 D6**
Coolidge Dam U.S.A. 33°10N 110°32W **169 K8**
Cooma Australia 36°12S 149°8E **153 D8**
Coon Rapids U.S.A. 45°9N 93°19W **172 C7**
Coonabarabran Australia 31°14S 149°18E **153 A8**
Coonalpyn Australia 35°43S 139°52E **152 C3**
Coonamble Australia 30°56S 148°27E **153 A8**
Coonana Australia 31°0S 123°0E **149 F3**
Coonana ⊙ Australia 30°51S 122°53E **149 F3**
Coondapoor India 13°42N 74°40E **127 H2**
Cooninnie, L. Australia 26°4S 139°59E **151 D2**
Coonoor India 11°21N 76°45E **127 J3**
Cooper U.S.A. 33°23N 95°42W **176 E7**
Cooper → U.S.A. 32°50N 79°56W **178 D9**
Cooper Cr. → Australia 28°29S 137°46E **151 D2**
Cooperstown N. Dak., U.S.A. 47°27N 98°8W **172 B4**
Cooperstown N.Y., U.S.A. 42°42N 74°56W **175 D10**
Coopracambra △ Australia 37°20S 149°20E **153 D8**
Coorabie Australia 31°54S 132°18E **149 F5**
Coorong, The Australia 35°50S 139°20E **152 C3**
Coorong △ Australia 36°0S 139°22E **152 C3**
Coorow Australia 29°53S 116°2E **149 E2**
Cooroy Australia 26°22S 152°54E **151 D5**
Coos Bay U.S.A. 43°22N 124°13W **168 E1**
Coosa → U.S.A. 32°30N 86°16W **177 E11**
Cootamundra Australia 34°36S 148°1E **153 C8**
Cootehill Ireland 54°4N 7°5W **64 B4**
Copahue Paso Argentina 37°49S 71°8W **190 D1**
Copainalá Mexico 17°4N 93°18W **181 D6**
Copake U.S.A. 42°7N 73°31W **175 D11**
Copalnic Mănăştur Romania 47°30N 23°41E **81 C8**
Copán Honduras 14°50N 89°9W **182 D2**
Copceac Moldova 45°51N 28°42E **81 E13**
Cope Colo., U.S.A. 39°40N 102°51W **168 G12**
Cope, C. Spain 37°26N 1°28W **91 H3**
Copeland U.S.A. 25°57N 81°22W **179 H7**
Copenhagen = København Denmark 55°40N 12°26E **63 J6**
Copenhagen U.S.A. 43°54N 75°41W **175 C9**
Copertino Italy 40°16N 18°3E **95 B11**
Copiapó Chile 27°30S 70°20W **190 B1**
Copiapó → Chile 27°19S 70°56W **190 B1**
Coplay U.S.A. 40°44N 75°29W **175 F9**
Copley Australia 30°36S 138°26E **152 A2**
Copo △ Argentina 25°53S 61°41W **190 B3**
Copp L. Canada 60°14N 114°40W **162 A6**
Copparo Italy 44°54N 11°49E **93 D8**
Coppename → Suriname 5°48N 55°55W **187 B7**
Copper Canyon = Barranca del Cobre △ Mexico 27°18N 107°40W **180 B3**
Copper Center U.S.A. 61°58N 145°18W **166 C10**
Copper Harbor U.S.A. 47°28N 87°53W **172 B10**
Copper Queen Zimbabwe 17°29S 29°18E **143 F2**
Copperas Cove U.S.A. 31°8N 97°54W **176 F6**
Copperbelt □ Zambia 13°15S 27°30E **143 E2**
Coppermine = Kugluktuk Canada 67°50N 115°5W **160 D8**
Coppermine → Canada 67°49N 116°4W **160 D8**
Copperopolis U.S.A. 37°58N 120°38W **170 H6**
Copşa Mică Romania 46°7N 24°15E **81 D9**
Coquet → U.K. 55°20N 1°32W **66 B6**
Coquille U.S.A. 43°11N 124°11W **168 E1**
Coquimbo Chile 30°0S 71°20W **190 B1**
Coquimbo □ Chile 31°0S 71°0W **190 C1**
Coquitlam Canada 49°17N 122°47W **170 A4**
Corabia Romania 43°48N 24°30E **81 G9**
Coração de Jesus Brazil 16°43S 44°22W **189 D2**
Coracora Peru 15°5S 73°45W **188 D3**
Coraki Australia 28°59S 153°17E **151 D5**
Coral U.S.A. 40°29N 79°14W **174 F5**
Coral Bay Australia 23°8S 113°46E **148 D1**
Coral Gables U.S.A. 25°45N 80°16W **179 J8**
Coral Harbour Canada 64°8N 83°10W **161 E15**
Coral Sea Pac. Oc. 15°0S 150°0E **150 C8**
Coral Sea Basin Pac. Oc. 14°0S 152°0E **156 J7**
Coral Sea Islands Terr. ☑ Australia 20°0S 155°0E **147 C4**
Coral Springs U.S.A. 26°16N 80°16W **179 H8**

Corangamite, L.
  Australia   38°5S 143°30E **152** E5
Corantijn = Courantyne ➤
  S. Amer.   5°50N 57°8W **186** B7
Coraopolis *U.S.A.*   40°31N 80°10W **174** F4
Corato *Italy*   41°9N 16°25E **95** A9
Corbeil-Essonnes *France*   48°36N 2°26E **71** D9
Corbett △ *India*   29°20N 79°0E **125** E8
Corbie *France*   49°54N 2°30E **71** C9
Corbières *France*   42°55N 2°35E **72** F6
Corbigny *France*   47°16N 3°40E **71** E10
Corbin *U.S.A.*   36°57N 84°6W **173** G11
Corbones ➤ *Spain*   37°36N 5°39W **89** H5
Corbu *Romania*   44°25N 28°39E **81** F13
Corby *U.K.*   52°30N 0°41W **67** E7
Corcaigh = Cork *Ireland*   51°54N 8°29W **64** E3
Corcoran *U.S.A.*   36°6N 119°33W **170** J7
Corcovado △ *Chile*   42°55N 72°45W **192** B2
Corcovado △ *Costa Rica*   8°33N 83°35W **182** E3
Cordele *U.S.A.*   31°58N 83°47W **178** D6
Cordell *U.S.A.*   35°17N 98°59W **176** D5
Cordès-sur-Ciel *France*   44°5N 1°57E **72** D5
Cordillera Azul △ *Peru*   7°30S 76°30W **188** B2
Cordisburgo *Brazil*   19°7S 44°21W **189** D2
Córdoba *Argentina*   31°20S 64°10W **190** C3
Córdoba *Mexico*   18°53N 96°56W **181** D5
Córdoba *Spain*   37°50N 4°50W **89** H6
Córdoba □ *Argentina*   31°22S 64°15W **190** C3
Córdoba □ *Spain*   38°5N 5°0W **89** G6
Córdoba, Sierra de
  Argentina   31°10S 64°25W **190** C3
Cordova *U.S.A.*   60°33N 145°45W **160** E2
Corella *Spain*   42°7N 1°48W **90** C3
Corella ➤ *Australia*   19°34S 140°47E **150** B3
Coremas *Brazil*   7°1S 37°58W **189** B3
Corentyne = Courantyne ➤
  S. Amer.   5°50N 57°8W **186** B7
Corfield *Australia*   21°40S 143°21E **150** C3
Corfu = Kerkyra *Greece*   39°38N 19°50E **101** A3
Corfu *U.S.A.*   42°57N 78°24W **164** C2
Corfu ✈ (CFU) *Greece*   39°35N 19°54E **98** B1
Corfu, Str. of = Kerkyras, Notio
  Steno *Greece*   39°34N 20°0E **101** A4
Corgo = O Corgo *Spain*   42°56N 7°25W **88** C3
Cori *Italy*   41°39N 12°55E **94** A5
Coria *Spain*   39°58N 6°33W **88** F4
Coria del Río *Spain*   37°16N 6°3W **89** H4
Coricudgy *Australia*   32°51S 150°24E **153** B9
Corigliano Cálabro *Italy*   39°36N 16°31E **95** C9
Coringa Is. *Australia*   16°58S 149°58E **150** B4
Corinth = Korinthos
  Greece   37°56N 22°55E **98** D4
Corinth *Miss., U.S.A.*   34°56N 88°31W **177** D10
Corinth *N.Y., U.S.A.*   43°15N 73°49W **175** C11
Corinth, G. of = Korinthiakos
  Kolpos *Greece*   38°16N 22°30E **98** C4
Corinth Canal *Greece*   37°58N 23°0E **98** D4
Corinto *Brazil*   18°20S 44°30W **189** D2
Corinto *Nic.*   12°30N 87°10W **182** D2
Cork *Ireland*   51°54N 8°29W **64** E3
Cork □ *Ireland*   51°57N 8°40W **64** E3
Cork Harbour *Ireland*   51°47N 8°16W **64** E3
Corlay *France*   48°20N 3°5W **70** D3
Corleone *Italy*   37°49N 13°18E **94** E6
Corleto Perticara *Italy*   40°23N 16°2E **95** B9
Çorlu *Turkey*   41°11N 27°49E **97** E11
Cormack L. *Canada*   60°56N 121°37W **162** A4
Cormòns *Italy*   45°58N 13°28E **93** C10
Cormorant *Canada*   54°14N 100°35W **163** C8
Cormorant L. *Canada*   54°15N 100°50W **163** C8
Corn Is. = Maíz, Is. del
  Nic.   12°15N 83°4W **182** D3
Cornalvo △ *Spain*   39°1N 6°13W **89** F4
Cornélio Procópio
  Brazil   23°7S 50°40W **191** A5
Corner Brook *Canada*   48°57N 57°58W **165** C8
Corner Inlet *Australia*   38°45S 146°20E **153** E7
Corner Seamounts
  Atl. Oc.   35°0N 52°0W **56** C6
Coreşti *Moldova*   47°21N 28°1E **81** C13
Corníglio *Italy*   44°29N 10°5E **92** D7
Corning *Ark., U.S.A.*   36°25N 90°35W **177** C9
Corning *Calif., U.S.A.*   39°56N 122°11W **168** G2
Corning *Iowa, U.S.A.*   40°59N 94°44W **172** E6
Corning *N.Y., U.S.A.*   42°9N 77°3W **174** D7
Corno Grande *Italy*   42°28N 13°34E **93** F10
Cornwall *Canada*   45°2N 74°44W **175** A10
Cornwall *U.K.*   40°17N 76°25W **174** F8
Cornwall □ *U.K.*   50°26N 4°40W **67** G3
Cornwall I. *Canada*   77°37N 94°38W **161** B13
Cornwallis I. *Canada*   75°8N 95°0W **161** B13
Cornwell *U.S.A.*   27°23N 81°6W **179** H8
Corny Pt. *Australia*   34°55S 137°0E **152** C2
Coro *Venezuela*   11°25N 69°41W **186** A4
Coroaci *Brazil*   18°35S 42°17W **189** D3
Coroatá *Brazil*   4°8S 44°0W **189** D2
Corocoro *Bolivia*   17°15S 68°28W **188** D4
Coroico *Bolivia*   16°0S 67°50W **188** D4
Coromandel *Brazil*   18°28S 47°13W **189** D2
Coromandel *N.Z.*   36°45S 175°31E **154** C4
Coromandel Coast *India*   12°30N 81°0E **127** H5
Coromandel Pen. *Australia*   37°0S 175°40E **154** D4
Coromandel Ra. *N.Z.*   37°0S 175°40E **154** D4
Corona *Calif., U.S.A.*   33°53N 117°34W **171** M9
Corona *N. Mex.,*
  U.S.A.   34°15N 105°36W **169** J11
Coronado *U.S.A.*   32°41N 117°10W **171** N9
Coronado, B. de
  Costa Rica   9°0N 83°40W **182** E3
Coronados, G. de los
  Chile   41°40S 74°0W **192** B2
Coronados, Is. Los
  Mexico   32°26N 117°19W **171** N9
Coronation *Canada*   52°5N 111°27W **162** C6
Coronation Gulf
  Canada   68°25N 110°0W **160** D10
Coronation I. *Antarctica*   60°45S 46°0W **55** C18
Coronation Is.
  Australia   14°57S 124°55E **148** B3
Coronda *Argentina*   31°58S 60°56W **190** C3
Coronel *Chile*   37°0S 73°10W **190** D1
Coronel Bogado
  Paraguay   27°11S 56°18W **190** B4
Coronel Dorrego
  Argentina   38°40S 61°10W **190** D3
Coronel Fabriciano
  Brazil   19°31S 42°38W **189** D2
Coronel Murta *Brazil*   16°37S 42°11W **189** D2
Coronel Oviedo
  Paraguay   25°24S 56°30W **190** B4

Coronel Pringles
  Argentina   38°0S 61°30W **190** D3
Coronel Suárez
  Argentina   37°30S 61°52W **190** D3
Coronel Vidal
  Argentina   37°28S 57°45W **190** D4
Coropuna, Nevado
  Peru   15°30S 72°41W **188** D3
Çorovodë *Albania*   40°31N 20°14E **96** F4
Corowa *Australia*   35°58S 146°21E **153** C7
Corozal □ *Belize*   18°23N 88°23W **181** D7
Corozal Pt.
  Trin. & Tob.   10°45N 61°37W **187** K15
Corps *France*   44°50N 5°56E **73** D9
Corpus *Argentina*   27°10S 55°30W **191** B4
Corpus Christi *U.S.A.*   27°47N 97°24W **176** H6
Corpus Christi, L.
  U.S.A.   28°2N 97°52W **176** G6
Corque *Bolivia*   18°20S 67°41W **188** D4
Corral *Chile*   39°52S 73°26W **192** A2
Corral de Almaguer
  Spain   39°45N 3°10W **88** F7
Corralejo *Canary Is.*   28°43N 13°53W **100** F6
Corraun Pen. *Ireland*   53°54N 9°54W **64** C2
Corréggio *Italy*   44°46N 10°47E **92** D7
Corrente *Brazil*   10°27S 45°10W **189** C1
Corrente ➤ *Brazil*   13°8S 43°28W **189** C2
Correntes, C. das
  Mozam.   24°6S 35°34E **145** B6
Correntina *Brazil*   13°20S 44°39W **189** C2
Corrèze □ *France*   45°20N 1°45E **72** C5
Corrèze ➤ *France*   45°10N 1°28E **72** C5
Corrib, L. *Ireland*   53°27N 9°16W **64** C2
Corridónia *Italy*   43°15N 13°30E **93** E10
Corrientes *Argentina*   27°30S 58°45W **190** B4
Corrientes □ *Argentina*   28°0S 57°0W **190** B4
Corrientes ➤
  Argentina   30°42S 59°38W **190** C4
Corrientes ➤ *Peru*   3°43S 74°35W **188** A3
Corrientes, C. *Colombia*   5°30N 77°34W **186** B3
Corrientes, C. *Cuba*   21°43N 84°30W **182** B3
Corrientes, C. *Mexico*   20°25N 105°42W **180** C3
Corrigan *U.S.A.*   31°0N 94°52W **176** F7
Corrigin *Australia*   32°20S 117°53E **149** F2
Corriverton *Guyana*   5°55N 57°20W **186** B7
Corry *U.S.A.*   41°55N 79°39W **174** E5
Corryong *Australia*   36°12S 147°53E **153** D7
Corse □ *France*   42°0N 9°0E **73** G13
Corse, C. *France*   43°1N 9°25E **73** E13
Corse ➤ *France*   42°14N 9°10E **73** F13
Corse-du-Sud □ *France*   41°45N 9°0E **73** G13
Corsica = Corse □ *France*   42°0N 9°0E **73** G13
Corsicana *U.S.A.*   32°6N 96°28W **176** E6
Corte *France*   42°19N 9°11E **73** F13
Corte Pinto *Portugal*   37°42N 7°29W **89** H3
Cortegana *Spain*   37°54N 6°49W **89** H4
Cortés, Mar de = California, G. de
  Mexico   27°0N 111°0W **180** B2
Cortez *U.S.A.*   37°21N 108°35W **169** H9
Córthaidh, Inis = Enniscorthy
  Ireland   52°30N 6°34W **64** D5
Cortina d'Ampezzo *Italy*   46°32N 12°8E **93** B9
Cortland *N.Y., U.S.A.*   42°36N 76°11W **175** D8
Cortland *Ohio, U.S.A.*   41°20N 80°44W **174** E4
Cortona *Italy*   43°16N 11°59E **93** E8
Corubal ➤ *Guinea-Biss.*   11°57N 15°5W **138** C2
Coruche *Portugal*   38°57N 8°30W **89** G2
Çoruh ➤ *Turkey*   41°38N 41°38E **87** K5
Çorum *Turkey*   40°30N 34°57E **104** B6
Çorum □ *Turkey*   40°40N 35°0E **104** B6
Corumbá *Brazil*   19°0S 57°30W **186** G7
Corumbá ➤ *Brazil*   18°19S 48°55W **189** D1
Corumbaíba *Brazil*   18°9S 48°34W **189** D1
Corund *Romania*   46°30N 25°13E **81** D10
Corunna = A Coruña
  Spain   43°20N 8°25W **88** B2
Corvallis *U.S.A.*   44°34N 123°16W **168** D2
Corvette, L. de la
  Canada   53°25N 74°3W **164** B5
Corvo *Azores*   39°43N 31°8W **134** a
Corydon *U.S.A.*   40°46N 93°19W **172** E7
Cosalá *Mexico*   24°23N 106°41W **180** C3
Cosamaloapan de Carpio
  Mexico   18°22N 95°48W **181** D5
Cosenza *Italy*   39°18N 16°15E **95** C9
Coşereni *Romania*   44°38N 26°35E **81** F11
Coshocton *U.S.A.*   40°16N 81°51W **174** F3
Cosmo Newberry
  Australia   28°0S 122°54E **149** E3
Cosmo Newberry ☉
  Australia   27°59S 122°53E **149** E3
Cosmonaut Sea *S. Ocean*   66°30S 40°0E **55** C5
Cosne-Cours-sur-Loire
  France   47°24N 2°54E **71** E9
Coso Junction *U.S.A.*   36°3N 117°57W **171** J9
Coso Pk. *U.S.A.*   36°13N 117°44W **171** J9
Cospeito = A Feira de Monte
  Spain   43°12N 7°34W **88** B3
Cosquín *Argentina*   31°15S 64°30W **190** C3
Cossato *Italy*   45°34N 8°10E **92** C5
Cossé-le-Vivien *France*   47°57N 0°54W **70** E6
Cosson ➤ *France*   47°30N 1°15E **70** E8
Costa Blanca *Spain*   38°25N 0°10W **91** G4
Costa Brava *Spain*   41°30N 3°0E **90** D8
Costa de la Luz *Spain*   36°15N 5°58W **89** J4
Costa del Sol *Spain*   36°30N 4°30W **89** J6
Costa dels Pins *Spain*   39°38N 3°26E **90** B10
Costa Mesa *U.S.A.*   33°38N 117°55W **171** M9
Costa Rica ■ *Cent. Amer.*   10°0N 84°0W **182** E3
Costa Teguise *Canary Is.*   29°0N 13°31W **100** F6
Costeşti *Romania*   44°40N 24°53E **81** F9
Costigliole d'Asti *Italy*   44°47N 8°11E **92** D5
Cosumnes ➤ *U.S.A.*   38°16N 121°26W **170** G5
Coswig *Sachsen, Germany*   51°7N 13°34E **76** D9
Coswig *Sachsen-Anhalt,*
  Germany   51°53N 12°27E **76** D8
Cotabato *Phil.*   7°14N 124°15E **119** C6
Cotacajes ➤ *Bolivia*   16°0S 67°1W **188** D4
Cotagaita *Bolivia*   20°45S 65°40W **190** A2
Côte d'Ivoire ■ *Africa*   7°30N 5°0W **138** D4
Côte-d'Or □ *France*   47°30N 4°50E **71** E11
Coteau des Prairies
  U.S.A.   45°20N 97°50W **172** C5
Coteau du Missouri
  U.S.A.   47°0N 100°0W **172** B4
Cotegipe *Brazil*   12°2S 44°15W **189** C2
Cotentin *France*   49°15N 1°30W **70** C5
Côtes-d'Armor □ *France*   48°25N 2°40W **70** D4
Côtes de Meuse *France*   49°15N 5°22E **71** C12
Côtes-du-Nord = Côtes-
  d'Armor □ *France*   48°25N 2°40W **70** D4
Cotiella *Spain*   42°31N 0°19E **90** C5

Cotiujeni *Moldova*   47°51N 28°33E **81** C13
Cotonou *Benin*   6°20N 2°25E **139** D5
Cotopaxi *Ecuador*   0°40S 78°30W **186** D2
Cotronei *Italy*   39°9N 16°47E **95** C9
Cotswold Hills *U.K.*   51°42N 2°10W **67** F5
Cottage Grove *U.S.A.*   43°48N 123°3W **168** E2
Cottageville *U.S.A.*   32°56N 80°29W **178** C9
Cottam *Canada*   42°8N 82°45W **174** D2
Cottbus *Germany*   51°45N 14°20E **76** D10
Cottingham *U.K.*   53°48N 0°25W **66** D7
Cottondale *U.S.A.*   30°48N 85°23W **178** F4
Cottonwood *Ala., U.S.A.*   31°3N 85°18W **178** D4
Cottonwood *Ariz.,*
  U.S.A.   34°45N 112°1W **169** J7
Cotulla *U.S.A.*   28°26N 99°14W **176** G5
Coubre, Pte. de la *France*   45°42N 1°15W **72** C2
Couches *France*   46°53N 4°30E **71** F11
Couço *Portugal*   38°59N 8°17W **89** G2
Coudersport *U.S.A.*   41°46N 78°1W **174** E6
Couedic, C. du *Australia*   36°5S 136°40E **152** D2
Couëron *France*   47°13N 1°44W **70** E5
Couesnon ➤ *France*   48°38N 1°32W **70** D5
Couhé *France*   46°17N 0°11E **72** B4
Coulanges-sur-Yonne
  France   47°31N 3°33E **71** E10
Coulee City *U.S.A.*   47°37N 119°17W **168** C4
Coulee Dam Nat. Recr. Area =
  Lake Roosevelt △
  U.S.A.   48°13N 118°14W **168** B4
Coulman I. *Antarctica*   73°35S 170°0E **55** D11
Coulommiers *France*   48°50N 3°3E **71** D10
Coulon ➤ *France*   43°51N 5°6E **73** E9
Coulonge ➤ *Canada*   45°52N 76°46W **164** C4
Coulonges-sur-l'Autize
  France   46°29N 0°36W **72** B3
Coulounieix-Chamiers
  France   45°11N 0°42E **72** C4
Coulterville *U.S.A.*   37°43N 120°12W **170** H6
Council *Alaska, U.S.A.*   64°53N 163°41W **166** C7
Council *Ga., U.S.A.*   30°37N 82°31W **178** F7
Council *Idaho, U.S.A.*   44°44N 116°26W **168** D5
Council Bluffs *U.S.A.*   41°16N 95°52W **172** E6
Council Grove *U.S.A.*   38°40N 96°29W **172** F5
Coupeville *U.S.A.*   48°13N 122°41W **170** B4
Courantyne ➤ *S. Amer.*   5°50N 57°8W **186** B7
Courcelles *Belgium*   50°28N 4°22E **69** D4
Courçon *France*   46°15N 0°50W **72** B3
Courchevel *France*   45°25N 6°36E **73** C10
Couronne, C. *France*   43°19N 5°3E **73** E9
Cours-la-Ville *France*   46°7N 4°19E **71** F11
Coursan *France*   43°14N 3°4E **72** E7
Courseulles-sur-Mer
  France   49°20N 0°29W **70** C6
Courtenay *Canada*   49°45N 125°0W **162** D4
Courtenay *France*   48°2N 3°3E **71** D10
Courtland *Canada*   42°51N 80°38W **174** D4
Courtland *U.S.A.*   38°20N 121°34W **170** G5
Courtrai = Kortrijk
  Belgium   50°50N 3°17E **69** D3
Courtright *Canada*   42°49N 82°28W **174** D2
Coushatta *U.S.A.*   32°1N 93°21W **176** E8
Coutances *France*   49°3N 1°28W **70** C5
Coutras *France*   45°2N 0°8W **72** C3
Coutts Crossing
  Australia   29°49S 152°55E **151** D5
Couva *Trin. & Tob.*   10°25N 61°27W **187** K15
Couvin *Belgium*   50°3N 4°29E **69** D4
Covarrubias *Spain*   42°4N 3°31W **88** C7
Covasna *Romania*   45°50N 26°10E **81** E11
Covasna □ *Romania*   45°50N 26°0E **81** E11
Cove I. *Canada*   45°17N 81°44W **174** A3
Coventry *U.K.*   52°25N 1°28W **67** E6
Coverdale *U.S.A.*   31°38N 83°58W **178** D6
Covilhã *Portugal*   40°17N 7°31W **88** E3
Covington *Ga., U.S.A.*   33°36N 83°51W **178** C6
Covington *Ky., U.S.A.*   39°5N 84°30W **173** F11
Covington *Tenn.,*
  U.S.A.   35°34N 89°39W **177** D10
Covington *Va., U.S.A.*   37°47N 79°59W **173** G14
Cowal, L. *Australia*   33°40S 147°25E **153** B7
Cowan, L. *Australia*   31°45S 121°45E **149** F3
Cowan L. *Canada*   54°0N 107°15W **163** C7
Cowangie *Australia*   35°12S 141°26E **152** C4
Cowansville *Canada*   45°14N 72°46W **175** A12
Coward Springs
  Australia   29°24S 136°49E **151** D2
Cowcowing Lakes
  Australia   30°55S 117°20E **149** F2
Cowdenbeath *U.K.*   56°7N 3°21W **65** E5
Cowell *Australia*   33°39S 136°56E **152** B2
Cowes *Australia*   38°28S 145°14E **153** E6
Cowes *U.K.*   50°45N 1°18W **67** G6
Cowichan L. *Canada*   48°53N 124°17W **170** B2
Cowlitz ➤ *U.S.A.*   46°6N 122°55W **170** D4
Cowra *Australia*   33°49S 148°42E **153** B8
Coxilha Grande *Brazil*   28°18S 51°30W **191** B5
Coxim *Brazil*   18°30S 54°55W **187** G8
Cox's Bazar *Bangla.*   21°26N 91°59E **123** J17
Coyah *Guinea*   9°42N 13°22E **138** D2
Coyote Wells *U.S.A.*   32°44N 115°58W **171** N11
Coyuca de Benitez
  Mexico   17°2N 100°4W **181** D4
Coyuca de Catalán
  Mexico   18°20N 100°39W **180** D4
Cozad *U.S.A.*   40°52N 99°59W **172** E4
Cozes *France*   45°34N 0°49W **72** C3
Cozia □ *Romania*   45°24N 24°16E **81** D9
Cozumel *Mexico*   20°31N 86°55W **181** C7
Cozumel, Isla *Mexico*   20°30N 86°40W **181** C7
Crab Hill *Barbados*   13°19N 59°38W **183** g
Cracow = Kraków
  Poland   50°4N 19°57E **83** H6
Cracow *Australia*   25°17S 150°17E **151** D5
Craddock Channel
  N.Z.   36°10S 175°13E **154** C4
Cradle Mt.-Lake St. Clair △
  Australia   41°49S 147°56E **151** G4
Cradock *Australia*   32°6S 138°31E **151** E2
Cradock *S. Africa*   32°8S 25°36E **144** C4
Crafers *Australia*   35°0S 138°42E **152** C3
Craig *U.S.A.*   40°31N 107°33W **168** F10
Craigavon *U.K.*   54°27N 6°23W **64** B5
Craigieburn *Australia*   37°36S 144°56E **153** D6
Craigmore *Zimbabwe*   20°28S 32°50E **143** G3
Craik *Canada*   51°3N 105°49W **163** C7
Crailsheim *Germany*   49°8N 10°5E **75** G6
Craiova *Romania*   44°21N 23°48E **81** F8
Cramsie *Australia*   23°20S 144°15E **150** C3
Cranberry L. *U.S.A.*   44°11N 74°50W **175** B10

Cranberry Portage
  Canada   54°35N 101°23W **163** C8
Cranbrook *Australia*   34°18S 117°33E **149** F2
Cranbrook *Canada*   49°30N 115°46W **162** D5
Crandon *U.S.A.*   45°34N 88°54W **172** C9
Crane *Oreg., U.S.A.*   43°25N 118°35W **168** E4
Crane *Tex., U.S.A.*   31°24N 102°21W **176** F3
Crane, The *Barbados*   13°6N 59°27W **183** g
Cranganore *India*   10°13N 76°13E **127** J3
Cranston *U.S.A.*   41°47N 71°26W **175** E13
Craon *France*   47°50N 0°58W **70** E6
Craonne *France*   49°27N 3°46E **71** C10
Craponne-sur-Arzon
  France   45°19N 3°51E **72** C7
Crasna *Romania*   46°32N 27°51E **81** D12
Crasna ➤ *Romania*   47°44N 22°35E **80** C7
Crasnei, Munţii *Romania*   47°0N 23°20E **81** C8
Crater L. *U.S.A.*   42°56N 122°6W **168** E2
Crater Lake △ *U.S.A.*   42°55N 122°10W **168** E2
Craters of the Moon △
  U.S.A.   43°25N 113°30W **168** E7
Crateús *Brazil*   5°10S 40°39W **189** B2
Crati ➤ *Italy*   39°43N 16°31E **95** C9
Crato *Brazil*   7°10S 39°25W **189** B3
Crato *Portugal*   39°16N 7°39W **89** F3
Craven, L. *Canada*   54°20N 76°56W **164** B4
Crawford *Ala., U.S.A.*   32°27N 85°11W **178** C4
Crawford *Nebr.,*
  U.S.A.   42°41N 103°25W **172** D2
Crawfordsville *U.S.A.*   40°2N 86°54W **172** E10
Crawfordville *Fla.,*
  U.S.A.   30°11N 84°23W **178** E5
Crawfordville *Ga.,*
  U.S.A.   33°33N 82°54W **178** B7
Crawley *U.K.*   51°7N 0°11W **67** F7
Crazy Mts. *U.S.A.*   46°12N 110°20W **168** C8
Crean L. *Canada*   54°5N 106°9W **163** B7
Crécy-en-Ponthieu
  France   50°15N 1°53E **71** B8
Crediton *Canada*   43°17N 81°33W **174** C3
Crediton *U.K.*   50°47N 3°40W **67** G4
Cree ➤ *Canada*   58°57N 105°47W **163** B7
Cree ➤ *U.K.*   54°55N 4°25W **65** G4
Cree L. *Canada*   57°30N 106°30W **163** B7
Creede *U.S.A.*   37°51N 106°56W **169** H10
Creekside *U.S.A.*   40°40N 79°11W **174** F5
Creel *Mexico*   27°45N 107°38W **180** B3
Creemore *Canada*   44°19N 80°6W **174** B4
Creighton *Canada*   54°45N 101°54W **163** C8
Creighton *U.S.A.*   42°28N 97°54W **172** D5
Creil *France*   49°15N 2°29E **71** C9
Crema *Italy*   45°22N 9°41E **92** C6
Cremona *Italy*   45°7N 10°2E **92** C7
Crepaja *Serbia*   45°1N 20°38E **80** E5
Crépy *France*   49°36N 3°32E **71** C10
Crépy-en-Valois *France*   49°14N 2°54E **71** C9
Cres *Croatia*   44°58N 14°25E **93** D11
Crescent Beach *U.S.A.*   29°46N 81°15W **178** F8
Crescent City *Calif.,*
  U.S.A.   41°45N 124°12W **168** F1
Crescent City *Fla.,*
  U.S.A.   29°26N 81°31W **179** F8
Crescent Group
  S. China Sea   16°30N 111°40E **118** A4
Crescent Hd.
  Australia   31°11S 152°59E **153** A10
Crescent L. *U.S.A.*   29°28N 81°30W **179** F8
Crescentino *Italy*   45°11N 8°6E **92** C5
Crespi d'Adda *Italy*   45°35N 9°32E **92** C6
Crespo *Argentina*   32°2S 60°19W **190** C3
Cresson *U.S.A.*   40°28N 78°36W **174** F6
Cressy *Australia*   38°2S 143°40E **152** E5
Crest *France*   44°44N 5°2E **73** D9
Crestline *Calif., U.S.A.*   34°14N 117°18W **171** L9
Crestline *Ohio, U.S.A.*   40°47N 82°44W **174** F2
Creston *Canada*   49°10N 116°31W **162** D5
Creston *Calif., U.S.A.*   35°32N 120°33W **170** K6
Creston *Iowa, U.S.A.*   41°4N 94°22W **172** E7
Crestview *Calif.,*
  U.S.A.   37°46N 118°58W **170** H8
Crestview *Fla., U.S.A.*   30°46N 86°34W **179** E3
Creswick *Australia*   37°25S 143°58E **152** D5
Crêt de la Neige *France*   46°16N 5°58E **71** F12
Crete = Kriti *Greece*   35°15N 25°0E **101** D7
Crete *U.S.A.*   40°38N 96°58W **172** E5
Crete, Sea of *Greece*   36°0N 25°0E **99** E7
Créteil *France*   48°47N 2°27E **71** D9
Creus, C. de *Spain*   42°20N 3°19E **90** C8
Creuse □ *France*   46°10N 2°0E **71** F9
Creuse ➤ *France*   47°0N 0°34E **72** B4
Creutzwald *France*   49°12N 6°42E **71** C13
Creuzburg *Germany*   51°3N 10°14E **76** D6
Crèvecœur-le-Grand
  France   49°37N 2°5E **71** C9
Crevillent *Spain*   38°12N 0°48W **91** G4
Crewe *U.K.*   53°6N 2°26W **66** D5
Crewkerne *U.K.*   50°53N 2°48W **67** G5
Crianlarich *U.K.*   56°24N 4°37W **65** E4
Criciúma *Brazil*   28°40S 49°23W **191** B6
Crieff *U.K.*   56°22N 3°50W **65** E5
Crikvenica *Croatia*   45°11N 14°40E **93** C11
Crimea □ *Ukraine*   45°30N 33°10E **85** K8
Crimean Pen. = Krymskyy
  Pivostriv *Ukraine*   45°0N 34°0E **85** K8
Crimmitschau *Germany*   50°48N 12°24E **76** E8
Cristino Castro *Brazil*   8°49S 44°13W **189** B2
Cristuru Secuiesc
  Romania   46°17N 25°2E **81** D10
Crişul Alb ➤ *Romania*   46°42N 21°17E **80** D6
Crişul Negru ➤
  Romania   46°42N 21°16E **80** D6
Crişul Repede ➤
  Romania   46°55N 20°59E **80** D5
Criuleni *Moldova*   47°13N 29°10E **81** C14
Crivitz *Germany*   53°34N 11°39E **76** B6
Crkvice *Montenegro*   42°34N 18°38E **96** D2
Crna ➤ *Macedonia*   41°33N 21°59E **96** E5
Crna Gora = Montenegro ■
  Europe   42°40N 19°20E **96** D3
Crna Gora *Macedonia*   42°10N 21°30E **96** D5
Crna Reka = Crna ➤
  Macedonia   41°33N 21°59E **96** E5
Crna Trava *Serbia*   42°49N 22°19E **96** C5
Crni Drim ➤ *Macedonia*   41°17N 20°40E **96** E4
Crni Timok ➤ *Serbia*   43°53N 22°15E **96** C6
Crnoljeva Planina = Zhar, Mali
  Kosovo   42°21N 20°60E **96** C4
Črnomelj *Slovenia*   45°33N 15°10E **93** C12
Croagh Patrick *Ireland*   53°46N 9°40W **64** C2

Croajingolong △
  Australia   37°45S 149°26E **153** D8
Croatia ■ *Europe*   45°20N 16°0E **93** C13
Crocker, Banjaran
  Malaysia   5°40N 116°30E **118** C5
Crockett *U.S.A.*   31°19N 95°27W **176** F7
Crocodile = Umgwenya ➤
  Mozam.   25°14S 32°18E **145** C5
Crocodile ➤ *S. Africa*   24°11S 26°53E **145** C4
Crocodile Is. *Australia*   12°3S 134°58E **150** A1
Crocq *France*   45°52N 2°21E **72** C6
Crohy Hd. *Ireland*   54°55N 8°26W **64** B3
Croix, L. La *Canada*   48°20N 92°15W **164** C1
Croix, Pte. du *France*   47°19N 2°31W **70** E4
Croker, C. *Australia*   10°58S 132°35E **148** B5
Croker, C. *Canada*   44°58N 80°59W **174** B4
Croker I. *Australia*   11°12S 132°32E **148** B5
Croker Islands Seas ☉
  Australia   11°20S 132°30E **148** B5
Cromarty *U.K.*   57°40N 4°2W **65** D4
Cromer *U.K.*   52°56N 1°17E **66** E9
Cromwell *N.Z.*   45°3S 169°14E **155** F2
Cromwell *U.S.A.*   41°36N 72°39W **175** E12
Cronat *France*   46°43N 3°47E **71** F10
Crook *U.K.*   54°43N 1°45W **66** C6
Crooked ➤ *Canada*   54°50N 122°54W **162** C4
Crooked ➤ *U.S.A.*   44°32N 121°16W **168** D3
Crooked I. *Bahamas*   22°50N 74°10W **183** B5
Crooked Island Passage
  Bahamas   22°55N 74°35W **183** B5
Crookston *Minn.,*
  U.S.A.   47°47N 96°37W **172** B5
Crookston *Nebr.,*
  U.S.A.   42°56N 100°45W **172** D3
Crookwell *Australia*   34°28S 149°24E **153** C8
Cropane-Micone □ *Italy*   38°31N 16°18E **95** D9
Crosby *U.K.*   53°30N 3°3W **66** D4
Crosby *N. Dak., U.S.A.*   48°55N 103°18W **172** A2
Crosby *Pa., U.S.A.*   41°45N 78°23W **174** E6
Crosbyton *U.S.A.*   33°40N 101°14W **176** E4
Crosia *Italy*   39°35N 16°45E **95** C9
Cross ➤ *Nigeria*   4°42N 8°21E **139** E6
Cross City *U.S.A.*   29°38N 83°7W **179** F6
Cross Fell *U.K.*   54°43N 2°28W **66** C5
Cross L. *Canada*   54°45N 97°30W **163** C9
Cross Lake *Canada*   54°37N 97°47W **163** C9
Cross River □ *Nigeria*   6°0N 8°0E **139** D6
Cross River △ *Nigeria*   5°50N 9°50E **139** D6
Cross Sound *U.S.A.*   58°0N 135°0W **160** F4
Crossett *U.S.A.*   33°8N 91°58W **176** E9
Crosshaven *Ireland*   51°47N 8°17W **64** E3
Crossley, Mt. *N.Z.*   42°50S 172°5E **155** C7
Crossmaglen *U.K.*   54°5N 6°36W **64** B5
Crossmolina *Ireland*   54°6N 9°20W **64** B2
Crossville *U.S.A.*   35°57N 85°2W **177** D12
Croswell *U.S.A.*   43°16N 82°37W **174** C2
Croton-on-Hudson
  U.S.A.   41°12N 73°55W **175** E11
Crotone *Italy*   39°5N 17°8E **95** C10
Crow ➤ *Canada*   59°41N 124°20W **162** B4
Crow Agency *U.S.A.*   45°36N 107°28W **168** D10
Crow Hd. *Ireland*   51°35N 10°9W **64** E1
Crowdy Bay △
  Australia   31°45S 152°45E **153** A10
Crowell *U.S.A.*   33°59N 99°43W **176** E5
Crowl Cr. ➤ *Australia*   32°0S 145°30E **153** B8
Crowley *U.S.A.*   30°13N 92°22W **176** F8
Crowley, L. *U.S.A.*   37°35N 118°42W **170** H8
Crown Point *Ind.*
  U.S.A.   41°25N 87°22W **172** E10
Crown Point *N.Y.,*
  U.S.A.   43°57N 73°26W **175** C11
Crown Pt. *Trin. & Tob.*   11°18N 60°51W **187** J16
Crownpoint *U.S.A.*   35°41N 108°9W **169** J9
Crows Landing *U.S.A.*   37°23N 121°6W **170** H5
Crows Nest *Australia*   27°16S 152°4E **151** D5
Crowsnest Pass
  Canada   49°40N 114°40W **162** D6
Croydon *Australia*   18°13S 142°14E **150** B3
Croydon □ *U.K.*   51°22N 0°5W **67** F7
Crozet, Îs. *Ind. Oc.*   46°27S 52°0E **146** H6
Crozet Basin *Ind. Oc.*   39°0S 60°0E **146** H5
Crozon *France*   48°15N 4°30W **70** D2
Cruce de Sardina
  Canary Is.   27°52S 15°22W **100** G4
Crusheen *Ireland*   52°57N 8°53W **64** D3
Cruz, C. *Cuba*   19°50N 77°50W **182** C4
Cruz Alta *Brazil*   28°45S 53°40W **191** B5
Cruz Bay *U.S. Virgin Is.*   18°20N 64°48W **183** e
Cruz das Almas *Brazil*   12°0S 39°6W **189** C3
Cruz del Eje *Argentina*   30°45S 64°50W **190** C3
Cruzeiro *Brazil*   22°33S 45°0W **191** A7
Cruzeiro do Oeste *Brazil*   23°46S 53°4W **191** A5
Cruzeiro do Sul *Brazil*   7°35S 72°35W **188** B3
Cry L. *Canada*   58°45N 129°0W **162** B3
Crystal B. *U.S.A.*   28°50N 82°45W **179** G7
Crystal Bay *U.S.A.*   39°15N 120°0W **170** F7
Crystal Brook
  Australia   33°21S 138°12E **152** B2
Crystal City *U.S.A.*   28°41N 99°50W **176** G5
Crystal Falls *U.S.A.*   46°5N 88°20W **172** B9
Crystal Lake *U.S.A.*   30°26N 85°42W **178** F4
Crystal River *U.S.A.*   28°54N 82°35W **179** G7
Crystal Springs *U.S.A.*   31°59N 90°21W **177** F9
Csenger *Hungary*   47°50N 22°41E **80** C7
Csongrád *Hungary*   46°43N 20°12E **80** E5
Csongrád □ *Hungary*   46°30N 20°15E **80** D5
Csorna *Hungary*   47°38N 17°18E **80** C2
Csurgo *Hungary*   46°16N 17°9E **80** D2
Cu Lao Hon *Vietnam*   10°54N 108°18E **121** G7
Cua Rao *Vietnam*   19°16N 104°27E **120** C5
Cuácua ➤ *Mozam.*   17°54S 37°0E **143** F4
Cuamato *Angola*   17°2S 15°7E **144** B2
Cuamba *Mozam.*   14°45S 36°22E **143** E4
Cuando ➤ *Angola*   17°30S 23°15E **144** B3
Cuangar *Angola*   17°36S 18°39E **144** B2
Cuango = Kwango ➤
  Dem. Rep. of the Congo   3°14S 17°22E **140** E3
Cuanza ➤ *Angola*   9°21S 13°9E **140** F2
Cuarto ➤ *Argentina*   33°25S 63°2W **190** C3
Cuatrociénegas *Mexico*   26°59N 102°5W **180** B4
Cuauhtémoc *Mexico*   28°25N 106°52W **180** B3
Cuba *Portugal*   38°10N 7°54W **89** G3
Cuba *N. Mex., U.S.A.*   36°1N 107°11W **169** H10
Cuba *N.Y., U.S.A.*   42°13N 78°17W **174** D6
Cuba ■ *W. Indies*   22°0N 79°0W **182** B4
Cubango ➤ *Africa*   18°50S 22°25E **144** B3
Çubuk *Turkey*   40°14N 33°3E **104** B5
Cuc Phuong △
  Vietnam   20°17N 105°38E **120** B5

Cuchillo-Co *Argentina*   38°20S 64°37W **192** A4
Cuchumatanes, Sierra de los
  Guatemala   15°35N 91°25W **182** C1
Cuckfield *U.K.*   51°1N 0°8W **67** F7
Cucuí *Brazil*   1°12N 66°50W **186** C5
Cucurpé *Mexico*   30°20N 110°43W **180** A2
Cúcuta *Colombia*   7°54N 72°31W **186** B4
Cudalbi *Romania*   45°46N 27°41E **81** E12
Cuddalore *India*   11°46N 79°45E **127** J4
Cuddapah = Kadapa
  India   14°30N 78°47E **127** G4
Cuddapan, L. *Australia*   25°45S 141°26E **150** D3
Cudgewa *Australia*   36°10S 147°42E **153** D7
Cudillero *Spain*   43°33N 6°9W **88** B4
Cue *Australia*   27°25S 117°54E **149** E2
Cuéllar *Spain*   41°23N 4°21W **88** D6
Cuenca *Ecuador*   2°50S 79°9W **186** D3
Cuenca *Spain*   40°5N 2°10W **90** E2
Cuenca □ *Spain*   40°0N 2°0W **90** E2
Cuenca, Serranía de
  Spain   39°55N 1°50W **90** F3
Cuenca Alta del Manzanares △
  Spain   40°30N 3°55W **88** E7
Cuerda del Pozo, Embalse de la
  Spain   41°51N 2°44W **90** D2
Cuernavaca *Mexico*   18°55N 99°15W **181** D5
Cuero *U.S.A.*   29°6N 97°17W **176** G6
Cuers *France*   43°14N 6°5E **73** E10
Cueva de la Quebrada del Toro △
  Venezuela   10°46N 69°3W **183** D6
Cuevas del Almanzora
  Spain   37°18N 1°58W **91** H3
Cuevo *Bolivia*   20°15S 63°30W **186** H6
Cugir *Romania*   45°48N 23°25E **81** E8
Cuglieri *Italy*   40°11N 8°34E **94** B1
Cugnaux *France*   43°32N 1°20E **72** E5
Cuhai-Bakony ➤
  Hungary   47°35N 17°54E **80** C2
Cuiabá *Brazil*   15°30S 56°0W **187** G7
Cuiabá ➤ *Brazil*   17°5S 56°36W **187** G7
Cuihangcun *China*   22°27N 113°32E **111** a
Cuijk *Neths.*   51°44N 5°50E **69** C5
Cuilco *Guatemala*   15°24N 91°58W **182** C1
Cuillin Hills *U.K.*   57°13N 6°15W **65** D2
Cuillin Sd. *U.K.*   57°4N 6°20W **65** D2
Cuilo = Kwilu ➤
  Dem. Rep. of the Congo   3°22S 17°22E **140** E3
Cuiseaux *France*   46°30N 5°22E **71** F12
Cuité *Brazil*   6°29S 36°9W **189** B3
Cuito ➤ *Angola*   18°1S 20°48E **144** A3
Cuitzeo, L. de *Mexico*   19°55N 101°5W **180** D4
Cujmir *Romania*   44°13N 22°57E **80** F7
Cukai *Malaysia*   4°13N 103°25E **121** K4
Çukurca *Turkey*   37°14N 43°36E **105** D10
Cukurova = Cicilia
  Turkey   36°30N 34°0E **104** D5
Culbertson *U.S.A.*   48°9N 104°31W **168** B11
Culburra *N.S.W.,*
  U.S.A.   34°45S 150°46E **153** C9
Culburra *S. Austral.,*
  Australia   35°50S 139°58E **152** C3
Culcairn *Australia*   35°41S 147°3E **153** C7
Culebra *Puerto Rico*   18°19N 65°18W **183** d
Culebra, Sierra de la
  Spain   41°55N 6°20W **88** D4
Culfa *Azerbaijan*   38°57N 45°38E **105** C11
Culgoa ➤ *Australia*   35°44S 143°6E **152** C5
Culgoa ➤ *Australia*   29°56S 146°20E **153** A8
Culgoa Flood Plain △
  Australia   28°58S 147°5E **151** D4
Culiacán *Mexico*   24°50N 107°23W **180** C3
Culiacán ➤ *Mexico*   24°30N 107°42W **180** C3
Culik *Indonesia*   8°21S 115°37E **119** J18
Culion *Phil.*   11°54N 119°58E **119** B6
Cúllar *Spain*   37°35N 2°34W **89** H8
Cullarin Ra. *Australia*   34°30S 149°30E **153** C8
Cullen *U.K.*   57°42N 2°49W **65** D6
Cullen Bullen *Australia*   33°18S 150°2E **153** B9
Cullen Pt. *Australia*   11°57S 141°54E **150** A3
Cullera *Spain*   39°9N 0°17W **91** F4
Cullman *U.S.A.*   34°11N 86°51W **177** D11
Culloden *U.S.A.*   32°52N 84°6W **178** C5
Cullompton *U.K.*   50°51N 3°24W **67** G4
Culoz *France*   45°47N 5°46E **73** C9
Culpeper *U.S.A.*   38°30N 78°0W **173** F14
Culuene ➤ *Brazil*   12°56S 52°51W **187** F8
Culver, Pt. *Australia*   32°54S 124°43E **149** F3
Culverden *N.Z.*   42°47S 172°49E **155** C7
Culverton *U.S.A.*   33°19N 82°54W **178** B7
Cumaná *Venezuela*   10°30N 64°5W **186** A6
Cumaovası *Turkey*   38°15S 27°9E **99** c
Cumari *Brazil*   18°16S 48°11W **189** D1
Cumberland *B.C.,*
  Canada   49°40N 125°0W **162** D4
Cumberland *Ont.,*
  Canada   45°29N 75°24W **175** A9
Cumberland *U.S.A.*   39°39N 78°46W **173** F14
Cumberland ➤ *U.S.A.*   37°9N 88°25W **172** G9
Cumberland, L. *U.S.A.*   36°52N 85°9W **173** G11
Cumberland Gap △
  U.S.A.   36°36N 83°40W **173** G12
Cumberland I. *U.S.A.*   30°50N 81°25W **178** E8
Cumberland Is.
  Australia   20°35S 149°10E **150** b
Cumberland Island △
  U.S.A.   30°12N 81°24W **178** E8
Cumberland L. *Canada*   54°3N 102°18W **163** C8
Cumberland Pen.
  Canada   67°0N 64°0W **161** D19
Cumberland Plateau
  U.S.A.   36°0N 85°0W **177** D12
Cumberland Sd.
  Canada   65°30N 66°0W **161** D18
Cumbernauld *U.K.*   55°57N 3°58W **65** F5
Cumborah *Australia*   29°40S 147°45E **151** D4
Cumbres de Majalca △
  Mexico   28°48N 106°30W **180** B3
Cumbres de Monterrey △
  Mexico   25°20N 100°25W **180** B4
Cumbres Mayores *Spain*   38°4N 6°39W **89** G4
Cumbria □ *U.K.*   54°42N 2°52W **66** C5
Cumbrian Mts. *U.K.*   54°30N 3°0W **66** C5
Cumbum *India*   15°40N 79°10E **127** G4
Cuminá ➤ *Brazil*   1°30S 56°0W **187** D7
Cummings Mt. *U.S.A.*   35°2N 118°34W **171** L8
Cummins *Australia*   34°16S 135°43E **151** E2
Cumnock *Australia*   32°59S 148°46E **153** B8
Cumnock *U.K.*   55°28N 4°17W **65** F4
Cumpas *Mexico*   30°0N 109°48W **180** B3
Cumplida, Pta.
  Canary Is.   28°50N 17°48W **100** F2

Çumra Turkey 37°34N 32°45E 104 D5
Cuncumén Chile 31°53S 70°38W 190 C1
Cundeelee ⊙ Australia 30°43S 123°25E 149 F3
Cunderdin Australia 31°37S 117°12E 149 F2
Cunene → Angola 17°20S 11°50E 144 A1
Cúneo Italy 44°23N 7°32E 92 D4
Cung Son Vietnam 13°2N 108°58E 120 F7
Çüngüş Turkey 38°13N 39°17E 128 B3
Cunillera, I. = Sa Conillera Spain 38°59N 1°13E 100 C7
Cunlhat France 45°38N 3°32E 72 C7
Cunnamulla Australia 28°2S 145°38E 151 D4
Cuorgnè Italy 45°23N 7°39E 92 C4
Cupar Canada 50°57N 104°10W 163 C8
Cupar U.K. 56°19N 3°1W 65 E5
Cupcini Moldova 48°6N 27°23E 81 B12
Cupertino U.S.A. 37°19N 122°2W 170 H4
Cupica, G. de Colombia 6°25N 77°30W 186 B3
Ćuprija Serbia 43°57N 21°26E 96 C5
Curaçá Brazil 8°59S 39°54W 189 B3
Curaçao W. Indies 12°10N 69°0W 183 D6
Curacautín Chile 38°26S 71°53W 192 A2
Curahuara de Carangas Bolivia 17°52S 68°26W 188 D4
Curanilahue Chile 37°29S 73°28W 190 D1
Curaray → Peru 2°20S 74°5W 186 D4
Cure → France 47°40N 3°41E 71 E10
Curepipe Mauritius 20°19S 57°31E 141 d
Curepto Chile 35°8S 72°1W 190 D1
Curia Portugal 40°22N 8°22W 88 E2
Curiapo Venezuela 8°33N 61°5W 186 B6
Curicó Chile 34°55S 71°20W 190 C1
Curieuse Seychelles 4°15S 55°44E 141 b
Curimatá Brazil 10°2S 44°17W 189 C2
Curinga Italy 38°49N 16°19E 95 D9
Curitiba Brazil 25°20S 49°10W 191 B6
Curitibanos Brazil 27°18S 50°36W 191 B5
Curlewis Australia 31°7S 150°16E 153 A9
Curonian Lagoon = Kurshskiy Zaliv Russia 55°9N 21°6E 82 C8
Curonian Spit Europe 55°20N 20°55E 82 C7
Currabubula Australia 31°16S 150°44E 153 A9
Currais Novos Brazil 6°13S 36°30W 189 B3
Curral Velho Cabo Verde 16°8N 22°48W 134 b
Curralinho Brazil 1°45S 49°46W 187 D9
Currane, L. Ireland 51°49N 10°4W 64 E1
Currant U.S.A. 38°44N 115°28W 168 G6
Curraweena Australia 30°47S 145°54E 153 A6
Currawinya △ Australia 28°55S 144°27E 151 D3
Current → U.S.A. 36°15N 90°55W 176 C9
Currie Australia 39°56S 143°53E 151 F3
Currie U.S.A. 40°16N 114°45W 168 F6
Curtea de Argeș Romania 45°12N 24°42E 81 E9
Curtici Romania 46°21N 21°18E 80 D6
Curtin Springs Australia 25°20S 131°45E 149 E5
Curtis U.S.A. 40°38N 100°31W 172 E3
Curtis Group Australia 39°30S 146°37E 151 F4
Curtis I. Australia 23°35S 151°10E 150 C5
Curuápanema → Brazil 2°25S 55°2W 187 D7
Curuçá Brazil 0°43S 47°50W 187 D9
Curuçá → Brazil 4°27S 71°23W 188 A3
Curuguaty Paraguay 24°31S 55°42W 191 A4
Çürüksu Çayi = Büyük Menderes → Turkey 37°28N 27°11E 99 D9
Curup Indonesia 3°26S 102°13E 118 E2
Cururupu Brazil 1°50S 44°50W 187 D10
Curuzú Cuatiá Argentina 29°50S 58°5W 190 B4
Curvelo Brazil 18°45S 44°27W 189 D2
Cusco Peru 13°32S 72°0W 188 C3
Cusco □ Peru 13°31S 71°59W 188 C3
Cushendall U.K. 55°5N 6°4W 64 A5
Cushing U.S.A. 35°59N 96°46W 176 D6
Cushing, Mt. Canada 57°35N 126°57W 162 B3
Cusihuiriáchic Mexico 28°14N 106°50W 180 B3
Cusna, Mte. Italy 44°17N 10°23E 92 D7
Cusset France 46°8N 3°28E 71 F10
Cusseta U.S.A. 32°18N 84°47W 178 C5
Custer U.S.A. 43°46N 103°36W 172 D2
Cut Bank U.S.A. 48°38N 112°20W 168 B7
Cutchogue U.S.A. 41°1N 72°30W 175 E12
Cutervo Peru 6°25S 78°55W 188 B2
Cuthbert U.S.A. 31°46N 84°48W 178 D5
Cutler U.S.A. 36°31N 119°17W 170 J7
Cutler Ridge U.S.A. 25°35N 80°20W 179 K9
Cutral-Có Argentina 38°58S 69°15W 192 A3
Cutro Italy 39°2N 16°59E 95 C9
Cuttaburra → Australia 29°43S 144°22E 151 D3
Cuttack India 20°25N 85°57E 126 D7
Cuvier, C. Australia 23°14S 113°22E 149 D1
Cuvier I. N.Z. 36°27S 175°50E 154 C4
Cuxhaven Germany 53°51N 8°41E 76 B4
Cuyahoga Falls U.S.A. 41°8N 81°29W 174 E3
Cuyahoga Valley △ U.S.A. 41°24N 81°33W 174 E3
Cuyo Phil. 10°51N 121°2E 119 B6
Cuyuni → Guyana 6°23N 58°41W 186 B7
Cuzco = Cusco Peru 13°32S 72°0W 188 C3
Cuzco Bolivia 20°0S 66°50W 186 H5
Čvrsnica Bos.-H. 43°36N 17°35E 80 G2
Cwmbran U.K. 51°39N 3°2W 67 F4
Cyangugu Rwanda 2°29S 28°54E 142 C2
Cybinka Poland 52°12N 14°46E 83 F1
Cyclades = Kyklades Greece 37°0N 24°30E 98 E6
Cygnet Australia 43°8S 147°1E 151 G4
Cynthiana U.S.A. 38°23N 84°18W 173 F11
Cypress Hills Canada 49°40N 109°30W 163 D7
Cypress Hills ⌂ Canada 49°40N 109°30W 163 D7
Cyprus ■ Asia 35°0N 33°0E 101 E12
Cyrenaica = Barqa Libya 27°0N 23°0E 135 C10
Cyrene Libya 32°53N 21°52E 135 B10
Czaplinek Poland 53°34N 16°14E 82 E3
Czar Canada 52°27N 110°50W 163 C6
Czarna → Łódzkie, Poland 51°18N 19°55E 83 G6
Czarna → Świętokrzyskie, Poland 50°28N 21°21E 83 H8
Czarna Białostocka Poland 53°18N 23°17E 83 E10
Czarna Woda Poland 53°51N 18°6E 82 E5
Czarne Poland 53°42N 16°58E 82 E3
Czarnków Poland 52°55N 16°38E 83 F3
Czech Rep. = Czechia ■ Europe 50°0N 15°0E 78 B8
Czechia ■ Europe 50°0N 15°0E 78 B8
Czechowice-Dziedzice Poland 49°54N 18°59E 83 J5
Czempiń Poland 52°9N 16°43E 83 F3
Czeremcha Poland 52°31N 23°21E 83 F10
Czerniejewo Poland 52°26N 17°30E 83 F4
Czersk Poland 53°46N 17°58E 82 E4
Czerwieńsk Poland 52°1N 15°23E 83 F2
Czerwionka-Leszczyny Poland 50°7N 18°37E 83 H5
Częstochowa Poland 50°49N 19°7E 83 H6
Człopa Poland 53°6N 16°6E 83 E3
Człuchów Poland 53°41N 17°22E 82 E4
Czyżew-Osada Poland 52°48N 22°19E 83 F9

D

Da → Vietnam 21°15N 105°20E 116 G5
Da Hinggan Ling China 48°0N 121°0E 111 B13
Da Lat Vietnam 11°56N 108°25E 121 G7
Da Nang Vietnam 16°4N 108°13E 120 D7
Da Qaidam China 37°50N 95°15E 110 D8
Da Yunhe → Hopei, China 39°10N 117°10E 115 E9
Da Yunhe → Jiangsu, China 34°25N 120°5E 115 H10
Da'an China 45°30N 124°7E 115 B13
Daan Viljoen ⌂ Namibia 22°2S 16°45E 144 B2
Dab'a, Ras el Egypt 31°3N 28°31E 137 E6
Daba Shan China 32°0N 109°0E 116 B7
Dabai Nigeria 11°25N 5°15E 139 C6
Dabakala Côte d'Ivoire 8°15N 4°20W 138 D4
Dabas Hungary 47°11N 19°19E 80 C4
Dabbagh, Jabal Si. Arabia 27°52N 35°45E 128 E2
Dabhoi India 22°10N 73°20E 124 H5
Dąbie Poland 52°5N 18°50E 83 F5
Dabie Shan China 31°20N 115°20E 117 B10
Dabilda Cameroon 12°45N 14°35E 139 C7
Dabnou Niger 14°10N 5°22E 139 C6
Dabola Guinea 10°50N 11°5W 138 C2
Dabou Côte d'Ivoire 5°20N 4°23W 138 D4
Daboya Ghana 9°30N 1°20W 139 D4
Dabravolya Belarus 52°55N 23°59E 83 F10
Dąbrowa Białostocka Poland 53°40N 23°21E 82 E10
Dąbrowa Górnicza Poland 50°15N 19°10E 83 H6
Dąbrowa Tarnowska Poland 50°10N 20°59E 83 H7
Dabu China 24°22N 116°41E 117 E11
Dabugam India 19°27N 82°26E 126 E6
Dabung Malaysia 5°23N 102°1E 121 K4
Dacca = Dhaka Bangla. 23°43N 90°26E 125 H14
Dachang China 32°13N 118°45E 117 A12
Dachaoshan Dam China 24°1N 100°22E 116 E3
Dachau Germany 48°15N 11°26E 77 G7
Dachigam △ India 34°10N 75°0E 124 B6
Dachstein, Hoher Austria 47°28N 13°35E 78 D6
Dačice Czechia 49°5N 15°26E 78 B8
Dacre Canada 45°22N 76°57W 174 A8
Dacula U.S.A. 33°59N 83°54W 178 B6
Dadanawa Guyana 2°50N 59°30W 186 C7
Daday Turkey 41°28N 33°27E 104 B5
Dade City U.S.A. 28°22N 82°11W 179 G7
Dadès, Oued → Morocco 30°58N 6°44W 136 B2
Dadeville U.S.A. 32°50N 85°46W 178 C4
Dadhar Pakistan 29°28N 67°39E 124 E2
Dadiya Nigeria 9°35N 11°24E 139 D7
Ḑadnah U.A.E. 25°32N 56°22E 129 E8
Dadra & Nagar Haveli □ India 20°5N 73°0E 126 D1
Dadri = Charkhi Dadri India 28°37N 76°17E 124 E7
Dadu Pakistan 26°45N 67°45E 124 F2
Dadu He → China 29°31N 103°46E 116 C4
Daegu S. Korea 35°50N 128°37E 115 G15
Daejeon S. Korea 36°20N 127°28E 115 F14
Daejeong S. Korea 33°8N 126°17E 115 H14
Daet Phil. 14°2N 122°55E 119 B6
Dafang China 27°9N 105°39E 116 D5
Dafeng China 33°3N 120°45E 115 H11
Dafnes Greece 35°13N 25°3E 101 D7
Dafni Greece 37°48N 22°1E 98 D4
Dağ Turkey 37°12N 30°31E 99 D12
Dagana Senegal 16°30N 15°35W 138 B1
Dagash Sudan 19°19N 33°25E 137 D3
Dagestan □ Russia 42°30N 47°0E 87 J8
Dagestanskiye Ogni Russia 42°6N 48°12E 87 J9
Dagg Sd. N.Z. 45°23S 166°45E 155 F1
Daggett U.S.A. 34°52N 116°52W 171 L10
Daghestan Republic = Dagestan □ Russia 42°30N 47°0E 87 J8
Daghfeli Sudan 19°18N 32°40E 137 D3
Dağlıq Qarabağ = Nagorno-Karabakh □ Azerbaijan 39°55N 46°45E 105 C12
Dagö = Hiiumaa Estonia 58°50N 22°45E 84 C2
Dagu China 38°59N 117°40E 115 E9
Daguan China 27°43N 103°56E 116 D4
Dagupan Phil. 16°3N 120°20E 119 A6
Daguragu Australia 17°33S 130°30E 148 C5
Daguragu ⊙ Australia 17°24S 130°48E 148 C5
Dahab Egypt 28°31N 34°31E 128 D2
Dahanu India 19°58N 72°44E 126 E1
Dahivadi India 17°43N 74°33E 126 F2
Dahlak Kebir Eritrea 15°50N 40°10E 131 D3
Dahlenburg Germany 53°11N 10°44E 76 B6
Dahlonega U.S.A. 34°32N 83°59W 177 D13
Dahme Germany 51°52N 13°25E 76 D9
Dahod India 22°50N 74°15E 124 H6
Dahong Shan China 31°25N 113°0E 117 B9
Dahongliutan China 35°45N 79°20E 125 B8
Dahra Libya 29°30N 17°50E 135 C9
Dahra Senegal 15°22N 15°30W 138 B1
Dahra, Massif de Algeria 36°7N 1°21E 136 A4
Dahshûr Egypt 29°45N 31°14E 137 F7
Dahūk Iraq 36°50N 43°1E 105 D10
Dahūk □ Iraq 36°50N 42°50E 105 D10
Dai Hao Vietnam 18°1N 106°25E 120 C6
Dai-Sen Japan 35°22N 133°32E 113 G6
Dai Shan China 30°25N 122°10E 117 B14
Dai Xian China 39°4N 112°58E 114 E7
Daicheng China 38°42N 116°38E 114 E9
Daikondi = Dāykondī □ Afghan. 34°0N 66°0E 122 C5
Dailekh Nepal 28°50N 81°44E 125 E9
Daimiel Spain 39°5N 3°35W 89 F7
Daingean Ireland 53°18N 7°17W 64 C4
Daingean, An = Dingle Ireland 52°9N 10°17W 64 D1
Dainkog China 32°30N 97°58E 116 A1
Daintree Australia 16°20S 145°20E 150 B4
Daintree △ Australia 16°8S 145°2E 150 B4
Daiō-Misaki Japan 34°15N 136°45E 113 G8
Dairût Egypt 27°34N 30°43E 137 B3
Daisen Japan 39°27N 140°29E 112 E10
Daisen-Oki △ Japan 35°23N 133°34E 113 G6
Daisetsu-Zan Japan 43°30N 142°57E 112 C11
Daisetsu-Zan △ Japan 43°30N 142°55E 112 C11
Daitari India 21°10N 85°46E 126 D7
Daiyun Shan China 25°50N 118°15E 117 E12
Dajarra Australia 21°42S 139°30E 150 C2
Dajiawa China 37°9N 119°0E 115 F10
Dajin Chuan → China 31°16N 101°59E 116 B3
Dajti △ Albania 41°22N 19°56E 96 E3
Dak Dam Cambodia 12°20N 107°21E 120 F6
Dak Nhe Vietnam 15°28N 107°48E 120 E6
Dak Pek Vietnam 15°4N 107°44E 120 E6
Dak Song Vietnam 12°19N 107°35E 121 F6
Dak Sui Vietnam 14°55N 107°43E 120 E6
Dakar Senegal 14°34N 17°29W 138 C1
Dakar □ Senegal 14°45N 17°20W 138 C1
Dakhla W. Sahara 23°50N 15°53W 134 D2
Dakhla, El Wâhât el Egypt 25°30N 28°50E 137 B2
Dakingari Nigeria 11°37N 4°1E 139 C5
Dakoank India 7°2N 93°43E 127 L11
Dakor India 22°45N 73°11E 124 H5
Dakoro Niger 14°31N 6°46E 139 C6
Dakota City U.S.A. 42°25N 96°25W 172 D5
Đakovica = Gjakovë Kosovo 42°22N 20°26E 96 D4
Đakovo Croatia 45°19N 18°24E 80 E3
Dala-Järna Sweden 60°33N 14°26E 62 D8
Dalaba Guinea 10°47N 12°12W 138 C2
Dalachi China 36°48N 105°0E 114 F3
Dalai Nur China 43°20N 116°45E 114 C9
Dālakī Iran 29°26N 51°17E 129 D6
Dalälven → Sweden 60°12N 16°43E 62 D10
Dalaman Turkey 36°48N 28°47E 99 E10
Dalaman → Turkey 36°41N 28°43E 99 E10
Dalandzadgad Mongolia 43°27N 104°30E 114 C3
Dalap-Uliga-Darrit = Majuro Marshall Is. 7°9N 171°12E 156 G9
Dalarna Sweden 61°0N 14°0E 62 D8
Dalarna □ Sweden 61°0N 14°15E 62 C8
Dalay Mongolia 43°28N 103°30E 114 C2
Dālbandīn Pakistan 29°0N 64°23E 122 E4
Dalbeattie U.K. 54°56N 3°50W 65 G5
Dalbeg Australia 20°16S 147°18E 150 C4
Dalbosjön Sweden 58°40N 12°45E 63 F6
Dalby Australia 27°10S 151°17E 151 D5
Dalby Sweden 55°40N 13°22E 63 J7
Dalby Söderskog △ Sweden 55°41N 13°21E 63 J7
Dale City U.S.A. 38°38N 77°19W 173 F15
Dale Hollow L. U.S.A. 36°32N 85°27W 177 C12
Daleville U.S.A. 31°19N 85°43W 178 D4
Dalga Egypt 27°39N 30°41E 137 B3
Dalgān Iran 27°31N 59°19E 129 E8
Dalgopol Bulgaria 43°3N 27°22E 97 C11
Dalhart U.S.A. 36°4N 102°31W 176 C3
Dalhousie Canada 48°5N 66°26W 165 C6
Dalhousie India 32°38N 75°58E 124 C6
Dali Shaanxi, China 34°48N 109°58E 114 G5
Dali Yunnan, China 25°40N 100°10E 116 E3
Dalian China 38°50N 121°40E 115 E11
Daliang Shan China 28°0N 102°45E 116 D4
Daling He → China 40°55N 121°40E 115 D11
Dāliyat el Karmel Israel 32°43N 35°2E 130 C4
Dalj Croatia 45°29N 18°59E 80 E3
Dalkeith U.K. 55°54N 3°4W 65 F5
Dalkeith U.S.A. 30°0N 85°9W 178 E4
Dalkey Ireland 53°16N 6°6W 64 C5
Dallas Ga., U.S.A. 33°55N 84°51W 178 B5
Dallas Oreg., U.S.A. 44°55N 123°19W 168 D2
Dallas Tex., U.S.A. 32°47N 96°48W 176 E6
Dallas-Fort Worth Int. ✕ (DFW) U.S.A. 32°54N 97°2W 176 E6
Dalles, The U.S.A. 45°36N 121°10W 168 D3
Dalmā U.A.E. 24°30N 52°20E 129 E7
Dalmacija Croatia 43°20N 17°0E 93 E13
Dalmas, L. Canada 53°30N 71°50W 165 B5
Dalmatia = Dalmacija Croatia 43°20N 17°0E 93 E13
Dalmau India 26°4N 81°2E 125 F9
Dalmellington U.K. 55°19N 4°23W 65 F4
Dalmeny Australia 36°10S 150°8E 153 D9
Dalnegorsk Russia 44°32N 135°33E 112 B7
Dalnerechensk Russia 45°50N 133°40E 112 B6
Dalnevostochnyy □ Russia 67°0N 140°0E 107 C14
Daloa Côte d'Ivoire 7°0N 6°30W 138 D3
Dalou Shan China 28°15N 107°0E 116 C6
Dalry U.K. 55°42N 4°43W 65 F4
Dalrymple, L. Australia 20°40S 147°0E 150 C4
Dalrymple, Mt. Australia 21°1S 148°39E 150 b
Dals Långed Sweden 58°56N 12°18E 63 F6
Dalsjöfors Sweden 57°46N 13°5E 63 G7
Dalsland Sweden 58°50N 12°15E 63 F6
Daltenganj India 24°0N 84°4E 125 H11
Dalton Ga., U.S.A. 34°46N 84°58W 177 D12
Dalton Mass., U.S.A. 42°28N 73°11W 175 D11
Dalton Nebr., U.S.A. 41°25N 102°58W 172 E2
Dalton, Kap Greenland 69°25N 24°3W 57 D8
Dalton-in-Furness U.K. 54°10N 3°11W 66 C4
Dalvík Iceland 65°58N 18°32W 60 D4
Dálvvadis = Jokkmokk Sweden 66°35N 19°50E 60 C18
Dalwallinu Australia 30°17S 116°40E 149 F2
Daly → Australia 13°35S 130°19E 148 B5
Daly City U.S.A. 37°42N 122°27W 170 H4
Daly L. Canada 56°32N 105°39W 163 B7
Daly River Australia 13°46S 130°42E 148 B5
Daly River-Port Keats ⊙ Australia 14°13S 129°36E 148 B4
Daly Waters Australia 16°15S 133°24E 150 B1
Dalyan Turkey 36°50N 28°39E 99 E10
Dam Doi Vietnam 8°50N 105°12E 121 H5
Dam Ha Vietnam 21°21N 107°36E 120 B6
Damachova Belarus 51°45N 23°36E 83 G10
Daman India 20°25N 72°57E 126 D1
Daman & Diu □ India 20°25N 72°58E 126 D1
Dāmaneh Iran 33°1N 50°29E 129 C6
Damanganga → India 20°25N 72°56E 126 D1
Damanhûr Egypt 31°0N 30°30E 137 E7
Damant L. Canada 61°45N 105°5W 163 A7
Damaq Iran 35°25N 48°49E 105 E13
Damar Indonesia 7°7S 128°40E 119 F7
Damara C.A.R. 4°58N 18°42E 140 D3
Damaraland Namibia 20°0S 15°0E 144 B2
Damascus = Dimashq Syria 33°30N 36°18E 130 B5
Damascus U.S.A. 31°18N 84°43W 178 D5
Damasi Greece 39°43N 22°11E 98 B4
Damaturu Nigeria 11°45N 11°55E 139 C7
Damāvand Iran 35°57N 52°7E 129 C7
Damāvand, Qolleh-ye Iran 35°57N 52°7E 129 C7
Damba Angola 6°44S 15°20E 140 F3
Damboa Nigeria 11°15N 12°55E 139 C7
Dâmboviţa □ Romania 45°0N 25°30E 81 F10
Dâmboviţa → Romania 44°12N 26°26E 81 F11
Dâmbovnic → Romania 44°28N 25°18E 81 F10
Dambulla Sri Lanka 7°51N 80°39E 127 L5
Dame Marie Haiti 18°34N 74°26W 183 C5
Dāmghān Iran 36°10N 54°17E 129 B7
Dămienesti Romania 46°44N 26°59E 81 D11
Damietta = Dumyât Egypt 31°24N 31°48E 137 E7
Daming China 36°15N 115°6E 114 F8
Damīr Qābū Syria 36°58N 41°51E 128 B4
Dammam = Ad Dammām Si. Arabia 26°20N 50°5E 129 E6
Dammarie-les-Lys France 48°31N 2°39E 71 D9
Dammartin-en-Goële France 49°3N 2°41E 71 C9
Damme Germany 52°32N 8°11E 76 C4
Damodar → India 23°17N 87°35E 125 H12
Damoh India 23°50N 79°28E 125 H8
Damous Algeria 36°31N 1°42E 136 A4
Dampier Australia 20°41S 116°42E 148 D2
Dampier, Selat Indonesia 0°40S 131°0E 119 E8
Dampier Arch. Australia 20°38S 116°32E 148 D2
Damrani Algeria 27°45N 2°56W 136 C3
Damrei, Chuor Phnum Cambodia 11°30N 103°0E 121 G4
Damvillers France 49°20N 5°21E 71 C12
Damyang S. Korea 35°19N 126°59E 115 G14
Dan-Gulbi Nigeria 11°40N 6°15E 139 C6
Dan-Sadau Nigeria 11°17N 6°29E 139 C6
Dana Indonesia 11°0S 121°15E 119 F6
Dana Jordan 30°41N 35°37E 130 E4
Dana Nepal 28°32N 83°37E 125 E10
Dana, L. Canada 50°53N 77°20W 164 B4
Dana, Mt. U.S.A. 37°54N 119°12W 170 H7
Danakil Desert Ethiopia 12°45N 41°0E 131 E3
Danané Côte d'Ivoire 7°16N 8°9W 138 D3
Danba China 30°54N 101°48E 116 B3
Danbury U.S.A. 41°24N 73°28W 175 E11
Danby L. U.S.A. 34°13N 115°5W 171 L11
Dand Afghan. 31°28N 65°32E 124 D1
Dande ⌂ Zimbabwe 15°56S 30°16E 143 F3
Dandeldhura Nepal 29°20N 80°35E 125 E9
Dandeli India 15°5N 74°30E 127 G2
Dandenong Australia 38°0S 145°15E 153 E6
Dandī Iran 36°32N 47°37E 105 D12
Dandīl Egypt 29°10N 31°2E 137 F7
Dandong China 40°10N 124°20E 115 D13
Daneborg Greenland 74°18N 20°14W 57 C8
Danfeng China 33°45N 110°25E 114 H6
Dangan Liedao China 22°2N 114°8E 117 F10
Dangé-St-Romain France 46°56N 0°36E 72 B4
Dângeni Romania 47°51N 26°58E 81 C11
Danger Is. = Pukapuka Cook Is. 10°53S 165°49W 157 J11
Danger Pt. S. Africa 34°40S 19°17E 144 D2
Dangla Shan = Tanggula Shan China 32°40N 92°10E 110 E7
Dangora Nigeria 11°30N 8°7E 139 C6
Dangouadougou Burkina Faso 10°9N 4°56W 138 D4
Dangrek, Mts. = Dangrek, Phnom Thailand 14°20N 104°0E 120 E5
Dangrek, Phnom Thailand 14°20N 104°0E 120 E5
Dangriga Belize 17°0N 88°13W 181 D7
Dangshan China 34°27N 116°22E 114 G9
Dangtu China 31°32N 118°25E 117 B12
Dangyang China 30°52N 111°44E 117 B8
Daniel U.S.A. 42°52N 110°4W 168 E8
Daniel's Harbour Canada 50°13N 57°35W 165 B8
Danielskuil S. Africa 28°11S 23°33E 144 C3
Danielson U.S.A. 41°48N 71°53W 175 E13
Danielsville U.S.A. 34°8N 83°13W 178 A6
Danilov Russia 58°16N 40°13E 84 C11
Danilovgrad Montenegro 42°38N 19°4E 96 D3
Danilovka Russia 50°25N 44°12E 86 E7
Daning China 36°28N 110°45E 114 F6
Danja Nigeria 11°21N 7°30E 139 C6
Danjiangkou China 32°31N 111°30E 117 A8
Danjiangkou Shuiku China 32°37N 111°30E 117 A8
Dank Oman 23°33N 56°16E 129 F8
Dankalwa Nigeria 11°52N 12°12E 139 C7
Dankama Nigeria 13°20N 7°44E 139 C6
Dankhar Gompa India 32°10N 78°10E 124 C8
Dankov Russia 53°20N 39°5E 84 F10
Danleng China 30°1N 103°31E 116 B4
Danlí Honduras 14°4N 86°35W 182 D2
Danmark = Denmark ■ Europe 55°45N 10°0E 63 J3
Danmark Fjord Greenland 81°30N 22°0W 57 A8
Danmarkshavn Greenland 76°45N 18°50W 57 B9
Dannemora U.S.A. 44°43N 73°44W 175 B11
Dannenberg Germany 53°6N 11°5E 76 B7
Dannevirke N.Z. 40°12S 176°8E 154 G5
Dannhauser S. Africa 28°0S 30°3E 145 C5
Dansville U.S.A. 42°34N 77°42W 174 D7
Danta India 24°11N 72°46E 124 G5
Dantan India 21°57N 87°20E 125 J12
Dante = Xaafuun Somalia 10°25N 51°16E 131 E5
Dantewara India 18°54N 81°21E 126 E5
Danube = Dunărea → Europe 45°20N 29°40E 81 E14
Danvers U.S.A. 42°34N 70°56W 175 D14
Danville Ga., U.S.A. 32°37N 83°15W 178 C6
Danville Ill., U.S.A. 40°8N 87°37W 172 E10
Danville Ky., U.S.A. 37°39N 84°46W 173 G11
Danville Pa., U.S.A. 40°58N 76°37W 175 F8
Danville Va., U.S.A. 36°36N 79°23W 173 G14
Danville Vt., U.S.A. 44°25N 72°9W 175 B12
Danyang China 32°0N 119°31E 117 B12
Danzhai China 26°11N 107°48E 116 D6
Danzhou China 19°31N 109°33E 117 a
Danzig = Gdańsk Poland 54°22N 18°40E 82 D5
Dão → Portugal 40°20N 8°11W 88 E2
Dao Xian China 25°36N 111°31E 117 E8
Daocheng China 29°0N 100°10E 116 C3
Daoud = Aïn Beïda Algeria 35°50N 7°29E 136 A5
Daoukro Côte d'Ivoire 7°10N 3°58W 138 D4
Dapaong Togo 10°55N 0°16E 139 C5
Dapchi Nigeria 12°32N 11°31E 139 C7
Dapoli India 17°46N 73°11E 126 F1
Daqing China 46°35N 125°0E 111 B13
Daqing Shan China 40°40N 111°0E 114 D6
Daqq-e Sorkh, Kavīr Iran 33°45N 52°50E 129 C7
Daqu Shan China 30°25N 122°20E 117 B14
Dar Banda Africa 8°0N 23°0E 132 F6
Dar el Beida = Casablanca Morocco 33°36N 7°36W 136 B2
Dar es Salaam Tanzania 6°50S 39°12E 142 D4
Dar Mazār Iran 29°14N 57°20E 129 D8
Dar'ā Syria 32°36N 36°7E 130 C5
Dar'ā □ Syria 32°55N 36°10E 130 C5
Dārāb Iran 28°50N 54°30E 129 D7
Daraban Pakistan 31°44N 70°20E 124 D4
Darabani Romania 48°10N 26°39E 81 B11
Daraj Libya 30°10N 10°28E 135 B8
Dārān Iran 32°59N 50°24E 129 C6
Daravica = Gjeravicë Kosovo 42°32N 20°8E 96 D4
Daraw Egypt 24°22N 32°51E 137 C3
Dārayyā Syria 33°28N 36°15E 130 B5
Darazo Nigeria 11°1N 10°24E 139 C7
Darband Pakistan 34°20N 72°50E 124 B5
Darband, Kūh-e Iran 31°34N 57°8E 129 D8
Darbhanga India 26°15N 85°55E 125 F11
D'Arcy Canada 50°33N 122°29W 162 C4
Darda Croatia 45°40N 18°41E 80 E3
Dardanë Kosovo 42°35N 21°35E 96 D5
Dardanelle Ark., U.S.A. 35°13N 93°9W 176 D8
Dardanelle Calif., U.S.A. 38°20N 119°50W 170 G7
Dardanelles = Çanakkale Boğazı Turkey 40°17N 26°32E 97 F10
Darende Turkey 38°31N 37°30E 104 C7
Dārestān Iran 29°9N 58°42E 129 D8
Darfield N.Z. 43°29S 172°7E 155 D7
Darfo-Boario Terme Italy 45°53N 10°11E 92 C7
Dârfûr Sudan 13°40N 24°0E 135 F10
Dargai Pakistan 34°25N 71°55E 124 B4
Dargaville N.Z. 35°57S 173°52E 154 B2
Dargol Niger 13°54N 1°22E 139 C5
Darhan Mongolia 49°37N 106°21E 110 B10
Darhan Muminggan China 41°40N 110°28E 114 D6
Darıca Turkey 40°45N 29°23E 104 B3
Darien U.S.A. 31°23N 81°26W 178 D8
Darién, G. del Caribbean 9°0N 77°0W 186 B3
Darién △ Panama 7°36N 77°57W 182 E4
Dariganga = Ovoot Mongolia 45°21N 113°45E 114 B7
Daringbadi India 19°54N 84°8E 126 E7
Darjeeling = Darjiling India 27°3N 88°18E 125 F13
Darjiling India 27°3N 88°18E 125 F13
Darkan Australia 33°20S 116°43E 149 F2
Darke Peak Australia 33°27S 136°12E 152 B2
Darkhana Pakistan 30°39N 72°11E 124 D5
Darkhazīneh Iran 31°54N 48°39E 129 D6
Darkot Pass Pakistan 36°45N 73°26E 125 A5
Darling → Australia 34°4S 141°54E 152 C4
Darling Downs Australia 27°30S 150°30E 151 D5
Darling Ra. Australia 32°30S 116°20E 149 F2
Darlington U.K. 54°32N 1°33W 66 C6
Darlington Fla., U.S.A. 30°57N 86°3W 178 E3
Darlington S.C., U.S.A. 34°18N 79°52W 177 D15
Darlington □ U.K. 54°32N 1°33W 66 C6
Darlington, L. S. Africa 33°10S 25°9E 144 D4
Darlington Point Australia 34°37S 146°1E 153 C7
Darlot, L. Australia 27°48S 121°35E 149 E3
Darłowo Poland 54°25N 16°25E 82 D3
Dărmănești Bacău, Romania 46°21N 26°33E 81 D11
Dărmănești Suceava, Romania 47°44N 26°9E 81 C11
Darmstadt Germany 49°51N 8°39E 77 F4
Darnah Libya 32°45N 22°45E 135 B10
Darnall S. Africa 29°23S 31°18E 145 C5
Darney France 48°5N 6°2E 71 D13
Darnick Australia 32°48S 143°38E 152 B5
Darnley Australia 9°35S 143°46E 150 a
Darnley, C. Antarctica 68°0S 69°0E 55 C6
Darnley B. Canada 69°30N 123°30W 160 D7
Daroca Spain 41°9N 1°25W 90 D3
Darou-Mousti Senegal 15°3N 16°3W 138 B1
Darr → Australia 23°39S 143°50E 150 C3
Darra Pezu Pakistan 32°19N 70°44E 124 C4
Darran Mts. N.Z. 44°37S 167°59E 155 E2
Darreh Shahr Iran 33°7N 47°22E 105 F12
Darrequeira Argentina 37°42S 63°10W 190 D3
Darrington U.S.A. 48°15N 121°36W 168 B3
Darsi India 15°46N 79°44E 127 G4
Darsser Ort Germany 54°28N 12°32E 76 A8
Dart → U.K. 50°24N 3°39W 67 G4
Dartford U.K. 51°26N 0°13E 67 F8
Dartmoor Australia 37°56S 141°19E 152 D4
Dartmoor U.K. 50°38N 3°57W 67 G4
Dartmoor △ U.K. 50°37N 3°59W 67 G4
Dartmouth Canada 44°40N 63°30W 165 D7
Dartmouth U.K. 50°21N 3°36W 67 G4
Dartmouth, L. Queens., Australia 26°4S 145°18E 151 D4
Dartmouth, L. Vic., Australia 36°34S 147°32E 153 D7
Dartuch, C. = Artrutx, C. de Spain 39°55N 3°49E 100 B10
Daruvar Croatia 45°35N 17°14E 80 E2
Darvel, Teluk = Lahad Datu, Teluk Malaysia 4°50N 118°20E 119 D5
Darvi Mongolia 46°27N 94°7E 109 C12
Darwen U.K. 53°42N 2°29W 66 D5
Darwendale Zimbabwe 17°41S 30°33E 145 A5
Darwha India 20°15N 77°45E 126 D3
Darwin Australia 12°25S 130°51E 148 B5
Darwin U.S.A. 36°15N 117°35W 171 J9
Darwin, Mt. Chile 54°47S 69°55W 192 D3
Darya Khan Pakistan 31°48N 71°6E 124 D4
Daryapur India 20°55N 77°20E 126 D3
Daryoi Amu = Amudarya → Uzbekistan 43°58N 59°34E 108 D5
Dās U.A.E. 25°20N 53°30E 129 E7
Dashen, Ras Ethiopia 13°8N 38°26E 131 E2
Dasher U.S.A. 30°45N 83°13W 178 E6
Dashetai China 41°0N 109°5E 114 D5
Dashiqiao China 40°38N 122°30E 115 D12
Dashkesan = Daşkäsän Azerbaijan 40°25N 46°0E 87 K7
Dashköpri Turkmenistan 36°16N 62°8E 129 B9
Dasht → Pakistan 25°10N 61°40E 122 G2
Daska Pakistan 32°20N 74°20E 124 C6
Daşkäsän Azerbaijan 40°25N 46°0E 87 K7
Daşoguz Turkmenistan 41°49N 59°58E 108 D5
Dassa Benin 7°46N 2°14E 139 D5
Dasuya India 31°49N 75°38E 124 D6
Datça Turkey 36°46N 27°40E 99 E9
Date Japan 42°28N 140°52E 112 C10
Datia India 25°39N 78°27E 125 G8
Datian China 25°40N 117°50E 117 E11
Datong Anhui, China 30°48N 117°44E 117 B11
Datong Qinghai, China 36°20N 102°50E 110 D9
Datong Shanxi, China 40°6N 113°18E 114 D7
Dattakhel Pakistan 32°54N 69°46E 124 C3
Dattapur = Dhamangaon India 20°48N 78°9E 126 D4
Datteln Germany 51°39N 7°21E 76 D3
Datu, Tanjung Indonesia 2°5N 109°39E 118 D3
Datu Piang Phil. 7°2N 124°30E 119 C6
Datuk, Tanjong = Datu, Tanjung Indonesia 2°5N 109°39E 118 D3
Daud Khel Pakistan 32°53N 71°34E 124 C4
Daudnagar India 25°2N 84°24E 125 G11
Daugava → Latvia 57°4N 24°3E 84 D3
Daugavpils Latvia 55°53N 26°32E 84 E4
Daulatabad India 19°57N 75°15E 126 E2
Daulpur India 26°45N 77°59E 124 F7
Daun Germany 50°11N 6°49E 77 E2
Daund India 18°26N 74°40E 126 E2
Daung Kyun Myanmar 12°13N 98°4E 121 F1
Dauphin Canada 51°9N 100°5W 163 C8
Dauphin U.S.A. 40°22N 76°56W 174 F8
Dauphin L. Canada 51°20N 99°45W 163 C9
Dauphiné France 45°15N 5°25E 73 C9
Daura Borno, Nigeria 11°31N 11°24E 139 C7
Daura Katsina, Nigeria 13°2N 8°21E 139 C6
Daurada, Costa Spain 41°12N 1°15E 90 D6
Dausa India 26°52N 76°20E 124 F7
Däväçi Azerbaijan 41°15N 48°57E 87 K9
Davangere India 14°25N 75°55E 127 G2
Davao Phil. 7°0N 125°40E 119 C7
Davao G. Phil. 6°30N 125°48E 119 C7
Dāvar Panāh = Sarāvān Iran 27°25N 62°15E 129 E9
Davenport Calif., U.S.A. 37°1N 122°12W 170 H4
Davenport Fla., U.S.A. 28°10N 81°36W 179 G8
Davenport Iowa, U.S.A. 41°32N 90°35W 172 E8
Davenport Wash., U.S.A. 47°39N 118°9W 168 C4
Davenport Ra. Australia 20°28S 134°0E 150 C1
Davenport Range △ Australia 20°36S 134°22E 150 C1
Daventry U.K. 52°16N 1°10W 67 E6
David Panama 8°30N 82°30W 182 E3
David City U.S.A. 41°15N 97°8W 172 E5
David Glacier Antarctica 75°20S 162°0E 55 D11
David Gorodok = Davyd Haradok Belarus 52°4N 27°8E 75 B14
Davidson Canada 51°16N 105°59W 163 C7
Davidson Mts. U.S.A. 68°41N 142°22W 166 B11
Davie U.S.A. 26°3N 80°14W 179 J9
Davis Antarctica 68°34S 77°55E 55 C6
Davis U.S.A. 38°33N 121°44W 170 G5
Davis Dam U.S.A. 35°12N 114°34W 171 K12
Davis Mts. U.S.A. 30°50N 103°55W 176 F3
Davis Sea Antarctica 66°0S 92°0E 55 C7
Davis Str. N. Amer. 65°0N 58°0W 161 D19
Davisboro U.S.A. 32°59N 82°36W 178 C7
Davlos Cyprus 35°25N 33°54E 101 D12
Davo → Côte d'Ivoire 5°0N 6°10W 138 D3
Davos Switz. 46°48N 9°49E 77 J5
Davutlar Turkey 37°43N 27°17E 99 D9
Davy L. Canada 58°53N 108°18W 163 B7
Davyd Haradok Belarus 52°4N 27°8E 75 B14
Dawaki Bauchi, Nigeria 9°25N 9°33E 139 D6
Dawaki Kano, Nigeria 12°5N 8°23E 139 C6
Dawei Myanmar 14°2N 98°12E 120 E2
Dawes Ra. Australia 24°40S 150°40E 150 C5
Dawlish U.K. 50°35N 3°28W 67 G4
Dawmat al Jandal Si. Arabia 29°55N 39°40E 128 D3
Dawna Ra. Myanmar 16°30N 98°30E 120 D2
Dawros Hd. Ireland 54°50N 8°33W 64 B3
Dawson U.S.A. 31°46N 84°27W 178 D5
Dawson, I. Chile 53°50S 70°50W 192 D2
Dawson B. Canada 52°53N 100°49W 163 C8
Dawson City Canada 64°10N 139°30W 160 E4
Dawson Creek Canada 55°45N 120°15W 162 B4
Dawson Inlet Canada 61°50N 93°25W 163 A10
Dawson Ra. Australia 24°30S 149°48E 150 C4
Dawu Hubei, China 31°34N 114°7E 117 B10
Dawu Sichuan, China 30°55N 101°10E 116 B3
Dax France 43°44N 1°3W 72 E2
Daxian China 31°15N 107°23E 116 B6
Daxin China 22°50N 107°11E 116 F6
Daxindian China 37°30N 120°50E 115 F11
Daxing China 39°47N 116°24E 114 E9
Daxinggou China 43°25N 129°40E 115 C15
Daxue Shan Sichuan, China 30°30N 101°30E 116 B3
Daxue Shan Yunnan, China 23°42N 99°48E 116 F2
Day U.S.A. 30°12N 83°17W 178 E6
Dayao China 25°43N 101°20E 116 E3
Daye China 30°6N 114°58E 117 B10
Dayet en Naharat Mali 17°39N 3°10W 138 B4
Dayi China 30°41N 103°29E 116 B4

Dāykondī □ *Afghan.* 34°0N 66°0E **122** C5
Daylesford *Australia* 37°21S 144°9E **152** D6
Dayong = Zhangjiajie
  China 29°11N 110°30E **117** C8
Dayr az Zawr *Syria* 35°20N 40°5E **105** E9
Dayr az Zawr □ *Syria* 34°50N 40°10E **105** E9
Daysland *Canada* 52°50N 112°20W **162** C6
Dayton *Nev., U.S.A.* 39°14N 119°36W **170** F7
Dayton *Ohio, U.S.A.* 39°45N 84°12W **173** F11
Dayton *Pa., U.S.A.* 40°53N 79°15W **174** F5
Dayton *Tenn., U.S.A.* 35°30N 85°1W **177** D12
Dayton *Wash., U.S.A.* 46°19N 117°59W **168** C5
Dayton *Wyo., U.S.A.* 44°53N 107°16W **168** D10
Daytona Beach *U.S.A.* 29°13N 81°1W **179** F8
Dayu *China* 25°24N 114°22E **117** E10
Dayville *U.S.A.* 44°28N 119°32W **168** D4
Dazhu *China* 30°41N 107°15E **116** B6
Dazkırı *Turkey* 37°57N 29°52E **99** D11
Dazu *China* 29°40N 105°42E **116** C5
De Aar *S. Africa* 30°39S 24°0E **144** D3
De Armanville *U.S.A.* 33°38N 85°45W **178** B4
De Bary *U.S.A.* 28°54N 81°18W **179** G8
De Funiak Springs
  U.S.A. 30°43N 86°7W **178** K3
De Grey → *Australia* 20°12S 119°13E **148** D2
De Haan *Belgium* 51°16N 3°2E **69** C3
De Hoop → *S. Africa* 30°20S 28°0E **144** D3
De Kalb Junction
  U.S.A. 44°30N 75°16W **175** B9
De Land *U.S.A.* 29°2N 81°18W **179** F8
De Leon *U.S.A.* 32°7N 98°32W **176** E5
De Leon Springs *U.S.A.* 29°7N 81°21W **179** F8
De Long Mts. *U.S.A.* 68°10N 163°30W **166** B7
De Panne *Belgium* 51°6N 2°34E **69** C2
De Pere *U.S.A.* 44°27N 88°4W **172** C9
De Queen *U.S.A.* 34°2N 94°21W **176** D7
De Quincy *U.S.A.* 30°27N 93°26W **176** F8
De Ruyters *U.S.A.* 42°45N 75°53W **175** D9
De Smet *U.S.A.* 44°23N 97°33W **172** C5
De Soto *U.S.A.* 38°8N 90°34W **172** F8
De Soto City *U.S.A.* 27°27N 81°24W **179** H8
De Tour Village *U.S.A.* 46°0N 83°56W **173** B12
De Witt *U.S.A.* 34°18N 91°20W **176** D9
Dead L. *Australia* 30°10N 85°10W **178** G4
Dead I. *Australia* 39°30S 147°20E **151** F4
Dealesville *S. Africa* 28°41S 25°44E **144** C4
de'an *China* 29°21N 115°46E **117** C10
Dean → *Canada* 52°49N 126°58W **162** C3
Dean, Forest of *U.K.* 51°45N 2°33W **67** F5
Dean Chan. *Canada* 52°30N 127°15W **162** C3
Deán Funes *Argentina* 30°20S 64°20W **190** C3
Dease → *Canada* 59°56N 128°32W **162** B3
Dease L. *Canada* 58°40N 130°5W **162** B2
Dease Lake *Canada* 58°25N 130°6W **162** B2
Death Valley *U.S.A.* 36°15N 116°50W **171** J10
Death Valley △ *U.S.A.* 36°29N 117°6W **171** J9
Death Valley Junction
  U.S.A. 36°20N 116°25W **171** J10
Deatnu = Tana →
  Norway 70°30N 28°14E **60** A23
Deauville *France* 49°23N 0°2E **70** C7
Deba *Spain* 43°18N 2°21W **90** B2
Deba Habe *Nigeria* 10°14N 11°20E **139** C7
Debagram *India* 23°41N 88°18E **125** H13
Debaltseve *Ukraine* 48°22N 38°26E **85** H10
Debao *China* 23°21N 106°46E **116** F6
Debar *Macedonia* 41°31N 20°30E **96** E4
Debden *Canada* 53°30N 106°50W **163** C7
Debdou *Morocco* 33°59N 3°0W **136** B5
Dębica *Poland* 50°2N 21°25E **83** H8
Dęblin *Poland* 51°34N 21°50E **83** G8
Dębno *Poland* 52°44N 14°41E **83** F1
Débo, L. *Mali* 15°14N 4°15W **138** B4
DeBolt *Canada* 55°12N 118°1W **162** B5
Deborah East, L.
  Australia 30°45S 119°30E **149** F2
Deborah West, L.
  Australia 30°45S 119°5E **149** F2
Debrc *Serbia* 44°38N 19°53E **96** B3
Debre Markos *Ethiopia* 10°20N 37°40E **131** E2
Debre Tabor *Ethiopia* 11°50N 38°26E **131** E2
Debre Zeyit *Ethiopia* 8°50N 39°0E **131** F2
Debrecen *Hungary* 47°33N 21°42E **80** C6
Debrzno *Poland* 53°33N 17°14E **82** E4
Debundscha *Cameroon* 4°7N 8°59E **139** E6
Deçan *Kosovo* 42°30N 20°18E **96** D4
Decatur *Ala., U.S.A.* 34°36N 86°59W **177** D11
Decatur *Ga., U.S.A.* 33°46N 84°16W **178** B4
Decatur *Ill., U.S.A.* 39°51N 88°57W **172** F9
Decatur *Ind., U.S.A.* 40°50N 84°56W **173** E11
Decatur *Tex., U.S.A.* 33°14N 97°35W **176** E6
Decazeville *France* 44°34N 2°15E **72** D6
Deccan *India* 18°0N 79°0E **126** F4
Deception, Mt.
  Australia 30°42S 138°16E **152** A3
Deception Bay
  Australia 27°10S 153°5E **151** D5
Deception I. *Antarctica* 63°0S 60°15W **55** C17
Deception I. *Canada* 56°33N 104°13W **163** B8
Dechang *China* 27°25N 102°11E **116** D4
Dechhu *India* 26°46N 72°20E **124** F5
Decimomannu *Italy* 39°19N 8°58E **94** C1
Decize *France* 46°50N 3°28E **73** F10
Deckerville *U.S.A.* 43°32N 82°44W **174** C2
Decollatura *Italy* 39°3N 16°21E **95** C9
Decorah *U.S.A.* 43°18N 91°48W **172** D8
Deda *Romania* 46°56N 24°50E **81** D9
Dedéagach = Alexandroupoli
  Greece 40°50N 25°54E **97** F9
Dedham *U.S.A.* 42°15N 71°10W **175** D13
Dédougou *Burkina Faso* 12°30N 3°25W **138** C4
Dedovichi *Russia* 57°32N 29°56E **84** D5
Dedza *Malawi* 14°20S 34°20E **143** E3
Dee → *Aberds., U.K.* 57°9N 2°5W **66** D6
Dee → *Dumf. & Gall., U.K.* 54°51N 4°3W **65** G4
Dee → *Wales, U.K.* 53°22N 3°17W **64** D4
Deep B. *Canada* 61°15N 116°35W **162** A5
Deep Bay = Shenzhen Wan
  China 22°27N 113°55E **111** a
Deep Lead *Australia* 37°0S 142°43E **152** D5
Deepwater *Australia* 29°25S 151°51E **151** D5
Deer → *Canada* 58°23N 94°13W **163** B10
Deer L. *Canada* 52°40N 94°20W **163** C10

Deer Lake *Nfld. & L.,*
  Canada 49°11N 57°27W **165** C8
Deer Lake *Ont.,*
  Canada 52°36N 94°20W **163** C10
Deer Lodge *U.S.A.* 46°24N 112°44W **168** C7
Deer Park *Fla., U.S.A.* 28°6N 80°54W **179** G9
Deer Park *Wash.,*
  U.S.A. 47°57N 117°28W **168** C5
Deer River *U.S.A.* 47°20N 93°48W **172** B7
Deergarail *Australia* 19°16S 146°33E **150** B4
Deerfield Beach *U.S.A.* 26°19N 80°6W **179** J9
Defiance *U.S.A.* 41°17N 84°22W **173** E11
Degana *India* 26°50N 74°20E **124** F6
Degê *China* 31°44N 98°39E **116** B3
Degebe → *Portugal* 38°13N 7°29W **89** G3
Degeberga *Sweden* 55°51N 14°5E **63** J8
Dégelis *Canada* 47°30N 68°35W **165** C6
Degerfors *Sweden* 59°15N 14°27E **62** E8
Degerhamn *Sweden* 56°20N 16°24E **63** H10
Deggendorf *Germany* 48°50N 12°57E **77** G8
Degh → *Pakistan* 31°3N 73°21E **124** D5
Değirmendere *Turkey* 40°42N 29°47E **97** F13
Değirmenlik = Kythréa
  Cyprus 35°15N 33°29E **101** D12
Deh Bīd *Iran* 30°39N 53°11E **129** D7
Deh Dasht *Iran* 30°47N 50°33E **129** D6
Deh-e Shīr *Iran* 31°29N 53°45E **129** D7
Dehaj *Iran* 30°42N 54°53E **129** D7
Dehak *Iran* 27°11N 62°37E **129** E9
Dehdez *Iran* 31°43N 50°17E **129** D6
Dehej *India* 21°44N 72°40E **124** J5
Dehestān *Iran* 28°30N 55°35E **129** D7
Dehgolān *Iran* 35°17N 47°25E **105** E12
Dehibat *Tunisia* 32°0N 10°47E **136** B6
Dehiwala *Sri Lanka* 6°50N 79°51E **127** L4
Dehlorān *Iran* 32°41N 47°16E **105** F12
Dehnow-e Kūhestān
  Iran 27°58N 58°32E **129** E8
Dehra Dun *India* 30°20N 78°4E **124** D8
Dehri *India* 24°50N 84°15E **125** G11
Dehua *China* 25°23N 118°1E **117** E12
Dehui *China* 44°30N 125°40E **115** B13
Deinze *Belgium* 50°59N 3°32E **69** D3
Deir al Balah *Gaza Strip* 31°25N 34°21E **130** D3
Dej *Romania* 47°10N 23°52E **81** C8
Deje *Sweden* 59°35N 13°29E **62** E7
Dejiang *China* 28°18N 108°7E **116** C7
Deka → *Zimbabwe* 18°4S 26°42E **144** A4
DeKalb *U.S.A.* 41°56N 88°46W **172** E9
Dekese
  Dem. Rep. of the Congo 3°24S 21°24E **140** E4
Del Caño Rise *Ind. Oc.* 45°15S 44°15E **146** J3
Del Mar *U.S.A.* 32°58N 117°16W **171** N9
Del Norte *U.S.A.* 37°41N 106°21W **169** H10
Del Rio *U.S.A.* 29°22N 100°54W **176** G4
Delambre I. *Australia* 20°26S 117°5E **148** D2
Delano *U.S.A.* 35°46N 119°15W **171** K7
Delano Peak *U.S.A.* 38°22N 112°22W **168** G7
Delareyville *S. Africa* 26°41S 25°26E **144** C4
Delaronde L. *Canada* 54°3N 107°3W **163** C7
Delavan *U.S.A.* 42°38N 88°39W **172** D9
Delaware *U.S.A.* 40°18N 83°4W **173** E12
Delaware □ *U.S.A.* 39°0N 75°20W **173** F16
Delaware → *U.S.A.* 39°15N 75°20W **173** F16
Delaware Water Gap △
  U.S.A. 41°10N 74°55W **175** D10
Delay → *Canada* 56°56N 71°28W **165** A5
Delbrück *Germany* 51°46N 8°34E **76** D5
Delčevo *Macedonia* 41°58N 22°46E **96** E6
Delegate *Australia* 37°4S 148°56E **153** D8
Delémont *Switz.* 47°22N 7°20E **77** H3
Delevan *U.S.A.* 42°29N 78°29W **174** D6
Delft *Neths.* 52°1N 4°22E **69** B4
Delft I. *Sri Lanka* 9°30N 79°40E **127** K4
Delfzijl *Neths.* 53°20N 6°55E **69** A6
Delgada, Punta *Chile* 52°28S 69°32W **192** D3
Delgado, C. *Mozam.* 10°45S 40°40E **143** E5
Delgerhet *Mongolia* 45°50N 110°30E **114** B6
Delgo *Sudan* 20°6N 30°40E **137** C3
Delhi *Canada* 42°51N 80°30W **174** D4
Delhi *India* 28°39N 77°13E **124** E7
Delhi *La., U.S.A.* 32°28N 91°30W **176** E9
Delhi *N.Y., U.S.A.* 42°17N 74°55W **175** D10
Deli Jovan *Serbia* 44°13N 22°9E **96** B6
Delia *Canada* 51°38N 112°23W **162** C6
Delice *Turkey* 39°54N 34°2E **104** C6
Delice → *Turkey* 40°45N 34°15E **104** B6
Delicias *Mexico* 28°13N 105°28W **186** B3
Deliján *Iran* 33°59N 50°40E **129** C6
Déline *Canada* 65°11N 123°25W **160** D7
Delingha *China* 37°23N 97°23E **110** D8
Delisle *Canada* 51°55N 107°8W **163** C7
Delitzsch *Germany* 51°31N 12°20E **76** D8
Deliverance I. *Australia* 9°31S 141°34E **150** a
Dell City *U.S.A.* 31°56N 105°12W **174** R8
Dell Rapids *U.S.A.* 43°50N 96°43W **172** D5
Delle *France* 47°30N 7°2E **71** E14
Dellys *Algeria* 36°57N 3°57E **136** A6
Delmar *U.S.A.* 42°37N 73°47W **175** D11
Delmenhorst *Germany* 53°3N 8°37E **76** B4
Delmiro Gouveia *Brazil* 9°24S 38°6W **189** B3
Delnice *Croatia* 45°23N 14°50E **93** C11
Delonga, Ostrova
  Russia 76°40N 149°20E **107** B15
Deloraine *Australia* 41°30S 146°40E **151** G4
Deloraine *Canada* 49°15N 100°29W **163** D8
Delos = Dilos *Greece* 37°23N 25°15E **99** D7
Delphi *Greece* 38°28N 22°30E **98** C4
Delphi *U.S.A.* 40°36N 86°41W **172** E10
Delphos *U.S.A.* 40°51N 84°21W **173** E11
Delportshoop *S. Africa* 28°22S 24°20E **144** C3
Delray Beach *U.S.A.* 26°28N 80°4W **179** J9
Delsbo *Sweden* 61°48N 16°32E **62** C10
Delta *Colo., U.S.A.* 38°44N 108°4W **168** G9
Delta *Utah, U.S.A.* 39°21N 112°35W **168** G7
Delta □ *Nigeria* 5°30N 6°0E **139** D6
Delta del Ebre △ *Spain* 40°43N 0°43E **90** E5
Delta del Po △ *Italy* 44°53N 12°15E **92** D9
Delta du Saloum △
  Senegal 13°42N 16°43W **138** C1
Delta Dunărea △
  Romania 45°45N 29°20E **81** E14
Delta Junction *U.S.A.* 64°2N 145°44W **160** C5
Deltebre *Spain* 40°43N 0°43E **90** E5
Deltona *U.S.A.* 28°54N 81°16W **179** G8
Delungra *Australia* 29°39S 150°51E **151** D5
Delvada *India* 20°46N 71°2E **124** K4
Delvinaki *Greece* 39°57N 20°32E **98** B2
Delvinë *Albania* 39°59N 20°6E **96** G4

Delyatyn *Ukraine* 48°32N 24°38E **81** B9
Demak *Indonesia* 6°53S 110°38E **119** G14
Demanda, Sierra de la
  Spain 42°15N 3°0W **90** C2
Dembia *C.A.R.* 4°56N 23°53E **142** B1
Dembia
  Dem. Rep. of the Congo 3°33N 25°48E **142** B2
Dembidolo *Ethiopia* 8°34N 34°50E **131** F1
Demchok *India* 32°42N 79°29E **125** C8
Demer → *Belgium* 50°57N 4°42E **69** D4
Demerara Abyssal Plain
  Atl. Oc. 0°0N 48°0W **56** F7
Demetrias *Greece* 39°22N 23°1E **98** B5
Demidov *Russia* 55°16N 31°30E **84** E6
Deming *N. Mex.,*
  U.S.A. 32°16N 107°46W **169** K10
Deming *Wash., U.S.A.* 48°50N 122°13W **170** B4
Demini → *Brazil* 0°46S 62°56W **186** D6
Demirci *Turkey* 39°2N 28°38E **99** B10
Demirköprü Barajı
  Turkey 38°42N 28°25E **99** C10
Demirköy *Turkey* 41°49N 27°45E **97** E11
Demmin *Germany* 53°54N 13°2E **76** B9
Demnate *Morocco* 31°44N 6°59W **136** B3
Demonte *Italy* 44°19N 7°17E **92** D4
Demopolis *U.S.A.* 32°31N 87°50W **177** E11
Dempo *Indonesia* 4°2S 103°15E **118** E2
Demyansk *Russia* 57°30N 32°27E **84** D7
Den Bosch = 's-Hertogenbosch
  Neths. 51°42N 5°17E **69** C5
Den Burg *Neths.* 53°3N 4°47E **69** A4
Den Chai *Thailand* 17°59N 100°4E **120** D3
Den Haag = 's-Gravenhage
  Neths. 52°7N 4°17E **69** B4
Den Helder *Neths.* 52°57N 4°45E **69** B4
Den Oever *Neths.* 52°56N 5°2E **69** B5
Denain *France* 50°20N 3°22E **71** B10
Denair *U.S.A.* 37°32N 120°48W **170** H6
Denali *U.S.A.* 63°4N 151°0W **160** E1
Denau = Denov
  Uzbekistan 38°16N 67°54E **109** F7
Denbigh *Canada* 45°8N 77°15W **174** A7
Denbigh *U.K.* 53°12N 3°25W **66** D4
Denbighshire □ *U.K.* 53°8N 3°22W **66** D4
Dendang *Indonesia* 3°7S 107°56E **118** E3
Dendermonde *Belgium* 51°2N 4°5E **69** C4
Dengchuan *China* 25°59N 100°3E **116** E3
Denge *Nigeria* 12°52N 5°21E **139** C6
Dengfeng *China* 34°25N 113°2E **114** C7
Dengi *Nigeria* 9°25N 9°55E **139** D7
Dengkou *China* 40°18N 106°55E **114** C4
Denguélé □ *Côte d'Ivoire* 9°45N 7°30W **138** D3
Dengzhou *China* 32°34N 112°4E **117** A9
Denham *Australia* 25°56S 113°31E **149** E1
Denham, Mt. *Jamaica* 18°13N 77°32W **182** a
Denham Ra. *Australia* 21°55S 147°46E **150** C4
Denham Sd. *Australia* 25°45S 113°15E **149** E1
Denholm *Canada* 52°39N 108°1W **163** C7
Denia *Spain* 38°49N 0°8E **91** G5
Denial B. *Australia* 32°14S 133°32E **151** E1
Deniliquin *Australia* 35°30S 144°58E **153** C6
Denimoo = Fort Resolution
  Canada 61°10N 113°40W **162** A6
Denison *Iowa, U.S.A.* 42°1N 95°21W **172** D6
Denison *Tex., U.S.A.* 33°45N 96°33W **176** E6
Denison, C. *Antarctica* 67°0S 142°40E **55** C10
Denison Plains
  Australia 18°35S 128°0E **148** C4
Denisovka *Kazakhstan* 52°27N 61°39E **108** B6
Deniyaya *Sri Lanka* 6°21N 80°33E **127** L5
Denizli *Turkey* 37°42N 29°2E **99** D11
Denizli □ *Turkey* 37°45N 29°0E **99** D11
Denman *Australia* 32°24S 150°42E **153** B9
Denman Glacier
  Antarctica 66°45S 100°0E **55** C8
Denmark *Australia* 34°59S 117°25E **149** F2
Denmark ■ *Europe* 55°45N 10°0E **63** J3
Denmark Str. *Atl. Oc.* 66°0N 30°0W **57** D8
Dennery *St. Lucia* 13°55N 60°54W **183** f
Dennison *U.S.A.* 40°24N 81°19W **174** F3
Denny *U.K.* 56°1N 3°55W **65** E5
Denov *Uzbekistan* 38°16N 67°54E **109** F7
Denpasar *Indonesia* 8°39S 115°13E **118** F5
Denpasar ✈ (DPS)
  Indonesia 8°44S 115°10E **119** K18
Denton *Mont., U.S.A.* 47°19N 109°57W **168** C9
Denton *Tex., U.S.A.* 33°13N 97°8W **176** E6
D'Entrecasteaux, Pt.
  Australia 34°50S 115°57E **149** F2
D'Entrecasteaux △
  Australia 34°20S 115°33E **149** F2
D'Entrecasteaux Is.
  Papua N. G. 9°0S 151°0E **147** B8
Dentsville *U.S.A.* 34°4N 80°58W **178** B6
Denu *Ghana* 6°4N 1°9E **139** D5
Denver *Colo., U.S.A.* 39°42N 104°59W **168** G11
Denver *Pa., U.S.A.* 40°14N 76°8W **175** F8
Denver City *U.S.A.* 32°58N 102°50W **176** E3
Denver Int. ✈ (DEN)
  U.S.A. 39°52N 104°40W **168** G11
Deoband *India* 29°42N 77°43E **124** E7
Deobhog *India* 19°53N 82°44E **125** E6
Deodrug *India* 16°26N 76°55E **127** F3
Deogarh *Odisha, India* 21°32N 84°45E **125** D7
Deogarh *Raj., India* 25°32N 73°54E **124** G5
Deoghar *India* 24°30N 86°42E **125** G12
Deolali *India* 19°58N 73°50E **126** E1
Deoli = Devli *India* 25°50N 75°20E **124** G6
Déols *France* 46°50N 1°43E **71** F8
Deori *India* 23°24N 79°1E **125** H8
Deoria *India* 26°31N 83°48E **125** F10
Deosai Mts. *Pakistan* 35°40N 75°0E **125** B6
Deosri *India* 26°40N 90°29E **125** F14
Depalpur *India* 22°51N 75°33E **124** H6
Deposit *U.S.A.* 42°4N 75°25W **175** D9
Depuch I. *Australia* 20°37S 117°44E **148** D2
Deputatskiy *Russia* 69°18N 139°54E **107** C14
Déqên *China* 28°34N 98°51E **116** C2
Deqing *China* 23°8N 111°42E **117** F8
Der-Chantecoq, L. du
  France 48°35N 4°40E **71** D11
Dera Ghazi Khan
  Pakistan 30°5N 70°43E **124** D4
Dera Ismail Khan
  Pakistan 31°50N 70°50E **124** D4
Derabugti *Pakistan* 29°2N 69°9E **124** E3
Derawar Fort *Pakistan* 28°46N 71°20E **124** E4
Derbent *Russia* 42°5N 48°15E **87** J9

Derbent *Turkey* 38°11N 28°33E **99** C10
Derby *Australia* 17°18S 123°38E **148** C3
Derby *U.K.* 52°56N 1°28W **66** E6
Derby *Conn., U.S.A.* 41°19N 73°5W **175** E11
Derby *Kans., U.S.A.* 37°33N 97°16W **172** G5
Derby *N.Y., U.S.A.* 42°41N 78°58W **174** D6
Derby City □ *U.K.* 52°56N 1°28W **66** E6
Derby Line *U.S.A.* 45°0N 72°6W **175** B12
Derbyshire □ *U.K.* 53°11N 1°38W **66** D6
Derdap □ *Serbia* 44°40N 22°23E **96** B6
Derdepoort *S. Africa* 24°38S 26°24E **144** B4
Derecske *Hungary* 47°20N 21°33E **80** C6
Dereham *U.K.* 52°41N 0°57E **67** E8
Dereköy *Turkey* 41°55N 27°21E **97** E11
Dereli *Turkey* 40°44N 38°26E **105** B8
Derg → *U.K.* 54°44N 7°26W **64** B4
Derg, L. *Ireland* 53°0N 8°20W **64** D3
Dergachi = Derhaci
  Ukraine 50°9N 36°11E **85** G9
Deridder *U.S.A.* 30°51N 93°17W **176** F8
Derik *Turkey* 37°21N 40°18E **105** D9
Derinkuyu *Turkey* 38°22N 34°45E **104** C6
Dermantsi *Bulgaria* 43°8N 24°17E **97** C8
Dermott *U.S.A.* 33°32N 91°26W **176** E9
Dêrong *China* 28°44N 99°9E **116** C2
Derrinallum *Australia* 37°57S 143°15E **152** D5
Derry = Londonderry
  U.K. 55°0N 7°20W **64** B4
Derry = Londonderry □
  U.K. 55°0N 7°20W **64** B4
Derry *N.H., U.S.A.* 42°53N 71°19W **175** D13
Derry *Pa., U.S.A.* 40°20N 79°18W **174** F5
Derryveagh Mts. *Ireland* 54°56N 8°11W **64** B3
Derval *France* 47°40N 1°41W **70** E5
Derveni *Greece* 38°8N 22°25E **98** C4
Derventa *Bos.-H.* 44°59N 17°55E **80** F2
Derwent → *Cumb., U.K.* 54°39N 3°9W **66** C4
Derwent → *Derby, U.K.* 52°57N 1°28W **66** E6
Derwent → *N. Yorks.,*
  U.K. 53°45N 0°58W **66** D7
Derwent Water *U.K.* 54°35N 3°9W **66** C4
Derzhavīnsk *Kazakhstan* 51°6N 66°19E **109** B7
Des Moines *Iowa,*
  U.S.A. 41°35N 93°37W **172** E7
Des Moines *N. Mex.,*
  U.S.A. 36°46N 103°50W **169** H12
Des Moines *Wash.,*
  U.S.A. 47°24N 122°19W **170** C4
Des Moines → *U.S.A.* 40°23N 91°25W **172** E8
Desa *Romania* 43°52N 23°2E **80** G8
Desaguadero *Peru* 16°34S 69°3W **188** D4
Desaguadero →
  Argentina 34°30S 66°46W **190** C2
Desaguadero →
  Bolivia 16°35S 69°5W **188** D4
Desantne *Ukraine* 45°34N 29°32E **81** E14
Desaru *Malaysia* 1°31N 104°17E **121** d
Descanso, Pta. *Mexico* 32°21N 117°3W **171** N9
Descartes *France* 46°59N 0°42E **72** B4
Deschaillons-sur-St-Laurent
  Canada 46°32N 72°7W **165** C5
Deschambault L.
  Canada 54°50N 103°30W **163** C8
Deschutes → *U.S.A.* 45°38N 120°55W **168** D3
Descobrimento △
  Brazil 16°53S 39°21W **189** D3
Dese *Ethiopia* 11°5N 39°40E **131** E2
Deseado, C. *Chile* 52°45S 74°42W **192** D2
Desenzano del Garda
  Italy 45°28N 10°32E **92** C7
Deseronto *Canada* 44°12N 77°3W **174** B7
Desert Center
  U.S.A. 33°43N 115°24W **171** M11
Desert Hot Springs
  U.S.A. 33°58N 116°30W **171** M10
Desfina *Greece* 38°25N 22°31E **98** C4
Deshnok *India* 27°48N 73°21E **124** F5
Desierto Central de Baja
  California □
  Mexico 29°40N 114°50W **180** B2
Deskati *Greece* 39°55N 21°49E **98** B3
Desna → *Ukraine* 50°33N 30°32E **75** C16
Desnățui → *Romania* 43°53N 23°35E **81** G8
Desnogorsk *Russia* 54°9N 33°17E **84** E7
Desolación, I. *Chile* 53°0S 74°0W **192** D2
Despeñaperros, Paso
  Spain 38°24N 3°30W **89** G7
Despeñaperros △ *Spain* 38°25N 3°32W **89** G7
Despotiko *Greece* 36°57N 24°58E **98** D6
Despotovac *Serbia* 44°6N 21°30E **96** B5
Dessau *Germany* 51°51N 12°14E **76** D8
Dessye = Dese *Ethiopia* 11°5N 39°40E **131** E2
Destin *U.S.A.* 30°24N 86°30W **178** G2
Destin → *U.S.A.* 30°24N 86°30W **178** G2
D'Estrees B. *Australia* 35°55S 137°45E **152** C2
Desuri *India* 25°18N 73°35E **124** G5
Desvres *France* 50°40N 1°48E **71** B8
Det Udom *Thailand* 14°54N 105°5E **120** E5
Deta *Romania* 45°24N 21°13E **80** E6
Dete *Zimbabwe* 18°38S 26°50E **144** A4
Detinja → *Serbia* 43°51N 20°5E **96** C4
Detmold *Germany* 51°56N 8°52E **76** D5
Detour, Pt. *U.S.A.* 45°40N 86°40W **172** C10
Detroit *U.S.A.* 42°19N 83°12W **174** D1
Detroit Lakes *U.S.A.* 46°49N 95°51W **172** B6
Detva *Slovakia* 48°34N 19°25E **79** C12
Deua △ *Australia* 35°30S 149°58E **153** C8
Deurne *Neths.* 51°27N 5°49E **69** C5
Deutsch-Luxemburgischer =
  Germany 49°58N 6°12E **77** F2
Deutsche Bucht *Germany* 54°15N 8°0E **76** A4
Deutschland = Germany ■
  Europe 51°0N 10°0E **76** E6
Deutschlandsberg
  Austria 46°49N 15°14E **78** E8
Deux-Sèvres □ *France* 46°35N 0°20W **70** F6
Deva *Romania* 45°53N 22°55E **80** E7
Devakottai *India* 9°55N 78°45E **127** K4
Devaprayag *India* 30°13N 78°35E **125** D8
Devarkonda *India* 16°40N 78°56E **126** F4
Dévaványa *Hungary* 47°2N 20°58E **80** C5
Deveci Dağları *Turkey* 40°16N 36°15E **104** B7
Devecikonağı *Turkey* 39°55N 28°34E **99** B10
Devecser *Hungary* 47°6N 17°26E **79** E9
Develi *Turkey* 38°25N 35°28E **104** C6
Deventer *Neths.* 52°15N 6°10E **69** B6
Devereux, L. *U.S.A.* 43°47N 80°13W **174** B3
Deveron → *U.K.* 57°41N 2°32W **65** D6
Devesel *Romania* 44°28N 22°41E **80** F7
Devgad I. *India* 16°0N 73°20E **126** F2
Devgadh Bariya *India* 22°40N 73°55E **124** H5
Devgarh *India* 25°39N 73°23E **127** F1

Devi → *India* 19°59N 86°24E **126** E8
Devikot *India* 26°42N 71°12E **124** F4
Devil River Pk. *N.Z.* 40°56S 172°37E **155** A7
Devils Den *U.S.A.* 35°46N 119°58W **170** K7
Devils Hole = Death Valley △
  U.S.A. 36°29N 117°6W **171** J9
Devils Lake *U.S.A.* 48°7N 98°52W **172** A4
Devils Paw *Canada* 58°47N 134°0W **162** B2
Devils Postpile △
  U.S.A. 37°37N 119°5W **170** H7
Devil's Pt. *Sri Lanka* 9°26N 80°6E **127** K5
Devils Tower *U.S.A.* 44°35N 104°42W **168** D11
Devils Tower △
  U.S.A. 44°48N 104°55W **168** D11
Devin *Bulgaria* 41°44N 24°24E **97** E8
Devine *U.S.A.* 29°8N 98°54W **176** G5
Devipattinam *India* 9°29N 78°54E **127** K4
Devizes *U.K.* 51°22N 1°58W **67** F6
Devli *India* 25°50N 75°20E **124** G6
Devnya *Bulgaria* 43°13N 27°33E **97** C11
Devoll → *Albania* 40°57N 20°15E **96** F4
Devon *Canada* 53°24N 113°44W **162** C6
Devon □ *U.K.* 50°50N 3°40W **67** G4
Devon I. *Canada* 75°10N 85°0W **161** B15
Devonport *Australia* 41°10S 146°22E **151** G4
Devonport *N.Z.* 36°49S 174°48E **155** B5
Devrek *Turkey* 41°7N 31°57E **104** B4
Devrekāni *Turkey* 41°36N 33°50E **104** B5
Devrez → *Turkey* 41°5N 34°25E **104** B6
Devrukh *India* 17°3N 73°37E **126** F1
Dewas *India* 22°59N 76°3E **124** H7
Dewetsdorp *S. Africa* 29°33S 26°39E **144** C4
Dewey *Puerto Rico* 18°18N 65°18W **183** d
Dexing *China* 28°46N 117°30E **117** C11
Dexter *Maine, U.S.A.* 45°1N 69°18W **173** C19
Dexter *Mo., U.S.A.* 36°48N 89°57W **172** G9
Dexter *N. Mex.,*
  U.S.A. 33°12N 104°22W **169** K11
Dey-Dey, L. *Australia* 29°12S 131°4E **149** E5
Deyang *China* 31°3N 104°27E **116** B5
Deyhūk *Iran* 33°15N 57°30E **129** C8
Deyyer *Iran* 27°55N 51°55E **129** E6
Dez → *Iran* 31°39N 48°52E **105** F6
Dezadeash L. *Canada* 60°28N 136°58W **162** A1
Dezfūl *Iran* 32°20N 48°30E **105** F13
Dezhneva, Mys
  Russia 66°5N 169°40W **107** C19
Dezhou *China* 37°26N 116°18E **114** F9
Dhadhar → *India* 24°56N 85°24E **125** G11
Dhahaban *Si. Arabia* 21°58N 39°3E **137** C4
Dhahiriya = Aẕ Ẕāhiriyah
  West Bank 31°25N 34°58E **130** D3
Dhahran = Aẕ Ẕahrān
  Si. Arabia 26°10N 50°7E **129** E6
Dhak *Pakistan* 32°25N 72°33E **124** C5
Dhaka *Bangla.* 23°43N 90°26E **125** H14
Dhaka □ *Bangla.* 24°30N 90°0E **125** H14
Dhali *Cyprus* 35°1N 33°25E **101** D12
Dhamangaon *India* 20°48N 78°9E **126** D4
Dhamār *Yemen* 14°30N 44°20E **131** E3
Dhampur *India* 29°19N 78°33E **125** E8
Dhamtari *India* 20°42N 81°35E **125** D5
Dhanbad *India* 23°50N 86°30E **125** H12
Dhangarhi *Nepal* 28°55N 80°40E **125** E9
Dhankuta *Nepal* 26°55N 87°40E **125** F12
Dhanora *India* 20°20N 80°22E **125** D5
Dhanushkodi *India* 9°11N 79°24E **127** K4
Dhar *India* 22°35N 75°26E **124** H6
Dharampur *India* 22°35N 75°18E **124** H6
Dharan *Nepal* 26°49N 87°17E **125** F12
Dharapuram *India* 10°45N 77°34E **127** J3
Dharawal △ *Australia* 34°12S 150°52E **153** C9
Dhariwal *India* 31°57N 75°19E **124** D6
Dharla → *Bangla.* 25°46N 89°42E **125** G13
Dharmapuri *India* 12°10N 78°10E **127** H4
Dharmavaram *India* 14°29N 77°44E **127** H3
Dharmjaygarh *India* 22°28N 83°13E **125** H10
Dharmsala *India* 32°16N 76°23E **124** C7
Dharni *India* 21°33N 76°53E **124** J7
Dharug △ *Australia* 33°20S 151°2E **153** B9
Dharur *India* 18°3N 76°8E **126** E3
Dharwad *India* 15°30N 75°4E **127** G2
Dhasan → *India* 25°48N 79°24E **125** G8
Dhaulagiri *Nepal* 28°39N 83°28E **125** E10
Dhebar, L. *India* 24°10N 74°0E **124** G6
Dheftera *Cyprus* 35°5N 33°16E **101** D12
Dhenkanal *India* 20°45N 85°35E **125** D7
Dherinia *Cyprus* 35°3N 33°57E **101** D12
Dheskáti = Deskati
  Greece 39°55N 21°49E **96** G5
Dhí Qār □ *Iraq* 31°0N 46°15E **105** G12
Dhiarrizos → *Cyprus* 34°41N 32°34E **101** E11
Dhībān *Jordan* 31°30N 35°46E **130** D4
Dhilwan *India* 31°31N 75°21E **124** D6
Dhimarkhera *India* 23°28N 80°22E **125** H9
Dholka *India* 22°44N 72°29E **124** H5
Dhomokós = Domokos
  Greece 39°10N 22°18E **98** B4
Dhond = Daund *India* 18°26N 74°40E **126** F2
Dhone *India* 15°25N 77°53E **127** G3
Dhoraji *India* 21°45N 70°37E **124** J4
Dhorpatan *Nepal* 28°29N 83°4E **125** E10
Dhragonísi = Tragonisi
  Greece 37°27N 25°29E **99** D7
Dhrangadhra *India* 22°59N 71°31E **124** H4
Dhrol *India* 22°33N 70°25E **124** H4
Dhuburi *India* 26°2N 89°59E **125** F16
Dhule *India* 20°58N 74°50E **126** D2
Di-ib, W. → *Sudan* 22°38N 36°6E **137** C4
Di Linh *Vietnam* 11°35N 108°4E **120** G7
Di Linh, Cao Nguyen
  Vietnam 11°30N 108°0E **120** G7
Dia *Greece* 35°28N 25°14E **101** D7
Diabakania *Guinea* 11°30N 9°0W **138** C2
Diablo Range *U.S.A.* 37°20N 121°25W **170** J5
Diafarabé *Mali* 14°9N 4°57W **138** C4
Diala *Mali* 14°10N 10°0W **138** C2
Dialakoro *Mali* 12°18N 7°54W **138** C3
Dialakoto *Senegal* 13°21N 13°19W **138** C2
Diallassagou *Mali* 13°47N 3°41W **138** C4
Diamante *Italy* 39°41N 15°49E **95** C8
Diamante *Argentina* 32°5S 60°40W **190** C3
Diamante → *Argentina* 34°30S 66°46W **190** C2
Diamantina *Brazil* 18°17S 43°40W **189** D2
Diamantina □
  Australia 26°45S 139°10E **151** D2

Diamantina △
  Australia 23°33S 141°23E **150** C3
Diamantino *Brazil* 14°30S 56°30W **187** F7
Diamond Bar *U.S.A.* 34°1N 117°48W **171** L9
Diamond Harbour
  India 22°11N 88°14E **125** H13
Diamond Is. *Australia* 17°25S 151°5E **150** B5
Diamond Mts. *U.S.A.* 39°40N 115°50W **168** G6
Diamond Springs
  U.S.A. 38°42N 120°49W **170** G6
Diamou *Mali* 14°5N 11°16W **138** C2
Dian Chi *China* 24°50N 102°43E **116** E4
Dianalund *Denmark* 55°32N 11°30E **63** J5
Dianbai *China* 21°33N 111°0E **117** G8
Diancheng *China* 21°30N 111°4E **117** G8
Diano Marina *Italy* 43°54N 8°5E **92** E5
Dianópolis *Brazil* 11°38S 46°50W **189** C1
Dianra *Côte d'Ivoire* 8°45N 6°14W **138** D3
Diaoyu Dao = Senkaku-Shotō
  E. China Sea 25°45N 123°30E **113** M1
Diaoyu Tai = Senkaku-Shotō
  E. China Sea 25°45N 123°30E **113** M1
Diapaga *Burkina Faso* 12°5N 1°46E **139** C5
Diapangou *Burkina Faso* 12°5N 0°10E **139** C5
Diariguila *Guinea* 10°35N 10°2W **138** C2
Diavolo, Mt. *India* 12°40N 92°56E **127** H11
Diba = Dibbā al Ḥiṣn
  U.A.E. 25°45N 56°16E **129** E8
Dibagah *Iraq* 35°52N 43°48E **105** E10
Dibai *India* 28°13N 78°15E **124** E8
Dibaya
  Dem. Rep. of the Congo 6°30S 22°57E **140** F4
Dibaya-Lubue
  Dem. Rep. of the Congo 4°12S 19°54E **140** E3
Dibbā al Ḥiṣn *U.A.E.* 25°45N 56°16E **129** E8
Dibbeen △ *Jordan* 32°20N 35°45E **130** C4
Dibër □ *Albania* 41°30N 20°20E **96** E4
D'Iberville, Lac *Canada* 55°55N 73°15W **164** A5
Dibete *Botswana* 23°45S 26°32E **144** B4
Dibrugarh *India* 27°29N 94°55E **123** F19
Dickens *U.S.A.* 33°37N 100°50W **176** E4
Dickinson *U.S.A.* 46°53N 102°47W **172** B2
Dickson *U.S.A.* 36°5N 87°23W **177** C11
Dickson City *U.S.A.* 41°28N 75°36W **175** E9
Dicle Baraji *Turkey* 38°20N 40°11E **105** D9
Dicle Nehri → *Turkey* 37°44N 41°10E **105** D9
Dicomano *Italy* 43°53N 11°31E **93** E8
Didiéni *Mali* 13°53N 8°6W **138** C3
Didim *Turkey* 37°22N 27°16E **99** D9
Didimóticho *Greece* 41°22N 26°29E **97** E10
Didsbury *Canada* 51°35N 114°10W **162** C6
Didwana *India* 27°23N 74°36E **124** F6
Die *France* 44°47N 5°22E **73** D9
Diébougou *Burkina Faso* 11°0N 3°15W **138** C4
Diecke *Guinea* 7°27N 8°54W **138** D3
Diefenbaker, L. *Canada* 51°0N 106°55W **163** C7
Diego de Almagro *Chile* 26°22S 70°3W **190** B1
Diego Garcia *Ind. Oc.* 7°50S 72°50E **146** E6
Diego Ramírez, Islas
  Chile 56°30S 68°44W **192** E3
Diego Suarez = Antsiranana
  Madag. 12°25S 49°20E **141** G9
Diekirch *Lux.* 49°52N 6°10E **69** E6
Diéma *Mali* 14°32N 9°12W **138** C3
Diembéring *Senegal* 12°29N 16°47W **138** C1
Diemelsee → *Germany* 51°20N 8°40E **76** D4
Dien Ban *Vietnam* 15°53N 108°16E **120** E7
Dien Bien Phu *Vietnam* 21°20N 103°0E **116** G4
Dien Chau, Vinh
  Vietnam 19°0N 105°55E **120** C5
Dien Khanh *Vietnam* 12°15N 109°6E **121** F7
Diepholz *Germany* 52°37N 8°22E **76** C4
Dieppe *France* 49°54N 1°4E **70** C8
Dierks *U.S.A.* 34°7N 94°1W **176** D7
Diest *Belgium* 50°58N 5°4E **69** D5
Dietikon *Switz.* 47°24N 8°24E **77** H4
Dieulefit *France* 44°32N 5°4E **73** D9
Dieuze *France* 48°49N 6°43E **71** D13
Dif *Somali Rep.* 0°59N 40°58E **131** G3
Diffa *Niger* 13°18N 12°36E **139** C8
Diffa □ *Niger* 14°0N 12°30E **139** C7
Differdange *Lux.* 49°31N 5°54E **69** E5
Dig *India* 27°28N 77°20E **124** F7
Digba
  Dem. Rep. of the Congo 4°25N 25°48E **142** B2
Digby *Canada* 44°38N 65°50W **165** D6
Digges Is. *Canada* 62°40N 77°50W **161** E16
Diggi *India* 26°22N 75°26E **124** F6
Dighinala *Bangla.* 23°15N 92°5E **123** H18
Dighton *U.S.A.* 38°29N 100°28W **172** F3
Digne-les-Bains *France* 44°5N 6°12E **73** D10
Digoin *France* 46°29N 4°1E **73** F11
Digor *Turkey* 40°22N 43°25E **105** B10
Digos *Phil.* 6°45N 125°20E **119** C7
Digranes *Iceland* 66°4N 14°44W **60** C6
Digras *India* 20°6N 77°45E **126** D4
Digul → *Indonesia* 7°7S 138°42E **119** F9
Digya △ *Ghana* 7°15N 0°5E **139** D5
Dihang = Brahmaputra →
  Asia 23°40N 90°35E **125** H13
Dijlah, Nahr → *Asia* 31°0N 47°25E **128** C5
Dijon *France* 47°20N 5°3E **71** E12
Dikhil *Djibouti* 11°8N 42°20E **131** E3
Dikili *Turkey* 39°4N 26°53E **99** B8
Dikirnis *Egypt* 31°6N 31°35E **137** B3
Dikodougou *Côte d'Ivoire* 9°4N 5°45W **138** D3
Diksmuide *Belgium* 51°2N 2°52E **69** C2
Dikson *Russia* 73°40N 80°5E **106** B9
Dikti Oros *Greece* 35°8N 25°30E **101** D7
Dikwa *Nigeria* 12°4N 13°30E **139** C8
Dila *Ethiopia* 6°21N 38°22E **131** F2
Dilek Yarimadisi △
  Turkey 37°40N 27°10E **99** D9
Dili *E. Timor* 8°39S 125°34E **119** F7
Diligent Strait *India* 12°11N 92°57E **127** H11
Dilijan *Armenia* 40°46N 44°57E **87** K7
Dilinata *Greece* 38°13N 20°31E **98** C2
Dilj *Croatia* 45°29N 18°1E **80** E3
Dillenburg *Germany* 50°44N 8°17E **76** E4
Dilley *U.S.A.* 28°40N 99°10W **176** G5
Dilli = Delhi *India* 28°39N 77°13E **124** E7
Dilli *Mali* 15°11N 7°44W **138** C4
Dillingen *Bayern,*
  Germany 48°36N 10°30E **77** G6
Dillingen *Saarland,*
  Germany 49°22N 6°43E **77** F2
Dillingham *U.S.A.* 59°3N 158°28W **166** D8
Dillon *Canada* 55°56N 108°35W **163** B7

Dillon *Mont., U.S.A.* 45°13N 112°38W **168** D7
Dillon *S.C., U.S.A.* 34°25N 79°22W **177** D15
Dillon → *Canada* 55°56N 108°56W **163** B7
Dillsburg *U.S.A.* 40°7N 77°2W **174** F7
Dilolo
 Dem. Rep. of the Congo 10°28S 22°18E **140** G4
Dilos *Greece* 37°23N 25°15E **99** D7
Dilove *Ukraine* 47°56N 24°11E **81** C9
Dimapur *India* 25°54N 93°45E **110** F7
Dimas *Mexico* 23°43N 106°47W **180** C3
Dimashq *Syria* 33°30N 36°18E **130** B5
Dimashq □ *Syria* 33°30N 36°30E **130** B5
Dimbaza *S. Africa* 32°50S 27°14E **145** D4
Dimboola *Australia* 36°28S 142°7E **152** D5
Dîmboviţa = Dâmboviţa →
 Romania 44°12N 26°26E **81** F11
Dimbulah *Australia* 17°8S 145°4E **150** B4
Dimitrovgrad *Bulgaria* 42°5N 25°35E **97** C8
Dimitrovgrad *Russia* 54°14N 49°39E **86** C9
Dimitrovgrad *Serbia* 43°2N 22°48E **96** C6
Dimitrovo = Pernik
 Bulgaria 42°35N 23°2E **96** D7
Dimitsana *Greece* 37°36N 22°3E **98** D4
Dimmitt *U.S.A.* 34°33N 102°19W **176** H3
Dimona *Israel* 31°2N 35°1E **130** D4
Dimovo *Bulgaria* 43°43N 22°50E **96** C6
Dinagat I. *Phil.* 10°10N 125°40E **119** F7
Dinajpur *Bangla.* 25°33N 88°43E **123** G16
Dinan *France* 48°28N 2°2W **70** D4
Dīnān Āb *Iran* 32°4N 56°49E **129** C8
Dinant *Belgium* 50°16N 4°55E **69** D4
Dinapur *India* 25°38N 85°5E **125** G11
Dinar *Turkey* 38°5N 30°10E **99** C12
Dīnār, Kūh-e *Iran* 30°42N 51°46E **129** D6
Dinara Planina *Croatia* 44°0N 16°30E **93** D13
Dinard *France* 48°38N 2°6W **70** D4
Dinaric Alps = Dinara Planina
 Croatia 44°0N 16°30E **93** D13
Dinbych = Denbigh
 U.K. 53°12N 3°25W **66** D4
Dinbych-y-Pysgod = Tenby
 U.K. 51°40N 4°42W **67** F3
Dindanko *Mali* 14°8N 9°30W **138** C3
Dindi → *India* 16°24N 78°15E **127** F4
Dindigul *India* 10°25N 78°0E **127** F4
Dindori *India* 22°57N 81°5E **125** H9
Ding Xian = Dingzhou
 China 38°30N 114°59E **114** E8
Dinga *Pakistan* 25°26N 67°10E **124** G2
Ding'an *China* 19°42N 110°19E **117** a
Dingbian *China* 37°35N 107°32E **114** F4
Dingelstädt *Germany* 51°18N 10°19E **76** D6
Dingle *Ireland* 52°9N 10°17W **64** D1
Dingle *Sweden* 58°32N 11°35E **63** F5
Dingle B. *Ireland* 52°3N 10°20W **64** D1
Dingle Pen. *Ireland* 52°12N 10°5W **64** D1
Dingmans Ferry
 U.S.A. 41°13N 74°55W **175** E10
Dingnan *China* 24°45N 115°0E **117** E10
Dingo *Australia* 23°38S 149°19E **150** C4
Dingolfing *Germany* 48°37N 12°30E **77** G8
Dingtao *China* 35°5N 115°35E **114** G8
Dinguiraye *Guinea* 11°18N 10°49W **138** C2
Dingwall *U.K.* 57°36N 4°26W **65** D4
Dingxi *China* 35°30N 104°33E **114** G3
Dingxiang *China* 38°30N 112°58E **114** E7
Dingyuan *China* 32°32N 117°41E **117** A11
Dingzhou *China* 38°30N 114°59E **114** E8
Dinh, Mui *Vietnam* 11°22N 109°1E **121** G7
Dinh Lap *Vietnam* 21°33N 107°6E **116** G6
Dinin → *Ireland* 52°43N 7°18W **64** D4
Dinira △ *Venezuela* 9°57N 70°6W **183** E6
Dinokwe *Botswana* 23°29S 26°37E **144** B4
Dinorwic *Canada* 49°41N 92°30W **163** D10
Dinosaur = *Canada* 50°47N 111°30W **162** C6
Dinosaur △ *U.S.A.* 40°30N 108°45W **168** F9
Dinuba *U.S.A.* 36°32N 119°23W **170** J7
Diö *Sweden* 56°37N 14°15E **63** H8
Dioïla *Mali* 12°23N 6°50W **138** C3
Dioka *Mali* 14°57N 10°4W **138** C2
Diongoï *Mali* 14°38N 8°34W **138** C3
Dionisiades *Greece* 35°20N 26°10E **101** D8
Diósgyör *Hungary* 48°7N 20°43E **80** B5
Diosig *Romania* 47°18N 22°2E **80** C7
Diougani *Mali* 14°19N 2°44W **138** C4
Diouloulou *Senegal* 13°5N 16°38W **138** C1
Dioura *Mali* 14°39N 5°12W **138** C3
Diourbel □ *Senegal* 14°30N 16°15W **138** C1
Diourbel *Senegal* 14°39N 16°12W **138** C1
Dipalpur *Pakistan* 30°40N 73°39E **124** D5
Dipkarpaz = Rizokarpaso
 Cyprus 35°36N 34°23E **101** D13
Diplo *Pakistan* 24°35N 69°35E **124** G3
Dipolog *Phil.* 8°36N 123°20E **119** G6
Dipperu △ *Australia* 21°56S 148°42E **150** C4
Dipton *N.Z.* 45°54S 168°22E **155** F2
Dir *Pakistan* 35°8N 71°59E **122** B7
Diré *Mali* 16°20N 3°25W **138** B4
Dire Dawa *Ethiopia* 9°35N 41°45E **131** F3
Dirfis Oros *Greece* 38°40N 23°54E **98** C5
Diriamba *Nic.* 11°51N 86°19W **182** D2
Dirk Hartog I. *Australia* 25°50S 113°5E **149** E1
Dirranbandi *Australia* 28°33S 148°17E **151** D4
Disa *India* 24°18N 72°10E **124** G5
Disappointment, C.
 U.S.A. 46°18N 124°5W **170** D2
Disappointment, L.
 Australia 23°20S 122°40E **148** D3
Disaster B. *Australia* 37°15S 149°58E **153** D8
Discovery B. *Australia* 38°10S 140°40E **152** E4
Discovery B. *China* 22°18N 114°1E **111** a
Discovery Bay △
 Australia 38°9S 141°16E **152** E4
Discovery Seamount
 Atl. Oc. 42°0S 0°10E **56** L12
Disentis Muster *Switz.* 46°42N 8°50E **77** J4
Dishna *Egypt* 26°9N 32°20E **135** C12
Disina *Nigeria* 11°35N 9°50E **139** C6
Disko = Qeqertarsuaq
 Greenland 69°45N 53°30W **57** D5
Disko Bugt *Greenland* 69°10N 52°0W **57** D5
Disna = Dzisna →
 Belarus 55°34N 28°12E **84** E5
Disneyland Hong Kong
 China 22°19N 114°2E **111** a
Diss *U.K.* 52°23N 1°7E **67** E9
Disteghil Sar *Pakistan* 36°20N 75°12E **125** A6
District of Columbia □
 U.S.A. 38°55N 77°0W **173** F15
Distrito Federal □
 Brazil 15°45S 47°45W **189** D1

Distrito Federal □
 Mexico 19°15N 99°10W **181** D5
Distúq *Egypt* 31°8N 30°35E **137** E7
Diu *India* 20°45N 70°58E **124** J4
Dīvāndarreh *Iran* 35°55N 47°2E **105** E12
Dives → *France* 49°18N 0°7W **70** C6
Dives-sur-Mer *France* 49°18N 0°8W **70** C6
Divi Pt. *India* 15°59N 81°9E **127** G5
Divichi = Dāvāçi
 Azerbaijan 41°15N 48°57E **87** K9
Divide *U.S.A.* 45°45N 112°45W **168** D7
Dividing Ra. *Australia* 27°45S 116°0E **149** E2
Divinópolis *Brazil* 20°10S 44°54W **189** E2
Divljake *Albania* 41°0N 19°32E **97** H1
Divnoye *Russia* 45°55N 43°21E **87** H6
Divo *Côte d'Ivoire* 5°48N 5°15W **138** D3
Divriği *Turkey* 39°23N 38°7E **105** C8
Dīwāl Kol *Afghan.* 34°23N 67°52E **124** B2
Dixie Mt. *U.S.A.* 39°55N 120°16W **170** F6
Dixon *Calif., U.S.A.* 38°27N 121°49W **170** G5
Dixon *Ill., U.S.A.* 41°50N 89°29W **172** E9
Dixon Entrance *U.S.A.* 54°30N 132°0W **160** G5
Dixville *Canada* 45°4N 71°46W **175** A13
Diyadin *Turkey* 39°33N 43°40E **105** C10
Diyālā □ *Iraq* 33°45N 44°50E **128** C5
Diyālā → *Iraq* 33°13N 44°30E **105** F11
Diyarbakir *Turkey* 37°55N 40°18E **105** D9
Diyarbakir □ *Turkey* 38°0N 40°10E **105** D9
Diyodar *India* 24°8N 71°50E **124** G4
Dizangué *Cameroon* 3°46N 9°59E **139** E6
Djakarta = Jakarta
 Indonesia 6°9S 106°52E **118** F3
Djamâa *Algeria* 33°32N 5°59E **136** B5
Djamba *Angola* 16°45S 13°58E **144** A1
Djambala *Congo* 2°32S 14°30E **140** E2
Djanet *Algeria* 24°35N 9°32E **136** D5
Djawa = Jawa *Indonesia* 7°0S 110°0E **118** F3
Djebel Tazzeka △
 Morocco 34°6N 4°11W **136** B3
Djebiniana *Tunisia* 35°1N 11°0E **136** A6
Djelfa *Algeria* 34°40N 3°15E **136** B4
Djelfa □ *Algeria* 34°20N 3°40E **136** B4
Djema *C.A.R.* 6°3N 25°15E **142** A2
Djémila *Algeria* 36°19N 5°44E **136** A5
Djenné *Mali* 14°0N 4°30W **138** C4
Djerba *Tunisia* 33°48N 10°54E **136** B6
Djerba, Î. de *Tunisia* 33°50N 10°48E **136** B6
Djerid, Chott *Tunisia* 33°42N 8°30E **136** B5
Djibo *Burkina Faso* 14°9N 1°35W **139** C4
Djibouti *Djibouti* 11°30N 43°5E **131** E3
Djibouti ■ *Africa* 12°0N 43°0E **131** E3
Djolu
 Dem. Rep. of the Congo 0°35N 22°5E **140** D4
Djougou *Benin* 9°40N 1°45E **139** D5
Djoum *Cameroon* 2°41N 12°35E **140** D2
Djourab, Erg du *Chad* 16°40N 18°50E **135** E9
Djugu
 Dem. Rep. of the Congo 1°55N 30°35E **142** B3
Djukbinj △ *Australia* 12°11S 131°2E **148** B5
Djúpivogur *Iceland* 64°39N 14°17W **60** D6
Djurås *Sweden* 60°34N 15°8E **62** D9
Djurdjura △ *Algeria* 36°20N 4°15E **136** A4
Djurö △ *Sweden* 58°52N 13°28E **63** F7
Djursland *Denmark* 56°27N 10°45E **63** H4
Dmitriya Lapteva, Proliv
 Russia 73°0N 140°0E **107** B15
Dmitriyev Lgovskiy
 Russia 52°10N 35°0E **85** F8
Dmitrov *Russia* 56°25N 37°32E **84** D9
Dmitrovsk-Orlovskiy
 Russia 52°29N 35°10E **85** F8
Dnepr = Dnipro →
 Ukraine 46°30N 32°18E **85** J7
Dneprodzerzhinsk =
 Dniprodzerzhynsk
 Ukraine 48°32N 34°37E **85** H8
Dneprodzerzhinskoye Vdkhr. =
 Dniprodzerzhynske Vdskh.
 Ukraine 48°32N 34°37E **85** H8
Dnepropetrovsk =
 Dnipropetrovsk
 Ukraine 48°30N 35°0E **85** H8
Dneprorudnoye = Dniprorudne
 Ukraine 47°21N 34°58E **85** J8
Dnestr = Dnister →
 Europe 46°18N 30°17E **75** E16
Dnieper = Dnipro →
 Ukraine 46°30N 32°18E **85** J7
Dniester = Dnister →
 Europe 46°18N 30°17E **75** E16
Dnipro → *Ukraine* 46°30N 32°18E **85** J7
Dniprodzerzhynsk
 Ukraine 48°32N 34°37E **85** H8
Dniprodzerzhynske Vdskh.
 Ukraine 48°32N 34°37E **85** H8
Dnipropetrovsk *Ukraine* 48°30N 35°0E **85** H8
Dnipropetrovsk □
 Ukraine 48°15N 34°50E **85** H8
Dniprorudne *Ukraine* 47°21N 34°58E **85** J8
Dnister → *Europe* 46°18N 30°17E **75** E16
Dnistrovskyy Lyman
 Ukraine 46°15N 30°17E **85** J6
Dno *Russia* 57°50N 29°58E **84** D5
Dnyapro = Dnipro →
 Ukraine 46°30N 32°18E **85** J7
Do Gonbadān = Gachsārān
 Iran 30°15N 50°45E **129** D6
Doaktown *Canada* 46°33N 66°8W **165** C6
Doan Hung *Vietnam* 21°30N 105°10E **116** G5
Doba *Chad* 8°40N 16°50E **135** G9
Dobandi *Pakistan* 31°13N 66°50E **124** D2
Dobbiaco *Italy* 46°44N 12°14E **93** B9
Dobbyn *Australia* 19°44S 140°2E **150** B3
Dobczyce *Poland* 49°52N 20°25E **83** D7
Doberai, Jazirah
 Indonesia 1°25S 133°0E **119** E8
Dobiegniew *Poland* 52°59N 15°45E **83** C4
Doblas *Argentina* 37°5S 64°0W **190** D3
Dobo *Indonesia* 5°45S 134°15E **119** F8
Doboj *Bos.-H.* 44°46N 18°4E **80** F3
Dobra *Wielkopolskie,*
 Poland 51°55N 18°37E **83** C5
Dobra *Zachodnio-Pomorskie,*
 Poland 53°34N 15°20E **82** B2

Dobra *Dâmboviţa,*
 Romania 44°52N 25°40E **81** F10
Dobra *Hunedoara,*
 Romania 45°54N 22°36E **80** E7
Dobra Miasto *Poland* 53°58N 20°26E **82** E7
Dobrich *Bulgaria* 43°37N 27°49E **97** C11
Dobrich □ *Bulgaria* 43°37N 27°49E **97** C11
Dobříš *Czechia* 49°46N 14°10E **78** B7
Dobrinishte *Bulgaria* 41°49N 23°34E **96** E7
Dobrodzień *Poland* 50°45N 18°25E **83** H5
Dobromyl *Ukraine* 49°34N 22°46E **83** J9
Dobron *Ukraine* 48°25N 22°23E **80** B7
Dobropole *Ukraine* 48°25N 37°2E **85** H9
Dobrovolsk *Russia* 54°46N 22°31E **82** D9
Dobruja *Europe* 44°30N 28°15E **81** F13
Dobrush *Belarus* 52°25N 31°22E **85** B16
Dobrzany *Poland* 53°22N 15°25E **82** B2
Dobrzyń nad Wisłą
 Poland 52°39N 19°22E **83** F6
Doc, Mui *Vietnam* 17°58N 106°30E **120** D6
Doce → *Brazil* 19°37S 39°49W **189** D3
Doctor Arroyo
 Mexico 23°40N 100°11W **180** C4
Doctor Pedro P. Peña
 Paraguay 22°27S 62°21W **190** A3
Doctors Inlet *U.S.A.* 30°6N 81°47W **178** E8
Doda *India* 33°10N 75°34E **125** C6
Doda, L. *Canada* 49°25N 75°13W **164** C4
Doda Betta *India* 11°24N 76°44E **127** G3
Dodballapur *India* 13°18N 77°32E **127** H3
Dodecanese = Dodekanisa
 Greece 36°35N 27°0E **99** E8
Dodekanisa *Greece* 36°35N 27°0E **99** E8
Dodge City *U.S.A.* 37°45N 100°1W **172** G3
Dodge L. *Canada* 59°50N 105°36W **163** B7
Dodgeville *U.S.A.* 42°58N 90°8W **172** D8
Dodo *Cameroon* 7°30N 12°3E **139** D7
Dodoma *Tanzania* 6°8S 35°45E **142** D4
Dodoma □ *Tanzania* 6°0S 36°0E **142** D4
Dodoni *Greece* 39°40N 20°46E **98** B2
Dodori □ *Kenya* 1°55S 41°7E **142** C5
Dodsland *Canada* 51°50N 108°45W **163** C7
Dodson *U.S.A.* 48°24N 108°15W **168** B9
Dodurga *Turkey* 39°49N 29°57E **99** B11
Doerun *U.S.A.* 31°19N 83°55W **178** D6
Doesburg *Neths.* 52°1N 6°9E **69** B6
Doetinchem *Neths.* 51°59N 6°18E **69** C6
Dog Creek *Canada* 51°35N 122°14W **162** C4
Dog I. *U.S.A.* 29°48N 84°36W **178** F5
Dog L. *Man., Canada* 51°2N 98°31W **163** C9
Dog L. *Ont., Canada* 48°48N 89°30W **164** C2
Doğanşehir *Turkey* 38°5N 37°53E **104** C7
Dogliani *Italy* 44°32N 7°56E **92** D4
Dogondoutchi *Niger* 13°38N 4°2E **139** C5
Dogons, Land of the =
 Bandiagara, Falaise de
 Mali 14°14N 3°29W **138** C4
Dogran *Pakistan* 31°48N 73°35E **124** D5
Doğubayazıt *Turkey* 39°31N 44°5E **105** C11
Doguéraoua *Niger* 14°0N 5°31E **139** C6
Doha = Ad Dawḩah
 Qatar 25°15N 51°35E **129** E6
Doha Int. ✈ (DOH)
 Qatar 25°16N 51°34E **129** E6
Dohazari *Bangla.* 22°10N 92°5E **123** H18
Dohrighat *India* 26°16N 83°31E **125** F10
Doi *Indonesia* 2°14N 127°49E **119** D7
Doi Inthanon *Thailand* 18°35N 98°29E **120** C2
Doi Inthanon △
 Thailand 18°33N 98°34E **120** C2
Doi Khuntan △
 Thailand 18°33N 99°11E **120** C2
Doi Luang *Thailand* 18°30N 101°0E **120** C3
Doi Luang △ *Thailand* 19°22N 99°35E **120** C2
Doi Phukha △ *Thailand* 19°8N 101°9E **120** C3
Doi Saket *Thailand* 18°52N 99°9E **120** C2
Doi Suthep Pui △
 Thailand 18°49N 98°53E **120** C2
Doi Toa *Thailand* 17°55N 98°30E **120** D2
Dois Irmãos, Sa. *Brazil* 9°0S 42°30W **189** D2
Dojransko Jezero
 Macedonia 41°13N 22°44E **96** D6
Dokdo = Liancourt Rocks
 Asia 37°15N 131°52E **113** F5
Dokkum *Neths.* 53°20N 5°59E **69** A5
Dokos *Greece* 37°20N 23°20E **98** D5
Dokri *Pakistan* 27°25N 68°7E **124** F3
Dokuchayevsk *Ukraine* 47°44N 37°40E **85** J10
Dol-de-Bretagne *France* 48°34N 1°47W **70** D5
Dolak, Pulau *Indonesia* 8°0S 138°30E **119** F9
Dolbeau-Mistassini
 Canada 48°53N 72°14W **165** C5
Dole *France* 47°7N 5°31E **71** E12
Dolenji Logatec = Logatec
 Slovenia 45°56N 14°15E **93** C11
Dolgellau *U.K.* 52°45N 3°53W **66** E4
Dolgelley = Dolgellau
 U.K. 52°45N 3°53W **66** E4
Dolhasca *Romania* 47°26N 26°36E **81** C11
Doliana *Greece* 39°54N 20°32E **98** B2
Dolianova *Italy* 39°22N 9°10E **94** C2
Dolinsk *Russia* 47°21N 142°48E **107** E15
Dolinskaya = Dolynska
 Ukraine 48°6N 32°46E **85** H7
Dolj □ *Romania* 44°10N 23°30E **81** F8
Dollard *Neths.* 53°20N 7°10E **69** A7
Dolna Banya *Bulgaria* 42°18N 23°44E **96** D7
Dolni Chiflik *Bulgaria* 42°59N 27°43E **97** D11
Dolni Dabnik *Bulgaria* 43°24N 24°26E **97** C8
Dolnośląskie □ *Poland* 51°10N 16°30E **83** G3
Dolný Kubín *Slovakia* 49°12N 19°18E **83** D6
Dolo *Ethiopia* 4°11N 42°3E **131** G3
Dolo *Italy* 45°25N 12°5E **93** C9
Dolomites = Dolomiti
 Italy 46°23N 11°51E **93** B8
Dolomiti *Italy* 46°23N 11°51E **93** B8
Dolomiti Bellunesi △
 Italy 46°10N 12°0E **93** B8
Dolores *Argentina* 36°20S 57°40W **190** D4
Dolores *Uruguay* 33°34S 58°15W **190** C4
Dolores *U.S.A.* 37°28N 108°30W **169** H9
Dolores → *U.S.A.* 38°49N 108°17W **168** G9
Dolovo *Serbia* 44°55N 20°52E **80** F5
Dolphin, C. *Falk. Is.* 51°10S 59°0W **192** G5
Dolphin and Union Str.
 Canada 69°5N 114°45W **160** D9
Dolsk *Poland* 51°59N 17°3E **83** G4

Dolyna *Ukraine* 48°58N 24°1E **81** B9
Dolynska *Ukraine* 48°6N 32°46E **85** H7
Dolynske *Ukraine* 46°21N 18°9E **80** D3
Dolzhanskaya *Russia* 46°37N 37°48E **85** J9
Dom Joaquim *Brazil* 18°57S 43°16W **189** D2
Dom Pedrito *Brazil* 31°0S 54°40W **191** C5
Dom Pedro *Brazil* 4°59S 44°27W **189** A2
Doma *Nigeria* 8°25N 8°18E **139** D6
Doma △ *Zimbabwe* 16°28S 30°12E **143** F3
Domanic *Turkey* 39°48N 29°36E **99** B11
Domariaganj → *India* 26°17N 83°44E **125** F10
Domasi *Malawi* 15°15S 35°22E **143** F4
Domažlice *Czechia* 49°28N 12°58E **78** B5
Dombarovskiy *Russia* 50°46N 59°32E **106** D6
Dombås *Norway* 62°4N 9°8E **60** E13
Dombasle-sur-Meurthe
 France 48°38N 6°21E **71** D13
Dombóvár *Hungary* 46°21N 18°9E **80** D3
Dombrád *Hungary* 48°13N 21°54E **80** B6
Dome Argus *Antarctica* 80°22N 29°55E **81** C14
Dome C. *Antarctica* 75°5S 123°37E **55** D9
Dome I. = Letsôk-aw Kyun
 Myanmar 11°30N 98°25E **121** G2
Domérat *France* 46°21N 2°32E **71** F9
Domett *N.Z.* 42°53S 173°12E **155** C4
Domeyko *Chile* 29°0S 71°0W **190** B1
Domeyko, Cordillera
 Chile 24°30S 69°0W **190** A2
Domfront *France* 48°37N 0°40W **70** D6
Domingos *Chile* 24°21S 69°20W **190** A2
Dominica ■ *W. Indies* 15°20N 61°20W **183** C7
Dominica Passage
 W. Indies 15°10N 61°20W **183** C7
Dominican Rep. ■
 W. Indies 19°0N 70°30W **183** C5
Dömitz *Germany* 53°8N 11°15E **76** B7
Domme *France* 44°48N 1°12E **72** D5
Dommel → *Neths.* 51°44N 5°28E **69** C5
Domneşti *Romania* 45°12N 24°50E **81** E9
Domodedovo *Russia* 55°26N 37°46E **84** E9
Domodedovo Int., Moscow ✈
 (DME) *Russia* 55°25N 37°54E **84** E9
Domodóssola *Italy* 46°7N 8°17E **92** B5
Domogled-Valea Cernei △
 Romania 44°52N 22°27E **80** F7
Domokos *Greece* 39°10N 22°18E **98** B4
Dompaire *France* 48°14N 6°14E **71** D13
Dompierre-sur-Besbre
 France 46°31N 3°41E **71** F10
Domville, Mt. *Australia* 28°1S 151°15E **151** D5
Domžale *Slovenia* 46°9N 14°35E **93** B11
Don → *India* 16°20N 76°15E **127** F3
Don → *Russia* 47°4N 39°18E **85** J10
Don → *Aberd., U.K.* 57°11N 2°5W **65** D6
Don → *S. Yorks., U.K.* 53°41N 0°52W **66** D7
Don, C. *Australia* 11°18S 131°46E **148** B5
Don Benito *Spain* 38°53N 5°51W **89** G5
Don Figuereroa Mts.
 Jamaica 18°5N 77°36W **182** a
Don Sak *Thailand* 9°18N 99°41E **121** b
Doña Ana = Nhamaabué
 Mozam. 17°25S 35°5E **143** F4
Doña Mencía *Spain* 37°33N 4°21W **89** H6
Donaghadee *U.K.* 54°39N 5°33W **64** B6
Donaghmore *Ireland* 52°52N 7°36W **64** D4
Donald *Australia* 36°23S 143°0E **152** D5
Donaldsonville *U.S.A.* 30°6N 90°59W **176** F9
Donalsonville *U.S.A.* 31°3N 84°53W **178** D5
Doñana △ *Spain* 36°59N 6°23W **89** J4
Donau = Dunărea →
 Europe 45°20N 29°40E **81** E14
Donau → *Austria* 48°10N 17°0E **79** C10
Donau Auen □ *Austria* 48°8N 16°44E **79** C9
Donaueschingen
 Germany 47°56N 8°29E **77** H4
Donauwörth *Germany* 48°43N 10°47E **77** G6
Doncaster *U.K.* 53°32N 1°6W **66** D6
Dondo *Angola* 9°45S 14°25E **140** F2
Dondo *Mozam.* 19°33S 34°46E **143** F3
Dondo, Teluk *Indonesia* 0°50N 120°30E **119** D6
Dondra Head *Sri Lanka* 5°55N 80°40E **127** M5
Donduşeni *Moldova* 48°14N 27°36E **81** B12
Donegal *Ireland* 54°39N 8°5W **64** B3
Donegal □ *Ireland* 54°53N 8°0W **64** B4
Donegal B. *Ireland* 54°31N 8°49W **64** B3
Donets → *Russia* 47°33N 40°55E **87** G5
Donets Basin *Ukraine* 48°0N 38°0E **58** F13
Donetsk *Ukraine* 48°0N 37°45E **85** J9
Donetsk □ *Ukraine* 48°30N 37°30E **85** J9
Dong Ba Thin *Vietnam* 12°8N 109°13E **121** F7
Dong Dang *Vietnam* 21°54N 106°42E **116** G6
Dong Giam *Vietnam* 19°25N 105°31E **120** C5
Dong Ha *Vietnam* 16°55N 107°8E **120** D6
Dong Hene *Laos* 16°40N 105°18E **120** D5
Dong Hoi *Vietnam* 17°29N 106°36E **120** D6
Dong Jiang → *China* 23°6N 114°0E **117** F10
Dong Khe *Vietnam* 22°26N 106°27E **120** A6
Dong Phayayen
 Thailand 14°20N 101°22E **120** E3
Dong Ujimqin Qi
 China 45°32N 116°55E **114** B9
Dong Van *Vietnam* 23°16N 105°22E **120** A5
Dong Xoai *Vietnam* 11°32N 106°55E **121** G6
Donga *Nigeria* 7°45N 10°2E **139** D7
Donga → *Nigeria* 8°20N 9°58E **139** D7
Dong'an *China* 26°23N 111°12E **117** D8
Dongara *Australia* 29°14S 114°57E **149** E1
Dongbei *China* 45°0N 125°0E **115** D13
Dongchuan *China* 26°8N 103°1E **116** D4
Dongen *Neths.* 51°38N 4°56E **69** C4
Dongfang *China* 18°50N 108°33E **116** D3
Dongfeng *China* 42°40N 125°34E **115** C13
Donggala *Indonesia* 0°30S 119°40E **119** E5
Donggan *China* 22°22N 105°9E **116** E5
Dongguang *China* 39°52N 124°10E **115** E13
Dongguan *China* 22°58N 113°44E **117** F9
Dongguang *China* 37°50N 116°30E **114** F9
Donghae *S. Korea* 37°29N 129°7E **115** F15
Donghai Dao *China* 21°0N 110°15E **117** G8
Dongjingcheng *China* 44°5N 129°12E **115** B15
Donglan *China* 24°30N 107°21E **116** E6
Dongliao He → *China* 42°58N 123°32E **115** C12
Dongliu *China* 30°13N 116°55E **117** B11

Dongmen *China* 22°20N 107°48E **116** F6
Dongning *China* 44°2N 131°5E **115** B16
Dongnyi *China* 28°3N 100°1E **116** D3
Dongola *Sudan* 19°9N 30°22E **137** D12
Dongshan *China* 23°43N 117°30E **117** F11
Dongsha Dao
 S. China Sea 20°45N 116°43E **111** G12
Dongsheng = Ordos
 China 39°50N 110°0E **114** E6
Dongtai *China* 32°51N 120°21E **117** A13
Dongting Hu *China* 29°18N 112°45E **117** C9
Dongtou *China* 27°50N 121°5E **117** D13
Dongxiang *China* 28°11N 116°34E **117** C11
Dongxing *China* 21°34N 108°0E **116** G7
Dongyang *China* 29°13N 120°15E **117** C13
Dongying *China* 37°37N 118°57E **115** F10
Dongyingang *China* 37°35N 118°58E **115** F10
Dongzhi *China* 30°12N 117°1E **117** B11
Donington, C. *Australia* 34°45S 136°0E **152** B2
Doniphan *U.S.A.* 36°37N 90°50W **172** G8
Donja Stubica *Croatia* 45°59N 15°59E **93** C12
Donji Dušnik *Serbia* 43°12N 22°5E **96** C6
Donji Miholjac *Croatia* 45°45N 18°10E **80** E3
Donji Milanovac *Serbia* 44°28N 22°6E **96** B6
Donji Vakuf *Bos.-H.* 44°8N 17°24E **80** F2
Dønna *Norway* 66°6N 12°30E **60** C15
Donna *U.S.A.* 26°9N 98°4W **176** M5
Donnaconna *Canada* 46°41N 71°41W **165** C5
Donnelly's Crossing
 N.Z. 35°42S 173°38E **154** B2
Donner Pass *U.S.A.* 39°19N 120°20W **170** F6
Donnybrook *Australia* 33°34S 115°48E **149** F2
Donnybrook *S. Africa* 29°59S 29°48E **145** D4
Donora *U.S.A.* 40°11N 79°52W **174** F5
Donostia = Donostia-San
 Sebastián *Spain* 43°17N 1°58W **90** B3
Donostia-San Sebastián
 Spain 43°17N 1°58W **90** B3
Donousa *Greece* 37°8N 25°48E **99** D7
Donskoy *Russia* 53°55N 38°15E **84** F10
Donwood *Canada* 44°19N 78°16W **174** B6
Donzère *France* 44°28N 4°43E **73** D8
Donzy *France* 47°20N 3°6E **71** E10
Doobie *Australia* 36°20S 145°41E **153** D6
Doomadgee *Australia* 17°56S 138°49E **150** B2
Doomadgee ◎
 Australia 17°56S 138°49E **150** B2
Doon → *U.K.* 55°27N 4°39W **65** F4
Doon Doon ◎
 Australia 16°18S 128°14E **148** C4
Dora, L. *Australia* 22°0S 123°0E **148** D3
Dora Báltea → *Italy* 45°11N 8°3E **92** C5
Dora Ripária → *Italy* 45°5N 7°44E **92** C4
Doran L. *Canada* 61°13N 108°6W **163** A7
Doraville *U.S.A.* 33°54N 84°17W **178** B5
Dorchester *U.K.* 50°42N 2°27W **67** G5
Dorchester, C. *Canada* 65°27N 77°27W **161** D16
Dordabis *Namibia* 22°52S 17°38E **144** B2
Dordogne □ *France* 45°2N 0°40E **72** C4
Dordogne → *France* 45°2N 0°36W **72** C3
Dordrecht *Neths.* 51°48N 4°39E **69** C4
Dordrecht *S. Africa* 31°20S 27°3E **144** E4
Dore → *France* 45°50N 3°35E **72** C7
Dore, Mts. *France* 45°32N 2°50E **72** C6
Doré L. *Canada* 54°46N 107°17W **163** C7
Dores do Indaiá *Brazil* 19°27S 45°36W **189** D2
Dorfen *Germany* 48°15N 12°7E **77** G8
Dorgali *Italy* 40°17N 9°35E **94** B2
Dori *Burkina Faso* 14°3N 0°2W **138** C4
Doring → *S. Africa* 31°54S 18°39E **144** D2
Doringbos *S. Africa* 31°59S 19°16E **144** D2
Dorking *U.K.* 51°14N 0°19W **67** F7
Dormaa-Ahenkro *Ghana* 7°15N 2°52W **138** D4
Dormans *France* 49°4N 3°38E **71** C10
Dornakal *India* 17°27N 80°10E **126** F5
Dornbirn *Austria* 47°25N 9°45E **78** D2
Dornes *France* 46°48N 3°18E **71** F10
Dorneşti *Romania* 47°52N 26°1E **81** C11
Dornie *U.K.* 57°17N 5°31W **65** D3
Dornoch *U.K.* 57°53N 4°2W **65** D4
Dornoch Firth *U.K.* 57°51N 4°4W **65** D4
Dornogovi □ *Mongolia* 44°0N 110°0E **114** C6
Doro *Mali* 16°9N 0°51W **138** B4
Doro, Kavo *Greece* 38°9N 24°38E **98** C6
Dorog *Hungary* 47°42N 18°45E **80** C3
Dorogobuzh *Russia* 54°50N 33°18E **84** E7
Dorohoi *Romania* 47°56N 26°23E **81** C11
Döröö Nuur *Mongolia* 48°0N 93°0E **114** B4
Dorr *Iran* 33°17N 50°38E **129** C6
Dorre I. *Australia* 25°13S 113°12E **149** E1
Dorrigo *Australia* 30°20S 152°44E **153** A10
Dorrigo △ *Australia* 30°22S 152°47E **153** A10
Dorris *U.S.A.* 41°58N 121°55W **168** F3
Dorset □ *Canada* 45°14N 78°54W **174** A6
Dorset *Ohio, U.S.A.* 41°40N 80°40W **174** E4
Dorset *Vt., U.S.A.* 43°15N 73°5W **175** C11
Dorset □ *U.K.* 50°45N 2°26W **67** G5
Dorsten *Germany* 51°40N 6°58E **76** D2
Dortmund *Germany* 51°30N 7°28E **76** D3
Dortmund-Ems-Kanal →
 Germany 51°50N 7°26E **76** D3
Dörtyol *Turkey* 36°50N 36°13E **104** D7
Dorum *Germany* 53°41N 8°34E **76** B4
Doruma
 Dem. Rep. of the Congo 4°42N 27°33E **142** B2
Dorūnēh *Iran* 35°10N 57°18E **129** C8
Dos Bahías, C.
 Argentina 44°58S 65°32W **192** E3
Dos Hermanas *Spain* 37°16N 5°55W **89** H5
Dos Palos *U.S.A.* 36°59N 120°37W **170** J6
Döşemealtı *Turkey* 37°0N 30°30E **99** E12
Dosso *Niger* 13°0N 3°13E **139** C5
Dosso □ *Niger* 12°36N 2°53E **139** C5
Dosso △ *Niger* 12°0N 3°30E **139** C5
Dostyq *Kazakhstan* 45°15N 82°29E **108** E9
Dothan *U.S.A.* 31°13N 85°24W **178** D4
Doty *U.S.A.* 46°38N 123°17W **170** D3
Douai *France* 50°21N 3°4E **71** B10
Douako *Guinea* 9°45N 10°8E **138** D2
Douala *Cameroon* 4°0N 9°45E **139** E6
Douarnenez *France* 48°6N 4°21W **70** D2
Doubabougou *Mali* 14°13N 7°50W **138** C3
Double Cone △ *N.Z.* 44°43S 168°49E **155** F2
Double Island Pt.
 Australia 25°56S 153°11E **151** D5
Double Mountain Fork →
 U.S.A. 33°16N 100°0W **176** E4
Doubrava → *Czechia* 50°8N 15°20E **78** A8
Doubs □ *France* 47°10N 6°20E **71** E13

Doubs → *France* 46°53N 5°1E **71** E12
Doubtful Sd. *N.Z.* 45°20S 166°49E **155** F1
Doubtless B. *N.Z.* 34°55S 173°26E **154** A2
Doudeville *France* 49°43N 0°47E **70** C7
Doué-la-Fontaine *France* 47°11N 0°15W **70** E6
Douentza *Mali* 14°58N 2°48W **138** C4
Douentza □ *Mali* 15°40N 2°25W **138** C4
Dougga *Tunisia* 36°25N 9°13E **136** A5
Doughboy B. *N.Z.* 47°25S 167°40E **155** F2
Douglas *I. of Man* 54°10N 4°28W **66** C3
Douglas *S. Africa* 29°4S 23°46E **144** D3
Douglas *Ariz., U.S.A.* 31°21N 109°33W **169** L9
Douglas *Ga., U.S.A.* 31°31N 82°51W **178** D7
Douglas *Wyo.,*
 U.S.A. 42°45N 105°24W **168** E11
Douglas Apsley △
 Australia 41°45S 148°11E **151** E4
Douglas Chan.
 Canada 53°40N 129°20W **162** C3
Douglas Pt. *Canada* 44°19N 81°37W **174** B3
Douglasville *U.S.A.* 33°45N 84°45W **178** B4
Douirat *Morocco* 33°2N 4°11W **136** B3
Doukaton, Akra *Greece* 38°34N 20°33E **98** C2
Doukkala-Abda □
 Morocco 32°10N 8°50W **136** B2
Doulevant-le-Château
 France 48°23N 4°55E **71** D11
Doullens *France* 50°10N 2°20E **71** B9
Doumen *China* 22°10N 113°18E **117** F9
Douna *Mali* 13°13N 6°0W **138** C3
Dounreay *U.K.* 58°35N 3°44W **65** C5
Dourada, Serra *Brazil* 13°10S 48°45W **189** C1
Dourados *Brazil* 22°9S 54°50W **191** A5
Dourados → *Brazil* 21°58S 54°18W **191** A5
Dourados, Serra dos
 Brazil 23°30S 53°30W **191** A5
Dourdan *France* 48°30N 2°1E **71** D9
Douro → *Europe* 41°8N 8°40W **88** D2
Douvaine *France* 46°19N 6°16E **71** F13
Douz *Tunisia* 33°25N 9°0E **136** B6
Douze → *France* 43°54N 0°30W **72** E3
Dove → *U.K.* 52°51N 1°36W **66** E6
Dove Creek *U.S.A.* 37°46N 108°54W **169** H9
Dover *Australia* 43°18S 147°2E **151** E4
Dover *U.K.* 51°7N 1°19E **67** F9
Dover *Del., U.S.A.* 39°10N 75°32W **173** F16
Dover *N.H., U.S.A.* 43°12N 70°56W **175** C14
Dover *N.J., U.S.A.* 40°53N 74°34W **175** F10
Dover *Ohio, U.S.A.* 40°32N 81°29W **174** F3
Dover, Pt. *Australia* 32°32S 125°32E **149** F4
Dover, Str. of *Europe* 51°0N 1°30E **67** G9
Dover-Foxcroft
 U.S.A. 45°11N 69°13W **173** C19
Dover Plains *U.S.A.* 41°43N 73°35W **175** E11
Dovey = Dyfi → *U.K.* 52°32N 4°3W **67** E3
Dovhe *Ukraine* 48°22N 23°17E **81** B8
Dovrefjell *Norway* 62°15N 9°33E **60** E13
Dovrefjell-Sunndalsfjella △
 Norway 62°23N 9°11E **60** E13
Dow Rūd *Iran* 33°28N 49°4E **129** C6
Dowa *Malawi* 13°38S 33°58E **143** E3
Dowagiac *U.S.A.* 41°59N 86°6W **172** E10
Dowerin *Australia* 31°12S 117°2E **149** F2
Dowgha'i *Iran* 36°54N 58°32E **129** B8
Dowlatābād *Kermān,*
 Iran 28°20N 56°40E **129** D8
Dowlatābād *Khorāsān,*
 Iran 34°30N 57°0E **129** C8
Dowling Park *U.S.A.* 30°15N 83°15W **178** E6
Down □ *U.K.* 54°23N 6°2W **64** B5
Downey *Calif., U.S.A.* 33°56N 118°9W **171** M8
Downey *Idaho, U.S.A.* 42°26N 112°7W **168** E7
Downham Market *U.K.* 52°37N 0°23E **67** E8
Downieville *U.S.A.* 39°34N 120°50W **170** F6
Downpatrick *U.K.* 54°20N 5°43W **64** B6
Downpatrick Hd. *Ireland* 54°20N 9°21W **64** B2
Downsville *U.S.A.* 42°5N 75°0W **175** D10
Downton, Mt. *Canada* 52°42N 124°52W **162** C4
Dowsārī *Iran* 28°25N 57°59E **129** D8
Doxato *Greece* 41°9N 24°16E **97** E8
Doyle *U.S.A.* 40°2N 120°6W **170** E6
Doylestown *U.S.A.* 40°21N 75°10W **175** F9
Dozois, Rés. *Canada* 47°30N 77°5W **164** C4
Dra Khel *Pakistan* 27°58N 66°45E **124** F2
Dra, C. *Morocco* 28°47N 11°0W **134** C3
Drăa, Hamada du *Algeria* 28°0N 7°0W **136** C2
Drâa, Oued →
 Morocco 28°40N 11°10W **136** C1
Drac → *France* 45°13N 5°41E **73** C9
Drac, Coves del *Spain* 39°31N 3°19E **100** B10
Dračevo *Macedonia* 41°56N 21°33E **96** E5
Drachten *Neths.* 53°7N 6°5E **69** A6
Drăgănești *Romania* 44°9N 24°32E **81** F9
Drăgănești-Olt *Romania* 44°9N 24°32E **81** F9
Drăgănești-Vlașca
 Romania 44°5N 25°33E **81** F10
Dragaš = Sharr *Kosovo* 42°5N 20°41E **96** D4
Drăgăşani *Romania* 44°39N 24°17E **81** F9
Dragichyn *Belarus* 52°15N 25°8E **83** E13
Dragocvet *Serbia* 43°58N 21°15E **96** C5
Dragon's Mouths
 Trin. & Tob. 11°0N 61°50W **187** K15
Dragovishtitsa *Bulgaria* 42°22N 22°39E **96** D6
Draguignan *France* 43°32N 6°27E **73** E10
Drahovo *Ukraine* 48°23N 23°33E **81** B8
Drain *U.S.A.* 43°40N 123°19W **168** E2
Drake *U.S.A.* 47°55N 100°23W **172** B3
Drake Passage *S. Ocean* 58°0S 68°0W **55** B17
Drakensberg *S. Africa* 31°0S 28°0E **145** D4
Drama *Greece* 41°9N 24°10E **97** E8
Drammen *Norway* 59°42N 10°12E **61** G14
Drangajökull *Iceland* 66°9N 22°15W **60** C2
Dranov, Ostrovul
 Romania 44°55N 29°30E **81** F15
Dras *India* 34°25N 75°48E **125** B6
Drastis, Akra *Greece* 39°48N 19°40E **101** A3
Drau = Drava →
 Croatia 45°33N 18°55E **80** E3
Drava → *Croatia* 45°33N 18°55E **80** E3
Dravograd *Slovenia* 46°36N 15°5E **93** B12
Drawa → *Poland* 52°52N 15°59E **83** E2
Drawieński △ *Poland* 53°6N 15°58E **83** E2
Drawno *Poland* 53°13N 15°46E **83** E2
Drawsko Pomorskie
 Poland 53°35N 15°50E **82** E2
Drayton *Canada* 43°46N 80°40W **174** C4
Drayton Valley
 Canada 53°12N 114°58W **162** C6

Drenthe □ *Neths.* 52°52N 6°40E **69** B6

Drepano, Akra *Greece* 35°28N 24°14E **101** D6
Drepanum, C. *Cyprus* 34°54N 32°19E **101** E11
Dresden *Canada* 42°35N 82°11W **174** D2
Dresden *Germany* 51°3N 13°44E **76** D9
Dresden *U.K.* 42°41N 76°57W **174** D8
Dreux *France* 48°44N 1°23E **70** D8
Drezdenko *Poland* 52°50N 15°49E **83** F2
Driffield *U.K.* 54°0N 0°26W **66** C7
Driftwood *U.S.A.* 41°20N 78°8W **174** E6
Driggs *U.S.A.* 43°44N 111°6W **168** E8
Drin → *Albania* 42°1N 19°38E **96** D3
Drin i Zi → *Albania* 41°37N 20°28E **96** E4
Drina → *Bos.-H.* 44°53N 19°21E **96** B3
Drincea → *Romania* 44°20N 22°55E **80** F7
Drinjača → *Bos.-H.* 44°15N 19°8E **80** F4
Driopida *Greece* 37°25N 24°26E **98** D6
Drissa = Vyerkhnyadzvinsk
   Belarus 55°45N 27°58E **84** E4
Drniš *Croatia* 43°51N 16°10E **93** E13
Drøbak *Norway* 59°39N 10°39E **61** G14
Drobeta-Turnu Severin
   Romania 44°39N 22°41E **80** F7
Drobin *Poland* 52°42N 19°58E **83** F6
Drochia *Moldova* 48°2N 27°48E **81** C12
Drogheda *Ireland* 53°43N 6°22W **64** C5
Drogichin = Dragichyn
   Belarus 52°15N 25°8E **75** B13
Drogobych = Drohobych
   Ukraine 49°20N 23°30E **83** J10
Drohiczyn *Poland* 52°24N 22°39E **83** F9
Drohobych *Ukraine* 49°20N 23°30E **83** J10
Droichead Átha = Drogheda
   Ireland 53°43N 6°22W **64** C5
Droichead na Bandan = Bandon
   Ireland 51°44N 8°44W **64** E3
Droichead Nua = Newbridge
   Ireland 53°11N 6°48W **64** C5
Droitwich *U.K.* 52°16N 2°8W **67** E5
Drôme □ *France* 44°38N 5°15E **73** D9
Drôme → *France* 44°46N 4°46E **73** D8
Dromedary, C.
   Australia 36°17S 150°10E **153** D9
Drömling △ *Germany* 52°29N 11°5E **76** C7
Dromore *Down, U.K.* 54°25N 6°9W **64** B5
Dromore *Tyrone, U.K.* 54°31N 7°28W **64** B4
Dromore West *Ireland* 54°15N 8°52W **64** B3
Dronero *Italy* 44°28N 7°22E **92** D4
Dronfield *U.K.* 53°19N 1°27W **66** D6
Dronne → *France* 45°2N 0°9W **72** C3
Dronning Ingrid Land
   Greenland 64°25N 52°5W **57** E5
Dronning Maud Land
   Antarctica 72°30S 12°0E **55** D3
Dronninglund *Denmark* 57°10N 10°19E **63** G4
Dronten *Neths.* 52°32N 5°43E **69** B5
Dropt → *France* 44°35N 0°6W **72** D3
Drosendorf *Austria* 48°52N 15°37E **78** C8
Droué *France* 48°3N 1°6E **70** D8
Drouin *Australia* 38°10S 145°53E **153** E6
Druk Yul = Bhutan ■
   Asia 27°25N 90°30E **123** F17
Drumbo *Canada* 43°16N 80°35W **174** C4
Drumcliff *Ireland* 54°20N 8°29W **64** B3
Drumheller *Canada* 51°25N 112°40W **162** C6
Drummond *U.S.A.* 46°40N 113°9W **168** C7
Drummond I. *U.S.A.* 46°1N 83°39W **173** B12
Drummond Pt.
   Australia 34°9S 135°16E **151** E2
Drummond Ra.
   Australia 23°45S 147°10E **150** C4
Drummondville
   Canada 45°55N 72°25W **164** C5
Drumright *U.S.A.* 35°59N 96°36W **176** D6
Druskininkai *Lithuania* 54°3N 23°58E **84** E2
Drut → *Belarus* 53°8N 30°5E **75** B16
Druya *Belarus* 55°45N 27°28E **84** E4
Druzhba *Bulgaria* 43°15N 28°1E **97** C12
Druzhina *Russia* 68°14N 145°18E **107** C15
Druzhkivka *Ukraine* 48°38N 37°32E **85** H9
Drvar *Bos.-H.* 44°21N 16°23E **93** D13
Drvenik *Croatia* 43°27N 16°3E **93** E13
Drweca → *Poland* 53°0N 18°42E **83** E5
Dry Harbour Mts.
   Jamaica 18°19N 77°24W **182** a
Dry Tortugas *U.S.A.* 24°38N 82°55W **177** J13
Dryander △ *Australia* 20°13S 148°34E **150** b
Dryanovo *Bulgaria* 42°59N 25°28E **97** D9
Dryden *Canada* 49°47N 92°50W **163** D10
Dryden *U.S.A.* 42°30N 76°18W **175** D8
Drygalski I. *Antarctica* 66°0S 92°0E **55** C7
Drygalski Ice Tongue
   Antarctica 75°24S 163°30E **55** D11
Drysdale → *Australia* 13°59S 126°51E **148** B4
Drysdale I. *Australia* 11°41S 136°0E **150** A2
Drysdale River △
   Australia 14°56S 127°2E **148** B4
Drzewica *Poland* 51°27N 20°29E **83** G7
Drzewiczka → *Poland* 51°36N 20°36E **83** G7
Dschang *Cameroon* 5°32N 10°3E **139** D7
Du Gué → *Canada* 57°21N 70°45W **164** A5
Du He → *China* 32°48N 110°40E **117** A8
Du Quoin *U.S.A.* 38°1N 89°14W **172** F9
Du'an *China* 23°59N 108°3E **116** F7
Duanesburg *U.S.A.* 42°45N 74°11W **175** D10
Duaringa *Australia* 23°42S 149°42E **150** C4
Duarte, Pico *Dom. Rep.* 19°2N 70°59W **183** C5
Dubai = Dubayy
   U.A.E. 25°18N 55°20E **129** E7
Dubăsari *Moldova* 47°15N 29°10E **81** C14
Dubăsari Vdkhr.
   Moldova 47°30N 29°0E **81** C13
Dubawnt → *Canada* 64°33N 100°6W **163** A8
Dubawnt L. *Canada* 63°8N 101°28W **163** A8
Dubayy *U.A.E.* 25°18N 55°20E **129** E7
Dubbo *Australia* 32°11S 148°35E **153** E4
Dube → *Liberia* 5°16N 7°29W **138** D3
Dubele
   Dem. Rep. of the Congo 2°56N 29°35E **142** B2
Dübendorf *Switz.* 47°24N 8°37E **77** H4
Dubica *Bos.-H.* 45°11N 16°48E **93** C13
Dubica *Croatia* 45°11N 16°48E **93** C13
Dublin *Ireland* 53°21N 6°15W **64** C5
Dublin *Ga., U.S.A.* 32°32N 82°54W **178** C7
Dublin *Tex., U.S.A.* 32°5N 98°21W **176** C5
Dublin □ *Ireland* 53°24N 6°20W **64** C5
Dublin ✈ (DUB) *Ireland* 53°26N 6°16W **64** C5
Dubna *Russia* 56°44N 37°10E **84** C9
Dubnica nad Váhom
   Slovakia 48°58N 18°11E **79** C11
Dubno *Ukraine* 50°25N 25°45E **75** C13
Dubois *Idaho, U.S.A.* 44°10N 112°14W **168** D7

DuBois *Pa., U.S.A.* 41°7N 78°46W **174** E6
Dubossary = Dubăsari
   Moldova 47°15N 29°10E **81** C14
Dubove *Ukraine* 48°10N 23°53E **81** B8
Dubovka *Russia* 49°5N 44°50E **87** F7
Dubovskoye *Russia* 47°28N 42°46E **87** G6
Dubrajpur *India* 23°48N 87°25E **125** H12
Dubréka *Guinea* 9°46N 13°31W **138** D2
Dubrovitsa = Dubrovytsya
   Ukraine 51°31N 26°35E **75** C14
Dubrovnik *Croatia* 42°39N 18°6E **96** C2
Dubrovytsya *Ukraine* 51°31N 26°35E **75** C14
Dubuque *U.S.A.* 42°30N 90°41W **172** D8
Dubysa → *Lithuania* 55°5N 23°26E **82** C10
Duc Tho *Vietnam* 18°32N 105°35E **120** C5
Duchang *China* 29°18N 116°12E **117** C11
Duchesne *U.S.A.* 40°10N 110°24W **168** F8
Duchess *Australia* 21°20S 139°50E **150** C2
Ducie I. *Pac. Oc.* 24°40S 124°48W **157** K15
Duck → *U.S.A.* 36°2N 87°52W **177** C11
Duck Cr. → *Australia* 22°37S 116°53E **148** D2
Duck Lake *Canada* 52°50N 106°16W **163** C7
Duck Mountain △
   Canada 51°45N 101°0W **163** C8
Duckwall, Mt. *U.S.A.* 37°58N 120°7W **170** H6
Duderstadt *Germany* 51°31N 10°15E **76** D6
Dudhi *India* 24°15N 83°10E **125** G10
Dudinka *Russia* 69°30N 86°13E **107** C9
Dudley *U.K.* 52°31N 2°5W **67** E5
Dudley *U.S.A.* 32°32N 83°5W **178** C6
Dudna → *India* 19°17N 76°54E **126** E3
Dudwa *India* 28°30N 80°41E **125** E9
Dudwa △ *India* 28°30N 80°40E **125** E9
Duékoué *Côte d'Ivoire* 6°40N 7°15W **138** D3
Dueñas *Spain* 41°52N 4°33W **88** D6
Duero = Douro →
   Europe 41°8N 8°40W **88** D2
Dufftown *U.K.* 57°27N 3°8W **65** D5
Dufourspitz *Switz.* 45°56N 7°52E **77** K3
Dugi Otok *Croatia* 44°0N 15°3E **93** D11
Dugo Selo *Croatia* 45°51N 16°18E **93** C13
Duisburg *Germany* 51°26N 6°45E **76** D2
Duiwelskloof = Modjadjiskloof
   S. Africa 23°42S 30°10E **145** B5
Dujiangyan *China* 31°2N 103°38E **116** B4
Dukat *Albania* 40°16N 19°32E **96** F3
Dūkdamīn *Iran* 35°59N 57°43E **129** C8
Dukelský Prùsmyk
   Slovakia 49°25N 21°42E **79** B14
Dukhān *Qatar* 25°25N 50°50E **129** E6
Dukhovshchina *Russia* 55°15N 32°27E **84** E7
Duki *Pakistan* 30°14N 68°25E **122** D6
Dukla *Poland* 49°30N 21°35E **83** J8
Duku *Bauchi, Nigeria* 10°43N 10°43E **139** C7
Duku *Sokoto, Nigeria* 11°11N 4°55E **139** C5
Dukuza = Stanger
   S. Africa 29°27S 31°14E **145** C5
Dulan *China* 36°0N 97°11E **110** D8
Dulce *U.S.A.* 36°56N 107°0W **169** H10
Dulce → *Argentina* 30°32S 62°33W **190** C3
Dulce, G. *Costa Rica* 8°40N 83°20W **182** E3
Dulf *Iraq* 35°7N 45°51E **128** C5
Duliu *China* 39°2N 116°55E **114** E9
Dullewala *Pakistan* 31°50N 71°25E **124** D4
Dullstroom *S. Africa* 25°27S 30°7E **145** C5
Dülmen *Germany* 51°49N 7°17E **76** D3
Dulovo *Bulgaria* 43°48N 27°9E **97** C11
Duluth *Ga., U.S.A.* 34°0N 84°9W **178** A5
Duluth *Minn., U.S.A.* 46°47N 92°6W **172** B7
Dum Dum *India* 22°39N 88°25E **125** H13
Dum Duma *India* 27°40N 95°40E **123** F19
Dūmā *Syria* 33°34N 36°24E **130** B5
Dumaguete *Phil.* 9°17N 123°15E **119** C6
Dumai *Indonesia* 1°35N 101°28E **118** D2
Dumaran *Phil.* 10°33N 119°50E **119** B5
Dumas *Ark., U.S.A.* 33°53N 91°29W **176** D9
Dumas *Tex., U.S.A.* 35°52N 101°58W **176** D4
Dumayr *Syria* 33°39N 36°42E **130** B5
Dumbarton *U.K.* 55°57N 4°33W **65** F4
Dumbleyung *Australia* 33°17S 117°42E **149** F2
Dumbrăveni *Romania* 46°14N 24°34E **81** D9
Dumfries *U.K.* 55°4N 3°37W **65** F5
Dumfries & Galloway □
   U.K. 55°9N 3°58W **65** F5
Dumitreşti *Romania* 45°33N 26°55E **81** E11
Dumka *India* 24°12N 87°15E **125** G12
Dumlupınar *Turkey* 38°53N 30°0E **99** C12
Dümmer *Germany* 52°31N 8°6E **76** C4
Dümmer △ *Germany* 52°31N 8°21E **76** C4
Dumoine → *Canada* 46°13N 77°51W **164** C4
Dumoine, L. *Canada* 46°55N 77°55W **164** C4
Dumont d'Urville
   Antarctica 66°40S 140°0E **55** C10
Dumont d'Urville Sea
   S. Ocean 63°30S 138°0E **55** C9
Dumyât *Egypt* 31°24N 31°48E **137** E7
Dumyât, Masabb *Egypt* 31°28N 31°51E **137** E7
Dún Dealgan = Dundalk
   Ireland 54°1N 6°24W **64** B5
Dún Garbhán = Dungarvan
   Ireland 52°5N 7°37W **64** D4
Dún Laoghaire *Ireland* 53°17N 6°8W **64** C5
Dún Laoghaire-Rathdown □
   Ireland 53°14N 6°11W **64** C5
Dun-le-Palestel *France* 46°18N 1°39E **71** F8
Dun-sur-Auron *France* 46°53N 2°33E **71** F9
Dun-sur-Meuse *France* 49°23N 5°11E **71** C12
Duna = Dunărea →
   Europe 45°20N 29°40E **81** E14
Duna-völgyi-főcsatorna
   Hungary 46°50N 18°57E **80** D3
Dunaföldvár *Hungary* 46°50N 18°57E **80** D3
Dunaj = Dunărea →
   Europe 45°20N 29°40E **81** E14
Dunajec → *Poland* 50°15N 20°44E **83** H7
Dunajská Streda
   Slovakia 48°0N 17°37E **79** G10
Dunakeszi *Hungary* 47°37N 19°8E **80** C4
Dunapataj *Hungary* 46°39N 18°57E **80** D4
Dunărea → *Europe* 45°20N 29°40E **81** E14
Dunaszekcső *Hungary* 46°6N 18°45E **80** E3
Dunaújváros *Hungary* 46°58N 18°57E **80** D3
Dunav = Dunărea →
   Europe 45°20N 29°40E **81** E14
Dunavaţu de Jos
   Romania 44°59N 29°13E **81** F14

Dunavtsi *Bulgaria* 43°57N 22°53E **96** C6
Dunay *Russia* 42°52N 132°22E **112** C6
Dunayivtsi *Ukraine* 48°54N 26°56E **81** B11
Dunback *N.Z.* 45°23S 170°36E **155** F5
Dunbar *U.K.* 56°0N 2°31W **65** E6
Dunblane *U.K.* 56°11N 3°58W **65** E5
Duncan *Canada* 48°45N 123°40W **170** B3
Duncan *Ariz., U.S.A.* 32°43N 109°6W **169** K9
Duncan *Okla., U.S.A.* 34°30N 97°57W **176** D6
Duncan, L. *Canada* 53°29N 77°58W **164** B4
Duncan L. *Canada* 62°51N 113°58W **162** A6
Duncan Passage *India* 11°0N 92°0E **127** J11
Duncan Town
   Bahamas 22°15N 75°45W **182** B4
Duncannon *U.S.A.* 40°23N 77°2W **174** F7
Duncansby Head *U.K.* 58°38N 3°1W **65** C5
Duncansville *U.S.A.* 40°25N 78°26W **174** F6
Dund-Us *Mongolia* 48°1N 91°38E **109** C12
Dundaga *Latvia* 57°33N 22°21E **82** A9
Dundalk *Canada* 44°10N 80°24W **174** B4
Dundalk *Ireland* 54°1N 6°24W **64** B5
Dundalk *U.S.A.* 39°15N 76°31W **173** F15
Dundalk Bay *Ireland* 53°55N 6°15W **64** C5
Dundas = Uummannaq
   Greenland 77°33N 68°52W **57** B4
Dundas *Canada* 43°17N 79°59W **174** C5
Dundas, L. *Australia* 32°35S 121°50E **149** F3
Dundas, L. *Australia* 32°35S 121°50E **149** F3
Dundas Str. *Australia* 11°15S 131°35E **148** B5
Dundee *S. Africa* 28°11S 30°15E **145** C5
Dundee *U.K.* 56°28N 2°59W **65** E6
Dundee *U.S.A.* 42°32N 76°59W **174** D8
Dundee City □ *U.K.* 56°30N 2°58W **65** E6
Dundgovĭ □ *Mongolia* 45°10N 106°0E **114** B4
Dundrum *U.K.* 54°16N 5°52W **64** B6
Dundrum B. *U.K.* 54°13N 5°47W **64** B6
Dunedin *N.Z.* 45°50S 170°33E **155** F5
Dunedin *U.S.A.* 28°1N 82°46W **179** D7
Dunedoo *Australia* 32°0S 149°25E **153** E4
Dunfanaghy *Ireland* 55°11N 7°58W **64** A4
Dunfermline *U.K.* 56°5N 3°27W **65** E5
Dungannon *Canada* 43°51N 81°36W **174** C3
Dungannon *U.K.* 54°31N 6°46W **64** B5
Dungarpur *India* 23°52N 73°45E **124** H5
Dungarvan *Ireland* 52°5N 7°37W **64** D4
Dungarvan Harbour
   Ireland 52°4N 7°35W **64** D4
Dungeness *U.K.* 50°54N 0°59E **67** G8
Dungiven *U.K.* 54°56N 6°56W **64** B5
Dungloe *Ireland* 54°57N 8°21W **64** B3
Dungo, L. do *Angola* 17°15S 19°0E **144** A2
Dungog *Australia* 32°22S 151°46E **153** B9
Dungu
   Dem. Rep. of the Congo 3°40N 28°32E **142** B2
Dungun *Malaysia* 4°45N 103°25E **121** K4
Dungunâb *Sudan* 21°10N 37°9E **137** C4
Dungunâb, Khalîg
   Sudan 21°5N 37°12E **137** C4
Dunhua *China* 43°20N 128°14E **115** C15
Dunhuang *China* 40°8N 94°36E **110** C7
Dunk I. *Australia* 17°59S 146°29E **150** B4
Dunkassa *Benin* 10°21N 3°10E **139** C5
Dunkeld *Queens.,
   Australia* 33°25S 149°29E **151** E4
Dunkeld *Vic., Australia* 37°40S 142°22E **152** D5
Dunkeld *U.K.* 56°34N 3°35W **65** E5
Dunkerque *France* 51°2N 2°20E **71** A9
Dunkery Beacon *U.K.* 51°9N 3°36W **67** F4
Dunkirk = Dunkerque
   France 51°2N 2°20E **71** A9
Dunkirk *U.S.A.* 42°29N 79°20W **174** D5
Dunkwa *Central, Ghana* 6°0N 1°47W **138** D4
Dunkwa *Central, Ghana* 5°30N 1°0W **139** D4
Dunleary = Dún Laoghaire
   Ireland 53°17N 6°8W **64** C5
Dunleer *Ireland* 53°50N 6°24W **64** C5
Dunmanus B. *Ireland* 51°31N 9°50W **64** E2
Dunmanway *Ireland* 51°43N 9°6W **64** E2
Dunmarra *Australia* 16°43S 133°25E **150** B1
Dunmore *U.S.A.* 41°25N 75°38W **175** E9
Dunmore East *Ireland* 52°9N 7°0W **64** D5
Dunmore Town
   Bahamas 25°30N 76°39W **182** A4
Dunn *U.S.A.* 35°19N 78°37W **177** D15
Dunnellon *U.S.A.* 29°3N 82°28W **179** F7
Dunnet Hd. *U.K.* 58°40N 3°21W **65** C5
Dunning *U.S.A.* 41°50N 100°6W **172** E3
Dunnville *Canada* 42°54N 79°36W **174** D5
Dunolly *Australia* 36°51S 143°44E **152** D5
Dunoon *U.K.* 55°57N 4°56W **65** F4
Dunqul *Egypt* 23°26N 31°37E **137** C3
Duns *U.K.* 55°47N 2°20W **65** F6
Dunseith *U.S.A.* 48°50N 100°3W **172** A3
Dunshaughlin *Ireland* 53°31N 6°48W **64** C5
Dunsmuir *U.S.A.* 41°13N 122°16W **168** F2
Dunstable *U.K.* 51°53N 0°32W **67** F7
Dunstan Mts. *N.Z.* 44°53S 169°35E **155** E4
Dunster *Canada* 53°8N 119°50W **162** C5
Duntroon *N.Z.* 44°51S 170°40E **155** E5
Dunvegan *U.K.* 57°27N 6°35W **65** D2
Dunvegan L. *Canada* 60°8N 107°10W **163** A7
Duolun *China* 42°12N 116°28E **114** C9
Duomula *China* 34°8N 82°29E **109** F10
Duong Dong *Vietnam* 10°13N 103°58E **121** G4
Dupree *U.S.A.* 45°4N 101°35W **172** C3
Dupuyer *U.S.A.* 48°13N 112°30W **168** B7
Duque de Caxias *Brazil* 22°46S 43°18W **191** A7
Duque de York, I.
   Chile 50°37S 75°25W **192** D1
Durack → *Australia* 15°33S 127°52E **148** C4
Durack Ra. *Australia* 16°50S 127°40E **148** C4
Durack River
   Australia 15°32S 127°39E **148** C4
Durağan *Turkey* 41°25N 35°3E **104** B6
Durak *Turkey* 39°47N 28°17E **99** B10
Durakovac = Gjurakoc
   Kosovo 42°43N 20°29E **96** C5
Durance → *France* 43°55N 4°45E **73** E8
Durand *U.S.A.* 42°55N 83°59W **178** B4
Durand *Wis., U.S.A.* 44°38N 91°58E **172** C8
Durango *Mexico* 24°3N 104°39W **180** C4
Durango *U.S.A.* 37°16N 107°53W **169** H10
Durango □ *Mexico* 24°50N 105°20W **180** C4
Durankulak *Bulgaria* 43°41N 28°32E **97** C12
Durant *Miss., U.S.A.* 33°4N 89°51W **177** E10
Durant *Okla., U.S.A.* 33°59N 96°25W **176** E6
Duratón → *Spain* 41°37N 4°7W **88** D6
Durazno *Uruguay* 33°25S 56°31W **190** C4
Durazzo = Durrës
   Albania 41°19N 19°28E **96** E3
Durban *France* 42°52N 2°49E **72** F6

Durban *S. Africa* 29°49S 31°1E **145** C5
Durban ✈ (DUR)
   S. Africa 29°37S 31°7E **145** C5
Durbuy *Belgium* 50°21N 5°28E **69** D5
Dúrcal *Spain* 36°59N 3°34W **89** J7
Đurđevac *Croatia* 46°2N 17°3E **93** C14
Düren *Germany* 50°48N 6°29E **76** E2
Durg = Bhilainagar-Durg
   India 21°13N 81°26E **126** D5
Durgapur *India* 23°30N 87°20E **125** H12
Durham *Canada* 44°10N 80°49W **174** B4
Durham *U.K.* 54°47N 1°34W **66** C6
Durham *Calif., U.S.A.* 39°39N 121°48W **170** F5
Durham *N.C., U.S.A.* 35°59N 78°54W **177** D15
Durham *N.H., U.S.A.* 43°8N 70°56W **175** C14
Durham □ *U.K.* 54°42N 1°45W **66** C6
Durlas = Thurles *Ireland* 52°41N 7°49W **64** D4
Dürleşti *Moldova* 47°1N 28°46E **81** C13
Durmã *Si. Arabia* 24°37N 46°5E **128** E5
Durmitor △ *Montenegro* 43°10N 19°0E **96** C2
Durmitor △ *Montenegro* 43°15N 19°5E **96** C3
Durness *U.K.* 58°34N 4°45W **65** C4
Durrës *Albania* 41°19N 19°28E **96** E3
Durrow *Ireland* 52°51N 7°24W **64** D4
Dursey I. *Ireland* 51°36N 10°12W **64** E1
Dursley *U.K.* 51°40N 2°21W **67** F5
Dursunbey *Turkey* 39°35N 28°37E **99** B10
Durtal *France* 47°40N 0°18W **70** E6
Duru
   Dem. Rep. of the Congo 4°14N 28°50E **142** B2
Duru Gölü *Turkey* 41°20N 28°35E **97** E12
Durusu *Turkey* 41°17N 28°41E **97** E12
Durūz, Jabal ad *Jordan* 32°35N 36°40E **130** C5
D'Urville, Tanjung
   Indonesia 1°28S 137°54E **119** E9
D'Urville I. *N.Z.* 40°50S 173°55E **155** A4
Duryea *U.S.A.* 41°20N 75°45W **175** E9
Dūsh *Egypt* 24°35N 30°41E **137** C3
Dushak *Turkmenistan* 37°13N 60°1E **129** B9
Dushan *China* 25°48N 107°30E **116** E6
Dushanbe *Tajikistan* 38°33N 68°48E **109** F7
Dusheti *Georgia* 42°10N 44°42E **87** J7
Dushore *U.S.A.* 41°31N 76°24W **175** E8
Dusky Sd. *N.Z.* 45°47S 166°30E **155** F1
Dussejour, C. *Australia* 14°45S 128°13E **148** B4
Düsseldorf *Germany* 51°14N 6°47E **76** D2
Düsseldorf Rhein-Ruhr ✈ (DUS)
   Germany 51°17N 6°46E **76** D2
Dusti *Tajikistan* 37°20N 68°40E **109** E7
Duszniki-Zdrój *Poland* 50°24N 16°24E **83** H3
Dutch Harbor *U.S.A.* 53°53N 166°32W **166** E6
Dutlwe *Botswana* 23°58S 23°46E **144** B3
Dutsan Wai *Nigeria* 10°50N 8°10E **139** C6
Dutse *Nigeria* 11°46N 9°20E **139** C6
Dutton *U.S.A.* 42°39N 81°30W **174** D3
Dutton → *Australia* 20°44S 143°10E **150** C3
Dutywa *S. Africa* 32°8S 28°18E **145** D4
Duved *Sweden* 63°23N 12°55E **62** A6
Düvertepe *Turkey* 39°14N 28°27E **99** B10
Duwayhin, Khawr
   U.A.E. 24°20N 51°25E **129** E6
Duyfken Pt. *Australia* 12°33S 141°38E **150** A3
Duyun *China* 26°18N 107°29E **116** D6
Düzağaç *Turkey* 38°48N 30°10E **99** C12
Duzce = Akhna *Cyprus* 35°3N 33°47E **101** D12
Düzce *Turkey* 40°50N 31°10E **104** B4
Düzce □ *Turkey* 40°50N 31°10E **104** B4
Düziçi *Turkey* 37°15N 36°28E **104** D7
Dve Mogili *Bulgaria* 43°35N 25°55E **97** C9
Dvina, Severnaya →
   Russia 64°32N 40°30E **58** C14
Dvinsk = Daugavpils
   Latvia 55°53N 26°32E **84** E4
Dvor *Croatia* 45°4N 16°22E **93** C13
Dvůr Králové nad Labem
   Czechia 50°27N 15°50E **78** A8
Dwarka *India* 22°18N 69°8E **124** H3
Dwellingup *Australia* 32°43S 116°4E **149** F2
Dwight *Canada* 45°20N 79°1W **174** A6
Dwight *U.S.A.* 41°5N 88°26W **172** E9
Dyakove *Ukraine* 48°1N 23°0E **80** B7
Dyatkovo *Russia* 53°40N 34°27E **84** F8
Dyatlovo = Dzyatlava
   Belarus 53°28N 25°28E **75** B13
Dyce *U.K.* 57°13N 2°12W **65** D6
Dyer, C. *Canada* 66°37N 61°16W **161** D19
Dyer Bay *Canada* 45°10N 81°20W **174** A3
Dyer Plateau
   Antarctica 70°45S 65°30W **55** D17
Dyersburg *U.S.A.* 36°3N 89°23W **177** C10
Dyfi → *U.K.* 52°32N 4°3W **67** E3
Dyje → *Czechia* 48°37N 16°56E **79** C9
Dykh Tau *Russia* 43°3N 43°8E **87** J6
Dymer *Ukraine* 50°47N 30°18E **75** C16
Dynów *Poland* 49°50N 22°11E **83** J9
Dysart *Australia* 22°32S 148°23E **150** C4
Dytiki Ellas □ *Greece* 38°20N 21°30E **98** C3
Dyviziya *Ukraine* 45°55N 29°59E **81** E14
Dzaoudzi *Mayotte* 12°47S 45°16E **141** a
Dzavhan Gol → *Mongolia* 48°0N 96°0E **109** C13
Dzavhan Gol →
   Mongolia 48°54N 93°23E **110** B7
Dzerzhinsk *Russia* 56°14N 43°30E **86** B6
Dzhalal-Abad = Jalal-Abad
   Kyrgyzstan 40°56N 73°0E **109** D8
Dzhalinda *Russia* 53°26N 124°0E **107** D13
Dzhambeyty *Kazakhstan* 50°16N 52°35E **88** B8
Dzhambul = Taraz
   Kazakhstan 42°54N 71°22E **109** D8
Dzhankoy *Ukraine* 45°40N 34°20E **85** K8
Dzhanybek *Kazakhstan* 49°30N 46°50E **86** E8
Dzhardzhan *Russia* 68°10N 124°10E **107** C13
Dzhezkazgan = Zhezqazghan
   Kazakhstan 47°44N 67°40E **108** E7
Dzhizak = Jizzax
   Uzbekistan 40°6N 67°50E **109** D7
Dzhugba *Russia* 44°30N 38°46E **87** H4
Dzhugdzur, Khrebet
   Russia 57°30N 138°0E **107** D14
Dzhulynka *Ukraine* 48°26N 29°45E **81** B14
Dzhumgoltau, Khrebet
   Kyrgyzstan 42°15N 74°30E **109** D8
Dzhungarskiye Vorota =
   Dzungarian Gate
   Asia 45°10N 82°0E **109** C10
Dzhurin *Ukraine* 48°41N 28°18E **81** B13
Dzhvari *Georgia* 42°42N 42°4E **87** J4
Dzhzekazgan = Zhezqazghan
   Kazakhstan 47°44N 67°40E **108** E7
Działdowo *Poland* 53°15N 20°15E **83** E7

Działoszyce *Poland* 50°22N 20°20E **83** H7
Działoszyn *Poland* 51°6N 18°50E **83** G5
Dzibilchaltún *Mexico* 21°10N 89°35W **181** C7
Dzierzgoń *Poland* 53°58N 19°20E **82** E6
Dzierżoniów *Poland* 50°45N 16°39E **83** H3
Dzilam de Bravo
   Mexico 21°24N 88°53W **181** C7
Dzioua *Algeria* 33°14N 5°14E **136** B5
Dzisna *Belarus* 55°34N 28°12E **84** E5
Dzisna → *Belarus* 55°34N 28°12E **84** E5
Dziwnów *Poland* 54°2N 14°45E **82** D1
Dzükija △ *Lithuania* 54°10N 24°30E **61** J21
Dzungaria = Junggar
   Pendi *China* 44°30N 86°0E **109** D11
Dzungarian Gate *Asia* 45°10N 82°0E **109** C10
Dzur *Mongolia* 49°39N 95°46E **109** C13
Dzüünbayan *Mongolia* 44°29N 110°2E **114** B6
Dzüünharaa
   Mongolia 48°52N 106°28E **110** B10
Dzüünmod *Mongolia* 47°45N 106°58E **110** B10
Dzyarzhynsk *Belarus* 53°40N 27°1E **75** B14
Dzyatlava *Belarus* 53°28N 25°28E **75** B13

E

E.C. Manning △
   Canada 49°5N 120°45W **162** D4
Eabamet L. *Canada* 51°30N 87°46W **164** B2
Eabametoong *Canada* 51°30N 88°0W **164** B2
Éadan Doire = Edenderry
   Ireland 53°21N 7°4W **64** C4
Eads *U.S.A.* 38°29N 102°47W **168** G12
Eagar *U.S.A.* 34°6N 109°17W **169** J9
Eagle *Alaska, U.S.A.* 64°47N 141°12W **160** E3
Eagle *Colo., U.S.A.* 39°39N 106°50W **168** G10
Eagle → *Canada* 53°36N 57°26W **165** B8
Eagle Butte *U.S.A.* 45°0N 101°10W **172** C3
Eagle Grove *U.S.A.* 42°40N 93°54W **172** D7
Eagle L. *Canada* 49°42N 93°13W **163** D10
Eagle L. *Calif., U.S.A.* 40°39N 120°45W **168** F3
Eagle L. *Maine, U.S.A.* 46°20N 69°22W **173** B19
Eagle Lake *Canada* 45°8N 78°29W **174** A6
Eagle Lake *Maine,
   U.S.A.* 47°3N 68°36W **173** B19
Eagle Lake *Tex., U.S.A.* 29°35N 96°20W **176** G6
Eagle Mountain
   U.S.A. 33°49N 115°27W **171** M11
Eagle Nest *U.S.A.* 36°33N 105°16W **169** H11
Eagle Pass *U.S.A.* 28°43N 100°30W **176** G4
Eagle Pk. *U.S.A.* 38°10N 119°25W **170** G7
Eagle Pt. *Australia* 16°11S 124°23E **148** C3
Eagle River *Mich.,
   U.S.A.* 47°25N 88°18W **172** B9
Eagle River *Wis.,
   U.S.A.* 45°55N 89°15W **172** C9
Eaglehawk *Australia* 36°44S 144°15E **152** D6
Eagles Mere *U.S.A.* 41°25N 76°33W **175** E8
Ealing □ *U.K.* 51°31N 0°20W **67** F7
Ear Falls *Canada* 50°38N 93°13W **163** C10
Earlimart *U.S.A.* 35°53N 119°16W **171** K7
Earlville *U.S.A.* 42°44N 75°32W **175** D9
Early Branch *U.S.A.* 32°45N 80°55W **178** D7
Earn → *U.K.* 56°21N 3°18W **65** E5
Earn, L. *U.K.* 56°23N 4°13W **65** E4
Earnslaw, Mt. *N.Z.* 44°32S 168°27E **155** E3
Earth *U.S.A.* 34°14N 102°24W **176** D3
Easley *U.S.A.* 34°50N 82°36W **177** D13
East Anglia *U.K.* 52°50N 1°0E **66** E9
East Angus *Canada* 45°30N 71°40W **165** C5
East Antarctica *Antarctica* 80°0S 90°0E **55** D7
East Aurora *U.S.A.* 42°46N 78°37W **174** D6
East Ayrshire □ *U.K.* 55°26N 4°11W **65** F4
East Bengal *Bangla.* 24°0N 90°0E **123** G17
East Beskids = Vychodné Beskydy
   Europe 49°20N 22°0E **79** B15
East Brady *U.S.A.* 40°59N 79°37W **174** F5
East Branch Clarion River L.
   U.S.A. 41°35N 78°35W **174** E6
East C. = Dezhneva, Mys
   Russia 66°5N 169°40W **107** C19
East C. *N.Z.* 37°42S 178°35E **154** D7
East Caroline Basin
   Pac. Oc. 4°0N 146°45E **156** G6
East Chicago *U.S.A.* 41°38N 87°27W **172** E10
East China Sea *Asia* 30°0N 126°0E **111** F14
East Coulee *Canada* 51°23N 112°27W **162** C6
East Dereham = Dereham
   U.K. 52°41N 0°57E **67** E8
East Dublin *U.S.A.* 32°32N 82°52W **178** C7
East Dunbartonshire □
   U.K. 55°57N 4°13W **65** F4
East Falkland *Falk. Is.* 51°30S 58°30W **192** D5
East Grand Forks
   U.S.A. 47°56N 97°1W **172** B5
East Greenwich
   U.S.A. 41°40N 71°27W **175** E13
East Grinstead *U.K.* 51°7N 0°0 **67** F8
East Hartford *U.S.A.* 41°46N 72°39W **175** E12
East Haydon *Australia* 18°0S 141°30E **150** B3
East Helena *U.S.A.* 46°35N 111°56W **168** C8
East Indies *Asia* 0°0 120°0E **102** J14
East Kavango □
   Namibia 18°0S 20°15E **144** A3
East Kilbride *U.K.* 55°47N 4°11W **65** F4
East Lamma Channel
   China 22°14N 114°9E **111** a
East Lansing *U.S.A.* 42°44N 84°29W **173** D11
East Liverpool *U.S.A.* 40°37N 80°35W **174** F4
East London *S. Africa* 33°0S 27°55E **145** D4
East Lothian □ *U.K.* 55°58N 2°44W **65** F6
East Main = Eastmain
   Canada 52°10N 78°30W **164** B4
East Mariana Basin
   Pac. Oc. 12°0N 153°0E **156** F7
East Naples *U.S.A.* 26°8N 81°46W **179** J8
East Northport *U.S.A.* 40°53N 73°19W **175** F11
East Orange *U.S.A.* 40°46N 74°12W **175** F10
East Pacific Rise
   Pac. Oc. 15°0S 110°0W **157** J17
East Palatka *U.S.A.* 29°39N 81°36W **179** F7
East Palestine *U.S.A.* 40°50N 80°33W **174** F4
East Pine *Canada* 55°48N 120°12W **162** B4
East Point *U.S.A.* 33°41N 84°27W **178** B4
East Providence
   U.S.A. 41°49N 71°23W **175** E13
East Pt. *Br. Virgin Is.* 18°40N 64°18W **183** a
East Renfrewshire □
   U.K. 55°46N 4°21W **65** F4

East Retford = Retford
   U.K. 53°19N 0°56W **66** D7
East Riding of Yorkshire □
   U.K. 53°55N 0°30W **66** D7
East Rochester *U.S.A.* 43°7N 77°29W **174** C7
East St. Louis *U.S.A.* 38°37N 90°9W **172** F8
East Schelde = Oosterschelde
   Neths. 51°33N 4°0E **69** C4
East Sea = Japan, Sea of
   Asia 40°0N 135°0E **112** E7
East Siberian Sea
   Russia 73°0N 160°0E **107** B17
East Stroudsburg *U.S.A.* 41°1N 75°11W **175** E9
East Sussex □ *U.K.* 50°56N 0°19E **67** G8
East Tasman Plateau
   Pac. Oc. 43°30S 152°0E **156** M7
East Tawas *U.S.A.* 44°17N 83°29E **173** C12
East Timor ■ *Asia* 8°50S 126°0E **119** F7
East Toorale *Australia* 30°27S 145°28E **151** E4
East Walker →
   U.S.A. 38°52N 119°10W **170** G7
East Windsor *U.S.A.* 40°17N 74°34W **175** F10
Eastbourne *N.Z.* 41°19S 174°55E **154** H3
Eastbourne *U.K.* 50°46N 0°18E **67** G8
Eastend *Canada* 49°32N 108°50W **163** D7
Easter Fracture Zone
   Pac. Oc. 25°0S 115°0W **157** K16
Easter I. = Pascua, I. de
   Chile 27°7S 109°23W **157** K17
Eastern □ *Ghana* 6°30N 0°30W **139** D4
Eastern □ *S. Leone* 8°15N 11°0W **138** D2
Eastern Cape □ *S. Africa* 32°0S 26°0E **144** D4
Eastern Cr. →
   Australia 20°40S 141°35E **150** C3
Eastern Desert = Sharqîya, Es
   Sahrâ esh *Egypt* 27°30N 32°30E **137** B3
Eastern Ghats *India* 14°0N 78°50E **127** H4
Eastern Group = Lau Group
   Fiji 17°0S 178°30W **154** a
Eastern Group
   Australia 33°30S 124°30E **149** F3
Eastern Guruma ☉
   Australia 22°0S 117°30E **148** D2
Eastern Transvaal =
   Mpumalanga □
   S. Africa 26°0S 30°0E **145** C5
Easterville *Canada* 53°8N 99°49W **163** C9
Easthampton *U.S.A.* 42°16N 72°40W **175** D12
Eastlake *U.S.A.* 41°40N 81°26W **174** E3
Eastland *U.S.A.* 32°24N 98°49W **176** C5
Eastleigh *U.K.* 50°58N 1°21W **67** G6
Eastmain *Canada* 52°10N 78°30W **164** B4
Eastmain → *Canada* 52°27N 78°26W **164** B4
Eastman *Canada* 45°18N 72°19W **175** A12
Eastman *U.S.A.* 32°12N 83°11W **178** C6
Easton *Md., U.S.A.* 38°47N 76°5W **173** F15
Easton *Pa., U.S.A.* 40°41N 75°13W **175** F9
Easton *Wash., U.S.A.* 47°14N 121°11W **170** C5
Eastover *U.S.A.* 33°52N 80°41W **178** D6
Eastpoint *U.S.A.* 29°44N 84°53W **178** F5
Eastport *U.S.A.* 44°56N 67°0W **173** C20
Eastsound *U.S.A.* 48°42N 122°55W **170** B4
Eaton *U.S.A.* 40°32N 104°42W **168** F11
Eatonia *Canada* 51°13N 109°25W **163** C17
Eatonton *U.S.A.* 33°20N 83°23W **178** B6
Eatontown *U.S.A.* 40°19N 74°4W **175** F10
Eatonville *U.S.A.* 46°52N 122°16W **170** D4
Eau Claire *U.S.A.* 44°49N 91°30W **172** C8
Eau Claire, L. à l'
   Canada 56°10N 74°25W **164** A5
Eauripik Rise *Pac. Oc.* 2°0N 142°0E **156** G6
Eauze *France* 43°53N 0°7E **72** E4
Eban *Nigeria* 9°40N 4°50E **139** D5
Ebano *Mexico* 22°13N 98°24W **181** C5
Ebbegebirge △ *Germany* 51°10N 7°55E **76** D3
Ebbw Vale *U.K.* 51°46N 3°12W **67** F4
Ebeltoft *Denmark* 56°12N 10°41E **63** H4
Ebeltoft Vig *Denmark* 56°10N 10°35E **63** H4
Ebensburg *U.S.A.* 40°29N 78°44W **174** F6
Ebensee *Austria* 47°48N 13°46E **78** D6
Eber Gölü *Turkey* 38°38N 31°11E **104** C4
Eberbach *Germany* 49°28N 9°59E **77** F4
Eberswalde-Finow
   Germany 52°50N 13°49E **76** C9
Ebetsu *Japan* 43°7N 141°34E **112** C10
Ebey's Landing
   U.S.A. 48°12N 122°41W **170** B4
Ebian *China* 29°11N 103°13E **116** C4
Ebingen = Albstadt
   Germany 48°13N 9°1E **77** G5
Ebinur Hu *China* 44°55N 82°55E **109** D10
Eboli *Italy* 40°39N 15°2E **95** B8
Ebolowa *Cameroon* 2°55N 11°10E **139** E7
Ebonda
   Dem. Rep. of the Congo 2°12N 22°21E **140** D4
Ebonyi □ *Nigeria* 6°20N 8°0E **139** D6
Ebrach *Germany* 49°50N 10°30E **77** F6
Ebre = Ebro → *Spain* 40°43N 0°54E **90** E5
Ébrié, Lagune
   Côte d'Ivoire 5°12N 4°26W **138** D4
Ebro → *Spain* 40°43N 0°54E **90** E5
Ebro, Embalse del *Spain* 43°0N 3°58W **88** C7
Ebstorf *Germany* 53°2N 10°24E **76** B6
Ecatepec de Morelos
   Mexico 19°36N 99°3W **181** D5
Ecbatana = Hamadān
   Iran 34°52N 48°32E **105** C13
Eceabat *Turkey* 40°11N 26°21E **97** F10
Ech Chéliff *Algeria* 36°10N 1°20E **136** A6
Ech Chéliff □ *Algeria* 36°15N 1°30E **136** A4
Echebonnee →
   U.S.A. 32°39N 83°36W **178** C6
Echigo-Sammyaku
   Japan 36°50N 139°50E **113** E9
Echinos *Greece* 41°16N 24°58E **97** E10
Échirolles *France* 45°8N 5°44E **73** C9
Echizen-Misaki *Japan* 35°59N 135°57E **113** G7
Echmiadzin = Ejmiatsin
   Armenia 40°12N 44°19E **87** K7
Echo *U.S.A.* 31°29N 85°28W **178** D4
Echo Bay *N.W.T.,
   Canada* 66°5N 117°55W **160** D8
Echo Bay *Ont., Canada* 46°29N 84°4W **164** D3
Echoing → *Canada* 55°51N 92°5W **164** B1
Echternach *Lux.* 49°49N 6°25E **69** E6
Echuca *Australia* 36°10S 144°45E **153** D6
Écija *Spain* 37°30N 5°10W **89** H5
Eckental *Germany* 49°35N 11°12E **77** F7

Eckernförde Germany 54°28N 9°50E 76 A5
Eclectic U.S.A. 32°38N 86°2W 178 C3
Eclipse I. Australia 35°5S 117°58E 149 G2
Eclipse Is. Australia 13°54S 126°19E 148 B4
Eclipse Sd. Canada 72°38N 79°0W 161 C16
Écommoy France 47°50N 0°17E 70 E7
Ecoporanga Brazil 18°23S 40°50W 189 D2
Écouché France 48°42N 0°10W 70 D6
Ecrins △ France 44°54N 6°18E 73 D10
Ecuador ■ S. Amer. 2°0S 78°0W 186 D3
Écueillé France 47°5N 1°21E 70 E8
Ed Sweden 58°55N 11°55E 63 F5
Ed Da'ein Sudan 11°26N 26°9E 140 B5
Ed Damazin Sudan 11°46N 34°21E 135 F12
Ed Dâmer Sudan 17°27N 34°0E 135 E12
Ed Dar el Beida = Casablanca Morocco 33°36N 7°36W 136 B2
Ed Debba Sudan 18°0N 30°51E 137 D3
Ed Déffa Egypt 30°40N 26°30E 137 A2
Ed Dueim Sudan 14°0N 32°10E 135 F12
Edam Canada 53°11N 108°46W 163 C7
Edam Neths. 52°31N 5°3E 69 B5
Edane Sweden 59°38N 12°49E 62 E6
Edapally India 11°19N 78°3E 127 J4
Eday U.K. 59°11N 2°47W 65 B6
Eddrachillis B. U.K. 58°17N 5°14W 65 C3
Eddystone U.K. 50°11N 4°16W 67 G3
Eddystone Pt. Australia 40°59S 148°20E 151 G4
Ede Neths. 52°4N 5°40E 69 B5
Ede Nigeria 7°45N 4°29E 139 D5
Édéa Cameroon 3°51N 10°9E 139 E7
Edebäck Sweden 60°4N 13°32E 62 D7
Edehon L. Canada 60°25N 97°15W 163 A9
Edelény Hungary 48°18N 20°44E 80 B5
Eden Australia 37°3S 149°55E 153 D8
Eden N.C., U.S.A. 36°29N 79°53W 177 C15
Eden N.Y., U.S.A. 42°39N 78°55W 174 D6
Eden Tex., U.S.A. 31°13N 99°51W 176 F5
Eden → U.K. 54°57N 3°1W 66 C4
Edenburg S. Africa 29°43S 25°58E 144 C4
Edendale N.Z. 46°19S 168°48E 155 G3
Edendale S. Africa 29°39S 30°18E 145 C5
Edenderry Ireland 53°21N 7°4W 64 C4
Edenhope Australia 37°4S 141°19E 152 D4
Edenton U.S.A. 36°4N 76°39W 177 C16
Edenville S. Africa 27°37S 27°34E 145 C4
Eder → Germany 51°12N 9°28E 76 D5
Eder-Stausee Germany 51°10N 8°57E 76 D4
Edessa Greece 40°48N 22°5E 96 F6
Edewecht Germany 53°8N 7°58E 76 B3
Edfu = Idfû Egypt 24°55N 32°49E 137 C3
Edgar U.S.A. 40°22N 97°58W 172 E5
Edgartown U.S.A. 41°23N 70°31W 175 E14
Edge Hill U.K. 52°8N 1°26W 67 E6
Edgecumbe N.Z. 37°59S 176°47E 154 D5
Edgefield U.S.A. 33°47N 81°56W 178 B8
Edgeley U.S.A. 46°22N 98°43W 172 B4
Edgemont U.S.A. 43°18N 103°50W 172 D2
Edgeøya Svalbard 77°45N 22°30E 54 B9
Edgewater U.S.A. 28°59N 80°54W 179 G9
Édhessa = Edessa Greece 40°48N 22°5E 96 F6
Edievale N.Z. 45°49S 169°22E 155 F4
Edina Liberia 6°0N 10°10W 138 D2
Edina U.S.A. 40°10N 92°11W 172 E7
Edinboro U.S.A. 41°52N 80°8W 174 E4
Edinburg U.S.A. 26°18N 98°10W 176 H5
Edinburgh U.K. 55°57N 3°13W 65 F5
Edinburgh ✕ (EDI) U.K. 55°54N 3°22W 65 F5
Edinburgh, City of □ U.K. 55°57N 3°17W 65 F5
Edineț Moldova 48°9N 27°18E 81 B12
Edirne Turkey 41°40N 26°34E 97 E10
Edirne □ Turkey 41°12N 26°30E 97 E10
Edison Ga., U.S.A. 31°34N 84°44W 178 D5
Edison Wash., U.S.A. 48°33N 122°27W 170 B4
Edisto → U.S.A. 32°29N 80°21W 178 C9
Edisto Beach U.S.A. 32°29N 80°20W 178 C9
Edisto I. U.S.A. 32°35N 80°20W 178 C9
Edithburgh Australia 35°5S 137°43E 152 C2
Edjeleh Algeria 28°38N 9°50E 136 C5
Edmeston U.S.A. 42°42N 75°15W 175 D9
Edmond U.S.A. 35°39N 97°29W 176 D6
Edmonds U.S.A. 47°48N 122°22W 170 C4
Edmonton Australia 17°2S 145°46E 150 B4
Edmonton Canada 53°30N 113°30W 162 C6
Edmund L. Canada 54°45N 93°17W 164 B1
Edmundston Canada 47°23N 68°20W 165 C6
Edna U.S.A. 28°59N 96°39W 176 G6
Edo □ Nigeria 6°30N 6°0E 139 D6
Edolo Italy 46°10N 10°21E 92 B7
Edremit Turkey 39°34N 27°0E 99 B9
Edremit Körfezi Turkey 39°30N 26°45E 99 B8
Edsbro Sweden 59°54N 18°29E 62 E12
Edsbruk Sweden 58°1N 16°29E 63 F10
Edsbyn Sweden 61°23N 15°49E 62 C9
Edson Canada 53°35N 116°28W 162 C5
Eduardo Castex Argentina 35°50S 64°18W 190 D3
Eduardo Frei Montalva = Frei Antarctica 62°30S 58°0W 55 C18
Edward → Australia 35°5S 143°30E 152 C5
Edward, L. Africa 0°25S 29°40E 142 C2
Edward VII Land Antarctica 80°0S 150°0W 55 E13
Edwards Calif., U.S.A. 34°50N 117°40W 171 L9
Edwards N.Y., U.S.A. 44°20N 75°15W 175 B9
Edwards Plateau U.S.A. 30°45N 101°20W 176 F4
Edwardsville U.S.A. 41°15N 75°56W 175 E9
Edzná Mexico 19°39N 90°19W 181 D6
Edzo = Behchoko Canada 62°50N 116°3W 162 A5
Eeklo Belgium 51°11N 3°33E 69 C3
Eenhana Namibia 17°30S 16°23E 144 A2
Eesti = Estonia ■ Europe 58°30N 25°30E 84 C3
Eferding Austria 48°18N 14°1E 78 C7
Effigy Mounds △ U.S.A. 43°5N 91°11W 172 D8
Effingham U.S.A. 39°7N 88°33W 172 F9
Eforie Romania 44°1N 28°37E 81 F13
Efxinoupoli Greece 39°12N 22°42E 98 B4
Ega → Spain 42°19N 1°55W 90 C3
Égadi, Ísole Italy 37°55N 12°16E 94 E5
Egan Range U.S.A. 39°35N 114°55W 168 G6
Eganville Canada 45°32N 77°5W 174 A7
Egedesminde = Aasiaat Greenland 68°43N 52°56W 57 D5
Eger = Cheb Czechia 50°9N 12°28E 78 A5
Eger Hungary 47°53N 20°27E 80 C5
Eger → Hungary 47°38N 20°50E 80 C5
Egersund Norway 58°26N 6°1E 61 G12
Egg L. Canada 55°5N 105°30W 163 B7
Eggegebirge Südlicher Teutoburger Wald △ Germany 51°40N 8°59E 76 D4
Eggenburg Austria 48°38N 15°50E 78 C8
Eggenfelden Germany 48°23N 12°46E 77 G8
Éghezée Belgium 50°35N 4°55E 69 D4
Egilsstaðir Iceland 65°16N 14°25W 60 D6
Egina Greece 37°45N 23°26E 98 D5
Eginio Greece 40°28N 22°28E 96 F6
Egio Greece 38°15N 22°5E 98 C4
Égletons France 45°24N 2°3E 72 C6
Eglinton I. Canada 75°48N 118°30W 161 B8
Egmont Canada 49°45N 123°56W 162 D4
Egmont, C. N.Z. 39°16S 173°45E 154 F2
Egmont, Mt. = Taranaki, Mt. N.Z. 39°17S 174°5E 154 F3
Egmont △ N.Z. 39°17S 174°4E 154 F3
Egra India 21°54N 87°32E 125 J12
Eğridir Turkey 37°52N 30°51E 104 D4
Eğridir Gölü Turkey 37°53N 30°50E 104 D4
Egtved Denmark 55°38N 9°18E 63 J3
Éguas → Brazil 13°26S 44°14W 189 C2
Éguzon-Chantôme France 46°27N 1°33E 71 F8
Egvekinot Russia 66°19N 179°50W 107 C19
Egyek Hungary 47°39N 20°52E 80 C5
Egypt ■ Africa 28°0N 31°0E 137 F7
Eha Amufu Nigeria 6°30N 7°46E 139 D6
Ehime □ Japan 33°30N 132°40E 113 H6
Ehingen Germany 48°16N 9°43E 77 G5
Ehrenberg U.S.A. 33°36N 114°31W 171 M12
Ehrhardt U.S.A. 33°6N 81°1W 178 B8
Ehrwald Austria 47°24N 10°56E 78 D3
Eibar Spain 43°11N 2°28W 90 B2
Eichstätt Germany 48°54N 11°11E 77 G7
Eider → Germany 54°19N 8°57E 76 A4
Eidsvold Australia 25°25S 151°12E 151 D5
Eidsvoll Norway 60°19N 11°14E 61 F14
Eielson U.S.A. 64°40N 147°4W 166 C10
Eifel Germany 50°15N 6°50E 77 E2
Eiffel Flats Zimbabwe 18°20S 30°0E 143 F3
Eiger Switz. 46°34N 8°1E 92 B5
Eigg U.K. 56°54N 6°10W 65 E2
Eighty Mile Beach Australia 19°30S 120°40E 148 C3
Eil, L. U.K. 56°51N 5°16W 65 E3
Eilat = Elat Israel 29°30N 34°56E 130 F3
Eildon Australia 37°14S 145°55E 153 D6
Eildon, L. Australia 37°10S 146°0E 153 D7
Eilean Siar □ U.K. 57°30N 7°10W 65 D1
Eilenburg Germany 51°27N 12°36E 76 D8
Einasleigh Australia 18°32S 144°5E 150 B3
Einasleigh → Australia 17°30S 142°17E 150 B3
Einbeck Germany 51°49N 9°53E 76 D5
Eindhoven Neths. 51°26N 5°28E 69 C5
Einsiedeln Switz. 47°7N 8°46E 77 H4
Eire = Ireland ■ Europe 53°50N 7°52W 64 C4
Eiríksjökull Iceland 64°46N 20°24W 60 D3
Eiriosgaigh = Eriskay U.K. 57°4N 7°18W 65 D1
Eirunepé Brazil 6°35S 69°53W 188 B4
Eiseb → Namibia 20°33S 20°59E 144 B2
Eisenach Germany 50°58N 10°19E 76 E6
Eisenberg Germany 50°58N 11°54E 76 E7
Eisenerz Austria 47°32N 14°54E 78 D7
Eisenhüttenstadt Germany 52°9N 14°38E 76 C10
Eisenkappel Austria 46°29N 14°36E 78 E7
Eisenstadt Austria 47°51N 16°31E 79 D9
Eisleben Germany 51°32N 11°32E 76 D7
Eislingen Germany 48°41N 9°42E 77 G5
Eivissa Spain 38°54N 1°26E 100 C7
Eixe, Serra do Spain 42°24N 6°54W 88 C4
Ejea de los Caballeros Spain 42°7N 1°9W 90 C3
Ejmiatsin Armenia 40°12N 44°19E 87 K7
Ejura Ghana 7°23N 1°15W 139 D4
Ejutla Mexico 16°34N 96°44W 181 D5
Ekalaka U.S.A. 45°53N 104°33W 168 D11
Ekaterinburg = Yekaterinburg Russia 56°50N 60°30E 106 D7
Ekenäs = Raasepori Finland 60°0N 23°26E 84 B2
Ekenässjön Sweden 57°28N 15°1E 63 G9
Ekerö Sweden 59°16N 17°45E 62 E11
Eket Nigeria 4°38N 7°56E 139 E6
Eketahuna N.Z. 40°38S 175°43E 154 G4
Ekibastuz Kazakhstan 51°50N 75°10E 109 B9
Ekiti □ Nigeria 7°25N 5°20E 139 D6
Ekoli Dem. Rep. of the Congo 0°23S 24°13E 142 C1
Ekoln Sweden 59°45N 17°37E 62 E11
Ekshärad Sweden 60°10N 13°30E 62 D7
Eksjö Sweden 57°40N 14°58E 63 G8
Ekuma → Namibia 18°40S 16°2E 144 A2
Ekwan → Canada 53°12N 82°15W 164 B3
Ekwan Pt. Canada 53°16N 82°7W 164 B3
El Aaiún W. Sahara 27°9N 13°12W 134 C3
El Abanico Chile 37°20S 71°31W 190 D1
El Abiodh-Sidi-Cheikh Algeria 32°53N 0°31E 136 B4
El Adeb Larache Algeria 27°22N 8°52E 136 C5
El 'Agrûd Egypt 30°14N 34°24E 130 E3
El Aioun Morocco 34°33N 2°30W 136 B3
El 'Aiyat Egypt 29°36N 31°15E 137 F7
El Alamein Egypt 30°48N 28°58E 137 E6
El Alto Peru 4°15S 81°14W 188 A1
El 'Aqaba, W. → Egypt 30°7N 33°54E 130 E2
El 'Arag Egypt 28°40N 26°20E 137 B2
El Aricha Algeria 34°13N 1°10W 136 B3
El Arîḥā West Bank 31°52N 35°27E 130 D4
El 'Arîsh Egypt 31°8N 33°50E 130 D2
El 'Arîsh, W. → Egypt 31°8N 33°47E 130 D2
El Arrouch Algeria 36°37N 6°53E 136 A5
El Asnam = Ech Chéliff Algeria 36°10N 1°20E 136 A4
El Astillero Spain 43°24N 3°49W 88 B7
El Badâri Egypt 27°4N 31°25E 137 B3
El Bahrein Egypt 28°30N 26°25E 137 B2
El Ballâs Egypt 26°2N 32°43E 137 B3
El Balyana Egypt 26°10N 32°3E 137 B3
El Baqeir Sudan 18°40N 33°40E 137 D3
El Barco de Ávila Spain 40°21N 5°31W 88 E5
El Barco de Valdeorras = O Barco Spain 42°23N 6°58W 88 C4
El Bauga Sudan 18°18N 33°52E 137 D3
El Bawiti Egypt 28°25N 28°45E 137 F6
El Bayadh Algeria 33°40N 1°1E 136 B4
El Bayadh □ Algeria 32°30N 1°10E 136 B4
El Bierzo Spain 42°45N 6°30W 88 C4
El Bluff Nic. 11°59N 83°40W 182 D3
El Bolsón Argentina 41°55S 71°30W 192 B2
El Bonillo Spain 38°57N 2°35W 91 G2
El Burgo de Osma Spain 41°35N 3°4W 90 D1
El Cain Argentina 41°38S 68°19W 192 B3
El Cajon U.S.A. 32°48N 116°58W 171 N10
El Calafate Argentina 50°19S 72°15W 192 D2
El Campello Spain 38°26N 0°24W 91 G4
El Campo U.S.A. 29°12N 96°16W 176 G6
El Capitan U.S.A. 37°44N 119°38E 170 H7
El Carbón Honduras 15°25N 85°32W 182 C2
El Carmen Colombia 9°43N 75°8W 186 B3
El Centro U.S.A. 32°48N 115°34W 171 N11
El Cerro Bolivia 17°30S 61°40W 186 G6
El Cerro de Andévalo Spain 37°45N 6°57W 89 H4
El Chaltén Argentina 49°19S 72°56W 192 C2
El Compadre Mexico 32°20N 116°14W 171 N10
El Corcovado Argentina 43°25S 71°35W 192 B2
El Coronil Spain 37°5N 5°38W 89 H5
El Cotillo Canary Is. 28°41N 14°1W 100 F5
El Cuy Argentina 39°55S 68°25W 192 A3
El Cuyo Mexico 21°31N 87°41W 181 C7
El Dab'a Egypt 31°0N 28°27E 137 E6
El Daheir Egypt 31°13N 34°10E 130 D3
El Deir Egypt 25°25N 32°20E 137 B3
El Descanso Mexico 32°12N 116°58W 171 N10
El Desemboque Mexico 30°33N 113°1W 180 A2
El Dilingat Egypt 30°50N 30°31E 137 E7
El Diviso Colombia 1°22N 78°14W 186 C3
El Djouf Mauritania 21°25N 6°40W 134 D4
El Dorado Mexico 24°17N 107°21W 180 C3
El Dorado Ark., U.S.A. 33°12N 92°40W 176 E8
El Dorado Kans., U.S.A. 37°49N 96°52W 172 G5
El Dorado Venezuela 6°55N 61°37W 186 B6
El Dorado Springs U.S.A. 37°52N 94°1W 172 G6
El Eglab Algeria 26°20N 4°30W 136 C3
El Ejido Spain 36°47N 2°49W 89 J8
El Escorial Spain 40°35N 4°7W 88 E6
El Espinar Spain 41°43N 4°15W 88 D6
El Eulma Algeria 36°9N 5°42E 136 A5
El Faiyûm Egypt 29°19N 30°50E 137 F7
El Faourar Tunisia 33°22N 8°45E 136 B5
El Fâsher Sudan 13°33N 25°26E 135 F11
El Fashn Egypt 28°50N 30°54E 137 F7
El Ferrol = Ferrol Spain 43°29N 8°15W 88 B2
El Fuerte Mexico 26°25N 108°39W 180 B3
El Gedida Egypt 25°40N 28°30E 137 B2
El Geneina = Al Junaynah Sudan 13°27N 22°45E 135 F10
El Gezira □ Sudan 15°0N 33°0E 135 F12
El Gir Sudan 19°50N 28°18E 137 D2
El Giza Egypt 30°0N 31°12E 137 F7
El Gogorrón △ Mexico 21°49N 100°57W 180 C4
El Goléa Algeria 30°30N 2°50E 136 B4
El Gouna Egypt 27°5N 33°47E 137 B3
El Guácharo △ Venezuela 10°8N 63°21W 183 D7
El Guache △ Venezuela 9°45N 69°30W 183 E6
El Hadjira Algeria 32°36N 5°30E 136 B5
El Hâi Egypt 29°39N 31°18E 137 F7
El Hajeb Morocco 33°43N 5°13W 136 B2
El Hamma Tunisia 33°54N 9°48E 136 B5
El Hammam Egypt 30°52N 29°25E 137 E6
El Homr Algeria 29°43N 1°45E 136 C4
El 'Idisât Egypt 25°30N 32°35E 137 B3
El Iskandarîya Egypt 31°13N 29°58E 137 H6
El Istiwa'iya Sudan 5°0N 28°0E 135 G11
El Jadida Morocco 33°11N 8°17W 136 B2
El Jardal Honduras 14°54N 88°50W 182 D2
El Jebha Morocco 35°11N 4°43W 136 A3
El Jem Tunisia 35°19N 10°41E 136 A6
El Kab Sudan 19°27N 32°46E 137 D3
El Kafr el Sharqi Egypt 31°16N 31°10E 137 E7
El Kala Algeria 36°53N 8°26E 136 A5
El Kantara Algeria 35°14N 5°45E 136 A5
El Kantara Tunisia 33°45N 10°58E 136 B6
El Karaba Sudan 18°32N 33°41E 137 D3
El Kef Tunisia 36°12N 8°47E 136 A5
El Kef □ Tunisia 36°0N 9°0E 136 A5
El Kelaâ de Srahna Morocco 32°4N 7°27W 136 B2
El Kelaâ M'Gouna Morocco 31°14N 6°7W 136 B2
El Khandaq Sudan 18°30N 30°30E 137 D3
El Khanka Egypt 30°13N 31°21E 137 E7
El Khârga Egypt 25°30N 30°33E 137 B3
El Khartûm Sudan 15°31N 32°35E 135 E12
El Khartûm Bahrî Sudan 15°40N 32°31E 135 E12
El Khroub Algeria 36°10N 6°55E 136 A5
El Kseur Algeria 36°46N 4°49E 136 A4
El Ksiba Morocco 32°45N 6°1W 136 B2
El Kuntilla Egypt 30°1N 34°45E 130 E3
El Leoncito △ Argentina 31°58S 69°10W 190 C2
El Lucero Mexico 30°37N 106°31W 180 A3
El Maestrazgo Spain 40°30N 0°25W 90 E4
El Maghra Egypt 30°15N 28°55E 137 E6
El Mahalla el Kubra Egypt 31°0N 31°0E 137 E7
El Mahârîq Egypt 25°35N 30°35E 137 B3
El Maîmûn Egypt 29°14N 31°12E 137 F7
El Maitén Argentina 42°3S 71°10W 192 B2
El Maiz Algeria 28°19N 0°9W 136 C3
El Maks el Bahari Egypt 24°30N 30°40E 137 C3
El Malpais △ U.S.A. 34°53N 108°0W 169 J10
El Manshâh Egypt 26°26N 31°50E 137 B3
El Mansour Algeria 27°47N 0°14W 136 C3
El Mansûra Egypt 31°0N 31°19E 137 E7
El Manzala Egypt 31°10N 31°50E 137 E7
El Marâgha Egypt 26°35N 31°10E 137 B3
El Masnou Spain 41°28N 2°20E 90 D7
El Matarîya Egypt 31°15N 32°0E 137 E8
El Medano Canary Is. 28°3N 16°32W 100 F3
El Meghaier Algeria 33°55N 5°58E 136 B5
El Ménia = El Goléa Algeria 30°30N 2°50E 136 B4
El Meraguen Algeria 28°0N 0°7W 136 C3
El Milagro Argentina 30°59S 65°59W 190 C2
El Milia Algeria 36°51N 6°13E 136 A5
El Minyâ Egypt 28°7N 30°33E 137 F7
El Monte U.S.A. 34°4N 118°1W 171 L8
El Montseny Spain 41°55N 2°25E 90 D7
El Mreyye Mauritania 18°0N 6°0W 138 B3
El Obeid Sudan 13°8N 30°10E 135 F12
El Odaiya Sudan 12°8N 28°12E 135 F11
El Oro Mexico 19°51N 100°7W 181 D4
El Oued Algeria 33°20N 6°58E 136 B5
El Oued □ Algeria 33°10N 7°15E 136 B5
El Palmar △ Argentina 32°10S 58°31W 190 C4
El Paso U.S.A. 31°45N 106°29W 176 F1
El Paso de Robles = Paso Robles U.S.A. 35°38N 120°41W 170 K6
El Pedernoso Spain 39°29N 2°45W 91 F2
El Pedroso Spain 37°51N 5°45W 89 H5
El Pinacate y Gran Desierto de Altar = Gran Desierto del Pinacate △ Mexico 31°51N 113°32W 180 A2
El Pobo de Dueñas Spain 40°46N 1°39W 90 E3
El Portal U.S.A. 37°41N 119°47W 170 H7
El Porvenir Mexico 31°15N 105°51W 180 A3
El Prat Barcelona ✕ (BCN) Spain 41°18N 2°5E 90 D7
El Prat de Llobregat Spain 41°19N 2°5E 90 D7
El Progreso Honduras 15°26N 87°51W 182 C2
El Pueblo Canary Is. 28°36N 17°47W 100 F2
El Puente del Arzobispo Spain 39°48N 5°10W 88 F5
El Puerto de Santa María Spain 36°36N 6°13W 89 J4
El Qâhira Egypt 30°2N 31°13E 137 E7
El Qantara Egypt 30°51N 32°20E 130 E1
El Qasr Egypt 25°44N 28°42E 137 B2
El Qubâbât Egypt 29°28N 31°16E 137 F7
El Quseima Egypt 30°40N 34°15E 130 E3
El Qusîya Egypt 27°29N 30°44E 137 B3
El Râshda Egypt 25°36N 28°57E 137 B2
El Real de Santa María Panama 8°0N 77°40W 186 B3
El Reno U.S.A. 35°32N 97°57W 167 H20
El Rey △ Argentina 24°40S 64°34W 190 A3
El Ridisiya Egypt 24°56N 32°51E 137 C3
El Rio U.S.A. 34°14N 119°10W 171 L7
El Ronquillo Spain 37°44N 6°10W 89 H4
El Roque, Pta. Canary Is. 28°10N 15°25W 100 F4
El Rosario Mexico 30°1N 115°45W 180 A1
El Rubio Spain 37°22N 5°0W 89 H5
El Saff Egypt 29°34N 31°16E 137 F7
El Salto Mexico 23°47N 105°22W 180 C3
El Salvador ■ Cent. Amer. 13°50N 89°0W 182 D2
El Sauce Nic. 13°0N 86°40W 182 D2
El Saucejo Spain 37°4N 5°6W 89 H5
El Shallal Egypt 24°0N 32°53E 137 C3
El Simbillawein Egypt 30°48N 31°13E 137 E7
El Suweis Egypt 29°58N 32°31E 137 F8
El Tabbîn Egypt 29°47N 31°18E 137 F7
El Tamarâni, W. → Egypt 30°7N 34°43E 130 E3
El Tarf Algeria 36°46N 8°19E 136 A5
El Tarf □ Algeria 36°45N 8°10E 136 A5
El Thamad Egypt 29°40N 34°28E 130 F3
El Tigre Venezuela 8°44N 64°15W 186 B6
El Tîh, Gebel Egypt 29°40N 33°50E 130 F2
El Tîna Egypt 31°3N 32°22E 130 D1
El Tofo Chile 29°22S 71°18W 190 B1
El Tránsito Chile 28°52S 70°17W 190 B1
El Tûr Egypt 28°14N 33°36E 128 D2
El Turbio Argentina 51°45S 72°5W 192 D2
El Uqsur Egypt 25°41N 32°38E 137 B3
El Valle △ Spain 37°56N 1°6W 91 H3
El Vendrell Spain 41°10N 1°30E 90 D6
El Vergel Mexico 26°28N 106°22W 180 B3
El Vigía Venezuela 8°38N 71°39W 186 B4
El Viso del Alcor Spain 37°23N 5°43W 89 H5
El Wabeira Egypt 29°34N 33°6E 130 F2
El Wuz Sudan 15°5N 30°7E 135 E12
Elafonisos Greece 36°29N 22°56E 98 E4
Elamanchili India 17°33N 82°50E 126 F6
Élancourt France 48°47N 1°58E 71 D8
Elands Australia 31°37S 152°20E 153 A10
Elasa Greece 35°18N 26°21E 99 F8
Elassona Greece 39°53N 22°12E 98 B4
Elat Israel 29°30N 34°56E 130 F3
Elatia Greece 38°37N 22°46E 98 C4
Elâzığ Turkey 38°37N 39°14E 105 C8
Elâzığ □ Turkey 38°40N 39°15E 105 C8
Elba Italy 42°46N 10°17E 92 F7
Elba U.S.A. 31°25N 86°4W 178 D3
Elbasan Albania 41°9N 20°9E 96 E4
Elbe U.S.A. 46°45N 122°10W 170 D4
Elbe → Europe 53°50N 9°0E 76 B4
Elbe-Seitenkanal Germany 52°45N 10°32E 76 C6
Elbert, Mt. U.S.A. 39°7N 106°27W 168 G10
Elberton U.S.A. 34°7N 82°52W 178 A7
Elbeuf France 49°17N 1°2E 70 C8
Elbing = Elbląg Poland 54°10N 19°25E 82 D6
Elbistan Turkey 38°13N 37°15E 104 C7
Elbląg Poland 54°10N 19°25E 82 D6
Elbow Canada 51°7N 106°35W 163 C7
Elbrus Russia 43°21N 42°30E 87 J6
Elbufer-Drawehn △ Germany 53°8N 10°58E 76 B6
Elburz Mts. = Alborz, Reshteh-ye Kūhhā-ye Iran 36°0N 52°0E 129 C7
Elche Spain 38°15N 0°42W 91 G4
Elche de la Sierra Spain 38°27N 2°3W 91 G2
Elcho I. Australia 11°55S 135°45E 150 A2
Elda Spain 38°29N 0°47W 91 G4
Eldama Ravine Kenya 0°3N 35°43E 142 B4
Elde → Germany 53°7N 11°15E 76 B7
Eldon Mo., U.S.A. 38°21N 92°35W 172 F7
Eldon Wash., U.S.A. 47°33N 123°3W 170 C3
Eldora U.S.A. 42°22N 93°5W 172 D7
Eldorado Argentina 26°28S 54°43W 191 B5
Eldorado Canada 44°35N 77°31W 174 B7
Eldorado Ill., U.S.A. 37°49N 88°26W 172 G9
Eldorado Tex., U.S.A. 30°52N 100°36W 176 F4
Eldorendo U.S.A. 31°3N 84°39W 178 D5
Eldoret Kenya 0°30N 35°17E 142 B4
Eldred U.S.A. 41°58N 78°23W 174 E6
Elea, C. Cyprus 35°19N 34°4E 101 D13
Eleanora, Pk. Australia 32°57S 121°9E 149 F3
Elefantes → Africa 24°10S 32°40E 145 B5
Elefantes, G. Chile 46°28S 73°49W 192 C2
Elefsina Greece 38°4N 23°26E 98 C5
Eleftherios Venizelos ✕ (ATH) Greece 37°56N 23°56E 98 D5
Elektrogorsk Russia 55°56N 38°50E 84 E10
Elektrostal Russia 55°41N 38°32E 84 E10
Elele Nigeria 5°5N 6°50E 139 D6
Elemi Triangle = Ilemi Triangle Africa 5°0N 35°20E 142 B4
Elena Bulgaria 42°55N 25°53E 97 D9
Elephant Butte Res. U.S.A. 33°9N 107°11W 169 K10
Elephant I. Antarctica 61°0S 55°0W 55 C18
Elephant Pass Sri Lanka 9°35N 80°25E 127 K5
Elesbão Veloso Brazil 6°13S 42°8W 189 B2
Eleshnitsa Bulgaria 41°52N 23°36E 96 E7
Eleşkirt Turkey 39°50N 42°50E 105 C10
Eleuthera I. Bahamas 25°0N 76°20W 182 B4
Eleutheroupoli Greece 40°52N 24°20E 97 F8
Elgeyo-Marakwet □ Kenya 0°50N 35°35E 142 B4
Elgin Canada 44°36N 76°13W 175 B8
Elgin U.K. 57°39N 3°19W 65 D5
Elgin Ill., U.S.A. 42°2N 88°17W 172 D9
Elgin N. Dak., U.S.A. 46°24N 101°51W 172 B3
Elgin Oreg., U.S.A. 45°34N 117°55W 168 D5
Elgin S.C., U.S.A. 34°10N 80°48W 178 A9
Elgin Tex., U.S.A. 30°21N 97°22W 176 F6
Elgoibar Spain 43°13N 2°24W 90 B2
Elgon, Mt. Africa 1°10N 34°30E 142 B3
Elhovo Bulgaria 42°10N 26°35E 97 D10
Eliase Indonesia 8°21S 130°48E 119 F8
Elikonos Oros Greece 38°18N 22°45E 98 C4
Elim Namibia 17°48S 15°31E 144 A2
Elim S. Africa 34°35S 19°45E 144 D2
Elin Pelin Bulgaria 42°40N 23°36E 96 D7
Elis = Ilia Greece 37°45N 21°35E 98 D3
Eliseu Martins Brazil 8°13S 43°42W 189 B2
Elista Russia 46°16N 44°14E 87 G7
Eliza, L. Australia 37°15S 139°50E 152 D3
Elizabeth Australia 34°42S 138°41E 152 C3
Elizabeth U.S.A. 40°39N 74°12W 175 F10
Elizabeth City U.S.A. 36°18N 76°14W 177 C16
Elizabethton U.S.A. 36°21N 82°13W 177 C13
Elizabethtown Ky., U.S.A. 37°42N 85°52W 173 G11
Elizabethtown N.Y., U.S.A. 44°13N 73°36W 175 B11
Elizabethtown Pa., U.S.A. 40°9N 76°36W 175 F8
Elizondo Spain 43°12N 1°30W 90 B3
Ełk Poland 53°50N 22°21E 82 E9
Elk → Canada 49°11N 115°14W 162 C5
Ełk → Poland 53°41N 22°28E 82 E9
Elk → U.S.A. 34°46N 87°16W 177 D11
Elk City U.S.A. 35°25N 99°25W 176 D5
Elk Creek U.S.A. 39°36N 122°32W 170 F4
Elk Grove U.S.A. 38°25N 121°22W 170 G5
Elk Island △ Canada 53°35N 112°59W 162 C6
Elk Lake Canada 47°40N 80°25W 164 C3
Elk Point Canada 53°54N 110°55W 163 C6
Elk River Idaho, U.S.A. 46°47N 116°11W 168 C5
Elk River Minn., U.S.A. 45°18N 93°35W 172 C7
Elkedra → Australia 21°8S 136°22E 150 C2
Elkhart Ind., U.S.A. 41°41N 85°58W 173 E11
Elkhart Kans., U.S.A. 37°0N 101°54W 172 G3
Elkhorn Canada 49°59N 101°14W 163 D8
Elkhorn → U.S.A. 41°8N 96°19W 172 E5
Elkin U.S.A. 36°15N 80°51W 177 C14
Elkins U.S.A. 38°55N 79°51W 173 F14
Elkland U.S.A. 41°59N 77°19W 174 E7
Elko Canada 49°20N 115°10W 162 D5
Elko U.S.A. 40°50N 115°46W 168 F6
Elkton U.S.A. 43°49N 83°11W 174 C1
Ellas = Greece ■ Europe 40°0N 23°0E 98 B3
Ellaville Fla., U.S.A. 30°23N 83°10W 178 E6
Ellaville Ga., U.S.A. 32°14N 84°19W 178 C5
Ellef Ringnes I. Canada 78°30N 102°2W 161 B11
Ellen, Mt. U.S.A. 44°9N 72°56W 175 B12
Ellenburg U.S.A. 44°54N 73°48W 175 B11
Ellendale U.S.A. 46°0N 98°32W 172 B4
Ellensburg U.S.A. 46°59N 120°34W 168 C3
Ellenville U.S.A. 41°43N 74°24W 175 E10
Ellerton Barbados 13°7N 59°33W 183 g
Ellery, Mt. Australia 37°28S 148°47E 153 D8
Ellesmere, L. N.Z. 43°47S 172°28E 155 D7
Ellesmere I. Canada 79°30N 80°0W 161 B16
Ellesmere Port U.K. 53°17N 2°54W 66 D5
Ellice Is. = Tuvalu ■ Pac. Oc. 8°0S 178°0E 147 B10
Ellicottville U.S.A. 42°17N 78°40W 174 D6
Ellington U.S.A. 42°13N 79°6W 174 D5
Elliot Australia 17°33S 133°32E 150 B1
Elliot S. Africa 31°22S 27°48E 145 D4
Elliot Lake Canada 46°25N 82°35W 164 C3
Elliotdale = Xhora S. Africa 31°55S 28°38E 145 D4
Elliott U.S.A. 34°6N 80°10W 178 A9
Elliott Key U.S.A. 25°27N 80°12W 179 K9
Ellis U.S.A. 38°56N 99°34W 172 F4
Elliston Australia 33°39S 134°53E 151 E1
Ellisville U.S.A. 31°36N 89°12W 177 F10
Ellon U.K. 57°22N 2°4W 65 D6
Ellora India 20°1N 75°10E 126 D2
Ellore = Eluru India 16°48N 81°8E 126 F5
Elloree U.S.A. 33°32N 80°34W 178 B9
Ellsworth Kans., U.S.A. 38°44N 98°14W 172 F4
Ellsworth Maine, U.S.A. 44°33N 68°25W 173 C19
Ellsworth Land Antarctica 76°0S 89°0W 55 D16
Ellsworth Mts. Antarctica 78°30S 85°0W 55 D16
Ellwangen Germany 48°57N 10°8E 77 G6
Ellwood City U.S.A. 40°52N 80°17W 174 F4
Ellzey U.S.A. 29°19N 82°48W 179 F7
Elm Switz. 46°54N 9°10E 77 J5
Elm-Lappwald △ Germany 52°15N 10°50E 76 C6
Elma Canada 49°52N 95°55W 163 D9
Elma U.S.A. 47°0N 123°25W 170 D3
Elmadağ Turkey 39°55N 33°14E 104 C5
Elmalı Turkey 36°44N 29°56E 99 E11
Elmhurst U.S.A. 41°53N 87°56W 172 E10
Elmina Ghana 5°5N 1°21W 139 D4
Elmira Canada 43°36N 80°33W 174 C4
Elmira U.S.A. 42°6N 76°48W 174 D8
Elmira Heights U.S.A. 42°8N 76°50W 174 D8
Elmodel U.S.A. 31°21N 84°29W 178 D5
Elmore Australia 36°30S 144°37E 152 D6
Elmore U.S.A. 32°32N 86°19W 178 C3
Elmshorn Germany 53°43N 9°40E 76 B5
Elmvale Canada 44°35N 79°52W 174 B5
Elne France 42°36N 2°58E 72 F6
Elora Canada 43°41N 80°26W 174 C4
Elos Greece 36°46N 22°43E 98 E4
Elounda Greece 35°16N 25°42E 101 D7
Eloy U.S.A. 32°45N 111°33W 169 K8
Éloyes France 48°6N 6°36E 71 D13
Elphin Canada 44°55N 76°37W 175 B8
Elpitiya Sri Lanka 6°17N 80°10E 127 L5
Elrose Canada 51°12N 108°0W 163 C7
Elsby △ Australia 14°55S 133°10E 148 B5
Elsdorf Germany 50°55N 6°34E 76 E2
Elsie U.S.A. 45°52N 123°36W 170 E3
Elsinore = Helsingør Denmark 56°2N 12°35E 63 H6
Elster → Germany 51°25N 11°57E 76 D7
Elsterwerda Germany 51°27N 13°31E 76 D9
Eltanin Fracture Zone System S. Ocean 54°0S 130°0W 55 B14
Eltham N.Z. 39°26S 174°19E 154 F3
Elton Russia 49°5N 46°52E 87 F8
Elton, Ozero Russia 49°5N 46°42E 87 F8
Eltville Germany 50°2N 8°7E 77 E4
Eluru India 16°48N 81°8E 126 F5
Elvas Portugal 38°50N 7°10W 89 G3
Elven France 47°44N 2°36W 70 E4
Elverum Norway 60°53N 11°34E 60 F14
Elvire → Australia 17°51S 128°11E 148 C4
Elvire, Mt. Australia 29°22S 119°36E 149 E2
Elvo → Italy 45°23N 8°21E 92 C5
Elwell, L. = Tiber Res. U.S.A. 48°19N 111°6W 168 B8
Elwood Ind., U.S.A. 40°17N 85°50W 173 E11
Elwood Nebr., U.S.A. 40°36N 99°52W 172 E4
Elx = Elche Spain 38°15N 0°42W 91 G4
Ely U.K. 52°24N 0°16E 67 E8
Ely Minn., U.S.A. 47°55N 91°51W 172 B8
Ely Nev., U.S.A. 39°15N 114°54W 168 G6
Elyria U.S.A. 41°22N 82°7W 174 E2
Elyros Greece 35°15N 23°45E 98 F5
Elz → Germany 48°18N 7°44E 77 G3
Emajõgi → Estonia 58°25N 27°20E 84 C4
eMakhazeni S. Africa 25°42S 30°2E 145 C5
eMalahleni S. Africa 25°51S 29°14E 145 C4
Emāmrūd Iran 36°30N 55°0E 129 B7
Emån → Sweden 57°8N 16°30E 63 G10
eMbalenhle S. Africa 26°32S 29°4E 145 C4
Embarcación Argentina 23°10S 64°0W 190 A3
Embetsu Japan 44°44N 141°47E 112 B10
Embi Kazakhstan 48°50N 58°8E 108 C5
Embi → Kazakhstan 46°55N 53°28E 108 C4
Embonas Greece 36°13N 27°51E 101 C9
Embro Canada 43°9N 80°54W 174 C4
Embrun France 44°34N 6°30E 73 D10
Embu Kenya 0°32S 37°38E 142 C4
Emden Germany 53°21N 7°12E 76 B3
Emecik Turkey 36°46N 27°49E 99 E9
Emei Shan China 29°32N 103°46E 116 C4
Emeishan China 29°31N 103°23E 116 C4
Emerald Australia 23°32S 148°10E 150 C4
Emerald I. Canada 76°48N 114°10W 161 B9
Émeraude, Côte d' France 48°45N 2°40W 70 D4
Emerson Canada 49°0N 97°10W 163 D9
Emerson U.S.A. 34°8N 84°45W 178 A5
Emet Turkey 39°20N 29°15E 99 B11
Emgwenya S. Africa 25°40S 30°18E 145 C5
Emi Koussi Chad 19°45N 18°55E 135 E9
Emilia-Romagna □ Italy 44°45N 11°0E 92 D8
Emilius, Mte. Italy 45°45N 7°20E 92 C4
Emin China 46°34N 83°36E 109 C10
Eminabad Pakistan 32°2N 74°8E 124 C6
Emine, Nos Bulgaria 42°40N 27°56E 97 D11
Emirdağ Turkey 39°2N 31°8E 104 C4
Emissi, Tarso Chad 21°27N 18°36E 135 D9
eMkhondo = Piet Retief S. Africa 27°1S 30°50E 145 C5
Emlenton U.S.A. 41°11N 79°43W 174 E5
Emlichheim Germany 52°37N 6°51E 76 C2
Emmaboda Sweden 56°37N 15°32E 63 H9
Emmalane U.S.A. 32°46N 82°0W 178 C7
Emmaus S. Africa 29°2S 25°15E 144 C4
Emmaus U.S.A. 40°32N 75°30W 175 F9
Emme → Switz. 47°14N 7°32E 77 H3
Emmeloord Neths. 52°44N 5°46E 69 B5
Emmen Neths. 52°48N 6°57E 69 B6
Emmen Switz. 47°5N 8°18E 77 H4
Emmendingen Germany 48°6N 7°51E 77 G3
Emmental Switz. 46°55N 7°40E 77 J3
Emmerich Germany 51°50N 6°14E 76 D2
Emmet Australia 24°45S 144°30E 150 C3
Emmetsburg U.S.A. 43°7N 94°41W 172 D6
Emmett Idaho, U.S.A. 43°52N 116°30W 168 E5
Emmett Mich., U.S.A. 42°59N 82°46W 174 D2
Emmiganuru = Yemmiganur India 15°44N 77°29E 127 G3
Emmonak U.S.A. 62°47N 164°31W 166 C7
Emo Canada 48°38N 93°50W 163 D10
Emőd Hungary 47°57N 20°47E 80 C5
Emona Bulgaria 42°43N 27°53E 97 D11
Empalme Mexico 27°58N 110°51W 180 B2
Empangeni S. Africa 28°50S 31°52E 145 C5
Empedrado Argentina 28°0S 58°46W 190 B4
Emperor Seamount Chain Pac. Oc. 40°0N 170°0E 156 D9
Emperor Trough Pac. Oc. 43°0N 175°30E 156 C9
Empire U.S.A. 32°21N 83°18W 178 C6
Empoli Italy 43°43N 10°57E 92 E7
Emporia Kans., U.S.A. 38°25N 96°11W 172 F5
Emporia Va., U.S.A. 36°42N 77°32W 173 G15
Emporium U.S.A. 41°31N 78°14W 174 E6
Empress Canada 50°57N 110°0W 163 C7
Empty Quarter = Rub' al Khālī Si. Arabia 19°0N 48°0E 131 D4
Ems → Germany 53°20N 7°12E 76 B3
Emsdale Canada 45°32N 79°19W 174 A5
Emsdetten Germany 52°10N 7°32E 76 C3
Emu China 43°40N 128°6E 115 C15
Emu Park Australia 23°13S 150°50E 150 C5
eMuziwezinto S. Africa 30°15S 30°45E 145 D5
'En 'Avrona Israel 29°43N 35°0E 130 F4
'En Boqeq Israel 31°12N 35°21E 130 D4
'En Gedi Israel 31°28N 35°25E 129 D4
En Nahud Sudan 12°45N 28°25E 135 F11
Ena Japan 35°25N 137°25E 113 G8
Enånger Sweden 61°30N 17°9E 62 C11
Enard B. U.K. 58°5N 5°20W 65 C3
Enare träsk = Inarijärvi Finland 69°0N 28°0E 60 B23
Enarotali Indonesia 3°55S 136°21E 119 E9
Encampment U.S.A. 41°12N 106°47W 168 F10
Encantadas, Serra Brazil 30°40S 53°0W 191 C5
Encarnación Paraguay 27°15S 55°50W 191 B4
Encarnación de Díaz Mexico 21°31N 102°13W 180 C4
Enchi Ghana 5°53N 2°48W 138 D4
Encinitas U.S.A. 33°3N 117°17W 171 M9
Encino U.S.A. 34°39N 105°28W 169 J11
Encounter B. Australia 35°45S 138°45E 152 C3
Encruzilhada Brazil 15°31S 40°54W 189 D2
Encs Hungary 48°20N 21°8E 80 B6

INDEX TO WORLD MAPS
Falconara Maríttima 219

Endako Canada 54°6N 125°2W 162 C3
Endau Kenya 1°18S 38°31E 142 C4
Endau Rompin △
Malaysia 2°27N 103°45E 121 L4
Ende Indonesia 8°45S 121°40E 119 F6
Endeavour Str.
Australia 10°45S 142°0E 150 A3
Endelave Denmark 55°46N 10°18E 63 J4
Enderbury Kiribati 3°8S 171°5W 156 H10
Enderby Canada 50°35N 119°10W 162 C5
Enderby Abyssal Plain
S. Ocean 60°0S 40°0E 55 C5
Enderby I. Australia 20°35S 116°30E 148 D2
Enderby Land Antarctica 66°0S 53°0E 55 C5
Enderlin U.S.A. 46°38N 97°36W 172 B5
Enderrocat, C. Spain 39°28N 2°43E 100 B9
Endicott U.S.A. 42°6N 76°4W 175 D8
Endicott Mts. U.S.A. 68°0N 152°0W 166 B9
Endimari → Brazil 8°46S 66°7W 188 B4
Endwell U.S.A. 42°6N 76°2W 175 D8
Endyalgout I. Australia 11°40S 132°35E 148 B5
Ené → Peru 11°10S 74°18W 188 C3
Eneabba Australia 29°49S 115°16E 149 E2
Enerhodar Ukraine 47°30N 34°28E 85 J8
Enewetak Atoll
Marshall Is. 11°30N 162°15E 156 F8
Enez Turkey 40°45N 26°5E 97 F10
Enfer, Pte. d' Martinique 14°22N 60°54W 182 c
Enfield Canada 44°56N 63°32W 165 D7
Enfield Conn., U.S.A. 41°58N 72°36W 175 E12
Enfield N.C., U.S.A. 36°11N 77°41W 177 C16
Enfield N.H., U.S.A. 43°39N 72°9W 175 C12
Engadin Switz. 46°45N 10°10E 77 J6
Engaño, C. Dom. Rep. 18°30N 68°20W 183 C6
Engaño, C. Phil. 18°35N 122°23E 119 A6
Engaru Japan 44°3N 143°31E 112 B11
Engcobo = Ngcobo
S. Africa 31°37S 28°0E 145 D4
Engelberg Switz. 46°48N 8°26E 77 J4
Engels Russia 51°28N 46°6E 86 E8
Engelsberg = Ängelsberg
Sweden 59°58N 16°0E 62 E10
Engemann L. Canada 58°0N 106°55W 163 B7
Enggano Indonesia 5°20S 102°40E 118 F2
England U.S.A. 34°33N 91°58W 176 D9
England □ U.K. 53°0N 2°0W 67 E5
Englee Canada 50°45N 56°5W 165 B8
Englehart Canada 47°49N 79°52W 164 C4
Englewood U.S.A. 26°58N 82°21W 179 J7
English → Canada 49°12N 91°5W 163 C10
English Bazar = Ingraj Bazar
India 24°58N 88°10E 125 G13
English Channel Europe 50°0N 2°0W 67 G6
English Company's Is., The
Australia 11°50S 136°32E 150 A2
English River Canada 49°14N 91°0W 164 C1
Engures ezers Latvia 57°16N 23°6E 82 A10
Enguri → Georgia 42°27N 41°38E 87 J5
Enid U.S.A. 36°24N 97°53W 176 C6
Enipeas → Greece 39°22N 22°17E 98 B4
Eniwa Japan 43°0N 141°30E 112 C10
Enkhuizen Neths. 52°42N 5°17E 69 B5
Enköping Sweden 59°37N 17°4E 62 E11
Enle China 24°0N 101°9E 116 F3
Enna Italy 37°34N 14°16E 95 E7
Ennadai L. Canada 60°58N 101°20W 163 A8
Ennedi Chad 17°15N 22°0E 135 E10
Enngonia Australia 29°21S 145°50E 151 D4
Ennigerloh Germany 51°50N 8°2E 76 D4
Ennis Ireland 52°51N 8°59W 64 D3
Ennis Mont., U.S.A. 45°21N 111°44W 168 D8
Ennis Tex., U.S.A. 32°20N 96°38W 176 E6
Enniscorthy Ireland 52°30N 6°34W 64 D5
Enniskillen U.K. 54°21N 7°39W 64 B4
Ennistymon Ireland 52°57N 9°17W 64 D2
Enns Austria 48°12N 14°28E 78 C7
Enns → Austria 48°14N 14°32E 78 C7
Eno Finland 62°47N 30°10E 60 E24
Enosburg Falls U.S.A. 44°55N 72°48W 175 B12
Enping China 22°16N 112°21E 117 F9
Enriquillo, L. Dom. Rep. 18°20N 71°40W 183 C5
Enschede Neths. 52°13N 6°53E 69 B6
Ensenada Argentina 34°55S 57°55W 190 C4
Ensenada Chile 41°12S 72°33W 192 B2
Ensenada Mexico 31°52N 116°37W 180 A1
Ensenada de los Muertos
Mexico 23°59N 109°51W 180 C2
Enshi China 30°18N 109°29E 116 B7
Ensiola, Pta. de n' Spain 39°7N 2°55E 100 B9
Ensisheim France 47°50N 7°20E 71 E14
Ensley U.S.A. 30°31N 87°16W 179 E2
Entebbe Uganda 0°4N 32°28E 142 B3
Enterprise Canada 60°47N 115°45W 162 A5
Enterprise Ala., U.S.A. 31°19N 85°51W 178 D4
Enterprise Oreg.,
U.S.A. 45°25N 117°17W 168 D5
Entiako ⌂ Canada 53°15N 125°26W 162 C3
Entorno de Doñana ⌂
Spain 37°0N 6°26W 89 J4
Entrance, The
Australia 33°21S 151°30E 153 B9
Entraygues-sur-Truyère
France 44°38N 2°35E 72 D6
Entre Ríos Bolivia 21°30S 64°25W 190 A3
Entre Rios Brazil 11°56S 38°5W 189 C3
Entre Ríos □ Argentina 30°30S 58°30W 190 C4
Entrepeñas, Embalse de
Spain 40°34N 2°42W 90 E2
Entroncamento Portugal 39°28N 8°28W 89 F2
Enugu Nigeria 6°30N 7°30E 139 D6
Enugu □ Nigeria 6°30N 7°45E 139 D6
Enugu Ezike Nigeria 7°0N 7°29E 139 D6
Enumclaw U.S.A. 47°12N 121°59W 170 C5
Envalira, Port d' Europe 42°33N 1°43E 90 C6
Envermeu France 49°53N 1°15E 70 C8
Enviken Sweden 60°49N 15°46E 62 D9
Envira Brazil 7°18S 70°13W 188 B3
Envira → Brazil 7°19S 70°15W 188 B3
Enying Hungary 46°56N 18°15E 80 D3
Enza → Italy 44°54N 10°31E 92 D7
Eochaill = Youghal
Ireland 51°56N 7°52W 64 E4
Eólie, Ís. Italy 38°30N 14°57E 95 D7
Epanomi Greece 40°25N 22°59E 96 F6
Epe Neths. 52°21N 5°59E 69 B5
Epe Nigeria 6°36N 3°59E 139 D5
Épernay France 49°3N 3°56E 71 C10
Épernon France 48°35N 1°40E 71 D8
Ephesus Turkey 37°55N 27°22E 99 D9
Ephraim U.S.A. 39°22N 111°35W 168 G8
Ephrata Pa., U.S.A. 40°11N 76°11W 175 F8
Ephrata Wash., U.S.A. 47°19N 119°33W 168 C4
Epidaurus = Epidavros
Greece 37°40N 23°7E 98 D5
Epidavros Greece 37°40N 23°7E 98 D5
Epidavros Limira Greece 36°46N 23°0E 98 E5
Épila Spain 41°36N 1°17W 90 D3
Épinac France 46°59N 4°31E 71 F11
Épinal France 48°10N 6°27E 71 D13
Epiros □ Greece 39°30N 20°30E 98 B2
Episkopi Cyprus 34°40N 32°54E 101 E11
Episkopi Greece 35°20N 24°20E 101 D6
Episkopi Bay Cyprus 34°35N 32°50E 101 E11
Epitalio Greece 37°37N 21°30E 98 D3
Eppalock, L. Australia 36°52S 144°34E 152 D6
Eppan = Appiano Italy 46°28N 11°15E 93 B8
Eppingen Germany 49°8N 8°53E 77 F4
Epsom U.K. 51°19N 0°16W 67 F7
Epukiro Namibia 21°40S 19°9E 144 B2
Equatoria = El Istiwa'iya
Sudan 5°0N 28°0E 135 G11
Equatorial Guinea ■ Africa 2°0N 8°0E 140 D1
Er Hai China 25°48N 100°11E 116 E3
Er Rachidia Morocco 31°58N 4°20W 136 B3
Er Rahad Sudan 12°45N 30°32E 135 F12
Er Rif Morocco 35°1N 4°1W 136 A3
Er Rogel Sudan 18°10N 35°25E 137 D4
Eraclea Italy 45°35N 12°40E 93 C9
Erandol India 20°56N 75°20E 126 D2
Erāwadī Myit = Ayeyawadi →
Myanmar 15°50N 95°6E 123 M19
Erāwadī Myitwanya = Irrawaddy,
Mouths of the
Myanmar 15°30N 95°0E 123 M19
Erawan △ Thailand 14°25N 98°58E 120 E2
Erba Italy 45°48N 9°15E 92 C6
Erba Sudan 19°5N 36°51E 137 D4
Erba, J. Sudan 20°48N 36°47E 137 C4
Erbaa Turkey 40°42N 36°36E 104 B7
Erbeng Shan China 42°50N 84°59E 109 D10
Erbeskopf Germany 49°44N 7°2E 77 F3
Erçek Turkey 38°39N 43°36E 128 B4
Erçis Turkey 39°2N 43°21E 105 C10
Erciyaş Dağı Turkey 38°30N 35°30E 128 B2
Érd Hungary 47°22N 18°56E 80 C3
Erdao Jiang → China 42°37N 128°0E 115 C14
Erdek Turkey 40°23N 27°47E 97 F11
Erdemli Turkey 36°36N 34°19E 104 D6
Erdene = Ulaan-Uul
Mongolia 46°4N 100°49E 110 B9
Erdenet Mongolia 49°2N 104°5E 110 B9
Erdenetsogt Mongolia 42°55N 106°5E 114 C4
Erding Germany 48°18N 11°54E 77 G7
Erdre → France 47°13N 1°32W 70 E5
Erebus, Mt. Antarctica 77°35S 167°0E 55 D11
Erechim Brazil 27°35S 52°15W 191 B5
Ereğli Konya, Turkey 37°31N 34°4E 104 D6
Ereğli Zonguldak, Turkey 41°15N 31°24E 104 B4
Erei, Monti Italy 37°20N 14°20E 95 E7
Erenhot China 43°48N 112°2E 114 C7
Eresma → Spain 41°26N 4°45W 88 D6
Eresos Greece 39°11N 25°57E 99 B7
Ereymentaū Kazakhstan 51°37N 73°6E 109 B8
Erfelek Turkey 41°53N 34°55E 104 B6
Erfenisdam S. Africa 28°30S 26°50E 144 C4
Erfoud Morocco 31°30N 4°15W 136 B3
Erfstadt Germany 50°50N 6°50E 76 E2
Erft → Germany 51°11N 6°44E 76 D2
Erfurt Germany 50°58N 11°2E 76 E7
Ergani Turkey 38°17N 39°49E 105 C8
Ergel Mongolia 43°8N 109°5E 114 C5
Ergene → Turkey 41°1N 26°22E 97 E10
Ergeni Vozvyshennost
Russia 47°0N 44°0E 87 G7
Ērgli Latvia 56°54N 25°38E 84 D3
Ergun He = Argun →
Russia 53°20N 121°28E 111 A13
Ergun Youqi China 50°15N 120°11E 111 A13
Erhlin Taiwan 23°54N 120°22E 117 F13
Eria → Spain 42°3N 5°44W 88 C5
Eriboll, L. U.K. 58°30N 4°42W 65 C4
Érice Italy 38°2N 12°35E 94 D5
Eridu U.S.A. 30°18N 83°45W 178 E6
Erie U.S.A. 42°8N 80°5W 174 D4
Erie, L. N. Amer. 42°15N 81°0W 174 D4
Erie Canal U.S.A. 43°5N 78°43W 174 C7
Erieau Canada 42°16N 81°57W 174 D3
Erigavo = Ceerigaabo
Somalia 10°35N 47°20E 131 E4
Erikoussa Greece 39°53N 19°34E 101 A3
Eriksdale Canada 50°52N 98°7W 163 C9
Erimanthos Greece 37°57N 21°50E 98 D3
Erimo-Misaki Japan 41°50N 143°15E 112 D11
Erin Canada 43°45N 80°7W 174 C4
Erin Pt. Trin. & Tob. 10°3N 61°39W 187 K15
Erinpura India 25°9N 73°3E 124 G5
Eriskay U.K. 57°4N 7°18W 65 D1
Erithres Greece 38°13N 23°20E 98 C5
Eritrea ■ Africa 14°0N 38°30E 131 D2
Erjas → Portugal 39°40N 7°1W 88 F3
Erkech-Tam Pass Asia 39°46N 74°2E 109 E8
Erkelenz Germany 51°4N 6°19E 76 D2
Erkner Germany 52°25N 13°44E 76 C9
Erlangen Germany 49°36N 11°0E 77 F6
Erldunda Australia 25°14S 133°12E 150 D1
Ermelo Neths. 52°18N 5°35E 69 B5
Ermelo S. Africa 26°31S 29°59E 145 C4
Ermenek Turkey 36°38N 33°0E 104 D5
Ermioni Greece 37°23N 23°15E 98 D5
Ermones Greece 39°37N 19°46E 101 A3
Ermoupoli Greece 37°28N 24°57E 98 D6
Ernakulam India 9°59N 76°22E 127 K3
Erne → Ireland 54°30N 8°16W 64 B3
Erne, Lower L. U.K. 54°28N 7°47W 64 B4
Erne, Upper L. U.K. 54°14N 7°32W 64 B4
Ernée France 48°18N 0°56W 70 D6
Ernest Giles Ra.
Australia 27°0S 123°45E 149 E3
Ernstberg Germany 50°13N 6°47E 77 E2
Erode India 11°24N 77°45E 127 J3
Eromanga Australia 26°40S 143°11E 151 D3
Erongo Namibia 21°39S 15°58E 144 B2
Erongo □ Namibia 22°20S 15°0E 144 B2
Erquy France 48°38N 2°29W 70 D4
Erramala Hills India 15°30N 78°15E 127 G4
Errentería Spain 43°19N 1°54W 90 B3
Errigal Ireland 55°2N 8°6W 64 A3
Errinundra △
Australia 37°20S 148°47E 153 D8
Erris Hd. Ireland 54°17N 10°0W 64 B1
Ersekë Albania 40°22N 20°40E 96 F4
Erskine U.S.A. 47°40N 96°0W 172 B6
Erstein France 48°25N 7°38E 71 D14
Ertai China 46°3N 90°5E 109 C12
Ertan Shuiku China 27°5N 101°52E 116 D3
Ertholmene Denmark 55°19N 15°11E 63 J9
Ertil Russia 51°55N 40°50E 86 E5
Ertis = Irtysh → Russia 61°4N 68°52E 106 C7
Ertis Kazakhstan 53°20N 75°27E 109 B9
Ertis → Kazakhstan 47°52N 84°16E 109 C10
Eruh Turkey 37°46N 42°13E 105 D10
Ervy-le-Châtel France 48°2N 3°55E 71 D10
Erwin U.S.A. 36°9N 82°25W 177 C13
Eryuan China 26°7N 99°57E 116 D2
Erzgebirge Germany 50°27N 12°55E 76 E8
Erzin Russia 50°15N 95°10E 109 B13
Erzincan Turkey 39°46N 39°30E 105 C8
Erzincan □ Turkey 39°45N 39°30E 105 C8
Erzurum Turkey 39°57N 41°15E 105 C9
Erzurum □ Turkey 39°55N 41°15E 105 C9
Es Caló Spain 38°40N 1°30E 100 C8
Es Canar Spain 39°2N 1°36E 100 B8
Es Mercadal Spain 39°59N 4°5E 100 B11
Es Migjorn Gran Spain 39°57N 4°3E 100 B11
Es Sînâ' Egypt 29°0N 34°0E 130 F2
Es Vedrà Spain 38°52N 1°12E 100 C7
Esambo
Dem. Rep. of the Congo 3°48S 23°30E 142 C1
Esan-Misaki Japan 41°40N 141°10E 112 D10
Esashi Hokkaidō, Japan 44°56N 142°35E 112 B11
Esashi Hokkaidō, Japan 41°52N 140°7E 112 D10
Esbjerg Denmark 55°29N 8°29E 63 J2
Esbo = Espoo Finland 60°12N 24°40E 84 B3
Escada Brazil 8°22S 35°8W 189 B3
Escalante U.S.A. 37°47N 111°36W 169 H8
Escalante → U.S.A. 37°24N 110°57W 169 H8
Escalón Mexico 26°45N 104°20W 180 B4
Escambia → U.S.A. 30°32N 87°11W 179 E2
Escanaba U.S.A. 45°45N 87°4W 172 C10
Escárcega Mexico 18°37N 90°43W 181 D6
Esch-sur-Alzette Lux. 49°32N 6°0E 69 E6
Eschede Germany 52°44N 10°14E 76 C6
Eschwege Germany 51°11N 10°2E 76 D6
Eschweiler Germany 50°49N 6°15E 76 E2
Escoma Bolivia 15°40S 69°8W 188 D4
Escondido U.S.A. 33°7N 117°5W 171 M9
Escravos → Nigeria 5°35N 5°10E 139 D6
Escuinapa de Hidalgo
Mexico 22°50N 105°50W 180 C3
Escuintla Guatemala 14°20N 90°48W 182 D1
Eséka Cameroon 3°41N 10°44E 139 E7
Eşen → Turkey 36°27N 29°16E 99 E11
Esenguly Turkmenistan 37°37N 53°59E 108 E4
Esens Germany 53°38N 7°36E 76 B3
Esentepe = Áyios Amvrósios
Cyprus 35°20N 33°35E 101 D12
Esenyurt Turkey 41°3N 28°48E 97 E12
Esera → Spain 42°6N 0°15E 90 C5
Eşfahān Iran 32°39N 51°43E 129 C6
Eşfahān □ Iran 32°50N 51°50E 129 C6
Esfarāyen Iran 37°4N 57°30E 129 B8
Esfideh Iran 33°39N 59°46E 129 C8
Esgueva → Spain 41°40N 4°43W 88 D6
Esh Sham = Dimashq
Syria 33°30N 36°18E 130 B5
Esh Shamâlîya □ Sudan 19°0N 29°0E 137 D2
Esha Ness U.K. 60°29N 1°38W 65 A7
Eshan China 24°11N 102°24E 116 E4
Esher U.K. 51°21N 0°20W 67 F7
Eshkāshem = Ishkashim
Tajikistan 36°44N 71°37E 109 E8
Eshkol △ Israel 31°20N 34°30E 130 D3
Eshowe S. Africa 28°50S 31°30E 145 C5
Esiama Ghana 4°56N 2°25W 138 E4
Esigodini Zimbabwe 20°18S 28°56E 145 B4
Esil = Ishim → Russia 57°45N 71°10E 106 D8
Esil Kazakhstan 51°57N 66°24E 109 B7
Esino → Italy 43°39N 13°22E 93 E10
Esk → Dumf. & Gall., U.K. 54°58N 3°2W 65 G5
Esk → N. Yorks., U.K. 54°30N 0°37W 66 C7
Eskān Iran 26°48N 63°9E 129 E9
Esker Siding Canada 53°53N 66°25W 165 B6
Eskifjörður Iceland 65°3N 13°55W 60 D7
Eskilsäter Sweden 58°57N 13°10E 63 F7
Eskilstuna Sweden 59°22N 16°32E 62 E10
Eskimalatya Turkey 38°24N 38°22E 105 C8
Eskimo Point = Arviat
Canada 61°6N 93°59W 163 A10
Eskişehir Turkey 39°50N 30°30E 99 B12
Eskişehir □ Turkey 39°40N 31°0E 99 B12
Esla → Spain 41°29N 6°3W 88 D4
Eslāmābād-e Gharb
Iran 34°10N 46°30E 105 E12
Eslāmshahr Iran 35°40N 51°10E 129 C6
Eslöv Sweden 55°50N 13°20E 63 J7
Eşme Turkey 38°23N 28°58E 99 C10
Esmeralda, I. Chile 48°55S 75°25W 192 C1
Esmeraldas Ecuador 1°0N 79°40W 186 C3
Esna = Isna Egypt 25°17N 32°30E 137 B3
Esnagi L. Canada 48°36N 84°33W 164 C3
Esom Hill U.S.A. 33°57N 85°23W 178 B4
Espalion France 44°32N 2°47E 72 D6
España = Spain ■ Europe 39°0N 4°0W 59 H5
Espanola Canada 46°15N 81°46W 164 C3
Espanola U.S.A. 35°59N 106°5W 169 J10
Esparreguera Spain 41°33N 1°52E 90 D6
Esparza Costa Rica 9°59N 84°40W 182 E3
Espelkamp Germany 52°24N 8°36E 76 C4
Esperança Brazil 7°1S 35°51W 189 B3
Esperance Australia 33°45S 121°55E 149 F3
Esperance B. Australia 33°48S 121°55E 149 F3
Esperance Harbour
St. Lucia 14°4N 60°55W 183 f
Esperantinópolis Brazil 4°53S 44°53W 189 A2
Esperanza Antarctica 65°0S 55°0W 55 C18
Esperanza Santa Cruz,
Argentina 51°1S 70°49W 192 D2
Esperanza Santa Fe,
Argentina 31°29S 61°3W 190 C3
Esperanza Puerto Rico 18°6N 65°28W 183 d
Espéraza France 42°56N 2°14E 72 F6
Espichel, C. Portugal 38°22N 9°16W 89 G1
Espiel Spain 38°11N 5°1W 89 G5
Espigão, Serra do
Brazil 26°35S 50°30W 191 B5
Espinar Peru 14°51S 71°24W 188 C3
Espinazo, Sierra del = Espinhaço,
Serra do Brazil 17°30S 43°30W 189 D2
Espinhaço, Serra do
Brazil 17°30S 43°30W 189 D2
Espinho Portugal 41°1N 8°38W 88 D2
Espinilho, Serra do
Brazil 28°30S 55°0W 191 B5
Espinosa de los Monteros
Spain 43°5N 3°34W 88 B7
Espírito Santo □ Brazil 20°0S 40°45W 189 E2
Espírito Santo do Pinhal
Brazil 22°10S 46°46W 191 A6
Espíritu Santo Vanuatu 15°15S 166°50E 147 C9
Espíritu Santo, B. del
Mexico 19°20N 87°35W 181 D7
Espíritu Santo, I.
Mexico 24°30N 110°22W 180 C2
Espita Mexico 21°1N 88°19W 181 C7
Espiye Turkey 40°56N 38°43E 105 B8
Esplanada Brazil 11°47S 37°57W 189 C3
Espoo Finland 60°12N 24°40E 84 B3
Espuña, Sierra de Spain 37°51N 1°35W 91 H3
Espungabera Mozam. 20°29S 32°45E 145 B5
Esquel Argentina 42°55S 71°20W 192 B2
Esquimalt Canada 48°26N 123°25W 170 B3
Esquina Argentina 30°0S 59°30W 190 C4
Essaouira Morocco 31°32N 9°42W 136 B2
Essen Belgium 51°28N 4°28E 69 C4
Essen Germany 51°28N 7°2E 76 D3
Essendon, Mt. Australia 25°0S 120°29E 149 E3
Essequibo → Guyana 6°50N 58°30W 186 B7
Essex Canada 42°10N 82°49W 174 D2
Essex Calif., U.S.A. 34°44N 115°15W 171 L11
Essex N.Y., U.S.A. 44°19N 73°21W 175 B11
Essex □ U.K. 51°54N 0°27E 67 F8
Essex Junction U.S.A. 44°29N 73°7W 175 B11
Esslingen Germany 48°44N 9°18E 77 G5
Essonne □ France 48°30N 2°20E 71 D9
Estaca de Bares, C. de
Spain 43°46N 7°42W 88 B3
Estación Camacho
Mexico 24°25N 102°18W 180 C4
Estación Simón
Mexico 24°42N 102°35W 180 C4
Estadilla Spain 42°4N 0°16E 90 C5
Estados, I. de Los
Argentina 54°40S 64°30W 192 D4
Estagel France 42°47N 2°40E 72 F6
Eşţahbānāt Iran 29°8N 54°4E 129 D7
Estância Brazil 11°16S 37°26W 189 C3
Estancia U.S.A. 34°46N 106°4W 169 J10
Estancia Monte León
Argentina 50°14S 68°55W 192 D3
Estārm Iran 28°21N 58°21E 129 D8
Estarreja Portugal 40°45N 8°35W 88 E2
Estats, Pic d' Spain 42°40N 1°24E 90 C6
Estcourt S. Africa 29°0S 29°53E 145 C4
Este Italy 45°14N 11°39E 93 C8
Este △ Dom. Rep. 18°14N 68°42W 183 C6
Estelí Nic. 13°9N 86°22W 182 D2
Estella Spain 42°40N 2°2W 90 C2
Estellencs Spain 39°39N 2°29E 100 B9
Estena → Spain 39°23N 4°44W 89 F6
Estepa Spain 37°17N 4°52W 89 H6
Estepona Spain 36°24N 5°7W 89 J5
Esterhazy Canada 50°37N 102°5W 163 C8
Esternay France 48°44N 3°33E 71 D10
Esterri d'Aneu Spain 42°38N 1°5E 90 C6
Estevan Canada 49°10N 102°59W 163 D8
Estevan Group Canada 53°3N 129°38W 162 C3
Estherville U.S.A. 43°24N 94°50W 172 D6
Estill U.S.A. 32°45N 81°15W 178 C8
Estissac France 48°16N 3°48E 71 D10
Eston Canada 51°8N 108°40W 163 C7
Estonia ■ Europe 58°30N 25°30E 84 C3
Estoril Portugal 38°42N 9°23W 89 G1
Estouk Mali 18°14N 1°2E 139 B5
Estreito Brazil 6°32S 47°25W 187 E9
Estreito Maranhão, Brazil 6°34S 47°27W 189 B1
Estrela, Serra da Portugal 40°10N 7°45W 88 E3
Estrella Spain 38°25N 3°35W 89 G7
Estremoz Portugal 38°51N 7°39W 89 G3
Estrondo, Serra do Brazil 7°20S 48°0W 187 E9
eSwatini = Swaziland ■
Africa 26°30S 31°30E 145 C5
Esztergom Hungary 47°47N 18°44E 80 C3
Et Tîdra Mauritania 19°45N 16°20W 138 B1
Etah India 27°35N 78°40E 125 F8
Étain France 49°13N 5°38E 71 C12
Étampes France 48°26N 2°10E 71 D9
Etanga Namibia 17°55S 13°0E 144 A1
Étaples France 50°30N 1°39E 71 B8
Etawah India 26°48N 79°6E 125 F8
Etawney L. Canada 57°50N 96°50W 163 B9
Etchojoa Mexico 26°55N 109°38W 180 B3
Ete Nigeria 7°2N 7°28E 139 D6
Etelä-Konneveden △
Finland 62°34N 26°39E 60 E22
eThekwini = Durban
S. Africa 29°49S 31°1E 145 C5
Ethel U.S.A. 46°32N 122°46W 170 D4
Ethelbert Canada 51°32N 100°25W 163 C8
Ethiopia ■ Africa 8°0N 40°0E 131 F3
Ethiopian Highlands
Ethiopia 10°0N 37°0E 131 F2
Etili Turkey 39°59N 26°54E 97 G10
Etive, L. U.K. 56°29N 5°10W 65 E3
Etna Italy 37°50N 14°55E 95 E7
Etoile
Dem. Rep. of the Congo 11°33S 27°30E 143 E2
Etoliko Greece 38°26N 21°21E 98 C3
Etolin Strait U.S.A. 60°20N 165°15W 166 C6
Etoloakarnania Greece 38°45N 21°18E 98 C3
Etosha △ Namibia 19°0S 16°0E 144 A2
Etosha Pan Namibia 18°40S 16°30E 144 A2
Etowah U.S.A. 35°20N 84°32W 177 D12
Étréchy France 48°30N 2°12E 71 D9
Etrek Turkmenistan 37°36N 54°46E 129 B7
Étrépagny France 49°18N 1°36E 71 C8
Étretat France 49°42N 0°12E 70 C7
Etropole Bulgaria 42°50N 24°0E 97 D8
Ettelbruck Lux. 49°51N 6°5E 69 E6
Ettlingen Germany 48°56N 8°25E 77 G4
Ettrick Water → U.K. 55°31N 2°55W 65 F6
Etuku
Dem. Rep. of the Congo 3°42S 25°45E 142 C2
Etulia Moldova 45°32N 28°27E 81 E13
Etzná-Tixmucuy = Edzná
Mexico 19°39N 90°19W 181 D6
Eu France 50°3N 1°26E 70 B8
Euboea = Evia Greece 38°30N 24°0E 98 C6
Euchareena Australia 32°57S 149°6E 153 B8
Eucla Australia 31°41S 128°52E 149 F4
Euclid U.S.A. 41°34N 81°32W 174 E3
Euclides da Cunha
Brazil 10°31S 39°1W 189 C3
Eucumbene, L.
Australia 36°2S 148°40E 153 D8
Eudora U.S.A. 33°7N 91°16W 176 E9
Eudunda Australia 34°12S 139°7E 152 C3
Eufaula Ala., U.S.A. 31°54N 85°9W 178 D4
Eufaula Okla., U.S.A. 35°17N 95°35W 176 D7
Eufaula L. U.S.A. 35°18N 95°21W 176 D7
Eugene U.S.A. 44°5N 123°4W 168 D2
Eugowra Australia 33°22S 148°24E 153 B8
Eulo Australia 28°10S 145°3E 151 D4
Eulonia U.S.A. 31°32N 81°26W 178 D8
Eumungerie Australia 31°56S 148°36E 153 A8
Eungella △ Australia 20°57S 148°40E 150 b
Eunice La., U.S.A. 30°30N 92°25W 176 F8
Eunice N. Mex.,
U.S.A. 32°26N 103°10W 169 K12
Eupen Belgium 50°37N 6°3E 69 D6
Euphrates = Furāt, Nahr al →
Asia 31°0N 47°25E 128 D5
Eure □ France 49°10N 1°0E 70 C8
Eure → France 49°18N 1°12E 70 C8
Eure-et-Loir □ France 48°22N 1°30E 70 D8
Eureka Canada 80°0N 85°56W 161 B14
Eureka Calif., U.S.A. 40°47N 124°9W 168 F1
Eureka Kans., U.S.A. 37°49N 96°17W 172 G5
Eureka Mont., U.S.A. 48°53N 115°3W 168 B6
Eureka Nev., U.S.A. 39°31N 115°58W 168 G6
Eureka S.C., U.S.A. 33°42N 81°46W 178 B8
Eureka S. Dak., U.S.A. 45°46N 99°38W 172 C4
Eureka, Mt. Australia 26°35S 121°35E 149 E3
Eureka Sd. Canada 79°0N 85°0W 161 B15
Eurelia Australia 32°33S 138°35E 152 B3
Eurinilla Cr. →
Australia 30°53S 140°11E 152 A4
Euroa Australia 36°44S 145°35E 153 D6
Euroairport, Basle ✈ (BSL)
France 47°36N 7°33E 71 E14
Europa, Île Ind. Oc. 22°20S 40°22E 145 B7
Europa, Picos de Spain 43°10N 4°49W 88 B6
Europa, Pt. Gib. 36°3N 5°21W 89 J5
Europe 50°0N 20°0E 58 E10
Europoort Neths. 51°57N 4°10E 69 C4
Euskadi = País Vasco □
Spain 42°50N 2°45W 90 C2
Euskirchen Germany 50°39N 6°48E 76 E2
Eustis U.S.A. 28°51N 81°41W 179 G8
Euston Australia 34°30S 142°46E 152 C5
Eutawville U.S.A. 33°24N 80°21W 178 B9
Eutin Germany 54°8N 10°36E 76 A6
Eutsuk L. Canada 53°20N 126°45W 162 C3
Evale Angola 16°33S 15°44E 144 A2
Evans U.S.A. 40°23N 104°41W 168 F11
Evans, L. Canada 50°50N 77°0W 164 B4
Evans City U.S.A. 40°46N 80°4W 174 F4
Evans Head Australia 29°7S 153°27E 151 D5
Evansburg Canada 53°36N 114°59W 162 C5
Evanston Ill., U.S.A. 42°3N 87°40W 172 D10
Evanston Wyo.,
U.S.A. 41°16N 110°58W 168 F8
Evansville U.S.A. 37°58N 87°35W 172 G10
Évaux-les-Bains France 46°12N 2°29E 71 F9
Evaz Iran 27°46N 53°59E 129 E7
Evciler Afyon, Turkey 38°4N 29°54E 99 C11
Evciler Çanakkale, Turkey 39°47N 26°44E 99 B8
Eveleth U.S.A. 47°28N 92°32W 172 B7
Evensk Russia 62°12N 159°30E 107 C16
Everard, L. Australia 31°30S 135°0E 151 E2
Everard Ranges
Australia 27°5S 132°28E 149 E5
Everest, Mt. Nepal 28°5N 86°58E 125 E12
Everett Ga., U.S.A. 31°24N 81°38W 178 D8
Everett Pa., U.S.A. 40°1N 78°23W 174 F6
Everett Wash., U.S.A. 47°59N 122°12W 170 C4
Everglades, The U.S.A. 25°50N 81°0W 179 K9
Everglades △ U.S.A. 25°30N 81°0W 179 K9
Everglades City U.S.A. 25°52N 81°23W 179 K8
Evergreen Ala., U.S.A. 31°26N 86°57W 177 F11
Evergreen Mont.,
U.S.A. 48°14N 114°17W 168 B6
Everöd Sweden 55°53N 14°5E 63 J8
Everton Australia 36°25S 146°33E 153 D7
Evertsberg Sweden 61°8N 13°58E 62 C7
Evesham U.K. 52°6N 1°56W 67 E6
Evia Greece 38°30N 24°0E 98 C6
Évian-les-Bains France 46°24N 6°35E 71 F13
Evinos → Greece 38°27N 21°40E 98 C3
Évisa France 42°15N 8°48E 73 F12
Evje Norway 58°36N 7°51E 61 G12
Évora Portugal 38°33N 7°57W 89 G3
Évora □ Portugal 38°33N 7°50W 89 G3
Evowghlī Iran 38°43N 45°13E 105 C11
Évreux France 49°3N 1°8E 70 C8
Evritania Greece 39°5N 21°30E 98 B3
Évron France 48°10N 0°24W 70 D6
Evros → Greece 41°40N 26°34E 97 F10
Evrotas → Greece 36°50N 22°40E 98 E4
Évry France 48°38N 2°27E 71 D9
Évvoia = Evia Greece 38°30N 24°0E 98 C6
Ewe, L. U.K. 57°49N 5°38W 65 D3
Ewing U.S.A. 42°16N 98°21W 172 D4
Ewo Congo 0°48S 14°45E 140 E2
Exaltación Bolivia 13°10S 65°20W 186 F5
Excelsior Springs
U.S.A. 39°20N 94°13W 172 F6
Excideuil France 45°20N 1°4E 72 C5
Exe → U.K. 50°41N 3°29W 67 G4
Exeter Canada 43°21N 81°29W 174 C3
Exeter U.K. 50°43N 3°31W 67 G4
Exeter Calif., U.S.A. 36°18N 119°9W 170 J7
Exeter N.H., U.S.A. 42°59N 70°57W 175 D14
Exmoor U.K. 51°12N 3°45W 67 F4
Exmoor △ U.K. 51°8N 3°42W 67 F4
Exmouth Australia 21°54S 114°10E 148 D1
Exmouth U.K. 50°37N 3°25W 67 G4
Exmouth G. Australia 22°15S 114°15E 148 D1
Exmouth Plateau
Ind. Oc. 19°0S 114°0E 156 J3
Expedition △ Australia 25°41S 149°7E 151 D4
Expedition Ra.
Australia 24°30S 149°12E 150 C4
Experiment = Highland Mills
U.S.A. 33°17N 84°17W 178 B5
Extremadura □ Spain 39°30N 6°5W 89 F4
Exuma Sound
Bahamas 24°30N 76°20W 182 B4
Eyasi, L. Tanzania 3°30S 35°0E 142 C4
Eye Pen. U.K. 58°13N 6°10W 65 C2
Eyemouth U.K. 55°52N 2°5W 65 F6
Eygues = Aigues →
France 44°7N 4°43E 73 D8
Eygurande France 45°40N 2°26E 71 G9
Eyjafjallajökull Iceland 63°38N 19°36W 60 E4
Eyjafjörður Iceland 66°15N 18°30W 60 C4
Eyl Somalia 8°0N 49°50E 131 F4
Eymet France 44°40N 0°25E 72 D4
Eymoutiers France 45°40N 1°45E 72 C5
Eynesil Turkey 41°4N 39°9E 105 B8
Eyre → France 44°39N 1°1W 72 D2
Eyre, L. = Kati Thanda-Lake Eyre
Australia 29°30S 137°26E 147 D6
Eyre Mts. N.Z. 45°25S 168°25E 155 F3
Eyre Pen. Australia 33°30S 136°17E 152 C1
Eysturoy Færoe Is. 62°13N 6°54W 60 E9
Eyvān = Jūy Zar Iran 33°50N 46°18E 105 F12
Eyvānkī Iran 35°24N 51°56E 129 C6
Ezcaray Spain 42°19N 3°0W 90 C1
Ežerėlis Lithuania 54°53N 23°37E 82 D10
Ezhou China 30°23N 114°50E 117 B10
Ezine Turkey 39°48N 26°20E 99 B8
Ezouza → Cyprus 34°44N 32°27E 101 E11

F

F.Y.R.O.M. = Macedonia ■
Europe 41°53N 21°40E 96 E5
Faaa Tahiti 17°34S 149°35W 155 b
Faaborg Denmark 55°6N 10°15E 63 J4
Faaone Tahiti 17°40S 149°21W 155 b
Fabala Guinea 9°44N 9°5W 138 D3
Fabens U.S.A. 31°30N 106°10W 176 F1
Fabero Spain 42°46N 6°37W 88 C4
Fabius U.S.A. 42°50N 75°59W 175 D9
Fabriano Italy 43°20N 12°54E 93 E9
Făcăeni Romania 44°32N 27°53E 81 F12
Faceville U.S.A. 30°45N 84°38W 178 E5
Fachi Niger 18°6N 11°34E 135 E8
Facundo Argentina 45°18S 69°58W 192 C3
Fada Chad 17°13N 21°34E 135 E10
Fada-n-Gourma
Burkina Faso 12°10N 0°30E 139 C5
Fadd Hungary 46°28N 18°49E 80 D3
Faddeyevskiy, Ostrov
Russia 76°0N 144°0E 107 B15
Fadghāmī Syria 35°53N 40°52E 105 E9
Faenza Italy 44°17N 11°53E 93 D8
Færingehavn =
Kangerluarsoruseq
Greenland 63°45N 51°27W 57 E5
Færoe Is. = Føroyar ☐
Atl. Oc. 62°0N 7°0W 60 F9
Fafa Mali 15°22N 0°48E 139 B5
Fafe Portugal 41°27N 8°11W 88 D2
Fagam Nigeria 11°1N 10°1E 139 C7
Făgăraş Romania 45°48N 24°58E 81 E9
Făgăraş, Munţii
Romania 45°40N 24°40E 81 E9
Fågelfors Sweden 57°12N 15°51E 63 H9
Fågelmara Sweden 56°16N 15°58E 63 H9
Fagerhult Sweden 57°8N 15°40E 63 G9
Fagersta Sweden 60°1N 15°46E 62 D9
Făget Romania 45°52N 22°10E 80 E7
Făget, Munţii Romania 47°40N 23°10E 81 C8
Faggo Nigeria 11°21N 9°57E 139 C6
Fagnano, L. Argentina 54°30S 68°0W 192 D3
Fagnières France 48°58N 4°20E 71 D11
Faguibine, L. Mali 16°45N 4°0W 138 B4
Fahlīān Iran 30°11N 51°28E 129 D6
Fahraj Kermān, Iran 29°0N 59°0E 129 D8
Fahraj Yazd, Iran 31°46N 54°36E 129 D7
Fai Tsi Long Vietnam 21°0N 107°30E 116 G6
Faial Azores 38°34N 28°42W 134 a
Faial Madeira 32°47N 16°53W 100 D3
Faichan Kangri India 35°48N 76°34E 125 B7
Fair Haven N.Y.,
U.S.A. 43°18N 76°42W 175 C8
Fair Haven Vt., U.S.A. 43°36N 73°16W 175 C11
Fair Hd. U.K. 55°14N 6°9W 64 A5
Fair Isle U.K. 59°32N 1°38W 68 B6
Fair Oaks U.S.A. 38°39N 121°16W 170 G5
Fairbanks Alaska,
U.S.A. 64°51N 147°43W 160 E2
Fairbanks Fla., U.S.A. 29°44N 82°16W 178 F7
Fairburn U.S.A. 33°34N 84°35W 178 B5
Fairbury U.S.A. 40°8N 97°11W 172 E5
Fairfax S.C., U.S.A. 32°59N 81°15W 178 C8
Fairfax Vt., U.S.A. 44°40N 73°1W 175 B11
Fairfield Australia 33°53S 150°57E 153 B9
Fairfield Calif., U.S.A. 38°15N 122°3W 170 G4
Fairfield Conn., U.S.A. 41°9N 73°16W 175 E11
Fairfield Idaho, U.S.A. 43°21N 114°44W 168 E6
Fairfield Ill., U.S.A. 38°23N 88°22W 172 F9
Fairfield Iowa, U.S.A. 40°56N 91°57W 172 E8
Fairfield Tex., U.S.A. 31°44N 96°10W 176 F6
Fairford Canada 51°37N 98°38W 163 C9
Fairhope U.S.A. 30°31N 87°54W 177 F11
Fairlie N.Z. 44°5S 170°49E 155 E5
Fairmead U.S.A. 37°5N 120°10W 170 H6
Fairmont Minn., U.S.A. 43°39N 94°28W 172 D6
Fairmont W. Va.,
U.S.A. 39°29N 80°9W 173 F13
Fairmount Calif.,
U.S.A. 34°45N 118°26W 171 L8
Fairmount N.Y., U.S.A. 43°5N 76°12W 175 C8
Fairplay U.S.A. 39°15N 106°2W 168 G10
Fairport U.S.A. 43°6N 77°27W 174 C7
Fairport Harbor U.S.A. 41°45N 81°17W 174 E3
Fairview Canada 56°5N 118°25W 162 B5
Fairview Mont.,
U.S.A. 47°51N 104°3W 168 C11
Fairview Okla., U.S.A. 36°16N 98°29W 176 C5
Fairweather, Mt.
U.S.A. 58°55N 137°32W 162 B1
Faisalabad Pakistan 31°30N 73°5E 124 D5
Faith U.S.A. 45°2N 102°2W 172 C2
Faizabad India 26°45N 82°10E 125 F10
Faizpur India 21°14N 75°49E 126 D2
Fajardo Puerto Rico 18°20N 65°39W 183 d
Fajr, W. → Si. Arabia 29°10N 38°10E 128 D3
Fakenham U.K. 52°51N 0°51E 66 E8
Fåker Sweden 63°0N 14°34E 62 A8
Fakfak Indonesia 2°55S 132°18E 119 E8
Fakiya Bulgaria 42°10N 27°6E 97 D11
Fakobli Côte d'Ivoire 7°23N 7°23W 138 D3
Fakse Denmark 55°15N 12°8E 63 J6
Fakse Bugt Denmark 55°11N 12°15E 63 J6
Fakse Ladeplads Denmark 55°11N 12°9E 63 J6
Faku China 42°32N 123°21E 115 C12
Falaba S. Leone 9°54N 11°22W 138 D2
Falaise France 48°54N 0°12W 70 D6
Falakro Oros Greece 41°15N 23°58E 96 E7
Falam Myanmar 23°0N 93°45E 123 H18
Fălciu Romania 46°17N 28°7E 81 D13
Falcó, C. des Spain 38°50N 1°23E 100 C7
Falcon, C. Algeria 35°50N 0°50W 136 A3
Falcón, Presa Mexico 26°35N 99°10W 181 B5
Falcon Lake Canada 49°42N 95°15W 163 D9
Falcon Res. U.S.A. 26°34N 99°10W 176 H5
Falconara Maríttima
Italy 43°37N 13°24E 93 E10

Falcone, C. del Italy 40°58N 8°12E 94 B1
Falconer U.S.A. 42°7N 79°12W 174 D5
Faléa Mali 12°16N 11°17W 138 C2
Falémé → Senegal 14°46N 12°14W 138 C2
Falerum Sweden 58°8N 16°13E 63 H10
Faleshty = Fălești Moldova 47°32N 27°44E 81 C12
Fălești Moldova 47°32N 27°44E 81 C12
Falfurrias U.S.A. 27°14N 98°9W 176 H5
Falher Canada 55°44N 117°15W 162 B5
Faliraki Greece 36°22N 28°12E 101 C10
Falkenberg Germany 51°35N 13°14E 76 D9
Falkenberg Sweden 56°54N 12°30E 63 H6
Falkensee Germany 52°34N 13°4E 76 C9
Falkirk U.K. 56°0N 3°47W 65 F5
Falkland U.K. 55°58N 3°49W 65 E5
Falkland, East, I. Falk. Is. 51°40S 58°30W 192 D5
Falkland, West, I. Falk. Is. 51°40S 60°0W 192 D5
Falkland Is. ☑ Atl. Oc. 51°30S 59°0W 192 D5
Falkland Plateau Atl. Oc. 51°0S 50°0W 56 M7
Falkland Ridge Atl. Oc. 49°20S 40°0W 56 L8
Falkland Sd. Falk. Is. 52°0S 60°0W 192 D5
Falkonera Greece 36°50N 23°52E 98 E5
Falköping Sweden 58°12N 13°33E 63 F7
Fall River U.S.A. 41°43N 71°10W 175 E13
Fallbrook U.S.A. 33°23N 117°15W 171 M9
Fallon U.S.A. 39°28N 118°47W 168 G4
Falls City U.S.A. 40°3N 95°36W 172 E6
Falls Creek U.S.A. 41°9N 78°48W 174 E6
Falmouth Jamaica 18°30N 77°40W 182 a
Falmouth U.K. 50°9N 5°5W 67 G2
Falmouth U.S.A. 41°33N 70°37W 175 E14
Falsa, Pta. Mexico 27°51N 115°3W 180 B1
False B. S. Africa 34°15S 18°40E 144 E2
False Divi Pt. India 15°43N 80°50E 127 G5
False Pt. India 20°18N 86°48E 126 D8
Falso, C. Honduras 15°12N 83°21W 182 C3
Falster Denmark 54°45N 11°55E 63 K5
Fălticeni Romania 47°21N 26°20E 81 C11
Falun Sweden 60°37N 15°37E 62 D9
Famagusta Cyprus 35°8N 33°55E 101 D12
Famagusta Bay Cyprus 35°15N 34°0E 101 D13
Famatina, Sierra de Argentina 27°30S 68°0W 190 B2
Famenin Iran 35°5N 48°58E 105 C13
Family L. Canada 51°54N 95°27W 163 C9
Famoso U.S.A. 35°37N 119°12W 171 K7
Fan Xian China 35°55N 115°38E 114 G8
Fana Mali 13°0N 6°56W 138 C3
Fana Hd. Ireland 55°17N 7°38W 64 A4
Fanari Greece 39°24N 21°47E 98 B3
Fánes-Sénnes-Braies △ Italy 46°38N 12°4E 93 B9
Fang Thailand 19°55N 99°13E 120 C2
Fang Xian China 32°3N 110°40E 117 A8
Fangchang China 31°5N 118°4E 117 B12
Fangcheng China 33°18N 112°59E 114 H7
Fangchenggang China 21°42N 108°21E 116 G7
Fangliao Taiwan 22°20N 120°38E 117 F13
Fangshan Beijing, China 39°41N 116°0E 114 E9
Fangshan Shanxi, China 38°3N 111°25E 114 E6
Fangzi China 36°33N 119°10E 115 F10
Fani i Madh → Albania 41°56N 20°16E 96 E4
Fanjiatun China 43°40N 125°15E 115 C13
Fanling China 22°30N 114°8E 111 a
Fannich, L. U.K. 57°38N 4°59W 65 D4
Fannūj Iran 26°35N 59°38E 129 E8
Fano Denmark 55°25N 8°25E 63 J2
Fano Italy 43°50N 13°1E 93 E10
Fanshi China 39°12N 113°20E 114 E7
Fao = Al Fāw Iraq 30°0N 48°30E 129 D6
Faqirwali Pakistan 29°27N 73°0E 124 E5
Fâqûs Egypt 30°44N 31°47E 137 E7
Far East = Dalnevostochnyy □ Russia 67°0N 140°0E 107 C14
Far East Asia 40°0N 130°0E 102 E14
Fara in Sabina Italy 42°12N 12°43E 93 F9
Faradje Dem. Rep. of the Congo 3°50N 29°45E 142 B2
Farafangana Madag. 22°49S 47°50E 141 C8
Farafenni Gambia 13°30N 15°34W 138 C1
Faráfra, El Wâhât el Egypt 27°15N 28°20E 137 B2
Farah Afghan. 32°20N 62°7E 122 C3
Farah □ Afghan. 32°25N 62°10E 122 C3
Faraid, Gebel Egypt 23°33N 35°19E 137 C4
Farako Côte d'Ivoire 9°35N 5°58W 138 D4
Faramana Burkina Faso 11°56N 4°45W 138 C4
Faranah Guinea 10°3N 10°45W 138 C2
Farap Turkmenistan 39°3N 63°36E 108 E6
Farasān, Jazā'ir St. Arabia 16°45N 41°55E 131 D3
Farasan Is. = Farasān, Jazā'ir St. Arabia 16°45N 41°55E 131 D3
Fardes → Spain 37°35N 3°0W 89 H7
Fareham U.K. 50°51N 1°11W 67 G6
Farewell, C. = Nunap Isua Greenland 59°48N 43°55W 57 F6
Farewell, C. N.Z. 40°29S 172°43E 155 E7
Farewell Spit N.Z. 40°35S 173°0E 155 A8
Färgelanda Sweden 58°34N 12°0E 63 F5
Fargo Ga., U.S.A. 30°41N 82°34W 178 E7
Fargo N. Dak., U.S.A. 46°53N 96°48W 172 B5
Farg'ona Uzbekistan 40°23N 71°19E 109 D8
Farg'ona □ Uzbekistan 40°30N 71°15E 109 D8
Farg'ona vodiysi Asia 40°46N 71°30E 109 D8
Fär'iah, W. al → West Bank 32°12N 35°27E 130 C4
Faribault U.S.A. 44°18N 93°16W 172 C7
Faridabad India 28°26N 77°19E 124 E6
Faridkot India 30°44N 74°45E 124 D6
Faridpur Bangla. 23°15N 89°55E 125 H13
Faridpur India 28°13N 79°33E 125 E8
Färila Sweden 61°48N 15°50E 62 D9
Farim Guinea-Biss. 12°27N 15°9W 138 C1
Farīmān Iran 35°40N 59°49E 129 C8
Farinha → Brazil 6°51S 47°30W 189 B1
Fariones, Pta. Canary Is. 29°13N 13°28W 188 E6
Fâriskûr Egypt 31°20N 31°43E 137 E7
Färjestaden Sweden 56°36N 16°27E 63 H10
Farkadona Greece 39°36N 22°4E 98 B4
Farleigh Australia 21°4S 149°8E 150 b
Farmakonisi Greece 37°17N 27°10E 99 C9
Farmerville U.S.A. 32°47N 92°24W 176 E8
Farmingdale U.S.A. 40°12N 74°10W 175 F10
Farmington Canada 55°54N 120°30W 162 B4
Farmington Calif., U.S.A. 37°55N 120°59W 170 H6
Farmington Ga., U.S.A. 33°47N 83°26W 178 D5
Farmington Maine, U.S.A. 44°40N 70°9W 173 C18
Farmington Mo., U.S.A. 37°47N 90°25W 172 G8
Farmington N.H., U.S.A. 43°24N 71°4W 175 C13
Farmington N. Mex., U.S.A. 36°44N 108°12W 169 H9
Farmington Utah, U.S.A. 40°59N 111°53W 168 F8
Farmington → U.S.A. 41°51N 72°38W 175 E12
Farmville U.S.A. 37°18N 78°24W 173 G14
Färnäs Sweden 61°0N 14°30E 62 D8
Farne Is. U.K. 55°38N 1°37W 66 B6
Färnebofjärden △ Sweden 60°10N 16°48E 62 D10
Farnham Canada 45°17N 72°59W 175 A12
Farnham, Mt. Canada 50°29N 116°30W 162 C5
Faro Brazil 2°10S 56°39W 188 D6
Faro Canada 62°11N 133°22W 160 E5
Faro Portugal 37°2N 7°55W 89 H3
Fårö Sweden 57°55N 19°5E 63 G13
Faro □ Portugal 37°2N 7°55W 89 H3
Fårösund Sweden 57°52N 19°2E 63 G13
Faro ✈ (FAO) Portugal 37°2N 7°57W 89 H3
Farquhar, C. Australia 23°50S 113°36E 149 D1
Farquhar Is. Seychelles 11°0S 52°0E 146 F4
Farrars Cr. → Australia 25°35S 140°43E 150 D3
Farrāshband Iran 28°57N 52°5E 129 D7
Farrell U.S.A. 41°13N 80°30W 174 E4
Farrell Flat Australia 33°48S 138°48E 152 B3
Farrokhī Iran 33°50N 59°31E 129 C8
Farruch, C. = Ferrutx, C. de Spain 39°47N 3°21E 100 B10
Farrukhabad India 27°24N 79°34E 124 A4
Fārs □ Iran 29°30N 55°0E 129 D7
Farsala Greece 39°17N 22°23E 98 B4
Fārsī Iran 27°58N 50°11E 129 E6
Farsø Denmark 56°46N 9°19E 63 H3
Farson U.S.A. 42°7N 109°26W 168 E9
Farsund Norway 58°5N 6°55E 61 G12
Fartak, Râs St. Arabia 28°5N 34°34E 128 D2
Fartak, Ra's Yemen 15°38N 52°15E 131 D5
Fartura, Serra da Brazil 26°21S 52°52W 191 B5
Faru Nigeria 12°48N 6°12E 139 C6
Fārūj Iran 37°14N 58°14E 129 B8
Fårup Denmark 56°33N 9°51E 63 H3
Farvel, Kap = Nunap Isua Greenland 59°48N 43°55W 57 F6
Farwell U.S.A. 34°23N 103°2W 176 D3
Färyāb □ Afghan. 36°0N 65°0E 109 F7
Fasā Iran 29°0N 53°39E 129 D7
Fasano Italy 40°50N 17°22E 95 B10
Fassa Mali 13°26N 8°15W 138 C3
Fassakoudé Mauritania 15°33N 5°31W 138 B3
Fastiv Ukraine 50°7N 29°57E 75 C15
Fastnet Rock Ireland 51°22N 9°37W 64 E2
Fastov = Fastiv Ukraine 50°7N 29°57E 75 C15
Fatagartuting, Tanjung Indonesia 2°46S 131°57E 119 E8
Fatehabad Haryana, India 29°31N 75°27E 124 E6
Fatehabad Ut. P., India 27°1N 78°19E 124 F8
Fatehgarh India 27°25N 79°35E 125 F8
Fatehpur Bihar, India 24°38N 85°14E 125 G11
Fatehpur Raj., India 28°0N 74°40E 124 F6
Fatehpur Ut. P., India 25°56N 81°13E 125 G9
Fatehpur Ut. P., India 27°10N 81°13E 125 F9
Fatehpur Sikri India 27°6N 77°40E 124 F6
Fatesh Russia 52°8N 35°57E 85 F8
Fathom Five △ Canada 45°17N 81°40W 174 A3
Fatick Senegal 14°19N 16°27W 138 C1
Fatick □ Senegal 14°15N 16°30W 138 C1
Fátima Portugal 39°37N 8°39W 89 F2
Fatoya Guinea 11°37N 9°10W 138 C3
Fatsa Turkey 41°2N 37°31E 104 B7
Faucille, Col de la France 46°22N 6°2E 71 F13
Faulkton U.S.A. 45°2N 99°8W 172 C4
Faulquemont France 49°3N 6°36E 71 C13
Faure I. Australia 25°52S 113°50E 149 E1
Făurei Romania 45°6N 27°19E 81 D11
Fauresmith S. Africa 29°44S 25°17E 144 C4
Fauske Norway 67°17N 15°25E 60 C16
Favara Italy 37°19N 13°39E 94 E6
Favàritx, C. de Spain 40°0N 4°15E 100 B11
Faverges France 45°45N 6°17E 73 C10
Favignana Italy 37°56N 12°20E 94 E5
Favignana, I. Italy 37°56N 12°19E 94 E5
Fawcett, Pt. Australia 11°46S 130°2E 148 B5
Fawn → Canada 55°20N 87°35W 164 A2
Fawnskin U.S.A. 34°16N 116°56W 171 L10
Faxaflói Iceland 64°29N 23°0W 60 D2
Faxälven → Sweden 63°13N 17°13E 62 A10
Faya-Largeau Chad 17°58N 19°6E 135 E9
Fayd Si. Arabia 27°1N 42°52E 128 E4
Fayence France 43°38N 6°42E 73 E10
Fayette Ala., U.S.A. 33°41N 87°50W 177 E11
Fayette Mo., U.S.A. 39°9N 92°41W 172 F7
Fayette N.Y., U.S.A. 42°48N 76°48W 175 D8
Fayetteville Ark., U.S.A. 36°4N 94°10W 176 C7
Fayetteville Ga., U.S.A. 33°27N 84°27W 178 D5
Fayetteville N.C., U.S.A. 35°3N 78°53W 177 D15
Fayetteville Tenn., U.S.A. 35°9N 86°34W 177 D11
Fayid Egypt 30°18N 32°16E 137 E8
Faylakah Kuwait 29°27N 48°20E 129 D6
Fayón Spain 41°15N 0°20E 90 D5
Fazao-Malfakassa △ Togo 8°45N 0°50E 139 D5
Fazilka India 30°27N 74°2E 124 D6
Fazilpur Pakistan 29°18N 70°29E 124 E4
Fdérik Mauritania 22°40N 12°45E 134 D3
Feakle Ireland 52°56N 8°40W 64 D3
Feale → Ireland 52°27N 9°37W 64 D2
Fear, C. U.S.A. 33°50N 77°58W 177 E16
Feather → U.S.A. 38°47N 121°36W 170 G5
Feather Falls U.S.A. 39°36N 121°16W 170 F5
Featherston N.Z. 41°6S 175°20E 154 H4
Featherstone Zimbabwe 18°42S 30°55E 143 F3
Fécamp France 49°45N 0°22E 70 B4
Fedala = Mohammedia Morocco 33°44N 7°21W 136 B4
Federación Argentina 31°0S 57°55W 190 C4
Féderal Argentina 30°57S 58°48W 190 C4
Federal Capital Terr. □ Nigeria 9°0N 7°10E 139 D6
Federal Way U.S.A. 47°18N 122°19W 170 D4
Fedeshküh Iran 28°49N 53°50E 129 D7
Fedorovka Kazakhstan 53°37N 62°42E 108 B6
Fehérgyarmat Hungary 47°58N 22°30E 80 C7
Fehmarn Germany 54°27N 11°7E 76 A7
Fehmarn Bælt Europe 54°35N 11°20E 63 K5
Fehmarn Belt = Fehmarn Bælt Europe 54°35N 11°20E 63 K5
Fei Xian China 35°18N 117°59E 115 G9
Feicheng China 36°14N 116°45E 114 F8
Feidong China 32°0N 117°35E 117 B11
Feijó Brazil 8°9S 70°21W 188 B3
Feilding N.Z. 40°13S 175°35E 154 G4
Feira de Santana Brazil 12°15S 38°57W 189 C3
Feixi China 31°43N 117°59E 117 B11
Feixiang China 36°30N 114°45E 114 F8
Fejaj, Chott el Tunisia 33°52N 9°14E 136 B8
Fejér □ Hungary 47°9N 18°30E 80 C3
Fejø Denmark 54°55N 11°30E 63 K5
Feke Turkey 37°48N 35°56E 104 D6
Fekete → Hungary 45°47N 18°10E 80 E3
Felanitx Spain 39°28N 3°9E 100 B10
Felda → U.S.A. 26°34N 81°26W 179 J8
Feldbach Austria 46°57N 15°52E 78 E8
Feldberg Baden-W., Germany 47°52N 8°0E 77 H3
Feldberg Mecklenburg-Vorpommern, Germany 53°20N 13°25E 76 B9
Feldkirch Austria 47°15N 9°37E 78 D2
Feldkirchen Austria 46°44N 14°6E 78 E7
Félicité Seychelles 4°19S 55°52E 141 b
Felipe Carrillo Puerto Mexico 19°38N 88°3W 181 D7
Felixburg Zimbabwe 19°29S 30°51E 145 A5
Felixlândia Brazil 18°47S 44°55W 189 D2
Felixstowe U.K. 51°58N 1°23E 67 F9
Felletin France 45°53N 2°11E 72 C6
Fellingsbro Sweden 59°26N 15°37E 62 E9
Fellsmere U.S.A. 27°46N 80°36W 179 H9
Felton U.S.A. 37°3N 122°4W 170 H4
Feltre Italy 46°1N 11°54E 93 B8
Femer Bælt = Fehmarn Bælt Europe 54°35N 11°20E 63 K5
Femø Denmark 54°58N 11°35E 63 K5
Femunden Norway 62°10N 11°53E 60 E14
Femundsmarka △ Norway 62°18N 12°6E 60 E15
Fen He → China 35°36N 110°42E 114 G6
Fene Spain 43°27N 8°9W 88 B2
Fenelon Falls Canada 44°32N 78°45W 174 B6
Fener Burnu Turkey 36°58N 27°18E 99 E9
Feng Xian Jiangsu, China 34°43N 116°35E 114 G9
Feng Xian Shaanxi, China 33°54N 106°40E 114 H4
Fengari Greece 40°25N 25°32E 97 F9
Fengcheng Jiangxi, China 28°12N 115°48E 117 C10
Fengcheng Liaoning, China 40°28N 124°5E 115 D13
Fengdu China 29°55N 107°48E 116 C6
Fengfeng China 36°28N 114°8E 114 F8
Fenggang China 27°57N 107°47E 116 D6
Fenghua China 29°40N 121°25E 117 C13
Fenghuang China 27°57N 109°29E 116 D7
Fengjie China 31°3N 109°31E 116 B7
Fengkai China 23°24N 111°30E 117 F9
Fengkang Taiwan 22°12N 120°41E 117 F13
Fengle China 31°29N 112°29E 117 B9
Fenglin Taiwan 23°45N 121°26E 117 F13
Fengning China 41°10N 116°33E 114 D9
Fengqing China 24°38N 99°55E 116 E2
Fengqiu China 35°2N 114°25E 114 G8
Fengrun China 39°48N 118°8E 115 E10
Fengshan Guangxi Zhuangzu, China 24°39N 109°15E 116 E7
Fengshan Guangxi Zhuangzu, China 24°31N 107°3E 116 E6
Fengshun China 23°46N 116°10E 117 F11
Fengtai China 32°50N 116°40E 117 A11
Fengtongzhai △ China 30°50N 102°54E 116 B4
Fengxiang China 34°29N 107°25E 114 G4
Fengxin China 28°41N 115°18E 117 C10
Fengyang China 32°51N 117°29E 117 A11
Fengyi China 25°37N 100°20E 116 E3
Fengyüan Taiwan 24°10N 120°42E 117 E13
Fengzhen China 40°25N 113°2E 114 D7
Feno, C. de France 41°58N 8°33E 73 G12
Fenoarivo Atsinanana Madag. 17°22S 49°25E 141 H9
Fens, The U.K. 52°38N 0°2W 66 E7
Fensmark Denmark 55°17N 11°48E 63 J5
Fenton U.S.A. 42°48N 83°42W 173 D12
Fenxi China 36°40N 111°31E 114 F6
Fenyang China 37°18N 111°48E 114 F6
Fenyi China 27°45N 114°47E 117 D10
Feodosiya Ukraine 45°2N 35°16E 85 K8
Fer, C. de Algeria 37°3N 7°10E 136 A6
Ferbane Ireland 53°16N 7°50W 64 C4
Ferdows Iran 33°58N 58°2E 129 C8
Fère-Champenoise France 48°45N 3°59E 71 D10
Fère-en-Tardenois France 49°10N 3°30E 71 C10
Ferentino Italy 41°42N 13°15E 93 G10
Feres Greece 40°53N 26°10E 97 F10
Ferfer Somalia 5°4N 45°9E 131 F4
Fergana = Farg'ona Uzbekistan 40°23N 71°19E 109 D8
Fergana Range Asia 40°30N 73°50E 109 D8
Fergus Canada 43°43N 80°24W 174 D4
Fergus Falls U.S.A. 46°17N 96°4W 172 B5
Fériana Tunisia 34°59N 8°33E 136 B5
Feričanci Croatia 45°32N 18°0E 80 E2
Ferihegy, Budapest ✈ (BUD) Hungary 47°26N 19°14E 80 C4
Ferizaj Kosovo 42°23N 21°10E 96 D5
Ferkane Algeria 34°37N 7°26E 136 B5
Ferkéssédougou Côte d'Ivoire 9°35N 5°6W 138 D3
Ferlach Austria 46°32N 14°18E 78 E7
Ferland Canada 50°19N 88°27W 164 B2
Ferlo, Vallée du Senegal 15°14N 15°14W 138 B2
Ferlo-Nord □ Senegal 15°43N 14°10W 138 B2
Ferlo-Sud □ Senegal 15°43N 14°0W 138 B2
Fermanagh □ U.K. 54°21N 7°40W 64 B4
Fermo Italy 43°9N 13°43E 93 E10
Fermont Canada 52°47N 67°5W 165 B6
Fermoselle Spain 41°19N 6°27W 88 D4
Fermoy Ireland 52°9N 8°16W 64 D3
Fernán Núñez Spain 37°40N 4°44W 89 H6
Fernández Argentina 27°55S 63°50W 190 B3
Fernandina Beach U.S.A. 30°40N 81°27W 178 E8
Fernando de Noronha Brazil 4°0S 33°10W 187 D12
Fernando Póo = Bioko Eq. Guin. 3°30N 8°40E 139 E6
Ferndale Canada 44°58N 81°17W 174 B3
Ferndale U.S.A. 48°51N 122°36W 170 B4
Fernie Canada 49°30N 115°5W 162 D5
Fernlees Australia 23°51S 148°7E 150 C4
Fernwood U.S.A. 43°16N 73°38W 175 C11
Feroke India 11°9N 75°46E 127 J2
Ferozepore = Firozpur India 30°55N 74°40E 124 D6
Ferrandina Italy 40°29N 16°27E 95 B9
Ferrara Italy 44°50N 11°35E 93 D8
Ferrato, C. Italy 39°18N 9°38E 94 C2
Ferreira do Alentejo Portugal 38°4N 8°6W 89 G2
Ferreñafe Peru 6°42S 79°50W 188 B2
Ferrerias Spain 39°59N 4°1E 100 B11
Ferret, C. France 44°38N 1°15W 72 D2
Ferrette France 47°30N 7°20E 71 E14
Ferriday U.S.A. 31°38N 91°33W 176 F9
Ferriere Italy 44°40N 9°30E 92 D6
Ferrières France 48°5N 2°48E 71 D9
Ferro, Capo Italy 41°9N 9°31E 94 A2
Ferrol Spain 43°29N 8°15W 88 A2
Ferrol, Pen. de Peru 9°10S 78°35W 188 B2
Ferron U.S.A. 39°5N 111°8W 168 G8
Ferros Brazil 19°14S 43°2W 189 D2
Ferrutx, C. de Spain 39°47N 3°21E 100 B10
Ferry Pass U.S.A. 30°31N 87°13W 179 E12
Ferryland Canada 47°2N 52°53W 165 C9
Fertő-Hanság △ Hungary 47°35N 16°53E 80 C1
Fertőszentmiklós Hungary 47°35N 16°53E 80 C1
Fès Morocco 34°0N 5°0W 136 B3
Fès □ Morocco 34°1N 5°0W 136 B3
Fessenden U.S.A. 47°39N 99°38W 172 B4
Festus U.S.A. 38°13N 90°24W 172 F8
Feté Bowé Senegal 14°56N 13°30W 138 C2
Fetești Romania 44°22N 27°51E 81 F12
Fethiye Turkey 36°36N 29°6E 99 E11
Fethiye Körfezi Turkey 36°40N 28°58E 99 E11
Fetlar U.K. 60°36N 0°52W 65 A8
Feuilles → Canada 58°47N 70°4W 161 F17
Feurs France 45°45N 4°13E 73 C8
Feyzābād Afghan. 37°7N 70°33E 109 E8
Fez = Fès Morocco 34°0N 5°0W 136 B3
Fezzan Libya 27°0N 13°0E 135 C8
Fiambalá Argentina 27°45S 67°37W 190 B2
Fianarantsoa Madag. 21°26S 47°5E 141 H9
Fianga Cameroon 9°55N 15°9E 135 G8
Fichtelgebirge Germany 50°8N 12°0E 77 E7
Ficksburg S. Africa 28°51S 27°53E 145 C4
Fidenza Italy 44°52N 10°3E 92 D7
Fidii Nigeria 7°45N 3°53E 139 D5
Field → Australia 23°48S 138°0E 150 C2
Field I. Australia 12°5S 132°23E 148 B5
Fieni Romania 45°8N 25°25E 81 E10
Fier Albania 40°43N 19°33E 96 F3
Fierzë Albania 42°25N 20°1E 96 D4
Fife □ U.K. 56°16N 3°1W 65 E5
Fife Ness U.K. 56°17N 2°35W 65 E6
Fifth Cataract Sudan 18°22N 33°50E 137 D3
Figari France 41°29N 9°7E 73 G13
Figeac France 44°37N 2°2E 72 D6
Figeholm Sweden 57°22N 16°33E 63 G10
Figline Valdarno Italy 43°37N 11°28E 93 E8
Figtree Zimbabwe 20°22S 28°20E 143 G2
Figueira Castelo Rodrigo Portugal 40°57N 6°58W 88 E4
Figueira da Foz Portugal 40°7N 8°54W 88 E2
Figueiró dos Vinhos Portugal 39°55N 8°16W 88 E2
Figueres Spain 42°18N 2°58E 90 C7
Figuig Morocco 32°5N 1°11W 136 B3
Fiji ■ Pac. Oc. 17°20S 179°0E 154 a
Fika Nigeria 11°15N 11°13E 139 C7
Filabres, Sierra de los Spain 37°13N 2°20W 89 H8
Filabusi Zimbabwe 20°34S 29°20E 145 B4
Filadelfia Bolivia 11°20S 68°46W 188 C4
Filadélfia Brazil 7°21S 47°30W 189 B1
Filadelfia Paraguay 22°21S 60°2W 190 A3
Fil'akovo Slovakia 48°17N 19°50E 79 C12
Filchner Ice Shelf Antarctica 79°0S 40°0W 5 D1
Filey U.K. 54°12N 0°18W 66 C7
Filey B. U.K. 54°12N 0°15W 66 C7
Filfla Malta 35°47N 14°24E 101 D1
Filiași Romania 44°32N 23°31E 81 F8
Filiates Greece 39°38N 20°16E 98 B2
Filiatrá Greece 37°9N 21°35E 98 D3
Filicudi Italy 38°35N 14°33E 95 D7
Filingué Niger 14°21N 3°22E 139 C5
Filiouri = Lissos → Greece 41°0N 25°40E 97 E10
Filipiada Greece 39°12N 20°53E 98 B2
Filipstad Sweden 59°43N 14°9E 62 E8
Filisur Switz. 46°41N 9°40E 77 J5
Filitosa France 41°45N 8°52E 73 G12
Fillmore Calif., U.S.A. 34°24N 118°55W 171 L8
Fillmore Utah, U.S.A. 38°58N 112°20W 168 G7
Filotio Greece 37°4N 25°27E 99 D9
Filottrano Italy 43°26N 13°21E 93 E10
Filyos Çayı → Turkey 41°35N 32°10E 104 B5
Fimbul Ice Shelf S. Ocean 69°30S 1°10W 5 D2
Fina Mali 13°15N 9°46E 138 C3
Finale Emília Italy 44°50N 11°18E 93 D8
Finale Lígure Italy 44°10N 8°20E 92 D5
Fiñana Spain 37°10N 2°50W 89 H8
Finch Canada 45°11N 75°7W 175 A9
Finch Hatton Australia 20°25S 148°39E 150 b
Findhorn → U.K. 57°38N 3°38W 65 D5
Findıklı Turkey 41°16N 41°8E 105 B9
Findlay U.S.A. 41°2N 83°39W 173 E12
Fine U.S.A. 44°14N 75°8W 175 B10
Fingal Ireland 53°28N 6°14W 64 C5
Finger L. Canada 53°33N 93°30W 164 B1
Finger Lakes U.S.A. 42°40N 76°30W 175 D8
Fingoè Mozam. 15°55S 31°50E 143 F3
Finike Turkey 36°21N 30°10E 99 E12
Finike Körfezi Turkey 36°17N 30°10E 99 E12
Finiq Albania 39°54N 20°3E 96 G4
Finistère □ France 48°20N 4°0W 70 D3
Finisterre = Fisterra Spain 42°54N 9°16W 88 C1
Finisterre, C. = Fisterra, C. Spain 42°50N 9°19W 88 C1
Finke Australia 25°34S 134°35E 150 D1
Finke Gorge △ Australia 24°8S 132°48E 148 D5
Finland ■ Europe 63°0N 27°0E 60 E22
Finland, G. of Europe 60°0N 26°0E 84 C3
Finlay → Canada 57°0N 125°10W 162 B3
Finley Australia 35°38S 145°35E 153 C6
Finley U.S.A. 47°31N 97°50W 172 B5
Finn → Ireland 54°51N 7°28W 64 B4
Finnerödja Sweden 58°57N 14°24E 63 F8
Finnigan, Mt. Australia 15°49S 145°17E 150 D4
Finniss, C. Australia 33°8S 134°51E 151 E1
Finnmark Norway 69°37N 23°57E 60 B20
Finnsnes Norway 69°14N 18°0E 60 B18
Finspång Sweden 58°43N 15°47E 63 F9
Finsteraarhorn Switz. 46°31N 8°10E 77 J4
Finsterwalde Germany 51°37N 13°42E 76 D9
Fiora → Italy 42°20N 11°34E 93 F8
Fiordland △ N.Z. 45°46S 167°0E 155 F2
Fiorenzuola d'Arda Italy 44°56N 9°55E 92 D6
Fiq Syria 32°46N 35°41E 130 C4
Firat = Furāt, Nahr al → Asia 31°0N 47°25E 128 D5
Fire Island △ U.S.A. 40°38N 73°8W 175 F11
Firebag → Canada 57°45N 111°21W 163 B6
Firebaugh U.S.A. 36°52N 120°27W 170 J6
Firedrake L. Canada 61°25N 104°30W 163 A8
Firenze Italy 43°46N 11°15E 93 E8
Firenze Amerigo Vespucci ✈ (FLR) Italy 43°49N 11°13E 93 E8
Firenze Pisa ✈ (PSA) Italy 43°40N 10°22E 92 E7
Firenzuola Italy 44°7N 11°23E 93 D8
Firk, Sha'ib → Iraq 30°59N 44°34E 128 D5
Firmi France 44°33N 2°19E 72 D6
Firminy France 45°23N 4°18E 73 C8
Firozabad India 27°10N 78°25E 125 F8
Firozpur India 30°55N 74°40E 124 D6
Firozpur-Jhirka India 27°48N 76°57E 124 F7
Fīrūzābād Iran 28°52N 52°35E 129 D7
Fīrūzkūh Iran 35°50N 52°50E 129 C7
Firvale Canada 52°27N 126°13W 162 C3
Fish → Namibia 28°7S 17°10E 144 D2
Fish → S. Africa 31°30S 20°16E 144 E3
Fish River Canyon Namibia 27°40S 17°35E 144 D2
Fisher B. Canada 51°35N 97°13W 163 C9
Fishers I. U.S.A. 41°15N 72°0W 175 E13
Fishguard U.K. 52°0N 4°58W 67 E3
Fishing L. Canada 52°10N 95°24W 163 C9
Fishkill U.S.A. 41°32N 73°54W 175 E11
Fiskardo Greece 38°28N 20°35E 98 C2
Fiskenæsset = Qeqertarsuatsiaat Greenland 63°50N 50°45W 57 E5
Fismes France 49°20N 3°40E 71 C10
Fisterra Spain 42°54N 9°16W 88 C1
Fisterra, C. Spain 42°50N 9°19W 88 C1
Fitchburg Mass., U.S.A. 42°35N 71°48W 175 D13
Fitchburg Wis., U.S.A. 42°58N 89°28W 172 D9
Fitz Roy Argentina 47°0S 67°0W 192 C3
Fitz Roy, Cerro Argentina 49°17S 73°5W 192 C2
Fitzgerald Canada 59°51N 111°36W 162 B6
Fitzgerald U.S.A. 31°43N 83°15W 178 D6
Fitzgerald River △ Australia 33°53S 119°55E 149 F3
Fitzmaurice → Australia 14°45S 130°5E 148 B5
Fitzroy → Queens., Australia 23°32S 150°52E 150 C5
Fitzroy → W. Austral., Australia 17°31S 123°35E 148 C3
Fitzroy Crossing Australia 18°9S 125°38E 148 C4
Fitzwilliam I. Canada 45°30N 81°45W 174 A3
Fiuggi Italy 41°48N 13°13E 93 G10
Fiume = Rijeka Croatia 45°20N 14°21E 93 C11
Fiumicino, Roma ✈ (FCO) Italy 41°46N 12°14E 94 A5
Fiumicino Italy 41°46N 12°14E 94 A5
Five Forks U.S.A. 36°26N 120°9W 170 J6
Five Points U.S.A. 36°26N 120°6W 170 J6
Fivizzano Italy 44°14N 10°8E 92 D7
Fizi Dem. Rep. of the Congo 4°17S 28°55E 142 C2
Fjällbacka Sweden 58°36N 11°17E 63 F5
Fjällnäs Sweden 62°36N 12°11E 62 B6
Fjärdhundra Sweden 59°47N 16°56E 62 E10
Fjellerup Denmark 56°29N 10°34E 63 H4
Fjerritslev Denmark 57°5N 9°15E 63 G3
Fjugesta Sweden 59°11N 14°52E 62 E8
Fkih ben Salah Morocco 32°32N 6°45W 136 B2
Flagler Beach U.S.A. 29°29N 81°8W 179 F8
Flagstaff U.S.A. 35°12N 111°39W 169 J8
Flagstaff L. U.S.A. 45°12N 70°18W 175 A14
Flaherty I. Canada 56°15N 79°15W 164 A4
Flåm Norway 60°50N 7°7E 60 F12
Flambeau → U.S.A. 45°18N 91°14W 172 C8
Flamborough Hd. U.K. 54°7N 0°5W 66 C7
Fläming Germany 52°0N 13°20E 76 C8
Flaming Gorge △ U.S.A. 41°10N 109°25W 168 F9
Flaming Gorge Res. U.S.A. 41°10N 109°25W 168 F9
Flamingo, Teluk Indonesia 5°30S 138°0E 119 F9
Flanders = Flandre Europe 50°50N 2°30E 71 B9
Flandre Europe 50°50N 2°30E 71 B9
Flandre-Occidentale = West-Vlaanderen □ Belgium 51°0N 3°0E 69 C2
Flandre-Orientale = Oost-Vlaanderen □ Belgium 51°5N 3°50E 69 C3
Flandreau U.S.A. 44°3N 96°36W 172 C5
Flanigan U.S.A. 40°10N 119°53W 170 F7
Flannan Is. U.K. 58°9N 7°52W 65 C1
Flåsjön Sweden 64°5N 15°40E 60 D16
Flat → Canada 61°33N 125°18W 162 A3
Flat I. Mauritius 19°53S 57°35E 141 d
Flat I. S. China Sea 10°49N 115°49E 118 B5
Flat Pt. N.Z. 41°14S 175°57E 154 H4
Flathead L. U.S.A. 47°51N 114°8W 168 C6
Flattery, C. Australia 14°58S 145°21E 150 A4
Flattery, C. U.S.A. 48°23N 124°29W 170 B2
Flatwoods U.S.A. 38°31N 82°43W 173 F12
Fleetwood U.K. 53°55N 3°1W 66 D4
Fleetwood U.S.A. 40°27N 75°49W 175 F9
Flekkefjord Norway 58°18N 6°39E 61 G12
Flemington U.S.A. 41°7N 77°28W 174 E7
Flemish Cap Atl. Oc. 47°0N 45°0W 56 B7
Flen Sweden 59°4N 16°35E 62 E10
Flensburg Germany 54°47N 9°27E 76 A5
Flers France 48°47N 0°33W 70 D6
Flesherton Canada 44°16N 80°33W 174 B4
Flesko, Tanjung Indonesia 0°29N 124°30E 119 D6
Fleurance France 43°52N 0°40E 72 E4
Fleurie, Côte France 49°25N 0°4W 70 C6
Fleurier Switz. 46°54N 6°35E 77 J2
Fleurieu Pen. Australia 35°40S 138°5E 152 C2
Flevoland □ Neths. 52°30N 5°30E 69 B5
Flin Flon Canada 54°46N 101°53W 163 C8
Flinders → Australia 17°36S 140°36E 150 B3
Flinders → Australia 17°36S 140°36E 150 B3
Flinders Chase △ Australia 35°50S 136°42E 152 C2
Flinders Group Australia 14°11S 144°15E 150 A3
Flinders I. S. Austral., Australia 33°44S 134°41E 151 E1
Flinders I. Tas., Australia 40°0S 148°0E 151 G4
Flinders Ranges Australia 31°30S 138°30E 152 A3
Flinders Ranges △ Australia 31°30S 138°30E 152 A3
Flinders Reefs Australia 17°37S 148°31E 150 B4
Flint U.K. 53°15N 3°8W 66 D4
Flint U.S.A. 43°1N 83°41W 173 D12
Flint → U.S.A. 30°57N 84°34W 178 E5
Flint I. Kiribati 11°26S 151°48W 157 J12
Flintshire □ U.K. 53°17N 3°17W 66 D4
Fliseryd Sweden 57°6N 16°15E 63 G10
Flix Spain 41°14N 0°32E 90 D5
Flixecourt France 50°1N 2°5E 71 B9
Floby Sweden 58°8N 13°20E 63 F7
Floda Sweden 57°49N 12°22E 63 G6
Flodden U.K. 55°37N 2°8W 66 B5
Flogny-la-Chapelle France 47°57N 3°57E 71 E10
Floodplains △ Sri Lanka 8°10N 81°10E 127 K5
Floodwood U.S.A. 46°56N 92°55W 172 B7
Flora U.S.A. 38°40N 88°29W 172 F9
Florac France 44°20N 3°37E 72 D7
Florahome U.S.A. 29°44N 81°54W 178 F8
Floral City U.S.A. 28°45N 82°17W 179 G7
Florala U.S.A. 31°0N 86°20W 177 F11
Florânia Brazil 6°8S 36°49W 189 B3
Florence = Firenze Italy 43°46N 11°15E 93 E8
Florence Ala., U.S.A. 34°48N 87°41W 177 D11
Florence Ariz., U.S.A. 33°2N 111°23W 169 K8
Florence Colo., U.S.A. 38°23N 105°8W 168 G11
Florence Oreg., U.S.A. 43°58N 124°7W 168 D1
Florence S.C., U.S.A. 34°12N 79°46W 177 D15
Florence, L. Australia 28°53S 138°9E 151 D2
Florencia Colombia 1°36N 75°36W 188 C2
Florennes Belgium 50°15N 4°35E 69 D4
Florensac France 43°23N 3°28E 72 E7
Florenville Belgium 49°40N 5°19E 69 E5
Flores Azores 39°26N 31°13W 134 a
Flores Brazil 7°51S 37°59W 189 B3
Flores Guatemala 16°59N 89°50W 182 C2
Flores Indonesia 8°35S 121°0E 119 F6
Flores I. Canada 49°20N 126°10W 162 D3
Flores Sea Indonesia 6°30S 120°0E 119 F6
Floresta Brazil 8°40S 37°26W 189 B3
Floresti Moldova 47°53N 28°17E 81 C13
Floresville U.S.A. 29°8N 98°10W 176 G5
Floriano Brazil 6°50S 43°0W 189 B2
Florianópolis Brazil 27°30S 48°30W 191 B6
Florida Cuba 21°32N 78°14W 182 B4
Florida Uruguay 34°7S 56°10W 191 C4
Florida □ U.S.A. 28°0N 82°0W 179 H8
Florida, Straits of U.S.A. 25°0N 80°0W 182 B4
Florida B. U.S.A. 25°0N 80°45W 179 K8
Florida City U.S.A. 25°27N 80°29W 179 J9
Florida Keys U.S.A. 24°40N 81°0W 179 K8
Floridia Italy 37°5N 15°9E 95 E8
Florin U.S.A. 38°30N 121°24W 170 G5
Florina Greece 40°48N 21°26E 96 G5
Florissant U.S.A. 38°47N 90°19W 172 F8
Florø Norway 61°35N 5°1E 60 F11
Flower Station Canada 45°10N 76°41W 175 A8
Flowerpot I. Canada 45°18N 81°38W 174 A3
Floydada U.S.A. 33°59N 101°20W 176 E4
Fluk Indonesia 1°42S 127°44E 119 E7
Flúmen → Spain 41°43N 0°9W 90 D4
Flumendosa → Italy 39°26N 9°38E 94 C2
Fluminimaggiore Italy 39°26N 8°30E 94 C1
Flushing = Vlissingen Neths. 51°26N 3°34E 69 C3
Fluvià → Spain 42°12N 3°7E 90 C8
Fly → Papua N. G. 8°25S 143°0E 147 B7
Flying Fish, C. Antarctica 72°6S 102°29W 5 D15
Foam Lake Canada 51°40N 103°32W 163 C8
Foča Bos.-H. 43°31N 18°47E 96 C2
Foça Turkey 38°39N 26°46E 99 B9
Focédontéa Guinea 10°50N 14°22W 138 C2
Fochabers U.K. 57°37N 3°6W 65 D5
Focșani Romania 45°41N 27°15E 81 E12
Fodécontéa Guinea 10°50N 14°22W 138 C2
Foggaret el Arab Algeria 27°13N 2°49E 136 C6
Foggaret ez Zoua Algeria 27°20N 2°53E 136 C6
Fóggia Italy 41°27N 15°34E 95 A8
Foglia → Italy 43°55N 12°54E 93 E9
Fogo Cabo Verde 15°5N 24°20W 134 b
Fogo Canada 49°43N 54°17W 165 C9
Fogo I. Canada 49°40N 54°5W 165 C9
Fohnsdorf Austria 47°12N 14°40E 78 D7
Fóia Portugal 37°19N 8°37W 89 H2
Foix France 42°58N 1°38E 72 F5
Fojnica Bos.-H. 43°59N 17°51E 80 G2
Fokida Greece 38°30N 22°15E 98 C4
Fokino Russia 53°30N 34°22E 84 E5
Fokku Nigeria 11°36N 4°32E 139 C5
Folda Nord-Trøndelag, Norway 64°32N 10°30E 60 D14
Folda Nordland, Norway 67°38N 14°50E 60 C16
Földeák Hungary 46°19N 20°30E 80 E5
Folegandros Greece 36°40N 24°55E 98 E6
Foley Botswana 21°34S 27°21E 145 A4

Foley Ala., U.S.A. 30°24N 87°41W 177 F11
Foley Fla., U.S.A. 30°4N 83°32W 178 E6
Foleyet Canada 48°15N 82°25W 164 C3
Folgefonna Norway 60°3N 6°23E 61 F12
Foligno Italy 42°57N 12°42E 93 F9
Folkestone U.K. 51°5N 1°12E 67 F9
Folkston U.S.A. 30°50N 82°0W 178 F5
Follansbee U.S.A. 40°19N 80°35W 174 F4
Follónica Italy 42°55N 10°45E 92 F7
Follónica, G. di Italy 42°54N 10°43E 92 F7
Folsom U.S.A. 38°40N 121°9W 170 G5
Folsom L. U.S.A. 38°42N 121°9W 170 G5
Foltești Romania 45°45N 28°3E 81 E13
Fomboni Comoros Is. 12°18S 43°46E 141 a
Fond-du-Lac Canada 59°19N 107°12W 163 B7
Fond du Lac U.S.A. 43°47N 88°27W 172 D9
Fond-du-Lac → Canada 59°17N 106°0W 163 B7
Fonda U.S.A. 42°57N 74°22W 175 D10
Fondi Italy 41°21N 13°25E 94 A6
Fonfría Spain 41°37N 6°9W 88 D4
Fongafale Tuvalu 8°31S 179°13E 147 B10
Fonni Italy 40°7N 9°15E 94 B2
Fonsagrada = A Fonsagrada
  Spain 43°8N 7°4W 88 B3
Fonseca, G. de
  Cent. Amer. 13°10N 87°40W 182 D2
Font-Romeu-Odeillo-Via
  France 42°31N 2°3E 72 F5
Fontaine-Française
  France 47°32N 5°21E 71 E12
Fontainebleau France 48°24N 2°40E 71 D9
Fontana U.S.A. 34°6N 117°26W 171 L9
Fontana, L. Argentina 44°55S 71°30W 192 B2
Fontas → Canada 58°14N 121°48W 162 B4
Fonte Boa Brazil 2°33S 66°0W 186 D5
Fontem Cameroon 5°32N 9°52E 139 D6
Fontenay-le-Comte
  France 46°28N 0°48W 72 B3
Fontenelle Res. U.S.A. 42°1N 110°3W 168 E8
Fontur Iceland 66°23N 14°32W 60 C6
Fonyód Hungary 46°44N 17°33E 80 D2
Foochow = Fuzhou
  China 26°5N 119°16E 117 D12
Foping China 33°41N 108°0E 114 H5
Foraker, Mt. U.S.A. 62°58N 151°24W 166 C5
Forbach France 49°10N 6°52E 71 C13
Forbes Australia 33°22S 148°5E 153 B8
Forbesganj India 26°17N 87°18E 125 F15
Forcados Nigeria 5°26N 5°26E 139 D6
Forcados → Nigeria 5°25N 5°19E 139 D6
Forcalquier France 43°58N 5°47E 73 E9
Forchheim Germany 49°43N 11°4E 77 F7
Ford City Calif., U.S.A. 35°9N 119°27W 171 K7
Ford City Pa., U.S.A. 40°46N 79°32W 174 F5
Førde Norway 61°27N 5°53E 60 F11
Fords Bridge Australia 29°41S 145°29E 151 D4
Fordyce U.S.A. 33°49N 92°25W 176 E8
Forécariah Guinea 9°28N 13°10W 138 D2
Forel, Mt. Greenland 66°52N 36°55W 57 D7
Foremost Canada 49°26N 111°34W 162 D6
Forest U.S.A. 32°22N 89°29W 177 E10
Forest Acres U.S.A. 34°1N 80°58W 178 A9
Forest City Iowa, U.S.A. 43°16N 93°39W 172 D7
Forest City N.C.,
  U.S.A. 35°20N 81°52W 177 D14
Forest City Pa., U.S.A. 41°39N 75°28W 175 E9
Forest Grove U.S.A. 45°31N 123°7W 170 E3
Forest Park U.S.A. 33°37N 84°22W 178 B5
Forestburg Canada 52°35N 112°1W 162 C6
Foreste Casentinesi-Monte
  Falterona-Campigna △
  Italy 43°50N 11°48E 93 E8
Foresthill U.S.A. 39°1N 120°49W 170 F6
Forestier Pen. Australia 43°0S 148°0E 151 G4
Forestville Canada 48°48N 69°2W 165 C6
Forestville Calif.,
  U.S.A. 38°28N 122°54W 170 G4
Forestville N.Y., U.S.A. 42°28N 79°10W 174 D5
Forêt d'Orient △ France 48°16N 4°25E 71 D11
Forez, Mts. du France 45°40N 3°50E 72 C7
Forfar U.K. 56°39N 2°53W 65 E6
Forillon △ Canada 48°46N 64°12W 165 C7
Forks U.S.A. 47°57N 124°23W 170 C2
Forksville U.S.A. 41°29N 76°35W 175 E8
Forlì Italy 44°13N 12°3E 93 D9
Forlì-Cesena □ Italy 43°10N 12°20E 93 D8
Forman U.S.A. 46°7N 97°38W 172 B5
Formazza Italy 46°22N 8°26E 92 B5
Formby Pt. U.K. 53°33N 3°6W 66 D4
Formentera Spain 38°43N 1°27E 100 C7
Formentor, C. de Spain 39°58N 3°13E 100 B10
Formentor, Pen. de
  Spain 39°56N 3°11E 100 B10
Former Yugoslav Republic of
  Macedonia = Macedonia ■
  Europe 41°53N 21°40E 96 E5
Fórmia Italy 41°15N 13°37E 94 A6
Formiga Brazil 20°27S 45°25W 189 E11
Formígine Italy 44°37N 10°51E 92 D7
Formosa = Taiwan ■
  Asia 23°30N 121°0E 117 F13
Formosa Argentina 26°15S 58°10W 190 B4
Formosa Brazil 15°32S 47°20W 189 D1
Formosa □ Argentina 25°0S 60°0W 190 B4
Formosa, Serra Brazil 12°0S 55°0W 187 F8
Formosa B. = Ungwana B.
  Kenya 2°45S 40°20E 142 C5
Formosa do Rio Prêto
  Brazil 11°2S 45°3W 189 C1
Fornells Spain 40°3N 4°7E 100 A11
Fornos de Algodres
  Portugal 40°38N 7°32W 88 E3
Fornovo di Taro Italy 44°42N 10°6E 92 D7
Forollhogna △ Norway 62°39N 10°41E 60 E14
Føroyar ☑ Atl. Oc. 62°0N 7°0W 60 B8
Forres U.K. 57°37N 3°37W 65 D5
Forrest Vic., Australia 38°33S 143°47E 152 E5
Forrest W. Austral.,
  Australia 30°51S 128°6E 149 F4
Forrest City U.S.A. 35°1N 90°47W 177 D9
Fors Sweden 60°14N 16°20E 62 D10
Forsayth Australia 18°33S 143°34E 150 B3
Forserum Sweden 57°42N 14°30E 63 G8
Forshaga Sweden 59°33N 13°29E 62 D7
Förslöv Sweden 56°21N 12°48E 63 H6
Forsmo Sweden 63°16N 17°11E 62 A11
Forssa Finland 60°49N 23°38E 63 E6
Forst Germany 51°45N 14°37E 76 D10
Forster Australia 32°12S 152°31E 153 B10

Forsvik Sweden 58°35N 14°26E 63 F8
Forsyth Ga., U.S.A. 33°2N 83°56W 178 B6
Forsyth Mont.,
  U.S.A. 46°16N 106°41W 168 C10
Forsyth I. N.Z. 40°58S 174°5E 155 M4
Fort Abbas Pakistan 29°12N 72°52E 124 E5
Fort Albany Canada 52°15N 81°35W 164 B3
Fort Assiniboine
  Canada 54°20N 114°45W 162 C6
Fort Augustus U.K. 57°9N 4°42W 65 D4
Fort Beaufort S. Africa 32°46S 26°40E 144 D4
Fort Benton U.S.A. 47°49N 110°40W 168 C8
Fort Bragg U.S.A. 39°26N 123°48W 168 G2
Fort Bridger U.S.A. 41°19N 110°23W 168 F8
Fort Caroline ☆ U.S.A. 30°23N 81°30W 178 E8
Fort Chipewyan
  Canada 58°42N 111°8W 163 B6
Fort Clatsop = Lewis and Clark △
  U.S.A. 46°8N 123°53W 170 D3
Fort Collins U.S.A. 40°35N 105°5W 168 F11
Fort-Coulonge Canada 45°50N 76°45W 164 C4
Fort Covington
  U.S.A. 44°59N 74°29W 175 B10
Fort Dauphin = Taolanaro
  Madag. 25°2S 47°0E 141 K9
Fort Davis Ala., U.S.A. 32°15N 85°43W 178 C4
Fort Davis Tex., U.S.A. 30°35N 103°54W 176 F3
Fort-de-France
  Martinique 14°36N 61°5W 182 c
Fort Defiance U.S.A. 35°45N 109°5W 169 J9
Fort Dodge U.S.A. 42°30N 94°11W 172 D6
Fort Drum U.S.A. 27°32N 80°48W 179 F6
Fort Edward U.S.A. 43°16N 73°35W 175 C11
Fort Erie Canada 42°54N 78°56W 174 D6
Fort Fairfield U.S.A. 46°46N 67°50W 173 B20
Fort Frances Canada 48°36N 93°24W 163 D10
Fort Franklin = Déline
  Canada 65°11N 123°25W 160 D7
Fort Frederica △
  U.S.A. 31°13N 81°23W 178 D8
Fort Gaines U.S.A. 31°36N 85°3W 178 D4
Fort Garland U.S.A. 37°26N 105°26W 169 H11
Fort George = Chisasibi
  Canada 53°50N 79°0W 164 B4
Fort Good Hope
  Canada 66°14N 128°40W 160 D6
Fort Hancock U.S.A. 31°18N 105°51W 176 F2
Fort Hope = Eabametoong
  Canada 51°30N 88°0W 164 B2
Fort Irwin U.S.A. 35°16N 116°41W 171 K10
Fort Kent U.S.A. 47°15N 68°36W 173 B19
Fort Klamath U.S.A. 42°42N 122°0W 168 D3
Fort Laramie U.S.A. 42°13N 104°31W 168 E11
Fort Lauderdale U.S.A. 26°7N 80°8W 179 J9
Fort Liard Canada 60°14N 123°30W 160 E7
Fort Liberté Haiti 19°42N 71°51W 183 C5
Fort Lupton U.S.A. 40°5N 104°49W 168 F11
Fort MacKay Canada 57°12N 111°41W 162 B6
Fort Macleod Canada 49°45N 113°30W 162 D6
Fort McMurray
  Canada 56°44N 111°7W 162 B6
Fort McPherson
  Canada 67°30N 134°55W 160 D5
Fort Madison U.S.A. 40°38N 91°27W 172 E8
Fort Matanzas △
  U.S.A. 29°43N 81°14W 178 F8
Fort Meade U.S.A. 27°45N 81°48W 179 H8
Fort Mitchell U.S.A. 32°20N 85°1W 178 C4
Fort Morgan U.S.A. 40°15N 103°48W 168 F12
Fort Myers U.S.A. 26°39N 81°52W 179 J8
Fort Myers Beach
  U.S.A. 26°26N 81°52W 179 J8
Fort Myers Villas
  U.S.A. 26°33N 81°52W 179 J8
Fort Nelson Canada 58°50N 122°44W 162 B4
Fort Nelson → Canada 59°32N 124°0W 162 B4
Fort Norman = Tulita
  Canada 64°57N 125°30W 160 E6
Fort Ogden U.S.A. 27°5N 81°57W 179 H8
Fort Payne U.S.A. 34°26N 85°43W 177 D12
Fort Peck U.S.A. 48°1N 106°27W 168 B10
Fort Peck Dam U.S.A. 48°0N 106°26W 168 C10
Fort Peck L. U.S.A. 48°0N 106°26W 168 C10
Fort Pierce U.S.A. 27°27N 80°20W 179 H9
Fort Pierre U.S.A. 44°21N 100°22W 172 C3
Fort Plain U.S.A. 42°56N 74°37W 175 D10
Fort Portal Uganda 0°40N 30°20E 142 B3
Fort Providence
  Canada 61°3N 117°40W 162 A5
Fort Pulaski △ U.S.A. 32°2N 80°56W 178 C9
Fort Qu'Appelle
  Canada 50°45N 103°50W 163 C8
Fort Resolution
  Canada 61°10N 113°40W 162 A6
Fort Rixon Zimbabwe 20°2S 29°17E 143 G2
Fort Ross U.S.A. 38°32N 123°13W 170 G3
Fort Rupert = Waskaganish
  Canada 51°30N 78°40W 164 B4
Fort St. James Canada 54°30N 124°10W 162 C4
Fort St. John Canada 56°15N 120°50W 162 B4
Fort Saskatchewan
  Canada 53°40N 113°15W 162 C6
Fort Scott U.S.A. 37°50N 94°42W 172 G6
Fort Severn Canada 56°0N 87°40W 164 A2
Fort Shevchenko
  Kazakhstan 44°35N 50°23E 87 H10
Fort Simpson Canada 61°45N 121°15W 162 A4
Fort Smith Canada 60°0N 111°51W 162 A6
Fort Smith U.S.A. 35°23N 94°25W 176 D7
Fort Stockton U.S.A. 30°53N 102°53W 176 F3
Fort Sumner U.S.A. 34°28N 104°15W 169 J11
Fort Thompson U.S.A. 44°3N 99°26W 172 C4
Fort Union △ U.S.A. 35°54N 105°1W 169 J11
Fort Valley U.S.A. 32°33N 83°53W 178 C6
Fort Vermilion Canada 58°24N 116°0W 162 B5
Fort Walton Beach
  U.S.A. 30°25N 86°36W 179 E3
Fort Ware Canada 57°26N 125°41W 162 B3
Fort Wayne U.S.A. 41°4N 85°9W 173 E11
Fort White U.S.A. 29°55N 82°43W 178 F7
Fort William U.K. 56°49N 5°7W 65 E3
Fort Worth U.S.A. 32°43N 97°19W 176 E6
Fort Yates U.S.A. 46°5N 100°38W 172 B3
Fort Yukon U.S.A. 66°34N 145°16W 166 D2
Fortaleza Bolivia 12°6S 66°49W 188 C4
Fortaleza Brazil 3°45S 38°35W 189 A4
Forteau Canada 51°28N 56°58W 165 B8
Fortescue → Australia 21°0S 116°4E 148 D2
Fortescue River Roadhouse
  Australia 21°17S 116°8E 148 D2
Forth → U.K. 56°9N 3°50W 65 E5
Forth, Firth of U.K. 56°5N 2°55W 65 E6

Forthassa Rharbia
  Algeria 32°52N 1°18W 136 B3
Fortín Uno Argentina 38°50S 65°18W 192 B3
Fortore → Italy 41°55N 15°17E 93 G12
Fortrose N.Z. 46°38S 168°45E 155 G3
Fortrose U.K. 57°35N 4°9W 65 D4
Fortuna Spain 38°11N 1°7W 91 G3
Fortuna Calif., U.S.A. 40°36N 124°9W 168 F1
Fortuna N. Dak.,
  U.S.A. 48°55N 103°47W 172 A2
Fortune Canada 47°4N 55°50W 165 C8
Fortune B. Canada 47°30N 55°22W 165 C8
Forūr Iran 26°17N 54°32E 129 E7
Fos-sur-Mer France 43°26N 4°56E 73 E8
Fosen Norway 63°50N 10°20E 60 E14
Foshan China 23°3N 113°9E 117 F9
Fosnavåg Norway 62°22N 5°38E 60 E11
Foso Ghana 5°43N 1°15W 139 D4
Fossano Italy 44°33N 7°43E 92 D4
Fossil U.S.A. 45°0N 120°9W 168 D3
Fossil Butte △ U.S.A. 41°50N 110°27W 168 F8
Fossombrone Italy 43°41N 12°48E 93 E9
Foster Australia 38°40S 146°15E 153 F7
Foster Canada 45°17N 72°30W 175 A12
Foster → Canada 55°47N 105°49W 163 B7
Fosters Ra. Australia 21°35S 133°48E 150 C1
Fostoria U.S.A. 41°10N 83°25W 173 E12
Fouesnant France 47°53N 4°1W 70 E2
Fougères France 48°21N 1°14W 70 D5
Foul Pt. Sri Lanka 8°35N 81°18E 127 K5
Foula U.K. 60°10N 2°5W 65 A6
Foulalaba Mali 10°40N 7°20W 138 C3
Foulness I. U.K. 51°36N 0°55E 67 F8
Foulwind, C. N.Z. 41°45S 171°28E 155 M6
Foum Zguid Morocco 30°2N 6°59W 136 B2
Foumban Cameroon 5°45N 10°50E 139 D7
Foumbot Cameroon 5°30N 10°35E 139 D7
Foumbouni Comoros Is. 11°51S 43°29E 141 a
Foumirate Algeria 20°3N 3°12W 136 C3
Foundiougne Senegal 14°5N 16°32W 138 C1
Fountain Colo.,
  U.S.A. 38°41N 104°42W 168 G11
Fountain Fla., U.S.A. 30°29N 85°25W 178 E4
Fountain Hills U.S.A. 33°37N 111°43W 169 K8
Fountain Springs
  U.S.A. 35°54N 118°51W 171 K8
Four Mountains, Is. of
  U.S.A. 53°0N 170°0W 166 E5
Fourchambault France 47°2N 3°3E 71 E10
Fouriesburg S. Africa 28°38S 28°14E 145 C4
Fourmies France 50°1N 4°2E 71 B11
Fourna Greece 39°3N 21°52E 98 B3
Fournoi Greece 37°36N 26°32E 99 D8
Fours France 46°50N 3°42E 71 F10
Fourth Cataract Sudan 18°47N 32°3E 135 E12
Fouta Djallon Guinea 11°20N 12°10W 138 C2
Foux, Cap-à- Haiti 19°43N 73°27W 183 C5
Foveaux Str. N.Z. 46°42S 168°10E 155 G3
Fowey U.K. 50°20N 4°39W 67 G3
Fowler Calif., U.S.A. 36°38N 119°41W 170 J7
Fowler Colo., U.S.A. 38°8N 104°2W 168 G11
Fowler, Pt. Australia 32°2S 132°3E 149 F5
Fowlers B. Australia 31°59S 132°34E 149 F5
Fowman Iran 37°13N 49°19E 105 D13
Fox → Canada 56°3N 93°18W 163 B10
Fox Creek Canada 54°24N 116°48W 162 C5
Fox Is. U.S.A. 53°0N 168°0W 166 E6
Fox Lake Canada 58°28N 114°31W 162 B6
Fox Valley Canada 50°30N 109°25W 163 C7
Foxboro Canada 44°14N 77°26W 174 B7
Foxboro U.S.A. 42°4N 71°16W 175 D13
Foxdale Australia 20°22S 148°35E 150 b
Foxe Basin Canada 66°0N 77°0W 161 D16
Foxe Chan. Canada 65°0N 80°0W 161 E16
Foxe Pen. Canada 65°0N 76°0W 161 E16
Foxen Sweden 59°25N 11°55E 62 E5
Foxford Ireland 53°59N 9°7W 64 C2
Foxton N.Z. 40°29S 175°18E 154 G4
Foyle, Lough U.K. 55°7N 7°4W 64 A4
Foynes Ireland 52°37N 9°7W 64 D2
Foz Spain 43°33N 7°20W 88 B3
Foz do Cunene Angola 17°15S 11°48E 144 A1
Foz do Gregório Brazil 6°47S 70°44W 188 B3
Foz do Iguaçu Brazil 25°30S 54°30W 191 B5
Frackville U.S.A. 40°47N 76°14W 175 F8
Fraga Spain 41°32N 0°21E 90 D5
Fraile Muerto Uruguay 32°31S 54°32W 191 C5
Framingham U.S.A. 42°18N 71°24W 175 D13
Frampol Poland 50°41N 22°40E 83 H9
Franca Brazil 20°33S 47°30W 189 E1
Francavilla al Mare
  Italy 42°25N 14°17E 93 F11
Francavilla Fontana
  Italy 40°32N 17°35E 95 B10
France ■ Europe 47°0N 3°0E 59 F6
Frances → Australia 36°41S 140°55E 152 D4
Frances → Canada 60°16N 129°10W 162 A3
Frances L. Canada 61°23N 129°30W 162 A3
Franceville Gabon 1°40S 13°32E 140 E2
Francis Case, L. U.S.A. 43°4N 98°34W 172 D4
Francisco Beltrão Brazil 26°5S 53°4W 191 B5
Francisco Ignacio Madero
  Coahuila, Mexico 25°48N 103°18W 180 B4
Francisco Ignacio Madero
  Durango, Mexico 24°26N 104°18W 180 C4
Francisco Sá Brazil 16°28S 43°30W 189 D2
Francistown Botswana 21°7S 27°33E 145 C4
Francofonte Italy 37°14N 14°53E 95 E7
François France 50°35N 56°45W 165 C8
François L. Canada 54°0N 125°30W 162 C3
Francois Peron △
  Australia 25°42S 113°33E 149 E1
Francs Pk. U.S.A. 43°58N 109°20W 168 E9
Franeker Neths. 53°12N 5°33E 69 A5
Frank Hann △
  Australia 32°52S 120°19E 149 F3
Frankenberg Germany 51°3N 8°48E 76 D4
Frankenhöhe
  Germany 49°20N 10°25E 77 F6
Frankenthal Germany 49°32N 8°21W 77 F5
Frankenwald Germany 50°18N 11°30E 77 E7
Frankford Canada 44°12N 77°36W 174 B7
Frankfort S. Africa 27°17S 28°30E 145 C4
Frankfort Ind., U.S.A. 40°17N 86°31W 172 E10
Frankfort Kans., U.S.A. 39°42N 96°25W 172 F5
Frankfort Ky., U.S.A. 38°12N 84°52W 173 F11
Frankfort N.Y., U.S.A. 43°2N 75°4W 175 D9
Frankfurt Brandenburg,
  Germany 52°20N 14°32E 76 C10

Frankfurt Hessen, Germany 50°7N 8°41E 77 E4
Frankfurt ✈ (FRA)
  Germany 50°1N 8°34E 77 E4
Fränkische Alb Germany 49°10N 11°23E 77 F7
Fränkische Rezat →
  Germany 49°11N 11°1E 77 F7
Fränkische Saale →
  Germany 50°3N 9°42E 77 E5
Fränkische Schweiz
  Germany 49°50N 11°16E 77 F7
Fränkische Schweiz-Veldensteiner
  Forst △ Germany 49°45N 11°22E 77 F7
Frankland → Australia 35°0S 116°48E 149 G2
Franklin Ga., U.S.A. 33°17N 85°6W 178 B4
Franklin Ky., U.S.A. 36°43N 86°35W 172 G10
Franklin La., U.S.A. 29°48N 91°30W 176 G9
Franklin Mass., U.S.A. 42°5N 71°24W 175 D13
Franklin N.H., U.S.A. 43°27N 71°39W 175 C13
Franklin N.Y., U.S.A. 42°20N 75°9W 175 D9
Franklin Nebr., U.S.A. 40°6N 98°57W 172 E4
Franklin Pa., U.S.A. 41°24N 79°50W 174 E5
Franklin Va., U.S.A. 36°41N 76°56W 173 G15
Franklin W. Va.,
  U.S.A. 38°39N 79°20W 173 F14
Franklin B. Canada 69°45N 126°0W 160 D6
Franklin D. Roosevelt L.
  U.S.A. 48°18N 118°9W 168 B4
Franklin-Gordon Wild Rivers △
  Australia 42°49S 145°51E 151 G4
Franklin Harb.
  Australia 33°43S 136°55E 152 B2
Franklin I. Antarctica 76°10S 168°30E 55 D11
Franklin I. Canada 45°24N 80°20W 174 A4
Franklin L. U.S.A. 40°25N 115°22W 168 F6
Franklin Mts. Canada 65°0N 125°0W 160 D6
Franklin Mts. N.Z. 44°55S 167°45E 155 L1
Franklin Str. Canada 72°0N 96°0W 160 C12
Franklinton U.S.A. 30°51N 90°9W 177 F9
Franklinville U.S.A. 42°20N 78°27W 174 D6
Frankston Australia 38°8S 145°8E 153 F6
Frånö Sweden 62°55N 17°50E 62 B11
Fransfontein Namibia 20°12S 15°1E 144 B2
Fränsta Sweden 62°30N 16°11E 62 B10
Frantsa Iosifa, Zemlya
  Arctic 82°0N 55°0E 106 A6
Franz Canada 48°25N 84°30W 164 C3
Franz Josef Land = Frantsa Iosifa,
  Zemlya Arctic 82°0N 55°0E 106 A6
Franz Josef Strauss ✈ (MUC)
  Germany 48°21N 11°47E 77 G7
Franzburg Germany 54°11N 12°51E 76 A8
Frascati Italy 41°48N 12°41E 93 G9
Fraser → B.C., Canada 49°7N 123°11W 170 A3
Fraser → Nfld. & L.,
  Canada 56°39N 62°10W 165 A7
Fraser, Mt. Australia 25°35S 118°20E 149 E2
Fraser I. Australia 25°15S 153°10E 151 D5
Fraser Lake Canada 54°0N 124°50W 162 C4
Fraserburg S. Africa 31°55S 21°30E 144 D3
Fraserburgh U.K. 57°42N 2°1W 65 D6
Fraserdale Canada 49°55N 81°37W 164 C3
Frasertown N.Z. 38°58S 177°28E 154 E6
Frashër Albania 40°23N 20°30E 96 F4
Frasne France 46°50N 6°10E 71 F13
Frătești Romania 43°58N 25°58E 81 G10
Frauenfeld Switz. 47°34N 8°54E 77 H4
Fray Bentos Uruguay 33°10S 58°15W 190 C4
Fray Jorge △ Chile 30°42S 71°40W 190 C1
Frazier Downs ◎
  Australia 18°48S 121°42E 148 C3
Frechilla Spain 42°8N 4°50W 88 C6
Fredericia Denmark 55°34N 9°45E 63 J3
Frederick Md., U.S.A. 39°25N 77°25W 173 F15
Frederick Okla., U.S.A. 34°23N 99°1W 176 D5
Frederick S. Dak.,
  U.S.A. 45°50N 98°31W 172 C4
Frederick E. Hyde Fjord
  Greenland 83°25N 29°0W 57 A8
Fredericksburg Pa.,
  U.S.A. 40°27N 76°26W 175 F8
Fredericksburg Tex.,
  U.S.A. 30°16N 98°52W 176 F5
Fredericksburg Va.,
  U.S.A. 38°18N 77°28W 173 F15
Fredericktown Mo.,
  U.S.A. 37°34N 90°18W 172 G8
Fredericktown Ohio,
  U.S.A. 40°29N 82°33W 174 F2
Frederico Westphalen
  Brazil 27°22S 53°24W 191 B5
Fredericton Canada 45°57N 66°40W 165 C6
Fredericton Junction
  Canada 45°41N 66°40W 165 C6
Frederikshåb = Paamiut
  Greenland 62°0N 49°43W 57 E6
Frederikshamn = Hamina
  Finland 60°34N 27°12E 84 B4
Frederikshavn Denmark 57°28N 10°31E 63 G4
Frederikssund Denmark 55°50N 12°3E 63 J6
Frederiksted
  U.S. Virgin Is. 17°43N 64°53W 183 C7
Frederiksværk Denmark 55°58N 12°4E 63 J6
Fredonia Ariz., U.S.A. 36°57N 112°32W 169 H7
Fredonia Kans., U.S.A. 37°32N 95°49W 172 G6
Fredonia N.Y., U.S.A. 42°26N 79°20W 174 D5
Fredrikstad Norway 59°13N 10°57E 63 E14
Free State □ S. Africa 28°30S 27°0E 144 C4
Freehold U.S.A. 40°16N 74°17W 175 F10
Freel Peak U.S.A. 38°52N 119°54W 170 G7
Freels, C. Nfld. & L.,
  Canada 49°15N 53°30W 165 C9
Freels, C. Nfld. & L.,
  Canada 46°37N 53°32W 165 C9
Freeman Calif., U.S.A. 35°35N 117°53W 171 K9
Freeman S. Dak.,
  U.S.A. 43°21N 97°26W 172 D5
Freeport Bahamas 26°30N 78°47W 182 A4
Freeport Fla., U.S.A. 30°30N 86°8W 178 E3
Freeport Ill., U.S.A. 42°17N 89°36W 172 D9
Freeport N.Y., U.S.A. 40°39N 73°35W 175 F11
Freeport Ohio, U.S.A. 40°12N 81°15W 174 F3
Freeport Pa., U.S.A. 40°41N 79°41W 174 F5
Freeport Tex., U.S.A. 28°57N 95°21W 176 G7
Freetown S. Leone 8°30N 13°17W 138 D2
Freeville U.S.A. 42°30N 76°20W 175 D8
Frégate, L. de la
  Canada 53°15N 74°45W 164 B5
Fregenal de la Sierra
  Spain 38°10N 6°39W 89 G4

Fregene Italy 41°51N 12°12E 93 G9
Fregon Australia 26°45S 132°1E 149 E5
Fréhel, C. France 48°40N 2°20W 70 D4
Frei Antarctica 62°30S 58°0W 55 C18
Freiberg Germany 50°55N 13°20E 76 E9
Freibourg = Fribourg
  Switz. 46°49N 7°9E 77 J3
Freiburg Baden-W.,
  Germany 47°59N 7°51E 77 H3
Freiburg Niedersachsen,
  Germany 53°49N 9°16E 76 B5
Freilassing Germany 47°50N 12°57E 77 H8
Freire Chile 38°54S 72°38W 192 A2
Freirina Chile 28°30S 71°10W 190 B1
Freising Germany 48°24N 11°45E 77 G7
Freistadt Austria 48°30N 14°30E 78 C7
Freital Germany 51°1N 13°40E 76 E9
Fréjus France 43°25N 6°44E 73 E10
Fremantle Australia 32°7S 115°47E 149 F2
Fremont Calif., U.S.A. 37°32N 121°57W 170 H4
Fremont Mich., U.S.A. 43°28N 85°57W 173 D11
Fremont Nebr., U.S.A. 41°26N 96°30W 172 E5
Fremont Ohio, U.S.A. 41°21N 83°7W 173 E12
Fremont → U.S.A. 38°24N 110°42W 168 G8
French Camp U.S.A. 37°53N 121°16W 170 H5
French Cays = Plana Cays
  Bahamas 22°38N 73°30W 183 B5
French Creek →
  U.S.A. 41°24N 79°50W 174 E5
French Frigate Shoals
  U.S.A. 23°45N 166°10W 167 L6
French Guiana ☑
  S. Amer. 4°0N 53°0W 187 C8
French I. Australia 38°20S 145°22E 153 E6
French Island △
  Australia 38°20S 145°22E 153 E6
French Pass N.Z. 40°55S 173°55E 155 M4
French Polynesia ☑
  Pac. Oc. 20°0S 145°0W 157 J13
French Riviera = Azur, Côte d'
  France 43°25N 7°10E 73 E11
Frenchman Cr. →
  N. Amer. 48°31N 107°10W 168 B10
Frenchman Cr. →
  U.S.A. 40°14N 100°50W 172 E3
Frenda Algeria 35°2N 1°1E 136 A4
Frenštát pod Radhoštěm
  Czechia 49°33N 18°13E 83 D11
Fresco Côte d'Ivoire 5°3N 5°31W 138 D3
Fresco → Brazil 7°15S 51°30W 187 E8
Freshfield, C.
  Antarctica 68°25S 151°10E 55 C10
Fresnay-sur-Sarthe France 48°17N 0°1E 70 D7
Fresnillo Mexico 23°10N 102°53W 180 C4
Fresno U.S.A. 36°44N 119°47W 170 J7
Fresno Alhándiga Spain 40°42N 5°37W 88 E5
Fresno Res. U.S.A. 48°36N 109°57W 168 B9
Freudenstadt Germany 48°27N 8°24E 77 G4
Frévent France 50°15N 2°17E 71 B9
Frew → Australia 20°0S 135°38E 150 C2
Frewsburg U.S.A. 42°3N 79°10W 174 D5
Freycinet △ Australia 42°11S 148°19E 151 G4
Freycinet Pen.
  Australia 42°10S 148°25E 151 G4
Freyming-Merlebach
  France 49°9N 6°48E 71 C13
Freyung Germany 48°48N 13°31E 77 G9
Fria Guinea 10°27N 13°38W 138 C2
Fria, C. Namibia 18°0S 12°0E 144 B1
Friant U.S.A. 36°59N 119°43W 170 J7
Frías Argentina 28°40S 65°5W 190 B2
Fribourg Switz. 46°49N 7°9E 77 J3
Fribourg □ Switz. 46°40N 7°0E 77 J3
Fridafors Sweden 56°25N 14°39E 63 H8
Friday Harbor U.S.A. 48°32N 123°1W 170 B3
Friedberg Bayern,
  Germany 48°21N 10°59E 77 G6
Friedberg Hessen,
  Germany 50°19N 8°45E 77 E4
Friedens U.S.A. 40°3N 78°59W 174 F6
Friedland Germany 53°40N 13°33E 76 B9
Friedrichshafen Germany 47°39N 9°30E 77 H5
Friedrichskoog Germany 54°1N 8°53E 76 A4
Friedrichstadt Germany 54°23N 9°6E 76 A5
Friendship U.S.A. 42°12N 78°8W 174 D6
Friesach Austria 46°57N 14°24E 78 E7
Friesack Germany 52°44N 12°34E 76 C8
Friesland □ Neths. 53°5N 5°50E 69 A5
Friesoythe Germany 53°1N 7°51E 76 B3
Frigate Seychelles 4°35S 55°56E 141 b
Friggesund Sweden 61°54N 16°32E 62 C10
Frillesås Sweden 57°20N 12°12E 63 G6
Frinnaryd Sweden 57°55N 14°50E 63 G8
Frio → U.S.A. 28°26N 98°11W 176 G5
Frio, C. Brazil 22°50S 41°50W 184 F6
Frisco U.S.A. 33°8N 96°49W 176 E6
Friona U.S.A. 34°38N 102°43W 176 D3
Fristad Sweden 57°50N 13°0E 63 G7
Fritch U.S.A. 35°38N 101°36W 176 D4
Fritsla Sweden 57°33N 12°47E 63 G6
Fritzlar Germany 51°7N 9°16E 76 D5
Friuli-Venézia Giulia □
  Italy 46°0N 13°0E 93 B9
Friza, Proliv Russia 45°30N 149°0E 107 E15
Frobisher B. = Iqaluit
  Canada 63°44N 68°31W 161 E18
Frobisher L. Canada 56°20N 108°15W 163 B7
Frohavet Norway 64°0N 9°30E 60 E13
Frohnleiten Austria 47°16N 15°19E 78 E8
Frolovo Russia 49°45N 43°40E 86 E7
Frombork Poland 54°21N 19°41E 83 A10
Frome U.K. 51°14N 2°19W 67 F5
Frome, L. Australia 30°45S 139°45E 152 A3
Frome Downs
  Australia 31°13S 139°45E 152 A3
Frómista Spain 42°16N 4°25W 88 C6
Front Range U.S.A. 40°25N 105°45W 168 F11
Front Royal U.S.A. 38°55N 78°12W 173 F14
Fronteira Portugal 39°3N 7°39W 89 F3
Fronteiras Brazil 7°5S 40°37W 189 B3
Frontenac △ Canada 44°20N 76°20W 175 B8
Frontera Canary Is. 27°47N 17°59W 100 G2
Frontera Mexico 18°30N 92°42W 181 D6
Fronteras Mexico 30°56N 109°31W 180 A3
Frontignan France 43°27N 3°34E 72 E7
Frosinone Italy 41°38N 13°19E 94 A6
Frostburg U.S.A. 39°39N 78°56W 173 F14
Frostisen Norway 68°14N 17°10E 60 B6
Frostproof U.S.A. 27°45N 81°32W 179 H8
Frouard France 48°47N 6°8E 71 D13

Frövi Sweden 59°28N 15°24E 62 E9
Frøya Norway 63°43N 8°40E 60 E13
Fruita U.S.A. 39°9N 108°44E 168 G9
Fruithurst U.S.A. 33°44N 85°26W 178 B4
Fruitland Park U.S.A. 28°51N 81°54W 178 G8
Frumoasa Romania 46°28N 25°48E 81 D10
Frunze = Bishkek
  Kyrgyzstan 42°54N 74°46E 109 D8
Frunzivka Ukraine 47°20N 29°45E 81 C14
Fruška Gora Serbia 45°7N 19°30E 80 E4
Fruška Gora △ Serbia 45°8N 19°40E 96 A3
Frutal Brazil 20°0S 49°0W 187 H9
Frutigen Switz. 46°35N 7°38E 77 J3
Frýdek-Místek Czechia 49°40N 18°20E 83 D11
Frýdlant Czechia 50°56N 15°9E 78 A8
Fryeburg U.S.A. 44°1N 70°59W 175 D14
Fryvaldov = Jeseník
  Czechia 50°14N 17°8E 79 A3
Fthiotída Greece 38°50N 22°25E 98 C4
Fu Jiang → China 30°0N 106°16E 116 C6
Fu Xian = Wafangdian
  China 39°38N 121°58E 115 E11
Fu'an China 27°11N 119°36E 117 D12
Fubian China 31°17N 102°22E 116 B4
Fucécchio Italy 43°44N 10°48E 92 E7
Fucheng China 37°50N 116°10E 114 F9
Fuchou = Fuzhou
  China 26°5N 119°16E 117 D12
Fuchū Japan 34°34N 133°14E 113 G6
Fuchuan China 24°50N 111°5E 117 E8
Fuchun Jiang → China 30°5N 120°5E 117 B13
Fúcino, Piana del Italy 42°2N 13°31E 93 F10
Fuding China 27°20N 120°12E 117 D13
Fuencaliente Canary Is. 28°28N 17°50W 100 G2
Fuencaliente Spain 38°25N 4°18W 89 G6
Fuencaliente, Pta.
  Canary Is. 28°27N 17°51W 100 G2
Fuengirola Spain 36°32N 4°41W 89 J6
Fuenlabrada Spain 40°17N 3°48W 88 E7
Fuensalida Spain 40°3N 4°12W 88 E6
Fuente-Álamo Spain 38°44N 1°24W 91 G3
Fuente Álamo de Murcia
  Spain 37°42N 1°6W 91 H3
Fuente de Cantos Spain 38°15N 6°18W 89 G4
Fuente del Maestre Spain 38°31N 6°28W 89 G4
Fuente el Fresno Spain 39°14N 3°46W 89 F7
Fuente Obejuna Spain 38°15N 5°25W 89 G5
Fuente Palmera Spain 37°42N 5°6W 89 H5
Fuentes de Andalucía
  Spain 37°28N 5°20W 89 H5
Fuentes de Ebro Spain 41°31N 0°38W 90 D4
Fuentes de León Spain 38°5N 6°32W 89 G4
Fuentes de Oñoro Spain 40°33N 6°52W 88 E4
Fuentesaúco Spain 41°15N 5°30W 88 D5
Fuerte → Mexico 25°54N 109°22W 180 B3
Fuerte Olimpo Paraguay 21°0S 57°51W 190 A4
Fuerteventura
  Canary Is. 28°30N 14°0W 100 F6
Fuerteventura ✈ (FUE)
  Canary Is. 28°24N 13°52W 100 F6
Fufeng China 34°22N 108°0E 114 G5
Fugong China 27°5N 98°47E 116 C2
Fugou China 34°3N 114°25E 114 G8
Fugu China 39°2N 111°3E 114 E6
Fuhai China 47°16N 132°1E 111 B15
Fuhaymī Iraq 34°16N 42°10E 105 C4
Fuhlsbüttel, Hamburg ✈ (HAM)
  Germany 53°35N 9°59E 76 B5
Fuidhaigh = Wiay U.K. 57°24N 7°13W 65 D1
Fuji Japan 35°9N 138°39E 113 G9
Fuji-Hakone-Izu △
  Japan 35°15N 138°45E 113 G9
Fuji-San Japan 35°22N 138°44E 113 G9
Fuji-Yoshida Japan 35°30N 138°46E 113 G9
Fujian □ China 26°0N 118°0E 117 E12
Fujin China 47°16N 132°1E 111 B15
Fujinomiya Japan 35°10N 138°40E 113 G9
Fujisawa Japan 35°22N 139°29E 113 G9
Fujiyama, Mt. = Fuji-San
  Japan 35°22N 138°44E 113 G9
Fukagawa Japan 43°43N 142°2E 112 C11
Fukang China 44°10N 87°58E 109 D11
Fukien = Fujian □
  China 26°0N 118°0E 117 E12
Fukuchiyama Japan 35°19N 135°9E 113 G7
Fukue Japan 32°41N 128°51E 113 H4
Fukue-Shima Japan 32°40N 128°45E 113 H4
Fukui Japan 36°5N 136°10E 113 F8
Fukui □ Japan 36°0N 136°12E 113 G8
Fukuoka Japan 33°39N 130°21E 113 H5
Fukuoka □ Japan 33°30N 131°0E 113 H5
Fukushima Japan 37°44N 140°28E 112 F10
Fukushima □ Japan 37°30N 140°15E 112 F10
Fukuyama Japan 34°35N 133°20E 113 G6
Fulacunda Guinea-Biss. 11°44N 15°3W 138 C1
Fulaga Fiji 19°8S 178°33W 154 a
Fulan → Sweden 61°18N 13°4E 62 C7
Fulda Germany 50°32N 9°40E 76 E5
Fulda → Germany 51°25N 9°39E 76 D5
Fuling China 29°40N 107°20E 116 C6
Fullerton Calif.,
  U.S.A. 33°53N 117°56W 171 M9
Fullerton Nebr., U.S.A. 41°22N 97°58W 172 E5
Fülöpszállás Hungary 46°49N 19°15E 80 D4
Fulton Mo., U.S.A. 38°52N 91°57W 172 F8
Fulton N.Y., U.S.A. 43°19N 76°25W 175 C8
Fulufjället Sweden 61°32N 12°41E 62 C6
Fumay France 49°58N 4°40E 71 C11
Fumel France 44°30N 0°58E 72 D4
Fumin China 25°10N 102°20E 116 E4
Funabashi Japan 35°45N 139°59E 113 G10
Funäsdalen Sweden 62°32N 12°34E 62 B6
Funchal Madeira 32°38N 16°54W 100 D3
Funchal ✈ (FNC)
  Madeira 32°42N 16°45W 100 D3
Fundación Colombia 10°31N 74°11W 186 A4
Fundão Brazil 19°55S 40°24W 189 E2
Fundão Portugal 40°8N 7°30W 88 E3
Fundu Moldovei
  Romania 47°32N 25°24E 81 C10
Fundulea Romania 44°28N 26°31E 81 F11
Fundy, B. of Canada 45°0N 66°0W 165 C6
Funing Hebei, China 39°53N 119°12E 115 E10

Funing Jiangsu, China 33°45N 119°50E 115 H10
Funing Yunnan, China 23°35N 105°45E 116 F5
Funiu Shan China 33°30N 112°20E 114 H7
Funsi Ghana 10°21N 1°54W 138 C4
Funtua Nigeria 11°30N 7°18E 139 C6
Fuping Hebei, China 38°48N 114°12E 114 E8
Fuping Shaanxi, China 34°42N 109°10E 114 G5
Fuqing China 25°41N 119°21E 117 E12
Fuquan China 26°40N 107°27E 116 D6
Furano Japan 43°21N 142°23E 112 C11
Furāt, Nahr al → Asia 31°0N 47°25E 128 D5
Fürg Iran 28°18N 55°13E 129 D7
Furman U.S.A. 32°41N 81°11W 178 C8
Furnás Spain 39°3N 1°32E 100 B8
Furnas, Represa de Brazil 20°50S 45°30W 191 A6
Furneaux Group Australia 40°10S 147°50E 151 G4
Furqlus Syria 34°36N 37°8E 130 A6
Fürstenau Germany 52°31N 7°40E 76 C3
Fürstenberg Germany 53°10N 13°8E 76 B9
Fürstenfeld Austria 47°3N 16°3E 78 D9
Fürstenfeldbruck Germany 48°11N 11°15E 77 G7
Fürstenwalde Germany 52°22N 14°3E 76 C10
Fürth Germany 49°28N 10°59E 77 F6
Fürth im Wald Germany 49°18N 12°50E 77 F8
Furtwangen Germany 48°2N 8°12E 77 G4
Furudal Sweden 61°10N 15°11E 62 C9
Furukawa = Ōsaki Japan 38°34N 140°58E 112 E10
Furulund Sweden 55°46N 13°6E 63 J7
Furuvik Sweden 61°38N 17°20E 62 D11
Fury and Hecla Str. Canada 69°56N 84°0W 161 D15
Fusagasugá Colombia 4°21N 74°22W 186 C4
Fuscaldo Italy 39°25N 16°2E 95 C9
Fushan Shandong, China 37°30N 121°15E 115 F11
Fushan Shanxi, China 35°58N 111°51E 114 G6
Fushë Arrëz Albania 42°4N 20°2E 96 D4
Fushë Kosovë Kosovo 42°40N 21°5E 96 D5
Fushë Kruja Albania 41°29N 19°43E 96 E3
Fushun Liaoning, China 41°50N 123°56E 115 D12
Fushun Sichuan, China 29°13N 104°52E 116 C5
Fusong China 42°20N 127°15E 115 C14
Füssen Germany 47°34N 10°42E 77 H6
Fustic Barbados 13°16N 59°38W 183 g
Fusui China 22°40N 107°56E 116 F6
Futian China 22°32N 114°4E 111 a
Futog Serbia 45°15N 19°42E 80 E4
Futrono Chile 40°8S 72°24W 192 B2
Fuwa Egypt 31°12N 30°33E 137 E7
Fuxian Hu China 24°30N 102°53E 116 E4
Fuxin China 42°5N 121°48E 115 C11
Fuyang Anhui, China 33°0N 115°48E 117 A10
Fuyang Zhejiang, China 30°5N 119°57E 117 B12
Fuyang He → China 38°12N 117°0E 114 E9
Fuying Dao China 26°34N 120°9E 117 D13
Fuyong China 22°40N 113°49E 111 a
Fuyu Heilongjiang, China 47°49N 124°27E 111 B13
Fuyu Jilin, China 45°12N 124°43E 115 B13
Fuyuan China 25°40N 104°16E 116 E5
Fuyun China 47°0N 89°28E 109 C11
Füzesgyarmat Hungary 47°6N 21°14E 80 C6
Fuzhou = Linchuan China 27°57N 116°15E 117 D11
Fuzhou China 26°5N 119°16E 117 D12
Füzuli Azerbaijan 39°36N 47°8E 105 C12
Fyn Denmark 55°20N 10°30E 63 J4
Fyne, L. U.K. 55°59N 5°23E 65 F3
Fynshav Denmark 54°50N 9°59E 63 K3

G

Ga Ghana 9°47N 2°30W 138 D4
Gaalkacyo Somalia 6°30N 47°30E 131 F4
Gaanda Nigeria 10°10N 12°27E 139 C6
Gabas → France 43°46N 0°42W 72 E3
Gabba Australia 9°45S 142°38E 150 a
Gabela Angola 11°0S 14°24E 140 G2
Gabès Tunisia 33°53N 10°2E 136 B6
Gabès □ Tunisia 33°35N 9°30E 136 B6
Gabès, G. de Tunisia 34°0N 10°30E 136 B6
Gabgaba, W. → Egypt 22°10N 33°5E 137 C3
Gabia la Grande Spain 37°8N 3°40W 89 H7
Gabin Poland 52°23N 19°41E 83 F6
Gabon ■ Africa 0°10S 10°0E 140 E2
Gaborone Botswana 24°45S 25°57E 144 B4
Gabriels U.S.A. 44°26N 74°12W 175 B10
Gābrīk Iran 25°44N 58°28E 129 E8
Gabrovo Bulgaria 42°52N 25°19E 97 D9
Gacé France 48°49N 0°20E 70 D7
Gāch Sār Iran 36°7N 51°19E 129 B6
Gachsārān Iran 30°15N 50°45E 129 D6
Gacko Bos.-H. 43°10N 18°33E 96 C2
Gad Hinglaj India 16°14N 74°21E 127 F2
Gadag India 15°30N 75°45E 127 G2
Gadap Pakistan 25°5N 67°28E 124 G2
Gadarwara India 22°50N 78°50E 125 H8
Gadebusch Germany 53°42N 11°7E 76 B7
Gadhada India 22°0N 71°35E 124 J4
Gádor, Sierra de Spain 36°57N 2°45W 89 J8
Gadra Pakistan 25°40N 70°38E 124 G4
Gadsden Ala., U.S.A. 34°1N 86°1W 178 B3
Gadsden S.C., U.S.A. 33°51N 80°46W 178 B9
Gadwal India 16°10N 77°50E 127 F3
Gadyach = Hadyach Ukraine 50°21N 34°0E 85 G8
Găeşti Romania 44°48N 25°19E 81 F10
Gaeta Italy 41°12N 13°35E 94 A6
Gaeta, G. di Italy 41°5N 13°30E 94 A6
Gaffney U.S.A. 35°5N 81°39W 177 D14
Gafsa Tunisia 34°24N 8°43E 136 B6
Gagarawa Nigeria 12°25N 9°32E 139 C6
Gagaria India 25°43N 70°46E 124 G4
Gagarin Russia 55°38N 35°0E 84 E8
Gagauz Moldova 46°10N 28°40E 81 E12
Gaggenau Germany 48°48N 8°18E 77 G4
Gagino Russia 55°15N 45°1E 86 C7
Gagliano del Capo Italy 39°50N 18°22E 95 C11
Gagnef Sweden 60°36N 15°5E 62 D9
Gagnoa Côte d'Ivoire 6°56N 6°16W 138 D3
Gagnon Canada 51°50N 68°5W 165 B6
Gagnon, L. Canada 62°3N 110°27W 163 A6
Gagra Georgia 43°20N 40°10E 87 A3
Gahini Rwanda 1°50S 30°30E 142 C3

Gahmar India 25°27N 83°49E 125 G10
Gahnpa = Ganta Liberia 7°15N 8°59W 138 D3
Gai Xian = Gaizhou China 40°22N 122°20E 115 D12
Gaidouronisi Greece 34°53N 25°41E 101 E7
Gail → Austria 46°36N 13°53E 78 E6
Gaillac France 43°54N 1°54E 72 E5
Gaillimh = Galway Ireland 53°17N 9°3W 64 C2
Gaillon France 49°10N 1°20E 70 C8
Gaimán Argentina 43°10S 65°25W 192 B3
Gaines U.S.A. 41°46N 77°35W 174 C7
Gainesville Fla., U.S.A. 29°40N 82°20W 179 F7
Gainesville Ga., U.S.A. 34°18N 83°50W 177 D13
Gainesville Mo., U.S.A. 36°36N 92°26W 172 G7
Gainesville Tex., U.S.A. 33°38N 97°8W 176 E6
Gainsborough U.K. 53°24N 0°46W 66 D7
Gairdner, L. Australia 31°30S 136°0E 152 A2
Gairloch U.K. 57°43N 5°41W 65 D3
Gairloch L. U.K. 57°43N 5°45W 65 D3
Gaizhou China 40°22N 122°20E 115 D12
Gaj Croatia 45°28N 17°3E 80 E2
Gaj = Pakistan 26°26N 67°21E 124 F2
Gajendragarh India 15°44N 75°59E 127 G2
Gakuch Pakistan 36°7N 73°45E 125 A5
Gal Oya → Sri Lanka 7°0N 81°30E 127 L5
Gal Oya Res. Sri Lanka 7°5N 81°30E 127 L5
Galabovo Bulgaria 42°8N 25°55E 97 D9
Galàla, Gebel el Egypt 29°21N 32°22E 137 E8
Galán, Cerro Argentina 25°55S 66°52W 190 B2
Galana → Kenya 3°9S 40°8E 142 C5
Galanta Slovakia 48°11N 17°45E 79 C10
Galapagar Spain 40°36N 3°58W 88 E7
Galápagos = Colón, Arch. de Ecuador 0°0 91°0W 184 D1
Galapagos Fracture Zone Pac. Oc. 3°0N 110°0W 157 G17
Galapagos Rise Pac. Oc. 15°0S 95°0W 157 J18
Galashiels U.K. 55°37N 2°49W 65 F6
Galatas Greece 37°30N 23°26E 98 D5
Galatea N.Z. 38°24S 176°45E 154 E5
Galateia Cyprus 35°25N 34°4E 101 D13
Galati Romania 45°27N 28°2E 81 E13
Galati □ Romania 45°45N 27°30E 81 E12
Galatia Turkey 39°30N 33°0E 104 C5
Galatina Italy 40°10N 18°10E 95 B11
Galátone Italy 40°9N 18°4E 95 B11
Galax U.S.A. 36°40N 80°56W 173 G13
Galaxídi Greece 38°22N 22°23E 98 C4
Galbîn Govĭ Mongolia 43°0N 107°0E 114 C4
Galcaio = Gaalkacyo Somalia 6°30N 47°30E 131 F4
Galdhøpiggen Norway 61°38N 8°18E 60 F13
Galeana Chihuahua, Mexico 30°7N 107°38W 180 A3
Galeana Nuevo León, Mexico 24°50N 100°4W 180 A3
Galela Indonesia 1°50N 127°49E 119 D7
Galera → India 16°50N 82°0E 126 C6
Galera, Pta. Chile 39°55S 73°43W 192 A2
Galera Pt. Trin. & Tob. 10°49N 60°54W 183 D7
Galesburg U.S.A. 40°57N 90°22W 172 E8
Galeton U.S.A. 41°44N 77°39W 174 C7
Galheirão → Brazil 12°23S 45°5W 189 C11
Gali Georgia 42°37N 41°46E 87 A5
Galicea Mare Romania 44°4N 23°19E 81 F8
Galich Russia 58°22N 42°24E 86 A6
Galiche Bulgaria 43°34N 23°53E 96 C7
Galicia □ Spain 42°43N 7°45W 88 C3
Galičica △ Macedonia 41°2N 20°55E 96 E4
Galilee = Hagalil Israel 32°53N 35°18E 130 C4
Galilee, L. Australia 22°20S 145°50E 150 C4
Galilee, Sea of = Yam Kinneret Israel 32°45N 35°35E 130 C4
Galim Cameroon 7°6N 12°25E 139 D7
Galina Pt. Jamaica 18°24N 76°58W 182 a
Galinoporni Cyprus 35°31N 34°18E 101 D13
Galion U.S.A. 40°44N 82°47W 174 F2
Galite, Îs. de la Tunisia 37°30N 8°59E 136 A5
Galiuro Mts. U.S.A. 32°30N 110°20W 169 K8
Galiwinku Australia 12°2S 135°34E 150 A2
Gallan Hd. U.K. 58°15N 7°2W 65 C1
Gallarate Italy 45°40N 8°48E 92 C5
Gallatin U.S.A. 36°24N 86°27W 177 C11
Galle Sri Lanka 6°5N 80°10E 127 L5
Gállego → Spain 41°39N 0°51W 90 D3
Gallegos → Argentina 51°35S 69°0W 192 D3
Galley Hd. Ireland 51°32N 8°55W 64 E3
Galliate Italy 45°29N 8°42E 92 C5
Gallinas, Pta. Colombia 12°28N 71°40W 186 A4
Gallipoli = Gelibolu Turkey 40°28N 26°43E 97 F10
Gallipoli Italy 40°3N 17°58E 95 B10
Gallipolis U.S.A. 38°49N 82°12W 173 F12
Gällivare Sweden 67°9N 20°40E 60 C19
Gallneukirchen Austria 48°21N 14°25E 78 C7
Gällö Sweden 62°55N 15°13E 62 B9
Gallo, C. Italy 38°13N 13°19E 94 D5
Gallocanta, L. de Spain 40°58N 1°30W 90 D3
Galloo I. U.S.A. 43°55N 76°25W 175 C8
Galloway U.K. 55°1N 4°29W 65 F4
Galloway, Mull of U.K. 54°39N 4°52W 65 G4
Gallup U.S.A. 35°32N 108°45W 169 J9
Gallur Spain 41°52N 1°19W 90 D3
Gallura Italy 41°5N 9°20E 94 A2
Galmudug Somalia 6°30N 48°0E 131 F4
Galong Australia 34°37S 148°34E 153 C8
Galoya Sri Lanka 8°10N 80°55E 127 K5
Galt U.S.A. 38°15N 121°18W 170 G5
Galten Denmark 56°9N 9°54E 63 H3
Galtür Austria 46°58N 10°11E 78 E3
Galty Mts. Ireland 52°22N 8°10W 64 D3
Galtymore Ireland 52°21N 8°11W 64 D3
Galugāh Iran 36°43N 53°48E 129 B7
Galva U.S.A. 41°10N 90°3W 172 E8
Galvarino Chile 38°24S 72°47W 192 A2
Galve de Sorbe Spain 41°13N 3°10W 90 D1
Galveston U.S.A. 29°18N 94°48W 176 E7
Galveston B. U.S.A. 29°36N 94°50W 176 E7
Gálvez Argentina 32°0S 61°14W 190 C3
Galway Ireland 53°17N 9°3W 64 C2
Galway □ Ireland 53°22N 9°1W 64 C2
Galway B. Ireland 53°13N 9°10W 64 C2
Gam → Vietnam 21°55N 105°12E 116 B5
Gamagōri Japan 34°50N 137°14E 113 G8
Gamawa Nigeria 12°10N 10°31E 139 C7
Gambaga Ghana 10°30N 0°28W 138 C4
Gambat Pakistan 27°17N 68°26E 124 F3

Gambhir → India 26°58N 77°27E 124 F6
Gambia ■ W. Afr. 13°25N 16°0W 138 C1
Gambia → W. Afr. 13°28N 16°34W 138 C1
Gambier U.S.A. 40°22N 82°23W 174 F2
Gambier, C. Australia 11°56S 130°57E 148 B5
Gambier, Îs. French Polynesia 23°8S 134°58W 157 K14
Gambier Is. Australia 35°3S 136°30E 152 C2
Gambo Canada 48°47N 54°13W 165 C9
Gamboli Pakistan 29°53N 68°24E 124 E3
Gamboma Congo 1°55S 15°52E 140 E3
Gamka → S. Africa 33°18S 21°39E 144 D3
Gamkab → Namibia 28°4S 17°54E 144 C2
Gamla Uppsala Sweden 59°54N 17°40E 62 E11
Gamlakarleby = Kokkola Finland 63°50N 23°8E 60 E20
Gamleby Sweden 57°54N 16°24E 63 G10
Gammon → Canada 51°24N 95°44W 163 C9
Gammon Ranges △ Australia 30°38S 139°8E 151 E2
Gamou Niger 14°20N 9°55E 139 C6
Gampaha Sri Lanka 7°5N 79°59E 127 L4
Gampola Sri Lanka 7°10N 80°34E 127 L5
Gamtoos → S. Africa 33°58S 25°1E 144 D4
Gamzigrad-Romuliana Serbia 43°53N 22°11E 96 C6
Gan France 43°12N 0°27W 72 E3
Gan Argentina 42°30S 68°10W 192 B3
Gan Goriama, Mts. Cameroon 7°44N 12°45E 139 D7
Gan Jiang → China 29°15N 116°0E 117 C11
Ganado U.S.A. 35°43N 109°33W 169 J9
Gananita Sudan 18°22N 33°50E 137 D3
Gananoque Canada 44°20N 76°10W 175 B8
Ganāveh Iran 29°35N 50°35E 129 D6
Gäncä Azerbaijan 40°45N 46°20E 87 K8
Gancheng China 18°51N 108°37E 117 a
Ganda Angola 13°3S 14°35E 141 G2
Gandajika Dem. Rep. of the Congo 6°46S 23°58E 140 F4
Gandak → India 25°39N 85°13E 125 G11
Gandava Pakistan 28°32N 67°32E 124 E2
Gander Canada 48°58N 54°35W 165 C9
Gander L. Canada 48°58N 54°35W 165 C9
Ganderowe Falls Zimbabwe 17°20S 29°10E 143 F2
Gandesa Spain 41°3N 0°26E 90 D5
Gandhi Sagar India 24°40N 75°40E 124 G6
Gandhinagar India 23°15N 72°45E 124 H5
Gandi Nigeria 12°55N 5°49E 139 C6
Gandino Italy 45°49N 9°54E 92 C6
Gando, Pta. Canary Is. 27°55N 15°22W 100 G4
Gandole Nigeria 8°28N 11°35E 139 D7
Gandu Brazil 13°45S 39°30W 189 C3
Gâneb Mauritania 12°39N 10°8W 138 B2
Ganedidalem = Gani Indonesia 0°48S 128°14E 119 E7
Ganga → India 23°20N 90°30E 125 H14
Ganga Sagar India 21°38N 88°5E 125 J13
Gangafani Mali 14°20N 2°20W 138 C4
Gangakher India 18°57N 76°45E 126 E3
Gangan → India 28°38N 78°58E 125 E8
Ganganagar India 29°56N 73°56E 124 E5
Gangapur Maharashtra, India 19°41N 75°1E 126 E2
Gangapur Raj., India 26°32N 76°49E 124 F7
Gangara Niger 14°35N 8°29E 139 C6
Gangaw Myanmar 22°5N 94°5E 123 H19
Gangawati India 15°30N 76°36E 127 G3
Gangdisê Shan China 31°20N 81°0E 125 D9
Ganges = Ganga → India 23°20N 90°30E 125 H14
Ganges Canada 48°51N 123°31W 162 D4
Ganges France 43°56N 3°42E 72 E7
Ganges, Mouths of the India 21°30N 90°0E 125 J14
Ganggyeong S. Korea 36°10N 127°0E 115 F14
Gânghester Sweden 57°42N 13°1E 63 G7
Gângiova Romania 43°54N 23°50E 81 G8
Gangneung S. Korea 37°45N 128°54E 115 F15
Gangoh India 29°46N 77°18E 124 E7
Gangotri △ India 30°50N 79°10E 125 D8
Gangseong S. Korea 38°24N 128°30E 115 E15
Gangtok India 27°20N 88°37E 125 F16
Gangu China 34°40N 105°15E 114 G3
Gangyao China 44°12N 126°37E 115 B14
Gani Indonesia 0°48S 128°14E 119 E7
Ganj India 27°45N 78°57E 125 F8
Ganluo China 28°58N 102°59E 116 C4
Ganmain Australia 34°47S 147°1E 153 C7
Gannan China 47°58N 123°30E 115 B13
Gannat France 46°7N 3°11E 71 F10
Gannett Peak U.S.A. 43°11N 109°39W 168 E9
Ganquan China 36°20N 109°20E 114 F5
Gänserdorf Austria 48°20N 16°43E 79 C9
Ganshui China 28°40N 106°40E 116 C6
Gansu □ China 36°0N 104°0E 114 G3
Ganta Liberia 7°15N 8°59W 138 D3
Gantheaume, C. Australia 36°4S 137°32E 152 D2
Gantheaume B. Australia 27°40S 114°10W 149 E1
Gantsevichi = Hantsavichy Belarus 52°49N 26°30E 75 B14
Ganyem = Genyem Indonesia 2°46S 140°12E 119 E10
Ganyu China 34°50N 119°8E 115 G10
Ganyushkino Kazakhstan 46°35N 49°20E 87 J10
Ganzhou China 25°51N 114°56E 117 E10
Gao Mali 16°15N 0°5W 138 B4
Gao Xian China 28°30N 104°32E 116 C5
Gao'an China 28°26N 115°17E 117 C10
Gaobeidian China 39°1N 115°51E 114 E8
Gaocheng China 38°2N 114°41E 114 E8
Gaohebu China 30°43N 114°9E 117 B11
Gaokeng China 27°40N 113°58E 117 D9
Gaolan China 21°55N 113°10E 111 a
Gaoligong Shan China 24°45N 98°18E 116 E2
Gaomi China 36°20N 119°42E 115 F10
Gaoping China 35°45N 112°55E 114 G7
Gaotang China 36°50N 116°15E 114 F9
Gaoua Burkina Faso 10°20N 3°8W 138 C4
Gaoual Guinea 11°45N 13°25W 138 C2

Gaoyang China 38°40N 115°45E 114 E8
Gaoyao China 23°3N 112°27E 117 F9
Gaoyou China 32°47N 119°26E 117 A12
Gaoyou Hu China 32°45N 119°20E 117 A12
Gaoyuan China 37°8N 117°58E 115 F9
Gaozhou China 21°58N 110°50E 117 G8
Gap France 44°33N 6°5E 73 D10
Gapat → India 24°30N 82°28E 125 G10
Gar China 32°10N 79°58E 110 E4
Gara, L. Ireland 53°57N 8°26W 64 C3
Garāb Iran 33°27N 47°16E 105 F12
Garabogazköl Aylagy Turkmenistan 41°0N 53°30E 108 D4
Garachico Canary Is. 28°22N 16°46W 100 F3
Garachiné Panama 8°0N 78°12W 182 E4
Garafia Canary Is. 28°48N 17°57W 100 F2
Garagum Turkmenistan 39°30N 60°0E 129 B8
Garah Australia 29°5S 149°38E 151 D4
Garajonay Canary Is. 28°7N 17°14W 100 F2
Garajonay △ Canary Is. 28°7N 17°14W 100 F2
Garamba △ Dem. Rep. of the Congo 4°0N 29°40E 142 B2
Garango Burkina Faso 11°48N 0°34W 139 C4
Garanhuns Brazil 8°50S 36°30W 189 B3
Garautha India 25°34N 79°18E 125 G8
Garawa → Australia 16°43S 136°51E 150 B2
Garawe Liberia 4°35N 8°0W 138 E3
Garba Tula Kenya 0°30N 38°32E 142 B4
Garberville U.S.A. 40°6N 123°48W 168 F2
Garbiyang India 30°8N 80°54E 125 D9
Garbsen Germany 52°26N 9°31E 76 C5
Garças → Brazil 8°43S 39°41W 189 B3
Gard → France 44°2N 4°10E 73 D8
Gard □ France 43°51N 4°37E 73 E8
Garda, L. di Italy 45°40N 10°41E 92 C7
Gardabani Georgia 41°27N 45°5E 87 K7
Gardanne France 43°27N 5°27E 73 E9
Gårdby Sweden 56°36N 16°38E 63 H10
Garde L. Canada 62°50N 106°13W 163 A7
Gardelegen Germany 52°32N 11°24E 76 C7
Garden City Ga., U.S.A. 32°6N 81°9W 178 C8
Garden City Kans., U.S.A. 37°58N 100°53W 172 G3
Garden City Tex., U.S.A. 31°52N 101°29W 176 F3
Garden Grove U.S.A. 33°47N 117°55W 171 M9
Gardens of Stone △ Australia 33°14S 150°11E 153 B9
Gardez Afghan. 33°37N 69°9E 124 C3
Gardiki Greece 38°50N 21°55E 98 C3
Gardiner Maine, U.S.A. 44°14N 69°47W 173 C19
Gardiner Mont., U.S.A. 45°2N 110°22W 168 D8
Gardiners I. U.S.A. 41°6N 72°6W 175 E12
Gardner Fla., U.S.A. 27°21N 81°48W 179 H8
Gardner Mass., U.S.A. 42°34N 71°59W 175 D13
Gardner Canal Canada 53°27N 128°8W 162 C3
Gardner Pinnacles U.S.A. 25°0N 168°0W 157 L6
Gardnerville U.S.A. 38°56N 119°45W 170 G7
Gardno, Jezioro Poland 54°40N 17°7E 82 A4
Gardo = Qardho Somalia 9°30N 49°6E 131 F4
Gardone Riviera Italy 45°37N 10°34E 92 C7
Gardone Val Trómpia Italy 45°41N 10°11E 92 C7
Gárdony Hungary 47°12N 18°39E 80 C3
Gares = Puente la Reina Spain 42°40N 1°49W 90 C3
Garešnica Croatia 45°36N 16°56E 93 C13
Garéssio Italy 44°12N 8°2E 92 D5
Garey U.S.A. 34°53N 120°19W 171 L6
Garfield U.S.A. 47°1N 117°9W 168 C5
Garforth U.K. 53°47N 1°24W 66 D6
Gargaliani Greece 37°4N 21°38E 98 D3
Gargan, Mt. France 45°37N 1°39E 72 C5
Gargano ∩ Italy 41°43N 15°52E 93 G12
Gargantua, C. Canada 47°36N 85°2W 173 B11
Gargett Australia 21°9S 148°46E 150 b
Gargouna Mali 15°56N 0°13E 139 B5
Gargždai Lithuania 55°43N 21°24E 84 B2
Garhchiroli India 20°10N 80°0E 126 D5
Garibaldi Canada 49°50N 122°40W 162 D4
Gariep, L. S. Africa 30°40S 25°40E 144 D3
Garies S. Africa 30°32S 17°59E 144 C2
Garig Gunak Barlu △ Australia 11°26S 131°58E 148 B5
Garigliano → Italy 41°13N 13°45E 94 A6
Garissa Kenya 0°25S 39°40E 142 C4
Garissa □ Kenya 0°20S 40°10E 142 C5
Garkida Nigeria 10°27N 12°36E 139 C7
Garko Nigeria 11°45N 8°35E 139 C6
Garland Tex., U.S.A. 32°54N 96°38W 176 E6
Garland Utah, U.S.A. 41°45N 112°10W 168 F7
Garlasco Italy 45°12N 8°55E 92 C5
Garliava Lithuania 54°49N 23°52E 82 D10
Garlin France 43°33N 0°16W 72 E3
Garmāb Semnān, Iran 35°25N 56°45E 128 C8
Garmāb Zanjān, Iran 35°50N 48°11E 105 E13
Garmisch-Partenkirchen Germany 47°30N 11°6E 77 H7
Garmsār Iran 35°20N 52°25E 129 C7
Garner U.S.A. 43°6N 93°36W 172 D7
Garnett U.S.A. 38°17N 95°14W 172 F6
Garnpung L. Australia 33°25S 143°10E 152 B5
Garo Hills India 25°30N 90°30E 125 G14
Garoe = Garoowe Somalia 8°25N 48°33E 131 F4
Garonne → France 45°2N 0°36W 72 C2
Garonne, Canal Latéral à la France 44°15N 0°18E 72 D4
Garoowe Somalia 8°25N 48°33E 131 F4
Garot India 24°19N 75°41E 124 G6
Garou, L. Mali 16°20N 3°9W 138 B4
Garoua Cameroon 9°19N 13°21E 139 D7
Garpenberg Sweden 60°19N 16°12E 62 D10
Garphyttan Sweden 59°18N 14°56E 62 E8
Garrauli India 25°5N 79°22E 125 G8
Garrel Germany 52°57N 8°1E 76 C4
Garrison Mont., U.S.A. 46°31N 112°49W 168 C7
Garrison N. Dak., U.S.A. 47°40N 101°25W 172 B3
Garrison Res. = Sakakawea, L. U.S.A. 47°30N 101°25W 172 B3
Garron Pt. U.K. 55°3N 5°59W 64 A6
Garrovillas de Alconétar Spain 39°43N 6°33W 89 F4
Garrucha Spain 37°11N 1°49W 91 H3
Garry → U.K. 56°44N 3°47W 65 E5
Garry, L. Canada 65°58N 100°18W 160 D11
Garrygala Turkmenistan 38°31N 56°29E 129 B8

Gàrsen Kenya 2°20S 40°5E 142 C5
Garson L. Canada 56°19N 110°2W 163 B6
Garstang U.K. 53°55N 2°46W 66 D5
Gartempe → France 46°47N 0°49E 72 B4
Gartz Germany 53°13N 14°22E 76 B10
Garu Ghana 10°55N 0°11W 139 C4
Garu India 23°40N 84°14E 125 H11
Garub Namibia 26°37S 16°0E 144 C2
Garut Indonesia 7°14S 107°53E 119 G12
Garvão Portugal 37°42N 8°21W 89 H2
Garvie Mts. N.Z. 45°30S 168°50E 155 F3
Garwa = Garoua Cameroon 9°19N 13°21E 139 D7
Garwa India 24°11N 83°47E 125 H11
Garwolin Poland 51°55N 21°38E 83 G8
Gary U.S.A. 41°36N 87°20W 172 E10
Garz Germany 54°19N 13°20E 76 A9
Garzê China 31°38N 100°1E 116 B3
Garzón Colombia 2°10N 75°40W 186 C3
Gas-San Japan 38°32N 140°1E 112 E10
Gasan Kuli = Esenguly Turkmenistan 37°37N 53°59E 108 E4
Gascogne France 43°45N 0°20E 72 E4
Gascogne, G. de Europe 44°0N 2°0W 72 E2
Gascony = Gascogne France 43°45N 0°20E 72 E4
Gascoyne → Australia 24°52S 113°37E 149 E1
Gascoyne Junction Australia 25°2S 115°17E 149 E2
Gascueña Spain 40°18N 2°31W 90 E2
Gashagar Nigeria 13°22N 12°47E 139 C7
Gashaka Nigeria 7°20N 11°29E 139 D7
Gashaka-Gumti △ Nigeria 7°23N 11°34E 139 D7
Gasherbrum Pakistan 35°40N 76°40E 125 B7
Gashua Nigeria 12°54N 11°0E 139 C7
Gaspar Str. = Gelasa, Selat Indonesia 2°20S 107°0E 118 E3
Gasparilla I. U.S.A. 26°46N 82°16W 179 J7
Gasparillo Trin. & Tob. 10°18N 61°26W 187 D7
Gaspé Canada 48°52N 64°30W 165 C7
Gaspé, C. de Canada 48°48N 64°7W 165 C7
Gaspé Pen. = Gaspésie, Pén. de la Canada 48°45N 65°40W 165 C6
Gaspésie, Pén. de la Canada 48°45N 65°40W 165 C6
Gaspésie △ Canada 48°55N 66°10W 165 C6
Gassan Burkina Faso 12°49N 3°12W 138 C4
Gassol Nigeria 8°34N 10°25E 139 D7
Gasteiz = Vitoria-Gasteiz Spain 42°50N 2°41W 90 C2
Gaston U.S.A. 33°49N 81°5W 178 B8
Gastonia U.S.A. 35°16N 81°11W 177 D14
Gastouni Greece 37°51N 21°15E 98 D3
Gastouri Greece 39°34N 19°54E 98 B1
Gastre Argentina 42°20S 69°15W 192 B3
Gästrikland Sweden 60°45N 16°40E 62 D10
Gata, C. Cyprus 34°34N 33°2E 101 E12
Gata, C. de Spain 36°41N 2°13W 91 J2
Gata, Sierra de Spain 40°20N 6°45W 88 E4
Gataga → Canada 58°35N 126°59W 162 B3
Gătaia Romania 45°26N 21°30E 80 E6
Gatchina Russia 59°35N 30°9E 84 C6
Gatehouse of Fleet U.K. 54°53N 4°12W 65 G4
Gates U.S.A. 43°9N 77°42W 174 C7
Gateshead I. Canada 70°36N 100°26W 160 C11
Gateshead U.K. 54°57N 1°35W 66 C6
Gatesville U.S.A. 31°26N 97°45W 176 F6
Gateway U.S.A. 40°38N 73°51W 175 F11
Gaths Zimbabwe 20°2S 30°32E 143 G3
Gâtinais France 48°5N 2°40E 70 D9
Gâtine, Hauteurs de France 46°35N 0°45W 72 B3
Gatineau Canada 45°29N 75°39W 175 A9
Gatineau → Canada 45°27N 75°42W 164 C4
Gatineau △ Canada 45°40N 76°0W 164 C4
Gattinara Italy 45°37N 8°22E 92 C5
Gatton Australia 27°32S 152°17E 151 D5
Gatún, L. Panama 9°7N 79°56W 182 E4
Gatwick, London ✈ (LGW) U.K. 51°10N 0°11W 67 F7
Gatyana S. Africa 32°16S 28°31E 145 D4
Gau Fiji 18°2S 179°18E 154 a
Gaucín Spain 36°31N 5°19W 89 J5
Gauer L. Canada 57°0N 97°50W 163 B9
Gauhati = Guwahati India 26°10N 91°45E 123 F17
Gauja → Latvia 57°10N 24°16E 84 B3

Gaula → Norway 63°21N 10°14E 60 E14
Gaurdak = Gowurdak Turkmenistan 37°50N 66°4E 109 F7
Gauri Phanta India 28°41N 80°36E 125 E9
Gauribidanur India 13°36N 77°22E 127 H3
Gaustatoppen Norway 59°48N 8°40E 61 C13
Gäväter Iran 25°10N 61°31E 129 E9
Gāvbandī Iran 27°12N 53°4E 129 E7
Gavdopoúla Greece 34°56N 24°0E 101 F6
Gávdos Greece 34°50N 24°5E 101 F6
Gaví Italy 44°41N 8°49E 92 D5
Gavião Portugal 39°28N 7°56W 89 F3
Gaviota U.S.A. 34°29N 120°13W 171 L6
Gāvkhūnī, Baţlāq-e Iran 32°6N 52°52E 129 C7
Gävle Sweden 60°40N 17°9E 62 D11
Gävleborg □ Sweden 61°30N 16°15E 62 C10
Gävlebukten Sweden 60°40N 17°20E 62 D11
Gavorrano Italy 42°55N 10°54E 92 E8
Gavrilov Yam Russia 57°18N 39°49E 86 B10
Gavrio Greece 37°54N 24°44E 98 D6
Gawachab Namibia 27°4S 17°55E 144 C2
Gawilgarh Hills India 21°15N 76°45E 126 D3
Gawler Australia 34°30S 138°42E 152 B2
Gawler Ranges Australia 32°30S 135°45E 152 B1
Gawu Nigeria 9°14N 6°52E 139 D6
Gaxun Nur China 42°22N 100°30E 110 C9
Gay Russia 51°27N 58°27E 108 B5
Gaya India 24°47N 85°4E 125 G11
Gaya Niger 11°52N 3°28E 139 C5
Gaya India 11°57N 9°0E 139 C6
Gayéri Burkina Faso 12°39N 0°29E 139 C5
Gaylord U.S.A. 45°2N 84°41W 173 C11
Gayndah Australia 25°35S 151°32E 151 D5
Gaysin = Haysyn Ukraine 48°57N 29°25E 81 B14
Gayvoron = Hayvoron Ukraine 48°22N 29°52E 81 B14
Gaza Gaza Strip 31°30N 34°28E 130 D3
Gaza □ Mozam. 23°10S 32°45E 145 C5
Gaza Strip □ Asia 31°29N 34°25E 130 D3
Gazanjyk = Bereket Turkmenistan 39°16N 55°32E 129 B7
Gazaoua Niger 13°32N 7°55E 139 C6
Gāzbor Iran 28°5N 58°51E 129 D8
Gazi Dem. Rep. of the Congo 1°3N 24°30E 142 B1
Gaziantep Turkey 37°6N 37°23E 104 D7
Gaziantep □ Turkey 37°0N 37°0E 104 D7
Gazimağusa = Famagusta Cyprus 35°8N 33°55E 101 D12
Gazipaşa Turkey 36°16N 32°18E 104 D5
Gazli Uzbekistan 40°14N 63°24E 108 E6
Gazojak Turkmenistan 41°11N 61°24E 108 D6
Gbadolite Dem. Rep. of the Congo 4°17N 21°1E 140 D4
Gbarnga Liberia 7°19N 9°13E 138 D3
Gboko Nigeria 7°17N 9°4E 139 D6
Gcowa Botswana 19°8S 24°18E 144 B3
Gcuwa S. Africa 32°20S 28°11E 145 D4
Gdańsk Poland 54°22N 18°40E 82 D5
Gdańsk ✈ (GDN) Poland 54°22N 18°30E 82 D5
Gdańsk B. = Gdańska, Zatoka Poland
Gdańska, Zatoka Poland 54°30N 19°20E 82 D6
Gdov Russia 58°48N 27°55E 84 C4
Gdynia Poland 54°35N 18°33E 82 D5
Geba → Guinea-Biss. 11°46N 15°36W 138 C1
Gebe Indonesia 0°5N 129°25E 119 D7
Gebeciler Turkey 38°46N 30°46E 99 C12
Gebeit Mine Sudan 21°3N 36°29E 137 C4
Gebel Abyad Sudan 19°0N 28°0E 137 D2
Gebel Iweibid Egypt 30°8N 32°13E 137 E8
Gebze Turkey 40°47N 29°25E 97 F13
Geçitkale = Lefkoniko Cyprus 35°18N 33°44E 101 D12
Gedaref Sudan 14°2N 35°28E 135 F13
Gede, Tanjung Indonesia 6°46S 105°12E 119 G11
Gediz Turkey 39°1N 29°24E 99 B11
Gediz → Turkey 38°35N 26°48E 99 C8
Gèdre France 42°47N 0°2E 72 F4
Gedser Denmark 54°35N 11°55E 63 K5
Gedung, Pulau Malaysia 5°17N 100°23E 121 c
Geegully Cr. → Australia 18°32S 123°41E 148 C3
Geel Belgium 51°10N 4°59E 69 C4
Geelong Australia 38°10S 144°22E 152 E6
Geelvink B. = Cenderawasih, Teluk Indonesia 3°0S 135°20E 119 E9
Geelvink Chan. Australia 28°30S 114°0E 149 E1
Geesthacht Germany 53°26N 10°22E 76 B6
Geidam Nigeria 12°57N 11°57E 139 C7
Geikie → Canada 57°45N 103°52W 163 B8
Geikie Gorge △ Australia 18°3S 125°41E 148 C4
Geilenkirchen Germany 50°57N 6°8E 76 E2
Geisingen Germany 47°54N 8°38E 77 H4
Geislingen Germany 48°37N 9°50E 77 G5
Geistown U.S.A. 40°18N 78°52W 174 F6
Geita Tanzania 2°48S 32°12E 142 C3
Geita □ Tanzania 2°50S 32°10E 142 C3
Geju China 23°20N 103°10E 116 F4
Gel, Meydān-e Iran 29°4N 54°50E 129 D7
Gela, G. di Italy 37°0N 14°8E 95 F7
Gela Italy 37°4N 14°15E 95 F7
Gelahun Liberia 7°55N 10°28W 138 D2
Gelang Patah Malaysia 1°27N 103°35E 121 d
Gelasa, Selat Indonesia 2°50S 107°0E 118 E3
Gelderland □ Neths. 52°5N 6°10E 69 B6
Geldern Germany 51°31N 6°20E 76 D2
Geldrop Neths. 51°25N 5°32E 69 C5
Gelehun S. Leone 8°20N 11°40W 138 D2
Gelendost Turkey 38°7N 31°1E 104 C4
Gelendzhik Russia 44°33N 38°0E 85 K10
Gelib = Jilib Somalia 0°29N 42°46E 131 G3
Gelibolu Turkey 40°28N 26°43E 97 F10
Gelibolu Yarımadası Turkey 40°26N 30°0E 97 F10
Gelidonya Burnu Turkey 36°12N 30°24E 104 D4
Gelnhausen Germany 50°11N 9°11E 77 E5
Gelnica Slovakia 48°51N 20°59E 83 G9
Gelsenkirchen Germany 51°32N 7°6E 76 D3
Gelting Germany 54°45N 9°53E 76 A5
Gelugur Malaysia 5°22N 100°18E 121 c
Gemas Malaysia 2°37N 102°36E 121 d
Gembloux Belgium 50°34N 4°43E 69 D4
Gembu Nigeria 6°42N 11°10E 139 D7
Gemena Dem. Rep. of the Congo 3°13N 19°48E 140 D3
Gemerek Turkey 39°15N 36°10E 104 C7
Gemikonağı = Karavostasi Cyprus 35°8N 32°50E 101 D11
Gemla Sweden 56°52N 14°39E 63 H8
Gemlik Turkey 40°26N 29°9E 97 F13
Gemlik Körfezi Turkey 40°25N 28°55E 97 F12
Gemona del Friuli Italy 46°16N 13°9E 93 B10
Gemsa Egypt 27°39N 33°35E 137 B3
Gemsbok △ Botswana 25°55S 21°1E 144 C3
Gemünden Germany 50°3N 9°42E 77 E5
Genadi Greece 36°2N 27°56E 101 C9
Genale → Ethiopia 6°2N 39°1E 135 G14
Genç Turkey 38°44N 40°34E 105 C9
Gençay France 46°23N 0°23E 72 B4
General Acha Argentina 37°20S 64°38W 190 D3
General Alvear B. Aires, Argentina 36°0S 60°0W 190 D4
General Alvear Mendoza, Argentina 35°0S 67°40W 190 D2
General Artigas Paraguay 26°52S 56°16W 190 B4
General Belgrano Argentina 36°35S 58°47W 190 D4
General Bernardo O'Higgins Antarctica 63°0S 58°3W 5 C18
General Cabrera Argentina 32°53S 63°52W 190 C3
General Carrera, L. S. Amer. 46°35S 72°0W 192 C2
General Cepeda Mexico 25°21N 101°22W 180 B4

General Conesa
  Argentina   40°6S 64°25W 192 B4
General Guido
  Argentina   36°40S 57°50W 190 D4
General Juan Madariaga
  Argentina   37°0S 57°0W 190 D4
General Lorenzo Vintter
  Argentina   40°45S 64°26W 192 B4
General MacArthur
  Phil.   11°18N 125°28E 119 B7
General Martín Miguel de Güemes
  Argentina   24°50S 65°0W 190 A3
General Pico Argentina 35°45S 63°50W 190 D3
General Pinedo
  Argentina   27°15S 61°20W 190 B3
General Pinto
  Argentina   34°45S 61°50W 190 C3
General Roca Argentina 39°2S 67°35W 192 A3
General Sampaio Brazil 4°2S 39°29W 189 A3
General Santos Phil.   6°5N 125°14E 119 C7
General Toshevo
  Bulgaria   43°42N 28°6E 97 C12
General Treviño
  Mexico   26°14N 99°29W 181 B5
General Trías Mexico 28°21N 106°22W 180 B3
General Viamonte
  Argentina   35°1S 61°3W 190 D3
General Villegas
  Argentina   35°5S 63°0W 190 D3
General Vintter, L.
  Argentina   43°55S 71°40W 192 B2
Genesee Idaho, U.S.A. 46°33N 116°56W 168 C5
Genesee Pa., U.S.A. 41°59N 77°54W 174 E7
Genesee → U.S.A.   43°16N 77°36W 174 C7
Geneseo Ill., U.S.A.   41°27N 90°9W 172 E8
Geneseo N.Y., U.S.A. 42°48N 77°49W 174 D7
Geneva = Genève Switz. 46°12N 6°9E 77 J2
Geneva Ala., U.S.A.   31°2N 85°52W 178 D4
Geneva Ga., U.S.A.   32°35N 84°33W 178 C5
Geneva N.Y., U.S.A.   42°52N 76°59W 174 D8
Geneva Nebr., U.S.A.   40°32N 97°36W 172 E5
Geneva Ohio, U.S.A.   41°48N 80°57W 174 E4
Geneva, L. = Léman, L.
  Europe   46°26N 6°30E 71 F13
Genève Switz.   46°12N 6°9E 77 J2
Gengenbach Germany   48°24N 8°1E 77 G4
Gengma China   23°32N 99°20E 118 F2
Genhe China   50°47N 121°31E 111 A13
Genichesk = Henichesk
  Ukraine   46°12N 34°50E 85 J8
Genil → Spain   37°42N 5°19W 89 H5
Genisea Greece   41°1N 24°57E 97 E8
Genk Belgium   50°58N 5°32E 69 D5
Genlis France   47°11N 5°12E 71 E12
Gennargentu, Mti. del
  Italy   40°1N 9°19E 94 B2
Gennes France   47°20N 0°17W 70 E6
Genoa = Génova Italy 44°25N 8°57E 92 D5
Genoa Australia   37°29S 149°35E 153 D8
Genoa N.Y., U.S.A.   42°40N 76°32W 175 D8
Genoa Nebr., U.S.A.   41°27N 97°44W 172 E5
Genoa Nev., U.S.A.   39°2N 119°50W 170 F7
Genoa → Argentina   44°55S 70°5W 192 B2
Génova Italy   44°25N 8°57E 92 D5
Génova ✈ (GOA) Italy 44°25N 8°56E 92 D5
Génova, G. di Italy   44°0N 9°0E 92 D6
Genriyetty, Ostrov
  Russia   77°6N 156°30E 107 B16
Gent Belgium   51°2N 3°42E 69 C3
Genteng Jawa Barat,
  Indonesia   7°22S 106°24E 119 G12
Genteng Jawa Timur,
  Indonesia   8°22S 114°9E 119 J17
Genthin Germany   52°25N 12°9E 76 C8
Gentio do Ouro Brazil 11°25S 42°30W 189 C2
Genyem Indonesia   2°46S 140°12E 119 E10
Genzano di Lucánia Italy 40°51N 16°2E 95 B9
Genzano di Roma Italy 41°42N 12°41E 93 G9
Geoagiu Romania   45°55N 23°12E 81 E8
Geochang S. Korea   35°41N 127°55E 115 G14
Geographe B. Australia 33°30S 115°15E 149 F2
Geographe Chan.
  Australia   24°30S 113°0E 149 D1
Geographical Society Ø
  Greenland   72°57N 23°15W 57 C8
Geoje S. Korea   34°51N 128°35E 115 G15
Geokchay = Göyçay
  Azerbaijan   40°42N 47°43E 87 K8
Georga, Zemlya Russia 80°30N 49°0E 106 A5
George S. Africa   33°58S 22°29E 144 E3
George → Canada   58°49N 66°10W 165 A6
George, L. N.S.W.,
  Australia   35°10S 149°25E 153 C8
George, L. S. Austral.,
  Australia   37°25S 140°0E 152 D4
George, L. W. Austral.,
  Australia   22°45S 123°40E 148 D3
George, L. Uganda   0°5N 30°10E 142 B3
George, L. Fla., U.S.A. 29°17N 81°36W 179 E6
George, L. N.Y.,
  U.S.A.   43°37N 73°33W 175 C11
George Bush Intercontinental,
  Houston ✈ (IAH)
  U.S.A.   29°59N 95°20W 176 E7
George Gill Ra.
  Australia   24°22S 131°45E 148 D5
George Pt. Australia 20°6S 148°36E 150 b
George River = Kangiqsualujjuaq
  Canada   58°30N 65°59W 161 F18
George Sound N.Z. 44°52S 167°25E 155 E1
George Town Australia 41°6S 146°49E 151 G4
George Town Bahamas 23°33N 75°47W 182 B4
George Town
  Cayman Is.   19°20N 81°24W 182 C3
George Town Malaysia 5°25N 100°20E 121 c
George V Land
  Antarctica   69°0S 148°0E 55 C10
George VI Sound
  Antarctica   71°0S 68°0W 55 D17
George West U.S.A. 28°20N 98°7W 176 G5
Georgetown = Janjanbureh
  Gambia   13°30N 14°47E 137 C2
Georgetown Australia 18°17S 143°33E 150 B3
Georgetown Ont.,
  Canada   43°40N 79°56W 174 C5
Georgetown P.E.I.,
  Canada   46°13N 62°24W 165 C17
Georgetown Guyana 6°50N 58°12W 186 B7
Georgetown Calif.,
  U.S.A.   38°54N 120°50W 170 G6

Georgetown Colo.,
  U.S.A.   39°42N 105°42W 168 G11
Georgetown Fla.,
  U.S.A.   29°23N 81°38W 179 F8
Georgetown Ga., U.S.A. 31°53N 85°6W 178 D4
Georgetown Ky.,
  U.S.A.   38°13N 84°33W 173 F11
Georgetown N.Y.,
  U.S.A.   42°46N 75°44W 175 D9
Georgetown Ohio,
  U.S.A.   38°52N 83°54W 173 F12
Georgetown S.C.,
  U.S.A.   33°23N 79°17W 177 E15
Georgetown Tex.,
  U.S.A.   30°38N 97°41W 176 F6
Georgia □ U.S.A.   32°50N 83°15W 178 C5
Georgia ■ Asia   42°0N 43°0E 87 J6
Georgia, Str. of
  N. Amer.   49°25N 124°0W 170 A3
Georgia Basin S. Ocean 50°45S 35°30W 55 B1
Georgian B. Canada 45°15N 81°0W 174 A4
Georgian Bay Islands △
  Canada   44°53N 79°52W 174 B5
Georgïevka
  Kazakhstan   49°19N 84°34E 109 C10
Georgina → Australia 23°30S 139°47E 150 C2
Georgina I. Canada   44°22N 79°17W 174 B5
Georgioupoli Greece 35°20N 24°15E 101 D6
Georgiyevsk Russia 44°12N 43°28E 87 H6
Georgsmarienhütte
  Germany   52°13N 8°3E 76 C4
Gera Germany   50°53N 12°4E 76 E8
Geraardsbergen Belgium 50°45N 3°53E 69 D3
Geraki Greece   37°4N 22°26E 98 D4
Geral, Serra Bahia, Brazil 14°0S 41°0W 189 C2
Geral, Serra Goiás,
  Brazil   11°15S 46°30W 189 C1
Geral, Serra Sta. Catarina,
  Brazil   26°25S 50°0W 191 B6
Geral de Goiás, Serra
  Brazil   12°0S 46°0W 189 C1
Geral do Paraná, Serra
  Brazil   15°0S 47°30W 189 D1
Geraldine N.Z.   44°5S 171°15E 155 G4
Geraldine Australia 28°48S 114°32E 149 E1
Geraldton Canada   49°44N 87°10W 164 C2
Geranium Australia 35°23S 140°11E 152 C4
Gérardmer France   48°3N 6°50E 71 D13
Gerçüş Turkey   37°34N 41°23E 105 D9
Gerdine, Mt. U.S.A. 61°35N 152°27W 166 C9
Gerede Turkey   40°45N 32°10E 104 B5
Gerês, Sierra do Portugal 41°48N 8°0W 88 D3
Gereshk Afghan.   31°47N 64°35E 122 D1
Geretsried Germany 47°51N 11°28E 77 H7
Gérgal Spain   37°7N 2°31W 89 H2
Gerik Malaysia   5°50N 101°15E 121 K3
Gering U.S.A.   41°50N 103°40W 172 E2
Gerlach U.S.A.   40°39N 119°21W 168 F14
Gerlachovský štít
  Slovakia   49°11N 20°7E 79 B13
German Bight = Deutsche Bucht
  Germany   54°15N 8°0E 76 A4
German Planina
  Macedonia   42°20N 22°0E 96 D6
Germania Land
  Greenland   77°5N 19°30W 57 B9
Germansen Landing
  Canada   55°43N 124°40W 162 B4
Germantown U.S.A. 35°5N 89°49W 177 D10
Germany ■ Europe 51°0N 10°0E 76 E6
Germencik Turkey 37°52N 27°37E 99 D9
Germering Germany 48°8N 11°22E 77 G7
Germersheim Germany 49°12N 8°22E 77 F4
Germí Iran   39°1N 48°3E 105 C13
Germiston S. Africa 26°13S 28°10E 145 C4
Gernika-Lumo Spain 43°19N 2°40W 90 B2
Gernsheim Germany 49°45N 8°30E 77 F4
Gero Japan   35°48N 137°14E 113 G8
Gerogery Australia 35°50S 147°1E 153 C7
Gerokgak Indonesia 8°11S 114°27E 119 J17
Gerolzhofen Germany 49°54N 10°21E 77 F6
Gerona = Girona Spain 41°58N 2°46E 90 D7
Geropotamos → Greece 35°3N 24°50E 101 D6
Gerrard Canada   50°30N 117°17W 162 C5
Gerringong Australia 34°46S 150°47E 153 C9
Gers □ France   43°35N 0°30E 72 E4
Gers → France   44°9N 0°39E 72 D4
Gersfeld Germany 50°27N 9°56E 76 E5
Gersoppa Falls India 14°12N 74°46E 127 G2
Gersthofen Germany 48°25N 10°53E 77 G6
Gertak Sanggul
  Malaysia   5°17N 100°12E 121 c
Gertak Sanggul, Tanjung
  Malaysia   5°16N 100°11E 121 c
Gerung Indonesia 8°43S 116°7E 119 K19
Gerzat France   45°48N 3°8E 72 C7
Gerze Turkey   41°48N 35°12E 104 B6
Geseke Germany   51°38N 8°31E 76 D4
Geser Indonesia   3°50S 130°54E 119 E8
Gesso → Italy   44°24N 7°33E 92 D4
Getafe Spain   40°18N 3°43W 88 E7
Getinge Sweden   56°49N 12°44E 63 H6
Gettysburg Pa., U.S.A. 39°50N 77°14W 173 F15
Gettysburg S. Dak.,
  U.S.A.   45°1N 99°57W 172 C4
Getxo = Algorta Spain 43°21N 2°59W 90 B2
Getz Ice Shelf Antarctica 75°0S 130°0W 55 D14
Geurie Australia   32°22S 148°50E 153 B8
Gevaş Turkey   38°15N 43°6E 105 C10
Gévaudan France   44°40N 3°40E 72 D7
Gévora → Spain   38°53N 6°57W 89 G4
Gevrai India   19°16N 75°45E 126 E2
Gex France   46°21N 6°3E 71 F13
Geyikli Turkey   39°48N 26°12E 99 B8
Geyser U.S.A.   47°16N 110°30W 168 C8
Geyserville U.S.A. 38°42N 122°54W 170 G4
Geyve Turkey   40°30N 30°18E 104 B4
Gezhouba Dam China 30°40N 111°20E 117 B8
Ghadāf, W. al → Iraq 32°56N 43°30E 105 F10
Ghadāmis Libya   30°11N 9°29E 136 B6
Ghaggar → India   29°30N 74°53E 124 E6
Ghaghara → India   25°45N 84°40E 125 G11
Ghaghat → Bangla. 25°19N 89°38E 125 G13
Ghagra India   23°17N 84°33E 125 H11
Ghagra → India   25°45N 84°40E 125 G11
Ghallamane Mauritania 23°15N 10°0W 134 D4
Ghana ■ W. Afr.   8°0N 1°0W 139 D4
Ghanpokhara Nepal 28°7N 84°14E 125 E11
Ghansor India   22°39N 80°1E 125 H9
Ghanzi Botswana   21°50S 21°34E 144 B3
Ghanzi □ Botswana 22°0S 23°0E 144 B3

Gharb-Chrarda-Beni Hssen □
  Morocco   35°35N 6°0W 136 A2
Gharbîya, Es Sahrâ el
  Egypt   27°40N 26°30E 137 B2
Ghardaïa Algeria   32°20N 3°37E 136 B6
Ghardaïa □ Algeria 31°5N 3°10E 136 B4
Ghârib, G. Egypt   28°6N 32°54E 137 B8
Gharm Tajikistan   39°0N 70°20E 106 F8
Gharyān Libya   32°10N 13°0E 135 B8
Ghāt Libya   24°59N 10°11E 135 D8
Ghatal India   22°40N 87°46E 125 H12
Ghatampur India   26°8N 80°13E 125 F9
Ghatgaon India   21°24N 85°53E 126 D7
Ghatprabha → India 16°15N 75°20E 127 F2
Ghats, Eastern India 14°0N 78°50E 127 H4
Ghats, Western India 14°0N 75°0E 127 H2
Ghatsila India   22°36N 86°29E 125 H12
Ghaṭṭī Si. Arabia   31°16N 37°31E 128 D3
Ghawdex = Gozo Malta 36°3N 14°15E 101 C1
Ghazal, Bahr el → Chad 13°0N 15°47E 135 F9
Ghazal, Bahr el →
  South Sudan   9°31N 30°25E 135 G12
Ghazaouet Algeria 35°8N 1°50W 136 A3
Ghaziabad India   28°42N 77°26E 124 E7
Ghazipur India   25°38N 83°35E 125 G10
Ghazni Afghan.   33°30N 68°28E 124 C3
Ghaznī □ Afghan.   32°10N 68°20E 122 C6
Ghedi Italy   45°24N 10°16E 92 C7
Ghelari Romania   45°38N 22°45E 80 E7
Ghent = Gent Belgium 51°2N 3°42E 69 C3
Gheorghe Gheorghiu-Dej = Oneşti
  Romania   46°28N 26°47E 81 D11
Gheorgheni Romania 46°43N 25°41E 81 D10
Gherla Romania   47°2N 23°57E 81 C8
Ghidigeni Romania 46°3N 27°30E 81 D12
Ghilarza Italy   40°7N 8°50E 94 B1
Ghimeş-Făget Romania 46°35N 26°2E 81 D11
Ghīnah, Wādī al →
  Si. Arabia   30°27N 38°14E 128 D3
Ghisonaccia France 42°1N 9°26E 73 F13
Ghisoni France   42°7N 9°12E 73 F13
Ghizar → Pakistan 36°15N 73°43E 125 A5
Ghod → India   18°30N 74°35E 126 E2
Ghogha India   21°40N 72°20E 126 D1
Ghot Ogrein Egypt 31°10N 25°20E 137 A2
Ghotaru India   27°20N 70°1E 124 F4
Ghotki Pakistan   28°5N 69°21E 124 E3
Ghowr □ Afghan.   34°0N 64°20E 122 C4
Ghughri India   22°39N 80°41E 125 H9
Ghugus India   19°58N 79°12E 126 E4
Ghulam Mohammad Barrage
  Pakistan   25°30N 68°20E 124 G3
Ghūrīān Afghan.   34°17N 61°25E 122 B2
Gia Lai = Plei Ku
  Vietnam   13°57N 108°0E 120 F7
Gia Nghia Vietnam 11°58N 107°42E 121 G6
Gia Ngoc Vietnam 14°50N 108°58E 120 E7
Gia Vuc Vietnam   14°42N 108°34E 120 E7
Giali Greece   36°41N 27°11E 99 E9
Gialtra Greece   38°51N 22°59E 98 C4
Giamama = Jamaame
  Somalia   0°4N 42°44E 131 G3
Gianitsa Greece   40°46N 22°24E 96 F5
Giannutri Italy   42°15N 11°6E 92 F8
Giant Forest U.S.A. 36°36N 118°43W 170 J8
Giant Sequoia □
  U.S.A.   36°10N 118°35W 170 K8
Giant's Causeway U.K. 55°16N 6°29W 64 A5
Giant's Tank Sri Lanka 8°51N 80°2E 127 K5
Gianyar Indonesia 8°32S 115°20E 119 K18
Giarabub = Al Jaghbūb
  Libya   29°42N 24°38E 135 C10
Giaros Greece   37°32N 24°40E 98 D6
Giarre Italy   37°43N 15°11E 95 E8
Giaveno Italy   45°2N 7°21E 92 C4
Gibara Cuba   21°9N 76°11W 182 B4
Gibbon U.S.A.   40°45N 98°51W 172 E4
Gibb River Australia 16°26S 126°26E 148 C4
Gibe III Ethiopia   7°0N 37°30E 131 F7
Gibellina Nuova Italy 37°47N 12°58E 94 E5
Gibeon Namibia   25°7S 17°45E 144 C2
Gibraleón Spain   37°23N 6°58W 89 H4
Gibraltar ☑ Europe 36°7N 5°22W 89 E5
Gibraltar, Str. of Medit. 35°55N 5°40W 89 K5
Gibraltar Range △
  Australia   29°31S 152°19E 151 E5
Gibson U.S.A.   33°14N 82°36W 178 D7
Gibson Desert Australia 24°0S 126°0E 148 D4
Gibsons Canada   49°24N 123°32W 162 D4
Gibsonton U.S.A.   27°51N 82°23W 179 H7
Gibsonville U.S.A.   39°46N 120°54W 170 F6
Giddalur India   15°20N 78°57E 127 G4
Giddings U.S.A.   30°11N 96°56W 176 F6
Giebelegäisi = Kebnekaise
  Sweden   67°53N 18°33E 60 C18
Gien France   47°40N 2°36E 71 E9
Giengen Germany   48°37N 10°14E 77 G6
Giessen Germany   50°34N 8°41E 76 E4
Gifan Iran   37°54N 57°28E 123 B8
Gifatin, Geziret Egypt 27°10N 33°50E 137 B8
Gifhorn Germany   52°30N 10°33E 76 C6
Gift Lake Canada   55°53N 115°49W 162 B5
Gifu Japan   35°30N 136°45E 113 G8
Gifu □ Japan   35°40N 137°0E 113 G8
Gigant Russia   46°28N 41°20E 87 G5
Giganta, Sa. de la
  Mexico   26°0N 111°39W 180 B2
Gigen Bulgaria   43°40N 24°28E 97 C8
Gigha U.K.   55°42N 5°44W 65 F3
Giglio Italy   42°20N 10°52E 92 F7
Gignac France   43°39N 3°32E 72 E7
Giğüela → Spain   39°8N 3°44W 89 F7
Gijón Spain   43°32N 5°42W 88 B5
Gikongoro Rwanda 2°28S 29°34E 142 C2
Gil I. Canada   53°12N 129°15W 162 C3
Gila → U.S.A.   32°43N 114°33W 169 K6
Gila Bend U.S.A.   32°57N 112°43W 169 K7
Gila Bend Mts. U.S.A. 33°10N 113°0W 169 K7
Gila Cliff Dwellings △
  U.S.A.   33°12N 108°16W 169 K9
Gīlān □ Iran   37°0N 50°0E 129 B6
Gīlān-e Gharb Iran 34°8N 45°55E 105 E11
Gilău Romania   46°45N 23°23E 81 D8
Gilbert → Australia 16°35S 141°15E 150 B3
Gilbert Is. Kiribati   1°0N 172°0E 147 A10
Gilbert River Australia 18°9S 142°52E 150 B3
Gilbert Seamounts
  Pac. Oc.   52°50N 150°10W 54 D18

Gilbués Brazil   9°5S 45°21W 189 B1
Gilead U.S.A.   44°24N 70°59W 175 B14
Gilf el Kebîr, Hadabat el
  Egypt   23°50N 25°50E 137 C2
Gilford I. Canada   50°40N 126°30W 162 C3
Gilgandra Australia 31°43S 148°39E 153 A8
Gilgil Kenya   0°30S 36°20E 142 C4
Gilgit India   35°50N 74°15E 125 B6
Gilgit → Pakistan 35°44N 74°37E 125 B6
Gilgit-Baltistan □
  Pakistan   35°50N 75°0E 125 B6
Gilgunnia Australia 32°26S 146°2E 153 B7
Gili □ Mozam.   16°39S 38°27E 143 F4
Gilimanuk Indonesia 8°10S 114°26E 119 J17
Giljeva Planina Europe 43°9N 20°0E 96 C3
Gillam Canada   56°20N 94°40W 163 B10
Gilleleje Denmark   56°8N 12°19E 63 H6
Gilles, L. Australia 32°50S 136°45E 152 B2
Gillespies Pt. N.Z.   43°24N 169°49E 155 E2
Gillette U.S.A.   44°18N 105°30W 168 D11
Gilliat Australia   20°40S 141°28E 150 C3
Gillingham U.K.   51°23N 0°33E 67 F8
Gilmer U.S.A.   32°44N 94°57W 176 E7
Gilmore, L. Australia 32°29S 121°37E 149 F3
Gilmour Canada   44°48N 77°37W 174 B7
Gilort → Romania 44°38N 23°32E 81 F8
Gilroy U.S.A.   37°1N 121°34W 170 H5
Gimcheon S. Korea 36°7N 128°9E 115 F14
Gimhae S. Korea   35°14N 128°53E 115 G15
Gimhwa S. Korea   38°17N 127°28E 115 E14
Gimie, Mt. St. Lucia 13°54N 61°0W 183 f
Gimje S. Korea   35°48N 126°45E 115 G14
Gimli Canada   50°40N 97°0W 163 C9
Gimo Sweden   60°11N 18°12E 62 D12
Gimone → France 44°0N 1°6E 72 E5
Gimont France   43°38N 0°52E 72 E4
Gin → Sri Lanka   6°5N 80°7E 127 G5
Gin Gin Australia   25°0S 151°58E 151 D5
Gînâh Egypt   25°21N 30°30E 137 B3
Gineifa Egypt   30°12N 32°25E 137 E8
Gingee India   12°15N 79°25E 127 H4
Gingin Australia   31°22S 115°54E 149 F2
Gingindlovu S. Africa 29°2S 31°30E 145 C5
Ginir Ethiopia   7°6N 40°40E 131 F5
Ginosa Italy   40°35N 16°45E 95 B9
Ginzo de Limia = Xinzo de Limia
  Spain   42°3N 7°47W 88 C3
Giofyros → Greece 35°20N 25°6E 101 D7
Giohar = Jawhar
  Somalia   2°48N 45°30E 131 G4
Gióia, G. di Italy   38°30N 15°45E 95 D8
Gióia del Colle Italy 40°48N 16°55E 95 B9
Gióia Táuro Italy   38°25N 15°54E 95 D8
Gioiosa Iónica Italy 38°10N 16°19E 95 D9
Gioiosa Marea Italy 38°10N 14°54E 95 D7
Giona, Oros Greece 38°38N 22°14E 98 C4
Giovi, Passo dei Italy 44°33N 8°57E 92 D5
Giovinazzo Italy   41°11N 16°40E 95 A9
Gippsland Australia 37°52S 147°0E 153 D7
Gipuzkoa □ Spain 43°12N 2°15W 90 B2
Gir → India   21°0N 71°0E 124 J4
Gir Hills India   21°0N 71°0E 124 J4
Girab India   26°2N 70°38E 124 F4
Girâfi, W. → Egypt 29°58N 34°39E 130 F3
Giraltovce Slovakia 49°7N 21°32E 79 B14
Girard St. Lucia   13°59N 60°57W 183 D7
Girard Ga., U.S.A.   33°3N 81°43W 178 D8
Girard Kans., U.S.A. 37°31N 94°51W 172 G6
Girard Ohio, U.S.A. 41°9N 80°42W 174 E4
Girard Pa., U.S.A.   42°0N 80°19W 174 E4
Girdle Ness U.K.   57°9N 2°3W 65 D6
Giresun Turkey   40°55N 38°30E 105 B8
Giresun □ Turkey 40°30N 38°30E 105 B8
Girga Egypt   26°17N 31°55E 137 B3
Giri → India   30°28N 77°41E 124 D7
Giridih India   24°10N 86°21E 125 G12
Girifalco Italy   38°49N 16°25E 95 D9
Giriftu Kenya   1°59N 39°46E 142 B4
Girilambone Australia 31°16S 146°57E 153 A7
Girne = Kyrenia
  Cyprus   35°20N 33°20E 101 D12
Giro Nigeria   11°7N 4°42E 139 C6
Giromagny France 47°45N 6°50E 71 E13
Giron = Kiruna Sweden 67°52N 20°15E 60 C19
Girona Spain   41°58N 2°46E 90 D7
Girona □ Spain   42°11N 2°30E 90 D7
Gironde □ France 44°45N 0°30W 72 D3
Gironde → France 45°32N 1°7W 72 C2
Gironella Spain   42°2N 1°53E 90 D6
Girraween △ Australia 28°46S 151°54E 151 D5
Girringun △ Australia 18°5S 145°49E 150 B4
Giru Australia   19°30S 147°5E 150 B4
Girvan U.K.   55°14N 4°51W 65 F4
Gisborne N.Z.   38°39S 178°5E 154 E7
Gisborne □ N.Z.   38°39S 178°0E 154 E7
Gisborne, Mt. N.Z. 43°55S 169°55E 155 E2
Gisenyi Rwanda   1°41S 29°15E 142 C2
Gislaved Sweden   57°19N 13°32E 63 G7
Gisors France   49°15N 1°47E 71 C8
Gitarama Rwanda 2°4S 29°45E 142 C2
Gitega Burundi   3°26S 29°56E 142 C2
Githio Greece   36°46N 22°34E 98 E4
Giuba = Juba →
  Somalia   1°30N 42°35E 131 G3
Giugliano in Campania
  Italy   40°56N 14°12E 95 B7
Giulianova Italy   42°45N 13°57E 93 F10
Giura Greece   39°23N 24°10E 98 B6
Giurgeni Romania 44°45N 27°48E 81 F12
Giurgiu Romania   43°52N 25°57E 81 G10
Giurgiu □ Romania 43°52N 25°57E 81 G10
Giurgiuleşti Moldova 45°29N 28°12E 81 E13
Give Denmark   55°51N 9°13E 63 J3
Givet France   50°8N 4°49E 71 B11
Givors France   45°35N 4°45E 73 C8
Givry France   46°41N 4°46E 71 F11
Giyani S. Africa   23°19S 30°43E 145 B5
Giza = El Gîza Egypt 30°0N 31°12E 137 F7
Giza Pyramids Egypt 29°58N 31°9E 137 F7
Gizab Afghan.   33°22N 66°17E 124 C1
Gizhiga Russia   62°3N 160°30E 107 C17
Gizhiginskaya Guba
  Russia   61°0N 158°0E 107 C16
Giżycko Poland   54°2N 21°48E 83 A12
Gizzeria Italy   38°59N 16°12E 95 D9
Gjakovë Kosovo   42°22N 20°26E 96 D4
Gjalicë e Lumës, Mal.
  Albania   42°2N 20°26E 96 D4
Gjegjan Albania   41°58N 20°3E 96 D4
Gjerdë Kosovo   42°32N 20°28E 96 D4
Gjilan Kosovo   42°28N 21°29E 96 D5

Gjirokastër Albania 40°7N 20°10E 96 F4
Gjoa Haven Canada 68°38N 95°53W 160 D12
Gjøvik Norway   60°47N 10°43E 60 F14
Gjuhës, Kep i Albania 40°28N 19°15E 96 F3
Gjurakovc Kosovo 42°43N 20°29E 96 C4
Glace Bay Canada 46°11N 59°58W 165 C8
Glacier △ U.S.A.   48°42N 113°48W 168 B7
Glacier Bay U.S.A. 58°40N 136°0W 160 F4
Glacier Bay △ U.S.A. 58°45N 136°30W 162 B1
Glacier Peak U.S.A. 48°7N 121°7W 168 B3
Gladewater U.S.A. 32°33N 94°56W 176 E7
Gladstone Queens.,
  Australia   23°52S 151°16E 150 C5
Gladstone S. Austral.,
  Australia   33°15S 138°22E 152 B3
Gladstone Canada 50°13N 98°57W 163 C9
Gladstone U.S.A.   45°51N 87°1W 172 C10
Gladwin U.S.A.   43°59N 84°29W 173 D11
Glafsfjorden Sweden 59°30N 12°37E 62 E6
Glagah Indonesia 8°13S 114°18E 119 J17
Glåma = Glomma →
  Norway   59°12N 10°57E 61 G14
Gláma Iceland   65°48N 23°0W 60 D2
Glamis U.S.A.   32°55N 115°5W 171 N11
Glamoč Bos.-H.   44°3N 16°51E 93 D13
Glamorgan, Vale of □
  U.K.   51°28N 3°25W 67 F4
Glamsbjerg Denmark 55°17N 10°6E 63 J4
Glarus Switz.   47°3N 9°4E 77 J5
Glarus □ Switz.   47°0N 9°5E 77 J5
Glasco Kans., U.S.A. 39°22N 97°50W 172 F5
Glasco N.Y., U.S.A. 42°3N 73°57W 175 D11
Glasgow U.K.   55°51N 4°15W 65 F4
Glasgow Ky., U.S.A. 37°0N 85°55W 173 G11
Glasgow Mont.,
  U.S.A.   48°12N 106°38W 168 B10
Glasgow City □ U.K. 55°51N 4°12W 65 F4
Glasgow Int. ✈ (GLA)
  U.K.   55°51N 4°21W 65 F4
Glaslyn Canada   53°22N 108°21W 163 C7
Glastonbury U.K.   51°9N 2°43W 67 F5
Glastonbury U.S.A. 41°43N 72°37W 175 E12
Glauchau Germany 50°49N 12°33E 76 E8
Glava Sweden   59°33N 12°35E 62 E6
Glavice Croatia   43°43N 16°41E 93 E13
Glazov Russia   58°9N 52°40E 86 A11
Gleichen Canada   50°52N 113°3W 162 C6
Gleisdorf Austria   47°6N 15°44E 78 D8
Gleiwitz = Gliwice
  Poland   50°22N 18°41E 83 H5
Glen U.S.A.   44°7N 71°11W 175 B13
Glen Affric U.K.   57°17N 5°1W 65 D3
Glen Afton N.Z.   37°3S 175°4E 154 D4
Glen Canyon U.S.A. 37°30N 110°40W 169 H8
Glen Canyon △ U.S.A. 37°15N 111°0W 169 H8
Glen Canyon Dam
  U.S.A.   36°57N 111°29W 169 H8
Glen Coe U.K.   56°40N 5°0W 65 E3
Glen Cove U.S.A.   40°52N 73°38W 175 F11
Glen Garry U.K.   57°3N 5°7W 65 D3
Glen Innes Australia 29°44S 151°44E 151 D5
Glen Lyon U.S.A.   41°10N 76°5W 175 E8
Glen Massey N.Z. 37°38S 175°12E 154 D4
Glen Mor U.K.   57°9N 4°37W 65 D4
Glen Moriston U.K. 57°11N 4°52W 65 D4
Glen Robertson
  Canada   45°22N 74°30W 175 A10
Glen Spean U.K.   56°53N 4°40W 65 E4
Glen Ullin U.S.A.   46°49N 101°50W 172 B3
Glenamaddy Ireland 53°37N 8°33W 64 C3
Glénan, Îs. de France 47°42N 4°0W 70 E3
Glenavy N.Z.   44°54S 171°7E 155 E3
Glenbeigh Ireland 52°3N 9°58W 64 D2
Glenburn Australia 27°25S 145°26E 151 D3
Glencoe Canada   42°45N 81°43W 174 D3
Glencoe S. Africa   28°11S 30°11E 145 C5
Glencoe Ala., U.S.A. 33°57N 85°56W 178 C4
Glencoe Minn., U.S.A. 44°46N 94°9W 172 C7
Glencolumbkille Ireland 54°43N 8°42W 64 B3
Glendale Ariz., U.S.A. 33°32N 112°11W 169 K7
Glendale Calif., U.S.A. 34°9N 118°15W 171 L8
Glendale Fla., U.S.A. 30°52N 86°7W 178 D3
Glendale Zimbabwe 17°22S 31°5E 143 F3
Glendive U.S.A.   47°7N 104°43W 168 C11
Glendo U.S.A.   42°30N 105°2W 168 E11
Glenelg Australia   34°58S 138°31E 152 C3
Glenelg → Australia 38°4S 140°59E 152 C4
Glenfield U.S.A.   43°43N 75°24W 175 C9
Glengad Hd. Ireland 55°20N 7°10W 64 A4
Glengarriff Ireland 51°45N 9°34W 64 E2
Glenham N.Z.   46°26S 168°52E 155 G2
Glenhope N.Z.   41°40S 172°39E 155 D4
Glenmary, Mt. N.Z. 43°55S 169°55E 155 E2
Glenmont U.S.A.   40°31N 82°6W 174 F3
Glenmorgan Australia 27°14S 149°42E 151 D4
Glenn U.S.A.   39°31N 122°1W 170 F4
Glennallen U.S.A. 62°7N 145°33W 166 D2
Glenns Ferry U.S.A. 42°57N 115°18W 168 E6
Glennville U.S.A.   31°56N 81°56W 179 E8
Glenora Canada   58°5N 131°35W 162 B2
Glenorchy Tas.,
  Australia   42°49S 147°18E 151 G4
Glenorchy Vic.,
  Australia   36°55S 142°41E 152 C5
Glenorchy N.Z.   44°51S 168°24E 155 E2
Glenore Australia 17°50S 141°12E 150 B3
Glenreagh Australia 30°2S 153°1E 151 E5
Glenrock U.S.A.   42°52N 105°52W 168 E11
Glenrothes U.K.   56°12N 3°10W 65 E5
Glenrowan Australia 36°29S 146°13E 153 D7
Glens Falls U.S.A. 43°19N 73°39W 175 C11
Glenside U.K.   40°6N 75°9W 175 F9
Glenthompson
  Australia   37°38S 142°35E 152 C5
Glenties Ireland   54°48N 8°17W 64 B3
Glenveagh △ Ireland 55°3N 8°1W 64 A4
Glenville U.S.A.   38°56N 80°50W 173 F13
Glenwood Canada 49°0N 54°58W 165 C9
Glenwood Ark., U.S.A. 34°20N 93°33W 176 D8
Glenwood Iowa, U.S.A. 41°3N 95°45W 172 E6
Glenwood Minn.,
  U.S.A.   45°39N 95°23W 172 C6
Glenwood Wash.,
  U.S.A.   46°1N 121°17W 170 D5
Glenwood Springs
  U.S.A.   39°33N 107°19W 168 G10

Glimåkra Sweden 56°19N 14°7E 63 H8
Glin Ireland   52°34N 9°17W 64 D2
Glina Croatia   45°20N 16°6E 93 C13
Glinojeck Poland   52°49N 20°21E 83 F7
Gliwice Poland   50°22N 18°41E 83 H5
Globe U.S.A.   33°24N 110°47W 169 K8
Glodeanu Siliştea
  Romania   44°50N 26°48E 81 F11
Glodeni Moldova   47°45N 27°31E 81 C12
Glödnitz Austria   46°53N 14°7E 78 E7
Gloggnitz Austria 47°41N 15°56E 78 D8
Głogów Poland   51°37N 16°5E 83 G3
Głogówek Poland 50°21N 17°53E 83 H4
Glomma → Norway 59°12N 10°57E 61 G14
Glorieuses, Îs. Ind. Oc. 11°30S 47°20E 141 G9
Glósa Greece   39°10N 23°45E 98 B5
Glossop U.K.   53°27N 1°56W 66 D6
Gloucester Australia 32°0S 151°59E 153 B9
Gloucester U.K.   51°53N 2°15W 67 F5
Gloucester U.S.A. 42°37N 70°40W 175 D14
Gloucester I. Australia 20°0S 148°30E 150 b
Gloucester Island △
  Australia   20°2S 148°30E 150 b
Gloucester Point
  U.S.A.   37°15N 76°30W 173 G15
Gloucestershire □ U.K. 51°46N 2°15W 67 F5
Gloversville U.S.A. 43°3N 74°21W 175 C10
Glovertown Canada 48°40N 54°3W 165 C9
Gloverville = Warrenville
  U.S.A.   33°33N 81°48W 178 D8
Glowno Poland   51°59N 19°42E 83 G6
Glubczyce Poland 50°13N 17°52E 83 H4
Glubokiy Russia   48°35N 40°25E 87 F5
Glúbokoe Kazakhstan 50°8N 82°18E 109 B10
Glubokoye = Hlybokaye
  Belarus   55°10N 27°45E 84 E4
Gluchołazy Poland 50°19N 17°24E 83 H4
Glücksburg Germany 54°50N 9°33E 76 A5
Glückstadt Germany 53°45N 9°25E 76 B5
Glukhov = Hlukhiv
  Ukraine   51°40N 33°58E 85 G7
Glusk Belarus   52°53N 28°41E 75 B13
Gluszyca Poland   50°41N 16°23E 83 H3
Glyfada = Glifada Greece 37°52N 23°45E 98 D5
Glyn Ebwy = Ebbw Vale
  U.K.   51°46N 3°12W 67 F4
Glyngøre Denmark 56°46N 8°52E 63 H2
Gmünd Kärnten, Austria 46°54N 13°31E 78 E6
Gmünd Niederösterreich,
  Austria   48°45N 15°0E 78 D8
Gmund Germany   47°55N 13°48E 78 D6
Gnarp Sweden   62°3N 17°16E 62 E11
Gnesta Sweden   59°3N 17°17E 62 E11
Gniew Poland   53°50N 18°50E 82 E5
Gniewkowo Poland 52°54N 18°25E 83 F5
Gniezno Poland   52°30N 17°35E 83 F4
Gnjilane = Gjilan Kosovo 42°28N 21°29E 96 D5
Gnoien Germany   53°58N 12°41E 76 B8
Gnosjö Sweden   57°22N 13°43E 63 G7
Gnowangerup
  Australia   33°58S 117°59E 149 F2
Go Cong Vietnam 10°22N 106°40E 121 G6
Gô-no-ura Japan   33°44N 129°40E 113 H4
Goa India   15°33N 73°59E 127 G1
Goa □ India   15°33N 73°59E 127 G1
Goalen Hd. Australia 36°33S 150°4E 153 D9
Goalpara India   26°10N 90°40E 123 F17
Goaltor India   22°43N 87°10E 125 H12
Goalundo Ghat
  Bangla.   23°50N 89°47E 125 H13
Goaso Ghana   6°48N 2°30W 138 D4
Goat Fell U.K.   55°38N 5°11W 65 F3
Goba Ethiopia   7°1N 39°59E 131 F2
Goba Mozam.   26°15S 32°13E 145 C5
Gobabis Namibia 22°30S 19°0E 144 C2
Göbel Turkey   40°20N 28°9E 99 B9
Gobernador Gregores
  Argentina   48°46S 70°15W 192 C2
Gobi Asia   44°0N 110°0E 114 C6
Gobichettipalayam
  India   11°31N 77°21E 127 J3
Gobō Japan   33°53N 135°10E 113 H7
Gobustan Azerbaijan 40°N 49°22E 105 B13
Göçbeyli Turkey   39°13N 27°29E 99 B9
Goch Germany   51°41N 6°9E 76 D2
Gochas Namibia   24°59S 18°55E 144 B2
Godalming U.K.   51°11N 0°36W 67 F7
Godavari → India   16°25N 82°18E 126 F6
Godavari Pt. India 17°0N 82°20E 126 F6
Godbout Canada   49°20N 67°38W 165 C16
Godda India   24°50N 87°13E 125 G12
Godech Bulgaria   43°1N 23°4E 96 C7
Goderich Canada 43°45N 81°41W 174 C3
Goderville France 49°38N 0°22E 70 C7
Godfrey Ra. Australia 24°0S 117°0E 149 D2
Godhavn = Qeqertarsuaq
  Greenland   69°15N 53°38W 57 D5
Godhra India   22°49N 73°40E 124 H5
Gödöllő Hungary   47°38N 19°25E 83 E10
Godoy Cruz Argentina 32°56S 68°52W 190 C2
Gods → Canada   56°22N 92°51W 164 A1
Gods L. Canada   54°40N 94°15W 164 B1
Gods River Canada 54°50N 94°5W 163 C10
Godthåb = Nuuk
  Greenland   64°10N 51°35W 57 C5
Goeie Hoop, Kaap die = Good
  Hope, C. of S. Africa 34°24S 18°30E 144 E2
Goéland, L. au Canada 49°50N 76°48W 164 C4
Goelands, L. aux
  Canada   55°27N 64°17W 165 A7
Goeree Neths.   51°50N 4°0E 69 C3
Goes Neths.   51°30N 3°55E 69 C3
Goffstown U.S.A. 43°1N 71°36W 175 C13
Gogama Canada   47°35N 81°43W 174 A3
Gogebic, L. U.S.A. 46°30N 89°35W 172 B9
Gogolin Poland   50°30N 18°0E 83 H5
Gogonou Benin   10°50N 2°50E 139 C5
Gogra = Ghaghara →
  India   25°45N 84°40E 125 G11
Gogrial South Sudan 8°30N 28°8E 135 G11
Gogui Mali   15°32N 9°25W 138 B3
Gôh-Djiboua □
  Côte d'Ivoire   6°2N 5°13W 138 D3
Gohana India   29°8N 76°42E 124 E7
Goharganj India   23°1N 77°41E 124 H7
Goi → India   22°4N 74°46E 124 H6
Goiana Brazil   7°33S 34°59W 189 D4
Goiânia Brazil   16°43S 49°20W 187 E9
Goiás Brazil   15°55S 50°10W 187 E8
Goiás □ Brazil   12°10S 48°0W 187 F9

Goiatins *Brazil* 7°42S 47°10W **189** B1
Goio-Erê *Brazil* 24°12S 53°1W **191** A5
Góis *Portugal* 40°10N 8°6W **88** E2
Gojō *Japan* 34°21N 135°42E **113** G2
Gojra *Pakistan* 31°10N 72°40E **126** D5
Gokak *India* 16°11N 74°52E **127** F2
Gokarn *India* 14°33N 74°17E **127** G2
Gökçe *Turkey* 40°10N 25°55E **97** F9
Gökçeada *Turkey* 40°10N 25°50E **97** F9
Gökçedağ *Turkey* 39°33N 28°56E **99** B10
Gökçen *Turkey* 38°7N 27°53E **99** D9
Gökçeören *Turkey* 38°37N 28°35E **99** C10
Gökçeyazı *Turkey* 39°40N 27°40E **99** B9
Gökırmak → *Turkey* 41°25N 35°58E **104** B6
Gökova *Turkey* 37°1N 28°17E **99** D10
Gökova Körfezi *Turkey* 36°55N 27°50E **99** D9
Göksu → *Turkey* 36°19N 34°5E **104** D6
Göksun *Turkey* 38°2N 36°30E **104** D6
Gokteik *Myanmar* 22°26N 97°0E **123** H20
Göktepe *Turkey* 37°25N 28°34E **99** D10
Gokurt *Pakistan* 29°40N 67°26E **124** E2
Gokwe *Zimbabwe* 18°7S 28°58E **145** A4
Gol Gol *Australia* 34°12S 142°14E **152** C5
Gola *India* 28°3N 80°32E **125** E9
Golakganj *India* 26°8N 89°52E **125** F13
Golan Heights = Hagolan
 Syria 33°0N 35°45E **130** C4
Golańcz *Poland* 52°57N 17°18E **83** F4
Goläshkerd *Iran* 27°59N 57°16E **129** E8
Golaya Pristen = Hola Prystan
 Ukraine 46°29N 32°32E **85** J7
Gölbaşı *Adıyaman,
 Turkey* 37°43N 37°25E **104** D7
Gölbaşı *Ankara, Turkey* 39°47N 32°49E **104** C5
Golconda *India* 17°24N 78°23E **126** F4
Golconda *U.S.A.* 40°58N 117°30W **168** F5
Gölcük *Kocaeli, Turkey* 40°42N 29°48E **97** F13
Gölcük *Niğde, Turkey* 38°14N 34°47E **104** C6
Gold *U.S.A.* 41°52N 77°50W **174** C7
Gold Beach *U.S.A.* 42°25N 124°25W **168** E1
Gold Coast *W. Afr.* 4°0N 1°40W **139** E4
Gold Hill *U.S.A.* 42°26N 123°3W **168** E2
Gold River *Canada* 49°46N 126°3W **162** D3
Goldap *Poland* 54°19N 22°18E **82** D9
Goldberg *Germany* 53°35N 12°4E **76** B8
Golden *Canada* 51°20N 116°59W **162** C5
Golden B. *N.Z.* 40°40S 172°50E **155** A7
Golden Gate Highlands △
 S. Africa 28°40S 28°40E **145** C4
Golden Hinde *Canada* 49°40N 125°44W **162** D3
Golden Lake *Canada* 45°34N 77°21W **174** A7
Golden Rock *India* 10°45N 78°48E **127** J4
Golden Spike ○
 U.S.A. 41°37N 112°33W **168** F7
Golden Vale *Ireland* 52°33N 8°17W **64** D3
Goldendale *U.S.A.* 45°49N 120°50W **168** D3
Goldfield *U.S.A.* 37°42N 117°14W **169** H5
Goldsand L. *Canada* 57°2N 101°8W **163** B8
Goldsboro *U.S.A.* 35°23N 77°59W **177** D16
Goldsmith *U.S.A.* 31°59N 102°37W **176** F3
Goldthwaite *U.S.A.* 31°27N 98°34W **176** F5
Golega *Portugal* 39°24N 8°29W **89** F2
Goleniów *Poland* 53°35N 14°50E **82** E1
Golestän □ *Iran* 37°20N 55°25E **129** B7
Golestának *Iran* 30°36N 54°14E **129** D7
Goleta *U.S.A.* 34°27N 119°50W **171** L7
Golfito *Costa Rica* 8°41N 83°5W **182** E3
Golfo Aranci *Italy* 40°59N 9°38E **94** B2
Golfo di Orosei e del
 Gennargentu △ *Italy* 40°5N 9°15E **94** B2
Gölgeli Dağları *Turkey* 37°10N 28°55E **99** D10
Gölhisar *Turkey* 37°8N 29°31E **99** D11
Goliad *U.S.A.* 28°40N 97°23W **176** G6
Golija *Montenegro* 43°5N 18°45E **96** C2
Golija *Serbia* 43°22N 20°15E **96** C4
Golina *Poland* 52°15N 18°4E **83** F5
Gölköy *Turkey* 40°41N 37°37E **104** B7
Göllersdorf *Austria* 48°29N 16°7E **78** C9
Gölmarmara *Turkey* 38°42N 27°55E **99** C9
Golmud *China* 36°25N 94°53E **110** D7
Golo → *France* 42°31N 9°32E **73** F13
Gölova *Turkey* 36°48N 30°5E **99** E12
Golpäyegän *Iran* 33°27N 50°18E **129** C6
Gölpazarı *Turkey* 40°16N 30°18E **104** B4
Golra *Pakistan* 33°37N 72°56E **124** C5
Golspie *U.K.* 57°58N 3°59W **65** D5
Golub-Dobrzyń *Poland* 53°7N 19°2E **83** E6
Golubac *Serbia* 44°38N 21°38E **96** B5
Golyama Kamchia →
 Bulgaria 43°10N 27°55E **97** C11
Goma
 Dem. Rep. of the Congo 1°37S 29°10E **142** C2
Gomal Pass *Pakistan* 31°56N 69°20E **124** D3
Gomati → *India* 25°32N 83°11E **125** G10
Gombari
 Dem. Rep. of the Congo 2°45N 29°3E **142** B2
Gombe *Nigeria* 10°19N 11°2E **139** C7
Gombe *Turkey* 36°33N 29°38E **99** E11
Gombe □ *Nigeria* 10°0N 11°10E **139** C7
Gombe → *Tanzania* 4°38S 31°40E **142** C3
Gombe Stream △
 Tanzania 4°42S 29°37E **142** C2
Gombi *Nigeria* 10°12N 12°30E **139** C7
Gomel = Homyel
 Belarus 52°28N 31°0E **75** B16
Gomera *Canary Is.* 28°7N 17°14W **100** F2
Gómez Palacio
 Mexico 25°34N 103°30W **180** B4
Gomfi *Greece* 39°26N 21°33E **98** B3
Gomishän *Iran* 37°4N 54°6E **129** B7
Gommern *Germany* 52°4N 11°50E **76** C7
Gomogomo *Indonesia* 6°39S 134°43E **117** F8
Gomoh *India* 23°52N 86°10E **125** H12
Gomotartsi *Bulgaria* 44°6N 22°57E **96** B6
Gompa = Ganta *Liberia* 7°15N 8°59W **138** D3
Gonābād *Iran* 34°15N 58°45E **129** C8
Gonaïves *Haiti* 19°20N 72°42W **183** C5
Gonarezhou △
 Zimbabwe 21°32S 31°55E **143** G3
Gonâve, G. de la *Haiti* 19°29N 72°42W **183** C5
Gonâve, Île de la *Haiti* 18°51N 73°3W **183** C5
Gonbad-e Kävüs *Iran* 37°20N 55°25E **129** B7
Gönc *Hungary* 48°28N 21°14E **80** B6
Gonda *India* 27°9N 81°58E **125** F9
Gondal *India* 21°58N 70°52E **124** J4
Gonder *Ethiopia* 12°39N 37°30E **137** E12
Gondia *India* 21°23N 80°10E **126** D5
Gondola *Mozam.* 19°10S 33°37E **143** F3
Gondomar *Portugal* 41°10N 8°35W **88** D2

Gondrecourt-le-Château
 France 48°31N 5°30E **71** D12
Gönen *Balıkesir, Turkey* 40°6N 27°39E **97** F11
Gönen *Isparta, Turkey* 37°57N 30°31E **99** D12
Gönen → *Turkey* 40°6N 27°39E **97** F11
Gong Xian *China* 28°23N 104°47E **116** C5
Gong'an *China* 30°7N 112°12E **117** B9
Gongbei *China* 22°12N 113°32E **111** a
Gongchangling *China* 41°7N 123°27E **115** D12
Gongcheng *China* 24°50N 110°49E **117** E8
Gongga Shan *China* 29°40N 101°55E **116** C3
Gongguan *China* 29°23N 91°7E **110** F7
Gonghe *China* 36°18N 100°32E **110** D9
Gongju *S. Korea* 36°27N 127°7E **115** F14
Gongliu *China* 43°28N 82°8E **110** C2
Gongming *China* 22°47N 113°53E **111** a
Gongola → *Nigeria* 9°30N 12°4E **139** D7
Gongolgon *Australia* 30°21S 146°54E **151** E4
Gongshan *China* 27°43N 98°29E **116** D2
Gongtan *China* 28°55N 108°20E **116** C7
Gongyi *China* 34°45N 112°58E **114** G7
Gongzhuling *China* 43°30N 124°40E **115** C13
Goni *Greece* 39°52N 22°29E **98** B4
Goniadz *Poland* 53°30N 22°44E **82** E9
Goniri *Nigeria* 11°30N 12°15E **139** C7
Gonnesa *Italy* 39°16N 8°28E **94** C1
Gonnosfanádiga *Italy* 39°29N 8°39E **94** C1
Gonzales *Calif., U.S.A.* 36°30N 121°26W **170** J5
Gonzales *Tex., U.S.A.* 29°30N 97°27W **176** G6
González *Mexico* 22°48N 98°25W **181** C5
Goobang △ *Australia* 33°0S 148°32E **153** B8
Good Hope, C. of
 S. Africa 34°24S 18°30E **144** D2
Good Hope Lake
 Canada 59°16N 129°18W **162** B3
Gooderham *Canada* 44°54N 78°21W **174** B6
Goodhouse *S. Africa* 28°57S 18°13E **144** C2
Gooding *U.S.A.* 42°56N 114°43W **168** E6
Goodland *U.S.A.* 39°21N 101°43W **172** F3
Goodlands *Mauritius* 20°2S 57°39E **141** d
Goodlow *Canada* 56°20N 120°8W **162** B4
Goodooga *Australia* 29°3S 147°28E **151** D4
Goodsprings *U.S.A.* 35°49N 115°27W **171** K11
Goodwater *U.S.A.* 33°4N 86°3W **178** B3
Goole *U.K.* 53°42N 0°53W **66** D7
Goolgowi *Australia* 33°58S 145°41E **153** B6
Goolwa *Australia* 35°30S 138°47E **152** C2
Goomalling *Australia* 31°15S 116°49E **149** F2
Goomeri *Australia* 26°12S 152°6E **151** D5
Goonda *Mozam.* 19°48S 33°57E **143** F3
Goondiwindi *Australia* 28°30S 150°21E **151** D5
Goongarrie, L. *Australia* 30°3S 121°9E **149** F3
Goongarrie △ *Australia* 30°7S 121°1E **149** F3
Goonyella *Australia* 21°47S 147°58E **150** C4
Goose → *Canada* 53°20N 60°35W **165** B8
Goose L. *U.S.A.* 41°56N 120°26W **168** F3
Gooty *India* 15°7N 77°41E **127** G3
Gopalganj *India* 26°28N 84°30E **125** F11
Gop *India* 22°5N 69°50E **124** H3
Göppingen *Germany* 48°42N 9°39E **77** G5
Gor *Spain* 37°23N 2°58W **89** H8
Góra Dolnośląskie, *Poland* 51°40N 16°31E **83** G3
Góra Mazowieckie, *Poland* 52°39N 20°6E **83** F7
Góra Kalwaria *Poland* 51°59N 21°14E **83** G8
Gorakhpur *India* 26°47N 83°23E **125** F10
Goražde *Bos.-H.* 43°38N 18°58E **80** G3
Gorbatov *Russia* 56°12N 43°2E **86** B6
Gorbea *Spain* 43°1N 2°50W **90** B2
Gorczański △ *Poland* 49°30N 20°10E **83** J7
Gorda, Pta. *Canary Is.* 28°45N 18°0W **100** F2
Gorda, Pta. *Nic.* 14°20N 83°10W **182** D3
Gordan B. *Australia* 11°35S 130°10E **148** B5
Gördes *Turkey* 38°54N 28°17E **99** C10
Gordon *Ga., U.S.A.* 32°54N 83°20W **178** C4
Gordon *Nebr., U.S.A.* 42°48N 102°12W **172** D3
Gordon → *Australia* 42°27S 145°30E **151** G4
Gordon, I. *Chile* 54°55S 69°30W **192** H3
Gordon Bay *Canada* 45°12N 79°47W **174** A5
Gordon L. *Alta.,
 Canada* 56°30N 110°25W **163** B6
Gordon L. *N.W.T.,
 Canada* 63°5N 113°11W **162** A6
Gordonvale *Australia* 17°5S 145°50E **150** B4
Goré *Chad* 7°59N 16°31E **135** G9
Gore *Ethiopia* 8°12N 35°32E **137** F12
Gore *N.Z.* 46°5S 168°58E **155** G3
Gore Bay *Canada* 45°57N 82°28W **164** C3
Gorée, Île de *Senegal* 14°40N 17°23W **138** C1
Görele *Turkey* 41°2N 39°0E **105** B8
Gorey *Ireland* 52°41N 6°18W **64** D5
Gorg *Iran* 29°29N 59°43E **129** D8
Gorgol □ *Mauritania* 15°45N 13°0W **138** B2
Gorgona *Italy* 43°26N 9°54E **92** E6
Gorgona, I. *Colombia* 3°0N 78°10W **186** C3
Gorgoram *Nigeria* 12°40N 10°45E **139** C7
Gorham *U.S.A.* 44°23N 71°10W **175** B13
Gori *Georgia* 42°0N 44°7E **87** J7
Goribidnur = Gauribidanur
 India 13°37N 77°32E **127** H3
Goriganga → *India* 29°45N 80°22E **125** E9
Gorinchem *Neths.* 51°50N 4°59E **69** C4
Goris *Armenia* 39°31N 46°22E **105** C12
Goritsy *Russia* 57°4N 36°43E **84** D9
Gorízia *Italy* 45°56N 13°37E **93** C10
Gorj □ *Romania* 45°5N 23°25E **81** E8
Gorkha *Nepal* 28°5N 84°40E **125** E11
Gorki = Horki *Belarus* 54°17N 30°59E **84** E6
Gorkiy = Nizhniy Novgorod
 Russia 56°20N 44°0E **86** B7
Gorkovskoye Vdkhr.
 Russia 57°2N 43°4E **86** B6
Gorlestone-on-Sea *U.K.* 52°35N 1°44E **67** E9
Gorlice *Poland* 49°35N 21°11E **83** J8
Görlitz *Germany* 51°9N 14°58E **76** D10
Gorlovka = Horlivka
 Ukraine 48°19N 38°5E **85** H10
Gorman *U.S.A.* 32°12N 98°41W **176** E5
Gorna Dzhumayo = Blagoevgrad
 Bulgaria 42°2N 23°5E **96** D7
Gorna Oryahovitsa
 Bulgaria 43°7N 25°40E **97** C10
Gornja Radgona
 Slovenia 46°40N 16°2E **93** B13
Gornja Tuzla *Bos.-H.* 44°35N 18°46E **80** F3
Gornji Grad *Slovenia* 46°20N 14°52E **93** B11
Gornji Milanovac *Serbia* 44°0N 20°29E **96** B4
Gornji Vakuf *Bos.-H.* 43°57N 17°34E **80** G2

Gorno Ablanovo
 Bulgaria 43°37N 25°43E **97** C9
Gorno-Altay □ *Russia* 51°0N 86°0E **109** D10
Gorno-Altaysk *Russia* 51°50N 86°5E **109** D11
Gorno-Badakhstan =
 Kühiston-Badakhshon □
 Tajikistan 38°30N 73°0E **109** F8
Gornozavodsk *Russia* 46°33N 141°50E **107** E15
Gornyak *Russia* 50°59N 81°27E **109** D10
Gornyatskiy *Russia* 48°18N 40°26E **87** F5
Gornyy *Primorsk,
 Russia* 44°57N 133°59E **112** B6
Gornyy *Saratov, Russia* 51°50N 48°30E **86** E9
Gorodenka = Horodenka
 Ukraine 48°41N 25°29E **81** B10
Gorodets *Russia* 56°38N 43°28E **86** B6
Gorodishche = Horodyshche
 Ukraine 49°17N 31°27E **85** H6
Gorodishche *Russia* 53°13N 45°40E **86** D7
Gorodnya = Horodnya
 Ukraine 51°55N 31°33E **85** G6
Gorodok = Haradok
 Belarus 55°30N 30°3E **84** E6
Gorodok = Horodok
 Ukraine 49°46N 23°32E **75** D12
Gorodovikovsk *Russia* 46°8N 41°58E **87** G5
Goroke *Australia* 36°43S 141°29E **152** D4
Gorokhov = Horokhiv
 Ukraine 50°30N 24°45E **75** C13
Gorokhovets *Russia* 56°13N 42°39E **86** B6
Gorom Gorom
 Burkina Faso 14°26N 0°14W **139** C4
Goromonzi *Zimbabwe* 17°52S 31°22E **143** F3
Gorong, Kepulauan
 Indonesia 3°59S 131°25E **119** E8
Gorongose → *Mozam.* 20°30S 34°40E **145** B5
Gorongosa *Mozam.* 18°44S 34°2E **143** F3
Gorongoza, Sa. da
 Mozam. 18°27S 34°2E **143** F3
Gorongoza △ *Mozam.* 18°50S 34°29E **145** A5
Gorontalo *Indonesia* 0°35N 123°5E **119** D6
Gorontalo □ *Indonesia* 0°50N 122°20E **119** D6
Goronyo *Nigeria* 13°29N 5°39E **139** C6
Górowo Iławeckie
 Poland 54°17N 20°30E **82** D7
Gorron *France* 48°25N 0°50W **70** D6
Gorshechnoye *Russia* 51°31N 38°2E **85** G10
Gort *Ireland* 53°3N 8°49W **64** C3
Gortis *Greece* 35°4N 24°58E **101** D6
Gorumahisani *India* 22°20N 86°24E **126** D8
Góry Bystrzyckie *Poland* 50°6N 16°33E **83** H3
Goryachiy Klyuch *Russia* 44°38N 39°8E **87** H4
Goryeong *S. Korea* 35°44N 128°15E **115** G15
Gorzkowice *Poland* 51°13N 19°36E **83** G6
Górzno *Poland* 53°12N 19°38E **83** E6
Gorzów Śląski *Poland* 51°3N 18°22E **83** G5
Gorzów Wielkopolski
 Poland 52°43N 15°15E **83** F2
Gosford *Australia* 33°23S 151°18E **153** B9
Goshen *Calif., U.S.A.* 36°21N 119°25W **170** J7
Goshen *Ind., U.S.A.* 41°35N 85°50W **173** E11
Goshen *N.Y., U.S.A.* 41°24N 74°20W **175** E10
Goshogawara *Japan* 40°48N 140°27E **112** D10
Goslar *Germany* 51°54N 10°25E **76** D6
Gospič *Croatia* 44°35N 15°23E **93** D12
Gosport *U.K.* 50°48N 1°9W **67** G6
Gossas *Senegal* 14°28N 16°0W **138** C1
Gosse → *Australia* 19°32S 134°37E **150** B1
Gossi *Mali* 15°48N 1°20W **139** B4
Gostivar *Macedonia* 41°48N 20°57E **96** E4
Gostyń *Poland* 51°50N 17°3E **83** G4
Gostynin *Poland* 52°26N 19°29E **83** F6
Göta älv → *Sweden* 57°42N 11°54E **63** G5
Göta kanal *Sweden* 58°30N 15°58E **63** F10
Götaland *Sweden* 57°30N 14°30E **63** G8
Göteborg *Sweden* 57°43N 11°59E **63** G5
Götene *Sweden* 58°32N 13°30E **63** F7
Goteşti *Moldova* 46°9N 28°10E **81** D13
Gotha *Germany* 50°56N 10°42E **76** E6
Gothenburg = Göteborg
 Sweden 57°43N 11°59E **63** G5
Gothenburg *U.S.A.* 40°56N 100°10W **172** E3
Gotland *Sweden* 57°30N 18°33E **63** G12
Gotland □ *Sweden* 57°15N 18°30E **63** G12
Gotō = Fukue *Japan* 32°41N 128°51E **113** H4
Gotō-Rettō *Japan* 32°55N 129°5E **113** H4
Gotse Delchev *Bulgaria* 41°36N 23°46E **96** E7
Gotska Sandön *Sweden* 58°24N 19°15E **63** F13
Gōtsu *Japan* 35°0N 132°14E **113** G6
Göttero, Monte *Italy* 44°22N 9°42E **92** D6
Göttingen *Germany* 51°31N 9°55E **76** D5
Gottskär *Sweden* 57°25N 12°0E **63** H6
Gottwald = Zmiyev
 Ukraine 49°39N 36°27E **85** H9
Gottwaldov = Zlín
 Czechia 49°14N 17°40E **79** B10
Goubangzi *China* 41°20N 121°52E **115** D11
Gouda *Neths.* 52°1N 4°42E **69** B4
Goudiri *Senegal* 14°15N 12°45W **138** C2
Goudoumaria *Niger* 13°40N 11°10E **139** C7
Goudouras, Akra *Greece* 34°59N 26°6E **101** E8
Gouèké *Guinea* 8°2N 8°43W **138** D3
Gough I. *Atl. Oc.* 40°10S 9°45W **56** L11
Gouin, Rés. *Canada* 48°35N 74°40W **164** C5
Goulard *Canada* 48°35N 74°40W **164** C5
Gouitafla *Côte d'Ivoire* 7°30N 5°53W **138** D3
Goulburn *Australia* 34°44S 149°44E **153** C8
Goulburn Is. *Australia* 11°40S 133°20E **150** A1
Goulburn River △
 Australia 32°19S 150°10E **153** B9
Goulds *U.S.A.* 25°33N 80°23W **179** K9
Goulia *Côte d'Ivoire* 10°1N 7°11W **138** C3
Goulmima *Morocco* 31°41N 4°57W **136** B5
Goumbou *Mali* 15°2N 7°25W **138** B3
Goumenissa *Greece* 40°56N 22°37E **96** F6
Goundam *Mali* 16°27N 3°40W **138** B4
Goura *Greece* 37°56N 22°20E **98** D4
Gouraya *Algeria* 36°31N 1°56E **136** A6
Gourbassi *Mali* 13°24N 11°38W **138** C2
Gourdon *France* 44°44N 1°23E **72** D5
Gouré *Niger* 14°0N 10°10E **139** C7
Gourin *France* 48°8N 3°37W **70** D3
Gourits → *S. Africa* 34°21S 21°52E **144** D3
Gourma-Rharous *Mali* 16°55N 1°50W **139** B4
Gournay-en-Bray *France* 49°29N 1°44E **71** C8
Gournes *Greece* 35°19N 25°1E **101** D7
Gourock Ra. *Australia* 36°0S 149°25E **153** D8
Gouverneur *U.S.A.* 44°20N 75°28W **175** B9
Gouviá *Greece* 39°39N 19°50E **101** A3

Gouzon *France* 46°12N 2°14E **71** F9
Gove Peninsula
 Australia 12°17S 136°49E **150** A2
Governador Valadares
 Brazil 18°15S 41°57W **189** D2
Governor's Harbour
 Bahamas 25°10N 76°14W **182** A4
Goviáltay □ *Mongolia* 45°30N 96°0E **109** C13
Govindgarh *India* 24°23N 81°18E **125** G9
Gowan Ra. *Australia* 25°0S 145°0E **150** D4
Gowanda *U.S.A.* 42°28N 78°56W **174** D6
Gower *U.K.* 51°35N 4°10W **67** F3
Gowers Corner *U.S.A.* 28°20N 82°30W **179** G7
Gowna, L. *Ireland* 53°51N 7°34W **64** C4
Gowurdak *Turkmenistan* 37°50N 66°4E **109** F7
Goya *Argentina* 29°10S 59°10W **190** B4
Goyang *S. Korea* 37°39N 126°50E **115** F14
Göyçay *Azerbaijan* 40°42N 47°43E **87** K8
Goyder Lagoon
 Australia 27°3S 138°58E **151** D2
Goygöl *Azerbaijan* 40°37N 46°12E **87** K8
Goyllarisquizga *Peru* 10°31S 76°24W **188** C3
Göynük *Antalya, Turkey* 36°41N 30°33E **99** E12
Göynük *Bolu, Turkey* 40°24N 30°48E **104** B4
Goz Beïda *Chad* 12°10N 21°20E **135** F10
Gozdnica *Poland* 51°28N 15°4E **83** G2
Gozo *Malta* 36°3N 14°15E **101** C1
Graaff-Reinet *S. Africa* 32°13S 24°32E **144** D3
Grabo *Côte d'Ivoire* 4°57N 7°30W **138** D3
Grabow *Germany* 53°17N 11°34E **76** B7
Grabów nad Prosną
 Poland 51°31N 18°7E **83** G5
Gračac *Croatia* 44°18N 15°57E **93** D12
Gračanica *Bos.-H.* 44°43N 18°18E **80** F3
Graçay *France* 47°10N 1°50E **71** E8
Graceville *U.S.A.* 30°58N 85°31W **178** E4
Gracewood *U.S.A.* 33°22N 82°2W **178** C5
Gracias a Dios, C.
 Honduras 15°0N 83°10W **182** D3
Graciosa *Azores* 39°4N 28°0W **134** a
Graciosa, I. *Canary Is.* 29°15N 13°32W **100** E6
Gradac *Montenegro* 42°33N 19°9E **96** C3
Gradačac *Bos.-H.* 44°52N 18°26E **80** F3
Gradeška Planina
 Macedonia 41°30N 22°15E **96** E6
Gradets *Bulgaria* 42°46N 26°30E **97** D10
Gradišče *Slovenia* 46°37N 15°3E **93** B12
Gradiška *Bos.-H.* 45°10N 17°15E **80** E2
Grădiştea de Munte
 Romania 45°37N 23°13E **81** E8
Grado *Italy* 45°40N 13°23E **93** C10
Grado *Spain* 43°23N 6°4W **88** B4
Grady *U.S.A.* 34°49N 103°19W **169** J12
Graeca, Lacul *Romania* 44°5N 26°10E **81** F11
Grafenau *Germany* 48°51N 13°22E **77** G9
Gräfenberg *Germany* 49°39N 11°14E **77** F7
Grafham Water *U.K.* 52°19N 0°18W **67** E7
Grafton *Australia* 29°38S 152°58E **151** D5
Grafton *N. Dak., U.S.A.* 48°25N 97°25W **172** A6
Grafton *W. Va., U.S.A.* 39°21N 80°2W **173** F13
Graham *Canada* 49°20N 90°30W **164** C1
Graham *Ga., U.S.A.* 31°50N 82°30W **178** D7
Graham *Tex., U.S.A.* 33°6N 98°35W **176** E5
Graham, Mt. *U.S.A.* 32°42N 109°52W **169** K9
Graham Bell, Ostrov = Greem-
 Bell, Ostrov *Russia* 81°0N 62°0E **106** A7
Graham I. *B.C.,
 Canada* 53°40N 132°30W **162** C2
Graham I. *Nunavut,
 Canada* 77°25N 90°30W **161** B13
Graham Land *Antarctica* 65°0S 64°0W **55** C17
Grahamstown *S. Africa* 33°19S 26°31E **144** D4
Grahamsville *U.S.A.* 41°51N 74°33W **175** E10
Grahovo *Montenegro* 42°40N 18°40E **96** D2
Graïba *Tunisia* 34°30N 10°13E **136** B6
Graie, Alpi *Europe* 45°30N 7°10E **73** C11
Grain Coast *W. Afr.* 4°20N 10°0W **138** E3
Grajagan *Indonesia* 8°35S 114°13E **119** K17
Grajaú *Brazil* 5°50S 46°4W **189** E1
Grajaú → *Brazil* 3°41S 44°48W **189** A2
Grajewo *Poland* 53°39N 22°30E **82** E9
Gramada *Bulgaria* 43°49N 22°39E **96** C6
Gramat *France* 44°48N 1°43E **72** D5
Grammichele *Italy* 37°13N 14°38E **95** F7
Grámmos, Óros *Greece* 40°18N 20°47E **96** F4
Grampian *U.S.A.* 40°58N 78°37W **174** F6
Grampian Highlands = Grampian
 Mts. *U.K.* 56°50N 4°0W **65** E5
Grampian Mts. *U.K.* 56°50N 4°0W **65** E5
Grampians, The
 Australia 37°15S 142°20E **152** D5
Grampians △
 Australia 37°15S 142°20E **152** D5
Gran Altiplanicie Central
 Argentina 49°0S 69°30W **192** C3
Gran Canaria
 Canary Is. 27°55N 15°35W **100** G4
Gran Chaco *S. Amer.* 25°0S 61°0W **190** B3
Gran Desierto del Pinacate △
 Mexico 31°51N 113°32W **180** A2
Gran Laguna Salada
 Argentina 44°24S 67°23W **192** E3
Gran Pajonal *Peru* 10°45S 74°30W **188** C3
Gran Paradiso *Italy* 45°33N 7°17E **92** C4
Gran Sasso d'Itália
 Italy 42°27N 13°42E **93** F10
Gran Sasso e Monti Della Laga △
 Italy 42°32N 13°22E **93** F10
Gran Tarajal *Canary Is.* 28°13N 14°1W **100** F5
Granada *Nic.* 11°58N 86°0W **182** D2
Granada *Spain* 37°10N 3°35W **89** H7
Granada *U.S.A.* 38°4N 102°19W **168** G12
Granada □ *Spain* 37°18N 3°0W **89** H7
Granadilla de Abona
 Canary Is. 28°7N 16°33W **100** F3
Granard *Ireland* 53°47N 7°30W **64** C4
Granbury *U.S.A.* 32°27N 97°47W **176** E6
Granby *Canada* 45°25N 72°45W **175** A12
Granby *U.S.A.* 40°5N 105°56W **168** F11
Grand → *Mo., U.S.A.* 39°23N 93°6W **172** F7
Grand → *S. Dak.,
 U.S.A.* 45°40N 100°45W **172** C3
Grand-Anse = Portsmouth
 Dominica 15°34N 61°27W **183** C7
Grand Bahama I.
 Bahamas 26°40N 78°30W **182** A4
Grand Baie *Mauritius* 20°0S 57°35E **141** d
Grand Bank *Canada* 47°6N 55°48W **165** C8
Grand Banks *Atl. Oc.* 45°0N 50°0W **56** C6

Grand Bassam
 Côte d'Ivoire 5°10N 3°49W **138** D4
Grand Bend *Canada* 43°18N 81°45W **174** C3
Grand Béréby
 Côte d'Ivoire 4°38N 6°55W **138** E3
Grand-Bourg
 Guadeloupe 15°53N 61°19W **182** b
Grand Canal = Da Yunhe →
 China 34°25N 120°5E **115** H10
Grand Canyon *U.S.A.* 36°3N 112°9W **169** H7
Grand Canyon △
 U.S.A. 36°15N 112°30W **169** H7
Grand Canyon-Parashant ○
 U.S.A. 36°30N 113°45W **169** H7
Grand Cayman
 Cayman Is. 19°20N 81°20W **182** C3
Grand Cess *Liberia* 4°40N 8°12W **138** E3
Grand Coulee *U.S.A.* 47°57N 119°0W **168** C4
Grand Coulee Dam
 U.S.A. 48°16N 100°47W **172** A3
Grand Est □ *France* 48°30N 5°0E **71** D12
Grand Falls *Canada* 47°3N 67°44W **165** C6
Grand Falls-Windsor
 Canada 48°56N 55°40W **165** C8
Grand Forks *Canada* 49°0N 118°30W **162** D5
Grand Forks *U.S.A.* 47°55N 97°3W **172** B5
Grand Gorge *U.S.A.* 42°21N 74°29W **175** D10
Grand Haven *U.S.A.* 43°4N 86°13W **172** D10
Grand I. *Mich., U.S.A.* 46°31N 86°40W **173** B10
Grand I. *N.Y., U.S.A.* 43°0N 78°58W **174** D6
Grand Island *U.S.A.* 40°55N 98°21W **172** E4
Grand Isle *La., U.S.A.* 29°14N 90°0W **177** G9
Grand Isle *Vt., U.S.A.* 44°43N 73°18W **175** B11
Grand Junction *U.S.A.* 39°4N 108°33W **168** G9
Grand L. *N.B., Canada* 45°57N 66°7W **165** D6
Grand L. *Nfld. & L.,
 Canada* 49°0N 57°30W **165** C8
Grand L. *Nfld. & L.,
 Canada* 53°40N 60°30W **165** B7
Grand L. *U.S.A.* 29°55N 92°47W **176** G8
Grand Lahou *Côte d'Ivoire* 5°10N 5°5W **138** D3
Grand Lake *U.S.A.* 40°15N 105°49W **168** F11
Grand-Lieu, L. de *France* 47°6N 1°40W **70** E5
Grand Manan I.
 Canada 44°45N 66°52W **165** D6
Grand Marais *Mich.,
 U.S.A.* 46°40N 85°59W **173** B11
Grand Marais *Minn.,
 U.S.A.* 47°45N 90°25W **164** C1
Grand-Mère *Canada* 46°36N 72°40W **164** C5
Grand Popo *Benin* 6°15N 1°57E **139** D5
Grand Portage *U.S.A.* 47°58N 89°41W **172** B9
Grand Prairie *U.S.A.* 32°44N 96°59W **176** E6
Grand Rapids *Canada* 53°12N 99°19W **163** C9
Grand Rapids *Mich.,
 U.S.A.* 42°58N 85°40W **173** D11
Grand Rapids *Minn.,
 U.S.A.* 47°14N 93°31W **172** B7
Grand Ridge *U.S.A.* 30°43N 85°1W **178** E4
Grand St-Bernard, Col du
 Europe 45°50N 7°10E **77** K3
Grand Staircase-Escalante ○
 U.S.A. 37°25N 111°33W **169** H8
Grand Teton *U.S.A.* 43°54N 110°50W **168** E8
Grand Teton △
 U.S.A. 43°50N 110°50W **168** E8
Grand Union Canal *U.K.* 52°7N 0°53W **67** E7
Grandas *Spain* 43°13N 6°53W **88** B4
Grande → *Jujuy,
 Argentina* 24°20S 65°2W **190** A2
Grande → *Mendoza,
 Argentina* 36°52S 69°45W **190** D2
Grande → *Bolivia* 15°51S 64°39W **186** G6
Grande → *Bahia,
 Brazil* 11°30S 44°30W **189** D2
Grande → *Minas Gerais,
 Brazil* 20°6S 51°4W **187** H8
Grande, B. *Argentina* 50°30S 68°20W **192** D3
Grande, Rio →
 N. Amer. 25°58N 97°9W **176** J6
Grande, Serra *Piauí,
 Brazil* 3°41S 44°48W **189** A2
Grande, Serra *Tocantins,
 Brazil* 8°0S 45°10W **189** B1
Grande Anse *Seychelles* 4°18S 55°45E **141** b
Grande Baleine →
 Canada 55°16N 77°47W **164** A4
Grande Cache *Canada* 53°53N 119°8W **162** C5
Grande Casse, Pte. de la
 France 45°24N 6°49E **73** C10
Grande Comore
 Comoros Is. 11°35S 43°20E **141** a
Grande-Entrée *Canada* 47°30N 61°40E **165** C7
Grande Prairie
 Canada 55°10N 118°50W **162** B5
Grande-Rivière *Canada* 48°26N 64°30W **165** C7
Grande-Vallée *Canada* 49°14N 65°8W **165** C6
Grande Vigie, Pte. de la
 Guadeloupe 16°32N 61°27W **182** b
Grandfalls *U.S.A.* 31°20N 102°51W **176** F3
Grândola *Portugal* 38°12N 8°35W **89** G2
Grandpré *France* 49°20N 4°50E **71** C11
Grands Causses △ *France* 44°5N 2°58E **72** D6
Grands-Jardins △
 Canada 47°41N 70°51W **165** C5
Grandview *Canada* 51°10N 100°42W **163** C8
Grandview *U.S.A.* 46°15N 119°54W **168** C4
Grandvilliers *France* 49°40N 1°57E **71** C8
Graneros *Chile* 34°5S 70°45W **190** C1
Grangemouth *U.K.* 56°1N 3°42W **65** E5
Granger *U.S.A.* 41°35N 109°58W **168** F9
Grangeville *U.S.A.* 45°56N 116°7W **168** D5
Granisle *Canada* 54°53N 126°13W **162** C3
Granit Rose, Côte *France* 48°50N 4°10W **70** D2
Granite City *U.S.A.* 38°42N 90°8W **172** F8
Granite Falls *U.S.A.* 44°49N 95°33W **172** C6
Granite L. *Canada* 48°8N 57°5W **165** C8
Granite Mt. *U.S.A.* 33°5N 116°28W **171** M10
Granite Pk. *U.S.A.* 45°10N 109°48W **168** D9
Granite S.C.
 U.S.A. 33°34N 81°49W **178** B6
Graniteville *Vt., U.S.A.* 44°8N 72°29W **175** B12
Granitola, C. *Italy* 37°34N 12°39E **94** F5
Granja *Brazil* 3°7S 40°50W **189** A3
Granja de Moreruela
 Spain 41°48N 5°44W **88** D5

Granja de Torrehermosa
 Spain 38°19N 5°35W **89** G5
Gränna *Sweden* 58°1N 14°28E **63** F8
Granollers *Spain* 41°39N 2°18E **90** D7
Gransee *Germany* 53°1N 13°8E **76** B8
Grant *Fla., U.S.A.* 27°56N 80°32W **179** H9
Grant *Nebr., U.S.A.* 40°50N 101°43W **172** E3
Grant, Mt. *U.S.A.* 38°34N 118°48W **168** G4
Grant City *U.S.A.* 40°29N 94°25W **172** E7
Grant I. *Australia* 11°10S 132°52E **148** B5
Grant Range *U.S.A.* 38°30N 115°25W **168** G6
Grantham *U.K.* 52°55N 0°38W **66** E7
Grantown-on-Spey *U.K.* 57°20N 3°36W **65** D5
Grants *U.S.A.* 35°9N 107°52W **169** J10
Grants Pass *U.S.A.* 42°26N 123°19W **168** E2
Grantsville *U.S.A.* 40°36N 112°28W **168** F7
Granville *France* 48°50N 1°35W **70** D5
Granville *N. Dak.,
 U.S.A.* 48°16N 100°47W **172** A3
Granville *N.Y., U.S.A.* 43°24N 73°16W **175** C11
Granville *Ohio, U.S.A.* 40°4N 82°31W **174** F2
Granville L. *Canada* 56°18N 100°30W **163** B8
Graskop *S. Africa* 24°56S 30°49E **145** B5
Gräsö *Sweden* 60°28N 18°35E **63** D12
Grass → *Canada* 56°3N 96°33W **163** B9
Grass Range *U.S.A.* 47°2N 108°48W **168** C9
Grass River △ *Canada* 54°40N 100°50W **163** C8
Grass Valley *Calif.,
 U.S.A.* 39°13N 121°4W **170** F6
Grass Valley *Oreg.,
 U.S.A.* 45°22N 120°47W **168** D3
Grassano *Italy* 40°38N 16°17E **95** B9
Grasse *France* 43°38N 6°56E **73** E10
Grassflat *U.S.A.* 41°0N 78°6W **174** E6
Grasslands △ *Canada* 49°11N 107°38W **163** D7
Grassy *Australia* 40°3S 144°5E **151** G3
Gråsten *Denmark* 54°55N 9°35E **63** K3
Grästorp *Sweden* 58°20N 12°40E **63** F7
Gratkorn *Austria* 47°8N 15°21E **78** D8
Graubünden □ *Switz.* 46°45N 9°30E **77** J5
Graulhet *France* 43°45N 1°59E **72** E5
Graus *Spain* 42°11N 0°20E **90** D5
Grave, Pte. de *France* 45°34N 1°4W **72** C2
Gravelbourg *Canada* 49°50N 106°35W **163** D7
Gravelines *France* 51°1N 2°10E **71** A9
's-Gravenhage *Neths.* 52°7N 4°17E **69** B4
Gravenhurst *Canada* 44°52N 79°20W **174** B5
Gravesend *Australia* 29°35S 150°20E **151** D5
Gravesend *U.K.* 51°26N 0°22E **67** F8
Gravina in Púglia *Italy* 40°49N 16°25E **95** B9
Gravois, Pointe-à- *Haiti* 16°2N 73°56W **183** C5
Gravona → *France* 41°58N 8°45E **73** G12
Gray *France* 47°27N 5°35E **71** E12
Gray *U.S.A.* 33°1N 83°32W **178** B6
Grayling *U.S.A.* 44°40N 84°43W **173** C11
Grays *U.K.* 51°28N 0°21E **67** F8
Grays Harbor *U.S.A.* 46°59N 124°1W **168** D2
Grays L. *U.S.A.* 43°4N 111°26W **168** E8
Grays River *U.S.A.* 46°21N 123°37W **170** D3
Grayvoron *Russia* 50°29N 35°41E **85** G8
Graz *Austria* 47°4N 15°27E **78** D8
Grdelica *Serbia* 42°55N 22°3E **96** C6
Greasy L. *Canada* 62°55N 122°12W **162** A4
Great Abaco I. = Abaco I.
 Bahamas 26°25N 77°10W **182** A4
Great Artesian Basin
 Australia 23°0S 144°0E **150** C3
Great Australian Bight
 Australia 33°30S 130°0E **149** F5
Great Bahama Bank
 Bahamas 23°15N 78°0W **182** B3
Great Barrier I. *N.Z.* 36°11S 175°25E **154** C4
Great Barrier Reef
 Australia 18°0S 146°50E **150** B4
Great Barrier Reef ○
 Australia 20°0S 150°0E **150** B4
Great Barrington
 U.S.A. 42°12N 73°22W **175** D11
Great Basalt Wall △
 Australia 19°52S 145°43E **150** B4
Great Basin *U.S.A.* 40°0N 117°0W **168** G5
Great Basin △ *U.S.A.* 38°56N 114°15W **168** G6
Great Basses *Sri Lanka* 6°11N 81°29E **127** L5
Great Bear → *Canada* 65°0N 126°0W **160** C7
Great Bear L. *Canada* 65°30N 120°0W **160** C8
Great Belt = Store Bælt
 Denmark 55°20N 11°0E **63** J4
Great Bend *Kans.,
 U.S.A.* 38°22N 98°46W **172** F4
Great Bend *Pa., U.S.A.* 41°58N 75°45W **175** E9
Great Blasket I. *Ireland* 52°6N 10°32W **64** D1
Great Britain *Europe* 54°0N 2°15W **58** E5
Great Camanoe
 Br. Virgin Is. 18°30N 64°35W **183** e
Great Channel *Asia* 6°0N 94°0E **127** L11
Great Coco I. = Koko Kyunzu
 Myanmar 14°7N 93°22E **127** G11
Great Codroy *Canada* 47°51N 59°16W **165** C8
Great Divide, The = Great
 Dividing Ra. *Australia* 23°0S 146°0E **150** C4
Great Divide Basin
 U.S.A. 42°0N 108°0W **168** E9
Great Dividing Ra.
 Australia 23°0S 146°0E **150** C4
Great Driffield = Driffield
 U.K. 54°0N 0°26W **66** C7
Great Exuma I.
 Bahamas 23°30N 75°50W **182** B4
Great Falls *Canada* 50°27N 96°1W **163** C9
Great Falls *U.S.A.* 47°30N 111°17W **168** C8
Great Fish = Groot-Vis →
 S. Africa 33°28S 27°5E **144** D4
Great Guana Cay
 Bahamas 24°0N 76°20W **182** B4
Great Himalayan △
 India 31°30N 77°30E **124** D7
Great Inagua I.
 Bahamas 21°0N 73°20W **183** B5
Great Indian Desert = Thar Desert
 India 28°0N 72°0E **124** F5
Great Karoo *S. Africa* 31°55S 21°0E **144** D3
Great Khingan Mts. = Da
 Hinggan Ling *China* 48°0N 121°0E **111** B13
Great Lake *Australia* 41°50S 146°40E **151** G4
Great Lakes *N. Amer.* 46°0N 84°0W **158** E11
Great Limpopo Transfrontier △
 Africa 23°30S 31°45E **145** B5
Great Malvern *U.S.A.* 37°27N 84°49W **173** F11
Great Miami → *U.S.A.* 39°7N 84°49W **173** F11
Great Nicobar *India* 7°0N 93°50E **127** L11
Great Ormes Head *U.K.* 53°20N 3°52W **66** D4

Great Otway △
  Australia 38°50S 143°50E **152** E5
Great Ouse → *U.K.* 52°48N 0°21E **66** E8
Great Palm I. *Australia* 18°45S 146°40E **150** B4
Great Pedro Bluff
  Jamaica 17°51N 77°44W **182** a
Great Pee Dee →
  U.S.A. 33°21N 79°10W **177** E15
Great Plains *N. Amer.* 47°0N 105°0W **158** E9
Great Ruaha →
  Tanzania 7°56S 37°52E **142** D4
Great Sacandaga L.
  U.S.A. 43°6N 74°16W **175** C10
Great Saint Bernard Pass = Grand
  St-Bernard, Col du
  Europe 45°50N 7°10E **77** K3
Great Salt Desert = Kavīr, Dasht-e
  Iran 34°30N 55°0E **129** C7
Great Salt L. *U.S.A.* 41°15N 112°40W **168** F7
Great Salt Lake Desert
  U.S.A. 40°50N 113°30W **168** F7
Great Salt Plains L.
  U.S.A. 36°45N 98°8W **176** C5
Great Sand Dunes △
  U.S.A. 37°48N 105°45W **169** H11
Great Sandy △
  Australia 26°13S 153°2E **151** D5
Great Sandy Desert
  Australia 21°0S 124°0E **148** D3
Great Sangi = Sangihe, Pulau
  Indonesia 3°35N 125°30E **119** D7
Great Scarcies → *S. Leone* 9°0N 13°0W **138** D2
Great Sea Reef *Fiji* 16°15S 179°0E **154** a
Great Sitkin I. *U.S.A.* 52°3N 176°6W **166** E4
Great Skellig *Ireland* 51°47N 10°33W **64** E1
Great Slave L. *Canada* 61°23N 115°38W **162** A5
Great Smoky Mts. △
  U.S.A. 35°40N 83°40W **177** D13
Great Stour = Stour →
  U.K. 51°18N 1°22E **67** F9
Great Victoria Desert
  Australia 29°30S 126°30E **149** E4
Great Wall *Antarctica* 62°30S 58°0W **55** C18
Great Wall *China* 38°30N 109°30E **114** E5
Great Whernside *U.K.* 54°10N 1°58W **66** C6
Great Yarmouth *U.K.* 52°37N 1°44E **67** E9
Great Zab = Zāb al Kabīr →
  Iraq 36°1N 43°24E **105** D10
Great Zimbabwe
  Zimbabwe 20°16S 30°54E **143** G3
Greater Antilles
  W. Indies 17°40N 74°0W **183** C5
Greater London □ *U.K.* 51°31N 0°6W **67** F7
Greater Manchester □
  U.K. 53°30N 2°15W **66** D5
Greater Sudbury
  Canada 46°30N 81°0W **164** C3
Greater Sunda Is.
  Indonesia 7°0S 112°0E **118** F4
Grebbestad *Sweden* 58°42N 11°15E **63** F5
Grebenka = Hrebenka
  Ukraine 50°9N 32°22E **85** G7
Greco, C. *Cyprus* 34°57N 34°5E **101** E13
Greco, Mte. *Italy* 41°48N 13°58E **93** G10
Gredos, Sierra de *Spain* 40°20N 5°0W **88** E6
Greece *Europe* 43°13N 77°41W **174** C7
Greece ■ *Europe* 40°0N 23°0E **98** B3
Greeley, Colo., U.S.A. 40°25N 104°42W **168** F11
Greeley, Nebr., U.S.A. 41°33N 98°32W **172** E4
Greeleyville *U.S.A.* 33°40N 79°59W **178** D10
Greely Fd. *Canada* 80°30N 85°0W **161** A15
Greem-Bell, Ostrov
  Russia 81°0N 62°0E **106** A7
Green →, Ky., U.S.A. 37°54N 87°30W **172** G10
Green →, Utah, U.S.A. 38°11N 109°53W **168** G9
Green B. *U.S.A.* 45°0N 87°30W **172** C10
Green Bay *U.S.A.* 44°31N 88°0W **172** C9
Green C. *Australia* 37°13S 150°1E **153** D9
Green Cove Springs
  U.S.A. 29°59N 81°42W **178** F8
Green I. = Lütao
  Taiwan 22°40N 121°30E **117** F13
Green Lake *Canada* 54°17N 107°47W **163** C7
Green Mts. *U.S.A.* 43°45N 72°45W **175** C12
Green Pond *U.S.A.* 32°44N 80°37W **178** C9
Green River *Wyo.,*
  U.S.A. 41°32N 109°28W **168** F9
Green River, *Utah, U.S.A.* 31°52N 109°56W **169** L8
Green Valley *U.S.A.* 31°52N 110°56W **169** L8
Greenacres *U.S.A.* 26°38N 80°7W **178** H9
Greenbank *U.S.A.* 48°6N 122°34W **170** B4
Greenbush *Mich.,*
  U.S.A. 44°35N 83°19W **174** B1
Greenbush *Minn.,*
  U.S.A. 48°42N 96°11W **172** A5
Greencastle *U.S.A.* 39°38N 86°52W **172** F9
Greene *U.S.A.* 42°20N 75°46W **175** D9
Greeneville *U.S.A.* 36°10N 82°50W **177** C13
Greenfield *Calif.,*
  U.S.A. 36°19N 121°15W **170** J5
Greenfield *Calif., U.S.A.* 35°15N 119°0W **171** K8
Greenfield *Ind., U.S.A.* 39°47N 85°46W **173** F11
Greenfield *Iowa, U.S.A.* 41°18N 94°28W **172** E6
Greenfield *Mass.,*
  U.S.A. 42°35N 72°36W **175** D12
Greenfield *Mo., U.S.A.* 37°25N 93°51W **172** G7
Greenfield Park
  Canada 45°29N 73°28W **175** A11
Greenland ☑ *N. Amer.* 66°0N 45°0W **57** D6
Greenland Sea *Arctic* 73°0N 10°0W **57** B10
Greenock *U.K.* 55°57N 4°46W **65** F4
Greenore *Ireland* 54°1N 6°9W **64** B5
Greenore Pt. *Ireland* 52°14N 6°19W **64** D5
Greenough →
  Australia 28°51S 114°38E **149** E1
Greenough Pt. *Canada* 44°58N 81°26W **174** B3
Greenport *U.S.A.* 41°6N 72°22W **175** E12
Greensboro *Fla., U.S.A.* 30°34N 84°45W **178** F6
Greensboro *Ga., U.S.A.* 33°35N 83°11W **178** B6
Greensboro *N.C.,*
  U.S.A. 36°4N 79°48W **177** C15
Greensboro *Vt.,*
  U.S.A. 44°36N 72°18W **175** B12
Greensburg *Ind.,*
  U.S.A. 39°20N 85°29W **173** F11
Greensburg *Kans.,*
  U.S.A. 37°36N 99°18W **172** G4
Greensburg *Pa., U.S.A.* 40°18N 79°33W **174** F5
Greenstone = Geraldton
  Canada 49°44N 87°10W **164** C2

Greenstone Pt. *U.K.* 57°55N 5°37W **65** D3
Greenvale *Australia* 18°59S 145°7E **150** B4
Greenville *Liberia* 5°1N 9°6W **138** D3
Greenville *Ala., U.S.A.* 31°50N 86°38W **177** F11
Greenville *Calif., U.S.A.* 40°8N 120°57W **170** E6
Greenville *Ga., U.S.A.* 33°2N 84°43W **178** B5
Greenville *Maine,*
  U.S.A. 45°28N 69°35W **173** C19
Greenville *Mich.,*
  U.S.A. 43°11N 85°15W **173** D11
Greenville *Miss., U.S.A.* 33°24N 91°4W **177** E9
Greenville *Mo., U.S.A.* 37°8N 90°27W **172** G8
Greenville *N.C.,*
  U.S.A. 35°37N 77°23W **177** D16
Greenville *N.H.,*
  U.S.A. 42°46N 71°49W **175** D13
Greenville *Ohio, U.S.A.* 40°6N 84°38W **173** E11
Greenville *Pa., U.S.A.* 41°24N 80°23W **174** E4
Greenville *S.C., U.S.A.* 34°51N 82°24W **177** D13
Greenville *Tex., U.S.A.* 33°8N 96°7W **176** E6
Greenwater Lake
  Canada 52°32N 103°30W **163** C8
Greenwich *Conn.,*
  U.S.A. 41°2N 73°38W **175** E11
Greenwich *N.Y.,*
  U.S.A. 43°5N 73°30W **175** C11
Greenwich *Ohio, U.S.A.* 41°2N 82°31W **174** E2
Greenwich □ *U.K.* 51°29N 0°1E **67** F8
Greenwood *Canada* 49°10N 118°40W **162** D5
Greenwood *Ark.,*
  U.S.A. 35°13N 94°16W **176** D7
Greenwood *Fla., U.S.A.* 30°52N 85°10W **178** F4
Greenwood *Ind., U.S.A.* 39°37N 86°7W **172** F10
Greenwood *Miss.,*
  U.S.A. 33°31N 90°11W **177** E9
Greenwood *S.C.,*
  U.S.A. 34°12N 82°10W **178** A7
Greenwood, Mt.
  Australia 13°48S 130°4E **148** B5
Gregbe *Côte d'Ivoire* 6°48N 6°43W **138** D3
Gregório → *Brazil* 6°50S 70°46W **188** B3
Gregory *U.S.A.* 43°14N 99°26W **172** D4
Gregory → *Australia* 17°53S 139°17E **150** B2
Gregory, L. *S. Austral.,*
  Australia 28°55S 139°0E **151** D2
Gregory, L. *W. Austral.,*
  Australia 20°0S 127°40E **148** D4
Gregory, L. *W. Austral.,*
  Australia 25°38S 119°58E **149** E2
Gregory → *Australia* 15°38S 131°15E **148** C5
Gregory Downs
  Australia 18°35S 138°45E **150** B2
Gregory Ra. *Queens.,*
  Australia 19°30S 143°40E **150** B3
Gregory Ra. *W. Austral.,*
  Australia 21°20S 121°12E **148** D3
Greiffenberg *Germany* 53°5N 13°57E **76** B9
Greifswald *Germany* 54°5N 13°23E **76** A9
Greifswalder Bodden
  Germany 54°12N 13°35E **76** A9
Grein *Austria* 48°14N 14°51E **78** C7
Greiz *Germany* 50°39N 12°10E **76** E8
Gremikha *Russia* 67°59N 39°47E **106** C4
Grenaa *Denmark* 56°25N 10°53E **63** H4
Grenada *U.S.A.* 33°47N 89°49W **177** E10
Grenada ■ *W. Indies* 12°10N 61°40W **183** D7
Grenade *France* 43°47N 1°17E **72** E5
Grenadier I. *U.S.A.* 44°3N 76°22W **175** B8
Grenadines, The
  St. Vincent 12°40N 61°20W **183** D7
Grenchen *Switz.* 47°12N 7°24E **77** H3
Grenen *Denmark* 57°44N 10°40E **63** G4
Grenfell *Australia* 33°52S 148°8E **153** B8
Grenfell *Canada* 50°30N 102°56W **163** C8
Grenoble *France* 45°12N 5°42E **73** C9
Grenville, C. *Australia* 12°0S 143°13E **150** A3
Grenville Chan.
  Canada 53°40N 129°46W **162** C3
Gréoux-les-Bains *France* 43°45N 5°52E **73** E9
Gresham *U.S.A.* 45°30N 122°25W **170** E4
Gresik *Indonesia* 7°13S 112°38E **119** G15
Gretna *U.K.* 55°0N 3°3W **65** F5
Gretna *Fla., U.S.A.* 30°37N 84°40W **178** F5
Gretna *La., U.S.A.* 29°54N 90°3W **177** F9
Greve Strand *Denmark* 55°34N 12°18E **63** J6
Greven *Germany* 52°6N 7°37E **76** D3
Grevena *Greece* 40°4N 21°25E **96** F5
Grevenbroich *Germany* 51°5N 6°35E **76** D2
Grevenmacher *Lux.* 49°41N 6°26E **69** E6
Grevesmühlen *Germany* 53°52N 11°12E **76** B7
Grey → *Canada* 47°34N 57°6W **165** C8
Grey → *N.Z.* 42°27S 171°12E **155** C6
Grey, C. *Australia* 13°0S 136°35E **150** A2
Grey Is. *Canada* 50°50N 55°35W **161** G20
Grey Ra. *Australia* 27°0S 143°30E **153** D3
Greybull *U.S.A.* 44°30N 108°3W **168** D9
Greymouth *N.Z.* 42°29S 171°13E **155** C6
Greystones *Ireland* 53°9N 6°5W **64** C5
Greytown *N.Z.* 41°5S 175°29E **154** H4
Greytown *S. Africa* 29°1S 30°36E **145** C5
Gribanovskiy *Russia* 51°28N 41°50E **86** E5
Gribbell I. *Canada* 53°23N 129°0W **162** C3
Gribës, Mal i *Albania* 40°17N 19°45E **96** F3
Gridley *U.S.A.* 39°22N 121°42W **170** F5
Griekwastad *S. Africa* 28°49S 23°15E **144** C3
Griesheim *Germany* 49°51N 8°33E **77** F4
Grieskirchen *Austria* 48°16N 13°48E **78** C6
Griffin *U.S.A.* 33°15N 84°16W **178** B5
Griffin, L. *U.S.A.* 28°52N 81°51W **178** G8
Griffith *Australia* 34°18S 146°2E **153** C7
Griffith *Canada* 45°15N 77°10W **174** B7
Griffith I. *Canada* 44°50N 80°55W **174** B4
Grignols *France* 44°26N 0°3W **72** D3
Grigoriopol *Moldova* 47°9N 29°18E **81** C14
Grimaylov = Hrymayliv
  Ukraine 49°20N 26°5E **75** D14
Grimes *U.S.A.* 39°4N 121°54W **170** F5
Grimma *Germany* 51°14N 12°43E **76** D8
Grimmen *Germany* 54°7N 13°3E **76** A9
Grimsay I. *U.K.* 57°29N 7°14E **65** D1
Grimsby *Canada* 43°12N 79°34W **174** C5
Grimsby *U.K.* 53°34N 0°5W **66** D7
Grímsey *Iceland* 66°33N 17°58W **60** C5
Grimshaw *Canada* 56°10N 117°40W **162** B5
Grimslöv *Sweden* 56°44N 14°34E **63** H6
Grimstad *Norway* 58°20N 8°35E **61** G13
Grindelwald *Switz.* 46°38N 8°2E **77** J4
Grindsted *Denmark* 55°46N 8°55E **63** J2
Grindstone I. *U.S.A.* 44°17N 76°27W **175** B8
Grindu *Romania* 44°44N 26°50E **81** F11

Grinnell *U.S.A.* 41°45N 92°43W **172** E7
Grinnell Pen. *Canada* 76°40N 95°0W **161** B13
Grintavec *Slovenia* 46°22N 14°32E **93** B11
Griomasaigh = Grimsay
  U.K. 57°29N 7°14E **65** D1
Gris-Nez, C. *France* 50°52N 1°35E **71** B8
Grise Fiord *Canada* 76°25N 82°57W **161** B15
Grisolles *France* 43°49N 1°19E **72** E5
Grisons = Graubünden □
  Switz. 46°45N 9°30E **77** J5
Grisslehamn *Sweden* 60°5N 18°49E **62** D12
Grmeč Planina *Bos.-H.* 44°43N 16°18E **93** D13
Groais I. *Canada* 50°55N 55°35W **165** B8
Grobiņa *Latvia* 56°35N 21°10E **82** B8
Groblersdal *S. Africa* 25°15S 29°25E **145** C4
Grobming *Austria* 47°27N 13°54E **78** D6
Grocka *Serbia* 44°40N 20°42E **96** B4
Gródek *Poland* 53°6N 23°40E **83** E10
Grodków *Poland* 50°43N 17°21E **83** H4
Grodno = Hrodna
  Belarus 53°42N 23°52E **82** E10
Grodzisk Mazowiecki
  Poland 52°7N 20°37E **83** F7
Grodzisk Wielkopolski
  Poland 52°15N 16°22E **83** F3
Grodzyanka = Hrodzyanka
  Belarus 53°31N 28°42E **75** B15
Groesbeck *U.S.A.* 31°31N 96°32W **176** F6
Groix *France* 47°38N 3°29W **70** E3
Groix, Î. de *France* 47°38N 3°28W **70** E3
Grójec *Poland* 51°50N 20°58E **83** G7
Gronau *Niedersachsen,*
  Germany 52°5N 9°47E **76** D5
Gronau *Nordrhein-Westfalen,*
  Germany 52°12N 7°2E **76** C3
Grong *Norway* 64°25N 12°8E **60** D15
Grönhögen *Sweden* 56°16N 16°24E **63** H7
Groningen *Neths.* 53°15N 6°35E **69** A6
Groningen □ *Neths.* 53°16N 6°40E **69** A6
Grønland △ *Greenland* 75°0N 35°0W **57** C7
Grønnedal = Kangilinnguit
  Greenland 61°14N 48°0W **57** E6
Groom *U.S.A.* 35°12N 101°6W **176** D4
Groot → *S. Africa* 33°45S 24°36E **144** D3
Groot-Berg → *S. Africa* 32°47S 18°8E **144** D2
Groot-Brakrivier
  S. Africa 34°2S 22°18E **144** D3
Groot Karasberge
  Namibia 27°20S 18°40E **144** C2
Groot-Kei → *S. Africa* 32°41S 28°22E **145** D4
Groot-Vis → *S. Africa* 33°28S 27°5E **145** D4
Grootdrink *S. Africa* 28°33S 21°42E **144** C3
Groote Eylandt
  Australia 14°0S 136°40E **150** A2
Groote Peel △ *Neths.* 51°22N 5°49E **69** C5
Grootfontein *Namibia* 19°31S 18°6E **144** A2
Grootlaagte → *Africa* 20°55S 21°27E **144** B3
Grootvloer → *S. Africa* 30°0S 20°40E **144** D3
Gros C. *Canada* 61°59N 113°32W **162** A6
Gros Islet *St. Lucia* 14°5N 60°58W **183** f
Gros Morne △ *Canada* 49°40N 57°50W **165** C8
Gros Piton *St. Lucia* 13°49N 61°5W **183** f
Gros Piton Pt. *St. Lucia* 13°49N 61°5W **183** f
Grósio *Italy* 46°18N 10°16E **92** D7
Grosne → *France* 46°42N 4°56E **71** F11
Grossa, Pta. *Spain* 39°6N 1°36E **108** B8
Grosse Point *U.S.A.* 42°23N 82°54W **174** D2
Grossenbrode *Germany* 54°21N 11°4E **76** A7
Grossenhain *Germany* 51°17N 13°32E **76** D9
Grosser Arber *Germany* 49°6N 13°8E **77** F9
Grosser Plöner See
  Germany 54°10N 10°22E **76** A6
Grosseto *Italy* 42°46N 11°8E **78** F5
Grossgerungs *Austria* 48°34N 14°57E **78** C7
Grossglockner *Austria* 47°5N 12°40E **78** D5
Grostwater B. *Canada* 54°20N 57°40W **165** B8
Groton *Conn., U.S.A.* 41°21N 72°5W **175** E12
Groton *N.Y., U.S.A.* 42°36N 76°22W **175** D8
Groton *S. Dak., U.S.A.* 45°27N 98°6W **172** C4
Grottáglie *Italy* 40°32N 17°26E **95** B10
Grottaminarda *Italy* 41°4N 15°2E **95** A8
Grottammare *Italy* 42°59N 13°52E **93** F10
Grotte Chauvet-Pont d'Arc
  France 44°23N 4°25E **73** D8
Grouard Mission
  Canada 55°33N 116°9W **162** B5
Grouin, Pte. du *France* 48°43N 1°51W **70** D5
Groulx, Mts. *Canada* 51°27N 68°41W **165** B6
Groundhog → *Canada* 48°45N 82°58W **164** C3
Grouw *Neths.* 53°5N 5°51E **69** A5
Grove City *Fla., U.S.A.* 26°56N 82°19W **178** J7
Grove City *Pa., U.S.A.* 41°10N 80°5W **174** E4
Grove Hill *U.S.A.* 31°42N 87°47W **177** F11
Groveland *Calif.,*
  U.S.A. 37°50N 120°14W **170** H6
Groveland *Fla., U.S.A.* 28°34N 81°51W **178** G8
Grover Beach *U.S.A.* 35°7N 120°37W **171** K6
Groveton *U.S.A.* 29°57N 93°54W **176** F7
Grovetown *U.S.A.* 44°36N 71°31W **175** B13
Grovetown *U.S.A.* 33°27N 82°12W **178** B7
Groznjan *Croatia* 45°22N 13°43E **93** C10
Groznyy *Russia* 43°20N 45°45E **87** J7
Grubišno Polje *Croatia* 45°44N 17°12E **80** E2
Grudovo = Sredets
  Bulgaria 42°21N 27°10E **97** D11
Grudusk *Poland* 53°3N 20°38E **83** E7
Grudziądz *Poland* 53°30N 18°47E **82** E5
Gruinard B. *U.K.* 57°56N 5°35W **65** D3
Gruissan *France* 43°8N 3°7E **72** E7
Grums *Sweden* 59°22N 13°5E **63** E6
Gründau *Germany* 50°10N 9°9E **77** E5
Grünberg *Germany* 50°36N 8°58E **76** E4
Grundy Center *U.S.A.* 42°22N 92°47W **172** D7
Grünstadt *Germany* 49°34N 8°9E **77** F4
Gruppo di Tessa △ *Italy* 46°30N 11°0E **92** B8
Gruvberget *Sweden* 61°6N 16°10E **62** D10
Gruver *U.S.A.* 36°16N 101°24W **176** C4
Gruyères *Switz.* 46°35N 7°4E **77** J3
Gruža *Serbia* 43°54N 20°46E **96** C4
Gryazi *Russia* 52°30N 39°58E **85** F10
Gryazovets *Russia* 58°50N 40°10E **84** C11
Grybów *Poland* 49°36N 20°55E **83** J7
Grycksbo *Sweden* 60°40N 15°29E **62** D9
Gryfice *Poland* 53°55N 15°13E **82** E2
Gryfino *Poland* 53°4N 14°29E **82** E1
Gryfów Śląski *Poland* 51°2N 15°24E **83** H2
Gryt *Sweden* 58°12N 16°48E **63** F8
Grythyttan *Sweden* 59°41N 14°32E **62** E8
Gryttjom *S. Georgia* 54°19S 36°50E **56** M8
Gstaad *Switz.* 46°28N 7°18E **77** J3
Gua *India* 22°18N 85°20E **125** H11
Gua Musang *Malaysia* 4°53N 101°58E **121** K3

Guabún, Pta. *Chile* 41°48S 74°2W **192** B2
Guacanayabo, G. de
  Cuba 20°40N 77°20W **182** B4
Guáchipas
  Argentina 25°40S 65°30W **190** B2
Guadajoz → *Spain* 37°50N 4°51W **89** H6
Guadalajara *Mexico* 20°40N 103°20W **180** C4
Guadalajara *Spain* 40°37N 3°12W **90** E1
Guadalajara □ *Spain* 40°47N 2°30W **90** E2
Guadalaviar = Turia →
  Spain 39°27N 0°19W **91** F4
Guadalcanal
  Solomon Is. 9°32S 160°12E **147** B9
Guadalcanal *Spain* 38°5N 5°52W **89** G5
Guadalén → *Spain* 38°5N 3°32W **89** G7
Guadales *Argentina* 34°30S 67°55W **190** C2
Guadalete → *Spain* 36°35N 6°13W **89** J4
Guadalhorce → *Spain* 36°41N 4°27W **89** J6
Guadalimar → *Spain* 38°5N 3°28W **89** G7
Guadalmena → *Spain* 38°19N 2°56W **89** G8
Guadalmez → *Spain* 38°46N 5°4W **89** G5
Guadalope → *Spain* 41°15N 0°3W **90** D4
Guadalquivir → *Spain* 36°47N 6°22W **89** J4
Guadalupe = Guadeloupe ☑
  W. Indies 16°15N 61°40W **182** b
Guadalupe *Brazil* 6°44S 43°47W **189** D10
Guadalupe *Mexico* 25°41N 100°15W **180** B4
Guadalupe *Spain* 39°27N 5°17W **89** F5
Guadalupe → *U.S.A.* 34°58N 120°34W **171** L6
Guadalupe → *U.S.A.* 28°27N 96°47W **176** G6
Guadalupe, Sierra de
  Spain 39°28N 5°30W **89** F5
Guadalupe de Bravo
  Mexico 31°23N 106°7W **180** A3
Guadalupe I. *Pac. Oc.* 29°0N 118°50W **158** G8
Guadalupe Mts. △
  U.S.A. 31°40N 104°30W **176** F2
Guadalupe Peak
  U.S.A. 31°50N 104°52W **176** F2
Guadalupe y Calvo
  Mexico 26°6N 106°58W **180** B3
Guadarrama, Sierra de
  Spain 41°0N 4°0W **88** E7
Guadeloupe ☑ *W. Indies* 16°15N 61°40W **182** b
Guadeloupe →
  Guadeloupe 16°10N 61°40W **182** b
Guadeloupe Passage
  W. Indies 16°50N 62°15W **183** C7
Guadeloupe *Peru* 7°15S 79°29W **188** B2
Guadiamar → *Spain* 36°55N 6°24W **89** J4
Guadiana → *Spain* 37°14N 7°22W **89** H3
Guadiana Menor →
  Spain 37°56N 3°15W **89** H7
Guadiaro → *Spain* 36°17N 5°17W **89** J5
Guadiato → *Spain* 37°48N 5°5W **89** H5
Guadiela → *Spain* 40°22N 2°49W **90** E2
Guadix *Spain* 37°18N 3°11W **89** H7
Guafo, Boca del *Chile* 43°35S 74°0W **192** B2
Guafo, I. *Chile* 43°35S 74°50W **192** B2
Guáhán = Guam ☑
  Pac. Oc. 13°27N 144°45E **156** F6
Guaico *Trin. & Tob.* 10°35N 61°9W **187** K15
Guainía → *Colombia* 2°1N 67°7W **186** C5
Guaíra *Brazil* 24°5S 54°10W **191** A5
Guaíra □ *Paraguay* 25°45S 56°30W **190** B4
Guaíre = Gorey *Ireland* 52°41N 6°18W **64** D5
Guaitecas, Is. *Chile* 44°0S 74°30W **192** B2
Guajará-Mirim *Brazil* 10°50S 65°20W **186** F5
Guajira, Pen. de la
  Colombia 12°0N 72°0W **186** A4
Gualán *Guatemala* 15°8N 89°22W **182** C2
Gualdo Tadino *Italy* 43°14N 12°47E **93** E9
Gualeguay *Argentina* 33°10S 59°14W **190** C4
Gualeguaychú
  Argentina 33°3S 59°31W **190** C4
Gualequay →
  Argentina 33°19S 59°39W **190** C4
Gualicho, Salina
  Argentina 40°25S 65°30W **192** B3
Gualjaina *Argentina* 42°45S 70°30W **192** B2
Guam ☑ *Pac. Oc.* 13°27N 144°45E **156** F6
Guamblin, I. *Chile* 44°50S 75°0W **192** B2
Guamini *Argentina* 37°1S 62°28W **190** D3
Guamúchil *Mexico* 25°28N 108°6W **180** B3
Guana I. *Br. Virgin Is.* 18°30N 64°30W **183** e
Guanabacoa *Cuba* 23°8N 82°18W **182** B3
Guanacaste, Cordillera de
  Costa Rica 10°40N 85°4W **182** D2
Guanacaste △
  Costa Rica 10°57N 85°30W **182** D2
Guanaceví *Mexico* 25°56N 105°57W **180** B3
Guanahani = San Salvador I.
  Bahamas 24°0N 74°40W **183** B5
Guanaja *Honduras* 16°30N 85°55W **182** C2
Guanajay *Cuba* 22°56N 82°42W **182** B3
Guanajuato *Mexico* 21°1N 101°15W **180** C4
Guanajuato □ *Mexico* 21°0N 101°0W **180** C4
Guanambi *Brazil* 14°13S 42°47W **189** F10
Guanacol *Argentina* 29°30S 68°40W **190** B2
Guandacol *Argentina* 29°30S 68°40W **190** B2
Guandi Shan *China* 37°53N 111°29E **114** F6
Guane *Cuba* 22°10N 84°7W **182** B3
Guang'an *China* 30°28N 106°35E **116** B6
Guangchang *China* 26°50N 116°21E **117** D11
Guangde *China* 30°54N 119°25E **117** B12
Guangdong □ *China* 23°0N 113°0E **117** F9
Guangfeng *China* 28°20N 118°15E **117** C12
Guangling *China* 39°47N 114°17E **116** B5
Guangnan *China* 24°5N 105°4E **116** E5
Guangning *China* 23°40N 112°22E **117** F9
Guangrao *China* 37°5N 118°25E **115** F10
Guangshui *China* 31°37N 114°0E **116** B9
Guangshun *China* 26°8N 106°21E **116** D6
Guangwu *China* 38°5N 105°57E **114** F3
Guangxi Zhuangzu Zizhiqu □
  China 24°0N 109°0E **116** F7
Guangyuan *China* 32°26N 105°51E **116** A5
Guangze *China* 27°30N 117°12E **117** D11
Guangzhou *China* 23°13N 113°18E **117** F9
Guangzhou Baiyun Int. ✈ (CAN)
  China 23°24N 113°18E **117** F9
Guanhães *Brazil* 18°47S 42°57W **189** D10
Guanica *Puerto Rico* 17°58N 66°55W **183** d
Guanipa → *Venezuela* 9°56N 62°26W **187** B6
Guanling *China* 25°38N 105°35E **116** E5
Guannan *China* 34°8N 119°21E **115** H10
Guantánamo *Cuba* 20°10N 75°14W **183** C7
Guantánamo B. *Cuba* 19°59N 75°10W **183** C7
Guantao *China* 36°42N 115°25E **114** F8
Guanyang *China* 25°30S 111°8E **117** E8
Guanyun *China* 34°20N 119°18E **115** G10

Guapay = Grande →
  Bolivia 15°51S 64°39W **186** G6
Guápiles *Costa Rica* 10°10N 83°46W **182** D3
Guapo B. *Trin. & Tob.* 10°12N 61°41W **187** K15
Guaporé *Brazil* 28°51S 51°54W **191** B5
Guaporé → *Brazil* 11°55S 65°4W **186** F5
Guaqui *Bolivia* 16°41S 68°54W **188** D4
Guara, Sierra de *Spain* 42°19N 0°15W **90** C4
Guarabira *Brazil* 6°51S 35°29W **189** B3
Guaramacal △
  Venezuela 9°13N 70°12W **183** E5
Guaraparí *Brazil* 20°40S 40°30W **192** D6
Guarapuava *Brazil* 25°20S 51°30W **191** B5
Guaratinguetá *Brazil* 22°49S 45°9W **191** A6
Guaratuba *Brazil* 25°53S 48°38W **191** B6
Guarda *Portugal* 40°32N 7°20W **88** E3
Guarda □ *Portugal* 40°40N 7°20W **88** E3
Guardafui, C. = Asir, Ras
  Somalia 11°55N 51°10E **131** E5
Guardamar del Segura
  Spain 38°5N 0°39W **91** G4
Guardavalle *Italy* 38°30N 16°30E **95** D9
Guárdia Sanframondi
  Italy 41°15N 14°36E **95** A7
Guardiagrele *Italy* 42°11N 14°13E **93** F11
Guardo *Spain* 42°47N 4°50W **88** C6
Guareña *Spain* 38°51N 6°6W **89** G4
Guareña → *Spain* 41°29N 5°23W **88** D5
Guárico □ *Venezuela* 8°40N 66°35W **186** B5
Guarujá *Brazil* 24°2S 46°25W **191** A6
Guarulhos *Brazil* 23°29S 46°33W **191** A6
Guasave *Mexico* 25°34N 108°27W **180** B3
Guasdualito *Venezuela* 7°15N 70°44W **186** B4
Guastalla *Italy* 44°55N 10°39E **92** D7
Guatemala *Guatemala* 14°40N 90°22W **182** D1
Guatemala ■
  Cent. Amer. 15°40N 90°30W **182** C1
Guatemala Basin
  Pac. Oc. 11°0N 95°0W **157** F18
Guatemala Trench
  Pac. Oc. 14°0N 95°0W **158** H10
Guatopo △ *Venezuela* 10°0N 66°30W **183** F6
Guatuaro Pt.
  Trin. & Tob. 10°19N 60°59W **187** K16
Guaviare → *Colombia* 4°3N 67°44W **186** C5
Guaxupé *Brazil* 21°10S 47°5W **191** A6
Guayaguayare
  Trin. & Tob. 10°8N 61°2W **187** K15
Guayama *Puerto Rico* 17°59N 66°7W **183** d
Guayaneco, Arch.
  Chile 47°45S 75°10W **192** C1
Guayaquil *Ecuador* 2°15S 79°52W **186** D3
Guayaquil *Mexico* 29°59N 115°4W **180** B1
Guayaquil, G. de *Ecuador* 3°10S 81°0W **186** D2
Guaymas *Mexico* 27°56N 110°54W **180** B2
Guba
  Dem. Rep. of the Congo 10°38S 26°27E **143** G5
Gûbâl, Madîq *Egypt* 27°30N 34°0E **137** B3
Gubbi *India* 13°19N 76°56E **127** H3
Gúbbio *Italy* 43°21N 12°35E **93** E9
Guben *Germany* 51°57N 14°43E **76** D10
Gubin *Poland* 51°57N 14°43E **83** G1
Gubio *Nigeria* 12°30N 12°42E **139** C7
Gubkin *Russia* 51°17N 37°32E **85** G9
Gubkinskiy *Russia* 64°27N 76°36E **106** C8
Guča *Serbia* 43°46N 20°15E **96** C4
Gucheng *China* 32°20N 111°30E **117** A8
Gudalur *India* 11°30N 76°29E **127** J3
Gudauta *Georgia* 43°7N 40°32E **87** J5
Gudbrandsdalen
  Norway 61°33N 10°10E **60** F14
Guddu Barrage
  Pakistan 28°30N 69°50E **124** E3
Gudena → *Denmark* 56°29N 10°13E **63** H4
Gudermes *Russia* 43°24N 46°5E **87** J8
Gudhjem *Denmark* 55°12N 14°58E **63** J8
Gudivada *India* 16°30N 81°3E **127** F5
Gudiyattam *India* 12°57N 78°55E **127** H4
Gudur *India* 14°12N 79°55E **127** G4
Guebwiller *France* 47°55N 7°12E **71** E14
Guecho = Algorta *Spain* 43°21N 2°59W **90** B2
Guékédou *Guinea* 8°40N 10°5W **138** D2
Guéle Mendouka
  Cameroon 4°23N 12°55E **139** E7
Guelma *Algeria* 36°25N 7°29E **136** A5
Guelma □ *Algeria* 36°25N 7°25E **136** A5
Guelmim *Morocco* 28°56N 10°0W **136** C3
Guelph *Canada* 43°35N 80°20W **174** C4
Guemar *Algeria* 33°30N 6°49E **136** B6
Guémené-Penfao *France* 47°38N 1°50W **70** E5
Guémené-sur-Scorff
  France 48°4N 3°13W **70** D3
Guéné *Benin* 11°44N 3°16E **139** C5
Güer Aike *Argentina* 51°39S 69°35W **192** D3
Guérande *France* 47°20N 2°26W **70** E4
Guercif *Morocco* 34°14N 3°21W **136** B5
Guéret *France* 46°11N 1°51E **71** F8
Guérigny *France* 47°5N 3°10E **71** E10
Guerneville *U.S.A.* 38°30N 123°0W **170** G4
Guernica = Gernika-Lumo
  Spain 43°19N 2°40W **90** B2
Guernsey *U.S.A.* 42°19N 104°45W **168** E11
Guernsey *U.K.* 49°26N 2°35W **67** H5
Guerra *Oasis, Algeria* 32°51N 4°22E **136** B4
Guerrara *Saoura, Algeria* 28°5N 0°8W **136** C5
Guerrero □ *Mexico* 17°40N 100°0W **181** D5
Guerzim *Algeria* 29°39N 1°40W **136** C4
Guéyo *Côte d'Ivoire* 5°25N 6°55W **138** D3
Gügher *Iran* 29°28N 56°27E **129** D8
Guglionesi *Italy* 41°55N 14°55E **93** G11
Gui Jiang → *China* 23°30N 111°15E **117** F8
Gui Xian = Guiping
  China 23°21N 110°2E **117** F8
Guia *Canary Is.* 28°8N 15°38W **105** F4
Guia de Isora
  Canary Is. 28°12N 16°46W **105** F3
Guia Lopes da Laguna
  Brazil 21°26S 56°7W **191** A4
Guiana Highlands
  S. Amer. 5°10N 60°40W **184** C4
Guibéroua *Côte d'Ivoire* 6°13N 5°56W **138** D3
Guichen B. *Australia* 37°10S 139°45E **152** C3
Guichi *China* 30°39N 117°27E **117** B11
Guider *Cameroon* 9°56N 13°57E **139** D7
Guidimaka □
  Mauritania 15°20N 12°0W **138** B2
Guidimouni *Niger* 13°42N 9°31E **139** C6
Guiding *China* 26°34N 107°11E **116** D6
Guidong *China* 26°7N 113°57E **117** D9

Guidónia-Montecélio
  Italy 42°1N 12°45E **93** F9
Guigang *China* 23°8N 109°35E **116** F7
Guiglo *Côte d'Ivoire* 6°45N 7°30W **138** D3
Guijá *Mozam.* 24°27S 33°0E **145** B5
Guijuelo *Spain* 40°33N 5°40W **88** E5
Guildford *U.K.* 51°14N 0°34W **67** F7
Guilford *U.S.A.* 41°17N 72°41W **175** E12
Guilin *China* 25°18N 110°15E **117** E8
Guillaume-Delisle, L.
  Canada 56°15N 76°17W **164** A4
Guillaumes *France* 44°5N 6°52E **73** D10
Guillestre *France* 44°39N 6°40E **73** D10
Guilvinec *France* 47°48N 4°17W **70** E2
Güimar *Canary Is.* 28°18N 16°24W **105** F3
Guimarães *Portugal* 41°28N 8°24W **88** D2
Guimaras □ *Phil.* 10°22N 122°37E **119** F6
Guinda *U.S.A.* 38°50N 122°12W **170** G4
Guinea *Africa* 8°0N 8°0E **132** F4
Guinea ■ *W. Afr.* 10°20N 11°30W **138** C2
Guinea, Gulf of *Atl. Oc.* 3°0N 2°30E **139** E5
Guinea Basin *Atl. Oc.* 0°0 5°0W **56** G11
Guinea-Bissau ■ *Africa* 12°0N 15°0W **138** C2
Güines *Cuba* 22°50N 82°0W **182** B3
Guingamp *France* 48°34N 3°10W **70** D3
Guinguinéo *Senegal* 14°20N 15°57W **138** C1
Guipavas *France* 48°26N 4°29W **70** D2
Guiping *China* 23°21N 110°2E **117** F8
Guir *Mali* 18°52N 2°52W **138** B4
Guir, O. → *Algeria* 31°29N 2°17W **136** B4
Guiratinga *Brazil* 16°21S 53°46W **187** H8
Güiria *Venezuela* 10°32N 62°18W **186** A6
Guiscard *France* 49°40N 3°1E **71** C10
Guise *France* 49°52N 3°35E **71** C10
Guissona *Spain* 41°47N 1°17E **90** D6
Guitiriz *Spain* 43°11N 7°50W **88** B3
Guitri *Côte d'Ivoire* 5°30N 5°14W **138** D3
Guiuan *Phil.* 11°5N 125°55E **119** B7
Guixi *China* 28°16N 117°15E **117** C11
Guiyang *Guizhou,*
  China 26°32N 106°40E **116** D6
Guiyang *Hunan, China* 25°46N 112°42E **117** E9
Guizhou □ *China* 27°0N 107°0E **116** D6
Gujan-Mestras *France* 44°38N 1°4W **72** D2
Gujar Khan *Pakistan* 33°16N 73°19E **124** C5
Gujarat □ *India* 23°20N 71°0E **124** H4
Gujiang *China* 27°11N 114°47E **117** D10
Gujiao *China* 37°54N 112°1E **114** F6
Gujō *Japan* 35°45N 136°57E **113** G8
Gujranwala *Pakistan* 32°10N 74°12E **124** C6
Gujrat *Pakistan* 32°40N 74°2E **124** C6
Gukovo *Russia* 48°1N 39°58E **87** F5
Gulargambone
  Australia 31°20S 148°30E **153** A8
Gulbarga = Kalaburagi
  India 17°20N 76°50E **126** F3
Gulbene *Latvia* 57°8N 26°52E **84** D4
Guledagudda *India* 16°3N 75°48E **127** F2
Gulf, The = Persian Gulf
  Asia 27°0N 50°0E **129** E6
Gulf Breeze *U.S.A.* 30°21N 87°9W **179** F2
Gulf Hammock *U.S.A.* 29°15N 82°43W **178** F7
Gulf Islands ○ *U.S.A.* 30°10N 87°10W **179** E2
Gulfport *Fla., U.S.A.* 27°44N 82°42W **178** H7
Gulfport *Miss., U.S.A.* 30°22N 89°6W **177** F10
Gulgong *Australia* 32°20S 149°49E **153** B8
Gulian *China* 52°56N 122°21E **111** A13
Gulin *China* 28°1N 105°50E **116** C5
Gulistan = Yining *China* 43°58N 81°10E **109** D10
Gull Lake *Canada* 50°10N 108°29W **163** C7
Gullbrandstorp *Sweden* 56°42N 12°43E **63** H6
Gullivan B. *U.S.A.* 25°45N 81°40W **178** K8
Gullspång *Sweden* 58°59N 14°6E **63** F8
Güllük *Turkey* 37°14N 27°35E **99** E9
Güllük Dağı △ *Turkey* 37°0N 30°30E **99** E12
Güllük Körfezi *Turkey* 37°12N 27°30E **99** E9
Gulma *India* 12°40N 4°23E **139** C5
Gulmarg *India* 34°3N 74°25E **125** B6
Gulnar *Turkey* 36°19N 33°24E **138** G5
Gulnare *Australia* 33°27S 138°27E **152** B3
Gülpınar *Turkey* 39°32N 26°7E **99** B8
Gülşehir *Turkey* 38°44N 34°37E **104** C6
Gülşat *Kazakhstan* 46°38N 74°12E **108** E8
Gulu *Uganda* 2°48N 32°17E **142** B3
Gulwe *Tanzania* 6°30S 36°25E **142** D4
Gulyaypole = Hulyaypole
  Ukraine 47°45N 36°21E **85** J9
Gum Lake *Australia* 32°42S 143°9E **152** B5
Gumal → *Pakistan* 31°40N 71°50E **124** D4
Gumbaz *Pakistan* 30°2N 69°0E **124** D3
Gumdag *Turkmenistan* 39°9N 54°56E **108** E4
Gumel *Nigeria* 12°39N 9°22E **139** C6
Gumi *S. Korea* 36°10N 128°12E **115** F15
Gumiel de Izán *Spain* 41°46N 3°41W **88** D7
Gumla *India* 23°3N 84°33E **125** H11
Gumlu *Australia* 19°53S 147°41E **150** B4
Gummersbach *Germany* 51°1N 7°34E **76** D3
Gummi *Nigeria* 12°4N 5°9E **139** C6
Gümüldür *Turkey* 38°3N 27°14E **99** C9
Gümüşçay *Turkey* 40°5N 27°22E **99** B9
Gümüşhacıköy *Turkey* 40°50N 35°18E **104** B6
Gümüşhane *Turkey* 40°30N 39°30E **105** B8
Gümüşsu *Turkey* 38°14N 29°16E **99** C11
Gümzai *Indonesia* 5°28S 134°42E **120** d
Guna *India* 24°40N 77°19E **124** G7
Gunbalanya *Australia* 12°20S 133°4E **148** B5
Gundagai *Australia* 35°3S 148°6E **153** C8
Gundarehi *India* 20°57N 81°17E **126** D5
Gundlakamma →
  India 15°30N 80°15E **127** G5
Gundlupet *India* 11°48N 76°41E **127** J3
Gunebang *Australia* 33°1S 146°38E **153** B7
Güney *Burdur, Turkey* 37°29N 29°34E **99** D11
Güney *Denizli, Turkey* 38°9N 29°4E **99** C11
Güneydoğu Toroslar
  Turkey 38°20N 40°30E **105** C9
Gungal *Australia* 32°22S 150°34E **153** B9
Gunisao → *Canada* 53°56N 97°53W **163** C9
Gunisao L. *Canada* 53°33N 96°15W **163** C9
Gunjur *Gambia* 13°12N 16°44W **138** C1
Gunjyal *Pakistan* 32°20N 71°55E **124** C4
Günlüce *Turkey* 36°50N 28°2E **99** E10
Gunma □ *Japan* 36°30N 138°20E **113** F9
Gunnarskog *Sweden* 59°49N 12°34E **62** E6

226 Gunnbjørn Fjeld
INDEX TO WORLD MAPS

Gunnbjørn Fjeld *Greenland* 68°55N 29°47W **57** D8
Gunnebo *Sweden* 57°44N 16°32E **63** G10
Gunnedah *Australia* 30°59S 150°15E **153** A9
Gunnewin *Australia* 25°59S 148°33E **151** D4
Gunningbar Cr. → *Australia* 31°14S 147°6E **153** A7
Gunnison *Colo., U.S.A.* 38°33N 106°56W **168** G10
Gunnison *Utah, U.S.A.* 39°9N 111°49W **168** G8
Gunnison → *U.S.A.* 39°4N 108°35W **168** G9
Gunsan *S. Korea* 35°59N 126°45E **115** G14
Guntakal *India* 15°11N 77°27E **127** G3
Gunter *Canada* 44°52N 77°32W **174** B7
Guntersville *U.S.A.* 34°21N 86°18W **177** D11
Guntong *Malaysia* 4°36N 101°3E **121** K3
Guntur *India* 16°23N 80°30E **127** F5
Gunung Ciremay △ *Indonesia* 6°53S 108°24E **119** G13
Gunungapi *Indonesia* 6°45S 126°30E **119** F7
Gunungsitoli *Indonesia* 1°15N 97°30E **118** D1
Gunupur *India* 19°5N 83°50E **126** E6
Günz → *Germany* 48°27N 10°16E **77** G6
Gunza *Angola* 10°50S 13°50E **140** G2
Günzburg *Germany* 48°26N 10°17E **77** G6
Gunzenhausen *Germany* 49°7N 10°44E **77** F6
Guo He → *China* 32°59N 117°10E **117** A11
Guoyang *China* 33°32N 116°12E **114** H9
Gupis *Pakistan* 36°15N 73°20E **125** A5
Gura Humorului *Romania* 47°35N 25°53E **81** C10
Gura-Teghii *Romania* 45°30N 26°25E **81** E11
Gurahonţ *Romania* 46°16N 22°21E **80** D7
Gurbantünggüt Shamo *China* 45°8N 87°20E **109** C11
Gurdaspur *India* 32°5N 75°31E **124** C6
Gurdon *U.S.A.* 33°55N 93°9W **176** E8
Güre *Balıkesir, Turkey* 39°36N 26°54E **99** B8
Güre *Uşak, Turkey* 38°39N 29°10E **99** C11
Gurgaon = Gurugram *India* 28°27N 77°1E **124** E7
Gürgentepe *Turkey* 40°51N 37°50E **104** B7
Gurghiu, Munţii *Romania* 46°41N 25°15E **81** D10
Gurgueia → *Brazil* 6°50S 43°24W **189** B2
Gurha *India* 25°12N 71°39E **124** G4
Guri, Embalse de *Venezuela* 7°50N 62°52W **186** B6
Gurin *Nigeria* 9°5N 12°54E **139** D7
Gurjaani *Georgia* 41°43N 45°52E **87** K7
Gurk → *Austria* 46°35N 14°31E **78** E7
Gurkha *Nepal* 28°5N 84°40E **125** E11
Gurla Mandhata = Naimona'nyi Feng *China* 30°26N 81°18E **125** D9
Gurley *Australia* 29°45S 149°48E **151** D4
Gurnet Point *U.S.A.* 42°1N 70°34W **175** D14
Guro *Mozam.* 17°26S 32°30E **143** F3
Güroymak *Turkey* 38°35N 42°1E **105** C10
Gürpınar *İstanbul, Turkey* 40°59N 28°37E **97** F12
Gürpınar *Van, Turkey* 38°18N 43°25E **105** C10
Gürsu *Turkey* 40°13N 29°11E **97** F13
Gurué *Mozam.* 15°25S 36°58E **143** F4
Gurugram *India* 28°27N 77°1E **124** E7
Gurun *Malaysia* 5°49N 100°27E **121** K3
Gürün *Turkey* 38°43N 37°15E **104** C7
Gurupá *Brazil* 1°25S 51°35W **187** D8
Gurupá, I. Grande de *Brazil* 1°25S 51°45W **187** D8
Gurupi *Brazil* 11°43S 49°4W **187** F9
Gurupi → *Brazil* 1°13S 46°6W **187** D9
Gurupi, Serra do *Brazil* 5°0S 47°50W **189** B1
Guruwe *Zimbabwe* 16°40S 30°42E **145** A5
Gurvan Sayhan Uul *Mongolia* 43°50N 104°0E **114** C3
Guryev = Atyraū *Kazakhstan* 47°5N 52°0E **108** C4
Guryevsk *Russia* 54°47N 20°38E **82** D7
Gus-Khrustalnyy *Russia* 55°42N 40°44E **86** C5
Gusau *Nigeria* 12°12N 6°40E **139** C6
Gusev *Russia* 54°35N 22°10E **82** D9
Gushan *China* 39°50N 123°35E **115** E12
Gushgy = Serhetabat *Turkmenistan* 35°20N 62°18E **129** C9
Gushi *China* 32°11N 115°41E **117** A10
Gushiago *Ghana* 9°55N 0°15W **139** D4
Gusinje *Montenegro* 42°35N 19°50E **96** D3
Gusinoozersk *Russia* 51°16N 106°27E **107** D11
Gùspini *Italy* 39°32N 8°37E **94** C1
Güssing *Austria* 47°3N 16°20E **79** D9
Gustav Holm, Kap *Greenland* 66°36N 34°15W **57** D7
Gustavus *U.S.A.* 58°25N 135°44W **162** B1
Gustine *U.S.A.* 37°16N 121°0W **170** H6
Güstrow *Germany* 53°47N 12°10E **76** B8
Gusum *Sweden* 58°16N 16°30E **63** F10
Guta = Kolárovo *Slovakia* 47°54N 18°0E **79** D10
Gütersloh *Germany* 51°54N 8°24E **76** D4
Gutha *Australia* 28°58S 115°55E **149** E2
Guthalungra *Australia* 19°52S 147°50E **150** B4
Guthrie *Canada* 44°28N 79°32W **174** B5
Guthrie *Okla., U.S.A.* 35°53N 97°25W **176** D6
Guthrie *Tex., U.S.A.* 33°37N 100°19W **176** E4
Gutian *China* 26°32N 118°43E **117** D12
Guttenberg *U.S.A.* 42°47N 91°6W **172** D8
Gutu *Zimbabwe* 19°41S 31°9E **145** A5
Guwahati *India* 26°10N 91°45E **123** F17
Guy Fawkes River △ *Australia* 30°0S 152°20E **151** D5
Guyana ■ *S. Amer.* 5°0N 59°0W **186** C7
Guyane française = French Guiana ☑ *S. Amer.* 4°0N 53°0W **187** C8
Guyang *China* 41°0N 110°5E **114** D6
Guyenne *France* 44°30N 0°40E **72** D4
Guymon *U.S.A.* 36°41N 101°29W **176** C4
Guyra *Australia* 30°15S 151°40E **151** E5
Guyton *U.S.A.* 32°20N 81°24W **178** C8
Guyuan *Hebei, China* 41°37N 115°40E **114** D8
Guyuan *Ningxia Huizu, China* 36°0N 106°20E **114** F4
Güzelbahçe *Turkey* 38°21N 26°54E **99** C8
Güzelyurt = Morphou *Cyprus* 35°12N 32°59E **101** D11
Guzhang *China* 28°42N 109°58E **116** C7
Guzhen *China* 33°22N 117°18E **115** H9
Guzmán, L. de *Mexico* 31°20N 107°30W **180** A3
G'uzor *Uzbekistan* 38°36N 66°15E **109** E7
Gvardeysk *Russia* 54°39N 21°5E **82** D8
Gvardeyskoye *Ukraine* 45°7N 34°1E **85** K8
Gwa *Myanmar* 17°36N 94°34E **123** L19
Gwaai *Zimbabwe* 19°15S 27°45E **143** F2
Gwaai → *Zimbabwe* 17°59S 26°52E **143** F2
Gwabegar *Australia* 30°37S 148°59E **153** A8
Gwadabawa *Nigeria* 13°28N 5°15E **139** C6
Gwādar *Pakistan* 25°10N 62°18E **122** G3
Gwagwada *Nigeria* 10°15N 7°15E **139** C6
Gwaii Haanas △ *Canada* 52°21N 131°26W **162** C2
Gwalior *India* 26°12N 78°10E **124** F8
Gwanara *Nigeria* 8°55N 3°9E **139** D5
Gwanda *Zimbabwe* 20°55S 29°0E **143** G2
Gwandu *Nigeria* 12°30N 4°41E **139** C5
Gwane *Dem. Rep. of the Congo* 4°45N 25°48E **142** B2
Gwangju *S. Korea* 35°9N 126°54E **115** G14
Gwangyang *S. Korea* 34°56N 127°41E **115** G14
Gwanju = Gwangju *S. Korea* 35°9N 126°54E **115** G14
Gwaram *Nigeria* 10°15N 10°25E **139** C7
Gwarzo *Nigeria* 12°20N 8°55E **139** C6
Gwasero *Nigeria* 9°29N 3°30E **139** D5
Gwda → *Poland* 53°3N 16°44E **83** E3
Gweebarra B. *Ireland* 54°51N 8°23W **64** B3
Gweedore *Ireland* 55°3N 8°14W **64** A3
Gweru *Zimbabwe* 19°28S 29°45E **143** F2
Gwi *Nigeria* 9°0N 7°10E **139** D6
Gwinn *U.S.A.* 46°19N 87°27W **172** B10
Gwio Kura *Nigeria* 12°40N 11°2E **139** C7
Gwoza *Nigeria* 11°5N 13°40E **139** C7
Gwydir → *Australia* 29°27S 149°48E **151** D4
Gwynedd □ *U.K.* 52°52N 4°10W **66** E3
Gyandzha = Gäncä *Azerbaijan* 40°45N 46°20E **87** K8
Gyangzê *China* 29°5N 89°47E **110** F6
Gyaring Hu *China* 34°50N 97°40E **110** E8
Gydanskiy Poluostrov *Russia* 70°0N 78°0E **106** C8
Gyeonggi-man *S. Korea* 37°0N 125°30E **115** F13
Gyeongju *S. Korea* 35°51N 129°14E **115** G15
Gyldenløve Fjord *Greenland* 64°15N 40°30W **57** E6
Gympie *Australia* 26°11S 152°38E **151** D5
Gyomaendrőd *Hungary* 46°56N 20°50E **80** D5
Gyöngyös *Hungary* 47°48N 19°56E **80** C4
Győr *Hungary* 47°41N 17°40E **80** C2
Győr-Moson-Sopron □ *Hungary* 47°40N 17°20E **80** C2
Gypsum Pt. *Canada* 61°53N 114°35W **162** A6
Gypsumville *Canada* 51°45N 98°40W **163** C9
Gyueshevo *Bulgaria* 42°14N 22°28E **96** D6
Gyula *Hungary* 46°38N 21°17E **80** D6
Gyumri *Armenia* 40°47N 43°50E **87** K6
Gyzylarbat = Serdar *Turkmenistan* 39°4N 56°23E **129** B8
Gyzyletrek = Etrek *Turkmenistan* 37°36N 54°46E **129** B7
Gyzylgaya *Turkmenistan* 40°40N 55°30E **108** D5
Gzhatsk = Gagarin *Russia* 55°38N 35°0E **84** E8

H

H. Neely Henry L. *U.S.A.* 33°55N 86°2W **178** B3
Ha 'Arava → *Israel* 30°50N 35°20E **130** E4
Ha Coi *Vietnam* 21°26N 107°46E **116** G6
Ha Dong *Vietnam* 20°58N 105°46E **116** G5
Ha Giang *Vietnam* 22°50N 104°59E **116** F5
Ha Karmel, Har *Israel* 32°44N 35°3E **130** C4
Ha Karmel △ *Israel* 32°45N 35°5E **130** C4
Ha Long = Hong Gai *Vietnam* 20°57N 107°5E **116** G6
Ha Long, Vinh *Vietnam* 20°56N 107°3E **120** B6
Ha Tien *Vietnam* 10°23N 104°29E **121** G5
Ha Tinh *Vietnam* 18°20N 105°54E **120** C5
Ha Trung *Vietnam* 19°58N 105°50E **120** C5
Haakon VII Topp = Beerenberg *Norway* 71°0N 8°20W **57** C10
Haaksbergen *Neths.* 52°9N 6°45E **69** B6
Haapsalu *Estonia* 58°56N 23°30E **84** C2
Haarby *Denmark* 55°13N 10°7E **63** J4
Haarlem *Neths.* 52°23N 4°39E **69** B4
Haast *N.Z.* 43°51S 169°1E **155** D4
Haast → *N.Z.* 43°50S 169°2E **155** D4
Haast Pass *N.Z.* 44°6S 169°21E **155** E4
Haasts Bluff *Australia* 23°22S 132°0E **148** D5
Haasts Bluff ✪ *Australia* 23°39S 130°34E **148** D5
Hab → *Pakistan* 24°53N 66°41E **124** G3
Hab Nadi Chauki *Pakistan* 25°0N 66°50E **124** G2
Habahe *China* 48°3N 86°23E **109** C11
Habaswein *Kenya* 1°2N 39°30E **142** B4
Habay *Canada* 58°50N 118°44W **162** B5
Ḩabbānīyah *Iraq* 33°17N 43°29E **105** F10
Ḩabbānīyah, Hawr al *Iraq* 33°17N 43°29E **105** F10
Habibas, Îles *Algeria* 35°44N 1°8W **91** K3
Habichtswald ⌂ *Germany* 51°15N 9°15E **76** D5
Habirag *China* 42°17N 115°42E **114** C8
Habo *Sweden* 57°55N 14°6E **63** G8
Haboro *Japan* 44°22N 141°42E **112** B10
Ḩabshān *U.A.E.* 23°50N 53°37E **129** F7
Hachenburg *Germany* 50°40N 7°49E **76** E3
Hachijō-Jima *Japan* 33°5N 139°45E **113** H9
Hachiman = Gujō *Japan* 35°45N 136°57E **113** G8
Hachinohe *Japan* 40°30N 141°29E **112** D10
Hachiōji *Japan* 35°40N 139°20E **113** G9
Hacı Zeynalabdin *Azerbaijan* 40°37N 49°33E **87** K9
Hacıbektaş *Turkey* 38°56N 34°33E **104** C6
Hacılar *Turkey* 38°38N 35°26E **104** C6
Hack, Mt. *Australia* 30°45S 138°55E **152** A3
Hackås *Sweden* 62°56N 14°30E **62** B8
Hackensack *U.S.A.* 40°52N 74°4W **175** F10
Hackettstown *U.S.A.* 40°51N 74°50W **175** F10
Håckrenmagasinet *Sweden* 63°15N 13°30E **62** C7
Hadali *Pakistan* 32°16N 72°11E **124** C5
Hadarba, Ras *Sudan* 22°4N 36°51E **137** C4
Hadarom □ *Israel* 31°0N 35°0E **130** E4
Ḩadd, Ra's al *Oman* 22°35N 59°50E **131** C6
Haddington *U.K.* 55°57N 2°47W **65** F6
Haddock *U.S.A.* 33°2N 83°26W **178** B6
Hadejia *Nigeria* 12°30N 10°5E **139** C7
Hadejia → *Nigeria* 12°50N 10°51E **139** C7
Ḩadera *Israel* 32°27N 34°55E **130** C3
Ḩadera, N. → *Israel* 32°28N 34°52E **130** C3
Haderslev *Denmark* 55°15N 9°30E **63** J3
Hadgaon *India* 19°30N 77°40E **126** E3
Hadhramaut = Ḩaḑramawt □ *Yemen* 15°30N 49°30E **131** D4
Hadīboh *Yemen* 12°39N 54°2E **131** E5
Hadilik *China* 37°56N 86°6E **109** E11
Hadım *Turkey* 36°58N 32°26E **104** D5
Ḩādīshahr *Iran* 38°51N 45°40E **105** C11
Hadjadj, O. el → *Algeria* 28°18N 5°20E **136** C5
Hadjeb el Aïoun *Tunisia* 35°21N 9°32E **136** A5
Hadley B. *Canada* 72°31N 108°12W **160** C10
Hadong *S. Korea* 35°5N 127°44E **115** G14
Ḩaḑramawt □ *Yemen* 15°30N 49°30E **131** D4
Ḩadrānīyah *Iraq* 35°38N 43°14E **128** C4
Hadrian's Wall *U.K.* 55°0N 2°30W **66** B5
Hadsten *Denmark* 56°19N 10°3E **63** H4
Hadsund *Denmark* 56°44N 10°8E **63** H4
Hadyach *Ukraine* 50°21N 34°0E **85** G8
Hae, Ko *Thailand* 7°44N 98°22E **121** a
Haeju *N. Korea* 38°3N 125°45E **115** E13
Hā'ena *U.S.A.* 22°14N 159°34W **167** L8
Haenam *S. Korea* 34°34N 126°35E **115** G14
Haenertsburg *S. Africa* 24°0S 29°50E **145** B4
Haerhpin = Harbin *China* 45°48N 126°40E **115** B14
Hafar al Bāţin *Si. Arabia* 28°32N 45°52E **128** D5
Hafik *Turkey* 39°51N 37°23E **104** C7
Ḩafīrat al 'Aydā *Si. Arabia* 26°26N 39°12E **128** E3
Ḩafit *Oman* 23°59N 55°49E **129** F7
Hafizabad *Pakistan* 32°5N 73°40E **124** C5
Haflong *India* 25°10N 93°5E **123** G18
Haft Gel *Iran* 31°30N 49°32E **129** D6
Hagalil *Israel* 32°53N 35°18E **130** C4
Hagari → *India* 15°40N 77°0E **127** G3
Hagby *Sweden* 56°34N 16°11E **63** H10
Hagemeister I. *U.S.A.* 58°39N 160°54W **166** D7
Hagen *Germany* 51°21N 7°27E **76** D3
Hagenow *Germany* 53°26N 11°12E **76** B7
Hagerman *U.S.A.* 33°7N 104°20W **169** K11
Hagerman Fossil Beds ⌂ *U.S.A.* 42°48N 114°57W **168** E6
Hagerstown *U.S.A.* 39°39N 77°43W **173** F15
Hagersville *Canada* 42°58N 80°3W **174** D4
Hagetmau *France* 43°39N 0°37W **72** E3
Hagfors *Sweden* 60°3N 13°45E **62** D7
Hagi *Japan* 34°30N 131°22E **113** G5
Hagolan *Syria* 33°0N 35°45E **130** C4
Hagondange *France* 49°16N 6°11E **71** C13
Hags Hd. *Ireland* 52°57N 9°28W **64** D2
Hague, C. de la *France* 49°44N 1°56W **70** C5
Hague, The = 's-Gravenhage *Neths.* 52°7N 4°17E **69** B4
Haguenau *France* 48°49N 7°47E **71** D14
Hahira *U.S.A.* 30°59N 83°22W **178** E6
Hai Duong *Vietnam* 20°56N 106°19E **116** G6
Hai'an *Guangdong, China* 20°18N 110°11E **117** a
Hai'an *Jiangsu, China* 32°37N 120°27E **117** A13
Haicheng *China* 40°50N 122°45E **115** D12
Haida Gwaii *Canada* 53°20N 132°10W **162** C2
Haidar Khel *Afghan.* 33°58N 68°38E **124** C3
Haidarâbâd = Hyderabad *India* 17°22N 78°29E **126** F4
Haidargarh *India* 26°37N 81°22E **125** F9
Haifa = Ḩefa *Israel* 32°46N 35°0E **130** C4
Haifeng *China* 22°58N 115°10E **117** F10
Haiger *Germany* 50°43N 8°12E **76** E4
Haikou *China* 20°1N 110°16E **117** a
Ḩā'il *Si. Arabia* 27°28N 41°45E **128** E4
Ḩā'il □ *Si. Arabia* 26°40N 41°40E **128** E4
Hailar *China* 49°10N 119°38E **111** B12
Hailey *U.S.A.* 43°31N 114°19W **168** E6
Haileybury *Canada* 47°30N 79°38W **164** C4
Hailin *China* 44°37N 129°30E **115** B15
Hailing Dao *China* 21°35N 111°47E **117** G8
Hailun *China* 47°28N 126°50E **111** B14
Hailuoto *Finland* 65°3N 24°45E **60** D21
Haimen *Guangdong, China* 23°15N 116°38E **117** F11
Haimen *Jiangsu, China* 31°52N 121°10E **117** B13
Hainan □ *China* 19°0N 109°30E **117** a
Hainan Dao *China* 19°0N 109°30E **117** a
Hainan Str. = Qiongzhou Haixia *China* 20°10N 110°15E **117** a
Hainaut □ *Belgium* 50°30N 4°0E **69** D4
Hainburg *Austria* 48°9N 16°56E **79** C9
Haines *Alaska, U.S.A.* 59°14N 135°26W **162** B1
Haines *Oreg., U.S.A.* 44°55N 117°56W **168** D5
Haines City *U.S.A.* 28°7N 81°38W **179** G8
Haines Junction *Canada* 60°45N 137°30W **162** A1
Hainfeld *Austria* 48°3N 15°48E **78** C8
Haining *China* 30°28N 120°40E **117** B13
Haiphong *Vietnam* 20°47N 106°41E **116** G6
Haitan Dao *China* 25°30N 119°45E **117** E12
Haiti ■ *W. Indies* 19°0N 72°30W **183** C5
Haiya *Sudan* 18°20N 36°21E **137** D4
Haiyan *Qinghai, China* 36°53N 100°59E **110** D9
Haiyan *Zhejiang, China* 30°28N 120°58E **117** B13
Haiyang *China* 36°47N 121°9E **115** F11
Haiyuan *Guangxi Zhuangzu, China* 22°8N 107°35E **116** F6
Haiyuan *Ningxia Huizu, China* 36°35N 105°52E **114** F3
Haizhou *China* 34°37N 119°7E **115** G10
Haizhou Wan *China* 34°50N 119°20E **115** G10
Hajdú-Bihar □ *Hungary* 47°30N 21°30E **80** C6
Hajdúböszörmény *Hungary* 47°40N 21°30E **80** C6
Hajdúdorog *Hungary* 47°48N 21°30E **80** C6
Hajdúhadház *Hungary* 47°40N 21°40E **80** C6
Hajdúnánás *Hungary* 47°50N 21°26E **80** C6
Hajdúsámson *Hungary* 47°37N 21°42E **80** C6
Hajdúszoboszló *Hungary* 47°27N 21°22E **80** C6
Haji Ibrahim *Iraq* 36°40N 44°30E **105** D11
Hajipur *India* 25°45N 85°13E **125** G11
Ḩājj Ali Qolī, Kavīr-e *Iran* 35°55N 54°50E **129** C7
Ḩajjah *Yemen* 15°42N 43°36E **131** D3
Ḩājjīābād *Hormozgān, Iran* 28°19N 55°55E **129** D7
Ḩājjīābād *Khorāsān, Iran* 33°37N 60°0E **129** C9
Ḩājjīābād-e Zarrīn *Iran* 33°9N 54°51E **129** C7
Hajnówka *Poland* 52°47N 23°35E **83** F10
Hakansson, Mts. *Dem. Rep. of the Congo* 8°40S 25°45E **143** D2
Hakataramea *N.Z.* 44°43S 170°30E **155** E5
Hakkâri *Turkey* 37°34N 43°44E **105** D10
Hakkâri □ *Turkey* 37°30N 44°0E **105** D10
Hakkâri Dağları *Turkey* 38°2N 42°58E **105** C10
Hakken-Zan *Japan* 34°10N 135°54E **113** G7
Hakkōda San *Japan* 40°50N 141°0E **112** D10
Hakodate *Japan* 41°45N 140°44E **112** D10
Hakos *Namibia* 23°13S 16°21E **144** B2
Håksberg *Sweden* 60°11N 15°12E **62** D9
Hakskeenpan *S. Africa* 26°48S 20°13E **144** C3
Haku-San *Japan* 36°9N 136°46E **113** F8
Haku-San △ *Japan* 36°15N 136°45E **113** F8
Hakui *Japan* 36°53N 136°47E **113** F8
Hakusan *Japan* 36°31N 136°34E **113** F8
Hala *Pakistan* 25°43N 68°20E **122** G6
Ḩalab *Syria* 36°10N 37°15E **104** D7
Ḩalab □ *Syria* 36°10N 37°10E **104** D7
Ḩalabjah *Iraq* 35°10N 45°58E **105** E11
Halaib *Sudan* 22°12N 36°30E **137** C4
Halaib Triangle *Africa* 22°30N 35°20E **137** C4
Ḩālat 'Ammār *Si. Arabia* 29°10N 36°4E **128** D3
Halbā *Lebanon* 34°34N 36°6E **130** A5
Halberstadt *Germany* 51°54N 11°3E **76** D7
Halcombe *N.Z.* 40°8S 175°30E **154** G4
Halcon, Mt. *Phil.* 13°16N 121°0E **119** B6
Halde Fjäll = Haltiatunturi *Finland* 69°17N 21°18E **60** B19
Halden *Norway* 59°9N 11°23E **61** G14
Haldensleben *Germany* 52°17N 11°24E **76** C7
Haldia *Bangla.* 22°1N 88°3E **125** H13
Haldwani *India* 29°31N 79°30E **125** E8
Hale → *Australia* 24°56S 135°53E **150** C2
Halesowen *U.K.* 52°27N 2°3W **67** E5
Halesworth *U.K.* 52°20N 1°31E **67** E9
Haleyville *U.S.A.* 34°14N 87°37W **177** D11
Half Assini *Ghana* 5°1N 2°50W **138** D4
Half Dome *U.S.A.* 37°44N 119°32E **170** H7
Halfeti *Turkey* 37°15N 37°52E **104** D7
Halfmoon Bay *N.Z.* 46°50S 168°5E **155** G3
Halfway → *Canada* 56°12N 121°32W **162** B4
Halia *India* 24°50N 82°19E **125** G10
Haliburton *Canada* 45°3N 78°30W **174** A6
Halifax *Australia* 18°32S 146°22E **150** B4
Halifax *Canada* 44°38N 63°35W **165** D7
Halifax *U.K.* 53°43N 1°52W **66** D6
Halifax *U.S.A.* 40°25N 76°55W **174** F8
Halifax B. *Australia* 18°50S 147°0E **150** B4
Halifax I. *Namibia* 26°38S 15°4E **144** C2
Halik Shan *China* 42°20N 81°22E **109** D10
Halīl → *Iran* 27°40N 58°30E **129** E8
Halimun △ *Indonesia* 6°42S 106°26E **119** G11
Halki = Chalki *Greece* 36°17N 27°35E **99** E9
Halkida = Chalkida *Greece* 38°27N 23°42E **98** C5
Halkidiki = Chalkidiki *Greece* 40°25N 23°20E **96** F7
Halkirk *U.K.* 58°30N 3°29W **65** C5
Hall Beach *Canada* 68°46N 81°12W **161** D15
Hall in Tirol *Austria* 47°17N 11°30E **78** D4
Hall Pen. *Canada* 63°30N 66°0W **161** E18
Hall Pt. *Australia* 15°40S 124°23E **148** C3
Hallabro *Sweden* 56°22N 15°5E **63** H9
Halland *Sweden* 57°8N 12°47E **61** H15
Halland □ *Sweden* 57°0N 12°48E **63** H6
Hallandale Beach *U.S.A.* 25°58N 80°8W **179** K9
Hallands Väderö *Sweden* 56°27N 12°34E **63** H6
Hallandsås *Sweden* 56°22N 13°0E **63** H7
Ḩallāniyat, Jazā'ir al *Oman* 17°30N 55°58E **131** D6
Hallasan *S. Korea* 33°22N 126°32E **115** H14
Hällbybrunn *Sweden* 59°24N 16°25E **62** E10
Halle *Belgium* 50°44N 4°13E **69** D4
Halle *Nordrhein-Westfalen, Germany* 52°3N 8°22E **76** C4
Halle *Sachsen-Anhalt, Germany* 51°30N 11°56E **76** D7
Hällefors *Sweden* 59°47N 14°31E **62** E8
Hälleforsnäs *Sweden* 59°10N 16°30E **62** E10
Hallein *Austria* 47°40N 13°5E **78** D6
Hällekis *Sweden* 58°38N 13°27E **63** F7
Hallen *Sweden* 63°11N 14°4E **62** A8
Hallett *Australia* 33°25S 138°55E **152** B3
Hallettsville *U.S.A.* 29°27N 96°57W **176** G6
Halley *Antarctica* 75°35S 26°39W **55** D1
Hallia → *India* 16°55N 79°20E **126** F4
Hallim *S. Korea* 33°24N 126°15E **115** H14
Hallingdalselva → *Norway* 60°23N 9°35E **60** F13
Hallingskarvet △ *Norway* 60°37N 7°45E **60** F12
Hallock *U.S.A.* 48°47N 96°57W **172** A5
Halls Creek *Australia* 18°16S 127°38E **148** C4
Halls Gap *Australia* 37°8S 142°34E **151** F3
Halls Lake *Canada* 45°7N 78°45W **174** A6
Hallsberg *Sweden* 59°5N 15°7E **62** E9
Hallstahammar *Sweden* 59°38N 16°15E **62** E10
Hallstatt *Austria* 47°33N 13°38E **78** D6
Hallstavik *Sweden* 60°5N 18°37E **62** D12
Hallstead *U.S.A.* 41°58N 75°45W **175** E9
Halmahera *Indonesia* 0°40N 128°0E **119** D7
Halmahera Sea *Indonesia* 2°0N 130°0E **119** D7
Halmeu *Romania* 47°57N 23°2E **80** C8
Halmstad *Sweden* 56°41N 12°52E **63** H6
Halong Bay = Ha Long, Vinh *Vietnam* 20°56N 107°3E **120** B6
Halq el Oued = La Goulette *Tunisia* 36°53N 10°18E **94** F3
Hals *Denmark* 57°0N 10°18E **63** H4
Hälsingborg = Helsingborg *Sweden* 56°3N 12°42E **63** H6
Hälsingland *Sweden* 61°40N 16°5E **62** C10
Halstead *U.K.* 51°57N 0°40E **67** F8
Haltern *Germany* 51°44N 7°11E **76** D3
Haltiatunturi *Finland* 69°17N 21°18E **60** B19
Halton □ *U.K.* 53°22N 2°45W **66** D5
Haltwhistle *U.K.* 54°58N 2°26W **66** C5
Ḩālūl *Qatar* 25°40N 52°40E **129** E7
Halvad *India* 23°1N 71°11E **124** H4
Ḩalvān *Iran* 33°57N 56°15E **129** C8
Ham *France* 49°45N 3°4E **71** C10
Hamab *Namibia* 28°7S 19°16E **144** C2
Hamada *Japan* 34°56N 132°4E **113** G6
Hamadān *Iran* 34°52N 48°32E **105** E13
Hamadān □ *Iran* 35°0N 49°0E **129** C6
Hamadia *Algeria* 35°28N 1°57E **136** A4
Ḩamāh *Syria* 35°5N 36°40E **104** E7
Ḩamāh □ *Syria* 35°10N 37°0E **104** E7
Hamale *Ghana* 10°56N 2°45W **138** C4
Hamamatsu *Japan* 34°45N 137°45E **113** G8
Hamar *Norway* 60°48N 11°7E **60** F14
Hamâta, Gebel *Egypt* 24°17N 35°0E **128** E2
Hamatonbetsu *Japan* 45°10N 142°20E **112** B11
Hambantota *Sri Lanka* 6°10N 81°10E **127** L5
Hamber ⌂ *Canada* 52°20N 118°0W **162** C5
Hamburg *Germany* 53°33N 9°59E **76** B5
Hamburg *Ark., U.S.A.* 33°14N 91°48W **176** E9
Hamburg *N.Y., U.S.A.* 42°43N 78°50W **174** D6
Hamburg *Pa., U.S.A.* 40°33N 75°59W **175** F9
Hamburg □ *Germany* 53°30N 10°0E **76** B5
Hamburg Fuhlsbüttel ✈ (HAM) *Germany* 53°35N 9°59E **76** B5
Ḩamḑ, W. al → *Si. Arabia* 24°55N 36°20E **128** E3
Hamden *U.S.A.* 41°23N 72°54W **175** E12
Hamdibey *Turkey* 39°50N 27°15E **99** B9
Häme *Finland* 61°38N 25°10E **60** F21
Hämeenlinna *Finland* 61°0N 24°28E **84** B3
Hamelin Pool *Australia* 26°22S 114°20E **149** E1
Hameln *Germany* 52°6N 9°21E **76** C5
Hamerkaz □ *Israel* 32°15N 34°55E **130** C3
Hamersley Ra. *Australia* 22°0S 117°45E **148** D2
Hamhŭng *N. Korea* 39°54N 127°30E **115** E14
Hami *China* 42°55N 93°25E **110** C7
Hamilton *Australia* 37°45S 142°2E **152** D5
Hamilton *Bermuda* 32°17N 64°47W **56** C5
Hamilton *Canada* 43°15N 79°50W **174** C5
Hamilton *N.Z.* 37°47S 175°19E **154** D4
Hamilton *U.K.* 55°46N 4°2W **65** F4
Hamilton *Ala., U.S.A.* 34°9N 87°59W **177** D11
Hamilton *Ga., U.S.A.* 32°45N 84°53W **178** C5
Hamilton *Mont., U.S.A.* 46°15N 114°10W **168** C6
Hamilton *N.Y., U.S.A.* 42°50N 75°33W **175** D9
Hamilton *Ohio, U.S.A.* 39°24N 84°34W **173** F11
Hamilton *Tex., U.S.A.* 31°42N 98°7W **176** F5
Hamilton → *Queens., Australia* 23°30S 139°47E **150** C2
Hamilton → *S. Austral., Australia* 26°40S 135°19E **151** D2
Hamilton City *U.S.A.* 39°45N 122°1W **170** F4
Hamilton I. *Australia* 20°21S 148°56E **150** b
Hamilton Inlet *Canada* 54°0N 57°30W **165** B8
Hamilton Mt. *U.S.A.* 43°25N 74°22W **175** C10
Hamina *Finland* 60°34N 27°12E **84** B4
Hamirpur *H.P., India* 31°41N 76°31E **124** D7
Hamirpur *Ut. P., India* 25°57N 80°9E **125** G9
Hamitabat *Turkey* 41°30N 27°17E **97** E11
Hamlet *U.S.A.* 34°53N 79°42W **177** D15
Hamley Bridge *Australia* 34°17S 138°35E **152** C3
Hamlin = Hameln *Germany* 52°6N 9°21E **76** C5
Hamlin *N.Y., U.S.A.* 43°17N 77°55W **174** C7
Hamlin *Tex., U.S.A.* 32°53N 100°8W **176** E4
Hamm *Germany* 51°40N 7°50E **76** D3
Hammām al 'Alīl *Iraq* 36°9N 43°15E **105** D10
Hammam Bouhadjar *Algeria* 35°23N 0°58W **136** A3
Hammamet *Tunisia* 36°24N 10°38E **136** A6
Ḩammār, Hawr al *Iraq* 30°50N 47°10E **128** D5
Hammarstrand *Sweden* 63°7N 16°20E **62** A10
Hammelburg *Germany* 50°6N 9°53E **77** E5
Hammeren *Denmark* 55°18N 14°47E **63** J8
Hammerfest *Norway* 70°39N 23°41E **60** A20
Hammerum *Denmark* 56°8N 9°3E **63** H3
Hamminkeln *Germany* 51°43N 6°35E **76** D2
Hammond *Ind., U.S.A.* 41°38N 87°30W **172** E10
Hammond *La., U.S.A.* 30°30N 90°28W **177** F9
Hammond *N.Y., U.S.A.* 44°27N 75°42W **175** B9
Hammondsport *U.S.A.* 42°25N 77°13W **174** D7
Hammonton *U.S.A.* 39°39N 74°48W **173** F16
Hampden *N.Z.* 45°18S 170°50E **155** F5
Hampi *India* 15°18N 76°28E **127** G3
Hampshire □ *U.K.* 51°7N 1°23W **67** F6
Hampshire Downs *U.K.* 51°15N 1°10W **67** F6
Hampton *N.B., Canada* 45°32N 65°51W **165** C6
Hampton *Ont., Canada* 43°58N 78°45W **174** C6
Hampton *Ark., U.S.A.* 33°32N 92°28W **176** E8
Hampton *Ga., U.S.A.* 33°23N 84°17W **178** B5
Hampton *Iowa, U.S.A.* 42°45N 93°13W **172** D7
Hampton *N.H., U.S.A.* 42°57N 70°50W **175** D14
Hampton *S.C., U.S.A.* 32°52N 81°7W **178** C8
Hampton *Va., U.S.A.* 37°2N 76°21W **173** G15
Hampton Bays *U.S.A.* 40°53N 72°30W **175** F12
Hampton Springs *U.S.A.* 30°5N 83°40W **178** E6
Hampton Tableland *Australia* 32°0S 127°0E **149** F4
Hamra *Sweden* 61°39N 14°59E **62** C8
Ḩamrīn, Jabal *Iraq* 34°30N 44°30E **105** E11
Hamur *Turkey* 39°37N 43°3E **105** C10
Hamyang *S. Korea* 35°32N 127°42E **115** G14
Han = Hangang → *S. Korea* 37°50N 126°30E **115** F14
Han i Hotit *Albania* 42°19N 19°27E **96** D3
Han Jiang → *China* 23°25N 116°40E **117** F11
Han Shui → *China* 30°34N 114°17E **117** B10
Hanahan *U.S.A.* 32°55N 80°0W **178** C10
Hanak *Si. Arabia* 25°32N 37°0E **128** E3
Hanak *Turkey* 41°14N 42°50E **105** B10
Hanamaki *Japan* 39°23N 141°7E **112** E10
Hanang *Tanzania* 4°30S 35°25E **142** C4
Hanau *Germany* 50°7N 8°56E **77** E4
Hanbogd = Ihbulag *Mongolia* 43°11N 107°10E **114** C4
Hançalar *Turkey* 38°8N 29°24E **99** C11
Hânceşti *Moldova* 46°50N 28°36E **81** D13
Hancheng *China* 35°31N 110°25E **114** G6
Hanchuan *China* 30°40N 113°50E **117** B9
Hancock *Mich., U.S.A.* 47°8N 88°35W **172** B9
Hancock *N.Y., U.S.A.* 41°57N 75°17W **175** E9
Hancock *Vt., U.S.A.* 43°55N 72°50W **175** C12
Handa *Japan* 34°53N 136°55E **113** G8
Handa I. *U.K.* 58°23N 5°11W **65** C3
Handan *China* 36°35N 114°28E **114** F8
Handeni *Tanzania* 5°25S 38°2E **142** D4
Handlová *Slovakia* 48°45N 18°35E **79** C11
Handub *Sudan* 19°15N 37°16E **137** D4
Handwara *India* 34°21N 74°20E **125** B6
Hanegev *Israel* 30°50N 35°0E **130** E4
Hanford *U.S.A.* 36°20N 119°39W **170** J7
Hanford Reach ⌂ *U.S.A.* 46°40N 119°30W **168** C4
Hang Chat *Thailand* 18°20N 99°21E **120** C2
Hangang → *S. Korea* 37°50N 126°30E **115** F14
Hangayn Nuruu *Mongolia* 47°30N 99°0E **110** B8
Hangchou = Hangzhou *China* 30°18N 120°11E **117** B13
Hanger *Sweden* 57°6N 13°58E **63** G7
Hanggin Houqi *China* 40°58N 107°4E **114** D4
Hanggin Qi *China* 39°52N 108°50E **114** E5
Hangu *China* 39°18N 117°53E **115** E9
Hangzhou *China* 30°18N 120°11E **117** B13
Hangzhou Wan *China* 30°15N 120°45E **117** B13
Hangzhou Xiaoshan Int. ✈ (HGH) *China* 30°14N 120°26E **117** B13
Hanh *Mongolia* 51°32N 100°35E **110** A9
Hanhöhiy Uul *Mongolia* 49°30N 94°30E **109** C12
Hanhongor *Mongolia* 43°55N 104°28E **114** C3
Hani *Turkey* 38°24N 40°23E **105** C9
Hania = Chania *Greece* 35°30N 24°4E **101** D6
Ḩanīdh *Si. Arabia* 26°35N 48°38E **129** E6
Ḩanīsh *Yemen* 13°45N 42°46E **131** E3
Haniska *Slovakia* 48°37N 21°15E **79** C14
Hanjiang *China* 25°26N 119°6E **117** E12
Hankinson *U.S.A.* 46°4N 96°54W **172** B5
Hankö *Finland* 59°50N 22°57E **84** C2
Hankou *China* 30°35N 114°30E **117** B10
Hanksville *U.S.A.* 38°22N 110°43W **168** G8
Hanle *India* 32°42N 79°4E **125** C8
Hanmer Springs *N.Z.* 42°32S 172°50E **155** C7
Hann → *Australia* 17°26S 126°17E **148** C4
Hann, Mt. *Australia* 15°45S 126°0E **148** C4
Hanna *Canada* 51°40N 111°54W **162** C6
Hanna *U.S.A.* 41°52N 106°34W **168** F10
Hannah B. *Canada* 51°40N 80°0W **164** B4
Hannibal *Mo., U.S.A.* 39°42N 91°22W **172** F8
Hannibal *N.Y., U.S.A.* 43°19N 76°35W **175** C8
Hannik *Sudan* 18°12N 32°20E **137** D3
Hannover *Germany* 52°22N 9°46E **76** C5
Hanö *Sweden* 56°1N 14°50E **63** H8
Hanöbukten *Sweden* 55°35N 14°30E **63** J8
Hanoi *Vietnam* 21°5N 105°55E **116** G5
Hanover = Hannover *Germany* 52°22N 9°46E **76** C5
Hanover *Canada* 44°9N 81°2W **174** B3
Hanover *S. Africa* 31°4S 24°29E **144** D3
Hanover *N.H., U.S.A.* 43°42N 72°17W **175** C12
Hanover *Ohio, U.S.A.* 40°4N 82°16W **174** F2
Hanover *Pa., U.S.A.* 39°48N 76°59W **173** F15
Hanover, I. *Chile* 51°0S 74°50W **192** D2
Hans Lollik I. *U.S. Virgin Is.* 18°24N 64°53W **183** e
Hansdiha *India* 24°36N 87°5E **125** G12
Hanshou *China* 28°56N 111°50E **117** C8
Hansi *H.P., India* 32°27N 77°50E **124** C7
Hansi *Haryana, India* 29°10N 75°57E **124** E6
Hanson, L. *Australia* 31°0S 136°15E **152** A2
Hanstholm *Denmark* 57°7N 8°36E **63** G2
Hanting *China* 36°46N 119°12E **115** F10
Hantsavichy *Belarus* 52°49N 26°30E **75** B14
Hanumangarh *India* 29°35N 74°19E **124** E6
Hanyin *China* 32°54N 108°28E **114** H5
Hanyuan *China* 29°21N 102°40E **116** C4
Hanzhong *China* 33°10N 107°1E **116** A6
Hanzhuang *China* 34°33N 117°23E **115** G9
Haora *India* 22°34N 88°18E **125** H13
Haoxue *China* 30°3N 112°24E **117** B9
Haparanda *Sweden* 65°52N 24°8E **60** D21
Haparanda Skärgård △ *Sweden* 65°35N 23°44E **60** D20
Hapeville *U.S.A.* 33°39N 84°24W **178** B5
Happy *U.S.A.* 34°45N 101°52W **176** D4
Happy Camp *U.S.A.* 41°48N 123°23W **168** F2
Happy Valley-Goose Bay *Canada* 53°15N 60°20W **165** B7
Hapsu *N. Korea* 41°13N 128°51E **115** D15
Hapur *India* 28°45N 77°45E **124** E7
Ḩaql *Si. Arabia* 29°10N 34°58E **130** F3
Haquira *Peru* 14°14S 72°12W **188** C3
Har *Indonesia* 5°16S 133°14E **119** F8
Har-Ayrag *Mongolia* 45°47N 109°16E **114** B5
Har Hu *China* 38°20N 97°38E **110** D8
Har Us Nuur *Mongolia* 48°0N 92°0E **109** C12
Har Yehuda *Israel* 31°35N 34°57E **130** D3
Ḩaraḑ *Si. Arabia* 24°22N 49°0E **131** C4
Haradok *Belarus* 55°30N 30°3E **84** E6
Häradsbäck *Sweden* 56°32N 14°26E **63** H8
Haramosh *Pakistan* 35°50N 74°54E **125** B6
Haranomachi = Minamisōma *Japan* 37°38N 140°58E **112** F10
Harar = Harer *Ethiopia* 9°20N 42°8E **131** F3
Harare *Zimbabwe* 17°43S 31°2E **143** F3
Harazé *Chad* 9°57N 20°48E **135** G10
Harbel *Liberia* 6°16N 10°20W **138** D2
Harbhanga *India* 20°38N 84°36E **126** D7
Harbin *China* 45°48N 126°40E **115** B14
Harbiye *Turkey* 36°10N 36°8E **104** D7
Harbo *Sweden* 60°7N 17°12E **62** D11
Harboøre *Denmark* 56°38N 8°10E **63** H2
Harbor Beach *U.S.A.* 43°51N 82°39W **174** C2
Harborcreek *U.S.A.* 42°9N 79°57W **174** D5
Harbour Breton *Canada* 47°29N 55°50W **165** C8
Harbour Deep *Canada* 50°25N 56°32W **165** B8
Harburg *Germany* 53°27N 9°58E **76** B5
Harburger Berge ⌂ *Germany* 53°26N 9°51E **76** B5
Harda *India* 22°27N 77°5E **124** H7
Hardangerfjorden *Norway* 60°5N 6°0E **61** F12
Hardangervidda *Norway* 60°7N 7°20E **60** F12
Hardap □ *Namibia* 24°0S 17°0E **144** B2
Hardap ⌂ *Namibia* 24°29S 17°45E **144** B2
Hardap Dam *Namibia* 24°32S 17°50E **144** B2
Hardeeville *U.S.A.* 32°17N 81°5W **178** C8
Harden *Australia* 34°32S 148°24E **153** C8
Hardenberg *Neths.* 52°34N 6°37E **69** B6
Harderwijk *Neths.* 52°21N 5°38E **69** B5
Hardey → *Australia* 22°45S 116°8E **148** D2
Hardin *U.S.A.* 45°44N 107°37W **168** D10
Harding *S. Africa* 30°35S 29°55E **145** D4
Harding, L. *U.S.A.* 32°40N 85°5W **178** C4
Harding Ra. *Australia* 16°17S 124°55E **148** C3
Hardisty *Canada* 52°40N 111°18W **162** C6
Hardoi *India* 27°26N 80°6E **125** F9
Hardwar = Haridwar *India* 29°58N 78°9E **124** E8
Hardwick *Ga., U.S.A.* 33°4N 83°14W **178** B6
Hardwick *Vt., U.S.A.* 44°30N 72°22W **175** B12
Hardwicke B. *Australia* 34°55S 137°20E **152** C2
Hardwood Lake *Canada* 45°12N 77°26W **174** A7
Hardy, Pen. *Chile* 55°30S 68°20W **192** E3
Hardy, Pte. *St. Lucia* 14°6N 60°56W **183** f
Hare B. *Canada* 51°15N 55°45W **165** B8
Hareid *Norway* 62°22N 6°1E **60** E12
Haren *Germany* 52°47N 7°13E **76** C3
Harer *Ethiopia* 9°20N 42°8E **131** F3
Harfleur *France* 49°30N 0°10E **70** C7
Hargeisa *Somalia* 9°30N 44°2E **131** F3
Harghita □ *Romania* 46°30N 25°30E **81** D10

Harghita, Munţii Romania 46°25N 25°35E 81 D10
Hargshamn Sweden 60°12N 18°30E 62 D12
Hari → Indonesia 1°16S 104°5E 118 E2
Haría Canary Is. 29°8N 13°32W 100 E6
Haridwar India 29°58N 78°9E 124 E8
Harihar India 14°32N 75°44E 127 G2
Harihari N.Z. 43°9S 170°33E 155 D5
Hariharpur Garhi Nepal 27°19N 85°29E 125 F11
Harim, Jabal al Oman 25°58N 56°14E 129 E8
Haringhata → Bangla. 22°0N 89°58E 123 J16
Haripad India 9°14N 76°28E 127 K3
Harīr, W. al → Syria 32°44N 35°59E 130 C4
Harīrūd → Asia 37°24N 60°38E 129 B9
Härjedalen Sweden 62°22N 13°5E 62 B7
Harlan Iowa, U.S.A. 41°39N 95°19W 172 E6
Harlan Ky., U.S.A. 36°51N 83°19W 173 G12
Hârlău Romania 47°23N 26°55E 81 C11
Harlech U.K. 52°52N 4°6W 66 E3
Harlem Ga., U.S.A. 33°25N 82°19W 178 B7
Harlem Mont., U.S.A. 48°32N 108°47W 168 B9
Hårlev Denmark 55°21N 12°14E 63 J6
Harleyville U.S.A. 33°13N 80°27W 178 B9
Harlingen Neths. 53°11N 5°25E 69 A5
Harlingen U.S.A. 26°12N 97°42W 176 H6
Harlow U.K. 51°46N 0°8E 67 F8
Harlowton U.S.A. 46°26N 109°50W 168 C9
Harmancık Turkey 39°41N 29°9E 99 B11
Harmånger Sweden 61°55N 17°20E 62 C11
Harmanli Bulgaria 41°55N 25°55E 97 E9
Harnai India 17°48N 73°6E 126 F1
Harnai Pakistan 30°6N 67°56E 124 D2
Harney, L. U.S.A. 28°45N 81°3W 179 G8
Harney Basin U.S.A. 43°0N 119°30W 168 E4
Harney L. U.S.A. 43°14N 119°8W 168 E4
Harney Peak U.S.A. 43°52N 103°32W 172 D2
Härnön Sweden 62°36N 18°0E 62 B12
Härnösand Sweden 62°38N 17°55E 62 B11
Haro Spain 42°35N 2°55W 90 C2
Harold U.S.A. 30°40N 86°53W 179 E3
Haroldswick U.K. 60°48N 0°50W 65 A8
Harp L. Canada 55°5N 61°50W 165 A7
Harpanahalli India 14°47N 76°2E 127 G3
Harper Liberia 4°25N 7°43W 138 E3
Harper, Mt. U.S.A. 64°14N 143°51W 166 C11
Harplinge Sweden 56°45N 12°45E 63 H6
Harrai India 22°37N 79°13E 125 H8
Harrand Pakistan 29°28N 70°3E 124 E4
Harricana → Canada 50°56N 79°32W 164 B4
Harriman U.S.A. 35°56N 84°33W 177 D12
Harrington Australia 31°52S 152°42E 153 A10
Harrington Harbour Canada 50°31N 59°30W 165 B8
Harris U.K. 57°50N 6°55W 65 D2
Harris, L. Australia 31°10S 135°10E 151 E2
Harris, L. U.S.A. 28°47N 81°49W 179 G8
Harris, Sd. of U.K. 57°44N 7°6W 65 D1
Harris Mts. N.Z. 44°49S 168°49E 155 E3
Harris Pt. Canada 43°6N 82°9W 174 C2
Harrisburg Ill., U.S.A. 37°44N 88°32W 172 G9
Harrisburg Nebr., U.S.A. 41°33N 103°44W 172 E2
Harrisburg Pa., U.S.A. 40°16N 76°53W 174 F8
Harrismith S. Africa 28°15S 29°8E 145 C4
Harrison Ark., U.S.A. 36°14N 93°7W 176 C8
Harrison Maine, U.S.A. 44°7N 70°39W 175 B14
Harrison Nebr., U.S.A. 42°41N 103°53W 172 D2
Harrison, C. Canada 54°55N 57°55W 165 B8
Harrison Bay U.S.A. 70°40N 151°0W 166 A9
Harrison L. Canada 49°33N 121°50W 162 D4
Harrisonburg U.S.A. 38°27N 78°52W 173 F14
Harrisonville U.S.A. 38°39N 94°21W 172 F6
Harriston Canada 43°57N 80°53W 174 C4
Harrisville Mich., U.S.A. 44°39N 83°17W 174 B1
Harrisville N.Y., U.S.A. 44°9N 75°19W 175 B9
Harrisville Pa., U.S.A. 41°8N 80°0W 174 E5
Harrodsburg U.S.A. 37°46N 84°51W 173 G11
Harrogate U.K. 54°0N 1°33W 66 C6
Harrow Australia 37°9S 141°35E 152 D4
Harrow Canada 42°2N 82°55W 174 D2
Harrow □ U.K. 51°35N 0°21W 67 F7
Harrowsmith Canada 44°24N 76°40W 175 B8
Harry S. Truman Res. U.S.A. 38°16N 93°24W 172 F7
Harsefeld Germany 53°27N 9°30E 76 B5
Harsewinkel Germany 51°56N 8°14E 76 D4
Harsīn Iran 34°18N 47°33E 105 E12
Hârşova Romania 44°40N 27°59E 81 F12
Harstad Norway 68°48N 16°30E 60 B17
Harsud India 22°6N 76°44E 124 H7
Hart U.S.A. 43°42N 86°22W 172 D10
Hart, L. Australia 31°10S 136°25E 152 A2
Hartbees → S. Africa 28°45S 20°32E 144 C3
Hartberg Austria 47°17N 15°58E 78 D8
Hartford Ala., U.S.A. 31°6N 85°42W 178 D4
Hartford Conn., U.S.A. 41°46N 72°41W 175 E12
Hartford Ky., U.S.A. 37°27N 86°55W 172 G10
Hartford S. Dak., U.S.A. 43°38N 96°57W 172 D5
Hartford Vt., U.S.A. 43°40N 72°20W 175 C12
Hartford Wis., U.S.A. 43°19N 88°22W 172 D9
Hartford City U.S.A. 40°27N 85°22W 173 E11
Hartland Canada 46°20N 67°32W 165 C6
Hartland Pt. U.K. 51°1N 4°32W 67 F3
Hartlepool U.K. 54°42N 1°13W 66 C6
Hartlepool □ U.K. 54°42N 1°17W 66 C6
Hartley Bay Canada 53°25N 129°15W 162 C3
Hartmannberge Namibia 17°0S 13°0E 144 A1
Hartney Canada 49°30N 100°35W 163 D8
Hârtop Moldova 46°39N 28°40E 81 D13
Harts → S. Africa 28°24S 24°17E 144 C3
Harts Range Australia 23°6S 134°55E 150 C1
Hartselle U.S.A. 34°27N 86°56W 177 D11
Hartsfield-Jackson Atlanta Int. ✈ (ATL) U.S.A. 33°38N 84°26W 178 B5
Hartshorne U.S.A. 34°51N 95°34W 176 D7
Hartstown U.S.A. 41°33N 80°23W 174 E4
Hartsville U.S.A. 34°23N 80°4W 177 D14
Hartswater S. Africa 27°34S 24°43E 144 C3
Hartwell U.S.A. 34°21N 82°56W 177 D13
Harunabad Pakistan 29°35N 73°8E 124 E5
Harur India 12°3N 78°29E 127 H4
Harvand Iran 28°25N 55°43E 129 D7
Harvey Australia 33°5S 115°54E 149 F2
Harvey Ill., U.S.A. 41°36N 87°50W 172 E10
Harvey N. Dak., U.S.A. 47°47N 99°56W 172 B4
Harwich U.K. 51°56N 1°17E 67 F9
Haryana □ India 29°0N 76°10E 124 E7
Haryn → Belarus 52°7N 27°17E 75 B14
Harz Germany 51°38N 10°44E 76 D6
Harz △ Germany 51°40N 10°18E 76 D6
Harzgerode Germany 51°38N 11°8E 76 D7
Hasa Si. Arabia 25°50N 49°0E 129 E6
Ḩasā, W. al → Jordan 31°4N 35°29E 130 D4
Ḩasanābād Iran 32°8N 52°44E 129 C7
Hasankeyf Turkey 37°42N 41°24E 105 D9
Hasanparti India 18°4N 79°32E 126 E4
Ḩasb, W. → Iraq 31°45N 44°17E 128 D5
Hasdo → India 21°44N 82°44E 125 J10
Haselünne Germany 52°40N 7°29E 76 C3
Hashimoto Japan 34°19N 135°37E 113 G7
Hashtjerd Iran 35°52N 50°40E 129 C6
Hashtpur = Tālesh Iran 37°58N 48°58E 105 D13
Hashtrud Iran 37°28N 47°4E 105 D12
Haskell U.S.A. 33°10N 99°44W 176 E5
Haskovo Bulgaria 41°56N 25°30E 97 E9
Haskovo □ Bulgaria 42°0N 25°40E 97 E9
Hasköy Turkey 41°38N 26°52E 97 E10
Haslach Germany 48°16N 8°5E 77 G4
Hasle Denmark 55°11N 14°44E 63 J8
Haslemere U.K. 51°5N 0°43W 67 F7
Haslev Denmark 55°18N 11°57E 63 J5
Hasparren France 43°24N 1°18W 72 E2
Hassa Turkey 36°48N 36°29E 104 D7
Hassan India 13°0N 76°5E 127 H3
Hassberge ⌂ Germany 50°8N 10°45E 77 E6
Hassela Sweden 62°7N 16°42E 62 B10
Hasselt Belgium 50°56N 5°21E 69 D5
Hassfurt Germany 50°2N 10°30E 77 E6
Hassi bel Guebbour Algeria 28°30N 6°41E 136 C5
Hassi bou Khelala Algeria 30°17N 0°18W 136 B3
Hassi Bourarchet Algeria 27°26N 9°19E 136 C5
Hassi Djafou Algeria 30°55N 3°35E 136 B4
Hassi el Hadjar Algeria 31°28N 4°45E 136 B4
Hassi Imoulaye Algeria 29°54N 9°10E 136 C5
Hassi Inifeg Algeria 28°15N 1°30W 136 C3
Hassi Inifel Algeria 29°50N 3°41E 136 C4
Hassi Mana Algeria 28°48N 2°37W 136 C3
Hassi Marroket Algeria 30°10N 3°0E 136 B4
Hassi Mengoub Algeria 29°49N 5°26W 136 C2
Hassi Messaoud Algeria 31°51N 6°1E 136 B5
Hassi Sougoued Algeria 26°50N 9°28E 136 C5
Hassi Tartrat Algeria 30°5N 6°28E 136 B5
Hassi Zerzour Morocco 30°51N 3°56W 136 B3
Hassi Zguilma Morocco 30°19N 6°10W 136 B2
Hässleholm Sweden 56°10N 13°46E 63 H7
Hasslö Sweden 56°7N 15°28E 63 H9
Hassloch Germany 49°22N 8°16E 77 F4
Hästholmen Sweden 58°17N 14°38E 63 F8
Hastings Australia 38°18S 145°12E 153 E6
Hastings N.Z. 39°39S 176°52E 154 F5
Hastings U.K. 50°51N 0°35E 67 G8
Hastings Fla., U.S.A. 29°43N 81°31W 178 F8
Hastings Mich., U.S.A. 42°39N 85°17W 173 D11
Hastings Minn., U.S.A. 44°44N 92°51W 172 C7
Hastings Nebr., U.S.A. 40°35N 98°23W 172 E4
Hastings Ra. Australia 31°15S 152°14E 153 A10
Hästveda Sweden 56°17N 13°55E 63 H7
Hat Ukraine 48°19N 22°38E 80 B7
Hat Head △ Australia 31°3S 153°1E 153 A10
Hat Lot Vietnam 21°15N 104°7E 120 B5
Hat Yai Thailand 7°1N 100°27E 121 J3
Hatanbulag = Ergel Mongolia 43°8N 109°5E 114 C5
Hatay Turkey 36°14N 36°10E 104 D7
Hatay □ Turkey 36°25N 36°15E 104 D7
Hatch U.S.A. 32°40N 107°9W 169 K10
Hatchet L. Canada 58°36N 103°40W 163 B8
Haţeg Romania 45°36N 22°55E 80 E7
Hateruma-Shima Japan 24°3N 123°47E 113 M1
Hatfield Australia 33°54S 143°49E 152 B5
Hatgal Mongolia 50°26N 100°9E 110 A9
Hathras India 27°36N 78°6E 124 F8
Hatia Bangla. 22°30N 91°5E 123 H17
Hatia Nepal 27°43N 87°21E 125 F12
Ḩāţibah, Ra's Si. Arabia 21°55N 38°57E 137 C4
Hatid India 17°17N 75°3E 126 F2
Hato Mayor Dom. Rep. 18°46N 69°15W 183 C6
Hatra = Al Ḩaḑr Iraq 35°35N 42°44E 105 E10
Hatta India 24°7N 79°36E 125 G8
Hatta U.A.E. 24°45N 56°4E 129 E8
Hattah Australia 34°48S 142°17E 152 C5
Hattah Kulkyne △ Australia 34°16S 142°33E 152 C5
Hatteras, C. U.S.A. 35°14N 75°32W 177 D17
Hatteras Abyssal Plain Atl. Oc. 28°0N 72°0W 56 D4
Hattiesburg U.S.A. 31°20N 89°17W 177 F10
Hattusa Turkey 40°0N 34°37E 104 B6
Hatvan Hungary 47°40N 19°45E 80 C4
Hau → Vietnam 9°30N 106°13E 121 H6
Haugesund Norway 59°23N 5°13E 61 G11
Hauhungaroa Ra. N.Z. 38°42S 175°40E 154 E4
Haukipudas Finland 65°12N 25°20E 60 D21
Haultain → Canada 55°51N 106°46W 163 B7
Hauraki G. N.Z. 36°35S 175°5E 154 C4
Hauroko L. N.Z. 45°59S 167°21E 155 F2
Hausruck Austria 48°6N 13°30E 78 C6
Haut Atlas Morocco 32°30N 5°0W 136 B3
Haut-Jura ⌂ France 46°23N 2°23E 71 F9
Haut-Katanga □ Dem. Rep. of the Congo 10°30S 27°30E 143 E2
Haut-Languedoc ⌂ France 43°30N 2°43E 72 E6
Haut-Niger △ Guinea 10°20N 10°20W 138 C2
Haut-Rhin □ France 48°0N 7°15E 71 E14
Haute-Corse □ France 42°30N 9°30E 73 F13
Haute-Garonne □ France 43°30N 1°30E 72 E5
Haute-Loire □ France 45°5N 3°50E 72 C7
Haute-Marne □ France 48°10N 5°20E 71 D12
Haute-Saône □ France 47°45N 6°10E 71 E13
Haute-Savoie □ France 46°0N 6°20E 73 C10
Haute-Vienne □ France 45°50N 1°10E 72 C5
Hautes-Alpes □ France 44°42N 6°20E 73 D10
Hautes-Fagnes = Hohes Venn Belgium 50°30N 6°5E 69 D6
Hautes-Pyrénées □ France 43°0N 0°10E 72 F4
Hauteville-Lompnès France 45°58N 5°36E 73 C9
Hautmont France 50°15N 3°55E 71 B10
Hauts-de-France □ France 50°30N 3°0E 71 B9
Hauts-de-Seine □ France 48°52N 2°15E 71 D9
Hauts Plateaux Algeria 35°0N 1°0E 136 B4
Hauzenberg Germany 48°40N 13°37E 77 G9
Havana = La Habana Cuba 23°8N 82°22W 182 B3
Havana Fla., U.S.A. 30°37N 84°25W 178 E5
Havana Ill., U.S.A. 40°18N 90°4W 172 E8
Havant U.K. 50°51N 0°58W 67 G7
Havârna Romania 48°4N 26°43E 81 B11
Havasor = Kığzı Turkey 38°18N 43°25E 128 B4
Havasu, L. U.S.A. 34°18N 114°28W 171 L12
Havdhem Sweden 57°10N 18°20E 63 G12
Havel → Germany 52°50N 12°3E 76 C8
Havelian Pakistan 34°2N 73°10E 124 B5
Havelock Canada 44°26N 77°53W 174 B7
Havelock N.Z. 41°17S 173°48E 155 B8
Havelock U.S.A. 34°53N 76°54W 177 D16
Havelock I. India 11°58N 93°0E 127 J11
Havelock North N.Z. 39°40S 176°53E 154 F5
Haverfordwest U.K. 51°48N 4°58W 67 F3
Haverhill U.K. 52°5N 0°28E 67 E8
Haverhill Fla., U.S.A. 26°42N 80°7W 179 J9
Haverhill Mass., U.S.A. 42°47N 71°5W 175 D13
Haveri India 14°53N 75°24E 127 G2
Havern Sweden 62°18N 15°7E 62 B9
Haverstraw U.S.A. 41°12N 73°58W 175 E11
Håverud Sweden 58°50N 12°28E 63 F6
Havirga Mongolia 45°41N 113°5E 114 B7
Havířov Czechia 49°46N 18°20E 79 B11
Havlíčkův Brod Czechia 49°36N 15°33E 78 B8
Havneby Denmark 55°5N 8°34E 63 J2
Havran Turkey 39°33N 27°6E 99 B9
Havre U.S.A. 48°33N 109°41W 168 B9
Havre-Aubert Canada 47°12N 61°56W 165 C7
Havre-St.-Pierre Canada 50°18N 63°33W 165 B7
Havsa Turkey 41°31N 26°48E 97 E10
Havza Turkey 41°0N 35°35E 104 B6
Haw → U.S.A. 35°36N 79°3W 177 D15
Hawai'i U.S.A. 19°30N 155°30W 167 M8
Hawai'i □ U.S.A. 19°30N 156°30W 167 M8
Hawaiian Is. Pac. Oc. 20°30N 156°0W 157 E12
Hawaiian Ridge Pac. Oc. 24°0N 165°0W 157 E11
Hawarden U.S.A. 43°0N 96°29W 172 D5
Hawea, L. N.Z. 44°28S 169°19E 155 E4
Hawea Flat N.Z. 44°40S 169°19E 155 E4
Hawera N.Z. 39°35S 174°19E 154 F3
Hawi U.S.A. 20°14N 155°50W 167 L8
Hawick U.K. 55°26N 2°47W 65 F6
Hawk Junction Canada 48°5N 84°38W 164 C3
Hawkdun Ra. N.Z. 44°53S 170°5E 155 E5
Hawke B. N.Z. 39°25S 177°20E 154 F6
Hawker Australia 31°59S 138°22E 152 A3
Hawke's Bay Canada 50°36N 57°10W 165 B8
Hawke's Bay □ N.Z. 39°45S 176°35E 154 F5
Hawkesbury Canada 45°37N 74°37W 164 C5
Hawkesbury I. Canada 53°37N 129°3W 162 C3
Hawkesbury Pt. Australia 11°55S 134°5E 150 A1
Hawkinsville U.S.A. 32°17N 83°28W 178 C6
Hawks Nest Australia 32°41S 152°11E 153 B10
Hawley Minn., U.S.A. 46°53N 96°19W 172 B5
Hawley Pa., U.S.A. 41°28N 75°11W 175 E9
Ḩawrān, W. → Iraq 33°58N 42°34E 105 F10
Hawsh Mūssá Lebanon 33°45N 35°55E 130 B4
Hawthorne Fla., U.S.A. 29°36N 82°5W 179 F7
Hawthorne Nev., U.S.A. 38°32N 118°38W 168 G4
Hay Australia 34°30S 144°51E 153 C6
Hay → Australia 24°50S 138°0E 150 C2
Hay → Canada 60°50N 116°26W 162 A5
Hay, C. Australia 14°5S 129°29E 148 B4
Hay I. Canada 44°53N 80°58W 174 B4
Hay L. Canada 58°50N 118°50W 162 B5
Hay-on-Wye U.K. 52°5N 3°8W 67 E4
Hay Point Australia 21°18S 149°17E 150 C4
Hay River Canada 60°51N 115°44W 162 A5
Hay Springs U.S.A. 42°41N 102°41W 172 D2
Hayachine-San Japan 39°34N 141°29E 112 E10
Hayange France 49°20N 6°2E 71 C13
Hayastan = Armenia ■ Asia 40°20N 45°0E 87 K7
Haydān, W. al → Jordan 31°29N 35°34E 130 D4
Haydarlı Turkey 38°16N 30°23E 99 C12
Hayden U.S.A. 40°30N 107°16W 168 F10
Hayes U.S.A. 44°23N 101°1W 172 C3
Hayes → Canada 57°3N 92°12W 164 A1
Hayes, Mt. U.S.A. 63°37N 146°43W 166 C10
Hayes Creek Australia 13°43S 131°22E 148 B5
Hayle U.K. 50°11N 5°26W 67 G2
Hayling I. U.K. 50°48N 0°59W 67 G7
Hayman I. Australia 20°4S 148°53E 150 b
Haymana Turkey 39°26N 32°31E 104 C5
Hayneville U.S.A. 32°23N 83°37W 178 C6
Hayrabolu Turkey 41°12N 27°5E 97 E11
Hays Canada 50°6N 111°48W 162 C6
Hays U.S.A. 38°53N 99°20W 172 F4
Haysyn Ukraine 48°57N 29°25E 81 B14
Hayvoron Ukraine 48°22N 29°52E 81 B14
Hayward Calif., U.S.A. 37°40N 122°4W 170 H4
Hayward Wis., U.S.A. 46°1N 91°29W 172 B8
Haywards Heath U.K. 51°0N 0°5W 67 G7
Hazafon □ Israel 32°40N 35°20E 130 C4
Hazar Turkmenistan 39°34N 53°16E 108 E4
Hazārān, Kūh-e Iran 29°35N 57°20E 129 D8
Hazard U.S.A. 37°15N 83°12W 173 G12
Hazaribag India 23°58N 85°26E 125 H11
Hazaribag Road India 24°12N 85°57E 125 G11
Hazebrouck France 50°42N 2°31E 71 B9
Hazelton Canada 55°20N 127°42W 162 B3
Hazelton U.S.A. 46°29N 100°17W 172 B3
Hazen U.S.A. 47°18N 101°38W 172 B3
Hazen, L. Canada 81°47N 71°1W 57 A3
Hazlehurst Ga., U.S.A. 31°52N 82°36W 178 D7
Hazlehurst Miss., U.S.A. 31°52N 90°24W 177 F9
Hazlet U.S.A. 40°25N 74°12W 175 F10
Hazleton U.S.A. 40°57N 75°59W 175 F9
Hazlett, L. Australia 21°30S 128°48E 148 D4
Hazro Turkey 38°15N 40°47E 128 B4
He Xian = Hezhou China 24°27N 111°30E 117 E8
He Xian China 31°45N 118°20E 117 B12
Head of Bight Australia 31°30S 131°25E 149 F5
Head-Smashed-In Buffalo Jump Canada 49°44N 113°37W 162 D6
Headland U.S.A. 31°21N 85°21W 178 D4
Headlands Zimbabwe 18°15S 32°2E 143 F3
Healdsburg U.S.A. 38°37N 122°52W 170 G4
Healdton U.S.A. 34°14N 97°29W 176 D6
Healesville Australia 37°35S 145°30E 153 D6
Healy U.S.A. 63°52N 148°58W 166 C10
Heany Junction Zimbabwe 20°6S 28°54E 145 B4
Heard I. Ind. Oc. 53°6S 72°36E 146 K6
Hearne U.S.A. 30°53N 96°36W 176 F6
Hearst Canada 49°40N 83°41W 164 C3
Heart → U.S.A. 46°46N 100°50W 172 B3
Heart's Content Canada 47°54N 53°27W 165 C9
Heath → Bolivia 12°31S 68°38W 188 C4
Heath, Pte. Canada 49°8N 61°40W 165 C7
Heath Mts. N.Z. 45°39S 167°9E 155 F2
Heathcote Australia 36°56S 144°45E 153 D6
Heathrow, London ✈ (LHR) U.K. 51°28N 0°27W 67 F7
Heavener U.S.A. 34°53N 94°36W 176 D7
Hebbronville U.S.A. 27°18N 98°41W 176 H5
Hebei □ China 39°0N 116°0E 114 E9
Hebel Australia 28°58S 147°47E 151 D4
Heber U.S.A. 32°44N 115°32W 171 N11
Heber Springs U.S.A. 35°30N 92°2W 176 D8
Hebgen L. U.S.A. 44°52N 111°20W 168 D8
Hebi China 35°57N 114°7E 114 G8
Hebrides U.K. 57°30N 7°0W 58 D4
Hebrides, Sea of the U.K. 57°5N 7°0W 65 D2
Hebron = Al Khalīl West Bank 31°32N 35°6E 130 D4
Hebron Canada 58°5N 62°30W 161 F19
Hebron N. Dak., U.S.A. 46°54N 102°3W 172 B2
Hebron Nebr., U.S.A. 40°10N 97°35W 172 E5
Heby Sweden 59°56N 16°53E 62 E10
Hecate Str. Canada 53°10N 130°30W 162 C2
Heceta I. U.S.A. 55°46N 133°40W 162 B2
Hechi China 24°40N 108°2E 116 E7
Hechingen Germany 48°21N 8°57E 77 G4
Hechuan China 30°2N 106°12E 116 B6
Hecla U.S.A. 45°53N 98°9W 172 C4
Hecla I. Canada 51°10N 96°43W 163 C9
Hedal Norway 60°37N 9°41E 62 D3
Hédé France 48°18N 1°49W 70 D5
Hede Sweden 62°23N 13°30E 62 B7
Hedemora Sweden 60°18N 15°58E 62 D9
Hedensted Denmark 55°46N 9°42E 63 J3
Hedesunda Sweden 60°24N 17°0E 62 D10
Hedgehope N.Z. 46°12S 168°34E 155 G3
Heerde Neths. 52°24N 6°2E 69 B6
Heerenveen Neths. 52°57N 5°55E 69 B5
Heerhugowaard Neths. 52°40N 4°51E 69 B4
Heerlen Neths. 50°55N 5°58E 69 D5
Ḩefa Israel 32°46N 35°0E 130 C4
Ḩefa □ Israel 32°40N 35°0E 130 C4
Hefei China 31°52N 117°18E 117 B11
Hefeng China 29°55N 109°52E 116 C7
Heflin U.S.A. 33°39N 85°35W 178 B4
Hegang China 47°20N 130°19E 111 B15
Heglig Sudan 10°0N 29°24E 135 G11
Hei Ling Chau China 22°15N 114°2E 111 a
Heichengzhen China 36°24N 106°3E 114 F4
Heide Germany 54°11N 9°6E 76 A5
Heidelberg Germany 49°24N 8°42E 77 F4
Heidelberg S. Africa 34°6S 20°59E 144 D3
Heidelburg S. Africa 26°30S 28°21E 145 C4
Heidenau Germany 50°57N 13°52E 76 E9
Heidenheim Germany 48°41N 10°9E 77 G6
Heihe China 50°10N 127°30E 111 A14
Heijing China 25°22N 101°44E 116 E3
Heilbad Heiligenstadt Germany 51°22N 10°8E 76 D6
Heilbron S. Africa 27°16S 27°59E 145 C4
Heilbronn Germany 49°9N 9°13E 77 F5
Heiligenblut Austria 47°2N 12°51E 78 D5
Heiligenhafen Germany 54°22N 10°59E 76 A6
Heilongjiang □ China 48°0N 126°0E 111 B14
Heiloo Neths. 52°36N 4°42E 69 B4
Heilprin Land Greenland 82°5N 33°0W 57 A7
Heilunkiang = Heilongjiang □ China 48°0N 126°0E 111 B14
Heimaey Iceland 63°26N 20°17W 60 E3
Heinola Finland 61°13N 26°2E 84 B4
Heinsberg Germany 51°3N 6°5E 76 D2
Heinze Chaung Myanmar 14°42N 97°52E 120 E1
Heinze Kyun Myanmar 14°25N 97°45E 120 E1
Heishan China 41°40N 122°5E 115 D12
Heishui Liaoning, China 42°8N 119°30E 115 C10
Heishui Sichuan, China 32°4N 103°2E 116 A4
Hejaz = Ḩijāz Si. Arabia 24°0N 40°0E 128 E3
Hejian China 38°25N 116°5E 114 E9
Hejiang China 28°43N 105°46E 116 C5
Hejin China 35°35N 110°42E 114 G6
Hejing China 42°18N 86°22E 109 D11
Hekimhan Turkey 38°50N 37°55E 104 C7
Hekla Iceland 63°56N 19°35W 60 E4
Hekou Gansu, China 36°10N 103°26E 114 F2
Hekou Guangdong, China 23°13N 112°45E 117 F9
Hekou Yunnan, China 22°30N 103°59E 116 F4
Hel Poland 54°37N 18°47E 82 D5
Helagsfjället Sweden 62°54N 12°25E 62 B6
Helan Shan China 38°30N 105°55E 114 E3
Helechosa de los Montes Spain 39°22N 4°53W 89 F6
Helen Atoll Palau 2°40N 132°0E 119 D8
Helena Ga., U.S.A. 32°5N 82°55W 178 C7
Helena Mont., U.S.A. 46°36N 112°2W 168 C7
Helena -West Helena U.S.A. 34°32N 90°36W 177 D9
Helendale U.S.A. 34°44N 117°19W 171 L9
Helensburgh Australia 34°11S 151°1E 153 C9
Helensburgh U.K. 56°1N 4°43W 65 E4
Helensville N.Z. 36°41S 174°29E 154 C3
Helenvale Australia 15°43S 145°14E 150 B4
Helgasjön Sweden 56°55N 14°50E 63 H8
Helgeland Norway 66°7N 13°29E 60 C15
Helgoland Germany 54°10N 7°53E 76 A3
Helheim Gletscher Greenland 66°24N 38°12W 57 D7
Heligoland = Helgoland Germany 54°10N 7°53E 76 A3
Heligoland B. = Deutsche Bucht Germany 54°15N 8°0E 76 A4
Heliopolis = Masr el Gedida Egypt 30°5N 31°21E 137 E7
Hell Hole Gorge △ Australia 25°31S 144°12E 150 D3
Hella Iceland 63°50N 20°24W 60 E3
Hellas = Greece ■ Europe 40°0N 23°0E 98 B3
Hellertown U.S.A. 40°35N 75°21W 175 F9
Hellespont = Çanakkale Boğazı Turkey 40°17N 26°32E 97 F10
Hellevoetsluis Neths. 51°50N 4°8E 69 C4
Hellín Spain 38°31N 1°40W 91 G3
Hells Canyon ⌂ U.S.A. 45°30N 117°45W 168 D5
Hell's Gate △ Kenya 0°54S 36°19E 142 C4
Helmand □ Afghan. 31°20N 64°0E 122 D4
Helmand → Afghan. 31°12N 61°34E 122 D2
Helme → Germany 51°20N 11°21E 76 D7
Helmeringhausen Namibia 25°54S 16°57E 144 C2
Helmond Neths. 51°29N 5°41E 69 C5
Helmsdale U.K. 58°7N 3°39W 65 C5
Helmsdale → U.K. 58°8N 3°43W 65 C5
Helmstedt Germany 52°12N 11°0E 76 C7
Helong China 42°40N 129°0E 115 C15
Helper U.S.A. 39°41N 110°51W 168 G8
Helsingborg Sweden 56°3N 12°42E 63 H6
Helsinge Denmark 56°2N 12°12E 63 H6
Helsingfors = Helsinki Finland 60°10N 24°55E 84 B3
Helsingør Denmark 56°2N 12°35E 63 H6
Helsinki Finland 60°10N 24°55E 84 B3
Helska, Mierzeja Poland 54°45N 18°40E 82 D5
Helston U.K. 50°6N 5°17W 67 G2
Helvellyn U.K. 54°32N 3°1W 66 C4
Helvetinjärvi △ Finland 62°5N 23°47E 60 E20
Helwân Egypt 29°50N 31°20E 137 F7
Hemavati → India 12°30N 76°20E 127 H3
Hemel Hempstead U.K. 51°44N 0°28W 67 F7
Hemet U.S.A. 33°45N 116°58W 171 M10
Hemingford U.S.A. 42°19N 103°4W 172 D2
Hemis △ India 34°10N 77°15E 124 B7
Hemmingford Canada 45°3N 73°35W 175 A11
Hempstead N.Y., U.S.A. 40°42N 73°37W 175 F11
Hempstead Tex., U.S.A. 30°6N 96°5W 176 F6
Hemse Sweden 57°15N 18°22E 63 G12
Hemsön Sweden 62°42N 18°5E 62 B12
Hen and Chickens Is. N.Z. 35°58S 174°45E 154 B3
Henån Sweden 58°14N 11°40E 63 F5
Henan □ China 34°0N 114°0E 114 H8
Henares → Spain 40°24N 3°30W 88 E7
Henashi-Misaki Japan 40°37N 139°51E 112 D9
Hendaye France 43°23N 1°47W 72 E2
Hendek Turkey 40°48N 30°44E 104 B4
Henderson Argentina 36°18S 61°43W 190 D3
Henderson Ga., U.S.A. 32°21N 83°47W 178 C6
Henderson Ky., U.S.A. 37°50N 87°35W 172 G10
Henderson N.C., U.S.A. 36°20N 78°25W 177 C15
Henderson N.Y., U.S.A. 43°50N 76°10W 175 C8
Henderson Nev., U.S.A. 36°2N 114°58W 171 J12
Henderson Tenn., U.S.A. 35°26N 88°38W 177 D10
Henderson Tex., U.S.A. 32°9N 94°48W 176 E7
Henderson I. Pac. Oc. 24°22S 128°19W 157 K15
Hendersonville N.C., U.S.A. 35°19N 82°28W 177 D13
Hendersonville Tenn., U.S.A. 36°18N 86°37W 177 C11
Hendījān Iran 30°14N 49°43E 129 D6
Hendorābī Iran 26°40N 53°37E 129 E7
Heng Jiang → China 28°40N 104°25E 116 C5
Heng Xian China 22°40N 109°17E 116 F7
Hengām Iran 26°38N 55°53E 129 E7
Hengcheng China 38°18N 106°28E 114 E4
Hëngch'un Taiwan 22°0N 120°44E 117 F13
Hengdaohezi China 44°52N 129°0E 115 B15
Hengduan Shan China 28°30N 98°50E 116 C2
Hengelo Neths. 52°16N 6°48E 69 B6
Henggang China 22°39N 114°12E 111 a
Hengmen China 22°33N 113°35E 111 a
Hengshan Hunan, China 27°16N 112°45E 117 D9
Hengshan Shaanxi, China 37°58N 109°5E 114 F5
Hengshui China 37°41N 115°40E 114 F8
Hengyang China 26°59N 112°22E 117 D9
Henichesk Ukraine 46°12N 34°50E 85 J8
Hénin-Beaumont France 50°25N 2°58E 71 B9
Henley-on-Thames U.K. 51°32N 0°54W 67 F7
Henlopen, C. U.S.A. 38°48N 75°6W 173 F16
Hennan Sweden 62°2N 15°54E 62 B9
Hennebont France 47°49N 3°19W 70 E3
Hennenman S. Africa 27°59S 27°1E 144 C4
Hennessey U.S.A. 36°6N 97°54W 176 C6
Hennigsdorf Germany 52°38N 13°12E 76 C9
Henri Pittier △ Venezuela 10°26N 67°37W 183 D6
Henrietta N.Y., U.S.A. 43°4N 77°37W 174 C7
Henrietta Tex., U.S.A. 33°49N 98°12W 176 E5
Henrietta, Ostrov = Genriyetty, Ostrov Russia 77°6N 156°30E 107 B16
Henrietta Maria, C. Canada 55°9N 82°20W 164 A3
Henry U.S.A. 41°7N 89°22W 172 E9
Henry Ice Rise Antarctica 80°35S 62°0W 55 E17
Henry Lawrence I. India 12°9N 93°5E 127 H11
Henryetta U.S.A. 35°27N 95°59W 176 D7
Henryville Canada 45°8N 73°11W 175 A11
Hensall Canada 43°26N 81°30W 174 C3
Henstedt-Ulzburg Germany 53°47N 10°0E 76 B6
Hentiesbaai Namibia 22°8S 14°18E 144 B1
Hentiyn Nuruu Mongolia 48°30N 108°30E 111 B10
Henty Australia 35°30S 147°3E 153 C7
Henzada = Hinthada Myanmar 17°38N 95°26E 123 L19
Hephaestia Greece 39°55N 25°14E 99 B7
Hephzibah U.S.A. 33°19N 82°6W 178 B7
Heping China 24°29N 115°0E 117 E10
Heppner U.S.A. 45°21N 119°33W 168 D4
Hepu China 21°40N 109°12E 116 G7
Hepworth Canada 44°37N 81°9W 174 B3
Heqing China 26°37N 100°11E 116 D3
Hequ China 39°20N 111°15E 114 E6
Heraðsflói Iceland 65°42N 14°12W 60 D6
Heraðsvötn → Iceland 65°45N 19°25W 60 D4
Heraklion = Iraklio Greece 35°20N 25°12E 101 D7
Herald Cays Australia 16°58S 149°9E 150 B4
Herangi Ra. N.Z. 38°33S 174°48E 154 E3
Herāt Afghan. 34°20N 62°7E 108 F6
Herāt □ Afghan. 35°0N 62°0E 122 B3
Hérault □ France 43°34N 3°15E 72 E7
Hérault → France 43°17N 3°26E 72 E7
Herbault France 47°36N 1°8E 70 E8
Herbert Canada 50°30N 107°10W 163 C7
Herbert → Australia 18°31S 146°17E 150 B4
Herbertabad India 11°43N 92°37E 127 J11
Herberton Australia 17°20S 145°25E 150 B4
Herbertsdale S. Africa 34°1S 21°46E 144 D3
Herbertville N.Z. 40°30S 176°33E 154 G5
Herbignac France 47°27N 2°18W 70 E4
Herborn Germany 50°40N 8°18E 76 E4
Herby Poland 50°45N 18°50E 83 H5
Herceg-Novi Montenegro 42°30N 18°33E 96 D2
Herchmer Canada 57°22N 94°10W 163 B10
Herðubreið Iceland 65°11N 16°21W 60 D5
Hereford U.K. 52°4N 2°43W 67 E5
Hereford U.S.A. 34°49N 102°24W 176 D3
Herefordshire □ U.K. 52°8N 2°40W 67 E5
Herekino N.Z. 35°18S 173°11E 154 B2
Herencia Spain 39°21N 3°22W 89 F7
Herentals Belgium 51°12N 4°51E 69 C4
Herford Germany 52°7N 8°39E 76 C4
Héricourt France 47°32N 6°45E 71 E13
Herington U.S.A. 38°40N 96°57W 172 F5
Herīs Iran 38°14N 47°6E 105 C12
Herisau Switz. 47°22N 9°17E 77 H5
Hérisson France 46°32N 2°42E 71 F9
Herkimer U.S.A. 43°2N 74°59W 175 D10
Herlen → Asia 48°48N 117°0E 111 B12
Herlong U.S.A. 40°8N 120°8W 170 E6
Herm U.K. 49°30N 2°28W 67 H5
Hermakivka Ukraine 48°42N 26°11E 81 B11
Hermann U.S.A. 38°42N 91°27W 172 F8
Hermannsburg Australia 23°57S 132°45E 148 D5
Hermannsburg Germany 52°50N 10°5E 76 C6
Hermanus S. Africa 34°27S 19°12E 144 D2
Herment France 45°45N 2°24E 72 C6
Hermidale Australia 31°30S 146°42E 153 A7
Hermiston U.S.A. 45°51N 119°17W 168 D4
Hermon Canada 45°6N 77°37W 174 A7
Hermon U.S.A. 44°28N 75°14W 175 B9
Hermon, Mt. = Shaykh, J. ash Lebanon 33°25N 35°50E 130 B4
Hermosillo Mexico 29°10N 111°0W 180 B2
Hernád → Hungary 47°56N 21°8E 80 C6
Hernandarias Paraguay 25°20S 54°40W 191 B5
Hernandez U.S.A. 36°24N 120°46W 170 J6
Hernando Argentina 32°28S 63°40W 190 C3
Hernando Fla., U.S.A. 28°54N 82°23W 179 G7
Hernando Miss., U.S.A. 34°50N 90°0W 177 D10
Hernando de Magallanes △ Chile 54°0S 72°40W 192 D2
Hernani Spain 43°16N 1°58W 90 B3
Herndon U.S.A. 40°43N 76°51W 174 F8
Herne Germany 51°32N 7°14E 76 D3
Herne Bay U.K. 51°21N 1°8E 67 F9
Herning Denmark 56°8N 8°58E 63 H2
Herod U.S.A. 31°42N 84°26W 178 D5
Heroica Caborca = Caborca Mexico 30°37N 112°6W 180 A2
Heroica Nogales = Nogales Mexico 31°19N 110°56W 180 A2
Heron Bay Canada 48°40N 86°25W 164 C2
Heron I. Australia 23°27S 151°55E 150 C5
Herradura, Pta. de la Canary Is. 28°26N 14°8W 100 F5
Herreid U.S.A. 45°50N 100°4W 172 C3
Herrenberg Germany 48°35N 8°52E 77 G4
Herrera Spain 37°26N 4°55W 89 H6
Herrera de Alcántara Spain 39°39N 7°25W 89 F3
Herrera de Pisuerga Spain 42°35N 4°20W 88 C6
Herrera del Duque Spain 39°10N 5°3W 89 F5
Herrestad Sweden 58°21N 11°50E 63 F5
Herrin U.S.A. 37°48N 89°2W 172 G9
Herriot Canada 56°22N 101°16W 163 B8
Herrljunga Sweden 58°5N 13°1E 63 F7
Hersbruck Germany 49°30N 11°26E 77 F7
Herschel I. Canada 69°35N 139°5W 54 C1
Hershey U.S.A. 40°17N 76°39W 175 F8
Herso = Cherso Greece 41°5N 22°47E 96 E6
Herstal Belgium 50°40N 5°38E 69 D5
Hertford U.K. 51°48N 0°4W 67 F7
Hertfordshire □ U.K. 51°51N 0°5W 67 F7
's-Hertogenbosch Neths. 51°42N 5°17E 69 C5
Hertsa Ukraine 48°9N 26°15E 81 B11
Hertzogville S. Africa 28°9S 25°30E 144 C4
Hervás Spain 40°16N 5°52W 88 E5
Hervey B. Australia 25°0S 152°52E 150 C5
Herzberg Brandenburg, Germany 51°41N 13°14E 76 D9
Herzberg Niedersachsen, Germany 51°38N 10°20E 76 D6
Herzliyya Israel 32°10N 34°50E 130 C3
Herzogenburg Austria 48°17N 15°41E 78 C8
Ḩeşār Fārs, Iran 29°52N 50°16E 129 D6
Ḩeşār Markazī, Iran 35°50N 49°12E 129 C6
Hesdin France 50°21N 2°2E 71 B9
Heshan Guangdong, China 22°34N 113°4E 117 F9
Heshan Guangxi Zhuangzu, China 23°50N 108°53E 116 F7
Heshui China 35°48N 108°0E 114 G5
Heshun China 37°22N 113°32E 114 F7
Hesperia U.S.A. 34°25N 117°18W 171 L9
Hesse = Hessen □ Germany 50°30N 9°0E 76 E4
Hessen □ Germany 50°30N 9°0E 76 E4
Hessenreuther und Manteler Wald ⌂ Germany 49°45N 12°1E 77 F8
Hessle U.K. 53°44N 0°24W 66 D7
Hesso Australia 32°8S 137°58E 152 B2
Hestra Sweden 57°26N 13°35E 63 G7
Hetauda Nepal 27°25N 85°2E 125 F11
Hetch Hetchy Aqueduct U.S.A. 37°29N 122°19W 170 H5
Hetta Enontekiö Finland 68°23N 23°37E 60 B20
Hettinger U.S.A. 46°0N 102°42W 172 B2
Hettstedt Germany 51°39N 11°31E 76 D7
Heuksando S. Korea 34°40N 125°30E 115 G13
Heunghae S. Korea 36°12N 129°21E 115 F15
Heuvelton U.S.A. 44°37N 75°25W 175 B9
Heves Hungary 47°36N 20°17E 80 C5
Heves □ Hungary 47°50N 20°0E 80 C5
Hewitt U.S.A. 31°28N 97°12W 176 F6
Hexham U.K. 54°58N 2°4W 66 C5
Hexi Yunnan, China 24°9N 102°38E 116 E4
Hexi Zhejiang, China 27°58N 119°38E 117 D12
Hexigten Qi China 43°18N 117°30E 115 C9
Ḩeydarābād Iran 30°33N 55°38E 129 D7
Heyfield Australia 37°59S 146°47E 153 D7
Heysham U.K. 54°3N 2°53W 66 C5
Heyuan China 23°39N 114°40E 117 F10
Heywood Australia 38°8S 141°37E 152 E4
Heze China 35°14N 115°20E 114 G8
Hezhang China 27°8N 104°41E 116 D5
Hezhou China 24°27N 111°30E 117 E8

Hi Vista U.S.A. 34°45N 117°46W 171 L9
Hialeah U.S.A. 25°51N 80°16W 179 K9
Hiawatha U.S.A. 39°51N 95°32W 172 F6
Hibbing U.S.A. 47°25N 92°56W 172 B7
Hibernia Reef Australia 12°0S 123°23E 148 B3
Hickman U.S.A. 36°34N 89°11W 172 G9
Hickory U.S.A. 35°44N 81°21W 177 D14
Hicks, Pt. Australia 37°49S 149°17E 153 D8
Hicks Bay N.Z. 37°34S 178°21E 154 D7
Hicks L. Canada 61°25N 100°0W 163 A9
Hicksville U.S.A. 40°46N 73°32W 175 F11
Hicpochee, L. U.S.A. 26°48N 81°9W 179 J8
Hida Romania 47°10N 23°19E 81 C8
Hida-Gawa → Japan 35°26N 137°3E 113 G8
Hida-Sammyaku Japan 36°30N 137°40E 113 F8
Hidaka Japan 42°30N 142°10E 112 C11
Hidaka-Sammyaku Japan 42°35N 142°45E 112 C11
Hidalgo □ Mexico 20°30N 99°0W 181 C5
Hidalgo del Parral Mexico 26°56N 105°40W 180 B3
Hiddensee Germany 54°32N 13°6E 76 A9
Hieflau Austria 47°36N 14°46E 78 D7
Hiendelaencina Spain 41°5N 3°0W 90 D2
Hierapolis-Pamukkale Turkey 37°55N 29°7E 99 D11
Hierro Canary Is. 27°44N 18°0W 100 G1
Higashiajima-San Japan 37°40N 140°10E 112 F10
Higashiōsaka Japan 34°39N 135°37E 113 G7
Higgins U.S.A. 36°7N 100°2W 176 C4
Higgins Corner U.S.A. 39°2N 121°5W 170 F5
High Bridge U.S.A. 40°40N 74°54W 175 F10
High Desert U.S.A. 43°40N 120°20W 168 E3
High Island Res. China 22°22N 114°21E 111 a
High Level Canada 58°31N 117°8W 162 B5
High Point U.S.A. 35°57N 80°0W 177 D15
High Prairie Canada 55°30N 116°30W 162 B5
High River Canada 50°30N 113°50W 162 C6
High Springs U.S.A. 29°50N 82°36W 178 F7
High Tatra = Tatry Slovakia 49°20N 20°0E 79 B13
High Veld Africa 27°0S 27°0E 132 J6
High Wycombe U.K. 51°37N 0°45W 67 F7
Highbank N.Z. 43°37S 171°45E 155 D6
Highland □ U.K. 57°17N 4°21W 65 D4
Highland City U.S.A. 27°58N 81°53W 179 H8
Highland Home U.S.A. 31°57N 86°19W 178 D3
Highland Mills U.S.A. 33°17N 84°17W 178 B5
Highland Park U.S.A. 42°11N 87°48W 172 D10
Highland View U.S.A. 29°50N 85°19W 178 F4
Highmore U.S.A. 44°31N 99°27W 172 C4
Highrock L. Canada 55°45N 100°30W 163 B8
Higüey Dom. Rep. 18°37N 68°42W 183 C6
Hihya Egypt 30°40N 31°36E 137 E7
Hiidenportti △ Finland 63°53N 29°0E 60 E23
Hiiumaa Estonia 58°50N 22°45E 84 C2
Híjar Spain 41°10N 0°27W 90 D4
Ḩijārah, Şaḩrā' al Iraq 30°25N 44°30E 128 D5
Ḩijāz Si. Arabia 24°0N 40°0E 128 E3
Hijo = Tagum Phil. 7°33N 125°53E 119 C7
Hikari Japan 33°58N 131°58E 113 H5
Hikkaduwa Sri Lanka 6°8N 80°6E 127 L5
Hikmak, Ras el Egypt 31°15N 27°51E 137 A2
Hiko U.S.A. 37°32N 115°14W 170 H11
Hikone Japan 35°15N 136°10E 113 G8
Hikurangi Gisborne, N.Z. 37°55S 178°4E 154 D7
Hikurangi Northland, N.Z. 35°36S 174°17E 154 B3
Hiland Park U.S.A. 30°12N 85°33W 178 E4
Hildburghausen Germany 50°25N 10°42E 76 E6
Hildesheim Germany 52°9N 9°56E 76 C5
Hill → Australia 30°23S 115°3E 149 F2
Hill City Idaho, U.S.A. 43°18N 115°3W 168 E6
Hill City Kans., U.S.A. 39°22N 99°51W 172 F4
Hill City Minn., U.S.A. 46°59N 93°36W 172 B7
Hill City S. Dak., U.S.A. 43°56N 103°35W 172 D2
Hill Island L. Canada 60°30N 109°50W 163 A7
Hillaby, Mt. Barbados 13°12N 59°35W 183 g
Hillared Sweden 57°37N 13°10E 63 G7
Hillcrest Barbados 13°13N 59°31W 183 g
Hillegom Neths. 52°18N 4°35E 69 B4
Hillerød Denmark 55°56N 12°19E 63 J6
Hillerstorp Sweden 57°20N 13°52E 63 G7
Hilliard U.S.A. 30°41N 81°55W 178 E8
Hillsboro Ga., U.S.A. 33°11N 83°38W 178 B6
Hillsboro Kans., U.S.A. 38°21N 97°12W 172 F5
Hillsboro N. Dak., U.S.A. 47°26N 97°3W 172 B5
Hillsboro Ohio, U.S.A. 39°12N 83°37W 173 F12
Hillsboro Oreg., U.S.A. 45°31N 122°59W 170 E4
Hillsboro Tex., U.S.A. 32°1N 97°8W 176 E6
Hillsboro Canal U.S.A. 26°30N 80°15W 179 J9
Hillsborough Grenada 12°28N 61°28W 183 D7
Hillsborough U.S.A. 43°7N 71°54W 175 C13
Hillsborough Channel Australia 20°56S 149°15E 150 b
Hillsdale Mich., U.S.A. 41°56N 84°38W 173 E11
Hillsdale N.Y., U.S.A. 42°11N 73°32W 175 D11
Hillsport Canada 49°27N 85°34W 164 C2
Hillston Australia 33°30S 145°31E 153 B6
Hilltonia U.S.A. 32°53N 81°40W 178 C8
Hilo U.S.A. 19°44N 155°5W 167 M8
Hilton U.S.A. 43°17N 77°48W 174 C7
Hilton Head Island U.S.A. 32°13N 80°45W 178 C9
Hilvan Turkey 37°34N 38°58E 105 D8
Hilversum Neths. 52°14N 5°10E 69 B5
Himachal Pradesh □ India 31°30N 77°0E 124 D7
Himalaya Asia 29°0N 84°0E 125 E11
Himalchuli Nepal 28°27N 84°38E 125 E11
Himarë Albania 40°8N 19°43E 96 F3
Himatnagar India 23°37N 72°57E 124 H5
Himeji Japan 34°50N 134°40E 113 G7
Himi Japan 36°50N 136°55E 113 F8
Himmerland Denmark 56°45N 9°30E 63 H3
Ḩimş Syria 34°40N 36°45E 130 A5
Ḩimş □ Syria 34°30N 37°0E 130 A6
Hin Khom, Laem Thailand 9°25N 99°56E 121 b
Hinche Haiti 19°9N 72°1W 183 C5
Hinchinbrook I. Australia 18°20S 146°15E 150 B4
Hinchinbrook Island △ Australia 18°14S 146°6E 150 B4
Hinckley U.K. 52°33N 1°22W 67 E6
Hinckley U.S.A. 46°1N 92°56W 172 B7
Hindaun India 26°44N 77°5E 124 F7
Hindmarsh, L. Australia 36°5S 141°55E 152 D4
Hindol India 20°40N 85°10E 126 D7
Hinds N.Z. 43°59S 171°36E 155 D6
Hindsholm Denmark 55°30N 10°40E 63 J4
Hindu Bagh Pakistan 30°56N 67°50E 124 D2
Hindu Kush Asia 36°0N 71°0E 109 E8
Hindupur India 13°49N 77°32E 127 H3
Hines Creek Canada 56°20N 118°40W 162 B5
Hinesville U.S.A. 31°51N 81°36W 178 D8
Hinganghat India 20°30N 78°52E 126 D4
Hingham U.S.A. 48°33N 110°25W 168 B8
Hingir India 21°57N 83°41E 125 J10
Hingoli India 19°41N 77°15E 126 E3
Hinis Turkey 39°22N 41°43E 105 C9
Hinna = Imi Ethiopia 6°28N 42°10E 131 F3
Hinna Nigeria 10°25N 11°35E 139 C7
Hinnerup Denmark 56°16N 10°4E 63 H4
Hinnøya Norway 68°35N 15°50E 60 B16
Hinojosa del Duque Spain 38°30N 5°9W 89 G5
Hinsdale U.S.A. 42°47N 72°29W 175 D12
Hinterrhein → Switz. 46°40N 9°25E 77 J5
Hinthada Myanmar 17°38N 95°26E 123 L19
Hinton Canada 53°26N 117°34W 162 C5
Hinton U.S.A. 37°40N 80°54W 173 G13
Hios = Chios Greece 38°27N 26°9E 99 C8
Hirado Japan 33°22N 129°33E 113 H4
Hirakud Dam India 21°32N 83°45E 126 D6
Hiran → India 23°6N 79°21E 125 H8
Hirapur India 24°22N 79°13E 125 G8
Hirara = Miyakojima Japan 24°48N 125°17E 113 M2
Hiratsuka Japan 35°19N 139°21E 113 G9
Hirekerur India 14°28N 75°23E 127 G2
Hirfanlı Barajı Turkey 39°18N 33°31E 104 C5
Hirhafok Algeria 23°49N 5°45E 136 D5
Hiroo Japan 42°17N 143°19E 112 C11
Hirosaki Japan 40°34N 140°28E 112 D10
Hiroshima Japan 34°24N 132°30E 113 G6
Hiroshima □ Japan 34°50N 133°0E 113 G6
Hirson France 49°55N 4°4E 71 C11
Hirtshals Denmark 57°36N 9°57E 63 G3
Hisar India 29°12N 75°45E 124 E6
Hisarcık Turkey 39°15N 29°14E 99 B11
Hisaria Bulgaria 42°30N 24°44E 97 D8
Hisb, Sha'ib = Ḩasb, W. → Iraq 31°45N 44°17E 128 D5
Ḩismá Si. Arabia 28°30N 36°0E 128 D3
Hispaniola W. Indies 19°0N 71°0W 183 C5
Hīt Iraq 33°38N 42°49E 105 F10
Hita Japan 33°20N 130°58E 113 H5
Hitachi Japan 36°36N 140°39E 113 F10
Hitan, W. el Egypt 29°19N 30°10E 137 F7
Hitchin U.K. 51°58N 0°16W 67 F7
Hitiaa Tahiti 17°36S 149°18W 155 b
Hitoyoshi Japan 32°13N 130°45E 113 H5
Hitra Norway 63°30N 8°45E 60 E13
Hitzacker Germany 53°9N 11°2E 76 B7
Hiva Oa French Polynesia 9°45S 139°0W 157 H14
Hixon Canada 53°25N 122°35W 162 C4
Ḩiyyon, N. → Israel 30°25N 35°10E 130 E4
Hjalmar L. Canada 61°33N 109°25W 163 A7
Hjälmaren Sweden 59°18N 15°40E 62 E9
Hjältevad Sweden 57°38N 15°20E 63 G9
Hjo Sweden 58°22N 14°17E 63 F8
Hjørring Denmark 57°29N 9°59E 63 G3
Hjort Trench S. Ocean 58°0S 157°30E 55 B10
Hjortkvarn Sweden 58°54N 15°26E 63 F9
Hkakabo Razi Myanmar 28°25N 97°23E 116 C1
Hkamti Myanmar 26°0N 95°39E 123 G19
Hlinsko Czechia 49°45N 15°54E 78 B8
Hlobane S. Africa 27°42S 31°0E 145 C5
Hlohovec Slovakia 48°26N 17°49E 79 C10
Hlučín Czechia 49°54N 18°11E 79 B11
Hluhluwe S. Africa 28°1S 32°15E 145 C5
Hluhluwe ⌂ S. Africa 22°10S 32°5E 145 B5
Hlukhiv Ukraine 51°40N 33°58E 85 G7
Hlyboka Ukraine 48°5N 25°56E 81 B10
Hlybokaye Belarus 55°10N 27°45E 84 E4
Hnúšt'a Slovakia 48°35N 19°58E 79 C12
Ho Ghana 6°37N 0°27E 139 D5
Ho Chi Minh City = Thanh Pho Ho Chi Minh Vietnam 10°58N 106°40E 121 G6
Ho Hoa Binh Vietnam 20°50N 105°0E 116 G5
Ho Thac Ba Vietnam 21°42N 105°1E 120 A5
Ho Thuong Vietnam 19°32N 105°48E 120 C5
Hoa Binh Vietnam 20°50N 105°20E 116 G5
Hoa Hiep Vietnam 11°34N 105°51E 121 G5
Hoai Nhon Vietnam 14°28N 109°1E 120 E7
Hoang Lien △ Vietnam 21°30N 105°32E 120 B5
Hoang Lien Son Vietnam 22°0N 104°0E 116 F4
Hoang Sa, Dao = Paracel Is. S. China Sea 15°50N 112°0E 118 A4
Hoanib → Namibia 19°27S 12°46E 144 A2
Hoare B. Canada 65°17N 62°30W 161 D19
Hoarusib → Namibia 19°3S 12°36E 144 A2
Hobart Australia 42°50S 147°21E 151 G4
Hobart U.S.A. 35°1N 99°6W 176 D5
Hobbs U.S.A. 32°42N 103°8W 169 K12
Hobbs Coast Antarctica 74°50S 131°0W 55 D14
Hobe Sound U.S.A. 27°4N 80°8W 179 H9
Hoboken Ga., U.S.A. 31°11N 82°8W 178 D7
Hoboken N.J., U.S.A. 40°44N 74°3W 175 F10
Hobro Denmark 56°39N 9°46E 63 H3
Hoburgen Sweden 56°55N 18°7E 63 H12
Hobyo Somalia 5°25N 48°30E 131 F4
Hocalar Turkey 38°36N 30°0E 99 C11
Hochfeld Namibia 21°28S 17°58E 144 B2
Hochharz △ Germany 51°48N 10°38E 76 D6
Hochschwab Austria 47°35N 15°0E 78 D8
Höchstadt Germany 49°42N 10°47E 77 F6
Hochtaunus ⌂ Germany 50°20N 8°30E 77 E4
Hockenheim Germany 49°19N 8°32E 77 F4
Hodaka-Dake Japan 36°17N 137°39E 113 F8
Hodeida = Al Ḩudaydah Yemen 14°50N 43°0E 131 E3
Hodgeville Canada 50°7N 106°58W 163 C7
Hodgson Canada 51°13N 97°36W 163 C9
Hodh El Gharbi □ Mauritania 16°30N 10°0W 138 B3
Hódmezővásárhely Hungary 46°28N 20°22E 80 D5
Hodna, Chott el Algeria 35°26N 4°43E 136 A4
Hodonín Czechia 48°50N 17°10E 79 C10
Hœdic, Î. de France 47°20N 2°53W 70 E4
Hoek van Holland Neths. 52°0N 4°7E 69 C4
Hoengseong S. Korea 37°29N 127°59E 115 F14
Hoeryong N. Korea 42°30N 129°45E 115 C15
Hoeyang N. Korea 38°43N 127°36E 115 E14
Hof Germany 50°19N 11°55E 77 E7
Hofgeismar Germany 51°29N 9°23E 76 D5
Hofheim Germany 50°5N 8°26E 77 E4
Hofmeyr S. Africa 31°39S 25°50E 144 D4
Höfn Iceland 64°15N 15°13W 60 D6
Hofors Sweden 60°31N 16°15E 62 D10
Hofsjökull Iceland 64°49N 18°48W 60 D4
Hōfu Japan 34°3N 131°34E 113 G5
Hogan Group Australia 39°13S 147°1E 151 F4
Höganäs Sweden 56°12N 12°33E 63 H6
Hogansville U.S.A. 33°10N 84°55W 178 B5
Hogarth, Mt. Australia 21°48S 136°58E 150 C2
Hoge Kempen △ Belgium 51°6N 5°35E 69 C5
Hoge Veluwe △ Neths. 52°5N 5°46E 69 B5
Hogenakai Falls India 12°6N 77°50E 127 H3
Hoggar = Ahaggar Algeria 23°0N 6°30E 136 D5
Högsäter Sweden 58°38N 12°5E 63 F6
Högsby Sweden 57°10N 16°1E 63 G10
Högsjö Sweden 59°4N 15°44E 62 E9
Hogsty Reef Bahamas 21°41N 73°48W 183 B5
Hoh → U.S.A. 47°45N 124°29W 170 C2
Hoh Xil Shan China 36°30N 89°0E 110 D6
Hohd ech Chargui □ Mauritania 19°0N 7°15W 138 B3
Hohe Acht Germany 50°22N 7°0E 77 E3
Hohe Tauern Austria 47°11N 12°40E 78 D5
Hohe Tauern △ Austria 47°5N 12°20E 78 D5
Hohenau Austria 48°36N 16°55E 79 C9
Hohenems Austria 47°22N 9°42E 78 D2
Hohenloher Ebene Germany 49°14N 9°36E 77 F5
Hohenwald U.S.A. 35°33N 87°33W 177 D11
Hohenwestedt Germany 54°5N 9°40E 76 A5
Hoher Rhön = Rhön Germany 50°24N 9°58E 76 E5
Hoher Vogelsberg ⌂ Germany 51°45N 9°35E 76 D5
Hohes Venn Belgium 50°30N 6°5E 69 D6
Hohes Venn-Eifel ⌂ Europe 50°30N 6°10E 76 E2
Hohhot China 40°52N 111°40E 114 D6
Hohoe Ghana 7°8N 0°32E 139 D5
Hoi An Vietnam 15°53N 108°19E 120 E7
Hoi Xuan Vietnam 20°25N 105°9E 116 G5
Hoisington U.S.A. 38°31N 98°47W 172 F4
Hojambaz Turkmenistan 38°7N 65°0E 108 E6
Højer Denmark 54°58N 8°42E 63 K2
Hōjō Japan 33°58N 132°46E 113 H6
Hok Sweden 57°31N 14°16E 63 G8
Hökensås Sweden 58°0N 14°5E 63 G8
Hökerum Sweden 57°51N 13°16E 63 G7
Hokianga Harbour N.Z. 35°31S 173°22E 154 B2
Hokitika N.Z. 42°42S 171°0E 155 C6
Hokkaidō □ Japan 43°30N 143°0E 112 C11
Hokuto Japan 41°49N 140°39E 112 D10
Hola Kenya 1°29S 40°2E 142 B4
Hola Prystan Ukraine 46°29N 32°32E 85 J7
Holakas Greece 35°57N 27°53E 101 D9
Holalkere India 14°2N 76°11E 127 G3
Holašovice Czechia 48°57N 14°15E 78 C7
Holbæk Denmark 55°43N 11°43E 63 J5
Holbrook Australia 35°42S 147°18E 153 C7
Holbrook U.S.A. 34°54N 110°10W 169 J8
Holcomb U.S.A. 42°54N 77°25W 174 D7
Holden U.S.A. 39°6N 112°16W 168 G7
Holdenville U.S.A. 35°5N 96°24W 176 D6
Holdich Argentina 45°57S 68°13W 192 C3
Holdrege U.S.A. 40°26N 99°23W 172 E4
Hole-Narsipur India 12°48N 76°16E 127 H3
Holešov Czechia 49°20N 17°35E 79 B10
Holetown Barbados 13°11N 59°38W 183 g
Holguín Cuba 20°50N 76°20W 182 B4
Holíč Slovakia 48°49N 17°10E 79 C10
Holice Czechia 50°5N 16°0E 78 A8
Holiday U.S.A. 28°11N 82°44W 179 G7
Höljes Sweden 60°50N 12°35E 62 D6
Hollabrunn Austria 48°34N 16°5E 78 C9
Hollams Bird I. Namibia 24°40S 14°30E 144 B1
Holland = Netherlands ■ Europe 52°0N 5°30E 69 C5
Holland Mich., U.S.A. 42°47N 86°7W 172 D10
Holland N.Y., U.S.A. 42°38N 78°32W 174 D6
Holland Centre Canada 44°23N 80°47W 174 B4
Holland Patent U.S.A. 43°14N 75°15W 175 C9
Hollandale U.S.A. 33°10N 90°51W 177 E9
Holley U.S.A. 43°14N 78°2W 174 C6
Hollfeld Germany 49°56N 11°18E 77 F7
Hollidaysburg U.S.A. 40°26N 78°24W 174 F6
Hollis U.S.A. 34°41N 99°55W 176 D5
Hollister Calif., U.S.A. 36°51N 121°24W 170 J5
Hollister Idaho, U.S.A. 42°21N 114°35W 168 E6
Höllviken Sweden 55°26N 12°58E 63 J6
Höllviksnäs = Höllviken Sweden 55°26N 12°58E 63 J6
Holly Hill Fla., U.S.A. 29°16N 81°3W 179 F8
Holly Hill S.C., U.S.A. 33°19N 80°25W 178 B9
Holly Springs Ga., U.S.A. 34°10N 84°30W 178 A5
Holly Springs Miss., U.S.A. 34°46N 89°27W 177 D10
Hollywood Ireland 53°6N 6°35W 64 B6
Hollywood U.S.A. 26°0N 80°8W 179 J9
Holman = Ulukhaktok Canada 70°44N 117°44W 160 C8
Hólmavík Iceland 65°42N 21°40W 60 D3
Holmen U.S.A. 43°58N 91°15W 172 D8
Holmes Beach U.S.A. 27°31N 82°43W 179 H7
Holmes Cr. → U.S.A. 30°30N 85°50W 178 E4
Holmes Reefs Australia 16°27S 148°0E 150 B4
Holmsjö Sweden 56°25N 15°32E 63 H9
Holmsjön Västernorrland, Sweden 62°41N 16°33E 62 B10
Holmsjön Västernorrland, Sweden 62°26N 15°20E 62 B9
Holmsland Klit Denmark 56°0N 8°5E 63 J2
Holmsund Sweden 63°41N 20°20E 60 E19
Holod Romania 46°49N 22°8E 80 D7
Holon Israel 32°0N 34°46E 130 C3
Holopaw U.S.A. 28°8N 81°5W 179 G8
Holovne Ukraine 51°20N 24°5E 83 G11
Holozubyntsi Ukraine 48°50N 26°55E 81 B11
Holroyd → Australia 14°10S 141°36E 150 A3
Holstebro Denmark 56°22N 8°37E 63 H2
Holsteinische Schweiz ⌂ Germany 54°8N 10°30E 76 A6
Holsteinsborg = Sisimiut Greenland 66°40N 53°30W 57 D5
Holsworthy U.K. 50°48N 4°22W 67 G3
Holt U.S.A. 30°43N 86°45W 179 E3
Holton Canada 54°31N 57°12W 165 B8
Holton U.S.A. 39°28N 95°44W 172 F6
Holtville U.S.A. 32°49N 115°23W 171 N11
Holwerd Neths. 53°22N 5°54E 69 A5
Holy Cross U.S.A. 62°12N 159°46W 166 C8
Holy I. Anglesey, U.K. 53°17N 4°37W 66 D3
Holy I. Northumberland, U.K. 55°40N 1°47W 66 B6
Holyhead U.K. 53°18N 4°38W 66 D3
Holyoke Colo., U.S.A. 40°35N 102°18W 168 F12
Holyoke Mass., U.S.A. 42°12N 72°37W 175 D12
Holyrood Canada 47°27N 53°8W 165 C9
Holzkirchen Germany 47°52N 11°42E 77 H7
Holzminden Germany 51°50N 9°28E 76 D5
Homa Bay Kenya 0°36S 34°30E 142 C3
Homalin Myanmar 24°55N 95°0E 123 G19
Homand Iran 32°28N 59°37E 129 C8
Homathko → Canada 51°0N 124°56W 162 C4
Homberg Germany 51°2N 9°25E 76 D5
Hombori Mali 15°20N 1°38W 139 B4
Hombori Tondo Mali 15°16N 1°40W 139 B4
Homburg Germany 49°28N 7°18E 77 F3
Home B. Canada 68°40N 67°10W 161 D18
Home Hill Australia 19°43S 147°25E 150 B4
Homedale U.S.A. 43°37N 116°56W 168 E5
Homeland U.S.A. 30°51N 82°1W 178 E7
Homer Alaska, U.S.A. 59°39N 151°33W 160 F1
Homer La., U.S.A. 32°48N 93°4W 176 E8
Homer N.Y., U.S.A. 42°38N 76°10W 175 D8
Homer City U.S.A. 40°32N 79°10W 174 F5
Homert ⌂ Germany 51°15N 8°0E 76 D4
Homerville U.S.A. 31°2N 82°45W 178 D7
Homestead Australia 20°20S 145°40E 150 C4
Homestead U.S.A. 25°28N 80°29W 179 K9
Homestead ⌂ U.S.A. 40°17N 96°50W 172 E5
Homnabad India 17°45N 77°11E 126 F3
Homoine Mozam. 23°55S 35°8E 145 B6
Homoljske Planina Serbia 44°10N 21°45E 96 B5
Homorod Romania 46°5N 25°15E 81 D10
Homosassa Springs U.S.A. 28°48N 82°35W 179 G7
Homs = Ḩimş Syria 34°40N 36°45E 130 A5
Homyel Belarus 52°28N 31°0E 75 B16
Homyel □ Belarus 52°40N 30°10E 85 F6
Hon Chong Vietnam 10°25N 104°30E 121 G5
Hon Hai Vietnam 10°0N 109°0E 121 H7
Hon Me Vietnam 19°23N 105°56E 120 C5
Honan = Henan □ China 34°0N 114°0E 114 H8
Honavar India 14°17N 74°27E 127 G2
Honaz Turkey 37°46N 29°18E 99 D11
Honbetsu Japan 43°7N 143°37E 112 C11
Honcut U.S.A. 39°20N 121°32W 170 F5
Hondarribia Spain 43°22N 1°47W 90 B3
Hondeklipbaai S. Africa 30°19S 17°17E 144 D2
Hondo Japan 32°27N 130°12E 113 H5
Hondo U.S.A. 29°21N 99°9W 176 G5
Hondo, Río → Belize 18°25N 88°21W 181 D7
Honduras ■ Cent. Amer. 14°40N 86°30W 182 D2
Honduras, G. de Caribbean 16°50N 87°0W 182 C2
Hønefoss Norway 60°10N 10°18E 61 F14
Honesdale U.S.A. 41°34N 75°16W 175 E9
Honey Harbour Canada 44°52N 79°49W 174 B5
Honey L. U.S.A. 40°15N 120°19W 170 E6
Honfleur France 49°25N 0°13E 70 C7
Høng Denmark 55°31N 11°18E 63 J5
Hong → Asia 20°16N 106°34E 120 B5
Hong Gai Vietnam 20°57N 107°5E 116 G6
Hong He → China 32°25N 115°35E 117 A10
Hong Hu China 29°54N 113°24E 117 C9
Hong Kong □ China 22°11N 114°14E 111 a
Hong Kong I. China 22°16N 114°12E 111 a
Hong Kong Int. ✈ (HKG) China 22°19N 113°57E 111 a
Hong'an China 31°20N 114°40E 117 B10
Hongcheon S. Korea 37°44N 127°53E 115 F14
Honghai Wan China 22°40N 115°0E 117 F10
Honghe China 23°25N 102°25E 116 F4
Honghu China 29°50N 113°30E 117 C9
Hongjiang China 27°7N 109°59E 116 D7
Hongliu He → China 38°0N 109°50E 114 F5
Hongor Mongolia 45°45N 112°50E 114 B7
Hongseong S. Korea 36°37N 126°38E 115 F14
Hongshan China 36°38N 117°58E 115 F9
Hongshui He → China 23°48N 109°30E 116 F7
Hongtong China 36°16N 111°40E 114 F6
Honguedo, Détroit d' Canada 49°15N 64°0W 165 C7
Hongwon N. Korea 40°0N 127°56E 115 E14
Hongya China 29°57N 103°22E 116 C4
Hongyuan China 32°51N 102°40E 116 A4
Hongze Hu China 33°15N 118°35E 115 H10
Honiara Solomon Is. 9°27S 159°57E 147 B8
Honiton U.K. 50°47N 3°11W 67 G4
Honjō = Yurihonjō Japan 39°23N 140°3E 112 E10
Honkorâb, Ras Egypt 24°35N 35°10E 137 C4
Honnali India 14°15N 75°40E 127 G2
Honningsvåg Norway 70°59N 25°59E 60 A21
Hönö Sweden 57°41N 11°39E 63 G5
Honolulu U.S.A. 21°19N 157°52W 167 L8
Honshū Japan 36°0N 138°0E 113 F9
Hontoria del Pinar Spain 41°50N 3°10W 90 D1
Hood, Mt. U.S.A. 45°23N 121°42W 168 D3
Hood, Pt. Australia 34°23S 119°34E 149 F2
Hood River U.S.A. 45°43N 121°31W 168 D3
Hoodsport U.S.A. 47°24N 123°9W 170 C3
Hooge Germany 54°34N 8°33E 76 A4
Hoogeveen Neths. 52°44N 6°28E 69 B6
Hoogezand-Sappemeer Neths. 53°9N 6°45E 69 A6
Hooghly = Hugli → India 21°56N 88°4E 125 J13
Hooghly-Chinsura = Chunchura India 22°53N 88°27E 125 H13
Hook Hd. Ireland 52°7N 6°56W 64 D5
Hook I. Australia 20°4S 149°0E 150 b
Hook of Holland = Hoek van Holland Neths. 52°0N 4°7E 69 C4
Hooker U.S.A. 36°52N 101°13W 176 C4
Hooker Creek = Lajamanu Australia 18°23S 130°38E 148 C5
Hooker Creek ✪ Australia 18°6S 130°23E 148 C5
Hoonah U.S.A. 58°7N 135°27W 162 B1
Hooper Bay U.S.A. 61°32N 166°6W 166 C6
Hoopeston U.S.A. 40°28N 87°40W 172 E10
Hoopstad S. Africa 27°50S 25°55E 144 C4
Höör Sweden 55°56N 13°33E 63 J7
Hoorn Neths. 52°38N 5°4E 69 B4
Hoover U.S.A. 33°24N 86°49W 177 E11
Hoover Dam U.S.A. 36°1N 114°44W 171 K12
Hooversville U.S.A. 40°9N 78°55W 174 F6
Hop Bottom U.S.A. 41°42N 75°46W 175 E9
Hopa Turkey 41°28N 41°30E 105 B9
Hope Canada 49°25N 121°25W 162 D4
Hope Ariz., U.S.A. 33°43N 113°42W 171 M13
Hope Ark., U.S.A. 33°40N 93°36W 176 E8
Hope, L. S. Austral., Australia 28°24S 139°18E 151 D2
Hope, L. W. Austral., Australia 32°35S 120°15E 149 F3
Hope, Pt. U.S.A. 68°21N 166°47W 158 C3
Hope I. Canada 44°55N 80°11W 174 B4
Hope Town Bahamas 26°35N 76°57W 182 A4
Hope Vale Australia 15°16S 145°20E 150 B4
Hope Vale ✪ Australia 15°8S 145°15E 150 B4
Hopedale Canada 55°28N 60°13W 165 A7
Hopedale U.S.A. 42°8N 71°33W 175 D13
Hopefield S. Africa 33°3S 18°22E 144 D2
Hopei = Hebei □ China 39°0N 116°0E 114 E9
Hopelchén Mexico 19°46N 89°51W 181 D7
Hopetoun Vic., Australia 35°42S 142°22E 152 C5
Hopetoun W. Austral., Australia 33°57S 120°7E 149 F3
Hopetown S. Africa 29°34S 24°3E 144 C3
Hopewell U.S.A. 37°18N 77°17W 173 G15
Hopfgarten Austria 47°27N 12°10E 78 D5
Hopkins, L. Australia 24°15S 128°35E 148 D4
Hopkinsville U.S.A. 36°52N 87°29W 172 G10
Hopland U.S.A. 38°58N 123°7W 170 G3
Hoquiam U.S.A. 46°59N 123°53W 170 D3
Hora Hoverla Ukraine 48°7N 24°41E 81 B9
Horana Sri Lanka 6°43N 80°4E 127 L5
Horasan Turkey 40°3N 42°11E 105 B10
Horažďovice Czechia 49°19N 13°42E 78 B6
Horb Germany 48°26N 8°47E 77 G4
Hörby Sweden 55°51N 13°40E 63 J7
Horcajo de Santiago Spain 39°50N 3°1W 90 F1
Hordern Hills Australia 20°15S 130°0E 148 D5
Horezu Romania 45°6N 24°0E 81 E8
Horgen Switz. 47°15N 8°35E 77 H4
Horgos China 44°10N 80°25E 109 D10
Horgoš Serbia 46°10N 20°0E 80 D4
Horinchove Ukraine 48°16N 23°26E 81 B8
Horinger China 40°28N 111°48E 114 D6
Horizontina Brazil 27°37S 54°19W 191 B5
Horki Belarus 54°17N 30°59E 84 E6
Horlick Mts. Antarctica 84°0S 102°0W 55 E15
Horlivka Ukraine 48°19N 38°5E 85 H10
Hormak Iran 29°58N 60°51E 129 D9
Hormoz Iran 27°35N 55°0E 129 E7
Hormoz, Jaz.-ye Iran 27°8N 56°28E 129 E8
Hormozgān □ Iran 27°30N 56°0E 129 E8
Hormuz, Kūh-e Iran 27°27N 55°10E 129 E7
Hormuz, Str. of The Gulf 26°30N 56°30E 129 E8
Horn Austria 48°39N 15°40E 78 C8
Horn Sweden 57°54N 15°51E 63 G9
Horn → Canada 61°30N 118°1W 162 A5
Horn, Cape = Hornos, C. de Chile 55°50S 67°30W 192 E3
Horn Head Ireland 55°14N 8°0W 64 A3
Horn I. Australia 10°37S 142°17E 150 A3
Horn Plateau Canada 62°15N 119°15W 162 A5
Hornachuelos Spain 37°50N 5°14W 89 H5
Hornavan Sweden 66°15N 17°30E 60 C17
Hornbeck U.S.A. 31°20N 93°24W 176 F8
Hornbrook U.S.A. 41°55N 122°33W 168 F2
Hornburg Germany 52°2N 10°37E 76 C6
Hornby N.Z. 43°33S 172°33E 155 D7
Horncastle U.K. 53°13N 0°7W 66 D7
Horndal Sweden 60°18N 16°23E 62 D10
Hornell U.S.A. 42°20N 77°40W 174 D7
Hornell L. Canada 62°20N 119°25W 162 A5
Hornepayne Canada 49°14N 84°48W 164 C3
Horní Planá Czechia 48°46N 14°2E 78 C7
Hornings Mills Canada 44°9N 80°12W 174 B4
Hornitos U.S.A. 37°30N 120°14W 170 H6
Hornopirén △ Chile 41°58S 72°17W 192 B2
Hornos, C. de Chile 55°50S 67°30W 192 E3
Hornoy-le-Bourg France 49°50N 1°54E 71 C8
Hornsby Australia 33°42S 151°2E 153 B9
Hornsea U.K. 53°55N 0°11W 66 D7
Hornslandet Sweden 61°35N 17°37E 62 C11
Hornslet Denmark 56°19N 10°19E 63 H4
Hörnum Germany 54°45N 8°17E 76 A4
Horobetsu = Noboribetsu Japan 42°24N 141°6E 112 C10
Horodenka Ukraine 48°41N 25°29E 81 B10
Horodnya Ukraine 51°55N 31°33E 85 G6
Horodok Khmelnytskyy, Ukraine 49°10N 26°34E 75 D14
Horodok Lviv, Ukraine 49°46N 23°32E 75 D12
Horodyshche Ukraine 49°17N 31°27E 85 H6
Horokhiv Ukraine 50°30N 24°45E 75 C13
Hořovice Czechia 49°48N 13°53E 78 B6
Horqin Youyi Qianqi China 46°5N 122°3E 115 A12
Horqin Zuoyi Zhongqi China 44°8N 123°18E 115 B12
Horqueta Paraguay 23°15S 56°55W 190 A4
Horred Sweden 57°22N 12°28E 63 G6
Horse Cr. → U.S.A. 41°57N 103°58W 168 F12
Horse I. Canada 53°20N 99°6W 163 C9
Horse Is. Canada 50°15N 55°50W 165 B8
Horsefly L. Canada 52°25N 121°0W 162 C4
Horseheads U.S.A. 42°10N 76°49W 174 D8
Horsens Denmark 55°52N 9°51E 63 J3
Horseshoe Bend ⌂ U.S.A. 32°59N 85°44W 178 C4
Horseshoe Lake Canada 45°17N 79°51W 174 A5
Horsham Australia 36°44S 142°13E 152 D5
Horsham U.K. 51°4N 0°20W 67 F7
Horšovský Týn Czechia 49°31N 12°58E 78 B5
Horta Azores 38°32N 28°38W 134 a
Horten Norway 59°25N 10°32E 61 G14
Hortense U.S.A. 31°20N 81°57W 178 D8
Horti India 17°7N 75°47E 126 F2
Hortobágy → Hungary 47°30N 21°6E 80 C6
Hortobágyi △ Hungary 47°36N 21°20E 80 C6
Horton U.S.A. 39°40N 95°32W 172 F6
Horton → Canada 69°56N 126°52W 160 D6
Horwood L. Canada 48°5N 82°20W 164 C3
Hosapete India 15°15N 76°20E 127 G3
Hosdrug = Kanhangad India 12°21N 74°58E 127 H2
Hosdurga India 13°49N 76°17E 127 H3
Ḩoseynābād Khuzestān, Iran 32°45N 48°20E 129 C6
Ḩoseynābād Kordestān, Iran 35°33N 47°8E 105 E12
Hosford U.S.A. 30°23N 84°48W 178 E5
Hôsh 'Îsa Egypt 30°55N 30°17E 137 E7
Hoshangabad India 22°45N 77°45E 124 H7
Hoshiarpur India 31°30N 75°58E 124 D6
Hoskote India 13°4N 77°48E 127 H3
Hospet = Hosapete India 15°15N 76°20E 127 G3
Hossegor France 43°39N 1°25W 72 E2
Hoste, I. Chile 55°0S 69°0W 192 E3
Hostens France 44°30N 0°40W 72 D3
Hosur India 12°43N 77°49E 127 H3
Hot Thailand 18°8N 98°29E 120 C2
Hot Creek Range U.S.A. 38°40N 116°20W 168 G5
Hot Springs Ark., U.S.A. 34°31N 93°3W 176 D8
Hot Springs S. Dak., U.S.A. 43°26N 103°29W 172 D2
Hot Springs △ U.S.A. 34°31N 93°3W 176 D8
Hotagen Sweden 63°59N 14°12E 60 E16
Hotan China 37°25N 79°55E 109 E9
Hotan He → China 40°22N 80°56E 109 D10
Hotazel S. Africa 27°17S 22°58E 144 C3
Hotchkiss U.S.A. 38°48N 107°43W 168 G10
Hotham, C. Australia 12°2S 131°18E 148 B5
Hoting Sweden 64°8N 16°15E 60 D17
Hotolisht Albania 41°10N 20°25E 96 E4
Hotspur Seamount Atl. Oc. 17°55S 35°55W 56 H8
Hotte, Massif de la Haiti 18°30N 73°45W 183 C5
Hottentotsbaai Namibia 26°8S 14°59E 144 C1
Hou Hai China 22°32N 113°56E 111 a
Houat, Î. de France 47°24N 2°58W 70 E4
Houdan France 48°48N 1°35E 71 D8
Houei Sai Laos 20°18N 100°26E 116 G3
Houeillès France 44°12N 0°2E 72 D4
Houffalize Belgium 50°8N 5°48E 69 D5
Houghton Mich., U.S.A. 47°7N 88°34W 172 B9
Houghton N.Y., U.S.A. 42°25N 78°10W 174 D6
Houghton L. U.S.A. 44°21N 84°44W 173 C11
Houghton-le-Spring U.K. 54°51N 1°28W 66 C6
Houhora Heads N.Z. 34°49S 173°9E 154 A2
Houlton U.S.A. 46°8N 67°51W 173 B20
Houma China 35°36N 111°20E 114 G6
Houma U.S.A. 29°36N 90°43W 177 G9
Houndé Burkina Faso 11°34N 3°31W 138 C4
Hourtin France 45°11N 1°4W 72 C2
Hourtin-Carcans, L. d' France 45°10N 1°6W 72 C2
Housatonic → U.S.A. 41°10N 73°7W 175 E11
Houston Canada 54°25N 126°39W 162 C3
Houston Fla., U.S.A. 30°15N 82°54W 178 E7
Houston Mo., U.S.A. 37°22N 91°58W 172 G8
Houston Tex., U.S.A. 29°45N 95°21W 176 G7
Houston George Bush Intercontinental ✈ (IAH) U.S.A. 29°59N 95°20W 176 G7
Hout = Mogwadi → S. Africa 23°4S 29°36E 145 B4
Houtkraal S. Africa 30°23S 24°5E 144 D3
Houtman Abrolhos Australia 28°43S 113°48E 149 E1
Hovd = Dund-Us Mongolia 48°1N 91°38E 109 C12
Hovd □ Mongolia 48°2N 91°37E 109 C12
Hove U.K. 50°50N 0°10W 67 G7
Hovenweep ⌂ U.S.A. 37°20N 109°0W 169 H9
Hoveyzeh Iran 31°27N 48°4E 129 D6
Hovgaard Ø Greenland 79°55N 18°50W 57 B9
Hovmantorp Sweden 56°47N 15°7E 63 H9
Hövsgöl Mongolia 43°37N 109°39E 114 C5
Hövsgöl Nuur Mongolia 51°0N 100°30E 110 A9
Hovsta Sweden 59°22N 15°15E 62 E9
Howar, Wadi → Sudan 17°30N 27°8E 135 E11
Howard Australia 25°16S 152°32E 151 D5
Howard Pa., U.S.A. 41°1N 77°40W 174 F7
Howard S. Dak., U.S.A. 44°1N 97°32W 172 C5
Howe U.S.A. 43°48N 113°0W 168 E7
Howe, C. Australia 37°30S 150°0E 153 D9
Howe, West Cape Australia 35°8S 117°36E 149 G2
Howe I. Canada 44°16N 76°17W 175 B8
Howell U.S.A. 42°36N 83°56W 173 D12
Howick Canada 45°11N 73°51W 175 A11
Howick N.Z. 36°54S 174°56E 154 C3
Howick S. Africa 29°28S 30°14E 145 C5
Howick Group Australia 14°20S 145°30E 150 A4
Howitt, L. Australia 27°40S 138°40E 151 D2
Howland I. Pac. Oc. 0°48N 176°38W 156 G10
Howlong Australia 35°59S 146°38E 153 C7
Howrah = Haora India 22°34N 88°18E 125 H13
Howth Ireland 53°23N 6°7W 64 C5
Howth Hd. Ireland 53°22N 6°4W 64 C5
Höxter Germany 51°46N 9°22E 76 D5
Hoxtolgay China 46°35N 85°59E 109 C11
Hoxud China 42°15N 86°51E 109 D11
Hoy U.K. 58°50N 3°15W 65 C5
Hoya Germany 52°49N 9°8E 76 C5
Høyanger Norway 61°13N 6°4E 60 F12
Hoyerswerda Germany 51°26N 14°14E 76 D10
Hoyos Spain 40°9N 6°45W 88 E4
Hpa-an = Pa-an Myanmar 16°51N 97°40E 123 L20
Hpunan Pass Asia 27°30N 96°55E 123 F20
Hpyu = Pyu Myanmar 18°30N 96°28E 123 K20
Hradec Králové Czechia 50°15N 15°50E 78 A8
Hrádek Czechia 48°46N 16°16E 79 C9
Hranice Czechia 49°34N 17°45E 79 B10
Hrazdan Armenia 40°30N 44°46E 87 K7
Hrebenka Ukraine 50°9N 32°22E 85 G7
Hrisoupoli = Chrisoupoli Greece 40°58N 24°42E 97 F8
Hrodna Belarus 53°42N 23°52E 84 F2
Hrodna □ Belarus 53°20N 24°45E 84 F3
Hrodzyanka Belarus 53°31N 28°42E 75 B15
Hron → Slovakia 47°49N 18°45E 79 D11
Hrubieszów Poland 50°49N 23°51E 83 H10
Hrubý Jeseník Czechia 50°5N 17°10E 79 A10
Hrvatska = Croatia ■ Europe 45°20N 16°0E 93 C13
Hrymayliv Ukraine 49°20N 26°5E 75 D14
Hrynyava Ukraine 47°59N 24°53E 81 C9
Hsenwi Myanmar 23°22N 97°55E 123 H20
Hsiamen = Xiamen China 24°25N 118°4E 117 E12
Hsian = Xi'an China 34°15N 109°0E 114 G5
Hsinchu Taiwan 24°48N 120°58E 117 E13

Hsinhailien = Lianyungang China 34°40N 119°11E 115 G10
Hsinkai = Bhamo Myanmar 24°15N 97°15E 123 G20
Hsinying Taiwan 23°21N 120°17E 117 F13
Hsopket Myanmar 23°11N 98°26E 116 F2
Hsüchou = Xuzhou China 34°18N 117°10E 115 G9
Htawei = Dawei Myanmar 14°2N 98°12E 120 E2
Hu Xian China 34°8N 108°42E 114 G5
Hua Hin Thailand 12°34N 99°58E 120 F2
Hua Muang Laos 20°13N 103°52E 120 B4
Hua Shan China 34°28N 110°4E 114 G6
Hua Xian Henan, China 35°30N 114°30E 114 G8
Hua Xian Shaanxi, China 34°30N 109°48E 114 G5
Hua'an China 25°1N 117°32E 117 E11
Huab → Namibia 20°52S 13°25E 144 A2
Huachacalla Bolivia 18°45S 68°17W 188 D4
Huacheng China 24°4N 115°37E 117 E10
Huachinera Mexico 30°9N 108°55W 180 A3
Huacho Peru 11°10S 77°35W 188 C2
Huachón Peru 10°35S 76°0W 188 C2
Huade China 41°55N 113°59E 114 D7
Huadian China 43°0N 126°40E 115 C14
Huadu China 23°22N 113°12E 117 F9
Huahine, Î. French Polynesia 16°46S 150°58W 157 J12
Huai Hat △ Thailand 16°52N 104°17E 120 D5
Huai He → China 33°0N 118°30E 117 A12
Huai Kha Khaeng ⌂ Thailand 15°20N 98°55E 120 E2
Huai Nam Dang △ Thailand 19°30N 98°30E 120 C2
Huai Yot Thailand 7°45N 99°37E 121 J2
Huai'an Hebei, China 40°30N 114°20E 114 D8
Huai'an Jiangsu, China 33°30N 119°10E 115 H10
Huaibei China 34°0N 116°48E 114 G9
Huaibin China 32°32N 115°27E 117 A10
Huaide = Gongzhuling China 43°30N 124°40E 115 C13
Huaidezhen China 43°48N 124°50E 115 C13
Huaihua China 27°32N 109°57E 116 D7
Huaiji China 23°55N 112°12E 117 F9
Huainan China 32°38N 116°58E 117 A11
Huaining China 30°24N 116°40E 117 B11
Huairen China 39°48N 113°20E 114 E7
Huairou China 40°20N 116°35E 114 D9
Huaiyang China 33°40N 114°52E 114 H8
Huaiyin China 33°30N 119°2E 115 H10
Huaiyuan Anhui, China 32°55N 117°10E 117 A11
Huaiyuan Guangxi Zhuangzu, China 24°31N 108°22E 116 E7
Huajuapán de León Mexico 17°48N 97°46W 181 D5
Hualapai Peak U.S.A. 35°5N 113°54W 171 K13
Hualien Taiwan 23°59N 121°36E 117 F13
Huallaga → Peru 5°15S 75°30W 188 B2
Huallanca Peru 8°50S 77°56W 188 B2
Huamachuco Peru 7°50S 78°5W 188 B2
Huambo Angola 12°42S 15°54E 141 G3
Huan Jiang → China 34°28N 109°0E 114 G5
Huan Xian China 36°33N 107°7E 114 F4
Huancabamba Peru 5°10S 79°15W 188 B2
Huancane Peru 15°10S 69°44W 188 D4
Huancapi Peru 13°40S 74°0W 188 C3
Huancavelica Peru 12°50S 75°5W 188 C2
Huancavelica □ Peru 13°0S 75°0W 188 C3
Huancayo Peru 12°5S 75°12W 188 C2
Huanchaca Bolivia 20°15S 66°40W 186 H5
Huang Hai = Yellow Sea China 35°0N 123°0E 115 G12
Huang He → China 37°55N 118°50E 115 F10
Huang Xian China 37°38N 120°30E 115 F11
Huangchuan China 32°15N 115°10E 117 A10
Huangdao China 36°0N 120°7E 115 G11
Huanggang China 30°29N 114°52E 117 B10
Huangguoshu China 26°0N 105°40E 116 E5
Huanghua China 38°22N 117°20E 115 E9
Huanghuagang China 38°20N 117°54E 115 E9
Huangling China 35°34N 109°15E 114 G5
Huanglong China 35°30N 109°59E 114 G5
Huanglong ⌂ China 32°44N 103°50E 116 A4
Huanglongtan China 32°40N 110°33E 117 A8
Huangmei China 30°5N 115°56E 117 B10
Huangpi China 30°50N 114°22E 117 B10
Huangping China 26°52N 107°54E 116 D6
Huangshan Anhui, China 30°8N 118°9E 117 B12
Huangshan Anhui, China 29°42N 118°25E 117 C12
Huangshi China 30°10N 115°3E 117 B10
Huangsongdian China 43°45N 127°25E 115 C14
Huangyan China 28°38N 121°19E 117 C13
Huangyangsi China 26°33N 111°39E 117 D8
Huaning China 24°17N 102°56E 116 E4
Huanjiang China 24°50N 108°18E 116 E7
Huanren China 41°23N 125°20E 115 D13
Huanta Peru 12°55S 74°20W 188 C3
Huantai China 36°58N 117°56E 115 F9
Huánuco Peru 9°55S 76°15W 188 B2
Huánuco □ Peru 9°55S 76°14W 188 B2
Huanzo, Cordillera de Peru 14°35S 73°20W 188 C3
Huaping China 26°46N 101°25E 116 D3
Huara Chile 19°59S 69°47W 188 D4
Huaral Peru 11°32S 77°13W 188 C2
Huaraz Peru 9°30S 77°32W 188 B2
Huari Peru 9°14S 77°14W 188 B2
Huarmey Peru 10°5S 78°5W 188 C2
Huarochiri Peru 12°9S 76°15W 188 C2
Huarocondo Peru 13°26S 72°14W 188 C3
Huarong China 29°29N 112°30E 117 C9
Huascarán, Nevado Peru 9°7S 77°37W 188 B2
Huasco Chile 28°30S 71°15W 190 B1
Huasco → Chile 28°27S 71°13W 190 B1
Huasna U.S.A. 35°6N 120°24W 171 K6
Huatabampo Mexico 26°50N 109°38W 180 B3
Huauchinango Mexico 20°12N 98°3W 181 C5
Huautla de Jiménez Mexico 18°8N 96°51W 181 D5
Huaxi China 26°25N 106°40E 116 D6
Huayhuash, Cordillera Peru 10°30S 76°45W 188 B2
Huayin China 34°35N 110°5E 114 G6
Huaying China 30°8N 106°44E 116 B6
Huayllay Peru 11°3S 76°21W 188 C2
Huayuan China 28°37N 109°29E 116 C7
Huazhou China 21°33N 110°33E 117 G8
Hubballi India 15°22N 75°15E 127 G2
Hubbard Ohio, U.S.A. 41°9N 80°34W 174 E4
Hubbard Tex., U.S.A. 31°51N 96°48W 176 F6
Hubbard Glacier Canada 60°18N 139°22W 160 E4
Hubbart Pt. Canada 59°21N 94°41W 163 B10
Hubei □ China 31°0N 112°0E 117 B9
Hubli = Hubballi India 15°22N 75°15E 127 G2
Huch'ang N. Korea 41°25N 127°2E 115 D14
Hucknall U.K. 53°3N 1°13W 66 D6
Huddersfield U.K. 53°39N 1°47W 66 D6
Huddinge Sweden 59°14N 18°0E 62 E12
Hude Germany 53°7N 8°26E 76 B4
Hudiksvall Sweden 61°43N 17°10E 62 C11
Hudson Canada 50°6N 92°9W 164 B1
Hudson Fla., U.S.A. 28°22N 82°42W 179 G7
Hudson Mass., U.S.A. 42°23N 71°34W 175 D13
Hudson N.Y., U.S.A. 42°15N 73°46W 175 D11
Hudson Wis., U.S.A. 44°58N 92°45W 172 C7
Hudson Wyo., U.S.A. 42°54N 108°35W 168 E9
Hudson → U.S.A. 40°42N 74°2W 175 F10
Hudson, C. Antarctica 68°21S 153°45E 55 C10
Hudson, Vol. Chile 46°4S 72°55W 192 C2
Hudson Bay Nunavut, Canada 60°0N 86°0W 161 F14
Hudson Bay Sask., Canada 52°51N 102°23W 163 C8
Hudson Falls U.S.A. 43°18N 73°35W 175 C11
Hudson Mts. Antarctica 74°32S 99°20W 55 D16
Hudson Str. Canada 62°0N 70°0W 161 E18
Hudson's Hope Canada 56°0N 121°54W 162 B4
Hue Vietnam 16°30N 107°35E 120 D6
Huebra → Spain 41°2N 6°48W 88 D4
Huedin Romania 46°52N 23°2E 80 D8
Huehuetenango Guatemala 15°20N 91°28W 182 C1
Huejúcar Mexico 22°21N 103°13W 180 C4
Huélamo Spain 40°17N 1°48W 90 E3
Huelgoat France 48°22N 3°46W 70 D3
Huelma Spain 37°39N 3°28W 89 H7
Huelva Spain 37°18N 6°57W 89 H4
Huelva □ Spain 37°40N 7°0W 89 H4
Huelva → Spain 37°27N 6°0W 89 H5
Huentelauquén Chile 31°38S 71°33W 190 C1
Huércal-Overa Spain 37°23N 1°57W 91 H3
Huerquehue △ Chile 39°6S 71°42W 192 A2
Huerta, Sa. de la Argentina 31°10S 67°30W 190 C2
Huertas, C. de las Spain 38°21N 0°24W 91 G4
Huerva → Spain 41°39N 0°52W 90 D4
Huesca Spain 42°8N 0°25W 90 C4
Huesca □ Spain 42°20N 0°1E 90 C5
Huéscar Spain 37°44N 2°35W 91 H2
Huetamo Mexico 18°35N 100°53W 180 D4
Huete Spain 40°10N 2°43W 90 E2
Huger U.S.A. 33°6N 79°48W 178 B10
Hugh → Australia 25°1S 134°1E 150 D1
Hughenden Australia 20°52S 144°10E 150 C3
Hughesville U.S.A. 41°14N 76°44W 175 E8
Hugli → India 21°56N 88°4E 125 J13
Hugo Colo., U.S.A. 39°8N 103°28W 168 G12
Hugo Okla., U.S.A. 34°1N 95°31W 176 D7
Hugoton U.S.A. 37°11N 101°21W 172 G3
Hui Xian = Huixian China 35°27N 113°12E 114 G7
Hui Xian China 33°50N 106°4E 114 H4
Hui'an China 25°1N 118°43E 117 E12
Hui'anbu China 37°28N 106°38E 114 F4
Huiarau Ra. N.Z. 38°45S 176°55E 154 E5
Huichang China 25°32N 115°45E 117 E10
Huichapan Mexico 20°23N 99°39W 181 C5
Huichon N. Korea 40°10N 126°16E 115 D14
Huidong Guangdong, China 22°58N 114°43E 117 F10
Huidong Sichuan, China 26°34N 102°35E 116 D4
Huifa He → China 43°0N 127°50E 115 C14
Huila, Nevado del Colombia 3°0N 76°0W 186 C3
Huilai China 23°0N 116°18E 117 F11
Huili China 26°35N 102°17E 116 D4
Huimin China 37°27N 117°28E 115 F9
Huinan China 42°40N 126°2E 115 C14
Huinca Renancó Argentina 34°51S 64°22W 190 C3
Huining China 35°38N 105°0E 114 G3
Huinong China 39°5N 106°35E 114 E4
Huiroa N.Z. 39°15S 174°30E 154 F3
Huishui China 26°7N 106°38E 116 D6
Huisne → France 47°59N 0°11E 70 E7
Huiting China 34°5N 116°5E 114 G9
Huitong China 26°51N 109°45E 116 D7
Huixian China 35°27N 113°12E 114 G7
Huixtla Mexico 15°9N 92°28W 181 D6
Huize China 26°24N 103°15E 116 D4
Huizhou China 23°0N 114°23E 117 F10
Hukawng Valley Myanmar 26°30N 96°30E 123 F20
Hukeri India 16°14N 74°36E 127 F2
Hukou China 29°45N 116°21E 117 C11
Hukuntsi Botswana 23°58S 21°45E 144 B3
Ḩulayfā' Si. Arabia 25°58N 40°45E 128 E4
Hulin China 45°48N 132°59E 111 B15
Hulin He → China 45°0N 122°10E 115 B12
Hull = Kingston upon Hull U.K. 53°45N 0°21W 66 D7
Hull Canada 45°26N 75°43W 175 A9
Hull → U.K. 53°44N 0°20W 66 D7
Hulst Neths. 51°17N 4°2E 69 C4
Hultsfred Sweden 57°30N 15°52E 63 G9
Huludao China 40°45N 120°50E 115 D11
Hulun Nur China 49°0N 117°30E 111 B12
Hulunbuir = Hailar China 49°10N 119°38E 111 B12
Hulyaypole Ukraine 47°45N 36°21E 85 J9
Huma, Tanjung Malaysia 5°29N 100°16E 121 c
Humacao Puerto Rico 18°9N 65°50W 183 d
Humahuaca Argentina 23°10S 65°25W 190 A2
Humaitá Brazil 7°35S 63°1W 186 E6
Humaitá Paraguay 27°2S 58°31W 190 B4
Humansdorp S. Africa 34°2S 24°46E 144 D3
Humbe Angola 16°40S 14°55E 144 A1
Humber → U.K. 53°42N 0°27W 66 D7
Humboldt Canada 52°15N 105°9W 163 C7
Humboldt Iowa, U.S.A. 42°44N 94°13W 172 D6
Humboldt Tenn., U.S.A. 35°50N 88°55W 177 D10
Humboldt → U.S.A. 39°59N 118°36W 168 G4
Humboldt Gletscher = Sermersuaq Greenland 79°30N 62°0W 57 B4
Humboldt Mts. N.Z. 44°30S 168°15E 155 E3
Hume U.S.A. 36°48N 118°54W 170 J8
Hume, L. Australia 36°0S 147°5E 153 D7
Humen China 22°50N 113°40E 111 a
Humenné Slovakia 48°55N 21°50E 79 C14
Hummelsta Sweden 59°34N 16°58E 62 E10
Humphreys, Mt. U.S.A. 37°17N 118°40W 170 H8
Humphreys Peak U.S.A. 35°21N 111°41W 169 J8
Humpolec Czechia 49°31N 15°20E 78 B8
Humptulips U.S.A. 47°14N 123°57W 170 C3
Humula Australia 35°30S 147°46E 153 C7
Hūn Libya 29°2N 16°0E 135 C9
Hun Jiang → China 40°50N 125°38E 115 D13
Húnaflói Iceland 65°50N 20°50W 60 D3
Hunan □ China 27°30N 112°0E 117 D9
Hunchun China 42°52N 130°28E 115 C16
Hundested Denmark 55°58N 11°52E 63 J5
Hundewali Pakistan 31°55N 72°38E 124 D5
Hundred Mile House Canada 51°38N 121°18W 162 C4
Hunedoara Romania 45°40N 22°50E 80 E7
Hunedoara □ Romania 45°50N 22°54E 80 E7
Hünfeld Germany 50°39N 9°46E 76 E5
Hung Yen Vietnam 20°39N 106°4E 116 G6
Hungary ■ Europe 47°20N 19°20E 79 D12
Hungary, Plain of Europe 47°0N 20°0E 58 F10
Hungerford Australia 28°58S 144°24E 151 D3
Hŭngnam N. Korea 39°49N 127°45E 115 E14
Hungt'ou Hsü = Lan Yü Taiwan 22°4N 121°25E 117 F13
Huni Valley Ghana 5°33N 1°56W 138 D4
Hunjiang China 41°54N 126°26E 115 D14
Hunneberg Sweden 58°18N 12°30E 63 F6
Hunnebostrand Sweden 58°27N 11°18E 63 F5
Hunsberge Namibia 27°45S 17°12E 144 C2
Hunsrück Germany 49°56N 7°27E 77 F3
Hunstanton U.K. 52°56N 0°29E 66 E8
Hunsur India 12°16N 76°16E 127 H3
Hunte → Germany 53°14N 8°28E 76 B4
Hunter N.Z. 44°36S 171°2E 155 E6
Hunter U.S.A. 42°13N 74°13W 175 D10
Hunter → Australia 32°52S 151°46E 153 B9
Hunter → N.Z. 44°21S 169°27E 155 E4
Hunter Hills, The N.Z. 44°26S 170°46E 155 E5
Hunter I. Australia 40°30S 144°45E 151 G3
Hunter I. Canada 51°55N 128°0W 162 C3
Hunter Mts. N.Z. 45°43S 167°25E 155 F2
Hunter Ra. Australia 32°45S 150°15E 153 B9
Hunters Road Zimbabwe 19°9S 29°49E 143 F2
Hunterville N.Z. 39°56S 175°35E 154 F4
Huntingburg U.S.A. 38°18N 86°57W 172 F10
Huntingdon U.K. 52°20N 0°11W 67 E7
Huntingdon U.S.A. 40°30N 78°1W 174 F6
Huntington Ind., U.S.A. 40°53N 85°30W 173 E11
Huntington N.Y., U.S.A. 40°52N 73°26W 175 F11
Huntington Oreg., U.S.A. 44°21N 117°16W 168 D5
Huntington Utah, U.S.A. 39°20N 110°58W 168 G8
Huntington W. Va., U.S.A. 38°25N 82°27W 173 F12
Huntington Beach U.S.A. 33°40N 118°5W 171 M9
Huntly N.Z. 37°34S 175°11E 154 D4
Huntly U.K. 57°27N 2°47W 65 D6
Huntsville Canada 45°20N 79°14W 174 A5
Huntsville Ala., U.S.A. 34°44N 86°35W 177 D11
Huntsville Tex., U.S.A. 30°43N 95°33W 176 F7
Hunyani → Zimbabwe 15°57S 30°39E 143 F3
Hunyuan China 39°42N 113°42E 114 E7
Hunza → India 35°54N 74°20E 125 B6
Huo Shan China 36°26N 111°52E 114 F6
Huo Xian = Huozhou China 36°36N 111°42E 114 F6
Huocheng China 44°0N 80°48E 109 D10
Huolin Gol China 45°32N 119°38E 115 B10
Huong Khe Vietnam 18°13N 105°41E 120 C5
Huonville Australia 43°0S 147°5E 151 G4
Huoqiu China 32°20N 116°12E 117 A11
Huoshan China 31°25N 116°20E 117 B11
Huoshao Dao = Lütao Taiwan 22°40N 121°30E 117 F13
Huozhou China 36°36N 111°42E 114 F6
Hupeh = Hubei □ China 31°0N 112°0E 117 B9
Ḩūr Iran 30°50N 57°7E 129 D8
Hurānd Iran 38°51N 47°22E 105 C12
Ḩuraymīla Si. Arabia 25°8N 46°8E 128 E5
Hurbanovo Slovakia 47°51N 18°11E 79 D11
Hurd, C. Canada 45°13N 81°44W 174 A3
Hure Qi China 42°45N 121°45E 115 C11
Hurezani Romania 44°49N 23°40E 81 F8
Hurghada Egypt 27°15N 33°50E 137 B3
Hurley N. Mex., U.S.A. 32°42N 108°8W 169 K9
Hurley Wis., U.S.A. 46°27N 90°11W 172 B8
Huron Calif., U.S.A. 36°12N 120°6W 170 J6
Huron Ohio, U.S.A. 41°24N 82°33W 174 E2
Huron S. Dak., U.S.A. 44°22N 98°13W 172 C4
Huron, L. U.S.A. 44°30N 82°40W 174 B2
Huron East Canada 43°37N 81°18W 174 C3
Hurricane U.S.A. 37°11N 113°17W 169 H7
Hurtsboro U.S.A. 32°15N 85°25W 178 C4
Hurungwe ⌂ Zimbabwe 16°7S 29°5E 143 F2
Hurunui → N.Z. 42°54S 173°18E 155 C8
Hurup Denmark 56°46N 8°25E 63 H2
Húsavík Iceland 66°3N 17°21W 60 C5
Huşi Romania 46°41N 28°7E 81 D13
Huskisson Australia 35°2S 150°41E 153 C9
Huskvarna Sweden 57°47N 14°15E 63 G8
Hustadvika Norway 63°0N 7°0E 60 E12
Hustontown U.S.A. 40°3N 78°2W 174 F6
Hustopeče Czechia 48°57N 16°43E 79 C9
Husum Germany 54°28N 9°4E 76 A5
Husum Sweden 63°21N 19°12E 62 A13
Hutchinson Kans., U.S.A. 38°5N 97°56W 172 F5
Hutchinson Minn., U.S.A. 44°54N 94°22W 172 C6
Hutiao Xia China 27°13N 100°9E 116 D3
Hutte Sauvage, L. de la Canada 56°15N 64°45W 165 A7
Hüttenberg Austria 46°56N 14°33E 78 E7
Hüttener Berge ⌂ Germany 54°24N 9°40E 76 A5
Hutton, Mt. Australia 25°51S 148°20E 151 D4
Huwaki Indonesia 7°55S 126°30E 119 F7
Huy Belgium 50°31N 5°15E 69 D5
Huzhou China 30°51N 120°8E 117 B13
Huzurabad India 18°12N 79°25E 126 E4
Huzurnagar India 16°54N 79°53E 126 F4
Hvalpsund Denmark 56°42N 9°11E 63 H3
Hvammstangi Iceland 65°24N 20°57W 60 D3
Hvar Croatia 43°11N 16°28E 93 E13
Hvarski Kanal Croatia 43°15N 16°35E 93 E13
Hvítá → Iceland 64°30N 21°58W 60 D3
Hvizdets Ukraine 48°35N 25°17E 81 B10
Hwacheon-Cheosuji S. Korea 38°5N 127°50E 115 E14
Hwang Ho = Huang He → China 37°55N 118°50E 115 F10
Hwange Zimbabwe 18°18S 26°30E 143 F2
Hwange △ Zimbabwe 19°0S 26°30E 144 A4
Hwlffordd = Haverfordwest U.K. 51°48N 4°58W 67 F3
Hyannis Mass., U.S.A. 41°39N 70°17W 173 E18
Hyannis Nebr., U.S.A. 42°0N 101°46W 172 D3
Hyargas Nuur Mongolia 49°0N 93°0E 109 C12
Hybo Sweden 61°49N 16°15E 62 C10
Hydaburg U.S.A. 55°15N 132°50W 162 B2
Hyde N.Z. 45°18S 170°16E 155 F5
Hyde Park U.S.A. 41°47N 73°56W 175 E11
Hyden Australia 32°24S 118°53E 149 F2
Hyder U.S.A. 55°55N 130°5W 162 B2
Hyderabad India 17°22N 78°29E 126 F4
Hyderabad Pakistan 25°23N 68°24E 124 G3
Hydra Greece 37°20N 23°28E 98 D5
Hyères France 43°8N 6°9E 73 F10
Hyères, Îs. d' France 43°0N 6°20E 73 F10
Hyesan N. Korea 41°20N 128°10E 115 D15
Hyland → Canada 59°52N 128°12W 162 B3
Hyltebruk Sweden 56°59N 13°15E 63 H7
Hyndman Peak U.S.A. 43°45N 114°8W 168 E6
Hyōgo □ Japan 35°15N 134°50E 113 G7
Hyrum U.S.A. 41°38N 111°51W 168 F8
Hysham U.S.A. 46°18N 107°14W 168 C10
Hythe U.K. 51°4N 1°5E 67 F9
Hyūga Japan 32°25N 131°35E 113 H5
Hyvinge = Hyvinkää Finland 60°38N 24°50E 84 B3
Hyvinkää Finland 60°38N 24°50E 84 B3

I

I-n-Akhmed Mali 19°49N 0°56W 139 B4
I-n-Azaoua Algeria 25°42N 6°54E 136 C5
I-n-Ezzane Algeria 23°29N 11°15E 136 D6
I-n-Gall Niger 16°51N 7°1E 139 B6
I-n-Kelemet Algeria 26°57N 5°47E 136 C5
I-n-Oudad Algeria 20°17N 4°38E 139 A5
I-n-Ouzzal Algeria 20°41N 2°34E 139 A5
I-n-Tadreft Niger 19°5N 6°38E 139 B6
Iabès, Erg Algeria 27°30N 2°2W 136 C3
Iablanița Romania 44°57N 22°19E 80 F7
Iaco → Brazil 9°3S 68°34W 188 B4
Iacobeni Romania 47°25N 25°20E 81 C10
Iaçu Brazil 12°45S 40°13W 189 C2
Ialissos Greece 36°24N 28°10E 101 C10
Ialomița □ Romania 44°30N 27°30E 81 F12
Ialomița → Romania 44°42N 27°51E 81 F12
Ialoveni Moldova 46°56N 28°47E 81 D13
Ialpug → Moldova 45°41N 28°35E 81 E13
Iamonia L. U.S.A. 30°38N 84°14W 178 E5
Ianca Romania 45°6N 27°29E 81 E12
Iara Romania 46°31N 23°35E 81 D8
Iargara Moldova 46°24N 28°23E 81 D13
Iași Romania 47°10N 27°40E 81 C12
Iași □ Romania 47°20N 27°0E 81 C12
Iasmos Greece 41°8N 25°11E 97 E9
Ib → India 21°34N 83°48E 125 J10
Iba Phil. 15°22N 120°0E 119 A6
Ibadan Nigeria 7°22N 3°58E 139 D5
Ibagué Colombia 4°20N 75°20W 186 C3
Iballë Albania 42°12N 20°2E 96 D4
Ibănești Botoșani, Romania 48°4N 26°22E 81 B11
Ibănești Mureș, Romania 46°45N 24°57E 81 D9
Ibar → Serbia 43°43N 20°45E 96 C4
Ibaraki □ Japan 36°10N 140°10E 113 F10
Ibarra Ecuador 0°21N 78°7W 186 C3
Ibb Yemen 14°2N 44°10E 131 E3
Ibbenbüren Germany 52°16N 7°43E 76 C3
Ibembo Dem. Rep. of the Congo 2°35N 23°35E 142 B1
Ibenga → Congo 2°19N 18°9E 140 D3
Ibera, L. Argentina 28°30S 57°9W 190 B4
Iberia Peru 11°21S 69°35W 188 C4
Iberian Peninsula Europe 40°0N 5°0W 58 H5
Iberville Canada 45°19N 73°17W 175 A11
Iberville, Mt. d' Canada 58°50N 63°50W 161 F19
Ibeto Nigeria 10°29N 5°8E 139 C6
Ibi Nigeria 8°15N 9°44E 139 D6
Ibi Spain 38°38N 0°34W 91 G4
Ibiá Brazil 19°30S 46°30W 189 D1
Ibiapaba, Sa. da Brazil 4°0S 41°30W 189 A2
Ibicaraí Brazil 14°51S 39°36W 189 C3
Ibicuí Brazil 14°51S 39°59W 189 C3
Ibicuí → Brazil 29°25S 56°47W 191 B4
Ibicuy Argentina 33°55S 59°10W 190 C4
Ibitiara Brazil 12°39S 42°13W 189 C2
Ibiza = Eivissa Spain 38°54N 1°26E 100 C7
Ibiza ✕ (IBZ) Spain 38°53N 1°22E 91 G6
Iblei, Monti Italy 37°15N 14°45E 95 E7
Ibo Mozam. 12°22S 40°40E 143 E5
Ibonma Indonesia 3°29S 133°31E 119 E8
Ibotirama Brazil 12°13S 43°12W 189 C2
Ibrāhīm → Lebanon 34°4N 35°38E 130 A4
'Ibrī Oman 23°14N 56°30E 131 C6
İbriktepe Turkey 41°0N 26°30E 97 E10
Ibshawâi Egypt 29°21N 30°40E 137 F7
Ibu Indonesia 1°35N 127°33E 119 D7
Ibusuki Japan 31°12N 130°40E 113 J5
Ica Peru 14°0S 75°48W 188 C2
Ica □ Peru 14°20S 75°30W 188 C2
Iça → Brazil 2°55S 67°58W 188 A4
Icacos Pt. Trin. & Tob. 10°3N 61°57W 187 K15
Içana Brazil 0°21N 67°19W 186 C5
Içana → Brazil 0°26N 67°19W 186 C5
Icatu Brazil 2°46S 44°4W 189 A2
İçel = Mersin Turkey 36°51N 34°36E 104 D6
Iceland ■ Europe 64°45N 19°0W 60 D4
Iceland Basin Atl. Oc. 61°0N 19°0W 54 C7
Icelandic Plateau Arctic 64°0N 10°0W 54 C7
İçeriçumra Turkey 37°34N 32°39E 104 D5
Ichalkaranji India 16°40N 74°33E 126 F2
Ich'ang = Yichang China 30°40N 111°20E 117 B8
Ichchapuram India 19°10N 84°40E 126 E7
Ichhawar India 23°1N 77°1E 124 H7
Ichigat Muja-Cordillera del Condor ⌂ Peru 4°20S 77°30W 188 A2
Ichihara Japan 35°28N 140°5E 113 G10
Ichikawa Japan 35°43N 139°54E 113 G9
Ichilo → Bolivia 15°57S 64°50W 186 G6
Ichinohe Japan 40°13N 141°17E 112 D10
Ichinomiya Japan 35°18N 136°48E 113 G8
Ichinoseki Japan 38°55N 141°8E 112 E10
Ichkeul △ Tunisia 37°5N 9°37E 136 A5
Ichnya Ukraine 50°52N 32°24E 85 G7
Icht Morocco 29°6N 8°54W 136 C2
Icó Brazil 6°24S 38°51W 189 B3
Icod Canary Is. 28°22N 16°43W 100 F3
İçoguz Turkmenistan 40°11N 58°24E 108 D5
Icy C. U.S.A. 70°20N 161°52W 158 B3
Ida Grove U.S.A. 42°21N 95°28W 172 D6
Idabel U.S.A. 33°54N 94°50W 176 E7
Idah Nigeria 7°5N 6°40E 139 D6
Idaho □ U.S.A. 45°0N 115°0W 168 D6
Idaho City U.S.A. 43°50N 115°50W 168 E6
Idaho Falls U.S.A. 43°30N 112°2W 168 E7
Idalia △ Australia 24°49S 144°36E 150 C3
Idanha-a-Nova Portugal 39°50N 7°15W 88 F3
Idar-Oberstein Germany 49°43N 7°16E 77 F3
Idelès Algeria 23°50N 5°53E 136 D5
Idensalmi = Iisalmi Finland 63°32N 27°10E 60 E22
Idfû Egypt 24°55N 32°49E 137 C3
Idi Indonesia 5°2N 97°37E 118 C1
Idi, Oros = Psiloritis, Oros Greece 35°15N 24°45E 101 D6
İdil Turkey 37°20N 41°53E 105 D9
Idiofa Dem. Rep. of the Congo 4°55S 19°42E 140 E3
Idkerberget Sweden 60°22N 15°15E 62 D9
Idku Egypt 31°18N 30°17E 137 E7
Idku, Bahra el Egypt 31°18N 30°18E 137 E7
Idlib Syria 35°55N 36°36E 104 E7
Idlib □ Syria 35°45N 36°45E 104 E7
Idomeni Greece 41°7N 22°31E 96 E6
Idra = Hydra Greece 37°20N 23°28E 98 D5
Idre Sweden 61°52N 12°42E 62 C6
Idria U.S.A. 36°25N 120°41W 170 J6
Idrija Slovenia 46°0N 14°5E 93 C11
Idritsa Russia 56°17N 28°53E 84 D5
Idutywa = Dutywa S. Africa 32°8S 28°18E 145 D4
Ieper Belgium 50°51N 2°53E 69 D2
Ierapetra Greece 35°1N 25°44E 101 E7
Ierissos Greece 40°22N 23°52E 96 F7
Ierissos Kolpos Greece 40°27N 23°57E 96 F7
Iernut Romania 46°27N 24°15E 81 D9
Iesi Italy 43°31N 13°14E 93 E10
Ifac, Penyal d' Spain 38°38N 0°5E 91 G5
Ifakara Tanzania 8°8S 36°41E 140 F7
'Ifāl, W. al → Si. Arabia 28°7N 35°3E 128 D2
Ife Nigeria 7°30N 4°31E 139 D5
Iférouâne Niger 19°5N 8°24E 139 B6
Ifetesene Algeria 25°30N 4°33E 136 C4
Iffley Australia 18°53S 141°12E 150 B3
Ifon Nigeria 6°58N 5°40E 139 D6
Iforas, Adrar des Africa 19°40N 1°40E 139 B5
Ifould, L. Australia 30°52S 132°6E 149 F5
Ifrane Morocco 33°33N 5°7W 136 B2
Igalo Montenegro 42°28N 18°30E 96 D2
Iganga Uganda 0°37N 33°28E 142 B3
Igarapava Brazil 20°3S 47°47W 189 E1
Igarka Russia 67°30N 86°33E 106 C9
Igatpuri India 19°40N 73°35E 126 E1
Igbetti Nigeria 8°44N 4°8E 139 D5
Igbo-Ora Nigeria 7°29N 3°15E 139 D5
Igboho Nigeria 8°53N 3°50E 139 D5
Igbor Nigeria 7°27N 8°34E 139 D6
Iğdır Turkey 39°55N 44°2E 105 C11
Igelfors Sweden 58°52N 15°41E 63 F9
Iggesund Sweden 61°39N 17°10E 62 C11
Ighil Izane = Relizane Algeria 35°44N 0°31E 136 A4
Iglésias Italy 39°19N 8°32E 94 C1
Igli Algeria 30°25N 2°19W 136 B3
Igloolik = Iglulik Canada 69°20N 81°49W 161 D15
Iglulligaarjuk = Chesterfield Inlet Canada 63°30N 90°45W 160 E13
Iglulik Canada 69°20N 81°49W 161 D15
'Igma, G. el Egypt 29°10N 34°0E 137 F8
Ignace Canada 49°30N 91°40W 164 C1
İğneada Turkey 41°52N 27°59E 97 E11
İğneada Burnu Turkey 41°53N 28°2E 97 E12
Igoumenitsa Greece 39°32N 20°18E 98 B2
Igrim Russia 63°12N 64°30E 106 C7
Iguaçu → Brazil 25°36S 54°36W 191 B5
Iguaçu, Cat. del Brazil 25°41S 54°26W 191 B5
Iguaçu △ Brazil 25°30S 54°0W 191 B5
Iguaçu Falls = Iguaçu, Cat. del Brazil 25°41S 54°26W 191 B5
Iguala Mexico 18°21N 99°32W 181 D5
Igualada Spain 41°37N 1°37E 90 D6
Iguassu = Iguaçu → Brazil 25°36S 54°36W 191 B5
Iguatu Brazil 6°20S 39°18W 189 B3
Iguazú △ Argentina 25°42S 54°22W 191 B5
Iguidi, Erg Africa 27°0N 6°0W 136 C2
Iharana Madag. 13°25S 50°0E 141 G10
Ihbulag Mongolia 43°11N 107°10E 114 C4
Iheya-Shima Japan 27°4N 127°58E 113 L3
Ihiala Nigeria 5°51N 6°55E 139 D6
Ihosy Madag. 22°24S 46°8E 141 J9
Ihugh Nigeria 7°2N 9°0E 139 D6
Ii Finland 65°19N 25°22E 60 D21
Ii-Shima Japan 26°43N 127°47E 113 L3
Iida Japan 35°35N 137°50E 113 G8
Iijoki → Finland 65°20N 25°20E 60 D21
Iisalmi Finland 63°32N 27°10E 60 E22
Iiyama Japan 36°51N 138°22E 113 F9
Iizuka Japan 33°38N 130°42E 113 H5
Ijâfene Mauritania 20°40N 8°0W 134 D4
Ijebu-Igbo Nigeria 6°56N 4°1E 139 D5
Ijebu-Ode Nigeria 6°47N 3°58E 139 D5
Ijevan Armenia 40°52N 45°8E 87 K7
IJmuiden Neths. 52°28N 4°35E 69 B4
Ijo älv = Iijoki → Finland 65°20N 25°20E 60 D21
IJssel → Neths. 52°35N 5°50E 69 B5
IJsselmeer Neths. 52°45N 5°20E 69 B5
Ijuí Brazil 28°23S 53°55W 191 B5
Ijuí → Brazil 27°58S 55°20W 191 B4
Ikamatua N.Z. 42°16S 171°41E 155 C6
Ikang Nigeria 4°49N 8°30E 139 E6
Ikanga Kenya 1°42S 38°4E 142 C4
Ikara Nigeria 11°12N 8°15E 139 C6
Ikare Nigeria 7°32N 5°40E 139 D6
Ikaria Greece 37°35N 26°10E 99 D8
Ikast Denmark 56°8N 9°10E 63 H3
Ikeda Japan 34°1N 133°48E 113 G6
Ikeja Nigeria 6°35N 3°20E 139 D5
Ikela Dem. Rep. of the Congo 1°6S 23°6E 140 E4
Ikere Nigeria 7°25N 5°19E 139 D6
Ikhtiman Bulgaria 42°27N 23°48E 96 D7
Iki Japan 33°45N 129°42E 113 H4
Ikimba L. Tanzania 1°30S 31°20E 142 C3
Ikire Nigeria 7°23N 4°15E 139 D5
İkizdere Turkey 40°46N 40°32E 105 B9
Ikom Nigeria 6°0N 8°42E 139 D6
Ikopa → Madag. 16°45S 46°40E 141 H9
Ikorongo ⌂ Tanzania 1°50S 34°53E 142 C3
Ikot Ekpene Nigeria 5°12N 7°40E 139 D6
Ikparjuk = Arctic Bay Canada 73°1N 85°7W 161 C14
Iksan S. Korea 35°59N 127°0E 115 G14
Ikungu Tanzania 1°33S 33°42E 142 C3
Ikuntji = Haasts Bluff Australia 23°22S 132°0E 148 D5
Ikurun Nigeria 7°54N 4°40E 139 D5
Ila Nigeria 8°0N 4°39E 139 D5
Ilagan Phil. 17°7N 121°53E 119 A6
Īlām Iran 33°36N 46°36E 105 F12
Ilam Nepal 26°58N 87°58E 125 F12
Īlām □ Iran 33°0N 47°0E 128 C5
Ilan Taiwan 24°45N 121°44E 117 E13
Ilanskiy Russia 56°14N 96°3E 107 D10
Ilaro Nigeria 6°53N 3°3E 139 D5
Ilatane Niger 16°30N 4°45E 139 B5
Ilave Peru 16°5S 69°40W 188 D4
Iława Poland 53°36N 19°34E 82 E6
Ilayangudi India 9°34N 78°37E 127 K4
Ile → Kazakhstan 45°53N 77°10E 109 C9
Île-à-la-Crosse Canada 55°27N 107°53W 163 B7
Île-à-la-Crosse, Lac Canada 55°40N 107°45W 163 B7
Ile-Alatau △ Kazakhstan 43°5N 77°5E 109 D9
Île-de-France □ France 49°0N 2°20E 71 D9
Ileanda Romania 47°20N 23°38E 81 C8
Ilebo Dem. Rep. of the Congo 4°17S 20°55E 140 E4
Ilek Russia 51°32N 53°21E 108 B4
Ilemi Triangle Africa 5°0N 35°20E 142 B4
Ilero Nigeria 8°0N 3°20E 139 D5
Ilesha Kwara, Nigeria 8°57N 3°28E 139 D5
Ilesha Oyo, Nigeria 7°37N 4°40E 139 D5
Ilford Canada 56°4N 95°35W 163 B9
Ilfov □ Romania 44°36N 26°7E 81 F11
Ilfracombe Australia 23°30S 144°30E 150 C3
Ilfracombe U.K. 51°12N 4°8W 67 F3
Ilgaz Turkey 40°55N 33°37E 104 B5
Ilgaz Dağları Turkey 41°10N 33°50E 104 B5
Ilgın Turkey 38°16N 31°55E 104 C4
Ilha Grande, Represa Brazil 23°10S 53°5W 191 A5
Ilha Grande △ Brazil 23°10S 53°20W 191 A5
Ílhavo Portugal 40°33N 8°43W 88 E2
Ilhéus Brazil 14°49S 39°2W 189 C3
Ili = Ile → Kazakhstan 45°53N 77°10E 109 C9
Ilia Greece 37°45N 21°35E 98 D3
Ilia Romania 45°57N 22°40E 80 E7
Iliamna L. U.S.A. 59°30N 155°0W 166 D8
Ilias, Profitis Greece 36°17N 27°56E 101 C9
Iliç Turkey 39°27N 38°33E 105 C8
Ilıca Turkey 39°52N 27°46E 99 B9
Iligan Phil. 8°12N 124°13E 119 C6
Ilion U.S.A. 43°1N 75°2W 175 D9
Ilirska-Bistrica Slovenia 45°34N 14°14E 93 C11
Ilkal India 15°57N 76°8E 127 G3
Ilkeston U.K. 52°58N 1°19W 66 E6
Ilkley U.K. 53°56N 1°48W 66 D6
Illampu = Ancohuma, Nevado Bolivia 16°0S 68°50W 188 D4
Illana B. Phil. 7°35N 123°45E 119 C6
Illapel Chile 32°0S 71°10W 190 C1
Ille-et-Vilaine □ France 48°10N 1°30W 70 D5
Ille-sur-Têt France 42°40N 2°38E 72 F6
Illéla Niger 14°32N 5°20E 139 C6
Iller → Germany 48°23N 9°58E 77 G5
Illertissen Germany 48°12N 10°7E 77 G6
Illes Balears = Baleares, Is. Spain 39°30N 3°0E 100 B10
Illescas Spain 40°8N 3°51W 88 E7
Illetas Spain 39°32N 2°35E 100 B9
Illichivsk Ukraine 46°20N 30°35E 85 J6
Illiers-Combray France 48°18N 1°15E 70 D8
Illimani, Nevado Bolivia 16°30S 67°50W 188 D4
Illinois □ U.S.A. 40°15N 89°30W 172 E9
Illinois → U.S.A. 38°58N 90°28W 172 F8
Illizi Algeria 26°31N 8°32E 136 C5
Illizi □ Algeria 26°50N 8°10E 136 C5
Illkirch-Graffenstaden France 48°34N 7°42E 71 D14
Íllora Spain 37°17N 3°53W 89 H7
Ilm → Germany 51°6N 11°40E 76 D7
Ilma, L. Australia 29°13S 127°46E 149 E4
Ilmajoki Finland 62°44N 22°34E 60 E20
Ilmen, Ozero Russia 58°15N 31°10E 84 C6
Ilmenau Germany 50°41N 10°54E 76 E6
Ilnytsya Ukraine 48°21N 23°5E 80 B8
Ilo Peru 17°40S 71°20W 188 D3
Ilobu Nigeria 7°45N 4°25E 139 D5
Iloilo Phil. 10°45N 122°33E 119 B6
Ilomantsi Finland 62°38N 30°57E 60 E24
Ilora Nigeria 7°45N 3°50E 139 D5
Ilorin Nigeria 8°30N 4°35E 139 D5
Ilovatka Russia 50°30N 45°50E 86 E7
Ilovlya Russia 49°15N 44°2E 87 F7
Ilovlya → Russia 49°14N 44°0E 87 F7
Ilowa Poland 51°30N 15°10E 83 G2
Ilulissat Greenland 69°12N 51°10W 57 D5
Ilva Mică Romania 47°17N 24°40E 81 C9
Ilwaco U.S.A. 46°19N 124°3W 170 D2
Ilyichevsk = Illichivsk Ukraine 46°20N 30°35E 85 J6
Iłża Poland 51°10N 21°15E 83 G8
Iłżanka → Poland 51°14N 21°48E 83 G8
Imabari Japan 34°4N 133°0E 113 G6
İmamoğlu Turkey 37°15N 35°38E 104 D6
Imandra, Ozero Russia 67°30N 33°0E 60 C25
Imari Japan 33°15N 129°52E 113 H4
Imatra Finland 61°12N 28°48E 84 B5
Iménas Mali 16°20N 0°40E 139 B5
imeni 26 Bakinskikh Komissarov = Neftçala Azerbaijan 39°19N 49°12E 105 C13
imeni 26 Bakinskikh Komissarov Turkmenistan 39°22N 54°10E 129 B7

imeni Ismail Samani, Pik Tajikistan 39°0N 72°2E 109 E8
imeni Karl Libknekhta Russia 51°40N 35°35E 85 G8
Imeri, Serra Brazil 0°50N 65°25W 186 C5
Imfolozi ⌂ S. Africa 28°18S 31°50E 145 C5
Imi Ethiopia 6°28N 42°10E 131 F3
Imişli Azerbaijan 39°55N 48°4E 87 L9
Imitek Morocco 29°43N 8°10W 136 C2
Imlay U.S.A. 40°40N 118°9W 168 F4
Imlay City U.S.A. 43°2N 83°5W 174 D1
Immenstadt Germany 47°33N 10°13E 77 H6
Immingham U.K. 53°37N 0°13W 66 D7
Immokalee U.S.A. 26°25N 81°25W 179 J8
Imo □ Nigeria 5°30N 7°10E 139 D6
Imo → Nigeria 4°36N 7°35E 139 E6
Ímola Italy 44°20N 11°42E 93 D8
Imotski Croatia 43°27N 17°12E 93 E14
Imperatriz Amazonas, Brazil 5°18S 67°11W 188 B4
Imperatriz Maranhão, Brazil 5°30S 47°29W 189 B1
Impéria Italy 43°53N 8°3E 92 E5
Imperial Canada 51°21N 105°28W 163 C7
Imperial Peru 13°4S 76°21W 188 C2
Imperial Calif., U.S.A. 32°51N 115°34W 171 N11
Imperial Nebr., U.S.A. 40°31N 101°39W 172 E3
Imperial Beach U.S.A. 32°35N 117°6W 171 N9
Imperial Dam U.S.A. 32°55N 114°25W 171 N12
Imperial Res. U.S.A. 32°53N 114°28W 171 N12
Imperial Valley U.S.A. 33°0N 115°30W 171 N11
Imperieuse Reef Australia 17°36S 118°50E 148 C2
Impfondo Congo 1°40N 18°0E 140 D3
Imphal India 24°48N 93°56E 123 G18
Imphy France 46°55N 3°16E 71 F10
İmranlı Turkey 39°54N 38°7E 105 C8
İmroz = Gökçeada Turkey 40°10N 25°50E 97 F9
Imst Austria 47°15N 10°44E 78 D3
Imuris Mexico 30°47N 110°52W 180 A2
Imuruan B. Phil. 10°40N 119°10E 119 B5
In Aleï Mali 17°42N 2°30W 138 B4
In Amenas Algeria 28°5N 9°33E 136 C5
In Amguel Algeria 23°41N 5°9E 136 D5
In Belbel Algeria 27°55N 1°12E 136 C4
In Delimane Mali 15°52N 1°31E 139 B5
In Ghar Algeria 27°10N 1°59E 136 C4
In Guezzam Algeria 19°37N 5°52E 139 B6
In Koufi Mali 19°11N 1°25E 139 B5
In Salah Algeria 27°10N 2°32E 136 C4
In Tallak Mali 16°19N 3°15E 139 B5
In Tebezas Mali 17°49N 1°53E 139 B5
Ina Japan 35°50N 137°55E 113 G8
Inaccessible I. Atl. Oc. 37°18S 12°40W 56 K10
Inagua △ Bahamas 21°5N 73°24W 183 B5
Inajá Brazil 8°54S 37°49W 189 B3
Inambari → Peru 12°41S 69°44W 188 C4
Inangahua N.Z. 41°52S 171°59E 155 B6
Inanwatan Indonesia 2°8S 132°10E 119 E8
Iñapari Peru 11°0S 69°40W 188 C4
Inari Finland 68°54N 27°1E 60 B22
Inarijärvi Finland 69°0N 28°0E 60 B23
Inawashiro-Ko Japan 37°29N 140°6E 112 F10
tInbhear Mór, An = Arklow Ireland 52°48N 6°10W 64 D5
Inca Spain 39°43N 2°54E 100 B9
Inca de Oro Chile 26°45S 69°54W 190 B2
Incahuasi Argentina 27°2S 68°18W 190 B2
Incahuasi Chile 29°12S 71°5W 190 B1
İnce Burun Turkey 42°7N 34°56E 104 A6
İncekum Burnu Turkey 36°13N 33°57E 104 D5
İncesu Turkey 38°38N 35°11E 104 C6
Incheon S. Korea 37°27N 126°40E 115 F14
Inchiri □ Mauritania 20°0N 15°0W 138 B2
Incio = A Cruz do Incio Spain 42°39N 7°21W 88 C3
İncirliova Turkey 37°50N 27°41E 99 D9
Incline Village U.S.A. 39°10N 119°58W 170 F7
Incomáti → Mozam. 25°46S 32°43E 145 C5
Incudine, Mte. France 41°50N 9°12E 73 G13
Indal Sweden 62°35N 17°5E 62 B11
Indalsälven → Sweden 62°36N 17°30E 62 B11
Indaw Myanmar 24°15N 96°5E 123 G20
Independence Calif., U.S.A. 36°48N 118°12W 170 J8
Independence Iowa, U.S.A. 42°28N 91°54W 172 D8
Independence Kans., U.S.A. 37°14N 95°42W 172 G6
Independence Ky., U.S.A. 38°57N 84°33W 173 F11
Independence Mo., U.S.A. 39°6N 94°25W 172 F6
Independence Fjord Greenland 82°10N 29°0W 57 A8
Independence Mts. U.S.A. 41°20N 116°0W 168 F5
Independência Brazil 5°23S 40°19W 189 B2
Independencia, I. Peru 14°16S 76°12W 188 C2
Independenţa Romania 45°25N 27°42E 81 E12
Înderbor Kazakhstan 48°33N 51°47E 108 C4
Index U.S.A. 47°50N 121°33W 170 C5
Indi India 17°10N 75°58E 126 F2
India ■ Asia 20°0N 78°0E 122 K11
Indialantic U.S.A. 28°6N 80°34W 179 G9
Indian → U.S.A. 27°59N 80°34W 179 G9
Indian Cabins Canada 59°52N 117°40W 162 B5
Indian Harbour Canada 54°27N 57°13W 165 B8
Indian Harbour Beach U.S.A. 28°10N 80°35W 179 G9
Indian Head Canada 50°30N 103°41W 163 C8
Indian L. U.S.A. 43°46N 74°16W 175 C10
Indian Lake U.S.A. 43°47N 74°16W 175 C10
Indian Ocean 5°0S 75°0E 146 E6
Indian Rocks Beach U.S.A. 27°52N 82°51W 179 H7
Indian Springs U.S.A. 36°35N 115°40W 171 J11
Indiana U.S.A. 40°37N 79°9W 174 F5
Indiana □ U.S.A. 40°0N 86°0W 173 F11
Indianapolis U.S.A. 39°46N 86°9W 172 F10
Indianola Iowa, U.S.A. 41°22N 93°34W 172 E7
Indianola Miss., U.S.A. 33°27N 90°39W 177 E9
Indiantown U.S.A. 27°1N 80°28W 179 H9
Indigirka → Russia 70°48N 148°54E 107 B15
Inđija Serbia 45°6N 20°7E 80 E5
Indio U.S.A. 33°43N 116°13W 171 M10
Indira Gandhi Canal India 28°0N 72°0E 124 F5
Indira Pt. India 6°44N 93°49E 127 L11
Indira Sagar India 22°15N 76°40E 124 H7
Indo-China Asia 15°0N 102°0E 102 G12
Indonesia ■ Asia 5°0S 115°0E 118 F5
Indore India 22°42N 75°53E 124 H6
Indramayu Indonesia 6°20S 108°19E 119 G13
Indravati → India 19°20N 80°20E 126 E5
Indre □ France 46°50N 1°39E 71 F8
Indre → France 47°16N 0°11E 70 E7
Indre-et-Loire □ France 47°20N 0°40E 70 E7
Indrio U.S.A. 27°31N 80°21W 179 H9
Indulkana Australia 26°58S 133°5E 151 D1
Indura Belarus 53°26N 23°53E 82 E10
Indus → Pakistan 24°20N 67°47E 124 G2
Indus, Mouths of the Pakistan 24°0N 68°0E 124 H3
İnebolu Turkey 41°55N 33°40E 104 B5
İnecik Turkey 40°56N 27°16E 97 F11
İnegöl Turkey 40°5N 29°31E 97 F13
Inés, Mt. Argentina 48°30S 69°40W 192 C3
Ineu Romania 46°26N 21°51E 80 D6
Inezgane Morocco 30°25N 9°29W 136 B2
Infantes = Villanueva de los Infantes Spain 38°43N 3°1W 89 G7
Infiernillo, Presa del Mexico 18°35N 101°50W 180 D4
Infiesto Spain 43°21N 5°21W 88 B5
Inga, Barrage d' Dem. Rep. of the Congo 5°39S 13°39E 140 F2
Ingaro Sweden 59°12N 18°45E 62 E12
Ingelstad Sweden 56°45N 14°56E 63 H8
Ingeniero Jacobacci Argentina 41°20S 69°36W 192 B3
Ingenio Canary Is. 27°55N 15°26W 100 G4
Ingenio Santa Ana Argentina 27°25S 65°40W 190 B2
Ingersoll Canada 43°4N 80°55W 174 C4
Ingham Australia 18°43S 146°10E 150 B4
Ingleborough U.K. 54°10N 2°22W 66 C5
Inglefield Land Greenland 78°30N 70°0W 57 B4
Inglewood Queens., Australia 28°25S 151°2E 151 D5
Inglewood Vic., Australia 36°29S 143°53E 152 D5
Inglewood N.Z. 39°9S 174°14E 154 F3
Inglewood U.S.A. 33°58N 118°21W 171 M8
Inglis U.S.A. 29°2N 82°40W 179 F7
Ingolf Fjord Greenland 80°35N 17°30W 57 A9
Ingólfshöfði Iceland 63°48N 16°39W 60 E5
Ingolstadt Germany 48°46N 11°26E 77 G7
Ingomar U.S.A. 46°35N 107°23W 168 C10
Ingonish Canada 46°42N 60°18W 165 C7
Ingore Guinea-Biss. 12°24N 15°48W 138 C1
Ingraj Bazar India 24°58N 88°10E 125 G13
Ingrid Christensen Coast Antarctica 69°30S 76°0E 55 C6
Ingul = Inhul → Ukraine 46°50N 32°0E 85 J7
Ingulec = Inhulec Ukraine 47°42N 33°14E 85 J7
Ingulets = Inhulets → Ukraine 46°46N 32°47E 85 J7
Inguri = Enguri → Georgia 42°27N 41°38E 87 J5
Ingushetia □ Russia 43°20N 44°50E 87 J7
Ingwavuma S. Africa 27°9S 31°59E 145 C5
Inhaca Mozam. 26°1S 32°57E 145 C5
Inhaca Pen. Mozam. 26°13S 32°55E 145 C5
Inhafenga Mozam. 20°36S 33°53E 145 B5
Inhambane Mozam. 23°54S 35°30E 145 B6
Inhambane □ Mozam. 22°30S 34°20E 145 B5
Inhambupe Brazil 11°47S 38°21W 189 C3
Inhaminga Mozam. 18°26S 35°0E 143 F4
Inharrime Mozam. 24°30S 35°0E 145 B6
Inharrime → Mozam. 24°30S 35°0E 145 B6
Inhisar Turkey 40°3N 30°23E 99 A12
Inhul → Ukraine 46°50N 32°0E 85 J7
Inhulec Ukraine 47°42N 33°14E 85 J7
Inhulets → Ukraine 46°46N 32°47E 85 J7
Inhuma Brazil 6°40S 41°42W 189 B2
Iniesta Spain 39°27N 1°45W 91 F3
Ining = Yining China 43°58N 81°10E 109 D10
Inirida → Colombia 3°55N 67°52W 186 C5
Inis = Ennis Ireland 52°51N 8°59W 64 D3
Inishbofin Ireland 53°37N 10°13W 64 C1
Inisheer Ireland 53°3N 9°32W 64 C2
Inishfree B. Ireland 55°4N 8°23W 64 A3
Inishkea North Ireland 54°9N 10°11W 64 B1
Inishkea South Ireland 54°7N 10°12W 64 B1
Inishmaan Ireland 53°5N 9°35W 64 C2
Inishmore Ireland 53°8N 9°45W 64 C2
Inishmurray Ireland 54°26N 8°39W 64 B3
Inishowen Pen. Ireland 55°14N 7°15W 64 A4
Inishshark Ireland 53°37N 10°16W 64 C1
Inishturk Ireland 53°42N 10°7W 64 C1
Inishvickillane Ireland 52°3N 10°37W 64 D1
Injāna Iraq 34°29N 44°38E 105 E11
Injinoo ✪ Australia 10°56S 142°15E 150 A3
Injune Australia 25°53S 148°32E 151 D4
Inklin → N. Amer. 58°50N 133°10W 162 B2
Inland Kaikoura Ra. N.Z. 41°59S 173°41E 155 B8
Inland Sea = Setonaikai Japan 34°20N 133°30E 113 G6
Inle L. Myanmar 20°30N 96°58E 123 J20
Inlet U.S.A. 43°45N 74°48W 175 C10
Inn → Austria 48°35N 13°28E 78 C6
Innamincka Australia 27°44S 140°46E 151 D3
Inner Hebrides U.K. 57°0N 6°30W 65 E2
Inner Mongolia = Nei Mongol Zizhiqu □ China 42°0N 112°0E 114 D7
Inner Sound U.K. 57°30N 5°55W 65 D3
Innerkip Canada 43°13N 80°42W 174 C4
Innes △ Australia 35°52S 136°53E 152 C2
Innetalling I. Canada 56°0N 79°0W 164 A4
Innisfail Australia 17°33S 146°5E 150 B4
Innisfail Canada 52°2N 113°57W 162 C6
In'noshima Japan 34°19N 133°10E 113 G6
Innsbruck Austria 47°16N 11°23E 78 D4
Innviertel Austria 48°15N 13°15E 78 C6
Inny → Ireland 53°32N 7°51W 64 C4
Inongo Dem. Rep. of the Congo 1°55S 18°30E 140 E3
İnönü Turkey 39°48N 30°9E 99 B12
Inoucdjouac = Inukjuak Canada 58°25N 78°15W 161 F16
Inousses Greece 38°33N 26°14E 99 C8
Inowrocław Poland 52°50N 18°12E 83 F5
Inquisivi Bolivia 16°50S 67°10W 188 D4
Inscription, C. Australia 25°29S 112°59E 149 E1
Insein Myanmar 16°50N 96°5E 123 L20
Insjön Sweden 60°41N 15°6E 62 D9
Ińsko Poland 53°25N 15°32E 82 E2
Însurăţei Romania 44°50N 27°40E 81 F12
Inta Russia 66°5N 60°8E 106 C6
Intendente Alvear Argentina 35°12S 63°32W 190 D3
İntepe Turkey 40°1N 26°20E 99 A8
Interlachen U.S.A. 29°37N 81°53W 179 F8
Interlaken Switz. 46°41N 7°50E 77 J3
Interlaken U.S.A. 42°37N 76°44W 175 D8
International Falls U.S.A. 48°36N 93°25W 172 A7
Interview I. India 12°55N 92°43E 127 H11
Intiyaco Argentina 28°43S 60°5W 190 B3
Întorsura Buzăului Romania 45°41N 26°2E 81 E11
Inukjuak Canada 58°25N 78°15W 161 F16
Inútil, B. Chile 53°30S 70°15W 192 D2
Inuvik Canada 68°16N 133°40W 160 D5
Inveraray U.K. 56°14N 5°5W 65 E3
Inverbervie U.K. 56°51N 2°17W 65 E6
Invercargill N.Z. 46°24S 168°24E 155 G3
Inverclyde □ U.K. 55°55N 4°49W 65 F4
Inverell Australia 29°45S 151°8E 151 D5
Invergordon U.K. 57°41N 4°10W 65 D4
Inverleigh Australia 38°6S 144°3E 152 E6
Inverloch Australia 38°38S 145°45E 151 F4
Invermere Canada 50°30N 116°2W 162 C5
Inverness Canada 46°15N 61°19W 165 C7
Inverness U.K. 57°29N 4°13W 65 D4
Inverness Ala., U.S.A. 32°1N 85°45W 178 C4
Inverness Fla., U.S.A. 28°50N 82°20W 179 G7
Inverurie U.K. 57°17N 2°23W 65 D6
Investigator Group Australia 34°45S 134°20E 151 E1
Investigator Ridge Ind. Oc. 11°30S 98°10E 146 F8
Investigator Str. Australia 35°30S 137°0E 152 C2
Inya Russia 50°28N 86°37E 109 B11
Inyanga Zimbabwe 18°12S 32°40E 143 F3
Inyangani Zimbabwe 18°5S 32°50E 143 F3
Inyantue Zimbabwe 18°33S 26°39E 144 A4
Inyo Mts. U.S.A. 36°40N 118°0W 170 J9
Inyokern U.S.A. 35°39N 117°49W 171 K9
Inyonga Tanzania 6°45S 32°5E 142 D3
Inza Russia 53°55N 46°25E 86 D8
Inzhavino Russia 52°22N 42°30E 86 D6
Iō-Jima Japan 30°48N 130°18E 113 J5
Ioannina Greece 39°42N 20°47E 98 B2
Iola U.S.A. 37°55N 95°24W 172 G6
Ion Corvin Romania 44°7N 27°50E 81 F12
Iona U.K. 56°20N 6°25W 65 E2
Ione U.S.A. 38°21N 120°56W 170 G6
Ionia U.S.A. 42°59N 85°4W 173 D11
Ionian Is. = Ionioi Nisoi Greece 38°40N 20°0E 98 C2
Ionian Sea Medit. S. 37°30N 17°30E 58 H9
Ionioi Nisoi Greece 38°40N 20°0E 98 C2
Ionioi Nisoi □ Greece 38°40N 20°0E 98 C2
Iony, Ostrov Russia 56°24N 143°22E 107 D15
Ios Greece 36°41N 25°20E 99 E7
Iowa □ U.S.A. 42°18N 93°30W 172 D7
Iowa → U.S.A. 41°10N 91°1W 172 E8
Iowa City U.S.A. 41°40N 91°32W 172 E8
Iowa Falls U.S.A. 42°31N 93°16W 172 D7
Iowa Park U.S.A. 33°57N 98°40W 176 E5
Ipala Tanzania 4°30S 32°52E 142 C3
Ipameri Brazil 17°44S 48°9W 189 D1
Ipanema Brazil 19°47S 41°44W 189 D2
Iparía Peru 9°17S 74°29W 188 B3
Ipati Greece 38°52N 22°14E 98 C4
Ipatinga Brazil 19°32S 42°30W 189 D2
Ipatovo Russia 45°45N 42°50E 87 H6
Ipel' → Europe 47°48N 18°53E 79 D11
Ipiales Colombia 0°50N 77°37W 186 C3
Ipiaú Brazil 14°8S 39°44W 189 C3
Ipin = Yibin China 28°45N 104°32E 116 C5
Ipirá Brazil 12°10S 39°44W 189 C3
Ipixuna Brazil 7°0S 71°40W 188 B3
Ipixuna → Brazil 7°11S 71°51W 188 B3
Ipoh Malaysia 4°35N 101°5E 121 K3
Ippy C.A.R. 6°5N 21°7E 140 C4
İpsala Turkey 40°55N 26°23E 97 F10
Ipsario, Oros Greece 40°40N 24°40E 97 F8
Ipswich Australia 27°35S 152°40E 151 D5
Ipswich U.K. 52°4N 1°10E 67 E9
Ipswich Mass., U.S.A. 42°41N 70°50W 175 D14
Ipswich S. Dak., U.S.A. 45°27N 99°2W 172 C4
Ipu Brazil 4°23S 40°44W 189 A2
Ipueiras Brazil 4°33S 40°43W 189 A2
Ipupiara Brazil 11°49S 42°37W 189 C2
Iqaluit Canada 63°44N 68°31W 161 E18
Iqaluktuutiaq = Cambridge Bay Canada 69°10N 105°0W 160 D11
Iquique Chile 20°19S 70°5W 188 E3
Iquitos Peru 3°45S 73°10W 186 D4
Irabu-Jima Japan 24°50N 125°10E 113 M2
Iracoubo Fr. Guiana 5°30N 53°10W 187 B8
Īrafshān Iran 26°42N 61°56E 129 E9
Iraklia Cyclades, Greece 36°50N 25°28E 99 E7
Iraklia Serres, Greece 41°10N 23°16E 96 E7
Iraklio Greece 35°20N 25°12E 101 D7
Iraklion = Iraklio Greece 35°20N 25°12E 101 D7
Irakliou, Kolpos Greece 35°23N 25°8E 101 D7
Irala Paraguay 25°55S 54°35W 191 B5
Iran ■ Asia 33°0N 53°0E 129 C7
Iran, Pegunungan Malaysia 2°20N 114°50E 118 D4
Iran Ra. = Iran, Pegunungan Malaysia 2°20N 114°50E 118 D4
Iranamadu Tank Sri Lanka 9°23N 80°29E 127 K5
Īrānshahr Iran 27°15N 60°40E 129 E9
Irapuato Mexico 20°41N 101°28W 180 C4
Iraq ■ Asia 33°0N 44°0E 105 F10
Irati Brazil 25°25S 50°38W 191 B5
Irazú, Volcan Costa Rica 9°59N 83°51W 182 D3
Irbes saurums Latvia 57°45N 22°5E 82 A9
Irbid Jordan 32°35N 35°48E 130 C4
Irbid □ Jordan 32°30N 35°50E 130 C5
Irbil = Arbīl Iraq 36°15N 44°5E 105 D11
Irebu Dem. Rep. of the Congo 0°40S 17°46E 140 E3
Irecê Brazil 11°18S 41°52W 189 C2
Iregua → Spain 42°27N 2°24E 90 C7
Ireland ■ Europe 53°50N 7°52W 64 C4
Irele Nigeria 7°40N 5°40E 139 D6
Irgiz = Yrghyz Kazakhstan 48°37N 61°16E 108 C6
Irgiz = Yrghyz → Kazakhstan 48°6N 62°30E 108 C6
Irgiz, Bolshaya → Russia 52°10N 49°10E 86 D9
Irharrhar, O. → Algeria 28°3N 6°15E 136 C5
Irherm Morocco 30°7N 8°18W 136 B2
Irhil M'Goun Morocco 31°30N 6°28W 136 B2
Iri = Iksan S. Korea 35°59N 127°0E 115 G14
Irian Jaya = Papua □ Indonesia 4°0S 137°0E 119 E9
Irian Jaya Barat □ Indonesia 2°5S 132°50E 119 E8
Irié Guinea 8°15N 9°10W 138 D3
Iriklinskoye Vdkhr. Russia 52°0N 59°0E 108 B5
Iringa Tanzania 7°48S 35°43E 142 D4
Iringa □ Tanzania 7°48S 35°43E 142 D4
Irinjalakuda India 10°21N 76°14E 127 J3
Iriomote △ Japan 24°29N 123°53E 113 M1
Iriomote-Jima Japan 24°19N 123°48E 113 M1
Iriona Honduras 15°57N 85°11W 182 C2
Iriri → Brazil 3°52S 52°37W 187 D8
Irish Sea Europe 53°38N 4°48W 66 D3
Irkeshtam Pass = Erkech-Tam Pass Asia 39°46N 74°2E 109 E8
Irkutsk Russia 52°18N 104°20E 110 A9
Irlığanlı Turkey 37°53N 29°12E 99 D11
Irma Canada 52°55N 111°14W 163 C6
Irō-Zaki Japan 34°36N 138°51E 113 G9
Iroise, Mer d' France 48°15N 4°45W 70 D2
Iron Baron Australia 32°58S 137°11E 152 B2
Iron Gate = Portile de Fier Europe 44°44N 22°30E 80 F7
Iron Knob Australia 32°46S 137°8E 152 B2
Iron Mountain U.S.A. 45°49N 88°4W 172 C9
Iron Range △ Australia 12°34S 143°18E 150 A3
Iron River U.S.A. 46°6N 88°39W 172 B9
Irondequoit U.S.A. 43°13N 77°35W 174 C7
Ironton Mo., U.S.A. 37°36N 90°38W 172 G8
Ironton Ohio, U.S.A. 38°32N 82°41W 173 F12
Ironwood U.S.A. 46°27N 90°9W 172 B8
Ironwood Forest △ U.S.A. 32°32N 111°28W 169 K8
Iroquois Canada 44°51N 75°19W 175 B9
Iroquois Falls Canada 48°46N 80°41W 164 C3
Irpin Ukraine 50°30N 30°15E 75 C16
Irrara Cr. → Australia 29°35S 145°31E 151 D4
Irrawaddy = Ayeyawadi → Myanmar 15°50N 95°6E 123 M19
Irrawaddy □ Myanmar 17°0N 95°0E 123 L19
Irrawaddy, Mouths of the Myanmar 15°30N 95°0E 123 M19
Irricana Canada 51°19N 113°37W 162 C6
Irrunytju Australia 26°3S 128°56E 149 E4
Irshava Ukraine 48°19N 23°3E 80 B8
Irsina Italy 40°45N 16°14E 95 B9
Irtysh → Russia 61°4N 68°52E 106 C7
Irumu Dem. Rep. of the Congo 1°32N 29°53E 142 B2
Irún Spain 43°20N 1°52W 90 B3
Irunea = Pamplona-Iruña Spain 42°48N 1°38W 90 C3
Irurzun Spain 42°55N 1°50W 90 C3
Irvine Canada 49°57N 110°16W 163 D6
Irvine U.K. 55°37N 4°41W 65 F4
Irvine Calif., U.S.A. 33°41N 117°46W 171 M9
Irvine Ky., U.S.A. 37°42N 83°58W 173 G12
Irvinestown U.K. 54°28N 7°39W 64 B4
Irving U.S.A. 32°48N 96°56W 176 E6
Irvona U.S.A. 40°46N 78°33W 174 F6
Irwin → Australia 29°15S 114°54E 149 E1
Irwinton U.S.A. 32°49N 83°10W 178 C6
Irwinville U.S.A. 31°39N 83°23W 178 D6
Irymple Australia 34°14S 142°8E 152 C5
Is, Jebel Sudan 22°3N 35°28E 137 C4
Is-sur-Tille France 47°30N 5°8E 71 E12
Isa Nigeria 13°14N 6°24E 139 C6
Isa Khel Pakistan 32°41N 71°17E 124 C4
Isaac → Australia 22°55S 149°20E 150 C4
Isabel U.S.A. 45°24N 101°26W 172 C3
Isabel, I. Mexico 21°51N 105°55W 180 C3
Isabela Phil. 6°40N 121°59E 119 C6
Isabela Puerto Rico 18°30N 67°2W 183 d
Isabella, Cord. Nic. 13°30N 85°25W 182 D2
Isabella Ra. Australia 21°0S 121°4E 148 D3
Isaccea Romania 45°16N 28°28E 81 E13
Isachsen, C. Canada 79°20N 105°28W 161 B10
Isachsen Mt. Antarctica 72°8S 26°5E 55 D4
Ísafjarðardjúp Iceland 66°10N 23°0W 60 C2
Ísafjörður Iceland 66°5N 23°9W 60 C2
Isagarh India 24°48N 77°51E 124 G7
Isahaya Japan 32°52N 130°2E 113 H5
Isaka Tanzania 3°56S 32°59E 142 C3
Işalniţa Romania 44°24N 23°44E 81 F8
Isan → India 26°51N 80°7E 125 F9
Isana = Içana → Brazil 0°26N 67°19W 186 C5
Isangano △ Zambia 11°8S 30°35E 143 E3
Isanlu Makutu Nigeria 8°20N 5°50E 139 D6
Isar → Germany 48°48N 12°57E 77 G8
Isarco → Italy 46°27N 11°18E 93 B8
Isaris Greece 37°22N 22°0E 98 D3
Ìscar Spain 41°22N 4°32W 88 D6
İscehisar Turkey 38°51N 30°45E 99 C12
Íschia Italy 40°44N 13°57E 94 B6
Ischigualasto △ Argentina 30°0S 68°0W 190 B2
Isdell → Australia 16°27S 124°51E 148 C3
Ise Japan 34°25N 136°45E 113 G8
Ise-Shima △ Japan 34°25N 136°48E 113 G8
Ise-Wan Japan 34°43N 136°43E 113 G8
Isefjord Denmark 55°53N 11°50E 63 J5
Isel → Austria 46°50N 12°47E 78 E5
Iseo Italy 45°39N 10°3E 92 C7
Iseo, L. d' Italy 45°43N 10°4E 92 C7
Iseramagazi Tanzania 4°37S 32°10E 142 C3
Isère □ France 45°15N 5°40E 73 C9
Isère → France 44°59N 4°51E 73 D8
Iserlohn Germany 51°22N 7°42E 76 D3
Isérnia Italy 41°36N 14°14E 95 A7
Iseyin Nigeria 8°0N 3°36E 139 D5
Isfahan = Eşfahān Iran 32°39N 51°43E 129 C6
Ishëm Albania 41°33N 19°34E 96 E3
Ishigaki Japan 24°26N 124°10E 113 M2
Ishigaki-Shima Japan 24°20N 124°10E 113 M2
Ishikari Japan 43°20N 141°15E 112 C10
Ishikari-Gawa → Japan 43°15N 141°23E 112 C10
Ishikari-Sammyaku Japan 43°30N 143°0E 112 C11
Ishikari-Wan Japan 43°25N 141°1E 112 C10
Ishikawa Japan 26°25N 127°49E 113 L3
Ishikawa □ Japan 36°30N 136°30E 113 F8
Ishim Russia 56°10N 69°30E 106 D7
Ishim → Russia 57°45N 71°10E 106 D8
Ishimbay Russia 53°28N 56°2E 108 B5
Ishinomaki Japan 38°32N 141°20E 112 E10
Ishioka Japan 36°11N 140°16E 113 F10
Ishkashim Tajikistan 36°44N 71°37E 109 E8
Ishkoman Pakistan 36°30N 73°50E 125 A5
Ishpeming U.S.A. 46°29N 87°40W 172 B10
Isigny-sur-Mer France 49°19N 1°6W 70 C5
Isıklar Dağı Turkey 40°45N 27°15E 97 F11
Işıklı Turkey 38°19N 29°51E 99 C11
Isil Kul Russia 54°55N 71°16E 109 B8
Ísili Italy 39°44N 9°6E 94 C2
iSimangaliso ⌂ S. Africa 27°50S 32°32E 145 C5
Isiolo Kenya 0°24N 37°33E 142 B4
Isiolo □ Kenya 1°0N 37°30E 142 B4
Isiro Dem. Rep. of the Congo 2°53N 27°40E 142 B2
Isisford Australia 24°15S 144°21E 150 C3
Iskar → Bulgaria 43°45N 24°25E 97 C8
İskele = Trikomo Cyprus 35°17N 33°52E 101 D12
İskenderun Turkey 36°32N 36°10E 104 D7
İskenderun Körfezi Turkey 36°40N 35°50E 104 D6
İskilip Turkey 40°45N 34°29E 104 B6
Iskitim Russia 54°38N 83°18E 109 B10
Iskŭr, Yazovir Bulgaria 42°23N 23°30E 96 D7
Iskut → Canada 56°45N 131°49W 162 B2
Isla → U.K. 56°32N 3°20W 65 E5
Isla Coiba △ Panama 7°33N 81°36W 182 E3
Isla Cristina Spain 37°13N 7°17W 89 H3
Isla de Salamanca △ Colombia 10°59N 74°40W 183 D5
Isla Gorge △ Australia 25°10S 149°57E 150 D4
Isla Guamblin △ Chile 44°50S 75°4W 192 B1
Isla Isabel △ Mexico 21°54N 105°58W 180 C3
Isla Magdalena △ Chile 44°20S 73°13W 192 B2
Isla Tiburón y San Esteban ⌂ Mexico 29°0N 112°27W 180 B2
Isla Vista U.S.A. 34°25N 119°53W 171 L7
İslahiye Turkey 37°0N 36°35E 104 D7
Islam Headworks Pakistan 29°49N 72°33E 124 E5
Islamabad Pakistan 33°40N 73°10E 124 C5
Islamgarh Pakistan 27°51N 70°48E 124 F4
Islamkot Pakistan 24°42N 70°13E 124 G4
Islamorada U.S.A. 24°56N 80°37W 179 L9
Islampur Bihar, India 25°9N 85°12E 125 G11
Islampur Maharashtra, India 17°2N 74°20E 126 F2
Islampur Paschimbanga, India 26°16N 88°12E 125 F13
Island = Iceland ■ Europe 64°45N 19°0W 60 D4
Island L. Canada 53°47N 94°25W 163 C10
Island Lagoon Australia 31°30S 136°40E 152 A2
Island Pond U.S.A. 44°49N 71°53W 175 B13
Islands, B. of Canada 49°11N 58°15W 165 C8
Islands, B. of N.Z. 35°15S 174°6E 154 B3
Islas Atlánticas de Galicia △ Spain 42°23N 8°55W 88 C2
Islay U.K. 55°46N 6°10W 65 F2
Isle → France 44°55N 0°15W 72 D3
Isle aux Morts Canada 47°35N 59°0W 165 C8
Isle of Hope U.S.A. 31°58N 81°5W 178 D8
Isle of Wight □ U.K. 50°41N 1°17W 67 G6
Isle Royale △ U.S.A. 48°0N 88°55W 172 B9
Isleton U.S.A. 38°10N 121°37W 170 G5
Ismail = Izmayil Ukraine 45°22N 28°46E 81 E13
Ismâ'ilîya Egypt 30°37N 32°18E 137 E8
Ismaning Germany 48°13N 11°40E 77 G7
Isna Egypt 25°17N 32°30E 137 B3
Isojärvi △ Finland 61°40N 25°0E 60 F21
Ísola del Liri Italy 41°41N 13°34E 93 G10
Ísola della Scala Italy 45°16N 11°0E 92 C8
Ísola di Capo Rizzuto Italy 38°58N 17°6E 95 D10
Isparta Turkey 37°47N 30°30E 99 D12
Isparta □ Turkey 38°0N 31°0E 104 D4
Isperih Bulgaria 43°43N 26°50E 97 C10
Íspica Italy 36°47N 14°55E 95 F7
İspir Turkey 40°28N 40°59E 105 B9
Israel ■ Asia 32°0N 34°50E 130 D3
Issakly Russia 54°8N 51°32E 86 C10
Issaouane, Erg Algeria 26°58N 8°42E 136 C5
Issia Côte d'Ivoire 6°33N 6°33W 138 D3
Issoire France 45°32N 3°15E 72 C7
Issoudun France 46°57N 1°59E 71 F8
Issyk-Kul = Balykchy Kyrgyzstan 42°26N 76°12E 109 D9
Issyk-Kul, Ozero = Ysyk-Köl Kyrgyzstan 42°25N 77°15E 109 D9
Ist Croatia 44°17N 14°47E 93 D11
Istállós-kő Hungary 48°4N 20°26E 80 B5
İstanbul Turkey 41°0N 28°58E 97 E12
İstanbul □ Turkey 41°0N 29°0E 97 E12
İstanbul ✈ (IST) Turkey 40°59N 28°49E 97 F12
İstanbul Boğazı Turkey 41°5N 29°3E 97 E13
Istaravshān Tajikistan 39°55N 69°1E 109 E7
Istiea Greece 38°57N 23°9E 98 C4
Isto, Mt. U.S.A. 69°12N 143°48W 166 B11
Istok = Burim Kosovo 42°45N 20°24E 96 D4
Istokpoga, L. U.S.A. 27°23N 81°17W 179 H8
Istra Croatia 45°10N 14°0E 93 C10
Istres France 43°31N 4°59E 73 E8
Istria = Istra Croatia 45°10N 14°0E 93 C10
Itá Paraguay 25°29S 57°21W 190 B4
Itabaiana Paraíba, Brazil 7°18S 35°19W 189 B3
Itabaiana Sergipe, Brazil 10°41S 37°37W 189 C3
Itabaianinha Brazil 11°16S 37°47W 189 C3
Itaberaba Brazil 12°32S 40°18W 189 C2
Itabira Brazil 19°37S 43°13W 189 D2
Itabirito Brazil 20°15S 43°48W 189 E2
Itabuna Brazil 14°48S 39°16W 189 C3
Itacajá Brazil 8°19S 47°46W 189 B1
Itacaunas → Brazil 5°21S 49°8W 187 E9
Itacoatiara Brazil 3°8S 58°25W 186 D7
Itaguaí Brazil 22°15S 43°46W 191 A7
Itaguari → Brazil 14°11S 44°40W 189 C2
Itaguatins Brazil 5°47S 47°29W 189 B1
Itaim → Brazil 7°2S 42°2W 189 B2
Itainópolis Brazil 7°24S 41°31W 189 B2
Itaipú, Represa de Brazil 25°30S 54°30W 191 B5
Itäisen Suomenlahti △ Finland 60°25N 27°15E 60 F22
Itaituba Brazil 4°10S 55°50W 187 D7
Itajaí Brazil 27°50S 48°39W 191 B6
Itajubá Brazil 22°24S 45°30W 191 A6
Itajuípe Brazil 14°41S 39°22W 189 C3
Itaka Tanzania 8°50S 32°49E 143 D3
Itala ⌂ S. Africa 27°30S 31°7E 145 C5
Italy ■ Europe 42°0N 13°0E 59 G8
Itamaraju Brazil 17°4S 39°32W 189 D3
Itamarati Brazil 6°24S 68°15W 188 B4
Itamataré Brazil 2°16S 46°24W 189 A1
Itambacuri Brazil 18°1S 41°42W 189 D2
Itambé Brazil 15°15S 40°37W 189 D2
Itanhém Brazil 17°9S 40°20W 189 D2
Itapagé Brazil 3°41S 39°34W 189 A3
Itaparica, I. de Brazil 12°54S 38°42W 189 C3
Itaparica, Represa de Brazil 11°3S 42°47W 189 C2
Itapebi Brazil 15°56S 39°32W 189 D3
Itapecuru Mirim Brazil 3°24S 44°20W 189 A2
Itaperuna Brazil 21°10S 41°54W 191 A7
Itapetinga Brazil 15°15S 40°15W 189 D2
Itapetininga Brazil 23°36S 48°7W 191 A6
Itapeva Brazil 23°59S 48°59W 191 A6
Itapicuru → Bahia, Brazil 11°47S 37°32W 189 C3
Itapicuru → Maranhão, Brazil 2°52S 44°12W 189 A2
Itapipoca Brazil 3°30S 39°35W 189 A3
Itapiúna Brazil 4°33S 38°57W 189 A3
Itaporanga Brazil 7°18S 38°0W 189 B3
Itapuá □ Paraguay 26°40S 55°40W 191 B4
Itaquai → Brazil 4°20S 70°12W 188 A3
Itaquí Maranhão, Brazil 2°34S 44°22W 189 A2
Itaquí Rio Grande do S., Brazil 29°8S 56°30W 190 B4
Itararé Brazil 24°6S 49°23W 191 A6
Itarsi India 22°36N 77°51E 124 H7
Itatí Argentina 27°16S 58°15W 190 B4
Itatiaia △ Brazil 22°22S 44°38W 191 A7
Itatira Brazil 4°30S 39°37W 189 A3
Itaueira Brazil 7°36S 43°2W 189 B2
Itaueira → Brazil 6°41S 42°55W 189 B2
Itaúna Brazil 20°4S 44°34W 189 E2
Itcha Ilgachuz ⌂ Canada 52°42N 124°58W 162 C3
Itchen → U.K. 50°55N 1°22W 67 G6
Ite Peru 17°55S 70°57W 188 D3
Itea Greece 38°25N 22°25E 98 C4
Itezhi Tezhi, L. Zambia 15°30S 25°30E 143 F2
Ithaca = Ithaki Greece 38°25N 20°40E 98 C2
Ithaca U.S.A. 42°27N 76°30W 175 D8
Ithaki Greece 38°25N 20°40E 98 C2
Iti △ Greece 38°50N 22°15E 98 C4
Itinga Brazil 16°36S 41°47W 189 D2
Itiquira → Brazil 17°18S 56°44W 187 G7
Itiruçu Brazil 13°31S 40°9W 189 C2
Itiúba Brazil 10°43S 39°51W 189 C3
Itiyuro → Argentina 22°40S 63°50W 190 A3
Itō Japan 34°58N 139°5E 113 G9
Itoigawa Japan 37°2N 137°51E 113 F8
Iton → France 49°9N 1°12E 70 C8
Itonamas → Bolivia 12°28S 64°24W 186 F6
Itri Italy 41°17N 13°32E 94 A6
Itsa Egypt 29°15N 30°47E 137 F7
Íttiri Italy 40°36N 8°34E 94 B1
Ittoqqortoormiit Greenland 70°20N 23°0W 57 C8
Itu Brazil 23°17S 47°15W 191 A6
Itu Nigeria 5°10N 7°58E 139 D6
Itu Aba I. S. China Sea 10°23N 114°21E 118 B4
Ituaçu Brazil 13°50S 41°18W 189 C2
Ituiutaba Brazil 19°0S 49°25W 187 G9
Itumbiara Brazil 18°20S 49°10W 187 G9
Ituna Canada 51°10N 103°24W 163 C8
Itunge Port Tanzania 9°40S 33°55E 143 D3
Iturbe Argentina 23°0S 65°25W 190 A2
Ituri Dem. Rep. of the Congo 2°30N 29°30E 142 B2
Ituri → Dem. Rep. of the Congo 1°40N 27°1E 142 B2
Iturup, Ostrov Russia 45°0N 148°0E 107 E15
Ituverava Brazil 20°20S 47°47W 189 E1
Ituxi → Brazil 7°18S 64°51W 186 E6
Itzehoe Germany 53°55N 9°31E 76 B5
Ivai → Brazil 23°18S 53°42W 191 A5
Ivalo Finland 68°38N 27°35E 60 B22
Ivalojoki → Finland 68°40N 27°40E 60 B22
Ivanava Belarus 52°7N 25°29E 75 B13
Ivančice Czechia 49°6N 16°23E 79 B9
Ivane-Puste Ukraine 48°39N 26°10E 81 B11
Ivăneşti Romania 46°39N 27°27E 81 D12
Ivangorod Russia 59°27N 28°13E 84 C5
Ivanhoe N.S.W., Australia 32°56S 144°20E 152 B6
Ivanhoe Vic., Australia 37°45S 145°3E 153 D6
Ivanhoe Canada 44°23N 77°28W 174 B7
Ivanhoe Calif., U.S.A. 36°23N 119°13W 170 J7
Ivanhoe Minn., U.S.A. 44°28N 96°15W 172 C5
Ivanhorod Ukraine 48°48N 29°50E 81 B14
Ivanić Grad Croatia 45°41N 16°25E 93 C13
Ivanjica Serbia 43°35N 20°12E 96 C4
Ivanjska Bos.-H. 44°55N 17°4E 80 F2
Ivankoyskoye Vdkhr. Russia 56°37N 36°32E 84 D9
Ivano-Frankivsk Ukraine 48°40N 24°40E 81 B9
Ivano-Frankivsk □ Ukraine 48°45N 24°30E 81 B9
Ivanovo = Ivanava Belarus 52°7N 25°29E 75 B13
Ivanovo Bulgaria 43°43N 25°58E 97 C9
Ivanovo Russia 57°5N 41°0E 84 D11
Ivanovo □ Russia 57°10N 41°50E 86 B5
Ivanšćica Croatia 46°12N 16°13E 93 B13
Ivatsevichy Belarus 52°43N 25°21E 75 B13
Ivaylovgrad Bulgaria 41°32N 26°8E 97 E10
Iveragh Pen. Ireland 51°52N 10°15W 64 E1
Ivinheima → Brazil 23°14S 53°42W 191 A5
Ivinhema Brazil 22°10S 53°37W 191 A5
Ivittuut Greenland 61°14N 48°12W 57 E6
Ivory Coast = Côte d'Ivoire ■ Africa 7°30N 5°0W 138 D4
Ivory Coast W. Afr. 4°20N 5°0W 138 E4
Ivösjön Sweden 56°8N 14°25E 63 H8
Ivrea Italy 45°28N 7°52E 92 C4
İvrindi Turkey 39°34N 27°30E 99 B9
Ivujivik Canada 62°24N 77°55W 161 E16
Ivvavik △ Canada 69°6N 139°30W 160 D4
Ivybridge U.K. 50°23N 3°56W 67 G4
Iwaizumi Japan 39°50N 141°45E 112 E10

Iwaki *Japan* 37°3N 140°55E **113** F10
Iwakuni *Japan* 34°15N 132°8E **113** G6
Iwamizawa *Japan* 43°12N 141°46E **112** C10
Iwanai *Japan* 42°58N 140°30E **112** C10
Iwata *Japan* 34°42N 137°51E **113** G8
Iwate □ *Japan* 39°30N 141°30E **112** E10
Iwate-San *Japan* 39°51N 141°0E **112** E10
Iwo *Nigeria* 7°39N 4°9E **139** D5
Iwŏn *N. Korea* 40°19N 128°39E **115** D15
Iwonicz-Zdrój *Poland* 49°37N 21°47E **83** J8
Ixiamas *Bolivia* 13°50S 68°5W **188** C4
Ixopo *S. Africa* 30°11S 30°5E **145** D5
Ixtepec *Mexico* 16°34N 95°6W **181** D5
Ixtlán del Río *Mexico* 21°2N 104°22W **180** C4
Iyo *Japan* 33°45N 132°45E **113** H6
Izabal, L. de *Guatemala* 15°30N 89°10W **182** C2
Izamal *Mexico* 20°56N 89°1W **181** C7
Izberbash *Russia* 42°35N 47°52E **87** J8
Izbica *Poland* 50°53N 23°10E **83** H10
Izbica Kujawska *Poland* 52°25N 18°40E **83** F5
Izbiceni *Romania* 43°45N 24°40E **81** G9
Izena-Shima *Japan* 26°56N 127°56E **113** L3
Izgrev *Bulgaria* 43°36N 26°58E **97** C10
Izhevsk *Russia* 56°51N 53°14E **106** D6
Izmayil *Ukraine* 45°22N 28°46E **81** E13
İzmir *Turkey* 38°25N 27°8E **99** C9
İzmir □ *Turkey* 38°15N 27°40E **99** C9
İzmir Adnan Menderes ✈ (ADB)
Turkey 38°23N 27°6E **99** C9
İzmir Körfezi *Turkey* 38°30N 26°50E **99** C8
İzmit = Kocaeli *Turkey* 40°45N 29°50E **97** F13
İznájar *Spain* 37°15N 4°19W **89** H6
İznalloz *Spain* 37°24N 3°30W **89** H7
İznik *Turkey* 40°23N 29°46E **104** B3
İznik Gölü *Turkey* 40°27N 29°30E **97** F13
Izobil'nyy *Russia* 45°25N 41°44E **87** H5
Izola *Slovenia* 45°32N 13°39E **93** C10
Izra *Syria* 32°51N 36°15E **130** C5
Iztochni Rodopi *Bulgaria* 41°45N 25°30E **97** E9
Izu-Hantō *Japan* 34°45N 139°0E **113** G9
Izu-Shotō *Japan* 34°30N 140°0E **113** G10
Izúcar de Matamoros
Mexico 18°36N 98°28W **181** D5
Izumi *Japan* 32°5N 130°22E **113** H5
Izumi-Sano *Japan* 34°23N 135°18E **113** G7
Izumo *Japan* 35°20N 132°46E **113** G6
Izyaslav *Ukraine* 50°5N 26°50E **75** C14
Izyum *Ukraine* 49°12N 37°19E **85** H9

J

J.F.K. Int. ✈ (JFK)
U.S.A. 40°38N 73°47W **175** F11
J.P. Koch Fjord *Greenland* 82°45N 44°0W **57** A6
J. Strom Thurmond L.
U.S.A. 33°40N 82°12W **178** B7
Ja-ela *Sri Lanka* 7°5N 79°53E **127** L4
Jabalón ➜ *Spain* 38°53N 4°5W **89** G6
Jabalpur *India* 23°9N 79°58E **125** H8
Jabālya *Gaza Strip* 31°32N 34°29E **130** D3
Jabbūl *Syria* 36°4N 37°30E **128** B3
Jabiru *Australia* 12°40S 132°53E **148** B5
Jablah *Syria* 35°20N 36°0E **104** E6
Jablanac *Croatia* 44°42N 14°56E **93** D11
Jablanica *Bos.-H.* 43°40N 17°45E **80** G2
Jablonec nad Nisou
Czechia 50°43N 15°10E **78** A8
Jablonica *Slovakia* 48°37N 17°26E **79** C10
Jabłonowo Pomorskie
Poland 53°23N 19°10E **82** E6
Jablunkov *Czechia* 49°35N 18°46E **79** B11
Jaboatão *Brazil* 8°7S 35°1W **189** B3
Jabotabek = Jakarta
Indonesia 6°9S 106°52E **118** F3
Jaboticabal *Brazil* 21°15S 48°17W **191** A6
Jabukovac *Serbia* 44°22N 22°21E **96** B6
Jaca *Spain* 42°35N 0°33W **90** C4
Jacaré ➜ *Brazil* 10°3S 42°13W **189** C2
Jacareí *Brazil* 23°20S 46°0W **191** A6
Jacarèzinho *Brazil* 23°5S 49°58W **191** A6
Jacinto *Brazil* 16°10S 40°17W **189** D2
Jack River △ *Australia* 14°58S 144°19E **150** A3
Jackman *U.S.A.* 45°37N 70°15W **173** C18
Jacksboro *U.S.A.* 33°13N 98°10W **176** E5
Jackson *Barbados* 13°7N 59°36W **183** g
Jackson *Ala., U.S.A.* 31°31N 87°53W **177** F11
Jackson *Calif., U.S.A.* 38°21N 120°46W **170** G6
Jackson *Ga., U.S.A.* 33°20N 83°57W **178** B6
Jackson *Ky., U.S.A.* 37°33N 83°23W **173** G12
Jackson *Mich., U.S.A.* 42°15N 84°24W **173** D11
Jackson *Minn., U.S.A.* 43°37N 95°1W **172** D6
Jackson *Miss., U.S.A.* 32°18N 90°12W **177** E9
Jackson *Mo., U.S.A.* 37°23N 89°40W **172** G9
Jackson *N.H., U.S.A.* 44°10N 71°11W **175** B13
Jackson *Ohio, U.S.A.* 39°3N 82°39W **173** F12
Jackson *S.C., U.S.A.* 33°20N 81°47W **178** B8
Jackson *Tenn., U.S.A.* 35°37N 88°49W **177** D10
Jackson *Wyo., U.S.A.* 43°29N 110°46W **168** E8
Jackson, C. *N.Z.* 40°59S 174°20E **155** A9
Jackson B. *N.Z.* 43°58S 168°42E **155** D3
Jackson Hd. *N.Z.* 43°58S 168°37E **155** D3
Jackson L. *Fla., U.S.A.* 30°30N 84°17W **178** E5
Jackson L. *Ga., U.S.A.* 33°19N 83°50W **178** B6
Jackson L. *Wyo.,*
U.S.A. 43°52N 110°36W **168** E8
Jacksons *N.Z.* 42°46S 171°32E **155** C6
Jackson's Arm *Canada* 49°52N 56°47W **165** C8
Jacksonville *Ala.,*
U.S.A. 33°49N 85°46W **178** B4
Jacksonville *Ark.,*
U.S.A. 34°52N 92°7W **176** D8
Jacksonville *Calif.,*
U.S.A. 37°52N 120°24W **170** H6
Jacksonville *Fla.,*
U.S.A. 30°20N 81°39W **178** E8
Jacksonville *Ga.,*
U.S.A. 31°49N 82°59W **178** D7
Jacksonville *Ill., U.S.A.* 39°44N 90°14W **172** F8
Jacksonville *N.C.,*
U.S.A. 34°45N 77°26W **177** D16
Jacksonville *Tex.,*
U.S.A. 31°58N 95°17W **176** F7
Jacksonville Beach
U.S.A. 30°17N 81°24W **178** E8
Jacksonville Int. ✈ (JAX)
U.S.A. 30°30N 81°41W **178** E8
Jacmel *Haiti* 18°14N 72°32W **183** C5
Jacob Lake *U.S.A.* 36°43N 112°13W **169** H7
Jacobabad *Pakistan* 28°20N 68°29E **124** E3
Jacobina *Brazil* 11°11S 40°30W **189** C2
Jacques-Cartier, Dét. de
Canada 50°0N 63°30W **165** C7
Jacques-Cartier, Mt.
Canada 48°57N 66°0W **165** C6
Jacques-Cartier △
Canada 47°15N 71°33W **165** C5
Jacqueville *Côte d'Ivoire* 5°12N 4°25W **138** D4
Jacuí ➜ *Brazil* 30°2S 51°15W **191** C5
Jacumba *U.S.A.* 32°37N 116°11W **171** N10
Jacundá ➜ *Brazil* 1°57S 50°26W **187** D8
Jadcherla *India* 16°46N 78°9E **126** F4
Jade *Germany* 53°20N 8°14E **76** B4
Jade, Côte de *France* 46°40N 2°0W **70** F4
Jade City *Canada* 59°15N 129°37W **162** B3
Jade Dragon Snow Mt. = Yulong
Xueshan *China* 27°6N 100°10E **116** D3
Jade Mt. = Yü Shan
Taiwan 23°25N 120°52E **117** F13
Jadebusen *Germany* 53°29N 8°12E **76** B4
Jadovnik *Serbia* 43°20N 19°45E **96** C3
Jadraque *Spain* 40°55N 2°55W **90** E2
Jaén *Peru* 5°25S 78°40W **188** B2
Jaén *Spain* 37°44N 3°43W **89** H7
Jaén □ *Spain* 37°50N 3°30W **89** H7
Jafarabad *India* 20°52N 71°22E **124** J4
Jaffa = Tel Aviv-Yafo
Israel 32°4N 34°48E **130** C3
Jaffa, C. *Australia* 36°58S 139°40E **152** D3
Jaffna *Sri Lanka* 9°45N 80°2E **127** K5
Jaffrey *U.S.A.* 42°49N 72°2W **175** D12
Jagadhri *India* 30°10N 77°20E **124** D7
Jagadishpur *India* 25°30N 84°21E **125** G11
Jagat *Nepal* 28°19N 84°53E **125** E11
Jagdalpur *India* 19°3N 82°0E **126** E6
Jagdaqi *China* 50°25N 124°7E **111** A13
Jagersfontein *S. Africa* 29°44S 25°27E **144** C4
Jaghīn ➜ *Iran* 27°17N 57°13E **129** E8
Jagodina *Serbia* 44°5N 21°15E **96** B5
Jagraon *India* 30°50N 75°25E **124** D6
Jagst ➜ *Germany* 49°14N 9°10E **77** F5
Jagtial *India* 18°50N 79°0E **126** E4
Jaguaquara *Brazil* 13°32S 39°58W **189** C3
Jaguariaiva *Brazil* 24°10S 49°50W **191** A6
Jaguaribe *Brazil* 5°53S 38°37W **189** B3
Jaguaribe ➜ *Brazil* 4°25S 37°45W **189** A3
Jaguaruana *Brazil* 4°50S 37°47W **189** A3
Jagüey Grande *Cuba* 22°35N 81°7W **182** B3
Jagungal, Mt. *Australia* 36°8S 148°22E **153** D8
Jahanabad *India* 25°13N 84°59E **125** G11
Jahazpur *India* 25°37N 75°17E **124** G6
Jahrom *Iran* 28°30N 53°31E **129** D7
Jaicós *Brazil* 7°21S 41°8W **189** B2
Jaigarh *India* 17°17N 73°13E **126** F1
Jaijon *India* 31°21N 76°9E **124** D7
Jailolo *Indonesia* 1°5N 127°30E **119** D7
Jailolo, Selat *Indonesia* 0°5N 129°5E **119** D7
Jaipur *India* 27°0N 75°50E **124** F6
Jais *India* 26°15N 81°32E **125** F9
Jaisalmer *India* 26°55N 70°54E **124** F4
Jaisinghnagar *India* 23°38N 78°34E **125** H8
Jaitaran *India* 26°12N 73°56E **124** F5
Jaithari *India* 23°14N 78°37E **125** H8
Jajarkot *Nepal* 28°42N 82°14E **125** E10
Jājarm *Iran* 36°58N 56°27E **129** B8
Jajce *Bos.-H.* 44°19N 17°17E **80** F2
Jajpur *India* 20°53N 86°22E **126** D8
Jakam ➜ *India* 23°54N 74°13E **124** H6
Jakarta *Indonesia* 6°9S 106°52E **118** F3
Jakarta Sukarno-Hatta Int. ✈
(CGK) *Indonesia* 6°7S 106°40E **119** G12
Jakhal *India* 29°48N 75°50E **124** E6
Jakhau *India* 23°13N 68°43E **124** H3
Jakobshavn = Ilulissat
Greenland 69°12N 51°10W **57** D5
Jakobstad = Pietarsaari
Finland 63°40N 22°43E **60** E20
Jakupica *Macedonia* 41°45N 21°22E **96** E5
Jal *U.S.A.* 32°7N 103°12W **169** K12
Jalājil *Si. Arabia* 25°40N 45°27E **128** E5
Jalal-Abad *Kyrgyzstan* 40°56N 73°0E **109** D8
Jalal-Abad □
Kyrgyzstan 41°30N 72°30E **109** D8
Jalālābād *Afghan.* 34°30N 70°29E **124** B4
Jalalabad *India* 27°41N 79°42E **125** F8
Jalalpur Jattan *Pakistan* 32°38N 74°11E **124** C6
Jalama *U.S.A.* 34°29N 120°29W **171** L6
Jalandhar *India* 31°20N 75°40E **124** D6
Jalapa *Guatemala* 14°39N 89°59W **182** D2
Jalapa Enríquez = Xalapa
Mexico 19°32N 96°55W **181** D5
Jalasjärvi *Finland* 62°29N 22°47E **60** E20
Jalaun *India* 26°8N 79°25E **125** F8
Jaldhaka ➜ *Bangla.* 26°16N 89°16E **125** F13
Jalesar *India* 27°29N 78°19E **124** F8
Jaleswar *Nepal* 26°38N 85°48E **125** F11
Jalgaon *India* 21°0N 75°42E **126** D2
Jalībah *Iraq* 30°35N 46°32E **128** D5
Jalingo *Nigeria* 8°55N 11°25E **139** D7
Jalisco □ *Mexico* 20°20N 103°40W **180** D4
Jalkot *Pakistan* 35°14N 73°24E **125** B5
Jalna *India* 19°48N 75°38E **126** E2
Jalón ➜ *Spain* 41°47N 1°4W **90** D3
Jalor *India* 25°21N 72°37E **124** G5
Jalpa *Mexico* 21°38N 102°58W **180** C4
Jalpaiguri *India* 26°32N 88°46E **123** F16
Jalpan *Mexico* 21°14N 99°29W **181** C5
Jaluit I. *Marshall Is.* 6°0N 169°30E **156** G8
Jalūlā *Iraq* 34°16N 45°10E **105** E11
Jamaame *Somalia* 0°4N 42°44E **131** G3
Jamaari *Nigeria* 11°44N 9°53E **139** C6
Jamaica ■ *W. Indies* 18°10N 77°30W **182** a
Jamalpur *Bangla.* 24°52N 89°56E **123** G16
Jamalpur *India* 25°18N 86°28E **125** G12
Jamalpurganj *India* 23°2N 87°59E **125** H13
Jamanxim ➜ *Brazil* 4°43S 56°18W **187** D7
Jamberwangi *Indonesia* 8°17S 114°7E **119** J17
Jambi *Indonesia* 1°38S 103°30E **118** E2
Jambi □ *Indonesia* 1°30S 102°30E **118** E2
Jambongan, Pulau
Malaysia 6°45N 117°20E **118** C5
Jambusar *India* 22°3N 72°51E **124** H5
James *U.S.A.* 32°58N 83°29W **178** C6
James ➜ *S. Dak.,*
U.S.A. 42°52N 97°18W **172** D5
James ➜ *Va., U.S.A.* 36°56N 76°27W **173** G15
James B. *Canada* 54°0N 80°0W **164** B3
James I. *Gambia* 13°19N 16°21W **138** C1
James Island *U.S.A.* 32°45N 79°55W **178** C10
James Ranges
Australia 24°10S 132°30E **148** D5
James Ross I.
Antarctica 63°58S 57°50W **55** C18
James Ross Str.
Canada 69°40N 96°10W **160** D12
Jamesabad *Pakistan* 25°17N 69°15E **124** G3
Jameson Land *Greenland* 71°0N 23°30W **57** C8
Jamestown *Australia* 33°10S 138°32E **152** B3
Jamestown *S. Africa* 31°6S 26°45E **144** D4
Jamestown *N. Dak.,*
U.S.A. 46°54N 98°42W **172** B4
Jamestown *N.Y., U.S.A.* 42°6N 79°14W **174** D5
Jamestown *Pa., U.S.A.* 41°29N 80°27W **174** E4
Jamestown *S.C.,*
U.S.A. 33°17N 79°42W **178** B10
Jamīlābād *Iran* 34°24N 48°28E **129** C6
Jamira ➜ *India* 21°35N 88°28E **125** J13
Jämjö *Sweden* 56°12N 15°49E **63** H9
Jamkhandi *India* 16°30N 75°15E **126** F2
Jamkhed *India* 18°43N 75°19E **126** E2
Jammalamadugu *India* 14°51N 78°25E **127** G4
Jammerbugten *Denmark* 57°15N 9°20E **63** G3
Jammu *India* 32°43N 74°54E **124** C6
Jammu & Kashmir □
India 34°25N 77°0E **125** B7
Jamnagar *India* 22°30N 70°6E **124** H4
Jamner *India* 20°45N 75°52E **126** D2
Jamni ➜ *India* 25°13N 78°35E **125** G8
Jampur *Pakistan* 29°39N 70°40E **124** E4
Jamrud *Pakistan* 33°59N 71°24E **124** C4
Jämsä *Finland* 61°53N 25°10E **84** B3
Jamshedpur *India* 22°44N 86°12E **125** H12
Jamtara *India* 23°59N 86°49E **125** H12
Jämtland *Sweden* 63°31N 14°0E **60** E16
Jämtland □ *Sweden* 63°0N 14°40E **62** B7
Jan L. *Canada* 54°56N 102°55W **163** C8
Jan Mayen *Arctic* 71°0N 9°0W **54** B7
Janakkala *Finland* 60°54N 24°36E **84** B3
Janakpur *Nepal* 26°42N 85°55E **126** A7
Janaúba *Brazil* 15°48S 43°19W **189** D2
Jand *Pakistan* 33°30N 72°6E **124** C5
Jandanku ⊙ *Australia* 16°20S 135°45E **150** B2
Jandaq *Iran* 34°3N 54°22E **129** C7
Jandia *Canary Is.* 28°6N 14°21W **100** F5
Jandía, Pta. de
Canary Is. 28°3N 14°31W **100** F5
Jandia △ *Canary Is.* 28°4N 14°19W **100** F5
Jandola *Pakistan* 32°20N 70°9E **124** C4
Jandowae *Australia* 26°45S 151°7E **151** D5
Jándula ➜ *Spain* 38°3N 4°6W **89** G6
Jane Pk. *N.Z.* 45°15S 168°20E **155** F3
Janesville *U.S.A.* 42°41N 89°1W **172** D9
Jang Bogo *Antarctica* 74°37S 164°12E **55** D11
Janga *Ghana* 10°5N 1°0W **139** C4
Jangamo *Mozam.* 24°6S 35°21E **145** B6
Janghai *India* 25°33N 82°19E **125** G10
Jangheung *S. Korea* 34°41N 126°52E **115** G14
Jangipur *India* 24°28N 88°4E **125** G12
Jangoon *India* 17°44N 79°5E **126** F4
Janikowo *Poland* 52°45N 18°7E **83** F5
Janja *Bos.-H.* 44°40N 19°14E **80** F4
Janjanbureh *Gambia* 13°30N 14°47W **138** C2
Janjevë *Kosovo* 42°35N 21°19E **96** D5
Janjgir *India* 22°1N 82°34E **125** J10
Janjina *Croatia* 42°58N 17°25E **93** F14
Janos *Mexico* 30°54N 108°10W **180** A3
Jánoshalma *Hungary* 46°18N 19°21E **80** D4
Jánosháza *Hungary* 47°8N 17°12E **80** C2
Jánossomorja *Hungary* 47°47N 17°11E **80** C2
Janów *Poland* 50°44N 19°27E **83** H6
Janów Lubelski *Poland* 50°48N 22°23E **83** H9
Janów Podlaski *Poland* 52°11N 23°11E **83** F10
Janowiec Wielkopolski
Poland 52°45N 17°30E **83** F4
Januária *Brazil* 15°25S 44°25W **189** D2
Janūb Sīnī □ *Egypt* 29°30N 33°50E **130** F2
Janubio *Canary Is.* 28°56N 13°50W **100** F6
Janville *France* 48°10N 1°50E **71** D8
Janwada *India* 18°0N 77°29E **126** E3
Janzé *France* 47°55N 1°28W **70** E5
Jaora *India* 23°40N 75°10E **124** H6
Japan ■ *Asia* 36°0N 136°0E **113** G8
Japan, Sea of *Asia* 40°0N 135°0E **112** E7
Japan Trench *Pac. Oc.* 32°0N 142°0E **156** D6
Japen = Yapen *Indonesia* 1°50S 136°0E **119** E9
Japiim *Brazil* 7°37S 72°54W **188** B3
Japla *India* 24°33N 84°1E **125** G11
Japurá ➜ *Brazil* 3°8S 65°46W **186** D5
Jaquarão *Brazil* 32°34S 53°23W **191** C5
Jaqué *Panama* 7°27N 78°8W **182** E4
Jarābulus *Syria* 36°49N 38°1E **105** D8
Jaraguá do Sul *Brazil* 26°29S 49°4W **191** B6
Jaraicejo *Spain* 39°40N 5°49W **89** F5
Jaraíz de la Vera *Spain* 40°4N 5°45W **88** E5
Jarama ➜ *Spain* 40°24N 3°32W **88** E7
Jaramānah *Syria* 33°29N 36°21E **104** F7
Jaramillo *Argentina* 47°10S 67°7W **192** C3
Jarandilla de la Vera *Spain* 40°8N 5°39W **88** E5
Jaranwala *Pakistan* 31°15N 73°26E **124** D5
Jarash *Jordan* 32°17N 35°54E **130** C4
Jarash □ *Jordan* 32°17N 35°54E **130** C4
Järbo *Sweden* 60°43N 16°36E **62** D10
Jardim *Brazil* 21°28S 56°2W **190** A4
Jardín ➜ *Spain* 38°50N 2°10W **91** G2
Jardín América
Argentina 27°3S 55°14W **191** B4
Jardine River △
Australia 11°9S 142°21E **150** A3
Jardines de la Reina, Arch. de los
Cuba 20°50N 78°50W **182** B4
Jargalang *China* 43°5N 122°55E **115** C12
Jari ➜ *Brazil* 1°9S 51°54W **187** D8
Jarīr, W. al ➜
Si. Arabia 25°38N 42°30E **128** E4
Järlåsa *Sweden* 59°53N 17°12E **62** E11
Jarmen *Germany* 53°54N 13°20E **76** B9
Järna *Sweden* 59°6N 17°34E **62** E11
Jarnac *France* 45°40N 0°11W **72** C3
Jarny *France* 49°9N 5°53E **71** C12
Jarocin *Poland* 51°59N 17°29E **83** G4
Jaroměř *Czechia* 50°22N 15°52E **78** A8
Jarosław *Poland* 50°2N 22°42E **83** H9
Järpås *Sweden* 58°23N 12°57E **63** F6
Järpen *Sweden* 63°21N 13°26E **62** A7
Jarrahdale *Australia* 32°24S 116°5E **149** F2
Jarrahi ➜ *Iran* 30°49N 48°48E **129** D6
Jartai *China* 39°45N 105°48E **114** E3
Jarud Qi *China* 44°28N 120°50E **115** B11
Järvenpää *Finland* 60°29N 25°5E **84** B3
Jarvis *Canada* 42°53N 80°6W **174** D4
Jarvis I. *Pac. Oc.* 0°15S 160°5W **157** H11
Jarvorník *Czechia* 50°23N 17°2E **79** A10
Järvsö *Sweden* 61°43N 16°10E **62** C10
Jarwa *India* 27°38N 82°30E **125** F10
Jaša Tomić *Serbia* 45°26N 20°50E **80** E5
Jasdan *India* 22°2N 71°12E **124** H4
Jashpurnagar *India* 22°54N 84°9E **125** H11
Jasidih *India* 24°31N 86°39E **125** G12
Jasień *Poland* 51°46N 15°0E **83** G2
Jāsimīyah *Iraq* 33°45N 44°41E **105** F11
Jasin *Malaysia* 2°20N 102°26E **121** L4
Jāsk *Iran* 25°38N 57°45E **129** E8
Jasliq *Uzbekistan* 43°58N 57°10E **108** D5
Jasło *Poland* 49°45N 21°30E **83** J8
Jasmund *Germany* 54°32N 13°35E **76** A9
Jasmund △ *Germany* 54°31N 13°38E **76** A9
Jaso *India* 24°30N 80°29E **125** G9
Jason Is. *Falk. Is.* 51°0S 61°0W **192** D4
Jasper *Alta., Canada* 52°55N 118°5W **162** C5
Jasper *Ont., Canada* 44°52N 75°57W **175** B9
Jasper *Ala., U.S.A.* 33°50N 87°17W **177** E11
Jasper *Fla., U.S.A.* 30°31N 82°57W **178** E7
Jasper *Ind., U.S.A.* 38°24N 86°56W **172** F10
Jasper *Tex., U.S.A.* 30°56N 94°1W **176** F7
Jasper △ *Canada* 52°50N 118°8W **162** C5
Jasrasar *India* 27°43N 73°49E **124** F5
Jassān *Iraq* 32°58N 45°52E **105** G11
Jastarnia *Poland* 54°42N 18°40E **82** D5
Jastrebarsko *Croatia* 45°41N 15°39E **93** C12
Jastrowie *Poland* 53°26N 16°49E **82** E3
Jastrzębie Zdrój *Poland* 49°57N 18°35E **83** J5
Jász-Nagykun-Szolnok □
Hungary 47°15N 20°30E **80** C5
Jászapáti *Hungary* 47°32N 20°10E **80** C5
Jászárokszállás *Hungary* 47°39N 19°58E **80** C4
Jászberény *Hungary* 47°30N 19°55E **80** C4
Jászkisér *Hungary* 47°27N 20°20E **80** C5
Jászladány *Hungary* 47°23N 20°10E **80** C5
Jataí *Brazil* 17°58S 51°48W **187** G8
Jath *India* 17°3N 75°13E **126** F2
Jati *Pakistan* 24°20N 68°19E **124** G3
Jatibarang *Indonesia* 6°28S 108°18E **119** G13
Jatiluwih *Indonesia* 8°23S 115°8E **119** J18
Jatinegara *Indonesia* 6°13S 106°52E **119** G12
Játiva = Xàtiva *Spain* 38°59N 0°32W **91** G4
Jättendal *Sweden* 61°58N 17°15E **62** C11
Jaú *Brazil* 22°10S 48°30W **191** A6
Jauja *Peru* 11°45S 75°15W **188** C2
Jaunpur *India* 25°46N 82°44E **125** G10
Java = Jawa *Indonesia* 7°0S 110°0E **118** F3
Java Sea *Indonesia* 4°35S 107°15E **118** E3
Java Trench *Ind. Oc.* 9°0S 105°0E **118** F3
Javadi Hills *India* 12°40N 78°40E **127** H4
Javalambre, Sa. de *Spain* 40°6N 1°0W **90** E4
Javānrud *Iran* 34°47N 46°31E **105** E12
Jávea *Spain* 38°48N 0°10E **91** G5
Javier, I. *Chile* 47°5S 74°25W **192** C2
Javla *India* 17°18N 75°9E **126** F2
Jawa *Indonesia* 7°0S 110°0E **118** F3
Jawa Barat □ *Indonesia* 7°0S 107°0E **119** G12
Jawa Tengah □
Indonesia 7°0S 110°0E **119** G14
Jawa Timur □ *Indonesia* 8°0S 113°0E **119** G15
Jawad *India* 24°36N 74°51E **124** G6
Jawhar *India* 19°55N 73°14E **126** E1
Jawhar *Somalia* 2°48N 45°30E **131** G4
Jawor *Poland* 51°4N 16°11E **83** G3
Jaworzno *Poland* 50°13N 19°11E **83** H6
Jaworzyna Śląska
Poland 50°55N 16°28E **83** H3
Jawoyn ⊙ *Australia* 14°16S 132°28E **148** B5
Jay *U.S.A.* 30°57N 87°9W **179** E2
Jay Peak *U.S.A.* 44°55N 72°32W **175** B12
Jaya, Puncak *Indonesia* 3°57S 137°17E **119** E9
Jayanca *Peru* 6°24S 79°50W **188** B2
Jayanti *India* 26°45N 89°40E **123** F16
Jayapura *Indonesia* 2°28S 140°38E **119** E10
Jayawijaya, Pegunungan
Indonesia 5°0S 139°0E **119** F9
Jaynagar *India* 26°43N 86°9E **125** F12
Jaypur = Jeypore *India* 18°50N 82°38E **126** E6
Jayrūd *Syria* 33°49N 36°44E **104** F7
Jayton *U.S.A.* 33°15N 100°34W **176** E4
Jāz Mūrīān, Hāmūn-e
Iran 27°20N 58°55E **129** E8
Jazīreh-ye Shīf *Iran* 29°4N 50°54E **129** D6
Jazminal *Mexico* 24°52N 101°24W **180** C4
Jazzīn *Lebanon* 33°31N 35°35E **130** B4
Jean *U.S.A.* 35°47N 115°20W **171** K11
Jean Marie River
Canada 61°32N 120°38W **162** A4
Jean-Rabel *Haiti* 19°50N 73°5W **183** C5
Jeanerette *U.S.A.* 29°55N 91°40W **176** G9
Jeannette, Ostrov = Zhannetty,
Ostrov *Russia* 76°43N 158°0E **107** B16
Jeannette *U.S.A.* 40°20N 79°36W **174** F5
Jebāl Bārez, Kūh-e *Iran* 28°30N 58°20E **129** D8
Jebba *Nigeria* 9°9N 4°48E **139** D5
Jebel, Bahr el ➜
South Sudan 9°30N 30°25E **135** G12
Jebel Ali = Minā' Jabal 'Alī
U.A.E. 25°2N 55°8E **129** E7
Jebel Elba △ *Egypt* 22°11N 36°22E **137** C4
Jeberos *Peru* 5°15S 76°10W **188** B2
Jecheon *S. Korea* 37°8N 128°12E **115** F15
Jedburgh *U.K.* 55°29N 2°33W **65** F6
Jedda = Jiddah
Si. Arabia 21°29N 39°10E **131** C2
Jeddore L. *Canada* 48°3N 55°55W **165** C8
Jedlicze *Poland* 49°43N 21°40E **83** J8
Jędrzejów *Poland* 50°35N 20°15E **83** H7
Jedwabne *Poland* 53°17N 22°18E **82** E9
Jeetzel ➜ *Germany* 53°9N 11°3E **76** B7
Jefferson *Ga., U.S.A.* 34°7N 83°35W **178** A6
Jefferson *Iowa, U.S.A.* 42°1N 94°23W **172** D6
Jefferson *Ohio, U.S.A.* 41°44N 80°46W **174** E4
Jefferson *Tex., U.S.A.* 32°46N 94°21W **176** E7
Jefferson, Mt. *Nev.,*
U.S.A. 38°47N 116°56W **168** G5
Jefferson, Mt. *Oreg.,*
U.S.A. 44°41N 121°48W **168** D3
Jefferson City *Mo.,*
U.S.A. 38°34N 92°10W **172** F7
Jefferson City *Tenn.,*
U.S.A. 36°7N 83°30W **177** C13
Jeffersontown *U.S.A.* 38°12N 85°35W **173** F11
Jeffersonville *Ga.,*
U.S.A. 32°41N 83°20W **178** C6
Jeffersonville *Ind.,*
U.S.A. 38°17N 85°44W **173** F11
Jeffrey City *U.S.A.* 42°30N 107°49W **168** E10
Jega *Nigeria* 12°15N 4°23E **139** C5
Jeju *S. Korea* 33°31N 126°32E **115** H14
Jeju-do *S. Korea* 33°29N 126°34E **115** H14
Jeju Haehyop
S. Korea 33°50N 126°30E **115** H14
Jēkabpils *Latvia* 56°29N 25°57E **84** D3
Jekyll I. *U.S.A.* 31°4N 81°25W **178** D8
Jelcz-Laskowice *Poland* 51°2N 17°19E **83** G4
Jelenia Góra *Poland* 50°50N 15°45E **83** H2
Jelgava *Latvia* 56°41N 23°49E **82** B10
Jelica *Serbia* 43°50N 20°17E **96** C4
Jelšava *Slovakia* 48°37N 20°15E **79** C13
Jemaluang *Malaysia* 2°16N 103°52E **121** L4
Jember *Indonesia* 8°11S 113°41E **119** H15
Jena *Germany* 50°54N 11°35E **76** E7
Jena *U.S.A.* 31°41N 92°8W **176** F8
Jenbach *Austria* 47°24N 11°47E **78** D4
Jendouba *Tunisia* 36°29N 8°47E **136** A5
Jendouba □ *Tunisia* 36°34N 8°52E **136** A5
Jengish Chokusu = Pobedy, Pik
Asia 42°0N 79°58E **109** D9
Jenīn *West Bank* 32°28N 35°18E **130** C4
Jenkins *U.S.A.* 37°10N 82°38W **173** G12
Jenner *U.S.A.* 38°27N 123°7W **170** G3
Jennings *Fla., U.S.A.* 30°36N 83°6W **178** E6
Jennings *La., U.S.A.* 30°13N 92°40W **176** F8
Jensen Beach *U.S.A.* 27°15N 80°14W **179** H9
Jeong-eup *S. Korea* 35°35N 126°50E **115** G14
Jeongseon *S. Korea* 37°20N 128°45E **115** F15
Jeonju *S. Korea* 35°50N 127°4E **115** G14
Jepara *Indonesia* 7°40S 109°14E **119** G14
Jeparit *Australia* 36°8S 142°1E **152** D5
Jequié *Brazil* 13°51S 40°5W **189** C2
Jequitaí ➜ *Brazil* 17°4S 44°50W **189** D2
Jequitinhonha *Brazil* 16°30S 41°0W **189** D2
Jequitinhonha ➜
Brazil 15°51S 38°53W **189** D3
Jerada *Morocco* 34°17N 2°10W **136** B3
Jerantut *Malaysia* 3°56N 102°22E **121** L4
Jerejak, Pulau *Malaysia* 5°19N 100°19E **121** c
Jérémie *Haiti* 18°40N 74°10W **183** C5
Jeremoabo *Brazil* 10°4S 38°21W **189** C3
Jerez, Pta. *Mexico* 22°58N 97°40W **181** C5
Jerez de García Salinas
Mexico 22°39N 103°0W **180** C4
Jerez de la Frontera *Spain* 36°41N 6°7W **89** J4
Jerez de los Caballeros
Spain 38°20N 6°45W **89** G4
Jericho = El Arīḥā
West Bank 31°52N 35°27E **130** D4
Jericho *Australia* 23°38S 146°6E **150** C4
Jerichow *Germany* 52°30N 12°1E **76** C8
Jerid, Chott el = Djerid, Chott
Tunisia 33°42N 8°30E **136** B5
Jerilderie *Australia* 35°20S 145°41E **153** C6
Jermyn *U.S.A.* 41°32N 75°33W **175** E9
Jerome *U.S.A.* 42°44N 114°31W **168** E6
Jerramungup *Australia* 33°55S 118°55E **149** F2
Jersey *U.K.* 49°11N 2°7W **67** H5
Jersey City *U.S.A.* 40°42N 74°4W **175** F10
Jersey Shore *U.S.A.* 41°12N 77°15W **174** E7
Jerseyville *U.S.A.* 39°7N 90°20W **172** F8
Jerumenha *Brazil* 7°5S 43°30W **189** B2
Jerusalem
Israel/West Bank 31°47N 35°10E **130** D4
Jervis B. *Australia* 35°8S 150°46E **153** C9
Jervis Bay △ *Australia* 35°9S 150°40E **153** C9
Jervis Inlet *Canada* 50°0N 123°57W **162** C4
Jerzu *Italy* 39°47N 9°31E **94** C2
Jesenice *Slovenia* 46°28N 14°3E **93** B11
Jeseník *Czechia* 50°14N 17°8E **79** A10
Jesenké *Slovakia* 48°20N 20°10E **79** C13
Jesi = Iesi *Italy* 43°31N 13°14E **93** E10
Jésolo *Italy* 45°32N 12°38E **93** C9
Jessnitz *Germany* 51°40N 12°18E **76** D8
Jessore *Bangla.* 23°10N 89°10E **123** H16
Jesup *U.S.A.* 31°36N 81°53W **178** D8
Jesup, L. *U.S.A.* 28°43N 81°14W **179** G8
Jesús *Peru* 7°15S 78°25W **188** B2
Jesús Carranza *Mexico* 17°26N 95°2W **181** D5
Jesús María *Argentina* 30°59S 64°5W **190** C3
Jetmore *U.S.A.* 38°4N 99°54W **172** F4
Jetpur *India* 21°45N 70°10E **124** J4
Jeumont *France* 50°18N 4°6E **71** B11
Jevnaker *Norway* 60°15N 10°26E **61** F14
Jewett *U.S.A.* 40°22N 81°2W **174** F3
Jewett City *U.S.A.* 41°36N 71°59W **175** E13
Jeyhūnābād *Iran* 34°58N 48°59E **129** C6
Jeypore *India* 18°50N 82°38E **126** E6
Jeziorak, Jezioro *Poland* 53°40N 19°35E **82** E6
Jeziorany *Poland* 53°58N 20°46E **82** E7
Jeziorka ➜ *Poland* 52°8N 21°9E **83** F8
Jha Jha *India* 24°46N 86°22E **125** G12
Jhaarkand = Jharkhand □
India 24°0N 85°50E **125** H11
Jhabua *India* 22°46N 74°36E **124** H6
Jhajjar *India* 28°37N 76°42E **124** E7
Jhal *Pakistan* 28°17N 67°27E **124** E2
Jhal Jhao *Pakistan* 26°20N 65°35E **122** F4
Jhalawar *India* 24°40N 76°10E **124** G7
Jhalida *India* 23°22N 85°58E **125** H11
Jhalrapatan *India* 24°33N 76°10E **124** G7
Jhang Maghiana
Pakistan 31°15N 72°22E **124** D5
Jhang Sadr = Jhang Maghiana
Pakistan 31°15N 72°22E **124** D5
Jhansi *India* 25°30N 78°36E **125** G8
Jhargram *India* 22°27N 86°59E **125** H12
Jharia *India* 23°45N 86°26E **125** H12
Jharkhand □ *India* 24°0N 85°50E **125** H11
Jharsuguda *India* 21°56N 84°5E **126** D7
Jhelum *Pakistan* 33°0N 73°45E **124** C5
Jhelum ➜ *Pakistan* 31°20N 72°10E **124** D5
Jhilmilli *India* 23°24N 82°51E **125** H10
Jhudo *Pakistan* 24°58N 69°18E **124** G3
Jhunjhunun *India* 28°10N 75°30E **124** E6
Ji-Paraná *Brazil* 10°52S 62°57W **186** F6
Ji Xian *China* 36°7N 110°40E **114** F6
Jia Xian *Henan, China* 33°59N 113°12E **114** H7
Jia Xian *Shaanxi, China* 38°12N 110°28E **114** E6
Jiahe *China* 25°38N 112°19E **117** E9
Jiaji = Qionghai *China* 19°15N 110°26E **117** a
Jialing Jiang ➜ *China* 29°30N 106°20E **116** C6
Jiamusi *China* 46°40N 130°26E **111** B15
Ji'an *Jiangxi, China* 27°6N 114°59E **117** D10
Ji'an *Jilin, China* 41°5N 126°10E **115** D14
Jianchang *China* 40°55N 120°35E **115** D11
Jianchuan *China* 26°38N 99°55E **116** D2
Jiande *China* 29°23N 119°15E **117** C12
Jiang'an *China* 28°40N 105°3E **116** C5
Jiangbei *China* 29°40N 106°34E **116** C6
Jiangcheng *China* 22°36N 101°52E **116** F3
Jiangchuan *China* 24°8N 102°39E **116** E4
Jiangdi *China* 26°57N 103°37E **116** D4
Jiangdu *China* 32°27N 119°36E **117** A12
Jiange *China* 32°4N 105°32E **116** A5
Jianghua *China* 25°0N 111°47E **117** E8
Jiangjin *China* 29°14N 106°14E **116** C6
Jiangkou *China* 27°40N 108°49E **116** D7
Jiangle *China* 26°42N 117°23E **117** D11
Jiangmen *China* 22°32N 113°0E **117** F9
Jiangning *China* 31°55N 118°50E **117** B12
Jiangshan *China* 28°40N 118°37E **117** C12
Jiangsu □ *China* 33°0N 120°0E **115** H11
Jiangxi □ *China* 27°30N 116°0E **117** D11
Jiangyan *China* 32°30N 120°7E **117** A13
Jiangyin *China* 31°54N 120°17E **117** B13
Jiangyong *China* 25°20N 111°22E **117** E8
Jiangyou *China* 31°44N 104°43E **116** B5
Jianhe *China* 26°37N 108°31E **116** D7
Jianli *China* 29°46N 112°56E **117** C9
Jianning *China* 26°50N 116°50E **117** D11
Jian'ou *China* 27°3N 118°17E **117** D12
Jianping *China* 41°53N 119°42E **115** D10
Jianshi *China* 30°37N 109°38E **116** B7
Jianshui *China* 23°36N 102°43E **116** F4
Jianyang *Fujian, China* 27°20N 118°5E **117** D12
Jianyang *Sichuan,*
China 30°24N 104°33E **116** B5
Jiao Xian = Jiaozhou
China 36°18N 120°1E **115** F11
Jiaohe *Hebei, China* 38°2N 116°20E **114** E9
Jiaohe *Jilin, China* 43°40N 127°22E **115** C14
Jiaoling *China* 24°41N 116°12E **117** E11
Jiaonan *China* 35°52N 119°58E **115** G10
Jiaozhou *China* 36°18N 120°1E **115** F11
Jiaozhou Wan *China* 36°5N 120°10E **115** F11
Jiaozuo *China* 35°16N 113°12E **114** G7
Jiawang *China* 34°28N 117°26E **115** G9
Jiaxiang *China* 35°25N 116°20E **114** G9
Jiaxing *China* 30°49N 120°45E **117** B13
Jiayu *China* 29°55N 113°55E **117** C9
Jiayuguan *China* 39°49N 98°18E **110** D8
Jibão, Serra do *Brazil* 14°48S 45°0W **189** C2
Jibiya *Nigeria* 13°5N 7°12E **139** C6
Jibou *Romania* 47°15N 23°17E **81** C8
Jibuti = Djibouti ■ *Africa* 12°0N 43°0E **131** E3
Jicarón, I. *Panama* 7°10N 81°50W **182** E3
Jičín *Czechia* 50°25N 15°28E **78** A8
Jiddah *Si. Arabia* 21°29N 39°10E **131** C2
Jido *India* 29°2N 94°58E **123** E19
Jieshou *China* 33°18N 115°22E **114** H8
Jiexiu *China* 37°2N 111°55E **114** F6
Jieyang *China* 23°35N 116°21E **117** F11
Jigalong *Australia* 23°21S 120°47E **148** D3
Jigalong ⊙ *Australia* 23°21S 120°46E **148** D3
Jigawa □ *Nigeria* 12°0N 9°45E **139** C6
Jigni *India* 25°45N 79°25E **125** G8
Jihlava *Czechia* 49°28N 15°35E **78** B8
Jihlava ➜ *Czechia* 48°55N 16°36E **79** C9
Jihočeský □ *Czechia* 49°8N 14°35E **78** B7
Jihomoravský □ *Czechia* 49°5N 16°30E **79** B9
Jijel *Algeria* 36°52N 5°50E **136** A5
Jijel □ *Algeria* 36°45N 6°0E **136** A5
Jijiga *Ethiopia* 9°20N 42°50E **131** F3
Jikamshi *Nigeria* 12°12N 7°45E **139** C6
Jilib *Somalia* 0°29N 42°46E **131** G3
Jilin *China* 43°44N 126°30E **115** C14
Jilin □ *China* 44°0N 127°0E **115** C14
Jiloca ➜ *Spain* 41°21N 1°39W **90** D3
Jim Thorpe *U.S.A.* 40°52N 75°44W **175** F9
Jima *Ethiopia* 7°40N 36°47E **131** F2
Jimbaran, Teluk
Indonesia 8°46S 115°9E **119** K18
Jimbolia *Romania* 45°47N 20°43E **80** E5
Jimena de la Frontera
Spain 36°27N 5°24W **89** J5
Jiménez *Mexico* 27°8N 104°54W **180** B4
Jimeta *Nigeria* 9°17N 12°28E **139** D7
Jimo *China* 36°23N 120°30E **115** F11
Jimsar *China* 43°59N 89°4E **109** D11
Jin Jiang ➜ *China* 28°24N 115°48E **117** C10
Jin Xian = Jinzhou
China 38°55N 121°42E **115** E11
Jinan *China* 36°38N 117°1E **114** F9
Jinchang *China* 38°30N 102°10E **110** D9
Jincheng *China* 35°29N 112°50E **114** G7
Jinchuan *China* 31°30N 102°3E **116** B4
Jind *India* 29°19N 76°22E **124** E7
Jindabyne *Australia* 36°25S 148°35E **153** D8
Jinding *China* 22°22N 113°33E **111** a
Jindo *S. Korea* 34°28N 126°15E **115** G14
Jindřichův Hradec
Czechia 49°10N 15°2E **78** B8
Jing He ➜ *China* 34°27N 109°4E **114** G5
Jing Shan *China* 31°20N 111°35E **117** B8
Jing Xian *China* 30°38N 118°25E **117** B12
Jing'an *China* 28°50N 115°17E **117** C10
Jingbian *China* 37°20N 108°30E **114** F5
Jingchuan *China* 35°20N 107°20E **114** G4
Jingde *China* 30°15N 118°27E **117** B12
Jingdezhen *China* 29°20N 117°11E **117** C11
Jingdong *China* 24°23N 100°47E **116** E3
Jinggangshan *China* 26°58N 114°15E **117** D10
Jinggu *China* 23°35N 100°41E **116** F3
Jinghai *Guangdong,*
China 22°59N 116°31E **117** F11
Jinghai *Tianjin, China* 38°55N 116°55E **114** E9
Jinghong *China* 22°0N 100°45E **116** G3
Jinghong Dam *China* 22°10N 100°46E **116** F3
Jingjiang *China* 32°2N 120°16E **117** A13
Jingle *China* 38°20N 111°55E **114** E6
Jingmen *China* 31°0N 112°10E **117** B9
Jingning *China* 35°30N 105°43E **114** G3
Jingpo Hu *China* 43°55N 128°55E **115** C15
Jingshan *China* 31°1N 113°7E **117** B9
Jingtai *China* 37°10N 104°6E **114** F3
Jingtang *China* 39°10N 119°5E **115** E10
Jingxi *China* 23°8N 106°27E **116** F6
Jingyang *China* 34°30N 108°50E **114** G5
Jingyu *China* 42°25N 126°45E **115** C14
Jingyuan *China* 36°30N 104°40E **114** F3
Jingzhou *Hubei, China* 30°21N 112°11E **117** B9
Jingzhou *Hunan, China* 26°33N 109°40E **116** D7
Jingziguan *China* 33°15N 111°0E **114** H6
Jinhua *China* 29°8N 119°38E **117** C12
Jining *Nei Monggol Zizhiqu,*
China 41°5N 113°0E **114** D7
Jining *Shandong, China* 35°22N 116°34E **114** G9
Jinja *Uganda* 0°25N 33°12E **142** B3
Jinjang *Malaysia* 3°13N 101°39E **121** L3
Jinji *China* 37°58N 106°8E **114** F4
Jinjiang *Fujian, China* 24°43N 118°33E **117** E12
Jinjiang *Yunnan, China* 26°14N 100°34E **116** D3
Jinjini *Ghana* 7°26N 2°42W **138** D4
Jinju *S. Korea* 35°12N 128°2E **115** G15
Jinkou *China* 30°20N 114°8E **117** B10
Jinkouhe *China* 29°18N 103°4E **116** C4
Jinmu Jiao *China* 18°9N 109°34E **117** a

Jinnah Barrage
  Pakistan 32°58N 71°33E 124 C4
Jinning China 24°38N 102°38E 116 E4
Jinotega Nic. 13°6N 85°59W 182 D2
Jinotepe Nic. 11°50N 86°10W 182 D2
Jinping Guizhou, China 26°41N 109°10E 116 D7
Jinping Yunnan, China 22°45N 103°18E 116 F4
Jinping Bend Dams
  China 28°1N 101°39E 116 C3
Jinsha China 27°29N 106°12E 116 D6
Jinsha Jiang → China 28°50N 104°36E 116 C5
Jinshi China 29°40N 111°50E 117 C9
Jintan China 31°42N 119°36E 117 B12
Jintur India 19°37N 76°42E 126 E3
Jinxi Jiangxi, China 27°56N 116°45E 117 D11
Jinxi Liaoning, China 40°52N 120°50E 115 D11
Jinxian China 28°26N 116°17E 117 C11
Jinxiang China 35°5N 116°22E 114 G9
Jinyang China 27°28N 103°5E 116 D4
Jinyun China 28°35N 120°5E 117 C13
Jinzhai China 31°40N 115°53E 117 B10
Jinzhong China 37°42N 112°46E 114 F7
Jinzhou Liaoning,
  China 38°55N 121°42E 115 E11
Jinzhou Liaoning, China 41°5N 121°3E 115 D11
Jiparaná Brazil 8°3S 62°52W 186 E6
Jipijapa Ecuador 1°0S 80°40W 186 D2
Jiquilpan Mexico 19°59N 102°43W 180 D4
Jirisan S. Korea 35°20N 127°44E 115 G14
Jiroft Iran 28°45N 57°50E 129 D8
Jishan China 35°34N 110°58E 114 G6
Jishou China 28°21N 109°43E 116 C7
Jishui China 27°13N 115°9E 117 D10
Jisr ash Shughūr Syria 35°49N 36°18E 104 E7
Jitarning Australia 32°48S 117°57E 149 F2
Jitra Malaysia 6°16N 100°25E 121 J3
Jiu → Romania 43°47N 23°48E 81 G8
Jiudengkou China 39°56N 106°40E 114 E4
Jiujiang Guangdong,
  China 22°50N 113°0E 117 F9
Jiujiang Jiangxi, China 29°42N 115°58E 117 C10
Jiuling Shan China 28°40N 114°40E 117 C10
Jiulong = Kowloon
  China 22°19N 114°11E 117 F10
Jiulong China 28°57N 101°31E 116 C3
Jiuquan China 39°50N 98°20E 110 D8
Jiutai China 44°10N 125°50E 115 B13
Jiuxincheng China 39°17N 115°59E 114 E8
Jiuzhaigou △ China 33°8N 103°52E 116 A4
Jiwani Pakistan 25°1N 61°44E 122 G2
Jixi Anhui, China 30°18N 118°34E 117 B12
Jixi Heilongjiang, China 45°20N 130°50E 115 B16
Jiyang China 37°0N 117°12E 115 F9
Jiyuan China 35°7N 112°57E 114 G7
Jīzān Si. Arabia 17°0N 42°20E 131 D3
Jize China 36°54N 114°54E 114 F8
Jizera → Czechia 50°10N 14°43E 78 A7
Jizhou China 37°35N 115°0E 114 F8
Jizl, Wādī al →
  Si. Arabia 25°39N 38°25E 128 E3
Jizō-Zaki Japan 35°34N 133°20E 113 G6
Jizzax Uzbekistan 40°6N 67°50E 108 E7
Jizzax □ Uzbekistan 40°20N 67°40E 109 D7
Joaçaba Brazil 27°5S 51°31W 191 B5
Joaima Brazil 16°39S 41°2W 189 D7
Joal Fadiout Senegal 14°9N 16°50W 138 C1
João Amaro Brazil 12°46S 40°22W 189 C2
João Câmara Brazil 5°32S 35°48W 189 B3
João Neiva Brazil 19°45S 40°24W 189 D2
João Pessoa Brazil 7°10S 34°52W 189 B4
João Pinheiro Brazil 17°45S 46°10W 189 C1
Joaquín V. González
  Argentina 25°10S 64°0W 190 B3
Jobat India 22°25N 74°34E 124 H6
Jobourg, Nez de France 49°41N 1°57W 70 C5
Jódar Spain 37°50N 3°21W 89 H7
Jodhpur India 26°23N 73°8E 124 F5
Jodiya India 22°42N 70°18E 124 H4
Joensuu Finland 62°37N 29°49E 60 E23
Jõetsu Japan 37°12N 138°10E 113 F9
Jœuf France 49°12N 6°0E 71 C12
Jofane Mozam. 21°15S 34°18E 145 B5
Jog Falls = Gersoppa Falls
  India 14°12N 74°46E 127 G2
Jogbani India 26°25N 87°15E 125 F12
Jõgeva Estonia 58°45N 26°24E 84 C4
Jogjakarta = Yogyakarta
  Indonesia 7°49S 110°22E 118 F4
Johannesburg S. Africa 26°11S 28°2E 145 D4
Johannesburg U.S.A. 35°22N 117°38W 171 K9
Johansfors Sweden 56°42N 15°32E 63 H9
Johilla → India 23°37N 81°14E 125 H9
John Crow Mts. Jamaica 18°5N 76°25W 182 a
John Day U.S.A. 44°25N 118°57W 168 D4
John Day → U.S.A. 45°44N 120°39W 168 D3
John Day Fossil Beds △
  U.S.A. 44°33N 119°38W 168 D4
John D'or Prairie
  Canada 58°30N 115°8W 162 B5
John F. Kennedy Space Center
  U.S.A. 28°40N 80°42W 179 G9
John H. Kerr Res.
  U.S.A. 36°36N 78°18W 177 C15
John o' Groats U.K. 58°38N 3°4W 65 C5
Johnnie U.S.A. 36°25N 116°5W 171 J10
Johns Creek U.S.A. 34°2N 84°12W 178 A5
Johns I. U.S.A. 32°47N 80°7W 178 C8
John's Ra. Australia 21°55S 133°23E 150 C1
Johnson U.S.A. 44°38N 72°41W 175 B12
Johnson City Kans.,
  U.S.A. 37°34N 101°45W 172 G3
Johnson City N.Y.,
  U.S.A. 42°7N 75°58W 175 D9
Johnson City Tenn.,
  U.S.A. 36°19N 82°21W 177 C13
Johnson City Tex.,
  U.S.A. 30°17N 98°25W 176 F5
Johnsonburg U.S.A. 41°29N 78°41W 174 E6
Johnsondale U.S.A. 35°58N 118°32W 171 K8
Johnsons Crossing
  Canada 60°29N 133°18W 162 A2
Johnsonville N.Z. 41°13S 174°48E 154 H3
Johnston U.S.A. 30°50N 81°48W 178 B2
Johnston, L. Australia 32°25S 120°30E 149 F3
Johnston Atoll
  Pac. Oc. 17°10N 169°8W 157 F11
Johnston Falls = Mambilima Falls
  Zambia 10°31S 28°45E 143 E2
Johnstone Str. Canada 50°28N 126°0W 162 C3
Johnstown Ireland 52°45N 7°33W 64 D4
Johnstown N.Y.,
  U.S.A. 43°0N 74°22W 175 C10

Johnstown Ohio, U.S.A. 40°9N 82°41W 174 F2
Johnstown Pa., U.S.A. 40°20N 78°55W 174 F6
Johor □ Malaysia 2°5N 103°20E 121 M4
Johor, Selat Asia 1°28N 103°47E 121 d
Johor Bahru Malaysia 1°28N 103°46E 121 d
Johor Port Malaysia 1°26N 103°53E 121 d
Jõhvi Estonia 59°22N 27°27E 84 C4
Joigny France 47°58N 3°20E 71 E10
Joinville Brazil 26°15S 48°55W 191 B6
Joinville France 48°27N 5°10E 71 D12
Joinville I. Antarctica 65°0S 55°30W 5 C18
Jojutla Mexico 18°37N 99°11W 181 D5
Jokkmokk Sweden 66°35N 19°50E 60 C18
Jökulsá á Bru →
  Iceland 65°40N 14°16W 60 D6
Jökulsá á Fjöllum →
  Iceland 66°10N 16°30W 60 C5
Jolfa Āzarbājān-e Sharqī,
  Iran 38°57N 45°38E 105 C11
Jolfa Eşfahan, Iran 32°58N 51°37E 129 C6
Joliet U.S.A. 41°32N 88°5W 172 E9
Joliette Canada 46°3N 73°24W 164 C5
Jolo Phil. 6°0N 121°0E 119 C6
Jolon U.S.A. 35°58N 121°9W 170 K5
Jombang Indonesia 7°33S 112°14E 119 G15
Jomda China 31°28N 98°12E 116 B2
Jonåker Sweden 58°45N 16°45E 63 F10
Jonava Lithuania 55°8N 24°12E 84 E3
Jones Sound Canada 76°0N 85°0W 161 B15
Jonesboro Ark., U.S.A. 35°50N 90°42W 177 D9
Jonesboro Ga., U.S.A. 33°31N 84°22W 178 B5
Jonesboro La., U.S.A. 32°15N 92°43W 176 E8
Jong → S. Leone 7°32N 12°23W 138 D2
Joniškis Lithuania 56°13N 23°35E 84 D3
Jönköping Sweden 57°45N 14°8E 63 G8
Jönköping □ Sweden 57°30N 14°30E 63 G8
Jonquière Canada 48°27N 71°14W 165 C5
Jonsered Sweden 57°45N 12°10E 63 d6
Jonzac France 45°27N 0°28W 72 C3
Joplin U.S.A. 37°6N 94°31W 172 G6
Jora India 26°20N 77°49E 124 F6
Jordan Mont., U.S.A. 47°19N 106°55W 168 C10
Jordan N.Y.,
  U.S.A. 43°4N 76°29W 175 C8
Jordan ■ Asia 31°0N 36°0E 130 E5
Jordan → Asia 31°48N 35°32E 130 D4
Jordan Valley U.S.A. 42°59N 117°3W 168 E5
Jordânia Brazil 15°55S 40°1W 189 D2
Jordanów Poland 49°41N 19°49E 83 J6
Jorge, C. Chile 51°4S 75°35W 192 D1
Jørgen Bronlund Fjord
  Greenland 82°30N 31°0W 57 A7
Jorhat India 26°45N 94°12E 123 F19
Jori → Norway 62°4N 9°5E 62 B3
Jörn Sweden 65°4N 20°1E 60 D19
Jorong Indonesia 3°58S 114°56E 118 E4
Jørpeland Norway 59°3N 6°1E 61 G12
Jorquera → Chile 28°3S 69°58W 190 B2
Joru S. Leone 7°41N 11°3W 138 D2
Jos Nigeria 9°53N 8°51E 139 D6
Jos Plateau Nigeria 9°55N 9°0E 139 D6
Jošanička Banja Serbia 43°24N 20°47E 96 C4
José Batlle y Ordóñez
  Uruguay 33°20S 55°10W 191 C4
José de San Martín
  Argentina 44°4S 70°26W 192 E2
Joseni Romania 46°42N 25°29E 81 D10
Joseph, L. Canada 45°10N 79°44W 174 A5
Joseph Banks Group
  Australia 34°36S 136°16E 152 C2
Joseph Bonaparte G.
  Australia 14°35S 128°50E 148 B4
Joseph City U.S.A. 34°57N 110°20W 169 J8
Joshinath India 30°34N 79°34E 125 D8
Joshinetsu-Kōgen △
  Japan 36°42N 138°32E 113 F9
Joshua Tree U.S.A. 34°8N 116°19W 171 L10
Joshua Tree △ U.S.A. 33°55N 116°0W 171 M10
Josselin France 47°57N 2°33W 70 E4
Jost Van Dyke I.
  Br. Virgin Is. 18°29N 64°47W 183 e
Jostedalsbreen Norway 61°40N 6°59E 60 F12
Jotunheimen Norway 61°35N 8°25E 60 F13
Joubertberg Namibia 18°30S 14°0E 144 A1
Joué-lès-Tours France 47°20N 0°40E 70 E7
Jourdanton U.S.A. 28°55N 98°33W 176 G5
Joutseno Finland 61°7N 28°31E 84 B5
Jovellanos Cuba 22°40N 81°10W 182 B3
Jowkār Iran 34°25N 48°40E 105 C13
Jowzjān □ Afghan. 36°10N 66°0E 109 E17
Joyeuse France 44°29N 4°16E 73 D8
Józefów Lubelskie, Poland 50°28N 23°2E 83 H10
Józefów Mazowieckie,
  Poland 52°10N 21°11E 83 F8
Ju Xian China 35°35N 118°20E 115 G10
Juan Aldama Mexico 24°19N 103°21W 180 C4
Juan Bautista Alberdi
  Argentina 34°26S 61°48W 190 C3
Juan de Fuca, Str. of.
  N. Amer. 48°15N 124°0W 170 B3
Juan de Nova Ind. Oc. 17°3S 43°45E 145 A7
Juan Fernández, Arch. de
  Pac. Oc. 33°50S 80°0W 184 G2
Juan José Castelli
  Argentina 25°27S 60°57W 190 B3
Juan L. Lacaze
  Uruguay 34°26S 57°25W 190 C4
Juanjuí Peru 7°10S 76°45W 188 B2
Juankoski Finland 63°3N 28°19E 60 E23
Juárez Mexico 27°37N 100°44W 180 B4
Juárez, Sa. de Mexico 32°0N 115°50W 180 A1
Juàzeiro Brazil 9°30S 40°30W 189 B3
Juàzeiro do Norte Brazil 7°10S 39°18W 189 B3
Juba South Sudan 4°50N 31°35E 135 H12
Juba → Somalia 1°30N 42°35E 135 G3
Jubail = Al Jubayl
  Si. Arabia 27°0N 49°50E 129 E6
Jubany = Carlini Base
  Antarctica 62°30S 58°0W 5 C18
Jubayl Lebanon 34°5N 35°39E 130 A4
Jubbah Si. Arabia 28°2N 40°56E 128 D4
Jubbal India 31°5N 77°40E 124 D7
Jubbulpore = Jabalpur
  India 23°9N 79°58E 125 H8
Jübek Germany 54°33N 9°22E 76 A5
Jubilee L. Australia 29°0S 126°50E 149 E4
Juby, C. Morocco 28°0N 12°59W 134 C3
Júcar = Xúquer → Spain 39°5N 0°10W 91 F4
Júcaro Cuba 21°37N 78°51W 182 B4
Juchitán de Zaragoza
  Mexico 16°26N 95°1W 181 D5

Judea = Har Yehuda
  Israel 31°35N 34°57E 130 D3
Judenburg Austria 47°12N 14°38E 78 D7
Judith → U.S.A. 47°44N 109°39W 168 C9
Judith, Pt. U.S.A. 41°22N 71°29W 175 E13
Judith Gap U.S.A. 46°41N 109°45W 168 C9
Juelsminde Denmark 55°43N 10°1E 63 J4
Juigalpa Nic. 12°6N 85°26W 182 D2
Juillac France 45°20N 1°19E 72 C5
Juist Germany 53°40N 6°59E 76 B3
Juiz de Fora Brazil 21°43S 43°19W 191 A7
Jujuy □ Argentina 23°20S 65°40W 190 A2
Julesburg U.S.A. 40°59N 102°16W 168 F12
Juli Peru 16°10S 69°25W 188 D4
Julia Cr. → Australia 20°0S 141°11E 150 C3
Julia Creek Australia 20°39S 141°44E 150 C3
Juliaca Peru 15°25S 70°10W 188 D3
Julian, L. Canada 54°25N 77°57W 164 B4
Julian U.S.A. 33°4N 116°38W 171 M10
Julian Alps = Julijske Alpe
  Slovenia 46°15N 14°1E 93 B11
Julianatop Suriname 3°40N 56°30W 187 C7
Julianehåb = Qaqortoq
  Greenland 60°43N 46°0W 57 E6
Jülich Germany 50°55N 6°22E 76 E2
Juliette U.S.A. 33°5N 83°50W 178 B6
Julijske Alpe Slovenia 46°15N 14°1E 93 B11
Julimes Mexico 28°25N 105°27W 180 B3
Jullundur = Jalandhar
  India 31°20N 75°40E 124 D6
Julu China 37°15N 115°2E 114 F8
Jumbo Zimbabwe 17°30S 30°58E 143 F3
Jumbo Pk. U.S.A. 36°12N 114°11W 171 J12
Jumentos Cays Bahamas 23°0N 75°40W 182 B4
Jumilla Spain 38°28N 1°19W 91 G3
Jumla Nepal 29°15N 82°13E 125 E10
Jumna = Yamuna →
  India 25°30N 81°53E 125 G9
Jumunjin S. Korea 37°55N 128°54E 115 F15
Junagadh India 21°30N 70°30E 124 J4
Junan China 35°12N 118°53E 115 G10
Junction Tex., U.S.A. 30°29N 99°46W 176 F5
Junction Utah, U.S.A. 38°14N 112°13W 169 G7
Junction B. Australia 11°52S 133°55E 150 A1
Junction City Ga.,
  U.S.A. 32°36N 84°28W 178 C5
Junction City Kans.,
  U.S.A. 39°2N 96°50W 172 F5
Junction City Oreg.,
  U.S.A. 44°13N 123°12W 168 D2
Junction Pt. Australia 11°45S 133°50E 150 A1
Jundah Australia 24°46S 143°2E 150 C3
Jundiaí Brazil 24°30S 47°0W 191 A6
Juneau U.S.A. 58°18N 134°25W 162 B22
Junee Australia 34°53S 147°35E 153 C7
Jungar Qi China 39°49N 110°57E 114 E6
Jungfrau Switz. 46°32N 7°58E 77 J3
Junggar Pendi China 44°30N 86°0E 109 D11
Jungshahi Pakistan 24°52N 67°44E 124 G2
Juniata → U.S.A. 40°24N 77°1W 174 F7
Junín Argentina 34°33S 60°57W 190 C3
Junín Peru 11°12S 76°0W 188 C2
Junín □ Peru 11°30S 75°0W 188 C2
Junín, L. de Peru 11°2S 76°6W 188 C2
Junín de los Andes
  Argentina 39°45S 71°0W 192 E2
Jūniyah Lebanon 33°59N 35°38E 130 B4
Junkerdal △ Norway 66°50N 15°50E 60 C16
Junlian China 28°8N 104°29E 116 C5
Junnar India 19°12N 73°58E 126 E1
Juno Beach U.S.A. 26°52N 80°3W 179 J10
Juntas Chile 28°24S 69°58W 190 B2
Juntura U.S.A. 43°45N 118°5W 168 E4
Juparanã, L. Brazil 19°16S 40°8W 189 D2
Jupiter U.S.A. 26°57N 80°6W 179 J10
Jur → South Sudan 8°45N 29°15E 135 G11
Jura = Jura, Mts. du
  Europe 46°40N 6°5E 71 F13
Jura = Schwäbische Alb
  Germany 48°20N 9°30E 77 G5
Jura U.K. 56°0N 5°50W 65 F3
Jura → France 46°47N 5°45E 71 F12
Jura □ Switz. 47°20N 7°20E 77 H3
Jūra → Lithuania 55°3N 22°9E 82 D9
Jura, Mts. du Europe 46°40N 6°5E 71 F13
Jura, Sd. of U.K. 55°57N 5°45W 65 F3
Jurassic Coast U.K. 50°42N 2°50W 67 G5
Jurbarkas Lithuania 55°4N 22°46E 82 C9
Jurien Bay Australia 30°18S 115°2E 149 F2
Jurilovca Romania 44°46N 28°52E 81 F13
Jūrmala Latvia 56°58N 23°34E 82 B10
Jurong China 31°57N 119°9E 117 B12
Jurong Singapore 1°19N 103°42E 121 d
Juruá → Brazil 2°37S 65°44W 186 D5
Juruena Brazil 13°0S 58°10W 186 F7
Juruena → Brazil 7°20S 58°3W 186 E7
Juruti Brazil 2°9S 56°4W 187 D7
Jussey France 47°50N 5°55E 71 E12
Justo Daract Argentina 33°52S 65°12W 190 C2
Jutaí Brazil 5°11S 68°54W 186 E4
Jutaí → Brazil 2°43S 66°57W 186 D5
Jüterbog Germany 51°59N 13°5E 76 D9
Juticalpa Honduras 14°40N 86°12W 182 D2
Jutland = Jylland
  Denmark 56°25N 9°30E 63 H3
Juuka Finland 63°13N 29°17E 60 E23
Juventud, I. de la Cuba 21°40N 82°40W 182 B3
Juvigny-sous-Andaine
  France 48°32N 0°30W 70 D6
Jūy Zar Iran 33°50N 46°18E 105 C12
Juye China 35°22N 116°5E 114 G9
Juzennecourt France 48°10N 4°58E 71 D11
Jvari Georgia 42°42N 42°4E 87 J6
Jwaneng Botswana 24°45S 24°50E 144 C4
Jyderup Denmark 55°40N 11°26E 63 J5
Jylland Denmark 56°25N 9°30E 63 H3
Jyväskylä Finland 62°14N 25°50E 84 A4

K

K2 Pakistan 35°58N 76°32E 125 B7
Ka → Nigeria 11°40N 4°10E 139 C5
Kaahka = Kaka
  Turkmenistan 37°21N 59°36E 129 B8
Kaap Plateau S. Africa 28°30S 24°0E 144 D3
Kaapkruis Namibia 21°55S 13°57E 144 B1
Kaapstad = Cape Town
  S. Africa 33°55S 18°22E 144 D2
Kaba Indonesia 3°15S 102°0E 119 E2
Kabaena Indonesia 5°15S 122°0E 119 F6
Kabala S. Leone 9°38N 11°37W 138 D2

Kabale Uganda 1°15S 30°0E 142 C3
Kabalo
  Dem. Rep. of the Congo 6°0S 27°0E 142 D2
Kabambare
  Dem. Rep. of the Congo 4°41S 27°39E 142 C2
Kabango
  Dem. Rep. of the Congo 8°35S 28°30E 143 D2
Kabanjahe Indonesia 3°6N 98°30E 118 D1
Kabankalan Phil. 9°59N 122°49E 119 C6
Kabara Fiji 18°59S 178°56W 154 a
Kabara Mali 16°40N 2°50W 138 B4
Kabardinka Russia 44°40N 37°57E 85 K10
Kabardino-Balkaria □
  Russia 43°30N 43°30E 87 J6
Kabarega Falls = Murchison Falls
  Uganda 2°15N 31°30E 142 B3
Kabarnet Kenya 0°30N 35°45E 142 B4
Kabasalan Phil. 7°47N 122°44E 119 C6
Kabat Indonesia 8°16S 114°19E 119 d
Kabba Nigeria 7°50N 6°3E 139 D6
Kabbani → India 12°13N 76°54E 127 H3
Kabin Buri Thailand 13°57N 101°43E 120 F3
Kabinakagami L.
  Canada 48°54N 84°25W 164 C3
Kabinda
  Dem. Rep. of the Congo 6°19S 24°20E 140 F4
Kabna Sudan 19°6N 32°40E 137 D3
Kabompo Zambia 13°36S 24°14E 143 E1
Kabompo → Zambia 14°11S 23°11E 141 G4
Kabondo
  Dem. Rep. of the Congo 8°58S 25°40E 143 D2
Kabongo
  Dem. Rep. of the Congo 7°22S 25°33E 142 D2
Kabot Guinea 10°48N 14°57W 138 C2
Kabrît, G. el Egypt 29°42N 33°16E 130 F2
Kabrousse Senegal 12°26N 16°45W 138 C1
Kabūd Gonbad Iran 37°5N 59°45E 129 B8
Kabudar Ahang Iran 35°11N 48°43E 105 C13
Kābul Afghan. 34°28N 69°11E 124 B3
Kābul □ Afghan. 34°30N 69°0E 109 F7
Kābul → Pakistan 33°55N 72°14E 124 C5
Kabunga
  Dem. Rep. of the Congo 1°38S 28°3E 142 C2
Kaburuang Indonesia 3°50N 126°30E 119 D7
Kabwe Zambia 14°30S 28°29E 143 E2
Kaçanik Kosovo 42°13N 21°12E 96 D5
Kačerginė Lithuania 54°56N 23°42E 82 D10
Kachar Kazakhstan 53°23N 62°55E 108 D8
Kachchh, Gulf of India 22°50N 69°15E 124 H3
Kachchh, Rann of India 24°0N 70°0E 124 H4
Kachchhidhana India 21°44N 78°46E 125 J8
Kachebera Zambia 13°50S 32°50E 143 E3
Kachia Nigeria 9°50N 7°55E 139 D6
Kachikau Botswana 18°8S 24°26E 144 A3
Kachin □ Myanmar 26°0N 97°30E 116 D1
Kachira, L. Uganda 0°40S 31°7E 142 C3
Kachīry Kazakhstan 53°10N 75°50E 108 D9
Kachnara India 23°50N 75°6E 124 H6
Kachot Cambodia 11°30N 103°3E 121 G4
Kaçkar Turkey 40°45N 41°10E 105 B9
Kadaiyanallur India 9°3N 77°22E 127 K3
Kadam, Mt. Uganda 1°45N 34°45E 142 B3
Kadan Czechia 50°23N 13°16E 78 A6
Kadan Kyun Myanmar 12°30N 98°20E 120 F2
Kadanai → Afghan. 31°22N 65°45E 124 D1
Kadapa India 14°30N 78°47E 127 G4
Kadavu Fiji 19°0S 178°15E 154 a
Kadavu Passage Fiji 18°45S 178°0E 154 a
Kade Ghana 6°7N 0°56W 138 D4
Kadhimain = Al Kāẓimīyah
  Iraq 33°22N 44°18E 105 F11
Kadi India 23°18N 72°23E 124 H5
Kadiana Mali 10°45N 6°30W 138 C3
Kadina Australia 33°55S 137°43E 152 B2
Kadinhanı Turkey 38°14N 32°13E 104 C5
Kadiolo Mali 10°35N 7°41W 138 C3
Kadipur India 26°10N 82°23E 125 F10
Kadirabad India 19°51N 75°54E 126 E2
Kadiri India 14°12N 78°13E 127 G4
Kadiyevka = Stakhanov
  Ukraine 48°35N 38°40E 85 H10
Kadmat I. India 11°14N 72°47E 127 J1
Kadoka U.S.A. 43°50N 101°31W 172 D3
Kadom Russia 54°37N 42°30E 86 C6
Kadoma Zimbabwe 18°20S 29°52E 143 F2
Kādugli Sudan 11°0N 29°45E 135 F11
Kaduna Nigeria 10°30N 7°21E 139 C6
Kaduna □ Nigeria 11°0N 7°30E 139 C6
Kaduna → Nigeria 8°45N 5°48E 139 D6
Kadur India 13°34N 76°1E 127 H3
Kaduy Russia 59°12N 37°9E 84 C9
Kaédi Mauritania 16°9N 13°28W 138 B2
Kaélé Cameroon 10°7N 14°27E 139 C7
Kaeng Khoi Thailand 14°35N 101°0E 120 E3
Kaeng Krachan △
  Thailand 12°57N 99°23E 120 F2
Kaeng Krung △
  Thailand 9°30N 98°50E 121 H2
Kaeng Tana △
  Thailand 15°25N 105°32E 120 E5
Kaeo N.Z. 35°6S 173°49E 154 B4
Kaesŏng N. Korea 37°58N 126°35E 115 F14
Kāf Si. Arabia 31°25N 37°29E 128 D3
Kafan = Kapan
  Armenia 39°18N 46°27E 105 C12
Kafanchan Nigeria 9°40N 8°20E 139 D6
Kafareti Nigeria 10°25N 11°12E 139 C7
Kaffrine Senegal 14°8N 15°36W 138 C1
Kafin Madaki Nigeria 10°41N 9°46E 139 C6
Kafireos, Stenon Greece 37°56N 24°32E 98 C5
Kafr el Battikh Egypt 31°25N 31°44E 137 H7
Kafr el Dauwâr Egypt 31°8N 30°8E 137 H7
Kafr el Sheikh Egypt 31°15N 30°50E 137 H7
Kafr el Zaiyât Egypt 30°49N 30°48E 137 H7
Kafue Zambia 15°46S 28°9E 143 F2
Kafue → Zambia 15°30S 29°0E 143 F2
Kafue △ Zambia 15°12S 25°25E 143 E1
Kafue Flats Zambia 15°40S 27°25E 143 E2
Kafulwe Zambia 9°0S 29°1E 143 D2
Kaga Afghan. 34°14N 70°10E 124 B4
Kaga Bandoro C.A.R. 7°0N 19°10E 135 G9
Kagarko Nigeria 9°36N 8°0E 139 D6
Kagawa □ Japan 34°15N 134°0E 113 G7
Kagera □ Tanzania 2°0S 31°30E 142 C3
Kagera → Tanzania 0°57S 31°47E 142 C3
Kağızman Turkey 40°5N 43°10E 105 B10
Kagoro Nigeria 9°36N 8°23E 139 D6

Kagoshima Japan 31°35N 130°33E 113 J5
Kagoshima □ Japan 31°30N 130°30E 113 J5
Kagul = Cahul Moldova 45°50N 28°15E 81 E13
Kahak Iran 36°6N 49°46E 129 B6
Kahama Tanzania 4°8S 32°30E 142 C3
Kahan Pakistan 29°18N 68°54E 124 E3
Kahang Malaysia 2°12N 103°32E 121 L4
Kahayan → Indonesia 3°40S 114°0E 118 E4
Kahe Tanzania 3°30S 37°25E 142 C4
Kahemba
  Dem. Rep. of the Congo 7°18S 18°55E 140 F3
Kaherekoau Mts. N.Z. 45°45S 167°15E 155 F2
Kahil, Djebel bou Algeria 34°26N 4°30E 136 B6
Kahnūj Iran 27°55N 57°40E 129 E8
Kahoka U.S.A. 40°25N 91°44W 172 E8
Kaho'olawe U.S.A. 20°33N 156°37W 167 M7
K'alak'unlun Shank'ou =
  Karakoram Pass
  Asia 35°33N 77°50E 125 B7
Kalam Pakistan 35°34N 72°30E 125 B5
Kalama
  Dem. Rep. of the Congo 2°52S 28°35E 142 C2
Kalama U.S.A. 46°1N 122°51W 170 E4
Kalamariá Greece 40°33N 22°55E 96 F6
Kalamáta Greece 37°3N 22°10E 98 D4
Kalamazoo U.S.A. 42°17N 85°35W 173 D11
Kalamazoo → U.S.A. 42°40N 86°10W 172 D10
Kalamb India 18°3N 74°48E 126 E2
Kalambaka Greece 39°42N 21°39E 98 B3
Kalambo Falls Tanzania 8°37S 31°35E 143 D3
Kalamnuri India 19°40N 77°20E 126 E3
Kálamos Attiki, Greece 38°17N 23°52E 98 C5
Kálamos Lefkada, Greece 38°37N 20°55E 98 C2
Kalan = Tunceli Turkey 39°6N 39°31E 105 C8
Kalangadoo Australia 37°34S 140°41E 152 C4
Kalankalan Guinea 10°7N 8°54W 138 C3
Kalannie Australia 30°22S 117°5E 149 F2
Kalāntarī Iran 32°10N 54°8E 129 C7
Kalao Indonesia 7°21S 121°0E 119 F6
Kalaotoa Indonesia 7°20S 121°50E 119 F6
Kalārne Sweden 62°59N 16°5E 62 E10
Kalasin Thailand 16°26N 103°30E 120 D4
Kālat Iran 25°29N 59°22E 129 E9
Kalat Pakistan 29°8N 66°31E 122 E5
Kalāteh Iran 36°33N 55°41E 129 B7
Kalāteh-ye Ganj Iran 27°31N 57°55E 129 E8
Kalathos Greece 36°9N 28°8E 99 C11
Kalavrita Greece 38°3N 22°8E 98 C4
Kalba U.A.E. 25°5N 56°22E 129 E8
Kalbarri Australia 27°40S 114°10E 149 E1
Kalbarri △ Australia 27°51S 114°30E 149 E1
Kalce Slovenia 45°54N 14°13E 74 F8
Kale Antalya, Turkey 36°14N 30°0E 99 E12
Kale Denizli, Turkey 37°26N 28°49E 99 D10
Kaleburnu = Galinoporni
  Cyprus 35°31N 34°18E 101 D13
Kalecik Turkey 40°4N 33°26E 104 B5
Kalegauk Kyun
  Myanmar 15°33N 97°35E 120 E1
Kalehe
  Dem. Rep. of the Congo 2°6S 28°50E 142 C2
Kalema Tanzania 1°12S 31°55E 142 C3
Kalemie
  Dem. Rep. of the Congo 5°55S 29°9E 142 D2
Kalety Poland 50°35N 18°52E 83 H5
Kalewa Myanmar 23°10N 94°15E 123 H19
Kaleybar Iran 38°47N 47°2E 105 C12
Kalghatgi India 15°11N 74°58E 127 G2
Kalgoorlie-Boulder
  Australia 30°40S 121°22E 149 F3
Kali → India 27°6N 79°55E 125 F8
Kali Sindh → India 25°32N 76°17E 124 G6
Kaliakra, Nos Bulgaria 43°21N 28°30E 97 C12
Kalianda Indonesia 5°50S 105°45E 118 F3
Kalibo Phil. 11°43N 122°22E 119 B6
Kalima
  Dem. Rep. of the Congo 2°33S 26°32E 142 C2
Kalimantan Indonesia 0°0 114°0E 118 E4
Kalimantan Barat □
  Indonesia 0°0 110°30E 118 E4
Kalimantan Selatan □
  Indonesia 2°30S 115°30E 118 E5
Kalimantan Tengah □
  Indonesia 2°0S 113°30E 118 E4
Kalimantan Timur □
  Indonesia 1°30N 116°30E 118 D5
Kálimnos Greece 37°0N 27°0E 99 D8
Kalimpong India 27°4N 88°35E 125 F13
Kalinadi → India 14°50N 74°7E 127 G2
Kaliningrad Russia 51°29N 44°18E 87 F7
Kaliningrad Russia 54°42N 20°32E 82 D7
Kaliningrad ✈ (KGD)
  Russia 54°45N 20°33E 82 D7
Kalininsk Russia 51°30N 44°40E 86 E7
Kalinkavichy Belarus 52°12N 29°20E 75 B15
Kalinkovichi = Kalinkavichy
  Belarus 52°12N 29°20E 75 B15
Kalinovik Bos.-H. 43°31N 18°25E 96 C2
Kalipetrovo Bulgaria 44°5N 27°14E 97 B11
Kaliráchi Greece 40°40N 24°35E 97 E8
Kalispell U.S.A. 48°12N 114°19W 168 B6
Kalisz Poland 51°45N 18°8E 83 G5
Kalisz Pomorski Poland 53°17N 15°55E 83 E2
Kalithéa Greece 37°56N 23°43E 98 D5
Kaliua Tanzania 5°5S 31°48E 142 D3
Kalivia Thorikou Greece 37°45N 23°59E 98 D5
Kalix Sweden 65°53N 23°12E 60 D20
Kalixälven → Sweden 65°50N 23°11E 60 D20
Kalka India 30°46N 76°57E 124 D7
Kalkan Turkey 36°15N 29°23E 99 E11
Kalkarindji Australia 17°30S 130°47E 148 C5
Kalkaska U.S.A. 44°44N 85°11W 173 C11
Kalkfeld Namibia 20°57S 16°14E 144 B2
Kalkfontein Botswana 22°4S 20°57E 144 B3
Kalkrand Namibia 24°1S 17°35E 144 B2
Kallakurichchi India 11°44N 79°1E 127 H4
Kallam India 18°36N 76°2E 126 E3
Kållands ö Sweden 58°40N 13°5E 63 F7
Kallavesi Finland 62°58N 27°30E 60 E22
Kallidaikurichi India 8°38N 77°31E 127 K3
Kallinge Sweden 56°15N 15°18E 63 H9
Kallmet Albania 41°51N 19°41E 96 B3
Kallsjön Sweden 63°38N 13°0E 62 D7
Kalmalo Nigeria 13°40N 5°20E 139 C6
Kalmar Sweden 56°40N 16°20E 63 H10
Kalmar □ Sweden 57°25N 16°15E 63 H10
Kalmar sund Sweden 56°40N 16°25E 63 H10

Kalmunai *Sri Lanka* 7°25N 81°49E **127** L5
Kalmykia □ *Russia* 46°5N 46°1E **87** G8
Kalna *India* 23°13N 88°25E **125** H13
Kalnai *India* 22°46N 83°30E **125** H10
Kalo Nero *Greece* 37°20N 21°38E **98** D3
Kalocsa *Hungary* 46°32N 19°0E **80** D4
Kalofer *Bulgaria* 42°37N 24°59E **97** C11
Kalokhorio *Cyprus* 34°51N 33°2E **101** E12
Kaloko
Dem. Rep. of the Congo 6°47S 25°48E **142** D2
Kalol *Gujarat, India* 22°37N 73°31E **124** H5
Kalol *Gujarat, India* 23°15N 72°33E **124** H5
Kalolimnos *Greece* 37°4N 27°5E **99** D9
Kalomo *Zambia* 17°0S 26°30E **143** F2
Kaloni *Greece* 39°14N 26°12E **99** B8
Kaloni, Kolpos *Greece* 39°10N 26°10E **99** B8
Kalpeni I. *India* 10°5N 73°38E **127** J1
Kalpi *India* 26°8N 79°47E **125** F8
Kalpitiya *Sri Lanka* 8°14N 79°46E **127** K4
Kalputhi I. *India* 10°49N 72°10E **127** J1
Kalrayan Hills *India* 11°45N 78°40E **127** J4
Kalsubai *India* 19°35N 73°45E **126** E1
Kaltag *U.S.A.* 64°20N 158°43W **166** C8
Kaltern = Caldaro *Italy* 46°25N 11°14E **93** B8
Kaltukatjara *Australia* 24°52S 129°5E **149** D4
Kaltungo *Nigeria* 9°48N 11°19E **139** D7
Kalu *Pakistan* 25°5N 67°39E **124** G2
Kaluga *Russia* 54°35N 36°10E **84** E9
Kaluga □ *Russia* 54°15N 34°50E **84** E8
Kalulushi *Zambia* 12°50S 28°3E **143** E2
Kalumburu *Australia* 13°55S 126°35E **148** B4
Kalumburu ◇
Australia 14°17S 126°38E **148** B4
Kalundborg *Denmark* 55°41N 11°5E **63** J5
Kalush *Ukraine* 49°3N 24°23E **75** D13
Kałuszyn *Poland* 52°13N 21°52E **83** F8
Kalutara *Sri Lanka* 6°35N 80°0E **127** L5
Kalwakurti *India* 16°41N 78°30E **126** F4
Kalyan = Basavakalyan
India 17°52N 76°57E **126** F3
Kalyan *Maharashtra,*
India 20°30N 74°3E **126** D2
Kalyan *Maharashtra,*
India 19°15N 73°9E **126** E1
Kalyandurg *India* 14°33N 77°6E **127** G3
Kalyansingapuram
India 19°30N 83°19E **126** E6
Kalyazin *Russia* 57°15N 37°55E **84** D9
Kam *Albania* 42°17N 20°18E **96** D4
Kam → *Nigeria* 8°15N 11°0E **139** D7
Kama
Dem. Rep. of the Congo 3°30S 27°5E **142** C2
Kama *Japan* 33°33N 130°49E **113** H5
Kama → *Russia* 55°45N 52°0E **86** D6
Kamachumu *Tanzania* 1°37S 31°37E **142** C3
Kamaishi *Japan* 39°16N 141°53E **112** E10
Kamalapuram *India* 14°35N 78°39E **127** G4
Kamalia *Pakistan* 30°44N 72°42E **124** D5
Kaman *India* 27°39N 77°16E **124** F6
Kaman *Turkey* 39°22N 33°44E **104** C5
Kamanjab *Namibia* 19°35S 14°51E **144** A2
Kamapanda *Zambia* 12°5S 24°0E **143** E1
Kamara *Mali* 14°38N 9°23W **138** C3
Kamarān *Yemen* 15°21N 42°35E **131** D3
Kamareddi *India* 18°19N 78°21E **126** E4
Kamativi *Zimbabwe* 18°20S 27°6E **144** A4
Kamba *Nigeria* 11°50N 3°45E **139** C5
Kambalda West
Australia 31°10S 121°37E **149** F3
Kambam *India* 9°45N 77°16E **127** K3
Kambangan, Nusa
Indonesia 7°40S 108°10E **119** G13
Kambar *Pakistan* 27°37N 68°1E **124** F3
Kambia *S. Leone* 9°3N 12°53W **138** D2
Kambolé *Togo* 8°43N 1°39E **139** D5
Kambolé *Zambia* 8°47S 30°48E **143** D3
Kambos *Cyprus* 35°2N 32°44E **101** D11
Kambove
Dem. Rep. of the Congo 10°51S 26°33E **143** E2
Kamchatka, Poluostrov
Russia 57°0N 160°0E **107** D17
Kamchatka Pen. = Kamchatka,
Poluostrov *Russia* 57°0N 160°0E **107** D17
Kamchia → *Bulgaria* 43°4N 27°44E **97** C11
Kameda-Hantō *Japan* 41°50N 141°0E **112** D10
Kamen *Russia* 53°50N 81°30E **109** B10
Kamen-Rybolov *Russia* 44°46N 132°2E **112** B5
Kamenica *Serbia* 43°27N 22°27E **96** C3
Kamenica *Serbia* 44°25N 19°45E **96** B3
Kamenice nad Lipou
Czechia 49°18N 15°2E **78** B8
Kamenjak, Rt *Croatia* 44°47N 13°55E **93** D10
Kamenka = Kamyanka
Ukraine 49°3N 32°6E **85** H7
Kamenka *Kazakhstan* 51°7N 50°19E **86** B6
Kamenka *Penza, Russia* 53°10N 44°5E **86** D6
Kamenka *Voronezh,*
Russia 50°47N 39°20E **85** G10
Kamenka Bugskaya =
Kamyanka-Buzka
Ukraine 50°8N 24°16E **75** C13
Kamenka Dneprovskaya =
Kamyanka-Dniprovska
Ukraine 47°29N 34°28E **85** J8
Kamennomostskiy
Russia 44°18N 40°13E **87** H5
Kameno *Bulgaria* 42°34N 27°18E **97** D11
Kamenolomni *Russia* 47°40N 40°14E **87** G5
Kamensk-Shakhtinskiy
Russia 48°23N 40°20E **87** F5
Kamensk Uralskiy
Russia 56°25N 62°2E **106** D7
Kamenskiy *Russia* 50°48N 45°30E **86** D8
Kamenskoye *Russia* 62°45N 165°30E **107** C17
Kamenyak *Bulgaria* 43°24N 26°57E **97** C10
Kamenz *Germany* 51°15N 14°5E **76** D10
Kameoka *Japan* 35°0N 135°35E **113** G7
Kamet *India* 30°55N 79°35E **125** D8
Kamiah *U.S.A.* 46°14N 116°2W **168** C5
Kamień Krajeński
Poland 53°32N 17°32E **82** E4
Kamień Pomorski
Poland 53°57N 14°43E **82** E1
Kamienna → *Poland* 51°6N 21°47E **83** G8
Kamienna Góra *Poland* 50°47N 16°2E **83** H3
Kamieskroon *S. Africa* 30°9S 17°56E **144** D2
Kamilukuak L.
Canada 62°22N 101°40W **163** A8

Kamin-Kashyrskyy
Ukraine 51°39N 24°56E **75** C13
Kamina
Dem. Rep. of the Congo 8°45S 25°0E **143** D2
Kaminak L. *Canada* 62°10N 95°0W **163** A10
Kaminoyama *Japan* 38°9N 140°17E **112** E10
Kamiros *Greece* 36°20N 27°56E **101** C9
Kamituga
Dem. Rep. of the Congo 3°2S 28°10E **142** C2
Kamla → *India* 25°35N 86°36E **125** G12
Kamloops *Canada* 50°40N 120°20W **162** C4
Kamnik *Slovenia* 46°14N 14°37E **93** B11
Kamo *Japan* 37°39N 139°3E **112** F9
Kamo *N.Z.* 35°42S 174°20E **154** B3
Kamoke *Pakistan* 32°4N 74°4E **124** C6
Kamp → *Austria* 48°23N 15°42E **78** C8
Kampala *Uganda* 0°20N 32°32E **142** B3
Kampar *Malaysia* 4°18N 101°9E **121** K3
Kampar → *Indonesia* 0°30N 103°8E **118** D2
Kampen *Neths.* 52°33N 5°53E **69** B5
Kampene
Dem. Rep. of the Congo 3°36S 26°40E **140** E5
Kamphaeng Phet
Thailand 16°28N 99°30E **120** C2
Kampinoski △ *Poland* 52°21N 20°40E **83** F7
Kampolombo, L.
Zambia 11°37S 29°42E **143** E2
Kampong Cham
Cambodia 12°0N 105°30E **121** G5
Kampong Chhnang
Cambodia 12°20N 104°35E **121** F5
Kampong Pengerang
Malaysia 1°22N 104°7E **121** d
Kampong Punggai
Malaysia 1°27N 104°18E **121** d
Kampong Saom
Cambodia 10°38N 103°30E **121** G4
Kampong Saom, Chaak
Cambodia 10°50N 103°32E **121** G4
Kampong Tanjong Langsat
Malaysia 1°28N 104°1E **121** d
Kampong Telok Ramunia
Malaysia 1°22N 104°15E **121** d
Kampot *Cambodia* 10°36N 104°10E **121** G5
Kampti *Burkina Faso* 10°7N 3°25W **138** C4
Kampuchea = Cambodia ■
Asia 12°15N 105°0E **120** F5
Kampung Air Putih
Malaysia 4°15N 103°10E **121** K4
Kampung Jerangau
Malaysia 4°50N 103°10E **121** K4
Kampung Raja
Malaysia 5°45N 102°35E **121** K4
Kampungbaru = Tolitoli
Indonesia 1°5N 120°50E **119** D6
Kamrau, Teluk
Indonesia 3°30S 133°36E **119** E8
Kamsack *Canada* 51°34N 101°54W **163** C8
Kamsar *Guinea* 10°40N 14°36W **138** C2
Kamskoye Ustye *Russia* 55°10N 49°20E **86** C9
Kamthi *India* 21°9N 79°19E **126** D4
Kamuchawie L.
Canada 56°18N 101°59W **163** B8
Kamui-Misaki *Japan* 43°20N 140°21E **112** C10
Kamyanets-Podilskyy
Ukraine 48°45N 26°40E **81** B11
Kamyanka *Ukraine* 49°3N 32°6E **85** H7
Kamyanka-Buzka
Ukraine 50°8N 24°16E **75** C13
Kamyanka-Dniprovska
Ukraine 47°29N 34°28E **85** J8
Kamyanyets *Belarus* 52°23N 23°49E **83** F11
Kamyanyuki *Belarus* 52°32N 23°49E **83** F11
Kāmyārān *Iran* 34°47N 46°56E **105** L12
Kamyshin *Russia* 50°10N 45°24E **87** F8
Kamyzyak *Russia* 46°4N 48°10E **87** G9
Kanaaupscow →
Canada 54°2N 76°30W **164** B4
Kanab *U.S.A.* 37°3N 112°32W **169** H7
Kanab Cr. → *U.S.A.* 36°24N 112°38W **169** H7
Kanacea *Lau Group, Fiji* 17°15S 179°6W **154** a
Kanacea *Taveuni, Fiji* 16°59S 179°56E **154** a
Kanaga I. *U.S.A.* 51°45N 177°22W **166** E4
Kanagi *Japan* 40°54N 140°27E **112** D10
Kanairiktok → *Canada* 55°2N 60°18W **165** A7
Kanakapura *India* 12°33N 77°28E **127** H3
Kanalia *Greece* 39°30N 22°53E **98** B4
Kananga
Dem. Rep. of the Congo 5°55S 22°18E **140** F4
Kanangra-Boyd △
Australia 33°57S 150°15E **153** B9
Kanash *Russia* 55°30N 47°32E **86** C8
Kanastraíon, Ákra = Paliouri,
Akra *Greece* 39°57N 23°45E **96** G7
Kanawha → *U.S.A.* 38°50N 82°9W **173** F12
Kanazawa *Japan* 36°30N 136°38E **113** F8
Kanchanaburi *Thailand* 14°2N 99°31E **120** E2
Kanchenjunga *Nepal* 27°50N 88°10E **125** F13
Kanchenjunga △ *India* 27°42N 88°8E **125** F13
Kanchipuram *India* 12°52N 79°45E **127** H4
Kańczuga *Poland* 49°59N 22°25E **83** J9
Kandaghat *India* 30°59N 77°7E **124** D7
Kandahār *Afghan.* 31°32N 65°43E **122** D4
Kandahār □ *Afghan.* 31°0N 65°0E **122** D4
Kandalaksha *Russia* 67°9N 32°30E **60** C25
Kandangan *Indonesia* 2°50S 115°20E **118** E5
Kandanos *Greece* 35°19N 23°44E **101** D5
Kandava *Latvia* 57°2N 22°46E **82** A9
Kandavu = Kadavu *Fiji* 19°0S 178°15E **154** a
Kandavu Passage = Kadavu
Passage *Fiji* 18°45S 178°0E **154** a
Kandé = Kanté *Togo* 9°57N 1°3E **139** D6
Kandhkot *Pakistan* 28°16N 69°8E **124** E3
Kandhla *India* 29°18N 77°19E **124** E7
Kandi *Benin* 11°7N 2°55E **139** C5
Kandi *India* 23°58N 88°5E **125** H13
Kandiaro *Pakistan* 27°4N 68°13E **124** F3
Kandila *Greece* 37°46N 22°22E **98** D4
Kandıra *Turkey* 41°4N 30°9E **104** B4
Kandla *India* 23°0N 70°10E **124** H4
Kandos *Australia* 32°45S 149°58E **153** B8
Kandy *Sri Lanka* 7°18N 80°43E **127** L5
Kane *U.S.A.* 41°40N 78°49W **174** E6
Kane Basin *Greenland* 79°1N 70°0W **57** B4
Kanel *Senegal* 15°30N 13°18W **138** B2
Kaneksaya *Russia* 46°3N 38°57E **87** G4
Kanfanar *Croatia* 45°7N 13°50E **93** D10
Kang *Botswana* 23°41S 22°50E **144** B3
Kangaamiut *Greenland* 65°50N 53°20W **57** D5
Kangaatsiaq *Greenland* 68°18N 53°28W **57** D5

Kangaba *Mali* 11°56N 8°25W **138** C3
Kangal *Turkey* 39°14N 37°23E **104** C7
Kangān *Fārs, Iran* 27°50N 52°3E **129** E7
Kangān *Hormozgān,*
Iran 25°48N 57°28E **129** E8
Kangar *Malaysia* 6°27N 100°12E **121** J3
Kangaré *Mali* 11°36N 8°4W **138** C3
Kangaroo I. *Australia* 35°45S 137°0E **152** C2
Kangaroo Mts.
Australia 23°29S 141°51E **150** C3
Kangasala *Finland* 61°28N 24°4E **84** B3
Kangāvar *Iran* 34°40N 48°0E **105** L12
Kangding *China* 30°2N 101°57E **116** B3
Kangdong *N. Korea* 39°9N 126°5E **115** E14
Kangean, Kepulauan
Indonesia 6°55S 115°23E **118** F5
Kangean Is. = Kangean,
Kepulauan *Indonesia* 6°55S 115°23E **118** F5
Kangerdlugssuak
Greenland 68°10N 32°20W **57** D7
Kangerluarsoruseq
Greenland 63°45N 51°27W **57** E5
Kangerluarsoruset =
Kangerluarsoruseq
Greenland 63°45N 51°27W **57** E5
Kangerlussuaq
Greenland 66°59N 50°40W **57** D5
Kangertittivaq = Scoresby Sund
Greenland 70°28N 21°46W **57** C8
Kanggye *N. Korea* 41°0N 126°35E **115** D14
Kangikajik *Greenland* 70°7N 22°0W **57** C8
Kangilinnguit *Greenland* 61°20N 47°57W **57** E6
Kangiqliniq = Rankin Inlet
Canada 62°30N 93°0W **160** E13
Kangiqsualujjuaq
Canada 58°30N 65°59W **161** F18
Kangiqsujuaq *Canada* 61°30N 72°0W **161** E17
Kangiqtugaapik = Clyde River
Canada 70°30N 68°30W **161** C18
Kangirsuk *Canada* 60°0N 70°0W **161** F17
Kangkar Chemaran
Malaysia 1°34N 104°12E **121** d
Kangkar Sungai Tiram
Malaysia 1°35N 103°55E **121** d
Kangkar Teberau
Malaysia 1°32N 103°51E **121** d
Kangping *China* 42°43N 123°18E **115** C12
Kangto *China* 27°50N 92°35E **123** F18
Kanha △ *India* 22°15N 80°40E **125** H9
Kanhan → *India* 21°4N 79°34E **126** D4
Kanhangad *India* 12°21N 74°58E **127** H2
Kanhar → *India* 24°28N 83°8E **125** G10
Kani *Côte d'Ivoire* 8°29N 6°36W **138** D3
Kaniama
Dem. Rep. of the Congo 7°30S 24°12E **142** D1
Kaniapiskau = Caniapiscau →
Canada 56°40N 69°30W **165** A6
Kaniapiskau, L. = Caniapiscau, L.
Canada 54°10N 69°55W **165** B6
Kaniere, L. *N.Z.* 42°50S 171°10E **155** C6
Kanigiri *India* 15°26N 79°43E **127** G4
Kanin, Poluostrov *Russia* 68°0N 45°0E **58** B14
Kanin Nos, Mys *Russia* 68°39N 43°32E **106** C5
Kanin Pen. = Kanin, Poluostrov
Russia 68°0N 45°0E **58** B14
Kaninë *Albania* 40°23N 19°30E **96** F3
Kaniva *Australia* 36°22S 141°18E **152** D4
Kanjiža *Serbia* 46°3N 20°4E **80** D5
Kanjut Sar *Pakistan* 36°7N 75°25E **125** A6
Kankaanpää *Finland* 61°44N 22°50E **84** B2
Kankakee *U.S.A.* 41°7N 87°52W **172** E10
Kankakee → *U.S.A.* 41°23N 88°15W **172** E9
Kankan *Guinea* 10°23N 9°15W **138** C3
Kankendy = Xankändi
Azerbaijan 39°52N 46°49E **105** C12
Kanker *India* 20°10N 81°40E **126** D5
Kankesanturai *Sri Lanka* 9°49N 80°2E **127** K5
Kankossa *Mauritania* 15°54N 11°31W **138** B2
Kankroli *India* 25°4N 73°53E **124** G5
Kanmaw Kyun
Myanmar 11°40N 98°28E **121** G2
Kannapolis *U.S.A.* 35°30N 80°37W **177** D14
Kannauj *India* 27°3N 79°56E **125** F8
Kanniyakumari *India* 8°5N 77°34E **127** K3
Kannod *India* 22°45N 76°40E **122** H10
Kannur *India* 11°53N 75°27E **127** J2
Kannyakumari *India* 8°3N 77°40E **127** K3
Kano *Nigeria* 12°2N 8°30E **139** C6
Kano □ *Nigeria* 11°30N 8°30E **139** C6
Kan'onji *Japan* 34°7N 133°39E **113** G6
Kanoroba *Côte d'Ivoire* 9°7N 6°8W **138** D3
Kanowit *Malaysia* 2°14N 112°20E **118** D4
Kanoya *Japan* 31°25N 130°50E **113** J5
Kanpetlet *Myanmar* 21°10N 93°59E **123** J18
Kanpur *India* 26°28N 80°20E **125** F9
Kansas □ *U.S.A.* 38°30N 99°0W **172** F4
Kansas → *U.S.A.* 39°7N 94°37W **172** F6
Kansas City *Kans.,*
U.S.A. 39°7N 94°38W **172** F6
Kansas City *Mo., U.S.A.* 39°6N 94°35W **172** F6
Kansenia
Dem. Rep. of the Congo 10°20S 26°0E **143** E2
Kansk *Russia* 56°20N 95°37E **107** D10
Kansu = Gansu □ *China* 36°0N 104°0E **114** G3
Kantaphor *India* 22°35N 76°34E **124** H7
Kantchari *Burkina Faso* 12°37N 1°37E **139** C5
Kantché *Niger* 13°31N 8°30E **139** C6
Kanté *Togo* 9°57N 1°3E **139** D6
Kantemirovka *Russia* 49°43N 39°55E **85** H10
Kantharalak *Thailand* 14°39N 104°39E **120** E5
Kanthi = Contai *India* 21°54N 87°46E **125** J12
Kanti → *India* 28°20N 75°30E **124** E6
Kantō □ *Japan* 36°15N 139°30E **113** F9
Kantō-Sanchi *Japan* 35°59N 138°50E **113** G9
Kanturk *Ireland* 52°11N 8°54W **64** D3
Kanuma *Japan* 36°34N 139°42E **113** F9
Kanus *Namibia* 27°50S 18°39E **144** D2
Kanye *Botswana* 24°55S 25°28E **144** B4
Kanzenze
Dem. Rep. of the Congo 10°30S 25°12E **128** G3
Kanzi, Ras *Tanzania* 7°1S 39°33E **142** D4
Kao Phara *Thailand* 8°5N 98°18E **121** a
Kaohsiung *Taiwan* 22°35N 120°16E **117** F13
Kaokoveld *Namibia* 19°15S 14°30E **144** B1
Kaolack *Senegal* 14°5N 16°8W **138** C1
Kaoloi △ *Senegal* 14°5N 15°15W **138** C1
Kaoshan *China* 44°38N 124°50E **115** B13
Kapa'a *U.S.A.* 22°5N 159°19W **167** L8
Kapadvanj *India* 23°5N 73°0E **124** H5

Kapaklı *Turkey* 41°19N 27°59E **97** E11
Kapan *Armenia* 39°18N 46°27E **105** C12
Kapanga
Dem. Rep. of the Congo 8°30S 22°40E **140** F4
Kapchagai = Qapshaghay
Kazakhstan 43°51N 77°14E **109** E9
Kapchagaiskoye Vdkhr. =
Qapshaghay Bögeni
Kazakhstan 43°45N 77°50E **109** E9
Kapedo *Kenya* 1°10N 36°5E **142** B4
Kapela = Velika Kapela
Croatia 45°10N 15°5E **93** C12
Kapellskär *Sweden* 59°44N 19°2E **62** E13
Kapelo, Akra *Greece* 36°9N 23°3E **98** E5
Kapema
Dem. Rep. of the Congo 10°45S 28°22E **143** E2
Kapenguria *Kenya* 1°14N 35°7E **142** B4
Kapfenberg *Austria* 47°26N 15°18E **78** D8
Kapı Dağı *Turkey* 40°28N 27°47E **99** B9
Kapiri Mposhi *Zambia* 13°59S 28°43E **143** E2
Kāpīsā □ *Afghan.* 35°0N 69°20E **122** B6
Kapiskau → *Canada* 52°47N 81°55W **164** B3
Kapit *Malaysia* 2°0N 112°55E **118** D4
Kapiti I. *N.Z.* 40°50S 174°56E **154** D5
Kaplan *U.S.A.* 30°0N 92°17W **176** F8
Kaplice *Czechia* 48°42N 14°30E **78** C7
Kapoe *Thailand* 9°34N 98°32E **121** H2
Kápolnásnyék *Hungary* 47°16N 18°41E **80** D3
Kaponga *N.Z.* 39°29S 174°9E **154** F3
Kapos → *Hungary* 46°44N 18°30E **80** D3
Kaposvár *Hungary* 46°25N 17°47E **80** D2
Kapowsin *U.S.A.* 46°59N 122°13W **170** D4
Kappeln *Germany* 54°40N 9°55E **76** A5
Kappelshamn *Sweden* 57°52N 18°47E **63** G12
Kapps *Namibia* 22°32S 17°18E **144** B2
Kaprije *Croatia* 43°42N 15°43E **93** E12
Kapsabet *Kenya* 0°12N 35°6E **142** B4
Kapsan *N. Korea* 41°4N 128°19E **115** D15
Kapsukas = Marijampolė
Lithuania 54°33N 23°19E **82** D10
Kaptai L. *Bangla.* 22°40N 92°20E **123** H18
Kapuas → *Indonesia* 0°25S 109°20E **118** E3
Kapuas Hulu, Pegunungan
Malaysia 1°30N 113°30E **118** D4
Kapuas Hulu Ra. = Kapuas Hulu,
Pegunungan
Malaysia 1°30N 113°30E **118** D4
Kapulo
Dem. Rep. of the Congo 8°18S 29°15E **143** D2
Kapunda *Australia* 34°20S 138°56E **152** C2
Kapuni *N.Z.* 39°29S 174°8E **154** F3
Kapurthala *India* 31°23N 75°25E **124** D6
Kapuskasing *Canada* 49°25N 82°30W **164** C3
Kapuskasing →
Canada 49°49N 82°0W **164** C3
Kapustin Yar *Russia* 48°37N 45°40E **87** F7
Kaputar, Mt. *Australia* 30°15S 150°10E **151** E5
Kaputir *Kenya* 2°5N 35°28E **142** B4
Kapuvár *Hungary* 47°36N 17°1E **80** C2
Kara *Russia* 69°10N 65°0E **106** C7
Karā, W. → *Si. Arabia* 20°45N 41°42E **137** C5
Kara Ada *Turkey* 36°58N 27°28E **99** E9
Kara-Balta *Kyrgyzstan* 42°50N 73°49E **109** D8
Kara Bogaz Gol, Zaliv =
Garabogazköl Aylagy
Turkmenistan 41°0N 53°30E **108** A7
Kara Burun *Turkey* 36°32N 27°58E **99** E9
Kara Kala = Garrygala
Turkmenistan 38°31N 56°29E **129** B8
Kara Kalpak Republic =
Qoraqalpog'iston □
Uzbekistan 43°0N 58°0E **108** D6
Kara-Köl *Kyrgyzstan* 41°40N 72°43E **109** D8
Kara Kum = Garagum
Turkmenistan 39°30N 60°0E **129** B8
Kara Sea *Russia* 75°0N 70°0E **106** B8
Karaadilli *Turkey* 38°18N 30°37E **99** C12
Karabiğa *Turkey* 40°23N 27°17E **99** F11
Karabük *Turkey* 41°12N 32°37E **104** B5
Karabük □ *Turkey* 41°10N 32°30E **104** B5
Karaburun *Albania* 40°25N 19°20E **96** F3
Karaburun *Turkey* 38°41N 26°28E **99** C8
Karaburun-Sazan △
Albania 40°19N 19°21E **96** F3
Karabutak = Qarabutaq
Kazakhstan 50°0N 60°14E **108** C6
Karacabey *Turkey* 40°12N 28°21E **99** F12
Karacakılavuz *Turkey* 41°8N 27°11E **97** F11
Karacaköy *Turkey* 41°24N 28°22E **97** F12
Karacasu *Turkey* 37°43N 28°35E **99** D10
Karachala = Qaraçala
Azerbaijan 39°45N 48°53E **87** L9
Karachayevsk *Russia* 43°50N 41°55E **87** J5
Karachev *Russia* 53°10N 35°5E **85** F8
Karachey-Cherkessia □
Russia 43°40N 41°30E **87** J5
Karachi *Pakistan* 24°50N 67°0E **124** G2
Karad *India* 17°15N 74°10E **126** F2
Karadeniz Boğazı *Turkey* 41°10N 29°10E **99** E13
Karaga *Ghana* 9°58N 0°28W **139** D4
Karaganda = Qaraghandy
Kazakhstan 49°50N 73°10E **109** E8
Karagayly = Qaraghayly
Kazakhstan 49°26N 76°0E **106** E8
Karaginskiy, Ostrov
Russia 58°45N 164°0E **107** D17
Karagola Road *India* 25°29N 87°23E **125** G12
Karagüney Dağları
Turkey 40°30N 34°40E **104** B6
Karaikal *India* 10°59N 79°50E **127** J4
Karaikkudi *India* 10°0N 78°45E **127** K4
Karaj *Iran* 35°48N 51°0E **129** B6
Karaj → *Iran* 35°4N 50°39E **129** B6
Karaitivu I. *Sri Lanka* 9°45N 79°52E **127** K4
Karaitivu I. *Sri Lanka* 8°22N 79°47E **127** K4
Karaj *Iran* 35°48N 51°0E **129** B6
Karajarri ◇ *Australia* 19°0S 122°30W **148** C3
Karak *Malaysia* 3°25N 102°2E **121** L4
Karakalpakstan =
Qoraqalpog'iston □
Uzbekistan 43°0N 58°0E **108** D6
Karakelong *Indonesia* 4°35N 126°50E **119** D7
Karakitang *Indonesia* 3°14N 125°20E **119** D7
Karakoçan *Turkey* 38°59N 40°4E **105** B9
Karakol *Kyrgyzstan* 42°30N 78°20E **109** D9
Karakoram Pass *Asia* 35°33N 77°50E **124** B7
Karakoram Ra. *Pakistan* 35°30N 77°0E **125** B7

Karakul = Qorako'l
Uzbekistan 39°32N 63°50E **108** E6
Karakul *Tajikistan* 39°2N 73°33E **109** E8
Karakul, Ozero
Ukraine 45°56N 33°0E **85** K7
Karakuwisa *Namibia* 18°56S 19°40E **144** A2
Karalon *Russia* 57°5N 115°50E **107** D12
Karama *Jordan* 31°57N 35°35E **138** D4
Karaman *Balkesir, Turkey* 39°39N 28°0E **99** B9
Karaman *Konya, Turkey* 37°14N 33°13E **104** D5
Karamanlı *Turkey* 37°23N 29°47E **99** D11
Karamay *China* 45°30N 84°58E **116** B6
Karambu *Indonesia* 3°53S 116°6E **118** E5
Karamea *N.Z.* 41°14S 172°6E **155** B7
Karamea *N.Z.* 41°13S 172°26E **155** B7
Karamea Bight *N.Z.* 41°22S 171°40E **155** B6
Karamnasa → *India* 25°31N 83°52E **125** G10
Karamürsel *Turkey* 40°41N 29°36E **99** F13
Karān *Si. Arabia* 27°43N 49°49E **129** E6
Karand *Iran* 34°16N 46°15E **128** C5
Karanganyar
Indonesia 7°38S 109°37E **119** G13
Karangana *Mali* 12°15N 5°4W **138** C3
Karanja *Maharashtra,*
India 21°11N 78°24E **126** D4
Karanja *Maharashtra,*
India 20°29N 77°31E **126** D3
Karanjanyar
Indonesia 7°35S 109°37E **119** G13
Karasburg *Namibia* 28°0S 18°44E **144** C2
Karasino *Russia* 66°50N 86°50E **106** C9
Karasjok *Norway* 69°27N 25°30E **60** B21
Karasuk *Russia* 53°44N 78°2E **109** B9
Karasuyama *Japan* 36°39N 140°9E **113** F10
Karataş *Adana, Turkey* 36°36N 35°21E **104** D6
Karataş *Manisa, Turkey* 38°33N 28°16E **99** C10
Karataş Burnu *Turkey* 36°31N 35°24E **104** D6
Karatau, Khrebet = Qarataū
Kazakhstan 43°30N 69°30E **108** D7
Karatax Shan *China* 35°57N 81°0E **109** E12
Karateki Shan *China* 40°40N 77°50E **116** C3
Karativu *Sri Lanka* 8°22N 79°47E **127** K4
Karatoprak = Turgutreis
Turkey 37°2N 27°15E **99** D9
Karatsu *Japan* 33°26N 129°58E **113** H5
Karaul *Russia* 70°6N 82°15E **106** B9
Karauli *India* 26°30N 77°4E **124** F7
Karavastaë △ *Albania* 40°55N 19°30E **96** F3
Karavastasë, L. e *Albania* 40°55N 19°30E **96** F3
Karavia *Greece* 36°49N 23°37E **98** E5
Karavostasi *Cyprus* 35°8N 32°50E **101** D11
Karawang *Indonesia* 6°30S 107°15E **119** G12
Karawanken *Europe* 46°30N 14°40E **78** E7
Karayazı *Turkey* 39°41N 42°9E **105** C10
Karazhal = Qarazhal
Kazakhstan 48°2N 70°49E **108** E8
Karbalā' *Iraq* 32°36N 44°3E **105** F11
Karbalā' □ *Iraq* 32°30N 43°50E **105** F10
Kârböle *Sweden* 61°59N 15°22E **62** C9
Karcag *Hungary* 47°19N 20°57E **80** C5
Karcha → *Pakistan* 34°45N 76°10E **124** B7
Karchana *India* 25°17N 81°56E **125** G9
Karczew *Poland* 52°5N 21°15E **83** F8
Kardam *Bulgaria* 43°45N 28°6E **97** C12
Kardamila *Greece* 38°35N 26°5E **99** C8
Kardamili *Greece* 36°53N 22°13E **98** E4
Kardeljevo = Ploče
Croatia 43°4N 17°26E **93** E14
Karditsa *Greece* 39°23N 21°54E **98** B3
Kärdla *Estonia* 59°0N 22°45E **84** C2
Kardzhali *Bulgaria* 41°38N 25°21E **97** B9
Kardzhali □ *Bulgaria* 41°38N 25°25E **97** B9
Kareeberge *S. Africa* 30°59S 21°50E **144** D3
Kareha → *India* 25°44N 86°21E **125** G12
Kareima *Sudan* 18°30N 31°49E **137** D11
Karelia □ *Russia* 65°30N 32°30E **106** C4
Karelian Republic = Karelia □
Russia 65°30N 32°30E **106** C4
Karera *India* 25°32N 78°9E **124** G8
Kārevāndar *Iran* 27°53N 60°44E **129** E9
Kargasok *Russia* 59°3N 80°53E **106** D9
Kargat *Russia* 55°10N 80°15E **106** D9
Kargi *Kenya* 2°31N 37°34E **142** B4
Kargıl *India* 34°32N 76°12E **124** B7
Kargopol *Russia* 61°30N 38°58E **84** B10
Kargowa *Poland* 52°5N 15°51E **83** F2
Karia ba Mohammed
Morocco 34°22N 5°12W **136** B2
Karīān *Iran* 26°57N 57°14E **129** E8
Kariba *Zimbabwe* 16°28S 28°50E **143** F2
Kariba, L. *Zimbabwe* 16°40S 28°25E **143** F2
Kariba Dam *Zimbabwe* 16°30S 28°35E **143** F2
Kariba Gorge *Zambia* 16°30S 28°50E **143** F2
Karibib *Namibia* 22°0S 15°56E **144** B2
Karies *Greece* 40°14N 24°19E **97** B8
Karīet *Iran* 35°15N 56°38E **137** D4
Kariya *Japan* 34°58N 137°1E **113** G8
Kariyangwe *Zimbabwe* 18°0S 27°38E **144** A4
Karjala *Finland* 62°0N 30°24E **84** B5
Karkal *India* 13°15N 74°56E **127** H2
Karkaralinsk = Qarqaraly
Kazakhstan 49°26N 75°30E **109** C9

Karkheh → *Iran* 31°2N 47°29E **128** D5
Karki *Azerbaijan* 39°47N 44°57E **105** C11
Karkinitska Zatoka
Ukraine 45°56N 33°0E **85** K7
Karkinitsky Zaliv = Karkinitska
Zatoka *Ukraine* 45°56N 33°0E **85** K7
Karkuk = Kirkūk
Iraq 35°30N 44°21E **105** E11
Karkur Tohl *Egypt* 22°5N 25°5E **137** C2
Karl Liebknecht = imeni Karl
Libknekhta *Russia* 51°35N 35°35E **85** G8
Karla, L. = Volvi, L.
Greece 40°40N 23°34E **96** F7
Karlantijpa North ◇
Australia 19°27S 133°33E **148** C5
Karlantijpa South ◇
Australia 20°31S 133°9E **148** C5
Karleby = Kokkola
Finland 63°50N 23°8E **60** E20
Karlholmsbruk *Sweden* 60°31N 17°37E **62** D11
Karlino *Poland* 54°3N 15°53E **82** D2
Karlova *Turkey* 39°17N 41°0E **105** C9
Karlivka *Ukraine* 49°29N 35°8E **85** H8
Karlobag *Croatia* 44°32N 15°5E **93** D12
Karlovac *Croatia* 45°31N 15°36E **93** C12
Karlovarský □ *Czechia* 50°13N 12°51E **78** A5
Karlovasi *Greece* 37°45N 26°42E **99** D8
Karlovka = Karlivka
Ukraine 49°29N 35°8E **85** H8
Karlovo *Bulgaria* 42°38N 24°47E **97** D8
Karlovy Vary *Czechia* 50°13N 12°51E **78** A5
Karlsbad = Karlovy Vary
Czechia 50°13N 12°51E **78** A5
Karlsborg *Sweden* 58°33N 14°33E **63** F8
Karlsena, Mys *Russia* 77°0N 67°42E **106** B7
Karlshamn *Sweden* 56°10N 14°51E **63** H8
Karlskoga *Sweden* 59°28N 14°33E **62** E8
Karlskrona *Sweden* 56°10N 15°35E **63** H9
Karlsruhe *Germany* 49°0N 8°23E **77** F4
Karlstad *Sweden* 59°23N 13°30E **62** E7
Karlstad *U.S.A.* 48°35N 96°31W **172** A5
Karlstadt *Germany* 49°57N 9°47E **77** F5
Karma *Niger* 13°38N 1°52E **139** C5
Karmala *India* 18°25N 75°12E **126** F2
Karmi'el *Israel* 32°55N 35°18E **130** C4
Karnak *Egypt* 25°43N 32°39E **137** B3
Karnal *India* 29°42N 77°2E **124** E7
Karnali = Ghaghara →
India 25°45N 84°40E **125** G11
Karnali → *Nepal* 28°45N 81°16E **125** E9
Karnaphuli Res. = Kaptai L.
Bangla. 22°40N 92°20E **123** H18
Karnaprayag *India* 30°16N 79°15E **124** D8
Karnes City *U.S.A.* 28°53N 97°54W **176** G6
Karnische Alpen *Europe* 46°36N 13°0E **78** E6
Karnobat *Bulgaria* 42°39N 26°59E **97** D10
Kärnten □ *Austria* 46°52N 13°30E **78** E7
Karo *Mali* 12°16N 3°18W **138** C4
Karoi *Zimbabwe* 16°48S 29°45E **143** F2
Karonga *Malawi* 9°57S 33°55E **143** D3
Karoo △ *S. Africa* 32°18S 22°27E **144** D3
Karoonda *Australia* 35°1S 139°59E **152** C3
Karor *Pakistan* 31°15N 70°59E **124** D5
Karora *Sudan* 17°44N 38°15E **135** E13
Karounga *Mali* 15°20N 7°35W **138** B3
Karousades *Greece* 39°47N 19°45E **98** B1
Karpacz *Poland* 50°46N 15°46E **83** H2
Karpasia *Cyprus* 35°32N 34°15E **101** D13
Karpathos *Greece* 35°37N 27°10E **99** F9
Karpathou, Stenon
Greece 36°0N 27°30E **99** F9
Karpatsky △ *Ukraine* 48°20N 24°35E **81** B9
Karpenisi *Greece* 38°55N 21°40E **98** C3
Karpuz Burnu = Apostolos
Andreas, C. *Cyprus* 35°42N 34°35E **101** D13
Karpuzlu *Turkey* 37°33N 27°51E **99** D9
Karratha *Australia* 20°44S 116°52E **148** D2
Kars *Turkey* 40°40N 43°5E **105** B10
Karsakpay *Kazakhstan* 47°55N 66°40E **108** E7
Karshi = Qarshi
Uzbekistan 38°53N 65°48E **108** F7
Karsiyang *India* 26°56N 88°18E **125** F13
Karsog *India* 31°23N 77°12E **124** D7
Karst = Kras *Slovenia* 45°35N 14°0E **93** C10
Kartal *Turkey* 40°53N 29°11E **99** F13
Kartala *Comoros Is.* 11°45S 43°21E **141** a
Kartaly *Russia* 53°3N 60°40E **108** D6
Kartapur *India* 31°27N 75°32E **124** D6
Karthaus *U.S.A.* 41°8N 78°9W **174** E6
Kartuzy *Poland* 54°22N 18°10E **82** D6
Karuah *Australia* 32°37S 151°56E **153** B9
Karufa *Indonesia* 3°50S 133°20E **119** E8
Karula △ *Estonia* 57°43N 26°30E **84** C4
Karuma *Uganda* 2°5N 32°15E **142** B3
Karumba *Australia* 17°31S 140°50E **150** B3
Karumo *Tanzania* 2°25S 32°50E **142** C3
Karumwa *Tanzania* 3°12S 32°38E **142** C3
Kärün → *Iran* 30°26N 48°10E **129** D6
Karungu *Kenya* 0°50S 34°10E **142** C3
Karup *Denmark* 56°19N 9°10E **63** H3
Karur *India* 10°59N 78°2E **127** J4
Karviná *Czechia* 49°53N 18°31E **79** B11
Karwan → *India* 27°26N 78°4E **124** F7
Karwar *India* 14°55N 74°13E **127** G2
Karwendel △ *Austria* 47°28N 11°25E **78** E6
Karwi *India* 25°12N 80°57E **125** G9
Karymskoye *Russia* 51°36N 114°21E **107** D12
Kaş *Turkey* 36°11N 29°37E **99** E11
Kasaba *Turkey* 36°39N 29°44E **99** E11
Kasache *Malawi* 13°25S 34°20E **143** E3
Kasai →
Dem. Rep. of the Congo 3°30S 16°10E **140** E3
Kasaji
Dem. Rep. of the Congo 10°25S 23°27E **143** E1
Kasama *Zambia* 10°16S 31°9E **143** E3
Kasan-dong *N. Korea* 41°18N 126°55E **115** D14
Kasane *Namibia* 17°34S 24°50E **144** A3
Kasanga *Tanzania* 8°30S 31°10E **143** D3
Kasanka △ *Zambia* 12°22S 30°15E **143** E3
Kasar, Ras *Sudan* 18°2N 38°36E **137** D4
Kasaragod *India* 12°30N 74°58E **127** H2
Kasba L. *Canada* 60°20N 102°10W **163** A8
Kasba Tadla *Morocco* 32°36N 6°17W **136** B2
Kasempa *Zambia* 13°30S 25°44E **143** E2
Kasenga
Dem. Rep. of the Congo 10°20S 28°45E **143** E2
Kasese *Uganda* 0°13N 30°3E **142** B3

Kasganj India 27°48N 78°42E 125 F8
Kashabowie Canada 48°40N 90°26W 164 C1
Kashaf Iran 35°58N 61°7E 129 C9
Kāshān Iran 34°5N 51°30E 129 C6
Kashechewan Canada 52°18N 81°37W 164 B3
Kashgan → Iran 33°5N 47°31E 105 F12
Kashgar = Kashi China 39°30N 76°2E 109 E9
Kashi China 39°30N 76°2E 109 E9
Kashimbo Dem. Rep. of the Congo 11°12S 26°19E 143 E2
Kashin Russia 57°20N 37°36E 84 D9
Kashipur Odisha, India 19°16N 83°3E 126 E6
Kashipur Uttarakhand, India 29°15N 79°0E 125 E8
Kashira Russia 54°45N 38°10E 84 E10
Kashiwazaki Japan 37°22N 138°33E 113 F9
Kashk-e Kohneh Afghan. 34°55N 62°30E 122 B3
Kashksaray Iran 38°27N 45°34E 105 C11
Kashkū'īyeh Iran 30°31N 55°40E 129 D7
Kāshmar Iran 35°16N 58°26E 129 C8
Kashmir Asia 34°0N 76°0E 125 C7
Kashmor Pakistan 28°28N 69°32E 124 E3
Kashpirovka Russia 53°0N 48°30E 86 D9
Kashun Noerh = Gaxun Nur China 42°22N 100°30E 110 C9
Kasiari India 22°8N 87°14E 125 H12
Kasimov Russia 54°55N 41°20E 86 C5
Kasinge Dem. Rep. of the Congo 6°15S 26°58E 142 D2
Kasiruta Indonesia 0°25S 127°12E 119 E7
Kaskaskia → U.S.A. 37°58N 89°57W 172 G9
Kaskattama → Canada 57°3N 90°4W 163 B10
Kaskinen Finland 62°22N 21°15E 60 E19
Kaskö = Kaskinen Finland 62°22N 21°15E 60 E19
Kaslo Canada 49°55N 116°55W 162 D5
Kasmere L. Canada 59°34N 101°10W 163 B8
Kasongo Dem. Rep. of the Congo 4°30S 26°33E 142 C2
Kasongo Lunda Dem. Rep. of the Congo 6°35S 16°49E 140 F3
Kasos Greece 35°20N 26°55E 99 F8
Kasou, Stenon Greece 35°30N 26°30E 99 F8
Kaspi Georgia 41°59N 44°26E 87 K7
Kaspichan Bulgaria 43°18N 27°11E 97 C11
Kaspiysk Russia 42°52N 47°40E 87 J8
Kaspiyskiy Russia 45°22N 47°23E 87 H8
Kassaba Egypt 22°40N 29°55E 137 C2
Kassalâ Sudan 15°30N 36°0E 135 E13
Kassandra Greece 40°0N 23°30E 96 F7
Kassandra Kolpos Greece 40°5N 23°30E 96 F7
Kassandras, Akra Greece 39°57N 23°30E 96 G7
Kassandria Greece 40°1N 23°27E 96 F7
Kassel Germany 51°18N 9°26E 76 D5
Kasserine Tunisia 35°10N 8°50E 136 A5
Kasserine □ Tunisia 35°10N 8°50E 136 A5
Kassinger Sudan 18°46N 31°51E 137 D3
Kassiopi Greece 39°48N 19°53E 101 A3
Kasson U.S.A. 44°2N 92°45W 172 C7
Kastamonu Turkey 41°25N 33°43E 104 B5
Kastamonu □ Turkey 41°20N 34°0E 104 B5
Kastav Croatia 45°22N 14°20E 93 C11
Kasteli = Kissamos Greece 35°29N 23°38E 101 D5
Kastelli Greece 35°12N 25°20E 101 D7
Kastellorizo = Megisti Greece 36°8N 29°34E 99 E11
Kastelo, Akra Greece 35°30N 27°15E 99 F9
Kasterlee Belgium 51°15N 4°59E 69 C4
Kastlösa Sweden 56°26N 16°25E 63 H10
Kastoria Greece 40°30N 21°19E 96 F5
Kastorias, L. Greece 40°30N 21°20E 96 F5
Kastorio Greece 37°10N 22°17E 98 D4
Kastornoye Russia 51°55N 38°2E 85 G10
Kastos Greece 38°35N 20°55E 98 C2
Kastro = Myrina Greece 39°53N 25°4E 99 B7
Kastrom Mefa'a = Umm al Rasas Jordan 31°30N 35°55E 130 D4
Kastrosikia Greece 39°6N 20°38E 98 B2
Kastrup, København ✈ (CPH) Denmark 55°37N 12°39E 63 J6
Kastsyukovichy Belarus 53°20N 32°4E 85 F7
Kasubi Tombs Uganda 0°20N 32°30E 142 B3
Kasulu Tanzania 4°37S 30°5E 142 C3
Kasumi Japan 35°38N 134°38E 113 G7
Kasumkent Russia 41°47N 48°15E 87 K9
Kasungu Malawi 13°0S 33°29E 143 E3
Kasungu △ Malawi 12°53S 33°9E 143 E3
Kasur Pakistan 31°5N 74°25E 124 D6
Kata, Ao Thailand 7°48N 98°18E 121 J2
Kata Archanes Greece 35°15N 25°10E 101 D7
Kata Tjuta Australia 25°20S 130°50E 149 E5
Kataba Zambia 16°5S 25°10E 143 F2
Katagum Nigeria 12°18N 10°21E 139 C7
Katahdin, Mt. U.S.A. 45°54N 68°56W 173 C19
Kataka = Cuttack India 20°25N 85°57E 126 D7
Katako Kombe Dem. Rep. of the Congo 3°25S 24°20E 142 C1
Katakolo Greece 37°38N 21°19E 98 D3
Katale Tanzania 4°52S 31°7E 142 C3
Katamatite Australia 36°6S 145°41E 153 D6
Katanda Katanga, Dem. Rep. of the Congo 7°52S 24°13E 142 D1
Katanda Nord-Kivu, Dem. Rep. of the Congo 0°55S 29°21E 142 C2
Katanga Dem. Rep. of the Congo 8°0S 25°0E 140 F5
Katangi India 21°56N 79°50E 126 D4
Katanning Australia 33°40S 117°33E 149 F2
Katastari Greece 37°50N 20°45E 98 D2
Katavi □ Tanzania 6°0S 31°0E 142 D3
Katavi △ Tanzania 6°51S 31°3E 142 D3
Katavi Swamp Tanzania 6°50S 31°10E 142 D3
Katchall India 7°57N 93°22E 127 L11
Katerini Greece 40°18N 22°37E 96 F6
Katghora India 22°30N 82°33E 125 H10
Katha Myanmar 24°10N 96°30E 123 G20
Katherîna, Gebel Egypt 28°30N 33°57E 128 D2
Katherine Australia 14°27S 132°20E 148 B5
Katherine Gorge = Nitmiluk △ Australia 14°6S 132°15E 148 B5
Kathi India 21°47N 74°3E 124 J6
Kathiawar India 22°20N 71°0E 124 H4
Kathikas Cyprus 34°55N 32°25E 101 E11
Kathleen U.S.A. 28°7N 82°2W 179 G7
Kathmandu Nepal 27°45N 85°20E 125 F11
Kathua India 32°23N 75°34E 124 C6
Kati Mali 12°41N 8°4W 138 C3
Kati Thanda-Lake Eyre Australia 29°30S 137°26E 147 D6
Kati Thanda-Lake Eyre (North) Australia 28°30S 137°20E 151 D2
Kati Thanda-Lake Eyre (South) Australia 29°18S 137°25E 151 D2
Katihar India 25°34N 87°36E 125 G12
Katikati N.Z. 37°32S 175°57E 154 D4
Katima Mulilo Namibia 17°28S 24°13E 144 A3
Katimbira Malawi 12°40S 34°0E 143 E3
Katingan = Mendawai → Indonesia 3°30S 113°0E 118 E4
Katiola Côte d'Ivoire 8°10N 5°10W 138 D3
Katiti ◎ Australia 25°1S 131°11E 149 E5
Katlabukh, Ozero Ukraine 45°28N 29°0E 81 E14
Katlanovo Macedonia 41°52N 21°40E 96 E5
Katmandu = Kathmandu Nepal 27°45N 85°20E 125 F11
Katni India 23°51N 80°24E 125 H9
Kato Achaia Greece 38°8N 21°33E 98 C3
Kato Chorio Greece 35°3N 25°47E 101 D7
Kato Korakiana Greece 39°42N 19°45E 101 A3
Kato Pyrgos Cyprus 35°11N 32°41E 101 D11
Katochi Greece 38°26N 21°15E 98 C3
Katol India 21°17N 78°38E 126 D4
Katompe Dem. Rep. of the Congo 6°2S 26°23E 142 D2
Katong Singapore 1°18N 103°53E 121 d
Katonga → Uganda 0°34N 31°50E 142 B3
Katoomba Australia 33°41S 150°19E 153 B9
Katouna Greece 38°47N 21°7E 98 C3
Katowice Poland 50°17N 19°5E 83 H6
Katrancı Dağı Turkey 37°27N 30°25E 99 D12
Katrine, L. U.K. 56°15N 4°30W 65 E4
Katrineholm Sweden 59°0N 16°12E 62 E10
Katsina Nigeria 13°0N 7°32E 139 C6
Katsina □ Nigeria 12°30N 7°30E 139 C6
Katsina Ala Nigeria 7°10N 9°30E 139 D6
Katsina Ala → Nigeria 7°10N 9°20E 139 D6
Katsumoto Japan 33°51N 129°42E 113 H4
Katsuura Japan 35°10N 140°20E 113 G10
Katsuyama Japan 36°3N 136°30E 113 F8
Kattaqo'rg'on Uzbekistan 39°55N 66°15E 109 E7
Kattavia Greece 35°57N 27°46E 101 D9
Kattegat Denmark 56°40N 11°20E 63 H5
Katthammarsvik Sweden 57°26N 18°51E 63 G12
Katumba Dem. Rep. of the Congo 7°40S 25°17E 142 D2
Katun → Russia 52°25N 85°1E 109 B11
Katwa India 23°30N 88°5E 125 H13
Katwijk Neths. 52°12N 4°24E 69 B4
Kąty Wrocławskie Poland 51°2N 16°45E 83 G3
Kau-Ye Kyun Myanmar 11°1N 98°32E 121 G2
Kaua'i U.S.A. 22°3N 159°30W 167 L8
Kaub Germany 50°5N 7°46E 77 E3
Kaudom ⌂ Namibia 18°45S 20°51E 144 A3
Kaufbeuren Germany 47°53N 10°37E 77 H6
Kaufman U.S.A. 32°35N 96°19W 176 E6
Kauhajoki Finland 62°25N 22°10E 60 E20
Kauhaneva-Pohjankangas △ Finland 62°13N 22°20E 60 E20
Kaukauna U.S.A. 44°17N 88°17W 172 C9
Kaukauveld Namibia 20°0S 20°15E 144 B3
Ka'ula I. U.S.A. 21°40N 160°33W 167 L7
Kaunas Lithuania 54°54N 23°54E 82 D10
Kaunas ✈ (KUN) Lithuania 54°57N 24°3E 82 D11
Kaunia Bangla. 25°46N 89°26E 125 G13
Kaunos Turkey 36°49N 28°39E 99 E10
Kaura Namoda Nigeria 12°37N 6°33E 139 C6
Kauru Nigeria 10°33N 8°12E 139 C6
Kautokeino Norway 69°0N 23°4E 60 B20
Kauwapur India 27°31N 82°18E 125 F10
Kavacha Russia 60°16N 169°51E 107 C17
Kavadarci Macedonia 41°26N 22°3E 96 E6
Kavajë Albania 41°11N 19°33E 96 E3
Kavak Turkey 41°4N 36°3E 104 B7
Kavak Dağı Turkey 37°10N 28°2E 99 D10
Kavaklı Turkey 41°39N 27°10E 97 E11
Kavaklıdere Turkey 37°27N 28°21E 99 D10
Kavala Greece 40°57N 24°28E 97 F8
Kavala Kolpos Greece 40°50N 24°25E 97 F8
Kavalerovo Russia 44°15N 135°4E 112 B7
Kavali India 14°55N 80°1E 127 G5
Kavango = Cubango → Africa 18°50S 22°25E 144 A3
Kavār Iran 29°11N 52°44E 129 D7
Kavaratti India 10°34N 72°37E 127 J1
Kavaratti I. India 10°33N 72°38E 127 J1
Kavarna Bulgaria 43°26N 28°22E 97 C12
Kaveri = Cauvery → India 11°9N 78°52E 127 J4
Kavi India 22°12N 72°38E 124 H5
Kavimba Botswana 18°2S 24°38E 144 A3
Kavīr, Dasht-e Iran 34°30N 55°0E 129 C7
Kavīr △ Iran 34°40N 52°0E 129 C7
Kävlinge Sweden 55°47N 13°9E 63 J7
Kavos Greece 39°23N 20°3E 101 B4
Kavousi Greece 35°7N 25°51E 99 F7
Kaw Fr. Guiana 4°30N 52°15W 187 C8
Kawagama L. Canada 45°18N 78°45W 174 A6
Kawagoe Japan 35°55N 139°29E 113 G9
Kawaguchi Japan 35°52N 139°45E 113 G9
Kawah Ijen △ Indonesia 8°3S 114°14E 119 H15
Kawakawa N.Z. 35°23S 174°6E 154 B3
Kawambwa Zambia 9°48S 29°3E 143 D2
Kawanoe = Shikokochūō Japan 34°1N 133°34E 113 G6
Kawardha India 22°0N 81°17E 125 J9
Kawasaki Japan 35°31N 139°43E 113 G9
Kawasi Indonesia 1°38S 127°28E 119 E7
Kawau I. N.Z. 36°25S 174°52E 154 C3
Kawawachikamach Canada 54°48N 66°50W 165 B6
Kaweka Ra. N.Z. 39°17S 176°19E 154 F5
Kawerau N.Z. 38°7S 176°42E 154 E5
Kawhia N.Z. 38°4S 174°49E 154 E3
Kawhia Harbour N.Z. 38°5S 174°51E 154 E3
Kawio, Kepulauan Indonesia 4°30N 125°30E 119 D7
Kawthaung Myanmar 10°5N 98°36E 121 H2
Kawthoolei = Kayin □ Myanmar 18°0N 97°30E 123 L20
Kawthule = Kayin □ Myanmar 18°0N 97°30E 123 L20
Kaxgar He → China 39°45N 78°24E 109 E9
Kaxholmen Sweden 57°51N 14°19E 63 G8
Kaya Burkina Faso 13°4N 1°10W 139 C4
Kayah □ Myanmar 19°15N 97°15E 123 K20
Kayak I. U.S.A. 59°56N 144°23W 166 D11
Kayalıköy Barajı Turkey 41°50N 27°5E 97 E11
Kayamkulam India 9°10N 76°33E 127 K3
Kayan → Indonesia 2°55N 117°35E 118 D5
Kaycee U.S.A. 43°43N 106°38W 168 E10
Kayeli Indonesia 3°20S 127°10E 119 E7
Kayenta U.S.A. 36°44N 110°15W 169 H8
Kayes Mali 14°25N 11°30W 138 C2
Kayes □ Mali 14°0N 11°0W 138 C2
Kayı Turkey 39°12N 30°46E 99 B12
Kayima S. Leone 8°54N 11°15W 138 D2
Kayin □ Myanmar 18°0N 97°30E 123 L20
Kaymakçı Turkey 38°10N 28°10E 99 C10
Kayoa Indonesia 0°1N 127°28E 119 D7
Kayombo Zambia 13°3S 23°51E 143 E1
Kaysatskoye Russia 49°47N 46°49E 86 F8
Kayseri Turkey 38°45N 35°30E 104 C6
Kayseri □ Turkey 38°40N 36°0E 104 C7
Kaysville U.S.A. 41°2N 111°56W 168 F8
Kayts Sri Lanka 9°42N 79°51E 127 K4
Kaz Dağı Turkey 39°42N 26°50E 99 B8
Kazachye Russia 70°52N 135°58E 107 B14
Kazakhstan ■ Asia 50°0N 70°0E 109 C8
Kazaly = Qazaly Kazakhstan 45°45N 62°6E 108 C6
Kazan Russia 55°50N 49°10E 86 C9
Kazan Turkey 40°14N 32°41E 104 B5
Kazan → Canada 64°2N 95°29W 163 A9
Kazan-Rettō Pac. Oc. 25°0N 141°0E 156 E6
Kazanlak Bulgaria 42°38N 25°20E 97 D9
Kazanskaya Russia 49°50N 41°10E 86 F5
Kazatin = Kozyatyn Ukraine 49°45N 28°50E 75 D15
Kazaure Nigeria 12°42N 8°28E 139 C6
Kazbek Russia 42°42N 44°30E 87 J7
Kāzerūn Iran 29°38N 51°40E 129 D6
Kazi Magomed = Qazımämmäd Azerbaijan 40°3N 49°0E 87 K9
Kazimierz Dolny Poland 51°19N 21°57E 83 G8
Kazimierza Wielka Poland 50°15N 20°30E 83 H7
Kazincbarcika Hungary 48°17N 20°36E 80 B5
Kazipet India 17°58N 79°30E 126 F4
Kazlų Rūda Lithuania 54°46N 23°30E 82 D10
Kaztalovka Kazakhstan 49°47N 48°43E 86 F9
Kazuma Pan △ Zimbabwe 18°20S 25°48E 143 F2
Kazuno Japan 40°10N 140°45E 112 D10
Kazym → Russia 63°54N 65°50E 106 C7
Kcynia Poland 53°0N 17°30E 83 F4
Ké-Macina Mali 13°58N 5°22W 138 C3
Kea Greece 37°35N 24°22E 98 D6
Keady U.K. 54°15N 6°42W 64 B5
Kearney U.S.A. 40°42N 99°5W 172 E4
Kearney ◎ Australia 20°10S 128°4E 148 D4
Kearny U.S.A. 33°3N 110°55W 169 K8
Kearsarge, Mt. U.S.A. 43°22N 71°50W 175 C13
Keban Turkey 38°50N 38°50E 105 C8
Keban Barajı Turkey 38°41N 38°33E 105 C8
Kebbi □ Nigeria 11°35N 4°0E 139 C5
Kébémèr Senegal 15°23N 16°34W 138 B1
Kébi Côte d'Ivoire 9°18N 6°37W 138 D3
Kébili Tunisia 33°47N 9°0E 136 B5
Kébili □ Tunisia 33°30N 8°50E 136 B5
Kebnekaise Sweden 67°53N 18°33E 60 C18
Kebri Dehar Ethiopia 6°45N 44°17E 131 F3
Kebumen Indonesia 7°42S 109°40E 119 G13
Kecel Hungary 46°31N 19°16E 80 D4
Kechika → Canada 59°41N 127°12W 162 B3
Keçiborlu Turkey 37°57N 30°18E 99 D12
Kecskemét Hungary 46°57N 19°42E 80 D4
Kedah □ Malaysia 5°50N 100°40E 121 K3
Kėdainiai Lithuania 55°15N 24°2E 82 C11
Kedarnath India 30°44N 79°4E 125 D8
Kedgwick Canada 47°40N 67°20W 165 C6
Kediri Indonesia 7°51S 112°1E 118 F4
Kedjebi Ghana 8°12N 0°25E 139 D5
Kédougou Senegal 12°35N 12°10W 138 C2
Kedros Oros Greece 35°11N 24°37E 101 D6
Kędzierzyn-Koźle Poland 50°20N 18°12E 83 H5
Keeler U.S.A. 36°29N 117°52W 170 J9
Keeley L. Canada 54°54N 108°8W 163 C7
Keeling Is. = Cocos Is. Ind. Oc. 12°10S 96°55E 146 F8
Keelung = Chilung Taiwan 25°3N 121°45E 117 E13
Keene Canada 44°15N 78°10W 174 B6
Keene Calif., U.S.A. 35°13N 118°33W 171 K8
Keene N.H., U.S.A. 42°56N 72°17W 175 D12
Keene N.Y., U.S.A. 44°16N 73°46W 175 B11
Keep River △ Australia 15°49S 129°8E 148 C4
Keeper Hill Ireland 52°45N 8°16W 64 D3
Keepit, L. Australia 30°50S 150°30E 153 A9
Keerweer, C. Australia 14°0S 141°32E 150 A3
Keeseville U.S.A. 44°29N 73°30W 175 B11
Keetmanshoop Namibia 26°35S 18°8E 144 C2
Keewatin Canada 49°46N 94°34W 163 D10
Keewatin → Canada 56°29N 100°46W 163 B8
Kefalonia Greece 38°15N 20°30E 98 C2
Kefalos Greece 36°45N 26°59E 99 E8
Kefamenanu Indonesia 9°28S 124°29E 119 F6
Kefar Sava Israel 32°11N 34°54E 130 C3
Keffi Nigeria 8°55N 7°43E 139 D6
Keffin Hausa Nigeria 12°13N 9°59E 139 C6
Keflavík Iceland 64°2N 22°35W 60 D2
Keg River Canada 57°54N 117°55W 162 B5
Kegalla Sri Lanka 7°15N 80°21E 127 L5
Kegaska Canada 50°9N 61°18W 165 B7
Kehancha Kenya 1°11S 34°37E 142 C3
Keheili Sudan 19°25N 32°50E 137 D3
Kehl Germany 48°34N 7°50E 77 G3
Keighley U.K. 53°52N 1°54W 66 D6
Keila Estonia 59°18N 24°25E 84 C3
Keimoes S. Africa 28°41S 20°59E 144 C3
Keita Niger 14°46N 5°56E 139 C6
Keitele Finland 63°10N 26°20E 60 E22
Keith Australia 36°6S 140°20E 152 D4
Keith U.K. 57°32N 2°57W 65 D6
Keiyasi Fiji 17°53S 177°46E 154 a
Keizer U.S.A. 44°57N 123°1W 168 D2
Kejimkujik △ Canada 44°25N 65°25W 165 D6
Kejserr Franz Joseph Fd. Greenland 73°30N 24°30W 57 C8
Kekri India 26°0N 75°10E 124 G6
Kelan China 38°43N 111°31E 114 E6
Kelang = Klang Malaysia 3°2N 101°26E 121 L3
Kelani Ganga → Sri Lanka 6°58N 79°50E 127 L4
Kelantan □ Malaysia 5°10N 102°0E 121 K3
Kelantan → Malaysia 6°13N 102°14E 121 J4
Këlcyrë Albania 40°20N 20°12E 96 F4
Kelekçi Turkey 37°15N 29°20E 99 D11
Keles Turkey 39°54N 29°14E 97 G13
Keleti-főcsatorna Hungary 47°45N 21°20E 80 C6
Kelheim Germany 48°54N 11°52E 77 G7
Kelibia Tunisia 36°50N 11°3E 136 A6
Kelkit Turkey 40°7N 39°16E 105 B8
Kelkit → Turkey 40°45N 36°32E 104 B7
Kellé Niger 14°16N 10°7E 139 C7
Keller U.S.A. 31°50N 81°15W 178 D8
Kellerberrin Australia 31°36S 117°38E 149 F2
Kellett, C. Canada 72°0N 126°0W 54 B1
Kelleys I. U.S.A. 41°36N 82°42W 174 E2
Kellogg U.S.A. 47°32N 116°7W 168 C5
Kells Ireland 53°44N 6°53W 64 C5
Kelmė Lithuania 55°38N 22°56E 82 C9
Kelmentsi Ukraine 48°28N 26°50E 81 B11
Kélo Chad 9°10N 15°45E 135 G9
Kelokedhara Cyprus 34°48N 32°39E 101 E11
Kelowna Canada 49°50N 119°25W 162 D5
Kelsey Creek Australia 20°26S 148°31E 150 b
Kelseyville U.S.A. 38°59N 122°50W 170 G4
Kelso N.Z. 45°54S 169°15E 155 F4
Kelso U.K. 55°36N 2°26W 65 F6
Kelso U.S.A. 46°9N 122°54W 170 D4
Keluang = Kluang Malaysia 2°3N 103°18E 121 L4
Kelud Indonesia 7°56N 112°18E 119 H15
Kelvington Canada 52°10N 103°30W 163 C8
Kem Russia 65°0N 34°38E 106 C4
Kem-Kem Morocco 30°40N 4°30W 136 B3
Kema Indonesia 1°22N 125°8E 119 D7
Kemah Turkey 39°32N 39°5E 105 C8
Kemaliye Erzincan, Turkey 39°16N 38°29E 105 C8
Kemaliye Manisa, Turkey 38°27N 28°25E 99 C10
Kemalpaşa Turkey 38°25N 27°27E 99 C9
Kemaman Malaysia 4°12N 103°18E 121 K4
Kemano Canada 53°35N 128°0W 162 C3
Kemasik Malaysia 4°25N 103°27E 121 K4
Kemer Antalya, Turkey 36°36N 30°34E 99 E12
Kemer Burdur, Turkey 37°21N 30°4E 99 D12
Kemer Muğla, Turkey 36°40N 29°22E 99 E11
Kemer Barajı Turkey 37°30N 28°37E 99 D10
Kemerovo Russia 55°20N 86°5E 106 D9
Kemerovo □ Russia 55°0N 86°0E 109 B11
Ķemeru △ Latvia 56°58N 23°25E 82 B10
Kemi Finland 65°44N 24°34E 60 D21
Kemi älv = Kemijoki → Finland 65°47N 24°32E 60 D21
Kemi träsk = Kemijärvi Finland 66°43N 27°22E 60 C22
Kemijärvi Finland 66°43N 27°22E 60 C22
Kemijoki → Finland 65°47N 24°32E 60 D21
Kemmerer U.S.A. 41°48N 110°32W 168 F8
Kemmuna = Comino Malta 36°1N 14°20E 101 C1
Kemp, L. U.S.A. 33°46N 99°9W 176 E5
Kemp Land Antarctica 69°0S 55°0E 55 C5
Kempas Malaysia 1°33N 103°42E 121 d
Kempsey Australia 31°1S 152°50E 153 A10
Kempt, L. Canada 47°25N 74°22W 164 C5
Kempten Germany 47°45N 10°17E 77 H6
Kempton Australia 42°31S 147°12E 151 G4
Kemptville Canada 45°0N 75°38W 175 B9
Ken → India 25°13N 80°27E 125 G9
Kenadsa Algeria 31°48N 2°26W 136 B3
Kenai U.S.A. 60°33N 151°16W 160 E1
Kenai Mts. U.S.A. 60°0N 150°0W 166 D9
Kenamuke Swamp South Sudan 5°55N 33°48E 142 A3
Kenansville U.S.A. 27°53N 80°59W 179 H9
Kendai India 22°45N 82°37E 125 H10
Kendal Indonesia 6°56S 110°14E 119 G14
Kendal U.K. 54°20N 2°44W 66 C5
Kendall Australia 31°35S 152°44E 153 A10
Kendall U.S.A. 25°40N 80°19W 179 K9
Kendall → Australia 14°4S 141°35E 150 A3
Kendallville U.S.A. 41°27N 85°16W 173 E11
Kendari Indonesia 3°50S 122°30E 119 E6
Kendawangan Indonesia 2°32S 110°17E 118 E4
Kende Nigeria 11°30N 4°12E 139 C5
Kendi, Pulau Malaysia 5°13N 100°11E 121 c
Kendrapara India 20°35N 86°30E 126 D8
Këndrevicës, Maja e Albania 40°15N 19°52E 96 F3
Kendrew S. Africa 32°32S 24°30E 144 D3
Kendrick U.S.A. 29°15N 82°10W 179 F7
Kene Thao Laos 17°44N 101°10E 120 D3
Kenedy U.S.A. 28°49N 97°51W 176 G6
Kenema S. Leone 7°50N 11°14W 138 D2
Keng Kok Laos 16°26N 105°12E 120 D5
Keng Tawng Myanmar 20°45N 98°18E 123 J21
Keng Tung Myanmar 21°18N 99°39E 120 B2
Kengeja Tanzania 5°26S 39°45E 142 D4
Kenhardt S. Africa 29°19S 21°12E 144 C3
Kéniéba Mali 12°54N 11°17W 138 C2
Kenitra Morocco 34°15N 6°40W 136 B2
Kenli China 37°30N 118°20E 115 F10
Kenmare Ireland 51°53N 9°36W 64 E2
Kenmare U.S.A. 48°41N 102°5W 172 A2
Kenmare River → Ireland 51°48N 9°51W 64 E2
Kennebago Lake U.S.A. 45°4N 70°40W 175 A14
Kennebec U.S.A. 43°54N 99°52W 172 D4
Kennebec → U.S.A. 43°45N 69°46W 173 D19
Kennebunk U.S.A. 43°23N 70°33W 175 C14
Kennedy Zimbabwe 18°52S 27°10E 144 A4
Kennedy Channel Arctic 80°50N 66°0W 57 A4
Kennedy Ra. Australia 24°45S 115°10E 149 D2
Kennedy Range △ Australia 24°34S 115°2E 149 D2
Kennedy Space Center U.S.A. 28°40N 80°42W 179 G9
Kennemerduinen △ Neths. 52°27N 4°33E 69 B4
Kenner U.S.A. 29°59N 90°14W 177 G9
Kennesaw U.S.A. 34°1N 84°37W 178 A5
Kennet → U.K. 51°27N 0°57W 67 F7
Kenneth Ra. Australia 23°50S 117°8E 149 D2
Kennett U.S.A. 36°14N 90°3W 172 G8
Kennewick U.S.A. 46°12N 119°7W 168 C4
Kennisis Lake Canada 45°13N 78°36W 174 A6
Kenogami → Canada 51°6N 84°28W 164 B3
Kenora Canada 49°47N 94°29W 163 D10
Kenosha U.S.A. 42°35N 87°49W 172 D10
Kenozersky △ Russia 62°5N 38°10E 106 C1
Kensington Canada 46°28N 63°34W 165 C7
Kent Ohio, U.S.A. 41°9N 81°22W 174 E3
Kent Tex., U.S.A. 31°4N 104°13W 176 F2
Kent Wash., U.S.A. 47°22N 122°14W 170 C4
Kent □ U.K. 51°12N 0°40E 67 F8
Kent Group Australia 39°30S 147°20E 151 F4
Kent Pen. Canada 68°30N 107°0W 160 D10
Kentaū Kazakhstan 43°32N 68°36E 109 D7
Kentland U.S.A. 40°46N 87°27W 172 E10
Kenton U.S.A. 40°39N 83°37W 173 E12
Kentucky □ U.S.A. 37°0N 84°0W 173 G11
Kentucky → U.S.A. 38°41N 85°11W 173 F11
Kentucky L. U.S.A. 37°1N 88°16W 172 G9
Kentville Canada 45°6N 64°29W 165 C7
Kentwood U.S.A. 30°56N 90°31W 177 F9
Kenya ■ Africa 1°0N 38°0E 142 B4
Kenya, Mt. Kenya 0°10S 37°18E 142 C4
Kenyir, Tasik Malaysia 5°1N 102°54E 121 K4
Keo Neua, Deo Vietnam 18°23N 105°10E 120 C5
Keokuk U.S.A. 40°24N 91°24W 172 E8
Keoladeo △ India 27°0N 77°20E 124 F7
Keonjhargarh India 21°28N 85°35E 125 J11
Kep Cambodia 10°29N 104°19E 121 G5
Kep Vietnam 21°24N 106°16E 120 B6
Kep △ Cambodia 10°30N 104°18E 121 G5
Kepala Batas Malaysia 5°31N 100°26E 121 c
Kepez Turkey 40°5N 26°24E 97 F10
Kepi Indonesia 6°32S 139°19E 119 F9
Kępice Poland 54°16N 16°51E 82 D3
Kepler Mts. N.Z. 45°25S 167°20E 155 F2
Kępno Poland 51°18N 17°58E 83 G4
Kepsut Turkey 39°40N 28°9E 99 B10
Kerala □ India 11°0N 76°15E 127 J3
Kerama-Rettō Japan 26°5N 127°15E 113 L3
Keramoti Greece 40°52N 24°42E 97 F8
Keran Pakistan 34°35N 73°59E 125 B5
Keran △ Togo 10°9N 0°41E 139 C5
Kerang Australia 35°40S 143°55E 152 C5
Keratea Greece 37°48N 23°58E 98 D5
Keraudren, C. Australia 19°58S 119°45E 148 C2
Kerava Finland 60°25N 25°5E 84 B3
Kerch Ukraine 45°20N 36°20E 85 K9
Kerchenskiy Proliv Black Sea 45°10N 36°30E 85 K9
Kerchoual Mali 17°12N 0°20E 139 B5
Kerempe Burnu Turkey 42°2N 33°20E 104 A5
Kerepakupai-Meru = Angel Falls Venezuela 5°57N 62°30W 186 B6
Kerewan Gambia 13°29N 16°10W 138 C1
Kerguelen Ind. Oc. 49°15S 69°10E 146 J5
Kerguelen Plateau S. Ocean 55°0S 75°0E 146 K6
Keri Greece 37°40N 20°49E 98 D2
Kerian, Kuala Malaysia 5°10N 100°25E 121 c
Kericho Kenya 0°22S 35°15E 142 C4
Kerikeri N.Z. 35°12S 173°59E 154 B2
Kerinci Indonesia 1°40S 101°15E 118 E2
Keriya He → China 38°30N 82°10E 109 E10
Kerkenna, Îs. Tunisia 34°48N 11°11E 136 B6
Kerki = Atamyrat Turkmenistan 37°50N 65°12E 109 E7
Kerkini, L. Greece 41°12N 23°10E 96 E7
Kerkouane Tunisia 36°58N 11°2E 94 F4
Kerkrade Neths. 50°53N 6°4E 69 D6
Kerkyra Greece 39°38N 19°50E 101 A3
Kerkyra ✈ (CFU) Greece 39°35N 19°54E 98 B1
Kerkyras, Notio Steno Greece 39°34N 20°0E 101 A4
Kerma Sudan 19°33N 30°32E 137 D3
Kermadec Is. Pac. Oc. 30°0S 178°15W 147 E11
Kermadec Trench Pac. Oc. 30°30S 176°0W 156 L10
Kermān Iran 30°15N 57°1E 129 D8
Kerman U.S.A. 36°43N 120°4W 170 J6
Kermān □ Iran 30°0N 57°0E 129 D8
Kermān, Bīābān-e Iran 28°45N 59°45E 129 D8
Kermānshāh Iran 34°23N 47°0E 105 E12
Kermānshāh □ Iran 34°0N 46°30E 128 C5
Kermen Bulgaria 42°30N 26°16E 97 D10
Kermit U.S.A. 31°52N 103°6W 176 F3
Kern → U.S.A. 35°16N 119°18W 171 K7
Kernavė Lithuania 54°53N 24°49E 84 E3
Kernhof Austria 47°49N 15°32E 78 D8
Kernow = Cornwall □ U.K. 50°26N 4°40W 67 G3
Kernville U.S.A. 35°45N 118°26W 171 K8
Keroh Malaysia 5°43N 101°1E 121 K3
Keros Greece 36°54N 25°40E 99 E7
Kérou Benin 10°50N 2°5E 139 C5
Kérouane Guinea 9°15N 9°0W 138 D3
Kerpen Germany 50°51N 6°41E 76 E2
Kerrera U.K. 56°24N 5°33W 65 E3
Kerrobert Canada 51°56N 109°8W 163 C7
Kerrville U.S.A. 30°3N 99°8W 176 F5
Kerry □ Ireland 52°7N 9°35W 64 D2
Kerry Hd. Ireland 52°25N 9°56W 64 D2
Kerulen = Herlen → Asia 48°48N 117°0E 111 B12
Kervo = Kerava Finland 60°25N 25°5E 84 B3
Kerzaz Algeria 29°29N 1°37W 136 C3
Kesagami → Canada 51°40N 79°45W 164 B4
Kesagami L. Canada 50°23N 80°15W 164 B3
Keşan Turkey 40°49N 26°38E 97 F10
Kesennuma Japan 38°54N 141°35E 112 E10
Keshāvar Iran 36°50N 46°22E 105 D12
Keshit Iran 29°43N 58°17E 129 D8
Kesigi = Kosgi India 15°51N 77°16E 127 G3
Keşiş Dağ Turkey 39°47N 39°46E 105 C8
Keskal India 20°5N 81°35E 126 D5
Keskin Turkey 39°40N 33°36E 104 C5
Kestenga Russia 65°50N 31°45E 60 D24
Keswick U.K. 54°36N 3°8W 66 C4
Keszthely Hungary 46°50N 17°15E 80 D2
Ket → Russia 58°55N 81°32E 106 D9
Keta Ghana 5°49N 1°0E 139 D5
Keta Lagoon Ghana 5°55N 1°0E 139 D5
Ketapang Jawa Timur, Indonesia 8°9S 114°23E 119 J17
Ketapang Kalimantan Barat, Indonesia 1°55S 110°0E 118 E4
Ketchenery Russia 47°18N 44°32E 87 G7
Ketchikan U.S.A. 55°21N 131°39W 162 B2
Ketchum U.S.A. 43°41N 114°22W 168 E6
Kete Krachi Ghana 7°46N 0°1W 139 D4
Keti Bandar Pakistan 24°8N 67°27E 124 G2
Kétou Benin 7°25N 2°45E 139 D5
Ketri India 28°1N 75°50E 124 E6
Kętrzyn Poland 54°7N 21°22E 82 D8
Kettering U.K. 52°24N 0°43W 67 E7
Kettering U.S.A. 39°41N 84°10W 173 F11
Kettle → Canada 56°40N 89°34W 163 B11
Kettle Falls U.S.A. 48°37N 118°3W 168 B4
Kettle Point Canada 43°10N 82°1W 174 C2
Kettle Pt. Canada 43°13N 82°1W 174 C2
Kettleman City U.S.A. 36°1N 119°58W 170 J7
Kęty Poland 49°51N 19°16E 83 J6
Keuka L. U.S.A. 42°30N 77°9W 174 D7
Keuruu Finland 62°16N 24°41E 84 A3
Kevelaer Germany 51°36N 6°15E 76 D2
Kewanee U.S.A. 41°14N 89°56W 172 E9
Keware Nepal 27°57N 83°47E 125 F10
Kewaunee U.S.A. 44°27N 87°31W 172 C10
Keweenaw B. U.S.A. 47°0N 88°15W 172 B9
Keweenaw Pen. U.S.A. 47°15N 88°15W 172 B9
Keweenaw Pt. U.S.A. 47°25N 87°43W 172 B10
Key, L. Ireland 54°0N 8°15W 64 C3
Key Colony Beach U.S.A. 24°45N 80°57W 179 L9
Key Lake Mine Canada 57°5N 105°32W 163 B7
Key Largo U.S.A. 25°5N 80°27W 179 K9
Key West U.S.A. 24°33N 81°48W 179 L8
Keynsham U.K. 51°24N 2°29W 67 F5
Keyser U.S.A. 39°26N 78°59W 173 F14
Keystone Heights U.S.A. 29°47N 82°2W 178 F7
Kezhma Russia 58°59N 101°9E 107 D11
Kezi Zimbabwe 20°58S 28°32E 145 B4
Kežmarok Slovakia 49°10N 20°28E 79 B13
Kgalagadi □ Botswana 24°30S 22°0E 144 B3
Kgalagadi Transfrontier ⌂ Africa 25°10S 21°0E 144 C3
Khabarovsk Russia 48°30N 135°5E 111 B16
Khabr △ Iran 28°51N 56°22E 129 D8
Khābūr → Syria 35°17N 40°35E 105 E9
Khachmas = Xaçmaz Azerbaijan 41°31N 48°42E 87 K9
Khachrod India 23°25N 75°20E 124 H6
Khadro Pakistan 26°11N 68°50E 124 F3
Khadyzhensk Russia 44°26N 39°32E 87 H4
Khadzhilyangar = Dahongliutan China 35°45N 79°20E 125 B8
Khaga India 25°47N 81°7E 125 G9
Khagaria India 25°30N 86°32E 125 G12
Khaipur Pakistan 29°34N 72°17E 124 E5
Khair India 27°57N 77°46E 124 F7
Khairabad India 27°33N 80°47E 125 F9
Khairagarh India 21°27N 81°2E 125 J9
Khairpur Pakistan 27°32N 68°49E 124 F3
Khairpur Nathan Shah Pakistan 27°6N 67°44E 124 F2
Khairwara India 23°58N 73°38E 124 H5
Khaisor → Pakistan 31°17N 68°59E 124 D3
Khajuraho India 24°51N 79°55E 125 G8
Khajuri Kach Pakistan 32°4N 69°51E 124 C3
Khakassia □ Russia 53°0N 90°0E 109 B12
Khakhea Botswana 24°48S 23°22E 144 B3
Khalafābād Iran 30°54N 49°24E 129 D6
Khalilabad India 26°48N 83°5E 125 F10
Khalīlī Iran 27°38N 53°17E 129 E7
Khalkhāl Iran 37°37N 48°32E 105 D13
Khalkís = Chalkida Greece 38°27N 23°42E 98 C5
Khalmer Yu Russia 67°58N 65°1E 106 C7
Khalūf Oman 20°30N 58°13E 131 C6
Kham Keut Laos 18°15N 104°43E 120 C5
Khamaria India 23°5N 80°48E 125 H9
Khambhaliya India 22°14N 69°41E 124 H3
Khambhat India 22°23N 72°33E 124 H5
Khambhat, G. of India 20°45N 72°30E 122 J8
Khamgaon India 20°42N 76°37E 126 D3
Khami Ruins = Kame Ruins Zimbabwe 20°7S 28°25E 143 G2
Khamīr Iran 26°57N 55°36E 129 E7
Khamir Yemen 16°2N 44°0E 131 D3
Khamīs Mushayṭ Si. Arabia 18°18N 42°44E 131 D3
Khammam India 17°11N 80°6E 126 F5
Khamsa Egypt 30°27N 32°23E 130 E1
Khan → Namibia 22°37S 14°56E 144 B2
Khān Abū Shāmat Syria 33°39N 36°53E 130 B5
Khān al Baghdādī Iraq 33°51N 42°32E 105 G10
Khān al Ḥammād Iraq 32°19N 44°16E 105 G11
Khān Azād Iraq 33°7N 44°22E 128 C5
Khān Mujiddah Iraq 32°21N 43°48E 128 C4
Khān Shaykhūn Syria 35°26N 36°38E 104 E7
Khan Tengri, Pik Asia 42°12N 80°10E 109 D10
Khān Yūnis Gaza Strip 31°21N 34°18E 130 D3
Khanai Pakistan 30°30N 67°8E 124 D2
Khānaqīn Iraq 34°23N 45°25E 105 E11
Khānbāghī Iran 36°10N 55°25E 129 B7
Khandwa India 21°49N 76°22E 126 D3
Khandyga Russia 62°42N 135°35E 107 C14
Khanewal Pakistan 30°20N 71°55E 124 D4
Khangah Dogran Pakistan 31°50N 73°37E 124 D5
Khangchendzonga = Kanchenjunga △ India 27°42N 88°8E 125 F13
Khanh Duong Vietnam 12°44N 108°44E 120 F7
Khaniá = Chania Greece 35°30N 24°4E 101 D6
Khaniadhana India 25°1N 78°8E 124 G8
Khanka, L. Asia 45°0N 132°24E 112 B6
Khankendy = Xankändi Azerbaijan 39°52N 46°49E 105 C12
Khanna India 30°42N 76°16E 124 D7
Khanozai Pakistan 30°37N 67°19E 124 D2
Khanpur Pakistan 28°42N 70°35E 124 E4
Khanty-Mansiysk Russia 61°0N 69°0E 106 C7
Khao Khitchakut △ Thailand 12°50N 102°10E 120 F4
Khao Laem △ Thailand 14°56N 98°31E 120 E2
Khao Laem Res. Thailand 14°50N 98°30E 120 E2
Khao Lak △ Malaysia 8°38N 98°18E 121 H2
Khao Luang △ Thailand 8°34N 99°42E 121 H2
Khao Nam Khang △ Thailand 6°32N 100°35E 121 J3
Khao Phlu Thailand 9°29N 99°59E 121 b
Khao Pu -Khao Ya △ Thailand 7°26N 99°57E 121 J2
Khao Sam Roi Yot △ Thailand 12°13N 99°57E 121 F2
Khao Sok △ Thailand 8°55N 98°38E 121 H2
Khao Yai △ Thailand 14°21N 101°29E 120 E3
Khaoen Si Nakarin △ Thailand 14°47N 99°0E 120 E2
Khapalu Pakistan 35°10N 76°20E 125 B7

Khapcheranga
Russia 49°42N 112°24E **107** E12
Khaptao △ *Nepal* 29°20N 81°10E **125** E9
Kharabali *Russia* 47°25N 47°15E **87** G8
Kharagauli *Georgia* 42°1N 43°12E **87** J6
Kharaghoda *India* 23°11N 71°46E **124** H4
Kharagpur *India* 22°20N 87°25E **125** H12
Kharan Kalat *Pakistan* 28°34N 65°21E **122** E4
Kharānaq *Iran* 32°20N 54°45E **127** C7
Kharda *India* 18°40N 75°34E **126** E2
Khardung La *India* 34°20N 77°43E **125** B7
Kharg = Khārk, Jazīreh-ye
Iran 29°15N 50°28E **129** D6
Khârga, El Wâhât el
Egypt 25°10N 30°35E **137** B3
Khargon *India* 21°45N 75°40E **126** D2
Khari → *India* 25°54N 74°31E **124** G6
Kharian *Pakistan* 32°49N 73°52E **124** C5
Khariar *India* 20°17N 82°46E **126** D6
Kharit, Wadi el →
Egypt 24°26N 33°3E **137** C3
Khārk, Jazīreh-ye *Iran* 29°15N 50°28E **129** D6
Kharkiv *Ukraine* 49°58N 36°20E **85** H9
Kharkiv □ *Ukraine* 48°20N 36°20E **85** H9
Kharkov = Kharkiv
Ukraine 49°58N 36°20E **85** H9
Kharovsk *Russia* 59°56N 40°13E **84** C11
Kharsawangarh *India* 22°48N 85°50E **125** H11
Kharta *Turkey* 40°55N 29°7E **104** B3
Khartoum = El Khartûm
Sudan 15°31N 32°35E **135** E12
Khartum *Canada* 45°15N 77°5W **174** A7
Khasan *Russia* 42°25N 130°40E **112** C5
Khasavyurt *Russia* 43°16N 46°40E **87** J8
Khāsh *Iran* 28°15N 61°15E **129** D9
Khashm el Girba
Sudan 14°59N 35°58E **135** F13
Khashuri *Georgia* 42°3N 43°35E **87** J6
Khat, Laem *Thailand* 8°6N 98°26E **121** a
Khatanga *Russia* 72°0N 102°20E **107** B11
Khatanga → *Russia* 72°55N 106°0E **107** B11
Khatauli *India* 29°17N 77°43E **124** E7
Khatlon □ *Tajikistan* 37°50N 69°0E **127** E7
Khatra *India* 22°59N 86°51E **125** H12
Khātūnābād *Iran* 30°1N 55°25E **129** D7
Khatyrka *Russia* 62°3N 175°15E **107** C18
Khavda *India* 23°51N 69°43E **124** H3
Khawr Fakkān *U.A.E.* 25°21N 56°22E **129** E8
Khay' *Si. Arabia* 18°45N 41°24E **137** D5
Khaybar, Ḥarrat
Si. Arabia 25°30N 39°45E **128** E4
Khāzimiyah *Iraq* 34°46N 43°37E **128** D4
Khe Bo *Vietnam* 19°8N 104°41E **120** C5
Khe Long *Vietnam* 21°29N 104°46E **120** B5
Khe Sanh *Vietnam* 16°37N 106°45E **120** D6
Khed *Maharashtra, India* 17°43N 73°27E **126** F1
Khed *Maharashtra, India* 18°51N 73°56E **124** E1
Khed Brahma *India* 24°7N 73°5E **124** G5
Khekra *India* 28°52N 77°20E **124** E7
Khemarak Phouminville = Krong
Kaoh Kong
Cambodia 11°37N 102°59E **121** G4
Khemisset *Morocco* 33°50N 6°1W **136** B2
Khemmarat *Thailand* 16°10N 105°15E **120** D5
Khenāmān *Iran* 30°27N 56°29E **129** D8
Khenchela *Algeria* 35°28N 7°11E **136** A5
Khenchela □ *Algeria* 35°0N 7°0E **136** B5
Khenifra *Morocco* 32°58N 5°46E **136** B3
Kherrata *Algeria* 36°27N 5°13E **136** A5
Khersān → *Iran* 31°33N 50°22E **129** D6
Kherson *Ukraine* 46°35N 32°35E **85** J7
Kherson □ *Ukraine* 46°15N 33°10E **85** J7
Kheta → *Russia* 71°54N 102°6E **107** B11
Khewari *Pakistan* 26°36N 68°52E **124** F3
Khilchipur *India* 24°2N 76°34E **124** G7
Khilok *Russia* 51°30N 110°45E **107** D12
Khimki *Russia* 55°50N 37°20E **84** B9
Khíos = Chios *Greece* 38°27N 26°9E **99** C8
Khirsadoh *India* 22°11N 78°47E **125** H8
Khiuma = Hiiumaa
Estonia 58°50N 22°45E **84** C2
Khiva = Xiva
Uzbekistan 41°30N 60°18E **108** D6
Khiwa = Xiva
Uzbekistan 41°30N 60°18E **108** D6
Khlebarovo *Bulgaria* 43°37N 26°15E **97** C10
Khlong Khlung
Thailand 16°12N 99°43E **120** D2
Khlong Lan △ *Thailand* 16°12N 99°17E **120** D2
Khlong Phanom △
Thailand 8°45N 98°38E **121** H2
Khmelnik *Ukraine* 49°33N 27°58E **75** D14
Khmelnytskyy *Ukraine* 49°23N 27°0E **75** D14
Khmelnytskyy □
Ukraine 49°23N 26°40E **75** D14
Khmer Rep. = Cambodia ■
Asia 12°15N 105°0E **120** F5
Khoai, Hon *Vietnam* 8°26N 104°50E **121** H5
Khobar = Al Khubar
Si. Arabia 26°17N 50°12E **129** E6
Khodoriv *Ukraine* 49°24N 24°19E **75** D13
Khodzent = Khŭjand
Tajikistan 40°17N 69°37E **109** D7
Khojak Pass *Afghan.* 30°51N 66°34E **124** D2
Khojayli = Xo'jayli
Uzbekistan 42°29N 59°31E **108** D5
Khok Kloi *Thailand* 8°17N 98°19E **121** a
Khok Pho *Thailand* 6°43N 101°6E **121** J3
Khok Samrong
Thailand 15°3N 100°43E **120** E3
Kholm *Afghan.* 36°45N 67°40E **109** E7
Kholm *Russia* 57°10N 31°15E **84** D0
Kholmärlu *Iran* 39°6N 47°5E **128** B5
Kholmsk *Russia* 47°40N 142°5E **107** E15
Khomas Hochland
Namibia 22°40S 16°0E **144** C2
Khombole *Senegal* 14°43N 16°42W **138** C1
Khomeyn *Iran* 33°40N 50°7E **129** C6
Khomeynī Shahr *Iran* 32°41N 51°31E **129** C6
Khomodino *Botswana* 22°46S 23°52E **144** B3
Khon Kaen *Thailand* 16°30N 102°47E **120** D4
Khong → *Cambodia* 13°32N 105°58E **120** F5
Khong Sedone *Laos* 15°34N 105°49E **120** E5
Khonuu *Russia* 66°30N 143°12E **107** C15
Khoper → *Russia* 49°30N 42°20E **86** F6
Khorāsān-e Janūb □
Iran 32°0N 59°0E **129** D8
Khorāsān-e Razavī □
Iran 35°0N 59°0E **129** C8
Khorāsān-e Shemālī □
Iran 37°0N 57°0E **129** B8

Khorat = Nakhon Ratchasima
Thailand 14°59N 102°12E **120** E4
Khorat, Cao Nguyen
Thailand 15°30N 102°50E **120** E4
Khorazm = Xorazm □
Uzbekistan 43°0N 60°0E **108** D6
Khorb el Ethel *Algeria* 28°30N 6°17W **136** C2
Khorixas *Namibia* 20°16S 14°59E **144** B1
Khorol *Ukraine* 49°48N 33°15E **85** H7
Khorramābād *Khorāsān,*
Iran 35°6N 57°57E **129** C8
Khorramābād *Lorestan,*
Iran 33°30N 48°25E **105** F13
Khorramdarreh *Iran* 36°11N 49°11E **105** D13
Khorramshahr *Iran* 30°29N 48°15E **129** D6
Khorugh *Tajikistan* 37°30N 71°36E **109** E8
Khosravī *Iran* 30°48N 51°28E **129** D6
Khosrowābād *Khuzestān,*
Iran 30°10N 48°25E **129** D6
Khosrowābād *Kordestān,*
Iran 35°31N 47°38E **105** E12
Khost *Pakistan* 30°13N 67°35E **124** D2
Khosūyeh *Iran* 28°32N 54°26E **127** D7
Khotang *Nepal* 27°1N 86°51E **125** F12
Khotyn *Ukraine* 48°31N 26°27E **81** B11
Khouribga *Morocco* 32°58N 6°57W **136** B2
Khowst *Afghan.* 33°22N 69°58E **124** C3
Khowst □ *Afghan.* 33°20N 70°0E **122** C6
Khoyniki *Belarus* 51°54N 29°55E **75** C15
Khram, Ko *Thailand* 12°42N 100°47E **120** F3
Khrami → *Georgia* 41°25N 45°0E **87** K7
Khrenovoye *Russia* 51°4N 40°16E **86** E5
Khromtaū *Kazakhstan* 50°17N 58°27E **108** B5
Khrysokhou B. *Cyprus* 35°6N 32°25E **101** D11
Khuan Wa *Thailand* 7°53N 98°17E **121** a
Khudzhand = Khŭjand
Tajikistan 40°17N 69°37E **109** D7
Khuff *Si. Arabia* 24°55N 44°53E **128** E5
Khūgīānī *Afghan.* 31°34N 66°32E **124** D2
Khuis *Botswana* 26°40S 21°49E **144** C3
Khuiyala *India* 27°9N 70°25E **124** F4
Khŭjand *Tajikistan* 40°17N 69°37E **109** D7
Khujner *India* 23°47N 76°36E **124** H7
Khukhan *Thailand* 14°42N 104°12E **120** E5
Khulna *Bangla.* 22°45N 89°34E **123** H16
Khulna □ *Bangla.* 22°25N 89°35E **123** H16
Khulo *Georgia* 41°33N 42°19E **87** K6
Khumago *Botswana* 20°26S 24°32E **144** B3
Khunjerab △ *Pakistan* 36°40N 75°30E **125** A6
Khunjerab Pass = Kinjirap Daban
Asia 36°40N 75°25E **109** E9
Khūnsorkh *Iran* 27°9N 56°7E **129** E8
Khunti *India* 23°5N 85°17E **125** H11
Khūr *Iran* 32°55N 58°18E **129** C8
Khurai *India* 24°3N 78°23E **124** G8
Khurayṣ *Si. Arabia* 25°6N 48°2E **129** E6
Khurda *India* 20°11N 85°37E **126** D7
Khurja *India* 28°15N 77°58E **124** E7
Khūrmāl *Iraq* 35°18N 46°2E **105** C12
Khurr, Wādī al *Iraq* 32°3N 43°52E **128** C4
Khūsf *Iran* 32°46N 58°53E **129** C8
Khushab *Pakistan* 32°20N 72°20E **124** C5
Khust *Ukraine* 48°10N 23°18E **81** B8
Khutse △ *Botswana* 23°31S 24°12E **144** B3
Khuzdar *Pakistan* 27°52N 66°30E **124** F2
Khūzestān □ *Iran* 31°0N 49°0E **129** D6
Khvāf *Iran* 34°33N 60°8E **129** C9
Khvājeh *Iran* 38°9N 46°35E **128** B5
Khvalynsk *Russia* 52°30N 48°2E **86** D9
Khvalynsky △ *Russia* 52°30N 48°0E **86** D9
Khvānsār *Iran* 29°56N 54°8E **129** D7
Khvatovka *Russia* 52°24N 46°32E **86** D8
Khvor *Iran* 33°45N 55°0E **129** C7
Khvorgū *Iran* 27°34N 56°27E **129** E8
Khvormūj *Iran* 28°40N 51°30E **129** D6
Khvoy *Iran* 38°35N 45°0E **105** C11
Khvoynaya *Russia* 58°58N 34°28E **84** C8
Khwae Noi → *Thailand* 14°1N 99°32E **120** E2
Khyber Pakhtunkhwa □
Pakistan 34°0N 72°0E **124** C5
Khyber Pass *Afghan.* 34°10N 71°8E **124** B4
Khyriv *Ukraine* 49°32N 22°58E **83** A9
Kia *Fiji* 16°16S 179°8E **154** a
Kiabukwa
Dem. Rep. of the Congo 8°40S 24°48E **143** D1
Kiadho → *India* 19°37N 77°40E **126** E3
Kiama *Australia* 34°40S 150°50E **153** C9
Kiamba *Phil.* 6°2N 124°46E **119** C6
Kiambi
Dem. Rep. of the Congo 7°15S 28°0E **142** D2
Kiambu *Kenya* 1°10S 36°56E **142** C4
Kiang West △ *Gambia* 13°25N 15°50W **138** C1
Kiangsi = Jiangxi □
China 27°30N 116°0E **117** D11
Kiangsu = Jiangsu □
China 33°0N 120°0E **115** H11
Kiato *Greece* 38°1N 22°45E **98** C4
Kibæk *Denmark* 56°2N 8°51E **63** H2
Kibale △ *Uganda* 0°16N 30°18E **142** B3
Kibanga Port *Uganda* 0°10N 32°58E **142** B3
Kibara *Tanzania* 2°8S 33°30E **142** C3
Kibare, Mts.
Dem. Rep. of the Congo 8°25S 27°10E **142** D2
Kibira △ *Burundi* 3°6S 30°24E **142** C2
Kibombo
Dem. Rep. of the Congo 3°57S 25°53E **142** C2
Kibondo *Tanzania* 3°35S 30°45E **142** C3
Kibre Mengist *Ethiopia* 5°54N 38°59E **137** F4
Kibumbu *Burundi* 3°32S 29°45E **142** C2
Kibungo *Rwanda* 2°10S 30°32E **142** C3
Kibuye *Burundi* 3°39S 29°59E **142** C2
Kibuye *Rwanda* 2°3S 29°21E **142** C2
Kibwesa *Tanzania* 6°30S 29°58E **142** D2
Kibwezi *Kenya* 2°27S 37°57E **142** C4
Kicevo *Macedonia* 41°31N 20°58E **98** A4
Kichha → *India* 28°41N 79°18E **125** E8
Kicking Horse Pass
Canada 51°28N 116°16W **162** C5
Kidal *Mali* 18°26N 1°22E **139** B5
Kidal □ *Mali* 18°26N 1°22E **139** B5
Kidderminster *U.K.* 52°24N 2°15W **67** E5
Kidepo Valley △ *Uganda* 3°50N 33°50E **142** B3
Kidete *Tanzania* 6°25S 37°17E **142** D4
Kidira *Senegal* 14°28N 12°13W **138** C2
Kidnappers, C. *N.Z.* 39°38S 177°5E **154** F6
Kidsgrove *U.K.* 53°5N 2°14W **66** D5
Kidston *Australia* 18°52S 144°8E **150** B3
Kidugallo *Tanzania* 6°49S 38°15E **142** D4
Kiel *Germany* 54°19N 10°8E **76** A6

Kiel Canal = Nord-Ostsee-Kanal
Germany 54°12N 9°32E **76** A5
Kielce *Poland* 50°52N 20°42E **83** H7
Kielder Water *U.K.* 55°11N 2°31W **66** B5
Kieler Bucht *Germany* 54°35N 10°25E **76** A6
Kiembara *Burkina Faso* 13°15N 2°44W **138** C4
Kienge
Dem. Rep. of the Congo 10°30S 27°30E **143** E2
Kiessé *Niger* 13°29N 4°1E **139** C5
Kiev = Kyyiv *Ukraine* 50°30N 30°28E **75** C16
Kifaya *Guinea* 12°10N 13°4W **138** C2
Kiffa *Mauritania* 16°37N 11°24W **138** B2
Kifisos → *Greece* 38°35N 23°20E **98** C5
Kifissia *Greece* 38°4N 23°49E **98** C5
Kifrī *Iraq* 34°45N 45°0E **105** E11
Kigali *Rwanda* 1°59S 30°4E **142** C3
Kigarama *Tanzania* 1°1S 31°50E **142** C3
Kigezi △ *Uganda* 0°34S 29°55E **142** C2
Kiği *Turkey* 39°18N 40°21E **105** C9
Kigoma □ *Tanzania* 5°0S 30°0E **142** D2
Kigoma-Ujiji *Tanzania* 4°55S 29°36E **142** C2
Kigomasha, Ras
Tanzania 4°58S 38°58E **142** C4
Kigosi △ *Tanzania* 4°10S 31°45E **142** C3
Kiğzı *Turkey* 38°18N 43°25E **128** B4
Kihikihi *N.Z.* 38°2S 175°22E **154** E4
Kihnu *Estonia* 58°9N 24°1E **84** C3
Kii-Sanchi *Japan* 34°20N 136°0E **113** G8
Kii-Suidō *Japan* 33°40N 134°45E **113** H7
Kiira Dam *Uganda* 0°25N 33°0E **142** B3
Kikaiga-Shima *Japan* 28°19N 129°59E **113** K4
Kikiak = Rigolet
Canada 54°10N 58°23W **165** B8
Kikinda *Serbia* 45°50N 20°30E **80** E5
Kikládhes = Kyklades
Greece 37°0N 24°30E **98** E6
Kikoira *Australia* 33°9S 146°40E **153** B7
Kikuchi *Japan* 32°59N 130°47E **113** H5
Kikuyu *Kenya* 1°1S 36°40E **142** C4
Kikwit
Dem. Rep. of the Congo 5°0S 18°45E **140** F3
Kil *Sweden* 59°30N 13°20E **62** E7
Kilafors *Sweden* 61°14N 16°36E **62** C10
Kilakkarai *India* 9°12N 78°47E **127** K4
Kilar *India* 33°6N 76°25E **124** C7
Kilbeggan *Ireland* 53°22N 7°30W **64** C4
Kilbrannan Sd. *U.K.* 55°37N 5°26W **65** F3
Kilbuck Mts. *U.S.A.* 60°36N 159°53W **166** C8
Kilchu *N. Korea* 40°57N 129°25E **115** D15
Kilcoy *Australia* 26°59S 152°30E **151** D5
Kildare *Ireland* 53°9N 6°55W **64** C5
Kildare □ *Ireland* 53°10N 6°50W **64** C5
Kildinstroy *Russia* 68°48N 33°6E **60** B25
Kilfinnane *Ireland* 52°21N 8°28W **64** D3
Kilgarvan *Ireland* 51°54N 9°27W **64** E2
Kilgore *U.S.A.* 32°23N 94°53W **176** E7
Kilgoris *Kenya* 1°0S 34°55E **142** C3
Kilibo *Benin* 8°32N 2°38E **139** D5
Kilifi *Kenya* 3°40S 39°48E **142** C4
Kilimanjaro *Tanzania* 3°7S 37°20E **142** C4
Kilimanjaro □ *Tanzania* 4°0S 38°0E **142** C4
Kilimanjaro □ *Tanzania* 3°2S 37°19E **142** C4
Kilimli *Turkey* 41°28N 31°50E **104** B4
Kilindini *Kenya* 4°4S 39°40E **142** C4
Kilinochchi *Sri Lanka* 9°24N 80°25E **127** K5
Kilis *Turkey* 36°50N 37°10E **104** D7
Kilis □ *Turkey* 36°50N 37°10E **104** D7
Kiliya *Ukraine* 45°28N 29°16E **81** E14
Kilkee *Ireland* 52°41N 9°39W **64** D2
Kilkeel *U.K.* 54°7N 5°55W **64** B5
Kilkenny *Ireland* 52°39N 7°15W **64** D4
Kilkenny □ *Ireland* 52°35N 7°15W **64** D4
Kilkieran B. *Ireland* 53°20N 9°41W **64** C2
Kilkis *Greece* 40°58N 22°57E **98** A4
Killala *Ireland* 54°13N 9°13W **64** B2
Killala B. *Ireland* 54°16N 9°8W **64** B2
Killaloe *Canada* 45°33N 77°25W **174** A7
Killaloe *Ireland* 52°48N 8°28W **64** D3
Killarney *Australia* 28°20S 152°18E **151** D5
Killarney *Canada* 49°10N 99°40W **163** D9
Killarney *Ireland* 52°4N 9°30W **64** D2
Killarney △ *Canada* 46°2N 81°35W **164** C3
Killarney □ *Canada* 52°0N 9°33W **64** D2
Killary Harbour *Ireland* 53°38N 9°52W **64** C2
Killdeer *U.S.A.* 47°22N 102°45W **172** B2
Killeberg *Sweden* 56°29N 14°5E **63** H8
Killeen *U.S.A.* 31°7N 97°44W **176** F6
Killin *U.K.* 56°28N 4°19W **65** E4
Killiney *Ireland* 53°15N 6°7W **64** C5
Killington Pk. *U.S.A.* 43°36N 72°49W **175** C12
Killini = Kyllini *Greece* 37°54N 22°25E **98** D3
Killini *Greece* 37°54N 22°25E **98** D4
Killiniq I. *Canada* 60°24N 64°37W **161** E19
Killorglin *Ireland* 52°6N 9°47W **64** D2
Killybegs *Ireland* 54°38N 8°26W **64** B3
Kilmarnock *U.K.* 55°37N 4°29W **65** F4
Kilmez *Russia* 56°58N 50°55E **86** B10
Kilmez → *Russia* 56°58N 50°28E **86** B10
Kilmore *Australia* 37°25S 144°53E **153** D8
Kilmore Quay *Ireland* 52°10N 6°36W **64** D5
Kilondo *Tanzania* 9°45S 34°20E **143** D3
Kilosa *Tanzania* 6°48S 37°0E **142** D4
Kilrush *Ireland* 52°38N 9°29W **64** D2
Kiltan I. *India* 11°29N 73°0E **127** J1
Kilwa Kisiwani *Tanzania* 8°58S 39°32E **143** D4
Kilwa Kivinje *Tanzania* 8°45S 39°25E **143** D4
Kilwa Masoko *Tanzania* 8°55S 39°30E **143** D4
Kilwinning *U.K.* 55°39N 4°43W **65** F4
Kim *U.S.A.* 37°15N 103°21W **169** H12
Kim → *Cameroon* 5°28N 11°7E **139** D7
Kimaam *Indonesia* 7°58S 138°53E **119** F9
Kimamba *Tanzania* 6°45S 37°10E **142** D4
Kimba *Australia* 33°8S 136°23E **152** B2
Kimball *Nebr., U.S.A.* 41°14N 103°40W **172** E2
Kimball *S. Dak., U.S.A.* 43°45N 98°57W **172** D4
Kimberley *B.C.,*
Canada 49°40N 115°59W **162** D5
Kimberley *Ont., Canada* 44°23N 80°32W **174** B4
Kimberley *S. Africa* 28°43S 24°46E **144** D3
Kimberly *U.S.A.* 42°32N 114°22W **168** E6
Kimch'aek *N. Korea* 40°40N 129°10E **115** D15
Kimhae = Gimhae
S. Korea 35°14N 128°53E **115** G15
Kimi *Greece* 38°38N 24°6E **98** C6
Kimmirut *Canada* 62°50N 69°50W **161** E19
Kimolos *Greece* 36°48N 24°37E **98** E6
Kimovsk *Russia* 54°0N 38°29E **84** E10
Kimparana *Mali* 12°48N 5°0W **138** C4
Kimpese
Dem. Rep. of the Congo 5°35S 14°26E **140** F2
Kimry *Russia* 56°55N 37°15E **84** D10

Kimstad *Sweden* 58°35N 15°58E **63** F9
Kinabalu, Gunung
Malaysia 6°3N 116°14E **118** C5
Kinango *Kenya* 4°8S 39°19E **142** C4
Kinard *U.S.A.* 30°16N 85°15W **178** E4
Kinaros *Greece* 36°59N 26°15E **99** E8
Kinaskan L. *Canada* 57°38N 130°8W **162** B2
Kinbasket L. *Canada* 52°0N 118°10W **162** C5
Kincardine *Canada* 44°10N 81°40W **174** B3
Kinchafoonee Cr. →
U.S.A. 31°38N 84°10W **178** D5
Kinchega △ *Australia* 32°27S 142°15E **152** B5
Kincolith *Canada* 55°0N 129°57W **162** C3
Kinda
Dem. Rep. of the Congo 9°18S 25°4E **143** D2
Kindberg *Austria* 47°30N 15°27E **78** D8
Kinde *U.S.A.* 43°56N 83°0W **174** C2
Kinder Scout *U.K.* 53°24N 1°52W **66** D6
Kindersley *Canada* 51°30N 109°10W **163** C7
Kindia *Guinea* 10°0N 12°52W **138** D2
Kindu
Dem. Rep. of the Congo 2°55S 25°50E **142** C2
Kinel *Russia* 53°15N 50°40E **86** D10
Kineshma *Russia* 57°30N 42°5E **86** B6
Kinesi *Tanzania* 1°25S 33°50E **142** C3
King, L. *Australia* 33°10S 119°35E **149** F2
King, Mt. *Australia* 25°10S 147°30E **150** D4
King Christian I.
Canada 77°48N 101°40W **161** B11
King Cr. → *Australia* 24°35S 139°30E **150** C2
King Edward →
Australia 14°14S 126°35E **148** B4
King Edward Point
S. Georgia 54°17S 36°30W **55** B1
King Frederick VI Land = Kong
Frederik VI.s Kyst
Greenland 63°0N 43°0W **57** E6
King George B.
Falk. Is. 51°30S 60°30W **192** D4
King George I. *Antarctica* 60°0S 60°0W **55** C18
King George Is.
Canada 57°20N 80°30W **161** F15
King George Sd.
Australia 35°5S 118°0E **149** G2
King I. = Kadan Kyun
Myanmar 12°30N 98°20E **120** F2
King I. *Australia* 39°50S 144°0E **151** F3
King I. *Canada* 52°10N 127°40W **162** C3
King Khalid Int. ✈ (RUH)
Si. Arabia 24°57N 46°42E **128** E4
King Khalid Military City =
Madinat al Malik Khālid al
Askarīyah *Si. Arabia* 27°54N 45°31E **128** E5
King Leopold Ranges
Australia 17°30S 125°45E **148** C4
King of Prussia *U.S.A.* 40°5N 75°23W **175** F9
King Sd. *Australia* 16°50S 123°20E **148** C3
King Sejong *Antarctica* 62°30S 58°0W **55** C18
King Shaka Int. ✈ (DUR)
S. Africa 29°37S 31°7E **145** C5
King William I.
Canada 69°10N 97°25W **160** D12
King William's Town
S. Africa 32°51S 27°22E **144** D4
Kingaok = Bathurst Inlet
Canada 66°50N 108°1W **160** D10
Kingaroy *Australia* 26°32S 151°51E **151** D5
Kingfisher *U.S.A.* 35°52N 97°56W **176** D6
Kingirbān *Iraq* 34°40N 44°54E **128** C5
Kingisepp = Kuressaare
Estonia 58°15N 22°30E **84** C2
Kingisepp *Russia* 59°25N 28°40E **84** C5
Kinglake △ *Australia* 37°30S 145°22E **153** D6
Kingman *Ariz., U.S.A.* 35°12N 114°4W **171** K12
Kingman *Kans., U.S.A.* 37°39N 98°7W **172** G4
Kingoonya *Australia* 30°55S 135°19E **151** E2
Kingri *Pakistan* 30°27N 69°49E **124** D3
Kings → *U.S.A.* 36°3N 119°50W **170** J7
Kings Canyon
Australia 24°15S 131°34E **148** D5
Kings Canyon △
U.S.A. 36°50N 118°40W **170** J8
King's Lynn *U.K.* 52°45N 0°24E **66** E8
Kings Park *U.S.A.* 40°53N 73°16W **175** F11
Kings Peak *U.S.A.* 40°46N 110°23W **168** F8
King's Trough *Atl. Oc.* 43°48N 22°0W **56** B9
Kingsbridge *U.K.* 50°17N 3°47W **67** G4
Kingsburg *U.S.A.* 36°31N 119°33W **170** J7
Kingscote *Australia* 35°40S 137°38E **152** C2
Kingscourt *Ireland* 53°54N 6°48W **64** C5
Kingsford *U.S.A.* 45°48N 88°4W **172** C9
Kingsland *U.S.A.* 30°48N 81°41W **178** E8
Kingsport *U.S.A.* 36°33N 82°33W **177** C13
Kingston *Canada* 44°14N 76°30W **175** B8
Kingston *Jamaica* 17°55N 76°50W **182** a
Kingston *N.Z.* 45°20S 168°43E **155** F3
Kingston *N.H., U.S.A.* 42°56N 71°3W **175** D13
Kingston *N.Y., U.S.A.* 41°56N 73°59W **175** E11
Kingston *Pa., U.S.A.* 41°16N 75°54W **175** E9
Kingston *R.I., U.S.A.* 41°29N 71°30W **175** E13
Kingston Pk. *U.S.A.* 35°44N 115°55W **171** K11
Kingston South East
Australia 36°51S 139°55E **152** D3
Kingston upon Hull
U.K. 53°45N 0°21W **66** D7
Kingston upon Hull □
U.K. 53°45N 0°21W **66** D7
Kingston-upon-Thames □
U.K. 51°24N 0°17W **67** F7
Kingstown *Australia* 30°29S 151°6E **153** B9
Kingstown *St. Vincent* 13°10N 61°10W **183** D7
Kingstree *U.S.A.* 33°40N 79°50W **178** D7
Kingsville *U.S.A.* 27°31N 97°52W **176** H6
Kingussie *U.K.* 57°6N 4°2W **65** D4
Kingwood *U.S.A.* 30°3N 95°16W **176** E7
Kınık *Antalya, Turkey* 36°20N 29°20E **99** E11
Kınık *İzmir, Turkey* 39°6N 27°24E **99** B9
Kinistino *Canada* 52°57N 105°2W **163** C7
Kinkala *Congo* 4°18S 14°49E **142** D2
Kinki □ *Japan* 33°45N 136°0E **113** H8
Kinleith *N.Z.* 38°20S 175°56E **154** E4
Kinmount *Canada* 44°48N 78°45W **174** B6
Kinna *Sweden* 57°32N 12°42E **63** F2
Kinnairds Hd. *U.K.* 57°43N 2°1W **65** D6
Kinnared *Sweden* 57°2N 13°7E **63** G7
Kinnarodden = Nordkinn
Norway 71°8N 27°40E **60** A22
Kinnarp *Sweden* 58°9N 13°32E **63** F7

Kinneviken *Sweden* 58°35N 13°15E **63** F7
Kinngait *Canada* 64°14N 76°32W **161** E16
Kinniyai *Sri Lanka* 8°29N 81°11E **127** K5
Kino Nuevo *Mexico* 28°52N 112°3W **180** B2
Kinoje → *Canada* 52°8N 81°25W **164** B3
Kinomoto *Japan* 35°30N 136°13E **113** G8
Kinoni *Uganda* 0°41S 30°28E **142** C3
Kinoosao *Canada* 57°5N 102°1W **163** B8
Kinross *U.K.* 56°13N 3°25W **65** E5
Kinsale *Ireland* 51°42N 8°31W **64** E3
Kinsale, Old Hd. of
Ireland 51°37N 8°33W **64** E3
Kinsha = Chang Jiang →
China 31°48N 121°10E **117** B13
Kinshasa
Dem. Rep. of the Congo 4°20S 15°15E **140** E3
Kinsley *U.S.A.* 37°55N 99°25W **172** G4
Kinsman *U.S.A.* 41°26N 80°35W **174** E4
Kinston *Ala., U.S.A.* 31°13N 86°10W **178** E3
Kinston *N.C., U.S.A.* 35°16N 77°35W **177** D16
Kintamani *Indonesia* 8°14S 115°19E **116** J18
Kintampo *Ghana* 8°5N 1°41W **139** D4
Kintore *U.K.* 57°14N 2°20W **65** D6
Kintore Ra. *Australia* 23°15S 128°47E **148** D5
Kintyre *U.K.* 55°30N 5°35W **65** F3
Kintyre, Mull of *U.K.* 55°17N 5°47W **65** F3
Kinushseo → *Canada* 55°15N 83°45W **164** A3
Kinuso *Canada* 55°20N 115°25W **162** B5
Kinvarra *Ireland* 53°8N 8°56W **64** C3
Kinwat *India* 19°38N 78°12E **126** E4
Kinyangiri *Tanzania* 4°25S 34°37E **142** C3
Kinyeti *South Sudan* 3°57N 32°54E **142** B3
Kinzig → *Germany* 48°36N 7°49E **77** G3
Kinzua *U.S.A.* 41°52N 78°58W **174** E6
Kioni *Greece* 38°27N 20°41E **98** C2
Kiosk *Canada* 46°6N 78°53W **164** C4
Kiowa *Kans., U.S.A.* 37°1N 98°29W **172** G4
Kiowa *Okla., U.S.A.* 34°43N 95°54W **176** D7
Kipahigan L. *Canada* 55°20N 101°55W **163** B8
Kipanga *Tanzania* 6°15S 35°20E **142** D4
Kiparissia *Greece* 37°15N 21°40E **98** D3
Kiparissiakos Kolpos
Greece 37°25N 21°25E **98** D3
Kipawa, L. *Canada* 46°50N 79°0W **164** C4
Kipembawe *Tanzania* 7°38S 33°27E **142** D3
Kipengere Ra. *Tanzania* 9°12S 34°15E **142** D3
Kipili *Tanzania* 7°28S 30°32E **142** D3
Kipini *Kenya* 2°30S 40°32E **142** C5
Kipling *Canada* 50°6N 102°38W **163** C8
Kippure *Ireland* 53°11N 6°21W **64** C5
Kipushi
Dem. Rep. of the Congo 11°48S 27°12E **143** E2
Kira *Uganda* 0°24N 32°38E **142** B3
Kira Panagia *Greece* 39°17N 24°4E **98** B6
Kirandul *India* 18°33N 81°10E **126** E5
Kirane *Mali* 15°20N 10°20W **138** C2
Kiraz *Turkey* 38°14N 28°13E **99** C10
Kirazlı *Turkey* 40°2N 26°41E **97** F10
Kirchhain *Germany* 50°47N 8°56E **76** E4
Kirchheim *Germany* 48°39N 9°27E **77** G5
Kirchheimbolanden
Germany 49°40N 8°0E **77** F3
Kirchschlag *Austria* 47°30N 16°19E **79** D9
Kireç *Turkey* 39°33N 28°22E **99** B10
Kirensk *Russia* 57°50N 107°55E **107** D11
Kirghiz Range = Qirghiz Range
Asia 42°40N 73°40E **109** D8
Kirghizia = Kyrgyzstan ■
Asia 42°0N 75°0E **109** D9
Kirgiziya Steppe *Eurasia* 50°0N 55°0E **108** C5
Kiri Buru *India* 22°0N 85°0E **126** D7
Kiri *Pac. Oc.* 3°0S 180°0E **147** B10
Kiribati ■ *Pac. Oc.* 3°0S 180°0E **147** B10
Kırıkhan *Turkey* 36°31N 36°21E **104** D7
Kırıkkale *Turkey* 39°51N 33°32E **104** C5
Kirikopuni *N.Z.* 35°50S 174°1E **154** B5
Kirillov *Russia* 59°49N 38°24E **84** C10
Kirin = Jilin *China* 43°44N 126°30E **115** C14
Kirindi Oya → *Sri Lanka* 6°15N 81°20E **127** L5
Kirinyaga = Kenya, Mt.
Kenya 0°10S 37°18E **142** C4
Kirinyaga □ *Kenya* 0°30S 37°20E **142** C4
Kirirom △ *Cambodia* 11°18N 104°5E **121** G5
Kirishi *Russia* 59°28N 32°0E **84** C7
Kirishima *Japan* 31°58N 130°51E **113** J5
Kirishima Yaku △
Japan 31°24N 130°50E **113** J5
Kiritimati *Kiribati* 1°58N 157°27W **157** G12
Kırka *Turkey* 39°17N 30°33E **99** B12
Kırkağaç *Turkey* 39°8N 27°40E **99** B9
Kirkby *U.K.* 53°30N 2°54W **66** D5
Kirkby-in-Ashfield *U.K.* 53°6N 1°14W **66** D6
Kirkby Lonsdale *U.K.* 54°12N 2°36W **66** C5
Kirkby Stephen *U.K.* 54°29N 2°21W **66** C5
Kirkcaldy *U.K.* 56°7N 3°9W **65** E5
Kirkcudbright *U.K.* 54°50N 4°2W **65** G4
Kirkenes *Norway* 69°40N 30°5E **60** B26
Kirkfield *Canada* 44°34N 78°59W **174** B6
Kirkintilloch *U.K.* 55°56N 4°8W **65** F4
Kirkjubæjarklaustur
Iceland 63°47N 18°4W **60** D4
Kirkkonummi *Finland* 60°8N 24°26E **63** B21
Kirkland Lake *Canada* 48°9N 80°2W **164** C3
Kırklareli *Turkey* 41°44N 27°15E **97** E11
Kırklareli □ *Turkey* 41°44N 27°15E **97** E11
Kirkliston Ra. *N.Z.* 44°25S 170°34E **155** E3
Kirkpatrick, Mt.
Antarctica 84°0S 166°25E **55** E11
Kirksville *U.S.A.* 40°12N 92°35W **172** E7
Kirkūk *Iraq* 35°30N 44°21E **105** E11
Kirkwall *U.K.* 58°59N 2°58W **65** C6
Kirkwood *S. Africa* 33°22S 25°15E **144** D4
Kirlampudi *India* 17°12N 82°12E **126** F6
Kirn *Germany* 49°47N 7°29E **77** F3
Kirov *Kaluga, Russia* 54°3N 34°20E **86** D4
Kirov *Kirov, Russia* 58°35N 49°40E **86** C10

Kirtachi *Niger* 12°52N 2°30E **139** C5
Kirthar △ *Pakistan* 25°45N 67°30E **124** F2
Kirthar Range *Pakistan* 27°0N 67°0E **124** F2
Kirtland *U.S.A.* 36°44N 108°21W **169** H9
Kiruna *Sweden* 67°52N 20°15E **60** C19
Kirundu
Dem. Rep. of the Congo 0°50S 25°35E **142** C2
Kirya *Russia* 55°8N 46°55E **86** C8
Kiryū *Japan* 36°24N 139°20E **113** F9
Kisaga *Tanzania* 4°30S 34°23E **142** C3
Kisalföld *Hungary* 47°30N 17°0E **80** C2
Kisanga
Dem. Rep. of the Congo 2°30S 26°35E **142** C2
Kisangani
Dem. Rep. of the Congo 0°35N 25°15E **142** B2
Kisar *Indonesia* 8°5S 127°10E **119** F7
Kisarawe *Tanzania* 6°53S 39°0E **142** D4
Kisarazu *Japan* 35°23N 139°55E **113** G9
Kisbér *Hungary* 47°30N 18°2E **80** C3
Kiselevsk *Russia* 54°5N 86°39E **109** B11
Kish = Qeys *Iran* 26°32N 53°58E **129** E7
Kishanganga →
Pakistan 34°18N 73°28E **125** B5
Kishanganj *India* 26°3N 88°14E **125** F13
Kishangarh *Raj., India* 26°34N 74°52E **124** F6
Kishangarh *Raj., India* 27°50N 70°30E **124** F4
Kishi *Nigeria* 9°1N 3°52E **139** D5
Kishinev = Chişinău
Moldova 47°2N 28°50E **81** C13
Kishiwada *Japan* 34°28N 135°22E **113** G7
Kishkeneköl
Kazakhstan 53°38N 72°20E **108** D8
Kishtwar *India* 33°20N 75°48E **124** C6
Kisielice *Poland* 53°36N 19°16E **82** E6
Kisigo → *Tanzania* 6°27S 34°17E **142** D3
Kisii *Kenya* 0°40S 34°45E **142** C3
Kisiju *Tanzania* 7°23S 39°19E **142** D4
Kisir → *Iran* 41°0N 43°5E **105** B10
Kisizi *Uganda* 1°0S 29°58E **142** C2
Kiska I. *U.S.A.* 51°59N 177°30E **166** E3
Kiskőmárom = Zalakomár
Hungary 46°33N 17°10E **80** D2
Kiskőrös *Hungary* 46°37N 19°20E **80** D4
Kiskőrös-viztároló
Hungary 47°31N 20°36E **80** C5
Kiskundorozsma
Hungary 46°16N 20°5E **80** D5
Kiskunfélegyháza
Hungary 46°42N 19°53E **80** D4
Kiskunhalas *Hungary* 46°28N 19°37E **80** D4
Kiskunmajsa *Hungary* 46°30N 19°30E **80** D4
Kiskunsági △ *Hungary* 46°53N 19°30E **80** D4
Kislovodsk *Russia* 43°50N 42°45E **87** J6
Kismaayo *Somalia* 0°22S 42°32E **131** H3
Kiso-Gawa → *Japan* 35°20N 136°45E **113** G8
Kiso-Sammyaku
Japan 35°45N 137°45E **113** G8
Kisofukushima *Japan* 35°52N 137°43E **113** G8
Kisoro *Uganda* 1°17S 29°48E **142** C2
Kissamos *Greece* 35°30N 23°38E **101** D5
Kissamou, Kolpos
Greece 35°30N 23°38E **101** D5
Kissidougou *Guinea* 9°5N 10°5W **138** D2
Kissimmee *U.S.A.* 28°18N 81°24W **179** G6
Kissimmee → *U.S.A.* 27°9N 80°52W **179** H8
Kissimmee, L. *U.S.A.* 27°57N 81°17W **179** H6
Kississing L. *Canada* 55°10N 101°20W **163** B8
Kissónerga *Cyprus* 34°49N 32°24E **101** E11
Kissu, J. *Sudan* 21°37N 25°10E **137** C2
Kisújszállás *Hungary* 47°12N 20°50E **80** C5
Kisumu *Kenya* 0°3S 34°45E **142** C3
Kisvárda *Hungary* 48°14N 22°4E **80** B7
Kiswani *Tanzania* 4°5S 37°57E **142** C4
Kiswere *Tanzania* 9°27S 39°30E **143** D4
Kit Carson *U.S.A.* 38°46N 102°48W **168** G12
Kita *Mali* 13°5N 9°25W **138** C3
Kitaibaraki *Japan* 36°50N 140°45E **113** F10
Kitakami *Japan* 39°20N 141°10E **112** E10
Kitakami-Gawa →
Japan 38°25N 141°19E **112** E10
Kitakata *Japan* 37°39N 139°52E **112** F9
Kitakyūshū *Japan* 33°50N 130°50E **113** H5
Kitale *Kenya* 1°0N 35°0E **142** B4
Kitami *Japan* 43°48N 143°54E **112** C11
Kitami-Sammyaku
Japan 44°22N 142°43E **112** B11
Kitangiri, L. *Tanzania* 4°5S 34°20E **142** C3
Kitaya *Tanzania* 10°38S 40°8E **143** E5
Kitchener *Canada* 43°27N 80°29W **174** C4
Kitee *Finland* 62°5N 30°8E **84** A6
Kitega = Gitega *Burundi* 3°26S 29°56E **142** C2
Kitengo
Dem. Rep. of the Congo 7°26S 24°8E **142** D1
Kitgum *Uganda* 3°17N 32°52E **142** B3
Kithira = Kythira *Greece* 36°8N 23°0E **98** E5
Kithnos = Kythnos
Greece 37°26N 24°27E **98** D6
Kiti *Cyprus* 34°50N 33°34E **101** E12
Kiti, C. *Cyprus* 34°48N 33°36E **101** E12
Kitikmeot *Canada* 70°0N 110°0W **160** D9
Kitinen → *Finland* 67°14N 27°27E **60** C22
Kitros *Greece* 40°22N 22°34E **96** F6
Kitsman *Ukraine* 48°26N 25°48E **81** D11
Kitsuki *Japan* 33°25N 131°37E **113** H5
Kittakittaooloo, L.
Australia 28°3S 138°14E **151** D2
Kittanning *U.S.A.* 40°49N 79°31W **174** F5
Kittatinny Mt. *U.S.A.* 41°19N 74°39W **175** F10
Kittery *U.S.A.* 43°5N 70°45W **175** D14
Kittilä *Finland* 67°40N 24°51E **60** C21
Kitui *Kenya* 1°17S 38°0E **142** C4
Kitui □ *Kenya* 1°30S 38°25E **142** C4
Kitwe *Zambia* 12°54S 28°13E **143** E2
Kitzbühel *Austria* 47°27N 12°24E **78** D6
Kitzbüheler Alpen
Austria 47°20N 12°20E **78** D6
Kitzingen *Germany* 49°44N 10°9E **77** F6
Kiunga Marine △ *Kenya* 2°1S 41°14E **142** C5
Kivalliq *Canada* 62°0N 95°0W **160** E12
Kivertsi *Ukraine* 50°50N 25°28E **75** C13
Kividhes *Cyprus* 34°46N 32°51E **101** E11
Kivik *Sweden* 55°41N 14°15E **63** J3
Kivotos *Greece* 40°13N 21°26E **96** F5
Kivu, L.
Dem. Rep. of the Congo 1°48S 29°0E **142** C2

Kiwirrkurra Australia 22°49S 127°45E 148 D4
Kiwirrkurra ✪ Australia 22°49S 127°45E 148 D4
Kiyev = Kyyiv Ukraine 50°30N 30°28E 75 C16
Kiyevskoye Vdkhr. = Kyyivske Vdskh. Ukraine 51°0N 30°25E 75 C16
Kıyıköy Turkey 41°38N 28°5E 97 E12
Kizhi, Ostrov Russia 62°4N 35°13E 84 B8
Kiziba-Baluba ⌂ Dem. Rep. of the Congo 11°50S 28°0E 143 E2
Kiziguru Rwanda 1°46S 30°23E 142 C3
Kızıl Adalar Turkey 40°52N 29°5E 97 F13
Kızıl Irmak → Turkey 41°44N 35°58E 104 B6
Kizil Jilga China 35°26N 78°50E 125 B8
Kizil Yurt Russia 43°13N 46°54E 87 J8
Kızılcabölük Turkey 37°37N 29°1E 99 D11
Kızılcadağ Turkey 37°1N 29°58E 99 D11
Kızılcahamam Turkey 40°30N 32°30E 104 B5
Kızıldağ △ Turkey 38°5N 31°20E 128 B1
Kızılhisar Turkey 37°32N 29°17E 104 D3
Kızılırmak Turkey 40°21N 33°59E 104 B5
Kızılkaya Turkey 37°18N 30°27E 99 D12
Kızılören Turkey 38°15N 30°10E 99 C12
Kızıltepe Turkey 37°12N 40°35E 105 D9
Kizimkazi Tanzania 6°28S 39°30E 142 D4
Kizlyar Russia 43°51N 46°40E 87 J8
Kizyl-Arvat = Serdar Turkmenistan 39°4N 56°23E 129 B8
Kjellerup Denmark 56°17N 9°25E 63 H3
Kjölur Iceland 64°50N 19°25W 60 D4
Kladanj Bos.-H. 44°14N 18°42E 80 F3
Kladnica Serbia 43°23N 20°2E 96 C4
Kladno Czechia 50°10N 14°7E 78 A7
Kladovo Serbia 44°36N 22°33E 96 B6
Klaeng Thailand 12°47N 101°39E 120 F3
Klagenfurt Austria 46°38N 14°20E 78 E7
Klaipėda Lithuania 55°43N 21°10E 82 C8
Klaipėda □ Lithuania 55°43N 21°7E 82 C8
Klaksvík Færoe Is. 62°14N 6°35W 60 E9
Klamath → U.S.A. 41°33N 124°5W 168 F1
Klamath Falls U.S.A. 42°13N 121°46W 168 E3
Klamath Mts. U.S.A. 41°50N 123°20W 168 F2
Klamono Indonesia 1°8S 131°30E 119 E8
Klang Malaysia 3°2N 101°26E 121 L3
Klanjec Croatia 46°3N 15°45E 93 B12
Klappan → Canada 58°0N 129°43W 162 B3
Klarälven → Sweden 59°23N 13°32E 62 E7
Klässbol Sweden 59°33N 12°45E 62 E6
Klatovy Czechia 49°23N 13°18E 78 B6
Klawer S. Africa 31°44S 18°36E 144 D2
Klazienaveen Neths. 52°44N 7°0E 69 B6
Klé Mali 12°0N 6°28W 138 C3
Klecko Poland 52°38N 17°25E 83 F4
Kleczew Poland 52°22N 18°9E 83 F5
Kleena Kleene Canada 52°0N 124°59W 162 C4
Klein-Karas Namibia 27°33S 18°7E 144 C2
Kleinbegin S. Africa 28°54S 21°40E 144 C3
Klekovača Bos.-H. 44°25N 16°32E 93 D13
Klembivka Ukraine 48°23N 28°25E 81 B13
Klenoec Macedonia 41°32N 20°49E 96 E4
Klenovec Slovakia 48°36N 19°54E 79 C12
Klerksdorp S. Africa 26°53S 26°38E 144 C4
Kleszczele Poland 52°35N 23°19E 83 F10
Kletnya Russia 53°23N 33°12E 84 F7
Kletsk = Klyetsk Belarus 53°5N 26°45E 75 B14
Kletskiy Russia 49°16N 43°11E 87 F6
Kleve Germany 51°47N 6°7E 76 D2
Klickitat U.S.A. 45°49N 121°9W 168 D3
Klickitat → U.S.A. 45°42N 121°17W 170 E5
Klidhes Cyprus 35°42N 34°36E 101 D13
Klimovichi Belarus 53°36N 32°0E 84 F6
Klimovsk Russia 55°21N 37°28E 84 E9
Klin Russia 56°20N 36°48E 84 D9
Klinaklini → Canada 51°21N 125°40W 162 C3
Klinë Kosovo 42°37N 20°35E 96 D4
Klintehamn Sweden 57°24N 18°12E 63 G12
Klintsy Russia 52°50N 32°10E 85 F7
Klip → S. Africa 27°3S 29°3E 145 C4
Klipdale S. Africa 34°19S 19°57E 144 D2
Klippan Sweden 56°8N 13°10E 63 H7
Klipplaat S. Africa 33°1S 24°22E 144 D3
Klishkivtsi Ukraine 48°26N 26°16E 81 B11
Klisura Bulgaria 42°40N 24°28E 97 D8
Kljajićevo Serbia 45°45N 19°17E 80 E4
Ključ Bos.-H. 44°32N 16°48E 93 D13
Klobuck Poland 50°55N 18°55E 83 H5
Klockestrand Sweden 62°53N 17°55E 62 B11
Kłodawa Poland 52°15N 18°55E 83 F5
Kłodzko Poland 50°28N 16°38E 83 H3
Klondike Canada 64°0N 139°26W 160 E4
Klong Wang Chao △ Thailand 16°20N 99°9E 120 D2
Klos Albania 41°28N 20°10E 96 E4
Klosterneuburg Austria 48°18N 16°19E 79 C9
Klosters Switz. 46°52N 9°52E 77 J5
Klötze Germany 52°37N 11°10E 76 C7
Klouto Togo 6°57N 0°44E 139 D5
Klövsjö Sweden 62°32N 14°11E 62 B8
Kluane △ Canada 60°45N 139°30W 162 A1
Kluane L. Canada 61°15N 138°40W 160 E4
Kluang Malaysia 2°3N 103°18E 121 L4
Kluczbork Poland 50°58N 18°12E 83 H5
Klukwan U.S.A. 59°24N 135°54W 162 B1
Klungkung Indonesia 8°32S 115°24E 119 K18
Klyetsk Belarus 53°5N 26°45E 75 B14
Klyuchevskaya, Sopka Russia 55°50N 160°30E 107 D17
Klyuchi Russia 56°18N 160°51E 107 D17
Knared Sweden 56°31N 13°19E 63 H7
Knaresborough U.K. 54°1N 1°28W 66 C6
Knee L. Man., Canada 55°3N 94°45W 164 A1
Knee L. Sask., Canada 55°51N 107°0W 163 B7
Kneïss, Îs. Tunisia 34°22N 10°18E 136 B6
Knezha Bulgaria 43°30N 24°5E 97 C8
Knight Inlet Canada 50°45N 125°40W 162 C3
Knighton U.K. 52°21N 3°3W 67 E4
Knights Ferry U.S.A. 37°50N 120°40W 170 H6
Knights Landing U.S.A. 38°48N 121°43W 170 G5
Knin Croatia 44°3N 16°17E 93 D13
Knislinge Sweden 56°12N 14°5E 63 H8
Knittelfeld Austria 47°13N 14°51E 78 D7
Knivsta Sweden 59°43N 17°48E 62 E11
Knjaževac Serbia 43°35N 22°18E 96 C6
Knob, C. Australia 34°32S 119°16E 149 F2
Knock Ireland 53°48N 8°55W 64 C3
Knockmealdown Mts. Ireland 52°14N 7°56W 64 D4
Knokke-Heist Belgium 51°21N 3°17E 69 C3
Knossos Greece 35°16N 25°10E 101 D7
Knowlton Canada 45°13N 72°31W 175 A12
Knox U.S.A. 41°18N 86°37W 172 E10
Knox Coast Antarctica 66°30S 108°0E 55 C8
Knoxville Ga., U.S.A. 32°47N 83°59W 178 C6
Knoxville Iowa, U.S.A. 41°19N 93°6W 172 E7
Knoxville Pa., U.S.A. 41°57N 77°27W 174 E7
Knoxville Tenn., U.S.A. 35°58N 83°55W 177 D13
Knud Rasmussen Land Greenland 78°0N 60°0W 57 B4
Knysna S. Africa 34°2S 23°2E 144 D3
Knyszyn Poland 53°20N 22°56E 82 E9
Ko Kha Thailand 18°11N 99°24E 120 C2
Ko Tarutao △ Thailand 6°31N 99°26E 121 J2
Ko Yao Thailand 8°7N 98°35E 121 a
Koani Tanzania 6°8S 39°17E 142 D4
Koartac = Quaqtaq Canada 60°55N 69°40W 161 E18
Koba Indonesia 6°37S 134°37E 119 F8
Kobarid Slovenia 46°15N 13°30E 93 B10
Kobayashi Japan 31°56N 130°59E 113 J5
Kōbe Japan 34°41N 135°13E 113 G7
Kobelyaky Ukraine 49°11N 34°9E 85 H8
København Denmark 55°40N 12°26E 63 J6
København ✈ (CPH) Denmark 55°37N 12°39E 63 J6
Kobenni Mauritania 15°58N 9°24W 138 B3
Kōbi-Sho E. China Sea 25°56N 123°41E 113 M1
Koblenz Germany 50°21N 7°36E 77 E3
Kobryn Belarus 52°15N 24°22E 75 B13
Kobuk → U.S.A. 66°54N 160°38W 166 B7
Kobuleti Georgia 41°55N 41°45E 87 K5
Kobyletska Polyana Ukraine 48°3N 24°4E 81 B9
Kobylin Poland 51°43N 17°12E 83 G4
Kobyłka Poland 52°20N 21°10E 83 F8
Kobylkino Russia 54°8N 43°56E 86 C6
Koca → Turkey 40°8N 27°57E 97 F11
Kocabaş Turkey 37°49N 29°20E 99 D11
Kocaeli Turkey 40°45N 29°50E 97 F13
Kocaeli □ Turkey 40°45N 29°55E 97 F13
Kočane Serbia 43°12N 21°52E 96 C5
Kočani Macedonia 41°55N 22°25E 96 E6
Koçarlı Turkey 37°45N 27°43E 99 D9
Koceljevo Serbia 44°28N 19°50E 96 B3
Kočevje Slovenia 45°39N 14°50E 93 C11
Koch Bihar India 26°22N 89°29E 123 F16
Kochas India 25°15N 83°56E 125 G10
Kocher → Germany 49°13N 9°12E 77 F5
Kochi India 9°58N 76°20E 127 K3
Kōchi Japan 33°30N 133°35E 113 H6
Kōchi □ Japan 33°40N 133°30E 113 H6
Kochiu = Gejiu China 23°20N 103°10E 116 F4
Kochkor Kyrgyzstan 42°13N 75°46E 109 D9
Kochubey Russia 44°23N 46°32E 87 H8
Kock Poland 51°38N 22°27E 83 G9
Kodala India 19°38N 84°57E 126 E7
Kodarma India 24°28N 85°36E 125 G11
Koddiyar B. Sri Lanka 8°33N 81°15E 127 K5
Kode Sweden 57°57N 11°51E 63 G5
Kodiak U.S.A. 57°47N 152°24W 166 D9
Kodiak I. U.S.A. 57°30N 152°45W 166 D9
Kodikkarai = Point Calimere India 10°17N 79°49E 127 J4
Kodinar India 20°46N 70°46E 124 J4
Kodinsk Russia 58°40N 99°10E 107 D10
Kodlipet India 12°48N 75°53E 127 H2
Kodori → Georgia 42°47N 41°10E 87 J5
Kodungallur = Cranganore India 10°13N 76°13E 127 J3
Kodyma Ukraine 48°6N 29°7E 81 B14
Koedoesberge S. Africa 32°40S 20°11E 144 D3
Koes Namibia 26°0S 19°15E 144 C2
Kofarnihon Tajikistan 38°33N 69°1E 109 E7
Kofçaz Turkey 41°58N 27°12E 97 E11
Koffiefontein S. Africa 29°30S 25°0E 144 C4
Kofiau Indonesia 1°11S 129°50E 119 E7
Köflach Austria 47°4N 15°5E 78 D8
Koforidua Ghana 6°3N 0°17W 139 D4
Kōfu Japan 35°40N 138°30E 113 G9
Koga Japan 36°11N 139°43E 113 F9
Kogaluc → Canada 56°12N 61°44W 165 A7
Køge Denmark 55°27N 12°11E 63 J6
Køge Bugt Denmark 55°34N 12°24E 63 J6
Kogi □ Nigeria 7°45N 6°45E 139 D6
Kogin Baba Nigeria 7°55N 11°35E 139 D7
Kogon Uzbekistan 39°43N 64°33E 108 E6
Koh-i-Khurd Afghan. 33°30N 65°59E 124 C1
Koh-i-Maran Pakistan 29°18N 66°50E 124 E2
Koh Ker Cambodia 13°47N 104°32E 120 F5
Koh Wai Thailand 11°54N 102°25E 121 H4
Kohat Pakistan 33°40N 71°29E 124 C4
Kohima India 25°35N 94°10E 123 G19
Kohkīlūyeh va Būyer Aḥmadi □ Iran 31°30N 50°30E 129 D6
Kohler Ra. Antarctica 77°0S 110°0W 55 D15
Kohlu Pakistan 29°54N 69°15E 124 E3
Kohtla-Järve Estonia 59°20N 27°20E 84 C4
Kohukohu N.Z. 35°22S 173°38E 154 B2
Kohylnyk → Ukraine 45°49N 29°40E 81 E14
Koi Sanjaq Iraq 36°5N 44°38E 105 D11
Koidu S. Leone 8°38N 10°59W 138 D2
Koihoa India 8°12N 93°29E 127 K11
Koilkuntla India 15°14N 78°19E 127 G4
Koillismaa Finland 65°44N 28°36E 60 D23
Koin N. Korea 40°28N 126°18E 115 D14
Koinare Bulgaria 43°21N 24°8E 97 C8
Koindu S. Leone 8°26N 10°19W 138 D2
Kojetín Czechia 49°21N 17°20E 79 B10
Kojŏ N. Korea 38°58N 127°58E 115 E14
Kojonup Australia 33°48S 117°10E 149 F2
Kojūr Iran 36°23N 51°43E 129 B6
Kokand = Qo'qon Uzbekistan 40°31N 70°56E 109 D8
Kokang Myanmar 23°45N 98°30E 116 F2
Kokas Indonesia 2°42S 132°26E 119 E8
Kokava Slovakia 48°35N 19°50E 79 C12
Kokcha → Afghan. 37°9N 69°24E 109 E7
Kokchetav = Kökshetaū Kazakhstan 53°20N 69°25E 109 B7
Kokemäenjoki → Finland 61°32N 21°44E 84 B1
Kokhma Russia 56°57N 41°8E 86 B5
Koki Senegal 15°30N 15°59W 138 B1
Kokkilai Sri Lanka 9°0N 80°57E 127 K5
Kokkola Finland 63°50N 23°8E 60 E20
Koko Nigeria 11°28N 4°29E 139 C5
Koko Kyunzu Myanmar 14°7N 93°22E 127 G11
Koko Nur = Qinghai Hu China 36°40N 100°10E 110 D9
Kokologo Burkina Faso 12°11N 1°53W 138 C4
Kokolopozo Côte d'Ivoire 5°8N 6°5W 138 D3
Kokomo U.S.A. 40°29N 86°8W 172 E10
Kokopo Papua N. G. 4°22S 152°19E 156 H7
Kokoro Niger 14°12N 0°55E 139 C5
Koksan N. Korea 38°46N 126°40E 115 E14
Kökshetaū Kazakhstan 53°20N 69°25E 109 B7
Koksoak → Canada 58°30N 68°10W 161 F18
Kokstad S. Africa 30°32S 29°29E 145 D4
Koktal Kazakhstan 44°8N 79°48E 109 D9
Kokubu = Kirishima Japan 31°44N 130°46E 113 J5
Kokyar China 37°23N 77°10E 109 E9
Kola Indonesia 5°35S 134°30E 119 F8
Kola Russia 68°45N 33°8E 60 B25
Kola Pen. = Kolskiy Poluostrov Russia 67°30N 38°0E 58 B13
Kolachel India 8°10N 77°15E 127 K3
Kolachi → Pakistan 27°8N 67°2E 124 F2
Kolahoi India 34°12N 75°22E 125 B6
Kolahun Liberia 8°15N 10°4W 138 D2
Kolaka Indonesia 4°3S 121°46E 119 E6
Kolar India 13°12N 78°15E 127 H4
Kolar Gold Fields India 12°58N 78°16E 127 H4
Kolaras India 25°14N 77°36E 124 G6
Kolari Finland 67°20N 23°48E 60 C20
Kolárovo Slovakia 47°54N 18°0E 79 D10
Kolašin Montenegro 42°50N 19°31E 96 D3
Kolayat India 27°50N 72°50E 124 F5
Kolbäck Sweden 59°34N 16°15E 62 E10
Kolbäcksån → Sweden 59°36N 16°16E 62 E10
Kolbermoor Germany 47°51N 12°4E 77 H8
Kolbuszowa Poland 50°15N 21°46E 83 H8
Kolchugino Russia 56°17N 39°22E 84 D10
Kolda Senegal 12°55N 14°57W 138 C2
Kolda □ Senegal 13°5N 14°50W 138 C2
Kolding Denmark 55°30N 9°29E 63 J3
Koléa Algeria 36°38N 2°46E 136 A4
Kolepom = Dolak, Pulau Indonesia 8°0S 138°30E 119 F9
Kolguyev, Ostrov Russia 69°20N 48°30E 106 C5
Kolhapur India 16°43N 74°15E 126 F2
Kolia Côte d'Ivoire 9°46N 6°28W 138 D3
Kolimbia Greece 36°15N 28°10E 101 C10
Kolín Czechia 50°2N 15°9E 78 A8
Kolind Denmark 56°21N 10°34E 63 H4
Kolkas rags Latvia 57°46N 22°37E 82 A9
Kolkata India 22°34N 88°21E 125 H13
Kollam India 8°50N 76°38E 127 K3
Kölleda Germany 51°11N 11°15E 76 D7
Kollegal India 12°9N 77°9E 127 H3
Kolleru L. India 16°40N 81°10E 126 F5
Kollum Neths. 53°17N 6°10E 69 A6
Kolmanskop Namibia 26°45S 15°14E 144 C2
Köln Germany 50°56N 6°57E 76 E2
Kolno Poland 53°25N 21°56E 82 E8
Koło Poland 52°14N 18°40E 83 F5
Kołobrzeg Poland 54°10N 15°35E 82 D2
Kolochava Ukraine 48°26N 23°41E 81 B8
Kolokani Mali 13°35N 7°45W 138 C3
Koloko Burkina Faso 11°5N 5°19W 138 C3
Kolomna Russia 55°8N 38°45E 84 E10
Kolomyya Ukraine 48°31N 25°2E 81 B10
Kolondiéba Mali 11°5N 6°54W 138 C3
Kolonodale Indonesia 2°0S 121°19E 119 E6
Kolonowskie Poland 50°39N 18°22E 83 H5
Kolpashevo Russia 58°20N 83°5E 106 D9
Kolpino Russia 59°44N 30°39E 84 C6
Kolpny Russia 52°17N 37°1E 85 F9
Kolskiy Poluostrov Russia 67°30N 38°0E 58 B13
Kolskiy Zaliv Russia 69°23N 34°0E 60 B26
Kolsva Sweden 59°36N 15°51E 62 E9
Kolubara → Serbia 44°35N 20°15E 96 B4
Koluszki Poland 51°45N 19°46E 83 G6
Kolwezi Dem. Rep. of the Congo 10°40S 25°25E 143 E2
Kolyma → Russia 69°30N 161°0E 107 C17
Kolymskoye Nagorye Russia 63°0N 157°0E 107 C16
Kôm Hamâda Egypt 30°46N 30°41E 137 E7
Kôm Ombo Egypt 24°25N 32°52E 137 C3
Koma Tou Yialou Cyprus 35°25N 34°8E 101 D13
Komadugu Gana → Nigeria 13°5N 12°24E 139 C7
Komandorskiye Is. = Komandorskiye Ostrova Russia 55°0N 167°0E 107 D17
Komandorskiye Ostrova Russia 55°0N 167°0E 107 D17
Komárno Slovakia 47°49N 18°5E 79 D11
Komarnyky Ukraine 48°59N 23°3E 80 B8
Komárom Hungary 47°43N 18°7E 80 C3
Komárom-Esztergom □ Hungary 47°35N 18°20E 80 C3
Komatipoort S. Africa 25°25S 31°55E 145 C5
Komatsu Japan 36°25N 136°30E 113 F8
Komatsushima Japan 34°0N 134°35E 113 H7
Kombissiri Burkina Faso 12°4N 1°20W 139 C4
Kombori Burkina Faso 13°26N 3°56W 138 C4
Komboti Greece 39°6N 21°5E 98 B3
Kome Channel Uganda 0°10S 32°35E 142 C3
Komen Slovenia 45°49N 13°45E 93 C10
Komenda Ghana 5°4N 1°28W 139 D4
Komi Cyprus 35°24N 34°0E 101 D13
Komi □ Russia 64°0N 55°0E 106 C6
Komiža Croatia 43°3N 16°11E 93 E13
Komló Hungary 46°15N 18°16E 80 D3
Kommamur Canal India 16°0N 80°25E 127 G5
Kommunarsk = Alchevsk Ukraine 48°30N 38°45E 85 H10
Kommunizma, Pik = imeni Ismail Samani, Pik Tajikistan 39°0N 72°2E 109 E8
Komodo Indonesia 8°37S 119°20E 119 F5
Komoran, Pulau Indonesia 8°18S 138°45E 119 F9
Komoro Japan 36°19N 138°26E 113 F9
Komotini Greece 41°9N 25°26E 97 E9
Komovi Montenegro 42°41N 19°39E 96 D3
Kompasberg S. Africa 31°45S 24°32E 144 D3
Kompong Chhnang = Kampong Chhnang Cambodia 12°20N 104°35E 121 F5
Kompong Chikreng Cambodia 13°5N 104°18E 120 F5
Kompong Kleang Cambodia 13°6N 104°8E 120 F5
Kompong Luong Cambodia 11°49N 104°48E 121 G5
Kompong Pranak Cambodia 13°35N 104°55E 120 F5
Kompong Som = Kampong Saom Cambodia 10°38N 103°30E 121 G4
Kompong Som, Chhung = Kampong Saom, Chaak Cambodia 10°50N 103°32E 121 G4
Kompong Speu Cambodia 11°26N 104°32E 121 G5
Kompong Sralau Cambodia 14°5N 105°46E 120 E5
Kompong Thom Cambodia 12°35N 104°51E 120 F5
Kompong Trabeck Cambodia 13°6N 105°14E 120 F5
Kompong Trach Cambodia 11°25N 105°48E 121 G5
Kompong Tralach Cambodia 11°54N 104°47E 121 G5
Komrat = Comrat Moldova 46°18N 28°40E 81 D13
Komsberg S. Africa 32°40S 20°45E 144 D3
Komsomolets = Qarabalyq Kazakhstan 53°45N 62°2E 108 B6
Komsomolets, Ostrov Russia 80°30N 95°0E 107 A10
Komsomolsk Russia 57°2N 40°20E 84 D11
Komsomolsk Ukraine 49°1N 33°38E 85 H7
Komsomolsk-na-Amur Russia 50°30N 137°0E 111 A16
Komsomolskiy Russia 54°27N 45°33E 86 C7
Komsomolskoe Kazakhstan 50°25N 60°5E 108 B6
Kömür Burnu Turkey 38°39N 26°12E 99 C8
Kon Ka Kinh △ Vietnam 14°19N 107°23E 120 E6
Kon Tum Vietnam 14°24N 108°0E 120 E7
Kon Tum, Plateau du Vietnam 14°30N 108°30E 120 E7
Kona Mali 14°57N 3°53W 138 C4
Kona Nigeria 8°57N 11°21E 139 D7
Konakovo Russia 56°40N 36°51E 84 D9
Konar □ Afghan. 34°30N 71°3E 122 B7
Konarak India 19°54N 86°7E 126 E8
Konārak Iran 25°21N 60°23E 129 E9
Konārī Iran 28°13N 51°36E 129 D6
Konch India 26°0N 79°10E 125 G8
Kondagaon India 19°35N 81°35E 126 E5
Konde Tanzania 4°57S 39°45E 142 C4
Kondias Greece 39°49N 25°10E 99 B7
Kondinin Australia 32°34S 118°8E 149 F2
Kondoa Tanzania 4°55S 35°50E 142 C4
Kondopoga Russia 62°12N 34°17E 84 A8
Kondoz Afghan. 36°50N 68°50E 109 E7
Kondoz → Afghan. 37°0N 68°16E 109 E7
Kondratyevo Russia 57°22N 98°15E 107 D10
Kondrovo Russia 54°48N 35°56E 84 E8
Konduga Nigeria 11°35N 13°26E 139 C7
Kondukur India 15°12N 79°57E 127 G4
Kondūz □ Afghan. 36°50N 68°50E 109 E7
Köneürgench Turkmenistan 42°19N 59°10E 108 D5
Konevo Russia 62°8N 39°20E 84 A10
Kong = Khong → Cambodia 13°32N 105°58E 120 F5
Kong Côte d'Ivoire 8°54N 4°36W 138 D4
Kong, Koh Cambodia 11°20N 103°0E 121 G4
Kong Christian IX.s Land Greenland 68°0N 36°0W 57 D7
Kong Christian X.s Land Greenland 74°0N 29°0W 57 C8
Kong Frederik IX.s Land Greenland 67°0N 52°0W 57 D5
Kong Frederik VI.s Kyst Greenland 63°0N 43°0W 57 E6
Kong Frederik VIII.s Land Greenland 78°30N 26°0W 57 B8
Kong Karls Land Svalbard 79°0N 28°0E 57 B13
Kong Oscar Fjord Greenland 72°20N 24°0W 57 C8
Kongeå → Denmark 55°23N 8°39E 63 J2
Kongernes Nordsjælland △ Denmark 56°5N 12°15E 63 H6
Kongerslev Denmark 56°54N 10°6E 63 H4
Konglu Myanmar 27°13N 97°57E 123 F20
Kongo Liberia 7°20N 11°6W 138 D2
Kongola Namibia 17°45S 23°20E 144 A3
Kongolo Kasai-Or., Dem. Rep. of the Congo 5°26S 24°49E 142 D1
Kongolo Katanga, Dem. Rep. of the Congo 5°22S 27°0E 142 D2
Kongossambougou ⌂ Mali 14°0N 8°30W 138 C3
Kongoussi Burkina Faso 13°19N 1°32W 139 C4
Kongsberg Norway 59°39N 9°39E 61 G13
Kongsvinger Norway 60°12N 12°2E 61 F15
Kongur Shan China 38°34N 75°18E 109 E9
Kongwa Tanzania 6°11S 36°26E 142 D4
Koni Dem. Rep. of the Congo 10°40S 27°11E 143 E2
Koniakari Mali 14°35N 10°50W 138 C2
Koniecpol Poland 50°46N 19°40E 83 H6
Königs Wusterhausen Germany 52°19N 13°38E 76 C9
Königsbrunn Germany 48°16N 10°54E 77 G6
Königslutter Germany 52°15N 10°49E 76 C6
Konin Poland 52°12N 18°15E 83 F5
Konispol Albania 39°42N 20°10E 96 G4
Konitsa Greece 40°5N 20°48E 98 A2
Köniz Switz. 46°56N 7°25E 77 J3
Konjic Bos.-H. 43°42N 17°58E 80 G2
Konkiep Namibia 26°49S 17°15E 144 C2
Konkouré → Guinea 9°50N 13°42W 138 D2
Könnern Germany 51°41N 11°47E 76 D7
Konnur India 16°14N 74°49E 127 F2
Kono S. Leone 8°30N 11°5W 138 D2
Konongo Ghana 6°40N 1°15W 139 D4
Konosha Russia 61°0N 40°5E 84 B11
Kōnosu Japan 36°3N 139°31E 113 F9
Konotop Ukraine 51°12N 33°7E 85 G7
Konqi He → China 40°45N 90°10E 109 D11
Konsankoro Guinea 9°2N 9°0W 138 D3
Końskie Poland 51°15N 20°23E 83 G7
Konstancin-Jeziorna Poland 52°5N 21°7E 83 F8
Konstantinovka = Kostyantynivka Ukraine 48°32N 37°39E 85 H9
Konstantinovsk Russia 47°33N 41°10E 87 G5
Konstantynów Łódzki Poland 51°45N 19°20E 83 G6
Konstanz Germany 47°40N 9°10E 77 H5
Kont Iran 26°55N 61°50E 129 E9
Konta India 17°48N 81°23E 126 F5
Kontagora Nigeria 10°23N 5°27E 139 C6
Kontcha Cameroon 7°59N 12°15E 139 D7
Kontiolahti Finland 62°46N 29°50E 60 E23
Kontokali Greece 39°38N 19°51E 101 A3
Konya Turkey 37°52N 32°35E 104 D5
Konya □ Turkey 37°46N 32°20E 104 D5
Konya Ovası Turkey 38°9N 33°5E 104 C5
Konz Germany 49°42N 6°34E 77 F2
Konza Kenya 1°45S 37°7E 142 C4
Koo-wee-rup Australia 38°13S 145°28E 153 E6
Koocanusa, L. Canada 49°20N 115°15W 168 B6
Kookynie Australia 29°17S 121°22E 149 E3
Koolyanobbing Australia 30°48S 119°36E 149 F2
Koondrook Australia 35°33S 144°8E 152 C6
Koonibba Australia 31°54S 133°25E 151 E1
Koorawatha Australia 34°2S 148°33E 153 C8
Koorda Australia 30°48S 117°35E 149 F2
Kooskia U.S.A. 46°9N 115°59W 168 C6
Kootenay → U.S.A. 49°19N 117°39W 162 D5
Kootenay △ Canada 51°0N 116°0W 162 C5
Kootenay L. Canada 49°45N 116°50W 168 B5
Kootingal Australia 31°3S 151°4E 153 A9
Kootjieskolk S. Africa 31°15S 20°21E 144 D3
Kopanovka Russia 47°28N 46°50E 87 G8
Kopaonik Serbia 43°10N 20°50E 96 C4
Kopaonik △ Serbia 43°20N 20°50E 96 C4
Kopargaon India 19°51N 74°28E 126 E2
Kópavogur Iceland 64°6N 21°55W 60 D3
Kopayhorod Ukraine 48°52N 27°53E 81 B12
Koper Slovenia 45°31N 13°44E 93 C10
Kopervik Norway 59°17N 5°17E 61 G11
Kopet Dagh Asia 38°0N 58°0E 129 B8
Kopeysk Russia 55°7N 61°37E 108 A6
Kopi Australia 33°24S 135°40E 151 E2
Köping Sweden 59°31N 16°3E 62 E10
Köpingsvik Sweden 56°53N 16°43E 63 H10
Kopište Croatia 42°48N 16°42E 93 F13
Koplik Albania 42°15N 19°25E 96 D3
Köpmanholmen Sweden 63°10N 18°35E 62 A12
Koppa India 13°33N 75°21E 127 H2
Koppal India 15°23N 76°5E 127 G3
Kopparberg Sweden 59°52N 15°0E 62 E9
Koppeh Dāgh = Kopet Dagh Asia 38°0N 58°0E 129 B8
Koppies S. Africa 27°20S 27°30E 145 C4
Koppom Sweden 59°43N 12°10E 62 E6
Koprivlen Bulgaria 41°31N 23°53E 96 E7
Koprivnica Croatia 46°12N 16°45E 93 B13
Kopřivnice Czechia 49°36N 18°9E 79 B11
Koprivshtitsa Bulgaria 42°40N 24°19E 97 D8
Köprübaşı Turkey 38°43N 28°23E 99 C10
Köprülü △ Turkey 37°20N 31°5E 128 B1
Kopychyntsi Ukraine 49°7N 25°58E 75 D13
Kora △ Kenya 0°14S 38°44E 142 C4
Korab Macedonia 41°44N 20°40E 96 E4
Koral India 21°50N 73°12E 124 J5
Korangal India 17°6N 77°38E 126 F3
Koraput India 18°50N 82°40E 126 E6
Korarou, L. Mali 15°15N 3°15W 138 B4
Korba India 22°20N 82°45E 125 H10
Korbach Germany 51°16N 8°52E 76 D4
Korbu, Gunung Malaysia 4°41N 101°18E 121 K3
Korçë Albania 40°37N 20°50E 96 F4
Korčula Croatia 42°56N 16°57E 93 F13
Korčulanski Kanal Croatia 43°3N 16°40E 93 E13
Kord Kūy Iran 36°48N 54°7E 129 B7
Kord Sheykh Iran 28°31N 52°53E 129 D7
Kordestan = Kurdistan Asia 37°20N 43°30E 105 D10
Kordestān □ Iran 36°0N 47°0E 128 C5
Kordié Burkina Faso 12°36N 2°22W 138 C4
Kordofân Sudan 13°0N 29°0E 135 F11
Koré Mayroua Niger 13°18N 3°55E 139 C5
Korea, North ■ Asia 40°0N 127°0E 115 E14
Korea, South ■ Asia 36°0N 128°0E 115 G15
Korea Bay Korea 39°0N 124°0E 115 E13
Korea Strait Asia 34°0N 129°30E 115 H15
Koregaon India 17°40N 74°10E 126 F2
Korenevo Russia 51°27N 34°55E 85 G8
Korenovsk Russia 45°30N 39°22E 87 H4
Korets Ukraine 50°40N 27°5E 75 C14
Korfantów Poland 50°29N 17°36E 83 H4
Körfez Turkey 40°47N 29°44E 97 F13
Korff Ice Rise Antarctica 79°0S 69°30W 55 D17
Korgalzhyn = Qorghalzhyn Kazakhstan 50°25N 69°11E 109 B7
Korgan Turkey 40°44N 37°13E 104 B7
Korgus Sudan 19°16N 33°29E 137 D3
Korhogo Côte d'Ivoire 9°29N 5°28W 138 D3
Koribundu S. Leone 7°41N 11°46W 138 D2
Korienzé Mali 15°22N 3°50W 138 B4
Korinthiakos Kolpos Greece 38°16N 22°30E 98 C4
Korinthos Greece 37°56N 22°55E 98 D4
Korioumé Mali 16°35N 3°0W 138 B4
Korissia, L. Greece 39°27N 19°53E 101 B3
Kōriyama Japan 37°24N 140°23E 112 F10
Korkino Russia 54°54N 61°23E 108 B6
Korkuteli Turkey 37°4N 30°13E 99 D12
Korla China 41°45N 86°4E 109 D11
Kormakiti, C. Cyprus 35°23N 32°56E 101 D11
Körmend Hungary 47°5N 16°35E 80 C1
Kormor Iraq 35°8N 44°50E 105 E11
Kornat Croatia 43°50N 15°20E 93 E12
Kornat △ Croatia 43°50N 15°12E 93 E12
Korneshty = Cornești Moldova 47°21N 28°1E 81 C13
Korneuburg Austria 48°20N 16°20E 79 C9
Kórnik Poland 52°15N 17°6E 83 F4
Koro Côte d'Ivoire 8°32N 7°30W 138 D3
Koro Fiji 17°19S 179°23E 154 a
Koro Mali 14°1N 2°58W 138 C4
Koro Sea Fiji 17°30S 179°45W 154 a
Korocha Russia 50°54N 37°19E 85 G9
Köroğlu Dağları Turkey 40°38N 33°0E 104 B5
Korogwe Tanzania 5°5S 38°25E 142 D4
Koroit Australia 38°18S 142°24E 152 E5
Koroleve Ukraine 48°9N 23°8E 81 B8
Korolevu Fiji 18°12S 177°46E 154 a
Korona U.S.A. 29°25N 81°12W 179 F8
Koronadal Phil. 6°12N 124°51E 119 C6
Korong Vale Australia 36°22S 143°45E 152 D5
Koroni Greece 36°48N 21°57E 98 E3
Koronia, L. Greece 40°47N 23°10E 96 F7
Koronos Greece 37°12N 25°35E 99 D7
Koronowo Poland 53°19N 17°55E 83 E4
Koropets Ukraine 48°56N 25°10E 81 B10
Körös → Hungary 46°43N 20°12E 80 D5
Körös Maros △ Hungary 47°8N 20°52E 80 C5
Köröstarcsa Hungary 46°53N 21°3E 80 D6
Korosten Ukraine 50°54N 28°36E 75 C15
Korostyshev Ukraine 50°19N 29°4E 75 C15
Korotoyak Russia 51°1N 39°2E 85 G10
Korovou Fiji 17°47S 178°32E 154 a
Koroyanitu △ Fiji 17°40S 177°35E 154 a
Korsakov Russia 46°36N 142°42E 107 E15
Korsberga Sweden 57°19N 15°7E 63 G9
Korshiv Ukraine 48°39N 25°1E 81 B10
Korshunovo Russia 58°37N 110°10E 107 D12
Korsør Denmark 55°20N 11°9E 63 J5
Korsun Shevchenkovskiy Ukraine 49°26N 31°16E 85 H6
Korsze Poland 54°11N 21°9E 82 D8
Korti Sudan 18°6N 31°33E 137 D3
Kortrijk Belgium 50°50N 3°17E 69 D3
Korucu Turkey 39°28N 27°22E 99 B9
Korumburra Australia 38°26S 145°50E 153 E6
Korwai India 24°7N 78°5E 124 G8
Koryakskoye Nagorye Russia 61°0N 171°0E 107 C18
Koryukovka Ukraine 51°46N 32°16E 85 G7
Kos Greece 36°50N 27°15E 99 E9
Kosan N. Korea 38°52N 127°25E 115 E14
Kosaya Gora Russia 54°10N 37°30E 84 E9
Kościan Poland 52°5N 16°40E 83 F3
Kościerzyna Poland 54°8N 17°59E 82 D4
Kosciusko U.S.A. 33°4N 89°35W 177 E10
Kosciuszko, Mt. Australia 36°27S 148°16E 153 D8
Kosciuszko △ Australia 36°30S 148°20E 153 D8
Kösély → Hungary 47°25N 21°5E 80 C6
Kosgi Andhra Pradesh, India 16°58N 77°43E 126 F3
Kosgi Andhra Pradesh, India 15°51N 77°16E 127 G3
Kosha Sudan 20°50N 30°30E 137 C3
Koshava Bulgaria 44°4N 23°2E 96 B7
K'oshih = Kashi China 39°30N 76°2E 109 E9
Koshiki-Rettō Japan 31°45N 129°49E 113 J4
Koshim → Kazakhstan 49°20N 50°30E 86 F10
Kosi India 27°48N 77°29E 124 F7
Kosi → India 28°41N 78°57E 125 E8
Košice Slovakia 48°42N 21°15E 79 C14
Košický □ Slovakia 48°45N 21°0E 79 C14
Kosiv Ukraine 48°19N 25°6E 81 B10
Kosjerić Serbia 44°0N 19°55E 96 B3
Köşk Turkey 37°50N 28°3E 99 D10
Koskinou Greece 36°23N 28°13E 101 C10
Koslan Russia 63°34N 49°14E 106 C5
Kosmach Ukraine 48°20N 24°50E 81 B9
Kosŏng N. Korea 38°40N 128°22E 115 E15
Kosovo ■ Europe 42°30N 21°0E 96 D4
Kosovo Polje = Fushë Kosovë Kosovo 42°40N 21°5E 96 D5
Kosovska Kamenica = Dardanë Kosovo 42°35N 21°35E 96 D5
Kosovska Mitrovica = Mitrovicë Kosovo 42°54N 20°52E 96 D4
Kossou, L. de Côte d'Ivoire 6°59N 5°31W 138 D3
Kosta Sweden 56°50N 15°24E 63 H9
Kostajnica Bos.-H. 45°11N 16°33E 93 C13
Kostajnica Croatia 45°17N 16°30E 93 C13
Kostanjevica Slovenia 45°51N 15°27E 93 C12
Kostenets Bulgaria 42°15N 23°52E 96 D7
Koster S. Africa 25°52S 26°54E 144 C4
Kôstî Sudan 13°8N 32°43E 135 F12
Kostinbrod Bulgaria 42°49N 23°13E 96 D7
Kostolac Serbia 44°37N 21°15E 96 B5
Kostomuksha Russia 64°41N 30°49E 60 D24
Kostopil Ukraine 50°51N 26°22E 75 C14
Kostroma Russia 57°50N 40°58E 84 D11
Kostromo □ Russia 58°10N 42°50E 86 A6
Kostromskoye Vdkhr. Russia 57°52N 40°49E 84 D11
Kostryzhivka Ukraine 48°39N 25°43E 81 B10
Kostrzyn Lubuskie, Poland 52°35N 14°39E 83 F1
Kostrzyn Wielkopolskie, Poland 52°24N 17°14E 83 F4
Kostyantynivka Ukraine 48°32N 37°39E 85 H9
Kostyukovichi = Kastsyukovichy Belarus 53°20N 32°4E 85 F7
Koszalin Poland 54°11N 16°8E 82 D3
Kőszeg Hungary 47°23N 16°33E 80 C1
Kot Addu Pakistan 30°30N 71°0E 124 D4
Kot Kapura India 30°35N 74°50E 124 D6
Kot Moman Pakistan 32°13N 73°0E 124 C5
Kot Sultan Pakistan 30°46N 70°56E 124 D4
Kota India 25°14N 75°49E 124 G6
Kota Barrage India 25°6N 75°51E 124 G6
Kota Belud Malaysia 6°21N 116°26E 118 C5
Kota Bharu Malaysia 6°7N 102°14E 121 J4
Kota I. = Loaita I. S. China Sea 10°41N 114°25E 118 B4
Kota Kinabalu Malaysia 6°0N 116°4E 118 C5
Kota Tinggi Malaysia 1°44N 103°53E 121 M4
Kotaagung Indonesia 5°38S 104°29E 118 F2
Kotabaru Indonesia 3°20S 116°20E 118 E5
Kotabumi Indonesia 4°49S 104°54E 118 E2
Kotamobagu Indonesia 0°57N 124°31E 119 D6
Kotapad India 19°9N 82°21E 126 E6
Kotapinang Indonesia 1°53N 100°5E 121 M3
Kotcho L. Canada 59°7N 121°12W 162 B4
Kotdwara India 29°45N 78°32E 125 E8
Kotel Bulgaria 42°52N 26°26E 97 D10
Kotelnich Russia 58°22N 48°24E 86 A9
Kotelnikovo Russia 47°38N 43°8E 87 G6
Kotelnyy, Ostrov Russia 75°10N 139°0E 107 B14
Kothapet India 19°21N 79°28E 126 E4
Kothari → India 25°20N 75°4E 124 G6
Köthen Germany 51°45N 11°59E 76 D7
Kothi Chhattisgarh, India 23°21N 82°3E 125 H10
Kothi Mad. P., India 24°45N 80°40E 125 G9
Kotiro Pakistan 26°17N 67°13E 124 F2
Kotka Finland 60°28N 26°58E 84 B4
Kotlas Russia 61°17N 46°43E 106 C5
Kotlenska Planina Bulgaria 42°56N 26°30E 97 D10
Kotli Pakistan 33°30N 73°55E 124 C5
Kotlik U.S.A. 63°2N 163°33W 166 C7
Kotma India 23°12N 81°58E 125 H9
Koton-Karifi Nigeria 8°0N 6°48E 139 D6
Kotonkoro Nigeria 11°3N 5°58E 139 C6
Kotor Montenegro 42°25N 18°47E 96 D2
Kotor Varoš Bos.-H. 44°38N 17°22E 80 F2
Kotoriba Croatia 46°23N 16°48E 93 B13
Kotovo Russia 50°22N 44°45E 86 E7
Kotovsk Russia 52°36N 41°32E 86 D5
Kotovsk Ukraine 47°45N 29°35E 75 E15
Kotputli India 27°43N 76°12E 124 F7

Kotri *Pakistan* 25°22N 68°22E **124** G3
Kotri → *India* 19°15N 80°35E **126** E5
Kotronas *Greece* 36°38N 22°29E **98** E4
Kötschach-Mauthen
　Austria 46°41N 13°1E **78** E6
Kottagudem *India* 17°30N 80°40E **126** F5
Kottayam *India* 9°35N 76°33E **127** K3
Kotto → *C.A.R.* 4°14N 22°2E **140** D4
Kottur *India* 10°34N 76°56E **127** J3
Kotturu *India* 14°45N 76°10E **127** G3
Kotuy → *Russia* 71°54N 102°6E **107** B11
Kotyuzhany *Ukraine* 48°48N 27°42E **81** B12
Kotzebue *U.S.A.* 66°53N 162°39W **166** B7
Kotzebue Sound
　U.S.A. 66°20N 163°0W **166** B7
Kouchibouguac △
　Canada 46°50N 65°0W **165** C6
Koudougou
　Burkina Faso 12°10N 2°20W **138** C4
Koufonísi *Iráklio, Greece* 34°56N 26°8E **101** E8
Koufonísi *Notío Aigaío,*
　Greece 36°57N 25°35E **99** E7
Kougaberge *S. Africa* 33°48S 23°50E **144** E3
Kouibli *Côte d'Ivoire* 7°15N 7°14W **138** D3
Kouilou → *Congo* 4°10S 12°5E **140** E2
Koukdjuak → *Canada* 66°43N 73°0W **161** D17
Koula *Greece* 41°23N 24°44E **98** D6
Koula Moutou *Gabon* 1°15S 12°25E **140** E2
Koulen = Kulen
　Cambodia 13°50N 104°40E **120** F5
Koulikoro *Mali* 12°40N 7°50W **138** C3
Koulikoro □ *Mali* 14°0N 7°45W **138** C3
Kouloúra *Greece* 39°42N 19°54E **101** A3
Koumala *Australia* 21°38S 149°15E **150** C4
Koumankou *Mali* 11°58N 6°6W **138** C3
Koumbia *Burkina Faso* 11°10N 3°50W **138** C4
Koumbia *Guinea* 11°48N 13°29W **138** C2
Koumboum *Guinea* 10°25N 13°0W **138** C2
Koumpenntoum
　Senegal 13°59N 14°34W **138** C2
Koumra *Chad* 8°50N 17°35E **135** G9
Koun-Fao *Côte d'Ivoire* 7°30N 3°15W **138** D4
Koundara *Guinea* 12°29N 13°18W **138** C2
Koungheul *Senegal* 14°0N 14°50W **138** C2
Kountze *U.S.A.* 30°22N 94°19W **176** F7
Koupéla *Burkina Faso* 12°11N 0°21W **139** C4
Kourémalé *Mali* 11°59N 8°42W **138** C3
Kouris → *Cyprus* 34°38N 32°54E **101** E11
Kourou *Fr. Guiana* 5°9N 52°39W **187** B8
Kourouba *Mali* 13°0N 10°57W **138** C2
Koûroudjel *Mauritania* 16°12N 11°30W **138** B2
Kouroukoto *Mali* 12°35N 10°5W **138** C2
Kourouma *Burkina Faso* 11°35N 4°50W **138** C4
Kourouninkoto *Mali* 13°52N 9°35W **138** C3
Kouroussa *Guinea* 10°45N 9°45W **138** C3
Koussanar *Senegal* 13°52N 14°14W **138** C2
Koussané *Mali* 14°53N 11°14W **138** C2
Koussané *Senegal* 14°10N 12°22W **138** C2
Kousseri *Cameroon* 12°0N 14°55E **135** F8
Koutiala *Mali* 12°25N 5°23W **138** C3
Kouto *Côte d'Ivoire* 9°53N 6°25W **138** D3
Kouvé *Togo* 6°25N 1°25E **139** D5
Kouvola *Finland* 60°52N 26°43E **60** B11
Kovačica *Serbia* 45°5N 20°38E **80** E5
Kovdor *Russia* 67°34N 30°24E **60** D24
Kovel *Ukraine* 51°11N 24°38E **75** C13
Kovilpatti *India* 9°10N 77°50E **127** K3
Kovin *Serbia* 44°44N 20°59E **80** F5
Kovrov *Russia* 56°25N 41°25E **86** B5
Kovur *Andhra Pradesh,*
　India 17°3N 81°39E **126** F5
Kovur *Andhra Pradesh,*
　India 14°30N 80°1E **127** G5
Kowal *Poland* 52°32N 19°7E **83** F6
Kowalewo Pomorskie
　Poland 53°10N 18°52E **83** E5
Kowanyama *Australia* 15°29S 141°44E **150** B3
Kowanyama ◯
　Australia 15°20S 141°47E **150** B3
Kowloon *China* 22°19N 114°11E **117** F10
Kowŏn *N. Korea* 39°26N 127°14E **115** E14
Koyampattur = Coimbatore
　India 11°2N 76°59E **127** J3
Köyceğiz *Turkey* 36°57N 28°40E **99** E10
Köyceğiz Gölü *Turkey* 36°56N 28°42E **99** E10
Koyukuk → *U.S.A.* 64°55N 157°32W **166** C8
Koyulhisar *Turkey* 40°18N 37°52E **104** B7
Koyunyeri *Turkey* 40°50N 26°52E **97** F10
Koza = Okinawa
　Japan 26°19N 127°46E **113** L3
Kozak *Turkey* 39°15N 27°6E **99** B9
Kozakli *Turkey* 39°13N 34°49E **104** C6
Kozan *Turkey* 37°26N 35°50E **104** D6
Kozani *Greece* 40°19N 21°47E **96** F5
Kozara *Bos.-H.* 45°0N 17°0E **93** D14
Kozara △ *Bos.-H.* 45°0N 17°0E **80** F2
Kozarac *Bos.-H.* 44°58N 16°48E **93** D13
Kozelets *Ukraine* 50°55N 31°7E **85** G6
Kozelsk *Russia* 54°2N 35°48E **84** E8
Kozhikode *India* 11°15N 75°43E **127** J2
Kozieglowy *Poland* 50°37N 19°8E **83** H6
Kozienice *Poland* 51°35N 21°34E **83** G8
Kozje *Slovenia* 46°5N 15°35E **93** B12
Kozloduy *Bulgaria* 43°45N 23°42E **96** C7
Kozlovets *Bulgaria* 43°30N 25°20E **97** C9
Kozlu *Russia* 55°52N 48°14E **86** C9
Kozlu *Turkey* 41°26N 31°45E **104** B4
Kozluk *Turkey* 38°11N 41°31E **105** C9
Koźmin *Poland* 51°48N 17°27E **83** G4
Koźmodemyansk *Russia* 56°20N 46°36E **86** B8
Kŏzu-Shima *Japan* 34°13N 139°10E **113** G9
Koźuchów *Poland* 51°45N 15°31E **83** G2
Kozyatyn *Ukraine* 49°45N 28°50E **75** D15
Kozyrevsk *Russia* 56°3N 159°51E **107** D16
Kpabia *Ghana* 9°10N 0°44E **139** D5
Kpalimé *Togo* 6°57N 0°44E **139** D5
Kpandae *Ghana* 8°30N 0°2W **139** D4
Kpessi *Togo* 8°4N 1°16E **139** D5
Kra, Isthmus of = Kra, Kho Khot
　Thailand 10°15N 99°30E **121** G2
Kra, Kho Khot *Thailand* 10°15N 99°30E **121** G2
Kra Buri *Thailand* 10°22N 98°46E **121** G2
Kraai → *S. Africa* 30°40S 26°45E **144** D4
Krabi *Thailand* 8°4N 98°55E **121** H2
Kracheh = Kratie
　Cambodia 12°32N 106°10E **120** F6
Kragan *Indonesia* 6°43S 111°38E **119** G14
Kragerø *Norway* 58°52N 9°25E **61** G13
Kragujevac *Serbia* 44°2N 20°56E **96** B4
Krajenka *Poland* 53°18N 16°59E **83** E3
Krakatau = Rakata, Pulau
　Indonesia 6°10S 105°20E **119** G11

Krakatoa = Rakata, Pulau
　Indonesia 6°10S 105°20E **119** G11
Krakor *Cambodia* 12°32N 104°12E **120** F5
Kraków *Poland* 50°4N 19°57E **83** H6
Kraków ✈ (KRK) *Poland* 50°7N 19°48E **83** H6
Kraksaan *Indonesia* 7°43S 113°23E **119** G16
Kralanh *Cambodia* 13°35N 103°25E **120** F4
Králíky *Czechia* 50°6N 16°45E **79** A9
Kraljevo *Serbia* 43°44N 20°41E **96** C4
Kraljuraja Sagar
　India 12°20N 76°30E **127** H3
Kralupy nad Vltavou
　Czechia 50°13N 14°20E **78** A7
Kramatorsk *Ukraine* 48°50N 37°30E **85** H9
Kramfors *Sweden* 62°55N 17°48E **62** B11
Kramis, C. *Algeria* 36°26N 0°45E **136** A4
Krania Elassonas *Greece* 39°53N 21°18E **96** G5
Kranidi *Greece* 37°20N 23°10E **98** D5
Kranj *Slovenia* 46°16N 14°22E **93** B11
Kranjska Gora *Slovenia* 46°29N 13°48E **93** B10
Krankskop *S. Africa* 28°0S 30°47E **145** C5
Krapina *Croatia* 46°10N 15°52E **93** B12
Krapina → *Croatia* 45°50N 15°50E **93** C12
Krapkowice *Poland* 50°29N 17°56E **83** H4
Kras *Slovenia* 45°35N 14°0E **93** C10
Krasió Res. *Thailand* 14°49N 99°30E **120** E2
Kraskino *Russia* 42°44N 130°48E **112** C5
Kräslava *Latvia* 55°54N 27°10E **84** H4
Kraslice *Czechia* 50°19N 12°31E **78** A5
Krasnaya Gorbatka
　Russia 55°52N 41°45E **86** C5
Krasnaya Polyana
　Russia 43°40N 40°13E **87** J5
Krasne *Ukraine* 46°7N 29°15E **81** D14
Krasni Okny *Ukraine* 47°32N 29°27E **81** C14
Kraśnik *Poland* 50°55N 22°15E **83** H9
Krasnoarmeisk *Ukraine* 48°18N 37°11E **85** H9
Krasnoarmeysk = Tayynsha
　Kazakhstan 53°50N 69°45E **109** B7
Krasnoarmeysk *Russia* 51°0N 45°42E **86** E7
Krasnoarmeyskiy *Russia* 47°0N 42°2E **87** G6
Krasnobrod *Poland* 50°33N 23°12E **83** H10
Krasnodar *Russia* 45°5N 39°0E **87** H4
Krasnodar □ *Russia* 45°30N 39°30E **87** G4
Krasnodon *Ukraine* 48°17N 39°44E **85** H10
Krasnogorskiy *Russia* 56°10N 48°28E **86** B9
Krasnograd = Krasnohrad
　Ukraine 49°27N 35°27E **85** H8
Krasnogvardeysk
　Ukraine 45°32N 34°16E **85** K8
Krasnogvardeyskoye
　Russia 45°52N 41°33E **87** H5
Krasnohrad *Ukraine* 49°27N 35°27E **85** H8
Krasnokamensk
　Russia 50°3N 118°0E **107** D12
Krasnokamsk *Russia* 50°10N 34°50E **85** G8
Krasnolesnyy *Russia* 51°53N 39°35E **85** G10
Krasnoperekopsk *Ukraine* 46°0N 33°54E **85** J7
Krasnorechenskiy
　Russia 44°41N 135°14E **112** B7
Krasnoselkup *Russia* 65°20N 82°10E **106** C9
Krasnoslobodsk *Mordvinia,*
　Russia 54°25N 43°45E **86** C6
Krasnoslobodsk *Volgograd,*
　Russia 48°42N 44°33E **87** F7
Krasnoturinsk *Russia* 59°46N 60°12E **106** D7
Krasnoyarsk *Russia* 56°8N 93°0E **107** D10
Krasnoyarskoye *Russia* 54°31N 21°56E **82** D8
Krasnoyarskoye Vdkhr.
　Russia 56°0N 92°30E **107** D10
Krasnoye = Krasnyy
　Russia 54°25N 31°30E **84** E6
Krasnoyilsk *Ukraine* 47°59N 25°38E **81** C10
Krasnozavodsk *Russia* 56°27N 38°25E **84** D10
Krasnoznamensk
　Russia 54°57N 22°30E **82** D9
Krasnystaw *Poland* 50°57N 23°5E **83** H10
Krasnyy *Russia* 54°25N 31°30E **84** E6
Krasnyy Kholm *Russia* 58°10N 37°10E **84** C9
Krasnyy Kut *Russia* 50°50N 47°0E **86** E8
Krasnyy Liman *Ukraine* 48°58N 37°50E **85** H9
Krasnyy Luch *Ukraine* 48°13N 39°0E **85** H10
Krasnyy Profintern
　Russia 57°45N 40°27E **84** D11
Krasnyy Sulin *Russia* 47°52N 40°8E **87** G5
Krasnyy Yar *Astrakhan,*
　Russia 46°43N 48°23E **87** G9
Krasnyy Yar *Samara,*
　Russia 53°30N 50°22E **86** D10
Krasnyy Yar *Volgograd,*
　Russia 50°42N 44°45E **87** F7
Krasnyye Baki *Russia* 57°8N 45°10E **86** B7
Krasnyyoskolske Vdskh.
　Ukraine 49°27N 37°40E **85** H9
Kraszna → *Hungary* 48°4N 22°20E **83** D10
Kratie *Cambodia* 12°32N 106°10E **120** F6
Kratovo *Macedonia* 42°6N 22°10E **96** D6
Krau *Indonesia* 3°19S 140°5E **119** E10
Kraulshavn = Nuussuaq
　Greenland 74°8N 57°3W **57** C5
Kravanh, Chuor Phnum
　Cambodia 12°0N 103°32E **121** G4
Krefeld *Germany* 51°20N 6°33E **76** D2
Kremaston, L. *Greece* 38°52N 21°30E **98** C3
Kremen *Croatia* 44°28N 15°53E **93** D12
Kremenchug = Kremenchuk
　Ukraine 49°5N 33°25E **85** H7
Kremenchuk *Ukraine* 49°5N 33°25E **85** H7
Kremenchuksk Vdskh.
　Ukraine 49°20N 32°30E **85** H7
Kremenets *Ukraine* 50°8N 25°43E **75** C13
Kremges = Svitlovodsk
　Ukraine 49°1N 38°10E **85** H7
Kremmen *Germany* 52°45N 13°1E **76** D7
Kremmling *U.S.A.* 40°4N 106°24W **168** F10
Kremnica *Slovakia* 48°45N 18°50E **79** C11
Krems an der Donau
　Austria 48°3N 15°36E **78** C8
Kremsmünster *Austria* 48°3N 14°8E **78** C7
Krestena *Greece* 37°37N 21°37E **98** D3
Kretinga *Lithuania* 55°53N 21°15E **82** C8
Krettamia *Algeria* 28°47N 3°27W **136** C5
Krettsy *Russia* 58°15N 32°30E **84** B7
Kreuzberg *Germany* 50°22N 9°58E **77** E5
Kreuztal *Germany* 50°57N 8°0E **76** E4
Kria Vrísi *Greece* 40°41N 22°18E **96** F6
Kribi *Cameroon* 2°57N 9°56E **139** G6
Krichem *Bulgaria* 42°8N 24°28E **97** D8

Krichev = Krychaw
　Belarus 53°40N 31°41E **75** B16
Kril'on, Mys *Russia* 45°53N 142°5E **112** B11
Krim *Slovenia* 45°53N 14°30E **93** C11
Krios, Ákra *Greece* 35°13N 23°34E **101** D5
Krishna → *India* 15°57N 80°59E **127** G5
Krishnagiri *India* 12°32N 78°16E **127** H4
Krishnanagar *India* 23°24N 88°33E **125** H13
Krishnaraja Sagar
　India 12°20N 76°30E **127** H3
Kristdala *Sweden* 57°24N 16°13E **63** G10
Kristiansand *Norway* 58°8N 8°1E **61** G13
Kristianstad *Sweden* 56°2N 14°9E **63** H8
Kristiansund *Norway* 63°7N 7°45E **60** E12
Kristiinankaupunki
　Finland 62°16N 21°21E **60** E19
Kristinehamn *Sweden* 59°18N 14°7E **62** E8
Kristinestad =
　Kristiinankaupunki
　Finland 62°16N 21°21E **60** E19
Kríti *Greece* 35°15N 25°0E **101** D7
Kritsa *Greece* 35°10N 25°41E **101** D7
Kriva → *Macedonia* 42°5N 21°47E **96** D5
Kriva Palanka
　Macedonia 42°11N 22°19E **96** D6
Krivaja → *Bos.-H.* 44°27N 18°9E **80** F3
Kriveli *Serbia* 44°10N 22°5E **96** B6
Křivoklátsko △ *Czechia* 50°1N 13°51E **78** A6
Krivoy Rog = Kryvyy Rih
　Ukraine 47°51N 33°20E **85** J7
Křiževci *Croatia* 46°3N 16°32E **93** B13
Krk *Croatia* 45°8N 14°40E **93** C11
Krk *Croatia* 45°8N 14°40E **93** C11
Krka → *Slovenia* 45°50N 15°30E **93** C12
Krka △ *Croatia* 43°53N 15°56E **93** E13
Krkonoše *Czechia* 50°50N 15°35E **78** A8
Krkonoše △ *Czechia* 50°43N 15°39E **78** A8
Krnov *Czechia* 50°5N 17°40E **79** A10
Krobia *Poland* 51°47N 16°59E **83** G3
Krokees *Greece* 36°53N 22°32E **98** E4
Krokek *Sweden* 58°40N 16°24E **63** F10
Krokodil = Umgwenya →
　Mozam. 25°14S 32°18E **145** C5
Krokom *Sweden* 63°20N 14°30E **62** A8
Krokowa *Poland* 54°47N 18°9E **82** D5
Kroleveis *Ukraine* 51°35N 33°20E **85** G7
Kroměříž *Czechia* 49°18N 17°21E **79** B10
Krompachy *Slovakia* 48°54N 20°52E **79** B13
Kromy *Russia* 52°48N 35°48E **85** F8
Kronach *Germany* 50°14N 11°19E **77** E7
Krong Kaoh Kong
　Cambodia 11°37N 102°59E **121** G4
Kronoberg □ *Sweden* 56°45N 14°30E **63** H8
Kronprins Christian Land
　Greenland 80°30N 22°0W **57** A8
Kronprins Frederik Land
　Greenland 81°0N 45°0W **57** A6
Kronprins Olav Kyst
　Antarctica 69°0S 42°0E **55** C5
Kronprinsesse Märtha Kyst
　Antarctica 73°30S 10°0W **55** D2
Kronshtadt *Russia* 59°57N 29°23E **84** B4
Kroonstad *S. Africa* 27°43S 27°19E **144** D4
Kröpelin *Germany* 54°4N 11°47E **76** A7
Kropotkin *Russia* 45°28N 40°28E **87** H5
Kropp *Germany* 54°24N 9°31E **76** A5
Krosna *Lithuania* 54°23N 23°33E **82** D10
Krośniewice *Poland* 52°15N 19°11E **83** F6
Krosno *Poland* 49°42N 21°46E **83** J8
Krosno Odrzańskie *Poland* 52°3N 15°7E **83** F2
Krotoszyn *Poland* 51°42N 17°23E **83** G4
Krotovka *Russia* 53°18N 51°10E **86** D10
Krousonas *Greece* 35°13N 24°59E **101** D6
Krrabë *Albania* 41°13N 20°0E **96** E4
Krško *Slovenia* 45°57N 15°30E **93** C12
Krstača *Serbia* 42°57N 20°8E **96** D4
Kruger △ *S. Africa* 24°50S 26°10E **145** B4
Krugersdorp *S. Africa* 26°5S 27°46E **145** C4
Kruisfontein *S. Africa* 33°59S 24°43E **144** D3
Krujë *Albania* 41°32N 19°46E **96** E3
Krulevshchina =
　Krulyewshchyna
　Belarus 55°5N 27°45E **84** E4
Krulyewshchyna *Belarus* 55°5N 27°45E **84** E4
Krumbach *Germany* 48°13N 10°22E **77** G6
Krumë *Albania* 42°14N 20°28E **96** D4
Krumovgrad *Bulgaria* 41°29N 25°38E **97** E9
Krung Thep = Bangkok
　Thailand 13°45N 100°35E **120** F3
Krupanj *Serbia* 44°25N 19°22E **96** B3
Krupina *Slovakia* 48°22N 19°5E **79** C12
Krupinica → *Slovakia* 48°4N 18°55E **79** C11
Krupki *Belarus* 54°19N 29°8E **75** A15
Kruševac *Serbia* 43°35N 21°28E **96** C5
Kruševo *Macedonia* 41°23N 21°19E **96** E4
Krushë e Madhe *Kosovo* 42°19N 20°39E **96** D4
Krushelnyksya *Ukraine* 49°7N 23°29E **83** J10
Kruszwica *Poland* 52°40N 18°20E **83** F5
Kruzenshterna, Proliv
　Russia 48°30N 154°0E **107** E16
Krychaw *Belarus* 53°40N 31°41E **75** B16
Krymsk *Russia* 44°50N 38°0E **85** K10
Krymskiy Poluostrov =
　Krymskyy Pivostriv
　Ukraine 45°0N 34°0E **85** K8
Krymskyy Pivostriv
　Ukraine 45°0N 34°0E **85** K8
Krynica *Poland* 49°25N 20°57E **83** J7
Krynica Morska *Poland* 54°23N 19°28E **82** D6
Krynki *Poland* 53°17N 23°43E **83** E10
Kryvyy Rih *Ukraine* 47°51N 33°20E **85** J7
Kryzhopil *Ukraine* 48°23N 28°35E **81** B13
Krzepice *Poland* 50°58N 18°50E **83** H5
Krzeszów *Poland* 50°24N 22°21E **83** H9
Krzywiń *Poland* 51°58N 16°50E **83** G3
Krzyż Wielkopolski
　Poland 52°52N 16°0E **83** F2
Ksabi *Morocco* 32°51N 4°13W **136** B5
Ksar Chellala *Algeria* 35°13N 2°19E **136** A6
Ksar el Boukhari *Algeria* 35°51N 2°52E **136** A4
Ksar el Kebir *Morocco* 35°0N 6°0W **136** B4
Ksar es Souk = Er Rachidia
　Morocco 31°58N 4°20W **136** B5
Ksar es Srhir *Morocco* 35°51N 5°34W **89** E3
Ksar Rhilane *Tunisia* 33°0N 9°39E **136** B8
Ksiąz Wielkopolski
　Poland 52°4N 17°14E **83** F4
Ksour, Mts. des *Algeria* 32°45N 0°30W **136** B4
Kstovo *Russia* 56°12N 44°13E **86** B7
Ku-Ring-Gai Chase △
　Australia 33°39S 151°14E **153** B9

Kuah *Malaysia* 6°19N 99°51E **121** J2
Kuala Belait *Malaysia* 4°35N 114°11E **118** D4
Kuala Berang *Malaysia* 5°5N 103°1E **121** K4
Kuala Dungun = Dungun
　Malaysia 4°45N 103°25E **121** K4
Kuala Kangsar
　Malaysia 4°46N 100°56E **121** K3
Kuala Kelawang
　Malaysia 2°56N 102°5E **121** L4
Kuala Kerai *Malaysia* 5°30N 102°12E **121** K4
Kuala Kubu Bharu
　Malaysia 3°34N 101°39E **121** L3
Kuala Lipis *Malaysia* 4°10N 102°3E **121** K4
Kuala Lumpur *Malaysia* 3°9N 101°41E **121** L3
Kuala Lumpur Int. ✈ (KUL)
　Malaysia 2°44N 101°42E **121** L3
Kuala Nerang *Malaysia* 6°16N 100°37E **121** J3
Kuala Pilah *Malaysia* 2°45N 102°15E **121** L4
Kuala Rompin
　Malaysia 2°49N 103°29E **121** L4
Kuala Selangor
　Malaysia 3°20N 101°15E **121** L3
Kuala Sepetang
　Malaysia 4°49N 100°28E **121** K3
Kuala Terengganu
　Malaysia 5°20N 103°8E **121** K4
Kualajelai *Indonesia* 2°58S 110°46E **118** E4
Kualakapuas *Indonesia* 2°55S 114°20E **118** E4
Kualakurun *Indonesia* 1°10S 113°50E **118** E4
Kualapembuang
　Indonesia 3°14S 112°38E **118** E4
Kualasimpang *Indonesia* 4°17N 98°3E **118** D1
Kuancheng *China* 40°37N 118°30E **115** D10
Kuandang *Indonesia* 0°56N 123°1E **119** D6
Kuandian *China* 40°45N 124°45E **115** D13
Kuando Kubango □
　Angola 16°25S 20°0E **144** A3
Kuangchou = Guangzhou
　China 23°6N 113°13E **117** F9
Kuanshan *Taiwan* 23°3N 121°9E **117** F13
Kuantan *Malaysia* 3°49N 103°20E **121** L4
Kuba = Quba *Azerbaijan* 41°21N 48°32E **87** K9
Kuban → *Russia* 45°20N 37°30E **85** K9
Kuban Depression =
　Prikubanskaya Nizmennost
　Russia 45°40N 38°33E **87** H4
Kubaysah *Iraq* 33°35N 42°37E **105** G10
Kubenskoye, Ozero
　Russia 59°40N 39°25E **84** C10
Kubokawa = Shimanto
　Japan 33°12N 133°8E **113** H6
Kubrat *Bulgaria* 43°49N 26°31E **97** C10
Kubu *Indonesia* 8°16S 115°35E **119** J18
Kubutambahan
　Indonesia 8°5S 115°10E **119** J18
Kucar, Tanjung
　Indonesia 8°39S 114°34E **119** K18
Kučevo *Serbia* 44°30N 21°40E **96** B5
Kuchaman *India* 27°13N 74°47E **124** F6
Kuchenspitze *Austria* 47°7N 10°12E **78** D3
Kuchinda *India* 21°44N 84°21E **125** J11
Kuching *Malaysia* 1°33N 110°25E **118** D4
Kuchino-eruba-Jima
　Japan 30°28N 130°12E **113** J5
Kuchino-Shima *Japan* 29°57N 129°55E **113** K4
Kuchinotsu *Japan* 32°36N 130°11E **113** H5
Kuchl *Austria* 47°37N 13°9E **78** D6
Kuchurhan → *Ukraine* 46°33N 29°57E **81** D14
Kucing = Kuching
　Malaysia 1°33N 110°25E **118** D4
Kuçovë *Albania* 40°47N 19°57E **96** F3
Kücükbahçe *Turkey* 38°33N 26°24E **99** C8
Kücükköy *Turkey* 39°16N 26°42E **99** B8
Kücükkuyu *Turkey* 39°33N 26°36E **99** B8
Kücükmenderes →
　Turkey 37°57N 27°16E **99** D9
Kud → *Pakistan* 26°5N 66°20E **124** F2
Kuda *India* 23°10N 71°15E **124** H4
Kudal *India* 16°2N 73°41E **127** F1
Kudalier → *India* 18°35N 79°48E **126** E4
Kudat *Malaysia* 6°55N 116°55E **118** C5
Kudirkos Naumiestis
　Lithuania 54°46N 22°53E **82** D9
Kudowa-Zdrój *Poland* 50°27N 16°15E **83** H3
Kudremukh *India* 13°15N 75°20E **127** H2
Kudus *Indonesia* 6°48S 110°51E **119** G14
Kudymkar *Russia* 59°1N 54°39E **106** D6
Kueiyang = Guiyang
　China 26°32N 106°40E **116** E6
Kufra Oasis = Al Kufrah
　Libya 24°17N 23°15E **135** D10
Kufstein *Austria* 47°35N 12°11E **78** D5
Kugaaruk = Pelly Bay
　Canada 68°38N 89°50W **161** D14
Kugluktuk *Canada* 67°50N 115°5W **160** D8
Kugong I. *Canada* 56°18N 79°50W **164** A4
Kŭh Dasht *Iran* 33°32N 47°36E **105** F12
Kŭh-e Sorkh *Iran* 35°30N 58°45E **108** E5
Kŭhak *Iran* 27°12N 63°10E **129** E9
Kŭhbonān *Iran* 31°23N 56°19E **129** D8
Kŭhestak *Iran* 26°47N 57°2E **129** E8
Kŭhīn *Iran* 36°22N 49°40E **108** E6
Kŭhīrī *Iran* 26°55N 61°2E **129** E9
Kūhiston-Badakhshon □
　Tajikistan 38°30N 73°0E **109** E8
Kuhmo *Finland* 64°7N 29°31E **60** D23
Kuhn Chae △ *Thailand* 19°8N 99°24E **120** C2
Kuhnsdorf *Austria* 36°47N 14°38E **78** E7
Kŭhpayeh *Esfahan, Iran* 32°44N 52°20E **129** C7
Kŭhpayeh, Kerman, Iran* 30°35N 57°15E **129** D8
Kŭhrān, Kŭh-e *Iran* 26°46N 58°12E **129** E8
Kui Buri *Thailand* 12°3N 99°52E **120** F2
Kuiburi △ *Thailand* 12°9N 99°37E **121** F2
Kuichong *China* 22°38N 114°25E **111** a
Kuiseb → *Namibia* 22°59S 14°31E **144** B1
Kuito *Angola* 12°22S 16°55E **141** G3
Kuiu I. *U.S.A.* 57°45N 134°10W **162** B2
Kujalleq = Greenland *Greenland* 61°0N 44°0W **57** E6
Kujang *N. Korea* 39°57N 126°1E **115** E14
Kujawsko-Pomorskie □
　Poland 53°0N 18°30E **82** E5
Kuji *Japan* 40°11N 141°46E **112** D10
Kuji-San *Japan* 33°5N 131°15E **113** H5
Kukava *Ukraine* 48°37N 27°45E **81** B12
Kukawa *Nigeria* 12°58N 13°27E **135** F8
Kukavica *Serbia* 42°48N 21°57E **96** D5
Kukės *Albania* 42°5N 20°27E **96** D4
Kukmor *Russia* 56°11N 50°54E **86** B10
Kukup *Malaysia* 1°20N 103°27E **121** d
Kukup, Pulau *Malaysia* 1°18N 103°25E **121** d

Kukvidze *Russia* 50°40N 43°0E **86** E6
Kula *Bulgaria* 43°52N 22°36E **96** C6
Kula *Serbia* 45°37N 19°32E **80** E4
Kula *Turkey* 38°32N 28°40E **99** C10
K'ula Shan *Bhutan* 28°14N 90°36E **110** F7
Kulachi *Pakistan* 31°56N 70°27E **124** D4
Kulai *Malaysia* 1°44N 103°35E **121** M4
Kulaly Aral *Kazakhstan* 45°0N 50°5E **87** H10
Kulasekarappattinam
　India 8°20N 78°5E **127** K4
Kulautuva *Lithuania* 54°56N 23°36E **82** D10
Kuldiga *Latvia* 56°58N 21°59E **82** B8
Kulebaki *Russia* 55°22N 42°25E **86** C6
Kulen *Cambodia* 13°50N 104°40E **120** F5
Kulen Vakuf *Bos.-H.* 44°35N 16°2E **93** D13
Kulgam *India* 33°36N 75°2E **126** B6
Kulgera *Australia* 25°50S 133°18E **150** D1
Kulim *Malaysia* 5°22N 100°34E **121** K3
Kulin *Australia* 32°40S 118°2E **149** F2
Kulittalai *India* 10°55N 78°25E **127** J4
Kulkayu = Hartley Bay
　Canada 53°25N 129°15W **162** C3
Kullen *Sweden* 56°18N 12°26E **63** H6
Kullu *India* 31°58N 77°6E **124** D7
Kulmbach *Germany* 50°6N 11°26E **77** E7
Külob *Tajikistan* 37°55N 69°50E **109** E7
Kulp *Turkey* 38°29N 41°2E **105** C9
Kulpawn → *Ghana* 10°20N 1°59W **139** D4
Kulsary = Qulsary
　Kazakhstan 46°59N 54°1E **108** C4
Kulti *India* 23°43N 86°50E **125** H12
Kulu *India* 39°5N 33°4E **104** C5
Kulunda *Russia* 52°35N 78°57E **109** B9
Kulundinskoye, Ozero
　Russia 53°0N 79°36E **109** B9
Kulungar *Afghan.* 34°0N 69°2E **124** C3
Kŭlvand *Iran* 31°21N 54°35E **129** D7
Kulwin *Australia* 35°2S 142°42E **152** C5
Kulyab = Külob
　Tajikistan 37°55N 69°50E **109** E7
Kuma → *Russia* 44°55N 47°0E **87** H8
Kumafşari *Turkey* 37°19N 29°32E **99** D11
Kumagami *Nigeria* 13°8N 10°38E **139** C7
Kumagaya *Japan* 36°9N 139°22E **113** F9
Kumai *Indonesia* 2°44S 111°43E **118** E4
Kumaly *Japan* 40°11N 141°46E **112** D10
Kumamba, Kepulauan
　Indonesia 1°36S 138°45E **119** E10
Kumamoto *Japan* 32°45N 130°45E **113** H5
Kumamoto □ *Japan* 32°55N 130°55E **113** H5
Kumanovo *Macedonia* 42°9N 21°42E **96** D5
Kumar → *Afghan.* 34°30N 70°28E **109** F8
Kumara *N.Z.* 42°37S 171°12E **155** C6
Kumarina Roadhouse
　Australia 24°41S 119°32E **149** D2
Kumasi *Ghana* 6°41N 1°38W **138** D4
Kumba *Cameroon* 4°36N 9°24E **139** H6
Kumbağ *Turkey* 40°51N 27°27E **97** F11
Kumbakonam *India* 10°58N 79°25E **127** J4
Kumbarilla *Australia* 27°15S 150°55E **151** D5
Kumbatine △
　Australia 31°8S 152°35E **153** A10
Kumbhalgarh △ *India* 25°10N 73°35E **124** G5
Kumbhraj *India* 24°22N 77°3E **124** G7
Kumbia *Australia* 26°41S 151°39E **151** D5
Kumbo *Cameroon* 6°15N 10°36E **139** D7
Kumbukkan Oya →
　Sri Lanka 6°35N 81°40E **127** L5
Kŭmch'on *N. Korea* 38°10N 126°29E **115** E14
Kume-Shima *Japan* 26°20N 126°47E **113** L3
Kumeny *Russia* 58°10N 49°47E **86** A9
Kumertau *Russia* 52°45N 55°57E **108** B5
Kumharsain *India* 31°19N 77°27E **124** D7
Kumi *Uganda* 1°30N 33°58E **142** B3
Kumkale *Turkey* 39°59N 26°11E **97** G10
Kumla *Sweden* 59°8N 15°10E **62** E9
Kumluca *Turkey* 36°22N 30°20E **99** E12
Kummerower See
　Germany 53°49N 12°51E **76** B8
Kumo *Nigeria* 10°1N 11°12E **139** C7
Kumo älv = Kokemäenjoki →
　Finland 61°32N 21°44E **84** B1
Kumon Bum
　Myanmar 26°30N 97°15E **123** F20
Kumta *India* 14°29N 74°25E **127** G2
Kumtag Shamo *China* 39°40N 92°0E **110** E7
Kumul = Hami *China* 42°55N 93°25E **110** C7
Kumyal = Koma Tou Yialou
　Cyprus 35°25N 34°8E **101** D13
Kumylzhenskaya *Russia* 49°51N 42°38E **86** E6
Kuna *U.S.A.* 43°30N 116°25W **168** E5
Kunágota *Hungary* 46°26N 21°3E **80** D6
Kunashir, Ostrov
　Russia 44°0N 146°0E **107** E15
Kunchha *Nepal* 28°8N 84°22E **125** E11
Kunda *Estonia* 59°30N 26°34E **84** C4
Kunda *India* 25°43N 81°31E **125** G9
Kundar → *Pakistan* 31°56N 69°19E **124** D3
Kundelungu △
　Dem. Rep. of the Congo 9°30S 27°40E **143** E2
Kundelungu Ouest △
　Dem. Rep. of the Congo 9°55S 27°17E **143** D2
Kundian *Pakistan* 32°27N 71°28E **124** C4
Kundla *India* 21°21N 71°25E **124** J4
Kunene □ *Namibia* 20°0S 14°0E **144** A1
Kung, Ao *Thailand* 8°5N 98°24E **121** a
Kunga → *Bangla.* 21°46N 89°30E **125** J13
Kungala *Australia* 29°58S 153°7E **151** D5
Kunghit I. *Canada* 52°6N 131°3W **162** C2
Kungrad = Qŭnghirot
　Uzbekistan 43°2N 58°50E **108** D5
Kungsängen *Sweden* 59°29N 17°45E **62** E11
Kungsbacka *Sweden* 57°30N 12°5E **63** H6
Kungshamn *Sweden* 58°22N 11°19E **63** F5
Kungsör *Sweden* 59°25N 16°5E **62** E10
Kungur *Russia* 57°25N 56°57E **86** B11
Kunhar → *Pakistan* 34°20N 73°30E **125** B5
Kunhegyes *Hungary* 47°22N 20°36E **80** C6
Kuningan *Indonesia* 6°59S 108°29E **119** G13
Kunlara *Australia* 34°54S 139°55E **152** C2
Kunlong *Myanmar* 23°20N 98°50E **125** H21
Kunlun Shan *Asia* 36°0N 86°30E **110** E6
Kunlun Shankou *China* 35°48N 94°0E **110** E7
Kunming *China* 25°1N 102°41E **116** E5
Kunming Changshui Int. ✈
　(KMG) *China* 25°6N 102°45E **116** E4
Kunmunya ◯
　Australia 15°26S 124°42E **148** C3

Kunnamkulam *India* 10°38N 76°7E **127** J3
Kunów *Poland* 50°57N 21°17E **83** H8
Kunshan *China* 31°22N 120°58E **117** B13
Kunszentmárton
　Hungary 46°50N 20°20E **80** D5
Kunszentmiklós *Hungary* 47°2N 19°8E **80** C4
Kuntaur *Senegal* 13°40N 14°48W **138** C2
Kununurra *Australia* 15°40S 128°50E **148** C4
Kunwari → *India* 26°26N 79°11E **125** F8
Kunya-Urgench = Köneürgench
　Turkmenistan 42°19N 59°10E **108** D5
Künzelsau *Germany* 49°17N 9°42E **77** F5
Kuopio *Finland* 62°53N 27°35E **60** E22
Kupa → *Croatia* 45°28N 16°24E **93** C13
Kupang *Indonesia* 10°19S 123°39E **119** F6
Kupreanof I. *U.S.A.* 56°50N 133°30W **162** B2
Kupres *Bos.-H.* 44°1N 17°15E **93** C7
Kupyansk *Ukraine* 49°52N 37°35E **85** H9
Kupyansk-Uzlovoi
　Ukraine 49°40N 37°43E **85** H9
Kuqa *China* 41°35N 82°30E **109** D10
Kür → *Azerbaijan* 39°29N 49°15E **105** C13
Kür Dili *Azerbaijan* 39°3N 49°13E **105** C13
Kura = Kür →
　Azerbaijan 39°29N 49°15E **105** C13
Kuranda *Australia* 16°48S 145°35E **150** B4
Kuranga *India* 22°4N 69°10E **124** H3
Kurashiki *Japan* 34°40N 133°50E **113** G6
Kurayn *Si. Arabia* 27°39N 49°50E **129** E6
Kurayoshi *Japan* 35°26N 133°50E **113** G6
Kürchatov *Kazakhstan* 50°45N 78°32E **109** B9
Kurchatov *Russia* 51°40N 35°39E **85** G8
Kürdämir *Azerbaijan* 40°25N 48°3E **87** K9
Kurdistan *Asia* 37°20N 43°30E **105** D10
Kurduvadi *India* 18°8N 75°29E **126** E2
Kure *Japan* 34°14N 132°32E **113** G6
Küre *Turkey* 41°36N 33°32E **104** B5
Küre Dağları *Turkey* 41°50N 34°10E **104** B6
Kure I. *U.S.A.* 28°25N 178°25W **167** K4
Kuressaare *Estonia* 58°15N 22°30E **84** C2
Kurgan *Russia* 55°26N 65°18E **108** A7
Kurgan-Tyube = Qŭrghonteppa
　Tajikistan 37°50N 68°47E **109** E7
Kurganinsk *Russia* 44°54N 40°34E **87** H5
Kurgannaya = Kurganinsk
　Russia 44°54N 40°34E **87** H5
Kuri *India* 26°37N 70°43E **124** F4
Kuria Maria Is. = Ḩallāniyat,
　Jazā'ir al *Oman* 17°30N 55°58E **131** D6
Kurichchi *India* 11°36N 77°35E **127** J3
Kuridala *Australia* 21°16S 140°29E **150** C3
Kurigram *Bangla.* 25°49N 89°39E **123** G16
Kurikka *Finland* 62°36N 22°24E **60** E20
Kuril Basin *Pac. Oc.* 47°0N 150°0E **54** E15
Kuril Is. = Kurilskiye Ostrova
　Russia 45°0N 150°0E **107** E16
Kuril-Kamchatka Trench
　Pac. Oc. 44°0N 153°0E **156** C7
Kurilsk *Russia* 45°14N 147°53E **107** E15
Kurilskiye Ostrova
　Russia 45°0N 150°0E **107** E16
Kurino *Japan* 31°57N 130°43E **113** J5
Kurinskaya Kosa = Kür Dili
　Azerbaijan 39°3N 49°13E **105** C13
Kurkheda *India* 20°37N 80°12E **126** D5
Kurkur *Egypt* 23°50N 32°0E **137** C3
Kurkuta △ *Australia* 24°0S 127°5E **148** D4
Kurlovskiy *Russia* 55°25N 40°40E **86** C5
Kurnool *India* 15°45N 78°0E **127** G4
Kuro-Shima *Kagoshima,*
　Japan 30°50N 129°57E **113** J4
Kuro-Shima *Okinawa,*
　Japan 24°14N 124°1E **113** M2
Kuror, J. *Sudan* 20°27N 31°30E **137** C3
Kurow *N.Z.* 44°44S 170°29E **155** E5
Kurów *Poland* 51°23N 22°12E **83** G9
Kurrajong *Australia* 33°33S 150°42E **153** B9
Kurram → *Pakistan* 32°36N 71°20E **124** C4
Kurri Kurri *Australia* 32°50S 151°28E **153** B9
Kurrimine *Australia* 17°47S 146°6E **150** B4
Kursavka *Russia* 44°29N 42°32E **87** H6
Kurse Korhi *India* 20°14N 80°46E **126** D5
Kurseong = Karsiyang
　India 26°56N 88°18E **125** F13
Kurshim *Kazakhstan* 48°34N 83°39E **109** C10
Kurshskaya Kosa △
　Russia 55°7N 20°45E **82** C7
Kurshskiy Zaliv *Russia* 55°9N 21°6E **82** C8
Kursk *Russia* 51°42N 36°11E **85** G9
Kursk □ *Russia* 51°50N 36°10E **85** G9
Kuršumlija *Serbia* 43°9N 21°11E **96** C5
Kuršumlijska Banja
　Serbia 43°3N 21°11E **96** C5
Kuršunlu *Bursa, Turkey* 40°30N 29°0E **97** F13
Kurşunlu *Çankırı,*
　Turkey 40°51N 33°15E **104** B5
Kurtalan *Turkey* 37°56N 41°44E **105** D9
Kurtbey *Turkey* 41°26N 26°36E **97** F10
Kurucaşile *Turkey* 41°49N 32°42E **104** B5
Kuruktag *China* 41°0N 89°0E **110** D9
Kuruman *S. Africa* 27°28S 23°28E **144** C3
Kuruman → *S. Africa* 26°56S 20°39E **144** C3
Kurume *Japan* 33°15N 130°30E **113** H5
Kurunegala *Sri Lanka* 7°30N 80°23E **127** L5
Kurya *Russia* 61°42N 57°9E **106** C6
Kus Gölü *Turkey* 40°10N 27°55E **97** F11
Kuşadası *Turkey* 37°52N 27°15E **99** D9
Kuşadası Körfezi *Turkey* 37°56N 27°0E **99** D8
Kusamba *Indonesia* 8°34S 115°27E **119** K18
Kusatsu *Japan* 35°3N 135°57E **113** G7
Kusawa L. *Canada* 60°20N 136°13W **162** A1
Kusel *Germany* 49°32N 7°24E **77** F3
Kushaka *Nigeria* 10°33N 8°55E **139** C7
Kushalgarh *India* 23°10N 74°27E **124** H6
Kushalnagar *India* 12°31N 75°57E **127** J2
Kushchevskaya *Russia* 46°33N 39°35E **87** G4
Kusheriki *Nigeria* 10°32N 6°35E **139** C6
Kushikino *Japan* 31°44N 130°16E **113** J5
Kushima *Japan* 31°29N 131°14E **113** J5
Kushimoto *Japan* 33°28N 135°47E **113** H7
Kushiro *Japan* 43°0N 144°25E **112** C12
Kushiro-Gawa →
　Japan 42°59N 144°23E **112** C12
Kushiro Shitsugen △
　Japan 43°9N 144°26E **112** C12

Kūshk *Iran* 28°46N 56°51E **129** D8
Kushka = Serhetabat *Turkmenistan* 35°20N 62°18E **129** C9
Kushmurun = Qusmuryn *Kazakhstan* 52°27N 64°36E **108** B6
Kushnytsya *Ukraine* 48°27N 23°15E **81** B8
Kushol *India* 33°40N 76°36E **125** C7
Kushtia *Bangla.* 23°55N 89°5E **123** H16
Kuskokwim → *U.S.A.* 60°5N 162°25W **166** C7
Kuskokwim B. *U.S.A.* 59°45N 162°25W **166** D7
Kuskokwim Mts. *U.S.A.* 62°30N 156°0W **166** C8
Kusmi *India* 23°17N 83°55E **125** H10
Kusŏng *N. Korea* 39°59N 125°15E **115** E13
Kussharo-Ko *Japan* 43°38N 144°21E **112** C12
Kustanay = Qostanay *Kazakhstan* 53°10N 63°35E **108** B6
Kut, Ko *Thailand* 11°40N 102°35E **121** G4
Kuta *Indonesia* 8°43S 115°11E **119** K18
Kütahya *Turkey* 39°30N 30°2E **99** B12
Kütahya □ *Turkey* 39°10N 29°30E **99** B11
Kutaisi *Georgia* 42°19N 42°40E **87** J6
Kutaraja = Banda Aceh *Indonesia* 5°35N 95°20E **118** C1
Kutch, Gulf of = Kachchh, Gulf of *India* 22°50N 69°15E **124** H3
Kutch, Rann of = Kachchh, Rann of *India* 24°0N 70°0E **124** H4
Kutina *Croatia* 45°29N 16°48E **93** C13
Kutiyana *India* 21°36N 70°2E **124** J4
Kutjevo *Croatia* 45°23N 17°55E **80** E2
Kutkashen = Qäbälä *Azerbaijan* 40°58N 47°47E **87** K8
Kutná Hora *Czechia* 49°57N 15°16E **78** B8
Kutno *Poland* 52°15N 19°23E **83** F6
Kutru *India* 19°5N 80°46E **126** E5
Kutse *Botswana* 21°7S 22°16E **144** B3
Kuttabul *Australia* 21°1S 148°54E **150** b
Kutu *Dem. Rep. of the Congo* 2°40S 18°11E **140** E3
Kutum *Sudan* 14°10N 24°40E **135** F10
Kúty *Slovakia* 48°40N 17°3E **79** C10
Kuty *Ukraine* 48°16N 25°11E **81** B10
Kuujjuaq *Canada* 58°6N 68°15W **161** F18
Kuujjuarapik *Canada* 55°20N 77°35W **164** A4
Kuusamo *Finland* 65°57N 29°8E **60** D23
Kuusankoski *Finland* 60°55N 26°38E **84** B4
Kuvshinovo *Russia* 57°2N 34°11E **84** D8
Kuwait = Al Kuwayt *Kuwait* 29°30N 48°0E **128** D5
Kuwait ■ *Asia* 29°30N 47°30E **128** D5
Kuwana *Japan* 35°5N 136°43E **113** G8
Kuwana → *India* 26°25N 83°15E **125** F10
Kuybyshev = Samara *Russia* 53°8N 50°6E **86** D10
Kuybyshev *Russia* 55°27N 78°19E **106** D8
Kuybyshevo *Ukraine* 47°25N 36°40E **85** J9
Kuybyshevskoye Vdkhr. *Russia* 55°2N 49°30E **86** C9
Kuye He → *China* 38°23N 110°46E **114** E6
Kūyeh *Iran* 38°45N 47°57E **128** B5
Kuyto, Ozero *Russia* 65°6N 31°20E **60** D24
Kuytun *China* 44°25N 85°0E **109** D11
Kuyucak *Turkey* 37°55N 28°28E **99** D10
Kuyumba *Russia* 60°58N 96°59E **107** C10
Kuzey Anadolu Dağları *Turkey* 41°0N 36°45E **104** B7
Kuzhithurai *India* 8°18N 77°11E **127** K3
Kuzmin *Serbia* 45°2N 19°25E **80** E4
Kuznetsk *Russia* 53°12N 46°40E **86** D8
Kuzomen *Russia* 66°22N 36°50E **106** C4
Kvænangen *Norway* 70°5N 21°15E **60** A19
Kværndrup *Denmark* 55°10N 10°31E **63** J4
Kvaløya *Norway* 69°40N 18°30E **60** B18
Kvänum *Sweden* 58°18N 13°11E **63** F7
Kvareli = Qvareli *Georgia* 41°57N 45°47E **87** K7
Kvarner *Croatia* 44°50N 14°10E **93** D11
Kvarnerič *Croatia* 44°43N 14°37E **93** D11
Kvicksund *Sweden* 59°27N 16°19E **62** E10
Kvillsfors *Sweden* 57°24N 15°29E **63** G9
Kvismare kanal *Sweden* 59°11N 15°35E **62** E9
Kvissleby *Sweden* 62°18N 17°22E **62** B11
Kvitøya *Svalbard* 80°8N 32°35E **57** A14
Kwabhaca *S. Africa* 30°51S 29°0E **145** D4
Kwae Noi = Khwae Noi → *Thailand* 14°1N 99°32E **120** E2
Kwajalein *Marshall Is.* 9°5N 167°20E **156** G8
Kwakhanai *Botswana* 21°39S 21°16E **144** B3
Kwakoegron *Suriname* 5°12N 55°25W **187** B7
Kwale *Kenya* 4°15S 39°31E **142** C4
Kwale *Nigeria* 5°46N 6°26E **139** D6
KwaMashu *S. Africa* 29°45S 30°58E **145** C5
Kwando → *Africa* 18°27S 23°32E **144** A3
Kwangchow = Guangzhou *China* 23°6N 113°13E **117** F9
Kwangdaeri *N. Korea* 40°34N 127°33E **115** D14
Kwango → *Dem. Rep. of the Congo* 3°14S 17°22E **140** E3
Kwangsi-Chuang = Guangxi Zhuangzu Zizhiqu □ *China* 24°0N 109°0E **116** F7
Kwangtung = Guangdong □ *China* 23°0N 113°0E **117** F9
Kwara □ *Nigeria* 8°45N 4°30E **139** D6
Kwataboahegan → *Canada* 51°9N 80°50W **164** B3
Kwatisore *Indonesia* 3°18S 134°50E **119** E8
KwaZulu Natal □ *S. Africa* 29°0S 30°0E **145** C5
Kweichow = Guizhou □ *China* 27°0N 107°0E **116** D6
Kwekwe *Zimbabwe* 18°58S 29°48E **143** F2
Kweneng □ *Botswana* 24°0S 25°0E **144** B3
Kwidzyn *Poland* 53°44N 18°55E **82** E5
Kwilu → *Dem. Rep. of the Congo* 3°22S 17°22E **140** E3
Kwinana *Australia* 32°15S 115°47E **149** F2
Kwisa → *Poland* 51°34N 15°24E **83** G2
Kwoka *Indonesia* 0°31S 132°27E **119** E8
Kwolla *Nigeria* 9°0N 9°15E **139** D6
Kwun Tong *China* 22°19N 114°13E **111** a
Kyabra Cr. → *Australia* 25°36S 142°55E **151** D3
Kyabram *Australia* 36°19S 145°4E **153** D6
Kyaikto *Myanmar* 17°20N 97°3E **120** D1
Kyaing Tong = Keng Tung *Myanmar* 21°18N 99°39E **120** B2
Kyakhta *Russia* 50°30N 106°25E **107** D11
Kyambura △ *Uganda* 0°7S 30°9E **142** C3
Kyancutta *Australia* 33°8S 135°33E **151** E2
Kyaukpadaung *Myanmar* 20°52N 95°8E **123** J19
Kyaukpyu *Myanmar* 19°28N 93°30E **123** K18
Kyaukse *Myanmar* 21°36N 96°10E **123** J20
Kybartai *Lithuania* 54°39N 22°45E **82** D9
Kyburz *U.S.A.* 38°47N 120°18W **170** G6
Kyelang *India* 32°35N 77°2E **124** C7
Kyenjojo *Uganda* 0°40N 30°37E **142** B3
Kyjov *Czechia* 49°1N 17°7E **79** B10
Kyklades *Greece* 37°0N 24°30E **98** E6
Kyle *Canada* 50°50N 108°2W **163** C7
Kyle *U.S.A.* 29°59N 97°53W **176** F6
Kyle Dam = Mutirikwe Dam *Zimbabwe* 20°15S 31°0E **143** G3
Kyle of Lochalsh *U.K.* 57°17N 5°44W **65** D3
Kyll → *Germany* 49°48N 6°41E **77** F2
Kyllburg *Germany* 50°2N 6°34E **77** E2
Kyllini *Greece* 37°55N 21°8E **98** D3
Kymijoki → *Finland* 60°30N 26°55E **84** B4
Kymmene älv = Kymijoki → *Finland* 60°30N 26°55E **84** B4
Kyneton *Australia* 37°10S 144°29E **152** D6
Kynuna *Australia* 21°37S 141°55E **150** C3
Kyō-ga-Saki *Japan* 35°45N 135°15E **113** G7
Kyoga, L. *Uganda* 1°35N 33°0E **142** B3
Kyogle *Australia* 28°40S 153°0E **151** D5
Kyŏngju = Gyeongju *S. Korea* 35°51N 129°14E **115** G15
Kyŏngsŏng *N. Korea* 41°35N 129°36E **115** D15
Kyonpyaw *Myanmar* 17°12N 95°10E **123** L19
Kyōto *Japan* 35°0N 135°45E **113** G7
Kyōto □ *Japan* 35°15N 135°45E **113** G7
Kyparissovouno *Cyprus* 35°19N 33°10E **101** D12
Kyperounda *Cyprus* 34°56N 32°58E **101** E11
Kypros = Cyprus ■ *Asia* 35°0N 33°0E **101** E12
Kyrenia *Cyprus* 35°20N 33°20E **101** D12
Kyrgyzstan ■ *Asia* 42°0N 75°0E **109** D9
Kyritz *Germany* 52°56N 12°24E **76** C8
Kyrkhult *Sweden* 56°22N 14°34E **63** H8
Kyrnasivka *Ukraine* 48°35N 28°58E **81** B13
Kyrnychky *Ukraine* 45°42N 29°4E **81** E14
Kyro älv = Kyrönjoki → *Finland* 63°14N 21°45E **60** E19
Kyrönjoki → *Finland* 63°14N 21°45E **60** E19
Kystatyam *Russia* 67°20N 123°10E **107** C13
Kysucké Nové Mesto *Slovakia* 49°18N 18°47E **79** B11
Kytay, Ozero *Ukraine* 45°40N 29°13E **81** E14
Kythira *Greece* 36°8N 23°0E **98** E5
Kythnos *Greece* 37°26N 24°27E **98** D6
Kythréa *Cyprus* 35°15N 33°29E **101** D12
Kyunhla *Myanmar* 23°25N 95°15E **123** H19
Kyuquot Sound *Canada* 50°2N 127°22W **162** D3
Kyurdamir = Kürdämir *Azerbaijan* 40°25N 48°3E **87** K9
Kyūshū *Japan* 33°0N 131°0E **113** H5
Kyūshū □ *Japan* 33°0N 131°0E **113** H5
Kyūshū-Palau Ridge *Pac. Oc.* 20°0N 136°0E **156** E5
Kyūshū-Sanchi *Japan* 32°35N 131°17E **113** H5
Kyustendil *Bulgaria* 42°16N 22°41E **96** D6
Kyustendil □ *Bulgaria* 42°16N 22°41E **96** D6
Kyusyur *Russia* 70°19N 127°30E **107** B13
Kywong *Australia* 34°58S 146°44E **153** C7
Kyyiv *Ukraine* 50°30N 30°28E **75** C16
Kyyiv □ *Ukraine* 50°5N 30°45E **85** G6
Kyyivske Vdskh. *Ukraine* 51°0N 30°25E **75** C16
Kyzyl *Russia* 51°50N 94°30E **109** B12
Kyzyl-Adyr *Kyrgyzstan* 42°39N 71°35E **109** D8
Kyzyl Kum *Uzbekistan* 42°30N 65°0E **109** D7
Kyzyl-Kyya *Kyrgyzstan* 40°16N 72°8E **109** D8
Kyzyl Orda = Qyzylorda *Kazakhstan* 44°48N 65°28E **108** D7
Kyzyl-Suu *Kyrgyzstan* 42°20N 78°0E **109** D9

L

La Albuera *Spain* 38°45N 6°49W **89** G4
La Alcarria *Spain* 40°31N 2°45W **90** E2
La Almarcha *Spain* 39°41N 2°24W **90** F2
La Almunia de Doña Godina *Spain* 41°29N 1°23W **90** D3
La Amistad △ *Cent. Amer.* 9°28N 83°18W **182** E3
La Asunción *Venezuela* 11°2N 63°51W **186** A6
La Baie *Canada* 48°19N 70°53W **165** C5
La Banda *Argentina* 27°45S 64°10W **190** B3
La Bañeza *Spain* 42°17N 5°54W **88** C5
La Barca *Mexico* 20°17N 102°34W **180** C4
La Barge *U.S.A.* 42°16N 110°12W **168** E8
La Barra *Nic.* 12°54N 83°33W **182** D3
La Bastide-Puylaurent *France* 44°35N 3°55E **72** D7
La Baule *France* 47°17N 2°24W **70** E4
La Belle *U.S.A.* 26°46N 81°26W **179** J8
La Biche → *Canada* 59°57N 123°50W **162** B4
La Biche, L. *Canada* 54°50N 112°3W **162** C6
La Bisbal d'Empordà *Spain* 41°58N 3°2E **90** D8
La Brea *Peru* 4°40S 81°7W **188** A1
La Brea *Trin. & Tob.* 10°15N 61°37W **187** K15
La Brède *France* 44°41N 0°32W **72** D3
La Bresse *France* 48°2N 6°53E **71** D13
La Bureba *Spain* 42°36N 3°24W **88** C7
La Calera *Chile* 32°50S 71°10W **190** C1
La Campana △ *Chile* 32°58S 71°14W **190** C1
La Campiña *Spain* 37°45N 4°45W **89** H6
La Canal = Sa Canal *Spain* 38°51N 1°23E **100** C7
La Cañiza = A Cañiza *Spain* 42°13N 8°16W **88** C2
La Canourgue *France* 44°26N 3°13E **72** D7
La Capelle *France* 49°59N 3°50E **71** C10
La Carlota *Argentina* 33°30S 63°20W **190** C3
La Carlota *Spain* 37°40N 4°56W **89** H6
La Carolina *Spain* 38°17N 3°38W **89** G7
La Cavalerie *France* 44°1N 3°10E **72** D7
La Ceiba *Honduras* 15°40N 86°50W **182** C2
La Chaise-Dieu *France* 45°18N 3°42E **72** C7
La Chapelle d'Angillon *France* 47°21N 2°25E **71** E9
La Chapelle-St-Luc *France* 48°20N 4°3E **71** D11
La Chapelle-sur-Erdre *France* 47°18N 1°34W **70** E5
La Charité-sur-Loire *France* 47°10N 3°1E **71** E10
La Chartre-sur-le-Loir *France* 47°44N 0°34E **70** E7
La Châtaigneraie *France* 46°39N 0°44W **72** B3
La Châtre *France* 46°35N 2°0E **71** F9
La Chaux-de-Fonds *Switz.* 47°7N 6°50E **77** H2
La Chorrera *Panama* 8°53N 79°47W **182** E4
La Ciotat *France* 43°10N 5°37E **73** E9
La Clayette *France* 46°17N 4°19E **71** F11
La Cocha *Argentina* 27°50S 65°40W **190** B2
La Concepción *Panama* 8°31N 82°37W **182** E3
La Concordia *Mexico* 16°5N 92°38W **181** D6
La Coruña = A Coruña *Spain* 43°20N 8°25W **88** B2
La Côte-St-André *France* 45°24N 5°15E **73** C9
La Courtine *France* 45°41N 2°15E **72** C6
La Crau *Bouches-du-Rhône, France* 43°32N 4°40E **73** E8
La Crau *Var, France* 43°9N 6°4E **73** E10
La Crescent *U.S.A.* 43°50N 91°18W **172** D8
La Crete *Canada* 58°11N 116°24W **162** B5
La Crosse *Fla., U.S.A.* 29°51N 82°24W **178** F7
La Crosse *Kans., U.S.A.* 38°32N 99°18W **172** F4
La Crosse *Wis., U.S.A.* 43°48N 91°15W **172** D8
La Cruz *Costa Rica* 11°4N 85°39W **182** D2
La Cruz *Mexico* 23°55N 106°54W **180** C3
La Désirade *Guadeloupe* 16°18N 61°3W **182** b
La Digue *Seychelles* 4°20S 55°51E **141** b
La Esperanza *Argentina* 40°26S 68°32W **192** B3
La Esperanza *Cuba* 22°46N 83°44W **182** B3
La Esperanza *Honduras* 14°15N 88°10W **182** D2
La Estrada = A Estrada *Spain* 42°43N 8°27W **88** C2
La Faouët *France* 48°2N 3°30W **70** D3
La Fayette *U.S.A.* 34°42N 85°17W **177** D12
La Fé *Cuba* 22°2N 84°15W **182** B3
La Fère *France* 49°39N 3°21E **71** C10
La Ferté-Bernard *France* 48°10N 0°40E **70** D7
La Ferté-Gaucher *France* 48°47N 3°19E **71** D10
La Ferté-Macé *France* 48°35N 0°22W **70** D6
La Ferté-St-Aubin *France* 47°42N 1°57E **71** E8
La Ferté-sous-Jouarre *France* 48°56N 3°8E **71** D10
La Ferté-Vidame *France* 48°37N 0°53E **70** D7
La Flèche *France* 47°42N 0°4W **70** E6
La Follette *U.S.A.* 36°23N 84°7W **177** C12
La Fregeneda *Spain* 40°58N 6°54W **88** E4
La Fuente de San Esteban *Spain* 40°49N 6°15W **88** E4
La Gacilly *France* 47°45N 2°8W **70** E4
La Gi *Vietnam* 10°40N 107°45E **121** G6
La Gineta *Spain* 39°8N 2°1W **91** F2
La Goulette *Tunisia* 36°53N 10°18E **94** F3
La Grand'Combe *France* 44°13N 4°2E **73** D8
La Grande *U.S.A.* 45°20N 118°5W **168** D4
La Grande → *Canada* 53°50N 79°0W **164** B5
La Grande 3, Rés. *Canada* 53°40N 75°10W **164** B4
La Grande 4, Rés. *Canada* 54°0N 73°15W **164** B5
La Grande-Motte *France* 43°23N 4°5E **73** E8
La Grange *Calif., U.S.A.* 37°42N 120°27W **170** H6
La Grange *Ga., U.S.A.* 33°2N 85°2W **178** B4
La Grange *Ky., U.S.A.* 38°24N 85°22W **173** F11
La Grange *Tex., U.S.A.* 29°54N 96°52W **176** G6
La Grave *France* 45°3N 6°18E **73** C10
La Guaira *Venezuela* 10°36N 66°56W **186** A5
La Guarda △ *Mexico* 29°20N 113°27W **180** B2
La Guardia = A Guarda *Spain* 41°56N 8°52W **88** D2
La Gudiña = A Gudiña *Spain* 42°4N 7°8W **88** C3
La Guerche-de-Bretagne *France* 47°57N 1°16W **70** E5
La Guerche-sur-l'Aubois *France* 46°58N 2°56E **71** F9
La Habana *Cuba* 23°8N 82°22W **182** B3
La Haute Vallée de Chevreuse △ *France* 48°35N 1°58E **71** D8
La Haye-du-Puits *France* 49°17N 1°33W **70** C5
La Horra *Spain* 41°44N 3°53W **88** D7
La Independencia *Mexico* 16°15N 92°1W **181** D6
La Isabela *Dom. Rep.* 19°58N 71°2W **183** C5
La Jonquera *Spain* 42°25N 2°53E **90** C7
La Joya *Peru* 16°43S 71°52W **188** D3
La Junta *U.S.A.* 37°59N 103°33W **168** H12
La Laguna = San Cristóbal de La Laguna *Canary Is.* 28°28N 16°18W **100** F3
La Libertad = Puerto Libertad *Mexico* 29°55N 112°43W **180** B2
La Libertad *Guatemala* 16°47N 90°7W **182** C1
La Libertad □ *Peru* 8°0S 78°30W **188** B2
La Ligua *Chile* 32°30S 71°16W **190** C1
La Línea de la Concepción *Spain* 36°15N 5°23W **89** J5
La Loche *Canada* 56°29N 109°26W **163** B7
La Londe-les-Maures *France* 43°8N 6°14E **73** E10
La Lora *Spain* 42°45N 4°0W **88** C7
La Loupe *France* 48°29N 1°0E **70** D8
La Louvière *Belgium* 50°27N 4°10E **69** D4
La Lune *Trin. & Tob.* 10°3N 61°22W **187** K15
La Machine *France* 46°54N 3°27E **71** F10
La Maddalena *Italy* 41°13N 9°24E **94** A2
La Malbaie *Canada* 47°40N 70°10W **165** C5
La Malinche △ *Mexico* 19°15N 98°3W **181** D5
La Mancha *Spain* 39°10N 2°54W **91** F2
La Mariña *Spain* 43°30N 7°40W **88** B3
La Martre, L. *Canada* 63°15N 117°55W **162** A5
La Merced *Peru* 11°3S 75°19W **188** C2
La Mercy ✕ (DUR) *S. Africa* 29°37S 31°7E **145** C5
La Mesa *Mexico* 32°30N 116°57W **171** N10
La Mesa *U.S.A.* 32°46N 117°1W **171** N9
La Mesilla *U.S.A.* 32°16N 106°48W **169** K10
La Mothe-Achard *France* 46°37N 1°40W **70** F5
La Motte-Chalançon *France* 44°30N 5°21E **73** D9
La Motte-du-Caire *France* 44°20N 6°3E **73** D10
La Motte-Servolex *France* 45°35N 5°53E **73** C9
La Moure *U.S.A.* 46°21N 98°18W **172** B4
La Muela *Spain* 41°36N 1°7W **90** D3
La Mure *France* 44°55N 5°48E **73** D9
La Negra *Chile* 23°46S 70°18W **190** A1
La Oliva *Canary Is.* 28°36N 13°57W **100** F6
La Oraya *Peru* 11°32S 75°54W **188** C2
La Orotava *Canary Is.* 28°22N 16°31W **100** F3
La Oroya *Peru* 11°32S 75°54W **188** C2
La Pacaudière *France* 46°11N 3°52E **71** F10
La Palma *Canary Is.* 28°40N 17°50W **100** F2
La Palma *Panama* 8°15N 78°0W **182** E4
La Palma del Condado *Spain* 37°21N 6°38W **89** H4
La Palmyre *France* 45°43N 1°9W **72** C2
La Paloma *Chile* 30°35S 71°0W **190** C1
La Pampa □ *Argentina* 36°50S 66°0W **190** D2
La Paragua *Venezuela* 6°50N 63°20W **186** B6
La Paz *Entre Ríos, Argentina* 30°50S 59°45W **190** C4
La Paz *San Luis, Argentina* 33°30S 67°20W **190** C2
La Paz *Bolivia* 16°20S 68°10W **188** D4
La Paz *Honduras* 14°20N 87°47W **182** D2
La Paz *Mexico* 24°10N 110°18W **180** C2
La Paz □ *Bolivia* 15°30S 68°0W **188** D4
La Paz Centro *Nic.* 12°20N 86°41W **182** D2
La Pedrera *Colombia* 1°18S 69°43W **186** D5
La Pérade *Canada* 46°35N 72°12W **165** C5
La Perla *Mexico* 28°18N 104°32W **180** B4
La Perouse Str. *Asia* 45°40N 142°0E **112** B11
La Pesca *Mexico* 23°46N 97°47W **181** C5
La Piedad *Mexico* 20°21N 102°0W **180** C4
La Pine *U.S.A.* 43°40N 121°30W **168** E3
La Plata *Argentina* 35°0S 57°55W **190** D4
La Plata, L. *Argentina* 44°55S 71°50W **192** B2
La Pobla de Lillet *Spain* 42°16N 1°59E **90** C6
La Pobla de Segur *Spain* 42°15N 0°58E **90** C5
La Pocatière *Canada* 47°22N 70°2W **165** C5
La Pola de Gordón *Spain* 42°51N 5°41W **88** C5
La Porta *France* 42°25N 9°21E **73** F13
La Porte *U.S.A.* 29°40N 95°1W **176** G7
La Presanella *Italy* 46°13N 10°40E **92** B7
La Puebla = Sa Pobla *Spain* 39°46N 3°1E **90** F8
La Puebla de Cazalla *Spain* 37°10N 5°20W **89** H5
La Puebla de los Infantes *Spain* 37°47N 5°24W **89** H5
La Puebla de Montalbán *Spain* 39°52N 4°22W **88** F6
La Puebla del Río *Spain* 37°16N 6°3W **89** H4
La Puerta de Segura *Spain* 38°22N 2°45W **89** G8
La Purísima *Mexico* 26°10N 112°4W **180** B2
La Push *U.S.A.* 47°55N 124°38W **170** C2
La Quiaca *Argentina* 22°5S 65°35W **190** A2
La Réole *France* 44°35N 0°1W **72** D3
La Restinga *Canary Is.* 27°38N 17°59W **100** G2
La Rinconada *Peru* 14°38S 69°27W **188** C4
La Rioja *Argentina* 29°20S 67°0W **190** B2
La Rioja □ *Argentina* 29°30S 67°0W **190** B2
La Rioja □ *Spain* 42°20N 2°20W **90** C2
La Robla *Spain* 42°50N 5°41W **88** C5
La Roche-Bernard *France* 47°31N 2°19W **70** E4
La Roche-Canillac *France* 45°12N 1°57E **72** C5
La Roche-en-Ardenne *Belgium* 50°11N 5°35E **69** D5
La Roche-sur-Foron *France* 46°4N 6°19E **71** F13
La Roche-sur-Yon *France* 46°40N 1°25W **70** F5
La Rochefoucauld *France* 45°44N 0°24E **72** C4
La Rochelle *France* 46°10N 1°9W **72** B2
La Roda *Spain* 39°13N 2°15W **91** F2
La Roda de Andalucía *Spain* 37°12N 4°46W **89** H6
La Romaine *Canada* 50°13N 60°40W **165** B7
La Romana *Dom. Rep.* 18°27N 68°57W **183** C6
La Ronge *Canada* 55°5N 105°20W **163** B7
La Rumorosa *Mexico* 32°34N 116°6W **171** N10
La Sabina = Sa Savina *Spain* 38°44N 1°25E **100** C7
La Sagra *Spain* 37°57N 2°35W **91** H2
La Salle *U.S.A.* 41°20N 89°6W **172** E9
La Sanabria *Spain* 42°0N 6°30W **88** C4
La Santa *Canary Is.* 29°5N 13°40W **100** E6
La Sarre *Canada* 48°45N 79°15W **164** C4
La Scie *Canada* 49°57N 55°36W **165** C8
La Selva *Spain* 42°0N 2°45E **90** C7
La Selva Beach *U.S.A.* 36°56N 121°51W **170** J5
La Selva del Camp *Spain* 41°13N 1°8E **90** D6
La Serena *Chile* 29°55S 71°10W **190** B1
La Serena *Spain* 38°45N 5°40W **89** G5
La Seu d'Urgell *Spain* 42°22N 1°23E **90** C6
La Seyne-sur-Mer *France* 43°7N 5°52E **73** E9
La Sila *Italy* 39°15N 16°35E **95** C9
La Solana *Spain* 38°59N 3°14W **89** G7
La Soufrière *St. Vincent* 13°20N 61°11W **183** D7
La Souterraine *France* 46°15N 1°30E **71** F8
La Spézia *Italy* 44°7N 9°50E **92** D6
La Suze-sur-Sarthe *France* 47°53N 0°2E **70** E7
La Tagua *Colombia* 0°3N 74°40W **186** C4
La Teste-de-Buch *France* 44°37N 1°8W **72** D2
La Tortuga, I. *Venezuela* 11°0N 65°22W **183** D6
La Tour-du-Pin *France* 45°33N 5°27E **73** C9
La Tranche-sur-Mer *France* 46°20N 1°27W **70** F5
La Tremblade *France* 45°46N 1°8W **72** C2
La Trinité *Martinique* 14°45N 60°58W **182** c
La Tuque *Canada* 47°30N 72°50W **164** C5
La Unión *Chile* 40°10S 73°0W **192** B2
La Unión *El Salv.* 13°20N 87°50W **182** D2
La Unión *Mexico* 17°58N 101°49W **180** D4
La Unión *Peru* 9°43S 76°45W **188** B2
La Unión *Spain* 37°38N 0°53W **91** H4
La Urbana *Venezuela* 7°8N 66°56W **186** B5
La Vache Pt. *Trin. & Tob.* 10°47N 61°28W **187** K15
La Vall d'Uixó *Spain* 39°49N 0°15W **90** F4
La Vecilla *Spain* 42°51N 5°27W **88** C5
La Vega *Dom. Rep.* 19°20N 70°30W **183** C5
La Vega *Peru* 10°41S 77°44W **188** C2
La Vela de Coro *Venezuela* 11°27N 69°34W **186** A5
La Veleta *Spain* 37°1N 3°22W **89** H7
La Venta *Mexico* 18°5N 94°3W **181** D6
La Vergne *U.S.A.* 36°1N 86°35W **177** C11
La Villa Joiosa = Villajoyosa *Spain* 38°30N 0°12W **91** G4
La Voulte-sur-Rhône *France* 44°48N 4°46E **73** D8
Laa an der Thaya *Austria* 48°43N 16°23E **79** C9
Laaber, Grosse → *Germany* 48°55N 12°30E **77** G8
Laage *Germany* 53°55N 12°21E **76** B8
Laascaanood = Las Anod *Somalia* 8°26N 47°19E **131** F4
Laatzen *Germany* 52°19N 9°48E **76** C5
Laba → *Russia* 45°11N 39°42E **87** H4
Labasa *Fiji* 16°30S 179°27E **154** a
Labastide-Murat *France* 44°39N 1°33E **72** D5
Labastide-Rouairoux *France* 43°28N 2°39E **72** E6
Labbézenga *Mali* 15°2N 0°48E **139** B5
Labdah = Leptis Magna *Libya* 32°40N 14°12E **135** B8
Labe = Elbe → *Europe* 53°50N 9°0E **76** B4
Labé *Guinea* 11°24N 12°16W **138** C2
Laberge, L. *Canada* 61°11N 135°12W **162** A1
Labin *Croatia* 45°5N 14°8E **93** C11
Labinsk *Russia* 44°40N 40°48E **87** H5
Labis *Malaysia* 2°22N 103°2E **121** L4
Łabiszyn *Poland* 52°57N 17°54E **83** F4
Laboe *Germany* 54°24N 10°13E **76** A6
Laborec → *Slovakia* 48°37N 21°58E **79** C14
Laborie *St. Lucia* 13°45N 61°2W **183** f
Labouheyre *France* 44°13N 0°55W **72** D3
Laboulaye *Argentina* 34°10S 63°30W **190** C3
Labrador *Canada* 53°20N 61°0W **165** B7
Labrador City *Canada* 52°57N 66°55W **165** B6
Labrador Sea *Atl. Oc.* 57°0N 54°0W **161** F21
Lábrea *Brazil* 7°15S 64°51W **186** E6
Labruguière *France* 43°31N 2°16E **72** E6
Labuan □ *Malaysia* 5°20N 115°12E **118** C4
Labuha *Indonesia* 0°30S 127°30E **119** E7
Labuhan *Indonesia* 6°22S 105°50E **119** G11
Labuhanbajo *Indonesia* 8°28S 119°54E **119** F6
Labuhanbilik *Indonesia* 2°31N 100°10E **121** L3
Labuk, Telok *Malaysia* 6°10N 117°50E **118** C5
Labyrinth, L. *Australia* 30°40S 135°11E **151** E2
Labytnangi *Russia* 66°39N 66°21E **106** C7
Laç *Albania* 41°38N 19°43E **96** E3
Lac-Bouchette *Canada* 48°16N 72°11W **165** C5
Lac-Édouard *Canada* 47°40N 72°16W **165** C5
Lac La Biche *Canada* 54°45N 111°58W **162** C6
Lac la Martre = Wha Ti *Canada* 63°8N 117°16W **160** E8
Lac La Ronge △ *Canada* 55°9N 104°41W **163** B7
Lac-Mégantic *Canada* 45°35N 70°53W **165** C5
Lac Thien *Vietnam* 12°25N 108°11E **120** F7
Lacanau *France* 44°58N 1°5W **72** D2
Lacanau, L. de *France* 44°58N 1°7W **72** D2
Lacantún → *Mexico* 16°36N 90°39W **181** D6
Lácara → *Spain* 38°55N 6°25W **89** G4
Lacaune *France* 43°43N 2°40E **72** E6
Lacaune, Mts. de *France* 43°43N 2°50E **72** E6
Laccadive Is. = Lakshadweep Is. *India* 10°0N 72°30E **127** J1
Lacepede B. *Australia* 36°40S 139°40E **152** D3
Lacepede Is. *Australia* 16°55S 122°0E **148** C3
Lacerdónia *Mozam.* 18°3S 35°35E **143** F4
Lacey *U.S.A.* 47°7N 122°49W **170** C4
Lachania *Greece* 35°58N 27°54E **101** D9
Lachay, Pta. *Peru* 11°17S 77°44W **188** C2
Lachhmangarh *India* 27°50N 75°4E **124** F6
Lachi *Pakistan* 33°25N 71°20E **124** C4
Lachine *Canada* 45°26N 73°42W **164** C5
Lachlan → *Australia* 34°22S 143°55E **152** C5
Lachoc *Peru* 12°50S 75°6W **188** C2
Lachute *Canada* 45°39N 74°21W **164** C5
Laçın *Azerbaijan* 39°38N 46°33E **105** C12
Lackagh Hills *Ireland* 54°16N 8°10W **64** B3
Lackawanna *U.S.A.* 42°50N 78°50W **174** D6
Lackawaxen *U.S.A.* 41°29N 74°59W **175** E10
Lacolle *Canada* 45°5N 73°22W **175** A11
Lacombe *Canada* 52°30N 113°44W **162** C6
Lacona *U.S.A.* 43°39N 76°10W **175** C8
Láconi *Italy* 39°54N 9°4E **94** C2
Laconia = Lakonia *Greece* 36°55N 22°30E **98** E4
Laconia *U.S.A.* 43°32N 71°28W **175** C13
Lacoochee *U.S.A.* 28°28N 82°11W **179** G7
Lacq *France* 43°25N 0°35W **72** E3
Lacs □ *Côte d'Ivoire* 7°1N 4°46W **138** D4
Ladakh Ra. *India* 34°0N 78°0E **125** C8
Lądek-Zdrój *Poland* 50°21N 16°53E **83** H3
Lâdik *Turkey* 40°57N 35°58E **104** B6
Ladismith *S. Africa* 33°28S 21°15E **144** D3
Ladispoli *Italy* 41°56N 12°5E **93** G9
Lādīz *Iran* 28°55N 61°15E **129** D9
Ladnun *India* 27°38N 74°25E **124** F6
Ladoga, L. = Ladozhskoye Ozero *Russia* 61°15N 30°30E **84** B6
Ladonas → *Greece* 37°40N 21°50E **98** D3
Ladozhskoye Ozero *Russia* 61°15N 30°30E **84** B6
Ladrillero, G. *Chile* 49°20S 75°35W **192** C1
Ladson *U.S.A.* 32°59N 80°6W **178** C9
Ladushkin *Russia* 54°34N 20°10E **82** D7
Lady Elliott I. *Australia* 24°7S 152°42E **150** C5
Lady Frere *S. Africa* 31°42S 27°14E **144** D4
Lady Grey *S. Africa* 30°43S 27°13E **144** D4
Lady Lake *U.S.A.* 28°55N 81°55W **179** G8
Ladybrand *S. Africa* 29°9S 27°29E **144** C4
Ladysmith *Canada* 49°0N 123°49W **170** B3
Ladysmith *S. Africa* 28°32S 29°46E **145** C4
Ladysmith *U.S.A.* 45°28N 91°12W **172** C8
Ladyzhyn *Ukraine* 48°40N 29°15E **81** B14
Lae *Papua N. G.* 6°40S 147°2E **147** B7
Laem Chabang *Thailand* 13°5N 100°53E **120** F3
Laem Ngop *Thailand* 12°10N 102°26E **121** F4
Laem Son △ *Thailand* 9°29N 98°24E **121** H2
Laerma *Greece* 36°9N 27°57E **101** C9
Læsø *Denmark* 57°15N 11°5E **63** G5
Læsø Rende *Denmark* 57°20N 10°45E **63** G4
Lafayette *Ala., U.S.A.* 32°54N 85°24W **178** C4
Lafayette *Ind., U.S.A.* 40°25N 86°54W **172** E10
Lafayette *La., U.S.A.* 30°14N 92°1W **176** F8
Lafayette *Tenn., U.S.A.* 36°31N 86°2W **177** C11
Laferte → *Canada* 61°53N 117°44W **162** A5
Lafia *Nigeria* 8°30N 8°34E **139** D6
Lafiagi *Nigeria* 8°52N 5°20E **139** D6
Lafkos *Greece* 39°9N 23°14E **98** B5
Lafleche *Canada* 49°45N 106°40W **163** D7
Laful *India* 7°10N 93°52E **127** L11
Lagan *Sweden* 56°56N 13°58E **63** H7
Lagan → *Sweden* 56°30N 12°58E **63** H6
Lagan → *U.K.* 54°36N 5°55W **64** B6
Lagarfljót → *Iceland* 65°40N 14°18W **60** D6
Lagarto *Brazil* 10°54S 37°41W **189** C3
Lagdo, L. de *Cameroon* 8°40N 14°0E **135** G8
Lage *Germany* 51°59N 8°48E **76** D4
Lågen → *Oppland, Norway* 61°8N 10°25E **60** F14
Lågen → *Vestfold, Norway* 59°3N 10°3E **61** G14
Lägerdorf *Germany* 53°53N 9°34E **76** B5
Lages *Brazil* 27°48S 50°20W **191** B5
Laghouat *Algeria* 33°50N 2°59E **136** B4
Laghouat □ *Algeria* 33°35N 2°40E **136** B4
Lagnieu *France* 45°55N 5°20E **73** C9
Lagny-sur-Marne *France* 48°52N 2°44E **71** D9
Lago *Italy* 39°10N 16°9E **95** C9
Lago de Sanabria y Entorno △ *Spain* 42°9N 6°45W **88** C4
Lago Posadas *Argentina* 47°30S 71°40W **192** C2
Lago Puela △ *Argentina* 42°30S 71°55W **192** B2
Lago Ranco *Chile* 40°19S 72°30W **192** B2
Lagôa *Portugal* 37°8N 8°27W **89** H2
Lagoa do Peixe △ *Brazil* 31°12S 50°55W **191** C5
Lagoa Vermelha *Brazil* 28°13S 51°32W **191** B5
Lagoaça *Portugal* 41°11N 6°44W **88** D4
Lagodekhi *Georgia* 41°50N 46°22E **87** K8
Lagónegro *Italy* 40°8N 15°45E **95** B8
Lagonoy G. *Phil.* 13°35N 123°50E **119** B6
Lagos *Greece* 41°1N 25°6E **97** E9
Lagos *Nigeria* 6°25N 3°27E **139** D5
Lagos *Portugal* 37°5N 8°41W **89** H2
Lagos □ *Nigeria* 6°28N 3°25E **139** D5
Lagos de Moreno *Mexico* 21°21N 101°55W **180** C4
Lagrange = Bidyadanga *Australia* 18°45S 121°43E **148** C3
Lagrange B. *Australia* 18°38S 121°42E **148** C3
Laguardia *Spain* 42°33N 2°35W **90** C2
Laguépie *France* 44°8N 1°57E **72** D5
Laguna *Brazil* 28°30S 48°50W **191** B6
Laguna *U.S.A.* 35°2N 107°25W **169** J10
Laguna, Sa. de la *Mexico* 23°35N 109°55W **180** C2
Laguna Beach *U.S.A.* 33°33N 117°47W **171** M9
Laguna Blanca △ *Argentina* 39°0S 70°5W **192** A2
Laguna de Duero *Spain* 41°35N 4°43W **88** D6
Laguna de la Restinga △ *Venezuela* 10°58N 64°0W **183** D6
Laguna de Lachuá △ *Guatemala* 15°55N 90°40W **182** C1
Laguna del Laja △ *Chile* 37°27S 71°20W **190** D1
Laguna del Tigre △ *Guatemala* 17°32N 90°56W **182** C1
Laguna Limpia *Argentina* 26°32S 59°45W **190** B4
Laguna San Rafael △ *Chile* 46°54S 73°31W **192** C2
Lagunas *Chile* 21°0S 69°45W **190** A2
Lagunas *Peru* 5°10S 75°35W **188** B2
Lagunas de Chacahua △ *Mexico* 16°0N 97°43W **181** D5
Lagunas de Montebello △ *Mexico* 16°4N 91°42W **181** D6
Lagunas de Ruidera △ *Spain* 38°57N 2°52W **91** G2
Lagunes □ *Côte d'Ivoire* 5°47N 4°12W **138** D4
Lahad Datu *Malaysia* 5°0N 118°20E **119** D5
Lahad Datu, Telok *Malaysia* 4°50N 118°20E **119** D5
Lahan Sai *Thailand* 14°25N 102°52E **120** E4
Lahanam *Laos* 16°16N 105°16E **120** D5
Lahar *India* 26°12N 78°57E **125** F8
Laharpur *India* 27°43N 80°56E **125** F9
Lahat *Indonesia* 3°45S 103°30E **118** E2
Lahewa *Indonesia* 1°22N 97°12E **118** D1
Lāhījān *Iran* 37°10N 50°6E **129** B6
Lahn → *Germany* 50°19N 7°37E **77** E3
Lahnstein *Germany* 50°19N 7°37E **77** E3
Laholm *Sweden* 56°30N 13°2E **63** H7
Laholmsbukten *Sweden* 56°30N 12°45E **63** H6
Lahore *Pakistan* 31°32N 74°22E **124** D6
Lahr *Germany* 48°20N 7°52E **77** G3
Lahri *Pakistan* 29°11N 68°13E **124** E3
Lāhrūd *Iran* 38°30N 47°52E **105** C12
Lahti *Finland* 60°58N 25°40E **84** B3
Lahtis = Lahti *Finland* 60°58N 25°40E **84** B3
Lahugala Kitulana △ *Sri Lanka* 6°50N 81°40E **127** L5
Laï *Chad* 9°25N 16°18E **135** G9
Lai Chau *Vietnam* 22°5N 103°3E **116** F4
Lai'an *China* 32°28N 118°30E **117** A12
Laibin *China* 23°42N 109°14E **116** F7
Laifeng *China* 29°27N 109°20E **116** C7
L'Aigle *France* 48°46N 0°38E **70** D7
Laignes *France* 47°50N 4°20E **71** E11
L'Aiguillon-sur-Mer *France* 46°20N 1°18W **72** B2
Laikipia □ *Kenya* 0°10N 36°40E **142** B4
Laila = Layla *Si. Arabia* 22°10N 46°40E **131** C4
Laingsburg *S. Africa* 33°9S 20°52E **144** D3
Lainioälven → *Sweden* 67°35N 22°40E **60** C20
Lairg *U.K.* 58°2N 4°24W **65** C4
Laisamis *Kenya* 1°36N 37°48E **142** B4
Laissac *France* 44°23N 2°50E **72** D6
Láives *Italy* 46°26N 11°20E **93** B8
Laiwu *China* 36°15N 117°40E **115** F9
Laixi *China* 36°50N 120°31E **115** F11
Laiyang *China* 36°59N 120°45E **115** F11
Laiyuan *China* 39°20N 114°40E **114** E8
Laizhou *China* 37°8N 119°57E **115** F10
Laizhou Wan *China* 37°30N 119°30E **115** F10
Lajamanu *Australia* 18°23S 130°38E **148** C5
Lajere *Nigeria* 12°10N 11°25E **139** C7
Lajes *Brazil* 5°41S 36°14W **189** B3
Lajinha *Brazil* 20°9S 41°37W **189** E2
Lajkovac *Serbia* 44°27N 20°14E **96** B4
Lajosmizse *Hungary* 47°3N 19°32E **80** C4
Lak Sao *Laos* 18°11N 104°59E **120** C5
Lakaband *Pakistan* 31°2N 69°15E **124** D3
Lakamané *Mali* 14°35N 9°44W **138** C3
Lake *U.S.A.* 44°33N 110°24W **168** D8
Lake Alfred *U.S.A.* 28°6N 81°44W **179** G8
Lake Alpine *U.S.A.* 38°29N 120°0W **170** G7
Lake Andes *U.S.A.* 43°9N 98°32W **172** D4
Lake Arthur *U.S.A.* 30°5N 92°41W **176** F8
Lake Bindegolly △ *Australia* 28°0S 144°12E **151** D3
Lake Boga *Australia* 35°26S 143°38E **152** C5
Lake Butler *U.S.A.* 30°1N 82°21W **178** E7
Lake Cargelligo *Australia* 33°15S 146°22E **153** B7
Lake Charles *U.S.A.* 30°14N 93°13W **176** F8
Lake City *Colo., U.S.A.* 38°2N 107°19W **168** G10
Lake City *Fla., U.S.A.* 30°11N 82°38W **178** E7
Lake City *Mich., U.S.A.* 44°20N 85°13W **173** C11
Lake City *Minn., U.S.A.* 44°27N 92°16W **172** C7
Lake City *Pa., U.S.A.* 42°1N 80°21W **174** D4
Lake City *S.C., U.S.A.* 33°52N 79°45W **178** B10
Lake Coleridge *N.Z.* 43°17S 171°30E **155** D6
Lake Cowichan *Canada* 48°49N 124°3W **162** D4
Lake District △ *U.K.* 54°30N 3°21W **66** C4
Lake Eildon △ *Australia* 37°10S 145°56E **153** D6

Lake Elsinore U.S.A. 33°38N 117°20W 171 M9
Lake Eyre △ Australia 28°40S 137°31E 151 D2
Lake Gairdner △
Australia 31°41S 135°51E 151 E2
Lake George U.S.A. 43°26N 73°43W 175 C11
Lake Grace Australia 33°7S 118°28E 149 F2
Lake Gregory ⊙
Australia 20°12S 127°27E 148 D4
Lake Harbor = Kimmirut
Canada 62°50N 69°50W 161 E18
Lake Havasu City
U.S.A. 34°27N 114°22W 171 L12
Lake Helen U.S.A. 28°59N 81°14W 179 G8
Lake Hughes U.S.A. 34°41N 118°26W 171 L8
Lake Isabella U.S.A. 35°38N 118°28W 171 K8
Lake Jackson U.S.A. 29°3N 95°27W 176 G7
Lake King Australia 33°5S 119°45E 149 F2
Lake Lenore Canada 52°24N 104°59W 163 C8
Lake Louise Canada 51°30N 116°10W 162 C5
Lake Mackay ⊙
Australia 21°48S 129°46E 148 D4
Lake Mburo △ Uganda 0°33S 30°56E 142 C3
Lake Mead △ U.S.A. 36°30N 114°22W 171 K12
Lake Meredith △
U.S.A. 35°50N 101°50W 176 D4
Lake Mills U.S.A. 43°25N 93°32W 172 D7
Lake Nakuru △ Kenya 0°21S 36°8E 142 C4
Lake Park Australia 30°19S 140°33E 152 C4
Lake Park Ga., U.S.A. 30°41N 83°11W 178 E6
Lake Placid Fla.,
U.S.A. 27°18N 81°22W 179 H8
Lake Placid N.Y.,
U.S.A. 44°17N 73°59W 175 B11
Lake Pleasant U.S.A. 43°28N 74°25W 175 C10
Lake Providence
U.S.A. 32°48N 91°10W 176 E9
Lake Pukaki N.Z. 44°11S 170°8E 155 E5
Lake Roosevelt △
U.S.A. 48°5N 118°14W 168 B4
Lake St. Peter Canada 45°18N 78°2W 174 A6
Lake Stevens U.S.A. 48°1N 122°4W 170 C4
Lake Superior △
Canada 47°45N 84°45W 164 C3
Lake Tekapo N.Z. 44°0S 170°30E 155 E5
Lake Torrens △
Australia 30°55S 137°40E 151 E2
Lake Village U.S.A. 33°20N 91°17W 176 E9
Lake Wales U.S.A. 27°54N 81°35W 179 H8
Lake Worth U.S.A. 26°37N 80°3W 179 J9
Lakeba Fiji 18°13S 178°47W 154 a
Lakeba Passage Fiji 18°15S 178°45W 154 a
Lakefield = Rinyirru △
Australia 15°24S 144°26E 150 B3
Lakefield Canada 44°25N 78°16W 174 B6
Lakehurst U.S.A. 40°1N 74°19W 175 F10
Lakeland Australia 15°49S 144°57E 150 B3
Lakeland Fla., U.S.A. 28°3N 81°57W 179 G8
Lakeland Ga., U.S.A. 31°2N 83°4W 178 D6
Lakemba = Lakeba
Fiji 18°13S 178°47W 154 a
Lakeport Calif., U.S.A. 39°3N 122°55W 170 F4
Lakeport Mich., U.S.A. 43°7N 82°30W 174 C2
Lakes Entrance
Australia 37°50S 148°0E 153 D8
Lakeside Calif.,
U.S.A. 32°52N 116°55W 171 N10
Lakeside Nebr., U.S.A. 42°3N 102°26W 172 D2
Lakeview U.S.A. 42°11N 120°21W 168 E3
Lakeville U.S.A. 44°39N 93°14W 172 C7
Lakewood Colo.,
U.S.A. 39°42N 105°4W 168 G11
Lakewood N.J., U.S.A. 40°6N 74°13W 175 F10
Lakewood N.Y., U.S.A. 42°6N 79°19W 174 D5
Lakewood Ohio, U.S.A. 41°28N 81°47W 174 E3
Lakewood Wash.,
U.S.A. 47°11N 122°32W 170 C4
Lakewood Park U.S.A. 27°33N 80°24W 179 H9
Lakha India 26°9N 70°54E 124 F4
Lakhimpur India 27°57N 80°46E 125 F9
Lakhisarai India 25°11N 86°5E 125 G12
Lakhnadon India 22°36N 79°36E 125 H8
Lakhnau = Lucknow
India 26°50N 81°0E 125 F9
Lakhonpheng Laos 15°54N 105°34E 120 E5
Lakhpat India 23°48N 68°47E 124 H3
Läki Azerbaijan 40°34N 47°22E 87 K8
Lakin U.S.A. 37°57N 101°15W 172 G4
Lakitusaki → Canada 54°21N 82°25W 164 B3
Lakki Greece 36°34N 23°57E 101 D5
Lakki Pakistan 32°36N 70°55E 124 C4
Lakonia Greece 36°55N 22°30E 98 E4
Lakonikos Kolpos
Greece 36°40N 22°40E 98 E4
Lakota Côte d'Ivoire 5°50N 5°30W 138 D4
Lakota U.S.A. 48°2N 98°21W 172 A4
Laksar India 29°46N 78°3E 124 E8
Laksefjorden Norway 70°45N 26°50E 60 A22
Lakselv Norway 70°2N 25°0E 60 A21
Laksettipet India 18°52N 79°13E 126 E4
Lakshadweep □ India 10°0N 72°30E 127 J1
Lakshadweep Is. India 10°0N 72°30E 127 G2
Lakshmanpur India 22°58N 83°3E 125 H10
Lakshmeshwar India 15°9N 75°28E 127 G2
Lakshmikantapur
India 22°5N 88°20E 125 H13
Lala Musa Pakistan 32°40N 73°57E 124 C5
Lalaghat India 24°30N 92°40E 125 G18
Lalapanzi Zimbabwe 19°20S 30°15E 143 F3
Lalapaşa Turkey 41°49N 26°44E 97 E10
Lalbenque France 44°19N 1°34E 72 D5
Lalganj India 25°52N 85°13E 125 G11
Lalgola India 24°25N 88°15E 125 G13
Lālī Iran 32°21N 49°6E 129 C6
Lalibela Ethiopia 12°3N 39°0E 131 E2
Lalin China 45°12N 127°0E 115 B14
Lalín Spain 42°40N 8°5W 88 C2
Lalinde France 44°50N 0°44E 72 D4
Lalitapur India 24°42N 78°28E 125 G8
Lalitpur Nepal 27°40N 85°20E 125 F11
Lalkua India 29°5N 79°31E 124 E8
Lalsot India 26°34N 76°20E 124 F7
Lam Nam Nan △
Thailand 17°55N 100°28E 120 D3

Lam Pao Res. Thailand 16°50N 103°15E 120 D5
Lama Kara Togo 9°30N 1°15E 139 D5
Lamae Thailand 9°51N 99°5E 121 H2
Lamaing Myanmar 15°25N 97°53E 120 E1
Lamar Colo., U.S.A. 38°5N 102°37W 168 G12
Lamar Mo., U.S.A. 37°30N 94°16W 172 G6
Lamarque Argentina 39°24S 65°40W 192 A3
Lamastre France 44°59N 4°35E 73 D8
Lamayuru India 34°25N 76°56E 125 B7
Lambach Austria 48°6N 13°51E 78 C6
Lambaré Gabon 0°41S 10°12E 140 E2
Lambaréné France 48°29N 2°31W 70 D4
Lambasa = Labasa Fiji 16°30S 179°27E 154 a
Lambay I. Ireland 53°29N 6°1W 64 C5
Lambayeque □ Peru 6°45S 80°0W 188 E3
Lambert's Bay S. Africa 32°5S 18°17E 144 D2
Lambesc France 43°39N 5°16E 73 E9
Lambeth Canada 42°54N 81°18W 174 D3
Lambia Greece 37°52N 21°53E 98 D3
Lambro → Italy 45°8N 9°32E 92 C6
Lame Nigeria 10°30N 9°20E 139 C6
Lame Deer U.S.A. 45°37N 106°40W 168 D10
Lamego Portugal 41°5N 7°52W 88 D3
Lameroo Australia 35°19S 140°33E 152 C4
Lamesa U.S.A. 32°44N 101°58W 176 E4
Lamezia Terme Italy 38°58N 16°16E 95 D9
Lamia Greece 38°55N 22°26E 98 C4
Lamington △
Australia 28°13S 153°12E 151 D5
Lamma I. China 22°12N 114°7E 111 a
Lammermuir Hills U.K. 55°50N 2°40W 65 F6
Lammhult Sweden 57°20N 14°35E 63 G8
Lamoille → U.S.A. 44°38N 73°13W 175 B11
Lamon B. Phil. 14°30N 122°20E 119 B6
Lamont Canada 53°46N 112°50W 162 C6
Lamont Calif., U.S.A. 35°15N 118°55W 171 K8
Lamont Fla., U.S.A. 30°23N 83°49W 178 E6
Lamont Wyo., U.S.A. 42°13N 107°29W 168 E10
Lamotte-Beuvron France 47°36N 2°2E 71 E9
Lampa Peru 15°22S 70°22W 188 D3
Lampang Thailand 18°16N 99°32E 120 C2
Lampasas U.S.A. 31°4N 98°11W 176 F5
Lampazos de Naranjo
Mexico 27°1N 100°31W 180 B4
Långsele Sweden 63°12N 17°4E 62 A11
Lampedusa Italy 35°36N 12°40E 94 G5
Lampeter U.K. 52°7N 4°4W 67 E3
Lampman Canada 49°25N 102°50W 163 D8
Lamprechtshausen
Austria 48°0N 12°58E 78 D5
Lampung □ Indonesia 5°30S 104°30E 118 F2
Lamta India 22°8N 80°7E 125 H9
Lamu Kenya 2°16S 40°55E 142 C5
Lamud Peru 6°10S 77°57W 188 E3
Lamy U.S.A. 35°29N 105°53W 169 J11
Lan Xian China 38°15N 111°35E 116 E6
Lan Yü Taiwan 22°4N 121°25E 117 F13
Lāna'i U.S.A. 20°50N 156°55W 167 L8
Lanak La China 34°27N 79°32E 125 B8
Lanak'o Shank'ou = Lanak La
China 34°27N 79°32E 125 B8
Lanark Canada 45°1N 76°22W 175 A8
Lanark U.K. 55°40N 3°47W 65 F5
Lanbi Kyun Myanmar 10°50N 98°20E 121 G2
Lancang China 22°36N 99°58E 116 F2
Lancang Jiang →
China 21°40N 101°10E 116 G3
Lancashire □ U.K. 53°50N 2°48W 66 D5
Lancaster Canada 45°10N 74°30W 175 A10
Lancaster U.K. 54°3N 2°48W 66 C5
Lancaster Calif., U.S.A. 34°42N 118°8W 171 L8
Lancaster Ky., U.S.A. 37°37N 84°35W 173 G11
Lancaster N.H.,
U.S.A. 44°29N 71°34W 175 B13
Lancaster Ohio, U.S.A. 39°43N 82°36W 173 F12
Lancaster Pa., U.S.A. 40°2N 76°19W 175 F8
Lancaster S.C., U.S.A. 34°43N 80°46W 177 D14
Lancaster Wis., U.S.A. 42°51N 90°43W 172 D8
Lancaster Sd. Canada 74°13N 84°0W 161 C15
Lancelin Australia 31°0S 115°18E 149 F2
Lanchow = Lanzhou
China 36°1N 103°52E 114 C7
Lanciano Italy 42°14N 14°23E 93 F11
Lanco Chile 39°24S 72°46W 192 A2
Lancones Peru 4°30S 80°30W 188 A1
Lancun China 36°25N 120°10E 115 F11
Lańcut Poland 50°10N 22°13E 83 H9
Land Between the Lakes □
U.S.A. 36°25N 88°0W 177 C11
Landau Bayern, Germany 48°40N 12°41E 77 G8
Landau Rhld.-Pfz., Germany 49°12N 8°6E 77 F8
Landeck Austria 47°9N 10°34E 78 B3
Lander U.S.A. 42°50N 108°44W 168 E9
Lander → Australia 22°0S 132°0E 148 D5
Landerneau France 48°28N 4°17W 70 D2
Landeryd Sweden 57°7N 13°15E 63 G7
Landes France 44°0N 1°0W 72 D3
Landes □ France 43°57N 0°48W 72 E3
Landes de Gascogne △
France 44°23N 0°50W 72 D3
Landete Spain 39°56N 1°25W 90 F3
Landfall I. India 13°40N 93°2E 127 H11
Landi Kotal Pakistan 34°7N 71°6E 124 B4
Landisburg U.S.A. 40°21N 77°19W 174 F7
Landivisiau France 48°31N 4°6W 70 D2
Landmannalaugar
Iceland 63°59N 19°4W 60 E4
Landquart Switz. 46°58N 9°32E 77 J5
Landrecies France 50°7N 3°40E 71 B10
Land's End U.K. 50°4N 5°44W 67 G2
Landsberg Germany 48°2N 10°53E 77 G6
Landsborough Cr. →
Australia 22°28S 144°35E 150 C3
Landsbro Sweden 57°24N 14°56E 63 G8
Landshut Germany 48°34N 12°8E 77 G8
Landskrona Sweden 55°53N 12°50E 63 H6
Landstuhl Germany 49°24N 7°33E 77 F3
Landvetter Sweden 57°41N 12°17E 63 G6
Lane U.S.A. 33°32N 79°53W 178 B10
Lanesboro U.S.A. 41°57N 75°34W 175 E9
Lanett U.S.A. 32°52N 85°12W 178 E4
Lang Shan China 41°0N 106°30E 114 C4
Lang Son Vietnam 21°52N 106°42E 116 G6
Lang Suan Thailand 9°57N 99°4E 121 H2
Langå Denmark 56°23N 9°54E 63 H3
La'nga Co China 30°45N 81°15E 125 D9
Langadás Greece 40°46N 23°3E 96 F7

Langadia Greece 37°43N 22°1E 98 D4
Långan → Sweden 63°19N 14°44E 62 A8
Langar Iran 35°23N 60°25E 129 C9
Langara I. Canada 54°14N 133°1W 162 C2
Langarūd Iran 37°11N 50°8E 129 B6
Långås Sweden 56°58N 12°26E 63 H6
Langdai China 26°6N 105°21E 116 D5
Langdon U.S.A. 48°45N 98°22W 172 A4
Länge Jan = Ölands södra udde
Sweden 56°12N 16°23E 63 H10
Langeac France 45°7N 3°29E 72 C7
Langeais France 47°20N 0°24E 70 E7
Langeb Baraka →
Sudan 17°28N 36°50E 137 D4
Langeberg S. Africa 33°55S 21°0E 144 D3
Langeberge S. Africa 28°15S 22°33E 144 C3
Langeland Denmark 54°56N 10°48E 63 K4
Langelands Bælt
Denmark 54°50N 10°55E 63 K4
Langen Hessen, Germany 49°59N 8°40E 77 F4
Langen Niedersachsen,
Germany 53°36N 8°36E 76 B4
Langenburg Canada 50°51N 101°43W 163 C8
Langeneß Germany 54°38N 8°36E 76 A4
Langenlois Austria 48°29N 15°40E 78 C8
Langeoog Germany 53°45N 7°32E 76 B3
Langeskov Denmark 55°22N 10°35E 63 H4
Langfang China 39°30N 116°41E 114 E9
Länghem Sweden 57°36N 13°14E 63 G7
Langhirano Italy 44°37N 10°16E 92 D7
Langholm U.K. 55°9N 3°0W 65 F5
Langjökull Iceland 64°39N 20°12W 60 D3
Langkawi, Pulau
Malaysia 6°25N 99°45E 121 J2
Langklip S. Africa 28°12S 20°20E 144 C3
Langkon Malaysia 6°30N 116°40E 118 C5
Langley Canada 49°7N 122°39W 170 A4
Langnau Switz. 46°56N 7°47E 77 J3
Langogne France 44°43N 3°50E 72 D7
Langon France 44°33N 0°16W 72 D3
Langøya Norway 68°45N 14°50E 60 B16
Langreo Spain 43°18N 5°40W 88 B5
Langres France 47°52N 5°20E 71 E12
Langres, Plateau de
France 47°45N 5°3E 71 E12
Langsa Indonesia 4°30N 97°57E 118 D1
Långsele Sweden 63°12N 17°4E 62 A11
Langtang △ Nepal 28°10N 85°30E 125 E11
Langtou China 40°1N 124°19E 115 D13
Langtry U.S.A. 29°49N 101°34W 176 G4
Langu Thailand 6°53N 99°47E 121 J2
Langue de Barbarie △
Senegal 14°54N 16°30W 138 C1
Languedoc France 43°58N 3°55E 72 E7
Langwang China 22°38N 113°27E 111 a
Langxi China 31°10N 119°12E 117 B12
Langzhong China 31°38N 105°58E 116 B5
Lanigan Canada 51°51N 105°2W 163 C7
Lanín △ Argentina 40°0S 71°58W 192 A2
Lanjigarh India 19°43N 83°23E 126 B6
Lankao China 34°48N 114°50E 114 G8
Länkäran Azerbaijan 38°48N 48°52E 105 C13
Lanmeur France 48°39N 3°43W 70 D3
Lannemezan France 43°8N 0°23E 72 E4
Lannilis France 48°35N 4°32W 70 D2
Lannion France 48°46N 3°29W 70 D3
L'Annonciade
Canada 46°25N 74°55W 164 C5
Lanouaille France 45°24N 1°9E 72 C5
Lanping China 26°28N 99°15E 116 D2
Lansang △ Thailand 16°45N 99°0E 120 D2
Lansdale U.S.A. 40°14N 75°17W 175 F9
Lansdowne Australia 31°48S 152°30E 153 A10
Lansdowne Canada 44°24N 76°1W 175 B8
Lansdowne India 29°50N 78°41E 125 E8
Lansdowne House = Neskantaga
Canada 52°14N 87°53W 164 B2
L'Anse U.S.A. 46°45N 88°27W 172 B9
L'Anse au Loup
Canada 51°32N 56°50W 165 B8
L'Anse aux Meadows
Canada 51°36N 55°32W 165 B8
Lansford U.S.A. 40°50N 75°53W 175 F9
Lanshan China 25°24N 112°10E 117 E9
Lanshantou China 35°5N 119°20E 115 G10
Länsi-Turunmaa
Finland 60°18N 22°18E 84 B2
Lansing U.S.A. 42°44N 84°33W 173 D11
Lanslebourg-Mont-Cenis
France 45°17N 6°52E 73 C10
Lanta, Ko Thailand 7°35N 99°3E 121 J2
Lantana U.S.A. 26°35N 80°3W 179 J9
Lantau I. China 22°15N 113°56E 111 a
Lantewa Nigeria 12°16N 11°44E 139 C7
Lantian China 34°11N 109°20E 114 G5
Lanus Argentina 34°42S 58°23W 190 C4
Lanusei Italy 39°52N 9°34E 94 C2
Lanxi China 29°13N 119°28E 117 C12
Lanzarote Canary Is. 29°0N 13°40W 100 F6
Lanzarote ✈ (ACE)
Canary Is. 28°57N 13°40W 100 F6
Lanzhou China 36°1N 103°52E 114 F2
Lanzo Torinese Italy 45°16N 7°28E 92 C4
Lao → Italy 39°47N 15°48E 95 C8
Lao Cai Vietnam 22°30N 103°57E 116 F4
Laoag Phil. 18°7N 120°34E 119 A6
Laoang Phil. 12°32N 125°8E 119 B7
Laoha He → China 43°25N 120°35E 115 C11
Laohekou China 32°22N 111°38E 117 A8
Laois □ Ireland 52°57N 7°27W 64 D4
Laon France 49°33N 3°35E 71 C10
Laona U.S.A. 45°34N 88°40W 172 C9
Laos ■ Asia 17°45N 105°0E 120 D5
Lapa Brazil 25°46S 49°44W 191 B6
Lapai Nigeria 9°5N 6°42E 139 D6
Lapalisse France 46°15N 3°38E 72 B7
Lapeer U.S.A. 43°3N 83°19W 173 D12
Lapeyrade France 44°4N 0°3W 72 D3
Lapithos Cyprus 35°21N 33°11E 101 D12
Lapland = Lappland
Europe 68°7N 24°0E 60 B21
LaPorte Ind., U.S.A. 41°36N 86°43W 172 E10
Laporte Pa., U.S.A. 41°25N 76°30W 175 E8
Lapleau France 45°24N 2°9E 72 C6
Lapoutroie France 48°9N 7°12E 72 D4
Lappeenranta Finland 61°3N 28°12E 63 C16
Lappland Myanmar 24°30N 96°55E 125 F20
Lappland Europe 68°7N 24°0E 60 B21
Lappo = Lapua Finland 62°58N 23°0E 60 E20
Laprida Argentina 37°34S 60°45W 190 D3
Lāpseki Turkey 40°20N 26°41E 97 F10
Lapta = Lapithos
Cyprus 35°21N 33°11E 101 D12
Langades Greece 35°21N 33°11E 101 D12

Laptev Sea Russia 76°0N 125°0E 107 B13
Lapua Finland 62°58N 23°0E 60 E20
Lāpuş → Romania 47°25N 23°40E 81 C8
Lăpuş, Munţii Romania 47°20N 23°50E 81 C8
Lăpuşna Moldova 46°53N 28°25E 81 D13
Laqiya Arba'in Sudan 20°1N 28°1E 137 D2
Laqiya Umran Sudan 19°55N 28°18E 137 D2
L'Áquila Italy 42°22N 13°22E 93 F10
Lār Iran 27°40N 54°14E 129 E7
Lara Australia 38°2S 144°26E 152 C6
Larabanga Ghana 9°16N 1°56W 138 D4
Larache Morocco 35°10N 6°5W 136 A2
Laragne-Montéglin
France 44°18N 5°49E 73 D9
Lārak Iran 26°51N 56°21E 129 E8
Laramie U.S.A. 41°19N 105°35W 168 F11
Laramie Mts. U.S.A. 42°0N 105°30W 168 F11
Laranjeiras do Sul
Brazil 25°23S 52°23W 191 B5
Larantuka Indonesia 8°21S 122°55E 119 F6
Larat Indonesia 7°0S 132°0E 119 F8
L'Arbresle France 45°50N 4°36E 73 C8
Lärbro Sweden 57°47N 18°50E 63 G12
Larde Mozam. 16°28S 39°43E 143 F4
Larder Lake Canada 48°5N 79°40W 164 C4
Lardos Greece 36°6N 28°1E 101 C10
Lardos, Ákra = Líndos, Ákra
Greece 36°4N 28°2E 101 C10
Lardos, Órmos Greece 36°4N 28°2E 101 C10
Lare Kenya 0°20N 37°56E 142 C4
Laredo Spain 43°26N 3°28W 88 B7
Laredo U.S.A. 27°30N 99°30W 176 H5
Laredo Sd. Canada 52°30N 128°53W 162 C3
Largentière France 44°34N 4°18E 73 D8
L'Argentière-la-Bessée
France 44°47N 6°33E 73 D10
Largo U.S.A. 27°54N 82°47W 179 H7
Largo, Key U.S.A. 25°15N 80°15W 179 K9
Largs U.K. 55°47N 4°52W 65 F4
Lari Italy 43°34N 10°35E 92 E7
Lariang Indonesia 1°26S 119°17E 119 E5
Larimore U.S.A. 47°54N 97°38E 172 B5
Larino Italy 41°48N 14°54E 93 G11
Lárisa Greece 39°36N 22°27E 98 B4
Larkana Pakistan 27°32N 68°18E 124 F6
Larnaca Cyprus 34°55N 33°38E 101 E12
Larnaca Bay Cyprus 34°53N 33°45E 101 E12
Larne U.K. 54°51N 5°51W 64 B6
Larned U.S.A. 38°11N 99°6W 172 F4
Laroquebrou France 44°58N 2°12E 72 D6
Larose U.S.A. 29°34N 90°23W 177 G9
Larrimah Australia 15°35S 133°12E 150 B5
Larsen Ice Shelf
Antarctica 67°0S 62°0W 55 C17
Laruns France 43°0N 0°26W 72 F3
Larvik Norway 59°4N 10°2E 63 G14
Larzac, Causse du France 43°50N 3°17E 72 E7
Las Alpujarras Spain 36°55N 3°20W 91 J1
Las Animas U.S.A. 38°4N 103°13W 168 G12
Las Anod Somalia 8°26N 47°19E 131 F4
Las Arenas Spain 43°17N 4°50W 88 B6
Las Batuecas △ Spain 40°30N 6°5W 88 E4
Las Brenãs Argentina 27°5S 61°7W 190 B3
Las Cabezas de San Juan
Spain 36°57N 5°58W 89 J5
Las Cañadas del Teide △
Canary Is. 28°15N 16°37W 100 F3
Las Cejas Argentina 26°53S 64°44W 190 B3
Las Chimeneas Mexico 32°8N 116°5W 171 N10
Las Coloradas
Argentina 39°34S 70°36W 192 A2
Las Cruces U.S.A. 32°19N 106°47W 169 K10
Las Flores Argentina 36°10S 59°7W 190 D4
Las Gabias = Gabia la Grande
Spain 37°8N 3°40W 89 H7
Las Heras Mendoza,
Argentina 32°51S 68°49W 190 C2
Las Heras Santa Cruz,
Argentina 46°33S 68°57W 192 C3
Las Horquetas
Argentina 48°14S 71°11W 192 C2
Las Lajas Argentina 38°30S 70°25W 192 A2
Las Lomas Peru 4°40S 80°10W 188 A1
Las Lomitas Argentina 24°43S 60°35W 190 A3
Las Manos, Cueva de
Argentina 47°9S 70°40W 192 C2
Las Marismas Spain 37°5N 6°20W 89 H4
Las Médulas Spain 42°28N 6°46W 88 C4
Las Minas Spain 38°20N 1°41W 91 G3
Las Navas de la Concepción
Spain 37°56N 5°30W 89 H5
Las Navas del Marqués
Spain 40°36N 4°20W 88 E6
Las Palmas →
Mexico 32°31N 116°58W 171 N10
Las Palmas ✈ (LPA)
Canary Is. 27°55N 15°25W 100 G4
Las Palmas de Gran Canaria
Canary Is. 28°7N 15°26W 100 F4
Las Pedroñeras Spain 39°26N 2°40W 91 F2
Las Piedras Uruguay 34°44S 56°14W 191 C4
Las Pipinas Argentina 35°30S 57°19W 190 D4
Las Plumas Argentina 43°40S 67°15W 192 B3
Las Rosas Argentina 32°30S 61°35W 190 C3
Las Rozas Spain 40°29N 3°52E 88 B7
Las Tablas Panama 7°49N 80°14W 182 E3
Las Toscas Argentina 28°21S 59°18W 190 B4
Las Tunas Cuba 20°58N 76°59W 182 B4
Las Varillas Argentina 31°50S 62°50W 190 C3
Las Vegas N. Mex.,
U.S.A. 35°36N 105°13W 169 J11
Las Vegas Nev., U.S.A. 36°10N 115°8W 171 J11
Las Vegas McCarran Int. ✈ (LAS)
U.S.A. 36°5N 115°9W 171 J11
Lasarte-Oria Spain 43°16N 2°1W 90 E2
Lascano Uruguay 33°35S 54°12W 191 C5
Lascelles Australia 35°34S 142°34E 152 C5
Lashburn Canada 53°10N 109°40W 163 C7
Lashio Myanmar 22°56N 97°45E 125 H20
Lashkar India 26°10N 78°10E 124 F8
Lasin Poland 53°30N 19°2E 82 E6
Lashkargah = Lashkar Gāh
Afghan. 31°45N 61°30E 122 D3
Lasithi Greece 35°11N 25°31E 101 D7
Läsjerd Iran 35°24N 53°4E 129 C7
Lask Poland 51°34N 19°8E 83 G6
Łaskarzew Poland 51°48N 21°36E 83 G8

Lavris Greece 35°25N 24°40E 101 D6
Laško Slovenia 46°10N 15°16E 93 B12
Lassance Brazil 17°54S 44°34W 189 D2
Lassay-les-Châteaux
France 48°27N 0°30W 70 D6
Lassen Pk. U.S.A. 40°29N 121°30W 168 F3
Lassen Volcanic △
U.S.A. 40°30N 121°20W 168 F3
Last Mountain L.
Canada 51°5N 105°14W 163 C7
Lastchance Cr. →
U.S.A. 40°2N 121°15W 170 E5
Lastoursville Gabon 0°55S 12°38E 140 E2
Lastovo Croatia 42°46N 16°55E 93 F13
Lastovski Kanal Croatia 42°50N 17°0E 93 F14
Lat Yao Thailand 15°45N 99°48E 120 E2
Latacunga Ecuador 0°50S 78°35W 188 D2
Latady I. Antarctica 70°45S 74°35W 55 D17
Latakia = Al Lādhiqīyah
Syria 35°30N 35°45E 104 D5
Latchford Canada 47°20N 79°50W 164 C4
Latehar India 23°45N 84°30E 125 H11
Laterza Italy 40°37N 16°48E 95 B9
Latham Australia 29°44S 116°20E 149 E2
Lathen Germany 52°52N 7°19E 76 C3
Lathi India 27°43N 71°23E 124 F4
Lathrop Wells U.S.A. 36°39N 116°24W 171 J10
Latiano Italy 40°33N 17°43E 95 B10
Latina Italy 41°28N 12°52E 94 A5
Latisana Italy 45°47N 13°0E 93 C10
Latium = Lazio □ Italy 42°10N 12°30E 93 F9
Laton U.S.A. 36°26N 119°41W 170 J7
Latorytsya → Slovakia 48°28N 21°50E 79 C14
Latouche Treville, C.
Australia 18°27S 121°49E 148 C3
Latrobe Australia 41°14S 146°30E 151 G4
Latrobe U.S.A. 40°19N 79°23W 174 F5
Latrónico Italy 40°5N 16°1E 95 B9
Latur India 18°25N 76°40E 126 E3
Latvia ■ Europe 56°50N 24°0E 84 D2
Lau Nigeria 9°11N 11°19E 139 D7
Lau Group Fiji 17°0S 178°30W 154 a
Lauca → Bolivia 19°9S 68°10W 188 D4
Lauchhammer Germany 51°29N 13°47E 76 D9
Lauda-Königshofen
Germany 49°33N 9°42E 77 F5
Laudio = Llodio Spain 43°9N 2°58W 90 E2
Lauenburg Germany 53°22N 10°32E 76 B6
Lauenburgische Seen △
Germany 53°38N 10°45E 76 B6
Lauf Germany 49°30N 11°17E 77 F7
Lauge Koch Kyst
Greenland 75°45N 57°45W 161 B20
Laughlin U.S.A. 35°10N 114°34W 171 K12
Lauhanvuori △ Finland 62°8N 22°6E 60 E20
Laujar de Andarax Spain 37°0N 2°54W 91 H2
Laukaa Finland 62°24N 25°56E 60 E21
Launceston Australia 41°24S 147°8E 151 G4
Launceston U.K. 50°38N 4°22W 67 G3
Laune → Ireland 52°7N 9°47W 64 D2
Launglon Bok
Myanmar 13°50N 97°54E 120 F1
Laupheim Germany 48°14N 9°52E 77 G5
Laura Queens.,
Australia 15°32S 144°32E 150 B3
Laura S. Austral.,
Australia 33°10S 138°18E 152 B3
Laureana di Borrello
Italy 38°30N 16°5E 95 D9
Laurel Fla., U.S.A. 27°8N 82°27W 179 H7
Laurel Miss., U.S.A. 31°41N 89°8W 177 F10
Laurel Mont., U.S.A. 45°40N 108°46W 168 D9
Laurel Bay U.S.A. 32°26N 80°43W 178 E5
Laurel Hill U.S.A. 40°14N 79°6W 174 F5
Laurencekirk U.K. 56°50N 2°28W 65 E6
Laurens U.S.A. 34°30N 82°1W 177 D13
Laurentian Plateau
Canada 52°0N 70°0W 165 B6
Lauria Italy 40°2N 15°50E 95 B8
Laurie L. Canada 56°35N 101°57W 163 B8
Laurinburg U.S.A. 34°47N 79°28W 177 D15
Laurium U.S.A. 47°14N 88°27W 172 B9
Lausanne Switz. 46°32N 6°38E 77 J2
Laut, Pulau Indonesia 4°45S 108°0E 118 D3
Lautaro Chile 38°31S 72°27W 192 A2
Lauterbach Germany 50°37N 9°24E 76 E5
Lauterecken Germany 49°38N 7°35E 77 F3
Lautoka Fiji 17°37S 177°27E 154 a
Lauwersmeer △ Neths. 53°22N 6°11E 69 A6
Lauzès France 44°34N 1°35E 72 D5
Lava → Russia 54°37N 21°14E 82 D8
Lava Beds △ U.S.A. 41°40N 121°30W 168 F3
Lavagh More Ireland 54°46N 8°6W 64 B3
Lavagna Italy 44°18N 9°20E 92 D6
Laval France 48°4N 0°48W 70 D6
Laval-des-Rapides
Canada 45°33N 73°42W 164 C5
Lavalle Argentina 28°15S 65°15W 190 B2
Lāvān Iran 26°48N 53°22E 129 E7
Lavant Canada 45°3N 76°42W 175 A8
Lāvar Meydān Iran 30°20N 54°30E 129 D7
Lavardac France 44°12N 0°20E 72 D4
Lavaur France 43°40N 1°49E 72 E5
Lavello Italy 41°3N 15°48E 95 A8
Lavers Hill Australia 38°40S 143°25E 152 C5
Laverton Australia 28°44S 122°29E 149 E3
Lavezzi, Is. France 41°22N 9°16E 73 G13
Lavis Italy 46°8N 11°7E 92 B8
Lavos Portugal 40°6N 8°49W 88 E2
Lavradio Portugal 38°40N 9°9W 89 G2
Lavras Brazil 21°20S 45°0W 191 A7
Lavre Portugal 38°46N 8°22W 89 G2
Lavrio Greece 37°40N 24°4E 98 D6

Lawrence Ind., U.S.A. 39°50N 86°2W 172 F10
Lawrence Kans., U.S.A. 38°58N 95°14W 172 F6
Lawrence Mass.,
U.S.A. 42°43N 71°10W 175 D13
Lawrenceburg Ind.,
U.S.A. 39°6N 84°52W 173 F11
Lawrenceburg Tenn.,
U.S.A. 35°14N 87°20W 177 D11
Lawrenceville Ga.,
U.S.A. 33°57N 83°59W 178 B6
Lawrenceville Pa.,
U.S.A. 41°59N 77°8W 174 E7
Laws U.S.A. 37°24N 118°20W 170 H8
Lawtey U.S.A. 30°3N 82°5W 178 E7
Lawton U.S.A. 34°37N 98°25W 176 D5
Lawu Indonesia 7°40S 111°13E 119 G14
Lawz, J. al Si. Arabia 28°39N 35°18E 137 B4
Laxá Sweden 58°59N 14°37E 63 F8
Laxford, L. U.K. 58°24N 5°6W 65 C3
Laxiwa Dam China 36°4N 101°11E 110 D9
Lay → France 46°18N 1°17W 72 B2
Layla Si. Arabia 22°10N 46°40E 131 C4
Laylän Iraq 35°18N 44°31E 128 C5
Layon → France 47°20N 0°45W 70 E6
Laysan I. U.S.A. 25°50N 171°50W 167 K5
Layton U.S.A. 24°50N 80°47W 179 L9
Layton Utah, U.S.A. 41°4N 111°58W 168 F8
Laytonville U.S.A. 39°41N 123°29W 168 G2
Lazarev Russia 52°13N 141°30E 107 D15
Lazarev Sea S. Ocean 67°30S 3°0W 55 C2
Lazarevskoye Russia 43°55N 39°21E 87 J4
Lázaro Cárdenas
Mexico 17°55N 102°11W 180 D4
Lazdijai Lithuania 54°14N 23°31E 82 D10
Lazhuglung China 34°52N 81°24E 109 F10
Lazio □ Italy 42°10N 12°30E 93 F9
Lazo Moldova 47°33N 28°2E 81 C13
Lazo Russia 43°25N 133°55E 112 C6
Le Beausset France 43°12N 5°48E 73 E9
Le Bic Canada 48°20N 68°41W 165 C6
Le Blanc France 46°37N 1°3E 72 B5
Le Bleymard France 44°30N 3°42E 72 D7
Le Bourgneuf-la-Fôret
France 48°10N 0°59W 70 D6
Le Bugue France 44°55N 0°56E 72 D4
Le Cateau Cambrésis
France 50°7N 3°32E 71 B10
Le Caylar France 43°53N 3°19E 72 E7
Le Chambon-Feugerolles
France 45°24N 4°19E 73 C8
Le Châtelet France 46°38N 2°16E 71 B9
Le Chesne France 49°30N 4°45E 71 C11
Le Cheylard France 44°55N 4°25E 73 D8
Le Conquet France 48°21N 4°46W 70 D2
Le Creusot France 46°48N 4°24E 71 F11
Le Croisic France 47°18N 2°30W 70 E4
Le Donjon France 46°22N 3°48E 72 B7
Le Dorat France 46°14N 1°5E 72 B5
Le François Martinique 14°38N 60°57W 182 c
Le Gosier Guadeloupe 16°14N 61°29W 182 b
Le Grand-Lucé France 47°52N 0°28E 70 E7
Le Grand-Pressigny
France 46°55N 0°48E 70 F7
Le Grand-Quevilly France 49°23N 1°4E 70 D7
Le Gris Gris Mauritius 20°31S 57°32E 141 d
Le Havre France 49°30N 0°5E 70 C7
Le Lamentin Martinique 14°35N 61°2W 182 c
Le Lavandou France 43°8N 6°22E 73 E10
Le Lion-d'Angers France 47°37N 0°43W 70 E6
Le Louroux-Béconnais
France 47°30N 0°55W 70 E6
Le Luc France 43°23N 6°21E 73 E10
Le Lude France 47°39N 0°9E 70 E7
Le Maire, Estr. de
Argentina 54°50S 65°0W 192 D4
Le Mans France 48°0N 0°10E 70 D7
Le Marin Martinique 14°27N 60°55W 182 c
Le Mars U.S.A. 42°47N 96°10W 172 D5
Le Mayet-de-Montagne
France 46°4N 3°40E 71 F10
Le Mêle-sur-Sarthe
France 48°31N 0°22E 70 D7
Le Monastier-sur-Gazeille
France 44°57N 3°59E 72 D7
Le Monêtier-les-Bains
France 44°58N 6°30E 73 D10
Le Mont-Dore France 45°35N 2°49E 72 C6
Le Mont-St-Michel
France 48°40N 1°30W 70 D5
Le Moule Guadeloupe 16°20N 61°22E 182 b
Le Moyne, L. Canada 56°45N 68°47W 165 A6
Le Muy France 43°28N 6°34E 73 E10
Le Palais France 47°20N 3°10W 70 E3
Le Perthus France 42°30N 2°53E 72 F6
Le Port Réunion 20°56S 55°18E 141 c
Le Prêcheur Martinique 14°50N 61°13W 182 c
Le Puy-en-Velay France 45°3N 3°52E 72 C7
Le Raysville U.S.A. 41°50N 76°10W 175 E8
Le Robert Martinique 14°40N 60°56W 182 c
Le Roy U.S.A. 42°58N 77°59W 174 D7
Le St-Esprit Martinique 14°34N 60°56W 182 c
Le Sueur U.S.A. 44°28N 93°55W 172 C7
Le Tampon Réunion 21°16S 55°32E 141 c
Le Teil France 44°33N 4°40E 73 D8
Le Teilleul France 48°32N 0°53W 70 D6
Le Theil France 48°16N 0°42E 70 D7
Le Thillot France 47°53N 6°46E 71 E13
Le Thuy Vietnam 17°14N 106°49E 120 D6
Le Touquet-Paris-Plage
France 50°30N 1°36E 71 B8
Le Tréport France 50°3N 1°20E 70 C7
Le Val-André France 48°35N 2°33W 70 D4
Le Val-d'Ajol France 47°55N 6°30E 71 E13
Le Verdon-sur-Mer
France 45°33N 1°4W 72 C3
Le Vigan France 43°59N 3°36E 72 E7
Lea → U.K. 51°31N 0°1E 67 F8
Leach Cambodia 12°21N 103°46E 120 F4
Lead U.S.A. 44°21N 103°46W 168 D2
Leader Canada 50°50N 109°30W 163 C7
Leadville U.S.A. 39°15N 106°18W 168 G10
Leaf → U.S.A. 30°59N 88°44W 177 F10
Leaf Rapids Canada 56°30N 99°59W 163 B8
Leaghur, L. Australia 33°35S 143°3E 152 B5
League City U.S.A. 29°31N 95°6W 176 G7
Leamington Canada 42°3N 82°36W 174 D2
Leamington N.Z. 37°55S 175°36E 154 a
Leamington U.S.A. 39°32N 112°17W 168 G7
Leamington Spa = Royal
Leamington Spa U.K. 52°18N 1°31W 67 E6

Le'an China 27°22N 115°48E **117** D10
Leander U.S.A. 30°34N 97°52W **176** F5
Leandro Norte Alem
  Argentina 27°34S 55°15W **191** B4
Leane, L. Ireland 52°2N 9°32W **64** D2
Learmonth Australia 22°13S 114°10E **148** D1
Leary U.S.A. 31°29N 84°31W **178** D5
Leask Canada 53°5N 106°45W **163** C7
Leatherhead U.K. 51°18N 0°20W **67** F7
Leavdnja = Lakselv
  Norway 70°2N 25°0E **60** A21
Leavenworth Kans.,
  U.S.A. 39°19N 94°55W **172** F6
Leavenworth Wash.,
  U.S.A. 47°36N 120°40W **168** C3
Leawood U.S.A. 38°58N 94°37W **172** F6
Leba Poland 54°45N 17°32E **82** D4
Leba → Poland 54°46N 17°33E **82** D4
Lebach Germany 49°25N 6°54E **77** F2
Lebam U.S.A. 46°34N 123°33W **170** D3
Lebane Serbia 42°56N 21°44E **96** D5
Lebanon Fla., U.S.A. 29°10N 82°37W **179** F7
Lebanon Ind., U.S.A. 39°3N 86°28W **172** E10
Lebanon Kans., U.S.A. 39°49N 98°33W **172** F4
Lebanon Ky., U.S.A. 37°34N 85°15W **173** G11
Lebanon Mo., U.S.A. 37°41N 92°40W **172** G8
Lebanon N.H., U.S.A. 43°39N 72°15W **175** C12
Lebanon Oreg., U.S.A. 44°32N 122°55W **168** D2
Lebanon Pa., U.S.A. 40°20N 76°26W **175** F8
Lebanon Tenn., U.S.A. 36°12N 86°18W **177** C11
Lebanon ■ Asia 34°0N 36°0E **130** B5
Lebap □ Turkmenistan 40°0N 63°0E **108** D6
Lebec U.S.A. 34°51N 118°52W **171** L8
Lebedyan Russia 53°0N 39°10E **85** F10
Lebedyn Ukraine 50°35N 34°30E **85** G10
Lebel-sur-Quévillon
  Canada 49°3N 76°59W **164** C4
Lebomboberge S. Africa 24°30S 32°0E **145** B5
Lebork Poland 54°33N 17°46E **82** D4
Lebowakgomo S. Africa 24°12S 29°30E **145** A4
Lebrija Spain 36°53N 6°5W **89** J4
Lebsko, Jezioro Poland 54°40N 17°25E **82** D4
Lebu Chile 37°40S 73°47W **190** D1
Leça da Palmeira
  Portugal 41°12N 8°42W **88** D2
Lecce Italy 40°23N 18°11E **95** B11
Lecco Italy 45°51N 9°23E **92** C6
Lecco, L. di Italy 45°55N 9°19E **92** C6
Lécera Spain 41°13N 0°43W **90** D4
Lech Austria 47°13N 10°9E **78** D3
Lech → Germany 48°43N 10°56E **77** G6
Lechang China 25°10N 113°20E **117** E9
Lechena Greece 37°57N 21°16E **98** D3
Lechtaler Alpen Austria 47°15N 10°30E **78** D3
Lecontes Mills U.S.A. 41°5N 78°17W **174** E6
Lectoure France 43°56N 0°38E **72** E4
Leczna Poland 51°18N 22°53E **83** G9
Leczyca Poland 52°5N 19°15E **83** F6
Ledang, Gunung
  Malaysia 2°22N 102°37E **121** L4
Ledesma Spain 41°6N 5°59W **88** D5
Lednice Czechia 48°46N 16°46E **79** C9
Ledong China 18°41N 109°5E **117** a
Leduc Canada 53°15N 113°30W **162** C6
Lee Fla., U.S.A. 30°25N 83°18W **178** E6
Lee Mass., U.S.A. 42°19N 73°15W **175** D11
Lee → Ireland 51°53N 8°56W **64** E3
Lee Vining U.S.A. 37°58N 119°7W **170** H7
Leech L. U.S.A. 47°10N 94°24W **172** B6
Leechburg U.S.A. 40°37N 79°36W **174** F5
Leeds U.K. 53°48N 1°33W **66** D6
Leeds U.S.A. 33°33N 86°33W **177** E11
Leek Neths. 53°10N 6°24E **69** A6
Leek U.K. 53°7N 2°1W **66** D5
Leeman Australia 29°57S 114°58E **149** E1
Leeper U.S.A. 41°22N 79°18W **174** E5
Leer Germany 53°13N 7°26E **76** B3
Leesburg Fla., U.S.A. 28°49N 81°53W **178** G8
Leesburg Ga., U.S.A. 31°44N 84°10W **178** D5
Leeston N.Z. 43°45S 172°19E **155** D7
Leesville U.S.A. 31°8N 93°16W **176** F8
Leeton Australia 34°33S 146°23E **153** C7
Leetonia U.S.A. 40°53N 80°45W **174** F4
Leeu Gamka S. Africa 32°47S 21°59E **144** D3
Leeuwarden Neths. 53°15N 5°48E **69** A5
Leeuwin, C. Australia 34°20S 115°9E **149** F2
Leeuwin Naturaliste △
  Australia 34°6S 115°3E **149** F2
Leeward Is. Atl. Oc. 16°30N 63°30W **183** C7
Lefka Cyprus 35°6N 32°51E **101** D11
Lefkada Greece 38°40N 20°43E **98** C2
Lefkimi Greece 39°25N 20°3E **101** B4
Lefkimis, Akra Greece 39°29N 20°4E **101** B4
Lefkoniko Cyprus 35°18N 33°44E **101** D12
Lefkosia = Nicosia
  Cyprus 35°10N 33°25E **101** D12
Lefroy Canada 44°16N 79°34W **174** B5
Lefroy, L. Australia 31°21S 121°40E **149** F3
Leg → Poland 50°42N 21°50E **83** H8
Leganés Spain 40°19N 3°45W **88** E7
Legazpi Phil. 13°10N 123°45E **119** B6
Lège-Cap-Ferret France 44°48N 1°9W **72** D2
Legendre I. Australia 20°22S 116°55E **148** D2
Leghorn = Livorno Italy 43°33N 10°19E **92** E7
Legian Indonesia 8°42S 115°10E **119** K18
Legionowo Poland 52°25N 20°50E **83** F7
Legnago Italy 45°11N 11°18E **93** C8
Legnano Italy 45°36N 8°54E **92** C5
Legnica Poland 51°12N 16°10E **83** G3
Legrad Croatia 46°17N 16°51E **93** B13
Leh India 34°9N 77°35E **125** B7
Lehigh Acres U.S.A. 26°36N 81°39W **179** J8
Lehighton U.S.A. 40°50N 75°43W **175** F9
Lehliu Romania 44°29N 26°50E **81** F11
Lehututu Botswana 23°54S 21°55E **144** B3
Lehrte Germany 52°22N 9°58E **76** B5
Lei Shui → China 26°55N 112°35E **117** D9
Leiah Pakistan 30°58N 70°58E **124** D4
Leibnitz Austria 46°47N 15°34E **78** E8
Leibo China 28°11N 103°34E **116** C4
Leicester U.K. 52°38N 1°8W **67** E6
Leicester City □ U.K. 52°38N 1°8W **67** E6
Leicestershire □ U.K. 52°41N 1°17W **67** E6
Leichhardt →
  Australia 17°35S 139°48E **150** B2
Leichhardt Ra.
  Australia 20°46S 147°40E **150** C4
Leiden Neths. 52°9N 4°30E **69** B4
Leie → Belgium 51°2N 3°45E **69** C3
Leifers = Láives Italy 46°26N 11°20E **93** B8
Leigh → Australia 38°18S 144°30E **152** E6

Leigh Creek Australia 30°38S 138°26E **152** A3
Leimen Germany 49°21N 8°41E **77** F4
Leimus Nic. 14°40N 84°3W **182** D3
Leine → Germany 52°43N 9°36E **76** C5
Leinefelde-Worbris
  Germany 51°23N 10°19E **76** D6
Leinster Australia 27°51S 120°36E **149** E3
Leinster □ Ireland 53°3N 7°8W **64** C4
Leinster, Mt. Ireland 52°37N 6°46W **64** D5
Leipalingis Lithuania 54°5N 23°51E **82** D10
Leipzig Germany 51°18N 12°22E **76** D8
Leiria Portugal 39°46N 8°53W **88** F2
Leiria □ Portugal 39°46N 8°53W **88** F2
Leirvik Norway 59°47N 5°28E **61** G11
Leishan China 26°15N 108°20E **116** D7
Leisler, Mt. Australia 23°23S 129°20E **148** D4
Leisure City U.S.A. 25°30N 80°26W **179** K9
Leith U.K. 55°59N 3°11W **65** F5
Leith Hill U.K. 51°11N 0°22W **67** F7
Leitha → Europe 47°50N 17°15E **79** D10
Leitir Ceanainn = Letterkenny
  Ireland 54°57N 7°45W **64** B4
Leitrim Ireland 54°0N 8°5W **64** B3
Leitrim □ Ireland 54°8N 8°0W **64** B4
Leitza Spain 43°5N 1°55W **90** B3
Leixlip Ireland 53°22N 6°30W **64** C5
Leiyang China 26°27N 112°45E **117** D9
Leizhou China 20°52N 110°8E **117** G8
Leizhou Bandao China 21°0N 110°0E **116** G7
Leizhou Wan China 20°50N 110°20E **117** G8
Lek → Neths. 51°54N 4°35E **69** C4
Leka Norway 65°5N 11°35E **60** D14
Lekani Greece 41°10N 24°35E **97** E8
Lekbibaj Albania 42°17N 19°56E **96** D3
Lekeitio Spain 43°20N 2°32W **90** B2
Lekki Lagoon Nigeria 6°30N 4°7E **139** D5
Leko Mali 13°37N 9°2W **138** C3
Lekoui Burkina Faso 12°37N 3°40W **138** C4
Leksand Sweden 60°44N 15°1E **62** D9
Leland Mich., U.S.A. 45°1N 85°45W **173** C11
Leland Miss., U.S.A. 33°24N 90°54W **177** E9
Lelâng Sweden 59°10N 12°5E **62** E6
Leleque Argentina 42°28S 71°0W **192** B2
Leling China 37°44N 117°13E **115** F9
Lélouma Guinea 11°11N 12°56W **138** C2
Lelystad Neths. 52°30N 5°25E **69** B5
Lem Denmark 56°1N 8°24E **63** H2
Lema Nigeria 12°58N 4°13E **139** C5
Lembar Indonesia 8°45S 116°4E **119** K19
Lembongan, Nusa
  Indonesia 8°40S 115°27E **119** K18
Lembuak Indonesia 8°36S 116°11E **119** K19
Lemera
  Dem. Rep. of the Congo 3°0S 28°55E **142** C2
Lemesós = Limassol
  Cyprus 34°42N 33°1E **101** E12
Lemhi Ra. U.S.A. 44°0N 113°0W **168** D7
Lemmenjoki △ Finland 68°40N 25°30E **60** B21
Lemmer Neths. 52°51N 5°43E **69** B5
Lemmon U.S.A. 45°57N 102°10W **172** C2
Lemon Grove U.S.A. 32°44N 117°1W **171** N9
Lemoore U.S.A. 36°18N 119°46W **170** J7
Lempdes-sur-Allagnon
  France 45°22N 3°17E **72** C7
Lemvig Denmark 56°33N 8°20E **63** H2
Lena → Russia 72°52N 126°40E **107** B13
Lena Pillars = Lenskiy Stolby
  Russia 60°55N 126°0E **107** C13
Lenadoon Pt. Ireland 54°18N 9°3W **64** B2
Lenart Slovenia 46°36N 15°48E **93** B12
Lenartovce Slovakia 48°18N 20°19E **79** C13
Lencloître France 46°50N 0°20E **70** F7
Lençóis Brazil 12°35S 41°24W **189** C2
Lençóis Maranhenses △
  Brazil 2°30S 43°0W **189** A2
Lendava Slovenia 46°35N 16°25E **93** B13
Lendinara Italy 45°5N 11°36E **93** C8
Lenger Kazakhstan 42°12N 69°54E **109** D7
Lengerich Germany 52°11N 7°52E **76** C3
Lenggong Malaysia 5°6N 100°58E **121** K3
Lenggries Germany 47°41N 11°34E **77** H7
Lengshuijiang China 27°40N 111°26E **117** D8
Lengshuitan China 26°27N 111°35E **117** D8
Lengua de Vaca, Pta.
  Chile 30°14S 71°38W **190** C1
Lengwe △ Malawi 16°14S 34°45E **143** F3
Lengyeltóti Hungary 46°40N 17°40E **80** D2
Lenhovda Sweden 57°0N 15°16E **63** G9
Lenina, Kanal → Russia 43°44N 45°17E **87** J7
Lenine Ukraine 45°17N 35°46E **85** K8
Leningrad □ Russia 59°40N 32°0E **84** C7
Leninogorsk = Ridder
  Kazakhstan 50°20N 83°30E **109** B10
Leninogorsk Russia 54°36N 52°30E **87** D17
Leninsk Russia 48°40N 45°15E **87** F7
Leninsk-Kuznetskiy
  Russia 54°44N 86°10E **109** B11
Leninskoye Russia 58°23N 47°3E **86** C8
Lenk Switz. 46°27N 7°28E **97** J3
Lenkoran = Länkäran
  Azerbaijan 38°48N 48°52E **105** C13
Lenmalu Indonesia 1°45S 130°15E **119** E8
Lennartsfors Sweden 59°20N 11°55E **62** E5
Lenne → Germany 51°25N 7°29E **76** D3
Lennestadt Germany 51°8N 8°2E **76** D4
Lennox U.S.A. 43°21N 96°53W **172** D5
Lennox, I. Chile 55°18S 66°50W **192** H3
Lennoxville Canada 45°22N 71°51W **175** A13
Leno Italy 45°22N 10°13E **92** C7
Lenoir U.S.A. 35°55N 81°32W **177** D14
Lenoir City U.S.A. 35°48N 84°16W **177** D12
Lenore L. Canada 52°30N 104°59W **163** C8
Lenox U.S.A. 31°16N 83°28W **178** D6
Lenox Mass., U.S.A. 42°22N 73°17W **175** D11
Lens France 50°26N 2°50E **71** B9
Lensahn Germany 54°13N 10°54E **76** A6
Lensk Russia 60°48N 114°55E **107** C12
Lenskiy Stolby Russia 60°55N 126°0E **107** C13
Lentas Greece 34°56N 24°56E **101** E6
Lentekhi Georgia 42°47N 42°45E **87** J6
Lenti Hungary 46°37N 16°33E **80** D1
Lentini Italy 37°17N 15°0E **95** E8
Lenwood U.S.A. 34°53N 117°7W **171** L9
Lenya Myanmar 11°33N 98°57E **121** G2
Lenzen Germany 53°5N 11°29E **76** B7
Léo Burkina Faso 11°3N 2°2W **138** C4
Leoben Austria 47°22N 15°5E **78** D8
Leodhais = Lewis U.K. 58°9N 6°40W **65** C2
Leola U.S.A. 45°43N 98°56W **172** C4
Leominster U.K. 52°14N 2°43W **67** E5
Leominster U.S.A. 42°32N 71°46W **175** D13

Léon France 43°53N 1°18W **72** E2
León Mexico 21°6N 101°41W **180** C4
León Nic. 12°27N 86°51W **182** D2
León Spain 42°38N 5°34W **88** C5
León □ Spain 42°40N 5°55W **88** C5
León → Spain 31°14N 97°28W **176** F6
León, Montes de Spain 42°30N 6°18W **88** C4
Leonardo da Vinci, Roma ✈ (FCO)
  Italy 41°48N 12°15E **93** G9
Leonardtown U.S.A. 38°17N 76°38W **173** F15
Leonardville Namibia 23°29S 18°49E **144** B2
Leonárisso Cyprus 35°28N 34°8E **101** D13
Leonberg Germany 48°48N 9°1E **77** G5
Leonding Austria 48°16N 14°15E **78** C7
Leonessa Italy 42°34N 12°58E **93** F9
Leonforte Italy 37°38N 14°23E **95** E7
Leongatha Australia 38°30S 145°58E **153** E6
Leonia U.S.A. 30°55N 86°1W **178** E3
Leonidio Greece 37°9N 22°52E **98** D4
Leonora Australia 28°49S 121°19E **149** E3
Leopoldina Brazil 21°28S 42°40W **191** A7
Leopoldo Bulhões
  Brazil 16°37S 48°46W **189** D1
Leopoldsburg Belgium 51°7N 5°13E **69** C5
Leoti U.S.A. 38°29N 101°21W **172** F3
Leova Moldova 46°28N 28°15E **81** E15
Leoville Canada 53°39N 107°33W **163** C7
Lepe Spain 37°15N 7°12W **89** H3
Lepel = Lyepyel Belarus 54°50N 28°40E **84** E4
Lepenou Greece 38°42N 21°17E **98** C3
Leping China 28°47N 117°7E **117** C11
Lépo, L. do Angola 17°0S 19°0E **144** A2
Lepontine, Alpi Italy 46°22N 8°27E **92** B5
Leposavić Kosovo 43°6N 20°48E **96** C4
Leppävirta Finland 62°29N 27°46E **60** E22
Lepsény Hungary 47°0N 18°15E **80** D3
Leptis Magna Libya 32°40N 14°12E **135** B8
Lequeitio = Lekeitio
  Spain 43°20N 2°32W **90** B2
Lercara Friddi Italy 37°45N 13°36E **94** E6
Léré Chad 9°39N 14°13E **139** D7
Léré Mali 15°45N 4°55W **138** B4
Lere Bauchi, Nigeria 9°43N 9°18E **139** D6
Lere Kaduna, Nigeria 10°23N 8°35E **139** C6
Leribe Lesotho 28°51S 28°3E **145** C4
Lérici Italy 44°4N 9°55E **92** D6
Lérida = Lleida Spain 41°37N 0°39E **90** D6
Lérins, Îs. de France 43°31N 7°3E **73** E11
Lerma Spain 42°0N 3°47W **88** C7
Leros Greece 37°10N 26°50E **99** D8
Lérouville France 48°44N 5°30E **71** D12
Lerum Sweden 57°46N 12°16E **63** G6
Lerwick U.K. 60°9N 1°9W **65** A7
Leş Romania 46°58N 21°50E **80** D6
Les Abrets France 45°32N 5°35E **73** C9
Les Andelys France 49°15N 1°25E **70** C8
Les Borges Blanques
  Spain 41°31N 0°52E **90** D5
Les Cayes Haiti 18°15N 73°46W **183** C5
Les Coteaux Canada 45°15N 74°13W **175** A10
Les Escoumins Canada 48°21N 69°24W **165** C6
Les Essarts France 46°47N 1°12W **70** F5
Les Herbiers France 46°52N 1°1W **70** F5
Les Minquiers, Plateau des
  Chan. Is. 48°58N 2°8W **70** D4
Les Pieux France 49°30N 1°48W **70** C5
Les Ponts-de-Cé France 47°25N 0°30W **70** E6
Les Riceys France 47°59N 4°22E **71** E11
Les Sables-d'Olonne
  France 46°30N 1°45W **72** B2
Les Vans France 44°25N 4°7E **73** D8
Lesbos Greece 39°10N 26°20E **99** B8
L'Escala Spain 42°7N 3°8E **90** C8
Leshan China 29°33N 103°41E **116** C4
Leshwe →
  Dem. Rep. of the Congo 12°45S 29°30E **143** E2
Lésina Italy 41°52N 15°21E **93** G12
Lésina, L. di Italy 41°53N 15°26E **93** G12
Lesjöfors Sweden 59°58N 14°11E **62** E8
Lesko Poland 49°30N 22°23E **83** J9
Leskov I. Antarctica 56°0S 28°0W **5** B1
Leskovac Serbia 43°0N 21°58E **96** C5
Leskovik Albania 40°10N 20°34E **96** F4
Leslie U.S.A. 31°57N 84°5W **178** D5
Lesná Poland 51°1N 15°15E **83** G2
Lesneven France 48°35N 4°20W **70** D2
Leśnica Poland 50°26N 18°11E **83** H5
Lešnica Serbia 44°39N 19°20E **96** B3
Lesnoye Russia 58°15N 35°18E **84** C8
Lesopilnoye Russia 46°44N 134°20E **112** A7
Lesosibirsk Russia 60°28N 90°0E **107** C10
Lesotho ■ Africa 29°40S 28°0E **145** C4
Lesozavodsk Russia 45°30N 133°29E **112** B6
Lesparre-Médoc France 45°18N 0°57W **72** C3
L'Espl:uga de Francolí
  Spain 41°24N 1°7E **90** D6
Lessay France 49°14N 1°30W **70** C5
Lesse → Belgium 50°15N 4°54E **69** D4
Lesse en Lomme △ Belgium 50°8N 5°9E **69** D5
Lessebo Sweden 56°45N 15°16E **63** H9
Lesser Antilles W. Indies 15°0N 61°0W **183** D7
Lesser Slave L. Canada 55°30N 115°25W **162** B5
Lesser Sunda Is. Indonesia 8°0S 120°0E **119** F6
Lessines Belgium 50°42N 3°50E **69** D3
Lester B. Pearson Int., Toronto ✈
  (YYZ) Canada 43°46N 79°35W **174** C5
Lestock Canada 51°19N 103°59W **163** C8
Lesuer L. Australia 13°50S 127°17E **148** B4
Lesueur △ Australia 30°11S 115°10E **149** F2
Lésvos = Lesbos Greece 39°10N 26°20E **99** B8
Leszno Poland 51°50N 16°30E **83** G3
Letaba S. Africa 23°59S 31°50E **145** B5
Letälven → Sweden 59°5N 14°20E **62** E8
Letávértes Hungary 47°23N 21°55E **80** C6

Letsôk-aw Kyun
  Myanmar 11°30N 98°25E **121** G2
Letterkenny Ireland 54°57N 7°45W **64** B4
Leu Romania 44°10N 24°0E **81** F9
Leucadia U.S.A. 33°4N 117°18W **171** M9
Leucate France 42°56N 3°3E **72** F7
Leucate, Étang de France 42°50N 3°0E **72** F7
Leuchars U.K. 56°24N 2°53W **65** E6
Leuk Switz. 46°19N 7°37E **77** J3
Leuser, Gunung
  Indonesia 3°46N 97°12E **118** D1
Leutkirch Germany 47°49N 10°1E **77** H6
Leuven Belgium 50°52N 4°42E **69** D4
Leuze-en-Hainaut
  Belgium 50°36N 3°37E **69** D3
Lev Tolstoy Russia 53°13N 39°29E **84** F10
Levan Albania 40°40N 19°28E **96** F3
Levanger Norway 63°45N 11°19E **60** E14
Levant, Î. du France 43°3N 6°28E **73** E10
Lévanzo Italy 38°0N 12°20E **94** D5
Levelland U.S.A. 33°35N 102°23W **176** E3
Leven U.K. 56°12N 3°0W **65** E5
Leven, L. U.K. 56°12N 3°22W **65** E5
Leveque C. Australia 16°20S 123°0E **148** C3
Leverano Italy 40°17N 18°0E **95** B10
Leverkusen Germany 51°1N 7°1E **76** D3
Levice Slovakia 48°13N 18°35E **79** C11
Lévico Terme Italy 46°0N 11°18E **93** C8
Levie France 41°40N 9°7E **73** G13
Levier France 46°58N 6°8E **71** F13
Levin N.Z. 40°37S 175°18E **154** G4
Lévis Canada 46°48N 71°9W **165** C5
Levis, L. Canada 62°37N 117°58W **162** A5
Levitha Greece 37°0N 26°28E **99** D8
Levittown N.Y.,
  U.S.A. 40°44N 73°31W **175** F11
Levittown Pa., U.S.A. 40°9N 74°51W **175** F10
Levka Bulgaria 41°52N 26°15E **97** E10
Levka Oros Greece 35°18N 24°3E **101** D6
Levkás = Lefkada Greece 38°40N 20°43E **98** C2
Levoča Slovakia 49°2N 20°35E **79** B13
Levroux France 46°59N 1°38E **71** F8
Levski Bulgaria 43°21N 25°10E **97** C9
Levskigrad = Karlovo
  Bulgaria 42°38N 24°47E **97** D8
Levuka Fiji 17°43S 179°0E **154** a
Lewes U.K. 50°52N 0°1E **67** G8
Lewes U.S.A. 38°46N 75°9W **173** F16
Lewin Brzeski Poland 50°45N 17°37E **83** H4
Lewis U.K. 58°9N 6°40W **65** C2
Lewis → U.S.A. 45°51N 122°48W **170** E4
Lewis, Butt of U.K. 58°31N 6°16W **65** C2
Lewis and Clark △
  U.S.A. 46°8N 123°53W **170** D3
Lewis Pass N.Z. 42°31S 172°11E **155** D7
Lewis Ra. Australia 20°3S 128°50E **148** D4
Lewis Range U.S.A. 48°5N 113°5W **168** B7
Lewis Run U.S.A. 41°52N 78°40W **174** E6
Lewisburg Pa., U.S.A. 40°58N 76°54W **174** F8
Lewisburg Tenn.,
  U.S.A. 35°27N 86°48W **177** D11
Lewisburg W. Va.,
  U.S.A. 37°48N 80°27W **173** G13
Lewisporte Canada 49°15N 55°3W **165** C8
Lewiston Idaho, U.S.A. 46°25N 117°1W **168** C5
Lewiston Maine, U.S.A. 44°6N 70°13W **173** C18
Lewiston N.Y., U.S.A. 43°11N 79°3W **174** C5
Lewistown Mont.,
  U.S.A. 47°4N 109°26W **168** C9
Lewistown Pa., U.S.A. 40°36N 77°34W **174** F7
Lexington Ga., U.S.A. 33°52N 83°7W **178** B6
Lexington Ill., U.S.A. 40°39N 88°47W **172** E9
Lexington Ky., U.S.A. 38°3N 84°30W **173** F11
Lexington Mich.,
  U.S.A. 43°16N 82°32W **174** C2
Lexington Mo., U.S.A. 39°11N 93°52W **172** F7
Lexington N.C.,
  U.S.A. 35°49N 80°15W **177** D14
Lexington N.Y.,
  U.S.A. 42°15N 74°22W **175** D10
Lexington Nebr., U.S.A. 40°47N 99°45W **172** E4
Lexington Ohio, U.S.A. 40°41N 82°35W **174** F2
Lexington S.C., U.S.A. 33°59N 81°11W **178** B8
Lexington Tenn.,
  U.S.A. 35°39N 88°24W **177** D10
Lexington Va., U.S.A. 37°47N 79°27W **173** G14
Lexington Park
  U.S.A. 38°16N 76°27W **173** F15
Leyburn U.K. 54°19N 1°48W **66** C6
Leye China 24°48N 106°29E **116** E6
Leyland U.K. 53°42N 2°43W **66** D5
Leyte □ Phil. 11°0N 125°0E **119** F7
Lezajsk Poland 50°16N 22°25E **83** H9
Lezay France 46°15N 0°1W **72** B3
Lezhë Albania 41°47N 19°39E **96** E3
Lezhi China 30°19N 104°58E **116** B5
Lézignan-Corbières
  France 43°13N 2°43E **72** E6
Lezoux France 45°49N 3°21E **72** C7
Lgov Russia 51°42N 35°16E **85** G8
Lhasa China 29°25N 90°58E **110** F7
Lhazê China 29°5N 87°38E **110** F6
L'Hermite, I. Chile 55°50S 68°0W **192** H3
Lhokkruet Indonesia 4°55N 95°24E **118** D1
Lhokseumawe Indonesia 5°10N 97°10E **118** C1
L'Hospitalet de Llobregat
  Spain 41°21N 2°6E **90** D7
Li Thailand 17°48N 98°57E **120** D2
Li Jiang → China 24°40N 110°40E **117** E8
Li Jiang △ China 24°38N 110°9E **117** E8
Li Shan China 35°30N 111°56E **114** G6
Li Shui → China 29°24N 112°1E **117** C9
Li Xian Gansu, China 34°10N 105°5E **114** H3
Li Xian Hebei, China 38°30N 115°35E **114** E8
Li Xian Hunan, China 29°36N 111°42E **117** C8

Lianjiang Fujian,
  China 26°12N 119°27E **117** D12
Lianjiang Guangdong,
  China 21°40N 110°0E **117** G8
Lianping China 24°26N 114°30E **117** E10
Lianshan China 24°38N 112°8E **117** E9
Lianshanguan China 40°53N 123°43E **115** D12
Lianshui China 33°42N 119°20E **115** H10
Lianyuan China 27°50N 111°40E **117** D8
Lianyungang China 34°40N 119°11E **115** G10
Lianzhou China 24°51N 112°22E **117** E9
Liao He → China 41°0N 121°50E **115** D11
Liaocheng China 36°28N 115°58E **114** F8
Liaodong Bandao
  China 40°0N 122°30E **115** E12
Liaodong Wan China 40°20N 121°10E **115** D11
Liaoning □ China 41°40N 122°30E **115** D11
Liaotung, G. of = Liaodong Wan
  China 40°20N 121°10E **115** D11
Liaoyang China 41°15N 122°58E **115** D12
Liaoyuan China 42°58N 125°2E **115** C13
Liaozhong China 41°23N 122°50E **115** D12
Liapades Greece 39°42N 19°40E **101** A3
Liard → Canada 61°51N 121°18W **162** A4
Liard River Canada 59°25N 126°5W **162** B3
Liari Pakistan 25°37N 66°30E **124** G2
Libanggaon Nepal 28°18N 82°38E **125** E10
Libau = Liepāja Latvia 56°30N 21°0E **82** B8
Libby U.S.A. 48°23N 115°33W **168** B6
Libenge
  Dem. Rep. of the Congo 3°40N 18°55E **140** D3
Liberal U.S.A. 37°3N 100°55W **172** G3
Liberdade Brazil 10°55S 70°20W **188** C3
Liberec Czechia 50°47N 15°7E **78** A8
Liberecký □ Czechia 50°45N 15°0E **78** A8
Liberia Costa Rica 10°40N 85°30W **182** D2
Liberia ■ W. Afr. 6°30N 9°30W **138** D3
Liberty □ Chile 34°15S 70°45W **190** C1
Liberty Mo., U.S.A. 39°15N 94°25W **172** F7
Liberty N.Y., U.S.A. 41°48N 74°45W **175** E10
Liberty Pa., U.S.A. 41°34N 77°6W **174** E7
Liberty Tex., U.S.A. 30°3N 94°48W **176** F7
Liberty-Newark Int. ✈ (EWR)
  U.S.A. 40°42N 74°10W **175** F10
Libiąż Poland 50°7N 19°21E **83** H6
Lībiya, Sahrâ' Africa 25°0N 25°0E **135** C10
Libo China 25°22N 107°53E **116** E6
Libobo, Tanjung
  Indonesia 0°54S 128°28E **119** E7
Libode S. Africa 31°33S 29°2E **145** D4
Libohovë Albania 40°3N 20°10E **96** F4
Libong, Ko Thailand 7°15N 99°23E **121** J2
Libourne France 44°55N 0°14W **72** D3
Libramont Belgium 49°55N 5°23E **69** E5
Librazhd Albania 41°12N 20°22E **96** E4
Libreville Gabon 0°25N 9°26E **140** D1
Libya ■ N. Afr. 27°0N 17°0E **135** C9
Libyan Desert = Lībiya, Sahrâ'
  Africa 25°0N 25°0E **135** C10
Libyan Plateau = Ed Déffa
  Egypt 30°40N 26°30E **137** A2
Licantén Chile 35°55S 72°0W **190** D1
Licata Italy 37°6N 13°56E **94** E6
Lice Turkey 38°27N 40°39E **105** C9
Licheng China 36°28N 113°20E **114** F7
Lichfield U.K. 52°41N 1°49W **67** E6
Lichinga Mozam. 13°13S 35°11E **143** E4
Lichtenburg S. Africa 26°8S 26°8E **144** C4
Lichtenfels Germany 50°8N 11°4E **77** E7
Lichuan Hubei, China 30°18N 108°57E **116** B7
Lichuan Jiangxi,
  China 27°18N 116°55E **117** D11
Licking → U.S.A. 39°6N 84°30W **173** F11
Licosa, Punta Italy 40°15N 14°54E **95** B7
Licungo → Mozam. 17°40S 37°15E **143** F4
Lida Belarus 53°53N 25°15E **75** B13
Liden Sweden 62°42N 16°48E **62** B10
Lidhult Sweden 56°50N 13°27E **63** H7
Lidköping Sweden 58°31N 13°7E **63** F7
Lido Niger 12°54N 3°44E **139** C5
Lido di Roma = Óstia, Lido di
  Italy 41°43N 12°17E **93** G9
Lidoriki Greece 38°32N 22°12E **98** C4
Lidzbark Poland 53°15N 19°49E **83** E6
Lidzbark Warmiński
  Poland 54°7N 20°34E **82** D7
Liebenwalde Germany 52°52N 13°24E **76** C9
Lieberose Germany 51°59N 14°17E **76** D10
Liebig, Mt. Australia 23°18S 131°22E **148** D5
Liebling Romania 45°36N 21°20E **80** E6
Liechtenstein ■ Europe 47°8N 9°35E **77** H5
Liège Belgium 50°38N 5°35E **69** D5
Liège □ Belgium 50°32N 5°35E **69** D5
Liegnitz = Legnica
  Poland 51°12N 16°10E **83** G3
Lieksa Finland 63°18N 30°2E **60** E24
Lienart
  Dem. Rep. of the Congo 3°3N 25°31E **142** B2
Lienyünchiangshih =
  Lianyungang
  China 34°40N 119°11E **115** G10
Lienz Austria 46°50N 12°46E **78** E5
Liepāja Latvia 56°30N 21°0E **82** B8
Liepājas ezers Latvia 56°27N 21°3E **82** B8
Lier Belgium 51°7N 4°34E **69** C4
Liernais France 47°13N 4°16E **71** E11
Lierne △ Norway 64°20N 13°50E **60** D15
Liesti Romania 45°38N 27°34E **81** E12
Lietuva = Lithuania ■
  Europe 55°30N 24°0E **84** E2
Liévin France 50°24N 2°47E **71** B9
Lièvre → Canada 45°31N 75°26W **164** C4
Liezen Austria 47°34N 14°15E **78** D7
Liffey → Ireland 53°21N 6°13W **64** C5
Lifford Ireland 54°51N 7°29W **64** B4
Liffré France 48°12N 1°30W **70** D5
Lifudzin Russia 44°21N 134°58E **112** B7
Lighthouse Point U.S.A. 26°15N 80°7W **179** J9
Lighthouse Pt. U.S.A. 29°54N 84°21W **178** F5
Lightning Ridge
  Australia 29°22S 148°0E **151** D4
Lignano Sabbiadoro
  Italy 45°42N 13°9E **93** C10
Ligny-en-Barrois France 48°36N 5°20E **71** D12
Lígonha → Mozam. 16°54S 39°9E **143** F4
Ligonier U.S.A. 40°15N 79°14W **174** F5
Ligourio Greece 37°37N 23°2E **98** D5
Liguria □ Italy 44°30N 8°50E **92** D5
Ligurian Sea Medit. S. 43°20N 9°0E **92** E6

Lihué Calel △ Argentina 38°0S 65°10W **190** D2
Lijiang China 26°55N 100°20E **116** D3
Lik → Laos 18°31N 102°30E **120** C4
Likasi
  Dem. Rep. of the Congo 10°55S 26°48E **143** E2
Likenäs Sweden 60°37N 13°3E **62** D7
Likhoslavl Russia 57°12N 35°30E **84** D8
Likhovskoy Russia 48°10N 40°10E **87** F5
Likoma I. Malawi 12°3S 34°45E **143** E3
Likumburu Tanzania 9°43S 35°8E **143** D4
L'Île-Bouchard France 47°7N 0°26E **70** E7
L'Île-Rousse France 42°38N 8°57E **73** F12
Liling China 27°42N 113°29E **117** D9
Lilla Edet Sweden 58°9N 12°8E **63** F6
Lille France 50°38N 3°3E **71** B10
Lille Bælt Denmark 55°20N 9°45E **63** J3
Lillebonne France 49°30N 0°32E **70** C7
Lillehammer Norway 61°8N 10°30E **63** D14
Lillesand Norway 58°15N 8°23E **63** G13
Lillhärdal Sweden 61°51N 14°5E **62** C8
Lillian Pt. Australia 27°40S 126°6E **149** E4
Lillo Spain 39°45N 3°20W **88** F7
Lillooet Canada 50°44N 121°57W **162** C4
Lillooet → Canada 49°15N 121°57W **162** C4
Lilongwe Malawi 14°0S 33°48E **143** E3
Liloy Phil. 8°4N 122°39E **119** C6
Lim → Europe 43°45N 19°15E **96** C3
Lim Chu Kang Singapore 1°26N 103°43E **121** d
Lima Indonesia 3°39S 127°58E **119** E7
Lima Peru 12°3S 77°2W **188** C2
Lima Mont., U.S.A. 44°38N 112°36W **168** D7
Lima N.Y., U.S.A. 42°54N 77°36W **174** D7
Lima Ohio, U.S.A. 40°44N 84°6W **173** E11
Lima → Portugal 41°41N 8°50W **88** D2
Liman Azerbaijan 38°53N 48°47E **105** C13
Liman Russia 45°45N 47°12E **87** H8
Limanowa Poland 49°42N 20°22E **83** J7
Limassol Cyprus 34°42N 33°1E **101** E12
Limavady U.K. 55°3N 6°56W **64** A5
Limay → Argentina 39°0S 68°0W **192** A3
Limay Mahuida
  Argentina 37°10S 66°45W **190** D2
Limbach-Oberfrohna
  Germany 50°52N 12°43E **76** E8
Limbang Malaysia 4°42N 115°6E **118** D5
Limbara, Mte. Italy 40°51N 9°10E **94** A2
Limbaži Latvia 57°31N 24°42E **84** D3
Limbdi India 22°34N 71°51E **124** H4
Limbe Cameroon 4°1N 9°10E **139** E6
Limburg Germany 50°22N 8°4E **77** E4
Limburg □ Belgium 51°2N 5°25E **69** C5
Limburg □ Neths. 51°20N 5°55E **69** C5
Limedsforsen Sweden 60°52N 13°25E **62** D7
Limeira Brazil 22°35S 47°28W **191** A6
Limenaria Greece 40°38N 24°32E **97** F8
Limenas = Thasos
  Greece 40°40N 24°40E **97** F8
Limenas Chersonisou
  Greece 35°18N 25°21E **99** F7
Limerick Ireland 52°40N 8°37W **64** D3
Limerick □ Ireland 52°30N 8°50W **64** D3
Limestone U.S.A. 42°2N 78°38W **174** D6
Limestone → Canada 56°31N 94°7W **163** B10
Limfjorden Denmark 56°55N 9°0E **63** H3
Limia = Lima →
  Portugal 41°41N 8°50W **88** D2
Limingen Norway 64°48N 13°35E **60** D15
Limmared Sweden 57°34N 13°20E **63** G7
Limmen ○ Australia 15°15S 135°30E **150** B2
Limmen Bight
  Australia 14°40S 135°35E **150** A2
Limmen Bight →
  Australia 15°7S 135°44E **150** B2
Limni Greece 38°43N 23°18E **98** C5
Limnos Greece 39°50N 25°5E **99** B7
Limoeiro Brazil 7°52S 35°27W **189** D3
Limoeiro do Norte Brazil 5°5S 38°0W **189** D3
Limoges Canada 45°20N 75°16W **175** A9
Limoges France 45°50N 1°15E **72** C5
Limón Costa Rica 10°0N 83°2W **182** E3
Limon U.S.A. 39°16N 103°41W **168** G12
Limone Piemonte Italy 44°12N 7°34E **92** D4
Limousin, Plateaux du
  France 45°45N 1°15E **72** C5
Limoux France 43°4N 2°12E **72** E6
Limpopo □ S. Africa 24°5S 29°0E **145** A4
Limpopo → Africa 25°5S 33°30E **145** C5
Limuru Kenya 1°2S 36°35E **140** E7
Lin Xian China 37°57N 110°58E **114** F6
Lin'an China 30°15N 119°42E **117** B12
Linares Chile 35°50S 71°40W **190** D1
Linares Mexico 24°52N 99°34W **181** C5
Linares Spain 38°10N 3°40W **89** G7
Linares □ Chile 35°50S 71°40W **190** D1
Lincang China 23°58N 100°1E **116** F3
Lincheng China 37°25N 114°30E **114** F8
Linchuan China 27°57N 116°15E **117** D11
Lincoln = Beamsville
  Canada 43°12N 79°28W **174** C5
Lincoln Argentina 34°55S 61°30W **190** C4
Lincoln N.Z. 43°38S 172°30E **155** D7
Lincoln U.K. 53°14N 0°32W **66** D7
Lincoln Calif., U.S.A. 38°54N 121°17W **170** G5
Lincoln Ill., U.S.A. 40°9N 89°22W **172** E9
Lincoln Kans., U.S.A. 39°3N 98°9W **172** F4
Lincoln Maine, U.S.A. 45°22N 68°30W **173** C19
Lincoln N.H., U.S.A. 44°3N 71°40W **175** B13
Lincoln N. Mex.,
  U.S.A. 33°30N 105°23W **169** K11
Lincoln Nebr., U.S.A. 40°49N 96°41W **172** E5
Lincoln City U.S.A. 44°57N 124°1W **168** D1
Lincoln Hav = Lincoln Sea
  Arctic 84°0N 55°0W **57** A5
Lincoln Park U.S.A. 42°15N 83°11W **174** D1
Lincoln Sea Arctic 84°0N 55°0W **57** A5
Lincolnshire □ U.K. 53°14N 0°32W **66** D7
Lincolnshire Wolds U.K. 53°26N 0°13W **66** D7
Lincolnton Ga., U.S.A. 33°48N 82°29W **178** B6
Lincolnton N.C.,
  U.S.A. 35°29N 81°16W **177** D14
Lind U.S.A. 46°58N 118°37W **168** C4
Linda U.S.A. 39°8N 121°34W **170** F5
Lindale U.S.A. 34°11N 85°11W **178** A4
Lindau Germany 47°33N 9°41E **77** H5
Lindeman I. Australia 20°27S 149°3E **150** C4

Lindeman Islands △
  Australia 20°28S 149°5E **150** b
Linden Guyana 6°0N 58°10W **186** B7
Linden Ala., U.S.A. 32°18N 87°48W **177** E11
Linden Calif., U.S.A. 38°1N 121°5W **170** G5
Linden Tex., U.S.A. 33°1N 94°22W **176** E7
Lindenhurst U.S.A. 40°41N 73°23W **175** F11
Lindenow Fjord
  Greenland 60°30N 43°25W **57** C6
Lindesberg Sweden 59°36N 15°15E **62** E9
Lindesnes Norway 57°58N 7°3E **61** H12
Lindi Tanzania 9°58S 39°38E **143** D4
Lindi □ Tanzania 9°40S 38°30E **143** D4
Lindi →
  Dem. Rep. of the Congo 0°33N 25°5E **142** B2
Lindley S. Africa 42°1N 77°8W **174** D7
Lindô Sweden 58°37N 16°15E **63** F10
Lindome Sweden 57°35N 12°5E **63** G6
Lindos Greece 36°6N 28°4E **101** C10
Lindos, Akra Greece 36°4N 28°10E **101** C10
Lindoso Portugal 41°52N 8°11W **88** D2
Lindsay Canada 44°22N 78°43W **174** B6
Lindsay Calif., U.S.A. 36°12N 119°5W **170** J7
Lindsay Okla., U.S.A. 34°50N 97°38W **176** D6
Lindsborg U.S.A. 38°35N 97°40W **172** F5
Lindsdal Sweden 56°46N 16°18E **63** H10
Line Islands Pac. Oc. 7°0N 160°0W **157** H12
Linesville U.S.A. 41°39N 80°26W **174** E4
Lineville U.S.A. 33°19N 85°45W **178** B4
Linfen China 36°3N 111°30E **114** F6
Ling Xian Hunan,
  China 26°29N 113°48E **117** D9
Ling Xian Shandong,
  China 37°22N 116°30E **114** F9
Lingal India 16°17N 78°31E **127** F4
Linganamakki Res.
  India 14°6N 74°52E **127** G2
Lingao China 19°56N 109°42E **117** a
Lingayen Phil. 16°1N 120°14E **119** A6
Lingayen G. Phil. 16°10N 120°15E **119** A6
Lingbao China 34°31N 110°51E **114** G6
Lingbi China 33°33N 117°33E **115** H9
Lingbo Sweden 61°3N 16°41E **62** C10
Lingchuan Guangxi Zhuangzu,
  China 25°26N 110°21E **117** E8
Lingchuan Shanxi,
  China 35°45N 113°12E **114** G7
Lingding Yang China 22°25N 113°44E **111** a
Lingen Germany 52°31N 7°19E **76** C3
Lingga Indonesia 0°12S 104°37E **118** E2
Lingga, Kepulauan
  Indonesia 0°10S 104°30E **118** E2
Lingga Arch. = Lingga,
  Kepulauan Indonesia 0°10S 104°30E **118** E2
Linghai China 41°11N 121°22E **115** D11
Linghed Sweden 60°48N 15°55E **62** D9
Linghem Sweden 58°26N 15°47E **63** F9
Lingle U.S.A. 42°8N 104°21W **168** E11
Lingqiu China 39°28N 114°22E **114** E8
Lingshi China 36°48N 111°48E **114** F6
Lingshou China 38°20N 114°20E **114** E8
Lingshui China 18°27N 110°0E **117** a
Lingsugur India 16°10N 76°31E **127** F3
Lingtai China 35°0N 107°40E **114** G4
Linguère Senegal 15°25N 15°5W **138** B1
Lingui China 25°12N 110°2E **117** E8
Lingwu China 38°6N 106°20E **114** E4
Lingyuan China 41°10N 119°15E **115** D10
Lingyun China 25°2N 106°35E **116** E6
Linhai China 28°50N 121°8E **117** C13
Linhares Brazil 19°25S 40°4W **189** D2
Linhe China 40°48N 107°20E **114** D4
Linjiang China 41°50N 127°0E **115** D14
Linköping Sweden 58°28N 15°36E **63** F9
Linkou China 45°15N 130°18E **115** B16
Linli China 29°27N 111°30E **117** C8
Linnansaari △ Finland 62°3N 28°40E **60** E23
Linnhe, L. U.K. 56°36N 5°25W **65** E3
Linqi China 35°45N 113°52E **114** G7
Linqing China 36°50N 115°42E **114** F8
Linqu China 36°25N 118°30E **115** F10
Linquan China 33°5N 115°17E **114** H8
Lins Brazil 21°40S 49°44W **191** A6
Linshu China 34°53N 118°38E **115** G10
Linshui China 30°21N 106°57E **116** B6
Linstead Jamaica 18°8N 77°2W **182** a
Lintao China 35°26N 103°58E **114** G2
Linth → Switz. 47°7N 9°7E **77** H5
Linthal Switz. 46°54N 9°0E **77** H5
Linton Ind., U.S.A. 39°2N 87°10W **172** F4
Linton N. Dak., U.S.A. 46°16N 100°14W **172** B4
Lintong China 34°20N 109°10E **114** G5
Linwood Canada 43°35N 80°43W **174** C4
Linwu China 25°19N 112°31E **117** E9
Linxi Hebei, China 39°42N 118°26E **115** E10
Linxi Liaoning, China 43°36N 118°2E **115** C10
Linxia China 35°36N 103°10E **110** D9
Linxiang China 29°28N 113°23E **117** C9
Linyanti → Africa 17°50S 25°5E **144** A4
Linyi Shandong, China 37°13N 116°54E **114** F9
Linyi Shandong, China 35°5N 118°21E **115** G10
Linying China 33°48N 113°56E **114** H7
Linz Austria 48°18N 14°18E **78** D7
Linz Germany 50°34N 7°17E **76** E3
Linzhenzhen China 36°30N 109°59E **114** F5
Linzhou China 36°4N 113°49E **114** F7
Linzi China 36°50N 118°20E **115** F10
Lion, G. du France 43°10N 4°0E **72** E7
Lioni Italy 40°52N 15°11E **95** B8
Lions, G. of = Lion, G. du
  France 43°10N 4°0E **72** E7
Lion's Den Zimbabwe 17°15S 30°5E **145** A5
Lion's Head Canada 44°58N 81°15W **174** B3
Liozno = Lyozna Belarus 55°0N 30°50E **84** E6
Lipa Phil. 13°57N 121°10E **119** E4
Lipali Mozam. 15°50S 35°50E **143** F4
Lipany Slovakia 49°9N 20°58E **79** B13
Lípari Italy 38°26N 14°58E **95** D7
Lípari, I. Italy 38°26N 14°58E **95** D7
Lípari, Is. = Eólie, Ís.
  Italy 38°30N 14°57E **95** D7
Lipcani Moldova 48°14N 26°48E **81** A11
Liperi Finland 62°31N 29°24E **60** E23
Lipetsk Russia 52°37N 39°35E **87** F10
Lipetsk □ Russia 52°50N 38°50E **86** D4
Lipiany Poland 53°2N 14°58E **83** E3
Liping China 26°15N 109°7E **116** D7
Lipisi Greece 37°19N 26°50E **99** D8
Lipjan Kosovo 42°31N 21°7E **96** D5

Lipkany = Lipcani
  Moldova 48°14N 26°48E **81** A11
Lipník nad Bečvou
  Czechia 49°32N 17°36E **79** B10
Lipno Poland 52°49N 19°15E **83** F6
Lipova Romania 46°8N 21°42E **80** D6
Lipovets Ukraine 49°12N 29°1E **75** D15
Lippe → Germany 51°39N 6°36E **76** D2
Lippstadt Germany 51°41N 8°22E **76** D4
Lipscomb U.S.A. 36°14N 100°16W **176** C4
Lipsk Poland 53°44N 23°24E **82** E10
Lipsko Poland 51°9N 21°40E **83** G8
Liptovský Hrádok
  Slovakia 49°2N 19°44E **79** B12
Liptovský Mikuláš
  Slovakia 49°6N 19°35E **79** B12
Liptrap, C. Australia 38°50S 145°55E **153** E6
Lipu China 24°30N 110°22E **117** E8
Lira Uganda 2°17N 32°57E **142** B3
Liri → Italy 41°25N 13°52E **94** A6
Liria = Llíria Spain 39°37N 0°35W **91** F4
Lisakovsk Kazakhstan 52°33N 62°37E **108** B6
Lisala
  Dem. Rep. of the Congo 2°12N 21°38E **140** D4
Lisboa Portugal 38°42N 9°8W **89** C1
Lisboa □ Portugal 39°0N 9°12W **89** C1
Lisboa ✈ (LIS) Portugal 38°46N 9°8W **89** C1
Lisbon = Lisboa Portugal 38°42N 9°8W **89** C1
Lisbon N. Dak., U.S.A. 46°27N 97°41W **172** B5
Lisbon N.H., U.S.A. 44°13N 71°55W **175** B13
Lisbon N.Y., U.S.A. 44°43N 75°19W **175** B9
Lisbon Ohio, U.S.A. 40°46N 80°46W **174** F4
Lisbon Falls U.S.A. 44°0N 70°4W **173** D18
Lisburn U.K. 54°31N 6°3W **64** B5
Lisburne, C. U.S.A. 68°53N 166°13W **166** B6
Liscannor B. Ireland 52°55N 9°24W **64** D2
Liscia → Italy 41°11N 9°9E **94** A2
Lisdoonvarna Ireland 53°2N 9°18W **64** C2
Lishe Jiang → China 24°15N 101°35E **116** E3
Lishi China 37°31N 111°8E **114** F6
Lishui Jiangsu, China 31°38N 119°2E **117** B12
Lishui Zhejiang, China 28°28N 119°54E **117** C12
Lisianski I. U.S.A. 26°2N 174°0W **167** K5
Lisichansk = Lysychansk
  Ukraine 48°55N 38°30E **85** H10
Lisieux France 49°10N 0°12E **70** C7
Liski Russia 51°3N 39°30E **85** G10
L'Isle-Jourdain Gers, France 43°36N 1°5E **72** E5
L'Isle-Jourdain Vienne,
  France 46°13N 0°31E **72** B4
L'Isle-sur-la-Sorgue France 43°54N 5°2E **73** E9
Lisle-sur-Tarn France 43°52N 1°49E **72** E5
Lismore Australia 28°44S 153°21E **151** D5
Lismore Ireland 52°8N 7°55W **64** D4
Lissos → Greece 41°15N 25°40E **97** E9
Lista Norway 58°7N 6°39E **61** G12
Lister, Mt. Antarctica 78°0S 162°0E **55** D11
Liston Australia 28°39S 152°6E **151** D5
Listowel Canada 43°44N 80°58W **174** C4
Listowel Ireland 52°27N 9°29W **64** D2
Lit Sweden 63°19N 14°51E **62** A8
Lit-et-Mixe France 44°2N 1°15W **72** D2
Litang Guangxi Zhuangzu,
  China 23°12N 109°8E **116** F7
Litang Sichuan, China 30°1N 100°17E **116** B3
Litang Qu → China 28°4N 101°32E **116** C3
Litani → Lebanon 33°20N 35°15E **130** B4
Litani → Lebanon 33°20N 35°15E **130** B4
Litchfield Australia 36°18S 142°52E **152** D5
Litchfield Calif., U.S.A. 40°24N 120°23W **170** E6
Litchfield Conn.,
  U.S.A. 41°45N 73°11W **175** E11
Litchfield Ill., U.S.A. 39°11N 89°39W **172** F9
Litchfield Minn., U.S.A. 45°8N 94°32W **172** C6
Litchfield △ Australia 13°14S 131°1E **148** B5
Liteni Romania 47°32N 26°32E **81** C11
Lithgow Australia 33°25S 150°8E **153** B9
Líthinos, Ákra Greece 34°55N 24°44E **101** E6
Lithuania ■ Europe 55°30N 24°0E **84** E2
Litija Slovenia 46°3N 14°50E **93** B11
Lititz U.S.A. 40°9N 76°18W **175** F8
Litochoro Greece 40°8N 22°34E **96** F6
Litoměřice Czechia 50°33N 14°10E **78** A7
Litomyšl Czechia 49°52N 16°20E **79** B9
Litschau Austria 48°58N 15°4E **78** C8
Little Abaco Bahamas 26°50N 77°30W **182** A4
Little Andaman I.
  India 10°45N 92°30E **127** J11
Little Aral Sea = Northern Aral
  Sea Kazakhstan 46°0N 61°0E **108** C6
Little Barrier I. N.Z. 36°12S 175°8E **154** C4
Little Basses Sri Lanka 6°24N 81°43E **127** L5
Little Belt Mts. U.S.A. 46°40N 110°45W **168** C8
Little Bighorn Battlefield △
  U.S.A. 45°34N 107°25W **168** D10
Little Blue → U.S.A. 39°42N 96°41W **172** F5
Little Buffalo →
  Canada 61°0N 113°46W **162** A6
Little Cayman
  Cayman Is. 19°41N 80°3W **182** C3
Little Churchill →
  Canada 57°30N 95°22W **163** B9
Little Coco I. Myanmar 14°0N 93°13E **127** H11
Little Colorado →
  U.S.A. 36°12N 111°48W **169** H8
Little Current Canada 45°55N 82°0W **164** D3
Little Current →
  Canada 50°57N 84°36W **164** B3
Little Desert △
  Australia 37°25S 141°30E **152** D4
Little Diomede I.
  U.S.A. 65°45N 168°56W **166** B6
Little Falls Minn.,
  U.S.A. 45°59N 94°22W **172** C6
Little Falls N.Y., U.S.A. 43°3N 74°51W **175** C10
Little Fork → U.S.A. 48°31N 93°35W **172** A7
Little Grand Rapids
  Canada 52°0N 95°29W **163** C9
Little Humboldt →
  U.S.A. 41°1N 117°43W **168** F5
Little Inagua I.
  Bahamas 21°40N 73°50W **183** B5
Little Karoo S. Africa 33°45S 21°0E **144** D3
Little Khingan Mts. = Xiao
  Hinggan Ling China 49°0N 127°0E **111** B14
Little Lake U.S.A. 35°56N 117°55W **171** K9
Little Laut Is. = Laut Kecil,
  Kepulauan Indonesia 4°45S 115°40E **118** E5
Little Mecatina = Petit-
  Mécatina → Canada 50°40N 59°30W **165** B8
Little Minch U.K. 57°35N 6°45W **65** D2

Little Missouri →
  U.S.A. 47°36N 102°25W **172** B2
Little Nicobar India 7°20N 93°40E **127** L11
Little Ouse → U.K. 52°22N 1°12E **67** E9
Little Rann India 23°25N 71°25E **124** H4
Little Red → U.S.A. 35°11N 91°27W **176** D9
Little River N.Z. 43°45S 172°49E **155** D15
Little Rock U.S.A. 34°45N 92°17W **176** D8
Little Ruaha → Tanzania 7°57S 37°53E **142** D4
Little Sable Pt. U.S.A. 43°38N 86°33W **172** D10
Little Scarcies →
  S. Leone 8°50N 13°10W **138** D2
Little Sioux → U.S.A. 41°48N 96°4W **172** E5
Little Smoky →
  Canada 54°44N 117°11W **162** C5
Little Snake →
  U.S.A. 40°27N 108°26W **168** F9
Little Tobago
  Trin. & Tob. 11°18N 60°30W **187** J16
Little Valley U.S.A. 42°15N 78°48W **174** D6
Little Wabash →
  U.S.A. 37°55N 88°5W **172** G9
Little White →
  U.S.A. 43°40N 100°40W **172** D3
Little Zab = Zāb aş Şaghīr →
  Iraq 35°17N 43°29E **105** E10
Littlefield U.S.A. 33°55N 102°20W **176** D3
Littlehampton U.K. 50°49N 0°32W **67** G7
Littleton U.S.A. 44°18N 71°46W **175** B13
Littoral □ Cameroon 4°0N 10°0E **139** E7
Litvínov Czechia 50°36N 13°37E **78** A6
Liu He → China 40°55N 121°35E **115** D11
Liu Jiang → China 23°55N 109°30E **116** F7
Liuba China 33°38N 106°55E **116** A6
Liucheng China 24°38N 109°14E **116** E7
Liugou China 40°57N 118°15E **115** D10
Liuhe China 42°17N 125°43E **115** C13
Liuheng Dao China 29°40N 122°5E **117** C14
Liujiang China 24°20N 120°18E **115** H11
Liukang Tenggaja = Sabalana,
  Kepulauan Indonesia 6°45S 118°50E **119** F5
Liuli Tanzania 11°3S 34°38E **143** E3
Liupan Shan China 35°39N 106°12E **114** G4
Liupanshui China 26°38N 104°48E **116** D5
Liuwa Plain Zambia 14°20S 22°30E **145** A4
Liuyang China 28°10N 113°37E **117** C9
Liuzhou China 24°22N 109°22E **116** E7
Liuzhuang China 33°12N 120°18E **115** H11
Livada Romania 47°52N 23°5E **80** C8
Livadero Greece 40°2N 21°57E **96** F5
Livadhia Cyprus 34°57N 33°38E **101** E12
Livadi Greece 40°8N 22°9E **98** A4
Livadia Greece 38°27N 22°54E **98** C4
Livarot France 48°58N 0°9E **70** D7
Live Oak Calif., U.S.A. 39°17N 121°40W **170** F5
Live Oak Fla., U.S.A. 30°18N 82°59W **178** F6
Lively Canada 46°26N 81°9W **173** B3
Livermore U.S.A. 37°41N 121°47W **170** H5
Livermore, Mt. U.S.A. 30°38N 104°11W **176** F2
Livermore Falls
  U.S.A. 44°29N 70°11W **173** C18
Liverpool Australia 33°54S 150°58E **153** B9
Liverpool Canada 44°5N 64°41W **165** D7
Liverpool U.K. 53°25N 3°0W **66** D4
Liverpool U.S.A. 43°6N 76°13W **175** C8
Liverpool Bay U.K. 53°30N 3°20W **66** D4
Liverpool Plains
  Australia 31°15S 150°15E **153** A9
Liverpool Ra. Australia 31°50S 150°30E **153** A9
Livigno Italy 46°35N 10°10E **92** B7
Livingston Guatemala 15°50N 88°50W **182** C2
Livingston U.K. 55°54N 3°30W **65** F5
Livingston Ala.,
  U.S.A. 32°35N 88°11W **177** E10
Livingston Calif.,
  U.S.A. 37°23N 120°43W **170** H6
Livingston Mont.,
  U.S.A. 45°40N 110°34W **168** D8
Livingston S.C., U.S.A. 33°38N 81°7W **178** D8
Livingston Tenn.,
  U.S.A. 36°23N 85°19W **177** C12
Livingston Tex., U.S.A. 30°43N 94°56W **176** F7
Livingston, L. U.S.A. 30°50N 95°10W **176** F7
Livingston Manor
  U.S.A. 41°54N 74°50W **175** E10
Livingstone Zambia 17°46S 25°52E **143** F2
Livingstone △
  Australia 35°22S 147°22E **153** C7
Livingstone Mts. N.Z. 45°15S 168°9E **155** F3
Livingstone Mts.
  Tanzania 9°40S 34°20E **143** D3
Livingstonia Malawi 10°38S 34°5E **143** E3
Livny Russia 52°30N 37°30E **85** F9
Livonia Mich., U.S.A. 42°23N 83°23W **173** D12
Livonia N.Y., U.S.A. 42°49N 77°40W **174** D7
Livorno Italy 43°33N 10°19E **92** E7
Livradois-Forez △ France 44°0N 3°0E **72** E7
Livramento Brazil 30°55S 55°30W **191** C4
Livramento do Brumado
  Brazil 13°39S 41°50W **189** C2
Livron-sur-Drôme France 44°46N 4°51E **73** D8
Liwonde Malawi 15°4S 35°13E **143** F4
Liwonde △ Malawi 14°48S 35°20E **143** E4
Lixi China 26°23N 101°59E **116** D3
Lixian China 31°23N 103°13E **116** B4
Lixin China 33°8N 116°13E **114** H9
Lixouri Greece 38°12N 20°26E **98** C2
Liyang China 31°26N 119°28E **117** B12
Lizard I. Australia 14°42S 145°30E **150** A4
Lizard Pt. U.K. 49°57N 5°13W **67** H2
Lizarda Brazil 9°36S 46°41W **189** B1
Lizarra = Estella Spain 42°40N 2°2W **90** C2
Lizzano Italy 40°23N 17°27E **95** B10
Ljig Serbia 44°13N 20°18E **96** B4
Ljubija Bos.-H. 44°55N 16°35E **93** D13
Ljubinje Bos.-H. 42°58N 18°5E **96** C2
Ljubišnja Europe 43°18N 18°16E **96** C2
Ljubljana Slovenia 46°4N 14°33E **93** B11
Ljubljana ✈ (LJU)
  Slovenia 46°14N 14°28E **93** B11
Ljubno Slovenia 46°25N 14°46E **78** E7
Ljubovija Serbia 44°11N 19°22E **96** B3
Ljugarn Sweden 57°20N 18°43E **63** G12
Ljung Sweden 57°59N 13°6E **63** F7
Ljungan → Sweden 62°18N 17°23E **62** B11
Ljungaverk Sweden 62°30N 16°5E **62** B10

Ljungby Sweden 56°49N 13°55E **63** H8
Ljungbyholm Sweden 56°39N 16°5E **63** H10
Ljungdalen Sweden 62°51N 12°47E **62** B6
Ljungsbro Sweden 58°31N 15°30E **63** F9
Ljungskile Sweden 58°14N 11°55E **63** F5
Ljusdal Sweden 61°46N 16°3E **62** C10
Ljusfallshammar Sweden 58°48N 15°30E **63** F9
Ljusnan → Sweden 61°12N 17°8E **62** C11
Ljusne Sweden 61°13N 17°7E **62** C11
Ljusterö Sweden 59°31N 18°37E **62** E12
Ljutomer Slovenia 46°31N 16°11E **93** B13
Llagostera Spain 41°50N 2°54E **90** D7
Llancanelo, Salina
  Argentina 35°40S 69°8W **190** D2
Llandeilo U.K. 51°53N 3°59W **67** F4
Llandovery U.K. 51°59N 3°48W **67** F4
Llandrindod Wells U.K. 52°14N 3°22W **67** E4
Llandudno U.K. 53°19N 3°50W **66** D4
Llanelli U.K. 51°41N 4°10W **67** F3
Llanes Spain 43°25N 4°50W **88** B6
Llanfair-ym-Muallt = Builth Wells
  U.K. 52°9N 3°25W **67** E4
Llangollen U.K. 52°58N 3°11W **66** E4
Llanidloes U.K. 52°27N 3°31W **67** E4
Llano U.S.A. 30°45N 98°41W **176** F5
Llano → U.S.A. 30°39N 98°26W **176** F5
Llano Estacado U.S.A. 33°30N 103°0W **176** E3
Llanos S. Amer. 5°0N 71°35W **186** C4
Llanos de Challe △ Chile 28°8S 71°1W **190** B1
Llanquihue, L. Chile 41°10S 72°50W **192** B1
Llanwrtyd Wells U.K. 52°7N 3°38W **67** E4
Llata Peru 9°25S 76°47W **188** B2
Llebeig, C. des Spain 39°33N 2°18E **100** B9
Lleida Spain 41°37N 0°39E **90** D5
Lleida □ Spain 42°6N 1°0E **90** C6
Llentrisca, C. Spain 38°52N 1°15E **100** C7
Llera de Canales Mexico 23°19N 99°1W **181** C5
Llerena Spain 38°17N 6°0W **89** C5
Lleyn Peninsula U.K. 52°51N 4°36W **66** E3
Llica Bolivia 19°52S 68°16W **188** D4
Llico Chile 34°46S 72°5W **190** C1
Lliria Spain 39°37N 0°35W **91** F4
Llívia Spain 42°28N 1°59E **72** F5
Llobregat → Spain 41°19N 2°5E **90** D7
Llodio Spain 43°9N 2°58W **90** B2
Llogara △ Albania 40°13N 19°35E **96** F3
Lloret de Mar Spain 41°41N 2°53E **90** D7
Lloseta Spain 39°43N 2°52E **100** B9
Lloyd B. Australia 12°45S 143°27E **150** A3
Lloyd L. Canada 57°22N 108°57W **163** B7
Lloydminster Canada 53°17N 110°0W **163** C7
Llubí Spain 39°42N 3°0E **100** B10
Lluchmayor = Llucmajor
  Spain 39°29N 2°53E **100** B9
Llucena del Cid Spain 40°9N 0°17W **90** E4
Llucmajor Spain 39°29N 2°53E **100** B9
Llullaillaco, Volcán
  S. Amer. 24°43S 68°30W **190** A2
Llullaillaco △ Chile 24°50S 68°51W **190** A2
Lo → Vietnam 21°18N 105°25E **120** B5
Loa U.S.A. 38°24N 111°39W **168** G8
Loa → Chile 21°26S 70°41W **190** A1
Loaita I. S. China Sea 10°41N 114°25E **118** B4
Loange →
  Dem. Rep. of the Congo 4°17S 20°2E **140** E4
Loano Italy 44°8N 8°15E **92** D5
Lobamba Swaziland 26°28S 31°12E **145** C5
Lobatse Botswana 25°12S 25°40E **144** C4
Löbau Germany 51°5N 14°40E **76** D10
Lobenstein Germany 50°25N 11°39E **76** E7
Lobería Argentina 38°10S 58°40W **190** D4
Löberöd Sweden 55°47N 13°31E **63** J7
Łobez Poland 53°38N 15°39E **82** E2
Lobito Angola 12°18S 13°35E **141** G2
Lobo → Côte d'Ivoire 6°2N 6°45W **138** D3
Loboc Phil. 9°35S 123°50E **118** D5
Lobos, I. Mexico 27°20N 110°36W **180** B2
Lobos, I. de Canary Is. 28°45N 13°50W **100** F6
Lobos de Afuera, Islas
  Peru 6°57S 80°42W **188** B1
Lobos de Tierra, I. Peru 6°27S 80°52W **188** B1
Łobżenica Poland 53°18N 17°15E **83** E4
Loc Binh Vietnam 21°46N 106°54E **120** B6
Loc Ninh Vietnam 11°50N 106°34E **121** G6
Locarno Switz. 46°10N 8°47E **77** J4
Loch Garman = Wexford
  Ireland 52°20N 6°28W **64** D5
Loch Lomond and the
  Trossachs △ U.K. 56°10N 4°40W **65** E4
Lochaber U.K. 56°59N 5°1W **65** E3
Locharbriggs U.K. 55°7N 3°35W **65** F5
Lochboisdale U.K. 57°9N 7°20W **65** D1
Loche, L. La Canada 56°30N 109°30W **163** B7
Lochem Neths. 52°9N 6°26E **69** B6
Loches France 47°7N 1°0E **70** E7
Lochgelly U.K. 56°7N 3°19W **65** E5
Lochgilphead U.K. 56°2N 5°26W **65** E3
Lochinvar △ Zambia 15°55S 27°15E **143** F2
Lochinver U.K. 58°9N 5°14W **65** C3
Lochloosa L. U.S.A. 29°30N 82°7W **179** F7
Lochmaddy U.K. 57°36N 7°10W **65** D1
Lochnagar Australia 23°33S 145°38E **150** C4
Lochnagar U.K. 56°57N 3°15W **65** E5
Łochów Poland 52°33N 21°42E **83** F8
Lochy, L. U.K. 57°0N 4°53W **65** E4
Lock Australia 33°34S 135°46E **151** E2
Lock Haven U.S.A. 41°8N 77°28W **174** E7
Lockeford U.S.A. 38°10N 121°9W **170** G5
Lockeport Canada 43°47N 65°4W **165** D6
Lockerbie U.K. 55°7N 3°21W **65** F5
Lockhart Australia 35°14S 146°40E **153** C7
Lockhart U.S.A. 29°53N 97°40W **176** G6
Lockhart, L. Australia 33°15S 119°3E **149** F2
Lockhart River
  Australia 12°58S 143°30E **150** A3
Lockhart River ◎
  Australia 12°47S 143°20E **150** A3
Lockney U.S.A. 34°7N 101°27W **176** D4
Lockport U.S.A. 43°10N 78°42W **174** C6
Locminé France 47°54N 2°51W **70** E4
Locri Italy 38°14N 16°16E **95** D9
Locronan France 48°7N 4°15W **70** D2
Locust Grove U.S.A. 36°12N 95°10W **176** C6
Lod Israel 31°57N 34°54E **130** D3
Lodeinoye Pole Russia 60°44N 33°33E **84** B8
Lodève France 43°44N 3°19E **72** E7
Lodge Bay Canada 52°14N 55°51W **165** B8
Lodge Grass U.S.A. 45°19N 107°22W **168** D10
Lodhran Pakistan 29°32N 71°30E **124** E4
Lodi Italy 45°19N 9°30E **92** C6
Lodi Calif., U.S.A. 38°8N 121°16W **170** G5
Lodi Ohio, U.S.A. 41°2N 82°1W **174** E3

Lodja
  Dem. Rep. of the Congo 3°30S 23°23E **142** C1
Lodosa Spain 42°25N 2°4W **90** C2
Lödöse Sweden 58°2N 12°9E **63** F6
Lodwar Kenya 3°7N 35°36E **142** B4
Łódź Poland 51°45N 19°27E **83** G6
Łódzkie □ Poland 51°30N 19°30E **83** G6
Loei Thailand 17°29N 101°35E **120** D3
Loengo
  Dem. Rep. of the Congo 4°48S 26°30E **142** C2
Loeriesfontein S. Africa 31°0S 19°26E **144** D2
Lofa → Liberia 6°35N 11°8W **138** D2
Lofa Mano △ Liberia 7°30S 37°55E **138** D2
Lofer Austria 47°35N 12°41E **78** E5
Lofoten Norway 68°30N 13°59E **60** B16
Lofsdalen Sweden 62°10N 13°27E **62** B7
Lofsen → Sweden 62°7N 13°57E **62** B7
Loftahammar Sweden 57°54N 16°41E **63** G10
Loga Niger 13°40N 3°15E **139** C5
Logan Iowa, U.S.A. 41°39N 95°47W **172** E6
Logan Ohio, U.S.A. 39°32N 82°25W **173** F12
Logan Utah, U.S.A. 41°44N 111°50W **168** F8
Logan W. Va., U.S.A. 37°51N 81°59W **173** G13
Logan, Mt. Canada 60°34N 140°23W **160** E3
Logan Martin L.
  U.S.A. 33°26N 86°20W **178** B3
Logandale U.S.A. 36°36N 114°29W **171** J12
Logansport Ind.,
  U.S.A. 40°45N 86°22W **172** E10
Logansport La., U.S.A. 31°58N 94°0W **176** F8
Loganville U.S.A. 33°50N 83°54W **178** B6
Logodoro Italy 40°35N 8°45E **94** B1
Logone → Chad 12°6N 15°2E **139** F9
Logroño Spain 42°28N 2°27W **90** C2
Logrosán Spain 39°20N 5°32W **89** F5
Løgstør Denmark 56°58N 9°14E **63** H3
Løgumkloster Denmark 55°4N 8°57E **63** J2
Lohals Denmark 55°8N 10°54E **63** J4
Lohardaga India 23°27N 84°45E **125** H11
Loharia India 23°45N 74°14E **124** H6
Loharu India 28°27N 75°49E **124** E6
Lohja Finland 60°12N 24°5E **64** B3
Lohne Germany 52°11N 8°40E **76** C4
Lohri Wah → Pakistan 27°27N 67°37E **124** F2
Loikaw Myanmar 19°40N 97°17E **123** K20
Loimaa Finland 60°50N 23°5E **64** B2
Loir → France 47°33N 0°32W **70** E6
Loir-et-Cher □ France 47°40N 1°20E **70** E8
Loire → France 47°16N 2°10W **70** E4
Loire □ France 45°40N 4°5E **73** C8
Loire-Anjou-Touraine △
  France 47°14N 0°5W **70** E6
Loire-Atlantique □
  France 47°25N 1°40W **70** E5
Loiret □ France 47°58N 2°10E **70** E9
Loitz Germany 53°58N 13°8E **76** B9
Loja Ecuador 3°59S 79°16W **188** A2
Loja Spain 37°10N 4°10W **89** H6
Loji = Kawasi Indonesia 1°38S 127°28E **119** E7
Lojo = Lohja Finland 60°12N 24°5E **64** B3
Løjt Kirkeby Denmark 55°7N 9°26E **63** J3
Lojung China 24°27N 109°36E **116** E7
Lokandu
  Dem. Rep. of the Congo 2°30S 25°45E **142** C2
Lokeren Belgium 51°6N 3°59E **69** C3
Lokgwabe Botswana 24°10S 21°50E **144** B3
Lokhvytsya Ukraine 50°25N 33°18E **85** G7
Lokichar Kenya 2°23N 35°39E **142** B4
Lokichokio Kenya 4°19N 34°13E **142** B3
Lokitaung Kenya 4°12N 35°48E **142** B4
Lokkan tekojärvi
  Finland 67°55N 27°35E **60** C22
Løkken Denmark 57°22N 9°41E **63** G3
Lokoja Nigeria 56°49N 30°4E **84** D6
Loknya Russia 56°49N 30°4E **84** D6
Loko Nigeria 8°35N 7°0E **139** D6
Lokoja Nigeria 7°47N 6°45E **139** D6
Lokolo →
  Dem. Rep. of the Congo 1°43S 18°23E **140** E3
Lokot Russia 52°34N 34°36E **85** F8
Lola Guinea 7°52N 8°29W **138** D3
Lola, Mt. U.S.A. 39°26N 120°22W **170** F6
Lolgorien Kenya 1°14S 34°48E **142** C3
Loliondo Tanzania 2°2S 35°39E **142** C4
Lolland Denmark 54°45N 11°30E **63** K5
Lollar Germany 50°37N 8°43E **76** E4
Lolo U.S.A. 46°45N 114°5W **168** C6
Lolodorf Cameroon 3°16N 10°49E **139** E7
Lom Bulgaria 43°48N 23°12E **96** C7
Lom → Bulgaria 43°45N 23°15E **96** C7
Lom Kao Thailand 16°53N 101°14E **120** D3
Lom Sak Thailand 16°47N 101°15E **120** D3
Loma U.S.A. 47°56N 110°30W **168** C8
Loma Mansa S. Leone 9°13N 11°7W **138** D2
Lomas S. Leone 9°13N 11°7W **138** D2
Lomaloma Fiji 17°17S 178°59W **154** a
Lomami →
  Dem. Rep. of the Congo 0°46N 24°16E **142** B1
Lomas de Zamora
  Argentina 34°45S 58°24W **190** C4
Lombadina Australia 16°31S 122°54E **148** C3
Lombárdia □ Italy 45°40N 9°30E **92** C6
Lombardy = Lombárdia □
  Italy 45°40N 9°30E **92** C6
Lombez France 43°29N 0°55E **72** E4
Lomblen Indonesia 8°30S 123°32E **119** F6
Lombok Indonesia 8°30S 116°30E **118** F5
Lombok, Selat
  Indonesia 8°30S 115°50E **119** K18
Lomé Togo 6°9N 1°20E **139** D5
Lomela
  Dem. Rep. of the Congo 2°19S 23°15E **140** E4
Lomela →
  Dem. Rep. of the Congo 0°15S 20°40E **140** E4
Lomma Sweden 55°43N 13°5E **63** J6
Lommel Belgium 51°14N 5°19E **69** C5
Lomond Canada 50°24N 112°36W **162** C6
Lomond, L. U.K. 56°8N 4°38W **65** E4
Lomonosov Ridge Arctic 88°0N 140°0E **54** A
Lomphat Cambodia 13°30N 106°59E **120** F6
Lompobatang Indonesia 5°24S 119°56E **119** F5
Lompoc U.S.A. 34°38N 120°28W **171** L6
Łomża Poland 53°10N 22°2E **83** E9
Lon, Ko Thailand 7°47N 98°23E **121** a
Lonaula India 18°46N 73°29E **126** D1
Loncoche Chile 39°20S 72°50W **192** A2
Loncopué Argentina 38°4S 70°37W **192** A2
Londa India 15°30N 74°30E **127** G2
Londiani Kenya 0°10S 35°33E **142** C4

Londinières France 49°50N 1°25E **70** C8
London Canada 42°59N 81°15W **174** D3
London U.K. 51°30N 0°3W **67** F7
London Ky., U.S.A. 37°8N 84°5W **173** G11
London Ohio, U.S.A. 39°53N 83°27W **173** F12
London, Greater □ U.K. 51°36N 0°5W **67** F8
London Gateway U.K. 51°31N 0°29E **67** F8
London Gatwick ✈ (LGW)
  U.K. 51°10N 0°11W **67** F7
London Heathrow ✈ (LHR)
  U.K. 51°28N 0°27W **67** F7
London Stansted ✈ (STN)
  U.K. 51°54N 0°14E **67** F8
Londonderry U.K. 55°0N 7°20W **64** B4
Londonderry □ U.K. 55°0N 7°20W **64** B4
Londonderry, C.
  Australia 13°45S 126°55E **148** B4
Londonderry, I. Chile 55°0S 71°0W **192** E2
Londres Argentina 27°43S 67°7W **190** B2
Londrina Brazil 23°18S 51°10W **191** A5
Lone Pine U.S.A. 36°36N 118°4W **170** J8
Lonely Mine Zimbabwe 19°30S 28°49E **145** A4
Long B. U.S.A. 33°35N 78°45W **177** E15
Long Beach Calif.,
  U.S.A. 33°46N 118°11W **171** M8
Long Beach N.Y.,
  U.S.A. 40°35N 73°39W **175** F11
Long Beach Wash.,
  U.S.A. 46°21N 124°3W **170** D2
Long Branch U.S.A. 40°18N 74°0W **175** F11
Long Creek U.S.A. 44°43N 119°6W **168** D4
Long Eaton U.K. 52°53N 1°15W **66** E6
Long I. Australia 20°22S 148°51E **150** b
Long I. Bahamas 23°20N 75°10W **183** B4
Long I. Canada 54°50N 79°20W **164** B4
Long I. Ireland 51°30N 9°34W **64** E2
Long I. U.S.A. 40°45N 73°30W **175** F11
Long Island Sd. U.S.A. 41°10N 73°0W **175** E12
Long L. Canada 49°30N 86°50W **164** C2
Long L. U.S.A. 44°0N 74°23W **175** C10
Long Lake U.S.A. 43°58N 74°25W **175** C10
Long Point Canada 42°34N 80°25W **174** D4
Long Point B. Canada 42°40N 80°10W **174** D4
Long Prairie U.S.A. 45°59N 94°52W **172** C6
Long Prairie → U.S.A. 46°20N 94°36W **172** B6
Long Pt., Ont., Canada 42°35N 80°2W **174** D4
Long Pt. Ont., Canada 43°56N 76°53W **175** C8
Long Pt. N.Z. 46°34S 169°36E **155** G4
Long Range Mts.
  Canada 49°30N 57°30W **165** C8
Long Reef Australia 14°1S 125°48E **148** B4
Long Str. = Longa, Proliv
  Russia 70°0N 175°0E **107** C18
Long Thanh Vietnam 10°47N 106°57E **121** G6
Long Xian China 34°55N 106°55E **114** G4
Long Xuyen Vietnam 10°19N 105°28E **121** G5
Longa Greece 36°53N 21°55E **98** D3
Longa, Proliv Russia 70°0N 175°0E **107** C18
Long'an China 23°10N 107°40E **116** F6
Longarone Italy 46°16N 12°18E **93** B9
Longbenton U.K. 55°1N 1°31W **66** B6
Longboat Key U.S.A. 27°23N 82°39W **179** M4
Longchang China 29°18N 105°15E **116** C5
Longchuan Guangdong,
  China 24°5N 115°17E **117** E10
Longchuan Yunnan,
  China 24°23N 97°58E **116** E1
Longde China 35°30N 106°20E **114** G4
Longeau-Percey France 47°47N 5°20E **71** E12
Longford Australia 41°32S 147°3E **151** G4
Longford Ireland 53°43N 7°49W **64** C4
Longford □ Ireland 53°42N 7°45W **64** C4
Longfort, An = Longford
  Ireland 53°43N 7°49W **64** C4
Longhai China 24°25N 117°46E **117** F11
Longhua Guangdong,
  China 22°39N 114°0E **111** a
Longhua Hebei, China 41°18N 117°45E **115** D9
Longhui China 27°7N 111°2E **117** D8
Longido Tanzania 2°43S 36°42E **142** C4
Longiram Indonesia 0°5S 115°45E **118** E5
Longjiang China 47°20N 123°12E **115** B12
Longkou Jiangxi, China 26°8N 115°10E **117** D10
Longkou Shandong,
  China 37°40N 120°18E **115** F11
Longlac China 49°45N 86°25W **164** C2
Longli China 26°25N 106°58E **116** D6
Longlin China 24°47N 105°20E **116** E5
Longling China 24°37N 98°39E **116** E1
Longmeadow U.S.A. 42°3N 72°34W **175** D12
Longmen Shiku China 34°28N 112°28E **114** G7
Longming China 22°59N 107°7E **116** F6
Longmont U.S.A. 40°10N 105°6W **168** F11
Longnan China 24°55N 114°47E **117** E10
Longnawan Indonesia 1°51N 114°55E **118** D4
Longobucco Italy 39°27N 16°37E **95** C9
Longquan China 28°7N 119°10E **117** C12
Longreach Australia 23°28S 144°14E **150** C3
Longshan China 29°29N 109°25E **116** C7
Longsheng China 25°48N 110°0E **117** E8
Longtan Dam China 25°7N 107°0E **116** E6
Longtan Shuiku China 25°10N 106°50E **116** E6
Longué-Jumelles France 47°22N 0°8W **70** E6
Longueau France 49°52N 2°21E **71** C9
Longueuil Canada 45°31N 73°29W **175** A11
Longuyon France 49°27N 5°35E **71** C12
Longvic France 47°17N 5°4E **71** E12
Longview Tex., U.S.A. 32°30N 94°44W **176** E7
Longview Wash.,
  U.S.A. 46°8N 122°57W **170** D4
Longwood U.S.A. 28°42N 81°21W **179** G8
Longwy France 49°30N 5°46E **71** C12
Longxi China 34°53N 104°40E **114** G3
Longxue Dao China 22°41N 113°38E **111** a
Longyearbyen Svalbard 78°13N 15°40E **54** B8
Longyou China 29°1N 119°8E **117** C12
Longzhou China 22°22N 106°50E **116** F6
Lonigo Italy 45°23N 11°23E **92** C8
Löningen Germany 52°44N 7°46E **76** C3
Lonja → Croatia 45°22N 16°40E **93** C13
Lonoke U.S.A. 34°47N 91°54W **176** D8
Lönsboda Sweden 56°24N 14°10E **63** H8
Lons-le-Saunier France 46°40N 5°31E **71** F12
Lontra Brazil 38°26S 71°14W **192** A2
Lookout, C. Canada 55°18N 83°56W **164** A3
Lookout, C. U.S.A. 34°35N 76°32W **177** D16
Loolmalasin Tanzania 3°0S 35°53E **142** C4

Loon → Alta., Canada 57°8N 115°3W **162** B5
Loon → Man., Canada 55°53N 101°59W **163** B8
Loon Lake Canada 54°2N 109°10W **163** C7
Loongana Australia 30°52S 127°5E **149** F4
Loop Hd. Ireland 52°34N 9°56W **64** D2
Lop China 37°3N 80°11E **109** E10
Lop Nor = Lop Nur China 40°20N 90°10E **109** D12
Lop Nur China 40°20N 90°10E **109** D12
Lopare Bos.-H. 44°39N 18°46E **80** F3
Lopatin Russia 43°50N 47°35E **87** J8
Lopatina, Gora Russia 50°47N 143°10E **107** D15
Lopatka, Mys Russia 50°52N 156°40E **107** D16
Lopburi Thailand 14°48N 100°37E **120** E3
Lopez U.S.A. 41°27N 76°20W **175** E8
Lopez, C. Gabon 0°47S 8°40E **140** E1
Lopphavet Norway 70°27N 21°15E **60** A19
Lora → Afghan. 31°35N 66°32E **122** D4
Lora, Hāmūn-i- Pakistan 29°38N 64°58E **122** E4
Lora Cr. → Australia 28°10S 135°22E **151** D2
Lora del Río Spain 37°39N 5°33W **89** H5
Lorain U.S.A. 41°28N 82°11W **174** E2
Lorca Spain 37°41N 1°42W **91** H3
Lord Howe I. Pac. Oc. 31°33S 159°6E **147** E8
Lord Howe Rise Pac. Oc. 30°0S 162°30E **156** L8
Lord Loughborough I. Myanmar 10°25N 97°54E **121** G1
Lordsburg U.S.A. 32°21N 108°43W **169** K9
Loreština □ Iran 33°30N 48°40E **129** C6
Loreto Brazil 7°5S 45°10W **189** B1
Loreto Italy 43°26N 13°36E **93** E10
Loreto Mexico 26°0N 111°21W **180** B2
Lorgues France 43°28N 6°22E **73** E10
Lorhosso = Loropéni Burkina Faso 10°17N 3°38W **138** C4
Lorient France 47°45N 3°23W **70** E3
Lőrinci Hungary 47°44N 19°41E **80** C4
Lormi India 22°17N 81°41E **125** H9
Lorn U.K. 56°26N 5°10W **65** E3
Lorn, Firth of U.K. 56°20N 5°40W **65** E3
Lorne Australia 38°33S 143°59E **152** E5
Loropéni Burkina Faso 10°17N 3°38W **138** C4
Lorovouno Cyprus 35°8N 32°36E **101** D11
Lörrach Germany 47°36N 7°40E **77** H3
Lorraine □ France 48°55N 5°50E **71** D12
Los Sweden 61°45N 15°10E **62** C9
Los, Îles de Guinea 9°30N 13°50W **138** D2
Los Alamos Calif., U.S.A. 34°44N 120°17W **171** L6
Los Alamos N. Mex., U.S.A. 35°53N 106°19W **169** J10
Los Alcornocales △ Spain 36°21N 5°32W **89** J5
Los Alerces △ Argentina 42°55S 71°55W **192** B2
Los Altos U.S.A. 37°23N 122°7W **170** H4
Los Andes Chile 32°50S 70°40W **190** C1
Los Angeles Chile 37°28S 72°23W **190** D1
Los Angeles U.S.A. 34°4N 118°15W **171** M8
Los Angeles Aqueduct U.S.A. 35°22N 118°5W **171** K9
Los Angeles Int. ✈ (LAX) U.S.A. 33°57N 118°25W **171** M8
Los Antiguos Argentina 46°35S 71°40W **192** C2
Los Banos U.S.A. 37°4N 120°51W **170** H6
Los Barrios Spain 36°11N 5°30W **89** J5
Los Blancos Argentina 23°40S 62°30W **190** A3
Los Cabos Int. ✈ (SJD) Mexico 23°9N 109°43W **180** C3
Los Cardones △ Argentina 25°8S 65°55W **190** B2
Los Chiles Costa Rica 11°2N 84°43W **182** D3
Los Corrales de Buelna Spain 43°16N 4°4W **88** B6
Los Cristianos Canary Is. 28°3N 16°42W **100** F3
Los Gallardos Spain 37°10N 1°57W **91** H3
Los Gatos U.S.A. 37°14N 121°59W **170** H5
Los Glaciares △ Argentina 50°0S 73°55W **192** C2
Los Haïtises △ Dom. Rep. 19°4N 69°30W **183** C6
Los Hermanos, Is. Venezuela 11°45N 64°25W **183** D7
Los Huemules △ Chile 46°10S 73°23W **192** C2
Los Islotes Canary Is. 29°4N 13°44W **100** E6
Los Lagos Chile 39°51S 72°50W **190** D1
Los Llanos de Aridane Canary Is. 28°38N 17°54W **100** F2
Los Loros Chile 27°50S 70°6W **190** B1
Los Lunas U.S.A. 34°48N 106°44W **169** J10
Los Menucos Argentina 40°50S 68°10W **192** B3
Los Mochis Mexico 25°45N 108°57W **180** B3
Los Monegros Spain 41°29N 0°13W **90** D4
Los Monos Argentina 46°1S 69°36W **192** C3
Los Muermos Chile 41°24S 73°29W **192** B2
Los Nietos Spain 37°36N 0°47W **91** H4
Los Olivos U.S.A. 34°40N 120°7W **171** L6
Los Palacios Cuba 22°35N 83°15W **182** B3
Los Palacios y Villafranca Spain 37°10N 5°55W **89** H5
Los Queñes Chile 35°1S 70°48W **190** D1
Los Reyes de Salgado Mexico 19°35N 102°29W **180** D4
Los Roques, Is. Venezuela 11°50N 66°45W **183** D6
Los Santos de Maimona Spain 38°27N 6°22W **89** G4
Los Teques Venezuela 10°21N 67°2W **186** A3
Los Testigos, Is. Venezuela 11°23N 63°6W **186** A6
Los Vilos Chile 32°10S 71°30W **190** C1
Los Yébenes Spain 39°36N 3°55W **89** F7
Losice Poland 52°13N 22°43E **83** F9
Lošinj Croatia 44°30N 14°30E **93** D11
Loskop Dam S. Africa 25°23S 29°20E **143** F2
Løsning Denmark 55°48N 9°42E **63** J3
Lossiemouth U.K. 57°42N 3°17W **65** D5
Lossen Sweden 62°26N 12°45E **62** B6
Lostwithiel U.K. 50°24N 4°41W **67** G3
Lot □ France 44°39N 1°40E **73** D4
Lot → France 44°18N 0°20E **72** D4
Lot-et-Garonne □ France 44°22N 0°30E **72** D4
Lota Chile 37°5S 73°10W **190** D1
Lotagipi Marsh Kenya 4°36N 34°55E **142** B3
Lotfābād Iran 37°32N 59°20E **129** B8
Lothair S. Africa 26°22S 30°27E **145** D5
Lotorp Sweden 58°44N 15°57E **63** F9
Lötschbergtunnel Switz. 46°26N 7°43E **77** J3
Lotta → Europe 68°42N 31°6E **60** B24

Lottefors Sweden 61°25N 16°24E **62** C10
Löttorp Sweden 57°10N 17°0E **63** G11
Lotung Taiwan 24°41N 121°46E **117** E13
Loubomo Congo 4°9S 12°47E **140** E2
Loudéac France 48°11N 2°47W **70** D4
Loudi China 27°42N 111°59E **117** D8
Loudonville U.S.A. 40°38N 82°14W **174** F2
Loudun France 47°3N 0°5E **70** E7
Louga Senegal 15°45N 16°5W **138** B1
Louga □ Senegal 15°20N 15°35W **138** B1
Loughborough U.K. 52°47N 1°11W **66** E6
Lougheed I. Canada 77°26N 105°6W **161** B10
Loughman U.S.A. 28°14N 81°34W **179** G8
Loughrea Ireland 53°12N 8°33W **64** C3
Loughros More B. Ireland 54°48N 8°32W **64** B3
Louhans France 46°38N 5°12E **71** F12
Louis Trichardt S. Africa 23°1S 29°43E **145** B4
Louis XIV, Pte. Canada 54°37N 79°45W **164** B4
Louisa U.S.A. 38°7N 82°36W **173** F12
Louisbourg Canada 45°55N 60°0W **165** C8
Louisburgh Ireland 53°46N 9°49W **64** C2
Louise I. Canada 52°55N 131°50W **162** C2
Louiseville Canada 46°20N 72°56W **164** C5
Louisiade Arch. Papua N. G. 11°10S 153°0E **147** C8
Louisiana U.S.A. 39°27N 91°3W **172** F8
Louisiana □ U.S.A. 30°50N 92°0W **176** F9
Louisville Ala., U.S.A. 31°47N 85°33W **178** D4
Louisville □ U.S.A. 33°0N 82°25W **178** B7
Louisville Ky., U.S.A. 38°15N 85°46W **173** F11
Louisville Miss., U.S.A. 33°7N 89°3W **177** E10
Louisville Ohio, U.S.A. 40°50N 81°16W **174** F3
Louisville Ridge Pac. Oc. 31°0S 172°30W **156** L10
Loulay France 46°3N 0°30W **72** B3
Loulé Portugal 37°9N 8°0W **89** H3
Loulouni Mali 10°54N 5°36W **138** C4
Loum Cameroon 4°42N 9°44E **139** E6
Louny Czechia 50°20N 13°48E **76** A6
Loup City U.S.A. 41°17N 98°58W **172** E4
Loups Marins, Lacs des Canada 56°30N 73°45W **164** A5
Lourdes France 43°6N 0°3W **72** E3
Lourdes-de-Blanc-Sablon Canada 51°24N 57°12W **165** B8
Lourinhã Portugal 39°14N 9°17W **89** F1
Louroujina Cyprus 35°0N 33°28E **101** E12
Lousã Portugal 40°7N 8°14W **88** E2
Louta Burkina Faso 13°30N 3°10W **138** C4
Louth Australia 30°30S 145°8E **153** A6
Louth Ireland 53°58N 6°32W **64** C5
Louth U.K. 53°22N 0°1W **66** D7
Louth □ Ireland 53°56N 6°34W **64** C5
Louth B. Australia 34°33S 135°56E **152** C1
Loutra Edipsou Greece 38°54N 23°2E **98** C4
Loutraki Greece 37°58N 22°57E **98** C4
Loutropoli Thermis Greece 39°11N 26°29E **99** B8
Louvain = Leuven Belgium 50°52N 4°42E **69** D4
Louvale U.S.A. 32°10N 84°50W **178** C5
Louviers France 49°12N 1°10E **70** C8
Louwsburg S. Africa 27°37S 31°7E **145** C5
Lovat → Russia 58°14N 31°28E **84** C6
Lovćen Montenegro 42°23N 18°51E **96** D2
Lovćen △ Montenegro 42°20N 18°50E **96** D2
Lovech Bulgaria 43°8N 24°42E **97** C8
Lovech □ Bulgaria 43°0N 24°45E **97** D8
Loveland U.S.A. 40°24N 105°5W **168** E2
Lovell U.S.A. 44°50N 108°24W **168** D9
Lovelock U.S.A. 40°11N 118°28W **168** F4
Lóvere Italy 45°49N 10°4E **92** C7
Lövestad Sweden 55°40N 13°54E **63** J7
Loviisa Finland 60°28N 26°12E **64** B4
Lovina Indonesia 8°9S 115°1E **119** J18
Loving U.S.A. 32°17N 104°6W **169** K11
Lovisa = Loviisa Finland 60°28N 26°12E **64** B4
Lovosice Czechia 50°30N 14°2E **78** A7
Lovran Croatia 45°18N 14°15E **93** C11
Lovrin Romania 45°58N 20°48E **80** E5
Lövstabruk Sweden 60°24N 17°53E **62** D11
Lövstabukten Sweden 60°35N 17°45E **62** D11
Low, L. Canada 52°29N 76°17W **164** B4
Low Pt. Australia 32°25S 127°25E **149** F4
Low Tatra = Nízké Tatry Slovakia 48°55N 19°30E **79** C12
Lowa Dem. Rep. of the Congo 1°25S 25°47E **142** C2
Lowa → Dem. Rep. of the Congo 1°24S 25°51E **142** C2
Lowell U.S.A. 42°38N 71°19W **175** D13
Lowellville U.S.A. 41°2N 80°32W **174** E4
Löwen → Namibia 26°51S 18°17E **144** C2
Lower Alkali L. U.S.A. 41°16N 120°2W **168** F3
Lower Arrow L. Canada 49°40N 118°5W **162** D5
Lower Austria = Niederösterreich □ Austria 48°25N 15°40E **78** C8
Lower California = Baja California Mexico 31°10N 115°12W **180** A1
Lower Glenelg △ Australia 38°4S 141°41E **152** E4
Lower Hutt N.Z. 41°10S 174°55E **154** F4
Lower Lake U.S.A. 38°55N 122°37W **170** G4
Lower Manitou L. Canada 49°15N 93°0W **163** D10
Lower Post Canada 59°58N 128°30W **162** B3
Lower Red L. U.S.A. 47°58N 95°0W **172** B6
Lower Saxony = Niedersachsen □ Germany 52°50N 9°0E **76** C4
Lower Tunguska = Tunguska, Nizhnyaya → Russia 65°48N 88°4E **107** C9
Lower Zambezi △ Zambia 15°25S 29°40E **143** F2
Lowestoft U.K. 52°29N 1°45E **67** E9
Lowgar □ Afghan. 34°0N 69°0E **122** C6
Lowicz Poland 52°6N 19°55E **83** F6
Lowly, Pt. Australia 33°0S 137°46E **152** B2
Lowther I. Canada 74°33N 97°3W **161** B11
Lowville U.S.A. 43°47N 75°29W **175** C9
Loxton S. Africa 31°30S 22°22E **144** D3
Loxton Australia 34°28S 140°31E **152** C4
Loyalton U.S.A. 39°41N 120°14W **170** F6
Loyalty Is. = Loyauté, Îs. N. Cal. 20°50S 166°30E **147** D9
Loyang = Luoyang China 34°40N 112°26E **114** G7
Loyauté, Îs. N. Cal. 20°50S 166°30E **147** D9

Loyev = Loyew Belarus 51°56N 30°46E **75** C16
Loyew Belarus 51°56N 30°46E **75** C16
Loyoro Uganda 3°22N 34°14E **142** B3
Lozère □ France 44°35N 3°30E **72** D7
Loznica Serbia 44°32N 19°12E **96** B3
Lozova Ukraine 49°0N 36°20E **85** H9
Ltalaltuma ◌ Australia 23°57S 132°25E **148** D5
Lü Shan China 29°30N 115°55E **117** C10
Lü Shan △ China 29°26N 115°52E **117** C10
Lü Wo China 22°33N 114°6E **111** a
Luachimo Angola 7°23S 20°48E **142** F4
Luajan → India 24°44N 85°1E **125** G11
Lualaba → Dem. Rep. of the Congo 0°26N 25°20E **142** B2
Luambe △ Zambia 12°30S 32°15E **143** E3
Luampa Zambia 15°4S 24°20E **143** F1
Lu'an China 31°45N 116°29E **116** H8
Luan Chau Vietnam 21°38N 103°24E **116** G4
Luan He → China 39°20N 119°5E **115** E10
Luan Xian China 39°40N 118°40E **115** E10
Luancheng Guangxi Zhuangzu, China 22°48N 108°55E **116** F7
Luancheng Hebei, China 37°53N 114°40E **114** F8
Luanco Spain 43°37N 5°48W **88** B5
Luanda Angola 8°58S 13°9E **142** F2
Luang, Doi Thailand 18°30N 101°15E **120** C3
Luang, Thale Thailand 7°30N 100°15E **121** J3
Luang Nam Tha Laos 20°58N 101°30E **116** G4
Luang Prabang Laos 19°52N 102°10E **116** H4
Luangwa Zambia 15°35S 30°16E **143** F3
Luangwa → Zambia 14°25S 30°25E **143** E3
Luangwa Valley Zambia 13°30S 31°30E **143** E3
Luangwe = Loange → Dem. Rep. of the Congo 4°17S 20°2E **140** F4
Luanne China 40°55N 117°40E **115** D9
Luanping China 40°53N 117°23E **115** D9
Luanshya Zambia 13°3S 28°28E **143** E2
Luapula □ Zambia 11°0S 29°0E **143** E2
Luapula → Africa 9°26S 28°33E **143** D2
Luarca Spain 43°32N 6°32W **88** B4
Luashi Dem. Rep. of the Congo 10°50S 23°36E **143** E1
Luau Angola 10°40S 22°10E **140** G4
Lubaczów Poland 50°10N 23°8E **83** H10
Lubań Poland 51°5N 15°15E **83** G2
Lubana, Ozero = Lubānas Ezers Latvia 56°45N 27°0E **84** D4
Lubānas Ezers Latvia 56°45N 27°0E **84** D4
Lubang Is. Phil. 13°50N 120°12E **119** B6
Lubango Angola 14°55S 13°30E **141** G2
Lubao Dem. Rep. of the Congo 5°17S 25°42E **142** D2
Lubartów Poland 51°28N 22°42E **83** G9
Lubawa Poland 53°30N 19°48E **82** E6
Lübbecke Germany 52°18N 8°37E **76** C4
Lübben Germany 51°56N 13°54E **76** D9
Lübbenau Germany 51°52N 13°57E **76** D9
Lubbock U.S.A. 33°35N 101°51W **176** E4
Lübeck Germany 53°52N 10°40E **76** B6
Lübecker Bucht Germany 54°3N 10°54E **76** A6
Lubefu Dem. Rep. of the Congo 4°47S 24°27E **142** C1
Lubefu → Dem. Rep. of the Congo 4°10S 23°0E **142** C1
Lubelskie □ Poland 51°20N 22°50E **83** G9
Lubero = Luofu Dem. Rep. of the Congo 0°1S 29°15E **142** C2
Luberon △ France 43°52N 5°25E **73** E9
Lubersac France 45°26N 1°23E **72** C5
Lubicon L. Canada 56°23N 115°56W **162** B5
Lubień Kujawski Poland 52°23N 19°9E **83** F6
Lubilash → Dem. Rep. of the Congo 6°2S 23°45E **140** F4
Lubin Poland 51°24N 16°11E **83** G3
Lublin Poland 51°12N 22°38E **83** G9
Lubliniec Poland 50°43N 18°45E **83** H5
Lubnān = Lebanon ■ Asia 34°0N 36°0E **130** B5
Lubnān, Jabal Lebanon 33°45N 35°40E **130** B4
Lubniewice Poland 52°31N 15°15E **83** F2
Lubny Ukraine 50°3N 32°58E **85** G7
Lubomierz Poland 51°1N 15°31E **83** G2
Luboń Poland 52°21N 16°51E **83** F3
Lubongola Dem. Rep. of the Congo 2°35S 27°50E **142** C2
L'ubotín Slovakia 49°17N 20°53E **79** B13
Lubraniec Poland 52°33N 18°50E **83** F5
Lubsko Poland 51°45N 14°57E **83** G1
Lübtheen Germany 53°18N 11°5E **76** B7
Lubudi Dem. Rep. of the Congo 9°57S 25°58E **140** F5
Lubudi → Dem. Rep. of the Congo 9°0S 25°35E **142** D2
Lubukbatang Indonesia 3°15S 102°55E **118** E2
Lubuksikaping Indonesia 0°10N 100°15E **118** D2
Lubumbashi Dem. Rep. of the Congo 11°40S 27°28E **143** E2
Lubunda Dem. Rep. of the Congo 5°12S 26°41E **142** D2
Lubungu Zambia 14°35S 26°24E **143** E2
Lubuskie □ Poland 52°10N 15°20E **83** F2
Lubutu Dem. Rep. of the Congo 0°45S 26°30E **142** C2
Luc-en-Diois France 44°36N 5°28E **73** D9
Lucan Canada 43°11N 81°24W **174** D3
Lucan Ireland 53°22N 6°28W **64** C5
Lucania, Mt. Canada 61°1N 140°27W **162** B1
Lucas Channel = Main Channel Canada 45°21N 81°45W **174** A3
Lucca Italy 43°50N 10°29E **92** E7
Lucé France 48°26N 1°27E **70** D8
Luce Bay U.K. 54°45N 4°48W **65** G4
Lucea Jamaica 18°27N 78°10W **182** a
Lucedale U.S.A. 30°56N 88°35W **178** E2
Lucena Phil. 13°56N 121°37E **119** B6
Lucena Spain 37°27N 4°31W **89** H6
Lučenec Slovakia 48°18N 19°42E **79** C12
Lucera Italy 41°30N 15°20E **95** A8
Lucerne = Luzern Switz. 47°3N 8°18E **77** H4
Lucerne U.S.A. 39°6N 122°48W **170** F4
Lucerne Valley U.S.A. 34°27N 116°57W **171** L10
Luchena → Spain 37°44N 1°50W **91** H3
Lucheng China 36°20N 113°11E **114** F7
Lucheringo → Mozam. 11°43S 36°17E **143** E4
Lüchow Germany 52°58N 11°9E **76** C7
Luchuan China 22°25N 110°12E **117** F8
Lucia U.S.A. 36°2N 121°33W **170** J5

Lucinda Australia 18°32S 146°20E **150** B4
Lucindale Australia 36°58S 140°26E **152** D4
Luckau Germany 51°50N 13°42E **76** D9
Luckenwalde Germany 52°5N 13°10E **76** C9
Luckhoff S. Africa 29°44S 24°43E **144** D3
Lucknow Canada 43°57N 81°31W **174** C3
Lucknow India 26°50N 81°0E **125** F9
Luçon France 46°28N 1°10W **72** B3
Lüda = Dalian China 38°50N 121°40E **115** E11
Luda Kamchia → Bulgaria 43°3N 27°29E **97** C11
Ludbreg Croatia 46°15N 16°38E **93** B13
Lüdenscheid Germany 51°13N 7°37E **76** D3
Lüderitz Namibia 26°41S 15°8E **144** C2
Lüderitzbaai Namibia 26°36S 15°8E **144** C2
Ludhiana India 30°57N 75°56E **124** D6
Ludian China 27°10N 103°33E **116** C4
Luding Qiao China 29°53N 102°12E **116** C4
Lüdinghausen Germany 51°46N 7°27E **76** D3
Ludington U.S.A. 43°57N 86°27W **172** D10
Ludlow U.K. 52°22N 2°42W **67** E5
Ludlow Calif., U.S.A. 34°43N 116°10W **171** L10
Ludlow Pa., U.S.A. 41°43N 78°56W **174** E6
Ludlow Vt., U.S.A. 43°24N 72°42W **175** C12
Ludowici U.S.A. 31°43N 81°45W **178** D8
Luduș Romania 46°29N 24°5E **81** D9
Ludvika Sweden 60°8N 15°14E **62** D7
Ludwigsburg Germany 48°53N 9°11E **77** G5
Ludwigsfelde Germany 52°17N 13°17E **76** C9
Ludwigshafen Germany 49°29N 8°26E **77** F4
Ludwigslust Germany 53°19N 11°30E **76** B7
Ludza Latvia 56°32N 27°43E **84** D4
Lue Australia 32°38S 149°50E **153** B8
Lueki Dem. Rep. of the Congo 3°20S 25°48E **142** C2
Luena Dem. Rep. of the Congo 9°28S 25°43E **143** D2
Luena Zambia 10°40S 30°25E **143** E3
Luena Flats Zambia 14°47S 23°17E **141** G4
Luenha = Ruenya → Africa 16°24S 33°48E **143** F3
Lüeyang China 33°22N 106°10E **116** A6
Lufeng Guangdong, China 22°57N 115°38E **117** F10
Lufeng Yunnan, China 25°0N 102°5E **116** E4
Lufira → Dem. Rep. of the Congo 9°30S 27°0E **143** D2
Lufkin U.S.A. 31°21N 94°44W **176** F7
Lufupa Dem. Rep. of the Congo 10°37S 24°56E **143** E1
Luga Russia 58°40N 29°55E **84** C5
Luga → Russia 59°40N 28°18E **84** C5
Lugano Switz. 46°1N 8°57E **77** J4
Lugano, L. di Switz. 46°0N 9°0E **92** C6
Lugansk = Luhansk Ukraine 48°38N 39°15E **85** H10
Lugard's Falls Kenya 3°6S 38°41E **142** C4
Lugela Mozam. 16°25S 36°43E **143** F4
Lugenda → Mozam. 11°25S 38°33E **143** E4
Lugh = Luuq Somalia 3°48N 42°34E **131** G3
Lugina e Valbonës △ Albania 42°27N 19°53E **96** D3
Lugnaquilla Ireland 52°58N 6°28W **64** D5
Lugnvik Sweden 62°56N 17°55E **62** B11
Lugo Italy 44°25N 11°54E **93** D8
Lugo Spain 43°2N 7°35W **88** B3
Lugo □ Spain 43°0N 7°30W **88** C3
Lugoj Romania 45°42N 21°57E **80** E6
Lugovoy = Qulan Kazakhstan 42°55N 72°43E **106** E8
Luhansk Ukraine 48°38N 39°15E **85** H10
Luhansk □ Ukraine 49°10N 38°40E **85** H10
Luhe China 32°19N 118°50E **117** A12
Luhe → Germany 53°23N 10°13E **76** B6
Luhuo China 31°21N 100°48E **116** B3
Lui → Angola 8°21S 17°33E **140** F3
Luiana Angola 17°25S 22°59E **144** A3
Luiana → Angola 17°24S 23°3E **141** H4
Luichow Pen. = Leizhou Bandao China 21°0N 110°0E **117** G7
Luimneach = Limerick Ireland 52°40N 8°37W **64** D3
Luing U.K. 56°14N 5°39W **65** E3
Luino Italy 45°59N 8°44E **92** C6
Luís Correia Brazil 3°0S 41°35W **189** A3
Luitpold Coast Antarctica 78°30S 32°0W **55** D1
Luiza Dem. Rep. of the Congo 7°40S 22°30E **140** F4
Luizi Dem. Rep. of the Congo 6°0S 27°25E **142** D2
Luján Argentina 34°45S 59°5W **190** C4
Lujiang China 31°20N 117°15E **117** B11
Lukang Taiwan 24°1N 120°22E **117** E13
Lukanga Swamp Zambia 14°30S 27°40E **143** E2
Lukavac Bos.-H. 44°33N 18°32E **80** F3
Lukenie → Dem. Rep. of the Congo 3°0S 18°50E **140** E3
Lukla Nepal 27°42N 86°43E **125** F12
Lukolela Dem. Rep. of the Congo 5°23S 24°32E **142** D1
Lukosi Zimbabwe 18°30S 26°30E **143** F2
Lukovë Albania 39°59N 19°54E **98** B2
Lukovit Bulgaria 43°13N 24°11E **97** C8
Łuków Poland 51°55N 22°23E **83** G9
Lukoyanov Russia 55°2N 44°29E **86** C7
Łukusuzi □ Zambia 12°43S 32°36E **143** E3
Lülang Shan China 38°0N 111°15E **114** F6
Luleå Sweden 65°35N 22°10E **60** D20
Luleälven → Sweden 65°35N 22°10E **60** D20
Lüleburgaz Turkey 41°23N 27°22E **97** E11
Luliang China 25°0N 103°40E **116** E4
Lulima Dem. Rep. of the Congo 7°40S 22°30E **142** D1
Luling U.S.A. 29°41N 97°39W **176** G6
Lulong China 39°53N 118°51E **115** E10
Lulonga → Dem. Rep. of the Congo 1°0N 18°10E **140** D3
Lulu → Dem. Rep. of the Congo 1°10N 23°0E **142** B1
Lulua → Dem. Rep. of the Congo 5°2S 21°4E **140** F4

Lumut Malaysia 4°13N 100°37E **121** K13
Lumut, Tanjung Indonesia 3°50S 105°58E **118** E3
Luna India 23°43N 69°16E **124** H3
Lunan China 24°40N 103°18E **116** E4
Lunavada India 23°8N 73°37E **124** H5
Lunca Corbului Romania 44°42N 24°45E **81** F9
Lund Sweden 55°44N 13°12E **63** J7
Lundazi Zambia 12°20S 33°7E **143** E3
Lunde Norway 62°53N 17°51E **62** B11
Lunderskov Denmark 55°29N 9°19E **63** J3
Lundi → Zimbabwe 21°43S 32°34E **143** F3
Lundu Malaysia 1°40N 109°50E **118** D3
Lundy U.K. 51°10N 4°41W **67** F3
Lüneburg Germany 53°15N 10°24E **76** B6
Lüneburg Heath = Lüneburger Heide Germany 53°10N 10°12E **76** B6
Lüneburger Heide Germany 53°10N 10°12E **76** B6
Lunel France 43°39N 4°9E **73** E8
Lünen Germany 51°37N 7°31E **76** D3
Lunenburg Canada 44°22N 64°18W **165** D7
Lunéville France 48°36N 6°30E **71** D13
Lunga → Zambia 14°34S 26°25E **143** E2
Lunga Lunga Kenya 4°33S 39°7E **142** C4
Lungi S. Leone 8°40N 13°17W **138** D2
Lunglei India 22°55N 92°45E **123** H18
Luni India 26°0N 73°6E **124** G5
Luni → India 24°41N 71°14E **124** G4
Luninets = Luninyets Belarus 52°15N 26°50E **75** B14
Luning U.S.A. 38°30N 118°11W **168** G4
Lunino Russia 53°38N 45°18E **86** D7
Luninyets Belarus 52°15N 26°50E **75** B14
Lunkaransar India 28°29N 73°44E **124** E5
Lunsar S. Leone 8°41N 12°32W **138** D2
Lunsemfwa → Zambia 14°54S 30°12E **143** E3
Lunsemfwa Falls Zambia 14°30S 29°6E **143** E2
Luntai China 41°46N 84°14E **109** D10
Luo He → China 34°35N 110°20E **114** G6
Luocheng China 24°48N 108°53E **116** E7
Luochuan China 35°45N 109°26E **114** G5
Luoci China 25°19N 102°18E **116** E4
Luodian China 25°24N 106°43E **116** E6
Luoding China 22°45N 111°40E **117** F8
Luofu Dem. Rep. of the Congo 0°10S 29°15E **142** C2
Luohe China 33°32N 114°2E **114** H8
Luojiang China 31°18N 104°33E **116** B5
Luonan China 34°5N 110°10E **114** G6
Luoning China 34°35N 111°40E **114** G6
Luoshan China 32°13N 114°30E **117** A10
Luotian China 30°46N 115°22E **117** B10
Luoxiao Shan China 26°30N 114°1E **117** D10
Luoyang China 34°40N 112°26E **114** G7
Luoyuan China 26°28N 119°30E **117** D12
Luoyunan China 24°29N 112°0E **117** E9
Luozigou China 43°42N 130°18E **115** C16
Lupeni Romania 45°21N 23°37E **81** E8
Lupilichi Mozam. 11°47S 35°13E **143** E4
Luputa Dem. Rep. of the Congo 5°58S 23°28E **142** D1
Łúras Italy 40°59N 9°10E **94** B2
Lure France 47°40N 6°30E **71** E13
Lurés △ Albania 41°47N 20°11E **96** E4
Lurgan U.K. 54°27N 6°20W **64** B5
Luribay Bolivia 17°6S 67°39W **188** G5
Lurín Peru 12°17S 76°52W **188** C2
Lúrio Mozam. 13°32S 40°30E **143** E5
Lúrio → Mozam. 13°36S 40°32E **143** E5
Lusaka Zambia 15°28S 28°16E **143** F2
Lusaka □ Zambia 15°30S 29°0E **143** F2
Lusambo Dem. Rep. of the Congo 4°58S 23°28E **142** C1
Lusangaye Dem. Rep. of the Congo 4°54S 26°0E **142** C2
Luseland Canada 52°5N 109°24W **163** C7
Lusenga Plain △ Zambia 9°22S 29°14E **143** D2
Lushan Henan, China 33°45N 112°55E **114** H7
Lushan Sichuan, China 30°12N 102°52E **116** B4
Lushi China 34°3N 111°3E **114** G6
Lushnjë Albania 40°55N 19°41E **96** F3
Lushoto Tanzania 4°47S 38°20E **142** C4
Lushui China 25°58N 98°44E **116** E2
Lüshun China 38°45N 121°15E **115** F11
Lusignan France 46°26N 0°8E **72** B4
Lusigny-sur-Barse France 48°16N 4°15E **71** D11
Lusk U.S.A. 42°46N 104°27W **168** E11
Lussac-les-Châteaux France 46°24N 0°43E **72** B4
Lustenau Austria 47°26N 9°39E **78** D2
Lüt, Dasht-e Iran 31°30N 58°0E **129** D8
Lüta = Dalian China 38°50N 121°40E **115** E11
Lütao Taiwan 22°40N 121°30E **117** F13
Lutherstadt Wittenberg Germany 51°53N 12°39E **76** D8
Luthersville U.S.A. 33°13N 84°45W **178** B5
Luton U.K. 51°53N 0°24W **67** F7
Luton □ U.K. 51°53N 0°24W **67** F7
Lutong Malaysia 4°28N 114°0E **118** D4
Lutsel K'e Canada 62°24N 110°44W **163** A6
Lutsk Ukraine 50°50N 25°15E **75** C13
Lutto = Lotta → Europe 68°42N 31°6E **60** B24
Lutz U.S.A. 28°9N 82°28W **179** G7
Lützow Holmbukta Antarctica 69°10S 37°30E **55** C4
Luuq Somalia 3°48N 42°34E **131** G3
Luverne Ala., U.S.A. 31°43N 86°16W **178** D3
Luverne Minn., U.S.A. 43°39N 96°13W **172** D5
Luvua Dem. Rep. of the Congo 8°48S 25°17E **143** D2
Luvua → Dem. Rep. of the Congo 6°50S 27°30E **142** D2
Luvuvhu → S. Africa 22°25S 31°18E **145** B5
Luwegu → Tanzania 8°31S 37°23E **142** D4
Luwuk Indonesia 0°56S 122°47E **119** E6
Luxembourg Lux. 49°37N 6°9E **69** E6
Luxembourg □ Belgium 49°58N 5°30E **69** E5
Luxembourg ■ (LUX) Lux. 49°45N 6°0E **69** E6
Luxeuil-les-Bains France 47°49N 6°24E **71** E13

Luxi Hunan, China 28°20N 110°7E **117** C8
Luxi Yunnan, China 24°40N 103°55E **116** E4
Luxi Yunnan, China 24°27N 98°36E **116** E2
Luxor = El Uqsur Egypt 25°41N 32°38E **137** C12
Luy-de-Béarn → France 43°39N 0°48W **72** E3
Luy-de-France → France 43°39N 0°48W **72** E3
Luyi China 33°50N 115°35E **114** H8
Luykau = Loikaw Myanmar 19°40N 97°17E **123** K20
Luz-St-Sauveur France 42°53N 0°0 **72** F4
Luzern Switz. 47°3N 8°18E **77** H4
Luzern □ Switz. 47°2N 7°55E **77** H3
Luzhai China 24°29N 109°42E **116** E7
Luzhany Ukraine 48°22N 25°47E **81** D9
Luzhi China 26°21N 105°10E **116** D5
Luzhou China 28°52N 105°20E **116** C5
Luziânia Brazil 16°20S 48°0W **188** E9
Luzilândia Brazil 3°28S 42°22W **189** D7
Lužnice → Czechia 49°14N 14°23E **78** B7
Luzon Phil. 16°0N 121°0E **119** A6
Luzon Strait Asia 21°0N 120°40E **117** G13
Luzy France 46°47N 3°58E **71** F10
Luzzi Italy 39°27N 16°17E **95** C9
Lviv Ukraine 49°50N 24°0E **75** D13
Lviv □ Ukraine 49°30N 23°45E **75** D12
Lvov = Lviv Ukraine 49°50N 24°0E **75** D13
Lwówek Poland 52°28N 16°10E **83** F3
Lwówek Śląski Poland 51°7N 15°38E **83** G2
Lyakhavichy Belarus 53°2N 26°32E **75** B14
Lyakhovskiye, Ostrova Russia 73°40N 141°0E **107** B15
Lyaki = Läki Azerbaijan 40°34N 47°22E **87** K8
Lyal I. Canada 44°57N 81°24W **174** B3
Lyall Mt. N.Z. 45°16S 167°32E **155** F2
Lyaskovets Bulgaria 43°6N 25°44E **97** C9
Lyasnaya → Belarus 52°9N 23°31E **83** F10
Lybster U.K. 58°18N 3°15W **65** C5
Lycaonia Turkey 38°0N 33°0E **104** D5
Lychen Germany 53°12N 13°18E **76** B9
Lychkova Russia 57°55N 32°24E **84** C7
Lycia Turkey 36°30N 29°30E **99** E11
Lyckebyån → Sweden 56°12N 15°39E **63** H9
Lycksele Sweden 64°38N 18°40E **60** D18
Lycosura Greece 37°20N 22°3E **98** D4
Lydda = Lod Israel 31°57N 34°54E **130** D3
Lydenburg S. Africa 25°10S 30°29E **145** C5
Lydia Turkey 38°48N 28°19E **99** C10
Łydynia → Poland 52°48N 20°40E **83** F7
Lyell N.Z. 41°48S 172°4E **155** B7
Lyell I. Canada 52°40N 131°35W **162** C2
Lyepyel Belarus 54°50N 28°40E **84** E5
Lygnern Sweden 57°30N 12°15E **63** G6
Lykens U.S.A. 40°34N 76°42W **175** F8
Lyman Ukraine 45°41N 29°45E **81** J11
Lyman U.S.A. 41°20N 110°18W **168** F8
Lymanske Ukraine 46°40N 29°58E **81** J10
Lyme B. U.K. 50°42N 2°53W **67** G4
Lyme Regis U.K. 50°43N 2°57W **67** G5
Lymington U.K. 50°45N 1°32W **67** G6
Łyna → Poland 54°37N 21°14E **82** D8
Lynchburg S.C., U.S.A. 34°3N 80°4W **178** B7
Lynchburg Va., U.S.A. 37°25N 79°9W **173** G14
Lynd → Australia 16°28S 143°18E **150** B3
Lynd Ra. Australia 25°30S 149°20E **154** D4
Lynden Canada 43°14N 80°9W **174** C4
Lynden U.S.A. 48°57N 122°27W **178** A3
Lyndhurst Australia 30°15S 138°18E **151** E2
Lyndon → Australia 23°29S 114°6E **149** D1
Lyndonville N.Y., U.S.A. 43°20N 78°23W **174** C6
Lyndonville Vt., U.S.A. 44°31N 72°1W **175** B12
Lyngen Norway 69°45N 20°30E **60** B19
Lynher Reef Australia 15°27S 121°55E **148** C3
Lynn U.S.A. 42°28N 70°57W **175** D14
Lynn Canal U.S.A. 58°50N 135°15W **166** D72
Lynn Haven U.S.A. 30°15N 85°39W **178** E4
Lynn Lake Canada 56°51N 101°3W **163** B8
Lynne U.S.A. 29°12N 81°59W **179** F9
Lynnwood U.S.A. 47°49N 122°18W **170** C4
Lynton U.K. 51°13N 3°50W **67** F4
Lyntupy Belarus 55°4N 26°23E **84** E4
Lynx L. Canada 62°25N 106°15W **163** A7
Lyon France 45°46N 4°50E **73** C8
Lyon St-Exupery ✈ (LYS) France 45°44N 5°2E **73** C9
Lyonnais France 45°45N 4°15E **73** C8
Lyons = Lyon France 45°46N 4°50E **73** C8
Lyons Ga., U.S.A. 32°12N 82°19W **178** C7
Lyons Kans., U.S.A. 38°21N 98°12W **172** F4
Lyons N.Y., U.S.A. 43°5N 77°0W **174** C8
Lyons → Australia 25°2S 115°9E **149** E2
Lyons Falls U.S.A. 43°37N 75°22W **175** C9
Lyozna Belarus 55°0N 30°50E **84** E6
Lys = Leie → Belgium 51°2N 3°45E **69** C3
Lysá nad Labem Czechia 50°11N 14°51E **78** A7
Lysekil Sweden 58°17N 11°26E **63** F5
Lysi Cyprus 35°6N 33°41E **101** D12
Lyskovo Russia 56°0N 45°3E **86** C7
Lystrup Denmark 56°14N 10°14E **63** H4
Lysvik Sweden 60°1N 13°9E **62** D6
Lysychansk Ukraine 48°55N 38°30E **85** H10
Lytham St. Anne's U.K. 53°45N 3°0W **66** D4
Lyttelton N.Z. 43°35S 172°44E **155** D5
Lytton Canada 50°13N 121°31W **162** C4
Lyuban Russia 59°16N 31°18E **84** C6
Lyubertsy Russia 55°40N 37°51E **84** E9
Lyubim Russia 58°50N 40°39E **86** B5
Lyubimets Bulgaria 41°50N 26°5E **97** E10
Lyubotyn Ukraine 50°0N 36°4E **85** G8
Lyubytino Russia 58°50N 33°16E **84** C7
Lyudinovo Russia 53°52N 34°28E **84** E8

M

M.R. Štefánik, Bratislava ✈ (BTS) Slovakia 48°11N 17°9E **79** C10
Ma → Vietnam 19°47N 105°56E **116** H5
Ma, O. el Algeria 27°45N 7°52E **136** C1
Ma On Shan China 22°23N 114°12E **111** a
Ma'adaba Jordan 31°43N 35°47E **130** D4
Ma'alot-Tarshiha Israel 33°1N 35°15E **130** B4
Maamba Zambia 17°17S 26°28E **144** A4
Ma'ān Jordan 30°12N 35°44E **130** E4
Ma'ān □ Jordan 30°0N 36°0E **130** F5
Maanselkä Finland 63°52N 28°0E **60** D24
Ma'anshan China 31°44N 118°29E **117** B12
Maarianhamina = Mariehamn Finland 60°5N 19°55E **61** F18

Maarmorilik *Greenland* 71°3N 51°0W 57 C5
Ma'arrat an Nu'mān *Syria* 35°43N 36°43E 104 E7
Maas → *Neths.* 51°45N 4°32E 69 C4
Maaseik *Belgium* 51°6N 5°45E 69 C5
Maasin *Phil.* 10°8N 124°50E 119 B6
Maastricht *Neths.* 50°50N 5°40E 69 D5
Maave *Mozam.* 21°4S 34°47E 145 B5
Mababe Depression *Botswana* 18°50S 24°15E 144 A3
Mabalane *Mozam.* 23°37S 32°31E 145 B5
Mabel L. *Canada* 50°35N 118°43W 162 C5
Mabenge *Dem. Rep. of the Congo* 4°15N 24°12E 142 B1
Maberly *Canada* 44°50N 76°32W 175 B8
Mabesi, L. *S. Leone* 7°10N 11°42W 138 D2
Mabian *China* 28°47N 103°37E 116 C4
Mablethorpe *U.K.* 53°20N 0°15E 66 D8
Mableton *U.S.A.* 33°49N 84°35W 178 B5
Mably *France* 46°5N 4°4E 71 F11
Maboma *Dem. Rep. of the Congo* 2°30N 28°10E 142 B2
Mabonto *S. Leone* 8°53N 11°50W 138 D2
Mabroûk *Mali* 19°29N 1°15W 139 B4
Mabuasehube ⌂ *Botswana* 25°5S 21°10E 144 C3
Mabuiag *Australia* 9°57S 142°11E 150 a
Mac Bac *Vietnam* 9°46N 106°7E 121 H6
Macachín *Argentina* 37°10S 63°43W 190 D3
Macaé *Brazil* 22°20S 41°43W 191 A7
Macael *Spain* 37°20N 2°18W 91 H2
Macaíba *Brazil* 5°51S 35°21W 189 B3
Macajuba *Brazil* 12°9S 40°22W 189 C2
McAlester *U.S.A.* 34°56N 95°46W 176 D7
McAllen *U.S.A.* 26°12N 98°14W 176 H5
McAlpin *U.S.A.* 30°8N 82°57W 178 E7
MacAlpine L. *Canada* 66°32N 102°45W 160 D11
Macamic *Canada* 48°45N 79°0W 164 C4
Macao = Macau *China* 22°12N 113°33E 117 F9
Macão *Portugal* 39°35N 7°59W 89 F3
Macapá *Brazil* 0°5N 51°4W 187 C8
Macarani *Brazil* 15°33S 40°24W 189 D2
Macarao △ *Venezuela* 10°22N 67°7W 183 D6
Macarthur *Australia* 38°5S 142°0E 152 E5
McArthur → *Australia* 15°54S 136°40E 150 B2
McArthur, Port *Australia* 16°4S 136°23E 150 B2
Macate *Peru* 8°48S 78°7W 188 B2
Macau *Brazil* 5°15S 36°40W 189 B3
Macau *China* 22°12N 113°33E 117 F9
Macaúbas *Brazil* 13°2S 42°42W 189 C2
McBride *Canada* 53°20N 120°19W 162 C4
McCall *U.S.A.* 44°55N 116°6W 168 D5
McCamey *U.S.A.* 31°8N 102°14W 176 F3
McCammon *U.S.A.* 42°39N 112°12W 168 E7
McCarran Int., Las Vegas ✕ (LAS) *U.S.A.* 36°5N 115°9W 171 J11
McCauley I. *Canada* 53°40N 130°15W 162 C2
McCleary *U.S.A.* 47°3N 123°16W 170 C3
Macclenny *U.S.A.* 30°17N 82°7W 178 E7
Macclesfield *U.K.* 53°15N 2°8W 66 D5
Macclesfield Bank *S. China Sea* 16°0N 114°30E 118 A4
M'Clintock Chan. *Canada* 72°0N 102°0W 160 C11
McClintock Ra. *Australia* 18°44S 127°38E 148 C4
McCloud *U.S.A.* 41°15N 122°8W 168 F2
McCluer I. *Australia* 11°5S 133°0E 148 B5
McClure *U.S.A.* 40°42N 77°19W 174 F7
McClure, L. *U.S.A.* 37°35N 120°16W 170 H6
M'Clure Str. *Canada* 75°0N 119°0W 161 C8
McClusky *U.S.A.* 47°29N 100°27W 172 B3
McComb *U.S.A.* 31°15N 90°27W 177 F9
McCook *U.S.A.* 40°12N 100°38W 172 E3
McCormick *U.S.A.* 33°55N 82°17W 178 B7
McCreary *Canada* 50°47N 99°29W 163 C9
McCullough Mt. *U.S.A.* 35°35N 115°13W 171 K11
McCusker → *Canada* 55°32N 108°39W 163 B7
McDavid *U.S.A.* 30°52N 87°19W 179 E2
McDermitt *U.S.A.* 41°59N 117°43W 168 F5
McDonald *U.S.A.* 40°22N 80°14W 174 F4
Macdonald, L. *Australia* 23°30S 129°0E 148 D4
McDonald Is. *Ind. Oc.* 53°0S 73°0E 146 K6
MacDonnell Ranges *Australia* 23°40S 133°0E 148 D5
McDonough *U.S.A.* 33°27N 84°9W 178 B5
McDougalls Well *Australia* 31°8S 141°15E 152 A4
MacDowell L. *Canada* 52°15N 92°45W 164 B1
Macduff *U.K.* 57°40N 2°31W 65 D6
Maceda *Spain* 42°16N 7°39W 88 C3
Macedonia *U.S.A.* 41°19N 81°31W 174 E3
Macedonia ■ *Europe* 41°53N 21°40E 96 E5
Maceió *Brazil* 9°40S 35°41W 189 B3
Maceira *Portugal* 39°41N 8°55W 88 F2
Macenta *Guinea* 8°35N 9°32W 138 D3
Macerata *Italy* 43°18N 13°27E 93 E10
McFarland *U.S.A.* 35°41N 119°14W 171 K7
McFarlane → *Canada* 59°12N 107°58W 163 B7
Macfarlane, L. *Australia* 32°0S 136°40E 152 B2
McGehee *U.S.A.* 33°38N 91°24W 176 E9
McGill *U.S.A.* 39°23N 114°47W 168 G6
Macgillycuddy's Reeks *Ireland* 51°58N 9°45W 64 E2
McGraw *U.S.A.* 42°36N 76°8W 175 D8
McGregor *U.S.A.* 43°1N 91°11W 172 D8
McGregor Ra. *Australia* 27°0S 142°45E 151 D3
McGuire, Mt. *Australia* 20°18S 148°23E 150 b
Mach *Pakistan* 29°50N 67°20E 124 E2
Māch Kowr *Iran* 25°48N 61°28E 129 E9
Machacalis *Brazil* 17°5S 40°45W 189 D2
Machado = Jiparaná → *Brazil* 8°3S 62°52W 186 E6
Machagai *Argentina* 26°56S 60°2W 190 B3
Machakos *Kenya* 1°30S 37°15E 142 C4
Machakos □ *Kenya* 1°15S 34°35E 142 C4
Machala *Ecuador* 3°20S 79°57W 186 D3
Machanga *Mozam.* 20°59S 35°0E 145 B6
Machattie, L. *Australia* 24°50S 139°48E 150 C2
Machault *France* 49°21N 4°29E 71 C11
Machava *Mozam.* 25°54S 32°28E 145 C5
Machecoul *France* 47°0N 1°49W 70 F5
Macheke *Zimbabwe* 18°5S 31°51E 145 A5
Macheng *China* 31°12N 115°2E 117 B10
Macherla *India* 16°29N 79°26E 126 F4
Machero *Spain* 39°21N 4°20W 89 F6
Machgaon *India* 20°5N 86°17E 126 D8
Machhu → *India* 23°6N 70°46E 124 H4
Machiara △ *Pakistan* 34°40N 73°30E 124 B5
Machias *Maine, U.S.A.* 44°43N 67°28W 173 C20
Machias *N.Y., U.S.A.* 42°25N 78°29W 174 D6
Machichi → *Canada* 57°3N 92°6W 163 B10
Machico *Madeira* 32°43N 16°44W 100 D3
Machilipatnam *India* 16°12N 81°8E 127 F5
Machiques *Venezuela* 10°4N 72°34W 186 A4
Machu Picchu *Peru* 13°8S 72°30W 188 C3
Machynlleth *U.K.* 52°35N 3°50W 67 E4
Macia *Mozam.* 25°2S 33°8E 145 C5
Maciejowice *Poland* 51°36N 21°26E 83 G8
McIlwraith Ra. *Australia* 13°50S 143°20E 150 A3
Măcin *Romania* 45°16N 28°8E 81 E13
Macina *Mali* 14°50N 5°0W 138 C4
McInnes L. *Canada* 52°13N 93°45W 163 C10
McIntosh *U.S.A.* 45°55N 101°21W 172 C3
McIntosh L. *Canada* 55°45N 105°0W 163 B8
Macintosh Ra. *Australia* 27°39S 125°32E 149 E4
Macintyre → *Australia* 28°37S 150°47E 151 D5
Macizo Galaico *Spain* 42°30N 7°30W 88 C3
Maçka *Turkey* 40°49N 39°36E 105 B8
Mackay *Australia* 21°8S 149°11E 150 K7
Mackay *U.S.A.* 43°55N 113°37W 168 E7
MacKay → *Canada* 57°10N 111°38W 162 B6
Mackay, L. *Australia* 22°30S 129°0E 148 D4
McKay Ra. *Australia* 23°0S 122°30E 148 D3
McKeesport *U.S.A.* 40°20N 79°51W 174 F5
McKellar *Canada* 45°30N 79°55W 174 A5
McKenna *U.S.A.* 46°56N 122°33W 170 D4
Mackenzie = Linden *Guyana* 6°0N 58°10W 186 B7
Mackenzie *Canada* 55°20N 123°5W 162 B4
McKenzie *U.S.A.* 36°8N 88°31W 177 C10
Mackenzie → *Australia* 23°38S 149°46E 150 C4
Mackenzie → *Canada* 69°10N 134°20W 160 D5
McKenzie → *U.S.A.* 44°7N 123°6W 168 D2
Mackenzie Bay *Canada* 69°0N 137°30W 158 C6
Mackenzie King I. *Canada* 77°45N 111°0W 161 B9
Mackenzie Mts. *Canada* 64°0N 130°0W 158 C6
Mackenzie Plains *N.Z.* 44°10S 170°25E 155 E5
McKerrow, L. *N.Z.* 44°25S 168°5E 155 E3
Mackinac, Straits of *U.S.A.* 45°50N 84°40W 173 C11
Mackinaw City *U.S.A.* 45°47N 84°44W 173 C11
McKinlay *Australia* 21°16S 141°18E 150 C3
McKinlay → *Australia* 20°50S 141°28E 150 C3
McKinley, Mt. = Denali *U.S.A.* 63°4N 151°0W 160 E1
McKinley Sea *Arctic* 82°0N 0°0 57 A11
McKinney *U.S.A.* 33°12N 96°37W 176 E6
Mackinnon Road *Kenya* 3°40S 39°1E 142 C4
McKittrick *U.S.A.* 35°18N 119°37W 171 K7
Macklin *Canada* 52°20N 109°56W 163 C7
Macksville *Australia* 30°40S 152°56E 153 A10
McLaren Vale *Australia* 35°13S 138°31E 152 C3
McLaughlin *U.S.A.* 45°49N 100°49W 172 C3
Maclean *Australia* 29°26S 153°16E 151 D5
McLean *U.S.A.* 35°14N 100°36W 176 D4
McLeansboro *U.S.A.* 38°6N 88°32W 172 F9
Maclear *S. Africa* 31°2S 28°23E 145 D4
Maclear, C. *Malawi* 13°58S 34°49E 143 E3
Macleay → *Australia* 30°56S 153°0E 153 A10
McLennan *Canada* 55°42N 116°50W 162 B5
McLeod → *Canada* 54°9N 115°44W 162 C5
MacLeod, L. *Australia* 24°9S 113°47E 149 D1
MacLeod B. *Canada* 62°53N 110°0W 163 A7
MacLeod Lake *Canada* 54°58N 123°0W 162 C4
McLoughlin, Mt. *U.S.A.* 42°27N 122°19W 168 E2
McMechen *U.S.A.* 39°57N 80°44W 174 G4
McMinnville *Oreg., U.S.A.* 45°13N 123°12W 168 D2
McMinnville *Tenn., U.S.A.* 35°41N 85°46W 177 D12
McMurdo *Antarctica* 77°51S 166°37E 55 D11
McMurdo Sd. *Antarctica* 77°0S 170°0E 55 D11
McMurray = Fort McMurray *Canada* 56°44N 111°7W 162 B6
McMurray *U.S.A.* 48°19N 122°14W 170 B4
Maçobere *Mozam.* 21°13S 32°47E 143 G3
Macodoene *Mozam.* 23°32S 35°5E 145 B6
Macomb *U.S.A.* 40°27N 90°40W 172 E8
Macomer *Italy* 40°16N 8°47E 94 B1
Mâcon *France* 46°19N 4°50E 71 F11
Macon *Ga., U.S.A.* 32°51N 83°38W 178 C6
Macon *Miss., U.S.A.* 33°7N 88°34W 177 E10
Macon *Mo., U.S.A.* 39°44N 92°28W 172 F7
Macossa *Mozam.* 17°55S 33°56E 143 F3
Macoun L. *Canada* 56°32N 103°40W 163 B8
Macovane *Mozam.* 21°30S 35°2E 145 B6
McPherson *U.S.A.* 38°22N 97°40W 172 F5
McPherson Pk. *U.S.A.* 34°53N 119°53W 171 L7
McPherson Ra. *Australia* 28°15S 153°15E 151 D5
Macquarie → *Australia* 30°7S 147°24E 153 A7
Macquarie Harbour *Australia* 42°15S 145°23E 151 G4
Macquarie I. *Pac. Oc.* 54°36S 158°55E 156 N7
Macquarie Ridge *S. Ocean* 57°0S 159°0E 55 B10
McRae *U.S.A.* 32°4N 82°54W 178 C7
MacRobertson Land *Antarctica* 71°0S 64°0E 55 D6
Macroom *Ireland* 51°54N 8°57W 64 E3
MacTier *Canada* 45°8N 79°47W 174 A5
Macubela *Mozam.* 16°53S 37°49E 143 F4
Macugnaga *Italy* 45°58N 7°58E 92 C4
Macuira △ *Colombia* 12°9N 71°21W 183 D5
Macumba → *Australia* 27°52S 137°12E 151 D2
Macuro *Venezuela* 10°42N 61°55W 187 K15
Macusani *Peru* 14°4S 70°29W 188 C3
Macuse *Mozam.* 17°45S 37°10E 143 F4
Macuspana *Mexico* 17°46N 92°36W 181 D6
Macusse *Angola* 17°48S 20°23E 144 A3
Mada → *Nigeria* 7°59N 7°55E 139 D6
Ma'dabā □ *Jordan* 31°43N 35°47E 130 D4
Madadeni *S. Africa* 27°43S 30°3E 145 C5
Madagali *Nigeria* 10°56N 13°33E 139 C7
Madagascar ■ *Africa* 20°0S 47°0E 141 J9
Madā'in Sālih *Si. Arabia* 26°46N 37°57E 128 E3
Madakasira *India* 13°56N 77°16E 127 H3
Madama *Niger* 22°0N 13°40E 135 D8
Madame, I. *Canada* 45°30N 60°58W 165 C7
Madan *Bulgaria* 41°30N 24°57E 97 E8
Madanapalle *India* 13°33N 78°28E 127 H4
Madang *Papua N. G.* 5°12S 145°49E 147 B7
Madaoua *Niger* 14°5N 6°27E 139 C6
Madara *Bulgaria* 43°17N 27°8E 97 C11
Madara *Nigeria* 11°45N 10°35E 139 C7
Madaripur *Bangla.* 23°19N 90°15E 123 H17
Madauk *Myanmar* 17°56N 96°52E 123 L20
Madawaska *Canada* 45°30N 78°0W 174 A7
Madawaska → *Canada* 45°27N 76°21W 174 A7
Madaya *Myanmar* 22°12N 96°10E 123 H20
Maddalena *Italy* 41°16N 9°23E 94 A2
Maddaloni *Italy* 41°2N 14°23E 95 A7
Maddur *India* 12°36N 77°4E 127 H3
Madeira *Atl. Oc.* 32°50N 17°0W 100 D3
Madeira → *Brazil* 3°22S 58°45W 186 D7
Madeleine, Îs. de la *Canada* 47°30N 61°40W 165 C7
Maden *Turkey* 38°23N 39°40E 105 C8
Madera *Mexico* 29°12N 108°7W 180 B3
Madera *Calif., U.S.A.* 36°57N 120°3W 170 J6
Madera *Pa., U.S.A.* 40°49N 78°26W 174 F6
Madgaon *India* 15°12N 73°58E 127 G1
Madha *India* 18°0N 75°30E 126 F2
Madhavpur *India* 21°15N 69°58E 124 J3
Madhepura *India* 26°11N 86°23E 125 F12
Madhira *India* 16°55N 80°22E 126 F5
Madhubani *India* 26°21N 86°7E 125 F12
Madhugiri *India* 13°40N 77°12E 127 H3
Madhupur *India* 24°16N 86°39E 125 G12
Madhya Pradesh □ *India* 22°50N 78°0E 124 J8
Madidi → *Bolivia* 12°32S 66°52W 188 C4
Madikeri *India* 12°30N 75°45E 127 H2
Madikwe ⌂ *S. Africa* 27°38S 32°15E 145 C5
Madill *U.S.A.* 34°6N 96°46W 176 D6
Madimba *Dem. Rep. of the Congo* 4°58S 15°5E 140 E3
Ma'din *Syria* 35°45N 39°36E 105 E8
Madina *Mali* 13°25N 8°50W 138 C3
Madinani *Côte d'Ivoire* 9°37N 6°57W 138 D3
Madīnat al Malik Khālid al Askarīyah *Si. Arabia* 27°54N 45°31E 128 E5
Madīnat ath Thawrah *Syria* 35°50N 38°32E 105 E8
Madīnat Masdar *U.A.E.* 24°26N 54°37E 129 E7
Madingou *Congo* 4°10S 13°33E 140 E2
Madison *Calif., U.S.A.* 38°41N 121°59W 170 G5
Madison *Fla., U.S.A.* 30°28N 83°25W 178 E6
Madison *Ga., U.S.A.* 33°36N 83°28W 178 B6
Madison *Ind., U.S.A.* 38°44N 85°23W 173 F11
Madison *Nebr., U.S.A.* 41°50N 97°27W 172 E5
Madison *Ohio, U.S.A.* 41°46N 81°3W 174 E3
Madison *S. Dak., U.S.A.* 44°0N 97°7W 172 C5
Madison *Wis., U.S.A.* 43°4N 89°24W 172 D9
Madison → *U.S.A.* 45°56N 111°31W 168 D8
Madison Heights *U.S.A.* 37°25N 79°8W 173 G14
Madisonville *Ky., U.S.A.* 37°20N 87°30W 172 G10
Madisonville *Tex., U.S.A.* 30°57N 95°55W 176 F7
Madista *Botswana* 21°15S 25°6E 144 B4
Madiun *Indonesia* 7°38S 111°32E 118 F4
Mado Gashi *Kenya* 0°44N 39°10E 142 B4
Madoc *Canada* 44°30N 77°28W 174 B7
Madoi *China* 34°46N 98°18E 110 E8
Madon → *France* 48°36N 6°2E 71 D13
Madona *Latvia* 56°53N 26°5E 84 D4
Madonie *Italy* 37°50N 13°50E 94 E6
Madonna di Campiglio *Italy* 46°14N 10°49E 92 B7
Madra Dağı *Turkey* 39°23N 27°12E 99 B9
Madrakah, Ra's al *Oman* 19°0N 57°50E 131 D6
Madras = Chennai *India* 13°8N 80°19E 127 H5
Madras = Tamil Nadu □ *India* 11°0N 77°0E 127 J3
Madras *U.S.A.* 44°38N 121°8W 168 D3
Madre, L. *U.S.A.* 26°50N 97°30W 176 J6
Madre, Sierra *Phil.* 17°0N 122°0E 119 A6
Madre de Dios □ *Peru* 12°0S 70°15W 188 C3
Madre de Dios → *Bolivia* 10°59S 66°8W 188 C4
Madre de Dios, I. *Chile* 50°20S 75°10W 192 D1
Madre del Sur, Sierra *Mexico* 17°30N 100°0W 181 D5
Madre Occidental, Sierra *Mexico* 27°0N 107°0W 180 B3
Madre Oriental, Sierra *Mexico* 25°0N 100°0W 180 C5
Madri *India* 24°16N 73°32E 124 G5
Madrid *Spain* 40°24N 3°42W 88 E7
Madrid *Ala., U.S.A.* 31°2N 85°24W 178 D4
Madrid *N.Y., U.S.A.* 44°45N 75°8W 175 B9
Madrid □ *Spain* 40°30N 3°45W 88 E7
Madrid Barajas ✕ (MAD) *Spain* 40°26N 3°34W 88 E7
Madridejos *Spain* 39°28N 3°33W 89 F7
Madrigal de las Altas Torres *Spain* 41°5N 5°0W 88 D6
Madrona, Sierra *Spain* 38°27N 4°16W 89 G6
Madroñera *Spain* 39°26N 5°42W 89 F5
Madula *Dem. Rep. of the Congo* 0°27N 25°22E 142 B2
Madura *Australia* 31°55S 127°0E 149 F4
Madura *Indonesia* 7°30S 114°0E 119 G15
Madura, Selat *Indonesia* 7°30S 113°20E 119 G15
Madura Oya △ *Sri Lanka* 7°20N 81°10E 127 L5
Madurai *India* 9°55N 78°10E 127 K4
Madurantakam *India* 12°30N 79°50E 127 H4
Madzhalis *Russia* 42°9N 47°47E 87 J8
Mae Chan *Thailand* 20°9N 99°52E 120 B2
Mae Charim △ *Thailand* 18°17N 100°59E 120 C3
Mae Hong Son *Thailand* 19°16N 97°56E 120 C2
Mae Khlong → *Thailand* 13°24N 100°0E 120 F3
Mae Moei △ *Thailand* 17°26N 98°7E 120 D2
Mae Phang △ *Thailand* 19°7N 99°13E 120 C2
Mae Phrik *Thailand* 17°27N 99°7E 120 D2
Mae Ping △ *Thailand* 17°37N 98°51E 120 D2
Mae Ramat *Thailand* 16°58N 98°31E 120 D2
Mae Rim *Thailand* 18°54N 98°57E 120 C2
Mae Sai *Thailand* 20°20N 99°55E 116 G2
Mae Sot *Thailand* 16°43N 98°34E 120 D2
Mae Suai *Thailand* 19°39N 99°33E 116 H2
Mae Tha *Thailand* 18°28N 99°8E 120 C2
Mae Tup Res. *Thailand* 17°52N 98°45E 120 D2
Mae Wa △ *Thailand* 17°23N 99°16E 120 D2
Mae Wong △ *Thailand* 15°54N 99°12E 120 E2
Mae Yom △ *Thailand* 18°43N 100°15E 120 C3
Maebaru *Japan* 33°33N 130°12E 113 H5
Maebashi *Japan* 36°24N 139°4E 113 F9
Maella *Spain* 41°8N 0°7E 90 D5
Maelpaeg L. *Canada* 48°20N 56°30W 165 C8
Maestra, Sierra *Cuba* 20°15N 77°0W 182 B4
Maevatanana *Madag.* 16°56S 46°49E 141 H9
Mafadi *S. Africa* 29°12S 29°21E 145 C4
Mafeking = Mafikeng *S. Africa* 25°50S 25°38E 144 C4
Mafeking *Canada* 52°40N 101°10W 163 C8
Maféré *Côte d'Ivoire* 5°30N 3°2W 138 D4
Mafeteng *Lesotho* 29°51S 27°15E 144 C4
Maffra *Australia* 37°53S 146°58E 153 D7
Mafia I. *Tanzania* 7°45S 39°50E 142 D4
Mafikeng *S. Africa* 25°50S 25°38E 144 C4
Mafra *Brazil* 26°10S 49°55W 191 B6
Mafra *Portugal* 38°55N 9°20W 89 G1
Mafungabusi Plateau *Zimbabwe* 18°30S 29°8E 143 F2
Magadan *Russia* 59°38N 150°50E 107 D16
Magadi *India* 12°58N 77°14E 127 H3
Magadi *Kenya* 1°54S 36°19E 142 C4
Magadi, L. *Kenya* 1°54S 36°19E 142 C4
Magaliesburg *S. Africa* 26°0S 27°32E 145 C4
Magallanes □ *Chile* 52°0S 72°0W 192 D2
Magallanes, Estrecho de *Chile* 52°30S 75°0W 192 D2
Magaluf *Spain* 39°29N 2°32E 91 F7
Magangué *Colombia* 9°14N 74°45W 186 B4
Magaria *Niger* 13°4N 9°5E 139 C6
Magburaka *S. Leone* 8°47N 12°0W 138 D2
Magdagachi *Russia* 53°27N 125°48E 107 D13
Magdalen Is. = Madeleine, Îs. de la *Canada* 47°30N 61°40W 165 C7
Magdalena *Argentina* 35°5S 57°30W 190 D4
Magdalena *Bolivia* 13°13S 63°57W 186 F6
Magdalena *U.S.A.* 34°7N 107°15W 169 J10
Magdalena → *Colombia* 11°6N 74°51W 186 A4
Magdalena, B. *Mexico* 24°35N 112°0W 180 C2
Magdalena, I. *Chile* 44°40S 73°0W 192 B2
Magdalena, I. *Mexico* 24°40N 112°15W 180 C2
Magdalena, Llano de *Mexico* 25°0N 111°25W 180 C2
Magdalena de Kino *Mexico* 30°38N 110°57W 180 A2
Magdeburg *Germany* 52°7N 11°38E 76 C7
Magdelaine Cays *Australia* 16°33S 150°18E 150 B5
Magee *U.S.A.* 31°52N 89°44W 177 F10
Magelang *Indonesia* 7°29S 110°13E 118 F4
Magellan's Str. = Magallanes, Estrecho de *Chile* 52°30S 75°0W 192 D2
Magenta *Italy* 45°28N 8°53E 92 C5
Magenta, L. *Australia* 33°30S 119°2E 149 F2
Magerøya *Norway* 71°3N 25°40E 60 A21
Maggea *Australia* 34°28S 140°2E 152 C4
Maggia → *Switz.* 46°18N 8°36E 77 J4
Maggiorasca, Mte. *Italy* 44°33N 9°29E 92 D6
Maggiore, L. *Italy* 45°57N 8°39E 92 B5
Maggotty *Jamaica* 18°9N 77°46W 182 a
Maghâgha *Egypt* 28°38N 30°50E 137 F7
Maghama *Mauritania* 15°32N 12°57W 138 B2
Maghera *U.K.* 54°51N 6°41W 64 B5
Magherafelt *U.K.* 54°45N 6°37W 64 B5
Maghnia *Algeria* 34°50N 1°43W 136 B3
Maghreb *N. Afr.* 32°0N 4°0W 132 C3
Magione *Italy* 43°8N 12°12E 93 E9
Magistralnyy *Russia* 56°16N 107°36E 107 D11
Maglaj *Bos.-H.* 44°33N 18°7E 80 F3
Magliano in Toscana *Italy* 42°36N 11°17E 93 F8
Máglie *Italy* 40°7N 18°18E 95 B11
Maglizh *Bulgaria* 42°37N 25°32E 97 D9
Magnac-Laval *France* 46°13N 1°11E 72 B5
Magnesia = Magnisía *Greece* 39°15N 23°0E 98 B5
Magnetic Pole (North) *Arctic* 85°9N 149°0W 54 A1
Magnetic Pole (South) *Antarctica* 64°8S 138°8E 55 C9
Magnisía *Greece* 39°15N 23°0E 98 B5
Magnitogorsk *Russia* 53°27N 59°4E 108 B5
Magnolia *Ark., U.S.A.* 33°16N 93°14W 176 E8
Magnolia *Miss., U.S.A.* 31°9N 90°28W 177 F9
Magny-en-Vexin *France* 49°9N 1°47E 71 C8
Mago *Fiji* 17°26S 179°8W 154 a
Magog *Canada* 45°18N 72°9W 175 A12
Magoro *Uganda* 1°45N 34°12E 142 B3
Magoulades *Greece* 39°45N 19°42E 101 A3
Magoye *Zambia* 16°1S 27°30E 143 F2
Magpie, L. *Canada* 51°0N 64°41W 165 B7
Magrath *Canada* 49°25N 112°50W 162 D6
Magre → *Spain* 39°11N 0°25W 91 F4
Magta Lahjar *Mauritania* 17°28N 13°17W 138 B2
Magu *Tanzania* 2°30S 33°30E 142 C3
Maguan *China* 23°0N 104°21E 116 F5
Maguarinho, C. *Brazil* 0°15S 48°30W 187 D9
Magude *Mozam.* 25°2S 32°40E 145 C5
Magurski △ *Poland* 49°30N 21°30E 83 J8
Mağusa = Famagusta *Cyprus* 35°8N 33°55E 101 D12
Maguse L. *Canada* 61°37N 95°10W 163 A9
Maguse Pt. *Canada* 61°20N 93°50W 163 A10
Magvana *India* 23°13N 69°22E 124 H3
Magway *Myanmar* 20°10N 95°0E 123 J19
Magyarorszag = Hungary ■ *Europe* 47°20N 19°20E 79 D12
Maha Oya *Sri Lanka* 7°31N 81°22E 127 L5
Maha Sarakham *Thailand* 16°12N 103°16E 120 D4
Mahābād *Iran* 36°50N 45°45E 105 D11
Mahabaleshwar *India* 17°58N 73°43E 126 F1
Mahabalipuram *India* 12°37N 80°11E 127 H5
Mahabharat Lekh *Nepal* 28°30N 82°0E 125 E10
Mahabo *Madag.* 20°23S 44°40E 141 J8
Mahad *India* 18°6N 73°29E 126 E1
Mahadeo Hills *India* 22°20N 78°30E 125 H8
Mahadeopur *India* 18°48N 80°0E 126 E5
Mahaffey *U.S.A.* 40°53N 78°44W 174 F6
Mahagi *Dem. Rep. of the Congo* 2°20N 31°0E 142 B3
Mahajan *India* 28°48N 73°56E 124 E5
Mahajanga *Madag.* 15°40S 46°25E 141 H9
Mahakam → *Indonesia* 0°35S 117°17E 118 E5
Mahalapye *Botswana* 23°1S 26°51E 144 B4
Mahale Mts. *Tanzania* 6°20S 30°0E 142 D3
Mahale Mts. △ *Tanzania* 6°10S 29°50E 142 D2
Maḩallāt *Iran* 33°55N 50°30E 129 C6
Māhān *Iran* 30°5N 57°18E 129 D8
Mahan → *India* 23°30N 82°50E 125 H10
Mahanadi → *India* 20°20N 86°25E 126 D8
Mahananda → *India* 25°12N 87°52E 125 G12
Mahanoro *Madag.* 19°54S 48°48E 141 H9
Mahanoy City *U.S.A.* 40°49N 76°9W 175 F8
Maharashtra □ *India* 20°30N 75°30E 126 D2
Maharès *Tunisia* 34°32N 10°29E 136 B6
Mahasamund *India* 21°6N 82°6E 126 D6
Mahasham, W. → *Egypt* 30°15N 34°10E 130 E3
Mahattat ash Shīdīyah *Jordan* 29°55N 35°55E 130 F4
Mahattat 'Unayzah *Jordan* 30°30N 35°47E 130 E4
Mahaweli Ganga → *Sri Lanka* 8°27N 81°13E 127 K5
Mahaxay *Laos* 17°22N 105°12E 120 D5
Mahbubabad *India* 17°42N 80°2E 126 F5
Mahbubnagar *India* 16°45N 77°59E 126 F3
Mahda *U.A.E.* 25°20N 56°15E 129 E8
Maḩḍah *Oman* 24°24N 55°59E 129 E7
Mahdia *Tunisia* 35°28N 11°0E 136 A6
Mahdia □ *Tunisia* 35°20N 10°35E 136 B6
Mahe *Jammu & Kashmir, India* 33°10N 78°32E 125 C8
Mahé *Puducherry, India* 11°42N 75°34E 127 J2
Mahé *Seychelles* 5°0S 55°30E 141 b
Mahé ✕ (SEZ) *Seychelles* 4°40S 55°31E 141 b
Mahébourg *Mauritius* 20°24S 57°42E 141 d
Mahendra Giri *India* 8°20N 77°30E 127 K3
Mahendragarh *India* 28°17N 76°14E 124 E7
Mahendranagar *Nepal* 28°55N 80°20E 125 E9
Mahenge *Tanzania* 8°45S 36°41E 143 D4
Maheno *N.Z.* 45°10S 170°50E 155 F5
Mahesana *India* 23°39N 72°26E 124 H5
Maheshwar *India* 22°11N 75°35E 124 H6
Mahgawan *India* 26°29N 78°37E 125 F8
Mahi → *India* 22°15N 72°55E 124 H5
Mahia Pen. *N.Z.* 39°9S 177°55E 154 F6
Mahikeng = Mafikeng *S. Africa* 25°50S 25°38E 144 C4
Mahilyow *Belarus* 53°55N 30°18E 75 B16
Mahilyow □ *Belarus* 54°10N 30°50E 84 E6
Mahim *India* 19°39N 72°44E 126 E1
Mahina *Tahiti* 17°30S 149°27W 155 b
Mahirija *Morocco* 34°0N 3°16W 136 B3
Mahmud Kot *Pakistan* 30°16N 71°0E 124 D4
Mahmudia *Romania* 45°5N 29°5E 81 E14
Mahmudiye *Turkey* 39°48N 30°15E 99 B12
Mahmutbey *Turkey* 41°3N 28°49E 97 E12
Māhneshān *Iran* 36°44N 47°39E 105 D12
Mahnomen *U.S.A.* 47°19N 95°58W 172 B6
Maho *Sri Lanka* 7°49N 80°16E 127 L5
Mahoba *India* 25°15N 79°55E 125 G8
Mahón = Maó *Spain* 39°53N 4°16E 100 B11
Mahon, Menorca ✕ (MAH) *Spain* 39°50N 4°16E 90 F9
Mahone Bay *Canada* 44°27N 64°23W 165 D7
Mahongo ⌂ *Namibia* 18°0S 23°15E 144 B3
Mahopac *U.S.A.* 41°22N 73°45W 175 E11
Mahuta *Nigeria* 11°32N 4°58E 139 C5
Mahuva *India* 21°5N 71°48E 124 J4
Mahya Daği *Turkey* 41°47N 27°36E 97 E11
Mai-Ndombe, L. *Dem. Rep. of the Congo* 2°0S 18°20E 140 E3
Mai Thon, Ko *Thailand* 7°40N 98°28E 121 a
Maia *Portugal* 41°14N 8°37W 88 D2
Maials *Spain* 41°22N 0°30E 90 D5
Maîche *France* 47°16N 6°48E 71 E13
Maicuru → *Brazil* 2°14S 54°17W 187 D8
Máida *Italy* 38°51N 16°22E 95 D9
Maidan Khula *Afghan.* 33°36N 69°50E 124 C3
Maidenhead *U.K.* 51°31N 0°42W 67 F7
Maidstone *Canada* 53°5N 109°20W 163 C7
Maidstone *U.K.* 51°16N 0°32E 67 F8
Maiduguri *Nigeria* 12°0N 13°20E 139 C7
Maiella △ *Italy* 42°5N 14°5E 93 F11
Măieruș *Romania* 45°53N 25°31E 81 E10
Maigatari *Nigeria* 12°46N 9°27E 139 C6
Maigh Nuad = Maynooth *Ireland* 53°23N 6°34W 64 C5
Maignelay Montigny *France* 49°32N 2°30E 71 C9
Maihar *India* 24°16N 80°45E 125 G9
Maikala Ra. *India* 22°0N 81°0E 126 D5
Maiko △ *Dem. Rep. of the Congo* 0°30S 27°50E 142 C2
Mailani *India* 28°17N 80°21E 125 E9
Maillezais *France* 46°22N 0°45W 72 B3
Mailsi *Pakistan* 29°48N 72°15E 124 E5
Main → *Germany* 50°0N 8°18E 77 F4
Main → *U.K.* 54°48N 6°18W 64 B5
Main Channel *Canada* 45°21N 81°45W 174 A3
Main Range △ *Australia* 28°11S 152°27E 151 D5
Main Ridge *Trin. & Tob.* 11°16N 60°40W 187 J16
Mainburg *Germany* 48°38N 11°47E 77 G7
Maindargi *India* 17°28N 76°18E 126 F3
Maine *France* 48°20N 0°15W 70 D6
Maine □ *U.S.A.* 45°20N 69°0W 173 C19
Maine → *Ireland* 52°9N 9°45W 64 D2
Maine, G. of *U.S.A.* 43°0N 68°30W 167 G26
Maine-et-Loire □ *France* 47°31N 0°30W 70 E6
Maïne-Soroa *Niger* 13°13N 12°2E 139 C7
Maingkwan *Myanmar* 26°15N 96°37E 123 F20
Mainistir na Corann = Midleton *Ireland* 51°55N 8°10W 64 E3
Mainit, L. *Phil.* 9°31N 125°30E 119 C7
Mainland *Orkney, U.K.* 58°59N 3°8W 65 C5
Mainland *Shet., U.K.* 60°15N 1°22W 65 A7
Mainpuri *India* 27°18N 79°4E 125 F8
Maintal *Germany* 50°7N 8°52E 77 E4
Maintenon *France* 48°35N 1°35E 71 D8
Maintirano *Madag.* 18°3S 44°1E 141 H8
Mainz *Germany* 50°1N 8°14E 77 E4
Maio *Cabo Verde* 15°10N 23°10W 134 b
Maipú *Argentina* 36°52S 57°50W 190 D4
Maiquetía *Venezuela* 10°36N 66°57W 186 A5
Máira → *Italy* 44°49N 7°38E 92 D4
Mairabari *India* 26°30N 92°22E 123 F18
Mairena del Aljarafe *Spain* 37°20N 6°6W 89 H4
Maisi *Cuba* 20°17N 74°9W 183 B5
Maisí, Pta. de *Cuba* 20°10N 74°10W 183 B5
Maitland *N.S.W., Australia* 32°33S 151°36E 153 B9
Maitland *S. Austral., Australia* 34°23S 137°40E 152 C2
Maitland → *Canada* 43°45N 81°43W 174 C3
Maitri *Antarctica* 70°0S 3°0W 55 D3
Maiyema *Nigeria* 12°5N 4°25E 139 C5
Maiyuan *China* 25°34N 117°28E 117 E11
Maiz, Is. del *Nic.* 12°15N 83°4W 182 D3
Maizuru *Japan* 35°25N 135°22E 113 G7
Majalengka *Indonesia* 6°50S 108°13E 119 G13
Majanji *Uganda* 0°16N 34°0E 142 B3
Majella = Maiella △ *Italy* 42°5N 14°5E 93 F11
Majene *Indonesia* 3°38S 118°57E 119 E5
Majete ⌂ *Malawi* 15°54S 34°34E 143 F3
Majevica *Bos.-H.* 44°45N 18°50E 80 F3
Majiang *China* 26°28N 107°32E 116 D6
Majorca = Mallorca *Spain* 39°30N 3°0E 100 B10
Majors Creek *Australia* 35°33S 149°45E 153 C8
Majuro *Marshall Is.* 7°9N 171°12E 156 G9
Mak, Ko *Thailand* 11°49N 102°29E 121 G4
Maka *Senegal* 13°40N 14°10W 138 C2
Makaha *Zimbabwe* 17°20S 32°39E 145 A5
Makak *Cameroon* 3°36N 11°0E 139 E7
Makalamabedi *Botswana* 20°19S 23°51E 144 B3
Makale *Indonesia* 3°6S 119°51E 119 E5
Makalu *Nepal* 27°55N 87°8E 125 F12
Makalu-Barun △ *Nepal* 27°45N 87°10E 125 F12
Makamba *Burundi* 4°8S 29°49E 142 C2
Makarewa Junction *N.Z.* 46°20S 168°21E 155 G3
Makari *Cameroon* 12°35N 10°27E 139 C7
Makarikari = Makgadikgadi Salt Pans *Botswana* 20°40S 25°45E 144 B4
Makarov Basin *Arctic* 87°0N 150°0W 54 A
Makarovo *Russia* 57°40N 107°45E 107 D11
Makarska *Croatia* 43°20N 17°2E 93 E14
Makaryev *Russia* 57°52N 43°50E 86 B6
Makassar *Indonesia* 5°10S 119°20E 119 F5
Makassar, Selat *Indonesia* 1°0S 118°20E 119 E5
Makassar, Str. of = Makassar, Selat *Indonesia* 1°0S 118°20E 119 E5
Makat = Maqat *Kazakhstan* 47°39N 53°19E 108 C4
Makedonija = Macedonia ■ *Europe* 41°53N 21°40E 96 E5
Makeni *S. Leone* 8°55N 12°5W 138 D2
Makeyevka = Makiyivka *Ukraine* 48°0N 38°0E 85 H9
Makgadikgadi △ *Botswana* 20°27S 24°47E 144 B3
Makgadikgadi Salt Pans *Botswana* 20°40S 25°45E 144 B4
Makhachkala *Russia* 43°0N 47°30E 87 J8
Makhado = Louis Trichardt *S. Africa* 23°1S 29°43E 145 B4
Makham, Ao *Thailand* 7°51N 98°25E 121 a
Makharadze = Ozurgeti *Georgia* 41°55N 42°0E 87 K5
Makhfar al Buşayyah *Iraq* 30°0N 46°10E 128 D5
Makhmūr *Iraq* 35°46N 43°35E 105 E10
Makhtal *India* 16°30N 77°31E 127 E3
Makian *Indonesia* 0°20N 127°20E 119 D7
Makindu *Kenya* 2°18S 37°50E 142 C4
Makīnsk *Kazakhstan* 52°37N 70°26E 109 B8
Makira = San Cristóbal *Solomon Is.* 10°30S 161°0E 147 C9
Makiyivka *Ukraine* 48°0N 38°0E 85 H9
Makkah *Si. Arabia* 21°30N 39°54E 137 C4
Makkovik *Canada* 55°10N 59°10W 165 A8
Makó *Hungary* 46°14N 20°33E 80 D5
Mako *Senegal* 12°52N 12°20W 138 C2
Makogai *Fiji* 17°28S 179°0E 154 a
Makokou *Gabon* 0°40N 12°50E 140 D2
Makongo *Dem. Rep. of the Congo* 3°25N 26°17E 142 B2
Makoro *Dem. Rep. of the Congo* 3°10N 29°59E 142 B2
Maków Mazowiecki *Poland* 52°52N 21°6E 83 F8
Maków Podhalański *Poland* 49°43N 19°45E 83 J6
Makra *Greece* 36°15N 25°54E 99 E7
Makrai *India* 22°2N 77°0E 124 H7
Makran Coast Range *Pakistan* 25°40N 64°0E 122 G4
Makrana *India* 27°2N 74°46E 124 F6
Makrany *Belarus* 51°48N 24°17E 83 G11
Makri *Greece* 40°52N 25°40E 97 F9
Makri *India* 19°46N 81°55E 126 E5
Makrigialos *Greece* 35°2N 25°59E 101 D7
Makthar *Tunisia* 35°48N 9°12E 136 A5
Mākū *Iran* 39°15N 44°31E 105 C11
Makueni □ *Kenya* 1°50S 37°40E 142 C4
Makunda *Botswana* 22°30S 20°7E 144 B3
Makung *Taiwan* 23°34N 119°34E 117 F12
Makurazaki *Japan* 31°15N 130°20E 113 J5
Makurdi *Nigeria* 7°43N 8°35E 139 D6
Makushin Volcano *U.S.A.* 53°53N 166°55W 166 E6
Makūyeh *Iran* 28°7N 53°9E 129 D7
Makwassie *S. Africa* 27°17S 26°0E 144 C4
Makwiro *Zimbabwe* 17°58S 30°25E 145 A5
Mâl *Mauritania* 16°58N 13°23W 138 B2
Mal B. *Ireland* 52°50N 9°30W 64 D2
Mala = Mallow *Ireland* 52°8N 8°39W 64 D3
Mala *Peru* 12°40S 76°38W 188 C2
Mala ✪ *Australia* 21°39S 130°45E 148 D5
Mala, Pta. *Panama* 7°28N 80°2W 182 E3
Malá Belozërka *Ukraine* 47°12N 34°56E 85 J8
Malá Fatra △ *Slovakia* 49°10N 19°0E 79 B12
Mala Kapela *Croatia* 44°45N 15°30E 93 D12
Mala Panew → *Poland* 50°43N 17°54E 83 H4
Mala Vyska *Ukraine* 48°39N 31°36E 85 H6
Malabar *U.S.A.* 28°0N 80°34W 179 H9
Malabar Coast *India* 11°0N 75°0E 127 J2
Malabu *Nigeria* 9°32N 12°48E 139 D7
Malacca, Straits of *Indonesia* 3°0N 101°0E 121 L3
Malacky *Slovakia* 48°27N 17°0E 79 C10
Malad City *U.S.A.* 42°12N 112°15W 168 E7
Maladeta *Spain* 42°39N 0°39E 90 C5
Maladzyechna *Belarus* 54°20N 26°50E 75 A14
Málaga *Spain* 36°43N 4°23W 89 J6
Málaga □ *Spain* 36°38N 4°58W 89 J6
Malagarasi *Tanzania* 5°5S 30°50E 142 D3
Malagarasi → *Tanzania* 5°12S 29°47E 142 D2
Malagasy Rep. = Madagascar ■ *Africa* 20°0S 47°0E 141 J9

Malagón Spain 39°11N 3°52W 89 F7
Malagón → Spain 37°35N 7°29W 89 H3
Malahide Ireland 53°26N 6°9W 64 C5
Malaimbandy Madag. 20°20S 45°36E 141 J9
Malaita Solomon Is. 9°0S 161°0E 147 B9
Malakal South Sudan 9°33N 31°40E 135 G12
Malakanagiri India 18°21N 81°54E 126 E5
Malakand Pakistan 34°40N 71°55E 124 B4
Malakula Vanuatu 16°15S 167°30E 147 C9
Malakwal Pakistan 32°34N 73°13E 124 C5
Malamala Indonesia 3°21S 120°55E 119 E6
Malanda Australia 17°22S 145°35E 150 B4
Malang Indonesia 7°59S 112°45E 118 F4
Malanga Mozam. 13°28S 36°7E 143 E4
Malangen Norway 69°24N 18°37E 60 B18
Malangwa Nepal 26°52N 85°34E 125 F11
Malanje Angola 9°36S 16°17E 140 F3
Malappuram India 11°7N 76°11E 127 J3
Mälaren Sweden 59°30N 17°10E 62 E11
Malargüe Argentina 35°32S 69°30W 190 D2
Malartic Canada 48°9N 78°9W 164 C4
Malaryta Belarus 51°50N 24°3E 83 G11
Malaspina Glacier U.S.A. 59°50N 140°30W 166 D11
Malatya Turkey 38°25N 38°20E 105 C6
Malatya □ Turkey 38°15N 38°0E 104 C7
Malawi ■ Africa 11°55S 34°0E 143 E3
Malawi, L. Africa 12°30S 34°30E 143 E3
Malay Pen. Asia 7°25N 100°0E 121 J3
Malaya Belozërka = Mala Belozërka Ukraine 47°12N 34°56E 85 J8
Malaya Vishera Russia 58°55N 32°25E 84 C7
Malaya Viska = Mala Vyska Ukraine 48°39N 31°36E 85 H6
Malaybalay Phil. 8°5N 125°7E 119 C7
Malãyer Iran 34°19N 48°51E 105 E13
Malaysia ■ Asia 5°0N 110°0E 118 D4
Malazgirt Turkey 39°10N 42°33E 105 C10
Malbaza Niger 13°59N 5°38E 139 C6
Malbon Australia 21°5S 140°17E 150 C3
Malbooma Australia 30°41S 134°11E 151 E1
Malbork Poland 54°3N 19°1E 82 D6
Malcésine Italy 45°46N 10°48E 92 C7
Malchin Germany 53°44N 12°44E 76 B8
Malchow Germany 53°28N 12°25E 76 B8
Malcolm Australia 28°51S 121°25E 149 E3
Malcolm, Pt. Australia 33°48S 123°45E 149 F3
Malczyce Poland 51°14N 16°29E 83 G3
Maldah India 25°2N 88°9E 125 G13
Maldegem Belgium 51°14N 3°26E 69 C3
Malden Mass., U.S.A. 42°26N 71°3W 175 D13
Malden Mo., U.S.A. 36°34N 89°57W 172 G9
Malden I. Kiribati 4°3S 155°1W 157 H12
Maldives ■ Ind. Oc. 5°0N 73°0E 103 H9
Maldon Australia 37°0S 144°6E 152 D6
Maldon U.K. 51°44N 0°42E 67 F8
Maldonado Uruguay 34°59S 55°0W 191 C5
Maldonado, Pta. Mexico 16°20N 98°33W 181 D5
Malè Italy 46°21N 10°55E 92 B7
Malé Maldives 4°10N 73°28E 146 D6
Malé Karpaty Slovakia 48°30N 17°20E 79 C10
Maleas, Akra Greece 36°28N 23°7E 98 E5
Malebo, Pool Africa 4°17S 15°20E 140 E3
Malegaon India 20°30N 74°38E 126 D2
Malei Mozam. 17°12S 36°58E 143 C6
Malek Kandĩ Iran 37°9N 46°6E 105 C12
Malela Dem. Rep. of the Congo 4°22S 26°8E 142 C2
Malema Mozam. 14°57S 37°20E 143 E4
Maleme Greece 35°31N 23°49E 101 D5
Maler Kotla India 30°32N 75°58E 124 D6
Måleräs Sweden 56°54N 15°34E 63 H8
Males Greece 35°6N 25°35E 101 D7
Malesherbes France 48°15N 2°24E 71 D9
Maleshevska Planina Europe 41°38N 23°7E 96 E7
Malesina Greece 38°37N 23°14E 98 C5
Malestroit France 47°49N 2°25W 70 E4
Malfa Italy 38°35N 14°50E 95 D7
Malgobek Russia 43°30N 44°34E 87 J7
Malgomaj Sweden 64°40N 16°30E 60 D17
Malgrat de Mar Spain 41°39N 2°46E 90 D7
Malha Sudan 15°8N 25°10E 135 E11
Malhada Brazil 14°15S 43°47W 189 C2
Malhargarh India 24°17N 74°59E 124 G6
Malheur → U.S.A. 44°4N 116°59W 168 E4
Malheur L. U.S.A. 43°20N 118°48W 168 E4
Mali Guinea 12°10N 12°20W 138 C2
Mali ■ Africa 17°0N 3°0W 138 B4
Mali → Myanmar 25°42N 97°30E 123 G20
Mali Kanal Serbia 45°36N 19°24E 80 E4
Mali Kyun Myanmar 13°0N 98°20E 128 C2
Malia Greece 35°17N 25°32E 101 D7
Malia, Kolpos Greece 35°19N 25°27E 101 D7
Malibu U.S.A. 34°2N 118°41W 171 L8
Maliku = Minicoy I. India 8°17N 73°2E 127 K1
Malili Indonesia 0°39S 123°16E 119 E6
Malili Indonesia 2°42S 121°6E 119 E6
Mälilla Sweden 57°23N 15°48E 63 G9
Malimba, Mts. Dem. Rep. of the Congo 7°30S 29°30E 142 D2
Malin Hd. Ireland 55°23N 7°23W 64 A4
Malin Pen. Ireland 55°20N 7°17W 64 A4
Malindi Kenya 3°12S 40°5E 142 C5
Malindi Marine △ Kenya 3°15S 40°7E 142 C5
Malines = Mechelen Belgium 51°2N 4°29E 69 C4
Malino Indonesia 1°0N 121°0E 119 D6
Malinyi Tanzania 8°56S 36°0E 143 D4
Malipo China 23°7N 104°42E 116 F5
Maliq Albania 40°45N 20°48E 96 F4
Malita Phil. 6°19N 125°39E 119 C7
Maliwun Myanmar 10°17N 98°40E 121 G2
Maliya India 23°5N 70°46E 124 H4
Maljenik Serbia 43°54N 21°43E 96 C5
Malka Mari △ Kenya 4°13N 40°20E 142 B5
Malkapur India 20°53N 76°12E 126 D3
Malkara Turkey 40°53N 26°53E 97 F10
Malkhangiri = Malakanagiri India 18°21N 81°54E 126 E5
Malkinia Górna Poland 52°42N 22°5E 83 E9
Malko Tarnovo Bulgaria 41°59N 27°31E 97 E11
Mallacoota Australia 37°40S 149°40E 153 D8
Mallacoota Inlet Australia 37°34S 149°40E 153 D8
Malladi U.K. 57°0N 5°59W 66 H6
Mallala Australia 34°26S 138°30E 152 C3
Mallaoua Niger 13°2N 9°36E 139 C6
Mallawan India 27°4N 80°12E 125 F9

Mallawi Egypt 27°44N 30°44E 137 B3
Mallee Cliffs △ Australia 34°16S 142°32E 152 C5
Mallemort France 43°43N 5°11E 73 E9
Málles Venosta Italy 46°41N 10°32E 92 B7
Mallicolo = Malakula Vanuatu 16°15S 167°30E 147 C9
Mallorca Spain 39°30N 3°0E 100 B10
Mallorytown Canada 44°29N 75°53W 175 B9
Mallow Ireland 52°8N 8°39W 64 D3
Malmbäck Sweden 57°34N 14°28E 63 G8
Malmberget Sweden 67°11N 20°40E 60 C19
Malmédy Belgium 50°25N 6°2E 69 D6
Malmesbury S. Africa 33°28S 18°41E 144 D2
Malmivaara = Malmberget Sweden 67°11N 20°40E 60 C19
Malmköping Sweden 59°8N 16°44E 62 E10
Malmö Sweden 55°36N 12°59E 63 J6
Malmslätt Sweden 58°27N 15°33E 63 F9
Malmyzh Russia 56°31N 50°41E 86 B10
Malnaš Romania 46°2N 25°49E 81 D10
Malo Konare Bulgaria 42°12N 24°24E 97 D8
Maloarkhangelsk Russia 52°28N 36°30E 85 F9
Malolo Fiji 17°45S 177°11E 154 a
Malolos Phil. 14°50N 120°49E 119 B6
Malolotja △ Swaziland 26°4S 31°6E 145 C5
Malombe L. Malawi 14°40S 35°15E 143 E4
Malomice Poland 51°34N 15°29E 83 G2
Malomir Bulgaria 42°16N 26°32E 97 D10
Malone Fla., U.S.A. 30°57N 85°10W 178 E4
Malone N.Y., U.S.A. 44°51N 74°18W 175 B10
Malong China 25°24N 103°34E 116 E4
Małopolskie □ Poland 49°50N 20°20E 83 J7
Malorad Bulgaria 43°28N 23°41E 96 C7
Maloti Mts. = Drakensberg S. Africa 31°0S 28°0E 145 D4
Måløy Norway 61°57N 5°6E 60 F11
Maloyaroslovets Russia 55°2N 36°20E 84 E9
Malpartida de Cáceres Spain 39°26N 6°30W 89 F4
Malpaso Canary Is. 27°43N 18°3W 100 G1
Malpaso, Presa = Netzahualcóyotl, Presa Mexico 17°8N 93°35W 181 D6
Malpelo, I. de Colombia 3°4N 81°35W 186 C2
Malpica de Bergantiños Spain 43°19N 8°50W 88 B2
Malprabha → India 16°20N 76°5E 127 F3
Malpur India 23°21N 73°27E 124 H5
Malpura India 26°17N 75°23E 124 F6
Mals = Málles Venosta Italy 46°41N 10°32E 92 B7
Malsiras India 17°52N 74°55E 126 F2
Malta Italy 6°54S 37°31W 189 B3
Malta Idaho, U.S.A. 42°18N 113°22W 168 E7
Malta Mont., U.S.A. 48°21N 107°52W 168 B10
Malta ■ Europe 35°55N 14°26E 101 D2
Maltahöhe Namibia 24°55S 17°0E 144 B2
Maltepe Turkey 40°55N 29°8E 97 F13
Malton Canada 43°42N 79°38W 174 C5
Malton U.K. 54°8N 0°49W 66 C7
Maluku Indonesia 1°0S 127°0E 119 E7
Maluku □ Indonesia 3°0S 128°0E 119 E7
Maluku Sea = Molucca Sea Indonesia 0°0 125°0E 119 E6
Malumfashi Nigeria 11°48N 7°39E 139 C6
Malung Sweden 60°42N 13°44E 62 D7
Malungsfors Sweden 60°44N 13°33E 62 D7
Malur India 13°0N 77°55E 127 H3
Maluwe Ghana 8°40N 2°17W 138 D4
Malvalli India 12°28N 77°8E 127 H3
Malvan India 16°2N 73°30E 127 F1
Malvern U.S.A. 34°22N 92°49W 176 D8
Malvern Hills U.K. 52°0N 2°19W 67 E5
Malvinas, Is. = Falkland Is. ☒ Atl. Oc. 51°30S 59°0W 192 D5
Malý Dunaj → Slovakia 47°45N 18°9E 79 D11
Malya Tanzania 3°5S 33°38E 142 C3
Malye Derbety Russia 47°57N 44°42E 87 G7
Malyn Ukraine 50°46N 29°3E 75 C15
Malyy Lyakhovskiy, Ostrov Russia 74°7N 140°36E 107 B15
Malyy Taymyr, Ostrov Russia 78°6N 107°15E 107 B11
Mama Russia 58°18N 112°54E 107 D12
Mamaku N.Z. 38°5S 176°8E 154 E5
Mamanguape Brazil 6°50S 35°4W 189 D4
Mamanuca Group Fiji 17°35S 177°5E 154 a
Mamarr Mitlā Egypt 30°2N 32°54E 130 E1
Mamasa Indonesia 2°55S 119°20E 119 E5
Mambasa Dem. Rep. of the Congo 1°22N 29°3E 142 B2
Mamberamo → Indonesia 2°0S 137°50E 119 E9
Mambilima Falls Zambia 10°31S 28°45E 143 E2
Mambirima Dem. Rep. of the Congo 11°25S 27°33E 143 E2
Mambo Tanzania 4°52S 38°22E 142 C4
Mambrui Kenya 3°5S 40°5E 142 C5
Mamburao Phil. 13°13N 120°39E 119 B6
Mamedkala Russia 42°10N 48°7E 87 J9
Mameigwess L. Canada 52°35N 87°50W 164 B2
Mamers France 48°21N 0°22E 70 D7
Mamfé Cameroon 5°50N 9°15E 139 D6
Mamili △ Namibia 18°2S 24°1E 144 A3
Mamiña Chile 20°5S 69°14W 188 E4
Mamlyutka Kazakhstan 54°56N 68°32E 109 B7
Mammoth U.S.A. 32°43N 110°39W 169 K8
Mammoth Cave △ U.S.A. 37°8N 86°13W 172 G10
Mammoth Lakes U.S.A. 37°39N 118°59W 170 H8
Mamonovo Russia 54°28N 19°55E 82 D6
Mamoré → Bolivia 10°23S 65°53W 187 F5
Mamou Guinea 10°15N 12°0W 138 C2
Mamoudzou Mayotte 12°48S 45°14E 141 a
Mampong Ghana 7°6N 1°26W 139 D4
Mamry, Jezioro Poland 54°5N 21°50E 82 D8
Mamuil Malal, Paso S. Amer. 39°35S 71°28W 192 A2
Mamuju Indonesia 2°41S 118°50E 119 E5
Mamuno Botswana 22°16S 20°1E 144 A3
Mamuras Albania 41°34N 19°41E 96 G2
Man Côte d'Ivoire 7°30N 7°40W 138 D3
Man, I. of U.K. 54°15N 4°30W 66 C3
Man-Bazar India 23°4N 86°39E 125 H12
Man Na Myanmar 23°27N 97°19E 123 H20
Mãnã U.S.A. 22°2N 159°47W 167 L8

Mana → Fr. Guiana 5°45N 53°55W 187 B8
Mana Pools △ Zimbabwe 15°56S 29°25E 143 F2
Manaar, G. of = Mannar, G. of Asia 8°30N 79°0E 127 K4
Manacapuru Brazil 3°16S 60°37W 186 D6
Manacor Spain 39°34N 3°13E 100 B10
Manado Indonesia 1°29N 124°51E 119 D6
Managua Nic. 12°6N 86°20W 182 D2
Managua, L. de Nic. 12°20N 86°30W 182 D2
Manaia N.Z. 39°33S 174°8E 154 F3
Manakara Madag. 22°8S 48°1E 141 J9
Manakau N.Z. 42°15S 173°42E 155 C8
Manali India 32°16N 77°10E 124 C7
Manama = Al Manāmah Bahrain 26°10N 50°30E 129 E6
Manangatang Australia 35°5S 142°54E 152 C5
Manantantely Madag. 21°13S 48°20E 141 J9
Manankory Madag. 10°28N 7°25W 138 C3
Manantali, L. de Mali 13°12N 10°28W 138 C2
Manantavadi India 11°49N 76°1E 127 J3
Manantenina Madag. 24°17S 47°19E 141 J9
Manaos = Manaus Brazil 3°0S 60°0W 186 D7
Manapire → Venezuela 7°42N 66°7W 186 B5
Manapouri N.Z. 45°34S 167°39E 155 F2
Manapouri, L. N.Z. 45°32S 167°32E 155 F2
Manapparai India 10°36N 78°22E 127 J4
Manar → India 18°50N 77°20E 126 E3
Manār, Jabal Yemen 14°2N 44°17E 131 E3
Manas China 44°17N 86°10E 109 D11
Manas → India 26°12N 90°40E 123 F17
Manas He → China 45°38N 85°12E 110 B6
Manas Hu China 45°45N 85°55E 109 C11
Manasa Nepal 28°33N 84°33E 125 E11
Manasquan U.S.A. 40°8N 74°3W 175 F10
Manassa U.S.A. 37°11N 105°56W 169 H11
Manassas U.S.A. 38°45N 77°29W 174 F7
Manati Puerto Rico 18°26N 66°29W 183 d
Manaus Brazil 3°0S 60°0W 186 D7
Manavgat Turkey 36°47N 31°26E 104 D4
Manawan L. Canada 55°24N 103°14W 163 B8
Manawatu → N.Z. 40°28S 175°12E 154 G4
Manawatu-Wanganui □ N.Z. 39°50S 175°30E 154 F4
Manbij Syria 36°31N 37°57E 130 D7
Mancha Real Spain 37°48N 3°39W 89 H7
Manche □ France 49°10N 1°20W 70 C5
Manchegorsk Russia 67°54N 32°58E 106 C4
Manchester U.K. 53°29N 2°12W 66 D5
Manchester Calif., U.S.A. 38°58N 123°41W 170 G3
Manchester Conn., U.S.A. 41°47N 72°31W 175 E12
Manchester Ga., U.S.A. 32°51N 84°37W 178 C5
Manchester Iowa, U.S.A. 42°29N 91°27W 172 D8
Manchester Ky., U.S.A. 37°9N 83°46W 173 G12
Manchester N.H., U.S.A. 42°59N 71°28W 175 D13
Manchester N.Y., U.S.A. 42°56N 77°16W 174 D7
Manchester Pa., U.S.A. 40°4N 76°43W 175 F8
Manchester Tenn., U.S.A. 35°29N 86°5W 177 D11
Manchester Vt., U.S.A. 43°10N 73°5W 175 C11
Manchester Int. ✈ (MAN) U.K. 53°21N 2°17W 66 D5
Manchhar L. Pakistan 26°25N 67°39E 124 F2
Manchuria = Dongbei China 45°0N 125°0E 115 D13
Manchurian Plain China 47°0N 124°0E 102 D14
Manciano Italy 42°35N 11°31E 93 F8
Máncora Peru 4°9S 81°1W 186 D1
Mand → India 21°42N 83°15E 125 J10
Mand → Iran 28°20N 52°30E 127 D7
Manda Ludewe, Tanzania 10°30S 34°40E 143 D3
Manda Mbeya, Tanzania 7°58S 32°29E 142 D3
Manda Mbeya, Tanzania 8°30S 32°49E 143 D3
Mandaguari Brazil 23°32S 51°42W 191 A5
Mandah = Töhöm Mongolia 44°27N 108°2E 114 B5
Mandal Norway 58°2N 7°25E 61 G12
Mandala, Puncak Indonesia 4°44S 140°20E 119 E10
Mandale = Mandalay Myanmar 22°0N 96°4E 123 J20
Mandalay Myanmar 22°0N 96°4E 123 J20
Mandalgarh India 25°12N 75°6E 124 G6
Mandalgovĭ Mongolia 45°45N 106°10E 114 B4
Mandali Iraq 33°43N 45°28E 105 F11
Mandan U.S.A. 46°50N 100°54W 172 B3
Mandar, Teluk Indonesia 3°32S 119°21E 119 E5
Mándas Italy 39°40N 9°8E 94 C2
Mandaue Phil. 10°20N 123°56E 119 B6
Mandelieu-la-Napoule France 43°34N 6°57E 73 E10
Mandera Kenya 3°55N 41°53E 142 B5
Mandera □ Kenya 3°20N 40°40E 142 B5
Mandeville Jamaica 18°2N 77°31W 182 a
Mandi India 31°39N 76°58E 124 D7
Mandi Burewala Pakistan 30°9N 72°41E 124 D5
Mandi Dabwali India 29°58N 74°42E 124 E6
Mandiana Guinea 10°37N 8°39W 138 C3
Mandimba Mozam. 14°20S 35°40E 143 E4
Mandioli Indonesia 0°40S 127°20E 119 E7
Mandla India 22°39N 80°30E 125 H9
Mandø Denmark 55°18N 8°33E 63 J2
Mandorah Australia 12°32S 130°42E 148 B5
Mandoudi Greece 38°48N 23°29E 98 C5
Mandra Greece 38°4N 23°30E 98 C5
Mandra Pakistan 33°23N 73°12E 124 C5
Mandritsara Madag. 15°50S 48°49E 141 H9
Mandsaur India 24°3N 75°8E 124 G6
Mandúria Italy 40°24N 17°38E 95 B10
Mandvi India 22°51N 69°22E 124 H3
Mandya India 12°30N 77°0E 127 J3
Mandzai Pakistan 30°55N 67°6E 124 D2
Mané Burkina Faso 12°59N 1°21W 139 C4
Maneh Iran 37°39N 57°7E 127 B8
Manengouba, Mts. Cameroon 5°0N 9°50E 139 E6
Maner → India 18°30N 79°40E 126 E4
Manerbio Italy 45°21N 10°8E 92 C7
Maneroo Cr. → Australia 23°21S 143°53E 150 C3
Manfalût Egypt 27°20N 30°52E 137 B3

Manfred Australia 33°19S 143°45E 152 B5
Manfredónia Italy 41°38N 15°55E 93 G12
Manfredónia, G. di Italy 41°35N 16°5E 93 G13
Manga Brazil 14°46S 43°56W 189 C2
Manga Burkina Faso 11°40N 1°4W 139 C4
Manga Niger 15°0N 14°0E 139 C7
Mangabeiras, Chapada das Brazil 10°0S 46°30W 189 C1
Mangaia Cook Is. 21°55S 157°55W 157 K12
Mangakino N.Z. 38°22S 175°47E 154 E4
Mangalagiri India 16°26N 80°36E 127 F5
Mangalia Romania 43°50N 28°35E 81 G13
Mangalore = Mangaluru India 12°55N 74°47E 127 H2
Mangaluru India 12°55N 74°47E 127 H2
Mangalvedha India 17°31N 75°28E 126 F2
Mangan India 27°31N 88°32E 125 F13
Mangaon India 18°15N 73°20E 126 E1
Mangarrayi ◌ Australia 15°5S 133°10E 150 B1
Mangawan India 24°41N 81°33E 125 G9
Mangaweka N.Z. 39°48S 175°47E 154 F4
Mangaweka, Mt. N.Z. 39°49S 176°5E 154 F5
Mangbo Indonesia 4°8S 133°32E 119 E8
Mangetti △ Namibia 18°43S 19°8E 144 A2
Manggar Indonesia 2°50S 108°10E 118 E3
Manggawitu Indonesia 4°8S 133°32E 119 E8
Mangghystaū Kazakhstan 43°40N 51°13E 108 D4
Mangghystaū □ Kazakhstan 45°0N 53°0E 108 D4
Mangghystaū Tübegi Kazakhstan 44°30N 52°30E 108 D4
Manggis Indonesia 8°29S 115°31E 119 J18
Mangkalihat, Tanjung Indonesia 1°2N 118°59E 119 D5
Mangkururpa ◌ Australia 20°35S 129°43E 148 D4
Mangla Pakistan 33°7N 73°39E 124 C5
Mangla Dam Pakistan 33°9N 73°44E 125 C5
Manglaur India 29°44N 77°49E 124 E7
Manglisi Georgia 41°41N 44°22E 87 K7
Mangnai China 37°52N 91°43E 110 D7
Mangnai Zhen China 38°24N 90°14E 109 E12
Mango Togo 10°20N 0°30E 139 C5
Mangoche Malawi 14°25S 35°16E 143 E4
Mangoky → Madag. 21°29S 43°41E 141 J8
Mangole Indonesia 1°50S 125°55E 119 E6
Mangombe Dem. Rep. of the Congo 1°20S 26°48E 142 C2
Mangonui N.Z. 35°1S 173°32E 154 B4
Mangrol Mad. P., India 21°7N 70°7E 124 J4
Mangrol Raj., India 25°20N 76°31E 124 G6
Mangrul Pir India 20°19N 77°21E 126 D3
Mangshi = Luxi China 24°27N 98°36E 116 E2
Mangualde Portugal 40°38N 7°48E 88 D3
Mangueira, L. da Brazil 33°0S 52°50W 191 C5
Mangui China 52°3N 122°3E 111 A13
Manguri Australia 28°58S 134°22E 151 A1
Mangyshlak, Poluostrov = Mangghystaū Tübegi Kazakhstan 44°30N 52°30E 108 D4
Manhattan U.S.A. 39°11N 96°35W 172 F5
Manhiça Mozam. 25°23S 32°49E 145 C5
Manhuaçu Brazil 20°15S 42°2W 189 E2
Manhumirim Brazil 20°22S 41°57W 189 E2
Maniago Italy 46°10N 12°43E 93 B9
Manica Mozam. 18°58S 32°59E 145 A5
Manica □ Mozam. 19°10S 33°45E 145 A5
Manicaland □ Zimbabwe 19°0S 32°30E 145 A5
Manicoré Brazil 5°48S 61°16W 186 E6
Manicouagan → Canada 49°30N 68°30W 165 C6
Manicouagan, Rés. Canada 51°5N 68°40W 165 B6
Maniema □ Dem. Rep. of the Congo 3°0S 26°0E 142 C2
Manifah Si. Arabia 27°44N 49°0E 129 E6
Manifold, C. Australia 22°41S 150°50E 150 C5
Maniganggo China 31°56N 99°10E 116 B2
Manigotagan Canada 51°6N 96°18W 163 C9
Manihari India 25°21N 87°38E 125 G12
Manihiki Cook Is. 10°24S 161°1W 157 J11
Manihiki Plateau Pac. Oc. 11°0S 164°0W 157 J11
Maniitsoq Greenland 65°26N 52°55W 57 D5
Manika, Plateau de la Dem. Rep. of the Congo 10°0S 25°5E 143 D2
Manikpur India 25°4N 81°7E 125 G9
Manila Phil. 14°35N 120°58E 119 B6
Manila U.S.A. 40°59N 109°43W 168 F9
Manila B. Phil. 14°40N 120°35E 119 B6
Manildra Australia 33°11S 148°41E 153 B8
Manilla Australia 30°45S 150°43E 153 A9
Manilva Spain 36°23S 5°15W 89 J5
Manimpé Mali 14°11N 5°28W 138 C3
Maningrida Australia 12°3S 134°13E 150 A1
Maninian Côte d'Ivoire 10°3N 7°52W 138 C3
Manipa, Selat Indonesia 3°20S 127°23E 119 E7
Manipur □ India 25°0N 94°0E 123 G19
Manipur → Myanmar 23°45N 94°20E 123 H19
Manisa Turkey 38°38N 27°30E 99 C9
Manisa □ Turkey 38°40N 28°0E 99 C9
Manistee U.S.A. 44°15N 86°19W 172 C10
Manistee → U.S.A. 44°15N 86°21W 172 C10
Manistique U.S.A. 45°57N 86°15W 172 C10
Manitoba □ Canada 55°30N 97°0W 163 B9
Manitoba, L. Canada 51°0N 98°45W 163 C9
Manitou Canada 49°15N 98°32W 163 D9
Manitou Is. U.S.A. 45°8N 86°0W 172 C10
Manitou L. Canada 52°43N 109°43W 163 C7
Manitou Springs U.S.A. 38°52N 104°55W 168 G11
Manitoulin I. Canada 45°40N 82°30W 164 C2
Manitouwadge Canada 49°8N 85°48W 164 C2
Manitowoc U.S.A. 44°5N 87°40W 172 C10
Maniyachi India 8°55N 77°55E 127 K3
Manizales Colombia 5°5N 75°32W 186 B3
Manja Madag. 21°26S 44°20E 141 J8
Manjacaze Mozam. 24°45S 34°0E 145 C5
Manjakandriana Madag. 18°55S 47°47E 141 H9
Manjhand Pakistan 25°50N 68°10E 124 G3
Manjimup Australia 34°15S 116°6E 149 F2
Manjra → India 18°49N 76°41E 126 E3
Mankato Kans., U.S.A. 39°47N 98°13W 172 F4
Mankato Minn., U.S.A. 44°10N 94°0W 172 C7
Mankayane Swaziland 26°40S 31°4E 145 C5

Mankera Pakistan 31°23N 71°26E 124 D4
Mankim Cameroon 5°6N 12°3E 139 D7
Mankono Côte d'Ivoire 8°1N 6°10W 138 D3
Mankota Canada 49°25N 107°5W 163 D7
Mankulam Sri Lanka 9°8N 80°26E 127 K5
Manlay = Üydzin Mongolia 44°9N 107°0E 114 B4
Manlleu Spain 42°2N 2°17E 90 C7
Manly Australia 33°47S 151°17E 153 B9
Manmad India 20°18N 74°28E 126 D2
Mann Ranges Australia 26°6S 130°5E 149 E5
Manna Indonesia 4°25S 102°55E 118 E2
Mannahill Australia 32°25S 140°0E 152 B4
Mannar Sri Lanka 9°1N 79°54E 127 K4
Mannar, G. of Asia 8°30N 79°0E 127 K4
Mannar I. Sri Lanka 9°5N 79°45E 127 K4
Mannargudi India 10°45N 79°51E 127 J4
Mannheim Germany 49°29N 8°27E 77 F4
Manning Canada 56°53N 117°39W 162 B5
Manning Oreg., U.S.A. 45°45N 123°13W 170 E3
Manning S.C., U.S.A. 33°42N 80°13W 178 C6
Manning → Australia 31°52S 152°43E 153 A10
Mannu → Italy 39°16N 9°0E 94 C2
Mannu, C. Italy 40°3N 8°21E 94 B1
Mannum Australia 34°50S 139°20E 152 C3
Mano S. Leone 8°3N 12°2W 138 D2
Mano → Liberia 6°56N 11°30W 138 D2
Manoharpur India 22°23N 85°12E 125 H11
Manokwari Indonesia 0°54S 134°0E 119 D8
Manolada Greece 38°4N 21°21E 98 C3
Manombo Madag. 22°57S 43°28E 141 J8
Manono Dem. Rep. of the Congo 7°15S 27°25E 142 D2
Manoppello Italy 42°15N 14°3E 93 F11
Manorhamilton Ireland 54°18N 8°11W 64 B3
Manosque France 43°49N 5°47E 73 E9
Manotick Canada 45°13N 75°41W 175 A9
Manouane → Canada 49°30N 71°10W 165 C5
Manouane, L. Canada 50°45N 70°45W 165 B5
Manp'o N. Korea 41°6N 126°24E 115 D14
Manpojin = Manp'o N. Korea 41°6N 126°24E 115 D14
Manpur Chhattisgarh, India 23°17N 83°35E 125 H10
Manpur Chhattisgarh, India 20°22N 80°43E 126 D5
Manpur Mad. P., India 22°26N 75°37E 124 H6
Manresa Spain 41°48N 1°50E 90 D6
Mansa Gujarat, India 23°27N 72°45E 124 H5
Mansa Punjab, India 30°0N 75°27E 124 E6
Mansa Zambia 11°13S 28°55E 143 E2
Mansa Konko Gambia 13°28N 15°33W 138 C1
Mansehra Pakistan 34°20N 73°15E 124 B5
Mansel I. Canada 62°0N 80°0W 161 E15
Mansfield U.K. 53°9N 1°11W 66 D6
Mansfield La., U.S.A. 32°2N 93°43W 176 E8
Mansfield Mass., U.S.A. 42°2N 71°13W 175 D13
Mansfield Ohio, U.S.A. 40°45N 82°31W 174 F2
Mansfield Pa., U.S.A. 41°48N 77°5W 174 E8
Mansfield Tex., U.S.A. 32°33N 97°8W 176 E6
Mansfield, Mt. U.S.A. 44°33N 72°49W 175 B12
Mansi Burma 10°43S 44°2W 189 C2
Mansilla de las Mulas Spain 42°30N 5°25W 88 C5
Mansle France 45°52N 0°12E 72 C4
Manso → Brazil 13°50S 47°0W 189 C1
Mansôa Guinea-Biss. 12°0N 15°20W 138 C1
Manson Creek Canada 55°37N 124°32W 162 B4
Mansoura Algeria 36°1N 4°31E 136 A4
Manta Ecuador 1°0S 80°40W 186 D1
Mantalingajan, Mt. Phil. 8°55N 117°45E 118 C5
Mantare Tanzania 2°42S 33°13E 142 C3
Mantaro → Peru 12°16S 73°57W 188 C3
Manteca U.S.A. 37°48N 121°13W 170 H5
Mantena Brazil 18°47S 40°59W 189 E2
Manteo U.S.A. 35°55N 75°40W 177 D17
Mantes-la-Jolie France 48°58N 1°41E 71 D8
Manthani India 18°40N 79°35E 126 E4
Manthani India 18°40N 79°35E 126 E4
Manti U.S.A. 39°16N 111°38W 168 G8
Mantiqueira, Serra da Brazil 22°0S 44°0W 191 A7
Manton U.S.A. 44°25N 85°24W 173 C11
Mantorp Sweden 58°21N 15°20E 63 F9
Mántova Italy 45°9N 10°48E 92 C7
Mänttä Vilppula Finland 62°2N 24°40E 64 A3
Mantua = Mántova Italy 45°9N 10°48E 92 C7
Manturovo Russia 58°23N 44°46E 86 A7
Manú Peru 12°10S 70°51W 188 C3
Manú → Peru 12°16S 70°55W 188 C3
Manuel Alves → Brazil 11°19S 48°28W 189 C1
Manuel Alves Grande → Brazil 7°27S 47°35W 189 D1
Manuel Urbano Brazil 8°53S 69°18W 188 B3
Manui Indonesia 3°35S 123°5E 119 E6
Manukau N.Z. 37°3S 174°52E 154 D3
Manukau Harbour N.Z. 37°3S 174°45E 154 D3
Manunui N.Z. 38°54S 175°21E 154 F4
Manuoha N.Z. 38°42S 177°20E 154 F6
Manuripi → Bolivia 11°6S 67°36W 188 C4
Manwath India 19°19N 76°32E 126 E3
Many U.S.A. 31°34N 93°29W 176 F8
Manyallaluk ◌ Australia 14°16S 132°49E 148 B5
Manyani Kenya 3°5S 38°30E 142 C4
Manyara, L. Tanzania 3°40S 35°50E 142 C4
Manyas Turkey 40°2N 27°59E 97 F11
Manych → Russia 47°13N 40°0E 87 G6
Manych-Gudilo, Ozero Russia 46°24N 42°38E 87 G6
Manyoni Tanzania 5°45S 34°55E 142 D3
Manzai Pakistan 32°12N 70°15E 124 C4
Manzanares Spain 39°2N 3°22W 89 F7

Manzaneda Spain 42°12N 7°15W 88 C3
Manzanillo Cuba 20°20N 77°31W 182 B4
Manzanillo Mexico 19°3N 104°20W 180 D4
Manzanillo, Pta. Panama 9°30N 79°40W 182 E4
Manzano Mts. U.S.A. 34°40N 106°20W 169 J10
Manzarîyeh Iran 34°53N 50°50E 129 C6
Manzhouli China 49°35N 117°25E 111 B13
Manzini Swaziland 26°30S 31°25E 145 C5
Manzouli = Manzhouli China 49°35N 117°25E 111 B13
Manzur Vadisi △ Turkey 39°10N 39°30E 128 B3
Mao Chad 14°4N 15°19E 135 F9
Maó Spain 39°53N 4°16E 100 B11
Maoke, Pegunungan Indonesia 3°40S 137°30E 119 E9
Maolin China 43°58N 123°30E 115 C12
Maoming China 21°50N 110°54E 117 G8
Maopi T'ou China 21°56N 120°43E 117 G13
Maoxian China 31°41N 103°49E 116 B4
Maoxing China 45°28N 124°40E 115 B13
Mapam Yumco China 30°45N 81°28E 125 D9
Mapastepec Mexico 15°26N 92°54W 181 D6
Maphrao, Ko Thailand 7°56N 98°26E 121 a
Mapia, Kepulauan Indonesia 0°50N 134°20E 119 D8
Mapimí Mexico 25°49N 103°51W 180 B4
Mapimí, Bolsón de Mexico 27°0N 104°15W 180 B4
Maping China 31°34N 113°32E 117 B9
Mapinga Tanzania 6°40S 39°12E 142 D4
Mapinhane Mozam. 22°20S 35°0E 145 C6
Maple Creek Canada 49°55N 109°29W 163 D7
Maple Valley U.S.A. 47°23N 122°3W 170 C4
Mapleton U.S.A. 44°2N 123°52W 168 D2
Mapoon ◌ Australia 11°44S 142°8E 150 A3
Mapourika, L. N.Z. 43°16S 170°12E 155 D3
Mapuca India 15°36N 73°46E 127 G1
Mapuera → Brazil 1°5S 57°2W 186 D7
Mapulanguene Mozam. 24°29S 32°6E 145 B5
Mapungubwe △ S. Africa 22°12S 29°22E 145 B4
Maputo Mozam. 25°58S 32°32E 145 C5
Maputo □ Mozam. 26°0S 32°25E 145 C5
Maputo, B. de Mozam. 25°50S 32°45E 145 C5
Maputo → Mozam. 26°23S 32°48E 145 C5
Maqanshy Kazakhstan 46°47N 82°1E 109 C10
Maqat Kazakhstan 47°39N 53°19E 108 C4
Maqên China 34°24N 100°6E 110 E8
Maqên Gangri China 34°55N 99°18E 110 E8
Maqiaohe China 44°40N 130°30E 115 B16
Maqnā Si. Arabia 28°25N 34°50E 128 D2
Maqteïr Mauritania 21°50N 11°40W 134 D3
Maqu China 34°1N 102°0E 110 E9
Maquan He = Brahmaputra → Asia 23°40N 90°35E 125 H13
Maqueda Spain 40°4N 4°22W 88 E6
Maquela do Zombo Angola 6°0S 15°15E 140 F3
Maquinchao Argentina 41°15S 68°50W 192 B3
Maquoketa U.S.A. 42°4N 90°40W 172 D8
Mar Canada 44°49N 81°12W 174 B3
Mar, Serra do Brazil 25°30S 49°0W 191 B6
Mar Chiquita, L. Argentina 30°40S 62°50W 190 C3
Mar del Plata Argentina 38°0S 57°30W 190 D4
Mar Menor Spain 37°40N 0°45W 91 H4
Mara Tanzania 1°30S 34°32E 142 C3
Mara □ Tanzania 1°45S 34°20E 142 C3
Maraã Brazil 1°52S 65°25W 186 D5
Maraa Tahiti 17°46S 149°34W 155 b
Marabá Brazil 5°20S 49°5W 189 D1
Maraboon, L. Australia 23°41S 148°0E 150 C4
Maracá, I. de Brazil 2°10N 50°30W 187 B8
Maracaibo Venezuela 10°40N 71°37W 186 A4
Maracaibo, L. de Venezuela 9°40N 71°30W 186 B4
Maracaju Brazil 21°38S 55°9W 191 A4
Maracanaú Brazil 3°52S 38°38W 189 D3
Maracás Brazil 13°26S 40°18W 189 C2
Maracas Bay Village Trin. & Tob. 10°46N 61°28W 187 D7
Maracay Venezuela 10°15N 67°28W 186 A5
Maracena Spain 37°13N 3°38W 89 H7
Marãdah Libya 29°15N 19°15E 135 C9
Maradi Niger 13°29N 7°20E 139 C6
Maradi □ Niger 14°15N 7°15E 139 C6
Marägheh Iran 37°30N 46°12E 105 D12
Maragogipe Brazil 12°46S 38°55W 189 C3
Marãh Si. Arabia 25°0N 45°35E 128 E5
Marahoué △ Côte d'Ivoire 8°0N 7°8W 138 D3
Marais du Cotentin et du Bessin △ France 49°10N 1°30W 70 C5
Marais Poitevin, Val de Sèvre et Vendée △ France 46°30N 0°35W 72 B3
Marajó, I. de Brazil 1°0S 49°30W 187 D9
Marãkand Iran 38°51N 45°16E 105 C12
Marakele △ S. Africa 24°30S 27°30E 145 B4
Maralal Kenya 1°0N 36°38E 142 B4
Maralinga Australia 30°13S 131°32E 149 F5
Maralinga Tjarutja ◌ Australia 29°30S 131°0E 149 E5
Marama Australia 35°10S 140°10E 152 C4
Maramaereğlisi Turkey 40°57N 27°57E 97 F11
Marambio Antarctica 64°0S 56°0W 5 C18
Maramureş □ Romania 47°45N 24°0E 81 C9
Maran Malaysia 3°35N 102°45E 121 L4
Maranboy Australia 14°40S 132°39E 150 A1
Maranchón Spain 41°6N 2°15W 90 D2
Marand Iran 38°30N 45°45E 105 C11
Marang Malaysia 5°12N 103°13E 121 K4
Maranguape Brazil 3°55S 38°50W 189 D3
Maranhão = São Luís Brazil 2°39S 44°15W 189 D2
Maranhão □ Brazil 5°0S 46°0W 189 D1
Marano, L. di Italy 45°44N 13°10E 93 C10
Maranoa → Australia 27°50S 148°37E 150 D4
Marañón → Peru 4°30S 73°35W 188 B3
Marão Mozam. 24°18S 34°2E 145 B5
Marari Brazil 5°43S 67°47W 188 B4
Maraş = Kahramanmaraş Turkey 37°37N 36°53E 104 D7
Mârãşeşti Romania 45°52N 27°14E 81 D12
Maratea Italy 39°59N 15°43E 95 C8
Marateca Portugal 38°34N 8°40W 89 G2
Marathasa Cyprus 34°59N 32°51E 101 E11

Marathokambos *Greece* 37°43N 26°42E **99** D8
Marathon *Australia* 20°51S 143°32E **150** C3
Marathon *Canada* 48°44N 86°23W **164** C2
Marathon *Fla., U.S.A.* 24°43N 81°5W **179** L8
Marathon *N.Y., U.S.A.* 42°27N 76°2W **175** D8
Marathon *Tex., U.S.A.* 30°12N 103°15W **176** F3
Marathonas *Greece* 38°11N 23°58E **98** C5
Marathóvounos
  Cyprus 35°13N 33°37E **101** D12
Maratua *Indonesia* 2°10N 118°35E **119** D5
Maraú *Brazil* 14°6S 39°0W **189** C3
Maraval *Trin. & Tob.* 10°42N 61°31W **187** K15
Maravatío *Mexico* 19°51N 100°25W **180** D4
Marāwih *U.A.E.* 24°18N 53°18E **129** E7
Marazliyivka *Ukraine* 46°8N 30°3E **81** D15
Marbella *Spain* 36°30N 4°57W **89** J6
Marble Bar *Australia* 21°9S 119°44E **148** D2
Marblehead *Mass.,*
  U.S.A. 42°29N 70°51W **175** D14
Marblehead *Ohio,*
  U.S.A. 41°32N 82°44W **174** E2
Marburg *Germany* 50°47N 8°46E **76** E4
Marca, Pta. do *Angola* 16°31S 11°43E **141** H2
Marcal → *Hungary* 47°41N 17°40E **80** C2
Marcali *Hungary* 46°35N 17°25E **80** D2
Marcapata *Peru* 13°31S 70°52W **188** C3
Marcaria *Italy* 45°7N 10°32E **92** C7
Mărcăuți *Moldova* 48°20N 27°14E **81** B12
March *U.K.* 52°33N 0°5E **67** E8
Marchand = Rommani
  Morocco 33°31N 6°40W **136** B2
Marche *France* 46°5N 1°20E **72** B5
Marche □ *Italy* 43°30N 13°15E **93** E10
Marche-en-Famenne
  Belgium 50°14N 5°19E **69** D5
Marchena *Spain* 37°18N 5°23W **89** H5
Marches = Marche □
  Italy 43°30N 13°15E **93** E10
Marchesale △ *Italy* 38°32N 16°13E **95** D9
Marciana Marina *Italy* 42°48N 10°12E **92** F7
Marcianise *Italy* 41°2N 14°17E **95** A7
Marcigny *France* 46°17N 4°2E **71** F11
Marcillat-en-Combraille
  France 46°12N 2°38E **71** F9
Marck *France* 50°57N 1°57E **71** B8
Marckolsheim *France* 48°10N 7°30E **71** D14
Marco Island *U.S.A.* 25°58N 81°44W **179** K8
Marcona *Peru* 15°10S 75°0W **188** D3
Marcos Juárez *Argentina* 32°42S 62°5W **190** C3
Mărculești *Moldova* 47°27N 28°15E **81** C13
Marcus Baker, Mt.
  U.S.A. 61°26N 147°45W **166** C10
Marcus I. = Minami-Tori-Shima
  Pac. Oc. 24°20N 153°58E **156** E7
Marcy, Mt. *U.S.A.* 44°7N 73°56W **175** B11
Mardan *Pakistan* 34°20N 72°0E **124** B5
Mardarivka *Ukraine* 47°38N 29°44E **81** C14
Mardie *Australia* 21°12S 115°59E **148** D2
Mardin *Turkey* 37°20N 40°43E **126** D9
Mårdsjö *Sweden* 63°18N 15°35E **62** A9
Mare e Brăila, I. *Romania* 44°44N 28°5E **83** F13
Marécchia → *Italy* 44°4N 12°34E **93** D9
Marechal Deodoro
  Brazil 9°43S 35°54W **189** B3
Maree, L. *U.K.* 57°40N 5°26W **65** D3
Mareeba *Australia* 16°59S 145°28E **150** B4
Mareetsane *S. Africa* 26°9S 25°25E **144** C4
Maremma *Italy* 42°30N 11°30E **93** F8
Maremma △ *Italy* 42°35N 11°8E **92** F8
Maréna *Kayes, Mali* 14°36N 10°45W **138** C2
Maréna *Koulikoro, Mali* 13°55N 7°20W **138** C3
Marengo *U.S.A.* 41°48N 92°4W **172** E7
Marennes *France* 45°49N 1°7W **72** C2
Maréttimo *Italy* 37°58N 12°4E **94** E5
Mareuil *France* 45°26N 0°29E **72** C4
Marfa *U.S.A.* 30°19N 104°1W **176** F7
Marfa Pt. *Malta* 35°59N 14°19E **101** D1
Marganets = Marhanets
  Ukraine 47°40N 34°40E **85** J8
Margao = Madgaon
  India 15°12N 73°58E **125** D1
Margaret → *Australia* 18°9S 125°41E **148** C4
Margaret Bay *Canada* 51°20N 127°35W **162** C3
Margaret L. *Canada* 58°56N 115°25W **162** B5
Margaret River
  Australia 33°57S 115°4E **149** F2
Margarita, I. de
  Venezuela 11°0N 64°0W **186** A6
Margariti *Greece* 39°22N 20°26E **98** B2
Margaritovo *Russia* 43°25S 134°45E **112** C7
Margate *S. Africa* 30°50S 30°20E **145** D5
Margate *U.K.* 51°23N 1°23E **67** F9
Margate *U.S.A.* 26°15N 80°12W **179** J9
Margeride, Mts. de la
  France 44°43N 3°38E **72** D7
Margherita di Savóia
  Italy 41°22N 16°9E **95** A9
Margherita Pk. *Uganda* 0°22N 29°51E **142** B3
Marghita *Romania* 47°22N 22°22E **83** E12
Marg'ilon *Uzbekistan* 40°27N 71°42E **109** D8
Margonin *Poland* 52°58N 17°5E **83** F4
Mārgow, Dasht-e
  Afghan. 30°40N 62°30E **122** D3
Marguerite *Canada* 52°30N 122°25W **162** C4
Marhanets *Ukraine* 47°40N 34°40E **85** J8
Marhoum *Algeria* 34°27N 0°11W **136** B3
Mari El □ *Russia* 56°30N 48°0E **86** B8
Mari Indus *Pakistan* 32°57N 71°34E **124** C4
Mari Republic = Mari El □
  Russia 56°30N 48°0E **86** B8
María, Sa. de *Spain* 37°39N 2°14W **91** H2
María de la Salut *Spain* 39°40N 3°5E **100** B10
María Elena *Chile* 22°18S 69°40W **190** A2
María Grande
  Argentina 31°45S 59°55W **190** C4
Maria I. N. Terr.,
  Australia 14°52S 135°45E **150** A2
Maria I. *Tas., Australia* 42°35S 148°0E **150** G4
Maria Island △
  Australia 42°38S 148°5E **151** G4
Maria van Diemen, C.
  N.Z. 34°29S 172°40E **154** A1
Mariager *Denmark* 56°40N 9°59E **63** H3
Mariager Fjord *Denmark* 56°42N 10°19E **63** H4
Mariakani *Kenya* 3°50S 39°27E **142** C4
Mariala △ *Australia* 25°57S 145°2E **151** D4
Marian L. *Canada* 63°0N 116°15W **162** A5
Marian Trench *Pac. Oc.* 13°0N 145°0E **156** F6
Mariana Ark., *U.S.A.* 34°46N 90°46W **177** D9
Marianna *Fla., U.S.A.* 30°46N 85°14W **178** E4
Mariannelund *Sweden* 57°37N 15°35E **63** G9

Mariánské Lázně
  Czechia 49°58N 12°41E **78** B5
Marias → *U.S.A.* 47°56N 110°30W **168** C8
Marías, Is. *Mexico* 21°25N 106°28W **180** C3
Mariato, Punta *Panama* 7°12N 80°52W **182** E3
Maribo *Denmark* 54°48N 11°30E **63** K5
Maribor *Slovenia* 46°36N 15°40E **93** B12
Marico → *Africa* 23°35S 26°57E **144** B4
Maricopa *Ariz., U.S.A.* 33°4N 112°3W **169** K7
Maricopa *Calif., U.S.A.* 35°4N 119°24W **171** K7
Marié → *Brazil* 0°27S 66°26W **186** D5
Marie Byrd Land
  Antarctica 79°30S 125°0W **55** D14
Marie-Galante
  Guadeloupe 15°56N 61°16W **182** b
Mariecourt = Kangiqsujuaq
  Canada 61°30N 72°0W **161** E17
Mariefred *Sweden* 59°15N 17°12E **62** E11
Mariehamn *Finland* 60°5N 19°55E **61** F18
Marieholm *Sweden* 55°53N 13°10E **63** J7
Marienbad = Mariánské Lázně
  Czechia 49°58N 12°41E **78** B5
Marienberg *Germany* 50°39N 13°9E **76** E9
Mariental *Namibia* 24°36S 18°0E **144** B2
Marienville *U.S.A.* 41°28N 79°8W **174** E5
Mariestad *Sweden* 58°43N 13°50E **63** F7
Marietta *Ga., U.S.A.* 33°57N 84°33W **178** B5
Marietta *Ohio, U.S.A.* 39°25N 81°27W **173** F13
Marieville *Canada* 45°26N 73°10W **175** A11
Mariga → *Nigeria* 9°40N 5°55E **138** D6
Marignane *France* 43°25N 5°13E **73** E9
Mariinsk *Russia* 56°10N 87°20E **110** D9
Mariinskiy Posad *Russia* 56°10N 47°45E **86** B8
Marijampolė *Lithuania* 54°33N 23°19E **82** D10
Marijampolė □
  Lithuania 54°34N 23°21E **82** D10
Marília *Brazil* 22°13S 50°0W **191** A6
Marín *Spain* 42°23N 8°42W **88** C2
Marina *U.S.A.* 36°41N 121°48W **170** J5
Marinduque *Phil.* 13°25N 122°0E **119** B6
Marine City *U.S.A.* 42°43N 82°30W **174** D2
Marineland *U.S.A.* 29°40N 81°13W **178** F6
Marineo *Italy* 37°57N 13°25E **94** E6
Marinette *U.S.A.* 45°6N 87°38W **172** C4
Maringá *Brazil* 23°26S 52°2W **191** A5
Marinha Grande
  Portugal 39°45N 8°56W **88** F2
Marinho dos Abrolhos △
  Brazil 17°50S 39°0W **189** D3
Marino *Italy* 41°46N 12°39E **93** G9
Marino di Campo *Italy* 42°46N 10°11E **92** F7
Marion *Ala., U.S.A.* 32°38N 87°19W **177** E11
Marion *Ark., U.S.A.* 35°13N 90°12W **177** D9
Marion *Ill., U.S.A.* 37°44N 88°56W **172** G3
Marion *Ind., U.S.A.* 40°32N 85°40W **173** E11
Marion *Iowa, U.S.A.* 42°2N 91°36W **172** E8
Marion *Kans., U.S.A.* 38°21N 97°1W **172** F6
Marion *N.C., U.S.A.* 35°41N 82°1W **177** D13
Marion *Ohio, U.S.A.* 40°35N 83°8W **173** E12
Marion *S.C., U.S.A.* 34°11N 79°24W **177** D15
Marion *Va., U.S.A.* 36°50N 81°31W **173** G13
Marion, L. *U.S.A.* 33°28N 80°10W **178** D5
Marion Bay *Australia* 35°12S 136°59E **152** C2
Marion I. *Ind. Oc.* 47°0S 38°0E **146** J7
Mariposa *U.S.A.* 37°29N 119°58W **170** H7
Mariscal Estigarribia
  Paraguay 22°3S 60°40W **190** A3
Maritime Alps = Maritimes, Alpes
  Europe 44°10N 7°10E **73** D11
Maritimes, Alpes *Europe* 44°10N 7°10E **73** D11
Maritsa = Evros →
  Greece 41°40N 26°34E **97** F10
Maritsa *Greece* 36°22N 28°8E **101** C10
Mariupol *Ukraine* 47°5N 37°31E **85** J9
Mariusa △ *Venezuela* 9°24N 61°27W **183** E7
Marīvān *Iran* 35°30N 46°25E **126** C12
Mariy Chodra △ *Russia* 56°10N 48°30E **86** B9
Marj 'Uyūn *Lebanon* 33°21N 35°34E **130** B4
Marka *Si. Arabia* 18°14N 41°19E **137** D5
Marka *Somalia* 1°48N 44°50E **131** G3
Markam *China* 29°42N 98°38E **116** C2
Markapur *India* 15°44N 79°19E **127** E4
Markaryd *Sweden* 56°28N 13°35E **63** H7
Markazī □ *Iran* 34°0N 49°30E **129** C6
Markdale *Canada* 44°19N 80°39W **174** B4
Marked Tree *U.S.A.* 35°32N 90°25W **177** D9
Markelsdorfer Huk
  Germany 54°33N 11°4E **76** A7
Market Drayton *U.K.* 52°54N 2°29W **66** E5
Market Harborough
  U.K. 52°29N 0°55W **67** E7
Market Rasen *U.K.* 53°24N 0°20W **66** D7
Markham *Canada* 43°52N 79°16W **174** C5
Markham, Mt.
  Antarctica 83°0S 164°0E **55** E11
Marki *Poland* 52°19N 21°2E **83** F8
Märkische Schweiz △
  Germany 52°34N 14°2E **76** C10
Markit *China* 38°54N 77°40E **109** E9
Markkleeberg *Germany* 51°16N 12°23E **76** D8
Markleeville *U.S.A.* 38°42N 119°47W **170** G7
Markopoulo *Greece* 37°53N 23°57E **98** D5
Markovac *Serbia* 44°14N 21°7E **96** B5
Markovo *Russia* 64°40N 170°24E **107** C17
Markoye *Burkina Faso* 14°39N 0°2E **139** C5
Marks *Russia* 51°45N 46°50E **86** E8
Marksville *U.S.A.* 31°8N 92°4W **176** F8
Markt Schwaben
  Germany 48°11N 11°52E **77** G7
Marktoberdorf *Germany* 47°45N 10°37E **77** H6
Marktredwitz *Germany* 50°1N 12°6E **77** E8
Marl *Germany* 51°39N 7°4E **76** D3
Marla *Australia* 27°19S 133°33E **151** D1
Marlbank *Canada* 44°26N 77°6W **174** B7
Marlboro *Australia* 22°46S 149°52E **150** C4
Marlborough *U.K.* 51°25N 1°43W **67** F6
Marlborough *U.S.A.* 42°21N 71°33W **175** D13
Marlborough □ *N.Z.* 41°40S 173°50E **155** B8
Marlborough Downs
  U.K. 51°27N 1°53W **67** F6
Marle *France* 49°43N 3°47E **71** C10
Marlin *U.S.A.* 31°18N 96°54W **176** F6
Marlow *Germany* 54°9N 12°34E **76** A8
Marlow *U.K.* 51°34N 0°46W **67** F7
Marlow *U.S.A.* 34°39N 97°58W **176** H6
Marmagao *India* 15°25N 73°56E **127** D1
Marmande *France* 44°30N 0°10E **72** D4
Marmara *Turkey* 40°35N 27°34E **97** F11

Marmara, Sea of = Marmara
  Denizi *Turkey* 40°45N 28°15E **97** F12
Marmara Denizi *Turkey* 40°45N 28°15E **97** F12
Marmara Gölü *Turkey* 38°37N 28°2E **99** C10
Marmaris *Turkey* 36°50N 28°14E **99** E10
Marmaris Limanı
  Turkey 36°50N 28°19E **99** E10
Marmion, Mt.
  Australia 29°16S 119°50E **149** E2
Marmion L. *Canada* 48°55N 91°20W **164** C1
Marmolada, Mte. *Italy* 46°26N 11°51E **93** B8
Marmolejo *Spain* 38°3N 4°13W **89** G6
Marmora *Canada* 44°28N 77°41W **174** B7
Mármora, La *Italy* 39°59N 9°20E **94** C2
Marnay *France* 47°16N 5°48E **71** E12
Marne *Germany* 53°57N 9°1E **76** A5
Marne □ *France* 48°50N 4°10E **71** D11
Marne → *France* 48°47N 2°29E **71** D9
Marneuli *Georgia* 41°30N 44°48E **87** K7
Marnoo *Australia* 36°40S 142°52E **152** D5
Maro Reef *U.S.A.* 25°25N 170°35W **157** L5
Maroantsetra *Madag.* 15°26S 49°44E **141** H9
Maroelaboom *Namibia* 19°15S 18°53E **144** A2
Maronea *Zimbabwe* 18°5S 31°42E **143** F3
Maroni → *Fr. Guiana* 5°30N 54°0W **187** B8
Maronne → *France* 45°5N 1°56E **72** C5
Maroochydore
  Australia 26°29S 153°5E **151** D5
Maroona *Australia* 37°27S 142°54E **152** D5
Maró □ *Hungary* 46°15N 20°13E **80** D5
Maróstica *Italy* 45°44N 11°40E **93** C8
Maroua *Cameroon* 10°40N 14°20E **139** C7
Marovoay *Madag.* 16°6S 46°39E **141** H9
Marqakōl *Kazakhstan* 48°45N 85°45E **109** C11
Marquard *S. Africa* 28°40S 27°28E **144** C4
Marquesas Fracture Zone
  Pac. Oc. 9°0S 125°0W **157** H15
Marquesas Is. = Marquises, Îs.
  French Polynesia 9°30S 140°0W **157** H14
Marquesas Keys
  U.S.A. 24°35N 82°10W **179** L7
Marquette *U.S.A.* 46°33N 87°24W **172** B10
Marquis *St. Lucia* 14°2N 60°54W **183** f
Marquise *France* 50°50N 1°40E **71** B8
Marquises, Îs.
  French Polynesia 9°30S 140°0W **157** H14
Marra, Djebel *Sudan* 13°10N 24°22E **135** F10
Marra Cr. → *Australia* 30°38S 147°15E **153** A7
Marra-Marra △
  Australia 33°30S 151°4E **153** B9
Marracuene *Mozam.* 25°45S 32°35E **145** C5
Marradi *Italy* 44°4N 11°37E **93** D8
Marrakech *Morocco* 31°9N 8°0W **136** B2
Marraxī *Spain* 39°39N 2°48E **90** F7
Marrawah *Australia* 40°55S 144°42E **151** G3
Marrecas, Serra das
  Brazil 9°0S 41°0W **189** B2
Marree *Australia* 29°39S 138°1E **151** D2
Marrero *U.S.A.* 29°53N 90°6W **177** G9
Marrimane *Mozam.* 22°58S 33°34E **145** B5
Marromeu *Mozam.* 18°15S 36°25E **145** A6
Marromeu △ *Mozam.* 19°0S 36°0E **145** A6
Marroquí, Punta *Spain* 36°0N 5°37W **89** K5
Marrowie Cr. →
  Australia 33°23S 145°40E **153** B6
Marrubane *Mozam.* 18°0S 37°0E **143** H7
Marrúbiu *Italy* 39°40N 8°35E **94** C1
Marrupa *Mozam.* 13°8S 37°30E **143** G7
Mars Hill *U.S.A.* 46°31N 67°52W **173** B20
Marsá 'Alam *Egypt* 25°5N 34°54E **137** D3
Marsá Matrûh *Egypt* 31°19N 27°9E **137** A2
Marsa Sha'b *Sudan* 22°52N 35°47E **137** C4
Marsabit *Kenya* 2°18N 38°0E **142** B4
Marsabit □ *Kenya* 3°0N 37°30E **142** B4
Marsabit △ *Kenya* 2°23N 37°56E **142** B4
Marsala *Italy* 37°48N 12°26E **94** E5
Marsalforn *Malta* 36°4N 14°16E **101** C1
Mârșani *Romania* 44°1N 24°1E **81** F9
Marsberg *Germany* 51°28N 8°52E **76** D4
Marsciano *Italy* 42°54N 12°20E **93** F9
Marsden *Australia* 33°47S 147°32E **153** B7
Marsden Point *N.Z.* 35°50S 174°31E **154** B3
Marseillan *France* 43°23N 3°31E **72** E7
Marseille *France* 43°18N 5°23E **73** E9
Marseille-Marignane ✈ (MRS)
  France 43°26N 5°14E **73** E9
Marseilles = Marseille
  France 43°18N 5°23E **73** E9
Marsh I. *U.S.A.* 29°34N 91°53W **176** G9
Marshall *Liberia* 6°8N 10°22W **138** D2
Marshall *Ark., U.S.A.* 35°55N 92°38W **176** D8
Marshall *Mich.,*
  U.S.A. 42°16N 84°58W **173** D11
Marshall *Minn., U.S.A.* 44°27N 95°47W **172** C6
Marshall *Mo., U.S.A.* 39°7N 93°12W **172** F7
Marshall *Tex., U.S.A.* 32°33N 94°23W **176** E7
Marshall → *Australia* 22°59S 136°59E **150** C2
Marshall Is. ■ *Pac. Oc.* 9°0N 171°0E **156** G9
Marshalltown *U.S.A.* 42°3N 92°55W **172** D7
Marshallville *U.S.A.* 32°27N 83°56W **178** D6
Marshbrook *Zimbabwe* 18°33S 31°9E **145** A5
Marshfield *Mo., U.S.A.* 37°15N 92°54W **172** G7
Marshfield *Vt., U.S.A.* 44°20N 72°20W **175** B12
Marshfield *Wis., U.S.A.* 44°40N 90°10W **172** C8
Marshūn *Iran* 36°19N 49°23E **129** B6
Mársico Nuovo *Italy* 40°25S 15°45E **95** B8
Märsta *Sweden* 59°37N 17°52E **62** E11
Marstal *Denmark* 54°51N 10°30E **63** K4
Marstrand *Sweden* 57°53N 11°35E **63** G5
Mart *U.S.A.* 31°33N 96°50W **176** F6
Marta → *Italy* 42°14N 11°42E **93** F8
Martaban *Myanmar* 16°30N 97°35E **123** L20
Martaban, G. of = Mottama, G. of
  Myanmar 16°5N 96°30E **123** L20
Martano *Italy* 40°12N 18°18E **95** B11
Martapura *Kalimantan Selatan,*
  Indonesia 3°22S 114°47E **118** E4
Martapura *Sumatera Selatan,*
  Indonesia 4°19S 104°22E **118** E2
Marte R. Gómez, Presa
  Mexico 26°10N 99°0W **181** B5
Martel *France* 44°57N 1°37E **72** D5
Martelange *Belgium* 49°49N 5°43E **69** E5
Martellago *Italy* 45°33N 12°9E **93** C9
Martés, Sierra *Spain* 39°20N 1°0W **91** F4
Martfü *Hungary* 47°1N 20°17E **80** C5
Marthaguy Cr. →
  Australia 30°16S 147°35E **153** A7
Marthapal *India* 19°2N 81°37E **126** E5

Martha's Vineyard
  U.S.A. 41°25N 70°38W **175** E14
Martigné-Ferchaud
  France 47°50N 1°20W **70** E5
Martigny *Switz.* 46°6N 7°3E **77** J2
Martigues *France* 43°24N 5°4E **73** E9
Martil *Morocco* 35°36N 5°15W **136** A2
Martin *Slovakia* 49°6N 18°58E **79** B11
Martin *S. Dak., U.S.A.* 43°11N 101°44W **172** D3
Martin *Tenn., U.S.A.* 36°21N 88°51W **177** C10
Martin → *Spain* 41°18N 0°19W **90** D4
Martin L. *U.S.A.* 32°41N 85°55W **178** C4
Martin Vaz *Atl. Oc.* 20°30S 28°51W **56** J9
Martina Franca *Italy* 40°42N 17°20E **95** B10
Martinborough *N.Z.* 41°14S 175°29E **154** B4
Martinez *Calif., U.S.A.* 38°1N 122°8W **170** G4
Martinez *Ga., U.S.A.* 33°31N 82°5W **178** B6
Martinho Campos
  Brazil 19°20S 45°13W **189** D1
Martinique ☑ *W. Indies* 14°40N 61°0W **182** c
Martinique Passage
  W. Indies 15°15N 61°0W **183** D7
Martino *Greece* 38°35N 23°12E **98** C5
Martinópolis *Brazil* 22°11S 51°12W **191** A5
Martins Bay *Barbados* 13°12N 59°29W **183** g
Martins Ferry *U.S.A.* 40°6N 80°44W **174** F4
Martinsburg *Pa.,*
  U.S.A. 40°19N 78°20W **174** F6
Martinsburg *W. Va.,*
  U.S.A. 39°27N 77°58W **173** F15
Martinsicuro *Italy* 42°54N 13°54E **93** F10
Martinsville *Ind.,*
  U.S.A. 39°26N 86°25W **172** F10
Martinsville *Va.,*
  U.S.A. 36°41N 79°52W **173** G14
Marton *N.Z.* 40°4S 175°23E **154** G4
Martorell *Spain* 41°28N 1°56E **90** D6
Martos *Spain* 37°44N 3°58W **89** H7
Martu △ *Australia* 22°30S 122°30E **148** D3
Martuni *Armenia* 40°8N 45°20E **87** K7
Maru *Nigeria* 12°22N 6°22E **139** C6
Marudi *Malaysia* 4°11N 114°19E **118** D4
Maruf *Afghan.* 31°30N 67°6E **122** D5
Marugame *Japan* 34°15N 133°40E **113** G6
Maruia → *N.Z.* 41°47S 172°13E **155** B7
Maruim *Brazil* 10°45S 37°5W **189** C3
Marulan *Australia* 34°43S 150°3E **153** C9
Marunga *Angola* 17°28S 20°2E **144** A3
Marungu, Mts.
  Dem. Rep. of the Congo 7°30S 30°0E **142** D3
Maruwa △ *Australia* 22°30S 127°30E **148** D4
Marv Dasht *Iran* 29°50N 52°40E **129** D7
Marvão *Portugal* 39°24N 7°20W **89** F3
Marvast *Iran* 30°30N 54°15E **129** D7
Marvejols *France* 44°33N 3°19E **72** D7
Marvel Loch *Australia* 31°28S 119°29E **149** F2
Marwar *India* 25°43N 73°45E **124** G5
Marwayne *Canada* 53°32N 110°20W **162** C6
Mary *Turkmenistan* 37°40N 61°50E **128** B9
Mary Esther *U.S.A.* 30°25N 86°40W **179** E3
Maryborough = Portlaoise
  Ireland 53°2N 7°18W **64** C4
Maryborough *Queens.,*
  Australia 25°31S 152°37E **151** D5
Maryborough *Vic.,*
  Australia 37°0S 143°44E **152** D5
Maryfield *Canada* 49°50N 101°35W **163** D8
Maryland □ *U.S.A.* 39°0N 76°30W **173** F15
Maryland Junction
  Zimbabwe 17°45S 30°31E **143** F3
Maryport *U.K.* 54°44N 3°28W **66** C4
Mary's Harbour
  Canada 52°18N 55°51W **165** B8
Marystown *Canada* 47°10N 55°10W **165** C8
Marysville *Calif., U.S.A.* 39°9N 121°35W **170** F5
Marysville *Kans.,*
  U.S.A. 39°51N 96°39W **172** F6
Marysville *Mich.,*
  U.S.A. 42°54N 82°29W **174** D2
Marysville *Ohio,*
  U.S.A. 40°14N 83°22W **173** E12
Marysville *Wash.,*
  U.S.A. 48°3N 122°11W **170** B4
Maryville *Mo., U.S.A.* 40°21N 94°52W **172** E6
Maryville *Tenn.,*
  U.S.A. 35°46N 83°58W **177** D13
Masada *Israel* 31°18N 35°21E **130** D4
Masahunga *Tanzania* 2°6S 33°18E **142** C3
Masai *Malaysia* 1°29N 103°55E **121** d
Masai Mara △ *Kenya* 1°25S 35°5E **142** C4
Masai Steppe *Tanzania* 4°30S 36°30E **142** C4
Masaka *Uganda* 0°21S 31°45E **142** C3
Masâl *Iran* 37°23N 49°9E **105** D12
Masalembo, Kepulauan
  Indonesia 5°35S 114°30E **118** F4
Masalima, Kepulauan
  Indonesia 5°4S 117°5E **118** F5
Masallı *Azerbaijan* 39°3N 48°40E **105** C13
Masamba *Indonesia* 2°30S 120°32E **119** E6
Masan *S. Korea* 35°11N 128°32E **115** G15
Masandam, Ra's *Oman* 26°30N 56°30E **129** D7
Masasi *Tanzania* 10°45S 38°52E **143** E4
Masaya *Nic.* 12°0N 86°7W **182** D2
Masba *Nigeria* 11°35N 13°1E **139** C7
Masbate *Phil.* 12°21N 123°36E **119** B6
Máscali *Italy* 37°45N 15°12E **95** E8
Mascara *Algeria* 35°26N 0°6E **136** A4
Mascara □ *Algeria* 35°25N 0°10E **136** A4
Mascarene Is. = Ind. Oc.
  22°0S 55°0E **132** J9
Mascota *Mexico* 20°32N 104°49W **180** C4
Masdar City = Madīnat Masdar
  U.A.E. 24°26N 54°37E **129** E7
Masela *Indonesia* 8°9S 129°51E **119** F7
Maseru *Lesotho* 29°18S 27°30E **144** C4
Mashaba *Zimbabwe* 20°3S 30°29E **143** G3
Mashābih *Si. Arabia* 25°35N 36°30E **126** E3
Mashan *China* 23°40N 108°11E **116** F7
Mashang *China* 35°48N 115°57E **114** G8
Mashatu △ *Botswana* 22°45S 29°5E **145** B4
Mashegu *Nigeria* 10°0N 5°40E **139** D6
Masherbrum *Pakistan* 35°38N 76°18E **125** B7
Mashhad *Iran* 36°20N 59°35E **129** B8
Mashi *Nigeria* 13°0N 7°54E **139** C6
Mashīz *Iran* 29°56N 56°37E **129** D8
Mäshkel, Hämûn-i-
  Pakistan 28°20N 62°56E **129** D9
Mashki Chāh *Pakistan* 29°5N 62°30E **122** E3
Mashonaland *Zimbabwe* 16°30S 31°0E **141** H6
Mashonaland Central □
  Zimbabwe 17°30S 31°0E **145** A5
Mashonaland East □
  Zimbabwe 18°0S 32°0E **145** A5

Mashonaland West □
  Zimbabwe 17°30S 29°30E **145** A4
Mashrakh *India* 26°7N 84°48E **125** F11
Masi Manimba
  Dem. Rep. of the Congo 4°40S 17°54E **140** E3
Masig *Australia* 9°45S 143°24E **150** a
Masindi *Uganda* 1°40N 31°43E **142** B3
Masindi Port *Uganda* 1°43N 32°2E **142** B3
Masinga Res. *Kenya* 0°58S 37°38E **142** C4
Masisi
  Dem. Rep. of the Congo 1°23S 28°49E **142** C2
Masjed Soleyman *Iran* 31°55N 49°18E **129** D6
Mask, L. *Ireland* 53°36N 9°22E **64** C2
Maski *India* 15°56N 76°46E **127** E3
Maskin *Oman* 23°44N 56°52E **129** F8
Maslen Nos *Bulgaria* 42°18N 27°48E **99** A10
Maslinica *Croatia* 43°24N 16°13E **93** E13
Masnou = El Masnou
  Spain 41°28N 2°20E **90** D7
Masoala, Tanjon' i
  Madag. 15°59S 50°13E **141** H10
Masohi = Amahai
  Indonesia 3°20S 128°55E **119** E7
Mason *Nev., U.S.A.* 38°56N 119°8W **170** G7
Mason *Tex., U.S.A.* 30°45N 99°14W **176** F5
Mason B. *N.Z.* 46°55S 167°45E **155** G2
Mason City *U.S.A.* 43°9N 93°12W **172** D7
Maspalomas *Canary Is.* 27°46N 15°35W **100** G4
Maspalomas, Pta.
  Canary Is. 27°43N 15°36W **100** G4
Masqat *Oman* 23°37N 58°36E **131** C6
Masr el Gedida *Egypt* 30°5N 31°21E **137** E7
Massa *Italy* 44°1N 10°9E **92** D7
Massa, O. → *Morocco* 30°2N 9°40W **136** B2
Massa e Carrara □ *Italy* 44°5N 10°10E **92** D7
Massa Marittima *Italy* 43°3N 10°52E **92** E7
Massachusetts □
  U.S.A. 42°30N 72°0W **175** D13
Massachusetts B.
  U.S.A. 42°25N 70°50W **175** D14
Massafra *Italy* 40°35N 17°7E **95** B10
Massakory *Chad* 13°0N 15°49E **135** F8
Massamba *Mozam.* 15°58S 33°31E **143** F3
Massanella *Spain* 39°48N 2°51E **100** B9
Massangena *Mozam.* 21°34S 33°0E **145** B5
Massango *Angola* 8°2S 16°21E **140** F3
Massapê *Brazil* 3°31S 40°19W **189** A2
Massat *France* 42°53N 1°21E **72** F5
Massawa = Mitsiwa
  Eritrea 15°35N 39°25E **131** D2
Massena *U.S.A.* 44°56N 74°54W **175** B10
Massenya *Chad* 11°21N 16°9E **135** F9
Masset *Canada* 54°2N 132°10W **162** C2
Masseube *France* 43°25N 0°34E **72** E4
Massiac *France* 45°15N 3°11E **72** C7
Massiah Street *Barbados* 13°9N 59°29W **183** g
Massif Central *France* 44°55N 3°0E **72** D7
Massif des Bauges △
  France 45°40N 6°10E **71** G13
Massigui *Mali* 11°48N 6°50W **138** C3
Massillon *U.S.A.* 40°48N 81°32W **174** F3
Massine, O. → *Algeria* 36°13N 2°12E **136** A4
Massinga *Mozam.* 23°15S 35°22E **145** B6
Massingir *Mozam.* 23°51S 32°4E **145** B5
Masson-Angers
  Canada 45°32N 75°25W **175** A9
Masson I. *Antarctica* 66°10S 93°20E **55** C7
Maştağa *Azerbaijan* 40°35N 50°1E **87** K10
Mastanli = Momchilgrad
  Bulgaria 41°33N 25°23E **97** F9
Masterton *N.Z.* 40°56S 175°39E **154** B4
Mastic *U.S.A.* 40°47N 72°54W **175** F12
Mastuj *Pakistan* 36°20N 72°36E **125** A5
Mastūng *Pakistan* 29°50N 66°56E **122** E5
Mastūrah *Si. Arabia* 23°7N 38°52E **137** C4
Masty *Belarus* 53°27N 24°38E **75** B13
Masuda *Japan* 34°40N 131°51E **113** G5
Masuku = Franceville
  Gabon 1°40S 13°32E **140** E2
Masurian Lakes = Mazurski,
  Pojezierze *Poland* 53°50N 21°0E **82** E7
Masvingo *Zimbabwe* 20°8S 30°49E **143** G3
Masvingo □ *Zimbabwe* 21°0S 31°30E **143** G3
Maswa □ *Tanzania* 2°58S 34°19E **142** C3
Maşyāf *Syria* 35°4N 36°20E **104** E7
Maszewo *Poland* 53°29N 15°3E **82** E2
Mat → *Albania* 41°40N 19°35E **96** E3
Mata-au = Clutha →
  N.Z. 46°20S 169°49E **155** G4
Mata de São João
  Brazil 12°31S 38°17W **189** C3
Matabeleland *Zimbabwe* 18°0S 27°0E **141** H5
Matabeleland North □
  Zimbabwe 19°0S 28°0E **143** F2
Matabeleland South □
  Zimbabwe 21°0S 29°0E **143** G2
Matachel → *Spain* 38°50N 6°17W **89** G4
Matachewan *Canada* 47°56N 80°39W **164** C3
Matadi
  Dem. Rep. of the Congo 5°52S 13°31E **140** F2
Matagalpa *Nic.* 13°0N 85°58W **182** D2
Matagami *Canada* 49°45N 77°34W **164** C4
Matagami, L. *Canada* 49°50N 77°40W **164** C4
Matagorda B. *U.S.A.* 28°40N 96°12W **176** G6
Matagorda I. *U.S.A.* 28°15N 96°30W **176** G6
Mataiea *Tahiti* 17°46S 149°25W **155** b
Matak *Indonesia* 3°18N 106°16E **118** D3
Matakana *Australia* 32°59S 145°54E **153** B6
Matakana *N.Z.* 36°21S 174°43E **154** B5
Matala *Greece* 34°59N 24°45E **101** E6
Matale *Sri Lanka* 7°30N 80°37E **127** L5
Matam *Senegal* 15°34N 13°17E **138** B2
Matamata *N.Z.* 37°48S 175°47E **154** B5
Matameye *Niger* 13°26N 8°28E **139** C6
Matamoros *Coahuila,*
  Mexico 25°32N 103°15W **180** B4
Matamoros *Tamaulipas,*
  Mexico 25°53N 97°30W **181** B5
Ma'tan as Sarra *Libya* 21°45N 22°0E **135** D10
Matane *Canada* 48°50N 67°33W **165** C6
Matang *China* 23°30N 104°7E **116** F5
Matankari *Niger* 13°46N 4°1E **139** C5
Matanomadh *India* 23°33N 68°57E **124** H3
Matanzas *Cuba* 23°0N 81°40W **182** B3
Matapa *Botswana* 23°11S 24°39E **144** B3

Matapan, C. = Tenaro, Akra
  Greece 36°22N 22°27E **98** E4
Matapédia *Canada* 48°0N 66°59W **165** C6
Matapo △ *Zimbabwe* 20°36S 29°40E **143** G2
Mataporquera *Spain* 42°52N 4°10W **88** C6
Matara *Sri Lanka* 5°58N 80°30E **127** M5
Mataram *Indonesia* 8°35S 116°7E **118** F5
Matarani *Peru* 17°0S 72°10W **188** D3
Mataranka *Australia* 14°55S 133°4E **148** B5
Matarma, Râs *Egypt* 30°27N 32°44E **130** E1
Mataró *Spain* 41°32N 2°29E **90** D7
Matarraña → *Spain* 41°14N 0°22E **90** D5
Mataruška Banja *Serbia* 43°40N 20°40E **96** C4
Matata *N.Z.* 37°54S 176°48E **154** B5
Matatiele *S. Africa* 30°20S 28°49E **145** D4
Matatila Dam *India* 25°25N 78°30E **125** G8
Mataura → *N.Z.* 46°11S 168°51E **155** G3
Mataura *N.Z.* 46°34S 168°44E **155** G3
Matavai, B. de *Tahiti* 17°30S 149°23W **155** b
Matehuala *Mexico* 23°39N 100°39W **180** C4
Mateke Hills *Zimbabwe* 21°48S 31°0E **143** G3
Matelot *Trin. & Tob.* 10°50N 61°7W **187** K15
Matera *Italy* 40°40N 16°36E **95** B9
Matese, Monti del *Italy* 41°27N 14°22E **95** A7
Matese △ *Italy* 41°24N 14°23E **95** A7
Mátészalka *Hungary* 47°58N 22°20E **80** C7
Mateur *Tunisia* 37°0N 9°40E **136** A6
Matfors *Sweden* 62°21N 17°2E **62** B11
Matha *France* 45°52N 0°20W **72** C3
Matheniko △ *Uganda* 2°49N 34°27E **142** B3
Mathis *U.S.A.* 28°6N 97°50W **176** G6
Mathoura *Australia* 35°50S 144°55E **153** C6
Mathraki *Greece* 39°48N 19°31E **101** A3
Mathura *India* 27°30N 77°40E **124** F7
Mati *Phil.* 6°55N 126°15E **119** C7
Matiakoali *Burkina Faso* 12°28N 1°2E **139** C5
Matiali *India* 26°56N 88°49E **125** F13
Matías Romero *Mexico* 16°53N 95°2W **181** D5
Matibane *Mozam.* 14°49S 40°45E **143** E5
Matiri Ra. *N.Z.* 41°38S 172°20E **155** B7
Matjiesfontein *S. Africa* 33°14S 20°35E **144** E3
Matla → *India* 21°40N 88°40E **125** J13
Matlamanyane
  Botswana 19°33S 25°57E **144** A4
Matli *Pakistan* 25°2N 68°39E **124** G3
Matlock *U.K.* 53°9N 1°33W **66** D6
Matmata *Tunisia* 33°37N 9°59E **136** B6
Mato Grosso □ *Brazil* 14°0S 55°0W **187** F8
Mato Grosso, Planalto do
  Brazil 15°0S 55°0W **187** G8
Mato Grosso do Sul □
  Brazil 18°0S 55°0W **187** G8
Matobo = Matapo △
  Zimbabwe 20°36S 29°40E **143** G2
Matochkin Shar, Proliv
  Russia 73°23N 55°12E **106** B6
Matola *Mozam.* 25°57S 32°27E **145** C5
Matopo Hills *Zimbabwe* 20°36S 28°20E **143** G2
Matopos *Zimbabwe* 20°20S 28°29E **143** G2
Matosinhos *Portugal* 41°11N 8°42W **88** D2
Matour *France* 46°19N 4°29E **71** F11
Matroosberg *S. Africa* 33°23S 19°40E **144** D2
Maţruḩ *Oman* 23°37N 58°30E **131** C6
Matsalu △ *Estonia* 58°45N 23°36E **84** C2
Matsena *Nigeria* 13°5N 10°5E **139** C7
Matsesta *Russia* 43°34N 39°51E **87** J4
Matsu Tao *Taiwan* 26°8N 119°56E **117** D12
Matsue *Japan* 35°25N 133°10E **113** G6
Matsum, Ko *Thailand* 9°22N 99°59E **121** b
Matsumae *Japan* 41°26N 140°7E **112** D10
Matsumae-Hantō
  Japan 41°30N 140°15E **112** D10
Matsumoto *Japan* 36°15N 138°0E **113** F9
Matsusaka *Japan* 34°34N 136°32E **113** G8
Matsushima *Japan* 38°20N 141°10E **112** E10
Matsuura *Japan* 33°20N 129°49E **113** H4
Matsuyama *Japan* 33°45N 132°45E **113** H6
Mattagami → *Canada* 50°43N 81°29W **164** B3
Mattancheri *India* 9°50N 76°15E **127** Q10
Mattawa *Canada* 46°20N 78°45W **164** C4
Matterhorn *Switz.* 45°58N 7°39E **77** J3
Mattersburg *Austria* 47°44N 16°24E **79** D9
Matthew Town
  Bahamas 20°57N 73°40W **183** B5
Matthews Ridge
  Guyana 7°37N 60°10W **186** B6
Mattice *Canada* 49°40N 83°20W **164** C3
Mattili *India* 18°33N 82°12E **126** E6
Mattituck *U.S.A.* 40°59N 72°32W **175** F12
Mattō = Hakusan
  Japan 36°31N 136°34E **113** F8
Mattoon *U.S.A.* 39°29N 88°23W **172** F3
Matuba *Mozam.* 24°28S 32°49E **145** B5
Matucana *Peru* 11°55S 76°25W **188** C2
Matugama *Sri Lanka* 6°31N 80°7E **127** L5
Matuku *Fiji* 19°10S 179°44E **154** a
Matūn = Khowst
  Afghan. 33°22N 69°58E **124** C3
Matura B. *Trin. & Tob.* 10°39N 61°1W **187** K15
Maturín *Venezuela* 9°45N 63°11W **186** B6
Matusadona △
  Zimbabwe 16°58S 28°42E **143** F2
Matveyev Kurgan
  Russia 47°35N 38°57E **85** J10
Matxitxako, C. *Spain* 43°28N 2°47W **90** B2
Mau *Ut. P., India* 26°17N 78°41E **125** F8
Mau *Ut. P., India* 25°56N 83°33E **125** G10
Mau *Ut. P., India* 25°17N 81°23E **125** G9
Mau Escarpment *Kenya* 0°40S 36°0E **142** C4
Mau Ranipur *India* 25°16N 79°8E **125** G8
Maua *Kenya* 0°14N 37°56E **142** C4
Maúa *Mozam.* 13°53S 37°10E **143** E4
Maubeuge *France* 50°17N 3°57E **71** B10
Maubin *Myanmar* 16°44N 95°39E **123** L19
Maubourguet *France* 43°28N 0°1E **72** E4
Maud, Pt. *Australia* 23°6S 113°45E **148** D1
Maud Rise *S. Ocean* 65°0S 3°0E **55** D3
Maude *Australia* 34°29S 144°18E **152** C6
Maudin Sun *Myanmar* 16°0N 94°30E **123** M19
Maués *Brazil* 3°20S 57°45W **186** D7
Mauganj *India* 24°50N 81°55E **125** G9
Maughold Hd. *I. of Man* 54°18N 4°18W **66** C3
Maui *U.S.A.* 20°48N 156°20W **157** a
Maulamyaing = Mawlamyine
  Myanmar 16°30N 97°40E **123** L20
Maule □ *Chile* 36°5S 72°30W **190** D1
Mauléon-Licharre
  France 43°14N 0°54W **72** E3
Maullín *Chile* 41°38S 73°37W **192** B2
Maumee *U.S.A.* 41°34N 83°39W **173** E12

Maumee → U.S.A. 41°42N 83°28W 173 E12
Maumere Indonesia 8°38S 122°13E 119 F6
Maumusson, Pertuis de France 45°48N 1°14W 72 C2
Maun Botswana 20°0S 23°26E 144 B3
Mauna Kea U.S.A. 19°50N 155°28W 167 M8
Mauna Loa U.S.A. 19°30N 155°35W 167 M8
Maunath Bhanjan = Mau India 25°56N 83°33E 125 G10
Maungaturoto N.Z. 36°6S 174°23E 154 C3
Maungmagan Kyunzu Myanmar 14°0N 97°48E 120 E1
Maungu Kenya 3°33S 38°45E 142 C4
Maupin U.S.A. 45°11N 121°5W 168 D3
Maure-de-Bretagne France 47°59N 1°58W 70 E5
Maurepas, L. U.S.A. 30°15N 90°30W 177 F9
Maures France 43°15N 6°15E 73 E10
Mauriac France 45°13N 2°19E 72 C6
Mauriceville N.Z. 40°45S 175°42E 154 G4
Mauricie △ Canada 46°45N 73°0W 164 C5
Mauritania ■ Africa 20°50N 10°0W 134 E3
Mauritius ■ Ind. Oc. 20°0S 57°0E 141 d
Mauron France 48°9N 2°18W 70 D4
Maurs France 44°43N 2°12E 72 D6
Mauston U.S.A. 43°48N 90°5W 172 D8
Mauterndorf Austria 47°9N 13°40E 78 E6
Mauthen Austria 46°40N 13°0E 78 E6
Mauvezin France 43°44N 0°53E 72 E4
Mauzé-sur-le-Mignon France 46°12N 0°41W 72 B3
Mavli India 24°45N 73°55E 124 G5
Mavoko = Athi River Kenya 1°28S 36°58E 142 C4
Mavrovë Albania 40°26N 19°32E 96 F3
Mavrovo △ Macedonia 41°36N 20°45E 96 E4
Mavuradonha Mts. Zimbabwe 16°30S 31°30E 143 F3
Mawa Dem. Rep. of the Congo 2°45N 26°40E 142 B2
Mawai India 22°30N 81°4E 125 H9
Mawana India 29°6N 77°58E 124 E7
Mawand Pakistan 29°33N 68°38E 124 E3
Mawat Iraq 35°54N 45°24E 105 E11
Mawjib, W. al → Jordan 31°28N 35°36E 130 D4
Mawkmai Myanmar 20°14N 97°37E 123 J20
Mawlaik Myanmar 23°40N 94°26E 123 H19
Mawlamyine Myanmar 16°30N 97°40E 123 L20
Mawqaq Si. Arabia 27°25N 41°8E 128 E4
Mawson Antarctica 67°30S 62°53E 55 C6
Mawson Coast Antarctica 68°30S 63°0E 55 C6
Mawson Pk. Heard I. 53°6S 73°31E 146 K6
Max U.S.A. 47°49N 101°18W 172 B3
Maxcanú Mexico 20°35N 90°0W 181 C6
Maxesibeni S. Africa 30°49S 29°23E 145 D4
Maxeys U.S.A. 33°53N 83°11W 178 B6
Maxhamish L. Canada 59°50N 123°17W 162 B4
Maxixe Mozam. 23°54S 35°17E 145 D6
Maxville Canada 45°17N 74°51W 175 A10
Maxwell N.Z. 39°51S 174°49E 154 F3
Maxwell U.S.A. 39°17N 122°11W 170 F4
Maxwelton Australia 20°43S 142°41E 150 C3
May, C. U.S.A. 38°56N 74°58W 175 F8
May Pen Jamaica 17°58N 77°15W 182 a
Maya → Russia 60°28N 134°28E 107 D14
Maya, Costa Mexico 18°44N 87°42W 181 D7
Maya Mts. Belize 16°30N 89°0W 181 D7
Mayabandar India 12°56N 92°56E 127 H11
Mayaguana I. Bahamas 22°30N 72°44W 183 B5
Mayaguana Passage Bahamas 22°32N 73°15W 183 B5
Mayaguéz Puerto Rico 18°12N 67°9W 183 d
Mayahi Niger 13°58N 7°40E 139 C6
Mayaky Ukraine 47°26N 29°33E 81 C14
Mayals = Maials Spain 41°22N 0°30E 90 D5
Mayang China 27°53N 109°49E 117 D8
Mayanup Australia 33°57S 116°27E 149 F2
Mayari Cuba 20°40N 75°41W 183 B4
Mayaro Trin. & Tob. 10°17N 61°1W 187 K15
Mayaro B. Trin. & Tob. 10°14N 60°59W 187 K16
Mayavaram = Mayiladuthurai India 11°3N 79°42E 127 J4
Maybell U.S.A. 40°31N 108°5W 168 F9
Maybole U.K. 55°21N 4°42W 65 F9
Maydān Iraq 34°55N 45°37E 105 E11
Maydan Ukraine 48°36N 23°29E 81 B8
Mayen Germany 50°19N 7°13E 77 E3
Mayenne France 48°20N 0°38W 70 D6
Mayenne □ France 48°10N 0°40W 70 D6
Mayenne → France 47°30N 0°32W 70 E6
Mayer U.S.A. 34°24N 112°14W 169 J7
Mayerthorpe Canada 53°57N 115°8W 162 C5
Mayesville U.S.A. 34°0N 80°12W 178 A4
Mayfield Ky., U.S.A. 36°44N 88°38W 172 G9
Mayfield N.Y., U.S.A. 43°6N 74°16W 175 C10
Mayhill U.S.A. 32°53N 105°29W 169 K11
Mayiladuthurai India 11°3N 79°42E 127 J4
Maykop Russia 44°35N 40°10E 87 H5
Mayma Russia 52°3N 85°55E 109 B11
Maymyo = Pyin-U-Lwin Myanmar 22°2N 96°28E 120 A1
Maynard Mass., U.S.A. 42°26N 71°27W 175 D13
Maynard Wash., U.S.A. 47°59N 122°55W 170 C4
Maynard Hills Australia 28°28S 119°49E 149 E2
Mayne → Australia 23°40S 141°55E 150 C3
Maynooth Canada 45°13N 77°56W 174 A7
Maynooth Ireland 53°23N 6°34W 64 C5
Mayo Canada 63°38N 135°57W 160 C6
Mayo U.S.A. 30°3N 83°10W 178 E6
Mayo □ Ireland 53°53N 9°3W 64 C2
Mayo → Argentina 45°45S 69°45W 192 C3
Mayo → Peru 6°38S 76°15W 188 B2
Mayo Daga Nigeria 6°59N 11°25E 139 D7
Mayo Faran Nigeria 8°57N 12°4E 139 D7
Mayon Volcano Phil. 13°15N 123°41E 119 B6
Mayor Buratovich Argentina 39°25S 62°37W 192 A4
Mayor I. N.Z. 37°16S 176°17E 154 D5
Mayorga Spain 42°10N 5°16W 88 C5
Mayotte ☑ Ind. Oc. 12°50S 45°10E 141 a
Mayqayyng Kazakhstan 51°27N 75°47E 109 B9

Maysān □ Iraq 31°55N 47°15E 128 D5
Mayskiy Russia 43°47N 44°2E 87 J7
Maysville U.S.A. 38°39N 83°46W 173 F12
Mayu Indonesia 1°30N 126°30E 119 D7
Mayumba = Mayiladuthurai India 11°3N 79°42E 127 J4
Mayville N. Dak., U.S.A. 47°30N 97°20W 172 B5
Mayville N.Y., U.S.A. 42°15N 79°30W 174 D5
Mazabuka Zambia 15°52S 27°44E 143 F2
Mazagán = El Jadida Morocco 33°11N 8°17W 136 B2
Mazagão Brazil 0°7S 51°16W 187 D8
Mazamet France 43°30N 2°20E 72 E6
Mazán Peru 3°30S 73°0W 186 D4
Māzandarān □ Iran 36°30S 52°0E 129 B7
Mazapil Mexico 24°39N 101°34W 180 C4
Mazar China 36°32N 77°1E 109 E9
Mazar, O. → Algeria 31°50N 1°36E 136 B4
Mazara del Vallo Italy 37°39N 12°35E 94 E5
Mazarredo Argentina 47°10S 66°50W 192 C3
Mazarrón Spain 37°38N 1°19W 91 H3
Mazarrón, G. de Spain 37°27N 1°19W 91 H3
Mazaruni → Guyana 6°25N 58°35W 186 B7
Mazatán Mexico 29°0N 110°8W 180 B2
Mazatenango Guatemala 14°35N 91°30W 182 D1
Mazatlán Mexico 23°13N 106°25W 180 C3
Mažeikiai Lithuania 56°20N 22°20E 82 B9
Māzhān Iran 32°30N 59°0E 129 C8
Mazinān Iran 36°19N 56°56E 129 B8
Mazo Cruz Peru 16°45S 69°44W 188 D4
Mazoe Mozam. 16°42S 33°7E 143 F3
Mazoe → Mozam. 16°20S 33°30E 143 F3
Mazowe Zimbabwe 17°28S 30°58E 143 F3
Mazowieckie □ Poland 52°40N 21°0E 83 F8
Mazurski, Pojezierze Poland 53°50N 21°0E 82 E7
Mazyr Belarus 51°59N 29°15E 75 B15
Mba Fiji 17°33S 177°41E 154 a
Mbaba Senegal 14°59N 16°44W 138 C1
Mbabane Swaziland 26°18S 31°6E 145 C5
Mbagne Mauritania 16°6N 14°47W 138 B2
M'bahiakro Côte d'Ivoire 7°33N 4°19W 138 D4
Mbaïki C.A.R. 3°53N 18°1E 140 D3
Mbala Zambia 8°46S 31°24E 143 D3
Mbalabala Zimbabwe 20°27S 29°3E 145 B4
Mbale Uganda 1°8N 34°12E 142 B3
Mbalmayo Cameroon 3°33N 11°33E 139 E7
Mbam → Cameroon 4°24N 11°17E 139 E7
Mbamba Bay Tanzania 11°13S 34°49E 143 E3
Mbandaka Dem. Rep. of the Congo 0°1N 18°18E 140 D3
Mbanga Cameroon 4°30N 9°33E 139 E6
Mbanza Congo Angola 6°18S 14°16E 140 F2
Mbanza Ngungu Dem. Rep. of the Congo 5°12S 14°53E 140 F2
Mbarangandu Tanzania 10°11S 36°48E 143 D4
Mbarara Uganda 0°35S 30°40E 142 C3
Mbatto Côte d'Ivoire 6°28N 4°22W 138 D4
Mbengga = Beqa Fiji 18°23S 178°8E 154 a
Mbenkuru → Tanzania 9°25S 39°50E 143 D4
Mberengwa Zimbabwe 20°29S 29°57E 143 G2
Mberengwa, Mt. Zimbabwe 20°37S 29°55E 143 G2
Mberubu Nigeria 6°10N 7°38E 139 D6
Mbesuma Zambia 10°0S 32°2E 143 E3
Mbeya Tanzania 8°54S 33°29E 143 D3
Mbeya □ Tanzania 8°15S 33°30E 143 D3
Mbhashe → S. Africa 32°15S 28°54E 145 D4
Mbinga Tanzania 10°50S 35°0E 143 E4
Mbini = Río Muni □ Eq. Guin. 1°30N 10°0E 140 D2
Mbizi Zimbabwe 21°23S 31°1E 143 G3
Mbombela S. Africa 25°29S 30°59E 145 C5
Mbomou = Bomu → C.A.R. 4°40N 22°30E 140 D4
M'bonge Cameroon 4°33N 9°5E 139 E6
Mboro Senegal 15°9N 16°54W 138 C1
Mbouda Cameroon 5°38N 10°15E 139 D7
M'boukou, L. de Cameroon 6°23N 12°50E 139 D7
Mboune Senegal 14°42N 13°34W 138 C2
Mbour Senegal 14°22N 16°54W 138 C1
Mbout Mauritania 16°1N 12°38W 138 B2
Mbuji-Mayi Dem. Rep. of the Congo 6°9S 23°40E 142 D1
Mbulu Tanzania 3°45S 35°30E 142 C4
Mburucuyá Argentina 28°1S 58°14W 190 B4
Mburucuyá △ Argentina 28°1S 58°12W 190 B4
Mcherrah Algeria 27°0N 4°30W 136 C3
Mchinga Tanzania 9°44S 39°45E 143 D4
Mchinji Malawi 13°47S 32°58E 143 E3
Mdantsane S. Africa 32°56S 27°46E 145 D4
Mead, L. U.S.A. 36°0N 114°44W 171 J12
Meade U.S.A. 37°17N 100°20W 172 G4
Meade River = Atqasuk U.S.A. 70°28N 157°24W 166 A8
Meadow Lake Canada 54°10N 108°26W 163 C7
Meadow Lake △ Canada 54°27N 109°0W 163 C7
Meadow Valley Wash → U.S.A. 36°40N 114°34W 171 J12
Meadville U.S.A. 41°39N 80°9W 174 E4
Meaford Canada 44°36N 80°35W 174 B4
Meakan Dake Japan 45°15N 144°0E 112 C11
Mealhada Portugal 40°22N 8°27W 88 E2
Mealy Mts. Canada 53°10N 58°0W 165 B8
Meander River Canada 59°2N 117°42W 162 B5
Meares, C. U.S.A. 45°37N 124°0W 168 D1
Mearim → Brazil 3°4S 44°35W 187 D10
Meath □ Ireland 53°40N 6°57W 64 C5
Meath Park Canada 53°27N 105°22W 163 C7
Meaulne France 46°36N 2°36E 71 F6
Meaux France 48°58N 2°50E 71 D9
Mebechi-Gawa → Japan 40°31N 141°31E 112 D10
Mebulu, Tanjung Indonesia 8°50S 115°5E 119 K18
Mecanhelas Mozam. 15°12S 35°54E 143 F4
Mecca = Makkah Si. Arabia 21°30N 39°54E 137 C4
Mecca U.S.A. 33°34N 116°5W 171 M10
Mechanicsburg U.S.A. 40°13N 77°1W 174 F7
Mechanicville U.S.A. 42°54N 73°41W 175 D11
Mechelen Belgium 51°2N 4°29E 68 C4
Mecheria Algeria 33°35N 0°18W 136 B3
Mechernich Germany 50°35N 6°39E 76 E1
Mechetinskaya Russia 46°45N 40°32E 87 G5

Mechra Bel Ksiri Morocco 34°34N 5°57W 136 B2
Mechra Benâbbou Morocco 32°39N 7°48W 136 B2
Mecitözü Turkey 40°32N 35°17E 104 B6
Mecklenburg Germany 53°33N 11°40E 74 B7
Mecklenburg-Vorpommern □ Germany 53°45N 12°15E 76 B8
Mecklenburger Bucht Germany 54°20N 11°40E 76 A7
Meconta Mozam. 14°59S 39°50E 143 E4
Mecubúri Mozam. 14°39S 38°54E 143 E4
Mecubúri → Mozam. 14°0S 40°30E 143 E4
Mecúfi Mozam. 13°20S 40°32E 143 E5
Mêda Portugal 40°57N 7°18W 88 E3
Medak India 18°1N 78°15E 126 E4
Medan Indonesia 3°40N 98°38E 118 D1
Médanos Argentina 38°50S 62°42W 192 A4
Médanos de Coro △ Venezuela 11°35N 69°44W 183 D6
Medanosa, Pta. Argentina 48°8S 66°0W 192 C3
Medart U.S.A. 30°5N 84°23W 178 E5
Medawachchiya Sri Lanka 8°30N 80°30E 127 K5
Medchal India 17°37N 78°29E 126 F4
Mede Italy 45°6N 8°44E 92 C5
Médéa Algeria 36°12N 2°50E 136 A4
Médéa □ Algeria 36°0N 3°0E 136 A4
Mededa Bos.-H. 43°44N 19°10E 80 G4
Medeiros Neto Brazil 17°20S 40°14W 189 D2
Medellín Colombia 6°15N 75°35W 186 B3
Medelpad Sweden 62°33N 16°30E 62 B10
Medemblik Neths. 52°46N 5°8E 68 B5
Médenine Tunisia 33°21N 10°30E 136 B8
Médenine □ Tunisia 32°20N 10°0E 136 B8
Mederdra Mauritania 17°0N 15°38W 138 B1
Medford Mass., U.S.A. 42°25N 71°7W 175 D13
Medford Oreg., U.S.A. 42°19N 122°52W 168 E2
Medford Wis., U.S.A. 45°9N 90°20W 172 C8
Medgidia Romania 44°15N 28°19E 81 F13
Media Agua Argentina 31°58S 68°25W 190 C2
Media Luna Argentina 34°45S 66°44W 190 C2
Medianeira Brazil 25°17S 54°5W 191 B5
Medias Romania 46°9N 24°22E 81 D9
Medicina Italy 44°28N 11°38E 93 D8
Medicine Bow U.S.A. 41°54N 106°12W 168 F10
Medicine Bow Mts. U.S.A. 40°40N 106°0W 168 F10
Medicine Hat Canada 50°0N 110°45W 163 D6
Medicine Lake U.S.A. 48°30N 104°30W 168 B11
Medicine Lodge U.S.A. 37°17N 98°35W 172 G4
Medina = Al Madīnah Si. Arabia 24°35N 39°52E 128 E3
Medina Brazil 16°15S 41°29W 189 D2
Medina N. Dak., U.S.A. 46°54N 99°18W 172 B4
Medina N.Y., U.S.A. 43°13N 78°23W 174 C6
Medina Ohio, U.S.A. 41°8N 81°52W 174 E3
Medina → U.S.A. 29°16N 98°29W 176 G5
Medina de Pomar Spain 42°56N 3°29W 88 C7
Medina de Rioseco Spain 41°53N 5°3W 88 D5
Medina del Campo Spain 41°18N 4°55W 88 D6
Médina Gounas Senegal 13°8N 13°45W 138 C2
Medina L. U.S.A. 29°32N 98°56W 176 G5
Medina Sidonia Spain 36°28N 5°57W 89 B5
Medinaceli Spain 41°12N 2°30W 90 D2
Medinipur India 22°25N 87°21E 125 H12
Medio-Campidano □ Italy 39°35N 8°30E 94 C1
Mediterranean Sea Europe 35°0N 15°0E 58 H7
Mednogorsk Russia 51°24N 57°37E 108 B5
Médoc France 45°10N 0°50W 72 C3
Medulin Croatia 44°49N 13°55E 93 D10
Medveda Serbia 42°50N 21°32E 96 E6
Medvedevo Russia 56°37N 47°47E 86 B8
Medveditsa → Tver, Russia 57°5N 37°30E 84 D1
Medveditsa → Volgograd, Russia 49°35N 42°41E 86 F6
Medvedok Russia 57°20N 50°1E 86 B10
Medvezhi, Ostrava Russia 71°0N 161°0E 107 B17
Medvezhyegorsk Russia 63°0N 34°25E 106 C4
Medway □ U.K. 51°25N 0°32E 67 F8
Medway → U.K. 51°27N 0°46E 67 F8
Medzev Slovakia 48°43N 20°55E 79 C13
Medzilaborce Slovakia 49°17N 21°52E 79 B14
Medžitlija Macedonia 40°56N 21°26E 96 F5
Meekatharra Australia 26°32S 118°29E 149 E2
Meeker U.S.A. 40°2N 107°55W 168 F10
Meeniyan Australia 38°35S 146°3E 153 F7
Meersburg Germany 47°41N 9°16E 77 H5
Meerut India 29°1N 77°42E 124 E7
Meeteetse U.S.A. 44°9N 108°52W 168 D9
Mega Ethiopia 3°57N 38°19E 131 G2
Megalo Chorio Greece 36°27N 27°24E 99 E9
Megalopoli Greece 37°25N 22°7E 98 D4
Meganisi Greece 38°38N 20°46E 98 C2
Megara Greece 37°58N 23°22E 98 D5
Megasini India 21°38N 86°21E 125 J12
Megdova = Tavropos → Greece 39°10N 21°45E 98 B3
Megève France 45°51N 6°37E 73 C10
Meghalaya □ India 25°50N 91°0E 123 G17
Meghna → Bangla. 22°50N 90°50E 123 H17
Megion Russia 61°3N 76°6E 106 C8
Mégiscane, L. Canada 48°35N 75°55W 164 C4
Megisti Greece 36°8N 29°34E 99 E11
Megra Russia 66°1N 37°14E 84 B9
Mehadia Romania 44°56N 22°23E 80 F7
Mehaïguene, O. → Algeria 32°15N 2°59E 136 B4
Meharry, Mt. Australia 22°59S 118°35E 148 D2
Mehedeby Sweden 60°27N 17°25E 62 A11
Mehedinţi □ Romania 44°40N 22°45E 80 F7
Meheisa Sudan 19°38N 32°57E 137 D3
Mehekar India 20°9N 76°34E 126 D3
Mehlville U.S.A. 38°31N 90°19W 172 F8
Mehmetçik = Galatea Cyprus 35°25N 34°4E 101 D13
Mehndawal India 26°58N 83°5E 125 F10
Mehr Jān Iran 33°50N 55°6E 129 C7
Mehrābād Iran 36°53N 47°55E 105 D12
Mehrābān Iran 38°4N 47°7E 105 C12
Mehrān Iran 33°7N 46°10E 128 C5
Mehrān → Iran 26°45N 55°26E 129 E7
Mehrgarh Pakistan 29°30N 67°30E 124 E2

Mehrīz Iran 31°35N 54°28E 129 D7
Mehun-sur-Yèvre France 47°10N 2°13E 71 E9
Mei Jiang → China 24°25N 116°35E 117 E11
Mei Xian China 34°18N 107°55E 114 G4
Meicheng China 29°29N 119°16E 117 C12
Meichengzhen China 28°9N 111°40E 117 C8
Meichuan China 30°8N 115°31E 117 B10
Meighen I. Canada 80°0N 99°30W 161 B12
Meigs U.S.A. 31°4N 84°6W 178 D5
Meigu China 28°16N 103°20E 116 C4
Meihekou China 42°32N 125°40E 115 C13
Meiktila Myanmar 20°53N 95°54E 123 J19
Meili Xue Shan China 28°30N 98°39E 116 C2
Meimyu = Pyin-U-Lwin Myanmar 22°2N 96°28E 120 A1
Meinerzhagen Germany 51°6N 7°38E 76 D3
Meiningen Germany 50°34N 10°25E 76 E6
Meio → Brazil 13°36S 44°57W 189 C2
Meira, Serra de Spain 43°15N 7°15W 88 B3
Meiringen Switz. 46°43N 8°12E 77 J4
Meishan China 30°3N 103°23E 116 B4
Meissen Germany 51°9N 13°29E 76 D9
Meissner Germany 51°14N 9°50E 76 D5
Meissner-Kaufunger Wald △ Germany 51°16N 9°45E 76 D5
Meizhou China 27°45N 107°29E 116 D6
Meja India 25°9N 82°7E 125 G10
Mejillones Chile 23°10S 70°30W 190 A1
Mékhé Senegal 15°7N 16°38W 138 B1
Mekhtar Pakistan 30°30N 69°15E 122 D6
Meknès Morocco 33°57N 5°33W 136 B2
Meknès-Tafilalet □ Morocco 33°30N 5°0W 136 B2
Meko Nigeria 7°27N 2°52E 139 D5
Mekong → Asia 9°30N 106°15E 121 H6
Mekongga Indonesia 3°39S 121°15E 119 E6
Mekrou → Benin 12°25N 2°50E 139 C5
Mekvari = Kür → Azerbaijan 39°29N 49°15E 105 C13
Mel Italy 46°4N 12°5E 93 B9
Melagiri Hills India 12°20N 77°30E 127 H3
Melah, Oued el → Algeria 32°20N 2°28E 136 B4
Melaka Malaysia 2°15N 102°15E 121 L4
Melaka □ Malaysia 2°15N 102°15E 121 L4
Melambes Greece 35°8N 24°40E 101 D6
Melanesia Pac. Oc. 4°0S 155°0E 156 H7
Melanesian Basin Pac. Oc. 0°5N 160°35E 156 G8
Melapalaiyam India 8°39N 77°44E 127 K3
Melaya Indonesia 8°17S 114°30E 119 J17
Melbourne Australia 37°48S 144°58E 153 F6
Melbourne U.S.A. 28°5N 80°37W 179 G9
Melchor Múzquiz Mexico 27°53N 101°31W 180 B4
Melchor Ocampo Mexico 24°51N 101°39W 180 C4
Méldola Italy 44°7N 12°4E 93 D9
Meldorf Germany 54°5N 9°5E 76 A5
Melegnano Italy 45°21N 9°19E 92 C6
Melekeok Palau 7°27N 134°38E 156 G5
Melenci Serbia 45°32N 20°20E 80 E5
Melenki Russia 55°20N 41°37E 86 C5
Mélèzes → Canada 57°40N 69°29W 164 A5
Melfi Italy 41°0N 15°39E 95 B8
Melfort Canada 52°50N 104°37W 163 C8
Melfort Zimbabwe 18°0S 31°25E 143 F3
Melgaço Portugal 42°7N 8°15W 88 C2
Melgar de Fernamental Spain 42°27N 4°17W 88 C6
Melhus Norway 63°17N 10°18E 60 E14
Melide Spain 42°55N 8°1W 88 C2
Meligales Greece 37°15N 21°59E 98 D3
Melilla N. Afr. 35°21N 2°57W 134 A5
Melilli Italy 37°11N 15°7E 95 E8
Melipilla Chile 33°42S 71°15W 190 C1
Melissa Canada 45°24N 79°14W 174 A5
Melissa, Akra Greece 35°6N 24°33E 101 D6
Melissa Oros Greece 37°32N 26°4E 99 D8
Mélito di Porto Salvo Italy 37°55N 15°47E 95 E8
Melitopol Ukraine 46°50N 35°22E 85 J8
Melk Austria 48°13N 15°20E 78 D8
Mellan Fryken Sweden 59°45N 13°10E 62 E7
Mellansel Sweden 63°26N 18°19E 60 E18
Mellbystrand Sweden 56°30N 12°56E 63 H6
Melle France 46°14N 0°10W 72 B3
Melle Germany 52°12N 8°20E 76 C4
Mellègue, O. → Tunisia 36°36N 9°14E 136 A5
Mellen U.S.A. 46°20N 90°40W 172 B8
Mellerud Sweden 58°41N 12°28E 63 F6
Mellette U.S.A. 45°9N 98°30W 172 C4
Mellid = Melide Spain 42°55N 8°1W 88 C2
Mellieha Malta 35°57N 14°22E 101 D1
Mellizo Sur, Cerro Chile 48°33S 73°10W 192 C2
Mellrichstadt Germany 50°25N 10°17E 76 E6
Melnik Bulgaria 41°30N 23°25E 96 E7
Mělník Czechia 50°22N 14°23E 78 A7
Melnytsya Podilska Ukraine 48°37N 26°10E 81 B11
Melo Uruguay 32°20S 54°10W 191 C5
Melolo Indonesia 9°53S 120°40E 119 F6
Melouprey Cambodia 13°48N 105°16E 120 F5
Melrhir, Chott Algeria 34°13N 6°30E 136 B6
Melrose Australia 32°42S 146°57E 153 E8
Melrose U.K. 55°36N 2°43W 65 F6
Melrose Minn., U.S.A. 45°40N 94°49W 172 C6
Melrose N. Mex., U.S.A. 34°26N 103°38W 169 J12
Melstone U.S.A. 46°36N 107°52W 168 C10
Melton U.K. 52°51N 1°16E 67 E9
Melton Mowbray U.K. 52°47N 0°54W 66 E7
Melun France 48°32N 2°39E 71 D9
Melung Nepal 27°31N 86°3E 125 F12
Melur India 10°2N 78°23E 127 J4
Melut Sudan 10°30N 32°13E 137 E3
Melville Canada 50°55N 102°50W 163 C8
Melville, C. Australia 14°11S 144°30E 150 A3
Melville, L. Canada 13°30S 139°50E 150 A2
Melville B. Australia 12°0S 136°45E 150 A2
Melville I. Australia 11°30S 131°0E 150 A1
Melville I. Canada 75°30N 112°0W 159 B8
Melville Pen. Canada 68°0N 84°0W 161 C11
Melvin, Lough Ireland 54°26N 8°10W 64 B3

Mélykút Hungary 46°11N 19°25E 80 D4
Memaliaj Albania 40°25N 19°56E 96 F3
Memba Mozam. 14°11S 40°30E 143 E5
Memberamo → Indonesia 8°13S 114°39E 119 J17
Membrilla Spain 38°59N 3°21W 89 G7
Memel = Klaipėda Lithuania 55°43N 21°10E 82 C8
Memel S. Africa 27°38S 29°36E 145 C4
Memmingen Germany 47°58N 10°10E 77 H6
Mempawah Indonesia 0°30N 109°5E 118 D3
Memphis Egypt 29°50N 31°12E 137 F7
Memphis Mich., U.S.A. 42°54N 82°46W 174 D2
Memphis Tenn., U.S.A. 35°8N 90°2W 177 D10
Memphis Tex., U.S.A. 34°44N 100°33W 176 D4
Memphrémagog, L. N. Amer. 45°8N 72°17W 175 B12
Mena Ukraine 51°31N 32°13E 85 G7
Mena U.S.A. 34°35N 94°15W 176 D7
Menai Strait U.K. 53°11N 4°13W 66 D3
Ménaka Mali 15°59N 2°18E 139 B5
Menan = Chao Phraya → Thailand 13°40N 100°31E 120 F3
Menard U.S.A. 30°55N 99°47W 176 F5
Menard Fracture Zone Pac. Oc. 43°0S 97°0W 157 M18
Mendaña Fracture Zone Pac. Oc. 16°0S 91°0W 157 J18
Mendawai → Indonesia 3°30S 113°0E 118 E4
Mende France 44°31N 3°30E 72 D7
Mendeleyev Ridge Arctic 80°0N 178°0W 54 B17
Menden Germany 51°26N 7°47E 76 D3
Menderes Turkey 38°14N 27°8E 99 C9
Mendhar India 33°35N 74°10E 125 C6
Mendip Hills U.K. 51°17N 2°40W 67 F5
Mendocino U.S.A. 39°19N 123°48W 168 G2
Mendocino, C. U.S.A. 40°26N 124°25W 168 F1
Mendocino Fracture Zone Pac. Oc. 40°0N 142°0W 157 D13
Mendooran Australia 31°50S 149°6E 153 E8
Mendota Calif., U.S.A. 36°45N 120°23W 170 J6
Mendota Ill., U.S.A. 41°33N 89°7W 172 E9
Mendoyo Indonesia 8°23S 114°42E 119 J17
Mendoza Argentina 32°50S 68°52W 190 C2
Mendoza □ Argentina 33°0S 69°0W 190 C2
Mene Grande Venezuela 9°49N 70°56W 186 B4
Menemen Turkey 38°34N 27°3E 99 C9
Menen Belgium 50°47N 3°7E 68 D3
Menéndez, L. Argentina 42°45S 71°51W 192 B2
Menfi Italy 37°36N 12°58E 94 E5
Mengcheng China 33°12N 116°33E 117 A11
Mengdingjie China 23°31N 98°58E 116 F2
Menggala Indonesia 4°30S 105°15E 118 E3
Menghai China 21°49N 100°16E 116 G3
Mengibar Spain 37°58N 3°48W 89 H7
Mengjin China 34°55N 112°45E 114 G7
Mengla China 21°20N 101°25E 116 G3
Menglian China 22°21N 99°27E 116 F2
Mengshan China 24°14N 110°55E 117 E8
Mengyin China 35°40N 117°58E 115 G9
Mengzhe China 22°2N 100°15E 116 F3
Mengzi China 23°20N 103°22E 116 F4
Menifee U.S.A. 33°41N 117°10W 171 M9
Menihek Canada 54°28N 56°36W 165 B6
Menihek L. Canada 54°0N 67°0W 165 B6
Menin = Menen Belgium 50°47N 3°7E 68 D3
Menindee Australia 32°20S 142°25E 152 E5
Menindee L. Australia 32°20S 142°25E 152 E5
Meningie Australia 35°50S 139°18E 152 F2
Menjangan, Pulau Indonesia 8°5S 114°31E 119 J17
Menkrour Algeria 26°27N 8°9E 136 C5
Menlo Park U.S.A. 37°27N 122°12W 170 H4
Menninee → Australia 22°15S 131°16E 148 C5
Menominee U.S.A. 45°6N 87°37W 172 C10
Menominee → U.S.A. 45°6N 87°36W 172 C10
Menomonie U.S.A. 44°53N 91°55W 172 C8
Menongue Angola 14°48S 17°52E 141 G3
Menorca Spain 40°0N 4°0E 100 B11
Menorca ✈ (MAH) Spain 39°50N 4°16E 90 F9
Mentakab Malaysia 3°29N 102°21E 121 L4
Mentawai, Kepulauan Indonesia 2°0S 99°0E 118 E1
Menton France 43°50N 7°29E 73 E11
Mentor U.S.A. 41°40N 81°21W 174 E3
Menzel-Bourguiba Tunisia 37°9N 9°49E 136 A5
Menzel-Chaker Tunisia 35°0N 10°26E 136 B6
Menzies Australia 29°40S 121°2W 149 E3
Meob B. Namibia 24°25S 14°34E 144 B1
Meoqui Mexico 28°17N 105°29W 180 B3
Mepaco Mozam. 15°57S 30°48E 143 F3
Meppel Neths. 52°42N 6°12E 68 B6
Meppen Germany 52°42N 7°17E 76 C3
Mequinenza Spain 41°22N 0°17E 90 D5
Mequinenza, Embalse de Spain 41°25N 0°15E 90 D5
Mer India 21°50N 70°15E 124 J4
Merak Indonesia 6°10N 106°26E 119 F12
Meramangye, L. Australia 28°25S 132°13E 149 E5
Meran = Merano Italy 46°40N 11°9E 93 B8
Merano Italy 46°40N 11°9E 93 B8
Merate Italy 45°42N 9°25E 92 C6
Merauke Indonesia 8°29S 140°24E 119 F10
Merbein Australia 34°10S 142°2E 152 E5
Merca = Marka Somalia 1°48N 44°50E 131 G3
Mercantour △ France 44°16N 6°43E 73 D10
Mercato Saraceno Italy 43°57N 12°12E 93 E9
Merced U.S.A. 37°18N 120°29W 170 H6
Merced → U.S.A. 37°21N 120°59W 170 H6
Merced Pk. U.S.A. 37°36N 119°24W 170 H7
Mercedes B. Aires, Argentina 34°40S 59°30W 190 C4
Mercedes Corrientes, Argentina 29°10S 58°5W 190 B4
Mercedes San Luis, Argentina 33°40S 65°21W 190 C2
Mercedes Uruguay 33°40S 58°0W 191 C4
Mercedes U.S.A. 26°9N 97°54W 177 H6
Merceditas Chile 28°20S 70°35W 190 B1
Mercer N.Z. 37°16S 175°5E 154 B5
Mercer U.S.A. 41°14N 80°15W 174 E4
Mercer Island U.S.A. 47°34N 122°13W 170 C4
Mercier Bolivia 10°42S 68°5W 188 C4
Mercury U.S.A. 36°40N 115°59W 171 J11
Mercury B. N.Z. 36°48S 175°45E 154 B5
Mercury Is. N.Z. 36°37S 175°52E 154 B5
Mercy, C. Canada 65°0N 63°30W 161 D13
Merdrignac France 48°11N 2°27W 70 D4

Mere U.K. 51°6N 2°16W 67 F5
Merebuk, Gunung Indonesia 8°13S 114°39E 119 J17
Meredith Australia 37°49S 144°5E 152 D6
Meredith, C. Falk. Is. 52°15S 60°40W 192 C4
Meredith U.S.A. 35°43N 101°33W 176 D4
Merefa Ukraine 49°48N 36°3E 85 H9
Merga = Nukheila Sudan 19°1N 26°21E 137 D2
Mergui Myanmar 12°26N 98°34E 120 E2
Mergui Arch. = Myeik Kyunzu Myanmar 11°30N 97°30E 121 G1
Meribah Australia 34°43S 140°51E 152 C4
Méribel-les-Alues France 45°25N 6°34E 73 C10
Meriç Turkey 41°11N 26°25E 97 E10
Meriç → Turkey 40°52N 26°12E 99 C7
Mérida Mexico 20°58N 89°37W 181 C7
Mérida Spain 38°55N 6°25W 89 G4
Mérida Venezuela 8°24N 71°8W 186 B4
Mérida, Cord. de Venezuela 9°0N 71°0W 186 B4
Meriden U.K. 52°26N 1°38W 67 E6
Meriden Calif., U.S.A. 41°32N 72°48W 175 E12
Meridian Ga., U.S.A. 32°29N 81°23W 178 C8
Meridian Idaho, U.S.A. 43°37N 116°24W 168 E5
Meridian Miss., U.S.A. 32°22N 88°42W 177 E10
Mérignac France 44°51N 0°39W 72 D3
Merimbula Australia 36°53S 149°54E 153 F8
Merinda Australia 20°2S 148°11E 150 C4
Mering Germany 48°16N 10°59E 77 G6
Meringa Nigeria 10°44N 12°9E 139 C7
Meringur Australia 34°20S 141°19E 152 C4
Merir Palau 4°10N 132°30E 119 D8
Meriruma Brazil 1°15N 54°50W 187 C8
Merkel U.S.A. 32°28N 100°1W 176 E4
Mermaid Reef Australia 17°6S 119°36E 148 C2
Meroë Sudan 16°56N 33°42E 137 D3
Merowe Sudan 18°29N 31°46E 137 D3
Merowe Dam Sudan 18°35N 31°56E 137 D3
Merredin Australia 31°28S 118°18E 149 F2
Merrick U.K. 55°8N 4°28W 65 F4
Merrickville Canada 44°55N 75°50W 175 B9
Merrill Oreg., U.S.A. 42°1N 121°36W 168 E3
Merrill Wis., U.S.A. 45°11N 89°41W 172 C9
Merrimack → U.S.A. 42°49N 70°49W 175 D14
Merriman U.S.A. 42°55N 101°42W 172 D3
Merritt Canada 50°10N 120°45W 162 D4
Merritt Island U.S.A. 28°21N 80°42W 179 G9
Merriwa Australia 32°6S 150°22E 153 E9
Merriwagga Australia 33°47S 145°43E 153 B6
Merry I. Canada 55°29N 77°31W 164 A4
Merrygoen Australia 31°51S 149°12E 153 A8
Merryville U.S.A. 30°45N 93°33W 176 F7
Mersch Lux. 49°44N 6°7E 69 E6
Merse → Italy 43°5N 11°22E 93 E8
Mersea I. U.K. 51°47N 0°58E 67 F8
Merseburg Germany 51°22N 11°59E 76 D7
Mersey → U.K. 53°25N 3°1W 66 D4
Merseyside □ U.K. 53°31N 3°2W 66 D4
Mersin Turkey 36°51N 34°36E 106 D6
Mersin □ Turkey 36°45N 34°0E 104 D5
Mersing Malaysia 2°25N 103°50E 121 L4
Merta India 26°39N 74°4E 124 F6
Merta Road India 26°43N 73°55E 124 F5
Merthyr Tydfil U.K. 51°45N 3°22W 67 F4
Merthyr Tydfil □ U.K. 51°46N 3°21W 67 F4
Merti Kenya 1°4N 38°40E 142 B4
Mértola Portugal 37°40N 7°40W 89 H3
Mertz Glacier Antarctica 67°30S 144°45E 55 C10
Mertzon U.S.A. 31°16N 100°49W 176 F4
Méru France 49°13N 2°8E 71 C9
Meru Kenya 0°3N 37°40E 142 B4
Meru Tanzania 3°15S 36°46E 142 C4
Meru □ Kenya 0°5N 38°10E 142 B4
Meru Betiri △ Indonesia 8°27S 113°51E 119 H15
Merville France 50°38N 2°38E 71 B9
Méry-sur-Seine France 48°31N 3°54E 71 D10
Merzifon Turkey 40°53N 35°32E 104 B6
Merzig Germany 49°26N 6°38E 77 F2
Merzouga, Erg Tin Algeria 24°0N 11°4E 136 D6
Mesa U.S.A. 33°25N 111°50W 169 K8
Mesa Verde △ U.S.A. 37°11N 108°29W 169 H9
Mesada = Masada Israel 31°18N 35°21E 130 D4
Mesagne Italy 40°34N 17°48E 95 B10
Mesanagros Greece 36°1N 27°49E 101 C12
Meschede Germany 51°20N 8°18E 76 D4
Mescit Turkey 40°21N 41°11E 105 B9
Mesgouez, L. Canada 51°20N 75°0W 164 B5
Meshchovsk Russia 54°22N 35°17E 84 E8
Meshchyora □ Russia 55°30N 40°20E 86 C5
Meshchyora → Russia 54°50N 41°10E 86 C5
Meshed = Mashhad Iran 36°20N 59°35E 129 B8
Meshgīn Shahr Iran 38°30N 47°45E 105 C12
Meshoppen U.S.A. 41°36N 76°3W 175 E8
Mesilinka → Canada 56°6N 124°30W 162 B4
Meslay-du-Maine France 47°58N 0°33W 70 E6
Mesocco Switz. 46°23N 9°12E 77 J5
Mesolongi Greece 38°21N 21°28E 98 C3
Mesongi Greece 39°22N 19°56E 101 B3
Mesopotamia = Al Jazirah Iraq 33°30N 44°0E 105 E10
Mesopotamia U.S.A. 41°27N 80°57W 174 E4
Mesoraca Italy 39°14N 20°32E 98 D2
Mésou Volimais = Volimes Greece 37°44N 20°40E 98 D2
Mesquite Nev., U.S.A. 36°48N 114°4W 169 H6
Mesquite Tex., U.S.A. 32°47N 96°36W 176 E6
Messaad Algeria 34°8N 3°30E 136 B4
Messac France 47°49N 1°50W 70 E5
Messalo → Mozam. 12°25S 39°15E 143 E4
Messaména Cameroon 3°48N 12°49E 139 E7
Messara, Kolpos Greece 35°6N 24°47E 101 D6
Messene Greece 37°4N 22°1E 98 D4
Messier, Canal Chile 48°20S 74°33W 192 C2
Messina = Musina S. Africa 22°20S 30°5E 145 B5
Messina Italy 38°11N 15°34E 95 D8
Messina, Str. di Italy 38°15N 15°35E 95 D8
Messiniakos Kolpos Greece 36°45N 22°5E 98 E4
Messkirch Germany 47°59N 9°7E 77 H5
Messlingen Sweden 62°40N 12°40E 62 A6

Mesta = Nestos → Europe 40°54N 24°49E **97** F8
Mesta, Akra *Greece* 38°16N 25°53E **99** C7
Mestanza *Spain* 38°35N 4°4W **89** G6
Mestersvig *Greenland* 72°10N 23°40W **57** C8
Mestre *Italy* 45°29N 12°15E **93** C9
Mestre, Espigão *Brazil* 12°30S 46°10W **189** C1
Mesudiye *Turkey* 40°28N 37°46E **104** B7
Meta → *S. Amer.* 6°12N 67°28W **186** B5
Meta Incognita Pen. *Canada* 62°45N 68°30W **161** E18
Metabetchouan *Canada* 48°26N 71°52W **165** C5
Metairie *U.S.A.* 29°59N 90°9W **177** G9
Metalici, Munţii *Romania* 46°15N 22°50E **80** D7
Metaline Falls *U.S.A.* 48°52N 117°22W **168** B5
Metallifere, Colline *Italy* 43°10N 11°0E **92** E8
Metán *Argentina* 25°30S 65°0W **190** B3
Metangula *Mozam.* 12°40S 34°50E **143** E3
Metauro → *Italy* 43°50N 13°3E **93** E10
Metcalf *U.S.A.* 30°43N 83°59W **178** E6
Metcalfe *Canada* 45°14N 75°28W **175** A9
Metema *Ethiopia* 12°58N 36°12E **131** E2
Metengobalame *Mozam.* 14°49S 34°30E **143** E3
Meteora *Greece* 39°43N 21°37E **98** B3
Methana *Greece* 37°35N 23°23E **98** D5
Methoni *Greece* 36°49N 21°42E **98** E3
Methven *N.Z.* 43°38S 171°40E **155** D6
Metil *Mozam.* 16°24S 39°0E **143** F4
Metkovets *Bulgaria* 43°37N 23°10E **96** C7
Metković *Croatia* 43°6N 17°39E **93** E14
Metlakatla *U.S.A.* 55°8N 131°35W **160** F5
Metlaoui *Tunisia* 34°24N 8°24E **136** B5
Metlika *Slovenia* 45°40N 15°20E **93** C12
Metlili Chaamba *Algeria* 32°16N 3°38E **136** B4
Metropolis *U.S.A.* 37°9N 88°44W **172** G9
Metropolitana □ *Chile* 33°30S 70°50W **190** C1
Metsovo *Greece* 39°48N 21°12E **98** B3
Metter *U.S.A.* 32°24N 82°3W **178** C7
Mettuppalaiyam *India* 11°18N 76°59E **127** J3
Mettur *India* 11°48N 77°47E **127** J3
Metu *Ethiopia* 8°18N 35°35E **131** F2
Metz *France* 49°8N 6°10E **71** C13
Metzingen *Germany* 48°31N 9°17E **77** G5
Meulaboh *Indonesia* 4°11N 96°3E **118** D1
Meung-sur-Loire *France* 47°50N 1°40E **71** E8
Meureudu *Indonesia* 5°19N 96°10E **118** C1
Meurthe → *France* 48°47N 6°9E **71** D13
Meurthe-et-Moselle □ *France* 48°52N 6°0E **71** D13
Meuse □ *France* 49°8N 5°25E **71** C12
Meuse → *Europe* 50°45N 5°41E **69** D5
Meuselwitz *Germany* 51°2N 12°17E **76** D8
Mexia *U.S.A.* 31°41N 96°29W **176** F6
Mexiana, I. *Brazil* 0°0 49°30W **187** D9
Mexicali *Mexico* 32°40N 115°30W **171** N11
Mexican Plateau *Mexico* 25°0N 104°0W **158** G9
Mexican Water *U.S.A.* 36°57N 109°32W **169** H9
Mexico *Maine, U.S.A.* 44°34N 70°33W **175** B14
Mexico *Mo., U.S.A.* 39°10N 91°53W **172** F8
Mexico *N.Y., U.S.A.* 43°28N 76°14W **175** C8
México □ *Mexico* 19°20N 99°30W **181** D5
Mexico ■ *Cent. Amer.* 25°0N 105°0W **180** C4
México, Ciudad de *Mexico* 19°24N 99°9W **181** D5
Mexico, G. of *Cent. Amer.* 25°0N 90°0W **181** C7
Mexico B. *U.S.A.* 43°35N 76°20W **175** C8
Mexico Beach *U.S.A.* 29°57N 85°25W **178** F4
Meydān-e Naftūn *Iran* 31°56N 49°18E **129** D6
Meydani, Ra's-e *Iran* 25°24N 59°6E **129** E8
Meyenburg *Germany* 53°18N 12°14E **76** B8
Meyers Chuck *U.S.A.* 55°45N 132°15W **162** B2
Meymac *France* 45°32N 2°10E **72** C6
Meymaneh *Afghan.* 35°53N 64°38E **108** E6
Meyrueis *France* 44°12N 3°27E **72** D7
Meyssac *France* 45°3N 1°40E **72** C5
Meyzieu *France* 45°46N 4°59E **73** C8
Mezdra *Bulgaria* 43°12N 23°42E **96** C7
Mèze *France* 43°27N 3°36E **72** E7
Mezen *Russia* 65°50N 44°20E **106** C5
Mezen → *Russia* 65°44N 44°22E **58** B14
Mézenc, Mt. *France* 44°54N 4°11E **73** D8
Mezeş, Munţii *Romania* 47°5N 23°5E **80** C8
Mezha → *Russia* 55°44N 31°33E **84** E6
Mezhdurechensk *Russia* 53°41N 88°3E **109** B11
Mezhdurechenskiy *Russia* 59°36N 65°56E **106** D7
Mézidon-Canon *France* 49°5N 0°1W **70** C6
Mézières-en-Brenne *France* 46°49N 1°13E **72** B5
Mézilhac *France* 44°49N 4°21E **73** D8
Mézin *France* 44°4N 0°16E **72** D4
Mezőberény *Hungary* 46°49N 21°3E **80** D6
Mezőfalva *Hungary* 46°55N 18°49E **80** D3
Mezőhegyes *Hungary* 46°19N 20°49E **80** D5
Mezőkövácsháza *Hungary* 46°25N 20°57E **80** D5
Mezőkövesd *Hungary* 47°49N 20°35E **80** C5
Mézos *France* 44°5N 1°10W **72** D2
Mezőtúr *Hungary* 47°1N 20°41E **80** C5
Mezquital *Mexico* 23°29N 104°23W **180** C4
Mezzolombardo *Italy* 46°13N 11°5E **92** B8
Mfolozi → *S. Africa* 28°25S 32°26E **145** C5
Mgeta *Tanzania* 8°22S 36°6E **143** D4
Mglin *Russia* 53°2N 32°50E **85** F7
Mhamid *Morocco* 29°49N 5°43W **136** C2
Mhlaba Hills *Zimbabwe* 18°30S 30°30E **143** F3
Mhow *India* 22°33N 75°50E **124** H6
Miahuatlán *Mexico* 16°20N 96°36W **181** D5
Miajadas *Spain* 39°9N 5°54W **89** F5
Miami *Fla., U.S.A.* 25°46N 80°11W **179** K9
Miami *Okla., U.S.A.* 36°53N 94°53W **176** C7
Miami *Tex., U.S.A.* 35°42N 100°38W **176** D4
Miami Beach *U.S.A.* 25°47N 80°7W **179** K9
Miami Canal *U.S.A.* 25°45N 80°12W **179** K9
Miami Gardens *U.S.A.* 25°56N 80°15W **179** C1
Miami Int. ✕ **(MIA)** *U.S.A.* 25°48N 80°17W **179** K9
Miami Shores *U.S.A.* 25°51N 80°11W **179** K9
Miami Springs *U.S.A.* 25°49N 80°17W **179** K9
Mian Xian *China* 33°10N 106°32E **116** A6
Mianchi *China* 34°48N 111°48E **114** G6
Mīāndarreh *Iran* 35°37N 53°39E **129** C7
Mīāndowāb *Iran* 37°0N 46°5E **105** D12
Miandrivazo *Madag.* 19°31S 45°29E **141** H9
Mīāneh *Iran* 37°30N 47°40E **105** D12
Mianning *China* 28°32N 102°9E **116** C4
Mianwali *Pakistan* 32°38N 71°28E **124** C4
Mianyang *China* 31°22N 104°47E **116** B5
Mianzhu *China* 31°22N 104°7E **116** B5
Miao Ling *China* 26°5N 107°30E **116** D6
Miaodao Qundao *China* 38°10N 120°45E **115** E11
Miaoli *Taiwan* 24°37N 120°49E **117** E13
Miass *Russia* 54°59N 60°6E **108** B6
Miasteczko Krajeńskie *Poland* 53°7N 17°1E **83** E4
Miastko *Poland* 54°0N 16°58E **82** E3
Mica *S. Africa* 24°10S 30°48E **145** B5
Micanopy *U.S.A.* 29°30N 82°17W **179** F7
Micăsasa *Romania* 46°7N 24°7E **81** D9
Micco *U.S.A.* 27°53N 80°30W **179** H9
Miccosukee *U.S.A.* 30°36N 84°3W **178** E5
Miccosukee, L. *U.S.A.* 30°33N 83°53W **178** E6
Michalovce *Slovakia* 48°47N 21°58E **79** C14
Michigan □ *U.S.A.* 44°0N 85°0W **173** C11
Michigan, L. *U.S.A.* 44°0N 87°0W **172** D10
Michigan City *U.S.A.* 41°43N 86°54W **172** E10
Michika *Nigeria* 10°36N 13°23E **139** C7
Michipicoten I. *Canada* 47°40N 85°40W **164** C2
Michoacán □ *Mexico* 19°10N 101°50W **180** D4
Michurin *Bulgaria* 42°9N 27°51E **97** D11
Michurinsk *Russia* 52°58N 40°27E **86** D5
Micoud *St. Lucia* 13°49N 60°54W **183** f
Micronesia *Pac. Oc.* 11°0N 160°0E **156** G7
Micronesia, Federated States of ■ *Pac. Oc.* 9°0N 150°0E **156** G7
Mid-Atlantic Ridge *Atl. Oc.* 0°0 20°0W **56** J10
Mid-Indian Ocean Basin *Ind. Oc.* 10°0S 80°0E **146** F7
Mid-Indian Ridge *Ind. Oc.* 30°0S 75°0E **146** H6
Mid-Oceanic Ridge *Ind. Oc.* 42°0S 90°0E **156** M1
Mid-Pacific Seamounts *Pac. Oc.* 18°0N 177°0W **156** F10
Midai *Indonesia* 3°0N 107°47E **118** D3
Midale *Canada* 49°25N 103°20W **163** D8
Middelburg *Neths.* 51°30N 3°36E **69** C3
Middelburg *Eastern Cape, S. Africa* 31°30S 25°0E **144** D4
Middelburg *Mpumalanga, S. Africa* 25°49S 29°28E **145** C4
Middelfart *Denmark* 55°30N 9°43E **63** J3
Middelpos *S. Africa* 31°55S 20°13E **144** D3
Middelwit *S. Africa* 24°51S 27°3E **144** B4
Middle Alkali L. *U.S.A.* 41°27N 120°5W **168** F3
Middle America Trench = Guatemala Trench *Pac. Oc.* 14°0N 95°0W **158** H10
Middle Andaman I. *India* 12°30N 92°50E **127** H11
Middle Bass I. *U.S.A.* 41°41N 82°48W **174** E2
Middle East *Asia* 35°0N 40°0E **102** E5
Middle Fork Feather → *U.S.A.* 38°33N 121°30W **170** F5
Middle I. *Australia* 34°6S 123°11E **149** F3
Middle Loup → *U.S.A.* 41°17N 98°24W **172** E4
Middleboro *U.S.A.* 41°54N 70°55W **175** E14
Middleburg *Fla., U.S.A.* 30°4N 81°52W **178** E8
Middleburg *Pa., U.S.A.* 40°47N 77°3W **174** F7
Middleburgh *U.S.A.* 42°36N 74°20W **175** D10
Middlebury *U.S.A.* 44°1N 73°10W **175** B11
Middlefield *U.S.A.* 41°27N 81°4W **174** E3
Middlemarch *N.Z.* 45°30S 170°9E **155** F5
Middlemount *Australia* 22°50S 148°40E **150** C4
Middleport *N.Y., U.S.A.* 43°13N 78°29W **174** C6
Middleport *Ohio, U.S.A.* 39°0N 82°3W **173** F12
Middlesboro *U.S.A.* 36°36N 83°43W **173** G12
Middlesbrough *U.K.* 54°35N 1°13W **66** C6
Middlesbrough □ *U.K.* 54°28N 1°13W **66** C6
Middlesex *Belize* 17°2N 88°31W **182** C2
Middlesex *N.J., U.S.A.* 40°36N 74°30W **175** F10
Middlesex *N.Y., U.S.A.* 42°42N 77°16W **174** D7
Middleton *Australia* 22°22S 141°32E **150** C3
Middleton *Canada* 44°57N 65°4W **165** D6
Middleton Cr. → *Australia* 22°35S 141°51E **150** C3
Middleton I. *U.S.A.* 59°26N 146°20W **166** D10
Middletown *U.K.* 54°17N 6°51W **64** B5
Middletown *Calif., U.S.A.* 38°45N 122°37W **170** G4
Middletown *Conn., U.S.A.* 41°34N 72°39W **175** E12
Middletown *N.Y., U.S.A.* 41°27N 74°25W **175** E10
Middletown *Ohio, U.S.A.* 39°31N 84°24W **173** F11
Middletown *Pa., U.S.A.* 40°12N 76°44W **175** F8
Midelt *Morocco* 32°46N 4°44W **136** B3
Midge Point *Australia* 20°39S 148°43E **150** b
Midhirst *N.Z.* 39°17S 174°18E **154** F3
Midhurst *Canada* 44°26N 79°43W **174** B5
Midhurst *U.K.* 50°59N 0°44W **67** G7
Midi, Canal du → *France* 43°45N 1°21E **72** E5
Midi d'Ossau, Pic du *France* 42°50N 0°26W **72** F3
Midland *Australia* 31°54S 116°1E **149** F2
Midland *Canada* 44°45N 79°50W **174** B5
Midland *Calif., U.S.A.* 33°52N 114°48W **171** M12
Midland *Mich., U.S.A.* 43°37N 84°14W **173** D11
Midland *Pa., U.S.A.* 40°39N 80°27W **174** F4
Midland *Tex., U.S.A.* 32°0N 102°3W **176** F3
Midlands □ *Zimbabwe* 19°40S 29°0E **143** F2
Midleton *Ireland* 51°55N 8°10W **64** E3
Midlothian □ *U.K.* 55°51N 3°5W **65** F5
Midnapore = Medinipur *India* 22°25N 87°21E **125** H12
Midou → *France* 43°54N 0°30W **72** E3
Midouze → *France* 43°48N 0°51W **72** E3
Midu *China* 25°18N 100°30E **116** E3
Midville *U.S.A.* 32°49N 82°14W **178** C7
Midway *Ala., U.S.A.* 32°5N 85°31W **178** C4
Midway *Fla., U.S.A.* 30°30N 84°27W **178** E5
Midway Is. *Pac. Oc.* 28°13N 177°22W **167** K4
Midway Wells *U.S.A.* 32°41N 115°7W **171** N11
Midwest *U.S.A.* 42°0N 90°0W **167** G22
Midwest *Wyo., U.S.A.* 43°25N 106°16W **168** E10
Midwest City *U.S.A.* 35°27N 97°24W **176** D6
Midyat *Turkey* 37°25N 41°23E **105** D9
Midžor *Bulgaria* 43°24N 22°40E **96** C6
Mie □ *Japan* 34°30N 136°10E **113** G8
Miechów *Poland* 50°21N 20°5E **83** H7
Miedwie, Jezioro *Poland* 53°17N 14°54E **83** E1
Międzybórz *Poland* 51°25N 17°34E **83** G4
Międzychód *Poland* 52°35N 15°53E **83** F2
Międzylesie *Poland* 50°8N 16°40E **83** H3
Międzyrzec Podlaski *Poland* 51°58N 22°45E **83** G9
Międzyrzecz *Poland* 52°26N 15°35E **83** F2
Międzyzdroje *Poland* 53°56N 14°26E **82** E1
Miejska Górka *Poland* 51°39N 16°58E **83** G3
Miélan *France* 43°27N 0°19E **72** E4
Mielec *Poland* 50°15N 21°25E **83** H8
Mienga *Angola* 17°12S 19°48E **144** A2
Miercurea-Ciuc *Romania* 46°21N 25°48E **81** D10
Miercurea Sibiului *Romania* 45°53N 23°48E **81** E8
Mieres *Spain* 43°18N 5°48W **88** B5
Mieroszów *Poland* 50°40N 16°11E **83** H3
Mieszkowice *Poland* 52°47N 14°30E **83** F1
Mifflintown *U.S.A.* 40°34N 77°24W **174** F7
Mifraz Ḥefa *Israel* 32°52N 35°0E **130** C4
Migang Shan *China* 35°32N 106°13E **114** G4
Migennes *France* 47°58N 3°31E **71** E10
Migliarino *Italy* 44°46N 11°56E **93** D8
Migliarino-San Rossore-Massaciuccoli △ *Italy* 43°44N 10°20E **92** E7
Migori *Kenya* 1°4S 34°28E **142** C3
Miguasha △ *Canada* 48°5N 66°26W **165** C6
Miguel Alemán, Presa *Mexico* 18°15N 96°32W **181** D5
Miguel Alves *Brazil* 4°11S 42°55W **189** A2
Miguel Calmon *Brazil* 11°26S 40°36W **189** C2
Miguel Hidalgo, Presa *Mexico* 26°30N 108°34W **180** B3
Migueltura *Spain* 38°58N 3°53W **89** G7
Mihăileni *Romania* 47°58N 26°9E **81** C11
Mihăileşti *Romania* 44°20N 25°54E **81** F10
Mihailovca *Moldova* 46°33N 28°56E **81** D13
Mihalgazi *Turkey* 40°2N 30°34E **99** A12
Mihalıççık *Turkey* 39°53N 31°30E **104** C4
Mihara *Japan* 34°24N 133°5E **113** G6
Miheşu de Cîmpie *Romania* 46°41N 24°9E **81** D9
Mijas *Spain* 36°36N 4°40W **89** J6
Mikese *Tanzania* 6°48S 37°55E **142** D4
Mikha-Tskhakaya = Senaki *Georgia* 42°15N 42°1E **87** J6
Mikhailovka = Mykhaylivka *Ukraine* 47°12N 35°15E **85** J8
Mikhaylov *Russia* 54°14N 39°0E **84** E10
Mikhaylovgrad = Montana *Bulgaria* 43°27N 23°16E **96** C7
Mikhaylovka *Russia* 50°3N 43°5E **86** E6
Mikhaylovsk *Russia* 45°8N 42°0E **87** H5
Mikhnevo *Russia* 55°4N 37°59E **84** E9
Mikkeli *Finland* 61°43N 27°15E **84** B4
Mikkwa → *Canada* 58°25N 114°46W **162** B6
Mikołajki *Poland* 53°49N 21°37E **82** E8
Míkonos = Mykonos *Greece* 37°30N 25°25E **99** D7
Mikri Prespa, L. *Greece* 40°47N 21°3E **96** F5
Mikro Derio *Greece* 41°19N 26°6E **97** E10
Mikstat *Poland* 51°32N 17°59E **83** G4
Mikulov *Czechia* 48°48N 16°39E **79** C9
Mikumi *Tanzania* 7°26S 37°0E **142** D4
Mikumi △ *Tanzania* 7°35S 37°15E **142** D4
Mila *Algeria* 36°27N 6°16E **136** A5
Mila □ *Algeria* 36°25N 6°10E **136** A5
Milaca *U.S.A.* 45°45N 93°39W **172** C7
Milagro *Ecuador* 2°11S 79°36W **186** D3
Milan = Milano *Italy* 45°28N 9°10E **92** C6
Milan *Ga., U.S.A.* 32°1N 83°4W **178** C6
Milan *Mo., U.S.A.* 40°12N 93°7W **172** E7
Milan *Tenn., U.S.A.* 35°55N 88°46W **177** D10
Milang *Australia* 35°24S 138°58E **152** C3
Milange *Mozam.* 16°3S 35°45E **143** F4
Milano *Italy* 45°28N 9°10E **92** C6
Milano Linate ✕ **(LIN)** *Italy* 45°27N 9°16E **92** C6
Milâs *Turkey* 37°20N 27°50E **99** D9
Milatos *Greece* 35°18N 25°34E **101** D7
Milazzo *Italy* 38°13N 15°15E **95** D8
Milbank *U.S.A.* 45°13N 96°38W **172** C5
Milbanke Sd. *Canada* 52°19N 128°33W **162** C3
Milden *Canada* 51°29N 107°32W **163** C7
Mildenhall *U.K.* 52°21N 0°32E **67** E8
Mildmay *Canada* 44°3N 81°7W **174** B3
Mildura *Australia* 34°13S 142°9E **152** C5
Mile *China* 24°28N 103°20E **116** E4
Miles *Australia* 26°40S 150°9E **151** D5
Miles City *U.S.A.* 46°25N 105°51W **168** C11
Mileşti *Moldova* 47°13N 28°3E **81** C13
Milestone *Canada* 49°59N 104°31W **163** D8
Mileto *Italy* 38°36N 16°4E **95** D9
Miletto, Mte. *Italy* 41°27N 14°22E **95** A7
Miletus *Turkey* 37°30N 27°18E **99** D9
Milevsko *Czechia* 49°27N 14°21E **78** B7
Milford *Calif., U.S.A.* 40°10N 120°22W **170** E6
Milford *Conn., U.S.A.* 41°14N 73°3W **175** E11
Milford *Del., U.S.A.* 38°55N 75°26W **173** F16
Milford *Mass., U.S.A.* 42°8N 71°31W **175** D13
Milford *N.H., U.S.A.* 42°50N 71°39W **175** D13
Milford *N.Y., U.S.A.* 42°35N 74°56W **175** D10
Milford *Pa., U.S.A.* 41°19N 74°48W **175** E10
Milford *Utah, U.S.A.* 38°24N 113°1W **168** G7
Milford Haven *U.K.* 51°42N 5°7W **67** F2
Milford Sd. *N.Z.* 44°41S 167°47E **155** E2
Milḩ, Baḩr al = Razāzah, Buḩayrat ar *Iraq* 32°40N 43°35E **105** F10
Miliana *Aïn Salah, Algeria* 27°20N 2°32E **136** C4
Miliana *Médéa, Algeria* 36°20N 2°15E **136** A4
Milicz *Poland* 51°31N 17°19E **83** G4
Milies *Greece* 39°20N 23°9E **98** B5
Milikapiti *Australia* 11°26S 130°40E **148** B5
Miling *Australia* 30°30S 116°17E **149** F2
Militello in Val di Catánia *Italy* 37°16N 14°48E **95** E7
Milk, Wadi el → *Sudan* 17°55N 30°20E **137** D3
Milk River *Canada* 49°10N 112°5W **162** D6
Mill → *U.S.A.* 42°57N 83°23W **174** D1
Mill I. *Antarctica* 66°0S 101°30E **55** C8
Mill I. *Canada* 63°58N 77°47W **161** E16
Mill Valley *U.S.A.* 37°54N 122°32W **170** H4
Millárs → *Spain* 39°55N 0°1W **90** F4
Millau *France* 44°8N 3°4E **72** D7
Millbridge *Canada* 44°41N 77°36W **174** B7
Millbrook *Canada* 44°10N 78°29W **174** B6
Millbrook *Ala., U.S.A.* 32°29N 86°22W **177** E11
Millbrook *N.Y., U.S.A.* 41°47N 73°42W **175** E11
Mille Lacs, L. des *Canada* 48°45N 90°35W **164** C1
Mille Lacs L. *U.S.A.* 46°15N 93°39W **172** B7
Milledgeville *U.S.A.* 33°5N 83°14W **178** B6
Millen *U.S.A.* 32°48N 81°57W **178** C8
Millennium I. = Caroline I. *Kiribati* 9°58S 150°13W **157** H12
Miller *U.S.A.* 44°31N 98°59W **172** C4
Miller Lake *Canada* 45°6N 81°26W **174** A3
Millerovo *Russia* 48°57N 40°28E **87** F5
Miller's Flat *N.Z.* 45°39S 169°23E **155** F4
Millersburg *Ohio, U.S.A.* 40°33N 81°55W **174** F3
Millersburg *Pa., U.S.A.* 40°32N 76°58W **174** F8
Millerton *N.Z.* 41°39S 171°54E **155** B6
Millerton *U.S.A.* 41°57N 73°31W **175** E11
Millerton L. *U.S.A.* 37°1N 119°41W **170** J7
Millet *St. Lucia* 13°55N 60°59W **183** f
Millevaches, Plateau de *France* 45°45N 2°0E **72** C6
Millheim *U.S.A.* 40°54N 77°29W **174** F7
Millicent *Australia* 37°34S 140°21E **152** D4
Milligan *U.S.A.* 30°45N 86°38W **179** E3
Millington *U.S.A.* 35°20N 89°53W **177** D10
Millinocket *U.S.A.* 45°39N 68°43W **173** C19
Millmerran *Australia* 27°53S 151°16E **151** D5
Millom *U.K.* 54°13N 3°16W **66** C4
Mills L. *Canada* 61°30N 118°20W **162** A5
Millsboro *U.S.A.* 40°0N 80°0W **174** G5
Millstream Chichester △ *Australia* 21°35S 117°6E **148** D2
Millstreet *Ireland* 52°4N 9°4W **64** D2
Millthorpe *Australia* 33°26S 149°12E **153** B8
Millville *N.J., U.S.A.* 39°24N 75°2W **173** F16
Millville *Pa., U.S.A.* 41°7N 76°32W **175** E8
Millwood L. *U.S.A.* 33°42N 93°58W **176** E8
Milna *Croatia* 43°20N 16°28E **93** E13
Milne → *Australia* 21°10S 137°33E **150** C2
Milne Land *Greenland* 70°40N 26°30W **57** C8
Milo *U.S.A.* 45°15N 68°59W **173** C19
Milo → *Guinea* 8°52N 9°0W **138** D3
Milon, Akra *Greece* 36°15N 28°11E **101** C10
Milos *Greece* 36°44N 24°25E **98** E6
Miłosław *Poland* 52°12N 17°32E **83** F4
Milot *Albania* 41°41N 19°43E **96** E3
Milparinka *Australia* 29°46S 141°57E **151** D3
Milpitas *U.S.A.* 37°26N 121°55W **170** H5
Miltenberg *Germany* 49°41N 9°16E **77** F5
Milton *Australia* 35°20S 150°27E **153** C9
Milton *N.S., Canada* 44°4N 64°45W **165** D7
Milton *Ont., Canada* 43°31N 79°53W **174** C5
Milton *N.Z.* 46°7S 169°59E **155** G4
Milton *Calif., U.S.A.* 38°3N 120°51W **170** G6
Milton *Fla., U.S.A.* 30°38N 87°3W **179** E2
Milton *Pa., U.S.A.* 41°1N 76°51W **174** F8
Milton *Vt., U.S.A.* 44°38N 73°7W **175** B11
Milton-Freewater *U.S.A.* 45°56N 118°23W **168** D4
Milton Keynes *U.K.* 52°1N 0°44W **67** E7
Milton Keynes □ *U.K.* 52°1N 0°44W **67** E7
Miltown Malbay *Ireland* 52°52N 9°24W **64** D2
Miluo *China* 29°0N 112°59E **117** C9
Milverton *Canada* 43°34N 80°55W **174** C4
Milwaukee *U.S.A.* 43°2N 87°54W **172** D10
Milwaukee Deep *Atl. Oc.* 19°50N 68°0W **183** C6
Milwaukie *U.S.A.* 45°26N 122°38W **170** E4
Mim *Ghana* 6°57N 2°33W **138** D4
Mimili *Australia* 27°0S 132°42E **149** E5
Mimizan *France* 44°12N 1°13W **72** D2
Mimoň *Czechia* 50°38N 14°43E **78** A7
Mimoso *Brazil* 15°10S 48°5W **189** D1
Mims *U.S.A.* 28°40N 80°51W **179** G9
Min Jiang → *Fujian, China* 26°0N 119°35E **117** E12
Min Jiang → *Sichuan, China* 28°45N 104°40E **116** C5
Min Xian *China* 34°25N 104°5E **114** G3
Mīnā' al Aḩmadī *Kuwait* 29°5N 48°10E **129** D6
Mīnā' Jabal 'Alī *U.A.E.* 25°2N 55°8E **129** E7
Mina Pirquitas *Argentina* 22°40S 66°30W **190** A2
Mīnā Su'ud *Si. Arabia* 28°45N 48°28E **129** D6
Minago → *Canada* 54°33N 98°59W **163** C9
Minaki *Canada* 49°59N 94°40W **163** D10
Minamata *Japan* 32°10N 130°30E **113** H5
Minami-Arapusa △ *Japan* 35°30N 138°9E **113** G9
Minami-Tori-Shima *Pac. Oc.* 24°20N 153°58E **156** E7
Minamiaizu *Japan* 37°12N 139°46E **113** F9
Minamiawaji *Japan* 34°10N 134°42E **113** G7
Minamisōma *Japan* 37°38N 140°58E **112** F10
Minas *Uruguay* 34°20S 55°10W **191** C4
Minas, Sierra de las *Guatemala* 15°9N 89°31W **182** C2
Minas Basin *Canada* 45°20N 64°12W **165** C7
Minas de Riotinto *Spain* 37°42N 6°35W **89** H4
Minas Gerais □ *Brazil* 18°50S 46°0W **189** D1
Minas Novas *Brazil* 17°15S 42°36W **189** D2
Minatitlán *Mexico* 17°59N 94°31W **181** D6
Minbu *Myanmar* 20°10N 94°52E **123** J19
Minchinabad *Pakistan* 30°10N 73°34E **124** D5
Mincio → *Italy* 45°4N 10°59E **92** C7
Minčol *Slovakia* 49°15N 20°58E **79** B13
Mindanao *Phil.* 8°0N 125°0E **119** C7
Mindanao Sea = Bohol Sea *Phil.* 9°0N 124°0E **119** C6
Mindanao Trench *Pac. Oc.* 12°0N 126°6E **119** B7
Mindel → *Germany* 48°31N 10°23E **77** G6
Mindelheim *Germany* 48°2N 10°29E **77** G6
Mindelo *Cabo Verde* 16°24N 25°0W **134** b
Minden *Canada* 44°55N 78°43W **174** B6
Minden *Germany* 52°17N 8°55E **76** C4
Minden *La., U.S.A.* 32°37N 93°17W **176** E8
Minden *Nev., U.S.A.* 38°57N 119°46W **170** G7
Mindibungu = Billiluna *Australia* 19°37S 127°41E **148** C4
Mindiptana *Indonesia* 5°55S 140°22E **119** F10
Mindona L. *Australia* 33°6S 142°6E **152** B5
Mindoro *Phil.* 13°0N 121°0E **119** B6
Mindoro Str. *Phil.* 12°30N 120°30E **119** B6
Mine *Japan* 34°12N 131°7E **113** G5
Minehead *U.K.* 51°12N 3°29W **67** F4
Mineola *N.Y., U.S.A.* 40°44N 73°38W **175** F11
Mineola *Tex., U.S.A.* 32°40N 95°29W **176** E7
Mineral King *U.S.A.* 36°27N 118°36W **170** J8
Mineral Wells *U.S.A.* 32°48N 98°7W **176** E5
Mineralnyye Vody *Russia* 44°15N 43°8E **87** H6
Miners Bay *Canada* 44°49N 78°46W **174** B6
Minersville *U.S.A.* 40°41N 76°16W **175** F8
Minerva *N.Y., U.S.A.* 43°47N 73°59W **175** C11
Minerva *Ohio, U.S.A.* 40°44N 81°6W **174** F3
Minervino Murge *Italy* 41°5N 16°5E **95** A9
Minetto *U.S.A.* 43°24N 76°28W **175** C8
Minfeng *China* 37°4N 82°46E **109** E10
Ming-Kush *Kyrgyzstan* 41°40N 74°28E **109** D8
Mingäçevir *Azerbaijan* 40°45N 47°0E **87** K8
Mingäçevir Su Anbarı *Azerbaijan* 40°57N 46°50E **87** K8
Mingan *Canada* 50°20N 64°0W **165** B7
Mingary *Australia* 32°8S 140°45E **152** B4
Mingechaur = Mingäçevir *Azerbaijan* 40°45N 47°0E **87** K8
Mingechaurskoye Vdkhr. = Mingäçevir Su Anbarı *Azerbaijan* 40°57N 46°50E **87** K8
Mingela *Australia* 19°52S 146°38E **150** B4
Mingenew *Australia* 29°12S 115°21E **149** E2
Mingera Cr. → *Australia* 20°38S 137°45E **150** C2
Minggang *China* 32°24N 114°3E **117** A10
Mingguang *China* 32°46N 117°59E **117** A11
Mingin *Myanmar* 22°50N 94°30E **123** H19
Mingir *Moldova* 46°40N 28°20E **81** D13
Minglanilla *Spain* 39°34N 1°38W **91** F3
Minglun *China* 25°10N 108°21E **116** E7
Mingo Junction *U.S.A.* 40°19N 80°37W **174** F4
Mingora *Pakistan* 34°48N 72°22E **125** B5
Mingorría *Spain* 40°45N 4°40W **88** E6
Mingshan *China* 30°6N 103°10E **116** B4
Mingteke Daban = Mintaka Pass *Pakistan* 37°0N 74°58E **125** A6
Mingxi *China* 26°18N 117°12E **117** D11
Mingyuegue *China* 43°2N 128°50E **115** C15
Minhe *China* 36°9N 102°45E **110** D9
Minho = Miño → *Spain* 41°52N 8°40W **88** D2
Minhou *China* 26°0N 119°15E **117** E12
Miničevo *Serbia* 43°42N 22°18E **80** G7
Minicoy I. *India* 8°17N 73°2E **127** K1
Minidoka *U.S.A.* 42°45N 113°29W **168** E7
Minigwal, L. *Australia* 29°31S 123°14E **149** E3
Minilya → *Australia* 23°45S 114°0E **149** D1
Minilya Roadhouse *Australia* 23°55S 114°0E **149** D1
Mininera *Australia* 37°37S 142°58E **152** D5
Minipi L. *Canada* 52°25N 60°45W **165** B7
Minjilang *Australia* 11°8S 132°33E **148** B5
Mink L. *Canada* 61°54N 117°40W **162** A5
Minlaton *Australia* 34°45S 137°35E **152** C2
Minna *Nigeria* 9°37N 6°30E **139** D6
Minneapolis *Kans., U.S.A.* 39°8N 97°42W **172** F5
Minneapolis *Minn., U.S.A.* 44°57N 93°16W **172** C7
Minneapolis-St. Paul Int. ✕ **(MSP)** *U.S.A.* 44°53N 93°13W **172** C7
Minnedosa *Canada* 50°14N 99°50W **163** C9
Minnesota □ *U.S.A.* 46°0N 94°15W **172** B6
Minnesota → *U.S.A.* 44°54N 93°9W **172** C7
Minnewaukan *U.S.A.* 48°4N 99°15W **172** A4
Minnipa *Australia* 32°51S 135°9E **151** E2
Minnitaki L. *Canada* 49°57N 92°10W **164** C1
Miño = A Carreira *Spain* 43°21N 8°12W **88** B2
Mino *Japan* 35°32N 136°55E **113** G8
Miño → *Spain* 41°52N 8°40W **88** D2
Minoa *Greece* 35°6N 25°45E **99** F7
Minorca = Menorca *Spain* 40°0N 4°0E **100** B11
Minore *Australia* 32°14S 148°27E **153** B8
Minot *U.S.A.* 48°14N 101°18W **172** A3
Minqin *China* 38°38N 103°20E **114** E2
Minqing *China* 26°15N 118°50E **117** D12
Minsen *Germany* 53°41N 7°58E **76** B3
Minsk *Belarus* 53°52N 27°30E **75** B14
Minsk □ *Belarus* 53°15N 27°30E **84** F4
Mińsk Mazowiecki *Poland* 52°10N 21°33E **83** F8
Mintabie *Australia* 27°15S 133°7E **151** D1
Mintaka Pass *Pakistan* 37°0N 74°58E **125** A6
Minto *Canada* 46°5N 66°5W **165** C6
Minto, L. *Canada* 57°13N 75°0W **164** A5
Minton *Canada* 49°10N 104°35W **163** D8
Minturn *U.S.A.* 39°35N 106°26W **168** G10
Minturno *Italy* 41°15N 13°45E **94** A6
Minudasht *Iran* 37°17N 56°7E **129** B8
Minûf *Egypt* 30°26N 30°52E **137** E7
Minusinsk *Russia* 53°43N 91°20E **109** B12
Minutang *India* 28°15N 96°30E **123** E20
Minvoul *Gabon* 2°9N 12°8E **140** D2
Minya el Qamh *Egypt* 30°31N 31°21E **137** E7
Minya Konka = Gongga Shan *China* 29°40N 101°55E **116** C3
Minyip *Australia* 36°29S 142°36E **152** D5
Minzhong *China* 22°37N 113°30E **111** a
Mionica *Bos.-H.* 44°51N 18°29E **80** F3
Mionica *Serbia* 44°14N 20°6E **96** B4
Mioveni *Romania* 44°56N 24°54E **81** F9
Miquelon *Canada* 49°25N 76°27W **164** C4
Miquelon *St-P. & M.* 47°8N 56°22W **165** C8
Mir *Belarus* 53°27N 26°28E **75** B14
Mir *Niger* 14°5N 11°59E **139** C7
Mīr Kūh *Iran* 26°22N 58°55E **129** E8
Mīr Shahdād *Iran* 26°15N 58°29E **129** E8
Mira *Italy* 45°26N 12°8E **93** C9
Mira *Portugal* 40°26N 8°44W **88** E2
Mira → *Portugal* 37°43N 8°47W **89** H2
Mira por vos Cay *Bahamas* 22°9N 74°30W **183** B5
Mirabella Eclano *Italy* 41°2N 14°59E **95** A7
Mirabello, Kolpos *Greece* 35°10N 25°50E **101** D7
Miracema do Norte *Brazil* 9°33S 48°24W **189** B1
Mirador *Brazil* 6°22S 44°22W **189** B2
Mirador-Río Azul △ *Guatemala* 17°45N 89°50W **182** C2
Miraj *India* 16°50N 74°45E **126** F2
Miram Shah *Pakistan* 33°0N 70°2E **124** C4
Miramar *Argentina* 38°15S 57°50W **190** D4
Miramar *Mozam.* 23°50S 35°35E **145** B6
Miramas *France* 43°33N 4°59E **73** E8
Mirambeau *France* 45°23N 0°35W **72** C3
Miramichi *Canada* 47°2N 65°28W **165** C6
Miramichi B. *Canada* 47°15N 65°0W **165** C7
Miramont-de-Guyenne *France* 44°37N 0°21E **72** D4
Miranda *Brazil* 20°10S 56°15W **187** H7
Miranda → *Brazil* 19°25S 57°20W **186** G7
Miranda de Ebro *Spain* 42°41N 2°57W **90** C2
Miranda do Corvo *Portugal* 40°6N 8°20W **88** E2
Miranda do Douro *Portugal* 41°30N 6°16W **88** D4
Mirande *France* 43°31N 0°25E **72** E4
Mirandela *Portugal* 41°32N 7°10W **88** D3
Mirándola *Italy* 44°53N 11°4E **92** D8
Mirandópolis *Brazil* 21°9S 51°6W **191** A5
Mirango *Malawi* 13°32S 34°58E **143** E3
Mirani *Australia* 21°8S 148°53E **150** b
Mirano *Italy* 45°30N 12°7E **93** C9
Miras *Albania* 40°30N 20°56E **96** F4
Mirassol *Brazil* 20°46S 49°28W **191** A6
Mirbāṭ *Oman* 17°0N 54°45E **131** D5
Mirboo North *Australia* 38°24S 146°10E **153** E7
Mirear *Egypt* 23°15N 35°41E **137** C4
Mirebeau *France* 46°49N 0°10E **70** F7
Mirebeau-sur-Bèze *France* 47°25N 5°20E **71** E12
Mirecourt *France* 48°20N 6°10E **71** D13
Mires *Greece* 35°4N 24°56E **101** D6
Mirgorod = Myrhorod *Ukraine* 49°58N 33°37E **85** H7
Miri *Malaysia* 4°23N 113°59E **118** D4
Mirialguda *India* 16°52N 79°35E **126** F4
Miriam Vale *Australia* 24°20S 151°33E **150** C5
Miribel *France* 45°50N 4°57E **71** G11
Mirigama *Sri Lanka* 7°15N 80°8E **127** L5
Mirim, L. *S. Amer.* 32°45S 52°50W **191** C5
Miriuwung Gajerrong ✪ *Australia* 15°0S 128°45E **148** C4
Mīrjāveh *Iran* 29°1N 61°30E **129** D9
Mirnyy *Antarctica* 66°50S 92°30E **55** C14
Mirnyy *Russia* 62°33N 113°53E **107** C12
Miroč *Serbia* 44°32N 22°16E **96** B6
Mirokhan *Pakistan* 27°46N 68°6E **124** F3
Mirond L. *Canada* 55°6N 102°47W **163** B8
Mirosławiec *Poland* 53°20N 16°5E **82** E3
Mirpur *Pakistan* 33°32N 73°56E **125** C5
Mirpur Batoro *Pakistan* 24°44N 68°16E **124** G3
Mirpur Bibiwari *Pakistan* 28°33N 67°44E **124** E2
Mirpur Khas *Pakistan* 25°30N 69°0E **124** G3
Mirpur Sakro *Pakistan* 24°33N 67°41E **124** G2
Mirria *Niger* 13°43N 9°7E **139** C6
Mirrool *Australia* 34°19S 147°10E **153** C7
Mirs Bay = Tai Pang Wan *China* 22°33N 114°24E **111** a
Mirsk *Poland* 50°58N 15°23E **83** H2
Mirtağ *Turkey* 38°23N 41°56E **128** B4
Mirtoo Sea *Greece* 37°0N 23°20E **98** D5
Miryang *S. Korea* 35°31N 128°44E **115** G15
Mirzaani *Georgia* 41°24N 46°5E **87** K8
Mirzapur *India* 25°10N 82°34E **125** G10
Mirzapur-cum-Vindhyachal = Mirzapur *India* 25°10N 82°34E **125** G10
Misantla *Mexico* 19°56N 96°50W **181** D5
Misawa *Japan* 40°41N 141°24E **112** D10
Miscou I. *Canada* 47°57N 64°31W **165** C7
Misha *India* 7°59N 93°20E **127** L10
Mish'āb, Ra's al *Si. Arabia* 28°15N 48°43E **129** D6
Mishagua → *Peru* 11°12S 72°58W **188** C3
Mishamo *Tanzania* 5°41S 30°41E **142** D3
Mishan *China* 45°37N 131°48E **112** B5
Mishawaka *U.S.A.* 41°40N 86°11W **172** E10
Mishbih, Gebel *Egypt* 22°38N 34°44E **137** C3
Mishima *Japan* 35°10N 138°52E **113** G9
Misión *Mexico* 32°6N 116°53W **171** N10
Misión Fagnano *Argentina* 54°32S 67°17W **192** D3
Misiones □ *Argentina* 27°0S 55°0W **191** B5
Misiones □ *Paraguay* 27°0S 56°0W **190** B4
Miskah *Si. Arabia* 24°49N 42°56E **128** E4
Miskitos, Cayos *Nic.* 14°26N 82°50W **182** D3
Miskolc *Hungary* 48°7N 20°50E **80** B5
Misoke *Dem. Rep. of the Congo* 0°42S 28°2E **142** C2
Misool *Indonesia* 1°52S 130°10E **119** E8
Miṣr = Egypt ■ *Africa* 28°0N 31°0E **137** F7
Miṣrātah *Libya* 32°24N 15°3E **135** B9
Missanabie *Canada* 48°20N 84°6W **164** C3
Missão Velha *Brazil* 7°15S 39°10W **189** B3
Missinaibi → *Canada* 50°43N 81°29W **164** B3
Missinaibi L. *Canada* 48°23N 83°40W **164** C3
Mission *Canada* 49°10N 122°15W **162** D4
Mission *S. Dak., U.S.A.* 43°18N 100°39W **172** D3
Mission *Tex., U.S.A.* 26°13N 98°20W **176** H5
Mission Beach *Australia* 17°53S 146°6E **150** B4
Mission Viejo *U.S.A.* 33°36N 117°40W **171** M9
Missirah *Senegal* 13°40N 16°30W **138** C1
Missisa L. *Canada* 52°20N 85°7W **164** B2
Missisicabi → *Canada* 51°14N 79°31W **164** B4
Mississagi → *Canada* 46°15N 83°9W **164** C3
Mississauga *Canada* 43°32N 79°35W **174** C5
Mississippi □ *U.S.A.* 33°0N 90°0W **177** E10
Mississippi → *U.S.A.* 29°9N 89°15W **177** G10
Mississippi L. *Canada* 45°5N 76°10W **175** A8
Mississippi River Delta *U.S.A.* 29°10N 89°15W **177** G10
Mississippi Sd. *U.S.A.* 30°20N 89°0W **177** F10
Missoula *U.S.A.* 46°52N 114°1W **168** C6
Missour *Morocco* 33°3N 4°0W **136** B3
Missouri □ *U.S.A.* 38°25N 92°30W **172** F7
Missouri → *U.S.A.* 38°49N 90°7W **172** F8
Missouri City *U.S.A.* 29°37N 95°32W **176** G7
Missouri Valley *U.S.A.* 41°34N 95°53W **172** E6
Mist *U.S.A.* 45°59N 123°15W **170** E3
Mistassibi → *Canada* 48°53N 72°13W **165** B5
Mistassini *Canada* 48°53N 72°12W **165** C5
Mistassini → *Canada* 48°42N 72°20W **165** C5
Mistassini, L. *Canada* 51°0N 73°30W **164** B5
Mistastin L. *Canada* 55°57N 63°20W **165** A7
Mistelbach *Austria* 48°34N 16°34E **79** C9
Misterbianco *Italy* 37°31N 15°1E **95** E8
Misti, Volcán *Peru* 16°18S 71°24W **188** D3
Mistinibi, L. *Canada* 55°56N 64°17W **165** A7
Mistissini *Canada* 48°53N 72°12W **165** C5
Mistras = Mystras *Greece* 37°4N 22°22E **98** D4
Mistretta *Italy* 37°56N 14°22E **95** E7
Misty L. *Canada* 58°53N 101°40W **163** B8
Misurata = Miṣrātah *Libya* 32°24N 15°3E **135** B9
Mit Ghamr *Egypt* 30°42N 31°12E **137** E7
Mitande *Mozam.* 14°6S 35°58E **143** E4
Mitchell *Australia* 26°29S 147°58E **151** D4
Mitchell *Canada* 43°28N 81°12W **174** C3
Mitchell *Ga., U.S.A.* 33°13N 82°42W **178** B7
Mitchell *Nebr., U.S.A.* 41°57N 103°49W **172** E2
Mitchell *Oreg., U.S.A.* 44°34N 120°9W **168** D3
Mitchell *S. Dak., U.S.A.* 43°43N 98°2W **172** D4
Mitchell → *Australia* 15°12S 141°35E **150** B3
Mitchell, Mt. *U.S.A.* 35°46N 82°16W **177** D13
Mitchell-Alice Rivers △ *Australia* 15°28S 142°5E **150** B3
Mitchell Ra. *Australia* 12°49S 135°36E **150** A2

Mitchell River △
  Australia 37°37S 147°22E **153 D7**
Mitchelstown *Ireland* 52°15N 8°16W **64 D3**
Mitha Tiwana *Pakistan* 32°13N 72°6E **124 C5**
Mithi *Pakistan* 24°44N 69°48E **124 G3**
Mithimna *Greece* 39°20N 26°12E **99 B8**
Mithrao *Pakistan* 27°28N 69°40E **124 F3**
Mitiamo *Australia* 36°12S 144°15E **152 D6**
Mitilini *Greece* 39°6N 26°35E **99 B8**
Mitilini □ *Greece* 37°42N 26°56E **99 D9**
Mitla Pass = Mamarr Mitlā
  Egypt 30°2N 32°54E **130 E1**
Mito *Japan* 36°20N 140°30E **113 F10**
Mitre, Mt. *N.Z.*
Mitrofanovka *Russia* 49°58N 39°42E **85 H10**
Mitrovicë *Kosovo* 42°54N 20°52E **96 D4**
Mitsamiouli *Comoros Is.* 11°20S 43°16E **141 a**
Mitsiwa *Eritrea* 15°35N 39°25E **131 D2**
Mitsukaidō *Japan* 36°1N 139°59E **113 F9**
Mittagong *Australia* 34°28S 150°29E **153 C9**
Mittelberg *Austria* 47°20N 10°10E **78 D3**
Mittelfranken □
  Germany 49°25N 10°40E **77 F6**
Mittellandkanal →
  Germany 52°20N 8°28E **76 C4**
Mittenwalde *Germany* 52°15N 13°31E **76 C9**
Mittersill *Austria* 47°16N 12°29E **78 D5**
Mitterteich *Germany* 49°57N 12°14E **77 F8**
Mittimatalik = Pond Inlet
  Canada 72°40N 77°0W **161 C12**
Mittweida *Germany* 50°59N 12°59E **76 E8**
Mitú *Colombia* 1°15N 70°13W **186 C4**
Mitumba *Tanzania* 7°8S 31°2E **142 D3**
Mitumba, Mts.
  Dem. Rep. of the Congo 7°0S 27°30E **142 D2**
Mitwaba
  Dem. Rep. of the Congo 8°2S 27°17E **143 D2**
Mityana *Uganda* 0°23N 32°2E **142 B3**
Mixteco → *Mexico* 18°11N 98°30W **181 D5**
Miyagi □ *Japan* 38°15N 140°45E **112 E10**
Miyah, W. el → *Egypt* 25°0N 33°23E **137 C3**
Miyah, W. el → *Syria* 34°44N 39°57E **128 C3**
Miyake-Jima *Japan* 34°5N 139°30E **113 G9**
Miyako *Japan* 39°40N 141°59E **112 E10**
Miyako-Jima *Japan* 24°45N 125°20E **113 M2**
Miyako-Rettō *Japan* 24°24N 125°0E **113 M2**
Miyakojima *Japan* 24°48N 125°17E **113 M2**
Miyakonojō *Japan* 31°40N 131°5E **113 J5**
Miyān Rahan *Iran* 34°34N 47°26E **105 E12**
Miyani *India* 21°50N 69°26E **124 J3**
Miyanoura-Dake
  Japan 30°20N 130°31E **113 J5**
Miyazaki *Japan* 31°56N 131°30E **113 J5**
Miyazaki □ *Japan* 32°30N 131°30E **113 H5**
Miyazu *Japan* 35°35N 135°10E **113 G7**
Miyet, Bahr el = Dead Sea
  Asia 31°30N 35°30E **130 D4**
Miyi *China* 26°47N 102°9E **116 D4**
Miyoshi *Japan* 34°48N 132°51E **113 G6**
Miyun *China* 40°28N 116°50E **114 D9**
Miyun Shuiku *China* 40°30N 117°0E **115 D9**
Mizdah *Libya* 31°30N 13°0E **135 B8**
Mizen Hd. *Cork, Ireland* 51°27N 9°50W **64 E2**
Mizen Hd. *Wicklow, Ireland* 52°51N 6°4W **64 D5**
Mizhhirya *Ukraine* 48°32N 23°30E **81 B8**
Mizhi *China* 37°47N 110°12E **114 F6**
Mizil *Romania* 44°59N 26°29E **81 F11**
Mizoram □ *India* 23°30N 92°40E **123 H18**
Mizpe Ramon *Israel* 30°34N 34°49E **130 E3**
Mizuho *Antarctica* 70°30S 41°0E **55 D5**
Mizusawa = Ōshū
  Japan 39°8N 141°8E **112 E10**
Mjällby *Sweden* 56°3N 14°40E **63 H8**
Mjöbäck *Sweden* 57°28N 12°53E **63 G6**
Mjölby *Sweden* 58°20N 15°10E **63 F9**
Mjörn *Sweden* 57°55N 12°25E **63 F6**
Mjøsa *Norway* 60°40N 11°0E **60 F14**
Mkata *Tanzania* 5°45S 38°20E **142 D4**
Mkhaya △ *Swaziland* 26°34S 31°45E **145 C5**
Mkhuze △ *S. Africa* 29°27S 29°30E **145 C4**
Mkoani *Tanzania* 5°0S 39°15E **142 D4**
Mkokotoni *Tanzania* 5°55S 39°15E **142 C4**
Mkomazi *Tanzania* 4°40S 38°7E **142 C4**
Mkomazi → *S. Africa* 30°12S 30°50E **145 C5**
Mkomazi △ *Tanzania* 4°4S 30°2E **142 C3**
Mkulwe *Tanzania* 8°37S 32°20E **143 D3**
Mkumbi, Ras *Tanzania* 7°38S 39°55E **142 D4**
Mkushi *Zambia* 14°25S 29°15E **143 E2**
Mkushi River *Zambia* 13°32S 29°45E **143 E2**
Mkuze *S. Africa* 27°10S 32°0E **145 C5**
Mladá Boleslav *Czechia* 50°27N 14°53E **78 A7**
Mladenovac *Serbia* 44°28N 20°44E **96 B4**
Mlala Hills *Tanzania* 6°50S 31°40E **142 D3**
Mlange = Mulanje, Mt.
  Malawi 16°2S 35°33E **143 H7**
Mlava → *Serbia* 44°45N 21°13E **96 B5**
Mława *Poland* 53°9N 20°25E **83 E7**
Mlawula △ *Swaziland* 26°12S 32°2E **145 C5**
Mlinište *Bos.-H.* 44°15N 16°50E **93 D13**
Mljet *Croatia* 42°43N 17°30E **93 F14**
Mljet △ *Croatia* 42°45N 17°25E **93 F14**
Mljetski Kanal *Croatia* 42°48N 17°35E **93 F14**
Mlynary *Poland* 54°12N 19°46E **83 D6**
Mmabatho *S. Africa* 25°49S 25°30E **144 D4**
Mme *Cameroon* 6°18N 10°14E **139 D7**
Mnichovo Hradiště
  Czechia 50°32N 14°59E **78 A7**
Mo i Rana *Norway* 66°20N 14°7E **60 C16**
Moa *Australia* 10°11S 142°16E **150 a**
Moa → *Africa*
Moa *Cuba* 20°40N 74°56W **183 B4**
Moa → *S. Leone* 6°59N 11°36W **138 D2**
Moab *U.S.A.* 38°35N 109°33W **168 G9**
Moaco → *Brazil* 7°41S 68°18W **188 E5**
Moala *Fiji* 18°36S 179°53E **154 a**
Moama *Australia* 25°36S 32°15E **145 C5**
Moamba *Mozam.* 25°36S 32°15E **145 C5**
Moapa *U.S.A.* 36°40N 114°37W **171 J12**
Moate *Ireland* 53°24N 7°44W **64 C4**
Moba
  Dem. Rep. of the Congo 7°0S 29°48E **142 D2**
Mobārakābād *Iran* 28°24N 53°20E **129 D7**
Mobaye *C.A.R.* 4°25N 21°5E **140 D4**
Moberly *U.S.A.* 39°25N 92°26W **172 F7**
Moberly Lake *Canada* 55°50N 121°44W **158 B4**
Mobile *U.S.A.* 30°41N 88°3W **177 F10**
Mobile B. *U.S.A.* 30°30N 88°0W **177 F11**
Mobridge *U.S.A.* 45°32N 100°26W **172 C3**
Moc Chau *Vietnam* 20°50N 104°38E **120 B5**
Moc Hoa *Vietnam* 10°46N 105°56E **121 G5**
Mocabe Kasari
  Dem. Rep. of the Congo 9°58S 26°12E **143 D2**

Moçambique = Mozambique ■
  Africa 19°0S 35°0E **143 H7**
Moçambique *Mozam.* 15°3S 40°42E **143 F5**
Mocanaqua *U.S.A.* 41°9N 76°8W **175 E8**
Moce *Fiji* 18°40S 178°29W **154 a**
Mocha, I. *Chile* 38°22S 73°56W **192 A2**
Mochima △ *Venezuela* 10°30N 64°5W **183 D7**
Mochos *Greece* 35°16N 25°27E **101 D7**
Mochudi *Botswana* 24°27S 26°7E **144 B4**
Mocimboa da Praia
  Mozam. 11°25S 40°20E **143 E5**
Mociu *Romania* 46°46N 24°3E **81 D9**
Möckeln *Sweden* 56°40N 14°15E **63 H8**
Mockfjärd *Sweden* 60°30N 14°57E **62 D8**
Moclips *U.S.A.* 47°14N 124°13W **170 C2**
Mocoa *Colombia* 1°7N 76°35W **186 C3**
Mococa *Brazil* 21°28S 47°0W **191 A6**
Mocorito *Mexico* 25°29N 107°55W **180 B3**
Moctezuma *Mexico* 29°48N 109°42W **180 B3**
Moctezuma → *Mexico* 21°59N 98°34W **181 C5**
Mocuba *Mozam.* 16°54S 36°57E **143 F4**
Modane *France* 45°12N 6°40E **73 C10**
Modasa *India* 23°30N 73°21E **124 H5**
Modder → *S. Africa* 29°2S 24°37E **144 C3**
Modderrivier *S. Africa* 29°2S 24°38E **144 C3**
Módena *Italy* 44°40N 10°55E **92 D7**
Modena *U.S.A.* 37°48N 113°56W **169 H7**
Modesto *U.S.A.* 37°39N 121°0W **170 H6**
Módica *Italy* 36°52N 14°46E **95 F7**
Modimolle *S. Africa* 24°42S 28°22E **145 B4**
Modjadjiskloof *S. Africa* 23°42S 30°10E **145 B5**
Mödling *Austria* 48°5N 16°17E **79 C9**
Modoc *U.S.A.* 33°44N 82°12W **178 B7**
Modra *Slovakia* 48°19N 17°20E **79 C10**
Modriča *Bos.-H.* 44°57N 18°17E **80 F3**
Moe *Australia* 38°12S 146°19E **153 E7**
Moebase *Mozam.* 17°3S 38°41E **143 F4**
Moëlan-sur-Mer *France* 47°49N 3°38W **70 E3**
Moengo *Suriname* 5°45N 54°20W **187 B8**
Moenjodaro = Mohenjodaro
  Pakistan 27°19N 68°7E **124 F3**
Moerewa *N.Z.* 35°8S 174°1E **154 B3**
Moers *Germany* 51°27N 6°36E **76 D2**
Moffat *U.K.* 55°21N 3°27W **65 F5**
Moga *India* 30°48N 75°8E **124 D6**
Mogadishu = Muqdisho
  Somalia 2°2N 45°25E **131 G4**
Mogador = Essaouira
  Morocco 31°32N 9°42W **136 B2**
Mogadouro *Portugal* 41°22N 6°47W **88 D4**
Mogalakwena →
  S. Africa 22°38S 28°40E **145 B4**
Mogami-Gawa →
  Japan 38°45N 140°0E **112 E10**
Mogán *Canary Is.* 27°53N 15°43W **100 G4**
Mogaung *Myanmar* 25°20N 97°0E **123 G20**
Mogente = Moixent
  Spain 38°52N 0°45W **91 G4**
Mogi-Mirim *Brazil* 22°29S 47°0W **187 H9**
Mogielnica *Poland* 51°42N 20°41E **83 G7**
Mogilev = Mahilyow
  Belarus 53°55N 30°18E **75 B16**
Mogilev-Podolskiy = Mohyliv-
  Podilskyy *Ukraine* 48°26N 27°48E **81 B12**
Mogilno *Poland* 52°39N 17°55E **83 F4**
Mogincual *Mozam.* 15°35S 40°25E **143 F5**
Mogliano Véneto *Italy* 45°33N 12°14E **93 C9**
Mogocha *Russia* 53°40N 119°50E **107 D12**
Mogoditshane
  Botswana 24°37S 25°51E **144 B4**
Mogok *Myanmar* 23°0N 96°40E **123 H20**
Mogollon Rim *U.S.A.* 34°10N 110°50W **169 J8**
Mógoro *Italy* 39°41N 8°47E **94 C1**
Mograt *Sudan* 19°28N 33°16E **137 D3**
Moguer *Spain* 37°15N 6°52W **89 H4**
Mogumber *Australia* 31°2S 116°3E **149 F2**
Mogwadi → *S. Africa* 23°4S 29°36E **145 B4**
Mohács *Hungary* 45°58N 18°41E **80 E3**
Mohaka → *N.Z.* 39°7S 177°12E **154 F6**
Mohala *India* 20°35N 80°44E **126 D5**
Mohales Hoek *Lesotho* 30°7S 27°26E **145 D4**
Mohali = Ajitgarh
  India 30°47N 76°41E **124 D7**
Mohall *U.S.A.* 48°46N 101°31W **172 A3**
Mohammadābād *Iran* 37°52N 59°5E **129 B8**
Mohammadia *Algeria* 35°33N 0°3E **136 A4**
Mohammedia *Morocco* 33°44N 7°21W **136 B2**
Mohana *India* 19°27N 84°16E **126 E7**
Mohana → *India* 24°43N 85°0E **125 G11**
Mohanlalganj *India* 26°41N 80°58E **125 F9**
Mohave, L. *U.S.A.* 35°12N 114°34W **171 K12**
Mohawk → *U.S.A.* 42°47N 73°41W **175 D11**
Moheda *Sweden* 57°1N 14°35E **63 G8**
Mohéli *Comoros Is.* 12°20S 43°40E **141 a**
Mohenjodaro *Pakistan* 27°19N 68°7E **124 F3**
Moher, Cliffs of *Ireland* 52°58N 9°27W **64 D2**
Mohican Res.
  U.S.A. 40°45N 82°9W **174 F2**
Möhne → *Germany* 51°29N 7°57E **76 D3**
Mohns Ridge *Arctic* 72°30S 5°0W **54 B7**
Mohoro *Tanzania* 8°6S 39°8E **142 D4**
Mohsenābād *Iran* 36°40N 59°35E **129 B8**
Mohyliv-Podilskyy
  Ukraine 48°26N 27°48E **81 B12**
Moidart, L. *U.K.* 56°47N 5°52W **65 E3**
Moinabad *India* 17°44N 77°16E **126 F3**
Moinești *Romania* 46°28N 26°31E **81 D11**
Moira → *Canada* 44°21N 77°24W **174 B7**
Moirans *France* 45°20N 5°33E **73 C9**
Moirans-en-Montagne
  France 46°26N 5°43E **71 F12**
Moisaküla *Estonia* 58°3N 25°12E **84 C3**
Moisie *Canada* 50°12N 66°1W **165 B6**
Moisie → *Canada* 50°14N 66°5W **165 B6**
Moissac *France* 44°7N 1°5E **72 D4**
Moita *Portugal* 38°38N 8°58W **89 G2**
Moixent *Spain* 38°52N 0°45W **91 G4**
Mojácar *Spain* 37°6N 1°55W **91 H3**
Mojados *Spain* 41°26N 4°40W **88 D6**
Mojave *U.S.A.* 35°3N 118°10W **171 K8**
Mojave Desert *U.S.A.* 35°0N 116°30W **171 L10**
Moji das Cruzes *Brazil* 23°31S 46°11W **191 A6**
Moji-Guaçu → *Brazil* 20°53S 48°10W **191 A6**
Mojiang *China* 23°37N 101°35E **116 F3**
Mojkovac *Montenegro* 42°58N 19°35E **96 D3**
Mojo *Bolivia* 21°48S 65°33W **190 A2**
Mojokerto *Indonesia* 7°28S 112°26E **119 G15**
Mokai *N.Z.* 38°32S 175°56E **154 E4**
Mokala △ *S. Africa* 29°10S 24°10E **144 C3**

Mokambo
  Dem. Rep. of the Congo 12°25S 28°20E **143 E2**
Mokameh *India* 25°24N 85°55E **125 G11**
Mokau *N.Z.* 38°42S 174°39E **154 E3**
Mokau → *N.Z.* 38°35S 174°35E **154 E3**
Mokelumne →
  U.S.A. 38°13N 121°28W **170 G5**
Mokelumne Hill
  U.S.A. 38°18N 120°43W **170 G6**
Mokhotlong *Lesotho* 29°22S 29°2E **145 C4**
Mokihinui → *N.Z.* 41°33S 171°58E **155 B6**
Möklinta *Sweden* 60°4N 16°33E **62 D10**
Moknine *Tunisia* 35°35N 10°58E **136 A6**
Mokoan, L. *Australia* 36°27S 146°5E **153 D7**
Mokokchung *India* 26°15N 94°30E **123 H19**
Mokolo *Cameroon* 10°49N 13°54E **137 C7**
Mokolo → *S. Africa* 23°14S 27°43E **145 B4**
Mokopane *S. Africa* 24°10S 28°55E **145 B4**
Mokpo *S. Korea* 34°50N 126°25E **115 G14**
Mokra Gora *Europe* 42°50N 20°30E **96 D4**
Mokronog *Slovenia* 45°57N 15°9E **93 C12**
Moksha → *Russia* 54°45N 41°53E **86 C6**
Mokshan *Russia* 53°25N 44°35E **86 D7**
Mokwa *Nigeria* 9°19N 5°0E **139 D6**
Mol *Belgium* 51°11N 5°5E **69 C5**
Mola di Bari *Italy* 41°4N 17°5E **95 A10**
Molai *Greece* 36°49N 22°56E **98 E4**
Molakalmuru *India* 14°55N 76°50E **127 G3**
Molaly *Kazakhstan* 45°2N 78°44E **109 C9**
Molara *Italy* 40°52N 9°43E **94 B2**
Molat *Croatia* 44°15N 14°50E **93 D11**
Molchanovo *Russia* 57°40N 83°50E **106 D9**
Mold *U.K.* 53°9N 3°8W **66 D4**
Moldava nad Bodvou
  Slovakia 48°38N 21°0E **79 C14**
Moldavia = Moldova ■
  Europe 47°0N 28°0E **81 C13**
Moldavia *Romania* 46°30N 27°0E **81 D12**
Molde *Norway* 62°45N 7°9E **60 E12**
Moldova ■ *Europe* 47°0N 28°0E **81 C13**
Moldova Nouă *Romania* 44°45N 21°41E **80 F6**
Moldoveanu, Vf.
  Romania 45°36N 24°45E **81 E9**
Moldovița *Romania* 47°41N 25°53E **81 C10**
Mole → *U.K.* 51°24N 0°21W **67 F7**
Mole △ *Ghana* 9°43N 1°44W **139 D4**
Molepolole *Botswana* 24°28S 25°28E **144 B4**
Molesworth *N.Z.* 42°5S 173°16E **155 C8**
Molfetta *Italy* 41°12N 16°36E **95 A9**
Molina de Aragón *Spain* 40°46N 1°52W **90 E3**
Molina de Segura *Spain* 38°3N 1°12W **91 G3**
Moline *U.S.A.* 41°30N 90°31W **172 E8**
Molinella *Italy* 44°37N 11°40E **93 D8**
Molino *U.S.A.* 30°43N 87°20W **179 D22**
Molinos *Argentina* 25°28S 66°15W **190 B2**
Moliro
  Dem. Rep. of the Congo 8°12S 30°30E **142 D3**
Moliterno *Italy* 40°14N 15°50E **95 B8**
Molivos = Mithimna
  Greece 39°20N 26°12E **99 B8**
Molkom *Sweden* 59°37N 13°44E **62 E7**
Mölle *Sweden* 56°17N 12°31E **63 H6**
Molledo *Spain* 43°8N 4°6W **88 B6**
Mollendo *Peru* 17°0S 72°0W **188 D3**
Mollerin, L. *Australia* 30°30S 117°35E **149 F2**
Mollerussa *Spain* 41°37N 0°54E **90 D6**
Mollina *Spain* 37°8N 4°38W **89 H6**
Mölln *Germany* 53°37N 10°41E **76 B6**
Mölltorp *Sweden* 58°30N 14°26E **63 F8**
Mölndal *Sweden* 57°40N 12°3E **63 G5**
Mölnlycke *Sweden* 57°40N 12°8E **63 G6**
Molo *Kenya* 0°15S 35°44E **142 C4**
Molochansk *Ukraine* 47°15N 35°35E **85 J8**
Molochnoye, Ozero
  Ukraine 46°30N 35°20E **85 J8**
Molodechno = Maladzyechna
  Belarus 54°20N 26°50E **75 A14**
Molodezhnaya
  Antarctica 67°40S 45°51E **55 C9**
Molodove *Ukraine* 46°13N 29°39E **81 D14**
Moloka'i *U.S.A.* 21°8N 157°0W **167 L8**
Molokai Fracture Zone
  Pac. Oc. 28°0N 125°0W **157 E15**
Molong *Australia* 33°5S 148°54E **153 B8**
Molopo → *Africa* 28°30S 20°12E **144 C3**
Molos *Greece* 38°47N 22°37E **98 C4**
Molsheim *France* 48°33N 7°29E **71 D14**
Molson L. *Canada* 54°22N 96°40W **163 C9**
Molteno *S. Africa* 31°22S 26°22E **144 E4**
Molu *Indonesia* 6°45S 131°40E **119 F8**
Molucca Sea *Indonesia* 0°0 125°0E **119 E6**
Moluccas = Maluku
  Indonesia 1°0S 127°0E **119 E7**
Moma
  Dem. Rep. of the Congo 1°35S 23°52E **142 C1**
Moma *Mozam.* 16°47S 39°4E **143 F4**
Momba *Australia* 30°58S 143°30E **152 A5**
Mombaça *Brazil* 5°43S 39°45W **189 D11**
Mombasa *Kenya* 4°3S 39°40E **142 C4**
Mombetsu *Japan* 44°21N 143°22E **112 B11**
Mombuey *Spain* 42°3N 6°20W **88 C4**
Momchilgrad *Bulgaria* 41°33N 25°23E **97 E9**
Momi
  Dem. Rep. of the Congo 1°42S 27°0E **142 C2**
Mompós *Colombia* 9°14N 74°26W **186 B4**
Møn *Denmark* 54°57N 12°20E **63 K6**
Mon □ *Myanmar* 16°0N 97°30E **123 L20**
Mona, Canal de la = Mona
  Passage *W. Indies* 18°30N 67°45W **183 C6**
Mona, Isla *Puerto Rico* 18°5N 67°54W **183 C6**
Mona, Pta. *Costa Rica* 9°37N 82°36W **182 E3**
Mona Passage
  W. Indies 18°30N 67°45W **183 C6**
Monaca *U.S.A.* 40°41N 80°17W **174 F4**
Monaco ■ *Europe* 43°46N 7°23E **73 E11**
Monadhliath Mts. *U.K.* 57°10N 4°4W **65 D4**
Monadnock, Mt.
  U.S.A. 42°52N 72°7W **175 D12**
Monaghan *Ireland* 54°15N 6°57W **64 B5**
Monaghan □ *Ireland* 54°11N 6°56W **64 B5**
Monahans *U.S.A.* 31°36N 102°54W **176 F3**
Monapo *Indonesia* 4°7S 123°15E **119 F6**
Monapo *Mozam.* 14°56S 40°19E **143 E5**
Monar, L. *U.K.* 57°26N 5°8W **65 D3**
Monaragala *Sri Lanka* 6°35N 81°10E **127 G5**
Monarch Mt. *Canada* 51°55N 125°57W **162 C3**
Monashee Mts. *Canada* 51°0N 118°43W **162 C5**
Monasterevin *Ireland* 53°8N 7°4W **64 C4**
Monastir = Bitola
  Macedonia 41°1N 21°20E **96 D5**
Monastir *Tunisia* 35°50N 10°49E **136 A6**
Monastir □ *Tunisia* 35°37N 10°45E **136 A6**

Monbetsu = Hidaka
  Japan 42°30N 142°10E **112 C11**
Moncalieri *Italy* 45°0N 7°41E **92 D4**
Moncalvo *Italy* 45°3N 8°16E **92 C5**
Monção *Portugal* 42°4N 8°27W **88 C2**
Moncarapacho *Portugal* 37°5N 7°46W **89 H3**
Moncayo, Sierra del
  Spain 41°48N 1°50W **90 D3**
Mönchengladbach
  Germany 51°11N 6°27E **76 D2**
Mónchique *Portugal* 37°19N 8°38W **89 H2**
Moncks Corner *U.S.A.* 33°12N 80°1W **178 B7**
Monclova *Mexico* 26°54N 101°25W **180 B4**
Moncontour *Canada* 48°22N 2°38W **70 D4**
Moncton *Canada* 46°7N 64°51W **165 C7**
Mondariz *Spain* 42°14N 8°27E **88 C2**
Mondego → *Portugal* 40°9N 8°52W **88 E2**
Mondego, C. *Portugal* 40°11N 8°54W **88 E2**
Mondeodo *Indonesia* 3°34S 122°9E **119 E6**
Mondeville *France* 49°10N 0°18W **70 C6**
Mondlo *S. Africa* 27°59S 30°43E **145 C5**
Mondolfo *Italy* 43°45N 13°6E **93 C10**
Mondoñedo *Spain* 43°25N 7°23W **88 B3**
Mondovì *Italy* 44°23N 7°49E **92 D4**
Mondragon = Arrasate
  Spain 43°4N 2°30W **90 B2**
Mondragone *Italy* 41°7N 13°53E **94 A6**
Mondrain I. *Australia* 34°9S 122°14E **149 F3**
Moneague *Jamaica* 18°16N 77°7W **182 a**
Moneron, Ostrov
  Russia 46°15N 141°16E **112 A10**
Monessen *U.S.A.* 40°9N 79°54W **174 F5**
Monesterio *Spain* 38°6N 6°15W **89 G4**
Monestier-de-Clermont
  France 44°55N 5°38E **73 D9**
Monett *U.S.A.* 36°55N 93°55W **172 G7**
Moneymore *U.K.* 54°41N 6°40W **64 B5**
Monfalcone *Italy* 45°49N 13°32E **93 C10**
Monflanquin *France* 44°32N 0°47E **72 D4**
Monforte *Portugal* 39°6N 7°25W **89 F3**
Monforte de Lemos *Spain* 42°31N 7°33W **88 C3**
Monfragüe △ *Spain* 39°48N 5°52W **88 F5**
Mong Hpayak
  Myanmar 20°52N 99°55E **120 B2**
Mong Hsat Shan,
  Myanmar 21°54N 98°30E **116 G2**
Mong Hsat Shan,
  Myanmar 20°31N 99°15E **120 B2**
Mong Kung *Myanmar* 21°35N 97°35E **123 J20**
Mong Nai *Myanmar* 20°32N 97°46E **123 J20**
Mong Ping *Myanmar* 21°22N 99°2E **116 G2**
Mong Tai = Shan □
  Myanmar 21°30N 98°30E **123 J21**
Mong Ton *Myanmar* 20°17N 98°45E **123 J21**
Mong Yai *Myanmar* 22°21N 98°3E **123 H21**
Mong Yang *Myanmar* 21°50N 99°41E **120 B2**
Mongalla *S. Sudan* 5°8N 31°42E **135 G12**
Mongers, L. *Australia* 29°25S 117°5E **149 E2**
Monghyr = Munger
  India 25°23N 86°30E **125 G12**
Mongibello = Etna *Italy* 37°50N 14°55E **95 E7**
Mongo *Chad* 12°14N 18°43E **135 F9**
Mongo → *S. Leone* 9°35N 12°10W **138 D2**
Mongolia ■ *Asia* 47°0N 103°0E **110 B9**
Mongolia, Plateau of
  Asia 45°0N 105°0E **102 D12**
Mongonu *Nigeria* 12°40N 13°32E **139 C7**
Mongu *Zambia* 15°16S 23°12E **141 H4**
Mongga *Angola* 16°43S 15°20E **144 A2**
Moniac *U.S.A.* 30°31N 82°14W **178 E7**
Monifieth *U.K.* 56°30N 2°48W **65 E6**
Monistrol-sur-Loire
  France 45°17N 4°11E **73 C8**
Monkey Bay *Malawi* 14°7S 35°1E **143 E4**
Monkey Mia *Australia* 25°48S 113°43E **149 E1**
Monkey River *Belize* 16°22N 88°29W **181 D7**
Mońki *Poland* 53°23N 22°48E **82 E9**
Monkland *Canada* 45°11N 74°52W **175 A10**
Monkoto
  Dem. Rep. of the Congo 1°38S 20°35E **140 E4**
Monkton *Canada* 43°35N 81°5W **174 C3**
Monmouth *U.K.* 51°48N 2°42W **67 F5**
Monmouth *Ill. U.S.A.* 40°55N 90°39W **172 E8**
Monmouth *Oreg.,*
  U.S.A. 44°51N 123°14W **168 D2**
Monmouthshire □ *U.K.* 51°48N 2°54W **67 F5**
Mono → *Togo* 6°17N 1°51E **139 D5**
Mono, Pta. *Nic.* 12°0N 83°30W **182 D3**
Mono L. *U.S.A.* 38°1N 119°1W **170 H7**
Monolith *U.S.A.* 35°7N 118°22W **171 K8**
Monolithos *Greece* 36°7N 27°45E **101 C9**
Monongahela *U.S.A.* 40°12N 79°56W **174 F5**
Monópoli *Italy* 40°57N 17°18E **95 B10**
Monor *Hungary* 47°21N 19°27E **80 C4**
Monos I. *Trin. & Tob.* 10°42N 61°44W **187 K15**
Monóvar *Spain* 38°28N 0°53W **91 G4**
Monowai *N.Z.* 45°53S 167°31E **155 F2**
Monowai, L. *N.Z.* 45°53S 167°25E **155 F2**
Monreal del Campo
  Spain 40°47N 1°20W **90 E3**
Monreale *Italy* 38°5N 13°17E **94 D6**
Monroe *Ga., U.S.A.* 33°47N 83°43W **178 B6**
Monroe *La., U.S.A.* 32°30N 92°7W **176 E8**
Monroe *Mich., U.S.A.* 41°55N 83°24W **173 E12**
Monroe *N.C., U.S.A.* 34°59N 80°33W **177 D14**
Monroe *N.Y., U.S.A.* 41°20N 74°11W **175 D10**
Monroe *Wash., U.S.A.* 47°51N 121°58W **168 C3**
Monroe *Wis., U.S.A.* 42°36N 89°38W **172 D9**
Monroe City *U.S.A.* 39°39N 91°44W **172 F8**
Monroeton *U.S.A.* 41°43N 76°29W **175 E8**
Monroeville *Ala.,*
  U.S.A. 31°31N 87°20W **177 F11**
Monroeville *Pa., U.S.A.* 40°26N 79°45W **174 F5**
Monrovia *Liberia* 6°18N 10°47W **138 D2**
Mons *Belgium* 50°27N 3°58E **69 D3**
Møns Klint *Denmark* 54°57N 12°33E **63 K6**
Monsaraz *Portugal* 38°28N 7°22W **89 G3**
Monse *Indonesia* 4°7S 123°15E **119 E6**
Monségur *France* 44°38N 0°4E **72 D4**
Mönsterås *Sweden* 57°3N 16°26E **63 G10**
Mont Cenis, Col du
  France 45°15N 6°55E **73 C10**
Mont-de-Marsan *France* 43°54N 0°31W **72 E3**
Mont-Joli *Canada* 48°37N 68°10W **165 C6**
Mont-Laurier *Canada* 46°35N 75°30W **164 C4**
Mont-Louis *Canada* 49°15N 65°44W **165 C6**

Mont Peko △ *Côte d'Ivoire* 9°5N 7°15W **138 D3**
Mont-roig del Camp *Spain* 41°5N 0°58E **90 D5**
Mont-St-Michel, Le
  France 48°40N 1°30W **70 D5**
Mont Sangbé △
  Côte d'Ivoire 8°0N 7°10W **138 D3**
Mont-Tremblant
  Canada 46°30N 74°30W **164 C5**
Montabaur *Germany* 50°25N 7°50E **76 E3**
Montagnac *France* 43°29N 3°28E **72 E7**
Montagnana *Italy* 45°14N 11°28E **92 C8**
Montagne de Reims △
  France 49°8N 4°0E **71 C11**
Montagnes
  Côte d'Ivoire 6°54N 7°50W **138 D3**
Montagu *S. Africa* 33°45S 20°8E **144 D3**
Montagu I. *Antarctica* 58°25S 26°20W **55 B1**
Montague *Canada* 46°10N 62°39W **165 C7**
Montague, I. *Mexico* 31°45N 114°48W **180 A2**
Montague I. *Australia* 36°16S 150°13E **153 D9**
Montague I. *U.S.A.* 60°0N 147°30W **166 D10**
Montague Ra.
  Australia 27°15S 119°30E **149 E2**
Montague Sd.
  Australia 14°28S 125°20E **148 B4**
Montaigu *France* 46°59N 1°18W **70 F5**
Montalbán *Spain* 40°50N 0°45W **90 E4**
Montalbano Iónico *Italy* 40°17N 16°34E **95 B9**
Montalbo *Spain* 39°53N 2°42W **90 E2**
Montalcino *Italy* 43°3N 11°29E **93 E8**
Montalegre *Portugal* 41°49N 7°47E **88 D3**
Montalto di Castro *Italy* 42°21N 11°37E **93 F8**
Montalto Uffugo *Italy* 39°24N 16°9E **95 C9**
Montalvo *U.S.A.* 34°15N 119°12W **171 L7**
Montamarta *Spain* 41°39N 5°49W **88 D5**
Montana *Bulgaria* 43°27N 23°16E **97 C7**
Montana *Peru* 6°0S 73°0W **188 B3**
Montana □ *Bulgaria* 43°30N 23°10E **97 C7**
Montana □ *U.S.A.* 47°0N 110°0W **168 C9**
Montaña Clara, I.
  Canary Is. 29°17N 13°33W **100 E6**
Montañas de Malaga △
  Spain 36°48N 4°32W **89 J6**
Montánchez *Spain* 39°15N 6°8W **89 F4**
Montargil *Portugal* 39°5N 8°10W **89 F2**
Montargis *France* 47°59N 2°43E **71 E9**
Montauban *France* 44°2N 1°21E **72 D5**
Montauk *U.S.A.* 41°3N 71°57W **175 E13**
Montauk Pt. *U.S.A.* 41°4N 71°51W **175 E13**
Montbard *France* 47°38N 4°20E **71 E11**
Montbarrey *France* 47°1N 5°39E **71 E12**
Montbéliard *France* 47°31N 6°48E **71 E13**
Montblanc *Spain* 41°23N 1°4E **90 D6**
Montbrison *France* 45°36N 4°3E **73 C8**
Montcalm, Pic de *France* 42°40N 1°25E **72 F5**
Montceau-les-Mines
  France 46°40N 4°23E **71 F11**
Montcenis *France* 46°47N 4°23E **73 B8**
Montchanin *France* 46°45N 4°28E **73 B8**
Montclair *U.S.A.* 40°49N 74°12W **175 F10**
Montcornet *France* 49°40N 4°1E **71 C11**
Montcuq *France* 44°21N 1°13E **72 D5**
Montdidier *France* 49°38N 2°35E **71 C9**
Monte Albán *Mexico* 17°2N 96°46W **181 D5**
Monte Alegre *Brazil* 2°0S 54°0W **187 D8**
Monte Alegre de Goiás
  Brazil 13°14S 47°10W **189 C1**
Monte Alegre do Piauí
  Brazil 9°46S 45°18W **189 B1**
Monte Azul *Brazil* 15°9S 42°53W **189 B2**
Monte Carmelo *Brazil* 18°43S 47°29W **189 D1**
Monte-Carlo *Monaco* 43°44N 7°25E **73 E11**
Monte Caseros
  Argentina 30°10S 57°50W **190 C4**
Monte Comán
  Argentina 34°40S 67°53W **190 C2**
Monte Cristi *Dom. Rep.* 19°52N 71°39W **183 C5**
Monte Cucco → *Italy* 43°22N 12°43E **93 E9**
Monte Dinero
  Argentina 52°18S 68°33W **192 G3**
Monte León *Argentina* 50°15S 69°0W **192 D3**
Monte Lindo →
  Paraguay 23°56S 57°12W **190 A4**
Monte Pascoal △
  Brazil 16°51S 39°21W **189 E3**
Monte Patria *Chile* 30°42S 70°58W **190 C1**
Monte Quemado
  Argentina 25°53S 62°41W **190 B3**
Monte Redondo *Portugal* 39°53N 8°50W **88 F2**
Monte Rio *U.S.A.* 38°28N 123°0W **170 G4**
Monte San Giovanni Campano
  Italy 41°38N 13°31E **94 A6**
Monte San Savino *Italy* 43°20N 11°43E **93 E8**
Monte Sant' Ángelo
  Italy 41°42N 15°59E **93 G12**
Monte Santu, C. di *Italy* 40°5N 9°44E **94 B2**
Monte Subásio △ *Italy* 43°5N 12°40E **93 E9**
Monte Vista *U.S.A.* 37°35N 106°9W **169 H10**
Monteagudo *Argentina* 27°14S 54°8W **191 B5**
Montealegre del Castillo
  Spain 38°48N 1°17W **91 G3**
Montebello *Canada* 45°40N 74°55W **164 C5**
Montebello Iónico *Italy* 37°59N 15°45E **95 E8**
Montebello Is.
  Australia 20°30S 115°45E **148 D2**
Montebelluna *Italy* 45°47N 12°3E **93 C9**
Montebourg *France* 49°30N 1°20W **70 C5**
Montecarlo *Argentina* 26°34S 54°47W **191 B5**
Montecastrilli *Italy* 42°39N 12°29E **93 F9**
Montecatini Terme *Italy* 43°53N 10°46E **92 E7**
Montecito *U.S.A.* 34°26N 119°40W **171 L7**
Montecristo *Italy* 42°20N 10°19E **92 F7**
Montefalco *Italy* 42°53N 12°39E **93 F9**
Montefiascone *Italy* 42°32N 12°2E **93 F9**
Montefrío *Spain* 37°19N 4°0W **89 H6**
Montego Bay *Jamaica* 18°28N 77°55W **182 a**
Montehermoso *Spain* 40°5N 6°21W **88 E4**
Monteiro *Brazil* 7°48S 37°0W **189 D11**
Montejícar *Spain* 37°33N 3°30W **89 H7**
Montélimar *France* 44°33N 4°45E **73 D8**
Montella *Italy* 40°50N 15°2E **95 B8**
Montellano *Spain* 36°59N 5°34W **89 J5**
Montello *U.S.A.* 43°48N 89°20W **172 D9**
Montemayor, Meseta de
  Argentina 44°20S 66°10W **192 E3**
Montemor-o-Novo
  Portugal 38°40N 8°12W **89 G2**
Montemor-o-Velho
  Portugal 40°11N 8°40W **88 E2**
Montemorelos *Mexico* 25°12N 99°49W **181 B5**

Montendre *France* 45°16N 0°26W **72 C3**
Montenegro *Brazil* 29°39S 51°29W **191 B5**
Montenegro ■ *Europe* 42°40N 19°20E **96 D3**
Montenero di Bisáccia
  Italy 41°57N 14°47E **93 G12**
Montepuez *Mozam.* 13°8S 38°59E **143 E4**
Montepuez → *Mozam.* 12°32S 40°27E **143 E5**
Montereale *Italy* 42°31N 13°15E **93 F10**
Montereau-Faut-Yonne
  France 48°22N 2°57E **71 D9**
Monterey *U.S.A.* 36°37N 121°55W **170 J5**
Monterey B. *U.S.A.* 36°45N 122°0W **170 J5**
Montería *Colombia* 8°46N 75°53W **186 B3**
Monteros *Argentina* 27°11S 65°30W **190 B2**
Monterotondo *Italy* 42°3N 12°37E **93 F9**
Monterrey *Mexico* 25°40N 100°19W **180 B4**
Montes Altos *Brazil* 5°50S 47°4W **189 D1**
Montes Azules △
  Mexico 16°21N 91°3W **181 D6**
Montes Claros *Brazil* 16°30S 43°50W **189 E2**
Montesano *U.S.A.* 46°59N 123°36W **170 D3**
Montesano sulla Marcellana
  Italy 40°16N 15°42E **95 B8**
Montesárchio *Italy* 41°4N 14°38E **95 A7**
Montescaglioso *Italy* 40°33N 16°40E **95 B9**
Montesilvano *Italy* 42°29N 14°8E **93 F11**
Montesinho △ *Portugal* 41°54N 6°52W **88 D4**
Montevarchi *Italy* 43°31N 11°34E **93 E8**
Montevideo *Uruguay* 34°50S 56°11W **191 C4**
Montevideo *U.S.A.* 44°57N 95°43W **172 C6**
Montezuma *Ga., U.S.A.* 32°18N 84°2W **178 C5**
Montezuma *Iowa,*
  U.S.A. 41°35N 92°32W **172 E7**
Montezuma Castle △
  U.S.A. 34°39N 111°45W **169 J8**
Montfaucon *France* 47°6N 1°7W **70 E5**
Montfaucon-d'Argonne
  France 49°16N 5°8E **71 C12**
Montfaucon-en-Velay
  France 45°11N 4°20E **73 C8**
Montfort-le-Gesnois
  France 48°3N 0°25E **70 D7**
Montfort-sur-Meu *France* 48°9N 1°58W **70 D5**
Montgenèvre *France* 44°56N 6°43E **73 D10**
Montgó △ *Spain* 38°48N 0°7W **91 G5**
Montgomery *U.K.* 52°34N 3°8W **67 E4**
Montgomery *Ala.,*
  U.S.A. 32°23N 86°19W **178 C3**
Montgomery *Pa.,*
  U.S.A. 41°10N 76°53W **174 E8**
Montgomery *W. Va.,*
  U.S.A. 38°11N 81°19W **173 F13**
Montgomery City
  U.S.A. 38°59N 91°30W **172 F8**
Montguyon *France* 45°12N 0°12W **72 C3**
Monthermé *France* 49°52N 4°42E **71 C11**
Monthey *Switz.* 46°15N 6°56E **77 J2**
Monthois *France* 49°19N 4°43E **71 C11**
Monti Lucrétili △ *Italy* 42°5N 12°50E **93 F9**
Monti Picentini △ *Italy* 40°45N 15°2E **95 B8**
Monti Sibillini △ *Italy* 42°55N 13°15E **93 F10**
Monti Simbruini △
  Italy 41°55N 13°13E **93 G10**
Monticelli d'Ongina *Italy* 45°5N 9°56E **92 C6**
Monticello *Ark., U.S.A.* 33°38N 91°47W **176 E9**
Monticello *Fla., U.S.A.* 30°33N 83°52W **178 E5**
Monticello *Ga., U.S.A.* 33°18N 83°40W **178 B5**
Monticello *Ind.,*
  U.S.A. 40°45N 86°46W **172 E10**
Monticello *Iowa,*
  U.S.A. 42°15N 91°12W **172 D8**
Monticello *Ky., U.S.A.* 36°50N 84°51W **173 G11**
Monticello *Minn.,*
  U.S.A. 45°18N 93°48W **172 C7**
Monticello *Miss., U.S.A.* 31°33N 90°7W **177 F9**
Monticello *N.Y.,*
  U.S.A. 41°39N 74°42W **175 E10**
Monticello *Utah,*
  U.S.A. 37°52N 109°21W **169 H9**
Montichiari *Italy* 45°28N 10°23E **92 C7**
Montier-en-Der *France* 48°30N 4°45E **71 D11**
Montignac *France* 45°4N 1°10E **72 C5**
Montigny-les-Metz
  France 49°7N 6°10E **71 C13**
Montigny-sur-Aube
  France 47°57N 4°45E **71 E11**
Montijo *Portugal* 38°41N 8°54W **89 G2**
Montijo *Spain* 38°52N 6°39W **89 G4**
Montilla *Spain* 37°36N 4°40W **89 H6**
Montivilliers *France* 49°33N 0°12E **70 C7**
Montluçon *France* 46°22N 2°36E **71 F9**
Montmagny *Canada* 46°58N 70°34W **165 C5**
Montmartre *Canada* 50°14N 103°27W **163 C8**
Montmédy *France* 49°30N 5°20E **71 C12**
Montmélian *France* 45°30N 6°4E **73 C10**
Montmirail *France* 48°51N 3°30E **71 D10**
Montmoreau-St-Cybard
  France 45°23N 0°8E **72 C4**
Montmorillon *France* 46°26N 0°50E **72 B4**
Montmort-Lucy *France* 48°55N 3°49E **71 D10**
Monto *Australia* 24°52S 151°6E **150 C5**
Montoire-sur-le-Loir
  France 47°45N 0°52E **70 E7**
Montongbuwoh
  Indonesia 8°33S 116°4E **119 K19**
Montório al Vomano
  Italy 42°35N 13°38E **93 F10**
Montoro *Spain* 38°1N 4°27W **89 G6**
Montour Falls *U.S.A.* 42°21N 76°51W **174 D8**
Montoursville *U.S.A.* 41°15N 76°55W **174 E8**
Montpelier *Idaho,*
  U.S.A. 42°19N 111°18W **168 E8**
Montpelier *Vt., U.S.A.* 44°16N 72°35W **175 B12**
Montpellier *France* 43°37N 3°52E **72 E7**
Montpezat-de-Quercy
  France 44°15N 1°30E **72 D5**
Montpon-Ménestérol
  France 45°0N 0°11E **72 D4**
Montréal *Canada* 45°30N 73°33W **175 A11**
Montréal *Aude, France* 43°13N 2°8E **72 E6**
Montréal *Gers, France* 43°57N 0°11E **72 E4**
Montréal → *Canada* 47°14N 84°39W **164 C3**
Montreal L. *Canada* 54°20N 105°45W **163 B7**
Montreal Lake *Canada* 54°3N 105°46W **163 C7**
Montredon-Labessonnié
  France 43°45N 2°18E **72 E6**
Montrésor *France* 47°10N 1°10E **70 E8**
Montret *France* 46°40N 5°7E **71 F12**

Montreuil *Pas-de-Calais, France* 50°27N 1°45E **71** B8
Montreuil *Seine-St-Denis, France* 48°51N 2°27E **71** D9
Montreuil-Bellay *France* 47°8N 0°9W **70** E6
Montreux *Switz.* 46°26N 6°55E **77** J2
Montrevel-en-Bresse *France* 46°21N 5°8E **71** F12
Montrichard *France* 47°20N 1°10E **70** E8
Montrose *U.K.* 56°44N 2°27W **65** E6
Montrose *Colo., U.S.A.* 38°29N 107°53W **168** G10
Montrose *Pa., U.S.A.* 41°50N 75°53W **175** E9
Monts, Pte. des *Canada* 49°20N 67°12W **165** C6
Montsalvy *France* 44°41N 2°30E **72** D6
Montsant, Serra de *Spain* 41°17N 1°0E **90** D6
Montsauche-les-Settons *France* 47°13N 4°2E **71** E11
Montsec, Serra del *Spain* 42°5N 0°45E **90** C5
Montseny △ *Spain* 41°43N 2°22W **90** D2
Montserrat *Spain* 41°36N 1°49E **90** D6
Montserrat ☑ *W. Indies* 16°40N 62°10W **183** C7
Montuenga *Spain* 41°3N 4°38W **88** D6
Montuïri *Spain* 39°34N 2°59E **90** B10
Monywa *Myanmar* 22°7N 95°11E **123** H19
Monza *Italy* 45°35N 9°16E **92** C6
Monza e Brianza □ *Italy* 45°30N 9°15E **92** C6
Monze *Zambia* 16°17S 27°29E **143** F2
Monze, C. *Pakistan* 24°47N 66°37E **124** G2
Monzón *Spain* 41°52N 0°10E **90** D5
Mooers *U.S.A.* 44°58N 73°35W **175** B11
Mooi → *S. Africa* 28°45S 30°34E **145** C5
Mooi River *S. Africa* 29°13S 29°50E **145** D4
Mookgopong *S. Africa* 24°31S 28°44E **145** B4
Moomba *Australia* 28°6S 140°12E **151** A3
Moonah → *Australia* 22°3S 138°33E **150** C2
Moonda, L. *Australia* 25°52S 140°25E **150** D3
Moonie *Australia* 27°46S 150°20E **151** D5
Moonie → *Australia* 29°19S 148°43E **151** D4
Moonta *Australia* 34°6S 137°32E **152** B2
Moora *Australia* 30°37S 115°58E **149** F2
Moorcroft *U.S.A.* 44°16N 104°57W **168** D11
Moore → *Australia* 31°22S 115°30E **149** F2
Moore, L. *Australia* 29°50S 117°35E **149** E2
Moore Falls *Canada* 44°48N 78°48W **174** B6
Moore Haven *U.S.A.* 26°50N 81°6W **179** J8
Moore Park *Australia* 24°43S 152°17E **150** C5
Moore Res. *U.S.A.* 44°20N 71°53W **175** B13
Moore River △ *Australia* 31°7S 115°39E **149** F2
Moorefield *U.S.A.* 39°4N 78°58W **173** F14
Moorhead *U.S.A.* 46°53N 96°45W **172** B5
Moormerland *Germany* 53°20N 7°20E **76** B3
Moornanyah L. *Australia* 33°15S 143°42E **152** B5
Mooroopna *Australia* 36°25S 145°22E **153** D6
Moorpark *U.S.A.* 34°17N 118°53W **171** L8
Moorreesburg *S. Africa* 33°6S 18°38E **144** D2
Moorrinya △ *Australia* 21°42S 144°58E **150** C3
Moosburg *Germany* 48°27N 11°56E **77** G7
Moose → *Canada* 51°20N 80°25W **164** B3
Moose → *U.S.A.* 43°38N 75°24W **175** C9
Moose Creek *Canada* 45°15N 74°58W **175** A10
Moose Factory *Canada* 51°16N 80°32W **164** B3
Moose Jaw *Canada* 50°24N 105°30W **163** C7
Moose Jaw → *Canada* 50°34N 105°18W **163** C7
Moose Lake *Canada* 53°46N 100°8W **163** C8
Moose Lake *U.S.A.* 46°27N 92°46W **172** B7
Moose Mountain △ *Canada* 46°29N 69°49W **173** C19
Moosehead L. *U.S.A.* 45°38N 69°40W **173** C19
Mooselookmeguntic L. *U.S.A.* 44°55N 70°49W **175** B14
Moosilauke, Mt. *U.S.A.* 44°3N 71°40W **175** B13
Moosomin *Canada* 50°9N 101°40W **163** C8
Moosonee *Canada* 51°17N 80°39W **164** B3
Moosup *U.S.A.* 41°43N 71°53W **175** E13
Mootwingee △ *Australia* 31°10S 142°30E **152** A5
Mopane *S. Africa* 22°37S 29°52E **145** B4
Mopeia Velha *Mozam.* 17°30S 35°40E **143** F4
Mopipi *Botswana* 21°6S 24°55E **144** B3
Mopoi *C.A.R.* 5°6N 26°54E **142** A2
Mopti *Mali* 14°30N 4°0W **138** C4
Mopti □ *Mali* 14°40N 4°0W **138** C4
Moqor *Afghan.* 32°50N 67°42E **124** C2
Moquegua *Peru* 17°15S 70°46W **188** D3
Moquegua □ *Peru* 16°0S 70°55W **188** D3
Mór *Hungary* 47°25N 18°12E **80** C3
Mora *Cameroon* 11°2N 14°7E **139** C7
Mora *Portugal* 38°55N 8°10W **89** G2
Mora *Spain* 39°41N 3°46W **89** F7
Mora *Sweden* 61°2N 14°38E **62** C8
Mora, Minn., U.S.A.* 45°53N 93°18W **172** C7
Mora, N. Mex., U.S.A.* 35°58N 105°20W **169** J11
Móra de Rubielos *Spain* 40°15N 0°45W **90** E4
Móra d'Ebre *Spain* 41°6N 0°38E **90** D5
Móra la Nova *Spain* 41°7N 0°39E **90** D5
Morača → *Montenegro* 42°20N 19°9E **98** B1
Morada Nova *Brazil* 5°7S 38°23W **189** B3
Morada Nova de Minas *Brazil* 18°37S 45°22W **189** D1
Moradabad *India* 28°50N 78°50E **125** E8
Morafenobe *Madag.* 17°50S 44°53E **141** H8
Morag *Poland* 53°55N 19°56E **82** E6
Moral de Calatrava *Spain* 38°51N 3°33W **89** G7
Moraleda, Canal *Chile* 44°30S 73°30W **192** B2
Moraleja *Spain* 40°6N 6°43W **88** E4
Moramanga *Madag.* 18°56S 48°12E **141** H9
Moran *Kans., U.S.A.* 37°55N 95°10W **172** G6
Moran *Wyo., U.S.A.* 43°50N 110°31W **168** E8
Moranbah *Australia* 22°1S 148°6E **150** C4
Morang = Biratnagar *Nepal* 26°27N 87°17E **125** F12
Morano Cálabro *Italy* 39°50N 16°8E **95** C9
Morant Bay *Jamaica* 17°53N 76°25W **182** a
Morant Cays *Jamaica* 17°22N 76°0W **182** C4
Morant Pt. *Jamaica* 17°55N 76°12W **182** a
Morar *India* 26°14N 78°14E **124** F8
Morar, L. *U.K.* 56°57N 5°40W **65** E3
Moratalla *Spain* 38°14N 1°49W **91** G3
Moratuwa *Sri Lanka* 6°45N 79°55E **127** L4
Morava → *Slovakia* 48°10N 16°59E **79** G9
Morava → *Serbia* 44°36N 21°4E **81** G11
Moravia *U.S.A.* 42°43N 76°25W **175** D8
Moravița *Romania* 45°17N 21°14E **80** E6
Moravská Třebová *Czechia* 49°45N 16°40E **79** B9
Moravské Budějovice *Czechia* 49°4N 15°49E **78** B8
Moravskoslezský □ *Czechia* 49°55N 17°58E **79** B10
Morawa *Australia* 29°13S 116°0E **149** E2
Morawhanna *Guyana* 8°30N 59°40W **186** B7
Moray □ *U.K.* 57°31N 3°18W **65** D5
Moray Firth *U.K.* 57°40N 3°52W **65** D5
Morbach *Germany* 49°48N 7°6E **77** F3
Morbegno *Italy* 46°8N 9°34E **92** B6
Morbi *India* 22°50N 70°42E **124** H4
Morbihan □ *France* 47°55N 2°50W **70** E4
Morcenx *France* 44°3N 0°55W **72** D3
Morcone *Italy* 41°20N 14°40E **95** A7
Mordelles *France* 48°5N 1°52W **70** D5
Morden *Canada* 49°15N 98°10W **163** D9
Mordogan *Turkey* 38°30N 26°37E **99** C8
Mordovian Republic = Mordvinia □ *Russia* 54°20N 44°30E **86** C7
Mordovo *Russia* 52°6N 40°50E **86** D5
Mordvinia □ *Russia* 54°20N 44°30E **86** C7
Mordy *Poland* 52°13N 22°31E **83** F9
Moreau → *U.S.A.* 45°18N 100°43W **172** C3
Morebeng *S. Africa* 23°30S 29°55E **145** B4
Morecambe *U.K.* 54°5N 2°52W **66** C5
Morecambe B. *U.K.* 54°7N 3°0W **66** C5
Moree *Australia* 29°28S 149°54E **151** D4
Morehead *U.S.A.* 38°11N 83°26W **173** F12
Morehead City *U.S.A.* 34°43N 76°43W **179** H7
Morel → *India* 26°13N 76°36E **124** F7
Moreland *U.S.A.* 33°17N 84°46W **178** E3
Morelia *Mexico* 19°42N 101°7W **180** D4
Morella *Australia* 23°0S 143°52E **150** C3
Morella *Spain* 40°35N 0°5W **90** E4
Morelos *Mexico* 26°42N 107°40W **180** B3
Morelos □ *Mexico* 18°45N 99°0W **181** D5
Morena *India* 26°30N 78°4E **124** F8
Morena, Sierra *Spain* 38°20N 4°0W **89** G7
Moreni *Romania* 44°59N 25°36E **83** F10
Moreno *Bolivia* 11°9S 66°15W **188** C4
Moreno Valley *U.S.A.* 33°56N 117°14W **171** M10
Moresby I. *Canada* 52°30N 131°40W **162** C2
Morestel *France* 45°40N 5°28E **73** C9
Moreton I. *Australia* 27°10S 153°25E **151** D5
Moreton Island △ *Australia* 27°2S 153°24E **151** D5
Moreuil *France* 49°46N 2°30E **71** C9
Morez *France* 46°31N 6°2E **71** F13
Morgan *Australia* 34°2S 139°35E **152** B2
Morgan, Ga., U.S.A.* 31°32N 84°36W **178** D5
Morgan City *U.S.A.* 29°42N 91°12W **179** G9
Morgan Hill *U.S.A.* 37°8N 121°39W **170** H5
Morganfield *U.S.A.* 37°41N 87°55W **172** G10
Morgan's Pt. *Trin. & Tob.* 29°40N 90°56W **176** G7
Morganton *U.S.A.* 35°45N 81°41W **177** D14
Morgantown *U.S.A.* 39°38N 79°57W **173** F14
Morgenzon *S. Africa* 26°45S 29°36E **145** C4
Morges *Switz.* 46°31N 6°29E **77** J2
Morghak *Iran* 29°7N 57°54E **129** D8
Morgongåva *Sweden* 59°57N 16°58E **62** E10
Morhange *France* 48°55N 6°38E **71** D13
Morhar → *India* 25°29N 85°11E **125** G11
Mori *China* 43°49N 90°11E **109** D12
Mori *Japan* 42°6N 140°35E **112** C10
Moriarty *U.S.A.* 34°59N 106°3W **169** J10
Moribaya *Guinea* 9°53N 9°32W **138** D3
Morice L. *Canada* 53°50N 127°40W **162** C3
Moriki *Nigeria* 12°52N 6°30E **139** C6
Morinville *Canada* 53°49N 113°41W **162** C6
Morioka *Japan* 39°45N 141°8E **112** E10
Moris *Mexico* 28°10N 108°32W **180** B3
Morisset *Australia* 33°6S 151°30E **153** B9
Morlaàs *France* 43°21N 0°18W **72** E3
Morlaix *France* 48°36N 3°52W **70** D3
Mörlunda *Sweden* 57°19N 15°52E **63** G9
Mormanno *Italy* 39°53N 15°59E **95** C8
Mormant *France* 48°37N 2°52E **71** D9
Mormugao = Marmagao *India* 15°25N 73°56E **127** G1
Mornington *Australia* 38°15S 145°5E **153** E6
Mornington, I. *Chile* 49°50S 75°30W **192** C1
Mornington I. *Australia* 16°30S 139°30E **150** B2
Mornington Peninsula △ *Australia* 38°28S 144°53E **153** E6
Mornos → *Greece* 38°25N 21°50E **98** C3
Moro *Pakistan* 26°40N 68°0E **124** F7
Moro → *Pakistan* 29°42N 67°22E **124** E2
Moro G. *Phil.* 6°30N 123°0E **119** C6
Moro Gulf = Moro G. *Phil.* 6°30N 123°0E **119** C6
Morocco ■ *N. Afr.* 32°0N 5°50W **134** B4
Morococha *Peru* 11°40S 76°5W **188** C2
Morogoro *Tanzania* 6°50S 37°40E **142** D4
Morogoro □ *Tanzania* 8°0S 37°0E **142** D4
Moroleón *Mexico* 20°8N 101°12W **180** C4
Morombe *Madag.* 21°45S 43°22E **141** J8
Moron *Argentina* 34°39S 58°37W **190** C4
Morón *Cuba* 22°8N 78°39W **182** B4
Mörön *Mongolia* 49°38N 100°9E **110** B9
Morón de Almazán *Spain* 41°29N 2°27W **90** D2
Morón de la Frontera *Spain* 37°6N 5°28W **89** H5
Morona → *Peru* 4°40S 77°10W **186** D3
Morondava *Madag.* 20°17S 44°17E **141** J8
Morondo *Côte d'Ivoire* 8°57N 6°47W **138** D3
Morongo Valley *U.S.A.* 34°3N 116°37W **171** L10
Moroni *Comoros Is.* 11°40S 43°16E **141** a
Moroni *U.S.A.* 39°32N 111°35W **168** G8
Morotai *Indonesia* 2°10N 128°30E **119** D7
Moroto *Uganda* 2°28N 34°42E **142** B3
Moroto, Mt. *Uganda* 2°30N 34°43E **142** B3
Morozov *Bulgaria* 42°30N 25°10E **97** D9
Morozovsk *Russia* 48°25N 41°50E **87** G6
Morpeth *Canada* 42°23N 81°50W **174** D3
Morpeth *U.K.* 55°10N 1°41W **66** B6
Morphou *Cyprus* 35°12N 32°59E **101** D11
Morphou Bay *Cyprus* 35°15N 32°50E **101** D11
Morrilton *U.S.A.* 35°9N 92°44W **176** D8
Morrinhos *Ceará, Brazil* 3°14S 40°7W **189** A2
Morrinhos *Minas Gerais, Brazil* 17°45S 49°10W **187** G9
Morrinsville *N.Z.* 37°40S 175°32E **154** D4
Morris *Canada* 49°25N 97°22W **163** D9
Morris, Ill., U.S.A.* 41°22N 88°26W **172** E9
Morris, Minn., U.S.A.* 45°35N 95°55W **172** C6
Morris, N.Y., U.S.A.* 42°33N 75°15W **175** D9
Morris, Pa., U.S.A.* 41°35N 77°17W **174** E7
Morris, Mt. *Australia* 26°9S 131°4E **149** E5
Morris Jesup, Kap *Greenland* 83°40N 34°0W **57** A7
Morrisburg *Canada* 44°55N 75°7W **175** D9
Morristown *Ariz., U.S.A.* 33°51N 112°37W **169** K7
Morristown *N.J., U.S.A.* 40°48N 74°29W **175** F10
Morristown *N.Y., U.S.A.* 44°35N 75°39W **175** B9
Morristown *Tenn., U.S.A.* 36°13N 83°18W **177** C13
Morrisville *N.Y., U.S.A.* 42°53N 75°35W **175** D9
Morrisville *Pa., U.S.A.* 40°13N 74°47W **175** F10
Morrisville *Vt., U.S.A.* 44°34N 72°36W **175** B12
Morro, Pta. *Chile* 27°6S 71°0W **190** B1
Morro Bay *U.S.A.* 35°22N 120°51W **170** K6
Morro Chico *Chile* 52°25S 71°26W **192** D2
Morro do Chapéu *Brazil* 11°33S 41°9W **189** D2
Morro Jable, Pta. de *Canary Is.* 28°2N 14°20W **100** F5
Morrocoy △ *Venezuela* 10°48N 68°13W **183** D6
Morros *Brazil* 2°52S 44°3W **189** A2
Morrosquillo, G. de *Colombia* 9°35N 75°40W **182** E4
Mörrum *Sweden* 56°12N 14°45E **63** H8
Morrumbene *Mozam.* 23°31S 35°16E **145** B6
Mörrumsån → *Sweden* 56°10N 14°45E **63** H8
Mors *Denmark* 56°50N 8°45E **63** H2
Morshansk *Russia* 53°28N 41°50E **86** D5
Morsi *India* 21°21N 78°0E **126** D4
Mörsil *Sweden* 63°19N 13°40E **62** A7
Mortagne → *France* 48°33N 6°27E **71** D13
Mortagne-au-Perche *France* 48°31N 0°33E **70** D7
Mortagne-sur-Gironde *France* 45°28N 0°47W **72** C3
Mortagne-sur-Sèvre *France* 47°0N 0°57W **70** F6
Mortain *France* 48°40N 0°57W **70** D6
Mortara *Italy* 45°15N 8°44E **92** C5
Morteau *France* 47°3N 6°36E **71** E13
Morteros *Argentina* 30°50S 62°0W **190** C3
Mortlach *Canada* 50°27N 106°4W **163** C7
Mortlake *Australia* 38°5S 142°50E **152** E5
Morton, Tex., U.S.A.* 33°44N 102°46W **176** E3
Morton, Wash., U.S.A.* 46°34N 122°17W **170** D4
Morton △ *Australia* 35°0S 150°12E **153** C9
Morundah *Australia* 34°57S 146°19E **153** C7
Moruya *Australia* 35°58S 150°3E **153** C9
Morvan *France* 47°5N 4°3E **71** E11
Morven *Australia* 26°22S 147°5E **151** D4
Morven *N.Z.* 44°50S 171°6E **155** E6
Morven *U.K.* 30°57N 83°30W **178** E6
Morvern *U.K.* 56°38N 5°44W **65** E3
Morwell *Australia* 38°10S 146°22E **153** E7
Morwell △ *Australia* 38°14S 146°23E **153** E7
Moryń *Poland* 52°51N 14°22E **83** F1
Morzine *France* 46°11N 6°42E **71** F13
Mosakahiken = Moose Lake *Canada* 53°46N 100°8W **163** C8
Mosalsk *Russia* 54°30N 34°55E **84** E8
Mosbach *Germany* 49°21N 9°9E **77** F5
Moščenice *Croatia* 45°17N 14°16E **93** C11
Mosciano Sant' Ángelo *Italy* 42°42N 13°52E **93** F10
Moscos Is. *Myanmar* 14°0N 97°30E **120** F1
Moscow = Moskva *Russia* 55°45N 37°37E **84** D9
Moscow, Idaho, U.S.A.* 46°44N 117°0W **168** C5
Moscow, Pa., U.S.A.* 41°20N 75°31W **175** E9
Moscow Domodedovo Int. ✈ (DME) *Russia* 55°24N 37°54E **84** E9
Mosel → *Europe* 50°22N 7°36E **71** B14
Moselle = Mosel → *Europe* 50°22N 7°36E **71** B14
Moselle □ *France* 48°59N 6°33E **71** D13
Moses Lake *U.S.A.* 47°8N 119°17W **168** C4
Mosgiel *N.Z.* 45°53S 170°21E **155** F5
Moshaweng → *S. Africa* 26°35S 22°50E **144** C3
Moshchnyy, Ostrov *Russia* 60°1N 27°50E **84** B4
Moshi *Tanzania* 3°22S 37°18E **142** C4
Moshi □ *Nigeria* 9°18N 4°38E **139** D5
Moshupa *Botswana* 24°46S 25°29E **144** B4
Mosi-oa-Tunya = Victoria Falls *Zimbabwe* 17°58S 25°52E **143** F2
Mosina *Poland* 52°15N 16°50E **83** F3
Mosjøen *Norway* 65°51N 13°12E **60** D15
Moskenesøya *Norway* 67°58N 13°0E **60** C15
Moskenstraumen *Norway* 67°47N 12°45E **60** C15
Moskva *Russia* 55°45N 37°37E **84** D9
Moskva → *Russia* 56°20N 37°20E **84** D9
Moskva → *Russia* 55°5N 38°51E **84** D10
Moslavačka Gora *Croatia* 45°40N 16°37E **93** C13
Mosomane *Botswana* 24°2S 26°19E **144** B4
Mosonmagyaróvár *Hungary* 47°52N 17°18E **80** C2
Mošorin *Serbia* 45°19N 20°4E **80** E5
Mospyne *Ukraine* 47°52N 38°0E **85** J9
Mosquera *Colombia* 2°35N 78°24W **186** C3
Mosquero *U.S.A.* 35°47N 103°58W **169** J12
Mosqueruela *Spain* 40°21N 0°27W **90** E4
Mosquitia *Honduras* 15°20N 84°10W **182** C3
Mosquito Creek L. *U.S.A.* 41°18N 80°46W **174** E4
Mosquito L. *Canada* 62°35N 103°20W **163** A8
Mosquitos, G. de los *Panama* 9°15N 81°10W **182** E3
Moss *Norway* 59°27N 10°40E **61** G14
Moss Vale *Australia* 34°32S 150°25E **153** C9
Mossaka *Congo* 11°3S 16°55W **138** E4
Mossbank *Canada* 49°56N 105°56W **163** D7
Mossburn *N.Z.* 45°41S 168°15E **155** F3
Mosselbaai *S. Africa* 34°11S 22°8E **144** D3
Mossendjo *Congo* 2°55S 12°42E **140** E2
Mossgiel *Australia* 33°15S 144°5E **152** B6
Mossingen *Germany* 48°24N 9°4E **77** G5
Mossman *Australia* 16°21S 145°15E **150** B4
Mossoró *Brazil* 5°10S 37°15W **189** B3
Mossuril *Mozam.* 14°58S 40°42E **143** E5
Mossy Head *U.S.A.* 30°45N 86°19W **179** E3
Mossy Point *Australia* 35°50S 150°11E **153** C9
Most *Czechia* 50°31N 13°38E **78** A6
Mosta *Malta* 35°55N 14°26E **101** D1
Mostaganem *Algeria* 35°54N 0°5E **136** A4
Mostaganem □ *Algeria* 35°40N 0°50E **136** A4
Mostar *Bos.-H.* 43°22N 17°50E **60** G2
Mostardas *Brazil* 31°2S 50°51W **191** C5
Mostiska = Mostyska *Ukraine* 49°48N 23°4E **83** J10
Móstoles *Spain* 40°19N 3°53W **88** E7
Mosty = Masty *Belarus* 53°27N 24°38E **75** B13
Mostyska *Ukraine* 49°48N 23°4E **83** J10
Mosul = Al Mawşil *Iraq* 36°15N 43°5E **105** D10
Mota del Cuervo *Spain* 39°30N 2°52W **91** F2
Mota del Marqués *Spain* 41°38N 5°11W **88** D5
Motagua → *Guatemala* 15°44N 88°14W **182** C2
Motala *Sweden* 58°32N 15°1E **63** F9
Motaze *Mozam.* 24°48S 32°52E **145** B5
Motça *Romania* 47°15N 26°37E **81** C11
Moth *India* 25°43N 78°57E **125** G8
Motherwell *U.K.* 55°47N 3°58W **65** F5
Motihari *India* 26°30N 84°55E **125** F11
Motilla del Palancar *Spain* 39°34N 1°55W **91** F3
Motiti I. *N.Z.* 37°38S 176°25E **154** D5
Motnik *Slovenia* 46°14N 14°54E **93** B11
Motovun *Croatia* 45°20N 13°50E **93** C10
Motozintla de Mendoza *Mexico* 15°22N 92°14W **181** D6
Motril *Spain* 36°31N 3°37W **89** J7
Motru *Romania* 44°48N 22°59E **80** F7
Motru → *Romania* 44°32N 23°31E **81** F8
Mott *U.S.A.* 46°23N 102°20W **172** B2
Mottama, G. of *Myanmar* 16°5N 96°30E **123** L20
Móttola *Italy* 40°38N 17°2E **95** B10
Motu → *N.Z.* 37°52S 177°36E **154** D6
Motueka *N.Z.* 41°7S 173°1E **155** D4
Motueka → *N.Z.* 41°5S 173°1E **155** D4
Motul *Mexico* 21°6N 89°17W **181** C7
Mouchalagane → *Canada* 50°56N 68°41W **165** B6
Mouding *China* 25°20N 101°28E **116** E3
Moudjeria *Mauritania* 17°50N 12°28W **138** B2
Moudon *Switz.* 46°40N 6°49E **77** J2
Moudros *Greece* 39°50N 25°18E **99** B7
Mougins *France* 43°36N 7°0E **73** E10
Mouhoun = Black Volta → *Africa* 8°41N 1°33W **138** D4
Mouila *Gabon* 1°50S 11°0E **140** E2
Moulamein *Australia* 35°3S 144°1E **152** C6
Moule à Chique, C. *St. Lucia* 13°43N 60°57W **183** f
Mouliana *Greece* 35°10N 25°59E **101** D7
Moulins *France* 46°35N 3°19E **71** F10
Moulmein = Mawlamyine *Myanmar* 16°30N 97°40E **123** L20
Moulouya, O. → *Morocco* 35°5N 2°25W **136** A3
Moultrie *U.S.A.* 31°11N 83°47W **178** D6
Moultrie, L. *U.S.A.* 33°20N 80°5W **178** B9
Mound City *Mo., U.S.A.* 40°7N 95°14W **172** E6
Mound City *S. Dak., U.S.A.* 45°44N 100°4W **172** C3
Moundou *Chad* 8°40N 16°10E **135** G9
Moundsville *U.S.A.* 39°55N 80°44W **174** G4
Moung *Cambodia* 12°46N 103°27E **120** F4
Mount Airy *U.S.A.* 36°31N 80°37W **177** C14
Mount Albert *Canada* 44°8N 79°19W **174** B5
Mount Aspiring △ *N.Z.* 44°19S 168°47E **155** E3
Mount Barker *S. Austral., Australia* 35°5S 138°52E **152** B2
Mount Barker *W. Austral., Australia* 34°38S 117°40E **149** F2
Mount Barnett Roadhouse *Australia* 16°39S 125°57E **148** C4
Mount Beauty *Australia* 36°47S 147°10E **153** D7
Mount Brydges *Canada* 42°54N 81°29W **174** D3
Mount Buffalo △ *Australia* 36°43S 146°46E **153** D7
Mount Burr *Australia* 37°34S 140°26E **151** F3
Mount Carleton △ *Canada* 47°25N 66°55W **165** C6
Mount Carmel = Ha Karmel △ *Israel* 32°45N 35°3E **130** C4
Mount Carmel Ill., U.S.A.* 38°25N 87°46W **172** F10
Mount Carmel Pa., U.S.A.* 40°47N 76°26W **175** F8
Mount Clemens *U.S.A.* 42°35N 82°53W **174** D2
Mount Cook *N.Z.* 43°44S 170°5E **155** D5
Mount Cook △ *N.Z.* 43°35S 170°15E **155** D5
Mount Coolon *Australia* 21°25S 147°25E **150** C4
Mount Darwin *Zimbabwe* 16°47S 31°38E **143** F3
Mount Desert I. *U.S.A.* 44°21N 68°20W **173** C19
Mount Dora *U.S.A.* 28°48N 81°38W **179** G8
Mount Ebenezer *Australia* 25°6S 132°34E **149** E5
Mount Eccles △ *Australia* 38°5S 141°54E **152** E4
Mount Edziza △ *Canada* 57°30N 130°45W **162** B2
Mount Elgon △ *E. Afr.* 1°9N 34°42E **142** B3
Mount Field △ *Australia* 42°39S 146°35E **151** G4
Mount Fletcher *S. Africa* 30°40S 28°30E **145** E4
Mount Forest *Canada* 43°59N 80°43W **174** C4
Mount Frankland △ *Australia* 34°47S 116°37E **149** F2
Mount Frederick △ *Australia* 19°39S 129°18E **148** C4
Mount Gambier *Australia* 37°50S 140°46E **152** E3
Mount Garnet *Australia* 17°37S 145°6E **150** B4
Mount Holly *U.S.A.* 39°59N 74°47W **175** G10
Mount Holly Springs *U.S.A.* 40°7N 77°12W **174** F7
Mount Hope *N.S.W., Australia* 32°51S 145°51E **153** B8
Mount Hope *S. Austral., Australia* 34°7S 135°23E **151** E2
Mount Isa *Australia* 20°42S 139°26E **150** C2
Mount James △ *Australia* 24°51S 116°54E **149** D2
Mount Jewett *U.S.A.* 41°44N 78°39W **174** E6
Mount Kaputar △ *Australia* 30°16S 150°10E **151** E5
Mount Kenya △ *Kenya* 0°7S 37°21E **142** C4
Mount Kisco *U.S.A.* 41°12N 73°44W **175** E11
Mount Laguna *U.S.A.* 32°52N 116°25W **171** N10
Mount Larcom *Australia* 23°48S 150°59E **150** C5
Mount Lofty Ranges *Australia* 34°35S 139°5E **152** C3
Mount Magnet *Australia* 28°2S 117°47E **149** E2
Mount Manara *Australia* 32°29S 143°58E **152** B5
Mount Maunganui *N.Z.* 37°40S 176°14E **154** D5
Mount Molloy *Australia* 16°42S 145°20E **150** B4
Mount Morgan *Australia* 23°40S 150°25E **150** C5
Mount Morris *U.S.A.* 42°44N 77°52W **174** D7
Mount Pearl *Canada* 47°31N 52°47W **165** C9
Mount Penn *U.S.A.* 40°20N 75°54W **175** F9
Mount Perry *Australia* 25°13S 151°42E **151** D5
Mount Pleasant *Iowa, U.S.A.* 40°58N 91°33W **172** E8
Mount Pleasant *Mich., U.S.A.* 43°36N 84°46W **173** D11
Mount Pleasant *Pa., U.S.A.* 40°9N 79°33W **174** F5
Mount Pleasant *S.C., U.S.A.* 32°47N 79°52W **178** C10
Mount Pleasant *Tenn., U.S.A.* 35°32N 87°12W **177** D11
Mount Pleasant *Tex., U.S.A.* 33°9N 94°58W **176** E7
Mount Pleasant *Utah, U.S.A.* 39°33N 111°27W **168** G8
Mount Pocono *U.S.A.* 41°7N 75°22W **175** E9
Mount Rainier △ *U.S.A.* 46°55N 121°50W **170** D5
Mount Remarkable △ *Australia* 32°47S 138°3E **152** B3
Mount Revelstoke △ *Canada* 51°5N 118°30W **162** C5
Mount Robson △ *Canada* 53°0N 119°0W **162** C5
Mount St. Helens △ *U.S.A.* 46°14N 122°11W **170** D4
Mount Selinda *Zimbabwe* 20°24S 32°43E **145** B5
Mount Shasta *U.S.A.* 41°19N 122°19W **168** F2
Mount Signal *U.S.A.* 32°39N 115°37W **171** N11
Mount Somers *N.Z.* 43°45S 171°27E **155** D6
Mount Sterling *Ill., U.S.A.* 39°59N 90°45W **172** F8
Mount Sterling *Ky., U.S.A.* 38°4N 83°56W **173** F12
Mount Surprise *Australia* 18°10S 144°17E **150** B3
Mount Union *U.S.A.* 40°23N 77°53W **174** F7
Mount Upton *U.S.A.* 42°26N 75°23W **175** D9
Mount Vernon *Ga., U.S.A.* 32°11N 82°36W **178** D7
Mount Vernon *Ill., U.S.A.* 38°19N 88°55W **172** F9
Mount Vernon *Ind., U.S.A.* 37°56N 87°54W **167** H22
Mount Vernon *N.Y., U.S.A.* 40°54N 73°49W **175** F11
Mount Vernon *Ohio, U.S.A.* 40°23N 82°29W **174** F2
Mount Vernon *Wash., U.S.A.* 48°25N 122°20W **170** B4
Mount Victor *Australia* 32°11S 139°44E **152** B3
Mount Wellington *N.Z.* 36°55S 174°52E **154** C3
Mount William △ *Australia* 40°45S 148°14E **151** G4
Mounta, Akra *Greece* 38°3N 20°47E **98** C2
Mountain Ash *U.K.* 51°40N 3°23W **67** F4
Mountain Center *U.S.A.* 33°42N 116°44W **171** M10
Mountain City *Nev., U.S.A.* 41°50N 115°58W **168** F6
Mountain City *Tenn., U.S.A.* 36°29N 81°48W **177** C14
Mountain Dale *U.S.A.* 41°41N 74°32W **175** E10
Mountain Grove *U.S.A.* 37°8N 92°16W **172** G7
Mountain Home *Ark., U.S.A.* 36°20N 92°23W **176** C8
Mountain Home *Idaho, U.S.A.* 43°8N 115°41W **168** E6
Mountain Iron *U.S.A.* 47°32N 92°37W **172** B7
Mountain Pass *U.S.A.* 35°29N 115°35W **171** K11
Mountain View *Ark., U.S.A.* 35°52N 92°7W **176** D8
Mountain View *Calif., U.S.A.* 37°23N 122°5W **170** H4
Mountain Zebra △ *S. Africa* 32°14S 25°27E **144** D4
Mountainair *U.S.A.* 34°31N 106°15W **169** J10
Mountbellew *Ireland* 53°28N 8°31W **64** C3
Mountlake Terrace *U.S.A.* 47°47N 122°18W **170** C4
Mountmellick *Ireland* 53°7N 7°20W **64** C4
Mountrath *Ireland* 53°0N 7°28W **64** C4
Moura *Australia* 24°35S 149°58E **150** C4
Moura *Brazil* 1°32S 61°38W **186** D6
Mourão *Portugal* 38°22N 7°22W **89** G3
Mourdi, Dépression du *Chad* 18°10N 23°0E **135** E10
Mourdiah *Mali* 14°35N 7°25W **138** C3
Mouri *Ghana* 5°6N 1°14W **139** D4
Mourilyan *Australia* 17°35S 146°3E **150** B4
Mourmelon-le-Grand *France* 49°8N 4°22E **71** C11
Mourne → *U.K.* 54°52N 7°26W **64** B4
Mourne Mts. *U.K.* 54°10N 6°0W **64** B5
Mournies *Greece* 35°29N 24°1E **101** D6
Mouscron *Belgium* 50°45N 3°12E **68** D3
Moussoro *Chad* 13°41N 16°35E **135** F9
Mouthe *France* 46°44N 6°12E **71** F13
Moutier *Switz.* 47°16N 7°21E **77** J3
Moûtiers *France* 45°29N 6°32E **73** C10
Moutong *Indonesia* 0°28N 121°13E **119** D6
Mouy *France* 49°18N 2°20E **71** C9
Mouydir, Monts du *Algeria* 25°30N 4°10E **136** C4
Mouzaki *Greece* 39°25N 21°37E **98** B3
Mouzon *France* 49°36N 5°3E **71** C12
Movas *Mexico* 28°10N 109°25W **180** B3
Moville *Ireland* 55°11N 7°3W **64** A4
Mowandjum *Australia* 17°22S 123°40E **148** C3
Moxotó → *Brazil* 9°19S 38°14W **189** B3
Moy → *Ireland* 54°8N 9°8W **64** B2
Moya *Comoros Is.* 12°18S 44°18E **141** a
Moyale *Ethiopia* 3°34N 39°5E **142** B4
Moyale *Kenya* 3°30N 39°4E **142** B4
Moyamba *S. Leone* 8°4N 12°30W **138** D2
Moyen Atlas *Morocco* 33°0N 5°0W **136** B3
Moyo *Indonesia* 8°10S 117°40E **118** F5
Moyobamba *Peru* 6°0S 77°0W **186** E3
Moyowosi △ *Tanzania* 3°50S 31°0E **142** C3
Møysalen △ *Norway* 68°20N 15°0E **60** B16
Moyu *China* 37°15N 79°44E **109** E9
Moyyero → *Russia* 68°44N 103°42E **107** C11
Moyynqum *Zhambyl, Kazakhstan* 44°17N 72°57E **109** D8
Moyynqum *Zhambyl, Kazakhstan* 44°12N 71°0E **109** D8
Moyynty *Kazakhstan* 47°10N 73°18E **109** C8
Mozambique = Moçambique *Mozam.* 15°3S 40°42E **143** F5
Mozambique ■ *Africa* 19°0S 35°0E **143** F4
Mozambique Basin *Ind. Oc.* 30°0S 40°0E **146** G2
Mozambique Chan. *Africa* 17°30S 42°30E **145** A7
Mozdok *Russia* 43°45N 44°48E **87** J7
Mozdūrān *Iran* 36°9N 60°35E **129** B9
Mozhaysk *Russia* 55°30N 36°2E **84** E9
Mozhga *Russia* 56°26N 52°15E **86** B11
Mozhnābād *Iran* 34°7N 60°6E **129** C9
Mozirje *Slovenia* 46°22N 14°58E **93** B11
Mozyr = Mazyr *Belarus* 51°59N 29°15E **75** B15
Mpanda *Tanzania* 6°23S 31°1E **142** D3
Mpésoba *Mali* 12°31N 5°39W **138** C3
Mphoeng *Zimbabwe* 21°10S 27°51E **143** G2
Mpika *Zambia* 11°51S 31°25E **143** E3
Mpulungu *Zambia* 8°51S 31°5E **143** D3
Mpumalanga *S. Africa* 29°50S 30°33E **145** D5
Mpumalanga □ *S. Africa* 26°0S 30°0E **145** C5
Mpwapwa *Tanzania* 6°23S 36°30E **142** D4
Mqandul *S. Africa* 31°49S 28°45E **145** D4
Mqinvartsveri = Kazbek *Russia* 42°42N 44°30E **87** J7
Mrągowo *Poland* 53°52N 21°18E **82** E8
Mramor *Serbia* 43°20N 21°45E **98** A2
Mrimina *Morocco* 29°50N 7°9W **136** C2
Mrkonjić Grad *Bos.-H.* 44°26N 17°4E **80** F2
Mrkopalj *Croatia* 45°21N 14°52E **93** C11
Mrocza *Poland* 53°16N 17°35E **83** E4
Msaken *Tunisia* 35°49N 10°33E **136** A4
Msambansovu *Zimbabwe* 15°50S 30°3E **143** F3
M'sila *Algeria* 35°46N 4°30E **136** A4
M'sila □ *Algeria* 35°46N 4°30E **136** A4
Msoro *Zambia* 13°35S 31°50E **143** E3
Msta → *Russia* 58°25N 31°20E **84** C6
Mstislavl = Mstsislaw *Belarus* 54°0N 31°50E **75** A16
Mstsislaw *Belarus* 54°0N 31°50E **75** A16
Mszana Dolna *Poland* 49°41N 20°5E **83** D7
Mszczonów *Poland* 51°58N 20°33E **83** G7
Mtama *Tanzania* 10°17S 39°21E **143** E4
Mtamvuna = Mthamvuna → *S. Africa* 31°6S 30°12E **145** D5
Mthamvuna → *S. Africa* 31°6S 30°12E **145** D5
Mtilikwe → *Zimbabwe* 21°9S 31°30E **143** G3
Mtirala △ *Georgia* 41°50N 42°2E **87** K6
Mtito Andei *Kenya* 2°41S 38°10E **142** C4
Mtsensk *Russia* 53°17N 36°36E **84** F9
Mtskheta *Georgia* 41°52N 44°45E **87** K7
Mtubatuba *S. Africa* 28°30S 32°8E **145** D5
Mtwalume *S. Africa* 30°30S 30°38E **145** D5
Mtwara □ *Tanzania* 10°20S 40°20E **143** E5
Mtwara-Mikindani *Tanzania* 10°20S 40°20E **143** E5
Mu Gia, Deo *Vietnam* 17°40N 105°47E **120** D5
Mu Ko Chang △ *Thailand* 11°59N 102°22E **121** G4
Mu Us Shamo *China* 39°0N 109°0E **114** E5
Muang Beng *Laos* 20°23N 101°46E **116** G3
Muang Chiang Rai = Chiang Rai *Thailand* 19°52N 99°50E **116** H2
Muang Et *Laos* 20°49N 104°1E **120** B5
Muang Hiam *Laos* 20°5N 103°22E **120** B4
Muang Hongsa *Laos* 19°43N 101°20E **120** B3
Muang Houn *Laos* 20°8N 101°23E **116** G3
Muang Kau *Laos* 15°6N 105°47E **120** E5
Muang Khao *Laos* 19°38N 103°32E **120** C4
Muang Khong *Laos* 14°7N 105°51E **120** E5
Muang Khoua *Laos* 21°5N 102°31E **116** G4
Muang Liap *Laos* 18°29N 101°40E **120** C3
Muang Mai *Thailand* 8°5N 98°21E **121** a
Muang May *Laos* 14°49N 106°56E **120** E6
Muang Na Mo *Laos* 20°36N 101°3E **116** G3
Muang Ngeun *Laos* 20°36N 101°3E **116** G3
Muang Ngoi *Laos* 20°43N 102°41E **116** G4
Muang Nong *Laos* 16°22N 106°30E **120** D6
Muang Ou Neua *Laos* 22°18N 101°48E **116** F3
Muang Ou Tay *Laos* 22°7N 101°48E **116** F3
Muang Pak Beng *Laos* 19°54N 101°8E **116** H3
Muang Phalane *Laos* 16°39N 105°34E **120** D5
Muang Phiang *Laos* 19°6N 101°32E **120** C3
Muang Phine *Laos* 16°32N 106°2E **120** D6
Muang Phonhong *Laos* 18°30N 102°25E **120** C4
Muang Saiapoun *Laos* 18°24N 101°31E **120** C3
Muang Sing *Laos* 21°11N 101°9E **116** G3
Muang Son *Laos* 20°27N 103°19E **120** B4
Muang Soui *Laos* 19°33N 102°52E **120** C4
Muang Va *Laos* 21°53N 102°19E **116** F4
Muang Va *Laos* 18°18N 101°20E **120** C3
Muang Xai *Laos* 20°42N 101°59E **116** G3
Muang Xamteu *Laos* 19°59N 104°38E **120** C5
Muar *Malaysia* 2°3N 102°34E **121** L4
Muarabungo *Indonesia* 1°28S 102°52E **118** E2
Muaraenim *Indonesia* 3°40S 103°50E **118** E2
Muarajuloi *Indonesia* 0°12S 114°3E **118** E4
Muarakaman *Indonesia* 0°2S 116°45E **118** E5
Muaratebo *Indonesia* 1°30S 102°26E **118** E2
Muaratembesi *Indonesia* 1°42S 103°8E **118** E2
Muaratewe *Indonesia* 0°58S 114°52E **118** E4
Mubarakpur *India* 26°6N 83°18E **125** F10

Mubarraz = Al Mubarraz
Sī. Arabia 25°30N 49°40E 129 E6
Mubende Uganda 0°33N 31°22E 142 B3
Mubi Nigeria 10°18N 13°16E 139 C7
Mucajaí → Brazil 2°25N 60°52W 186 C6
Muchachos, Roque de los
Canary Is. 28°44N 17°52W 100 F2
Müchen Germany 51°17N 11°47E 76 D7
Muchinga Mts. Zambia 11°30S 31°30E 143 E3
Muchinga □ Zambia 12°0S 31°30E 143 E3
Muchkapskiy Russia 51°52N 42°28E 86 E6
Muchuan China 28°57N 103°55E 116 C5
Muck U.K. 56°50N 6°15W 65 E2
Muckadilla Australia 26°35S 148°23E 151 D4
Muckalee Cr. → U.S.A. 31°38N 84°9W 178 D5
Muckaty ○ Australia 18°37S 133°52E 150 B1
Muckle Flugga U.K. 60°51N 0°54W 65 A8
Mucugê Brazil 13°0S 41°23W 189 C2
Mucur Turkey 39°3N 34°22E 104 C6
Mucuri Brazil 18°0S 39°36W 189 D3
Mucurici Brazil 18°6S 40°31W 189 D2
Mucusso Angola 18°1S 21°25E 144 A3
Muda Canary Is. 28°34N 13°57W 100 F6
Mudanjiang China 44°38N 129°30E 115 B15
Mudanya Turkey 40°25N 28°50E 97 F12
Muddebihal India 16°20N 76°8E 127 F3
Muddus △ Sweden 66°58N 20°10E 60 C19
Muddy Cr. → U.S.A. 38°24N 110°42W 168 G8
Mudgee Australia 32°32S 149°31E 153 B8
Mudhol Karnataka, India 16°21N 75°17E 127 F2
Mudhol Telangana, India 18°58N 77°55E 126 E3
Mudigere India 13°8N 75°38E 127 H2
Mudjatik → Canada 56°1N 107°36W 163 B7
Mudumu △ Namibia 18°17S 23°37E 144 A3
Mudurnu Turkey 40°27N 31°12E 104 B4
Muecate Mozam. 14°55S 39°40E 143 E4
Mueda Mozam. 11°36S 39°28E 143 E4
Mueller Ranges
Australia 18°18S 126°46E 148 C4
Muende Mozam. 14°28S 33°0E 143 E3
Muerto, Mar Mexico 16°10N 94°10W 181 D6
Mufu Shan China 29°20N 114°30E 117 C10
Mufulira Zambia 12°32S 28°15E 143 E2
Mufumbiro Range
Africa 1°25S 29°30E 142 C2
Mugardos Spain 43°27N 8°15W 88 B2
Muge → Portugal 39°8N 8°44W 89 F2
Múggia Italy 45°36N 13°46E 93 C10
Mughal Sarai India 25°18N 83°7E 125 G10
Mughalzhar Taūy
Kazakhstan 49°0N 58°40E 108 C3
Mughayrā' Sī. Arabia 29°17N 37°41E 128 D3
Mugi Japan 33°40N 134°25E 113 H7
Mugia = Muxía Spain 43°3N 9°10W 88 B1
Mugila, Mts.
Dem. Rep. of the Congo 7°0S 28°50E 142 D2
Muğla Turkey 37°15N 28°22E 99 D10
Muğla □ Turkey 37°15N 28°0E 99 D10
Mugodzhary = Mughalzhar Taūy
Kazakhstan 49°0N 58°40E 108 C3
Mugu Nepal 29°45N 82°30E 125 E10
Mugu Karnali →
Nepal 29°38N 81°51E 125 E10
Muhala
Dem. Rep. of the Congo 5°40S 28°43E 142 D2
Muhammad, Râs Egypt 27°44N 34°16E 128 E2
Muhammad Qol Sudan 20°53N 37°9E 137 C4
Muhammadabad India 26°4N 83°25E 125 F10
Muḥayil Sī. Arabia 18°33N 42°3E 131 D3
Muhesi → Tanzania 7°0S 35°20E 142 D4
Mühlacker Germany 48°57N 8°51E 77 G4
Mühldorf Germany 48°14N 12°32E 77 G8
Mühlhausen Germany 51°12N 10°27E 76 D6
Mühlig Hofmann fjell
Antarctica 72°30S 5°0E 55 D3
Mühlviertel Austria 48°30N 14°10E 78 C7
Muhos Finland 64°47N 25°59E 60 D21
Muhu Estonia 58°36N 23°11E 84 C2
Muhutwe Tanzania 1°35S 31°45E 142 C3
Mui Wo China 22°16N 114°0E 111 a
Muileann gCearr, An = Mullingar
Ireland 53°31N 7°21W 64 C4
Muine Bheag = Bagenalstown
Ireland 52°42N 6°58W 64 D5
Muineachán = Monaghan
Ireland 54°15N 6°57W 64 B5
Muir, L. Australia 34°30S 116°40E 149 F2
Muir of Ord U.K. 57°32N 4°28W 65 D4
Mujeres, I. Mexico 21°13N 86°43W 182 B2
Muka, Tanjung
Malaysia 5°28N 100°11E 121 c
Mukacheve Ukraine 48°27N 22°45E 80 D7
Mukachevo = Mukacheve
Ukraine 48°27N 22°45E 80 D7
Mukah Malaysia 2°55N 112°5E 118 D4
Mukandwara India 24°49N 75°59E 124 G6
Mukawwa, Geziret
Egypt 23°55N 35°53E 137 C4
Mukawwar Sudan 20°50N 37°17E 137 C4
Mukdahan Thailand 16°32N 104°43E 120 D5
Mukdahan △ Thailand 16°26N 104°45E 120 D5
Mukden = Shenyang
China 41°48N 123°27E 115 D12
Mukerian India 31°57N 75°37E 124 D6
Mukhavets → Belarus 52°29N 23°39E 83 F10
Mukher India 18°42N 77°22E 126 E3
Mukhtolovo Russia 55°29N 43°15E 86 C6
Mukinbudin Australia 30°55S 118°5E 149 F2
Mukishi
Dem. Rep. of the Congo 8°30S 24°44E 143 D1
Muko Phetra △ Thailand 6°59N 99°33E 121 d2
Mukomuko Indonesia 2°30S 101°10E 118 E2
Mukomwenze
Dem. Rep. of the Congo 6°49S 27°15E 142 D2
Mukono Uganda 0°21N 32°45E 142 B3
Muktinath Nepal 28°49N 83°53E 125 E10
Muktsar India 30°30N 74°30E 124 D6
Mukur = Moqor
Afghan. 32°50N 67°42E 124 C2
Mukutuwa → Canada 53°10N 97°24W 163 C9
Mukwela Zambia 17°0S 26°40E 143 F2
Mul India 20°4N 79°40E 126 D4
Mula Spain 38°3N 1°33W 91 G3
Mula → India 18°34N 74°21E 126 D2
Mula → Pakistan 27°57N 67°36E 124 F2
Mulange
Dem. Rep. of the Congo 3°40S 27°10E 142 C2
Mulanje, Mt. Malawi 16°5S 35°33E 143 F4
Mulbagal India 13°15N 78°13E 127 H3
Mulberry U.S.A. 27°54N 81°59W 179 H8
Mulchatna → U.S.A. 59°40N 157°7W 166 D8

Mulchén Chile 37°45S 72°20W 190 D1
Mulde → Germany 51°53N 12°15E 76 D8
Mule Creek Junction
U.S.A. 43°23N 104°13W 168 E11
Muleba Tanzania 1°50S 31°37E 142 C3
Mulegé Mexico 26°53N 111°59W 180 B2
Muleshoe U.S.A. 34°13N 102°43W 176 H3
Mulgrave Canada 45°38N 61°31W 165 C7
Mulgrave I. = Badu
Australia 10°7S 142°11E 150 a
Mulhacén Spain 37°4N 3°20W 89 H7
Mülheim Germany 51°25N 6°54E 76 D2
Mulhouse France 47°40N 7°20E 71 E14
Muli China 27°52N 101°8E 116 D3
Muling China 44°35N 130°10E 115 B16
Mulki India 13°6N 74°48E 127 H2
Mull U.K. 56°25N 5°56W 65 E3
Mull, Sound of U.K. 56°30N 5°50W 65 E3
Mullach Íde = Malahide
Ireland 53°26N 6°9W 64 C5
Mullaittivu Sri Lanka 9°15N 80°49E 127 L5
Mullan U.S.A. 42°3N 101°1W 172 D3
Mullengudgery
Australia 31°43S 147°23E 151 B4
Mullens U.S.A. 37°35N 81°23W 173 G13
Muller, Pegunungan
Indonesia 0°30N 113°30E 118 D4
Mullet Pen. Ireland 54°13N 10°2W 64 B1
Mullewa Australia 28°29S 115°30E 149 E2
Müllheim Germany 47°47N 7°36E 77 H3
Mulligan → Australia 25°0S 139°0E 150 D2
Mullingar Ireland 53°31N 7°21W 64 C4
Mullins U.S.A. 34°12N 79°15W 177 D15
Mullsjö Sweden 57°56N 13°55E 63 G7
Mullumbimby
Australia 28°30S 153°30E 151 D5
Mulobezi Zambia 16°45S 25°7E 143 F2
Mulonga Plain Zambia 16°20S 22°40E 141 H4
Mulroy B. Ireland 55°15N 7°46W 64 A4
Mulshi L. India 18°30N 73°48E 126 E1
Multai India 21°50N 78°21E 126 D4
Multan Pakistan 30°15N 71°36E 124 D4
Mulug India 18°11N 79°57E 126 E4
Mulumbe, Mts.
Dem. Rep. of the Congo 8°40S 27°30E 143 D2
Mulungushi Dam
Zambia 14°48S 28°48E 143 E2
Mulurulu L. Australia 33°15S 143°20E 152 B5
Mulwad Sudan 18°45N 30°39E 137 D3
Mulwala Australia 35°59S 146°0E 153 D5
Mulwala, L. Australia 35°59S 146°1E 151 C4
Mumbai India 18°56N 72°50E 126 E1
Mumbwa Zambia 15°0S 27°0E 143 F2
Mumias Kenya 0°20N 34°29E 142 C4
Mummel Gulf △
Australia 31°17S 151°51E 153 A9
Mumra Russia 45°45N 47°41E 87 H8
Mun → Thailand 15°19N 105°30E 120 E5
Munabao India 25°45N 70°17E 124 G4
Munamagi Estonia 57°43N 27°4E 84 D4
Munaung Myanmar 18°45N 93°40E 123 K18
Munaung I. = Cheduba I.
Myanmar 18°45N 93°40E 123 K18
Muncan Indonesia 8°34S 115°11E 119 K18
Munch'ŏn N. Korea 39°14N 127°19E 115 E14
Muncie U.S.A. 40°12N 85°23W 173 E11
Muncoonie L. West
Australia 25°12S 138°40E 150 D2
Mundabbera Australia 25°36S 151°18E 151 D5
Mundakayam India 9°30N 76°50E 127 K3
Mundal Sri Lanka 7°48N 79°48E 127 L4
Munday U.S.A. 33°27N 99°38W 176 E5
Mundemba Cameroon 4°57N 8°52E 139 E6
Münden Germany 51°25N 9°38E 76 D5
Münden = Hann. Münden
Germany 51°25N 9°38E 76 D5
Mundiwindi Australia 23°47S 120°9E 148 D3
Mundo → Spain 38°30N 1°15W 91 G2
Mundo Novo Brazil 11°50S 40°29W 189 C2
Mundra India 22°54N 69°48E 124 H3
Mundrabilla Australia 31°52S 127°51E 149 F4
Munera Spain 39°2N 2°29W 91 F2
Muneru → India 16°45N 80°3E 126 F5
Mungallala Australia 26°28S 147°34E 151 D4
Mungallala Cr. →
Australia 28°53S 147°5E 151 D4
Mungana Australia 17°8S 144°27E 150 B3
Mungaoli India 24°24N 78°7E 124 G8
Mungari Mozam. 17°12S 33°30E 143 F3
Mungbere
Dem. Rep. of the Congo 2°36N 28°28E 142 B2
Mungeli India 22°4N 81°41E 125 H9
Munger India 25°23N 86°30E 125 G12
Mungerannie Australia 28°1S 138°39E 151 A2
Mungilli △ Australia 25°14S 124°17E 149 E3
Mungkan Kandju △
Australia 13°35S 142°52E 150 A3
Mungkarta ◎ Australia 20°22S 134°2E 150 C1
Mungo, L. Australia 33°45S 143°0E 152 B5
Mungo △ Australia 33°44S 143°6E 152 B5
Munich = München
Germany 48°8N 11°34E 77 G7
Munising U.S.A. 46°25N 86°40W 172 B10
Munka-Ljungby Sweden 56°16N 12°58E 63 H6
Munkebo Denmark 55°27N 10°34E 63 J4
Munkedal Sweden 58°28N 11°40E 63 F5
Munkfors Sweden 59°47N 13°30E 62 E7
Munku-Sardyk
Russia 51°45N 100°20E 107 D11
Münnerstadt Germany 50°14N 10°12E 77 E6
Munnsville U.S.A. 42°59N 75°35W 175 D9
Muñoz Gamero, Pen.
Chile 52°30S 73°5W 192 D2
Munroe L. Canada 59°13N 98°35W 163 B9
Munsan S. Korea 37°51N 126°48E 115 F14
Munson U.S.A. 30°52N 86°52W 179 D12
Münster France 48°2N 7°8E 71 D14
Münster Niedersachsen,
Germany 52°59N 10°5E 76 C6
Münster Nordrhein-Westfalen,
Germany 51°58N 7°37E 76 D3

Munster □ Ireland 52°18N 8°44W 64 D3
Muntadgin Australia 31°45S 118°33E 149 F2
Muntele Mare, Vf.
Romania 46°30N 23°12E 81 D8
Muntok Indonesia 2°5S 105°10E 118 E3
Munzur Dağları Turkey 39°30N 39°10E 105 C8
Muong Nhie Vietnam 22°12N 102°28E 116 F4
Muong Sen Vietnam 19°24N 104°8E 120 C5
Muong Te Vietnam 22°24N 102°49E 116 F4
Muong Xia Vietnam 20°50N 104°44E 120 B5
Muonio Finland 67°57N 23°40E 60 C20
Muonio älv = Muonionjoki →
Finland 67°11N 23°34E 60 C20
Muonioälven = Muonionjoki →
Finland 67°11N 23°34E 60 C20
Muonionjoki →
Finland 67°11N 23°34E 60 C20
Mupa → Mozam. 18°58S 35°54E 143 F4
Muping China 37°22N 121°36E 115 F11
Muqdisho Somalia 2°2N 45°25E 131 G4
Mur → Austria 48°18N 16°52E 79 E9
Muradiye Manisa, Turkey 38°39N 27°21E 99 C9
Muradiye Van, Turkey 38°59N 43°44E 105 C10
Murakami Japan 38°14N 139°29E 112 E9
Muralag = Prince of Wales I.
Australia 10°40S 142°10E 150 A3
Murallón, Cerro Chile 49°48S 73°30W 192 C2
Muranda Rwanda 1°52S 29°20E 142 C2
Murang'a Kenya 0°45S 37°9E 142 C4
Murashi Russia 59°30N 49°0E 106 D5
Murat France 45°7N 2°53E 72 C6
Murat → Turkey 38°46N 40°0E 105 C9
Murat Dağı Turkey 38°55N 29°43E 99 C11
Muratlı Turkey 41°10N 27°29E 97 F11
Murato France 42°35N 9°20E 73 F13
Murau Austria 47°6N 14°10E 78 D7
Murava Belarus 52°39N 24°15E 83 F11
Muravera Italy 39°25N 9°34E 94 C2
Murayama Japan 38°30N 140°25E 112 E10
Murça Portugal 41°24N 7°28W 88 D3
Murchison N.Z. 41°49S 172°21E 155 D5
Murchison → Australia 27°45S 114°0E 149 E1
Murchison, Mt.
Antarctica 73°25S 166°20E 55 D11
Murchison, Mt. N.Z. 43°0S 171°22E 155 D6
Murchison Falls Uganda 2°15N 31°30E 142 B3
Murchison Falls △
Uganda 2°17N 31°48E 142 B3
Murchison Mts. N.Z. 45°13S 167°23E 155 F2
Murchison Ra.
Australia 20°0S 134°10E 150 C1
Murchison Rapids
Malawi 15°55S 34°35E 143 F3
Murchison Roadhouse
Australia 27°39S 116°14E 149 E2
Murcia Spain 38°5N 1°10W 91 G3
Murcia □ Spain 37°50N 1°30W 91 H3
Murdo U.S.A. 43°53N 100°43W 172 D3
Murdoch Pt. Australia 14°37S 144°55E 150 A3
Mürefte Turkey 40°40N 27°14E 97 F11
Mureş → Romania 46°45N 24°40E 81 D8
Mureş □ Romania 46°15N 20°13E 80 D5
Mureşul = Mureş →
Romania 46°15N 20°13E 80 D5
Muret France 43°30N 1°20E 72 E5
Murewa Zimbabwe 17°39S 31°47E 145 A5
Murfreesboro N.C.,
U.S.A. 36°27N 77°6W 177 C16
Murfreesboro Tenn.,
U.S.A. 35°51N 86°24W 177 D11
Murgap Tajikistan 38°10N 74°2E 109 E8
Murgap → Turkmenistan 38°18N 61°12E 129 B9
Murgenella Australia 11°34S 132°56E 148 B5
Murgeni Romania 46°12N 28°1E 81 D13
Murgha Kibzai
Pakistan 30°44N 69°25E 124 D3
Murghob = Murgap
Tajikistan 38°10N 74°2E 109 E8
Murgon Australia 26°15S 151°54E 151 D5
Muri India 23°22N 85°52E 125 H11
Muria Indonesia 6°36S 110°53E 119 L14
Muriaé Brazil 21°8S 42°23W 191 A7
Murias de Paredes Spain 42°52N 6°11W 88 C4
Murici Brazil 9°19S 35°56W 189 B3
Muriel Mine Zimbabwe 17°14S 30°40E 143 D5
Müritz Germany 53°25N 12°42E 76 B8
Müritz □ Germany 53°22N 12°55E 76 B8
Muriwai Beach N.Z. 36°50S 174°26E 154 C3
Murliganj India 25°54N 86°59E 125 G12
Murmansk Russia 68°57N 33°10E 60 B25
Murmashi Russia 68°47N 32°42E 60 B25
Muro France 42°34N 8°54E 73 F12
Muro, C. di France 41°44N 8°37E 73 G12
Muro de Alcoy Spain 38°46N 0°26W 91 G4
Muro Lucano Italy 40°45N 15°29E 95 B8
Murom Russia 55°35N 42°3E 86 C6
Muroran Japan 42°25N 141°0E 112 C10
Muros Spain 42°45N 9°5W 88 C1
Muros e Noya, Ría de →
Spain 42°45N 9°0W 88 C1
Muroto Japan 33°18N 134°9E 113 H7
Muroto-Misaki Japan 33°15N 134°10E 113 H7
Murovani Kurylivtsi
Ukraine 48°44N 27°31E 81 B12
Murowana Goślina
Poland 52°35N 17°0E 83 F3
Murphy U.S.A. 43°13N 116°33W 168 E5
Murphys U.S.A. 38°8N 120°28W 170 G6
Murrat Sudan 18°51N 29°33E 137 D2
Murrat Wells Sudan 21°30N 32°55E 137 C3
Murray Ky., U.S.A. 36°37N 88°19W 172 G9
Murray Utah, U.S.A. 40°40N 111°53W 168 E8
Murray → Australia 35°20S 139°22E 152 C2
Murray, L. U.S.A. 34°3N 81°13W 178 A8
Murray Bridge
Australia 35°6S 139°14E 152 C2
Murray Fracture Zone
Pac. Oc. 35°0N 130°0W 157 D14
Murray Harbour
Canada 46°0N 62°28W 165 C7
Murray River △
Australia 34°23S 140°32E 151 E3
Murray-Sunset △
Australia 34°45S 141°30E 152 C4
Murraysburg S. Africa 31°58S 23°47E 144 E3
Murree Pakistan 33°56N 73°28E 124 C5
Murrieta U.S.A. 33°33N 117°13W 171 M9

Murro di Porco, Capo
Italy 37°0N 15°20E 95 F8
Murrumbateman
Australia 34°58S 149°0E 153 C8
Murrumbidgee →
Australia 34°43S 143°12E 152 C5
Murrumburrah
Australia 34°32S 148°22E 153 C8
Murrundi Australia 31°42S 150°51E 153 A9
Murrupula Mozam. 15°25S 38°52E 143 E4
Murshid Sudan 21°40N 31°10E 137 C3
Murshidabad India 24°11N 88°19E 125 G13
Murska Sobota
Slovenia 46°39N 16°12E 93 B13
Murtazapur India 20°40N 77°25E 126 D3
Murtle L. Canada 52°8N 119°38W 162 C5
Murtoa Australia 36°35S 142°28E 152 C5
Murtosa Portugal 40°44N 8°40E 88 E2
Muru → Brazil 8°9S 70°45W 188 B3
Murud India 18°19N 72°58E 126 E1
Murungu Tanzania 4°12S 31°10E 142 C3
Murupara N.Z. 38°28S 176°42E 154 E5
Mururoa
French Polynesia 21°52S 138°55W 157 K14
Murwara India 23°46N 80°28E 125 H9
Murwillumbah
Australia 28°18S 153°27E 151 D5
Mürz → Austria 47°30N 15°25E 78 D8
Murzüq Libya 25°53N 13°57E 135 C8
Murzuq, Idehän Libya 24°50N 13°51E 135 D8
Mürzzuschlag Austria 47°36N 15°41E 78 D8
Muş Turkey 9°14N 92°47E 127 K11
Muş □ Turkey 38°45N 41°30E 105 C10
Muş □ Turkey 38°45N 41°0E 105 C10
Mûsa, Gebel Egypt 28°33N 33°59E 128 D2
Musa Khel Pakistan 30°59N 69°52E 124 D3
Mûsa Qal'eh Afghan. 32°20N 64°50E 124 C4
Musafirkhana India 26°22N 81°48E 125 F9
Musala Bulgaria 42°13N 23°37E 96 D7
Musala Indonesia 1°41N 98°28E 118 D1
Musan N. Korea 42°12N 129°12E 115 C15
Musangu
Dem. Rep. of the Congo 10°28S 23°55E 143 E1
Musasa Tanzania 3°25S 31°30E 142 C3
Muscat = Masqat
Oman 23°37N 58°36E 131 C6
Muscatine U.S.A. 41°25N 91°3W 172 E8
Muscle Shoals U.S.A. 34°45N 87°40W 177 D11
Musengezi = Unsengedsi →
Zimbabwe 15°43S 31°14E 143 F3
Musgrave Harbour
Canada 49°27N 53°58W 165 C9
Musgrave Ranges
Australia 26°0S 132°0E 149 E5
Mushie
Dem. Rep. of the Congo 2°56S 16°55E 140 C3
Mushin Nigeria 6°31N 3°21E 139 D5
Musi → India 16°41N 79°40E 126 F4
Musi → Indonesia 2°20S 104°56E 118 E2
Musina S. Africa 22°20S 30°5E 145 B5
Musiri India 10°56N 78°27E 127 J4
Muskeg → Canada 60°20N 123°20W 162 A4
Muskegon U.S.A. 43°14N 86°16W 172 D9
Muskegon → U.S.A. 43°14N 86°21W 172 D9
Muskegon Heights
U.S.A. 43°12N 86°16W 172 D10
Muskogee U.S.A. 35°45N 95°22W 176 D7
Muskoka, L. Canada 45°0N 79°25W 174 B5
Muskoka Falls Canada 44°59N 79°17W 174 B5
Muskwa → Canada 58°47N 122°48W 162 B4
Muslimiyah Syria 36°19N 37°12E 128 B3
Musmar Sudan 18°13N 35°40E 137 D4
Musofu Zambia 13°30S 29°0E 143 E2
Musoma Tanzania 1°30S 33°48E 142 C3
Musquaro, L. Canada 50°38N 61°5W 165 B7
Musquodoboit Harbour
Canada 44°50N 63°9W 165 D7
Musselburgh U.K. 55°57N 3°2W 65 F5
Musselshell →
U.S.A. 47°21N 107°57W 168 C10
Mussende Angola 10°32S 16°5E 140 G3
Mussidan France 45°2N 0°22E 72 C4
Mussomeli Italy 37°35N 13°45E 94 E6
Mussoorie India 30°27N 78°6E 124 D8
Mussuco Angola 17°2S 19°3E 144 A2
Mustafakemalpaşa
Turkey 40°2N 28°24E 97 F12
Mustang Nepal 29°10N 83°55E 125 E10
Musters, L. Argentina 45°20S 69°25W 192 C3
Musudan N. Korea 40°50N 129°43E 115 D15
Muswellbrook
Australia 32°16S 150°56E 153 B9
Muszyna Poland 49°22N 20°55E 83 J7
Mût Egypt 25°28N 28°58E 137 B2
Mut Turkey 36°40N 33°28E 104 D5
Mutanda Mozam. 21°0S 33°34E 145 B5
Mutanda Zambia 12°24S 26°13E 143 E2
Mutare Zimbabwe 18°58S 32°38E 143 F3
Mutawintji △
Australia 31°10S 142°30E 151 E3
Mutha Kenya 1°48S 38°26E 142 C4
Muting Indonesia 7°23S 140°20E 119 F10
Mutirikwe Dam
Zimbabwe 20°15S 31°0E 143 G3
Mutki = Mirtağ Turkey 38°23N 41°56E 128 B4
Mutoko Zimbabwe 17°24S 32°13E 145 A5
Mutomo Kenya 1°51S 38°12E 142 C4
Mutoray Russia 60°56N 101°0E 107 C11
Mutsamudu Comoros Is. 12°10S 44°25E 141 a
Mutshatsha
Dem. Rep. of the Congo 10°35S 24°20E 143 E1
Mutsu Japan 41°5N 140°55E 112 D10
Mutsu-Wan Japan 41°5N 140°55E 112 D10
Muttaburra Australia 22°38S 144°29E 150 C3
Muttalip Turkey 39°50N 30°32E 99 B12
Mutton I. Ireland 52°49N 9°32W 64 D2
Mutual U.S.A. 14°16N 80°6E 127 G5
Mutum Biyu Nigeria 8°40N 10°50E 139 D7
Mutur Sri Lanka 8°27N 81°16E 127 K5
Muweilih Egypt 30°42N 34°19E 128 E3
Muxía Spain 43°9N 9°10W 88 B1
Muy Muy Nic. 12°39N 85°36W 182 E3
Muyinga Burundi 3°14S 30°33E 142 C3
Muynoq Uzbekistan 43°44N 59°10E 108 D6
Muyunkum, Peski = Moyynqum
Kazakhstan 44°12N 71°0E 108 C8
Muz Tag China 36°25N 87°25E 109 E11
Muzaffarabad Pakistan 34°25N 73°30E 124 C5
Muzaffargarh Pakistan 30°5N 71°14E 124 D4
Muzaffarnagar India 29°26N 77°40E 124 E7

Muzaffarpur India 26°7N 85°23E 125 F11
Muzaffirpur Pakistan 30°58N 69°9E 124 D3
Mużakowski, Park =
Muskauer
Park Europe 51°34N 14°43E 76 D10
Muzhi Russia 65°25N 64°40E 106 C7
Muzillac France 47°35N 2°30W 70 E4
Muztagh-Ata China 38°17N 75°7E 109 E9
Mvadi Gabon 1°13N 13°12E 140 D2
Mvam Zimbabwe 19°16S 30°30E 143 F3
Mvuma Zimbabwe 17°0S 30°57E 143 F3
Mvurwi Zimbabwe 17°0S 30°57E 143 F3
Mwabvi △ Malawi 16°42S 35°0E 143 F3
Mwadui Tanzania 3°26S 33°32E 142 C3
Mwali = Mohéli
Comoros Is. 12°20S 43°40E 141 a
Mwambo Tanzania 10°30S 40°22E 143 E5
Mwandi Zambia 17°30S 24°51E 143 F1
Mwanza
Dem. Rep. of the Congo 7°55S 26°43E 142 D2
Mwanza Tanzania 2°30S 32°58E 142 C3
Mwanza Zambia 16°58S 24°28E 143 F1
Mwanza □ Tanzania 2°0S 33°0E 142 C3
Mwaya Tanzania 9°32S 33°55E 143 D3
Mweelrea Ireland 53°39N 9°49W 64 C2
Mweka
Dem. Rep. of the Congo 4°50S 21°34E 140 C4
Mwenezi Zimbabwe 21°15S 30°48E 143 G3
Mwenezi → Mozam. 22°40S 31°50E 143 G3
Mwenga
Dem. Rep. of the Congo 3°1S 28°28E 142 C2
Mweru, L. Zambia 9°0S 28°40E 143 D2
Mweru Wantipa △
Zambia 8°39S 29°25E 143 D2
Mweza Range Zimbabwe 21°0S 30°0E 143 G3
Mwilambwe
Dem. Rep. of the Congo 8°7S 25°5E 142 D2
Mwimbi Tanzania 8°38S 31°39E 143 D3
Mwingi Kenya 0°56S 38°4E 142 C4
Mwinilunga Zambia 11°43S 24°25E 143 E1
My Son Vietnam 15°48N 108°7E 120 E7
My Tho Vietnam 10°29N 106°23E 120 G6
Mya, O. → Algeria 30°46N 4°54E 136 B4
Myajlar India 26°15N 70°20E 124 F4
Myall Lakes △
Australia 32°25S 152°30E 153 B10
Myanaung Myanmar 18°18N 95°22E 123 K19
Myanmar ■ Asia 21°0N 96°30E 123 J20
Myaungmya
Myanmar 16°30N 94°40E 123 L19
Mycenæ = Mykenes
Greece 37°43N 22°46E 98 D4
Myedna Belarus 52°52N 23°42E 83 G10
Myeik = Mergui
Myanmar 12°26N 98°34E 120 F2
Myeik Kyunzu
Myanmar 11°30N 97°30E 121 G1
Myerstown U.S.A. 40°22N 76°19W 175 F8
Myingyan Myanmar 21°30N 95°20E 123 J19
Myitkyina Myanmar 25°24N 97°26E 123 G20
Myjava Slovakia 48°41N 17°37E 79 C10
Mykenes Greece 37°43N 22°46E 98 D4
Mykhaylivka Ukraine 47°12N 35°15E 85 J8
Mykines Faroe Is. 62°7N 7°35W 60 E9
Mykolayiv Ukraine 46°58N 32°0E 85 J7
Mykolayiv □ Ukraine 47°20N 31°50E 85 J6
Mykonos Greece 37°30N 25°25E 98 D7
Mylius Erichsen Land
Greenland 81°30N 27°0W 57 A8
Mymensingh Bangla. 24°45N 90°24E 123 G17
Mynydd Du U.K. 51°52N 3°50W 67 F4
Mýrdalsjökull Iceland 63°40N 19°6W 60 E4
Myrhorod Ukraine 49°58N 33°37E 85 H7
Myrina Greece 39°53N 25°4E 99 B7
Myrtle Beach U.S.A. 33°42N 78°53W 177 E15
Myrtle Creek U.S.A. 43°1N 123°17W 168 E2
Myrtle Grove U.S.A. 30°23N 87°17W 179 E2
Myrtle Point U.S.A. 43°4N 124°8W 168 E1
Myrtleford Australia 36°34S 146°44E 153 D7
Myrtou = Mirtoo Sea
Greece 37°0N 23°20E 98 D5
Myrtou Cyprus 35°18N 33°4E 101 D12
Myrviken Sweden 62°58N 14°20E 62 E8
Mysia Turkey 39°50N 27°0E 97 G11
Myślenice Poland 49°51N 19°57E 83 J6
Myślibórz Poland 52°55N 14°50E 83 F1
Mysłowice Poland 50°15N 19°12E 83 G6
Mysore = Karnataka □
India 13°15N 77°0E 127 H3
Mysore = Mysuru
India 12°17N 76°41E 127 H3
Mystic U.S.A. 41°21N 71°58W 175 E13
Mystras Greece 37°4N 22°25E 98 D4
Mysuru India 12°17N 76°41E 127 H3
Myszków Poland 50°45N 19°22E 83 H6
Mytilene = Mitilini
Greece 39°6N 26°35E 99 B10
Mytishchi Russia 55°50N 37°50E 84 B6
Mývatn Iceland 65°36N 17°0W 60 D5
M'zab, Oued = M'zab, Oued →
Algeria 32°15N 5°0E 136 B5
Mže → Czechia 49°46N 13°24E 78 B6
Mzimba Malawi 11°55S 33°39E 143 E3
Mzimkulu → S. Africa 30°44S 30°28E 145 E5
Mzimvubu → S. Africa 31°38S 29°33E 145 D4
Mzuzu Malawi 11°30S 33°55E 143 E3

N

Na Clocha Liatha = Greystones
Ireland 53°9N 6°4W 64 C5
Na Haeo △ Thailand 17°31N 100°58E 120 D3
Na Hearadh = Harris
U.K. 57°50N 6°55W 65 D2
Na Hearadh, Caolas = Harris, Sd.
of U.K. 57°44N 7°6W 65 D1
Na Noi Thailand 18°19N 100°43E 120 D3
Na Phao Laos 17°35N 105°44E 120 D5
Na Sam Vietnam 22°3N 106°37E 116 F6
Na Sceiri = Skerries
Ireland 53°35N 6°8W 64 C5
Na Thon Thailand 9°32N 99°56E 121 b
Naab → Germany 49°1N 12°2E 77 F8
Naama Algeria 33°30N 0°23W 136 B4
Naama □ Algeria 33°15N 0°15W 136 B4
Naantali Finland 60°29N 22°2E 84 B1
Naas Ireland 53°13N 6°40W 64 C5
Nababeep S. Africa 29°36S 17°46E 144 D2

Nabadwip = Navadwip
India 23°34N 88°20E 125 H13
Nabawa Australia 28°30S 114°48E 149 E1
Nabberu, L. Australia 25°50S 120°30E 149 E3
Nabburg Germany 49°27N 12°11E 77 F8
Naberezhnyye Chelny
Russia 55°42N 52°19E 86 C11
Nabeul Tunisia 36°30N 10°44E 136 A6
Nabeul □ Tunisia 36°30N 10°44E 136 A6
Nabha India 30°26N 76°14E 124 D7
Nabid Iran 29°40N 57°38E 129 D8
Nabire Indonesia 3°15S 135°26E 119 E9
Nabisar Pakistan 25°8N 69°40E 124 G3
Nabisipi → Canada 50°14N 62°13W 165 B7
Nablus = Nābulus
West Bank 32°14N 35°15E 130 C4
Naboomspruit S. Africa 24°32S 28°40E 145 C4
Nabou Burkina Faso 11°25N 2°50W 138 C4
Nabouwalu Fiji 17°0S 178°45E 154 a
Nābulus West Bank 32°14N 35°15E 130 C4
Nacala Mozam. 14°32S 40°34E 143 E5
Nacaome Honduras 13°31N 87°30W 182 D2
Nacaroa Mozam. 14°22S 39°56E 143 E4
Naches U.S.A. 46°44N 120°42W 168 C4
Naches → U.S.A. 46°38N 120°31W 170 D6
Nachicapau, L. Canada 56°40N 68°5W 165 A6
Nachingwea Tanzania 10°23S 38°49E 143 E4
Nachna India 27°34N 71°41E 124 F4
Náchod Czechia 50°25N 16°8E 78 A9
Nachuge India 10°47N 92°21E 127 J11
Nacimiento, L. U.S.A. 35°46N 120°53W 170 K6
Nacka Sweden 59°18N 18°10E 62 E12
Nackara Australia 32°48S 139°12E 152 B3
Naco Mexico 31°19N 109°56W 180 A3
Nacogdoches U.S.A. 31°36N 94°39W 176 F7
Nácori Chico Mexico 29°40N 108°57W 180 B3
Nacozari de García
Mexico 30°25N 109°38W 180 A3
Nacula Fiji 16°54S 177°27E 154 a
Nada = Danzhou China 19°31N 109°33E 117 a
Nådendal = Naantali
Finland 60°29N 22°2E 84 B1
Nadi Fiji 17°42S 177°20E 154 a
Nadi Sudan 18°40N 33°41E 137 D3
Nadiad India 22°41N 72°56E 124 H5
Nădlac Romania 46°10N 20°50E 80 D5
Nador Morocco 35°14N 2°58W 136 A3
Nadur Malta 36°2N 14°18E 101 C1
Nadvirna Ukraine 48°37N 24°30E 81 B9
Nadvornaya = Nadvirna
Ukraine 48°37N 24°30E 81 B9
Nadym Russia 65°35N 72°42E 106 C8
Nadym → Russia 66°12N 72°0E 106 C8
Nærbø Norway 58°40N 5°39E 63 G11
Næstved Denmark 55°13N 11°44E 63 J5
Nafada Nigeria 11°8N 11°20E 139 C7
Nafarroa = Navarra □
Spain 42°40N 1°40W 90 C3
Nafpaktos Greece 38°24N 21°50E 98 C3
Nafplio Greece 37°33N 22°50E 98 D4
Naft-e Safid Iran 31°40N 49°17E 129 D6
Naftshahr Iran 34°0N 45°30E 105 E11
Nafud Desert = An Nafūd
Sī. Arabia 28°15N 41°0E 128 D4
Nag Hammâdi Egypt 26°2N 32°18E 137 B3
Naga Phil. 13°38N 123°15E 119 B6
Naga, Kreb en Africa 24°12N 6°0W 136 D2
Nagagami → Canada 50°23N 84°20W 164 B3
Nagahama Japan 35°23N 136°16E 113 G8
Nagai Japan 38°6N 140°2E 112 E10
Nagaland □ India 26°0N 94°30E 123 G19
Nagambie Australia 36°47S 145°10E 153 D6
Nagano Japan 36°40N 138°10E 113 F9
Nagano □ Japan 36°15N 138°0E 113 F9
Nagaoka Japan 37°27N 138°51E 113 F9
Nagaon India 26°20N 92°50E 123 F18
Nagappattinam India 10°46N 79°51E 127 J4
Nagar → Bangla. 24°27N 89°12E 125 G13
Nagar Karnul India 16°29N 78°20E 127 F4
Nagar Parkar Pakistan 24°28N 70°46E 124 G4
Nagaram India 18°21N 80°26E 126 E5
Nagarhole △ India 12°0N 76°10E 127 J3
Nagari Hills India 13°3N 79°45E 127 H4
Nagarjuna Sagar India 16°30N 79°13E 127 F4
Nagasaki Japan 32°47N 129°50E 113 H4
Nagasaki □ Japan 32°50N 129°40E 113 H4
Nagato Japan 34°19N 131°5E 113 G5
Nagaur India 27°15N 73°45E 124 F5
Nagbhir India 20°34N 79°55E 126 D4
Nagda India 23°27N 75°25E 124 H6
Nagercoil India 8°12N 77°26E 127 K3
Nagina India 29°30N 78°30E 124 E8
Nagîneh Iran 34°20N 57°15E 129 C8
Nagir Pakistan 36°12N 74°42E 124 A5
Naglarby Sweden 60°25N 15°34E 62 D9
Nagles Mts. Ireland 52°8N 8°30W 64 D3
Nagod India 24°34N 80°35E 125 G9
Nagold Germany 48°32N 8°43E 77 G4
Nagold → Germany 48°52N 8°42E 77 G4
Nagoorin Australia 24°17S 151°15E 150 C5
Nagorno-Karabakh □
Azerbaijan 39°55N 46°45E 105 C12
Nagornyy Russia 55°58N 124°57E 107 D13
Nagoya Japan 35°10N 136°50E 113 G8
Nagoya ✈ (NGO)
Japan 34°53N 136°45E 113 G8
Nagpur India 21°8N 79°10E 126 D4
Nagqu China 31°29N 92°3E 110 E7
Nagua Dom. Rep. 19°23N 69°50W 183 C6
Naguabo Puerto Rico 18°13N 65°44W 183 d
Nagurunguru
Australia 16°45S 129°45E 148 C4
Nagyatád Hungary 46°14N 17°22E 80 E2
Nagyecsed Hungary 47°53N 22°24E 80 C7
Nagykálló Hungary 47°53N 21°51E 80 C6
Nagykanizsa Hungary 46°28N 17°0E 80 C2
Nagykáta Hungary 47°23N 19°48E 80 C4
Nagykőrös Hungary 47°5N 19°48E 80 C4
Naha Japan 26°13N 127°42E 113 L3
Nahan India 30°33N 77°18E 124 D7
Nahanni △ Canada 61°15N 125°48W 162 A3
Nahanni Butte Canada 61°2N 123°31W 162 A4
Nahargarh Mad. P.,
India 24°10N 75°14E 124 G6
Nahargarh Raj., India 24°55N 76°50E 124 G7
Nahariyya Israel 33°1N 35°5E 130 B4
Nahāvand Iran 34°10N 48°22E 105 E13
Nahe → Germany 49°58N 7°57E 77 F3
Nahīya, W. → Egypt 28°55N 31°0E 137 C3

Nahuel Huapi, L. Argentina 41°0S 71°32W 192 B2
Nahuel Huapi △ Argentina 41°3S 71°59W 192 B2
Nahuelbuta △ Chile 37°44S 72°57W 190 D1
Nahunta U.S.A. 31°12N 81°59W 178 D8
Nai Yong Thailand 8°14N 98°22E 121 a
Naicá Mexico 27°53N 105°31W 180 B3
Naicam Canada 52°30N 104°30W 163 C8
Naikoon ⌓ Canada 53°55N 131°55W 162 C2
Naikul India 21°20N 84°58E 126 D7
Naila Germany 50°19N 11°42E 77 E7
Naimisharanya India 27°21N 80°30E 125 F9
Naimona'nyi Feng China 30°26N 81°18E 125 D9
Nain Canada 56°34N 61°40W 165 A7
Nā'īn Iran 32°54N 53°0E 129 C7
Naini Tal India 29°30N 79°30E 125 E8
Nainpur India 22°30N 80°10E 125 H9
Naintré France 46°46N 0°29E 70 F7
Nainwa India 25°46N 75°51E 124 G6
Naipu Romania 44°12N 25°47E 81 F10
Nairai Fiji 17°49S 179°15E 154 a
Nairn U.K. 57°35N 3°53W 65 D5
Nairobi Kenya 1°17S 36°48E 142 C4
Nairobi △ Kenya 1°22S 36°50E 142 C4
Naissaar Estonia 59°34N 24°29E 84 C3
Naitaba Fiji 17°0S 179°16W 154 a
Naivasha Kenya 0°40S 36°30E 142 C4
Naivasha, L. Kenya 0°48S 36°20E 142 C4
Najac France 44°14N 1°58E 72 D5
Najaf = An Najaf Iraq 32°3N 44°15E 105 G11
Najafābād Iran 32°40N 51°15E 129 C6
Najd Si. Arabia 26°30N 42°0E 131 B3
Nájera Spain 42°26N 2°48W 90 C2
Najerilla → Spain 42°32N 2°48W 90 C2
Najibabad India 29°40N 78°20E 124 E8
Najin N. Korea 42°12N 130°15E 115 C16
Najmah Si. Arabia 26°42N 50°6E 129 E6
Najrān Si. Arabia 17°34N 44°18E 131 D3
Naju S. Korea 35°3N 126°43E 115 G14
Nakadōri-Shima Japan 32°57N 129°4E 113 H4
Nakalagba Dem. Rep. of the Congo 2°50N 27°58E 142 B2
Nakambé = White Volta → Ghana 9°10N 1°15W 139 D4
Nakaminato Japan 36°21N 140°36E 113 F10
Nakamura = Shimanto Japan 32°59N 132°56E 113 H6
Nakano Japan 36°45N 138°22E 113 F9
Nakano-Shima Japan 29°51N 129°52E 113 K4
Nakashibetsu Japan 43°33N 144°59E 112 C12
Nakfa Eritrea 16°40N 38°32E 131 D2
Nakha Yai, Ko Thailand 8°3N 98°28E 121 a
Nakhichevan = Naxçıvan Azerbaijan 39°12N 45°15E 105 C11
Nakhichevan Rep. = Naxçıvan □ Azerbaijan 39°25N 45°26E 105 C11
Nakhl Egypt 29°55N 33°43E 130 F2
Nakhl-e Taqī Iran 27°28N 52°36E 129 E7
Nakhodka Russia 42°53N 132°54E 112 C6
Nakhon Nayok Thailand 14°12N 101°13E 120 E3
Nakhon Pathom Thailand 13°49N 100°3E 120 F3
Nakhon Phanom Thailand 17°23N 104°43E 120 D5
Nakhon Ratchasima Thailand 14°59N 102°12E 120 E4
Nakhon Sawan Thailand 15°35N 100°10E 120 E3
Nakhon Si Thammarat Thailand 8°29N 100°0E 121 H3
Nakhon Thai Thailand 17°5N 100°44E 120 D3
Nakhtarana India 23°20N 69°15E 124 H3
Nakina Canada 50°10N 86°40W 164 B2
Nakło nad Notecią Poland 53°9N 17°38E 83 E4
Nako Burkina Faso 10°40N 3°4W 138 C4
Nakodar India 31°8N 75°31E 124 D6
Nakskov Denmark 54°50N 11°8E 63 K5
Naktong → S. Korea 35°7N 128°57E 115 G15
Nakuru Kenya 0°15S 36°4E 142 C4
Nakuru, L. Kenya 0°23S 36°5E 142 C4
Nakusp Canada 50°20N 117°45W 162 C5
Nal Pakistan 27°40N 66°12E 124 F2
Nal → Pakistan 25°20N 65°30E 124 G1
Nalázi Mozam. 24°3S 33°20E 145 B5
Nalchik Russia 43°30N 43°33E 87 J6
Nałęczów Poland 51°17N 22°9E 83 G9
Nalerigu Ghana 10°35N 0°25W 139 C4
Nalgonda India 17°6N 79°15E 126 F4
Nalhati India 24°17N 87°52E 125 G12
Naliya India 23°16N 68°50E 124 H3
Nallamalai Hills India 15°30N 78°50E 127 G4
Nallıhan Turkey 40°11N 31°20E 104 B4
Nalón → Spain 43°32N 6°4W 88 B4
Nalubaale Dam Uganda 0°30N 33°5E 142 B3
Nalumasortoq Greenland 60°23N 44°28W 57 E6
Nam Can Vietnam 8°46N 104°59E 121 H5
Nam-ch'on N. Korea 38°15N 126°26E 115 E14
Nam Co China 30°30N 90°45E 110 E7
Nam Dinh Vietnam 20°25N 106°5E 116 G6
Nam Du, Quan Dao Vietnam 9°41N 104°21E 121 H5
Nam Hka → Myanmar 21°34N 95°41E 116 G2
Nam Loi → Myanmar 21°3N 98°27E 116 G3
Nam Nao △ Thailand 16°44N 101°32E 120 D3
Nam Ngum Res. Laos 18°35N 102°34E 120 C4
Nam Phan Vietnam 10°30N 106°0E 121 G6
Nam Phong Thailand 16°42N 102°52E 120 D4
Nam Theun Res. Laos 17°51N 105°3E 120 D5
Nam Tok Thailand 14°21N 99°4E 120 E2
Nam Un Res. Thailand 17°13N 103°44E 120 D4
Namacunde Angola 17°18S 15°50E 144 A2
Namacurra Mozam. 17°30S 36°50E 145 A6
Namadgi △ Australia 35°42S 149°0E 153 C8
Namak, Daryācheh-ye Iran 34°30N 52°0E 129 C7
Namak, Kavir-e Iran 34°30N 57°30E 129 C8
Namakkal India 11°13N 78°13E 127 J4
Namakzār, Daryācheh-ye Iran 34°0N 60°30E 129 C9
Namaland Namibia 26°0S 17°0E 144 B2
Namanga Kenya 2°33S 36°47E 142 C4
Namangan Uzbekistan 41°0N 71°40E 109 D8
Namangan □ Uzbekistan 41°0N 71°15E 109 D8
Namapa Mozam. 13°43S 39°50E 143 E4
Namaqua △ S. Africa 30°0S 17°30E 144 D2
Namaqualand S. Africa 30°0S 17°25E 144 D2
Namasagali Uganda 1°2N 33°0E 142 B3
Namber Indonesia 1°2S 134°49E 119 E8
Nambour Australia 26°32S 152°58E 151 D5
Nambouwalu = Nabouwalu Fiji 17°0S 178°45E 154 a
Nambucca Heads Australia 30°37S 153°0E 153 A10
Nambung △ Australia 30°30S 115°5E 149 F2
Namcha Barwa China 29°40N 95°10E 110 F8
Namche Bazar Nepal 27°51N 86°47E 125 F12
Namchonjŏm = Nam-ch'on N. Korea 38°15N 126°26E 115 E14
Namecunda Mozam. 14°54S 37°37E 143 E4
Namenalala Fiji 17°8S 179°9E 154 a
Nameponda Mozam. 15°50S 39°50E 143 F4
Náměšť nad Oslavou Czechia 49°12N 16°10E 79 B9
Námestovo Slovakia 49°24N 19°25E 79 B12
Nametil Mozam. 15°40S 39°21E 143 F4
Namew L. Canada 54°14N 101°56W 163 C8
Namgia India 31°48N 78°40E 125 D8
Namhkam Myanmar 23°50N 97°41E 116 E1
Namialo Mozam. 14°55S 39°59E 143 E4
Namib Desert Namibia 22°30S 15°0E 144 B2
Namib-Naukluft ⌓ Namibia 24°40S 15°16E 144 B2
Namibe Angola 15°7S 12°11E 141 H2
Namibe □ Angola 16°35S 12°30E 144 A1
Namibia ■ Africa 22°0S 18°9E 144 B2
Namibia Abyssal Plain Atl. Oc. 30°0S 5°30E 56 J12
Namibwoestyn = Namib Desert Namibia 22°30S 15°0E 144 B2
Namīn Iran 38°25N 48°30E 105 C13
Naminüs = Lubango Angola 14°55S 13°30E 141 G2
Naminüs = Lüderitz Namibia 26°41S 15°8E 144 C2
Namjeju S. Korea 33°14N 126°33E 115 H14
Namlea Indonesia 3°18S 127°5E 119 E7
Namoi → Australia 30°12S 149°30E 153 A9
Namous, O. en → Algeria 31°0N 0°15W 136 B3
Nampa U.S.A. 43°34N 116°34W 168 E5
Nampala Mali 15°20N 5°30W 138 B3
Namp'o N. Korea 38°52N 125°10E 115 E13
Nampō-Shotō Japan 32°0N 140°0E 113 J10
Nampula Mozam. 15°6S 39°15E 143 F4
Namrole Indonesia 3°46S 126°46E 119 E7
Namse Shankou China 30°0N 82°25E 125 E10
Namsen → Norway 64°28N 11°37E 60 D14
Namsos Norway 64°29N 11°30E 60 D14
Namtok Chat Trakan △ Thailand 17°17N 100°40E 120 D3
Namtok Huay Yang △ Thailand 11°35N 99°30E 121 G2
Namtok Mae Surin △ Thailand 18°55N 98°2E 120 C2
Namtok Ngao △ Thailand 9°58N 98°46E 121 H2
Namtok Phlew △ Thailand 12°32N 102°13E 120 F4
Namtok Yong △ Thailand 8°15N 98°45E 121 H2
Namtsy Russia 62°43N 129°37E 107 C13
Namtu Myanmar 23°5N 97°28E 123 H20
Namtumbo Tanzania 10°30S 36°4E 143 E4
Namu Canada 51°52N 127°50W 162 C3
Namuka-i-Lau Fiji 18°53S 178°37W 154 a
Namur Belgium 50°27N 4°52E 69 D4
Namur □ Belgium 50°17N 5°0E 69 D4
Namuruputh Kenya 4°34N 35°57E 142 B4
Namutoni Namibia 18°49S 16°55E 144 A2
Namwala Zambia 15°44S 26°30E 143 F2
Namwon S. Korea 35°23N 127°23E 115 G14
Namyang N. Korea 42°57N 129°52E 115 C15
Namyit I. S. China Sea 10°11N 114°22E 118 C4
Namysłów Poland 51°6N 17°42E 83 G4
Nan Thailand 18°48N 100°46E 120 C3
Nan → Thailand 15°42N 100°9E 120 E3
Nan Ling China 25°0N 112°30E 117 E9
Nan Xian China 29°20N 112°22E 117 C9
Nana Romania 44°17N 26°34E 81 F11
Nana Kru Liberia 4°55N 8°45W 138 E3
Nanaimo Canada 49°10N 124°0W 162 D4
Nānākuli U.S.A. 21°24N 158°9W 167 L8
Nanam N. Korea 41°44N 129°40E 115 D15
Nan'an China 24°59N 118°21E 117 E12
Nanango Australia 26°40S 152°0E 151 D5
Nan'ao China 23°28N 117°5E 117 F11
Nanao Japan 37°0N 137°0E 113 F8
Nanbu China 31°18N 106°3E 116 B6
Nanchang China 28°42N 115°55E 117 C10
Nancheng China 27°33N 116°35E 117 D11
Nanching = Nanjing China 32°2N 118°47E 117 A12
Nanchong China 30°43N 106°2E 116 B6
Nanchuan China 29°9N 107°6E 116 C6
Nancowry India 7°59N 93°32E 127 L11
Nancy France 48°42N 6°12E 71 D13
Nanda Devi India 30°23N 79°59E 125 D8
Nanda Devi △ India 30°30N 79°50E 125 D8
Nanda Kot India 30°17N 80°5E 125 D9
Nandan = Minamiawaji Japan 34°10N 134°42E 113 G7
Nandan China 24°58N 107°29E 116 E6
Nanded India 19°10N 77°20E 126 E3
Nandewar Ra. Australia 30°15S 150°35E 151 E5
Nandgaon India 20°19N 74°39E 126 D2
Nandi = Nadi Fiji 17°42S 177°20E 154 a
Nandi Zimbabwe 20°58S 31°44E 143 G3
Nandi □ Kenya 0°10N 35°10E 142 B4
Nandigama India 16°47N 80°18E 126 F5
Nandigram India 22°1N 87°58E 125 H12
Nandikotkur India 15°52N 78°18E 127 G4
Nandura India 20°52N 76°25E 126 D3
Nandurbar India 21°20N 74°15E 126 D2
Nandyal India 15°30N 78°30E 127 G4
Nanfeng Guangdong, China 23°45N 111°47E 117 F8
Nanfeng Jiangxi, China 27°12N 116°28E 117 D11
Nang Rong Thailand 14°38N 102°48E 120 E4
Nanga-Eboko Cameroon 4°41N 12°22E 139 E7
Nanga Parbat Pakistan 35°10N 74°35E 125 B6
Nangade Mozam. 11°5S 39°36E 143 E4
Nangapinoh Indonesia 0°20S 111°44E 118 E4
Nangar △ Australia 33°23S 148°3E 153 B8
Nangarhār □ Afghan. 34°20N 70°0E 122 B7
Nangatayap Indonesia 1°32S 110°34E 118 E4
Nangbéto, L. de Togo 7°26N 1°25E 139 D5
Nangeya Mts. Uganda 3°30N 33°30E 142 B3
Nangis France 48°33N 3°1E 71 D10
Nangong China 37°23N 115°22E 114 F8
Nanguneri India 8°29N 77°40E 127 K3
Nangwarry Australia 37°33S 140°48E 152 D4
Nanhua China 25°13N 101°21E 116 E3
Nanhuang China 36°58N 121°48E 115 F11
Nanhui China 31°5N 121°44E 117 B13
Nanisivik Canada 73°2N 84°33W 161 C15
Nanjangud India 12°6N 76°43E 127 H3
Nanji Shan China 27°27N 121°4E 117 D13
Nanjian China 25°2N 100°25E 116 E3
Nanjiang China 32°28N 106°51E 116 A6
Nanjing Fujian, China 24°25N 117°20E 117 E11
Nanjing Jiangsu, China 32°2N 118°47E 117 A12
Nanjirinji Tanzania 9°41S 39°5E 143 D4
Nankana Sahib Pakistan 31°27N 73°38E 124 D5
Nankang China 25°40N 114°45E 117 E10
Nanking = Nanjing China 32°2N 118°47E 117 A12
Nankoku Japan 33°39N 133°44E 113 H6
Nanlang China 22°30N 113°32E 111 a
Nanling China 30°55N 118°20E 117 B12
Nannial India 19°4N 79°38E 126 E4
Nanning China 22°48N 108°20E 116 F7
Nannup Australia 33°59S 115°48E 149 F2
Nanortalik Greenland 60°10N 45°17W 57 E6
Nanpan Jiang → China 25°10N 106°5E 116 E6
Nanpara India 27°52N 81°33E 125 F9
Nanping Fujian, China 26°38N 118°10E 117 D12
Nanping Henan, China 29°55N 112°3E 117 C9
Nanri Dao China 25°15N 119°25E 117 E12
Nansei-Shotō = Ryūkyū-Rettō Japan 26°0N 126°0E 113 M3
Nansen Basin Arctic 84°0N 50°0E 54 A10
Nansen Land Greenland 83°0N 43°0W 57 A6
Nansen Sd. Canada 81°0N 91°0W 161 A13
Nansha China 22°45N 113°34E 111 a
Nansha Port China 22°40N 113°40E 111 a
Nanshan China 18°19N 109°10E 117 a
Nanshan I. S. China Sea 10°45N 115°49E 118 B5
Nansio Tanzania 2°3S 33°4E 142 C3
Nant France 44°1N 3°18E 72 D7
Nantawarrinna ⚙ Australia 30°49S 138°58E 151 B2
Nanterre France 48°53N 2°12E 71 D9
Nantes France 47°12N 1°33W 70 E5
Nantiat France 46°1N 1°11E 72 B5
Nanticoke U.S.A. 41°12N 76°0W 175 E8
Nanton Canada 50°21N 113°46W 162 C6
Nantong China 32°1N 120°52E 117 A13
Nantou China 22°32N 113°55E 111 a
Nant'ou Taiwan 23°55N 120°41E 117 F13
Nantua France 46°10N 5°35E 71 F12
Nantucket U.S.A. 41°17N 70°6W 173 E18
Nantucket I. U.S.A. 41°16N 70°5W 173 E18
Nantulo Mozam. 12°32S 38°45E 143 E4
Nantwich U.K. 53°4N 2°31W 66 D5
Nanty Glo U.S.A. 40°28N 78°50W 174 F6
Nanuku Passage Fiji 16°45S 179°15W 154 a
Nanuque Brazil 17°50S 40°21W 189 D2
Nanusa, Kepulauan Indonesia 4°45N 127°1E 119 D7
Nanutarra Roadhouse Australia 22°32S 115°30E 148 D2
Nanxi China 28°54N 104°59E 116 C5
Nanxiong China 25°6N 114°15E 117 E10
Nanyang China 33°11N 112°30E 114 H7
Nanyi Hu China 31°5N 119°0E 117 B12
Nanyuan China 39°47N 116°24E 114 E9
Nanyuki Kenya 0°2N 37°4E 142 B4
Nanzhang China 31°45N 111°50E 117 B8
Nanzhao China 33°30N 112°20E 114 H7
Nao, C. de la Spain 38°44N 0°14E 91 G5
Naococane, L. Canada 52°50N 70°45W 165 B5
Naoussa Cyclades, Greece 37°7N 25°14E 99 D7
Naoussa Imathia, Greece 40°42N 22°9E 96 F6
Naozhou Dao China 20°55N 110°20E 117 G8
Napa U.S.A. 38°18N 122°17W 170 G4
Napa → U.S.A. 38°10N 122°19W 170 G4
Napanee Canada 44°15N 77°0W 174 B8
Napanoch U.S.A. 41°44N 74°22W 175 E10
Nape Laos 18°18N 105°6E 120 C5
Nape Pass = Keo Neua, Deo Vietnam 18°23N 105°10E 120 C5
Napier N.Z. 39°30S 176°56E 154 F5
Napier Broome B. Australia 14°2S 126°37E 148 B4
Napier Pen. Australia 12°4S 135°43E 150 A2
Napierville Canada 45°11N 73°25W 175 A11
Naples = Nápoli Italy 40°50N 14°15E 95 B7
Naples U.S.A. 26°8N 81°48W 179 J8
Naples Park U.S.A. 26°17N 81°46W 179 J8
Napo China 23°22N 105°50E 116 F5
Napo → Peru 3°20S 72°40W 186 D4
Napoleon N. Dak., U.S.A. 46°30N 99°46W 172 B4
Napoleon Ohio, U.S.A. 41°23N 84°8W 173 E11
Nápoli Italy 40°50N 14°15E 95 B7
Nápoli, G. di Italy 40°43N 14°10E 95 B7
Nápoli Capodichino ✕ (NAP) Italy 40°53N 14°16E 95 B7
Napopo Dem. Rep. of the Congo 4°15N 28°0E 142 B2
Napperby Australia 33°9S 138°7E 152 B3
Naqadeh Iran 36°57N 45°23E 105 D11
Naqb, Ra's an Jordan 29°48N 35°44E 130 F4
Naqqāsh Iran 35°40N 49°6E 129 C6
När Sweden 57°15N 18°35E 63 G10
Nara Japan 34°40N 135°49E 113 G7
Nara Mali 15°10N 7°20W 138 B3
Nara □ Japan 34°30N 136°0E 113 G8
Nara Canal Pakistan 24°30N 69°20E 124 G3
Nara Visa U.S.A. 35°37N 103°6W 169 J12
Naracoorte Australia 36°58S 140°45E 152 D4
Naradhan Australia 33°34S 146°17E 153 B7
Naraini India 25°11N 80°29E 125 G9
Naranjos Mexico 21°21N 97°41W 181 C5
Narasannapeta India 18°25N 84°3E 126 E7
Narasapur India 16°26N 81°40E 127 F5
Narasaraopet India 16°14N 80°4E 127 F5
Narathiwat Thailand 6°30N 101°48E 121 J3
Narayanapatnam India 18°53N 83°10E 126 E6
Narayangadh = Bharatpur Nepal 27°34N 84°10E 125 F11
Narayanganj Bangla. 23°40N 90°33E 123 H17
Narayanpet India 16°45N 77°30E 126 F3
Narberth U.K. 51°47N 4°44W 67 F3
Narbonne France 43°11N 3°0E 72 E7
Narcea → Spain 43°33N 6°44W 88 B4
Narcondam I. India 13°20N 94°16E 127 H12
Nardīn Iran 37°3N 55°59E 129 B7
Nardò Italy 40°11N 18°2E 95 B11
Narembeen Australia 32°7S 118°24E 149 F2
Nares Abyssal Plain Atl. Oc. 22°0N 67°0W 56 D5
Nares Str. Arctic 80°0N 70°0W 57 B3
Naretha Australia 31°0S 124°45E 149 F3
Narew → Poland 52°26N 20°41E 83 F7
Nari → Pakistan 28°0N 67°40E 124 F2
Narin Afghan. 36°5N 69°0E 122 A6
Narita Japan 35°47N 140°19E 113 G10
Nariva Swamp Trin. & Tob. 10°26N 61°4W 187 K15
Närke Sweden 59°10N 15°0E 62 E8
Narmada → India 21°38N 72°36E 124 J5
Narmada Canal India 22°20N 73°45E 126 C1
Narman Turkey 40°26N 41°57E 105 B9
Narnaul India 28°5N 76°11E 124 E7
Narni Italy 42°30N 12°30E 93 F9
Naro Ghana 10°22N 2°27W 138 C4
Naro Fominsk Russia 55°23N 36°43E 84 E9
Narochanski △ Belarus 54°55N 26°50E 84 E4
Narodnaya Russia 65°5N 59°58E 58 B17
Narok Kenya 1°55S 35°52E 142 C4
Narok □ Kenya 1°15S 35°40E 142 C4
Narón Spain 43°32N 8°9W 88 B2
Narooma Australia 36°14S 150°4E 153 D9
Narowal Pakistan 32°6N 74°54E 124 C6
Narrabri Australia 30°19S 149°46E 151 E4
Narran → Australia 28°37S 148°12E 151 D4
Narrandera Australia 34°42S 146°31E 153 C7
Narrogin Australia 32°58S 117°14E 149 F2
Narromine Australia 32°12S 148°12E 153 B8
Narrow Hills ⌓ Canada 54°0N 104°37W 163 C8
Narsampet India 17°57N 79°58E 126 F4
Narsaq Greenland 60°57N 46°4W 57 E6
Narsimhapur India 22°54N 79°14E 125 H8
Narsinghgarh India 23°45N 76°40E 124 H7
Narsinghpur India 20°28N 85°5E 126 D7
Narsipatnam India 17°40N 82°37E 126 F6
Nartes, L. e Albania 40°32N 19°25E 96 F3
Nartkala Russia 43°33N 43°51E 87 J6
Narutō = Sanmu Japan 34°11N 134°37E 113 G7
Narva Estonia 59°23N 28°12E 84 C5
Narva → Russia 59°27N 28°2E 84 C4
Narva Bay = Narva Laht Estonia 59°35N 27°35E 61 G22
Narva Laht Estonia 59°35N 27°35E 61 G22
Narvik Norway 68°28N 17°26E 60 B17
Narvskoye Vdkhr. Russia 59°18N 28°14E 84 C5
Narwana India 29°39N 76°6E 124 E7
Narwiański △ Poland 52°5N 22°53E 83 F9
Narwinbi ⚙ Australia 16°7S 136°17E 150 B2
Naryan-Mar Russia 67°42N 53°12E 106 C6
Naryn Russia 59°0N 81°30E 106 D9
Naryn Kyrgyzstan 41°26N 75°58E 109 D9
Naryn □ Kyrgyzstan 41°26N 75°58E 109 D9
Naryn → Uzbekistan 40°52N 71°36E 109 D8
Naryn Qum Kazakhstan 47°30N 49°0E 87 G9
Nás, An = Naas Ireland 53°12N 6°40W 64 C5
Nasa Norway 66°29N 15°23E 60 C16
Nasarawa Nigeria 8°32N 7°41E 139 D6
Nasarawa □ Nigeria 8°30N 8°20E 139 D6
Nasau Fiji 17°19S 179°27E 154 a
Năsăud Romania 47°19N 24°29E 81 C9
Nasca Peru 14°50S 74°57W 188 C3
Nasca Ridge Pac. Oc. 20°0S 80°0W 157 K19
Naseby N.Z. 45°1S 170°10E 155 F5
Naselle U.S.A. 46°22N 123°49W 170 D3
Naser, Buheirat en Egypt 23°0N 32°30E 137 C3
Nashik = Nasik India 19°58N 73°50E 126 E1
Nashua Mont., U.S.A. 48°8N 106°22W 168 B10
Nashua N.H., U.S.A. 42°45N 71°28W 175 D13
Nashville Ark., U.S.A. 33°57N 93°51W 176 E8
Nashville Ga., U.S.A. 31°12N 83°15W 178 D6
Nashville Tenn., U.S.A. 36°10N 86°47W 177 C11
Našice Croatia 45°32N 18°4E 80 E3
Nasielsk Poland 52°35N 20°50E 83 F7
Nasik India 19°58N 73°50E 126 E1
Nasirabad India 26°15N 74°45E 124 F6
Nasirabad Pakistan 28°23N 68°24E 124 E3
Nasiri = Ahvāz Iran 31°20N 48°40E 129 D6
Nasiriyah = An Nāşirīyah Iraq 31°0N 46°15E 128 D5
Naskaupi → Canada 53°47N 60°51W 165 B7
Naso Italy 38°7N 14°47E 95 D7
Naşrābād Iran 34°8N 51°26E 129 C6
Naşriān-e Pā'īn Iran 32°52N 46°52E 128 C5
Nass → Canada 55°0N 129°40W 162 C3
Nassau Bahamas 25°5N 77°20W 182 A4
Nassau U.S.A. 42°31N 73°37W 175 D11
Nassau, B. Chile 55°20S 68°0W 192 E3
Nasser, L. = Naser, Buheirat en Egypt 23°0N 32°30E 137 C3
Nassian Côte d'Ivoire 8°28N 3°28W 138 D4
Nässjö Sweden 57°39N 14°42E 63 G8
Nastapoka → Canada 56°55N 76°33W 164 A4
Nastapoka, Is. Canada 56°55N 76°50W 164 A4
Näsum Sweden 56°10N 14°29E 63 H8
Nasushiobara Japan 36°58N 140°3E 113 F10
Näsviken Sweden 61°46N 16°52E 62 C10
Nata Botswana 20°12S 26°12E 144 B4
Nata → Botswana 20°14S 26°10E 144 B4
Natal Brazil 5°47S 35°13W 189 B3
Natal Indonesia 0°35N 99°7E 118 D1
Natal Drakensberg = uKhahlamba Drakensberg ⌓ S. Africa 29°27S 29°30E 145 C4
Natalinci Serbia 44°15N 20°49E 80 F5
Naṭanz Iran 33°30N 51°55E 129 C6
Natashquan Canada 50°14N 61°46W 165 B7
Natashquan → Canada 50°7N 61°50W 165 B7
Natchez U.S.A. 31°34N 91°24W 176 F9
Natchitoches U.S.A. 31°46N 93°5W 176 F8
Natewa B. Fiji 16°35S 179°40E 154 a
Nathalia Australia 36°1S 145°13E 153 D6
Nathdwara India 24°55N 73°50E 124 G5
Nati, Pta. Spain 40°3N 3°50E 100 A10
Natimuk Australia 36°42S 142°0E 152 D5
Nation → Canada 55°30N 123°32W 162 B4
National City U.S.A. 32°40N 117°5W 171 N9
Natitingou Benin 10°20N 1°26E 139 C5
Natividad, I. Mexico 27°52N 115°11W 180 B1
Natividade Brazil 11°43S 47°47W 189 C1
Natkyizin Myanmar 14°57N 97°59E 120 E1
Natron, L. Tanzania 2°20S 36°0E 142 C4
Natrona Heights U.S.A. 40°37N 79°44W 174 F5
Natrûn, W. el → Egypt 30°25N 30°13E 137 E7
Nattai △ Australia 34°12S 150°22E 153 C9
Nättraby Sweden 56°13N 15°31E 63 H9
Natuashish Canada 55°55N 61°8W 165 A7
Natukanaoka Pan Namibia 18°40S 15°45E 144 A2
Natuna Besar, Kepulauan Indonesia 4°0N 108°15E 118 D3
Natuna Is. = Natuna Besar, Kepulauan Indonesia 4°0N 108°15E 118 D3
Natuna Selatan, Kepulauan Indonesia 2°45N 109°0E 118 D3
Natural Bridge U.S.A. 44°5N 75°30W 175 B9
Natural Bridges ⌓ U.S.A. 37°36N 110°0W 169 H9
Naturaliste, C. Tas., Australia 40°50S 148°15E 151 G4
Naturaliste, C. W. Austral., Australia 33°32S 115°0E 149 F2
Naturaliste Plateau Ind. Oc. 34°0S 112°0E 156 L3
Nau Qala Afghan. 34°5N 68°5E 124 B3
Naucelle France 44°13N 2°20E 72 D6
Nauders Austria 46°54N 10°30E 78 E3
Nauen Germany 52°36N 12°52E 76 C8
Naugatuck U.S.A. 41°30N 73°3W 175 E11
Naujaat = Repulse Bay Canada 66°30N 86°30W 161 D14
Naujoji Akmenė Lithuania 56°19N 22°54E 82 B9
Naumburg Germany 51°9N 11°47E 76 D7
Naupada India 18°34N 84°18E 126 E7
Nauru ■ Pac. Oc. 1°0S 166°0E 147 B9
Naushahra = Nowshera Pakistan 34°0N 72°0E 122 C8
Naushahro Pakistan 26°50N 68°7E 124 F3
Naushon I. U.S.A. 41°29N 70°45W 175 E14
Nausori Fiji 18°2S 178°32E 154 a
Nauta Peru 4°31S 73°35W 186 D4
Nautanwa India 27°20N 83°25E 125 F10
Naute ⌓ Namibia 26°55S 17°57E 144 C2
Nautla Mexico 20°13N 96°47W 181 C5
Nava Mexico 28°25N 100°45W 180 B4
Nava Spain 43°21N 5°31W 88 B5
Nava del Rey Spain 41°22N 5°6W 88 D5
Navadwip India 23°34N 88°20E 125 H13
Navahermosa Spain 39°41N 4°28W 89 F6
Navahrudak Belarus 53°40N 25°50E 75 B13
Navajo Res. U.S.A. 36°48N 107°36W 169 H10
Navalcarnero Spain 40°17N 4°5W 88 E6
Navalgund India 15°34N 75°22E 127 G2
Navalmoral de la Mata Spain 39°52N 5°33W 88 F5
Navalvillar de Pela Spain 39°9N 5°24W 89 F5
Navan Ireland 53°39N 6°41W 64 C5
Navapolatsk Belarus 55°32N 28°37E 84 E5
Navarin, Mys Russia 62°15N 179°5E 107 C18
Navarino, I. Chile 55°0S 67°40W 192 E3
Navarra □ Spain 42°40N 1°40W 90 C3
Navarre Fla., U.S.A. 30°24N 86°52W 179 E3
Navarre Ohio, U.S.A. 40°43N 81°31W 174 F3
Navarro → U.S.A. 39°11N 123°45W 170 F3
Navas de San Juan Spain 38°30N 3°19W 89 G7
Navasota U.S.A. 30°23N 96°5W 176 F6
Navassa I. W. Indies 18°30N 75°0W 183 C5
Nävekvarn Sweden 58°38N 16°49E 63 F10
Naver → U.K. 58°32N 4°14W 65 C4
Navi Mumbai India 19°5N 73°0E 126 E1
Navia Spain 43°35N 6°42W 88 B4
Navia → Spain 43°15N 6°50W 88 B4
Navia de Suarna = A Pobre Spain 42°58N 7°3W 88 C3
Navibandar India 21°26N 69°48E 124 J3
Navidad Chile 33°57S 71°50W 190 C1
Naviraí Brazil 23°8S 54°13W 191 A5
Naviti Fiji 17°7S 177°15E 154 a
Navlakhi India 22°58N 70°28E 124 H4
Navlya Russia 52°53N 34°30E 85 F8
Năvodari Romania 44°19N 28°36E 81 F13
Navoiy Uzbekistan 40°9N 65°22E 108 D7
Navojoa Mexico 27°6N 109°26W 180 B3
Navolato Mexico 24°47N 107°42W 180 C3
Navrongo Ghana 10°51N 1°3W 139 C4
Navsari India 20°57N 72°59E 126 D1
Navua Fiji 18°12S 178°11E 154 a
Nawa Kot Pakistan 28°21N 71°24E 124 E4
Nawab Khan Pakistan 30°17N 69°12E 124 D3
Nawabganj Ut. P., India 26°56N 81°14E 125 F9
Nawabganj Ut. P., India 28°32N 79°40E 125 E8
Nawabshah Pakistan 26°15N 68°25E 124 F3
Nawada India 24°50N 85°33E 125 G11
Nawakot Nepal 27°55N 85°10E 125 F11
Nawalgarh India 27°50N 75°15E 124 F6
Nawanshahr India 32°33N 74°48E 125 C6
Nawapara India 20°46N 82°33E 126 D6
Nawar, Dasht-i- Afghan. 33°52N 68°0E 124 C3
Nawāsīf, Ḥarrat Si. Arabia 21°20N 42°10E 137 C5
Nawi Sudan 18°32N 30°50E 137 D3
Nawoiy = Navoiy Uzbekistan 40°9N 65°22E 108 D7
Naxçıvan Azerbaijan 39°12N 45°15E 105 C11
Naxçıvan □ Azerbaijan 39°25N 45°26E 105 C11
Naxos Greece 37°8N 25°25E 99 D7
Nay France 43°10N 0°18W 72 E3
Nay, Mui Vietnam 12°54N 109°26E 120 F7
Nāy Band Būshehr, Iran 27°20N 52°40E 129 E7
Nāy Band Khorāsān, Iran 32°20N 57°34E 129 C8
Nay Pyi Taw = Naypyidaw Myanmar 19°44N 96°12E 110 H8
Nayagarh India 20°8N 85°6E 126 D7
Nayakhan Russia 61°56N 159°0E 107 C16
Nayarit □ Mexico 22°0N 105°0W 180 C4
Nayau Fiji 18°6S 178°10E 154 a
Nayé Senegal 14°28N 12°12W 138 C2
Nayong China 26°50N 105°20E 116 D5
Nayoro Japan 44°21N 142°28E 112 B11
Naypyidaw Myanmar 19°44N 96°12E 110 H8
Nayudupeta India 13°54N 79°54E 127 H4
Nayyāl, W. → Si. Arabia 28°35N 39°4E 128 D3
Nazar Kahrīzī Iran 37°20N 46°45E 105 D12
Nazaré Bahia, Brazil 13°2S 39°0W 189 C3
Nazaré Tocantins, Brazil 6°23S 47°40W 189 B1
Nazaré Portugal 39°36N 9°4W 89 F1
Nazareth = Nazerat Israel 32°42N 35°17E 130 C4
Nazareth U.S.A. 40°44N 75°19W 175 F9
Nazarovo Russia 57°2N 90°40E 107 D10
Nazas Mexico 25°14N 104°8W 180 B4
Nazas → Mexico 25°12N 104°12W 180 B4
Nazca = Nasca Peru 14°50S 74°57W 188 C3
Naze, The U.K. 51°53N 1°18E 67 F9
Nazerat Israel 32°42N 35°17E 130 C4
Nāzīk Iran 39°1N 45°4E 105 C11
Nazilli Turkey 37°55N 28°15E 99 D10
Nazinon = Red Volta → Africa 10°34N 0°30W 139 C4
Nazko Canada 53°1N 123°37W 162 C4
Nazko → Canada 53°7N 123°34W 162 C4
Nāzlu Iran 37°41N 45°0E 105 D11
Nazret Ethiopia 8°32N 39°22E 131 F2
Nchanga Zambia 12°30S 27°49E 143 E2
Ncheu Malawi 14°50S 34°47E 143 E3
Ndala Tanzania 4°45S 33°15E 142 C3
Ndalatando Angola 9°12S 14°48E 140 F2
Ndali Benin 9°50N 2°46E 139 D5
Ndareda Tanzania 4°12S 35°30E 142 C4
Ndélé C.A.R. 8°25N 20°36E 140 C4
Ndiael ⌓ Senegal 16°15N 16°0W 138 B1
Ndikinimeki Cameroon 4°46N 10°50E 139 E7
N'Dioum Senegal 16°31N 14°39W 138 B2
Ndjamena Chad 12°10N 15°0E 135 F8
Ndola Zambia 13°0S 28°34E 143 E2
Ndomo ⌓ S. Africa 26°52S 32°15E 145 C5
Ndoto Mts. Kenya 2°0N 37°0E 142 B4
Nduguti Tanzania 4°18S 34°41E 142 C3
Nea Alikarnassos Greece 35°19N 25°11E 99 F7
Nea Anchialos Greece 39°16N 22°49E 98 B4
Nea Artaki Greece 38°31N 23°38E 98 C5
Nea Epidavros Greece 37°40N 23°7E 98 D5
Nea Ionia Greece 39°21N 22°56E 98 B4
Nea Kalikratia Greece 40°21N 23°3E 96 F7
Nea Makri Greece 38°5N 23°59E 98 C5
Nea Moudania Greece 40°15N 23°17E 96 F7
Nea Peramos Attiki, Greece 38°0N 23°26E 98 C5
Nea Peramos Kavala, Greece 40°50N 24°18E 97 F8
Nea Visa Greece 41°34N 26°33E 97 E10
Nea Zichni Greece 41°2N 23°49E 96 E7
Neagh, Lough U.K. 54°37N 6°25W 64 B5
Neah Bay U.S.A. 48°22N 124°37W 170 B2
Neale, L. Australia 24°15S 130°0E 148 D5
Neales → Australia 28°8S 136°47E 151 D2
Neamţ □ Romania 47°0N 26°20E 81 C11
Neapoli Kozani, Greece 40°20N 21°24E 96 F5
Neapoli Kriti, Greece 35°15N 25°37E 101 D7
Neapoli Lakonia, Greece 36°27N 23°8E 98 E5
Near Is. U.S.A. 52°30N 174°0E 166 E2
Neath U.K. 51°39N 3°48W 67 F4
Neath Port Talbot □ U.K. 51°42N 3°45W 67 F4
Nebbi Uganda 2°28N 31°6E 142 B3
Nebbou Burkina Faso 11°9N 1°51W 139 C4
Nebine Cr. → Australia 29°27S 146°56E 151 D4
Nebitdag = Balkanabat Turkmenistan 39°30N 54°22E 129 B7
Nebka Algeria 27°28N 3°12W 136 C3
Nebo Australia 21°42S 148°42E 150 C4
Nebolchy Russia 59°8N 33°18E 84 C7
Nebraska □ U.S.A. 41°30N 99°30W 172 E4
Nebraska City U.S.A. 40°41N 95°52W 172 E6
Nébrodi, Monti Italy 37°54N 14°35E 95 E7
Necedah U.S.A. 44°2N 90°4W 172 C8
Nechako → Canada 53°55N 122°42W 162 C4
Neches → U.S.A. 29°58N 93°51W 176 G8
Neckar → Germany 49°27N 8°29E 77 F4
Neckartal-Odenwald ⌓ Germany 49°30N 9°5E 77 F5
Necker I. U.S.A. 23°35N 164°42W 167 L7
Necochea Argentina 38°30S 58°50W 190 D4
Nectar Brook Australia 32°43S 137°57E 152 B2
Neda Spain 43°30N 8°9W 88 B2
Neda → Greece 37°25N 21°45E 98 D3
Nedelino Bulgaria 41°27N 25°5E 97 E9
Nedelišće Croatia 46°23N 16°22E 93 B13
Nederland = Netherlands ■ Europe 52°0N 5°30E 69 C5
Nedoboyivtsi Ukraine 48°26N 26°21E 81 B11
Nedroma Algeria 35°1N 1°45W 136 A3
Needles Canada 49°53N 118°7W 162 D5
Needles U.S.A. 34°51N 114°37W 171 L12
Needles, The U.K. 50°39N 1°35W 67 G6
Needles Pt. N.Z. 36°3S 175°25E 154 C4
Neembucú □ Paraguay 27°0S 58°0W 190 B4
Neemuch = Nimach India 24°30N 74°56E 124 G6
Neenah U.S.A. 44°11N 88°28W 172 C9
Neepawa Canada 50°15N 99°30W 163 C9
Neeses U.S.A. 33°33N 81°7W 178 B8
Nefta Tunisia 33°53N 7°50E 136 B5
Neftçala Azerbaijan 39°19N 49°12E 105 C13
Neftegorsk Krasnodar, Russia 44°25N 39°45E 87 H4
Neftegorsk Sakhalin, Russia 53°1N 142°58E 107 D15
Neftekumsk Russia 44°46N 44°50E 87 H7
Nefteyugansk Russia 61°5N 72°42E 106 C8
Nefyn U.K. 52°56N 4°31W 66 E3
Négala Mali 12°52N 8°30W 138 C3
Negapatam = Nagappattinam India 10°46N 79°51E 127 J4
Negara Indonesia 8°22S 114°37E 119 J17
Negaunee U.S.A. 46°30N 87°36W 172 B10
Negele Ethiopia 5°20N 39°36E 131 F2
Negeri Sembilan □ Malaysia 2°45N 102°10E 121 L4
Negev Desert = Hanegev Israel 30°50N 35°0E 130 E4
Negoiul, Vf. Romania 45°38N 24°35E 81 E9
Negombo Sri Lanka 7°12N 79°50E 127 L4
Negotin Serbia 44°16N 22°37E 96 B6
Negotino Macedonia 41°29N 22°7E 96 E6
Negra, Peña Spain 42°11N 6°30W 88 C4
Negra, Pta. Mauritania 22°54N 16°18W 134 D2
Negra, Pta. Peru 6°6S 81°10W 188 B1
Negrais, C. = Maudin Sun Myanmar 16°0N 94°30E 123 M19
Negreşti Romania 46°50N 27°30E 81 D12
Negreşti-Oaş Romania 47°52N 23°26E 81 C8
Negril Jamaica 18°22N 78°20W 182 a
Négrine Algeria 34°30N 7°30E 136 B5
Negro → Argentina 41°2S 62°47W 192 B4
Negro → Brazil 3°0S 60°0W 186 D7
Negro → Uruguay 33°24S 58°22W 190 C4
Negro, C. = Tarf, Ras Morocco 35°40N 5°11W 136 A2
Negros Phil. 9°30N 122°40E 119 C6
Negru Vodă Romania 43°47N 28°21E 81 G13
Neguac Canada 47°15N 65°5W 165 C6
Nehalem → U.S.A. 45°40N 123°56W 170 E3
Nehāvand Iran 35°56N 49°31E 129 C6

Nehbandān Iran 31°35N 60°5E 129 D9
Nehe China 48°29N 124°50E 111 B13
Nehoiu Romania 45°24N 26°20E 81 E11
Nei Mongol Zizhiqu □
China 42°0N 112°0E 114 D7
Neiges, Piton des Réunion 21°5S 55°29E 141 c
Neijiang China 29°35N 104°55E 116 C5
Neilingding Dao China 22°25N 113°48E 111 a
Neill I. India 11°50N 93°12E 127 J11
Neillsville U.S.A. 44°34N 90°36W 172 C8
Neilton U.S.A. 47°25N 123°53W 170 C3
Neiqiu China 37°15N 114°30E 114 F8
Neiva Colombia 2°56N 75°18W 186 C3
Neixiang China 33°10N 111°52E 114 H6
Nejanilini L. Canada 59°33N 97°48W 163 B9
Nekā Iran 36°39N 53°19E 129 B7
Nekemte Ethiopia 9°4N 36°30E 131 F2
Nekheb Egypt 25°10N 32°48E 63 J9
Nekso Denmark 55°4N 15°8E 63 J9
Nelamangala India 13°6N 77°24E 127 H3
Nelas Portugal 40°32N 7°52E 88 B2
Nelia Australia 20°39S 142°12E 150 C3
Nelidovo Russia 56°13N 32°49E 84 D7
Neligh U.S.A. 42°8N 98°2W 172 E4
Nelkan Russia 57°40N 136°4E 107 D14
Nellikuppam India 11°46N 79°43E 127 J4
Nellore India 14°27N 79°59E 127 H4
Nelson Canada 49°30N 117°20W 162 D5
Nelson N.Z. 41°18S 173°16E 155 B8
Nelson U.K. 53°50N 2°13W 66 D5
Nelson Ariz., U.S.A. 35°31N 113°19W 169 J7
Nelson Nev., U.S.A. 35°42N 114°49W 171 K12
Nelson □ N.Z. 41°20S 173°20E 155 B8
Nelson → Canada 54°33N 98°2E 163 C9
Nelson, C. Australia 38°26S 141°32E 152 E4
Nelson Bay Australia 32°43S 152°9E 153 B10
Nelson Forks Canada 59°30N 124°0W 162 B4
Nelson House Canada 55°48N 98°51W 163 B9
Nelson L. Canada 55°48N 100°7W 163 B8
Nelson Lakes △ N.Z. 41°55S 172°44E 155 B8
Nelspoort S. Africa 32°7S 23°0E 144 D3
Nelspruit = Mbombela
S. Africa 25°29S 30°59E 145 C5
Néma Mauritania 16°40N 7°15W 138 B3
Neman = Nemunas →
Lithuania 55°25N 21°10E 82 C8
Neman Russia 55°2N 22°2E 82 C9
Nembe Nigeria 4°32N 6°24E 139 E6
Nembrala Indonesia 10°45S 122°48E 148 B3
Nemea Greece 37°49N 22°40E 98 D4
Nemeiben L. Canada 55°20N 105°20W 163 B7
Nemercke, Mal Albania 40°15N 20°15E 96 F4
Nemira, Vf. Romania 46°17N 26°19E 81 D11
Nemiscau Canada 51°18N 76°54W 164 B4
Nemiscau, L. Canada 51°25N 76°40W 164 B4
Nemours France 48°16N 2°40E 71 D9
Nemrut Dağı △ Turkey 38°0N 38°55E 105 C8
Nemšová Slovakia 48°58N 18°7E 79 C11
Nemunas → Lithuania 55°25N 21°10E 82 C8
Nemuro Japan 43°20N 145°35E 112 C12
Nemuro-Kaikyō
Japan 43°30N 145°30E 112 C12
Nemyriv Ukraine 50°7N 23°27E 83 H10
Nen Jiang → China 45°28N 124°30E 115 B13
Nenagh Ireland 52°52N 8°11W 64 D3
Nenana U.S.A. 64°34N 149°5W 166 C10
Nenasi Malaysia 3°9N 103°23E 121 L4
Nene → U.K. 52°49N 0°11E 67 E8
Nenita Greece 38°14N 26°6E 99 C8
Nenjiang China 49°10N 125°10E 111 B14
Neno Malawi 15°25S 34°40E 143 F3
Neo Chori Greece 38°25N 21°17E 98 C3
Neochori Greece 39°4N 21°0E 98 C3
Neodesha U.S.A. 37°25N 95°41W 172 G6
Neon Petritsi Greece 41°16N 23°15E 96 E7
Neópolis Brazil 10°18S 36°35W 189 E11
Neora Valley △ India 27°0N 88°45E 125 F13
Neos Marmaras Greece 40°6N 23°47E 96 F7
Neosho U.S.A. 36°52N 94°22W 172 G6
Neosho → U.S.A. 36°48N 95°18W 176 C7
Nepal ■ Asia 28°0N 84°30E 125 F11
Nepalganj Nepal 28°5N 81°40E 125 E9
Nepalganj Road India 28°1N 81°41E 125 E9
Nepean B. Australia 35°42S 137°37E 152 C2
Nephi U.S.A. 39°43N 111°50W 168 G8
Nephin Ireland 54°1N 9°22W 64 B2
Nephin Beg Range Ireland 54°0N 9°40W 64 C2
Nepi Italy 42°14N 12°21E 93 F9
Nepomuk Czechia 49°29N 13°35E 78 B6
Neptune U.S.A. 40°13N 74°2W 175 F10
Neptune Is. Australia 35°17S 136°10E 152 C2
Neqāb Iran 36°42N 57°25E 129 B8
Nera → Italy 42°26N 12°24E 93 F9
Nera → Romania 44°48N 21°25E 80 F6
Nérac France 44°8N 0°21E 72 D4
Nerang Australia 27°58S 153°20E 151 D5
Neratovice Czechia 50°16N 14°31E 78 A7
Nereju Romania 45°43N 26°43E 81 E11
Nerekhta Russia 57°26N 40°38E 84 D11
Neresnytsya Ukraine 48°7N 23°46E 81 B8
Néret, L. Canada 54°45N 70°44W 165 B5
Neretvanski Kanal
Croatia 43°7N 17°10E 93 E14
Neringa Lithuania 55°20N 21°5E 82 C8
Neris → Lithuania 55°8N 24°16E 84 E3
Nerja Spain 36°43N 3°55W 89 J7
Nerl → Russia 56°11N 40°34E 84 D11
Nerpio Spain 38°11N 2°16W 91 G2
Nerva Spain 37°42N 6°30W 89 H4
Nervi Italy 44°23N 9°2E 92 D6
Neryungri Russia 57°38N 124°28E 107 D13
Nescopeck U.S.A. 41°3N 76°12W 175 E8
Nesebŭr Bulgaria 42°41N 27°46E 97 D11
Neskantaga Canada 52°14N 87°53W 164 B2
Neskaupstaður Iceland 65°9N 13°42W 60 D7
Ness, L. U.K. 57°15N 4°32W 65 D4
Ness City U.S.A. 38°27N 99°54W 172 F4
Nessebar = Nesebŭr
Bulgaria 42°41N 27°46E 97 D11
Nesterov = Zhovkva
Ukraine 50°4N 23°58E 75 C12
Nestório Greece 22°25N 113°5E 82 D9
Nestos → Europe 40°54N 24°49E 97 F8
Nesvady Slovakia 47°56N 18°7E 79 D11
Nesvizh = Nyasvizh
Belarus 53°14N 26°38E 83 D14
Netanya Israel 32°30N 34°51E 130 C3
Netarhat India 23°29N 84°16E 125 H11

Nete → Belgium 51°7N 4°14E 69 C4
Netherdale Australia 21°10S 148°33E 150 b
Netherlands ■ Europe 52°0N 5°30E 69 C5
Netherlands Antilles = ABC
Islands W. Indies 12°15N 69°0W 183 D6
Neto → Italy 39°12N 17°9E 95 C10
Netrang India 21°39N 73°21E 124 J5
Nettancourt France 48°51N 4°57E 71 D11
Nettilling L. Canada 66°30N 71°0W 161 D17
Nettuno Italy 41°27N 12°39E 94 A5
Netzahualcóyotl, Presa
Mexico 17°8N 93°35W 181 D6
Neu-Isenburg Germany 50°3N 8°42E 77 E4
Neu-Ulm Germany 48°22N 10°0E 77 G6
Neubrandenburg
Germany 53°33N 13°15E 76 B9
Neubukow Germany 54°2N 11°39E 76 A7
Neuburg Germany 48°44N 11°11E 77 G7
Neuchâtel Switz. 47°0N 6°55E 77 J2
Neuchâtel □ Switz. 47°0N 6°55E 77 J2
Neuchâtel, Lac de Switz. 46°53N 6°50E 77 J2
Neudau Austria 47°11N 16°6E 78 D9
Neuenhagen Germany 52°32N 13°58E 76 C9
Neuenhaus Germany 52°30N 6°58E 76 C2
Neuf-Brisach France 48°1N 7°30E 71 D14
Neufahrn Bayern,
Germany 48°41N 12°11E 77 G8
Neufahrn Bayern,
Germany 48°18N 11°40E 77 G7
Neufchâteau Belgium 49°50N 5°25E 69 E5
Neufchâteau France 48°21N 5°40E 71 D12
Neufchâtel-en-Bray
France 49°44N 1°26E 70 C8
Neufchâtel-sur-Aisne
France 49°26N 4°1E 71 C11
Neuhaus Germany 53°17N 10°56E 76 B6
Neuillé-Pont-Pierre
France 47°33N 0°33E 70 E7
Neuilly-St-Front France 49°10N 3°15E 71 C10
Neukalen Germany 53°49N 12°46E 76 B8
Neumarkt Germany 49°26N 11°27E 77 F7
Neumayer III Antarctica 71°0S 68°30W 55 D2
Neumünster Germany 54°4N 9°58E 76 A5
Neung-sur-Beuvron
France 47°30N 1°50E 71 E8
Neunkirchen Austria 47°43N 16°4E 78 D9
Neunkirchen Germany 49°20N 7°9E 77 F3
Neuquén Argentina 38°55S 68°0W 192 A3
Neuquén □ Argentina 38°0S 69°50W 190 D2
Neuquén → Argentina 38°59S 68°0W 192 A3
Neuruppin Germany 52°55N 12°48E 76 C8
Neusäss Germany 48°24N 10°50E 77 G6
Neuse → U.S.A. 35°6N 76°29W 177 D16
Neusiedl Austria 47°57N 16°50E 79 D9
Neusiedler See Austria 47°50N 16°47E 79 D9
Neusiedler See-Seewinkel △
Austria 47°50N 16°45E 79 D9
Neuss Germany 51°11N 6°42E 76 D2
Neussargues-Moissac
France 45°9N 3°0E 72 C7
Neustadt Bayern,
Germany 49°44N 12°10E 77 F8
Neustadt Bayern,
Germany 48°48N 11°46E 77 G7
Neustadt Bayern, Germany 50°19N 11°7E 77 E7
Neustadt Brandenburg,
Germany 52°50N 12°27E 76 C8
Neustadt Hessen, Germany 50°51N 9°9E 76 E5
Neustadt Sachsen,
Germany 51°2N 14°12E 76 D10
Neustadt Schleswig-Holstein,
Germany 54°6N 10°49E 76 A6
Neustadt Thüringen,
Germany 50°45N 11°43E 76 E7
Neustadt am Rübenberge
Germany 52°30N 9°30E 76 C5
Neustadt an der Weinstrasse
Germany 49°21N 8°10E 77 F4
Neustrelitz Germany 53°21N 13°4E 76 B9
Neuvic France 45°23N 2°16E 72 C6
Neuville-sur-Saône
France 45°52N 4°51E 73 C8
Neuville-le-Roi France 47°36N 0°36E 70 E7
Neuvy-St-Sépulchre
France 46°35N 1°48E 71 F8
Neuvy-sur-Barangeon
France 47°20N 2°15E 71 E9
Neuwerk Germany 53°55N 8°30E 76 B4
Neuwied Germany 50°26N 7°29E 76 E3
Neva → Russia 59°56N 30°20E 84 C6
Nevada Iowa, U.S.A. 42°1N 93°27W 172 D7
Nevada Mo., U.S.A. 37°51N 94°22W 172 G6
Nevada □ U.S.A. 39°0N 117°0W 168 G5
Nevada, Cerro
Chile 27°13S 69°5W 190 B2
Nevado de Colima = Volcán de
Colima △ Mexico 19°30N 103°40W 180 D4
Nevado de Tres Cruces △
Chile 27°13S 69°5W 190 B2
Nevasa India 19°34N 75°0E 124 E2
Nevel Russia 56°0N 29°55E 84 D5
Nevelsk Russia 46°40N 141°51E 107 E15
Nevers France 47°0N 3°9E 71 F10
Nevertire Australia 31°50S 147°44E 153 A7
Nevesinje Bos.-H. 43°14N 18°6E 96 C2
Neville Canada 49°58N 107°39W 163 D7
Nevinnomyssk Russia 44°40N 42°0E 87 H6
Nevis St. Kitts & Nevis 17°0N 62°30W 183 C7
Nevrokop = Gotse Delchev
Bulgaria 41°36N 23°46E 96 E7
Nevşehir Turkey 38°33N 34°40E 104 C6
Nevşehir □ Turkey 38°50N 34°40E 104 C6
Nevyansk Russia 54°32N 22°39E 80 D11
New → U.S.A. 38°10N 81°12W 173 F13
New Aiyansh Canada 55°12N 129°4W 162 B3
New Albany Ind.,
U.S.A. 38°18N 85°49W 173 F11
New Albany Miss.,
U.S.A. 34°29N 89°0W 177 D10
New Albany Pa.,
U.S.A. 41°36N 76°27W 175 E8
New Amsterdam
Guyana 6°15N 57°36W 186 B7
New Atlas = Akhali Atoni
Georgia 43°7N 40°50E 87 J5
New Baltimore U.S.A. 42°41N 82°44W 174 D2
New Berlin N.Y.,
U.S.A. 42°37N 75°20W 175 D9

New Berlin Pa., U.S.A. 40°50N 76°57W 174 F8
New Bern U.S.A. 35°7N 77°3W 177 D16
New Bethlehem U.S.A. 41°0N 79°20W 174 F5
New Bight Bahamas 24°19N 75°24W 183 B4
New Bloomfield U.S.A. 40°25N 77°11W 174 F7
New Boston U.S.A. 33°28N 94°25W 176 E7
New Braunfels U.S.A. 29°42N 98°8W 176 G5
New Brighton N.Z. 43°29S 172°43E 155 D7
New Brighton U.S.A. 40°42N 80°19W 174 F4
New Britain Papua N. G. 5°50S 150°20E 147 B8
New Britain U.S.A. 41°40N 72°47W 175 E12
New Brockton U.S.A. 31°23N 85°56W 178 D4
New Brunswick
U.S.A. 40°30N 74°27W 175 F10
New Brunswick □
Canada 46°50N 66°30W 165 C6
New Bussa Nigeria 9°53N 4°31E 139 D5
New Caledonia ☑
Pac. Oc. 21°0S 165°0E 147 D9
New Caledonia Trough
Pac. Oc. 30°0S 165°0E 156 L8
New Castle = Castilla-La
Mancha □ Spain 39°30N 3°30W 89 F7
New Castle Ind.,
U.S.A. 39°55N 85°22W 173 F11
New Castle Pa., U.S.A. 41°0N 80°21W 174 F4
New Chitose ✈ (CTS)
Japan 42°46N 141°41E 112 C10
New City U.S.A. 41°9N 73°59W 175 E11
New Concord U.S.A. 39°59N 81°54W 174 G3
New Cumberland
U.S.A. 40°30N 80°36W 174 F4
New Cuyama U.S.A. 34°57N 119°38W 171 L7
New Delhi India 28°36N 77°11E 124 E7
New Denver Canada 50°0N 117°25W 162 D5
New Don Pedro Res.
U.S.A. 37°43N 120°24W 170 H6
New Ellenton U.S.A. 33°28N 81°41W 178 B8
New England U.S.A. 46°32N 102°52W 172 B2
New England △
Australia 30°25S 152°30E 153 A10
New England Ra.
Australia 30°20S 151°45E 151 E5
New England Seamounts
Atl. Oc. 38°0N 63°0W 56 C5
New Forest △ U.K. 50°53N 1°34W 67 G6
New Galloway U.K. 55°5N 4°9W 65 F4
New Glasgow Canada 45°35N 62°36W 165 C7
New Guinea Oceania 4°0S 136°0E 147 B6
New Hamburg Canada 43°23N 80°42W 174 C4
New Hampshire □
U.S.A. 44°0N 71°30W 175 C13
New Hampton U.S.A. 43°3N 92°19W 172 D7
New Hanover S. Africa 29°22S 30°31E 145 C5
New Hartford U.S.A. 43°4N 75°18W 175 C9
New Haven Conn.,
U.S.A. 41°18N 72°55W 175 E12
New Haven Mich.,
U.S.A. 42°44N 82°48W 174 D2
New Haven N.Y.,
U.S.A. 43°28N 76°18W 175 C8
New Hazelton Canada 55°20N 127°30W 162 B3
New Hebrides = Vanuatu ■
Pac. Oc. 15°0S 168°0E 147 C9
New Holland U.S.A. 40°6N 76°5W 175 F8
New Iberia U.S.A. 30°1N 91°49W 176 F9
New Ireland
Papua N. G. 3°20S 151°50E 147 B8
New Jersey □ U.S.A. 40°0N 74°30W 173 F16
New Kensington
U.S.A. 40°34N 79°46W 174 F5
New Lexington
U.S.A. 39°43N 82°13W 173 F12
New Liskeard Canada 47°31N 79°41W 164 C4
New London Conn.,
U.S.A. 41°22N 72°6W 175 E12
New London Ohio,
U.S.A. 41°5N 82°24W 174 E2
New London Wis.,
U.S.A. 44°23N 88°45W 172 C9
New Madrid U.S.A. 36°36N 89°32W 172 G9
New Martinsville
U.S.A. 39°39N 80°52W 173 F13
New Meadows U.S.A. 44°58N 116°18W 168 D5
New Melones L.
U.S.A. 37°57N 120°31W 170 H6
New Mexico □ U.S.A. 34°30N 106°0W 169 J11
New Milford Conn.,
U.S.A. 41°35N 73°25W 175 E11
New Milford Pa.,
U.S.A. 41°52N 75°44W 175 E9
New Mumbai = Navi Mumbai
India 19°5N 73°0E 126 E1
New Norcia Australia 30°57S 116°13E 149 F2
New Norfolk Australia 42°46S 147°2E 151 G4
New Orleans U.S.A. 29°57N 90°4W 177 G9
New Philadelphia
U.S.A. 40°30N 81°27W 174 F3
New Plymouth N.Z. 39°4S 174°5E 154 F3
New Plymouth
U.S.A. 43°58N 116°49W 168 D5
New Port Richey
U.S.A. 28°16N 82°43W 179 D7
New Providence
Bahamas 25°25N 77°35W 182 A4
New Quay U.K. 52°13N 4°21E 67 E3
New Radnor U.K. 52°15N 3°9W 67 E4
New Richmond
Canada 48°15N 65°45W 165 C6
New Richmond U.S.A. 45°7N 92°32W 172 C7
New River Gorge △
U.S.A. 37°53N 81°5W 173 G13
New Roads U.S.A. 30°42N 91°26W 176 F9
New Rochelle U.S.A. 40°55N 73°46W 175 F11
New Rockford U.S.A. 47°41N 99°8W 172 B4
New Romney U.K. 50°59N 0°57E 67 G8
New Ross Ireland 52°23N 6°57W 64 D5
New Salem U.S.A. 46°51N 101°25W 172 B3
New Scone = Scone U.K. 56°25N 3°24W 65 E5
New Siberian I. = Novaya Sibir,
Ostrov Russia 75°10N 150°0E 107 B16
New Siberian Is. = Novosibirskiye
Ostrova Russia 75°0N 142°0E 107 B15
New Smyrna Beach
U.S.A. 29°1N 80°56W 179 D7
New South Wales □
Australia 33°0S 146°0E 153 B7
New Tecumseth = Alliston
Canada 44°9N 79°52W 174 B5
New Town U.S.A. 47°59N 102°30W 172 B2

New Ulm U.S.A. 44°19N 94°28W 172 C6
New Waterford Canada 46°13N 60°4W 165 C7
New Westminster
Canada 49°13N 122°55W 170 A4
New York U.S.A. 40°43N 74°0W 175 F11
New York □ U.S.A. 43°0N 75°0W 175 D9
New York J.F. Kennedy Int. ✈
(JFK) U.S.A. 40°38N 73°47W 175 F11
New Zealand ■ Oceania 40°0S 176°0E 154 G5
Newa → India 24°24N 76°49E 124 G7
Newala Tanzania 10°58S 39°18E 143 E4
Newark Del., U.S.A. 39°41N 75°46W 173 F16
Newark N.J., U.S.A. 40°44N 74°10W 175 F10
Newark N.Y., U.S.A. 43°3N 77°6W 174 C7
Newark Ohio, U.S.A. 40°3N 82°24W 174 F2
Newark Liberty Int. ✈ (EWR)
U.S.A. 40°42N 74°10W 175 F10
Newark-on-Trent U.K. 53°5N 0°48W 66 D7
Newark Valley U.S.A. 42°14N 76°11W 175 D8
Newberg U.S.A. 45°18N 122°58W 168 D2
Newberry Fla., U.S.A. 29°39N 82°37W 179 F7
Newberry Mich.,
U.S.A. 46°21N 85°30W 173 B11
Newberry S.C., U.S.A. 34°17N 81°37W 177 D14
Newberry Springs
U.S.A. 34°50N 116°41W 171 L10
Newboro L. Canada 44°38N 76°20W 175 B8
Newbridge Ireland 53°11N 6°48W 64 C5
Newburgh Canada 44°19N 76°52W 175 B8
Newburgh U.S.A. 41°30N 74°1W 175 E10
Newbury U.K. 51°24N 1°20W 67 F6
Newbury N.H., U.S.A. 43°19N 72°3W 175 B12
Newbury Vt., U.S.A. 44°5N 72°4W 175 B12
Newburyport U.S.A. 42°49N 70°53W 175 D14
Newcastle Australia 33°0S 151°46E 153 B9
Newcastle N.B., Canada 47°1N 65°38W 165 C6
Newcastle Ont., Canada 43°55N 78°35W 164 D4
Newcastle Ireland 52°27N 9°3W 64 D2
Newcastle S. Africa 27°45S 29°58E 145 C4
Newcastle Calif., U.S.A. 38°53N 121°8W 170 G5
Newcastle Wyo.,
U.S.A. 43°50N 104°11W 168 E11
Newcastle Emlyn U.K. 52°2N 4°28W 67 E3
Newcastle Ra.
Australia 15°45S 130°15E 148 C5
Newcastle-under-Lyme
U.K. 53°1N 2°14W 66 D5
Newcastle-upon-Tyne
U.K. 54°58N 1°36W 66 C6
Newcastle Waters
Australia 17°30S 133°28E 150 B1
Newcomb U.S.A. 43°58N 74°10W 175 C10
Newcomerstown
U.S.A. 40°16N 81°36W 174 F3
Newdegate Australia 33°6S 119°0E 149 F2
Newell Australia 16°20S 145°16E 150 B4
Newell U.S.A. 44°43N 103°25W 172 C2
Newenham, C. U.S.A. 58°39N 162°11W 166 D7
Newfane U.S.A. 43°17N 78°43W 174 C6
Newfield U.S.A. 42°18N 76°33W 175 D8
Newfound L. U.S.A. 43°40N 71°47W 175 C13
Newfoundland Canada 49°0N 55°0W 165 C8
Newfoundland U.S.A. 41°18N 75°19W 175 E9
Newfoundland & Labrador □
Canada 52°0N 58°0W 165 B8
Newhaven U.K. 50°47N 0°3E 67 G8
Newington U.S.A. 32°35N 81°30W 178 C8
Newkirk U.S.A. 36°53N 97°3W 176 C6
Newlyn U.K. 50°6N 5°34W 67 G2
Newman Australia 23°18S 119°45E 148 D2
Newman U.S.A. 37°19N 121°1W 170 H5
Newmarket Canada 44°3N 79°28W 174 B5
Newmarket Ireland 52°13N 9°0W 64 D2
Newmarket U.K. 52°15N 0°25E 67 E8
Newnan U.S.A. 33°23N 84°48W 178 B5
Newport Ireland 53°53N 9°33W 64 C2
Newport I. of W., U.K. 50°42N 1°17W 67 G6
Newport Newport, U.K. 51°35N 3°0W 67 F5
Newport Ark., U.S.A. 35°37N 91°16W 176 D9
Newport Ky., U.S.A. 39°5N 84°29W 173 F11
Newport N.H., U.S.A. 43°22N 72°10W 175 C12
Newport N.Y., U.S.A. 43°11N 75°1W 175 C9
Newport Oreg., U.S.A. 44°39N 124°3W 168 D1
Newport R.I., U.S.A. 41°29N 71°19W 175 E13
Newport Tenn., U.S.A. 35°58N 83°11W 177 D13
Newport Vt., U.S.A. 44°56N 72°13W 175 B12
Newport Wash., U.S.A. 48°11N 117°3W 168 B5
Newport □ U.K. 51°33N 3°1W 67 F4
Newport Beach
U.S.A. 33°37N 117°56W 171 M9
Newport News U.S.A. 36°58N 76°25W 173 G15
Newport Pagnell U.K. 52°5N 0°43W 67 E7
Newquay U.K. 50°25N 5°6W 67 G2
Newry U.K. 54°11N 6°21W 64 B5
Newry Islands △
Australia 20°51S 148°56E 150 b
Newton Ga., U.S.A. 31°19N 84°20W 178 D5
Newton Ill., U.S.A. 38°59N 88°10W 172 F9
Newton Iowa, U.S.A. 41°42N 93°3W 172 E7
Newton Kans., U.S.A. 38°3N 97°21W 172 F5
Newton Mass., U.S.A. 42°21N 71°12W 175 D14
Newton Miss., U.S.A. 32°19N 89°10W 177 E10
Newton N.C., U.S.A. 35°40N 81°13W 177 D14
Newton N.J., U.S.A. 41°3N 74°45W 175 E10
Newton Tex., U.S.A. 30°51N 93°46W 176 F8
Newton Abbot U.K. 50°32N 3°37W 67 G4
Newton Aycliffe U.K. 54°37N 1°34W 66 C6
Newton Falls N.Y.,
U.S.A. 44°12N 74°59W 175 B10
Newton Falls Ohio,
U.S.A. 41°11N 80°59W 174 E4
Newton Stewart U.K. 54°57N 4°30W 65 G4
Newtonmore U.K. 57°4N 4°8W 65 D4
Newtontoppen Svalbard 79°0N 17°30E 57 B12
Newtown U.K. 52°31N 3°19W 67 E4
Newtownabbey U.K. 54°40N 5°56W 64 B6
Newtownards U.K. 54°36N 5°42W 64 B6
Newtownbarry = Bunclody
Ireland 52°39N 6°40W 64 D5
Newtownstewart U.K. 54°43N 7°23W 64 B4
Neville U.K. 54°17N 0°4W 66 C7
Nexon France 45°41N 1°11E 72 C5
Neya Russia 58°21N 43°49E 86 A6
Neyriz Iran 29°15N 54°19E 129 D7
Neyshābūr Iran 36°10N 58°50E 129 B8
Neyveli India 11°32N 79°29E 127 J4
Neyyattinkara India 8°26N 77°5E 127 K3
Nezhin = Nizhyn Ukraine 51°5N 31°55E 85 G6

Nezperce U.S.A. 46°14N 116°14W 168 C5
Nezvysko Ukraine 48°46N 25°15E 81 B10
Nga, Laem Thailand 7°55N 98°27E 121 a
Ngaanyatjarra ◌
Australia 22°40S 127°0E 148 D4
Ngabang Indonesia 0°23N 109°55E 118 D3
Ngabordamlu, Tanjung
Indonesia 6°56S 134°11E 119 F8
N'Gage Angola 7°46S 15°15E 140 F3
Ngala Nigeria 12°20N 14°11E 139 C7
Ngaliwurru Nungali ◌
Australia 15°42S 130°4E 148 C5
Ngambé Centre,
Cameroon 5°48N 11°29E 139 D7
Ngambé Littoral,
Cameroon 4°21N 10°40E 139 E7
Ngami Depression
Botswana 20°30S 22°46E 144 B3
Ngamo Zimbabwe 19°3S 27°32E 143 F2
Ngamring China 29°14N 87°10E 110 F6
Nganbéto, L. de Togo 7°26N 1°25E 139 D5
Nganglong Kangri China 33°0N 81°0E 125 C9
Ngao Thailand 18°46N 99°59E 120 C2
Ngaoundéré Cameroon 7°15N 13°35E 140 C2
Ngapara N.Z. 44°57S 170°46E 155 E3
Ngara Tanzania 2°29S 30°40E 142 C5
Ngarluma ◌ Australia 21°30S 117°0E 148 D2
Ngaruawahia N.Z. 37°42S 175°11E 154 D4
Ngaruroro → N.Z. 39°34S 176°55E 154 F5
Ngatapa N.Z. 38°33S 177°43E 154 E6
Ngauruhoe, Mt. N.Z. 39°13S 175°45E 154 F5
Ngawi Indonesia 7°24S 111°26E 119 G14
Ngcobo S. Africa 31°37S 28°0E 145 D4
Ngerulmud = Melekeok
Palau 7°27N 134°38E 156 G5
Nghia Lo Vietnam 21°33N 104°28E 120 B5
Ngoma Malawi 13°8S 33°45E 143 E3
Ngomahura Zimbabwe 20°26S 30°43E 143 G3
Ngomba Tanzania 8°20S 32°53E 143 D3
Ngomeni, Ras Kenya 2°59S 40°14E 142 C5
Ngongotaha N.Z. 38°5S 176°12E 154 E5
Ngoring Hu China 34°55N 97°5E 110 E8
Ngorkou Mali 15°40N 3°41W 138 B4
Ngorongoro Tanzania 3°11S 35°32E 142 C4
Ngorongoro ◌ Tanzania 2°40S 35°30E 142 C4
Ngozi Burundi 2°54S 29°50E 142 C2
Ngudu Tanzania 2°58S 33°25E 142 C3
Nguigmi Niger 14°20N 13°20E 135 F8
Nguila Cameroon 4°41N 11°43E 139 E7
Nguiu Australia 11°46S 130°38E 148 B5
Ngukurr Australia 14°44S 134°44E 150 A1
Ngum → Laos 18°31N 102°32E 120 C4
Ngundu Zimbabwe 18°11S 31°15E 143 F3
Ngunga Tanzania 3°37S 33°37E 142 C3
Nguru Nigeria 12°56N 10°29E 139 C7
Nguru Mts. Tanzania 6°0S 37°30E 142 D4
Ngusi Malawi 14°0S 34°50E 143 E3
Nguyen Binh Vietnam 22°39N 105°56E 120 A5
Ngwakwase ◌ Botswana 25°0S 25°0E 144 C3
Nha Bang Vietnam 10°37N 105°0E 121 G5
Nha Trang Vietnam 12°16N 109°10E 121 F7
Nhacoongo Mozam. 24°18S 35°14E 145 B6
Nhamaabué Mozam. 17°25S 35°5E 143 F4
Nhamundá → Brazil 2°12S 56°41W 187 D7
Nhangulaze, L. Mozam. 24°0S 34°30E 145 B5
Nharnuwangga, Wajarri and
Ngarlawangga ◌
Australia 24°50S 118°0E 149 E2
Nhill Australia 36°18S 141°40E 153 C5
Nho Quan Vietnam 20°18N 105°45E 116 G5
Nhulunbuy Australia 12°10S 137°20E 150 A2
Nia-nia
Dem. Rep. of the Congo 1°30N 27°40E 142 B2
Niafounké Mali 16°0N 4°5W 138 B4
Niagara Falls Canada 43°7N 79°5W 174 C5
Niagara Falls U.S.A. 43°5N 79°4W 174 C6
Niagara-on-the-Lake
Canada 43°15N 79°4W 174 C5
Niah Malaysia 3°58N 113°46E 118 D4
Niamey Niger 13°27N 2°6E 139 C5
Niamtougou Togo 9°46N 1°6E 139 D5
Niandan-Koro Guinea 11°5N 9°15W 138 C3
Nianforando Guinea 9°37N 10°36W 138 D2
Niangara
Dem. Rep. of the Congo 3°42N 27°50E 142 B2
Niangay, L. Mali 15°50N 3°0W 138 B4
Niangbo Côte d'Ivoire 8°49N 5°10W 138 D3
Niangoloko
Burkina Faso 10°15N 4°55W 138 C4
Niantic U.S.A. 41°20N 72°11W 175 E12
Nias Indonesia 1°0N 97°30E 118 D1
Niassa □ Mozam. 13°30S 36°0E 143 E4
Niassa, L. = Malawi, L.
Africa 12°30S 34°30E 143 E3
Niassa △ Mozam. 12°4S 36°57E 143 E4
Nibāk Si. Arabia 24°25N 50°50E 129 E7
Nibe Denmark 56°59N 9°38E 63 H3
Nicaragua ■
Cent. Amer. 11°40N 85°30W 182 D2
Nicaragua, L. de Nic. 12°0N 85°30W 182 D2
Nicastro Italy 38°59N 16°19E 95 D9
Nice France 43°42N 7°14E 73 E11
Nice-Côte-d'Azur ✈ (NCE)
France 43°41N 7°12E 73 E11
Niceville U.S.A. 30°31N 86°30W 178 D4
Nichicun, L. Canada 53°5N 71°0W 165 B5
Nichinan Japan 31°38N 131°23E 113 K4
Nicholás, Canal
Caribbean 23°30N 80°5W 182 B3
Nicholas Channel = Nicholás,
Canal Caribbean 23°30N 80°5W 182 B3
Nicholasville U.S.A. 37°53N 84°34W 173 G11
Nicholls U.S.A. 31°31N 82°38W 178 D7
Nicholson Australia 18°2S 128°54E 148 C4
Nicholson U.S.A. 41°37N 75°47W 175 E9
Nicholson Ra.
Australia 27°15S 116°45E 149 E2
Nicholville U.S.A. 44°41N 74°39W 175 B10
Nicobar Is. Ind. Oc. 9°0N 93°0E 127 L11
Nicola Canada 50°12N 120°40W 162 C4
Nicolet Canada 46°17N 72°35W 165 C5
Nicosia Cyprus 35°10N 33°25E 101 D12
Nicosia Italy 37°45N 14°24E 95 E7
Nicótera Italy 38°33N 15°56E 95 D8
Nicoya Costa Rica 10°9N 85°27W 182 E2
Nicoya, G. de Costa Rica 10°0N 85°0W 182 E3

Nicoya, Pen. de
Costa Rica 9°45N 85°40W 182 E2
Nida Lithuania 55°20N 21°4E 82 C8
Nidd → U.K. 53°59N 1°23W 66 C6
Nidda Germany 50°23N 9°1E 77 E5
Nidda → Germany 50°17N 8°48E 77 E4
Nidwalden □ Switz. 46°50N 8°25E 77 J4
Nidzica Poland 53°25N 20°28E 83 B7
Niebüll Germany 54°46N 8°48E 76 A4
Nied → Germany 49°23N 6°40E 71 C13
Niederaula Germany 50°47N 9°36E 76 E5
Niederbayern □
Germany 48°40N 12°50E 77 G8
Niederbronn-les-Bains
France 48°57N 7°39E 71 D14
Niedere Tauern Austria 47°20N 14°0E 78 D7
Niederlausitz Germany 51°50N 13°10E 76 D9
Niederösterreich □
Austria 48°25N 15°40E 78 C8
Niedersachsen □ Germany 52°50N 9°0E 76 C4
Niedersächsisches Wattenmeer △
Germany 53°45N 7°30E 76 B3
Niekerkshoop S. Africa 29°19S 22°51E 144 C3
Niellé Côte d'Ivoire 10°5N 5°38W 138 C3
Niemba
Dem. Rep. of the Congo 5°58S 28°24E 142 D2
Niemen = Nemunas →
Lithuania 55°25N 21°10E 82 C8
Niemodlin Poland 50°38N 17°38E 83 H4
Niemur Australia 35°17S 144°9E 152 C6
Nienburg Germany 52°39N 9°13E 76 C5
Niepolomice Poland 50°3N 20°13E 83 H7
Niers → Germany 51°43N 5°57E 76 D1
Niesky Germany 51°17N 14°49E 76 D10
Nieszawa Poland 52°52N 18°50E 83 F5
Nieu Bethesda S. Africa 31°51S 24°34E 144 D3
Nieuw Amsterdam
Suriname 5°53N 55°5W 187 B7
Nieuw Nickerie Suriname 6°0N 56°59W 187 B7
Nieuwoudtville S. Africa 31°23S 19°7E 144 D2
Nieuwpoort Belgium 51°8N 2°45E 69 C2
Nieves, Pico de las
Canary Is. 27°57N 15°35W 100 G4
Nièvre □ France 47°10N 3°40E 71 E10
Niğa Mali 13°38N 5°27W 138 C3
Niğde Turkey 37°58N 34°40E 104 C6
Niğde □ Turkey 38°0N 34°30E 104 C6
Nigel S. Africa 26°27S 28°25E 145 C4
Niger □ Nigeria 10°0N 5°30E 139 D6
Niger ■ W. Afr. 17°30N 10°0E 139 B7
Niger → W. Afr. 5°33N 6°33E 139 E6
Niger Delta Africa 5°0N 6°0E 139 E6
Nigeria ■ W. Afr. 8°30N 8°0E 139 D6
Nighasin India 28°14N 80°52E 125 E9
Nightcaps N.Z. 45°57S 168°2E 155 F2
Nigrita Greece 40°56N 23°29E 96 F7
Nihoa U.S.A. 23°6N 161°58W 167 L7
Nihon = Japan ■ Asia 36°0N 136°0E 113 G8
Nii-Jima Japan 34°20N 139°15E 113 G9
Niigata Japan 37°58N 139°0E 113 F9
Niigata □ Japan 37°15N 138°45E 113 F9
Niihama Japan 33°55N 133°16E 113 H6
Ni'ihau U.S.A. 21°54N 160°9W 167 L7
Niimi Japan 34°59N 133°28E 113 G6
Niitsu Japan 37°48N 139°7E 112 F9
Nijar Spain 36°53N 2°15W 91 J2
Nijil Jordan 30°32N 35°33E 130 E4
Nijkerk Neths. 52°13N 5°30E 69 B5
Nijmegen Neths. 51°50N 5°52E 69 C5
Nijverdal Neths. 52°22N 6°28E 69 B6
Nik Pey Iran 36°50N 48°10E 105 D13
Nikaweratiya Sri Lanka 7°45N 80°7E 127 L5
Nike Nigeria 6°26N 7°29E 139 E6
Nikel Russia 69°24N 30°13E 60 B24
Nikiniki Indonesia 9°49S 124°30E 148 B4
Nikisiani Greece 40°57N 24°9E 97 F8
Nikiti Greece 40°13N 23°43E 96 F7
Nikkō Japan 9°58N 31°12E 139 D5
Nikkō Japan 36°45N 139°35E 113 F9
Nikolayev = Mykolayiv
Ukraine 46°58N 32°0E 85 J7
Nikolayevsk Russia 50°0N 45°35E 86 E7
Nikolayevsk-na-Amur
Russia 53°8N 140°44E 107 D15
Nikolsk Russia 53°49N 46°4E 86 D8
Nikolskoye Russia 55°12N 166°0E 107 D17
Nikopol Bulgaria 43°43N 24°54E 97 D8
Nikopol Greece 47°35N 34°25E 85 J8
Nikopolis Greece 39°5N 20°43E 98 B2
Niksar Turkey 40°31N 37°2E 104 B7
Nikshahr Iran 26°15N 60°10E 129 E9
Nikšić Montenegro 42°50N 18°57E 96 D2
Nil, Nahr en → Africa 30°10N 31°6E 137 C7
Nil el Abyad → Sudan 15°38N 32°31E 135 E12
Nil el Azraq → Sudan 15°38N 32°31E 135 E12
Nila Indonesia 6°44S 129°31E 119 F7
Nilakkottai India 10°10N 77°52E 127 L4
Niland U.S.A. 33°14N 115°31W 171 M11
Nilanga India 18°6N 76°46E 126 E3
Nile = Nil, Nahr en →
Africa 30°10N 31°6E 137 C7
Nile Delta Egypt 31°0N 31°0E 137 E7
Niles Mich., U.S.A. 41°50N 86°15W 172 E10
Niles Ohio, U.S.A. 41°11N 80°46W 174 E4
Nileshwar India 12°15N 75°6E 127 H2
Nilgiri Hills India 11°30N 76°30E 127 J3
Nilo Peçanha Brazil 13°37S 39°6W 189 D3
Nilüfer → Turkey 40°18N 28°27E 99 B3
Nim Ka Thana India 27°44N 75°48E 124 F6
Nimach India 24°30N 74°56E 124 G6
Nimba, Mt. Africa 7°37N 8°25E 138 D3
Nimbahera India 24°37N 74°45E 124 G6
Nîmes France 43°50N 4°23E 73 E8
Nimfaíon, Ákra = Pines, Akra
Greece 40°5N 24°20E 97 F8
Nimmitabel Australia 36°29S 149°15E 153 D8
Nin Croatia 44°16N 15°12E 93 D12
Nīnawá Iraq 36°25N 43°10E 105 D10
Nīnawá □ Iraq 36°15N 43°0E 108 B4
Nindigully Australia 28°21S 148°50E 151 D4
Nine Degree Channel
India 9°0N 73°0E 127 K1
Ninepin Group China 22°16N 114°21E 111 a
Ninety Mile Beach N.Z. 34°48S 173°0E 154 B4
Ninety Mile Beach, The
Australia 38°15S 147°24E 153 E7
Ninety Six U.S.A. 34°11N 82°1W 178 B8
Nineveh = Nīnawá
Iraq 36°25N 43°10E 105 D10
Ning Xian China 35°30N 107°58E 114 G4

Ningaloo Marine ○ Australia 22°23S 113°32E 148 D1
Ning'an China 44°22N 129°20E 115 B15
Ningbo China 29°51N 121°28E 117 C13
Ningcheng China 41°32N 119°53E 115 D10
Ningde China 26°38N 119°23E 117 D12
Ningdu China 26°25N 115°59E 117 D10
Ninggang China 26°42N 113°56E 117 D9
Ningguo China 30°35N 119°0E 117 B12
Ninghai China 29°15N 121°28E 117 C13
Ninghua China 26°14N 116°45E 117 D11
Ningi Nigeria 10°55N 9°30E 139 C6
Ningjin China 37°35N 114°57E 114 F8
Ningjing Shan China 31°0N 98°20E 116 C2
Ninglang China 27°20N 100°55E 116 D3
Ningling China 34°25N 115°22E 114 G8
Ningming China 22°8N 107°4E 116 F6
Ningnan China 27°0N 102°36E 116 D4
Ningpo = Ningbo
China 29°51N 121°28E 117 C13
Ningqiang China 32°47N 106°15E 114 H4
Ningshan China 33°21N 108°21E 116 A7
Ningsia Hui A.R. = Ningxia Huizu
Zizhiqu □ China 38°0N 106°0E 114 F4
Ningwu China 39°0N 112°18E 114 E7
Ningxia Huizu Zizhiqu □
China 38°0N 106°0E 114 F4
Ningxiang China 28°15N 112°30E 117 C9
Ningyang China 35°47N 116°45E 114 G9
Ningyuan China 25°37N 111°57E 117 D8
Ninh Binh Vietnam 20°15N 105°55E 116 G5
Ninh Giang Vietnam 20°44N 106°24E 116 B6
Ninh Hoa Vietnam 12°30N 109°7E 120 F7
Ninh Ma Vietnam 12°48N 109°21E 120 F7
Nini-Suhien △ Ghana 5°20N 2°34W 138 D4
Ninove Belgium 50°51N 4°2E 69 D4
Nioaque Brazil 21°5S 55°50W 191 A4
Niobrara U.S.A. 42°45N 98°2W 172 D4
Niobrara → U.S.A. 42°46N 98°3W 172 D5
Niokolo-Koba △ Senegal 13°3N 13°2W 138 C2
Niono Mali 14°15N 6°0W 138 C3
Nionsamoridougou
Guinea 8°45N 8°50W 138 D3
Nioro du Rip Senegal 13°40N 15°50W 138 C1
Nioro du Sahel Mali 15°15N 9°30W 138 B3
Niort France 46°19N 0°29W 72 B3
Nipani India 16°20N 74°25E 127 F2
Nipawin Canada 53°20N 104°0W 163 C8
Nipfjället Sweden 61°59N 12°50E 62 C6
Nipigon Canada 49°0N 88°17W 164 C2
Nipigon, L. Canada 49°50N 88°30W 164 C2
Nipishish L. Canada 54°12N 60°45W 165 B7
Nipissing, L. Canada 46°20N 80°0W 164 C4
Nipomo U.S.A. 35°3N 120°29W 171 K6
Nippon = Japan ■ Asia 36°0N 136°0E 113 G8
Nipton U.S.A. 35°28N 115°16W 171 K11
Niquelândia Brazil 14°33S 48°23W 189 C1
Nir Iran 38°2N 47°59E 105 C12
Nira → India 17°58N 75°8E 126 F2
Nirasaki Japan 35°42N 138°27E 113 G9
Nirmal India 19°3N 78°20E 126 E4
Nirmali India 26°20N 86°35E 125 F12
Niš Serbia 43°19N 21°58E 96 C5
Nisa Portugal 39°30N 7°41W 89 F3
Nisa Turkmenistan 37°59N 58°11E 129 B8
Niṣāb Si. Arabia 29°11N 44°43E 128 D5
Niṣāb Yemen 14°25N 46°29E 131 E4
Nišava → Serbia 43°20N 21°46E 96 C5
Niscemi Italy 37°9N 14°23E 95 E7
Nishinomiya Japan 34°45N 135°20E 113 G7
Nishino'omote Japan 30°43N 130°59E 113 J5
Nishiwaki Japan 34°59N 134°58E 113 G7
Niška Banja Serbia 43°18N 22°1E 96 C6
Niskibi → Canada 56°29N 88°9W 164 A2
Nisko Poland 50°35N 22°7E 83 H9
Nisporeni Moldova 47°4N 28°10E 81 C13
Nisqually → U.S.A. 47°7N 122°42W 170 C4
Nissaki Greece 39°43N 19°52E 101 A3
Nissan → Sweden 56°40N 12°51E 63 H6
Nissiros Greece 36°35N 27°12E 99 E9
Nissum Bredning
Denmark 56°40N 8°20E 63 H2
Nissum Fjord Denmark 56°20N 8°11E 63 H2
Nistru = Dnister →
Europe 46°18N 30°17E 75 E16
Nisutlin → Canada 60°14N 132°34W 162 A2
Nitchequon Canada 53°10N 70°58W 165 B5
Niterói Brazil 22°53S 43°7W 191 A7
Nith → Canada 43°12N 80°23W 174 C4
Nith → U.K. 55°14N 3°33W 65 F5
Nitmiluk △ Australia 14°6S 132°15E 148 B5
Nitra Slovakia 48°19N 18°4E 79 C11
Nitra → Slovakia 47°46N 18°10E 79 D11
Nittenau Germany 49°12N 12°16E 77 D8
Niue ☑ Pac. Oc. 19°2S 169°54W 157 J11
Niulan Jiang → China 27°30N 103°5E 116 D4
Niut Indonesia 0°55N 109°54E 118 D4
Niutou Shan China 29°5N 121°59E 117 C13
Niuzhuang China 40°58N 122°28E 115 D12
Nivala Finland 63°56N 24°57E 60 E21
Nivelles Belgium 50°35N 4°20E 69 D4
Nivernais France 47°15N 3°30E 71 E10
Niverville Canada 49°36N 97°3W 163 D9
Niwas India 23°3N 80°26E 125 H9
Nixa U.S.A. 37°3N 93°18W 172 G7
Nixon U.S.A. 29°16N 97°46W 176 G6
Nizam Sagar India 18°10N 77°58E 126 E3
Nizamabad India 18°45N 78°7E 126 E4
Nizamghat India 28°20N 95°45E 123 E19
Nizhne-Kolymsk
Russia 68°34N 160°55E 107 C17
Nizhne-Svirskiy ○
Russia 60°30N 32°55E 84 B7
Nizhnegorskiy = Nyzhnohirskyy
Ukraine 45°27N 34°38E 85 K8
Nizhnekamsk Russia 55°38N 51°49E 86 C10
Nizhneudinsk Russia 54°54N 99°3E 107 D10
Nizhnevartovsk Russia 60°56N 76°38E 106 C8
Nizhniy Bestyakh
Russia 61°57N 129°54E 107 C13
Nizhniy Chir Russia 48°22N 43°5E 87 F6
Nizhniy Lomov Russia 53°34N 43°38E 86 D6
Nizhniy Novgorod Russia 56°20N 44°0E 86 B7
Nizhniy Novgorod □
Russia 56°30N 44°20E 86 B7
Nizhniy Tagil Russia 57°55N 59°57E 106 D6
Nizhyn Ukraine 51°5N 31°55E 85 G6
Nizina Mazowiecka
Poland 52°30N 21°0E 83 F8
Nizip Turkey 37°5N 37°50E 104 D7
Nizké Tatry Slovakia 48°55N 19°30E 79 C12

Nízke Tatry △ Slovakia 48°55N 19°37E 79 C12
Nízký Jeseník Czechia 49°50N 17°30E 79 B10
Nizwá Oman 22°56N 57°32E 131 C6
Njakwa Malawi 11°35S 33°56E 143 D3
Njazidja = Grande Comore
Comoros Is. 11°35S 43°20E 141 a
Njegoš Montenegro 42°53N 18°45E 96 C2
Njeru Uganda 0°27N 33°10E 142 B3
Njinjo Tanzania 8°48S 38°54E 143 D4
Njombe Tanzania 9°20S 34°50E 143 D3
Njombe Tanzania 9°10S 34°50E 143 D3
Njombe → Tanzania 6°56S 35°6E 142 D4
Njurundabommen
Sweden 62°15N 17°25E 62 B11
Nkambe Cameroon 6°35N 10°40E 139 D7
Nkana Zambia 12°50S 28°8E 143 E2
Nkandla S. Africa 28°37S 31°5E 145 D5
Nkawkaw Ghana 6°36N 0°49W 139 D4
Nkayi Zimbabwe 19°41S 29°20E 143 F2
Nkhotakota Malawi 12°56S 34°15E 143 E3
Nkhotakota △ Malawi 12°50S 34°0E 143 E3
Nkondwe Tanzania 5°51S 30°51E 142 D3
Nkongsamba Cameroon 4°55N 9°55E 139 E6
Nkoteng Cameroon 4°31N 12°2E 139 E7
Nkurenkuru Namibia 17°42S 18°32E 144 A2
Nkwanta Ghana 6°10N 2°10W 138 D4
Nmai → Myanmar 25°30N 97°25E 116 F2
Noakhali Bangla. 22°48N 91°10E 123 H17
Nobel Canada 45°25N 80°6W 174 A4
Nobeoka Japan 32°36N 131°41E 113 H5
Noblejas Spain 39°58N 3°26E 89 F7
Noblesville U.S.A. 40°3N 86°1W 172 E10
Noboribetsu Japan 42°24N 141°6E 112 C10
Nocatee U.S.A. 27°10N 81°53W 179 H8
Nocera Inferiore Italy 40°44N 14°38E 95 B7
Nocera Umbra Italy 43°5N 12°47E 93 E9
Noci Italy 40°48N 17°7E 95 B10
Nocona U.S.A. 33°47N 97°44W 176 E6
Nocrich Romania 45°55N 24°26E 81 E9
Noda Japan 35°56N 139°52E 113 G9
Nogales Mexico 31°19N 110°56W 180 A2
Nogales U.S.A. 31°21N 110°56W 169 L8
Nogaro France 43°45N 0°2W 72 E3
Nogat → Poland 54°17N 19°17E 82 D6
Nōgata Japan 33°48N 130°44E 113 H5
Nogent France 48°1N 5°20E 71 D12
Nogent-le-Rotrou France 48°20N 0°50E 70 D7
Nogent-sur-Seine
France 48°30N 3°30E 71 D10
Noggerup Australia 33°32S 116°5E 149 F2
Noginsk Russia 64°30N 90°50E 107 C10
Nogliki Russia 51°50N 143°10E 107 D15
Nogoa → Australia 23°40S 147°55E 150 C4
Nogoyá Argentina 32°24S 59°48W 190 C4
Nógrád □ Hungary 48°0N 19°30E 80 C4
Noguera Pallaresa →
Spain 41°55N 0°55E 90 D5
Noguera Ribagorçana →
Spain 41°40N 0°43E 90 D5
Nohar India 29°11N 74°49E 124 E6
Nohfelden Germany 49°35N 7°7E 77 F3
Nohta India 23°40N 79°34E 125 H8
Noia Spain 42°48N 8°53W 89 A1
Noida India 28°36N 77°19E 124 E7
Noire, Montagne France 43°28N 2°18E 72 E6
Noires, Mts. France 48°11N 3°40W 70 D3
Noirétable France 45°48N 3°46E 72 C7
Noirmoutier, Î. de France 46°58N 2°10W 70 E4
Noirmoutier-en-l'Île
France 47°0N 2°14W 70 F4
Nojane Botswana 23°15S 20°14E 144 B3
Nojima-Zaki Japan 34°54N 139°53E 113 G9
Nok Kundi Pakistan 28°50N 62°45E 122 E3
Nok Ta Phao, Ko
Thailand 9°23N 99°40E 121 b
Nokaneng Botswana 19°40S 22°17E 144 A3
Nokia Finland 61°30N 23°30E 84 B2
Nokomis Canada 51°35N 105°0W 163 C8
Nokomis U.S.A. 27°7N 82°27W 179 H7
Nokomis L. Canada 57°0N 103°0W 163 B8
Nola C.A.R. 3°35N 16°4E 140 D3
Nola Italy 40°55N 14°33E 95 B7
Nolinsk Russia 57°28N 49°57E 86 B9
Noma U.S.A. 30°59N 85°37W 178 F12
Noma Omuramba →
Namibia 18°52S 20°53E 144 A3
Nombre de Dios Panama 9°34N 79°28W 182 E4
Nome U.S.A. 64°30N 165°25W 166 C6
Nomgon Mongolia 42°50N 105°8E 114 C3
Nomo-Zaki Japan 32°35N 129°44E 113 H4
Nonacho L. Canada 61°42N 109°40W 163 A7
Nonancourt France 48°47N 1°11E 70 D8
Nonda Australia 20°40S 142°28E 150 C3
None Italy 44°56N 7°32E 92 D4
Nong Chang Thailand 15°23N 99°51E 120 D2
Nong Han Res.
Thailand 17°11N 104°9E 120 D5
Nong Het Laos 19°29N 103°59E 120 C4
Nong Khai Thailand 17°50N 102°46E 120 D4
Nong'an China 44°25N 125°5E 115 B13
Nongoma S. Africa 27°58S 31°35E 145 C5
Nongsa Indonesia 1°11N 104°8E 121 d
Nonoava Mexico 27°28N 106°44W 180 B3
Nonsan S. Korea 36°12N 127°5E 115 F14
Nonthaburi Thailand 13°50N 100°29E 120 F3
Nontron France 45°31N 0°40E 72 C4
Nonza France 42°47N 9°21E 73 F13
Noonamah Australia 12°40S 131°4E 148 B5
Noondie, L. Australia 28°30S 119°30E 149 E2
Noonkanbah ○
Australia 18°30S 124°50E 148 C3
Noord Brabant □ Neths. 51°40N 5°0E 69 C5
Noord Holland □ Neths. 52°30N 4°45E 69 B4
Noordbeveland Neths. 51°35N 3°50E 69 C3
Noordoostpolder Neths. 52°45N 5°45E 69 B5
Noordwijk Neths. 52°14N 4°26E 69 B4
Noosa Heads Australia 26°25S 153°6E 151 D5
Nootka I. Canada 49°32N 126°42W 162 D3
Nopiming ○ Canada 50°30N 95°37W 163 C9
Nora Sweden 59°32N 15°2E 63 E9
Noralee Canada 53°59N 126°26W 162 C3
Noranda = Rouyn-Noranda
Canada 48°20N 79°0W 164 C4
Norberg Sweden 60°4N 15°56E 62 D9
Nórcia Italy 42°48N 13°5E 93 F10
Norco U.S.A. 33°56N 117°33W 171 M9

Nord □ Cameroon 8°30N 14°0E 139 D7
Nord □ France 50°15N 3°30E 71 B10
Nord-Kivu □
Dem. Rep. of the Congo 1°0S 29°0E 142 C2
Nord-Ostsee-Kanal
Germany 54°12N 9°32E 76 A5
Nord-Ouest □ Cameroon 6°0N 10°0E 139 D7
Nordaustlandet Svalbard 79°14N 23°0E 54 B9
Nordborg Denmark 55°5N 9°50E 63 J3
Nordby Denmark 55°27N 8°24E 63 J2
Norddeich Germany 53°36N 7°9E 76 B3
Nordegg Canada 52°29N 116°5W 162 C5
Nordenham Germany 53°30N 8°30E 76 B4
Nordenham Germany 53°30N 8°30E 76 B4
Norderney Germany 53°42N 7°9E 76 B3
Norderstedt Germany 53°42N 10°1E 76 B6
Nordfjord Norway 61°55N 5°30E 60 F11
Nordfriesische Inseln
Germany 54°40N 8°20E 76 A4
Nordhausen Germany 51°30N 10°47E 76 D6
Nordhorn Germany 52°26N 7°4E 76 C3
Nordkinn = Kinnarodden
Norway 71°8N 27°40E 58 A11
Nordøyane Norway 71°10N 25°50E 58 A11
Nordkapp Norway 71°10N 25°50E 60 A21
Nordkapp Svalbard 80°31N 20°0E 54 A9
Nordkinn Norway 71°8N 27°40E 60 A22
Nordkinnhalvøya
Norway 70°55N 27°40E 60 A22
Nordland □ Norway 65°40N 13°0E 58 E10
Nördlingen Germany 48°48N 10°30E 77 G6
Nordostrundingen
Greenland 81°22N 11°40W 57 A5
Nordre Strømfjord
Greenland 67°10N 53°35W 57 D5
Nordrhein-Westfalen □
Germany 51°45N 7°30E 76 D3
Nordstrand Germany 54°30N 8°52E 76 A4
Nordvik Russia 74°2N 111°32E 107 B12
Nore → Ireland 52°25N 6°58E 64 D4
Noreland Canada 44°43N 78°48W 174 B6
Norfolk = Simcoe
Canada 42°50N 80°23W 174 D4
Norfolk N.Y., U.S.A. 44°48N 74°59W 175 B10
Norfolk Nebr., U.S.A. 42°2N 97°25W 172 D5
Norfolk Va., U.S.A. 36°50N 76°17W 173 G15
Norfolk □ U.K. 52°45N 0°54E 67 E8
Norfolk Broads △ U.K. 52°45N 1°30E 67 E9
Norfolk I. Pac. Oc. 28°58S 168°3E 147 D9
Norfolk Ridge Pac. Oc. 29°0S 168°0E 156 K8
Norfork L. U.S.A. 36°15N 92°14W 176 E8
Norge = Norway ■
Europe 63°0N 11°0E 60 E14
Norilsk Russia 69°20N 88°6E 107 C9
Norma, Mt. Australia 20°55S 140°42E 150 C3
Normal U.S.A. 40°31N 88°59W 172 E9
Norman U.S.A. 35°13N 97°26W 176 D6
Norman → Australia 19°18S 141°51E 150 B3
Norman Park U.S.A. 31°16N 83°41W 178 D6
Norman Wells
Canada 65°17N 126°51W 160 D6
Normanby → N.Z. 39°32S 174°18E 154 F3
Normanby →
Australia 14°23S 144°10E 150 A3
Normandie □ France 49°0N 0°0 70 D7
Normandie-Maine □
France 48°30N 0°20W 70 D6
Normandin Canada 48°49N 72°31W 164 C5
Normanhurst, Mt.
Australia 25°4S 122°30E 149 E3
Normanton Australia 17°40S 141°10E 150 B3
Normanville Australia 35°27S 138°18E 152 C3
Normétal Canada 49°0N 79°22W 164 C4
Norquay Canada 51°53N 102°5W 163 C8
Norquinco Argentina 41°51S 70°55W 192 B2
Norra Kvill △ Sweden 57°46N 15°35E 63 G9
Norra Ulvön Sweden 63°3N 18°40E 62 A12
Norrahammar Sweden 57°43N 14°7E 63 G8
Norrbottens län □
Sweden 66°50N 20°0E 60 C19
Nørre Aaby Denmark 55°27N 9°52E 63 J3
Nørre Alslev Denmark 54°54N 11°52E 63 K5
Nørresundby Denmark 57°5N 9°52E 63 G3
Norrhult-Klavreström
Sweden 57°1N 15°10E 63 G9
Norris Point Canada 49°31N 57°53W 165 C8
Norristown Ga., U.S.A. 32°30N 82°30W 178 C7
Norristown Pa., U.S.A. 40°7N 75°21W 175 D9
Norrköping Sweden 58°37N 16°11E 63 F10
Norrland Sweden 62°15N 15°45E 60 E16
Norrsundet Sweden 60°56N 17°8E 62 D11
Norrtälje Sweden 59°46N 18°42E 62 E12
Norseman Australia 32°8S 121°43E 149 F3
Norsewood N.Z. 40°3S 176°13E 154 G5
Norsk Russia 52°30N 130°5E 107 D14
Norte, Pta. Argentina 42°5S 63°46W 192 B4
Norte, Pta. del
Canary Is. 27°51N 17°57W 100 G2
Norte, Serra do Brazil 11°20S 59°0W 188 F7
Norte □ S. Africa 33°37N 81°6W 178 B8
North, C. Canada 47°2N 60°20W 165 C7
North Adams U.S.A. 42°42N 73°7W 175 D11
North America 40°0N 100°0W 158 F10
North Andaman I.
India 13°15N 92°55E 127 H11
North Arm Canada 62°0N 114°30W 162 A5
North Augusta U.S.A. 33°30N 81°59W 178 B8
North Australian Basin
Ind. Oc. 14°30S 116°30E 146 F10
North Ayrshire □ U.K. 55°45N 4°44W 65 F4
North Bass I. U.S.A. 41°40N 82°50W 174 E2
North Battleford
Canada 52°50N 108°17W 163 C7
North Bay Canada 46°20N 79°30W 164 C4
North Belcher Is.
Canada 56°50N 79°50W 164 A4
North Bend Oreg.
U.S.A. 43°24N 124°14W 168 E1
North Bend Pa., U.S.A. 41°20N 77°42W 174 E7
North Bend Wash.
U.S.A. 47°30N 121°47W 170 C5
North Bennington
U.S.A. 42°56N 73°15W 175 D11
North Berwick U.K. 56°4N 2°42W 65 E6
North Berwick U.S.A. 43°18N 70°44W 175 C14
North Branch Canada 46°20N 79°0W 164 C4
North Brother I. India 10°59N 92°40E 127 H11
North C. Canada 47°5N 64°0W 165 C7
North C. N.Z. 34°23N 173°4E 154 A2

North Canadian →
U.S.A. 35°22N 95°37W 176 D7
North Canton U.S.A. 40°53N 81°24W 174 F3
North Cape = Nordkapp
Norway 71°10N 25°50E 60 A21
North Caribou L.
Canada 52°50N 90°40W 164 B1
North Carolina □
U.S.A. 35°30N 80°0W 177 D15
North Cascades △
U.S.A. 48°45N 121°10W 168 B3
North Channel Canada 46°0N 83°0W 164 C3
North Channel U.K. 55°13N 5°52W 65 F3
North Charleston
U.S.A. 32°53N 79°58W 178 C10
North Chicago U.S.A. 42°19N 87°51W 172 D10
North Collins U.S.A. 42°35N 78°56W 174 D6
North Creek U.S.A. 43°42N 73°59W 175 C11
North Dakota □
U.S.A. 47°30N 100°15W 172 B3
North Downs U.K. 51°19N 0°21E 67 F8
North East U.K. 42°13N 79°50W 174 D5
North East □ Botswana 20°45S 27°30E 145 B4
North East Frontier Agency =
Arunachal Pradesh □
India 28°0N 95°0E 123 F19
North East Lincolnshire □
U.K. 53°34N 0°2W 66 D7
North Esk → U.K. 56°46N 2°24W 65 E6
North European Plain
Europe 55°0N 25°0E 58 E10
North Foreland U.K. 51°22N 1°28E 67 F9
North Fork U.S.A. 37°14N 119°21W 170 H7
North Fork American →
U.S.A. 38°57N 120°59W 170 G5
North Fork Edisto →
U.S.A. 33°16N 80°54W 178 B9
North Fork Feather →
U.S.A. 38°33N 121°30W 170 G5
North Fork Grand →
U.S.A. 45°47N 102°16W 172 C2
North Fork Red →
U.S.A. 34°24N 99°14W 176 D5
North Fort Myers
U.S.A. 26°41N 81°53W 179 J8
North Frisian Is. = Nordfriesische
Inseln Germany 54°40N 8°20E 76 A4
North Gower Canada 45°8N 75°43W 175 A9
North Hd. Australia 30°14S 114°59E 149 F1
North Henik L. Canada 61°45N 97°40W 163 A9
North Highlands
U.S.A. 38°40N 121°23W 170 G5
North Horr Kenya 3°20N 37°8E 142 B4
North Horr Kenya 3°20N 37°8E 142 B4
North I. India 10°8N 72°20E 127 J1
North I. Kenya 4°5N 36°5E 142 B4
North I. N.Z. 38°0S 175°0E 154 E4
North I. Seychelles 4°25S 55°13E 141 b
North Kingsville
U.S.A. 41°54N 80°42W 174 E4
North Kitui △ Kenya 0°15S 38°29E 142 C4
North Knife →
Canada 58°53N 94°45W 163 B10
North Koel → India 24°45N 83°50E 125 G10
North Korea ■ Asia 40°0N 127°0E 115 E14
North L. Australia 32°30S 143°5E 152 B5
North Lakhimpur India 27°14N 94°7E 123 F19
North Lanarkshire □
U.K. 55°52N 3°56W 65 F5
North Las Vegas
U.S.A. 36°11N 115°7W 171 J11
North Lincolnshire □
U.K. 53°36N 0°30W 66 D7
North Little Rock
U.S.A. 34°45N 92°16W 176 D8
North Loup → U.S.A. 41°17N 98°24W 172 E4
North Luangwa △
Zambia 11°49S 32°9E 143 E3
North Magnetic Pole
Arctic 85°9N 149°0W 54 A1
North Mankato U.S.A. 44°10N 94°1W 172 C7
North Miami U.S.A. 25°53N 80°11W 179 K9
North Miami Beach
U.S.A. 25°55N 80°9W 179 K9
North Minch U.K. 58°5N 5°55W 65 C3
North Moose L. Canada 54°4N 100°12W 163 C8
North Myrtle Beach
U.S.A. 33°48N 78°42W 177 E15
North Nahanni →
Canada 62°15N 123°20W 162 A4
North Naples U.S.A. 26°12N 81°48W 179 J8
North New River Canal
U.S.A. 26°30N 80°30W 179 J9
North Olmsted U.S.A. 41°25N 81°56W 174 E3
North Ossetia-Alaniya □
Russia 43°30N 44°30E 87 J7
North Pagai, I. = Pagai Utara,
Pulau Indonesia 2°35S 100°0E 118 E2
North Palisade U.S.A. 37°6N 118°31W 170 H8
North Paravar India 10°13N 76°14E 127 J3
North Platte U.S.A. 41°8N 100°46W 172 E3
North Platte → U.S.A. 41°7N 100°42W 172 E3
North Point Canada 47°2N 64°0W 165 C7
North Pole Arctic 90°0N 0°0 54 A
North Portal Canada 49°0N 102°33W 163 D8
North Powder U.S.A. 45°2N 117°55W 168 D5
North Pt. Barbados 13°20N 59°37W 183 g
North Pt. Trin. & Tob. 11°21N 60°31W 187 J16
North Pt. U.S.A. 45°2N 83°16W 174 A1
North Reef I. India 13°15N 92°43E 127 H11
North Rhine Westphalia =
Nordrhein-Westfalen □
Germany 51°45N 7°30E 76 D3
North River Canada 53°49N 57°6W 165 B8
North Rona U.K. 59°7N 5°49W 64 B4
North Ronaldsay U.K. 59°22N 2°26W 65 B6
North Saskatchewan →
Canada 53°15N 105°5W 163 C7
North Sea Europe 56°0N 4°0E 58 D6
North Seal → Canada 58°50N 98°7W 163 B9
North Sentinel I. India 11°33N 92°15E 127 J11
North Shields
Australia 34°38S 135°52E 152 C1
North Slope U.S.A. 69°15N 151°0W 166 A4
North Somerset □ U.K. 51°24N 2°45W 67 F5
North Sydney Canada 46°12N 60°15W 165 C7
North Syracuse U.S.A. 43°8N 76°7W 175 C8
North Taranaki Bight
N.Z. 38°50S 174°15E 154 E3
North Thompson →
Canada 50°40N 120°20W 162 C4
North Tonawanda
U.S.A. 43°2N 78°53W 174 C6

North Troy U.S.A. 45°0N 72°24W 175 B12
North Twin I. Canada 53°20N 80°0W 164 B4
North Tyne → U.K. 55°0N 2°8W 66 B5
North Uist U.K. 57°40N 7°15W 65 D1
North Vancouver
Canada 49°19N 123°4W 170 A3
North Vernon U.S.A. 39°0N 85°38W 173 F11
North Wabasca L.
Canada 56°0N 113°55W 162 B6
North Walsham U.K. 52°50N 1°22E 66 E9
North West = Severo-Zapadnyy □
Russia 65°0N 40°0E 106 C4
North West □ Botswana 19°0S 22°30E 144 A3
North-West □ S. Africa 27°0S 25°0E 144 D4
North West C. Australia 21°45S 114°9E 148 D1
North West Christmas I. Ridge
Pac. Oc. 6°30N 165°0W 157 F11
North West Frontier = Khyber
Pakhtunkhwa □
Pakistan 34°0N 72°0E 124 C5
North West Highlands
U.K. 57°33N 4°58W 65 D4
North West River
Canada 53°30N 60°10W 165 B7
North Western □
Zambia 13°30S 25°30E 143 E2
North Wildwood
U.S.A. 39°0N 74°48W 173 F16
North York Moors U.K. 54°23N 0°53W 66 C7
North York Moors △
U.K. 54°27N 0°51W 66 C7
North Yorkshire □ U.K. 54°15N 1°25W 66 C6
Northallerton U.K. 54°20N 1°26W 66 C6
Northam Australia 31°35S 116°42E 149 F2
Northam S. Africa 24°56S 27°18E 144 B4
Northampton
Australia 28°27S 114°33E 149 E1
Northampton U.K. 52°15N 0°53W 67 E7
Northampton Mass.,
U.S.A. 42°19N 72°38W 175 D12
Northampton Pa.,
U.S.A. 40°41N 75°30W 175 F9
Northamptonshire □
U.K. 52°16N 0°55W 67 E7
Northbridge U.S.A. 42°9N 71°39W 175 D13
Northbrook Australia 34°44N 77°9W 174 B7
Northcliffe Australia 34°39S 116°7E 149 F2
Northeast Pacific Basin
Pac. Oc. 32°0N 145°0W 157 D13
Northeast Providence Channel
W. Indies 26°0N 76°0W 182 A4
Northeim Germany 51°42N 10°0E 76 D6
Northern = Limpopo □
S. Africa 24°5S 29°0E 145 B4
Northern □ Ghana 9°30N 1°0W 139 D4
Northern □ Malawi 11°0S 34°0E 143 E3
Northern □ S. Leone 9°15N 11°30W 138 D2
Northern □ Zambia 10°30S 30°30E 143 E3
Northern Aral Sea
Kazakhstan 46°20N 60°30E 108 C6
Northern Cape □
S. Africa 30°0S 20°0E 144 C3
Northern Circars India 17°30N 82°30E 126 F6
Northern Dvina = Severnaya
Dvina → Russia 64°32N 40°30E 58 C14
Northern Indian L.
Canada 57°20N 97°20W 163 B9
Northern Ireland □ U.K. 54°45N 7°0W 64 B5
Northern Lau Group
Fiji 17°30S 178°59W 154 a
Northern Light L.
Canada 48°15N 90°39W 164 C1
Northern Marianas ☑
Pac. Oc. 17°0N 145°0E 156 F6
Northern Province □
S. Africa 24°0S 29°0E 145 B4
Northern Range
Trin. & Tob. 10°46N 61°15W 187 K15
Northern Sporades = Voreioi
Sporades Greece 39°15N 23°30E 98 B5
Northern Territory □
Australia 20°0S 133°0E 148 D5
Northfield Minn., U.S.A. 44°27N 93°9W 172 C7
Northfield Vt., U.S.A. 44°9N 72°40W 175 B12
Northgate Canada 49°0N 102°16W 163 D8
Northland □ N.Z. 35°30S 173°30E 154 B2
Northome U.S.A. 47°52N 94°17W 172 B6
Northport Ala., U.S.A. 33°14N 87°35W 177 E11
Northport Wash.,
U.S.A. 48°55N 117°48W 168 B5
Northport N.Y.,
U.S.A. 40°54N 73°21W 175 F11
Northumberland, C.
Australia 38°5S 140°40E 152 E4
Northumberland Is.
Australia 21°30S 149°50E 150 C4
Northumberland Str.
Canada 46°20N 64°0W 165 C7
Northumberland □
U.K. 55°12N 2°0W 66 B6
Northville U.S.A. 43°13N 74°11W 175 C10
Northwest Atlantic Mid-Ocean
Canyon Atl. Oc. 56°0N 46°0W 58 A7
Northwest Pacific Basin
Pac. Oc. 32°0N 165°0E 156 D8
Northwest Providence Channel
W. Indies 26°0N 78°0W 182 A4
Northwest Territories □
Canada 63°0N 118°0W 160 E8
Northwich U.K. 53°15N 2°31W 66 D5
Northwood Iowa,
U.S.A. 43°27N 93°13W 172 D7
Northwood N. Dak.,
U.S.A. 47°44N 97°34W 172 B5
Norton U.S.A. 39°50N 99°53W 172 F4
Norton Zimbabwe 17°52S 30°40E 143 F3
Norton Sd. U.S.A. 63°50N 164°0W 166 C7
Nortorf Germany 54°10N 9°50E 76 A5
Norwalk Calif., U.S.A. 33°54N 118°4W 171 M8
Norwalk Conn., U.S.A. 41°7N 73°22W 175 E11
Norwalk Iowa, U.S.A. 41°29N 93°41W 172 E7
Norwalk Ohio, U.S.A. 41°15N 82°37W 174 E2
Norway Maine, U.S.A. 44°13N 70°32W 175 B14
Norway Mich., U.S.A. 45°47N 87°55W 172 C10
Norway ■ Europe 63°0N 11°0E 60 E14
Norway House Canada 53°59N 97°50W 163 C9
Norwegian B. Canada 77°30N 90°0W 161 B14
Norwegian Basin Atl. Oc. 68°0N 2°0E 54 C8
Norwegian Sea Atl. Oc. 66°0N 1°0E 58 B6
Norwich Canada 42°59N 80°36W 174 D4

Norwich U.K. 52°38N 1°18E 67 E9
Norwich Conn., U.S.A. 41°31N 72°5W 175 E12
Norwich N.Y., U.S.A. 42°32N 75°32W 175 D9
Norwood Canada 44°23N 77°59W 174 B7
Norwood U.S.A. 44°45N 75°0W 175 B10
Nosappu-Misaki
Japan 45°26N 141°39E 112 C12
Noshiro Japan 40°12N 140°0E 112 D10
Nosivka Ukraine 50°50N 31°37E 85 G6
Nosovka = Nosivka
Ukraine 50°50N 31°37E 85 G6
Noṣratābād Iran 29°55N 60°0E 129 D8
Noss Hd. U.K. 58°28N 3°3W 65 C5
Nossa Senhora da Glória
Brazil 10°14S 37°25W 189 C3
Nossa Senhora das Dores
Brazil 10°29S 37°13W 189 C3
Nossa Senhora do Socorro
Brazil 10°52S 37°7W 189 C3
Nossebro Sweden 58°12N 12°43E 63 F6
Nossob → S. Africa 26°55S 20°45E 144 C3
Nossombougou Mali 13°5N 7°55W 138 C3
Nosy Varika Madag. 20°35S 48°32E 141 J9
Notasulga U.S.A. 32°34N 85°41W 178 D4
Noteć → Poland 52°44N 15°26E 83 F2
Notikewin → Canada 57°2N 117°38W 162 B5
Notio Aigaio □ Greece 36°52N 25°34E 99 E7
Notios Aiyáion = Notio Aigaio □
Greece 36°52N 25°34E 99 E7
Notios Evvoikos Kolpos
Greece 38°20N 24°0E 98 C5
Noto Italy 36°53N 15°4E 95 F8
Noto, G. di Italy 36°50N 15°12E 95 F8
Noto, Val di Italy 37°14N 14°31E 95 F7
Noto-Hantō Japan 37°15N 136°40E 113 F8
Notodden Norway 59°35N 9°17E 61 G13
Notre Dame B. Canada 49°45N 55°30W 165 C8
Notre-Dame-de-Koartac =
Quaqtaq Canada 60°55N 69°40W 161 E18
Notre-Dame-des-Bois
Canada 45°24N 71°4W 175 A13
Notre-Dame-d'Ivugivic = Ivujivik
Canada 62°24N 77°55W 161 E16
Notre-Dame-du-Nord
Canada 47°36N 79°30W 164 C4
Notsé Togo 7°0N 1°17E 139 D5
Nottawasaga B.
Canada 44°35N 80°15W 174 B4
Nottaway → Canada 51°22N 78°55W 164 B4
Nottingham U.K. 52°58N 1°10W 66 E6
Nottingham, City of □
U.K. 52°58N 1°10W 66 E6
Nottingham I. Canada 63°20N 77°55W 161 E16
Nottinghamshire □ U.K. 53°10N 1°3W 66 D6
Nottoway → U.S.A. 36°33N 76°55W 173 G15
Notwane → U.S.A. 23°35S 26°58E 144 B4
Nouâdhibou Mauritania 20°54N 17°0W 134 D2
Nouâdhibou, Râs
Mauritania 20°50N 17°0W 134 D2
Nouakchott Mauritania 18°9N 15°58W 138 B1
Nouâmghâr
Mauritania 19°20N 16°20W 138 B1
Nouméa N. Cal. 22°17S 166°30E 147 D9
Nouna Burkina Faso 12°45N 3°52W 138 C4
Noupoort S. Africa 31°10S 24°57E 144 D3
Nouveau Comptoir = Wemindji
Canada 53°0N 78°49W 164 B4
Nouvelle Amsterdam, Î.
Ind. Oc. 38°30S 77°30E 146 H6
Nouvelle-Aquitaine □
France 45°0N 0°30E 72 C4
Nouvelle-Calédonie = New
Caledonia ☑ Pac. Oc. 21°0S 165°0E 147 D9
Nouzonville France 49°48N 4°44E 71 C11
Nová Baňa Slovakia 48°28N 18°39E 79 C10
Nová Bystřice Czechia 49°2N 15°8E 78 B8
Nova Cruz Brazil 6°28S 35°39W 189 B3
Nova Era Brazil 19°45S 43°3W 189 C2
Nova Esperança Brazil 23°8S 52°24W 191 A5
Nova Friburgo Brazil 22°16S 42°30W 191 A7
Nova Gorica Slovenia 45°55N 13°39E 93 C10
Nova Gradiška Croatia 45°17N 17°28E 80 E2
Nova Iguaçu Brazil 22°45S 43°28W 191 A7
Nova Iorque Brazil 7°0S 44°5W 189 B2
Nova Kakhovka Ukraine 46°42N 33°27E 85 J7
Nova Lamego
Guinea-Biss. 12°19N 14°11W 138 C2
Nova Lusitânia Mozam. 19°50S 34°34E 143 F3
Nova Mambone Mozam. 21°0S 35°3E 143 B6
Nova Odesa Ukraine 47°19N 31°47E 85 J6
Nova Paka Czechia 50°29N 15°30E 78 A8
Nova Pavova Serbia 44°56N 20°14E 80 F5
Nova Ponte Brazil 19°8S 47°41W 189 D1
Nova Russas Brazil 4°42S 40°34W 189 A4
Nova Scotia □ Canada 45°10N 63°0W 165 C7
Nova Siri Italy 40°10N 16°35E 95 B9
Nova Sofala Mozam. 20°7S 34°42E 145 B5
Nova Ushytsya Ukraine 48°50N 27°17E 81 B12
Nova Varoš Serbia 43°29N 19°48E 96 C3
Nova Venécia Brazil 18°45S 40°24W 189 D2
Nova Zagora Bulgaria 42°32N 26°1E 97 D10
Novaci Macedonia 41°5N 21°29E 96 E5
Novaci Romania 45°10N 23°42E 81 E8
Novafeltria Italy 43°53N 12°17E 93 E9
Novar Canada 45°27N 79°15W 174 A5
Novara Italy 45°28N 8°38E 92 C5
Novato U.S.A. 38°6N 122°35W 170 G4
Novaya Kakhovka = Nova
Kakhovka Ukraine 46°42N 33°27E 85 J7
Novaya Kazanka = Zhangqala
Kazakhstan 48°56N 49°36E 87 F9
Novaya Ladoga Russia 60°7N 32°16E 84 B7
Novaya Lyalya Russia 59°4N 60°45E 106 D7
Novaya Sibir, Ostrov
Russia 75°10N 150°0E 107 B16
Novaya Zemlya Russia 75°0N 56°0E 106 B6
Nové Mesto na Moravě
Czechia 49°34N 16°5E 78 B8
Nové Mesto nad Metují
Czechia 50°20N 16°10E 79 A8
Nové Mesto nad Váhom
Slovakia 48°45N 17°50E 79 C10
Novelda Spain 38°24N 0°45W 91 G4
Novellara Italy 44°51N 10°44E 92 D7
Noventa Vicentina Italy 45°18N 11°32E 93 C8
Novgorod = Velikiy Novgorod
Russia 58°30N 31°25E 84 C6
Novgorod □ Russia 58°30N 32°30E 84 C6
Novgorod-Severskiy = Novhorod-
Siverskyy Ukraine 52°2N 33°10E 85 G7

Novhorod-Siverskyy
  Ukraine 52°2N 33°10E 85 G7
Novi Bečej Serbia 45°36N 20°10E 86 B5
Novi Grad Bos.-H. 45°2N 16°22E 93 C13
Novi Iskar Bulgaria 42°48N 23°21E 96 D7
Novi Kneževac Serbia 46°4N 20°8E 80 D5
Novi Ligure Italy 44°46N 8°47E 92 D5
Novi Pazar Bulgaria 43°25N 27°15E 97 C11
Novi Pazar Serbia 43°12N 20°28E 96 C4
Novi Sad Serbia 45°18N 19°52E 80 E4
Novi Slankamen Serbia 45°8N 20°15E 80 E5
Novi Travnik Bos.-H. 44°10N 17°40E 80 F2
Novi Vinodolski Croatia 45°10N 14°48E 93 C11
Novigrad Istra, Croatia 45°19N 13°33E 93 C10
Novigrad Zadar, Croatia 44°10N 15°32E 93 D12
Novigradsko More
  Croatia 44°12N 15°33E 93 D12
Novo Acôrdo Brazil 10°10S 46°48W 189 C1
Novo Cruzeiro Brazil 17°29S 41°53W 189 D2
Novo Hamburgo Brazil 29°37S 51°7W 191 B5
Novo Ivanivka Ukraine 45°55N 29°5E 81 E14
Novo Mesto Slovenia 45°47N 15°12E 93 C12
Novo Miloševo Serbia 45°42N 20°20E 80 E5
Novoaleksandrovsk
  Russia 45°29N 41°17E 87 H5
Novoaleksandrovskaya =
  Novoaleksandrovsk
  Russia 45°29N 41°17E 87 H5
Novoaltaysk Russia 53°30N 84°0E 109 B10
Novoanninskiy Russia 50°32N 42°39E 86 E6
Novoazovsk Ukraine 47°15N 38°4E 85 J10
Novocheboksarsk Russia 56°5N 47°27E 86 B8
Novocherkassk Russia 47°27N 40°15E 87 G5
Novodevichye Russia 53°37N 48°50E 86 D9
Novodvinsk Russia 64°25N 40°42E 106 C5
Novogrudok = Navahrudak
  Belarus 53°40N 25°50E 75 B13
Novohrad-Volynskyy
  Ukraine 50°34N 27°35E 75 C14
Novokachalinsk Russia 45°5N 132°0E 112 B5
Novokhopersk Russia 51°5N 41°39E 86 E5
Novokuybyshevsk
  Russia 53°7N 49°58E 86 D9
Novokuznetsk Russia 53°45N 87°10E 109 B11
Novolazarevskaya
  Antarctica 71°0S 12°0E 55 D3
Novomoskovsk Russia 54°5N 38°15E 84 E10
Novomoskovsk Ukraine 48°33N 35°17E 85 H8
Novomyrhorod Ukraine 48°45N 31°33E 85 H6
Novopolotsk = Navapolatsk
  Belarus 55°32N 28°37E 84 E5
Novorossiysk Russia 44°43N 37°46E 85 K9
Novorybnoye Russia 72°50N 105°50E 107 B11
Novorzhev Russia 57°3N 29°25E 84 D5
Novosej Albania 41°56N 20°35E 96 E4
Novoselytsya Ukraine 48°14N 26°15E 81 E11
Novoshakhtinsk Russia 47°46N 39°58E 85 J10
Novosibirsk Russia 55°0N 83°5E 109 B10
Novosibirskiye Ostrova
  Russia 75°0N 142°0E 107 B15
Novosibirskoye Vdkhr.
  Russia 54°35N 82°35E 109 B10
Novosil Russia 52°59N 37°2E 85 F9
Novosokolniki Russia 56°20N 30°8E 84 D6
Novotitarovskaya Russia 45°17N 39°2E 87 H4
Novotroitsk Russia 51°10N 58°15E 108 B5
Novotroitskoye = Töle Bī
  Kazakhstan 43°42N 73°46E 109 D8
Novoukrayinka Ukraine 48°25N 31°30E 85 H6
Novoulyanovsk Russia 54°8N 48°24E 86 D8
Novouzensk Russia 50°32N 48°17E 86 E9
Novovolynsk Ukraine 50°45N 24°4E 83 H11
Novovoronezh Russia 51°39N 39°13E 85 G10
Novoyavoriske Ukraine 49°53N 23°33E 83 J10
Novozybkov Russia 52°30N 31°55E 84 E6
Novska Croatia 45°19N 17°0E 93 C14
Nový Bor Czechia 50°46N 14°35E 78 A7
Novy Bug = Novyy Buh
  Ukraine 47°34N 32°29E 85 J7
Nový Bydžov Czechia 50°14N 15°29E 78 A8
Nový Dvor Belarus 52°50N 24°21E 83 H11
Novy Dwór Mazowiecki
  Poland 52°26N 20°44E 83 F7
Nový Jičín Czechia 49°30N 18°2E 79 B11
Novyy Buh Ukraine 47°34N 32°29E 85 J7
Novyy Oskol Russia 50°44N 37°55E 85 G9
Novyy Port Russia 67°40N 72°30E 106 C8
Novyy Urengoy Russia 65°48N 76°52E 106 C8
Nowa Deba Poland 50°26N 21°41E 83 H8
Nowa Nowa Australia 37°44S 148°3E 153 D8
Nowa Ruda Poland 50°35N 16°30E 83 H3
Nowa Sarzyna Poland 50°21N 22°21E 83 H9
Nowa Sól Poland 51°48N 15°44E 82 H2
Nowata U.S.A. 36°42N 95°38W 176 C7
Nowbarān Iran 35°8N 49°42E 129 C6
Nowe Poland 53°41N 18°44E 82 E6
Nowe Miasteczko
  Poland 51°42N 15°42E 83 G2
Nowe Miasto Poland 51°38N 20°34E 83 G7
Nowe Miasto Lubawskie
  Poland 53°27N 19°33E 82 E6
Nowe Skalmierzyce
  Poland 51°43N 18°0E 83 G4
Nowe Warpno Poland 53°42N 14°18E 82 E1
Nowendoc Australia 31°32S 151°44E 153 A9
Nowendoc △ Australia 31°33S 151°44E 153 A9
Nowghāb Iran 33°53N 59°4E 129 C8
Nowgong = Nagaon
  India 26°20N 92°50E 123 F18
Nowgong India 25°4N 79°27E 125 G8
Nowogard Poland 53°41N 15°10E 82 E2
Nowogród Poland 53°14N 21°53E 83 E8
Nowogród Bobrzanski
  Poland 51°48N 15°15E 83 G2
Nowra Australia 34°53S 150°35E 153 C9
Nowrangapur India 19°14N 82°33E 126 E6
Nowshera Pakistan 34°0N 72°0E 122 C4
Nowy Dwór Gdański
  Poland 54°13N 19°7E 82 D6
Nowy Sącz Poland 49°40N 20°41E 83 J7
Nowy Staw Poland 54°13N 19°2E 82 D6
Nowy Targ Poland 49°29N 20°2E 83 J7
Nowy Tomyśl Poland 52°19N 16°10E 83 F3
Nowy Wiśnicz Poland 49°55N 20°27E 83 J7
Noxen U.S.A. 41°25N 76°4W 175 E8
Noyabr'sk Russia 64°34N 76°21E 106 C8
Noyant France 47°30N 0°6E 70 E4
Noyers France 47°40N 4°0E 71 E10
Noyon France 49°34N 2°59E 71 C6
Noyon Mongolia 43°2N 102°4E 114 C2
Nozay France 47°34N 1°38W 70 E1

Nqutu S. Africa 28°13S 30°32E 145 D5
Nsa, O. en → Algeria 32°28N 5°24E 136 B5
Nsanje Malawi 16°55S 35°12E 143 F4
Nsawam Ghana 5°50N 0°24W 139 D4
Nseluka Zambia 9°58S 31°16E 143 D3
Nsomba Zambia 10°45S 29°51E 143 E2
Nsukka Nigeria 6°51N 7°29E 139 D6
Ntaria ⊙ Australia 24°0S 132°41E 148 D5
Ntui Cameroon 4°27N 11°38E 139 E7
Ntungamo Uganda 0°56S 30°17E 142 C3
Nu Jiang → China 29°58N 97°25E 116 E2
Nu Shan China 26°0N 99°20E 116 E2
Nuba Mts. = Nubah, Jibalan
  Sudan 12°0N 31°0E 135 F12
Nubah, Jibalan Sudan 12°0N 31°0E 135 F12
Nubia Africa 21°0N 32°0E 132 D7
Nubian Desert = Nûbîya, Es Sahrâ
  en Sudan 21°30N 33°30E 137 C3
Nûbîya, Es Sahrâ en
  Sudan 21°30N 33°30E 137 C3
Nubledo Spain 43°31N 5°52W 88 B5
Nuboai Indonesia 2°10S 136°30E 119 E9
Nubra → India 34°35N 77°35E 125 B7
Nucet Romania 46°28N 22°35E 80 D7
Nueces → U.S.A. 27°51N 97°30W 176 H6
Nueltin L. Canada 60°30N 99°30W 163 A9
Nuestra Señora del Rosario de
  Caá-Catí Argentina 27°45S 57°36W 190 B4
Nueva, I. Chile 55°13S 66°30W 192 E3
Nueva Carteya Spain 37°35N 4°28W 89 H6
Nueva Ciudad Guerrero
  Mexico 26°34N 99°12W 181 B5
Nueva Gerona Cuba 21°53N 82°49W 182 B3
Nueva Imperial Chile 38°45S 72°58W 192 A2
Nueva Palmira
  Uruguay 33°52S 58°20W 190 C4
Nueva Rosita Mexico 27°57N 101°13W 180 B4
Nueva San Salvador
  El Salv. 13°40N 89°18W 182 D2
Nueva Tabarca Spain 38°17N 0°30W 91 G4
Nuéve de Julio
  Argentina 35°30S 61°0W 190 D3
Nuevitas Cuba 21°30N 77°20W 182 B4
Nuevo, G. Argentina 43°0S 64°30W 192 A4
Nuevo Casas Grandes
  Mexico 30°25N 107°55W 180 A3
Nuevo Laredo Mexico 27°30N 99°31W 181 B5
Nuevo León □ Mexico 25°20N 100°0W 180 C5
Nuevo Mundo, Cerro
  Bolivia 21°55S 66°53W 188 E4
Nuevo Rocafuerte
  Ecuador 0°55S 75°27W 186 D3
Nugget Pt. N.Z. 46°27S 169°50E 155 G4
Nugrus, Gebel Egypt 24°47N 34°35E 137 C3
Nuhaka N.Z. 39°3S 177°45E 154 F6
Nuits-St-Georges France 47°10N 4°56E 71 E11
Nukey Bluff Australia 32°26S 135°29E 151 E2
Nukhayb Iraq 32°4N 42°3E 105 F10
Nuku Hiva
  French Polynesia 8°54S 140°6W 157 H13
Nuku'alofa Tonga 21°10S 175°12W 147 D11
Nukus Uzbekistan 42°27N 59°41E 108 D5
Nulato U.S.A. 64°43N 158°6W 166 C8
Nules Spain 39°51N 0°9W 90 F4
Nullagine Australia 21°53S 120°7E 148 D3
Nullagine → Australia 21°20S 120°20E 148 D3
Nullarbor Australia 31°28S 130°55E 149 F5
Nullarbor △ Australia 31°10S 131°0E 149 F5
Nullarbor Plain
  Australia 31°10S 129°0E 149 F4
Numalla, L. Australia 28°43S 144°20E 151 D3
Numan Nigeria 9°29N 12°3E 139 D7
Numata Japan 36°45N 139°4E 113 F9
Numaykoos Lake △
  Canada 57°52N 95°58E 163 B9
Numazu Japan 35°7N 138°51E 113 G9
Numbulwar Australia 14°15S 135°45E 150 A2
Numfoor Indonesia 1°0S 134°50E 119 E8
Numurkah Australia 36°5S 145°26E 153 D6
Nunap Isua Greenland 59°48N 43°55W 57 F6
Nunatsiavut Canada 55°30N 62°0W 165 A7
Nunavik Canada 56°30N 71°0W 161 F17
Nunavik Greenland 71°50N 54°35W 57 J2
Nunavut □ Canada 66°0N 85°0W 161 D15
Nunda U.S.A. 42°35N 77°56W 174 D7
Nungarin Australia 31°12S 118°6E 149 F2
Nungo Mozam. 13°23S 37°43E 143 E4
Nungwe Tanzania 2°48S 32°2E 142 C3
Nunivak I. U.S.A. 60°10N 166°30W 166 C6
Nunkun India 33°57N 76°2E 125 C7
Núoro Italy 40°20N 9°20E 94 B2
Nuozhadu Dam China 22°39N 100°25E 116 F3
Nūr Iran 36°33N 52°1E 129 B7
Nura → Kazakhstan 50°30N 69°59E 109 B7
Nūrābād Hormozgân,
  Iran 27°47N 57°12E 129 E8
Nūrābād Lorestân, Iran 34°4N 47°58E 105 E12
Nure → Italy 45°3N 9°49E 92 C6
Nuremberg = Nürnberg
  Germany 49°27N 11°3E 77 F7
Nuri Mexico 28°5N 109°22W 180 B3
Nuri Sudan 18°29N 31°59E 137 D3
Nuriootpa Australia 34°27S 139°0E 152 C3
Nuristān □ Afghan. 35°20N 71°0E 109 E8
Nurlat Russia 54°29N 50°45E 86 C10
Nurmes Finland 63°33N 29°10E 60 E23
Nürnberg Germany 49°27N 11°3E 77 F7
Nurpur Pakistan 31°53N 71°54E 124 D4
Nurra, La Italy 40°45N 8°15E 94 B1
Nurran, L. = Terewah, L.
  Australia 29°52S 147°35E 149 E8
Nurrari Lakes Australia 29°1S 130°5E 149 E5
Nurri Italy 39°43N 9°14E 94 C2
Nürtingen Germany 48°37N 9°19E 77 G5
Nurzec → Poland 52°37N 22°25E 83 F9
Nus Italy 45°45N 7°28E 92 C4
Nusa Dua Indonesia 8°48S 115°14E 119 K18
Nusa Tenggara Barat □
  Indonesia 8°50S 117°30E 118 F5
Nusa Tenggara Timur □
  Indonesia 9°30S 122°0E 119 F6
Nusaybin Turkey 37°3N 41°10E 105 D9
Nuşeirat Gaza Strip 31°27N 34°24E 138 D3
Nushki Pakistan 29°35N 66°0E 124 E2
Nuuk Greenland 64°10N 51°35W 57 E5
Nuussuaq Greenland 74°8N 57°3W 57 C5
Nuwakot Nepal 28°10N 83°55E 125 E10
Nuwara Eliya Sri Lanka 6°58N 80°48E 127 L5

Nuwayb'ī, W. an →
  Si. Arabia 29°18N 34°57E 130 F3
Nuweiba' Egypt 28°59N 34°39E 130 D2
Nuwerus S. Africa 31°8S 18°24E 144 D2
Nuweveldberge
  S. Africa 32°10S 21°45E 144 D3
Nuyts, Pt. Australia 35°4S 116°38E 149 G2
Nuyts Arch. Australia 32°35S 133°20E 151 E1
Nuyts Land Australia 32°2S 132°21E 149 F5
Ny-Ålesund Svalbard 78°55N 11°56E 57 B12
Nyaake Liberia 4°52N 7°37W 138 E3
Nyabing Australia 33°33S 118°9E 149 F2
Nyack U.S.A. 41°5N 73°55W 175 E11
Nyagan Russia 62°30N 65°38E 106 C7
Nyah West Australia 35°16S 143°21E 152 C5
Nyahanga Tanzania 2°20S 33°37E 142 C3
Nyahua Tanzania 5°25S 33°23E 142 D3
Nyahururu Kenya 0°2N 36°27E 142 B4
Nyaingêntanglha Shan
  China 30°0N 90°0E 110 F7
Nyakanazi Tanzania 3°2S 31°10E 142 C2
Nyakrom Ghana 5°40N 0°50W 139 D4
Nyålå Sudan 12°2N 24°58E 135 F10
Nyalam China 28°32N 86°4E 110 F6
Nyalam Zimbabwe 19°55S 28°16E 143 F2
Nyambiti Tanzania 2°48S 33°27E 142 C3
Nyamira Kenya 0°36S 34°52E 142 B4
Nyamwaga Tanzania 1°27S 34°33E 142 C3
Nyandekwa Tanzania 3°57S 32°32E 142 C3
Nyandoma Russia 61°40N 40°12E 84 B11
Nyandrua □ Kenya 0°30S 36°35E 142 C4
Nyanga △ Zimbabwe 18°17S 32°44E 143 F3
Nyanga Namibia 18°0S 20°40E 144 A3
Nyanguge Tanzania 2°30S 33°12E 142 C3
Nyanji Zambia 14°25S 31°46E 143 E3
Nyankpala Ghana 9°21N 0°58W 139 D4
Nyanza Rwanda 2°20S 29°42E 142 C2
Nyanza-Lac Burundi 4°21S 29°36E 142 C2
Nyasa, L. = Malawi, L.
  Africa 12°30S 34°30E 143 E3
Nyasvizh Belarus 53°14N 26°38E 75 B14
Nyaungdon = Yandoon
  Myanmar 17°0N 95°40E 123 L19
Nyazura Zimbabwe 18°40S 32°16E 143 F3
Nyazwidzi → Zimbabwe 20°0S 31°17E 143 G3
Nyborg Denmark 55°18N 10°47E 63 J4
Nybro Sweden 56°44N 15°55E 63 H9
Nyda → Russia 66°45N 69°30E 106 C7
Nyeboe Land Greenland 82°0N 57°0W 57 A5
Nyeri Kenya 0°23S 36°56E 142 C4
Nyhammar Sweden 60°17N 14°58E 62 D8
Nyika △ Malawi 10°30S 33°53E 143 E3
Nyimba Zambia 14°33S 30°50E 143 E3
Nyinahin Ghana 6°43N 2°3W 138 D4
Nyingchi China 29°32N 94°25E 110 F7
Nyíradony Hungary 47°41N 21°55E 80 C6
Nyiragongo
  Dem. Rep. of the Congo 1°30S 29°15E 142 C2
Nyirbátor Hungary 47°49N 22°9E 80 C7
Nyíregyháza Hungary 47°58N 21°47E 80 C6
Nyiru, Mt. Kenya 2°8N 36°50E 142 B4
Nykarleby = Uusikaarlepyy
  Finland 63°32N 22°31E 60 E20
Nykøbing Nordjylland,
  Denmark 56°48N 8°51E 63 H2
Nykøbing Sjælland,
  Denmark 54°56N 11°52E 63 K5
Nykøbing Sjælland,
  Denmark 55°55N 11°40E 63 J5
Nyköping Sweden 58°45N 17°1E 63 F11
Nykroppa Sweden 59°37N 14°18E 62 E8
Nykvarn Sweden 59°11N 17°25E 62 E11
Nyland Sweden 63°1N 17°45E 62 A11
Nylstroom = Modimolle
  S. Africa 24°42S 28°22E 145 B4
Nymagee Australia 32°7S 146°20E 153 B7
Nymboida △ Australia 29°38S 152°26E 151 D5
Nymburk Czechia 50°10N 15°1E 78 A8
Nynäshamn Sweden 58°54N 17°57E 63 F11
Nyngan Australia 31°30S 147°8E 153 B7
Nyoma Rap India 33°10N 78°40E 125 C8
Nyoman = Nemunas →
  Lithuania 55°25N 21°10E 62 C8
Nyon Switz. 46°23N 6°14E 77 J2
Nyong → Cameroon 3°17N 9°54E 139 E6
Nyons France 44°22N 5°10E 73 D9
Nyou Burkina Faso 12°42N 1°51W 138 C4
Nýrsko Czechia 49°18N 13°9E 78 B6
Nysa Poland 50°30N 17°22E 83 H4
Nysa → Europe 52°4N 14°46E 76 C10
Nysa Kłodzka → Poland 50°49N 17°40E 83 H4
Nysäter Sweden 59°17N 12°47E 62 E6
Nyslott = Savonlinna
  Finland 61°52N 28°53E 84 B5
Nyssa U.S.A. 43°53N 117°0W 168 E5
Nystad = Uusikaupunki
  Finland 60°47N 21°25E 84 B1
Nysted Denmark 54°40N 11°44E 63 K5
Nyunzu
  Dem. Rep. of the Congo 5°57S 27°58E 142 D2
Nyurba Russia 63°17N 118°28E 107 C12
Nyzhankovychi Ukraine 49°40N 22°49E 83 J9
Nyzhnohirskyy Ukraine 45°37N 34°38E 85 K8
Nyzhny Vorota Ukraine 48°46N 23°6E 80 B8
Nzébéla Guinea 8°9N 9°7W 138 D3
Nzega Tanzania 4°10S 33°12E 142 C3
Nzérékoré Guinea 7°49N 8°48E 138 D3
Nzeto Angola 7°10S 12°52E 140 F2
Nzilo, Chutes de
  Dem. Rep. of the Congo 10°18S 25°27E 143 E2
N'zo → Côte d'Ivoire 6°15N 7°3W 138 D3
N'zo △ Côte d'Ivoire 6°45N 7°15W 138 D3
Nzubuka Tanzania 4°45S 32°50E 142 C3
Nzwani = Anjouan
  Comoros Is. 12°15S 44°20E 141 a

O

O Barco Spain 42°23N 6°58W 88 C4
O Carballiño Spain 42°26N 8°5W 88 C2
O Castro de Ferreira
  Spain 42°31N 7°37W 88 C3
O Convento Spain 42°28N 8°41W 88 C2
O Corgo Spain 42°56N 7°25W 88 C3
O Pedrouzo Spain 42°56N 8°22W 88 C2
O Pino = O Pedrouzo
  Spain 42°56N 8°22W 88 C2
O Porriño Spain 42°10N 8°37W 88 C2
O Real Spain 43°20N 8°19W 88 B2

O Seixo Spain 41°59N 8°46W 88 C2
Ō-Shima Hokkaidō,
  Japan 41°30N 139°22E 112 D9
Ō-Shima Shizuoka,
  Japan 34°44N 139°24E 113 G9
O.R. Tambo Int. ✈ (JNB)
  S. Africa 26°8S 28°15E 145 C4
Oa, Mull of U.K. 55°35N 6°20W 65 F2
Oacoma U.S.A. 43°48N 99°24W 172 D4
Oahe, L. U.S.A. 44°27N 100°24W 172 C3
Oahe Dam U.S.A. 44°27N 100°24W 172 C3
O'ahu U.S.A. 21°28N 157°58W 167 L8
Oak Harbor U.S.A. 48°18N 122°39W 170 B4
Oak Hill Fla., U.S.A. 28°52N 80°51W 178 G5
Oak Hill W. Va., U.S.A. 37°59N 81°9W 173 G13
Oak Island U.S.A. 33°55N 78°10W 177 E15
Oak Park U.S.A. 32°22N 82°19W 178 E5
Oak Ridge U.S.A. 36°1N 84°16W 177 C12
Oak View U.S.A. 34°24N 119°18W 171 L7
Oakan-Dake Japan 43°27N 144°10E 112 C12
Oakbank Australia 33°4S 140°33E 152 B4
Oakdale Calif., U.S.A. 37°46N 120°51W 170 H6
Oakdale La., U.S.A. 30°49N 92°40W 176 F8
Oakes U.S.A. 46°8N 98°6W 172 B4
Oakesdale U.S.A. 47°8N 117°15W 168 C5
Oakey Australia 27°25S 151°43E 151 D5
Oakfield Ga., U.S.A. 31°47N 83°58W 178 D6
Oakfield N.Y., U.S.A. 43°4N 78°16W 174 C6
Oakham U.K. 52°40N 0°43W 67 E7
Oakhurst U.S.A. 37°19N 119°40W 170 H7
Oakland Calif., U.S.A. 37°48N 122°16W 170 H4
Oakland Oreg., U.S.A. 41°57N 75°36W 174 F1
Oakland Park U.S.A. 26°10N 80°7W 179 J9
Oaklands Australia 35°34S 146°10E 153 C7
Oakley Idaho, U.S.A. 42°15N 113°53W 168 E7
Oakley Kans., U.S.A. 39°8N 100°51W 172 F3
Oakover → Australia 21°0S 120°40E 148 D3
Oakridge U.S.A. 43°45N 122°28W 168 E2
Oaks, The Australia 34°3S 150°34E 153 C9
Oakville Canada 43°27N 79°41W 174 C5
Oakville U.S.A. 46°51N 123°14W 170 D3
Oamaru N.Z. 45°5S 170°59E 155 F5
Oancea Romania 45°21N 27°42E 81 E12
Oasis Calif., U.S.A. 37°29N 117°55W 170 H9
Oasis Calif., U.S.A. 33°28N 116°6W 171 M10
Oates Land Antarctica 69°0S 160°0E 55 C11
Oatman U.S.A. 35°1N 114°19W 171 K12
Oaxaca Mexico 17°3N 96°43W 181 D5
Oaxaca □ Mexico 17°0N 96°30W 181 D5
Ob → Russia 66°45N 69°30E 106 C7
Oba Canada 49°4N 84°7W 164 C3
Obala Cameroon 4°9N 11°32E 139 E7
Obama Japan 35°30N 135°45E 113 G7
Oban Nigeria 5°17N 8°33E 139 D6
Oban U.K. 56°25N 5°29W 65 E3
Oberá Argentina 27°21S 55°2W 191 B4
Oberammergau Germany 47°36N 11°4E 77 H7
Oberasbach Germany 49°25N 10°57E 77 F6
Oberbayern □ Germany 48°5N 11°50E 77 G7
Oberdrauburg Austria 46°44N 12°58E 78 E5
Obere Donau △ Germany 48°5N 9°0E 77 G5
Oberer Bayerischer Wald △
  Germany 49°15N 12°40E 77 F8
Oberfranken □ Germany 50°10N 11°20E 77 E7
Oberhausen Germany 51°28N 6°51E 76 D2
Oberkirch Germany 48°31N 8°4E 77 G4
Oberlausitz Germany 51°16N 14°18E 76 D10
Oberlin Kans., U.S.A. 39°49N 100°32W 172 F3
Oberlin La., U.S.A. 30°37N 92°46W 176 F8
Oberlin Ohio, U.S.A. 41°18N 82°13W 174 E2
Obernai France 48°28N 7°30E 71 D14
Oberndorf Germany 48°17N 8°34E 77 G4
Oberon Australia 33°45S 149°52E 153 B8
Oberösterreich □ Austria 48°10N 14°0E 78 C7
Oberpfalz □ Germany 49°30N 12°25E 77 F8
Oberpfälzer Wald
  Germany 49°30N 12°25E 77 F8
Oberpfälzer Wald △
  Germany 49°40N 12°22E 77 F8
Oberstdorf Germany 47°25N 10°16E 77 H6
Obertyn Ukraine 48°42N 25°10E 81 D10
Oberursel Germany 50°11N 8°35E 77 E4
Oberwart Austria 47°17N 16°12E 79 D9
Obi, Kepulauan
  Indonesia 1°23S 127°45E 119 E7
Obiaruku Nigeria 5°51N 6°9E 139 D6
Óbidos Brazil 1°50S 55°30W 187 D7
Óbidos Portugal 39°19N 9°10W 89 F1
Obihiro Japan 42°56N 143°12E 112 C11
Obilatu Indonesia 1°25S 127°20E 119 E7
Obilnoye Russia 47°32N 44°30E 87 G7
Obing Germany 48°0N 12°24E 77 G8
Objat France 45°16N 1°24E 72 C5
Obluchye Russia 49°1N 131°4E 107 E14
Obninsk Russia 55°8N 36°37E 84 E9
Obo C.A.R. 5°20N 26°32E 142 A2
Obodivka Ukraine 48°24N 29°15E 81 D14
Oborniki Poland 52°39N 16°50E 83 F3
Oborniki Śląskie Poland 51°18N 16°53E 83 G3
Oboyan Russia 51°15N 36°21E 85 G9
Obozerskaya = Obozerskiy
  Russia 63°34N 40°21E 106 C5
Obozerskiy Russia 63°34N 40°21E 106 C5
Obrenovac Serbia 44°40N 20°11E 96 B4
O'Brien U.S.A. 30°2N 82°57W 178 F3
Obrovac Croatia 44°11N 15°41E 93 D12
Obruk Turkey 38°7N 33°12E 104 C5
Obrzycko Poland 52°46N 16°23E 83 F3
Observatory Inlet
  Canada 55°10N 129°54W 162 B3
Obshchi Syrt Russia 52°0N 53°0E 58 E16
Obskaya Guba Russia 69°0N 73°0E 106 C8
Obuasi Ghana 6°17N 1°40W 139 D4
Obubra Nigeria 6°8N 8°20E 139 D6
Obudu Nigeria 6°38N 9°5E 139 D6
Obwalden □ Switz. 46°58N 8°15E 77 J4
Obzor Bulgaria 42°50N 27°52E 97 D11
Ocala U.S.A. 29°11N 82°8W 178 F7
Ocampo Chihuahua,
  Mexico 28°11N 108°23W 180 B3
Ocampo Tamaulipas,
  Mexico 22°50N 99°20W 181 C5
Ocaña Spain 39°55N 3°30W 88 F7
Occidental, Cordillera
  Colombia 5°0N 76°0W 186 C3
Occidental, Cordillera
  Peru 14°0S 74°0W 188 D3
Occidental, Grand Erg
  Algeria 30°20N 1°0E 136 B6
Occitanie □ France 44°0N 2°0E 72 E5
Ocean City Md., U.S.A. 38°20N 75°5W 173 F16

Ocean City N.J.,
  U.S.A. 39°17N 74°35W 173 F16
Ocean City Wash.,
  U.S.A. 47°4N 124°10W 170 C2
Ocean Falls Canada 52°18N 127°48W 162 C3
Ocean I. = Banaba
  Kiribati 0°45S 169°50E 156 H8
Ocean Park U.S.A. 46°30N 124°3W 170 D2
Oceano U.S.A. 35°6N 120°37W 171 K6
Oceanport U.S.A. 40°19N 74°1W 175 F10
Oceanside U.S.A. 33°12N 117°23W 171 M9
Ochagavía Spain 42°55N 1°5W 90 C3
Ochakiv Ukraine 46°37N 31°33E 85 J6
Ochamchire Georgia 42°46N 41°32E 87 A6
Ochi, Oros Greece 38°5N 24°25E 98 D6
Ochil Hills U.K. 56°14N 3°40W 65 E5
Ochlocknee U.S.A. 30°58N 84°3W 178 F5
Ochlocknee →
  U.S.A. 29°59N 84°26W 178 F5
Ocho Rios Jamaica 18°24N 77°6W 182 a
Ochopee U.S.A. 25°54N 81°18W 179 K8
Ochsenfurt Germany 49°40N 10°4E 77 F6
Ochsenhausen Germany 48°4N 9°57E 77 G5
Ocilla U.S.A. 31°36N 83°15W 178 D6
Ockelbo Sweden 60°54N 16°45E 62 D10
Ocmulgee → U.S.A. 31°58N 82°33W 178 E4
Ocmulgee △ U.S.A. 32°49N 83°37W 178 D6
Ocna Mureş Romania 46°23N 23°55E 81 D8
Ocna Sibiului Romania 45°52N 24°2E 81 E8
Ocnele Mari Romania 45°8N 24°18E 81 E9
Ocnița Moldova 48°25N 27°30E 81 B12
Ocoña Peru 16°26S 73°8W 188 D3
Ocoña → Peru 16°26S 73°8W 188 D3
Oconee, L. U.S.A. 33°58N 83°15W 178 D7
Oconee → U.S.A. 31°58N 82°33W 178 E4
Oconomowoc U.S.A. 43°7N 88°30W 172 D9
Oconto U.S.A. 44°53N 87°52W 172 C10
Oconto Falls U.S.A. 44°52N 88°9W 172 C9
Ocosingo Mexico 16°53N 92°6W 181 D6
Ocotal Nic. 13°41N 86°31W 182 D2
Ocotlán Jalisco,
  México 20°21N 102°46W 180 C4
Ocotlán Oaxaca, Mexico 16°48N 96°40W 181 D5
Ocreza → Portugal 39°32N 7°50W 89 F3
Ocsa Hungary 47°17N 19°15E 80 C4
Oda Ghana 5°50N 0°51W 139 D4
Ōda Japan 35°11N 132°30E 113 G6
Oda, J. Sudan 20°21N 36°39E 137 C4
Ódáðahraun Iceland 65°5N 17°0W 60 D5
Ōdaejin N. Korea 41°34N 129°40E 112 D10
Ōdate Japan 40°16N 140°34E 112 D10
Odawara Japan 35°20N 139°6E 113 G9
Odda Norway 60°3N 6°35E 61 F12
Odder Denmark 55°58N 10°10E 63 J4
Odei → Canada 56°6N 96°54W 163 B9
Odemira Portugal 37°35N 8°40W 89 H2
Ödemiş Turkey 38°15N 28°0E 99 D9
Odendaalsrus S. Africa 27°48S 26°45E 144 C4
Odense Denmark 55°22N 10°23E 63 J4
Odenwald Germany 49°35N 9°0E 77 F5
Oder → Europe 53°33N 14°38E 76 B10
Oder-Havel Kanal
  Germany 52°52N 14°2E 76 C10
Oderzo Italy 45°47N 12°29E 93 C9
Odesa Ukraine 46°30N 30°45E 85 J6
Odessa = Odesa Ukraine 46°30N 30°45E 85 J6
Odessa Canada 44°17N 76°43W 175 B8
Odessa Tex., U.S.A. 31°52N 102°23W 176 F3
Odessa Wash., U.S.A. 47°20N 118°41W 168 C4
Odiakwe Botswana 20°12S 25°17E 144 B4
Odiel → Spain 37°10N 6°55W 89 H4
Odienné Côte d'Ivoire 9°30N 7°34W 138 D3
Odintsovo Russia 55°40N 37°16E 84 E9
Odisha □ India 20°0N 84°0E 126 E7
Odobeşti Romania 45°43N 27°4E 81 E12
Odolanów Poland 51°34N 17°40E 83 G4
O'Donnell Pt. Canada 45°5N 80°5W 174 A4
Odorheiu Secuiesc
  Romania 46°21N 25°21E 81 D10
Odoyevo Russia 53°56N 36°42E 84 F9
Odra = Oder → Europe 53°33N 14°38E 76 B10
Odra → Spain 42°14N 4°17W 88 C6
Odum U.S.A. 31°40N 82°2W 178 D7
Odžaci Serbia 45°30N 19°17E 80 E4
Odžak Bos.-H. 45°3N 18°18E 80 E3
Odzi Zimbabwe 19°0S 32°20E 145 A5
Odzi → Zimbabwe 19°45S 32°23E 145 A5
Oeiras Brazil 7°0S 42°8W 189 B2
Oeiras Portugal 38°41N 9°18W 89 G1
Oelrichs U.S.A. 43°11N 103°14W 172 D2
Oelsnitz Germany 50°24N 12°10E 77 E8
Oelwein U.S.A. 42°41N 91°55W 172 D8
Oeno I. Pac. Oc. 24°0S 131°0W 157 K14
Oenpelli = Gunbalanya
  Australia 12°20S 133°4E 148 B5
Oetz Austria 47°13N 10°53E 78 D3
Of Turkey 40°59N 40°23E 105 E9
Ofanto → Italy 41°22N 16°13E 95 A8
Offa Nigeria 8°13N 4°42E 139 D5
Offaly □ Ireland 53°15N 7°30W 64 C4
Offenbach Germany 50°6N 8°44E 77 E4
Offenburg Germany 48°28N 7°56E 77 G3
Officer Cr. → Australia 27°46S 132°30E 149 E5
Offida Italy 42°56N 13°41E 93 F10
Ofidousa Greece 36°33N 26°8E 99 E8
Ofotfjorden Norway 68°27N 16°40E 60 B17
Ofunato Japan 39°4N 141°43E 112 E10
Oga Japan 39°55N 139°50E 112 E9
Oga-Hantō Japan 39°58N 139°47E 112 E9
Ōgaki Japan 35°21N 136°37E 113 G8
Ogallala U.S.A. 41°8N 101°43W 172 E3
Ogasawara Gunto
  Pac. Oc. 27°0N 142°0E 156 E6
Ogbomosho Nigeria 8°1N 4°11E 139 D5
Ogden U.S.A. 41°13N 111°58W 168 F8
Ogdensburg U.S.A. 44°42N 75°30W 175 A9
Ogea Driki Fiji 19°12S 178°27W 154 a
Ogea Levu Fiji 19°8S 178°24W 154 a
Ogeechee → U.S.A. 31°50N 81°3W 178 E8
Ogilby U.S.A. 32°49N 114°50W 171 N12
Oglethorpe U.S.A. 32°18N 84°4W 178 D5

Ogliastra □ Italy 39°50N 9°35E 94 C2
Óglio → Italy 45°2N 10°39E 92 C7
Óglio Nord △ Italy 45°22N 9°54E 92 C6
Óglio Sud △ Italy 45°8N 10°25E 92 C7
Ogmore Australia 22°37S 149°35E 150 C4
Ognon → France 47°16N 5°28E 71 E12
Ogoja Nigeria 6°38N 8°39E 139 D6
Ogoki Canada 51°38N 85°58W 164 B2
Ogoki → Canada 51°38N 85°57W 164 B2
Ogoki L. Canada 50°50N 87°10W 164 B2
Ogoki Res. Canada 50°45N 88°15W 164 B2
Ogooué → Gabon 1°0S 9°0E 140 E1
Ogosta → Bulgaria 43°48N 23°55E 96 C7
Ogou → Togo 7°22N 1°27E 139 D5
Ogowe = Ogooué → Gabon 1°0S 9°0E 140 E1
Ograzden Macedonia 41°30N 22°50E 96 B6
Ogulin Croatia 45°16N 15°16E 93 C12
Ogun □ Nigeria 7°0N 3°0E 139 D5
Ogurja Ada
  Turkmenistan 38°55N 53°2E 129 B7
Oguta Nigeria 5°44N 6°44E 139 D6
Ogwashi-Uku Nigeria 6°15N 6°30E 139 D6
Ogwe Nigeria 5°0N 7°14E 139 E6
Ohai N.Z. 45°55S 168°0E 155 F3
Ohakune N.Z. 39°24S 175°24E 154 F4
Ohanet Algeria 28°44N 8°46E 136 C5
Ohangwena □ Namibia 17°30S 17°0E 144 A2
Ohata Japan 41°24N 141°10E 112 D10
Ohatchee U.S.A. 33°47N 86°0W 178 D4
Ohau, L. N.Z. 44°15S 169°53E 155 E4
Ohaupo N.Z. 37°56S 175°20E 154 C4
Ohio □ U.S.A. 40°15N 82°45W 174 F2
Ohio → U.S.A. 36°59N 89°8W 172 G9
Ohiwa Harbour N.Z. 37°59S 177°10E 154 D6
Ohře → Czechia 50°30N 14°10E 78 A7
Ohře → Germany 52°18N 11°46E 76 C7
Ohrid Macedonia 41°8N 20°52E 96 E4
Ohridsko Jezero
  Macedonia 41°8N 20°52E 96 E4
Ohrigstad S. Africa 24°39S 30°36E 145 B5
Öhringen Germany 49°12N 9°31E 77 F5
Ohura N.Z. 38°51S 174°59E 154 E3
Oi Qu → China 28°37N 98°16E 116 C2
Oiapoque Brazil 3°50N 51°50W 187 B8
Oikou China 38°35N 117°42E 115 E9
Oil City U.S.A. 41°26N 79°42W 174 E5
Oil Springs Canada 42°47N 82°7W 174 D2
Oildale U.S.A. 35°25N 119°1W 171 K7
Oinousa = Inousses
  Greece 38°33N 26°14E 99 C8
Oise □ France 49°28N 2°30E 71 C9
Oise → France 49°0N 2°4E 71 C9
Oistins Barbados 13°4N 59°33W 183 g
Oistins B. Barbados 13°4N 59°33W 183 g
Ōita Japan 33°14N 131°36E 113 H5
Ōita □ Japan 33°15N 131°30E 113 H5
Oiticica Brazil 5°3S 41°5W 189 B2
Ojai U.S.A. 34°27N 119°15W 171 L7
Ojcowski △ Poland 50°15N 19°50E 83 H6
Ojhar India 20°6N 73°56E 126 D1
Ojinaga Mexico 29°34N 104°25W 180 B4
Ojiya Japan 37°18N 138°48E 113 F9
Ojo Caliente Mexico 22°34N 102°15W 180 C4
Ojo de Liebre, L.
  Mexico 27°45N 114°15W 180 B2
Ojos del Salado, Cerro
  Argentina 27°0S 68°40W 190 B2
Oka → Russia 56°20N 43°59E 86 B7
Okaba Indonesia 8°6S 139°42E 119 F9
Okahandja Namibia 22°0S 16°59E 144 B2
Okahukura N.Z. 38°48S 175°14E 154 E4
Okaihau N.Z. 35°19S 173°47E 154 B4
Okakarara Namibia 20°35S 17°27E 144 B2
Okanagan L. Canada 50°0N 119°30W 162 D5
Okandja Gabon 0°35S 13°45E 140 E2
Okanogan U.S.A. 48°22N 119°35W 168 B4
Okanogan → U.S.A. 48°6N 119°44W 168 B4
Okanogan Range
  N. Amer. 49°0N 119°55W 162 D5
Okany Hungary 46°52N 21°21E 80 D6
Okapi
  Dem. Rep. of the Congo 2°30N 27°20E 142 B2
Okaputa Namibia 20°5S 17°0E 144 B2
Okara Pakistan 30°50N 73°31E 124 D5
Okarito N.Z. 43°15S 170°9E 155 D3
Okarukambe = Steinhausen
  Namibia 21°49S 18°20E 144 B2
Okato N.Z. 39°12S 173°53E 154 F2
Okaukuejo Namibia 19°10S 16°0E 144 A2
Okavango = Cubango →
  Africa 18°50S 22°25E 144 A3
Okavango Delta
  Botswana 18°45S 22°45E 144 A3
Okavango Swamp = Okavango
  Delta Botswana 18°45S 22°45E 144 A3
Okaya Japan 36°5N 138°10E 113 F9
Okayama Japan 34°40N 133°54E 113 G6
Okayama □ Japan 35°0N 133°50E 113 G6
Oke-Iho Nigeria 8°1N 3°18E 139 D5
Okęcie, Warszawa ✈ (WAW)
  Poland 52°20N 20°59E 83 F7
Okeechobee U.S.A. 27°15N 80°50W 179 F9
Okeechobee, L. U.S.A. 27°0N 80°50W 179 F9
Okefenokee △ U.S.A. 30°45N 82°18W 178 E7
Okefenokee Swamp
  U.S.A. 30°40N 82°20W 178 F7
Okehampton U.K. 50°44N 4°0W 67 G4
Okene Nigeria 7°32N 6°11E 139 D6
Oker → Germany 52°32N 10°22E 76 C6
Okha India 22°27N 69°4E 124 H3
Okha Russia 53°40N 143°0E 107 D15
Okhotsk Russia 59°20N 143°10E 107 D15
Okhotsk, Sea of Asia 55°0N 145°0E 107 D15
Okhotskiy Perevoz
  Russia 61°52N 135°35E 107 C14
Okhtyrka Ukraine 50°25N 35°0E 85 G8
Oki-Shotō Japan 36°5N 133°15E 113 F6
Okiep S. Africa 29°39S 17°53E 144 C2
Okigwi Nigeria 5°52N 7°20E 139 D6
Okija Nigeria 5°54N 6°55E 139 D6
Okinawa Japan 26°40N 128°0E 113 L3
Okinawa □ Japan 26°40N 128°0E 113 L3
Okinawa-Guntō Japan 26°40N 128°0E 113 L3
Okinawa-Jima Japan 26°32N 128°0E 113 L4
Okino-erabu-Shima
  Japan 27°21N 128°33E 113 L4
Okitipupa Nigeria 6°31N 4°50E 139 D5
Oklahoma □ U.S.A. 35°20N 97°30W 176 C6

Oklahoma City U.S.A. 35°30N 97°30W 176 D6
Oklawaha → U.S.A. 29°28N 81°41W 179 F8
Okmulgee U.S.A. 35°37N 95°58W 176 D7
Oknitsa = Ocniţa
  Moldova 48°25N 27°30E 81 B12
Oko, W. → Sudan 21°15N 35°56E 137 C4
Okolo Uganda 2°37N 31°8E 142 B3
Okombahe Namibia 21°23S 15°22E 144 C2
Okonek Poland 53°32N 16°51E 82 E3
Okotoks Canada 50°43N 113°58W 162 C6
Okrika Nigeria 4°40N 7°10E 139 E6
Oktyabrsk = Qandyaghash
  Kazakhstan 49°28N 57°25E 108 C5
Oktyabrsk Russia 53°11N 48°40E 86 D9
Oktyabrskiy = Aktsyabrski
  Belarus 52°38N 28°53E 75 B15
Oktyabrskiy Bashkortostan,
  Russia 54°28N 53°28E 108 B4
Oktyabrskiy Kamchatka,
  Russia 52°39N 156°14E 107 D16
Oktyabrskiy Rostov,
  Russia 47°30N 40°4E 87 G5
Oktyabrskoy Revolyutsii, Ostrov
  Russia 79°30N 97°0E 107 B10
Oktyabrskoye = Zhovtneve
  Ukraine 46°54N 32°3E 85 J7
Okulovka Russia 58°25N 33°19E 84 C7
Okuru N.Z. 43°55S 168°55E 155 D3
Okushiri-Tō Japan 42°15N 139°30E 112 C9
Okuta Nigeria 9°14N 3°12E 139 D5
Okwa → Botswana 22°30S 23°0E 144 C3
Ola Russia 59°35N 151°17E 107 D16
Ola U.S.A. 35°2N 93°13W 176 D8
Ólafsfjörður Iceland 66°4N 18°39W 60 C4
Ólafsvík Iceland 64°53N 23°43W 60 D2
Olaine Latvia 56°48N 23°59E 82 B10
Olancha U.S.A. 36°17N 118°1W 171 J8
Olancha Pk. U.S.A. 36°16N 118°7W 171 J8
Olanchito Honduras 15°30N 86°30W 182 C2
Öland Sweden 56°45N 16°38E 63 H10
Ölands norra udde
  Sweden 57°22N 17°5E 63 G11
Ölands södra udde
  Sweden 56°12N 16°23E 63 H10
Olanta U.S.A. 33°56N 79°56W 178 B10
Olar U.S.A. 33°11N 81°11W 178 B8
Olargues France 43°34N 2°53E 72 E6
Olary Australia 32°18S 140°19E 152 B4
Olascoaga Argentina 35°15S 60°39W 190 D3
Olathe U.S.A. 38°53N 94°49W 172 F6
Olavarría Argentina 36°55S 60°20W 190 D4
Oława Poland 50°57N 17°20E 83 H4
Olbernhau Germany 50°40N 13°19E 76 E9
Ólbia Italy 40°55N 9°31E 94 B2
Ólbia, G. di Italy 40°55N 9°39E 94 B2
Olching Germany 48°12N 11°21E 77 G7
Olcott U.S.A. 43°20N 78°42W 174 C6
Old Bahama Chan. = Bahama,
  Canal Viejo de
  W. Indies 22°10N 77°30W 182 B4
Old Baldy Pk. = San Antonio, Mt.
  U.S.A. 34°17N 117°38W 171 L9
Old Bar Australia 31°58S 152°35E 153 A10
Old Bridge U.S.A. 40°25N 74°22W 175 F10
Old Castile = Castilla y León □
  Spain 42°0N 5°0W 88 D6
Old Crow Canada 67°30N 139°55W 160 D4
Old Dale U.S.A. 34°8N 115°47W 171 L11
Old Forge N.Y., U.S.A. 43°43N 74°58W 175 C10
Old Forge Pa., U.S.A. 41°22N 75°45W 175 E9
Old Mapoon ○
  Australia 11°5S 142°22E 150 A3
Old Perlican Canada 48°5N 53°1W 165 C9
Old Shinyanga Tanzania 3°33S 33°27E 142 C3
Old Speck Mt. U.S.A. 44°34N 70°57W 175 B14
Old Town U.S.A. 29°36N 82°59W 179 F7
Old Town Maine,
  U.S.A. 44°56N 68°39W 173 C19
Old Washington U.S.A. 40°2N 81°27W 174 F3
Old Wives L. Canada 50°5N 106°0W 163 C7
Oldbury U.K. 51°38N 2°33W 67 F5
Oldcastle Ireland 53°46N 7°10W 64 C4
Oldeani Tanzania 3°22S 35°35E 142 C4
Oldenburg Niedersachsen,
  Germany 53°9N 8°13E 76 B4
Oldenburg Schleswig-Holstein,
  Germany 54°17N 10°52E 76 A6
Oldenzaal Neths. 52°19N 6°53E 69 B6
Oldham U.K. 53°33N 2°7W 66 D5
Oldman → Canada 49°57N 111°42W 162 D6
Oldmeldrum U.K. 57°20N 2°19W 65 D6
Olds Canada 51°50N 114°10W 162 C6
Oldsmar U.S.A. 28°2N 82°39W 179 D7
Olduvai Gorge Tanzania 2°57S 35°25E 142 C4
Oldziyt Mongolia 44°40N 109°1E 114 B5
Ole Rømer Land
  Greenland 74°10N 24°30W 57 C8
Olean U.S.A. 42°5N 78°26W 174 D6
Oleby Sweden 60°8N 13°2E 62 D7
Olecko Poland 54°2N 22°31E 82 D9
Oléggio Italy 45°36N 8°38E 92 C5
Oleiros = O Real Spain 43°20N 8°19W 88 A2
Oleiros Portugal 39°56N 7°56W 88 F3
Olekma → Russia 60°22N 120°42E 107 C13
Olekminsk Russia 60°25N 120°30E 107 C13
Oleksandrivka Ukraine 48°55N 32°20E 85 H7
Oleksandriya Kirovohrad,
  Ukraine 48°42N 33°3E 85 H7
Oleksandriya Rivne,
  Ukraine 50°37N 26°19E 75 C14
Olema U.S.A. 38°3N 122°47W 170 G4
Olenegorsk Russia 68°9N 33°18E 60 B25
Olenek Russia 68°28N 112°18E 107 C12
Olenek → Russia 73°0N 120°10E 107 B13
Olga, L. Canada 49°47N 77°15W 164 C4
Olgas, The = Kata Tjuta
  Australia 25°20S 130°50E 149 E5
Ölgiy Mongolia 48°56N 89°57E 114 B6
Ölgod Denmark 55°49N 8°36E 63 J2
Olhão Portugal 37°3N 7°48W 89 H3
Olhopil Ukraine 48°12N 29°30E 81 B14
Olhovatka Russia 54°30N 37°48E 81 B13
Olib Croatia 44°23N 14°44E 93 D11
Oliena Italy 40°16N 9°24E 94 B2
Oliete Spain 41°1N 0°41W 90 D4

Olifants = Elefantes →
  Africa 24°10S 32°40E 145 B5
Olifants → Namibia 25°30S 19°30E 144 B2
Olifantshoek S. Africa 27°57S 22°42E 144 C3
Ólimbos Greece 40°6N 22°23E 96 F6
Olímpia Brazil 20°44S 48°54W 191 A6
Olimpos-Beydaglari △
  Turkey 36°36N 30°30E 99 E12
Olinda Brazil 8°1S 34°51W 189 B4
Olite Spain 42°29N 1°40W 90 C3
Oliva Argentina 32°0S 63°38W 190 C3
Oliva Spain 38°58N 0°9W 91 G4
Oliva de la Frontera
  Spain 38°17N 6°54W 89 G4
Olivares, Cerro los
  Argentina 30°18S 69°55W 190 C2
Olivares de Júcar Spain 39°46N 2°20W 90 F2
Olive Branch U.S.A. 34°57N 89°49W 177 D10
Olivehurst U.S.A. 39°6N 121°34W 170 F5
Oliveira Brazil 20°39S 44°50W 189 E2
Oliveira de Azeméis
  Portugal 40°49N 8°29W 88 E2
Oliveira do Douro Portugal 41°5N 8°2W 88 D2
Oliveira dos Brejinhos
  Brazil 12°19S 42°54W 189 C2
Olivenza Spain 38°41N 7°9W 89 G3
Oliver Canada 49°13N 119°37W 162 D5
Oliver L. Canada 56°56N 103°22W 163 B8
Olivet France 47°51N 1°55E 71 E4
Olivine Ra. N.Z. 44°15S 168°30E 155 D3
Olkhovka Russia 49°48N 44°32E 86 F7
Olkusz Poland 50°18N 19°33E 83 H6
Ollagüe Chile 21°15S 68°10W 190 A2
Olmaliq Uzbekistan 40°50N 69°35E 109 D7
Olmedo Spain 41°20N 4°43W 88 D6
Olmeto France 41°43N 8°55E 73 G12
Olmos Peru 5°59S 79°46W 188 B2
Olney Ill., U.S.A. 38°44N 88°5W 172 F9
Olney Tex., U.S.A. 33°22N 98°45W 176 E5
Olofström Sweden 56°17N 14°32E 63 H8
Oloitokitok Kenya 2°56S 37°30E 142 C4
Oloma Cameroon 3°29N 11°19E 134 D2
Olomane → Canada 50°14N 60°37W 165 B7
Olomouc Czechia 49°38N 17°12E 79 B10
Olomoucký □ Czechia 49°45N 17°5E 79 B10
Olonets Russia 61°0N 32°54E 84 B7
Olongapo Phil. 14°50N 120°18E 119 B6
Olonkinbyen Norway 70°55N 8°43W 57 C10
Olonne-sur-Mer France 46°32N 1°47W 72 B2
Oloron, Gave d' → France 43°33N 1°5W 72 E2
Oloron-Ste-Marie France 43°11N 0°38W 72 E3
Olosenga = Swains I.
  Amer. Samoa 11°1S 171°4W 157 J11
Olot Spain 42°11N 2°30E 90 C7
Olovo Bos.-H. 44°8N 18°35E 80 F3
Olovyannaya Russia 50°58N 115°35E 107 D12
Oloy → Russia 66°29N 159°29E 107 C16
Olsberg Germany 51°21N 8°31E 76 D4
Olshammar Sweden 58°45N 14°48E 63 F8
Olshanka Ukraine 48°16N 30°58E 85 H6
Olshany Ukraine 50°3N 35°53E 85 G8
Olsztyn Poland 53°48N 20°29E 82 E7
Olsztynek Poland 53°34N 20°19E 82 E7
Olt □ Romania 44°20N 24°30E 81 F9
Olt → Romania 43°43N 24°51E 81 G9
Olten Switz. 47°21N 7°53E 77 H3
Olteniţa Romania 44°7N 26°42E 81 F11
Olton U.S.A. 34°11N 102°8W 176 D3
Oltu Turkey 40°35N 41°58E 105 B9
Oluan Pi Taiwan 21°53N 120°51E 117 G13
Olula del Río Spain 37°21N 2°18W 91 H2
Olur Turkey 40°49N 42°8E 105 B10
Olustee U.S.A. 30°12N 82°26W 178 E7
Olvega Spain 41°47N 2°0W 90 D2
Olvera Spain 36°55N 5°18W 89 J5
Olymbos Cyprus 35°21N 33°45E 101 D12
Olymbos Oros Greece 40°6N 22°23E 96 F6
Olympia Greece 37°39N 21°39E 98 D3
Olympia U.S.A. 47°3N 122°53W 170 D4
Olympic △ U.S.A. 47°45N 123°43W 170 C3
Olympic Dam
  Australia 30°30S 136°55E 152 A2
Olympic Mts. U.S.A. 47°55N 123°45W 170 C3
Olympus Cyprus 34°56N 32°52E 101 E11
Olympus, Mt. = Olymbos Oros
  Greece 40°6N 22°23E 96 F6
Olympus, Mt. = Uludağ
  Turkey 40°4N 29°13E 97 F13
Olympus, Mt. U.S.A. 47°48N 123°43W 170 C3
Olyphant U.S.A. 41°27N 75°36W 175 E9
Olyutorskiy, Mys
  Russia 59°55N 170°27E 107 D18
Om → Russia 54°59N 73°22E 109 B8
Ōma Japan 41°45N 141°5E 112 D10
Ōmachi Japan 36°30N 137°52E 113 F8
Omae-Zaki Japan 34°36N 138°14E 113 G9
Ōmagari = Daisen
  Japan 39°27N 140°29E 112 E10
Omagh U.K. 54°36N 7°19W 64 B4
Omagh □ U.K. 54°35N 7°15W 64 B4
Omaha U.S.A. 41°17N 95°58W 172 E6
Omaheke □ Namibia 21°30S 21°0E 144 B3
Omak U.S.A. 48°25N 119°31W 168 B4
Omalos Greece 35°19N 23°55E 100 E6
Oman ■ Asia 23°0N 58°0E 131 C6
Oman, G. of Asia 24°30N 58°30E 129 E8
Omapere N.Z. 35°37S 173°25E 154 B2
Omaruru Namibia 21°26S 16°0E 144 B2
Omaruru → Namibia 22°7S 14°15E 144 B1
Omate Peru 16°45N 70°45W 188 D3
Ombai, Selat Indonesia 8°30S 124°50E 119 F6
Omboué Gabon 1°35S 9°15E 140 E1
Omdurmân Sudan 15°40N 32°28E 135 E12
Omega Italy 45°53N 8°24E 92 C5
Omemee Canada 44°18N 78°33W 174 B6
Omeo Australia 37°6S 147°36E 153 D7
Omeonga
  Dem. Rep. of the Congo 3°40S 24°22E 142 C1
Ometepe, I. de Nic. 11°32N 85°35W 182 D2
Ometepec Mexico 16°41N 98°25W 180 D5
Ominato Japan 41°17N 141°10E 112 D10
Omineca → Canada 56°4N 124°16W 162 B4
Omineca Mts. Canada 56°30N 125°0W 162 B3
Omiš Croatia 43°28N 16°40E 93 E13
Omišalj Croatia 45°13N 14°32E 93 C11

Omitara Namibia 22°16S 18°2E 144 B2
Ōmiya = Saitama
  Japan 35°54N 139°38E 113 G9
Omme Å → Denmark 55°56N 8°32E 63 J2
Ommen Neths. 52°31N 6°26E 69 B6
Omnōgovĭ □ Mongolia 43°15N 104°0E 114 C2
Omo → Ethiopia 6°25N 36°10E 137 F4
Omodeo, L. Italy 40°8N 8°56E 94 B1
Omodhos Cyprus 34°51N 32°48E 101 E11
Omoko Nigeria 5°19N 6°40E 139 D6
Omolon → Russia 68°42N 158°36E 107 C16
Omono-Gawa →
  Japan 39°46N 140°3E 112 E10
Ompha Canada 45°0N 76°50W 175 B8
Omsk Russia 55°0N 73°12E 109 B8
Omsukchan Russia 62°32N 155°48E 107 C16
Ōmu Japan 44°34N 142°58E 112 B11
Omul, Vf. Romania 45°27N 25°29E 81 E10
Omulew → Poland 53°5N 21°32E 82 E8
Ōmura Japan 32°56N 129°57E 113 H4
Omuramba Omatako →
  Namibia 17°45S 20°25E 144 A2
Omuramba Ovambo →
  Namibia 18°45S 16°59E 144 A2
Omurtag Bulgaria 43°8N 26°26E 97 C10
Omusati □ Namibia 18°30S 15°0E 144 A1
Ōmuta Japan 33°5N 130°26E 113 H5
Omuthiya Namibia 17°43S 16°13E 144 A2
Oña Spain 42°43N 3°25W 88 C7
Ona U.S.A. 27°29N 81°55W 179 E7
Onaga U.S.A. 39°29N 96°10W 172 F5
Onalaska U.S.A. 43°53N 91°14W 172 D8
Onancock U.S.A. 37°43N 75°45W 173 G16
Onangue, L. Gabon 0°57S 10°4E 140 E2
Onaping L. Canada 47°3N 81°30W 164 C3
Oñati Spain 43°3N 2°25W 90 B2
Onavas Mexico 28°31N 109°35W 180 B3
Onawa U.S.A. 42°2N 96°6W 172 D5
Oncócua Angola 16°30S 13°25E 144 A1
Onda Spain 39°55N 0°17W 90 F4
Ondangwa Namibia 17°57S 16°4E 144 A2
Ondarroa Spain 43°19N 2°25W 90 B2
Ondas → Brazil 12°8S 44°55W 189 C2
Ondava → Slovakia 48°27N 21°48E 79 C14
Ondjiva Angola 16°48S 15°50E 144 A2
Ondo □ Nigeria 7°4N 4°47E 139 D5
Ondo □ Nigeria 6°45N 5°0E 139 D6
Öndörhaan Mongolia 47°19N 110°39E 111 B11
Öndverðarnes Iceland 64°52N 24°0W 60 D2
One Arm Point
  Australia 16°26S 123°3E 148 C3
One Arm Point ○
  Australia 16°31S 122°53E 148 C3
One Tree Australia 34°11S 144°43E 151 E3
Oneata Fiji 18°26S 178°25W 154 a
Oneco U.S.A. 27°25N 82°31W 179 H7
Onega Russia 63°58N 38°2E 58 C13
Onega, L. = Onezhskoye Ozero
  Russia 61°44N 35°22E 84 B8
Onega → Russia 63°58N 38°2E 58 C13
Onehunga N.Z. 36°55S 174°48E 154 C3
Oneida U.S.A. 43°6N 75°39W 175 C9
Oneida L. U.S.A. 43°12N 75°54W 175 C9
O'Neill U.S.A. 42°27N 98°39W 172 D4
Onekotan, Ostrov
  Russia 49°25N 154°45E 107 E16
Onema
  Dem. Rep. of the Congo 4°35S 24°30E 142 C1
Oneonta U.S.A. 42°27N 75°4W 175 D9
Onerahi N.Z. 35°45S 174°22E 154 B3
Oneşti Romania 46°17N 26°47E 81 D11
Onezhskoye Ozero
  Russia 61°44N 35°22E 84 B8
Ongarue N.Z. 38°42S 175°19E 154 E4
Ongea Levu = Ogea Levu
  Fiji 19°8S 178°24W 154 a
Ongers → S. Africa 31°4S 23°13E 144 D3
Ongerup Australia 33°58S 118°28E 149 F2
Ongi Mongolia 45°27N 103°54E 114 B2
Ongjin N. Korea 37°56N 125°21E 115 F13
Ongkharak Thailand 14°8N 101°1E 120 E3
Ongniud Qi China 43°0N 118°38E 115 C10
Ongoka
  Dem. Rep. of the Congo 1°20S 26°0E 142 C2
Ongole India 15°33N 80°2E 127 G5
Ongon = Havirga
  Mongolia 45°41N 113°5E 114 B7
Ongtüstik Qazaqstan □
  Kazakhstan 43°0N 68°0E 109 D7
Ongwediva Namibia 17°47S 15°46E 144 A2
Oni Georgia 42°33N 43°26E 87 J6
Onida U.S.A. 44°42N 100°4W 172 C3
Onilahy → Madag. 23°34S 43°45E 141 J8
Onitsha Nigeria 6°6N 6°42E 139 D6
Onne Nigeria 4°47N 7°9E 139 E6
Ono Fiji 18°55S 178°29E 154 a
Onoda Japan 33°59N 131°11E 113 H5
Onoke, L. N.Z. 41°22S 175°8E 154 H4
Ons, I. de Spain 42°23N 8°55W 88 C2
Onsala Sweden 57°26N 12°0E 63 G6
Onslow Australia 21°40S 115°12E 148 D2
Onslow B. U.S.A. 34°20N 77°15W 177 D16
Ontake-San Japan 35°53N 137°29E 113 G8
Ontario Calif., U.S.A. 34°4N 117°39W 171 L9
Ontario Oreg., U.S.A. 44°2N 116°58W 168 D5
Ontario □ Canada 48°0N 83°0W 164 B2
Ontario, L. N. Amer. 43°20N 78°0W 174 C7
Ontinyent Spain 38°50N 0°35W 91 G4
Ontonagon U.S.A. 46°52N 89°19W 172 B9
Ontur Spain 38°38N 1°29W 91 G3
Onyx U.S.A. 35°41N 118°14W 171 K8
Oodaaq Greenland 83°40N 30°40W 57 A7
Oodnadatta Australia 27°33S 135°30E 151 D2
Ooldea Australia 30°27S 131°50E 149 F5
Oombulgurri Australia 15°15S 127°45E 148 C4
Oombulgurri ○
  Australia 15°10S 127°50E 148 C4
Oorindi Australia 20°40S 141°1E 150 D3
Oost-Vlaanderen □
  Belgium 51°5N 3°50E 69 C3
Oostende Belgium 51°15N 2°54E 69 C2
Oosterhout Neths. 51°39N 4°47E 69 C4
Oosterschelde → Neths. 51°33N 4°0E 69 C4
Oosterwolde Neths. 53°0N 6°17E 69 B6
Oostvaardersplassen ○
  Neths. 52°27N 5°22E 69 B5
Ootacamund = Udagamandalam
  India 11°30N 76°44E 127 J3
Ootha Australia 33°6S 147°29E 153 B8
Ootsa L. Canada 53°50N 126°2W 162 C3

Ooty = Udagamandalam
  India 11°30N 76°44E 127 J3
Op Luang △ Thailand 18°12N 98°32E 120 C2
Opaka Bulgaria 43°28N 26°10E 97 C10
Opala
  Dem. Rep. of the Congo 0°40S 24°20E 142 C1
Opâle, Côte d' France 50°30N 1°30E 70 B8
Opalenica Poland 52°18N 16°24E 83 F3
Opan Bulgaria 42°13N 25°41E 97 D9
Opanake Sri Lanka 6°35N 80°40E 127 L5
Opapa N.Z. 39°47S 176°42E 154 F5
Opasatika Canada 49°30N 82°50W 164 C3
Opasquia □ Canada 53°33N 93°5W 164 B1
Opatija Croatia 45°21N 14°17E 93 C11
Opatów Poland 50°50N 21°27E 83 H8
Opava Czechia 49°57N 17°58E 79 B10
Opelika U.S.A. 32°39N 85°23W 178 C4
Opelousas U.S.A. 30°32N 92°5W 176 F8
Opémisca, L. Canada 48°51N 106°24W 168 B10
Opheim U.S.A. 48°51N 106°24W 168 B10
Ophthalmia Ra.
  Australia 23°15S 119°30E 148 D2
Opi Nigeria 6°36N 7°28E 139 D6
Opinaca → Canada 52°15N 78°2W 164 B4
Opinaca, Rés. Canada 52°39N 76°20W 164 B4
Opinnagau → Canada 54°12N 82°25W 164 B3
Opiscotéo, L. Canada 53°10N 68°10W 165 B6
Opobo Nigeria 4°35N 7°34E 139 E6
Opochka Russia 56°42N 28°45E 84 D5
Opoczno Poland 51°22N 20°18E 83 G7
Opole Poland 50°42N 17°58E 83 H4
Opole Lubelskie Poland 51°9N 21°58E 83 G8
Opolskie □ Poland 50°30N 18°0E 83 H5
Oponono L. Namibia 18°8S 15°45E 144 A2
Opornyy = Borankul
  Kazakhstan 46°11N 54°25E 108 C4
Oporto = Porto Portugal 41°8N 8°40W 88 D2
Opotiki N.Z. 38°1S 177°19E 154 E6
Opp U.S.A. 31°17N 86°16W 178 D3
Oppland □ Norway 61°15N 9°40E 63 E5
Opportunity U.S.A. 47°39N 117°15W 168 C5
Oprişor Romania 44°17N 23°5E 80 F8
Oprtalj Croatia 45°23N 13°50E 93 C10
Opua N.Z. 35°19S 174°9E 154 B3
Opunake N.Z. 39°26S 173°52E 154 F2
Opuwo Namibia 18°3S 13°45E 144 A1
Opuzen Croatia 43°1N 17°34E 93 E14
Or → Kazakhstan 51°11N 58°32E 108 B5
Or, Côte d' France 47°10N 4°50E 71 E11
Ora Cyprus 34°51N 33°12E 101 E12
Oracle U.S.A. 32°37N 110°46W 169 K8
Oradea Romania 47°2N 21°58E 80 C7
Orahovac = Rahovec
  Kosovo 42°24N 20°40E 96 C4
Orahovica Croatia 45°35N 17°52E 80 E2
Orai India 25°58N 79°30E 125 G8
Oraiokastro Greece 40°44N 22°55E 96 F6
Oraison France 43°55N 5°55E 73 E9
Oral = Zhayyq →
  Kazakhstan 47°0N 51°48E 108 C4
Oral Kazakhstan 51°20N 51°20E 86 E10
Oran Algeria 35°45N 0°39W 136 A3
Oran □ Algeria 35°0N 0°45W 136 A3
Orange Australia 33°15S 149°7E 153 B8
Orange France 44°8N 4°47E 73 D8
Orange Calif., U.S.A. 33°47N 117°51W 171 M9
Orange Mass., U.S.A. 42°35N 72°19W 175 D12
Orange Tex., U.S.A. 30°6N 93°44W 176 F7
Orange Va., U.S.A. 38°15N 78°7W 173 F14
Orange → S. Africa 28°41S 16°28E 144 C2
Orange, C. Brazil 4°20N 51°30W 187 B8
Orange City U.S.A. 28°57N 81°18W 179 G8
Orange Cove U.S.A. 36°38N 119°19W 170 J7
Orange Free State = Free State □
  S. Africa 28°30S 27°0E 144 C4
Orange Grove U.S.A. 27°58N 97°56W 176 H6
Orange L. U.S.A. 29°25N 82°13W 179 F7
Orange Park U.S.A. 30°10N 81°42W 178 E8
Orange Walk Belize 18°6N 88°33W 181 D7
Orangeburg U.S.A. 33°30N 80°52W 178 B9
Orangeville Canada 43°55N 80°5W 174 C4
Orango Guinea-Biss. 11°5N 16°0W 138 C1
Orani Italy 40°15N 9°11E 94 B2
Oranienburg Germany 52°45N 13°14E 76 C9
Oranje = Orange →
  S. Africa 28°41S 16°28E 144 C2
Oranjemund Namibia 28°38S 16°29E 144 C2
Oranjerivier S. Africa 29°40S 24°12E 144 C3
Oranjestad Aruba 12°32N 70°2W 183 D5
Orapa Botswana 21°15S 25°30E 141 A5
Oras Phil. 12°9N 125°28E 119 B7
Orašje Bos.-H. 45°1N 18°42E 80 E3
Orăştie Romania 45°50N 23°10E 81 E8
Orava → Slovakia 49°9N 19°8E 79 B12
Orava, Vodná nádrž
  Slovakia 49°25N 19°35E 79 B12
Oraviţa Romania 45°2N 21°43E 80 E6
Orawia N.Z. 46°1S 167°50E 155 G2
Orb → France 43°15N 3°18E 72 E7
Orba → Italy 44°53N 8°37E 92 D5
Ørbæk Denmark 55°17N 10°39E 63 J4
Orbe Switz. 46°43N 6°32E 77 J2
Orbec France 49°1N 0°23E 70 C7
Orbetello Italy 42°27N 11°13E 93 F8
Órbigo → Spain 42°5N 5°42W 88 C5
Orbisonia U.S.A. 40°15N 77°54W 174 F7
Orbost Australia 37°40S 148°29E 153 D8
Örbyhus Sweden 60°15N 17°43E 62 D11
Orcadas Antarctica 60°44S 44°37W 5 C18
Orcas I. U.S.A. 48°42N 122°56E 170 B4
Orce Spain 37°44N 2°28W 91 H2
Orce → Spain 37°44N 2°28W 91 H2
Orchard City U.S.A. 38°50N 107°58W 168 G10
Orchard Homes U.S.A. 46°52N 114°2W 168 C6
Orchid I. = Lan Yü
  Taiwan 22°4N 121°25E 117 F13
Orchies France 50°28N 3°14E 71 B10
Orchila, I. Venezuela 11°48N 66°10W 183 D6
Orchilla, Pta.
  Canary Is. 27°42N 18°10W 100 G1
Orco → Italy 45°10N 7°52E 92 C4
Orcopampa Peru 15°20S 72°20W 188 D3
Orcutt U.S.A. 34°52N 120°27W 171 L6
Ord → Australia 15°33S 128°15E 148 C4
Ord, Mt. Australia 17°20S 125°34E 148 C4
Ord Mts. U.S.A. 34°39N 116°45W 171 L10
Ordenes = Ordes Spain 43°5N 8°29W 88 B2
Orderville U.S.A. 37°17N 112°38W 169 H7

Ordes Spain 43°5N 8°29W 88 B2
Ordesa y Monte Perdido △
  Spain 42°40N 0°10W 90 C4
Ording = Sankt Peter-Ording
  Germany 54°20N 8°36E 76 A4
Ordos = Mu Us Shamo
  China 39°0N 109°0E 114 E5
Ordu Turkey 40°55N 37°53E 104 B7
Ordu □ Turkey 40°50N 37°40E 104 B7
Ordubad Azerbaijan 38°54N 46°1E 105 C12
Orduña, Álava, Spain 42°58N 2°58W 90 C2
Orduña Granada, Spain 37°20N 3°30W 89 H7
Ordway U.S.A. 38°13N 103°46W 168 G12
Ordzhonikidze = Denisovka
  Kazakhstan 52°27N 61°39E 108 B6
Ordzhonikidze Ukraine 47°39N 34°3E 85 J8
Ore Dem. Rep. of the Congo 3°17N 29°30E 142 B2
Ore Mts. = Erzgebirge
  Germany 50°27N 12°55E 76 E8
Orebić Croatia 43°0N 17°11E 93 F14
Örebro Sweden 59°20N 15°18E 62 E9
Örebro □ Sweden 59°27N 15°0E 62 E8
Orecchiella △ Italy 44°16N 10°22E 92 D7
Oregon U.S.A. 42°1N 89°20W 172 D9
Oregon □ U.S.A. 44°0N 121°0W 168 E3
Oregon City U.S.A. 45°21N 122°36W 170 E4
Oregon Dunes △
  U.S.A. 43°40N 124°10W 168 E1
Øregrund Sweden 60°21N 18°30E 62 D12
Öregrundsgrepen
  Sweden 60°25N 18°15E 62 D12
Orekhov = Orikhiv
  Ukraine 47°30N 35°48E 85 J8
Orekhovo-Zuyevo
  Russia 55°50N 38°55E 84 E10
Orel Russia 52°57N 36°3E 85 F9
Orel → Russia 52°30N 36°40E 85 F9
Orellana, Canal de Spain 39°2N 6°0W 89 F5
Orellana, Embalse de
  Spain 39°5N 5°10W 89 F5
Orellana la Vieja Spain 39°1N 5°32W 89 F5
Orem U.S.A. 40°19N 111°42W 168 F8
Ören Turkey 37°3N 27°57E 99 D9
Orenburg Russia 51°45N 55°6E 108 B5
Orencik Turkey 39°16N 29°33E 99 B11
Orense = Ourense Spain 42°19N 7°55W 88 C3
Orepuki N.Z. 46°19S 167°46E 155 G2
Orestes Pereyra
  Mexico 26°30N 105°39W 180 B3
Orestiada Greece 41°30N 26°33E 97 E10
Øresund Europe 55°45N 12°40E 63 J6
Oreti → N.Z. 46°28S 168°14E 155 G2
Orfanos Kolpos Greece 40°33N 24°0E 96 F7
Orford Ness U.K. 52°5N 1°35E 67 E9
Organ Pipe Cactus △
  U.S.A. 32°12N 112°52W 169 K7
Organos, Pta. de los
  Canary Is. 28°12N 17°17W 100 F2
Organyà Spain 42°13N 1°20E 90 C6
Orgaz Spain 39°39N 3°53W 89 F7
Orgeyev = Orhei
  Moldova 47°24N 28°50E 81 C13
Orgiva Spain 36°53N 3°24W 89 J7
Orhaneli Turkey 39°54N 28°59E 99 B11
Orhaneli → Turkey 39°50N 28°58E 99 B11
Orhangazi Turkey 40°29N 29°18E 99 F13
Orhei Moldova 47°24N 28°50E 81 C13
Orhon Gol →
  Mongolia 50°21N 106°0E 110 A10
Ória Italy 40°30N 17°38E 95 B10
Oria Spain 37°30N 2°30W 91 H2
Oriental □ Morocco 33°0N 2°0W 136 B5
Oriental, Cordillera
  Colombia 6°0N 73°0W 186 B4
Oriental, Grand Erg
  Algeria 30°0N 6°30E 136 B5
Oriente Argentina 38°44S 60°37W 190 D3
Orihuela Spain 38°7N 0°55W 91 G4
Orihuela del Tremedal
  Spain 40°33N 1°39W 90 E3
Orikhiv Ukraine 47°30N 35°48E 85 J8
Orikum Albania 40°20N 19°26E 98 D1
Oril → Ukraine 48°40N 34°39E 85 H8
Orillia Canada 44°40N 79°24W 174 B5
Orinoco → Venezuela 9°15N 61°30W 186 B6
Orion Canada 49°27N 110°49W 163 D6
Oriska U.S.A. 46°56N 97°47W 172 B5
Oriskany N.Y., U.S.A. 43°9N 75°20W 175 C9
Orissa = Odisha □ India 20°0N 84°0E 126 D8
Orissaare Estonia 58°34N 23°5E 63 F8
Oristano Italy 39°54N 8°36E 94 C1
Oristano, G. di Italy 39°50N 8°29E 94 C1
Orizaba Mexico 18°51N 97°6W 181 D5
Orizaba, Pico de
  Mexico 18°58N 97°15W 181 D5
Orizare Bulgaria 42°44N 27°39E 97 D11
Orizona Brazil 17°3S 48°18W 189 D1
Orjen Bos.-H. 42°35N 18°34E 96 D2
Orjiva = Orgiva Spain 36°53N 3°24W 89 J7
Orkanger Norway 63°18N 9°52E 60 E13
Orkelljunga Sweden 56°17N 13°17E 63 H7
Örken Sweden 57°6N 15°1E 63 H9
Örkény Hungary 47°9N 19°26E 80 C4
Orkhon = Orhon Gol →
  Mongolia 50°21N 106°0E 110 A10
Orkla → Norway 63°18N 9°51E 60 E13
Orkney S. Africa 26°58S 26°40E 144 C4
Orkney □ U.K. 59°2N 3°13W 65 B5
Orkney Is. U.K. 59°0N 3°0W 65 B6
Orland U.S.A. 39°45N 122°12W 170 F4
Orlando U.S.A. 28°32N 81°22W 179 G8
Orlando, C. d' Italy 38°10N 14°43E 95 D7
Orlando Int. ✈ (MCO)
  U.S.A. 28°26N 81°19W 179 G8
Orléanais France 48°0N 2°0E 71 E5
Orléans France 47°54N 1°52E 71 E4
Orleans U.S.A. 44°49N 72°12W 175 B12
Orléans, Î. d' Canada 46°54N 70°58W 165 C5
Orlice → Czechia 50°13N 15°58E 78 A8
Orlik Russia 52°30N 99°55E 107 D10
Orlivka Ukraine 49°17N 20°51E 79 B13
Orlov Slovakia 49°17N 20°51E 79 B13
Orlov Gay Russia 50°56N 48°19E 86 E8
Orlová Czechia 49°51N 18°27E 79 B11
Orlovat Serbia 45°14N 20°33E 80 E5
Orlovskoye Polesye △
  Russia 58°30N 33°0E 84 F9
Orly, Paris ✈ (ORY)
  France 48°44N 2°23E 71 D9
Ormara Pakistan 25°16N 64°33E 122 G4
Ormea Italy 44°9N 7°54E 92 D4
Ormília Greece 40°16N 23°39E 96 F6
Ormoc Phil. 11°0N 124°37E 119 B6

Ormond N.Z. 38°33S 177°56E 154 E6
Ormond Beach U.S.A. 29°17N 81°3W 179 F8
Ormond-by-the-Sea
  U.S.A. 29°21N 81°4W 179 F8
Ormondville N.Z. 40°5S 176°19E 154 G5
Ormož Slovenia 46°25N 16°10E 93 B13
Ormskirk U.K. 53°35N 2°54W 66 D5
Ormstown Canada 45°8N 74°0W 175 A11
Ornans France 47°7N 6°10E 71 E13
Orne □ France 48°40N 0°5E 70 D7
Orne → France 49°18N 0°15W 70 C6
Orneta Poland 54°8N 20°9E 82 D7
Ornö Sweden 59°4N 18°24E 62 E12
Örnsköldsvik Sweden 63°17N 18°40E 62 A12
Oro N. Korea 40°1N 127°27E 115 D14
Oro → Mexico 25°35N 105°2W 180 B3
Oro Grande U.S.A. 34°36N 117°20W 171 L9
Oro Valley U.S.A. 32°21N 110°58W 169 K8
Orobie, Alpi Italy 46°7N 10°0E 92 B6
Orobie Bergamasche △
  Italy 46°0N 9°45E 92 C6
Orobie Valtellinesi △ Italy 46°5N 9°45E 92 B6
Orocué Colombia 4°48N 71°20W 186 C4
Orodara Burkina Faso 11°0N 4°55W 138 C4
Orodo Nigeria 5°34N 7°4E 139 D6
Orofino U.S.A. 46°29N 116°15W 168 C5
Orohena, Mt. Tahiti 17°37S 149°28W 155 b
Orol Dengizi = Aral Sea
  Asia 45°0N 58°20E 108 C5
Oromocto Canada 45°54N 66°29W 165 C6
Oron Nigeria 4°48N 8°14E 139 E6
Orono Canada 43°59N 78°37W 174 C6
Orono U.S.A. 44°53N 68°40W 173 C19
Oronsay U.K. 56°1N 6°15W 65 E2
Oropesa Spain 39°57N 5°10W 88 F5
Oroquieta Phil. 8°32N 123°44E 119 C6
Orós Brazil 6°15S 38°55W 189 B4
Orosei Italy 40°23N 9°42E 94 B2
Orosei, G. di Italy 40°15N 9°44E 94 B2
Orosháza Hungary 46°32N 20°42E 80 D5
Oroszlány Hungary 47°29N 18°19E 80 C3
Orotukan Russia 62°16N 151°42E 107 C16
Oroville Calif., U.S.A. 39°31N 121°33W 170 F5
Oroville Wash., U.S.A. 48°56N 119°26W 168 B4
Oroville, L. U.S.A. 39°33N 121°29W 170 F5
Orrefors Sweden 56°50N 15°45E 63 H9
Orroroo Australia 32°43S 138°38E 152 B3
Orrviken Sweden 63°6N 14°26E 62 A8
Orrville U.S.A. 40°50N 81°46W 174 F3
Orsa Sweden 61°7N 14°37E 62 C8
Orsara di Púglia Italy 41°17N 15°16E 95 A8
Orsasjön Sweden 61°7N 14°37E 62 C8
Orsha Belarus 54°30N 30°25E 84 E6
Orsières Switz. 46°2N 7°9E 92 A4
Orsjö Sweden 56°42N 15°45E 63 H9
Orsk Russia 51°12N 58°34E 108 B5
Ørsta Norway 62°12N 6°9E 63 E5
Orşova Romania 44°41N 22°25E 80 F7
Ørsted Denmark 56°30N 10°20E 63 H4
Örsundsbro Sweden 59°44N 17°18E 62 E11
Orta, L. d' Italy 45°48N 8°21E 92 C5
Orta Nova Italy 41°19N 15°42E 95 A8
Ortaca Turkey 36°49N 28°45E 99 E10
Ortakent Turkey 37°5N 27°21E 99 D9
Ortaklar Turkey 37°52N 27°35E 99 D9
Ortaköy Çorum, Turkey 40°16N 35°15E 104 B6
Ortaköy Niğde, Turkey 38°44N 34°3E 104 B6
Orte Italy 42°27N 12°23E 93 F9
Ortegal, C. Spain 43°43N 7°52W 88 B3
Orthez France 43°29N 0°48W 72 E3
Ortigueira Spain 43°40N 7°50W 88 B3
Ortigueira, Ria de Spain 43°42N 7°45W 88 B3
Orting U.S.A. 47°6N 122°12W 170 C4
Ortisei Italy 46°34N 11°40E 93 B8
Ortles Italy 46°31N 10°33E 92 B7
Ortón → Bolivia 10°50S 67°0W 188 C4
Ortona Italy 42°21N 14°24E 93 F11
Ortonville U.S.A. 45°19N 96°27W 172 C5
Orūmīyeh Iran 37°40N 45°0E 105 D11
Orūmīyeh, Daryācheh-ye
  Iran 37°50N 45°30E 105 D11
Orune Italy 40°24N 9°22E 94 B2
Oruro Bolivia 18°0S 67°9W 188 D4
Oruro □ Bolivia 18°40S 67°30W 188 D4
Orust Sweden 58°10N 11°40E 63 F5
Oruzgān □ Afghan. 33°0N 66°0E 122 C5
Orvault France 47°17N 1°38W 70 E5
Orvieto Italy 42°43N 12°7E 93 F9
Orwell N.Y., U.S.A. 43°35N 75°50W 175 C9
Orwell Ohio, U.S.A. 41°32N 80°52W 174 E4
Orwell → U.K. 51°59N 1°18E 67 F9
Orwigsburg U.S.A. 40°39N 76°6W 175 E8
Orynyn Ukraine 48°46N 26°24E 81 B11
Oryol = Orel Russia 52°57N 36°3E 85 F9
Orzinuovi Italy 45°24N 9°55E 92 C6
Orzyc → Poland 52°46N 21°14E 83 F8
Orzysz Poland 53°50N 21°58E 82 E8
Osa, Pen. de Costa Rica 8°0N 84°0W 182 E3
Osage U.S.A. 43°17N 92°49W 172 D7
Osage → U.S.A. 38°36N 91°57W 172 F7
Osage City U.S.A. 38°38N 95°50W 172 F6
Ōsaka Japan 34°42N 135°30E 113 G7
Osakarovka Kazakhstan 50°33N 72°34E 109 B8
Ōsaki Japan 38°34N 140°58E 112 E10
Osam → Bulgaria 43°42N 24°51E 97 C8
Osawatomie U.S.A. 38°31N 94°57W 172 F6
Osborn Plateau Ind. Oc. 14°45S 87°0E 146 F7
Osborne U.S.A. 39°26N 98°42W 172 F4
Osby Sweden 56°23N 13°59E 63 H7
Osceola Ark., U.S.A. 35°42N 89°58W 177 D10
Osceola Iowa, U.S.A. 41°2N 93°46W 172 E7
Oschatz Germany 51°17N 13°6E 76 D9
Oschersleben Germany 52°2N 11°13E 76 C7
Óschiri Italy 40°43N 9°6E 94 B2
Osečina Serbia 44°23N 19°34E 96 B3
Ösel = Saaremaa
  Estonia 58°30N 22°30E 63 F7
Osery Russia 54°52N 38°28E 84 E10
Osgoode Canada 45°8N 75°36W 175 A9
Osh Kyrgyzstan 40°37N 72°49E 109 D8
Oshakati Namibia 17°45S 15°40E 144 A1
Oshana □ Namibia 17°45S 15°40E 144 A1
Oshawa Canada 43°50N 78°50W 174 C6
Oshika-Hantō Japan 38°20N 141°30E 112 E10
Oshikoto □ Namibia 18°30S 17°0E 144 A2
Oshivelo Namibia 18°37S 17°10E 144 A2
Oshkosh Nebr., U.S.A. 41°24N 102°21W 172 E2
Oshkosh Wis., U.S.A. 44°1N 88°33W 172 C9

Oshmyany = Ashmyany
  Belarus 54°26N 25°52E **75** A13
Oshnovīyeh Iran 37°2N 45°6E **105** D11
Oshogbo Nigeria 7°48N 4°37E **139** D5
Oshtorīnān Iran 34°1N 48°38E **105** E13
Ōshū Japan 39°8N 141°8E **112** E10
Oshwe
  Dem. Rep. of the Congo 3°25S 19°28E **140** E3
Osi Nigeria 8°8N 5°14E **139** D6
Osieczna Poland 51°55N 16°40E **83** G3
Osijek Croatia 45°34N 18°41E **80** E3
Ósilo Italy 40°45N 8°40E **94** B1
Ósimo Italy 43°28N 13°30E **93** E10
Osintorf Belarus 54°40N 30°39E **84** E6
Osipovichi = Asipovichy
  Belarus 53°19N 28°33E **75** B15
Osiyan India 26°43N 72°55E **124** F5
Osizweni S. Africa 27°49S 30°7E **145** C5
Oskaloosa U.S.A. 41°18N 92°39W **172** E7
Oskarshamn Sweden 57°15N 16°27E **63** G10
Oskarström Sweden 56°48N 12°58E **63** H6
Osklánéo Canada 58°45N 75°15W **164** C4
Öskemen Kazakhstan 50°0N 82°36E **109** C10
Oskol → Ukraine 49°6N 37°25E **85** H9
Oslo Norway 59°54N 10°43E **61** G14
Oslofjorden Norway 59°20N 10°35E **61** G14
Otero de Rey = Outeiro de Rei
  Spain 43°6N 7°36W **88** B3
Osmanabad India 18°5N 76°10E **126** E3
Osmancık Turkey 40°58N 34°47E **104** B6
Osmaniye Turkey 37°5N 36°10E **104** D7
Osmanlı Turkey 41°35N 26°51E **107** B9
Osmannagar India 18°32N 79°20E **126** E4
Ösmo Sweden 58°58N 17°55E **62** F11
Osnabrück Germany 52°17N 8°3E **76** C4
Ošno Lubuskie Poland 52°28N 14°51E **83** F1
Osoblaha Czechia 50°17N 17°44E **79** A10
Osogbo = Oshogbo
  Nigeria 7°48N 4°37E **139** D5
Osogovska Planina
  Macedonia 42°10N 22°30E **96** D6
Osor Italy 44°42N 14°24E **93** D11
Osório Brazil 29°53S 50°17W **191** B5
Osorno Chile 40°25S 73°0W **192** D2
Osorno Spain 42°24N 4°22W **88** C6
Osorno → Chile 40°34S 73°9W **192** D2
Osorno, Vol. Chile 41°0S 72°30W **192** D2
Osoyoos Canada 49°0N 119°30W **162** D5
Óspika → Canada 56°20N 124°0W **162** B4
Osprey → Australia 27°12N 82°29W **179** H7
Osprey Reef Australia 13°52S 146°36E **150** A4
Oss Neths. 51°46N 5°32E **65** C5
Ossa, Mt. Australia 41°52S 146°3E **151** G4
Ossa, Oros Greece 39°47N 22°42E **98** B4
Ossa de Montiel Spain 38°58N 2°45W **91** G2
Ossabaw I. U.S.A. 31°50N 81°5W **178** E5
Ossabaw Sd. U.S.A. 31°50N 81°6W **178** D5
Osse → France 44°7N 0°17E **72** D4
Osse → Nigeria 6°10N 5°20E **139** D6
Ossi Italy 40°40N 8°35E **94** B1
Ossining U.S.A. 41°10N 73°55W **175** E11
Ossipee U.S.A. 43°41N 71°7W **175** C13
Ossokmanuan L.
  Canada 53°25N 65°0W **165** B7
Ossora Russia 59°20N 163°13E **107** D17
Ostashkov Russia 57°4N 33°2E **84** D7
Östavall Sweden 62°26N 15°29E **62** B9
Oste → Germany 53°49N 9°2E **76** B5
Ostend = Oostende
  Belgium 51°15N 2°54E **65** C2
Ostend N.Z. 36°48S 175°2E **154** C4
Oster Ukraine 50°57N 30°53E **75** C16
Österbotten = Pohjanmaa □
  Finland 62°58N 22°50E **60** E20
Osterburg Germany 52°47N 11°45E **76** C7
Osterburg U.S.A. 40°16N 78°31W **174** F6
Osterburken Germany 49°25N 9°26E **77** F5
Österbybruk Sweden 60°13N 17°55E **62** D11
Österbymo Sweden 57°49N 15°15E **63** G9
Österdalälven → Sweden 60°30N 15°7E **62** C7
Österdalen Norway 61°40N 10°50E **62** C4
Österforse Sweden 63°9N 17°3E **62** A11
Östergötland □ Sweden 58°35N 15°45E **63** F9
Osterholz-Scharmbeck
  Germany 53°13N 8°47E **76** B4
Østerild Denmark 57°2N 8°51E **63** G2
Östermyra = Seinäjoki
  Finland 62°40N 22°51E **60** E20
Osterode Germany 51°43N 10°15E **76** D6
Österreich = Austria ■
  Europe 47°0N 14°0E **78** E7
Östersund Sweden 63°10N 14°38E **62** A8
Östervåla Sweden 60°11N 17°11E **62** D11
Ostfriesische Inseln
  Germany 53°42N 7°0E **76** B3
Ostfriesland Germany 53°20N 7°30E **76** B3
Östhammar Sweden 60°16N 18°22E **62** D12
Óstia, Lido di Italy 41°43N 12°17E **93** G9
Östmark Sweden 60°17N 12°45E **62** D6
Östra Husby Sweden 58°35N 16°33E **63** F10
Ostrava Czechia 49°51N 18°18E **79** B11
Ostróda Poland 53°42N 19°58E **82** E6
Ostrogozhsk Russia 50°55N 39°7E **85** G10
Ostroh Ukraine 50°20N 26°30E **75** C14
Ostrołęka Poland 53°4N 21°32E **83** E8
Ostrov Bulgaria 43°40N 24°9E **97** C11
Ostrov Czechia 50°18N 12°57E **78** A5
Ostrov Romania 44°6N 27°24E **81** F12
Ostrov Russia 57°25N 28°20E **84** D5
Ostrów Lubelski Poland 51°29N 22°51E **83** G9
Ostrów Mazowiecka
  Poland 52°50N 21°51E **83** F8
Ostrów Wielkopolski
  Poland 51°36N 17°44E **83** G4
Ostrowiec-Świętokrzyski
  Poland 50°55N 21°22E **83** H8
Ostrožac Bos.-H. 43°43N 17°49E **80** G2
Ostrzeszów Poland 51°25N 17°52E **83** G4
Ostseebad Kühlungsborn
  Germany 54°8N 11°44E **76** A7
Osttirol □ Austria 46°50N 12°30E **78** E5
Ostuni Italy 40°44N 17°35E **95** B10
Osum → Albania 40°40N 20°10E **96** E4
Ōsumi-Kaikyō Japan 30°55N 131°0E **113** J5
Ōsumi-Shotō Japan 30°30N 130°0E **113** J5
Osun □ Nigeria 7°30N 4°30E **139** D5
Osuna Spain 37°14N 5°8W **89** H5
Oswegatchie →
  U.S.A. 44°42N 75°30W **175** B9
Oswego U.S.A. 43°27N 76°31W **175** C8

Oswego → U.S.A. 43°27N 76°30W **175** C8
Oswestry U.K. 52°52N 3°3W **66** E4
Oświęcim Poland 50°2N 19°11E **83** H6
Otago □ N.Z. 45°15S 170°0E **155** F5
Otago Harbour N.Z. 45°47S 170°42E **155** F5
Otago Pen. N.Z. 45°48S 170°39E **155** F5
Otaheite B.
  Trin. & Tob. 10°15N 61°30W **187** K15
Otahuhu N.Z. 36°56S 174°51E **154** C3
Ōtake Japan 34°12N 132°13E **113** G6
Otaki N.Z. 40°45S 175°10E **154** G4
Otane N.Z. 39°54S 176°39E **154** F5
Otaru Japan 43°10N 141°0E **112** C10
Otaru-Wan = Ishikari-Wan
  Japan 43°25N 141°1E **112** C10
Otautau N.Z. 46°9S 168°1E **155** H2
Otava → Czechia 49°26N 14°12E **78** B7
Otavalo Ecuador 0°13N 78°20W **186** C2
Otavi Namibia 19°40S 17°24E **144** A2
Ōtawara Japan 36°50N 140°5E **113** F10
Otchinjau Angola 16°30S 13°56E **144** A1
Otego U.S.A. 42°23N 75°10W **175** D9
Otelec Romania 45°36N 20°50E **80** E5
Oteluc Roşu Romania 45°30N 22°22E **80** E7
Otepää Estonia 58°4N 26°30E **62** B4
Othello U.S.A. 46°50N 119°10W **168** C4
Othoni Greece 39°52N 19°22E **98** B1
Othris, Oros Greece 39°2N 22°37E **98** B4
Oti → Africa 7°48N 0°18E **139** D5
Oti → Togo 8°40N 0°35E **139** C5
Otira N.Z. 42°49S 171°35E **155** C6
Otira Gorge N.Z. 42°53S 171°33E **155** C6
Otish, Mts. Canada 52°22N 70°30W **165** B5
Otishi △ Peru 11°40S 73°5W **188** D4
Otjinene Namibia 21°8S 18°46E **144** B2
Otjiwarongo Namibia 20°30S 16°33E **144** B2
Otjondjupa □ Namibia 21°0S 17°0E **144** B2
Otmuchów Poland 50°28N 17°10E **83** H4
Otočac Croatia 44°53N 15°12E **93** D12
Otoineppu Japan 44°44N 142°16E **112** B11
Otok Croatia 45°10N 16°44E **93** E13
Otopeni, Bucureşti ✈ (OTP)
  Romania 44°30N 26°11E **81** F11
Otorohanga N.Z. 38°12S 175°14E **154** E4
Otoskwin → Canada 52°13N 88°6W **164** B2
Otra → Norway 58°9N 8°1E **61** G13
Otradniy Russia 53°22N 51°21E **86** D10
Otranto Italy 40°9N 18°28E **95** B11
Otranto, C. d' Italy 40°7N 18°30E **95** B11
Otranto, Str. of Italy 40°15N 18°40E **95** B11
Otrokovice Czechia 49°12N 17°32E **79** B10
Otse S. Africa 25°2S 25°45E **144** C4
Otsego L. U.S.A. 42°45N 74°53W **175** D10
Ōtsu Japan 35°0N 135°50E **113** G7
Ōtsuki Japan 35°36N 138°57E **113** G9
Ottapalam India 10°46N 76°23E **127** J3
Ottawa = Outaouais →
  Canada 45°27N 74°8W **164** C5
Ottawa Canada 45°26N 75°42W **175** A9
Ottawa Ill., U.S.A. 41°21N 88°51W **172** E9
Ottawa Kans., U.S.A. 38°37N 95°16W **172** F6
Ottawa Is. Canada 59°35N 80°10W **161** F15
Ottélé Cameroon 3°38N 11°19E **139** E7
Ottensheim Austria 48°21N 14°12E **78** C7
Otter Cr. U.S.A. 44°13N 73°17W **175** B11
Otter Creek U.S.A. 29°19N 82°46W **179** F7
Otter Lake Canada 45°17N 79°56W **174** A5
Otterbäcken Sweden 58°57N 14°3E **63** F8
Otterndorf Germany 53°48N 8°53E **76** B4
Otterup Denmark 55°30N 10°22E **63** J4
Otterville Canada 42°55N 80°36W **174** D4
Ottery St. Mary U.K. 50°44N 3°17W **67** G4
Otto Beit Bridge
  Zimbabwe 15°59S 28°56E **143** F2
Ottosdal S. Africa 26°46S 25°59E **144** C4
Ottumwa U.S.A. 41°1N 92°25W **172** E7
Otukpa Nigeria 7°9N 7°41E **139** D6
Oturkpo Nigeria 7°16N 8°8E **139** D6
Otway, B. Chile 53°30S 74°0W **192** D2
Otway, C. Australia 38°52S 143°30E **152** E5
Otway, Seno de Chile 53°0S 71°30W **192** D2
Otway △ Australia 38°47S 143°34E **152** E5
Otwock Poland 52°5N 21°20E **83** F8
Otyniya Ukraine 48°44N 24°51E **81** B9
Ötztaler Ache →
  Austria 47°14N 10°50E **78** E3
Ötztaler Alpen Austria 46°56N 11°0E **78** E3
Ou → Laos 20°4N 102°13E **120** B4
Ou-Sammyaku Japan 39°20N 140°35E **112** E10
Ouachita → U.S.A. 31°38N 91°49W **176** F9
Ouachita, L. U.S.A. 34°34N 93°12W **176** D8
Ouachita Mts. U.S.A. 34°30N 94°30W **176** D7
Ouagadougou
  Burkina Faso 12°25N 1°30W **139** C4
Ouahigouya
  Burkina Faso 13°31N 2°25W **138** C4
Oualâta Mauritania 17°20N 6°55W **138** B3
Ouallam Niger 14°23N 2°10E **139** C5
Ouallene Algeria 24°41N 1°11E **136** D6
Ouarâne Mauritania 21°0N 10°30W **134** D3
Ouargaye Burkina Faso 11°40N 0°5E **139** C5
Ouargla Algeria 31°59N 5°16E **136** B7
Ouargla □ Algeria 30°0N 5°0E **136** C7
Ouarkoye Burkina Faso 12°5N 3°40W **138** C4
Ouarkziz, Djebel Algeria 28°50N 7°20W **136** C4
Ouarra → C.A.R. 5°0N 24°26E **140** C4
Ouarzazate Morocco 30°55N 6°50W **136** B4
Ouassouas Mali 16°10N 1°23E **139** B5
Ouatagouna Mali 15°11N 0°43E **139** B5
Oubangi →
  Dem. Rep. of the Congo 0°30S 17°50E **140** E3
Oubarakai, O. → Algeria 27°20N 9°0E **136** C7
Ouche → France 47°6N 5°16E **71** E12
Ouddorp Neths. 51°50N 3°57E **65** C3
Oude Rijn → Neths. 52°12N 4°24E **65** B4
Oudeíka Mali 19°10N 1°40W **139** B4
Oudenaarde Belgium 50°50N 3°37E **65** D3
Oudon → France 47°41N 0°53W **70** E6
Oudtshoorn S. Africa 33°35S 22°14E **144** E3
Ouellé Côte d'Ivoire 7°26N 4°1W **138** D4
Ouéma → Benin 6°0N 3°30W **139** D5
Ouenza Algeria 35°57N 8°4E **136** A5
Ouessa Burkina Faso 11°4N 2°47W **138** C4
Ouessant, Î. d' France 48°28N 5°6W **70** D1
Ouesso Congo 1°37N 16°5E **140** D3

Ouest □ Cameroon 5°30N 10°30E **139** D7
Ouest, Pte. de l' Canada 49°52N 64°40W **165** C7
Ouezzane Morocco 34°51N 5°35W **136** B2
Ougarou Burkina Faso 12°10N 0°58E **139** C5
Oughter, L. Ireland 54°1N 7°28W **64** B4
Oughterard Ireland 53°26N 9°18W **64** C2
Ouidah Benin 6°25N 2°0E **139** D5
Ouidi Niger 14°10N 5°0E **139** C7
Oujda Morocco 34°41N 1°55W **136** B3
Oujeft Mauritania 20°2N 13°0W **138** A2
Oulainen Finland 64°17N 24°47E **60** D21
Oulanka △ Finland 66°26N 29°25E **60** C23
Ould Yenjé Mauritania 15°38N 12°16E **138** B2
Ouled Djellal Algeria 34°28N 5°2E **136** B5
Ouled Naïl, Mts. des
  Algeria 34°30N 3°30E **136** B4
Oullins France 45°43N 4°49E **73** C8
Oulmès Morocco 33°17N 6°0W **136** B2
Oulu Finland 65°1N 25°29E **60** D21
Oulujärvi Finland 64°25N 27°15E **60** D22
Oulujoki → Finland 65°1N 25°30E **60** D21
Oulx Italy 45°1N 6°50E **94** C1
Oum Chalouba Chad 15°48N 20°46E **135** E10
Oum-el-Bouaghi Algeria 35°55N 7°9E **136** A5
Oum-el-Bouaghi □
  Algeria 35°50N 7°5E **136** A5
Oum el Ksi Algeria 29°4N 6°59W **136** C2
Oum-er-Rbia, O. →
  Morocco 33°19N 8°21W **136** B2
Oum Hadjer Chad 13°18N 19°41E **135** F9
Oumé Côte d'Ivoire 6°21N 5°27W **138** D3
Ounane, Dj. Algeria 25°4N 7°19E **136** D5
Ounasjoki → Finland 66°31N 25°40E **60** C21
Ounguati Namibia 22°0S 15°46E **144** B2
Ounianga Kébir Chad 19°4N 20°29E **135** E10
Our → Lux. 49°55N 6°5E **69** E6
Oura, Akra Greece 38°10N 26°2E **99** C8
Ouranoupoli Greece 40°20N 23°59E **96** F7
Ourârène Niger 19°30N 7°10E **139** B6
Ouray U.S.A. 38°1N 107°40W **169** G10
Ourém Portugal 39°40N 8°35W **88** F2
Ourense Spain 42°19N 7°55W **88** C3
Ourense □ Spain 42°15N 7°51W **88** C3
Ouricuri Brazil 7°53S 40°5W **189** B2
Ourinhos Brazil 23°0S 49°54W **191** A6
Ourique Portugal 37°38N 8°16W **89** H2
Ouro Fino Brazil 22°16S 46°25W **191** A6
Ouro-Ndia Mali 15°8N 4°35W **138** B4
Ouro Prêto Brazil 20°20S 43°30W **191** A7
Ouro Sogui Senegal 15°36N 13°19W **138** B2
Oursi Burkina Faso 14°41N 0°27W **139** C4
Ourthe → Belgium 50°29N 5°35E **65** D5
Ouse → E. Sussex, U.K. 50°47N 0°4E **67** G8
Ouse → N. Yorks., U.K. 53°44N 0°55W **66** D7
Oust France 42°52N 1°13E **72** F5
Oust → France 47°35N 2°6W **70** E4
Outamba-Kilimi △
  S. Leone 9°50N 12°40W **138** D2
Outaouais → Canada 45°27N 74°8W **164** C5
Outapi Namibia 17°30S 15°0E **144** A2
Outardes → Canada 49°24N 69°30W **165** C6
Outat Oulad el Haj
  Morocco 33°22N 3°42W **136** B3
Outeiro de Rei Spain 43°6N 7°36W **88** B3
Outer Hebrides U.K. 57°30N 7°15W **65** D1
Outes = A Serra de Outes
  Spain 42°52N 8°55W **88** C2
Outjo Namibia 20°5S 16°7E **144** B2
Outlook Canada 51°30N 107°0W **163** C7
Outokumpu Finland 62°43N 29°1E **60** E23
Outreau France 50°40N 1°36E **71** B8
Ouvèze → France 43°59N 4°51E **73** E8
Ouyen Australia 35°1S 142°22E **152** C5
Ouzouer-le-Marché
  France 47°54N 1°32E **71** E8
Ovada Italy 44°38N 8°38E **93** D8
Ovalau Fiji 17°40S 178°48E **154** a
Ovalle Chile 30°33S 71°18W **190** C1
Ovamboland Namibia 18°30S 16°0E **144** A2
Ovanäker Sweden 61°22N 15°53E **62** C9
Ovar Portugal 40°51N 8°40W **88** E2
Overath Germany 50°56N 7°17E **76** E3
Overflakkee Neths. 51°44N 4°10E **65** C4
Overijssel □ Neths. 52°25N 6°35E **65** B6
Overland Park U.S.A. 38°58N 94°40W **172** F7
Overland Roadhouse
  Australia 26°19S 114°28E **149** E1
Overton U.S.A. 36°33N 114°27W **171** J12
Övertorneå Sweden 66°23N 23°38E **60** C20
Överum Sweden 58°0N 16°20E **63** F10
Ovid U.S.A. 42°41N 76°49W **175** D8
Ovidiopol Ukraine 46°15N 30°30E **85** J6
Oviedu Romania 44°16N 28°34E **81** F13
Oviedo Spain 43°25N 5°50W **88** B5
Oviedo □ Spain 28°40N 81°13W **179** G8
Oviksfjällen Sweden 63°0N 13°49E **62** A7
Ovoot Mongolia 45°21N 113°45E **114** B7
Övör Hangay □
  Mongolia 45°0N 102°30E **114** B2
Ovoro Nigeria 5°26N 7°16E **139** D6
Øvre Anárjohka △
  Norway 68°30N 24°40E **60** B21
Øvre Ärdal Norway 61°19N 7°48E **60** F12
Øvre Dividal △ Norway 68°43N 19°50E **60** B18
Øvre Fryken Sweden 60°0N 13°7E **62** E7
Øvre Pasvik △ Norway 69°6N 28°54E **60** B23
Ovruch Ukraine 51°25N 28°45E **75** C15
Owaka N.Z. 46°27S 169°40E **155** G4
Owambo = Ovamboland
  Namibia 18°30S 16°0E **144** A2
Owasco L. U.S.A. 42°50N 76°31W **175** D8
Owase Japan 34°7N 136°12E **113** G8
Owatonna U.S.A. 44°5N 93°14W **172** C7
Owbeh Afghan. 34°28N 63°10E **122** B3
Owego U.S.A. 42°6N 76°16W **175** D8
Owen Australia 34°15S 138°32E **152** B2
Owen, Mt. N.Z. 41°35S 172°33E **155** D5
Owen Falls Dam = Nalubaale
  Dam Uganda 0°23N 33°2E **142** B3
Owen Sound Canada 44°35N 80°55W **174** B4
Owen Stanley Ra.
  Papua N. G. 8°30S 147°0E **148** f7
Oweniny → Ireland 54°8N 9°34W **64** B2
Owens → U.S.A. 36°32N 117°59W **170** J9
Owens L. U.S.A. 36°26N 117°57W **170** J9
Owensboro U.S.A. 37°46N 87°7W **172** G9
Owerri Nigeria 5°29N 7°0E **139** D6
Owhango N.Z. 39°0S 175°23E **154** F4

Owl → Canada 57°51N 92°44W **163** B10
Owo Nigeria 7°10N 5°39E **139** D6
Owosso U.S.A. 43°0N 84°10W **173** D11
Owyhee U.S.A. 41°57N 116°6W **168** F5
Owyhee → U.S.A. 43°49N 117°2W **168** E5
Owyhee, L. U.S.A. 43°38N 117°14W **168** E5
Ox Mts. = Slieve Gamph
  Ireland 54°6N 9°0W **64** B3
Oxapampa Peru 10°33S 75°26W **188** C2
Öxarfjörður Iceland 66°15N 16°45W **60** C5
Oxbow Canada 49°14N 102°10W **163** D8
Oxelösund Sweden 58°43N 17°5E **63** F11
Oxford N.Z. 43°18S 172°11E **155** D7
Oxford U.K. 51°46N 1°15W **67** F6
Oxford Ala., U.S.A. 33°36N 85°51W **178** D4
Oxford Mass., U.S.A. 42°7N 71°52W **175** D13
Oxford Miss., U.S.A. 34°22N 89°31W **177** D10
Oxford N.C., U.S.A. 36°19N 78°35W **177** C15
Oxford N.Y., U.S.A. 42°27N 75°36W **175** D9
Oxford Ohio, U.S.A. 39°31N 84°45W **173** F11
Oxford L. Canada 54°51N 95°37W **163** C9
Oxfordshire □ U.K. 51°48N 1°16W **67** F6
Oxia Greece 38°18N 21°6E **98** C3
Oxie Sweden 55°33N 13°6E **63** J7
Oxilithos Greece 38°35N 24°7E **98** C6
Oxnard U.S.A. 34°12N 119°11W **171** L7
Oxsjövålen Sweden 62°34N 13°57E **62** B7
Oxus = Amudarya →
  Uzbekistan 43°58N 59°34E **108** D5
Oya Malaysia 2°55N 111°55E **118** D4
Oyama Japan 36°18N 139°48E **113** F9
Oyambre △ Spain 43°22N 4°21W **88** B6
Oyem Gabon 1°34N 11°31E **140** D2
Oyen Canada 51°22N 110°28W **163** C6
Oykel → U.K. 57°56N 4°26W **65** D4
Oymyakon Russia 63°25N 142°44E **107** C15
Oyo Nigeria 7°46N 3°56E **139** D5
Oyo Sudan 21°58N 36°10E **137** C4
Oyo □ Nigeria 8°15N 3°30E **139** D5
Oyón Peru 10°37S 76°47W **188** C2
Oyonnax France 46°16N 5°40E **73** F12
Öyübari Japan 43°1N 142°5E **112** C11
Oyyl → Kazakhstan 49°4N 54°40E **108** C4
Özalp Turkey 38°39N 43°59E **105** C10
Ozamiz Phil. 8°15N 123°50E **119** C6
Ozar = Ojhar India 20°6N 73°56E **126** D1
Ozark Ala., U.S.A. 31°28N 85°39W **178** D4
Ozark Ark., U.S.A. 35°29N 93°50W **176** D8
Ozark Mo., U.S.A. 37°1N 93°12W **172** G7
Ozark Plateau U.S.A. 37°20N 91°40W **172** G8
Ozarks, L. of the U.S.A. 38°12N 92°38W **172** F7
Ożarów Poland 50°52N 21°40E **83** H8
Ózd Hungary 48°14N 20°15E **83** J7
Ozernoye Russia 51°46N 51°28E **86** E10
Ozersk Russia 54°25N 22°0E **82** D8
Ozette L. U.S.A. 48°6N 124°38W **168** B1
Ozieri Italy 40°35N 9°0E **94** B2
Ozimek Poland 50°41N 18°11E **83** H5
Ozinki Russia 51°12N 49°44E **86** E9
Ozona U.S.A. 30°43N 101°12W **176** F4
Ozorków Poland 51°57N 19°16E **83** G6
Ozren Bos.-H. 43°55N 18°29E **80** G3
Ozuluama Mexico 21°40N 97°51W **181** C5
Ozun Romania 45°47N 25°50E **81** E10
Ozurgeti Georgia 41°55N 42°0E **87** K5

P

Pa Burkina Faso 11°33N 3°19W **138** C4
Pa-an Myanmar 16°51N 97°40E **123** L20
Pa Mong Dam Thailand 18°0N 102°22E **120** D4
Pa Sak → Thailand 15°30N 101°0E **120** E3
Paamiut Greenland 62°0N 49°43W **57** E6
Paanayarvi △ Russia 66°16N 30°10E **60** C24
Paar → Germany 48°46N 11°36E **77** G7
Paarl S. Africa 33°45S 18°56E **144** D2
Pab Hills Pakistan 26°30N 66°45E **124** F7
Pabaidh = Pabbay U.K. 57°46N 7°14W **65** D1
Pabbay U.K. 57°46N 7°14W **65** D1
Pabianice Poland 51°40N 19°20E **83** G6
Pabna Bangla. 24°1N 89°18E **123** G16
Pabo Uganda 3°1N 32°10E **142** B3
Pacaipampa Peru 5°35S 79°39W **188** B2
Pacaja → Brazil 1°56S 50°50W **187** D8
Pacajus Brazil 4°10S 38°31W **189** A4
Pacaraima, Sa. S. Amer. 4°0N 62°30W **186** C6
Pacarán Peru 12°55S 76°33W **188** C2
Pacaraos Peru 11°12S 76°42W **188** C2
Pacasmayo Peru 7°20S 79°35W **188** B2
Pace U.S.A. 30°36N 87°11W **179** G2
Paceco Italy 37°59N 12°33E **94** E5
Pachacamac Peru 12°14S 77°53W **188** C2
Pachia Greece 36°17N 25°50W **99** F7
Pachino Italy 36°43N 15°5E **95** F8
Pachitea → Peru 8°46S 74°33W **188** B3
Pachiza Peru 7°16S 76°46W **188** B2
Pachmarhi India 22°28N 78°26E **125** H8
Pachnes Greece 35°16N 24°4E **101** D6
Pachora India 20°38N 75°29E **126** D2
Pachpadra India 25°58N 72°10E **124** G8
Pachuca Mexico 20°7N 98°44W **181** C5
Pacific Antarctic Ridge
  Pac. Oc. 43°0S 115°0W **55** B13
Pacific Grove U.S.A. 36°38N 121°56W **170** J5
Pacific Ocean 10°0N 140°0W **157** G14
Pacific Rim △ Canada 48°40N 124°45W **170** a
Pacifica U.S.A. 37°37N 122°27W **170** H4
Pacitan Indonesia 8°12S 111°7E **119** H14
Packsaddle Australia 30°36S 141°58E **152** A4
Packwood U.S.A. 46°36N 121°40W **170** D5
Pacov Czechia 49°27N 15°0E **78** B8
Pacuí → Brazil 16°46S 45°1W **189** F3
Pacy-sur-Eure France 49°1N 1°23E **70** C8
Padaido, Kepulauan
  Indonesia 1°15S 136°30E **119** E9
Padampur India 20°59N 83°4E **126** D6
Padang Riau, Indonesia 1°30N 102°30E **120** M4
Padang Sumatera Barat,
  Indonesia 1°0S 100°20E **118** E2
Padang Endau
  Malaysia 2°40N 103°38E **121** L4
Padangpanjang
  Indonesia 0°40S 100°20E **118** E2
Padangsidempuan
  Indonesia 1°30N 99°15E **118** D1
Padborg Denmark 54°49N 9°21E **63** K3

Paderborn Germany 51°42N 8°45E **76** D4
Paderoo India 18°5N 82°40E **126** E6
Padeş, Vf. Romania 45°40N 22°22E **80** E7
Padina Romania 44°50N 27°8E **81** F12
Pádova Italy 45°25N 11°53E **93** C8
Padra India 22°15N 73°7E **124** H5
Padrauna India 26°54N 83°59E **125** F10
Padre I. U.S.A. 27°10N 97°25W **176** H6
Padre Island △ U.S.A. 27°0N 97°25W **176** H6
Padrón Spain 42°41N 8°39W **88** C2
Padstow U.K. 50°33N 4°58W **67** G3
Padthaway Australia 36°36S 140°31E **152** D4
Padua = Pádova Italy 45°25N 11°53E **93** C8
Paducah Ky., U.S.A. 37°5N 88°37W **172** G9
Paducah Tex., U.S.A. 34°1N 100°18W **176** D4
Padukka Sri Lanka 6°50N 80°5E **127** L5
Padul Spain 37°1N 3°38W **89** H7
Padwa India 18°27N 82°47E **126** E6
Paea Tahiti 17°41S 149°35W **155** b
Paekakariki N.Z. 40°59S 174°58E **154** G3
Paektu-san N. Korea 41°59N 128°4E **115** D15
Paengaroa N.Z. 37°23S 176°29E **154** D5
Paeroa N.Z. 37°23S 175°41E **154** D4
Paesana Italy 44°41N 7°16E **92** D4
Pafúri Mozam. 22°28S 31°17E **145** B5
Pag Croatia 44°25N 15°3E **93** D12
Paga Ghana 11°1N 1°9W **139** C4
Pagadian Phil. 7°55N 123°30E **119** C6
Pagai Selatan, Pulau
  Indonesia 3°0S 100°15E **118** E2
Pagai Utara, Pulau
  Indonesia 2°35S 100°0E **118** E2
Pagalu = Annobón
  Atl. Oc. 1°25S 5°36E **133** G4
Pagara India 24°22N 80°1E **125** G9
Pagastikos Kolpos Greece 39°15N 23°0E **98** B5
Pagatan Indonesia 3°33S 115°59E **118** E5
Page U.S.A. 36°57N 111°27W **169** H8
Pagégiai Lithuania 55°9N 21°54E **82** C9
Paget, Mt. S. Georgia 54°26S 36°31W **194** H6
Paget I. India 14°26N 93°22E **127** H11
Pagosa Springs
  U.S.A. 37°16N 107°1W **169** H10
Pagri China 27°45N 89°10E **110** F6
Pagwa River Canada 50°2N 85°14W **164** B2
Pāhala U.S.A. 19°12N 155°29W **167** M8
Pahang □ Malaysia 3°30N 102°45E **121** L4
Pahang → Malaysia 3°30N 103°9E **121** L4
Pahia Pt. N.Z. 46°20S 167°41E **155** G2
Pahiatua N.Z. 40°27S 175°50E **154** G4
Pahokee U.S.A. 26°50N 80°40W **179** H8
Pahrump U.S.A. 36°12N 115°59W **171** J11
Pahute Mesa U.S.A. 37°20N 116°45W **170** H10
Pai Thailand 19°19N 98°27E **120** C2
Paicines U.S.A. 36°44N 121°17W **170** J5
Paide Estonia 58°53N 25°33E **84** C3
Paignton U.K. 50°26N 3°35W **67** G4
Paihia N.Z. 35°17S 174°6E **154** B3
Paiho Taiwan 23°21N 120°25E **117** F13
Paiján Peru 7°42S 79°20W **188** B2
Päijänne Finland 61°30N 25°30E **84** B3
Pailani India 25°45N 80°26E **125** G9
Pailin Cambodia 12°46N 102°36E **120** F4
Paimpol France 48°48N 3°4W **70** D3
Painan Indonesia 1°21S 100°34E **118** E2
Paine Grande, Cerro
  Chile 51°0S 73°0W **192** D2
Painesville U.S.A. 41°43N 81°15W **174** E3
Paint Hills = Wemindji
  Canada 53°0N 78°49W **164** B4
Paint L. Canada 55°28N 97°57W **163** B9
Painted Desert U.S.A. 36°0N 111°0W **169** H8
Paintsville U.S.A. 37°49N 82°48W **173** G12
País Vasco □ Spain 42°50N 2°45W **90** C2
Paisley Canada 44°18N 81°16W **174** B3
Paisley U.K. 55°50N 4°25W **65** F4
Paita Peru 5°11S 81°9W **188** B1
Paithan India 19°29N 75°23E **126** E2
Paiva → Portugal 41°4N 8°16W **88** D2
Pajares Spain 43°1N 5°46W **88** B5
Pajares, Puerto de Spain 42°58N 5°46W **88** C5
Pajęczno Poland 51°10N 19°0E **83** G5
Pak Lay Laos 18°15N 101°27E **120** C3
Pak Ou Laos 20°3N 102°13E **120** B3
Pak Phanang Thailand 8°21N 100°12E **121** H3
Pak Sane Laos 18°22N 103°39E **120** C4
Pak Song Laos 15°11N 106°14E **120** E6
Pak Suang Laos 19°58N 102°15E **120** C4
Pak Tam Chung China 22°24N 114°19E **111** a
Pak Thong Chai
  Thailand 14°43N 102°1E **120** E4
Pakala India 13°29N 79°8E **127** H4
Pakaur India 24°38N 87°51E **125** G12
Pakch'ŏn N. Korea 39°44N 125°35E **115** E13
Pakenham Australia 38°6S 145°30E **153** E6
Pakhuis S. Africa 32°9S 19°5E **144** E2
Pakistan ■ Asia 30°0N 70°0E **124** E4
Pakkading Laos 18°19N 103°59E **120** C4
Paklenica △ Croatia 44°20N 15°39E **93** D12
Pakokku Myanmar 21°20N 95°0E **123** J19
Pakokku □ Myanmar 52°48N 98°7E **123** J19
Pakowki L. Canada 49°20N 111°0W **163** D6
Pakpattan Pakistan 30°25N 73°27E **124** D5
Pakrac Croatia 45°27N 17°12E **80** E2
Pakruojis Lithuania 55°58N 23°52E **82** C10
Paks Hungary 46°38N 18°55E **80** D3
Paktia □ Afghan. 33°30N 69°15E **122** C3
Paktīkā □ Afghan. 32°30N 69°0E **122** C3
Pakse Laos 15°5N 105°52E **120** E5
Pakwach Uganda 2°28N 31°27E **142** B3
Pakwe → Botswana 23°22S 115°58E **148** D2
Pala Chad 9°25N 15°5E **135** G8
Pala U.S.A. 33°22N 117°5W **171** M9
Palabek Uganda 3°22N 32°33E **142** B3
Palacios U.S.A. 28°42N 96°13W **176** G6
Palafrugell Spain 41°55N 3°10E **90** D8
Palagiano Italy 40°35N 17°2E **95** B10
Palagonia Italy 37°19N 14°45E **95** E7
Palagruža Croatia 42°24N 16°15E **93** G13
Palaiseau France 48°42N 2°14E **71** D9
Palakkad India 10°46N 76°42E **127** J3
Palakkollu India 16°31N 81°46E **127** F5
Palalankwe India 10°6N 92°29E **127** J11

Paderborn Germany 51°42N 8°45E **76** D4
Palam India 19°0N 77°0E **126** E3
Palamás Greece 39°26N 22°4E **98** B4
Palamós Spain 41°50N 3°10E **90** D8
Palampur India 32°10N 76°30E **124** C7
Palamut Turkey 38°59N 27°41E **99** C9
Palana Australia 39°45S 147°55E **151** F4
Palana Russia 59°10N 159°59E **107** D16
Palanan Phil. 17°8N 122°29E **119** A4
Palanan Pt. Phil. 17°17N 122°30E **119** A4
Palandri Pakistan 33°42N 73°40E **125** C5
Palanga Lithuania 55°58N 21°3E **82** C8
Palangkaraya Indonesia 2°16S 113°56E **118** E4
Palani India 10°30N 77°30E **127** J3
Palani Hills India 10°14N 77°33E **127** J3
Palanpur India 24°10N 72°25E **124** G8
Palapye Botswana 22°30S 27°7E **144** C4
Palar → India 12°27N 80°13E **127** H5
Palas Pakistan 35°4N 73°14E **125** B5
Palas de Rey Spain 42°52N 7°52W **88** C3
Palasbari India 21°47N 85°34E **125** J11
Palasponga India 21°47N 85°34E **125** J11
Palatka Russia 60°6N 150°54E **107** C16
Palatka U.S.A. 29°39N 81°38W **178** F7
Palau ■ Palau 7°30N 134°30E **156** G5
Palauk Myanmar 13°10N 98°40E **120** F2
Palaw Myanmar 12°58N 98°39E **120** F2
Palawan Phil. 9°30N 118°30E **118** C5
Palayankottai India 8°45N 77°45E **127** K3
Palazzo, Pte. France 42°28N 8°30E **73** F12
Palazzo San Gervásio
  Italy 40°56N 15°59E **95** B8
Palazzolo Acréide Italy 37°4N 14°54E **95** E7
Palca Chile 19°7S 69°9W **188** D3
Paldiski Estonia 59°23N 24°9E **84** C3
Pale Bos.-H. 43°50N 18°38E **80** G3
Palekastro Greece 35°12N 26°15E **101** D8
Paleleh Indonesia 1°10N 121°50E **119** D6
Palembang Indonesia 3°0S 104°50E **118** E2
Palena → Italy 43°50S 73°50W **192** E2
Palena, L. Chile 43°55S 71°40W **192** E2
Palencia Spain 42°0N 4°34W **88** C6
Palencia □ Spain 42°31N 4°33W **88** C6
Palenque Mexico 17°29N 92°1W **181** D6
Paleochora Greece 35°16N 23°39W **101** D5
Paleokastrítsa Greece 39°40N 19°41E **101** A3
Paleometokho Cyprus 35°7N 33°11E **101** D12
Paleopoli Greece 37°49N 24°50E **98** D6
Palermo Italy 38°7N 13°22E **94** D6
Palermo U.S.A. 39°26N 121°33W **170** F5
Palermo ✈ (PMO) Italy 38°11N 13°5E **94** D6
Paleros Greece 38°50N 20°42E **98** C2
Palestina Chile 23°50S 69°47W **190** A2
Palestine Asia 32°0N 35°0E **130** D4
Palestine U.S.A. 31°46N 95°38W **176** F7
Palestrina Italy 41°50N 12°53E **93** G9
Paletwa Myanmar 21°10N 92°50E **123** J18
Palghat = Palakkad
  India 10°46N 76°42E **127** J3
Palgrave, Mt.
  Australia 23°22S 115°58E **148** D2
Palhoça Brazil 27°38S 48°40W **191** B6
Pali India 25°50N 73°20E **124** G8
Pali-Aike △ Chile 52°6S 69°44W **192** D3
Palikir Micronesia 6°55N 158°9E **156** G7
Palinuro Italy 40°2N 15°17E **95** B8
Palinuro, C. Italy 40°1N 15°16E **95** B8
Paliouri, Akra Greece 39°57N 23°45E **96** F7
Palisades Res. U.S.A. 43°20N 111°12W **168** E8
Paliseul Belgium 49°54N 5°8E **65** F5
Palitana India 21°32N 71°49E **124** J4
Palizada Mexico 18°15N 92°5W **181** D6
Palk Bay Asia 9°30N 79°15E **127** K4
Palk Strait Asia 10°0N 79°45E **127** K4
Palkānhah Iraq 35°49N 44°26E **128** C5
Palkonda India 18°36N 83°48E **126** E6
Palkonda Ra. India 13°50N 79°20E **127** H4
Palkot India 22°53N 84°39E **125** H11
Pallanza = Verbánia
  Italy 45°56N 8°33E **92** C5
Pallarenda Australia 19°12S 146°46E **150** B4
Pallas-Yllästunturi △
  Finland 68°8N 24°15E **60** B21
Pallasovka Russia 50°4N 47°0E **86** E8
Palleru → India 16°45N 80°2E **126** F5
Pallès, Bishti i Albania 41°24N 19°24E **96** E1
Pallinup → Australia 34°27S 118°50E **149** F2
Pallisa Uganda 1°12N 33°43E **142** B3
Palliser, C. N.Z. 41°37S 175°14E **154** H4
Palliser B. N.Z. 41°26S 175°5E **154** H4
Pallu India 28°59N 74°14E **124** E6
Palm Bay U.S.A. 28°2N 80°35W **179** G8
Palm Beach U.S.A. 26°43N 80°2W **179** H9
Palm Coast U.S.A. 29°35N 81°12W **179** F8
Palm Desert U.S.A. 33°43N 116°22W **171** M10
Palm-Grove △
  Australia 24°57S 149°21E **150** C4
Palm Harbor U.S.A. 28°5N 82°46W **179** G7
Palm Is. Australia 18°40S 146°35E **150** B4
Palm Springs U.S.A. 33°50N 116°33W **171** M10
Palm Valley U.S.A. 30°11N 81°23W **178** E8
Palma Mozam. 10°46S 40°29E **143** E5
Palma → Brazil 12°33S 47°52W **189** D1
Palma, B. de Spain 39°30N 2°39E **89** B9
Palma de Mallorca
  Spain 39°35N 2°39E **89** B9
Palma de Mallorca ✈ (PMI)
  Spain 39°34N 2°43E **91** F7
Palma del Río Spain 37°43N 5°17W **89** H5
Palma di Montechiaro
  Italy 37°11N 13°46E **94** E6
Palma Nova = Palmanova
  Spain 39°32N 2°34E **100** B9
Palma Soriano Cuba 20°15N 76°0W **182** B4
Palmanova Spain 39°32N 2°34E **100** B9
Palmanova Italy 45°54N 13°19E **93** C10
Palmares Brazil 8°41S 35°28W **189** B3
Palmarola Italy 40°56N 12°51E **94** B5
Palmas Paraná, Brazil 26°29S 52°0W **191** B5
Palmas Tocantins, Brazil 10°13S 48°16W **189** D1
Palmas, C. Liberia 4°27N 7°46W **138** E3
Pálmas, G. di Italy 39°0N 8°30E **94** D1
Palmas de Monte Alto
  Brazil 14°16S 43°10W **189** D2
Palmdale Calif., U.S.A. 34°35N 118°7W **171** L8
Palmdale Fla., U.S.A. 26°57N 81°19W **179** H7
Palmeira das Missões
  Brazil 27°55S 53°17W **191** B5
Palmeira dos Índios
  Brazil 9°25S 36°37W **189** D3
Palmeiras Brazil 12°31S 41°34W **189** D2
Palmeiras → Brazil 12°22S 47°8W **189** D1

Palmela *Portugal* 38°32N 8°57W **89** G2
Palmer *Antarctica* 64°35S 65°0W **55** C17
Palmer *U.S.A.* 61°36N 149°7W **160** E2
Palmer → *Australia* 16°0S 142°26E **150** B3
Palmer Arch. *Antarctica* 64°15S 65°0W **55** C17
Palmer Lake *U.S.A.* 39°7N 104°55W **168** G11
Palmer Land *Antarctica* 73°0S 63°0W **55** D18
Palmerston *Australia* 12°31S 130°59E **148** B5
Palmerston *Canada* 43°50N 80°51W **174** C4
Palmerston *N.Z.* 45°29S 170°43E **155** F5
Palmerston North *N.Z.* 40°21S 175°39E **154** G4
Palmerton *U.S.A.* 40°48N 75°37W **175** F9
Palmetto *Fla., U.S.A.* 27°31N 82°34W **179** H7
Palmetto *Ga., U.S.A.* 33°31N 84°40W **178** B5
Palmi *Italy* 38°21N 15°51E **95** D8
Palmira *Argentina* 32°59S 68°34W **190** C2
Palmira *Colombia* 3°32N 76°16W **186** C3
Palmyra = Tudmur *Syria* 34°36N 38°15E **105** E8
Palmyra *Mo., U.S.A.* 39°48N 91°32W **172** F8
Palmyra *N.J., U.S.A.* 40°0N 75°1W **175** F9
Palmyra *N.Y., U.S.A.* 43°5N 77°18W **174** C7
Palmyra *Pa., U.S.A.* 40°18N 76°36W **175** F8
Palmyra Is. *Pac. Oc.* 5°52N 162°5W **157** G11
Palmyras Pt. *India* 20°46N 87°1E **126** D8
Palo Alto *U.S.A.* 37°27N 122°10W **170** H4
Palo Seco *Trin. & Tob.* 10°4N 61°36W **187** K15
Palo Verde *U.S.A.* 33°26N 114°44W **171** M12
Palo Verde △ *Costa Rica* 10°21N 85°21W **182** D2
Palomar Mt. *U.S.A.* 33°22N 116°50W **171** M10
Palopo *Indonesia* 3°0S 120°16E **119** E6
Palos, C. de *Spain* 37°38N 0°40W **91** H4
Palos de la Frontera *Spain* 37°14N 6°53W **89** H4
Palos Verdes, Pt. *U.S.A.* 33°46N 118°25W **171** M8
Palos Verdes Estates *U.S.A.* 33°48N 118°23W **171** M8
Palpa *Peru* 14°30S 75°15W **188** C2
Pålsboda *Sweden* 59°3N 15°22E **62** E9
Palu *Indonesia* 1°0S 119°52E **119** E5
Palu *Turkey* 38°45N 40°0E **105** C9
Paluke *Liberia* 5°2N 8°5W **138** D3
Paluma Ra. *Australia* 19°9S 146°22E **150** B4
Paluzza *Italy* 46°32N 13°1E **93** B10
Palwal *India* 28°8N 77°19E **124** E7
Pama *Burkina Faso* 11°19N 0°44E **139** C5
Pama ⌂ *Burkina Faso* 11°27N 0°40E **139** C5
Pamanukan *Indonesia* 6°16S 107°49E **119** G12
Pamban I. *India* 9°15N 79°20E **127** K4
Pamekasan *Indonesia* 7°10S 113°28E **119** G15
Pamenang *Indonesia* 8°24S 116°6E **119** J19
Pamiers *France* 43°7N 1°39E **72** E5
Pamir *Tajikistan* 37°40N 73°0E **109** E8
Pamlico → *U.S.A.* 35°20N 76°28W **177** D16
Pamlico Sd. *U.S.A.* 35°20N 76°0W **177** D17
Pampa *U.S.A.* 35°32N 100°58W **176** D4
Pampa de Agma *Argentina* 43°45S 69°40W **192** B3
Pampa de las Salinas *Argentina* 32°1S 66°58W **190** C2
Pampa Hermosa *Peru* 7°7S 75°4W **188** B2
Pampanua *Indonesia* 4°16S 120°8E **119** E6
Pampas *Argentina* 35°0S 63°0W **190** D3
Pampas *Peru* 12°20S 74°50W **188** C3
Pampas → *Peru* 13°24S 73°12W **188** C3
Pamphylia *Turkey* 37°0N 31°20E **104** D4
Pamplona *Colombia* 7°23N 72°39W **186** B4
Pamplona-Iruña *Spain* 42°48N 1°38W **90** C3
Pampoenpoort *S. Africa* 31°3S 22°40E **144** D3
Pamukçu *Turkey* 39°30N 27°54E **99** B9
Pamukkale *Turkey* 37°55N 29°8E **99** D11
Pan de Azúcar *Chile* 24°5S 68°10W **190** A2
Pan de Azúcar △ *Chile* 26°0S 70°40W **190** B1
Pan Xian *China* 25°46N 104°38E **116** E5
Pana *U.S.A.* 39°23N 89°5W **172** F9
Panaca *U.S.A.* 37°47N 114°23W **169** H6
Panacea *U.S.A.* 30°2N 84°23W **178** E5
Panadura *Sri Lanka* 6°47N 79°53E **127** L4
Panagyurishte *Bulgaria* 42°30N 24°15E **97** D8
Panaitan *Indonesia* 6°36S 105°12E **119** G11
Panaji *India* 15°25N 73°50E **127** G1
Panamá *Panama* 9°0N 79°25W **182** E4
Panama *Sri Lanka* 6°45N 81°48E **127** L5
Panama ■ *Cent. Amer.* 8°48N 79°55W **182** E4
Panamá, G. de *Panama* 8°4N 79°20W **182** E4
Panama, Isthmus of *Cent. Amer.* 9°0N 79°0W **182** E4
Panama Basin *Pac. Oc.* 5°0N 83°30W **157** G19
Panama Canal *Panama* 9°10N 79°37W **182** E4
Panama City *U.S.A.* 30°10N 85°40W **178** E4
Panama City Beach *U.S.A.* 30°11N 85°48W **178** E4
Panamint Range *U.S.A.* 36°20N 117°20W **171** J9
Panamint Springs *U.S.A.* 36°20N 117°28W **171** J9
Panão *Peru* 9°55S 75°55W **188** B2
Panare *Thailand* 6°51N 101°30E **121** J3
Panarea *Italy* 38°38N 15°4E **95** D8
Panaro → *Italy* 44°55N 11°25E **93** D8
Panay *Phil.* 11°10N 122°30E **119** B6
Panay G. *Phil.* 11°0N 122°30E **119** B6
Pančevo *Serbia* 44°52N 20°41E **80** F5
Panch'iao *Taiwan* 25°1N 121°27E **117** E13
Panciu *Romania* 45°54N 27°8E **81** E12
Pancorbo, Desfiladero *Spain* 42°32N 3°5W **88** C7
Pâncota *Romania* 46°20N 21°45E **80** D6
Panda *Mozam.* 24°2S 34°45E **145** B5
Pandan *Malaysia* 1°32N 103°46E **121** d
Pandan *Phil.* 11°45N 122°10E **119** B6
Pandan, Selat *Singapore* 1°15N 103°44E **121** d
Pandan Tampoi = Tampoi *Malaysia* 1°30N 103°39E **121** d
Pandegelang *Indonesia* 6°25S 106°5E **119** G12
Pandhana *India* 21°42N 76°13E **124** J7
Pandharkawada *India* 20°1N 78°32E **126** D4
Pandharpur *India* 17°41N 75°20E **126** F2
Pandhurna *India* 21°36N 78°35E **126** D4
Pando *Uruguay* 34°44S 56°0W **191** C4
Pando □ *Bolivia* 11°20S 67°40W **188** C4
Pando, L. = Hope, L. *Australia* 28°24S 139°18E **151** D2
Pandokratoras *Greece* 39°45N 19°50E **101** A3
Pandora *Costa Rica* 9°43N 83°3W **182** E3
Pandrup *Denmark* 57°14N 9°40E **63** G3
Panevéggio-Pale di San Martino ⌂ *Italy* 46°14N 11°46E **93** B8
Panevėžys *Lithuania* 55°42N 24°25E **84** E3
Panfilovo *Russia* 50°25N 42°46E **86** E6
Pang Sida △ *Thailand* 14°5N 102°17E **120** E4
Panga *Dem. Rep. of the Congo* 1°52N 26°18E **142** B2
Pangaíon Óros *Greece* 40°50N 24°0E **97** F8
Pangandaran *Indonesia* 7°40S 108°39E **119** G13
Pangandaran △ *Indonesia* 7°43S 108°42E **119** G13
Pangani *Tanzania* 5°25S 38°58E **142** D4
Pangani → *Tanzania* 5°26S 38°58E **142** D4
Pangar Djeréme ⌂ *Cameroon* 5°50N 13°10E **139** D7
Pangfou = Bengbu *China* 32°58N 117°20E **117** A11
Pangga, Tanjung *Indonesia* 8°54S 116°2E **119** K19
Panghsang = Bangkang *Myanmar* 22°4N 99°1E **116** F2
Pangil *Dem. Rep. of the Congo* 3°10S 26°35E **142** C2
Pangjiabu *China* 40°38N 115°26E **114** D8
Pangkah, Tanjung *Indonesia* 6°51S 112°33E **119** G15
Pangkai *Myanmar* 22°49N 98°39E **116** F2
Pangkajene *Indonesia* 4°46S 119°34E **119** E5
Pangkalanbrandan *Indonesia* 4°1N 98°20E **118** D1
Pangkalanbuun *Indonesia* 2°41S 111°37E **118** E4
Pangkalpinang *Indonesia* 2°10S 106°10E **118** E3
Pangkor, Pulau *Malaysia* 4°13N 100°34E **121** K3
Pangniqtuuq = Pangnirtung *Canada* 66°8N 65°43W **161** D18
Pangnirtung *Canada* 66°8N 65°43W **161** D18
Pangody *Russia* 65°52N 74°27E **106** C8
Pangong Tso = Bangong Co *China* 33°45N 78°43E **125** C8
Panguipulli *Chile* 39°38S 72°20W **192** A2
Panguitch *U.S.A.* 37°50N 112°26W **169** H7
Pangutaran Group *Phil.* 6°18N 120°34E **119** C6
Panhala *India* 16°49N 74°7E **126** F2
Panhandle *U.S.A.* 35°21N 101°23W **176** D4
Pani Mines *India* 22°29N 73°50E **124** H5
Pania-Mutombo *Dem. Rep. of the Congo* 5°11S 23°51E **142** D1
Panikota I. *India* 20°46N 71°21E **124** J4
Panipat *India* 29°25N 77°2E **124** E7
Panjakent *Tajikistan* 39°29N 67°37E **109** E7
Panjal Range = Pir Panjal Range *India* 32°30N 76°50E **124** C7
Panjgur *Pakistan* 27°0N 64°5E **122** F4
Panjhra → *India* 21°13N 74°57E **126** D2
Panjim = Panaji *India* 15°25N 73°50E **127** G1
Panjin *China* 41°3N 122°2E **115** D12
Panjnad → *Pakistan* 28°57N 70°30E **124** E4
Panjnad Barrage *Pakistan* 29°22N 71°15E **124** E4
Panjshīr □ *Afghan.* 35°50N 69°45E **109** E7
Panjwai *Afghan.* 31°26N 65°27E **124** D1
Pankisi Gorge = Pankisis Kheoba *Georgia* 42°7N 45°15E **87** J7
Pankisis Kheoba *Georgia* 42°7N 45°15E **87** J7
Pankshin *Nigeria* 9°16N 9°25E **139** D6
Panmunjŏm *N. Korea* 37°59N 126°38E **115** F14
Panna *India* 24°40N 80°15E **125** G9
Panna △ *India* 24°40N 80°0E **125** G8
Panna Hills *India* 24°40N 81°15E **125** G9
Pannawonica *Australia* 21°39S 116°19E **148** D2
Pano Akil *Pakistan* 27°51N 69°7E **124** F3
Pano Lefkara *Cyprus* 34°53N 33°20E **101** E12
Pano Panayia *Cyprus* 34°55N 32°38E **101** E11
Panorama *Brazil* 21°21S 51°51W **191** A5
Panormos *Greece* 35°25N 24°41E **101** D6
Panruti *India* 11°46N 79°35E **127** J4
Pansemal *India* 21°39N 74°42E **124** J6
Panshan = Panjin *China* 41°3N 122°2E **115** D12
Panshi *China* 42°58N 126°5E **115** C14
Pantanal *Brazil* 17°30S 57°40W **186** H7
Pantanos de Centla ⌂ *Mexico* 18°25N 92°25W **181** D6
Pantar *Indonesia* 8°28S 124°10E **119** F6
Pante Macassar *E. Timor* 9°30S 123°58E **119** F6
Pantelleria *Italy* 36°50N 11°57E **94** F4
Pantón = O Castro de Ferreira *Spain* 42°31N 7°37W **88** C3
Pánuco *Mexico* 22°3N 98°10W **181** C5
Panvel *India* 18°59N 73°4E **126** E1
Panyam *Nigeria* 9°27N 9°8E **139** D6
Panyu *China* 23°1N 113°21E **117** F9
Panzhihua *China* 26°33N 101°44E **116** D3
Páola *Italy* 39°21N 16°2E **95** C9
Paola *Malta* 35°52N 14°30E **101** D2
Paola *U.S.A.* 38°35N 94°53W **172** F6
Paonia *U.S.A.* 38°52N 107°36W **168** G10
Paoting = Baoding *China* 38°50N 115°28E **114** E8
Paot'ou = Baotou *China* 40°32N 110°2E **114** D6
Paoua *C.A.R.* 7°9N 16°20E **140** C3
Pápa *Hungary* 47°22N 17°30E **80** C2
Papa Stour *U.K.* 60°20N 1°42W **65** A7
Papa Westray *U.K.* 59°20N 2°55W **65** B6
Papagayo → *Mexico* 16°46N 99°43W **181** D5
Papagayo, G. de *Costa Rica* 10°30N 85°50W **182** D2
Papagni → *India* 15°35N 77°45E **127** G3
Papakura *N.Z.* 37°4S 174°59E **154** D3
Papantla *Mexico* 20°27N 97°19W **181** C5
Papar *Malaysia* 5°45N 116°0E **118** C5
Papara *Tahiti* 17°43S 149°31W **155** b
Paparoa *N.Z.* 36°6S 174°16E **154** C3
Paparoa △ *N.Z.* 42°7S 171°26E **155** C6
Paparoa Ra. *N.Z.* 42°5S 171°35E **155** C6
Papatoetoe *N.Z.* 36°59S 174°51E **154** C3
Papeete *Tahiti* 17°32S 149°34W **155** b
Papenburg *Germany* 53°5N 7°23E **76** B3
Papenoo *Tahiti* 17°30S 149°25W **155** b
Papenoo → *Tahiti* 17°30S 149°25W **155** b
Paphlagonia *Turkey* 41°30N 33°0E **104** B5
Paphos *Cyprus* 34°46N 32°25E **101** E11
Papikio Oros *Greece* 41°15N 25°13E **97** E9
Paposo *Chile* 25°0S 70°30W **190** B1
Papoutsa *Cyprus* 34°54N 33°4E **101** E12
Papua □ *Indonesia* 4°0S 137°0E **119** E9
Papua, G. of *Papua N. G.* 9°0S 144°50E **147** B7
Papua New Guinea ■ *Oceania* 8°0S 145°0E **147** B7
Papudo *Chile* 32°29S 71°27W **190** C1
Papuk *Croatia* 45°30N 17°30E **80** E2
Papun *Myanmar* 18°2N 97°30E **123** K20
Papunya *Australia* 23°15S 131°54E **148** D5
Pará = Belém *Brazil* 1°20S 48°30W **187** D9
Pará □ *Brazil* 3°20S 52°0W **187** D8
Paraburdoo *Australia* 23°14S 117°32E **148** D2
Paracas, Pen. de *Peru* 13°53S 76°20W **188** C2
Paracatu *Brazil* 17°10S 46°50W **189** D1
Paracatu → *Brazil* 16°30S 45°4W **189** D1
Paracel Is. *S. China Sea* 15°50N 112°0E **118** A4
Parachilna *Australia* 31°10S 138°21E **152** A3
Parachinar *Pakistan* 33°55N 70°5E **124** C4
Paraćin *Serbia* 43°54N 21°27E **96** C5
Paracuru *Brazil* 3°24S 39°4W **189** A3
Parada, Punta *Peru* 15°22S 75°11W **188** D2
Paradas *Spain* 37°18N 5°29W **89** H5
Paradela *Spain* 42°44N 7°37W **88** C3
Paradip *India* 20°15N 86°35E **126** D8
Paradise *Calif., U.S.A.* 39°46N 121°37W **170** F5
Paradise *Nev., U.S.A.* 36°5N 115°8W **171** J11
Paradise → *Canada* 53°27N 57°19W **165** B8
Paradise Hill *Canada* 53°32N 109°28W **163** C7
Paradise River *Canada* 53°27N 57°17W **165** B8
Paradise Valley *U.S.A.* 41°30N 117°32W **168** F5
Paradisi *Greece* 36°18N 28°7E **101** C10
Paragould *U.S.A.* 36°3N 90°29W **177** C9
Paragua → *Venezuela* 6°55N 62°55W **186** B6
Paraguaçú → *Brazil* 12°45S 38°54W **189** C3
Paraguaçu Paulista *Brazil* 22°22S 50°35W **191** A5
Paraguaná, Pen. de *Venezuela* 12°0N 70°0W **186** A5
Paraguarí *Paraguay* 25°36S 57°0W **190** B4
Paraguarí □ *Paraguay* 26°0S 57°10W **190** B4
Paraguay ■ *S. Amer.* 23°0S 57°0W **190** A4
Paraguay → *Paraguay* 27°18S 58°38W **190** B4
Paraíba = João Pessoa *Brazil* 7°10S 34°52W **189** B4
Paraíba □ *Brazil* 7°0S 36°0W **189** B3
Paraíba do Sul → *Brazil* 21°37S 41°3W **191** A7
Paraíso *Mexico* 18°24N 93°14W **181** D6
Parak *Iran* 27°38N 52°25E **129** E7
Parakhino Paddubye *Russia* 58°26N 33°10E **84** C7
Parakou *Benin* 9°25N 2°40E **139** D5
Parakylia *Australia* 30°24S 136°25E **152** A2
Paralimni *Cyprus* 35°2N 33°58E **101** D12
Paralio Astros *Greece* 37°25N 22°45E **98** D4
Paralkote *India* 19°47N 80°41E **126** E5
Paramaribo *Suriname* 5°50N 55°10W **187** B7
Parambu *Brazil* 6°13S 40°43W **189** B2
Paramirim *Brazil* 13°26S 42°15W **189** C2
Paramirim → *Brazil* 11°34S 43°18W **189** C2
Paramithia *Greece* 39°30N 20°35E **98** B2
Paramonga *Peru* 10°40S 77°50W **188** C2
Páramos del Batallón y La Negra △ *Venezuela* 8°2N 71°55W **183** E5
Paramushir, Ostrov *Russia* 50°24N 156°0E **107** D16
Paran → *Israel* 30°20N 35°10E **130** E4
Paraná *Argentina* 31°45S 60°30W **190** C3
Paraná *Brazil* 12°30S 47°48W **189** C1
Paraná □ *Brazil* 24°30S 51°0W **191** A5
Paraná → *Argentina* 33°43S 59°15W **190** C4
Paraná → *Brazil* 12°30S 48°14W **189** C1
Paranaguá *Brazil* 25°30S 48°30W **191** B6
Paranaíba *Brazil* 19°40S 51°11W **187** G8
Paranaíba → *Brazil* 20°6S 51°4W **187** H8
Paranal, Cerro *Chile* 24°38S 70°24W **190** A1
Paranapanema → *Brazil* 22°40S 53°9W **191** A5
Paranapiacaba, Serra do *Brazil* 24°31S 48°35W **191** A6
Paranavaí *Brazil* 23°4S 52°56W **191** A5
Parang *Maguindanao, Phil.* 7°23N 124°16E **119** C6
Parang *Sulu, Phil.* 5°55N 120°54E **119** C6
Parangippettai *India* 11°30N 79°38E **127** J4
Parângul Mare, Vf. *Romania* 45°20N 23°37E **81** E8
Paranthan *Sri Lanka* 9°26N 80°24E **127** K5
Paraparaumu *N.Z.* 40°57S 175°3E **154** G4
Paraspori, Akra *Greece* 35°55N 27°15E **99** F9
Paratinga *Brazil* 12°40S 43°10W **189** C2
Paratoo *Australia* 32°42S 139°20E **152** B3
Parauapebas *Brazil* 6°4S 49°54W **187** E9
Paray-le-Monial *France* 46°27N 4°7E **71** F11
Parbati → *Mad. P., India* 25°50N 76°30E **124** G7
Parbati → *Raj., India* 26°54N 77°53E **124** F7
Parbhani *India* 19°8N 76°52E **126** E3
Parchim *Germany* 53°26N 11°52E **76** B7
Parczew *Poland* 51°40N 22°52E **83** G9
Pardes Hanna-Karkur *Israel* 32°28N 34°57E **130** C3
Pardilla *Spain* 41°33N 3°43W **88** D7
Pardo → *Bahia, Brazil* 15°40S 39°0W **189** D3
Pardo → *Mato Grosso, Brazil* 21°46S 52°9W **191** A5
Pardo → *Minas Gerais, Brazil* 15°48S 44°48W **189** D2
Pardoo Roadhouse *Australia* 20°6S 119°3E **148** D2
Pardubice *Czechia* 50°3N 15°45E **78** A8
Pardubický □ *Czechia* 49°50N 16°0E **78** B8
Pare *Indonesia* 7°43S 112°12E **119** G15
Pare Mts. *Tanzania* 4°0S 37°45E **142** C4
Parecis, Serra dos *Brazil* 13°0S 60°0W **186** F7
Paredes de Nava *Spain* 42°9N 4°42W **88** C6
Parelhas *Brazil* 6°41S 36°39W **189** B3
Paren *Russia* 62°30N 163°15E **107** C17
Parenda *India* 18°16N 75°28E **126** E2
Parengarenga Harbour *N.Z.* 34°31S 173°0E **154** A2
Parent *Canada* 47°55N 74°35W **164** C5
Parent, L. *Canada* 48°31N 77°1W **164** C4
Parentis-en-Born *France* 44°21N 1°4W **72** D2
Parepare *Indonesia* 4°0S 119°40E **119** E5
Parfino *Russia* 57°59N 31°34E **84** D6
Parga *Greece* 39°15N 20°29E **98** B2
Pargas = Länsi-Turunmaa *Finland* 60°18N 22°18E **84** B2
Pargi *India* 17°11N 77°53E **126** E3
Pargo, Pta. do *Madeira* 32°49N 17°17W **100** D2
Parham *Canada* 44°39N 76°43W **175** B8
Paria → *U.S.A.* 36°52N 111°36W **169** H8
Paria, G. de *Venezuela* 10°30N 61°40W **187** K14
Pariaguán *Venezuela* 8°51N 64°34W **186** B6
Paricutín, Cerro *Mexico* 19°28N 102°15W **180** D4
Parigi *Indonesia* 0°50S 120°5E **119** E6
Parika *Guyana* 6°50N 58°20W **186** B7
Parikia *Greece* 37°6N 25°11E **99** D7
Parikkala *Finland* 61°33N 29°31E **84** B5
Parima, Serra *Brazil* 2°30N 64°0W **186** C6
Parinari *Peru* 4°35S 74°25W **188** A3
Pariñas, Pta. *Peru* 4°30S 82°0W **188** A1
Parincea *Romania* 46°27N 27°9E **81** D12
Paringa *Australia* 34°10S 140°46E **152** C4
Parintins *Brazil* 2°40S 56°50W **187** D7
Pariparit Kyun *Myanmar* 14°52N 93°41E **127** G11
Paris *Canada* 43°12N 80°25W **174** C4
Paris *France* 48°53N 2°20E **71** D9
Paris *Idaho, U.S.A.* 42°14N 111°24W **168** E8
Paris *Ky., U.S.A.* 38°13N 84°15W **173** F11
Paris *Tenn., U.S.A.* 36°18N 88°19W **177** C10
Paris *Tex., U.S.A.* 33°40N 95°33W **176** E7
Paris, Ville de □ *France* 48°50N 2°20E **71** D9
Paris Charles de Gaulle ✕ (CDG) *France* 49°0N 2°32E **71** D9
Paris Orly ✕ (ORY) *France* 48°44N 2°23E **71** D9
Parish *U.S.A.* 43°25N 76°8W **175** C8
Parishville *U.S.A.* 44°38N 74°49W **175** B10
Pariti *Indonesia* 10°1S 123°45E **148** B3
Park *U.S.A.* 48°45N 122°18W **170** B4
Park City *U.S.A.* 37°48N 97°20W **172** G5
Park Falls *U.S.A.* 45°56N 90°27W **172** C8
Park Head *Canada* 44°36N 81°9W **174** B3
Park Hills *U.S.A.* 37°51N 90°51W **172** G8
Park Range *U.S.A.* 40°41N 106°41W **168** F10
Park Rapids *U.S.A.* 46°55N 95°4W **172** B6
Park River *U.S.A.* 48°24N 97°45W **172** A5
Park Rynie *S. Africa* 30°25S 30°45E **145** D5
Parkā Bandar *Iran* 25°55N 59°35E **129** E8
Parkano *Finland* 62°1N 23°0E **84** A2
Parkent *Uzbekistan* 41°18N 69°40E **109** D7
Parker *Ariz., U.S.A.* 34°9N 114°17W **171** L12
Parker *Pa., U.S.A.* 41°5N 79°41W **174** E5
Parker Dam *U.S.A.* 34°18N 114°8W **171** L12
Parkersburg *U.S.A.* 39°16N 81°34W **173** F13
Parkes *Australia* 33°9S 148°11E **153** B8
Parkfield *U.S.A.* 35°54N 120°26W **170** K6
Parkhill *Canada* 43°15N 81°38W **174** C3
Parkland *U.S.A.* 47°9N 122°26W **170** C4
Parkston *U.S.A.* 43°24N 97°59W **172** D5
Parksville *Canada* 49°20N 124°21W **162** D4
Parkway *U.S.A.* 38°32N 121°26W **170** G5
Parla *Spain* 40°14N 3°46W **88** E7
Parlakimidi *India* 18°45N 84°5E **126** E7
Parli *India* 18°50N 76°35E **126** E3
Pârliţa *Moldova* 47°19N 27°52E **81** C12
Parma *Italy* 44°48N 10°20E **92** D7
Parma *Idaho, U.S.A.* 43°47N 116°57W **168** E5
Parma *Ohio, U.S.A.* 41°24N 81°43W **174** E3
Parma → *Italy* 44°56N 10°26E **92** D7
Parnaguá *Brazil* 10°10S 44°38W **189** C2
Parnaíba *Brazil* 2°54S 41°47W **189** A2
Parnaíba → *Brazil* 3°0S 41°50W **189** A2
Parnamirim *Pernambuco, Brazil* 8°5S 39°34W **189** B3
Parnamirim *Rio Grande do N., Brazil* 5°55S 35°15W **189** B3
Parnarama *Brazil* 5°31S 43°6W **189** B2
Parnassos *Greece* 38°35N 22°30E **98** C4
Parnassus *N.Z.* 42°42S 173°23E **155** C8
Parndana *Australia* 35°48S 137°12E **152** C2
Parner *India* 19°0N 74°26E **126** E2
Parnitha *Greece* 38°14N 23°45E **98** C5
Parnitha △ *Greece* 38°12N 23°44E **98** C5
Parnonas Oros *Greece* 37°15N 22°45E **98** D4
Pärnu *Estonia* 58°28N 24°33E **84** C3
Pärnu → *Estonia* 58°28N 24°33E **84** C3
Paro Dzong *Bhutan* 27°32N 89°53E **125** F13
Parola *India* 20°47N 75°7E **126** D2
Paroo → *Australia* 31°28S 143°32E **152** A5
Paros *Greece* 37°5N 25°12E **99** D7
Parowan *U.S.A.* 37°51N 112°50W **169** H7
Parpaillon *France* 44°30N 6°40E **73** D10
Parral *Chile* 36°10S 71°52W **190** D1
Parramatta *Australia* 33°48S 151°1E **153** B9
Parras *Mexico* 25°25N 102°11W **180** B4
Parrett → *U.K.* 51°12N 3°1W **67** F4
Parris I. *U.S.A.* 32°20N 80°41W **178** C9
Parrish *U.S.A.* 27°35N 82°26W **179** H7
Parrott *U.S.A.* 31°54N 84°31W **178** D5
Parrsboro *Canada* 45°30N 64°25W **165** C7
Parry Channel *Canada* 74°15N 94°0W **161** C13
Parry I. *Canada* 45°18N 80°10W **174** A4
Parry Is. *Canada* 77°0N 110°0W **161** B10
Parry Sound *Canada* 45°20N 80°0W **174** A5
Parsābād *Iran* 39°39N 47°50E **105** C12
Parsaloi *Kenya* 1°16N 36°51E **142** B4
Parsberg *Germany* 49°10N 11°43E **77** F7
Parsęta → *Poland* 54°11N 15°34E **82** D2
Parsnip → *Canada* 55°10N 123°2W **162** B4
Parsons *U.S.A.* 37°20N 95°16W **172** G6
Parsons Ra. *Australia* 13°30S 135°15E **150** A2
Partabpur *India* 20°0N 80°42E **126** E5
Partanna *Italy* 37°43N 12°53E **94** E5
Partenio ⌂ *Italy* 40°56N 14°38E **95** B7
Parthenay *France* 46°38N 0°16W **70** F6
Partinico *Italy* 38°3N 13°7E **94** D6
Partizansk *Russia* 43°8N 133°9E **107** E14
Partizánske *Slovakia* 48°38N 18°23E **79** C11
Partridge I. *Canada* 55°59N 87°37W **164** A2
Partry Mts. *Ireland* 53°40N 9°28W **64** C2
Partur *India* 19°40N 76°14E **126** E3
Paru → *Brazil* 1°33S 52°38W **187** D8
Parur = North Paravar *India* 10°13N 76°14E **127** J3
Paruro *Peru* 13°45S 71°50W **188** C3
Parvān □ *Afghan.* 35°0N 69°0E **109** F7
Parvatipuram *India* 18°50N 83°25E **126** E6
Parvatsar *India* 26°52N 74°49E **124** F6
Parvomay *Bulgaria* 42°8N 25°17E **97** D9
Påryd *Sweden* 56°34N 15°55E **63** H9
Parys *S. Africa* 26°52S 27°29E **144** C4
Pas, Pta. des *Spain* 38°46N 1°26E **100** C7
Pas, The *Canada* 53°45N 101°15W **163** C8
Pas-de-Calais □ *France* 50°30N 2°10E **71** B9
Pasada *Spain* 43°23N 5°40W **88** B5
Pasadena *Canada* 49°1N 57°36W **165** C8
Pasadena *Calif., U.S.A.* 34°9N 118°8W **171** L8
Pasadena *Tex., U.S.A.* 29°43N 95°13W **176** G7
Pasaje → *Argentina* 25°39S 63°56W **190** B3
Paşalimanı *Turkey* 40°29N 27°36E **97** F11
Pasar *Indonesia* 8°27S 114°54E **119** J17
Pasargadae *Iran* 30°11N 53°10E **129** D7
Pascagoula *U.S.A.* 30°21N 88°33W **177** F10
Pascagoula → *U.S.A.* 30°23N 88°37W **177** F10
Paşcani *Romania* 47°14N 26°45E **81** C11
Paschimbanga □ *India* 23°0N 88°0E **125** H13
Pasco *U.S.A.* 46°14N 119°6W **168** C4
Pasco □ *Peru* 10°40S 75°0W **188** C3
Pasco I. *Australia* 20°57S 115°20E **148** D2
Pascoag *U.S.A.* 41°57N 71°42W **175** E13
Pascua, I. de *Chile* 27°7S 109°23W **157** K17
Pasewalk *Germany* 53°30N 13°58E **76** B9
Pasfield L. *Canada* 58°24N 105°20W **163** B7
Pasha → *Russia* 60°29N 32°55E **84** B7
Pasinler *Turkey* 39°59N 41°41E **105** C9
Pasir Mas *Malaysia* 6°2N 102°8E **121** J4
Pasir Panjang *Singapore* 1°18N 103°46E **121** d
Pasir Putih *Malaysia* 5°50N 102°24E **121** K4
Påskallavik *Sweden* 57°10N 16°26E **63** G10
Paskūh *Iran* 27°34N 61°39E **129** E9
Pasłęk *Poland* 54°3N 19°41E **82** D6
Pasłęka → *Poland* 54°26N 19°46E **82** D6
Pasley, C. *Australia* 33°52S 123°35E **149** F3
Pašman *Croatia* 43°58N 15°20E **93** E12
Pasmore → *Australia* 31°5S 139°49E **152** A3
Pasni *Pakistan* 25°15N 63°27E **122** G3
Paso Bravo △ *Paraguay* 22°32S 57°5W **190** A4
Paso Cantinela *Mexico* 32°33N 115°47W **171** N11
Paso de Indios *Argentina* 43°55S 69°0W **192** B3
Paso de los Indios *Argentina* 38°32S 69°25W **192** A3
Paso de los Libres *Argentina* 29°44S 57°10W **190** B4
Paso de los Toros *Uruguay* 32°45S 56°30W **190** C4
Paso Flores *Argentina* 40°35S 70°38W **192** B2
Paso Robles *U.S.A.* 35°38N 120°41W **170** K6
Paspébiac *Canada* 48°3N 65°17W **165** C6
Pasrur *Pakistan* 32°16N 74°43E **124** C6
Passage East *Ireland* 52°14N 7°0W **64** D5
Passage West *Ireland* 51°52N 8°21W **64** E3
Passaic *U.S.A.* 40°51N 74°7W **175** F10
Passau *Germany* 48°34N 13°28E **77** G9
Passero, C. *Italy* 36°41N 15°10E **95** F8
Passo Fundo *Brazil* 28°10S 52°20W **191** B5
Passos *Brazil* 20°45S 46°37W **189** E1
Passow *Germany* 53°8N 14°6E **76** B10
Passy *France* 45°55N 6°41E **73** C10
Pastavy *Belarus* 55°4N 26°50E **84** E4
Pastaza → *Peru* 4°50S 76°52W **186** D3
Pasto *Colombia* 1°13N 77°17W **186** C3
Pastos Bons *Brazil* 6°36S 44°5W **189** B2
Pastrana *Spain* 40°27N 2°53W **90** E2
Pasuruan *Indonesia* 7°40S 112°44E **119** G15
Pasym *Poland* 53°48N 20°49E **82** E7
Pásztó *Hungary* 47°52N 19°43E **80** C4
Patag I. = Flat I. *S. China Sea* 10°49N 115°49E **118** B5
Patagonia *Argentina* 45°0S 69°0W **192** C3
Patagonia *U.S.A.* 31°33N 110°45W **169** L8
Patambar *Iran* 29°45N 60°17E **129** D9
Patan = Lalitpur *Nepal* 27°40N 85°20E **125** F11
Patan = Somnath *India* 20°53N 70°22E **124** J4
Patan *Gujarat, India* 23°54N 72°14E **124** H5
Patan *Maharashtra, India* 17°22N 73°57E **126** F1
Patani *Indonesia* 0°20N 128°50E **119** D7
Pătârlagele *Romania* 45°19N 26°21E **81** E11
Pataudi *India* 28°18N 76°48E **124** E7
Patchewollock *Australia* 35°22S 142°12E **152** C5
Patchogue *U.S.A.* 40°46N 73°1W **175** F11
Pate *Kenya* 2°10S 41°0E **142** C5
Patea *N.Z.* 39°45S 174°30E **154** F3
Pategi *Nigeria* 8°50N 5°45E **139** D6
Patensie *S. Africa* 33°46S 24°49E **144** D3
Paterna *Spain* 39°30N 0°26W **91** F4
Paternion *Austria* 46°43N 13°38E **78** E6
Paternò *Italy* 37°34N 14°54E **95** E7
Pateros *U.S.A.* 48°3N 119°54W **168** B4
Paterson *Australia* 32°35S 151°36E **153** B9
Paterson *U.S.A.* 40°54N 74°9W **175** F10
Paterson Inlet *N.Z.* 46°56S 168°12E **155** G3
Paterson Ra. *Australia* 21°45S 122°10E **148** D3
Pathankot *India* 32°18N 75°45E **124** C6
Pathardi *India* 19°10N 75°11E **126** E2
Pathein *Myanmar* 16°45N 94°30E **123** L19
Pathfinder Res. *U.S.A.* 42°28N 106°51W **168** E10
Pathiu *Thailand* 10°42N 99°19E **121** G2
Pathri *India* 19°15N 76°27E **126** E3
Pathum Thani *Thailand* 14°1N 100°32E **120** E3
Pati *Indonesia* 6°45S 111°1E **119** G14
Patía → *Colombia* 2°13N 78°40W **186** C3
Patiala *Punjab, India* 30°23N 76°26E **124** D7
Patiala *Ut. P., India* 27°43N 79°1E **125** F8
Patine Kouka *Senegal* 12°45N 13°45W **138** C2
Patitiri *Greece* 39°8N 23°50E **98** B5
Patkai Bum *India* 27°0N 95°30E **123** F19
Patmos *Greece* 37°21N 26°36E **99** D8
Patna *India* 25°35N 85°12E **125** G11
Patnagarh *India* 20°43N 83°9E **126** D6
Patnos *Turkey* 39°13N 42°51E **105** C10
Pato Branco *Brazil* 26°13S 52°40W **191** B5
Patong, Ao *Thailand* 7°54N 98°17E **121** a
Patonga *Uganda* 2°45N 33°15E **142** B3
Patos *Albania* 40°42N 19°38E **96** F3
Patos *Brazil* 6°55S 37°16W **189** B3
Patos, L. dos *Brazil* 31°20S 51°0W **191** C5
Patos, Río de los → *Argentina* 31°18S 69°25W **190** C2
Patos de Minas *Brazil* 18°35S 46°32W **189** D1
Patquía *Argentina* 30°2S 66°55W **190** C2
Patra *Greece* 38°14N 21°47E **98** C3
Patraikos Kolpos *Greece* 38°17N 21°30E **98** C3
Patras = Patra *Greece* 38°14N 21°47E **98** C3
Patricio Lynch, I. *Chile* 48°35S 75°30W **192** C1
Patrocínio *Brazil* 18°57S 47°0W **189** D1
Pattada *Italy* 40°35N 9°6E **94** B2
Pattadakal *India* 16°1N 75°42E **127** F2
Pattani *Thailand* 6°48N 101°15E **121** J3
Pattaya *Thailand* 12°52N 100°55E **120** F3
Patten *U.S.A.* 46°0N 68°38W **173** B19
Patterson *Calif., U.S.A.* 37°28N 121°8W **170** H5
Patterson *Ga., U.S.A.* 31°23N 82°8W **178** D7
Patterson *La., U.S.A.* 29°42N 91°18W **176** G9
Patterson, Mt. *U.S.A.* 38°29N 119°20W **170** G7
Patti *Punjab, India* 31°17N 74°54E **124** D6
Patti *Ut. P., India* 25°55N 82°12E **125** G10
Patti *Italy* 38°8N 14°58E **95** D7
Pattoki *Pakistan* 31°5N 73°52E **124** D5
Patton *U.S.A.* 40°38N 78°39W **174** F6
Pattukkattai *India* 10°25N 79°20E **127** J4
Patu *Brazil* 6°6S 37°38W **189** B3
Patuakhali *Bangla.* 22°20N 90°25E **123** H17
Patuanak *Canada* 55°55N 107°43W **163** B7
Patuca → *Honduras* 15°50N 84°18W **182** C3
Patuca, Punta *Honduras* 15°49N 84°14W **182** C3
Patuca △ *Honduras* 14°30N 85°30W **182** D2
Pătulele *Romania* 44°21N 22°47E **80** F7
Patur *India* 20°27N 76°56E **126** D3
Patvinsuo △ *Finland* 63°7N 30°45E **60** E24
Pátzcuaro *Mexico* 19°31N 101°38W **180** D4
Pau *France* 43°19N 0°25W **72** E3
Pau, Gave de → *France* 43°33N 1°12W **72** E2
Pau dos Ferros *Brazil* 6°7S 38°10W **189** B3
Pauanui *N.Z.* 37°1S 175°52E **154** D4
Paucartambo *Peru* 13°19S 71°35W **188** C3
Paudash *Canada* 44°59N 77°58W **174** B7
Pauillac *France* 45°11N 0°46W **72** C3
Pauini *Brazil* 7°40S 66°58W **188** B4
Pauk *Myanmar* 21°27N 94°30E **123** J19
Paul I. *Canada* 56°30N 61°20W **165** A7
Paul Smiths *U.S.A.* 44°26N 74°15W **175** B10
Paulatuk *Canada* 69°25N 124°0W **160** D7
Paulding Bay *S. Ocean* 66°0S 118°0E **55** C8
Paulhan *France* 43°33N 3°28E **72** E7
Paulista *Brazil* 7°57S 34°53W **189** B4
Paulistana *Brazil* 8°9S 41°9W **189** B2
Paulistrӧm *Sweden* 57°28N 15°31E **63** G9
Paulo Afonso *Brazil* 9°21S 38°15W **189** B3
Paulpietersburg *S. Africa* 27°23S 30°50E **145** C5
Pauls Valley *U.S.A.* 34°44N 97°13W **176** D6
Pauma Valley *U.S.A.* 33°16N 116°58W **171** M10
Pauni *India* 20°48N 79°40E **126** D4
Pauri *India* 30°9N 78°47E **125** D8
Pausa *Peru* 15°16S 73°22W **188** D3
Pavagada *India* 14°6N 77°16E **127** G3
Pāveh *Iran* 35°3N 46°22E **105** E12
Pavelets *Russia* 53°49N 39°14E **84** F10
Pavia *Italy* 45°7N 9°8E **92** C6
Pavilion *U.S.A.* 42°52N 78°1W **174** D6
Pavilly *France* 49°34N 0°57E **70** C7
Pāvilosta *Latvia* 56°53N 21°14E **82** B8
Pavlikeni *Bulgaria* 43°14N 25°20E **97** C9
Pavlodar *Kazakhstan* 52°33N 77°0E **109** B9
Pavlograd = Pavlohrad *Ukraine* 48°30N 35°52E **85** H8
Pavlohrad *Ukraine* 48°30N 35°52E **85** H8
Pavlovo *Russia* 55°58N 43°5E **86** C6
Pavlovsk *Russia* 50°26N 40°5E **86** E5
Pavlovskaya *Russia* 46°17N 39°47E **87** G4
Pavlovskiy-Posad *Russia* 55°47N 38°42E **84** E10
Pavo *U.S.A.* 30°58N 83°45W **178** E6
Pavullo nel Frignano *Italy* 44°20N 10°50E **92** D7
Pawai, Pulau *Singapore* 1°11N 103°44E **121** d
Pawayan *India* 28°4N 80°6E **125** E9
Pawhuska *U.S.A.* 36°40N 96°20W **176** C6
Pawling *U.S.A.* 41°34N 73°36W **175** E11
Pawnee *U.S.A.* 36°20N 96°48W **176** C6
Pawnee City *U.S.A.* 40°7N 96°9W **172** E5
Pawtucket *U.S.A.* 41°53N 71°23W **175** E13
Paxi *Greece* 39°14N 20°12E **98** B2
Paximadia *Greece* 35°0N 24°35E **101** E6
Paxton *U.S.A.* 40°27N 88°6W **172** E9
Payakumbuh *Indonesia* 0°20S 100°35E **118** E2
Payerne *Switz.* 46°49N 6°56E **77** J2
Payette *U.S.A.* 44°5N 116°56W **168** D5
Paymogo *Spain* 37°44N 7°21W **89** H3
Payne Bay = Kangirsuk *Canada* 60°0N 70°0W **161** F18
Payne L. *Canada* 59°30N 74°30W **161** F17
Paynes Find *Australia* 29°15S 117°42E **149** E2
Paynesville *Liberia* 6°20N 10°45W **138** D2
Paynesville *U.S.A.* 45°23N 94°43W **172** C6
Pays de la Loire □ *France* 47°45N 0°25W **70** E6
Paysandú *Uruguay* 32°19S 58°8W **190** C4
Payson *Ariz., U.S.A.* 34°14N 111°20W **169** J8
Payson *Utah, U.S.A.* 40°3N 111°44W **168** F8
Paz → *Guatemala* 13°44N 90°10W **182** D1
Paz, B. de la *Mexico* 24°9N 110°25W **180** C2
Pāzanān *Iran* 30°35N 49°59E **129** D6
Pazar *Turkey* 41°10N 40°50E **105** B9
Pazarcık *Turkey* 37°30N 37°17E **104** D7
Pazardzhik *Bulgaria* 42°12N 24°20E **97** D8
Pazardzhik □ *Bulgaria* 42°12N 24°20E **97** D8
Pazarköy *Turkey* 39°51N 27°24E **99** B9
Pazarlar *Turkey* 39°0N 29°7E **99** C11
Pazaryeri *Turkey* 40°0N 29°56E **99** B11
Pazaryolu *Turkey* 40°21N 40°47E **105** B9
Pazin *Croatia* 45°14N 13°56E **93** C10
Pazña *Bolivia* 18°36S 66°55W **188** D4
Pčinja → *Macedonia* 41°50N 21°45E **96** E5
Pe Ell *U.S.A.* 46°34N 123°18W **170** D3
Pea → *U.S.A.* 31°1N 85°51W **178** D4
Peabody *U.S.A.* 42°31N 70°56W **175** D14
Peace → *Canada* 59°0N 111°25W **162** B6
Peace → *U.S.A.* 26°56N 82°6W **179** J7
Peace Point *Canada* 59°7N 112°27W **162** B6
Peace River *Canada* 56°15N 117°18W **162** B5
Peach Springs *U.S.A.* 35°32N 113°25W **169** J7
Peachland *Canada* 49°47N 119°45W **162** D5
Peachtree City *U.S.A.* 33°25N 84°35W **178** B5
Peak, The = Kinder Scout *U.K.* 53°24N 1°52W **66** D6
Peak Charles △ *Australia* 32°42S 121°10E **149** F3
Peak District △ *U.K.* 53°24N 1°46W **66** D6
Peak Hill *Australia* 32°47S 148°11E **153** B8
Peak Ra. *Australia* 22°50S 148°20E **150** C4
Peake *Australia* 35°25S 139°55E **152** C3
Peake Cr. → *Australia* 28°2S 136°7E **151** D2
Peal de Becerro *Spain* 37°55N 3°7W **89** H7
Peale, Mt. *U.S.A.* 38°26N 109°14W **168** G9
Pearblossom *U.S.A.* 34°30N 117°55W **171** L9
Pearl → *U.S.A.* 30°11N 89°32W **177** F10
Pearl and Hermes Reef *U.S.A.* 27°55N 175°45W **167** K4
Pearl Banks *Sri Lanka* 8°45N 79°45E **127** K4
Pearl River = Zhu Jiang → *China* 22°45N 113°37E **117** F9
Pearl River *U.S.A.* 41°4N 74°2W **175** E10
Pearl River Bridge *China* 22°15N 113°48E **111** a
Pearsall *U.S.A.* 28°54N 99°6W **176** G5
Pearson *U.S.A.* 31°18N 82°51W **178** D7
Pearson Int. Toronto ✕ (YYZ) *Canada* 43°46N 79°35W **174** C5
Peary Chan. *Canada* 79°40N 101°30W **161** B11

Peary Land Greenland 82°40N 33°0W 57 A7
Pease → U.S.A. 34°12N 99°2W 176 D5
Peawanuck Canada 55°15N 85°12W 164 A2
Pebane Mozam. 17°10S 38°8E 143 F4
Pebas Peru 3°10S 71°46W 186 D4
Pebble, I. Falk. Is. 51°20S 59°40W 192 D5
Pebble Beach U.S.A. 36°34N 121°57W 170 J5
Peć = Pejë Kosovo 42°40N 20°17E 96 D4
Peçanha Brazil 18°33S 42°34W 189 D2
Péccioli Italy 43°33N 10°43E 92 C7
Pechea Romania 45°36N 27°49E 81 E12
Pechenga Russia 69°29N 31°4E 60 B24
Pechenizhyn Ukraine 48°30N 24°48E 81 B9
Pechiguera, Pta.
 Canary Is. 28°51N 13°53W 100 F6
Pechnezhskoye Vdkhr.
 Ukraine 50°5N 36°54E 85 G9
Pechora Russia 65°10N 57°11E 106 C6
Pechora → Russia 68°13N 54°15E 58 B16
Pechorskaya Guba
 Russia 68°40N 54°0E 106 C6
Pechory Russia 57°48N 27°40E 84 D4
Pecica Romania 46°10N 21°3E 80 D6
Pecka Serbia 44°18N 19°33E 96 B3
Pécora, C. Italy 39°27N 8°23E 94 C1
Pecos N. Mex., U.S.A. 35°35N 105°41W 169 J11
Pecos Tex., U.S.A. 31°26N 103°30W 176 F4
Pecos → U.S.A. 29°42N 101°22W 176 G4
Pécs Hungary 46°5N 18°15E 80 D3
Pedasí Panama 7°32N 80°2W 182 E3
Pedda Bellala India 19°4N 78°49E 126 E4
Peddapalli India 18°40N 79°24E 126 E4
Peddapuram India 17°6N 82°8E 126 F6
Pedder, L. Australia 42°55S 146°10E 151 G4
Peddie S. Africa 33°14S 27°7E 145 D4
Pedernales Dom. Rep. 18°2N 71°44W 183 C5
Pedieos → Cyprus 35°10N 33°54E 101 D12
Pedirka Desert
 Australia 26°47S 134°11E 151 A1
Pedra Azul Brazil 16°2S 41°17W 189 D2
Pedra Grande, Recifes de
 Brazil 17°45S 38°58W 189 D3
Pedra Lume Cabo Verde 16°40N 22°52W 134 b
Pedreguer Spain 38°48N 0°3E 91 G5
Pedreiras Brazil 4°32S 44°40W 189 D2
Pedro Afonso Brazil 9°0S 48°10W 189 E1
Pedro Cays Jamaica 17°5N 77°48W 182 C4
Pedro de Valdivia Chile 22°55S 69°38W 190 A2
Pedro Juan Caballero
 Paraguay 22°30S 55°40W 191 A4
Pedro Muñoz Spain 39°25N 2°56W 89 F8
Pedrógão Grande Portugal 39°55N 8°9W 88 F2
Pee Dee = Great Pee Dee →
 U.S.A. 33°21N 79°10W 177 E15
Peebinga Australia 34°52S 140°57E 152 C4
Peebles U.K. 55°40N 3°11W 65 F5
Peekskill U.S.A. 41°17N 73°55W 175 E11
Peel I. of Man 54°13N 4°40W 66 C3
Peel → Australia 30°50S 150°29E 153 A9
Peel → Canada 67°0N 135°0W 160 D5
Peel Sd. Canada 73°0N 96°0W 160 C12
Peene → Germany 54°9N 13°46E 76 A9
Peera Peera Poolanna L.
 Australia 26°30S 138°0E 151 D2
Peerless Lake Canada 56°37N 114°40W 162 B6
Peers Canada 53°40N 116°0W 162 C5
Peery L. Australia 30°45S 143°35E 152 A5
Pegasus Bay N.Z. 43°20S 173°10E 155 D8
Peggau Austria 47°12N 15°21E 78 D8
Pegnitz Germany 49°44N 11°31E 77 F7
Pegnitz → Germany 49°30N 10°59E 77 F6
Pego Spain 38°51N 0°8W 91 G4
Pegu = Bago Myanmar 17°20N 96°29E 123 L20
Pegu Yoma Myanmar 19°0N 96°0E 123 K20
Pehčevo Macedonia 41°41N 22°55E 96 E6
Pehlivanköy Turkey 41°20N 26°55E 97 E10
Pehuajó Argentina 35°45S 62°0W 190 D3
Pei Xian China 34°44N 116°55E 114 G9
Peikang Taiwan 23°34N 120°18E 117 F13
Peine Chile 23°45S 68°8W 190 A2
Peine Germany 52°19N 10°14E 76 C6
Peip'ing = Beijing
 China 39°53N 116°21E 114 E9
Peipus, L. = Chudskoye, Ozero
 Russia 58°13N 27°30E 84 C4
Peissenberg Germany 47°48N 11°4E 77 H7
Peitz Germany 51°51N 14°24E 76 D10
Peixe Brazil 12°0S 48°40W 189 C1
Peixe → Brazil 21°31S 51°58W 187 H8
Pejë Kosovo 42°40N 20°17E 96 D4
Pek → Serbia 44°45N 21°29E 96 B5
Pekalongan Indonesia 6°53S 109°40E 118 F3
Pekan Malaysia 3°30N 103°25E 121 L4
Pekan Nenas Malaysia 1°31N 103°31E 121 d
Pekanbaru Indonesia 0°30N 101°15E 118 D2
Peking = Beijing
 China 39°53N 116°21E 114 E9
Pekutatan Indonesia 8°25S 114°49E 119 J17
Pela Greece 40°46N 22°23E 96 F6
Pelabuhan Ratu, Teluk
 Indonesia 7°5S 106°30E 119 G12
Pélagos = Kira Panagia
 Greece 39°17N 24°4E 98 B6
Pelaihari Indonesia 3°55S 114°45E 118 E4
Pelat, Mt. France 44°16N 6°42E 73 D10
Pelczyce Poland 53°3N 15°16E 83 E2
Peleaga, Vf. Romania 45°22N 22°55E 80 E7
Pelechuco Bolivia 14°48S 69°4W 188 D4
Pelée, Mt. Martinique 14°48N 61°10W 182 c
Pelee, Pt. Canada 41°54N 82°31W 164 D3
Pelee I. Canada 41°47N 82°40W 164 D3
Pelejo Peru 6°10S 75°49W 188 B2
Pelekech Kenya 3°52N 35°8E 142 B4
Peleng Indonesia 1°20S 123°30E 119 E6
Pelentong Malaysia 1°32N 103°49E 121 d
Pélézi Côte d'Ivoire 7°17N 6°54W 138 D3
Pelham U.S.A. 31°8N 84°9W 177 F12
Pelhřimov Czechia 49°24N 15°12E 78 B8
Pelican U.S.A. 57°58N 136°14W 162 B1
Pelican L. Canada 52°28N 100°20W 163 C8
Pelican Narrows
 Canada 55°10N 102°56W 163 B8
Pelion U.S.A. 33°46N 81°15W 178 B8
Pelister = Macedonia 41°0N 21°10E 96 E5
Pelješac Croatia 42°55N 17°25E 93 F14
Pelkosenniemi Finland 67°6N 27°28E 60 C22
Pell City U.S.A. 33°35N 86°17W 178 B3
Pella Greece 40°52N 22°0E 96 F6
Pella S. Africa 29°1S 19°6E 144 D2
Pella U.S.A. 41°25N 92°55W 172 E7
Pello Finland 66°47N 23°59E 60 C20

Pellworm Germany 54°31N 8°39E 76 A4
Pelly → Canada 62°47N 137°19W 162 A1
Pelly Bay Canada 58°38N 89°50W 161 D14
Peloponnesos □ Greece 37°10N 22°0E 98 D4
Peloritani, Monti Italy 38°3N 15°20E 95 D8
Pelorus → N.Z. 41°6S 173°45E 155 B8
Pelorus Sd. N.Z. 40°59S 173°59E 155 A8
Pelotas Brazil 31°42S 52°23W 191 C5
Pelotas → Brazil 27°28S 51°55W 191 B5
Pelovo Bulgaria 43°26N 24°17E 97 C8
Pelplin Poland 53°55N 18°42E 82 E5
Pelvoux, Massif du
 France 44°52N 6°20E 73 D10
Pemalang Indonesia 6°53S 109°23E 119 G13
Pemanggil, Pulau
 Malaysia 2°37N 104°21E 121 L5
Pematangsiantar
 Indonesia 2°57N 99°5E 118 D1
Pemba Mozam. 12°58S 40°30E 143 E5
Pemba Zambia 16°30S 27°28E 143 F2
Pemba Channel Tanzania 5°0S 39°37E 142 D4
Pemba I. Tanzania 5°0S 39°45E 142 D4
Pemberton Australia 34°30S 116°0E 149 F2
Pemberton Canada 50°25N 122°50W 162 C4
Pembina → Canada 54°45N 114°17W 162 C6
Pembroke Canada 45°50N 77°7W 164 C4
Pembroke U.K. 51°41N 4°55W 67 F3
Pembroke U.S.A. 32°8N 81°37W 178 C8
Pembroke Pines U.S.A. 26°0N 80°13W 179 J9
Pembrokeshire □ U.K. 51°52N 4°56W 67 F3
Pembrokeshire Coast △
 U.K. 51°50N 5°2W 67 F2
Pen India 18°45N 73°5E 126 E6
Pen-y-bont ar Ogwr = Bridgend
 U.K. 51°30N 3°34W 67 F4
Pen-y-Ghent U.K. 54°10N 2°14W 66 C5
Peña, Sierra de la Spain 42°32N 0°45W 90 C4
Peña de Francia, Sierra de la
 Spain 40°32N 6°10W 88 E4
Peñafiel Portugal 41°12N 8°17W 88 D2
Peñafiel Spain 41°35N 4°7W 88 D6
Peñaflor Spain 37°43N 5°21W 89 H5
Penal Trin. & Tob. 10°9N 61°29W 187 K15
Peñalara Spain 40°51N 3°57W 88 E7
Penalva Brazil 3°18S 45°10W 189 A1
Penamacôr Portugal 40°10N 7°10W 88 E3
Penang = Pinang
 Malaysia 5°25N 100°15E 121 c
Penápolis Brazil 21°30S 50°0W 191 A6
Peñaranda de Bracamonte
 Spain 40°53N 5°13W 88 E5
Peñarroya Spain 40°25N 0°40W 90 C4
Peñarroya-Pueblonuevo
 Spain 38°19N 5°16W 89 G5
Penarth U.K. 51°26N 3°11W 67 F4
Peñas, C. de Spain 43°42N 5°52W 88 A5
Peñas, G. de Chile 47°0S 75°0W 192 C2
Peñas de San Pedro Spain 38°44N 2°0W 91 G3
Peñas del Chache
 Canary Is. 29°6N 13°33W 100 E6
Peñausende Spain 41°17N 5°52W 88 D5
Pench → India 21°17N 79°10E 126 D4
Pench △ India 21°45N 79°20E 125 J8
Pench'i = Benxi
 China 41°20N 123°48E 115 D12
Pend Oreille → U.S.A. 49°4N 117°37W 168 B5
Pend Oreille, L.
 U.S.A. 48°10N 116°21W 168 B5
Pendalofos Greece 40°14N 21°12E 96 F5
Pendembu Eastern,
 S. Leone 8°10N 10°42W 138 D2
Pendembu Northern,
 S. Leone 9°7N 11°14W 138 D2
Pendências Brazil 5°15S 36°43W 189 B3
Pender B. Australia 16°45S 122°42E 148 C3
Pendik Turkey 40°53N 29°13E 97 F13
Pendjari → Benin 10°55N 0°50E 139 C5
Pendjari △ Benin 11°15N 1°32E 139 C5
Pendleton U.S.A. 45°40N 118°47W 168 D4
Pendra India 22°46N 81°57E 125 H9
Pendzhikent = Panjakent
 Tajikistan 39°29N 67°37E 109 E7
Penedo Brazil 10°15S 36°36W 189 C3
Penedono Portugal 41°57N 8°15W 88 D2
Penelokan Indonesia 8°17S 115°22E 119 J18
Penetanguishene
 Canada 44°50N 79°55W 174 B5
Penfield U.S.A. 41°13N 78°35W 174 E6
Penfro = Pembroke U.K. 51°41N 4°55W 67 F3
Peng Chau China 22°17N 114°2E 111 a
Peng'an China 31°2N 106°22E 116 B6
Penganga → India 19°53N 79°9E 126 E4
Penge Eastern Cape Or.,
 Dem. Rep. of the Congo 5°30S 24°33E 142 D1
Penge Sud-Kivu,
 Dem. Rep. of the Congo 4°27S 28°25E 142 C2
P'enghu Ch'üntou
 Taiwan 23°34N 119°30E 117 F12
Penglai China 37°48N 120°42E 115 F11
Pengshan China 30°14N 103°58E 116 B4
Pengshui China 29°17N 108°12E 116 C7
Penguin Australia 41°8S 146°6E 151 G4
Pengxi China 30°44N 105°45E 116 B5
Pengze China 29°52N 116°32E 117 C11
Pengzhou China 31°4N 103°32E 116 B4
Penhalonga Zimbabwe 18°52S 32°40E 143 F3
Peniche Portugal 39°19N 9°22W 89 F1
Penicuik U.K. 55°50N 3°13W 65 F5
Penida, Nusa Indonesia 8°45S 115°30E 118 F5
Peninnes, Alpes = Pennine, Alpi
 Alps 46°4N 7°30E 77 J3
Peninsular Malaysia □
 Malaysia 4°0N 102°0E 121 L4
Peñíscola Spain 40°22N 0°24E 90 E5
Penitente, Serra do
 Brazil 8°45S 36°0W 189 C1
Pēnjwīn Iraq 35°37N 45°56E 105 C11
Penkridge U.K. 52°44N 2°6W 66 E5
Penmarch France 47°49N 4°21W 70 E2
Penmarch, Pte. de
 France 47°48N 4°22W 70 E2
Penn Hills U.S.A. 40°28N 79°52W 174 F5
Penn Yan U.S.A. 42°40N 77°3W 174 D7
Penna, Punta della
 Italy 42°10N 14°43E 93 F11
Pennant Canada 50°32N 108°14W 163 C7
Penne Italy 42°27N 13°50E 93 F10
Penner → India 14°35N 80°10E 127 G5
Penneshaw Australia 35°44S 137°56E 152 C2
Pennine, Alpi Alps 46°4N 7°30E 77 J3
Pennines U.K. 54°45N 2°27W 66 C5
Pennington U.S.A. 39°15N 121°47W 170 F5

Pennington → Nigeria 4°45N 5°35E 139 E6
Pennino, Mte. Italy 43°6N 12°53E 93 E9
Pennsburg U.S.A. 40°23N 75°29W 175 F9
Pennsylvania □
 U.S.A. 40°45N 77°30W 173 E15
Penny Canada 53°51N 121°20W 162 C4
Peno Russia 57°2N 32°49E 84 D7
Penobscot → U.S.A. 44°30N 68°48W 173 C19
Penobscot B. U.S.A. 44°35N 68°50W 173 C19
Penola Australia 37°25S 140°48E 152 C3
Penong Australia 31°56S 133°1E 149 F5
Penonomé Panama 8°31N 80°21W 182 E3
Penrhyn Cook Is. 9°0S 158°0W 157 H12
Penrith Australia 33°43S 150°38E 153 B9
Penrith U.K. 54°40N 2°45W 66 C5
Penryn U.K. 50°9N 5°7W 67 G2
Pensacola U.S.A. 30°25N 87°13W 179 F22
Pensacola B. U.S.A. 30°25N 87°5W 179 F22
Pensacola Mts. Antarctica 84°0S 40°0W 55 E1
Pense Canada 50°25N 104°59W 163 C8
Penshurst Australia 37°49S 142°20E 152 C3
Pentadaktylos Cyprus 35°20N 33°20E 101 D12
Pentecostes Brazil 3°48S 39°17W 189 A3
Penticton Canada 49°30N 119°38W 162 D5
Pentland Australia 20°32S 145°25E 150 C4
Pentland Firth U.K. 58°43N 3°10W 65 C5
Pentland Hills U.K. 55°48N 3°25W 65 F5
Penukonda India 14°5N 77°38E 127 G3
Penza Russia 53°15N 45°5E 86 D7
Penza □ Russia 52°50N 44°50E 86 D7
Penzance U.K. 50°7N 5°33W 67 G2
Penzberg Germany 47°45N 11°22E 77 H7
Penzhino Russia 63°30N 167°55E 107 C17
Penzhinskaya Guba
 Russia 61°30N 163°0E 107 C17
Penzlin Germany 53°30N 13°5E 76 B9
Peoria Ariz., U.S.A. 33°35N 112°14W 169 K7
Peoria Ill., U.S.A. 40°42N 89°36W 172 E9
Pepacton Res. U.S.A. 42°5N 74°58W 175 D10
Pepani → S. Africa 25°49S 22°47E 144 D3
Pepel S. Leone 8°40N 13°5W 138 D2
Pera Hd. Australia 12°55S 141°37E 150 A3
Perabumilih Indonesia 3°27S 104°15E 118 E2
Perachora Greece 38°2N 22°56E 98 C4
Perak □ Malaysia 5°0N 101°0E 121 K3
Perak → Malaysia 4°0N 100°50E 121 K3
Perales del Alfambra
 Spain 40°38N 1°0W 90 E4
Perales del Puerto Spain 40°10N 6°40W 88 E4
Peralta Spain 42°20N 1°48W 90 C3
Perama Epiros, Greece 39°42N 20°51E 98 B2
Perama Kerkyra, Greece 39°34N 19°54E 101 A3
Perama Kriti, Greece 35°20N 24°40E 101 D6
Perämeri → Finland 65°35N 24°22E 60 D21
Perancak Indonesia 8°24S 114°37E 119 J17
Peräpohjola Finland 66°16N 26°10E 60 C22
Perast Montenegro 42°31N 18°47E 96 D2
Percé Canada 48°31N 64°13W 165 C7
Perche France 48°31N 1°1E 70 D8
Perche △ France 48°24N 0°46E 70 D7
Perchtoldsdorf Austria 48°7N 16°17E 79 C9
Percival Lakes Australia 21°25S 125°0E 148 D4
Percy Is. Australia 21°39S 150°16E 150 C5
Perdido → Argentina 42°55S 67°0W 192 B3
Perdido, Mte. Spain 42°40N 0°5E 90 C6
Perdu, Mt. = Perdido, Mte.
 Spain 42°40N 0°5E 90 C6
Perechyn Ukraine 48°44N 22°28E 80 B7
Perehinske Ukraine 48°49N 24°11E 81 B9
Pereira Colombia 4°49N 75°43W 186 C3
Perejil Spain 35°55N 5°25W 89 K5
Perelazovsky Russia 49°8N 42°35E 87 F6
Perelik Bulgaria 41°36N 24°33E 97 E8
Peremul Par India 11°10N 72°4E 127 J1
Perené → Peru 11°9S 74°14W 188 C2
Perenjori Australia 29°26S 116°16E 149 E2
Peresecina Moldova 47°16N 28°46E 81 C13
Pereslavl-Zalesskiy
 Russia 56°45N 38°50E 84 D10
Peretu Romania 44°3N 25°5E 81 F10
Pereyaslav-Khmelnytskyy
 Ukraine 50°3N 31°28E 85 G6
Pereyma Ukraine 48°4N 29°30E 81 B14
Pérez, I. Mexico 22°24N 89°42W 181 C7
Perg Austria 48°15N 14°38E 78 C7
Pergamino Argentina 33°52S 60°30W 190 C3
Pergamon Turkey 39°8N 27°11E 99 B9
Pergau → Malaysia 5°23N 102°2E 121 K3
Pérgine Valsugana Italy 46°4N 11°14E 93 B8
Pérgola Italy 43°34N 12°50E 93 E9
Perham U.S.A. 46°36N 95°34W 172 B6
Perhentian, Kepulauan
 Malaysia 5°54N 102°42E 121 K4
Peri → Turkey 38°53N 39°52E 105 C8
Periam Romania 46°2N 20°52E 80 D5
Perico Argentina 24°20S 65°5W 190 A2
Pericos Mexico 25°3N 107°42W 180 B3
Périers France 49°11N 1°25W 70 C5
Périgord France 45°0N 0°40E 72 D4
Périgord-Limousin △
 France 45°40N 0°50E 72 C4
Périgueux France 45°10N 0°42E 72 C4
Perijá, Sierra de Colombia 9°30N 73°3W 186 B4
Perijá △ Venezuela 9°30N 72°55W 183 E5
Peringat Malaysia 6°2N 102°17E 121 J4
Perisher Valley
 Australia 36°27S 148°25E 153 D8
Peristera → Greece 39°15N 23°58E 98 B6
Peristerona → Cyprus 35°8N 33°5E 101 D12
Perito Moreno
 Argentina 46°36S 70°56W 192 C2
Perito Moreno △
 Argentina 47°49S 72°17W 192 C2
Peritoró Brazil 4°20S 44°18W 189 A2
Perivol = Dragovishtitsa
 Bulgaria 42°22N 22°39E 96 D6
Periyakulam India 10°5N 77°30E 127 J3
Periyar → India 10°15N 76°10E 127 J3
Periyar, L. India 9°25N 77°10E 127 K3
Periyar △ India 9°25N 77°0E 127 K3
Perkasie U.S.A. 40°22N 75°18W 175 F9
Perković Croatia 43°41N 16°10E 93 E13
Perlas, Arch. de las
 Panama 8°41N 79°7W 182 E4
Perlas, Punta de Nic. 12°30N 83°30W 182 D3
Perleberg Germany 53°5N 11°52E 76 B7

Perlez Serbia 45°11N 20°22E 80 E5
Perlis □ Malaysia 6°30N 100°15E 121 J2
Perm Russia 58°0N 56°10E 106 D6
Përmet Albania 40°15N 20°21E 96 F4
Pernambuco = Recife
 Brazil 8°0S 35°0W 189 C4
Pernambuco □ Brazil 8°0S 37°0W 189 B3
Pernambuco Abyssal Plain
 Atl. Oc. 5°0S 24°0W 56 G9
Pernatty Lagoon
 Australia 31°30S 137°12E 152 A2
Pernik Bulgaria 42°35N 23°2E 96 D7
Pernik □ Bulgaria 42°35N 23°2E 96 D7
Peron Is. Australia 13°9S 130°4E 148 B5
Peron Pen. Australia 26°0S 113°10E 149 E1
Péronne France 49°55N 2°57E 71 C9
Perosa Argentina Italy 44°58N 7°10E 92 D4
Perow Canada 54°35N 126°10W 162 C3
Perpignan France 42°42N 2°53E 72 F6
Perrine U.S.A. 25°36N 80°21W 179 K9
Perris U.S.A. 33°47N 117°14W 171 M9
Perros-Guirec France 48°49N 3°28W 70 D3
Perry Fla., U.S.A. 30°7N 83°35W 178 E6
Perry Ga., U.S.A. 32°28N 83°44W 178 D6
Perry Iowa, U.S.A. 41°51N 94°6W 172 E6
Perry N.Y., U.S.A. 42°42N 78°0W 174 D7
Perry Okla., U.S.A. 36°17N 97°14W 176 C6
Perryton U.S.A. 36°24N 100°48W 176 C4
Perryville U.S.A. 37°43N 89°52W 172 G9
Persan France 49°9N 2°16E 71 C9
Persberg Sweden 59°47N 14°15E 62 E8
Persembe Turkey 41°5N 37°46E 104 B7
Persepolis Iran 29°55N 52°50E 107 C18
Pershotravensk
 Ukraine 50°13N 27°40E 75 C14
Pershotravensk
 Ukraine 48°13N 36°7E 85 H8
Persia = Iran ■ Asia 33°0N 53°0E 129 C7
Persian Gulf Asia 27°0N 50°0E 129 E6
Perstorp Sweden 56°10N 13°25E 63 H7
Pertek Turkey 38°51N 39°19E 105 C8
Perth Australia 31°57S 115°52E 149 F2
Perth Canada 44°55N 76°15W 175 B8
Perth U.K. 56°24N 3°26W 65 E5
Perth & Kinross □ U.K. 56°45N 3°55W 65 E5
Perth Amboy U.S.A. 40°30N 74°15W 175 F10
Perth-Andover Canada 46°44N 67°42W 165 C6
Perth Basin Ind. Oc. 30°0S 108°0E 156 L2
Pertuis France 43°42N 5°30E 73 E9
Pertusato, C. France 41°21N 9°11E 73 G13
Peru Ind., U.S.A. 40°45N 86°4W 172 E10
Peru N.Y., U.S.A. 44°35N 73°32W 175 B11
Peru ■ S. Amer. 4°0S 75°0W 186 D4
Peru Basin Pac. Oc. 20°0S 95°0W 157 J18
Peru-Chile Trench
 Pac. Oc. 20°0S 72°0W 186 G3
Perugia Italy 43°7N 12°23E 93 E9
Perušić Croatia 44°40N 15°22E 93 D12
Pervomaysk Russia 54°56N 43°58E 86 D6
Pervomaysk Ukraine 48°10N 30°46E 85 H5
Pervomayskiy
 Kazakhstan 50°16N 82°0E 109 E10
Pervouralsk Russia 56°59N 59°59E 106 D6
Pésaro Italy 43°54N 12°55E 93 E9
Pésaro e Urbino □ Italy 43°45N 12°40E 93 E9
Pescadores = P'enghu Ch'üntou
 Taiwan 23°34N 119°30E 117 F12
Pescara Italy 42°28N 14°13E 93 F11
Pescara → Italy 42°28N 14°13E 93 F11
Peschanokopskoye
 Russia 46°14N 41°4E 87 G5
Péscia Italy 43°54N 10°41E 92 E7
Pescina Italy 42°2N 13°39E 93 F10
Peshawar Pakistan 34°2N 71°37E 124 B4
Peshkopi Albania 41°41N 20°25E 96 E4
Peshtera Bulgaria 42°2N 24°18E 97 D8
Peshtigo U.S.A. 45°3N 87°45W 172 C10
Peski Russia 51°14N 42°29E 86 E6
Peski Turkmenistan 38°11N 62°55E 108 E6
Pêso da Régua Portugal 41°10N 7°47W 88 D3
Pesqueira Brazil 8°20S 36°42W 189 B3
Pessac France 44°48N 0°37W 72 D3
Pest □ Hungary 47°29N 19°5E 80 C4
Pesto = Paestum Italy 40°22N 15°0E 95 B7
Pestovo Russia 58°33N 35°42E 84 D8
Pestravka Russia 52°28N 49°57E 86 D9
Petah Tiqwa Israel 32°6N 34°53E 130 C3
Petalidi Greece 36°57N 21°55E 98 E3
Petalioi Greece 38°5N 24°15E 98 D6
Petaling Jaya Malaysia 3°4N 101°42E 121 L3
Petaloudes Greece 36°18N 28°5E 101 C10
Petaluma U.S.A. 38°14N 122°39W 170 G4
Pétange Lux. 49°33N 5°55E 69 E5
Petaro Pakistan 25°31N 68°18E 124 G3
Petas Greece 39°10N 21°2E 98 B3
Petatlán Mexico 17°31N 101°16W 180 D4
Petauke Zambia 14°14S 31°20E 143 E3
Petawawa Canada 45°54N 77°17W 164 C4
Petén Itzá, L.
 Guatemala 16°58N 89°50W 182 C2
Peter I. Br. Virgin Is. 18°22N 64°35W 183 e
Peter I. Øy Antarctica 69°0S 91°0W 55 C16
Peter Pond L. Canada 55°55N 108°44W 163 B7
Peterbell Canada 48°36N 83°21W 164 C3
Peterborough
 Australia 32°58S 138°51E 152 B3
Peterborough Canada 44°20N 78°20W 174 B6
Peterborough U.K. 52°35N 0°15W 67 E7
Peterborough □ U.K. 52°35N 0°15W 67 E7
Peterculter U.K. 57°6N 2°16W 65 D6
Peterhead U.K. 57°31N 1°48W 65 D7
Peterlee U.K. 54°47N 1°20W 66 C6
Petermann ○ Australia 24°58S 130°0E 149 E4
Petermann Bjerg
 Greenland 73°7N 28°25W 57 C8
Petermann Gletscher
 Greenland 80°30N 60°0W 57 A4
Petermann Ranges
 Australia 26°0S 130°30E 149 E5
Petersburg Alaska,
 U.S.A. 56°48N 132°58W 160 F5
Petersburg Pa., U.S.A. 40°34N 78°3W 174 F6
Petersburg Va., U.S.A. 37°14N 77°24W 173 G15
Petersburg W. Va.,
 U.S.A. 39°1N 79°5W 173 F14
Petersfield U.K. 51°1N 0°56W 67 F7
Petershagen Germany 52°23N 8°58E 76 C4
Petília Policastro Italy 39°7N 16°48E 95 C9
Petilia de Aragón Spain 42°28N 1°6W 90 C3
Philadelphia Miss.,
 U.S.A. 32°46N 89°7W 177 E10

Petit-Mécatina →
 Canada 50°40N 59°30W 165 B8
Petit-Mécatina, Î. du
 Canada 50°30N 59°25W 165 B8
Petit Piton St. Lucia 13°51N 61°5W 183 f
Petit-Saguenay Canada 48°15N 70°4W 165 C5
Petit Saint Bernard, Col du
 Italy 45°40N 6°52E 73 C10
Petitcodiac Canada 45°57N 65°11W 165 C6
Petite Terre, Îles de la
 Guadeloupe 16°13N 61°9W 182 b
Petitot → Canada 60°14N 123°29W 162 A4
Petitsikapau L. Canada 54°37N 66°25W 165 B6
Petlad India 22°30N 72°45E 124 H7
Peto Mexico 20°8N 88°55W 181 C7
Petone N.Z. 41°13S 174°53E 155 B5
Petorca Chile 32°15S 70°56W 190 C1
Petoskey U.S.A. 45°22N 84°57W 173 C11
Petra Jordan 30°20N 35°22E 130 E4
Petra Spain 39°37N 3°6E 100 B10
Petra, Ostrov Russia 76°15N 118°30E 107 B12
Petra Velikogo, Zaliv
 Russia 42°40N 132°0E 112 C6
Petre, Pt. Canada 43°50N 77°9W 174 C7
Petrel = Petrer Spain 38°30N 0°46W 91 G4
Petrella, Monte Italy 41°18N 13°40E 94 A6
Petrer Spain 38°30N 0°46W 91 G4
Petreto-Bicchisano
 France 41°47N 8°58E 73 G12
Petrich Bulgaria 41°24N 23°13E 96 E7
Petrified Forest △
 U.S.A. 35°0N 109°30W 169 J9
Petrijanec Croatia 46°23N 16°17E 93 B13
Petrila Romania 45°29N 23°29E 81 E8
Petrinja Croatia 45°28N 16°18E 93 C13
Petrolândia Brazil 9°5S 38°20W 189 B3
Petrolia Canada 42°54N 82°9W 174 D2
Petrolina Brazil 9°24S 40°30W 189 B3
Petropavl Kazakhstan 54°53N 69°13E 108 D7
Petropavlovsk = Petropavl
 Kazakhstan 54°53N 69°13E 108 D7
Petropavlovsk-Kamchatskiy
 Russia 53°3N 158°43E 107 D16
Petropavlovskiy = Akhtubinsk
 Russia 48°13N 46°7E 87 F8
Petrópolis Brazil 22°33S 43°9W 191 A7
Petroşani Romania 45°28N 23°20E 81 E8
Petrova Gora Croatia 45°15N 15°45E 93 C12
Petrovac Montenegro 42°13N 18°57E 96 D2
Petrovaradin Serbia 45°16N 19°55E 80 E4
Petrovsk Russia 52°22N 45°19E 86 D7
Petrovsk-Zabaykalskiy
 Russia 51°20N 108°55E 107 D11
Petrovskaya Russia 45°25N 37°58E 85 K9
Petrozavodsk Russia 61°41N 34°20E 84 B8
Petrus Steyn S. Africa 27°38S 28°8E 145 C4
Petrusburg S. Africa 29°4S 25°26E 144 C4
Petukhovo Russia 55°6N 67°58E 108 D7
Petzeck Austria 46°57N 12°48E 78 E5
Peumo Chile 34°21S 71°12W 190 C1
Peureulak Indonesia 4°48N 97°45E 118 D1
Pevek Russia 69°41N 171°19E 107 C18
Peveragno Italy 44°20N 7°37E 92 D4
Peyrehorade France 43°34N 1°7W 72 E2
Peyruis France 44°1N 5°56E 73 D9
Pézenas France 43°28N 3°24E 72 E7
Pezinok Slovakia 48°17N 17°17E 79 C10
Pfaffenhofen Germany 48°31N 11°31E 77 G7
Pfälzerwald △ Germany 49°18N 9°55E 77 F5
Pfarrkirchen Germany 48°25N 12°56E 77 G8
Pfeffenhausen Germany 48°39N 11°58E 77 G7
Pforzheim Germany 48°52N 8°41E 77 G4
Pfullendorf Germany 47°55N 9°15E 77 H5
Pfungstadt Germany 49°48N 8°35E 77 F4
Pha Taem △ Thailand 15°32N 105°30E 120 E5
Phaestos Greece 35°2N 24°50E 101 D6
Phagwara India 31°10N 75°40E 124 D6
Phala Botswana 23°45S 26°50E 144 C4
Phalaborwa S. Africa 23°57S 31°7E 145 B5
Phalera = Phulera
 India 26°52N 75°16E 124 F6
Phalodi India 27°12N 72°24E 124 F5
Phalsbourg France 48°46N 7°15E 71 D14
Phaltan India 17°59N 74°26E 126 F2
Phaluai, Ko Thailand 9°32N 99°41E 121 b
Phan Thailand 19°28N 99°43E 120 C2
Phan Rang -Thap Cham
 Vietnam 11°34N 109°0E 121 G7
Phan Ri Cua Vietnam 11°16N 108°40E 121 G7
Phan Si Pan Vietnam 22°18N 103°46E 120 A4
Phan Thiet Vietnam 11°1N 108°9E 121 G7
Phan Thiet, Vinh
 Vietnam 10°53N 108°5E 121 G7
Phanae Greece 38°8N 25°57E 99 C7
Phanat Nikhom
 Thailand 13°27N 101°11E 120 F3
Phangan, Ko Thailand 9°45N 100°0E 121 H3
Phangnga Thailand 8°28N 98°30E 121 H2
Phangnga, Ao Thailand 8°16N 98°33E 121 a
Phanom Sarakham
 Thailand 13°45N 101°21E 120 F3
Phaphund India 26°36N 79°28E 125 F8
Pharenda India 27°5N 83°17E 125 F10
Pharr U.S.A. 26°12N 98°11W 176 H5
Phatthalung Thailand 7°39N 100°6E 121 J3
Phayam, Ko Thailand 9°45N 98°19E 121 H2
Phayao Thailand 19°11N 99°55E 120 C2
Phelps U.S.A. 42°58N 77°3W 174 D7
Phelps L. U.S.A. 35°46N 76°28W 177 D16
Phenix City U.S.A. 32°28N 85°1W 178 C4
Phet Buri = Phetchaburi
 Thailand 13°1N 99°55E 120 F2
Phetchabun Thailand 16°25N 101°8E 120 D3
Phetchabun, Thiu Khao
 Thailand 16°0N 101°20E 120 E3
Phetchaburi Thailand 13°1N 99°55E 120 F2
Phi Phi, Ko Thailand 7°45N 98°46E 121 J2
Phiafay Laos 14°48N 106°0E 120 E6
Phibun Mangsahan
 Thailand 15°14N 105°14E 120 E5
Phichai Thailand 17°22N 100°10E 120 D3
Phichit Thailand 16°26N 100°22E 120 D3
Philadelphia Miss.,
 U.S.A. 32°46N 89°7W 177 E10
Philadelphia N.Y.,
 U.S.A. 44°9N 75°43W 175 B9
Philadelphia Pa., U.S.A. 39°57N 75°9W 175 G9

Philadelphia Int. ✕ (PHL)
 U.S.A. 39°51N 75°18W 175 G9
Philip U.S.A. 44°2N 101°40W 172 C3
Philip Smith Mts.
 U.S.A. 68°0N 148°0W 166 B10
Philippi Greece 41°1N 24°16E 97 E8
Philippeville Belgium 50°12N 4°33E 69 D4
Philippi U.S.A. 39°9N 80°3W 173 F13
Philippi L. Australia 24°20S 138°55E 150 C2
Philippine Basin Pac. Oc. 17°0N 132°0E 156 F5
Philippine Sea Pac. Oc. 18°0N 125°0E 156 F4
Philippine Trench = Mindanao
 Trench Pac. Oc. 12°0N 126°6E 119 E7
Philippines ■ Asia 12°0N 123°0E 119 B6
Philippolis S. Africa 30°15S 25°16E 144 D4
Philippolis = Plovdiv
 Bulgaria 42°8N 24°44E 97 D8
Philipsburg Canada 45°2N 73°5W 175 A11
Philipsburg Mont.,
 U.S.A. 46°20N 113°18W 168 C7
Philipsburg Pa., U.S.A. 40°54N 78°13W 174 F6
Philipstown = Daingean
 Ireland 53°18N 7°17W 64 C4
Philipstown S. Africa 30°28S 24°30E 144 D3
Phillip I. Australia 38°30S 145°12E 153 D8
Phillips U.S.A. 45°42N 90°24W 172 C8
Phillipsburg Ga.,
 U.S.A. 31°25N 83°30W 178 D6
Phillipsburg Kans.,
 U.S.A. 39°45N 99°19W 172 F4
Phillipsburg N.J.,
 U.S.A. 40°42N 75°12W 175 F9
Philmont U.S.A. 42°15N 73°39W 175 D11
Philomath Ga., U.S.A. 33°44N 82°59W 178 B7
Philomath Oreg.,
 U.S.A. 44°32N 123°22W 168 D2
Phimai Thailand 15°13N 102°30E 120 E4
Phitsanulok Thailand 16°50N 100°12E 120 D3
Phnom Kulen △
 Cambodia 13°38N 104°15E 120 F5
Phnom Penh
 Cambodia 11°33N 104°55E 121 G5
Phnom Penh = Phnom Penh
 Cambodia 11°33N 104°55E 121 G5
Pho, Laem Thailand 6°55N 101°19E 121 J3
Phocis = Fokida Greece 38°30N 22°15E 98 C4
Phoenicia U.S.A. 42°5N 74°14W 175 D10
Phoenix Mauritius 20°17S 57°30E 141 d
Phoenix Ariz., U.S.A. 33°26N 112°4W 169 K7
Phoenix N.Y., U.S.A. 43°14N 76°18W 175 C8
Phoenix Is. Kiribati 3°30S 172°0W 156 H10
Phoenix Sky Harbour Int. ✕
 (PHX) U.S.A. 33°26N 112°5W 169 K7
Phoenixville U.S.A. 40°8N 75°31W 175 F9
Phon Thailand 15°49N 102°36E 120 D4
Phong → Thailand 16°23N 102°56E 120 D4
Phong Nha -Ke Bang △
 Vietnam 17°30N 106°10E 120 D6
Phong Saly Laos 21°42N 102°9E 116 G4
Phong Tho Vietnam 22°32N 103°21E 116 G4
Phonsavan Laos 19°27N 103°10E 120 C4
Phonum Thailand 8°49N 98°48E 121 H2
Phosphate Hill
 Australia 21°53S 139°58E 150 C2
Photharam Thailand 13°41N 99°51E 120 F2
Phra Nakhon Si Ayutthaya
 Thailand 14°25N 100°30E 120 E3
Phra Pradaeng
 Thailand 13°39N 100°33E 120 F3
Phra Thong, Ko Thailand 9°5N 98°17E 121 H2
Phrae Thailand 18°7N 100°9E 120 C3
Phrom Phiram
 Thailand 17°2N 100°12E 120 D3
Phrygia Turkey 38°40N 30°0E 104 C4
Phthiotis = Fthiotida
 Greece 38°50N 22°25E 98 C4
Phu Bia Laos 19°10N 103°0E 120 C4
Phu Chong -Na Yoi △
 Thailand 14°25N 105°30E 120 E5
Phu Hin Rong Kla △
 Thailand 17°0N 100°59E 120 D3
Phu Kao -Phu Phan Kham △
 Thailand 16°50N 102°31E 120 D4
Phu Kradung △
 Thailand 17°2N 101°44E 120 D3
Phu Loi Laos 20°14N 103°14E 120 B4
Phu Luang △ Thailand 17°15N 101°29E 120 D3
Phu Ly Vietnam 20°35N 105°50E 116 G5
Phu My Vietnam 14°15N 109°0E 121 E7
Phu Pha Man △
 Thailand 16°43N 101°50E 120 D3
Phu Phan △ Thailand 17°0N 103°56E 120 D4
Phu Quoc, Dao
 Vietnam 10°20N 104°0E 121 G4
Phu Sa Dok Bua △
 Thailand 16°11N 104°45E 120 D5
Phu Sang △ Thailand 19°35N 100°19E 120 C3
Phu Tho Vietnam 21°24N 105°13E 116 G5
Phu Wiang △
 Thailand 16°39N 102°23E 120 D4
Phuc Yen Vietnam 21°16N 105°45E 116 G5
Phuket Thailand 7°53N 98°24E 121 a
Phuket, Ko Thailand 8°0N 98°22E 121 a
Phul India 30°19N 75°14E 124 D6
Phulad India 26°36N 73°49E 124 G5
Phulbani India 20°28N 84°14E 125 J10
Phulchari Bangla. 25°11N 89°37E 125 G13
Phulera India 26°52N 75°16E 124 F6
Phulpur India 25°31N 82°49E 125 G10
Phun Phin Thailand 9°7N 99°12E 121 H2
Phuntsholing Bhutan 26°51N 89°23E 125 F13
Phuphrabat Thailand 17°38N 102°40E 120 D4
Phuthaditjhaba
 S. Africa 28°29S 28°48E 145 C4
Phyu = Pyu Myanmar 18°30N 96°28E 123 K20
Pia Italy 10°24S 36°25W 189 C3
Piaçabuçu Brazil 10°24S 36°25W 189 C3
Piacenza Italy 45°1N 9°40E 92 C6
Piai, Tanjung Malaysia 1°17N 103°30E 121 d
Piako → N.Z. 37°12S 175°30E 154 C4
Pian Cr. → Australia 30°2S 148°12E 153 A8
Pian-Upe ○ Uganda 1°44N 34°20E 142 B3
Piana France 42°15N 8°34E 73 F12
Piangil Australia 35°5S 143°20E 152 B6
Pianella Italy 42°24N 14°2E 93 F11
Pianosa Puglia, Italy 42°12N 15°44E 93 F12
Pianosa Toscana, Italy 42°35N 10°5E 92 F7
Piao'ertun China 41°50N 123°47E 115 C12
Piapot Canada 49°59N 109°8W 163 D7
Pias Portugal 38°1N 7°29W 89 G3

Piaseczno Poland 52°5N 21°2E 83 F8
Piaski Poland 51°8N 22°52E 83 G9
Piastów Poland 52°12N 20°48E 83 F7
Piatã Brazil 13°9S 41°48W 189 C2
Piatra Romania 43°51N 25°9E 81 G10
Piatra Craiului △ Romania 45°30N 25°12E 81 G10
Piatra Neamț Romania 46°56N 26°21E 81 D11
Piatra Olt Romania 44°22N 24°16E 81 F9
Piauí □ Brazil 7°0S 43°0W 189 B2
Piauí → Brazil 6°38S 42°42W 189 B2
Piave → Italy 45°32N 12°44E 93 C9
Piazza Ármerina Italy 37°21N 14°20E 95 E7
Pibor Post South Sudan 6°47N 33°3E 135 G12
Pic St-Loup France 43°47N 3°48E 72 E7
Pica Chile 20°35S 69°25W 188 E4
Picardie, Plaine de France 50°0N 2°0E 71 C9
Picayune U.S.A. 30°32N 89°41W 177 F10
Picerno Italy 40°38N 15°38E 95 B8
Pichhor India 25°58N 78°20E 125 G8
Pichilemu Chile 34°22S 72°0W 190 C1
Pichor India 25°11N 78°11E 124 G8
Pickerel L. Canada 48°40N 91°25W 164 C1
Pickering U.K. 54°15N 0°46W 66 C7
Pickering, Vale of U.K. 54°14N 0°45W 66 C7
Pickle Lake Canada 51°30N 90°12W 164 B1
Pickwick L. U.S.A. 35°4N 88°15W 177 D10
Pico Azores 38°28N 28°20W 134 a
Pico Bonito △ Honduras 15°34N 86°48W 182 C2
Pico Truncado Argentina 46°40S 68°0W 192 C3
Picos Brazil 7°5S 41°28W 189 B2
Picos, Pta. dos Spain 43°53N 8°88W 88 A1
Picos de Europa △ Spain 43°14N 4°59W 88 B6
Picota Peru 6°54S 76°24W 188 B2
Picton Australia 34°12S 150°34E 153 C9
Picton Canada 44°1N 77°9W 174 B7
Picton N.Z. 41°18S 174°3E 155 B9
Picton, I. Chile 55°2S 66°57W 192 E3
Pictou Canada 45°41N 62°42W 165 C7
Picture Butte Canada 49°55N 112°45W 162 D6
Pictured Rocks △ U.S.A. 46°30N 86°30W 172 B10
Picuí Brazil 6°31S 36°21W 189 B3
Picún Leufú Argentina 39°30S 69°5W 192 C3
Pidbuzh Ukraine 49°19N 23°14E 83 J10
Pidurutalagala Sri Lanka 7°10N 80°50E 127 L5
Piechowice Poland 50°51N 15°36E 83 H2
Piedimonte Matese Italy 41°22N 14°22E 95 A7
Piedmont = Piemonte □ Italy 45°0N 8°0E 92 D5
Piedmont Ala., U.S.A. 33°55N 85°37W 178 B4
Piedmont S.C., U.S.A. 34°42N 82°28W 158 F11
Piedra → Spain 41°18N 1°47W 90 D3
Piedra del Águila Argentina 40°2S 70°4W 192 B2
Piedra del Águila, Embalse Argentina 40°12S 70°4W 192 B2
Piedrabuena Spain 39°0N 4°10W 89 G6
Piedrahita Spain 40°28N 5°23W 88 E5
Piedralaves Spain 40°24N 4°27W 88 E6
Piedras, R. de las → Peru 12°30S 69°15W 188 C4
Piedras Blancas Spain 43°33N 5°58W 88 B5
Piedras Negras Mexico 28°42N 100°31W 180 B4
Piekary Śląskie Poland 50°24N 18°57E 83 H5
Pieksämäki Finland 62°18N 27°10E 60 E22
Pielinen Finland 63°15N 29°40E 60 E23
Pieljekaise △ Sweden 66°20N 16°45E 60 C17
Piemonte □ Italy 45°0N 8°0E 92 D5
Pienaarsrivier S. Africa 25°15S 28°18E 145 C4
Pieniężno Poland 54°14N 20°8E 82 D7
Pieninský △ Europe 49°25N 20°25E 79 B13
Pieńsk Poland 51°16N 15°2E 83 G2
Pienza Italy 43°4N 11°40E 92 F8
Piercefield U.S.A. 44°13N 74°35W 175 B10
Pierceland Canada 54°20N 109°46W 163 C7
Pieria Greece 40°13N 22°25E 96 F6
Pierpont U.S.A. 41°45N 80°34W 174 E4
Pierre U.S.A. 44°22N 100°21W 172 C3
Pierre-Buffière France 45°41N 1°22E 72 C5
Pierre-de-Bresse France 46°54N 5°13E 71 F12
Pierrefonds Canada 45°29N 73°51W 175 A11
Pierrefontaine-les-Varans France 47°14N 6°32E 71 E13
Pierrefort France 44°55N 2°50E 72 D6
Pierrelatte France 44°23N 4°43E 73 D8
Pierson U.S.A. 29°14N 81°28W 179 F14
Piešťany Slovakia 48°36N 17°50E 79 C10
Piesting → Austria 48°6N 16°40E 79 C9
Pieszyce Poland 50°43N 16°33E 83 H3
Piet Retief S. Africa 27°1S 30°50E 145 C5
Pietarsaari Finland 63°40N 22°43E 60 E20
Pietermaritzburg S. Africa 29°35S 30°25E 145 C5
Pietersburg = Polokwane S. Africa 23°54S 29°25E 145 B4
Pietragalla Italy 40°45N 15°53E 95 B8
Pietrasanta Italy 43°57N 10°14E 92 E7
Pietroșița Romania 45°11N 25°26E 81 E10
Pietrosul, Vf. Maramureș, Romania 47°35N 24°43E 81 C9
Pietrosul, Vf. Suceava, Romania 47°12N 25°18E 81 C10
Pieve di Cadore Italy 46°26N 12°22E 93 B9
Pieve di Teco Italy 44°3N 7°56E 92 D4
Pievepélago Italy 44°12N 10°37E 92 D7
Pigadítsa Greece 39°59N 21°23E 96 G5
Pigeon L. India 14°2N 74°20E 127 G2
Pigeon L. Canada 44°27N 78°30W 174 B6
Piges Greece 39°17N 21°25E 96 B3
Pigna Italy 43°56N 7°40E 92 D4
Pigüe Argentina 37°36S 62°25W 190 D3
Piha N.Z. 36°57S 174°28E 154 C13
Pihani India 27°36N 80°15E 125 F9
Pihlajavesi Finland 61°45N 28°45E 64 B5
Pijijiapan Mexico 15°42N 93°14W 181 D6
Pikalevo Russia 59°37N 34°0E 84 B9
Pikangikum Canada 51°49N 94°0W 163 C10
Pikes Peak U.S.A. 38°50N 105°3W 168 G11
Piketberg S. Africa 32°55S 18°40E 144 D2
Pikeville U.S.A. 37°29N 82°31W 173 G12
Pikou China 39°18N 122°22E 115 E12
Pikwitonei Canada 55°35N 97°9W 163 B9
Piła Poland 53°10N 16°48E 83 E3
Pilani India 28°22N 75°33E 124 E6
Pilar Brazil 9°36S 35°56W 189 B3

Pilar Paraguay 26°50S 58°20W 190 B4
Pilar de la Horadada Spain 37°52N 0°47W 91 H4
Pilat, Dune du France 44°35N 1°13W 72 D2
Pilat △ France 45°20N 4°30E 73 C8
Pilawa Poland 51°57N 21°32E 83 G8
Pilbara Australia 21°15S 118°16E 148 D2
Pilcomayo → Paraguay 25°21S 57°42W 190 B4
Pilea Greece 40°32N 22°59E 96 F6
Pilgrim's Rest S. Africa 24°55S 30°44E 145 B5
Pilgrimstad Sweden 62°56N 15°2E 62 B9
Pili Greece 36°50N 27°15E 99 E9
Pilibhit India 28°40N 79°50E 125 E8
Pilica → Poland 51°52N 21°17E 83 G8
Pilio, Oros Greece 39°27N 23°3E 98 B5
Pilipinas = Philippines ■ Asia 12°0N 123°0E 119 B6
Pilis Hungary 47°17N 19°35E 80 C4
Pilisvörösvár Hungary 47°38N 18°56E 80 C3
Pilkhawa India 28°43N 77°42E 124 E7
Pilliga Australia 30°21S 148°54E 151 E4
Pilos Greece 36°55N 21°42E 98 E3
Pilot Mound Canada 49°15N 98°54W 163 D9
Pilot Point U.S.A. 33°24N 96°58W 176 E6
Pilot Rock U.S.A. 45°29N 118°50W 168 D4
Pilštanj Slovenia 46°8N 15°39E 93 B12
Piltene Latvia 57°13N 21°40E 82 A8
Pilzno Poland 49°58N 21°16E 83 J8
Pima U.S.A. 32°54N 109°50W 169 K9
Pimba Australia 31°18S 136°46E 152 B2
Pimenta Bueno Brazil 11°35S 61°10W 186 F6
Pimentel Peru 6°45S 79°55W 188 B2
Pimpri Chinchwad India 18°37N 73°47E 126 E1
Pin Valley △ India 31°50N 77°50E 124 C7
Pina de Ebro Spain 41°29N 0°33W 90 D4
Pinang Malaysia 5°25N 100°15E 121 c
Pinang □ Malaysia 5°20N 100°20E 121 K3
Pinar, C. des Spain 39°53N 3°12E 100 B10
Pinar del Río Cuba 22°26N 83°40W 182 B3
Pınarbaşı Çanakkale, Turkey 39°53N 26°15E 99 B8
Pınarbaşı Kayseri, Turkey 38°43N 36°23E 104 C7
Pınarhisar Turkey 41°37N 27°30E 97 E11
Pinatubo, Mt. Phil. 15°8N 120°21E 119 A6
Pinawa Canada 50°9N 95°50W 163 C10
Pincehely Hungary 46°41N 18°27E 80 D3
Pinchang China 31°36N 107°3E 116 B6
Pincher Creek Canada 49°30N 113°57W 162 D6
Pinchi L. Canada 54°38N 124°30W 162 C4
Pinckard U.S.A. 31°19N 85°33W 178 D4
Pinckneyville U.S.A. 38°5N 89°23W 172 F9
Pińczów Poland 50°32N 20°32E 83 H7
Pind Dadan Khan Pakistan 32°36N 73°7E 109 F8
Pindar Australia 28°30S 115°47E 149 E2
Pindaré → Brazil 3°17S 44°47W 189 A2
Pindaré-Mirim Brazil 3°37S 45°21W 189 A1
Pindera Downs ○ Australia 29°24S 142°37E 151 A3
Pindi Gheb Pakistan 33°14N 72°21E 124 C5
Pindiga Nigeria 9°58N 10°53E 139 D7
Pindos △ Greece 39°52N 21°11E 98 B3
Pindos Oros Greece 40°0N 21°0E 98 B3
Pindus Mts. = Pindos Oros Greece 40°0N 21°0E 98 B3
Pine → B.C., Canada 56°8N 120°43W 162 B4
Pine → Sask., Canada 58°50N 105°38W 163 B7
Pine Bluff U.S.A. 34°13N 92°1W 176 D8
Pine Bluffs U.S.A. 41°11N 104°4W 168 F11
Pine City U.S.A. 45°50N 92°59W 172 C7
Pine Cr. → U.S.A. 41°10N 77°16W 174 E7
Pine Creek Australia 13°50S 131°50E 148 B5
Pine Falls Canada 50°34N 96°11W 163 C9
Pine Flat L. U.S.A. 36°50N 119°20W 170 J7
Pine Grove Australia 40°33N 76°23W 175 F8
Pine Hill U.S.A. 23°38S 146°57E 150 C4
Pine Hills U.S.A. 28°33N 81°27W 179 G8
Pine I. U.S.A. 26°36N 82°7W 179 J7
Pine Island Glacier Antarctica 76°0S 100°0W 55 D15
Pine Level U.S.A. 32°4N 86°4W 178 C3
Pine Mountain U.S.A. 32°49N 84°51W 178 C5
Pine Pass Canada 55°25N 122°42W 162 B4
Pine Ridge Australia 31°30S 150°28E 153 A9
Pine Ridge U.S.A. 43°2N 102°33W 172 D2
Pine River Canada 51°45N 100°30W 163 C8
Pine River U.S.A. 46°43N 94°24W 172 B6
Pine Valley U.S.A. 32°50N 116°32W 171 N10
Pinecrest U.S.A. 38°12N 120°1W 170 G6
Pineda de Mar Spain 41°37N 2°40E 90 D7
Pinedale Calif., U.S.A. 36°50N 119°48W 170 J7
Pinedale Wyo., U.S.A. 42°52N 109°52W 168 E9
Pinega → Russia 64°30N 44°19E 106 C5
Pinehouse L. Canada 55°32N 106°35W 163 B7
Pineimuta → Canada 52°8N 88°33W 164 B2
Pinellas Park U.S.A. 27°50N 82°41W 179 H7
Pinerolo Italy 44°53N 7°21E 92 D4
Pines, Akra Greece 40°5N 24°20E 97 F8
Pineville La., U.S.A. 31°19N 92°26W 176 F8
Pineville S.C., U.S.A. 33°26N 80°1W 178 B9
Pinewood U.S.A. 33°44N 80°27W 178 B9
Piney France 48°22N 4°21E 71 D11
Piney → Thailand 13°10N 100°0E 120 E3
Pingaring Australia 32°40S 118°32E 149 F2
Pingba China 26°23N 106°12E 116 D6
Pingbian China 23°0N 103°45E 116 F4
Pingchuan China 27°47N 113°38E 114 F7
Pingdingshan China 33°43N 113°27E 114 H7
Pingdu China 36°42N 119°59E 115 F10
Pingguo China 23°19N 107°21E 117 E11
Pinghai China 30°40N 121°2E 117 B13
Pingjiang China 28°45N 113°36E 117 C9
Pingle China 24°40N 110°40E 117 D8
Pingli China 32°27N 109°22E 116 A7
Pingliang China 35°35N 106°31E 114 G4
Pingluo China 38°52N 106°30E 114 E4
Pingnan Fujian, China 26°55N 119°0E 117 D12

Pingnan Guangxi Zhuangzu, China 23°33N 110°22E 117 F8
Pingquan China 41°1N 118°37E 115 D10
Pingrup Australia 33°32S 118°29E 149 F2
Pingshan China 28°39N 104°3E 116 C5
Pingtan China 25°31N 119°47E 117 E12
Pingtang China 25°49N 107°17E 116 E6
P'ingtung Taiwan 22°38N 120°30E 117 F13
Pingwu China 32°25N 104°30E 114 H3
Pingxiang Guangxi Zhuangzu, China 22°6N 106°46E 116 F6
Pingxiang Jiangxi, China 27°43N 113°48E 117 D9
Pingyao China 37°12N 112°10E 114 F7
Pingyi China 35°30N 117°35E 115 G9
Pingyin China 36°20N 116°25E 114 F9
Pingyuan Guangdong, China 24°37N 115°57E 117 E10
Pingyuan Shandong, China 37°10N 116°22E 114 F9
Pingyuanjie China 23°45N 103°48E 116 F4
Pinhal Novo Portugal 38°38N 8°55W 89 G2
Pinheiro Brazil 2°31S 45°5W 189 A1
Pinheiro Machado Brazil 31°34S 53°23W 191 C5
Pinhel Portugal 40°50N 7°1W 88 E3
Pini Indonesia 0°10N 98°40E 118 D1
Pinios → Ilia, Greece 37°48N 21°20E 98 D3
Pinios → Trikala, Greece 39°55N 22°41E 98 B4
Pinjarra Australia 32°37S 115°52E 149 F2
Pink Mountain Canada 57°3N 122°52W 162 B4
Pinkafeld Austria 47°22N 16°9E 79 D9
Pinnacle Is. = Senkaku-Shotō E. China Sea 25°45N 123°30E 113 M1
Pinnacles U.S.A. 36°25N 121°12W 170 J5
Pinnaroo Australia 35°17S 140°53E 152 C4
Pinneberg Germany 53°40N 9°48E 76 B5
Pino Hachado, Paso S. Amer. 38°39S 70°54W 192 A2
Pinon Hills U.S.A. 34°26N 117°39W 171 L9
Pinos Mexico 22°18N 101°34W 180 C4
Pinos, Mt. U.S.A. 34°49N 119°8W 171 L7
Pinos Pt. U.S.A. 36°38N 121°57W 169 H3
Pinos Puente Spain 37°15N 3°45W 89 H7
Pinrang Indonesia 3°46S 119°41E 119 E5
Pins, Pte. aux Canada 42°15N 81°51W 174 D3
Pinsk Belarus 52°10N 26°1E 75 B14
Pintados Chile 20°35S 69°40W 188 E4
Pinturas → Argentina 46°30S 70°20W 192 C2
Pinyang China 27°42N 120°31E 117 D13
Pinyug Russia 60°5N 48°0E 106 C5
Pio XII Brazil 3°53S 45°17W 189 A1
Pioche U.S.A. 37°56N 114°27W 169 H6
Piombino Italy 42°55N 10°32E 92 F7
Piombino, Canale di Italy 42°53N 10°30E 92 F7
Pioner, Ostrov Russia 79°50N 92°0E 107 B10
Pionerskiy Russia 54°56N 20°14E 82 D7
Pionki Poland 51°29N 21°28E 83 G8
Piopiotaki = Milford Sd. N.Z. 44°41S 167°47E 155 E2
Piorini, L. Brazil 3°15S 62°35W 186 D6
Piotrków Trybunalski Poland 51°23N 19°43E 83 G6
Piove di Sacco Italy 45°18N 12°2E 93 C9
Pip Iran 26°45N 60°10E 129 E9
Pipar India 26°25N 73°31E 124 F5
Pipar Road India 26°27N 73°27E 124 F5
Piparia Mad. P., India 22°45N 78°23E 124 H8
Piparia Mad. P., India 21°49N 77°37E 124 J7
Piperi Greece 39°20N 24°19E 98 B6
Pipestone U.S.A. 44°0N 96°19W 172 D5
Pipestone → Canada 52°53N 89°23W 164 B2
Pipestone Cr. → Canada 49°38N 100°15W 163 D8
Pipiriki N.Z. 39°28S 175°5E 154 F4
Piplan Pakistan 32°17N 71°21E 124 C4
Piploda India 23°37N 74°56E 124 H6
Pippingarra Australia 20°27S 118°42E 148 D2
Pipriac France 47°49N 1°58W 70 E5
Piqua U.S.A. 40°9N 84°15W 173 E11
Piquet Carneiro Brazil 5°48S 39°25W 189 B3
Piquiri → Brazil 24°3S 54°14W 191 A5
Pir Panjal Range India 32°30N 76°50E 124 C7
Pir Sohráb Iran 25°44N 60°54E 129 E9
Pira Benin 8°28N 1°48E 139 D5
Piracicaba Brazil 22°45S 47°40W 191 A6
Piracuruca Brazil 3°50S 41°50W 189 A2
Pirae Tahiti 17°31S 149°32W 155 b
Piræus = Pireas Greece 37°57N 23°42E 98 D5
Piraiévs = Pireas Greece 37°57N 23°42E 98 D5
Pirajuí Brazil 21°59S 49°29W 191 A6
Piram I. India 21°36N 72°21E 124 J5
Piran Slovenia 45°31N 13°33E 93 C10
Pirané Argentina 25°42S 59°6W 190 B4
Piranhas Brazil 9°27S 37°46W 189 B3
Pirano = Piran Slovenia 45°31N 13°33E 93 C10
Pīränshahr Iran 36°41N 45°8E 105 D11
Pirapemas Brazil 3°43S 44°14W 189 A2
Pirapora Brazil 17°18S 44°56W 187 F10
Pirawa India 24°10N 76°2E 124 G7
Pirdop Bulgaria 42°40N 24°10E 97 D8
Pireas Greece 37°57N 23°42E 98 D5
Pires do Rio Brazil 17°18S 48°17W 189 D1
Pirgi Greece 38°13N 25°59E 99 C7
Pirgos Ilia, Greece 37°40N 21°27E 98 D3
Pirgos Kriti, Greece 35°0N 25°43E 97 F9
Pirgovo Bulgaria 43°44N 25°43E 97 C9
Piribebuy Paraguay 25°26S 57°2W 190 B4
Pirimapun Indonesia 6°20S 138°24E 119 F9
Pirin △ Bulgaria 41°48N 23°22E 96 E7
Pirin Planina Bulgaria 41°40N 23°30E 96 E7
Pirineos = Pyrénées Europe 42°45N 0°18E 72 F4
Piripiri Brazil 4°15S 41°46W 189 A2
Pirlangimpi Australia 11°24S 130°26E 148 B5
Pirmasens Germany 49°12N 7°36E 77 D3
Pirna Germany 50°57N 13°56E 76 C9
Pirot Serbia 43°9N 22°33E 80 D6
Piru Indonesia 3°4S 128°12E 119 E7
Piru U.S.A. 34°25N 118°48W 171 L8
Piryatin = Pyryatyn Ukraine 50°15N 32°25E 86 G7
Pisa Italy 43°43N 10°23E 92 E7
Pisa → Poland 53°14N 21°52E 83 E8
Pisa, Firenze ✈ (PSA) Italy 43°40N 10°22E 92 E7
Pisa Ra. Peru 13°25S 71°50W 188 C3
Pisagua Chile 19°40S 70°15W 188 D3

Pisarovina Croatia 45°35N 15°50E 93 C12
Pisco Peru 13°50S 76°12W 188 C2
Piscu Romania 45°30N 27°43E 81 E12
Pishan China 37°30N 78°33E 109 E9
Pishchanka Ukraine 48°12N 28°54E 81 B13
Pishin Iran 26°6N 61°47E 129 E9
Pishin Pakistan 30°35N 67°0E 124 D2
Pishin Lora → Pakistan 29°9N 64°5E 124 E1
Pishion Indonesia 5°8S 121°53E 119 F6
Pisidia Turkey 37°30N 31°0E 104 D4
Pismo Beach U.S.A. 35°9N 120°38W 171 K6
Piso, L. Liberia 6°50N 11°15W 138 D2
Pisogne Italy 45°45N 10°10E 92 C7
Pissila Burkina Faso 13°7N 0°50W 139 C4
Pissis, Cerro Argentina 27°45S 68°48W 190 B2
Pisses France 44°19N 0°49W 72 D3
Pissouri Cyprus 34°40N 32°42E 101 E11
Pisticci Italy 40°23N 16°33E 95 B9
Pistóia Italy 43°55N 10°54E 92 E7
Pistol B. Canada 62°25N 92°37W 163 A10
Pisuerga → Spain 41°33N 4°52W 88 D6
Pisz Poland 53°38N 21°49E 82 E8
Pita Guinea 11°5N 12°15W 138 C2
Pitangui Brazil 19°40S 44°54W 189 D2
Pitarpunga L. Australia 34°24S 143°30E 152 C5
Pitch L. Trin. & Tob. 10°1N 61°39W 187 K15
Piteå Sweden 65°20N 21°25E 60 D19
Piteälven → Sweden 65°20N 21°25E 60 D19
Piterka Russia 50°41N 47°29E 86 E8
Pitești Romania 44°52N 24°54E 81 E9
Pithapuram India 17°10N 82°15E 126 F6
Pithara Australia 30°20S 116°35E 149 F2
Pithio Greece 41°24N 26°40E 97 E10
Pithora India 21°16N 82°31E 126 D6
Pithoragarh India 29°35N 80°13E 125 E9
Pithoro Pakistan 25°31N 69°23E 124 G3
Pitigliano Italy 42°38N 11°40E 93 F8
Pitkyaranta Russia 61°34N 31°37E 84 B6
Pitlochry U.K. 56°42N 3°44W 65 E5
Pitrufquén Chile 38°59S 72°39W 192 A2
Pitsilia Cyprus 34°55N 33°0E 101 E12
Pitsunda = Bichvinta Georgia 43°9N 40°21E 87 J5
Pitt I. Canada 53°30N 129°50W 162 C3
Pitti I. India 10°50N 72°38E 127 J1
Pittsburg Calif., U.S.A. 38°2N 121°53W 170 G5
Pittsburg Kans., U.S.A. 37°25N 94°42W 172 G6
Pittsburg Tex., U.S.A. 33°0N 94°59W 176 E7
Pittsburgh U.S.A. 40°26N 79°58W 174 E5
Pittsfield Maine, U.S.A. 44°47N 69°23W 173 C19
Pittsfield Ill., U.S.A. 39°36N 90°49W 172 F8
Pittsfield Mass., U.S.A. 42°27N 73°15W 175 D11
Pittsfield N.H., U.S.A. 43°18N 71°20W 175 C13
Pittston U.S.A. 41°19N 75°47W 175 E9
Pittsview U.S.A. 32°11N 85°10W 178 D4
Pittsworth Australia 27°41S 151°37E 151 D5
Pituri → Australia 22°35S 138°30E 150 C2
Piumhi Brazil 20°28S 45°58W 189 E1
Piura Peru 5°15S 80°38W 188 B1
Piura □ Peru 5°10S 80°0W 188 B1
Piuthan Nepal 28°7N 82°56E 125 E10
Piva → Montenegro 43°20N 18°50E 96 C2
Pixian China 30°48N 103°52E 116 B4
Pixley U.S.A. 35°58N 119°18W 170 K7
Pizarra Spain 36°36N 4°42W 89 J6
Pizhou = Pei Xian China 34°44N 116°55E 114 G9
Pizhou China 34°18N 117°57E 115 G9
Pizzo Italy 38°44N 16°10E 95 D9
Placentia Canada 47°20N 54°0W 165 C9
Placentia B. Canada 47°0N 54°40W 165 C9
Placerville U.S.A. 38°44N 120°48W 170 G6
Placetas Cuba 22°15N 79°44W 182 B4
Plácido de Castro Brazil 10°20S 67°11W 188 C4
Plačkovica Macedonia 41°45N 22°30E 96 E6
Plaine des Jarres Laos 19°27N 103°10E 120 C4
Plainfield N.J., U.S.A. 40°37N 74°25W 175 F10
Plainfield Ohio, U.S.A. 40°13N 81°43W 174 F3
Plainfield Vt., U.S.A. 44°17N 72°26W 175 B12
Plains Mont., U.S.A. 47°28N 114°53W 168 C6
Plains Tex., U.S.A. 33°11N 102°50W 176 E3
Plainview Nebr., U.S.A. 42°21N 97°47W 172 D5
Plainview Tex., U.S.A. 34°11N 101°43W 176 E4
Plainwell U.S.A. 42°27N 85°38W 173 D11
Plaisance France 43°36N 0°3E 72 E4
Plaistow U.S.A. 42°50N 71°6W 175 D13
Plaka Greece 40°0N 25°24E 99 B7
Plaka, Akra Greece 35°11N 26°19E 101 D8
Plakenska Planina Macedonia 41°14N 21°2E 96 E5
Planá Czechia 49°50N 12°44E 78 B5
Plana Cays Bahamas 22°38N 73°30W 183 B5
Planada U.S.A. 37°16N 120°19W 170 H6
Planchón Peru 12°14S 69°11W 188 C4
Plandiște Serbia 45°16N 21°10E 80 B5
Plano U.S.A. 33°1N 96°42W 176 E6
Plant City U.S.A. 28°1N 82°7W 179 G7
Plantation U.S.A. 26°7N 80°14W 179 J9
Plaquemine U.S.A. 30°17N 91°14W 176 F9
Plasencia Spain 40°3N 6°8W 88 E4
Plaški Croatia 45°4N 15°22E 93 C12
Plast Russia 54°22N 60°50E 106 D11
Plaster City U.S.A. 32°47N 115°51W 171 N11
Plaster Rock Canada 46°53N 67°22W 165 C6
Plastun Russia 44°45N 136°19E 110 B8
Plasy Czechia 49°56N 13°24E 78 B6
Plata, Río de la → S. Amer. 34°45S 57°30W 190 D4
Plátani → Italy 37°23N 13°16E 94 E6
Platanos Greece 35°28N 23°33E 101 D5
Plateau □ Nigeria 8°30N 9°0E 139 D6
Platí, Akra Greece 40°27N 24°0E 97 F8
Platja d'Aro Spain 41°49N 3°4E 92 D8
Plato Colombia 9°47N 74°47W 186 B4
Platte U.S.A. 43°23N 98°51W 172 D4
Platte → Mo., U.S.A. 39°16N 94°50W 172 F6
Platte → Nebr., U.S.A. 41°4N 95°53W 172 E6
Platteville U.S.A. 42°44N 90°29W 172 D8
Plattling Germany 48°46N 12°53E 77 G8
Plattsburgh U.S.A. 44°42N 73°28W 175 B11
Plattsmouth U.S.A. 41°1N 95°53W 172 E6
Plau Germany 53°27N 12°16E 76 B8
Plauen Germany 50°30N 12°8E 76 C8

Plauer See Germany 53°28N 12°17E 76 B8
Plav Montenegro 42°38N 19°57E 96 D3
Plavinas Latvia 56°35N 25°46E 84 D3
Plavnica Montenegro 42°20N 19°13E 96 D3
Plavno Croatia 44°9N 16°10E 93 D13
Plavsk Russia 53°40N 37°18E 84 F9
Playa Blanca Canary Is. 28°51N 13°50W 100 F6
Playa de las Americas Canary Is. 28°5N 16°43W 100 F3
Playa de Mogán Canary Is. 27°48N 15°47W 100 G4
Playa del Carmen Mexico 20°37N 87°4W 181 C7
Playa del Inglés Canary Is. 27°45N 15°33W 100 G4
Playgreen L. Canada 54°0N 98°15W 163 C9
Pleasant Bay Canada 46°51N 60°48W 165 C7
Pleasant Hill U.S.A. 38°47N 94°16W 172 F6
Pleasant Mount U.S.A. 41°44N 75°26W 175 E9
Pleasanton Calif., U.S.A. 37°39N 121°52W 170 H5
Pleasanton Tex., U.S.A. 28°58N 98°29W 176 G5
Pleasantville N.J., U.S.A. 39°24N 74°32W 173 F16
Pleasantville Pa., U.S.A. 41°35N 79°34W 174 E5
Pléaux France 45°8N 2°13E 72 C6
Plei Ku Vietnam 13°57N 108°0E 120 F7
Plélan-le-Grand France 48°0N 2°7W 70 D4
Pleniţa Romania 44°14N 23°10E 81 F8
Plenty → Australia 23°25S 136°31E 150 C2
Plenty, B. of N.Z. 37°45S 177°0E 154 D6
Plentywood U.S.A. 48°47N 104°34W 168 B11
Plérin France 48°32N 2°46W 70 D4
Pleshcheyevo Ozero ○ Russia 56°45N 38°50E 84 D10
Plessisville Canada 46°14N 71°47W 165 C5
Plestin-les-Grèves France 48°40N 3°39W 70 D3
Pleszew Poland 51°53N 17°47E 83 G4
Pleternica Croatia 45°17N 17°48E 80 G2
Plétipi, L. Canada 51°44N 70°6W 165 B5
Pleven Bulgaria 43°26N 24°37E 97 C8
Pleven □ Bulgaria 43°26N 24°37E 97 C8
Plevna Canada 44°58N 76°59W 174 B8
Plitvice Lakes = Plitvička Jezera △ Croatia 44°54N 15°35E 93 D12
Plitvička Jezera △ Croatia 44°54N 15°35E 93 D12
Plješevica Croatia 44°45N 15°45E 93 D12
Pljevlja Montenegro 43°21N 19°21E 96 C3
Ploče Croatia 43°4N 17°26E 93 E14
Plock Poland 52°32N 19°40E 83 F6
Plöckenpass Italy 46°37N 12°57E 93 B9
Plöckenstein Germany 48°46N 13°51E 77 G9
Ploemeur France 47°44N 3°26W 70 E3
Ploërmel France 47°55N 2°26W 70 E4
Ploiești Romania 44°57N 26°5E 81 F11
Plomari Greece 38°59N 26°22E 99 C8
Plombières-les-Bains France 47°58N 6°27E 71 E13
Plomin Croatia 45°8N 14°10E 93 C11
Plonge, Lac la Canada 55°8N 107°20W 163 B7
Płońsk Poland 52°37N 20°21E 83 F7
Plopeni Romania 45°4N 25°59E 81 E10
Plopișului, Munții Romania 47°5N 22°30E 80 C7
Ploty Poland 53°48N 15°18E 82 E2
Plouaret France 48°37N 3°28W 70 D3
Plouay France 47°55N 3°21W 70 E3
Ploučnice → Czechia 50°46N 14°13E 78 A7
Ploudalmézeau France 48°34N 4°41W 70 D2
Plouescat France 48°40N 4°0W 70 D2
Plougastel-Daoulas France 48°22N 4°17W 70 D2
Plouguerneau France 48°36N 4°30W 70 D2
Plouha France 48°41N 2°57W 70 D4
Plouhinec France 48°0N 4°29W 70 E2
Plovdiv Bulgaria 42°8N 24°44E 97 D8
Plovdiv □ Bulgaria 42°8N 24°44E 97 D8
Plover Cove Res. China 22°28N 114°15E 111 a
Plum U.S.A. 40°29N 79°47W 174 F5
Plum I. U.S.A. 41°11N 72°12W 175 E12
Plumas U.S.A. 39°45N 120°4W 170 F6
Plummer U.S.A. 47°20N 116°53W 168 C5
Plumridge Lakes Australia 29°26S 125°16E 149 E4
Plumtree Zimbabwe 20°27S 27°55E 143 G2
Plunge Lithuania 55°53N 21°59E 82 C8
Pluvigner France 47°46N 3°1W 70 E3
Plužine Montenegro 43°8N 18°51E 96 C2
Plymouth Trin. & Tob. 11°14N 60°48W 187 J16
Plymouth U.K. 50°22N 4°10W 67 G3
Plymouth Ind., U.S.A. 41°21N 86°19W 172 E10
Plymouth Mass., U.S.A. 41°57N 70°40W 175 E14
Plymouth N.C., U.S.A. 35°52N 76°43W 177 D16
Plymouth N.H., U.S.A. 43°46N 71°41W 175 C13
Plymouth Pa., U.S.A. 41°14N 75°57W 175 E9
Plymouth Wis., U.S.A. 43°45N 87°59W 172 D10
Plympton-Wyoming = Wyoming Canada 42°57N 82°7W 174 D2
Plynlimon = Pumlumon Fawr U.K. 52°28N 3°46W 67 E4
Plyusa Russia 58°23N 29°27E 84 C5
Plyussa → Russia 59°4N 28°6E 84 C5
Plzeň Czechia 49°45N 13°22E 78 B6
Plzeňský □ Czechia 49°35N 13°0E 78 B6
Pmere Nyente Australia 24°15S 136°10E 150 C2
Pniewy Poland 52°31N 16°16E 83 F3
Pô Burkina Faso 11°14N 1°5W 139 C4
Po → Italy 44°57N 12°4E 93 C9
Po, Foci del Italy 44°55N 12°30E 93 C10
Pô, Parc National de △ Burkina Faso 11°25N 1°5W 139 C4
Po Hai = Bo Hai China 39°0N 119°0E 115 E10
Po Toi China 22°10N 114°16E 111 a
Pobé Benin 7°0N 2°56E 139 D5
Pobé Burkina Faso 13°53N 1°42W 139 C4
Pobeda Russia 65°12N 146°12E 107 C15
Pobedy, Pik Asia 42°0N 79°58E 108 D7
Pobiedziska Poland 52°29N 17°11E 83 F4
Poblet, Monasterio de Spain 41°22N 1°4E 90 D6

Pobra de Trives Spain 42°20N 7°10W 88 C3
Pocahontas Ark., U.S.A. 36°16N 90°58W 177 C9
Pocahontas Iowa, U.S.A. 42°44N 94°40W 172 D6
Pocatello U.S.A. 42°52N 112°27W 168 E7
Počátky Czechia 49°15N 15°14E 78 B8
Pochep Russia 52°58N 33°29E 85 F7
Pochinki Russia 54°41N 44°59E 86 C7
Pochinok Russia 54°28N 32°29E 84 E7
Pöchlarn Austria 48°12N 15°12E 78 C8
Pocinhos Brazil 7°4S 36°3W 189 B3
Pocking Germany 48°23N 13°19E 77 G9
Poções Brazil 14°31S 40°21W 189 C2
Pocomoke City U.S.A. 38°5N 75°34W 173 F16
Poços de Caldas Brazil 21°50S 46°33W 191 A6
Podbořany Czechia 50°14N 13°25E 78 A6
Poddębice Poland 51°54N 18°58E 83 G5
Poděbrady Czechia 50°9N 15°8E 78 A8
Podensac France 44°40N 0°22W 72 D3
Podenzano Italy 44°57N 9°41E 92 D6
Podgorač Croatia 45°27N 18°13E 80 E3
Podgorica Montenegro 42°30N 19°19E 96 D3
Podgorie Albania 40°49N 20°48E 96 E4
Podile India 15°37N 79°37E 127 G4
Podlaská Vysochyna Ukraine 49°0N 28°0E 81 B13
Podkarpackie □ Poland 50°0N 22°0E 83 H9
Podkova Bulgaria 41°24N 25°24E 97 E9
Podlabača Croatia 44°37N 15°47E 93 D12
Podlaskie □ Poland 53°10N 23°0E 83 E10
Podoleni Romania 46°46N 26°39E 81 D11
Podolinec Slovakia 49°16N 20°31E 79 B13
Podolsk Russia 55°25N 37°30E 84 E13
Podor Senegal 16°40N 15°2W 138 B1
Podporozhye Russia 60°55N 34°2E 84 B10
Podu Iloaiei Romania 47°13N 27°16E 81 C12
Podu Turcului Romania 46°11N 27°25E 81 D12
Podujevo = Besianë Kosovo 42°54N 21°10E 96 D5
Podyjí △ Czechia 48°51N 15°57E 78 C8
Poel Germany 54°0N 11°25E 76 B6
Pofadder S. Africa 29°10S 19°22E 144 C2
Poggiardo Italy 40°3N 18°23E 95 B11
Poggibonsi Italy 43°28N 11°9E 92 E8
Pöggio Mirteto Italy 42°16N 12°41E 93 F9
Pogoanele Romania 44°55N 27°0E 81 F12
Pogorzela Poland 51°50N 17°12E 83 G4
Pogradec Albania 40°54N 20°37E 96 E4
Pogranichnyy Russia 44°25N 131°24E 112 B5
Poh Indonesia 0°46S 122°51E 119 E6
Pohang S. Korea 36°1N 129°23E 115 F15
Pohjanmaa □ Finland 62°58N 22°50E 60 E20
Pohnpei Micronesia 6°55N 158°10E 156 G7
Pohořelice Czechia 48°59N 16°31E 79 C9
Pohorje Slovenia 46°30N 15°0E 93 B12
Pohri India 25°32N 77°22E 124 G6
Poiana Mare Romania 43°57N 23°5E 80 G8
Poiana Ruscăi, Munții Romania 45°45N 22°25E 80 E7
Poiana Stampei Romania 47°19N 25°7E 81 C10
Poinsett, C. Antarctica 65°42S 113°18E 55 C8
Point Arena U.S.A. 38°55N 123°41W 170 G3
Point Baker U.S.A. 56°21N 133°37W 162 B2
Point Calimere India 10°17N 79°49E 127 J4
Point Fortin Trin. & Tob. 10°10N 61°42W 187 K15
Point Hope U.S.A. 68°21N 166°47W 166 B6
Point L. Canada 65°15N 113°4W 160 D9
Point Lisas Trin. & Tob. 10°24N 61°29W 187 K15
Point Pedro Sri Lanka 9°50N 80°15E 127 K5
Point Pelee △ Canada 41°57N 82°31W 174 E2
Point Pleasant N.J., U.S.A. 40°5N 74°4W 175 F10
Point Pleasant W. Va., U.S.A. 38°51N 82°8W 173 F12
Point Reyes △ U.S.A. 38°10N 122°55W 170 G4
Pointe-à-Pitre Guadeloupe 16°15N 61°32W 182 b
Pointe-au-Pic = La Malbaie Canada 47°40N 70°10W 165 C5
Pointe-Claire Canada 45°26N 73°50W 175 A11
Pointe-Gatineau Canada 45°27N 75°41W 175 A9
Pointe-Noire Congo 4°48S 11°53E 142 E2
Pointe-Noire Guadeloupe 16°14N 61°47W 182 b
Poio = O Convento Spain 42°28N 8°41W 88 C2
Poipet Cambodia 13°39N 102°33E 120 F4
Poirino Italy 44°56N 7°48E 92 D4
Poisonbush Ra. Australia 22°30S 121°30E 148 D3
Poissonnier Pt. Australia 19°57S 119°10E 148 D2
Poitiers France 46°35N 0°20E 70 F7
Poitou France 46°40N 0°10W 72 B3
Poix-de-Picardie France 49°47N 1°58E 71 C8
Poix-Terron France 49°39N 4°38E 71 C11
Pojoaque U.S.A. 35°54N 106°1W 169 J11
Pokaran India 27°0N 71°50E 124 F4
Pokataroo Australia 29°30S 148°36E 151 D4
Pokhara Nepal 28°14N 83°58E 125 E10
Pokhvistnevo Russia 53°36N 52°6E 86 D11
Poko Dem. Rep. of the Congo 3°7N 26°52E 142 D5
Pokrovka = Kyzyl-Suu Kyrgyzstan 42°20N 78°0E 109 D9
Pokrovsk Russia 61°29N 129°0E 107 C13
Pokrovskoye Russia 47°25N 38°54E 85 J10
Pol-e Dokhtar Iran 33°9N 47°42E 105 E11
Pol-e Zahāb Iran 34°27N 45°51E 105 E11
Pola = Pula Croatia 44°54N 13°57E 93 D10
Pola Russia 57°55N 32°0E 84 D7
Pola de Allande Spain 43°16N 6°37W 88 B4
Pola de Lena Spain 43°9N 5°49W 88 B5
Pola de Siero Spain 43°24N 5°39W 88 B5
Pola de Somiedo Spain 43°6N 6°15W 88 B4
Polacca U.S.A. 35°50N 110°23W 169 J8
Poland ■ Europe 52°0N 20°0E 83 G8
Polanica-Zdrój Poland 50°24N 16°32E 83 H3
Polaniec Poland 50°26N 21°17E 83 H8
Polar Bear △ Canada 55°0N 83°45W 164 A3
Polatlı Turkey 39°36N 32°9E 104 C5
Polatsk Belarus 55°30N 28°50E 84 D5
Polavaram India 17°15N 81°38E 126 F5
Polcura Chile 37°17S 71°43W 190 D1

Połczyn-Zdrój *Poland* 53°47N 16°5E **82** E3
Poldasht *Iran* 39°20N 45°4E **105** C11
Poleski △ *Poland* 51°29N 23°5E **83** G10
Polessk *Russia* 54°50N 21°8E **82** D8
Polesye = Pripet Marshes
Europe 52°10N 27°10E **75** B15
Polgar *Hungary* 47°54N 21°6E **80** C6
Poli *Cameroon* 8°34N 13°15E **139** C7
Policastro, G. di *Italy* 40°0N 15°35E **95** C8
Police *Poland* 53°33N 14°33E **82** E1
Police, Pte. *Seychelles* 4°51S 55°32E **141** b
Polichnitos *Greece* 39°6N 26°10E **99** B8
Polička *Czechia* 49°43N 16°15E **79** B9
Policoro *Italy* 40°13N 16°41E **95** B9
Poliegos *Greece* 36°45N 24°38E **98** E6
Poligiros *Greece* 40°23N 23°25E **96** F7
Polignano a Mare *Italy* 41°0N 17°13E **95** A9
Poligny *France* 46°50N 5°42E **71** F12
Polillo Is. *Phil.* 14°56N 122°0E **119** B6
Polis *Cyprus* 35°2N 32°26E **101** D11
Polistena *Italy* 38°24N 16°4E **95** D9
Polk *U.S.A.* 41°22N 79°56W **174** E5
Polkowice *Poland* 51°29N 16°3E **83** G3
Polla *Italy* 40°31N 15°29E **95** B8
Pollachi *India* 10°35N 77°0E **127** J3
Pollença *Spain* 39°54N 3°1E **100** B10
Pollença, B. de *Spain* 39°53N 3°8E **100** B10
Póllica *Italy* 40°11N 15°3E **95** B8
Pollino, Mte. *Italy* 39°55N 16°11E **95** C9
Pollino △ *Italy* 40°0N 16°12E **95** C9
Polna *Russia* 58°31N 28°5E **84** C5
Polnovat *Russia* 63°50N 65°54E **106** C7
Pology *Ukraine* 47°29N 36°15E **85** J9
Polokwane *S. Africa* 23°54S 29°25E **145** B4
Polokwane ➝ *S. Africa* 22°25S 30°5E **145** B5
Polonnaruwa *Sri Lanka* 7°56N 81°0E **127** L5
Polonne *Ukraine* 50°6N 27°30E **75** C14
Polonnoye = Polonne
Ukraine 50°6N 27°30E **75** C14
Polski Trambesh
Bulgaria 43°20N 25°38E **97** C9
Polsko Kosovo *Bulgaria* 43°23N 25°38E **97** C9
Polson *U.S.A.* 47°41N 114°9W **168** C6
Poltár *Slovakia* 48°26N 19°48E **79** C12
Poltava *Ukraine* 49°35N 34°35E **85** H8
Poltava □ *Ukraine* 50°15N 33°15E **85** G7
Põltsamaa *Estonia* 58°39N 25°58E **84** C3
Polunochnoye *Russia* 60°52N 60°25E **106** C7
Polur *India* 12°32N 79°11E **127** H4
Põlva *Estonia* 58°3N 27°3E **84** C4
Polyana *Ukraine* 48°38N 22°58E **80** B7
Polyarny *Russia* 69°8N 33°20E **60** B25
Polyarnyye Zori *Russia* 67°22N 32°30E **60** C25
Polykastro *Greece* 41°0N 22°34E **96** E6
Polynesia *Pac. Oc.* 10°0S 162°0W **157** F11
Polynésie française = French
Polynesia ☑ *Pac. Oc.* 20°0S 145°0W **157** J13
Pomabamba *Peru* 8°50S 77°28W **188** B2
Pomarance *Italy* 43°18N 10°52E **92** E7
Pombal *Brazil* 6°45S 37°50W **189** B3
Pombal *Portugal* 39°55N 8°40W **88** F2
Pombia *Greece* 35°0N 24°51E **101** E6
Pomene *Mozam.* 22°53S 35°33E **145** B6
Pomeroy *Ohio, U.S.A.* 39°2N 82°2W **173** F12
Pomeroy *Wash.,*
U.S.A. 46°28N 117°36W **168** C5
Pomézia *Italy* 41°40N 12°30E **94** A5
Pomichna *Ukraine* 48°13N 31°36E **85** H6
Pomona *Australia* 26°22S 152°52E **151** D5
Pomona *U.S.A.* 34°4N 117°45W **171** L9
Pomona Park *U.S.A.* 29°30N 81°36W **179** F8
Pomorie *Bulgaria* 42°32N 27°41E **97** D11
Pomorskie □ *Poland* 54°30N 18°0E **82** D5
Pomorskie, Pojezierze
Poland 53°40N 16°37E **82** E3
Pomos *Cyprus* 35°9N 32°33E **101** D11
Pomos, C. *Cyprus* 35°10N 32°33E **101** D11
Pompano Beach *U.S.A.* 26°14N 80°7W **179** J9
Pompei *Italy* 40°45N 14°30E **95** B7
Pompey *France* 48°46N 6°6E **71** D13
Pompeys Pillar
U.S.A. 45°59N 107°57W **168** D10
Pompeys Pillar ⌂
U.S.A. 46°0N 108°0W **168** D10
Pompton Lakes *U.S.A.* 41°0N 74°17W **175** F10
Ponape = Pohnpei
Micronesia 6°55N 158°10E **156** G7
Ponask L. *Canada* 54°0N 92°41W **164** B1
Ponca *U.S.A.* 42°34N 96°43W **172** D5
Ponca City *U.S.A.* 36°42N 97°5W **176** C6
Ponce *Puerto Rico* 18°1N 66°37W **183** d
Ponce de Leon *U.S.A.* 30°44N 85°56W **178** E4
Ponce de Leon B.
U.S.A. 25°15N 81°10W **179** K8
Ponchatoula *U.S.A.* 30°26N 90°26W **177** F9
Poncheville, L. *Canada* 50°10N 76°55W **164** B4
Pond *U.S.A.* 35°43N 119°20W **171** K7
Pond Inlet *Canada* 72°40N 77°0W **161** C16
Pondicherry = Puducherry
India 11°59N 79°50E **127** J4
Ponds, I. of *Canada* 53°27N 55°52W **165** B8
Ponferrada *Spain* 42°32N 6°35W **88** C4
Poniatowa *Poland* 51°11N 22°3E **83** G9
Poniec *Poland* 51°48N 16°50E **83** G3
Ponikva *Slovenia* 46°16N 15°26E **93** B12
Ponnaiyar ➝ *India* 11°50N 79°45E **127** J4
Ponnani *India* 10°45N 75°59E **127** J2
Ponneri *India* 13°20N 80°15E **127** H5
Ponnuru *India* 16°5N 80°34E **127** F5
Ponoka *Canada* 52°42N 113°40W **162** C6
Ponorogo *Indonesia* 7°52S 111°27E **119** G14
Pons = Ponts *Spain* 41°55N 1°12E **90** D6
Pons *France* 45°35N 0°34W **72** C3
Ponsul ➝ *Portugal* 39°40N 7°31W **88** F3
Pont-à-Mousson *France* 48°54N 6°1E **71** D13
Pont-Audemer *France* 49°21N 0°30E **70** C7
Pont-Aven *France* 47°51N 3°47W **70** E3
Pont Canavese *Italy* 45°25N 7°36E **92** C4
Pont-d'Ain *France* 46°3N 5°21E **71** F12
Pont-de-Roide *France* 47°23N 6°45E **71** E13
Pont-de-Salars *France* 44°18N 2°44E **72** D6
Pont-de-Vaux *France* 46°26N 4°56E **71** F11
Pont-de-Veyle *France* 46°17N 4°53E **71** F11
Pont-du-Château *France* 45°47N 3°15E **71** G10
Pont du Gard *France* 43°57N 4°32E **73** E8
Pont-l'Abbé *France* 47°52N 4°15W **70** E2
Pont-l'Évêque *France* 49°18N 0°11E **70** C7
Pont-St-Esprit *France* 44°16N 4°40E **73** D8
Pont-St-Martin *Italy* 45°36N 7°48E **92** C4
Pont-Ste-Maxence *France* 49°18N 2°36E **71** C9
Pont-sur-Yonne *France* 48°18N 3°10E **71** D10
Ponta Delgada *Azores* 37°44N 25°40W **134** a
Ponta do Sol *Madeira* 32°42N 17°7W **100** D2
Ponta Grossa *Brazil* 25°7S 50°10W **191** B5
Ponta Porã *Brazil* 22°20S 55°35W **191** A4
Pontacq *France* 43°11N 0°8W **72** E3
Pontailler-sur-Saône
France 47°13N 5°25E **71** E12
Pontal ➝ *Brazil* 9°8S 40°12W **189** B2
Pontardawe *U.K.* 51°43N 3°51W **67** F3
Pontarlier *France* 46°54N 6°20E **71** F13
Pontassieve *Italy* 43°46N 11°26E **93** E8
Pontaumur *France* 45°52N 2°40E **72** C6
Pontcharra *France* 45°26N 6°1E **73** C10
Pontchartrain, L. *U.S.A.* 30°5N 90°5W **177** F9
Pontchâteau *France* 47°25N 2°5W **70** E4
Ponte Alta, Serra do
Brazil 19°42S 47°40W **189** D1
Ponte Alta do Norte
Brazil 10°45S 47°34W **189** C1
Ponte da Barca *Portugal* 41°48N 8°25W **88** D2
Ponte de Lima *Portugal* 41°46N 8°35W **88** D2
Ponte de Sor *Portugal* 39°17N 8°1W **89** F2
Ponte dell'Ólio *Italy* 44°52N 9°39E **92** D6
Ponte di Legno *Italy* 46°16N 10°31E **92** B7
Ponte do Pungué
Mozam. 19°30S 34°33E **143** F3
Ponte-Leccia *France* 42°28N 9°13E **73** F13
Ponte nelle Alpi *Italy* 46°11N 12°16E **93** B9
Ponte Nova *Brazil* 20°25S 42°54W **189** E2
Ponte Vedra Beach
U.S.A. 30°15N 81°23W **178** E8
Ponteareas *Spain* 42°10N 8°28W **88** C2
Pontebba *Italy* 46°30N 13°18E **93** B10
Ponteceso *Spain* 43°15N 8°54W **88** B2
Pontecorvo *Italy* 41°27N 13°40E **94** A6
Pontedeume *Spain* 43°24N 8°10W **88** B2
Ponteix *Canada* 49°46N 107°29W **163** D7
Pontevedra *Spain* 42°26N 8°40W **88** C2
Pontevedra □ *Spain* 42°25N 8°39W **88** C2
Pontevedra, R. de ➝
Spain 42°22N 8°45W **88** C2
Pontevico *Italy* 45°16N 10°5E **92** C7
Pontiac *Ill., U.S.A.* 40°53N 88°38W **172** E9
Pontiac *Mich., U.S.A.* 42°38N 83°18W **173** D12
Pontian Kechil *Malaysia* 1°29N 103°23E **121** d
Pontianak *Indonesia* 0°3S 109°15E **118** E3
Pontine Is. = Ponziane, Ísole
Italy 40°55N 12°57E **94** B5
Pontine Mts. = Kuzey Anadolu
Dağları *Turkey* 41°0N 36°45E **104** B7
Pontínia *Italy* 41°25N 13°2E **94** A6
Pontivy *France* 48°5N 2°58W **70** D4
Pontoise *France* 49°3N 2°5E **71** C9
Ponton ➝ *Canada* 58°27N 116°11W **162** B5
Pontorson *France* 48°34N 1°30W **70** D5
Pontrémoli *Italy* 44°22N 9°53E **92** D6
Pontrieux *France* 48°42N 3°10W **70** D3
Ponts *Spain* 41°55N 1°12E **90** D6
Pontypool *Canada* 44°6N 78°38W **174** B6
Pontypool *U.K.* 51°42N 3°2W **67** F4
Pontypridd *U.K.* 51°36N 3°20W **67** F4
Ponza *Italy* 40°54N 12°58E **94** B5
Ponziane, Ísole *Italy* 40°55N 12°57E **94** B5
Poochera *Australia* 32°43S 134°51E **151** E1
Poole *U.K.* 50°43N 1°59W **67** G6
Poole □ *U.K.* 50°43N 1°59W **67** G6
Pooler *U.S.A.* 32°7N 81°15W **178** C8
Poona = Pune *India* 18°29N 73°57E **126** E1
Poonamallee *India* 13°3N 80°10E **127** H5
Pooncarie *Australia* 33°22S 142°31E **152** B5
Poopelloe L. *Australia* 31°40S 144°0E **152** A6
Poopó *Bolivia* 18°23S 66°59W **188** D4
Poopó, L. de *Bolivia* 18°30S 67°35W **188** D4
Poor Knights Is. *N.Z.* 35°29S 174°43E **154** B3
Popayán *Colombia* 2°27N 76°36W **186** C3
Poperinge *Belgium* 50°51N 2°42E **69** D2
Popiltah L. *Australia* 33°10S 141°42E **152** B4
Popina *Bulgaria* 44°7N 26°57E **97** B10
Popio L. *Australia* 33°10S 141°52E **152** B4
Poplar *U.S.A.* 48°7N 105°12W **168** B11
Poplar ➝ *Canada* 53°0N 97°19W **163** C9
Poplar Bluff *U.S.A.* 36°46N 90°24W **172** G8
Poplarville *U.S.A.* 30°51N 89°32W **177** F10
Popocatépetl, Volcán
Mexico 19°2N 98°38W **181** D5
Popokabaka
Dem. Rep. of the Congo 5°41S 16°40E **140** F3
Pópoli *Italy* 42°10N 13°50E **93** F10
Popovača *Croatia* 45°30N 16°41E **93** C13
Popovo *Bulgaria* 43°21N 26°18E **97** C10
Poppberg *Germany* 49°26N 11°37E **77** F7
Poppi *Italy* 43°43N 11°46E **93** E8
Poprad *Slovakia* 49°3N 20°18E **79** B13
Poprad ➝ *Slovakia* 49°38N 20°42E **79** B13
Porali ➝ *Pakistan* 25°58N 66°26E **124** G2
Porangaba *Brazil* 8°48S 70°36W **188** B3
Porangahau *N.Z.* 40°17S 176°37E **154** G5
Porbandar *India* 21°44N 69°43E **124** J3
Porcher I. *Canada* 53°50N 130°30W **162** C2
Porcos ➝ *Brazil* 12°42S 45°7W **189** C1
Porcuna *Spain* 37°52N 4°11W **89** H6
Porcupine ➝ *Canada* 59°11N 104°46W **163** B8
Porcupine ➝ *U.S.A.* 66°34N 145°19W **160** D2
Porcupine Abyssal Plain
Atl. Oc. 48°0N 8°0W **56** B10
Porcupine Gorge △
Australia 20°22S 144°26E **150** C3
Pordenone *Italy* 45°57N 12°39E **93** C9
Pordim *Bulgaria* 43°23N 24°51E **97** C8
Poreč *Croatia* 45°14N 13°36E **93** C10
Poretskoye *Russia* 55°9N 46°21E **86** C8
Pori *Finland* 61°29N 21°48E **84** B1
Pori *Greece* 35°58N 23°13E **98** F5
Porkhov *Russia* 57°45N 29°38E **84** D5
Porlamar *Venezuela* 10°57N 63°51W **186** A6
Porlezza *Italy* 46°2N 9°7E **92** B6
Porma ➝ *Spain* 42°49N 5°28W **88** C5
Pormpuraaw *Australia* 14°59S 141°26E **150** A3
Pormpuraaw ✪
Australia 14°55S 141°47E **150** A3
Pornic *France* 47°7N 2°5W **70** E4
Poronaysk *Russia* 49°13N 143°0E **111** B17
Poros *Greece* 37°30N 23°30E **98** D5
Poroshiri-Dake *Japan* 42°41N 142°52E **112** C11
Poroszló *Hungary* 47°39N 20°40E **80** C5
Poroto Mts. *Tanzania* 9°0S 33°30E **143** D3
Porpoise B. *Antarctica* 66°0S 127°0E **55** C9
Porquerolles, Î. de *France* 43°0N 6°13E **73** F10
Porrentruy *Switz.* 47°25N 7°6E **77** H3
Porreres *Spain* 39°31N 3°2E **100** B10
Porsangerfjorden
Norway 70°40N 25°40E **60** A21
Porsgrunn *Norway* 59°10N 9°40E **61** G13
Port Adelaide
Australia 34°50S 138°30E **152** C3
Port Alberni *Canada* 49°14N 124°50W **162** D4
Port Albert *Australia* 38°42S 146°42E **153** E7
Port Alfred *S. Africa* 33°36S 26°55E **144** D4
Port Alice *Canada* 50°20N 127°25W **162** C3
Port Allegany *U.S.A.* 41°48N 78°17W **174** E6
Port Allen *U.S.A.* 30°27N 91°12W **176** F9
Port Alma *Australia* 23°38S 150°53E **150** C5
Port Alma *Canada* 42°10N 82°14W **174** D2
Port Angeles *U.S.A.* 48°7N 123°27W **170** B3
Port Antonio *Jamaica* 18°10N 76°26W **182** a
Port Aransas *U.S.A.* 27°50N 97°4W **176** H6
Port Arthur *Australia* 43°7S 147°50E **151** G4
Port Arthur *U.S.A.* 29°54N 93°56W **176** G8
Port au Choix *Canada* 50°43N 57°22W **165** B8
Port au Port B. *Canada* 48°40N 58°50W **165** C8
Port-au-Prince *Haiti* 18°40N 72°20W **183** C5
Port Augusta *Australia* 32°30S 137°50E **152** B2
Port Austin *U.S.A.* 44°3N 83°1W **174** B2
Port-aux-Français
Kerguelen 49°21S 70°13E **146** J6
Port Blair *India* 11°40N 92°45E **127** J11
Port Blandford *Canada* 48°20N 54°10W **165** C9
Port-Bouët *Côte d'Ivoire* 5°16N 3°57W **138** D4
Port Bradshaw
Australia 12°30S 137°20E **150** A2
Port Broughton
Australia 33°37S 137°56E **152** B2
Port Bruce *Canada* 42°39N 81°0W **174** D4
Port Burwell *Canada* 42°40N 80°48W **174** D4
Port Campbell *Australia* 38°37S 143°1E **152** E5
Port Campbell *India* 11°56N 92°37E **127** J11
Port Campbell △
Australia 38°8S 143°6E **152** E5
Port Canning *India* 22°23N 88°40E **125** H13
Port Carling *Canada* 45°7N 79°35W **174** A5
Port-Cartier *Canada* 50°2N 66°50W **165** B6
Port Chalmers *N.Z.* 45°49S 170°30E **155** F5
Port Charles *N.Z.* 36°33S 175°30E **154** C4
Port Charlotte *U.S.A.* 26°59N 82°6W **179** J7
Port Chester *U.S.A.* 41°0N 73°40W **175** F11
Port Clements *Canada* 53°40N 132°10W **162** C2
Port Clinton *U.S.A.* 41°31N 82°56W **173** E12
Port Colborne *Canada* 42°50N 79°10W **174** D5
Port Coquitlam
Canada 49°15N 122°45W **170** A4
Port Cornwallis *India* 13°17N 93°5E **127** H11
Port Credit *Canada* 43°33N 79°35W **174** C5
Port-Cros △ *France* 43°0N 6°24E **73** F10
Port Curtis *Australia* 23°57S 151°20E **150** C5
Port d'Alcúdia *Spain* 39°50N 3°7E **100** B10
Port Dalhousie *Canada* 43°13N 79°16W **174** C5
Port d'Andratx *Spain* 39°32N 2°23E **100** B9
Port Darwin *Australia* 12°24S 130°45E **148** B5
Port Darwin *Falk. Is.* 51°50S 59°0W **192** D5
Port Davey *Australia* 43°16S 145°55E **151** G4
Port-de-Bouc *France* 43°24N 4°59E **73** E8
Port-de-Paix *Haiti* 19°50N 72°50W **183** C5
Port de Pollença *Spain* 39°54N 3°4E **100** B10
Port de Sóller *Spain* 39°48N 2°42E **100** B9
Port Dickson *Malaysia* 2°30N 101°49E **121** L3
Port Douglas *Australia* 16°30S 145°30E **150** B4
Port Dover *Canada* 42°47N 80°12W **174** D4
Port Edward *Canada* 54°12N 130°10W **162** C2
Port Elgin *Canada* 44°25N 81°25W **174** B3
Port Elizabeth *S. Africa* 33°58S 25°40E **144** D4
Port Ellen *U.K.* 55°38N 6°11W **65** F2
Port Elliot *Australia* 35°32S 138°41E **152** C3
Port-en-Bessin-Huppain
France 49°21N 0°45W **70** C6
Port Erin *I. of Man* 54°5N 4°45W **66** C3
Port Essington
Australia 11°15S 132°10E **148** B5
Port Ewen *U.S.A.* 41°54N 73°59W **175** E11
Port Fairy *Australia* 38°22S 142°12E **152** E5
Port Fitzroy *N.Z.* 36°8S 175°20E **154** C4
Port Fouâd = Bûr Fuad
Egypt 31°15N 32°20E **137** E8
Port Gamble *U.S.A.* 47°51N 122°34W **170** C4
Port-Gentil *Gabon* 0°40S 8°50E **140** E1
Port Germein *Australia* 33°1S 138°1E **151** E2
Port Ghalib *Egypt* 25°20N 34°50E **128** E2
Port Gibson *U.S.A.* 31°58N 90°59W **176** F9
Port Glasgow *U.K.* 55°56N 4°41W **65** F4
Port Harcourt *Nigeria* 4°40N 7°10E **139** E6
Port Hardy *Canada* 50°41N 127°30W **162** C3
Port Harrison = Inukjuak
Canada 58°25N 78°15W **161** F16
Port Hawkesbury
Canada 45°36N 61°22W **165** C7
Port Hedland *Australia* 20°25S 118°35E **148** D2
Port Henry *U.S.A.* 44°3N 73°28W **175** B11
Port Hood *Canada* 46°0N 61°32W **165** C7
Port Hope *Canada* 43°56N 78°20W **174** C6
Port Hope *U.S.A.* 43°57N 82°43W **174** C2
Port Hope Simpson
Canada 52°33N 56°18W **165** B8
Port Hueneme *U.S.A.* 34°7N 119°12W **171** L7
Port Huron *U.S.A.* 42°58N 82°26W **174** D2
Port Iliç = Liman
Azerbaijan 38°53N 48°47E **105** C13
Port Jefferson *U.S.A.* 40°57N 73°3W **175** F11
Port Jervis *U.S.A.* 41°22N 74°41W **175** E10
Port-Joinville *France* 46°45N 2°23W **70** F4
Port Katon *Russia* 46°52N 38°46E **85** J10
Port Kavkaz *Russia* 45°20N 36°40E **85** K9
Port Kembla *Australia* 34°52S 150°49E **153** C9
Port Kenny *Australia* 33°10S 134°41E **151** E1
Port Klang *Malaysia* 3°0N 101°35E **121** L3
Port-la-Nouvelle *France* 43°1N 3°3E **72** E7
Port Láirge = Waterford
Ireland 52°15N 7°8W **64** D4
Port Lavaca *U.S.A.* 28°37N 96°38W **176** G6
Port Leyden *U.S.A.* 43°35N 75°21W **175** C9
Port Lincoln *Australia* 34°42S 135°52E **152** C1
Port Loko *S. Leone* 8°48N 12°46W **138** D2
Port Louis *France* 47°42N 3°22W **70** E3
Port-Louis *Guadeloupe* 16°28N 61°32W **182** b
Port Louis *Mauritius* 20°10S 57°30E **141** d
Port MacDonnell
Australia 38°5S 140°48E **152** E4
Port McNeill *Canada* 50°35N 127°6W **162** C3
Port Macquarie
Australia 31°25S 152°25E **153** A10
Port Maria *Jamaica* 18°22N 76°54W **182** a
Port Mathurin
Rodrigues 19°41S 63°25E **146** F5
Port Matilda *U.S.A.* 40°48N 78°3W **174** F6
Port Mayaca *U.S.A.* 26°59N 80°36W **179** J9
Port McNicoll *Canada* 44°44N 79°48W **174** B5
Port Mellon *Canada* 49°32N 123°31W **162** D4
Port-Menier *Canada* 49°51N 64°15W **165** C7
Port Moody *Canada* 49°17N 122°51W **170** A4
Port Morant *Jamaica* 17°54N 76°19W **182** a
Port Moresby
Papua N. G. 9°24S 147°8E **147** B7
Port Muhammed Bin Qasim =
Port Qasim *Pakistan* 24°46N 67°20E **124** G2
Port Musgrave
Australia 11°55S 141°50E **150** A3
Port-Navalo *France* 47°34N 2°54W **70** E4
Port Neches *U.S.A.* 30°0N 93°59W **176** G8
Port Nicholson *N.Z.* 41°20S 174°52E **154** H3
Port Nolloth *S. Africa* 29°17S 16°52E **144** C2
Port Nouveau-Québec =
Kangiqsualujjuaq
Canada 58°30N 65°59W **161** F18
Port of Climax *Canada* 49°10N 108°20W **163** D7
Port of Coronach
Canada 49°7N 105°31W **163** D7
Port of Spain
Trin. & Tob. 10°40N 61°31W **183** D7
Port Orange *U.S.A.* 29°9N 80°59W **179** F9
Port Orchard *U.S.A.* 47°32N 122°38W **170** C4
Port Orford *U.S.A.* 42°45N 124°30W **168** E1
Port Pegasus *N.Z.* 47°12S 167°41E **155** H2
Port Perry *Canada* 44°6N 78°56W **174** B6
Port Phillip B.
Australia 38°10S 144°50E **153** E6
Port Pirie *Australia* 33°10S 138°1E **152** B3
Port Qasim *Pakistan* 24°46N 67°20E **124** G2
Port Renfrew *Canada* 48°30N 124°20W **170** B2
Port Roper *Australia* 14°45S 135°25E **150** A2
Port Rowan *Canada* 42°40N 80°30W **174** D4
Port Royal Sd. *U.S.A.* 32°15N 80°40W **178** C9
Port Safaga = Bûr Safâga
Egypt 26°43N 33°57E **128** E2
Port Said = Bûr Sa'îd
Egypt 31°16N 32°18E **137** E8
Port St. Joe *U.S.A.* 29°49N 85°18W **178** F4
Port St. John *U.S.A.* 28°29N 80°47W **179** G9
Port St. Johns = Umzimvubu
S. Africa 31°38S 29°33E **145** D4
Port-St-Louis-du-Rhône
France 43°23N 4°49E **73** E8
Port St. Lucie *U.S.A.* 27°18N 80°21W **179** H9
Port-Ste-Marie *France* 44°15N 0°25E **72** D4
Port Salerno *U.S.A.* 27°9N 80°12W **179** H9
Port Sanilac *U.S.A.* 43°26N 82°33W **174** C2
Port Severn *Canada* 44°48N 79°43W **174** B5
Port Shepstone *S. Africa* 30°44S 30°28E **145** D5
Port Simpson *Canada* 54°30N 130°20W **162** C2
Port Stanley = Stanley
Falk. Is. 51°40S 59°51W **192** D5
Port Stanley *Canada* 42°40N 81°10W **174** D3
Port Sudan = Bûr Sûdân
Sudan 19°32N 37°9E **137** D4
Port Sulphur *U.S.A.* 29°29N 89°42W **177** G10
Port-sur-Saône *France* 47°42N 6°2E **71** E13
Port Talbot *U.K.* 51°35N 3°47W **67** F4
Port Taufiq = Bûr Taufiq
Egypt 29°54N 32°32E **137** F8
Port Townsend *U.S.A.* 48°7N 122°45W **170** B4
Port-Vendres *France* 42°32N 3°8E **72** F7
Port Victoria *Australia* 34°30S 137°29E **152** C2
Port Vila *Vanuatu* 17°45S 168°18E **147** C9
Port Vladimir *Russia* 69°25N 33°6E **60** B25
Port Wakefield
Australia 34°12S 138°10E **152** C3
Port Washington
U.S.A. 43°23N 87°53W **172** D10
Port Wentworth *U.S.A.* 32°9N 81°10W **178** C8
Porta Orientalis *Romania* 45°6N 22°18E **75** F12
Portacloy *Ireland* 54°20N 9°46W **64** B2
Portadown *U.K.* 54°25N 6°27W **64** B5
Portaferry *U.K.* 54°23N 5°33W **64** B6
Portage *Pa., U.S.A.* 40°23N 78°41W **174** F6
Portage *Wis., U.S.A.* 43°33N 89°28W **172** D9
Portage la Prairie
Canada 49°58N 98°18W **163** D9
Portageville *U.S.A.* 36°26N 89°42W **172** G9
Portal *U.S.A.* 32°33N 81°56W **178** C8
Portalegre *Portugal* 39°19N 7°25W **89** F3
Portalegre □ *Portugal* 39°20N 7°40W **89** F3
Portales *U.S.A.* 34°11N 103°20W **169** J12
Portarlington *Ireland* 53°9N 7°14W **64** C4
Portbou *Spain* 42°25N 3°9E **90** C8
Porteirinha *Brazil* 15°44S 43°2W **189** D2
Portel *Portugal* 38°19N 7°41W **89** G3
Portela, Lisboa ✕ (LIS)
Portugal 38°46N 9°8W **89** G1
Porter L. *N.W.T.,*
Canada 61°41N 108°5W **163** A7
Porter L. *Sask., Canada* 56°20N 107°20W **163** B7
Porterville *S. Africa* 33°0S 19°0E **144** D2
Porterville *U.S.A.* 36°4N 119°1W **170** J8
Portes-lès-Valence *France* 44°52N 4°54E **73** D8
Porth Tywyn = Burry Port
U.K. 51°41N 4°15W **67** F3
Porthcawl *U.K.* 51°29N 3°42W **67** F4
Porthill *U.S.A.* 48°59N 116°30W **168** B5
Porthmadog *U.K.* 52°55N 4°8W **66** E3
Portile de Fier *Europe* 44°44N 22°30E **80** F7
Portimão *Portugal* 37°8N 8°32W **89** H2
Portishead *U.K.* 51°29N 2°46W **67** F5
Portiței, Gura *Romania* 44°41N 29°0E **81** F14
Portknockie *U.K.* 57°42N 2°51W **65** D6
Portland *N.S.W.,*
Australia 33°20S 150°0E **153** B9
Portland *Vic., Australia* 38°20S 141°35E **152** E4
Portland *Canada* 44°42N 76°12W **175** B8
Portland *Conn., U.S.A.* 41°34N 72°38W **175** E12
Portland *Fla., U.S.A.* 30°31N 86°12W **178** E3
Portland *Maine,*
U.S.A. 43°39N 70°16W **173** D18
Portland *Mich., U.S.A.* 42°52N 84°54W **173** D11
Portland *Oreg., U.S.A.* 45°32N 122°37W **170** E4
Portland *Pa., U.S.A.* 40°55N 75°6W **175** F9
Portland *Tex., U.S.A.* 27°53N 97°20W **176** H6
Portland, I. of *U.K.* 50°33N 2°26W **67** G5
Portland B. *Australia* 38°15S 141°45E **152** E4
Portland Bight *Jamaica* 17°52N 77°5W **182** a
Portland Bill *U.K.* 50°31N 2°28W **67** G5
Portland Canal *U.S.A.* 55°56N 130°0W **162** B2
Portland I. *N.Z.* 39°20S 177°51E **154** F6
Portland Int. ✕ (PDX)
U.S.A. 45°35N 122°36W **170** E4
Portland Pt. *Jamaica* 17°42N 77°11W **182** a
Portlaoise *Ireland* 53°2N 7°18W **64** C4
Portmadoc = Porthmadog
U.K. 52°55N 4°8W **66** E3
Portmore *Jamaica* 17°53N 76°53W **182** a
Porto *Brazil* 3°54S 42°42W **189** A2
Porto *France* 42°16N 8°42E **73** F12
Porto *Portugal* 41°8N 8°40W **88** D2
Porto □ *Portugal* 41°8N 8°20W **88** D2
Porto, G. de *France* 42°17N 8°34E **73** F12
Porto Acre *Brazil* 9°34S 67°31W **188** B4
Pôrto Alegre *Brazil* 30°5S 51°10W **191** C5
Porto Azzurro *Italy* 42°46N 10°24E **92** F7
Porto Cervo *Italy* 41°8N 9°33E **94** A2
Porto Colom *Spain* 39°26N 3°15E **100** B10
Porto Cristo *Spain* 39°33N 3°20E **100** B10
Pôrto da Fôlha *Brazil* 9°55S 37°17W **189** B3
Porto de Moz *Brazil* 1°41S 52°13W **187** D8
Porto de Pedras *Brazil* 9°10S 35°17W **189** B3
Porto Empédocle *Italy* 37°17N 13°32E **94** E6
Porto Esperança *Brazil* 19°37S 57°29W **186** G7
Porto Franco *Brazil* 6°20S 47°24W **189** B1
Porto Inglês = Vila do Maio
Cabo Verde 15°21N 23°10W **134** b
Porto Mendes *Brazil* 24°30S 54°15W **191** A5
Porto Moniz *Madeira* 32°52N 17°11W **100** D2
Porto Murtinho *Brazil* 21°45S 57°55W **186** H7
Porto Nacional *Brazil* 10°40S 48°30W **189** C1
Porto-Novo *Benin* 6°23N 2°42E **139** D5
Porto Primavera, Represa
Brazil 22°10S 52°45W **191** A5
Porto San Giórgio *Italy* 43°11N 13°48E **93** E10
Porto Santo, I. de
Madeira 33°45N 16°25W **134** B2
Porto Sant' Elpídio
Italy 43°15N 13°43E **93** E10
Porto Santo Stéfano *Italy* 42°26N 11°7E **92** F8
Pôrto São José *Brazil* 22°43S 53°10W **191** A5
Porto Seguro *Brazil* 16°26S 39°5W **189** D3
Porto Tolle *Italy* 44°56N 12°22E **93** D9
Porto Tórres *Italy* 40°50N 8°24E **94** B1
Pôrto União *Brazil* 26°10S 51°10W **191** B5
Porto-Vecchio *France* 41°35N 9°16E **73** G13
Pôrto Velho *Brazil* 8°46S 63°54W **186** E6
Porto Viro *Italy* 45°1N 12°13E **93** C9
Porto Walter *Brazil* 8°15S 72°40W **188** B3
Portobelo *Panama* 9°35N 79°42W **182** E4
Portoferráio *Italy* 42°48N 10°20E **92** F7
Portofino *Italy* 44°18N 9°12E **92** D6
Portogruaro *Italy* 45°47N 12°50E **93** C9
Portola *U.S.A.* 39°49N 120°28W **170** F6
Portomaggiore *Italy* 44°42N 11°48E **93** D8
Portopetro *Spain* 39°22N 3°13E **100** B10
Portoscuso *Italy* 39°12N 8°24E **94** C1
Portovénere *Italy* 44°3N 9°51E **92** D6
Portoviejo *Ecuador* 1°7S 80°28W **186** D2
Portpatrick *U.K.* 54°51N 5°7W **65** G3
Portree *U.K.* 57°25N 6°12W **65** D2
Portrush *U.K.* 55°12N 6°40W **64** A5
Portsmouth *Dominica* 15°34N 61°27W **183** C7
Portsmouth *U.K.* 50°48N 1°6W **67** G6
Portsmouth *N.H.,*
U.S.A. 43°5N 70°45W **175** C14
Portsmouth *Ohio,*
U.S.A. 38°44N 82°57W **173** F12
Portsmouth *R.I.,*
U.S.A. 41°36N 71°15W **175** E13
Portsmouth *Va.,*
U.S.A. 36°58N 76°23W **173** G15
Portsmouth □ *U.K.* 50°48N 1°6W **67** G6
Portsoy *U.K.* 57°41N 2°41W **65** D6
Portstewart *U.K.* 55°11N 6°43W **64** A5
Porttipahdan tekojärvi
Finland 68°5N 26°40E **60** B22
Portugal ■ *Europe* 40°0N 8°0W **88** F3
Portugalete *Spain* 43°19N 3°4W **90** B1
Portumna *Ireland* 53°6N 8°14W **64** C3
Portville *U.S.A.* 42°3N 78°20W **174** D6
Poruma *Australia* 10°2S 143°4E **150** a
Porvenir *Bolivia* 11°10S 68°50W **188** C4
Porvenir *Chile* 53°10S 70°16W **192** D2
Porvoo *Finland* 60°24N 25°40E **84** B3
Porzuna *Spain* 39°9N 4°9W **89** F6
Posada *Italy* 40°38N 9°43E **94** B2
Posada ➝ *Italy* 40°39N 9°45E **94** B2
Posadas *Argentina* 27°30S 55°50W **191** B4
Posadas *Spain* 37°47N 5°11W **89** H5
Poschiavo *Switz.* 46°19N 10°4E **77** J6
Posets *Spain* 42°39N 0°25E **90** C5
Poshan = Boshan *China* 36°28N 117°49E **115** F9
Posht-e Badam *Iran* 33°2N 55°23E **129** C7
Posidium *Greece* 35°30N 27°10E **99** F9
Poso *Indonesia* 1°20S 120°55E **119** E6
Poso, Danau *Indonesia* 1°52S 120°35E **119** E6
Posof *Turkey* 41°30N 42°43E **105** B10
Pospelikha *Russia* 51°57N 81°46E **109** B10
Posse *Brazil* 14°4S 46°18W **189** C1
Possession I. *Antarctica* 72°4S 172°0E **55** D11
Pössneck *Germany* 50°42N 11°35E **76** E7
Possum Kingdom L.
U.S.A. 32°52N 98°26W **176** E5
Post *U.S.A.* 33°12N 101°23W **176** E4
Post Falls *U.S.A.* 47°43N 116°57W **168** C5
Postavy = Pastavy
Belarus 55°4N 26°50E **84** E4
Poste-de-la-Baleine =
Kuujjuarapik
Canada 55°20N 77°35W **164** A4
Postmasburg *S. Africa* 28°18S 23°5E **144** C3
Postojna *Slovenia* 45°46N 14°12E **93** C11
Poston *U.S.A.* 34°0N 114°24W **171** M12
Postville *Canada* 54°54N 59°47W **165** B8
Posyet *Russia* 42°39N 130°48E **112** C5
Potamos *Antikythira,*
Greece 35°52N 23°15E **98** F5
Potamos *Kythira, Greece* 36°15N 22°58E **98** E4
Potchefstroom *S. Africa* 26°41S 27°7E **144** C4
Potcoava *Romania* 44°30N 24°39E **81** F9
Poté *Brazil* 17°49S 41°49W **189** D2
Poteau *U.S.A.* 35°3N 94°37W **176** D7
Poteet *U.S.A.* 29°2N 98°35W **176** G5
Potenza *Italy* 40°38N 15°48E **95** B8
Potenza ➝ *Italy* 43°25N 13°40E **93** E10
Potenza Picena *Italy* 43°22N 13°37E **93** E10
Poteriteri, L. *N.Z.* 46°5S 167°10E **155** G2
Potgietersrus = Mokopane
S. Africa 24°10S 28°55E **145** B4
Poti *Georgia* 42°10N 41°38E **87** J5
Potiraguá *Brazil* 15°36S 39°53W **189** D3
Potiskum *Nigeria* 11°39N 11°2E **139** C7
Potlogi *Romania* 44°34N 25°34E **81** F10
Potomac ➝ *U.S.A.* 38°0N 76°23W **173** F14
Potosí *Bolivia* 19°38S 65°50W **186** G5
Potosi Mt. *U.S.A.* 35°57N 115°29W **171** K11
Pototan *Phil.* 10°54N 122°38E **119** B6
Potrerillos *Chile* 26°30S 69°30W **190** B2
Potsdam *Germany* 52°23N 13°3E **76** C9
Potsdam *U.S.A.* 44°40N 74°59W **175** B10
Pottangi *India* 18°34N 82°58E **126** E6
Pottenstein *Germany* 49°46N 11°24E **77** F7
Pottersville *U.S.A.* 43°43N 73°50W **175** C11
Pottstown *U.S.A.* 40°15N 75°39W **175** F9
Pottsville *U.S.A.* 40°41N 76°12W **175** F8
Pottuvil *Sri Lanka* 6°55N 81°50E **127** L5
P'otzu *Taiwan* 23°28N 120°15E **117** F13
Pouancé *France* 47°44N 1°10W **70** E5
Pouce Coupé *Canada* 55°40N 120°10W **162** B4
Poughkeepsie *U.S.A.* 41°42N 73°56W **175** E11
Pouilly-sur-Loire *France* 47°17N 2°57E **71** E9
Poulan *U.S.A.* 31°31N 83°47W **178** D6
Poulaphouca Res. *Ireland* 53°8N 6°30W **64** C5
Poulsbo *U.S.A.* 47°44N 122°38W **170** C4
Poultney *U.S.A.* 43°31N 73°14W **175** C11
Poulton-le-Fylde *U.K.* 53°51N 2°58W **66** D5
Pouso Alegre *Brazil* 22°14S 45°57W **191** A6
Pout *Senegal* 14°45N 17°0W **138** C1
Pouthisat *Cambodia* 12°34N 103°50E **120** F4
Pouytenga *Burkina Faso* 12°15N 0°25W **139** C4
Pouzauges *France* 46°47N 0°50W **70** F6
Považská Bystrica
Slovakia 49°8N 18°27E **79** B11
Poverty B. *N.Z.* 38°43S 178°2E **154** E7
Poverty Point Nat. Monument ⌂
U.S.A. 32°39N 91°24W **176** E9
Povlen *Serbia* 44°9N 19°44E **96** B3
Póvoa de Lanhosa
Portugal 41°33N 8°15W **88** D2
Póvoa de Santa Iria
Portugal 38°51N 9°4W **89** G1
Póvoa de Varzim
Portugal 41°25N 8°46W **88** D2
Povorino *Russia* 51°12N 42°5E **86** E6
Povorotnyy, Mys
Russia 42°40N 133°2E **112** C6
Povungnituk = Puvirnituq
Canada 60°2N 77°10W **161** E16
Powassan *Canada* 46°5N 79°25W **164** C4
Poway *U.S.A.* 32°58N 117°2W **171** N9
Powder ➝ *U.S.A.* 46°45N 105°26W **168** C11
Powder River *U.S.A.* 43°2N 106°59W **168** E10
Powder Springs *U.S.A.* 33°52N 84°41W **178** B5
Powell *U.S.A.* 44°45N 108°46W **168** D9
Powell, L. *U.S.A.* 36°57N 111°29W **169** H8
Powell River *Canada* 49°50N 124°35W **162** D4
Powelton *U.S.A.* 33°26N 82°52W **178** B7
Powers *U.S.A.* 45°41N 87°32W **172** C10
Pownal *U.S.A.* 42°45N 73°14W **175** D11
Powys □ *U.K.* 52°20N 3°20W **67** E4
Poyang Hu *China* 29°5N 116°20E **117** C11
Poyarkovo *Russia* 49°36N 128°41E **107** E13
Poysdorf *Austria* 48°40N 16°37E **79** C9
Poza de la Sal *Spain* 42°35N 3°31W **88** C7
Poza Rica *Mexico* 20°33N 97°27W **181** C5
Pozantı *Turkey* 37°25N 34°50E **104** D6
Požarevac *Serbia* 44°35N 21°18E **96** B5
Pozazal, Puerto *Spain* 42°56N 4°10W **88** C6
Požega *Croatia* 45°20N 17°40E **80** E2
Požega *Serbia* 43°53N 20°2E **96** C4
Poznań *Poland* 52°25N 16°55E **83** F3
Poznań ✕ (POZ) *Poland* 52°26N 16°45E **83** F3
Pozo *U.S.A.* 35°20N 120°24W **171** K6
Pozo Alcón *Spain* 37°42N 2°56W **89** H8
Pozo Almonte *Chile* 20°10S 69°50W **188** E4
Pozo Colorado
Paraguay 23°30S 58°45W **190** A4
Pozo Negro *Canary Is.* 28°19N 13°55W **100** F6
Pozoblanco *Spain* 38°23N 4°51W **89** G6
Pozuzo *Peru* 10°5S 75°35W **188** C2
Pozzallo *Italy* 36°43N 14°51E **95** F7
Pozzomaggiore *Italy* 40°24N 8°39E **94** B1
Pozzuoli *Italy* 40°49N 14°7E **95** B7
Pra ➝ *Ghana* 5°1N 1°37W **139** D4
Prabuty *Poland* 53°47N 19°15E **82** E6
Prača *Bos.-H.* 43°47N 18°43E **80** G3
Prachatice *Czechia* 49°1N 14°0E **78** B6
Prachin Buri *Thailand* 14°0N 101°25E **120** F3
Prachuap Khirikhan
Thailand 11°49N 99°48E **121** G2
Pradelles *France* 44°46N 3°52E **72** D7
Prades *France* 42°38N 2°23E **72** F6
Prado *Brazil* 17°20S 39°13W **189** D3
Prado del Rey *Spain* 36°48N 5°33W **89** J5
Præstø *Denmark* 55°8N 12°2E **63** J6
Pragersko *Slovenia* 46°27N 15°42E **93** B12
Prague = Praha *Czechia* 50°4N 14°25E **78** A7
Praha *Czechia* 50°4N 14°25E **78** A7
Praha ✕ (PRG) *Czechia* 50°6N 14°16E **78** A7
Prahecq *France* 46°19N 0°26W **72** B3
Prahita ➝ *India* 19°0N 79°55E **126** E4
Prahova □ *Romania* 45°10N 26°0E **81** E10
Prahova ➝ *Romania* 44°50N 25°50E **81** F10
Prahovo *Serbia* 44°18N 22°39E **96** B6
Praia *Cabo Verde* 15°2N 23°34W **134** b
Praia a Mare *Italy* 39°50N 15°45E **95** C8
Praid *Romania* 46°32N 25°10E **81** D10
Prainha *Brazil* 1°45S 53°30W **187** D8
Prainha Nova *Brazil* 7°10S 60°30W **186** E6
Prairie *Australia* 20°50S 144°35E **150** C3
Prairie City *U.S.A.* 44°28N 118°43W **168** D4
Prairie Dog Town Fork Red ➝
U.S.A. 34°34N 99°58W **176** D5
Prairie du Chien *U.S.A.* 43°3N 91°9W **172** D8
Prairies, L. of the
Canada 51°16N 101°32W **163** C8
Pramanda *Greece* 39°32N 21°8E **98** B3
Prambanan △
Indonesia 7°45S 110°28E **119** G14
Prampram *Ghana* 5°43N 0°8E **139** D5
Pran Buri *Thailand* 12°23N 99°55E **120** F2
Prang *Ghana* 8°1N 0°56W **139** D4
Prapat *Indonesia* 2°41N 98°58E **118** D1
Praslin *Seychelles* 4°18S 55°45E **141** b
Prasonisi, Akra *Greece* 35°42N 27°46E **101** D9
Praszka *Poland* 51°5N 18°31E **83** G5
Prata *Brazil* 19°25S 48°54W **187** G9
Pratabpur *India* 23°28N 83°15E **125** H10
Pratapgarh *Raj., India* 24°2N 74°40E **124** G6
Pratapgarh *Ut. P., India* 25°56N 81°59E **125** G9
Pratas I. = Dongsha Dao
S. China Sea 20°45N 116°43E **111** G12
Prato *Italy* 43°53N 11°6E **92** E8
Prátola Peligna *Italy* 42°6N 13°52E **93** F10
Prats-de-Mollo-la-Preste
France 42°25N 2°27E **72** F6
Pratt *U.S.A.* 37°39N 98°44W **172** G4
Prattville *U.S.A.* 32°28N 86°29W **177** E11
Pravara ➝ *India* 19°35N 74°45E **126** E2
Pravdinsk *Kaliningrad,*
Russia 54°27N 21°1E **82** D8
Pravdinsk *Nizhniy Novgorod,*
Russia 56°29N 43°28E **86** B6

Pravets *Bulgaria* 42°53N 23°55E **96** D7
Pravia *Spain* 43°30N 6°12W **88** B4
Praya *Indonesia* 8°39S 116°17E **118** F5
Prayag = Allahabad
  India 25°25N 81°58E **125** G9
Pre-delta △ *Argentina* 32°10S 60°40W **190** C3
Pré-en-Pail *France* 48°28N 0°12W **70** D6
Preah Seihanu = Kampong Saom
  Cambodia 10°38N 103°30E **121** G4
Preah Vihear
  Cambodia 14°23N 104°41E **120** E5
Preble *U.S.A.* 42°44N 76°8W **175** D8
Precipice △ *Australia* 25°18S 150°5E **151** D5
Precordillera *Argentina* 30°0S 69°1W **190** C2
Predáppio *Italy* 44°6N 11°59E **93** D8
Predazzo *Italy* 46°19N 11°36E **93** B8
Predeal *Romania* 45°30N 25°34E **81** E10
Predejane *Serbia* 42°51N 22°9E **96** D6
Preeceville *Canada* 51°57N 102°40W **163** C8
Preeta *Germany* 54°14N 10°18E **76** A6
Pregolya → *Russia* 54°41N 20°22E **82** D7
Pregrada *Croatia* 46°11N 15°45E **93** B12
Preili *Latvia* 56°18N 26°43E **84** D4
Preko *Croatia* 44°7N 15°10E **93** D12
Prelog *Croatia* 46°18N 16°32E **93** B13
Premer *Australia* 31°29S 149°56E **153** A8
Prémery *France* 47°10N 3°18E **71** E10
Premià de Mar *Spain* 41°29N 2°22E **90** D7
Premont *U.S.A.* 27°22N 98°7W **176** H5
Premuda *Croatia* 44°20N 14°36E **93** D11
Prentice *U.S.A.* 45°33N 90°17W **172** C8
Prenzlau *Germany* 53°19N 13°50E **76** B9
Preobrazheniye
  Russia 42°54N 133°54E **112** C6
Preparis I. = Pariparit Kyun
  Myanmar 14°52N 93°41E **127** G11
Preparis North Channel
  Ind. Oc. 15°27N 94°5E **127** G11
Preparis South Channel
  Ind. Oc. 14°33N 93°30E **127** G11
Přerov *Czechia* 49°28N 17°27E **79** B10
Prescott *Canada* 44°45N 75°30W **175** B9
Prescott *Ariz., U.S.A.* 34°33N 112°28W **169** J7
Prescott *Ark., U.S.A.* 33°48N 93°23W **176** E8
Prescott Valley *U.S.A.* 34°40N 112°18W **169** J7
Preservation Inlet *N.Z.* 46°8S 166°35E **155** G1
Preševo *Serbia* 42°19N 21°39E **96** D5
Presho *U.S.A.* 43°54N 100°3W **172** D3
Presicce *Italy* 39°54N 18°16E **95** C11
Presidencia de la Plaza
  Argentina 27°0S 59°50W **190** B4
Presidencia Roque Sáenz Peña
  Argentina 26°45S 60°30W **190** B3
Presidente Dutra *Brazil* 5°15S 44°30W **189** B2
Presidente Epitácio
  Brazil 21°56S 52°6W **187** H8
Presidente Hayes □
  Paraguay 24°0S 59°0W **190** A4
Presidente Prudente
  Brazil 22°5S 51°25W **191** A5
Presidente Ríos, L.
  Chile 46°28S 74°25W **192** C2
Presidio *U.S.A.* 29°34N 104°22W **176** G2
Presláv *Bulgaria* 43°10N 26°52E **97** C10
Preslavska Planina
  Bulgaria 43°10N 26°45E **97** C10
Prešov *Slovakia* 49°0N 21°15E **79** B14
Prešovský □ *Slovakia* 49°10N 21°0E **79** B13
Prespa *Bulgaria* 41°44N 24°55E **97** E8
Prespa, L. = Prespansko Jezero
  Macedonia 40°55N 21°0E **96** F5
Prespa △ *Europe* 40°48N 21°4E **96** F4
Prespansko Jezero
  Macedonia 40°55N 21°0E **96** F5
Presque I. *U.S.A.* 42°10N 80°6W **174** D4
Presque Isle *U.S.A.* 46°41N 68°1W **173** B19
Prestatyn *U.K.* 53°20N 3°24W **66** E4
Prestea *Ghana* 5°22N 2°7W **138** D4
Presteigne *U.K.* 52°17N 3°0W **67** E5
Přeštice *Czechia* 49°34N 13°20E **78** B6
Preston *Canada* 43°23N 80°21W **174** C4
Preston *U.K.* 53°46N 2°42W **66** D5
Preston *Ga., U.S.A.* 32°4N 84°32W **178** C5
Preston *Idaho, U.S.A.* 42°6N 111°53W **168** E8
Preston *Minn., U.S.A.* 43°40N 92°5W **172** D7
Preston, C. *Australia* 20°51S 116°12E **148** D2
Prestonsburg *U.S.A.* 37°40N 82°47W **173** G12
Prestrand *Norway* 59°6N 9°4E **62** E3
Prestwick *U.K.* 55°29N 4°37W **65** F4
Prêto → *Brazil* 11°21S 43°52W **187** F10
Pretoria *S. Africa* 25°44S 28°12E **145** C4
Preuilly-sur-Claise *France* 46°51N 0°56E **70** F7
Prévaza *Greece* 38°57N 20°45E **98** C2
Prey Veng *Cambodia* 11°35N 105°29E **121** G5
Priazovskoye *Ukraine* 46°44N 35°40E **85** J8
Pribaykalsky △
  Russia 52°30N 106°0E **107** D11
Pribilof Is. *U.S.A.* 57°0N 170°0W **166** D6
Priboj *Serbia* 43°35N 19°32E **96** C3
Příbram *Czechia* 49°41N 14°2E **78** B7
Price *U.S.A.* 39°36N 110°49W **168** G8
Price, C. *India* 13°34N 93°3E **127** H11
Price I. *Canada* 52°23N 128°41W **162** C3
Prichard *U.S.A.* 30°44N 88°5W **177** F10
Priego *Spain* 40°26N 2°21W **90** E2
Priego de Córdoba *Spain* 37°27N 4°12W **89** H6
Priekule *Latvia* 56°26N 21°35E **82** B8
Priekule *Lithuania* 55°33N 21°19E **82** C8
Prielbrusye △ *Russia* 43°27N 42°37E **87** A6
Prien *Germany* 47°51N 12°20E **77** H8
Prienai *Lithuania* 54°38N 23°57E **82** D10
Prieska *S. Africa* 29°40S 22°42E **144** C3
Priest L. *U.S.A.* 48°35N 116°52W **168** B5
Priest River *U.S.A.* 48°11N 116°55W **168** B5
Priest Valley *U.S.A.* 36°10N 120°39W **170** J6
Prievidza *Slovakia* 48°46N 18°36E **79** C11
Prignitz *Germany* 53°6N 11°45E **76** B7
Prijedor *Bos.-H.* 44°58N 16°41E **93** D13
Prijepolje *Serbia* 43°27N 19°40E **96** C3
Prikaspiyskaya Nizmennost =
  Caspian Depression
  Eurasia 47°0N 48°0E **87** D8
Prikro *Côte d'Ivoire* 7°40N 3°59W **138** D4
Prikubanskaya Nizmennost
  Russia 45°39N 38°33E **87** H4
Prilep *Macedonia* 41°21N 21°32E **96** E5
Priluki = Pryluky
  Ukraine 50°30N 32°24E **85** G7
Prime Hd. *Antarctica* 63°12S 48°57W **55** C18
Prime Seal I. *Australia* 40°3S 147°43E **151** G4
Primeira Cruz *Brazil* 2°30S 43°26W **189** A2
Primo Tapia *Mexico* 32°16N 116°54W **171** N10

Primorsk *Kaliningrad,*
  Russia 54°44N 20°0E **82** D6
Primorsk *St. Petersburg,*
  Russia 60°22N 28°37E **84** B5
Primorskiy Kray □
  Russia 45°0N 135°0E **112** B7
Primorsko *Bulgaria* 42°15N 27°44E **97** D11
Primorsko-Akhtarsk
  Russia 46°2N 38°10E **85** C8
Primrose L. *Canada* 54°55N 109°45W **163** C7
Prince Albert *Canada* 53°15N 105°50W **163** C7
Prince Albert *S. Africa* 33°12S 22°2E **144** D3
Prince Albert □
  Canada 54°0N 106°25W **163** C7
Prince Albert Mts.
  Antarctica 76°0S 161°30E **55** D11
Prince Albert Pen.
  Canada 72°30N 116°0W **160** C8
Prince Albert Sd.
  Canada 70°25N 115°0W **160** C9
Prince Alfred, C.
  Canada 74°20N 124°40W **54** B1
Prince Charles I.
  Canada 67°47N 76°12W **161** D16
Prince Charles Mts.
  Antarctica 72°0S 67°0E **55** D6
Prince Edward Fracture Zone
  Ind. Oc. 46°0S 35°0E **55** A4
Prince Edward I. □
  Canada 46°20N 63°20W **165** C7
Prince Edward Is.
  Ind. Oc. 46°35S 38°0E **146** J2
Prince George *Canada* 53°55N 122°50W **162** C4
Prince of Wales, C.
  U.S.A. 65°36N 168°5W **166** B6
Prince of Wales I.
  Australia 10°40S 142°10E **150** A3
Prince of Wales I.
  Canada 73°0N 99°0W **160** C12
Prince of Wales I.
  U.S.A. 55°47N 132°50W **160** F5
Prince of Wales Icefield
  Canada 78°15N 79°0W **161** B16
Prince of Wales Str.
  Canada 73°0N 117°0W **160** C8
Prince Patrick I. *Canada* 77°0N 120°0W **161** B8
Prince Regent Inlet
  Canada 73°0N 90°0W **161** C14
Prince Rupert *Canada* 54°20N 130°20W **162** C2
Prince William Sd.
  U.S.A. 60°40N 147°0W **160** E2
Princes Town
  Trin. & Tob. 10°16N 61°23W **187** K15
Princesa Isabel *Brazil* 7°44S 38°0W **189** B3
Princess Charlotte B.
  Australia 14°25S 144°0E **150** A3
Princess Elizabeth Trough
  S. Ocean 64°10S 83°0E **55** C7
Princess May Ranges
  Australia 15°30S 125°30E **148** C4
Princess Royal I.
  Canada 53°0N 128°40W **162** C3
Princeton *Canada* 49°27N 120°30W **162** D4
Princeton *Calif., U.S.A.* 39°24N 122°1W **170** F4
Princeton *Ill., U.S.A.* 41°23N 89°28W **172** E9
Princeton *Ind., U.S.A.* 38°21N 87°34W **172** F10
Princeton *Ky., U.S.A.* 37°7N 87°53W **172** G10
Princeton *Mo., U.S.A.* 40°24N 93°35W **172** E7
Princeton *N.J., U.S.A.* 40°21N 74°39W **175** F10
Princeton *W. Va.,*
  U.S.A. 37°22N 81°6W **173** G13
Príncipe
  São Tomé & Príncipe 1°37N 7°25E **132** F4
Príncipe da Beira
  Brazil 12°20S 64°30W **186** F6
Prineville *U.S.A.* 44°18N 120°51W **168** D3
Prins Christian Sund
  Greenland 60°4N 43°10W **57** E6
Prins Harald Kyst
  Antarctica 70°0S 35°1E **55** D4
Prins Karls Forland
  Svalbard 78°30N 11°0E **57** B12
Prinsesse Astrid Kyst
  Antarctica 70°45S 12°30E **55** D3
Prinsesse Ragnhild Kyst
  Antarctica 70°15S 27°30E **55** D4
Prinzapolca *Nic.* 13°20N 83°35W **182** D3
Prior, C. *Spain* 43°34N 8°17W **88** B2
Priozersk *Russia* 61°2N 30°7E **84** B6
Pripet = Prypyat →
  Europe 51°20N 30°15E **75** C16
Pripet Marshes *Europe* 52°10N 27°10E **75** B15
Pripet = Prypyat →
  Europe 51°20N 30°15E **75** C16
Pripyat Marshes = Pripet Marshes
  Europe 52°10N 27°10E **75** B15
Pripyats = Prypyat →
  Europe 51°20N 30°15E **75** C16
Prishtinë *Kosovo* 42°40N 21°13E **96** D5
Prislop, Pasul *Romania* 47°37N 24°48E **81** C9
Pristen *Russia* 51°15N 36°44E **85** G9
Priština = Prishtinë
  Kosovo 42°40N 21°13E **96** D5
Pritzwalk *Germany* 53°9N 12°10E **76** B8
Privas *France* 44°45N 4°37E **73** D8
Priverno *Italy* 41°28N 13°11E **94** A6
Privolzhsk *Russia* 57°23N 41°16E **86** B5
Privolzhskaya Vozvyshennost
  Russia 51°0N 46°0E **86** E7
Privolzhskiy *Russia* 51°25N 46°3E **86** E8
Privolzhskoye □ *Russia* 56°0N 50°0E **106** D6
Privolzhye *Russia* 52°52N 48°33E **86** D9
Priyutnoye *Russia* 46°12N 43°40E **87** G6
Prizren *Kosovo* 42°13N 20°45E **96** D4
Prizzi *Italy* 37°43N 13°26E **94** B5
Prnjavor *Bos.-H.* 44°52N 17°43E **80** F2
Probolinggo *Indonesia* 7°46S 113°13E **119** G15
Prochowice *Poland* 51°16N 16°20E **83** G3
Proctor *U.S.A.* 43°40N 73°2W **175** C11
Proddatur *India* 14°45N 78°30E **127** G4
Prodhromos *Cyprus* 34°57N 32°50E **101** E11
Proença-a-Nova *Portugal* 39°45N 7°54W **88** F3
Profilia *Greece* 36°5N 27°51E **101** C9
Profondeville *Belgium* 50°23N 4°52E **69** D4
Progreso *Coahuila,*
  Mexico 27°28N 100°59W **180** B4
Progreso *Yucatán,*
  Mexico 21°20N 89°40W **181** C7
Progress *Antarctica* 69°20S 76°20E **55** C6
Progress *Russia* 49°45N 129°37E **107** E13
Prokhladnyy *Russia* 43°50N 44°2E **87** J7
Prokhorovka *Russia* 51°2N 36°44E **86** E3
Prokletije *Albania* 42°30N 19°45E **96** D3
Prokopyevsk *Russia* 54°0N 86°45E **109** B11

Prokuplje *Serbia* 43°16N 21°36E **96** C5
Proletarsk *Russia* 46°42N 41°50E **87** G5
Prome = Pye
  Myanmar 18°49N 95°13E **123** K19
Prophet → *Canada* 58°48N 122°40W **162** B4
Prophet River *Canada* 58°6N 122°43W **162** B4
Propriá *Brazil* 10°13S 36°51W **189** C3
Propriano *France* 41°41N 8°52E **73** G12
Proserpine *Australia* 20°21S 148°36E **150** b
Prosna → *Poland* 52°6N 17°44E **83** F4
Prospect *U.S.A.* 43°18N 75°9W **175** C9
Prosperity *U.S.A.* 30°51N 85°56W **178** F4
Prosser *U.S.A.* 46°12N 119°46W **168** C4
Prostějov *Czechia* 49°30N 17°9E **79** B10
Prostki *Poland* 53°42N 22°25E **82** E9
Proston *Australia* 26°8S 151°32E **151** D5
Proszowice *Poland* 50°13N 20°16E **83** H7
Proti *Greece* 37°5N 21°32E **98** D3
Provadiya *Bulgaria* 43°12N 27°30E **97** C11
Provadiyska →
  Bulgaria 43°12N 27°42E **97** C11
Provence *France* 43°40N 5°46E **73** E9
Provence-Alpes-Côte d'Azur □
  France 44°0N 6°0E **73** E10
Providence *Ky.,*
  U.S.A. 37°24N 87°46W **172** G10
Providence *R.I.,*
  U.S.A. 41°49N 71°24W **175** E13
Providence, C. *N.Z.* 45°59S 166°29E **155** F1
Providence Bay
  Canada 45°41N 82°15W **164** C3
Providence Mts.
  U.S.A. 35°10N 115°15W **171** K11
Providencia, I. de
  Caribbean 13°25N 81°26W **182** D3
Provideniya *Russia* 64°23N 173°18W **107** C19
Provincetown *U.S.A.* 42°3N 70°11W **173** D18
Provins *France* 48°33N 3°15E **71** D10
Provo *U.S.A.* 40°14N 111°39W **168** F8
Provost *Canada* 52°25N 110°20W **163** C6
Prozor *Bos.-H.* 43°50N 17°34E **80** G2
Prrenjas *Albania* 41°4N 20°32E **96** E4
Prudhoe Bay *U.S.A.* 70°18N 148°22W **166** A10
Prudhoe I. *Australia* 21°19S 149°41E **150** C4
Prud'homme *Canada* 52°20N 105°54W **163** C7
Prudnik *Poland* 50°20N 17°38E **83** H4
Prüm *Germany* 50°12N 6°25E **77** E2
Prundu *Romania* 44°6N 26°14E **81** F11
Prundu Bârgăului
  Romania 47°13N 24°46E **81** C9
Pruszcz Gdański *Poland* 54°17N 18°40E **82** D5
Pruszków *Poland* 52°9N 20°49E **83** F7
Prut → *Romania* 45°28N 28°10E **81** E13
Pružany *Belarus* 52°33N 24°28E **75** B13
Prvić *Croatia* 44°55N 14°47E **93** D11
Prydz B. *Antarctica* 69°0S 74°0E **55** C6
Pryluky *Ukraine* 50°30N 32°24E **85** G7
Prymorske *Ukraine* 46°48N 36°20E **85** J9
Pryor *U.S.A.* 36°19N 95°19W **176** C7
Prypyat → *Europe* 51°20N 30°15E **75** C16
Prypyatsky △ *Belarus* 52°0N 28°0E **75** C14
Przasnysz *Poland* 53°2N 20°54E **83** E7
Przedbórz *Poland* 51°6N 19°53E **83** G6
Przedecz *Poland* 52°20N 18°53E **83** F5
Przemków *Poland* 51°31N 15°48E **83** G2
Przemyśl *Poland* 49°50N 22°45E **83** J9
Przeworsk *Poland* 50°6N 22°32E **83** H9
Przewóz *Poland* 51°28N 14°57E **83** G1
Przhevalsk = Karakol
  Kyrgyzstan 42°30N 78°20E **109** D9
Przysucha *Poland* 51°22N 20°38E **83** G7
Psachna *Greece* 38°34N 23°35E **98** C5
Psara *Greece* 38°37N 25°38E **99** C7
Psathoura *Greece* 39°30N 24°12E **98** B6
Pserimos *Greece* 36°56N 27°8E **99** E9
Psiloritis, Oros *Greece* 35°15N 24°45E **101** D6
Psira *Greece* 35°12N 25°52E **101** D7
Pskem → *Uzbekistan* 41°38N 70°1E **109** D7
Pskov *Russia* 57°50N 28°25E **84** D5
Pskov □ *Russia* 57°20N 29°0E **84** D5
Pskovskoye, Ozero
  Russia 58°0N 27°58E **84** D5
Psol → *Ukraine* 49°10N 33°37E **85** H7
Psunj *Croatia* 45°25N 17°19E **80** E2
Pteleos *Greece* 39°3N 22°57E **98** B4
Ptich → Ptsich →
  Belarus 52°9N 28°52E **75** B15
Ptichia = Vidos *Greece* 39°38N 19°55E **101** A3
Ptolemaida *Greece* 40°30N 21°43E **96** F5
Ptsich → *Belarus* 52°9N 28°52E **75** B15
Ptuj *Slovenia* 46°28N 15°50E **93** B12
Ptujska Gora *Slovenia* 46°23N 15°47E **93** B12
Pu Xian *China* 36°24N 111°6E **114** F6
Pua *Thailand* 19°11N 100°55E **120** C3
Puán *Argentina* 37°30S 62°45W **190** D3
Pu'an *China* 25°46N 104°57E **116** E5
Pubei *China* 22°16N 109°31E **116** F7
Pucallpa *Peru* 8°25S 74°30W **188** B3
Pucará *Cajamarca, Peru* 6°0S 79°7W **188** B2
Pucará *Puno, Peru* 15°5S 70°24W **188** B3
Pucarani *Bolivia* 16°23S 68°30W **188** D4
Pucheng *China* 27°59N 118°31E **117** D12
Pucheni *Romania* 45°12N 25°17E **81** E10
Puchheim *Germany* 48°9N 11°21E **77** G7
Puch'on = Bucheon
  S. Korea 37°28N 126°45E **115** F14
Púchov *Slovakia* 49°3N 18°20E **79** B11
Pucioasa *Romania* 45°5N 25°25E **81** E10
Pučišća *Croatia* 43°22N 16°43E **93** E13
Puck *Poland* 54°45N 18°23E **82** D5
Pucka, Zatoka *Poland* 54°30N 18°40E **82** D5
Pucol *Spain* 39°37N 0°18W **91** F4
Pudasjärvi *Finland* 65°23N 26°53E **60** D22
Puding *China* 26°18N 105°44E **116** D5
Pudozh *Russia* 61°48N 36°32E **84** A9
Pudu = Suizhou *China* 31°42N 113°24E **117** B9
Pudukkottai *India* 10°28N 78°47E **127** J4
Puebla *Mexico* 19°3N 98°12W **181** D5
Puebla □ *Mexico* 18°50N 98°0W **181** D5
Puebla de Alcocer *Spain* 38°59N 5°14W **89** G5
Puebla de Don Fadrique
  Spain 37°58N 2°25W **91** H2
Puebla de Don Rodrigo
  Spain 39°5N 4°37W **89** F6
Puebla de Guzmán *Spain* 37°37N 7°15W **89** H3
Puebla de la Calzada
  Spain 38°54N 6°37W **89** G4
Puebla de Sanabria *Spain* 42°4N 6°38W **88** C4
Puebla de Trives = Pobra de
  Trives *Spain* 42°20N 7°10W **88** C3
Pueblo *U.S.A.* 38°16N 104°37W **168** G11

Puelches *Argentina* 38°5S 65°51W **190** D2
Puelén *Argentina* 37°32S 67°38W **190** D2
Puente Alto *Chile* 33°32S 70°35W **190** C1
Puente-Genil *Spain* 37°22N 4°47W **89** H6
Puente la Reina *Spain* 42°40N 1°49W **90** C3
Puente San Miguel *Spain* 43°21N 4°5W **88** B6
Puenteareas = Ponteareas
  Spain 42°10N 8°28W **88** C2
Puentedeume = Pontedeume
  Spain 43°24N 8°10W **88** B2
Puentes de Garcia Rodriguez = As
  Pontes de García Rodríguez
  Spain 43°27N 7°50W **88** B3
Pu'er *China* 23°20N 101°15E **116** F3
Puerca, Pta. *Puerto Rico* 18°13N 65°36W **183** d
Puerco → *U.S.A.* 34°22N 107°50W **169** J10
Puerto Acosta *Bolivia* 15°32S 69°15W **188** D4
Puerto Aisén *Chile* 45°27S 73°0W **192** C2
Puerto Ángel *Mexico* 15°40N 96°29W **181** D5
Puerto Arista *Mexico* 15°56N 93°48W **181** D6
Puerto Armuelles
  Panama 8°20N 82°51W **182** E3
Puerto Ayacucho
  Venezuela 5°40N 67°35W **186** B5
Puerto Barrios
  Guatemala 15°40N 88°32W **182** C2
Puerto Bermejo
  Argentina 26°55S 58°34W **190** B4
Puerto Bermúdez *Peru* 10°20S 74°58W **188** C3
Puerto Bolívar *Ecuador* 3°19S 79°55W **186** D3
Puerto Cabello
  Venezuela 10°28N 68°1W **186** A5
Puerto Cabezas *Nic.* 14°0N 83°30W **182** D3
Puerto Cabo Gracias á Dios
  Nic. 15°0N 83°10W **182** D3
Puerto Carreño
  Colombia 6°12N 67°22W **186** B5
Puerto Castilla *Honduras* 16°0N 86°0W **182** C2
Puerto Chicama *Peru* 7°45S 79°20W **188** B2
Puerto Cisnes *Chile* 44°45S 72°42W **192** C2
Puerto Coig *Argentina* 50°54S 69°15W **192** D3
Puerto Cortés *Honduras* 15°51N 88°0W **182** C2
Puerto Cumarebo
  Venezuela 11°29N 69°30W **186** A5
Puerto de Alcudia = Port
  d'Alcúdia *Spain* 39°50N 3°7E **100** B10
Puerto de Cabrera *Spain* 39°8N 2°56E **100** B9
Puerto de la Cruz
  Canary Is. 28°24N 16°32W **100** F3
Puerto de los Angeles △
  Mexico 23°39N 105°45W **180** C3
Puerto de Mazarrón
  Spain 37°34N 1°15W **91** H3
Puerto de Sóller = Port de Sóller
  Spain 39°48N 2°42E **100** B9
Puerto de Somosierra
  Spain 41°9N 3°35W **88** D7
Puerto del Carmen
  Canary Is. 28°55N 13°38W **100** F6
Puerto del Rosario
  Canary Is. 28°30N 13°52W **100** F6
Puerto Deseado
  Argentina 47°55S 66°0W **192** C3
Puerto Escondido
  Mexico 15°50N 97°3W **181** D5
Puerto Heath *Bolivia* 12°34S 68°39W **188** C4
Puerto Inca *Peru* 9°22S 74°54W **188** B3
Puerto Inírida *Colombia* 3°53N 67°52W **186** C5
Puerto Juárez *Mexico* 21°11N 86°49W **181** C7
Puerto La Cruz
  Venezuela 10°13N 64°38W **186** A6
Puerto Leguízamo
  Colombia 0°12S 74°46W **186** D4
Puerto Lempira
  Honduras 15°16N 83°46W **182** C3
Puerto Libertad
  Mexico 29°55N 112°43W **180** B2
Puerto Limón *Colombia* 3°23N 73°30W **186** C4
Puerto Lobos *Argentina* 42°0S 65°3W **192** B3
Puerto Lumbreras *Spain* 37°34N 1°48W **91** H3
Puerto Madryn
  Argentina 42°48S 65°4W **192** B3
Puerto Maldonado
  Peru 12°30S 69°10W **188** C4
Puerto Manatí *Cuba* 21°22N 76°50W **182** B4
Puerto Montt *Chile* 41°28S 73°0W **192** B2
Puerto Morazán *Nic.* 12°51N 87°11W **182** D2
Puerto Morelos *Mexico* 20°50N 86°52W **181** C7
Puerto Natales *Chile* 51°45S 72°15W **192** D2
Puerto Oscuro *Chile* 31°24S 71°35W **190** C1
Puerto Padre *Cuba* 21°13N 76°35W **182** B4
Puerto Páez *Venezuela* 6°13N 67°28W **186** B5
Puerto Peñasco
  Mexico 31°20N 113°33W **180** A2
Puerto Pinasco
  Paraguay 22°36S 57°50W **190** A4
Puerto Pirámides
  Argentina 42°35S 64°20W **192** B3
Puerto Plata *Dom. Rep.* 19°48N 70°45W **183** C5
Puerto Pollensa = Port de
  Pollença *Spain* 39°54N 3°4E **100** B10
Puerto Portillo *Peru* 9°55S 72°42W **188** B3
Puerto Princesa *Phil.* 9°46N 118°45E **119** C5
Puerto Quepos *Costa Rica* 9°29N 84°6W **182** E3
Puerto Real *Spain* 36°33N 6°12W **89** J4
Puerto Rico *Bolivia* 11°5S 67°38W **188** C4
Puerto Rico ☑ *Canary Is.* 27°47N 15°42W **100** G4
Puerto Rico ☑ *W. Indies* 18°15N 66°45W **183** d
Puerto Rico Trench
  Atl. Oc. 19°50N 66°0W **183** C6
Puerto Saavedra *Chile* 38°47S 73°24W **192** A2
Puerto San Julián
  Argentina 49°15S 67°45W **192** C3
Puerto Santa Cruz
  Argentina 50°0S 68°32W **192** D3
Puerto Sastre *Paraguay* 22°2S 57°55W **190** A4
Puerto Serrano *Spain* 36°56N 5°33W **89** J5
Puerto Suárez *Bolivia* 18°58S 57°52W **188** G7
Puerto Supe *Peru* 11°0S 77°30W **188** C2
Puerto Vallarta
  Mexico 20°37N 105°15W **180** C3
Puerto Wilches *Colombia* 7°21N 73°54W **186** B4
Puerto Williams *Chile* 54°50S 68°30W **192** E3
Puertollano *Spain* 38°43N 4°7W **89** G6
Puertомarín *Spain* 42°48N 7°37W **88** C3
Pueu *Tahiti* 17°44S 149°13W **155** b
Pueyrredón, L.
  Argentina 47°20S 72°0W **192** C2
Puffin I. *Ireland* 51°50N 10°24W **64** E1
Pugачev *Russia* 52°0N 48°49E **86** D9

Pugal *India* 28°30N 72°48E **124** E5
Puge *China* 27°20N 102°31E **116** D4
Puge *Tanzania* 4°45S 33°11E **142** C3
Puget Sound *U.S.A.* 47°50N 122°30W **170** C4
Puget-Théniers *France* 43°58N 6°53E **73** E10
Púglia □ *Italy* 41°15N 16°15E **95** A9
Pugо̀dong *N. Korea* 42°5N 130°0E **115** C16
Pugu *Tanzania* 6°55S 39°4E **142** D4
Pŭgŭnzi *Iran* 25°49N 59°10E **129** E8
Puha *N.Z.* 38°30S 177°50E **154** F6
Pui *Romania* 45°30N 23°4E **80** E8
Puica *Peru* 15°5S 72°33W **188** D3
Puieşti *Romania* 46°25N 27°33E **81** D12
Puig Major *Spain* 39°48N 2°47E **100** B9
Puigcerdà *Spain* 42°24N 1°50E **90** C6
Puigmal *Spain* 42°23N 2°7E **90** C7
Puijiang *China* 30°14N 103°30E **116** B4
Puisaye, Collines de la
  France 47°37N 3°20E **71** E10
Puisseaux *France* 48°11N 2°30E **71** D9
Pujehun *S. Leone* 7°23N 11°45W **138** D2
Pujiang *China* 29°29N 119°54E **117** C12
Pujols *France* 44°48N 0°2W **72** D3
Pujon-ho *N. Korea* 40°35N 127°35E **115** D14
Pukaki, L. *N.Z.* 44°4S 170°1E **155** J11
Pukapuka *Cook Is.* 10°53S 165°49W **157** J11
Pukaskwa △ *Canada* 48°20N 86°0W **164** C2
Pukatawagan *Canada* 55°45N 101°20W **163** B8
Pukchin *N. Korea* 40°12N 125°45E **115** D13
Pukch'ŏng *N. Korea* 40°14N 128°19E **115** D15
Pukë *Albania* 42°2N 19°53E **96** D3
Pukearuhe *N.Z.* 38°55S 174°31E **154** C3
Puketeraki Ra. *N.Z.* 42°58S 172°13E **155** C7
Puketoi Ra. *N.Z.* 40°35S 176°5E **154** G5
Pukeuri *N.Z.* 45°4S 171°2E **155** F6
Pukhrayan *India* 26°14N 79°51E **125** F8
Puksoobaek-san
  N. Korea 40°42N 127°45E **115** D14
Pula *Croatia* 44°54N 13°57E **93** D10
Pula *Italy* 39°1N 9°0E **94** C1
Pulacayo *Bolivia* 20°25S 66°41W **188** E4
Pulandian *China* 39°25N 121°58E **115** E11
Pulaski *N.Y., U.S.A.* 43°34N 76°8W **175** C8
Pulaski *Tenn., U.S.A.* 35°12N 87°2W **177** D11
Pulaski *Va., U.S.A.* 37°3N 80°47W **173** G13
Pulau → *Indonesia* 5°50S 138°15E **119** F9
Pulau Gili *Indonesia* 8°21S 116°1E **119** J19
Pulawy *Poland* 51°23N 21°59E **83** G9
Pulga *China* 35°48N 121°29W **170** D5
Pulgaon *India* 20°44N 78°21E **126** D4
Pulicat *India* 13°25N 80°19E **127** H5
Pulicat L. *India* 13°40N 80°15E **127** H5
Pulivendla *India* 14°25N 78°14E **127** G4
Puliyangudi *India* 9°11N 77°24E **127** K3
Pullman *U.S.A.* 46°44N 117°10W **168** C5
Pulog, Mt. *Phil.* 16°40N 120°50E **119** A6
Pulpí *Spain* 37°24N 1°44W **91** H3
Pultusk *Poland* 52°43N 21°6E **83** F8
Pülümür *Turkey* 39°30N 39°51E **105** C8
Pumlumon Fawr *U.K.* 52°28N 3°46W **67** E4
Pumpunang → *India* 25°31N 85°18E **125** G11
Puná, I. *Ecuador* 2°55S 80°5W **186** D2
Punaauia *Tahiti* 17°37S 149°34W **155** b
Punakha Dzong
  Bhutan 27°42N 89°52E **123** F16
Punalur *India* 9°0N 76°56E **127** K3
Punasar *India* 27°6N 73°6E **124** F5
Punata *Bolivia* 17°32S 65°50W **188** G5
Punch *India* 33°48N 74°4E **126** C5
Punch → *Pakistan* 33°12N 73°40E **124** C5
Punda Maria *S. Africa* 22°40S 31°5E **145** B5
Pune *India* 18°29N 73°57E **126** F2
Pungue, Ponte de *Mozam.* 19°0S 34°0E **143** H6
Puning *China* 23°20N 116°12E **117** F11
Punjab □ *India* 31°0N 76°0E **124** D7
Punjab □ *Pakistan* 32°0N 72°30E **124** E6
Puno *Peru* 15°55S 70°3W **188** D3
Puno □ *Peru* 14°30S 70°0W **188** D3
Punpun → *India* 25°31N 85°18E **125** G11
Punta, Cerro de
  Puerto Rico 18°10N 66°37W **183** d
Punta Alta *Argentina* 38°53S 62°4W **192** A4
Punta Arenas *Chile* 53°10S 71°0W **192** D2
Punta Coles *Peru* 17°43S 71°23W **188** D3
Punta de Bombón
  Peru 17°10S 71°48W **188** D3
Punta del Díaz *Chile* 28°0S 70°45W **190** B1
Punta del Hidalgo
  Canary Is. 28°33N 16°19W **100** F3
Punta Delgada
  Argentina 42°43S 63°38W **192** B4
Punta Gorda *Belize* 16°10N 88°45W **181** D7
Punta Gorda *U.S.A.* 26°56N 82°3W **179** J7
Punta Prieta *Mexico* 28°58N 114°17W **180** B2
Punta Prima *Spain* 39°48N 4°16E **100** B11
Punta Umbría *Spain* 37°10N 6°56W **89** H4
Puntarenas *Costa Rica* 10°0N 84°50W **182** E3
Puntland *Somalia* 9°0N 50°0E **131** F4
Punto Fijo *Venezuela* 11°50N 70°13W **186** A4
Punxsutawney *U.S.A.* 40°57N 78°59W **174** F6
Puan *Indonesia* 0°35S 119°18E **119** E6
Puqi *China* 29°40N 113°50E **117** C9
Puquio *Peru* 14°45S 74°10W **188** C3
Pur → *Russia* 67°31N 77°55E **106** C8
Purace, Vol. *Colombia* 2°21N 76°23W **186** C3
Puracíc *Bos.-H.* 44°33N 18°28E **80** F3
Puralia = Puruliya
  India 23°17N 86°24E **125** H12
Puranpur *India* 28°31N 80°9E **125** E9
Purbalingga *Indonesia* 7°23S 109°21E **119** G13
Purbeck, Isle of *U.K.* 50°39N 1°59W **67** G5
Purcell *U.S.A.* 35°1N 97°22W **176** D6
Purcell Mts. *Canada* 49°55N 116°15W **162** D5
Purdy *Canada* 45°0N 77°40W **174** B7
Puri *India* 19°50N 85°58E **126** E7
Purmerend *Neths.* 52°32N 4°58E **69** B4
Purna → *India* 19°6N 77°2E **126** E3
Purnia *India* 25°45N 87°31E **125** G12
Purnululu △ *Australia* 17°20S 128°20E **148** C4
Pursat = Pouthisat
  Cambodia 12°34N 103°50E **120** F4
Purukcahu *Indonesia* 0°35S 114°35E **118** E4
Puruliya *India* 23°17N 86°24E **125** H12
Purus → *Brazil* 3°42S 61°28W **186** D6
Puruvesi *Finland* 61°46N 29°14E **63** B9
Purvis *U.S.A.* 31°9N 89°25W **177** F10
Purwa *India* 26°28N 80°47E **125** F9
Purwakarta *Indonesia* 6°35S 107°29E **119** G12
Purwo, Tanjung
  Indonesia 8°44S 114°21E **119** K18

Purwodadi *Indonesia* 7°7S 110°55E **119** G14
Purwokerto *Indonesia* 7°25S 109°14E **119** G13
Puryŏng *N. Korea* 42°5N 129°43E **115** C15
Pus → *India* 19°55N 77°55E **126** E3
Pusa *India* 25°59N 85°41E **125** G11
Pusad *India* 19°56N 77°36E **126** E3
Pusan = Busan
  S. Korea 35°5N 129°0E **115** G15
Pushkin *Russia* 59°45N 30°25E **84** C6
Pushkino *Moskva, Russia* 56°2N 37°49E **84** C9
Pushkino *Saratov, Russia* 51°16N 47°0E **86** E8
Püspökladány *Hungary* 47°19N 21°6E **80** C6
Pustoshka *Russia* 56°20N 29°30E **84** D5
Put-in-Bay *U.S.A.* 41°39N 82°49W **174** E2
Putahow L. *Canada* 59°54N 100°40W **163** B8
Putao *Myanmar* 27°28N 97°30E **123** F20
Putaruru *N.Z.* 38°2S 175°50E **154** E4
Putbus *Germany* 54°22N 13°28E **76** A9
Puteran *Indonesia* 7°5S 114°0E **119** G15
Putian *China* 25°23N 119°0E **117** E12
Putignano *Italy* 40°51N 17°7E **95** B10
Puting, Tanjung
  Indonesia 3°31S 111°46E **118** E4
Putlitz *Germany* 53°15N 12°2E **76** B8
Putna *Romania* 47°50N 25°33E **81** C10
Putna → *Romania* 45°42N 27°26E **81** E12
Putnam *U.S.A.* 41°55N 71°55W **175** E13
Putney *U.S.A.* 31°29N 84°8W **178** D5
Putnok *Hungary* 48°18N 20°26E **80** B5
Putorana, Gory *Russia* 69°0N 95°0E **107** C10
Putorino *N.Z.* 39°4S 176°58E **154** F5
Putrajaya *Malaysia* 2°55N 101°40E **121** L3
Putre *Chile* 18°12S 69°35W **188** G5
Puttalam *Sri Lanka* 8°1N 79°55W **127** K5
Puttalam Lagoon
  Sri Lanka 8°15N 79°45E **127** K4
Puttgarden *Germany* 54°30N 11°10E **76** A7
Püttlingen *Germany* 49°17N 6°53E **77** F2
Puttur *Andhra Pradesh,*
  India 13°27N 79°33E **127** H4
Puttur *Karnataka, India* 12°46N 75°12E **127** H2
Putty *Australia* 32°57S 150°42E **153** B9
Putumayo → *S. Amer.* 3°7S 67°58W **186** D5
Putuo *China* 29°56N 122°20E **117** C14
Putussibau *Indonesia* 0°50N 112°56E **118** D4
Pututahi *N.Z.* 38°39S 177°53E **154** E6
Putyla *Ukraine* 48°0N 25°5E **81** B10
Puvirnituq *Canada* 60°2N 77°10W **161** E16
Puy-de-Dôme *France* 45°46N 2°57E **72** C6
Puy-de-Dôme □ *France* 45°40N 3°5E **72** C7
Puy-l'Évêque *France* 44°31N 1°9E **72** D5
Puyallup *U.S.A.* 47°12N 122°18W **170** C4
Puyang *China* 35°40N 115°1E **114** G8
Puyehue *Chile* 40°40S 72°37W **192** B2
Puyehue △ *Chile* 40°27S 72°6W **192** B2
Puylaurens *France* 43°35S 2°0E **72** E6
Puysegur Pt. *N.Z.* 46°9S 166°37E **155** G1
Pūzeh Rīg *Iran* 27°20N 58°40E **129** E8
Puzhaykove *Ukraine* 48°7N 29°50E **81** A14
Pwani □ *Tanzania* 7°0S 39°0E **142** D4
Pweto
  Dem. Rep. of the Congo 8°25S 28°51E **143** D2
Pwllheli *U.K.* 52°53N 4°25W **66** E3
Pyana → *Russia* 55°43N 46°1E **86** C8
Pyaozero, Ozero *Russia* 66°5N 30°58E **60** C24
Pyapon *Myanmar* 16°20N 95°40E **123** L19
Pyasina → *Russia* 73°30N 87°0E **107** B9
Pyatigorsk *Russia* 44°2N 43°6E **87** H6
Pyatykhatky *Ukraine* 48°28N 33°38E **85** H7
Pyay = Pye *Myanmar* 18°49N 95°13E **123** K19
Pydna *Greece* 40°20N 22°34E **96** F6
Pye *Myanmar* 18°49N 95°13E **123** K19
Pyeongtaek *S. Korea* 37°1N 127°4E **115** F14
Pyetrikaw *Belarus* 52°11N 28°29E **75** B15
Pyhäjoki *Finland* 64°28N 24°14E **60** D21
Pyhäntürri *Finland* 63°21N 27°5E **60** C22
Pyin-U-Lwin *Myanmar* 22°2N 96°28E **123** H20
Pyinmana *Myanmar* 19°45N 96°12E **123** K20
Pyla, C. *Cyprus* 34°56N 33°51E **101** E12
Pymatuning Res.
  U.S.A. 41°30N 80°28W **174** E4
Pyŏktong *N. Korea* 40°50N 125°50E **115** D13
P'yŏnggang *N. Korea* 38°24N 127°17E **115** E14
P'yŏngsong *N. Korea* 39°14N 125°52E **115** E13
Pyote *U.S.A.* 31°32N 103°8W **176** F3
Pyramid L. *U.S.A.* 40°1N 119°35W **168** F4
Pyramid Pk. *U.S.A.* 36°25N 116°37W **171** J10
Pyramids *Egypt* 29°58N 31°9E **137** C12
Pyrénées *Europe* 42°45N 0°18E **72** F4
Pyrénées → *France* 42°52N 0°10W **72** F3
Pyrénées-Atlantiques □
  France 43°10N 0°50W **72** E3
Pyrénées-Orientales □
  France 42°35N 2°26E **72** F6
Pyryatyn *Ukraine* 50°15N 32°25E **85** G7
Pyrzyce *Poland* 53°10N 14°55E **83** E1
Pyskowice *Poland* 50°24N 18°38E **83** H5
Pytalovo *Russia* 57°5N 27°55E **84** D4
Pyu *Myanmar* 18°30N 96°28E **123** K20
Pyzdry *Poland* 52°11N 17°42E **83** F4

Q

Qaanaaq *Greenland* 77°30N 69°10W **57** B4
Qaasuitsup □ *Greenland* 74°0N 52°0W **57** C5
Qäbälä *Azerbaijan* 40°58N 47°47E **87** K8
Qabanbay *Kazakhstan* 45°50N 80°37E **109** C10
Qabirri → *Azerbaijan* 41°3N 46°17E **87** K8
Qachasnek *S. Africa* 30°6S 28°42E **145** D4
Qādiriyah, Buhayrat al
  Iraq 34°20N 42°12E **105** C4
Qa'el Jafr *Jordan* 30°20N 36°25E **130** E5
Qa'emābād *Iran* 31°44N 60°2E **129** D9
Qā'emshahr *Iran* 36°30N 52°53E **129** B7
Qafē-Shtamē △ *Albania* 41°31N 19°54E **96** E3
Qagan *Nur Jilin,*
  China 45°45N 124°18E **115** B13
Qagan Nur *Nei Monggol Zizhiqu,*
  China 43°30N 114°55E **114** C8
Qahar Youyi Zhongqi
  China 41°12N 112°40E **114** C7
Qahremānshahr = Kermānshāh
  Iran 34°23N 47°0E **105** C12
Qaidam Pendi *China* 37°0N 95°0E **110** D8
Qaiyara *Iraq* 35°48N 43°17E **105** B10
Qajarīyeh *Iran* 31°1N 48°22E **129** D6
Qala, Ras il *Malta* 36°2N 14°20E **101** C1

Qala-i-Jadid = Spīn Būldak Afghan. 31°1N 66°25E 124 D2
Qala Point = Qala, Ras il Malta 36°2N 14°20E 101 C1
Qala Viala Pakistan 30°49N 67°17E 124 D2
Qala Yangi Afghan. 34°20N 66°30E 124 B2
Qalaikhum = Kalaikhum Tajikistan 38°28N 70°46E 109 E8
Qal'at al Akhḍar Si. Arabia 28°4N 37°9E 128 E3
Qal'at Bīshah Si. Arabia 20°0N 42°36E 137 C5
Qal'at Dīzah Iraq 36°11N 45°7E 105 D11
Qal'at Ṣāliḥ Iraq 31°31N 47°16E 128 D5
Qal'at Sukkar Iraq 31°51N 46°5E 105 G12
Qal'eh-ye Now Afghan. 35°0N 63°5E 108 F6
Qalyûb Egypt 30°12N 31°11E 137 E7
Qamani'tuaq = Baker Lake Canada 64°20N 96°3W 160 E12
Qamdo China 31°15N 97°6E 116 B1
Qamea Fiji 16°45S 179°45W 154 a
Qamruddin Karez Pakistan 31°45N 68°20E 124 D3
Qandahār = Kandahār Afghan. 31°32N 65°43E 122 D4
Qandahār = Kandahār □ Afghan. 31°0N 65°0E 122 D4
Qandyaghash Kazakhstan 49°28N 57°25E 108 C5
Qapān Iran 37°40N 55°47E 129 B7
Qapqal China 43°48N 81°5E 109 D10
Qapshaghay Kazakhstan 43°51N 77°14E 109 D9
Qapshaghay Bögeni Kazakhstan 43°45N 77°50E 109 D9
Qaqortoq Greenland 60°43N 46°0W 57 E6
Qâra Egypt 29°38N 26°30E 137 B2
Qara Dāgh Iraq 35°18N 45°18E 105 E11
Qara Qash → China 35°0N 78°30E 125 B8
Qarabalyq Kazakhstan 53°45N 62°2E 108 B6
Qarabutaq Kazakhstan 50°0N 60°14E 108 C6
Qaraçala Azerbaijan 39°45N 48°53E 87 L9
Qaraçuxar Azerbaijan 40°25N 50°1E 87 K10
Qaraghandy Kazakhstan 49°50N 73°10E 109 C8
Qaraghayly Kazakhstan 49°26N 76°0E 106 E8
Qārah Si. Arabia 29°55N 40°3E 128 D4
Qarah Āghāj Iran 37°8N 46°58E 105 D12
Qaraoba Kazakhstan 47°6N 56°15E 108 C5
Qaraqīya Oyysy Kazakhstan 43°27N 51°45E 108 D4
Qaraqosh Iraq 36°16N 43°22E 105 D10
Qarataū Ongtüstik Qazaqstan, Kazakhstan 43°30N 69°30E 109 D7
Qarataū Zhambyl, Kazakhstan 43°10N 70°28E 109 D8
Qarazhal Kazakhstan 48°2N 70°49E 106 E8
Qarchak Iran 35°25N 51°34E 129 C6
Qardho Somalia 9°30N 49°6E 131 F4
Qareh → Iran 39°25N 47°22E 105 C12
Qareh Tekān Iran 36°38N 49°29E 129 B6
Qarnein U.A.E. 24°56N 52°52E 129 E7
Qarokŭl = Karakul, Ozero Tajikistan 39°5N 73°25E 109 E8
Qarqan He → China 39°30N 88°30E 109 E11
Qarqaraly Kazakhstan 49°26N 75°30E 109 C9
Qarshi Uzbekistan 38°53N 65°48E 109 E7
Qartabā Lebanon 34°4N 35°50E 130 A4
Qārūh Kuwait 28°49N 48°46E 129 D6
Qaryat al Gharab Iraq 31°27N 44°48E 128 D5
Qaryat al 'Ulyā Si. Arabia 27°33N 47°42E 128 E5
Qarynzharyq Oyysy Kazakhstan 42°55N 54°25E 108 D4
Qashqadaryo □ Uzbekistan 38°35N 66°0E 109 E7
Qasigiannguit Greenland 68°50N 51°18W 57 D5
Qasr 'Amra Jordan 31°48N 36°35E 128 D3
Qaṣr-e Qand Iran 26°15N 60°45E 129 E9
Qaṣr-e Shīrīn Iran 34°31N 45°35E 105 E11
Qasr Farâfra Egypt 27°0N 28°1E 137 B2
Qasuittuq = Resolute Canada 74°42N 94°54W 161 C13
Qatanā Syria 33°26N 36°4E 130 B5
Qatar ■ Asia 25°30N 51°15E 129 E6
Qatlīsh Iran 37°50N 57°19E 129 B8
Qattâra Egypt 30°12N 27°3E 137 A2
Qattâra, Munkhafed el Egypt 29°30N 27°30E 137 B2
Qattâra Depression = Qattâra, Munkhafed el Egypt 29°30N 27°30E 137 B2
Qausuittuq △ Canada 76°0N 101°0W 161 B11
Qawām al Ḥamzah = Al Ḥamzah Iraq 31°43N 44°58E 128 D5
Qāyen Iran 33°40N 59°10E 129 C8
Qaynar Kazakhstan 49°12N 77°22E 109 C9
Qazaly Kazakhstan 45°45N 62°6E 108 C6
Qazaqstan = Kazakhstan ■ Asia 50°0N 70°0E 109 C8
Qazaqtyng Usaqshogylyghy Kazakhstan 50°0N 72°0E 109 C8
Qazax Azerbaijan 41°5N 45°21E 87 K7
Qazımämmäd Azerbaijan 40°3N 49°0E 87 K9
Qazvīn Iran 36°15N 50°0E 129 B6
Qazvīn □ Iran 36°20N 50°0E 129 B6
Qazyghurt Kazakhstan 41°45N 69°23E 109 D7
Qena Egypt 26°10N 32°43E 137 B3
Qena, W. → Egypt 26°12N 32°44E 137 B3
Qeqertarsuaq Qaasuitsup, Greenland 69°45N 53°30W 57 D5
Qeqertarsuaq Qaasuitsup, Greenland 69°15N 53°38W 57 D5
Qeqertarsuatsiaat Greenland 63°5N 50°45W 57 E5
Qeqqata □ Greenland 66°30N 48°0W 57 D6
Qeshlāq Iran 34°55N 46°28E 105 E12
Qeshm Iran 26°55N 56°10E 129 E8
Qeydār Iran 36°6N 48°35E 105 D13
Qeys Iran 26°32N 53°58E 129 E7
Qezel Owzen → Iran 36°45N 49°22E 129 B6
Qezi'ot Israel 30°52N 34°26E 130 E3
Qi Xian China 34°40N 114°48E 114 G8
Qian Gorlos China 45°5N 124°42E 115 B13
Qian Hai China 22°32N 113°54E 111 a
Qian Xian China 34°31N 108°15E 114 G5
Qian'an China 40°0N 118°41E 115 E10
Qiancheng China 27°12N 109°50E 116 D7
Qianjiang Guangxi Zhuangzu, China 23°38N 108°58E 116 F7
Qianjiang Hubei, China 30°24N 112°55E 117 B9
Qianjiang Sichuan, China 29°33N 108°47E 116 C7
Qianjin China 47°34N 133°4E 111 B15
Qianshan Anhui, China 30°37N 116°35E 117 B11
Qianshan Guangdong, China 22°15N 113°31E 111 a
Qianwei China 29°13N 103°56E 116 C4
Qianxi China 27°3N 106°3E 116 D6
Qianyang Hunan, China 27°18N 110°10E 117 D8
Qianyang Shaanxi, China 34°40N 107°8E 114 G4
Qianyang Zhejiang, China 30°11N 119°25E 117 B12
Qi'ao China 22°25N 113°39E 111 a
Qi'ao Dao China 22°25N 113°38E 111 a
Qiaocun China 39°56N 112°55E 114 E7
Qiaojia China 26°56N 102°58E 116 D4
Qichun China 30°18N 115°25E 117 B10
Qidong Hunan, China 26°49N 112°7E 117 D9
Qidong Jiangsu, China 31°48N 121°38E 117 B13
Qiemo China 38°8N 85°32E 109 E11
Qijiang China 28°57N 106°35E 116 C6
Qijiaojing China 43°28N 91°36E 109 D12
Qikiqtaaluk = Baffin I. Canada 68°0N 75°0W 161 D17
Qikiqtarjuaq Canada 67°33N 63°0W 161 D19
Qila Saifullāh Pakistan 30°45N 68°17E 124 D3
Qilian Shan China 38°30N 96°0E 110 D8
Qimen China 29°50N 117°42E 117 C11
Qin He → China 35°1N 113°22E 114 G7
Qin Jiang → Guangxi Zhuangzu, China 21°53N 108°35E 116 F7
Qin Jiang → Jiangxi, China 26°15N 115°55E 117 D10
Qin Ling = Qinling Shandi China 33°50N 108°10E 114 H5
Qin'an China 34°48N 105°40E 114 G3
Qing Xian China 38°35N 116°45E 114 E9
Qingcheng China 37°15N 117°40E 115 F9
Qingcheng Shan China 30°58N 103°31E 116 B4
Qingchuan China 32°36N 105°9E 114 H3
Qingdao China 36°5N 120°20E 115 F11
Qingfeng China 35°52N 115°8E 114 G8
Qinghai □ China 36°0N 98°0E 110 D8
Qinghai Hu China 36°40N 100°10E 110 D9
Qinghe China 46°37N 90°25E 109 C12
Qinghecheng China 41°28N 124°15E 115 D13
Qinghemen China 41°48N 121°25E 115 D11
Qingjian China 37°8N 110°8E 114 F6
Qingjiang = Huaiyin China 33°30N 119°2E 115 H10
Qingliu China 26°11N 116°48E 117 D11
Qinglong China 25°49N 105°12E 116 E5
Qingping China 26°39N 107°47E 116 D6
Qingshui China 34°48N 106°8E 114 G4
Qingshuihe China 39°55N 111°35E 114 E6
Qingtian China 28°12N 120°15E 117 C13
Qingtongxia China 38°2N 106°3E 114 E4
Qingtongxia Shuiku China 37°50N 105°58E 114 F3
Qingxi China 27°8N 108°43E 116 D7
Qingxu China 37°34N 112°22E 114 F7
Qingyang Anhui, China 30°38N 117°50E 117 B11
Qingyang Gansu, China 36°2N 107°55E 114 F4
Qingyi Jiang → China 29°32N 103°44E 116 C4
Qingyuan Guangdong, China 23°40N 112°59E 117 F9
Qingyuan Liaoning, China 42°10N 124°55E 115 C13
Qingyuan Zhejiang, China 27°36N 119°3E 117 D12
Qingyun China 37°45N 117°20E 115 F9
Qingzhen China 26°31N 106°25E 116 D6
Qinhuangdao China 39°56N 119°30E 115 E10
Qinling Shandi China 33°50N 108°10E 114 H5
Qinshui China 35°40N 112°8E 114 G7
Qinyang = Jiyuan China 35°7N 112°57E 114 G7
Qinyang China 35°5N 112°56E 114 G7
Qinyuan China 36°29N 112°20E 114 F7
Qinzhou China 21°58N 108°38E 116 G7
Qionghai China 19°15N 110°26E 117 a
Qionglai China 30°25N 103°31E 116 B4
Qionglai Shan China 31°0N 102°30E 116 B4
Qiongshan China 19°51N 110°26E 117 a
Qiongzhou Haixia China 20°10N 110°15E 117 a
Qiqihar China 47°26N 124°0E 111 B13
Qira China 37°0N 80°48E 109 E10
Qiraîya, W. → Egypt 30°27N 34°0E 130 E3
Qiryat Ata Israel 32°47N 35°6E 130 C4
Qiryat Gat Israel 31°32N 34°46E 130 D3
Qiryat Mal'akhi Israel 31°44N 34°44E 130 D3
Qiryat Shemona Israel 33°13N 35°35E 130 B4
Qiryat Yam Israel 32°51N 35°4E 130 C4
Qishan China 34°25N 107°38E 114 G4
Qitai China 44°2N 89°35E 109 D11
Qitaihe China 45°48N 130°51E 112 B5
Qiubei China 24°2N 104°12E 116 E5
Qixia China 37°17N 120°52E 115 F11
Qiyang China 26°35N 111°50E 117 D8
Qızılağac Körfäzi Azerbaijan 39°9N 49°0E 105 C13
Qobda Kazakhstan 50°55N 54°31E 108 B4
Qods Iran 35°45N 51°15E 129 C6
Qojūr Iran 36°12N 47°55E 128 B5
Qom Iran 34°40N 51°0E 129 C6
Qom □ Iran 34°40N 51°0E 129 C6
Qomolangma Feng = Everest, Mt. Nepal 28°5N 86°58E 125 E12
Qomsheh Iran 32°0N 51°55E 129 D6
Qong Muztag China 35°42N 82°22E 109 E10
Qoqek = Tacheng China 46°40N 82°58E 109 C10
Qoqon = Qo'qon Uzbekistan 40°31N 70°56E 109 D8
Qo'qon Uzbekistan 40°31N 70°56E 109 D8
Qorako'l Uzbekistan 39°32N 63°50E 108 E6
Qoraqalpog'istan □ Uzbekistan 43°0N 58°0E 108 D5
Qorghalzhyn Kazakhstan 50°25N 69°11E 109 B7
Qorveh Iran 35°10N 47°48E 105 E12
Qosshaghyl Kazakhstan 46°40N 54°0E 108 C4
Qostanay Kazakhstan 53°10N 63°35E 108 B6
Qotanqaraghay Kazakhstan 49°10N 85°36E 109 C11
Qoṭūr Iran 38°28N 44°25E 105 C11
Qu Jiang → China 30°1N 106°24E 116 B6
Qu Xian China 30°48N 106°58E 116 B6
Quabbin Res. U.S.A. 42°20N 72°20W 175 D12
Quairading Australia 32°0S 117°21E 149 F2
Quakenbrück Germany 52°41N 7°57E 76 C3
Quakertown U.S.A. 40°26N 75°21W 175 F9
Qualicum Beach Canada 49°22N 124°26W 162 D4
Quambatook Australia 35°49S 143°34E 152 C5
Quambone Australia 30°57S 147°53E 153 A7
Quamby Australia 20°22S 140°17E 150 C3
Quan Long = Ca Mau Vietnam 9°7N 105°8E 121 H5
Quanah U.S.A. 34°18N 99°44W 176 D5
Quandialla Australia 34°1S 147°47E 153 C7
Quang Ngai Vietnam 15°13N 108°58E 120 E7
Quang Tri Vietnam 16°45N 107°13E 120 D6
Quang Yen Vietnam 20°56N 106°52E 116 G6
Quannan China 24°45N 114°33E 117 E10
Quantock Hills U.K. 51°8N 3°10W 67 F4
Quanyang China 42°21N 127°32E 115 C14
Quanzhou Fujian, China 24°55N 118°34E 117 E12
Quanzhou Guangxi Zhuangzu, China 25°57N 111°5E 117 E8
Qu'Appelle → Canada 50°33N 103°53W 163 C8
Quaqtaq Canada 60°55N 69°40W 161 E18
Quarai Brazil 30°15S 56°20W 190 C4
Quarré-les-Tombes France 47°21N 4°0E 71 E11
Quarteira Portugal 37°4N 8°6W 89 H2
Quartu Sant'Elena Italy 39°15N 9°10E 94 C2
Quartzsite U.S.A. 33°40N 114°13W 171 M12
Quatre Bornes Mauritius 20°15S 57°28E 141 d
Quatsino Sd. Canada 50°25N 127°58W 162 C3
Quba Azerbaijan 41°21N 48°32E 87 K9
Qūchān Iran 37°10N 58°27E 129 B8
Queanbeyan Australia 35°17S 149°14E 153 C8
Québec Canada 46°52N 71°13W 165 C5
Québec □ Canada 48°0N 74°0W 164 B6
Quebo Guinea-Biss. 11°20N 14°56W 138 C2
Quebrada del Condorito △ Argentina 31°49S 64°40W 190 C3
Quedlinburg Germany 51°47N 11°8E 76 D7
Queen Alexandra Ra. Antarctica 85°0S 170°0E 55 E11
Queen Charlotte B. Falk. Is. 51°50S 60°40W 192 D4
Queen Charlotte City Canada 53°15N 132°2W 162 C2
Queen Charlotte Is. = Haida Gwaii Canada 53°20N 132°10W 162 C2
Queen Charlotte Sd. Canada 51°0N 128°0W 162 C3
Queen Charlotte Sd. N.Z. 41°10S 174°15E 155 B9
Queen Charlotte Strait Canada 50°45N 127°10W 162 C3
Queen Elizabeth △ Uganda 0°0 30°0E 142 C3
Queen Elizabeth Is. Canada 76°0N 95°0W 161 B13
Queen Elizabeth Land Antarctica 85°0S 60°0W 55 E17
Queen Mary Land Antarctica 70°0S 95°0E 55 D7
Queen Maud G. Canada 68°15N 102°30W 160 D11
Queen Maud Land = Dronning Maud Land Antarctica 72°30S 12°0E 55 D3
Queen Maud Mts. Antarctica 86°0S 160°0W 55 E12
Queens Channel Australia 15°0S 129°30E 148 C4
Queenscliff Australia 38°16S 144°39E 152 E6
Queensland U.S.A. 31°46N 83°14W 178 D6
Queensland □ Australia 22°0S 142°0E 150 C3
Queenstown Australia 42°4S 145°35E 151 G4
Queenstown N.Z. 45°1S 168°40E 155 F3
Queenstown Singapore 1°18N 103°48E 121 d
Queenstown S. Africa 31°52S 26°52E 144 D4
Queets U.S.A. 47°32N 124°19W 170 C2
Queguay Grande → Uruguay 32°9S 58°9W 190 C4
Queimadas Brazil 11°0S 39°38W 189 C3
Quelimane Mozam. 17°53S 36°58E 143 F4
Quellón Chile 43°7S 73°37W 192 B2
Quelpart = Jeju-do S. Korea 33°29N 126°34E 115 H14
Queluz Portugal 38°45N 9°14W 89 G1
Quemado N. Mex., U.S.A. 34°20N 108°30W 169 J9
Quemado Tex., U.S.A. 28°56N 100°37W 176 G4
Quemoy = Chinmen Taiwan 24°26N 118°19E 117 E12
Quemú-Quemú Argentina 36°3S 63°36W 190 D3
Quepem India 15°13N 74°3E 127 G2
Quequén Argentina 38°30S 58°30W 190 D4
Querco Peru 13°50S 74°52W 188 C3
Querétaro Mexico 20°36N 100°23W 180 C4
Querétaro □ Mexico 21°0N 99°55W 180 C5
Querfurt Germany 51°23N 11°35E 76 D7
Quérigut France 42°42N 2°6E 72 F6
Querqueville France 49°40N 1°42W 70 C5
Quesada Spain 37°51N 3°4W 89 H7
Queshan China 32°55N 114°2E 117 A10
Quesnel Canada 53°0N 122°30W 162 C4
Quesnel → Canada 52°58N 122°29W 162 C4
Quesnel L. Canada 52°30N 121°20W 162 C4
Questa U.S.A. 36°42N 105°36W 169 H11
Questembert France 47°40N 2°28W 70 E4
Quetico △ Canada 48°30N 91°45W 164 C1
Quetrequile Argentina 41°33S 69°22W 192 B3
Quetta Pakistan 30°15N 66°55E 124 D2
Quetzaltenango Guatemala 14°50N 91°30W 182 D1
Queulat △ Chile 44°29S 72°24W 192 B2
Queyras △ France 44°45N 6°50E 73 D10
Quezon City Phil. 14°37N 121°2E 119 B6
Qufār Si. Arabia 27°26N 41°37E 128 E4
Qufu China 35°36N 116°58E 114 G9
Qui Nhon Vietnam 13°40N 109°13E 120 F7
Quibala Angola 10°46S 14°59E 140 G2
Quibaxe Angola 8°24S 14°27E 140 F2
Quibdó Colombia 5°42N 76°40W 186 B3
Quiberon France 47°29N 3°9W 70 E3
Quiberon, Presqu'île de France 47°30N 3°8W 70 E3
Quickborn Germany 53°42N 9°52E 76 B5
Quiet L. Canada 61°5N 133°5W 162 A2
Quiindy Paraguay 25°58S 57°14W 190 B4
Quilá Mexico 24°23N 107°13W 180 C3
Quilán, C. Chile 43°15S 74°30W 192 B2
Quilcene U.S.A. 47°49N 122°53W 170 C4
Quilimarí Chile 32°5S 71°30W 190 C1
Quilino Argentina 30°14S 64°29W 190 C3
Quillabamba Peru 12°50S 72°50W 188 C3
Quillagua Chile 21°40S 69°40W 190 A2
Quillan France 42°53N 2°10E 72 F6
Quillota Chile 32°54S 71°16W 190 C1
Quilmes Argentina 34°43S 58°15W 190 C4
Quilon = Kollam India 8°50N 76°38E 127 K3
Quilpie Australia 26°35S 144°11E 151 D3
Quilpué Chile 33°5S 71°33W 190 C1
Quilua Mozam. 16°17S 39°54E 143 F4
Quime Bolivia 17°2S 67°15W 188 D4
Quimili Argentina 27°40S 62°30W 190 B3
Quimper France 48°0N 4°9W 70 E2
Quimperlé France 47°53N 3°33W 70 E3
Quinault → U.S.A. 47°21N 124°18W 170 C2
Quince Mil Peru 13°15S 70°40W 188 C3
Quincy Calif., U.S.A. 39°56N 120°57W 170 F6
Quincy Fla., U.S.A. 30°35N 84°34W 178 E5
Quincy Ill., U.S.A. 39°56N 91°23W 172 F8
Quincy Mass., U.S.A. 42°14N 71°0W 175 D14
Quincy Wash., U.S.A. 47°14N 119°51W 168 C4
Quines Argentina 32°13S 65°48W 190 C2
Quinga Mozam. 15°49S 40°15E 143 F5
Quingey France 47°7N 5°52E 71 E12
Quinhámel Guinea-Biss. 11°53N 15°51W 138 C1
Quintana de la Serena Spain 38°45N 5°40W 89 G5
Quintana Roo □ Mexico 19°40N 88°30W 181 D7
Quintana Roo △ Quintana Roo, Mexico 20°15N 87°45W 181 C7
Quintanar de la Orden Spain 39°36N 3°5W 89 F7
Quintanar de la Sierra Spain 41°57N 2°55W 90 D2
Quintanar del Rey Spain 39°21N 1°56W 91 F3
Quintero Chile 32°45S 71°30W 190 C1
Quintin France 48°26N 2°56W 70 D4
Quinto Spain 41°25N 0°32W 90 D4
Quípar → Spain 38°15N 1°40W 91 G3
Quirihue Chile 36°15S 72°35W 190 D1
Quirimbas △ Mozam. 12°30S 40°15E 143 E5
Quirindi Australia 31°28S 150°40E 153 A9
Quirinópolis Brazil 18°32S 50°30W 187 G8
Quiroga Spain 42°28N 7°18W 88 C3
Quiruvilca Peru 8°1S 78°19W 188 B2
Quissac France 43°55N 4°0E 73 E8
Quissanga Mozam. 12°24S 40°28E 143 E5
Quissico Mozam. 24°42S 34°44E 145 B5
Quitilipi Argentina 26°50S 60°13W 190 B3
Quitman U.S.A. 30°47N 83°34W 178 E6
Quito Ecuador 0°15S 78°35W 186 D3
Quitralco △ Chile 45°43S 73°25W 192 C2
Quixadá Brazil 4°55S 39°0W 189 A3
Quixaxe Mozam. 15°17S 40°4E 143 F5
Quixeramobim Brazil 5°12S 39°17W 189 B3
Qujing China 25°32N 103°41E 116 E4
Qulan Kazakhstan 42°55N 72°43E 106 E8
Qul'ân, Jazâ'ir Egypt 24°22N 35°31E 128 E2
Qulsary Kazakhstan 46°59N 54°1E 108 C4
Qumbu S. Africa 31°10S 28°48E 145 D4
Quneitra = Al Qunayṭirah Syria 33°5N 35°45E 130 B4
Qŭnghirot Uzbekistan 43°2N 58°50E 108 D5
Qu'nyido China 31°15N 98°6E 116 B2
Quoin I. Australia 14°54S 129°32E 148 B4
Quoin Pt. S. Africa 34°46S 19°37E 144 D2
Quorn Australia 32°25S 138°5E 152 B3
Qŭrghonteppa Tajikistan 37°50N 68°47E 109 E7
Qurimbas △ Mozam. 12°20S 40°10E 143 E5
Qurnat as Sawdā' Lebanon 34°18N 36°6E 130 A5
Quryq Kazakhstan 43°12N 51°39E 108 D4
Qûs Egypt 25°55N 32°50E 137 B3
Qusar Azerbaijan 41°25N 48°26E 87 K9
Quşaybā' Si. Arabia 26°53N 43°35E 128 E4
Qusaybah Iraq 34°24N 40°59E 105 E9
Quseir Egypt 26°7N 34°16E 128 E2
Quseir Amra = Qasr 'Amra Jordan 31°48N 36°35E 128 D3
Qūshchī Iran 37°59N 45°3E 105 D11
Qusmuryn Kazakhstan 52°27N 64°36E 108 B6
Qusmuryn Köli Kazakhstan 52°41N 64°48E 108 B6
Qutang Gorge = Qutang Xia China 31°0N 109°40E 116 B7
Qutang Xia China 31°0N 109°40E 116 B7
Quthing Lesotho 30°25S 27°36E 145 D4
Qūṭīābād Iran 35°47N 48°30E 105 E13
Quttinirpaaq = Ellesmere I. Canada 79°30N 80°0W 161 B16
Quttinirpaaq △ Canada 82°13N 72°13W 161 A17
Quwo China 35°38N 111°25E 114 G6
Quyang China 38°35N 114°40E 114 E8
Quynh Nhai Vietnam 21°49N 103°33E 120 B4
Quyon Canada 45°31N 76°14W 175 A8
Quzhou China 28°57N 118°54E 117 C12
Quzi China 36°20N 107°20E 114 F4
Qvareli Georgia 41°57N 45°47E 87 K7
Qyzylorda Kazakhstan 44°48N 65°28E 108 D7
Qyzylorda □ Kazakhstan 45°0N 65°0E 108 D6
Qyzylzhar Kazakhstan 48°17N 69°38E 109 C7

R

Ra, Ko Thailand 9°13N 98°16E 121 H2
Raab Austria 48°21N 13°39E 78 C6
Raahe Finland 64°40N 24°28E 60 D21
Raalte Neths. 52°23N 6°16E 69 B6
Raas Indonesia 7°8S 114°33E 119 G16
Raasay U.K. 57°25N 6°4W 65 D2
Raasay, Sd. of U.K. 57°30N 6°8W 65 D2
Raasepori Finland 60°0N 23°26E 84 B2
Rab Croatia 44°45N 14°45E 93 D11
Rába → Hungary 47°38N 17°38E 80 C2
Raba → Poland 50°8N 20°30E 83 H7
Rabaçal → Portugal 41°30N 7°12W 88 D3
Rabah Nigeria 13°5N 5°30E 139 C6
Rabai Kenya 3°50S 39°31E 142 C4
Rabastens France 43°50N 1°43E 72 E5
Rabastens-de-Bigorre France 43°23N 0°9E 72 E4
Rabat = Victoria Malta 36°3N 14°14E 101 C1
Rabat Malta 35°53N 14°24E 101 D1
Rabat Morocco 34°2N 6°48W 136 B2
Rabat □ Morocco 34°10N 6°45W 136 B2
Rabaul Papua N. G. 4°24S 152°18E 147 B8
Rabbit Flat Australia 20°11S 130°1E 148 D5
Rabbit Lake Mine Canada 58°4N 104°5W 163 B8
Rabi Fiji 16°30S 179°59W 154 a
Rābigh Si. Arabia 22°50N 39°5E 131 C2
Rabka Poland 49°37N 19°59E 83 J6
Râbniţa = Rîbniţa Moldova 47°45N 29°0E 81 C14
Rābor Iran 29°17N 56°55E 129 D8
Rabwah = Chenab Nagar Pakistan 31°45N 72°55E 124 D5
Rača Serbia 44°14N 21°0E 96 B4
Răcăciuni Romania 46°20N 26°59E 81 D11
Răcăşdia Romania 44°59N 21°36E 80 F6
Racconigi Italy 44°46N 7°46E 92 D4
Race, C. Canada 46°40N 53°5W 165 C9
Race Pond U.S.A. 31°1N 82°8W 178 D7
Rach Gia Vietnam 10°5N 105°5E 121 G5
Rach Soi Vietnam 9°57N 105°7E 121 H5
Racha Noi, Ko Thailand 7°30N 98°19E 121 J2
Racha Yai, Ko Thailand 7°36N 98°21E 121 J2
Rachid Mauritania 18°45N 11°35W 138 B2
Raciąż Poland 52°46N 20°10E 83 F7
Racibórz Poland 50°7N 18°18E 83 H5
Racichy Belarus 53°44N 23°42E 82 E10
Racine U.S.A. 42°44N 87°47W 172 D10
Rackerby U.S.A. 39°26N 121°22W 170 F5
Råda Sweden 60°0N 13°36E 62 E7
Radan Serbia 42°59N 21°29E 96 D5
Rădăuţi Romania 47°50N 25°59E 81 C10
Rădăuţi-Prut Romania 48°14N 26°48E 81 B11
Radbuza → Czechia 49°45N 13°22E 78 B6
Radcliff U.S.A. 37°51N 85°57W 173 G11
Radeberg Germany 51°7N 13°53E 76 D9
Radebeul Germany 51°6N 13°39E 76 D9
Radeče Slovenia 46°5N 15°14E 93 B12
Radekhiv Ukraine 50°25N 24°32E 75 C13
Radekhov = Radekhiv Ukraine 50°25N 24°32E 75 C13
Radenthein Austria 46°48N 13°43E 78 E6
Radew → Poland 54°2N 15°52E 82 D2
Radford U.S.A. 37°8N 80°34W 173 G13
Radhanpur India 23°50N 71°38E 124 H4
Radhwa, Jabal Si. Arabia 24°34N 38°18E 128 E3
Radika → Macedonia 41°38N 20°37E 96 E4
Radisson Qué., Canada 53°47N 77°37W 164 B4
Radisson Sask., Canada 52°30N 107°20W 163 C7
Radium Hot Springs Canada 50°35N 116°2W 162 C5
Radlje ob Dravi Slovenia 46°38N 15°13E 93 B12
Radnevo Bulgaria 42°17N 25°58E 97 D9
Radnice Czechia 49°51N 13°35E 78 B6
Radnor Forest U.K. 52°17N 3°10W 67 E4
Radolfzell Germany 47°39N 8°59E 77 H4
Radom Poland 51°23N 21°12E 83 G8
Radomir Bulgaria 42°37N 22°59E 96 D6
Radomka → Poland 51°43N 21°28E 83 G8
Radomsko Poland 51°5N 19°28E 83 G6
Radomyshl Ukraine 50°30N 29°12E 75 C15
Radomyśl Wielki Poland 50°14N 21°15E 83 H8
Radoszyce Poland 51°4N 20°15E 83 G7
Radoviš Macedonia 41°38N 22°28E 96 E6
Radovljica Slovenia 46°22N 14°12E 93 B11
Radstadt Austria 47°24N 13°28E 78 D6
Radstock, C. Australia 33°12S 134°20E 151 E1
Răducăneni Romania 46°58N 27°54E 81 D12
Raduša Macedonia 42°7N 21°15E 96 D5
Raduzhnyy Russia 62°5N 77°28E 106 C8
Radvanichy Belarus 52°1N 24°0E 83 F11
Radviliškis Lithuania 55°49N 23°33E 82 C10
Radville Canada 49°30N 104°15W 163 D8
Radwā, J. Si. Arabia 24°34N 38°18E 137 C4
Radymno Poland 49°59N 22°52E 83 J9
Radzanów Poland 52°56N 20°8E 83 F7
Radziejów Poland 52°40N 18°30E 83 F5
Radzyń Chełmiński Poland 53°23N 18°55E 82 E5
Radzyń Podlaski Poland 51°47N 22°37E 83 G9
Rae = Behchoko Canada 62°50N 116°3W 162 A5
Rae Bareli India 26°18N 81°20E 125 F9
Rae Isthmus Canada 66°40N 87°30W 161 D14
Raeren Belgium 50°41N 6°7E 69 D6
Raeside, L. Australia 29°20S 122°0E 149 E3
Raetihi N.Z. 39°25S 175°17E 154 F4
Rafaela Argentina 31°10S 61°30W 190 C3
Rafah Gaza Strip 31°18N 34°14E 130 D3
Rafai C.A.R. 4°59N 23°58E 142 B1
Raffadali Italy 37°24N 13°32E 94 E6
Rafḥā Si. Arabia 29°35N 43°35E 128 D4
Rafina Greece 38°2N 24°0E 98 C6
Rafsanjān Iran 30°30N 56°5E 129 D8
Raft Pt. Australia 16°4S 124°26E 148 C3
Raga South Sudan 8°28N 25°41E 135 G11
Ragachow Belarus 53°8N 30°5E 75 B16
Ragama Sri Lanka 7°0N 79°50E 122 R11
Ragged, Mt. Australia 33°27S 123°25E 149 F3
Ragged Pt. Barbados 13°10N 59°26W 183 g
Raghunathpalli India 22°14N 84°48E 125 H11
Raghunathpur India 23°33N 86°40E 125 H12
Raglan N.Z. 37°55S 174°55E 154 D3
Raglan Harbour N.Z. 37°47S 174°50E 154 D3
Ragland U.S.A. 33°45N 86°9W 178 B3
Ragusa Italy 36°55N 14°44E 95 F7
Raha Indonesia 4°55S 123°0E 119 E6
Rahaeng = Tak Thailand 16°52N 99°8E 120 D2
Rahat Israel 31°24N 34°45E 130 D3
Rahat, Ḥarrat Si. Arabia 23°0N 40°5E 137 C5
Rahatgarh India 23°47N 78°22E 125 H8
Rahden Germany 52°26N 8°36E 76 C4
Rahimyar Khan Pakistan 28°30N 70°25E 124 E4
Rāhjerd Iran 34°22N 50°22E 129 C6
Rahole △ Kenya 0°5N 38°57E 142 B4
Rahon India 31°3N 76°7E 124 D7
Rahotu N.Z. 39°20S 173°49E 154 F2
Rahovec Kosovo 42°24N 20°40E 96 D4
Rahuri India 19°23N 74°39E 126 E2
Rai, Hon Vietnam 9°48N 104°38E 121 H5
Raiatéa, Î. French Polynesia 16°50S 151°25W 157 J12
Raichur India 16°10N 77°20E 127 F3
Raiford U.S.A. 30°4N 82°14W 178 E7
Raiganj India 25°37N 88°10E 125 G13
Raigarh India 21°56N 83°25E 126 D6
Raighar India 19°51N 82°6E 126 E6
Raijua Indonesia 10°37S 121°36E 119 F6
Raikot India 30°41N 75°42E 124 D6
Railton Australia 41°25S 146°28E 151 G4
Rainbow Bridge △ U.S.A. 37°5N 110°58W 169 H8
Rainbow City U.S.A. 33°57N 86°5W 178 B3
Rainbow Lake Canada 58°30N 119°23W 162 B5
Rainier U.S.A. 46°53N 122°41W 170 D4
Rainier, Mt. U.S.A. 46°52N 121°46W 170 D5
Rainy L. Canada 48°42N 93°10W 163 D10
Rainy River Canada 48°43N 94°29W 163 D10
Raippaluoto Finland 63°13N 21°14E 60 E19
Raipur India 21°17N 81°45E 126 D5
Rairakhol India 21°4N 84°21E 126 D7
Ra'is Si. Arabia 23°33N 38°43E 137 C4
Raisen India 23°20N 77°48E 124 H8
Raisio Finland 60°28N 22°11E 84 B2
Raj Nandgaon India 21°5N 81°5E 126 D5
Raj Nilgiri India 21°28N 86°46E 125 J12
Raja, Ujung Indonesia 3°40N 96°25E 118 D1
Raja Ampat, Kepulauan Indonesia 0°30S 130°0E 119 E8
Rajahmahendravaram India 17°1N 81°48E 126 F5
Rajahmundry = Rajahmahendravaram India 17°1N 81°48E 126 F5
Rajaji △ India 30°10N 78°20E 124 D8
Rajampet India 14°11N 79°10E 127 G4
Rajang → Malaysia 2°30N 112°0E 118 D4
Rajanpur Pakistan 29°6N 70°19E 124 E4
Rajapalaiyam India 9°25N 77°35E 127 K3
Rajapur India 16°40N 73°31E 126 F1
Rajasthan □ India 26°45N 73°30E 124 F5
Rajasthan Canal = Indira Gandhi Canal India 28°0N 72°0E 124 F5
Rajauri India 33°25N 74°21E 125 C6
Rajendranagar India 17°18N 78°27E 126 F4
Rajgarh Mad. P., India 24°2N 76°45E 124 G7
Rajgarh Raj., India 27°14N 76°38E 124 F7
Rajgarh Raj., India 28°40N 75°25E 124 E6
Rajghat Dam India 24°45N 78°20E 126 B4
Rajgir India 25°2N 85°25E 125 G11
Rajgród Poland 53°42N 22°42E 82 E9
Rajim India 20°58N 81°53E 126 D5
Rajkot India 22°15N 70°56E 124 H4
Rajmahal Hills India 24°30N 87°30E 125 G12
Rajpipla India 21°50N 73°30E 126 D1
Rajpur India 22°18N 74°21E 124 H6
Rajpura India 30°25N 76°32E 124 D7
Rajsamand = Kankroli India 25°4N 73°53E 124 G5
Rajshahi Bangla. 24°22N 88°39E 123 G16
Rajshahi □ Bangla. 25°0N 89°0E 125 G13
Rajula India 21°3N 71°26E 124 J4
Rajur India 20°7N 78°55E 126 D4
Rajura India 19°47N 79°22E 126 E4
Rakaia N.Z. 43°45S 172°1E 155 D7
Rakaia → N.Z. 43°36S 172°15E 155 D7
Rakan, Ra's Qatar 26°10N 51°20E 129 E6
Rakaposhi Pakistan 36°10N 74°25E 125 A6
Rakata, Pulau Indonesia 6°10S 105°20E 119 G11
Rakbah, Sahl Si. Arabia 22°15N 41°0E 137 C5
Rakhine □ Myanmar 19°0N 94°15E 123 K18
Rakhiv Ukraine 48°3N 24°12E 81 B9
Rakhni Pakistan 30°4N 69°56E 124 D3
Rakhni → Pakistan 29°31N 69°36E 124 E3
Rakhny-Lisovi Ukraine 48°47N 28°29E 81 B13
Rakiraki Fiji 17°22S 178°11E 154 a
Rakitnoye Russia 45°36N 134°17E 112 B7
Rakitnoye Russia 50°57N 35°56E 85 G8
Rakitovo Bulgaria 41°59N 24°5E 97 E8
Rakiura = Stewart I. N.Z. 46°58S 167°54E 155 G2
Rakoniewice Poland 52°10N 16°16E 83 F3
Rakops Botswana 21°1S 24°28E 144 B3
Rakovica Croatia 44°59N 15°38E 93 D12
Rakovník Czechia 50°6N 13°42E 78 A6
Rakovski Bulgaria 42°21N 24°57E 97 D8
Rakvere Estonia 59°20N 26°25E 84 C4
Raleigh Fla., U.S.A. 29°25N 82°32W 179 F7
Raleigh N.C., U.S.A. 35°47N 78°39W 177 D15
Ralik Chain Pac. Oc. 8°0N 168°0E 156 G8
Ralja Serbia 44°33N 20°34E 96 B4
Rälla Sweden 56°40N 16°30E 63 H10
Ralls U.S.A. 33°41N 101°24W 176 E4
Ralston U.S.A. 41°30N 76°57W 174 E8
Ram → Canada 62°1N 123°41W 162 A4
Rām Allāh West Bank 31°55N 35°10E 130 D4
Rama Nic. 12°9N 84°15W 182 D3
Ramacca Italy 37°23N 14°42E 95 E7
Ramachandrapuram India 16°50N 82°4E 126 F6
Ramagiri Udayagiri India 19°5N 84°18E 126 E7
Ramagundam India 18°55N 79°15E 126 E4
Ramakona India 21°43N 78°50E 125 J8
Ramalho, Serra do Brazil 13°45S 44°0W 189 C2
Rāmallāh = Rām Allāh West Bank 31°55N 35°10E 130 D4
Raman Thailand 6°29N 101°18E 121 J3
Ramanathapuram India 9°25N 78°55E 127 K4
Ramanujganj India 23°48N 83°42E 125 H10
Ramas C. India 15°5N 73°55E 127 G1
Ramat Gan Israel 32°4N 34°48E 130 C3
Ramatlhabama S. Africa 25°37S 25°33E 144 C4
Ramban India 33°14N 75°12E 125 C6
Rambervillers France 48°20N 6°38E 71 D13
Rambi = Rabi Fiji 16°30S 179°59W 154 a
Rambipuji Indonesia 8°12S 113°37E 119 H15
Rambouillet France 48°39N 1°50E 71 D8
Ramdurg India 15°58N 75°22E 127 G2
Rame Hd. Australia 37°47S 149°30E 153 D8
Ramechhap Nepal 27°25N 86°10E 125 F12
Ramelton Ireland 55°2N 7°39W 64 A4
Ramenskoye Russia 55°32N 38°15E 84 E10
Ramer U.S.A. 32°3N 86°13W 178 C3
Rameswaram India 9°17N 79°18E 127 K4
Ramganga → India 27°5N 79°58E 125 F8
Ramgarh Jharkhand, India 23°40N 85°35E 125 H11
Ramgarh Raj., India 27°16N 75°14E 124 F6
Ramgarh Raj., India 27°30N 70°36E 124 F4
Rāmhormoz Iran 31°15N 49°35E 129 D6
Ramīān Iran 37°3N 55°16E 129 B7
Ramingining Australia 12°19S 135°3E 150 A2
Ramla Israel 31°55N 34°52E 130 D3
Ramm = Rum Jordan 29°39N 35°26E 130 F4
Ramm, Jabal Jordan 29°35N 35°24E 130 F4
Râmna → Romania 45°36N 27°3E 81 E12

Ramnad = Ramanathapuram
India 9°25N 78°55E **127** K4
Ramnagar Jammu & Kashmir,
India 32°47N 75°18E **125** C6
Ramnagar Uttarakhand,
India 29°24N 79°7E **125** E8
Ramnäs Sweden 59°46N 16°12E **62** E10
Râmnicu Sărat Romania 45°26N 27°3E **81** E12
Râmnicu Vâlcea Romania 45°9N 24°21E **81** E9
Ramnous Greece 38°12N 24°3E **98** C6
Ramon Russia 51°55N 39°21E **85** G10
Ramona U.S.A. 33°2N 116°52W **171** M10
Ramonville-St-Agne
France 43°33N 1°28E **72** E5
Ramore Canada 48°30N 80°25W **164** C3
Ramos → Nigeria 5°8N 5°22E **139** D6
Ramotswa Botswana 24°50S 25°52E **144** B4
Rampur H.P., India 31°26N 77°43E **124** D7
Rampur Mad. P., India 23°25N 73°53E **124** H5
Rampur Odisha, India 21°48N 83°58E **126** D6
Rampur Ut. P., India 28°50N 79°5E **125** E8
Rampur Hat India 24°10N 87°50E **125** G12
Rampura India 24°30N 75°27E **124** G6
Ramrama Tola India 21°52N 79°55E **125** J8
Ramree I. Myanmar 19°0N 93°40E **123** K19
Râmsar Iran 36°53N 50°41E **129** B6
Ramsey I. of Man 54°20N 4°22W **64** C3
Ramsey U.S.A. 41°4N 74°9W **175** E10
Ramsey L. Canada 47°13N 82°15W **164** C3
Ramsgate U.K. 51°20N 1°25E **67** F9
Ramsjö Sweden 62°11N 15°37E **62** B9
Ramstein Germany 49°27N 7°32E **77** F3
Ramtek India 21°20N 79°15E **126** D4
Ramu Kenya 3°55N 41°10E **142** B5
Ramvik Sweden 62°49N 17°51E **62** B11
Rana Pratap Sagar Dam
India 24°58N 75°38E **124** G6
Ranaghat India 23°15N 88°35E **125** H13
Ranahu Pakistan 25°55N 69°45E **124** G3
Ranau Malaysia 6°2N 116°40E **118** C5
Rancagua Chile 34°10S 70°50W **190** C1
Rance → France 48°34N 1°59W **70** D5
Rancheria → Canada 60°13N 129°7W **162** A3
Ranchester U.S.A. 44°54N 107°10W **168** D10
Ranchi India 23°19N 85°27E **125** H11
Rancho Cordova
U.S.A. 38°36N 121°18W **170** G5
Rancho Cucamonga
U.S.A. 34°10N 117°30W **171** L9
Ranco, L. Chile 40°15S 72°25W **192** B2
Rand Australia 35°33S 146°32E **153** C7
Randalstown U.K. 54°45N 6°19W **64** B5
Randan France 46°3N 3°21E **71** F10
Randazzo Italy 37°53N 14°57E **95** E7
Rander India 21°14N 72°47E **126** D1
Randers Denmark 56°29N 10°1E **63** H4
Randers Fjord Denmark 56°37N 10°20E **63** H4
Randfontein S. Africa 26°8S 27°45E **145** C4
Randle U.S.A. 46°32N 121°57W **170** D5
Randolph Mass.,
U.S.A. 42°10N 71°2W **175** D14
Randolph N.Y., U.S.A. 42°10N 78°59W **174** D6
Randolph Utah,
U.S.A. 41°40N 111°11W **168** F8
Randolph Vt., U.S.A. 43°55N 72°40W **175** C12
Randsburg U.S.A. 35°22N 117°39W **171** K9
Rânealven → Sweden 65°50N 22°20E **60** D20
Ranfurly N.Z. 45°7S 170°6E **155** F5
Rangae Thailand 6°19N 101°44E **121** J3
Rangataua N.Z. 39°26S 175°28E **154** F4
Rangaunu B. N.Z. 34°51S 173°15E **154** A2
Range, The Zimbabwe 19°2S 31°2E **143** F3
Rangeley U.S.A. 44°58N 70°39W **175** B14
Rangeley L. U.S.A. 44°55N 70°43W **175** B14
Rangely U.S.A. 40°5N 108°48W **168** F9
Ranger U.S.A. 32°28N 98°41W **176** E5
Rangia India 26°28N 91°38E **123** F17
Rangiora N.Z. 43°19S 172°36E **155** D7
Rangitaiki N.Z. 38°52S 176°24E **154** D6
Rangitaiki → N.Z. 37°54S 176°49E **154** D5
Rangitata → N.Z. 43°45S 171°15E **155** D6
Rangitikei → N.Z. 40°17S 175°15E **154** G4
Rangitoto ke te tonga = D'Urville
I. N.Z. 40°50S 173°55E **155** A8
Rangitoto Ra. N.Z. 38°25S 175°35E **154** E4
Rangkasbitung
Indonesia 6°21S 106°15E **119** G12
Rangon = Yangôn
Myanmar 16°45N 96°20E **123** L20
Rangpur Bangla. 25°42N 89°22E **123** G16
Rangsang Indonesia 1°20N 103°5E **121** M4
Rani-ki-Vav India 23°51N 72°6E **124** H4
Ranibennur India 14°35N 75°30E **127** G2
Raniganj Paschimbanga,
India 23°40N 87°5E **125** H15
Raniganj Ut. P., India 27°3N 82°13E **125** F9
Ranikhet India 29°39N 79°25E **125** E8
Ranippettai India 12°56N 79°23E **127** H4
Raniwara India 24°50N 72°10E **124** G5
Rāniyah Iraq 36°15N 44°53E **105** D11
Ranka India 23°59N 83°47E **125** H10
Ranken → Australia 20°31S 137°36E **150** C2
Rankin U.S.A. 31°13N 101°56W **176** F4
Rankin Inlet Canada 62°30N 93°0W **160** B10
Rankins Springs
Australia 33°49S 146°14E **153** B7
Rankweil Austria 47°17N 9°39E **78** D2
Rannoch, L. U.K. 56°41N 4°20W **65** E4
Rannoch Moor U.K. 56°38N 4°48W **65** E4
Ranohira Madag. 22°29S 45°24E **141** J9
Ranong Thailand 9°56N 98°40E **121** H2
Ranpur India 20°5N 85°25E **126** D7
Rânsa Iran 33°39N 48°18E **129** C6
Ransiki Indonesia 1°30S 134°10E **119** E8
Rantau Abang
Malaysia 4°52N 103°24E **121** K4
Rantauprapat Indonesia 2°15N 99°50E **118** D1
Rantemario △ India 3°15S 119°57E **119** E5
Ranthambore △ India 26°10N 76°30E **124** F7
Rantoul U.S.A. 40°19N 88°9W **172** E1
Ranum Denmark 56°54N 9°14E **63** H3
Ranyah, W. →
Si. Arabia 21°18N 43°20E **137** C5
Raohe China 46°47N 134°0E **112** A7
Raon l'Étape France 48°24N 6°50E **71** D13
Raoping China 23°42N 117°1E **117** F11
Raoui, Erg er Algeria 29°0N 2°0W **136** C5
Raoyang China 38°15N 115°45E **114** E8
Rap, Ko Thailand 9°19N 99°58E **121** b
Rapa French Polynesia 27°35S 144°20W **157** K13
Rapa Nui = Pascua, I. de
Chile 27°7S 109°23W **157** K17

Rapallo Italy 44°21N 9°14E **92** D6
Rapar India 23°34N 70°38E **124** H4
Räpch Iran 25°40N 59°15E **129** E8
Rapel, Lago Chile 34°20S 71°14W **190** C1
Raper, C. Canada 69°44N 67°6W **161** D18
Rapid City U.S.A. 44°5N 103°14W **172** C2
Rapid River U.S.A. 45°55N 86°58W **172** C4
Rapla Estonia 59°1N 24°52E **84** C3
Rapti → India 26°18N 83°41E **125** F10
Raquette → U.S.A. 45°0N 74°42W **175** B10
Raquette Lake U.S.A. 43°49N 74°40W **175** C10
Rara △ Nepal 29°30N 82°10E **125** E10
Rarotonga Cook Is. 21°30S 160°0W **157** K12
Ra's al 'Ayn Syria 36°45N 40°12E **105** D9
Ra's Al Khair Si. Arabia 27°27N 49°18E **129** E6
Ra's al Khaymah
U.A.E. 25°50N 55°59E **129** E7
Ra's aţ Ţib Tunisia 37°1N 11°2E **96** F4
Râs el Ma Algeria 34°26N 0°50W **136** B3
Râs el Mâ Mali 16°35N 4°30W **138** B4
Râs el Oued Algeria 35°57N 5°2E **136** A5
Râs Ghârib Egypt 28°6N 33°18E **137** F8
Râs Muhammad △
Egypt 27°45N 34°16E **137** F8
Râs Sudr Egypt 29°40N 32°42E **137** F8
Rasa, Pta. B. Aires,
Argentina 36°20S 56°41W **190** D4
Rasa, Pta. Río Negro,
Argentina 40°50S 62°15W **192** B4
Rasca, Pta. de la
Canary Is. 27°59N 16°41W **100** G3
Râșcani Moldova 47°58N 27°13E **81** C14
Raseiniai Lithuania 55°25N 23°5E **82** C10
Rashid Egypt 31°21N 30°22E **137** D7
Rashid, Masabb Egypt 31°22N 30°17E **137** E7
Rashmi India 25°4N 74°22E **124** G6
Rasht Iran 37°20N 49°40E **105** D13
Rasi Salai Thailand 15°20N 104°9E **120** E5
Rasipuram India 11°30N 78°15E **127** J4
Râška Serbia 43°19N 20°39E **96** C4
Raskot Nepal 29°14N 81°39E **125** E9
Rason L. Australia 28°45S 124°25E **149** E3
Rasony Belarus 44°15N 27°55E **81** F12
Rasovo Bulgaria 43°42N 23°17E **96** C7
Rasra India 25°50N 83°50E **125** G10
Rasskazovo Russia 52°35N 41°50E **86** D5
Rast Romania 43°53N 23°16E **81** G8
Rastatt Germany 48°50N 8°11E **77** G4
Rastede Germany 53°15N 8°12E **76** B4
Râstoliţa Romania 46°59N 24°58E **81** D9
Rasua Garhi Nepal 28°17N 85°23E **125** E11
Rasul Pakistan 32°42N 73°34E **124** C5
Raszków Poland 51°43N 17°40E **83** G4
Rat → Canada 49°35N 97°10W **163** D9
Rat Buri = Ratchaburi
Thailand 13°30N 99°54E **120** F2
Rat Islands U.S.A. 52°0N 178°0E **166** E3
Rat L. Canada 56°10N 99°40W **163** B9
Ratak Chain Pac. Oc. 1°0N 170°0E **156** G8
Rätan Sweden 62°29N 14°33E **62** B8
Ratangarh India 28°5N 74°35E **124** E6
Raţāwī Iraq 30°38N 47°13E **128** D5
Ratcatchers L.
Australia 32°30S 143°12E **152** B5
Ratchaburi Thailand 13°30N 99°54E **120** F2
Rath India 25°36N 79°37E **125** G8
Rath Luirc = Charleville
Ireland 52°21N 8°40W **64** D3
Rathangan Ireland 53°14N 7°0W **64** C4
Rathdrum Ireland 52°56N 6°14W **64** D5
Rathenow Germany 52°37N 12°19E **76** C8
Rathkeale Ireland 52°32N 8°56W **64** D3
Rathlin I. U.K. 55°18N 6°14W **64** A5
Ratibor = Racibórz
Poland 50°7N 18°18E **83** H5
Rätikon Austria 47°0N 9°55E **78** D2
Ratingen Germany 51°18N 6°52E **76** D2
Ratlam India 23°20N 75°0E **124** H6
Ratmanova, Ostrov
Russia 65°46N 169°6W **166** B6
Ratnagiri India 16°57N 73°18E **126** F1
Ratnapura Sri Lanka 6°40N 80°20E **127** L5
Ratodero Pakistan 27°48N 68°18E **124** F3
Raton U.S.A. 36°54N 104°24W **169** H11
Rattaphum Thailand 7°8N 100°16E **121** J3
Ratten Austria 47°28N 15°44E **78** D8
Rattray Hd. U.K. 57°38N 1°50W **65** D7
Rättvik Sweden 60°52N 15°7E **62** D9
Ratz, Mt. Canada 57°23N 132°12W **162** B2
Ratzeburg Germany 53°40N 10°46E **76** B6
Raub Malaysia 3°47N 101°52E **121** L3
Rauch Argentina 36°45S 59°5W **190** D4
Raudales Mexico 17°27N 93°39W **181** D6
Raufarhöfn Iceland 66°27N 15°57W **60** C6
Raufoss Norway 60°44N 10°37E **60** F14
Raukumara Ra. N.Z. 38°5S 177°55E **154** E7
Raul Soares Brazil 20°5S 42°22W **189** E2
Rauma Finland 61°10N 21°30E **84** B1
Raumo = Rauma
Finland 61°10N 21°30E **84** B1
Raung, Gunung
Indonesia 8°8S 114°3E **119** J17
Raurkela India 22°14N 84°50E **125** H11
Rausu-Dake Japan 44°4N 145°7E **112** B12
Răut → Moldova 47°15N 28°49E **81** D15
Rava-Ruska Ukraine 50°15N 23°42E **83** H10
Rava Russkaya = Rava-Ruska
Ukraine 50°15N 23°42E **83** H10
Ravalli U.S.A. 47°17N 114°11W **168** C6
Ravānsar Iran 34°43N 46°40E **105** E12
Ravanusa Italy 37°16N 13°58E **94** E6
Rāvar Iran 31°20N 56°51E **129** D8
Ravena U.S.A. 42°28N 73°49W **175** D11
Ravenel U.S.A. 32°46N 80°15W **178** C9
Ravenna Italy 44°25N 12°12E **93** D9
Ravenna Nebr., U.S.A. 41°1N 98°55W **172** E4
Ravenna Ohio, U.S.A. 41°9N 81°15W **174** E3
Ravensburg Germany 47°46N 9°36E **77** H5
Ravenshoe Australia 17°37S 145°29E **150** B4
Ravensthorpe Australia 33°35S 120°2E **149** F3
Ravenswood Australia 20°6S 146°54E **150** C4
Ravenswood U.S.A. 38°57N 81°46W **173** F13
Ravensworth Australia 32°26S 151°4E **153** B9
Raver India 21°15N 76°2E **126** D3
Ravi → Pakistan 30°35N 71°49E **124** D4
Ravna Gora Croatia 45°24N 14°50E **95** C11
Ravna Reka Serbia 44°1N 21°33E **96** B5
Ravne na Koroškem
Slovenia 46°36N 14°58E **93** B11
Rawa Mazowiecka
Poland 51°46N 20°12E **83** G7

Rawalpindi Pakistan 33°38N 73°8E **124** C5
Rawang Malaysia 3°20N 101°35E **121** L3
Rawene N.Z. 35°25S 173°32E **154** B2
Rawi, Ko Thailand 6°33N 99°14E **121** J2
Rawicz Poland 51°36N 16°52E **83** G3
Rawka → Poland 52°9N 20°8E **83** F7
Rawlinna Australia 30°58S 125°28E **149** F4
Rawlins U.S.A. 41°47N 107°14W **168** F10
Rawlinson Ra.
Australia 24°40S 128°30E **149** D4
Rawson Argentina 43°15S 65°5W **192** B3
Raxaul India 26°59N 84°51E **125** F11
Ray, C. Canada 47°33N 59°15W **165** C8
Ray, U.S.A. 48°21N 103°10W **172** A2
Ray City U.S.A. 31°5N 83°11W **178** D6
Ray Mts. U.S.A. 66°0N 152°0W **166** B9
Raya Ring, Ko Thailand 8°18N 98°29E **121** a
Rayachoti India 14°4N 78°50E **127** G3
Rayadurg India 14°40N 76°50E **127** G3
Rayagada India 19°15N 83°20E **126** E6
Raychikhinsk Russia 49°46N 129°25E **107** E13
Râyen Iran 34°24N 57°26E **129** D8
Rayle U.S.A. 33°48N 82°54W **178** B7
Raymond Calif.,
U.S.A. 37°13N 119°54W **170** H7
Raymond N.H., U.S.A. 43°2N 71°11W **175** C13
Raymond Wash.,
U.S.A. 46°41N 123°44W **170** D3
Raymond Terrace
Australia 32°45S 151°44E **153** B9
Raymondville U.S.A. 26°29N 97°47W **176** H6
Raymore Canada 51°25N 104°31W **163** C8
Rayón Mexico 29°43N 110°35W **180** B2
Rayong Thailand 12°40N 101°20E **120** F3
Raystown L. U.S.A. 40°25N 78°5W **174** F6
Rayville U.S.A. 32°29N 91°46W **176** E9
Raz, Pte. du France 48°2N 4°47W **70** D2
Razan Iran 35°23N 49°2E **105** E13
Ražana Serbia 44°6N 19°55E **96** B4
Razanj Serbia 43°40N 21°31E **96** C5
Razāzah, Buḩayrat ar
Iraq 32°40N 43°35E **105** F10
Razdelna Bulgaria 43°13N 27°41E **97** C11
Razdel'naya = Rozdilna
Ukraine 46°50N 30°2E **81** D15
Razdolnoye Russia 43°30N 131°52E **112** C5
Razdolnoye Ukraine 45°46N 33°29E **85** K7
Razeh Iran 32°47N 48°9E **129** C6
Razgrad Bulgaria 43°33N 26°34E **97** C10
Razgrad □ Bulgaria 43°30N 26°34E **97** C10
Razhevo Konare
Bulgaria 42°23N 24°46E **97** D8
Razim, Lacul Romania 44°50N 29°0E **81** F14
Razlog Bulgaria 41°53N 23°28E **96** E7
Razmak Pakistan 32°45N 69°50E **124** C3
Răznas Ezers △ Latvia 56°30N 27°30E **84** D4
Razzaza, L. = Razāzah, Buḩayrat
ar Iraq 32°40N 43°35E **105** F10
Re, Cu Lao Vietnam 15°22N 109°8E **120** E7
Ré, Î. de France 46°12N 1°30W **72** F2
Reading U.K. 51°27N 0°58W **67** F7
Reading U.S.A. 40°20N 75°56W **175** F9
Reading □ U.K. 51°27N 0°58W **67** F7
Real, Cordillera Bolivia 17°0S 67°10W **188** G4
Realicó Argentina 35°0S 64°15W **190** D3
Réalmont France 43°48N 2°10E **72** E6
Ream Cambodia 10°34N 103°39E **121** G4
Ream → Cambodia 10°30N 103°45E **121** G4
Reay Forest U.K. 58°22N 4°55W **65** C4
Rebais France 48°50N 3°10E **71** D10
Rebecca, L. Australia 30°0S 122°15E **149** F3
Rebi Indonesia 6°23S 134°7E **119** F8
Rebiana, Sahrâ' Libya 24°30N 21°0E **135** D10
Reboly Russia 63°49N 30°47E **60** E24
Rebun-Tō Japan 45°23N 141°2E **112** B10
Recanati Italy 43°24N 13°32E **93** E10
Recaş Romania 45°46N 21°30E **80** E6
Recco Italy 44°22N 9°9E **92** D6
Recherche, Arch. of the
Australia 34°15S 122°50E **149** F3
Rechna Doab Pakistan 31°35N 73°30E **124** D5
Rechytsa Belarus 52°21N 30°24E **75** D6
Recife Brazil 8°0S 35°0W **189** B4
Recife Seychelles 4°36S 55°42E **141** b
Recklinghausen Germany 51°37N 7°12E **76** D3
Reckong Peo India 31°32N 78°16E **124** D8
Reconquista Argentina 29°10S 59°45W **190** B4
Recreo Argentina 29°25S 65°10W **190** B2
Recuay Peru 9°43S 77°28W **188** E3
Recz Poland 53°16N 15°31E **83** E2
Red → Hong = Asia 20°16N 106°34E **120** B5
Red → U.S.A. 31°1N 91°45W **176** F9
Red → Canada 50°24N 96°48W **163** C9
Red Bank U.S.A. 40°21N 74°5W **175** E10
Red Bay Canada 51°44N 56°25W **165** B8
Red Bluff U.S.A. 40°11N 122°15W **170** F4
Red Bluff Res. U.S.A. 31°54N 103°55W **169** L12
Red Cliffs Australia 34°19S 142°11E **152** C5
Red Cloud U.S.A. 40°5N 98°32W **172** E4
Red Creek U.S.A. 43°14N 76°45W **175** C8
Red Deer Canada 52°20N 113°50W **162** C6
Red Deer → Alta.,
Canada 50°58N 110°0W **163** C7
Red Deer → Man.,
Canada 52°53N 101°1W **163** C8
Red Deer L. Canada 52°55N 101°20W **163** C8
Red Hook U.S.A. 41°55N 73°53W **175** E11
Red Indian L. Canada 48°35N 57°0W **165** C8
Red L. Canada 51°3N 93°49W **163** C10
Red Lake Canada 51°3N 93°49W **163** C10
Red Lake Falls U.S.A. 47°53N 96°16W **172** B5
Red Lake Road
Canada 49°59N 93°25W **163** C10
Red Lodge U.S.A. 45°11N 109°15W **168** D9
Red Mountain U.S.A. 35°37N 117°38W **171** K9
Red Oak U.S.A. 41°1N 95°14W **172** E6
Red River of the North →
N. Amer. 49°0N 97°15W **172** A6
Red Rock Canada 48°55N 88°15W **164** C2
Red Rock, L. U.S.A. 41°22N 92°59W **172** E7
Red Rocks Pt.
Australia 32°13S 127°32E **149** F4
Red Sea Asia 25°0N 36°0E **131** C2
Red Slate Mt. U.S.A. 37°31N 118°52W **170** H8
Red Sucker L. Canada 54°9N 93°40W **164** B1
Red Tower Pass = Turnu Roşu, P.
Romania 45°33N 24°17E **81** E9
Red Volta → Africa 10°58N 0°35W **138** C4
Red Wing U.S.A. 44°34N 92°31W **172** C7
Reda Poland 54°40N 18°19E **82** B5
Redang, Pulau Malaysia 5°49N 103°2E **121** K4

Redange Lux. 49°46N 5°52E **69** E5
Redbridge □ U.K. 51°35N 0°7E **67** F8
Redcar U.K. 54°37N 1°4W **66** C6
Redcar & Cleveland □
U.K. 54°29N 1°0W **66** C7
Redcliff Canada 50°10N 110°50W **168** A8
Redcliffe Australia 27°12S 153°6E **151** D5
Redcliffe, Mt. Australia 28°30S 121°30E **149** E3
Redcliffe, Mt. Australia 28°30S 121°30E **149** E3
Redding U.S.A. 40°35N 122°24W **168** F2
Reddick U.S.A. 29°22N 82°12W **179** F7
Redditch U.K. 52°18N 1°55W **67** E6
Redenção Brazil 4°13S 38°43W **189** A3
Redfield U.S.A. 44°53N 98°31W **172** C4
Redford U.S.A. 44°38N 73°48W **175** B11
Redhead Trin. & Tob. 10°44N 60°58W **187** K16
Redkino Russia 56°39N 36°16E **84** D9
Redlands U.S.A. 34°4N 117°11W **171** M9
Redmond Oreg.,
U.S.A. 44°17N 121°11W **168** D3
Redmond Wash.,
U.S.A. 47°40N 122°7W **170** C4
Redon France 47°40N 2°6W **70** E4
Redonda Antigua & B. 16°58N 62°19W **183** C7
Redondela Spain 42°15N 8°38W **88** C2
Redondo Portugal 38°39N 7°37W **89** G3
Redondo Beach
U.S.A. 33°50N 118°23W **171** M8
Redoubt Volcano
U.S.A. 60°29N 152°45W **166** C9
Redruth U.K. 50°14N 5°14W **67** G2
Redvers Canada 49°35N 101°40W **163** D8
Redwater Canada 53°55N 113°6W **162** C6
Redwood U.S.A. 44°18N 75°48W **175** B9
Redwood △ U.S.A. 41°40N 124°5W **168** F1
Redwood City U.S.A. 37°30N 122°15W **170** H4
Redwood Falls U.S.A. 44°32N 95°7W **172** C6
Ree, L. Ireland 53°35N 8°0W **64** C3
Reed City U.S.A. 43°53N 85°31W **173** D11
Reed L. Canada 54°38N 100°30W **163** C8
Reedley U.S.A. 36°36N 119°27W **170** J7
Reedsburg U.S.A. 43°32N 90°0W **172** D8
Reedsport U.S.A. 43°42N 124°6W **168** E1
Reedsville U.S.A. 40°39N 77°35W **174** F7
Reedy Creek Australia 36°58S 140°2E **152** D4
Reefton N.Z. 42°6S 171°51E **155** C6
Rees Germany 51°46N 6°24E **76** D2
Reese → U.S.A. 40°48N 117°4W **168** F5
Reetfale Sweden 57°11N 13°35E **63** G7
Refugio U.S.A. 28°18N 97°17W **176** G6
Reftele Sweden 57°11N 13°35E **63** G7
Rega → Poland 54°10N 15°18E **82** D2
Regalbuto Italy 37°40N 14°38E **95** E7
Regana, C. de Spain 39°25N 2°43E **100** B9
Regen Germany 48°58N 13°8E **77** G9
Regen → Germany 49°1N 12°6E **77** F8
Regeneração Brazil 6°15S 42°41W **189** B2
Regensburg Germany 49°1N 12°6E **77** F8
Regenstauf Germany 49°7N 12°8E **77** F8
Réggâne = Zaouiet Reggâne
Algeria 26°32N 0°3E **136** C6
Reggello Italy 43°41N 11°32E **93** E8
Réggio di Calábria Italy 38°6N 15°39E **95** E8
Réggio nell'Emília Italy 44°43N 10°36E **92** D7
Reghin Romania 46°46N 24°42E **81** D9
Regina Canada 50°27N 104°35W **163** C8
Regina Beach Canada 50°47N 105°0W **163** C8
Register U.S.A. 32°22N 81°53W **178** C8
Registro Brazil 24°29S 47°49W **191** A6
Reguengos de Monsaraz
Portugal 38°25N 7°32W **89** G3
Rehar → India 23°55N 82°40E **125** H10
Rehli India 23°38N 79°5E **125** H8
Rehoboth Namibia 23°15S 17°4E **144** B2
Rehovot Israel 31°54N 34°48E **130** D3
Rei, Costa Italy 39°15N 9°40E **94** C2
Reichenbach Germany 50°37N 12°17E **76** E8
Reid Australia 30°49S 128°26E **149** F4
Reidsville G., U.S.A. 32°6N 82°7W **178** C7
Reidsville N.C., U.S.A. 36°21N 79°40W **177** C15
Reigate U.K. 51°14N 0°12W **67** F7
Reillo Spain 39°54N 1°53W **90** F3
Reims France 49°15N 4°1E **71** C11
Reina Adelaida, Arch.
Chile 52°20S 74°0W **192** D2
Reina Sofia, Tenerife ✕ (TFS)
Canary Is. 28°3N 16°33W **100** F3
Reinbek Germany 53°30N 10°7E **76** B6
Reindeer → Canada 55°36N 103°11W **163** B8
Reindeer I. Canada 52°30N 98°0W **163** C9
Reindeer L. Canada 57°15N 102°15W **163** B8
Reinga, C. N.Z. 34°25S 172°43E **154** A1
Reinheimen △ Norway 62°15N 7°45E **60** E12
Reinosa Spain 43°2N 4°15W **88** B6
Reitz S. Africa 27°48S 28°29E **145** C4
Reivilo S. Africa 27°36S 24°8E **144** C3
Rejmyre Sweden 58°50N 15°55E **63** F9
Rejowiec Fabryczny
Poland 51°5N 23°17E **83** G10
Reka → Slovenia 45°40N 14°0E **93** C11
Rekovac Serbia 43°51N 21°3E **96** C5
Rekwa → Canada 60°0N 109°20W **163** A7
Relizane Algeria 35°44N 0°31E **136** A4
Relizane □ Algeria 35°45N 0°50E **136** A4
Remad, Oued →
Algeria 33°28N 1°20W **136** B3
Rémalard France 48°26N 0°47E **70** D7
Remanso Brazil 9°41S 42°4W **189** B2
Remarkable, Mt.
Australia 32°48S 138°10E **152** B3
Remarkables, The
N.Z. 45°10S 168°50E **155** F3
Rembang Indonesia 6°42S 111°21E **119** G14
Remchi Algeria 35°2N 1°26E **136** A3
Remedios Panama 8°15N 81°50W **182** E3
Remeshk Iran 26°55N 58°50E **129** E8
Remetea Romania 46°45N 25°29E **81** D10
Remich Lux. 49°32N 6°22E **69** E6
Remiremont France 48°2N 6°36E **71** D13
Remontnoye Russia 46°34N 43°37E **87** G6
Remoulins France 43°55N 4°35E **73** E8
Rémuzat France 44°19N 5°19E **73** D9
Ren Xian China 37°8N 114°40E **114** F8
Rendang Indonesia 8°26S 115°25E **119** J18
Rende Italy 39°20N 16°11E **95** C9
Rendina Greece 39°4N 21°58E **98** B3
Rendsburg Germany 54°17N 9°39E **76** A5
Rene Russia 66°2N 179°25W **107** C19
René-Levasseur, Î.
Canada 51°20N 68°40W **165** B6
Renfrew Canada 45°30N 76°40W **175** A8
Renfrewshire □ U.K. 55°49N 4°38W **65** F4
Reneca Argentina 29°35S 67°30W **190** B3
Reng, C. = Reni = Europe 51°52N 6°2E **69** C6
Rheden Germany 52°0N 6°2E **76** D2

Rengat Indonesia 0°30S 102°45E **118** E2
Rengo Chile 34°24S 70°50W **190** C1
Renhua China 25°5N 113°40E **117** E9
Renhuai China 27°48N 106°24E **116** D6
Reni = Taranagar India 28°43N 74°50E **124** E6
Reni Ukraine 45°28N 28°15E **81** E13
Reniguta India 13°38N 79°30E **127** H4
Renland Greenland 71°10N 26°30W **57** C8
Renmark Australia 34°11S 140°43E **152** C4
Renneil Sd. Canada 53°23N 132°35W **162** C2
Renner Springs
Australia 18°20S 133°47E **150** B1
Rennes France 48°7N 1°41W **70** D5
Rennick Glacier
Antarctica 70°30S 161°45E **55** D11
Rennie L. Canada 61°32N 105°35W **163** A7
Reno → Italy 44°38N 12°16E **93** D9
Reno U.S.A. 39°31N 119°48W **170** F7
Renovo U.S.A. 41°20N 77°45W **174** E7
Renqiu China 38°43N 116°5E **114** E9
Rens Denmark 54°54N 9°5E **63** K3
Renshou China 29°59N 104°9E **116** C5
Rensselaer Ind., U.S.A. 40°57N 87°9W **172** E10
Rensselaer N.Y.,
U.S.A. 42°38N 73°45W **175** D11
Renton U.S.A. 47°28N 122°12W **170** C4
Renukoot India 24°12N 83°2E **125** G10
Renwick N.Z. 41°30S 173°51E **155** B8
Réo Burkina Faso 12°28N 2°35W **138** C4
Reocín = Puente San Miguel
Spain 43°21N 4°5W **88** B6
Reotipur India 25°33N 83°45E **125** G10
Repalle India 16°2N 80°45E **127** F5
Repcelak Hungary 47°24N 17°1E **80** C2
Republic Mo., U.S.A. 37°7N 93°29W **177** D7
Republic Wash.,
U.S.A. 48°39N 118°44W **168** B4
Republican → U.S.A. 39°4N 96°48W **172** F5
Republika Srpska □
Bos.-H. 44°56N 17°11E **93** D14
Repulse B. Australia 20°35S 148°46E **150** b
Repulse Bay Canada 66°30N 86°30W **161** D14
Requena Peru 5°5S 73°52W **188** B3
Requena Spain 39°30N 1°4W **91** F3
Réquista France 44°1N 2°32E **72** D6
Reşadiye Muğla, Turkey 36°45N 27°39E **99** E9
Reşadiye Tokat, Turkey 40°23N 37°20E **104** B7
Reşadiye Yarımadası
Turkey 36°40N 27°45E **99** E9
Resavica Serbia 44°4N 21°31E **96** B5
Reserve U.S.A. 33°43N 108°45W **169** K9
Resht = Rasht Iran 37°20N 49°40E **105** D13
Resistencia Argentina 27°30S 59°0W **190** B4
Reşiţa Romania 45°18N 21°53E **80** E6
Resko Poland 53°47N 15°25E **82** E2
Reso = Raisio Finland 60°28N 22°11E **84** B2
Resolute Canada 74°42N 94°54W **161** C13
Resolution I. Canada 61°30N 65°0W **161** E19
Resolution I. N.Z. 45°40S 166°40E **155** F1
Resplandes Brazil 6°17S 45°13W **189** B1
Resplendor Brazil 19°20S 41°15W **189** E2
Ressano Garcia Mozam. 25°25S 32°0E **145** D5
Reston U.S.A. 49°33N 101°6W **163** D8
Reszel Poland 54°4N 21°10E **82** D8
Retalhuleu Guatemala 14°33N 91°46W **182** D1
Retenue, L. de
Dem. Rep. of the Congo 11°0S 27°0E **143** E2
Retezat, Munţii Romania 45°25N 23°0E **80** E8
Retezat △ Romania 45°23N 22°56E **80** E7
Retford U.K. 53°19N 0°56W **66** D7
Rethel France 49°30N 4°20E **71** C11
Rethem Germany 52°47N 9°22E **76** C5
Réthimno Greece 35°18N 24°30E **101** D6
Réthimno □ Greece 35°23N 24°28E **101** D6
Retiche, Alpi Switz. 46°30N 10°0E **77** J6
Retiers France 47°55N 1°23W **70** E5
Retortillo Spain 40°48N 6°21W **88** E4
Rétság Hungary 47°58N 19°10E **80** C4
Réunion ☐ Ind. Oc. 21°0S 56°0E **141** c
Reus Spain 41°10N 1°5E **90** B6
Reutlingen Germany 48°29N 9°12E **77** G5
Reutte Austria 47°29N 10°42E **78** D3
Reval = Tallinn Estonia 59°22N 24°48E **84** C3
Revel France 43°28N 2°1E **72** E6
Revelganj India 25°50N 84°40E **125** G11
Revelstoke Canada 51°0N 118°10W **162** C5
Reventazón Peru 6°10S 80°58W **188** B1
Revigny-sur-Ornain
France 48°49N 4°59E **71** D11
Revilla Gigedo, Is. de
Pac. Oc. 18°40N 112°0W **180** D2
Revillagigedo Archipelago △
Mexico 18°40N 112°0W **180** D2
Revin France 49°55N 4°39E **71** C11
Revúca Slovakia 48°41N 20°7E **83** G5
Revuè → Mozam. 19°50S 34°0E **143** F3
Rewa India 24°33N 81°25E **125** G9
Rewari India 28°15N 76°40E **124** E7
Rexburg U.S.A. 43°49N 111°47W **168** E8
Rey Iran 35°35N 51°25E **105** C13
Rey, I. del Panama 8°20N 78°30W **182** E4
Rey, L. del Mexico 27°1N 103°26W **180** B4
Rey Malabo Eq. Guin. 3°45N 8°50E **139** E6
Reyes Bolivia 14°19S 67°23W **188** G5
Reyes, Pt. U.S.A. 38°0N 123°0W **168** G2
Reyhanlı Turkey 36°16N 36°35E **104** D7
Reykjahlíð Iceland 65°40N 16°55W **60** D6
Reykjanes Iceland 63°48N 22°40W **60** E2
Reykjanes Ridge Atl. Oc. 59°0N 31°0W **56** D8
Reykjavík Iceland 64°10N 21°57W **60** D3
Reynolds Ra. Australia 22°30S 133°0E **150** D1
Reynolds Ga.,
U.S.A. 32°33N 84°6W **178** D5
Reynoldsville U.S.A. 41°6N 78°53W **174** E6
Reynosa Mexico 26°7N 98°18W **181** B5
Rēzekne Latvia 56°30N 27°17E **84** D4
Rezina Moldova 47°45N 28°58E **81** C13
Rezovo Bulgaria 42°0N 28°0E **97** E12
Rezvān Iran 27°34N 56°6E **129** E8
Rezvānshahr Iran 37°32N 49°7E **105** D13
Rgotina Serbia 44°1N 22°18E **96** B6
Rharbi, Zahrez Algeria 34°50N 2°55E **136** B6
Rharis, O. → Algeria 26°0N 5°4E **136** C6
Rhayader U.K. 52°18N 3°29W **67** E4
Rheda-Wiedenbrück
Germany 51°50N 8°20E **76** D4
Rhede Germany 51°50N 6°42E **76** D2
Rhein → Europe 51°52N 6°2E **69** C6
Rhein-Main-Donau-Kanal
Germany 49°1N 11°27E **77** F7
Rhein-Ruhr, Düsseldorf ✕ (DUS)
Germany 51°17N 6°46E **76** D2
Rhein-Taunus △
Germany 50°10N 8°10E **77** E4
Rhein-Westerwald △
Germany 50°32N 7°20E **76** E3
Rheinbach Germany 50°38N 6°57E **76** E2
Rheine Germany 52°17N 7°26E **76** C3
Rheinfelden Germany 47°33N 7°47E **77** H4
Rheinland-Pfalz □ Germany 50°0N 7°0E **76** E2
Rheinsberg Germany 53°6N 12°54E **76** B8
Rheris, Oued →
Morocco 30°50N 4°34W **136** B3
Rhin = Rhein → Europe 51°52N 6°2E **69** C6
Rhine = Rhein → Europe 51°52N 6°2E **69** C6
Rhine U.S.A. 31°59N 83°12W **178** D6
Rhinebeck U.S.A. 41°56N 73°55W **175** E11
Rhineland-Palatinate =
Rheinland-Pfalz □
Germany 50°0N 7°0E **77** E2
Rhinelander U.S.A. 45°38N 89°25W **172** C9
Rhinns Pt. U.K. 55°40N 6°29W **65** F2
Rhino Camp Uganda 3°0N 31°22E **142** B3
Rhir, Cap Morocco 30°38N 9°54W **136** B2
Rho Italy 45°31N 9°2E **92** C6
Rhode Island □
U.S.A. 41°40N 71°30W **175** E13
Rhodes Greece 36°15N 28°10E **101** C10
Rhodes ✕ (RHO) Greece 36°23N 28°12E **99** G10
Rhodope Mts. = Rodopi Planina
Bulgaria 41°40N 24°20E **97** E8
Rhön Germany 50°24N 9°58E **76** E5
Rhondda U.K. 51°39N 3°31W **67** F4
Rhondda Cynon Taff □
U.K. 51°42N 3°27W **67** F4
Rhône □ France 45°54N 4°35E **73** C8
Rhône → France 43°28N 4°42E **73** E8
Rhum = Rùm U.K. 57°0N 6°20W **65** E2
Rhydaman = Ammanford
U.K. 51°48N 3°59W **67** F4
Rhyl U.K. 53°20N 3°29W **66** D4
Ri-Aba Eq. Guin. 3°28N 8°40E **139** E6
Ria Formosa △ Portugal 37°1N 7°48W **89** H3
Riachão Brazil 7°20S 46°37W **189** B1
Riacho de Santana
Brazil 13°37S 42°57W **189** D2
Riang, Laem Thailand 8°7N 98°27E **121** a
Riaño Spain 42°59N 4°59W **88** B6
Rians France 43°37N 5°44E **73** E9
Riansáres → Spain 39°32N 3°18W **89** F7
Riasi India 33°10N 74°50E **125** C6
Riau □ Indonesia 0°0 102°35E **118** E2
Riau, Kepulauan □
Indonesia 0°30N 104°20E **118** D2
Riau Arch. = Riau, Kepulauan □
Indonesia 0°30N 104°20E **118** D2
Riaza Spain 41°18N 3°30W **88** D7
Riaza → Spain 41°42N 3°55W **88** D7
Riba de Saelices Spain 40°55N 2°17W **90** D2
Riba-roja de Túria Spain 39°33N 0°34W **91** F4
Ribadavia Spain 42°17N 8°8W **88** C2
Ribadeo Spain 43°35N 7°5W **88** B3
Ribadesella Spain 43°30N 5°7W **88** B5
Ribado Nigeria 9°16N 12°47E **139** D7
Ribamar Brazil 2°33S 44°3W **189** A2
Ribao Cameroon 6°32N 11°30E **139** D7
Ribas = Ribes de Freser
Spain 42°19N 2°15E **90** C7
Ribas do Rio Pardo
Brazil 20°27S 53°46W **187** H8
Ribauè Mozam. 14°57S 38°17E **143** E4
Ribble → U.K. 53°52N 2°25W **66** E5
Ribe Denmark 55°19N 8°44E **63** J2
Ribécourt-Dreslincourt
France 49°30N 2°56E **71** C9
Ribeira Spain 42°36N 8°58W **88** C2
Ribeira Brava Madeira 32°41N 17°4W **100** D3
Ribeira do Pombal
Brazil 10°50S 38°32W **189** C3
Ribeira Grande Cabo Verde 17°0N 25°4W **134** b
Ribeirão Prêto Brazil 21°10S 47°50W **191** A6
Ribeiro Gonçalves
Brazil 7°32S 45°14W **189** B1
Ribemont France 49°47N 3°27E **71** C10
Ribera Italy 37°30N 13°16E **94** E6
Ribérac France 45°15N 0°20E **72** C4
Ribeirão Bolívia 11°0S 66°0W **186** F5
Ribes de Freser Spain 42°19N 2°15E **90** C7
Ribnica Slovenia 45°54N 14°45E **93** C11
Ribniţa Moldova 47°45N 29°0E **81** C14
Ribnitz-Damgarten
Germany 54°15N 12°27E **76** A8
Říčany Czechia 50°0N 14°40E **78** B7
Riccarton N.Z. 43°32S 172°37E **155** D7
Riccia Italy 41°30N 14°50E **95** A7
Riccione Italy 44°0N 12°39E **93** E9
Rice U.S.A. 34°5N 114°51W **171** L12
Rice L. Canada 44°12N 78°10W **174** B6
Rice Lake U.S.A. 45°30N 91°44W **172** C8
Riceboro U.S.A. 31°44N 81°26W **178** E8
Rich, C. Canada 44°43N 80°38W **174** B4
Richard Toll Senegal 16°28N 15°41W **138** B1
Richards Bay S. Africa 28°48S 32°6E **145** C5
Richardson →
Canada 58°25N 111°14W **163** B6
Richardson Lakes
U.S.A. 44°46N 70°58W **173** C18
Richardson Mts. N.Z. 44°49S 168°34E **155** E3
Richardson Springs
U.S.A. 39°51N 121°46W **170** F5
Riche, C. Australia 34°36S 118°47E **149** F2
Richelieu France 47°0N 0°20E **70** E7
Richey U.S.A. 47°39N 105°4W **168** C11
Richfield U.S.A. 38°46N 112°5W **168** G7
Richfield Springs
U.S.A. 42°51N 74°59W **175** C10
Richford U.S.A. 45°0N 72°40W **175** B12
Richibucto Canada 46°42N 64°54W **165** C7
Richland Ga., U.S.A. 32°5N 84°40W **178** D5
Richland Wash.,
U.S.A. 46°17N 119°18W **168** C4
Richland Center
U.S.A. 43°21N 90°23W **172** D8
Richlands U.S.A. 37°6N 81°48W **173** G13
Richmond N.S.W.,
Australia 33°35S 150°42E **153** B9

264 Richmond
INDEX TO WORLD MAPS

Richmond Queens., Australia 20°43S 143°8E 150 C3
Richmond N.Z. 41°20S 173°12E 155 B8
Richmond U.K. 54°25N 1°43W 66 C6
Richmond Calif., U.S.A. 37°56N 122°21W 170 H4
Richmond Ind., U.S.A. 39°50N 84°53W 173 F11
Richmond Ky., U.S.A. 37°45N 84°18W 173 G11
Richmond Mich., U.S.A. 42°49N 82°45W 174 D2
Richmond Mo., U.S.A. 39°17N 93°58W 172 F7
Richmond Tex., U.S.A. 29°35N 95°46W 176 G7
Richmond Utah, U.S.A. 41°56N 111°48W 168 F8
Richmond Va., U.S.A. 37°33N 77°27W 173 G15
Richmond Vt., U.S.A. 44°24N 72°59W 175 B12
Richmond, Mt. N.Z. 41°32S 173°22E 155 B8
Richmond Hill Canada 43°52N 79°27W 174 C5
Richmond Hill U.S.A. 31°56N 81°18W 178 D8
Richmond Ra. Australia 29°0S 152°45E 151 D5
Richmond Ra. N.Z. 41°32S 173°22E 155 B8
Richmondville U.S.A. 42°38N 74°33W 175 D10
Richtersveld △ S. Africa 28°15S 17°10E 144 C2
Richville U.S.A. 44°25N 75°23W 175 B9
Richwood U.S.A. 38°14N 80°32W 173 F13
Ricla Spain 41°31N 1°24W 90 D3
Ridder Kazakhstan 50°20N 83°30E 109 B10
Riddlesburg U.S.A. 40°9N 78°15W 174 F6
Rideau → Canada 45°27N 75°42W 175 A9
Ridge Spring U.S.A. 33°51N 81°40W 178 B8
Ridgecrest U.S.A. 35°38N 117°40W 171 K9
Ridgefield Conn., U.S.A. 41°17N 73°30W 175 E11
Ridgefield Wash., U.S.A. 45°49N 122°45W 170 E4
Ridgeland Miss., U.S.A. 32°26N 90°8W 177 E9
Ridgeland S.C., U.S.A. 32°29N 80°59W 178 C9
Ridgetown Canada 42°26N 81°52W 174 D3
Ridgeville U.S.A. 33°6N 80°19W 178 B9
Ridgewood U.S.A. 40°59N 74°7W 175 F10
Ridgway U.S.A. 41°25N 78°44W 174 E6
Riding Mountain △ Canada 50°50N 100°0W 163 C9
Ridley, Mt. Australia 33°12S 122°7E 149 F3
Riebeek-Oos S. Africa 33°10S 26°10E 144 D4
Ried Austria 48°14N 13°30E 78 C6
Riedlingen Germany 48°9N 9°28E 77 G5
Riedstadt Germany 49°45N 8°30E 77 F4
Rienza → Italy 46°49N 11°47E 93 B8
Riesa Germany 51°17N 13°17E 76 D9
Riesco, I. Chile 52°55S 72°40W 192 D2
Riesi Italy 37°17N 14°5E 95 E7
Riet → S. Africa 29°0S 23°54E 144 C3
Rietavas Lithuania 55°44N 21°56E 82 C8
Rietbron S. Africa 32°54S 23°10E 144 D3
Rietfontein Namibia 21°58S 20°58E 144 B3
Rieti Italy 42°24N 12°51E 93 F9
Rieupeyroux France 44°19N 2°12E 72 D6
Riez France 43°49N 6°6E 73 E10
Rif = Er Rif Morocco 35°1N 4°1W 136 A3
Riffe L. U.S.A. 46°32N 122°26W 170 D4
Rifle U.S.A. 39°32N 107°47W 168 G10
Rift Valley Africa 7°0N 30°0E 132 G7
Rīga Latvia 56°53N 24°8E 82 B11
Riga ✈ (RIX) Latvia 56°54N 23°59E 82 B10
Riga, G. of Latvia 57°40N 23°45E 82 A10
Rigacikun Nigeria 10°40N 7°28E 139 C6
Rīgān Iran 28°37N 58°58E 129 D8
Rīgas Jūras Līcis = Riga, G. of Latvia 57°40N 23°45E 82 A10
Rigaud Canada 45°29N 74°18W 175 A10
Rigby U.S.A. 43°40N 111°55W 168 E8
Rīgestān Afghan. 30°15N 65°0E 122 D4
Riggins U.S.A. 45°25N 116°19W 168 D5
Rignac France 44°25N 2°16E 72 D6
Rigolet Canada 54°10N 58°23W 165 B8
Rigu Ghana 9°59N 0°48W 139 D4
Rihand Dam India 24°9N 83°2E 125 G10
Riihimäki Finland 60°45N 24°48E 84 B3
Riiser-Larsen-halvøya Antarctica 68°0S 35°0E 55 C4
Riiser-Larsen Ice Shelf S. Ocean 74°0S 19°0W 55 D2
Riiser-Larsen Sea S. Ocean 67°30S 22°0E 55 C4
Riisitunturi △ Finland 66°27N 28°27E 60 C23
Rijau Nigeria 11°8N 5°17E 139 C6
Rijeka Croatia 45°20N 14°21E 93 C11
Rijeka Crnojevića Montenegro 42°24N 19°1E 96 D3
Rijssen Neths. 52°19N 6°31E 69 B6
Rika → Ukraine 48°11N 23°16E 81 B8
Rikuchū-Kaigan △ Japan 39°20N 142°0E 112 E11
Rikuzentakata Japan 39°0N 141°40E 112 E10
Rila Bulgaria 42°7N 23°7E 96 D7
Rila Planina Bulgaria 42°10N 23°20E 96 D7
Riley U.S.A. 43°32N 119°28W 168 E4
Rima → Nigeria 13°4N 5°10E 139 C6
Rimah, Wadi ar → Si. Arabia 26°5N 41°30E 128 E4
Rimau, Pulau Malaysia 5°15N 100°16E 121 c
Rimavská Sobota Slovakia 48°22N 20°2E 79 C13
Rimbey Canada 52°35N 114°15W 162 C6
Rimbo Sweden 59°44N 18°21E 62 E12
Rimersburg U.S.A. 41°3N 79°30W 174 E5
Rimforsa Sweden 58°6N 15°43E 63 F9
Rímini Italy 44°3N 12°33E 93 D9
Rimouski Canada 48°27N 68°30W 165 C6
Rimrock U.S.A. 46°40N 121°7W 170 D5
Rinca Indonesia 8°45S 119°35E 119 F5
Rincon U.S.A. 32°18N 81°14W 178 C8
Rincón de Anchuras = Anchuras Spain 39°29N 4°50W 89 F6
Rincón de la Victoria Spain 36°43N 4°18W 89 J6
Rincón de Romos Mexico 22°14N 102°18W 180 C4
Rinconada Argentina 22°26S 66°10W 190 A2
Rind → India 25°53N 80°33E 125 G9
Ringarum Sweden 58°21N 16°26E 63 F10
Ringas India 27°21N 75°34E 124 F6
Ringe Denmark 55°13N 10°28E 63 J4
Ringgold Is. Fiji 16°15S 179°25W 154 a
Ringim Nigeria 12°13N 9°10E 139 C6
Ringkøbing Denmark 56°5N 8°15E 63 H2
Ringkøbing Fjord Denmark 56°0N 8°15E 63 H2
Ringsjön Sweden 55°55N 13°30E 63 J7
Ringsted Denmark 55°25N 11°46E 63 J5
Ringvassøya Norway 69°56N 19°15E 60 B18
Ringwood U.S.A. 41°7N 74°15W 175 E10
Rinia Greece 37°23N 25°13E 99 D7
Rinjani, Gunung Indonesia 8°24S 116°28E 118 F5
Rinteln Germany 52°10N 9°8E 76 C5
Rinyirru △ Australia 15°24S 144°26E 150 B3
Rio, Punta del Spain 36°49N 2°24W 91 J2
Rio Branco Brazil 9°58S 67°49W 188 B4
Río Branco Uruguay 32°40S 53°40W 191 C5
Río Bravo Mexico 25°59N 98°6W 181 B5
Río Bravo ⌂ N. Amer. 29°2N 102°45W 180 B4
Río Bravo del Norte → Mexico 25°57N 97°9W 181 B5
Rio Brilhante Brazil 21°48S 54°33W 191 A5
Río Bueno Chile 40°19S 72°58W 192 B2
Rio Claro Brazil 22°19S 47°35W 191 A6
Rio Claro Trin. & Tob. 10°20N 61°10W 183 D7
Río Colorado Argentina 39°0S 64°0W 192 A4
Río Cuarto Argentina 33°10S 64°25W 190 C3
Rio das Pedras Mozam. 23°8S 35°28E 145 B6
Rio de Contas Brazil 13°36S 41°48W 189 C2
Rio de Janeiro Brazil 22°54S 43°12W 191 A7
Rio de Janeiro □ Brazil 22°50S 43°0W 191 A7
Rio do Prado Brazil 16°35S 40°34W 189 D2
Rio do Sul Brazil 27°13S 49°37W 191 B6
Rio Dulce △ Guatemala 15°43N 88°50W 182 C2
Río Gallegos Argentina 51°35S 69°15W 192 D3
Río Grande Argentina 53°50S 67°45W 192 D3
Rio Grande Bolivia 20°51S 67°17W 188 E4
Rio Grande Brazil 32°0S 52°20W 191 C5
Río Grande Mexico 23°50N 103°2W 180 C4
Río Grande Puerto Rico 18°23N 65°50W 183 d
Rio Grande → N. Amer. 25°58N 97°9W 176 J6
Rio Grande City U.S.A. 26°23N 98°49W 176 H5
Río Grande de Santiago → Mexico 21°36N 105°26W 180 C3
Rio Grande do Norte □ Brazil 5°40S 36°0W 189 B3
Rio Grande do Sul □ Brazil 30°0S 53°0W 191 C5
Rio Grande Rise Atl. Oc. 31°0S 35°0W 56 K8
Río Hato Panama 8°22N 80°10W 182 E3
Río Lagartos Mexico 21°36N 88°10W 181 C7
Rio Largo Brazil 9°28S 35°50W 189 B3
Rio Maior Portugal 39°19N 8°57W 89 F2
Rio Marina Italy 42°49N 10°25E 92 F7
Río Mayo Argentina 45°40S 70°15W 192 C2
Río Mulatos Bolivia 19°40S 66°50W 188 D4
Río Muni □ Eq. Guin. 1°30N 10°0E 140 D2
Rio Negro Brazil 26°0S 49°55W 191 B6
Río Negro Chile 40°47S 73°14W 192 B2
Rio Pardo Brazil 30°0S 52°30W 191 C5
Río Pico Argentina 44°0S 70°22W 192 B2
Río Pilcomayo △ Argentina 25°5S 58°5W 190 B4
Río Plátano ⌂ Honduras 15°45N 85°0W 182 C3
Rio Rancho U.S.A. 35°14N 106°41W 169 J10
Rio Real Brazil 11°28S 37°56W 189 C3
Río Segundo Argentina 31°40S 63°59W 190 C3
Río Simpson △ Chile 45°27S 73°30W 192 C2
Río Tercero Argentina 32°15S 64°8W 190 C3
Rio Tinto Brazil 6°48S 35°5W 189 B3
Rio Tinto Portugal 41°11N 8°34W 88 D2
Río Turbio Argentina 51°32S 72°18W 192 D2
Rio Verde Brazil 17°50S 51°0W 187 G8
Río Verde Mexico 21°56N 99°59W 181 C5
Rio Vista U.S.A. 38°10N 121°42W 170 G5
Riobamba Ecuador 1°50S 78°45W 186 D3
Riohacha Colombia 11°33N 72°55W 186 A4
Rioja Peru 6°11S 77°5W 188 B2
Riom France 45°54N 3°7E 72 C7
Riom-ès-Montagnes France 45°17N 2°39E 72 C6
Rion-des-Landes France 43°55N 0°56W 72 E3
Rionero in Vúlture Italy 40°55N 15°40E 95 B8
Rioni → Georgia 42°14N 41°44E 87 J5
Riós Spain 41°58N 7°16W 88 D3
Ríosucio Colombia 7°27N 77°7W 186 B3
Riou L. Canada 59°7N 106°25W 163 B7
Rioz France 47°26N 6°5E 71 E13
Ripatransone Italy 42°59N 13°46E 93 F10
Ripley Canada 44°4N 81°35W 174 B3
Ripley Calif., U.S.A. 33°32N 114°39W 171 M12
Ripley N.Y., U.S.A. 42°16N 79°43W 174 D5
Ripley Tenn., U.S.A. 35°45N 89°32W 177 D10
Ripley W. Va., U.S.A. 38°49N 81°43W 173 F13
Ripoll Spain 42°15N 2°13E 90 C7
Ripon U.K. 54°9N 1°31W 66 C6
Ripon Calif., U.S.A. 37°44N 121°7W 170 H5
Ripon Wis., U.S.A. 43°51N 88°50W 172 D9
Riposto Italy 37°44N 15°12E 95 E8
Risan Montenegro 42°32N 18°42E 96 D2
Riscle France 43°39N 0°5W 72 E3
Rishā', W. ar → Si. Arabia 25°33N 44°5E 128 E5
Rishikesh India 30°7N 78°19E 124 D8
Rishiri-Rebun-Sarobetsu △ Japan 45°26N 141°30E 112 B10
Rishiri-Tō Japan 45°11N 141°15E 112 B10
Rishon le Ziyyon Israel 31°58N 34°48E 130 D3
Risle → France 49°26N 0°23E 70 C7
Risnjak △ Croatia 45°25N 14°36E 93 C11
Rison U.S.A. 33°58N 92°11W 176 E8
Risør Norway 58°43N 9°13E 61 G13
Rissani Morocco 31°18N 4°12W 136 B3
Rita Blanca Cr. → U.S.A. 35°40N 102°29W 176 D3
Ritchie's Arch. India 12°14N 93°10E 127 H11
Riti Nigeria 7°57N 9°41E 139 D6
Ritter, Mt. U.S.A. 37°41N 119°12W 170 H7
Rittman U.S.A. 40°58N 81°47W 174 F3
Ritzville U.S.A. 47°8N 118°23W 168 C4
Riva del Garda Italy 45°53N 10°50E 92 C7
Riva Ligure Italy 43°50N 7°50E 92 E4
Rivadavia B. Aires, Argentina 35°29S 62°59W 190 D3
Rivadavia Mendoza, Argentina 33°13S 68°30W 190 C2
Rivadavia Salta, Argentina 24°5S 62°54W 190 A3
Rivadavia Chile 29°57S 70°35W 190 B1
Rivarolo Canavese Italy 45°19N 7°43E 92 C4
Rivas Nic. 11°30N 85°50W 182 D2
Rivash Iran 35°28N 58°26E 129 C8
Rive-de-Gier France 45°32N 4°37E 73 C8
River Cess Liberia 5°30N 9°32W 138 D3
River Jordan Canada 48°26N 124°3W 170 B2
Rivera Argentina 37°12S 63°14W 190 D3
Rivera Uruguay 31°0S 55°50W 191 C4
Riverbank U.S.A. 37°44N 120°56W 170 H6
Riverdale Calif., U.S.A. 36°26N 119°52W 170 J7
Riverdale Ga., U.S.A. 33°34N 84°25W 178 B5
Riverhead U.S.A. 40°55N 72°40W 175 F12
Riverhurst Canada 50°55N 106°50W 163 C7
Rivers Canada 50°2N 100°14W 163 C8
Rivers □ Nigeria 4°30N 7°10E 139 E6
Rivers Inlet Canada 51°42N 127°15W 162 C3
Riversdale Canada 44°5N 81°20W 174 B3
Riversdale N.Z. 45°54S 168°44E 155 F3
Riversdale S. Africa 34°7S 21°15E 144 D3
Riverside U.S.A. 33°59N 117°22W 171 M9
Riversleigh Australia 19°5S 138°40E 150 B2
Riverton Australia 34°10S 138°46E 152 C3
Riverton Canada 51°1N 97°0W 163 C9
Riverton N.Z. 46°21S 168°0E 155 G3
Riverton U.S.A. 43°2N 108°23W 168 E9
Riverview Fla., U.S.A. 27°52N 82°20W 179 H7
Riverview Fla., U.S.A. 30°32N 87°12W 179 E2
Rives France 45°21N 5°31E 73 C9
Rivesaltes France 42°47N 2°50E 72 F6
Riviera = Azur, Côte d' France 43°25N 7°10E 73 E11
Riviera U.S.A. 35°4N 114°35W 171 K12
Riviera Beach U.S.A. 26°47N 80°3W 179 J9
Riviera di Levante Italy 44°15N 9°30E 92 D6
Riviera di Ponente Italy 44°10N 8°20E 92 D5
Rivière-au-Renard Canada 48°59N 64°23W 165 C7
Rivière-du-Loup Canada 47°50N 69°30W 165 C6
Rivière-Pentecôte Canada 49°57N 67°1W 165 C6
Rivière-Pilote Martinique 14°26N 60°53W 182 c
Rivière St-Paul Canada 51°28N 57°45W 165 B8
Rivière-Salée Martinique 14°31N 61°0W 182 c
Rivne Odesa, Ukraine 46°1N 29°10E 81 D14
Rivne Rivne, Ukraine 50°40N 26°10E 75 C14
Rivne □ Ukraine 51°15N 26°30E 75 C14
Rívoli Italy 45°3N 7°31E 92 C4
Rivoli B. Australia 37°32S 140°3E 152 D4
Riwaka N.Z. 41°5S 172°59E 155 B7
Rixheim France 47°40N 7°24E 71 E14
Riyadh = Ar Riyāḍ Si. Arabia 24°41N 46°42E 128 E5
Riza Greece 40°31N 23°15E 96 F7
Rize Turkey 41°0N 40°30E 105 B9
Rize □ Turkey 41°0N 40°30E 105 B9
Rizhao China 35°25N 119°30E 115 G10
Rizokarpaso Cyprus 35°36N 34°23E 101 D13
Rizzuto, C. Italy 38°53N 17°5E 95 D10
Rjukan Norway 59°54N 8°33E 61 G13
Rkîz, L. Mauritania 16°50N 15°23W 138 B1
Ro Greece 36°9N 29°33E 99 E11
Roa Spain 41°41N 3°56W 88 D7
Road Town Br. Virgin Is. 18°27N 64°37W 183 e
Roan Plateau U.S.A. 39°20N 109°20W 168 G9
Roanne France 46°3N 4°4E 71 F11
Roanoke Ala., U.S.A. 33°9N 85°22W 178 B4
Roanoke Va., U.S.A. 37°16N 79°56W 173 G14
Roanoke → U.S.A. 35°57N 76°42W 177 D16
Roanoke I. U.S.A. 35°53N 75°39W 177 D17
Roanoke Rapids U.S.A. 36°28N 77°40W 177 C16
Roatán Honduras 16°18N 86°35W 182 C2
Robāṭ Iran 34°16N 46°47E 105 E12
Robāṭ Sang Iran 35°35N 59°10E 129 C8
Robāṭkarīm Iran 35°25N 50°59E 129 C6
Robben I. S. Africa 33°46S 18°22E 144 D2
Robbins I. Australia 40°42S 145°0E 151 G4
Róbbio Italy 45°17N 8°35E 92 C5
Robe Australia 37°11S 139°45E 152 D3
Robe → Australia 21°42S 116°15E 148 D2
Röbel Germany 53°22N 12°35E 76 B8
Robert Bourassa, Rés. Canada 53°40N 76°55W 164 B4
Robert Lee U.S.A. 31°54N 100°29W 176 F4
Roberta U.S.A. 32°43N 84°1W 178 C5
Robertsdale U.S.A. 40°11N 78°6W 174 F6
Robertsganj India 24°44N 83°4E 125 G10
Robertson S. Africa 33°46S 19°50E 144 D2
Robertson I. Antarctica 65°15S 59°30W 55 C18
Robertson Ra. Australia 23°15S 121°0E 148 D3
Robertsport Liberia 6°45N 11°26W 138 D2
Robertstown Australia 33°58S 139°5E 152 B3
Roberval Canada 48°32N 72°15W 165 C5
Robeson Chan. N. Amer. 82°0N 61°30W 57 A4
Robesonia U.S.A. 40°21N 76°8W 175 F8
Robinson U.S.A. 39°0N 87°44W 172 F10
Robinson → Australia 16°3S 137°16E 150 B2
Robinson Crusoe I. Pac. Oc. 33°38S 78°52W 184 F2
Robinson Ra. Australia 25°40S 119°0E 149 E2
Robinvale Australia 34°40S 142°45E 152 C5
Robledo Spain 38°46N 2°26W 91 G2
Roblin Canada 51°14N 101°21W 163 C8
Roboré Bolivia 18°10S 59°45W 186 G7
Robson, Mt. Canada 53°10N 119°10W 162 C5
Robstown U.S.A. 27°47N 97°40W 176 H6
Roca, C. da Portugal 38°40N 9°31W 89 G1
Roca Partida, I. Mexico 19°1N 112°2W 180 D2
Rocamadour France 44°48N 1°37E 72 D5
Rocas, Atol das Brazil 4°0S 34°1W 187 D12
Rocca San Casciano Italy 44°3N 11°50E 93 D8
Roccadáspide Italy 40°27N 15°10E 95 B8
Roccastrada Italy 43°0N 11°10E 93 F8
Roccella Iónica Italy 38°19N 16°24E 95 D9
Rocciamelone, Mte. Italy 45°12N 7°5E 73 C11
Rocha Uruguay 34°30S 54°25W 191 C5
Rochdale U.K. 53°38N 2°9W 66 D5
Roche Melon = Rocciamelone, Mte. Italy 45°12N 7°5E 73 C11
Rochechouart France 45°50N 0°49E 72 C4
Rochefort Belgium 50°9N 5°12E 69 D5
Rochefort France 45°56N 0°57W 72 C3
Rochefort-en-Terre France 47°42N 2°22W 70 E4
Rochelle Ga., U.S.A. 31°57N 83°27W 178 D6
Rochelle Ill., U.S.A. 41°56N 89°4W 172 E9
Rocher River Canada 61°23N 112°44W 162 A6
Rocheservière France 46°57N 1°30W 70 F5
Rochester Australia 36°22S 144°41E 152 D6
Rochester U.K. 51°23N 0°31E 67 F8
Rochester Ind., U.S.A. 41°4N 86°13W 172 E10
Rochester Minn., U.S.A. 44°1N 92°28W 172 C7
Rochester N.H., U.S.A. 43°18N 70°59W 175 C14
Rochester N.Y., U.S.A. 43°10N 77°37W 174 C7
Rociu Romania 44°43N 25°2E 81 F10
Rock → Canada 60°7N 127°7W 162 A3
Rock, The Australia 35°15S 147°2E 153 C7
Rock Creek U.S.A. 41°40N 80°52W 174 E4
Rock Falls U.S.A. 41°47N 89°41W 172 E9
Rock Flat Australia 36°21S 149°13E 153 D8
Rock Hill U.S.A. 34°56N 81°1W 177 D14
Rock Island U.S.A. 41°30N 90°34W 172 E8
Rock Port U.S.A. 40°25N 95°31W 172 E6
Rock Rapids U.S.A. 43°26N 96°10W 172 D5
Rock Sound Bahamas 24°54N 76°12W 182 B4
Rock Springs Mont., U.S.A. 46°49N 106°15W 168 C10
Rock Springs Wyo., U.S.A. 41°35N 109°14W 168 F9
Rock Valley U.S.A. 43°12N 96°18W 172 D5
Rockall Atl. Oc. 57°37N 13°42W 58 D3
Rockall Trough Atl. Oc. 57°0N 12°0W 56 A10
Rockdale Tex., U.S.A. 30°39N 97°0W 176 F6
Rockdale Wash., U.S.A. 47°22N 121°28W 170 C5
Rockeby = Mungkan Kandju △ Australia 13°35S 142°52E 150 A3
Rockefeller Plateau Antarctica 76°0S 130°0W 55 E14
Rockford Ala., U.S.A. 32°53N 86°13W 178 C3
Rockford Ill., U.S.A. 42°16N 89°6W 172 D9
Rockglen Canada 49°11N 105°57W 163 D7
Rockhampton Australia 23°22S 150°32E 150 C5
Rockingham Australia 32°15S 115°38E 149 F2
Rockingham N.C., U.S.A. 34°57N 79°46W 177 D15
Rockingham Vt., U.S.A. 43°11N 72°29W 175 C12
Rockingham B. Australia 18°5S 146°10E 150 B4
Rocklake U.S.A. 48°47N 99°15W 172 A4
Rockland Canada 45°33N 75°17W 175 A9
Rockland Idaho, U.S.A. 42°34N 112°53W 168 E7
Rockland Maine, U.S.A. 44°6N 69°7W 173 C19
Rockland Mich., U.S.A. 46°44N 89°11W 172 B9
Rocklands Reservoir Australia 37°15S 142°5E 152 D5
Rockledge U.S.A. 28°20N 80°43W 179 G9
Rocklin U.S.A. 38°48N 121°14W 170 G5
Rockly B. Trin. & Tob. 11°9N 60°46W 187 J16
Rockmart U.S.A. 34°1N 85°3W 178 A4
Rockport Mass., U.S.A. 42°39N 70°37W 175 D14
Rockport Tex., U.S.A. 28°2N 97°3W 176 G6
Rocksprings U.S.A. 30°1N 100°13W 176 F4
Rockville Conn., U.S.A. 41°52N 72°28W 175 E12
Rockville Md., U.S.A. 39°5N 77°9W 173 F15
Rockwall U.S.A. 32°56N 96°28W 176 E6
Rockwell City U.S.A. 42°24N 94°38W 172 D6
Rockwood Canada 43°37N 80°8W 174 C4
Rockwood Maine, U.S.A. 45°41N 69°45W 173 C19
Rockwood Tenn., U.S.A. 35°52N 84°41W 177 D12
Rocky Ford U.S.A. 38°3N 103°43W 168 G12
Rocky Gully Australia 34°30S 116°57E 149 F2
Rocky Harbour Canada 49°36N 57°55W 165 C8
Rocky Island L. Canada 46°55N 83°0W 164 C3
Rocky Lane Canada 58°31N 116°22W 162 B5
Rocky Mount U.S.A. 35°57N 77°48W 177 D16
Rocky Mountain △ U.S.A. 40°25N 105°45W 168 F11
Rocky Mountain House Canada 52°22N 114°55W 162 C6
Rocky Mts. N. Amer. 49°0N 115°0W 168 B6
Rocky Point Namibia 19°3S 12°30E 144 A2
Rocroi France 49°55N 4°30E 71 C11
Rod Pakistan 28°10N 63°5E 122 E3
Roda Greece 39°48N 19°46E 101 A3
Rødby Denmark 54°41N 11°23E 63 K5
Rødbyhavn Denmark 54°39N 11°22E 63 K5
Roddickton Canada 50°51N 56°8W 165 B8
Rødding Denmark 55°23N 9°3E 63 J3
Rödeby Sweden 56°15N 15°37E 63 H9
Rødekro Denmark 55°4N 9°20E 63 J3
Rodenkirchen Germany 53°23N 8°26E 76 B4
Rodez France 44°21N 2°33E 72 D6
Ródhos = Rhodes Greece 36°15N 28°10E 101 C10
Rodi Garganico Italy 41°55N 15°53E 93 G12
Rodia Greece 35°22N 25°1E 101 D7
Rodina Kazakhstan 50°16N 66°53E 109 B7
Rodna Romania 47°25N 24°50E 81 C9
Rodna ✪ Australia 23°45S 132°4E 148 D5
Rodnei, Munţii Romania 47°35N 24°35E 81 C9
Rodney Canada 42°34N 81°41W 174 D3
Rodney, C. N.Z. 36°17S 174°50E 154 C3
Rodniki Russia 57°7N 41°47E 86 B5
Rodolivos Greece 40°55N 24°0E 96 F7
Rodonit, Kepi i Albania 41°35N 19°27E 96 E3
Rodopi Greece 41°5N 25°30E 97 E9
Rodopi Planina Bulgaria 41°40N 24°20E 97 E8
Rodopos Greece 35°34N 23°45E 101 D5
Rodrigues Ind. Oc. 19°45S 63°20E 146 F5
Roe → U.K. 55°6N 6°59W 64 A5
Roebling U.S.A. 40°7N 74°47W 175 F10
Roebourne Australia 20°44S 117°9E 148 D2
Roebuck B. Australia 18°5S 122°20E 148 C3
Roebuck Roadhouse Australia 17°59S 122°36E 148 C3
Roermond Neths. 51°12N 6°0E 69 C6
Roes Welcome Sd. Canada 65°0N 87°0W 161 E14
Roeselare Belgium 50°57N 3°7E 69 D3
Rogachev = Ragachow Belarus 53°8N 30°5E 75 B16
Rogačica Serbia 44°4N 19°40E 96 B3
Rogagua, L. Bolivia 13°43S 66°50W 188 C4
Rogaška Slatina Slovenia 46°15N 15°42E 93 B12
Rogatec Slovenia 46°15N 15°46E 93 B12
Rogatica Bos.-H. 43°47N 19°0E 80 G4
Rogatyn Ukraine 49°24N 24°36E 75 D13
Rogen Sweden 62°20N 12°20E 62 B6
Rogers U.S.A. 36°20N 94°7W 176 C7
Rogers City U.S.A. 45°25N 83°49W 173 C12
Rogersville Canada 46°44N 65°26W 165 C6
Roggan → Canada 54°24N 79°25W 164 B4
Roggan L. Canada 54°8N 77°50W 164 B4
Roggeveen Basin Pac. Oc. 31°30S 95°30W 157 L18
Roggeveldberge S. Africa 32°10S 20°10E 144 D3
Roggiano Gravina Italy 39°37N 16°9E 95 C9
Rogliano France 42°57N 9°30E 73 F13
Rogliano Italy 39°10N 16°19E 95 C9
Rogoaguado, L. Bolivia 13°0S 65°30W 186 F5
Rogojampi Indonesia 8°19S 114°17E 119 J17
Rogoźno Poland 52°45N 16°59E 83 F3
Rogue → U.S.A. 42°26N 124°26W 168 E1
Roha India 18°26N 73°7E 126 E1
Rohan France 48°4N 2°45W 70 D4
Rohnert Park U.S.A. 38°16N 122°40W 170 G4
Rohri Pakistan 27°45N 68°51E 124 F3
Rohri Canal Pakistan 26°15N 68°27E 124 F3
Rohtak India 28°55N 76°43E 124 E7
Roi Et Thailand 16°4N 103°40E 120 D4
Roja Latvia 57°29N 22°43E 82 A9
Rojas Argentina 34°10S 60°45W 190 C3
Rojiște Romania 44°4N 24°38E 81 F8
Rojo, C. Mexico 21°33N 97°20W 181 C5
Rokan → Indonesia 2°0N 100°50E 118 D2
Rokel → S. Leone 8°30N 12°48W 138 D2
Rokiškis Lithuania 55°55N 25°35E 84 E3
Rokua △ Finland 64°30N 26°15E 60 D22
Rokycany Czechia 49°43N 13°35E 78 B6
Rolândia Brazil 23°18S 51°23W 191 A5
Rolla Mo., U.S.A. 37°57N 91°46W 172 G8
Rolla N. Dak., U.S.A. 48°52N 99°37W 172 A4
Rolleston Australia 24°28S 148°35E 150 C4
Rolleston N.Z. 43°35S 172°24E 155 D7
Rollingstone Australia 19°2S 146°24E 150 B4
Roma Australia 26°32S 148°49E 151 D4
Roma Italy 41°54N 12°28E 93 G9
Roma Sweden 57°32N 18°26E 63 G12
Roma Fiumicino ✈ (FCO) Italy 41°48N 12°15E 93 G9
Roma-Los Saenz U.S.A. 26°24N 99°1W 176 H5
Romain, C. U.S.A. 33°0N 79°22W 177 E15
Romaine → Canada 50°18N 63°47W 165 B7
Roman Bulgaria 43°8N 23°57E 96 C7
Roman Romania 46°57N 26°55E 81 D11
Roman-Kosh, Gora Ukraine 44°37N 34°15E 85 K8
Romanche → France 45°5N 5°43E 73 C9
Romang Indonesia 7°30S 127°20E 119 F7
Români Egypt 30°59N 32°38E 130 E1
Romania ■ Europe 46°0N 25°0E 81 D10
Romanija Bos.-H. 43°50N 18°45E 80 G3
Romano, C. U.S.A. 25°51N 81°41W 179 K8
Romano, Cayo Cuba 22°0N 77°30W 182 B4
Romans-sur-Isère France 45°3N 5°3E 73 C9
Romanshorn Switz. 47°33N 9°22E 77 H5
Romanzof C. U.S.A. 61°49N 166°6W 166 C6
Romblon Phil. 12°33N 122°17E 119 B6
Rome = Roma Italy 41°54N 12°28E 93 G9
Rome Ga., U.S.A. 34°15N 85°10W 177 D12
Rome N.Y., U.S.A. 43°13N 75°27W 175 C9
Rome Pa., U.S.A. 41°51N 76°21W 175 E8
Rometta Italy 38°10N 15°25E 95 D8
Romilly-sur-Seine France 48°31N 3°44E 71 D10
Romiton Uzbekistan 39°56N 64°23E 108 E6
Rommani Morocco 33°31N 6°40W 136 B2
Romney U.S.A. 39°21N 78°45W 173 F14
Romney Marsh U.K. 51°2N 0°54E 67 F8
Romny Ukraine 50°48N 33°28E 85 G7
Rømø Denmark 55°10N 8°30E 63 J2
Romodan Ukraine 49°55N 33°15E 85 G7
Romodanovo Russia 54°26N 45°23E 86 C7
Romont Switz. 46°42N 6°54E 77 J2
Romorantin-Lanthenay France 47°21N 1°45E 71 E8
Rompin → Malaysia 2°49N 103°29E 121 L4
Romsdalen Norway 62°25N 7°52E 60 E12
Romsey U.K. 51°0N 1°29W 67 G6
Ron India 15°40N 75°44E 127 G2
Ron Vietnam 17°53N 106°27E 120 D6
Rona U.K. 57°34N 5°59W 65 D3
Ronan U.S.A. 47°32N 114°6W 168 C6
Roncador, Cayos Caribbean 13°32N 80°4W 182 D3
Roncador, Serra do Brazil 12°30S 52°30W 187 F8
Ronciglione Italy 42°17N 12°13E 93 F9
Ronco → Italy 44°24N 12°12E 93 D9
Ronda Spain 36°46N 5°12W 89 J5
Ronda, Serranía de Spain 36°44N 5°3W 89 J5
Rondane Norway 61°57N 9°50E 60 F13
Rondônia □ Brazil 11°0S 63°0W 186 F6
Rondonópolis Brazil 16°28S 54°38W 187 G8
Rondu Pakistan 35°32N 75°10E 125 B6
Rong, Koh Cambodia 10°45N 103°15E 121 G4
Rong Jiang → China 24°35N 109°20E 116 E7
Rong Xian China 22°50N 110°31E 117 F8
Rong'an China 25°14N 109°22E 116 E7
Rongchang China 29°20N 105°32E 116 C5
Rongcheng China 37°9N 122°23E 115 F12
Ronge, L. la Canada 55°6N 105°17W 163 B7
Rongjiang China 25°57N 108°28E 116 E7
Rongotea N.Z. 40°19S 175°25E 154 G4
Rongshui China 25°5N 109°12E 116 E7
Rongxian China 29°23N 104°22E 116 C5
Rønne Denmark 55°6N 14°43E 63 J8
Ronne Ice Shelf Antarctica 77°30S 60°0W 55 D18
Ronneby Sweden 56°12N 15°17E 63 H9
Ronnebyån → Sweden 56°11N 15°18E 63 H9
Rönneshytta Sweden 58°56N 15°2E 63 F9
Ronsard, C. Australia 24°46S 113°10E 149 D1
Ronse Belgium 50°45N 3°35E 69 D3
Roodepoort S. Africa 26°11S 27°54E 145 C4
Roof Butte U.S.A. 36°28N 109°5W 169 H9
Rooiboklaagte → Namibia 20°50S 21°0E 144 B3
Rooniu, Mt. Tahiti 17°49S 149°12W 155 b
Roopville U.S.A. 33°27N 85°8W 178 B4
Roorkee India 29°52N 77°59E 124 E7
Roosendaal Neths. 51°32N 4°29E 69 C4
Roosevelt U.S.A. 40°18N 109°59W 168 F9
Roosevelt → Brazil 7°35S 60°20W 186 E6
Roosevelt, Mt. Canada 58°26N 125°20W 162 B3
Roosevelt I. Antarctica 79°30S 162°0W 55 D12
Ropczyce Poland 50°4N 21°38E 83 H8
Roper → Australia 14°43S 135°27E 150 A2
Roper Bar Australia 14°44S 134°44E 150 A1
Roper River = St. Vidgeon's ✪ Australia 14°47S 134°53E 150 A1
Roque Pérez Argentina 35°25S 59°24W 190 D4
Roquefort France 44°2N 0°20W 72 D3
Roquemaure France 44°3N 4°48E 73 D8
Roquetas de Mar Spain 36°46N 2°36W 91 J2
Roquetes Spain 40°50N 0°30E 90 E5
Roquevaire France 43°20N 5°36E 73 E9
Roraima □ Brazil 2°0N 61°30W 186 C6
Roraima, Mt. Venezuela 5°10N 60°40W 186 B6
Røros Norway 62°35N 11°23E 60 E14
Rorschach Switz. 47°28N 9°28E 77 H5
Ros Comáin = Roscommon Ireland 53°38N 8°11W 64 C3
Ros Mhic Thriúin = New Ross Ireland 52°23N 6°57W 64 D5
Rosa Zambia 9°33S 31°15E 143 D3
Rosa, C. Algeria 37°0N 8°16E 136 A5
Rosa, Monte Europe 45°57N 7°53E 92 C4
Rosal de la Frontera Spain 37°59N 7°13W 89 H3
Rosalia U.S.A. 47°14N 117°22W 168 C5
Rosamond U.S.A. 34°52N 118°10W 171 L8
Rosans France 44°24N 5°29E 73 D9
Rosario Argentina 33°0S 60°40W 190 C3
Rosário Brazil 3°0S 44°15W 189 A2
Rosario Mexico 22°58N 105°53W 180 C3
Rosario Paraguay 24°30S 57°35W 190 A4
Rosario de la Frontera Argentina 25°50S 65°0W 190 B3
Rosario de Lerma Argentina 24°59S 65°35W 190 A2
Rosario del Tala Argentina 32°20S 59°10W 190 C4
Rosário do Sul Brazil 30°15S 54°55W 191 C5
Rosarito Baja Calif., Mexico 32°20N 117°2W 171 N9
Rosarito Baja Calif., Mexico 28°38N 114°1W 180 B2
Rosarno Italy 38°29N 15°58E 95 D8
Rosas = Roses Spain 42°19N 3°10E 90 C8
Roscoe U.S.A. 41°56N 74°55W 175 E10
Roscoff France 48°44N 3°58W 70 D3
Roscommon Ireland 53°38N 8°11W 64 C3
Roscommon □ Ireland 53°49N 8°23W 64 C3
Roscrea Ireland 52°57N 7°49W 64 D4
Rose → Australia 14°16S 135°45E 150 A2
Rose, L. Bahamas 21°0N 73°30W 183 B5
Rose Belle Mauritius 20°24S 57°36E 141 d
Rose Blanche Canada 47°38N 58°45W 165 C8
Rose Hill Mauritius 20°14S 57°27E 141 d
Rose Pt. Canada 54°11N 131°39W 162 C2
Rose Valley Canada 52°19N 103°49W 163 C8
Roseau Dominica 15°17N 61°24W 183 C7
Roseau U.S.A. 48°51N 95°46W 172 A6
Rosebery Australia 41°46S 145°33E 151 G4
Rosebud Australia 38°21S 144°54E 152 E6
Rosebud S. Dak., U.S.A. 43°14N 100°51W 172 D3
Rosebud Tex., U.S.A. 31°4N 96°59W 176 F6
Roseburg U.S.A. 43°13N 123°20W 168 E2
Rosedale U.S.A. 33°51N 91°2W 177 E9
Rosehearty U.K. 57°42N 2°7W 65 D6
Roseires Res. Sudan 11°51N 34°23E 135 F12
Roseland U.S.A. 38°25N 122°43W 170 G4
Rosemary Canada 50°46N 112°5W 162 C6
Rosenberg U.S.A. 29°34N 95°49W 176 G7
Rosendaël France 51°3N 2°24E 71 A9
Rosenheim Germany 47°51N 12°7E 77 H8
Roses Spain 42°19N 3°10E 90 C8
Roses, G. de Spain 42°10N 3°15E 90 C8
Roseto degli Abruzzi Italy 42°41N 14°1E 93 F11
Rosetown Canada 51°35N 107°59W 163 C7
Rosetta = Rashîd Egypt 31°21N 30°22E 137 E7
Roseville Calif., U.S.A. 38°45N 121°17W 170 G5
Roseville Mich., U.S.A. 42°30N 82°56W 174 D2
Roseville Pa., U.S.A. 41°51N 76°57W 175 E8
Rosewood Australia 27°38S 152°36E 151 D5
Roshkhvār Iran 34°58N 59°37E 129 C8
Rosières-en-Santerre France 49°49N 2°42E 71 C9
Rosignano Maríttimo Italy 43°24N 10°28E 92 E7
Rosignol Guyana 6°15N 57°30W 186 B7
Roşiori de Vede Romania 44°9N 25°0E 81 F10
Rositsa Bulgaria 43°57N 27°57E 97 C11
Rositsa → Bulgaria 43°10N 25°30E 97 C9
Roskilde Denmark 55°38N 12°3E 63 J6
Roskovec Albania 40°44N 19°43E 96 F3
Roslavl Russia 53°57N 32°55E 84 F7
Rosmaninhal Portugal 39°44N 7°5W 88 F3
Rosmead S. Africa 31°29S 25°8E 144 D4
Røsnæs Denmark 55°44N 10°55E 63 J4
Rosolini Italy 36°49N 14°57E 95 F7
Rosporden France 47°57N 3°50W 70 E3
Ross Australia 42°2S 147°30E 151 G4
Ross N.Z. 42°53S 170°49E 155 C5
Ross Béthio Mauritania 16°15N 16°8W 138 B1
Ross Dependency Antarctica 76°0S 170°0W 55 D12
Ross I. Antarctica 77°30S 168°0E 55 D11
Ross Ice Shelf Antarctica 80°0S 180°0E 55 E12
Ross L. U.S.A. 48°44N 121°4W 168 B3
Ross-on-Wye U.K. 51°54N 2°34W 67 F5
Ross River Australia 23°44S 134°30E 150 C1
Ross River Canada 62°30N 131°30W 162 A2
Ross Sea Antarctica 74°0S 178°0E 55 D11
Rossall Pt. U.K. 53°55N 3°3W 66 D4
Rossan Pt. Ireland 54°42N 8°47W 64 B3
Rossano Italy 39°36N 16°39E 95 C9
Rossburn Canada 50°40N 100°49W 163 C8
Rosseau Canada 45°16N 79°39W 174 A5
Rosseau, L. Canada 45°10N 79°35W 174 A5
Rosses, The Ireland 55°2N 8°20W 64 A3
Rossignol, L. Canada 52°43N 73°40W 164 B5
Rossignol L. Canada 44°12N 65°10W 165 D6
Rossiya = Russia ■ Eurasia 62°0N 105°0E 107 C11
Rossland Canada 49°6N 117°50W 162 D5
Rosslare Ireland 52°17N 6°24W 64 D5
Rosslare Europort = Rosslare Harbour Ireland 52°15N 6°20W 64 D5
Rosslare Harbour Ireland 52°15N 6°20W 64 D5
Rosslau Germany 51°52N 12°15E 76 D8
Rossmore Canada 44°8N 77°23W 174 B7
Rosso Mauritania 16°40N 15°45W 138 B1
Rosso, C. France 42°13N 8°32E 73 F12
Rossosh Russia 50°15N 39°28E 85 G10
Røssvatnet Norway 65°45N 14°5E 60 D16
Røst Norway 67°32N 12°10E 60 C15
Rosthern Canada 52°40N 106°20W 163 C7
Rostock Germany 54°5N 12°8E 76 A8
Rostov Don, Russia 47°15N 39°45E 85 J10
Rostov Yaroslavl, Russia 57°14N 39°25E 84 D10
Rostov □ Russia 48°50N 41°10E 87 F5
Rostrenen France 48°14N 3°21W 70 D3
Roswell Ga., U.S.A. 34°2N 84°22W 178 A5
Roswell N. Mex., U.S.A. 33°24N 104°32W 169 K11
Rota Spain 36°37N 6°20W 89 J4
Rotan U.S.A. 32°51N 100°28W 176 E4
Rote Indonesia 10°50S 123°0E 119 F6
Rotenburg Hessen, Germany 50°59N 9°44E 76 E5
Rotenburg Niedersachsen, Germany 53°6N 9°25E 76 B5
Roth Germany 49°15N 11°5E 77 F7

Rothaargebirge *Germany* 51°2N 8°13E **76 D4**
Rothaargebirge △
  Germany 51°0N 8°15E **76 E4**
Rothenburg ob der Tauber
  Germany 49°23N 10°11E **77 F6**
Rothera *Antarctica* 67°34S 68°8W **5 C17**
Rotherham *U.K.* 53°26N 1°20W **66 D6**
Rothes *U.K.* 57°32N 3°13W **65 D5**
Rothesay *Canada* 45°23N 66°0W **165 C6**
Rothesay *U.K.* 55°50N 5°3W **65 F3**
Roti = Rote *Indonesia* 10°50S 123°0E **119 F6**
Rotja, Pta. *Spain* 38°38N 1°35E **91 G6**
Roto *Australia* 33°0S 145°30E **153 B6**
Rotoaira, L. *N.Z.* 39°3S 175°45E **154 F4**
Rotoehu, L. *N.Z.* 38°1S 176°32E **154 E5**
Rotoiti, L. *Bay of Plenty,*
  N.Z. 38°2S 176°30E **154 E5**
Rotoiti, L. *W. Coast,*
  N.Z. 41°51S 172°49E **155 B7**
Rotoma, L. *N.Z.* 38°2S 176°35E **154 E5**
Rotondo, Mte. *France* 42°14N 9°8E **73 F13**
Rotorua, L. *N.Z.* 41°55S 172°39E **155 B7**
Rotorua *N.Z.* 38°9S 176°16E **154 E5**
Rotorua, L. *N.Z.* 38°5S 176°18E **154 E5**
Rott → *Germany* 48°27N 13°25E **77 G9**
Rottenburg *Germany* 48°28N 8°55E **77 G4**
Rottenmann *Austria* 47°31N 14°22E **78 D7**
Rotterdam *Neths.* 51°55N 4°30E **69 C4**
Rotterdam *U.S.A.* 42°48N 74°1W **175 D10**
Rottne *Sweden* 57°1N 14°54E **63 G8**
Rottnest I. *Australia* 32°0S 115°27E **149 F2**
Rottumeroog *Neths.* 53°33N 6°34E **69 A6**
Rottweil *Germany* 48°9N 8°38E **77 G4**
Rotuma *Fiji* 12°25S 177°5E **147 C10**
Roubaix *France* 50°40N 3°10E **71 B10**
Roudnice nad Labem
  Czechia 50°25N 14°15E **78 A7**
Rouen *France* 49°27N 1°4E **70 C4**
Rouergue *France* 44°15N 2°0E **72 D5**
Rough Ridge *N.Z.* 45°10S 169°55E **155 F4**
Rouillac *France* 45°47N 0°4W **72 C3**
Rouissat *Algeria* 31°55N 5°20E **136 B6**
Rouleau *Canada* 50°10N 104°56W **163 C8**
Roulpmaulpma ○
  Australia 23°52S 133°0E **148 D5**
Round I. *Mauritius* 19°51S 57°45E **141 d**
Round Mountain
  U.S.A. 38°43N 117°4W **168 G5**
Round Mt. *Australia* 30°26S 152°16E **153 A4**
Round Rock *U.S.A.* 30°31N 97°41W **176 F6**
Roundup *U.S.A.* 46°27N 108°33W **168 C9**
Rousay *U.K.* 59°10N 3°2W **65 B5**
Rouses Point *U.S.A.* 44°59N 73°22W **175 B11**
Rouseville *U.S.A.* 41°28N 79°42W **174 E5**
Rousse = Ruse *Bulgaria* 43°48N 25°59E **97 C9**
Roussenski Lom △
  Bulgaria 43°40N 26°10E **97 C10**
Roussillon *Isère, France* 45°24N 4°49E **73 C8**
Roussillon *Pyrénées-Or.,*
  France 42°30N 2°35E **72 F6**
Rouxville *S. Africa* 30°25S 26°50E **144 D4**
Rouyn-Noranda *Canada* 48°20N 79°0W **164 C4**
Rovaniemi *Finland* 66°29N 25°41E **60 C21**
Rovato *Italy* 45°34N 10°0E **92 C7**
Rovenki *Ukraine* 48°5N 39°21E **85 H10**
Rovereto *Italy* 45°53N 11°3E **92 C8**
Rovigo *Italy* 45°4N 11°47E **92 C8**
Rovinj *Croatia* 45°5N 13°40E **93 C10**
Rovno = Rivne *Ukraine* 50°40N 26°10E **75 C14**
Rovnoye *Russia* 50°52N 46°3E **86 E8**
Rovuma = Ruvuma →
  Tanzania 10°29S 40°28E **143 E5**
Row'ān *Iran* 35°8N 48°51E **129 C6**
Rowena *Australia* 29°48S 148°55E **151 D4**
Rowley I. *Canada* 69°6N 77°52W **161 D16**
Rowley Shoals
  Australia 17°30S 119°0E **148 C2**
Roxa *Guinea-Biss.* 11°15N 15°45W **138 C1**
Roxas *Phil.* 11°36N 122°49E **119 B6**
Roxboro *U.S.A.* 36°24N 78°59W **177 C15**
Roxborough
  Trin. & Tob. 11°15N 60°35W **187 J16**
Roxburgh *N.Z.* 45°33S 169°19E **155 F4**
Roxbury *N.Y., U.S.A.* 42°17N 74°33W **175 D10**
Roxbury *Pa., U.S.A.* 40°6N 77°39W **174 F7**
Roxby Downs
  Australia 30°43S 136°46E **151 E2**
Roxen *Sweden* 58°30N 15°40E **63 F9**
Roy *Mont., U.S.A.* 47°20N 108°58W **168 C9**
Roy *N. Mex., U.S.A.* 35°57N 104°12W **169 J11**
Roy *Utah, U.S.A.* 41°10N 112°2W **168 F7**
Roy Hill *Australia* 22°41S 119°57E **148 D3**
Royal △ *Australia* 34°5S 151°5E **153 C9**
Royal Bardia △ *Nepal* 28°20N 81°20E **125 E9**
Royal Canal *Ireland* 53°30N 7°13W **64 C4**
Royal Chitawan △
  Nepal 26°30N 84°30E **125 F11**
Royal Geographical Society Is.
  Canada 68°56N 100°15W **160 D11**
Royal Leamington Spa
  U.K. 52°18N 1°31W **67 E6**
Royal Natal △ *S. Africa* 28°43S 28°51E **145 C4**
Royal Palm Beach
  U.S.A. 26°42N 80°14W **179 J9**
Royal Tunbridge Wells
  U.K. 51°7N 0°16E **67 F8**
Royale, Isle *U.S.A.* 48°0N 88°54W **172 B9**
Royalla *Australia* 35°30S 149°9E **153 C8**
Royan *France* 45°37N 1°2W **72 C2**
Roye *France* 49°42N 2°48E **71 C9**
Royston *U.K.* 52°3N 0°0 **67 E7**
Rožaj *Montenegro* 42°50N 20°11E **96 D4**
Rózan *Poland* 52°52N 21°25E **85 E8**
Rozay-en-Brie *France* 48°41N 2°58E **71 D9**
Rozdilna *Ukraine* 46°50N 30°2E **81 D15**
Rozhnyativ *Ukraine* 48°55N 24°9E **81 B9**
Rozhyshche *Ukraine* 50°54N 25°15E **75 C13**
Rožmitál pod Třemšinem
  Czechia 49°35N 13°53E **78 B6**
Rožňava *Slovakia* 48°37N 20°35E **79 C13**
Rozogi *Poland* 53°28N 21°19E **82 E8**
Rozoy-sur-Serre *France* 49°40N 4°8E **71 C11**
Roztoczański △ *Poland* 50°37N 23°0E **83 H10**
Rozzano *Italy* 45°26N 9°10E **92 C6**
Rrëshen *Albania* 41°47N 19°49E **96 E3**
Rrogozhinë *Albania* 41°4N 19°50E **96 E3**
Rtanj *Serbia* 43°45N 21°50E **96 C5**
Rtishchevo *Russia* 52°18N 43°46E **86 D6**
Rúa = A Rúa *Spain* 42°24N 7°6W **88 C3**
Ruacaná *Namibia* 17°27S 14°21E **144 A1**

Ruaha △ *Tanzania* 7°41S 34°30E **142 D3**
Ruahine Ra. *N.Z.* 39°55S 176°2E **154 F5**
Ruamahanga → *N.Z.* 41°24S 175°8E **154 H4**
Ruapehu *N.Z.* 39°17S 175°35E **154 F4**
Ruapuke I. *N.Z.* 46°46S 168°31E **155 G3**
Ruâq, W. → *Egypt* 30°30N 33°49E **130 F2**
Ruatoria *N.Z.* 37°55S 178°20E **154 C7**
Ruawai *N.Z.* 36°8S 173°59E **154 C2**
Rub' al Khālī *Si. Arabia* 19°0N 48°0E **131 D4**
Rubeho Mts. *Tanzania* 6°50S 36°25E **142 D4**
Rubezhnoye = Rubizhne
  Ukraine 49°6N 38°25E **85 H10**
Rubh a' Mhail *U.K.* 55°56N 6°8W **65 F2**
Rubha Hunish *U.K.* 57°42N 6°20W **65 D2**
Rubha Robhanais = Lewis, Butt of
  U.K. 58°31N 6°16W **65 C2**
Rubi *Spain* 41°29N 2°2E **90 D7**
Rubicon → *U.S.A.* 38°53N 121°4W **170 G5**
Rubicone → *Italy* 44°8N 12°28E **93 D9**
Rubik *Albania* 41°46N 19°47E **96 E3**
Rubino *Côte d'Ivoire* 6°4N 4°18W **138 D4**
Rubio *Venezuela* 7°43N 72°22W **186 B4**
Rubizhne *Ukraine* 49°6N 38°25E **85 H10**
Rubondo △ *Tanzania* 2°18S 31°58E **142 C3**
Rubtsovsk *Russia* 51°30N 81°10E **109 B10**
Ruby L. *U.S.A.* 40°10N 115°28W **168 F6**
Ruby Mts. *U.S.A.* 40°30N 115°20W **168 F6**
Rubyvale *Australia* 23°25S 147°42E **150 C4**
Rucheng *China* 25°33N 113°38E **117 E9**
Ruciane-Nida *Poland* 53°40N 21°32E **82 E8**
Rūd Sar *Iran* 37°8N 50°18E **129 B6**
Ruda *Sweden* 57°6N 16°7E **63 G10**
Ruda Śląska *Poland* 50°16N 18°50E **83 H5**
Rudall *Australia* 33°43S 136°17E **152 B2**
Rudall → *Australia* 22°34S 122°13E **148 D3**
Rudall River △
  Australia 22°38S 122°30E **148 D3**
Rudbar *Iran* 36°48N 49°23E **129 B6**
Rüdersdorf *Germany* 52°27N 13°47E **76 C9**
Rudewa *Tanzania* 10°7S 34°40E **143 E3**
Rudkøbing *Denmark* 54°56N 10°41E **63 K4**
Rudky *Ukraine* 49°38N 23°29E **83 J10**
Rudna *Poland* 51°30N 16°17E **83 G3**
Rudnik *Bulgaria* 42°36N 27°30E **97 D11**
Rudnik *Poland* 50°26N 22°15E **83 H9**
Rudnik *Serbia* 44°7N 20°35E **96 B4**
Rudnya *Russia* 54°55N 31°7E **84 E6**
Rudnytsya *Ukraine* 48°16N 28°54E **81 B13**
Rudnyy *Kazakhstan* 52°57N 63°7E **108 B6**
Rudo *Bos.-H.* 43°41N 19°23E **80 G4**
Rudolfa, Ostrov *Russia* 81°45N 58°30E **106 A6**
Rudolstadt *Germany* 50°44N 11°19E **76 E7**
Rudong *China* 32°20N 121°12E **117 A13**
Rudozem *Bulgaria* 41°29N 24°51E **97 E8**
Rudrapur *India* 28°59N 79°24E **125 E8**
Rudyard *U.S.A.* 46°14N 84°36W **173 B11**
Rue *France* 50°15N 1°40E **71 B8**
Ruenya → *Africa* 16°24S 33°48E **143 F3**
Rufiji → *Tanzania* 7°50S 39°15E **142 D4**
Ruffling Pt. *Br. Virgin Is.* 18°44N 64°27W **183 e**
Rufiji → *Tanzania* 7°50S 39°15E **142 D4**
Rufino *Argentina* 34°20S 62°50W **190 C3**
Rufisque *Senegal* 14°40N 17°15W **138 C1**
Rufunsa *Zambia* 15°4S 29°34E **143 F2**
Rui Barbosa *Brazil* 12°18S 40°27W **189 C2**
Rui'an *China* 27°47N 120°40E **117 D13**
Ruichang *China* 29°40N 115°39E **117 C10**
Ruidoso *U.S.A.* 33°20N 105°41W **169 K11**
Ruijin *China* 25°48N 116°0E **117 E10**
Ruili *China* 24°6N 97°46E **116 E1**
Ruiru *Kenya* 1°9S 36°58E **142 C4**
Ruivo, Pico *Madeira* 32°45N 16°56W **100 D3**
Ruj *Bulgaria* 42°52N 22°34E **96 C6**
Rujen *Macedonia* 42°9N 22°30E **96 D6**
Rujm Tal'at al Jamā'ah
  Jordan 30°24N 35°30E **130 E4**
Ruk *Pakistan* 27°50N 68°42E **124 F3**
Rukhla *Pakistan* 32°27N 71°57E **124 C4**
Ruki →
  Dem. Rep. of the Congo 0°5N 18°17E **140 E3**
Rukumkot *Nepal* 28°37N 82°37E **125 E10**
Rukwa □ *Tanzania* 7°0S 31°30E **142 D3**
Rukwa, L. *Tanzania* 8°0S 32°20E **142 D3**
Rulenge *Burundi* 2°43S 30°37E **142 C3**
Rulhieres, C. *Australia* 13°56S 127°22E **148 B4**
Rum *Jordan* 29°39N 35°26E **130 F4**
Rùm *U.K.* 57°0N 6°20W **65 E2**
Rum Cay *Bahamas* 23°40N 74°58W **183 B5**
Rum Jungle *Australia* 13°0S 130°59E **148 B5**
Ruma △ *Kenya* 0°39S 34°18E **142 C3**
Rumāḥ *Si. Arabia* 25°29N 47°10E **128 E5**
Rumania = Romania ■
  Europe 46°0N 25°0E **81 D10**
Rumaylah *Iraq* 30°47N 47°37E **128 D5**
Rumaylah, 'Urūq ar
  Si. Arabia 22°0N 48°30E **131 C4**
Rumbek *South Sudan* 6°54N 29°37E **135 G11**
Rumburk *Czechia* 50°57N 14°32E **78 A8**
Rumford *U.S.A.* 44°33N 70°33W **175 B14**
Rumia *Poland* 54°37N 18°30E **82 D5**
Rumilly *France* 45°53N 5°56E **73 C9**
Rumoi *Japan* 43°56N 141°39E **112 C10**
Rumonge *Burundi* 3°59S 29°26E **142 C2**
Rumphi *Malawi* 11°1S 33°52E **143 E3**
Rumson *U.S.A.* 40°23N 74°0W **175 F11**
Rumuruti *Kenya* 0°17N 36°32E **142 B4**
Runan *China* 33°0N 114°30E **117 A10**
Runanga *N.Z.* 42°25S 171°15E **155 C6**
Runaway, C. *N.Z.* 37°32S 177°59E **154 B6**
Runaway Bay *Jamaica* 18°27N 77°20W **182 a**
Runcorn *U.K.* 53°21N 2°44W **66 D5**
Rundu *Namibia* 17°52S 19°43E **144 A2**
Rungwa *Tanzania* 6°55S 33°32E **142 D3**
Rungwa → *Tanzania* 7°36S 31°50E **142 D3**
Rungwa △ *Tanzania* 6°53S 34°2E **142 D3**
Rungwe *Tanzania* 9°11S 33°32E **143 D3**
Rungwe, Mt. *Tanzania* 9°8S 33°40E **143 D3**
Runka *Nigeria* 12°28N 7°20E **139 C6**
Runn *Sweden* 60°30N 15°40E **62 D9**

Runton Ra. *Australia* 23°31S 123°6E **148 D3**
Ruo Shui → *China* 41°0N 100°16E **110 C9**
Ruokolahti *Finland* 61°17N 28°50E **84 B5**
Ruoqiang *China* 38°55N 88°10E **109 E11**
Rupa *India* 27°15N 92°21E **123 F18**
Rupar *India* 31°2N 76°38E **124 D7**
Rupat *Indonesia* 1°45N 101°40E **118 D2**
Rupea *Romania* 46°2N 25°13E **81 D10**
Rupen → *India* 23°28N 71°31E **124 H4**
Rupert *U.S.A.* 42°37N 113°41W **168 E7**
Rupert → *Canada* 51°29N 78°45W **164 B4**
Rupert B. *Canada* 51°35N 79°0W **164 B4**
Rupert House = Waskaganish
  Canada 51°30N 78°40W **164 B4**
Rupnagar = Rupar
  India 31°2N 76°38E **124 D7**
Rupsa *India* 21°37N 87°1E **125 J12**
Rur → *Neths.* 51°12N 6°3E **69 C6**
Rus → *Spain* 39°30N 2°30W **91 F2**
Rusambo *Zimbabwe* 16°30S 32°4E **143 F3**
Rusape *Zimbabwe* 18°35S 32°8E **143 F3**
Ruschuk = Ruse
  Bulgaria 43°48N 25°59E **97 C9**
Ruse *Bulgaria* 43°48N 25°59E **97 C9**
Ruse → *Bulgaria* 43°35N 25°40E **97 C9**
Ruşeţu *Romania* 44°57N 27°14E **81 F12**
Rush *Ireland* 53°31N 6°6W **64 C5**
Rushden *U.K.* 52°18N 0°35W **67 E7**
Rushikulya → *India* 19°23N 85°5E **126 E7**
Rushmore, Mt.
  U.S.A. 43°53N 103°28W **172 D2**
Rushville *Ill., U.S.A.* 40°7N 90°34W **172 E8**
Rushville *Ind., U.S.A.* 39°37N 85°27W **173 F11**
Rushville *Nebr.,*
  U.S.A. 42°43N 102°28W **172 D2**
Rushworth *Australia* 36°32S 145°1E **153 D6**
Ruskin *U.S.A.* 27°43N 82°26W **179 H7**
Russas *Brazil* 4°55S 37°50W **189 A3**
Russell *Canada* 50°50N 101°20W **163 C8**
Russell *N.Z.* 35°16S 174°10E **154 B3**
Russell *Fla., U.S.A.* 30°3N 81°45W **178 E8**
Russell *Kans., U.S.A.* 38°54N 98°52W **172 F4**
Russell *N.Y., U.S.A.* 44°27N 75°9W **175 B9**
Russell *Pa., U.S.A.* 41°56N 79°8W **174 E5**
Russell Cave △
  U.S.A. 34°59N 85°49W **177 D12**
Russell L. *Man.,*
  Canada 56°15N 101°30W **163 B8**
Russell L. *N.W.T.,*
  Canada 63°5N 115°44W **162 A5**
Russellkonda *India* 19°57N 84°42E **126 E7**
Russellville *Ala.,*
  U.S.A. 34°30N 87°44W **177 D11**
Russellville *Ark., U.S.A.* 35°17N 93°8W **176 D8**
Russellville *Ky.,*
  U.S.A. 36°51N 86°53W **172 G10**
Rüsselsheim *Germany* 49°59N 8°25E **77 F4**
Russi *Italy* 44°22N 12°2E **93 D9**
Russia ■ *Eurasia* 62°0N 105°0E **107 C11**
Russian → *U.S.A.* 38°27N 123°8W **170 G3**
Russkaya Arktika △
  Russia 73°40N 55°55E **106 B6**
Russkiy, Ostrov *Russia* 43°0N 131°50E **112 C5**
Russky Sever △ *Russia* 59°57N 38°34E **84 B10**
Rust *Austria* 47°49N 16°42E **79 D9**
Rustam Shahr *Pakistan* 26°58N 66°6E **124 F2**
Rustavi *Georgia* 41°30N 45°0E **87 K7**
Rustenburg *S. Africa* 25°41S 27°14E **144 C4**
Ruston *U.S.A.* 32°32N 92°38W **176 E8**
Ruta *Spain* 37°19N 4°23W **89 H6**
Rutana *Burundi* 3°55S 30°0E **142 C3**
Ruteng *Indonesia* 8°35S 120°30E **119 F6**
Rutenga *Zimbabwe* 21°15S 30°44E **143 G3**
Ruth *U.S.A.* 43°42N 82°45W **174 C2**
Rutherford *Australia* 38°54N 77°29W **173 F15**
Rutherglen *Australia* 36°5S 146°29E **153 D7**
Rutland □ *U.K.* 52°38N 0°40W **67 E7**
Rutland *U.S.A.* 43°37N 72°58W **175 C12**
Rutland I. *U.K.* 11°25N 92°10E **127 J11**
Rutland Water *U.K.* 52°39N 0°38W **67 E7**
Rutledge → *Canada* 61°4N 112°0W **163 A6**
Rutledge L. *Canada* 61°33N 110°47W **163 A6**
Rutog *China* 33°27N 79°42E **125 E9**
Rutqa, W. → *Syria* 34°30N 41°3E **105 E9**
Rutshuru
  Dem. Rep. of the Congo 1°13S 29°25E **142 C2**
Ruvo di Púglia *Italy* 41°7N 16°29E **95 A9**
Ruvu *Tanzania* 6°49S 38°43E **142 D4**
Ruvu → *Tanzania* 6°23S 38°52E **142 D4**
Ruvuba △ *Burundi* 3°3S 29°33E **142 C2**
Ruvuma □ *Tanzania* 10°20S 36°0E **143 E4**
Ruvuma → *Tanzania* 10°29S 40°28E **143 E5**
Ruwais *U.A.E.* 24°5N 52°50E **129 E7**
Ruwenzori *Africa* 0°30N 29°55E **142 B2**
Ruwenzori △ *Uganda* 0°20N 30°0E **142 B2**
Ruya → *Zimbabwe* 16°27S 32°5E **145 A5**
Ruyang *China* 34°9N 112°27E **116 A7**
Ruyigi *Burundi* 3°29S 30°15E **142 C3**
Ruyuan *China* 24°46N 113°16E **117 E9**
Růžavevka *Kazakhstan* 52°49N 66°56E **108 B7**
Ruzayevka *Russia* 54°4N 45°0E **86 C7**
Ruzhou *China* 34°11N 112°52E **116 A7**
Ružomberok *Slovakia* 49°3N 19°17E **79 B12**
Ruzyně, Praha ✈ (PRG)
  Czechia 50°6N 14°16E **78 A7**
Rwanda ■ *Africa* 2°0S 30°0E **142 C3**
Ryakhovo *Bulgaria* 43°58N 26°18E **97 C10**
Ryan, L. *U.K.* 55°0N 5°2W **65 G3**
Ryazan *Russia* 54°40N 39°40E **84 E10**
Ryazhsk *Russia* 53°45N 40°3E **84 E11**
Rybachiy Poluostrov
  Russia 69°43N 32°0E **60 B25**
Rybachiy
  = Balykchy
  Kyrgyzstan 42°26N 76°12E **108 D9**
Rybinsk *Russia* 58°5N 38°50E **84 C10**
Rybinskoye Vdkhr.
  Russia 58°30N 38°25E **84 C10**
Rybnik *Poland* 50°6N 18°32E **83 H5**
Rybnitsa = Râbnița
  Moldova 47°45N 29°0E **81 C14**
Rybnoye *Russia* 54°45N 39°30E **86 C10**
Rychnov nad Kněžnou
  Czechia 50°10N 16°17E **79 A9**
Rychwał *Poland* 52°4N 18°10E **83 F5**
Rycroft *Canada* 55°45N 118°40W **162 B5**
Ryd *Sweden* 56°27N 14°42E **63 H8**
Rydaholm *Sweden* 56°59N 14°18E **63 H8**

Ryde *U.K.* 50°43N 1°9W **67 G6**
Ryderwood *U.S.A.* 46°23N 123°3W **170 D3**
Rydzyna *Poland* 51°47N 16°39E **83 G3**
Rye *U.K.* 50°57N 0°45E **67 G8**
Rye → *U.K.* 54°11N 0°44W **66 C7**
Rye Bay *U.K.* 50°52N 0°49E **67 G8**
Rye Patch Res. *U.S.A.* 40°28N 118°19W **168 F4**
Ryegate *U.S.A.* 46°18N 109°15W **168 C9**
Ryki *Poland* 51°38N 21°56E **83 G8**
Ryley *Canada* 53°17N 112°26W **162 C6**
Rylsk *Russia* 51°36N 34°43E **85 G8**
Rylstone *Australia* 32°46S 149°58E **153 B8**
Rymanów *Poland* 49°35N 21°51E **83 J8**
Ryn *Poland* 53°57N 21°34E **82 E8**
Ryn Peski = Naryn Qum
  Kazakhstan 47°30N 49°0E **87 H9**
Ryōtsu *Japan* 38°5N 138°26E **112 E9**
Rypin *Poland* 53°3N 19°25E **83 E6**
Ryssby *Sweden* 56°52N 14°10E **63 H8**
Rysy *Europe* 49°10N 20°4E **79 B13**
Ryūgasaki *Japan* 35°54N 140°11E **113 G10**
Ryukyu Is. = Ryūkyū-Rettō
  Japan 26°0N 126°0E **113 M3**
Ryūkyū-Rettō *Japan* 26°0N 126°0E **113 M3**
Rzepin *Poland* 52°20N 14°49E **83 F1**
Rzeszów *Poland* 50°5N 21°58E **83 H8**
Rzhev *Russia* 56°20N 34°20E **84 D8**

S

Sa Cabaneta *Spain* 39°37N 2°45E **100 B9**
Sa Canal *Spain* 38°51N 1°23E **100 C7**
Sa Conillera *Spain* 38°59N 1°13E **100 C7**
Sa Dec *Vietnam* 10°20N 105°46E **121 G5**
Sa Dragonera *Spain* 39°35N 2°19E **100 B9**
Sa Kaeo *Thailand* 13°49N 102°4E **120 F4**
Sa Mesquida *Spain* 39°55N 4°16E **100 B11**
Sa Pa *Vietnam* 22°20N 103°47E **120 A4**
Sa Pobla *Spain* 39°46N 3°1E **90 F8**
Sa Savina *Spain* 38°44N 1°25E **100 C7**
Sa'ādat Shahr *Iran* 30°10N 53°5E **129 D7**
Sa'ādatābād *Hormozgān,*
  Iran 28°3N 55°53E **129 D7**
Sa'ādatābād *Kermān,*
  Iran 29°40N 55°51E **129 D7**
Saale → *Germany* 51°56N 11°54E **76 D7**
Saaler Bodden *Germany* 54°20N 12°27E **76 A8**
Saalfeld *Germany* 50°38N 11°21E **76 E7**
Saalfelden *Austria* 47°25N 12°51E **78 D5**
Saane → *Switz.* 47°8N 7°10E **77 H3**
Saanich *Canada* 48°29N 123°26W **170 B3**
Saar → *Europe* 49°41N 6°32E **69 E6**
Saar-Hunsrück △
  Germany 49°30N 6°50E **77 F2**
Saarbrücken *Germany* 49°14N 6°59E **77 F2**
Saarburg *Germany* 49°36N 6°32E **77 F2**
Saaremaa *Estonia* 58°30N 22°30E **84 C2**
Saarijärvi *Finland* 62°43N 25°16E **60 E21**
Saarland □ *Germany* 49°20N 7°0E **77 F2**
Saarlouis *Germany* 49°18N 6°45E **77 F2**
Saath *Azerbaijan* 39°55N 48°22E **105 C13**
Sab 'Ābar *Syria* 33°46N 37°41E **104 F7**
Saba *W. Indies* 17°38N 63°14W **183 C7**
Šabac *Serbia* 44°48N 19°42E **96 B3**
Sabadell *Spain* 41°28N 2°7E **90 D7**
Sabah □ *Malaysia* 6°0N 117°0E **118 C5**
Sabak Bernam
  Malaysia 3°46N 100°58E **121 L3**
Sabalān, Kūhhā-ye
  Iran 38°15N 47°45E **105 C12**
Sabalana, Kepulauan
  Indonesia 6°45S 118°50E **119 F5**
Sabana de la Mar
  Dom. Rep. 19°7N 69°24W **183 C6**
Sábanalarga *Colombia* 10°38N 74°55W **186 A4**
Sabang *Indonesia* 5°50N 95°15E **118 C1**
Şabanözü *Turkey* 40°28N 33°16E **104 B5**
Săbăoani *Romania* 47°1N 26°51E **81 C11**
Sabari → *India* 17°35N 81°16E **126 H5**
Sabarmati → *India* 22°18N 72°22E **124 H5**
Sabattis *U.S.A.* 44°6N 74°40W **175 B10**
Sábáudia *Italy* 41°18N 13°1E **94 A6**
Sabaya *Bolivia* 19°1S 68°23W **188 D4**
Saberania *Indonesia* 2°5S 138°18E **119 E9**
Sabhā *Libya* 27°9N 14°29E **135 C8**
Sabi → *India* 28°29N 76°44E **124 E7**
Sabidana, J. *Sudan* 18°4N 36°50E **137 D4**
Sabie *S. Africa* 25°10S 30°48E **145 D5**
Sabinal *U.S.A.* 29°19N 99°28W **176 G5**
Sabiñánigo *Spain* 42°31N 0°22W **89 A5**
Sabinar, Punta del *Spain* 36°43N 2°44W **91 J2**
Sabinas *Mexico* 27°51N 101°7W **180 B4**
Sabinas → *Mexico* 27°37N 100°42W **180 B4**
Sabinas Hidalgo
  Mexico 26°30N 100°10W **180 B4**
Sabine → *U.S.A.* 29°59N 93°47W **176 G8**
Sabine L. *U.S.A.* 29°53N 93°51W **176 G8**
Sabine Pass *U.S.A.* 29°44N 93°54W **176 G8**
Sabinópolis *Brazil* 18°40S 43°6W **189 D2**
Sabinov *Slovakia* 49°6N 21°5E **83 J8**
Sabirabad *Azerbaijan* 40°5N 48°30E **87 K9**
Sablayan *Phil.* 12°50N 120°50E **119 E6**
Sable *Canada* 55°30N 68°21W **165 A6**
Sable, C. *Canada* 43°29N 65°38W **165 D6**
Sable, C. *U.S.A.* 25°9N 81°8W **179 K8**
Sable I. *Canada* 44°0N 60°0W **165 D8**
Sablé-sur-Sarthe *France* 47°50N 0°20W **68 E6**
Saboeiro *Brazil* 6°32S 39°54W **189 B3**
Sabonkafi *Niger* 14°40N 8°45E **139 C6**
Sabou *Burkina Faso* 12°1N 2°15W **138 C4**
Sabres *France* 44°9N 0°43W **72 D3**
Sabrina Coast *Antarctica* 68°0S 120°0E **5 C9**
Sabugal *Portugal* 40°20N 7°5W **88 E3**
Sabulubek *Indonesia* 1°36S 98°40E **118 E1**
Sabuncu *Turkey* 38°29N 31°27E **104 C4**
Sabzevār *Iran* 36°15N 57°40E **129 B8**
Sabzvārān = Jiroft *Iran* 28°45N 57°50E **129 D8**
Sac City *U.S.A.* 42°25N 95°0W **172 D6**
Sacedón *Spain* 40°29N 2°41W **90 E2**
Săcele *Romania* 45°37N 25°41E **81 D10**
Sachigo → *Canada* 55°6N 88°58W **164 A2**
Sachigo, L. *Canada* 53°50N 92°12W **164 B1**
Sachimbo *Angola* 6°0S 20°16E **140 F4**
Sachin *India* 21°5N 72°55E **126 D7**
Sachkhere *Georgia* 42°25N 43°15E **87 K6**
Sachsen □ *Germany* 50°55N 13°10E **76 E9**
Sachsen-Anhalt □
  Germany 52°0N 12°0E **76 D7**

Sächsische Schweiz △
  Germany 50°55N 14°10E **76 E10**
Sacile *Italy* 45°57N 12°30E **93 C9**
Sackets Harbor *U.S.A.* 43°57N 76°7W **175 C8**
Sackville *Canada* 45°54N 64°22W **165 C7**
Saco *Maine, U.S.A.* 43°30N 70°27W **175 C14**
Saco *Mont., U.S.A.* 48°28N 107°21W **168 B10**
Sacramento *Brazil* 19°53S 47°27W **189 D1**
Sacramento *U.S.A.* 38°35N 121°29W **170 G5**
Sacramento → *U.S.A.* 38°3N 121°56W **170 G5**
Sacramento Mts.
  U.S.A. 32°30N 105°30W **169 K11**
Sacramento Valley
  U.S.A. 39°30N 122°0W **170 G5**
Sacratif, C. *Spain* 36°42N 3°28W **89 J7**
Săcueni *Romania* 47°20N 22°5E **80 C7**
Sada *Spain* 43°22N 8°15W **88 B2**
Sada-Misaki *Japan* 33°20N 132°5E **113 H6**
Sadabad *India* 27°27N 78°3E **124 F8**
Sa'dah *Yemen* 16°15N 43°37E **131 D3**
Sadani *Tanzania* 5°58S 38°35E **142 D4**
Sadao *Thailand* 6°38N 100°26E **121 J3**
Sadani △ *Tanzania* 6°3S 38°47E **142 D4**
Sadao *Thailand* 6°38N 100°26E **121 J3**
Sadd el Aali *Egypt* 23°54N 32°54E **137 C3**
Saddle Mt. *U.S.A.* 45°58N 123°41W **170 E3**
Saddle Pk. *U.S.A.* 13°9N 93°1E **127 H11**
Sade *Nigeria* 11°22N 10°45E **139 C7**
Sadimi
  Dem. Rep. of the Congo 9°25S 23°32E **143 D1**
Sadiola *Mali* 13°50N 11°40W **138 C2**
Sa'dīyah, Hawr as
  Iraq 32°15N 46°30E **105 F12**
Sado *Japan* 38°0N 138°25E **112 F9**
Sado → *Portugal* 38°29N 8°55W **89 G2**
Sadon *Russia* 42°52N 43°58E **87 J7**
Sadovoye *Russia* 47°47N 44°31E **87 G7**
Sadra *India* 23°21N 72°43E **124 H5**
Sadrazamköy = Liveras
  Cyprus 35°23N 32°57E **101 D11**
Sadri *India* 25°11N 73°26E **124 G5**
Sæby *Denmark* 57°21N 10°30E **63 G4**
Saedinenie *Bulgaria* 42°16N 24°33E **97 D8**
Saegertown *U.S.A.* 41°43N 80°9W **174 E4**
Saelices *Spain* 39°55N 2°49W **90 F2**
Safaalan *Turkey* 41°26N 28°6E **97 E12**
Šafárik = Tornal'a
  Slovakia 48°25N 20°20E **79 C13**
Säffle *Sweden* 59°8N 12°55E **62 E6**
Safford *U.S.A.* 32°50N 109°43W **169 K9**
Saffron Walden *U.K.* 52°1N 0°16E **67 E8**
Safi *Morocco* 32°18N 9°20W **136 B2**
Ṣafiābād *Iran* 36°45N 57°58E **129 B8**
Safid Dasht *Iran* 33°27N 48°11E **129 C6**
Safid Kūh *Afghan.* 34°45N 63°0E **108 F6**
Safid Rūd → *Iran* 37°23N 50°11E **129 B6**
Safipur *India* 26°44N 80°21E **125 F9**
Safonovo *Russia* 55°4N 33°16E **84 E7**
Safranbolu *Turkey* 41°15N 32°41E **104 B5**
Saft Rashīn *Egypt* 28°58N 30°55E **137 C2**
Ṣafwān *Iraq* 30°7N 47°43E **128 D5**
Sag Harbor *U.S.A.* 41°0N 72°18W **175 E12**
Saga *Japan* 33°15N 130°16E **113 H5**
Saga □ *Japan* 33°15N 130°20E **113 H5**
Sagae *Japan* 38°22N 140°17E **112 E10**
Sagaing *Myanmar* 21°52N 95°59E **123 J19**
Sagala *Mali* 14°9N 6°38W **138 C4**
Sagamore *U.S.A.* 40°46N 79°14W **174 F5**
Saganaga L. *Canada* 48°14N 90°52W **172 A8**
Saganthit Kyun
  Myanmar 11°56N 98°29E **121 G2**
Sagar *Karnataka, India* 16°38N 76°48E **126 F3**
Sagar *Karnataka, India* 14°14N 75°6E **127 G2**
Sagar *Mad. P., India* 23°50N 78°44E **125 H8**
Sagara, L. *Tanzania* 5°20S 31°0E **142 D3**
Sagarejo *Georgia* 41°44N 45°19E **87 K7**
Sagarmatha = Everest, Mt.
  Nepal 28°5N 86°58E **125 E12**
Sagarmatha △ *Nepal* 27°55N 86°45E **125 E12**
Saginaw *U.S.A.* 43°26N 83°56W **173 D12**
Saginaw B. *U.S.A.* 43°50N 83°40W **173 D12**
Sagleipie *Liberia* 7°0N 8°52W **138 D3**
Sagone = Salluit
  Canada 62°14N 75°38W **161 E16**
Sagone *France* 42°7N 8°42E **73 F12**
Sagone, G. de *France* 42°4N 8°40E **73 F12**
Sagres *Portugal* 37°0N 8°58W **89 J2**
Sagua la Grande *Cuba* 22°50N 80°10W **182 B3**
Saguache *U.S.A.* 38°5N 106°8W **168 G10**
Saguaro △ *U.S.A.* 32°12N 110°38W **169 K8**
Saguenay → *Canada* 48°22N 71°0W **165 C5**
Sagunt = Sagunto *Spain* 39°42N 0°18W **90 F4**
Sagunto *Spain* 39°42N 0°18W **90 F4**
Sagwara *India* 23°41N 74°1E **124 H6**
Sahaba *Sudan* 18°57N 30°25E **137 D3**
Sahagún *Spain* 42°18N 5°2W **88 C5**
Ṣaḥam al Jawlān *Syria* 32°45N 35°55E **130 C4**
Sahand, Kūh-e *Iran* 37°44N 46°27E **105 C12**
Sahara *Africa* 23°0N 5°0E **134 D6**
Saharan Atlas = Saharien, Atlas
  Algeria 33°30N 1°0E **136 B6**
Saharan Seamounts
  Atl. Oc. 25°30N 19°50W **50 D3**
Saharanpur *India* 29°58N 77°33E **124 E7**
Saharien, Atlas *Algeria* 33°30N 1°0E **136 B6**
Saharsa *India* 25°53N 86°36E **125 G12**
Sahaswan *India* 28°5N 78°45E **124 E8**
Saheira, W. el → *Egypt* 30°5N 33°25E **130 E2**
Sahel *Africa* 16°0N 5°0E **134 E5**
Sahel, Canal du *Mali* 14°20N 6°0W **138 C4**
Sahibganj *India* 25°12N 87°40E **125 G12**
Ṣāḥilīyah *Iraq* 33°43N 42°42E **105 F10**
Sahiwal *Pakistan* 30°45N 73°8E **124 D5**
Şahneh *Iran* 34°29N 47°41E **105 E12**
Sahrawi = Western Sahara ■
  Africa 25°0N 13°0W **134 D3**
Sahuaripa *Mexico* 29°3N 109°14W **180 B3**
Sahuarita *U.S.A.* 31°57N 110°58W **169 L8**
Sahuayo de Díaz
  Mexico 20°4N 102°43W **180 C4**
Şahy *Slovakia* 48°4N 18°55E **79 C11**
Sai → *India* 25°39N 82°47E **125 G10**
Sai Buri *Thailand* 6°43N 101°45E **121 J3**
Sai Kung *China* 22°23N 114°16E **111 a**
Sai Thong △ *Thailand* 15°56N 101°10E **120 E3**
Sai Yok △ *Thailand* 14°25N 98°50E **120 E2**
Saibai I. *Australia* 9°25S 142°40E **150 a**
Ṣa'id Bundas
  South Sudan 8°24N 24°48E **135 G10**

Saïda *Algeria* 34°50N 0°11E **136 B4**
Saïda □ *Algeria* 34°40N 0°20E **136 B4**
Sa'īdābād = Sīrjān *Iran* 29°30N 55°45E **129 D7**
Sa'īdābād *Iran* 36°8N 54°11E **129 B7**
Saïdia *Morocco* 35°5N 2°14W **136 A4**
Saidpur *Bangla.* 25°48N 89°0E **123 G16**
Saidpur *India* 25°33N 83°11E **125 G10**
Saidu Sharif *Pakistan* 34°43N 72°24E **125 B5**
Saignes *France* 45°20N 2°31E **72 C6**
Saigō *Japan* 36°12N 133°20E **113 F6**
Saigon = Thanh Pho Ho Chi Minh
  Vietnam 10°58N 106°40E **121 G6**
Saijō *Japan* 33°55N 133°11E **113 H6**
Saikai △ *Japan* 33°12N 129°36E **113 H4**
Saikhoa Ghat *India* 27°50N 95°40E **123 F19**
Saiki *Japan* 32°58N 131°51E **113 H5**
Sailana *India* 23°28N 74°55E **124 H6**
Saillans *France* 44°42N 5°12E **73 D9**
Sailolof *Indonesia* 1°15S 130°46E **126 E3**
Sailu *India* 19°28N 76°28E **126 E3**
Saimaa *Finland* 61°15N 28°15E **84 B5**
Saimen = Saimaa
  Finland 61°15N 28°15E **84 B5**
Sa'in Dezh *Iran* 36°40N 46°25E **105 D12**
St. Abb's Head *U.K.* 55°55N 2°8W **65 F6**
St. Affrique *France* 43°57N 2°53E **72 E6**
St-Agrève *France* 45°0N 4°23E **73 C8**
St-Aignan *France* 47°16N 1°22E **70 E8**
St. Alban's *Canada* 47°51N 55°50W **165 C8**
St. Albans *U.K.* 51°45N 0°19W **67 F7**
St. Albans *W. Va.,*
  U.S.A. 44°49N 73°5W **175 B11**
St. Alban's Head *U.K.* 50°34N 2°4W **67 G5**
St. Albert *Canada* 53°37N 113°32W **162 C6**
St-Amand-en-Puisaye
  France 47°32N 3°5E **71 E10**
St-Amand-les-Eaux
  France 50°27N 3°25E **71 B10**
St-Amand-Montrond
  France 46°43N 2°30E **71 F9**
St-Amarin *France* 47°54N 7°2E **71 E14**
St-Amour *France* 46°26N 5°21E **71 F12**
St-André *Réunion* 20°57S 55°39E **141 c**
St-André-de-Cubzac
  France 44°59N 0°26W **72 D3**
St-André-les-Alpes
  France 43°58N 6°30E **73 E10**
St. Andrew Sd. *U.S.A.* 30°58N 81°25W **178 F5**
St. Andrew's *Canada* 47°45N 59°15W **165 C8**
St. Andrews *N.Z.* 44°33S 171°10E **155 E4**
St. Andrews *U.K.* 56°20N 2°47W **65 E6**
St. Anicet *Canada* 45°8N 74°22W **175 A10**
St. Annes *Canada* 49°40N 96°39W **163 D9**
St. Ann's B. *Canada* 46°22N 60°25W **165 C7**
St. Ann's Bay *Jamaica* 18°26N 77°12W **182 a**
St. Anthony *Canada* 51°22N 55°35W **165 B8**
St. Anthony *U.S.A.* 43°58N 111°41W **168 E8**
St-Antoine *Canada* 46°22N 64°45W **165 C7**
St-Antonin-Noble-Val
  France 44°10N 1°45E **72 D5**
St. Arnaud *Australia* 36°40S 143°16E **152 D5**
St. Arnaud Ra. *N.Z.* 42°1S 172°53E **155 D5**
St-Astier *France* 45°8N 0°31E **72 C4**
St-Aubin-du-Cormier
  France 48°15N 1°26W **70 D5**
St-Augustin *Canada* 51°13N 58°38W **165 B8**
St-Augustin →
  Canada 51°16N 58°40W **165 B8**
St. Augustine *U.S.A.* 29°54N 81°19W **178 F8**
St. Augustine Beach
  U.S.A. 29°51N 81°16W **178 F8**
St-Aulaye *France* 45°12N 0°9E **72 C4**
St. Austell *U.K.* 50°20N 4°47W **67 G3**
St-Avold *France* 49°6N 6°43E **71 C13**
St. Barbe *Canada* 51°12N 56°46W **165 B8**
St-Barthélemy ☑
  W. Indies 17°50N 62°50W **183 C7**
St. Barts = St-Barthélemy ☑
  W. Indies 17°50N 62°50W **183 C7**
St. Bathans *N.Z.* 44°53S 169°50E **155 E4**
St. Bathan's, Mt. *N.Z.* 44°45S 169°45E **155 E4**
St-Béat *France* 42°55N 0°41E **72 F4**
St. Bees Hd. *U.K.* 54°31N 3°38W **66 C4**
St. Bees I. *Australia* 20°56S 149°26E **150 b**
St-Benoît *Réunion* 21°2S 55°43E **141 c**
St-Benoît-du-Sault
  France 46°26N 1°24E **72 B5**
St-Bonnet-en-Champsaur
  France 44°40N 6°5E **73 D10**
St-Brevin-les-Pins *France* 47°14N 2°10W **70 E4**
St-Brice-en-Coglès
  France 48°25N 1°22W **70 D5**
St. Bride's *Canada* 46°56N 54°10W **165 C9**
St. Brides B. *U.K.* 51°49N 5°9W **67 F2**
St-Brieuc *France* 48°30N 2°46W **70 D4**
St-Calais *France* 47°55N 0°45E **70 E7**
St-Cast-le-Guildo *France* 48°37N 2°18W **70 D4**
St. Catharines *Canada* 43°10N 79°15W **174 C5**
St. Catherines I. *U.S.A.* 31°40N 81°10W **178 F5**
St. Catherine's Pt. *U.K.* 50°34N 1°18W **67 G6**
St-Céré *France* 44°51N 1°54E **72 D5**
St-Cergue *Switz.* 46°27N 6°10E **77 J2**
St-Cernin *France* 45°5N 2°25E **72 C6**
St-Chamond *France* 45°28N 4°31E **73 C8**
St. Charles *Ill., U.S.A.* 41°54N 88°19W **172 E8**
St. Charles *Md.,*
  U.S.A. 38°36N 76°56W **173 F15**
St. Charles *Mo., U.S.A.* 38°47N 90°29W **172 F8**
St. Charles *Va., U.S.A.* 36°48N 83°4W **173 G12**
St-Chély-d'Apcher *France* 44°48N 3°17E **72 D7**
St-Chinian *France* 43°25N 2°56E **72 E6**
St. Christopher-Nevis = St. Kitts &
  Nevis ■ *W. Indies* 17°20N 62°40W **183 C7**
St-Ciers-sur-Gironde
  France 45°17N 0°37W **72 C3**
St. Clair *Mich., U.S.A.* 42°50N 82°30W **174 D2**
St. Clair *Pa., U.S.A.* 40°43N 76°12W **175 F8**
St. Clair → *N. Amer.* 42°38N 82°31W **174 D2**
St. Clair, L. *Australia* 42°8S 146°10E **150 d**
St. Clair, L. *N. Amer.* 42°27N 82°39W **174 D2**
St. Clairsville *U.S.A.* 40°5N 80°54W **174 F4**
St-Claud *France* 45°54N 0°28E **72 C4**
St. Claude *Canada* 49°40N 98°20W **163 D9**
St-Claude *France* 46°22N 5°52E **71 F12**
St-Clet *Canada* 45°21N 74°13W **175 A10**
St. Cloud *Fla., U.S.A.* 28°15N 81°17W **179 G8**
St. Cloud *Minn., U.S.A.* 45°34N 94°10W **172 C6**

St. Cricq, C. *Australia* 25°17S 113°6E **149** E1
St. Croix *U.S. Virgin Is.* 17°45N 64°45W **183** C7
St. Croix ➤ *U.S.A.* 44°45N 92°48W **172** C7
St. Croix Falls *U.S.A.* 45°24N 92°38W **172** C7
St-Cyprien *France* 42°37N 3°2E **72** F7
St-Cyr-sur-Mer *France* 43°11N 5°43E **73** E9
St. David's *Canada* 48°12N 58°52W **165** C8
St. David's *U.K.* 51°53N 5°16W **67** F2
St. David's Head *U.K.* 51°54N 5°19W **67** F2
St-Denis *France* 48°56N 2°20E **71** D9
St-Denis *Réunion* 20°52S 55°27E **141** c
St-Denis ✈ (RUN)
  Réunion 20°53S 55°32E **141** c
St-Dié-en-Vosges *France* 48°17N 6°56E **71** D13
St-Dizier *France* 48°38N 4°56E **71** D11
St-Égrève *France* 45°14N 5°41E **73** C9
St. Elias, Mt. *U.S.A.* 60°18N 140°56W **160** E3
St. Elias Mts. *N. Amer.* 60°33N 139°28W **162** A1
St-Éloy-les-Mines *France* 46°10N 2°51E **71** F9
St-Émilion *France* 44°53N 0°9W **72** D3
St-Étienne *France* 45°27N 4°22E **73** C8
St-Étienne-de-Tinée
  France 44°16N 6°56E **73** D10
St-Étienne-du-Rouvray
  France 49°23N 1°6E **70** D8
St. Eugène *Canada* 45°30N 74°28W **175** A10
St. Eustatius *W. Indies* 17°20N 63°0W **183** C7
St-Exupéry, Lyon ✈ (LYS)
  France 45°44N 5°2E **73** C9
St-Fargeau *France* 47°39N 3°4E **71** E10
St-Félicien *Canada* 48°40N 72°25W **164** C5
St-Florent *France* 42°41N 9°18E **73** F13
St-Florent, G. de *France* 42°47N 9°12E **73** F13
St-Florent-sur-Cher
  France 46°59N 2°15E **71** F9
St-Florentin *France* 48°0N 3°45E **71** E10
St-Flour *France* 45°2N 3°6E **72** C7
St. Francis *U.S.A.* 39°47N 101°48W **172** F7
St. Francis ➤ *U.S.A.* 34°38N 90°36W **177** D9
St. Francis, C. *S. Africa* 34°14S 24°49E **144** E3
St. Francisville *U.S.A.* 30°47N 91°23W **177** F9
St-François, L. *Canada* 45°10N 74°22W **175** A10
St-Fulgent *France* 46°50N 1°10W **70** F5
St-Gabriel *Canada* 46°17N 73°24W **164** C5
St. Gallen = Sankt Gallen
  Switz. 47°26N 9°22E **77** H5
St-Galmier *France* 45°35N 4°19E **71** G11
St-Gaudens *France* 43°6N 0°44E **72** E4
St-Gaultier *France* 46°39N 1°26E **70** F8
St-Gengoux-le-National
  France 46°37N 4°40E **71** F11
St-Geniez-d'Olt *France* 44°27N 2°58E **72** D6
St. George *Australia* 28°1S 148°30E **151** D4
St. George *N.B., Canada* 45°11N 66°50W **165** C6
St. George *Ont., Canada* 43°15N 80°15W **174** C4
St. George *Ga., U.S.A.* 30°31N 82°2W **178** E7
St. George *S.C., U.S.A.* 33°11N 80°35W **178** B9
St. George *Utah, U.S.A.* 37°6N 113°35W **169** H7
St. George, C. *Canada* 48°30N 59°16W **165** C8
St. George, C. *U.S.A.* 29°40N 85°5W **178** F4
St. George I. *Alaska,*
  U.S.A. 56°35N 169°35W **166** D6
St. George I. *Fla.,*
  U.S.A. 29°35N 84°55W **178** F5
St. George Ra. *Australia* 18°40S 125°0E **148** C4
St. George's *Canada* 48°26N 58°31W **165** C8
St. George's *Canada* 46°8N 70°40W **165** C5
St. George's *Grenada* 12°5N 61°43W **183** D7
St. George's B. *Canada* 48°24N 58°53W **165** C8
St. Georges Basin *N.S.W.,*
  Australia 35°7S 150°36E **153** C9
St. Georges Basin *W. Austral.,*
  Australia 15°23S 125°2E **148** C4
St. George's Channel
  Europe 52°0N 6°0W **64** E6
St. George's Channel
  India 7°15N 93°43E **127** L11
St. Georges Hd.
  Australia 35°12S 150°42E **153** C9
St-Georges-lès-Baillargeaux
  France 46°40N 0°22E **72** B4
St-Germain-de-Calberte
  France 44°13N 3°48E **72** D7
St-Germain-en-Laye
  France 48°53N 2°4E **71** D9
St-Germain-Lembron
  France 45°27N 3°14E **72** C7
St-Gervais-d'Auvergne
  France 46°4N 2°50E **71** F9
St-Gervais-les-Bains
  France 45°53N 6°42E **73** C10
St-Gildas, Pte. de *France* 47°8N 2°14W **70** E4
St-Gilles *France* 43°40N 4°26E **72** E8
St-Girons *France* 42°59N 1°8E **72** F5
St. Gotthard P. = San Gottardo, P.
  del *Switz.* 46°33N 8°33E **77** J4
St. Helena *Atl. Oc.* 15°58S 5°42W **132** H3
St. Helena *U.S.A.* 38°30N 122°28W **170** G4
St. Helena, Mt. *U.S.A.* 38°40N 122°36W **170** G4
St. Helena B. *S. Africa* 32°40S 18°10E **144** D2
St. Helena Sd. *U.S.A.* 32°15N 80°25W **178** C9
St. Helens *Australia* 41°20S 148°15E **151** G4
St. Helens *U.K.* 53°27N 2°44W **66** D5
St. Helens *U.S.A.* 45°52N 122°48W **170** E4
St. Helens, Mt. *U.S.A.* 46°12N 122°12W **170** D4
St. Helier *U.K.* 49°10N 2°7W **67** H5
St-Herblain *France* 47°13N 1°40W **70** E5
St-Hilaire-du-Harcouët
  France 48°35N 1°5W **70** D5
St-Hilaire-de-Riez
  France 46°43N 1°57W **72** B2
St-Hippolyte *France* 47°19N 6°50E **71** E13
St-Hippolyte-du-Fort
  France 43°58N 3°52E **72** E7
St-Honoré-les-Bains
  France 46°54N 3°50E **71** F10
St-Hubert *Canada* 45°29N 73°25W **175** A11
St-Hyacinthe *Canada* 45°40N 72°58W **164** C5
St. Ignace *U.S.A.* 45°52N 84°44W **173** C11
St. Ignace I. *Canada* 48°45N 88°0W **164** C2
St. Ignatius *U.S.A.* 47°19N 114°6W **168** C6
St-Imier *Switz.* 47°9N 6°58E **77** H2
St. Ives *Cambs., U.K.* 52°20N 0°4W **67** E7
St. Ives *Corn., U.K.* 50°12N 5°30W **67** G2
St. James *France* 48°31N 1°20W **70** D5
St. James *U.S.A.* 43°59N 94°38W **172** D6
St-Jean ➤ *Canada* 50°17N 64°20W **165** B7
St-Jean, L. *Canada* 48°40N 72°0W **165** C5
St-Jean-d'Angély *France* 45°57N 0°31W **72** C3
St-Jean-de-Braye *France* 47°53N 1°58E **71** E8
St-Jean-de-Luz *France* 43°23N 1°39W **72** E2

St-Jean-de-Maurienne
  France 45°16N 6°21E **73** C10
St-Jean-de-Monts *France* 46°47N 2°4W **70** F4
St-Jean-du-Gard *France* 44°7N 3°52E **72** D7
St-Jean-en-Royans *France* 45°1N 5°18E **73** C9
St-Jean-Pied-de-Port
  France 43°10N 1°14W **72** E2
St-Jean-Port-Joli
  Canada 47°15N 70°13W **165** C5
St-Jérôme *Canada* 45°47N 74°0W **164** C5
St. John *Canada* 45°20N 66°8W **165** C6
St. John *U.S.A.* 38°0N 98°46W **172** F4
St. John ➤ *Liberia* 6°4N 9°10W **138** D2
St. John ➤ *N. Amer.* 45°12N 66°5W **173** C20
St. John I. *U.S. Virgin Is.* 18°20N 64°42W **183** e
St. John's *Antigua & B.* 17°6N 61°51W **183** C7
St. John's *Canada* 47°35N 52°40W **165** C9
St. Johns *Ariz., U.S.A.* 34°30N 109°22W **169** J9
St. Johns *Mich., U.S.A.* 43°0N 84°33W **173** D11
St. Johns ➤ *U.S.A.* 30°24N 81°24W **178** D7
St. John's Pt. *Ireland* 54°34N 8°27W **64** B3
St. Johnsbury *U.S.A.* 44°25N 72°1W **175** B12
St. Johnsville *U.S.A.* 43°0N 74°43W **175** C10
St. Joseph *Canada* 43°24N 81°42W **174** C3
St-Joseph *Martinique* 14°39N 61°4W **182** c
St-Joseph *Réunion* 21°22S 55°37E **141** c
St. Joseph *La., U.S.A.* 31°55N 91°14W **177** E9
St. Joseph *Mo., U.S.A.* 39°46N 94°50W **176** F6
St. Joseph ➤ *U.S.A.* 42°7N 86°29W **172** D10
St. Joseph, I. *Canada* 46°12N 83°58W **164** C3
St. Joseph, L. *Canada* 51°10N 90°35W **164** B1
St. Joseph Pt. *U.S.A.* 29°52N 85°24W **178** F4
St-Juéry *France* 43°57N 2°12E **72** E6
St-Julien-Chapteuil *France* 45°2N 4°4E **73** C8
St-Julien-de-Vouvantes
  France 47°38N 1°13W **70** E5
St-Julien-en-Genevois
  France 46°9N 6°5E **71** F13
St-Just-en-Chaussée
  France 49°30N 2°25E **71** C9
St-Just-en-Chevalet
  France 45°55N 3°50E **72** C7
St. Kilda *N.Z.* 45°53S 170°31E **155** F5
St. Kilda *U.K.* 57°49N 8°34W **68** C2
St. Kitts & Nevis ■
  W. Indies 17°20N 62°40W **183** C7
St. Laurent *Canada* 50°25N 97°58W **163** C9
St-Laurent-de-la-Salanque
  France 42°46N 2°59E **72** F6
St-Laurent-du-Pont
  France 45°23N 5°45E **73** C9
St-Laurent-en-Grandvaux
  France 46°35N 5°58E **71** F12
St-Laurent-Médoc *France* 45°8N 0°49W **72** C3
St. Lawrence *Australia* 22°16S 149°31E **150** C4
St. Lawrence *Canada* 46°54N 55°23W **165** C8
St. Lawrence ➤ *Canada* 49°30N 66°0W **165** C6
St. Lawrence, Gulf of
  Canada 48°25N 62°0W **165** C7
St. Lawrence I. *U.S.A.* 63°30N 170°30W **166** C5
St. Lawrence Islands △
  Canada 44°27N 75°52W **175** B9
St. Léonard *Canada* 47°12N 67°58W **165** C6
St-Léonard-de-Noblat
  France 45°49N 1°29E **72** C5
St-Leu *Réunion* 21°9S 55°17E **141** c
St. Lewis ➤ *Canada* 52°26N 56°11W **165** B8
St-Lô *France* 49°7N 1°5W **70** C5
St-Louis *France* 47°30N 7°34E **71** E14
St-Louis *Guadeloupe* 15°56N 61°19W **182** b
St-Louis *Réunion* 21°16S 55°25E **141** c
St-Louis *Senegal* 16°8N 16°27W **138** B1
St. Louis *U.S.A.* 38°37N 90°11W **172** F8
St-Louis □ *Senegal* 16°50N 15°50W **138** B2
St. Louis ➤ *U.S.A.* 46°44N 92°9W **172** B7
St-Loup-sur-Semouse
  France 47°53N 6°16E **71** E13
St-Luc *Canada* 45°22N 73°18W **175** A11
St. Lucia ■ *W. Indies* 14°0N 60°57W **183** f
St. Lucia, L. *S. Africa* 28°5S 32°30E **145** C5
St. Lucia △ *S. Africa* 28°6S 32°27E **145** C5
St. Lucia Channel
  W. Indies 14°15N 61°0W **183** D7
St. Lucia Canal *U.S.A.* 27°10N 80°18W **179** H9
St. Maarten ☑ *W. Indies* 18°2N 63°5W **183** C7
St. Magnus B. *U.K.* 60°25N 1°35W **65** A7
St-Maixent-l'École
  France 46°24N 0°12W **72** B3
St-Malo *France* 48°39N 2°1W **70** D4
St-Malo, G. de *France* 48°50N 2°30W **70** D4
St-Mandrier-sur-Mer
  France 43°4N 5°57E **73** E9
St-Marc *Haiti* 19°10N 72°41W **183** C5
St-Marcellin *France* 45°9N 5°20E **73** C9
St-Marcouf, Îs. *France* 49°30N 1°10W **70** C5
St. Maries *U.S.A.* 47°19N 116°35W **168** C5
St. Marks *U.S.A.* 30°9N 84°12W **178** E6
St-Martin ☑ *W. Indies* 18°5N 63°5W **183** C7
St-Martin, C. *Martinique* 14°52N 61°14W **182** c
St-Martin, L. *Canada* 51°40N 98°30W **163** C9
St-Martin-de-Crau *France* 43°38N 4°48E **73** E8
St-Martin-de-Ré *France* 46°12N 1°21W **72** B2
St-Martin-d'Hères *France* 45°9N 5°45E **73** C9
St-Martin-Vésubie *France* 44°4N 7°15E **73** D11
St. Martins *Barbados* 13°5N 59°28W **183** g
St-Martory *France* 43°9N 0°56E **72** E4
St. Mary Is. *India* 13°20N 74°35E **127** H2
St. Mary Pk. *Australia* 31°32S 138°34E **152** G2
St. Marys *Australia* 41°35S 148°11E **151** G4
St. Marys *U.S.A.* 30°44N 81°33W **178** E8
St. Marys *Pa., U.S.A.* 41°26N 78°34W **174** E6
St. Marys ➤ *U.S.A.* 30°43N 81°27W **178** E8
St. Marys, C. *Canada* 46°50N 54°12W **165** C9
St. Mary's Bay *Canada* 44°25N 66°10W **165** D6
St. Matthew I. *U.S.A.* 60°24N 172°42W **166** C5
St. Matthews *U.S.A.* 33°40N 80°46W **178** B9
St. Maurice ➤ *Canada* 46°21N 72°31W **164** C5
St. Mawes *U.K.* 50°10N 5°2W **67** G2
St-Maximin-la-Ste-Baume
  France 43°27N 5°52E **73** E9
St-Médard-en-Jalles
  France 44°53N 0°43W **72** D3

St-Méen-le-Grand
  France 48°11N 2°12W **70** D4
St-Mihiel *France* 48°54N 5°32E **71** D12
St-Nazaire *France* 47°17N 2°12W **70** E4
St. Neots *U.K.* 52°14N 0°15N **67** E7
St-Nicolas-de-Port
  France 48°38N 6°18E **71** D13
St-Omer *France* 50°45N 2°15E **71** B9
St-Palais-sur-Mer *France* 45°38N 1°5W **72** C2
St-Pamphile *Canada* 46°58N 69°48W **165** C6
St-Pardoux-la-Rivière
  France 45°29N 0°45E **72** C4
St-Pascal *Canada* 47°32N 69°48W **165** C6
St. Paul *Canada* 54°0N 111°17W **162** C6
St. Paul *Réunion* 20°59S 55°17E **141** c
St. Paul *Minn., U.S.A.* 44°56N 93°5W **172** C7
St. Paul *Nebr., U.S.A.* 41°13N 98°27W **172** E4
St. Paul ➤ *Canada* 51°27N 57°42W **165** B8
St. Paul ➤ *Liberia* 6°25N 10°48W **138** D2
St. Paul, Î. *Ind. Oc.* 38°55S 77°34E **146** H6
St. Paul I. *Canada* 47°12N 60°9W **165** C7
St-Paul-lès-Dax *France* 43°44N 1°3W **72** E2
St-Paul-sur-Ubaye
  France 44°31N 6°45E **73** D10
St-Péray *France* 44°57N 4°50E **73** D8
St. Pete Beach *U.S.A.* 27°43N 82°44W **179** H7
St. Peter *U.S.A.* 44°20N 93°57W **172** C7
St. Peter Port *U.K.* 49°26N 2°33W **67** H5
St. Peters *N.S., Canada* 45°40N 60°53W **165** C7
St. Peters *P.E.I., Canada* 46°25N 62°35W **165** C7
St. Petersburg *U.S.A.* 27°46N 82°41W **179** H7
St. Petersburg = Sankt-Peterburg
  Russia 59°55N 30°20E **84** C6
St. Petersburg ✈ *U.S.A.* 27°54N 82°41W **179** H7
St-Philbert-de-Grand-Lieu
  France 47°2N 1°39W **70** E5
St-Phillipe *Réunion* 21°21S 55°44E **141** c
St-Pie *Canada* 45°30N 72°54W **175** A12
St-Pierre *Martinique* 14°45N 61°10W **182** c
St-Pierre *Réunion* 21°19S 55°28E **141** c
St-Pierre *St-P. & M.* 46°46N 56°12W **165** C8
St-Pierre, L. *Canada* 46°12N 72°52W **164** C5
St-Pierre-d'Oléron
  France 45°57N 1°19W **72** C2
St-Pierre-en-Port *France* 49°48N 0°30E **70** C7
St-Pierre-et-Miquelon ☑
  N. Amer. 46°55N 56°10W **165** C8
St-Pierre-le-Moûtier
  France 46°47N 3°7E **71** F10
St-Pierre-sur-Dives *France* 49°2N 0°1W **70** C6
St-Pol-de-Léon *France* 48°41N 4°0W **70** D3
St-Pol-sur-Mer *France* 51°1N 2°20E **71** A9
St-Pol-sur-Ternoise
  France 50°23N 2°20E **71** B9
St-Pons *France* 43°30N 2°45E **72** E6
St-Pourçain-sur-Sioule
  France 46°18N 3°18E **71** F10
St-Priest *France* 45°42N 4°57E **73** C8
St-Quay-Portrieux
  France 48°39N 2°51W **70** D4
St-Quentin *Canada* 47°30N 67°23W **165** C6
St-Quentin *France* 49°50N 3°16E **71** C10
St-Raphaël *France* 43°25N 6°46E **73** E10
St. Regis *U.S.A.* 47°18N 115°6W **168** C6
St. Regis Falls *U.S.A.* 44°40N 74°32W **175** B10
St-Renan *France* 48°26N 4°37W **70** D2
St-Saëns *France* 49°41N 1°16E **70** C8
St-Savin *France* 46°34N 0°53E **72** B4
St-Savinien *France* 45°53N 0°42W **72** C3
St-Seine-l'Abbaye
  France 47°26N 4°47E **71** E11
St-Sernin-sur-Rance
  France 43°54N 2°35E **72** E6
St-Sever *France* 43°45N 0°35W **72** E3
St-Siméon *Canada* 47°51N 69°54W **165** C6
St. Simons I. *U.S.A.* 31°12N 81°15W **178** E8
St. Simons Island
  U.S.A. 31°9N 81°22W **178** D8
St. Stephen *Canada* 45°16N 67°17W **165** C6
St. Stephen *U.S.A.* 33°24N 79°55W **178** B10
St-Sulpice *France* 43°46N 1°41E **72** E5
St-Sulpice-Laurière *France* 46°3N 1°29E **72** B5
St-Sulpice-les-Feuilles
  France 46°19N 1°21E **72** B5
St-Syprien = St-Cyprien
  France 42°37N 3°2E **72** F7
St. Teresa *U.S.A.* 29°55N 84°27W **178** F5
St-Thégonnec *France* 48°31N 3°57W **70** D3
St. Thomas *Canada* 42°45N 72°34W **164** C4
St. Thomas I.
  U.S. Virgin Is. 18°20N 64°55W **183** e
St-Tite *Canada* 46°45N 72°34W **164** C5
St-Trond = Sint-Truiden
  Belgium 50°48N 5°10E **69** D5
St-Tropez *France* 43°17N 6°38E **73** E10
St-Vaast-la-Hougue
  France 49°35N 1°17W **70** C5
St-Valery-en-Caux
  France 49°52N 0°43E **70** C7
St-Valéry-sur-Somme
  France 50°11N 1°38E **71** B8
St-Vallier *France* 46°38N 4°22E **71** F11
St-Vallier-de-Thiey
  France 43°42N 6°51E **73** E10
St-Varent *France* 46°53N 0°13W **70** F6
St-Vaury *France* 46°12N 1°46E **72** B5
St. Videgon's ○
  Australia 14°47S 134°53E **150** A1
St. Vincent = São Vicente
  Cabo Verde 17°0N 25°0W **134** b
St. Vincent *Italy* 45°45N 7°39E **92** C4
St. Vincent, G. *Australia* 35°0S 138°0E **152** C3
St. Vincent & the Grenadines ■
  W. Indies 13°0N 61°10W **183** D7
St-Vincent-de-Tyrosse
  France 43°39N 1°19W **72** E2
St. Vincent I. *U.S.A.* 29°42N 85°3W **179** F4
St. Vincent Passage
  W. Indies 13°30N 61°0W **183** D7
St-Vith *Belgium* 50°17N 6°9E **69** D6
St-Vivien-de-Médoc
  France 45°26N 1°2W **72** C2
St. Walburg *Canada* 53°39N 109°12W **163** C7
St-Yrieix-la-Perche
  France 45°31N 1°12E **72** C5
Saintala *India* 20°26N 83°20E **126** D6
Ste-Agathe-des-Monts
  Canada 46°3N 74°17W **164** C5
Ste-Anne *Guadeloupe* 16°13N 61°24W **182** b

Ste-Anne *Seychelles* 4°36S 55°31E **141** b
Ste-Anne, L. *Canada* 50°0N 67°42W **165** B6
Ste-Anne-des-Monts
  Canada 49°8N 66°30W **165** C6
Ste-Croix *Switz.* 46°49N 6°34E **77** J2
Ste-Énimie *France* 44°22N 3°26E **72** D7
Ste-Foy-la-Grande *France* 44°50N 0°13E **72** D4
Ste. Genevieve *U.S.A.* 37°59N 90°2W **172** G8
Ste-Hermine *France* 46°32N 1°4W **72** B2
Ste-Livrade-sur-Lot
  France 44°24N 0°36E **72** D4
Ste-Marguerite ➤
  Canada 50°9N 66°36W **165** B6
Ste-Marie *Martinique* 14°48N 61°1W **182** c
Ste-Marie *Réunion* 20°53S 55°33E **141** c
Ste-Marie, Ile = Boraha, Nosy
  Madag. 16°50S 49°55E **141** H9
Ste-Marie-aux-Mines
  France 48°15N 7°12E **71** D14
Ste-Maxime *France* 43°19N 6°39E **73** E10
Ste-Menehould *France* 49°5N 4°54E **71** C11
Ste-Mère-Église *France* 49°24N 1°19W **70** C5
Ste-Rose *Guadeloupe* 16°20N 61°45W **182** b
Ste-Rose *Réunion* 21°8S 55°45E **141** c
Ste. Rose du Lac *Canada* 51°4N 99°30W **163** C9
Ste-Savine *France* 48°18N 4°3E **71** D11
Ste-Sigolène *France* 45°15N 4°14E **73** C8
Saintes *France* 45°45N 0°37W **72** C3
Saintes, Îs. des
  Guadeloupe 15°50N 61°35W **182** b
Stes-Maries-de-la-Mer
  France 43°26N 4°26E **73** E8
Saintfield *U.K.* 54°28N 5°49W **64** B6
Saintonge *France* 45°40N 0°50W **72** C3
Saipal *Nepal* 29°50N 81°40E **125** E9
Saipan *N. Marianas* 15°12N 145°45E **156** F6
Sairang *India* 23°50N 92°45E **123** H18
Sairecábur, Cerro
  Bolivia 22°43S 67°54W **190** A2
Sāitah *Si. Arabia* 16°36N 42°56E **131** D3
Saitama *Japan* 35°54N 139°38E **113** G9
Saitama □ *Japan* 36°25N 139°30E **113** F9
Saiteli = Kadınhanı
  Turkey 38°14N 32°13E **104** C5
Saiti *Moldova* 46°30N 29°24E **81** D14
Saiyid *Pakistan* 33°7N 73°2E **124** C5
Saja-Besaya △ *Spain* 43°10N 4°9W **88** B6
Sajama *Bolivia* 18°7S 69°0W **188** D4
Sajama, Nevado *Bolivia* 18°6S 68°54W **188** D4
Sajan *Serbia* 45°50N 20°20E **80** E5
Sajó ➤ *Hungary* 47°56N 21°7E **80** C6
Sajószentpéter *Hungary* 48°12N 20°44E **80** B5
Sajum *India* 33°20N 79°0E **125** C8
Sak ➤ *S. Africa* 30°52S 20°25E **144** D3
Saka *Kenya* 0°9S 39°20E **142** C4
Sakaba *Nigeria* 11°4N 5°35E **138** C6
Sakai *Japan* 34°34N 135°27E **113** G7
Sakaide *Japan* 34°19N 133°50E **113** G6
Sakaiminato *Japan* 35°38N 133°11E **113** G6
Sakākah *Si. Arabia* 30°0N 40°8E **128** D4
Sakakawea, L. *U.S.A.* 47°30N 101°25W **172** B3
Sakami ➤ *Canada* 53°40N 76°40W **164** B4
Sakami, L. *Canada* 53°15N 77°0W **164** B4
Sâkâne, 'Erg i-n *Mali* 20°30N 1°30W **139** A4
Sakania
  Dem. Rep. of the Congo 12°43S 28°30E **143** E2
Sakartvelo = Georgia ■
  Asia 42°0N 43°0E **87** J6
Sakarya *Turkey* 40°48N 30°25E **104** B4
Sakarya *Turkey* 40°45N 30°25E **104** B4
Sakarya ➤ *Turkey* 41°7N 30°39E **104** B4
Sakashima-Guntō
  Japan 24°46N 124°0E **113** M2
Sakassou *Côte d'Ivoire* 7°29N 5°19W **138** D3
Sakata *Japan* 38°55N 139°50E **112** E9
Sakchu *N. Korea* 40°23N 125°2E **115** D13
Sakété *Benin* 6°40N 2°45E **139** D5
Sakha □ *Russia* 66°0N 130°0E **107** C14
Sakhalin *Russia* 51°0N 143°0E **107** D15
Sakhalinskiy Zaliv
  Russia 54°0N 141°0E **107** D15
Sakhi Gopal *India* 19°58N 85°50E **126** E7
Şaki *Azerbaijan* 41°10N 47°5E **87** K8
Šakiai *Lithuania* 54°59N 23°2E **82** D10
Sakmara ➤ *Russia* 51°46N 55°1E **108** B5
Sakoli *India* 21°5N 79°59E **126** D4
Sakon Nakhon
  Thailand 17°10N 104°9E **120** D5
Sakrand *Pakistan* 26°10N 68°15E **124** F3
Sakri *Maharashtra, India* 26°13N 86°52E **125** F12
Sakri *Maharashtra, India* 21°2N 74°20E **126** D2
Sakrivier *S. Africa* 30°54S 20°28E **144** D3
Saksköbing *Denmark* 54°49N 11°39E **63** K5
Sakti *India* 22°2N 82°58E **125** H10
Sakuma *Japan* 35°3N 137°49E **113** G8
Sakurai *Japan* 34°30N 135°51E **113** G7
Saky *Ukraine* 45°9N 33°34E **85** K7
Sal *Cabo Verde* 16°45N 22°55W **134** b
Sal ➤ *Russia* 47°31N 40°45E **87** G5
Sal Rei *Cabo Verde* 16°11N 22°53W **134** b
Sal'a *Slovakia* 48°10N 17°50E **79** C10
Sala *Sweden* 59°58N 16°35E **62** E10
Sala Consilina *Italy* 40°23N 15°36E **95** B8
Sala-y-Gómez
  Pac. Oc. 26°28S 105°28W **157** K17
Sala-y-Gómez Ridge
  Pac. Oc. 25°0S 98°0W **157** K18
Salaberry-de-Valleyfield
  Canada 45°15N 74°8W **175** A10
Salacgrīva *Latvia* 57°45N 24°21E **82** A11
Salada, L. *Mexico* 32°20N 115°40W **169** K6
Saladas *Argentina* 28°15S 58°40W **190** B4
Saladillo *Argentina* 35°40S 59°55W **190** D4
Salado ➤ *B. Aires,*
  Argentina 35°44S 57°22W **190** D4
Salado ➤ *La Pampa,*
  Argentina 37°30S 67°0W **190** D3
Salado ➤ *Rio Negro,*
  Argentina 37°30S 65°3W **190** D3
Salado ➤ *Santa Fe,*
  Argentina 31°40S 60°41W **190** C4
Salado ➤ *Mexico* 26°52N 99°19W **176** H5
Salaga *Ghana* 8°31N 0°31W **139** D4
Sālah *Syria* 32°40N 36°45E **130** C5
Şalāh ad Dīn □ *Iraq* 34°35N 43°35E **128** C4
Salaj □ *Romania* 47°15N 23°0E **80** B8
Salakos *Greece* 36°17N 27°57E **101** C9
Salala *Liberia* 6°42N 10°7W **138** D2
Salala *Sudan* 21°17N 36°16E **137** C4

Salālah *Oman* 16°56N 53°59E **131** D5
Salamajärvi △ *Finland* 63°12N 24°56E **63** E21
Salamanca *Chile* 31°46S 70°59W **190** C1
Salamanca *Spain* 40°58N 5°39W **88** E5
Salamanca *U.S.A.* 42°10N 78°43W **174** D6
Salamanca □ *Spain* 40°57N 5°40W **88** E5
Salāmatābād *Iran* 35°39N 47°50E **128** C5
Salamina *Greece* 37°56N 23°30E **98** D5
Salamina □ *Greece* 37°56N 23°30E **98** D5
Salar de Atacama
  Chile 23°30S 68°25W **190** A2
Salar de Uyuni *Bolivia* 20°30S 67°45W **188** E4
Salard *Romania* 47°12N 22°3E **80** C7
Salas *Spain* 43°25N 6°15W **88** A4
Salas de los Infantes *Spain* 42°2N 3°17W **88** C7
Salatiga *Indonesia* 7°19S 110°30E **119** G14
Salavat *Russia* 53°21N 55°55E **108** B5
Salaverry *Peru* 8°15S 79°0W **182** G3
Salawati *Indonesia* 1°7S 130°52E **119** E8
Salawin □ *Thailand* 18°18N 97°40E **120** C1
Salaya *India* 22°19N 69°35E **124** H3
Salayar *Indonesia* 6°7S 120°30E **119** F6
Salazar ➤ *Spain* 42°40N 1°20W **90** C3
Salbris *France* 47°25N 2°3E **71** E9
S'Albufera *Spain* 39°47N 3°7E **100** B10
Salcantay, Nevado
  Peru 13°19S 72°33W **188** C3
Salcia *Romania* 43°56N 24°55E **81** G9
Sālciua *Romania* 46°24N 23°26E **81** D8
Salcombe *U.K.* 50°14N 3°47W **67** G4
Saldaña *Spain* 42°32N 4°48W **88** C6
Saldanha *S. Africa* 33°0S 17°58E **144** D2
Saldanha B. *S. Africa* 33°6S 18°0E **144** D2
Saldus *Latvia* 56°38N 22°30E **82** B9
Sale *Australia* 38°6S 147°6E **153** E7
Sale *Italy* 44°59N 8°48E **92** D5
Salé *Morocco* 34°3N 6°48W **136** B2
Sale *U.K.* 53°26N 2°19W **66** D5
Sale City *U.S.A.* 31°16N 84°1W **178** D5
Salekhard *Russia* 66°30N 66°35E **106** C7
Salem *India* 11°40N 78°11E **127** J4
Salem *Fla., U.S.A.* 29°53N 83°25W **178** F6
Salem *Ill., U.S.A.* 38°38N 88°57W **172** F9
Salem *Ind., U.S.A.* 38°36N 86°6W **172** F10
Salem *Mass., U.S.A.* 42°31N 70°53W **175** D14
Salem *Mo., U.S.A.* 37°39N 91°32W **172** G8
Salem *N.H., U.S.A.* 42°45N 71°12W **175** D13
Salem *N.J., U.S.A.* 39°34N 75°28W **173** F16
Salem *N.Y., U.S.A.* 43°10N 73°20W **175** C11
Salem *Ohio, U.S.A.* 40°54N 80°52W **174** E4
Salem *Oreg., U.S.A.* 44°56N 123°2W **168** D2
Salem *S. Dak., U.S.A.* 43°44N 97°23W **172** D5
Salem *Va., U.S.A.* 37°18N 80°3W **173** G13
Salemi *Italy* 37°49N 12°48E **94** F5
Sälen *Sweden* 61°20N 13°10E **62** C7
Salernes *France* 43°34N 6°15E **73** E10
Salerno *Italy* 40°41N 14°47E **95** B7
Salerno, G. di *Italy* 40°35N 14°45E **95** B7
Salford *U.K.* 53°30N 2°18W **66** D5
Salgótarján *Hungary* 48°5N 19°47E **80** B4
Salgueiro *Brazil* 8°4S 39°6W **189** E11
Salher *India* 20°40N 73°55E **126** D1
Salhus *Ukraine* 45°38N 35°1E **85** K8
Salibabu *Indonesia* 3°51N 126°40E **119** D7
Salibea = Salybia
  Trin. & Tob. 10°43N 61°2W **183** K15
Salida *U.S.A.* 38°32N 106°0W **168** G11
Salies-de-Béarn *France* 43°28N 0°56W **72** E3
Salihli *Turkey* 38°28N 28°8E **104** C3
Salihorsk *Belarus* 52°51N 27°27E **83** F14
Salima *Malawi* 13°47S 34°28E **141** G6
Salina *Italy* 38°34N 14°50E **95** B7
Salina *Kans., U.S.A.* 38°50N 97°37W **172** F5
Salina *Utah, U.S.A.* 38°58N 111°51W **168** G8
Salina Cruz *Mexico* 16°10N 95°12W **181** D5
Salina di Margherita di Savóia ○
  Italy 41°23N 16°4E **95** A9
Salinas *Brazil* 16°10S 42°10W **189** G10
Salinas *Ecuador* 2°10S 80°58W **186** D2
Salinas *U.S.A.* 36°40N 121°39W **170** J5
Salinas ➤ *Guatemala* 16°28N 90°31W **181** D6
Salinas ➤ *U.S.A.* 36°45N 121°48W **170** J5
Salinas, B. de *Nic.* 11°4N 85°45W **182** D2
Salinas, Pampa de las
  Argentina 31°58S 66°42W **190** C3
Salinas Ambargasta
  Argentina 29°0S 65°0W **190** B3
Salinas de Hidalgo
  Mexico 22°38N 101°43W **180** C4
Salinas Grandes
  Argentina 30°0S 65°0W **190** C3
Salinas Pueblo Missions
  U.S.A. 34°6N 106°4W **169** J10
Salinas Valley *U.S.A.* 36°15N 121°15W **170** J5
Saline ➤ *Ark., U.S.A.* 33°10N 92°8W **176** E8
Saline ➤ *Kans., U.S.A.* 38°52N 97°30W **172** F5
Saline di Trapani e Paceco ○
  Italy 37°59N 12°28E **94** E5
Salines, C. des *Spain* 39°16N 3°4E **100** B10
Salinópolis *Brazil* 0°40S 47°20W **187** D9
Salins-les-Bains *France* 46°58N 5°52E **71** F12
Salir *Portugal* 37°14N 8°2W **89** H2
Salisbury *Australia* 34°46S 138°38E **152** C3
Salisbury *U.K.* 51°4N 1°47W **67** F6
Salisbury *Md., U.S.A.* 38°22N 75°36W **175** F16
Salisbury *N.C., U.S.A.* 35°40N 80°29W **177** D14
Salisbury I. *Canada* 63°30N 77°0W **161** C16
Salisbury Plain *U.K.* 51°14N 1°55W **67** F6
Sālişte *Romania* 45°54N 23°56E **81** D8
Salitre ➤ *Brazil* 9°29S 40°39W **189** D10
Salkehatchie ➤
  U.S.A. 45°15N 74°8W **175** A10
Şalkhad *Syria* 32°29N 36°43E **130** C5
Salkove *Ukraine* 48°15N 29°59E **81** B14
Salla *Finland* 66°50N 28°49E **63** D23
Sallanches *France* 45°56N 6°38E **73** C10
Sallent *Spain* 41°49N 1°54E **90** D6
Salles-Curan *France* 44°11N 2°48E **72** D6
Salliq = Coral Harbour
  Canada 64°8N 83°10W **161** E15
Sallisaw *U.S.A.* 35°28N 94°47W **176** D7
Sallom *Sudan* 19°17N 37°6E **137** D4
Salluit *Canada* 62°14N 75°38W **161** E16
Sallyana *Nepal* 28°22N 82°10E **125** E9
Salmerón *Spain* 40°33N 2°29W **90** E2
Salmo *Canada* 49°10N 117°20W **168** B5
Salmon *U.S.A.* 45°11N 113°54W **168** D7
Salmon ➤ *Canada* 54°3N 122°40W **162** C4

Salmon ➤ *U.S.A.* 45°51N 116°47W **168** D5
Salmon Arm *Canada* 50°40N 119°15W **162** C5
Salmon Gums
  Australia 32°59S 121°38E **149** F3
Salmon Pt. *Canada* 43°52N 77°15W **174** C7
Salmon River Mts.
  U.S.A. 44°50N 115°30W **168** D6
Salmon River Res.
  U.S.A. 43°32N 75°55W **175** C9
Salo *Finland* 60°22N 23°10E **84** B2
Salò *Italy* 45°36N 10°31E **92** C7
Salobreña *Spain* 36°44N 3°35W **89** J7
Salome *U.S.A.* 33°47N 113°37W **171** M13
Salon *India* 26°2N 81°27E **125** F9
Salon-de-Provence *France* 43°39N 5°6E **73** E9
Salonica = Thessaloniki
  Greece 40°38N 22°58E **96** F6
Salonta *Romania* 46°49N 21°42E **80** D6
Salor ➤ *Spain* 39°39N 7°3W **89** F3
Salou *Spain* 41°4N 1°10E **90** D6
Salou, C. de *Spain* 41°3N 1°10E **90** D6
Saloum ➤ *Senegal* 13°50N 16°43E **138** C1
Salpausselkä 3 *Finland* 61°3N 26°15E **84** B4
Salsacate *Argentina* 31°20S 65°5W **190** C2
Salses *France* 42°50N 2°55E **72** F6
Salsette I. *India* 19°2N 72°53E **126** E1
Salsk *Russia* 46°28N 41°30E **87** G5
Salso ➤ *Italy* 37°6N 13°57E **94** E6
Salsomaggiore Terme
  Italy 44°49N 9°59E **92** D6
Salt *Spain* 41°58N 2°47E **90** D7
Salt ➤ *Canada* 60°0N 112°25W **162** B6
Salt ➤ *U.S.A.* 33°23N 112°19W **169** K7
Salt Fork Red ➤
  U.S.A. 34°27N 99°21W **176** D5
Salt L. *Australia* 30°6S 142°8E **151** E3
Salt Lake City *U.S.A.* 40°45N 111°53W **168** F8
Salt Lake City Int. ✈ (SLC)
  U.S.A. 40°47N 111°58W **168** F7
Salt Range *Pakistan* 32°30N 72°25E **124** C5
Salt Springs *U.S.A.* 29°21N 81°44W **179** F8
Salta *Argentina* 24°57S 65°25W **190** A2
Salta □ *Argentina* 24°48S 65°30W **190** A2
Saltara *Italy* 43°45N 12°50E **93** E9
Saltash *U.K.* 50°24N 4°14W **67** G3
Saltburn-by-the-Sea
  U.K. 54°35N 0°58W **66** C7
Saltcoats *U.K.* 55°38N 4°47W **65** F4
Saltee Is. *Ireland* 52°7N 6°37W **64** D5
Salters *U.S.A.* 33°36N 79°51W **178** B10
Saltfjellet *Norway* 66°40N 15°15E **60** C16
Saltfjellet-Svartisen △
  Norway 66°45N 15°10E **60** C16
Saltfjorden *Norway* 67°15N 14°10E **60** C16
Saltholm *Denmark* 55°38N 12°43E **63** J6
Saltillo *Mexico* 25°25N 101°0W **180** B4
Salto *Argentina* 34°20S 60°15W **190** C4
Salto *Uruguay* 31°27S 57°50W **190** C4
Salto da Divisa *Brazil* 16°0S 39°57W **189** G11
Salto del Guaíra
  Paraguay 24°3S 54°17W **191** A5
Salton City *U.S.A.* 33°18N 115°57W **171** M11
Salton Sea *U.S.A.* 33°15N 115°45W **171** M11
Saltpond *Ghana* 5°15N 1°3W **139** D4
Saltsburg *U.S.A.* 40°29N 79°27W **174** F5
Saltsjöbaden *Sweden* 59°15N 18°20E **62** E11
Saltville *U.S.A.* 36°54N 81°46W **178** A8
Saltö ➤ *U.S.A.* 34°1N 81°4W **178** B8
Saluda ➤ *U.S.A.* 34°1N 81°4W **178** B8
Salue Timpaus, Selat
  Indonesia 1°50S 123°50E **119** E6
Sālūm *Egypt* 31°31N 25°7E **137** A2
Salūm, Khâlig el *Egypt* 31°30N 25°24E **137** A2
Salur *India* 18°27N 83°18E **126** E6
Saluzzo *Italy* 44°39N 7°29E **92** D4
Salvacíon, B. *Chile* 50°50S 75°0W **192** D2
Salvador *Brazil* 13°0S 38°30W **189** F11
Salvador, El ■
  Cent. Amer. 13°50N 89°0W **182** D2
Salvador, L. *U.S.A.* 29°43N 90°15W **177** G9
Salvaterra de Magos
  Portugal 39°1N 8°47W **89** F2
Sálvora, I. de *Spain* 42°30N 8°58W **88** C2
Salween ➤ *Myanmar* 16°31N 97°37E **123** L20
Salyan *Azerbaijan* 39°33N 48°59E **105** C13
Salybia *Trin. & Tob.* 10°43N 61°2W **183** K15
Salza ➤ *Austria* 47°40N 14°43E **78** E7
Salzach ➤ *Austria* 48°12N 12°56E **78** D6
Salzburg *Austria* 47°48N 13°2E **78** D6
Salzburg □ *Austria* 47°15N 13°0E **78** D6
Salzgitter *Germany* 52°9N 10°19E **76** B6
Salzkotten *Germany* 51°40N 8°37E **76** D4
Salzwedel *Germany* 52°52N 11°10E **76** D7
Sam *India* 26°50N 70°31E **124** F4
Sam Neua *Laos* 20°29N 104°5E **116** G5
Sam Ngao *Thailand* 17°18N 99°0E **120** D2
Sam Rayburn Res.
  U.S.A. 31°4N 94°5W **176** F7
Sam Rong, Laem *Thailand* 9°35N 100°1E **121** b
Sam Son *Vietnam* 19°44N 105°54E **120** C5
Sama de Langreo = Langreo
  Spain 43°18N 5°40W **88** B5
Samac Bos.-H. *Bos.-H.* 45°3N 18°29E **80** E3
Samagaltay *Russia* 50°36N 95°3E **109** D11
Samales Group *Phil.* 6°0N 121°0E **119** C6
Samalga Pass *U.S.A.* 52°50N 169°0W **166** E6
Samalkot *India* 17°3N 82°13E **126** F6
Samâlût *Egypt* 28°20N 30°42E **137** C12
Samana *India* 30°10N 76°13E **124** D7
Samana Cays *Bahamas* 23°3N 73°45W **183** B5
Samandağı *Turkey* 36°5N 35°59E **104** D6
Samangān □ *Afghan.* 36°15N 68°3E **109** E7
Samangwa
  Dem. Rep. of the Congo 4°23S 24°10E **142** C1
Samani *Japan* 42°7N 142°56E **112** C11
Samar *Phil.* 12°0N 125°0E **119** B7
Samara *Russia* 53°8N 50°6E **86** D10
Samara ➤ *Russia* 53°10N 50°4E **86** D10
Samaria △ *Greece* 35°17N 23°58E **101** D5
Samarinda *Indonesia* 0°30S 117°9E **118** E5
Samarkand = Samarqand
  Uzbekistan 39°40N 66°55E **109** E7
Samarqand *Uzbekistan* 39°40N 66°55E **109** E7
Samarqand □
  Uzbekistan 39°35N 66°35E **109** E7
Sāmarrā *Iraq* 34°12N 43°52E **105** E10
Samarskaya Luka △
  Russia 53°30N 49°30E **86** D9

Samastipur *India* 25°50N 85°50E **125** G11
Şamaxı *Azerbaijan* 40°38N 48°37E **87** K9
Samba
Dem. Rep. of the Congo 4°38S 26°22E **142** C2
Sambaíba *India* 32°32N 75°10E **125** C6
Sambaíba *Brazil* 7°8S 45°21W **189** B1
Sambalpur *India* 21°28N 84°4E **126** D7
Sambar, Tanjung
Indonesia 2°59S 110°19E **118** E4
Sambas *Indonesia* 1°20N 109°20E **118** D3
Sambawizi *Zimbabwe* 18°24S 26°13E **143** F2
Sambhajinagar = Aurangabad
India 19°50N 75°23E **126** E2
Sambhal *India* 28°35N 78°37E **125** E8
Sambhar *India* 26°52N 75°6E **124** F6
Sambhar L. *India* 26°55N 75°12E **124** F6
Sambir *Ukraine* 49°30N 23°10E **83** J10
Sambor *Cambodia* 12°46N 106°0E **120** F6
Sambor Prei Kuk
Cambodia 12°46N 105°58E **120** F5
Samborombón, B.
Argentina 36°5S 57°20W **190** D4
Sambuca di Sicília *Italy* 37°39N 13°7E **94** E6
Samburu □ *Kenya* 1°10N 36°40E **142** B4
Samburu △ *Kenya* 0°37N 37°31E **142** B4
Samcheok *S. Korea* 37°26N 129°10E **115** F15
Same *Tanzania* 4°2S 37°38E **142** C4
Samer *France* 50°38N 1°44E **71** B8
Samet, Ko *Thailand* 12°34N 101°27E **120** F3
Samfya *Zambia* 11°22S 29°31E **143** E2
Sami *Greece* 38°15N 20°39E **98** C2
Şämkir *Azerbaijan* 40°50N 46°0E **87** K8
Samland = Zemlandskiy
Poluostrov *Russia* 54°50N 20°20E **82** D7
Şamlı *Turkey* 39°48N 27°51E **99** B9
Sammanturai *Sri Lanka* 7°36N 81°39E **127** L5
Samnah *Si. Arabia* 25°10N 37°15E **128** E3
Samo Alto *Chile* 30°22S 71°0W **190** C1
Samoa ■ *Pac. Oc.* 14°0S 172°0W **147** C11
Samobor *Croatia* 45°47N 15°44E **93** C12
Samoëns *France* 46°5N 6°45E **71** F13
Samokov *Bulgaria* 42°18N 23°35E **97** C10
Šamorín *Slovakia* 48°2N 17°19E **79** C10
Samorogouan
Burkina Faso 11°21N 4°57W **138** C4
Samos *Greece* 37°45N 26°50E **99** D8
Samoš *Serbia* 45°13N 20°46E **80** E5
Samos *Spain* 42°44N 7°20W **88** C3
Samoset *U.S.A.* 27°28N 82°33W **179** H7
Samothráki = Mathraki
Greece 39°48N 19°31E **101** A3
Samothraki *Greece* 40°28N 25°28E **97** F9
Samoylovka *Russia* 51°12N 43°43E **86** E6
Sampa *Ghana* 8°0N 2°36W **138** D4
Sampacho *Argentina* 33°20S 64°50W **190** C3
Sampalan *Indonesia* 8°41S 115°34E **119** K18
Sampang *Indonesia* 7°11S 113°13E **119** G15
Samper de Calanda
Spain 41°11N 0°28W **90** D4
Sampéyre *Italy* 44°34N 7°1E **92** D4
Sampit *Indonesia* 2°34S 113°0E **118** E4
Sampit, Teluk *Indonesia* 3°5S 113°3E **118** E4
Samrong *Cambodia* 14°15N 103°30E **120** E4
Samsø *Denmark* 55°50N 10°35E **63** J4
Samsø Bælt *Denmark* 55°45N 10°45E **63** J4
Samson *U.S.A.* 31°7N 86°3W **178** D3
Samsun *Turkey* 41°15N 36°22E **104** B7
Samsun □ *Turkey* 41°10N 36°10E **104** B7
Samtredia *Georgia* 42°7N 42°24E **87** J6
Samui, Ko *Thailand* 9°30N 100°0E **121** b
Samur → *Azerbaijan* 41°53N 48°32E **87** K9
Samurskiy Khrebet
Russia 41°55N 47°11E **87** K8
Samusole
Dem. Rep. of the Congo 10°2S 24°0E **143** E1
Samut Prakan
Thailand 13°40N 100°36E **120** F3
Samut Sakhon
Thailand 13°32N 100°17E **120** F3
Samut Songkhram
Thailand 13°24N 100°1E **120** F3
Samwari *Pakistan* 28°30N 66°46E **124** E2
San *Mali* 13°15N 4°57W **138** C4
San → *Cambodia* 13°32N 105°57E **120** F5
San → *Poland* 50°45N 21°51E **83** H8
San Adrián *Spain* 42°20N 1°56W **90** C3
San Adrián, C. de *Spain* 43°21N 8°50W **88** B2
San Agustin *S. Phil.* 6°20N 126°13E **119** C7
San Agustín de Valle Fértil
Argentina 30°35S 67°30W **190** C2
San Ambrosio *Pac. Oc.* 26°28S 79°53W **184** F3
San Andreas *U.S.A.* 38°12N 120°41W **170** G6
San Andrés, I. de
Caribbean 12°42N 81°46W **182** D3
San Andrés del Rabanedo
Spain 42°37N 5°36W **88** C5
San Andres Mts.
U.S.A. 33°0N 106°30W **169** K10
San Andrés Tuxtla
Mexico 18°27N 95°13W **181** D5
San Angelo *U.S.A.* 31°28N 100°26W **176** F4
San Anselmo *U.S.A.* 37°59N 122°34W **170** H4
San Antonio *Belize* 16°15N 89°2W **182** C2
San Antonio *Chile* 33°40S 71°40W **190** C1
San Antonio *N. Mex.,*
U.S.A. 33°55N 106°52W **169** K10
San Antonio *Tex.,*
U.S.A. 29°25N 98°29W **176** G5
San Antonio →
U.S.A. 28°30N 96°54W **176** G6
San Antonio, C.
Argentina 36°15S 56°40W **190** D4
San Antonio, C. de
Cuba 21°50N 84°57W **182** B3
San Antonio, C. de *Spain* 38°48N 0°12E **91** G5
San Antonio, Mt.
U.S.A. 34°17N 117°38W **171** L9
San Antonio de los Baños
Cuba 22°54N 82°31W **182** B3
San Antonio de los Cobres
Argentina 24°10S 66°17W **190** A2
San Antonio Oeste
Argentina 40°40S 65°0W **192** B4
San Ardo *U.S.A.* 36°1N 120°54W **170** J6
San Augustín
Canary Is. 27°47N 15°32W **100** G4
San Augustine *U.S.A.* 31°32N 94°7W **176** F17
San Bartolomé
Canary Is. 28°59N 13°37W **100** F6
San Bartolomé de Tirajana
Canary Is. 27°54N 15°34W **100** G4

San Bartolomeo in Galdo
Italy 41°24N 15°1E **95** A8
San Benedetto del Tronto
Italy 42°57N 13°53E **93** F10
San Benedetto Po *Italy* 45°2N 10°55E **92** C7
San Benedicto, I.
Mexico 19°18N 110°49W **180** D2
San Benito *U.S.A.* 26°8N 97°38W **176** H6
San Benito → *U.S.A.* 36°53N 121°34W **170** J5
San Benito Mt. *U.S.A.* 36°22N 120°37W **170** J6
San Bernardino *U.S.A.* 34°7N 117°19W **171** L9
San Bernardino Mts.
U.S.A. 34°10N 116°45W **171** L10
San Bernardino Str.
Phil. 12°30N 124°10E **119** B7
San Bernardo *Chile* 33°40S 70°50W **190** C1
San Bernardo, I. de
Colombia 9°45N 75°50W **186** B3
San Blas *Mexico* 26°5N 108°46W **180** B3
San Blas, Arch. de
Panama 9°50N 78°31W **182** E4
San Blas, C. *U.S.A.* 29°40N 85°21W **178** F3
San Bonifacio *Italy* 45°24N 11°16E **93** C8
San Borja *Bolivia* 14°50S 66°52W **188** C4
San Buenaventura = Ventura
U.S.A. 34°17N 119°18W **171** L7
San Buenaventura
Bolivia 14°28S 67°35W **188** C4
San Buenaventura
Mexico 27°5N 101°32W **180** B4
San Carlos = Sant Carles
Spain 39°3N 1°34E **100** B8
San Carlos *Argentina* 33°50S 69°0W **190** C2
San Carlos *Chile* 36°10S 72°0W **190** D1
San Carlos *Baja Calif. S.,*
Mexico 24°47N 112°7W **180** C2
San Carlos *Coahuila,*
Mexico 29°1N 100°51W **180** B4
San Carlos *Nic.* 11°12N 84°50W **182** D3
San Carlos *Phil.* 10°29N 123°25E **119** B6
San Carlos *Uruguay* 34°46S 54°58W **191** C5
San Carlos *U.S.A.* 33°21N 110°27W **169** K8
San Carlos *Venezuela* 9°40N 68°36W **186** B5
San Carlos de Bariloche
Argentina 41°10S 71°25W **192** B2
San Carlos de Bolívar
Argentina 36°15S 61°6W **190** D3
San Carlos de la Rápita = Sant
Carles de la Ràpita *Spain* 40°37N 0°35E **90** E5
San Carlos del Zulia
Venezuela 9°1N 71°55W **186** B4
San Carlos L. *U.S.A.* 33°11N 110°32W **169** K8
San Carlos Park *U.S.A.* 26°28N 81°49W **179** J8
San Cataldo *Italy* 37°29N 13°59E **94** E6
San Celoni = Sant Celoni
Spain 41°42N 2°30E **90** D7
San Clemente *Spain* 39°24N 2°25W **91** F2
San Clemente *U.S.A.* 33°26N 117°37W **171** M9
San Clemente I.
U.S.A. 32°53N 118°29W **171** N8
San Cristóbal = Es Migjorn Gran
Spain 39°57N 4°3E **100** B11
San Cristóbal *Argentina* 30°20S 61°10W **190** C3
San Cristóbal *Dom. Rep.* 18°25N 70°6W **183** C5
San Cristóbal
Solomon Is. 10°30S 161°0E **147** C9
San Cristóbal *Venezuela* 7°46N 72°14W **186** B4
San Cristóbal de La Laguna
Canary Is. 28°28N 16°18W **100** F3
San Cristóbal de las Casas
Mexico 16°45N 92°38W **181** D6
San Damiano d'Asti *Italy* 44°50N 8°4E **92** D5
San Daniele del Friuli
Italy 46°9N 13°1E **93** B10
San Diego *Calif., U.S.A.* 32°42N 117°9W **171** N9
San Diego *Tex., U.S.A.* 27°46N 98°14W **176** H5
San Diego, C. *Argentina* 54°40S 65°10W **192** D3
San Diego de la Unión
Mexico 21°28N 100°52W **180** C4
San Diego Int. ✈ (SAN)
U.S.A. 32°44N 117°11W **171** N9
San Dimitri, Ras *Malta* 36°4N 14°11E **101** C1
San Dimitri Point = San Dimitri,
Ras *Malta* 36°4N 14°11E **101** C1
San Donà di Piave *Italy* 45°38N 12°34E **93** C9
San Estanislao
Paraguay 24°39S 56°26W **190** A4
San Esteban de Gormaz
Spain 41°34N 3°13W **90** D1
San Felice Circeo *Italy* 41°14N 13°5E **94** A6
San Felice sul Panaro
Italy 44°50N 11°8E **93** D8
San Felipe *Chile* 32°43S 70°42W **190** C1
San Felipe *Mexico* 31°1N 114°52W **180** A2
San Felipe *Venezuela* 10°20N 68°44W **186** A5
San Felipe → *U.S.A.* 33°10N 115°49W **171** M11
San Félix *Chile* 28°56S 70°28W **190** B1
San Félix *Pac. Oc.* 26°23S 80°0W **184** F2
San Fernando = Sant Ferran
Spain 38°42N 1°28E **100** C7
San Fernando *Chile* 34°30S 71°0W **190** C1
San Fernando *Mexico* 24°51N 98°10W **181** C5
San Fernando *La Union,*
Phil. 16°40N 120°23E **119** A6
San Fernando *Pampanga,*
Phil. 15°5N 120°37E **119** A6
San Fernando *Spain* 36°28N 6°17W **89** J4
San Fernando
Trin. & Tob. 10°16N 61°28W **183** D7
San Fernando *U.S.A.* 34°17N 118°26W **171** L8
San Fernando de Apure
Venezuela 7°54N 67°15W **186** B5
San Fernando de Atabapo
Venezuela 4°3N 67°42W **186** C5
San Fernando di Púglia
Italy 41°18N 16°5E **95** A9
San Francisco *Argentina* 31°30S 62°5W **190** C3
San Francisco *Peru* 12°36S 73°49W **186** D3
San Francisco *U.S.A.* 37°46N 122°23W **170** H4
San Francisco →
U.S.A. 32°59N 109°22W **169** K9
San Francisco, C. de
Colombia 6°18N 77°29W **184** C3
San Francisco, Paso de
S. Amer. 27°0S 68°0W **190** B2
San Francisco de Macorís
Dom. Rep. 19°19N 70°15W **183** C5
San Francisco del Monte de Oro
Argentina 32°36S 66°8W **190** C2

San Francisco del Oro
Mexico 26°52N 105°51W **180** B3
San Francisco Int. ✈ (SFO)
U.S.A. 37°37N 122°22W **170** H4
San Francisco Javier = Sant
Francesc de Formentera
Spain 38°42N 1°26E **100** C7
San Fratello *Italy* 38°1N 14°36E **95** D7
San Gabriel *Chile* 33°47S 70°15W **190** C1
San Gabriel Chilac
Mexico 18°19N 97°21W **181** D5
San Gabriel Mts.
U.S.A. 34°17N 117°38W **171** L9
San Gavino Monreale
Italy 39°33N 8°47E **94** C1
San German *Puerto Rico* 18°4N 67°4W **183** d
San Gimignano *Italy* 43°28N 11°2E **92** E8
San Giórgio di Nogaro
Italy 45°50N 13°13E **93** C10
San Giórgio Iónico
Italy 40°27N 17°23E **95** B10
San Giovanni Bianco
Italy 45°52N 9°39E **92** C6
San Giovanni in Fiore
Italy 39°15N 16°42E **95** C9
San Giovanni in Persiceto
Italy 44°38N 11°11E **93** D8
San Giovanni Rotondo
Italy 41°42N 15°44E **93** G12
San Giovanni Valdarno
Italy 43°34N 11°32E **93** E8
San Giuliano Terme
Italy 43°46N 10°26E **92** E7
San Gorgonio Mt.
U.S.A. 34°6N 116°50W **171** L10
San Gottardo, P. del
Switz. 46°33N 8°33E **77** J4
San Gregorio *Uruguay* 32°37S 55°40W **191** C4
San Gregorio *U.S.A.* 37°20N 122°23W **170** H4
San Guillermo △
Argentina 27°50S 69°45W **190** B2
San Guiseppe Jato *Italy* 37°57N 13°11E **94** E6
San Ignacio *Belize* 17°10N 89°5W **181** D7
San Ignacio *Bolivia* 16°20S 60°55W **186** G6
San Ignacio *Mexico* 27°27N 112°51W **180** B2
San Ignacio *Paraguay* 26°52S 57°3W **190** B4
San Ignacio *Peru* 5°8S 78°59W **188** B2
San Ignacio, L.
Mexico 26°54N 113°13W **180** B2
San Isidro *Argentina* 34°29S 58°31W **190** C4
San Jacinto *U.S.A.* 33°47N 116°57W **171** M10
San Jaime = Sant Jaume
Spain 39°54N 4°4E **100** B11
San Javier *Misiones,*
Argentina 27°55S 55°5W **191** B4
San Javier *Santa Fe,*
Argentina 30°40S 59°55W **190** C4
San Javier *Bolivia* 16°18S 62°30W **186** G6
San Javier *Chile* 35°40S 71°45W **190** D1
San Javier *Spain* 37°49N 0°50W **91** H4
San Jerónimo Taviche
Mexico 16°44N 96°35W **181** D5
San Joaquín *U.S.A.* 36°36N 120°11W **170** J6
San Joaquin → *U.S.A.* 38°4N 121°51W **170** G5
San Joaquin Valley
U.S.A. 37°20N 121°0W **170** J6
San Jon *U.S.A.* 35°6N 103°20W **169** J12
San Jordi = Sant Jordi
Spain 39°33N 2°46E **100** B9
San Jorge *Argentina* 31°54S 61°50W **190** C3
San Jorge, B. *Mexico* 31°20N 113°20W **180** A2
San Jorge, G. *Argentina* 46°0S 66°0W **192** C3
San José = San Josep
Spain 38°55N 1°18E **100** C7
San José *Costa Rica* 9°55N 84°2W **182** E3
San José *Guatemala* 14°0N 90°50W **182** D1
San Jose *Mind. Occ.,*
Phil. 12°27N 121°4E **119** B6
San Jose *Nueva Ecija,*
Phil. 15°45N 120°55E **119** A6
San Jose *U.S.A.* 37°20N 121°53W **170** H5
San Jose → *U.S.A.* 34°25N 106°45W **169** J10
San Jose, G. *Argentina* 42°20S 64°18W **192** B4
San Jose, I. *Mexico* 25°0N 110°38W **180** C2
San Jose de Buenavista
Phil. 10°45N 121°56E **119** B6
San Jose de Chiquitos
Bolivia 17°53S 60°50W **186** G6
San José de Feliciano
Argentina 30°26S 58°46W **190** C4
San José de Jáchal
Argentina 30°15S 68°46W **190** C2
San José de Mayo
Uruguay 34°27S 56°40W **191** C4
San José de Uchapiamonas
Bolivia 14°13S 68°5W **188** C4
San José del Cabo
Mexico 23°3N 109°41W **180** C3
San José del Guaviare
Colombia 2°35N 72°38W **186** C4
San Josep *Spain* 38°55N 1°18E **100** C7
San Juan *Argentina* 31°30S 68°30W **190** C2
San Juan *Peru* 15°22S 75°7W **188** D2
San Juan *Puerto Rico* 18°28N 66°7W **183** d
San Juan *Trin. & Tob.* 10°39N 61°29W **187** K15
San Juan □ *Argentina* 31°9S 69°0W **190** C2
San Juan → *Argentina* 32°20S 67°25W **190** C2
San Juan → *Nic.* 10°56N 83°42W **182** D3
San Juan → *U.S.A.* 37°16N 110°26W **169** H8
San Juan → *Venezuela* 9°55N 64°44W **187** B7
San Juan Bautista = Sant Joan de
Labritja *Spain* 39°5N 1°31E **100** B8
San Juan Bautista
Paraguay 26°37S 57°6W **190** B4
San Juan Bautista
U.S.A. 36°51N 121°32W **170** J5
San Juan Capistrano
U.S.A. 33°30N 117°40W **171** M9
San Juan Cr. →
U.S.A. 35°40N 120°22W **170** J5
San Juan de Guadalupe
Mexico 24°38N 102°44W **180** C4
San Juan de la Costa
Mexico 24°20N 110°41W **180** C2
San Juan de los Lagos
Mexico 21°15N 102°18W **180** C4
San Juan de los Morros
Venezuela 9°55N 67°21W **186** B5
San Juan del Norte
Nic. 10°58N 83°40W **182** D3

San Juan del Norte, B. de
Nic. 11°0N 83°40W **182** D3
San Juan del Río
Mexico 20°23N 100°0W **181** C5
San Juan del Sur *Nic.* 11°20N 85°51W **182** D2
San Juan Island △
U.S.A. 48°35N 123°8W **170** B4
San Juan Mts. *U.S.A.* 37°30N 107°0W **169** H10
San Just, Sierra de *Spain* 40°45N 0°49W **90** E4
San Justo *Argentina* 30°47S 60°30W **190** C3
San Kamphaeng
Thailand 18°45N 99°8E **120** C2
San Lázaro, C. *Mexico* 24°50N 112°18W **180** C2
San Leandro *U.S.A.* 37°44N 122°9W **170** H4
San Leonardo de Yagüe
Spain 41°51N 3°5W **90** D1
San Lorenzo = Sant Llorenç des
Cardassar *Spain* 39°37N 3°17E **100** B10
San Lorenzo *Argentina* 32°45S 60°45W **190** C3
San Lorenzo *Ecuador* 1°15N 78°50W **186** C2
San Lorenzo *Paraguay* 25°20S 57°32W **190** B4
San Lorenzo →
Mexico 24°15N 107°24W **180** C3
San Lorenzo, I.
Mexico 28°38N 112°51W **180** B2
San Lorenzo, I. *Peru* 12°7S 77°15W **188** D2
San Lorenzo, Mte.
Argentina 47°40S 72°20W **192** C2
San Lorenzo de la Parrilla
Spain 39°51N 2°22W **90** F2
San Lorenzo de Morunys = Sant
Llorenç de Morunys
Spain 42°8N 1°35E **90** C6
San Lucas = Cabo San Lucas
Mexico 22°53N 109°54W **180** C3
San Lucas *Bolivia* 20°5S 65°7W **186** H5
San Lucas *Mexico* 27°10N 112°14W **180** B2
San Lucas *U.S.A.* 36°8N 121°1W **170** J5
San Lucas, C. *Mexico* 22°52N 109°53W **180** C3
San Lúcido *Italy* 39°18N 16°3E **95** C9
San Luis *Argentina* 33°20S 66°20W **190** C2
San Luis *Cuba* 20°13N 75°50W **182** B4
San Luis *Guatemala* 16°14N 89°27W **182** C2
San Luis *Ariz., U.S.A.* 32°29N 114°47W **169** K6
San Luis *Colo., U.S.A.* 37°12N 105°25W **169** H11
San Luis □ *Argentina* 34°0S 66°0W **190** C2
San Luis, I. *Mexico* 29°58N 114°26W **180** B2
San Luis, Sierra de
Argentina 32°30S 66°10W **190** C2
San Luis de la Paz
Mexico 21°18N 100°31W **180** C4
San Luis Obispo
U.S.A. 35°17N 120°40W **171** K6
San Luis Potosí *Mexico* 22°9N 100°59W **180** C4
San Luis Potosí □
Mexico 23°0N 101°0W **180** C4
San Luis Res. *U.S.A.* 37°4N 121°5W **170** H5
San Luis Río Colorado
Mexico 32°29N 114°58W **180** A2
San Manuel *U.S.A.* 32°36N 110°38W **169** K8
San Marco, C. *Italy* 39°51N 8°26E **94** C1
San Marco Argentano
Italy 39°33N 16°7E **95** C9
San Marco in Lámis
Italy 41°43N 15°38E **93** G12
San Marcos *Calif.,*
U.S.A. 33°9N 117°10W **171** M9
San Marcos *Tex.,*
U.S.A. 29°53N 97°56W **176** G5
San Marcos, I. *Mexico* 27°13N 112°6W **180** B2
San Marino ■ *Europe* 43°56N 12°25E **93** E9
San Marino *San Marino* 43°55N 12°30E **93** E9
San Martín *Antarctica* 68°11S 67°0W **55** C17
San Martín *Argentina* 33°5S 68°28W **190** C2
San Martín □ *Peru* 7°0S 76°50W **188** B2
San Martín → *Bolivia* 13°8S 63°43W **186** F6
San Martín, L.
Argentina 48°50S 72°50W **192** C2
San Martín de la Vega
Spain 40°13N 3°34W **88** E7
San Martín de los Andes
Argentina 40°10S 71°20W **192** B2
San Martín de Valdeiglesias
Spain 40°21N 4°24W **88** E6
San Mateo = Sant Mateu
Baleares,
Spain 39°3N 1°23E **100** B7
San Mateo = Sant Mateu
Valencia,
Spain 40°28N 0°10E **90** E5
San Mateo *U.S.A.* 37°34N 122°19W **170** H4
San Matías *Bolivia* 16°25S 58°20W **186** G7
San Matías, G.
Argentina 41°30S 64°0W **192** B4
San Miguel = Sant Miquel
Spain 39°3N 1°26E **100** B7
San Miguel *Brazil* 28°30S 54°33W **191** B5
San Miguel *El Salv.* 13°30N 88°12W **182** D2
San Miguel *Panama* 8°27N 78°55W **182** E4
San Miguel *U.S.A.* 35°45N 120°42W **170** K6
San Miguel → *Bolivia* 13°52S 63°56W **186** F6
San Miguel de Huachi
Bolivia 15°40S 67°15W **188** C4
San Miguel de Tucumán
Argentina 26°50S 65°20W **190** B2
San Miguel del Monte
Argentina 35°23S 58°50W **190** D4
San Miguel I. *U.S.A.* 34°2N 120°23W **171** L6
San Millán de la Cogolla
Spain 42°19N 2°51W **90** C2
San Miniato *Italy* 43°41N 10°51E **92** E7
San Nicandro Gargánico
Italy 41°50N 15°34E **93** G12
San Nicolás *Canary Is.* 27°58N 15°47W **100** G4
San Nicolás de los Arroyos
Argentina 33°25S 60°10W **190** C3
San Nicolas I. *U.S.A.* 33°15N 119°30W **171** M7
San Onofre *U.S.A.* 33°22N 117°34W **171** M9
San Páolo di Civitate
Italy 41°44N 15°15E **93** G12
San Pedro B. Aires,
Argentina 33°40S 59°40W **190** C4
San Pedro *Côte d'Ivoire* 4°50N 6°33W **138** E3
San Pedro *Misiones,*
Argentina 26°30S 54°10W **191** B5
San Pedro *Chile* 33°54S 71°28W **190** C1
San Pedro *Mexico* 23°55N 110°17W **180** C2
San Pedro *Peru* 14°49S 74°5W **188** D3
San Pedro □ *Paraguay* 24°0S 57°0W **190** A4
San Pedro → *Chihuahua,*
Mexico 28°21N 105°25W **180** B3

San Pedro → *Nayarit,*
Mexico 21°45N 105°30W **180** C3
San Pedro → *U.S.A.* 32°59N 110°47W **169** K8
San Pedro, Pta. *Chile* 25°30S 70°38W **190** B1
San Pedro, Sierra de
Spain 39°18N 6°40W **89** F4
San Pedro Channel
U.S.A. 33°30N 118°25W **171** M8
San Pedro de Atacama
Chile 22°55S 68°15W **190** A2
San Pedro de Jujuy
Argentina 24°12S 64°55W **190** A3
San Pedro de las Colonias
Mexico 25°45N 102°59W **180** B4
San Pedro de Lloc *Peru* 7°15S 79°28W **188** B2
San Pedro de Macorís
Dom. Rep. 18°30N 69°18W **183** C6
San Pedro del Norte
Nic. 13°4N 84°33W **182** D3
San Pedro del Paraná
Paraguay 26°43S 56°13W **190** B4
San Pedro del Pinatar
Spain 37°50N 0°50W **91** H4
San Pedro Mártir, Sa. de
Mexico 30°45N 115°13W **180** A1
San Pedro Ocampo = Melchor
Ocampo *Mexico* 24°51N 101°39W **180** C4
San Pedro Pochutla
Mexico 15°44N 96°28W **181** D5
San Pedro Sula
Honduras 15°30N 88°0W **182** C2
San Pietro *Italy* 39°8N 8°17E **94** C1
San Pietro Vernótico
Italy 40°29N 18°0E **95** B11
San Rafael *Argentina* 34°40S 68°21W **190** C2
San Rafael *Calif.,*
U.S.A. 37°58N 122°32W **170** H4
San Rafael *N. Mex.,*
U.S.A. 35°7N 107°53W **169** J10
San Rafael Mt. *U.S.A.* 34°41N 119°52W **171** L7
San Rafael Mts.
U.S.A. 34°40N 119°50W **171** L7
San Ramón de la Nueva Orán
Argentina 23°10S 64°20W **190** A3
San Remo *Italy* 43°49N 7°46E **92** E4
San Roque *Argentina* 28°25S 58°45W **190** B4
San Roque *Spain* 36°17N 5°21W **89** J5
San Rosendo *Chile* 37°16S 72°43W **190** D1
San Saba *U.S.A.* 31°12N 98°43W **176** F5
San Salvador *El Salv.* 13°40N 89°10W **182** D2
San Salvador I.
Bahamas 24°0N 74°30W **183** B5
San Salvo *Italy* 42°3N 14°44E **93** F11
San Salvador de Jujuy
Argentina 24°10S 64°48W **190** A3
San Sebastián = Donostia-San
Sebastián *Spain* 43°17N 1°58W **90** B3
San Sebastián
Argentina 53°10S 68°30W **192** D3
San Sebastián
Puerto Rico 18°20N 66°59W **183** d
San Sebastián de la Gomera
Canary Is. 28°5N 17°7W **100** F2
San Serra = Son Serra
Spain 39°43N 3°13E **100** B10
San Serverino Marche
Italy 43°13N 13°10E **93** E10
San Severo *Italy* 41°41N 15°23E **93** G12
San Simeon *U.S.A.* 35°39N 121°11W **170** K5
San Simon *U.S.A.* 32°16N 109°14W **169** K9
San Stéfano di Cadore
Italy 46°34N 12°33E **93** B9
San Stino di Livenza
Italy 45°44N 12°41E **93** C9
San Telmo = Sant Elm
Spain 39°35N 2°21E **100** B9
San Telmo *Mexico* 30°58N 116°6W **180** A1
San Teodoro *Italy* 40°46N 9°40E **94** B2
San Tiburcio *Mexico* 24°8N 101°32W **180** C4
San Valentin, Mte.
Chile 46°30S 73°30W **192** C2
San Vicente de Alcántara
Spain 39°22N 7°8W **89** F3
San Vicente de Cañete
Peru 13°8S 76°30W **188** D2
San Vicente de la Barquera
Spain 43°23N 4°29W **88** B6
San Vicenzo *Spain* 42°58N 8°46W **88** C2
San Vincenzo *Italy* 43°6N 10°32E **92** E7
San Vito *Costa Rica* 8°50N 82°58W **182** E3
San Vito *Italy* 39°26N 9°32E **94** C2
San Vito, C. *Italy* 38°11N 12°41E **94** D5
San Vito al Tagliamento
Italy 45°54N 12°52E **93** C9
San Vito Chietino *Italy* 42°18N 14°27E **93** F11
San Vito dei Normanni
Italy 40°39N 17°42E **95** B10
Sana → = Şan'a' *Yemen* 15°27N 44°12E **131** D3
Saña *Peru* 6°54S 79°36W **188** B2
Şan'a' *Yemen* 15°27N 44°12E **131** D3
Sana → *Bos.-H.* 45°3N 16°23E **93** C13
Sanaa = Şan'a' *Yemen* 15°27N 44°12E **131** D3
Sanaba *Burkina Faso* 12°25N 3°47W **138** C4
Sanae IV *Antarctica* 70°0S 9°0W **55** D2
Şanafir *Si. Arabia* 27°56N 34°42E **137** B3
Sanaga → *Cameroon* 3°35N 9°38E **139** G6
Sanak I. *U.S.A.* 54°25N 162°40W **166** F7
Sanalona, Presa
Mexico 24°49N 107°7W **180** C3
Sanana *Indonesia* 2°4S 125°58E **119** E7
Sanand *India* 22°59N 72°25E **124** H8
Sananduva *Bolivia* 27°57S 51°48W **191** B5
Sanandaj *Iran* 35°18N 47°1E **105** E12
Sanary-sur-Mer *France* 43°7N 5°49E **73** E9
Sanawad *India* 22°11N 76°5E **124** H7
Sancellas = Sencelles
Spain 39°39N 2°54E **100** B9
Sancergues *France* 47°10N 2°54E **71** E9
Sancerre *France* 47°20N 2°50E **71** E9
Sancerrois, Collines du
France 47°20N 2°40E **71** E9
Sancha He → *China* 26°48N 106°7E **116** D6
Sanchahe *China* 44°50N 126°2E **115** B14
Sánchez *Dom. Rep.* 19°15N 69°36W **183** C6
Sanchi *India* 23°28N 77°44E **124** H7
Sanchor *India* 24°45N 71°55E **124** G4
Sancoins *France* 46°47N 2°55E **71** F9
Sancti Spíritus *Cuba* 21°52N 79°33W **182** B4
Sancy, Puy de *France* 45°32N 2°50E **72** C6

Sand = Polokwane →
S. Africa 22°25S 30°5E **145** B5
Sand Hills *U.S.A.* 42°10N 101°30W **172** D3
Sand Lakes △ *Canada* 57°51N 98°32W **163** B9
Sand Springs *U.S.A.* 36°9N 96°7W **176** C6
Sanda *Japan* 34°53N 135°14E **113** G7
Sandakan *Malaysia* 5°53N 118°4E **118** C5
Sandalwood *Australia* 34°55S 140°9E **152** C4
Sandan = Sambor
Cambodia 12°46N 106°0E **120** F6
Sandanski *Bulgaria* 41°35N 23°16E **96** E7
Sandaré *Mali* 14°40N 10°15W **138** C2
Sandared *Sweden* 57°43N 12°47E **63** G6
Sandarne *Sweden* 61°16N 17°9E **62** C11
Sanday *U.K.* 59°16N 2°31W **55** B6
Sanday *U.K.* 59°0N 10°12E **62** E4
Sandefjord *Norway* 59°10N 10°15E **61** G14
Sanders *U.S.A.* 35°13N 109°20W **169** J9
Sanderson *Fla., U.S.A.* 30°15N 82°16W **178** F7
Sanderson *Tex., U.S.A.* 30°9N 102°24W **176** E3
Sandersville *U.S.A.* 32°59N 82°48W **178** C7
Sandfire Roadhouse
Australia 19°45S 121°15E **148** C3
Sandfly L. *Canada* 55°43N 106°6W **163** B7
Sandfontein *Namibia* 23°48S 19°1E **144** B2
Sandhammaren *Sweden* 55°23N 14°14E **63** J8
Sandheads, The *India* 21°10N 88°20E **125** J13
Sandia *Peru* 14°10S 69°30W **188** C4
Sandikh *Turkey* 38°28N 30°17E **99** C12
Sandila *India* 27°5N 80°31E **125** F9
Sandnes *Norway* 58°50N 5°45E **61** G11
Sandnessjøen *Norway* 66°2N 12°38E **60** C15
Sandoa
Dem. Rep. of the Congo 9°41S 23°0E **140** F4
Sandomierz *Poland* 50°40N 21°43E **83** H8
Sândominic *Romania* 46°35N 25°47E **81** D10
Sandover → *Australia* 21°43S 136°32E **150** C2
Sandoway = Thandwe
Myanmar 18°20N 94°30E **123** K19
Sandoy *Færoe Is.* 61°52N 6°46W **60** F9
Sandpoint *U.S.A.* 48°17N 116°33W **168** B5
Sandray *U.K.* 56°53N 7°31W **65** E1
Sandringham *U.K.* 52°51N 0°31E **66** E8
Sandstone *Australia* 27°59S 119°16E **149** E2
Sandu *China* 26°0N 107°52E **116** E6
Sandur *India* 15°6N 76°33E **127** F3
Sandusky *Mich.,*
U.S.A. 43°25N 82°50W **174** C2
Sandusky *Ohio, U.S.A.* 41°27N 82°42W **174** C2
Sandveld *Namibia* 21°25S 20°0E **144** B3
Sandvig *Denmark* 55°18N 14°47E **63** J8
Sandviken *Sweden* 60°38N 16°46E **62** D10
Sandwich, C. *Australia* 18°14S 146°18E **150** B4
Sandwich B. *Canada* 53°40N 57°15W **165** B8
Sandwich B. *Namibia* 23°25S 14°20E **144** B1
Sandy *Oreg., U.S.A.* 45°24N 122°16W **170** E4
Sandy *Pa., U.S.A.* 41°6N 78°46W **174** E6
Sandy *Utah, U.S.A.* 40°32N 111°50W **168** F8
Sandy Bay *Canada* 55°31N 102°19W **163** B8
Sandy Bight *Australia* 33°50S 123°20E **149** F3
Sandy C. *Queens.,*
Australia 24°42S 153°15E **150** C5
Sandy C. *Tas., Australia* 41°25S 144°45E **151** G3
Sandy Cay *Bahamas* 23°13N 75°18W **183** B4
Sandy Cr. → *Australia* 31°54S 145°18E **151** B4
Sandy Cr. → *U.S.A.* 41°51N 109°47W **168** F9
Sandy Creek *U.S.A.* 43°38N 76°5W **175** C8
Sandy L. *Canada* 53°2N 93°0W **164** B1
Sandy Lake *Canada* 53°0N 93°15W **164** B1
Sandy Point *India* 10°32N 92°22E **127** J11
Sandy Springs *U.S.A.* 33°56N 84°23W **178** B5
Sandy Valley *U.S.A.* 35°49N 115°38W **171** K11
Sânfjället △ *Sweden* 62°17N 13°35E **62** B7
Sanford *Fla., U.S.A.* 28°48N 81°16W **179** G8
Sanford *Maine, U.S.A.* 43°27N 70°47W **175** C14
Sanford *N.C., U.S.A.* 35°29N 79°10W **177** D15
Sanford → *Australia* 27°22S 115°53E **149** E2
Sanford, Mt. *U.S.A.* 62°13N 144°8W **166** D5
Sang-i-Masha *Afghan.* 33°8N 67°27E **124** C2
Sanga *Mozam.* 12°22S 35°21E **143** E4
Sanga → *Congo* 1°5S 17°0E **140** E3
Sangamner *India* 19°37N 74°15E **126** E2
Sangān *Iran* 34°23N 60°15E **129** C9
Sanganeb Atoll △
Sudan 19°33N 37°11E **137** D4
Sangar *Afghan.* 32°56N 65°30E **124** C1
Sangar *Russia* 64°2N 127°31E **107** C13
Sangar Sarai *Afghan.* 34°27N 70°35E **124** B4
Sangareddi *India* 17°38N 78°7E **126** F4
Sangarh → *Pakistan* 30°43N 70°44E **124** D4
Sangasso *Mali* 12°5N 5°35W **138** C3
Sangatte *France* 50°56N 1°44E **71** B8
Sangaw *Iraq* 35°17N 45°10E **105** E11
Sangay *Ecuador* 2°0S 78°20W **186** D3
Sangbé *Cameroon* 4°58N 13°6E **139** D7
Sange
Dem. Rep. of the Congo 6°58S 28°21E **142** D2
Sangeang *Indonesia* 8°12S 119°6E **119** F5
Sângeorz-Bãi *Romania* 47°22N 24°41E **81** C9
Sanger *U.S.A.* 36°42N 119°33W **170** J7
Sângera *Moldova* 46°55N 28°51E **81** D13
Sangerhausen *Germany* 51°28N 11°18E **76** D7
Sanggan He → *China* 38°12N 117°15E **114** C9
Sanggau *Indonesia* 0°5N 110°30E **118** D4
Sanghar *Pakistan* 26°2N 68°57E **124** F3
Sangihe, Kepulauan
Indonesia 3°0N 125°30E **119** D7
Sangihe, Pulau
Indonesia 3°35N 125°30E **119** D7
Sangiran △ *Indonesia* 7°27S 110°50E **119** G14
Sangju *S. Korea* 36°25N 128°10E **115** F15
Sangkapura *Indonesia* 5°52S 112°40E **118** F4
Sangkha *Thailand* 14°57N 103°52E **120** E4
Sangkhla Buri *Thailand* 14°57N 98°28E **120** E2
Sangkulirang *Indonesia* 1°0N 117°58E **118** D5
Sangla *Pakistan* 31°43N 73°23E **124** D5
Sangli *India* 16°55N 74°33E **126** F2
Sangmélima *Cameroon* 2°57N 12°1E **139** E7
Sango *Zimbabwe* 18°44S 31°44E **143** F3
Sangod *India* 24°55N 76°17E **124** G7
Sangole *India* 17°26N 75°12E **126** F2
Sangre de Cristo Mts.
U.S.A. 37°30N 105°20W **169** H11
Sangre Grande
Trin. & Tob. 10°35N 61°8W **187** K15
Sangro → *Italy* 42°14N 14°32E **93** F11
Sangrur *India* 30°14N 75°50E **124** D6
Sangudo *Canada* 53°50N 114°54W **162** C6
Sangue → *Brazil* 11°1S 58°39W **186** F7
Sangüesa *Spain* 42°37N 1°17W **90** C3
Sanguinaires, Îs. *France* 41°51N 8°36E **73** G12

Sangzhi China 29°25N 110°12E 117 C8
Sanhala Côte d'Ivoire 10°3N 6°51W 138 C3
Sanibel U.S.A. 26°27N 82°1W 179 J7
Sanibel I. U.S.A. 26°26N 82°6W 179 J7
Sanikluaq Canada 56°32N 79°14W 164 A4
Sanin-Kaigan △ Japan 35°39N 134°37E 113 G7
Sanirajak = Hall Beach
  Canada 68°46N 81°12W 161 D15
Sanjawi Pakistan 30°17N 68°21E 124 D3
Sanje Uganda 0°49S 31°30E 142 C3
Sanjiang China 25°48N 109°37E 116 E7
Sanjo Japan 37°37N 138°57E 112 F9
Sankarankovil India 9°10N 77°35E 127 K3
Sankeshwar India 16°23N 74°32E 127 F2
Sankh → India 22°15N 84°48E 125 H11
Sankt Andrä Austria 46°46N 14°50E 78 E7
Sankt Anton Austria 40°10N 10°16E 77 H6
Sankt Augustin Germany 50°45N 7°10E 76 E3
Sankt Blasien Germany 47°47N 8°7E 77 H4
Sankt Gallen Switz. 47°26N 9°22E 77 H5
Sankt Gallen □ Switz. 47°25N 9°22E 77 H5
Sankt Goar Germany 50°12N 7°43E 77 E3
Sankt Ingbert Germany 49°16N 7°6E 77 F3
Sankt Johann im Pongau
  Austria 47°22N 13°12E 78 D6
Sankt Johann in Tirol
  Austria 47°30N 12°25E 78 D5
Sankt Michel = Mikkeli
  Finland 61°43N 27°15E 84 B4
Sankt Moritz Switz. 46°30N 9°51E 77 J5
Sankt Peter-Ording
  Germany 54°20N 8°36E 76 A4
Sankt-Peterburg Russia 59°55N 30°20E 84 C6
Sankt Pölten Austria 48°12N 15°38E 78 C8
Sankt Ulrich = Ortisei
  Italy 46°34N 11°40E 93 B8
Sankt Valentin Austria 48°11N 14°33E 78 C7
Sankt Veit an der Glan
  Austria 46°47N 14°22E 78 E7
Sankt Wendel Germany 49°27N 7°9E 77 F3
Sankt Wolfgang Austria 47°43N 13°27E 78 D6
Sankuru →
  Dem. Rep. of the Congo 4°17S 20°25E 140 E4
Sanliurfa Turkey 37°12N 38°50E 105 D8
Sanliurfa □ Turkey 37°0N 39°0E 105 D8
Sanlúcar de Barrameda
  Spain 36°46N 6°21W 89 J4
Sanluri Italy 39°34N 8°54E 94 C1
Sânmartin Romania 46°19N 25°58E 81 D10
Sanmen China 29°5N 121°35E 117 C13
Sanmenxia China 34°47N 111°12E 114 G6
Sanming China 26°15N 117°40E 117 D11
Sanmu Japan 35°11N 134°37E 113 G7
Sanndraigh = Sandray
  U.K. 56°53N 7°31W 65 E1
Sânnicolau Mare
  Romania 46°5N 20°39E 80 D5
Sannieshof S. Africa 26°30S 25°47E 144 C4
Sannin, J. Lebanon 33°57N 35°52E 130 B4
Sanniquellie Liberia 7°19N 8°38W 138 D3
Sannûr, W. → Egypt 28°59N 31°3E 137 F7
Sano Japan 36°19N 139°35E 113 F9
Sanok Poland 49°35N 22°10E 83 J9
Sanqingshan △ China 28°54N 118°3E 117 C12
Sanquhar U.K. 55°22N 3°54W 65 F5
Sanremo = San Remo
  Italy 43°49N 7°46E 92 E4
Sans Souci Trin. & Tob. 10°50N 61°0W 187 K16
Sansanding Mali 13°48N 6°0W 138 C3
Sansané Niger 13°50N 1°36E 139 C5
Sansepolcro Italy 43°34N 12°8E 93 E9
Sansha China 26°58N 120°12E 117 D13
Sanshui China 23°10N 112°56E 117 F9
Sanski Most Bos.-H. 44°46N 16°40E 93 D13
Sansui China 26°58N 108°39E 116 D7
Sant Antoni de Portmany
  Spain 38°59N 1°19E 100 C7
Sant Boi de Llobregat
  Spain 41°20N 2°2E 90 D7
Sant Carles Spain 39°3N 1°34E 100 B8
Sant Carles de la Ràpita
  Spain 40°37N 0°35E 90 E5
Sant Celoni Spain 41°42N 2°30E 90 D7
Sant Elm Spain 39°35N 2°21E 100 B9
Sant Feliu de Guíxols
  Spain 41°45N 3°1E 90 D8
Sant Feliu de Llobregat
  Spain 41°22N 2°2E 90 D7
Sant Ferran Spain 38°42N 1°28E 100 C7
Sant Francesc de Formentera
  Spain 38°42N 1°26E 100 C7
Sant Jaume Spain 39°54N 4°4E 100 B11
Sant Joan Spain 39°36N 3°4E 100 B10
Sant Joan d'Alacant
  Spain 38°24N 0°26W 91 G4
Sant Joan de Labritja
  Spain 39°5N 1°31E 100 B8
Sant Jordi Ibiza, Spain 38°53N 1°24E 100 C7
Sant Jordi Mallorca, Spain 39°33N 2°46E 100 B9
Sant Jordi, G. de Spain 40°53N 1°2E 90 E6
Sant Llorenç de Morunys
  Spain 42°8N 1°35E 90 C6
Sant Llorenç del Munt y l'Obac △
  Spain 41°39N 1°55W 90 D3
Sant Llorenç des Cardassar
  Spain 39°37N 3°17E 100 B10
Sant Mateu Baleares,
  Spain 39°3N 1°23E 100 B7
Sant Mateu Valencia,
  Spain 40°28N 0°10E 90 E5
Sant Miquel Spain 39°3N 1°26E 100 B7
Sant Pere de Ribes Spain 41°16N 1°46E 90 D6
Sant Salvador Spain 39°27N 3°11E 100 B10
Sant Vicent del Raspeig
  Spain 38°24N 0°31W 91 G4
Santa Peru 9°0S 78°40W 188 E3
Sant' Ágata Militello Italy 38°2N 14°8E 95 D7
Santa Agnés Spain 39°3N 1°21E 100 B7
Santa Ana Beni, Bolivia 13°50S 65°40W 186 F5
Santa Ana La Paz,
  Bolivia 15°31S 67°30W 188 D4
Santa Ana El Salv. 14°0N 89°31W 182 D2
Santa Ana Mexico 30°33N 111°7W 180 A2
Santa Ana U.S.A. 33°46N 117°52W 171 M9
Santa Ana de los Rios de Cuenca
  = Cuenca Ecuador 2°50S 79°9W 186 D3
Santa Bárbara Chile 37°40S 72°1W 190 D1
Santa Bárbara
  Honduras 14°53N 88°14W 182 D2
Santa Bárbara Mexico 26°48N 105°49W 180 B3
Santa Bárbara Spain 40°42N 0°29E 90 E5
Santa Barbara U.S.A. 34°25N 119°42W 171 L7

Santa Bárbara, Mt.
  Spain 37°23N 2°50W 91 H2
Santa Barbara Channel
  U.S.A. 34°15N 120°0W 171 L7
Santa Barbara I.
  U.S.A. 33°29N 119°2W 171 M7
Santa Catalina, Gulf of
  U.S.A. 33°10N 117°50W 171 N9
Santa Catalina, I.
  Mexico 25°40N 110°47W 180 B2
Santa Cataliña de Armada
  Spain 43°2N 8°49W 88 B2
Santa Catalina I.
  U.S.A. 33°23N 118°25W 171 M8
Santa Catarina □
  Brazil 27°25S 48°30W 191 B6
Santa Catarina, I. de
  Brazil 27°30S 48°40W 191 B6
Santa Caterina di Pittinuri
  Italy 40°6N 8°27E 94 B1
Santa Caterina Villarmosa
  Italy 37°35N 14°2E 95 E7
Santa Cecília Brazil 26°56S 50°18W 191 B5
Santa Clara Cuba 22°20N 80°0W 182 B4
Santa Clara Calif.,
  U.S.A. 37°21N 121°57W 170 H5
Santa Clara N.Y.,
  U.S.A. 44°38N 74°27W 175 B10
Santa Clara Utah,
  U.S.A. 37°8N 113°39W 169 H7
Santa Clara → Mexico 29°51N 107°6W 180 A3
Santa Clara de Olimar
  Uruguay 32°50S 54°54W 191 C5
Santa Clara Valley
  U.S.A. 36°50N 121°30W 170 J5
Santa Clarita U.S.A. 34°24N 118°33W 171 L8
Santa Clotilde Peru 2°33S 73°45W 186 D4
Santa Coloma de Farners
  Spain 41°50N 2°39E 90 D7
Santa Coloma de Gramenet
  Spain 41°27N 2°13E 90 D7
Santa Comba = Santa Cataliña de
  Armada Spain 43°2N 8°49W 88 B2
Santa Croce Camerina
  Italy 36°50N 14°31E 95 F7
Santa Croce di Magliano
  Italy 41°42N 14°59E 93 G11
Santa Cruz Bolivia 17°43S 63°10W 186 G6
Santa Cruz Brazil 6°13S 36°1W 189 B3
Santa Cruz Chile 34°38S 71°27W 190 C1
Santa Cruz Costa Rica 10°15N 85°35W 182 D2
Santa Cruz Madeira 32°42N 16°46W 100 D3
Santa Cruz Peru 5°40S 75°56W 188 E3
Santa Cruz Phil. 14°20N 121°24E 119 B6
Santa Cruz □ Argentina 49°0S 70°0W 192 C3
Santa Cruz →
  Argentina 50°10S 68°20W 192 D3
Santa Cruz Cabrália
  Brazil 16°17S 39°2W 189 D3
Santa Cruz de la Palma
  Canary Is. 28°41N 17°46W 100 F2
Santa Cruz de la Palma ✈ (SPC)
  Canary Is. 28°41N 17°46W 100 F2
Santa Cruz de Mompox =
  Mompós Colombia 9°14N 74°26W 186 B4
Santa Cruz de Mudela
  Spain 38°39N 3°28W 89 G7
Santa Cruz de Tenerife
  Canary Is. 28°28N 16°15W 100 F3
Santa Cruz del Norte
  Cuba 23°9N 81°55W 182 B3
Santa Cruz del Retamar
  Spain 40°8N 4°14W 88 E6
Santa Cruz del Sur Cuba 20°44N 78°0W 182 B4
Santa Cruz do Rio Pardo
  Brazil 22°54S 49°37W 191 A6
Santa Cruz do Sul
  Brazil 29°42S 52°25W 191 B5
Santa Cruz I. U.S.A. 34°1N 119°43W 171 M7
Santa Cruz Is.
  Solomon Is. 10°30S 166°0E 147 C9
Santa Cruz Mts. Jamaica 17°58N 77°43W 182 a
Santa Elena Argentina 30°58S 59°47W 190 C4
Santa Elena, C.
  Costa Rica 10°54N 85°56W 182 D2
Santa Eufémia, G. di Italy 38°51N 16°4E 95 D9
Santa Eulària des Riu
  Spain 38°59N 1°32E 100 C8
Santa Fé Argentina 31°35S 60°41W 190 C3
Santa Fé □ Argentina 31°50S 60°55W 190 C3
Santa Fe U.S.A. 35°41N 105°57W 169 J11
Santa Fé do Sul Brazil 20°13S 50°56W 187 H8
Santa Filomena Brazil 9°6S 45°50W 189 B1
Santa Fiora Italy 42°50N 11°35E 93 F8
Santa Gertrudis Spain 39°0N 1°26E 100 C7
Santa Giulia France 41°32N 9°17E 73 G13
Santa Giustina Italy 46°10N 12°3E 93 B9
Santa Helena Brazil 2°14S 45°18W 189 A1
Santa Inês Bahia, Brazil 13°17S 39°48W 189 C3
Santa Inês Maranhão,
  Brazil 3°39S 45°22W 189 A1
Santa Inés Spain 38°32N 5°37W 89 G5
Santa Inés, I. Chile 54°0S 73°0W 192 D2
Santa Isabel Argentina 36°10S 66°54W 190 D2
Santa Isabel do Morro
  Brazil 11°34S 50°40W 187 F8
Santa Lucía Corrientes,
  Argentina 28°58S 59°5W 190 B4
Santa Lucía San Juan,
  Argentina 31°30S 68°30W 190 C2
Santa Lucia Spain 37°35N 0°58W 91 H4
Santa Lucía Uruguay 34°27S 56°24W 190 C4
Santa Lucia Range
  U.S.A. 36°0N 121°20W 170 K5
Santa Luzia Brazil 19°47S 43°52W 189 D2
Santa Luzia Cabo Verde 16°50N 24°35W 134 b
Santa Margalida Spain 39°42N 3°6E 100 B10
Santa Margarita
  Argentina 38°28S 61°35W 190 D3
Santa Margarita
  U.S.A. 35°23N 120°37W 170 K6
Santa Margarita →
  U.S.A. 33°13N 117°23W 171 M9
Santa Margarita, I.
  Mexico 24°27N 111°50W 180 C2
Santa Margherita Italy 38°58N 8°58E 94 D1
Santa Margherita Ligure
  Italy 44°20N 9°11E 92 D6
Santa María Argentina 26°40S 66°0W 190 B2
Santa Maria Azores 36°58N 25°6W 134 a

Santa Maria Brazil 29°40S 53°48W 191 B5
Santa Maria Cabo Verde 16°31N 22°53W 134 b
Santa Maria U.S.A. 34°57N 120°26W 171 L6
Santa Maria →
  Mexico 31°0N 107°14W 180 A3
Santa María, B. de
  Mexico 25°4N 108°6W 180 B3
Santa Maria, C. de
  Portugal 36°58N 7°53W 89 J3
Santa María, Vol.
  Guatemala 14°45N 91°33W 182 D1
Santa María Cápua Vétere
  Italy 41°5N 14°15E 95 A7
Santa Maria da Feira
  Portugal 40°55N 8°35W 88 E2
Santa Maria da Vitória
  Brazil 13°24S 44°12W 189 C2
Santa María de Guadalupe =
  Guadalupe Spain 39°27N 5°17W 89 F5
Santa Maria del Camí
  Spain 39°38N 2°47E 100 B9
Santa Maria di Léuca, C.
  Italy 39°47N 18°22E 95 C11
Santa Maria do Suaçuí
  Brazil 18°12S 42°25W 189 D2
Santa María la Real de Nieva
  Spain 41°4N 4°24W 88 D6
Santa Marinella Italy 42°2N 11°51E 93 F8
Santa Marta Colombia 11°15N 74°13W 186 A4
Santa Marta, Sierra Nevada de
  Colombia 10°55N 73°50W 186 A4
Santa Marta de Tormes
  Spain 40°57N 5°38W 88 E5
Santa Marta Grande, C.
  Brazil 28°43S 48°50W 191 B6
Santa Maura = Lefkada
  Greece 38°40N 20°43E 98 C2
Santa Monica U.S.A. 34°1N 118°29W 171 M8
Santa Monica Mts. △
  U.S.A. 34°4N 118°44W 171 L8
Santa Olalla Spain 40°2N 4°25W 88 E6
Santa Olalla del Cala
  Spain 37°54N 6°14W 89 H4
Santa Paula U.S.A. 34°21N 119°4W 171 L7
Santa Pola Spain 38°13N 0°35W 91 G4
Santa Ponça Spain 39°30N 2°28E 100 B9
Santa Quitéria Brazil 4°20S 40°10W 189 A3
Santa Rita Brazil 7°8S 34°58W 189 B4
Santa Rita de Cássia
  Brazil 11°0S 44°32W 189 C2
Santa Rosa La Pampa,
  Argentina 36°40S 64°17W 190 D3
Santa Rosa San Luis,
  Argentina 32°21S 65°10W 190 C2
Santa Rosa Beni,
  Bolivia 14°10S 66°53W 188 C4
Santa Rosa Pando,
  Bolivia 10°36S 67°20W 188 C4
Santa Rosa Brazil 27°52S 54°29W 191 B5
Santa Rosa Peru, Peru 14°30S 70°50W 186 G4
Santa Rosa San Martin,
  Peru 6°41S 76°37W 188 B2
Santa Rosa Calif.,
  U.S.A. 38°26N 122°43W 170 G4
Santa Rosa N. Mex.,
  U.S.A. 34°57N 104°41W 169 J11
Santa Rosa and San Jacinto
  Mts. △ U.S.A. 33°28N 116°20W 171 M10
Santa Rosa Beach
  U.S.A. 30°22N 86°14W 178 E3
Santa Rosa de Copán
  Honduras 14°47N 88°46W 182 D2
Santa Rosa de Río Primero
  Argentina 31°8S 63°20W 190 C3
Santa Rosa del Sara
  Bolivia 17°7S 63°35W 186 G6
Santa Rosa I. Calif.,
  U.S.A. 33°58N 120°6W 171 M6
Santa Rosa I. Fla.,
  U.S.A. 30°20N 86°50W 179 E3
Santa Rosa Range
  U.S.A. 41°45N 117°40W 168 F5
Santa Rosalía Mexico 27°19N 112°17W 180 B2
Santa Sylvina
  Argentina 27°50S 61°10W 190 B3
Santa Tecla = Nueva San
  Salvador El Salv. 13°40N 89°18W 182 D2
Santa Teresa Argentina 33°25S 60°47W 190 C3
Santa Teresa Australia 24°8S 134°22E 150 C1
Santa Teresa Brazil 19°55S 40°36W 189 D3
Santa Teresa Mexico 25°17N 97°51W 181 B5
Santa Teresa △
  Uruguay 33°57S 53°31W 190 C5
Santa Teresa di Riva
  Italy 37°57N 15°22E 95 E8
Santa Teresa Gallura
  Italy 41°14N 9°11E 94 A2
Santa Teresita
  Argentina 36°32S 56°41W 190 D4
Santa Uxía de Ribeira = Ribeira
  Spain 42°36N 8°58W 88 C2
Santa Vitória do Palmar
  Brazil 33°32S 53°25W 191 C5
Santa Ynez → U.S.A. 34°41N 120°36W 171 L6
Santa Ynez Mts.
  U.S.A. 34°30N 120°0W 171 L6
Santa Ysabel U.S.A. 33°7N 116°40W 171 M10
Santadi Italy 39°5N 8°43E 94 C1
Santaella Spain 37°34N 4°51W 89 H6
Santai China 31°5N 104°58E 116 B5
Santaluz Brazil 11°15S 39°22W 189 C3
Santana Brazil 13°2S 44°5W 189 C2
Santana Madeira 32°48N 16°52W 100 D3
Sântana Romania 46°20N 21°30E 80 D6
Santana, Coxilha de
  Brazil 30°50S 55°35W 191 B5
Santana do Ipanema
  Brazil 9°22S 37°14W 189 B3
Santana do Livramento
  Brazil 30°55S 55°30W 191 C4
Santander Spain 43°27N 3°51W 88 B7
Santander Jiménez
  Mexico 24°11N 98°29W 181 C5
Santanilla, Is.
  Honduras 17°22N 83°57W 182 C3
Santanyí Spain 39°20N 3°5E 100 B10
Santaquin U.S.A. 39°59N 111°47W 168 G8
Santarcángelo di Romagna
  Italy 44°4N 12°26E 93 D9
Santarém Brazil 2°25S 54°42W 187 D8
Santarém Portugal 39°12N 8°42W 89 F2
Santarém □ Portugal 39°10N 8°40W 89 F2

Santaren Channel
  W. Indies 24°0N 79°30W 182 B4
Santee U.S.A. 32°50N 116°58W 171 N10
Santee → U.S.A. 33°7N 79°17W 177 E15
Santerno → Italy 44°43N 11°58E 93 D8
Santhià Italy 45°22N 8°10E 92 C5
Santi-Quaranta = Sarandë
  Albania 39°52N 19°55E 96 G3
Santiago = Río Grande de
  Mexico 21°36N 105°26W 180 C3
Santiago = São Tiago
  Cabo Verde 15°0N 23°40W 134 b
Santiago Brazil 29°11S 54°52W 191 B5
Santiago Canary Is. 28°2N 17°12W 100 F2
Santiago Chile 33°26S 70°40W 190 C1
Santiago Panama 8°0N 81°0W 182 E3
Santiago Peru 14°11S 75°43W 188 C2
Santiago Phil. 16°41N 121°33E 119 A6
Santiago → Peru 4°27S 77°38W 186 D3
Santiago, C. Chile 50°46S 75°27W 192 D1
Santiago, Punta de
  Eq. Guin. 3°12N 8°40E 139 E6
Santiago de Chuco Peru 8°9S 78°11W 188 E3
Santiago de Compostela
  Spain 42°52N 8°37W 88 C2
Santiago de Cuba Cuba 20°0N 75°49W 182 C4
Santiago de los Caballeros
  Dom. Rep. 19°30N 70°40W 183 C5
Santiago del Estero
  Argentina 27°50S 64°15W 190 B3
Santiago del Estero □
  Argentina 27°40S 63°15W 190 B3
Santiago del Teide
  Canary Is. 28°17N 16°48W 100 F3
Santiago do Cacém
  Portugal 38°1N 8°42W 89 G2
Santiago Ixcuintla
  Mexico 21°49N 105°13W 180 C3
Santiago Jamiltepec
  Mexico 16°17N 97°49W 181 D5
Santiago Papasquiaro
  Mexico 25°3N 105°25W 180 C3
Santiago Pinotepa Nacional
  Mexico 16°19N 98°1W 181 D5
Santiaguillo, L. de
  Mexico 24°48N 104°48W 180 C4
Santillana del Mar Spain 43°24N 4°6W 88 B6
Santisteban del Puerto
  Spain 38°17N 3°15W 89 G7
Santo → Peru 8°56S 78°37W 188 E2
Santo Amaro Brazil 12°30S 38°43W 189 C3
Santo Anastácio Brazil 21°58S 51°39W 191 A5
Santo André Brazil 23°39S 46°29W 191 A6
Santo Ângelo Brazil 28°15S 54°15W 191 B5
Sant' Ángelo Lodigiano
  Italy 45°14N 9°25E 92 C6
Santo Antão Cabo Verde 16°52N 25°10W 134 b
Sant' Antíoco Italy 39°4N 8°27E 94 C1
Santo Antônio de Jesus
  Brazil 12°58S 39°16W 189 C3
Santo Antônio do Içá
  Brazil 3°5S 67°57W 186 D5
Santo Antônio do Leverger
  Brazil 15°52S 56°5W 187 G7
Santo Domingo
  Dom. Rep. 18°30N 69°59W 183 C6
Santo Domingo
  Mexico 25°29N 111°55W 180 B2
Santo Domingo Nic. 12°14N 84°59W 182 D3
Santo Domingo, Cay
  Bahamas 21°25N 75°45W 182 B4
Santo Domingo de la Calzada
  Spain 42°26N 2°57W 90 C2
Santo Domingo de los Colorados
  Ecuador 0°15S 79°9W 186 D3
Santo Domingo Pueblo
  U.S.A. 35°31N 106°22W 169 J10
Santo Domingo Tehuantepec =
  Tehuantepec
  Mexico 16°19N 95°13W 181 D5
Sant' Egídio alla Vibrata
  Italy 42°49N 13°42E 93 F10
Santo Stéfano di Camastro
  Italy 38°1N 14°22E 95 D7
Santo Tirso Portugal 41°21N 8°28W 88 D2
Santo Tomás Mexico 31°33N 116°24W 180 A1
Santo Tomás Peru 14°26S 72°8W 186 G4
Santo Tomé Argentina 28°40S 56°5W 191 B4
Santo Tomé de Guayana = Ciudad
  Guayana Venezuela 8°0N 62°30W 186 B6
Santoña Spain 43°29N 3°27W 88 B7
Santoríni Greece 36°23N 25°27E 99 E7
Santos Brazil 24°0S 46°20W 191 A6
Santos, Sierra de los Spain 38°7N 5°12W 89 G5
Santos Dumont Brazil 22°55S 43°10W 191 A7
Santuario de Aves Laguna
  Colorada △ Bolivia 22°10S 67°45W 190 A2
Sanur Indonesia 8°41S 115°15E 119 K18
Sanwer India 22°59N 75°50E 124 H6
Sanxenxo Spain 42°24N 8°49W 88 C2
Sanxia Shuiku China 30°3N 107°58E 116 B4
Sanxiang China 22°21N 113°25E 111 a
Sanya China 18°14N 109°29E 117 J ...
Sanyuan China 34°35N 108°58E 114 G5
São Bartolomeu de Messines
  Portugal 37°15N 8°17W 89 H2
São Benedito Brazil 4°3S 40°53W 189 A3
São Bento Brazil 2°42S 44°50W 189 A2
São Bento do Norte Brazil 5°4S 36°2W 189 B3
São Bernardo do Campo
  Brazil 23°45S 46°34W 191 A6
São Borja Brazil 28°39S 56°0W 191 B4
São Brás de Alportel
  Portugal 37°8N 7°37W 89 H3
São Caitano Brazil 8°21S 36°6W 189 B3
São Carlos Brazil 22°0S 47°50W 191 A6
São Cristóvão Brazil 11°1S 37°15W 189 C3
São Domingos Brazil 13°25S 46°19W 189 C2
São Domingos
  Guinea-Biss. 12°19N 16°13W 138 C1
São Domingos do Maranhão
  Brazil 5°42S 44°22W 189 B2
São Filipe Cabo Verde 15°2N 24°30W 134 b
São Francisco Brazil 16°0S 44°50W 189 D2
São Francisco →
  Brazil 10°30S 36°24W 189 C3

São Francisco do Maranhão
  Brazil 6°15S 42°52W 189 B2
São Francisco do Sul
  Brazil 26°15S 48°36W 191 B6
São Gabriel Brazil 30°20S 54°20W 191 C5
São Gabriel da Palha
  Brazil 18°45S 40°39W 189 D2
São Gonçalo Brazil 22°48S 43°5W 191 A7
São Gotardo Brazil 19°19S 46°3W 189 D1
Sao Hill Tanzania 8°20S 35°12E 143 D4
São João Guinea-Biss. 11°32N 15°25W 138 C1
São João da Boa Vista
  Brazil 22°0S 46°52W 191 A6
São João da Madeira
  Portugal 40°54N 8°30W 88 E2
São João da Pesqueira
  Portugal 41°8N 7°24W 88 D3
São João da Ponte
  Brazil 15°56S 44°1W 189 D2
São João del Rei Brazil 21°8S 44°15W 191 A7
São João do Araguaia
  Brazil 5°23S 48°46W 187 E9
São João do Paraíso
  Brazil 15°19S 42°1W 189 D2
São João do Piauí Brazil 8°21S 42°15W 189 B2
São João dos Patos
  Brazil 6°30S 43°42W 189 B2
São Joaquim Brazil 28°18S 49°56W 191 B6
São Joaquim △ Brazil 28°12S 49°37W 191 B6
São Joaquim da Barra
  Brazil 20°45S 47°53W 189 E1
São Jorge Azores 38°38N 28°3W 134 a
São Jorge, Pta. de
  Madeira 32°50N 16°53W 100 D3
São José Brazil 27°38S 48°39W 191 B5
São José da Laje Brazil 9°1S 36°3W 189 B3
São José de Mipibu Brazil 6°5S 35°14W 189 B4
São José do Norte Brazil 32°1S 52°3W 191 C5
São José do Peixe Brazil 7°24S 42°34W 189 B2
São José do Rio Preto
  Brazil 20°50S 49°20W 189 E1
São José dos Campos
  Brazil 23°7S 45°52W 191 A6
São Leopoldo Brazil 29°50S 51°10W 191 B5
São Lourenço Brazil 22°7S 45°3W 191 A6
São Lourenço →
  Brazil 17°53S 57°27W 187 G7
São Lourenço, Pta. de
  Madeira 32°44N 16°39W 100 D3
São Lourenço do Sul
  Brazil 31°22S 51°58W 191 C5
São Luís Brazil 2°39S 44°15W 189 A2
São Luís de Curu Brazil 3°40S 39°14W 189 A3
São Luís Gonzaga Brazil 28°25S 55°0W 191 B5
São Marcos → Brazil 18°15S 47°37W 189 D1
São Marcos, B. de Brazil 2°0S 44°0W 189 A2
São Martinho da Cortiça
  Portugal 40°18N 8°8W 88 E2
São Mateus Brazil 18°44S 39°50W 189 D3
São Mateus → Brazil 18°35S 39°44W 189 D3
São Mateus do Sul
  Brazil 25°52S 50°23W 191 B5
São Miguel Azores 37°47N 25°30W 134 a
São Miguel do Oeste
  Brazil 26°45S 53°34W 191 B5
São Miguel dos Campos
  Brazil 9°47S 36°5W 189 B3
São Nicolau Cabo Verde 16°20N 24°20W 134 b
São Nicolau → Brazil 5°45S 42°2W 189 B2
São Paulo Atl. Oc. 0°56N 29°22W 56 F9
São Paulo Brazil 23°32S 46°38W 191 A6
São Paulo □ Brazil 22°0S 49°0W 191 A6
São Paulo de Olivença
  Brazil 3°27S 68°48W 186 D5
São Pedro Atl. Oc. 0°56N 29°22W 56 F9
São Pedro do Sul Portugal 40°46N 8°4W 88 E2
São Rafael Brazil 5°47S 36°55W 189 B3
São Raimundo das Mangabeiras
  Brazil 7°1S 45°29W 189 B1
São Raimundo Nonato
  Brazil 9°1S 42°42W 189 B2
São Romão Brazil 16°22S 45°4W 189 D2
São Roque Madeira 32°46N 16°48W 100 D3
São Roque, C. de Brazil 5°30S 35°16W 189 B3
São Sebastião, I. de
  Brazil 23°50S 45°18W 191 A6
São Sebastião do Paraíso
  Brazil 20°54S 46°59W 191 A6
São Teotónio Portugal 37°30N 8°42W 89 H2
São Tiago Cabo Verde 15°0N 23°40W 134 b
São Tomé Brazil 5°58S 36°4W 189 B3
São Tomé
  São Tomé & Príncipe 0°10N 6°39E 132 F4
São Tomé, C. de Brazil 22°0S 40°59W 189 E2
São Tomé & Príncipe ■
  Africa 0°12N 6°39E 133 F4
São Vicente Brazil 23°57S 46°23W 191 A6
São Vicente Cabo Verde 16°50N 25°0W 134 b
São Vicente Madeira 32°48N 17°3W 100 D3
São Vicente, C. de Portugal 37°0N 9°0W 89 H1
Saona, I. Dom. Rep. 18°10N 68°40W 183 C6
Saône → France 45°44N 4°50E 71 G11
Saône-et-Loire □ France 46°30N 4°50E 71 F11
Saonek Indonesia 0°22S 130°55E 119 E8
Saoura, O. → Algeria 29°0N 0°55W 134 B4
Sapam, Ao Thailand 8°0N 98°26E 121 a
Sapanca Turkey 40°41N 30°16E 104 B4
Sapão → Brazil 11°1S 45°32W 189 C1
Saparua Indonesia 3°33S 128°40E 119 E7
Sapé Brazil 7°6S 35°13W 189 B3
Sapele Nigeria 5°50N 5°40E 139 D6
Sapelo I. U.S.A. 31°25N 81°12W 177 F14
Sapelo Sound U.S.A. 31°30N 81°10W 178 F14
Sapes Greece 41°2N 25°43E 97 E9
Saphane Turkey 39°1N 29°15E 105 C3
Sapi △ Zimbabwe 15°48S 29°42E 143 F2
Sapienza Greece 36°45N 21°43E 98 E3
Sapo △ Liberia 5°15N 8°30W 138 D3
Sapone Burkina Faso 12°3N 1°35W 138 C4
Saposoa Peru 6°55S 76°45W 188 E2
Sapotskina Belarus 53°49N 23°40E 82 D11
Sapouy Burkina Faso 11°34N 1°34W 138 C4
Sapozhok Russia 53°59N 40°41E 86 D5
Sapphire Australia 23°28S 147°43E 154 C4
Sappho U.S.A. 48°4N 124°16W 170 B2
Sapporo Japan 43°0N 141°21E 112 C10
Sapporo New Chitose ✈ (CTS)
  Japan 42°46N 141°41E 112 C10
Sapri Italy 40°4N 15°38E 95 B8
Sapt Kosi → Nepal 26°30N 86°56E 125 F12
Sapudi Indonesia 7°6S 114°20E 119 G16

Sapulpa U.S.A. 35°59N 96°5W 176 H6
Saqqez Iran 36°15N 46°20E 105 D12
Sar Dasht Äzarbäyjän-e Gharbi,
  Iran 36°9N 45°28E 105 D11
Sar Dasht Khuzestän,
  Iran 32°32N 48°52E 129 C6
Sar-e Pol Afghan. 36°10N 66°0E 129 F7
Sar-e Pol □ Afghan. 36°20N 65°50E 109 F7
Sar Gachineh = Yāsūj
  Iran 30°31N 51°31E 129 D6
Sar Planina Macedonia 42°0N 21°0E 96 C4
Sara Burkina Faso 11°40N 3°53W 138 C4
Šara △ Serbia 42°12N 21°0E 96 C5
Sara Buri = Saraburi
  Thailand 14°30N 100°55E 120 E3
Sarāb Iran 37°55N 47°40E 105 D12
Sarābādī Iraq 33°1N 44°48E 128 C5
Sarābleh Iran 33°44N 46°34E 105 F12
Saraburi Thailand 14°30N 100°55E 120 E3
Saradiya India 21°34N 70°2E 124 J4
Sarafére Mali 15°50N 3°40W 138 B4
Saragossa = Zaragoza
  Spain 41°39N 0°53W 90 D4
Saraguro Ecuador 3°35S 79°16W 186 D3
Sarahs Turkmenistan 36°32N 61°13E 129 B9
Sarai Naurang Pakistan 32°50N 70°47E 124 C4
Saraikela India 22°42N 85°56E 125 H11
Saraipali India 21°20N 82°59E 126 D6
Saraiu Romania 44°43N 28°10E 81 F13
Sarajevo Bos.-H. 43°52N 18°26E 80 G3
Sarakhs = Sarahs
  Turkmenistan 36°32N 61°13E 129 B9
Sarakhs Iran 36°32N 61°9E 108 E6
Saran, Gunung
  Indonesia 0°30S 111°25E 118 D4
Saranac Lake U.S.A. 44°20N 74°10W 175 B11
Saranac Lakes U.S.A. 44°20N 74°28W 175 B10
Saranda Tanzania 5°45S 34°59E 142 D3
Sarandë Albania 39°52N 19°55E 96 G3
Sarandí del Yí Uruguay 33°18S 55°38W 191 C4
Sarandí Grande
  Uruguay 33°44S 56°20W 190 C4
Sarangani B. Phil. 6°0N 125°13E 119 C7
Sarangani Is. Phil. 5°25N 125°25E 119 C7
Sarangarh India 21°30N 83°5E 126 D6
Saransk Russia 54°10N 45°10E 86 C7
Sarapul Russia 56°28N 53°48E 106 C6
Sarasota U.S.A. 27°20N 82°32W 179 H7
Sarata Ukraine 46°1N 29°40E 81 E14
Sarata → Ukraine 45°51N 29°41E 81 E14
Saratoga Calif., U.S.A. 37°16N 122°2W 170 H4
Saratoga Wyo.,
  U.S.A. 41°27N 106°49W 168 F10
Saratoga △ U.S.A. 43°0N 73°38W 175 D11
Saratoga L. U.S.A. 43°1N 73°44W 175 C11
Saratoga Springs
  U.S.A. 43°5N 73°47W 175 C11
Saratok Malaysia 1°55N 111°17E 118 D4
Saratov Russia 51°30N 46°2E 86 E7
Saratov □ Russia 51°30N 46°20E 86 E8
Saratovskoye Vdkhr.
  Russia 53°10N 48°35E 86 D9
Sarāvān Iran 27°25N 62°15E 129 E9
Saravane Laos 15°43N 106°25E 120 E6
Sarawak □ Malaysia 2°0N 113°0E 118 D4
Saray Tekirdağ, Turkey 41°26N 27°55E 97 E11
Saray Van, Turkey 38°38N 44°9E 105 C11
Saraya Senegal 12°50N 11°45W 138 C2
Saraycık Turkey 39°1N 29°9E 105 C3
Sarayköy Turkey 37°55N 28°54E 99 D10
Saraylar Turkey 40°39N 27°67E 97 E11
Sarayönü Turkey 38°16N 32°24E 104 C5
Sarbāz Iran 26°38N 61°19E 129 E9
Sarbīsheh Iran 32°30N 59°40E 129 C8
Sárbogárd Hungary 46°50N 18°40E 80 D3
Sarca → Italy 45°52N 10°52E 92 C7
Sarcelles France 49°1N 2°23E 71 D9
Sarda → India 27°21N 81°23E 125 F9
Sardar Sarovar Dam
  India 21°50N 73°50E 126 D7
Sardarshahr India 28°30N 74°29E 124 E6
Sardegna □ Italy 40°0N 9°0E 94 B1
Sardhana India 29°9N 77°39E 124 E7
Sardina, Pta. Canary Is. 28°9N 15°44W 100 F4
Sardinia = Sardegna □
  Italy 40°0N 9°0E 94 B1
Sardis Turkey 38°28N 27°58E 99 C10
Sardis U.S.A. 32°58N 81°46W 178 E4
Sārdūīyeh = Dar Mazār
  Iran 29°14N 57°20E 129 D8
Sarek △ Sweden 67°22N 17°35E 86 C17
Saren Indonesia 8°26S 115°34E 119 J17
S'Arenal Spain 39°30N 2°45E 100 B9
Sarentino Italy 46°38N 11°21E 93 B8
Sarera, G. of Indonesia 2°0S 135°0E 147 B6
Saréyamou Mali 16°7N 3°10W 138 B4
Sargasso Sea Atl. Oc. 27°0N 72°0W 158 G13
Sargent U.S.A. 33°26N 84°52W 178 E3
Sargodha Pakistan 32°10N 72°40E 124 C5
Sarh Chad 9°5N 18°23E 135 G9
Sarhala Côte d'Ivoire 8°22N 6°9W 138 D3
Sarhro, Jebel Morocco 31°6N 5°0W 134 B3
Sārī Iran 36°30N 53°4E 129 B7
Sari d'Orcino France 42°3N 8°49E 73 F12
Saria Greece 35°54N 27°17E 99 F9
Saria India 21°38N 83°22E 126 D6
Sariab Pakistan 30°6N 66°59E 124 D2
Saribeyler Turkey 39°24N 27°35E 99 B9
Sarıgöl Turkey 38°14N 28°41E 104 C3
Sarikaya Turkey 39°29N 35°22E 104 C6
Sarikei Malaysia 2°8N 111°30E 118 D4
Sarıköy Turkey 40°12N 27°37E 97 F11
Sarila India 25°46N 79°41E 125 G8
Sarina Australia 21°22S 149°13E 150 C4
Sariñena Spain 41°47N 0°11W 90 D4
Sarıoğlan Turkey 39°5N 35°59E 104 C6
Sarita U.S.A. 27°13N 97°47W 181 B5
Sariwŏn N. Korea 38°31N 125°46E 115 E13
Sariyar Barajı Turkey 40°0N 31°33E 104 B4
Sarıyer Turkey 41°10N 29°3E 104 B3
Sarju → India 27°21N 81°23E 125 F9
Sark U.K. 49°25N 2°22W 67 H5
Sarkad Hungary 46°47N 21°23E 80 E6
Sarkari Tala India 27°39N 70°52E 124 F4
Şarkışla Turkey 39°21N 36°25E 104 C7
Şarköy Turkey 40°36N 27°6E 97 F11
Sarlat-la-Canéda France 44°54N 1°13E 72 D5
Särmaşag Romania 47°22N 22°51E 80 C7
Sărmaşu Romania 46°45N 24°13E 81 D8
Sarmi Indonesia 1°49S 138°44E 119 G16

Sarmiento *Argentina* 45°35S 69°5W **192** C3
Sarmiento, Mt. *Chile* 54°27S 70°50W **192** D2
Sarmizegetusa *Romania* 45°31N 22°47E **80** E7
Särna *Sweden* 61°41N 13°8E **62** C7
Sarnano *Italy* 43°2N 13°18E **93** B8
Sarnen *Switz.* 46°53N 8°13E **77** J4
Sarnia *Canada* 42°58N 82°23W **174** D2
Sarno *Italy* 40°49N 14°37E **95** B7
Sarnthein = Sarentino
Italy 46°38N 11°21E **93** B8
Särö *Sweden* 57°31N 11°57E **63** G5
Sarolangun *Indonesia* 2°19S 102°42E **118** E2
Saronikos Kolpos *Greece* 37°45N 23°45E **98** D5
Saronno *Italy* 45°38N 9°2E **92** C6
Saros Körfezi *Turkey* 40°30N 26°15E **97** F10
Sárospatak *Hungary* 48°18N 21°33E **80** A6
Sarov *Russia* 54°56N 43°19E **86** C6
Sarpsborg *Norway* 59°16N 11°7E **61** G14
Sarqan *Kazakhstan* 45°24N 79°55E **109** E9
Sarracín *Spain* 42°15N 3°45W **88** C7
Sarralbe *France* 49°1N 7°1E **71** D14
Sarre = Saar → *Europe* 49°41N 6°32E **69** E6
Sarre *Italy* 45°40N 7°15E **92** C4
Sarre-Union *France* 48°57N 7°4E **71** D14
Sarrebourg *France* 48°43N 7°3E **71** D14
Sarreguemines *France* 49°5N 7°4E **71** C14
Sarria *Spain* 42°49N 7°29W **88** C3
Sarrión *Spain* 40°9N 0°49W **90** E4
Sarro *Mali* 13°40N 5°15W **138** C3
Sarroch *Italy* 39°4N 9°1E **94** C2
Sarsing *Iraq* 37°2N 43°20E **105** D10
Sarstedt *Germany* 52°14N 9°52E **76** C5
Sartell *U.S.A.* 45°37N 94°12W **172** C6
Sartène *France* 41°38N 8°58E **73** G12
Sarthe □ *France* 48°10N 0°10E **70** D7
Sarthe → *France* 47°33N 0°31W **70** E6
Sartilly *France* 48°45N 1°28W **70** D5
Saruhanlı *Turkey* 38°44N 27°36E **99** C9
Sărulești *Romania* 44°25N 26°39E **81** F11
Saruna → *Pakistan* 26°31N 67°7E **124** F2
Särur *Azerbaijan* 39°22N 45°5E **105** C11
Sárvár *Hungary* 47°15N 16°56E **80** C1
Sarvar *India* 26°4N 75°0E **124** F6
Sarvestān *Iran* 29°20N 53°10E **129** D7
Särvfjället *Sweden* 62°42N 13°30E **62** B7
Sárviz → *Hungary* 46°24N 18°41E **80** D3
Sary-Tash *Kyrgyzstan* 39°44N 73°15E **109** E8
Sarych, Mys *Ukraine* 44°25N 33°45E **85** K7
Saryesik-Atyraū Qumy
Kazakhstan 45°30N 76°0E **109** C9
Sarykamyshskoye, Ozero =
Saryqamysh Köli
Turkmenistan 41°56N 57°25E **108** D5
Sarykemer *Kazakhstan* 43°0N 71°30E **109** D8
Sarykenggir →
Kazakhstan 48°22N 67°59E **109** C7
Saryköl *Kazakhstan* 53°20N 65°12E **108** D7
Sarykolskiy Khrebet
Tajikistan 38°30N 74°30E **109** E8
Saryözek *Kazakhstan* 44°22N 77°59E **109** D9
Saryqamysh Köli
Turkmenistan 41°56N 57°25E **108** D5
Saryshaghan
Kazakhstan 46°12N 73°38E **109** C8
Sarysü → *Kazakhstan* 45°12N 66°36E **109** C7
Sarzana *Italy* 44°7N 9°58E **92** D6
Sarzeau *France* 47°31N 2°48W **70** E4
Sasan Gir *India* 21°10N 70°36E **124** J4
Sasaram *India* 24°57N 84°5E **125** G11
Sasebo *Japan* 33°10N 129°43E **113** H4
Saser Kangri *India* 34°50N 77°50E **114** B7
Saskatchewan □
Canada 54°40N 106°0W **163** C7
Saskatchewan →
Canada 53°37N 100°40W **163** C8
Saskatoon *Canada* 52°10N 106°38W **163** C7
Saskylakh *Russia* 71°55N 114°1E **107** B12
Saslaya △ *Nic.* 13°45N 85°4W **182** D2
Sasolburg *S. Africa* 26°46S 27°49E **145** C4
Sason *Turkey* 38°19N 41°24E **105** C9
Sasovo *Russia* 54°25N 41°55E **86** C5
Sassandra *Côte d'Ivoire* 4°55N 6°8W **138** E3
Sassandra → *Côte d'Ivoire* 4°58N 6°5W **138** E3
Sassandra-Marahoué □
Côte d'Ivoire 6°58N 6°26W **138** D3
Sássari *Italy* 40°43N 8°34E **94** B1
Sassie *Australia* 10°2S 142°51E **150** a
Sassnitz *Germany* 54°29N 13°39E **76** A9
Sasso Marconi *Italy* 44°24N 11°15E **93** D8
Sassocorvaro *Italy* 43°47N 12°20E **93** E9
Sassoferrato *Italy* 43°26N 12°51E **93** E9
Sassuolo *Italy* 44°33N 10°47E **92** D7
Sástago *Spain* 41°19N 0°21W **90** D4
Sastamala *Finland* 61°20N 22°54E **84** B2
Sastown *Liberia* 4°45N 8°27W **138** E3
Sasvad *India* 18°20N 74°2E **126** E2
Sasyk, Ozero *Ukraine* 45°45N 29°40E **81** E14
Sasyqköl *Kazakhstan* 46°35N 81°0E **109** C10
Sata-Misaki *Japan* 31°0N 130°40E **113** J5
Satadougou *Mali* 12°25N 11°25W **138** C2
Satakunta □ *Finland* 61°45N 23°0E **60** F20
Satama-Soukoura
Côte d'Ivoire 7°55N 4°27W **138** D4
Satara *India* 17°44N 73°58E **126** F1
Satara *S. Africa* 24°29S 31°47E **145** B5
Sätbaev *Kazakhstan* 48°10N 67°31E **109** C7
Satbarwa *India* 23°55N 84°16E **125** H11
Satellite Beach *U.S.A.* 28°10N 80°36W **179** D6
Säter *Sweden* 60°21N 15°45E **62** A8
Satevó *Mexico* 27°57N 106°7W **180** B3
Satilla → *U.S.A.* 30°59N 81°29W **178** E8
Satipo *Peru* 11°15S 74°25W **188** C3
Satka *Russia* 55°3N 59°1E **108** A5
Satluj = Sutlej →
Pakistan 29°23N 71°3E **124** E4
Satmala Hills *Maharashtra,*
India 20°15N 74°40E **126** D2
Satmala Hills *Telangana,*
India 19°45N 78°45E **126** E4
Satna *India* 24°35N 80°50E **125** G9
Šator *Bos.-H.* 44°11N 16°37E **93** D13
Sátoraljaújhely *Hungary* 48°25N 21°41E **80** B6
Satpura □ *India* 22°40N 78°15E **124** J7
Satpura Ra. *India* 21°25N 76°10E **124** J6
Satsuma *Germany* 54°41N 9°36E **76** A5
Satsuma-Sendai *Japan* 31°50N 130°20E **113** J5
Satsunan-Shotō *Japan* 30°0N 130°0E **113** K5
Sattahip *Thailand* 12°41N 100°54E **120** F3
Sattenapalle *India* 16°25N 80°6E **127** F5
Satu Mare *Romania* 47°46N 22°55E **80** C7
Satu Mare □ *Romania* 47°45N 23°0E **80** C8
Satui *Indonesia* 3°50S 115°27E **118** E5

Satun *Thailand* 6°43N 100°2E **121** J3
Saturnina → *Brazil* 12°15S 58°10W **186** F7
Sauce *Argentina* 30°5S 58°46W **190** C4
Sauceda *Mexico* 25°46N 101°19W **180** B4
Saucillo *Mexico* 28°1N 105°17W **180** B3
Sauda *Norway* 59°40N 6°20E **61** G12
Sauðarkrókur *Iceland* 65°45N 19°40W **60** D4
Saudi Arabia ■ *Asia* 26°0N 44°0E **128** B3
Sauerland *Germany* 51°12N 7°59E **74** C4
Saugeen → *Canada* 44°30N 81°22W **174** B3
Saugerties *U.S.A.* 42°5N 73°57W **175** D11
Saugues *France* 44°58N 3°32E **72** D7
Saugus *U.S.A.* 34°25N 118°32W **171** L8
Saujon *France* 45°41N 0°55W **72** C3
Sauk Centre *U.S.A.* 45°44N 94°57W **172** C6
Sauk Rapids *U.S.A.* 45°35N 94°10W **172** C6
Sault *France* 44°6N 5°24E **73** D9
Sault Ste. Marie
Canada 46°30N 84°20W **164** C3
Sault Ste. Marie
U.S.A. 46°30N 84°21W **173** B11
Saumalkol *Kazakhstan* 53°17N 68°6E **109** B7
Saumlaki *Indonesia* 7°55S 131°20E **119** F8
Saumur *France* 47°15N 0°5W **70** E6
Saundatti *India* 15°47N 75°7E **127** D2
Saunders, C. *N.Z.* 45°53S 170°45E **155** F5
Saunders I. *Antarctica* 57°48S 26°28W **55** B1
Saunders Pt. *Australia* 27°52S 125°38E **149** E4
Sauri *Nigeria* 11°42N 6°44E **139** C6
Saurimo *Angola* 9°40S 20°12E **140** F4
Sausalito *U.S.A.* 37°51N 122°29W **170** H4
Sauvage, Côte *France* 45°50N 1°30W **72** C2
Sauveterre-de-Béarn
France 43°24N 0°57W **72** E3
Sauzé-Vaussais *France* 46°8N 0°8E **72** B4
Savá *Honduras* 15°32N 86°15W **182** C2
Sava → *Serbia* 44°50N 20°26E **80** F5
Sava *Italy* 40°24N 17°33E **95** B10
Savage *U.S.A.* 47°27N 104°21W **168** C11
Savage I. = Niue ☑
Pac. Oc. 19°2S 169°54W **157** J11
Savage River *Australia* 41°31S 145°14E **151** G4
Savai'i *Samoa* 13°28S 172°24W **147** C11
Savalou *Benin* 7°57N 1°58E **139** D5
Savane *Mozam.* 19°37S 35°8E **143** F4
Savanes □ *Côte d'Ivoire* 9°30N 6°0W **138** C3
Savanna *U.S.A.* 42°5N 90°8W **172** D8
Savanna-la-Mar
Jamaica 18°10N 78°10W **182** a
Savannah *Ga., U.S.A.* 32°5N 81°6W **178** C8
Savannah *Mo., U.S.A.* 39°56N 94°50W **172** F6
Savannah *Tenn.,*
U.S.A. 35°14N 88°15W **177** D10
Savannah → *U.S.A.* 32°2N 80°53W **178** C9
Savannah Beach = Tybee Island
U.S.A. 32°1N 80°51W **178** C9
Savannakhet *Laos* 16°30N 104°49E **120** D5
Savant L. *Canada* 50°16N 90°44W **164** B1
Savant Lake *Canada* 50°14N 90°40W **164** B1
Savantvadi *India* 15°55N 73°54E **127** G1
Savanur *India* 14°59N 75°21E **127** G2
Savarkundla = Kundla
India 21°21N 71°25E **124** J4
Sāvārşin *Romania* 46°1N 22°14E **80** D7
Savaştepe *Turkey* 39°22N 27°42E **99** B9
Savda *India* 21°9N 75°56E **126** D2
Savé *Benin* 8°2N 2°29E **139** D5
Save → *France* 43°47N 1°17E **72** E5
Save → *Mozam.* 21°16S 34°0E **145** B5
Säveh *Iran* 35°2N 50°20E **129** C6
Savelugu *Ghana* 9°38N 0°54W **139** D4
Savenay *France* 47°20N 1°55W **70** E5
Săveni *Romania* 47°57N 26°52E **81** C11
Saverdun *France* 43°14N 1°34E **72** E5
Saverne *France* 48°43N 7°20E **71** D14
Savigliano *Italy* 44°38N 7°40E **92** D4
Savigny-sur-Braye
France 47°53N 0°49E **70** E7
Sávio → *Italy* 44°19N 12°20E **93** D9
Šavnik *Montenegro* 42°59N 19°10E **96** D3
Savo *Finland* 62°45N 27°30E **60** E22
Savoie □ *France* 45°26N 6°25E **73** C10
Savolax = Savo *Finland* 62°45N 27°30E **60** E22
Savona *Italy* 44°17N 8°30E **92** D5
Savona *U.S.A.* 42°17N 77°13W **174** D7
Savonlinna *Finland* 61°52N 28°53E **84** B5
Savoy = Savoie □
France 45°26N 6°25E **73** C10
Savsat *Turkey* 41°15N 42°20E **105** B10
Sävsjö *Sweden* 57°20N 14°40E **63** G8
Savur *Turkey* 37°34N 40°53E **128** B4
Savusavu *Fiji* 16°34S 179°15E **154** a
Savusavu B. *Fiji* 16°45S 179°15E **154** a
Savuti *Botswana* 18°37S 24°5E **144** A3
Sawahlunto *Indonesia* 0°40S 100°52E **118** E2
Sawai *Indonesia* 3°0S 129°5E **119** E7
Sawai Madhopur *India* 26°0N 76°25E **124** G7
Sawaleke *Fiji* 17°39S 179°18E **154** a
Sawang Daen Din
Thailand 17°28N 103°28E **120** D4
Sawankhalok *Thailand* 17°19N 99°50E **120** D2
Sawara *Japan* 35°55N 140°30E **113** G10
Sawatch Range
U.S.A. 39°0N 106°30W **168** G10
Sawel Mt. *U.K.* 54°50N 7°2W **64** B4
Sawi *Thailand* 10°14N 99°5E **121** G2
Sawla *Ghana* 9°17N 2°25W **138** D4
Sawmills *Zimbabwe* 19°30S 28°2E **143** F2
Sawtell *Australia* 30°19S 153°6E **153** A10
Sawtooth △ *U.S.A.* 44°0N 114°50W **168** D6
Sawtooth Range
U.S.A. 44°3N 114°58W **168** D6
Sawu *Indonesia* 10°35S 121°50E **119** F6
Sawu Sea *Indonesia* 9°30S 121°50E **119** F6
Saxby → *Australia* 18°25S 140°53E **150** B3
Saxmundham *U.K.* 52°13N 1°30E **67** E9
Saxon Switzerland = Sächsische
Schweiz △ *Germany* 50°55N 14°10E **76** E10
Saxony = Sachsen □
Germany 50°55N 13°10E **76** E9
Saxony, Lower =
Niedersachsen □
Germany 52°50N 9°0E **76** C4
Say *Mali* 13°50N 4°57W **138** C4
Say *Niger* 13°8N 2°22E **139** C5
Saya *Nigeria* 9°26N 6°3E **139** D6
Sayabec *Canada* 48°35N 67°41W **165** D6
Sayaboury *Laos* 19°15N 101°45E **120** C3

Sayán *Peru* 11°8S 77°12W **188** C2
Sayan, Vostochnyy
Russia 54°0N 96°0E **107** D10
Sayan, Zapadnyy
Russia 52°30N 94°0E **109** B12
Sayanogorsk *Russia* 53°5N 91°22E **109** B12
Sayano-Shushenskoye Vdkhr.
Russia 52°50N 91°22E **109** B12
Sayda *Lebanon* 33°35N 35°25E **130** B4
Sayhandulaan = Öldziyt
Mongolia 44°40N 109°1E **114** B5
Sayhūt *Yemen* 15°12N 51°10E **128** D5
Saykhin *Kazakhstan* 48°50N 46°47E **87** F8
Saylac *Somalia* 11°21N 43°30E **131** E3
Saynshand = Buyant-Uhaa
Mongolia 44°55N 110°11E **114** B6
Sayre *Okla., U.S.A.* 35°18N 99°38W **176** D5
Sayre *Pa., U.S.A.* 41°59N 76°32W **175** E8
Sayreville *U.S.A.* 40°28N 74°22W **175** E10
Sayula *Mexico* 19°52N 103°36W **180** D4
Say'ūn *Yemen* 15°56N 48°47E **131** D4
Sayward *Canada* 50°21N 125°55W **162** C3
Sazanit *Albania* 40°30N 19°20E **98** B1
Săzava → *Czechia* 49°53N 14°24E **78** B7
Sazin *Pakistan* 35°35N 73°30E **125** B5
Sazlika → *Bulgaria* 41°59N 25°50E **97** E9
Sbeïtla *Tunisia* 35°12N 9°7E **136** A5
Scaër *France* 48°2N 3°42E **70** D3
Scafell Pike *U.K.* 54°27N 3°14W **66** C4
Scalea *Italy* 39°49N 15°47E **95** C8
Scalloway *U.K.* 60°9N 1°17W **65** A7
Scalpay *U.K.* 57°18N 6°0W **65** D3
Scandia *Canada* 50°20N 112°2W **162** C6
Scandiano *Italy* 44°36N 10°43E **92** D7
Scandicci *Italy* 43°45N 11°11E **93** E8
Scandinavia *Europe* 64°0N 12°0E **60** E15
Scansano *Italy* 42°41N 11°20E **93** F8
Scapa Flow *U.K.* 58°53N 3°3W **65** E5
Scarámia, Capo *Italy* 36°47N 14°29E **95** F7
Scarba *U.K.* 56°11N 5°43W **66** E3
Scarborough
Trin. & Tob. 11°11N 60°42W **183** D7
Scarborough *U.K.* 54°17N 0°24W **66** C7
Scargill *N.Z.* 42°56S 172°58E **155** C7
Scariff I. *Ireland* 51°44N 10°15W **64** E1
Scarp *U.K.* 58°1N 7°8W **65** C1
Scarpe-Escaut □ *France* 50°26N 3°23E **71** B10
Scarsdale *Australia* 37°41S 143°39E **152** D5
Scebeli = Shabeelle →
Somalia 2°0N 44°0E **131** G3
Šcedro *Croatia* 43°6N 16°43E **93** E13
Schaal See *Germany* 53°36N 10°55E **76** B6
Schaalsee △ *Germany* 53°40N 10°59E **76** B6
Schaffhausen *Switz.* 47°42N 8°39E **77** H4
Schagen *Neths.* 52°49N 4°48E **69** B4
Schaghticoke *U.S.A.* 42°54N 73°35W **175** D11
Schärding *Austria* 48°27N 13°27E **78** C6
Scharhörn *Germany* 53°57N 8°24E **76** B4
Scheessel *Germany* 53°10N 9°29E **76** B5
Schefferville *Canada* 54°48N 66°50W **165** B6
Scheibbs *Austria* 48°1N 15°9E **78** D8
Schelde → *Belgium* 51°15N 4°16E **69** C4
Schell Creek Ra.
U.S.A. 39°25N 114°40W **168** G6
Schellsburg *U.S.A.* 40°3N 78°39W **174** F6
Schenectady *U.S.A.* 42°49N 73°57W **175** D11
Schenevus *U.S.A.* 42°33N 74°50W **175** D10
Scherfede *Germany* 51°32N 9°2E **76** D5
Schesslitz *Germany* 49°58N 11°1E **77** F7
Schiedam *Neths.* 51°55N 4°25E **69** C4
Schiermonnikoog *Neths.* 53°30N 6°15E **69** A6
Schiermonnikoog △
Neths. 53°30N 6°15E **69** A6
Schiltigheim *France* 48°35N 7°45E **71** D14
Schinousa *Greece* 36°53N 25°31E **99** E7
Schio *Italy* 45°43N 11°21E **93** C8
Schiphol, Amsterdam ✈ (AMS)
Neths. 52°18N 4°45E **69** B4
Schiza *Greece* 36°41N 21°40E **98** E3
Schladming *Austria* 47°23N 13°41E **78** D6
Schlanders = Silandro
Italy 46°38N 10°46E **92** B7
Schlei → *Germany* 54°40N 10°0E **76** A5
Schleiden *Germany* 50°31N 6°28E **76** E2
Schleiz *Germany* 50°35N 11°49E **76** E7
Schleswig *Germany* 54°31N 9°34E **76** A5
Schleswig-Holstein □
Germany 54°30N 9°30E **76** A5
Schlüchtern *Germany* 50°21N 9°31E **77** E5
Schmalkalden *Germany* 50°43N 10°26E **76** E6
Schmölln *Germany* 50°54N 12°19E **76** E8
Schneeberg *Austria* 47°45N 15°48E **78** D8
Schneeberg *Germany* 50°35N 12°38E **76** E8
Schneverdingen *Germany* 53°7N 9°48E **76** B5
Schoelcher *Martinique* 14°36N 61°7W **182** c
Schoharie *U.S.A.* 42°40N 74°19W **175** D10
Schoharie Cr. →
U.S.A. 42°57N 74°18W **175** D10
Schokland *Netherlands* 52°38N 5°46E **69** B5
Scholls *U.S.A.* 45°24N 122°56W **170** E4
Schönberg
Mecklenburg-Vorpommern,
Germany 53°52N 10°56E **76** B6
Schönberg *Schleswig-Holstein,*
Germany 54°23N 10°21E **76** A6
Schönbuch △ *Germany* 48°35N 9°2E **77** G5
Schönebeck *Germany* 52°2N 11°44E **76** C7
Schöngau *Germany* 47°47N 10°53E **77** H6
Schöningen *Germany* 52°8N 10°58E **76** C6
Schopfheim *Germany* 47°39N 7°49E **77** H3
Schorndorf *Germany* 48°47N 9°32E **77** G5
Schortens *Germany* 53°31N 7°56E **76** B3
Schouten I. *Australia* 42°20S 148°20E **151** G4
Schouten Is. = Supiori
Indonesia 1°0S 136°0E **119** E9
Schouwen *Neths.* 51°43N 3°45E **69** C3
Schramberg *Germany* 48°13N 8°22E **77** G4
Schrankogel *Austria* 47°3N 11°7E **78** D4
Schreiber *Canada* 48°45N 87°20W **164** C2
Schrems *Austria* 48°49N 15°4E **78** C8
Schrobenhausen
Germany 48°34N 11°16E **77** G7
Schroffenstein *Namibia* 27°11S 18°42E **144** C2
Schroon Lake *U.S.A.* 43°50N 73°46W **175** C11
Schruns *Austria* 47°5N 9°55E **76** K2
Schuler *Canada* 50°20N 110°6W **163** C6
Schumacher *Canada* 48°30N 81°16W **164** C3
Schurz *U.S.A.* 38°57N 118°49W **168** G4
Schuyler *U.S.A.* 41°27N 97°4W **172** E5
Schuylerville *U.S.A.* 43°6N 73°35W **175** C11
Schuylkill → *U.S.A.* 39°53N 75°12W **175** G9

Schuylkill Haven
U.S.A. 40°37N 76°11W **175** F8
Schwabach *Germany* 49°19N 11°2E **77** F7
Schwaben □ *Germany* 48°15N 10°30E **77** G6
Schwäbisch-Fränkischer Wald △
Germany 49°0N 9°30E **77** G5
Schwäbisch Gmünd
Germany 48°48N 9°47E **77** G5
Schwäbisch Hall *Germany* 49°6N 9°44E **77** F5
Schwäbische Alb
Germany 48°20N 9°30E **77** G5
Schwabmünchen
Germany 48°11N 10°45E **77** G6
Schwalmstadt *Germany* 50°55N 9°10E **76** E5
Schwandorf *Germany* 49°20N 12°7E **77** F8
Schwaner, Pegunungan
Indonesia 1°0S 112°30E **118** E4
Schwanewede *Germany* 53°14N 8°35E **76** B4
Schwarmstedt *Germany* 52°39N 9°38E **76** C5
Schwarze Elster →
Germany 51°48N 12°50E **76** D8
Schwarzenberg *Germany* 50°32N 12°47E **76** E8
Schwarzrand *Namibia* 25°37S 16°50E **144** C2
Schwarzwald *Germany* 48°30N 8°20E **77** G4
Schwatka Mts.
U.S.A. 67°20N 156°30W **166** B8
Schwaz *Austria* 47°20N 11°44E **78** D4
Schwechat *Austria* 48°8N 16°28E **79** C9
Schwechat, Wien ✈ (VIE)
Austria 48°7N 16°35E **79** C9
Schwedt *Germany* 53°3N 14°16E **76** B10
Schweinfurt *Germany* 50°3N 10°14E **77** E6
Schweiz = Switzerland ■
Europe 46°30N 8°0E **77** J4
Schweizer-Reneke
S. Africa 27°11S 25°18E **144** C4
Schwenningen = Villingen-
Schwenningen *Germany* 48°3N 8°26E **77** G4
Schwerin *Germany* 53°36N 11°22E **76** B7
Schweriner See *Germany* 53°45N 11°26E **76** B7
Schwetzingen *Germany* 49°23N 8°35E **77** F4
Schwyz *Switz.* 47°2N 8°39E **77** H4
Schwyz □ *Switz.* 47°2N 8°39E **77** H4
Sciacca *Italy* 37°31N 13°3E **94** E6
Scicli *Italy* 36°47N 14°42E **95** F7
Sciliar-Catinaccio △
Italy 46°28N 11°35E **93** B8
Scilla *Italy* 38°15N 15°43E **95** D8
Scilly, Isles of *U.K.* 49°56N 6°22W **67** H1
Scione *Greece* 39°57N 23°36E **98** D6
Scioto → *U.S.A.* 38°44N 83°1W **173** F12
Scituate *U.S.A.* 42°12N 70°44W **175** D14
Scobey *U.S.A.* 48°47N 105°25W **168** B11
Scone *Australia* 32°5S 150°52E **153** B9
Scone *U.K.* 56°25N 3°24W **65** E5
Scordia *Italy* 37°18N 14°51E **95** E7
Scoresby Sund
Greenland 70°28N 21°46W **57** C8
Scoresbysund = Ittoqqortoormiit
Greenland 70°20N 23°0W **57** C8
Scornicesti *Romania* 44°34N 24°33E **81** F8
Scotia *Calif., U.S.A.* 40°29N 124°6W **168** F1
Scotia *N.Y., U.S.A.* 42°50N 73°58W **175** D11
Scotia Sea *Antarctica* 56°5S 56°0W **55** B18
Scotland *Canada* 43°1N 80°22W **174** C4
Scotland □ *U.K.* 57°0N 4°0W **66** E5
Scott *Antarctica* 77°0S 166°45E **55** D11
Scott, C. *Australia* 13°30S 129°49E **148** B4
Scott City *U.S.A.* 38°29N 100°54W **172** F3
Scott Glacier *Antarctica* 66°15S 100°5E **55** C8
Scott I. *Antarctica* 67°0S 179°0E **55** C11
Scott Is. *Canada* 50°48N 128°40W **162** C2
Scott L. *Canada* 59°55N 106°18W **163** B7
Scott Reef *Australia* 14°0S 121°50E **148** B3
Scottburgh *S. Africa* 30°15S 30°47E **145** D5
Scottdale *U.S.A.* 40°6N 79°35W **174** F5
Scottish Borders □ *U.K.* 55°35N 2°50W **66** F6
Scotts Head *Australia* 30°45S 153°0E **153** A10
Scotts Valley *U.S.A.* 41°52N 103°40W **172** E2
Scottsboro *U.S.A.* 34°40N 86°2W **177** D11
Scottsburg *U.S.A.* 38°41N 85°47W **173** F11
Scottsdale *Australia* 41°9S 147°31E **151** G4
Scottsdale *U.S.A.* 33°40N 111°53W **169** K8
Scottsville *Ky., U.S.A.* 36°45N 86°11W **172** G10
Scottsville *N.Y., U.S.A.* 43°2N 77°47W **174** C7
Scottville *U.S.A.* 43°58N 86°17W **172** D9
Scranton *U.S.A.* 41°25N 75°40W **175** E9
Screven *U.S.A.* 31°29N 82°1W **178** D7
Scugog, L. *Canada* 44°10N 78°55W **174** B6
Scunthorpe *U.K.* 53°36N 0°39W **66** D7
Scuol Schuls *Switz.* 46°48N 10°17E **77** J6
Scutari = Shkodër
Albania 42°4N 19°32E **96** D3
Scutari = Üsküdar *Turkey* 41°1N 29°0E **97** F13
Sea Lake *Australia* 35°28S 142°55E **152** C5
Seabra *Brazil* 12°25S 41°46W **189** C2
Seabrook, L. *Australia* 30°55S 119°40E **149** F2
Seaford *U.K.* 50°47N 0°7E **67** G8
Seaford *U.S.A.* 38°39N 75°37W **175** F16
Seaforth *Australia* 20°55S 148°57E **150** b
Seaforth *Canada* 43°35N 81°25W **174** C3
Seaforth, L. *U.K.* 57°52N 6°36W **65** D2
Seaham *U.K.* 54°50N 1°20W **66** C6
Seal → *Canada* 59°4N 94°48W **163** B10
Seal L. *Canada* 54°20N 61°30W **165** B7
Seale *U.S.A.* 32°18N 85°10W **178** C4
Sealy *U.S.A.* 29°47N 96°9W **176** G6
Searchlight *U.S.A.* 35°28N 114°55W **171** K12
Searcy *U.S.A.* 35°15N 91°44W **177** D8
Searles L. *U.S.A.* 35°44N 117°21W **171** K9
Seascale *U.K.* 54°24N 3°29W **66** C4
Seaside *Calif., U.S.A.* 36°37N 121°50W **170** J5
Seaside *Oreg., U.S.A.* 46°0N 123°56W **170** E3
Seaspray *Australia* 38°25S 147°15E **153** D7
Seattle *U.S.A.* 47°36N 122°19W **170** C4
Seattle-Tacoma Int. ✈ (SEA)
U.S.A. 47°27N 122°18W **170** C4
Seaward Kaikoura Ra.
N.Z. 42°10S 173°44E **155** C6
Seba *Indonesia* 10°29S 121°50E **119** F6
Sebago L. *U.S.A.* 43°52N 70°34W **175** C14
Sebago Lake *U.S.A.* 43°51N 70°34W **175** C14
Sebastián Vizcaíno, B.
Mexico 28°0N 114°30W **180** B2
Sebastopol = Sevastopol
Ukraine 44°35N 33°30E **85** K7

Sebastopol *U.S.A.* 38°24N 122°49W **170** G4
Sebba *Burkina Faso* 13°35N 0°32E **139** C5
Sebdou *Algeria* 34°38N 1°19W **136** B3
Seben *Turkey* 40°24N 31°34E **104** B4
Sebeş *Romania* 45°58N 23°40E **81** E8
Sebewaing *U.S.A.* 43°44N 83°27W **173** D12
Sebezh *Russia* 56°14N 28°22E **84** D5
Sebha = Sabhā *Libya* 27°9N 14°29E **135** C8
Sébi *Mali* 15°50N 4°12W **138** B4
Sebinkarahisar *Turkey* 40°22N 38°28E **105** B8
Sebino = Iseo, L. d'
Italy 45°43N 10°4E **92** C7
Sebiş *Romania* 46°23N 22°13E **80** D7
Sebnitz *Germany* 50°58N 14°15E **76** E10
Sebou, Oued →
Morocco 34°16N 6°40W **136** B2
Sebring *Fla., U.S.A.* 27°30N 81°27W **179** H8
Sebring *Ohio, U.S.A.* 40°55N 81°2W **174** F3
Sebringville *Canada* 43°24N 81°4W **174** C3
Sebta = Ceuta *N. Afr.* 35°52N 5°18W **134** A4
Sebuku *Indonesia* 3°30S 116°25E **118** E5
Sečanj *Serbia* 45°25N 20°47E **80** E5
Secchia → *Italy* 45°4N 11°0E **92** C8
Sechelt *Canada* 49°25N 123°42W **162** D4
Sechura *Peru* 5°39S 80°50W **188** B1
Sechura, Desierto de
Peru 6°0S 80°30W **188** B1
Seclin *France* 50°33N 3°2E **71** B10
Secondigny *France* 46°37N 0°26W **70** F6
Sečovce *Slovakia* 48°42N 21°40E **79** C14
Secretary I. *N.Z.* 45°15S 166°56E **155** F1
Secunderabad *India* 17°28N 78°30E **126** F4
Sedalia *U.S.A.* 38°42N 93°14W **172** F7
Sedam *India* 17°11N 77°17E **126** E3
Sedan *Australia* 34°34S 139°19E **152** C3
Sedan *France* 49°43N 4°57E **71** C11
Sedan *U.S.A.* 37°8N 96°11W **172** G5
Sedano *Spain* 42°43N 3°49W **88** C7
Sedbergh *U.K.* 54°20N 2°31W **66** C5
Seddon *N.Z.* 41°40S 174°7E **155** B9
Seddonville *N.Z.* 41°33S 172°1E **155** B7
Sedé Boqér *Israel* 30°52N 34°47E **130** E3
Sedeh *Fārs, Iran* 30°45N 52°11E **129** D7
Sedeh *Khorāsān, Iran* 33°20N 59°14E **129** C8
Séderon *France* 44°12N 5°32E **73** D9
Sédhiou *Senegal* 12°44N 15°30W **138** C1
Sedico *Italy* 46°8N 12°6E **93** B9
Sedlčany *Czechia* 49°40N 14°25E **78** B7
Sedley *Canada* 50°10N 104°0W **163** C8
Sedona *U.S.A.* 34°52N 111°46W **169** J8
Sedova, Pik *Russia* 73°29N 54°58E **86** A6
Sedrata *Algeria* 36°7N 7°31E **136** A5
Sedro-Woolley *U.S.A.* 48°30N 122°14W **170** B4
Seduva *Lithuania* 55°45N 23°45E **84** C12
Sedziszów *Poland* 50°35N 20°4E **83** H7
Sędziszów Małopolski
Poland 50°5N 21°45E **83** H8
Seebad Ahlbeck
Germany 53°56N 14°10E **76** B10
Seefeld in Tirol *Austria* 47°19N 11°13E **78** D4
Seehausen *Germany* 52°54N 11°45E **76** C7
Seeheim *Namibia* 26°50S 17°45E **144** C2
Seeheim-Jugenheim
Germany 49°49N 8°40E **77** F4
Seeis *Namibia* 22°29S 17°39E **144** D2
Seekoei → *S. Africa* 30°18S 25°1E **144** D4
Seeley's Bay *Canada* 44°29N 76°14W **175** B8
Seelow *Germany* 52°32N 14°22E **76** C10
Seemandhra = Andhra Pradesh □
India 18°0N 79°0E **126** F4
Sées *France* 48°38N 0°10E **70** D7
Seesen *Germany* 51°54N 10°10E **76** D6
Seevetal *Germany* 53°26N 10°1E **76** B6
Seewinkel = Neusiedler See-
Seewinkel △ *Austria* 47°50N 16°45E **79** D9
Şefaatli *Turkey* 39°30N 34°45E **104** C6
Seferihisar *Turkey* 38°10N 26°50E **99** C8
Séfeto *Mali* 14°9N 9°49W **138** C3
Sefophe *Botswana* 22°11S 27°58E **145** B4
Sefrou *Morocco* 33°52N 4°52W **136** B3
Sefton *U.K.* 43°15N 172°41E **155** D7
Sefwi Bekwai *Ghana* 6°10N 2°25W **138** D4
Segamat *Malaysia* 2°30N 102°50E **121** L4
Segezha *Russia* 63°44N 34°19E **86** B4
Segorbe *Spain* 39°50N 0°30W **90** E4
Ségou *Mali* 13°30N 6°16W **138** C3
Ségou □ *Mali* 14°0N 6°0W **138** C3
Segovia = Coco →
Cent. Amer. 15°0N 83°8W **182** D3
Segovia *Spain* 40°57N 4°10W **88** E6
Segovia □ *Spain* 40°55N 4°10W **88** E6
Segré *France* 47°40N 0°52W **70** E6
Segre → *Spain* 41°40N 0°43E **90** D5
Séguéla *Côte d'Ivoire* 7°55N 6°40W **138** D3
Séguéla □ *Côte d'Ivoire* 8°0N 6°40W **138** D3
Séguénéga *Burkina Faso* 13°25N 1°58W **139** C4
Segundo → *Argentina* 30°53S 62°44W **190** C3
Segura → *Spain* 38°3N 0°44W **91** G4
Segura, Sierra de *Spain* 38°5N 2°45W **91** G2
Seh Qal'eh *Iran* 33°40N 58°24E **129** C8
Sehitwa *Botswana* 20°30S 22°30E **144** B3
Sehlabathebe △ *Lesotho* 29°53S 29°7E **145** C4
Sehore *India* 23°10N 77°5E **124** H7
Sehwan *Pakistan* 26°28N 67°53E **124** F2
Seia *Portugal* 40°25N 7°43W **88** E3
Şeica Mare *Romania* 46°1N 24°10E **81** E8
Seikan Tunnel *Japan* 41°28N 140°10E **112** D10
Seil *U.K.* 56°17N 5°40W **66** E3
Seiland *Norway* 70°25N 23°15E **60** A20
Seilhac *France* 45°23N 1°45E **72** C5
Seiling *U.S.A.* 36°9N 98°56W **176** C5
Seinäjoki *Finland* 62°40N 22°51E **60** E20
Seine → *France* 49°26N 0°26E **70** C7
Seine, B. de la *France* 49°40N 0°40W **70** C6
Seine-et-Marne □ *France* 48°45N 3°0E **71** D10
Seine-Maritime □ *France* 49°40N 1°0E **70** C7
Seine-St-Denis □ *France* 48°58N 2°24E **71** D9
Seini *Romania* 47°44N 23°21E **81** C8
Seirijai *Lithuania* 54°14N 23°49E **84** D12
Seistan = Sīstān *Asia* 30°50N 61°0E **129** D9
Seistan, Daryācheh-ye = Sīstān,
Daryācheh-ye *Iran* 31°0N 61°0E **129** D9
Seitseminen △ *Finland* 61°55N 23°25E **60** F20
Sejerø △ *Denmark* 55°54N 11°9E **63** J5
Sejerø Bugt *Denmark* 55°53N 11°15E **63** J5
Sejny *Poland* 54°6N 23°21E **83** E10
Sekayu *Indonesia* 2°51S 103°51E **118** E2
Seke *Tanzania* 3°20S 33°31E **142** C3
Sekenke *Tanzania* 4°18S 34°11E **142** C3
Sekhira *Tunisia* 34°20N 10°5E **136** B6
Seki *Turkey* 36°38N 29°33E **99** E11
Sekondi-Takoradi *Ghana* 4°58N 1°45W **138** E4
Sekseūil *Kazakhstan* 47°5N 61°9E **108** C6
Seksna *Russia* 59°13N 38°30E **84** C10
Sekudai *Malaysia* 1°32N 103°39E **121** d
Sekuma *Botswana* 24°36S 23°50E **144** B3
Selah *U.S.A.* 46°39N 120°32E **168** C3
Selama *Malaysia* 5°12N 100°42E **121** K3
Selangor □ *Malaysia* 3°10N 101°30E **121** L3
Selárgius *Italy* 39°16N 9°10E **94** C2
Selaru *Indonesia* 8°9S 131°0E **119** F8
Selatan, Selat *Malaysia* 5°15N 100°20E **121** c
Selawik L. *U.S.A.* 66°30N 160°45W **166** B7
Selb *Germany* 50°10N 12°7E **77** E8
Selby *U.K.* 53°47N 1°5W **66** D6
Selby *U.S.A.* 45°31N 100°2W **172** C3
Selca *Croatia* 43°20N 16°50E **93** E13
Selçuk *Turkey* 37°56N 27°22E **99** D9
Selden *U.S.A.* 39°33N 100°34W **172** F3
Sele → *Italy* 40°29N 14°56E **95** B7
Selebi-Phikwe
Botswana 21°58S 27°48E **145** B4
Selemdzha → *Russia* 51°42N 128°53E **107** D13
Selendi *Manisa, Turkey* 38°43N 28°50E **99** C10
Selendi *Manisa, Turkey* 38°46N 27°53E **99** C9
Selenga = Selenge Mörön →
Asia 52°16N 106°16E **110** A10
Selenge Mörön →
Asia 52°16N 106°16E **110** A10
Selenicë *Albania* 40°33N 19°39E **96** E1
Selenter See *Germany* 54°18N 10°26E **76** A6
Sélestat *France* 48°16N 7°26E **71** D14
Seletan, Tanjung
Indonesia 4°10S 114°40E **118** E4
Selevac *Serbia* 44°28N 20°52E **96** B4
Sélibabi *Mauritania* 15°10N 12°15W **138** B2
Seliger, Ozero *Russia* 57°15N 33°0E **84** D7
Seligman *U.S.A.* 35°20N 112°53W **169** J7
Şelim *Turkey* 40°30N 42°46E **105** B10
Sélima *Sudan* 21°22N 29°19E **137** C2
Selimiye *Turkey* 37°24N 27°40E **99** D9
Selinda Spillway →
Botswana 18°35S 23°10E **144** A3
Sélingué, L. de *Mali* 11°37N 8°14W **138** C3
Selinsgrove *U.S.A.* 40°48N 76°52W **174** F8
Selizharovo *Russia* 56°51N 33°27E **84** D7
Selkirk *Man., Canada* 50°10N 96°55W **163** C9
Selkirk *Ont., Canada* 42°49N 79°56W **174** D5
Selkirk *U.K.* 55°33N 2°50W **65** F6
Selkirk I. = Horse I.
Canada 53°20N 99°6W **163** C9
Selkirk Mts. *Canada* 51°15N 117°40W **160** G8
Sellafield *U.K.* 54°25N 3°29W **66** C4
Sellia *Greece* 35°12N 24°23E **101** D6
Sellières *France* 46°50N 5°32E **71** F12
Sells *U.S.A.* 31°55N 111°53W **169** L8
Sellye *Hungary* 45°52N 17°51E **80** E2
Selma *Ala., U.S.A.* 32°25N 87°1W **177** E11
Selma *Calif., U.S.A.* 36°34N 119°37W **170** J7
Selma *N.C., U.S.A.* 35°32N 78°17W **177** D15
Selmer *U.S.A.* 35°10N 88°36W **177** D10
Selongey *France* 47°36N 5°11E **71** E12
Selouane *Morocco* 35°7N 2°55E **136** A3
Selous □ *Tanzania* 8°37S 37°42E **143** D4
Selowandoma Falls
Zimbabwe 21°15S 31°50E **143** G3
Selpele *Indonesia* 0°1S 130°5E **119** E8
Selsey Bill *U.K.* 50°43N 0°47W **67** G7
Seltso *Russia* 53°22N 34°4E **84** F8
Seltz *France* 48°54N 8°4E **71** D15
Selu *Indonesia* 7°32S 130°55E **119** F8
Sélune → *France* 48°38N 1°22W **70** D5
Selva = La Selva del Camp
Spain 41°13N 1°8E **90** D6
Selva *Argentina* 29°50S 62°0W **190** B3
Selva *Spain* 39°46N 2°54E **100** B9
Selva Lancandona = Montes
Azules △ *Mexico* 16°21N 91°3W **181** D6
Selvagens, Ilhas
Madeira 30°5N 15°55W **134** B2
Selvas *Brazil* 6°30S 67°0W **188** B3
Selwyn L. *Canada* 60°0N 104°30W **163** B8
Selwyn Mts. *Canada* 63°0N 130°0W **160** C5
Selwyn Ra. *Australia* 21°10S 140°0E **150** C3
Selyatyn *Ukraine* 47°51N 25°12E **81** C10
Seman → *Albania* 40°47N 19°30E **96** F1
Semarang *Indonesia* 7°0S 110°26E **118** F4
Semarapura = Klungkung
Indonesia 8°32S 115°24E **119** K18
Sembabule *Uganda* 0°4S 31°25E **142** C3
Sembung *Indonesia* 1°27N 103°52E **121** d
Sembung *Indonesia* 8°28S 115°11E **119** J18
Şemdinli *Turkey* 37°18N 44°35E **105** D11
Sémé *Senegal* 13°41N 13°41W **138** B2
Semenic-Cheile Caraşului △
Romania 45°8N 22°5E **80** F7
Semenivka *Chernihiv,*
Ukraine 52°8N 32°36E **85** F7
Semenivka *Kremenchuk,*
Ukraine 49°37N 33°10E **85** H7
Semenov *Russia* 56°43N 44°30E **86** B7
Semeru *Indonesia* 8°4S 112°55E **119** H15
Semey *Kazakhstan* 50°30N 80°10E **109** B10
Semikarakorsk *Russia* 47°31N 40°48E **87** G5
Semiluki *Russia* 51°41N 39°2E **85** G10
Seminoe Res. *U.S.A.* 42°9N 106°55W **168** E10
Seminole *Fla., U.S.A.* 27°50N 82°47W **179** H7
Seminole *Okla., U.S.A.* 35°14N 96°41W **176** D6
Seminole *Tex., U.S.A.* 32°43N 102°39W **176** E3
Seminole, L. *U.S.A.* 30°45N 84°52W **178** E5
Seminole Draw →
U.S.A. 32°27N 102°20W **176** E3

Semipalatinsk = Semey
  Kazakhstan 50°30N 80°10E 109 B10
Semirara Is. Phil. 12°0N 121°20E 119 B6
Semisopochnoi I.
  U.S.A. 51°55N 179°36E 166 E3
Semitau Indonesia 0°29N 111°57E 118 D4
Semliki → Uganda 0°49N 30°4E 142 B3
Semmering P. Austria 47°41N 15°45E 78 D8
Semnān Iran 35°40N 53°23E 129 C7
Semnān □ Iran 36°0N 54°0E 129 C7
Semporna Malaysia 4°30N 118°33E 119 D5
Semuda Indonesia 2°51S 112°58E 118 E4
Semur-en-Auxois France 47°30N 4°20E 71 E11
Sen → Cambodia 12°32N 104°28E 120 F5
Sena Bolivia 11°32S 67°11W 188 C4
Senā Iran 28°27N 51°36E 129 D6
Sena Mozam. 17°25S 35°0E 143 F4
Sena → Bolivia 11°31S 67°11W 188 C4
Sena Madureira Brazil 9°5S 68°45W 188 B4
Senador Pompeu Brazil 5°40S 39°20W 189 B3
Senaki Georgia 42°15N 42°1E 87 J6
Senang, Pulau Singapore 1°11N 103°52E 121 d
Senanga Zambia 16°7S 23°16E 141 H4
Senatobia U.S.A. 34°37N 89°58W 177 D10
Sencelles Spain 39°39N 2°54E 100 B9
Sendai = Satsuma-Sendai
  Japan 31°50N 130°20E 113 J5
Sendai Japan 38°15N 140°53E 112 E10
Sendai-Wan Japan 38°15N 141°0E 112 E10
Senden Bayern, Germany 48°19N 10°4E 77 G6
Senden Nordrhein-Westfalen,
  Germany 51°52N 7°22E 76 D3
Sendhwa India 21°41N 75°6E 124 J6
Sendurjana India 21°32N 78°17E 126 D4
Sene → Ghana 7°30N 0°33W 139 D4
Senec Slovakia 48°12N 17°23E 79 C10
Seneca U.S.A. 34°41N 82°57W 177 D13
Seneca Falls U.S.A. 42°55N 76°48W 175 D8
Seneca L. U.S.A. 42°40N 76°54W 174 D8
Senecaville L. U.S.A. 39°55N 81°25W 174 G3
Senegal ■ W. Afr. 14°30N 14°30W 138 C2
Sénégal → W. Afr. 15°48N 16°32W 138 B1
Senegambia Africa 12°45N 12°0W 132 E2
Senekal S. Africa 28°20S 27°36E 145 D4
Senftenberg Germany 51°32N 14°0E 76 D10
Senga Hill Zambia 9°19S 31°11E 143 D3
Senge Khambab = Indus →
  Pakistan 24°20N 67°47E 124 G2
Sengerema Tanzania 2°42S 32°35E 142 C3
Senggigi Indonesia 8°29S 116°2E 119 J19
Sengiley Russia 53°58N 48°46E 86 D9
Sengua → Zimbabwe 17°7S 28°5E 143 F2
Senguerr → Argentina 45°35S 68°50W 192 C3
Senhor-do-Bonfim
  Brazil 10°30S 40°10W 189 C2
Senica Slovakia 48°41N 17°25E 79 C10
Senigállia Italy 43°43N 13°13E 93 C5
Senio → Italy 44°35N 12°15E 93 D9
Senirkent Turkey 38°6N 30°33E 99 C12
Senise Italy 40°9N 16°17E 95 B9
Senj Croatia 45°0N 14°58E 93 D11
Senja Norway 69°25N 17°30E 60 B17
Senkaku-Shotō
  E. China Sea 25°45N 123°30E 113 M1
Senlis France 49°13N 2°35E 71 C9
Senmonorom
  Cambodia 12°27N 107°12E 120 F6
Senneterre Canada 48°25N 77°15W 164 C4
Senno Belarus 54°45N 29°43E 84 E5
Sénnori Italy 40°47N 8°35E 94 B1
Seno Laos 16°35N 104°50E 120 D5
Senoia U.S.A. 33°18N 84°33W 178 B5
Senonches France 48°34N 1°2E 70 D8
Senorbì Italy 39°32N 9°8E 94 C2
Senožeče Slovenia 45°43N 14°3E 93 C11
Senqu → Orange →
  S. Africa 28°41S 16°28E 144 C2
Sens France 48°11N 3°15E 71 D10
Senta Serbia 45°55N 20°3E 80 E5
Sentery →
  Dem. Rep. of the Congo 5°17S 25°42E 142 D2
Sentinel U.S.A. 32°52N 113°13W 169 K7
Šentjur Slovenia 46°14N 15°24E 93 D12
Sentosa Singapore 1°16N 103°50E 121 d
Senwabarona S. Africa 23°17S 29°7E 145 B4
Senya Beraku Ghana 5°28N 0°31W 139 D4
Seo de Urgel = La Seu d'Urgell
  Spain 42°22N 1°23E 90 C6
Seogwipo S. Korea 33°13N 126°34E 115 H14
Seohara India 29°15N 78°33E 125 E8
Seonath → India 21°44N 82°28E 125 J10
Seondha India 26°9N 78°48E 125 F8
Seongnam S. Korea 37°26N 127°8E 115 F14
Seoni India 22°5N 79°30E 125 H8
Seoni Malwa India 22°27N 77°28E 124 H8
Seonsan S. Korea 36°14N 128°17E 115 F15
Seoriuarayan India 21°45N 82°34E 126 D6
Seosan S. Korea 36°47N 126°27E 115 F14
Seoul S. Korea 37°31N 126°58E 115 F14
Sepang Malaysia 2°57N 101°44E 121 L3
Separation Pt. N.Z. 40°47S 172°59E 155 A7
Sepīdān Iran 30°20N 52°5E 129 D7
Sepo-ri N. Korea 38°57N 127°25E 115 E14
Sepólno Krajeńskie
  Poland 53°26N 17°30E 82 E4
Sepone Laos 16°45N 106°13E 120 D6
Sepopol Poland 54°16N 21°2E 82 D8
Septemvri Bulgaria 42°13N 24°6E 97 D8
Sepúlveda Spain 41°18N 3°45W 88 D7
Sequeros Spain 40°31N 6°2W 88 E4
Sequim U.S.A. 48°5N 123°6W 168 B3
Sequoia △ U.S.A. 36°30N 118°30W 170 J8
Serafimovich Russia 49°36N 42°43E 85 F6
Seraing Belgium 50°35N 5°32E 69 D5
Serakhis → Cyprus 35°13N 32°55E 102 D11
Seram Indonesia 3°10S 129°0E 119 E7
Seram Sea Indonesia 2°30S 128°30E 119 E7
Serampore = Shrirampur
  India 22°44N 88°21E 125 H13
Serang Indonesia 6°8S 106°10E 119 G12
Serangoon Singapore 1°23N 103°54E 121 d
Serasan Indonesia 2°29N 109°4E 118 D3
Seravezza Italy 43°59N 10°13E 92 C7
Şerbettar Turkey 41°27N 26°4E 107 B10
Serbia ■ Europe 43°20N 20°0E 96 C4
Şercaia Romania 45°49N 25°9E 81 E10
Serdar Turkmenistan 39°4N 56°23E 129 A9
Serdobsk Russia 52°28N 44°10E 86 D7
Serebryansk
  Kazakhstan 49°41N 83°17E 109 E10
Sered' Slovakia 48°17N 17°44E 79 C10

Seredka Russia 58°12N 28°10E 84 C5
Serednye Ukraine 48°32N 22°30E 80 B7
Şereflikoçhisar Turkey 38°56N 33°32E 104 C5
Seregno Italy 45°39N 9°12E 92 C6
Seremban Malaysia 2°43N 101°53E 121 L3
Serengeti □ Tanzania 2°11S 35°0E 142 C3
Serengeti Plain Tanzania 2°40S 35°0E 142 C4
Serenje Zambia 13°14S 30°15E 143 E3
Seret → Ukraine 48°37N 25°52E 81 B10
Sereth = Siret →
  Romania 45°24N 28°1E 81 E12
Sergach Russia 55°30N 45°30E 86 C7
Sergeevka Kazakhstan 53°52N 67°24E 109 B7
Sergen Turkey 41°41N 27°42E 97 E11
Sergeya Kirova, Ostrova
  Russia 77°30N 89°0E 107 B10
Sergino Russia 62°25N 65°12E 106 C7
Sergipe □ Brazil 10°30S 37°30W 189 C3
Sergiyev Posad Russia 56°20N 38°10E 84 D10
Serhetabat
  Turkmenistan 35°20N 62°18E 129 C9
Seria Brunei 4°37N 114°23E 118 D4
Serian Malaysia 1°10N 110°31E 118 D4
Seriate Italy 45°41N 9°43E 92 C6
Sericho Kenya 1°5N 39°5E 142 B4
Sérifontaine France 49°20N 1°45E 71 C8
Sérifos Greece 37°9N 24°30E 98 D6
Sérignan France 43°17N 3°17E 72 E7
Sérigny → Canada 56°47N 66°0W 165 A6
Serik Turkey 36°55N 31°7E 104 D4
Seringapatam Reef
  Australia 13°38S 122°5E 148 B3
Serinhisar Turkey 37°36N 29°18E 99 D11
Serir Indonesia 8°12S 114°56E 119 J17
Serishābād Iran 35°14N 47°30E 105 E12
Serkout Algeria 23°56N 6°47E 136 D5
Sermaize-les-Bains
  France 48°47N 4°54E 71 D11
Sermata Indonesia 8°15S 128°50E 119 F7
Sermersooq □ Greenland 60°0N 40°0W 57 D7
Sermersuaq Greenland 79°30N 62°0W 57 B4
Sérmide Italy 45°0N 11°18E 93 D8
Sernovodsk Russia 53°58N 51°16E 86 D10
Sernur Russia 56°52N 49°2E 86 B9
Serock Poland 52°31N 21°4E 83 F8
Serón Spain 37°20N 2°29W 91 H2
Seròs Spain 41°27N 0°24E 90 D5
Serouenout Algeria 24°18N 7°25E 136 D5
Serov Russia 59°29N 60°35E 106 C10
Serowe Botswana 22°25S 26°43E 144 B4
Serpa Portugal 37°57N 7°38W 89 H3
Serpeddì, Pta. Italy 39°22N 9°18E 94 C2
Serpentara Italy 39°8N 9°36E 94 C2
Serpentine Lakes
  Australia 28°30S 129°10E 149 E4
Serpent's Mouth = Sierpe, Bocas
  de la Venezuela 10°0N 61°30W 187 L15
Serpis → Spain 38°59N 0°9W 91 G4
Serpneve Ukraine 46°18N 29°1E 81 D14
Serpukhov Russia 54°55N 37°28E 84 E9
Serra Brazil 20°7S 40°18W 189 E2
Serra da Canastra △
  Brazil 20°3S 46°50W 189 E1
Serra da Capivara △
  Brazil 8°42S 42°15W 189 B2
Serra da Estrela
  Portugal 40°27N 7°33W 88 E3
Serra das Confusões △
  Brazil 8°50S 43°50W 189 B2
Serra de Mesa, Barragem de
  Brazil 13°35S 48°30W 189 C1
Serra do Cipó △ Brazil 19°14S 43°23W 189 E1
Serra do Divisor △ Brazil 8°3S 73°29W 188 B3
Serra do Navio Brazil 0°59N 52°3W 187 C8
Serra do Salitre Brazil 19°6S 46°41W 189 E1
Serra San Bruno Italy 38°35N 16°20E 95 D9
Serra Talhada Brazil 7°59S 38°18W 189 B3
Serradilla Spain 39°50N 6°9W 88 F4
Serramanna Italy 39°25N 8°55E 94 C1
Serrania San Luís □
  Paraguay 22°35S 57°22W 190 A4
Serrania San Rafael △
  Paraguay 26°30S 56°0W 191 B4
Serras d'Aire e Candeeiros □
  Portugal 39°31N 8°48W 89 F2
Serravalle Scrívia Italy 44°43N 8°51E 92 D5
Serre-Ponçon, L. de
  France 44°22N 6°20E 73 D10
Serréjon Spain 39°49N 5°48W 88 F5
Serres France 44°26N 5°43E 73 D9
Serres Greece 41°5N 23°31E 96 E7
Serrezuela Argentina 30°40S 65°20W 190 C2
Serrinha Brazil 11°39S 39°0W 189 D3
Serrita Brazil 7°56S 39°19W 189 B3
Sersale Italy 39°1N 16°43E 95 C9
Sertânia Brazil 8°5S 37°20W 189 B3
Sertanópolis Brazil 23°4S 51°2W 191 A5
Sêrtar China 32°20N 100°41E 116 A3
Serua Indonesia 6°18S 130°1E 119 F8
Serui Indonesia 1°53S 136°10E 119 E9
Serule Botswana 21°57S 27°20E 144 B4
Servia Greece 40°11N 22°0E 96 F6
Serzedelo Portugal 41°24N 8°14W 88 D2
Ses Salines Spain 39°21N 3°3E 100 B10
Sese Is. Uganda 0°20S 32°20E 142 C3
Sesepe Indonesia 1°30S 127°59E 119 E7
Sesfontein Namibia 19°7S 13°39E 144 A1
Sesheke Zambia 17°29S 24°13E 144 A3
Sésia → Italy 45°5N 8°37E 92 C5
Sesimbra Portugal 38°28N 9°6W 89 G1
Sessa Aurunca Italy 41°14N 13°56E 94 A6
S'Espalmador Spain 38°47N 1°26E 100 C7
S'Espardell Spain 38°48N 1°29E 100 C7
S'Estanyol Spain 39°22N 2°54E 100 B9
Sestao Spain 43°18N 3°0W 90 B2
Sesto Calende Italy 45°44N 8°37E 92 C5
Sesto San Giovanni Italy 45°31N 9°13E 92 C6
Sestri Levante Italy 44°16N 9°24E 92 D6
Sestriere Italy 44°57N 6°56E 92 D3
Sestroretsk Russia 60°5N 29°58E 84 B6
Sestrunj Croatia 44°10N 15°0E 93 D11
Sestu Italy 39°18N 9°5E 94 C2
Setana Japan 42°26N 139°51E 112 C9
Sète France 43°25N 3°42E 72 E7
Sete Cidades △ Brazil 4°0S 41°37W 189 A2
Sete Lagoas Brazil 19°27S 44°16W 189 E2
Setermoen Norway 68°50N 18°19E 60 B15
Sétif Algeria 36°9N 5°26E 136 A5
Sétif □ Algeria 36°10N 5°26E 136 A5
Seto Japan 35°14N 137°6E 113 G8

Setonaikai Japan 34°20N 133°30E 113 G6
Setonaikai △ Japan 34°15N 133°15E 113 G6
Settat Morocco 33°0N 7°40W 136 B2
Séttimo Torinese Italy 45°9N 7°46E 92 C4
Setting L. Canada 55°0N 98°38W 163 C9
Settle U.K. 54°5N 2°16W 66 C5
Settlement, The
  Br. Virgin Is. 18°43N 64°22W 183 e
Settlers S. Africa 25°2S 28°30E 145 C4
Setúbal Portugal 38°30N 8°58W 89 G2
Setúbal □ Portugal 38°25N 8°35W 89 G2
Setúbal, B. de Portugal 38°40N 8°56W 89 G2
Seugne → France 45°42N 0°32W 72 C3
Seul, Lac Canada 50°20N 92°30W 164 B1
Seurre France 47°0N 5°8E 71 F12
Sevan Armenia 40°33N 44°56E 87 K7
Sevan, Ozero = Sevana Lich
  Armenia 40°30N 45°20E 87 K7
Sevana Lich Armenia 40°30N 45°20E 87 K7
Sevastopol Ukraine 44°35N 33°30E 85 K7
Seven Sisters Canada 54°56N 128°10W 162 C3
Sévérac-le-Château France 44°20N 3°5E 72 D7
Severn → Canada 56°2N 87°36W 164 A2
Severn → U.K. 51°35N 2°40W 67 F5
Severnaya Zemlya
  Russia 79°0N 100°0E 107 B11
Severno Kosovo Kosovo 43°29N 21°27E 96 C4
Severo-Kurilsk Russia 50°40N 156°8E 107 D16
Severo-Yeniseyskiy
  Russia 60°22N 93°1E 107 C10
Severo-Zapadnyy □
  Russia 65°0N 40°0E 106 C4
Severobaykalsk
  Russia 55°39N 109°19E 107 D11
Severočeský □ Czechia 50°30N 14°0E 78 A7
Severodonetsk = Syeverodonetsk
  Ukraine 48°58N 38°35E 85 H10
Severodvinsk Russia 64°27N 39°58E 106 C4
Severomoravský □
  Czechia 49°38N 17°40E 79 B10
Severomorsk Russia 69°5N 33°27E 60 B25
Seversk Russia 56°34N 84°49E 106 D9
Sevier → U.S.A. 39°4N 113°6W 168 G7
Sevier Desert U.S.A. 39°40N 112°45W 168 G7
Sevier L. U.S.A. 38°54N 113°9W 168 G7
Sevilla Spain 37°23N 5°58W 89 H5
Sevilla □ Spain 37°25N 5°30W 89 H5
Seville = Sevilla Spain 37°23N 5°58W 89 H5
Seville Fla., U.S.A. 29°19N 81°30W 179 F6
Seville Ohio, U.S.A. 41°1N 81°52W 174 E3
Sevlievo Bulgaria 43°2N 25°6E 97 C9
Sevnica Slovenia 46°2N 15°19E 93 B12
Sèvre-Nantaise →
  France 47°12N 1°33W 70 E5
Sèvre-Niortaise →
  France 46°28N 0°50W 72 B3
Sevsk Russia 52°10N 34°30E 85 F8
Sewa → S. Leone 7°20N 12°10W 138 D2
Sewani India 28°58N 75°39E 124 E6
Seward Alaska, U.S.A. 60°7N 149°27W 160 E2
Seward Nebr., U.S.A. 40°55N 97°6W 172 E5
Seward P., U.S.A. 40°25N 79°1W 174 F5
Seward Peninsula
  U.S.A. 65°30N 166°0W 166 B6
Sewell Chile 34°10S 70°23W 190 C1
Sewer Indonesia 5°53S 134°40E 119 F8
Sewickley U.S.A. 40°32N 80°12W 174 F4
Sexsmith Canada 55°21N 118°47W 162 B5
Seychelles ■ Ind. Oc. 5°0S 56°0E 141 b
Seyðisfjörður Iceland 65°16N 13°57W 60 D7
Seydişehir Turkey 37°25N 31°51E 104 D4
Seydvān Iran 38°34N 45°2E 105 C11
Seyhan → Turkey 36°43N 34°53E 104 D6
Seyhan Baraji Turkey 37°20N 35°18E 104 D6
Seyitgazi Turkey 39°27N 30°43E 99 B12
Seyitömer Turkey 39°34N 29°52E 99 B11
Seym → Ukraine 51°27N 32°34E 85 G7
Seymen Turkey 41°6N 27°57E 97 E11
Seymour Australia 37°2S 145°10E 153 D6
Seymour S. Africa 32°33S 26°46E 145 D4
Seymour Conn., U.S.A. 41°24N 73°4W 175 E11
Seymour Ind., U.S.A. 38°58N 85°53W 173 F11
Seymour Tex., U.S.A. 33°35N 99°16W 176 E5
Seyne France 44°21N 6°22E 73 D10
Seyssel France 45°57N 5°50E 73 C9
Sežana Slovenia 45°43N 13°41E 93 C10
Sézanne France 48°40N 3°40E 71 D10
Sezze Italy 41°30N 13°3E 94 A6
Sfântu Gheorghe Covasna,
  Romania 45°52N 25°48E 81 E10
Sfântu Gheorghe Tulcea,
  Romania 44°53N 29°36E 81 F14
Sfântu Gheorghe, Brațul →
  Romania 44°51N 29°36E 81 F14
Sfax Tunisia 34°49N 10°48E 136 B6
Sfax □ Tunisia 34°40N 10°20E 136 B6
Sha Tau Kok China 22°33N 114°13E 111 a
Sha Tin China 22°23N 114°12E 111 a
Sha Xi → China 26°35N 118°0E 117 D12
Sha Xian China 26°23N 117°45E 117 D11
Shaanxi □ China 35°0N 109°0E 114 G5
Shaba = Katanga □
  Dem. Rep. of the Congo 8°0S 25°0E 140 F5
Shaba → Kenya 0°38N 37°48E 142 B4
Shabeelle → Somalia 2°0N 44°0E 131 G3
Shabestar Iran 38°11N 45°41E 105 C11
Shabla Bulgaria 43°31N 28°32E 97 C12
Shabogamo L. Canada 53°15N 66°30W 165 B6
Shabunda
  Dem. Rep. of the Congo 2°40S 27°16E 142 C2
Shache China 38°20N 77°10E 109 E9
Shackleton Fracture Zone
  S. Ocean 60°0S 60°0W 55 E18
Shackleton Ice Shelf
  Antarctica 66°0S 100°0E 55 C8
Shackleton Inlet
  Antarctica 83°0S 160°0E 55 E11
Shādegān Iran 30°40N 48°38E 129 D6
Shadi China 26°7N 114°47E 117 D10
Shadi India 33°24N 77°14E 124 C7
Shadrinsk Russia 56°5N 63°32E 106 D7
Shady Dale U.S.A. 33°24N 83°34W 178 B6
Shady Grove U.S.A. 30°17N 83°38W 178 E6
Shadyside U.S.A. 39°58N 80°45W 174 G4
Shaffa Nigeria 10°30N 12°6E 139 C7
Shafter U.S.A. 35°30N 119°16W 171 K7
Shaftesbury U.K. 51°0N 2°11W 67 F5
Shaftsbury U.S.A. 43°0N 73°11W 175 D11
Shag Pt. N.Z. 45°29N 170°52E 155 B3
Shag Rocks Atl. Oc. 53°0S 41°0W 56 M7
Shagamu Nigeria 6°51N 3°39E 139 D5

Shagram Pakistan 36°24N 72°20E 125 A5
Shah Alam Malaysia 3°5N 101°32E 121 L3
Shah Alizai Pakistan 29°25N 66°33E 124 E2
Shah Bunder Pakistan 24°13N 67°56E 124 G2
Shahabad Karnataka,
  India 17°10N 76°54E 126 C3
Shahabad Punjab, India 30°10N 76°55E 124 D7
Shahabad Raj., India 25°15N 77°11E 124 G7
Shahabad Ut. P., India 27°36N 79°56E 125 F8
Shahada India 21°33N 74°30E 126 D2
Shahadpur Pakistan 25°55N 68°35E 124 G3
Shahapur India 15°50N 74°34E 127 G2
Shahba' Syria 32°52N 36°38E 130 C5
Shahdād Iran 30°30N 57°40E 129 D8
Shahdād, Namakzār-e
  Iran 30°20N 58°20E 129 D8
Shahdadkot Pakistan 27°50N 67°55E 124 F2
Shahdol India 23°19N 81°26E 125 H9
Shahe China 37°0N 114°32E 116 F8
Shahganj India 26°3N 82°44E 125 F10
Shahgarh India 27°15N 69°50E 124 F3
Shahid Rajaee Port = Bandar
  Shahid Rajaee Iran 27°7N 56°4E 129 E8
Shāhīn Shahr Iran 32°49N 51°32E 129 C6
Shahjahanpur India 27°54N 79°57E 125 F8
Shahpur = Salmās
  Iran 38°11N 44°47E 105 C11
Shahpur Karnataka,
  India 16°40N 76°48E 126 C3
Shahpur Mad. P., India 22°12N 77°58E 124 H7
Shahpur Baluchistan,
  Pakistan 28°46N 68°27E 124 E3
Shahpur Punjab,
  Pakistan 32°17N 72°26E 124 C5
Shahpur Chakar
  Pakistan 26°9N 68°39E 124 F3
Shahpura Mad. P., India 23°10N 80°45E 125 H9
Shahpura Raj., India 25°38N 74°56E 124 G6
Shahr-e Bābak Iran 30°7N 55°9E 129 D7
Shahr-e Kord Iran 32°15N 50°55E 129 C6
Shahr-I Sokhta Iran 30°34N 61°21E 129 D9
Shahrakht Iran 33°38N 60°16E 129 C9
Shahrezā = Qomsheh
  Iran 32°0N 51°55E 129 D6
Shahrig Pakistan 30°15N 67°40E 124 D2
Shahrisyabz Uzbekistan 39°3N 66°50E 109 F7
Shāhrud = Emāmrūd
  Iran 36°30N 55°0E 129 B7
Shahukou China 40°20N 112°18E 114 D7
Shaikhabad Afghan. 34°2N 68°45E 124 B3
Shajapur India 23°27N 76°21E 124 H7
Shajing China 22°44N 113°48E 111 a
Shakargarh Pakistan 32°17N 75°10E 124 C6
Shakawe Botswana 18°28S 21°49E 144 A3
Shaker Heights U.S.A. 41°28N 81°32W 174 E3
Shakhrisabz = Shahrisabz
  Uzbekistan 39°3N 66°50E 109 F7
Shakhtersk Russia 49°10N 142°8E 107 E15
Shakhty Russia 47°40N 40°16E 85 H5
Shakhunya Russia 57°40N 46°46E 86 B8
Shaki Nigeria 8°41N 3°21E 139 D5
Shakir Egypt 27°30N 33°59E 137 B3
Shakotan-Hantō
  Japan 43°10N 140°30E 112 C10
Shaksam Valley Asia 36°0N 76°20E 125 A7
Shali Russia 43°9N 45°55E 87 J7
Shalkar Köli
  Kazakhstan 50°35N 51°47E 86 E10
Shallow Lake Canada 44°36N 81°5W 174 B3
Shalqar Kazakhstan 47°48N 59°39E 108 C5
Shalqar Köli Kazakhstan 50°33N 51°40E 108 A4
Shalskiy Russia 61°48N 35°58E 84 B8
Shaluli Shan China 30°40N 99°55E 116 B2
Shām Iran 26°39N 57°21E 129 E8
Shām, Bādiyat ash Asia 32°0N 40°0E 128 C3
Shamāl Sīnī □ Egypt 30°30N 33°30E 130 C2
Shamattawa Canada 55°51N 92°5W 164 A1
Shamattawa → Canada 55°1N 85°23W 164 A2
Shamil Iran 27°30N 56°55E 129 E8
Shamkhor = Şämkir
  Azerbaijan 40°50N 46°0E 87 K8
Shāmkūh Iran 35°47N 57°50E 129 C8
Shamli India 29°32N 77°18E 124 E7
Shammar, Jabal
  Si. Arabia 27°40N 41°0E 128 E4
Shamo = Gobi Asia 44°0N 110°0E 114 C6
Shamo, L. Ethiopia 5°45N 37°30E 131 F2
Shamokin U.S.A. 40°47N 76°34W 175 F8
Shamrock Canada 45°23N 76°50W 175 A8
Shamrock U.S.A. 35°13N 100°15W 176 C4
Shamva Zimbabwe 17°20S 31°32E 143 F3
Shan □ Myanmar 21°30N 98°30E 123 J21
Shan Xian China 26°50N 116°5E 114 H8
Shanchengzhen
  China 42°20N 125°20E 115 C13
Shāndak Iran 28°28N 60°27E 129 D9
Shandan China 38°45N 101°15E 110 D9
Shandon U.S.A. 35°39N 120°23W 170 K6
Shandong □ China 36°0N 118°0E 115 G10
Shandong Bandao
  China 37°0N 121°0E 115 F11
Shandur Pass Pakistan 36°4N 72°31E 125 A5
Shang Xian = Shangzhou
  China 33°50N 109°58E 114 H5
Shangalowe
  Dem. Rep. of the Congo 10°50S 26°30E 143 E2
Shangani Zimbabwe 19°41S 29°20E 145 A4
Shangani → Zimbabwe 18°41S 27°10E 143 F2
Shangbancheng
  China 40°50N 118°1E 115 D10
Shangcheng China 31°47N 115°26E 117 B10
Shangchuan Dao
  China 21°40N 112°50E 117 G9
Shangdu China 41°30N 113°30E 114 C7
Shanggao China 28°17N 114°55E 117 C10
Shanghai China 31°15S 121°26E 117 B13
Shanghai Shi □ China 31°10N 121°30E 117 B13
Shanghang China 25°2N 116°23E 117 D11
Shanghe China 37°20N 117°10E 115 F9
Shangluo China 33°32N 114°35E 116 H8
Shangqiu China 34°26N 115°36E 116 G8
Shangrao China 28°25N 117°59E 117 C11
Shangri-La = Zhongdian
  China 28°0N 99°42E 116 D2
Shangshui China 33°32N 114°32E 116 H8
Shangsi China 22°0N 107°57E 116 F6
Shangyou China 25°48N 114°32E 117 D10
Shangyu China 30°0N 120°35E 117 C13
Shangzhi China 45°22N 127°56E 115 B14
Shangzhou China 33°50N 109°58E 114 H5

Shani Nigeria 10°14N 12°2E 139 C7
Shānidar Iraq 36°48N 44°14E 105 D11
Shanklin U.K. 50°38N 1°11W 67 G6
Shannon N.Z. 40°33S 175°25E 154 E4
Shannon → Ireland 52°35N 9°30W 64 D2
Shannon ✕ (SNN)
  Ireland 52°42N 8°57W 64 D3
Shannon, Mouth of the
  Ireland 52°30N 9°55W 64 D2
Shannon ∆ Canada 34°35S 116°25E 149 F2
Shannonbridge Ireland 53°17N 8°3W 64 C3
Shannontown U.S.A. 33°55N 80°21W 178 B9
Shanshan China 42°52N 90°10E 110 E7
Shansi = Shanxi □
  China 37°0N 112°0E 114 F7
Shantar, Ostrov Bolshoy
  Russia 55°9N 137°40E 107 D14
Shantipur India 23°17N 88°25E 125 H13
Shantou China 23°18N 116°40E 117 F11
Shantung = Shandong □
  China 36°0N 118°0E 115 G10
Shanwei China 22°48N 115°22E 117 F10
Shanxi □ China 37°0N 112°0E 114 F7
Shanyang China 33°31N 109°55E 114 H5
Shanyin China 39°25N 112°56E 114 F7
Shaodong China 27°15N 111°43E 117 D8
Shaoguan China 24°48N 113°35E 117 E9
Shaoshan China 27°55N 112°33E 117 D9
Shaowu China 27°22N 117°28E 117 D11
Shaoxing China 30°0N 120°35E 117 C13
Shaoyang China 27°14N 111°25E 117 D8
Shap U.K. 54°32N 2°40W 66 C5
Shapinsay U.K. 59°3N 2°51W 65 B6
Shaqlāwah Iraq 36°23N 44°20E 105 D11
Shaqra' Si. Arabia 25°15N 45°16E 128 E5
Shar Kazakhstan 49°35N 81°2E 109 E10
Sharafkhāneh Iran 38°11N 45°29E 105 C11
Sharashova Belarus 52°34N 24°12E 83 F11
Sharavati → India 14°20N 74°25E 127 G2
Sharbaqty Kazakhstan 51°23N 78°17E 109 B9
Sharbot Lake Canada 44°46N 76°41W 175 B8
Shardara, Step
  Kazakhstan 42°20N 68°0E 109 E7
Sharhorod Ukraine 48°45N 28°5E 81 B13
Shari Japan 43°55N 144°40E 112 C12
Sharjah = Ash Shāriqah
  U.A.E. 25°23N 55°26E 129 E7
Shark B. Australia 25°30S 113°32E 149 E1
Shark Bay △ Australia 25°30S 113°30E 149 E1
Sharm el Sheikh Egypt 27°53N 34°18E 137 B3
Sharon U.S.A. 44°56N 72°6W 174 B5
Sharon Mass., U.S.A. 42°7N 71°11W 175 D13
Sharon Pa., U.S.A. 41°14N 80°31W 174 E4
Sharon Springs Kans.,
  U.S.A. 38°54N 101°45W 172 F3
Sharon Springs N.Y.,
  U.S.A. 42°48N 74°37W 175 D10
Sharp Pt. Australia 10°58S 142°43E 150 A3
Sharpe L. Canada 54°24N 93°40W 164 B1
Sharpes U.S.A. 28°26N 80°46W 179 F6
Sharpsville U.S.A. 41°15N 80°29W 174 E4
Sharqi, Al Jabal ash
  Lebanon 33°40N 36°10E 130 B5
Sharqīya, Es Sahrâ esh
  Egypt 27°30N 32°30E 137 B3
Sharr Kosovo 42°5N 20°41E 96 D4
Sharya Russia 58°22N 45°20E 86 A7
Shashemene Ethiopia 7°13N 38°33E 131 F2
Shashi Africa 21°14S 29°20E 143 G2
Shashi Botswana 21°15S 27°27E 145 B4
Shashi → Africa 21°14S 29°20E 143 G2
Shasta, Mt. U.S.A. 41°25N 122°12W 168 F2
Shasta L. U.S.A. 40°43N 122°25W 168 F2
Shatsk Russia 54°5N 41°45E 86 C5
Shatsk Ukraine 51°29N 23°55E 83 G10
Shatsky Rise Pac. Oc. 34°0N 157°0E 156 D7
Shatskyy △ Ukraine 51°30N 23°52E 83 G10
Shatt al Arab Asia 29°57N 48°34E 129 D6
Shatura Russia 55°33N 39°21E 84 E10
Shaumyani = Shulaveri
  Georgia 41°22N 44°45E 87 K7
Shaunavon Canada 49°35N 108°25W 163 D7
Shaver L. U.S.A. 37°9N 119°18W 170 H7
Shaw → Australia 20°21S 119°17E 148 D2
Shaw I. Australia 20°30S 149°2E 150 b
Shawanaga Canada 45°31N 80°17W 174 A4
Shawangunk Mts.
  U.S.A. 41°35N 74°30W 175 E10
Shawano U.S.A. 44°47N 88°36W 172 C9
Shawinigan Canada 46°35N 72°50W 164 C5
Shawmari, J. ash
  Jordan 30°35N 36°35E 130 E5
Shawnee Ga., U.S.A. 32°29N 81°25W 178 C8
Shawnee Okla., U.S.A. 35°20N 96°55W 176 D6
Shay Gap Australia 20°30S 120°10E 148 D3
Shayang China 30°42N 112°29E 117 B9
Shaybārā Si. Arabia 25°26N 36°47E 128 E3
Shayib el Banat, Gebel
  Egypt 26°59N 33°29E 137 B3
Shaykh, J. ash Lebanon 33°25N 35°50E 130 B4
Shaykh Miskīn Syria 32°49N 36°9E 130 C5
Shaykh Sa'd Iraq 32°34N 46°17E 105 F12
Shaykh 'Uthmān
  Yemen 12°52N 44°59E 131 E3
Shāzand Iran 33°56N 49°24E 129 C6
Shazud Tajikistan 37°45N 72°26E 109 F8
Shchekino Russia 54°1N 37°34E 84 E9
Shchigry Russia 51°55N 36°58E 85 F9
Shchors Ukraine 51°48N 31°56E 85 G6
Shchūchīnsk
  Kazakhstan 52°56N 70°12E 109 B8
She Xian Anhui,
  China 29°50N 118°25E 117 C12
She Xian Hebei, China 36°35N 113°48E 116 F8
Shebekino Russia 50°28N 36°54E 85 G9
Shebele = Shabeelle →
  Somalia 2°0N 44°0E 131 G3
Shebenik-Jabllanicë △
  Albania 41°12N 20°28E 96 E4
Sheberghān Afghan. 36°40N 65°45E 109 F7
Sheboygan U.S.A. 43°46N 87°45W 172 D10
Shebshi Mts. Nigeria 8°30N 12°0E 139 D7
Shediac Canada 46°14N 64°32W 165 C7
Sheelin, L. Ireland 53°48N 7°20W 64 C4
Sheenjek → U.S.A. 66°45N 144°33W 166 B11
Sheep Haven Ireland 55°11N 7°52W 64 A4
Sheep Range U.S.A. 36°35N 115°15W 171 J11
Sheerness U.K. 51°26N 0°47E 67 F8
Sheet Harbour Canada 44°56N 62°31W 165 D7
Sheffield N.Z. 43°23S 172°1E 155 D7

Sheffield U.K. 53°23N 1°28W 66 E6
Sheffield Ala., U.S.A. 34°46N 87°41W 177 D11
Sheffield Mass., U.S.A. 42°5N 73°21W 175 D11
Sheffield Pa., U.S.A. 41°42N 79°3W 174 E5
Shegaon India 20°48N 76°47E 126 D3
Shehong China 30°54N 105°18E 116 B5
Shehuen → Argentina 49°35S 69°34W 192 C3
Sheikh Zayed Canal
  Egypt 23°30N 30°15E 137 C2
Sheikhpura India 25°9N 85°53E 125 G11
Shekhupura Pakistan 31°42N 73°58E 124 D5
Sheki = Şaki Azerbaijan 41°10N 47°0E 87 K8
Shekou China 22°30N 113°55E 111 a
Shelburne N.S., Canada 43°47N 65°20W 165 D6
Shelburne Ont., Canada 44°4N 80°15W 174 B4
Shelburne B. Australia 11°50S 142°50E 150 A3
Shelburne Falls
  U.S.A. 42°36N 72°45W 175 D12
Shelby Mich., U.S.A. 43°37N 86°22W 172 D10
Shelby Miss., U.S.A. 33°57N 90°46W 177 E9
Shelby Mont., U.S.A. 48°30N 111°51W 168 B8
Shelby N.C., U.S.A. 35°17N 81°32W 177 D14
Shelby Ohio, U.S.A. 40°53N 82°40W 174 F2
Shelbyville Ill., U.S.A. 39°24N 88°48W 172 F9
Shelbyville Ind.,
  U.S.A. 39°31N 85°47W 173 F11
Shelbyville Ky., U.S.A. 38°13N 85°14W 173 F11
Shelbyville Tenn.,
  U.S.A. 35°29N 86°28W 177 D11
Sheldon Iowa, U.S.A. 43°11N 95°51W 172 D6
Sheldon S.C., U.S.A. 32°36N 80°48W 178 C9
Sheldrake Canada 50°20N 64°51W 165 B7
Shelek Kazakhstan 43°33N 78°17E 109 E9
Shelikhova, Zaliv
  Russia 59°30N 157°0E 107 D16
Shelikof Strait U.S.A. 57°30N 155°0W 166 D9
Shell Lakes Australia 29°20S 127°30E 149 E4
Shellbrook Canada 53°13N 106°24W 163 C7
Shellharbour Australia 34°31S 150°51E 153 C9
Shellman U.S.A. 31°46N 84°37W 178 D5
Shelon → Russia 58°13N 30°47E 84 C6
Shelton Conn., U.S.A. 41°19N 73°5W 175 E11
Shelton Wash., U.S.A. 47°13N 123°6W 170 C3
Shemakha = Şamaxı
  Azerbaijan 40°38N 48°37E 87 K9
Shemonaïkha
  Kazakhstan 50°37N 81°54E 109 B10
Shemsi Sudan 19°2N 29°57E 137 D2
Shen Xian China 36°15N 115°40E 114 F8
Shenandoah Iowa,
  U.S.A. 40°46N 95°22W 172 E6
Shenandoah Pa.,
  U.S.A. 40°49N 76°12W 175 F8
Shenandoah Va.,
  U.S.A. 38°29N 78°37W 173 F14
Shenandoah →
  U.S.A. 39°19N 77°44W 173 F15
Shenandoah △
  U.S.A. 38°35N 78°22W 173 F14
Shenchi China 39°8N 112°10E 114 E7
Shencottah India 8°59N 77°18E 127 K3
Shendam Nigeria 8°49N 9°30E 139 D6
Shendi Sudan 16°46N 33°22E 135 E12
Shendurni India 20°39N 75°36E 126 D2
Shenge S. Leone 7°54N 12°55W 138 D2
Shengfang China 39°3N 116°42E 114 E9
Shëngjergj Albania 41°17N 20°10E 96 E4
Shëngjin Albania 41°50N 19°35E 96 E3
Shengzhou China 29°35N 120°50E 117 C13
Shenjingzi China 44°40N 124°30E 115 B13
Shenmu China 38°50N 110°29E 114 E6
Shennongjia China 31°43N 110°4E 117 B8
Shenqiu China 33°25N 115°5E 114 H8
Shensi = Shaanxi □
  China 35°0N 109°0E 114 G5
Shenyang China 41°48N 123°27E 115 D12
Shenzhen China 22°32N 114°5E 117 F10
Shenzhen Bao'an Int. ✕ (SZX)
  China 22°31N 113°49E 111 a
Shenzhen Shuiku China 22°34N 114°11E 111 a
Shenzhen Wan China 22°27N 113°55E 111 a
Sheo India 26°11N 71°15E 124 F4
Sheopur Kalan India 25°40N 76°40E 124 G6
Shepetivka Ukraine 50°10N 27°10E 75 C14
Shepparton Australia 36°23S 145°26E 153 D6
Sheppey, I. of U.K. 51°25N 0°48E 67 F8
Shepton Mallet U.K. 51°11N 2°33W 67 F5
Sheqi China 33°12N 112°57E 114 H7
Sher Qila Pakistan 36°7N 74°2E 125 A6
Sherborne U.K. 50°57N 2°31W 67 G5
Sherbro → S. Leone 7°45N 12°55W 138 D2
Sherbro I. S. Leone 7°30N 12°40W 138 D2
Sherbrooke N.S., Canada 45°8N 61°59W 165 C7
Sherbrooke Qué.,
  Canada 45°28N 71°57W 175 A13
Sherburne U.S.A. 42°41N 75°30W 175 D9
Shereik Sudan 18°44N 33°47E 137 D3
Shergarh India 26°20N 72°18E 124 F4
Sherghati India 24°34N 84°47E 125 G11
Sheridan Ark., U.S.A. 34°19N 92°24W 176 D8
Sheridan Wyo.,
  U.S.A. 44°48N 106°58W 168 D10
Sheringham U.K. 52°56N 1°13E 66 E9
Sherkin I. Ireland 51°28N 9°26W 64 E2
Sherkot India 29°22N 78°35E 125 E8
Sherlovaya Gora
  Russia 50°34N 116°15E 107 D12
Sherman N.Y., U.S.A. 42°9N 79°35W 174 D5
Sherman Tex., U.S.A. 33°38N 96°36W 176 E6
Sherobod Uzbekistan 37°40N 67°1E 109 F7
Sherpur India 25°34N 83°47E 125 G10
Sherridon Canada 55°8N 101°5W 163 B8
Sherwood Forest U.K. 53°6N 1°7W 66 D6
Sherwood Park
  Canada 53°31N 113°19W 162 C6
Sheslay → Canada 58°48N 132°5W 162 B2
Shethanei L. Canada 58°48N 97°50W 163 B9
Shetland □ U.K. 60°30N 1°30W 65 A7
Shetland Is. U.K. 60°30N 1°30W 65 A7
Shetpe Kazakhstan 44°10N 52°7E 108 E4
Shetrunji → India 21°58N 72°12E 124 J5
Sheung Shui China 22°31N 114°7E 111 a
Shevaroy Hills India 11°58N 78°12E 127 J4
Shevchenko Ukraine 43°35N 29°20E 81 E14
Shevgaon India 19°21N 75°14E 126 D2
Shevishe Iran 35°21N 46°40E 105 E12

Shey-Phoksundo △
Nepal 29°30N 82°45E 125 E10
Sheyang China 33°48N 120°29E 115 H11
Sheyenne → U.S.A. 47°2N 96°50W 172 B5
Shiashkotan, Ostrov
Russia 48°49N 154°6E 107 E16
Shibām Yemen 15°59N 48°36E 131 D4
Shibata Japan 37°57N 139°20E 112 F9
Shibecha Japan 43°17N 144°36E 112 C12
Shibetsu Hokkaidō,
Japan 43°30N 145°10E 112 C12
Shibetsu Hokkaidō,
Japan 44°10N 142°23E 112 B11
Shibīn el Kôm Egypt 30°31N 30°55E 137 E7
Shibīn el Qanâtir Egypt 30°19N 31°19E 137 E7
Shibing China 27°2N 108°7E 116 D7
Shibogama L. Canada 53°35N 88°15W 164 B2
Shibushi Japan 31°25N 131°8E 113 G5
Shicheng China 26°22N 116°20E 117 D11
Shickshinny U.S.A. 41°9N 76°9W 175 E8
Shickshock Mts. = Chic-Chocs,
Mts. Canada 48°55N 66°0W 165 C6
Shidao China 36°50N 122°25E 115 F12
Shiderti → Kazakhstan 52°32N 74°50E 109 B8
Shidian China 24°40N 99°56E 116 E2
Shido = Sanuki Japan 34°19N 134°10E 113 G7
Shiel, L. U.K. 56°48N 5°34W 65 E3
Shieli Kazakhstan 44°20N 66°15E 109 D7
Shifang China 31°8N 104°10E 116 B5
Shiga □ Japan 35°20N 136°0E 113 G8
Shigu China 26°51N 99°56E 116 D2
Shiguaigou China 40°52N 110°15E 114 D6
Shihchiachuangi = Shijiazhuang
China 38°2N 114°28E 114 E8
Shihezi China 44°15N 86°2E 109 E11
Shijak Albania 41°21N 19°33E 96 E3
Shijiazhuang China 38°2N 114°28E 114 E8
Shijiu Hu China 31°25N 118°50E 117 B12
Shikarpur India 28°17N 78°7E 124 E8
Shikarpur Pakistan 27°57N 68°39E 124 F3
Shikohabad India 27°6N 78°36E 125 F8
Shikokochūō Japan 34°1N 133°34E 113 G6
Shikoku □ Japan 33°30N 133°30E 113 H6
Shikoku-Sanchi Japan 33°30N 133°30E 113 H6
Shikotan, Ostrov
Asia 43°47N 146°44E 107 E15
Shikotsu-Ko Japan 42°45N 141°25E 112 C10
Shikotsu-Tōya △ Japan 44°4N 145°8E 112 C10
Shiliguri India 26°45N 88°25E 125 F7
Shiliu = Changjiang
China 19°20N 108°55E 117 a
Shilka Russia 52°0N 115°55E 107 D12
Shilka → Russia 53°20N 121°26E 107 D12
Shillelagh Ireland 52°45N 6°32W 64 D5
Shillington U.S.A. 40°18N 75°58W 175 F9
Shillong India 25°35N 91°53E 123 G17
Shilo West Bank 32°4N 35°18E 130 C4
Shilong China 23°5N 113°52E 117 F9
Shilou China 37°0N 110°48E 114 F6
Shilovo Russia 54°25N 40°57E 86 C5
Shimabara Japan 32°48N 130°20E 113 H5
Shimada Japan 34°49N 138°10E 113 G9
Shimane □ Japan 35°0N 132°30E 113 G6
Shimanovsk Russia 52°15N 127°30E 107 D13
Shimanto Kōchi, Japan 33°12N 133°8E 113 H6
Shimanto Kōchi, Japan 32°59N 132°56E 113 H6
Shimba Hills → Kenya 4°14S 39°25E 142 C4
Shimbiris Somalia 10°44N 47°14E 131 E4
Shimen China 29°35N 111°20E 117 C8
Shimenjie China 29°29N 116°48E 117 C11
Shimian China 29°12N 102°23E 116 C4
Shimizu Japan 35°0N 138°30E 113 G9
Shimla India 31°2N 77°9E 124 D7
Shimodate Japan 36°20N 139°55E 113 F9
Shimoga = Shivamogga
India 13°57N 75°32E 127 H2
Shimokita-Hantō
Japan 41°20N 141°0E 112 D10
Shimoni Kenya 4°38S 39°20E 142 C4
Shimonoseki Japan 33°58N 130°55E 113 H5
Shimpuru Rapids
Namibia 17°45S 19°55E 144 A2
Shimsha → India 13°15N 77°10E 127 H3
Shimsk Russia 58°15N 30°50E 84 C6
Shin, L. U.K. 58°5N 4°30W 65 C4
Shinan China 22°44N 109°53E 116 F7
Shinano-Gawa →
Japan 36°50N 138°30E 113 F9
Shinās Oman 24°46N 56°28E 134 E8
Shindand Afghan. 33°12N 62°8E 122 C3
Shinglehouse U.S.A. 41°58N 78°12W 174 E6
Shingū Japan 33°40N 135°55E 113 H7
Shingwidzi S. Africa 23°5S 31°25E 145 B5
Shinjō Japan 38°46N 140°18E 112 E10
Shinkafe Nigeria 13°8N 6°29E 139 C6
Shinkolobwe
Dem. Rep. of the Congo 11°10S 26°40E 140 G5
Shinshār Syria 34°36N 36°43E 130 A5
Shintuya Peru 12°41S 71°15W 188 C3
Shinyanga Tanzania 3°45S 33°27E 142 C3
Shinyanga □ Tanzania 3°50S 33°30E 142 C3
Shio-no-Misaki Japan 33°25N 135°45E 113 H7
Shiogama Japan 38°19N 141°1E 112 E10
Shiojiri Japan 36°6N 137°58E 113 F8
Shipchenski Prokhod
Bulgaria 42°45N 25°15E 97 D9
Shiphoirt, L. = Seaforth, L.
U.K. 57°52N 6°36W 65 D2
Shiping China 23°45N 102°23E 116 F4
Shippagan Canada 47°45N 64°45W 165 C7
Shippensburg U.S.A. 40°3N 77°31W 174 F7
Shippenville U.S.A. 41°15N 79°28W 174 E5
Shiprock U.S.A. 36°47N 108°41W 169 H9
Shiqian China 27°32N 108°13E 116 D7
Shiqma, N. → Israel 31°37N 34°30E 130 D3
Shiquan China 33°5N 108°15E 116 A7
Shiquan He = Indus →
Pakistan 24°20N 67°47E 124 G2
Shīr Kūh Iran 31°39N 54°3E 129 D7
Shira'awh Qatar 25°2N 52°14E 129 E7
Shirabad = Sherobod
Uzbekistan 37°40N 67°1E 109 F7
Shiragami-Misaki
Japan 41°24N 140°12E 112 D10
Shirakawa Fukushima,
Japan 37°7N 140°13E 113 F10
Shirakawa Gifu, Japan 36°17N 136°56E 113 F8
Shirane-San Gumma,
Japan 36°48N 139°22E 113 F9
Shirane-San Yamanashi,
Japan 35°42N 138°9E 113 G9

Shiraoi Japan 42°33N 141°21E 112 C10
Shīrāz Iran 29°42N 52°30E 129 D7
Shirbīn Egypt 31°11N 31°32E 137 E7
Shire → Africa 17°42S 35°19E 143 F4
Shiretoko △ Japan 44°15N 145°15E 112 B12
Shiretoko-Misaki
Japan 44°21N 145°20E 112 B12
Shirinab → Pakistan 30°15N 66°28E 124 D2
Shiriya-Zaki Japan 41°25N 141°30E 112 D10
Shiroishi Japan 38°0N 140°37E 112 F10
Shirol India 16°47N 74°41E 126 F2
Shiroro Res. Nigeria 9°56N 6°54E 139 D6
Shirpur India 21°21N 74°57E 126 D2
Shirshov Ridge Pac. Oc. 58°0N 170°0E 156 B8
Shīrvān Iran 37°30N 57°50E 129 B8
Shirwa, L. = Chilwa, L.
Malawi 15°15S 35°40E 143 F4
Shishaldin Volcano
U.S.A. 54°45N 163°58W 166 E7
Shishi China 24°44N 118°37E 117 E12
Shishou China 29°38N 112°22E 117 C9
Shitai China 30°12N 117°25E 117 B11
Shivamogga India 13°57N 75°32E 127 H2
Shivpuri India 25°26N 77°42E 124 G7
Shixian China 43°5N 129°50E 115 C15
Shixing China 24°46N 114°5E 117 E10
Shiyan Guangdong,
China 22°42N 113°56E 111 a
Shiyan Hubei, China 32°35N 110°45E 117 A8
Shiyan Shuiku China 22°42N 113°54E 111 a
Shiyata Egypt 29°25N 25°7E 137 B2
Shizhu China 29°58N 108°7E 116 C7
Shizong China 24°50N 104°0E 116 E5
Shizuishan China 39°15N 106°50E 114 E4
Shizuoka Japan 34°57N 138°24E 113 G9
Shizuoka □ Japan 35°15N 138°40E 113 G9
Shkhara Georgia 43°0N 43°8E 105 A10
Shklov = Shklow
Belarus 54°16N 30°15E 75 A14
Shklow Belarus 54°16N 30°15E 75 A16
Shkodër Albania 42°4N 19°32E 96 D3
Shkumbini → Albania 41°2N 19°31E 96 E3
Shmidta, Ostrov Russia 81°0N 91°0E 107 A10
Shō-Gawa → Japan 36°47N 137°4E 113 F8
Shoal L. Canada 49°33N 95°1W 163 D9
Shoal Lake Canada 50°30N 100°35W 163 C8
Shōdo-Shima Japan 34°30N 134°15E 113 G7
Sholapur = Solapur
India 17°43N 75°56E 126 F2
Shōmron West Bank 32°15N 35°13E 130 C4
Shonzhy Kazakhstan 43°32N 79°28E 109 D9
Shoranur India 10°46N 76°19E 127 J3
Shorapur India 16°31N 76°48E 127 F3
Shoreham U.S.A. 43°53N 73°18W 175 C11
Shoreham-by-Sea U.K. 50°50N 0°16W 67 G7
Shori → Pakistan 28°29N 69°44E 124 E3
Shorkot Pakistan 30°50N 72°2E 124 D4
Shorkot Road Pakistan 30°47N 72°15E 124 D5
Shorsky △ Russia 52°40N 88°0E 109 E11
Shorter U.S.A. 32°24N 85°57W 178 E4
Shortt's I. India 20°47N 87°2E 126 D8
Shoshone Calif.,
U.S.A. 35°58N 116°16W 171 K10
Shoshone Idaho,
U.S.A. 42°56N 114°25W 168 E6
Shoshone L. U.S.A. 44°22N 110°43W 168 D8
Shoshone Mts. U.S.A. 39°20N 117°25W 168 G5
Shoshong Botswana 22°56S 26°31E 144 B4
Shoshoni U.S.A. 43°14N 108°7W 168 E9
Shostka Ukraine 51°57N 33°32E 85 G7
Shotover → N.Z. 44°59S 168°41E 155 E3
Shou Xian China 32°37N 116°42E 117 A11
Shouchang China 29°18N 119°12E 117 C12
Shouguang China 37°0N 118°45E 115 F10
Shouning China 27°27N 119°33E 117 D12
Shouyang China 37°54N 113°8E 114 F7
Show Low U.S.A. 34°15N 110°2W 169 J8
Showt Iran 39°12N 44°49E 105 C11
Shpola Ukraine 49°1N 31°30E 85 H6
Shpykiv Ukraine 48°47N 28°34E 81 B13
Shqipëria = Albania ■
Europe 41°0N 20°0E 96 E4
Shreveport U.S.A. 32°31N 93°45W 176 E8
Shrewsbury U.K. 52°43N 2°45W 67 E5
Shri Mohangarh India 27°17N 71°18E 124 F4
Shrigonda India 18°37N 74°41E 126 E2
Shrirampur India 22°44N 88°21E 125 H13
Shropshire □ U.K. 52°36N 2°45W 67 E5
Shtërpcë Kosovo 42°14N 21°1E 96 D5
Shū Kazakhstan 43°36N 73°42E 109 D8
Shū → Kazakhstan 45°0N 67°44E 109 D7
Shuangcheng China 45°20N 126°15E 115 B14
Shuangcheng China 29°12N 112°11E 117 D9
Shuanggou China 34°2N 117°30E 115 G9
Shuangjiang China 23°26N 99°58E 116 F2
Shuangliao China 43°29N 123°30E 115 C12
Shuangshanzi China 40°20N 119°50E 115 D10
Shuangyang China 43°28N 125°40E 115 C13
Shuangyashan China 46°28N 131°5E 115 B15
Shubarqudyq
Kazakhstan 49°13N 56°34E 108 C5
Shubarshī Kazakhstan 48°39N 57°11E 108 C5
Shubrâ el Kheima Egypt 30°6N 31°15E 137 E7
Shubrâ Khît Egypt 31°2N 30°42E 137 E7
Shugozero Russia 59°54N 34°10E 84 C8
Shuguri Falls Tanzania 8°33S 37°22E 143 D4
Shuiding = Huocheng
China 44°8N 80°48E 109 D10
Shuiji China 27°13N 118°12E 117 D12
Shujalpur India 23°18N 76°46E 124 H7
Shukpa Kunzang India 34°22N 78°22E 124 B7
Shulan China 44°28N 127°0E 115 B14
Shulaveri Georgia 41°22N 44°43E 129 D7
Shule China 39°25N 76°3E 109 E9
Shule He → China 40°20N 92°50E 114 B7
Shumagin Is. U.S.A. 55°7N 160°30W 166 D7
Shumanay Uzbekistan 42°33N 58°56E 108 D5
Shumen Bulgaria 43°18N 26°55E 97 C10
Shumerlya Russia 55°10N 46°25E 86 C8
Shunan Japan 34°3N 131°50E 113 G5
Shunde China 22°42N 113°14E 117 F9
Shungay Kazakhstan 48°30N 46°45E 87 F8
Shungnak U.S.A. 66°52N 157°9W 166 B8

Shuo Xian = Shuozhou
China 39°20N 112°33E 114 E7
Shuozhou China 39°20N 112°33E 114 E7
Shuqrā' Yemen 13°22N 45°44E 131 E4
Shūr → Fārs, Iran 30°52N 57°37E 129 D8
Shūr → Kermān, Iran 30°52N 57°37E 129 D8
Shūr → Yazd, Iran 31°45N 55°15E 129 D7
Shūr Āb Iran 34°23N 51°11E 129 C6
Shūr Gaz Iran 29°10N 59°20E 129 D8
Shūrāb Iran 33°43N 56°29E 129 C8
Shūrjestān Iran 31°24N 52°25E 129 D7
Shurugwi Zimbabwe 19°40S 30°0E 143 F3
Shūsf Iran 31°50N 60°5E 129 D9
Shūsh Iran 32°11N 48°15E 105 F13
Shushenskoye Russia 53°19N 91°56E 109 B12
Shushensky Bor △
Russia 52°40N 91°15E 109 B12
Shūshtar Iran 32°0N 48°50E 129 D6
Shuswap L. Canada 50°55N 119°3W 162 C5
Shute Harbour △
Australia 20°17S 148°47E 150 b
Shuya Russia 56°50N 41°28E 86 B5
Shuyang China 34°10N 118°42E 115 G10
Shūzū Iran 29°52N 54°30E 129 D7
Shwebo Myanmar 22°30N 95°45E 123 H19
Shwegu Myanmar 24°15N 96°26E 123 G20
Shweli → Myanmar 23°45N 96°45E 123 H20
Shyamnagar India 13°21N 92°57E 127 H11
Shyghanaq Kazakhstan 45°6N 73°59E 109 C8
Shyghys Qazaqstan □
Kazakhstan 48°30N 82°0E 109 D10
Shymkent Kazakhstan 42°18N 69°36E 109 D7
Shyok India 34°13N 78°12E 125 B8
Shyok → Pakistan 35°13N 75°53E 125 B6
Shyroke Odesa, Ukraine 45°59N 30°5E 81 E15
Shyroke Ternopil, Ukraine 48°13N 23°6E 80 B8
Si Kiang = Xi Jiang →
China 22°5N 113°20E 117 F9
Si Lanna △ Thailand 19°17N 99°12E 120 C2
Si Nakarin Res. Thailand 14°35N 99°0E 120 E2
Si-ngan = Xi'an China 34°15N 109°0E 114 G5
Si Phangnga Thailand 9°8N 98°29E 121 H2
Si Prachan Thailand 14°37N 100°9E 120 E3
Si Racha Thailand 13°10N 100°48E 120 F3
Sa Ket Thailand 15°8N 104°23E 120 E5
Siachen Glacier Asia 35°20N 77°30E 125 B7
Sīah Cheshmeh Iran 39°3N 44°25E 105 C11
Siahaf → Pakistan 29°3N 68°57E 124 E3
Siahan Range Pakistan 27°30N 64°40E 124 F2
Siak Sri Indrapura
Indonesia 0°51N 102°0E 118 D2
Sialkot Pakistan 32°32N 74°30E 124 C6
Siam = Thailand ■ Asia 16°0N 102°0E 120 E4
Sian = Xi'an China 34°15N 109°0E 114 G5
Sian Ka'an → Mexico 19°35N 87°40W 181 D7
Sianów Poland 54°13N 16°18E 82 D3
Siantan Indonesia 3°10N 106°15E 118 D3
Siäreh Iran 28°5N 60°14E 129 D9
Siargao I. Phil. 9°52N 126°3E 119 C7
Siasi Phil. 5°34N 120°50E 119 C6
Siatista Greece 40°15N 21°33E 96 F5
Siau Indonesia 2°50N 125°25E 119 D7
Šiauliai Lithuania 55°56N 23°15E 82 C10
Šiauliai □ Lithuania 55°56N 23°15E 82 C10
Siavonga Zambia 16°33S 28°42E 145 A4
Siaya Kenya 0°4N 34°17E 142 B3
Siazan = Siyäzän
Azerbaijan 41°3N 49°10E 87 K9
Sībā, Gebel el Egypt 25°45N 34°10E 128 E2
Sibang Indonesia 8°34S 115°13E 119 K18
Sibay Russia 52°42N 58°39E 108 B5
Sibayi, L. S. Africa 27°20S 32°45E 145 D5
Šibenik Croatia 43°48N 15°54E 93 E12
Siberia = Sibirskiy □
Russia 58°0N 90°0E 107 D10
Siberia Russia 60°0N 100°0E 102 B12
Siberut Indonesia 1°30S 99°0E 118 E1
Sibi Pakistan 29°30N 67°54E 124 E2
Sibiloi △ Kenya 4°0N 36°20E 142 B4
Sibirskiy □ Russia 58°0N 90°0E 107 D10
Sibirtsevo Russia 44°12N 132°26E 112 B5
Sibiti Congo 3°38S 13°19E 140 E2
Sibiu Romania 45°45N 24°9E 81 E9
Sibiu □ Romania 45°50N 24°15E 81 E9
Sibley U.S.A. 43°24N 95°45W 172 D6
Sibo Sweden 61°13N 16°37E 62 C10
Sibolga Indonesia 1°42N 98°45E 118 D1
Siborongborong
Indonesia 2°13N 98°58E 121 L2
Sibsagar = Sivasagar
India 27°0N 94°36E 123 F19
Sibu Malaysia 2°18N 111°49E 118 D4
Sibuco Phil. 7°20N 122°10E 119 C6
Sibuguey B. Phil. 7°50N 122°45E 119 C6
Sibut C.A.R. 5°46N 19°10E 140 D3
Sibutu Phil. 4°45N 119°30E 119 D5
Sibutu Passage E. Indies 4°50N 120°0E 119 D6
Sibuyan I. Phil. 12°25N 122°40E 119 B6
Sibuyan Sea Phil. 12°30N 122°20E 119 B6
Sic Romania 46°56N 23°53E 81 D8
Sicamous Canada 50°49N 119°0W 162 C5
Sicasica Bolivia 17°22S 67°45W 188 D4
Siccus → Australia 31°55S 139°17E 152 A3
Sichon Thailand 9°0N 99°54E 121 H2
Sichuan □ China 30°30N 103°0E 116 B5
Sichuan Pendi China 31°0N 105°0E 116 B5
Sicilia Italy 37°30N 14°30E 95 E7
Sicily = Sicilia Italy 37°30N 14°30E 95 E7
Sicily, Str. of Medit. S. 37°35N 11°56E 94 F4
Sico → Honduras 15°58N 84°58W 182 C3
Sicuani Peru 14°21S 71°10W 188 D3
Šid Serbia 45°8N 19°14E 80 E4
Sidaoutet Niger 15°36N 7°51E 139 D7
Sidari Greece 39°47N 19°41E 101 A3
Siddhapur India 23°56N 72°25E 124 H5
Siddipet India 18°5N 78°51E 126 E4
Sidensjö Sweden 63°17N 18°17E 62 E12
Sidéradougou
Burkina Faso 10°42N 4°12W 138 C4
Siderno Italy 38°16N 16°18E 95 D9
Sideros, Akra Greece 35°19N 26°19E 101 D8
Sidhauli India 27°17N 80°50E 125 F9
Sidhi India 24°25N 81°53E 125 G9
Sidi Abd el Rahman
Egypt 30°55N 29°44E 137 E6
Sidi Barrâni Egypt 31°38N 25°58E 137 B6
Sidi-bel-Abbès Algeria 35°13N 0°39W 136 A5
Sidi-bel-Abbès □
Algeria 34°0N 0°30W 136 B5
Sidi Bennour Morocco 32°40N 8°25W 136 B3
Sidi Boubekeur Algeria 35°1N 0°4E 136 A4

Sidi Bouzid Tunisia 35°1N 9°16E 136 B5
Sidi Bouzid □ Tunisia 35°0N 9°30E 136 B5
Sidi Haneish Egypt 31°10N 27°35E 137 A6
Sidi Ifni Morocco 29°29N 10°12W 134 C3
Sidi Kacem Morocco 34°12N 5°42W 136 B2
Sidi Omar Egypt 31°24N 24°57E 137 A1
Sidi Slimane Morocco 34°16N 5°56W 136 B2
Sidi Smaïl Morocco 32°50N 8°31W 136 B2
Sidikalang Indonesia 2°45N 98°19E 118 D1
Sidirokastro Greece 41°13N 23°24E 96 E7
Sidlaw Hills U.K. 56°32N 3°2W 65 E5
Sidley, Mt. Antarctica 77°2S 126°2W 55 D14
Sidmouth, C. Australia 13°25S 143°36E 150 A3
Sidmouth U.K. 50°40N 3°15W 67 G4
Sidney Canada 48°39N 123°24W 170 B3
Sidney N.Y., U.S.A. 42°19N 75°24W 175 D9
Sidney Nebr., U.S.A. 41°8N 102°59W 172 E2
Sidney Ohio, U.S.A. 40°17N 84°9W 173 E11
Sidney Lanier, L. U.S.A. 34°10N 84°4W 178 A5
Sido Mali 11°37N 7°29W 138 C3
Sidoarjo Indonesia 7°27S 112°43E 119 G15
Sidon = Saydā Lebanon 33°35N 35°25E 130 B4
Sidra = Surt Libya 31°11N 16°39E 135 B9
Sidra, G. of = Surt, Khalīj
Libya 31°40N 18°30E 135 B9
Siedlce Poland 52°10N 22°20E 83 F9
Sieg → Germany 50°46N 7°6E 76 E3
Siegburg Germany 50°47N 7°12E 76 E3
Siegen Germany 50°51N 8°0E 76 E4
Siem Pang Cambodia 14°7N 106°23E 120 E6
Siem Reap = Siemreab
Cambodia 13°20N 103°52E 120 F4
Siemiatycze Poland 52°27N 22°53E 83 F9
Siemreab Cambodia 13°20N 103°52E 120 F4
Siena Italy 43°19N 11°21E 93 E8
Sieniawa Poland 50°11N 22°38E 83 G5
Sieradz Poland 51°37N 18°41E 83 G5
Sieraków Poland 52°39N 16°2E 83 F3
Sierck-les-Bains France 49°26N 6°20E 71 C13
Sierning Austria 48°2N 14°18E 78 C7
Sierpc Poland 52°55N 19°43E 83 F6
Sierpe, Bocas de la
Venezuela 10°0N 61°30W 187 L15
Sierra Blanca U.S.A. 31°11N 105°22W 176 F2
Sierra Blanca Peak
U.S.A. 33°23N 105°49W 169 K11
Sierra Colorada
Argentina 40°35S 67°50W 192 B3
Sierra de Agalta △
Honduras 15°1N 85°48W 182 C2
Sierra de Andújar △
Spain 38°20N 3°50W 89 G7
Sierra de Aracena y Picos de
Aroche △ Spain 37°53N 6°41W 89 H4
Sierra de Bahoruco △
Dom. Rep. 18°10N 71°25W 183 C5
Sierra de Baza △ Spain 37°20N 2°48W 91 H2
Sierra de Castril △ Spain 37°54N 2°50W 91 H2
Sierra de Espuña △
Spain 37°50N 1°31W 91 H3
Sierra de Grazalema △
Spain 36°31N 5°28W 89 J5
Sierra de Gredos △ Spain 40°17N 5°17W 88 E5
Sierra de Guadarrama △
Spain 40°50N 4°0W 88 E7
Sierra de Hornachuelos △
Spain 37°56N 5°14W 89 H5
Sierra de Huétor △ Spain 37°14N 3°30W 89 H7
Sierra de La Culata △
Venezuela 8°45N 71°10W 183 E5
Sierra de Lancandón △
Guatemala 16°59N 90°23W 182 C1
Sierra de las Nieves △
Spain 36°42N 5°0W 89 J6
Sierra de las Quijadas △
Argentina 32°29S 67°5W 190 C2
Sierra de María-Los Vélez △
Spain 37°41N 2°10W 91 H2
Sierra de San Luis △
Venezuela 11°20N 69°43W 183 D6
Sierra de San Pedro Mártir △
Mexico 31°0N 115°30W 180 A1
Sierra de Yeguas Spain 37°7N 4°52W 89 H6
Sierra del São Mamede △
Portugal 39°17N 7°18W 89 F3
Sierra Gorda Chile 22°50S 69°15W 190 A2
Sierra Grande
Argentina 41°36S 65°22W 192 B3
Sierra Leone ■ W. Afr. 9°0N 12°0W 138 D2
Sierra Leone Basin Atl. Oc. 5°0N 17°0W 56 F10
Sierra Leone Rise Atl. Oc. 7°0N 22°0W 56 F9
Sierra Madre Mexico 16°0N 93°0W 181 D6
Sierra Madre Occidental
Mexico 27°0N 101°0W 180 B3
Sierra Madre Oriental
Mexico 25°0N 100°0W 180 C5
Sierra Mágina △ Spain 37°44N 3°28W 89 H7
Sierra Mojada Mexico 27°18N 103°41W 180 B4
Sierra Nevada U.S.A. 39°0N 120°30W 170 H6
Sierra Nevada Spain 37°3N 3°15W 89 H7
Sierra Nevada △ Spain 37°4N 3°7W 89 H7
Sierra Nevada △
Venezuela 8°35N 70°45W 183 E5
Sierra Nevada de Santa Marta △
Colombia 10°56N 73°36W 183 D5
Sierra Norte de Sevilla △
Spain 37°55N 5°46W 89 H5
Sierra Subbéticas △
Spain 37°26N 4°18W 89 H6
Sierra Vista U.S.A. 31°33N 110°18W 169 L8
Sierras de Cardeña y Montoro △
Spain 38°20N 4°15W 89 G6
Sierras de Cazorla, Segura y las
Villas △ Spain 37°59N 2°45W 91 J2
Sierraville U.S.A. 39°36N 120°22W 170 F6
Sifié Côte d'Ivoire 8°0N 7°31E 77 D3
Sifnos Greece 37°0N 24°45E 98 E6
Sifton Canada 51°21N 100°8W 163 C8
Sifton Pass Canada 57°52N 126°15W 162 B3
Sig Algeria 35°32N 0°12W 136 A3
Sigatoka Fiji 18°5S 177°32E 154 a
Sigean France 43°2N 2°58E 72 E6
Sighetu-Marmaţiei
Romania 47°57N 23°52E 81 D8
Sighişoara Romania 46°12N 24°50E 81 D9
Sigiriya Sri Lanka 7°57N 80°45E 127 L5
Sigli Indonesia 5°25N 96°0E 118 C1
Siglufjörður Iceland 66°12N 18°55W 60 C4
Sigmaringen Germany 48°5N 9°12E 77 G5

Signa Italy 43°45N 11°10E 92 E8
Signakhi = Tsnori
Georgia 41°40N 45°57E 87 K7
Signal de Botrang Belgium 50°29N 6°4E 69 D6
Signal Pk. U.S.A. 33°20N 114°2W 171 M12
Signy I. Antarctica 60°43S 45°36W 55 C18
Signy-l'Abbaye France 49°40N 4°25E 71 C11
31°16N 83°52W 178 D6
Sigsbee Deep
Gulf of Mexico 25°0N 92°0W 56 D1
Sigsig Ecuador 3°0S 78°50W 186 D3
Sigtuna Sweden 59°36N 17°44E 62 E11
Sigüenza Spain 41°3N 2°40W 90 D2
Siguiri Guinea 11°31N 9°10W 138 C3
Sigulda Latvia 57°10N 24°55E 84 D3
Siguniangshan China 31°15N 103°10E 116 B4
Sihawa India 20°19N 81°55E 126 D5
Sihong China 33°27N 118°16E 115 H10
Sihora India 23°29N 80°6E 125 H9
Sihuas Peru 8°40S 77°40W 188 B2
Sihui China 23°20N 112°40E 117 F9
Siikajoki → Finland 64°50N 24°43E 60 D21
Siilinjärvi Finland 63°4N 27°39E 60 E22
Siirt Turkey 37°57N 41°55E 105 D9
Siirt □ Turkey 37°50N 41°50E 105 D9
Sijarira Ra. = Chizarira Ra.
Zimbabwe 17°36S 27°45E 143 F2
Sika India 22°26N 69°47E 124 H3
Sikanni Chief →
Canada 57°47N 122°15W 162 B4
Sikao Thailand 7°34N 99°21E 121 J2
Sikar India 27°33N 75°10E 124 F6
Sikasso Mali 11°18N 5°35W 138 C3
Sikasso □ Mali 10°55N 7°0W 138 C3
Sikeston U.S.A. 36°53N 89°35W 172 G9
Sikhote Alin, Khrebet
Russia 45°0N 136°0E 112 B8
Sikhote Alin Ra. = Sikhote Alin,
Khrebet Russia 45°0N 136°0E 112 B8
Sikia Greece 40°2N 23°56E 96 F7
Sikinos Greece 36°40N 25°8E 99 E7
Sikkim □ India 27°50N 88°30E 123 F16
Siklós Hungary 45°50N 18°19E 80 E3
Sil → Spain 42°27N 7°43W 88 C3
Silacayoapan Mexico 17°30N 98°9W 181 D5
Silale Lithuania 55°28N 22°12E 82 C9
Silandro Italy 46°38N 10°46E 92 B7
Silawad India 21°54N 74°54E 124 J6
Silba Croatia 44°24N 14°41E 93 D11
Silchar India 24°49N 92°48E 123 G18
Şile Turkey 41°10N 29°37E 97 E13
Silent Valley △ India 11°10N 76°20E 127 J3
Siler City U.S.A. 35°44N 79°28W 177 D15
Sileru → India 17°49N 81°24E 126 F5
Silesia = Śląsk Poland 51°0N 16°30E 76 C9
Siletitengiz Köli
Kazakhstan 53°20N 73°10E 109 B8
Silgarhi Doti Nepal 29°15N 81°0E 125 E9
Silghat India 26°35N 93°0E 123 F18
Silhouette Seychelles 4°29S 55°12E 141 b
Sili Burkina Faso 11°37N 2°30W 138 C4
Siliana Tunisia 36°5N 9°22E 136 A6
Siliana □ Tunisia 36°0N 9°20E 136 A6
Silicon Valley = Santa Clara
Valley U.S.A. 36°50N 121°30W 170 J5
Silifke Turkey 36°22N 33°58E 104 D5
Siliguri = Shiliguri
India 26°45N 88°25E 123 F16
Siling Co China 31°50N 89°20E 110 E6
Silistea Nouă Romania 44°23N 25°1E 81 F10
Silistra Bulgaria 44°6N 27°19E 97 B11
Silistra □ Bulgaria 44°6N 27°19E 97 B11
Silivri Turkey 41°4N 28°14E 97 C12
Siljan Sweden 60°55N 14°45E 62 D8
Siljansnäs Sweden 60°47N 14°52E 62 D8
Silkeborg Denmark 56°10N 9°32E 63 H3
Silkwood Australia 17°45S 146°2E 150 B4
Silla Spain 39°22N 0°25W 91 F4
Sillajhuay, Cordillera
Chile 19°46S 68°40W 188 D5
Sillamäe Estonia 59°24N 27°45E 64 A4
Sillé-le-Guillaume France 48°10N 0°8W 70 D6
Silloth U.K. 54°52N 3°23W 66 C4
Sillustani Peru 15°50S 70°7W 188 D3
Silo Greece 41°10N 25°53E 97 E9
Siloam Springs U.S.A. 36°11N 94°32W 176 B6
Silopi Turkey 37°15N 42°27E 105 D10
Siluko Nigeria 6°35N 5°10E 139 D6
Šilutė Lithuania 55°21N 21°33E 82 C8
Silvan Turkey 38°7N 41°0E 105 D9
Silvassa India 20°18N 73°0E 125 D5
Silver City U.S.A. 32°46N 108°17W 169 K9
Silver Cr. → U.S.A. 43°16N 119°13W 168 E4
Silver Creek U.S.A. 42°33N 79°10W 174 D5
Silver L. U.S.A. 38°39N 120°6W 170 G6
Silver Lake Calif.,
U.S.A. 35°21N 116°7W 171 K10
Silver Lake Oreg., U.S.A. 43°8N 121°3W 168 E3
Silver Springs U.S.A. 29°13N 82°3W 179 F7
Silverdalen Sweden 57°32N 15°45E 63 G9
Silvermine Mts. Ireland 52°47N 8°15W 64 D3
Silverton Australia 31°52S 141°10E 152 A4
Silverton Colo.,
U.S.A. 37°49N 107°40W 169 H10
Silverton Tex., U.S.A. 34°28N 101°19W 176 D4
Silves Portugal 37°11N 8°26W 89 H2
Silvi Marina Italy 42°34N 14°5E 93 F11
Silvies → U.S.A. 43°34N 119°2W 168 E4
Silvretta Switz. 46°50N 10°6E 92 B7
Silwa Bahari Egypt 24°45N 32°55E 137 C3
Silz Austria 47°16N 10°56E 78 D8
Sim, C. Morocco 31°26N 9°51W 136 B2
Simaltala India 24°43N 86°33E 125 G12
Simanggang = Bandar Sri Aman
Malaysia 1°15N 111°32E 118 D4
Simao China 22°47N 101°5E 116 F3
Simão Dias Brazil 10°44S 37°49W 189 D11
Simard, L. Canada 47°40N 78°40W 164 C4
Sīmareh → Iran 33°9N 47°41E 105 F12
Simav Turkey 39°4N 28°58E 98 B3
Simav → Turkey 40°23N 28°31E 97 E12
Simav Dağları Turkey 39°30N 29°5E 98 B4
Simba Tanzania 2°10S 37°36E 142 C4
Simbirsk = Ulyanovsk
Russia 54°20N 48°25E 86 C8
Simbo Tanzania 4°51S 29°41E 142 C2
Simcoe Canada 42°50N 80°20W 164 D4
Simcoe, L. Canada 44°25N 79°20W 164 D5

Simdega India 22°37N 84°31E 125 H11
Simeonovgrad Bulgaria 42°1N 25°50E 97 D9
Simeria Romania 45°51N 23°1E 80 E8
Simeto → Italy 37°24N 15°6E 95 E8
Simeulue Indonesia 2°45N 95°45E 118 D1
Simferopol Ukraine 44°55N 34°3E 85 K8
Simi Greece 36°35N 27°50E 99 E9
Simi Valley U.S.A. 34°16N 118°47W 171 L8
Simikot Nepal 30°0N 81°50E 125 E9
Simineh → Iran 36°59N 45°54E 105 D11
Simitli Bulgaria 41°52N 23°7E 96 E7
Simiyu □ Tanzania 2°55S 34°20E 142 C3
Simla = Shimla India 31°2N 77°9E 124 D7
Simlångsdalen Sweden 56°43N 13°6E 63 H7
Simleu-Silvaniei
Romania 47°17N 22°50E 80 C7
Similpal △ India 21°45N 86°30E 125 J12
Simmern Germany 49°59N 7°30E 77 F3
Simmie Canada 49°56N 108°6W 163 D7
Simmler U.S.A. 35°21N 119°59W 171 K7
Simnas Lithuania 54°24N 23°39E 82 D10
Simo älv = Simojoki →
Finland 65°35N 25°1E 60 D21
Simões Brazil 7°36S 40°49W 189 D10
Simojoki → Finland 65°35N 25°1E 60 D21
Simojovel Mexico 17°8N 92°38W 181 D6
Simonette → Canada 55°9N 118°15W 162 B5
Simonstown S. Africa 34°14S 18°26E 144 E2
Simontornya Hungary 46°45N 18°33E 80 D3
Simpang Empat
Malaysia 5°27N 100°29E 121 c
Simplicio Mendes Brazil 7°51S 41°54W 189 D10
Simplonpass Switz. 46°15N 8°3E 77 J4
Simplontunnel Switz. 46°15N 8°7E 77 J4
Simpson Desert
Australia 25°0S 137°0E 150 D2
Simpson Desert △
Australia 24°59S 138°21E 150 C2
Simpson Pen. Canada 68°34N 88°45W 161 D14
Simrishamn Sweden 55°33N 14°22E 63 J8
Simsbury U.S.A. 41°53N 72°48W 175 E12
Simushir, Ostrov
Russia 46°50N 152°30E 107 E16
Sin Cowe I. S. China Sea 9°53N 114°19E 118 C4
Sina → India 17°30N 75°55E 126 F2
Sina Dhago Somalia 5°50N 47°0E 131 F4
Sinabang Indonesia 2°30N 96°24E 118 D1
Sinai = Sînā □ Egypt 29°0N 34°0E 130 F2
Sinai, Mt. = Mûsa, Gebel
Egypt 28°33N 33°59E 128 D2
Sinaia Romania 45°21N 25°38E 81 E10
Sinaloa □ Mexico 25°0N 107°30W 180 C3
Sinaloa de Leyva
Mexico 25°50N 108°14W 180 B3
Sinalunga Italy 43°12N 11°44E 93 E8
Sinan China 27°56N 108°13E 116 D7
Sînandrei Romania 45°52N 21°13E 80 E6
Sinarades Greece 39°34N 19°51E 101 A3
Sincan Turkey 39°36N 32°36E 104 B5
Sincanlı Turkey 38°45N 30°15E 99 C12
Sincelejo Colombia 9°18N 75°24W 186 B3
Sinch'ang N. Korea 40°7N 128°28E 115 D15
Sinch'ŏn N. Korea 38°17N 125°21E 115 E13
Sinclair U.S.A. 41°47N 107°7W 168 F10
Sinclair, L. U.S.A. 33°8N 83°12W 178 B6
Sinclair Mills Canada 54°5N 121°40W 162 C4
Sinclair's B. U.K. 58°31N 3°5W 65 C5
Sinclairville U.S.A. 42°16N 79°16W 174 D5
Sincorá, Serra do
Brazil 13°10S 41°20W 189 C2
Sind = Sindh □ Pakistan 26°0N 69°0E 124 F3
Sind → Jammu & Kashmir,
India 34°18N 74°45E 125 B6
Sind → Mad. P., India 26°26N 79°13E 125 F8
Sind Sagar Doab
Pakistan 32°0N 71°30E 124 D4
Sindal Denmark 57°28N 10°10E 63 G4
Sindangan Phil. 8°10N 123°5E 119 C6
Sindangbarang
Indonesia 7°27S 107°1E 119 G12
Sinde Zambia 17°28S 25°51E 143 F2
Sindelfingen Germany 48°42N 9°0E 77 G4
Sindewahi India 20°17N 79°39E 126 D4
Sindgi India 16°55N 76°14E 126 F3
Sindh = Indus →
Pakistan 24°20N 67°47E 124 G2
Sindh □ Pakistan 26°0N 69°0E 124 F3
Sindhnur India 15°47N 76°46E 127 F3
Sindhuli Garhi Nepal 26°55N 85°58E 125 F11
Sindi India 20°48N 78°52E 126 D4
Sındırgı Turkey 39°14N 28°10E 99 B3
Sindou Burkina Faso 10°35N 5°4W 138 C3
Sine → Senegal 14°10N 16°28W 138 C1
Sinegorskiy Russia 47°55N 40°52E 87 G5
Sinekli Turkey 41°14N 28°12E 97 E12
Sinelnikovo = Synelnykove
Ukraine 48°25N 35°30E 85 H8
Sinendé Benin 10°20N 2°22E 139 C5
Sines Portugal 37°56N 8°51W 89 H2
Sines, C. de Portugal 37°58N 8°53W 89 H2
Sineu Spain 39°38N 3°1E 100 B10
Sinfra Côte d'Ivoire 6°35N 5°56W 138 D3
Sing Buri Thailand 14°53N 100°25E 120 E3
Singa Sudan 13°10N 33°57E 135 F12
Singalila △ India 27°10N 88°5E 125 F13
Singanallur India 11°2N 77°1E 127 J3
Singapore ■ Asia 1°17N 103°51E 121 d
Singapore Changi ✈ (SIN)
Singapore 1°23N 103°59E 121 M4
Singaraja Indonesia 8°7S 115°6E 118 J18
Singatoka = Sigatoka
Fiji 18°8S 177°32E 154 a
Singen Germany 47°45N 8°50E 77 H4
Singida Tanzania 4°49S 34°48E 142 C3
Singida □ Tanzania 6°0S 34°30E 142 D3
Singkaki Indonesia 1°0N 108°57E 118 D3
Singkawang Indonesia 1°0N 108°57E 118 D3
Singkep Indonesia 0°30S 104°25E 118 E2
Singkil Indonesia 2°17N 97°49E 121 L1
Singkuang Indonesia 1°3N 98°55E 121 L2
Singleton Australia 32°33S 151°0E 153 B9
Singleton, Mt. N. Terr.,
Australia 22°0S 130°46E 150 D5
Singleton, Mt. W. Austral.,
Australia 29°27S 117°15E 149 E2
Singö Sweden 60°12N 18°45E 62 D12
Singoli India 25°0N 75°22E 124 G6
Singora = Songkhla
Thailand 7°13N 100°37E 121 J3
Singrauli India 24°7N 82°23E 125 G10

Sinh Ton, Dao = Sin Cowe I.
S. China Sea 9°53N 114°19E 118 C4
Sinharaja Sri Lanka 6°25N 80°30E 127 L5
Sinhgarh India 18°22N 73°45E 126 E1
Sinhŭng N. Korea 40°11N 127°34E 115 D14
Sinis Italy 38°55N 8°25E 94 C1
Siniscóla Italy 40°34N 9°41E 94 B2
Sinj Croatia 43°42N 16°39E 93 E13
Sinjai Indonesia 5°7S 120°20E 119 F6
Sinjajevina Montenegro 42°57N 19°22E 96 D3
Sinjär Iraq 36°19N 41°52E 105 D9
Sinjär, Jabal Iraq 36°23N 41°47E 105 D9
Sinkat Sudan 18°55N 36°49E 137 D4
Sinkiang = Xinjiang Uygur
Zizhiqu □ China 42°0N 86°0E 109 D11
Sinko Guinea 8°53N 8°16W 138 D3
Sinmak N. Korea 38°25N 126°14E 115 E14
Sinmi-do N. Korea 39°33N 124°53E 115 E13
Sinnai Italy 39°18N 9°13E 94 C2
Sinnamary Fr. Guiana 5°25N 53°0W 187 B8
Sinnar India 19°48N 74°0E 126 E2
Sinni → Italy 40°8N 16°41E 95 B9
Sinnuris Egypt 29°26N 30°31E 137 F7
Sinoie, Lacul Romania 44°35N 28°50E 81 F13
Sinop Turkey 42°1N 35°11E 104 A6
Sinop □ Turkey 42°0N 35°0E 104 B6
Sinor India 21°55N 73°20E 124 J5
Sinp'o N. Korea 40°0N 128°13E 115 E15
Sinsheim Germany 49°15N 8°52E 77 F4
Sinsk Russia 61°8N 126°48E 107 C13
Sint-Hubert Belgium 50°2N 5°23E 69 D5
Sint-Niklaas Belgium 51°10N 4°8E 69 C4
Sint-Truiden Belgium 50°48N 5°10E 69 D5
Sintang Indonesia 0°5N 111°35E 118 D4
Sinton U.S.A. 28°2N 97°31W 176 G6
Sintra Portugal 38°47N 9°25W 89 G1
Sintra-Cascais △
Portugal 38°50N 9°25W 89 G1
Sinŭiju N. Korea 40°5N 124°24E 115 D13
Sinyukha → Ukraine 48°3N 30°51E 85 H6
Sinzig Germany 50°32N 7°14E 76 E3
Sio → Hungary 46°20N 18°53E 80 D3
Siocon Phil. 7°40N 122°10E 119 C6
Siófok Hungary 46°54N 18°3E 80 D3
Sion Switz. 46°14N 7°20E 77 J3
Sion Mills U.K. 54°48N 7°29W 64 B4
tSionainn, An = Shannon →
Ireland 52°35N 9°30W 64 D2
Sioux Center U.S.A. 43°5N 96°11W 172 D5
Sioux City U.S.A. 42°30N 96°24W 172 D5
Sioux Falls U.S.A. 43°33N 96°44W 172 D5
Sioux Lookout Canada 50°10N 91°50W 164 B1
Sioux Narrows
Canada 49°25N 94°10W 163 D10
Sipadan Malaysia 4°18N 118°38E 119 D5
Šipan Croatia 42°45N 17°52E 96 D1
Siparia Trin. & Tob. 10°8N 61°31W 187 K15
Sipil Daği □ Turkey 38°35N 27°30E 99 C9
Siping China 43°8N 124°21E 115 C13
Sipiwesk L. Canada 55°5N 97°35W 163 B9
Siple I. Antarctica 73°40S 125°10W 55 D14
Šipovo Bos.-H. 44°16N 17°6E 80 F2
Sipra → India 23°55N 75°28E 124 H6
Sipsongpanna = Xishuangbanna
China 22°5N 101°1E 116 F3
Sipur India 21°11N 85°9E 126 D7
Sipura Indonesia 2°18S 99°40E 118 E1
Siquijor Phil. 9°12N 123°35E 119 C6
Siquirres Costa Rica 10°6N 83°30W 182 D3
Siquia → Nic. 12°10N 84°20W 182 D3
Şīr Abu Nu'ayr U.A.E. 25°20N 54°20E 129 E7
Sir Banī Yās U.A.E. 24°19N 52°37E 129 E7
Sir Edward Pellew Group
Australia 15°40S 137°10E 150 B2
Sir Graham Moore Is.
Australia 13°53S 126°34E 148 B4
Sir James MacBrien, Mt.
Canada 62°7N 127°41W 160 E6
Sira India 13°41N 76°49E 127 H3
Sira → Norway 58°23N 6°34E 63 G12
Siracusa Italy 37°4N 15°17E 95 E8
Sirajganj Bangla. 24°25N 89°47E 125 G13
Sirakoro Mali 12°41N 9°14W 138 C3
Şiran Turkey 40°11N 39°7E 105 B8
Sirasso Côte d'Ivoire 9°16N 6°6W 138 D3
Sirathu India 25°39N 81°19E 125 G9
Sirdān Iran 36°39N 49°12E 105 D13
Sirdaryo □ Uzbekistan 40°30N 68°45E 109 D7
Siren U.S.A. 45°47N 92°24W 172 C7
Sirente-Velino □ Italy 42°10N 13°32E 93 F10
Sirer Spain 38°56N 1°22E 100 C7
Siret Romania 47°55N 26°5E 81 C11
Siret → Romania 45°24N 28°1E 81 E12
Sirghāyā Syria 33°51N 36°8E 130 B5
Şiria Romania 46°16N 21°38E 80 D6
Sirikit Res. Thailand 17°45N 100°34E 120 C3
Sirinat □ Thailand 8°6N 98°17E 121 a
Sirino, Mte. Italy 40°7N 15°50E 95 B8
Sirjan Iran 29°30N 55°45E 129 D7
Sirkali = Sirkazhi India 11°15N 79°41E 127 J4
Sirkazhi India 11°15N 79°41E 127 J4
Sirmans U.S.A. 30°21N 83°39W 178 E6
Sirmaur India 24°51N 81°23E 125 G9
Sirmilik △ Canada 72°50N 80°35W 161 C15
Sirmione Italy 45°30N 10°36E 92 C7
Sirna Greece 36°22N 26°42E 99 E8
Şırnak Turkey 37°32N 42°28E 105 D10
Sirohi India 24°52N 72°53E 124 G5
Sironj India 24°5N 77°39E 124 G7
Siros = Ermoupoli
Greece 37°28N 24°57E 98 D6
Sirpur India 19°29N 79°36E 126 E4
Sirr, Nafud as Si. Arabia 25°33N 44°35E 128 E5
Sirretta Pk. U.S.A. 35°56N 118°19W 171 K8
Sirrī Iran 25°55N 54°32E 129 E7
Sirsa India 29°33N 75°4E 124 E6
Sirsa → India 26°51N 79°4E 125 F8
Sirsi India 14°40N 74°49E 127 M3
Sirsilla India 18°23N 78°50E 126 E4
Sirte = Surt Libya 31°11N 16°39E 135 B9
Siruela Spain 38°58N 5°3W 89 C5
Siruguppa India 15°38N 76°54E 127 F3
Sirur India 18°50N 74°12E 126 F2
Şirvan Azerbaijan 39°59N 48°52E 87 L9
Sirvän → Iran 35°4N 46°50E 105 C12
Sisak Croatia 45°30N 16°21E 93 C13
Sisante Spain 39°25N 2°12W 91 F2
Sisargas, Is. Spain 43°21N 8°50W 88 A2
Sishen S. Africa 27°47S 22°59E 144 C3
Sishui India 35°42N 111°18E 116 D6
Sisian Armenia 39°31N 46°11E 105 C12
Sisimiut Greenland 66°40N 53°30W 57 D5

Sisipuk L. Canada 55°45N 101°50W 163 B8
Sisophon Cambodia 13°38N 102°59E 120 F4
Sisseton U.S.A. 45°40N 97°3W 172 C5
Sissonne France 49°34N 3°51E 71 C10
Sīstān Asia 30°50N 61°0E 129 D9
Sīstān, Daryācheh-ye
Iran 31°0N 61°0E 129 D9
Sīstān va Balūchestān □
Iran 27°0N 62°0E 129 E9
Sisteron France 44°12N 5°57E 73 D9
Sisters U.S.A. 44°18N 121°33W 168 D3
Sisters, The Seychelles 4°16S 55°52E 141 b
Siswa Bazar India 27°9N 83°46E 125 F10
Sitakili Mali 13°7N 11°14W 138 C2
Sitamarhi India 26°37N 85°30E 125 F11
Sitapur India 27°38N 80°45E 125 F9
Siteki Swaziland 26°32S 31°58E 145 C5
Sitges Spain 41°17N 1°47E 90 D6
Sithonia Greece 40°0N 23°45E 96 F7
Sitia Greece 35°13N 26°6E 101 D8
Sítio da Abadia Brazil 14°48S 46°16W 189 C1
Sítio-Ozima Ridge
Pac. Oc. 23°0N 143°0E 156 E6
Sitka U.S.A. 57°3N 135°20W 162 B1
Sitkaing = Sagaing
Myanmar 21°52N 95°59E 123 J19
Sitoti Botswana 23°15S 23°40E 144 B3
Sitra Egypt 28°40N 26°53E 137 B2
Sittang Myit →
Myanmar 17°20N 96°45E 123 L20
Sittard Neths. 51°0N 5°52E 69 C5
Sittensen Germany 53°17N 9°32E 76 B5
Sittingbourne U.K. 51°21N 0°45E 67 F8
Sittoung = Sittang Myit →
Myanmar 17°20N 96°45E 123 L20
Sittwe Myanmar 20°18N 92°45E 123 J18
Situbondo Indonesia 7°42S 113°56E 119 G16
Siuna Nic. 13°37N 84°45W 182 D3
Siuri India 23°50N 87°34E 125 H12
Siutghiol, Lacul
Romania 44°15N 28°35E 81 F13
Sivaganga India 9°50N 78°28E 127 K4
Sivagiri India 9°16N 77°26E 127 K3
Sivakasi India 9°24N 77°47E 127 K3
Sivand Iran 30°5N 52°55E 129 D7
Sivas Turkey 39°43N 36°58E 104 C7
Sivas □ Turkey 39°45N 37°0E 104 C7
Sivasagar India 27°0N 94°36E 123 F19
Sivasamudram India 12°16N 77°12E 127 H3
Sivash Turkey 38°31N 29°42E 99 C11
Siverek Turkey 37°50N 39°19E 105 D8
Sivrihisar Turkey 39°30N 31°35E 104 C4
Siwa, El Wâhât es
Egypt 29°10N 25°30E 137 B2
Siwa Oasis = Sīwa, El Wâhât es
Egypt 29°10N 25°30E 137 B2
Siwalik Range Nepal 28°0N 83°0E 125 F10
Siwan India 26°13N 84°21E 125 F11
Siwana India 25°38N 72°25E 124 G5
Six Cross Roads Barbados 13°7N 59°28W 183 g
Six-Fours-les-Plages
France 43°6N 5°49E 73 E9
Sixian China 33°30N 117°50E 115 H9
Sixmilebridge Ireland 52°44N 8°46W 64 D3
Sixth Cataract Sudan 16°20N 32°42E 135 E12
Siyabuswa S. Africa 25°7S 29°3E 145 C4
Siyah Kuh, Kavīr-e
Iran 32°55N 53°55E 129 C7
Siyāl, Jazā'ir Egypt 22°49N 36°12E 137 C4
Siyang China 33°42N 118°40E 115 H10
Siyāzän Azerbaijan 41°3N 49°10E 87 K9
Siziwang Qi China 41°25N 111°40E 114 D6
Sjælland Denmark 55°30N 11°30E 63 D5
Sjællands Odde Denmark 55°58N 11°24E 63 J5
Sjenica Serbia 43°16N 20°0E 96 C3
Sjeverni Velebit △
Croatia 44°30N 15°15E 93 D12
Sjöbo Sweden 55°37N 13°45E 63 J7
Sjötofta Sweden 57°22N 13°17E 63 G7
Sjötorp Sweden 58°50N 14°0E 63 F8
Sjumen = Shumen
Bulgaria 43°18N 26°55E 97 C10
Sjuntorp Sweden 58°12N 12°13E 63 F6
Skadarsko Jezero Europe 42°10N 19°20E 96 D3
Skadarsko Jezero △
Montenegro 42°10N 19°20E 96 D3
Skadovsk Ukraine 46°17N 32°52E 85 J7
Skælskör Denmark 55°15N 11°18E 63 J5
Skærbæk Denmark 55°9N 8°45E 63 J2
Skaftafell △ Iceland 64°1N 17°0W 60 D5
Skagafjörður Iceland 65°54N 19°35W 60 D4
Skagastølstindane
Norway 61°28N 7°52E 60 F12
Skagaströnd Iceland 65°50N 20°19W 60 D3
Skagen Denmark 57°43N 10°35E 63 G4
Skagern Sweden 59°0N 14°20E 62 E8
Skagerrak Denmark 57°30N 9°0E 63 G2
Skagit → U.S.A. 48°23N 122°22W 170 B4
Skagway U.S.A. 59°28N 135°19W 160 F4
Skala-Podilska Ukraine 48°50N 26°15E 81 B11
Skalat Ukraine 49°23N 25°55E 75 D13
Skalbmierz Poland 50°20N 20°25E 83 D11
Skälderviken Sweden 56°22N 12°30E 63 H6
Skalica Slovakia 48°50N 17°15E 79 C10
Skallingen Denmark 55°32N 8°13E 63 J2
Skalni Dol = Kamenyak
Bulgaria 43°24N 26°57E 97 C10
Skanderborg Denmark 56°2N 9°55E 63 H3
Skåne Sweden 55°59N 13°30E 63 J7
Skåne □ Sweden 56°15N 14°0E 63 H7
Skaneateles U.S.A. 42°57N 76°26W 175 D8
Skaneateles L. U.S.A. 42°51N 76°22W 175 D8
Skänninge Sweden 58°24N 15°5E 63 F9
Skanör med Falsterbo
Sweden 55°24N 12°50E 63 J6
Skantzoura Greece 39°5N 24°6E 98 B6
Skara Sweden 58°25N 13°30E 63 F7
Skärblacka Sweden 58°35N 15°54E 63 F9
Skardu Pakistan 35°20N 75°44E 125 B6
Skärhamn Sweden 58°0N 11°35E 63 F5
Skärhamn Sweden 57°59N 11°34E 63 G5
Skarszewy Poland 54°4N 18°25E 82 B8
Skarvan og Roltdalen △
Norway 63°16N 11°31E 60 E14
Skaryszew Poland 51°19N 21°15E 83 D8
Skarżysko-Kamienna
Poland 51°7N 20°52E 83 G7
Skattkärr Sweden 59°25N 13°40E 62 E7
Skattungbyn Sweden 61°14N 14°56E 62 C8
Skawina Poland 49°58N 19°48E 83 J6
Skebobruk Sweden 59°58N 18°36E 62 C12

Skee Sweden 58°56N 11°19E 63 F5
Skeena → Canada 54°9N 130°5W 162 C2
Skeena Mts. Canada 56°40N 128°30W 162 B3
Skegness U.K. 53°9N 0°20E 66 E8
Skeleton Coast Namibia 20°0S 13°0E 141 J2
Skeleton Coast △
Namibia 20°0S 13°0E 144 A1
Skellefteå Sweden 64°45N 20°50E 60 D19
Skellefteälven →
Sweden 64°45N 21°10E 60 D19
Skelleftehamn Sweden 64°40N 21°9E 60 D19
Skellig Michael = Great Skellig
Ireland 51°47N 10°33W 64 E1
Skender Vakuf Bos.-H. 44°29N 17°22E 80 F2
Skënderaj Kosovo 42°45N 20°47E 96 D4
Skerries Ireland 53°35N 6°8W 64 C5
Skerries, The U.K. 53°25N 4°36W 66 D3
Skidegate Canada 53°15N 132°1W 162 C2
Skidra Greece 40°46N 22°10E 96 F6
Skien Norway 59°12N 9°35E 61 G13
Skierniewice Poland 51°58N 20°10E 83 G7
Skikda Algeria 36°50N 6°58E 136 A7
Skikda □ Algeria 36°45N 6°50E 136 A5
Skillingaryd Sweden 57°27N 14°5E 63 G8
Skillinge Sweden 55°30N 14°16E 63 J8
Skilloura Cyprus 35°14N 33°10E 101 D12
Skinari, Akra Greece 37°56N 20°42E 98 D2
Skinnskatteberg Sweden 59°50N 15°42E 62 E9
Skipton Australia 37°39S 143°40E 152 D5
Skipton U.K. 53°58N 2°3W 66 E5
Skiring, C. Senegal 12°26N 16°46W 138 C1
Skírmish Pt. Australia 11°59S 134°17E 150 A1
Skíros = Skyros Greece 38°55N 24°34E 98 B6
Skivarp Sweden 55°26N 13°34E 63 J7
Skive Denmark 56°33N 9°2E 63 H3
Skjálfandafljót →
Iceland 65°59N 17°25W 60 D5
Skjálfandi Iceland 66°5N 17°30W 60 C5
Skjern Denmark 55°57N 8°30E 63 J2
Skjern → Denmark 55°50N 8°30E 63 H2
Škocjanske Jame
Slovenia 45°40N 14°0E 93 C10
Skoczów Poland 49°49N 18°45E 83 J5
Škofja Loka Slovenia 46°9N 14°19E 93 B11
Skoghall Sweden 59°20N 13°30E 62 E7
Skogstorp Sweden 59°19N 16°29E 62 E10
Skoki Poland 52°40N 17°11E 83 F4
Skole Ukraine 49°3N 23°30E 75 D12
Skopelos Greece 39°9N 23°47E 98 B5
Skopi Greece 35°11N 26°2E 101 D8
Skopin Russia 53°55N 39°32E 84 F10
Skopje Macedonia 42°1N 21°26E 96 D5
Skopje ✈ (SKP)
Macedonia 41°59N 21°29E 96 E5
Skórcz Poland 53°47N 18°30E 82 E5
Skørping Denmark 56°50N 9°53E 63 H3
Skövde Sweden 58°24N 13°50E 63 F7
Skovorodino Russia 54°0N 124°0E 107 D13
Skowhegan U.S.A. 44°46N 69°43W 173 C19
Skradin Croatia 43°52N 15°53E 93 E12
Skrea Sweden 56°53N 12°34E 63 H6
Skrunda Latvia 56°41N 22°1E 82 B9
Skrwa → Poland 52°35N 19°32E 83 F6
Skuleskogen △ Sweden 63°6N 18°30E 62 A12
Skull Ireland 51°32N 9°34W 64 E2
Skultorp Sweden 58°24N 13°51E 63 F7
Skultuna Sweden 59°43N 16°25E 62 E10
Skunk → U.S.A. 40°42N 91°7W 172 E8
Skuodas Lithuania 56°16N 21°33E 82 B8
Skurup Sweden 55°28N 13°30E 63 J7
Skutskär Sweden 60°37N 17°25E 62 B11
Skvyra Ukraine 49°44N 29°40E 75 D15
Skwierzyna Poland 52°33N 15°30E 83 F2
Skye U.K. 57°15N 6°10W 65 D2
Skykomish U.S.A. 47°42N 121°22W 168 C3
Skyring, Seno Chile 52°35S 72°0W 192 D3
Skyropoula Greece 38°50N 24°4E 98 C6
Skyros Greece 38°55N 24°34E 98 B6
Skyttorp Sweden 60°5N 17°44E 62 C11
Slade Point Australia 21°4S 149°13E 150 b
Slade Pt. Australia 21°4S 149°13E 150 b
Slættaratindur Faroe Is. 62°18N 7°1W 60 E9
Slagelse Denmark 55°23N 11°19E 63 J5
Slamet Indonesia 7°16S 109°8E 119 G13
Slanchev Bryag
Bulgaria 42°40N 27°41E 97 D11
Slane Ireland 53°42N 6°33W 64 C5
Slaney → Ireland 52°26N 6°33W 64 D5
Slangberge S. Africa 31°32S 20°48E 144 D3
Slánic Romania 45°14N 25°58E 81 E10
Slano Croatia 42°48N 17°53E 96 D1
Slantsy Russia 59°7N 28°5E 84 C5
Slaný Czechia 50°13N 14°6E 78 A7
Śląsk Poland 51°0N 16°30E 74 C9
Śląskie □ Poland 50°30N 19°0E 83 H6
Slătbaken Sweden 58°25N 16°48E 63 F9
Slate Is. Canada 48°40N 87°0W 164 C2
Slatina Croatia 45°42N 17°45E 80 E2
Slatina Romania 44°28N 24°22E 81 F9
Slatina Timiş Romania 45°15N 22°17E 80 E7
Slatington U.S.A. 40°45N 75°37W 175 F9
Slaton U.S.A. 33°26N 101°39W 176 E4
Slave → Canada 61°18N 113°39W 162 A6
Slave Coast W. Afr. 6°0N 2°30E 139 D5
Slave Lake Canada 55°17N 114°43W 162 A5
Slave River Canada 61°11N 115°56W 162 A5
Slavgorod Russia 53°1N 78°37E 109 D9
Slavinja Serbia 43°5N 22°50E 96 C7
Slavkov u Brna Czechia 49°10N 16°52E 79 B9
Slavkovský Les □ Czechia 50°10N 12°43E 78 A5
Slavonia = Slavonija Europe 45°20N 17°40E 80 E2
Slavonski Brod Croatia 45°11N 18°1E 80 E3
Slavsk Russia 55°3N 21°41E 82 C8
Slavske Ukraine 48°51N 23°27E 81 B8
Slavuta Ukraine 50°15N 27°2E 75 C14
Slavyanka Russia 42°53N 131°21E 112 C5
Slavyanovo Bulgaria 43°28N 24°53E 97 C8
Slavyansk = Slovyansk
Ukraine 48°55N 37°36E 85 H9
Slavyansk-na-Kubani
Russia 45°15N 38°11E 85 K10
Sława Poland 51°52N 16°2E 83 G3
Slawharad Belarus 53°27N 31°0E 75 B16

Sławno Poland 54°20N 16°41E 82 D3
Sławoborze Poland 53°55N 15°42E 82 E2
Slea Hd. Ireland 52°6N 10°27W 64 D1
Sleaford U.K. 53°0N 0°24W 66 D7
Sleaford B. Australia 34°55S 135°45E 151 E2
Sleat, Sd. of U.K. 57°5N 5°47W 65 D3
Sleeper Is. Canada 58°30N 81°0W 161 F15
Sleeping Bear Dunes △
U.S.A. 44°50N 86°5W 172 C10
Sleepy Eye U.S.A. 44°18N 94°43W 172 C6
Slemon L. Canada 63°13N 116°4W 162 A5
Ślesin Poland 52°22N 18°14E 83 F5
Slide Mt. U.S.A. 42°0N 74°25W 175 E10
Slidell U.S.A. 30°17N 89°47W 177 F10
Sliema Malta 35°55N 14°30E 101 D2
Slieve Aughty Ireland 53°4N 8°30W 64 C3
Slieve Bloom Ireland 53°4N 7°40W 64 C4
Slieve Donard U.K. 54°11N 5°55W 64 B6
Slieve Gamph Ireland 54°6N 9°0W 64 B3
Slieve Gullion U.K. 54°7N 6°26W 64 B5
Slieve League Ireland 54°40N 8°42W 64 B3
Slieve Mish Ireland 52°12N 9°50W 64 D2
Slievenamon Ireland 52°25N 7°34W 64 D4
Sligeach = Sligo Greece 54°16N 8°28W 64 B3
Sligo Ireland 54°16N 8°28W 64 B3
Sligo U.S.A. 41°6N 79°29W 174 E5
Sligo □ Ireland 54°8N 8°42W 64 B3
Sligo B. Ireland 54°18N 8°40W 64 B3
Slippery Rock U.S.A. 41°4N 80°3W 174 E4
Slite Sweden 57°42N 18°48E 63 H13
Sliters □ Latvia 57°41N 22°21E 82 A9
Sliven Bulgaria 42°42N 26°19E 97 D10
Slivnitsa Bulgaria 42°50N 23°0E 96 C7
Sljeme Croatia 45°57N 15°58E 93 C12
Sloan U.S.A. 35°57N 115°13W 171 K11
Sloansville U.S.A. 42°45N 74°22W 175 D10
Slobidka Ukraine 47°54N 29°21E 81 C14
Slobozia Moldova 46°45N 29°42E 81 D14
Slobozia Arges, Romania 44°30N 25°14E 81 F10
Slobozia Ialomița,
Romania 44°34N 27°23E 81 F12
Slocan Canada 49°48N 117°28W 162 D5
Slochteren Neths. 53°12N 6°48E 69 A6
Slomniki Poland 50°16N 20°4E 83 H7
Slonim Belarus 53°4N 25°19E 75 B13
Slonim Belarus 53°4N 25°19E 75 B13
Slough U.K. 51°30N 0°36W 67 F7
Slough □ U.K. 51°30N 0°36W 67 F7
Sloughhouse U.S.A. 38°26N 121°12W 170 G5
Slovak Rep. = Slovakia ■
Europe 48°30N 20°0E 79 C13
Slovakia ■ Europe 48°30N 20°0E 79 C13
Slovakian Ore Mts. = Slovenské
Rudohorie Slovakia 48°45N 20°0E 79 C12
Slovenia ■ Europe 45°58N 14°30E 93 C11
Slovenija = Slovenia ■
Europe 45°58N 14°30E 93 C11
Slovenj Gradec Slovenia 46°31N 15°5E 93 B12
Slovenska = Slovakia ■
Europe 48°30N 20°0E 79 C13
Slovenska Bistrica
Slovenia 46°24N 15°35E 93 B12
Slovenské Konjice
Slovenia 46°20N 15°28E 93 B12
Slovenské Rudohorie
Slovakia 48°45N 20°0E 79 C12
Slovyansk Ukraine 48°55N 37°36E 85 H9
Słowiński △ Poland 54°43N 17°26E 82 D4
Słubice Poland 52°22N 14°35E 83 F1
Sluch → Ukraine 51°37N 26°38E 75 C14
Sluis Neths. 51°18N 3°23E 69 C3
Slunj Croatia 45°6N 15°33E 93 C12
Słupca Poland 52°15N 17°52E 83 F4
Słupia → Poland 54°35N 16°51E 82 D3
Słupsk Poland 54°30N 17°3E 82 D4
Slurry S. Africa 25°49S 25°42E 144 C4
Slutsk Belarus 53°2N 27°31E 75 B14
Slyudyanka Russia 51°40N 103°40E 107 D11
Småland Sweden 57°15N 15°25E 63 H9
Smålandsfarvandet
Denmark 55°10N 11°20E 63 J5
Smålandsstenar Sweden 57°10N 13°25E 63 H7
Smalltree L. Canada 61°0N 105°0W 163 A8
Smallwood Res. Canada 54°5N 64°30W 165 B7
Smarhon Belarus 54°20N 26°24E 75 A14
Smarje Slovenia 46°15N 15°34E 93 B12
Smartt Syndicate Dam
S. Africa 30°45S 23°10E 144 D3
Smartville U.S.A. 39°13N 121°18W 170 F5
Smeaton Canada 53°30N 104°49W 163 C8
Smedby Sweden 56°41N 16°13E 63 H10
Smederevo Serbia 44°40N 20°57E 96 B4
Smederevska Palanka
Serbia 44°22N 20°58E 96 B4
Smedjebacken Sweden 60°8N 15°25E 62 D9
Smela = Smila Ukraine 49°15N 31°58E 85 H6
Smeralda, Costa Italy 41°5N 9°35E 94 A2
Smerwick Harbour
Ireland 52°12N 10°23W 64 D1
Smethport U.S.A. 41°49N 78°27W 174 E6
Smidovich Russia 48°36N 133°49E 107 E14
Šmigiel Poland 52°1N 16°32E 83 F3
Smith Canada 55°10N 114°0W 162 B6
Smith Center U.S.A. 39°47N 98°47W 172 F4
Smith I. Canada 60°45N 78°25W 161 E16
Smith I. U.S.A. 38°0N 76°0W 174 F8
Smith Islands △
Australia 20°40S 149°9E 150 b
Smith River △ U.S.A. 41°55N 124°0W 168 F2
Smith Sd. N. Amer. 78°25N 74°0W 57 B3
Smithburne →
Australia 17°3S 140°57E 150 B3
Smithers Canada 54°45N 127°10W 162 C3
Smithfield S. Africa 30°9S 26°30E 145 D4
Smithfield N.C.,
U.S.A. 35°31N 78°21W 177 D11
Smithfield Utah,
U.S.A. 41°50N 111°50W 168 F8
Smiths Falls Canada 44°55N 76°0W 165 E15
Smithton Australia 40°53S 145°6E 151 G4
Smithville Canada 43°6N 79°33W 174 C5
Smithville Ga., U.S.A. 31°54N 84°15W 178 E5
Smithville Tex., U.S.A. 30°1N 97°10W 176 F6
Smoke Creek Desert
U.S.A. 40°30N 119°40W 168 F4
Smoky → Canada 56°10N 117°21W 162 B5

Smoky Bay Australia 32°22S 134°13E 151 E1
Smoky Hill → U.S.A. 39°4N 96°48E 172 F6
Smoky Hills U.S.A. 39°15N 99°30W 172 F4
Smoky Lake Canada 54°10N 112°30W 162 C6
Smøla Norway 63°23N 8°3E 60 E13
Smolensk Russia 54°45N 32°5E 84 E7
Smolensk □ Russia 55°20N 33°0E 84 E7
Smolenskoye Poozerye △
Russia 55°35N 31°50E 84 E6
Smolikas, Oros Greece 40°9N 20°58E 96 F4
Smolnik Slovakia 48°43N 20°44E 79 C13
Smolny △ Russia 55°17N 85°10W 177 D12
Smolyan Bulgaria 41°36N 24°38E 97 E8
Smolyan □ Bulgaria 41°36N 24°38E 97 E8
Smooth Rock Falls
Canada 49°17N 81°37W 164 C3
Smoothstone L.
Canada 54°40N 106°50W 163 C7
Smorgon = Smarhon
Belarus 54°20N 26°24E 75 A14
Smotrych Ukraine 48°57N 26°33E 81 B11
Smotrych → Ukraine 48°36N 26°39E 81 B11
Smulți Romania 45°57N 27°44E 81 E12
Smyadovo Bulgaria 43°2N 27°1E 97 C11
Smygehamn Sweden 55°21N 13°22E 63 J7
Smygehuk Sweden 55°20N 13°20E 63 J7
Smyley I. Antarctica 72°55S 78°0W 55 D17
Smyrna = İzmir Turkey 38°25N 27°8E 99 C9
Smyrna Del., U.S.A. 39°18N 75°36W 173 F16
Smyrna Ga., U.S.A. 33°53N 84°31W 178 B5
Snæfell Iceland 64°48N 15°34W 60 D6
Snaefell I. of Man 54°16N 4°27W 66 C3
Snæfellsjökull Iceland 64°49N 23°46W 60 D2
Snake → U.S.A. 46°12N 119°2W 168 C4
Snake I. = Zmiinyi, Ostriv
Black Sea 45°15N 30°12E 85 K6
Snake I. Australia 38°47S 146°33E 153 E7
Snake Range U.S.A. 39°0N 114°20W 168 G6
Snake River Plain
U.S.A. 42°50N 114°0W 168 E7
Snasahögarna Sweden 63°13N 12°21E 62 A6
Snåsavatnet Norway 64°12N 12°0E 60 D15
Snedsted Denmark 56°55N 8°32E 63 H2
Sneek Neths. 53°2N 5°40E 69 A5
Sneem Ireland 51°50N 9°54W 64 E2
Sneeuberge S. Africa 31°46S 24°20E 144 D3
Snejbjerg Denmark 56°8N 8°54E 63 H2
Snelling Calif., U.S.A. 37°31N 120°26W 170 H6
Snelling S.C., U.S.A. 33°15N 81°17W 178 B8
Snells Beach N.Z. 36°25S 174°44E 154 C3
Sneznoye Ukraine 48°0N 38°58E 85 J10
Snežka Europe 50°41N 15°50E 83 A8
Snežnik Slovenia 45°36N 14°35E 93 C11
Śniadowo Poland 53°2N 22°0E 83 E8
Śniardwy, Jezioro Poland 53°48N 21°50E 82 E8
Śnieżka Europe 50°44N 15°44E 78 A8
Snigirevka = Snihurivka
Ukraine 47°2N 32°49E 85 J7
Snihurivka Ukraine 47°2N 32°49E 85 J7
Snina Slovakia 48°58N 22°9E 79 C15
Snizort, L. U.K. 57°33N 6°28E 65 D2
Snøhetta Norway 62°19N 9°16E 60 E13
Snohomish U.S.A. 47°55N 122°6W 170 C4
Snoqualmie U.S.A. 47°31N 121°49W 170 C5
Snoqualmie Pass
U.S.A. 47°25N 121°25W 170 C5
Snoul Cambodia 12°4N 106°26E 121 F6
Snover U.S.A. 43°27N 82°58W 173 D12
Snow Hill U.S.A. 38°11N 75°24W 173 F16
Snow Lake Canada 54°52N 100°3W 163 C8
Snow Mt. Calif.,
U.S.A. 39°23N 122°45W 170 F4
Snow Mt. Maine,
U.S.A. 45°18N 70°48W 175 A14
Snow Shoe U.S.A. 41°2N 77°57W 174 E7
Snowbird L. Canada 60°45N 103°0W 163 A8
Snowdon U.K. 53°4N 4°5W 66 D3
Snowdonia △ U.K. 53°7N 3°59W 66 D4
Snowdoun U.S.A. 32°15N 86°18W 178 C3
Snowdrift = Lutsel K'e
Canada 62°24N 110°44W 163 A6
Snowflake U.S.A. 34°30N 110°5W 169 J8
Snowshoe Pk. U.S.A. 48°13N 115°41W 168 B6
Snowtown Australia 33°46S 138°14E 152 B3
Snowville U.S.A. 41°58N 112°43W 168 F7
Snowy → Australia 37°46S 148°30E 153 D8
Snowy Mt. U.S.A. 43°42N 74°23W 175 C10
Snowy Mts. Australia 36°30S 148°20E 153 D8
Snowy River △
Australia 37°15S 147°29E 153 D7
Snug Corner Bahamas 22°33N 73°52W 183 B5
Snug Harbour Canada 45°22N 80°17W 174 A4
Snyatyn Ukraine 48°27N 25°38E 81 B10
Snyder Okla., U.S.A. 34°40N 98°57W 176 D5
Snyder Tex., U.S.A. 32°44N 100°55W 176 E4
Soalala Madag. 16°6S 45°20E 141 H9
Soan → Pakistan 33°1N 71°44E 124 C4
Soar → Romania 45°56N 24°55E 81 E9
Soba Nigeria 10°58N 8°4E 139 C6
Sobat → South Sudan 9°22N 31°33E 135 G12
Sobëslav Czechia 49°16N 14°45E 78 B7
Sobhapur India 22°47N 78°17E 124 H8
Sobinka Russia 56°0N 40°0E 84 C11
Sobótka Poland 50°54N 16°44E 83 H3
Sobra Croatia 42°44N 17°34E 93 F14
Sobradinho, Represa de
Brazil 9°30S 42°0W 189 B2
Sobral Brazil 3°50S 40°20W 188 B3
Sobrance Slovakia 48°45N 22°11E 79 C15
Sobreira Formosa
Portugal 39°46N 7°51W 88 F3
Soc Giang Vietnam 22°54N 106°1E 116 F6
Soc Trang Vietnam 9°37N 105°50E 121 H5
Soča → Europe 46°20N 13°40E 78 E6
Sochaczew Poland 52°15N 20°13E 83 F7
Soch'e = Shache China 38°20N 77°10E 109 E8
Sochi Russia 43°35N 39°40E 87 A3
Sochi ✈ (AER) Russia 43°27N 39°57E 87 A3
Sochos Greece 40°49N 23°22E 96 F6
Social Circle U.S.A. 33°41N 83°43W 178 B6
Société, Îs. de la
French Polynesia 17°0S 151°0W 157 J12
Society Hill U.S.A. 34°30N 79°33W 174 C5
Society Is. = Société, Îs. de la
French Polynesia 17°0S 151°0W 157 J12
Socompa, Portezuelo de
Chile 24°27S 68°18W 190 A2
Socorro N. Mex.,
U.S.A. 34°4N 106°54W 169 J10

Socorro Tex., U.S.A. 31°39N 106°18W 176 F1
Socorro, I. Mexico 18°45N 110°58W 180 D2
Socotra Yemen 12°30N 54°0E 131 E5
Socovos Spain 38°20N 1°58W 91 G3
Socuéllamos Spain 39°16N 2°47W 91 F2
Soda U.S.A. 35°10N 116°4W 171 K10
Soda Plains India 35°30N 79°0E 125 B8
Soda Springs U.S.A. 42°39N 111°36W 168 E8
Sodankylä Finland 67°29N 26°40E 60 C22
Soddy-Daisy U.S.A. 35°17N 85°10W 177 D12
Söderala Sweden 61°17N 16°55E 62 C10
Söderåsen △ Sweden 56°2N 13°13E 63 H7
Söderbärke Sweden 60°5N 15°33E 62 D9
Söderfors Sweden 60°23N 17°25E 62 D11
Söderhamn Sweden 61°18N 17°10E 62 C11
Söderköping Sweden 58°31N 16°35E 63 F9
Södermanland □
Sweden 59°10N 16°30E 62 E10
Södertälje Sweden 59°12N 17°39E 62 E11
Sodiri Sudan 14°27N 29°0E 135 F11
Södra Finnskoga Sweden 60°42N 12°34E 62 D6
Södra Sandby Sweden 55°43N 13°21E 63 J7
Södra Ulvön Sweden 62°59N 18°38E 62 B12
Södra Vi Sweden 57°45N 15°45E 63 G9
Sodražica Slovenia 45°45N 14°39E 93 C11
Sodus U.S.A. 43°14N 77°4W 174 C7
Sodwana Bay △
S. Africa 27°35S 32°43E 145 C5
Soe Indonesia 9°52S 124°17E 148 A3
Soekmekaar = Morebeng
S. Africa 23°30S 29°55E 145 B4
Soest Germany 51°34N 8°7E 76 D4
Soest Neths. 52°9N 5°19E 69 B5
Sofades Greece 39°20N 22°4E 98 B4
Sofala □ Mozam. 19°30S 34°30E 145 A5
Sofara Mali 13°59N 4°9W 138 C4
Sofia Bulgaria 42°45N 23°20E 96 C7
Sofia → Madag. 15°27S 47°23E 141 H9
Sofia ✈ (SOF) Bulgaria 42°35N 23°20E 96 D7
Sofia-Grad □ Bulgaria 42°45N 23°20E 96 C7
Sofievka Ukraine 48°6N 33°55E 85 H7
Sofiko Greece 37°47N 23°3E 98 D5
Sofiya = Sofia Bulgaria 42°45N 23°20E 96 C7
Sofrana Greece 36°36N 26°24E 99 E8
Sōfu-Gan Japan 29°49N 140°21E 113 K10
Sogakofe Ghana 6°2N 0°39E 139 D5
Sogamoso Colombia 5°43N 72°56W 186 B4
Sogār Iran 25°53N 58°6E 129 E8
Sögel Germany 52°50N 7°31E 76 C3
Sogndalsfjøra Norway 61°14N 7°5E 60 F12
Søgne Norway 58°5N 7°48E 61 G12
Sognefjorden Norway 61°10N 5°50E 61 F11
Söğüt Bilecik, Turkey 40°2N 30°11E 99 A12
Söğüt Burdur, Turkey 37°5N 29°55E 99 D11
Söğüt Dağı Turkey 37°50N 29°55E 99 D11
Söğütküy Turkey 36°40N 28°8E 99 E10
Soh Iran 33°26N 51°27E 129 C6
Sohâg Egypt 26°33N 31°43E 137 B3
Sohagpur India 22°42N 78°12E 124 H8
Sohar = Şuḥār Oman 24°20N 56°40E 129 E8
Sohela India 21°18N 83°24E 126 D6
Soheuksando S. Korea 34°4N 125°7E 115 G13
Sohm Abyssal Plain
Atl. Oc. 36°0N 55°0W 56 C6
Soignies Belgium 50°35N 4°5E 69 D4
Soin Burkina Faso 12°47N 3°50W 138 C4
Soissons France 49°25N 3°19E 71 C10
Sōja Japan 34°40N 133°45E 113 G6
Sojat India 25°55N 73°45E 124 G5
Sok → Russia 53°24N 50°8E 86 D10
Sokal Ukraine 50°31N 24°15E 75 C13
Sokcho S. Korea 38°12N 128°36E 115 E15
Söke Turkey 37°48N 27°28E 99 D9
Sokelo
Dem. Rep. of the Congo 9°55S 24°36E 143 D1
Sokhumi Georgia 43°0N 41°0E 87 J5
Sokki, Oued In →
Algeria 29°30N 3°42E 136 C4
Soko Banja Serbia 43°40N 21°51E 96 C5
Soko Is. China 22°10N 113°54E 111 a
Sokodé Togo 9°0N 1°11E 139 D5
Sokol Russia 59°30N 40°5E 84 C11
Sokolac Bos.-H. 43°56N 18°48E 80 G3
Sokółka Poland 53°25N 23°30E 82 E10
Sokolo Ségou, Mali 14°53N 6°8W 138 C3
Sokolo Sikasso, Mali 10°52N 6°59W 138 C3
Sokolov Czechia 50°12N 12°40E 78 A5
Sokołów Małopolski
Poland 50°12N 22°7E 83 H9
Sokołów Podlaski
Poland 52°25N 22°15E 83 F9
Sokoły Poland 52°59N 22°42E 83 E9
Sokoto Nigeria 13°2N 5°16E 139 C6
Sokoto □ Nigeria 12°30N 6°10E 139 C5
Sokoto → Nigeria 11°20N 4°10E 139 C5
Sokyrnytsya Ukraine 48°7N 23°23E 81 B8
Sokyryany Ukraine 48°27N 27°25E 81 A12
Sol, Costa del Spain 36°30N 4°30W 89 d
Sol Iletsk Russia 51°10N 55°0E 108 D6
Sola → Poland 50°4N 19°15E 83 J6
Solai Kenya 0°2N 36°12E 142 D4
Solan India 30°55N 77°7E 124 D7
Solana Beach U.S.A. 32°58N 117°16W 171 N9
Solander I. N.Z. 46°34S 166°54E 155 G1
Solapur India 17°43N 75°56E 124 F7
Solca Romania 47°40N 25°50E 81 C10
Soldănești Moldova 47°49N 28°48E 81 C13
Soldeu Andorra 42°35N 1°40E 90 D6
Soldotna U.S.A. 60°29N 151°3W 160 D1
Soléa Cyprus 35°5N 33°4E 101 D12
Solec Kujawski Poland 53°5N 18°14E 83 E5
Soledad Colombia 10°55N 74°46W 186 A4
Soledad U.S.A. 36°26N 121°20W 170 H5
Soledad Venezuela 8°10N 63°34W 186 B6
Solent, The U.K. 50°45N 1°25W 67 G6
Solenzara France 41°53N 9°23E 73 G13
Solesmes France 50°10N 3°30E 71 B10
Solferino Italy 45°22N 10°34E 92 C7
Solfonntaggen Norway 60°2N 6°57E 61 F12
Solhan Turkey 38°57N 41°3E 105 C9
Solikamsk Russia 59°38N 56°50E 86 D6
Solila Madag.
Solimões = Amazonas →
S. Amer. 0°5S 50°0W 187 D8
Solin Croatia 43°33N 16°30E 93 E13
Solingen Germany 51°10N 7°5E 76 D3
Söll Austria 47°30N 12°11E 77 H8
Sollebrunn Sweden 58°8N 12°32E 63 F6

Solleftea Sweden 63°12N 17°20E 62 A11
Sollentuna Sweden 59°25N 17°56E 62 E11
Söller Spain 39°46N 2°43E 100 B9
Solleron Sweden 60°55N 14°37E 62 D8
Solling Germany 51°42N 9°38E 76 D5
Solling-Vogler △ Germany 51°45N 9°32E 76 D5
Solnechnogorsk Russia 56°10N 36°57E 84 D9
Solo = Indonesia 6°47S 112°22E 119 G15
Solofra Italy 40°50N 14°51E 95 B7
Sologne France 47°40N 1°45E 71 E8
Solok Indonesia 0°45S 100°40E 118 E2
Sololá Guatemala 14°49N 91°10W 182 D1
Sololo Kenya 3°33N 38°39E 142 B4
Solomon, N. Fork → U.S.A. 39°29N 98°26W 172 F4
Solomon, S. Fork → U.S.A. 39°25N 99°12W 172 F4
Solomon Is. ■ Pac. Oc. 6°0S 155°0E 147 B8
Solomon Rise Pac. Oc. 1°0N 157°0E 156 G7
Solon China 46°32N 121°10E 111 B13
Solon Springs U.S.A. 46°22N 91°49W 172 B8
Solonópole Brazil 5°44S 39°1W 189 D3
Solor Indonesia 8°27S 123°0E 119 F6
Solotcha Russia 54°48N 39°53E 84 E10
Solothurn Switz. 47°13N 7°32E 77 H3
Solothurn □ Switz. 47°18N 7°40E 77 H3
Solotvyn Ukraine 48°42N 24°25E 81 B9
Solsona Spain 42°0N 1°31E 90 C6
Solt Hungary 46°45N 19°1E 80 D4
Šolta Croatia 43°24N 16°15E 93 E13
Soltānābād Khorāsān, Iran 34°13N 59°58E 129 C8
Soltānābād Khorāsān, Iran 36°29N 58°5E 129 B8
Soltāniyeh Iran 36°26N 48°47E 105 D13
Soltau Germany 52°59N 9°50E 76 C5
Soltsy Russia 58°10N 30°30E 84 C6
Soltüstik Qazaqstan □ Kazakhstan 54°0N 70°0E 109 B8
Solunska Glava Macedonia 41°44N 21°31E 96 E5
Solvang U.S.A. 34°36N 120°8W 171 L6
Solvay U.S.A. 43°3N 76°13W 175 C8
Sölvesborg Sweden 56°5N 14°35E 63 H6
Solwezi Zambia 12°11S 26°21E 143 E2
Sōma Japan 37°30N 140°50E 112 F10
Soma Turkey 39°10N 27°35E 99 B9
Somabhula Zimbabwe 19°42S 29°40E 145 A4
Somali Pen. Africa 7°0N 46°0E 132 F8
Somalia ■ Africa 7°0N 47°0E 131 F4
Somaliland □ Somalia 10°0N 46°0E 131 F4
Sombernon France 47°20N 4°40E 71 E11
Sombra Canada 42°43N 82°29W 174 D2
Sombrerete Mexico 23°38N 103°39W 180 C4
Sombrero Anguilla 18°37N 63°30W 183 C7
Sombrero Channel India 7°41N 93°35E 127 L11
Şomcuta Mare Romania 47°31N 23°28E 81 C8
Someido △ Spain 43°5N 6°11W 88 B4
Somers U.S.A. 48°5N 114°13W 168 B6
Somerset Ky., U.S.A. 37°5N 84°36W 173 G11
Somerset Mass., U.S.A. 41°47N 71°8W 175 E13
Somerset Pa., U.S.A. 40°1N 79°5W 174 F5
Somerset □ U.K. 51°9N 3°0W 67 F5
Somerset East S. Africa 32°42S 25°35E 144 D4
Somerset I. Canada 73°30N 93°0W 160 C13
Somerset West S. Africa 34°8S 18°50E 144 D2
Somersworth U.S.A. 43°16N 70°52W 175 C14
Somerton U.S.A. 32°36N 114°43W 169 K6
Somerville U.S.A. 40°35N 74°38W 175 F10
Someş → Romania 47°49N 22°43E 80 C7
Someşul Mare → Romania 47°9N 23°55E 81 C8
Somme □ France 49°57N 2°20E 71 C9
Somme → France 50°11N 1°38E 71 B8
Somme, B. de la France 50°14N 1°33E 70 B8
Sommen Jönköping, Sweden 58°12N 14°58E 63 F8
Sommen Östergötland, Sweden 58°0N 15°15E 63 F9
Sommepy-Tahure France 49°15N 4°31E 71 C11
Sömmerda Germany 51°9N 11°7E 76 D7
Sommesous France 48°44N 4°12E 71 C11
Sommières France 43°47N 4°6E 73 E8
Somnath India 20°53N 70°22E 124 J4
Somogy □ Hungary 46°19N 17°30E 80 D2
Somogyszob Hungary 46°18N 17°20E 80 D2
Somosomo Fiji 16°47S 179°58W 154 a
Somosomo Str. Fiji 16°0S 180°0E 154 a
Somoto Nic. 13°28N 86°37W 182 D2
Sompolno Poland 52°26N 18°30E 83 F5
Somport, Túnel de Spain 42°48N 0°31W 90 C4
Somuncurá, Meseta de Argentina 41°30S 67°0W 192 E3
Somvarpet India 12°36N 75°52E 127 H2
Son → India 25°42N 84°52E 125 G11
Son, Laem Thailand 7°59N 98°16E 121 a
Son Ha Vietnam 15°3N 108°34E 120 E7
Son La Vietnam 21°20N 103°50E 116 B4
Son Morrell Spain 39°44N 3°20E 100 B10
Son Rapinya Spain 39°35N 2°37E 100 B9
Son Sardina Spain 39°37N 2°40E 100 B9
Son Serra Spain 39°43N 3°13E 100 B10
Son Servera Spain 39°37N 3°21E 100 B10
Son Tay Vietnam 21°8N 105°30E 116 G5
Son Tinh Vietnam 15°10N 108°40E 120 E7
Soná Panama 8°0N 81°20W 182 E3
Sonamarg India 34°18N 75°21E 125 B6
Sonamukhi India 23°18N 87°27E 125 H12
Sonar → India 24°24N 79°56E 124 G4
Sönch'ŏn N. Korea 39°48N 124°55E 115 E13
Sondags → S. Africa 33°44S 25°51E 144 D4
Söndalo Italy 46°20N 10°19E 92 B7
Sønder Felding Denmark 55°57N 8°47E 63 J2
Sønder Omme Denmark 55°50N 8°54E 63 J2
Sønderborg Denmark 54°55N 9°49E 63 K3
Sondershausen Germany 51°22N 10°51E 76 D6
Søndre Strømfjord = Kangerlussuaq Greenland 66°59N 50°40W 57 D5
Sondur → India 20°40N 82°1E 126 D6
Sone Mozam. 17°23S 34°55E 143 F3
Sonepur India 20°55N 83°50E 126 D6
Sonfi Brazil 6°0S 67°52W 188 B4
Song Nigeria 9°49N 12°39E 139 D7
Song Thailand 18°28N 100°11E 120 C3

Song Cau Vietnam 13°27N 109°18E 120 F7
Song-Köl Kyrgyzstan 41°50N 75°12E 109 D9
Song Ma Vietnam 20°56N 103°53E 116 G4
Song Xian China 34°12N 112°8E 114 G7
Songadh India 21°9N 73°33E 126 D1
Songea Tanzania 10°40S 35°40E 143 G4
Songgeons France 49°32N 1°50E 71 C8
Songgang China 22°46N 113°50E 111 a
Songhua Hu China 43°35N 126°50E 115 C14
Songhua Jiang → China 47°45N 132°30E 111 B15
Songimvelo △ S. Africa 25°50S 31°2E 145 C5
Songjiang China 31°1N 121°12E 117 B13
Songjianghe China 42°10N 127°29E 115 C14
Söngjin = Kimch'aek N. Korea 40°40N 129°10E 115 D15
Songkan China 28°35N 106°52E 116 C6
Songkhla Thailand 7°13N 100°37E 121 J3
Songming China 25°12N 103°2E 116 E4
Songnim N. Korea 38°45N 125°39E 115 E13
Songo Mozam. 15°34S 32°38E 145 A5
Songpan China 32°40N 103°30E 116 A4
Songtao China 28°11N 109°10E 116 C7
Songwe Dem. Rep. of the Congo 3°20S 26°16E 142 C2
Songwe → Africa 9°44S 33°58E 143 D3
Songxi China 27°31N 118°44E 117 C12
Songzi China 30°12N 111°45E 117 B8
Sonhat India 23°29N 82°31E 125 H10
Sonid Youqi China 42°45N 112°48E 114 C7
Sonid Zuoqi China 43°50N 113°42E 114 C7
Sonipat India 29°0N 77°5E 124 E7
Sonkach India 22°59N 76°21E 124 H7
Sonkovo Russia 57°50N 37°5E 84 D9
Sonmiani Pakistan 25°25N 66°40E 124 G2
Sonmiani B. Pakistan 25°15N 66°30E 124 G2
Sonneberg Germany 50°21N 11°10E 77 F7
Sonnino Italy 41°25N 13°14E 94 A6
Sono → Minas Gerais, Brazil 17°2S 45°32W 189 D1
Sono → Tocantins, Brazil 9°58S 48°11W 189 D1
Sonoma U.S.A. 38°18N 122°28W 170 G4
Sonora Calif., U.S.A. 37°59N 120°23W 170 H6
Sonora Tex., U.S.A. 30°34N 100°39W 176 F4
Sonora □ Mexico 29°20N 110°40W 180 B2
Sonora → Mexico 29°5N 110°55W 180 B2
Sonoran Desert U.S.A. 33°40N 113°30W 171 L12
Sonoyta Mexico 31°51N 112°50W 180 A2
Sonqor Iran 34°47N 47°36E 105 E12
Sonseca Spain 39°42N 3°57W 89 F7
Sonsonate El Salv. 13°43N 89°44W 182 D2
Sonstorp Sweden 58°44N 15°38E 63 F9
Sonthofen Germany 47°30N 10°16E 77 H6
Soochow = Suzhou China 31°19N 120°38E 117 B13
Sooke Canada 48°13N 123°43W 170 B3
Soomaaliya = Somalia ■ Africa 7°0N 47°0E 131 F4
Sop Hao Laos 20°33N 104°27E 116 G5
Sop Prap Thailand 17°53N 99°20E 120 D2
Sopchoppy U.S.A. 30°4N 84°29W 178 E5
Sopelana Spain 43°23N 2°58W 90 B2
Sopi Indonesia 2°34N 128°28E 119 D7
Sopot Bulgaria 42°39N 24°45E 97 C8
Sopot Poland 54°27N 18°31E 82 D5
Sopron Hungary 47°45N 16°32E 80 C1
Sopur India 34°18N 74°27E 125 B6
Sør-Rondane Antarctica 72°0S 25°0E 55 D4
Sora Italy 41°43N 13°37E 93 G10
Sorab India 14°23N 75°6E 127 G2
Sorada India 19°45N 84°26E 126 E7
Söråker Sweden 62°30N 17°32E 62 B11
Sorang Kazakhstan 49°46N 72°51E 109 C8
Sorano Italy 42°41N 11°43E 93 H8
Soraon India 25°37N 81°51E 125 G9
Sorata Bolivia 15°50S 68°40W 188 D4
Sorbas Spain 37°6N 2°7W 91 H2
Sörbygden Sweden 62°48N 16°12E 62 B10
Sord = Swords Ireland 53°28N 6°13W 64 C5
Sordellen Sweden 68°16N 16°43E 62 C10
Sore France 44°18N 0°35W 72 D3
Sorel-Tracy Canada 46°0N 73°10W 164 C5
Soresina Italy 45°17N 9°51E 92 C6
Sörforsa Sweden 61°43N 16°58E 62 A11
Sórgono Italy 40°1N 9°6E 94 B2
Sorgues France 44°1N 4°53E 73 D8
Sorgun Turkey 39°46N 35°11E 104 C6
Soria Spain 41°43N 2°32W 90 D2
Soria □ Spain 41°46N 2°28W 90 D2
Soriano Uruguay 33°24S 58°19W 190 C4
Soriano nel Cimino Italy 42°25N 12°14E 93 F9
Sorkh, Kuh-e Iran 35°40N 58°30E 129 C8
Sorkheh Iran 55°26N 11°32E 63 J5
Soro Denmark 55°26N 11°32E 63 J5
Soro Guinea 10°9N 9°48W 138 C3
Soroca Moldova 48°8N 28°12E 81 B13
Sorocaba Brazil 23°31S 47°27W 191 A6
Sorochinsk Russia 52°26N 53°10E 108 B4
Soroki = Soroca Moldova 48°8N 28°12E 81 B13
Sorong Indonesia 0°55S 131°15E 119 E8
Soroni Greece 36°21N 28°1E 101 C10
Soroti Uganda 1°43N 33°35E 142 B3
Søroya Norway 70°40N 22°30E 60 A20
Søroysundet Norway 70°25N 23°0E 60 A20
Sorraia → Portugal 38°55N 8°53W 89 G2
Sorrell Australia 42°47S 147°34E 151 G4
Sorrento Italy 40°37N 14°22E 95 B7
Sorsele Sweden 65°31N 17°30E 60 D17
Sorso Italy 40°48N 8°34E 94 B1
Sorsogon Phil. 13°0N 124°0E 119 E6
Sortavala Russia 61°42N 30°41E 84 B6
Sortino Italy 37°9N 15°2E 95 E7
Sortland Norway 68°42N 15°25E 60 B16
Sortot Sudan 19°3N 30°28E 137 D3
Sørvågen Norway 67°53N 13°1E 60 C15
Sorvizhi Russia 57°52N 48°32E 86 B9
Sos del Rey Católico Spain 42°30N 1°13W 90 C3
Soscumica, L. Canada 50°15N 77°27W 164 B4
Sösdala Sweden 56°2N 13°41E 63 H7
Sosnovka Kirov, Russia 56°17N 51°17E 86 B10
Sosnovka Tambov, Russia 53°13N 41°24E 86 D5
Sosnovyy Bor Russia 59°55N 29°6E 84 C5

Sosnowiec Poland 50°20N 19°10E 83 H6
Sospel France 43°52N 7°27E 73 E11
Sossus Vlei Namibia 24°40S 15°23E 144 B2
Šoštanj Slovenia 46°23N 15°4E 93 B12
Sōsura N. Korea 42°16N 130°36E 115 C16
Sot → India 27°27N 79°37E 125 F8
Sotavento Cabo Verde 15°0N 24°0W 134 b
Soto Spain 43°32N 6°4W 88 B4
Soto la Marina Mexico 23°46N 98°13W 181 C5
Soto la Marina → Mexico 23°46N 97°45W 181 C5
Soto y Amío Spain 42°46N 5°53W 88 C5
Sotouboua Togo 8°34N 0°59E 139 D5
Sotrondio Spain 43°17N 5°36W 88 B5
Sotuta Mexico 20°36N 89°1W 181 C7
Souanké Congo 2°10N 14°3E 140 D2
Souderton U.S.A. 40°19N 75°19W 175 F9
Soudas, Ormos Greece 35°25N 24°10E 101 D6
Soufli Greece 41°12N 26°18E 97 E10
Soufrière Guadeloupe 16°5N 61°40W 182 b
Soufrière St. Lucia 13°51N 61°3W 183 f
Soufrière Bay Dominica 15°13N 61°22W 183 f
Souillac France 44°53N 1°29E 72 D5
Souilly France 49°3N 5°17E 71 C12
Souk-Ahras Algeria 36°23N 7°57E 136 A5
Souk-Ahras □ Algeria 36°17N 7°55E 136 A5
Souk el Arba du Rharb Morocco 34°43N 5°59W 136 B2
Soukhouma Laos 14°38N 105°48E 120 E5
Sŏul = Seoul S. Korea 37°31N 126°58E 115 F14
Soulac-sur-Mer France 45°30N 1°7W 72 C2
Soulougou Burkina Faso 13°1N 0°25E 139 C5
Soultz-sous-Forêts France 48°57N 7°52E 71 D14
Sound, The = Øresund Europe 55°45N 12°40E 63 J6
Sound, The U.K. 50°20N 4°10W 67 G3
Sound I. India 12°58N 92°59E 127 H11
Sounio, Akra Greece 37°37N 24°1E 98 D6
Sour el Ghozlane Algeria 36°10N 3°45E 136 A4
Sources, Mt. aux Lesotho 28°45S 28°50E 145 C4
Soure Brazil 0°35S 48°30W 187 D9
Soure Portugal 40°4N 8°38W 88 E2
Souris Man., Canada 49°40N 100°20W 163 D8
Souris P.E.I., Canada 46°21N 62°15W 165 C7
Souris → N. Amer. 49°40N 99°34W 172 A4
Sourou → Burkina Faso 12°45N 3°25E 138 C4
Sourpi Greece 39°6N 22°54E 98 B4
Sous, O. → Morocco 30°27N 9°31W 136 B2
Sous-Massa △ Morocco 30°26N 9°35W 136 B2
Sous-Massa-Drâa □ Morocco 30°45N 6°30W 136 B2
Sousa Brazil 6°45S 38°10W 189 B3
Sousel Portugal 38°57N 7°40W 89 G3
Sousse Tunisia 35°50N 10°38E 136 A6
Sousse □ Tunisia 35°40N 10°30E 136 A6
Soustons France 43°45N 1°19W 72 E2
Sout → S. Africa 31°35S 18°24E 144 D2
South Africa ■ Africa 32°0S 23°0E 144 D3
South America 10°0S 60°0W 184 E5
South Andaman India 11°45N 92°10E 127 J11
South Aulatsivik I. Canada 56°45N 61°30W 165 A7
South Australia □ Australia 32°0S 139°0E 152 B3
South Australian Basin Ind. Oc. 38°0S 126°0E 156 L4
South Ayrshire □ U.K. 55°18N 4°41W 66 F4
South Baldy Pk. U.S.A. 34°6N 107°11W 169 J10
South Bass I. U.S.A. 41°39N 82°49W 174 E2
South Bay U.S.A. 26°40N 80°43W 179 J9
South Bend Ind., U.S.A. 41°41N 86°15W 172 E10
South Bend Wash., U.S.A. 46°40N 123°48W 170 D3
South Boston U.S.A. 36°42N 78°54W 173 G14
South Branch Canada 47°55N 59°2W 165 C8
South Brook Canada 49°26N 56°5W 165 C8
South Brother I. India 9°26N 93°10E 127 J11
South Bruny I. Australia 43°20S 147°15E 151 G4
South Carolina □ U.S.A. 34°0N 81°0W 177 E14
South Charleston U.S.A. 38°22N 81°44W 173 F13
South China Sea Asia 10°0N 113°0E 118 C4
South Congaree U.S.A. 33°53N 81°9W 178 B8
South Cumberland Is. △ Australia 20°42S 149°11E 150 C4
South Dakota □ U.S.A. 44°15N 100°0W 172 D5
South Dayton U.S.A. 42°21N 79°3W 174 D5
South Deerfield U.S.A. 42°29N 72°37W 175 D12
South Downs U.K. 50°52N 0°25W 67 G7
South Downs △ U.K. 50°50N 0°50W 67 G7
South Dublin □ Ireland 53°16N 6°24W 64 C5
South East □ Botswana 25°0S 25°40E 144 C4
South East C. Australia 43°40S 146°50E 151 G4
South East Forest △ Australia 37°0S 149°30E 153 D8
South East Is. Australia 34°17S 123°30E 149 F3
South Esk → U.K. 56°43N 2°31W 66 E6
South Fiji Basin Pac. Oc. 26°0S 175°0E 156 K9
South Foreland U.K. 51°8N 1°24E 67 F9
South Fork American → U.S.A. 38°57N 121°5W 170 G5
South Fork Edisto → U.S.A. 33°16N 80°54W 178 B9
South Fork Feather → Australia 31°12S 119°15E 149 F2
South Fork Grand → U.S.A. 45°43N 102°17W 172 C2
South Fork Milk → U.S.A. 48°4N 106°19W 168 B10
South Fork Republican → U.S.A. 40°3N 101°31W 172 E3
South Georgia Antarctica 54°30S 37°0W 55 B1
South Gloucestershire □ U.K. 51°32N 2°28W 67 F5
South Hadley U.S.A. 42°16N 72°35W 175 D12
South Haven U.S.A. 42°24N 86°16W 172 D10
South Henik L. Canada 61°30N 97°30W 163 A9
South Horr Kenya 2°3N 36°56E 142 B4
South I. India 10°0S 72°17E 127 J1

South I. Kenya 2°35N 36°35E 142 B4
South I. N.Z. 44°0S 170°0E 155 E5
South Indian Lake Canada 56°47N 98°56W 163 B9
South Invercargill N.Z. 46°26S 168°23E 155 G3
South Island △ Kenya 2°39N 36°35E 142 B4
South Kitui △ Kenya 1°48S 38°46E 142 C4
South Knife → Canada 58°55N 94°37W 163 B10
South Koel → India 22°32N 85°14E 125 H11
South Korea ■ Asia 36°0N 128°0E 115 G15
South Lake Tahoe U.S.A. 38°57N 119°59W 170 G6
South Lanarkshire □ U.K. 55°37N 3°53W 66 F5
South Loup → U.S.A. 41°4N 98°39W 172 E4
South Luangwa △ Zambia 13°0S 31°20E 143 E3
South Magnetic Pole Antarctica 64°8S 138°8E 55 C9
South Miami U.S.A. 25°42N 80°17W 179 K9
South Milwaukee U.S.A. 42°55N 87°52W 172 D10
South Molton U.K. 51°1N 3°51W 67 F4
South Moose L. Canada 53°49N 100°1W 163 C8
South Nahanni → Canada 61°3N 123°21W 162 A4
South Nation → Canada 45°34N 75°6W 175 A9
South Natuna Is. = Natuna Selatan, Kepulauan Indonesia 2°45N 109°0E 118 D3
South Negril Pt. Jamaica 18°16N 78°22W 182 a
South Newport U.S.A. 31°38N 81°24W 178 D8
South Orkney Is. Antarctica 63°0S 45°0W 55 C18
South Ossetia □ Georgia 42°21N 44°2E 87 J7
South Otselic U.S.A. 42°38N 75°46W 175 D9
South Pagai, I. = Pagai Selatan, Pulau Indonesia 3°0S 100°15E 118 E2
South Paris U.S.A. 44°14N 70°31W 175 B14
South Pittsburg U.S.A. 35°1N 85°42W 177 D12
South Platte → U.S.A. 41°7N 100°42W 172 E3
South Pole Antarctica 90°0S 0°0 55 E
South Ponte Vedra Beach U.S.A. 30°3N 81°20W 178 E8
South Porcupine Canada 48°30N 81°12W 164 C3
South Portland U.S.A. 43°38N 70°15W 173 D18
South Pt. Barbados 13°2N 59°32W 183 g
South Pt. U.S.A. 44°52N 83°19W 174 B1
South River Canada 45°52N 79°23W 164 C4
South River U.S.A. 40°27N 74°23W 175 F10
South Ronaldsay U.K. 58°48N 2°58W 65 C6
South Rukuru → Malawi 10°44S 34°14E 143 E3
South Sandwich Is. Antarctica 57°0S 27°0W 55 B1
South Sandwich Trench Atl. Oc. 56°0S 24°0W 55 B1
South Saskatchewan → Canada 53°15N 105°5W 163 C7
South Seal → Canada 58°48N 98°8W 163 B9
South Sentinel I. India 10°59N 92°14E 127 J11
South Shetland Is. Antarctica 62°0S 59°0W 55 C18
South Shields U.K. 55°0N 1°25W 66 C6
South Sioux City U.S.A. 42°28N 96°24W 172 D5
South Sister U.S.A. 44°4N 121°51W 168 D3
South Sudan ■ Africa 8°0N 30°0E 135 G11
South Taranaki Bight N.Z. 39°40S 174°5E 154 F3
South Tasman Rise S. Ocean 48°0S 146°0E 55 A10
South Thompson → Canada 50°40N 120°20W 162 C4
South Twin I. Canada 53°7N 79°52W 164 B4
South Tyne → U.K. 54°59N 2°8W 66 C5
South Uist U.K. 57°20N 7°15W 65 D1
South Valley U.S.A. 35°1N 106°41W 169 J10
South Venice U.S.A. 27°3N 82°25W 179 H7
South Wellesley Is. Australia 16°58S 139°17E 150 B2
South West C. Australia 43°34S 146°3E 151 G4
South West C. N.Z. 47°17S 167°28E 155 H2
South West Rocks Australia 30°52S 153°3E 153 A10
South Williamsport U.S.A. 41°13N 77°0W 174 E8
South Yorkshire □ U.K. 53°27N 1°36W 66 D6
Southampton Canada 44°30N 81°25W 164 D3
Southampton U.K. 50°54N 1°23W 67 G6
Southampton U.S.A. 40°53N 72°23W 175 F12
Southampton □ U.K. 50°54N 1°23W 67 G6
Southampton I. Canada 64°30N 84°0W 161 E15
Southaven U.S.A. 34°59N 90°0W 177 D9
Southbank Canada 54°2N 125°46W 162 C3
Southbridge N.Z. 43°48S 172°16E 155 D7
Southbridge U.S.A. 42°5N 72°2W 175 D12
Southeast Indian Ridge Ind. Oc. 43°0S 80°0E 146 J10
Southend Canada 56°19N 103°22W 163 B8
Southend-on-Sea U.K. 51°32N 0°44E 67 F8
Southend-on-Sea □ U.K. 51°32N 0°44E 67 F8
Southern □ Malawi 15°0S 35°0E 143 F4
Southern □ S. Leone 8°0N 12°30W 138 D2
Southern □ Zambia 16°20S 26°20E 143 F2
Southern Alps N.Z. 43°41S 170°11E 155 D6
Southern Aral Sea Asia 45°0N 58°0E 108 C5
Southern Cross Australia 31°12S 119°15E 149 F2
Southern Indian L. Canada 57°10N 98°30W 163 B9
Southern Lau Group Fiji 18°40S 178°40W 154 a
Southern Ocean 62°0S 60°0E 55 C6
Southern Pines U.S.A. 35°11N 79°24W 177 D15
Southern Uplands U.K. 55°28N 3°52W 66 F5
Southington U.S.A. 41°36N 72°53W 175 E12
Southland □ N.Z. 45°30S 168°0E 155 F3
Southold U.S.A. 41°4N 72°26W 175 E12
Southport Australia 27°58S 153°25E 153 D5
Southport U.K. 53°39N 3°0W 66 D4
Southport Fla., U.S.A. 30°17N 85°38W 178 E4
Southport N.Y., U.S.A. 42°3N 76°49W 174 D8

Southwest △ Australia 43°8S 146°5E 151 G4
Southwest Pacific Basin Pac. Oc. 40°0S 140°0W 55 A12
Southwold U.K. 52°20N 1°41E 67 E9
Southwood △ Australia 27°48S 150°8E 151 D5
Soutpansberg S. Africa 23°0S 29°30E 145 B4
Souvigny France 46°33N 3°10E 71 F10
Sovata Romania 46°35N 25°3E 81 D10
Soverato Italy 38°41N 16°33E 95 D9
Sovetsk Kaliningrad, Russia 55°6N 21°50E 82 C8
Sovetsk Kirov, Russia 57°38N 48°53E 86 B9
Sovetskaya Gavan Russia 48°58N 140°18E 107 E15
Sovicille Italy 43°17N 11°13E 93 E8
Soweto S. Africa 26°14S 27°52E 145 C4
Sowma'eh Sarā Iran 37°17N 49°18E 105 D13
Söya-Kaikyō = La Perouse Str. Asia 45°40N 142°0E 112 B11
Söya-Misaki Japan 45°30N 141°55E 112 B10
Soyaux France 45°39N 0°12E 72 C4
Soyo Angola 6°13S 12°20E 140 F2
Sozaq Kazakhstan 44°8N 68°28E 109 D7
Sozh → Belarus 51°57N 30°48E 75 B16
Sozopol Bulgaria 42°23N 27°42E 97 D11
Spa Belgium 50°29N 5°53E 69 D5
Spaatz I. Antarctica 73°10S 75°0W 55 D17
Spain ■ Europe 39°0N 4°0W 59 H5
Spalding Australia 33°30S 138°37E 152 B3
Spalding U.K. 52°48N 0°9W 66 E7
Spanaway U.S.A. 47°6N 122°26W 170 C4
Spangler U.S.A. 40°39N 78°48W 174 F6
Spanish Canada 46°12N 82°20W 164 C3
Spanish Fork U.S.A. 40°7N 111°39W 168 F8
Spanish Town Br. Virgin Is. 18°26N 64°26W 183 e
Spanish Town Jamaica 18°0N 76°57W 182 a
Sparks Ga., U.S.A. 31°11N 83°26W 178 D6
Sparks Nev., U.S.A. 39°32N 119°45W 170 G7
Sparreholm Sweden 59°4N 16°49E 62 E10
Sparta = Sparti Greece 37°5N 22°25E 98 D4
Sparta Ga., U.S.A. 33°17N 82°58W 178 B7
Sparta Mich., U.S.A. 43°10N 85°42W 173 D11
Sparta N.J., U.S.A. 41°2N 74°38W 175 E10
Sparta Wis., U.S.A. 43°56N 90°49W 172 D8
Spartanburg U.S.A. 34°56N 81°57W 177 D14
Spartel, C. Morocco 35°47N 5°56W 136 A2
Sparti Greece 37°5N 22°25E 98 D4
Spartivento, C. Calabria, Italy 37°55N 16°4E 95 F9
Spartivento, C. Sard., Italy 38°53N 8°50E 94 D1
Sparwood Canada 49°44N 114°53W 162 D6
Spas-Demensk Russia 54°20N 34°0E 84 E7
Spas-Klepiki Russia 55°10N 40°10E 84 E11
Spassk-Dalniy Russia 44°40N 132°48E 112 B6
Spassk-Ryazanskiy Russia 54°24N 40°25E 84 E11
Spatha, Akra Greece 35°42N 23°43E 101 D5
Spatsizi → Canada 57°42N 128°7W 162 B3
Spatsizi Plateau Wilderness △ Canada 57°40N 128°0W 162 B3
Spean → U.K. 56°55N 4°59W 65 E4
Spearfish U.S.A. 44°30N 103°52W 172 C2
Spearman U.S.A. 36°12N 101°12W 176 C4
Speculator U.S.A. 43°30N 74°22W 175 C10
Speed Australia 35°21S 142°27E 152 C5
Speia Moldova 46°59N 29°19E 81 D14
Speightstown Barbados 13°15N 59°39W 183 g
Speke Gulf Tanzania 2°20S 32°50E 142 C3
Spello Italy 42°59N 12°40E 93 F9
Spence Bay = Taloyoak Canada 69°32N 93°32W 160 D13
Spencer Idaho, U.S.A. 44°22N 112°11W 168 D7
Spencer Iowa, U.S.A. 43°9N 95°9W 172 D6
Spencer N.Y., U.S.A. 42°13N 76°30W 175 D8
Spencer, C. Australia 35°20S 136°53E 152 C2
Spencer B. Namibia 25°30S 14°47E 144 C1
Spencer G. Australia 34°0S 137°20E 152 C2
Spencerville Canada 44°51N 75°33W 175 B9
Spences Bridge Canada 50°25N 121°20W 162 C4
Spennymoor U.K. 54°42N 1°36W 66 C6
Spenser Mts. N.Z. 42°15S 172°45E 155 D5
Spentrup Denmark 56°33N 10°2E 63 H4
Sperchios → Greece 38°57N 22°3E 98 C4
Sperrgebiet △ Namibia 27°38S 15°56E 144 C2
Sperrin Mts. U.K. 54°50N 7°0W 64 B5
Spessart Germany 49°56N 9°18E 77 F5
Spetses Greece 37°15N 23°10E 98 D5
Spey → U.K. 57°40N 3°6W 65 D5
Speyer Germany 49°29N 8°25E 77 F4
Spezand Pakistan 29°59N 67°0E 124 E2
Spezzano Albanese Italy 39°40N 16°19E 95 C9
Spiddal Ireland 53°15N 9°18W 64 C2
Spiekeroog Germany 53°46N 7°42E 76 B3
Spiez Switz. 46°40N 7°40E 77 J3
Spili Greece 35°13N 24°31E 101 D6
Spilimbergo Italy 46°7N 12°54E 93 B9
Spin Būldak Afghan. 31°1N 66°25E 124 D2
Spinalonga Greece 35°18N 25°44E 101 D7
Spinazzola Italy 40°58N 16°5E 95 B9
Spineni Romania 44°43N 24°37E 81 F9
Spinifex △ Australia 28°30S 128°30E 149 E4
Spirit Lake U.S.A. 46°15N 122°9W 170 D4
Spirit River Canada 55°45N 118°50W 162 B5
Spiritwood Canada 53°24N 107°33W 163 C7
Spišská Nová Ves Slovakia 48°58N 20°34E 79 C13
Spišské Podhradie Slovakia 49°0N 20°48E 79 B13
Spital Austria 46°48N 13°31E 78 E6
Spjelkavik Norway 62°28N 6°22E 60 E12
Split Croatia 43°31N 16°26E 93 E13
Split × (SPU) Croatia 43°33N 16°18E 93 E13
Split L. Canada 56°8N 96°15W 163 B9
Split Lake Canada 56°8N 96°15W 163 B9
Splitski Kanal Croatia 43°31N 16°20E 93 E13
Splügenpass Switz. 46°30N 9°20E 77 J5
Spofford U.S.A. 29°10N 100°25W 176 G4
Spokane U.S.A. 47°40N 117°24W 168 C5
Spoleto Italy 42°44N 12°44E 93 F9
Spooner U.S.A. 45°50N 91°53W 172 C8
Sporyy Navolok, Mys Russia 75°50N 68°40E 106 B7

Spratly I. S. China Sea 8°38N 111°55E 118 C4
Spratly Is. S. China Sea 8°20N 112°0E 118 C4
Spray U.S.A. 44°50N 119°48W 168 D4
Spreča → Bos.-H. 44°44N 18°6E 80 F3
Spree → Germany 52°32N 13°12E 76 C9
Spreewald Germany 51°58N 13°51E 76 D9
Spremberg Germany 51°34N 14°22E 76 D10
Sprengisandur Iceland 64°52N 18°7W 60 D4
Spring City U.S.A. 40°11N 75°33W 175 F9
Spring Cr. → U.S.A. 30°54N 84°45W 178 F5
Spring Creek U.S.A. 40°44N 115°35W 168 F6
Spring Garden U.S.A. 39°52N 120°47W 170 F6
Spring Hall Barbados 13°18N 59°36W 183 g
Spring Hill Ala., U.S.A. 31°42N 85°58W 178 D4
Spring Hill Fla., U.S.A. 28°27N 82°41W 179 G7
Spring Mts. U.S.A. 36°0N 115°45W 171 J11
Spring Temple Buddha China 33°46N 112°27E 114 H7
Spring Valley Calif., U.S.A. 32°44N 116°59W 171 N10
Spring Valley Nev., U.S.A. 36°6N 115°14W 171 J11
Springbok S. Africa 29°42S 17°54E 144 C2
Springboro U.S.A. 41°48N 80°22W 174 E4
Springdale Canada 49°30N 56°6W 165 C8
Springdale U.S.A. 36°11N 94°8W 176 C7
Springe Germany 52°13N 9°33E 76 C5
Springer U.S.A. 36°22N 104°36W 169 H11
Springerville U.S.A. 34°8N 109°17W 169 J9
Springfield Canada 42°50N 80°56W 174 D4
Springfield N.Z. 43°19S 171°56E 155 D6
Springfield Colo., U.S.A. 37°24N 102°37W 169 H12
Springfield Fla., U.S.A. 30°10N 85°37W 178 E4
Springfield Ga., U.S.A. 32°22N 81°18W 178 C8
Springfield Ill., U.S.A. 39°48N 89°39W 172 F9
Springfield Mass., U.S.A. 42°6N 72°35W 175 D12
Springfield Mo., U.S.A. 37°13N 93°17W 172 G7
Springfield Ohio, U.S.A. 39°55N 83°49W 173 F12
Springfield Oreg., U.S.A. 44°3N 123°1W 168 D2
Springfield S.C., U.S.A. 33°30N 81°17W 178 B8
Springfield Tenn., U.S.A. 36°31N 86°53W 177 C11
Springfield Vt., U.S.A. 43°18N 72°29W 175 C12
Springfontein S. Africa 30°15S 25°40E 144 D4
Springhill Canada 45°40N 64°4W 165 C7
Springhill U.S.A. 33°0N 93°28W 176 E8
Springhouse Canada 51°56N 122°7W 162 C4
Springlands = Corriverton Guyana 5°55N 57°20W 186 B7
Springs S. Africa 26°13S 28°25E 145 C4
Springsure Australia 24°8S 148°6E 150 C4
Springvale Qld., U.S.A. 31°50N 84°53W 178 D5
Springvale Maine, U.S.A. 43°28N 70°48W 175 C14
Springville Calif., U.S.A. 36°8N 118°49W 170 J8
Springville N.Y., U.S.A. 42°31N 78°40W 174 D6
Springville Utah, U.S.A. 40°10N 111°37W 168 F8
Springwater U.S.A. 42°38N 77°35W 174 D7
Spruce-Creek U.S.A. 40°36N 78°9W 174 F6
Spruce Knob-Seneca Rocks △ U.S.A. 38°50N 79°30W 173 F14
Spruce Mt. U.S.A. 44°12N 72°19W 175 B12
Sprucedale Canada 45°29N 79°28W 174 A5
Spur U.S.A. 33°28N 100°52W 176 E4
Spurn Hd. U.K. 53°35N 0°8E 66 D8
Spuž Montenegro 42°32N 19°10E 96 D3
Spuzzum Canada 49°37N 121°23W 162 D4
Squam L. U.S.A. 43°45N 71°32W 175 C13
Squamish Canada 49°45N 123°10W 162 D4
Square Islands Canada 52°47N 55°47W 165 B8
Squillace, G. di Italy 38°45N 16°50E 95 D9
Squinzano Italy 40°26N 18°2E 95 B11
Squires, Mt. Australia 26°14S 127°28E 149 E4
Srbac Bos.-H. 45°7N 17°30E 80 E2
Srbica = Skënderaj Kosovo 42°45N 20°47E 96 D4
Srbija = Serbia ■ Europe 43°20N 20°0E 96 C4
Srbobran Serbia 45°32N 19°48E 80 E4
Sre Ambel Cambodia 11°8N 103°46E 121 G4
Sre Khtum Cambodia 12°10N 106°52E 121 F6
Sre Umbell = Sre Ambel Cambodia 11°8N 103°46E 121 G4
Srebarna Bulgaria 44°6N 27°4E 97 B11
Srebrenica Bos.-H. 44°6N 19°18E 80 F4
Sredinnyy Khrebet Russia 57°0N 160°0E 107 D17
Sredinnyy Ra. = Sredinnyy Khrebet Russia 57°0N 160°0E 107 D17
Središče Slovenia 46°24N 16°17E 93 B13
Sredna Gora Bulgaria 42°40N 24°20E 97 C8
Srednekolymsk Russia 67°27N 153°40E 107 C16
Sredni Rodopi Bulgaria 41°40N 24°45E 97 E8
Srednogorie Bulgaria 42°43N 24°10E 97 C8
Śrem Poland 52°6N 17°2E 83 F4
Sremska Mitrovica Serbia 44°59N 19°38E 80 F4
Sremski Karlovci Serbia 45°12N 19°56E 80 E4
Srepok → Cambodia 13°33N 106°16E 120 F6
Sretensk Russia 52°10N 117°40E 107 D12
Sri Aman = Bandar Sri Aman Malaysia 1°15N 111°32E 118 D4
Sri Kalahasti India 13°45N 79°44E 127 H4
Sri Lanka ■ Asia 7°30N 80°50E 127 L5
Sri Pada = Adam's Peak Sri Lanka 6°48N 80°30E 127 L5
Sriharikota I. India 13°40N 80°30E 127 H5
Srikakulam India 18°14N 83°58E 126 E6
Srinagar India 34°5N 74°50E 125 B6
Srivardhan India 18°4N 73°3E 126 E1
Srivilliputtur India 9°31N 77°40E 127 L3
Środa Śląska Poland 51°10N 16°36E 83 G3
Środa Wielkopolski Poland 52°15N 17°19E 83 F4
Srono Indonesia 8°24S 114°16E 119 J17
Srpska Crnja Serbia 45°38N 20°44E 80 E5
Srpski Itebej Serbia 45°35N 20°42E 80 E5
Srungavarapukota India 18°7N 83°10E 126 E6
Ssese Is. = Sese Is. Uganda 0°20S 32°20E 142 C3
Staaten → Australia 16°24S 141°17E 150 B3
Staaten River △ Australia 16°15S 142°40E 150 B3
Stabbursdalen △ Norway 70°5N 24°15E 60 A21
Staberhuk Germany 54°23N 11°18E 76 A7
Stade Germany 53°35N 9°29E 76 B5

Stadskanaal Neths. 53°4N 6°55E 69 A6
Stadtallendorf Germany 50°48N 9°1E 76 E5
Stadthagen Germany 52°19N 9°13E 76 C5
Stadtlohn Germany 51°59N 6°55E 76 D2
Stadtroda Germany 50°52N 11°44E 76 E7
Staffa U.K. 56°27N 6°21W 65 E2
Staffanstorp Sweden 55°39N 13°13E 63 J7
Stafford U.K. 52°49N 2°7W 66 E5
Stafford U.S.A. 37°58N 98°36W 172 G4
Stafford, L. U.S.A. 29°20N 82°29W 179 F7
Stafford Springs U.S.A. 41°57N 72°18W 175 E12
Staffordshire □ U.K. 52°53N 2°10W 66 E5
Stagnone Italy 37°53N 12°26E 94 E5
Stagnone di Marsala ⌓ Italy 37°52N 12°26E 94 E5
Staines-upon-Thames U.K. 51°26N 0°29W 67 F7
Stainz Austria 46°53N 15°17E 78 E8
Stakhanov Ukraine 48°35N 38°40E 85 H10
Stalać Serbia 43°43N 21°28E 96 C5
Stalida Greece 35°17N 25°25E 101 D7
Stallarholmen Sweden 59°22N 17°12E 62 E11
Ställdalen Sweden 59°56N 14°56E 62 E8
Stalowa Wola Poland 50°34N 22°3E 83 H9
Stalybridge U.K. 53°28N 2°3W 66 D5
Stamford Australia 21°15S 143°46E 150 C3
Stamford U.K. 52°39N 0°29W 67 E7
Stamford Conn., U.S.A. 41°3N 73°32W 175 E11
Stamford N.Y., U.S.A. 42°25N 74°38W 175 D10
Stamford Tex., U.S.A. 32°57N 99°48W 176 E5
Stampriet Namibia 24°20S 18°28E 144 B2
Stamps U.S.A. 33°22N 93°30W 176 E8
Stančevo = Kalipetrovo Bulgaria 44°5N 27°14E 97 B11
Standerton S. Africa 26°55S 29°7E 145 C4
Standish U.S.A. 43°59N 83°57W 173 D12
Stanford S. Africa 34°26S 19°29E 144 D2
Stanford U.S.A. 47°9N 110°13W 168 C8
Stånga Sweden 57°17N 18°29E 63 G12
Stanger S. Africa 29°27S 31°14E 145 C5
Stängselåsen = Salpausselkä Finland 61°3N 26°15E 84 B4
Stanhope Australia 36°27S 144°59E 153 D6
Stanišić Serbia 45°56N 19°10E 80 E4
Stanislaus → U.S.A. 37°40N 121°14W 170 H5
Stanisławów Poland 52°18N 21°33E 83 F8
Stanley Australia 40°46S 145°19E 151 G4
Stanley China 22°13N 114°12E 111 a
Stanley Falk. Is. 51°40S 59°51W 192 D5
Stanley U.K. 54°53N 1°41W 66 C6
Stanley Idaho, U.S.A. 44°13N 114°56W 168 D6
Stanley N. Dak., U.S.A. 48°19N 102°23W 172 A2
Stanley N.Y., U.S.A. 42°48N 77°6W 174 D7
Stanley Mission Canada 55°25N 104°33W 163 B8
Stanley Res. India 11°50N 77°40E 127 J3
Stannards U.S.A. 42°5N 77°55W 174 D7
Stanovoy Khrebet Russia 55°0N 130°0E 107 D14
Stanovoy Ra. = Stanovoy Khrebet Russia 55°0N 130°0E 107 D14
Stansmore Ra. Australia 21°23S 128°33E 148 D4
Stansted, London ✕ (STN) U.K. 51°54N 0°14E 67 F8
Stanthorpe Australia 28°36S 151°59E 151 D5
Stanton U.S.A. 32°8N 101°48W 176 E4
Stanwood U.S.A. 48°15N 122°23W 170 B4
Staples Canada 42°10N 82°35W 174 D2
Staples U.S.A. 46°21N 94°48W 172 B6
Stapleton U.S.A. 41°29N 100°31W 172 E3
Stapodia Greece 37°24N 25°34E 99 D7
Stąporków Poland 51°9N 20°31E 83 G7
Star City Canada 52°50N 104°20W 163 C8
Star Lake U.S.A. 44°10N 75°2W 175 B9
Stará L'ubovňa Slovakia 49°18N 20°42E 79 B13
Stara Moravica Serbia 45°50N 19°30E 80 E4
Stara Pazova Serbia 44°58N 20°10E 80 F5
Stara Planina Bulgaria 43°15N 23°0E 96 C7
Stara Sil Ukraine 49°29N 22°58E 83 J9
Stará Turá Slovakia 48°47N 17°42E 79 C10
Stara Ushytsya Ukraine 48°35N 27°8E 81 B12
Stara Zagora Bulgaria 42°26N 25°39E 97 D9
Stara Zagora □ Bulgaria 42°26N 25°39E 97 D9
Starachowice Poland 51°3N 21°2E 83 G8
Staraya Russa Russia 57°58N 31°23E 84 D6
Starbuck I. Kiribati 5°37S 155°55W 157 H12
Starchiojd Romania 45°19N 26°11E 81 E11
Starcke △ Australia 14°56S 145°2E 150 A4
Stargard Szczeciński Poland 53°20N 15°0E 82 E2
Stari Bar Montenegro 42°7N 19°10E 96 D3
Stari Grad Croatia 43°10N 16°38E 93 E13
Stari Trg Slovenia 45°29N 15°7E 93 C12
Staritsa Russia 56°33N 34°55E 84 D8
Starke U.S.A. 29°57N 82°7W 178 F7
Starkville U.S.A. 33°28N 88°49W 177 E10
Starnberg Germany 48°0N 11°21E 77 H7
Starnberger See Germany 47°54N 11°19E 77 H7
Staro Oryakhovo Bulgaria 42°59N 27°47E 97 D11
Starobilsk Ukraine 49°16N 39°0E 85 H10
Starodub Russia 52°30N 32°50E 85 F7
Starogard Gdański Poland 53°59N 18°30E 82 E5
Starokonstantinov = Starokonstyantyniv Ukraine 49°48N 27°10E 75 D14
Starokonstyantyniv Ukraine 49°48N 27°10E 75 D14
Starokozache Ukraine 46°20N 29°59E 81 D14
Starominskaya Russia 46°33N 39°0E 87 G4
Staroshcherbinovskaya Russia 46°40N 38°53E 87 G4
Starrs Mill U.S.A. 33°19N 84°31W 178 B5
Start Pt. U.K. 50°13N 3°39W 67 G4
Stary Sącz Poland 49°33N 20°35E 83 J7
Staryy Biryuzyak Russia 44°46N 46°50E 87 H8
Staryy Chartoriysk Ukraine 51°15N 25°54E 75 C13
Staryy Krym Ukraine 45°3N 35°8E 85 K8
Staryy Oskol Russia 51°19N 37°55E 85 G9
Staryy Sambir Ukraine 49°27N 22°59E 83 J9
Stassfurt Germany 51°51N 11°35E 76 D7
Staszów Poland 50°33N 21°10E 83 H8
State College U.S.A. 40°48N 77°52W 174 F7
Stateline U.S.A. 38°57N 119°56W 170 G7
Staten, I. = Estados, I. de Los Argentina 54°40S 64°30W 192 D4
Staten I. U.S.A. 40°35N 74°9W 175 F10
Statesboro U.S.A. 32°27N 81°47W 178 C8
Statesville U.S.A. 35°47N 80°53W 177 D14
Statham U.S.A. 33°58N 83°35W 178 B6
Statia = St. Eustatius W. Indies 17°20N 63°0W 183 C7
Stauffer U.S.A. 34°45N 119°3W 171 L7
Staunton Ill., U.S.A. 39°1N 89°47W 172 F9
Staunton Va., U.S.A. 38°9N 79°4W 173 F14
Stavanger Norway 58°57N 5°40E 61 G11
Stavelot Belgium 50°23N 5°55E 69 D5
Stavern Norway 59°0N 10°1E 61 G14
Stavoren Neths. 52°53N 5°22E 69 B5
Stavropol Russia 45°5N 42°0E 87 H6
Stavropol □ Russia 47°20N 42°50E 87 G6
Stavros Cyprus 35°1N 32°38E 101 D11
Stavros Kriti, Greece 35°12N 24°45E 101 D6
Stavros Thessaloniki, Greece 40°39N 23°43E 96 F7
Stavros, Akra Greece 35°26N 24°58E 101 D6
Stavroupoli Greece 41°12N 24°45E 97 E8
Stawell Australia 37°5S 142°47E 152 D5
Stawell → Australia 20°20S 142°55E 150 C3
Stawiski Poland 53°22N 22°9E 82 E9
Stawiszyn Poland 51°56N 18°4E 83 G5
Stayner Canada 44°25N 80°5W 174 B4
Stayton U.S.A. 44°48N 122°48W 168 D2
Steamboat Springs U.S.A. 40°29N 106°50W 168 F10
Steblevë Albania 41°23N 20°33E 96 E4
Steele Ala., U.S.A. 33°56N 86°12W 178 B3
Steele N. Dak., U.S.A. 46°51N 99°55W 172 B4
Steelton U.S.A. 40°14N 76°50W 174 F8
Steen River Canada 59°40N 117°12W 162 B5
Steens Mt. U.S.A. 42°35N 118°40W 168 E4
Steenstrup Gletscher Greenland 75°15N 57°0W 57 B5
Steenwijk Neths. 52°47N 6°7E 69 B6
Steep Pt. Australia 26°8S 113°8E 149 E1
Steep Rock Canada 51°30N 98°48W 163 C9
Ştefan Vodă Moldova 46°27N 29°42E 81 D14
Ştefăneşti Romania 47°44N 27°15E 81 C12
Stefanie L. = Chew Bahir Ethiopia 4°40N 36°50E 131 G2
Stefansson Bay Antarctica 67°20S 59°8E 55 C5
Stefansson I. Canada 73°20N 105°45W 161 C10
Stege Denmark 54°59N 12°18E 63 K6
Ştei Romania 46°32N 22°27E 80 D7
Steiermark □ Austria 47°26N 15°0E 78 D8
Steigerwald Germany 49°44N 10°26E 77 F6
Steigerwald ⌓ Germany 49°50N 10°30E 77 F6
Steilacoom U.S.A. 47°10N 122°36W 170 C4
Steilrandberge Namibia 17°45S 13°20E 144 A1
Steinbach Canada 49°32N 96°40W 163 D9
Steinfurt Germany 52°9N 7°20E 76 C3
Steinhatchee U.S.A. 29°40N 83°23W 178 F6
Steinhausen Namibia 21°49S 18°20E 144 B2
Steinheim Germany 51°51N 9°5E 76 D5
Steinhuder Meer Germany 52°29N 9°21E 76 C5
Steinhuder Meer ⌓ Germany 52°30N 9°16E 76 C5
Steinkjer Norway 64°1N 11°31E 60 D14
Steinkopf S. Africa 29°18S 17°43E 144 C2
Steinwald ⌓ Germany 49°55N 12°8E 77 F8
Stellarton Canada 45°32N 62°30W 165 C7
Stellenbosch S. Africa 33°58S 18°50E 144 D2
Stélvio, Paso dello Italy 46°32N 10°27E 92 B7
Stenay France 49°29N 5°12E 71 C12
Stendal Germany 52°36N 11°53E 76 C7
Stende Latvia 57°11N 22°33E 82 A9
Stenhamra Sweden 59°20N 17°41E 62 E11
Stenshuvud △ Sweden 55°39N 14°15E 63 J8
Stenstorp Sweden 58°17N 13°45E 63 F7
Stenungsund Sweden 58°6N 11°50E 63 F5
Steornabhaigh = Stornoway U.K. 58°13N 6°23W 65 C2
Stepanakert = Xankändi Azerbaijan 39°52N 46°49E 105 C12
Stepanavan Armenia 41°1N 44°23E 87 K7
Stephens, C. N.Z. 40°42S 173°58E 155 A8
Stephens Creek Australia 31°50S 141°30E 152 A4
Stephens I. Canada 54°10N 130°45W 162 C2
Stephens I. N.Z. 40°40S 174°1E 155 A9
Stephens L. Canada 56°32N 95°0W 163 B9
Stephenville Canada 48°31N 58°35W 165 C8
Stephenville U.S.A. 32°13N 98°12W 176 E5
Stepnica Poland 53°38N 14°36E 82 E1
Stepnogorsk Kazakhstan 52°21N 71°53E 109 B8
Steppe Asia 50°0N 50°0E 102 C7
Sterea Ellas □ Greece 38°50N 23°0E 98 C4
Sterkstroom S. Africa 31°32S 26°32E 144 D4
Sterling Colo., U.S.A. 40°37N 103°13W 168 F12
Sterling Ga., U.S.A. 31°16N 81°34W 178 D8
Sterling Ill., U.S.A. 41°48N 89°42W 172 E9
Sterling Kans., U.S.A. 38°13N 98°12W 172 F4
Sterling City U.S.A. 31°51N 101°0W 176 F4
Sterling Heights U.S.A. 42°35N 83°2W 173 D12
Sterling Run U.S.A. 41°25N 78°12W 174 E6
Sterlitamak Russia 53°40N 56°0E 108 B5
Sternberg Germany 53°42N 11°50E 76 B7
Šternberk Czechia 49°45N 17°15E 79 B10
Sternes Greece 35°30N 24°9E 101 D6
Sterzing = Vipiteno Italy 46°54N 11°26E 93 B8
Stettin = Szczecin Poland 53°27N 14°27E 82 E1
Stettiner Haff Germany 53°47N 14°15E 76 B10
Stettler Canada 52°19N 112°40W 162 C6
Steubenville U.S.A. 40°22N 80°37W 174 F4
Stevenage U.K. 51°55N 0°13W 67 F7
Stevens Point U.S.A. 44°31N 89°34W 172 C9
Stevens Pottery U.S.A. 32°57N 83°17W 178 C6
Stevenson U.S.A. 45°42N 121°53W 170 E5
Stevenson → Australia 27°6S 135°33E 151 D2
Stevenson L. Canada 53°55N 96°0W 163 C9
Stevensville U.S.A. 46°30N 114°5W 168 C6
Stevns Klint Denmark 55°17N 12°28E 63 J6
Stewart Canada 55°56N 129°57W 162 B3
Stewart Ga., U.S.A. 33°25N 83°52W 178 B6
Stewart Nev., U.S.A. 39°5N 119°46W 170 F7
Stewart → Canada 63°19N 139°26W 160 E4
Stewart, C. Australia 11°57S 134°56E 150 A1
Stewart, I. Chile 54°50S 71°15W 192 D2
Stewart I. N.Z. 46°58S 167°54E 155 G2
Stewarts Point U.S.A. 38°39N 123°24W 170 G3
Stewartville U.S.A. 43°51N 92°29W 172 D7
Stewiacke Canada 45°9N 63°22W 165 C7
Steynsburg S. Africa 31°15S 25°49E 144 D4
Steyr Austria 48°3N 14°25E 78 C7
Steyr → Austria 48°3N 14°25E 78 C7
Steytlerville S. Africa 33°17S 24°19E 144 D3
Stia Italy 43°48N 11°42E 93 E8
Stigler U.S.A. 35°15N 95°8W 176 D7
Stigliano Italy 40°24N 16°14E 95 B9
Stigtomta Sweden 58°47N 16°48E 63 F10
Stikine → Canada 56°40N 132°30W 162 B2
Stilfontein S. Africa 26°51S 26°50E 144 C4
Stilida Greece 38°55N 22°47E 98 C4
Stillmore U.S.A. 32°27N 82°13W 178 C7
Stillwater N.Y., U.S.A. 42°55N 73°41W 175 D11
Stillwater Okla., U.S.A. 36°7N 97°4W 176 C6
Stillwater Range U.S.A. 39°50N 118°5W 168 G4
Stillwater Res. U.S.A. 43°54N 75°3W 175 C9
Stilo, Pta. Italy 38°25N 16°35E 95 D9
Stilwell U.S.A. 35°49N 94°38W 176 D7
Stînga Nistrului = Transnistria □ Moldova 47°20N 29°15E 81 C14
Štip Macedonia 41°42N 22°10E 96 E6
Stira Greece 38°9N 24°14E 98 C6
Stirling Canada 44°18N 77°33W 174 B7
Stirling N.Z. 46°14S 169°49E 155 G4
Stirling U.K. 56°8N 3°57W 65 E5
Stirling □ U.K. 56°12N 4°18W 65 E4
Stirling Ra. Australia 34°23S 118°0E 149 F2
Stirling Range △ Australia 34°26S 118°20E 149 F2
Stittsville Canada 45°15N 75°55W 175 A9
Stjernøya Norway 70°20N 22°40E 60 A20
Stjørdalshalsen Norway 63°29N 10°51E 60 E14
Stock Island U.S.A. 24°32N 81°34W 179 L8
Stocka Sweden 61°53N 17°20E 62 C11
Stockach Germany 47°50N 9°1E 77 H5
Stockaryd Sweden 57°19N 14°36E 63 G8
Stockbridge U.S.A. 33°33N 84°14W 178 B5
Stockerau Austria 48°24N 16°12E 79 C9
Stockholm Sweden 59°19N 18°4E 62 E12
Stockholm □ Sweden 59°30N 18°20E 62 E12
Stockholm Arlanda ✕ (ARN) Sweden 59°41N 17°56E 62 E11
Stockport U.K. 53°25N 2°9W 66 D5
Stocksbridge U.K. 53°29N 1°35W 66 D6
Stockton Calif., U.S.A. 37°58N 121°17W 170 H5
Stockton Kans., U.S.A. 39°26N 99°16W 172 F4
Stockton Mo., U.S.A. 37°42N 93°48W 172 G7
Stockton-on-Tees U.K. 54°35N 1°19W 66 C6
Stockton-on-Tees □ U.K. 54°35N 1°19W 66 C6
Stockton Plateau U.S.A. 30°30N 102°30W 176 F3
Stoczek Łukowski Poland 51°58N 21°58E 83 G8
Stöde Sweden 62°28N 16°35E 62 B10
Stoeng Treng Cambodia 13°31N 105°58E 120 F5
Stoer, Pt. of U.K. 58°16N 5°23W 65 C3
Stogovo Macedonia 41°31N 20°38E 96 E4
Stoholm Denmark 56°30N 9°8E 63 H3
Stoke N.Z. 41°19S 173°14E 155 B8
Stoke-on-Trent U.K. 53°1N 2°11W 66 D5
Stoke-on-Trent □ U.K. 53°1N 2°11W 66 D5
Stokes △ Australia 33°45S 121°11E 149 F3
Stokes Bay Canada 45°0N 81°28W 174 B3
Stokes Pt. Australia 40°10S 143°56E 151 G3
Stokes Ra. Australia 15°50S 130°50E 148 C5
Stokksnes Iceland 64°14N 14°58W 60 D6
Stokmarknes Norway 68°34N 14°54E 60 B16
Stolac Bos.-H. 43°5N 17°59E 96 C1
Stolberg Germany 50°47N 6°13E 76 E2
Stolbovoy, Ostrov Russia 74°44N 135°14E 107 B14
Stolbtsy = Stowbtsy Belarus 53°30N 26°43E 75 B14
Stolin Belarus 51°53N 26°50E 75 C14
Stöllet Sweden 60°26N 13°15E 62 D7
Stolnici Romania 44°31N 24°48E 81 F9
Stomio Greece 35°21N 23°32E 101 D5
Ston Croatia 42°51N 17°43E 93 F14
Stone U.K. 52°55N 2°9W 66 E5
Stone Mountain U.S.A. 33°49N 84°10W 178 B5
Stoneboro U.S.A. 41°20N 80°7W 174 E4
Stonehaven U.K. 56°59N 2°12W 65 E6
Stonehenge Australia 24°22S 143°17E 150 C3
Stonehenge U.K. 51°9N 1°45W 67 F6
Stonewall Canada 50°10N 97°19W 163 C9
Stony I. U.S.A. 43°53N 76°19W 175 C8
Stony L. Man., Canada 58°51N 98°40W 163 B9
Stony L. Ont., Canada 44°30N 78°5W 174 B6
Stony Point U.S.A. 41°14N 73°59W 175 E11
Stony Pt. U.S.A. 43°50N 76°18W 175 C8
Stony Rapids Canada 59°16N 105°50W 163 B7
Stony Tunguska = Tunguska, Podkamennaya → Russia 61°50N 90°13E 107 C10
Stonyford U.S.A. 39°23N 122°33W 170 F4
Stopnica Poland 50°27N 20°57E 83 H7
Storå Sweden 59°42N 15°6E 62 E9
Storå → Denmark 56°20N 8°19E 63 H2
Stora Gla Sweden 59°30N 12°30E 62 E6
Stora Le Sweden 59°5N 11°55E 62 E5
Stora Lulevatten Sweden 67°10N 19°30E 60 C18
Stora Sjöfallet △ Sweden 67°36N 17°45E 60 C17
Storavan Sweden 65°45N 18°10E 60 D18
Stord Norway 59°52N 5°23E 61 G11
Store Bælt Denmark 55°20N 11°0E 63 J4
Store Heddinge Denmark 55°18N 12°23E 63 J6
Store Koldewey Greenland 76°30N 19°0W 57 B9
Store Mosse △ Sweden 57°18N 13°55E 63 G7
Storebro Sweden 57°35N 15°52E 63 G9
Storfors Sweden 59°32N 14°17E 62 E8
Storkerson Pen. Canada 72°30N 106°30W 160 C10
Storlien Sweden 63°19N 12°6E 62 A6
Storm B. Australia 43°10S 147°30E 151 G4
Storm Lake U.S.A. 42°39N 95°13W 172 D6
Stormberge S. Africa 31°16S 26°17E 144 D4
Stormsrivier S. Africa 33°59S 23°52E 144 D3
Stornoway U.K. 58°13N 6°23W 65 C2
Storo Italy 45°51N 10°35E 92 C7
Storozhinets = Storozhynets Ukraine 48°14N 25°45E 81 B10
Storozhynets Ukraine 48°14N 25°45E 81 B10
Storrs U.S.A. 41°49N 72°15W 175 E12
Storsjön Gävleborg, Sweden 60°35N 16°45E 62 D10
Storsjön Jämtland, Sweden 62°48N 13°7E 62 B7
Storsjön Jämtland, Sweden 63°9N 14°30E 62 A8
Storstrømmen Greenland 76°17N 22°25W 57 B8
Storuman Sweden 65°5N 17°10E 60 D17
Storuman, L. Sweden 65°13N 16°50E 60 D17
Storvätteshågna Sweden 62°6N 12°30E 62 B6
Storvik Sweden 60°35N 16°33E 62 D10
Storvreta Sweden 59°58N 17°44E 62 E11
Stouffville Canada 43°58N 79°15W 174 C5
Stoughton Canada 49°40N 103°0W 163 D8
Stour → Dorset, U.K. 50°43N 1°47W 67 G6
Stour → Kent, U.K. 51°18N 1°22E 67 F9
Stour → Suffolk, U.K. 51°57N 1°4E 67 F9
Stourbridge U.K. 52°28N 2°8W 67 E5
Stout L. Canada 52°0N 94°40W 163 C10
Stove Pipe Wells Village U.S.A. 36°35N 117°11W 171 J9
Støvring Denmark 56°54N 9°50E 63 H3
Stow U.S.A. 41°10N 81°27W 174 E3
Stowbtsy Belarus 53°30N 26°43E 75 B14
Stowmarket U.K. 52°12N 1°0E 67 E9
Strabane U.K. 54°50N 7°27W 64 B4
Stracin Macedonia 42°13N 22°2E 96 D6
Stradella Italy 45°5N 9°18E 92 C6
Strahan Australia 42°9S 145°20E 151 G4
Strajitsa Bulgaria 43°14N 25°58E 97 C9
Strakonice Czechia 49°15N 13°53E 78 B6
Straldzha Bulgaria 42°35N 26°40E 97 D10
Stralsund Germany 54°18N 13°4E 76 A9
Strand S. Africa 34°9S 18°48E 144 D2
Stranda Møre og Romsdal, Norway 62°19N 6°58E 60 E12
Stranda Nord-Trøndelag, Norway 63°33N 10°14E 60 E14
Strandby Denmark 57°30N 10°29E 63 G4
Strangford L. U.K. 54°30N 5°37W 64 B6
Strängnäs Sweden 59°23N 17°2E 62 E11
Stranorlar Ireland 54°48N 7°46W 64 B4
Stranraer U.K. 54°54N 5°1W 65 G3
Strasbourg Canada 51°4N 104°55W 163 C8
Strasbourg France 48°35N 7°42E 71 D14
Strasburg Germany 53°30N 13°43E 76 B9
Străşeni Moldova 47°8N 28°36E 81 C13
Strássa Sweden 59°44N 15°12E 62 E9
Stratford N.S.W., Australia 32°7S 151°55E 153 B9
Stratford Vic., Australia 37°59S 147°7E 153 D7
Stratford Canada 43°23N 81°0W 174 C4
Stratford N.Z. 39°20S 174°19E 154 F3
Stratford Calif., U.S.A. 36°11N 119°49W 170 J7
Stratford Conn., U.S.A. 41°12N 73°8W 175 E11
Stratford Tex., U.S.A. 36°20N 102°4W 176 C3
Stratford-upon-Avon U.K. 52°12N 1°42W 67 E6
Strath Spey U.K. 57°9N 3°49W 65 D5
Strathalbyn Australia 35°13S 138°53E 152 C3
Strathaven U.K. 55°40N 4°5W 65 F4
Strathcona ⌓ Canada 49°38N 125°40W 162 D3
Strathmore Canada 51°5N 113°18W 162 C6
Strathmore U.K. 56°37N 3°7W 65 E5
Strathmore U.S.A. 36°9N 119°4W 170 J7
Strathnaver Canada 53°20N 122°33W 162 C4
Strathpeffer U.K. 57°35N 4°32W 65 D4
Strathroy Canada 42°58N 81°38W 174 D3
Strathy Pt. U.K. 58°36N 4°1W 65 C4
Stratoni Greece 40°31N 23°49E 96 F7
Strattanville U.S.A. 41°12N 79°19W 174 E5
Stratton U.S.A. 45°8N 70°26W 175 A14
Stratton Mt. U.S.A. 43°4N 72°55W 175 C12
Straubing Germany 48°52N 12°34E 77 G8
Straumnes Iceland 66°26N 23°8W 60 C2
Strausberg Germany 52°35N 13°54E 76 C9
Strawberry → U.S.A. 40°10N 110°24W 168 F8
Strážnice Czechia 48°54N 17°19E 79 C10
Streaky B. Australia 32°48S 134°13E 151 E1
Streaky Bay Australia 32°51S 134°18E 151 E1
Streator U.S.A. 41°8N 88°50W 172 E9
Středočeský □ Czechia 49°55N 14°30E 78 B7
Streetsboro U.S.A. 41°14N 81°21W 174 E3
Streetsville Canada 43°35N 79°42W 174 C5
Strehaia Romania 44°37N 23°10E 81 F8
Strelcha Bulgaria 42°25N 24°19E 97 D8
Streng → Cambodia 13°12N 103°37E 120 F4
Stresa Italy 45°52N 8°28E 92 C5
Streymoy Færoe Is. 62°8N 7°5W 60 E9
Strezhevoy Russia 60°42N 77°34E 106 C8
Stříbro Czechia 49°44N 13°0E 78 A6
Strilky Ukraine 49°20N 22°59E 83 J9
Strimonas → Greece 40°46N 23°51E 96 F7
Stroeder Argentina 40°12S 62°37W 192 B4
Strofades Greece 37°15N 21°0E 98 D3
Strokestown Ireland 53°47N 8°5W 64 C3
Stroma U.K. 58°41N 3°7W 65 C5
Stromberg-Heuchelberg ⌓ Germany 49°2N 8°50E 77 F4
Strómboli Italy 38°47N 15°13E 95 D8
Stromeferry U.K. 57°21N 5°33W 65 D3
Stromness U.K. 58°58N 3°17W 65 C5
Strömsbruk Sweden 61°52N 17°18E 62 C11
Stromsburg U.S.A. 41°7N 97°36W 172 E5
Strömsnäsbruk Sweden 56°35N 13°45E 63 H7
Strömstad Sweden 58°56N 11°10E 63 F5
Strömsund Sweden 63°51N 15°33E 60 E16
Strongili Greece 36°6N 29°42E 99 E11
Strongoli Italy 39°16N 17°3E 95 C10
Strongsville U.S.A. 41°19N 81°50W 174 E3
Stronie Śląskie Poland 50°18N 16°53E 83 H3
Stronsay U.K. 59°7N 2°35W 65 B6
Stropkov Slovakia 49°13N 21°39E 79 B14
Stroud U.K. 51°45N 2°13W 67 F5
Stroud Road Australia 32°18S 151°57E 153 B9
Stroudsburg U.S.A. 40°59N 75°12W 175 F9
Stroumbi Cyprus 34°53N 32°29E 101 E11
Štrpce = Shtërpcë Kosovo 42°14N 21°1E 96 D5
Struer Denmark 56°30N 8°35E 63 H2
Struga Macedonia 41°11N 20°44E 96 E4
Strugi Krasnyye Russia 58°21N 29°1E 84 C5
Strumica Macedonia 41°28N 22°41E 96 E6
Strumica → Europe 41°20N 23°22E 96 E7
Strumok Ukraine 45°43N 29°27E 81 E14
Struthers U.S.A. 41°4N 80°39W 174 E4
Stryama Bulgaria 42°16N 24°54E 97 D8
Stryker U.S.A. 48°41N 114°46W 168 B6
Stryków Poland 51°55N 19°33E 83 G6
Stryy Ukraine 49°16N 23°48E 75 D12
Strzegom Poland 50°58N 16°20E 83 H3
Strzelce Krajeńskie Poland 52°52N 15°33E 83 F2
Strzelce Opolskie Poland 50°31N 18°18E 83 H5
Strzelecki Cr. → Australia 29°37S 139°59E 151 D2
Strzelecki Desert Australia 29°30S 140°0E 151 D3
Strzelin Poland 50°46N 17°2E 83 H4
Strzelno Poland 52°35N 18°9E 83 F5
Strzybnica Poland 50°28N 18°48E 83 H5
Strzyżów Poland 49°52N 21°47E 83 J8
Stuart Fla., U.S.A. 27°12N 80°15W 179 H9
Stuart Nebr., U.S.A. 42°36N 99°8W 172 D4
Stuart → Canada 54°0N 123°35W 162 C4
Stuart Bluff Ra. Australia 22°50S 131°52E 148 D5
Stuart I. U.S.A. 63°35N 162°30W 166 C7
Stuart L. Canada 54°30N 124°30W 162 C4
Stuart Mts. N.Z. 45°2S 167°39E 155 F2
Stuart Ra. Australia 29°10S 134°56E 151 D1
Stubbekøbing Denmark 54°53N 12°9E 63 K6
Stuben Austria 47°10N 10°8E 78 D3
Studen Kladenets, Yazovir Bulgaria 41°37N 25°30E 97 E9
Studenica Serbia 43°29N 20°32E 96 C4
Studenka Czechia 49°44N 18°5E 79 B11
Studholme N.Z. 44°42S 171°9E 155 E6
Stugun Sweden 63°10N 15°40E 62 A9
Stuhr Germany 53°5N 8°44E 76 B4
Stull L. Canada 54°24N 92°34W 164 B1
Stung Treng = Stoeng Treng Cambodia 13°31N 105°58E 120 F5
Stupart → Canada 56°0N 93°25W 164 A1
Stupava Slovakia 48°17N 17°2E 79 C10
Stupino Russia 54°57N 38°2E 84 E10
Sturge I. Antarctica 67°26S 164°47E 55 C11
Sturgeon B. Canada 52°0N 97°50W 163 C9
Sturgeon Bay U.S.A. 44°50N 87°23W 172 C10
Sturgeon Falls Canada 46°25N 79°57W 164 C4
Sturgeon L. Alta., Canada 55°6N 117°32W 162 B5
Sturgeon L. Ont., Canada 50°0N 90°45W 164 C1
Sturgeon L. Ont., Canada 44°28N 78°43W 174 B6
Sturgis Canada 51°56N 102°36W 163 C8
Sturgis Mich., U.S.A. 41°48N 85°25W 173 E11
Sturgis S. Dak., U.S.A. 44°25N 103°31W 172 C2
Sturkö Sweden 56°5N 15°42E 63 H9
Štúrovo Slovakia 47°48N 18°41E 79 D11
Sturt △ Australia 29°17S 141°37E 151 D3
Sturt Cr. → Australia 19°8S 127°50E 148 C4
Sturt Stony Desert Australia 28°30S 141°0E 151 D3
Sturts Meadows Australia 31°18S 141°42E 152 A4
Stutterheim S. Africa 32°33S 27°28E 144 D4
Stuttgart Germany 48°48N 9°11E 77 G5
Stuttgart U.S.A. 34°30N 91°33W 176 D9
Stuttgart Echterdingen ✕ (STR) Germany 48°42N 9°11E 77 G5
Stuyvesant U.S.A. 42°23N 73°45W 175 D11
Stykkishólmur Iceland 65°2N 22°40W 60 D2
Styria = Steiermark □ Austria 47°26N 15°0E 78 D8
Styrsö Sweden 57°37N 11°46E 63 G5
Su Xian = Suzhou China 33°41N 116°59E 114 H9
Suakin Sudan 19°8N 37°20E 137 D4
Suakin Archipelago Sudan 18°42N 38°30E 137 D4
Suamico U.S.A. 44°38N 88°2W 172 C9
Suan N. Korea 38°42N 126°22E 115 E14
Suana Indonesia 8°44S 115°36E 119 K18
Suape Brazil 8°24S 35°0W 189 B3
Suar India 29°2N 79°3E 125 E8
Şubā Si. Arabia 27°10N 35°40E 128 E2
Subang Indonesia 6°34S 107°45E 119 G12
Subansiri → India 26°48N 93°50E 123 F18
Subarnagiri India 19°50N 83°51E 126 E6
Subarnarekha → India 22°34N 87°24E 125 H12
Subay', Urūq Si. Arabia 22°15N 43°5E 137 C5
Subayhah Si. Arabia 30°2N 38°50E 128 D3
Subcetate Romania 45°36N 23°0E 80 E8
Subi Indonesia 2°58N 108°50E 118 D3
Subiaco Italy 41°56N 13°5E 93 G10
Subotica Serbia 46°6N 19°39E 80 D4
Suceava Romania 47°38N 26°16E 81 C11
Suceava □ Romania 47°37N 25°40E 81 C10
Suceava → Romania 47°32N 26°32E 81 C11
Sucha-Beskidzka Poland 49°44N 19°35E 83 J6
Suchan = Partizansk Russia 43°8N 133°9E 107 E14
Suchań Poland 53°18N 15°18E 83 E2
Suchedniów Poland 51°3N 20°49E 83 G7
Suchil Mexico 23°39N 103°54W 180 C4
Suchou = Suzhou China 31°19N 120°38E 117 B13
Süchow = Xuzhou China 34°18N 117°10E 115 G9
Suchowola Poland 53°33N 23°3E 82 E10
Suck → Ireland 53°17N 8°3W 64 C3
Sucre Bolivia 19°0S 65°15W 186 G5
Sućuraj Croatia 43°10N 17°8E 93 E14
Sucuriú → Brazil 20°47S 51°38W 187 H8
Sud □ Cameroon 2°30N 11°45E 139 E7
Sud, Pte. du Canada 49°3N 62°14W 165 C7
Sud-Kivu □ Dem. Rep. of the Congo 3°0S 28°30E 142 C2
Sud-Ouest □ Cameroon 5°25N 9°20E 139 D6
Sud-Ouest, Pte. Canada 49°23N 63°36W 165 C7
Sud Ouest, Pte. Mauritius 20°28S 57°18E 141 d
Suda → Russia 59°0N 37°40E 84 C9
Sudak Ukraine 44°51N 34°57E 85 K8
Sudan U.S.A. 34°4N 102°31W 176 D3
Sudan ■ Africa 15°0N 30°0E 135 E11
Sudbury U.K. 52°2N 0°45E 67 E8
Sudd South Sudan 8°20N 30°0E 135 G12
Sudeifel = Deutsch-Luxemburgischer ⌓ Germany 49°58N 6°12E 77 F2
Süderbrarup Germany 54°38N 9°45E 76 A5
Süderlügum Germany 54°52N 8°54E 76 A4
Süderoogsand Germany 54°27N 8°28E 76 A4
Sudeten Mts. = Sudety Europe 50°20N 16°45E 79 A9
Sudety Europe 50°20N 16°45E 79 A9
Südheide ⌓ Germany 52°46N 10°10E 76 C6
Suðuroy Færoe Is. 61°32N 6°50W 60 F9
Sudi Tanzania 10°11S 39°57E 143 E4
Sudirman, Pegunungan Indonesia 4°30S 137°0E 119 E9
Sudiţi Romania 44°35N 27°38E 81 F12
Sudogda Russia 55°55N 40°50E 86 C5
Sudong, Pulau Singapore 1°13N 103°44E 121 d
Sudova Vyshnya Ukraine 49°46N 23°22E 83 J10
Sudzha Russia 51°14N 35°17E 85 G8
Sueca Spain 39°12N 0°21W 91 F4
Suemez I. U.S.A. 55°15N 133°20W 162 B2
Suez = El Suweis Egypt 29°58N 32°31E 137 F8
Suez, G. of = Suweis, Khalîg el Egypt 28°40N 33°0E 137 F8
Suez Canal = Suweis, Qanâ es Egypt 31°0N 32°20E 137 E8
Suffield Canada 50°12N 111°10W 162 C6
Suffolk U.S.A. 36°44N 76°35W 173 G15
Suffolk □ U.K. 52°16N 1°0E 67 E9
Şufiān Iran 38°16N 45°58E 105 C11
Şugag Romania 45°47N 23°37E 81 E8
Sugaing = Sagaing Myanmar 21°52N 95°59E 123 J19
Sugar Grove U.S.A. 41°59N 79°20W 174 E5
Sugar Hill U.S.A. 34°6N 84°2W 178 A5
Sugarcreek U.S.A. 41°25N 79°52W 174 E5
Sugarive → India 26°16N 86°24E 125 F12
Sughd □ Tajikistan 40°0N 69°0E 109 E7
Suğla Gölü Turkey 37°20N 32°0E 104 D5
Sugluk = Salluit Canada 62°14N 75°38W 161 E16
Sugun China 39°53N 76°47E 109 E9
Suha Reke = Therandë Kosovo 42°21N 20°50E 96 D4
Suhaia, Lacul Romania 43°45N 25°15E 81 G10
Şuḩār Oman 24°20N 56°40E 129 E8
Sühbaatar Mongolia 50°17N 106°10E 110 A10
Sühbaatar □ Mongolia 45°30N 114°0E 114 B8
Suheli Par India 10°5N 72°17E 127 J1
Suhl Germany 50°36N 10°42E 76 E6
Şuhut Turkey 38°31N 30°32E 99 C12
Sui Pakistan 28°37N 69°19E 124 E3
Sui Xian China 34°25N 115°2E 114 G8
Šuica Bos.-H. 43°52N 17°11E 80 G2
Suichang China 28°29N 119°15E 117 C12
Suichuan China 26°20N 114°32E 117 D10
Suide China 37°30N 110°12E 114 F6
Suifenhe China 44°25N 131°10E 115 B16
Suihua China 46°32N 126°55E 111 B14
Suijiang China 28°40N 103°59E 116 C4
Suining Hunan, China 26°35N 110°10E 117 D8
Suining Jiangsu, China 33°56N 117°58E 115 H9
Suining Sichuan, China 30°26N 105°35E 116 B5
Suiping China 33°10N 113°59E 114 H7
Suippes France 49°8N 4°30E 71 C11
Suir → Ireland 52°16N 7°9W 64 D4
Suisse = Switzerland ■ Europe 46°30N 8°0E 77 J4
Suisun City U.S.A. 38°15N 122°2W 170 G4
Suixi China 21°19N 110°18E 117 G8
Suiyang Guizhou, China 27°58N 107°18E 116 D6
Suiyang Heilongjiang, China 44°30N 130°56E 115 B16
Suizhong China 40°21N 120°20E 115 D11
Suizhou China 31°42N 113°24E 117 B9
Sujangarh India 27°42N 74°31E 124 F6
Sujiatun China 41°39N 123°20E 115 D12
Sukabumi Indonesia 6°56S 106°50E 119 G12
Sukadana Indonesia 1°10S 110°0E 118 E4
Sukagawa Japan 37°17N 140°23E 113 F10
Sukamade Indonesia 8°30S 113°52E 119 H15
Sukaraja Indonesia 2°28S 110°25E 118 E4
Sukarno-Hatta Int., Jakarta ✕ (CGK) Indonesia 6°7S 106°40E 119 G12
Sukawati Indonesia 8°35S 115°17E 119 K18
Sukch'ŏn N. Korea 39°22N 125°35E 115 E13
Sukhindol Bulgaria 43°11N 25°10E 97 C9
Sukhinichi Russia 54°8N 35°10E 84 E8
Sukhona → Russia 61°15N 46°39E 106 D4
Sukhothai Thailand 17°1N 99°49E 120 D2
Sukhumi = Sokhumi Georgia 43°0N 41°0E 87 J5
Sukkertoppen = Maniitsoq Greenland 65°26N 52°55W 57 D5
Sukkur Pakistan 27°42N 68°54E 124 F3
Sukkur Barrage Pakistan 27°40N 68°50E 124 F3
Sukma India 18°24N 81°45E 126 E5
Sukovo Serbia 43°4N 22°37E 96 C6
Sukri → India 25°4N 71°43E 124 G4
Sukumo Japan 32°56N 132°44E 113 H6
Sukunka → Canada 55°45N 121°15W 162 B4
Sula → Ukraine 49°40N 32°41E 85 H7
Sula, Kepulauan Indonesia 1°45S 125°0E 119 E7
Sulaco → Honduras 15°2N 87°44W 182 C2
Sulaiman Range Pakistan 30°30N 69°50E 124 D3
Sulaiman-Too Kyrgyzstan 40°31N 72°46E 109 D8
Sulak → Russia 43°20N 47°34E 87 J8
Sulakyurt Turkey 40°9N 33°43E 104 B5
Sūlār Iran 31°53N 51°54E 129 D6
Sulawesi Indonesia 2°0S 120°0E 119 E6
Sulawesi Barat □ Indonesia 3°0S 119°0E 119 E5
Sulawesi Sea = Celebes Sea Indonesia 3°0N 123°0E 119 D6
Sulawesi Selatan □ Indonesia 2°30S 120°0E 119 E6
Sulawesi Tengah □ Indonesia 1°30S 121°0E 119 E6
Sulawesi Tenggara □ Indonesia 3°50S 122°0E 119 E6
Sulawesi Utara □ Indonesia 1°0N 124°0E 119 D6
Sulechów Poland 52°5N 15°40E 83 F2
Sulęcin Poland 52°26N 15°10E 83 F2
Suleja Nigeria 9°10N 7°10E 139 D6
Sulejów Poland 51°26N 19°53E 83 G6
Sulejówek Poland 52°13N 21°17E 83 F8
Süleymanlı Turkey 38°58N 27°49E 99 C9
Sulima S. Leone 6°58N 11°32W 138 D2
Sulina Romania 45°10N 29°40E 81 E14
Sulina, Braţul → Romania 45°10N 29°20E 81 E14
Sulingen Germany 52°41N 8°48E 76 C4
Suliţa Romania 47°39N 26°59E 81 C11
Sulitjelma Norway 67°9N 16°3E 60 C17
Sulkowice Poland 49°50N 19°49E 83 J6
Sullana Peru 4°52S 80°39W 188 A1
Süller Turkey 38°9N 29°29E 99 C11
Sullivan Ill., U.S.A. 39°36N 88°37W 172 F9
Sullivan Ind., U.S.A. 39°6N 87°24W 172 F10
Sullivan Mo., U.S.A. 38°13N 91°10W 172 F8
Sullivan Bay Canada 50°55N 126°50W 162 C3

Sullivan I. = Lanbi Kyun
Myanmar 10°50N 98°20E 121 G2
Sullom Voe U.K. 60°27N 1°20W 65 A7
Sullorsuaq Greenland 70°5N 53°0W 57 C5
Sully-sur-Loire France 47°45N 2°20E 78 E5
Sulmona Italy 42°3N 13°55E 93 F10
Süloğlu Turkey 41°44N 26°53E 97 E10
Sulphur La., U.S.A. 30°14N 93°23W 176 F8
Sulphur Okla., U.S.A. 34°31N 96°58W 176 D6
Sulphur Pt. Canada 60°56N 114°48W 162 A6
Sulphur Springs U.S.A. 33°8N 95°36W 176 E7
Sultan Canada 47°36N 82°47W 164 C3
Sultan U.S.A. 47°52N 121°49W 170 C5
Sultan Hamud Kenya 2°1S 37°20E 142 C4
Sultan Dağları Turkey 38°20N 31°20E 104 C4
Sultanabad = Arāk Iran 34°0N 49°40E 129 C6
Sultanhisar Turkey 37°53N 28°9E 99 D10
Sultaniça Turkey 40°37N 26°8E 97 F10
Sultaniye Turkey 40°32N 28°44E 99 C10
Sultanpur Mad. P., India 23°9N 77°56E 124 H8
Sultanpur Punjab, India 31°13N 75°11E 124 D6
Sultanpur U. P., India 26°18N 82°4E 125 F10
Sulu Arch. Phil. 6°0N 121°0E 119 C6
Sulu Sea E. Indies 8°0N 120°0E 119 C6
Sülüklü Turkey 38°53N 32°20E 104 C5
Suluova Turkey 40°46N 35°32E 104 B6
Sulūq Libya 31°44N 20°14E 135 B10
Suluru India 13°42N 80°1E 127 H5
Sulzbach Germany 49°18N 7°3E 77 F3
Sulzbach-Rosenberg
   Germany 49°30N 11°44E 77 F7
Sulzberger Ice Shelf
   Antarctica 78°0S 150°0W 55 E13
Sumalata Indonesia 1°0N 122°31E 119 D6
Sumampa Argentina 29°25S 63°29W 190 B3
Sumatera Indonesia 0°40N 100°20E 118 D2
Sumatera Barat □
   Indonesia 1°0S 101°0E 118 E2
Sumatera Selatan □
   Indonesia 3°0S 104°0E 118 E2
Sumatera Utara □
   Indonesia 2°30N 98°0E 118 D1
Sumatra = Sumatera
   Indonesia 0°40N 100°20E 118 D2
Sumatra U.S.A. 30°1N 84°59W 178 E5
Sumava △ Czechia 49°0N 13°49E 78 C6
Sumba Indonesia 9°45S 119°35E 119 F5
Sumba, Selat Indonesia 9°0S 118°40E 119 F5
Sumbawa Indonesia 8°26S 117°30E 118 F5
Sumbawa Besar
   Indonesia 8°30S 117°26E 118 F5
Sumbawanga Tanzania 8°0S 31°30E 140 F6
Sumbe Angola 11°10S 13°48E 140 G2
Sumbu △ Zambia 8°43S 30°22E 143 D3
Sumburgh Hd. U.K. 59°52N 1°17W 65 B7
Sumdeo India 31°26N 78°44E 125 D8
Sumdo China 35°6N 78°41E 125 B8
Sumé Brazil 7°39S 36°55W 189 D11
Sumedang Indonesia 6°52S 107°55E 119 G12
Sümeg Hungary 46°59N 17°20E 80 D2
Sumen = Shumen
   Bulgaria 43°18N 26°55E 97 C10
Sumenep Indonesia 7°1S 113°52E 119 G15
Sumgait = Sumqayıt
   Azerbaijan 40°34N 49°38E 87 K9
Summer L. U.S.A. 42°50N 120°45W 168 E3
Summerland Canada 49°32N 119°41W 162 D5
Summerland Key
   U.S.A. 24°40N 81°27W 179 L8
Summerside Canada 46°24N 63°47W 165 C7
Summersville U.S.A. 38°17N 80°51W 173 F13
Summerton U.S.A. 33°36N 80°20W 178 B9
Summertown U.S.A. 35°25N 82°16W 178 C7
Summerville Ga.,
   U.S.A. 34°29N 85°21W 177 D12
Summerville S.C.,
   U.S.A. 33°1N 80°11W 178 B9
Summit Lake Canada 54°20N 122°40W 162 C4
Summit Peak U.S.A. 37°21N 106°42W 169 H10
Sumner N.Z. 43°35S 172°48E 155 D7
Sumner Iowa, U.S.A. 42°51N 92°6W 172 D7
Sumner Wash., U.S.A. 47°12N 122°14W 170 C4
Sumner, L. N.Z. 42°42S 172°15E 155 C7
Sumoto Japan 34°21N 134°54E 113 G7
Šumperk Czechia 49°59N 16°59E 79 B9
Sumqayıt Azerbaijan 40°34N 49°38E 87 K9
Sumter U.S.A. 33°55N 80°21W 178 B9
Sumxi China 34°35N 80°22E 109 F10
Sumy Ukraine 50°57N 34°50E 85 G8
Sumy □ Ukraine 50°50N 34°0E 85 G8
Sun City S. Africa 25°17S 27°3E 144 C4
Sun City Center U.S.A. 27°43N 82°18W 179 M4
Sun Kosi → Nepal 26°59N 87°8E 125 F12
Sun Lakes U.S.A. 33°10N 111°52W 169 K8
Sun Valley U.S.A. 43°42N 114°21W 168 E6
Sunagawa Japan 43°29N 141°55E 112 C10
Sunan N. Korea 39°15N 125°40E 115 E13
Sunart, L. U.K. 56°42N 5°43W 65 E3
Sunburst U.S.A. 48°53N 111°55W 168 A8
Sunbury Australia 37°35S 144°44E 153 D6
Sunbury U.S.A. 40°52N 76°48W 175 E8
Sunchales Argentina 30°58S 61°35W 190 C3
Suncheon S. Korea 34°52N 127°31E 115 G14
Suncho Corral
   Argentina 27°55S 63°27W 190 B3
Sunch'on N. Korea 39°25N 125°56E 115 E13
Suncook U.S.A. 43°8N 71°27W 175 C13
Sunda, Selat Indonesia 6°20S 105°30E 118 F3
Sunda Is. Indonesia 5°0S 105°0E 156 H2
Sunda Str. = Sunda, Selat
   Indonesia 6°20S 105°30E 118 F3
Sunda Trench = Java Trench
   Ind. Oc. 9°0S 105°0E 118 F3
Sundance Canada 56°32N 94°4W 163 B10
Sundance U.S.A. 44°24N 104°23W 168 D11
Sundar Nagar India 31°32N 76°53E 124 D7
Sundarbans Asia 22°0N 89°0E 123 J16
Sundarbans △ India 22°0N 89°0E 125 J13
Sundargarh India 22°4N 84°5E 126 C7
Sundays = Sondags →
   S. Africa 33°44S 25°51E 144 D4
Sunderland Canada 44°16N 79°4W 164 B5
Sunderland U.K. 54°55N 1°23W 66 C6
Sundown △ Australia 28°49S 151°38E 151 D5
Sundre Canada 51°49N 114°38W 162 C6
Sunds Denmark 56°13N 9°1E 63 F3
Sundsvall Sweden 62°23N 17°17E 62 B11
Sundsvallsbukten
   Sweden 62°21N 17°25E 62 B11
Sungai Acheh Malaysia 5°8N 100°30E 121 c
Sungai Kolok Thailand 6°2N 101°58E 121 J3

Sungai Lembing
   Malaysia 3°55N 103°3E 121 L4
Sungai Petani Malaysia 5°37N 100°30E 121 K3
Sungaigerong Indonesia 2°59S 104°52E 118 E2
Sungailiat Indonesia 1°51S 106°8E 118 E3
Sungaipenuh Indonesia 2°1S 101°20E 118 E2
Sungari = Songhua Jiang →
   China 47°45N 132°30E 111 B15
Sunghua Chiang = Songhua
   Jiang → China 47°45N 132°30E 111 B15
Sungurlu Turkey 40°12N 34°21E 104 B6
Sunja Croatia 45°21N 16°35E 93 C13
Sunland Park U.S.A. 31°50N 106°40W 169 L10
Sunnansjö Sweden 60°13N 14°58E 62 D8
Sunndalsøra Norway 62°40N 8°33E 60 E13
Sunne Sweden 59°52N 13°5E 62 E7
Sunnemo Sweden 59°53N 13°44E 62 E7
Sunnyside U.S.A. 46°20N 120°0W 168 C4
Sunnyvale U.S.A. 37°23N 122°2W 170 H4
Sunrise U.S.A. 26°8N 80°14W 179 J9
Sunrise Manor U.S.A. 36°12N 115°4W 171 J11
Suntar Russia 62°15N 117°30E 107 C12
Sunyani Ghana 7°21N 2°22W 138 D4
Suomenselkä Finland 62°52N 24°0E 60 E21
Suomi = Finland ■
   Europe 63°0N 27°0E 60 E22
Suomussalmi Finland 64°54N 29°10E 60 D23
Suoyarvi Russia 62°3N 32°20E 84 A7
Supai U.S.A. 36°15N 112°41W 169 H7
Supaul India 26°10N 86°40E 125 F12
Superior Ariz., U.S.A. 33°18N 111°6W 169 K8
Superior Mont., U.S.A. 47°12N 114°53W 168 C6
Superior Nebr., U.S.A. 40°1N 98°4W 172 E4
Superior Wis., U.S.A. 46°44N 92°6W 172 B7
Superior, L. N. Amer. 47°0N 87°0W 164 C2
Supetar Croatia 43°25N 16°32E 93 E13
Suphan Buri Thailand 14°14N 100°10E 120 E3
Suphan Dağı Turkey 38°54N 42°48E 105 C10
Supiori Indonesia 1°0S 136°0E 119 D9
Suprasl Poland 53°13N 23°19E 83 E10
Supraśl → Poland 53°11N 22°57E 83 E9
Supsa → Georgia 42°2N 41°49E 87 J5
Supung Shuiku
   China 40°35N 124°50E 115 D13
Süq ash Shuyūkh Iraq 30°53N 46°28E 128 D5
Süq Suwayq Si. Arabia 24°23N 38°27E 128 E3
Suqian China 33°54N 118°8E 115 H10
Suquṭra = Socotra
   Yemen 12°30N 54°0E 131 E5
Şūr Lebanon 33°19N 35°16E 130 B4
Şūr Oman 22°34N 59°32E 131 C6
Sur, Pt. U.S.A. 36°18N 121°54W 170 J5
Sura → Russia 56°6N 46°0E 86 C8
Surab Pakistan 28°25N 66°15E 124 E2
Surabaja = Surabaya
   Indonesia 7°17S 112°45E 118 F4
Surabaya Indonesia 7°17S 112°45E 118 F4
Surahammar Sweden 59°43N 16°13E 62 E10
Suraia Romania 45°40N 27°25E 81 E12
Surakarta Indonesia 7°35S 110°48E 118 F4
Šurany Slovakia 48°6N 18°10E 79 C11
Surat Australia 27°10S 149°6E 151 D4
Surat India 21°12N 72°55E 126 D1
Surat Thani Thailand 9°6N 99°20E 121 H2
Suratgarh India 29°18N 73°55E 124 E5
Surathkal India 12°58N 74°46E 127 H2
Suraxanı = Qaraçuxar
   Azerbaijan 40°25N 50°1E 87 K10
Şuraymilā Si. Arabia 25°7N 46°7E 128 E5
Suraż Poland 52°57N 22°57E 83 F9
Surazh Belarus 55°25N 30°44E 84 E6
Surazh Russia 53°5N 32°27E 85 F7
Surduc Romania 47°15N 23°25E 81 E8
Surduc Pasul Romania 45°21N 23°23E 81 E8
Surdulica Serbia 42°41N 22°11E 96 B6
Surendranagar India 22°45N 71°40E 124 H4
Surf U.S.A. 34°41N 120°36W 171 L6
Surfers Paradise
   Australia 28°0S 153°25E 151 D5
Surfside U.S.A. 25°52N 80°7W 179 K9
Surgana India 20°34N 73°37E 126 D1
Surgères France 46°7N 0°47W 72 B3
Surgut Russia 61°14N 73°20E 106 C8
Sùria Spain 41°50N 1°45E 90 D6
Suriapet India 17°10N 79°40E 126 F4
Surigao Phil. 9°47N 125°29E 119 C7
Surin Thailand 14°50N 103°34E 120 E4
Surinam = Suriname ■
   S. Amer. 4°0N 56°0W 187 C7
Suriname ■ S. Amer. 4°0N 56°0W 187 C7
Suriname → Suriname 5°50N 55°15W 187 B7
Surjagarh India 19°36N 80°25E 126 E5
Sürmaq Iran 31°3N 52°48E 129 D7
Sürmene Turkey 41°0N 40°1E 105 B9
Surovikino Russia 48°32N 42°55E 87 F6
Surprise U.S.A. 33°38N 112°19W 169 K7
Surrency U.S.A. 31°44N 82°12W 178 D7
Surrey □ Canada 49°7N 122°45W 170 A4
Surrey □ U.K. 51°15N 0°31W 67 F7
Sursand India 26°39N 85°43E 125 F11
Sursar → India 26°14N 87°3E 125 F12
Sursee Switz. 47°11N 8°6E 77 H4
Sursk Russia 53°3N 45°40E 86 D7
Surskoye Russia 54°30N 46°44E 86 C8
Surt Libya 31°11N 16°39E 135 B9
Surt, Khalīj Libya 31°40N 18°30E 135 B9
Surtanahu Pakistan 26°22N 70°0E 124 F4
Surte Sweden 57°50N 12°1E 63 G6
Surtsey Iceland 63°20N 20°30W 60 E3
Surubim Brazil 7°50S 35°45W 189 D11
Sürüç Turkey 36°58N 38°25E 105 D8
Suruga-Wan Japan 34°45N 138°30E 113 G9
Surxondaryo □
   Uzbekistan 38°0N 67°30E 109 E7
Susa Italy 45°8N 7°3E 92 C4
Şuşa Azerbaijan 39°46N 46°45E 105 C12
Susá → Denmark 55°12N 11°42E 63 G5
Susak Croatia 44°30N 14°18E 93 D11
Süsangerd Iran 31°35N 48°6E 105 G13
Susaki Japan 33°22N 133°17E 113 H6
Susanville U.S.A. 40°25N 120°39W 168 F4
Suşehri Turkey 40°10N 38°6E 105 B8
Susice Czechia 49°17N 13°30E 78 B6
Susleni Moldova 47°25N 28°59E 81 C13
Susner India 23°57N 76°7E 124 H7
Susong China 30°10N 116°55E 117 B11
Susquehanna
   U.S.A. 39°33N 76°5W 175 G8
Susquehanna →
   U.S.A. 39°33N 76°5W 175 G8
Susques Argentina 23°35S 66°25W 190 A2
Sussex Canada 45°45N 65°37W 165 C6
Sussex U.S.A. 41°13N 74°37W 175 E10
Sussex, East □ U.K. 51°0N 0°20E 67 G8
Sussex, West □ U.K. 51°0N 0°30W 67 G7
Sussex Inlet Australia 35°10S 150°36E 153 C9
Sustut → Canada 56°20N 127°30W 162 B3
Susuman Russia 62°47N 148°10E 107 C15
Susunu Indonesia 3°7S 133°39E 119 E8
Susurluk Turkey 39°54N 28°8E 99 B10
Susuz Turkey 40°46N 43°8E 105 B10
Sutay Uul Asia 46°35N 93°38E 110 B7
Sütçüler Turkey 37°29N 30°57E 104 D4
Suțești Romania 45°13N 27°27E 81 E12
Sutherland Australia 34°2S 151°4E 153 C9
Sutherland S. Africa 32°24S 20°40E 144 D3
Sutherland U.K. 58°12N 4°50W 65 C4
Sutherland Falls N.Z. 44°48S 167°46E 155 E2
Sutherlin U.S.A. 43°23N 123°19W 168 E2
Suthri India 23°3N 68°55E 124 H3
Sutjeska △ Bos.-H. 43°50N 18°32E 80 G3
Sutlej → Pakistan 29°23N 71°3E 124 E4
Sutter U.S.A. 39°10N 121°45W 170 F5
Sutter Buttes U.S.A. 39°12N 121°49W 170 F5
Sutter Creek U.S.A. 38°24N 120°48W 170 G6
Sutton Canada 45°6N 72°37W 175 A12
Sutton N.Z. 45°34S 170°8E 155 F5
Sutton W. Va., U.S.A. 38°40N 80°43W 173 F13
Sutton → Canada 55°15N 83°45W 164 A3
Sutton Coldfield U.K. 52°35N 1°49W 67 E6
Sutton in Ashfield U.K. 53°8N 1°16W 66 D6
Sutton L. Canada 54°15N 84°42W 164 B3
Suttor → Australia 21°36S 147°2E 150 C4
Sutwik I. U.S.A. 56°34N 157°12W 166 D8
Suva Fiji 18°6S 178°30E 154 a
Suva Gora Macedonia 41°45N 21°3E 96 E5
Suva Planina Serbia 43°10N 22°5E 96 C6
Suva Reka = Therandë
   Kosovo 42°21N 20°50E 96 D4
Suvorov Russia 54°7N 36°30E 84 E9
Suvorov Is. = Suwarrow Is.
   Cook Is. 13°15S 163°5W 157 J11
Suvorove Ukraine 45°35N 28°59E 81 E13
Suvorovo Bulgaria 43°20N 27°35E 97 C11
Suwałki Poland 54°8N 22°59E 83 D9
Suwannaphum
   Thailand 15°33N 103°47E 120 E4
Suwannee U.S.A. 29°20N 83°9W 179 F6
Suwannee → U.S.A. 29°17N 83°10W 179 F6
Suwannee Sd. U.S.A. 29°20N 83°15W 179 F6
Suwanose-Jima Japan 29°38N 129°43E 113 K4
Suwarrow Is. Cook Is. 13°15S 163°5W 157 J11
Suwayqīyah, Hawr as
   Iraq 32°40N 46°3E 105 G12
Suweis, Khalîg el Egypt 28°40N 33°0E 137 F8
Suweis, Qanâ es Egypt 31°0N 32°20E 137 E8
Suwon S. Korea 37°17N 127°1E 115 F14
Suzdal Russia 56°29N 40°26E 84 B11
Suzhou Anhui, China 33°41N 116°59E 114 H9
Suzhou Jiangsu, China 31°19N 120°38E 117 B13
Suzu Japan 37°25N 137°17E 113 F8
Suzu-Misaki Japan 37°31N 137°21E 113 F8
Suzuka Japan 34°55N 136°36E 113 G8
Suzun Russia 53°47N 82°18E 109 B10
Suzzara Italy 44°59N 10°45E 92 D7
Svalbard Arctic 78°0N 17°0E 57 B12
Svalbard Radio = Longyearbyen
   Svalbard 78°13N 15°40E 54 B8
Svalöv Sweden 55°57N 13°8E 63 J7
Svalyava Ukraine 48°33N 22°59E 80 B7
Svaneke Denmark 55°8N 15°8E 63 J9
Svaneti Georgia 42°50N 42°45E 105 A10
Svängsta Sweden 56°16N 14°47E 63 H8
Svanskog Sweden 59°11N 12°33E 62 E6
Svappavaara Sweden 67°40N 21°3E 60 C19
Svärdsjö Sweden 60°45N 15°54E 62 D9
Svartå Sweden 59°8N 14°32E 62 E8
Svartisen Norway 66°40N 13°59E 60 C15
Svartvik Sweden 62°19N 17°24E 62 B11
Svatove Ukraine 49°35N 38°11E 85 H10
Svay Chek Cambodia 13°48N 102°58E 120 F4
Svay Rieng Cambodia 11°9N 105°45E 121 G5
Svealand Sweden 60°20N 15°0E 62 D9
Svedala Sweden 55°30N 13°15E 63 J7
Sveg Sweden 62°2N 14°21E 62 B8
Svendborg Denmark 55°4N 10°35E 63 J4
Svenljunga Sweden 57°29N 13°5E 63 G7
Svenstavik Sweden 62°45N 14°26E 62 B8
Svenstrup Denmark 56°58N 9°50E 63 H3
Svenhorodka Ukraine 49°4N 30°56E 85 H6
Sverdlovsk Ukraine 48°5N 39°47E 85 H10
Sverdrup Chan.
   Canada 79°56N 96°25W 161 B12
Sverdrup Is. Canada 79°0N 97°0W 158 B10
Sverige = Sweden ■
   Europe 57°0N 15°0E 61 H16
Sveshtari Bulgaria 43°40N 26°40E 97 C10
Svetac Croatia 43°3N 15°43E 93 E12
Sveti Nikola, Prokhad
   Europe 43°27N 22°6E 96 C6
Sveti Nikole Macedonia 41°51N 21°56E 96 E5
Sveti Rok Croatia 44°22N 15°39E 93 D12
Svetlaya Russia 46°33N 138°18E 112 A9
Svetlogorsk = Svyetlahorsk
   Belarus 52°38N 29°46E 75 D15
Svetlograd Russia 45°25N 42°58E 87 H6
Svetlovodsk = Svitlovodsk
   Ukraine 49°2N 33°13E 85 H7
Svetly Kaliningrad, Russia 54°41N 20°8E 83 D5
Svetly Orenburg, Russia 50°48N 60°51E 108 B6
Svidník Slovakia 49°20N 21°37E 81 B14
Svilaja Planina Croatia 43°49N 16°31E 93 E13
Svilajnac Serbia 44°15N 21°11E 96 C5
Svilengrad Bulgaria 41°49N 26°12E 97 C10
Svir → Russia 60°30N 32°48E 84 A7
Sviritsa Russia 60°30N 32°51E 84 A7
Svishtov Bulgaria 43°36N 25°23E 97 C9
Svislach Belarus 53°3N 24°2E 83 E11
Svitava → Czechia 49°11N 16°37E 79 B9
Svitavy Czechia 49°47N 16°28E 79 B9
Svitlovodsk Ukraine 49°2N 33°13E 85 H7
Svity → Asia 50°8N 38°0E 85 H10
Svobodnyy Russia 51°20N 128°0E 107 D13
Svoge Bulgaria 42°59N 23°23E 96 D7
Svolvær Norway 68°15N 14°34E 60 B16
Svratka → Czechia 49°11N 16°38E 79 B9
Svrljig Serbia 43°25N 22°6E 96 C6
Svyetlahorsk Belarus 52°38N 29°46E 75 D15
Swabian Alps = Schwäbische Alb
   Germany 48°20N 9°30E 77 G5
Swaffham U.K. 52°39N 0°42E 67 E8
Swains I. Amer. Samoa 11°11S 171°4W 157 J11
Swainsboro U.S.A. 32°36N 82°20W 178 D6
Swakop → Namibia 22°38S 14°36E 144 B2
Swakopmund Namibia 22°37S 14°30E 144 B1
Swale → U.K. 54°5N 1°20W 66 C6
Swamihalli India 14°52N 76°38E 127 G3
Swan → Australia 32°3S 115°45E 149 F2
Swan → Canada 52°30N 100°45W 163 C8
Swan Hill Australia 35°20S 143°33E 152 C5
Swan Hills Canada 54°43N 115°24W 162 C5
Swan Is. = Santanilla, Is.
   Honduras 17°22N 83°57W 182 C3
Swan L. =
   Kalajun-Ku'erdening △
   China 43°10N 81°50E 109 D10
Swan L. Man., Canada 52°30N 100°40W 163 C8
Swan L. Ont., Canada 54°16N 91°11W 164 B1
Swan Ra. U.S.A. 48°0N 113°45W 168 C7
Swan Reach Australia 34°35S 139°37E 152 C3
Swan River Canada 52°10N 101°16W 163 C8
Swanage U.K. 50°36N 1°58W 67 G6
Swansea N.S.W.,
   Australia 33°3S 151°35E 153 B9
Swansea Tas., Australia 42°8S 148°4E 150 G4
Swansea U.K. 51°38N 3°57W 67 F4
Swansea U.K. 33°44N 81°6W 178 B8
Swansea → U.K. 51°37N 3°57W 67 F4
Swansea □ U.K. 51°38N 4°3W 67 F4
Swartberg S. Africa 30°20S 29°0E 145 E4
Swartmodder S. Africa 28°1S 20°32E 144 C3
Swartnossob → Namibia 23°8S 18°42E 144 B2
Swartruggens S. Africa 25°39S 26°42E 144 C4
Swarzędz Poland 52°25N 17°4E 83 F9
Swastika Canada 48°7N 80°6W 164 C3
Swat → Pakistan 34°40N 72°5E 125 B5
Swatow = Shantou
   China 23°18N 116°40E 117 F11
Swaziland ■ Africa 26°30S 31°30E 145 C5
Sweden ■ Europe 57°0N 15°0E 61 H16
Swedru Ghana 5°32N 0°41W 139 D4
Sweet Grass U.S.A. 48°59N 111°58W 168 D8
Sweet Home U.S.A. 44°24N 122°44W 168 D2
Sweetwater Nev.,
   U.S.A. 38°27N 119°9W 170 G7
Sweetwater Tenn.,
   U.S.A. 35°36N 84°28W 177 D12
Sweetwater Tex.,
   U.S.A. 32°28N 100°25W 176 E4
Sweetwater →
   U.S.A. 42°31N 107°2W 168 E10
Swellendam S. Africa 34°1S 20°26E 144 E3
Swider → Poland 52°6N 21°14E 83 F8
Świdnica Poland 50°50N 16°30E 83 H3
Świdnik Poland 51°13N 22°39E 83 G9
Świdwin Poland 53°47N 15°49E 82 E2
Świebodzice Poland 50°51N 16°20E 83 H3
Świebodzin Poland 52°15N 15°31E 83 F2
Świecie Poland 53°25N 18°30E 82 E5
Świerzawa Poland 51°1N 15°54E 83 G2
Swift Current Canada 50°50N 107°45W 163 C7
Swift Current →
   Canada 50°38N 107°44W 163 C7
Swifts Creek Australia 37°15S 147°44E 153 D7
Swilly, L. Ireland 55°12N 7°33W 64 A4
Swindon U.K. 51°34N 1°46W 67 F6
Swindon □ U.K. 51°34N 1°46W 67 F6
Swinemünde = Świnoujście
   Poland 53°54N 14°16E 82 E1
Swinford Ireland 53°57N 8°58W 64 C3
Świnoujście Poland 53°54N 14°16E 82 E1
Switzerland ■ Europe 46°30N 8°0E 77 J4
Swords Ireland 53°28N 6°13W 64 C5
Swoyerville U.S.A. 41°18N 75°53W 175 E9
Syasstroy Russia 60°9N 32°33E 84 B7
Sychevka Russia 55°59N 34°16E 84 E8
Syc(̊)ow Poland 51°19N 17°40E 83 G4
Sydenham → Canada 42°33N 82°25W 174 D2
Sydney Australia 33°52S 151°12E 153 B9
Sydney Canada 46°7N 60°7W 165 C7
Sydney L. Canada 50°41N 94°25W 163 C10
Sydney Mines Canada 46°18N 60°15W 165 C7
Sydprøven = Alluitsup Paa
   Greenland 60°30N 45°35W 57 E6
Sydra, G. of = Surt, Khalīj
   Libya 31°40N 18°30E 135 B9
Syeverodonetsk
   S. Africa 33°58S 18°28E 144 E2
Table Mt. S. Africa 33°58S 18°26E 144 E2
Table Rock L. U.S.A. 36°36N 93°19W 172 G7
Tabletop, Mt. Australia 23°24S 147°11E 150 C4
Tábor Czechia 49°25N 14°39E 78 B7
Tabora Tanzania 5°2S 32°50E 142 D3
Tabora □ Tanzania 5°0S 33°0E 142 D3
Tabou Côte d'Ivoire 4°30N 7°20W 138 E3
Tabrīz Iran 38°7N 46°20E 105 C12
Tabuaeran Kiribati 3°51N 159°22W 157 G12
Tabuenca Spain 41°42N 1°33W 90 D3
Tabūk Si. Arabia 28°23N 36°36E 128 D3
Taburno-Camposauro △
   Italy 41°8N 14°37E 95 A7
Tacámbaro de Codallos
   Mexico 19°14N 101°28W 180 D4
Tacheng China 46°40N 82°58E 109 C10
Tach'i Taiwan 24°53N 121°17E 117 E13
Tachia Taiwan 24°25N 120°37E 117 E13
Tachikleks Myanmar 20°29N 99°55E 120 B2
Tach'ing Shan = Daqing Shan
   China 40°40N 111°0E 114 D6
Tachov Czechia 49°47N 12°39E 78 B5
Tácina → Italy 38°57N 16°55E 95 C9
Tacloban Phil. 11°15N 124°58E 119 B6
Tacna Peru 18°0S 70°20W 188 D3
Tacna □ Peru 18°0S 70°20W 188 D3
Tacoma U.S.A. 47°14N 122°26W 170 C4
Tacuarembó Uruguay 31°45S 56°0W 191 C4
Tademaït, Plateau du
   Algeria 28°30N 2°30E 136 C6
Tādepallegudem India 16°50N 81°30E 126 F5
Tadio, L. Côte d'Ivoire 5°10N 5°15W 138 D3
Tadjerdjeri, O. → Algeria 26°0N 8°0E 136 C5
Tadjerouna Algeria 33°31N 2°3E 136 B4
Tadjmout Laghouat,
   Algeria 33°52N 2°30E 136 B4
Tadjmout Saoura, Algeria 25°37N 3°48E 136 C4
Tadjourah Djibouti 11°50N 42°55E 131 E3
Tadla-Azilal □ Morocco 32°0N 6°30W 136 B2
Tadmor N.Z. 41°27S 172°45E 155 B7
Tadoba △ India 20°30N 79°28E 126 D4
Tadoule L. Canada 58°36N 98°20W 163 B9
Tadoussac Canada 48°11N 69°42W 165 C6
Tadpatri India 14°55N 78°1E 127 G4
Tadrés → Niger 16°0N 7°10E 138 B7
Tadzhikistan = Tajikistan ■
   Asia 38°30N 70°0E 109 E8
Taegu = Daegu
   S. Korea 35°50N 128°37E 115 G15
Taegwan N. Korea 40°13N 125°12E 115 D13
Tejŏn = Daejeon
   S. Korea 36°20N 127°28E 115 F14
Taen, Ko Thailand 9°22N 99°57E 121 b
Tafalla Spain 42°30N 1°41W 90 C3
Tafelbaai = Table B.
   S. Africa 33°35S 18°25E 144 D2
Tafelney, C. Morocco 31°3N 9°51W 136 B2
Tafermaar Indonesia 6°47S 134°10E 119 F8
Taffermit Morocco 29°37N 9°15W 136 C2
Tafi Viejo Argentina 26°43S 65°17W 190 B2
Tafīhān Iran 29°25N 52°39E 129 D7
Tafilalet Morocco 31°20N 4°45W 136 B3
Tafire Côte d'Ivoire 9°4N 5°4W 138 D3
Tafo Ghana 6°15N 0°20W 139 D4
Tafraoute Morocco 29°50N 8°58W 136 C2
Tafresh Iran 34°45N 49°57E 129 C6
Taft Iran 31°45N 54°14E 129 D7
Taft Phil. 11°57N 125°30E 119 B7
Taft U.S.A. 35°8N 119°28W 171 K7
Taftan Pakistan 29°0N 61°30E 122 E2
Taftān, Kūh-e Iran 28°40N 61°0E 129 D9
Tafwap India 7°23N 93°43E 127 L11
Taga Dzong Bhutan 27°5N 89°55E 123 F16
Taganay △ Russia 55°15N 59°48E 108 L11
Taganrog Russia 47°12N 38°50E 85 J10
Taganrogskiy Zaliv
   Russia 47°0N 38°30E 85 J10
Tagânt □ Mauritania 19°0N 10°0W 138 B3
Tagbilaran Phil. 9°39N 123°51E 119 C6
Tággia Italy 43°52N 7°51E 92 E4
Taghit Algeria 30°57N 2°4W 136 B4
Tagish Canada 60°19N 134°16W 162 A2
Tagish L. Canada 60°10N 134°20W 162 A2
Tagliacozzo Italy 42°4N 13°14E 93 F10
Tagliamento → Italy 45°38N 13°5E 93 C10
Táglio di Po Italy 45°0N 12°12E 93 D9
Tagomago Spain 39°2N 1°39E 100 B5
Tagourâret Mauritania 17°45N 7°45W 138 B3
Taguatinga Distrito Federal,
   Brazil 15°51S 48°4W 189 F7
Taguatinga Tocantins,
   Brazil 12°27S 46°22W 189 C1
Tagum Phil. 7°33N 125°53E 119 C7
Tagus = Tejo → Europe 38°40N 9°24W 89 F2
Tahakopa N.Z. 46°30S 169°23E 155 G4
Tahala Morocco 34°0N 4°28W 136 B3
Tahan, Gunung
   Malaysia 4°34N 102°17E 121 K4
Tahat Algeria 23°18N 5°33E 136 D6
Tāherī Iran 27°43N 52°20E 129 E7
Tahifet Algeria 22°40N 5°57E 136 D6
Tahlequah U.S.A. 35°55N 94°58W 176 D7
Tahoe, L. U.S.A. 39°6N 120°2W 170 F6
Tahoe City U.S.A. 39°10N 120°9W 170 F6
Tahoka U.S.A. 33°10N 101°48W 176 E4
Taholah U.S.A. 47°21N 124°17W 170 C2
Tahora N.Z. 39°2S 174°49E 154 F3
Tahoua Niger 14°57N 5°16E 139 C6
Tahrūd Iran 29°26N 57°49E 129 D8
Tahsis Canada 49°55N 126°40E 162 D3
Tahta Egypt 26°44N 31°32E 137 B3
Tahtaköprü Turkey 39°57N 29°39E 97 G13
Tahtalı Dağları Turkey 38°20N 36°50E 104 C7
Tahuamanú → Bolivia 11°6S 67°36W 188 C4
Tahulandang Indonesia 2°27N 125°23E 119 D7
Tahuna Indonesia 3°38N 125°30E 119 D7
Tai Côte d'Ivoire 5°55N 7°30W 138 D3
Tai △ Côte d'Ivoire 5°25N 7°5W 138 D3
Tai Hu China 31°5N 120°10E 117 B13
Tai Mo Shan China 22°25N 114°7E 111 a
Tai O China 22°15N 113°52E 111 a
Tai Pang Wan China 22°33N 114°24E 111 a
Tai Po China 22°27N 114°10E 111 a
Tai Rom Yen △ Thailand 8°45N 99°30E 121 H2
Tai Shan China 36°25N 117°20E 115 F9
Tai Yue Shan = Lantau I.
   China 22°15N 113°56E 111 a
Tai'an China 36°12N 117°8E 115 F9
Taiarapu, Presqu'île de
   Tahiti 17°47S 149°14W 155 b
Taibai Shan China 33°57N 107°45E 114 H4
Taibique Canary Is. 27°42N 17°58W 100 G2
Taibus Qi China 41°54N 115°22E 114 D8
Taicang China 31°30N 121°5E 117 B13
T'aichung Taiwan 24°9N 120°37E 117 E13
Taieri → N.Z. 46°3S 170°12E 155 G5
Taigu China 37°28N 112°30E 114 F7
Taihang Shan China 36°0N 113°30E 114 F7
Taihape N.Z. 39°41S 175°48E 154 F4
Taihe Anhui, China 33°20N 115°42E 116 A9
Taihe Jiangxi, China 26°47N 114°52E 117 D10
Taihu China 30°22N 116°20E 117 B10
Taijiang China 26°39N 108°21E 116 D7
Tailem Bend Australia 35°12S 139°29E 152 C3
Taillfingen Germany 48°15N 9°1E 77 G5
T'ailuko Taiwan 24°8N 121°37E 117 E13
Taimyr Peninsula = Taymyr,
   Poluostrov Russia 75°0N 100°0E 107 B11
Tain U.K. 57°49N 4°4W 65 D4
T'ainan Taiwan 23°17N 120°18E 117 F13
Taining China 26°54N 117°9E 117 D11
Taiobeiras Brazil 15°49S 42°14W 189 D2
Taipa China 22°13N 113°35E 111 a
T'aipei Taiwan 25°4N 121°29E 117 E13
Taiping China 34°11N 114°14E 116 A10
Taiping Malaysia 4°51N 100°44E 121 K3
Taiping Dao = Itu Aba I.
   S. China Sea 10°23N 114°21E 118 B4
Taipingchuan China 44°23N 123°11E 115 B12

Taipingzhen China 33°35N 111°42E 114 H6
Taipu Brazil 5°37S 35°36W 189 B3
Tairua N.Z. 37°0S 175°51E 154 D4
Taishan China 22°14N 112°41E 117 F9
Taishun China 27°30N 119°42E 117 D12
Taita Hills Kenya 3°25S 38°15E 142 C4
Taitao, C. Chile 45°53S 75°5W 192 C1
Taitao, Pen. de Chile 46°30S 75°0W 192 C1
Ta'itung Taiwan 22°43N 121°4E 117 F13
Taivalkoski Finland 65°33N 28°12E 60 D23
Taiwan ■ Asia 23°30N 121°0E 117 F13
Taiwan Strait Asia 24°40N 120°0E 117 E12
Taixing China 32°11N 120°0E 117 H10
Taiyiba Israel 32°36N 35°27E 130 C4
Taiyuan China 37°52N 112°33E 114 F7
Taizhou Jiangsu, China 32°28N 119°55E 117 A12
Taizhou Zhejiang, China 28°40N 121°24E 117 C13
Taizhou Liedao China 28°30N 121°51E 117 C13
Ta'izz Yemen 13°35N 44°2E 131 E3
Taj Mahal India 27°10N 78°2E 124 F8
Tājābād Iran 30°2N 54°24E 129 D7
Tajikistan ■ Asia 38°30N 70°0E 109 E8
Tajima = Minamiaizu Japan 37°12N 139°46E 113 F9
Tajo = Tejo → Europe 38°40N 9°24W 89 F2
Tajrīsh Iran 35°48N 51°25E 129 C6
Tak Thailand 16°52N 99°8E 120 D2
Takāb Iran 36°24N 47°7E 105 C12
Takachiho Japan 32°42N 131°18E 113 H5
Takachu Botswana 22°37S 21°58E 144 B3
Takada Japan 37°7N 138°15E 113 F9
Takahagi Japan 36°43N 140°45E 113 F10
Takaka N.Z. 40°51S 172°50E 155 A7
Takamaka Seychelles 4°50S 55°30E 141 b
Takamatsu Japan 34°20N 134°5E 113 G7
Takaoka Japan 36°47N 137°0E 113 F8
Takapau N.Z. 40°2S 176°21E 154 G5
Takapuna N.Z. 36°47S 174°47E 154 C3
Takasaki Japan 36°20N 139°0E 113 F9
Takatsuki Japan 34°51N 135°37E 113 G7
Takaungu Kenya 3°38S 39°52E 142 C4
Takayama Japan 36°18N 137°11E 113 F8
Take-Shima Japan 30°49N 130°26E 113 J5
Takefu = Echizen Japan 35°50N 136°10E 113 G8
Takengon Indonesia 4°45N 96°50E 118 D1
Takeo Cambodia 10°59N 104°47E 121 G5
Takeo Japan 33°12N 130°1E 113 H5
Tåkern Sweden 58°22N 14°45E 63 F8
Takeshima = Liancourt Rocks Asia 37°15N 131°52E 113 F5
Tākestān Iran 36°0N 49°40E 129 C6
Taketa Japan 32°58N 131°24E 113 H5
Takh India 33°6N 77°32E 125 C7
Takhār □ Afghan. 36°40N 70°0E 109 E7
Takhiyatas Uzbekistan 42°20N 59°33E 108 D5
Takhmau Cambodia 11°29N 104°57E 121 G5
Takht-e Soleyman Iran 36°36N 47°14E 105 D12
Takht-Sulaiman Pakistan 31°40N 69°58E 124 D3
Takiéta Niger 13°41N 8°32E 139 C6
Takikawa Japan 43°33N 141°54E 112 C10
Takla L. Canada 55°15N 125°45W 162 B3
Takla Landing Canada 55°30N 125°50W 162 B3
Taklamakan China 38°0N 83°0E 109 E10
Taklamakan Shamo = Taklamakan China 38°0N 83°0E 109 E10
Taksimo Russia 56°20N 114°52E 107 D12
Taku → Canada 58°30N 133°50W 162 B2
Takua Thung Thailand 8°24N 98°27E 121 a
Takum Nigeria 7°18N 9°36E 139 D6
Tal Halāl Iran 28°54N 55°1E 129 D7
Tala Uruguay 34°21S 55°46W 191 C4
Talachyn Belarus 54°25N 29°42E 84 E5
Talagang Pakistan 32°55N 72°25E 124 C5
Talagante Chile 33°40S 70°50W 190 C1
Talahouhait Algeria 24°52N 1°5E 136 A4
Talaimannar Sri Lanka 9°6N 79°43E 127 K4
Talaïnt Morocco 29°41N 9°40W 136 C2
Talak Niger 18°0N 5°0E 139 B6
Talamanca, Cordillera de Cent. Amer. 9°20N 83°20W 182 E3
Talampaya △ Argentina 29°43S 67°42W 190 B2
Talant France 47°19N 4°58E 71 E11
Talara Peru 4°38S 81°18W 188 A1
Talaud Australia 34°45S 117°37E 149 F2
Talas Kyrgyzstan 42°30N 72°13E 109 D8
Talas Turkey 38°41N 35°33E 104 C6
Talas → Kyrgyzstan 42°20N 72°0E 109 D8
Talas → Kazakhstan 44°0N 70°20E 108 D7
Talas Ala Too Kyrgyzstan 42°15N 72°0E 109 D8
Talasskiy Alatau = Talas Ala Too Kyrgyzstan 42°15N 72°0E 109 D8
Talâta Egypt 30°36N 32°20E 130 E1
Talata Mafara Nigeria 12°38N 6°4E 139 C6
Talaud, Kepulauan Indonesia 4°30N 126°50E 119 D7
Talaud Is. = Talaud, Kepulauan Indonesia 4°30N 126°50E 119 D7
Talavera de la Reina Spain 39°55N 4°46W 88 F6
Talavera la Real Spain 38°53N 6°46W 89 G4
Talayan Phil. 6°52N 124°24E 119 C6
Talayuela Spain 39°59N 5°36W 88 F5
Talbandh India 22°3N 86°20E 125 H12
Talbert, Sillon de France 48°53N 3°5W 70 D3
Talbot Australia 37°10S 143°44E 152 D5
Talbot, C. Australia 13°48S 126°43E 150 B4
Talbotton U.S.A. 32°41N 84°32W 178 C5
Talbragar → Australia 32°12S 148°37E 153 E8
Talca Chile 35°28S 71°40W 190 D1
Talcahuano Chile 36°40S 73°10W 190 D1
Talcher India 21°0N 85°18E 126 D7
Talcho Niger 14°44N 3°28E 139 C5
Taldy Kurgan = Taldyqorghan Kazakhstan 45°10N 78°45E 109 C9
Taldyqorghan Kazakhstan 45°10N 78°45E 109 C9
Tålesh Iran 37°58N 48°58E 105 D13
Tålesh, Kūhhā-ye Iran 37°42N 48°55E 105 D13
Talgar = Talghar Kazakhstan 43°19N 77°15E 109 D9
Talghar Kazakhstan 43°19N 77°15E 109 D9
Talguharai Sudan 18°19N 35°56E 137 D4
Talguppa India 14°13N 74°56E 127 G9

Tali Post South Sudan 5°55N 30°44E 135 G12
Taliabu Indonesia 1°50S 125°0E 119 E6
Talibon Phil. 10°9N 124°20E 119 B6
Talihina U.S.A. 34°45N 95°3W 176 D7
Talikota India 16°29N 76°17E 127 F3
Talipparamba India 12°3N 75°21E 127 F2
Talkha Egypt 31°3N 31°22E 137 E7
Talkot Nepal 29°37N 81°19E 125 E9
Tall 'Afar Iraq 36°22N 42°27E 105 D10
Tall Kalakh Syria 34°41N 36°15E 130 A5
Tall Kayf Iraq 36°29N 43°7E 105 D10
Talla Egypt 28°5N 30°43E 137 F7
Talladega U.S.A. 33°26N 86°6W 178 B3
Tallaganda △ Australia 35°29S 149°37E 153 C8
Tallahassee U.S.A. 30°27N 84°17W 178 E5
Tallangatta Australia 36°15S 147°19E 153 D7
Tallapoosa U.S.A. 33°45N 85°17W 178 B4
Tallapoosa → U.S.A. 32°30N 86°16W 178 C3
Tallard France 44°28N 6°3E 73 D10
Tallarook Australia 37°5S 145°6E 153 D6
Tallassee U.S.A. 32°32N 85°54W 178 C4
Tällberg Sweden 60°51N 15°2E 62 D9
Talli Pakistan 29°32N 68°8E 124 E3
Tallinn Estonia 59°22N 24°48E 84 C3
Tallmadge U.S.A. 41°6N 81°27W 174 E3
Tallulah U.S.A. 32°25N 91°11W 176 E9
Tålmaciu Romania 45°38N 24°19E 81 E9
Talmest Morocco 31°48N 9°21W 136 B2
Talmont-St-Hilaire France 46°27N 1°37W 72 B2
Talnakh Russia 69°29N 88°22E 107 C9
Talne Ukraine 48°50N 30°44E 85 H6
Talnoye = Talne Ukraine 48°50N 30°44E 85 H6
Taloda India 21°34N 74°11E 126 D2
Taloqān Afghan. 36°44N 69°33E 109 E7
Talovaya Russia 51°6N 40°45E 86 F5
Taloyoak Canada 69°32N 93°32W 160 D13
Talpa de Allende Mexico 20°23N 104°51W 180 C4
Talparo Trin. & Tob. 10°30N 61°17W 187 K15
Talquin, L. U.S.A. 30°23N 84°39W 178 E5
Talsi Latvia 57°10N 22°30E 82 A9
Talsint Morocco 32°33N 3°27W 136 B3
Taltal Chile 25°23S 70°33W 190 B1
Taltson → Canada 61°24N 112°46W 162 A6
Talwood Australia 28°29S 149°29E 151 D4
Talyawalka Cr. → Australia 32°28S 142°22E 152 B5
Tam Dao △ Vietnam 21°45N 105°45E 120 B5
Tam Ky Vietnam 15°34N 108°29E 120 D7
Tam Quan Vietnam 14°35N 109°3E 120 E7
Tama U.S.A. 41°58N 92°35W 172 E7
Tama Abu, Banjaran Malaysia 3°50N 115°5E 118 D5
Tamale Ghana 9°22N 0°50W 139 D4
Taman Russia 45°14N 36°41E 85 K9
Taman Negara △ Malaysia 4°38N 102°26E 121 K4
Tamanar Morocco 31°1N 9°46W 136 B2
Tamano Mali 13°20N 6°50W 138 C3
Tamano Japan 34°29N 133°59E 113 G6
Tamanrasset Algeria 22°50N 5°30E 136 D5
Tamanrasset □ Algeria 23°45N 4°40E 136 D4
Tamaqua U.S.A. 40°48N 75°58W 175 F9
Tamar → U.K. 50°27N 4°15W 67 G3
Tamarac U.S.A. 26°12N 80°15W 179 J9
Tamarin Mauritius 20°19S 57°20E 141 d
Tamarite de Litera Spain 41°52N 0°25E 90 D5
Tamashima Japan 34°32N 133°40E 113 G6
Tamási Hungary 46°40N 18°18E 80 D3
Tamaské Niger 14°49N 5°43E 139 C6
Tamatave = Toamasina Madag. 18°10S 49°25E 141 H9
Tamaulipas □ Mexico 24°0N 98°45W 181 C5
Tamaulipas, Sierra de Mexico 23°30N 98°20W 181 C5
Tamazula Mexico 24°57N 106°57W 180 C4
Tamazunchale Mexico 21°16N 98°47W 181 C5
Tamba-Dabatou Guinea 11°50N 10°40W 138 C2
Tambach Kenya 0°36N 35°31E 142 B4
Tambacounda Senegal 13°45N 13°40W 138 C2
Tambacounda □ Senegal 14°0N 13°0W 138 C2
Tambaram India 12°55N 80°7E 127 H5
Tambelan, Kepulauan Indonesia 1°0N 107°30E 118 D3
Tambellup Australia 34°4S 117°37E 149 F2
Tambo Australia 24°54S 146°14E 150 C4
Tambo Peru 12°57S 74°1W 188 C3
Tambo → Peru 10°42S 73°47W 188 C3
Tambo de Mora Peru 13°30S 76°8W 188 C2
Tambobamba Peru 13°54S 72°9W 188 C3
Tambopata → Peru 12°21S 69°36W 188 C4
Tamboritha, Mt. Australia 37°31S 146°40E 153 D7
Tamboura C.A.R. 5°10N 25°12E 142 A2
Tambov Russia 52°45N 41°28E 86 D5
Tambov □ Russia 52°50N 41°20E 86 D5
Tambre → Spain 42°49N 8°53W 88 C2
Tambuku Indonesia 7°8S 113°40E 119 G15
Tâmchekket Mauritania 17°25N 10°40W 138 B2
Tâmega → Portugal 41°5N 8°21W 88 D2
Tamegroute Morocco 30°15N 5°39W 136 B3
Tamelelt Morocco 31°50N 7°32W 136 B3
Tamenglong India 25°0N 93°35E 123 G18
Tamerza Tunisia 34°23N 7°58E 136 B5
Tamgué, Massif du Guinea 12°0N 12°18W 138 C2
Tamiahua, L. de Mexico 21°35N 97°35W 181 C5
Tamiami Canal U.S.A. 25°50N 81°0W 179 H7
Tamil Nadu □ India 11°0N 77°0E 127 J3
Tamis → Serbia 44°51N 20°39E 80 F5
Tamiya Egypt 29°29N 30°58E 137 F7
Tamlelt, Plaine de Morocco 32°30N 2°20W 136 B3
Tamluk India 22°18N 87°58E 125 H12
Tammerfors = Tampere Finland 61°30N 23°50E 84 B2
Tämnaren Sweden 60°10N 17°25E 62 D11
Tampa, Tanjung Indonesia 8°55S 116°12E 119 K19
Tampa U.S.A. 27°50N 82°30W 179 H7
Tampa Int. ✈ (TPA) U.S.A. 27°59N 82°32W 179 H7

Tampere Finland 61°30N 23°50E 84 B2
Tampico Mexico 22°13N 97°51W 181 C5
Tampin Malaysia 2°28N 102°13E 121 L4
Tampoi Malaysia 1°30N 103°39E 121 d
Tamri Morocco 30°49N 9°50W 136 B2
Tamsagbulag Mongolia 47°14N 117°21E 111 B12
Tamsweg Austria 47°7N 13°49E 78 D6
Tamu Myanmar 24°13N 94°12E 123 G19
Tamuja → Spain 39°38N 6°29W 89 F4
Tamworth Australia 31°7S 150°58E 153 A9
Tamworth Canada 44°29N 77°0W 174 B8
Tamworth U.K. 52°39N 1°41W 67 E6
Tan An Vietnam 10°32N 106°25E 121 G6
Tan Chau Vietnam 10°48N 105°12E 121 G5
Tan Hiep Vietnam 10°27N 106°21E 121 G6
Tan Iddah Sudan 13°13N 29°10E 137 F7
Tan-Tan Morocco 28°29N 11°1W 134 C3
Tan Yen Yen Vietnam 21°55N 104°22E 120 B5
Tana → Kenya 2°32S 40°31E 142 C5
Tana → Norway 70°30N 28°14E 60 A23
Tana, L. Ethiopia 13°5N 37°30E 137 E4
Tana River □ Kenya 1°30S 39°30E 142 C5
Tana River Primate △ Kenya 1°55S 40°7E 142 C5
Tanabe Japan 33°44N 135°22E 113 H7
Tanafjorden Norway 70°45N 28°25E 60 A23
Tanaga I. U.S.A. 51°48N 177°53W 166 E4
Tanah Merah Malaysia 5°48N 102°9E 121 K4
Tanahbala Indonesia 0°30S 98°30E 118 E1
Tanahgrogot Indonesia 1°55S 116°15E 118 E5
Tanahjampea Indonesia 7°10S 120°35E 119 F6
Tanahmasa Indonesia 0°12S 98°39E 118 E1
Tanahmerah Indonesia 6°5S 140°16E 119 F10
Tanakpur India 29°5N 80°7E 125 E9
Tanamalwila Sri Lanka 6°26N 81°8E 127 L5
Tanami Desert Australia 18°50S 132°0E 148 C5
Tanana U.S.A. 65°10N 152°4W 166 B9
Tanana → U.S.A. 65°10N 151°58W 166 B9
Tananarive = Antananarivo Madag. 18°55S 47°31E 141 H9
Tanannt Morocco 31°54N 6°56W 136 B3
Tánaro → Italy 44°55N 8°40E 92 D5
Tancheng China 34°25N 118°20E 115 G10
Tanch'ŏn N. Korea 40°27N 128°54E 115 D15
Tanda Côte d'Ivoire 7°48N 3°10W 138 D4
Tanda Ut. P., India 26°33N 82°35E 125 F10
Tanda Ut. P., India 28°57N 78°56E 125 E8
Tandag Phil. 9°4N 126°9E 119 C7
Tandaia Tanzania 9°25S 34°15E 143 D3
Tândārei Romania 44°39N 27°40E 81 F12
Tandaué Angola 16°58S 18°5E 144 A2
Tandil Argentina 37°15S 59°6W 190 D4
Tandil, Sa. del Argentina 37°30S 59°0W 190 D4
Tandlianwala Pakistan 31°3N 73°9E 124 D5
Tando Adam Pakistan 25°45N 68°40E 124 G3
Tando Allahyar Pakistan 25°28N 68°43E 124 G3
Tando Bago Pakistan 24°47N 68°58E 124 G3
Tando Mohommed Khan Pakistan 25°8N 68°32E 124 G3
Tandou L. Australia 32°40S 142°5E 152 B5
Tandoureh △ Iran 37°50N 59°0E 129 B8
Tandragee U.K. 54°21N 6°24W 64 B5
Tandsjöborg Sweden 61°42N 14°43E 62 C8
Tandula → India 21°6N 81°14E 126 D5
Tandula Tank India 20°6N 81°12E 126 D5
Tandur Telangana, India 19°11N 79°30E 126 E4
Tandur Telangana, India 17°14N 77°35E 126 F3
Tane-ga-Shima Japan 30°30N 131°0E 113 J5
Taneatua N.Z. 38°4S 177°1E 154 E6
Tanen Tong Dan = Dawna Ra. Myanmar 16°30N 98°30E 120 D2
Tanew → Poland 50°29N 22°16E 83 H9
Tanezrouft Algeria 23°9N 0°11E 134 D6
Tang, Koh Cambodia 10°16N 103°7E 121 G4
Tang, Ra's-e Iran 25°21N 59°52E 129 E8
Tang Krasang Cambodia 12°34N 105°3E 120 F5
Tanga Tanzania 5°5S 39°2E 142 D4
Tanga □ Tanzania 5°20S 38°0E 142 D4
Tangalla Sri Lanka 6°1N 80°48E 127 L5
Tanganyika Dem. Rep. of the Congo 6°30S 28°0E 142 D2
Tanganyika, L. Africa 6°40S 30°0E 142 D2
Tangasseri India 8°53N 76°35E 127 K3
Tangaza Nigeria 13°19N 4°55E 139 C5
Tanger Morocco 35°50N 5°49W 136 A3
Tanger-Med Morocco 35°53N 5°30W 89 K5
Tanger-Tétouan □ Morocco 35°50N 5°50W 136 A2
Tangerang Indonesia 6°11S 106°37E 119 G12
Tangerhütte Germany 52°26N 11°48E 76 C7
Tangermünde Germany 52°33N 11°58E 76 C7
Tanggu China 39°2N 117°40E 115 E9
Tanggula Shan China 32°40N 92°10E 110 E7
Tanggula Shankou China 32°42N 92°27E 110 D7
Tanghe China 32°47N 112°50E 117 A9
Tanghla Range = Tanggula Shan China 32°40N 92°10E 110 D7
Tangi India 19°50N 85°24E 126 E7
Tangier = Tanger Morocco 35°50N 5°49W 136 A2
Tangjia China 22°22N 113°35E 111 a
Tangjia Wan China 22°21N 113°36E 111 a
Tangorin Australia 21°47S 144°12E 150 C3
Tangra Yumco China 31°0N 86°38E 110 E6
Tangshan China 39°38N 118°10E 115 E10
Tangtou China 35°28N 118°30E 115 G10
Tanguen-Dassouri Burkina Faso 12°16N 1°42W 139 C4
Tanguiéta Benin 10°35N 1°21E 139 C5
Tangxi China 29°3N 119°25E 117 C12
Tangyan He → China 28°54N 108°19E 116 C7
Tangyin China 35°54N 114°21E 114 G8
Taniantaweng Shan China 31°20N 98°0E 116 D2
Tanimbar, Kepulauan Indonesia 7°30S 131°30E 119 F8
Tanimbar Is. = Tanimbar, Kepulauan Indonesia 7°30S 131°30E 119 F8
Tanintharyi = Taninthayi Myanmar 12°6N 99°3E 121 F2
Taninthayi Myanmar 12°6N 99°3E 121 F2
Tanjay Phil. 9°30N 123°5E 119 C6
Tanjore = Thanjavur India 10°48N 79°12E 127 J4
Tanjung Kalimantan Selatan, Indonesia 2°10S 115°25E 118 E5

Tanjung Nusa Tenggara Barat, Indonesia 8°21S 116°9E 119 J19
Tanjung Malim Malaysia 3°42N 101°31E 121 L3
Tanjung Pelepas Malaysia 1°21N 103°33E 121 d
Tanjung Tokong Malaysia 5°28N 100°18E 121 c
Tanjungbalai Indonesia 2°55N 99°44E 118 D1
Tanjungbatu Indonesia 2°23N 118°3E 118 D5
Tanjungkarang Telukbetung = Bandar Lampung Indonesia 5°20S 105°10E 118 F3
Tanjungpandan Indonesia 2°43S 107°38E 118 E3
Tanjungpinang Indonesia 1°5N 104°30E 118 D2
Tanjungredeb Indonesia 2°9N 117°29E 118 D5
Tanjungselor Indonesia 2°55N 117°25E 118 D5
Tank Pakistan 32°14N 70°25E 124 C4
Tankhala India 21°58N 73°47E 124 J5
Tankwa-Karoo △ S. Africa 32°14S 19°50E 144 D2
Tännäs Sweden 62°26N 12°42E 62 B6
Tannersville U.S.A. 41°3N 75°18W 175 E9
Tannis Bugt Denmark 57°40N 10°15E 63 F5
Tannu Ola Asia 51°0N 94°0E 109 D10
Tannum Sands Australia 23°57S 151°22E 150 C5
Tano → Ghana 5°7N 2°56W 138 D4
Tanombella Algeria 25°30N 5°49E 136 C5
Tanout Niger 14°50N 8°55E 139 C6
Tanquinho Brazil 11°58S 39°6W 189 D3
Tanshui Taiwan 25°10N 121°28E 117 E13
Tansilla Burkina Faso 12°25N 4°23W 138 C4
Tansing Nepal 27°52N 83°33E 125 F10
Tanta Egypt 30°45N 30°57E 137 E7
Tantoyuca Mexico 21°21N 98°14W 181 C5
Tantung = Dandong China 40°10N 124°20E 115 D13
Tanuku India 16°45N 81°44E 126 F5
Tanumshede Sweden 58°42N 11°20E 63 F5
Tanunda Australia 34°30S 139°0E 152 C2
Tanur India 11°1N 75°52E 127 J2
Tanus France 44°8N 2°19E 72 D6
Tanzania ■ Africa 6°0S 34°0E 142 D3
Tanzhou China 22°16N 113°28E 111 a
Tanzilla → Canada 58°8N 130°43W 162 B2
Tao, Ko Thailand 10°5N 99°52E 121 G2
Tao'an = Taonan China 45°22N 122°40E 115 B12
Tao'er He → China 45°45N 124°5E 115 B13
Taohua Dao China 29°50N 122°20E 117 C14
Taolanaro Madag. 25°2S 47°0E 141 K9
Taole China 38°48N 106°40E 114 E4
Taonan China 45°22N 122°40E 115 B12
Taormina Italy 37°51N 15°17E 95 E8
Taos U.S.A. 36°24N 105°35W 169 H11
Taoudenni Mali 22°40N 3°55W 134 D5
Taoudrart, Adrar Algeria 24°25N 2°24E 136 D4
Taounate Morocco 34°25N 4°41W 136 B3
Taourirt Algeria 26°37N 0°20E 136 C4
Taourirt Morocco 34°25N 2°53W 136 B3
Taouz Morocco 30°53N 4°0W 136 B3
Taoyuan China 28°55N 111°16E 117 C8
T'aoyüan Taiwan 25°0N 121°4E 117 E13
Tapa Estonia 59°15N 25°50E 61 G21
Tapa Shan = Daba Shan China 32°0N 109°0E 116 B7
Tapachula Mexico 14°54N 92°17W 181 E6
Tapah Malaysia 4°12N 101°15E 121 K3
Tapajós → Brazil 2°24S 54°41W 187 D8
Tapaktuan Indonesia 3°15N 97°10E 118 D1
Tapanahoni → Suriname 4°20N 54°25W 187 C8
Tapanui N.Z. 45°56S 169°18E 155 F4
Tapauá Brazil 5°40S 64°21W 186 E6
Tapauá → Brazil 5°40S 64°21W 186 E6
Tapes Brazil 30°40S 51°23W 191 C5
Tapeta Liberia 6°29N 8°52W 138 D3
Taphan Hin Thailand 16°13N 100°26E 120 D3
Tapia de Casariego Spain 43°34N 6°56W 88 B4
Tapirapé, Serra Brazil 19°52S 46°1W 189 D1
Tapirapecó, Serra Venezuela 1°10N 65°0W 186 C5
Taplan Australia 34°33S 140°52E 152 C4
Taplejung Nepal 27°1N 86°16E 125 F12
Tapo-Capara △ Venezuela 7°55N 71°15W 183 E5
Tapolca Hungary 46°53N 17°29E 80 D2
Tapti → India 21°8N 72°41E 126 D1
Tapuae-o-Uenuku N.Z. 42°0S 173°39E 155 C8
Tapul Group Phil. 5°35N 120°50E 119 C6
Tapurucuará Brazil 0°24S 65°2W 186 D5
Taqtaq Iraq 35°53N 44°35E 105 E11
Taquara Brazil 29°36S 50°46W 191 B5
Taquari → Brazil 19°15S 57°17W 186 G7
Tara Canada 44°28N 81°9W 174 B3
Tara Russia 56°55N 74°24E 106 D8
Tara Zambia 16°58S 26°45E 143 F2
Tara → Montenegro 43°21N 18°51E 96 C2
Tara △ Serbia 43°55N 19°30E 81 C8
Taraba □ Nigeria 8°0N 10°0E 139 D7
Taraba → Nigeria 8°30N 10°15E 139 D7
Tarābulus Lebanon 34°31N 35°50E 130 A4
Tarābulus Libya 32°49N 13°7E 135 B8
Tarābulus Libya 31°0N 13°0E 135 B8
Taraclia Taraclia, Moldova 45°54N 28°40E 81 E13
Taraclia Tighina, Moldova 46°34N 29°7E 81 D14
Taradale N.Z. 39°33N 176°36E 154 F5
Taradehi India 23°18N 79°21E 125 H8
Tarajalejo Canary Is. 28°12N 14°7W 100 F5
Tarakan Indonesia 3°20N 117°35E 118 D5
Tarakit, Mt. Kenya 2°2N 35°10E 142 B4
Taralga Australia 34°26S 149°52E 153 C8
Tarama-Jima Japan 24°39N 124°42E 113 M2
Taramakau → N.Z. 42°34S 171°8E 155 C6
Taran, Mys Russia 54°56N 19°59E 82 D6
Taranagar India 28°43N 74°50E 124 E6
Taranaki □ N.Z. 39°25S 174°30E 154 F3
Taranaki, Mt. N.Z. 39°17S 174°5E 154 F3
Tarancón Spain 40°1N 3°1W 89 E7
Tarangire △ Tanzania 4°15S 36°7E 142 C4
Taransay U.K. 57°54N 7°0W 65 D1
Táranto Italy 40°28N 17°14E 95 B10
Táranto, G. di Italy 40°8N 17°20E 95 B10
Tarapacá Colombia 2°56S 69°46W 186 D5
Tarapacá □ Chile 20°45S 69°30W 190 A2
Tarapoto Peru 6°30S 76°20W 188 B2
Tarare France 45°54N 4°26E 73 C8

Tararua Ra. N.Z. 40°45S 175°25E 154 G4
Tarascon France 43°48N 4°39E 73 E8
Tarascon-sur-Ariège France 42°50N 1°36E 72 F5
Tarashcha Ukraine 49°30N 30°31E 85 H16
Tarata Peru 17°27S 70°2W 188 D3
Tarauacá Brazil 8°6S 70°48W 188 B3
Tarauacá → Brazil 6°42S 69°48W 188 B3
Taravao Tahiti 17°43S 149°19W 155 b
Taravao, Isthme de Tahiti 17°43S 149°19W 155 b
Taravo → Tahiti 41°42N 8°49E 73 G12
Tarawa Kiribati 1°30N 173°0E 156 G9
Tarawera N.Z. 39°2S 176°36E 154 F5
Tarawera, L. N.Z. 38°13S 176°27E 154 E5
Tarawera, Mt. N.Z. 38°14S 176°32E 154 E5
Taraz Kazakhstan 42°54N 71°22E 109 D8
Tarazona Spain 41°55N 1°43W 90 D3
Tarazona de la Mancha Spain 39°16N 1°55W 91 F3
Tarbagatay, Khrebet Kazakhstan 48°0N 83°0E 109 C10
Tarbat Ness U.K. 57°52N 3°47W 65 D5
Tarbela Dam Pakistan 34°8N 72°52E 124 B5
Tarbert Argyll & Bute, U.K. 55°52N 5°25W 65 F3
Tarbert W. Isles, U.K. 57°54N 6°49W 65 D2
Tarbes France 43°15N 0°3E 72 E4
Tarboro U.S.A. 35°54N 77°32W 177 D16
Tarcento Italy 46°13N 13°13E 93 B10
Tarcoola Australia 30°44S 134°36E 151 E1
Tarcoon Australia 30°15S 146°43E 151 E4
Tarcutta Australia 35°5S 147°44E 153 C7
Tardoire → France 45°52N 0°14E 72 C4
Taredjerdja Algeria 25°12N 2°32E 136 C4
Taree Australia 31°50S 152°30E 153 A10
Tarf, Ras Morocco 35°40N 5°11W 136 A2
Tarfa, W. el → Egypt 28°25N 30°50E 137 C7
Tarfaya Morocco 27°55N 12°55W 134 C3
Targoviste Bulgaria 43°17N 26°38E 97 C10
Târgoviste Romania 44°55N 25°27E 81 F10
Târgu Bujor Romania 45°52N 27°54E 81 E12
Târgu Cărbunești Romania 44°57N 23°31E 81 E8
Târgu Frumos Romania 47°12N 27°2E 81 C12
Târgu Jiu Romania 45°5N 23°19E 81 E8
Târgu Lăpuș Romania 47°27N 23°52E 81 C8
Târgu Mureș Romania 46°31N 24°38E 81 C9
Târgu Neamț Romania 47°12N 26°25E 81 C11
Târgu Ocna Romania 46°16N 26°39E 81 C11
Târgu Secuiesc Romania 46°0N 26°10E 81 E11
Tarhbalt Morocco 30°39N 5°20W 136 B3
Tarhmanant Algeria 24°23N 1°55E 136 D4
Tarhūnah Libya 32°30N 13°20E 135 B8
Tarif U.A.E. 24°3N 53°46E 129 E7
Tarifa Spain 36°1N 5°36W 89 J5
Tarija Bolivia 21°30S 64°40W 190 A3
Tarija □ Bolivia 21°30S 63°30W 190 A3
Tariku → Indonesia 2°55S 138°26E 119 E9
Tarim Yemen 16°3N 49°0E 131 D4
Tarim Basin = Tarim Pendi China 40°0N 84°0E 109 E10
Tarim He → China 41°5N 86°40E 109 E11
Tarim Pendi China 40°0N 84°0E 109 E10
Tarka → S. Africa 32°10S 26°0E 144 G4
Tarka La Bhutan 27°12N 89°44E 125 F13
Tarkastad S. Africa 32°0S 26°16E 144 D4
Tarkhankut, Mys Ukraine 45°25N 32°30E 85 K7
Tarko Sale Russia 64°55N 77°50E 106 C8
Tarkwa Ghana 5°20N 2°0W 138 D4
Tarlac Phil. 15°29N 120°35E 119 A6
Tarm Denmark 55°56N 8°31E 63 G2
Tarma Peru 11°25S 75°45W 188 C2
Tarmiya Iraq 33°40N 44°23E 105 G11
Tarn □ France 43°49N 2°8E 72 E6
Tarn → France 44°5N 1°6E 72 D5
Tarn-et-Garonne □ France 44°8N 1°20E 72 D5
Tarna → Hungary 47°31N 19°59E 80 C4
Târnava Mare → Romania 46°9N 23°43E 81 E8
Târnava Mică → Romania 46°25N 24°13E 81 E9
Târnăveni Romania 46°19N 24°13E 81 E9
Tarnica Poland 49°4N 22°44E 83 J9
Tarnobrzeg Poland 50°35N 21°41E 83 H8
Tarnogród Poland 50°22N 22°45E 83 H9
Tarnos France 43°32N 1°28W 72 E2
Târnova Moldova 48°10N 27°40E 81 B12
Tarnów Poland 50°3N 21°0E 83 H8
Tarnowskie Góry Poland 50°27N 18°54E 83 H5
Tärnsjö Sweden 60°9N 16°56E 62 D10
Táro → Italy 45°2N 10°15E 92 C7
Tarom Iran 28°11N 55°46E 129 D7
Taroom Australia 25°36S 149°48E 151 D4
Taroudannt Morocco 30°30N 8°52W 136 B2
Tarp Germany 54°39N 9°24E 76 A5
Tarpeena Australia 37°37S 140°47E 152 D4
Tarpon Springs U.S.A. 28°9N 82°45W 179 G7
Tarquínia Italy 42°15N 11°45E 93 F8
Tarra Bulga △ Australia 38°27S 146°31E 153 E7
Tarrafal Cabo Verde 15°18N 23°39W 100 b
Tarragona Spain 41°5N 1°17E 90 D6
Tarragona □ Spain 41°5N 1°0E 90 C6
Tarraleah Australia 42°17S 146°26E 155 G4
Tarrasa = Terrassa Spain 41°34N 2°1E 90 D7
Tàrrega Spain 41°39N 1°9E 90 D6
Tarrytown Ga., U.S.A. 32°19N 82°34W 178 D7
Tarrytown N.Y., U.S.A. 41°4N 73°52W 175 E11
Tårs Denmark 57°23N 10°7E 63 G4
Tarsus Turkey 36°58N 34°55E 104 D6
Tartagal Argentina 22°30S 63°50W 190 A3
Tartu Estonia 58°20N 26°44E 84 C4
Tarțăr → Azerbaijan 40°20N 46°58E 87 K8
Tartūs Syria 34°55N 35°55E 104 C6
Ţarţūs □ Syria 34°55N 36°0E 130 A4
Tarumirim Brazil 19°16S 41°59W 189 D3
Tarumizu Japan 31°29N 130°42E 113 J5

Tarusa Russia 54°44N 37°10E 84 D10
Tarutao = Ko Tarutao △ Thailand 6°31N 99°26E 121 J2
Tarutao, Ko Thailand 6°33N 99°40E 121 J2
Tarutung Indonesia 2°0N 98°54E 118 D1
Tarutyne Ukraine 46°12N 29°9E 81 E15
Tarvisio Italy 46°30N 13°35E 93 B10
Tasaret, O. → Algeria 26°25N 1°59E 136 C4
Tasböget Kazakhstan 44°46N 65°33E 108 D7
Taseko → Canada 52°8N 123°45W 162 C4
Tasgaon India 17°2N 74°39E 126 F2
Tash-Kömür Kyrgyzstan 41°40N 72°10E 109 D8
Tashauz = Daşoguz Turkmenistan 41°49N 59°58E 108 D6
Tashi Chho Dzong = Thimphu Bhutan 27°31N 89°45E 123 F16
Tashk, Daryācheh-ye Iran 29°45N 53°35E 129 D7
Tashkent = Toshkent Uzbekistan 41°20N 69°10E 109 D7
Tashtagol Russia 52°47N 87°53E 109 D11
Tasiilaq Greenland 65°40N 37°20W 57 D7
Tasikmalaya Indonesia 7°18S 108°12E 119 G13
Tåsinge Denmark 55°0N 10°35E 63 J4
Tåsjön Sweden 64°15N 15°40E 60 E7
Task Niger 14°56N 10°46E 139 C7
Taskan Russia 62°59N 150°20E 107 C16
Taşkent Turkey 36°55N 32°29E 104 D5
Taşköprü Turkey 41°30N 34°15E 104 B6
Taşlaç Moldova 47°4N 29°24E 81 C14
Taşlıçay Turkey 39°38N 43°22E 105 C10
Tasman □ N.Z. 41°30S 172°40E 155 D7
Tasman → N.Z. 43°48S 170°8E 155 D5
Tasman, Mt. N.Z. 43°34S 170°12E 155 D5
Tasman B. N.Z. 40°59S 173°25E 155 D6
Tasman Basin Pac. Oc. 46°0S 158°0E 156 M7
Tasman Glacier N.Z. 43°37S 170°12E 155 D5
Tasman Mts. N.Z. 41°3S 172°25E 155 D6
Tasman Pen. Australia 43°10S 148°0E 151 G4
Tasman Sea Pac. Oc. 36°0S 160°0E 147 E9
Tasmania □ Australia 42°0S 146°30E 151 G4
Tasmanian Wilderness World Heritage Area △ Australia 43°0S 146°0E 151 G4
Tåşnad Romania 47°30N 22°33E 81 C8
Taşova Turkey 40°45N 36°19E 104 B7
Tassili n'Ajjer △ Algeria 25°47N 8°1E 136 D5
Tassili n' Ajjer △ Algeria 26°5N 6°0E 136 C5
Tassili-oua-n-Ahaggar Algeria 20°41N 5°30E 134 D7
Tassili Ti-n-Rerhoh Algeria 20°5N 3°55E 139 A5
Tassū Iran 38°18N 45°23E 105 C11
Tat Ton △ Thailand 15°57N 102°2E 120 E4
Tata Hungary 47°37N 18°19E 80 C3
Tata Morocco 29°46N 7°56W 136 C3
Tatabánya Hungary 47°32N 18°25E 80 C3
Tataouine Tunisia 32°57N 10°29E 136 B6
Tataouine □ Tunisia 32°0N 10°30E 136 C6
Tatar Republic = Tatarstan □ Russia 55°30N 51°30E 86 C10
Tatarbunary Ukraine 45°50N 29°39E 81 E14
Tatarsk Russia 55°14N 76°0E 109 D9
Tatarskiy Proliv Russia 50°0N 141°0E 107 E15
Tatarstan □ Russia 55°30N 51°30E 86 C10
Tatatua, Pte. Tahiti 17°44S 149°8W 155 b
Tateyama Japan 35°0N 139°50E 113 G9
Tathlina L. Canada 60°33N 117°39W 162 A5
Tathra Australia 36°44S 149°59E 153 D8
Tatinnai L. Canada 60°55N 97°40W 163 A9
Tatla Lake Canada 52°0N 124°20W 162 C4
Tatlisu = Akanthou Cyprus 35°22N 33°45E 101 D12
Tatlısu Turkey 40°24N 27°55E 101 B11
Tatnam, C. Canada 57°16N 91°0W 163 B10
Tatra = Tatry Slovakia 49°20N 20°0E 79 B13
Tatranský □ Slovakia 49°10N 20°0E 79 B13
Tatry Slovakia 49°20N 20°0E 79 B13
Tatshenshini → Canada 59°28N 137°45W 162 B1
Tatshenshini-Alsek △ Canada 59°55N 137°45W 162 B1
Tatsuno Japan 34°52N 134°33E 113 G7
Tatta = Thatta Pakistan 24°42N 67°55E 124 G2
Tatuī Brazil 23°25S 47°53W 191 A6
Tatum U.S.A. 33°16N 103°19W 169 K12
Tat'ung = Datong China 40°6N 113°18E 114 D7
Tatura Australia 36°29S 145°16E 153 D6
Tatvan Turkey 38°31N 42°15E 105 C10
Tauá Brazil 6°1S 40°26W 189 B2
Taubaté Brazil 23°0S 45°36W 191 A6
Tauberbischofsheim Germany 49°37N 9°39E 77 F5
Taucha Germany 51°23N 12°29E 76 D8
Tauern Austria 47°15N 12°40E 74 E7
Tauern-tunnel Austria 47°0N 13°12E 78 D6
Taulé France 48°37N 3°55W 70 D3
Taumarunui N.Z. 38°53S 175°15E 154 E4
Taumaturgo Brazil 8°54S 72°51W 188 B3
Taung S. Africa 27°33S 24°47E 144 C3
Taungdwingyi Myanmar 20°1N 95°40E 123 J19
Taunggyi Myanmar 20°50N 97°0E 123 J20
Taungoo = Toungoo Myanmar 19°0N 96°30E 123 K20
Taungup Myanmar 18°51N 94°14E 123 K19
Taunsa Pakistan 30°42N 70°39E 124 D4
Taunsa Barrage Pakistan 30°42N 70°50E 124 D4
Taunton U.K. 51°1N 3°5W 67 F4
Taunton U.S.A. 41°54N 71°6W 175 E13
Taunus Germany 50°13N 8°34E 74 C5
Taupo N.Z. 38°41S 176°7E 154 E5
Taupo, L. N.Z. 38°46S 175°55E 154 E5
Taurage Lithuania 55°14N 22°16E 82 C9
Tauragė □ Lithuania 55°25N 22°30E 82 C9
Tauranga N.Z. 37°42S 176°11E 154 E5
Tauranga Harb. N.Z. 37°30S 176°5E 154 E5
Taureau, Rés. Canada 46°46N 73°50W 173 B17
Tauro, Mte. Italy 38°21N 16°1E 95 D9
Taurus Mts. = Toros Dağları Turkey 37°0N 32°30E 104 D5
Tauste Spain 41°58N 1°18W 90 D3
Tautira Tahiti 17°44S 149°9W 155 b
Tauyskaya Guba Russia 59°20N 150°20E 107 D16
Tavan Bogd Uul Mongolia 49°10N 87°49E 109 C11

Tavares U.S.A. 28°48N 81°44W 179 G8
Tavas Turkey 37°34N 29°4E 99 D11
Tavastehus = Hämeenlinna Finland 61°0N 24°28E 84 B3
Tavda Russia 58°7N 65°8E 106 D7
Tavda → Russia 57°47N 67°18E 106 D7
Taverner B. Canada 67°12N 72°25W 161 D17
Tavernes de la Valldigna Spain 39°5N 0°13W 91 F4
Tavernier U.S.A. 25°1N 80°31W 179 K9
Taveta Kenya 3°23S 37°37E 142 C4
Taveuni Fiji 16°51S 179°58W 154 a
Taviano Italy 39°59N 18°5E 95 C11
Tavignano → France 42°7N 9°33E 73 F13
Tavira Portugal 37°8N 7°40W 89 H3
Tavistock Canada 43°19N 80°50W 174 C4
Tavistock U.K. 50°33N 4°9W 67 G3
Tavolara Italy 40°54N 9°42E 94 B2
Távora → Portugal 41°8N 7°35W 88 D3
Tavoy = Dawei Myanmar 14°2N 98°12E 120 E2
Tavoy Pt. Myanmar 13°32N 98°10E 120 F2
Tavrichanka Russia 43°18N 131°59E 112 C5
Tavropos → Greece 39°10N 21°45E 98 B3
Tavşanlı Turkey 39°32N 29°30E 99 B11
Tavua Fiji 17°37S 177°5E 154 a
Tavuki Fiji 19°7S 178°8E 154 a
Taw → U.K. 51°4N 4°4W 67 F3
Tawa → India 22°48N 77°48E 124 H8
Tawa Res. India 22°35N 78°5E 126 C4
Tawas City U.S.A. 44°16N 83°31W 173 C12
Tawau Malaysia 4°20N 117°55E 118 D5
Tawi-tawi I. Phil. 5°10N 120°15E 119 C6
Tawu Taiwan 22°22N 120°54E 117 F13
Tāwūq Iraq 35°8N 44°26E 105 E11
Taxco Mexico 18°33N 99°36W 181 D5
Taxila Pakistan 33°42N 72°52E 124 C5
Taxkorgan Tajik Zizhixian China 37°49N 75°14E 109 E9
Tay → U.K. 56°37N 3°38W 65 E5
Tay, Firth of U.K. 56°25N 3°8W 65 E5
Tay, L. Australia 32°55S 120°48E 149 F3
Tay, L. U.K. 56°32N 4°8W 65 E4
Tay ⌓ U.K. 56°43N 3°59W 65 E5
Tay Ninh Vietnam 11°20N 106°5E 121 G6
Tayabamba Peru 8°15S 77°16W 188 B2
Taygetos Oros Greece 37°0N 22°23E 98 D4
Taylakova Russia 59°13N 74°0E 106 D8
Taylor Canada 56°13N 120°40W 162 B4
Taylor Fla., U.S.A. 30°26N 82°18W 178 E7
Taylor Nebr., U.S.A. 41°46N 99°23W 172 E4
Taylor Pa., U.S.A. 41°23N 75°43W 175 E9
Taylor Tex., U.S.A. 30°34N 97°25W 176 F6
Taylor, Mt. N.Z. 43°30S 171°20E 155 D6
Taylor, Mt. U.S.A. 35°14N 107°37W 169 J10
Taylorville U.S.A. 39°33N 89°18W 172 F9
Taymā Si. Arabia 27°35N 38°45E 128 E3
Taymyr, Oz. Russia 74°20N 102°0E 107 B11
Taymyr, Poluostrov Russia 75°0N 100°0E 107 B11
Tayport U.K. 56°27N 2°52W 65 E6
Tayrona △ Colombia 11°20N 74°2W 183 D5
Tayshet Russia 55°58N 98°1E 107 D10
Taytay Phil. 10°45N 119°30E 119 B5
Tāyyebād Iran 34°45N 60°45E 129 C9
Tāyyebād □ Iran 34°44N 60°44E 129 C9
Tayynsha Kazakhstan 53°50N 69°45E 109 B7
Taz → Russia 67°32N 78°40E 106 C8
Taza Morocco 34°16N 4°6W 136 B3
Taza-Al Hoceïma-Taounate □ Morocco 34°15N 3°20W 136 B3
Tāza Khurmātū Iraq 35°18N 44°20E 105 E11
Taza-Taou □ Morocco 34°15N 4°10W 136 B3
Tazawa-Ko Japan 39°43N 140°40E 112 E10
Tazenakht Morocco 30°35N 7°12W 136 B2
Tazerbo Libya 25°45N 21°0E 135 C10
Tazin → Canada 59°48N 109°55W 163 B7
Tazin L. Canada 59°44N 108°42W 163 B7
Tazoult Algeria 35°29N 6°11E 136 A5
Tazovskiy Russia 67°30N 78°44E 106 C8
Tazrouk Algeria 23°24N 6°15E 136 D5
Tbilisi Georgia 41°43N 44°50E 87 K7
Tchad = Chad ■ Africa 15°0N 17°15E 135 F8
Tchad, L. Chad 13°30N 14°30E 135 F8
Tchaourou Benin 8°58N 2°40E 139 D5
Tch'eng-tou = Chengdu China 30°38N 104°2E 116 B5
Tchentlo L. Canada 55°15N 125°0W 162 B4
Tchetti Benin 7°50N 1°40E 139 D5
Tchibanga Gabon 2°45S 11°0E 140 E2
Tchien Liberia 5°59N 8°15W 138 D3
Tchin Tabaraden Niger 15°58N 5°56E 139 B6
Tchogha Zanbil = Choghā Zanbīl Iran 32°1N 48°32E 129 C6
Tch'ong-k'ing = Chongqing China 29°35N 106°25E 116 C6
Tczew Poland 54°8N 18°50E 82 D5
Te Anau N.Z. 45°25S 167°43E 155 F2
Te Anau, L. N.Z. 45°15S 167°45E 155 F2
Te Araroa N.Z. 37°39S 178°25E 154 D7
Te Aroha N.Z. 37°32S 175°44E 154 D4
Te Awamutu N.Z. 38°1S 175°20E 154 E4
Te Ika-a-Māui = North I. N.Z. 38°0S 175°0E 154 E4
Te Kaha N.Z. 37°44S 177°52E 154 D6
Te Karaka N.Z. 38°26S 177°53E 154 E6
Te Kauwhata N.Z. 37°25S 175°9E 154 D4
Te Kopuru N.Z. 36°2S 173°56E 154 C2
Te Kuiti N.Z. 38°20S 175°11E 154 E4
Te-n-Dghâmcha, Sebkhet Mauritania 18°30N 15°55W 138 B1
Te Puke N.Z. 37°46S 176°22E 154 D5
Te Teko N.Z. 38°2S 176°48E 154 E5
Te Waewae B. N.Z. 46°13S 167°33E 155 G2
Te Waipounamu = South I. N.Z. 44°0S 170°0E 155 E5
Teaca Romania 46°55N 24°30E 81 D9
Teague U.S.A. 31°38N 96°17W 176 F6
Teahupoo Tahiti 17°50S 149°16W 155 b
Teano Italy 41°15N 14°4E 95 A7
Teapa Mexico 17°33N 92°57W 181 D6
Teba Spain 36°59N 4°55W 89 J6
Tebakang Malaysia 1°6N 110°30E 118 D4
Tébarat Niger 14°49N 4°27E 139 C5
Teberau → Malaysia 1°30N 103°42E 121 d
Teberda Russia 43°30N 41°46E 87 J5
Tébessa Algeria 35°22N 8°8E 136 A5
Tébessa □ Algeria 35°0N 7°50E 136 B5
Tebicuary → Paraguay 26°36S 58°16W 190 B4
Tebingtinggi Riau, Indonesia 1°0N 102°45E 118 E2
Tebingtinggi Sumatera Utara, Indonesia 3°20N 99°9E 118 D1
Tébourba Tunisia 36°49N 9°51E 136 A5
Téboursouk Tunisia 36°29N 9°10E 136 A5
Tebulos Georgia 42°36N 45°17E 87 J7
Tecate Mexico 32°34N 116°38W 171 N10
Tecer Dağları Turkey 39°27N 37°27E 104 C7
Tech → France 42°36N 3°3E 72 F7
Techiman Ghana 7°35N 1°58W 138 D4
Techirghiol Romania 44°4N 28°32E 81 F13
Tecka Argentina 43°29S 70°48W 192 B2
Tecomán Mexico 18°55N 103°53W 180 D4
Tecopa U.S.A. 35°51N 116°13W 171 K10
Tecoripa Mexico 28°37N 109°57W 180 B3
Tecuala Mexico 22°23N 105°27W 180 C3
Tecuci Romania 45°51N 27°27E 81 E12
Tecumseh Canada 42°19N 82°54W 174 D2
Tecumseh Mich., U.S.A. 42°0N 83°57W 173 D12
Tecumseh Okla., U.S.A. 35°15N 96°56W 176 D6
Tedzhen = Tejen Turkmenistan 37°23N 60°31E 108 E6
Tees → U.K. 54°37N 1°10W 66 C6
Tees B. U.K. 54°40N 1°9W 66 C6
Teeswater Canada 43°59N 81°17W 174 C3
Tefé Brazil 3°25S 64°50W 186 D6
Tefenni Turkey 37°18N 29°45E 99 D11
Tegal Indonesia 6°52S 109°8E 118 F3
Tegallalang Indonesia 8°27S 115°17E 119 J18
Tegalsari Indonesia 8°25S 114°8E 119 J17
Tegel, Berlin ✕ (TXL) Germany 52°35N 13°14E 76 C9
Tegernsee Germany 47°43N 11°46E 77 H7
Teggiano Italy 40°23N 15°32E 95 B8
Tegid, L. = Bala, L. U.K. 52°53N 3°37W 66 E4
Tegina Nigeria 10°5N 6°11E 139 C6
Tegucigalpa Honduras 14°5N 87°14W 182 D2
Teguidda i-n-Tessoum Niger 17°25N 6°37E 139 B6
Tehachapi U.S.A. 35°8N 118°27W 171 K8
Tehachapi Mts. U.S.A. 35°0N 118°30W 171 L8
Tehamiyam Sudan 18°20N 36°32E 137 D4
Teheran = Tehrān Iran 35°41N 51°25E 129 C6
Téhini Côte d'Ivoire 9°39N 3°40W 138 D4
Tehoru Indonesia 3°23S 129°30E 119 E7
Tehrān Iran 35°41N 51°25E 129 C6
Tehrān □ Iran 35°30N 51°30E 129 C6
Tehri India 30°23N 78°29E 125 D8
Tehuacán Mexico 18°27N 97°23W 181 D5
Tehuantepec Mexico 16°21N 95°13W 181 D5
Tehuantepec, G. de Mexico 15°50N 95°12W 181 D5
Tehuantepec, Istmo de Mexico 17°15N 94°30W 181 D6
Teide, Pico del Canary Is. 28°15N 16°38W 100 F3
Teifi → U.K. 52°5N 4°41W 67 E3
Teigebyen Norway 60°12N 11°0E 62 D5
Teign → U.K. 50°32N 3°32W 67 G4
Teignmouth U.K. 50°33N 3°31W 67 G4
Teijo △ Finland 60°13N 22°56E 84 B2
Teinainano = Tarawa Kiribati 1°30N 173°0E 156 G9
Teiuş Romania 46°12N 23°40E 81 D8
Teixeira Brazil 7°13S 37°15W 189 B3
Teixeira Pinto Guinea-Biss. 12°3N 16°0W 138 C1
Tejakula Indonesia 8°8S 115°20E 119 J18
Tejen Turkmenistan 37°23N 60°31E 108 E6
Tejen → Turkmenistan 37°24N 60°38E 129 B9
Tejo → Europe 38°40N 9°24W 89 F2
Tejon Pass U.S.A. 34°49N 118°53W 171 L8
Tekamah U.S.A. 41°47N 96°13W 172 E5
Tekapo → N.Z. 44°13S 170°21E 155 E5
Tekapo, L. N.Z. 43°53S 170°33E 155 D5
Tekax Mexico 20°12N 89°17W 181 C7
Teke Turkey 41°4N 29°39E 97 E13
Tekeli Kazakhstan 44°50N 79°0E 109 D9
Tekeze Dam Ethiopia 13°10N 38°45E 131 E2
Tekija Serbia 44°42N 22°26E 96 B6
Tekirdağ Turkey 40°58N 27°30E 97 F11
Tekirdağ □ Turkey 41°0N 27°0E 97 E11
Tekirova Turkey 36°30N 30°32E 99 E12
Tekkali India 18°37N 84°15E 126 E7
Tekke Turkey 40°42N 36°12E 104 B7
Tekman Turkey 39°38N 41°29E 105 C9
Tekoa U.S.A. 47°14N 117°4W 168 C5
Tekong Besar, Pulau Singapore 1°25N 104°3E 121 d
Tel → India 20°50N 83°54E 126 D6
Tel Aviv ✕ (TLV) Israel 32°5N 34°49E 130 C3
Tel Aviv-Yafo Israel 32°4N 34°48E 130 C3
Tel Lakhish Israel 31°34N 34°51E 130 D3
Tel Megiddo Israel 32°35N 35°11E 130 C4
Tela Honduras 15°40N 87°28W 182 C2
Télagh Algeria 34°51N 0°32W 136 B3
Telanaipura = Jambi Indonesia 1°38S 103°30E 118 E2
Telangana □ India 17°30N 78°30E 126 F4
Telaščica ⌓ Croatia 43°55N 15°10E 93 E12
Telavi Georgia 42°0N 45°30E 87 J7
Telč Czechia 49°11N 15°28E 78 B8
Telciu Romania 47°25N 24°24E 81 C9
Telde Canary Is. 27°59N 15°25W 100 G4
Telegraph Creek Canada 58°0N 131°10W 162 B2
Telekhany = Tsyelyakhany Belarus 52°30N 25°46E 75 B13
Telemark Norway 59°15N 7°40E 61 G12
Télemsès Niger 15°37N 4°44E 139 B5
Telén Argentina 36°15S 65°31W 190 D2
Teleneşti Moldova 47°30N 28°22E 81 C13
Teleng Iran 25°47N 61°3E 129 E9
Teleño Spain 42°23N 6°22W 88 C4
Teleorman □ Romania 44°0N 25°0E 81 G10
Teleorman → Romania 43°52N 25°26E 81 G10
Telerhteba, Djebel Algeria 24°10N 6°51E 136 D5
Teles Pires → Brazil 7°21S 58°3W 186 E7
Telescope Pk. U.S.A. 36°10N 117°5W 171 J9
Teletaye Mali 16°31N 1°30E 139 B5
Teletskoye, Oz. Russia 51°40N 87°30E 109 B11
Telford U.K. 52°40N 2°27W 67 E5
Telford and Wrekin □ U.K. 52°45N 2°27W 66 E5
Telfs Austria 47°19N 11°4E 78 D4
Télimélé Guinea 10°54N 13°2W 138 C2
Telkwa Canada 54°41N 127°5W 162 C3
Tell City U.S.A. 37°57N 86°46W 172 G10
Teller U.S.A. 65°16N 166°22W 166 B6
Tellicherry = Thalassery India 11°45N 75°30E 127 J2
Telluride U.S.A. 37°56N 107°49W 169 H10
Teloloapán Mexico 18°21N 99°51W 181 D5
Telpos Iz Russia 63°16N 59°13E 58 C17
Telsen Argentina 42°30S 66°50W 192 B3
Telšiai Lithuania 55°59N 22°14E 82 C9
Telšiai □ Lithuania 55°59N 22°15E 82 C9
Teltow Germany 52°23N 13°17E 76 C9
Teluk Anson = Teluk Intan Malaysia 4°3N 101°0E 121 K3
Teluk Bahang Malaysia 5°28N 100°13E 121 c
Teluk Betung = Bandar Lampung Indonesia 5°20S 105°10E 118 F3
Teluk Intan Malaysia 4°3N 101°0E 121 K3
Teluk Kumbar Malaysia 5°18N 100°14E 121 c
Telukbutun Indonesia 4°13N 108°12E 118 D3
Telukdalam Indonesia 0°33N 97°50E 118 D1
Tema Ghana 5°41N 0°0 139 D5
Temagami, L. Canada 47°0N 80°10W 164 C3
Temax Mexico 21°9N 88°56W 181 C7
Temba S. Africa 25°20S 28°17E 145 C4
Tembagapura Indonesia 4°20S 137°0E 119 E9
Tembe Dem. Rep. of the Congo 0°16S 28°14E 142 C2
Tembe ⌓ S. Africa 26°51S 32°24E 145 C5
Tembleque Spain 39°41N 3°30W 88 F7
Temblor Range U.S.A. 35°20N 119°50W 171 K7
Teme → U.K. 52°11N 2°13W 67 E5
Temecula U.S.A. 33°30N 117°9W 171 M9
Temengor, Tasik Malaysia 5°24N 101°18E 121 K3
Temerloh Malaysia 3°27N 102°25E 121 L4
Teminabuan Indonesia 1°26S 132°1E 119 E8
Temir Kazakhstan 49°1N 57°14E 108 C5
Temirtau Kazakhstan 50°5N 72°56E 109 B8
Temirtau Russia 53°10N 87°30E 109 B11
Témiscamie → Canada 50°59N 73°5W 165 B5
Témiscaming Canada 46°44N 79°5W 164 C4
Témiscamingue, L. Canada 47°10N 79°25W 164 C4
Temnikov Russia 54°40N 43°11E 86 C6
Temo → Italy 40°17N 8°28E 94 B1
Temora Australia 34°30S 147°30E 153 C7
Temosachic Mexico 28°57N 107°51W 180 B3
Tempe U.S.A. 33°24N 111°54W 169 K8
Témpio Pausánia Italy 40°54N 9°6E 94 B2
Tempiute U.S.A. 37°39N 115°38W 170 H11
Temple U.S.A. 31°6N 97°21W 176 F6
Temple B. Australia 12°15S 143°3E 150 A3
Temple Terrace U.S.A. 28°2N 82°23W 179 G7
Templemore Ireland 52°47N 7°51W 64 D4
Templeton U.S.A. 35°33N 120°42W 170 K6
Templeton → Australia 21°0S 138°40E 150 C2
Templin Germany 53°7N 13°28E 76 B9
Tempoal de Sánchez Mexico 21°31N 98°23W 181 C5
Temryuk Russia 45°15N 37°24E 85 K9
Temska → Serbia 43°17N 22°33E 96 C6
Temuco Chile 38°45S 72°40W 192 A2
Temuka N.Z. 44°14S 171°17E 155 E6
Ten Degree Channel India 10°0N 92°30E 127 K11
Ten Thousand Is. U.S.A. 25°55N 81°45W 179 K8
Tenabo Mexico 20°3N 90°14W 181 C6
Tenaha U.S.A. 31°57N 94°15W 176 F7
Tenakee Springs U.S.A. 57°47N 135°13W 162 B1
Tenali India 16°15N 80°35E 127 F5
Tenancingo Mexico 18°58N 99°38W 181 D5
Tenango del Valle Mexico 19°7N 99°33W 181 D5
Tenaro, Akra Greece 36°22N 22°27E 98 E4
Tenasserim = Taninthayi Myanmar 12°6N 99°3E 121 F2
Tenasserim □ Myanmar 14°0N 98°30E 120 F2
Tenasserim → Myanmar 12°24N 98°37E 120 F2
Tenby U.K. 51°40N 4°42W 67 F3
Tenda, Colle di France 44°7N 7°36E 73 D11
Tendaho Ethiopia 11°48N 40°54E 131 E3
Tende France 44°5N 7°35E 73 D11
Tendjedi, Adrar Algeria 23°41N 7°32E 136 D5
Tendō Japan 38°20N 140°30E 112 E10
Tendrara Morocco 33°3N 1°58W 136 B3
Tendrovskaya Kosa Ukraine 46°16N 31°35E 85 J6
Tendukhera India 23°24N 79°33E 125 H8
Teneguía, Volcán Canary Is. 28°28N 17°51W 100 F2
Teneida Egypt 25°30N 29°19E 137 B2
Tenenkou Mali 14°28N 4°55W 138 C4
Ténéré Niger 19°0N 10°30E 139 B7
Ténéré, Erg du Niger 17°35N 10°55E 135 E8
Tenerife Canary Is. 28°15N 16°35W 100 F3
Tenerife, Pico Canary Is. 27°43N 18°1W 100 G1
Tenerife Norte ✕ (TFN) Canary Is. 28°28N 16°17W 100 F3
Tenerife Sur ✕ (TFS) Canary Is. 28°3N 16°33W 100 F3
Ténès Algeria 36°31N 1°14E 136 A4
Teng Xian Guangxi Zhuangzu, China 23°21N 110°56E 117 F8
Teng Xian Shandong, China 35°5N 117°10E 115 G9
Tengah, Kepulauan Indonesia 7°5S 118°15E 118 F5
Tengchong China 25°0N 98°28E 116 E2
Tengchowfu = Penglai China 37°48N 120°42E 115 F11
Tenggarong Indonesia 0°24S 116°58E 118 E5
Tengger Feng China 43°12N 86°48E 109 D11
Tengger Shamo China 38°0N 104°10E 114 F3
Tenggol, Pulau Malaysia 4°48N 103°41E 121 K4
Tengiz Köli Kazakhstan 50°30N 69°0E 109 B7
Tengzhou China 35°4N 117°9E 115 G9
Tenhult Sweden 57°41N 14°20E 63 G8
Teniente Enciso △ Paraguay 21°5S 61°8W 190 A3
Tenille U.S.A. 29°46N 83°19W 178 F6
Tenino U.S.A. 46°51N 122°51W 170 D4
Tenkasi India 8°55N 77°20E 127 K3
Tenke Katanga, Dem. Rep. of the Congo 11°22S 26°40E 143 E2
Tenke Katanga, Dem. Rep. of the Congo 10°32S 26°7E 143 E2
Tenkodogo Burkina Faso 11°54N 0°19W 139 C4
Tenna → Italy 43°14N 13°47E 93 E10
Tennant Creek Australia 19°30S 134°15E 150 B1
Tennessee □ U.S.A. 36°0N 86°30W 177 D11
Tennessee → U.S.A. 37°4N 88°34W 177 C10
Tennille U.S.A. 32°56N 82°48W 178 C7
Teno, Pta. de Canary Is. 28°21N 16°55W 100 F3
Tenojoki = Tana → Norway 70°30N 28°14E 60 A23
Tenom Malaysia 5°4N 115°57E 118 C5
Tenosique Mexico 17°29N 91°26W 181 D6
Tenryū-Gawa → Japan 35°39N 137°48E 113 G8
Tensift, Oued → Morocco 32°3N 9°28W 136 B2
Tenterden U.K. 51°4N 0°42E 67 F8
Tenterfield Australia 29°0S 152°0E 151 D5
Teo = A Ramallosa Spain 42°45N 8°30W 88 C2
Teófilo Otoni Brazil 17°50S 41°30W 189 D2
Tepa Indonesia 7°52S 129°31E 119 F7
Tepalcatepec → Mexico 18°35N 101°59W 180 D4
Tepecik Bursa, Turkey 40°7N 28°25E 97 F12
Tepecik Kütahya, Turkey 39°32N 29°28E 99 B11
Tepehuanes Mexico 25°21N 105°44W 180 B3
Tepelenë Albania 40°17N 20°2E 96 F4
Tepetongo Mexico 22°28N 103°9W 180 C4
Tepic Mexico 21°30N 104°54W 180 C4
Teplá Czechia 49°59N 12°52E 78 B5
Teplice Czechia 50°40N 13°48E 78 A6
Teplyk Ukraine 48°40N 29°44E 81 B14
Tequila Mexico 20°54N 103°47W 180 C4
Ter → Spain 42°2N 3°12E 90 C8
Ter Apel Neths. 52°53N 7°5E 69 B7
Téra Niger 14°0N 0°45E 139 C5
Tera → Spain 41°54N 5°44W 88 D5
Teraina Kiribati 4°43N 160°25W 157 G12
Téramo Italy 42°39N 13°42E 93 F10
Terang Australia 38°15S 142°55E 152 E5
Terang, Teluk Indonesia 8°44S 116°0E 119 K19
Terawhiti, C. N.Z. 41°16S 174°38E 154 H3
Terazit, Massif de Niger 20°2N 8°30E 139 A6
Tercan Turkey 39°47N 40°23E 105 C9
Terceira Azores 38°43N 27°13W 134 a
Tercero → Argentina 32°58S 61°47W 190 C3
Terdal India 16°33N 75°3E 126 F2
Terebovlya Ukraine 49°18N 25°44E 75 D13
Teregova Romania 45°10N 22°16E 80 E7
Terek → Russia 44°0N 47°30E 87 J8
Terengganu □ Malaysia 4°55N 103°0E 121 K4
Terepaima △ Venezuela 9°58N 69°17W 183 E6
Tereshka → Russia 51°48N 46°26E 86 E8
Teresina Brazil 5°9S 42°45W 189 B2
Terespol Poland 52°5N 23°37E 83 F10
Teressa India 8°15N 93°10E 127 K11
Teresva Ukraine 48°0N 23°42E 81 B8
Terewah, L. Australia 29°52S 147°35E 151 D4
Terges → Portugal 37°49N 7°41W 89 H3
Tergnier France 49°40N 3°17E 71 C10
Teridgerie Cr. → Australia 30°25S 148°50E 153 A8
Terlizzi Italy 41°8N 16°32E 95 A9
Termas de Río Hondo Argentina 27°29S 64°52W 190 B3
Terme Turkey 41°11N 37°0E 104 B7
Términi Imerese Italy 37°59N 13°42E 94 E6
Términos, L. de Mexico 18°37N 91°33W 181 D6
Termiz Uzbekistan 37°15N 67°15E 109 E7
Térmoli Italy 42°0N 15°0E 93 F12
Ternate Indonesia 0°45N 127°25E 119 D7
Terneuzen Neths. 51°20N 3°50E 69 C3
Terney Russia 45°3N 136°37E 112 B8
Terni Italy 42°34N 12°37E 93 F9
Ternitz Austria 47°43N 16°2E 78 D9
Ternivka Ukraine 48°32N 29°58E 81 B14
Ternopil Ukraine 49°30N 25°40E 75 D13
Ternopil □ Ukraine 48°10N 25°10E 75 D13
Ternopol = Ternopil Ukraine 49°30N 25°40E 75 D13
Terowie Australia 33°8S 138°55E 152 B3
Terpni Greece 40°55N 23°26E 96 F7
Terra Bella U.S.A. 35°58N 119°3W 171 K7
Terra Nova △ Canada 48°33N 53°55W 165 C9
Terrace Canada 54°30N 128°35W 162 C3
Terrace Bay Canada 48°47N 87°5W 164 C2
Terracina Italy 41°17N 13°15E 94 A6
Terralba Italy 39°43N 8°39E 94 C1
Terrasini Italy 38°10N 13°4E 94 D6
Terrassa Spain 41°34N 2°1E 90 D7
Terrasson-la-Villedieu France 45°8N 1°18E 72 C5
Terre Haute U.S.A. 39°28N 87°25W 172 F10
Terrebonne B. U.S.A. 29°5N 90°35W 177 G9
Terrecht Mali 19°35N 0°22E 139 B5
Terrenceville Canada 47°40N 54°44W 165 C9
Terrick Terrick △ Australia 36°8S 144°13E 152 D6
Terry U.S.A. 46°47N 105°19W 168 C11
Terryville U.S.A. 41°41N 73°3W 175 E11
Terschelling Neths. 53°25N 5°20E 69 A5
Tersko-Kumskiy Kanal Russia 44°32N 44°38E 87 H7
Tertenía Italy 39°42N 9°34E 94 C2
Terter = Tärtär → Azerbaijan 40°26N 47°20E 87 K8
Teruel Spain 40°22N 1°8W 90 E3
Teruel □ Spain 40°48N 1°0W 90 E4
Tervel Bulgaria 43°45N 27°28E 97 C11
Tervola Finland 66°6N 24°49E 60 C21
Teryaweynya L. Australia 32°18S 143°22E 152 B5
Tešanj Bos.-H. 44°38N 18°1E 80 F3
Tesha → Russia 55°38N 42°9E 86 C6
Teshio Japan 44°53N 141°44E 112 B10
Teshio-Gawa → Japan 44°53N 141°45E 112 B10
Tešica Serbia 43°27N 21°45E 96 C5
Tesiyn Gol → Mongolia 50°40N 93°20E 110 A7
Teslić Bos.-H. 44°37N 17°54E 80 F2
Teslin Canada 60°10N 132°43W 162 A2
Teslin → Canada 61°34N 134°35W 162 A2
Teslin L. Canada 60°15N 132°57W 162 A2
Tessalit Mali 20°12N 1°0E 139 A5
Tessaoua Niger 13°47N 7°56E 139 C6
Tessin Germany 54°2N 12°26E 76 A8
Tessit Mali 15°13N 0°18E 139 B5
Test → U.K. 50°56N 1°29W 67 G6
Testa del Gargano Italy 41°50N 16°10E 93 G13
Testigos, Is. Los Venezuela 11°23N 63°7W 183 D7
Tét Hungary 47°30N 17°33E 80 C2
Têt → France 42°44N 3°2E 72 F7
Tetachuck L. Canada 53°18N 125°55W 162 C3
Tetas, Pta. Chile 23°31S 70°38W 190 A1
Tete Mozam. 16°13S 33°33E 143 F3
Tete □ Mozam. 15°15S 32°40E 143 F3
Teterev → Ukraine 51°1N 30°5E 75 C16
Teterow Germany 53°46N 12°34E 76 B8
Teteven Bulgaria 42°58N 24°17E 97 D8
Tethul → Canada 60°35N 112°12W 162 A6
Tetiyev Ukraine 49°22N 29°38E 75 D15
Tetlit Zheh = Fort McPherson Canada 67°30N 134°55W 160 D5
Teton → U.S.A. 47°56N 110°31W 168 C8
Tétouan Morocco 35°35N 5°21W 136 A2
Tetovo Macedonia 42°1N 20°59E 96 D4
Tetufera, Mt. Tahiti 17°40S 149°26W 155 b
Tetyushi Russia 54°55N 48°49E 86 C9
Teuco → Argentina 25°35S 60°11W 190 B3
Teulada Italy 38°58N 8°46E 94 D1
Teulon Canada 50°23N 97°16W 163 C9
Teun Indonesia 6°59S 129°8E 119 F7
Teuri-Tō Japan 44°26N 141°19E 112 B10
Teutoburger Wald Germany 52°5N 8°22E 76 C4
Tevere → Italy 41°44N 12°14E 93 G9
Tevere ⌓ Italy 42°46N 12°14E 93 F9
Teverya Israel 32°47N 35°32E 130 C4
Teviot → U.K. 55°29N 2°38W 65 F6
Tewantin Australia 26°27S 153°3E 151 D5
Tewkesbury U.K. 51°59N 2°9W 67 F5
Texada I. Canada 49°40N 124°25W 162 D4
Texarkana Ark., U.S.A. 33°26N 94°2W 176 E7
Texarkana Tex., U.S.A. 33°26N 94°3W 176 E7
Texas Australia 28°49S 151°9E 151 D5
Texas □ U.S.A. 31°40N 98°30W 176 F5
Texas City U.S.A. 29°24N 94°54W 176 G7
Texel Neths. 53°5N 4°50E 69 A4
Texline U.S.A. 36°23N 103°2W 176 C3
Texoma, L. U.S.A. 33°50N 96°34W 176 E6
Teyateyaneng Lesotho 29°7S 27°34E 141 K5
Teykovo Russia 56°55N 40°30E 84 D11
Teza → Russia 56°32N 41°53E 86 B5
Tezin Afghan. 34°24N 69°30E 124 B3
Teziutlán Mexico 19°49N 97°21W 181 D5
Tezpur India 26°40N 92°45E 123 F18
Tezzeron L. Canada 54°43N 124°30W 162 C4
Tha-anne → Canada 60°31N 94°37W 163 A10
Tha Deua Laos 17°57N 102°53E 120 D4
Tha Deua Laos 19°26N 101°50E 120 C3
Tha Li Thailand 17°37N 101°25E 120 D3
Tha Pla Thailand 17°48N 100°32E 120 D3
Tha Rua Thailand 14°34N 100°44E 120 E3
Tha Sala Thailand 8°40N 99°56E 121 H2
Tha Song Yang Thailand 17°34N 97°55E 120 D1
Thaba Putsoa Lesotho 29°45S 28°0E 145 C4
Thaba-Tseka Lesotho 29°32S 28°36E 145 C4
Thabana Ntlenyana Lesotho 29°30S 29°16E 145 C4
Thabazimbi S. Africa 24°40S 27°21E 145 B4
Thādiq Si. Arabia 25°18N 45°52E 128 E5
Thai Binh Vietnam 20°35N 106°1E 116 G6
Thai Muang Thailand 8°24N 98°16E 121 H2
Thai Nguyen Vietnam 21°35N 105°55E 116 G5
Thailand ■ Asia 16°0N 102°0E 120 E4
Thailand, G. of Asia 11°30N 101°0E 121 G3
Thakhek Laos 17°25N 104°45E 120 D5
Thal Pakistan 33°28N 70°33E 124 C4
Thal Desert Pakistan 31°10N 71°30E 124 D4
Thala Tunisia 35°35N 8°40E 136 A5
Thala La = Hkakabo Razi Myanmar 28°25N 97°23E 116 C1
Thalabarivat Cambodia 13°33N 105°57E 120 F5
Thalang = Amphoe Thalang Thailand 8°1N 98°20E 121 a
Thalara Nepal 29°29N 80°59E 125 E9
Thalassery India 11°45N 75°30E 127 J2
Thale Sap Songkhla Thailand 7°12N 100°28E 121 J3
Thallon Australia 28°39S 148°49E 151 D4
Thalu, Ko Thailand 9°26N 99°54E 121 b
Thalwil Switz. 47°17N 8°35E 77 H4
Tham Lot Thailand 19°34N 98°16E 120 C2
Thamarīt Oman 17°39N 54°2E 131 D5
Thames N.Z. 37°7S 175°34E 154 D4
Thames → Canada 42°20N 82°25W 174 D2
Thames → U.K. 51°29N 0°34E 67 F8
Thames → U.S.A. 41°18N 72°5W 175 E12
Thames, Firth of N.Z. 37°0S 175°25E 154 D4
Thames Estuary U.K. 51°29N 0°52E 67 F8
Thamesford Canada 43°4N 81°0W 174 C4
Thamesville Canada 42°33N 81°59W 174 D3
Than India 22°34N 71°11E 124 H4
Than Kyun Myanmar 9°49N 98°4E 121 H1
Than Uyen Vietnam 22°0N 103°54E 120 B4
Thana Gazi India 27°25N 76°19E 124 F7
Thandla India 23°0N 74°34E 124 H6
Thandwe Myanmar 18°20N 94°30E 123 K19
Thane India 19°12N 72°59E 126 E1
Thanesar India 30°1N 76°52E 124 D7
Thanet, I. of U.K. 51°21N 1°20E 67 F9
Thangool Australia 24°38S 150°42E 150 C5
Thanh Hoa Vietnam 19°48N 105°46E 120 C5
Thanh Hung Vietnam 9°55N 105°43E 121 H5
Thanh Pho Ho Chi Minh Vietnam 10°58N 106°40E 121 G6
Thanh Thuy Vietnam 22°55N 104°51E 120 A5
Thanjavur India 10°48N 79°12E 127 J4
Thanlwin = Salween → Myanmar 16°31N 97°37E 123 L20
Thann France 47°48N 7°5E 71 E14
Thano Bula Khan Pakistan 25°22N 67°50E 124 G2
Thanya Buri Thailand 14°1N 100°45E 120 E3
Thaoge → Botswana 20°27S 22°36E 144 B3
Thaolintoa L. Canada 61°30N 96°25W 163 A9
Thaon-les-Vosges France 48°15N 6°24E 71 D13
Thap Lan △ Thailand 14°15N 102°16E 120 E4
Thap Sakae Thailand 11°30N 99°37E 121 G2
Thap Than Thailand 15°27N 99°54E 120 E2
Thar Desert India 28°0N 72°0E 124 F5
Tharad India 24°30N 71°44E 124 G4
Tharaka-Nithi □ Kenya 0°20S 38°0E 142 C4
Thargomindah Australia 27°58S 143°46E 151 D3
Tharp Fracture Zone S. Ocean 54°0S 135°0W 55 B14
Tharrawaddy Myanmar 17°38N 95°48E 123 L19
Tharthār, Buḩayrat ath Iraq 34°0N 43°15E 105 E10
Tharthar, L. = Tharthār, Buḩayrat ath Iraq 34°0N 43°15E 105 E10
Tharthār, W. ath → Iraq 34°32N 43°4E 105 E10
Thasopoula Greece 40°49N 24°45E 97 F8
Thasos Greece 40°40N 24°40E 97 F8
That Khe Vietnam 22°16N 106°28E 116 F6
Thatcher Ariz., U.S.A. 32°51N 109°46W 169 K9
Thatcher Colo., U.S.A. 37°33N 104°7W 169 H11
Thaton Myanmar 16°55N 97°22E 123 L20
Thatta Pakistan 24°42N 67°55E 124 G2
Thau, Bassin de France 43°23N 3°36E 72 E7
Thaungdut Myanmar 24°30N 94°40E 123 G19
Thayawthadangy Kyun Myanmar 12°19N 98°0E 120 F1
Thayer U.S.A. 36°31N 91°33W 172 G8
Thayetmyo Myanmar 19°20N 95°10E 123 K19
Thazi Myanmar 21°0N 96°5E 123 J20
Thbeng Meanchey Cambodia 13°49N 104°58E 120 F5
The Bahamas ■ N. Amer. 24°0N 75°0W 183 B5
The Broads U.K. 52°45N 1°30E 66 E9
The Everglades U.S.A. 25°50N 81°0W 179 K9
The Gambia ■ W. Afr. 13°25N 16°0W 138 C1
The Gulf = Persian Gulf Asia 27°0N 50°0E 129 E6
The Hague = 's-Gravenhage Neths. 52°7N 4°17E 69 B4
The Pas Canada 53°45N 101°15W 163 C8
The Wash U.K. 52°58N 0°20E 66 E8
The Weald U.K. 51°4N 0°20E 67 F8
Thebes = Thiva Greece 38°19N 23°19E 98 C5
Thebes Egypt 25°40N 32°35E 137 B3
Thedford U.S.A. 41°59N 100°35W 172 E3
Theebine Australia 25°57S 152°34E 151 D5
Thekulthili L. Canada 61°3N 110°0W 163 A7
Thelon → Canada 64°16N 96°4W 163 A8
Thénezay France 46°44N 0°2W 70 F6
Thenon France 45°9N 1°4E 72 C5
Theodore Australia 24°55S 150°3E 150 C5
Theodore Canada 51°26N 102°55W 163 C8
Theodore U.S.A. 30°33N 88°10W 177 F10
Theodore Roosevelt △ U.S.A. 47°0N 103°25W 172 B2
Theodore Roosevelt L. U.S.A. 33°40N 111°10W 169 K8
Thepha Thailand 6°52N 100°58E 121 J3
Thérain → France 49°15N 2°27E 71 C9
Therandë Kosovo 42°21N 20°50E 96 D4
Theresa U.S.A. 44°13N 75°48W 175 B9
Theressa U.S.A. 29°50N 82°4W 178 F7
Thermaïkos Kolpos Greece 40°15N 22°45E 96 F6
Thermopolis U.S.A. 43°39N 108°13W 168 E9
Thermopylæ Greece 38°48N 22°35E 98 C4
Thesprotia Greece 39°27N 20°22E 98 B2
Thessalon Canada 46°20N 83°30W 164 C3
Thessalonica, Gulf of = Thermaïkos Kolpos Greece 40°15N 22°45E 96 F6
Thessaloniki Greece 40°38N 22°58E 96 F6
Thessaloniki ✕ (SKG) Greece 40°30N 23°0E 96 F7
Thessaly □ Greece 39°25N 22°0E 98 B4
Thetford U.K. 52°25N 0°45E 67 E8
Thetford Mines Canada 46°8N 71°18W 165 C5
Thethi △ Albania 42°24N 19°46E 96 D3
Theun → Laos 18°19N 104°0E 120 C5
Theunissen S. Africa 28°26S 26°43E 144 C4
Thevenard Australia 32°9S 133°38E 151 E1
Thiamis → Greece 39°15N 20°6E 98 B2
Thiberville France 49°8N 0°27E 70 C7
Thibodaux U.S.A. 29°48N 90°49W 177 G9
Thicket Portage Canada 55°19N 97°42W 163 B9
Thief River Falls U.S.A. 48°7N 96°10W 172 A5
Thiel Mts. Antarctica 85°15S 91°0W 55 E16
Thiene Italy 45°42N 11°29E 93 C8
Thiérache France 49°51N 3°45E 71 C10
Thiers France 45°52N 3°33E 72 C7
Thiès Senegal 14°50N 16°51W 138 C1
Thiès □ Senegal 14°45N 16°50W 138 C1
Thiesi Italy 40°31N 8°43E 94 B1
Thika Kenya 1°1S 37°5E 142 C4
Thille-Boubacar Senegal 16°31N 15°5W 138 B1
Thimphu Bhutan 27°31N 89°45E 123 F16
Thina → S. Africa 31°18S 29°13E 145 D4
Þingvallavatn Iceland 64°11N 21°9W 60 D3
Thionville France 49°20N 6°10E 71 C13
Thira = Santorini Greece 36°23N 25°27E 99 E7
Thirasia Greece 36°26N 25°21E 99 E7
Third Cataract Sudan 19°42N 30°20E 137 D3
Thirsk U.K. 54°14N 1°19W 66 C6
Thiruvananthapuram India 8°41N 77°0E 127 K3
Thiruvarur India 10°46N 79°38E 127 J4
Thisted Denmark 56°58N 8°40E 63 H2
Thistle I. Australia 35°0S 136°8E 152 C2
Thithia = Cicia Fiji 17°45S 179°18W 154 a
Thitu I. S. China Sea 11°3N 114°17E 118 B4
Thiva Greece 38°19N 23°19E 98 C5
Thiviers France 45°25N 0°54E 72 C4
Þjórsá → Iceland 63°47N 20°48W 60 E3
Thlewiaza → Canada 60°29N 94°40W 163 A10
Thmar Puok Cambodia 13°57N 103°4E 120 F4
Tho Chu, Dao Vietnam 9°20N 103°28E 121 H4
Tho Vinh Vietnam 19°16N 105°42E 120 C5
Thoa → Canada 60°31N 109°47W 163 A7
Thoen Thailand 17°43N 99°12E 120 D2
Thoeng Thailand 19°41N 100°12E 120 C3
Thohoyandou S. Africa 22°58S 30°29E 141 J6
Thomas U.S.A. 35°45N 98°45W 176 D5
Thomas, L. Australia 26°4S 137°58E 151 D2
Thomas Hubbard, C. Canada 82°0N 94°25W 161 A13
Thomaston U.S.A. 32°53N 84°20W 178 C5
Thomasville Ala., U.S.A. 31°55N 87°44W 177 F11
Thomasville Ga., U.S.A. 30°50N 83°59W 178 E6
Thomasville N.C., U.S.A. 35°53N 80°5W 177 D14
Thompson Canada 55°45N 97°52W 163 B9
Thompson U.S.A. 41°52N 75°31W 175 E9
Thompson → Canada 50°15N 121°24W 162 C4
Thompson → U.S.A. 39°46N 93°37W 172 F7
Thompson Falls U.S.A. 47°36N 115°21W 168 C6
Thompson Pk. U.S.A. 41°0N 123°2W 168 F2
Thompson Sd. N.Z. 45°8S 166°46E 155 F1
Thompson Springs U.S.A. 38°58N 109°43W 168 G9
Thompsontown U.S.A. 40°33N 77°14W 174 F7
Thomson U.S.A. 33°28N 82°30W 178 B7
Thomson → Australia 25°11S 142°53E 150 C3
Thon Buri Thailand 13°45N 100°29E 120 F3

Thônes France 45°54N 6°18E 73 C10
Thong Yang Thailand 9°28N 99°56E 121 b
Thonon-les-Bains
  France 46°22N 6°29E 71 F13
Thoothukudi = Tuticorin
  India 8°50N 78°12E 127 K4
Thorez Ukraine 48°4N 38°34E 85 H10
Þórisvatn Iceland 64°20N 18°55W 60 D4
Thornaby on Tees U.K. 54°33N 1°18W 66 C6
Thornbury Canada 44°34N 80°26W 174 B4
Thornbury N.Z. 46°17S 168°9E 155 G3
Thorne U.K. 53°37N 0°57W 66 D7
Thornton Canada 44°16N 79°43W 174 B5
Thornton U.S.A. 39°52N 104°58W 168 G11
Thorold Canada 43°7N 79°12W 174 C5
Þórshöfn Iceland 66°12N 15°20W 60 C6
Thouarcé France 47°17N 0°30W 70 E6
Thouars France 47°0N 0°15W 70 F6
Thouet → France 47°17N 0°6W 70 E6
Thouin, C. Australia 20°20S 118°10E 148 D2
Thousand Islands
  U.S.A. 44°20N 76°0W 175 B9
Thousand Oaks
  U.S.A. 34°10N 118°50W 171 L8
Thrace Europe 41°0N 27°0E 97 F10
Thrace, Sea of Greece 40°30N 25°0E 97 F8
Thredbo Australia 36°31S 148°20E 153 D8
Three Forks U.S.A. 45°54N 111°33W 168 D8
Three Gorges Dam
  China 30°45N 111°15E 117 B8
Three Gorges Res. = Sanxia
  Shuiku China 30°3N 107°58E 116 B6
Three Hills Canada 51°43N 113°15W 162 C6
Three Hummock I.
  Australia 40°25S 144°55E 151 G3
Three Pagodas Pass
  Asia 15°20N 98°30E 120 E2
Three Points, C. Ghana 4°42N 2°6W 138 E4
Three Rivers Calif.,
  U.S.A. 36°26N 118°54W 170 J8
Three Rivers Tex.,
  U.S.A. 28°28N 98°11W 176 L5
Three Springs
  Australia 29°32S 115°45E 149 E2
Thrissur India 10°30N 76°18E 127 J3
Throssell, L. Australia 27°33S 124°10E 149 E3
Throssell Ra. Australia 22°3S 121°43E 148 D3
Thruxton △ Australia 17°47S 147°40E 151 D4
Thu Dau Mot Vietnam 10°58N 106°39E 121 G6
Thua → Kenya 1°31S 39°30E 142 C4
Thuamal Rampur India 19°23N 82°56E 126 E6
Thuan Hoa Vietnam 8°58N 105°30E 121 H5
Thubun Lakes Canada 61°30N 112°0W 163 A6
Thueyts France 44°41N 4°9E 73 D8
Thugga = Dougga
  Tunisia 36°25N 9°13E 136 A5
Thuin Belgium 50°20N 4°17E 69 D4
Thuir France 42°38N 2°45E 72 F6
Thule = Qaanaaq
  Greenland 77°30N 69°10W 57 B4
Thule Air Base = Uummannaq
  Greenland 77°33N 68°52W 57 B4
Thun Switz. 46°45N 7°38E 77 J3
Thunder B. U.S.A. 45°0N 83°20W 174 B1
Thunder Bay Canada 48°20N 89°15W 164 C2
Thunderbolt U.S.A. 32°3N 81°4W 178 C8
Thunersee Switz. 46°43N 7°39E 77 J3
Thung Salaeng Luang △
  Thailand 16°43N 100°50E 120 D3
Thung Song Thailand 8°10N 99°40E 121 H2
Thungyai △ Thailand 15°30N 98°40E 120 D2
Thunkar Bhutan 27°55N 91°0E 123 F17
Thuong Tra Vietnam 16°2N 107°42E 120 D6
Thur → Switz. 47°32N 9°10E 77 H5
Thurgau □ Switz. 47°34N 9°10E 77 H5
Thüringen □ Germany 51°0N 11°0E 76 D6
Thüringer Wald Germany 50°35N 11°0E 76 D5
Thuringowa △
  Australia 19°18S 146°43E 150 B4
Thurles Ireland 52°41N 7°49W 64 D4
Thurn P. Austria 47°20N 12°25E 78 D5
Thurrock □ U.K. 51°31N 0°23E 67 F8
Thursday I. Australia 10°30S 142°3E 150 A3
Thurso Canada 45°36N 75°15W 164 C4
Thurso U.K. 58°36N 3°32W 65 C5
Thurso → U.K. 58°36N 3°32W 65 C5
Thurston I. Antarctica 72°0S 100°0W 55 D16
Thury-Harcourt France 48°59N 0°30W 70 D6
Thutade L. Canada 57°0N 126°55W 162 B3
Thy Denmark 56°52N 8°25E 63 H2
Thy △ Denmark 56°55N 8°25E 63 H2
Thyborøn Denmark 56°42N 8°12E 63 H2
Thyolo Malawi 16°7S 35°5E 143 F4
Ti-n-Amzi → Niger 13°38N 4°58E 139 B5
Ti-n-Barraouene, O. →
  Africa 18°40N 4°5E 139 B5
Ti-n-Tanetfirt Algeria 24°49N 3°48E 136 D4
Ti-n-Zaouatene Algeria 19°55N 2°55E 136 E4
Ti-Tree Australia 22°5S 133°22E 150 C1
Tiadiaye Senegal 14°25N 16°40W 138 C1
Tiahuanaco Bolivia 16°33S 68°42W 188 D4
Tian Shan Asia 40°30N 76°0E 109 D9
Tianchang China 32°40N 119°0E 117 A12
Tiandeng China 23°6N 107°7E 116 F6
Tiandong China 23°36N 107°8E 116 F6
Tian'e China 25°1N 107°9E 116 E6
Tianguá Brazil 3°44S 40°59W 189 A2
Tianhe China 24°48N 108°40E 116 E7
Tianjin China 39°7N 117°12E 115 E9
Tianjin Shi □ China 39°8N 117°12E 115 E9
Tianjun China 38°0N 98°30E 110 D8
Tiankoura Burkina Faso 10°47N 3°17W 138 C4
Tianlin China 24°21N 106°12E 116 E6
Tianmen China 30°39N 113°9E 116 B8
Tianquan China 30°7N 102°43E 116 B4
Tianshifu China 41°17N 124°22E 115 D13
Tianshui China 34°32N 105°40E 114 C3
Tiantai China 29°10N 121°2E 117 C13
Tianya China 18°16N 109°20E 117 a
Tianyang China 23°42N 106°53E 116 F6
Tianyar Indonesia 8°12S 115°30E 119 J18
Tianzhen China 40°24N 114°5E 114 D8
Tianzhuangtai China 40°43N 122°5E 115 D12
Tiarei Tahiti 17°32S 149°20W 155 b
Tiaret Algeria 35°20N 1°21E 136 A6
Tiaret □ Algeria 34°30N 1°30E 136 B6
Tiassalé Côte d'Ivoire 5°58N 4°57W 138 D4
Tibagi Brazil 24°30S 50°24W 191 A5
Tibagi → Brazil 22°47S 51°1W 191 A5
Tibastī, Sarīr Libya 22°50N 18°30E 135 D9
Tibati Cameroon 6°22N 12°30E 139 D7

Tiber = Tevere → Italy 41°44N 12°14E 93 G9
Tiber Res. U.S.A. 48°19N 111°6W 168 B8
Tiberias = Teverya
  Israel 32°47N 35°32E 130 C4
Tiberias, L. = Yam Kinneret
  Israel 32°45N 35°35E 130 C4
Tibesti Chad 21°0N 17°30E 135 D9
Tibet = Xizang Zizhiqu □
  China 32°0N 88°0E 110 E6
Tibet, Plateau of Asia 32°0N 86°0E 102 E10
Tibiri Niger 13°34N 7°4E 139 C6
Tibles, Vf. Romania 47°32N 24°15E 81 C9
Tiblesului, Munții
  Romania 47°38N 24°5E 81 C9
Tibnī Syria 35°36N 39°50E 105 E8
Tibooburra Australia 29°26S 142°1E 151 D3
Tibrikot Nepal 29°3N 82°48E 125 E10
Tibro Sweden 58°28N 14°10E 63 F8
Tiburón, I. Mexico 29°0N 112°25W 180 B2
Tice U.S.A. 26°40N 81°49W 179 J8
Tîchît Mauritania 18°21N 9°29W 138 B3
Ticino □ Switz. 46°20N 8°45E 77 J4
Ticino → Italy 45°9N 9°14E 92 C6
Ticleni Romania 44°53N 23°24E 81 F8
Ticonderoga U.S.A. 43°51N 73°26W 175 C11
Ticul Mexico 20°24N 89°32W 181 C7
Tidaholm Sweden 58°12N 13°58E 63 F7
Tidan Sweden 58°34N 14°1E 63 F8
Tiddim Myanmar 23°28N 93°45E 123 H18
Tiden India 7°15N 93°33E 127 L11
Tidioute U.S.A. 41°41N 79°24W 174 E5
Tidjikja Mauritania 18°29N 11°35W 138 B2
Tidore Indonesia 0°40N 127°25E 119 D7
Tiébissou Côte d'Ivoire 7°9N 5°10W 138 D3
Tiefa China 42°28N 123°26E 115 C12
Tiegang Shuiku China 22°37N 113°53E 111 a
Tiel Neths. 51°53N 5°26E 69 C5
Tiel Senegal 14°55N 15°5W 138 C1
Tieli China 46°57N 128°3E 111 B14
Tieling China 42°20N 123°55E 115 C12
Tielt Belgium 51°0N 3°20E 69 C3
Tiemenguan China 41°49N 85°39E 109 D11
Tien Shan = Tian Shan
  Asia 40°30N 76°0E 109 D9
Tien-tsin = Tianjin
  China 39°7N 117°12E 115 E9
Tien Yen Vietnam 21°20N 107°24E 120 B6
T'ienching = Tianjin
  China 39°7N 117°12E 115 E9
Tienen Belgium 50°48N 4°57E 69 D4
Tiénigbé Côte d'Ivoire 8°11N 5°43W 138 D3
Tientsin = Tianjin
  China 39°7N 117°12E 115 E9
Tieri Australia 23°2S 148°21E 150 C4
Tierp Sweden 60°20N 17°30E 62 D11
Tierra Amarilla Chile 27°28S 70°18W 190 B1
Tierra Amarilla
  U.S.A. 36°42N 106°33W 169 H10
Tierra Colorada
  Mexico 17°11N 99°32W 181 D5
Tierra de Barros Spain 38°40N 6°30W 89 G4
Tierra de Campos Spain 42°10N 4°50W 88 C6
Tierra del Fuego □
  Argentina 54°0S 67°45W 192 D3
Tierra del Fuego, I. Grande de
  Argentina 54°0S 69°0W 192 D3
Tierra del Fuego △
  Argentina 54°50S 68°23W 192 D3
Tiétar → Spain 39°50N 6°1W 88 F4
Tietê Brazil 23°6S 47°41W 191 A6
Tietê → Brazil 20°40S 51°35W 191 A5
Tiffin U.S.A. 41°7N 83°11W 173 E12
Tiflèt Morocco 33°54N 6°20W 136 B4
Tifton U.S.A. 31°27N 83°31W 178 D6
Tifu Indonesia 3°39S 126°24E 119 E7
Tiga Res. Nigeria 11°35N 8°30E 139 C6
Tiger Leaping Gorge = Hutiao Xia
  China 27°13N 100°9E 116 D3
Tigharghar, Adrar Mali 19°30N 1°13E 139 B5
Tighina = Bendery
  Moldova 46°50N 29°30E 81 D14
Tigil Russia 57°49N 158°40E 107 D16
Tigiria India 20°29N 85°31E 126 D7
Tignall U.S.A. 33°52N 82°44W 178 B7
Tignish Canada 46°58N 64°2W 165 C7
Tigre → Peru 4°30S 74°10W 188 A3
Tigre → Venezuela 9°20N 62°30W 186 B6
Tigris = Dijlah, Nahr →
  Asia 31°0N 47°25E 128 D5
Tiguentourine Algeria 27°52N 9°8E 136 C5
Tigveni Romania 45°10N 24°31E 81 E9
Tigyaing Myanmar 23°45N 96°10E 123 H20
Tîh, Gebel el Egypt 29°32N 33°26E 137 F8
Tihāmah Asia 15°3N 41°55E 131 D3
Tihodaine, Erg de
  Algeria 25°15N 7°15E 136 C5
Tiilikka △ Finland 63°40N 28°15E 60 E23
Tijara India 27°56N 76°31E 124 F7
Tijuana Mexico 32°32N 117°1W 171 N9
Tikal Guatemala 17°13N 89°24W 182 C2
Tikal △ Guatemala 17°13N 89°34W 182 C2
Tikamgarh India 24°44N 78°50E 125 G8
Tikchik Lakes U.S.A. 60°0N 159°0W 166 D8
Tikhoretsk Russia 45°56N 40°5E 87 H5
Tikhvin Russia 59°35N 33°30E 84 C7
Tikirarjuaq = Whale Cove
  Canada 62°10N 92°34W 163 A10
Tikkadouine, Adrar
  Algeria 24°28N 1°30E 136 D4
Tikmehdāsh Iran 37°16N 46°54E 105 D12
Tiko Cameroon 4°4N 9°20E 139 E6
Tikrīt Iraq 34°35N 43°37E 105 E10
Tiksi Russia 71°40N 128°45E 107 B13
Tilāʾ al ʿAlī Jordan 32°0N 35°52E 130 D4
Tilamuta Indonesia 0°32N 122°23E 119 D6
Tilburg Neths. 51°31N 5°6E 69 C5
Tilbury Canada 42°17N 82°23W 174 D2
Tilcara Argentina 23°36S 65°23W 190 A2
Tilden U.S.A. 28°27N 98°33W 176 L5
Tilemsi, Vallée du Mali 17°42N 0°15E 139 B5
Tilhar India 28°0N 79°45E 125 F8
Tilia, O. → Algeria 27°1N 0°2W 136 C5
Tilichiki Russia 60°27N 166°5E 107 C17
Tililane Algeria 27°49N 0°6E 136 C4
Tilissos Greece 35°20N 25°1E 101 D7
Till → U.K. 55°41N 2°13W 66 B5
Tillabéri Niger 14°28N 1°28E 139 C5
Tillamook U.S.A. 45°27N 123°51W 168 D2
Tillanchong I. India 8°30N 93°37E 127 K11
Tillberga Sweden 59°48N 16°39E 62 E10

Tillia Niger 16°8N 4°47E 139 B5
Tillman U.S.A. 32°28N 81°6W 178 C8
Tillsonburg Canada 42°53N 80°44W 174 D4
Tillyeria Cyprus 35°6N 32°40E 101 D11
Tilogne Senegal 16°0N 13°40W 138 B2
Tilos Greece 36°27N 27°27E 99 E9
Tilpa Australia 30°57S 144°24E 152 A6
Tilrhemt Algeria 33°9N 3°22E 136 B6
Tilt → U.K. 56°46N 3°51W 65 E5
Tilton U.S.A. 43°27N 71°36W 175 C13
Tiltonsville U.S.A. 40°10N 80°41W 174 F4
Tim Denmark 56°12N 8°19E 63 H2
Tima Egypt 26°54N 31°25E 137 B3
Timanfaya △ Canary Is. 29°0N 13°46W 100 F6
Timaru N.Z. 44°23S 171°14E 155 G6
Timashevo Russia 53°22N 51°9E 86 D11
Timashevsk Russia 45°35N 39°0E 87 H4
Timau Kenya 0°4N 37°15E 142 B4
Timbaki Greece 35°4N 24°45E 101 D6
Timbaúba Brazil 7°31S 35°19W 189 E3
Timbedgha Mauritania 16°17N 8°16W 138 B3
Timber Creek
  Australia 15°40S 130°29E 148 C5
Timber Lake U.S.A. 45°26N 101°5W 172 C3
Timber Mt. U.S.A. 37°6N 116°28W 170 H10
Timbo Guinea 10°35N 11°50W 138 D2
Timbo Liberia 5°35N 9°45W 138 D3
Timboon Australia 38°30S 142°58E 152 E5
Timbué, Ponta Mozam. 18°47S 36°22E 143 F4
Timbuktu = Tombouctou
  Mali 16°50N 3°0W 138 B4
Timeïaouine Algeria 20°27N 1°50E 139 A5
Timellouline Algeria 28°29N 8°55E 136 C5
Timétrine Mali 19°19N 0°34W 139 B4
Timétrine, Mts. Mali 19°25N 1°10W 139 B4
Timfi Oros Greece 39°59N 20°45E 98 B2
Timfristos, Oros Greece 38°57N 21°50E 98 C3
Timgad Algeria 35°28N 6°28E 136 A5
Timhadit Morocco 33°15N 5°4W 136 B4
Timi Cyprus 34°44N 32°31E 101 E11
Tîmia Niger 18°4N 8°40E 139 B6
Timika Indonesia 4°47S 136°32E 119 E9
Timimoun Algeria 29°14N 0°16E 136 C4
Timimoun, Sebkha de
  Algeria 28°50N 0°46E 136 C4
Timiris, Râs Mauritania 19°21N 16°30W 138 B1
Timiş = Tamis → Serbia 44°51N 20°39E 98 B5
Timiş □ Romania 45°40N 21°30E 80 E6
Timiskaming, L. =
  Témiscamingue, L.
  Canada 47°10N 79°25W 164 C4
Timişoara Romania 45°43N 21°15E 80 E6
Timmersdala Sweden 58°32N 13°46E 63 F7
Timmins Canada 48°28N 81°25W 164 C3
Timmonsville U.S.A. 34°8N 79°57W 178 A10
Timok → Serbia 44°10N 22°40E 96 B6
Timoleague Ireland 51°39N 8°46W 64 E3
Timon Brazil 5°8S 42°52W 189 B2
Timor Asia 9°0S 125°0E 119 F7
Timor Leste = East Timor ■
  Asia 8°50S 126°0E 119 F7
Timor Sea Ind. Oc. 12°0S 127°0E 148 B4
Timrå Sweden 62°29N 17°18E 62 B11
Timucuan △ U.S.A. 30°23N 81°27W 178 E8
Tin Alkoum Algeria 24°42N 10°17E 136 D5
Tin Atanai Algeria 25°52N 1°37E 136 C4
Tin Can Bay Australia 25°52N 153°0E 151 D5
Tin Ethisane Mali 19°3N 0°52W 139 B4
Tin Gornai Mali 16°38N 0°38W 139 B4
Tin Mt. U.S.A. 36°50N 117°10W 170 J9
Tin Shui Wai China 22°28N 114°0E 111 a
Tina → S. Africa 31°18S 29°13E 145 D4
Tina, Khalig el Egypt 31°10N 32°40E 130 D1
Tinaca Pt. Phil. 5°30N 125°25E 117 D7
Tinajo Canary Is. 29°4N 13°42W 100 E6
Tinca Romania 46°46N 21°58E 80 D6
Tindal Australia 14°31S 132°22E 148 B5
Tindivanam India 12°15N 79°41E 127 H4
Tindouf Algeria 27°42N 8°10W 136 C2
Tindouf □ Algeria 27°25N 5°0W 136 C2
Tinée → France 43°55N 7°11E 73 E11
Tineo Spain 43°21N 6°27W 88 B4
Tinerhir Morocco 31°29N 5°31W 136 B2
Tinfouchi Algeria 28°52N 5°49W 136 C3
Tinfunque △ Paraguay 23°55S 60°17W 190 A3
Ting Jiang → China 24°45N 116°35E 117 E11
Tinggi, Pulau Malaysia 2°18N 104°7E 121 L5
Tingi Mts. S. Leone 8°55N 10°55W 138 D2
Tinglev Denmark 54°57N 9°13E 63 A2
Tingo María Peru 9°10S 75°54W 188 B2
Tingrela Côte d'Ivoire 10°27N 6°25W 138 C3
Tingri China 28°34N 86°38E 110 F6
Tingsryd Sweden 56°31N 15°0E 63 H6
Tinh Bien Vietnam 10°36N 104°57E 121 G5
Tinharé, I. de Brazil 13°30S 38°58W 189 D3
Tinian N. Marianas 15°0N 145°38E 156 F6
Tinkisso → Guinea 11°21N 9°10W 138 C2
Tinnevelly = Tirunelveli
  India 8°45N 77°45E 127 K3
Tinogasta Argentina 28°5S 67°32W 190 B2
Tinos Greece 37°33N 25°8E 99 D7
Tiñoso, C. Spain 37°32N 1°6W 91 H3
Tinpahar India 24°59N 87°44E 125 G12
Tinrhert, Plateau du
  Algeria 29°30N 9°0E 136 C6
Tinta Peru 14°3S 71°20W 188 C3
Tintâne Mauritania 16°18N 10°10W 138 B2
Tintina Argentina 27°2S 62°45W 190 B3
Tintinara Australia 35°48S 140°2E 152 C4
Tintioulé Guinea 10°13N 9°12W 138 D3
Tinto → Spain 37°12N 6°55W 89 H4
Tinui N.Z. 40°52S 176°5E 154 G5
Tinwald N.Z. 43°55S 171°43E 155 G6

Tiptur India 13°15N 76°26E 127 H3
Tiquina Bolivia 16°13S 68°50W 188 D4
Tiracambu, Serra do
  Brazil 3°15S 46°30W 189 A1
Tirahart, O. → Algeria 23°45N 3°10E 136 D4
Tirān Iran 32°45N 51°8E 129 C6
Tīrān Si. Arabia 27°57N 34°23E 137 C13
Tiranë Albania 41°18N 19°49E 96 E3
Tiranë × (TIA) Albania 41°57N 19°42E 96 E3
Tirano Italy 46°13N 10°10E 92 B7
Tirari Desert Australia 28°22S 138°7E 151 D2
Tiratimine Algeria 25°56N 3°37E 136 D4
Tiraspol Moldova 46°55N 29°35E 81 D14
Tirau N.Z. 37°58S 175°46E 154 D4
Tirdout Mali 16°7N 1°5W 139 B4
Tire Turkey 38°5N 27°45E 99 C9
Tirebolu Turkey 40°58N 38°45E 105 B8
Tiree U.K. 56°31N 6°55W 65 E2
Tiree, Passage of U.K. 56°30N 6°30W 65 E2
Tîrgoviște = Târgoviște
  Romania 44°55N 25°27E 81 F10
Tîrgu Jiu = Târgu Jiu
  Romania 45°5N 23°19E 81 E8
Tîrgu Mureş = Târgu Mureş
  Romania 46°31N 24°38E 81 D9
Tirich Mir Pakistan 36°15N 71°55E 109 E8
Tiriolo Italy 38°57N 16°30E 95 D9
Tiririca, Serra da Brazil 17°6S 47°6W 189 D1
Tiriro Guinea 10°27N 8°40W 138 C3
Tiritiri o te Moana = Southern
  Alps N.Z. 43°41S 170°11E 155 D5
Tirna → India 18°4N 76°57E 126 E3
Tirnavos Greece 39°45N 22°18E 98 B4
Tirodi India 21°40N 79°44E 126 D4
Tirol □ Austria 47°3N 10°43E 78 D3
Tiros Brazil 19°0S 45°58W 189 D1
Tirrukkovil Sri Lanka 7°7N 81°51E 127 L5
Tirschenreuth Germany 49°53N 12°19E 77 F8
Tiruchchendur India 8°30N 78°11E 127 K4
Tiruchchirappalli India 10°45N 78°45E 127 J4
Tirukkoyilur India 11°57N 79°12E 127 J4
Tirumangalam India 9°49N 77°58E 127 K3
Tirumayam India 10°14N 78°45E 127 J4
Tirunelveli India 8°45N 77°45E 127 K3
Tirupati India 13°39N 79°25E 127 H4
Tiruppattur Tamil Nadu,
  India 10°8N 78°37E 127 J4
Tiruppattur Tamil Nadu,
  India 12°30N 78°30E 127 H4
Tiruppur India 11°5N 77°22E 127 J3
Tirur India 10°54N 75°55E 127 J2
Tiruttani India 13°11N 79°58E 127 H4
Tiruvadaimarudur India 10°32N 79°41E 127 J4
Tiruvallur India 9°23N 76°54E 127 K3
Tiruvannamalai India 12°15N 79°45E 127 H4
Tiruvettipuram India 12°39N 79°33E 127 H4
Tiruvottiyur India 13°10N 80°22E 127 H5
Tisa → Serbia 45°15N 20°17E 80 E5
Tisdale Canada 52°50N 104°0W 163 C8
Tishomingo U.S.A. 34°14N 96°41W 176 D6
Tisjön Sweden 60°56N 13°0E 62 D7
Tisnaren Sweden 58°58N 15°56E 63 F9
Tišnov Czechia 49°21N 16°25E 79 B9
Tisovec Slovakia 48°41N 19°56E 79 C12
Tissamaharama
  Sri Lanka 6°17N 81°17E 127 L5
Tissemsilt Algeria 35°35N 1°50E 136 A6
Tissemsilt □ Algeria 35°45N 1°45E 136 A6
Tissint Morocco 29°57N 7°16W 136 C2
Tisza = Tisa → Serbia 45°15N 20°17E 80 E5
Tiszaföldvár Hungary 46°58N 20°14E 80 D5
Tiszafüred Hungary 47°38N 20°50E 80 C5
Tiszalök Hungary 48°1N 21°20E 80 C6
Tiszavasvári Hungary 47°58N 21°18E 80 C6
Tit Ahaggar, Algeria 23°0N 5°10E 136 D5
Tit Tademait, Algeria 27°0N 1°29E 136 C4
Tit-Ary Russia 71°55N 127°2E 107 B13
Titaguas Spain 39°53N 1°6W 90 F3
Titao Burkina Faso 13°46N 2°5W 138 C4
Titel Serbia 45°10N 20°18E 80 E5
Tithwal Pakistan 34°21N 73°50E 125 B5
Titicaca, L. S. Amer. 15°30S 69°30W 188 D4
Titisee Germany 47°54N 8°10E 77 H4
Titita Hd. N.Z. 43°36S 169°25E 155 D4
Titiwa Nigeria 12°14N 12°53E 139 C7
Titlagarh India 20°15N 83°11E 126 D6
Tito Italy 40°35N 15°40E 95 B8
Titova Korenica
  Croatia 44°45N 15°41E 93 D12
Titu Romania 44°39N 25°32E 81 F10
Titule
  Dem. Rep. of the Congo 3°15N 25°31E 142 B2
Titusville Fla., U.S.A. 28°37N 80°49W 179 G9
Titusville Pa., U.S.A. 41°38N 79°41W 174 E5
Tivaouane Senegal 14°56N 16°45W 138 C1
Tivat Montenegro 42°28N 18°43E 96 D2
Tivedens △ Sweden 58°45N 14°35E 63 F8
Tiverton Canada 44°16N 81°32W 174 B3
Tiverton U.S.A. 50°54N 3°29W 67 G4
Tivoli Italy 41°58N 12°45E 93 G9
Tiwanaku = Tiahuanaco
  Bolivia 16°33S 68°42W 188 D4
Tiwi ◊ Australia 11°33S 130°42E 148 B5
Tizga Morocco 32°1N 5°9W 136 B3
Ti'zi N'Isli Morocco 32°28N 5°47W 136 B3
Tizi-Ouzou Algeria 36°42N 4°3E 136 A4
Tizi-Ouzou □ Algeria 36°35N 4°5E 136 A4
Tizimín Mexico 21°9N 88°9W 181 C7
Tiznap He → China 38°21N 77°20E 109 C5
Tiznit Morocco 29°48N 9°45W 136 C3
Tjæreborg Denmark 55°28N 8°36E 63 J2
Tjällmo Sweden 58°43N 15°21E 63 F9
Tjeggelvas Sweden 66°37N 17°45E 60 C17
Tjeggelvas = Tjeggelvas
Tjirebon = Cirebon
  Indonesia 6°45S 108°32E 118 F3
Tjirrkarli ◊ Australia 26°0S 125°28E 149 E3
Tjluring Indonesia 8°5S 114°13E 119 J17
Tjörn Sweden 58°0N 11°35E 63 F5
Tjukayirla Roadhouse
  Australia 27°9S 124°24E 149 E3
Tjurabalan ◊ Australia 19°50S 128°0E 148 C4

Tkvarcheli = Tqvarcheli
  Georgia 42°47N 41°42E 87 J5
Tlacotalpan Mexico 18°37N 95°40W 181 D5
Tlahualilo de Zaragoza
  Mexico 26°7N 103°27W 180 B4
Tlaquepaque Mexico 20°39N 103°19W 180 C4
Tlaxcala Mexico 19°19N 98°14W 181 D5
Tlaxcala □ Mexico 19°25N 98°10W 181 D5
Tlaxiaco Mexico 17°25N 97°35W 181 D5
Tlemcen Algeria 34°52N 1°21W 136 B3
Tlemcen □ Algeria 34°38N 1°30W 136 B3
Tleta Sidi Bouguedra
  Morocco 32°16N 9°59W 136 B2
Tlokweng Botswana 24°40S 25°58E 144 F4
Tlumach Ukraine 48°51N 25°0E 81 D7
Tłuszcz Poland 52°25N 21°25E 77 B11
Tlyarata Russia 42°9N 46°26E 87 J8
To Bong Vietnam 12°45N 109°16E 120 F7
Toa Payoh Singapore 1°20N 103°51E 121 d
Toad → Canada 59°25N 124°57W 162 B4
Toad River Canada 58°51N 125°14W 162 B3
Toamasina Madag. 18°10S 49°25E 141 H9
Toamasina □ Madag. 18°0S 49°0E 141 H9
Toay Argentina 36°43S 64°38W 190 D3
Toba China 31°19N 97°12E 116 B1
Toba Japan 34°30N 136°51E 113 G8
Toba, Danau Indonesia 2°30N 98°30E 118 D1
Toba Kakar Pakistan 31°30N 69°0E 124 D3
Toba Tek Singh
  Pakistan 30°55N 72°25E 124 D5
Tobago Trin. & Tob. 11°10N 60°30W 183 D7
Tobarra Spain 38°37N 1°44W 91 G3
Tobelo Indonesia 1°45N 127°56E 119 D7
Tobercurry Ireland 54°3N 8°44W 64 B3
Tobermory Canada 45°12N 81°40W 174 A3
Tobermory U.K. 56°38N 6°5W 65 E2
Tobi Palau 2°40N 131°10E 119 D8
Tobi-Shima Japan 42°12N 139°34E 112 D9
Tobin, L. Australia 21°45S 125°49E 148 D4
Tobin, L. Canada 53°35N 103°30W 163 C8
Toboali Indonesia 3°0S 106°25E 118 E3
Tobol → Russia 58°10N 68°10E 106 D7
Toboli Indonesia 0°38S 120°5E 119 E6
Tobolsk Russia 58°15N 68°10E 106 D7
Tobor Senegal 12°40N 16°15W 138 C1
Tobruk = Tubruq
  Libya 32°7N 23°55E 135 B10
Tobyhanna U.S.A. 41°11N 75°25W 175 E9
Tobyl = Tobol →
  Russia 58°10N 68°12E 106 D7
Tobyl Kazakhstan 52°41N 62°34E 108 D6
Tocache Nuevo Peru 8°9S 76°9W 188 B2
Tocantínia Brazil 9°33S 48°22W 189 B1
Tocantinópolis Brazil 6°20S 47°25W 189 B1
Tocantins □ Brazil 10°0S 48°0W 187 F9
Tocantins → Brazil 1°45S 49°10W 187 D9
Toccoa U.S.A. 34°35N 83°19W 177 D13
Toce → Italy 45°56N 8°29E 92 C5
Tochi → Pakistan 32°49N 70°41E 124 C4
Tochigi Japan 36°25N 139°45E 113 F9
Tochigi □ Japan 36°45N 139°45E 113 F9
Tocina Spain 37°37N 5°44W 89 H5
Töcksfors Sweden 59°31N 11°50E 62 E5
Toco Chile 22°5S 69°35W 188 E4
Toco Trin. & Tob. 10°49N 60°57W 187 K16
Toconao Chile 23°11S 68°1W 190 A2
Tocopilla Chile 22°5S 70°10W 190 A1
Tocumwal Australia 35°51S 145°31E 153 C4
Tocuyo → Venezuela 11°3N 68°23W 186 A5
Todd → Australia 24°52S 135°48E 150 C2
Todeli Indonesia 1°40S 124°29E 119 E6
Todenyang Kenya 4°35N 35°56E 142 B4
Todgarh India 25°42N 73°58E 124 G5
Todi Italy 42°47N 12°24E 93 F9
Todos os Santos, B. de
  Brazil 12°48S 38°38W 189 D3
Todos Santos Mexico 23°26N 110°13W 180 C2
Todtnau Germany 47°49N 7°56E 77 H3
Toe Hd. U.K. 57°50N 7°8W 65 D1
Toecé Burkina Faso 11°50N 1°16W 139 C4
Toetoes B. N.Z. 46°42S 168°41E 155 G2
Tofield Canada 53°25N 112°40W 162 C6
Tofino Canada 49°11N 125°55W 162 D3
Töfsingdalen △ Sweden 62°10N 12°28E 62 B6
Tōgane Japan 35°33N 140°22E 113 G10
Togba Mauritania 17°26N 10°12W 138 B2
Togian, Kepulauan
  Indonesia 0°20S 121°50E 119 E6
Togliatti Russia 53°32N 49°24E 86 D9
Togo ■ W. Afr. 8°30N 1°35E 139 D5
Togtöng Mongolia 47°25N 92°13E 109 C12
Togtoh China 40°15N 111°10E 114 D6
Tohma → Turkey 38°29N 38°23E 104 C3
Tōhōku □ Japan 39°50N 141°45E 112 E10
Tōhōm Mongolia 44°27N 108°2E 114 B5
Tohopekaliga, East L.
  U.S.A. 28°18N 81°15W 179 G8
Tohopekaliga, L.
  U.S.A. 28°11N 81°24W 179 G8
Toibalewe India 10°30N 92°30E 127 J11
Toinya South Sudan 6°17N 29°46E 135 G11
Toiyabe Range U.S.A. 39°30N 117°0W 168 G5
Tojikiston = Tajikistan ■
  Asia 38°30N 70°0E 108 F8
Tōjō Japan 34°53N 133°16E 113 G6
Tok U.S.A. 63°20N 142°59W 166 D11
Tokaanu N.Z. 38°58S 175°46E 154 E4
Tokachi-Dake Japan 43°17N 142°5E 112 C11
Tokachi-Gawa →
  Japan 42°44N 143°42E 112 C11
Tokaj Hungary 48°8N 21°27E 80 B6
Tokala Indonesia 1°30S 121°40E 119 E6
Tōkamachi Japan 37°8N 138°43E 113 F9
Tokanui N.Z. 46°34S 168°56E 155 G2
Tokar Sudan 18°27N 37°56E 135 E13
Tokara-Rettō Japan 29°37N 129°43E 113 K4
Tokarahi N.Z. 44°56S 170°39E 155 F3
Tokashiki-Shima
  Japan 26°11N 127°21E 113 L3
Tokat Turkey 40°22N 36°35E 104 B7
Tokat □ Turkey 40°15N 36°30E 104 B7
Tŏkch'ŏn N. Korea 39°45N 126°18E 115 E14
Tokdo = Liancourt Rocks
  Asia 37°15N 131°52E 113 F5
Tokelau Is. ◊ Pac. Oc. 9°0S 171°45W 156 G10
Tokmak Kyrgyzstan 42°49N 75°15E 108 E8
Tokmak Ukraine 47°16N 35°42E 85 J8
Toko Ra. Australia 23°5S 138°20E 150 C2
Tokmaru Bay N.Z. 38°8S 178°22E 154 E7
Tokoro-Gawa → Japan 44°7N 144°5E 112 B12

Tokoroa N.Z. 38°13S 175°50E 154 E4
Toksun China 42°47N 88°38E 109 D11
Toktogul Kyrgyzstan 41°50N 72°50E 108 D8
Tokuno-Shima Japan 27°56N 128°55E 113 L4
Tokushima Japan 34°4N 134°34E 113 G7
Tokushima □ Japan 33°55N 134°0E 113 H7
Tokuyama = Shunan
  Japan 34°3N 131°50E 113 G5
Tōkyō Japan 35°43N 139°45E 113 G9
Tolaga Bay N.Z. 38°21S 178°20E 154 E7
Tolbo Mongolia 48°25N 90°17E 109 C12
Tolbukhin = Dobrich
  Bulgaria 43°37N 27°49E 97 C11
Tôle Kazakhstan 43°42N 73°46E 108 E8
Toledo Brazil 24°44S 53°45W 191 A5
Toledo Spain 39°50N 4°2W 88 F6
Toledo Ohio, U.S.A. 41°39N 83°33W 173 E12
Toledo Oreg., U.S.A. 44°37N 123°56W 168 D2
Toledo Wash., U.S.A. 46°26N 122°51W 170 D4
Toledo, Montes de Spain 39°33N 4°20W 89 F6
Toledo Bend Res.
  U.S.A. 31°11N 93°34W 176 F3
Tolentino Italy 43°12N 13°17E 93 E10
Tolfa Italy 42°9N 11°56E 93 F8
Tolga Algeria 34°40N 5°22E 136 B5
Tolga Australia 17°15S 145°29E 150 B4
Tolhuaca △ Chile 38°15S 71°50W 192 A2
Toli China 45°57N 83°37E 109 C10
Toliara Madag. 23°21S 43°40E 141 J8
Toliara □ Madag. 21°0S 45°0E 141 J8
Tolima Colombia 4°40N 75°19W 186 C2
Tolitoli Indonesia 1°5N 120°50E 119 D6
Tolkmicko Poland 54°19N 19°31E 82 D6
Tollarp Sweden 55°55N 13°58E 63 J7
Tollensee Germany 53°30N 13°13E 76 B9
Tollhouse U.S.A. 37°1N 119°24W 170 H7
Tolmachevo Russia 58°56N 29°51E 84 C5
Tolmezzo Italy 46°24N 13°1E 93 B10
Tolmin Slovenia 46°11N 13°45E 93 B10
Tolna Hungary 46°25N 18°48E 80 D3
Tolna □ Hungary 46°30N 18°30E 80 D3
Tolo, Teluk Indonesia 2°0S 122°10E 119 E6
Tolo Harbour China 22°25N 114°13E 111 a
Tolochin = Talachyn
  Belarus 54°25N 29°42E 84 E5
Tolosa Spain 43°8N 2°5W 90 B2
Tolox Spain 36°41N 4°54W 89 J6
Toltén Chile 39°13S 73°2W 192 A2
Toltén → Chile 39°13S 74°14W 192 A2
Toluca Mexico 19°17N 99°40W 181 D5
Tolyatti = Togliatti
  Russia 53°32N 49°24E 86 D9
Tom Burke S. Africa 23°5S 28°0E 145 A4
Tom Price Australia 22°40S 117°48E 148 D2
Toma Burkina Faso 12°45N 2°53W 138 C4
Tomah U.S.A. 43°59N 90°30W 172 C9
Tomahawk U.S.A. 45°28N 89°44W 172 C9
Tomai Moldova 46°34N 28°19E 81 D13
Tomakomai Japan 42°38N 141°36E 112 C10
Tomales U.S.A. 38°15N 122°53W 170 G4
Tomales B. U.S.A. 38°15N 123°58W 170 G3
Tomanivi Fiji 17°37S 178°1E 154 a
Tomar Portugal 39°36N 8°25W 89 F2
Tomaros, Oros Greece 39°29N 20°48E 98 B2
Tomarza Turkey 38°27N 35°48E 104 C6
Tomás Barrón Bolivia 17°35S 67°31W 188 D4
Tomashevka Belarus 51°33N 23°36E 83 G10
Tomashpil Ukraine 48°32N 28°31E 81 B13
Tomaszów Lubelski
  Poland 50°27N 23°25E 83 H10
Tomaszów Mazowiecki
  Poland 51°30N 20°2E 83 G7
Tomatlán Mexico 19°56N 105°15W 180 D3
Tombador, Serra do
  Brazil 12°0S 58°0W 186 F7
Tombigbee → U.S.A. 31°8N 87°57W 177 F11
Tombouctou Mali 16°50N 3°0W 138 B4
Tombouctou □ Mali 20°0N 3°0W 138 B4
Tombstone U.S.A. 31°43N 110°4W 169 L8
Tombua Angola 15°55S 11°55E 144 B1
Tomé Chile 36°36S 72°57W 190 D1
Tome Japan 38°40N 141°20E 112 E10
Tomelilla Sweden 55°33N 13°58E 63 J7
Tomelloso Spain 39°10N 3°2W 89 F7
Tomingley Australia 32°26S 148°16E 153 B8
Tominian Mali 13°17N 4°35W 138 C4
Tomini Indonesia 0°30N 120°30E 119 D6
Tomini, Teluk Indonesia 0°10S 121°0E 119 E6
Tomiño = O Seixo Spain 41°59N 8°46W 88 D2
Tomintoul U.K. 57°15N 3°23W 65 D5
Tomislavgrad Bos.-H. 43°42N 17°13E 80 G2
Tomkinson Ranges
  Australia 26°11S 129°5E 149 E4
Tommot Russia 59°4N 126°20E 107 D13
Tomnop Ta Suos
  Cambodia 11°20N 104°15E 121 G5
Tomo → Colombia 5°20N 67°48W 186 B5
Tomorri ◊ Albania 40°43N 20°8E 96 E4
Toms Place U.S.A. 37°34N 118°41W 170 H8
Toms River U.S.A. 39°58N 74°12W 175 G10
Tomsk Russia 56°30N 85°5E 106 D9
Tomtabacken Sweden 57°30N 14°30E 63 G8
Tomür Feng = Pobedy, Pik
  Asia 42°0N 79°58E 108 D9
Tonalá Chiapas, Mexico 16°4N 93°45W 181 D6
Tonalá Jalisco, Mexico 20°37N 103°14W 180 C4
Tonale, Passo del Italy 46°16N 10°35E 92 B7
Tonantins Brazil 2°45S 67°45W 186 D5
Tonasket U.S.A. 48°42N 119°26W 168 B4
Tonawanda U.S.A. 43°1N 78°53W 174 D6
Tonb U.A.E. 26°15N 55°15E 129 E7
Tonbridge U.K. 51°11N 0°17E 67 F8
Tondano Indonesia 1°35N 124°54E 119 D6
Tondela Portugal 40°31N 8°5W 88 E2
Tønder Denmark 54°58N 8°50E 63 K2
Tondi India 9°45N 79°4E 127 K4
Tondi Kiwindi Niger 14°28N 2°2E 139 C5
Tondibi Mali 16°39N 0°14W 139 B4
Tondoro Namibia 17°45S 18°50E 144 A2
Tone → Australia 34°25S 116°25E 149 F2
Tone-Gawa → Japan 35°44N 140°51E 113 F9
Tonekābon Iran 36°45N 51°12E 129 B6
Tong Xian China 39°55N 116°35E 114 E9
Tong-yeong S. Korea 34°50N 128°20E 115 G15
Tonga ■ Pac. Oc. 19°50S 174°30W 154 c
Tonga Trench Pac. Oc. 18°0S 175°0W 156 J10
Tongaat S. Africa 29°33S 31°9E 145 D5
Tong'an China 24°38N 118°8E 117 E12
Tongareva = Penrhyn
  Cook Is. 9°0S 158°0W 157 H12

Tongariro, Mt. N.Z. 39°8S 175°38E 154 F4
Tongariro △ N.Z. 39°8S 175°33E 154 F4
Tongatapu Group Tonga 21°0S 175°0W 147 D11
Tongbai China 32°20N 113°23E 117 A9
Tongcheng Anhui, China 31°4N 116°56E 117 B11
Tongcheng Hubei, China 29°15N 113°50E 117 C9
Tongchuan China 35°6N 109°3E 114 G5
Tongdao China 26°10N 109°42E 116 D7
Tongeren Belgium 50°47N 5°28E 69 D5
Tonggu China 28°31N 114°20E 117 C10
Tonggu Jiao China 22°22N 113°37E 111 a
Tongguan China 34°40N 110°25E 114 G6
Tonghai China 24°10N 102°53E 116 E4
Tonghua China 41°42N 125°58E 115 D13
Tongjiang Heilongjiang, China 47°40N 132°27E 111 B15
Tongjiang Sichuan, China 31°58N 107°11E 116 B6
Tongjosŏn-man N. Korea 39°30N 128°0E 115 E15
Tongking, G. of = Tonkin, G. of Asia 20°0N 108°0E 120 C7
Tongliang China 29°50N 106°3E 116 C6
Tongliao China 43°38N 122°18E 115 C12
Tongling China 30°55N 117°48E 117 B11
Tonglu China 29°45N 119°37E 117 C12
Tongnan = Anyue China 30°9N 105°50E 116 B5
Tongoy Chile 30°16S 71°31W 190 C1
Tongren Guizhou, China 27°43N 109°11E 116 D7
Tongren Qinghai, China 35°25N 102°5E 110 D9
Tongres = Tongeren Belgium 50°47N 5°28E 69 D5
Tongsa Dzong Bhutan 27°31N 90°31E 123 F17
Tongshi China 18°50N 109°20E 117 a
Tongue U.K. 58°29N 4°25W 65 C4
Tongue → U.S.A. 46°25N 105°52W 168 C11
Tongwei China 35°0N 105°5E 114 G3
Tongxiang China 30°39N 120°34E 117 B13
Tongxin China 36°59N 105°58E 114 F3
Tongyang N. Korea 39°9N 126°53E 115 E14
Tongyu China 44°45N 123°4E 115 B12
Tongzhou China 32°12N 121°2E 117 A13
Tongzi China 28°9N 106°49E 116 C6
Tonj South Sudan 7°20N 28°44E 135 G11
Tonk India 26°6N 75°54E 124 F6
Tonkawa U.S.A. 36°41N 97°18W 176 C6
Tonkin = Bac Phan Vietnam 22°0N 105°0E 116 G5
Tonkin, G. of Asia 20°0N 108°0E 120 C7
Tonlé Sap Cambodia 13°0N 104°0E 120 F5
Tonnay-Charente France 45°56N 0°55W 72 C3
Tonneins France 44°23N 0°19E 72 D4
Tonnerre France 47°51N 3°59E 71 E10
Tönning Germany 54°19N 8°56E 76 A4
Tono Japan 39°19N 141°32E 112 E10
Tonopah U.S.A. 38°4N 117°14W 169 G5
Tonosí Panama 7°20N 80°20W 182 E3
Tons → Haryana, India 30°30N 77°39E 124 D7
Tons → Ut. P., India 26°1N 83°33E 125 F10
Tønsberg Norway 59°19N 10°25E 61 G14
Tonto △ U.S.A. 33°39N 111°7W 169 K8
Tonya Turkey 40°53N 39°16E 105 B8
Toobanna Australia 18°42S 146°9E 150 B4
Toodyay Australia 31°34S 116°28E 149 F2
Tooele U.S.A. 40°32N 112°18W 168 F7
Toompine Australia 27°15S 144°19E 151 D3
Toomsboro U.S.A. 32°50N 83°5W 178 C6
Toora Australia 38°39S 146°23E 153 E7
Toora-Khem Russia 52°28N 96°17E 109 B13
Toowoomba Australia 27°32S 151°56E 151 D5
Top Springs Australia 16°37S 131°51E 148 C5
Topalu Romania 44°31N 28°3E 81 F13
Topaz U.S.A. 38°41N 119°30W 170 G7
Topeka U.S.A. 39°3N 95°40W 172 F6
Topl'a → Slovakia 48°45N 21°45E 79 C14
Topley Canada 54°49N 126°18W 162 C3
Toplica → Serbia 43°15N 21°49E 96 C5
Toplița Romania 46°55N 25°20E 81 D10
Topocalma, Pta. Chile 34°10S 72°2W 190 C1
Topock U.S.A. 34°46N 114°29W 171 L12
Topola Serbia 44°17N 20°41E 96 B4
Topolčani Macedonia 41°14N 21°25E 96 E5
Topol'čany Slovakia 48°35N 18°12E 79 C11
Topolnitsa → Bulgaria 42°11N 24°18E 97 D8
Topolobampo Mexico 25°36N 109°3W 180 B3
Topoloveni Romania 44°49N 25°5E 81 F10
Topolovgrad Bulgaria 42°5N 26°20E 97 D10
Topolvățu Mare Romania 45°46N 21°41E 80 E6
Topozero, Ozero Russia 65°35N 32°0E 60 D25
Toppenish U.S.A. 46°23N 120°19W 168 C3
Topraisar Romania 44°1N 28°27E 81 F13
Topusko Croatia 45°18N 15°59E 93 C12
Toquepala Peru 17°24S 70°25W 188 D3
Toqyraŭyn → Kazakhstan 46°48N 75°24E 109 C9
Torà Spain 41°49N 1°25E 90 D6
Torata Peru 17°23S 70°1W 188 D3
Torbalı Turkey 38°10N 27°21E 99 C9
Torbat-e Heydārīyeh Iran 35°15N 59°12E 129 C8
Torbat-e Jām Iran 35°16N 60°35E 129 C9
Torbay Canada 47°40N 52°42W 165 C9
Torbay □ U.K. 50°26N 3°31W 67 G4
Torbjörntorp Sweden 58°12N 13°36E 63 F7
Tordesillas Spain 41°30N 5°0W 88 D6
Töreboda Sweden 58°41N 14°7E 63 F8
Torekov Sweden 56°26N 12°37E 63 H6
Torellò Spain 42°3N 2°16E 90 C7
Toreno Spain 42°42N 6°30W 88 C4
Torfaen □ U.K. 51°43N 3°3W 67 F4
Torgau Germany 51°34N 13°0E 76 D8
Torgelow Germany 53°37N 14°1E 76 B10
Torghay Kazakhstan 49°38N 63°29E 108 C6
Torghay → Kazakhstan 48°1N 62°45E 108 C6
Torghay Ustirti Asia 51°0N 63°0E 108 B6
Torghay Zhylghasy Kazakhstan 52°0N 64°30E 108 B6
Torhamn Sweden 56°6N 15°50E 63 H9
Torhout Belgium 51°5N 3°7E 69 C3
Torhovytsya Ukraine 48°36N 25°26E 81 B10
Tori-Shima Japan 30°29N 140°19E 113 J10
Torigni-sur-Vire France 49°3N 0°58W 70 C6
Torija Spain 40°44N 3°2W 90 E1
Torilla Pen. Australia 22°29S 150°5E 150 C5
Torino Italy 45°3N 7°40E 92 C4
Torit South Sudan 4°27N 32°31E 135 H12
Torkamān Iran 37°35N 47°23E 105 D12
Torkovichi Russia 58°51N 30°21E 84 C6
Tormac Romania 45°30N 21°30E 80 E6
Tormes → Spain 41°18N 6°29W 88 D4
Tornado Mt. Canada 49°55N 114°40W 162 D6
Tornal'a Slovakia 48°25N 20°20E 79 C13
Torneå = Tornio Finland 65°50N 24°12E 60 D21
Torneälven → Europe 65°50N 24°12E 60 D21
Torneträsk Sweden 68°24N 19°15E 60 B18
Torngat Mountains Nat. Park △ Canada 59°0N 63°40W 161 F19
Torngat Mts. Canada 59°0N 63°40W 161 F19
Tornio Finland 65°50N 24°12E 60 D21
Tornionjoki = Torneälven → Europe 65°50N 24°12E 60 D21
Tornquist Argentina 38°8S 62°15W 190 D3
Toro Baleares, Spain 39°59N 4°8E 100 B11
Toro Zamora, Spain 41°35N 5°24W 88 D5
Torö Sweden 58°48N 17°50E 63 F11
Toro, Cerro del Chile 29°10S 69°50W 190 B2
Toro ⌂ Uganda 1°5N 30°22E 142 C3
Toro Pk. U.S.A. 33°34N 116°24W 171 M10
Torodi Niger 13°7N 1°47E 139 C5
Törökszentmiklós Hungary 47°11N 20°27E 80 C5
Toronto Australia 33°0S 151°30E 153 B9
Toronto Canada 43°39N 79°20W 174 C5
Toronto U.S.A. 40°28N 80°36W 174 F4
Toronto Lester B. Pearson Int. ✈ (YYZ) Canada 43°46N 79°35W 174 C5
Toropets Russia 56°30N 31°40E 84 D6
Tororo Uganda 0°45N 34°12E 142 B3
Toros Dağları Turkey 37°0N 32°30E 104 D5
Torpa India 22°57N 85°6E 125 H11
Torquay Australia 38°20S 144°19E 152 E6
Torquay U.K. 50°27N 3°32W 67 G4
Torquemada Spain 42°2N 4°19W 88 C6
Torrance U.S.A. 33°50N 118°20W 171 M8
Torrão Portugal 38°16N 8°11W 89 G2
Torre Annunziata Italy 40°45N 14°27E 95 B7
Torre de Moncorvo Portugal 41°12N 7°8W 88 D3
Torre del Campo Spain 37°46N 3°53W 89 H7
Torre del Greco Italy 40°47N 14°22E 95 B7
Torre del Mar Spain 36°44N 4°6W 89 J6
Torre-Pacheco Spain 37°44N 0°57W 91 H4
Torre Péllice Italy 44°49N 7°13E 92 D4
Torreblanca Spain 40°14N 0°12E 90 E5
Torrecampo Spain 38°29N 4°41W 89 G6
Torrecilla en Cameros Spain 42°15N 2°38W 90 C2
Torredembarra Spain 41°9N 1°24E 90 D6
Torredonjimeno Spain 37°46N 3°57W 89 H7
Torrejón de Ardoz Spain 40°27N 3°29W 88 E7
Torrejoncillo Spain 39°54N 6°28W 88 F4
Torrelaguna Spain 40°50N 3°38W 88 E7
Torrelavega Spain 43°20N 4°5W 88 B6
Torremaggiore Italy 41°41N 15°17E 93 G12
Torremolinos Spain 36°38N 4°30W 89 J6
Torrens, L. Australia 31°0S 137°50E 152 A2
Torrens Cr. → Australia 22°23S 145°9E 150 C4
Torrens Creek Australia 20°48S 145°3E 150 C4
Torrent Spain 39°27N 0°28W 91 F4
Torrenueva Spain 38°38N 3°22W 89 G7
Torreón Mexico 25°33N 103°26W 180 B4
Torreperogil Spain 38°2N 3°17W 89 G7
Torres Brazil 29°21S 49°44W 191 B5
Torres Mexico 28°46N 110°47W 180 B2
Torres del Paine △ Chile 51°3S 72°58W 192 D2
Torres Novas Portugal 39°27N 8°33W 89 F2
Torres Strait Australia 9°50S 142°20E 150 a
Torres Vedras Portugal 39°5N 9°15W 89 F1
Torrevieja Spain 37°59N 0°42W 91 H4
Torrey U.S.A. 38°18N 111°25W 168 G8
Torridge → U.K. 51°0N 4°13W 67 G3
Torridon, L. U.K. 57°35N 5°50W 65 D3
Torrijos Spain 39°59N 4°18W 88 F6
Tørring Denmark 55°52N 9°29E 63 J3
Torrington Conn., U.S.A. 41°48N 73°7W 175 E11
Torrington Wyo., U.S.A. 42°4N 104°11W 168 E11
Torroella de Montgrí Spain 42°2N 3°8E 90 C8
Torrox Spain 36°46N 3°57W 89 J7
Torsås Sweden 56°24N 16°0E 63 H9
Torsby Sweden 60°7N 13°0E 62 D6
Torshälla Sweden 59°25N 16°28E 62 E10
Tórshavn Færoe Is. 62°5N 6°56W 60 E9
Torslanda Sweden 57°44N 11°45E 63 G5
Torsö Sweden 58°48N 13°45E 63 F7
Tortola Br. Virgin Is. 18°19N 64°45W 183 e
Tórtoles de Esgueva Spain 41°49N 4°2W 88 D6
Tortolì Italy 39°55N 9°39E 94 C2
Tortona Italy 44°54N 8°52E 92 D5
Tortorici Italy 38°2N 14°49E 95 D7
Tortosa Spain 40°49N 0°31E 90 E5
Tortosa, C. Spain 40°41N 0°52E 90 E5
Tortosendo Portugal 40°15N 7°31W 88 E3
Tortue, Î. de la Haiti 20°5N 72°57W 183 B5
Tortuguero △ Costa Rica 10°31N 83°29W 182 D3
Tortum Turkey 40°19N 41°35E 105 B9
Torūd Iran 35°25N 55°5E 129 C7
Torul Turkey 40°34N 39°18E 105 B8
Toruń Poland 53°2N 18°39E 83 E5
Torun Ukraine 48°40N 23°34E 81 B8
Tory Hill Canada 44°58N 78°16W 174 B6
Tory I. Ireland 55°16N 8°13W 64 A3
Torysa → Slovakia 48°39N 21°21E 79 C14
Torzhok Russia 57°5N 34°55E 84 D8
Torzym Poland 52°19N 15°5E 83 F2
Tosa Japan 33°24N 133°23E 113 H6
Tosa-Shimizu Japan 32°52N 132°58E 113 H6
Tosa-Wan Japan 33°15N 133°30E 113 H6
Toscana □ Italy 43°25N 11°0E 92 E8
Toscano, Arcipelago Italy 42°30N 10°30E 92 F7
Toshka Egypt 22°30N 31°53E 137 C3
Toshka, Buheirat en Egypt 22°50N 31°0E 137 C3
Toshkent Uzbekistan 41°20N 69°10E 109 D7
Toshkent □ Uzbekistan 41°0N 69°40E 109 D7
Tosno Russia 59°38N 30°46E 84 C6
Tossa de Mar Spain 41°43N 2°56E 90 D7
Tösse Sweden 58°58N 12°39E 63 F6
Tostado Argentina 29°15S 61°50W 190 B3
Tostedt Germany 53°17N 9°42E 76 B5
Tostón, Pta. de Canary Is. 28°42N 14°2W 100 F5
Tosu Japan 33°22N 130°31E 113 H5
Tosya Turkey 41°1N 34°2E 104 B6
Toszek Poland 50°27N 18°32E 83 H5
Totana Spain 37°45N 1°30W 91 H3
Totebo Sweden 57°38N 16°12E 63 G10
Toteng Botswana 20°22S 22°58E 144 B3
Tôtes France 49°41N 1°2E 70 C8
Tótkomlós Hungary 46°24N 20°45E 80 D5
Totma Russia 60°0N 42°40E 106 D5
Totnes U.K. 50°26N 3°42W 67 G4
Totness Suriname 5°53N 56°19W 187 B7
Toto Nigeria 8°26N 7°5E 139 D6
Totonicapán Guatemala 14°58N 91°12W 182 D1
Totoya, I. Fiji 18°57S 179°50W 154 a
Totten Glacier Antarctica 66°45S 116°10E 55 C8
Tottenham Australia 32°14S 147°21E 153 B7
Tottenham Canada 44°1N 79°49W 174 B5
Tottori Japan 35°30N 134°15E 113 G7
Tottori □ Japan 35°30N 134°12E 113 G7
Touâret Niger 20°17N 7°8E 139 A6
Touat Algeria 27°27N 0°30E 136 C4
Touba Côte d'Ivoire 8°22N 7°40W 138 D3
Touba Senegal 14°50N 15°55W 138 C1
Toubkal, Djebel Morocco 31°0N 8°0W 136 B2
Toubkal △ Morocco 31°0N 8°2W 136 B2
Toucy France 47°44N 3°15E 71 E10
Tougan Burkina Faso 13°11N 2°58W 138 C4
Touggourt Algeria 33°6N 6°4E 136 B5
Tougouri Burkina Faso 13°20N 0°30W 139 C4
Tougué Guinea 11°25N 11°50W 138 C2
Toukoto Mali 13°27N 9°52W 138 C3
Toul France 48°40N 5°53E 71 D12
Toulepleu Côte d'Ivoire 6°32N 8°24W 138 D3
Touliu Taiwan 23°42N 120°31E 117 F13
Toulon France 43°10N 5°55E 73 E9
Toulouse France 43°37N 1°27E 72 E5
Toulouse Blagnac ✈ (TLS) France 43°37N 1°22E 72 E5
Toummo Niger 22°45N 14°8E 135 D8
Toumodi Côte d'Ivoire 6°32N 5°4W 138 D3
Tounan Taiwan 23°41N 120°28E 117 F13
Tounassine, Hamada Algeria 28°48N 5°0W 136 C3
Toungoo Myanmar 19°0N 96°30E 123 K20
Toungo Nigeria 8°20N 12°3E 139 D7
Touques → France 49°22N 0°8E 70 C7
Touraine France 47°20N 0°30E 70 E7
Touran = Tūrān △ Iran 35°45N 56°30E 129 C8
Tourcoing France 50°42N 3°10E 71 B10
Touriñán, C. Spain 43°3N 9°18W 88 B1
Tournai Belgium 50°35N 3°25E 69 D3
Tournan-en-Brie France 48°44N 2°46E 71 D9
Tournay France 43°13N 0°13E 72 E4
Tournon-St-Martin France 46°45N 0°58E 70 F7
Tournon-sur-Rhône France 45°4N 4°50E 73 C8
Tournus France 46°35N 4°54E 71 F11
Touros Brazil 5°12S 35°28W 189 B3
Tours France 47°22N 0°40E 70 E7
Toussoro, Mt. C.A.R. 9°7N 23°14E 140 C4
Touws → S. Africa 33°45S 21°11E 144 D3
Touwsrivier S. Africa 33°20S 20°2E 144 D3
Tovarkovskiy Russia 53°40N 38°14E 84 F10
Tovste Ukraine 48°50N 25°44E 81 B10
Tovuz Azerbaijan 41°0N 45°40E 87 K7
Towada Japan 40°37N 141°13E 112 D10
Towada-Hachimantai △ Japan 40°20N 140°55E 112 D10
Towada-Ko Japan 40°28N 140°55E 112 D10
Towanda U.S.A. 41°46N 76°27W 175 E8
Towarri △ Australia 31°50S 150°37E 153 A9
Tower U.S.A. 47°48N 92°17W 172 B7
Towerhill Cr. → Australia 22°28S 144°35E 150 C3
Towner U.S.A. 48°21N 100°25W 172 A3
Townsend Ga., U.S.A. 31°33N 81°31W 178 D8
Townsend Mont., U.S.A. 46°19N 111°31W 168 C8
Townshend I. Australia 22°10S 150°31E 150 C5
Townsville Australia 19°15S 146°45E 150 B4
Towot South Sudan 6°12N 34°25E 142 A3
Towraghondī Afghan. 35°13N 62°16E 108 E6
Towson U.S.A. 39°24N 76°36W 173 F15
Towuti, Danau Indonesia 2°45S 121°32E 119 E6
Toxkan He → China 41°8N 80°11E 109 D10
Tōya-Ko Japan 42°35N 140°51E 112 C10
Toyama Japan 36°40N 137°15E 113 F8
Toyama □ Japan 36°45N 137°30E 113 F8
Toyama-Wan Japan 37°0N 137°30E 113 F8
Toyapakeh Indonesia 8°41S 115°29E 119 K18
Toyohashi Japan 34°45N 137°25E 113 G8
Toyokawa Japan 34°48N 137°27E 113 G8
Toyonaka Japan 34°46N 135°28E 113 G7
Toyooka Japan 35°35N 134°48E 113 G7
Toyota Japan 35°3N 137°7E 113 G8
Tozeur Tunisia 33°56N 8°8E 136 B5
Tozeur □ Tunisia 34°0N 8°5E 136 B5
Tqibuli Georgia 42°26N 43°0E 87 J6
Tqvarcheli Georgia 42°47N 41°42E 87 J5
Trá Li = Tralee Ireland 52°16N 9°42W 64 D2
Trá Mhór = Tramore Ireland 52°10N 7°10W 64 D4
Tra On Vietnam 9°58N 105°55E 121 H5
Tra Vinh Vietnam 9°50N 106°15E 121 H6
Trabancos → Spain 41°36N 5°15W 88 D5
Traben-Trarbach Germany 49°57N 7°7E 77 F3
Trabzon Turkey 41°0N 39°45E 105 B8
Trabzon □ Turkey 41°10N 39°45E 105 B8
Tracadie Canada 47°30N 64°55W 165 C7
Tracy Canada 46°1N 73°9W 164 C5
Tracy Calif., U.S.A. 37°44N 121°26W 170 H5
Tracy Minn., U.S.A. 44°14N 95°37W 172 C6
Tradate Italy 45°43N 8°54E 92 C5
Trade Town Liberia 5°40N 9°50W 138 D3
Trafalgar Australia 38°14S 146°12E 153 E7
Trafalgar, C. Spain 36°10N 6°2W 89 J4
Tragonhsi Greece 37°27N 25°29E 99 D7
Traian Brăila, Romania 45°11N 27°44E 81 E12
Traian Tulcea, Romania 45°2N 28°15E 81 E13
Traiguén Chile 38°15S 72°41W 192 A2
Trail Canada 49°5N 117°40W 162 D5
Traill Ø Greenland 72°30N 23°0W 57 C8
Trainor L. Canada 60°24N 120°17W 162 A4
Trakai △ Lithuania 54°30N 25°10E 61 J21
Trákhonas Cyprus 35°12N 33°21E 101 D12
Tralee Ireland 52°16N 9°42W 64 D2
Tralee B. Ireland 52°17N 9°55W 64 D2
Tram Chim △ Vietnam 10°43N 105°31E 121 G5
Tramore Ireland 52°10N 7°10W 64 D4
Tramore B. Ireland 52°9N 7°10W 64 D4
Tramuntana, Serra de Spain 39°48N 2°54E 100 B9
Tran Bulgaria 42°51N 22°38E 96 D6
Tran Ninh, Cao Nguyen Laos 19°30N 103°10E 120 C4
Tranås Sweden 58°3N 14°59E 63 F8
Tranbjerg Denmark 56°6N 10°9E 63 H4
Trancas Argentina 26°11S 65°20W 190 B2
Trancoso Portugal 40°49N 7°21W 88 E3
Tranebjerg Denmark 55°51N 10°36E 63 J4
Tranemo Sweden 57°30N 13°20E 63 G7
Trang Thailand 7°33N 99°38E 121 J2
Trangan Indonesia 6°40S 134°20E 119 F8
Trangie Australia 32°4S 148°0E 153 B8
Trångsviken Sweden 63°19N 13°59E 62 A7
Trani Italy 41°17N 16°25E 95 A9
Tranoroa Madag. 24°42S 45°4E 141 J9
Tranqueras Uruguay 31°13S 55°45W 191 C4
Trans-Nzoia □ Kenya 1°10N 34°55E 142 B3
Transantarctic Mts. Antarctica 85°0S 170°0W 55 E12
Transcarpathia = Zakarpattya □ Ukraine 48°20N 23°20E 81 B8
Transilvania Romania 46°30N 24°0E 81 D9
Transilvanian Alps = Carpații Meridionali Romania 45°30N 25°0E 81 E9
Transnistria □ Moldova 47°20N 29°15E 81 C14
Transtrand Sweden 61°6N 13°20E 62 C7
Transtrandsfjällen Sweden 61°8N 13°0E 62 C6
Transylvania = Transilvania Romania 46°30N 24°0E 81 D9
Trápani Italy 38°1N 12°29E 94 D5
Trapper Pk. U.S.A. 45°54N 114°18W 168 D6
Traralgon Australia 38°12S 146°34E 153 E7
Traryd Sweden 56°35N 13°45E 63 H7
Trarza □ Mauritania 18°0N 15°0W 138 B2
Trasacco Italy 41°57N 13°32E 93 G10
Trăscău, Munții Romania 46°14N 23°14E 81 D8
Trasimeno, L. Italy 43°8N 12°6E 93 E9
Träslövsläge Sweden 57°4N 12°16E 63 G6
Trastenik Bulgaria 43°31N 24°28E 97 C8
Trasvase Tajo-Segura, Canal de Spain 40°15N 2°55W 90 E2
Trat Thailand 12°14N 102°33E 121 F4
Tratani → Pakistan 29°19N 68°20E 124 E3
Traun Austria 48°14N 14°15E 78 C7
Traunreut Germany 47°57N 12°36E 77 H8
Traunsee Austria 47°55N 13°50E 78 D6
Traunstein Germany 47°52N 12°37E 77 H8
Travellers L. Australia 33°20S 142°0E 152 B5
Travemünde Germany 53°57N 10°52E 76 B6
Travers, Mt. N.Z. 42°1S 172°45E 155 C7
Traverse City U.S.A. 44°46N 85°38W 173 C11
Travis, L. U.S.A. 30°24N 97°55W 176 F6
Travnik Bos.-H. 44°17N 17°39E 80 F2
Trawbreaga B. Ireland 55°20N 7°25W 64 A4
Trbovlje Slovenia 46°12N 15°5E 93 B12
Treasure Island U.S.A. 27°46N 82°46W 179 H7
Trébbia → Italy 45°4N 9°41E 92 C6
Trebel → Germany 53°54N 13°2E 76 B9
Trébeurden France 48°46N 3°35W 70 D3
Trebević △ Bos.-H. 43°20N 18°45E 80 G3
Třebíč Czechia 49°14N 15°55E 78 B8
Trebinje Bos.-H. 42°44N 18°22E 96 D2
Trebisacce Italy 39°52N 16°32E 95 C9
Trebišnjica → Bos.-H. 42°47N 18°8E 96 D2
Trebišov Slovakia 48°38N 21°41E 79 C14
Trebižat → Bos.-H. 43°15N 17°30E 93 E14
Trebnje Slovenia 45°54N 15°1E 93 C12
Třeboň Czechia 49°1N 14°48E 78 B7
Trebonne Australia 18°37S 146°5E 150 B4
Třeboňsko ⌂ Czechia 49°1N 14°49E 78 B7
Trebujena Spain 36°52N 6°11W 89 J4
Trecate Italy 45°26N 8°44E 92 C5
Trefaldwyn = Montgomery U.K. 52°34N 3°8W 67 E4
Trefynwy = Monmouth U.K. 51°48N 2°42W 67 F5
Tregaron U.K. 52°14N 3°56W 67 E4
Tregnago Italy 45°31N 11°10E 93 C8
Tregrosse Is. Australia 17°41S 150°43E 150 B5
Tréguier France 48°47N 3°16W 70 D3
Trégunc France 47°51N 3°51W 70 E3
Treherne Canada 49°38N 98°42W 163 D9
Tréia Italy 43°19N 13°19E 93 E10
Treignac France 45°32N 1°48E 72 C5
Treinta y Tres Uruguay 33°16S 54°17W 191 C5
Treis-karden Germany 50°10N 7°18E 77 E3
Treklyano Bulgaria 42°33N 22°36E 96 D6
Trelawney Zimbabwe 17°30S 30°30E 145 A5
Trélazé France 47°26N 0°30W 70 E6
Trelew Argentina 43°10S 65°20W 192 B3
Trélissac France 45°11N 0°47E 72 C4
Trelleborg Sweden 55°20N 13°10E 63 J7
Tremadog Bay U.K. 52°51N 4°18W 66 E3
Trémiti Italy 42°8N 15°30E 93 F12
Tremonton U.S.A. 41°43N 112°10W 168 F7
Tremp Spain 42°10N 0°52E 90 C5
Trenche → Canada 47°46N 72°53W 164 C5
Trenčiansky □ Slovakia 48°45N 18°20E 79 C11
Trenčín Slovakia 48°52N 18°4E 79 C11
Trenggalek Indonesia 8°3S 111°43E 119 H14
Trenque Lauquen Argentina 36°5S 62°45W 190 D3
Trent → Canada 44°6N 77°34W 174 B7
Trent → U.K. 53°41N 0°42W 66 D7
Trentino-Alto Adige □ Italy 46°30N 11°20E 93 B8
Trento Italy 46°4N 11°8E 92 B8
Trenton Canada 44°10N 77°34W 174 B7
Trenton Fla., U.S.A. 29°37N 82°49W 179 F7
Trenton Mo., U.S.A. 40°5N 93°37W 172 E7
Trenton N.J., U.S.A. 40°14N 74°46W 175 F10
Trenton Nebr., U.S.A. 40°11N 101°1W 172 E3
Trenton S.C., U.S.A. 33°45N 81°51W 178 B8
Trepassey Canada 46°43N 53°25W 165 C9
Trepuzzi Italy 40°24N 18°4E 95 B11
Tres Arroyos Argentina 38°26S 60°20W 190 D3
Três Corações Brazil 21°44S 45°15W 191 A6
Três Lagoas Brazil 20°50S 51°43W 187 H8
Tres Lagos Argentina 49°35S 71°25W 192 C2
Tres Lomas Argentina 36°27S 62°51W 190 D3
Três Marias, Represa Brazil 18°12S 45°15W 189 D1
Tres Montes, C. Chile 46°50S 75°30W 192 C1
Tres Pinos U.S.A. 36°48N 121°19W 170 J5
Três Pontas Brazil 21°23S 45°29W 191 A6
Tres Puentes Chile 27°50S 70°15W 190 B1
Tres Puntas, C. Argentina 47°0S 66°0W 192 C3
Três Rios Brazil 22°6S 43°15W 191 A7
Tres Valles Mexico 18°15N 96°8W 181 D5
Tresco U.K. 49°57N 6°20W 67 H1
Treska → Macedonia 42°0N 21°20E 96 E5
Treskavica Bos.-H. 43°40N 18°20E 80 G3
Trespaderne Spain 42°47N 3°24W 88 C7
Tresticklan △ Sweden 59°0N 11°42E 63 F5
Trets France 43°27N 5°41E 73 E9
Treuchtlingen Germany 48°58N 10°54E 77 G6
Treuenbrietzen Germany 52°5N 12°52E 76 C8
Trevi Italy 42°52N 12°45E 93 F9
Treviglio Italy 45°31N 9°35E 92 C6
Trevinca, Peña Spain 42°15N 6°46W 88 C4
Treviño Spain 42°44N 2°45W 88 C8
Treviso Italy 45°40N 12°15E 93 C9
Trgovište Serbia 42°20N 22°10E 96 D6
Triabunna Australia 42°30S 147°55E 151 G4
Triangle Zimbabwe 21°2S 31°28E 145 B5
Triaucourt-en-Argonne France 48°59N 5°2E 71 D12
Tribal Areas □ Pakistan 33°0N 70°0E 124 C4
Tribsees Germany 54°5N 12°44E 76 A8
Tribulation, C. Australia 16°5S 145°29E 150 B4
Tribune U.S.A. 38°28N 101°45W 172 F3
Tricárico Italy 40°37N 16°9E 95 B9
Tricase Italy 39°56N 18°22E 95 C11
Trichinopoly = Tiruchchirappalli India 10°45N 78°45E 127 J4
Trichonida, L. Greece 38°34N 21°30E 98 C3
Trichur = Thrissur India 10°30N 76°18E 127 J3
Trichy = Tiruchchirappalli India 10°45N 78°45E 127 J4
Trida Australia 33°1S 145°1E 153 B6
Trier Germany 49°45N 6°38E 77 F2
Trieste Italy 45°40N 13°46E 93 C10
Trieste, G. di Italy 45°40N 13°35E 93 C10
Trieux → France 48°43N 3°9W 70 D3
Triggiano Italy 41°4N 16°55E 95 A9
Triglav Slovenia 46°21N 13°50E 93 B10
Triglavski △ Slovenia 46°20N 13°50E 93 B10
Trigno → Italy 42°4N 14°48E 93 F11
Trigueros Spain 37°24N 6°50W 89 H4
Trikala Greece 39°34N 21°47E 98 B3
Trikeri Greece 39°6N 23°5E 98 B5
Trikomo Cyprus 35°17N 33°52E 101 D12
Trikora, Puncak Indonesia 4°15S 138°45E 119 E9
Trilby U.S.A. 28°28N 82°12W 179 G7
Trilj Croatia 43°38N 16°42E 93 E13
Trillo Spain 40°42N 2°35W 90 E2
Trim Ireland 53°33N 6°48W 64 C5
Trimbak India 19°56N 73°33E 126 E1
Trimmu Dam Pakistan 31°10N 72°8E 124 D5
Trincomalee Sri Lanka 8°38N 81°15E 127 K5
Trindade Atl. Oc. 20°20S 29°50W 56 J9
Trindade Brazil 16°40S 49°30W 187 G9
Třinec Czechia 49°41N 18°39E 79 B11
Trinidad Bolivia 14°46S 64°50W 186 F6
Trinidad Cuba 21°48N 80°0W 182 B4
Trinidad Paraguay 27°7S 55°47W 191 B4
Trinidad Trin. & Tob. 10°30N 61°15W 183 D7
Trinidad Uruguay 33°30S 56°50W 190 C4
Trinidad U.S.A. 37°10N 104°31W 169 H11
Trinidad, G. Chile 49°55S 75°25W 192 C1
Trinidad, I. Argentina 39°10S 62°0W 192 A4
Trinidad & Tobago ■ W. Indies 10°30N 61°20W 186 A6
Trinitápoli Italy 41°21N 16°5E 95 A9
Trinity Canada 48°59N 53°55W 165 C9
Trinity U.S.A. 30°57N 95°22W 176 F7
Trinity → Calif., U.S.A. 41°11N 123°42W 168 F2
Trinity → Tex., U.S.A. 29°45N 94°43W 176 G7
Trinity B. Canada 48°20N 53°10W 165 C9
Trinity Hills Trin. & Tob. 10°7N 61°7W 187 K15
Trinity Is. U.S.A. 56°33N 154°25W 166 D9
Trinity Range U.S.A. 40°10N 118°40W 168 F4
Trinkat India 8°5N 93°30E 127 K11
Trinkitat Sudan 18°45N 37°51E 137 D4
Trino Italy 45°12N 8°18E 92 C5
Trinway U.S.A. 40°9N 82°1W 174 F2
Triolet Mauritius 20°4S 57°32E 141 d
Trionto, C. Italy 39°37N 16°43E 95 C9
Triora Italy 44°1N 7°46E 92 D4
Tripoli = Tarābulus Lebanon 34°31N 35°50E 130 A4
Tripoli = Tarābulus Libya 32°49N 13°7E 135 B8
Tripoli Greece 37°31N 22°25E 98 D4
Tripolitania = Tarābulus Libya 31°0N 13°0E 135 B8
Tripura □ India 24°0N 92°0E 123 H18
Tripylos Cyprus 34°59N 32°41E 101 E11
Trischen Germany 54°3N 8°40E 76 A4
Tristan da Cunha Atl. Oc. 37°6S 12°20W 133 K2
Trisul India 30°19N 79°47E 125 D8
Triton I. S. China Sea 15°47N 111°12E 118 A4
Trivandrum = Thiruvananthapuram India 8°41N 77°0E 127 K3
Trivento Italy 41°47N 14°33E 93 G11
Trizina Greece 37°25N 23°15E 98 D5
Trnava Slovakia 48°23N 17°35E 79 C10
Trnavský □ Slovakia 48°30N 17°45E 79 C10
Troarn France 49°11N 0°11W 70 C6
Trochu Canada 51°50N 113°13W 162 C6
Trodely I. Canada 52°15N 79°26W 164 B4
Troebratskiy Kazakhstan 54°25N 66°4E 109 B7
Trogir Croatia 43°32N 16°15E 93 E13
Troglav Croatia 43°56N 16°36E 93 E13
Tróia Italy 41°22N 15°18E 95 A8
Troilus, L. Canada 50°50N 74°35W 164 B5
Troina Italy 37°47N 14°36E 95 E7
Trois Fourches, Cap des Morocco 35°26N 2°58W 136 A3
Trois-Pistoles Canada 48°5N 69°10W 165 C6
Trois-Rivières Canada 46°25N 72°34W 164 C5
Trois-Rivières Guadeloupe 15°57N 61°40W 182 b
Troisdorf Germany 50°48N 7°11E 76 E3
Troitsk Russia 54°10N 61°35E 108 B6
Troitsko Pechorsk Russia 62°40N 56°10E 106 C6
Troitskoye Russia 46°26N 44°15E 87 G7
Troll Antarctica 72°0S 2°30E 55 D3
Trölladyngja Iceland 64°54N 17°16W 60 D5
Trollhättan Sweden 58°17N 12°20E 63 F6
Trollheimen Norway 62°46N 9°1E 60 E13
Trombetas → Brazil 1°55S 55°35W 187 D7
Tromelin I. Ind. Oc. 15°52S 54°25E 146 F4
Tromsø Norway 69°40N 18°56E 60 B18
Tron Thailand 17°28N 100°7E 120 D3
Trona U.S.A. 35°46N 117°23W 171 K9
Tronador, Mte. Argentina 41°10S 71°50W 192 B2
Trøndelag Norway 64°17N 11°50E 60 D14
Trondheim Norway 63°36N 10°25E 60 E14
Trondheimsfjorden Norway 63°35N 10°30E 60 E14
Trönninge Sweden 56°37N 12°51E 63 H6
Tronto → Italy 42°54N 13°55E 93 F10
Troodos Cyprus 34°55N 32°52E 101 E11
Troon U.K. 55°33N 4°39W 65 F4
Tropea Italy 38°41N 15°54E 95 D8
Tropic U.S.A. 37°37N 112°5W 169 H7
Tropojë Albania 42°23N 20°10E 96 D4
Trosa Sweden 58°54N 17°33E 63 F11
Trostan U.K. 55°3N 6°10W 64 A5
Trostberg Germany 48°1N 12°33E 77 G8
Trostyanets Sumy, Ukraine 50°33N 34°59E 85 G8
Trostyanets Vinnyts'ka, Ukraine 48°31N 29°11E 81 B14
Trou Gras Pt. St. Lucia 13°51N 60°53W 183 f
Trout → Canada 61°19N 119°51W 162 A5
Trout L. N.W.T., Canada 60°40N 121°14W 162 A4
Trout L. Ont., Canada 51°20N 93°15W 163 C10
Trout Lake Canada 56°30N 114°32W 162 B6
Trout Lake U.S.A. 46°0N 121°32W 170 E5
Trout River Canada 49°29N 58°8W 165 C8
Trout Run U.S.A. 41°23N 77°3W 174 E7
Trouville-sur-Mer France 49°21N 0°5E 70 C7
Trowbridge U.K. 51°18N 2°12W 67 F5
Troy Turkey 39°57N 26°12E 99 B8
Troy Ala., U.S.A. 31°48N 85°58W 178 D4
Troy Kans., U.S.A. 39°47N 95°5W 172 F6
Troy Mo., U.S.A. 38°59N 90°59W 172 F8
Troy Mont., U.S.A. 48°28N 115°53W 168 B6
Troy N.Y., U.S.A. 42°44N 73°41W 175 D11
Troy Ohio, U.S.A. 40°2N 84°12W 173 E11
Troy Pa., U.S.A. 41°47N 76°47W 175 E8
Troyan Bulgaria 42°57N 24°43E 97 D8
Troyes France 48°19N 4°3E 71 D11
Trpanj Croatia 43°1N 17°15E 93 E14
Trstenik Serbia 43°36N 21°0E 96 C5
Trubchevsk Russia 52°33N 33°47E 85 F7
Truchas Pk. U.S.A. 35°58N 105°39W 169 J11
Trucial States = United Arab Emirates ■ Asia 23°50N 54°0E 129 F7
Truckee U.S.A. 39°20N 120°11W 170 F6
Trudfront Russia 45°56N 47°40E 87 H8
Trudovoye Russia 43°17N 132°5E 112 C6
Trujillo Honduras 16°0N 86°0W 182 C2
Trujillo Peru 8°6S 79°0W 188 B2
Trujillo Spain 39°28N 5°55W 89 F5
Trujillo U.S.A. 35°32N 104°42W 169 J11
Trujillo Venezuela 9°22N 70°38W 186 B4
Truk Micronesia 7°25N 151°46E 156 G7
Trumann U.S.A. 35°41N 90°31W 177 D9
Trumansburg U.S.A. 42°33N 76°40W 175 D8
Trumbull, Mt. U.S.A. 36°25N 113°19W 169 H7
Trun France 48°50N 0°2E 70 D7
Trundle Australia 32°53S 147°35E 153 B7
Trung Lon, Hon Vietnam 8°36N 106°8E 121 H6
Trung Phan Vietnam 17°0N 109°0E 120 D6
Truong Sa, Dao = Spratly I. S. China Sea 8°38N 111°55E 118 C4
Truro Australia 34°24S 139°9E 152 C3
Truro Canada 45°21N 63°14W 165 C7
Truro U.K. 50°16N 5°4W 67 G2
Truskavets Ukraine 49°17N 23°30E 75 D12
Trustrup Denmark 56°20N 10°46E 63 H4
Trutch Canada 57°44N 122°57W 162 B4
Truth or Consequences U.S.A. 33°8N 107°15W 169 K10
Trutnov Czechia 50°37N 15°54E 78 A8
Truyère → France 44°38N 2°34E 72 D6
Tryavna Bulgaria 42°54N 25°25E 97 D9
Tryonville U.S.A. 41°42N 79°48W 174 E5
Tryphena N.Z. 36°18S 175°28E 154 C4
Trzcianka Poland 53°3N 16°25E 83 E3
Trzciel Poland 52°23N 15°50E 83 F2
Trzcińsko Zdrój Poland 52°58N 14°35E 83 F1
Trzebiatów Poland 54°3N 15°18E 82 D2
Trzebiez Poland 53°38N 14°31E 82 E1
Trzebnica Poland 51°20N 17°1E 83 G4
Trzemeszno Poland 52°33N 17°48E 83 F4
Tržič Slovenia 46°22N 14°18E 93 B11
Tsagaannur Mongolia 49°32N 89°42E 109 C11
Tsagan Aman Russia 47°34N 46°43E 87 G8
Tsala Apopka L. U.S.A. 28°53N 82°19W 179 G7
Tsamandas Greece 39°46N 20°21E 98 B2
Tsandi Namibia 17°42S 14°50E 144 A1
Tsaratanana Madag. 16°47S 47°39E 141 G9
Tsarevo Bulgaria 42°28N 25°52E 97 D9
Tsaritsani Greece 39°53N 22°14E 98 B4
Tsau Botswana 20°8S 22°22E 144 B3
Tsavo Kenya 2°59S 38°28E 142 C4
Tsavo East △ Kenya 2°44S 38°47E 142 C4
Tsavo West △ Kenya 3°19S 37°57E 142 C4
Tsentralen Balkan △ Bulgaria 42°40N 24°45E 97 D8
Tsentralnyy □ Russia 52°0N 40°0E 106 D4
Tses Namibia 25°58S 18°8E 144 C2
Tsetserleg Mongolia 47°36N 101°32E 110 B9
Tseung Kwan China 22°19N 114°15E 111 a
Tsévié Togo 6°25N 1°20E 139 D5
Tshabong Botswana 26°2S 22°29E 144 C3
Tshane Botswana 24°5S 21°54E 144 B3
Tshela Dem. Rep. of the Congo 4°57S 13°4E 140 E2
Tshesebe Botswana 21°51S 27°32E 145 B4
Tshibeke Dem. Rep. of the Congo 2°40S 28°35E 142 C2
Tshibinda Dem. Rep. of the Congo 2°23S 28°43E 142 C2
Tshikapa Dem. Rep. of the Congo 6°28S 20°48E 140 F4
Tshilenge Dem. Rep. of the Congo 6°17S 23°48E 142 D1
Tshinsenda Dem. Rep. of the Congo 12°20S 28°0E 143 E2
Tshofa Dem. Rep. of the Congo 5°13S 25°16E 142 D2
Tshwane = Pretoria S. Africa 25°44S 28°12E 145 C4

Tshwane *Botswana* 22°24S 22°1E **144** B3
Tsigara *Botswana* 20°22S 25°54E **144** B4
Tsihombe *Madag.* 25°10S 45°41E **141** K9
Tsiigehtchic *Canada* 67°15N 134°00W **160** D5
Ts'il-os △ *Canada* 51°9N 123°59W **162** C4
Tsimlyansk *Russia* 47°40N 42°6E **87** G6
Tsimlyansk Res. = Tsimlyanskoye
  Vdkhr. *Russia* 48°0N 43°0E **87** F6
Tsimlyanskoye Vdkhr.
  Russia 48°0N 43°0E **87** F6
Tsinan = Jinan *China* 36°38N 117°1E **114** F9
Tsineng *S. Africa* 27°5S 23°5E **144** D3
Tsing Yi *China* 22°21N 114°6E **111** a
Tsinghai = Qinghai □
  China 36°0N 98°0E **110** D8
Tsingtao = Qingdao
  China 36°5N 120°20E **115** F11
Tsirigo = Kythira *Greece* 36°8N 23°0E **98** E5
Tsiteli-Tsqaro = Dedoplis Tsqaro
  Georgia 41°33N 46°0E **87** K8
Tsitsikamma △ *S. Africa* 34°3S 23°40E **144** E3
Tsivilsk *Russia* 55°50N 47°25E **86** C8
Tskhinvali *Georgia* 42°14N 44°1E **87** J7
Tsna → *Russia* 54°55N 41°58E **86** D6
Tsnori *Georgia* 41°40N 45°57E **87** K7
Tso Moriri, L. *India* 32°50N 78°20E **125** C8
Tsobis *Namibia* 19°27S 17°30E **144** A2
Tsodilo Hills *Botswana* 18°49S 21°43E **144** A3
Tsogttsetsiy = Baruunsuu
  Mongolia 43°43N 105°35E **114** C3
Tsolo *S. Africa* 31°18S 28°37E **145** D4
Tsomo *S. Africa* 32°0S 27°42E **145** D4
Tsu *Japan* 34°45N 136°25E **113** G8
Tsu L. *Canada* 60°40N 111°52W **162** A6
Tsuchiura *Japan* 36°5N 140°15E **113** F10
Tsuen Wan *China* 22°22N 114°6E **111** a
Tsugaru-Hantō *Japan* 41°0N 140°30E **112** D10
Tsugaru-Kaikyō
  Japan 41°35N 141°0E **112** D10
Tsumeb *Namibia* 19°9S 17°44E **144** A2
Tsumis *Namibia* 23°39S 17°29E **144** B2
Tsuruga *Japan* 35°45N 136°2E **113** G8
Tsurugi-San *Japan* 33°51N 134°6E **113** H7
Tsuruoka *Japan* 38°44N 139°50E **112** E9
Tsushima *Gifu, Japan* 35°10N 136°43E **113** G8
Tsushima *Nagasaki,*
  Japan 34°20N 129°20E **113** G4
Tsuyama *Japan* 35°3N 134°0E **113** G7
Tsvetkovo *Ukraine* 49°8N 31°33E **85** H6
Tsyelyakhany *Belarus* 52°30N 25°46E **75** B13
Tua → *Portugal* 41°13N 7°26W **88** D3
Tuaheni Pt. *N.Z.* 38°43S 178°4E **154** E7
Tuai *N.Z.* 38°47S 177°10E **154** E6
Tuaim = Tuam *Ireland* 53°31N 8°51W **64** C3
Tuakau *N.Z.* 37°16S 174°59E **154** D6
Tual *Indonesia* 5°38S 132°44E **119** F8
Tuam *Ireland* 53°31N 8°51W **64** C3
Tuamarina *N.Z.* 41°25S 173°59E **155** B8
Tuamotu, Îs.
  French Polynesia 17°0S 144°0W **157** J13
Tuamotu Arch. = Tuamotu, Îs.
  French Polynesia 17°0S 144°0W **157** J13
Tuamotu Ridge
  Pac. Oc. 20°0S 138°0W **157** K14
Tuan Giao *Vietnam* 21°35N 103°25E **120** B4
Tuanfeng *China* 30°38N 114°52E **117** B10
Tuanxi *China* 27°28N 107°8E **116** D6
Tuao *Phil.* 17°45N 121°22E **119** A6
Tuapse *Russia* 44°5N 39°10E **87** H4
Tuas *Singapore* 1°19N 103°39E **121** d
Tuatapere *N.Z.* 46°8S 167°41E **155** G2
Tuba City *U.S.A.* 36°8N 111°14W **169** H8
Tuban *Indonesia* 6°54S 112°3E **119** G15
Tubani *Botswana* 24°46S 24°18E **144** B3
Tubarão *Brazil* 28°30S 49°0W **191** B6
Tübäs *West Bank* 32°20N 35°22E **130** C4
Tubas → *Namibia* 22°54S 14°35E **144** B2
Tübingen *Germany* 48°31N 9°4E **77** G5
Tubmanburg = Bomi
  Liberia 7°1N 10°38W **138** D2
Tubou *Fiji* 18°13S 178°48W **154** a
Tubruq *Libya* 32°7N 23°55E **135** B10
Tubuaï, Îs.
  French Polynesia 25°0S 150°0W **157** K13
Tuc Trung *Vietnam* 11°1N 107°12E **121** G6
Tucacas *Venezuela* 10°48N 68°19W **186** A4
Tucano *Brazil* 10°58S 38°48W **189** C3
T'uch'ang *Taiwan* 24°35N 121°27E **117** E13
Tuchitua *Canada* 60°55N 129°13W **162** A3
Tuchodi → *Canada* 58°17N 123°42W **162** B4
Tuchola *Poland* 53°33N 17°52E **82** E4
Tuchów *Poland* 49°54N 21°1E **83** J8
Tuckanarra *Australia* 27°7S 118°5E **149** E2
Tucker *U.S.A.* 33°51N 84°13W **178** B5
Tucson *U.S.A.* 32°13N 110°58W **169** K8
Tucumán □ *Argentina* 26°48S 66°2W **190** B2
Tucumcari *U.S.A.* 35°10N 103°44W **169** J12
Tucupita *Venezuela* 9°2N 62°3W **186** B6
Tucuruí *Brazil* 3°42S 49°44W **187** D9
Tucuruí, Represa de
  Brazil 4°0S 49°30W **187** D9
Tuczno *Poland* 53°13N 16°10E **83** E3
Tudela *Spain* 42°4N 1°39W **90** C3
Tudmur *Syria* 34°36N 38°15E **108** E6
Tudor, L. *Canada* 55°50N 65°25E **165** A6
Tudora *Romania* 47°31N 26°45E **81** C11
Tuella → *Portugal* 41°30N 7°12W **88** D3
Tuen Mun *China* 22°23N 113°57E **111** a
Tufanbeyli *Turkey* 38°15N 36°13E **104** C7
Tug Hill Plateau
  U.S.A. 43°45N 75°50W **173** C9
Tugela → *S. Africa* 29°14S 31°30E **145** D5
Tugela Falls *S. Africa* 28°48S 28°51E **145** D4
Tuguegarao *Phil.* 17°35N 121°42E **119** A6
Tugur *Russia* 53°44N 136°45E **107** D14
Tui *Spain* 42°3N 8°39W **88** C2
Tuineje *Canary Is.* 28°19N 14°3W **100** F5
Tukangbesi, Kepulauan
  Indonesia 6°0S 124°0E **119** F6
Tukarak I. *Canada* 56°15N 96°0W **161** E11
Tukayyid *Iraq* 29°47N 44°55E **128** D5
Tūkh *Egypt* 30°21N 31°12E **137** E7
Tukhlya *Ukraine* 48°55N 23°28E **81** B8
Tukituki → *N.Z.* 39°36S 176°56E **154** E6
Tukobo *Ghana* 5°1N 2°47W **138** E4
Tuktoyaktuk *Canada* 69°27N 133°2W **160** C6
Tuktut Nogait △
  Canada 69°15N 122°0W **160** D7
Tukums *Latvia* 56°58N 23°10E **82** A10
Tukuyu *Tanzania* 9°17S 33°35E **143** D3

Tula *Hidalgo, Mexico* 20°3N 99°21W **181** C5
Tula *Tamaulipas, Mexico* 23°0N 99°43W **181** C5
Tula *Nigeria* 9°51N 11°27E **139** D7
Tula *Russia* 54°13N 37°38E **84** E9
Tula → *Russia* 54°53N 37°30E **84** F9
Tulach Mhór = Tullamore
  Ireland 53°16N 7°31W **64** C4
Tulancingo *Mexico* 20°5N 98°22W **181** C5
Tulare *Serbia* 42°48N 21°28E **96** D5
Tulare *U.S.A.* 36°13N 119°21W **170** J7
Tulare Lake Bed
  U.S.A. 36°0N 119°48W **170** K7
Tularosa *U.S.A.* 33°5N 106°1W **169** K10
Tulbagh *S. Africa* 33°16S 19°6E **144** D2
Tulcán *Ecuador* 0°48N 77°43W **186** C3
Tulcea *Romania* 45°13N 28°46E **81** E13
Tulcea □ *Romania* 45°0N 28°30E **81** E13
Tulchyn *Ukraine* 48°41N 28°49E **81** B13
Tūledi Araldary
  Kazakhstan 45°2N 50°16E **87** H10
Tūleh *Iran* 34°35N 52°33E **129** C7
Tulemalu L. *Canada* 62°58N 99°25W **163** A9
Tulghes *Romania* 46°58N 25°45E **81** D10
Tuli *Zimbabwe* 21°58S 29°13E **143** C2
Tulia *U.S.A.* 34°32N 101°46W **176** D4
Tuliszków *Poland* 52°5N 18°18E **83** F5
Tulita *Canada* 64°57N 125°30W **160** E6
Tůlkarm *West Bank* 32°19N 35°2E **130** C4
Tulla *Ireland* 52°53N 8°46W **64** D3
Tullahoma *U.S.A.* 35°22N 86°13W **177** D11
Tullamore *Australia* 32°39S 147°36E **153** B7
Tullamore *Ireland* 53°16N 7°31W **64** C4
Tulle *France* 45°16N 1°46E **72** C5
Tulln an der Donau
  Austria 48°20N 16°4E **78** C9
Tullow *Ireland* 52°49N 6°45W **64** D5
Tully *Australia* 17°56S 145°55E **150** B4
Tully *U.S.A.* 42°48N 76°7W **175** D8
Tulnici *Romania* 45°51N 26°38E **81** E11
Tuloma → *Russia* 68°56N 33°0E **92** B13
Tulsa *U.S.A.* 36°10N 95°55W **176** C7
Tulsequah *Canada* 58°39N 133°35W **162** B2
Tuluá *Colombia* 4°6N 76°11W **186** C3
Tulucești *Romania* 45°34N 28°2E **81** E13
Tulun *Mexico* 20°13N 87°28W **181** C7
Tulua *Russia* 54°32N 100°35E **107** D11
Tulungagung *Indonesia* 8°5S 111°54E **119** H14
Tuma → *Nic.* 13°6N 84°35W **182** D3
Tumacacori △ *U.S.A.* 31°35N 111°6W **169** L8
Tumaco *Colombia* 1°50N 78°45W **186** C3
Tumakuru *India* 13°18N 77°6E **127** H3
Tumatumari *Guyana* 5°20N 58°55W **186** B7
Tumba *Sweden* 59°12N 17°48E **62** E11
Tumba, L.
  Dem. Rep. of the Congo 0°50S 18°0E **140** E3
Tumbarumba *Australia* 35°44S 148°0E **153** C8
Tumbaya *Argentina* 23°50S 65°26W **190** A2
Tumbes *Peru* 3°37S 80°27W **188** A1
Tumbes □ *Peru* 3°50S 80°30W **188** A1
Tumbler Ridge *Canada* 55°8N 121°0W **162** B4
Tumbwe
  Dem. Rep. of the Congo 11°25S 27°15E **143** E2
Tumby Bay *Australia* 34°21S 136°8E **152** C2
Tumd Youqi *China* 40°30N 110°30E **114** D6
Tumen *China* 43°0N 129°50E **112** C4
Tumen Jiang →
  China 42°20N 130°35E **115** C16
Tumeremo *Venezuela* 7°18N 61°30W **186** B6
Tumiritinga *Brazil* 18°58S 41°38W **189** D2
Tumkur = Tumakuru
  India 13°18N 77°6E **127** H3
Tump *Pakistan* 26°7N 62°16E **122** F3
Tumpat *Malaysia* 6°11N 102°10E **121** J4
Tumu *Ghana* 10°56N 1°56W **138** C4
Tumucumaque, Serra
  Brazil 2°0N 55°0W **187** C8
Tumupasa *Bolivia* 14°9S 67°55W **188** C4
Tumut *Australia* 35°16S 148°13E **153** C8
Tumwater *U.S.A.* 47°1N 122°54W **170** C4
Tumxuk *China* 41°22N 79°58E **109** D9
Tun Sweden *Sweden* 58°26N 12°43E **63** F6
Tunapuna
  Trin. & Tob. 10°38N 61°24W **187** K15
Tunas de Zaza *Cuba* 21°39N 79°34W **184** B4
Tunbridge Wells = Royal
  Tunbridge Wells *U.K.* 51°7N 0°16E **67** F8
Tunçbilek *Turkey* 39°37N 29°29E **99** B11
Tunceli *Turkey* 39°6N 39°31E **105** C8
Tunceli □ *Turkey* 39°5N 39°35E **105** C8
Tunchang *China* 19°21N 110°5E **117** a
Tuncurry *Australia* 32°17S 152°29E **153** B10
Tundla *India* 27°12N 78°17E **124** F8
Tundubai *Sudan* 18°36N 28°53E **137** D2
Tunduru *Tanzania* 11°8S 37°25E **143** E4
Tundzha → *Bulgaria* 41°40N 26°35E **97** E10
Tung Chung *China* 22°17N 113°57E **111** a
Tung Lung Chau *China* 22°15N 114°17E **111** a
Tungabhadra → *India* 15°57N 78°15E **127** G2
Tungabhadra Dam
  India 15°0N 75°50E **127** G2
Tungla *Nic.* 13°24N 84°21W **182** D3
Tungsha Tao = Dongsha Dao
  S. China Sea 20°45N 116°43E **111** G12
Tungshih *Taiwan* 24°12N 120°43E **117** E13
Tungsten *Canada* 61°57N 128°16W **162** A3
Tunguska, Nizhnyaya →
  Russia 65°48N 88°4E **107** C9
Tunguska, Podkamennaya →
  Russia 61°50N 90°13E **107** C10
Tuni *India* 17°22N 82°36E **126** F6
Tunica *U.S.A.* 34°41N 90°23W **177** D9
Tunis *Tunisia* 36°50N 10°11E **136** A6
Tunis □ *Tunisia* 36°50N 10°11E **136** A6
Tunis, Golfe de *Tunisia* 37°0N 10°30E **136** A6
Tunis ✈ (TUN) *Tunisia* 36°52N 10°14E **94** F3
Tunisia ■ *Africa* 33°30N 9°10E **136** B6
Tunja *Colombia* 5°33N 73°25E **186** B4
Tunkhannock *U.S.A.* 41°32N 75°57W **175** E9
Tunkinsky △ *Russia* 51°45N 102°10E **107** D11
Tunliu *China* 36°13N 112°52E **114** F7
Tunnel Creek △
  Australia 17°41S 125°18E **148** C4
Tunnsjøen *Norway* 64°45N 13°25E **60** D5
Tunungayualok I.
  Canada 56°0N 61°0W **165** A7
Tunuyán *Argentina* 33°35S 69°0W **190** C2

Tunuyán → *Argentina* 33°33S 67°30W **190** C2
Tunxi = Huangshan
  China 29°42N 118°25E **117** C12
Tuo Jiang → *China* 28°50N 105°35E **116** C5
Tuolumne *U.S.A.* 37°58N 120°15W **170** H6
Tuolumne → *U.S.A.* 37°36N 121°13W **170** H5
Tūp Āghāj *Iran* 36°3N 47°50E **105** D12
Tupã *Brazil* 21°57S 50°28W **191** A5
Tupaciguara *Brazil* 18°35S 48°42W **189** D1
Tupelo *U.S.A.* 34°16N 88°43W **177** D10
Tupik *Russia* 54°26N 119°57E **107** D12
Tupinambarana, I. *Brazil* 3°0S 58°0W **186** D7
Tupirama *Brazil* 8°58S 48°12W **189** B1
Tupiratins *Brazil* 8°23S 48°8W **189** B1
Tupiza *Bolivia* 21°30S 65°40W **190** A2
Tupman *U.S.A.* 35°18N 119°21W **171** K7
Tupper *Canada* 55°32N 120°1W **162** B4
Tupper L. *U.S.A.* 44°10N 74°32W **175** B10
Tupper Lake *U.S.A.* 44°14N 74°28W **175** B10
Tūpqarghan Muyis
  Kazakhstan 44°40N 50°19E **87** H10
Tupungato, Cerro
  S. Amer. 33°15S 69°50W **190** C2
Tuquan *China* 45°18N 121°38E **115** B11
Túquerres *Colombia* 1°5N 77°37W **186** C3
Tura *Russia* 64°20N 100°17E **107** C11
Turabah *Ḥā'il,*
  Si. Arabia 28°20N 43°15E **128** D4
Turabah *Makkah,*
  Si. Arabia 21°15N 41°34E **137** C5
Turakina *N.Z.* 40°3S 175°16E **154** D4
Turakina → *N.Z.* 40°5S 175°8E **154** C4
Turakirae Hd. *N.Z.* 41°26S 174°56E **154** H3
Tūran *Iran* 35°39N 56°42E **129** C8
Turan *Russia* 51°55N 94°0E **109** D12
Tūrān △ *Iran* 35°45N 56°30E **129** C8
Turan Lowland *Asia* 43°0N 62°0E **108** D6
Turangi *N.Z.* 38°59S 175°48E **154** E5
Ţurayf *Si. Arabia* 31°41N 38°39E **128** D3
Turbaco *Colombia* 10°20N 75°25W **186** A3
Turbat *Pakistan* 26°0N 63°20E **122** F3
Turbe *Bos.-H.* 44°15N 17°35E **80** F2
Turbeville *U.S.A.* 33°54N 80°1W **178** B9
Turbo *Colombia* 8°6N 76°43W **186** B3
Turčianske Teplice
  Slovakia 48°52N 18°52E **79** C11
Turco *Bolivia* 18°10S 68°11W **188** D4
Turcoaia *Romania* 45°7N 28°11E **81** E13
Turda *Romania* 46°34N 23°47E **81** D8
Turek *Poland* 52°3N 18°30E **83** F5
Turén *Venezuela* 9°17N 69°6W **186** B5
Turfan = Turpan
  China 43°58N 89°10E **109** D11
Turfan Basin = Turpan Pendi
  China 42°40N 89°25E **109** D11
Turfan Depression = Turpan
  Pendi *China* 42°40N 89°25E **109** D11
Turgayskaya Stolovaya Strana =
  Torghay Ustirti *Kazakhstan* 51°0N 63°0E **108** B6
Turgeon → *Canada* 50°0N 78°56W **164** C4
Turgut *Turkey* 37°22N 28°4E **99** D10
Turgutlu *Turkey* 38°30N 27°43E **99** C9
Turgutreis *Turkey* 37°0N 27°15E **99** D9
Turgwe → *Zimbabwe* 21°31S 32°15E **145** B5
Turhal *Turkey* 40°24N 36°5E **104** B7
Turia → *Spain* 39°27N 0°19W **91** F4
Turiaçu *Brazil* 1°40S 45°19W **187** D9
Turiaçu → *Brazil* 1°36S 45°19W **187** D9
Turiec → *Slovakia* 49°7N 18°55E **79** B11
Turin = Torino *Italy* 45°3N 7°40E **92** C4
Turka *Ukraine* 49°10N 23°2E **83** J10
Turkana □ *Kenya* 3°10N 35°20E **142** B4
Turkana, L. *Africa* 3°30N 36°5E **142** B4
Türkeli *Turkey* 40°30N 27°30E **97** F11
Turkestan = Türkistan
  Kazakhstan 43°17N 68°16E **109** D7
Turkestan Range *Asia* 39°35N 69°0E **109** D7
Türkeve *Hungary* 47°6N 20°44E **80** C5
Turkey ■ *Eurasia* 39°0N 36°0E **104** C7
Turkey Creek = Warmun
  Australia 17°2S 128°12E **148** C4
Turki *Russia* 52°0N 43°15E **86** E7
Türkistan *Kazakhstan* 43°17N 68°16E **109** D7
Türkmenabat
  Turkmenistan 39°6N 63°34E **129** B9
Türkmenbashi
  Turkmenistan 40°5N 53°5E **129** A7
Turkmenistan ■ *Asia* 39°0N 59°0E **108** E5
Türkmenli *Turkey* 39°45N 26°30E **99** B8
Türkoğlu *Turkey* 37°23N 36°50E **104** D7
Turks & Caicos Is. ☑
  W. Indies 21°20N 71°20W **183** B5
Turks Island Passage
  Turks & Caicos 21°25N 71°19W **183** B5
Turku *Finland* 60°30N 22°19E **84** B2
Turkwel → *Kenya* 3°6N 36°6E **142** B4
Turlock *U.S.A.* 37°30N 120°51W **170** H6
Turnagain → *Canada* 59°12N 127°35W **162** B3
Turnagain, C. *N.Z.* 40°28S 176°38E **154** G5
Turneffe Is. *Belize* 17°20N 87°50W **182** C2
Turner *Australia* 19°13S 128°12E **148** C4
Turner *U.S.A.* 48°51N 108°24W **168** B9
Turner Pt. *Australia* 11°47S 133°32E **150** A1
Turner Valley *Canada* 50°40N 114°17W **162** C6
Turners Falls *U.S.A.* 42°36N 72°33W **175** D12
Turner's Pen. *S. Leone* 8°1N 13°0W **138** D2
Turnhout *Belgium* 51°19N 4°57E **74** C4
Türnitz *Austria* 47°55N 15°29E **78** D8
Turnor L. *Canada* 56°35N 108°35W **163** B7
Turnov *Czechia* 50°34N 15°10E **78** A8
Turnu Măgurele
  Romania 43°46N 24°56E **81** G9
Turnu Roșu, P. *Romania* 45°33N 24°17E **81** E9
Turobin *Poland* 50°50N 22°44E **83** H9
Tuross Head *Australia* 36°3S 150°7E **153** C9
Turpan *China* 43°58N 89°10E **109** D11
Turpan Pendi *China* 42°40N 89°25E **109** D11
Turrawan *Australia* 30°28S 149°53E **153** A4
Turrës, Kala e *Albania* 41°10N 19°28E **96** D1
Turriff *U.K.* 57°32N 2°27W **65** D9
Tursãq *Iraq* 33°27N 45°47E **105** F11
Tursi *Italy* 40°15N 16°28E **95** B9
Tursunzoda *Tajikistan* 38°30N 68°14E **108** D7
Turtle Head I.
  Australia 10°56S 142°37E **150** A3
Turtle Is. *S. Leone* 7°40N 13°0W **138** D2
Turtle L. *Canada* 53°36N 108°38W **163** C7
Turtle Lake *U.S.A.* 47°31N 100°53W **172** B3
Turtleford *Canada* 53°23N 108°57W **162** C7

Turua *N.Z.* 37°14S 175°35E **154** D4
Turuépano △
  Venezuela 10°34N 62°43W **183** D7
Turukhansk *Russia* 65°21N 88°5E **107** C9
Turzovka *Slovakia* 49°25N 18°35E **79** B11
Tuscaloosa *U.S.A.* 33°12N 87°34W **177** E11
Tuscany = Toscana □
  Italy 43°25N 11°0E **93** C4
Tuscarawas → *U.S.A.* 40°24N 81°25W **174** F3
Tuscarora Mt. *U.S.A.* 40°55N 77°55W **174** F7
Tuscola *Ill., U.S.A.* 39°48N 88°17W **172** F10
Tuscola *Tex., U.S.A.* 32°12N 99°48W **176** E5
Tuscumbia *U.S.A.* 34°44N 87°42W **177** D11
Tuskegee *U.S.A.* 32°25N 85°42W **178** C4
Tuszyn *Poland* 51°36N 19°33E **83** G6
Tutak *Turkey* 39°31N 42°46E **105** C10
Tutayev *Russia* 57°53N 39°32E **84** B10
Tutia *India* 8°50N 78°12E **127** K4
Tutóia *Brazil* 2°45S 42°20W **189** B3
Tutong *Brunei* 4°47N 114°40E **118** D4
Tutova → *Romania* 46°7N 27°30E **81** D12
Tutrakan *Bulgaria* 44°2N 26°40E **97** B10
Tuttle Creek L. *U.S.A.* 39°15N 96°36W **172** F5
Tuttlingen *Germany* 47°58N 8°48E **77** H4
Tutuala *E. Timor* 8°25S 127°15E **119** F7
Tutuko, Mt. *N.Z.* 44°35S 168°1E **155** E3
Tutume *Botswana* 20°30S 27°5E **143** C1
Tutun *Egypt* 29°9N 30°46E **137** F7
Tuul Gol → *Mongolia* 48°30N 104°25E **110** B9
Tuva □ *Russia* 51°30N 95°0E **109** D10
Tuvalu ■ *Pac. Oc.* 8°0S 178°0E **147** B10
Tuvuca *Fiji* 17°40S 178°48W **154** a
Tuxer Alpen *Austria* 47°10N 11°45E **78** D4
Tuxpan *Mexico* 20°57N 97°24W **181** C5
Tuxtla Gutiérrez *Mexico* 16°45N 93°7W **181** D6
Tuy = Tui *Spain* 42°3N 8°39W **88** C2
Tuy Duc *Vietnam* 12°15N 107°27E **121** F6
Tuy Phong *Vietnam* 11°14N 108°43E **121** G7
Tuya L. *Canada* 59°7N 130°35W **162** B2
Tuyen Hoa *Vietnam* 17°50N 106°10E **120** D6
Tuyen Quang *Vietnam* 21°50N 105°10E **116** G5
Tuymazy *Russia* 54°36N 53°42E **108** B4
Tūysarkān *Iran* 34°33N 48°27E **105** E13
Tuz Gölü *Turkey* 38°42N 33°18E **104** C5
Tūz Khurmātū *Iraq* 34°56N 44°38E **105** E11
Tuzi *Montenegro* 42°22N 19°20E **96** D3
Tuzigoot △ *U.S.A.* 34°46N 112°2W **169** J7
Tuzla *Bos.-H.* 44°34N 18°41E **80** F3
Tuzlov → *Russia* 47°17N 39°57E **85** J10
Tuzluca *Turkey* 40°3N 43°39E **105** B10
Tuzly *Ukraine* 45°54N 30°6E **81** C16
Tvååker *Sweden* 57°4N 12°25E **63** G6
Tvardiţa *Moldova* 46°9N 28°58E **81** D10
Tvarditsa *Bulgaria* 42°42N 25°53E **97** D9
Tver *Russia* 56°55N 35°59E **84** D8
Tver □ *Russia* 56°50N 35°0E **84** D8
Tvrdošín *Slovakia* 49°21N 19°35E **79** B12
Tvrdošovce *Slovakia* 48°6N 18°4E **79** C11
Twain *U.S.A.* 40°1N 121°3W **170** E5
Twain Harte *U.S.A.* 38°2N 120°14W **170** G6
Twardogóra *Poland* 51°23N 17°28E **83** G4
Twee → *Namibia* 25°27S 19°27E **144** D2
Twee Rivier *Namibia* 25°27S 19°27E **144** D2
Tweed *Canada* 44°29N 77°19W **174** B7
Tweed → *U.K.* 55°45N 2°0W **65** F6
Tweed Heads *Australia* 28°10S 153°31E **151** D5
Tweedsmuir △ *Canada* 53°0N 126°20W **162** C3
Twentynine Palms
  U.S.A. 34°8N 116°3W **171** L10
Twillingate *Canada* 49°42N 54°45W **165** C9
Twin Bridges *U.S.A.* 45°33N 112°20W **168** D7
Twin City *U.S.A.* 32°35N 82°10W **178** C7
Twin Falls *Canada* 53°30N 64°32W **165** B7
Twin Falls *U.S.A.* 42°34N 114°28W **168** E6
Twin Lakes *U.S.A.* 30°43N 83°13W **178** E6
Twin Valley *U.S.A.* 47°16N 96°16W **172** B5
Twinsburg *U.S.A.* 41°19N 81°26W **174** E3
Twistringen *Germany* 52°48N 8°37E **76** C4
Twitchell Res. *U.S.A.* 34°59N 120°19W **171** L6
Two Harbors *U.S.A.* 47°2N 91°40W **172** B8
Two Hills *Canada* 53°43N 111°52W **162** C6
Two Rivers *U.S.A.* 44°9N 87°34W **172** C10
Two Rocks *Australia* 31°30S 115°35E **149** F2
Two Thumb Ra. *N.Z.* 43°45S 170°44E **155** D5
Twofold B. *Australia* 37°8S 149°59E **153** D8
Twyfelfontein *Namibia* 20°34S 14°22E **144** B1
Ty Ty *U.S.A.* 31°28N 83°39W **178** D6
Tyachiv *Ukraine* 48°1N 23°35E **75** D12
Tybee Island *U.S.A.* 32°1N 80°51W **178** C9
Tychy *Poland* 50°9N 18°59E **83** H5
Tyczyn *Poland* 49°58N 22°2E **83** J9
Tykocin *Poland* 53°13N 22°46E **83** D9
Tyler *Minn., U.S.A.* 44°17N 96°8W **172** C5
Tyler *Tex., U.S.A.* 32°21N 95°18W **176** E7
Tyligul → *Ukraine* 47°4N 30°57E **85** J6
Tynda *Russia* 55°10N 124°43E **107** D13
Tyndall *U.S.A.* 43°0N 97°50W **172** D5
Tyne → *U.K.* 54°59N 1°32W **66** C6
Tyne & Wear □ *U.K.* 55°6N 1°17W **66** C6
Tynec nad Sázavou
  Czechia 49°50N 14°36E **78** B7
Tynemouth *U.K.* 55°1N 1°26W **66** B6
Tyre = Sūr *Lebanon* 33°19N 35°16E **130** B4
Tyresta *Sweden* 59°12N 18°14E **62** E12
Tyrifjorden *Norway* 60°2N 10°8E **61** F14
Tyringe *Sweden* 56°9N 13°35E **63** H7
Tyrol = Tirol □ *Austria* 47°3N 10°43E **78** E3
Tyrone *Australia* 40°40N 78°14W **174** F6
Tyrone □ *U.K.* 54°38N 7°11W **64** B4
Tyrrell → *Australia* 35°26S 142°51E **152** C5
Tyrrell, L. *Australia* 35°20S 142°50E **152** C5
Tyrrell L. *Canada* 63°7N 105°27W **163** A7
Tyrrhenian Sea *Medit. S.* 40°0N 12°30E **58** G8
Tysfjorden *Norway* 68°7N 16°25E **60** B17
Tysmenytsya *Ukraine* 48°54N 24°51E **81** B9
Tystberga *Sweden* 58°51N 17°15E **63** F11
Tytuvėnai *Lithuania* 55°36N 23°12E **82** C10
Tyub Karagan, Mys =
  Tūpqarghan Muyis
  Kazakhstan 44°40N 50°19E **87** H10
Tyulenii, Ostrova = Tūledi
  Araldary *Kazakhstan* 45°2N 50°16E **87** H10
Tyuleniy, Mys
  Azerbaijan 40°28N 50°29E **87** K9
Tyuleniy *S. Africa* 34°4N 19°50E **144** E2
Tyumen *Russia* 57°11N 65°29E **108** D7
Tyup = Tūp *Kyrgyzstan* 42°45N 78°20E **109** D9
Tywi → *U.K.* 51°48N 4°21W **67** F3

Tywyn *U.K.* 52°35N 4°5W **67** E3
Tzaneen *S. Africa* 23°47S 30°9E **145** B5
Tzermiado *Greece* 35°12N 25°29E **101** D7
Tzoumérka, Óros = Athamanon
  Oros *Greece* 39°30N 21°26E **98** B3
Tzukong = Zigong
  China 29°15N 104°48E **116** C5

U

U.S.A. = United States of
  America ■ *N. Amer.* 37°0N 96°0W **167** H20
U.S. Virgin Is. ☑
  W. Indies 18°20N 65°0W **183** e
Uaimh, An = Navan
  Ireland 53°39N 6°41W **64** C5
Uainn Uen = Wanleweyne
  Somalia 2°37N 44°54E **131** G3
Uasin Gishu □ *Kenya* 0°30N 35°15E **142** D4
Uatumã → *Brazil* 2°26S 57°37W **186** D7
Uauá *Brazil* 9°50S 39°28W **189** B3
Uaupés *Brazil* 0°8S 67°5W **186** D5
Uaupés → *Brazil* 0°2N 67°16W **186** C5
Uaxactún *Guatemala* 17°25N 89°29W **182** C2
Ub *Serbia* 44°28N 20°6E **96** B4
Ubá *Brazil* 21°8S 43°0W **191** A7
Uba *Nigeria* 10°29N 13°13E **139** C7
Ubaitaba *Brazil* 14°18S 39°20W **189** D3
Ubajara △ *Brazil* 3°55S 40°50W **189** A2
Ubangi = Oubangi →
  Dem. Rep. of the Congo 0°30S 17°50E **140** E3
Ubauro *Pakistan* 28°15N 69°45E **124** E3
Ubaye → *France* 44°28N 6°18E **73** D10
Ubayyiḍ, W. al →
  Iraq 32°34N 43°48E **105** F10
Ube *Japan* 33°56N 131°15E **113** H5
Úbeda *Spain* 38°3N 3°23W **89** G7
Uberaba *Brazil* 19°50S 47°55W **189** D1
Uberlândia *Brazil* 19°0S 48°20W **189** D1
Überlingen *Germany* 47°46N 9°10E **77** H4
Ubiaja *Nigeria* 6°41N 6°22E **139** D6
Ubin, Pulau *Singapore* 1°24N 103°57E **121** d
Ubly *U.S.A.* 43°42N 82°55W **174** C2
Ubolratna Res.
  Thailand 16°45N 102°30E **120** D4
Ubombo *S. Africa* 27°31S 32°4E **145** C5
Ubon Ratchathani
  Thailand 15°15N 104°50E **120** E5
Ubondo
  Dem. Rep. of the Congo 0°55S 25°42E **142** C2
Ubort → *Belarus* 52°6N 28°30E **75** B15
Ubrique *Spain* 36°41N 5°27W **89** J5
Ubud *Indonesia* 8°30S 115°16E **119** J18
Ubundu
  Dem. Rep. of the Congo 0°22S 25°30E **142** C2
Ucar *Azerbaijan* 40°31N 47°39E **87** K8
Ucayali → *Peru* 4°30S 73°30W **188** A3
Uchab *Namibia* 19°47S 17°42E **144** A2
Uchiura-Wan *Japan* 42°25N 140°40E **112** C10
Uchiza *Peru* 8°25S 76°20W **188** B2
Uchquduq *Uzbekistan* 41°50N 62°50E **108** D6
Uchte *Germany* 52°30N 8°54E **76** C4
Uchur → *Russia* 58°48N 130°35E **107** D14
Uckermark *Germany* 53°5N 13°30E **76** B9
Ucluelet *Canada* 48°57N 125°32W **162** D3
Uda → *Russia* 54°42N 135°14E **107** D14
Uda Walawe △ *Sri Lanka* 6°20N 81°0E **127** L5
Udachny *Russia* 66°25N 112°24E **107** C12
Udagamandalam *India* 11°30N 76°44E **127** H3
Udainagar *India* 24°36N 76°44E **124** H7
Udaipur *India* 24°36N 73°44E **124** G5
Udaipur Garhi *Nepal* 27°0N 86°35E **125** F12
Udala *India* 21°35N 86°34E **125** J12
Udayagiri *Andhra Pradesh,*
  India 14°52N 79°19E **127** G4
Udayagiri *Odisha, India* 20°8N 84°22E **125** K11
Udbina *Croatia* 44°31N 15°47E **93** D12
Uddeholm *Sweden* 60°1N 13°38E **62** D7
Uddevalla *Sweden* 58°21N 11°55E **63** F5
Uddheden *Sweden* 59°57N 12°54E **62** E6
Uddjaure *Sweden* 65°57N 17°49E **60** D17
Udegeyskaya Legenda △
  Russia 45°45N 135°30E **112** B7
Uden *Neths.* 51°40N 5°37E **69** C5
Udgir *India* 18°25N 77°5E **126** E3
Udhampur *India* 33°0N 75°5E **125** C6
Udi *Nigeria* 6°17N 7°21E **139** D6
Údine *Italy* 46°3N 13°14E **93** B10
Udintsev Fracture Zone
  S. Ocean 57°0S 145°0W **96** S13
Udmurtia □ *Russia* 57°30N 52°30E **86** C9
Udon Thani *Thailand* 17°29N 102°46E **120** D4
Udong *Cambodia* 11°48N 104°45E **121** G5
Udskaya Guba
  Russia 54°50N 135°45E **107** D14
Udu Pt. *Fiji* 16°9S 179°57W **154** a
Udumalaippettai *India* 10°35N 77°15E **127** J3
Udupi *India* 13°25N 74°42E **127** H2
Udva *India* 20°5N 73°0E **126** D1
Udvoy Balkan *Bulgaria* 42°50N 26°50E **97** D10
Udzungwa △ *Tanzania* 7°52S 36°35E **142** D4
Udzungwa Range
  Tanzania 9°30S 35°10E **143** D3
Ueckermünde *Germany* 53°44N 14°1E **76** B10
Ueda *Japan* 36°24N 138°16E **113** F9
Uedineniya, Os. *Russia* 78°0N 85°0E **54** B17
Uele →
  Dem. Rep. of the Congo 3°45N 24°45E **140** D4
Uelen *Russia* 66°10N 170°0W **107** C19
Uelzen *Germany* 52°57N 10°32E **76** B6
Uetersen *Germany* 53°40N 9°40E **76** B5
Uetze *Germany* 52°28N 10°11E **76** C6
Ufa *Russia* 54°45N 55°55E **86** D10
Ufa → *Russia* 54°40N 56°0E **108** B4
Uffenheim *Germany* 49°32N 10°14E **76** G6
Ugab → *Namibia* 20°55S 13°30E **144** B1
Ugalla → *Tanzania* 5°8S 30°42E **142** D3
Ugalla River △ *Tanzania* 5°50S 31°54E **142** D3
Uganda ■ *Africa* 2°0N 32°0E **142** B3
Ugarchin *Bulgaria* 43°6N 24°9E **97** C8
Ugento *Italy* 39°55N 18°10E **95** C11
Ughelli *Nigeria* 5°33N 6°0E **139** D6
Ugie *S. Africa* 31°10S 28°13E **145** D4
Ugíjar *Spain* 36°58N 3°7W **89** H7
Ugine *France* 45°45N 6°25E **73** C10
Uglegorsk *Russia* 49°5N 142°2E **107** E15
Uglich *Russia* 57°33N 38°20E **84** C10
Ugljan *Croatia* 44°12N 15°10E **93** D12
Ugljane *Croatia* 43°35N 16°46E **93** E13
Ugljevik *Bos.-H.* 44°40N 19°20E **81** F4
Ugol'noye = Beringovskiy
  Russia 63°3N 179°19E **107** C18
Ugolnye Kopi *Russia* 64°44N 177°42E **107** C18
Ugra → *Russia* 54°30N 36°7E **84** E9

Ugra △ *Russia* 54°45N 35°30E **84** D9
Uh → *Slovakia* 48°37N 22°0E **79** C15
Uherské Hradiště
  Czechia 49°4N 17°30E **79** B10
Uherský Brod *Czechia* 49°1N 17°40E **79** B10
Úhlava → *Czechia* 49°45N 13°24E **78** B6
Uhlenhorst *Namibia* 23°45S 17°55E **144** B2
Uhniv *Ukraine* 50°22N 23°45E **83** H10
Uhrichsville *U.S.A.* 40°24N 81°21W **174** F3
Uibhist a Deas = South Uist
  U.K. 57°20N 7°15W **65** D1
Uibhist a Tuath = North Uist
  U.K. 57°40N 7°15W **65** D1
Uíge *Angola* 7°30S 14°40E **140** F2
Uijeongbu *S. Korea* 37°48N 127°0E **115** F14
Ŭiju *N. Korea* 40°15N 124°35E **115** D13
Uinta Mts. *U.S.A.* 40°45N 110°30W **168** F8
Uiseong *S. Korea* 36°21N 128°45E **115** F15
Uitenhage *S. Africa* 33°40S 25°28E **144** E4
Uithuizen *Neths.* 53°24N 6°41E **69** A6
Ujazd *Poland* 50°23N 18°21E **83** H5
Újfehértó *Hungary* 47°49N 21°41E **80** C6
Ujh → *India* 32°10N 75°18E **124** C6
Ujhani *India* 28°0N 79°6E **125** E8
Uji-guntō *Japan* 31°15N 129°25E **113** J4
Ujjain *India* 23°9N 75°43E **124** H6
Uiście *Poland* 53°3N 16°58E **83** E3
Ujście Warty △ *Poland* 52°35N 14°44E **83** F1
Újszász *Hungary* 47°19N 20°7E **80** C5
Ujung Kulon △
  Indonesia 6°46S 105°19E **119** G11
Ujung Pandang = Makassar
  Indonesia 5°10S 119°20E **119** F5
Uka *Russia* 57°50N 162°0E **107** D17
Ukai Sagar *India* 21°20N 73°43E **126** D1
Ukara I. *Tanzania* 1°50S 33°0E **142** C3
Uke-Shima *Japan* 28°2N 129°14E **113** K4
Ukerewe I. *Tanzania* 2°0S 33°0E **142** C3
uKhahlamba Drakensberg →
  S. Africa 29°27S 29°30E **145** D4
Ukholovo *Russia* 53°47N 40°30E **86** D5
Ukhrul *India* 25°10N 94°25E **123** G19
Ukhta *Russia* 63°34N 53°41E **106** C6
Ukiah *U.S.A.* 39°9N 123°13W **170** F3
Ukkusiksalik △
  Canada 65°20N 89°30W **160** D14
Ukmergė *Lithuania* 55°15N 24°45E **84** E3
Ukraine ■ *Europe* 49°0N 32°0E **85** H7
Ukwi *Botswana* 23°29S 20°30E **144** B3
Ula *Turkey* 37°6N 28°25E **104** D3
Ulaan Nuur *Mongolia* 44°30N 103°40E **114** B2
Ulaan-Uul *Mongolia* 46°4N 100°49E **110** B9
Ulaanbaatar
  Mongolia 47°55N 106°53E **110** B10
Ulaangom *Mongolia* 50°5N 92°10E **109** B12
Ulaanjirem *Mongolia* 45°5N 105°30E **114** B3
Ulak I. *U.S.A.* 51°22N 178°57W **166** E4
Ulamambri *Australia* 31°19S 149°23E **153** A8
Ulamba
  Dem. Rep. of the Congo 9°3S 23°38E **143** D1
Ulan Bator = Ulaanbaatar
  Mongolia 47°55N 106°53E **110** B10
Ulan Erge *Russia* 46°19N 44°53E **87** G7
Ulan Khol *Russia* 45°18N 47°4E **87** H8
Ulan Ude *Russia* 51°45N 107°40E **111** A10
Ulanhad = Chifeng
  China 42°18N 118°58E **115** C12
Ulanhot = Horqin Youyi Qianqi
  China 46°32N 122°3E **115** A12
Ulanów *Poland* 50°30N 22°16E **83** H9
Ulansuhai Nur *China* 40°53N 108°51E **114** D5
Ulas *Sivas, Turkey* 39°26N 37°2E **104** C7
Ulaş *Tekirdağ, Turkey* 41°14N 27°42E **97** F11
Ulaya *Morogoro, Tanzania* 7°3S 36°55E **142** D4
Ulaya *Tabora, Tanzania* 4°25S 33°30E **142** C3
Ulcinj *Montenegro* 41°58N 19°10E **96** E3
Ulco *S. Africa* 28°21S 24°15E **144** C3
Ule älv = Oulujoki →
  Finland 65°1N 25°30E **60** D21
Ule träsk = Oulujärvi
  Finland 64°25N 27°15E **60** D22
Uleåborg = Oulu *Finland* 65°1N 25°29E **60** D21
Ulefoss *Norway* 59°17N 9°16E **61** G13
Ulëz *Albania* 41°46N 19°54E **96** E3
Ulfborg *Denmark* 56°16N 8°20E **63** H2
Ulhasnagar *India* 19°15N 73°10E **126** E1
Uliastay *Mongolia* 47°56N 97°28E **110** B8
Uljin *S. Korea* 36°59N 129°24E **115** F15
Uljma *Serbia* 45°2N 21°10E **80** E6
Ülken Kazakhstan *Kazakhstan* 45°12N 73°58E **109** E8
Ülken Borsyq Qumy
  Kazakhstan 47°0N 59°11E **108** C5
Ulla → *Spain* 42°39N 8°44W **88** C2
Ulladulla *Australia* 35°21S 150°29E **153** C9
Ullal *India* 12°48N 74°51E **127** H2
Ullapool *U.K.* 57°54N 5°9W **65** D3
Ullared *Sweden* 57°8N 12°42E **63** G6
Ulldecona *Spain* 40°36N 0°20E **90** E5
Ulleungdo *S. Korea* 37°30N 130°30E **113** F5
Ullswater *Canada* 45°12N 79°29W **174** A5
Ullswater *U.K.* 54°34N 2°52W **66** C5
Ulm *Germany* 48°23N 9°58E **77** G5
Ulmarra *Australia* 29°37S 153°4E **151** D5
Ulmeni *Buzău, Romania* 45°4N 26°40E **81** E11
Ulmeni *Maramureș,*
  Romania 47°28N 23°18E **81** C8
Ulongué *Mozam.* 14°37S 34°19E **143** E3
Ulricehamn *Sweden* 57°46N 13°26E **63** G7
Ulrika *Sweden* 58°5N 15°23E **63** F9
Ulsan *S. Korea* 35°20N 129°15E **115** G15
Ulsta *U.K.* 60°30N 1°9W **65** A7
Ulster □ *U.K.* 54°30N 6°30W **64** B5
Ulstrem *Bulgaria* 42°22N 26°41E **97** D10
Ultima *Australia* 35°30S 143°18E **152** C5
Ulua → *Honduras* 15°48N 87°46W **182** C2
Ulubat Gölü *Turkey* 40°9N 28°35E **97** F12
Ulubey *Turkey* 38°4N 29°33E **99** C11
Uluborlu *Turkey* 38°4N 30°28E **99** C12
Uluçınar *Turkey* 36°25N 35°53E **104** D6
Uludağ *Turkey* 40°4N 29°13E **97** F13
Uludağ △ *Turkey* 40°5N 29°12E **97** F13
Uludere *Turkey* 37°28N 42°42E **105** D10
Uluguru Mts. *Tanzania* 7°15S 37°40E **142** D4
Ulukhaktok *Canada* 70°44N 117°44W **160** C8
Uluki§la *Turkey* 37°35N 34°36E **104** D6
Ulul *Micronesia* 8°25S 149°4E ...
Ulungur He → *China* 47°1N 87°24E **109** C6
Ulungur Hu *China* 47°20N 87°10E **109** B6

Uluru *Australia* 25°23S 131°5E **149** E5
Uluru-Kata Tjuta △
  Australia 25°19S 131°1E **149** E5
Uluwatu *Indonesia* 8°50S 115°5E **119** K18
Ulva *U.K.* 56°29N 6°13W **66** C2
Ulverston *U.K.* 54°13N 3°5W **66** C4
Ulverstone *Australia* 41°11S 146°11E **151** G4
Ulya *Russia* 59°10N 142°0E **107** D15
Ulyanovo *Russia* 54°50N 22°6E **82** D9
Ulyanovsk *Russia* 54°20N 48°25E **86** C9
Ulyanovsk □ *Russia* 54°5N 48°5E **86** C9
Ulyasutay = Uliastay
  Mongolia 47°56N 97°28E **110** B8
Ulysses *Kans., U.S.A.* 37°35N 101°22W **172** G3
Ulysses *Pa., U.S.A.* 41°54N 77°46W **174** E7
Ulysses, Mt. *Canada* 57°20N 124°5W **162** B4
Ulytau *Kazakhstan* 48°39N 67°1E **109** C7
Ulyzhylanshyq →
  Kazakhstan 48°51N 63°46E **108** C6
Umag *Croatia* 45°26N 13°31E **93** C10
Umala *Bolivia* 17°25S 68°5W **188** D4
'Umān = Oman ■ *Asia* 23°0N 58°0E **131** C6
Uman *Ukraine* 48°40N 30°12E **75** D16
Umaria *India* 23°35N 80°50E **125** H9
Umarkhed *India* 19°37N 77°46E **126** E3
Umarkot *Pakistan* 25°15N 69°40E **124** G3
Umarpada *India* 21°27N 73°30E **124** J5
Umatilla *U.S.A.* 45°55N 119°21W **168** D4
Umbagog L. *U.S.A.* 44°46N 71°3W **175** B13
Umbakumba *Australia* 13°47S 136°50E **150** A2
Umbértide *Italy* 43°18N 12°20E **93** E9
Umbrella Mts. *N.Z.* 45°35S 169°5E **155** F4
Umbria □ *Italy* 42°45N 12°30E **93** F9
Umeå *Sweden* 63°45N 20°20E **60** E19
Umeälven → *Sweden* 63°45N 20°20E **60** E19
Umera *Indonesia* 0°12S 129°37E **119** E7
Umfuli → *Zimbabwe* 17°30S 29°23E **143** F2
Umfurudzi △ *Zimbabwe* 17°6S 31°40E **143** F3
Umgusa *Zimbabwe* 19°29S 27°52E **143** F2
Umgwenya → *Mozam.* 25°14S 32°18E **145** C5
Umiujaq *Canada* 56°33N 76°33W **164** A4
Umka *Serbia* 44°40N 20°19E **96** B4
Umkomaas *S. Africa* 30°13S 30°48E **145** D5
Umlazi *S. Africa* 29°59S 30°54E **141** L6
Umm ad Daraj, J.
  Jordan 32°18N 35°48E **130** C4
Umm al Khashab
  Si. Arabia 17°23N 42°32E **137** D5
Umm al Qaywayn
  U.A.E. 25°30N 55°35E **129** E7
Umm al Qittayn *Jordan* 32°18N 36°40E **130** C5
Umm al Rasas *Jordan* 31°30N 35°55E **130** D4
Umm Bāb *Qatar* 25°12N 50°48E **129** E6
Umm Birkah *Si. Arabia* 27°44N 36°31E **137** B4
Umm Durman = Omdurmân
  Sudan 15°40N 32°28E **135** E12
Umm el Fahm *Israel* 32°31N 35°9E **130** C4
Umm el Kert, Khalig
  Egypt 23°40N 35°35E **128** F2
Umm Keddada *Sudan* 13°33N 26°35E **135** F11
Umm Lajj *Si. Arabia* 25°0N 37°23E **128** E3
Umm Qasr *Iraq* 30°1N 47°58E **128** D5
Umm Ruwaba *Sudan* 12°50N 31°20E **135** F12
Umm Sa'id *Qatar* 25°0N 51°33E **129** E6
Umm Tais △ *Qatar* 26°7N 51°15E **129** E6
Umm Urūmah
  Si. Arabia 25°43N 36°35E **137** B4
Umm Zehetir *Egypt* 28°48N 32°31E **137** F8
Umnak I. *U.S.A.* 53°15N 168°20W **166** E6
Umniati → *Zimbabwe* 16°49S 28°45E **143** F2
Umpqua → *U.S.A.* 43°40N 124°12W **168** E1
Umred *India* 20°51N 79°18E **126** D4
Umreth *India* 22°41N 73°4E **124** H5
Umri *India* 17°30N 77°39E **126** E3
Umtata = Mthatha
  S. Africa 31°36S 28°49E **145** D4
Umuahia *Nigeria* 5°31N 7°26E **139** D6
Umuarama *Brazil* 23°45S 53°20W **191** A5
Umurbey *Turkey* 40°13N 26°36E **97** F10
Umvukwe Ra.
  Zimbabwe 16°45S 30°45E **143** F3
Umzimvubu → *S. Africa* 31°38S 29°33E **145** D4
Umzingwane →
  Zimbabwe 22°12S 29°56E **143** G2
Umzinto = eMuziwezinto
  S. Africa 30°15S 30°45E **145** D5
Una → *Bos.-H.* 20°46N 71°8E **124** J4
Unac → *Bos.-H.* 44°30N 16°9E **93** D13
Unadilla *Ga., U.S.A.* 32°16N 83°44W **178** C6
Unadilla *N.Y., U.S.A.* 42°20N 75°19W **175** D9
Unaí *Brazil* 16°23S 46°53W **189** D1
Unalakleet *U.S.A.* 63°52N 160°47W **166** C7
Unalaska *U.S.A.* 53°53N 166°32W **166** E6
Unalaska I. *U.S.A.* 53°35N 166°50W **166** E6
'Unayzah *Si. Arabia* 26°6N 43°58E **128** E4
'Unayzah, J. *Asia* 32°12N 39°18E **105** E8
Uncastillo *Spain* 42°21N 1°8W **90** C3
Uncía *Bolivia* 18°25S 66°40W **186** G5
Uncompahgre Peak
  U.S.A. 38°4N 107°28W **168** G10
Uncompahgre Plateau
  U.S.A. 38°20N 108°15W **168** G9
Undara Volcanic △
  Australia 18°14S 144°41E **150** B3
Unden *Sweden* 58°45N 14°25E **63** F8
Underbool *Australia* 35°10S 141°51E **152** C4
Undersåker *Sweden* 63°19N 13°21E **62** A7
Underwood *Canada* 44°18N 81°29W **174** B3
Unecha *Russia* 52°50N 32°37E **85** F7
Ungarie *Australia* 33°38S 146°56E **153** B7
Ungarra *Australia* 34°12S 136°2E **152** B2
Ungava, Pén. d' *Canada* 60°0N 74°0W **161** F17
Ungava B. *Canada* 59°30N 67°30W **161** F18
Ungeny = Ungheni
  Moldova 47°11N 27°51E **81** C12
Unggi *N. Korea* 42°16N 130°28E **116** C5
Ungheni *Moldova* 47°11N 27°51E **81** C12
Unguja = Zanzibar
  Tanzania 6°12S 39°12E **142** D4
Ungwana B. *Kenya* 2°45S 40°20E **142** C5
Uni *Russia* 57°46N 51°31E **86** B10
União *Brazil* 4°35S 42°52W **189** A2
União da Vitória *Brazil* 26°13S 51°5W **191** B5
União dos Palmares
  Brazil 9°10S 36°2W **189** B3
Uničov *Czechia* 49°46N 17°8E **83** D9
Uniejów *Poland* 51°59N 18°46E **83** G5
Unije *Croatia* 44°40N 14°15E **93** D11
Unimak I. *U.S.A.* 54°45N 164°0W **166** E7
Unimak Pass. *U.S.A.* 54°15N 164°30W **166** E7
Union *Miss., U.S.A.* 32°34N 89°7W **177** E10

Union *Mo., U.S.A.* 38°27N 91°0W **172** F8
Union *S.C., U.S.A.* 34°43N 81°37W **177** D14
Union City *Calif.,*
  U.S.A. 37°36N 122°1W **170** H4
Union City *Ga., U.S.A.* 33°35N 84°33W **178** B5
Union City *N.J., U.S.A.* 40°45N 74°2W **175** F10
Union City *Pa., U.S.A.* 41°54N 79°51W **174** E5
Union City *Tenn.,*
  U.S.A. 36°26N 89°3W **177** C10
Union Dale *U.S.A.* 41°43N 75°29W **175** E9
Union Gap *U.S.A.* 46°33N 120°28W **168** C3
Union Park *U.S.A.* 28°34N 81°17W **179** G8
Union Point *U.S.A.* 33°37N 83°4W **178** B6
Union Springs *Ala.,*
  U.S.A. 32°9N 85°43W **178** E4
Union Springs *N.Y.,*
  U.S.A. 42°50N 76°41W **175** D8
Uniondale *S. Africa* 33°39S 23°7E **144** D3
Uniontown *U.S.A.* 39°54N 79°44W **173** F14
Unionville *Ga., U.S.A.* 31°26N 83°30W **178** D6
Unionville *Mo., U.S.A.* 40°29N 93°1W **172** E7
Unirea *Romania* 44°15N 27°35E **81** F12
United Arab Emirates ■
  Asia 23°50N 54°0E **129** F7
United Kingdom ■ *Europe* 53°0N 2°0W **68** E6
United States of America ■
  N. Amer. 37°0N 96°0W **167** H20
Unity *Canada* 52°30N 109°5W **163** C7
Universales, Mtes. *Spain* 40°18N 1°33W **90** E3
University Park
  U.S.A. 32°17N 106°45W **169** K10
University Place
  U.S.A. 47°14N 122°33W **170** C4
Unjha *India* 23°46N 72°24E **124** H5
Unna *Germany* 51°32N 7°42E **76** D3
Unnao *India* 26°35N 80°30E **125** F9
Uno, Ilha *Guinea-Biss.* 11°15N 16°13W **138** C1
Unsengedsi →
  Zimbabwe 15°43S 31°14E **143** F3
Unst *U.K.* 60°44N 0°53W **65** A8
Unstrut → *Germany* 51°10N 11°48E **76** D7
Unterfranken □ *Germany* 50°0N 10°0E **77** F5
Unterschleissheim
  Germany 48°17N 11°34E **77** G7
Unuk → *Canada* 56°5N 131°3W **162** B2
Ünye *Turkey* 41°5N 37°15E **104** B7
Unzen-Amakusa △
  Japan 32°15N 130°10E **113** H5
Unzha *Russia* 58°0N 44°0E **86** A7
Unzha → *Russia* 57°49N 43°47E **86** B6
Uong Bi *Vietnam* 21°2N 106°47E **120** B6
Uotsuri-Shima
  E. China Sea 25°45N 123°29E **113** M1
Uozu *Japan* 36°48N 137°24E **113** A5
Upata *Venezuela* 8°1N 62°24W **186** B6
Upatoi Cr. → *U.S.A.* 32°22N 84°58W **178** C5
Upemba, L.
  Dem. Rep. of the Congo 8°30S 26°20E **143** D2
Upemba △
  Dem. Rep. of the Congo 9°0S 26°35E **143** D2
Upernavik *Greenland* 72°49N 56°20W **57** C5
Upington *S. Africa* 28°25S 21°15E **144** D3
Upleta *India* 21°46N 70°16E **124** J4
'Upolu *Samoa* 13°58S 172°0W **147** C11
Upper Alkali L. *U.S.A.* 41°47N 120°8W **168** F3
Upper Arrow L.
  Canada 50°30N 117°50W **162** C5
Upper Daly △ *Australia* 14°26S 131°3E **148** B5
Upper Darby *U.S.A.* 39°55N 75°16W **173** F16
Upper East □ *Ghana* 10°30N 1°0W **139** C4
Upper Foster L.
  Canada 56°47N 105°20W **163** B7
Upper Hutt *N.Z.* 41°8S 175°5E **154** H4
Upper Klamath L.
  U.S.A. 42°25N 121°55W **168** E3
Upper Lake *U.S.A.* 39°10N 122°54W **170** F4
Upper Liard *Canada* 60°3N 128°54W **162** A3
Upper Manilla
  Australia 30°38S 150°40E **153** A9
Upper Manzanilla
  Trin. & Tob. 10°31N 61°4W **187** K15
Upper Missouri Breaks △
  U.S.A. 47°50N 109°55W **168** C9
Upper Musquodoboit
  Canada 45°10N 62°58W **165** C7
Upper Red L. *U.S.A.* 48°8N 94°45W **172** A6
Upper Sandusky
  U.S.A. 40°50N 83°17W **173** E12
Upper Volta = Burkina Faso ■
  Africa 12°0N 1°0W **138** C4
Upper West □ *Ghana* 10°30N 2°20W **138** C4
Upphärad *Sweden* 58°9N 12°19E **63** F6
Uppland *Sweden* 59°59N 17°48E **62** C12
Upplands-Väsby
  Sweden 59°31N 17°54E **62** C11
Uppsala *Sweden* 59°53N 17°38E **62** E11
Uppsala □ *Sweden* 60°0N 17°30E **62** D11
Upshi *India* 33°48N 77°52E **125** C7
Upton *U.S.A.* 44°6N 104°38W **168** D11
Uqsuqtuuq = Gjoa Haven
  Canada 68°38N 95°53W **160** D12
Ur *Iraq* 30°55N 46°25E **128** D5
Ura-Tyube = Istaravshān
  Tajikistan 39°55N 69°1E **109** E7
Urad Qianqi *China* 40°40N 108°30E **114** D5
Uraricoera *Brazil* 42°50N 143°40E **112** C11
Urakawa *Japan* 42°9N 142°47E **112** C11
Ural = Uralskiy □ *Russia* 60°0N 59°0E **58** C10
Ural = Zhayyq →
  Kazakhstan 47°0N 51°48E **108** C4
Ural *Australia* 33°21S 146°12E **153** B7
Ural Mts. = Uralskie Gory
  Eurasia 60°0N 59°0E **58** C17
Uralla *Australia* 30°37S 151°29E **153** A9
Uralsk = Oral
  Kazakhstan 51°20N 51°20E **86** E10
Uralskie Gory *Eurasia* 60°0N 59°0E **58** C17
Uralskiy □ *Russia* 64°0N 70°0E **106** C7
Urambo *Tanzania* 5°4S 32°0E **142** D3
Urana *Australia* 35°15S 146°21E **153** C7
Urana, L. *Australia* 35°16S 146°10E **152** C6
Urandangi *Australia* 21°32S 138°14E **150** C2
Uranga *Australia* 30°31S 153°1E **153** A10
Uranium City *Canada* 59°34N 108°37W **163** B7
Urapuntja = Utopia
  Australia 22°14S 134°33E **150** C1
Uraricoera → *Brazil* 3°2N 60°30W **186** C6
Urasoe *Japan* 26°15N 127°43E **113** L3
Uravakonda *India* 14°57N 77°12E **127** G3
Urawa = Saitama
  Japan 35°54N 139°38E **113** G9
Uray *Russia* 60°5N 65°15E **106** C7

'Uray'irah *Si. Arabia* 25°57N 48°53E **129** E6
Urbana *Ill., U.S.A.* 40°7N 88°12W **172** E9
Urbana *Ohio, U.S.A.* 40°7N 83°45W **173** E12
Urbandale *U.S.A.* 41°38N 93°43W **172** E7
Urbánia *Italy* 43°40N 12°31E **93** E9
Urbano Santos *Brazil* 3°12S 43°23W **189** A2
Urbino *Italy* 43°43N 12°38E **93** E9
Urbión, Picos de *Spain* 42°1N 2°52W **90** C2
Urcos *Peru* 13°40S 71°38W **188** C3
Urdinarrain *Argentina* 32°37S 58°52W **190** C4
Urdos *France* 42°51N 0°35W **73** F3
Ure → *U.K.* 54°5N 1°20W **66** C6
Uren *Russia* 57°35N 45°55E **86** B7
Urengoy *Russia* 65°58N 78°22E **106** C8
Ures *Mexico* 29°26N 110°24W **180** B2
Urewera △ *N.Z.* 38°29S 177°7E **154** C6
Urfa = Sanliurfa *Turkey* 37°12N 38°50E **105** D8
Urganch *Uzbekistan* 41°40N 60°41E **108** D6
Urgench = Urganch
  Uzbekistan 41°40N 60°41E **108** D6
Ürgüp *Turkey* 38°38N 34°56E **104** C6
Urho Kekkonen △
  Finland 68°20N 27°40E **60** B22
Uri *India* 34°8N 74°2E **125** B6
Uri □ *Switz.* 46°43N 8°35E **77** J4
Uribia *Colombia* 11°43N 72°16W **186** A4
Uricani *Romania* 45°20N 23°9E **80** E8
Uriondo *Bolivia* 21°41S 64°41W **190** A3
Urique *Mexico* 27°13N 107°55W **180** B3
Urique → *Mexico* 26°29N 107°58W **180** B3
Urk *Neths.* 52°39N 5°36E **69** B5
Urkiola △ *Spain* 43°6N 1°2W **90** B3
Urla *Turkey* 38°20N 26°47E **99** C8
Urlaţi *Romania* 44°59N 26°15E **81** F11
Urmia = Orūmīyeh
  Iran 37°40N 45°0E **105** D11
Uromi *Nigeria* 6°42N 6°20E **139** D6
Uroševac = Ferizaj
  Kosovo 42°23N 21°10E **96** D5
Urrampinyi Iltjiltarri ◇
  Australia 24°20S 132°10E **148** D5
Urshult *Sweden* 56°31N 14°50E **63** H8
Uru Uru, L. *Bolivia* 18°6S 67°8W **188** D4
Uruaçu *Brazil* 14°30S 49°10W **187** F9
Uruapan *Mexico* 19°24N 102°3W **180** D4
Urubamba *Peru* 13°20S 72°10W **188** C3
Urubamba → *Peru* 10°43S 73°48W **188** C3
Urucará *Brazil* 2°32S 57°45W **186** D7
Uruçui *Brazil* 7°20S 44°28W **189** B2
Uruçui, Serra do *Brazil* 9°0S 44°45W **189** B2
Uruçui Prêto → *Brazil* 7°25S 44°38W **189** B2
Urucuia → *Brazil* 16°8S 45°9W **189** E2
Uruguai → *Brazil* 26°0S 53°30W **191** B5
Uruguaiana *Brazil* 29°50S 57°0W **190** B4
Uruguay ■ *S. Amer.* 32°30S 56°30W **190** C4
Uruguay → *S. Amer.* 34°12S 58°18W **190** C4
Urumchi = Ürümqi
  China 43°45N 87°45E **108** D11
Ürümqi *China* 43°45N 87°45E **108** D11
Uruna △ *Australia* 24°3S 133°1E **148** D5
Urup → *Russia* 45°0N 41°10E **87** H5
Urup, Ostrov *Russia* 46°0N 151°0E **107** E16
Urus-Martan *Russia* 43°8N 45°33E **87** J7
Urutaí *Brazil* 17°28S 48°12W **189** D1
Uryupinsk *Russia* 50°45N 41°58E **86** E5
Ürzhar *Kazakhstan* 47°5N 81°38E **109** C10
Urzhum *Russia* 57°10N 49°56E **86** B9
Urziceni *Romania* 44°40N 26°42E **81** F11
Usa → *Russia* 66°16N 59°49E **106** C6
Uşak *Turkey* 38°43N 29°28E **99** C11
Uşak □ *Turkey* 38°30N 29°0E **99** C11
Usakos *Namibia* 21°54S 15°31E **144** B2
Usborne, Mt. *Falk. Is.* 51°40S 59°55W **192** D5
Ušče *Serbia* 43°30N 20°40E **96** C4
Usedom *Germany* 53°55N 14°2E **76** B10
Usedom □ *Germany* 53°55N 14°0E **76** B10
Useless Loop *Australia* 26°8S 113°23E **149** E1
'Usfān *Si. Arabia* 21°58N 39°27E **137** C4
Ushakova, Ostrov *Russia* 82°0N 80°0E **107** A8
Ushakovo *Russia* 54°37N 20°16E **82** D7
Ushant = Ouessant, Î. d'
  France 48°28N 5°6W **70** D1
Ūsharal *Kazakhstan* 46°10N 80°56E **109** C10
Ushashi *Tanzania* 1°59S 33°57E **142** C3
'Ushayrah *Ar Riyāḍ,*
  Si. Arabia 25°35N 45°47E **128** E5
'Ushayrah *Makkah,*
  Si. Arabia 21°46N 40°42E **137** C5
Ushibuka *Japan* 32°11N 130°1E **113** H5
Ūshtöbe *Kazakhstan* 45°16N 78°0E **109** C9
Ushuaia *Argentina* 54°50S 68°23W **192** G3
Ushumun *Russia* 52°47N 126°32E **107** D13
Ushytsya → *Ukraine* 48°35N 27°8E **81** B12
Usinsk *Russia* 65°57N 57°27E **106** C6
Usk *Canada* 54°38N 128°26W **162** C3
Usk → *U.K.* 51°33N 2°58W **67** F5
Usk *India* 27°12N 83°7E **125** F10
Üsküdar *Turkey* 41°1N 29°0E **97** F13
Uslar *Germany* 51°39N 9°38E **76** D5
Usman *Russia* 52°5N 39°48E **85** F10
Usoke *Tanzania* 5°8S 32°24E **142** D3
Usolye-Sibirskoye
  Russia 52°48N 103°40E **107** D11
Usoro *Russia* 55°33N 6°11E **139** D6
Uspallata, P. de
  Argentina 32°37S 69°22W **190** C2
Ussel *France* 45°32N 2°18E **72** D5
Usson-du-Poitou *France* 46°16N 0°31E **72** B4
Ussuriysk *Russia* 43°48N 131°59E **112** C5
Ussurka *Russia* 45°12N 133°31E **112** B6
Ust-Buzulukskaya *Russia* 50°8N 42°11E **86** E6
Ust-Chaun *Russia* 68°47N 170°30E **107** C18
Ust-Chorna *Ukraine* 48°19N 23°56E **81** B8
Ust-Donetskiy *Russia* 47°35N 40°55E **87** G5
Ust-Ilimsk *Russia* 58°3N 102°39E **107** D11
Ust-Ishim *Russia* 57°45N 71°10E **106** D8
Ust-Kamchatsk
  Russia 56°10N 162°28W **107** D17
Ust-Kamenogorsk = Öskemen
  Kazakhstan 50°0N 82°36E **109** C10
Ust-Khayryuzovo
  Russia 57°15N 156°45E **107** D16
Ust-Kut *Russia* 56°50N 105°42E **107** D11
Ust-Kuyga *Russia* 70°1N 135°43E **107** B14
Ust-Labinsk *Russia* 45°15N 39°41E **87** H4
Ust-Luga *Russia* 59°35N 28°20E **84** C5

Ust-Maya *Russia* 60°30N 134°28E **107** C14
Ust-Mil *Russia* 59°40N 133°11E **107** D14
Ust-Nera *Russia* 64°35N 143°15E **107** C15
Ust-Nyukzha *Russia* 56°34N 121°37E **107** D13
Ust-Olenek *Russia* 73°0N 120°5E **107** B12
Ust-Omchug *Russia* 61°9N 149°38E **107** C15
Ust-Port *Russia* 69°40N 84°26E **106** C9
Ust-Tsilma *Russia* 65°28N 52°11E **106** C6
Ust-Urt = Ustyurt Plateau
  Asia 44°0N 55°0E **108** D5
Ustaritz *France* 43°24N 1°27W **72** E2
Ústecký □ *Czechia* 50°30N 14°0E **78** A7
Uster *Switz.* 47°22N 8°43E **77** H4
Ústí nad Labem *Czechia* 50°41N 14°3E **78** A7
Ústí nad Orlicí *Czechia* 49°58N 16°24E **79** B9
Ústica *Italy* 38°42N 13°11E **94** D6
Ustinov = Izhevsk
  Russia 56°51N 53°14E **106** D6
Ustka *Poland* 54°35N 16°55E **82** B3
Ustroń *Poland* 49°43N 18°48E **83** D5
Ustrzyki Dolne *Poland* 49°27N 22°40E **83** J9
Ustyluh *Ukraine* 50°51N 24°10E **83** H11
Ustyurt Plateau *Asia* 44°0N 55°0E **108** D5
Ustyuzhna *Russia* 58°50N 36°32E **84** C9
Usu *China* 44°27N 84°40E **109** D10
Usuki *Japan* 33°8N 131°49E **113** H5
Usulután *El Salv.* 13°25N 88°28W **182** D2
Usumacinta →
  Mexico 18°24N 92°38W **181** D6
Usumbura = Bujumbura
  Burundi 3°16S 29°18E **142** C2
Usure *Tanzania* 4°40S 34°22E **142** C3
Usutuo → *Mozam.* 26°48S 32°7E **145** C5
Uta *Indonesia* 4°33S 136°0E **119** E9
Utah □ *U.S.A.* 39°20N 111°30W **168** G8
Utah L. *U.S.A.* 40°12N 111°48W **168** F8
Utansjö *Sweden* 62°46N 17°55E **62** B11
Utara, Selat *Malaysia* 5°28N 100°20E **121** c
Utarni *India* 26°5N 71°58E **124** F4
Utatlan *Guatemala* 15°2N 91°11W **182** C1
Ute Creek → *U.S.A.* 35°21N 103°50W **169** J12
Utebo *Spain* 41°43N 1°0W **90** D3
Utena *Lithuania* 55°27N 25°40E **84** E3
Utete *Tanzania* 8°0S 38°45E **142** D4
Uthai Thani *Thailand* 15°22N 100°3E **120** E3
Uthal *Pakistan* 25°44N 66°40E **124** G2
Utiariti *Brazil* 13°0S 58°10W **186** F7
Utica *N.Y., U.S.A.* 43°6N 75°14W **175** C9
Utica *Ohio, U.S.A.* 40°14N 82°27W **174** F2
Utiel *Spain* 39°37N 1°11W **91** F3
Utikuma L. *Canada* 55°50N 115°30W **162** B5
Utila *Honduras* 16°6N 86°56W **182** C2
Utinga *Brazil* 12°6S 41°9W **189** C3
Utkela *India* 20°6N 83°10E **126** D6
Utländen *Sweden* 56°2N 15°48E **63** H9
Utnur *India* 19°22N 78°46E **126** E4
Utō *Sweden* 58°56N 18°16E **62** F12
Utopia *Australia* 22°14S 134°33E **150** C1
Utraula *India* 27°19N 82°25E **125** F10
Utrecht *Neths.* 52°5N 5°8E **69** B5
Utrecht *S. Africa* 27°38S 30°20E **145** C5
Utrecht □ *Neths.* 52°6N 5°7E **69** B5
Utrera *Spain* 37°12N 5°48W **89** H5
Utsjoki *Finland* 69°51N 26°59E **60** B22
Utsunomiya *Japan* 36°30N 139°50E **113** F9
Uttar Pradesh □ *India* 27°0N 80°0E **125** F9
Uttaradit *Thailand* 17°36N 100°5E **120** D3
Uttarakhand □ *India* 30°0N 79°30E **125** D8
Utterson *Canada* 45°12N 79°19W **174** A5
Uttoxeter *U.K.* 52°54N 1°52W **66** E6
Utuado *Puerto Rico* 18°16N 66°42W **183** d
Uummannaq, Greenland
  Greenland 70°58N 52°17W **54** B5
Uummannaq Qaasuitsup,
  Greenland 77°33N 68°52W **57** B4
Uummannarsuaq = Nunap Isua
  Greenland 59°48N 43°55W **57** F6
Uunartoq Qeqertoq
  Greenland 71°33N 21°47W **57** C8
Uusikaarlepyy *Finland* 63°32N 22°31E **60** E20
Uusikaupunki *Finland* 60°47N 21°25E **64** B1
Uva *Russia* 56°59N 52°36E **86** B11
Uvac → *Serbia* 43°35N 19°30E **96** C3
Uvalda *U.S.A.* 32°2N 82°31W **178** D7
Uvalde *U.S.A.* 29°13N 99°47W **176** G5
Uvarovo *Russia* 51°59N 42°14E **86** E6
Uvat *Russia* 59°5N 68°50E **106** D7
Uvinza *Tanzania* 5°5S 30°24E **142** D3
Uvira
  Dem. Rep. of the Congo 3°22S 29°3E **142** C2
Uvs → *Mongolia* 49°30N 92°0E **110** B4
Uvs Nuur *Mongolia* 50°20N 92°30E **109** B12
'Uwairidh, Ḥarrat al
  Si. Arabia 26°50N 38°0E **128** E3
Uwajima *Japan* 33°10N 132°35E **113** H6
Uwanda △ *Tanzania* 7°46S 32°0E **142** D3
Uweinat, Jebel *Sudan* 21°54N 24°58E **135** D10
Uxbridge *Canada* 44°6N 79°7W **174** B5
Uxin Qi *China* 38°50N 109°5E **114** E5
Uxmal *Mexico* 20°22N 89°46W **181** C7
Üydzin *Mongolia* 44°9N 107°0E **114** B4
Uyo *Nigeria* 5°1N 7°53E **139** D6
Üyük Tepe *Turkey* 37°5N 27°21E **99** D9
Uyûn Mûsa *Egypt* 29°53N 32°40E **130** F1
Uyuni *Bolivia* 20°28S 66°47W **188** E4
Uzbekistan ■ *Asia* 41°30N 65°0E **109** D7
Uzboy → *Turkmenistan* 39°30N 55°0E **129** B7
Uzen, Mal → *Kazakhstan* 49°4N 49°44E **87** F9
Uzerche *France* 45°25N 1°34E **72** C5
Uzès *France* 44°1N 4°26E **73** D8
Uzh → *Ukraine* 51°15N 30°12E **75** C16
Uzhgorod = Uzhhorod
  Ukraine 48°36N 22°18E **80** A7
Uzhhorod *Ukraine* 48°36N 22°18E **80** A7
Uzhok *Ukraine* 48°59N 22°52E **80** B7
Užice *Serbia* 43°55N 19°50E **96** C4
Uzlovaya *Russia* 54°0N 38°5E **84** F10
Üzümlü *Turkey* 36°44N 29°14E **99** E11
Uzunköprü *Turkey* 41°16N 26°43E **97** F10
Uzunkuyu *Turkey* 38°17N 26°33E **99** C8

V

Vaal → *S. Africa* 29°4S 23°38E **144** C3
Vaal Dam *S. Africa* 27°0S 28°14E **145** C4
Vaalwater *S. Africa* 24°15S 28°8E **145** B4
Vaasa *Finland* 63°6N 21°38E **60** E19
Vabre *France* 43°42N 2°24E **72** E6
Vác *Hungary* 47°49N 19°10E **80** C4
Vacaria *Brazil* 28°31S 50°52W **191** B5
Vacaville *U.S.A.* 38°21N 121°59W **170** G5

Vaccarès, Étang de
  France 43°32N 4°34E **73** E8
Vach = Vakh →
  Russia 60°45N 76°45E **106** C8
Vacha *Bulgaria* 42°10N 24°26E **97** D8
Vache, Î. à *Haiti* 18°2N 73°35W **183** C5
Väckelsång *Sweden* 56°37N 14°58E **63** H8
Vacoas *Mauritius* 20°18S 57°29E **141** d
Vada *India* 19°39N 73°8E **126** E1
Vadakara *India* 11°35N 75°40E **127** J2
Väddö *Sweden* 60°0N 18°50E **62** D12
Vadehavet △ *Denmark* 55°20N 8°30E **63** J2
Väderstad *Sweden* 58°19N 14°55E **63** F8
Vadnagar *India* 23°47N 72°40E **124** H5
Vado Ligure *Italy* 44°17N 8°26E **92** D5
Vadodara *India* 22°20N 73°10E **124** H5
Vadsø *Norway* 70°3N 29°50E **60** A23
Vadstena *Sweden* 58°28N 14°48E **63** F8
Vaduj *India* 17°36N 74°27E **126** F2
Vaduz *Liech.* 47°8N 9°31E **77** H5
Vværøy *Norway* 67°40N 12°40E **60** C15
Vágar *Færoe Is.* 62°5N 7°15W **60** E9
Vaggeryd *Sweden* 57°30N 14°10E **63** G8
Vaghia *Greece* 38°19N 23°11E **98** C5
Vagia, Akra *Greece* 36°15N 28°11E **101** C10
Vagney *France* 48°1N 6°43E **71** D13
Vagnhärad *Sweden* 58°57N 17°33E **63** F11
Vagos *Portugal* 40°33N 8°42W **88** E2
Vágsfjorden *Norway* 68°50N 16°50E **60** B17
Váh → *Slovakia* 47°43N 18°7E **79** D11
Vahsel B. *Antarctica* 75°0S 35°0W **55** D1
Váhtjer = Gällivare
  Sweden 67°9N 20°40E **60** C19
Vai *Greece* 35°15N 26°18E **101** D8
Vaiaku = Fongafale
  Tuvalu 8°31S 179°13E **147** B10
Vaigai → *India* 9°15N 79°10E **127** K4
Vaiges *France* 48°2N 0°30W **70** D6
Vaihingen *Germany* 48°54N 8°57E **77** G4
Vaihiria, L. *Tahiti* 17°40S 149°25W **155** b
Vaijapur *India* 19°58N 74°45E **126** E2
Vaikam *India* 9°45N 76°25E **127** K3
Vail *U.S.A.* 39°40N 106°20W **168** G10
Vailly-sur-Aisne *France* 49°24N 3°31E **71** C10
Vaippar → *India* 9°0N 78°25E **127** K4
Vairao *Tahiti* 17°47S 149°17W **155** b
Vaisali → *India* 26°28N 78°53E **125** F8
Vaison-la-Romaine *France* 44°14N 5°4E **73** D9
Vajpur *India* 21°24N 73°17E **126** D1
Vakarai *Sri Lanka* 8°8N 81°26E **127** K5
Vakarel *Bulgaria* 42°35N 23°40E **96** D7
Vakfikebir *Turkey* 41°2N 39°17E **105** B8
Vakh → *Russia* 60°45N 76°45E **106** C8
Vakhsh → *Tajikistan* 37°6N 68°18E **109** F7
Vakhtan *Russia* 57°53N 46°47E **86** B8
Vál *Hungary* 47°22N 18°40E **80** C3
Val Camónica *Italy* 46°0N 10°20E **92** B7
Val-de-Marne □ *France* 48°45N 2°28E **71** D9
Val-d'Isère *France* 45°27N 6°59E **73** C10
Val-d'Oise □ *France* 49°5N 2°10E **71** C9
Val-d'Or *Canada* 48°7N 77°47W **164** C4
Val Grande △ *Italy* 46°3N 8°25E **92** B5
Val Marie *Canada* 49°15N 107°45W **163** D7
Val Thorens *France* 45°20N 6°33E **73** C10
Valaam *Russia* 61°22N 30°57E **84** B6
Valadares *Portugal* 41°5N 8°38W **88** D2
Valahia *Romania* 44°35N 25°0E **81** F9
Valaichenai *Sri Lanka* 7°54N 81°32E **127** L5
Valais □ *Switz.* 46°12N 7°45E **77** J3
Valais, Alpes du *Switz.* 46°5N 7°35E **77** J3
Valandovo *Macedonia* 41°19N 22°34E **96** E6
Valašské Meziříčí
  Czechia 49°29N 17°59E **79** B10
Valatie *U.S.A.* 42°24N 73°40W **175** D11
Valaxa *Greece* 38°50N 24°29E **98** C6
Válberg *Sweden* 59°23N 13°11E **62** E7
Valbo *Sweden* 60°40N 17°0E **62** D7
Valbondione *Italy* 46°2N 10°1E **92** B7
Valcheta *Argentina* 40°40S 66°8W **192** E3
Valdagno *Italy* 45°39N 11°18E **93** C8
Valdahon *France* 47°8N 6°21E **71** E13
Valdai Hills = Valdayskaya
  Vozvyshennost *Russia* 57°0N 33°30E **84** D7
Valdayskaya Vozvyshennost
  Russia 57°0N 33°30E **84** D7
Valdecañas, Embalse de
  Spain 39°45N 5°25W **88** F5
Valdemarsvik *Sweden* 58°14N 16°40E **63** F10
Valdemoro *Spain* 40°12N 3°40W **88** E7
Valdepeñas *Spain* 38°43N 3°25W **89** G7
Valderaduey → *Spain* 41°31N 5°42W **88** D5
Valderrobres *Spain* 40°53N 0°9E **90** E5
Valdés, Pen. *Argentina* 42°30S 63°45W **192** E4
Valdez *U.S.A.* 61°7N 146°16W **160** E2
Valdivia *Chile* 39°50S 73°14W **192** D2
Valdivia Abyssal Plain
  S. Ocean 62°30S 70°0E **55** C6
Valdobbiádene *Italy* 45°53N 12°0E **93** C8
Valdosta *U.S.A.* 30°50N 83°17W **178** E6
Valdoviño = Aviño *Spain* 43°36N 8°8W **88** B2
Vale *Georgia* 41°35N 42°58E **87** K6
Vale *U.S.A.* 43°59N 117°15W **168** E5
Vale of Glamorgan □
  U.K. 51°28N 3°25W **67** F4
Valea lui Mihai *Romania* 47°32N 22°11E **80** C7
Valea Mărului *Romania* 45°54N 27°42E **81** E12
Valemount *Canada* 52°50N 119°15W **162** C5
Valença *Brazil* 13°20S 39°5W **189** C3
Valença *Portugal* 42°1N 8°34W **88** C2
Valença do Piauí *Brazil* 6°20S 41°45W **189** B2
Valençay *France* 47°9N 1°34E **71** E8
Valence *France* 44°57N 4°54E **73** D8
Valence d'Agen *France* 44°6N 0°53E **72** D4
Valencia *Spain* 39°27N 0°23W **91** F4
Valencia *Venezuela* 10°11N 68°0W **186** A5
Valencia □ *Spain* 39°20N 0°40W **91** F4
Valencia, G. de *Spain* 39°30N 0°20E **91** F5
Valencia Trin. & Tob. 10°19N 61°13W **187** K15
Valencia □ *Spain* 34°40N 106°43W **169** J10
Valencia *Venezuela* 10°11N 68°0W **186** A5
Valencia ✕ (VLC) *Spain* 39°29N 0°28W **91** F4
Valencia, G. de *Spain* 39°30N 0°20E **91** F5

Valencia de Alcántara
  Spain 39°25N 7°14W **89** F3
Valencia de Don Juan
  Spain 42°17N 5°31W **88** C5
Valencia I. *Ireland* 51°54N 10°22W **64** E1
Valenciennes *France* 50°20N 3°34E **71** B10
Văleni *Romania* 44°15N 24°45E **81** F9
Vălenii de Munte
  Romania 45°11N 26°2E **81** E11
Valensole *France* 43°50N 5°59E **73** E9
Valentigney *France* 47°27N 6°51E **71** E13
Valentim, Sa. do *Brazil* 6°0S 43°30W **189** B2
Valentin *Russia* 43°8N 134°17E **112** C7
Valentine *Nebr.,*
  U.S.A. 42°52N 100°33W **172** D3
Valentine *Tex., U.S.A.* 30°35N 104°30W **176** F2
Valenza *Italy* 45°1N 8°38E **92** C5
Valera *Venezuela* 9°19N 70°37W **186** B4
Valga *Estonia* 57°47N 26°2E **84** C4
Valguarnera Caropepe
  Italy 37°30N 14°23E **95** E7
Valier *U.S.A.* 48°18N 112°16W **168** B7
Valinco, G. de *France* 41°40N 8°52E **73** G12
Valjevo *Serbia* 44°18N 19°53E **96** B3
Valka *Latvia* 57°42N 25°57E **84** C4
Valkeakoski *Finland* 61°16N 24°2E **84** B2
Valkenswaard *Neths.* 51°21N 5°29E **69** C5
Vall de Uxó = La Vall d'Uixó
  Spain 39°49N 0°15W **90** F4
Valla *Sweden* 59°2N 16°20E **62** E10
Valladolid *Mexico* 20°41N 88°12W **181** C7
Valladolid *Spain* 41°38N 4°43W **88** D6
Valladolid □ *Spain* 41°38N 4°43W **88** D6
Vallata *Italy* 41°2N 15°15E **95** A8
Valldemossa *Spain* 39°43N 2°37E **100** B9
Valle d'Aosta □ *Italy* 45°45N 7°15E **92** C4
Valle de la Pascua
  Venezuela 9°13N 66°0W **186** B5
Valle de las Palmas
  Mexico 32°20N 116°43W **171** N10
Valle de Santiago
  Mexico 20°23N 101°12W **180** C4
Valle de Villaverde *Spain* 43°15N 3°15W **88** B7
Valle de Zaragoza
  Mexico 27°25N 105°50W **180** B3
Valle del Ticino △ *Italy* 45°22N 9°0E **92** C6
Valle Fértil, Sierra del
  Argentina 30°20S 68°0W **190** C2
Valle Gran Rey
  Canary Is. 28°5N 17°20W **100** F2
Valle Hermoso *Mexico* 25°35N 97°40W **181** B5
Valle Nacional *Mexico* 17°47N 96°18W **181** D5
Valledupar *Colombia* 10°29N 73°15W **186** A4
Vallée du Bandama □
  Côte d'Ivoire 8°0N 5°0W **138** D3
Vallehermoso
  Canary Is. 28°10N 17°15W **100** F2
Vallejo *U.S.A.* 38°7N 122°14W **170** G4
Vallenar *Chile* 28°30S 70°50W **190** B1
Vallentuna *Sweden* 59°32N 18°5E **62** E12
Valleraugue *France* 44°6N 3°39E **72** D7
Vallet *France* 47°10N 1°15W **70** E5
Valletta *Malta* 35°54N 14°31E **101** D2
Valley Center *U.S.A.* 33°13N 117°2W **171** M9
Valley City *U.S.A.* 46°55N 98°0W **172** B5
Valley Falls *Oreg.,*
  U.S.A. 42°29N 120°17W **168** E3
Valley Falls *R.I.,*
  U.S.A. 41°54N 71°24W **175** E13
Valley of Flowers △
  India 30°50N 79°40E **125** D8
Valley of the Kings
  Egypt 25°41N 32°34E **137** B3
Valley Springs *U.S.A.* 38°12N 120°50W **170** G6
Valley View *U.S.A.* 40°39N 76°33W **175** F8
Valley Wells *U.S.A.* 35°27N 115°46W **171** K11
Valleyview *Canada* 55°5N 117°17W **162** B5
Valli di Comácchio *Italy* 44°40N 12°15E **93** D9
Vallimanca, Arroyo
  Argentina 35°40S 59°10W **190** D4
Vallo della Lucánia *Italy* 40°14N 15°16E **95** B8
Vallon-Pont-d'Arc *France* 44°24N 4°24E **73** D8
Vallorbe *France* 46°42N 6°20E **77** J2
Valls *Spain* 41°18N 1°15E **90** D6
Vallvik *Sweden* 61°11N 17°10E **62** C11
Valmaseda = Balmaseda
  Spain 43°11N 3°12W **90** B1
Valmiera *Latvia* 57°37N 25°29E **84** D3
Valnera *Spain* 43°9N 3°40W **88** B7
Valognes *France* 49°30N 1°28W **70** C5
Valona = Vlorë *Albania* 40°32N 19°28E **96** F3
Valongo *Portugal* 41°8N 8°30W **88** D2
Valozhyn *Belarus* 54°3N 26°30E **75** A14
Valpaços *Portugal* 41°36N 7°17W **88** D3
Valparai *India* 10°22N 76°58E **127** J3
Valparaíso *Chile* 33°2S 71°40W **190** C1
Valparaíso *Mexico* 22°46N 103°34W **180** C4
Valparaíso *Fla., U.S.A.* 30°29N 86°30W **179** E3
Valparaiso *Ind., U.S.A.* 41°28N 87°4W **172** E9
Valparaíso □ *Chile* 33°2S 71°40W **190** C1
Valpovo *Croatia* 45°39N 18°25E **80** E3
Valpoy *India* 15°32N 74°8E **127** G2
Valréas *France* 44°24N 5°0E **73** D9
Vals → *S. Africa* 27°23S 26°30E **144** C4
Vals, Tanjung *Indonesia* 8°26S 137°25E **119** F9
Vals-les-Bains *France* 44°42N 4°24E **73** D8
Valsad *India* 20°40N 72°58E **126** D1
Valtellina *Italy* 46°11N 9°55E **92** B6
Valuyki *Russia* 50°10N 38°5E **85** G10
Valverde *Canary Is.* 27°48N 17°55W **100** G2
Valverde del Camino
  Spain 37°35N 6°47W **89** H4
Valverde del Fresno
  Spain 40°15N 6°51W **88** E4
Vama *Romania* 47°34N 25°42E **81** C9
Vambori *India* 19°17N 74°44E **126** E2
Vamdrup *Denmark* 55°25N 9°17E **63** J3
Vámhus *Sweden* 61°7N 14°29E **62** C8
Vamizi, I. *Mozam.* 11°2S 40°40E **143** E5
Vammala = Sastamala
  Finland 61°20N 22°54E **84** B2
Vamos *Greece* 35°24N 24°13E **101** D6
Vamsadhara → *India* 18°21N 84°8E **126** E7
Van *Turkey* 38°30N 43°20E **105** C10
Van □ *Turkey* 38°30N 43°20E **105** C10
Van, L. = Van Gölü
  Turkey 38°30N 43°0E **105** C10
Van Alstyne *U.S.A.* 33°25N 96°35W **176** E6
Van Blommestein Meer
  Suriname 4°45N 55°5W **187** C7
Van Buren *Canada* 47°10N 67°55W **165** C6

Van Buren *Ark., U.S.A.* 35°26N 94°21W **176** D7
Van Buren *Maine,*
  U.S.A. 47°10N 67°58W **173** B20
Van Buren *Mo., U.S.A.* 37°0N 91°1W **172** G8
Van Canh *Vietnam* 13°37N 109°0E **120** F7
Van Diemen, C. *N. Terr.,*
  Australia 11°9S 130°24E **148** B5
Van Diemen, C. *Queens.,*
  Australia 16°30S 139°46E **150** B2
Van Diemen G.
  Australia 11°45S 132°0E **148** B5
Van Gölü *Turkey* 38°30N 43°0E **105** C10
Van Horn *U.S.A.* 31°3N 104°50W **176** F2
Van Ninh *Vietnam* 12°42N 109°14E **120** F7
Van Rees, Pegunungan
  Indonesia 2°35S 138°15E **119** E9
Van Tivu *India* 8°51N 78°15E **127** K4
Van Wert *U.S.A.* 40°52N 84°35W **173** E11
Van Yen *Vietnam* 21°4N 104°42E **116** G5
Van Zylsrus *S. Africa* 26°52S 22°4E **144** C3
Vanadzor *Armenia* 40°48N 44°30E **87** K7
Vanavara *Russia* 60°22N 102°16E **107** C11
Vancouver *Canada* 49°15N 123°7W **170** A3
Vancouver *U.S.A.* 45°38N 122°40W **170** A3
Vancouver, C. *Australia* 35°2S 118°11E **149** G2
Vancouver I. *Canada* 49°50N 126°0W **170** A2
Vancouver Int. ✈ (YVR)
  Canada 49°10N 123°10W **170** A3
Vanda = Vantaa *Finland* 60°18N 24°56E **84** B3
Vandalia *Ill., U.S.A.* 38°58N 89°6W **172** F9
Vandalia *Mo., U.S.A.* 39°19N 91°29W **172** F8
Vandavasi *India* 12°30N 79°30E **127** H4
Vandellòs *Spain* 41°0N 0°55E **90** E5
Vandeloos B. *Sri Lanka* 8°0N 81°45E **127** L5
Vandenberg Village
  U.S.A. 34°43N 120°28W **171** L6
Vanderbijlpark
  S. Africa 26°42S 27°54E **145** C4
Vandergrift *U.S.A.* 40°36N 79°34W **174** F5
Vanderhoof *Canada* 54°0N 124°0W **162** C4
Vanderkloof Dam
  S. Africa 30°4S 24°40E **144** D3
Vanderlin I. *Australia* 15°44S 137°2E **150** B2
Vänern *Sweden* 58°47N 13°30E **63** F7
Vänersborg *Sweden* 58°26N 12°19E **63** F6
Vang Vieng *Laos* 18°58N 102°32E **120** C4
Vanga *Kenya* 4°35S 39°12E **142** C4
Vangaindrano *Madag.* 23°21S 47°36E **141** J9
Vänge *Sweden* 49°55N 107°20W **163** D7
Vanguard *Canada* 49°55N 107°20W **163** D7
Vanino *Russia* 48°50N 140°5E **107** E15
Vanivilasa Sagara
  India 13°45N 76°30E **127** H3
Vaniyambadi *India* 12°46N 78°44E **127** H4
Vankleek Hill *Canada* 45°32N 74°40W **175** A10
Vännäs *Sweden* 63°58N 19°48E **60** E18
Vannes *France* 47°40N 2°47W **70** E4
Vannøya *Norway* 70°6N 19°50E **60** C18
Vanoise, Massif de la
  France 45°25N 6°40E **73** C10
Vanrhynsdorp *S. Africa* 31°36S 18°44E **144** D2
Vansada *India* 20°47N 73°25E **126** D1
Vansbro *Sweden* 60°32N 14°15E **62** D8
Vansittart B. *Australia* 14°3S 126°17E **148** B4
Vansittart I. *Canada* 65°50N 84°0W **161** D15
Vantaa *Finland* 60°18N 24°56E **84** B3
Vanua Balavu *Fiji* 17°12S 178°55W **154** a
Vanua Levu *Fiji* 16°33S 179°15E **154** a
Vanua Vara *Fiji* 17°26S 179°31W **154** a
Vanuatu ■ *Pac. Oc.* 15°0S 168°0E **147** C9
Vanwyksvlei *S. Africa* 30°18S 21°49E **144** D3
Vapi *India* 20°22N 72°49E **126** D1
Vapnyarka *Ukraine* 48°32N 28°45E **81** B13
Var □ *France* 43°27N 6°18E **73** E10
Var → *France* 43°39N 7°12E **73** E11
Vara *Sweden* 58°16N 12°55E **63** F6
Varada → *India* 15°0N 75°40E **127** G2
Varades *France* 47°25N 1°1W **70** E5
Varáita → *Italy* 44°9N 7°53E **92** D4
Varalé *Côte d'Ivoire* 9°40N 3°17W **138** D4
Varallo *Italy* 45°49N 8°15E **92** C5
Varāmīn *Iran* 35°20N 51°39E **129** C6
Varāmīn □ *Iran* 35°18N 51°50E **129** B6
Varanasi *India* 25°22N 83°0E **125** G10
Varangerfjorden
  Norway 70°3N 29°25E **60** A23
Varangerhalvøya
  Norway 70°25N 29°30E **60** A23
Varano, Lago di *Italy* 41°53N 15°45E **93** G12
Varazze *Italy* 44°22N 8°34E **92** D5
Varberg *Sweden* 57°6N 12°20E **63** G6
Varbitsa *Bulgaria* 42°59N 26°40E **97** C11
Vardak □ *Afghan.* 34°0N 68°0E **130** B5
Vardar = Axios →
  Greece 40°57N 22°35E **96** F6
Varde *Denmark* 55°38N 8°29E **63** J2
Varde Å → *Denmark* 55°35N 8°19E **63** J2
Vardenis *Armenia* 40°10N 45°43E **87** K7
Vardø *Norway* 70°23N 31°5E **60** A24
Varel *Germany* 53°23N 8°8E **76** B4
Varella, Mui = Nay, Mui
  Vietnam 12°54N 109°26E **120** F7
Varèna *Lithuania* 54°12N 24°30E **84** E3
Varennes-sur-Allier
  France 46°19N 3°24E **71** F10
Varennes-Vauzelles *France* 47°3N 3°9E **71** E10
Vareš *Bos.-H.* 44°12N 18°23E **80** F3
Varese *Italy* 45°48N 8°50E **92** C5
Vårfurile *Romania* 46°19N 22°31E **80** D7
Vårgårda *Sweden* 58°2N 12°49E **63** F6
Vargem Bonita *Brazil* 20°20S 46°22W **189** E2
Vargem Grande *Brazil* 3°33S 43°56W **189** A2
Varginha *Brazil* 21°33S 45°25W **191** A6
Varillas *Chile* 24°0S 70°10W **190** A1
Varkaus *Finland* 62°19N 27°50E **84** A4
Värmdölandet *Sweden* 59°18N 18°33E **62** E12
Värmeln *Sweden* 59°35N 12°54E **62** E6
Värmland □ *Sweden* 60°0N 13°20E **62** E6
Värmlandsbro *Sweden* 59°11N 13°0E **62** E7
Varna *Bulgaria* 43°13N 27°56E **97** C11
Varna □ *Bulgaria* 43°20N 27°30E **97** C11
Varna → *India* 16°48N 74°32E **126** F2
Värnamo *Sweden* 57°10N 14°3E **63** G8
Várnjárga = Varangerhalvøya
  Norway 70°25N 29°30E **60** A23
Varnsdorf *Czechia* 50°55N 14°35E **78** A7
Varnville *U.S.A.* 32°51N 81°5W **178** E4
Várpalota *Hungary* 47°12N 18°8E **80** C3
Vars *Canada* 45°21N 75°21W **175** A9

Vars *France* 44°37N 6°42E **73** D10
Varto *Turkey* 39°10N 41°27E **105** C9
Varvarin *Serbia* 43°43N 21°20E **96** C5
Varysburg *U.S.A.* 42°46N 78°19W **174** D6
Varzaneh *Iran* 32°25N 52°40E **129** C7
Varzaqān *Iran* 38°29N 46°40E **105** C12
Várzea Alegre *Brazil* 6°47S 39°17W **189** B3
Várzea da Palma
  Brazil 17°36S 44°44W **189** D2
Varzi *Italy* 44°49N 9°12E **92** D6
Varzo *Italy* 46°12N 8°15E **92** B5
Varzy *France* 47°22N 3°20E **71** E10
Vas □ *Hungary* 47°10N 16°55E **80** C1
Vasa = Vaasa *Finland* 63°6N 21°38E **60** E19
Vasa Barris → *Brazil* 11°10S 37°10W **189** C3
Vásárosnamény *Hungary* 48°9N 22°19E **80** B7
Vascão → *Portugal* 37°31N 7°31W **89** H3
Vașcău *Romania* 46°28N 22°30E **80** D7
Vascongadas = País Vasco □
  Spain 42°50N 2°45W **90** C2
Vashkivtsi *Ukraine* 48°23N 25°31E **81** B10
Vasht = Khāsh *Iran* 28°15N 61°15E **129** D9
Vasilevichi *Belarus* 52°15N 29°50E **75** B16
Vasilika *Greece* 40°29N 23°8E **96** F7
Vasiliki *Greece* 38°37N 20°36E **98** C2
Vasiliko *Greece* 38°25N 23°40E **98** C5
Vasilkov = Vasylkiv
  Ukraine 50°7N 30°15E **75** C16
Väskinde *Sweden* 57°40N 18°20E **63** G10
Vaslui *Romania* 46°38N 27°42E **81** D12
Vaslui □ *Romania* 46°30N 27°45E **81** D12
Väsman *Sweden* 60°9N 15°5E **62** D9
Vassar *Canada* 49°10N 95°55W **163** D9
Vassar *U.S.A.* 43°22N 83°35W **173** D12
Västerås *Sweden* 59°37N 16°38E **62** E10
Västerbotten *Sweden* 64°36N 20°4E **60** D19
Västerdalälven →
  Sweden 60°30N 15°7E **62** D8
Västergötland *Sweden* 58°0N 13°10E **63** F7
Västerhaninge *Sweden* 59°7N 18°6E **62** E12
Västervik *Sweden* 57°43N 16°33E **63** G10
Västmanland *Sweden* 60°10N 16°20E **61** G17
Västmanland □ *Sweden* 59°45N 16°20E **62** E10
Vasto *Italy* 42°8N 14°40E **93** F11
Västra Götaland □ *Sweden* 58°0N 13°0E **63** F6
Vasvár *Hungary* 47°3N 16°47E **80** C1
Vasylkiv *Ukraine* 50°7N 30°15E **75** C16
Vat Phou *Laos* 14°51N 105°49E **120** E5
Vatan *France* 47°4N 1°50E **71** E8
Vatersay *U.K.* 56°55N 7°32W **65** E1
Vathia *Greece* 36°29N 22°29E **98** E4
Vati *Greece* 36°3N 27°53E **101** C9
Vatican City ■ *Europe* 41°54N 12°27E **93** G9
Vaticano, C. *Italy* 38°37N 15°50E **95** D8
Vatili *Cyprus* 35°6N 33°40E **101** D12
Vatin *Serbia* 45°12N 21°20E **80** E6
Vatiu = Atiu *Cook Is.* 20°0S 158°10W **157** J12
Vatnajökull *Iceland* 64°30N 16°48W **64** D5
Vatnajökull △ *Iceland* 64°24N 16°48W **64** D5
Vato *Sweden* 59°50N 19°0E **62** E12
Vatolakkos *Greece* 35°27N 23°53E **101** D5
Vatra-Dornei *Romania* 47°22N 25°22E **81** C10
Vatrak → *India* 23°9N 73°2E **124** H5
Vattern *Sweden* 58°25N 14°30E **63** F8
Vatu Vara *Fiji* 17°26S 179°31W **154** a
Vatulele *Fiji* 18°33S 177°37E **154** a
Vaucluse □ *France* 43°50N 5°20E **73** E9
Vaucouleurs *France* 48°37N 5°40E **71** D12
Vaud □ *Switz.* 46°35N 6°30E **77** J2
Vaudreuil-Dorion
  Canada 45°23N 74°3W **175** A10
Vaughn *Mont., U.S.A.* 47°33N 111°33W **168** C8
Vaughn *N. Mex.,*
  U.S.A. 34°36N 105°13W **169** J11
Vaujours L. *Canada* 55°27N 74°15W **164** A5
Vaupés □ *Brazil* 0°2N 67°16W **186** C5
Vaupés = Uaupés →
  Brazil 0°2N 67°16W **186** C5
Vaupés □ *Colombia* 1°0N 71°0W **186** C4
Vauvert *France* 43°42N 4°17E **73** E8
Vauxhall *Canada* 50°5N 112°9W **162** C6
Vav *India* 24°22N 71°31E **124** G4
Vavoua *Côte d'Ivoire* 7°23N 6°29W **138** D3
Vavuniya *Sri Lanka* 8°45N 80°30E **127** K5
Vawkavysk *Belarus* 53°9N 24°30E **75** B13
Vaxholm *Sweden* 59°25N 18°20E **62** E12
Växjö *Sweden* 56°52N 14°50E **63** H8
Våxtorp *Sweden* 56°25N 13°8E **63** H7
Vaypalad *India* 13°39N 78°38E **127** H4
Vaygach, Ostrov *Russia* 70°0N 60°0E **106** C7
Veadeiros *Brazil* 14°7S 47°31W **189** C1
Veaikevárri = Svappavaara
  Sweden 67°40N 21°3E **60** C19
Vechelde *Germany* 52°16N 10°22E **76** C6
Vechta *Germany* 52°44N 8°17E **76** C4
Vechte → *Neths.* 52°34N 6°6E **69** B6
Vecsés *Hungary* 47°26N 19°19E **80** C4
Vedaranniyam *India* 10°25N 79°50E **127** J4
Veddige *Sweden* 57°17N 12°20E **63** G6
Vedea → *Romania* 43°42N 25°41E **81** C10
Vedia *Argentina* 34°30S 61°31W **190** C3
Vedrette di Ries-Aurina △
  Italy 46°54N 12°5E **93** B9
Vedum *Sweden* 58°11N 13°0E **63** F7
Vejer de la Frontera
  Spain 36°15N 5°59W **89** J5
Vejle *Denmark* 55°43N 9°30E **63** J3
Vejle Fjord *Denmark* 55°40N 9°50E **63** J3
Velachha *India* 21°26N 73°16E **126** D1
Velanai I. *Sri Lanka* 9°45N 79°45E **127** K4
Velas, C. *Costa Rica* 10°21N 85°52W **182** D2
Velasco, Sierra de
  Argentina 29°20S 67°10W **190** B2
Velay, Mts. du *France* 45°0N 3°40E **72** D7
Velddrif *S. Africa* 32°42S 18°11E **144** D2

Velebit Planina *Croatia* 44°50N 15°20E **93** D12
Velebitski Kanal
  Croatia 44°45N 14°55E **93** D11
Veleka → *Bulgaria* 42°4N 27°58E **97** D11
Velenci-tó *Hungary* 47°13N 18°36E **80** C3
Velenje *Slovenia* 46°23N 15°8E **93** B12
Veles *Macedonia* 41°46N 21°47E **96** E5
Velestino *Greece* 39°23N 22°43E **98** B4
Vélez-Málaga *Spain* 36°48N 4°5W **89** J6
Vélez Rubio *Spain* 37°41N 2°5W **91** H2
Velhas → *Brazil* 17°13S 44°49W **189** D2
Velika *Croatia* 45°27N 17°40E **80** E2
Velika Gorica *Croatia* 45°44N 16°5E **93** C13
Velika Kapela *Croatia* 45°10N 15°5E **93** C12
Velika Kladuša *Bos.-H.* 45°11N 15°48E **93** C12
Velika Kruša = Krushë e Madhe
  Kosovo 42°19N 20°39E **96** D4
Velika Morava → *Serbia* 44°43N 21°3E **96** B5
Velika Plana *Serbia* 44°20N 21°4E **96** B5
Veliki Gradište *Serbia* 44°46N 21°29E **96** B5
Veliki Kanal *Serbia* 45°45N 19°15E **80** E4
Veliki Popović *Serbia* 44°8N 21°18E **96** B5
Velikiy Novgorod *Russia* 58°30N 31°25E **84** C6
Velikiye Luki *Russia* 56°25N 30°32E **84** D6
Veliko Tarnovo *Bulgaria* 43°5N 25°41E **97** C9
Veliko Tarnovo □
  Bulgaria 43°5N 25°41E **97** C9
Velikonda Range *India* 14°45N 79°10E **127** G4
Velingara *Kolda, Senegal* 13°12N 14°55W **138** C2
Velingara *Louga, Senegal* 15°0N 14°40W **138** C2
Velingrad *Bulgaria* 42°4N 23°58E **96** D7
Velino, Mte. *Italy* 42°9N 13°23E **93** F10
Velizh *Russia* 55°36N 31°11E **84** E6
Vel'ké Kapušany
  Slovakia 48°34N 22°5E **79** C15
Velké Karlovice *Czechia* 49°20N 18°17E **79** B11
Velké Meziříčí *Czechia* 49°21N 16°1E **78** B9
Vel'ký Javorník
  Slovakia 49°19N 18°22E **79** B11
Vel'ký Krtíš *Slovakia* 48°13N 19°21E **79** C12
Vel'ký Meder *Slovakia* 47°52N 17°46E **79** D10
Vel'ký Tribeč *Slovakia* 48°28N 18°15E **79** C11
Vellar → *India* 11°30N 79°36E **127** J4
Velletri *Italy* 41°41N 12°47E **94** A5
Vellinge *Sweden* 55°29N 13°2E **63** J6
Vellmar *Germany* 51°22N 9°28E **76** D5
Vellore *India* 12°57N 79°10E **127** H4
Velopoula *Greece* 36°55N 23°27E **98** E5
Velsen-Noord *Neths.* 52°27N 4°40E **69** B4
Velsk *Russia* 61°10N 42°0E **84** B11
Velten *Germany* 52°42N 13°10E **76** C9
Veluwezoom △ *Neths.* 52°5N 6°0E **69** B6
Velva *U.S.A.* 48°4N 100°56W **172** A3
Velvendos *Greece* 40°15N 22°6E **96** F6
Velyka Mykhaylivka
  Ukraine 47°4N 29°52E **81** C14
Velyki Luchky *Ukraine* 48°25N 22°34E **80** B7
Velykyy Bereznyy
  Ukraine 48°54N 22°28E **80** B7
Velykyy Bychkiv *Ukraine* 47°58N 24°1E **81** C9
Vemb *Denmark* 56°21N 8°21E **63** H2
Vembanad L. *India* 9°36N 76°15E **127** K3
Vemdalen *Sweden* 62°27N 13°51E **62** B7
Ven *Sweden* 55°55N 12°45E **63** J6
Venado *Mexico* 22°56N 101°6W **180** C4
Venado Tuerto
  Argentina 33°50S 62°0W **190** C3
Venafro *Italy* 41°29N 14°2E **95** A7
Venaria-les-Laumes
  France 47°32N 4°26E **71** E11
Venaria *Italy* 45°8N 7°38E **92** C4
Vence *France* 43°43N 7°6E **73** E11
Vendas Novas *Portugal* 38°39N 8°27W **89** G2
Vendée □ *France* 46°50N 1°35W **70** F5
Vendée → *France* 46°20N 1°10W **70** F5
Vendéen, Bocage *France* 46°50N 1°20W **72** B2
Vendeuvre-sur-Barse
  France 48°14N 4°28E **71** D11
Vendicari *Italy* 36°49N 15°6E **95** F8
Vendôme *France* 47°47N 1°3E **70** E8
Vendrell = El Vendrell
  Spain 41°10N 1°30E **90** D6
Vendsyssel *Denmark* 57°22N 10°0E **63** G4
Vendychany *Ukraine* 48°37N 28°48E **81** B12
Venelles *France* 43°35N 5°28E **73** E9
Veneta, L. *Italy* 45°23N 12°25E **93** C9
Véneto □ *Italy* 45°30N 12°0E **93** C9
Venev *Russia* 54°22N 38°17E **84** E10
Venézia *Italy* 45°27N 12°21E **93** C9
Venézia, G. di *Italy* 45°15N 13°0E **93** C10
Venézia Lido *Italy* 45°25N 12°22E **93** C9
Venezuela ■ *S. Amer.* 8°0N 66°0W **186** B5
Venezuela, G. de
  Venezuela 11°30N 71°0W **186** A4
Vengurla *India* 15°53N 73°45E **127** G1
Vengurla Rocks *India* 15°55N 73°22E **127** G1
Venice = Venézia *Italy* 45°27N 12°21E **93** C9
Venice *U.S.A.* 27°6N 82°27W **179** H7
Vénissieux *France* 45°42N 4°53E **73** C8
Venjan *Sweden* 60°57N 13°53E **62** D7
Venjansjön *Sweden* 60°54N 14°0E **62** D8
Venkatagiri *India* 14°0N 79°35E **127** H4
Venkatapuram *India* 18°20N 80°30E **126** E5
Venlo *Neths.* 51°22N 6°11E **69** C6
Vennachar Junction
  Canada 45°5N 77°14W **174** A7
Vengadeo *Spain* 43°27N 7°4W **88** B3
Vegoritida, L. *Greece* 40°45N 21°45E **96** F5
Vegreville *Canada* 53°30N 112°5W **162** C6
Veinge *Sweden* 56°33N 13°4E **63** H7
Veisiejai *Lithuania* 54°6N 23°42E **82** D10
Vejbystrand *Sweden* 56°19N 12°45E **63** H6
Vejen *Denmark* 55°30N 9°9E **63** J3
Vejer de la Frontera
  Spain 36°15N 5°59W **89** J5

Ventura *U.S.A.* 34°17N 119°18W **171** L7
Venus *U.S.A.* 27°4N 81°22W **179** H8
Venus, Pte. *Tahiti* 17°29S 149°29W **155** b
Venus B. *Australia* 38°40S 145°42E **153** E6
Venustiano Carranza
  Mexico 30°25N 115°53W **180** A1
Venustiano Carranza, Presa
  Mexico 27°30N 100°37W **180** B4
Vera *Argentina* 29°30S 60°20W **190** B3
Vera *Spain* 37°15N 1°51W **91** H3
Veracruz *Mexico* 19°11N 96°8W **181** D5
Veracruz □ *Mexico* 19°0N 96°15W **181** D5
Veraval *India* 20°53N 70°27E **124** J4
Verbánia *Italy* 45°56N 8°33E **92** C5
Verbano, L. di = Maggiore, L.
  Italy 45°57N 8°39E **92** B5
Verbano Cusio Ossola □
  Italy 45°40N 8°30E **92** C5
Verbicaro *Italy* 39°45N 15°55E **95** C8
Verbier *Switz.* 46°6N 7°13E **77** J3
Vercelli *Italy* 45°19N 8°25E **92** C5
Verchovchevo *Ukraine* 48°32N 34°10E **85** H8
Verdalsøra *Norway* 63°48N 11°30E **60** E14
Verde → *Argentina* 41°56N 65°5W **190** E4
Verde → *Goiás, Brazil* 18°1S 50°14W **187** G8
Verde → *Mato Grosso do Sul,*
  Brazil 21°25S 52°20W **187** H8
Verde → *Chihuahua,*
  Mexico 26°29N 107°11W **180** B3
Verde → *Jalisco,*
  Mexico 20°42N 103°14W **180** C4
Verde → *Oaxaca,*
  Mexico 15°59N 97°50W **181** D5
Verde → *Paraguay* 23°9S 57°37W **190** A4
Verde → *U.S.A.* 33°33N 111°40W **169** K8
Verde, Cay *Bahamas* 23°0N 75°5W **182** B4
Verde Grande →
  Brazil 16°13S 43°49W **189** D2
Verde Pequeno →
  Brazil 14°48S 43°31W **189** D2
Verden *Germany* 52°55N 9°14E **76** C5
Verdi *U.S.A.* 39°31N 119°59W **170** F7
Verdikoussa *Greece* 39°47N 21°59E **98** B3
Verdon → *France* 43°43N 5°46E **73** E9
Verdun *France* 45°50N 6°5E **73** C10
Verdun *France* 49°9N 5°24E **71** C12
Verdun-sur-le-Doubs
  France 46°54N 5°2E **71** F12
Vereeniging *S. Africa* 26°38S 27°57E **145** C4
Verendrye △ *Canada* 47°20N 76°40W **164** C4
Verga, C. *Guinea* 10°30N 14°10W **138** C2
Vergara = Bergara *Spain* 43°9N 2°28W **90** B2
Vergara *Uruguay* 32°56S 53°57W **191** C5
Vergato *Italy* 44°17N 11°7E **92** D8
Vergemont Cr. →
  Australia 24°16S 143°16E **150** C3
Vergennes *U.S.A.* 44°10N 73°15W **175** B11
Vergina = Aigai *Greece* 40°28N 22°19E **96** F6
Vergt *France* 45°2N 0°43E **72** C4
Véria *Greece* 40°34N 22°12E **96** F6
Verín *Spain* 41°57N 7°27W **88** D3
Verkhnedvinsk =
  Vyerkhnyadzvinsk
  Belarus 55°45N 27°58E **84** E4
Verkhnetulomskoye Vdkhr.
  Russia 68°36N 31°12E **60** B24
Verkhnevilyuysk
  Russia 63°27N 120°18E **107** C13
Verkhniy Baskunchak
  Russia 48°14N 46°44E **87** F8
Verkhovye *Russia* 52°55N 37°15E **85** F9
Verkhovyna *Ukraine* 48°9N 24°47E **81** B9
Verkhoyansk *Russia* 67°35N 133°25E **107** C14
Verkhoyansk Ra. =
  Verkhoyanskiy Khrebet
  Russia 66°0N 129°0E **107** C13
Verkhoyanskiy Khrebet
  Russia 66°0N 129°0E **107** C13
Vermeille, Côte *France* 42°30N 3°20E **72** F7
Vermenton *France* 47°40N 3°42E **71** E10
Vermilion *Canada* 53°20N 110°50W **162** C6
Vermilion *U.S.A.* 41°25N 82°22W **174** E2
Vermilion → *Canada* 53°22N 110°51W **162** C6
Vermilion B. *U.S.A.* 29°42N 92°0W **179** H6
Vermilion Bay *Canada* 49°51N 93°34W **163** D10
Vermilion Cliffs Nat.
  Monument △
  U.S.A. 36°54N 112°5W **169** H7
Vermilion L. *U.S.A.* 47°53N 92°26W **172** B7
Vermillion *U.S.A.* 42°47N 96°56W **172** D5
Vermillion → *Canada* 47°38N 72°56W **164** C5
Vermont □ *U.S.A.* 44°0N 73°0W **175** C12
Vermosh *Albania* 42°35N 19°42E **96** D3
Verna *Bulgaria* 43°13N 27°56E **97** C11
Vernal *U.S.A.* 40°27N 109°32W **168** F9
Vernalis *U.S.A.* 37°36N 121°17W **170** H5
Verner *Canada* 46°25N 80°8W **164** C3
Verneuil-sur-Avre *France* 48°45N 0°55E **70** D7
Verneukpan *S. Africa* 30°0S 21°0E **144** D3
Vernet *Switz.* 46°11N 6°12E **77** J2
Vernon *Canada* 50°20N 119°15W **162** C5
Vernon *France* 49°5N 1°30E **70** C8
Vernon *U.S.A.* 34°9N 99°17W **176** D5
Vernonia *U.S.A.* 45°52N 123°11W **170** D3
Vero Beach *U.S.A.* 27°38N 80°24W **179** H9
Véroia = Veria *Greece* 40°34N 22°12E **96** F6
Véroli *Italy* 41°41N 13°25E **93** G10
Verona *Canada* 44°29N 76°42W **175** B8
Verona *Italy* 45°27N 10°59E **92** C7
Verona *U.S.A.* 45°40N 72°2E **172** D8
Versailles *France* 48°48N 2°7E **71** D9
Versmold *Germany* 52°2N 8°9E **76** C4
Vert, C. *Senegal* 14°45N 17°30W **138** C1
Vertou *France* 47°10N 1°28W **70** E5
Vertus *France* 48°54N 4°2E **71** D11
Verulam *S. Africa* 29°38S 31°2E **145** C5
Verviers *Belgium* 50°37N 5°52E **69** D5
Vervins *France* 49°50N 3°53E **71** C10
Verzej *Slovenia* 46°34N 16°13E **93** B13
Verzy *France* 49°9N 4°10E **71** C11
Vescovato *France* 42°30N 9°27E **73** F13
Veseli nad Lužnicí
  Czechia 49°12N 14°43E **78** B7
Veselovskoye Vdkhr.
  Russia 46°58N 41°25E **87** G5
Veselie *Bulgaria* 42°18N 27°38E **97** D11

Vessigebro *Sweden* 56°58N 12°40E **63** H6
Vesterålen *Norway* 68°45N 15°0E **60** B16
Vestfjorden *Norway* 67°55N 14°0E **60** C16
Vestmannaeyjar *Iceland* 63°27N 20°15W **64** E3
Vestvågøya *Norway* 68°18N 13°50E **60** B15
Vesuvio *Italy* 40°49N 14°26E **95** B7
Vesuvius, Mt. = Vesuvio
  Italy 40°49N 14°26E **95** B7
Vetlanda *Sweden* 57°24N 15°3E **63** G9
Vetluga *Russia* 57°53N 45°45E **86** B7
Vetlugu → *Russia* 56°36N 46°4E **86** B7
Vetovo *Bulgaria* 43°42N 26°16E **97** C10
Vetralla *Italy* 42°20N 12°2E **93** F9
Vetren *Bulgaria* 42°15N 24°3E **97** D8
Vettore, Mte. *Italy* 42°49N 13°16E **93** F10
Veurne *Belgium* 51°5N 2°40E **69** C2
Vevey *Switz.* 46°28N 6°51E **77** J2
Vevi *Greece* 40°47N 21°38E **96** F5
Veynes *France* 44°32N 5°49E **73** D9
Veys *Iran* 31°30N 49°0E **129** D6
Vézelay *France* 47°27N 3°45E **71** E10
Vézelise *France* 48°30N 6°5E **71** D13
Vézère → *France* 44°53N 0°53E **72** D4
Vezhen *Bulgaria* 42°50N 24°20E **97** D8
Vezirköprü *Turkey* 41°8N 35°27E **104** B6
Vezzani *France* 42°14N 9°18E **73** F13
Vi Thanh *Vietnam* 9°42N 105°26E **121** H5
Viacha *Bolivia* 16°39S 68°18W **188** D4
Viadana *Italy* 44°56N 10°31E **92** D7
Viamão *Brazil* 30°5S 51°0W **191** C5
Viana *Brazil* 3°13S 44°55W **189** A2
Viana *Spain* 42°31N 2°22W **90** C2
Viana do Alentejo
  Portugal 38°17N 7°59W **89** G3
Viana do Bolo *Spain* 42°11N 7°6W **88** C3
Viana do Castelo
  Portugal 41°42N 8°50W **88** D2
Viana do Castelo □
  Portugal 41°50N 8°30W **88** D2
Vianden *Lux.* 49°56N 6°12E **69** E6
Viangchan = Vientiane
  Laos 17°58N 102°36E **120** D4
Vianópolis *Brazil* 16°40S 48°35W **189** D1
Vianos *Greece* 35°2N 25°21E **101** D7
Viar → *Spain* 37°36N 5°50W **89** H5
Viaréggio *Italy* 43°52N 10°14E **92** E7
Viaur → *France* 44°8N 1°58E **72** D5
Vibble *Sweden* 57°37N 18°16E **63** G12
Vibo Valéntia *Italy* 38°40N 16°6E **95** D9
Viborg *Denmark* 56°27N 9°23E **63** H3
Vibraye *France* 48°3N 0°44E **70** D7
Vic *Spain* 41°58N 2°19E **90** D7
Vich = Vic *Spain* 41°58N 2°19E **90** D7
Vichada □ *Colombia* 4°55N 67°50W **186** C5
Vichuga *Russia* 57°12N 41°55E **86** B6
Vichy *France* 46°9N 3°26E **71** F10
Vicksburg *Ariz.,*
  U.S.A. 33°45N 113°45W **171** M13
Vicksburg *Miss., U.S.A.* 32°21N 90°53W **177** E9
Vico *France* 42°10N 8°48E **73** F12
Vico, L. di *Italy* 42°19N 12°10E **93** F9
Vico del Gargano *Italy* 41°54N 15°57E **93** G12
Viçosa *Brazil* 9°28S 36°14W **189** B3
Viçosa do Ceará *Brazil* 3°34S 41°5W **189** A2
Vicovu de Sus *Romania* 47°56N 25°41E **81** C10
Victor *India* 21°0N 71°30E **124** J4
Victor Harbor
  Australia 35°30S 138°37E **152** C3
Victoria *Argentina* 32°40S 60°10W **190** C3
Victoria *Canada* 48°30N 123°25W **170** B3
Victoria *Chile* 38°13S 72°20W **190** D2
Victoria *China* 22°17N 114°11E **111** a
Victoria *Guinea* 10°50N 14°32W **138** C2
Victoria *Malta* 36°3N 14°14E **101** C1
Victoria *Romania* 45°44N 24°41E **81** E9
Victoria *Seychelles* 4°38S 55°28E **141** b
Victoria *Kans., U.S.A.* 38°52N 99°9W **172** F4
Victoria *Tex., U.S.A.* 28°48N 97°0W **176** G6
Victoria → *Australia* 15°10S 129°40E **148** C4
Victoria □ *Australia* 37°0S 144°0E **152** D6
Victoria, Grand L.
  Canada 47°31N 77°30W **164** C4
Victoria, L. *Africa* 1°0S 33°0E **142** C3
Victoria, L. *Australia* 33°57S 141°15E **152** B4
Victoria, Mt. *Myanmar* 21°15N 93°55W **123** J18
Victoria Beach *Canada* 50°40N 96°35W **163** C9
Victoria de Durango = Durango
  Mexico 24°3N 104°39W **180** C4
Victoria de las Tunas = Las Tunas
  Cuba 20°58N 76°59W **182** B4
Victoria Falls *Zimbabwe* 17°58S 25°52E **143** F2
Victoria Fjord *Greenland* 82°10N 46°0W **57** A6
Victoria Harbour
  Canada 44°45N 79°45W **174** B5
Victoria I. *Canada* 71°0N 111°0W **160** C9
Victoria Ld. *Antarctica* 75°0S 160°0E **55** D11
Victoria Nile → *Uganda* 2°14N 31°26E **142** D2
Victoria River *Australia* 16°25S 131°0E **148** C5
Victoria Str. *Canada* 69°31N 100°30W **160** D11
Victoria West *S. Africa* 31°25S 23°4E **144** D3
Victoriaville *Canada* 46°4N 71°56W **165** C5
Victorica *Argentina* 36°20S 65°30W **190** D2
Victorville *U.S.A.* 34°32N 117°18W **171** L9
Vicuña *Chile* 30°0S 70°50W **190** C1
Vicuña Mackenna
  Argentina 33°53S 64°25W **190** C3
Vidal *U.S.A.* 34°7N 114°31W **171** L12
Vidalia *U.S.A.* 32°13N 82°25W **178** E4
Vidamlya *Belarus* 52°19N 23°47E **83** F10
Vidauban *France* 43°25N 6°27E **73** E10

Viddolatno = Vindelälven →
  Sweden 63°55N 19°50E **60** E18
Videbæk *Denmark* 56°6N 8°38E **63** H2
Videle *Romania* 44°17N 25°31E **81** F10
Vidette *U.S.A.* 33°2N 82°15W **178** B7
Vidigueira *Portugal* 38°12N 7°48W **89** G3
Vidin *Bulgaria* 43°59N 22°50E **96** C6
Vidin □ *Bulgaria* 43°59N 22°50E **96** C6
Vidio, C. *Spain* 43°35N 6°14W **88** B4
Vidisha *India* 23°28N 77°53E **124** H7
Vidos *Greece* 39°38N 19°55E **101** A3
Vidra *Romania* 45°56N 26°55E **81** E11
Viduša *Bos.-H.* 42°55N 18°21E **96** D2
Vidzy *Belarus* 55°23N 26°37E **84** E4
Viechtach *Germany* 49°4N 12°53E **77** F8
Viedma *Argentina* 40°50S 63°0W **190** E3
Viedma, L. *Argentina* 49°30S 72°30W **192** C2
Vieira do Minho *Portugal* 41°38N 8°8W **88** D2
Vielha *Spain* 42°43N 0°44E **90** C5
Viella = Vielha *Spain* 42°43N 0°44E **90** C5
Vielle-St-Girons *France* 43°56N 1°18W **72** E2
Vielsalm *Belgium* 50°17N 5°54E **69** D5
Vienenburg *Germany* 51°57N 10°34E **76** D6
Vieng Pou Kha *Laos* 20°41N 101°4E **116** G3
Vienna = Wien *Austria* 48°12N 16°22E **79** C9
Vienna *Ga., U.S.A.* 32°6N 83°47W **178** C6
Vienna *Ill., U.S.A.* 37°25N 88°54W **172** G9
Vienna *Mo., U.S.A.* 38°11N 91°57W **172** F8
Vienne *France* 45°31N 4°53E **73** C8
Vienne □ *France* 46°30N 0°42E **72** B4
Vienne → *France* 47°13N 0°5E **70** E7
Vientiane *Laos* 17°58N 102°36E **120** D4
Vientos, Paso de los
  Caribbean 20°0N 74°0W **183** C5
Vieques *Puerto Rico* 18°8N 65°25W **183** d
Vierge Pt. *St. Lucia* 13°49N 60°53W **183** f
Viernheim *Germany* 49°31N 8°35E **77** F4
Viersen *Germany* 51°15N 6°23E **76** D2
Vierwaldstättersee *Switz.* 46°57N 8°30E **77** J4
Vierzon *France* 47°13N 2°5E **71** E9
Vieste *Italy* 41°53N 16°10E **93** G13
Viet Quang *Vietnam* 22°30N 104°48E **116** F5
Viet Tri *Vietnam* 21°18N 105°25E **120** B5
Vietnam ■ *Asia* 19°0N 106°0E **120** C6
Vieux-Boucau-les-Bains
  France 43°48N 1°23W **72** E2
Vieux Fort *St. Lucia* 13°46N 60°58W **183** f
Vif *France* 45°5N 5°41E **73** C9
Vigan *Phil.* 17°35N 120°28E **119** A6
Vigévano *Italy* 45°19N 8°51E **92** C5
Vigia *Brazil* 0°50S 48°5W **187** D9
Viglas, Akra *Greece* 35°54N 27°51E **101** D9
Vignemale *France* 42°47N 0°10W **72** F3
Vigneulles-lès-Hattonchâtel
  France 48°59N 5°43E **71** D12
Vignola *Italy* 44°29N 11°1E **92** D8
Vigo *Spain* 42°12N 8°41W **88** C2
Vigo, Ría de *Spain* 42°15N 8°45W **88** C2
Vihiers *France* 47°10N 0°30W **70** E6
Vihiga *Kenya* 0°3N 34°44E **142** B3
Vihowa *Pakistan* 31°8N 70°30E **124** D4
Vihowa → *Pakistan* 31°8N 70°41E **124** D4
Vijayadurg *India* 16°30N 73°25E **126** F1
Vijayapura *India* 16°50N 75°55E **126** F2
Vijayawada *India* 16°31N 80°39E **126** F5
Vijosë → *Albania* 40°37N 19°24E **96** F3
Vík *Iceland* 63°25N 19°1W **60** E4
Vika *Sweden* 60°57N 14°28E **62** D8
Vikarabad *India* 17°20N 77°54E **124** L10
Vikarbyn *Sweden* 60°55N 15°1E **62** D9
Vikeke = Viqueque
  E. Timor 8°52S 126°23E **119** F7
Viken *Skåne, Sweden* 56°9N 12°34E **63** H6
Viken *Västra Götaland,*
  Sweden 58°39N 14°20E **63** F8
Viking *Canada* 53°7N 111°50W **162** C6
Vikmanshyttan *Sweden* 60°18N 15°50E **62** D9
Vikna *Norway* 64°55N 10°58E **60** D14
Vikos-Aoos △ *Greece* 40°0N 20°45E **98** B2
Vila Bela da Santíssima Trindade
  Brazil 15°0S 59°57W **186** G7
Vila da Maganja
  Mozam. 17°18S 37°30E **143** F4
Vila da Ribeira Brava
  Cabo Verde 16°32N 24°25W **134** b
Vila de Rei *Portugal* 39°41N 8°9W **88** F2
Vila do Bispo *Portugal* 37°5N 8°53W **89** H2
Vila do Conde *Portugal* 41°21N 8°45W **88** D2
Vila do Maio *Cabo Verde* 15°21N 23°10W **134** b
Vila Franca de Xira
  Portugal 38°57N 8°59W **89** G2
Vila Gamito *Mozam.* 14°12S 33°0E **143** E3
Vila Gomes da Costa
  Mozam. 24°20S 33°37E **145** B5
Vila Machado *Mozam.* 19°15S 34°14E **143** F3
Vila Mouzinho *Mozam.* 14°48S 34°25E **143** E3
Vila Nova de Famalicão
  Portugal 41°25N 8°32W **88** D2
Vila Nova de Foz Côa
  Portugal 41°5N 7°9W **88** D3
Vila Nova de Gaia
  Portugal 41°8N 8°37W **88** D2
Vila Pouca de Aguiar
  Portugal 41°30N 7°38W **88** D3
Vila Real *Portugal* 41°17N 7°48W **88** D3
Vila Real *Spain* 39°55N 0°3W **90** F4
Vila Real □ *Portugal* 41°36N 7°35W **88** D3
Vila Real de Santo António
  Portugal 37°10N 7°28W **89** H3
Vila-seca *Spain* 41°7N 1°9E **90** D6
Vila Vasco da Gama
  Mozam. 14°54S 32°14E **143** E3
Vila Velha *Espírito Santo,*
  Brazil 20°20S 40°17W **189** E2
Vila Velha *Sergipe, Brazil* 11°20S 36°59W **189** C3
Vila Viçosa *Portugal* 38°45N 7°27W **89** G3

Vilaseca-Salou = Vila-seca
 Spain 41°7N 1°9E 90 D6
Vilbjerg Denmark 56°12N 8°46E 63 H2
Vilcabamba, Cordillera
 Peru 13°0S 72°0W 188 C3
Vilcanchos Peru 13°40S 74°25W 188 C3
Vilcheka, Ostrov Russia 80°0N 58°31E 106 B6
Vilcheka, Zemlya
 Russia 80°30N 60°30E 54 A11
Vilches Spain 38°12N 3°30W 89 G7
Vileyka Belarus 54°30N 26°53E 75 A14
Vilhelmina Sweden 64°35N 16°39E 60 D17
Vilhena Brazil 12°40S 60°5W 186 F6
Viliya = Neris →
 Lithuania 55°8N 24°16E 84 E3
Viljandi Estonia 58°28N 25°30E 84 C3
Vilkaviškis Lithuania 54°39N 23°2E 82 D10
Vilkija Lithuania 55°3N 23°35E 82 C10
Vilkitskogo, Proliv
 Russia 78°0N 103°0E 107 B11
Vilkovo = Vylkove
 Ukraine 45°28N 29°32E 81 E14
Villa Abecia Bolivia 21°0S 68°18W 190 A2
Villa Ana Argentina 28°28S 59°40W 190 B4
Villa Angela Argentina 27°34S 60°45W 190 B3
Villa Bella Bolivia 10°25S 65°22W 186 F5
Villa Cañás Argentina 34°0S 61°35W 190 C3
Villa Constitución
 Argentina 33°15S 60°20W 190 C3
Villa de Arriaga
 Mexico 21°56N 101°20W 180 C4
Villa de María
 Argentina 29°55S 63°43W 190 B3
Villa de Méndez Mexico 25°7N 98°34W 181 B5
Villa del Rio Spain 37°59N 4°17W 89 H6
Villa Dolores Argentina 31°58S 65°15W 190 C2
Villa Gesell Argentina 37°15S 56°55W 190 D4
Villa Guillermina
 Argentina 28°15S 59°29W 190 B4
Villa Hayes Paraguay 25°5S 57°20W 190 B4
Villa Hidalgo Mexico 24°15N 99°26W 181 C5
Villa Iris Argentina 38°12S 63°12W 190 D3
Villa Las Estrellas = Frei
 Antarctica 62°30S 58°0W 55 C18
Villa María Argentina 32°20S 63°10W 190 C3
Villa Mazán Argentina 28°40S 66°30W 190 B3
Villa Minozzo Italy 44°22N 10°28E 92 D7
Villa Montes Bolivia 21°10S 63°30W 190 A3
Villa Ocampo
 Argentina 28°30S 59°20W 190 B4
Villa Ocampo Mexico 26°27N 105°31W 180 B3
Villa Ojo de Agua
 Argentina 29°30S 63°44W 190 B3
Villa Regina Argentina 39°6S 67°4W 192 A3
Villa Rica U.S.A. 33°44N 84°55W 178 B5
Villa San Giovanni Italy 38°13N 15°38E 95 D8
Villa San Martín
 Argentina 28°15S 64°9W 190 B3
Villa Santina Italy 46°24N 12°55E 93 B9
Villa Unión Mexico 23°12N 106°14W 180 C3
Villablino Spain 42°57N 6°19W 88 C4
Villacarlos Spain 39°53N 4°17E 100 B11
Villacarrillo Spain 43°14N 3°48W 88 B7
Villacarrillo Spain 38°7N 3°3W 89 G7
Villacastín Spain 40°46N 4°25W 88 E6
Villach Austria 46°37N 13°51E 78 E6
Villacidro Italy 39°27N 8°44E 94 C1
Villada Spain 42°15N 4°59W 88 C6
Villadiego Spain 42°31N 4°1W 88 C6
Villadóssola Italy 46°4N 8°16E 92 B5
Villafeliche Spain 41°10N 1°30W 90 D3
Villafranca Spain 42°17N 1°46W 90 C3
Villafranca de Bonany
 Spain 39°34N 3°5E 100 B10
Villafranca de los Barros
 Spain 38°35N 6°18W 89 G4
Villafranca de los Caballeros
 Spain 39°26N 3°21W 89 F7
Villafranca del Cid Spain 40°26N 0°16W 90 E4
Villafranca del Panadés =
 Vilafranca del Penedès
 Spain 41°21N 1°40E 90 D6
Villafranca di Verona
 Italy 45°21N 10°50E 92 C7
Villafranca Tirrena Italy 38°20N 15°25E 95 D8
Villagrán Mexico 24°29N 99°29W 181 C5
Villaguay Argentina 32°0S 59°0W 190 C4
Villaharta Spain 38°9N 4°54W 89 G6
Villahermosa Mexico 17°59N 92°55W 181 D6
Villahermosa Spain 38°46N 2°52W 91 G2
Villaines-la-Juhel France 48°20N 0°20W 70 D6
Villajoyosa Spain 38°30N 0°12W 91 G4
Villalba Spain 43°26N 7°40W 88 B3
Villalba de Guardo Spain 42°42N 4°49W 88 C6
Villalón de Campos Spain 42°5N 5°4W 88 C5
Villalpando Spain 41°51N 5°25W 88 D5
Villaluenga de la Sagra
 Spain 40°2N 3°54W 88 E7
Villamanán Spain 42°19N 5°35W 88 C5
Villamartín Spain 36°52N 5°38W 89 J5
Villamayor de Santiago
 Spain 39°50N 2°59W 90 F2
Villamblard France 45°2N 0°32E 72 C4
Villanova Monteleone
 Italy 40°30N 8°28E 94 B1
Villanueva U.S.A. 35°16N 105°22W 169 J11
Villanueva de Castellón
 Spain 39°5N 0°31W 91 F4
Villanueva de la Fuente
 Spain 38°42N 2°42W 91 G2
Villanueva de la Serena
 Spain 38°59N 5°50W 89 G5
Villanueva de la Sierra
 Spain 40°12N 6°24W 88 E4
Villanueva de los Castillejos
 Spain 37°30N 7°15W 89 H3
Villanueva de los Infantes
 Spain 38°43N 3°1W 89 G7
Villanueva del Arzobispo
 Spain 38°10N 3°0W 91 G2
Villanueva del Fresno
 Spain 38°23N 7°10W 89 G3
Villanueva y Geltrú = Vilanova i
 la Geltrú Spain 41°13N 1°40E 90 D6
Villaquilambre Spain 42°39N 5°33E 88 C5
Villar del Arzobispo
 Spain 39°44N 0°50W 90 F4
Villar del Rey Spain 39°7N 6°50W 89 F4
Villard-de-Lans France 45°3N 5°33E 73 C9

Villarramiel Spain 42°2N 4°55W 88 C6
Villarreal = Vila-Real
 Spain 39°55N 0°3W 90 F4
Villarrica Chile 39°15S 72°15W 192 A2
Villarrica Paraguay 25°40S 56°30W 190 B4
Villarrica △ Chile 39°24S 71°46W 192 A2
Villarrobledo Spain 39°18N 2°36W 91 F2
Villarroya de la Sierra
 Spain 41°27N 1°46W 90 D3
Villarrubia de los Ojos
 Spain 39°14N 3°36W 89 F7
Villarroya de los Gamitos
 Spain 41°2N 6°7W 88 D4
Villasimius Italy 39°8N 9°31E 94 C2
Villastar Spain 40°17N 1°9W 90 E3
Villatobas Spain 39°54N 3°20W 88 F7
Villavicencio Argentina 32°28S 69°0W 190 C2
Villavicencio Colombia 4°9N 73°37W 186 C4
Villaviciosa Spain 43°32N 5°27W 88 B5
Villazón Bolivia 22°0S 65°35W 190 A2
Ville-Marie Canada 47°20N 79°30W 164 C4
Ville Platte U.S.A. 30°41N 92°17W 176 F8
Villedieu-les-Poêles
 France 48°50N 1°13W 70 D5
Villefort France 44°28N 3°56E 72 D7
Villefranche-de-Lauragais
 France 43°25N 1°44E 72 E5
Villefranche-de-Rouergue
 France 44°21N 2°2E 72 D6
Villefranche-du-Périgord
 France 44°38N 1°5E 72 D5
Villefranche-sur-Saône
 France 45°59N 4°43E 73 C8
Villel Spain 40°14N 1°12W 90 E3
Villemur-sur-Tarn France 43°51N 1°31E 72 E5
Villena Spain 38°39N 0°52W 91 G4
Villenauxe-la-Grande
 France 48°35N 3°33E 71 D10
Villeneuve-d'Ornon
 France 44°46N 0°33W 72 D3
Villeneuve-d'Ascq France 50°38N 3°9E 71 B10
Villeneuve-l'Archevêque
 France 48°14N 3°32E 71 D10
Villeneuve-lès-Avignon
 France 43°58N 4°49E 73 E8
Villeneuve-sur-Allier
 France 46°40N 3°13E 71 F10
Villeneuve-sur-Lot
 France 44°24N 0°42E 72 D4
Villeneuve-sur-Yonne
 France 48°5N 3°18E 71 D10
Villeréal France 44°38N 0°45E 72 D4
Villers-Bocage France 49°3N 0°40W 70 C6
Villers-Cotterêts France 49°15N 3°4E 71 C10
Villers-sur-Mer France 49°21N 0°2W 70 C6
Villersexel France 47°33N 6°26E 71 E13
Villerupt France 49°28N 5°55E 71 C12
Villeurbanne France 45°46N 4°55E 73 C8
Villiers S. Africa 27°2S 28°36E 145 C4
Villingen-Schwenningen
 Germany 48°3N 8°26E 77 G4
Villmanstrand = Lappeenranta
 Finland 61°3N 28°12E 84 B5
Villupuram India 11°59N 79°31E 127 J4
Vilna Canada 54°7N 111°55W 162 C6
Vilnius Lithuania 54°38N 25°19E 84 E3
Vils Austria 47°33N 10°38E 78 D3
Vils → Bayern, Germany 48°37N 13°11E 77 G8
Vils → Bayern, Germany 49°10N 11°57E 77 F7
Vilsandi △ Estonia 58°23N 21°52E 84 C1
Vilsbiburg Germany 48°26N 12°22E 77 G8
Vilshofen Germany 48°37N 13°11E 77 G8
Vilusi Montenegro 42°44N 18°34E 96 D2
Vilvoorde Belgium 50°56N 4°26E 69 D4
Vilyuchinsk Russia 52°55N 158°24E 107 D16
Vilyuy → Russia 64°24N 126°26E 107 C13
Vilyuysk Russia 63°40N 121°35E 107 C13
Vilyuyskoye Vdkhr.
 Russia 63°0N 112°0E 107 C12
Vimianzo Spain 43°7N 9°2W 88 B1
Vimioso Portugal 41°35N 6°31W 88 D4
Vimmerby Sweden 57°40N 15°55E 63 G9
Vimoutiers France 48°57N 0°10E 70 D7
Vimperk Czechia 49°3N 13°46E 76 D6
Viña del Mar Chile 33°0S 71°30W 190 C1
Vinarós Spain 40°30N 0°27E 90 E6
Vincennes U.S.A. 38°41N 87°32W 172 F10
Vincennes Bay S. Ocean 66°0S 109°0E 55 C8
Vincent U.S.A. 34°33N 118°11W 171 L8
Vinchina Argentina 28°45S 68°15W 190 B2
Vindelälven → Sweden 63°55N 19°50E 60 E18
Vindeln Sweden 64°12N 19°43E 60 D18
Vinderup Denmark 56°29N 8°45E 63 H2
Vindhya Ra. India 22°50N 77°0E 124 H7
Vineland U.S.A. 39°29N 75°2W 173 F16
Vineuil France 47°35N 1°22E 70 E8
Vinga Romania 46°1N 21°14E 80 D6
Vingåker Sweden 59°2N 15°52E 62 E9
Vinh Vietnam 18°45N 105°38E 120 C5
Vinh Long Vietnam 10°16N 105°57E 121 G5
Vinh Moc Vietnam 21°18N 105°1E 120 B5
Vinh Yen Vietnam 21°21N 105°35E 116 G5
Vinhais Portugal 41°50N 7°5W 88 D3
Vinica Macedonia 41°53N 22°32E 96 E6
Vinica Slovenia 45°28N 15°16E 93 C12
Vinita U.S.A. 36°39N 95°9W 176 C7
Vinkovci Croatia 45°19N 18°48E 80 E3
Vinnytsia = Vinnytsya
 Ukraine 49°15N 28°30E 75 D15
Vinnytsya Ukraine 49°15N 28°30E 75 D15
Vinnytsya □ Ukraine 49°20N 28°15E 75 D15
Vinslöv Sweden 56°7N 13°55E 63 H7
Vinson Massif
 Antarctica 78°35S 85°25W 55 D16
Vintjärn Sweden 60°56N 16°4E 62 F10
Vinton Calif., U.S.A. 39°48N 120°10W 170 F6
Vinton Iowa, U.S.A. 42°10N 92°1W 172 D8
Vinton La., U.S.A. 30°11N 93°35W 176 F8
Vințu de Jos Romania 46°0N 23°30E 81 E12
Vinukonda India 16°5N 79°45E 127 F4
Viöl Germany 54°34N 9°11E 64 A5
Violet Town Australia 36°38S 145°42E 153 D6
Violet Valley ◎
 Australia 17°10S 127°55E 148 C4
Vioolsdrif S. Africa 28°46S 17°39E 144 C2
Viotia □ Greece 38°20N 23°0E 98 C5
Vipava Slovenia 45°51N 13°58E 93 C10
Vipiteno Italy 46°54N 11°26E 93 B8
Viqueque E. Timor 8°52S 126°23E 119 F7

Vir Croatia 44°17N 15°3E 93 D12
Virac Phil. 13°30N 124°20E 119 B6
Virachey Cambodia 14°15N 106°48E 120 F6
Virachey △ Cambodia 14°14N 106°55E 120 E6
Virago Sd. Canada 54°20N 132°30W 162 C2
Virajpet = Virarajendrapet
 India 12°10N 75°50E 127 H2
Viramgam India 23°5N 72°0E 124 H5
Virananşehir Turkey 37°13N 39°45E 105 D8
Virarajendrapet India 12°10N 75°50E 127 H2
Virawah Pakistan 24°31N 70°46E 124 G4
Virbalis Lithuania 54°39N 22°49E 82 D9
Virden Canada 49°50N 100°56W 163 D8
Vire France 48°50N 0°53W 70 D6
Vire → France 49°20N 1°7W 70 C5
Virgem da Lapa Brazil 16°49S 42°21W 189 D2
Virgenes, C. Argentina 52°19S 68°21W 192 D3
Virgin → U.S.A. 36°28N 114°21W 169 H6
Virgin Gorda
 Br. Virgin Is. 18°30N 64°26W 183 a
Virgin Is. (British) ☑
 W. Indies 18°30N 64°30W 183 a
Virgin Is. (U.S.) ☑
 W. Indies 18°20N 65°0W 183 a
Virgin Islands △
 U.S. Virgin Is. 18°21N 64°43W 183 C7
Virginia S. Africa 28°8S 26°55E 144 C4
Virginia U.S.A. 47°31N 92°32W 172 B7
Virginia □ U.S.A. 37°30N 78°45W 173 G14
Virginia Beach U.S.A. 36°49N 76°9W 173 F16
Virginia City Mont.,
 U.S.A. 45°18N 111°56W 168 D8
Virginia City Nev.,
 U.S.A. 39°19N 119°39W 170 F7
Virginia Falls Canada 61°38N 125°42W 162 A3
Virginiatown Canada 48°9N 79°36W 164 C4
Virje Croatia 46°4N 16°59E 93 B13
Viroqua U.S.A. 43°34N 90°53W 172 D8
Virovitica Croatia 45°51N 17°21E 80 E2
Virpazar Montenegro 42°14N 19°6E 96 D3
Virpur India 21°51N 70°42E 124 J4
Virsbo Sweden 59°52N 16°12E 62 E10
Virserum Sweden 57°20N 15°35E 63 G9
Virton Belgium 49°35N 5°32E 69 E5
Virtsu Estonia 58°32N 23°33E 84 C2
Virú Peru 8°25S 78°45W 188 B2
Virudhunagar India 9°30N 77°58E 127 K3
Virunga △
 Dem. Rep. of the Congo 0°5N 29°38E 142 B2
Vis Croatia 43°4N 16°10E 93 E13
Visalia U.S.A. 36°20N 119°18W 170 J7
Visayan Sea Phil. 11°30N 123°30E 119 B6
Visby Sweden 57°37N 18°18E 63 G12
Viscount Melville Sd.
 Canada 74°10N 108°0W 161 C10
Visé Belgium 50°44N 5°41E 69 D5
Vise, Ostrov Russia 79°33N 76°50E 106 B8
Višegrad Bos.-H. 43°47N 19°17E 80 G4
Viseu Brazil 1°10S 46°5W 187 D9
Viseu Portugal 40°40N 7°55W 88 E3
Viseu □ Portugal 40°40N 7°55W 88 E3
Vişeu de Sus Romania 47°45N 24°25E 81 C9
Vishakhapatnam India 17°45N 83°20E 126 F6
Vişina Romania 43°52N 24°27E 81 G9
Vişineşti Moldova 46°20N 28°27E 81 D13
Visingsö Sweden 58°2N 14°20E 63 F8
Viskafors Sweden 57°37N 12°50E 63 G6
Viskan → Sweden 57°14N 12°12E 63 G6
Viški Kanal Croatia 43°4N 16°5E 93 E13
Vislanda Sweden 56°46N 14°30E 63 H8
Visnagar India 23°45N 72°32E 124 H5
Višnja Gora Slovenia 45°58N 14°45E 93 C11
Viso, Mte. Italy 44°38N 7°5E 92 D4
Viso del Marqués Spain 38°32N 3°34W 89 G7
Visoko Bos.-H. 43°58N 18°10E 80 G3
Visokoi I. Antarctica 56°43S 27°15W 55 B1
Visp Switz. 46°17N 7°52E 77 J3
Vissefjärda Sweden 56°32N 15°35E 63 H9
Visselhövede Germany 52°59N 9°34E 76 C5
Vissenbjerg Denmark 55°23N 10°7E 63 J4
Vista U.S.A. 33°12N 117°14W 171 M9
Vistonida, L. Greece 41°0N 25°7E 97 E9
Vistonikos, Ormos = Vistonida, L.
 Greece 41°0N 25°7E 97 E9
Vistula = Wisła →
 Poland 54°22N 18°55E 82 D5
Vistula Spit Europe 54°25N 19°35E 82 D6
Vit → Bulgaria 43°37N 24°45E 81 C11
Vita India 17°17N 74°33E 126 F2
Vitanje Slovenia 46°25N 15°18E 93 B12
Vitebsk = Vitsyebsk
 Belarus 55°10N 30°15E 84 E6
Viterbo Italy 42°25N 12°6E 93 F9
Vitez Bos.-H. 44°10N 17°48E 80 F2
Viti Levu Fiji 17°30S 177°30E 154 a
Vitigudino Spain 41°1N 6°26W 88 D4
Vitim Russia 59°28N 112°35E 107 D12
Vitim → Russia 59°26N 112°34E 107 D12
Vitina Bos.-H. 43°17N 17°29E 93 E14
Vitina Greece 37°40N 22°10E 98 D4
Vítkov Czechia 49°46N 17°45E 79 B10
Vitória da Conquista
 Brazil 14°51S 40°51W 189 D2
Vitória Brazil 20°20S 40°22W 189 C2
Vitória de Santo Antão
 Brazil 8°10S 35°20W 189 B3
Vitoria-Gasteiz Spain 42°50N 2°41W 90 C2
Vitória Seamount Atl. Oc. 20°0S 44°0W 56 J8
Vitorino Freire Brazil 4°4S 45°10W 189 A1
Vitosha △ Bulgaria 42°36N 23°18E 96 D7
Vitré France 48°8N 1°12W 70 D5
Vitry-le-François France 48°43N 4°33E 71 D11
Vitry-sur-Seine France 48°47N 2°23E 71 D9
Vitsand Sweden 60°20N 13°0E 62 D7
Vitsi, Oros Greece 40°40N 21°25E 96 F5
Vitsyebsk Belarus 55°10N 30°15E 84 E6
Vitsyebsk □ Belarus 55°10N 29°30E 84 E5
Vittangi Sweden 67°49N 21°40E 60 C19
Vittaryd Sweden 56°58N 13°57E 63 H7
Vittel France 48°12N 5°57E 71 E12
Vittória Italy 36°57N 14°32E 95 F7
Vittório Véneto Italy 45°59N 12°18E 93 C9
Vittsjö Sweden 56°20N 13°42E 63 H7
Viveiro Spain 43°39N 7°38W 88 A3
Vivian U.S.A. 32°53N 93°59W 176 E8
Viviers France 44°30N 4°40E 73 D8
Vivonne Australia 35°59S 137°9E 152 C2
Vivonne France 46°36N 0°15E 72 B4
Vivonne B. Australia 35°58S 137°9E 152 C2
Viwa Fiji 17°10S 177°58E 154 a
Vizcaíno, Desierto de
 Mexico 27°30N 113°45W 180 B2

Vizcaíno, Sierra
 Mexico 27°30N 114°0W 180 B2
Vize Turkey 41°34N 27°45E 97 E11
Vizianagaram India 18°6N 83°30E 126 E6
Vizille France 45°5N 5°46E 73 C9
Viziñada Croatia 45°20N 13°46E 93 C10
Viziru Romania 45°0N 27°43E 81 E12
Vizzini Italy 37°10N 14°45E 95 E7
Vjosa → Albania 40°37N 19°42E 96 G2
Vlaardingen Neths. 51°55N 4°21E 69 C4
Vlachiotis Greece 36°50N 22°45E 98 E4
Vlădeasa, Vf. Romania 46°47N 22°50E 80 D7
Vladichin Han Serbia 42°42N 22°1E 96 C8
Vladikavkaz Russia 43°0N 44°35E 87 J7
Vladimir Russia 56°15N 40°30E 84 D11
Vladimir □ Russia 56°5N 40°10E 86 B10
Vladimirci Serbia 44°36N 19°50E 96 B3
Vladimirovac Serbia 45°1N 20°53E 80 E5
Vladimirovka Russia 48°27N 46°10E 87 E8
Vladimirovo Bulgaria 43°32N 23°22E 96 C7
Vladislavovka Ukraine 45°12N 35°29E 85 K8
Vladivostok Russia 43°10N 131°53E 112 C5
Vlăhița Romania 46°21N 25°31E 81 D10
Vlasenica Jezero Serbia 42°44N 22°22E 96 D6
Vlasotince Serbia 42°59N 22°7E 96 D6
Vlieland Neths. 53°16N 4°55E 69 A4
Vlissingen Neths. 51°26N 3°34E 69 C3
Vlkolínec Slovakia 49°1N 19°16E 79 B12
Vlorë Albania 40°32N 19°28E 96 F3
Vlorës, Gjiri i Albania 40°29N 19°27E 96 F3
Vltava → Czechia 50°21N 14°30E 78 A7
Vo Dat Vietnam 11°9N 107°31E 121 G6
Vočin Croatia 45°37N 17°33E 80 E2
Vöcklabruck Austria 48°1N 13°39E 78 C6
Vodice Croatia 43°47N 15°47E 93 E12
Vodlozersky △ Russia 62°40N 37°5E 106 C1
Vodňany Czechia 49°9N 14°11E 78 B7
Vodnjan Croatia 44°59N 13°52E 93 D10
Voe U.K. 60°21N 1°16W 65 A7
Vogan Togo 6°23N 1°30E 139 D6
Vogel Pk. Nigeria 8°24N 11°47E 139 D7
Vogelkop = Doberai, Jazirah
 Indonesia 1°25S 133°0E 119 E8
Vogelsberg Germany 50°31N 9°12E 76 E5
Voghera Italy 44°59N 9°1E 92 D6
Vohibinany Madag. 18°49S 49°4E 141 H9
Vohimarina = Iharana
 Madag. 13°25S 50°0E 141 G10
Vohimena, Tanjon' i
 Madag. 25°36S 45°8E 141 K9
Vohipeno Madag. 22°22S 47°51E 141 J9
Voi Kenya 3°25S 38°32E 142 C4
Void-Vacon France 48°40N 5°36E 71 D12
Voineşti Iaşi, Romania 47°5N 27°27E 81 C12
Voineşti Prahova,
 Romania 45°5N 25°14E 81 E10
Voinjama Liberia 8°25N 9°44W 138 D3
Voiron France 45°22N 5°35E 73 C9
Voisey B. Canada 56°15N 61°50W 165 A7
Voitsberg Austria 47°3N 15°9E 78 D8
Vojens Denmark 55°16N 9°18E 63 J3
Vojmsjön Sweden 65°0N 16°24E 60 D17
Vojnić Croatia 45°19N 15°43E 93 C12
Vojnik Slovenia 46°18N 15°19E 93 B12
Vojvodina □ Serbia 45°20N 20°0E 80 E5
Vokhtoga Russia 58°46N 41°8E 84 C11
Volary Czechia 48°54N 13°52E 78 C6
Volborg U.S.A. 45°51N 105°41W 168 D2
Volcán de Colima △
 Mexico 19°30N 103°40W 180 D4
Volcano Is. = Kazan-Rettō
 Pac. Oc. 25°0N 141°0E 156 E6
Volcans △ Rwanda 1°30S 29°26E 142 C2
Volcans d'Auvergne △
 France 45°20N 2°40E 72 C6
Volchansk = Vovchansk
 Ukraine 50°17N 36°58E 85 G9
Volchikha Russia 52°0N 80°23E 109 B10
Volchya → Ukraine 48°32N 36°0E 85 H8
Volda Norway 62°9N 6°5E 60 E12
Volga = Privolzhskiy □
 Russia 56°0N 50°0E 86 C9
Volga Russia 57°58N 38°16E 84 C10
Volga → Russia 46°0N 48°30E 87 G9
Volga Hts. = Privolzhskaya
 Vozvyshennost Russia 51°0N 46°0E 86 E7
Volgo-Baltiyskiy Kanal
 Russia 60°0N 38°0E 84 B9
Volgo-Donskoy Kanal
 Russia 48°40N 43°37E 87 F7
Volgodonsk Russia 47°33N 42°5E 87 G6
Volgograd Russia 48°40N 44°25E 87 F7
Volgogradskoye Vdkhr.
 Russia 50°0N 45°20E 86 E8
Volgorechensk Russia 57°28N 41°14E 86 B5
Volimes Greece 37°52N 20°39E 98 D2
Volintiri Moldova 46°26N 29°37E 81 D14
Volissos Greece 38°29N 25°54E 99 C7
Volkach Germany 49°52N 10°14E 77 F6
Völkermarkt Austria 46°39N 14°39E 78 E7
Volkhov → Russia 60°8N 32°20E 84 B7
Völklingen Germany 49°15N 6°50E 77 F2
Volkovysk = Vawkavysk
 Belarus 53°9N 24°30E 75 B13
Volksrust S. Africa 27°24S 29°53E 145 C4
Volnovakha Ukraine 47°35N 37°30E 85 J9
Volochanka Russia 71°0N 94°28E 107 B10
Volodarsk Russia 56°12N 43°15E 86 B6
Volodymyr-Volynskyy
 Ukraine 50°50N 24°18E 75 C13
Vologda Russia 59°10N 39°45E 84 C10
Vologda □ Russia 59°40N 40°0E 84 C11
Volokolamsk Russia 56°5N 35°57E 84 D8
Volokonovka Russia 50°33N 37°52E 85 G9
Volos Greece 39°24N 22°59E 98 B4
Volosovo Russia 59°27N 29°32E 84 C5
Volovets Ukraine 48°43N 23°11E 81 B8
Volozhin = Valozhyn
 Belarus 54°3N 26°30E 75 A14
Volsk Russia 52°5N 47°22E 86 D8
Volta □ Ghana 7°30N 0°15E 139 D5
Volta → Ghana 5°46N 0°41E 139 D5
Volta, L. Ghana 7°30N 0°0 139 D5
Volta Blanche = White Volta →
 Ghana 9°10N 1°15W 139 D4

Volta Redonda Brazil 22°31S 44°5W 191 A7
Voltaire, C. Australia 14°16S 125°35E 148 B4
Volterra Italy 43°24N 10°51E 92 E7
Voltri Italy 44°26N 8°45E 92 D5
Volturno → Italy 41°1N 13°55E 94 A6
Volubilis Morocco 34°2N 5°33W 136 B2
Voluntar Romania 44°30N 26°11E 81 F11
Volvi, L. Greece 40°40N 23°34E 96 F7
Volyn □ Ukraine 51°15N 24°30E 75 C13
Volyně Czechia 49°10N 13°53E 78 B6
Volzhsk Russia 55°57N 48°23E 86 C9
Volzhskiy Russia 48°56N 44°46E 87 F7
Vomo Fiji 17°30S 177°15E 154 a
Vonitsa Greece 38°45N 21°0E 98 C3
Vopnafjörður Iceland 65°45N 14°50W 60 D6
Vorarlberg □ Austria 47°20N 10°0E 78 D2
Voras Oros Greece 40°57N 21°45E 96 F5
Vorbasse Denmark 55°39N 9°6E 63 J3
Vorchdorf Austria 48°0N 13°55E 78 C6
Vorderrhein → Switz. 46°49N 9°25E 77 J5
Vordingborg Denmark 55°0N 11°54E 63 J5
Vorë Albania 41°23N 19°39E 96 E3
Voreio Aigaio □ Greece 38°50N 25°30E 99 C7
Voreies Sporades Greece 39°15N 23°30E 98 B5
Vorë Albania 41°23N 19°39E 96 E3
Voria Ellas Greece 35°4N 24°49E 98 F6
Vorios Evoikos Kolpos
 Greece 38°45N 23°15E 98 C5
Vorkuta Russia 67°48N 64°20E 106 C7
Vormsi Estonia 59°1N 23°13E 84 C2
Vorona → Russia 51°22N 42°3E 86 E6
Voronezh Russia 51°40N 39°10E 85 G10
Voronezh □ Russia 51°30N 39°30E 86 E4
Voronezh → Russia 51°56N 37°17E 85 G9
Vorontsovo-Aleksandrovskoye =
 Zelenokumsk Russia 44°24N 44°0E 87 H6
Vorpommersche
 Boddenlandschaft △
 Germany 54°25N 12°32E 76 A8
Vorskla → Ukraine 48°50N 34°10E 85 H8
Võrts järv Estonia 58°16N 26°3E 84 C4
Võru Estonia 57°48N 26°54E 84 D4
Vosges France 48°20N 7°10E 71 D14
Vosges □ France 48°12N 6°20E 71 D13
Voskopojë Albania 40°35N 20°33E 96 F4
Voskresensk Russia 55°19N 38°43E 84 E10
Voskresenskoye Russia 56°51N 45°30E 86 B7
Voss Norway 60°38N 6°26E 60 F12
Vostochnyy Port
 Russia 42°44N 133°4E 112 C6
Vostok Antarctica 78°30S 106°50E 55 D8
Vostok I. Kiribati 10°5S 152°23W 157 J12
Votice Czechia 49°38N 14°39E 78 B7
Vouga → Portugal 40°41N 8°40W 88 E2
Vouillé France 46°38N 0°10E 70 F7
Vouxa, Akra Greece 35°37N 23°32E 101 D5
Vouzela Portugal 40°43N 8°7W 88 E2
Vouziers France 49°22N 4°40E 71 C11
Vovchansk Ukraine 50°17N 36°58E 85 G9
Vovchyn Belarus 52°18N 23°18E 83 F10
Voxna Sweden 61°20N 15°40E 62 F9
Voyageurs △ U.S.A. 48°32N 93°0W 172 A7
Voynitsa Russia 65°10N 30°20E 60 D24
Voyvozh Russia 62°56N 54°56E 106 C9
Vozhe, Ozero Russia 60°45N 39°0E 84 B10
Vozhega Russia 60°29N 40°12E 84 B11
Voznesenye Russia 61°0N 35°28E 84 B8
Vozrozhdeniya I. Asia 45°10N 59°20E 108 C5
Vráble Slovakia 48°15N 18°16E 79 C11
Vraćevšnica Serbia 44°2N 20°34E 96 B4
Vrachneika Greece 38°10N 21°40E 98 C3
Vrancea □ Romania 46°0N 26°30E 81 E11
Vrancei, Munţii
 Romania 46°0N 26°30E 81 E11
Vrangel Russia 42°43N 133°5E 112 C6
Vrangelya, Ostrov
 Russia 71°0N 180°0E 107 B18
Vranica Bos.-H. 43°55N 17°50E 80 G2
Vranje Serbia 42°34N 21°54E 96 D6
Vranjska Banja Serbia 42°34N 22°1E 96 D6
Vranov nad Topl'ou
 Slovakia 48°53N 21°40E 79 C14
Vransko Slovenia 46°17N 14°58E 93 B11
Vransko Jezero Croatia 43°53N 15°34E 93 E12
Vrapčište Macedonia 41°50N 20°53E 96 E4
Vratsa Bulgaria 43°15N 23°30E 96 C7
Vratsa □ Bulgaria 43°15N 23°30E 96 C7
Vrbas Serbia 45°40N 19°40E 80 E4
Vrbas → Bos.-H. 45°8N 17°29E 80 E2
Vrbnik Croatia 45°4N 14°40E 93 C11
Vrbovec Croatia 45°53N 16°28E 93 C13
Vrbovsko Croatia 45°24N 15°5E 93 C12
Vrchlabí Czechia 50°38N 15°37E 78 A8
Vrede S. Africa 27°24S 29°6E 145 C4
Vredefort S. Africa 27°0S 27°22E 144 C4
Vredenburg S. Africa 32°56N 17°59E 144 C2
Vredendal S. Africa 31°41S 18°35E 144 D2
Vretstorp Sweden 59°1N 14°53E 62 E8
Vrgorac Croatia 43°12N 17°20E 93 E14
Vrhnika Slovenia 45°58N 14°15E 93 C11
Vriddhachalam India 11°30N 79°20E 127 J4
Vridi Côte d'Ivoire 5°15N 4°3W 138 E4
Vrigstad Sweden 57°21N 14°28E 63 G8
Vrindavan India 27°37N 77°40E 124 F7
Vrises Greece 35°23N 24°13E 101 D6
Vrnograč Bos.-H. 45°10N 15°57E 93 C12
Vrondádes Greece 38°25N 26°7E 99 C8
Vrpolje Croatia 45°13N 18°24E 80 E3
Vršac Serbia 45°8N 21°0E 80 E5
Vrsacki Kanal Serbia 45°15N 21°0E 80 E5
Vrútky Slovakia 49°8N 18°55E 79 B11
Vryburg S. Africa 26°55S 24°45E 144 C3
Vryheid S. Africa 27°45S 30°47E 145 C5
Vsetín Czechia 49°20N 18°0E 79 B10
Vu Liet Vietnam 18°43N 105°23E 120 C5
Vučitrn = Vushtrri
 Kosovo 42°49N 20°59E 96 D6
Vukovar Croatia 45°21N 18°59E 80 E3
Vuktyl Russia 63°52N 57°0E 106 C6
Vulcan Canada 50°25N 113°15W 162 D6
Vulcan Romania 45°23N 23°17E 81 E8
Vulcăneşti Moldova 45°41N 28°18E 81 E13
Vulkaneshty = Vulcăneşti
 Moldova 45°41N 28°18E 81 E13
Vulcano Italy 38°24N 14°58E 95 E7
Vulkan → Mozam. 18°56S 34°1E 143 F3
Vung Tau Vietnam 10°21N 107°4E 121 G6
Vunidawa Fiji 17°50S 178°21E 154 a

Vunisea Fiji 19°3S 178°10E 154 a
Vuntut △ Canada 68°25N 139°41W 160 D4
Vurshets Bulgaria 43°13N 23°23E 96 C7
Vushtrri Kosovo 42°49N 20°59E 96 D6
Vutcani Romania 46°26N 27°59E 81 D12
Vuzlove Ukraine 48°22N 22°24E 80 B7
Vwaza △ Malawi 10°58S 33°25E 143 E3
Vyara India 21°8N 73°28E 126 D1
Vyartsilya Russia 62°8N 30°45E 84 A6
Vyatka = Kirov Russia 58°35N 49°40E 86 B8
Vyatka → Russia 55°37N 51°28E 86 C10
Vyatskiye Polyany
 Russia 56°14N 51°5E 86 B10
Vyazemskiy Russia 47°32N 134°45E 107 E14
Vyazma Russia 55°10N 34°15E 84 E8
Vyazniki Russia 56°10N 42°10E 86 B6
Vyborg Russia 60°43N 28°47E 84 B5
Vychegda → Russia 61°18N 46°36E 106 C5
Vychodné Beskydy
 Europe 49°20N 22°0E 79 B15
Vyerkhnyadzvinsk
 Belarus 55°45N 27°58E 84 E4
Vyhoda Ukraine 48°50N 23°59E 81 B8
Vyksa Russia 55°19N 42°11E 86 C6
Vylkove Ukraine 45°28N 29°32E 81 E14
Vylok Ukraine 48°6N 22°50E 80 B7
Vynohradiv Ukraine 48°9N 23°2E 80 B8
Vypin India 10°10N 76°15E 127 J3
Vyrnwy, L. U.K. 52°48N 3°31W 66 E4
Vyshhiv Ukraine 48°44N 23°39E 81 B8
Vyshkove Ukraine 48°3N 23°25E 81 B8
Vyshniy Volochek
 Russia 57°30N 34°30E 84 D8
Vyshzha = imeni 26 Bakinskikh
 Komissarov
 Turkmenistan 39°22N 54°10E 129 B7
Vyškov Czechia 49°17N 17°0E 79 B9
Vysočina □ Czechia 49°30N 15°30E 78 B8
Vysokaye Belarus 52°22N 23°22E 83 F10
Vysoké Mýto Czechia 49°58N 16°10E 79 B9
Vysokovsk Russia 56°22N 36°30E 84 D9
Vyšší Brod Czechia 48°37N 14°19E 78 C7
Vytegra Russia 61°0N 36°27E 84 B9
Vyzhnytsya Ukraine 48°15N 25°11E 81 B10

W

W du Benin △ Benin 11°57N 2°43E 139 C5
W du Burkina Faso △
 Burkina Faso 11°52N 2°50E 139 C5
W du Niger △ Niger 13°31N 2°28E 139 C5
W.A.C. Bennett Dam
 Canada 56°2N 122°6W 162 B4
Wa Ghana 10°7N 2°25W 138 C4
Waal → Neths. 51°37N 5°0E 69 C5
Waalwijk Neths. 51°42N 5°4E 69 C5
Waanyi-Garawa ◎
 Australia 18°2S 137°33E 150 B2
Wabakimi △ Canada 50°43N 89°30W 164 C2
Wabana Canada 47°40N 53°0W 165 C9
Wabasca → Canada 58°22N 115°20W 162 B5
Wabasca-Desmarais
 Canada 55°57N 113°56W 162 B6
Wabash U.S.A. 40°48N 85°49W 173 E11
Wabash → U.S.A. 37°48N 88°2W 172 G9
Wabasso U.S.A. 27°45N 80°26W 179 M5
Wabigoon L. Canada 49°44N 92°44W 163 D10
Wabowden Canada 54°55N 98°38W 163 C9
Wąbrzeźno Poland 53°16N 18°57E 83 E5
Wabu Hu China 32°20N 116°50E 117 A11
Wabuk Pt. Canada 55°20N 85°5W 164 A2
Wabush Canada 52°55N 66°52W 165 B6
Waccasassa B. U.S.A. 29°10N 82°50W 179 F7
Wachau Austria 48°21N 15°26E 78 C8
Wąchock Poland 51°4N 21°1E 83 G8
Wächtersbach Germany 50°14N 9°17E 77 E5
Wacissa U.S.A. 30°22N 83°59W 178 G6
Waco U.S.A. 31°33N 97°9W 176 F6
Waconichi, L. Canada 50°8N 74°0W 164 B5
Wad Hamid Sudan 16°30N 32°45E 135 E12
Wad Medani Sudan 14°28N 33°30E 135 F12
Wad Thana Pakistan 27°22N 66°23E 124 F2
Wadayama Japan 35°19N 134°52E 113 G7
Wadbilliga △ Australia 36°25S 149°35E 153 D8
Waddeneilanden Neths. 53°25N 5°10E 69 A5
Waddenzee Neths. 53°6N 5°10E 69 A5
Waddi, Chappal Nigeria 7°2N 11°43E 139 D7
Waddington U.S.A. 44°52N 75°12W 173 A17
Waddington, Mt.
 Canada 51°23N 125°15W 162 C4
Waddy Pt. Australia 24°58S 153°21E 151 C5
Wadebridge U.K. 50°31N 4°51W 67 G3
Wadena Canada 51°57N 103°47W 163 C8
Wadena U.S.A. 46°26N 95°8W 172 B6
Wädenswil Switz. 47°14N 8°40E 77 H4
Wadern Germany 49°32N 6°53E 77 F2
Wadeye Australia 14°28S 129°52E 148 B4
Wadgaon India 18°44N 73°39E 126 F1
Wadhams Canada 51°30N 127°30W 162 C3
Wadhwan India 22°42N 71°41E 124 H4
Wadi India 17°4N 76°59E 126 F3
Wādī as Sīr Jordan 31°56N 35°49E 130 D4
Wadi Gemâl, J. Egypt 24°35N 35°10E 137 C4
Wadi Halfa Sudan 21°53N 31°19E 137 C3
Wādī Rum △ Jordan 29°30N 35°20E 130 F4
Wadian China 32°42N 112°29E 117 A9
Wadlew Poland 51°31N 19°23E 83 G6
Wadley Ala., U.S.A. 33°7N 85°34W 178 B4
Wadley Ga., U.S.A. 32°52N 82°24W 178 D6
Wadowice Poland 49°52N 19°30E 83 J6
Wadsworth Nev.,
 U.S.A. 39°38N 119°17W 168 G4
Wadsworth Ohio, U.S.A. 41°2N 81°44W 174 E13
Waegwan S. Korea 35°59N 128°23E 115 G15
Wafangdian China 39°38N 121°58E 116 E11
Wafrah Kuwait 28°33N 47°56E 131 F9
Wagait ◎ Australia 13°1S 130°5E 148 B5
Wagener U.S.A. 33°39N 81°22W 178 D7
Wageningen Neths. 51°58N 5°40E 69 C5
Wager B. Canada 65°26N 88°40W 161 D14
Wagga Wagga
 Australia 35°7S 147°24E 153 C7
Waghai India 20°46N 73°28E 126 D1
Wagin Australia 33°17S 117°25E 149 F2
Wagner U.S.A. 43°5N 98°18W 172 D4
Wagon Mound
 U.S.A. 36°1N 104°42W 169 H11
Wagoner U.S.A. 35°58N 95°22W 176 D7
Wągrowiec Poland 52°48N 17°11E 83 F4

Wah Pakistan 33°45N 72°40E 124 C5
Wahai Indonesia 2°48S 129°35E 119 E7
Waharoa N.Z. 37°46S 175°45E 154 D4
Wāḥid Egypt 30°48N 32°21E 130 E1
Wahnai Afghan. 32°40N 65°50E 124 C1
Wahoo U.S.A. 41°13N 96°37W 172 E5
Wahpeton U.S.A. 46°16N 96°36W 172 B5
Wai India 17°56N 73°57E 126 F1
Waialua U.S.A. 21°34N 158°9W 167 L8
Waiapu → N.Z. 37°4S 178°29E 154 D7
Waiau N.Z. 42°39S 173°5E 155 E4
Waiau → Canterbury, N.Z. 42°47S 173°22E 155 C8
Waiau → Southland, N.Z. 46°12S 167°38E 155 G2
Waiawe Ganga → Sri Lanka 6°15N 81°0E 127 L5
Waibeem Indonesia 0°30S 132°59E 119 E8
Waiblingen Germany 48°49N 9°18E 77 G5
Waidhofen an der Thaya Austria 48°49N 15°17E 78 C8
Waidhofen an der Ybbs Austria 47°57N 14°46E 78 D7
Waigeo Indonesia 0°20S 130°40E 119 E8
Waihao → N.Z. 44°45S 171°10E 155 E6
Waihao Downs N.Z. 44°45S 171°1E 155 E6
Waiheke I. N.Z. 36°48S 175°6E 154 C4
Waihi N.Z. 37°23S 175°52E 154 D4
Waihola N.Z. 46°1S 170°8E 155 G5
Waihola L. N.Z. 45°59S 170°8E 155 F5
Waihou → N.Z. 37°15S 175°40E 154 D4
Waika Dem. Rep. of the Congo 2°22S 25°42E 142 C2
Waikabubak Indonesia 9°45S 119°25E 119 F5
Waikaia N.Z. 45°44S 168°51E 155 F3
Waikaka N.Z. 45°55S 169°1E 155 F3
Waikare, L. N.Z. 37°26S 175°13E 154 D4
Waikareiti, L. N.Z. 38°43S 177°10E 154 E6
Waikaremoana N.Z. 38°42S 177°7E 154 E6
Waikaremoana, L. N.Z. 38°49S 177°9E 154 E6
Waikari N.Z. 42°58S 172°41E 155 C7
Waikato → N.Z. 37°23S 174°43E 154 D3
Waikelo Indonesia 9°24S 119°19E 148 A2
Waikerie Australia 34°9S 140°0E 152 C4
Waikiekie N.Z. 35°57S 174°16E 154 B3
Waikokopu N.Z. 39°3S 177°52E 154 F6
Waikouaiti N.Z. 45°36S 170°41E 155 F5
Waikouaiti Downs N.Z. 45°30S 170°30E 155 F5
Waimakariri → N.Z. 43°24S 172°42E 155 D7
Waimangaroa N.Z. 41°43S 171°46E 155 B6
Waimarie N.Z. 41°35S 171°58E 155 B6
Waimate N.Z. 44°45S 171°3E 155 E6
Waimea Plain N.Z. 45°55S 168°35E 155 F3
Wainganga → India 18°50N 79°55E 126 E4
Waingapu Indonesia 9°35S 120°11E 119 F6
Waini → Guyana 8°20N 59°50W 186 B7
Wainuiomata N.Z. 41°17S 174°56E 154 F3
Wainwright Canada 52°50N 110°50W 163 C6
Wainwright U.S.A. 70°38N 160°2W 166 A7
Waiotapu N.Z. 38°21S 176°25E 154 E5
Waiouru N.Z. 39°28S 175°41E 154 E4
Waipa → N.Z. 38°16S 175°21E 154 D4
Waipahi N.Z. 46°6S 169°15E 155 G4
Waipapa Pt. N.Z. 46°40S 168°51E 155 G3
Waipara N.Z. 43°3S 172°46E 155 D7
Waipawa N.Z. 39°56S 176°38E 154 F5
Waipiro N.Z. 38°2S 178°22E 154 E7
Waipiro Bay N.Z. 38°1S 178°21E 154 E7
Waipoua Forest N.Z. 35°39S 173°33E 154 B2
Waipu N.Z. 35°59S 174°26E 154 B3
Waipukurau N.Z. 40°1S 176°33E 154 G5
Wairakei N.Z. 38°37S 176°6E 154 E5
Wairarapa, L. N.Z. 41°14S 175°15E 154 F3
Wairau → N.Z. 41°32S 174°7E 155 B9
Wairio N.Z. 45°59S 168°3E 155 F3
Wairoa → N.Z. 39°3S 177°25E 154 F6
Wairoa → Hawke's Bay, N.Z. 39°4S 177°25E 154 F6
Wairoa → Northland, N.Z. 36°5S 173°59E 154 C2
Waitaki → N.Z. 44°56S 171°7E 155 E6
Waitaki Plains N.Z. 44°22S 170°0E 155 E5
Waitangi N.Z. 35°16S 174°5E 154 B3
Waitara N.Z. 38°59S 174°15E 154 E3
Waitara → N.Z. 38°59S 174°14E 154 E3
Waitiki Landing N.Z. 34°31S 172°50E 154 A1
Waitoa N.Z. 37°36S 175°37E 154 D4
Waitomo Caves N.Z. 38°16S 175°7E 154 E4
Waitotara N.Z. 39°49S 174°44E 154 E3
Waitotara → N.Z. 39°51S 174°41E 154 F3
Waitsburg U.S.A. 46°16N 118°9W 168 C4
Waiuku N.Z. 37°15S 174°44E 154 D3
Wajima Japan 37°30N 137°0E 113 F8
Wajir Kenya 1°42N 40°5E 142 B5
Wajir □ Kenya 1°45N 40°5E 142 B5
Wakasa Japan 35°20N 134°24E 113 G7
Wakasa-Wan Japan 35°40N 135°30E 113 G7
Wakatipu, L. N.Z. 45°5S 168°33E 155 F3
Wakaw Canada 52°39N 105°44W 163 C7
Wakaya Fiji 17°37S 179°0E 154 a
Wakayama Japan 34°15N 135°15E 113 G7
Wakayama □ Japan 33°50N 135°30E 113 H7
Wake Forest U.S.A. 35°59N 78°30W 177 D15
Wake I. Pac. Oc. 19°18N 166°36E 156 F8
WaKeeney U.S.A. 39°1N 99°53W 172 F4
Wakefield Jamaica 18°26N 77°42W 182 a
Wakefield N.Z. 41°24S 173°5E 155 B8
Wakefield U.K. 53°41N 1°29W 66 D6
Wakefield Mass., U.S.A. 42°30N 71°5W 175 D13
Wakefield Mich., U.S.A. 46°29N 89°56W 172 B9
Wakkanai Japan 45°28N 141°35E 112 B10
Wakkerstroom S. Africa 27°24S 30°10E 145 C5
Wakool Australia 35°28S 144°23E 153 C3
Wakool → Australia 35°5S 143°33E 152 C5
Wakre Indonesia 0°19S 131°5E 119 E8
Wakuach, L. Canada 55°34N 67°32W 165 A6
Wakulla U.S.A. 30°14N 84°14W 178 E5
Walagunya ○ Australia 23°10S 124°31E 148 D3
Walamba Zambia 13°30S 28°42E 143 E2
Wałbrzych Poland 50°45N 16°18E 83 H3
Walbury Hill U.K. 51°21N 1°28W 67 F6
Walcha Australia 30°55S 151°31E 153 A9
Walchen Neths. 51°30N 3°35E 69 C3
Walcott U.S.A. 41°46N 106°51W 168 F10
Wałcz Poland 53°17N 16°27E 83 E3
Waldbröl Germany 50°52N 7°37E 76 E3

Waldburg Ra. Australia 24°40S 117°35E 149 D2
Waldeck Germany 51°12N 9°4E 76 D5
Walden Colo., U.S.A. 40°44N 106°17W 168 F10
Walden N.Y., U.S.A. 41°34N 74°11W 175 E10
Waldkirch Germany 48°5N 7°58E 77 G3
Waldkirchen Germany 48°43N 13°36E 77 G9
Waldkraiburg Germany 48°11N 12°24E 77 G8
Waldo U.S.A. 29°48N 82°10W 178 F7
Waldport U.S.A. 44°26N 124°4W 168 D1
Waldron U.S.A. 34°54N 94°5W 176 D7
Waldviertel Austria 48°30N 15°30E 78 C8
Walebing Australia 30°41S 116°13E 149 F2
Walembele Ghana 10°30N 1°58W 138 C4
Walgett Australia 30°0S 148°5E 151 E4
Walgreen Coast Antarctica 75°15S 105°0W 55 D15
Walhalla Australia 37°56S 146°29E 153 D7
Walker 47°6N 94°35W 172 B7
Walker, L. Canada 50°20N 67°11W 165 B6
Walker L. Canada 54°42N 95°57W 163 C10
Walker L. U.S.A. 38°42N 118°43W 168 G4
Walkerston Australia 21°11S 149°8E 150 b
Walkerton Canada 44°10N 81°10W 174 B3
Wall U.S.A. 44°0N 102°8W 172 C2
Walla Walla Australia 35°45S 146°54E 153 C7
Walla Walla U.S.A. 46°4N 118°20W 168 C4
Wallace Idaho, U.S.A. 47°28N 115°56W 168 C6
Wallace N.C., U.S.A. 34°44N 77°59W 177 D16
Wallaceburg Canada 42°34N 82°23W 174 D2
Wallacetown N.Z. 46°21S 168°19E 155 G3
Wallachia = Valahia Romania 44°35N 25°0E 81 F9
Wallal Australia 26°32S 146°7E 151 D4
Wallam Cr. → Australia 28°40S 147°20E 151 D4
Wallambin, L. Australia 30°57S 117°35E 149 F2
Wallan Australia 37°26S 144°59E 153 D6
Wallangarra Australia 28°56S 151°58E 151 D5
Wallaroo Australia 33°56S 137°39E 152 B2
Wallasey U.K. 53°25N 3°2W 66 D4
Walldürn Germany 49°34N 9°22E 77 F5
Wallenhorst Germany 52°21N 8°1E 76 C4
Wallenpaupack, L. U.S.A. 41°25N 75°15W 175 E9
Wallerawang Australia 33°25S 150°4E 153 B9
Wallingat △ Australia 32°14S 152°25E 153 B10
Wallingford Conn., U.S.A. 41°27N 72°50W 175 E12
Wallingford Vt., U.S.A. 43°28N 72°58W 175 C12
Wallis & Futuna, Îs. ☑ Pac. Oc. 13°18S 176°10W 147 C11
Wallowa U.S.A. 45°34N 117°32W 168 D5
Wallowa Mts. U.S.A. 45°20N 117°30W 168 D5
Walls U.K. 60°14N 1°33W 65 A7
Walls of Jerusalem △ Australia 41°56S 146°15E 151 G4
Wallsend Australia 32°55S 151°40E 153 B9
Wallula U.S.A. 46°5N 118°54W 168 C4
Wallumbilla Australia 26°33S 149°9E 151 D4
Walmsley L. Canada 63°25N 108°36W 163 A7
Walney, I. of U.K. 54°6N 3°15W 66 C4
Walnut Canyon △ U.S.A. 35°15N 111°20W 169 J8
Walnut Creek U.S.A. 37°54N 122°4W 170 H4
Walnut Grove U.S.A. 34°4N 86°18W 178 A3
Walnut Hill U.S.A. 30°53N 87°30W 179 E2
Walnut Ridge U.S.A. 36°4N 90°57W 177 C9
Walpeup Australia 35°7S 142°2E 152 C5
Walpole Australia 34°58S 116°44E 149 F2
Walpole U.S.A. 42°9N 71°15W 175 D13
Walpole-Nornalup △ Australia 35°0S 116°45E 149 G2
Wals Austria 47°47N 12°58E 78 D5
Walsall U.K. 52°35N 1°58W 67 E6
Walsenburg U.S.A. 37°38N 104°47W 169 H11
Walsh U.S.A. 37°23N 102°17W 169 H12
Walsh → Australia 16°31S 143°42E 150 B3
Walsingham Canada 42°40N 80°31W 174 D4
Walsrode Germany 52°51N 9°36E 76 C5
Walt Disney World Resort U.S.A. 28°22N 81°33W 179 G8
Waltair India 17°44N 83°23E 126 F6
Walter F. George Res. U.S.A. 31°38N 85°4W 178 D4
Walterboro U.S.A. 32°55N 80°40W 178 C9
Walters U.S.A. 34°22N 98°19W 176 D5
Waltershausen Germany 50°54N 10°33E 76 E6
Waltershausen Gletscher Greenland 73°54N 24°25W 57 C8
Waltham U.S.A. 42°23N 71°14W 175 D13
Waltman U.S.A. 43°4N 107°12W 168 E10
Walton U.S.A. 42°10N 75°8W 175 D9
Walton-on-the-Naze U.K. 51°51N 1°17E 67 F9
Walvis Bay Namibia 23°0S 14°28E 144 B1
Walvis Ridge Atl. Oc. 26°0S 5°0E 56 J12
Walvisbaai = Walvis Bay Namibia 23°0S 14°28E 144 B1
Walwa Australia 35°59S 147°44E 153 C7
Wamba Dem. Rep. of the Congo 2°10N 27°57E 142 B2
Wamba Kenya 0°58N 37°19E 142 B4
Wamba Nigeria 8°57N 8°42E 139 D6
Wambardi ○ Australia 16°2S 130°55E 148 C5
Wamego U.S.A. 39°12N 96°18W 172 F5
Wamena Indonesia 4°4S 138°57E 119 E9
Wampana Karlantijpa ○ Australia 17°45S 132°10E 148 C5
Wampaya ○ Australia 17°20S 135°0E 150 B2
Wamsutter U.S.A. 41°40N 107°58W 168 F10
Wamulan Indonesia 3°27S 126°7E 119 E7
Wan Tup Myanmar 21°13N 98°42E 116 G2
Wan Xian China 38°47N 115°7E 114 E8
Wana Pakistan 32°20N 69°32E 124 C3
Wanaaring Australia 29°38S 144°9E 151 D3
Wanaka N.Z. 44°42S 169°9E 155 E4
Wanaka, L. N.Z. 44°33S 169°7E 155 E4
Wan'an China 26°26N 114°49E 117 D10
Wanapitei L. Canada 46°45N 80°40W 164 C3
Wanbi Australia 34°46S 140°17E 152 C4
Wandel Sea = McKinley Sea Arctic 82°0N 0°0 57 A11
Wandérama Côte d'Ivoire 8°37N 4°25W 138 D4

Wandhari Pakistan 27°42N 66°48E 124 F2
Wanding China 24°5N 98°4E 116 E2
Wandoan Australia 26°5S 149°55E 151 D4
Wandur Marine △ India 11°30N 92°30E 127 J11
Wanfu China 40°8N 122°38E 115 D12
Wang → Thailand 17°8N 99°2E 120 D2
Wang Noi Thailand 14°13N 100°44E 120 D3
Wang Saphung Thailand 17°18N 101°46E 120 D3
Wang Thong Thailand 16°50N 100°26E 120 D3
Wanga Dem. Rep. of the Congo 2°58N 29°12E 142 B2
Wanganella Australia 35°6S 144°49E 153 C6
Wanganui N.Z. 39°56S 175°3E 154 F4
Wanganui □ W. Coast., N.Z. 39°35S 175°3E 154 F4
Wanganui → Wanganui-Manawatu, N.Z. 37°55S 175°4E 154 F4
Wangaratta Australia 36°21S 146°19E 153 D7
Wangary Australia 34°35S 135°29E 152 B2
Wangcang China 32°18N 106°20E 116 A6
Wangcun China 28°22N 112°49E 117 C9
Wangcun China 36°41N 117°41E 115 F9
Wangdu China 38°40N 115°7E 114 E8
Wangen Germany 47°41N 9°50E 77 H5
Wangerooge Germany 53°47N 7°54E 76 B3
Wangiwangi Indonesia 5°22S 123°37E 119 F6
Wangjiang China 30°10N 116°42E 117 B11
Wangmo China 25°11N 106°5E 116 E6
Wangolodougou Côte d'Ivoire 9°55N 5°10W 138 D3
Wangqing China 43°12N 129°42E 115 C15
Wani India 20°5N 78°55E 126 D4
Wanimiyn ○ Australia 15°55S 130°49E 148 C5
Wanjina Wunggurr Wilinggin ○ Australia 16°15S 125°49E 149 E2
Wankaner India 22°35N 71°0E 124 H4
Wanless Canada 54°11N 101°21W 163 C8
Wanleweyne Somalia 2°37N 44°54E 131 G3
Wanneroo Australia 31°42S 115°46E 149 F2
Wannian China 28°42N 117°4E 117 C11
Wanning China 18°48N 110°22E 117 a
Wannoo Billabong Roadhouse Australia 27°15S 115°49E 149 E2
Wanon Niwat Thailand 17°38N 103°46E 120 D4
Wanqinsha China 22°43N 113°33E 111 a
Wanquan China 40°50N 114°40E 114 D8
Wanrong China 35°25N 110°50E 114 G6
Wanshan China 27°30N 109°12E 116 D7
Wanshan Qundao China 21°57N 113°45E 111 a
Wansheng China 28°57N 106°53E 116 C6
Wanstead N.Z. 40°8S 176°30E 154 G5
Wantage U.K. 51°35N 1°25W 67 F6
Wanxian China 30°42N 108°20E 116 B7
Wanyuan China 32°4N 108°3E 116 A7
Wanzai Guangdong, China 22°12N 113°31E 111 a
Wanzai Jiangxi, China 28°7N 114°30E 117 C10
Wapakoneta U.S.A. 40°34N 84°12W 173 E11
Wapato U.S.A. 46°27N 120°25W 168 C3
Wapawekka L. Canada 54°55N 104°40W 163 C8
Wapikopa L. Canada 52°56N 87°53W 164 B2
Wapiti → Canada 55°5N 118°18W 162 B5
Wappingers Falls U.S.A. 41°36N 73°55W 175 E11
Wapsipinicon → U.S.A. 41°44N 90°19W 172 E8
Wapusk △ Canada 57°46N 93°22W 163 B10
Warakurna Australia 24°59S 128°17E 149 D4
Warangal India 17°58N 79°35E 126 F4
Waraseoni India 21°45N 80°2E 125 J9
Waratah Australia 41°30S 145°30E 151 G4
Waratah B. Australia 38°54S 146°5E 153 E7
Warburg Germany 51°28N 9°11E 76 D5
Warburton Vic., Australia 37°47S 145°42E 153 D6
Warburton W. Austral., Australia 26°8S 126°35E 149 E4
Warburton → Australia 28°4S 137°28E 151 D2
Warburton Groove Australia 28°18S 137°8E 151 A2
Warburton Ra. Australia 25°55S 126°28E 149 E4
Ward N.Z. 41°49S 174°11E 155 B9
Ward → Australia 26°28S 146°6E 151 D4
Ward Mt. U.S.A. 37°12N 118°54W 170 H8
Wardang I. Australia 34°30S 137°20E 152 C2
Warden S. Africa 27°50S 29°0E 145 C4
Wardha India 20°45N 78°39E 126 D4
Wardha → India 19°57N 79°11E 124 H6
Wardsville Canada 42°39N 81°45W 174 D3
Ware U.K. 51°49N 0°0 67 F8
Ware U.S.A. 42°16N 72°14W 175 D12
Waregem Belgium 50°53N 3°27E 69 D3
Wareham U.S.A. 41°46N 70°43W 175 E14
Waremme Belgium 50°43N 5°15E 69 D5
Waren Germany 53°30N 12°41E 76 B8
Warendorf Germany 51°57N 8°1E 76 D4
Waresboro U.S.A. 31°15N 82°29W 178 E7
Warialda Australia 29°29S 150°33E 151 D5
Warin Chamrap Thailand 15°12N 104°53E 120 E5
Warka Poland 51°47N 21°12E 83 G8
Warkopi Indonesia 1°12S 134°9E 119 E8
Warkworth N.Z. 36°24S 174°41E 154 C3
Warm Springs Ga., U.S.A. 32°53N 84°41W 178 C5
Warm Springs Nev., U.S.A. 38°10N 116°20W 169 G5
Warman Canada 52°19N 106°30W 163 C7
Warmbad = Bela Bela S. Africa 24°51S 28°19E 145 B4
Warmbad Namibia 28°25S 18°42E 144 C2
Warming I. = Uunartoq Qeqertaq Greenland 71°33N 21°47W 57 C8
Warmiński-Mazurskie □ Poland 53°55N 21°0E 83 E8
Warminster U.K. 51°12N 2°10W 67 F5
Warminster U.S.A. 40°12N 75°6W 175 F9
Warmun Australia 17°2S 128°12E 148 C4
Warnemünde Germany 54°10N 12°4E 76 A8
Warner Robins U.S.A. 32°37N 83°36W 178 D6
Warner Mts. U.S.A. 41°40N 120°15W 168 F3
Warnow → Germany 54°6N 12°9E 76 A8
Waroona Australia 32°50S 115°58E 149 F2

Warora India 20°14N 79°1E 126 D4
Warrabah △ Australia 30°31S 150°56E 153 A10
Warrabri ○ Australia 21°1S 134°19E 150 C1
Warracknabeal Australia 36°9S 142°26E 152 D5
Warragul Australia 38°10S 145°58E 153 E6
Warrego → Australia 30°24S 145°21E 151 E4
Warrego Ra. Australia 24°58S 146°0E 150 C4
Warren Australia 31°42S 147°51E 153 A7
Warren Ark., U.S.A. 33°37N 92°4W 176 E8
Warren Mich., U.S.A. 42°28N 83°1W 172 D4
Warren Minn., U.S.A. 48°12N 96°46W 172 A5
Warren Ohio, U.S.A. 41°14N 80°49W 174 E4
Warren Pa., U.S.A. 41°51N 79°9W 174 E5
Warrenpoint U.K. 54°6N 6°15W 64 B5
Warrensburg Mo., U.S.A. 38°46N 93°44W 172 F7
Warrensburg N.Y., U.S.A. 43°29N 73°46W 175 C11
Warrenton S. Africa 28°9S 24°47E 144 C3
Warrenton Ga., U.S.A. 33°24N 82°40W 178 B7
Warrenton Oreg., U.S.A. 46°10N 123°56W 170 D3
Warrenville U.S.A. 33°33N 81°48W 178 B8
Warri Nigeria 5°30N 5°41E 139 D6
Warrington N.Z. 45°43S 170°35E 155 F5
Warrington U.K. 53°24N 2°35W 66 D5
Warrington U.S.A. 30°23N 87°17W 179 E2
Warrnambool Australia 38°25S 142°30E 152 E5
Warroad U.S.A. 48°54N 95°19W 172 A6
Warrumbungle △ Australia 31°18S 149°1E 153 A8
Warruwi Australia 11°36S 133°20E 150 A1
Warsak Dam Pakistan 34°11N 71°19E 124 B4
Warsaw = Warszawa Poland 52°14N 21°0E 83 F8
Warsaw Ind., U.S.A. 41°14N 85°51W 173 E11
Warsaw N.Y., U.S.A. 42°45N 78°8W 174 D6
Warsaw Ohio, U.S.A. 40°20N 82°0W 174 F3
Warsaw Chopin ✈ (WAW) Poland 52°9N 20°59E 83 F7
Warstein Germany 51°26N 8°22E 76 D4
Warszawa Poland 52°14N 21°0E 83 F8
Warta Poland 51°43N 18°38E 83 G5
Warta → Poland 52°35N 14°39E 83 F1
Warthe = Warta → Poland 52°35N 14°39E 83 F1
Warthen Germany 33°6N 82°48W 178 B7
Waru Indonesia 3°30S 130°36E 119 E8
Warud India 21°30N 78°16E 126 D4
Warumungu ○ Australia 19°15S 134°44E 150 B1
Warwick Australia 28°10S 152°1E 151 D5
Warwick U.K. 52°18N 1°35W 67 E6
Warwick Ga., U.S.A. 31°50N 83°57W 178 D6
Warwick N.Y., U.S.A. 41°16N 74°22W 175 E10
Warwick R.I., U.S.A. 41°42N 71°28W 175 E13
Warwickshire □ U.K. 52°14N 1°38W 67 E6
Wasaga Beach Canada 44°31N 80°1W 174 B4
Wasagaming Canada 50°39N 99°58W 163 C9
Wasatch Ra. U.S.A. 40°0N 111°30W 168 F8
Wasbank S. Africa 28°15S 30°9E 145 C5
Wasco Calif., U.S.A. 35°36N 119°20W 171 K7
Wasco Oreg., U.S.A. 45°36N 120°42W 168 D3
Wase Nigeria 9°4N 9°54E 139 D6
Waseca U.S.A. 44°5N 93°30W 172 C7
Wasekamio L. Canada 56°45N 108°45E 163 B7
Wasgomura △ Sri Lanka 7°45N 81°0E 127 L5
Wash, The U.K. 52°58N 0°20E 66 E8
Washago Canada 44°45N 79°20W 174 B5
Washburn N. Dak., U.S.A. 47°17N 101°2W 172 B3
Washburn Wis., U.S.A. 46°40N 90°54W 172 B8
Washim India 20°3N 77°0E 126 D3
Washington U.K. 54°55N 1°30W 66 C6
Washington D.C., U.S.A. 38°53N 77°2W 173 F15
Washington Ga., U.S.A. 33°44N 82°44W 178 B7
Washington Ind., U.S.A. 38°40N 87°10W 172 F10
Washington Iowa, U.S.A. 41°18N 91°42W 172 E8
Washington Mo., U.S.A. 38°33N 91°1W 172 F8
Washington N.C., U.S.A. 35°33N 77°3W 177 D16
Washington N.J., U.S.A. 40°46N 74°59W 175 F10
Washington Pa., U.S.A. 40°10N 80°15W 174 F4
Washington Utah, U.S.A. 37°8N 113°31W 169 H7
Washington, Mt. U.S.A. 44°16N 71°18W 175 B13
Washington Court House U.S.A. 39°32N 83°26W 173 F12
Washington Dulles Int. ✈ (IAD) U.S.A. 38°57N 77°27W 173 F15
Washington I. U.S.A. 45°23N 86°54W 172 C10
Washington Land Greenland 80°30N 66°0W 57 A4
Washougal U.S.A. 45°35N 122°21W 170 E4
Washpool △ Australia 29°22S 152°20E 151 D5
Wasian Indonesia 1°47S 133°19E 119 E8
Wasilków Poland 53°12N 23°13E 83 E10
Wasilla U.S.A. 61°35N 149°26W 160 E2
Wasini Marine △ Kenya 4°39S 39°14E 142 C4
Wasior Indonesia 2°43S 134°30E 119 E8
Wāsiṭ □ Iraq 32°50N 45°50E 105 F11
Waskaganish Canada 51°30N 78°40W 164 B4
Waskaiowaka L. Canada 56°33N 96°23W 163 B9
Waskesiu Lake Canada 53°55N 106°5W 163 C7
Wasserburg Germany 48°3N 12°14E 77 G8
Wasserkuppe Germany 50°29N 9°55E 76 E5
Wassy France 48°30N 4°58E 71 D11
Wasur △ Indonesia 8°41S 140°4E 119 F10
Waswanipi Canada 49°40N 76°29W 164 C4
Waswanipi, L. Canada 49°35N 76°40W 164 C4
Watagans △ Australia 33°0S 151°28E 153 B9
Watampone Indonesia 4°29S 120°25E 119 E6
Watamu Kenya 3°23S 40°0E 142 C5
Watarrka △ Australia 24°20S 131°30E 148 D5
Water Park Pt. Australia 22°56S 150°47E 150 C5

Water Valley U.S.A. 34°10N 89°38W 177 D10
Waterberg Plateau Namibia 20°25S 17°18E 144 B2
Waterberge S. Africa 24°10S 28°0E 145 A4
Waterbury Conn., U.S.A. 41°33N 73°3W 175 E11
Waterbury Vt., U.S.A. 44°20N 72°46W 175 B12
Waterbury L. Canada 58°10N 104°22W 163 B8
Waterdown Canada 43°20N 79°53W 174 C5
Wateree → U.S.A. 33°45N 80°37W 178 D8
Waterford Canada 42°56N 80°17W 174 D4
Waterford Ireland 52°15N 7°8W 64 D4
Waterford Calif., U.S.A. 37°38N 120°46W 170 H6
Waterford Pa., U.S.A. 41°57N 79°59W 174 E5
Waterford □ Ireland 52°10N 7°40W 64 D4
Waterford Harbour Ireland 52°8N 6°58W 64 D5
Waterhen L. Canada 52°10N 99°40W 163 C9
Waterloo Belgium 50°43N 4°25E 69 D4
Waterloo Ont., Canada 43°30N 80°32W 174 C4
Waterloo Qué., Canada 45°22N 72°32W 175 A12
Waterloo S. Leone 8°26N 13°8W 138 D2
Waterloo Ill., U.S.A. 38°20N 90°9W 172 F8
Waterloo Iowa, U.S.A. 42°30N 92°21W 172 D7
Waterloo N.Y., U.S.A. 42°54N 76°52W 175 D8
Watersmeet U.S.A. 46°16N 89°11W 172 B9
Waterton Lakes △ Canada 48°45N 115°0W 162 D6
Watertown Conn., U.S.A. 41°36N 73°7W 175 E11
Watertown N.Y., U.S.A. 43°59N 75°55W 175 C9
Watertown S. Dak., U.S.A. 44°54N 97°7W 172 C5
Watertown Wis., U.S.A. 43°12N 88°43W 172 D9
Waterval-Boven = Emgwenya S. Africa 25°40S 30°18E 145 C5
Waterville Canada 45°16N 71°54W 175 A13
Waterville Maine, U.S.A. 44°33N 69°38W 173 C19
Waterville N.Y., U.S.A. 42°56N 75°23W 175 D9
Waterville Pa., U.S.A. 41°19N 77°21W 174 E7
Waterville Wash., U.S.A. 47°39N 120°4W 168 C3
Watervliet U.S.A. 42°44N 73°42W 175 D11
Wates Indonesia 7°51S 110°10E 119 G14
Watford Canada 42°57N 81°53W 174 D3
Watford U.K. 51°40N 0°24W 67 F7
Watford City U.S.A. 47°48N 103°17W 172 B2
Wathaman → Canada 57°16N 102°59W 163 B8
Wathaman L. Canada 56°58N 103°43W 163 B8
Watheroo Australia 30°15S 116°5E 149 F2
Watheroo △ Australia 30°19S 115°48E 149 F2
Wating China 35°40N 106°38E 114 G4
Watkins Glen U.S.A. 42°23N 76°52W 174 D8
Watkinsville U.S.A. 33°52N 83°25W 178 B6
Watling I. = San Salvador I. Bahamas 24°0N 74°30W 183 B5
Watonga U.S.A. 35°51N 98°25W 176 D5
Watrous Canada 51°40N 105°25W 163 C7
Watrous U.S.A. 35°48N 104°59W 169 J11
Watsa Dem. Rep. of the Congo 3°4N 29°30E 142 B2
Watseka U.S.A. 40°47N 87°44W 172 E10
Watson Canada 52°10N 104°30W 163 C8
Watson Lake Canada 60°6N 128°49W 162 A3
Watsontown U.S.A. 41°5N 76°52W 174 E8
Watsonville U.S.A. 36°55N 121°45W 170 J5
Wattamolla Cr. → Australia 28°57S 136°10E 151 D2
Wattiwarriganna Cr. → Australia 28°57S 136°10E 151 D2
Wattwil Switz. 47°18N 9°6E 77 H5
Watuata = Batuata Indonesia 6°12S 122°42E 119 F6
Watubela, Kepulauan Indonesia 4°28S 131°35E 119 E8
Watubela Is. = Watubela, Kepulauan Indonesia 4°28S 131°35E 119 E8
Wau South Sudan 7°45N 28°1E 135 G11
Waubamik Canada 45°27N 80°1W 174 A4
Waubay U.S.A. 45°20N 97°18W 172 C5
Waubra Australia 37°21S 143°39E 152 D5
Wauchope N.S.W., Australia 31°28S 152°45E 153 A10
Wauchope N. Terr., Australia 20°36S 134°15E 150 C1
Wauchula U.S.A. 27°33N 81°49W 179 H8
Waukarlycarly, L. Australia 21°18S 121°56E 148 D3
Waukeenah U.S.A. 30°25N 83°57W 178 E6
Waukegan U.S.A. 42°22N 87°50W 172 D10
Waukesha U.S.A. 43°1N 88°14W 172 D9
Waukon U.S.A. 43°16N 91°29W 172 D8
Waupaca U.S.A. 44°21N 89°5W 172 C9
Waupun U.S.A. 43°38N 88°44W 172 D9
Waurika U.S.A. 34°10N 98°0W 176 D6
Wausau Fla., U.S.A. 30°38N 85°35W 178 E4
Wausau Wis., U.S.A. 44°58N 89°38W 172 C9
Wautoma U.S.A. 44°4N 89°18W 172 C9
Wauwatosa U.S.A. 43°2N 88°0W 172 D9
Wave Hill = Kalkarindji Australia 17°30S 130°47E 148 C5
Wave Rock ○ Australia 32°26S 118°53E 149 F2
Waveney → U.K. 52°35N 1°39E 67 E9
Waverley N.Z. 39°46S 174°37E 154 F3
Waverly Ala., U.S.A. 32°44N 85°35W 178 B4
Waverly Fla., U.S.A. 27°59N 81°37W 179 H8
Waverly Iowa, U.S.A. 42°44N 92°29W 172 D7
Waverly N.Y., U.S.A. 42°1N 76°32W 175 D8
Waverly Hall U.S.A. 32°41N 84°44W 178 C5
Wavre Belgium 50°43N 4°38E 69 D4
Wâw = Wau South Sudan 7°45N 28°1E 135 G11
Wâw al Kabīr Libya 25°20N 16°43E 137 C9
Wawa Nigeria 9°54N 4°27E 139 D5
Wawa Sudan 20°30N 30°22E 137 D13
Wawanesa Canada 49°36N 99°40W 163 D9
Wawona U.S.A. 37°32N 119°39W 170 H7
Waxahachie U.S.A. 32°24N 96°51W 176 E6
Waxxari China 38°41N 87°19E 113 C11
Way, L. Australia 26°45S 120°16E 149 E3
Waya Fiji 17°19S 177°10E 154 a
Waycross U.S.A. 31°13N 82°21W 178 E6
Wayland U.S.A. 42°34N 77°35W 174 D7
Wayne Nebr., U.S.A. 42°14N 97°1W 172 D5

Wayne W. Va., U.S.A. 38°13N 82°27W 173 F12
Waynesboro Ga., U.S.A. 33°6N 82°1W 178 B7
Waynesboro Miss., U.S.A. 31°40N 88°39W 177 F10
Waynesboro Pa., U.S.A. 39°45N 77°35W 173 F15
Waynesboro Va., U.S.A. 38°4N 78°53W 173 F14
Waynesburg U.S.A. 39°54N 80°11W 173 F13
Waynesville U.S.A. 35°28N 82°58W 177 D12
Waynoka U.S.A. 36°35N 98°53W 176 C5
Wayside U.S.A. 33°4N 83°37W 178 B6
Wazirabad Pakistan 32°30N 74°8E 124 C6
Waziristan Pakistan 33°0N 70°0E 124 C4
Wda → Poland 53°18N 18°29E 82 E5
We Indonesia 5°51N 95°18E 118 C1
Weald, The U.K. 51°4N 0°20E 67 F8
Wear → U.K. 54°55N 1°23W 66 C6
Weatherford Okla., U.S.A. 35°32N 98°43W 176 D5
Weatherford Tex., U.S.A. 32°46N 97°48W 176 E6
Weaverville U.S.A. 40°44N 122°56W 168 F2
Webb City U.S.A. 37°9N 94°28W 172 G6
Webequie Canada 52°59N 87°21W 164 B2
Weber → N.Z. 40°24S 176°20E 154 G6
Webo = Nyaake Liberia 4°52N 7°37W 138 E3
Webster Mass., U.S.A. 42°3N 71°53W 175 D13
Webster N.Y., U.S.A. 43°13N 77°26W 174 C7
Webster S. Dak., U.S.A. 45°20N 97°31W 172 C5
Webster City U.S.A. 42°28N 93°49W 172 D7
Webster Springs U.S.A. 38°29N 80°25W 173 F13
Webuye Kenya 0°37N 34°46E 142 B3
Weda Indonesia 0°21N 127°50E 119 D7
Weda, Teluk Indonesia 0°20N 128°0E 119 D7
Weddell Abyssal Plain S. Ocean 65°0S 20°0W 55 C2
Weddell I. Falk. Is. 51°50S 61°0W 192 D4
Weddell Sea Antarctica 72°30S 40°0W 55 D1
Wedderburn Australia 36°26S 143°33E 152 D5
Weddin Mts. △ Australia 33°59S 148°0E 153 C8
Wedel Germany 53°34N 9°42E 76 B5
Wedemark Germany 52°32N 9°43E 76 C5
Wedgeport Canada 43°44N 65°59W 165 D6
Wedowee U.S.A. 33°19N 85°29W 178 B4
Wedza Zimbabwe 18°40S 31°33E 143 F3
Wee Waa Australia 30°11S 149°26E 151 E4
Weed U.S.A. 41°25N 122°23W 168 F2
Weed Heights U.S.A. 38°59N 119°13W 170 G7
Weedsport U.S.A. 43°2N 76°33W 175 C8
Weedville U.S.A. 41°17N 78°30W 174 E6
Weeki Wachee U.S.A. 28°32N 82°35W 179 G7
Weenen S. Africa 28°48S 30°7E 145 C5
Weener Germany 53°9N 7°20E 76 B3
Weerribben △ Neths. 52°47N 5°58E 69 B5
Weert Neths. 51°15N 5°43E 69 C5
Węgierska-Górka Poland 49°36N 19°7E 83 J6
Węgliniec Poland 51°18N 15°10E 83 G2
Węgorzewo Poland 54°13N 21°43E 82 D8
Węgorzyno Poland 53°32N 15°33E 82 E2
Węgrów Poland 52°24N 22°0E 83 F9
Wei He → Hebei, China 36°10N 115°45E 114 F8
Wei He → Shaanxi, China 34°38N 110°15E 114 G6
Weichang China 41°58N 117°49E 115 D9
Weichuan China 34°20N 113°59E 114 G7
Weida Germany 50°46N 12°2E 76 E8
Weiden Germany 49°41N 12°10E 77 F8
Weifang China 36°44N 119°7E 115 F10
Weihai China 37°30N 122°6E 115 F12
Weihui China 35°25N 114°3E 114 G8
Weil Germany 47°35N 7°37E 77 H3
Weilburg Germany 50°28N 8°17E 76 E4
Weilheim Germany 47°50N 11°9E 77 H7
Weimar Germany 50°58N 11°19E 76 E7
Weinan China 34°31N 109°29E 114 G5
Weingarten Germany 47°49N 9°38E 77 H5
Weinheim Germany 49°32N 8°39E 77 F4
Weining China 26°50N 104°17E 116 D5
Weipa Australia 12°40S 141°50E 150 A3
Weir → Australia 28°20S 149°50E 151 D4
Weir → Canada 56°54N 93°21W 163 B10
Weir River Canada 56°49N 94°6W 163 B10
Weirsdale U.S.A. 28°59N 81°55W 179 G8
Weirton U.S.A. 40°24N 80°35W 174 F4
Weiser U.S.A. 44°15N 116°58W 168 D5
Weishan Shandong, China 34°47N 117°5E 115 G9
Weishan Yunnan, China 25°12N 100°20E 116 E3
Weishan Hu China 34°35N 117°14E 115 G9
Weissenburg Germany 49°2N 10°58E 77 F6
Weissenfels Germany 51°11N 12°0E 76 D7
Weisswasser Germany 51°30N 14°36E 76 D10
Wéitra Austria 48°41N 14°54E 78 C7
Weixi China 27°10N 99°10E 116 D2
Weixin China 27°48N 105°3E 116 D5
Weiyuan Gansu, China 35°7N 104°10E 114 G3
Weiyuan Sichuan, China 29°35N 104°36E 116 C5
Weiz Austria 47°13N 15°39E 78 D8
Weizhou Dao China 21°0N 109°5E 116 G7
Wejherowo Poland 54°35N 18°12E 82 D5
Wekusko L. Canada 54°40N 99°50W 163 C9
Welch U.S.A. 37°26N 81°35W 173 G13
Welford △ Australia 25°5S 143°16E 150 D3
Welkom S. Africa 28°0S 26°46E 144 C4
Welland Canada 43°0N 79°15W 174 D5
Welland → U.K. 52°51N 0°5W 66 E7
Wellawaya Sri Lanka 6°44N 81°6E 127 L5
Wellesley Is. Australia 16°42S 139°30E 150 B2
Wellingborough U.K. 52°19N 0°41W 67 E7
Wellington Australia 32°35S 148°59E 153 B8
Wellington N.Z. 41°19S 174°46E 154 H1
Wellington Somst., U.K. 50°58N 3°13W 67 G4
Wellington Telford & Wrekin, U.K. 52°42N 2°30W 67 E5
Wellington Colo., U.S.A. 40°42N 105°0W 168 E11
Wellington Fla., U.S.A. 26°39N 80°15W 179 H8
Wellington Kans., U.S.A. 37°16N 97°24W 172 G5

Wellington *Nev.*,
 U.S.A. 38°45N 119°23W **170** G7
Wellington *Ohio*,
 U.S.A. 41°10N 82°13W **174** E2
Wellington *Tex.*,
 U.S.A. 34°51N 100°13W **176** D4
Wellington □ *N.Z.* 41°0S 175°30E **154** H4
Wellington, I. *Chile* 49°30S 75°0W **192** C2
Wellington, L. *Australia* 38°6S 147°20E **153** E7
Wellington Chan.
 Canada 75°0N 93°0W **161** C13
Wells *U.K.* 51°13N 2°39W **67** F5
Wells *Maine, U.S.A.* 43°20N 70°35W **175** C14
Wells *N.Y., U.S.A.* 43°24N 74°17W **175** C10
Wells *Nev., U.S.A.* 41°7N 114°58W **168** F6
Wells, L. *Australia* 26°44S 123°15E **149** E3
Wells, Mt. *Australia* 17°25S 127°8E **148** C4
Wells Gray △ *Canada* 52°30N 120°15W **162** C4
Wells-next-the-Sea *U.K.* 52°57N 0°51E **66** E8
Wells River *U.S.A.* 44°9N 72°4W **175** B12
Wellsboro *U.S.A.* 41°45N 77°18W **174** E7
Wellsburg *U.S.A.* 40°16N 80°37W **174** F4
Wellsford *N.Z.* 36°16S 174°32E **154** C3
Wellsville *N.Y., U.S.A.* 42°7N 77°57W **174** D7
Wellsville *Ohio, U.S.A.* 40°36N 80°39W **174** F4
Wellsville *Utah, U.S.A.* 41°38N 111°56W **168** F8
Wellton *U.S.A.* 32°40N 114°8W **169** K6
Wels *Austria* 48°9N 14°1E **78** C7
Welshpool *Australia* 38°42S 146°26E **153** E7
Welshpool *U.K.* 52°39N 3°8W **67** E4
Welwyn Garden City
 U.K. 51°48N 0°12W **67** F7
Wem *U.K.* 52°52N 2°44W **66** E5
Wembere → *Tanzania* 4°10S 34°15E **142** C3
Wemindji *Canada* 53°0N 78°49W **164** B4
Wemyss *Canada* 44°52N 76°23W **175** B8
Wen Xian *Gansu,*
 China 32°43N 104°36E **114** H3
Wen Xian *Henan, China* 34°55N 113°5E **114** G7
Wenatchee *U.S.A.* 47°25N 120°19W **168** C3
Wenchang *China* 19°38N 110°42E **117** J4
Wencheng *China* 27°46N 120°4E **117** D13
Wenchi *China* 7°46N 2°8W **138** D4
Wenchow = Wenzhou
 China 28°0N 120°38E **117** D13
Wenchuan *China* 31°22N 103°35E **116** B4
Wenden *U.S.A.* 33°49N 113°33W **171** M13
Wendeng *China* 37°15N 122°5E **115** F12
Wendover *U.S.A.* 40°44N 114°2W **168** F6
Weng'an *China* 27°5N 107°25E **116** D6
Wengcheng *China* 24°22N 113°50E **117** E9
Wengen *Switz.* 46°37N 7°55E **71** F14
Wengyuan *China* 24°20N 114°2E **117** E10
Wenling *China* 28°21N 121°20E **117** C13
Wenlock → *Australia* 12°2S 141°55E **150** A3
Wenshan *China* 23°20N 104°18E **116** F5
Wenshang *China* 35°45N 116°30E **114** G9
Wenshui *China* 37°26N 112°1E **114** F7
Wensleydale *U.K.* 54°17N 2°0W **66** C6
Wensu *China* 41°15N 80°10E **109** D10
Wensum → *U.K.* 52°40N 1°15E **66** E8
Wentworth *Australia* 34°2S 141°54E **152** C4
Wentzel L. *Canada* 59°2N 114°28W **162** B6
Wenut *Indonesia* 3°11S 133°19E **119** E8
Wenxi *China* 35°20N 111°10E **114** G6
Wenzhou *China* 28°0N 120°38E **117** D13
Weott *U.S.A.* 40°20N 123°55W **168** F2
Wepener *S. Africa* 29°42S 27°3E **144** C4
Werda *Botswana* 25°24S 23°15E **144** D3
Werdau *Germany* 50°44N 12°22E **76** E8
Werder *Germany* 52°23N 12°55E **76** C8
Werdohl *Germany* 51°15N 7°46E **76** D3
Weri *Indonesia* 3°10S 132°38E **119** E8
Werneck *Germany* 49°58N 10°5E **77** F6
Wernigerode *Germany* 51°50N 10°47E **76** D6
Werra → *Germany* 51°24N 9°39E **76** D5
Werribee *Australia* 37°54S 144°40E **152** D6
Werrikimbe △
 Australia 31°11S 152°15E **153** A10
Werrimull *Australia* 34°25S 141°38E **152** C4
Werris Creek *Australia* 31°18S 150°38E **153** A9
Wertach → *Germany* 48°22N 10°54E **77** G6
Wertheim *Germany* 49°45N 9°32E **77** F5
Wertingen *Germany* 48°33N 10°41E **77** G6
Wesel *Germany* 51°39N 6°37E **76** D2
Weser → *Germany* 53°36N 8°28E **76** B4
Weserbergland *Germany* 52°12N 9°7E **76** C5
Weserbergland Schaumburg
 Hameln □ *Germany* 52°6N 9°20E **76** C5
Weslaco *U.S.A.* 26°10N 97°58W **176** H6
Weslemkoon L. *Canada* 45°2N 77°25W **174** A7
Wesleyville *Canada* 49°9N 53°33W **165** C9
Wesleyville *U.S.A.* 42°9N 80°1W **174** D4
Wessel, C. *Australia* 10°59S 136°46E **150** A2
Wessel Is. *Australia* 11°10S 136°45E **150** A2
Wesselburen *Germany* 54°13N 8°54E **76** A4
Wessex □ *U.K.* 51°0N 2°0W **67** F5
Wessington Springs
 U.S.A. 44°5N 98°34W **172** C4
West *U.S.A.* 31°48N 97°6W **176** F6
West → *U.S.A.* 42°52N 72°33W **175** D12
West Allis *U.S.A.* 43°1N 88°0W **172** D9
West Antarctica
 Antarctica 80°0S 90°0W **55** D15
West Baines →
 Australia 15°38S 129°59E **148** C4
West Bank □ *Asia* 32°6N 35°13E **108** C4
West Bend *U.S.A.* 43°25N 88°11W **172** D9
West Bengal = Paschimbanga □
 India 23°0N 88°0E **125** H13
West Berkshire □ *U.K.* 51°25N 1°17W **67** F6
West Beskids = Západné Beskydy
 Europe 49°30N 19°0E **79** B12
West Branch *U.S.A.* 44°17N 84°14W **173** C11
West Branch Susquehanna →
 U.S.A. 40°53N 76°48W **175** F8
West Bromwich *U.K.* 52°32N 1°59W **67** E6
West Burra *U.K.* 60°5N 1°21W **65** A7
West Canada Cr. →
 U.S.A. 43°1N 74°58W **175** C10
West Caroline Basin
 Pac. Oc. 4°0N 138°0E **156** G5
West Chazy *U.S.A.* 44°49N 73°28W **175** B11
West Chester *U.S.A.* 39°58N 75°36W **175** G9
West Coast △ *Canada* 43°15S 170°30E **155** D6
West Coast △ *Namibia* 21°53S 14°14E **144** B1
West Coast △ *S. Africa* 33°13S 18°0E **144** D2
West Columbia *S.C.,*
 U.S.A. 33°59N 81°4W **177** B8
West Columbia *Tex.,*
 U.S.A. 29°9N 95°39W **176** G7
West Covina *U.S.A.* 34°4N 117°54W **171** L9
West Des Moines
 U.S.A. 41°35N 93°43W **172** E7
West Dunbartonshire □
 U.K. 55°59N 4°30W **65** F4
West End *Bahamas* 26°41N 78°58W **182** A4
West Falkland *Falk. Is.* 51°40S 60°0W **192** D5
West Fargo *U.S.A.* 46°52N 96°54W **172** B5
West Fiji Basin *Pac. Oc.* 17°0S 173°0E **156** J9
West Fjord = Vestfjorden
 Norway 67°55N 14°0E **60** C16
West Fork Trinity →
 U.S.A. 32°48N 96°54W **176** E6
West Frankfort *U.S.A.* 37°54N 88°55W **172** G9
West Grand L. *U.S.A.* 45°14N 67°51W **173** C20
West Green *U.S.A.* 31°37N 82°44W **178** D7
West Hartford *U.S.A.* 41°45N 72°44W **175** E12
West Haven *U.S.A.* 41°17N 72°57W **175** E12
West Hazleton *U.S.A.* 40°58N 76°0W **175** F9
West Hurley *U.S.A.* 41°59N 74°7W **175** E10
West I. *India* 13°35S 92°54E **127** H11
West Ice Shelf *Antarctica* 67°0S 85°0E **55** C7
West Indies *Cent. Amer.* 15°0N 65°0W **183** D7
West Jordan *U.S.A.* 40°36N 111°56W **168** F8
West Kavango □
 Namibia 18°0S 18°30E **144** A2
West Lamma Channel
 China 22°14N 114°4E **111** a
West Linn *U.S.A.* 45°21N 122°36W **170** E4
West Lorne *Canada* 42°36N 81°36W **174** D3
West Lothian □ *U.K.* 55°54N 3°36W **65** F5
West Lunga → *Zambia* 13°6S 24°39E **143** E1
West MacDonnell △
 Australia 23°38S 132°59E **148** D5
West Mariana Basin
 Pac. Oc. 15°0N 137°0E **156** F5
West Memphis *U.S.A.* 35°8N 90°10W **177** D9
West Midlands □ *U.K.* 52°26N 2°0W **67** E6
West Mifflin *U.S.A.* 40°21N 79°52W **174** F5
West Milford *U.S.A.* 41°8N 74°22W **175** E10
West Milton *U.S.A.* 41°1N 76°50W **174** E8
West Monroe *U.S.A.* 32°31N 92°9W **176** E8
West Newton *U.S.A.* 40°14N 79°46W **174** F5
West Nicholson
 Zimbabwe 21°2S 29°20E **143** G2
West Odessa *U.S.A.* 31°50N 102°30W **176** E3
West Palm Beach
 U.S.A. 26°43N 80°3W **179** J9
West Palm Beach Canal
 U.S.A. 26°40N 80°15W **179** J9
West Pensacola *U.S.A.* 30°25N 87°16W **179** E2
West Plains *U.S.A.* 36°44N 91°51W **172** G8
West Point *Ga., U.S.A.* 32°53N 85°11W **178** C4
West Point *Miss.,*
 U.S.A. 33°36N 88°39W **177** E10
West Point *N.Y.,*
 U.S.A. 41°24N 73°58W **175** E11
West Point *Nebr.,*
 U.S.A. 41°51N 96°43W **172** E5
West Point *Va.,*
 U.S.A. 37°32N 76°48W **173** G15
West Point L. *U.S.A.* 33°8N 85°0W **178** C4
West Pokot □ *Kenya* 1°15N 35°10E **142** B4
West Pt. = Ouest, Pte. de l'
 Canada 49°52N 64°40W **165** C7
West Pt. *Australia* 35°1S 135°56E **152** C1
West Road → *Canada* 53°18N 122°53W **162** C4
West Rutland *U.S.A.* 43°36N 73°3W **175** C11
West Schelde = Westerschelde
 Neths. 51°25N 3°25E **69** C3
West Seneca *U.S.A.* 42°51N 78°48W **174** D6
West Siberian Plain
 Russia 62°0N 75°0E **102** B9
West Sussex □ *U.K.* 50°55N 0°30W **67** G7
West-Terschelling *Neths.* 53°22N 5°13E **69** A5
West Valley City
 U.S.A. 40°42N 111°58W **168** F8
West Virginia □
 U.S.A. 38°45N 80°30W **173** F13
West-Vlaanderen □
 Belgium 51°0N 3°0E **69** D2
West Walker →
 U.S.A. 38°54N 119°9W **170** G7
West Wyalong
 Australia 33°56S 147°10E **153** B7
West Yellowstone
 U.S.A. 44°40N 111°6W **168** D8
West Yorkshire □ *U.K.* 53°45N 1°40W **66** D6
Westall, Pt. *Australia* 32°55S 134°4E **151** E1
Westbay *N.Z.* 42°18N 85°52W **178** E4
Westbrook *U.S.A.* 43°41N 70°22W **173** D18
Westbury *Australia* 41°30S 146°51E **151** G4
Westby *U.S.A.* 48°52N 104°3W **168** B11
Westend *U.S.A.* 35°42N 117°24W **171** K9
Westerland *Germany* 54°54N 8°17E **76** A4
Westerly *U.S.A.* 41°22N 71°50W **175** E13
Western □ *Ghana* 5°30N 2°30W **138** D4
Western □ *S. Leone* 8°30N 13°20W **138** D2
Western □ *Zambia* 15°0S 24°4E **143** F1
Western Australia □
 Australia 25°0S 118°0E **149** E2
Western Cape □ *S. Africa* 34°0S 20°0E **144** D3
Western Dvina = Daugava →
 Latvia 57°4N 24°3E **84** D3
Western Ghats *India* 14°0N 75°0E **127** H2
Western Isles = Eilean Siar □
 U.K. 57°30N 7°10W **65** D1
Western Sahara ■
 Africa 25°0N 13°0W **134** D3
Western Samoa = Samoa ■
 Pac. Oc. 14°0S 172°0W **147** C11
Western Sierra Madre = Madre
 Occidental, Sierra
 Mexico 27°0N 107°0W **180** B3
Westernport *U.S.A.* 39°29N 79°3W **173** F14
Westerschelde → *Neths.* 51°25N 3°25E **69** C3
Westerstede *Germany* 53°15N 7°55E **76** B3
Westerwald *Germany* 50°38N 7°56E **76** E3
Westfield *Mass., U.S.A.* 42°7N 72°45W **175** D12
Westfield *N.Y., U.S.A.* 42°20N 79°35W **174** D5
Westfield *Pa., U.S.A.* 41°55N 77°32W **174** E7
Westhill *U.K.* 57°9N 2°19W **65** D6
Westhope *U.S.A.* 48°55N 101°1W **172** A3
Westland Bight *N.Z.* 42°55S 170°5E **155** C5
Westland Tai Poutini △
 N.Z. 43°16S 170°16E **155** D5
Westlock *Canada* 54°9N 113°55W **162** C6
Westmar *Australia* 27°55S 149°44E **151** D4
Westmeath □ *Ireland* 53°33N 7°34W **64** C4
Westminster *Calif.,*
 U.S.A. 33°45N 118°0W **171** M8
Westminster *Colo.,*
 U.S.A. 39°50N 105°2W **168** G11
Westminster *Md.,*
 U.S.A. 39°34N 76°59W **173** F15
Westmont *U.S.A.* 40°19N 78°58W **174** F6
Westmoreland *Barbados* 13°13N 59°37W **183** g
Westmorland *U.S.A.* 33°2N 115°37W **171** M11
Weston *Oreg., U.S.A.* 45°49N 118°26W **168** D4
Weston *W. Va., U.S.A.* 39°2N 80°28W **173** F13
Weston I. *Canada* 52°33N 79°36W **164** B4
Weston-super-Mare
 U.K. 51°21N 2°58W **67** F5
Westover *U.S.A.* 40°45N 78°40W **174** F6
Westport *Canada* 44°40N 76°25W **175** B8
Westport *Ireland* 53°48N 9°31W **64** C2
Westport *N.Z.* 41°46S 171°37E **155** B6
Westport *N.Y., U.S.A.* 44°11N 73°26W **175** B11
Westport *Oreg., U.S.A.* 46°8N 123°23W **170** D3
Westport *Wash., U.S.A.* 46°53N 124°6W **170** D2
Westray *Canada* 53°36N 101°24W **163** C8
Westray *U.K.* 59°18N 3°0W **65** B5
Westree *Canada* 47°26N 81°34W **164** C3
Westville *Calif., U.S.A.* 39°8N 120°42W **170** F6
Westville *Fla., U.S.A.* 30°46N 85°51W **178** E4
Westwood *U.S.A.* 40°18N 121°0W **168** F3
Westwood Lake *U.S.A.* 25°44N 80°23W **179** K9
Wetar *Indonesia* 7°48S 126°30E **119** F7
Wetaskiwin *Canada* 52°55N 113°24W **162** C6
Wete *Tanzania* 5°4S 39°43E **140** F7
Wetherby *U.K.* 53°56N 1°23W **66** D6
Wethersfield *U.S.A.* 41°42N 72°40W **175** E12
Wetteren *Belgium* 51°0N 3°53E **69** D3
Wetumka *U.S.A.* 35°14N 96°13W **176** D6
Wetumpka *U.S.A.* 32°32N 86°13W **178** C3
Wetzlar *Germany* 50°32N 8°31E **76** E4
Wewahitchka *U.S.A.* 30°7N 85°12W **178** E4
Wewoka *U.S.A.* 35°9N 96°30W **176** D6
Wexford *Ireland* 52°20N 6°28W **64** D5
Wexford □ *Ireland* 52°20N 6°25W **64** D5
Wexford Harbour *Ireland* 52°20N 6°25W **64** D5
Weyburn *Canada* 49°40N 103°50W **163** D8
Weyer Markt *Austria* 47°51N 14°40E **78** D7
Weyhe *Germany* 52°58N 8°49E **76** C4
Weymouth *Canada* 44°30N 66°1W **165** D6
Weymouth *U.K.* 50°37N 2°28W **67** G5
Weymouth *U.S.A.* 42°13N 70°58W **175** D14
Weymouth, C.
 Australia 12°37S 143°27E **150** A3
Wha Ti *Canada* 63°8N 117°16W **160** E8
Whakaari *N.Z.* 37°30S 177°13E **154** B6
Whakamaru *N.Z.* 38°23S 175°50E **154** E4
Whakatane *N.Z.* 37°57S 177°1E **154** D6
Whakatane → *N.Z.* 37°57S 177°1E **154** D6
Whale = Baleine →
 Canada 58°15N 67°40W **165** A6
Whale B. *Myanmar* 11°37N 98°38E **121** G2
Whale Cove *Canada* 62°10N 92°34W **163** A10
Whale Valley = Hitan, W. el
 Egypt 29°19N 30°10E **137** F2
Whales, B. of *Antarctica* 78°0S 160°0W **55** D12
Whalsay *U.K.* 60°22N 0°59W **65** A8
Whangaehu → *N.Z.* 40°3S 175°6E **154** G4
Whangamata *N.Z.* 37°12S 175°53E **154** D6
Whangamomona *N.Z.* 39°8S 174°44E **154** F3
Whanganui *N.Z.* 39°17S 174°53E **154** F3
Whangaparaoa Pen.
 N.Z. 36°40S 174°45E **154** C3
Whangarei *N.Z.* 35°43S 174°21E **154** B3
Whangarei Harb. *N.Z.* 35°45S 174°28E **154** B3
Whangaroa Harb. *N.Z.* 35°4S 173°46E **154** B2
Whangaruru Harb.
 N.Z. 35°24S 174°32E **154** B3
Wharanui *N.Z.* 41°55S 174°6E **155** B9
Wharekauri = Chatham Is.
 Pac. Oc. 43°55S 176°40W **155** c
Wharfe → *U.K.* 53°51N 1°9W **66** D6
Wharfedale *U.K.* 54°6N 2°1W **66** C5
Wharton *N.J., U.S.A.* 40°54N 74°35W **175** F10
Wharton *Pa., U.S.A.* 41°31N 78°1W **174** E6
Wharton *Tex., U.S.A.* 29°19N 96°6W **176** G6
Wharton Basin *Ind. Oc.* 22°0S 99°0E **146** G9
Whataroa *N.Z.* 43°18S 170°24E **155** D5
Whataroa → *N.Z.* 43°7S 170°16E **155** D5
Wheatland *Calif.,*
 U.S.A. 39°1N 121°25W **170** F5
Wheatland *Wyo.,*
 U.S.A. 42°3N 104°58W **168** E11
Wheatley *Canada* 42°6N 82°27W **174** D2
Wheaton *Md., U.S.A.* 39°3N 77°3W **173** F15
Wheaton *Minn., U.S.A.* 45°48N 96°30W **172** C5
Wheelbarrow Pk.
 U.S.A. 37°26N 116°5W **170** H10
Wheeler *Oreg., U.S.A.* 45°41N 123°53W **168** D2
Wheeler *Tex., U.S.A.* 35°27N 100°16W **176** D4
Wheeler → *Canada* 57°2N 67°13W **165** A6
Wheeler L. *U.S.A.* 34°48N 87°23W **177** D11
Wheeler Pk. *N. Mex.,*
 U.S.A. 36°34N 105°25W **169** H11
Wheeler Pk. *Nev.,*
 U.S.A. 38°57N 114°15W **168** G6
Wheeler Ridge *U.S.A.* 35°0N 118°57W **171** L8
Wheelersburg *U.S.A.* 38°44N 82°51W **173** F12
Wheeling *U.S.A.* 40°4N 80°43W **174** F4
Whernside *U.K.* 54°14N 2°24W **66** C5
Whiddy I. *Ireland* 51°41N 9°31W **64** E2
Whim Creek *Australia* 20°50S 117°49E **148** D2
Whiskey Jack L.
 Canada 58°23N 101°55W **163** B8
Whiskeytown-Shasta-Trinity △
 U.S.A. 40°45N 122°15W **168** F2
Whistleduck Cr. →
 Australia 20°15S 135°18E **150** C2
Whistler *Canada* 50°7N 122°58W **162** C4
Whitby *Canada* 43°52N 78°56W **174** C6
Whitby *U.K.* 54°29N 0°37W **66** C7
Whitcombe Pass *N.Z.* 43°13S 170°55E **155** D5
White → *Ark., U.S.A.* 33°57N 91°5W **176** D8
White → *Ind., U.S.A.* 38°25N 87°45W **172** F10
White → *S. Dak.,*
 U.S.A. 43°42N 99°27W **172** D4
White → *Utah, U.S.A.* 40°4N 109°41W **168** F9
White → *Vt., U.S.A.* 43°37N 72°20W **175** C12
White → *Wash.,*
 U.S.A. 47°12N 122°15W **170** C4
White B. *Canada* 21°9S 128°56E **148** D4
White Bird *U.S.A.* 45°46N 116°18W **168** D5
White Butte *U.S.A.* 46°23N 103°18W **172** B2
White City *Fla., U.S.A.* 29°53S 85°13W **178** F7
White City *Oreg.,*
 U.S.A. 42°26N 122°51W **168** E2
White Cliffs *Australia* 30°50S 143°10E **152** A5
White Desert = Beida, Es Sahrâ al
 Egypt 27°50N 28°45E **137** B2
White Hall *U.S.A.* 39°26N 90°24W **172** F8
White Haven *U.S.A.* 41°4N 75°47W **175** E9
White Horse, Vale of
 U.K. 51°37N 1°30W **67** F6
White I. = Whakaari
 N.Z. 37°30S 177°13E **154** D6
White L. *Canada* 45°18N 76°31W **175** A8
White L. *U.S.A.* 29°44N 92°30W **176** G8
White Lake *Canada* 45°21N 76°29W **175** A8
White Mountain Peak
 U.S.A. 37°38N 118°15W **170** H8
White Mts. *Calif.,*
 U.S.A. 37°30N 118°15W **170** H8
White Mts. *N.H.,*
 U.S.A. 44°15N 71°15W **175** B13
White Mts. △
 Australia 20°43S 145°12E **150** C4
White Nile = Nil el Abyad →
 Sudan 15°38N 32°31E **135** E12
White Oak *U.S.A.* 32°31N 81°43W **178** D8
White Otter L. *Canada* 49°5N 91°55W **164** C1
White Pass *U.S.A.* 46°38N 121°24W **170** D4
White Plains *Ga., U.S.A.* 33°28N 83°11W **178** B6
White Plains *N.Y.,*
 U.S.A. 41°2N 73°46W **175** E11
White River *Canada* 48°35N 85°20W **164** C2
White River *U.S.A.* 43°34N 100°45W **172** D3
White Rock *Canada* 49°2N 122°48W **170** A4
White Rock *U.S.A.* 35°50N 106°12W **169** J10
White Rocks Nat. Recr. Area △
 U.S.A. 43°22N 72°55W **175** C12
White Russia = Belarus ■
 Europe 53°30N 27°0E **75** B14
White Sands △
 U.S.A. 32°46N 106°20W **169** K10
White Sea = Beloye More
 Russia 66°30N 38°0E **58** B13
White Springs *U.S.A.* 30°20N 82°45W **178** E7
White Sulphur Springs *Mont.,*
 U.S.A. 46°33N 110°54W **168** C8
White Sulphur Springs *W. Va.,*
 U.S.A. 37°48N 80°18W **173** G13
White Swan *U.S.A.* 46°23N 120°44W **170** D6
White Volta → *Ghana* 9°10N 1°15W **139** D4
Whitecliffs *N.Z.* 43°26S 171°55E **155** D6
Whitecourt *Canada* 54°10N 115°45W **162** C5
Whiteface Mt. *U.S.A.* 44°22N 73°54W **175** B11
Whitefield *U.S.A.* 44°23N 71°37W **175** B13
Whitefish *U.S.A.* 48°25N 114°20W **168** B6
Whitefish B. *U.S.A.* 46°40N 84°55W **164** C3
Whitefish L. *Canada* 62°41N 106°48W **163** A7
Whitefish Pt. *U.S.A.* 46°45N 84°59W **173** B11
Whitegull, L. = Goélands, L. aux
 Canada 55°27N 64°17W **165** A7
Whitehall *Mich.,*
 U.S.A. 43°24N 86°21W **172** D10
Whitehall *Mont.,*
 U.S.A. 45°52N 112°6W **168** D7
Whitehall *N.Y.,*
 U.S.A. 43°33N 73°24W **175** C11
Whitehall *Wis., U.S.A.* 44°22N 91°19W **172** C8
Whitehaven *U.K.* 54°33N 3°35W **66** C4
Whitehorse *Canada* 60°43N 135°3W **162** A1
Whitemark *Australia* 40°7S 148°3E **151** G4
Whiteriver *U.S.A.* 33°50N 109°58W **169** K9
Whitesand → *Canada* 60°9N 115°45W **162** A5
Whitesands *S. Africa* 34°23S 20°50E **144** D3
Whitesboro *N.Y., U.S.A.* 43°7N 75°18W **175** C9
Whitesboro *Tex.,*
 U.S.A. 33°39N 96°54W **176** E6
Whiteshell △ *Canada* 50°0N 95°40W **163** D9
Whiteside, Canal *Chile* 53°55S 70°15W **192** D2
Whiteville *U.S.A.* 34°20N 78°42W **177** D15
Whitewater *U.S.A.* 42°50N 88°44W **172** D9
Whitewater B. *U.S.A.* 25°15N 81°0W **179** K9
Whitewater Baldy
 U.S.A. 33°20N 108°39W **169** K9
Whitewater L. *Canada* 50°50N 89°10W **164** B2
Whitewood *Australia* 21°28S 143°30E **150** C3
Whitewood *Canada* 50°20N 102°20W **163** C8
Whitfield *Australia* 36°42S 146°24E **153** D7
Whithorn *U.K.* 54°44N 4°26W **65** G4
Whitianga *N.Z.* 36°47S 175°41E **154** C4
Whitman *U.S.A.* 42°5N 70°56W **175** D14
Whitmore Mts.
 Antarctica 82°35S 104°30W **55** E15
Whitney *Canada* 45°31N 78°14W **174** A6
Whitney, Mt. *U.S.A.* 36°35N 118°18W **170** J8
Whitney Point *U.S.A.* 42°20N 75°58W **175** D9
Whitstable *U.K.* 51°21N 1°3E **67** F9
Whitsunday I. *Australia* 20°15S 149°4E **150** b
Whitsunday Islands △
 Australia 20°15S 149°0E **150** b
Whittier *Alaska,*
 U.S.A. 60°47N 148°41W **166** C10
Whittier *Calif., U.S.A.* 33°58N 118°2W **171** M8
Whittlesea *Australia* 37°27S 145°9E **153** D6
Wholdaia L. *Canada* 60°43N 104°20W **163** A8
Whyalla *Australia* 33°2S 137°30E **152** B2
Wiang Kosai △
 Thailand 17°54N 99°29E **120** D2
Wiang Sa *Thailand* 18°34N 100°45E **120** C3
Wiarton *Canada* 44°40N 81°10W **174** B3
Wiawso *Ghana* 6°10N 2°25W **138** D4
Wiay *U.K.* 57°24N 7°13W **65** D1
Wiązów *Poland* 50°50N 17°10E **83** H4
Wibaux *U.S.A.* 46°59N 104°11W **168** C11
Wichian Buri *Thailand* 15°39N 101°7E **120** E3
Wichita *U.S.A.* 37°42N 97°20W **172** G5
Wichita Falls *U.S.A.* 33°54N 98°30W **176** E5
Wick *U.K.* 58°26N 3°5W **65** C5
Wickenburg *U.S.A.* 33°58N 112°44W **169** K7
Wickepin *Australia* 32°50S 117°30E **149** F2
Wickham *Australia* 20°42S 117°11E **148** D2
Wickham, C. *Australia* 39°35S 143°57E **151** F3
Wickliffe *U.S.A.* 41°36N 81°28W **174** E3
Wicklow *Ireland* 52°59N 6°3W **64** D5
Wicklow □ *Ireland* 52°57N 6°25W **64** D5
Wicklow Hd. *Ireland* 52°58N 6°0W **64** D6
Wicklow Mts. *Ireland* 52°58N 6°26W **64** C5
Wicklow Mts. △ *Ireland* 53°6N 6°21W **64** C5
Widawa *Poland* 51°27N 18°51E **83** G5
Widawka → *Poland* 51°27N 19°52E **83** G5
Widgeegoara Cr. →
 Australia 28°51S 146°34E **151** D4
Widgiemooltha
 Australia 31°30S 121°34E **149** F3
Widnes *U.K.* 53°23N 2°45W **66** D5
Więcbork *Poland* 53°21N 17°30E **83** E4
Wiehengebirge = Nördlicher
 Teutoburger
 Wald-Wiehengebirge △
 Germany 52°18N 8°10E **76** C4
Wiehl *Germany* 50°56N 7°34E **76** E3
Wiek *Germany* 54°37N 13°17E **76** A9
Wielbark *Poland* 53°24N 20°55E **82** E7
Wieleń *Poland* 52°53N 16°9E **83** F3
Wielichowo *Poland* 52°7N 16°2E **83** F3
Wielkopolski △ *Poland* 52°18N 16°45E **83** F3
Wielkopolskie □ *Poland* 52°10N 17°30E **83** F4
Wieluń *Poland* 51°15N 18°34E **83** G5
Wien *Austria* 48°12N 16°22E **79** C9
Wiener Neustadt
 Austria 47°49N 16°16E **79** D9
Wieprz → *Poland* 51°34N 21°49E **83** G8
Wieprza → *Poland* 54°26N 16°35E **82** D3
Wieruszów *Poland* 51°19N 18°9E **83** G5
Wiesbaden *Germany* 50°4N 8°14E **77** E4
Wiesental *Germany* 49°13N 8°31E **77** F4
Wiesloch *Germany* 49°18N 8°41E **77** F4
Wiesmoor *Germany* 53°24N 7°47E **76** B3
Wieżyca *Poland* 54°14N 18°8E **82** D5
Wigan *U.K.* 53°33N 2°38W **66** D5
Wiggins *Colo., U.S.A.* 40°14N 104°4W **168** F11
Wiggins *Miss., U.S.A.* 30°51N 89°8W **177** F10
Wight, I. of *U.K.* 50°41N 1°17W **67** G6
Wigierski △ *Poland* 54°5N 23°5E **82** D10
Wigston *U.K.* 52°35N 1°6W **67** E6
Wigton *U.K.* 54°50N 3°10W **66** C4
Wigtown *U.K.* 54°53N 4°27W **65** G4
Wigtown B. *U.K.* 54°46N 4°15W **65** G4
Wik and Wikway People ◇
 Australia 13°55S 142°28E **150** A3
Wil *Switz.* 47°28N 9°3E **75** H5
Wilamowice *Poland* 49°55N 19°9E **83** J6
Wilber *U.S.A.* 40°29N 96°58W **172** E5
Wilberforce *Canada* 45°2N 78°13W **174** A6
Wilberforce, C.
 Australia 11°54S 136°35E **150** A2
Wilburton *U.S.A.* 34°55N 95°19W **176** D7
Wilcannia *Australia* 31°30S 143°26E **152** A5
Wilcox *U.S.A.* 41°35N 78°41W **174** E6
Wildbad *Germany* 48°44N 8°33E **77** G4
Wildeshausen *Germany* 52°54N 8°27E **76** C4
Wildhauser Geest ○
 Germany 52°54N 8°30E **76** C4
Wildomar *U.S.A.* 33°36N 117°16W **171** M9
Wildon *Austria* 46°52N 15°31E **78** E8
Wildrose *U.S.A.* 36°14N 117°11W **171** J9
Wildspitze *Austria* 46°53N 10°53E **78** E3
Wildwood *U.S.A.* 28°52N 82°2W **179** G2
Wilga → *Poland* 51°52N 21°18E **83** G8
Wilge → *S. Africa* 27°3S 28°20E **145** C4
Wilhelm II Coast
 Antarctica 68°0S 90°0E **55** C7
Wilhelmsburg *Austria* 48°6N 15°36E **78** C8
Wilhelmshaven *Germany* 53°31N 8°7E **76** B4
Wilhelmstal *Namibia* 21°58S 16°21E **144** B2
Wilis *Indonesia* 7°51S 111°48E **119** G15
Wilkes-Barre *U.S.A.* 41°15N 75°53W **175** E9
Wilkes Land *Antarctica* 69°0S 120°0E **55** D9
Wilkie *Canada* 52°27N 108°42W **163** C7
Wilkins Ice Shelf
 Antarctica 70°30S 72°0W **55** C17
Wilkinsburg *U.S.A.* 40°26N 79°52W **174** F5
Wilkinson Lakes
 Australia 29°40S 132°39E **149** E5
Willacoochee *U.S.A.* 31°20N 83°3W **178** D6
Willandra △ *Australia* 33°12S 145°0E **153** B6
Willandra Creek →
 Australia 33°22S 145°52E **153** B6
Willapa B. *U.S.A.* 46°40N 124°0W **170** D3
Willapa Hills *U.S.A.* 46°35N 123°25W **170** D3
Willard *U.S.A.* 41°3N 82°44W **174** E2
Willare Bridge Roadhouse
 Australia 17°43S 123°38E **148** C3
Willbriggie *Australia* 34°28S 146°2E **153** C7
Willcox *U.S.A.* 32°15N 109°50W **169** K9
Willemstad *Curaçao* 12°5N 68°55W **183** D6
Willi Willi △
 Australia 30°57S 152°27E **153** A10
William → *Canada* 59°8N 109°19W **163** B7
William 'Bill' Dannelly Res.
 U.S.A. 32°6N 87°24W **177** E11
William Creek
 Australia 28°58S 136°22E **151** D2
Williams *Australia* 33°2S 116°52E **149** F2
Williams *Ariz., U.S.A.* 35°15N 112°11W **169** J7
Williams *Calif., U.S.A.* 39°9N 122°9W **170** F4
Williams Harbour
 Canada 52°33N 55°47W **165** B8
Williams Lake *Canada* 52°10N 122°10W **162** C4
Williamsburg *Ky.,*
 U.S.A. 36°44N 84°10W **173** G11
Williamsburg *Pa.,*
 U.S.A. 40°28N 78°12W **174** F6
Williamsburg *Va.,*
 U.S.A. 37°16N 76°43W **173** G15
Williamson *N.Y.,*
 U.S.A. 43°14N 77°11W **174** C7
Williamson *W. Va.,*
 U.S.A. 37°41N 82°17W **173** G12
Williamsport *Pa.,*
 U.S.A. 41°15N 77°1W **174** E7
Williamston *U.S.A.* 35°51N 77°4W **177** D16
Williamstown
 Australia 37°51S 144°52E **153** F5
Williamstown *Ky.,*
 U.S.A. 38°38N 84°34W **173** F11
Williamstown *Mass.,*
 U.S.A. 42°43N 73°12W **175** D11
Williamstown *N.Y.,*
 U.S.A. 43°26N 75°53W **175** C9
Willimantic *U.S.A.* 41°43N 72°13W **175** E12
Willingboro *U.S.A.* 40°3N 74°54W **175** F10
Williston *S. Africa* 31°20S 20°53E **144** D3
Williston *Fla., U.S.A.* 29°23N 82°27W **179** F2
Williston *N. Dak.,*
 U.S.A. 48°9N 103°37W **168** A12
Williston L. *Canada* 56°0N 124°0W **162** B4
Willits *U.S.A.* 39°25N 123°21W **168** G2
Willmar *U.S.A.* 45°7N 95°3W **172** C6
Willmore Wilderness △
 Canada 53°45N 119°30W **162** C5
Willoughby *U.S.A.* 41°39N 81°24W **174** E3
Willow Bunch
 Canada 49°20N 105°35W **163** D7
Willow L. *Canada* 62°10N 119°8W **162** A5
Willow Tree *Australia* 31°40S 150°45E **153** A9
Willow Wall, The
 China 42°10N 122°0E **115** C12
Willowick *U.S.A.* 41°38N 81°28W **174** E3
Willowlake → *Canada* 62°42N 123°8W **162** A4
Willowmore *S. Africa* 33°15S 23°30E **144** D3
Willows *U.S.A.* 39°31N 122°12W **170** F4
Willowvale = Gatyana
 S. Africa 32°16S 28°31E **145** D4
Wills, L. *Australia* 21°25S 128°51E **148** D4
Wills Cr. → *Australia* 22°43S 140°2E **150** C3
Willsboro *U.S.A.* 44°21N 73°24W **175** B11
Willunga *Australia* 35°15S 138°30E **152** C2
Wilma *U.S.A.* 30°9N 84°58W **178** E5
Wilmette *U.S.A.* 42°4N 87°42W **172** D10
Wilmington *Australia* 32°39S 138°7E **152** B3
Wilmington *Del.,*
 U.S.A. 39°45N 75°33W **173** F16
Wilmington *N.C.,*
 U.S.A. 34°14N 77°55W **177** D16
Wilmington *Ohio,*
 U.S.A. 39°27N 83°50W **173** F12
Wilmington *Vt.,*
 U.S.A. 42°52N 72°52W **175** D12
Wilmslow *U.K.* 53°19N 2°13W **66** D5
Wilpattu △ *Sri Lanka* 8°20N 79°50E **127** K4
Wilpena *Australia* 31°31S 138°37E **152** A2
Wilpena Cr. →
 Australia 31°25S 139°29E **152** A3
Wilsall *U.S.A.* 45°59N 110°38W **168** D8
Wilson *N.C., U.S.A.* 35°44N 77°55W **177** D16
Wilson *N.Y., U.S.A.* 43°19N 78°50W **174** C6
Wilson *Pa., U.S.A.* 40°41N 75°15W **175** F9
Wilson → *Australia* 16°48S 128°16E **148** C4
Wilson Bluff *Australia* 31°41S 129°0E **149** F4
Wilson Inlet *Australia* 35°0S 117°22E **149** G2
Wilsons Promontory
 Australia 38°59S 146°23E **153** E7
Wilsons Promontory △
 Australia 38°59S 146°23E **153** D7
Wilster *Germany* 53°55N 9°23E **76** B5
Wilton *U.S.A.* 47°10N 100°47W **172** B3
Wilton → *Australia* 14°45S 134°33E **150** A1
Wiltshire □ *U.K.* 51°18N 1°53W **67** F6
Wiltz *Lux.* 49°57N 5°55E **69** E5
Wiluna *Australia* 26°36S 120°14E **149** E3
Wimborne Minster *U.K.* 50°48N 1°59W **67** G6
Wimereux *France* 50°45N 1°37E **71** B8
Wimmera → *Australia* 36°8S 141°56E **152** D4
Winam G. *Kenya* 0°20S 34°15E **142** C3
Winburg *S. Africa* 28°30S 27°2E **144** C4
Winchelsea *Australia* 38°10S 144°1E **152** E6
Winchendon *U.S.A.* 42°41N 72°3W **175** D12
Winchester *N.Z.* 44°11S 171°17E **155** E6
Winchester *U.K.* 51°4N 1°18W **67** F6
Winchester *Conn.,*
 U.S.A. 41°53N 73°9W **175** E11
Winchester *Idaho,*
 U.S.A. 46°14N 116°38W **168** C5
Winchester *Ind.,*
 U.S.A. 40°10N 84°59W **173** E11
Winchester *Ky.,*
 U.S.A. 37°59N 84°11W **173** G11
Winchester *N.H.,*
 U.S.A. 42°46N 72°23W **175** D12
Winchester *Nev.,*
 U.S.A. 36°7N 115°7W **171** J11
Winchester *Tenn.,*
 U.S.A. 35°11N 86°7W **177** D11
Winchester *Va.,*
 U.S.A. 39°11N 78°10W **173** F14
Wind → *U.S.A.* 43°12N 108°12W **168** E9
Wind Cave △ *U.S.A.* 43°32N 103°17W **172** D2
Wind River Range
 U.S.A. 43°0N 109°30W **168** E9
Windamere, L.
 Australia 32°48S 149°51E **153** B8
Windau = Ventspils
 Latvia 57°25N 21°32E **82** A8
Windber *U.S.A.* 40°14N 78°50W **174** F6
Winder *U.S.A.* 34°0N 83°45W **178** A6
Windermere *U.K.* 54°23N 2°55W **66** C5
Windermere *U.S.A.* 28°29N 81°32W **179** G8
Windhoek *Namibia* 22°35S 17°4E **144** B2
Windidda △ *Australia* 26°23S 122°12E **149** E3
Windischgarsten
 Austria 47°42N 14°21E **78** D7
Windjana Gorge △
 Australia 17°51S 125°0E **148** C3
Windom *U.S.A.* 43°52N 95°7W **172** D6
Windorah *Australia* 25°24S 142°36E **150** D3
Window Rock *U.S.A.* 35°41N 109°3W **169** J9
Windrush → *U.K.* 51°43N 1°24W **67** F6
Windsor *Australia* 33°37S 150°50E **153** B9
Windsor *N.S., Canada* 44°59N 64°5W **165** D7
Windsor *Ont., Canada* 42°18N 83°0W **174** D2
Windsor *N.Z.* 44°59S 170°49E **155** E5
Windsor *U.K.* 51°29N 0°36W **67** F7
Windsor *Calif., U.S.A.* 38°33N 122°49W **170** G4
Windsor *Colo., U.S.A.* 40°29N 104°54W **168** F11
Windsor *Conn., U.S.A.* 41°50N 72°39W **175** E12
Windsor *Mo., U.S.A.* 38°32N 93°31W **172** F7
Windsor *N.Y., U.S.A.* 42°5N 75°37W **175** D9
Windsor *Vt., U.S.A.* 43°29N 72°24W **175** C12
Windsor & Maidenhead □
 U.K. 51°29N 0°40W **67** F7
Windsorton *S. Africa* 28°16S 24°44E **144** D3
Windward Is. *W. Indies* 13°0N 61°0W **183** D7
Windward Passage = Vientos,
 Paso de los *Caribbean* 20°0N 74°0W **183** C5
Winefred L. *Canada* 55°30N 110°30E **163** B6
Winfield *U.S.A.* 37°15N 96°59W **172** G5
Wingate Mts.
 Australia 14°25S 130°40E **148** B5
Wingellina = Irruntyju
 Australia 26°3S 128°56E **149** E4
Wingham *Australia* 31°48S 152°22E **153** A10
Wingham *Canada* 43°55N 81°20W **174** C3
Winisk → *Canada* 55°17N 85°5W **164** A2
Winisk L. *Canada* 52°55N 87°22W **164** B2
Wink *U.S.A.* 31°45N 103°9W **176** E3
Winkler *Canada* 49°10N 97°56W **163** D9
Winklern *Austria* 46°52N 12°52E **78** E5
Winlock *U.S.A.* 46°30N 122°56W **170** D4
Winneba *Ghana* 5°25N 0°36W **138** D4
Winnebago, L. *U.S.A.* 44°0N 88°26W **172** D9
Winnecke Cr. →
 Australia 18°35S 131°34E **148** C5

Winnemucca U.S.A. 40°58N 117°44W **168 F5**
Winnemucca L. U.S.A. 40°7N 119°21W **168 F4**
Winner U.S.A. 43°22N 99°52W **172 D4**
Winnett U.S.A. 47°0N 108°21W **168 C9**
Winnfield U.S.A. 31°56N 92°38W **176 F8**
Winnibigoshish, L.
  U.S.A. 47°27N 94°13W **172 B8**
Winnipeg Canada 49°54N 97°9W **163 C9**
Winnipeg → Canada 50°38N 96°19W **163 C9**
Winnipeg, L. Canada 52°0N 97°0W **163 C9**
Winnipeg Beach
  Canada 50°30N 96°58W **163 C9**
Winnipegosis Canada 51°39N 99°55W **163 C9**
Winnipegosis L.
  Canada 52°30N 100°0W **163 C9**
Winnipesaukee, L.
  U.S.A. 43°38N 71°21W **175 C13**
Winnisquam L.
  U.S.A. 43°33N 71°31W **175 C13**
Winnsboro La., U.S.A. 32°10N 91°43W **176 E9**
Winnsboro S.C., U.S.A. 34°23N 81°5W **177 D14**
Winnsboro Tex., U.S.A. 32°58N 95°17W **176 E7**
Winokapau, L. Canada 53°15N 62°50W **165 B7**
Winona Minn., U.S.A. 44°3N 91°39W **172 C8**
Winona Miss., U.S.A. 33°29N 89°44W **177 E10**
Winooski U.S.A. 44°29N 73°11W **175 B11**
Winooski → U.S.A. 44°32N 73°17W **175 B11**
Winschoten Neths. 53°9N 7°3E **69 A7**
Winsen Germany 53°22N 10°13E **76 B6**
Winsford U.K. 53°12N 2°31W **66 D5**
Winslow = Bainbridge Island
  U.S.A. 47°38N 122°32W **170 C4**
Winslow U.S.A. 35°2N 110°42W **169 J8**
Winsted U.S.A. 41°55N 73°4W **175 E11**
Winston-Salem U.S.A. 36°6N 80°15W **177 C14**
Winter Garden U.S.A. 28°34N 81°35W **179 G8**
Winter Haven U.S.A. 28°1N 81°44W **179 G8**
Winter Park U.S.A. 28°36N 81°20W **179 G8**
Winterberg Germany 51°11N 8°33E **76 D4**
Winterhaven U.S.A. 32°44N 114°38W **171 N12**
Winters U.S.A. 38°32N 121°58W **170 G5**
Winterset U.S.A. 41°20N 94°1W **172 E6**
Winterswijk Neths. 51°58N 6°43E **69 C6**
Winterthur Switz. 47°30N 8°44E **77 H4**
Winthrop U.S.A. 48°28N 120°10W **168 B3**
Winton Australia 22°24S 143°3E **150 C3**
Winton N.Z. 46°8S 168°20E **155 G3**
Wipper → Germany 51°16N 11°12E **76 D7**
Wirlyajarrayi ◎
  Australia 21°45S 132°35E **148 D5**
Wirraminna Australia 31°12S 136°13E **152 A2**
Wirrulla Australia 32°24S 134°31E **151 E1**
Wisbech U.K. 52°41N 0°9E **67 E8**
Wisconsin □ U.S.A. 44°45N 89°30W **172 C9**
Wisconsin → U.S.A. 43°0N 91°15W **172 D8**
Wisconsin Rapids
  U.S.A. 44°23N 89°49W **172 C9**
Wisdom U.S.A. 45°37N 113°27W **168 D7**
Wiseman U.S.A. 67°25N 150°6W **166 B9**
Wishaw U.K. 55°46N 3°54W **65 F5**
Wishek U.S.A. 46°16N 99°33W **172 B4**
Wisła Poland 49°38N 18°53E **83 J5**
Wisła → Poland 54°22N 18°55E **82 D5**
Wiślany, Zalew Poland 54°20N 19°50E **82 D6**
Wisłok → Poland 50°13N 22°32E **83 H9**
Wisłoka → Poland 50°27N 21°23E **83 H8**
Wismar Germany 53°54N 11°29E **76 B7**
Wisner U.S.A. 41°59N 96°55W **172 E5**
Wissant France 50°52N 1°40E **71 B8**
Wissembourg France 49°2N 7°57E **71 C14**
Wisznice Poland 51°48N 23°13E **83 G10**
Witbank = eMalahleni
  S. Africa 25°51S 29°14E **145 C4**
Witches Gorge = Wu Xia
  China 31°2N 110°10E **117 B8**
Witdraai S. Africa 26°58S 20°48E **144 C3**
Witham U.K. 51°48N 0°40E **67 F8**
Witham → U.K. 52°59N 0°2W **67 E7**
Withernsea U.K. 53°44N 0°1E **66 D8**
Withlacoochee → Fla.,
  U.S.A. 30°24N 83°10W **178 E6**
Withlacoochee → Fla.,
  U.S.A. 29°0N 82°45W **179 G7**
Witjira △ Australia 26°22S 135°37E **151 D2**
Witkowo Poland 52°26N 17°45E **83 F4**
Witless Bay Canada 47°17N 52°50W **165 C9**
Witney U.K. 51°48N 1°28W **67 F6**
Witnica Poland 52°40N 14°54E **83 F1**
Witnossob → Namibia 23°55S 18°45E **144 C2**
Witriver S. Africa 25°20S 31°0E **145 C5**
Wittdün Germany 54°38N 8°23E **76 A4**
Wittelsheim France 47°48N 7°14E **71 E14**
Witten Germany 51°26N 7°20E **76 D3**
Wittenberge Germany 53°0N 11°45E **76 B7**
Wittenburg Germany 53°31N 11°4E **76 B7**
Wittenoom Australia 22°15S 118°20E **148 D2**
Wittingen Germany 52°44N 10°44E **76 C6**
Wittlich Germany 49°59N 6°53E **77 F2**
Wittmund Germany 53°34N 7°46E **76 B3**
Wittow Germany 54°38N 13°26E **76 A9**
Wittstock Germany 53°10N 12°28E **76 B8**
Witu Kenya 2°23S 40°26E **142 C5**
Witvlei Namibia 22°23S 18°32E **144 B2**
Witzenhausen Germany 51°20N 9°51E **76 D5**
Wiwon N. Korea 40°54N 126°3E **115 D14**
Wkra → Poland 52°27N 20°44E **83 F7**
Władysławowo Poland 54°48N 18°25E **82 D5**
Wleń Poland 51°2N 15°39E **83 G2**
Wlingi Indonesia 8°5S 112°25E **119 H15**
Włocławek Poland 52°40N 19°3E **83 F6**
Włodawa Poland 51°33N 23°31E **83 G10**
Włoszczowa Poland 50°50N 19°55E **83 H6**
Woburn U.S.A. 42°29N 71°9W **175 D13**
Wodian China 32°50N 112°35E **114 H7**
Wodonga Australia 36°5S 146°50E **153 D7**
Wodzisław Śląski Poland 50°1N 18°26E **83 H5**
Wœrth France 48°57N 7°45E **71 D14**
Woinbogoin China 32°51N 98°39E **116 A2**
Woippy France 49°10N 6°8E **71 C13**
Wojcieszow Poland 50°58N 15°55E **83 H2**
Wokam Indonesia 5°45S 134°28E **119 F8**
Woking U.K. 51°19N 0°34W **67 F7**
Wokingham U.K. 51°24N 0°49W **67 F7**
Wokingham □ U.K. 51°25N 0°51W **67 F7**
Woko △ Australia 31°46S 151°49E **153 A3**
Wolbrom Poland 50°24N 19°45E **83 H6**
Wołczyn Poland 51°1N 18°3E **83 G5**
Woldegk Germany 53°27N 13°35E **76 B8**
Wolf → Canada 60°17N 132°33W **162 A2**
Wolf Creek U.S.A. 47°0N 112°4W **168 C7**
Wolf L. Canada 60°24N 131°40W **162 A2**

Wolf Point U.S.A. 48°5N 105°39W **168 B11**
Wolfe Creek Crater △
  Australia 19°10S 127°47E **148 C4**
Wolfe I. Canada 44°7N 76°20W **175 B8**
Wolfeboro U.S.A. 43°35N 71°13W **175 C13**
Wolfenbüttel Germany 52°10N 10°33E **76 C6**
Wolfratshausen
  Germany 47°54N 11°24E **77 H7**
Wolfsberg Austria 46°50N 14°52E **78 E7**
Wolfsburg Germany 52°25N 10°48E **76 C6**
Wolhusen Switz. 47°4N 8°4E **71 F14**
Wolin Poland 53°50N 14°37E **82 E1**
Woliński △ Poland 53°57N 14°28E **82 E1**
Wollaston Forland
  Greenland 74°26N 19°40W **57 C9**
Wollaston L. Canada 58°7N 103°10W **163 B8**
Wollaston Lake
  Canada 58°3N 103°33W **163 B8**
Wollaston Pen. Canada 69°30N 115°0W **160 D9**
Wollongong Australia 34°25S 150°54E **153 C5**
Wolmaransstad
  S. Africa 27°12S 25°59E **144 C4**
Wolmirstedt Germany 52°14N 11°37E **76 C7**
Wolomin Poland 52°19N 21°15E **83 F8**
Wołów Poland 51°20N 16°38E **83 G3**
Wolseley Australia 36°23S 140°54E **152 D4**
Wolseley S. Africa 33°26S 19°7E **144 D2**
Wolsey U.S.A. 44°25N 98°28W **172 C4**
Wolstenholme, C.
  Canada 62°35N 77°30W **158 C12**
Wolsztyn Poland 52°8N 16°5E **83 F3**
Wolvega Neths. 52°52N 6°0E **69 B6**
Wolverhampton U.K. 52°35N 2°7W **67 E5**
Wondai Australia 26°5S 151°49E **151 D5**
Wongalarroo L.
  Australia 31°32S 144°0E **152 A4**
Wongan Hills
  Australia 30°51S 116°37E **149 F2**
Wonju S. Korea 37°22N 127°58E **115 F14**
Wonosari Indonesia 7°58S 110°36E **119 G14**
Wonosobo Indonesia 7°22S 109°54E **119 G13**
Wonowon Canada 56°44N 121°48W **162 B4**
Wŏnsan N. Korea 39°11N 127°27E **115 E14**
Wonthaggi Australia 38°37S 145°37E **153 E6**
Wood Buffalo △
  Canada 59°0N 113°41W **162 B6**
Wood Is. Australia 16°24S 123°19E **148 C3**
Wood L. Canada 55°17N 103°17W **163 B8**
Woodah, I. Australia 13°27S 136°10E **150 A2**
Woodbine U.S.A. 30°58N 81°44W **178 E8**
Woodbourne U.S.A. 41°46N 74°36W **175 E10**
Woodbridge Canada 43°47N 79°36W **174 C5**
Woodbridge U.K. 52°6N 1°20E **67 E9**
Woodburn Australia 29°6S 153°23E **151 A5**
Woodburn U.S.A. 45°9N 122°51W **168 D2**
Woodbury U.S.A. 32°59N 84°35W **178 C5**
Woodenbong
  Australia 28°24S 152°39E **151 D5**
Woodend Australia 37°20S 144°33E **152 D6**
Woodford Australia 26°58S 152°47E **151 D5**
Woodfords U.S.A. 38°47N 119°50W **170 G7**
Woodlake U.S.A. 36°25N 119°6W **170 J7**
Woodland Calif.,
  U.S.A. 38°41N 121°46W **170 G5**
Woodland Maine,
  U.S.A. 45°9N 67°25W **173 C20**
Woodland Pa., U.S.A. 41°0N 78°21W **174 F6**
Woodland Wash.,
  U.S.A. 45°54N 122°45W **170 E4**
Woodland Caribou △
  Canada 51°0N 94°45W **163 C10**
Woodlands Singapore 1°26N 103°46E **121 d**
Woodlands, The U.S.A. 30°9N 95°29W **176 F7**
Woodonga Australia 36°10S 146°50E **153 C7**
Woodridge Canada 49°20N 96°9W **163 D9**
Woodroffe, Mt.
  Australia 26°20S 131°45E **149 E5**
Woods, L. Australia 17°50S 133°30E **150 B1**
Woods, L. of the
  N. Amer. 49°15N 94°45W **163 D10**
Woods Bay Canada 45°8N 79°59W **174 A5**
Woodside S. Austral.,
  Australia 34°58S 138°52E **152 C2**
Woodside Vic.,
  Australia 38°31S 146°52E **153 E7**
Woodstock N.S.W.,
  Australia 33°45S 148°53E **153 B8**
Woodstock Queens.,
  Australia 19°35S 146°50E **150 B4**
Woodstock N.B.,
  Canada 46°11N 67°37W **165 C6**
Woodstock Ont.,
  Canada 43°10N 80°45W **174 C4**
Woodstock U.K. 51°51N 1°20W **67 F6**
Woodstock Ill., U.S.A. 42°19N 88°27W **172 D9**
Woodstock N.Y., U.S.A. 42°2N 74°7W **175 D10**
Woodstock Vt.,
  U.S.A. 43°37N 72°31W **175 C12**
Woodsville U.S.A. 44°9N 72°2W **175 B12**
Woodview Canada 44°35N 78°6W **174 B6**
Woodville N.Z. 40°20S 175°53E **154 D5**
Woodville Fla., U.S.A. 30°19N 84°15W **178 E5**
Woodville Ga., U.S.A. 33°40N 83°7W **178 B6**
Woodville Miss., U.S.A. 31°6N 91°18W **176 F9**
Woodville Tex., U.S.A. 30°47N 94°25W **176 F7**
Woodward U.S.A. 36°26N 99°24W **176 C5**
Woody U.S.A. 35°42N 118°50W **171 K8**
Woody → Canada 52°40N 101°51W **163 C8**
Woody I. S. China Sea 16°50N 112°20E **118 A4**
Woolacombe U.K. 51°10N 4°13W **67 F3**
Woolamai, C. Australia 38°30S 145°23E **153 E6**
Woolbrook Australia 30°55S 151°15E **153 A5**
Wooler U.K. 55°33N 2°1W **66 B5**
Woolgoolga Australia 30°6S 153°11E **151 E5**
Woomargama △
  Australia 35°50S 147°15E **153 C7**
Woomera Australia 31°5S 136°50E **152 A2**
Woonsocket R.I.,
  U.S.A. 42°0N 71°31W **175 E13**
Woonsocket S. Dak.,
  U.S.A. 44°3N 98°17W **172 C4**
Wooramel →
  Australia 25°47S 114°10E **149 E1**
Wooramel Roadhouse
  Australia 25°45S 114°17E **149 E1**
Wooroonooran △
  Australia 17°25S 146°1E **150 B4**
Wooster U.S.A. 40°48N 81°56W **174 F3**
Worcester S. Africa 33°39S 19°27E **144 D2**

Worcester U.K. 52°11N 2°12W **67 E5**
Worcester Mass.,
  U.S.A. 42°16N 71°48W **175 D13**
Worcester N.Y.,
  U.S.A. 42°36N 74°45W **175 D10**
Worcestershire □ U.K. 52°13N 2°10W **67 E5**
Wörgl Austria 47°29N 12°3E **78 D5**
Workington U.K. 54°39N 3°33W **66 C4**
Worksop U.K. 53°18N 1°7W **66 D6**
Workum Neths. 52°59N 5°26E **69 B5**
Worland U.S.A. 44°1N 107°57W **168 D10**
Wormhout France 50°52N 2°28E **71 B9**
Worms Germany 49°37N 8°21E **77 F4**
Woroba ◎ Côte d'Ivoire 8°19N 7°5W **138 D3**
Worsley Canada 56°31N 119°8W **162 B5**
Wörth Germany 49°1N 12°24E **77 F8**
Wortham U.S.A. 31°47N 96°28W **176 F6**
Wörther See Austria 46°37N 14°10E **78 E7**
Worthing Barbados 13°5N 59°35W **183 g**
Worthing U.K. 50°49N 0°21W **67 G7**
Worthington Minn.,
  U.S.A. 43°37N 95°36W **172 D6**
Worthington Pa.,
  U.S.A. 40°50N 79°38W **174 F5**
Wosi Indonesia 0°15S 128°0E **119 E7**
Wote Kenya 1°47S 37°38E **142 C4**
Wotjalum ◎ Australia 16°30S 123°45E **148 C3**
Wotjobaluk ◎ Australia 37°0S 142°0E **151 C3**
Wou-han = Wuhan
  China 30°31N 114°18E **117 B10**
Wousi = Wuxi China 31°33N 120°18E **117 B13**
Wowoni Indonesia 4°5S 123°5E **119 E6**
Woy Woy Australia 33°30S 151°19E **153 B9**
Wrangel I. = Vrangelya, Ostrov
  Russia 71°0N 180°0E **107 B18**
Wrangell U.S.A. 56°28N 132°23W **162 B2**
Wrangell Mts. U.S.A. 61°30N 142°0W **160 C5**
Wrath, C. U.K. 58°38N 5°1W **65 C3**
Wray U.S.A. 40°5N 102°13W **168 F12**
Wrekin, The U.K. 52°41N 2°32W **67 E5**
Wrens U.S.A. 33°12N 82°23W **178 B7**
Wrexham U.K. 53°3N 3°0W **66 D4**
Wrexham □ U.K. 53°1N 2°58W **66 D5**
Wriezen Germany 52°42N 14°7E **76 C10**
Wright U.S.A. 30°27N 86°38W **178 F3**
Wright Wyo., U.S.A. 43°45N 105°28W **168 E11**
Wright Pt. Canada 43°48N 81°44W **174 C3**
Wrightmyo India 11°47N 92°43E **127 J11**
Wrightson, Mt.
  U.S.A. 31°42N 110°51W **169 L8**
Wrightsville U.S.A. 32°44N 82°43W **178 C7**
Wrightwood U.S.A. 34°22N 117°38W **171 L9**
Wrigley Canada 63°16N 123°37W **160 C7**
Wrocław Poland 51°5N 17°5E **83 G4**
Wronki Poland 52°41N 16°21E **83 F3**
Września Poland 52°21N 17°36E **83 F4**
Wschowa Poland 51°48N 16°20E **83 G3**
Wu Jiang → China 29°40N 107°20E **116 C6**
Wu Kau Tang China 22°30N 114°14E **111 a**
Wu Xia China 31°2N 110°10E **117 B8**
Wu'an China 36°40N 114°15E **114 F6**
Wubalawun ◎
  Australia 15°28S 133°1E **148 C5**
Wubin Australia 30°6S 116°37E **149 F2**
Wubu China 37°28N 110°42E **114 F6**
Wuchang China 44°55N 127°5E **115 B14**
Wucheng China 37°12N 116°20E **114 F6**
Wuchuan Guangdong,
  China 21°33N 110°43E **117 G8**
Wuchuan Guizhou,
  China 28°25N 108°3E **116 C7**
Wuchuan Nei Monggol Zizhiqu,
  China 41°5N 111°28E **114 D6**
Wuda China 39°29N 106°42E **114 E4**
Wudang Shan China 32°23N 111°2E **117 A8**
Wudi China 37°40N 117°35E **115 F9**
Wuding China 25°24N 102°21E **116 E4**
Wuding He → China 37°2N 110°23E **114 F6**
Wudinna Australia 33°0S 135°22E **151 E2**
Wudongde Dam
  China 26°20N 102°15E **116 D4**
Wudu China 33°22N 104°54E **114 H3**
Wufeng China 30°12N 110°42E **117 B8**
Wugang China 26°44N 110°35E **117 C8**
Wugong Shan China 27°30N 114°0E **117 D9**
Wuguishan China 22°25N 113°25E **111 a**
Wuhai China 39°39N 106°48E **114 E4**
Wuhan China 30°31N 114°18E **117 B10**
Wuhe China 33°10N 117°50E **115 H9**
Wuhsi = Wuxi China 31°33N 120°18E **117 B13**
Wuhu China 31°22N 118°21E **117 B12**
Wujiang China 31°10N 120°38E **117 B13**
Wujiaqu China 44°12N 87°33E **109 E6**
Wukari Nigeria 7°51N 9°42E **139 D7**
Wulajie China 44°6N 126°33E **115 B14**
Wulanbulang China 41°5N 110°55E **114 D6**
Wular L. India 34°20N 74°30E **125 B6**
Wulehe Ghana 8°39N 0°0 **139 D5**
Wulff Land Greenland 82°0N 49°0W **57 A6**
Wulian China 35°40N 119°12E **115 G10**
Wulian Feng China 26°0N 104°0E **116 E4**
Wulian Shan China 21°0N 100°0E **116 G3**
Wuliaru Indonesia 7°27S 131°0E **119 F8**
Wuling Shan China 30°0N 110°0E **116 C7**
Wulingyuan △ China 29°22N 110°43E **116 C7**
Wulong China 29°22N 107°43E **116 C6**
Wulong △ China 31°8N 103°5E **116 B4**
Wulumuchi = Ürümqi
  China 43°45N 87°45E **109 D11**
Wum Cameroon 6°24N 10°2E **139 D7**
Wumeng Shan China 26°48N 104°0E **116 D5**
Wuming China 23°12N 108°0E **116 F7**
Wunnanyi Kenya 3°24S 38°22E **142 C4**
Wuning China 29°17N 115°5E **117 C10**
Wunna → India 20°18N 78°48E **126 D4**
Wunnummin L.
  Canada 52°55N 89°10W **164 B2**
Wunsiedel Germany 50°2N 12°0E **77 E8**
Wunstorf Germany 52°25N 9°29E **76 C5**
Wuntho Myanmar 23°55N 95°45E **134 H9**
Wupatki △ U.S.A. 35°35N 111°20W **169 J8**
Wuping China 25°5N 116°5E **117 E11**
Wuppertal Germany 51°16N 7°12E **76 D3**
Wuppertal S. Africa 32°13S 19°12E **144 D2**
Wuqia China 39°40N 75°7E **109 E3**
Wuqing China 39°23N 117°4E **115 E9**
Wurralilla ◎ Australia 15°43S 135°11E **150 B2**
Wurtsboro U.S.A. 41°35N 74°29W **175 E10**
Würzburg Germany 49°46N 9°55E **77 F5**
Wurzen Germany 51°22N 12°44E **76 D8**

Wushan China 34°43N 104°53E **114 G3**
Wushi China 41°9N 79°13E **109 D9**
Wushishi Nigeria 9°46N 6°7E **139 D6**
Wutach → Germany 47°37N 8°15E **77 H4**
Wutai China 38°40N 113°12E **114 E7**
Wutai Shan China 39°3N 113°32E **114 E7**
Wuting = Huimin
  China 37°27N 117°28E **115 F9**
Wutong China 25°24N 110°4E **117 E8**
Wutonghaolai China 42°50N 120°5E **115 C11**
Wutongqiao China 29°22N 103°50E **116 C4**
Wuwei Anhui, China 31°18N 117°54E **117 B11**
Wuwei Gansu, China 37°57N 102°34E **110 D9**
Wuxi Jiangsu, China 31°33N 120°18E **117 B13**
Wuxi Sichuan, China 31°23N 109°35E **116 B7**
Wuxiang China 36°49N 112°50E **114 F7**
Wuxuan China 23°34N 109°38E **116 F7**
Wuxue China 29°52N 115°30E **117 C10**
Wuyang China 33°25N 113°35E **114 H7**
Wuyi Hebei, China 37°46N 115°56E **114 F8**
Wuyi Zhejiang, China 28°52N 119°50E **117 C12**
Wuyi Shan China 27°0N 117°0E **117 D11**
Wuyishan China 27°45N 118°0E **117 D12**
Wuyishan △ China 27°55N 117°54E **117 D11**
Wuyo Nigeria 10°23N 11°50E **139 C7**
Wuyuan Jiangxi,
  China 29°15N 117°50E **117 C11**
Wuyuan Nei Monggol Zizhiqu,
  China 41°2N 108°20E **114 D5**
Wuzhai China 38°54N 111°48E **114 E6**
Wuzhi Shan China 18°45N 109°30E **117 a**
Wuzhishan = Tongshi
  China 18°50N 109°20E **117 a**
Wuzhong China 38°2N 106°12E **114 E4**
Wuzhou China 23°30N 111°18E **117 F8**
Wyaaba Cr. →
  Australia 16°27S 141°35E **150 B3**
Wyalkatchem Australia 31°8S 117°22E **149 F2**
Wyalusing U.S.A. 41°40N 76°16W **175 E8**
Wyandotte U.S.A. 42°12N 83°9W **173 D12**
Wyandra Australia 27°12S 145°56E **151 D4**
Wyangala, L. Australia 33°54S 149°0E **153 B8**
Wyara, L. Australia 28°42S 144°14E **151 D3**
Wycheproof Australia 36°5S 143°17E **152 D5**
Wycliffe Well Australia 20°48S 134°14E **150 C1**
Wye → U.K. 51°38N 2°40W **67 F5**
Wyemandoo Australia 28°28S 118°29E **149 E2**
Wyk Germany 54°41N 8°33E **76 A4**
Wymondham U.K. 52°35N 1°7E **67 E9**
Wymore U.S.A. 40°7N 96°40W **172 E5**
Wyndham Australia 15°33S 128°3E **148 C4**
Wyndham N.Z. 46°20S 168°51E **155 G3**
Wynne U.S.A. 35°14N 90°47W **177 D9**
Wynyard Australia 41°5S 145°44E **155 G4**
Wynyard Canada 51°45N 104°10W **163 C8**
Wyola L. Australia 29°8S 130°17E **149 E5**
Wyoming Canada 42°57N 82°7W **174 D2**
Wyoming □ U.S.A. 43°0N 107°30W **168 E10**
Wyomissing U.S.A. 40°20N 75°59W **175 F9**
Wyong Australia 33°14S 151°24E **153 B9**
Wyperfeld △ Australia 35°35S 141°42E **152 C4**
Wyrzysk Poland 53°10N 17°17E **83 E4**
Wyśmierzyce Poland 51°37N 20°50E **83 G7**
Wysoka Poland 53°13N 17°2E **83 E4**
Wysokie Poland 50°55N 22°40E **83 H9**
Wysokie Mazowieckie
  Poland 52°55N 22°30E **83 F9**
Wyszków Poland 52°36N 21°25E **83 F8**
Wyszogród Poland 52°23N 20°9E **83 F7**
Wytheville U.S.A. 36°57N 81°5W **173 G13**
Wyżyna Małopolska
  Poland 50°45N 20°0E **83 H7**

X

Xaafuun Somalia 10°25N 51°16E **131 E5**
Xaafuun, Ras Somalia 10°27N 51°24E **131 E5**
Xàbia = Jávea Spain 38°48N 0°10E **91 G5**
Xaçmaz Azerbaijan 41°31N 48°42E **87 K9**
Xai-Xai Mozam. 25°6S 33°31E **145 C5**
Xaidulla China 36°28N 77°59E **109 E9**
Xaignabouri = Sayaboury
  Laos 19°15N 101°45E **120 C3**
Xainza China 30°58N 88°35E **118 C6**
Xalapa Mexico 19°32N 96°55W **181 D5**
Xallas → Spain 42°54N 9°8W **88 C1**
Xangongo Angola 16°45S 15°5E **144 A2**
Xankändi Azerbaijan 39°52N 46°49E **105 C2**
Xanlar = Goygöl
  Azerbaijan 40°37N 46°12E **87 K8**
Xanten Germany 51°39N 6°26E **76 D2**
Xanthi Greece 41°10N 24°58E **97 E8**
Xanthos Turkey 36°19N 29°18E **99 E11**
Xanxerê Brazil 26°53S 52°23W **191 B5**
Xapuri Brazil 10°35S 68°35W **188 C4**
Xar Moron He →
  China 43°25N 120°35E **115 C11**
Xarrë Albania 39°44N 20°3E **96 G4**
Xátiva Spain 38°59N 0°32W **91 G4**
Xau, L. Botswana 21°15S 24°44E **144 B3**
Xavantina Brazil 21°15S 52°48W **191 A5**
Xayar China 41°33N 82°48E **109 D10**
Xebert China 44°2N 122°0E **115 B12**
Xenia U.S.A. 39°41N 83°56W **173 F12**
Xeraco Spain 39°2N 0°13W **91 F4**
Xertigny France 48°3N 6°24E **71 D13**
Xhora S. Africa 31°55S 28°38E **145 D4**
Xhumo Botswana 21°7S 24°35E **144 B3**
Xi Jiang → China 22°5N 113°20E **117 F9**
Xi Ujimqin Qi China 44°32N 117°40E **115 B9**
Xi Xian Henan, China 32°20N 114°43E **117 A10**
Xi Xian Shanxi, China 36°41N 110°58E **114 F6**
Xiachengzi China 44°40N 130°18E **115 B16**
Xiachuan Dao China 21°40N 112°40E **117 G9**
Xiajiang China 27°30N 115°10E **117 D10**
Xiajin China 36°56N 116°0E **114 F8**
Xiamen China 24°25N 118°4E **117 E12**
Xiamen Gaoqi Int. ✕ (XMN)
  China 24°33N 118°7E **117 E12**
Xi'an China 34°15N 109°0E **114 G5**
Xianfeng China 29°40N 109°8E **116 C7**
Xiang Jiang → China 28°55N 112°50E **117 C9**
Xiang Khouang Laos 19°17N 103°25E **120 C4**

Xiangcheng Henan,
  China 33°50N 113°27E **114 H7**
Xiangcheng Sichuan,
  China 28°53N 99°47E **116 C2**
Xiangdu China 23°13N 106°58E **116 F6**
Xiangfan China 32°2N 112°8E **117 A9**
Xianggang = Hong Kong □
  China 22°11N 114°14E **111 a**
Xianghuang Qi China 42°2N 113°50E **114 C7**
Xiangjiaba Dam China 28°37N 104°17E **116 C5**
Xiangning China 35°58N 110°50E **114 F6**
Xiangquan China 36°30N 113°1E **114 F7**
Xiangquan He = Sutlej →
  Pakistan 29°23N 71°3E **124 E4**
Xiangshan China 29°29N 121°51E **117 C13**
Xiangshui China 34°12N 119°33E **115 G10**
Xiangtan China 27°51N 112°54E **117 D9**
Xiangxiang China 27°43N 112°28E **117 D9**
Xiangyang China 32°1N 112°8E **117 A9**
Xiangyun China 25°34N 100°35E **116 E3**
Xiangzhou China 23°58N 109°40E **116 F7**
Xianju China 28°51N 120°44E **117 C13**
Xianning China 29°51N 114°16E **117 C10**
Xianshui He → China 30°10N 100°59E **116 B3**
Xiantao China 30°25N 113°25E **117 B9**
Xianyang China 34°20N 108°40E **114 G5**
Xianyou China 25°22N 118°38E **117 E12**
Xiao Hinggan Ling
  China 49°0N 127°0E **111 B14**
Xiao Xian China 34°15N 116°55E **114 G8**
Xiaofeng China 30°56N 119°22E **117 B12**
Xiaogan China 30°52N 113°55E **117 B9**
Xiaojin China 30°59N 102°21E **116 B4**
Xiaolan China 22°38N 113°13E **117 F9**
Xiaoshan China 30°12N 120°18E **117 B13**
Xiaowan Dam China 24°42N 100°5E **116 E3**
Xiaowutai Shan China 39°51N 114°59E **114 E8**
Xiaoyi China 37°8N 111°48E **114 F6**
Xiashui China 29°2N 114°33E **117 C10**
Xiashan = Zhanjiang
  China 21°15N 110°20E **117 G8**
Xiawa China 42°35N 120°38E **115 C11**
Xiayi China 34°15N 116°10E **114 G8**
Xichang China 27°51N 102°19E **116 D4**
Xichou China 23°25N 104°42E **116 F5**
Xichuan China 33°0N 111°30E **114 H6**
Xide China 28°8N 102°19E **116 D4**
Xiemahe China 31°38N 111°12E **117 B8**
Xifei He → China 32°45N 116°40E **117 A11**
Xifeng Gansu, China 35°40N 107°40E **114 G4**
Xifeng Guizhou, China 27°7N 106°42E **116 D6**
Xifeng Liaoning, China 42°42N 124°45E **115 C13**
Xifengzhen = Xifeng
  China 35°40N 107°40E **114 G4**
Xigazê China 29°5N 88°45E **110 F6**
Xihe China 34°2N 105°20E **114 G3**
Xihua China 33°45N 114°30E **114 H8**
Xilaganni Greece 40°58N 25°28E **97 D9**
Xili Shuiku China 22°36N 113°57E **111 a**
Xiliao He → China 43°32N 123°35E **115 C12**
Xilin China 24°30N 105°6E **116 E5**
Xiling Gorge = Xiling Xia
  China 30°54N 110°48E **117 B8**
Xiling Xia China 30°54N 110°48E **117 B8**
Xilinhot China 43°52N 116°2E **114 C9**
Xilokastro Greece 38°5N 22°38E **98 C4**
Xiluodu Dam China 28°13N 103°38E **116 C5**
Ximana Mozam. 19°24S 33°58E **143 F3**
Xime Guinea-Biss. 11°59N 14°57W **138 C2**
Ximeng China 22°50N 99°27E **116 F2**
Ximiao China 40°59N 100°12E **110 B9**
Xin Jiang → China 28°45N 116°35E **117 C11**
Xin Xian = Xinzhou
  China 38°22N 112°46E **114 E7**
Xin'anjiang Shuiku
  China 29°33N 118°56E **117 C12**
Xinavane Mozam. 25°2S 32°47E **145 C5**
Xinbin China 41°40N 125°2E **115 D13**
Xincai China 32°43N 114°58E **117 A10**
Xincheng Guangxi Zhuangzu,
  China 24°5N 108°39E **116 E7**
Xincheng Jiangxi,
  China 26°48N 114°6E **117 D10**
Xinfeng Guangdong,
  China 24°5N 114°16E **117 E10**
Xinfeng Jiangxi, China 27°7N 116°11E **117 D11**
Xinfeng Jiangxi, China 25°27N 114°58E **117 E10**
Xinfengjiang Shuiku
  China 23°52N 114°30E **117 F10**
Xing Xian China 38°27N 111°7E **114 E6**
Xing'an Guangxi Zhuangzu,
  China 25°38N 110°40E **117 E8**
Xingan Jiangxi, China 27°46N 115°20E **117 D10**
Xingcheng China 40°40N 120°45E **115 D11**
Xingguo China 26°21N 115°21E **117 D10**
Xinghe China 40°55N 113°55E **114 D7**
Xinghua China 32°58N 119°48E **117 A12**
Xinghua Wan China 25°15N 119°20E **117 E12**
Xingning China 24°3N 115°42E **117 E10**
Xingping China 34°20N 108°28E **114 G5**
Xingren China 25°24N 105°11E **116 E5**
Xingshan China 31°15N 110°45E **117 B8**
Xingtai China 37°3N 114°32E **114 F8**
Xingu → Brazil 1°30S 51°53W **187 D8**
Xingwen China 28°22N 104°54E **116 C5**
Xingxingxia China 41°47N 95°0E **110 B7**
Xingyang China 34°45N 112°52E **114 G7**
Xingyi China 25°3N 104°59E **116 E5**
Xinhe Hebei, China 37°30N 115°15E **114 F8**
Xinhe Xinjiang Uygur,
  China 41°33N 82°37E **109 D10**
Xinhua China 27°42N 111°13E **117 C8**
Xinhui China 22°25N 113°0E **117 F9**
Xining China 36°34N 101°40E **110 D9**
Xinji China 37°55N 115°13E **114 F8**
Xinjiang China 35°34N 111°11E **114 G6**
Xinjiang Uygur Zizhiqu □
  China 42°0N 86°0E **109 D11**
Xinjin = Pulandian
  China 39°25N 121°58E **115 E11**
Xinjin China 30°24N 103°47E **116 B4**
Xinkai He → China 43°32N 123°35E **115 C12**
Xinken China 22°39N 113°36E **111 a**
Xinle China 38°25N 114°40E **114 E8**
Xinlitun China 42°0N 122°8E **115 C12**
Xinlong China 30°30N 100°22E **116 B3**
Xinmi China 34°30N 113°25E **114 G7**

Xinmin China 41°59N 122°50E **115 D12**
Xinning China 26°28N 110°50E **117 D8**
Xinping China 24°5N 101°59E **116 E3**
Xinshao China 27°21N 111°26E **117 D8**
Xintai China 35°55N 117°45E **115 G9**
Xintian China 25°55N 112°13E **117 E9**
Xinwan China 22°47N 113°40E **111 a**
Xinxiang China 35°18N 113°50E **114 G7**
Xinxing China 22°35N 112°15E **117 F9**
Xinyang China 32°6N 114°3E **117 A10**
Xinye China 32°30N 112°21E **117 A9**
Xinyi Guangdong, China 22°25N 110°56E **117 F8**
Xinyi Nei Monggol Zizhiqu,
  China 34°23N 118°21E **115 G10**
Xinyu China 27°49N 114°58E **117 D10**
Xinzhan China 43°50N 127°18E **115 C14**
Xinzheng China 34°20N 113°45E **114 G7**
Xinzhou Hainan, China 19°43N 109°17E **117 a**
Xinzhou Hubei, China 30°50N 114°48E **117 B10**
Xinzhou Shanxi, China 38°22N 112°46E **114 E7**
Xinzo de Limia Spain 42°3N 7°47W **88 C3**
Xiongyuecheng China 40°12N 122°5E **115 D12**
Xiping Henan, China 33°22N 114°5E **114 H8**
Xiping Henan, China 33°25N 111°8E **114 H6**
Xiping Zhejiang, China 28°16N 119°2E **117 C12**
Xique-Xique Brazil 10°50S 42°40W **189 D10**
Xirdalan Azerbaijan 40°27N 49°45E **105 B13**
Xiruá → Brazil 6°3S 67°50W **188 C4**
Xisha Qundao = Paracel Is.
  S. China Sea 15°50N 112°0E **118 A4**
Xishuangbanna China 22°5N 101°1E **116 F3**
Xishui Guizhou, China 28°19N 106°9E **116 C6**
Xishui Hubei, China 30°30N 115°15E **117 B10**
Xitole Guinea-Biss. 11°43N 14°50W **138 C2**
Xiu Shui → China 29°13N 116°0E **117 C10**
Xiuning China 29°45N 118°10E **117 C12**
Xiuren China 24°27N 110°12E **117 E8**
Xiushan China 28°25N 108°57E **116 C7**
Xiushui China 29°2N 114°33E **117 C10**
Xiuwen China 26°49N 106°32E **116 D6**
Xiuyan China 40°18N 123°11E **115 D12**
Xiva Uzbekistan 41°30N 60°18E **108 C7**
Xixabangma Feng
  China 28°20N 85°40E **125 D11**
Xixia China 33°25N 111°29E **114 H6**
Xixiang Guangdong,
  China 22°34N 113°52E **111 a**
Xixiang Shaanxi, China 33°0N 107°44E **114 H4**
Xixón = Gijón Spain 43°32N 5°42W **88 B5**
Xiyang China 37°38N 113°38E **114 F7**
Xizang Zizhiqu □ China 32°0N 88°0E **110 E6**
Xlendi Malta 36°1N 14°12E **101 D1**
Xochob Mexico 19°21N 89°48W **181 D7**
Xo'jayli Uzbekistan 42°32N 59°31E **108 D5**
Xorazm □ Uzbekistan 43°0N 60°0E **108 D6**
Xu Jiang → China 28°0N 116°25E **117 D11**
Xuan Loc Vietnam 10°56N 107°14E **121 G6**
Xuan'en China 30°0N 109°30E **116 C7**
Xuanhan China 31°18N 107°38E **116 B6**
Xuanhua China 40°40N 115°2E **114 D8**
Xuanwei China 26°15N 103°59E **116 D5**
Xuanzhou China 30°56N 118°43E **117 B12**
Xuchang China 34°2N 113°48E **114 G7**
Xudat Azerbaijan 41°38N 48°41E **87 K9**
Xuefeng Shan China 27°5N 110°35E **117 C8**
Xun Jiang → China 31°9N 110°16E **117 B8**
Xun Xian China 35°42N 114°33E **114 G8**
Xundian China 25°36N 103°15E **116 E4**
Xunwu China 24°54N 115°37E **117 E10**
Xunyang China 32°48N 109°22E **114 H5**
Xunyi China 35°8N 108°20E **114 G5**
Xupu China 27°53N 110°32E **117 D8**
Xúquer → Spain 39°5N 0°10W **91 F4**
Xushui China 39°2N 115°40E **114 E8**
Xuwen China 20°20N 110°10E **117 G8**
Xuyi China 32°55N 118°32E **117 A12**
Xuyong China 28°10N 105°22E **116 C5**
Xuzhou China 34°18N 117°10E **115 G9**
Xylophagou Cyprus 34°54N 33°51E **101 E12**

Y

Y Drenewydd = Newtown
  U.K. 52°31N 3°19W **67 E4**
Y Fenni = Abergavenny
  U.K. 51°49N 3°1W **67 F4**
Y Gelli Gandryll = Hay-on-Wye
  U.K. 52°5N 3°8W **67 E4**
Y Trallwng = Welshpool
  U.K. 52°39N 3°8W **67 E4**
Ya Xian = Sanya China 18°14N 109°29E **117 a**
Yaamba Australia 23°8S 150°22E **150 C5**
Ya'an China 29°58N 103°5E **116 C4**
Yaapeet Australia 35°45S 142°3E **152 C5**
Yabassi Cameroon 4°30N 9°57E **139 E6**
Yabayo Côte d'Ivoire 5°56N 6°36W **138 D3**
Yablanitsa Bulgaria 43°2N 24°5E **97 C8**
Yablonovskiy Russia 44°59N 38°57E **87 H4**
Yablonovyy Khrebet
  Russia 53°0N 114°0E **107 D12**
Yablonovyy Ra. = Yablonovyy
  Khrebet Russia 53°0N 114°0E **107 D12**
Yabluniv Ukraine 48°24N 24°57E **81 B9**
Yablunytsya Ukraine 48°19N 24°29E **81 B9**
Yabrai Shan China 39°40N 103°0E **114 E2**
Yabrūd Syria 33°58N 36°39E **130 B5**
Yabucoa Puerto Rico 18°3N 65°53W **183 d**
Yacambú △ Venezuela 9°42N 69°27W **183 E6**
Yacata Fiji 17°15S 179°31W **154 a**
Yacheng China 18°22N 109°6E **117 a**
Yackandandah
  Australia 36°18S 146°52E **153 D7**
Yacuiba Bolivia 22°0S 63°43W **190 A3**
Yacuma → Bolivia 13°38S 65°23W **186 F5**
Yacurí △ Ecuador 4°42S 79°29W **186 D2**
Yadgir India 16°45N 77°5E **126 F3**
Yadkin → U.S.A. 35°23N 80°4W **177 D14**
Yadrin Russia 55°57N 46°38E **73 C8**
Yadua Fiji 16°49S 178°18E **154 a**
Yaeyama-Rettō Japan 24°30N 123°40E **113 M1**
Yagaba Ghana 10°14N 1°20W **138 C4**
Yagasa Cluster Fiji 18°57S 178°28W **154 a**
Yağcılar Turkey 39°25N 28°23E **99 B10**
Yagodnoye Russia 62°33N 149°40E **107 C15**
Yahila
  Dem. Rep. of the Congo 0°13N 24°28E **142 B1**
Yahk Canada 49°6N 116°10W **162 D5**
Yahotyn Ukraine 50°17N 31°46E **85 G6**
Yahuma
  Dem. Rep. of the Congo 1°0N 23°10E **140 D4**

Yahyalı Turkey 38°5N 35°2E 104 C6
Yaita Japan 36°48N 139°56E 113 F9
Yaiza Canary Is. 28°57N 13°46W 100 F6
Yajiang China 30°2N 100°57E 116 B3
Yajua Nigeria 11°27N 12°49E 139 C7
Yakeshi China 49°17N 120°44E 111 B13
Yakima U.S.A. 46°36N 120°31W 168 C3
Yakima → U.S.A. 46°15N 119°14W 168 C4
Yakishiri-Jima Japan 44°26N 141°25E 112 B10
Yako Burkina Faso 12°59N 2°15W 138 C4
Yakobi I. U.S.A. 58°0N 136°30W 162 B1
Yakoruda Bulgaria 42°1N 23°39E 96 D7
Yakovlevka Russia 44°26N 133°28E 112 B6
Yaku-Shima Japan 30°20N 130°30E 113 J5
Yakumo Japan 42°15N 140°16E 112 C10
Yakutat U.S.A. 59°33N 139°44W 160 F4
Yakutat B. U.S.A. 59°45N 140°45W 166 D11
Yakutia = Sakha □ Russia 66°0N 130°0E 107 C14
Yakutsk Russia 62°5N 129°50E 107 C13
Yakymivka Ukraine 46°44N 35°0E 85 J8
Yala Thailand 6°33N 101°18E 121 J3
Yala △ Sri Lanka 6°20N 81°30E 127 L5
Yalata Australia 31°59S 132°26E 149 F5
Yalata ✪ Australia 31°35S 132°7E 149 F5
Yalboroo Australia 20°50S 148°40E 150 b
Yale U.S.A. 43°8N 82°48W 174 C2
Yalgorup △ Australia 32°39S 115°38E 149 F2
Yalinga C.A.R. 6°33N 23°10E 140 C4
Yalkabul, Pta. Mexico 21°32N 88°37W 181 C7
Yalleroi Australia 24°3S 145°42E 150 C4
Yalobusha → U.S.A. 33°33N 90°10W 177 E9
Yalong China 18°12N 109°42E 117 a
Yalong Jiang → China 26°40N 101°55E 116 D3
Yalova Turkey 40°41N 29°15E 97 F13
Yalpirakinu ✪ Australia 22°24S 132°15E 148 D5
Yalpuh, Ozero Ukraine 45°30N 28°41E 81 E13
Yalta Ukraine 44°30N 34°10E 85 K8
Yalu Jiang → China 39°55N 124°19E 115 E13
Yalvaç Turkey 38°17N 31°10E 104 C4
Yam Australia 9°54S 142°46E 150 a
Yam Ha Melah = Dead Sea Asia 31°30N 35°30E 130 D4
Yam Kinneret Israel 32°45N 35°35E 130 C4
Yamada = Kama Japan 33°33N 130°49E 113 H5
Yamagata Japan 38°15N 140°15E 112 E10
Yamagata □ Japan 38°30N 140°0E 112 E10
Yamaguchi Japan 34°10N 131°32E 113 G5
Yamaguchi □ Japan 34°20N 131°40E 113 G5
Yamal, Poluostrov Russia 71°0N 70°0E 106 B8
Yamal Pen. = Yamal, Poluostrov Russia 71°0N 70°0E 106 B8
Yamanashi □ Japan 35°40N 138°40E 113 G9
Yamantau, Gora Russia 54°15N 58°6E 108 B5
Yamato Ridge Sea of Japan 39°20N 135°0E 112 E7
Yamba Australia 29°26S 153°23E 151 D5
Yambarran Ra. Australia 15°10S 130°25E 148 C5
Yambéring Guinea 11°50N 12°18W 138 C2
Yambio South Sudan 4°35N 28°16E 135 H11
Yambol Bulgaria 42°30N 26°30E 97 D10
Yambol □ Bulgaria 42°30N 26°30E 97 D10
Yamburg Russia 68°21N 77°8E 106 C8
Yamdena Indonesia 7°45S 131°20E 119 F8
Yame Japan 33°13N 130°35E 113 H5
Yamethin Myanmar 20°29N 96°18E 123 J20
Yamma Yamma, L. Australia 26°16S 141°20E 151 D3
Yamoussoukro Côte d'Ivoire 6°49N 5°17W 138 D3
Yamoussoukro □ Côte d'Ivoire 6°47N 5°14W 138 D3
Yampa → U.S.A. 40°32N 108°59W 168 F9
Yampi Sd. Australia 16°8S 123°38E 148 C3
Yampil Moldova 48°15N 28°15E 75 D15
Yampol = Yampil Moldova 48°15N 28°15E 75 D15
Yamrat Nigeria 10°11N 9°55E 139 C6
Yamrukchal = Botev Bulgaria 42°44N 24°52E 97 D8
Yamu, Laem Thailand 7°59N 98°26E 121 a
Yamuna → India 25°30N 81°53E 125 G9
Yamunanagar India 30°7N 77°17E 124 D7
Yamzho Yumco China 28°48N 90°35E 110 F7
Yan Nigeria 10°5N 12°11E 139 C7
Yan Oya → Sri Lanka 9°0N 81°10E 127 K5
Yana → Russia 71°30N 136°0E 107 B14
Yanagawa Japan 33°10N 130°24E 113 H5
Yanai Japan 33°58N 132°7E 113 H6
Yan'an China 36°35N 109°26E 114 F5
Yanbian China 26°47N 101°31E 116 D3
Yanbu 'al Baḩr Si. Arabia 24°5N 38°5E 128 E3
Yanchang China 36°43N 110°1E 114 F6
Yancheng Henan, China 33°35N 114°0E 114 H8
Yancheng Jiangsu, China 33°23N 120°8E 115 H11
Yanchep Australia 31°33S 115°37E 149 F2
Yanchi China 37°48N 107°20E 114 F4
Yanchuan China 36°51N 110°10E 114 F6
Yanco Australia 34°38S 146°27E 153 C7
Yanco Cr. → Australia 35°14S 145°35E 153 C6
Yandang Shan China 28°0N 120°25E 117 D13
Yandeyarra ✪ Australia 21°17S 118°24E 148 D2
Yandicoogina Australia 22°49S 119°12E 148 D2
Yandoon Myanmar 17°0N 95°40E 123 L19
Yanfeng China 25°52N 101°8E 116 E3
Yanfolila Mali 11°11N 8°9W 138 C3
Yang Xian China 33°15N 107°30E 116 A6
Yang-yang S. Korea 38°4N 128°38E 115 E15
Yang-Yang Senegal 15°30N 15°20W 138 B1
Yangambi Dem. Rep. of the Congo 0°47N 24°24E 142 B1
Yangbi China 25°41N 99°58E 116 E2
Yangcheng China 35°28N 112°22E 114 G7
Yangch'ü = Taiyuan China 37°52N 112°33E 114 F7
Yangchun China 22°11N 111°48E 117 F8
Yanggao China 40°21N 113°55E 114 D7
Yanggu China 36°8N 115°43E 114 F8
Yangiyŭl Uzbekistan 41°0N 69°3E 109 D7
Yangjiang China 21°50N 111°59E 117 G8
Yangliuqing China 39°2N 117°5E 115 E9
Yangôn Myanmar 16°45N 96°20E 123 L20
Yangping China 31°12N 111°25E 117 B8
Yangpingguan China 32°58N 106°5E 116 A6
Yangquan China 37°58N 113°31E 114 F7
Yangshan Guangdong, China 24°30N 112°40E 117 E9
Yangshan Shanghai, China 30°37N 122°4E 117 B14
Yangshuo China 24°48N 110°29E 117 E8
Yangtse = Chang Jiang → China 31°48N 121°10E 117 B13
Yangtze Kiang = Chang Jiang → China 31°48N 121°10E 117 B13
Yangxin China 29°50N 115°12E 117 C10
Yangyuan China 40°1N 114°10E 114 D8
Yangzhong China 32°22N 119°22E 117 A12
Yangzhou China 32°21N 119°26E 117 A12
Yanhe China 28°31N 108°29E 116 C7
Yanji China 42°59N 129°30E 115 C15
Yanjin China 28°5N 104°18E 116 C5
Yanjing China 29°7N 98°33E 116 C2
Yankari △ Nigeria 9°50N 10°28E 139 D7
Yankton U.S.A. 42°53N 97°23W 172 D5
Yankunytjatjara-Antakirinja ✪ Australia 27°20S 134°30E 151 A1
Yanonge Dem. Rep. of the Congo 0°35N 24°38E 142 B1
Yanqi China 42°5N 86°35E 109 D11
Yanqing China 40°30N 115°58E 114 D8
Yanshan Hebei, China 38°4N 117°22E 115 E9
Yanshan Jiangxi, China 28°15N 117°41E 117 C11
Yanshan Yunnan, China 23°35N 104°20E 116 F5
Yanshou China 45°28N 128°22E 115 B15
Yantabulla Australia 29°21S 145°0E 151 D4
Yantai China 37°34N 121°22E 115 F11
Yantarnyy Russia 54°52N 19°57E 82 D6
Yantian China 22°35N 114°16E 111 a
Yanting China 31°11N 105°24E 116 B5
Yantongshan China 43°17N 126°0E 115 C14
Yantra → Bulgaria 43°40N 25°37E 97 C9
Yanuca Fiji 18°24S 178°0E 154 a
Yanununbeyan △ Australia 35°29S 149°24E 153 C8
Yanwa China 27°35N 98°55E 116 D2
Yanyuan China 27°25N 101°30E 116 D3
Yanzhou China 35°35N 116°49E 114 G9
Yao Xian China 34°55N 108°59E 114 G5
Yao Yai, Ko Thailand 8°7N 98°37E 121 a
Yao'an China 25°31N 101°18E 116 E3
Yaoundé Cameroon 3°50N 11°35E 139 E7
Yaowan China 34°15N 118°3E 115 G10
Yap Pac. Oc. 9°30N 138°10E 156 G5
Yapei Ghana 9°10N 1°10W 139 D4
Yapen Indonesia 1°50S 136°0E 119 E9
Yapen, Selat Indonesia 1°20S 136°10E 119 E9
Yapero Indonesia 4°59S 137°11E 119 E9
Yappar → Australia 18°22S 141°16E 150 B3
Yapuparra ✪ Australia 27°15S 126°20E 149 E4
Yaqaga Fiji 16°35S 178°36E 154 a
Yaqui → Mexico 27°37N 110°39W 180 B2
Yar Çalli = Naberezhnyye Chelny Russia 55°42N 52°19E 86 C11
Yar-Sale Russia 66°50N 70°50E 106 C8
Yaraka Australia 24°53S 144°3E 150 C3
Yaransk Russia 57°22N 47°49E 86 B8
Yarbasan Turkey 38°59N 28°49E 99 C10
Yardımcı Burnu Turkey 36°13N 30°25E 99 E12
Yare → U.K. 52°35N 1°38E 67 E9
Yaremcha Ukraine 48°27N 24°33E 81 B9
Yarensk Russia 62°11N 49°15E 106 C5
Yarfa Si. Arabia 24°37N 38°35E 137 C4
Yari → Colombia 0°20S 72°20W 186 D4
Yarkand = Shache China 38°20N 77°10E 109 E9
Yarkant He → China 40°26N 80°59E 109 D10
Yarker Canada 44°23N 76°46W 175 B8
Yarkhun → Pakistan 36°17N 72°30E 125 A5
Yarlung Ziangbo Jiang = Brahmaputra → Asia 23°40N 90°35E 125 H13
Yarmouth Canada 43°50N 66°7W 165 D6
Yarmük → Syria 32°42N 35°40E 130 C4
Yaroslavl Russia 57°35N 39°55E 84 D10
Yaroslavl □ Russia 59°20N 38°50E 84 C10
Yarqa, W. → Egypt 30°0N 33°49E 130 F2
Yarra Ranges △ Australia 37°40S 146°3E 153 D7
Yarra Yarra Lakes Australia 29°40S 115°45E 149 E2
Yarram Australia 38°29S 146°39E 153 E7
Yarraman Australia 26°50S 152°0E 151 D5
Yarras Australia 31°25S 152°20E 153 A10
Yarrawonga Australia 36°0S 146°0E 153 D7
Yarrie Australia 20°40S 120°12E 148 D3
Yartsevo Sib., Russia 60°20N 90°0E 107 C10
Yartsevo Smolensk, Russia 55°6N 32°43E 84 E7
Yarumal Colombia 6°58N 75°24W 186 B3
Yasawa Fiji 16°47S 177°31E 154 a
Yasawa Group Fiji 17°0S 177°23E 154 a
Yaselda Belarus 52°7N 26°28E 75 B14
Yasen Ukraine 48°45N 24°10E 81 B9
Yashi Nigeria 12°23N 7°54E 139 C6
Yashikera Nigeria 9°44N 3°29E 139 D5
Yashkul Russia 46°11N 45°21E 87 G7
Yasin Pakistan 36°24N 73°23E 125 A5
Yasinovataya Ukraine 48°7N 37°57E 85 H9
Yasinski, L. Canada 53°16N 77°35W 164 B4
Yasinya Ukraine 48°16N 24°21E 81 B9
Yasnyy Russia 51°1N 59°58E 108 B5
Yasothon Thailand 15°50N 104°10E 120 E5
Yass Australia 34°49S 148°54E 153 C8
Yāsūj Iran 30°31N 51°31E 129 D6
Yatağan Turkey 37°20N 28°10E 99 D10
Yatakala Niger 14°50N 0°22E 139 C5
Yates Center U.S.A. 37°53N 95°44W 172 G6
Yates Pt. N.Z. 44°29S 167°49E 155 E2
Yathkyed L. Canada 62°40N 98°0W 163 A9
Yathong Australia 32°37S 145°33E 153 B6
Yatsushiro Japan 32°30N 130°40E 113 H5
Yatta Plateau Kenya 2°0S 38°0E 142 C4
Yauca Peru 15°39S 74°35W 188 D3
Yauco Puerto Rico 18°2N 66°51W 183 d
Yauri Peru 14°47S 71°25W 188 C3
Yauya Peru 8°59S 77°17W 188 B2
Yauyos Peru 12°19S 75°50W 188 C2
Yaval India 21°10N 75°42E 126 D2
Yavari → Peru 4°21S 70°2W 188 A3
Yávaros Mexico 26°42N 109°31W 180 B3
Yavatmal India 20°20N 78°15E 126 D4
Yavero → Peru 12°6S 72°57W 188 C3
Yavne Israel 31°52N 34°45E 130 D3
Yavoriv Ukraine 49°55N 23°20E 75 D12
Yavorov = Yavoriv Ukraine 49°55N 23°20E 75 D12
Yavuzeli Turkey 37°18N 37°24E 104 D7
Yawatahama Japan 33°27N 132°24E 113 H6
Yawri B. S. Leone 8°22N 13°0W 138 D2
Yaxi China 27°33N 106°41E 116 D6
Yaxian = Sanya China 18°14N 109°29E 117 a
Yayladağı Turkey 35°54N 36°3E 104 E7
Yazd Iran 31°55N 54°27E 129 D7
Yazd □ Iran 32°0N 55°0E 129 D7
Yazd-e Khvāst Iran 31°31N 52°7E 129 D7
Yazıköy Turkey 36°40N 27°20E 99 E9
Yazman Pakistan 29°8N 71°45E 124 E4
Yazoo → U.S.A. 32°22N 90°54W 177 E9
Yazoo City U.S.A. 32°51N 90°25W 177 E9
Ybbs Austria 48°12N 15°4E 78 C8
Ybycuí △ Paraguay 26°5S 56°46W 190 B4
Ybytyruzú △ Paraguay 25°51S 56°11W 191 B4
Ye Myanmar 15°15N 97°15E 120 E1
Ye Xian China 33°35N 113°25E 114 H7
Yea Australia 37°14S 145°26E 153 D6
Yebyu Myanmar 14°15N 98°13E 120 E2
Yecheng China 37°54N 77°26E 109 E9
Yecheon S. Korea 36°39N 128°27E 115 F15
Yecla Spain 38°35N 1°5W 91 G3
Yécora Mexico 28°20N 108°58W 180 B3
Yedintsy = Edineț Moldova 48°9N 27°18E 81 B12
Yedigöller △ Turkey 40°55N 31°55E 104 B4
Yedseram → Nigeria 12°30N 14°5E 139 C7
Yefremov Russia 53°8N 38°3E 84 F10
Yeghegnadzor Armenia 39°44N 45°19E 105 C11
Yegorlyk → Russia 46°35N 41°57E 87 G5
Yegorlykskaya Russia 46°35N 40°35E 87 G5
Yegoryevsk Russia 55°27N 38°55E 84 E10
Yegros Paraguay 26°20S 56°25W 190 B4
Yehbuah Indonesia 8°23S 114°45E 119 J17
Yehuda, Midbar Israel 31°35N 35°15E 130 D4
Yei South Sudan 4°9N 30°40E 135 H12
Yeji Ghana 8°13N 0°39W 139 D4
Yejmiadzin = Ejmiatsin Armenia 40°12N 44°19E 87 K7
Yekaterinburg Russia 56°50N 60°30E 106 D7
Yekateriny, Proliv Russia 44°30N 146°30E 107 E15
Yelabuga Russia 55°46N 52°2E 86 C11
Yelan Russia 50°55N 43°43E 86 E6
Yelandur India 12°6N 77°0E 127 H3
Yelarbon Australia 28°33S 150°38E 151 D5
Yelatma Russia 55°0N 41°45E 86 C5
Yelcho, L. Chile 43°18S 72°18W 192 B2
Yelets Russia 52°40N 38°30E 85 F10
Yélimané Mali 15°9N 10°34W 138 B2
Yelin = Lingshui China 18°27N 110°0E 117 a
Yelizavetgrad = Kirovohrad Ukraine 48°35N 32°20E 85 H7
Yelizovo Russia 53°11N 158°23E 107 D16
Yell U.K. 60°35N 1°5W 65 A7
Yell Sd. U.K. 60°33N 1°15W 65 A7
Yellamanchilli = Elamanchili India 17°33N 82°50E 126 F6
Yellandu India 17°39N 80°23E 126 F5
Yellapur India 14°58N 74°43E 127 G2
Yellareddi India 18°12N 78°2E 126 E4
Yellow = Huang He → China 37°55N 118°50E 115 F10
Yellow → U.S.A. 30°30N 87°0W 179 E3
Yellow Sea China 35°0N 123°0E 115 G12
Yellowhead Pass Canada 52°53N 118°25W 162 C5
Yellowknife Canada 62°27N 114°29W 162 A6
Yellowknife → Canada 62°31N 114°19W 162 A6
Yellowstone → U.S.A. 47°59N 103°59W 168 C12
Yellowstone △ U.S.A. 44°40N 110°30W 168 D8
Yellowstone L. U.S.A. 44°27N 110°22W 168 D8
Yelnya Russia 54°35N 33°15E 84 E7
Yelsk Belarus 51°50N 29°10E 75 C15
Yelwa Nigeria 10°49N 4°41E 139 C5
Yemanzhelinsk Russia 54°58N 61°18E 108 B6
Yemassee U.S.A. 32°41N 80°51W 178 C9
Yemen ■ Asia 15°0N 44°0E 131 E3
Yemmiganur India 15°44N 77°29E 127 G3
Yen Bai Vietnam 21°42N 104°52E 116 G5
Yenagoa Nigeria 4°58N 6°16E 139 E6
Yenakiieve Ukraine 48°15N 38°15E 85 H10
Yenakiyevo = Yenakiieve Ukraine 48°15N 38°15E 85 H10
Yenangyaung Myanmar 20°30N 95°0E 123 J19
Yenbo = Yanbu 'al Baḩr Si. Arabia 24°5N 38°5E 128 E3
Yenda Australia 34°13S 146°14E 153 C7
Yende Millimou Guinea 8°55N 10°10W 138 D2
Yendegaia △ Chile 54°50S 68°45W 192 D3
Yendéré Burkina Faso 10°12N 4°59W 138 C4
Yendi Ghana 9°29N 0°1W 139 D4
Yengisar China 38°56N 76°9E 109 E9
Yengo △ Australia 33°0S 150°55E 153 B9
Yéni Niger 13°30N 3°1E 139 C5
Yeni Erenköy = Yialousa Cyprus 35°32N 34°10E 101 D13
Yenibogaziçi = Áyios Seryios Cyprus 35°12N 33°53E 101 D12
Yenice Ankara, Turkey 39°14N 32°42E 104 C5
Yenice Aydın, Turkey 37°49N 28°35E 99 D10
Yenice Çanakkale, Turkey 39°55N 27°17E 99 B9
Yenice Edirne, Turkey 40°42N 26°9E 97 F10
Yenice → Turkey 37°37N 35°33E 104 D6
Yenifoça Turkey 38°44N 26°51E 99 C8
Yenihisar = Didim Turkey 37°22N 27°16E 99 D9
Yeniköy Bursa, Turkey 40°31N 29°22E 97 F13
Yeniköy Çanakkale, Turkey 39°55N 26°10E 99 B8
Yeniköy Kütahya, Turkey 38°52N 29°17E 99 C11
Yenipazar Turkey 37°49N 28°11E 99 D10
Yenişehir Turkey 40°16N 29°38E 97 F13
Yenisey → Russia 71°50N 82°40E 106 B9
Yeniseysk Russia 58°27N 92°13E 107 D10
Yeniseyskiy Zaliv Russia 72°20N 81°0E 106 B9
Yenne France 45°43N 5°44E 73 C9
Yenotayevka Russia 47°15N 47°0E 87 G8
Yenyuka Russia 57°57N 121°15E 107 D13
Yeo → U.K. 51°2N 2°49W 67 G5
Yeo, L. Australia 28°0S 124°30E 149 E3
Yeo I. Canada 45°24N 81°48W 174 A3
Yeola India 20°2N 74°30E 126 D2
Yeong-wol S. Korea 37°11N 128°28E 115 F15
Yeongcheon S. Korea 35°58N 128°56E 115 G15
Yeongdeok S. Korea 36°24N 129°22E 115 F15
Yeongdong S. Korea 36°10N 127°46E 115 F14
Yeongju S. Korea 36°50N 128°40E 115 F15
Yeosu S. Korea 34°47N 127°45E 115 G14
Yeotmal = Yavatmal India 20°20N 78°15E 126 D4
Yeovil U.K. 50°57N 2°38W 67 G5
Yepes Spain 39°55N 3°39W 88 F7
Yeppoon Australia 23°5S 150°47E 150 C5
Yerbent Turkmenistan 39°19N 58°36E 129 B8
Yerbogachen Russia 61°16N 108°0E 107 C11
Yerevan Armenia 40°10N 44°31E 87 K7
Yerington U.S.A. 38°59N 119°10W 168 G4
Yerkesik Turkey 37°7N 28°19E 99 D10
Yerköy Turkey 39°38N 34°28E 104 C6
Yerla → India 16°50N 74°30E 126 F2
Yermo U.S.A. 34°54N 116°50W 171 L10
Yerolakkos Cyprus 35°11N 33°15E 101 D12
Yeropol Russia 65°15N 168°40E 107 C17
Yeroskipos Cyprus 34°46N 32°28E 101 E11
Yershov Russia 51°23N 48°27E 86 E9
Yerupajá, Cerro Peru 10°16S 76°55W 188 C2
Yerushalayim = Jerusalem Israel/West Bank 31°47N 35°10E 130 D4
Yerville France 49°40N 0°53E 70 C7
Yes Tor U.K. 50°41N 4°0W 67 G4
Yesan S. Korea 36°41N 126°51E 115 F14
Yeşilhisar Turkey 38°20N 35°5E 104 C6
Yeşilırmak → Turkey 41°22N 36°37E 104 B7
Yeşilkent Turkey 36°57N 36°12E 104 D7
Yeşilova Turkey 37°31N 29°46E 99 D11
Yeşilyurt Manisa, Turkey 38°22N 28°40E 99 C10
Yeşilyurt Muğla, Turkey 37°10N 28°20E 99 D10
Yesnogorsk Russia 54°32N 37°38E 84 E9
Yeso U.S.A. 34°26N 104°37W 169 J11
Yessentuki Russia 44°5N 42°53E 87 H6
Yessey Russia 68°29N 102°10E 107 C11
Yeste Spain 38°22N 2°19W 91 G2
Yetman Australia 28°56S 150°48E 151 D5
Yeu, Î. d' France 46°42N 2°20W 70 F4
Yevlax Azerbaijan 40°39N 47°7E 87 K8
Yevpatoriya Ukraine 45°15N 33°20E 85 K7
Yeya → Russia 46°40N 38°40E 87 G4
Yeysk Russia 46°40N 38°12E 85 J10
Yezd = Yazd Iran 31°55N 54°27E 129 D7
Yezerishche Belarus 55°50N 30°0E 84 E6
Ygatimi Paraguay 24°5S 55°40W 191 A4
Yhati Paraguay 25°45S 56°35W 190 B4
Yhú Paraguay 25°0S 56°0W 191 B4
Yí → Uruguay 33°7S 57°8W 190 C4
Yi 'Allaq, G. Egypt 30°21N 33°31E 130 E2
Yi He → China 34°10N 118°8E 115 G10
Yi Xian Anhui, China 29°55N 117°57E 117 C11
Yi Xian Hebei, China 39°20N 115°30E 114 E8
Yi Xian Liaoning, China 41°30N 121°22E 115 D11
Yialiás → Cyprus 35°9N 33°44E 101 D12
Yialousa Cyprus 35°32N 34°10E 101 D13
Yibin China 28°45N 104°32E 116 C5
Yichang China 30°40N 111°20E 117 B8
Yicheng Henan, China 31°41N 112°12E 117 B9
Yicheng Shanxi, China 35°42N 111°40E 114 G6
Yichuan China 36°2N 110°10E 114 F6
Yichun Heilongjiang, China 47°44N 128°52E 111 B14
Yichun Jiangxi, China 27°48N 114°22E 117 D10
Yidu China 36°43N 118°28E 115 F10
Yidun China 30°22N 99°21E 116 B2
Yifeng China 28°22N 114°45E 117 C10
Yihuang China 27°30N 116°12E 117 D11
Yijun China 35°28N 109°8E 114 G5
Yıldız Dağları Turkey 41°48N 27°36E 97 E11
Yıldızeli Turkey 39°51N 36°36E 104 C7
Yilehuli Shan China 51°20N 124°20E 111 A13
Yiliang Yunnan, China 27°38N 104°2E 116 D5
Yiliang Yunnan, China 24°56N 103°11E 116 E4
Yılmazköy = Skilloura Cyprus 35°14N 33°10E 101 D12
Yilong China 31°34N 106°23E 116 B6
Yima China 34°44N 111°53E 114 G6
Yimen China 24°40N 102°10E 116 E4
Yimianpo China 45°7N 128°2E 115 B15
Yin Xu China 36°7N 114°18E 114 F8
Yi'nan China 35°31N 118°24E 115 G10
Yinchuan China 38°30N 106°15E 114 E4
Yindarlgooda, L. Australia 30°40S 121°52E 149 F3
Yindjibarndi ✪ Australia 22°0S 118°35E 148 D2
Ying He → China 32°30N 116°30E 117 A11
Ying Xian China 39°32N 113°10E 114 E7
Yingcheng China 30°56N 113°35E 117 B9
Yingde China 24°10N 113°25E 117 E9
Yingjiang China 24°41N 97°55E 116 E1
Yingjing China 29°41N 102°52E 116 C4
Yingkou China 40°37N 122°18E 115 D12
Yingpanshui China 37°26N 104°18E 114 F3
Yingshan Hubei, China 30°41N 115°32E 117 B10
Yingshan Sichuan, China 31°4N 106°35E 116 B6
Yingshang China 32°38N 116°12E 117 A11
Yingtan China 28°12N 117°0E 117 C11
Yingualyalya ✪ Australia 18°49S 129°12E 148 C4
Yining China 43°58N 81°10E 109 D10
Yiningarra ✪ Australia 20°53S 129°27E 148 D4
Yinjiang China 28°1N 108°21E 116 C7
Yinmabin Myanmar 22°10N 94°55E 123 H19
Yioúra = Giaros Greece 37°32N 24°40E 98 D6
Yipinglang China 25°10N 101°52E 116 E3
Yirga Alem Ethiopia 6°48N 38°22E 131 F2
Yirrkala Australia 12°14S 136°56E 150 A2
Yishan China 24°28N 108°38E 116 E7
Yishui China 35°47N 118°30E 115 G10
Yishun Singapore 1°26N 103°51E 121 d
Yitong China 43°13N 125°20E 115 C13
Yiwu China 29°20N 120°3E 117 C13
Yixing China 31°21N 119°48E 117 B12
Yiyang Henan, China 34°27N 112°10E 114 G7
Yiyang Hunan, China 28°35N 112°18E 117 C9
Yiyang Jiangxi, China 28°22N 117°20E 117 C11
Yizhang China 25°27N 112°57E 117 E9
Yizheng China 32°18N 119°10E 117 A12
Yli-Kitka Finland 66°8N 28°30E 60 C23
Yliki, L. Greece 38°24N 23°15E 98 C5
Ylitornio Finland 66°19N 23°39E 60 C20
Ylivieska Finland 64°4N 24°28E 60 D21
Ymer Ø Greenland 73°9N 24°20W 57 C8
Yngaren Sweden 58°50N 16°35E 63 F10
Yoakum U.S.A. 29°17N 97°9W 176 G6
Yobe □ Nigeria 12°0N 11°30E 139 C7
Yog Pt. Phil. 14°6N 124°12E 119 B6
Yoğuntaş Turkey 41°50N 27°4E 97 E11
Yogyakarta Indonesia 7°49S 110°22E 118 F4
Yogyakarta □ Indonesia 7°48S 110°22E 119 G14
Yoho △ Canada 51°25N 116°30W 162 C5
Yojoa, L. de Honduras 14°53N 88°0W 182 D2
Yok Don △ Vietnam 12°50N 107°40E 120 F6
Yokadouma Cameroon 3°26N 14°55E 140 D2
Yokkaichi Japan 34°55N 136°38E 113 G8
Yoko Cameroon 5°32N 12°20E 139 D7
Yokohama Japan 35°27N 139°28E 113 G9
Yokosuka Japan 35°20N 139°40E 113 G9
Yokote Japan 39°20N 140°30E 112 E10
Yola Nigeria 9°10N 12°29E 139 D7
Yolaina, Cordillera de Nic. 11°30N 84°0W 182 D3
Ýolöten Turkmenistan 37°18N 62°21E 129 B9
Yom → Thailand 15°35N 100°1E 120 E3
Yonago Japan 35°25N 133°19E 113 G6
Yonaguni-Jima Japan 24°27N 123°0E 113 M1
Yŏnan N. Korea 37°55N 126°11E 115 F14
Yonezawa Japan 37°57N 140°4E 112 F10
Yong-in S. Korea 37°14N 127°12E 115 F14
Yong Peng Malaysia 2°0N 103°3E 121 M4
Yong Sata Thailand 7°8N 99°41E 121 J2
Yong'an China 25°59N 117°25E 117 E11
Yongamp'o N. Korea 39°56N 124°23E 115 E13
Yongchang China 38°17N 102°7E 110 D9
Yongcheng China 33°55N 116°20E 114 H9
Yongchuan China 29°17N 105°55E 116 C5
Yongchun China 25°16N 118°20E 117 E12
Yongde China 24°5N 99°25E 116 E2
Yongdeng China 36°38N 103°25E 114 F2
Yongding China 24°43N 116°45E 117 E11
Yongfeng China 27°20N 115°22E 117 D10
Yongfu China 24°59N 109°59E 116 E7
Yonghe China 36°46N 110°38E 114 F6
Yŏnghŭng N. Korea 39°31N 127°18E 115 E14
Yongji Jilin, China 43°33N 126°13E 115 C14
Yongji Shanxi, China 34°52N 110°28E 114 G6
Yongjia China 28°10N 120°45E 117 C13
Yongkang Yunnan, China 24°9N 99°20E 116 E2
Yongkang Zhejiang, China 28°55N 120°2E 117 C13
Yongnian China 36°47N 114°29E 114 F8
Yongning Guangxi Zhuangzu, China 22°44N 108°28E 116 F7
Yongning Ningxia Huizu, China 38°15N 106°14E 114 E4
Yongping China 25°27N 99°38E 116 E2
Yongren China 26°4N 101°40E 116 D3
Yongshan China 28°11N 103°35E 116 C4
Yongsheng China 26°38N 100°46E 116 D3
Yongshun China 29°2N 109°51E 116 C7
Yongtai China 25°49N 118°58E 117 E12
Yongxin = Jinggangshan China 26°58N 114°15E 117 D10
Yongxing China 26°9N 113°8E 117 D9
Yongxing Dao = Woody I. S. China Sea 16°50N 112°20E 118 A4
Yongxiu China 29°2N 115°42E 117 C10
Yongzhou China 26°17N 111°37E 117 D8
Yonibana S. Leone 8°30N 12°19W 138 D2
Yonkers U.S.A. 40°56N 73°52W 175 F11
Yonne □ France 47°50N 3°40E 71 E10
Yonne → France 48°23N 2°58E 71 D9
York Australia 31°52S 116°47E 149 F2
York U.K. 53°58N 1°6W 66 D6
York Ala., U.S.A. 32°29N 88°18W 177 E10
York Nebr., U.S.A. 40°52N 97°36W 172 E5
York Pa., U.S.A. 39°58N 76°44W 173 F15
York, C. Australia 10°42S 142°31E 150 A3
York, City of □ U.K. 53°58N 1°6W 66 D6
York, Kap Greenland 75°55N 66°25W 57 B4
York, Vale of U.K. 54°15N 1°25W 66 C6
York Sd. Australia 15°0S 125°5E 148 C4
Yorke Pen. Australia 34°50S 137°40E 152 C2
Yorketown Australia 35°2S 137°33E 152 C2
Yorkshire Dales △ U.K. 54°12N 2°10W 66 C5
Yorkshire Wolds U.K. 54°8N 0°31W 66 C7
Yorkton Canada 51°11N 102°28W 163 C8
Yorkville Calif., U.S.A. 38°52N 123°13W 170 G3
Yorkville Ga., U.S.A. 33°55N 84°58W 178 B5
Yoro Honduras 15°9N 87°7W 182 C2
Yoron-Jima Japan 27°2N 128°26E 113 L4
Yorosso Mali 12°17N 4°55W 138 C4
Yos Sudarso, Pulau = Dolak, Pulau Indonesia 8°0S 138°30E 119 F9
Yosemite △ U.S.A. 37°45N 119°40W 170 H7
Yosemite Village U.S.A. 37°45N 119°35W 170 H7
Yoshino-Kumano △ Japan 34°12N 135°55E 113 H8
Yoshkar Ola Russia 56°38N 47°55E 86 B8
Yotvata Israel 29°55N 35°2E 130 F4
You Jiang → China 22°50N 108°6E 116 F6
You Xian China 27°1N 113°17E 117 D9
Youbou Canada 48°53N 124°13W 170 B2
Youghal Ireland 51°56N 7°52W 64 E4
Youghal B. Ireland 51°55N 7°49W 64 E4
Youkounkoun Guinea 12°35N 13°11W 138 C2
Young Australia 34°19S 148°18E 153 C8
Young Canada 51°47N 105°45W 163 C7
Young Uruguay 32°44S 57°36W 190 C4
Young I. Antarctica 66°25S 162°24E 55 C11
Young Ra. N.Z. 44°10S 169°30E 155 E4
Younghusband, L. Australia 30°50S 136°5E 152 A2
Younghusband Pen. Australia 36°0S 139°25E 152 D3
Youngstown Canada 51°35N 111°10W 163 C6
Youngstown Fla., U.S.A. 30°22N 85°26W 178 E4
Youngstown N.Y., U.S.A. 43°15N 79°3W 174 C5
Youngstown Ohio, U.S.A. 41°6N 80°39W 174 E4
Youngsville U.S.A. 41°51N 79°19W 174 E5
Youngwood U.S.A. 40°14N 79°34W 174 F5
Youssoufia Morocco 32°16N 8°31W 136 B2
Youxi China 26°10N 118°13E 117 D12
Youyang China 28°47N 108°42E 116 C7
Youyu China 40°10N 112°20E 114 D7
Yozgat Turkey 39°51N 34°47E 104 C6
Yozgat □ Turkey 39°30N 35°0E 104 C6
Ypacaraí △ Paraguay 25°18S 57°19W 190 B4
Ypané → Paraguay 23°29S 57°19W 190 A4
Yport France 49°45N 0°15E 70 C7
Ypres = Ieper Belgium 50°51N 2°53E 69 D2
Yr Wyddgrug = Mold U.K. 53°9N 3°8W 66 D4
Yreka U.S.A. 41°44N 122°38W 168 F2
Yrghyz Kazakhstan 48°37N 61°16E 108 C6
Yrghyz → Kazakhstan 48°6N 62°30E 108 C6
Yssingeaux France 45°9N 4°8E 73 C8
Ystad Sweden 55°26N 13°50E 63 J7
Ystradgynlais U.K. 51°47N 3°46W 67 F4
Ysyk-Köl = Balykchy Kyrgyzstan 42°26N 76°12E 109 D9
Ysyk-Köl Kyrgyzstan 42°25N 77°15E 109 D9
Ysyk-Köl □ Kyrgyzstan 42°0N 78°0E 109 D9
Ythan → U.K. 57°19N 1°59W 65 D7
Ytteran Sweden 63°16N 14°7E 62 A8
Ytterhogdal Sweden 62°12N 14°56E 62 B8
Yttermalung Sweden 60°35N 13°51E 62 D7
Ytyk-Kyuyel Russia 62°30N 133°45E 107 C14
Yu Jiang → China 23°22N 110°3E 116 F7
Yü Shan Taiwan 23°25N 120°52E 117 F13
Yu Xian = Yuzhou China 34°10N 113°28E 114 G7
Yu Xian Hebei, China 39°50N 114°35E 114 E8
Yu Xian Shanxi, China 38°5N 113°20E 114 E7
Yuan Jiang = Hong → Asia 20°16N 106°34E 120 B5
Yuan Jiang → Hunan, China 28°55N 111°50E 117 C8
Yuan Jiang → Yunnan, China 22°20N 103°59E 116 F4
Yuan'an China 31°3N 111°34E 117 B8
Yuanjiang Hunan, China 28°47N 112°21E 117 C9
Yuanjiang Yunnan, China 23°32N 102°0E 116 F4
Yüanli Taiwan 24°27N 120°39E 117 E13
Yüanlin Taiwan 23°58N 120°30E 117 F13
Yuanling China 28°29N 110°22E 117 C8
Yuanmou China 25°42N 101°53E 116 E3
Yuanping China 38°42N 112°46E 114 E7
Yuanqu China 35°18N 111°40E 114 G6
Yuanyang Henan, China 35°3N 113°58E 114 G7
Yuanyang Yunnan, China 23°10N 102°43E 116 F4
Yuba → U.S.A. 39°8N 121°36W 170 F5
Yuba City U.S.A. 39°8N 121°37W 170 F5
Yūbari Japan 43°4N 141°59E 112 C10
Yūbetsu Japan 44°13N 143°50E 112 B11
Yucatán □ Mexico 20°50N 89°0W 181 C7
Yucatán, Canal de Caribbean 22°0N 86°30W 182 B2
Yucatán, Península de Mexico 19°30N 89°0W 158 H11
Yucatan Basin Cent. Amer. 19°0N 86°0W 181 D7
Yucatan Channel = Yucatán, Canal de Caribbean 22°0N 86°30W 182 B2
Yucca U.S.A. 34°52N 114°9W 171 L12
Yucca Valley U.S.A. 34°8N 116°27W 171 L10
Yucheng China 36°55N 116°32E 114 F9
Yuci = Jinzhong China 37°42N 112°46E 114 F7
Yudu China 25°59N 115°30E 117 E10
Yuechi China 30°34N 106°25E 116 B6
Yuen Long China 22°26N 114°2E 111 a
Yuendumu Australia 22°16S 131°49E 148 D5
Yuendumu ✪ Australia 22°21S 131°40E 148 D5
Yueqing China 28°9N 120°59E 117 C13
Yueqing Wan China 28°5N 121°20E 117 C13
Yuexi Anhui, China 30°50N 116°20E 117 B11
Yuexi Sichuan, China 28°37N 102°26E 116 C4
Yueyang China 29°21N 113°5E 117 C9
Yugan China 28°43N 116°37E 117 C11
Yugorenok Russia 59°47N 137°40E 107 D14
Yugyd Va △ Russia 62°25N 58°45E 106 C6
Yuhuan China 28°9N 121°12E 117 C13
Yuhuan Dao China 28°5N 121°15E 117 C13
Yujiang China 28°10N 116°43E 117 C11
Yukhary Askipara Azerbaijan 41°4N 45°1E 105 B11
Yukhnov Russia 54°44N 35°15E 84 E8
Yukon U.S.A. 35°31N 97°45W 176 D6
Yukon □ Canada 63°0N 135°0W 160 E5
Yukon → U.S.A. 62°32N 163°54W 166 C7
Yukon Flats U.S.A. 66°40N 145°45W 166 B10
Yüksekova Turkey 37°34N 44°16E 105 D11
Yukta Russia 63°26N 105°42E 107 C11
Yukuhashi Japan 33°44N 130°59E 113 H5
Yulara Australia 25°10S 130°55E 149 E5
Yule → Australia 20°41S 118°17E 148 D2
Yuleba Australia 26°37S 149°24E 151 D4
Yulee U.S.A. 30°38N 81°36W 178 E8
Yuli China 41°19N 86°15E 109 D11
Yuli Nigeria 9°44N 10°12E 139 D7
Yüli Taiwan 23°20N 121°18E 117 F13
Yulin Guangxi Zhuangzu, China 22°40N 110°8E 117 F8
Yulin Hainan, China 18°10N 109°31E 117 a
Yulin Shaanxi, China 38°20N 109°30E 114 E5
Yulong Xueshan China 27°6N 100°10E 116 D3
Yuma Ariz., U.S.A. 32°43N 114°37W 171 N12
Yuma Colo., U.S.A. 40°8N 102°43W 168 F12
Yuma, B. de Dom. Rep. 18°20N 68°35W 183 C6
Yumali Australia 35°32S 139°45E 152 C3
Yumbe Uganda 3°28N 31°15E 142 B3
Yumbi Dem. Rep. of the Congo 1°12S 26°15E 142 C2
Yumen China 39°50N 97°30E 110 D8
Yumurtalık Turkey 36°45N 35°48E 104 D6
Yun Gui Gaoyuan China 26°0N 104°0E 116 E3
Yun Ling Shan China 27°0N 99°20E 116 D2
Yun Xian Hubei, China 32°50N 110°46E 117 A8
Yun Xian Yunnan, China 24°27N 100°8E 116 E3
Yuna Australia 28°20S 115°0E 149 E2
Yunak Turkey 38°49N 31°43E 104 C4
Yunan China 23°12N 111°30E 117 F8
Yuncheng Henan, China 35°36N 115°57E 114 G8
Yuncheng Shanxi, China 35°2N 111°0E 114 G6
Yunfu China 22°50N 112°5E 117 F9
Yungang Shiku China 40°6N 113°7E 114 D7
Yungas Bolivia 17°0S 66°0W 186 G5
Yungay Chile 37°10S 72°5W 190 D1
Yungay Peru 9°2S 77°45W 188 B2
Yunhe China 28°8N 119°33E 117 C12
Yunkai Dashan China 22°30N 111°0E 117 F8
Yunkanjini ✪ Australia 22°33S 131°6E 148 D5
Yunling Shan China 28°30N 98°50E 110 F8
Yunlong China 25°57N 99°13E 116 E2
Yunmeng China 31°2N 113°43E 117 B9
Yunnan □ China 25°0N 102°0E 116 E4
Yunquera de Henares Spain 40°47N 3°11W 90 E1
Yunt Dağı Turkey 38°56N 27°13E 99 C9
Yunta Australia 32°34S 139°36E 151 E2
Yunxi China 33°0N 110°22E 117 A8
Yunxiao China 23°59N 117°18E 117 F11

Yunyang Chongqing,
China 31°2N 108°51E 116 B7
Yunyang Henan, China 33°26N 112°42E 117 A9
Yupanqui Basin
Pac. Oc. 19°0S 101°0W 157 J17
Yuping China 27°13N 108°56E 116 D7
Yuqing China 27°13N 107°58E 116 D6
Yuraygir △ Australia 29°45S 153°15E 151 E5
Yurihonjō Japan 39°23N 140°3E 112 E10
Yurimaguas Peru 5°55S 76°7W 188 B2
Yurkiyka Ukraine 48°24N 28°35E 81 B13
Yurubí △ Venezuela 10°26N 68°42W 183 D6
Yurungkax He →
China 38°5N 80°34E 109 E10
Yuryev-Polskiy Russia 56°30N 39°40E 84 D10
Yuryevets Russia 57°25N 43°2E 86 B6
Yuscarán Honduras 13°58N 86°45W 182 D2
Yûsef, Bahr → Egypt 28°25N 30°35E 137 F7
Yushan China 28°42N 118°10E 117 C12
Yushanzhen China 29°28N 108°22E 116 C7
Yushe China 37°4N 112°58E 114 F7
Yushu Jilin, China 44°43N 126°38E 115 B14
Yushu Qinghai, China 33°5N 96°55E 110 E18
Yusufeli Turkey 40°50N 41°33E 105 B9
Yutai China 35°0N 116°45E 114 G9
Yutian Hebei, China 39°53N 117°45E 115 C9
Yutian Sinkiang-Uigur,
China 36°52N 81°42E 109 E10
Yuxari Qarabağ =
Nagorno-Karabakh □
Azerbaijan 39°55N 46°45E 105 C12
Yuxi China 24°30N 102°35E 116 E4
Yuyao China 30°3N 121°10E 117 B13
Yuzawa Japan 39°10N 140°30E 112 E10
Yuzha Russia 56°34N 42°1E 86 B6
Yuzhno-Kurilsk
Russia 44°1N 145°51E 107 E15
Yuzhno-Sakhalinsk
Russia 46°58N 142°45E 111 B17
Yuzhno-Sukhokumsk
Russia 44°40N 45°35E 87 H7
Yuzhnoukrainsk
Ukraine 47°49N 31°11E 85 J6
Yuzhnouralsk Russia 54°26N 61°15E 108 B6
Yuzhnyy □ Russia 44°0N 40°0E 106 E5
Yuzhou China 34°10N 113°28E 114 G7
Yvelines □ France 48°40N 1°45E 71 D8
Yverdon-les-Bains Switz. 46°47N 6°39E 77 J2
Yvetot France 49°37N 0°44E 70 C7
Yzeure France 46°33N 3°22E 71 F10

Z

Zaanstad Neths. 52°27N 4°50E 69 B4
Zab, Monts du Algeria 34°55N 5°0E 136 B5
Záb al Kabir → Iraq 36°1N 43°24E 105 D10
Záb aş Şaghīr → Iraq 35°17N 43°29E 105 E10
Žabalj Serbia 45°21N 20°5E 98 B5
Žabari Serbia 44°22N 21°15E 98 B5
Zabaykalsk Russia 49°40N 117°25E 107 E12
Zabaykalsky △ Russia 53°40N 109°0E 107 D11
Zabki Poland 52°17N 21°6E 83 F8
Ząbkowice Śląskie
Poland 50°35N 16°50E 83 H3
Žabljak Montenegro 43°18N 19°5E 96 C2
Zabłudów Poland 53°0N 23°19E 83 F9
Żabno Poland 50°9N 20°53E 83 H7
Zābol Iran 31°0N 61°32E 129 D9
Zābol □ Afghan. 32°0N 67°0E 122 D5
Zāboli Iran 27°10N 61°35E 129 E9
Zabolotiv Ukraine 48°28N 25°18E 81 B10
Zabolottya Ukraine 51°38N 24°16E 83 G11
Zabré Burkina Faso 11°12N 0°36W 139 C4
Zábřeh Czechia 52°53N 16°52E 79 B9
Zabrze Poland 50°18N 18°50E 83 H5
Zabuzhzhya Ukraine 51°21N 23°42E 83 G10
Zabzuga Ghana 9°20N 0°30E 139 D5
Zacapa Guatemala 14°59N 89°31W 182 D2
Zacatecas Mexico 22°47N 102°35W 180 C4
Zacatecas □ Mexico 23°0N 103°0W 180 C4
Zacatecoluca El Salv. 13°29N 88°51W 182 D2
Zacharo Greece 37°30N 21°39E 98 D3
Zachary U.S.A. 30°39N 91°9W 176 F9
Zachodnio-Pomorskie □
Poland 53°40N 15°50E 82 E2
Zacoalco de Torres
Mexico 20°14N 103°33W 180 C4
Zacualtipán Mexico 20°39N 98°36W 181 C5
Zadar Croatia 44°8N 15°14E 93 D12
Zadawa Nigeria 11°33N 10°19E 139 C7
Zadetkyi Kyun
Myanmar 10°0N 98°25E 121 G2
Zadonsk Russia 52°25N 38°56E 85 F10
Zafarqand Iran 33°11N 52°29E 127 E7
Zafra Spain 38°26N 6°30W 89 G4
Żagań Poland 51°39N 15°22E 83 G2
Zagaoua Chad 15°30N 22°24E 135 E10
Žagarė Lithuania 56°21N 23°15E 82 B10
Zagazig Egypt 30°40N 31°30E 137 E7
Zâgheh Iran 33°30N 48°42E 129 C6
Zaghouan Tunisia 36°23N 10°10E 136 A6
Zaghouan □ Tunisia 36°20N 10°10E 136 A6
Zaglou Algeria 27°17N 0°3W 136 C3
Zagnanado Benin 7°18N 2°28E 139 D5
Zagora Greece 39°27N 23°6E 98 B5
Zagora Morocco 30°22N 5°51W 136 B4
Zagorje ob Savi Slovenia 46°8N 15°0E 93 B11
Zagórów Poland 52°10N 17°54E 83 F4
Zagórz Poland 49°30N 22°14E 83 J9
Zagreb Croatia 45°50N 15°58E 93 C12
Zagreb ✈ (ZAG) Croatia 45°45N 16°4E 93 C13
Zagros, Kühhā-ye = Zāgros, Kühhā-ye
Iran 33°45N 48°5E 129 C6
Zagros Mts. = Zāgros, Kühhā-ye
Iran 33°45N 48°5E 129 C6
Žagubica Serbia 44°15N 21°47E 98 B5
Zaguinaso Côte d'Ivoire 10°1N 6°14W 138 C3
Zagyva → Hungary 47°11N 20°11E 80 C5
Zāhedān Fārs, Iran 28°46N 53°52E 129 D7
Zāhedān Sīstān va Balūchestān,
Iran 29°30N 60°50E 129 D9
Zahirabad India 17°43N 77°37E 126 F3
Zahlah Lebanon 33°52N 35°50E 130 B4
Zahna Germany 51°54N 12°47E 79 C8
Żahony Hungary 48°25N 22°11E 80 B7
Zaḥrān al Janub
Sī. Arabia 17°40N 43°30E 131 D3
Zainsk Russia 55°18N 52°4E 86 C11
Zaïre = Congo → Africa 6°4S 12°24E 140 F12
Zaječar Serbia 43°53N 22°18E 96 C6

Zaka Zimbabwe 20°20S 31°29E 145 B5
Zakamensk Russia 50°23N 103°17E 107 D11
Zakarpattya □ Ukraine 48°20N 23°20E 81 B8
Zākhū Iraq 37°10N 42°50E 105 D10
Zakinthos = Zakynthos
Greece 37°47N 20°54E 98 D2
Zakopane Poland 49°18N 19°57E 83 J6
Zakroczym Poland 52°26N 20°38E 83 F7
Zakros Greece 35°6N 26°10E 101 D8
Zakynthos Greece 37°47N 20°54E 98 D2
Zala □ Hungary 46°42N 16°50E 80 D1
Zala → Hungary 46°33N 17°12E 80 D1
Zalaegerszeg Hungary 46°53N 16°47E 80 D1
Zalakomár Hungary 46°33N 17°12E 80 D1
Zalalövö Hungary 46°51N 16°35E 80 D1
Zalamea de la Serena
Spain 38°40N 5°38W 89 G5
Zalamea la Real Spain 37°41N 6°38W 89 H4
Zalantun China 48°0N 122°43E 111 B13
Zalari Russia 53°33N 102°30E 107 D11
Zalău Romania 47°12N 23°3E 80 C8
Žalec Slovenia 46°16N 15°10E 93 B12
Zaleshchiki = Zalishchyky
Ukraine 48°45N 25°45E 81 B10
Zalesye Russia 54°50N 21°31E 82 D8
Zalewo Poland 53°50N 19°41E 82 E6
Zalingei Sudan 12°51N 23°29E 135 F10
Zalishchyky Ukraine 48°45N 25°45E 81 B10
Zama L. Canada 58°45N 119°5W 162 B5
Zambeke
Dem. Rep. of the Congo 2°8N 25°17E 142 B2
Zambeze → Africa 18°35S 36°20E 143 F4
Zambezi = Zambeze →
Africa 18°35S 36°20E 143 F4
Zambezi Zambia 13°30S 23°15E 141 G4
Zambezi □ Namibia 18°0S 23°30E 144 A3
Zambezi △ Zimbabwe 17°54S 25°41E 143 F2
Zambezia □ Mozam. 16°15S 37°30E 143 F4
Zambia ■ Africa 15°0S 28°0E 143 F2
Zamboanga Phil. 6°59N 122°3E 119 C6
Zambrów Poland 52°59N 22°14E 83 F9
Zamfara □ Nigeria 12°10N 6°0E 139 C6
Zamfara → Nigeria 12°5N 4°2E 139 C5
Zamora Mexico 19°59N 102°16W 180 D4
Zamora Spain 41°30N 5°45W 88 D5
Zamora □ Spain 41°30N 5°46W 88 D5
Zamość Poland 50°43N 23°15E 83 H10
Zamtang China 32°26N 101°6E 116 A3
Zan Ghana 9°26N 0°17W 139 D4
Záncara → Spain 39°18N 3°18W 91 F1
Zanda China 31°32N 79°50E 110 E4
Zandvoort Neths. 52°22N 4°32E 69 B4
Zanesville U.S.A. 39°56N 82°1W 174 G2
Zangābād Iran 38°26N 46°44E 128 B5
Zangliveri Greece 40°36N 23°15E 98 B4
Zangoza = Sangüesa
Spain 42°37N 1°17W 90 C3
Zangue → Mozam. 17°50S 35°21E 143 F4
Zanjan Iran 36°40N 48°35E 105 D13
Zanjan □ Iran 37°8N 47°47E 129 B6
Zannone Italy 40°58N 13°3E 94 B6
Zante = Zakynthos
Greece 37°47N 20°54E 98 D2
Zanthus Australia 31°2S 123°34E 149 F3
Zanzan □ Côte d'Ivoire 8°30N 3°30W 138 D4
Zanzibar Tanzania 6°12S 39°12E 142 D4
Zaouatallaz Algeria 24°52N 8°26E 137 D6
Zaouiet El-Kala = Bordj Omar
Driss Algeria 28°10N 6°40E 136 C5
Zaouiet Reggâne Algeria 26°32N 0°3E 136 C4
Zaoyang China 32°10N 112°45E 117 A9
Zaozernyy Kazakhstan 53°6N 71°9E 109 B8
Zaozhuang China 34°50N 117°35E 115 G9
Zap Suyu = Záb al Kabir →
Iraq 36°1N 43°24E 105 D10
Zapadna Morava →
Serbia 43°38N 21°30E 96 C5
Zapadnaya Dvina = Daugava →
Latvia 57°4N 24°3E 84 D3
Zapadnaya Dvina Russia 56°15N 32°3E 84 D7
Západné Beskydy
Europe 49°30N 19°0E 79 B12
Západní Rodopi Bulgaria 41°50N 24°40E 98 H7
Západočeský □ Czechia 49°35N 13°0E 78 B6
Zapala Argentina 39°0S 70°5W 192 A2
Zapaleri, Cerro Bolivia 22°49S 67°11W 190 A2
Zapata U.S.A. 26°55N 99°16W 176 H5
Zapatón → Spain 39°0N 6°49W 89 F4
Zapolyarnyy Russia 69°26N 30°51E 60 B24
Zaporizhzhya Ukraine 47°50N 35°10E 85 J8
Zaporizhzhya □ Ukraine 46°55N 35°50E 85 J8
Zaporozhye = Zaporizhzhya
Ukraine 47°50N 35°10E 85 J8
Zaqatala Azerbaijan 41°38N 46°35E 87 K8
Zara Turkey 39°58N 37°43E 104 C7
Zarafshon Uzbekistan 41°34N 64°12E 108 D6
Zaragoza Coahuila,
Mexico 28°29N 100°55W 180 B4
Zaragoza Nuevo León,
Mexico 23°58N 99°46W 181 C5
Zaragoza Spain 41°39N 0°53W 90 D4
Zaragoza □ Spain 41°35N 1°0W 90 D4
Zarand Kermān, Iran 30°46N 56°34W 128 C4
Zarand Markazi, Iran 35°18N 50°25E 129 C6
Zărandului, Munţii
Romania 46°14N 22°7E 80 D7
Zaranj Afghan. 30°55N 61°55E 122 D2
Zarasai Lithuania 55°40N 26°20E 84 E4
Zárate Argentina 34°7S 59°0W 190 C4
Zarautz Spain 43°17N 2°10W 90 D2
Zard, Kūh-e Iran 32°22N 50°4E 128 C5
Zārehriy Russia 58°54N 61°20E 86 D7
Zārēh Iran 35°7N 49°9E 129 C6
Zari Nigeria 13°4N 12°45E 139 C7
Zaria Nigeria 11°0N 7°40E 139 C6
Zarineh → Iran 36°17N 46°26E 105 D12
Żarki Poland 53°43N 84°55E 109 B9
Żarko Poland 50°38N 19°23E 83 H6
Zarneh Iran 33°55N 46°10E 128 C5
Zărneşti Romania 45°33N 25°18E 81 D10
Żarów Poland 50°56N 16°29E 83 H3
Zarqā', Nahr az →
Jordan 32°10N 35°37E 130 C4

Zarrīn Iran 32°46N 54°37E 129 C7
Zarrīnābād Iran 36°25N 48°17E 105 D13
Zaruma Ecuador 3°40S 79°38W 188 D3
Żary Poland 51°37N 15°10E 83 G2
Zarza de Granadilla Spain 40°14N 6°3W 88 E4
Zarzaïtine Algeria 28°15N 9°34E 136 C5
Zarzis Tunisia 33°31N 11°2E 136 B6
Zas Spain 43°4N 8°53W 88 B2
Zashaghan Kazakhstan 51°11N 51°20E 88 B4
Zaskar → India 34°13N 77°20E 125 B7
Zaskar Mts. India 33°15N 77°30E 125 C7
Zastavna Ukraine 48°31N 25°51E 81 B10
Zastron S. Africa 30°18S 27°7E 144 D4
Žatec Czechia 50°20N 13°32E 78 A6
Zaterechnyy Russia 44°48N 45°11E 87 H7
Zator Poland 49°59N 19°28E 83 J6
Zatyshshya Ukraine 47°20N 29°51E 81 C14
Zavala Bos.-H. 42°50N 17°59E 96 D1
Zavāreh Iran 33°29N 52°28E 129 C7
Zave Zimbabwe 17°6S 30°1E 145 A5
Zavetnoye Russia 47°13N 43°50E 87 G6
Zavidovići Bos.-H. 44°27N 18°10E 96 B3
Zavodovski I. Antarctica 56°0S 27°45W 55 B1
Zavolzhsk Russia 57°30N 42°3E 86 B6
Zavolzhye Russia 56°37N 43°26E 86 B6
Zawadzkie Poland 50°37N 18°28E 83 H5
Zawichost Poland 50°48N 21°51E 83 H8
Zawidów Poland 51°1N 15°1E 83 G2
Zawiercie Poland 50°30N 19°24E 83 H6
Zāwiyat al Baydā = Al Baydā
Libya 32°50N 21°44E 135 B10
Zâwyet Shammâs
Egypt 31°30N 26°37E 137 A2
Zâwyet Um el Rakham
Egypt 31°18N 27°1E 137 A2
Zâwyet Ungeîla Egypt 31°23N 26°42E 137 A2
Zāyā Iraq 33°33N 44°13E 128 C5
Zāyandeh → Iran 32°35N 52°0E 129 C7
Zaysan Kazakhstan 47°28N 84°52E 109 C10
Zaysan Köli Kazakhstan 48°0N 83°0E 109 C10
Zayü China 28°48N 97°27E 123 E20
Zázrivá Slovakia 49°16N 19°7E 78 B9
Zbarazh Ukraine 49°43N 25°44E 75 D13
Zbąszyń Poland 52°14N 15°56E 83 F2
Zbąszynek Poland 52°16N 15°51E 83 F2
Zblewo Poland 53°56N 18°19E 82 E5
Zbruch → Ukraine 48°32N 26°27E 81 B11
Żdár nad Sázavou
Czechia 49°34N 15°57E 78 B8
Zdolbuniv Ukraine 50°30N 26°15E 75 C14
Ždrelo Serbia 44°16N 21°28E 98 B5
Zduńska Wola Poland 51°37N 18°59E 83 G5
Zduny Poland 51°39N 17°21E 83 G4
Zeballos Canada 49°59N 126°50W 162 D23
Zebediela S. Africa 24°20S 29°17E 145 B4
Zebila Ghana 10°55N 0°30W 139 C4
Zebulon U.S.A. 33°6N 84°21W 178 B5
Zeebrugge Belgium 51°19N 3°12E 69 C3
Zeehan Australia 41°52S 145°25E 151 G4
Zeeland □ Neths. 51°30N 3°50E 69 C3
Zeerust S. Africa 25°31S 26°4E 144 C4
Zefat Israel 32°58N 35°29E 130 C4
Zegdou Algeria 29°51N 4°45W 136 C3
Zeggemar, Iracher Mali 16°49N 2°16E 139 B5
Zégoua Mali 10°32N 5°35W 138 C3
Zehak Iran 30°53N 61°42E 129 D9
Zehdenick Germany 52°58N 13°20E 76 C9
Zeil, Mt. Australia 23°30S 132°23E 148 E5
Zeila = Saylac Somalia 11°21N 43°30E 131 E3
Zeist Neths. 52°5N 5°15E 69 B5
Zeitz Germany 51°2N 12°7E 76 D8
Żelechów Poland 51°49N 21°54E 83 G8
Zelena Ukraine 48°3N 24°45E 81 B9
Zelená Hora Czechia 49°34N 15°56E 78 B8
Zelengora Bos.-H. 43°22N 18°30E 96 C2
Zelenodolsk Russia 55°55N 48°30E 86 C9
Zelenogorsk Russia 60°12N 29°43E 84 B5
Zelenograd Russia 56°1N 37°12E 84 D9
Zelenogradsk Russia 54°53N 20°29E 82 D7
Zelenokumsk Russia 44°24N 44°0E 87 H6
Železná Ruda Czechia 49°8N 13°15E 78 B6
Železnik Serbia 44°43N 20°23E 96 B4
Zelfana Algeria 32°27N 4°15E 136 B4
Zelienople U.S.A. 40°48N 80°8W 174 F4
Zelina Croatia 45°57N 16°16E 93 C13
Zell Baden-W., Germany 47°42N 7°52E 77 H3
Zell Rhld-Pfz., Germany 50°1N 7°10E 77 E3
Zell am See Austria 47°19N 12°47E 78 D5
Zella-Mehlis Germany 50°39N 10°40E 76 E6
Zelów Poland 51°28N 19°14E 83 G6
Zeltweg Austria 47°11N 14°45E 78 D7
Zémaičiu △ Lithuania 56°2N 21°55E 82 B8
Zemetchino Russia 53°30N 42°30E 86 D6
Zémio C.A.R. 5°2N 25°5E 142 A2
Zemlandskiy Poluostrov
Russia 54°50N 20°20E 82 D7
Zemmora Algeria 35°44N 0°51E 136 A4
Zemoul, O. → Algeria 29°15N 7°0W 136 C2
Zemplén-hegység
Hungary 48°25N 21°25E 80 B6
Zemplínska šírava
Slovakia 48°48N 22°0E 79 C15
Zempoala Mexico 19°27N 96°23W 181 D5
Zemun Serbia 44°51N 20°25E 96 B4
Zengbé Cameroon 5°46N 11°3E 139 D7
Zengcheng China 23°13N 113°52E 117 F9
Zenica Bos.-H. 44°10N 17°57E 96 B2
Zephyrhills U.S.A. 28°14N 82°11W 179 G7
Zepu China 38°11N 77°16E 109 E9
Zerbst Germany 51°58N 12°4E 76 C8
Zerhamra Algeria 29°58N 2°30W 136 B3
Żerków Poland 52°4N 17°32E 83 F4
Zermatt Switz. 46°2N 7°46E 77 J3
Zernez Switz. 46°42N 10°7E 77 J6
Zernograd Russia 46°52N 40°19E 87 G5
Zestaponi Georgia 42°6N 43°0E 87 J6
Zetel Germany 53°25N 7°58E 76 B3
Zeulenroda-Triebes
Germany 50°39N 11°59E 76 E7
Zeven Germany 53°17N 9°17E 76 B5
Zevenaar Neths. 51°56N 6°5E 69 C6
Zévio Italy 45°22N 11°8E 92 C8
Zeya Russia 51°42N 128°53E 107 D13
Zeya → Russia 51°42N 128°53E 107 D13
Zeyskoye Vdkhr.
Russia 54°30N 127°0E 107 D13
Zeytinbaği Turkey 40°24N 28°47E 97 F12
Zeytindağ Turkey 38°58N 27°4W 99 E9
Zghartā Lebanon 34°21N 35°53E 130 A4

Zgierz Poland 51°50N 19°27E 83 G6
Zgorzelec Poland 51°10N 15°0E 83 G2
Zgurița Moldova 48°8N 28°1E 81 B13
Zhabinka Belarus 52°13N 24°2E 83 F11
Zhabokrych Ukraine 48°23N 28°59E 81 B13
Zhalaghash Kazakhstan 45°5N 64°40E 108 C6
Zhalpaqtal Kazakhstan 49°42N 49°26E 88 B3
Zhaltyr Kazakhstan 51°37N 69°49E 108 B7
Zhambyl = Taraz
Kazakhstan 42°54N 71°22E 109 D8
Zhambyl □ Kazakhstan 44°0N 72°0E 109 D8
Zhanatas Kazakhstan 43°35N 69°35E 109 D7
Zhangaly Kazakhstan 47°1N 50°37E 87 G10
Zhangaözen Kazakhstan 43°18N 52°48E 88 C4
Zhangaqala Kazakhstan 48°56N 49°36E 88 B4
Zhangatas = Zhanatas
Kazakhstan 43°35N 69°35E 109 D7
Zhangbei China 41°10N 114°45E 114 D8
Zhanggucai Ling
China 45°0N 129°0E 115 B15
Zhangjiabian China 22°33N 113°28E 111 a
Zhangjiagang China 31°55N 120°30E 117 B13
Zhangjiajie China 29°11N 110°30E 117 C8
Zhangjiakou China 40°48N 114°55E 114 D8
Zhangping China 25°17N 117°23E 117 E11
Zhangpu China 24°8N 117°35E 117 E11
Zhangshu China 28°4N 115°29E 117 C10
Zhangye China 38°50N 100°23E 110 D9
Zhangzhou China 24°30N 117°35E 117 E11
Zhanhua China 37°40N 118°8E 115 F10
Zhänibek Kazakhstan 49°25N 46°50E 86 F8
Zhanjiang China 21°15N 110°20E 117 G8
Zhannetty, Ostrov
Russia 76°43N 158°0E 107 B16
Zhanyi China 25°38N 103°48E 116 E4
Zhanyu China 44°30N 122°30E 115 B12
Zhao Xian China 37°43N 114°45E 114 F8
Zhao'an China 23°41N 117°10E 117 F11
Zhaocheng China 36°22N 111°38E 114 F6
Zhaodong China 46°4N 125°59E 111 B13
Zhaojue China 28°1N 102°49E 116 C4
Zhaoping China 24°11N 110°48E 117 E8
Zhaoqing China 23°0N 112°20E 117 F9
Zhaotong China 27°20N 103°44E 116 D4
Zhaoyang Hu China 35°4N 116°47E 114 G9
Zhaoyuan Heilongjiang,
China 45°27N 125°0E 115 B13
Zhaoyuan Shandong,
China 37°20N 120°23E 115 F11
Zhari Namco China 31°6N 85°36E 110 E6
Zharkent Kazakhstan 44°10N 80°0E 109 D10
Zharkovskiy Russia 55°56N 32°19E 84 E7
Zhashui China 33°40N 109°8E 114 H5
Zhaslyk = Jasliq
Uzbekistan 43°58N 57°10E 108 D5
Zhayrang Kazakhstan 48°20N 70°10E 109 C8
Zhayyq → Kazakhstan 47°0N 51°48E 108 C4
Zhdanov = Mariupol
Ukraine 47°5N 37°31E 85 J9
Zhecheng China 34°7N 115°20E 114 G8
Zhegao China 31°46N 117°45E 117 B11
Zhejiang □ China 29°0N 120°0E 117 C13
Zhelezinka
Russia 54°22N 21°19E 82 D8
Zheleznogorsk Russia 52°22N 35°23E 85 F8
Zheleznogorsk-Ilimskiy
Russia 56°34N 104°8E 107 D11
Zheltyye Vody = Zhovti Vody
Ukraine 48°21N 33°31E 85 H7
Zhen'an China 33°27N 109°9E 116 C6
Zhenba China 32°34N 107°58E 116 A6
Zhenfeng China 25°22N 105°40E 116 E5
Zheng'an China 28°32N 107°21E 116 C6
Zhengding China 38°8N 114°32E 114 E8
Zhenghe China 27°20N 118°50E 117 D12
Zhengyang China 32°37N 114°22E 117 A10
Zhengyangguan
China 32°30N 116°29E 117 A11
Zhengzhou China 34°45N 113°34E 114 G7
Zhenhai China 29°59N 121°42E 117 C13
Zhenjiang China 32°11N 119°26E 117 A12
Zhenkang China 23°58N 99°0E 116 F2
Zhenlai China 45°50N 123°5E 115 B12
Zhenning China 26°4N 105°45E 116 D5
Zhenping Henan, China 33°10N 112°16E 114 H7
Zhenping Shaanxi,
China 31°59N 109°31E 116 B7
Zhenxiong China 27°27N 104°50E 116 D5
Zhenyuan Gansu,
China 35°35N 107°30E 114 G4
Zhenyuan Yunnan,
China 23°51N 100°59E 116 F3
Zherdevka Russia 51°56N 41°29E 86 E5
Zherebkove Ukraine 47°52N 29°52E 81 C14
Zherong China 27°15N 119°52E 117 D12
Zhetiqara Kazakhstan 52°11N 61°12E 108 B6
Zhezdi Kazakhstan 48°3N 67°30E 108 C7
Zhezqazghan
Kazakhstan 47°44N 67°40E 109 C7
Zhicheng China 30°25N 111°27E 117 B8
Zhidan China 36°48N 108°48E 114 F5
Zhigansk Russia 66°48N 123°27E 107 C13
Zhigulevsk Russia 53°28N 49°30E 86 D8
Zhijiang Hubei, China 30°28N 111°45E 117 B8
Zhijiang Hunan, China 27°27N 109°42E 116 D7
Zhijin China 26°37N 105°45E 116 D5
Zhilinda Russia 70°0N 114°20E 107 C12
Zhirnovsk Russia 50°57N 44°49E 86 E7
Zhitomir = Zhytomyr
Ukraine 50°20N 28°40E 75 C15
Zhizdra Russia 53°45N 34°40E 84 F8
Zhlobin Belarus 52°55N 30°0E 75 B16
Zhmerinka = Zhmerynka
Ukraine 49°2N 28°2E 81 B13
Zhob Pakistan 31°20N 69°31E 124 C2
Zhob → Pakistan 32°4N 69°50E 124 C2
Zhodzina Belarus 54°5N 28°17E 75 A15
Zhokhova, Ostrov
Russia 76°4N 152°40E 107 B16
Zhongba China 29°39N 84°10E 110 F6
Zhongdian China 27°49N 99°47E 116 D2
Zhongdong China 22°48N 107°47E 116 F6
Zhongjian Dao = Triton I.
S. China Sea 15°47N 111°12E 118 A4
Zhongning China 37°29N 105°40E 114 F3

Zhongsha Qundao = Macclesfield
Bank S. China Sea 16°0N 114°30E 118 A4
Zhongshan Antarctica 69°0S 39°50E 55 C6
Zhongshan Guangdong,
China 22°26N 113°20E 117 F9
Zhongshan Guangxi Zhuangzu,
China 24°29N 111°18E 117 E8
Zhongshankong China 22°35N 113°29E 111 a
Zhongtiao Shan China 35°0N 111°10E 114 G6
Zhongwei China 37°30N 105°12E 114 F3
Zhongxian China 30°18N 107°58E 116 B6
Zhongxiang China 31°12N 112°34E 117 B9
Zhongyang China 37°20N 111°11E 114 F6
Zhorany Ukraine 51°19N 23°58E 83 G10
Zhosaly Kazakhstan 45°29N 64°4E 108 C6
Zhoucun China 36°47N 117°48E 115 F9
Zhoukou China 33°41N 114°38E 114 H8
Zhoukoudian China 39°41N 115°56E 114 E8
Zhouning China 27°12N 119°20E 117 D12
Zhoushan China 30°1N 122°6E 117 B14
Zhoushan Dao China 30°5N 122°10E 117 B14
Zhouzhi China 34°10N 108°12E 114 G5
Zhovkva Ukraine 50°4N 23°58E 75 C12
Zhovti Vody Ukraine 48°21N 33°31E 85 H7
Zhovtneve Lubelskie,
Ukraine 50°42N 24°12E 83 H11
Zhovtneve Mykolayiv,
Ukraine 46°54N 32°3E 85 J7
Zhu Jiang → China 22°45N 113°37E 117 F9
Zhuanghe China 39°40N 123°0E 115 E12
Zhucheng China 36°0N 119°27E 115 G10
Zhugqu China 33°40N 104°30E 116 A3
Zhuhai China 22°17N 113°34E 117 F9
Zhuji China 29°40N 120°10E 117 C13
Zhujiang Kou China 22°20N 113°45E 111 a
Zhukovka Russia 53°35N 33°50E 84 F7
Zhumadian China 32°59N 114°2E 117 A10
Zhuo Xian = Zhuozhou
China 39°28N 115°58E 114 E8
Zhuolu China 40°20N 115°12E 114 D8
Zhuozhou China 39°28N 115°58E 114 E8
Zhuozi China 41°0N 112°25E 114 D7
Zhur Kosovo 42°13N 20°34E 96 D4
Zhushan China 32°15N 110°3E 117 A8
Zhuxi China 32°25N 109°40E 116 A7
Zhuzhou China 27°49N 113°12E 117 D9
Zhvanets Ukraine 48°33N 26°30E 81 B11
Zhympity Kazakhstan 50°15N 52°35E 108 B4
Zhytomyr Ukraine 50°20N 28°40E 75 C15
Zhytomyr □ Ukraine 50°50N 28°10E 75 C14
Zi Shui → China 28°40N 112°40E 117 C9
Zibo China 36°47N 118°3E 115 F10
Zichang China 37°18N 109°40E 114 F5
Zidarovo Bulgaria 42°20N 27°24E 97 D11
Zidi = Wandhari
Pakistan 27°42N 66°48E 124 C2
Zièbice Poland 50°37N 17°2E 83 H4
Zielona Góra Poland 51°57N 15°31E 83 G2
Zierikzee Neths. 51°40N 3°55E 69 C3
Ziesar Germany 52°16N 12°17E 76 C8
Zifta Egypt 30°43N 31°14E 137 E7
Zigong China 29°15N 104°48E 116 C5
Ziguéy Chad 14°43N 15°50E 135 F9
Ziguinchor Senegal 12°35N 16°20W 138 C1
Ziguinchor □ Senegal 12°45N 16°20W 138 C1
Zihuatanejo Mexico 17°39N 101°33W 180 D4
Zijin China 23°33N 115°1E 117 F10
Zile Turkey 40°15N 35°52E 104 B6
Žilina Slovakia 49°12N 18°42E 79 B11
Zillah Libya 28°30N 17°33E 135 C9
Zillertaler Alpen Austria 47°6N 11°45E 78 D4
Zima Russia 54°0N 102°5E 107 D11
Zimapán Mexico 20°45N 99°21W 181 C5
Zimba Zambia 17°20S 26°11E 143 F2
Zimbabwe Zimbabwe 20°16S 30°54E 143 G3
Zimbabwe ■ Africa 19°0S 30°0E 143 F2
Zimmi S. Leone 7°20N 11°20W 138 D2
Zimnicea Romania 43°40N 25°22E 81 G10
Zimovniki Russia 47°10N 42°25E 87 G6
Zinave △ Mozam. 21°35S 33°40E 145 C5
Zinder Niger 13°48N 9°0E 139 C6
Zinder □ Niger 15°0N 10°30E 139 C7
Zinga Tanzania 9°16S 38°49E 143 D4
Zingaro △ Italy 38°6N 12°53E 94 D5
Zingst Germany 54°26N 12°40E 76 A7
Ziniaré Burkina Faso 12°35N 1°18W 139 C4
Zinnowitz Germany 54°4N 13°54E 76 A8
Zion △ U.S.A. 37°15N 113°5W 169 H7
Zionsville U.S.A. 39°57N 86°16W 172 E10
Zirbitzkogel Austria 47°4N 14°34E 78 D7
Zirc Hungary 47°17N 17°52E 80 C3
Žiri Slovenia 46°5N 14°8E 93 B11
Žirje Croatia 43°39N 15°42E 93 E12
Zirl Austria 47°17N 11°14E 78 D4
Zirndorf Germany 49°27N 10°57E 76 F6
Ziros Greece 35°5N 26°8E 101 D8
Zirreh, Gowd-e Afghan. 29°45N 62°0E 122 E3
Zisterdorf Austria 48°33N 16°45E 78 D9
Zitácuaro Mexico 19°24N 100°22W 180 D4
Žitava → Slovakia 48°14N 18°21E 79 C11
Žitište Serbia 45°30N 20°32E 98 A5
Zitong China 31°37N 105°10E 116 B5
Zitsa Greece 39°47N 20°40E 98 B2
Zittau Germany 50°57N 14°44E 76 D10
Zitundo Mozam. 26°48S 32°47E 145 C5
Živinice Bos.-H. 44°27N 18°36E 96 B3
Ziwa Magharibi = Kagera □
Tanzania 2°0S 31°30E 142 C3
Ziway, L. Ethiopia 8°0N 38°50E 132 F2
Zixi China 27°45N 117°4E 117 D11
Zixing China 25°58N 113°27E 117 D9
Ziyamet = Leonárisso
Cyprus 35°28N 34°8E 101 D13
Ziyang Shaanxi, China 32°32N 108°31E 114 H5
Ziyang Sichuan, China 30°6N 104°37E 116 B5
Ziyuan China 26°0N 110°28E 117 D8
Ziyun China 25°45N 106°5E 116 E6
Ziz, Oued → Morocco 31°40N 4°15W 136 B3
Zizhong China 29°48N 104°47E 116 C5
Zizur Mayor Spain 42°47N 1°41W 90 C3
Zlarin Croatia 43°42N 15°49E 93 E12
Zlatar Serbia 43°25N 19°47E 96 C3
Zlatar Bulgaria 43°22N 26°50E 97 C10
Zlataritsa Bulgaria 43°2N 25°57E 97 C9
Zlatibor Serbia 43°45N 19°43E 96 C3
Zlatitsa Bulgaria 42°41N 24°7E 97 D8
Zlatna Romania 46°8N 23°11E 81 D8
Zlatna Panega Bulgaria 43°8N 24°18E 97 C8
Zlatni Pyasŭtsi Bulgaria 43°17N 28°3E 97 C12

Zlatograd Bulgaria 41°22N 25°7E 97 D8
Zlatoust Russia 55°10N 59°40E 108 A5
Zletovo Macedonia 41°59N 22°17E 96 A6
Zlín Czechia 49°14N 17°40E 79 B10
Zlínský □ Czechia 49°20N 17°40E 79 B10
Złochew Poland 51°24N 18°35E 83 G5
Złoczew Poland 51°24N 18°35E 83 G5
Zlot Serbia 44°1N 21°58E 96 B5
Złotoryja Poland 51°8N 15°55E 83 G2
Złotów Poland 53°22N 17°2E 82 E4
Zmeinogorsk
Kazakhstan 51°10N 82°13E 109 B10
Żmigród Poland 51°28N 16°53E 83 G3
Zmiinyi, Ostriv Black Sea 45°15N 30°12E 85 K6
Zmiyev Ukraine 49°39N 36°27E 85 H9
Znamenka = Znamyanka
Ukraine 48°45N 32°30E 85 H7
Znamensk = Kapustin Yar
Russia 48°35N 45°40E 87 F7
Znamensk Russia 54°36N 21°16E 82 D8
Znamyanka Ukraine 48°45N 32°30E 85 H7
Żnin Poland 52°51N 17°44E 83 F4
Znojmo Czechia 48°50N 16°2E 78 C9
Zobeyri Iran 34°10N 46°40E 128 C5
Zobia
Dem. Rep. of the Congo 3°0N 25°59E 142 B2
Zoetermeer Neths. 52°3N 4°30E 69 B4
Zogang China 29°55N 97°42E 116 C1
Zogno Italy 45°48N 9°40E 92 C6
Zohreh → Iran 30°16N 51°15E 129 D6
Zolfo Springs U.S.A. 27°30N 81°48W 179 H6
Zolochiv Ukraine 49°45N 24°51E 75 D13
Zolotonosha Ukraine 49°39N 32°5E 85 H7
Zolotyy Potik Ukraine 48°54N 25°20E 81 B10
Zomba Malawi 15°22S 35°19E 143 F4
Zongo
Dem. Rep. of the Congo 4°20N 18°35E 140 D3
Zonguldak Turkey 41°28N 31°50E 104 B4
Zongyang □ Turkey 41°28N 31°45E 104 B4
Zongyang China 30°42N 117°12E 117 B11
Zonqor Pt. Malta 35°52N 14°34E 92 D2
Zonza France 41°45N 9°11E 73 G13
Zorgo Burkina Faso 12°15N 0°35W 139 C4
Zorita Spain 39°17N 5°39W 89 F5
Zorleni Romania 46°14N 27°44E 81 C12
Zornitsa Bulgaria 42°23N 26°58E 97 D10
Zorritos Peru 3°43S 80°40W 188 A1
Żory Poland 50°3N 18°44E 83 H5
Zorzor Liberia 7°46N 9°28W 138 D3
Zossen Germany 52°13N 13°27E 76 C9
Zou Xiang China 35°30N 116°58E 114 G9
Zouan-Hounien
Côte d'Ivoire 6°55N 8°15W 138 D3
Zouar Chad 20°30N 16°32E 135 D9
Zouérate = Zouîrât
Mauritania 22°44N 12°21W 134 D3
Zouîrât Mauritania 22°44N 12°21W 134 D3
Zourika Niger 19°16N 7°52E 139 B6
Zourma Burkina Faso 12°10N 0°25W 139 C4
Zoushan U.S.A. 38°6N 12°53E 94 D5
Zov Tigra △ Russia 43°25N 134°10E 112 C7
Zrenjanin Serbia 45°22N 20°23E 80 E5
Zuba Nigeria 9°11N 7°12E 139 D6
Zubin Potok Kosovo 42°54N 20°41E 96 D4
Zubtsov Russia 56°10N 34°34E 84 D8
Zuénoula Côte d'Ivoire 7°34N 6°3W 138 D3
Zuera Spain 41°51N 0°49W 90 D4
Zufar Oman 17°40N 54°0E 131 D5
Zug Switz. 47°10N 8°31E 77 H4
Zugdidi Georgia 42°30N 41°55E 87 J5
Zugersee Switz. 47°7N 8°35E 77 H4
Zugspitze Germany 47°25N 10°59E 77 H6
Zuid-Holland □ Neths. 52°0N 4°35E 69 C4
Zuidbeveland Neths. 51°30N 3°50E 69 C3
Zuidhorn Neths. 53°15N 6°23E 69 A6
Zújar Spain 37°34N 2°50W 89 H8
Zújar → Spain 39°1N 5°47W 89 G5
Zukowo Poland 54°21N 18°22E 82 D5
Zula Eritrea 15°17N 39°40E 131 D2
Zülpich Germany 50°41N 6°39E 76 E2
Zumaia Spain 43°19N 2°15W 90 C2
Zumárraga Spain 43°5N 2°19W 90 C2
Zumbo Mozam. 15°35S 30°26E 143 F3
Zummo Nigeria 9°51N 12°59E 139 D7
Zumpango Mexico 19°48N 99°6W 181 D5
Zungeru Nigeria 9°48N 6°8E 139 D6
Zuni Pueblo U.S.A. 35°4N 108°51W 169 J9
Zunyi China 27°42N 106°53E 116 D6
Zuo Jiang → China 22°50N 108°6E 116 F6
Zuoquan China 37°1N 113°27E 114 F7
Zuozhou China 22°24N 107°27E 116 F6
Županja Croatia 45°4N 18°43E 80 E3
Zürbätīyah Iraq 33°9N 46°3E 105 F12
Zürich Switz. 47°22N 8°32E 77 H4
Zürich □ Switz. 47°26N 8°40E 77 H4
Zürich ✈ (ZRH) Switz. 47°27N 8°34E 77 H4
Zürichsee Switz. 47°18N 8°40E 77 H4
Żuromin Poland 53°4N 19°51E 83 E6
Žut Croatia 43°52N 15°17E 93 E12
Zutphen Neths. 52°9N 6°12E 69 B6
Zuurberg △ S. Africa 33°12S 25°32E 144 E4
Zuwārah Libya 32°58N 12°1E 135 B8
Zūzan Iran 34°22N 59°53E 129 C8
Žužemberk Slovenia 45°50N 14°56E 93 C11
Zvečan Kosovo 42°54N 20°50E 96 D4
Zvenigorodka = Svenyhorodka
Ukraine 48°30N 56°6E 75 H6
Zvezdets Bulgaria 42°6N 27°26E 97 D11
Zvishavane Zimbabwe 20°17S 30°2E 143 G3
Zvolen Slovakia 48°33N 19°10E 79 C12
Zvonce Serbia 42°57N 22°34E 96 C6
Zvornik Bos.-H. 44°26N 19°5E 80 F4
Zwedru = Tchien Liberia 5°59N 8°15W 138 D3
Zweibrücken Germany 49°15N 7°21E 77 F3
Zwenkau Germany 51°13N 12°19E 76 D8
Zwettl Austria 48°35N 15°9E 78 C8
Zwickau Germany 50°44N 12°30E 76 E8
Zwierzyniec Poland 50°36N 22°58E 83 H9
Zwiesel Germany 49°1N 13°13E 77 F9
Zwischenahn, Bad
Germany 53°11N 8°0E 76 B4
Zwolle Neths. 52°31N 6°6E 69 B6
Zwolle U.S.A. 31°38N 93°39W 176 F8
Żychlin Poland 52°15N 19°37E 83 F6
Zyrardów Poland 52°3N 20°28E 83 F7
Zyrya Kazakhstan 49°43N 84°20E 109 C10
Zyryanovsk = Zyryan
Kazakhstan 49°43N 84°20E 109 C10
Żyrzyn Poland 51°29N 22°7E 83 G9
Zyuratkul △ Russia 54°50N 58°56E 108 B5
Żywiec Poland 49°42N 19°10E 83 J6